DATE DUE

DEMCO 38-296

THE CQ Researcher

JANUARY— DECEMBER 1998

Published by Congressional Quarterly Inc. 1414 22nd Street, N.W., Washington, D.C. 20037
Congressional Quarterly offers a complete line of publications and research services.
For subscription information, call (202) 887-6279 or (800) 432-2250 ext. 279.

ISBN 1-56802-261-1
ISSN 1056-2036

...ts of The CQ Researcher

Subscribers to *The CQ Researcher* receive 48 reports per year. Each report provides background on a current topic of widespread interest. Designed as a starting place for research, the reports define the issues and include a chronology and extensive bibliographies. A feature called "At Issue," which quotes opposing viewpoints from two experts, also is a part of each report.

The publication is available in various formats.

THE REPORT

The report, about 12,000 words in length, is issued on Friday four times a month. Each report treats a subject that is in the news or likely to be in the news in the near future.

BOUND REPORTS

The weekly reports are bound into quarterly paperback editions and an annual hardbound cumulation.

INDEX

A subject index to the reports is published each quarter and cumulated annually. The latest index may be found at the back of this volume.

CITATION

Recommended format for citing these reports in a bibliography, based on The Modern Language Association of America's *Handbook for Writers of Research Papers,* 3rd edition, follows.

Clark, Charles S. "The Obscenity Debate." *The CQ Researcher* 20 Dec. 1991: 969-992.

THE CQ Researcher

CONTENTS JANUARY — DECEMBER 1998

The CQ Researcher

PUBLISHED BY CONGRESSIONAL QUARTERLY INC.

Foster Care Reform

Can new approaches stem the crisis?

O n the last day of the 1997 legislative session, Congress passed what has been hailed as the most significant overhaul of the foster care system in nearly 20 years. The Adoption and Safe Families Act is designed to hasten the adoption of children in foster care by putting more emphasis on children's safety rather than returning them to dangerous family situations. In doing so, the legislation addresses one of the leading criticisms of existing child-protective law — that it overemphasizes family preservation rather than protecting abused and neglected children. The legislation also gives states new financial incentives to find adoptive parents. But critics question whether the law can increase the underfunded child-welfare system's ability to cope with acute societal problems caused by drugs, AIDS and poverty.

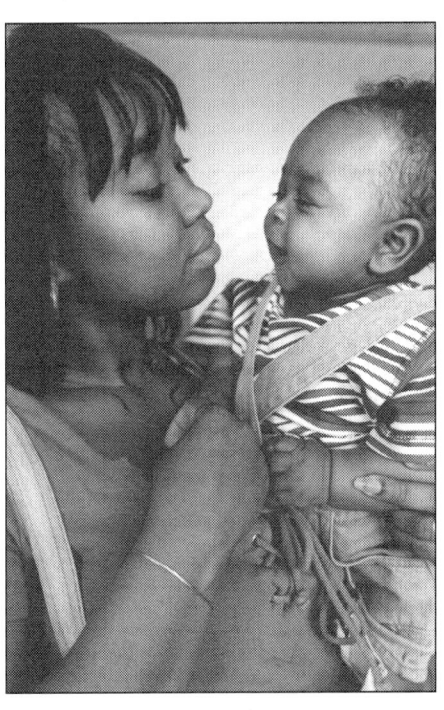

C_Q   **Jan. 9, 1998**   •   **Volume 8, No. 1**   •   **Pages 1-24**

Formerly Editorial Research Reports

CQ Researcher

January 9, 1998
Volume 8, No. 1

EDITOR
Sandra Stencel

MANAGING EDITOR
Thomas J. Colin

ASSOCIATE EDITOR
Sarah M. Magner

STAFF WRITERS
Mary H. Cooper
Kenneth Jost
David Masci

PRODUCTION EDITOR
Melissa Hall

EDITORIAL ASSISTANT
Vanessa E. Furlong

PUBLISHED BY
Congressional Quarterly Inc.

CHAIRMAN
Andrew Barnes

VICE CHAIRMAN
Andrew P. Corty

PRESIDENT AND PUBLISHER
Robert W. Merry

EXECUTIVE EDITOR
David Rapp

The CQ Researcher (ISSN 1056-2036). Formerly Editorial Research Reports. Published weekly, except Jan. 2, May 29, July 3, Oct. 30, by Congressional Quarterly Inc., 1414 22nd St., N.W., Washington, D.C. 20037. Annual subscription rate for libraries, businesses and government is $340. Additional rates furnished upon request. Periodicals postage paid at Washington, D.C., and additional mailing offices. POSTMASTER: Send address changes to The CQ Researcher, 1414 22nd St., N.W., Washington, D.C. 20037.

COVER: SINCE 1992, THE ANNIE E. CASEY FOUNDATION IN BALTIMORE, MD., HAS FUNDED "FAMILY TO FAMILY" PROGRAMS IN SIX STATES TO DEVELOP LINKS BETWEEN BIRTH AND FOSTER PARENTS. (LIZZIE HIMMEL, COURTESY OF THE CASEY FOUNDATION)

Foster Care Reform

BY RACHEL S. COX

THE ISSUES

Who is to blame for the death of Sabrina Green, age 9, found dead in her home on Nov. 8 from untreated burns, gangrene and blows to her head?

Sabrina's older half-sister and legal guardian, Yvette, and her boyfriend, Daryl Stephens, have been charged with manslaughter. But what about the New York City school officials who failed to investigate Sabrina's repeated absences from school? What about the Family Court judge who, in a March hearing lasting just a few minutes, awarded custody of Sabrina to Yvette, 31, who lived on welfare with her own 10 children and two dogs in a four-bedroom Bronx apartment?

And what of the caseworkers who had investigated Yvette three times between 1984 and 1994 for not caring for her own children adequately but had failed to prevent her from getting custody of Sabrina?

Sabrina and other child victims tear at our hearts from the front pages all too regularly. How is it that the child-protective system, which employs thousands of workers and spends billions of dollars per year, cannot intervene more effectively?

In theory, foster care provides a social safety net for children whose biological families cannot care for them, or may be harming them. Sabrina Green spent her short life deeply involved with the social welfare system. Born drug-addicted, she was abandoned in the hospital for two months by her mother, Joanne Coleman. But the city child-welfare agency investigated and allowed Coleman to keep Sabrina and her other children. It was at least the third investigation of Coleman, including one prompted by the earlier death of her 2-year-old son, who was scalded

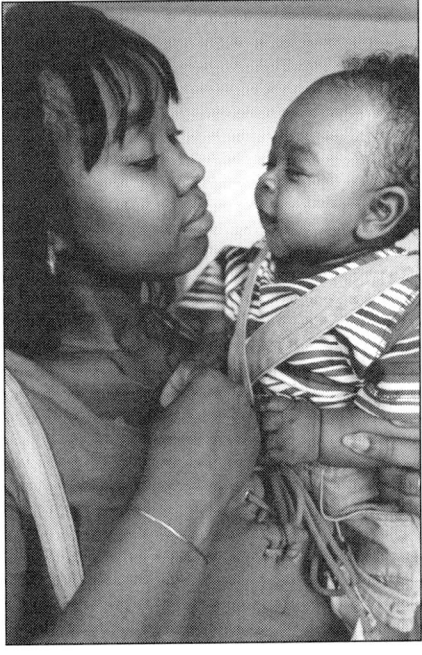

to death at a family friend's apartment.

After Coleman died, Sabrina was placed with Yvette. Of all Sabrina's 10 brothers and sisters, only her younger sister Saleena, also born drug-addicted, was successfully placed in foster care and later adopted.

Saleena's adoption represents an alternative scenario favored by numerous child advocates and critics of the child-protective system: rapidly moving children from abusive homes to caring foster families, followed as soon as possible by adoption.

In December 1996, President Clinton made adoption a national priority, instructing the Department of Health and Human Services (HHS) to double the number of children adopted or placed in permanent homes annually from the foster care system by the year 2002. There were 27,000 such placements in 1996. [1]

"No child should be trapped in the limbo of foster care," Clinton told radio listeners in a holiday-season address. "No child should be uncertain about what the word 'family' or 'parent' or 'home' means, particularly

when there are open arms waiting to welcome these children into safe and strong households where they can build good, caring lives."

Yet for most children removed from their birth families, adoption remains an unlikely outcome. Each year, about 60 percent of the children in foster care return home, most within a year of placement. [2] Nationwide, eight of every 1,000 children, or roughly 500,000 youths, were in substitute care at the end of fiscal 1996. [3] Of those half-million children, about 100,000 have been judged unable to return home without jeopardizing their health, safety and development. [4] For the majority of these children, the goal is adoption or other permanent placement. Many have been in foster care for two years or more.

According to the HHS, more than 25,000 children in the foster care system were legally available for adoption in 1996. [5] But Conna Craig, president of the Institute for Children in Cambridge, Mass., and a leading critic of the current foster care system, asserted in a recent state-by-state survey that twice that number were legally free for adoption at the start of fiscal 1997. [6]

The number of children in foster care is the highest in 20 years, and the number has almost doubled since the mid-1980s. [7] (*See graph, p. 4.*) Some of the increase can be attributed to societal factors. Reports of child abuse and neglect are at record levels. Drug addiction, teenage pregnancy, the AIDS epidemic — all have pushed up the number of children orphaned, abandoned or removed from their families and placed in alternative care. [8]

Yet Craig, like other adoption advocates, asserts that "the growth in the substitute-care population has been influenced more by declines in exit rates than increases in the number of children entering care. Fewer

Number of Children in Foster Care Rose

The number of children in foster care plummeted after passage of the 1980 Adoption Assistance and Child Welfare Act but then began rising steadily in the wake of the AIDS and crack cocaine epidemics. *

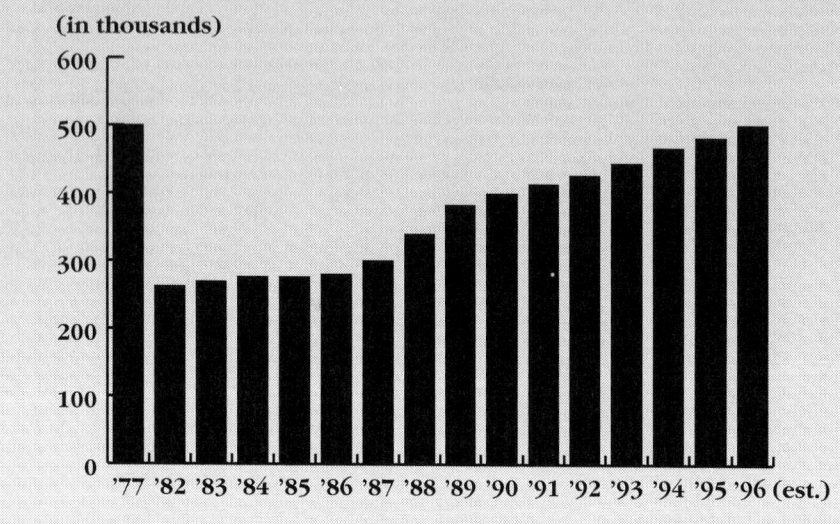

(in thousands)

'77 '82 '83 '84 '85 '86 '87 '88 '89 '90 '91 '92 '93 '94 '95 '96 (est.)

* Based on voluntary reporting by 38 states.

Source: American Public Welfare Association.

children are leaving foster care than are coming in." [9]

Many critics of the foster care system blame the sluggishness with which children are legally severed from their families and made available for adoption on the law that has governed federal foster care policy for the last 18 years. Under the Adoption Assistance and Child Welfare Act, the states have primary responsibility for administering child-welfare services and setting policy. But the federal government is largely responsible for establishing the conditions for financial compensation to states for certain foster care and adoption costs, exerting a heavy influence on state policies.

Others point at a bureaucratic system so overburdened, underfunded and poorly managed that good decisions about child custody are rare. Indeed, during the last decade, 21

state systems have been placed in court receivership because they had failed to protect children effectively. [10]

Proposed solutions are many and varied. Proponents of "privatization" point to examples of efficient private adoption agencies and tout the efficacy of the free market as the answer (*see p. 9*). Traditionally liberal child-welfare proponents advocate more federal and state spending for salaries, training and support services for families. And a growing number of workers in the field promote efforts to reorganize the child-protective system along more community-based, family-friendly lines as an approach that promises better health and safety for children without creating more bureaucracy.

Most observers agree that change is essential, and that passage in late 1997 of the Adoption and Safe Families Act, designed to hasten the adoption of children in foster care, sug-

gests that the political will to act is finally present. [11] In essence, the new statute changes existing law to give more emphasis to protecting children's safety rather than seeking to reunite them with troubled families. And it gives states new financial incentives to find adoptive parents for children in foster care.

There is unanimous agreement that promoting permanency for children caught in the foster care system, and increasing the number of parentless children adopted, are laudable goals. But most would also agree that meeting them depends, to a large extent, on dealing with a host of problems ranging from the lack of community-based family support services to chronic social problems such as teen pregnancy and drug addiction.

As the nation struggles with the foster care dilemma, these are some of the questions being asked:

Should the adoption of children from the foster care system be made easier?

Passage of the Adoption Assistance and Child Welfare Act in 1980 marked the federal government's first attempt to level the financial playing field for adoptions, reimbursing states for adoption expenses just as it did for foster care costs. Since then, federal and state foster care policies have supported adoption for foster children once the determination was made that they cannot return to their biological families. The new Adoption and Safe Families Act reiterated federal support for adoption, created financial incentives for states to promote it, took steps to remove financial and bureaucratic barriers and required states to document and report adoption efforts in order to remain eligible for federal funding (*see p. 18*).

Maureen Hogan, executive director of Adopt a Special Kid/America, in Washington, D.C., thinks the president's goal of doubling the number of children adopted from foster care by 2002 doesn't go far enough. "I wish the president had set the bar higher," she said. "This is an infinitesimal response to a huge problem." [12]

Pro-adoption advocates often focus on horror stories — kids living with loving foster families who want to adopt them but can't because social workers and the courts keep trying to reunite them with their abusive biological parents. "It is hard being a child in today's world, but being a child today that doesn't really belong to any one family must be torturous," says Janice Mink, of Hear My Voice, an adoption advocacy group based in Ann Arbor, Mich. "These children deserve a chance at life."

Rep. Barbara B. Kennelly, D-Conn., helped craft the Adoption and Safe Families Act in the House. "In the best of all worlds," she said, "we all agree the best place for a child is with his or her parents. But we must also recognize there are times when a child's safety is threatened by living at home."

"Our foster care system is an extremely valuable safety net," she added, "but it should not be a way of life for children."

In the Senate, Mike DeWine, R-Ohio, said that "far too many children are spending their most important, formative years in a legal limbo that denies them their chance to be adopted. These children are being denied what all children should have — the chance to be loved and cared for by parents." He added that "too few of the children who are available for adoption are actually adopted."

While few child-welfare advocates

argue against adoption as a desirable outcome for children who never will be able to return home safely, they do reject the view of adoption as a cure-all for the overburdened foster care system. An overemphasis on adoption, according to the Child Welfare League of America, can obscure the fact that "many vulnerable families, with appropriate support, can and do

The Annie E. Casey Foundation's "Family to Family" program seeks foster families from the child's community and trains foster parents to work closely with the birth parents.

provide nurturing homes." And it warns that "without efforts that will promote and carry out good decisions, many children may end up with parental rights terminated, but without a permanent home." [13]

"There are no more important deci-

sions for a child," said Mary Lee Allen, director of the Children's Defense Fund's (CDF) Child Welfare and Mental Health Division, "than the decision to remove a child from familiar surroundings or the decision to permanently sever a child's parental ties, especially when there is no assurance that a new family will follow." [14]

What's more, the judicial procedure that precedes adoption, termination of parental rights (TPR), involves a profound judgment about the rights of the parents as well as about the best interests of the child. Ronald K. Henry, an attorney from Washington, D.C., worries that a rush to terminate parental rights in the interest of promoting permanency will shortchange the interests of non-custodial parents.

"Many groups are concerned about reports of abuse of governmental power in removing children from their families," he said. Indeed, he argues that a simple change of custody [from the custodial parent to a non-custodial parent] offers an alternative to foster care that is too rarely considered by caseworkers. [15]

Another reason given for not always pushing ahead on TPR is concern about the child's loss of certain inheritable rights, such as veterans' benefits and Social Security, even if the child cannot live with a parent.

Other observers warn that adoption advocates may be painting a rosier view of adoption than the reality suggests. "Many of these kids are very difficult to place," says Nancy Smith, a Washington, D.C., foster

Will Overburdened Family Courts . . .

When Nancy Smith recounts the tribulations and rewards of being a foster parent for three children, one person stands out as a stalwart ally — the family court judge who oversees the children placed with Smith and her husband.

For example, when the District of Columbia terminated payments to the private school that one of their learning-disabled children attended, the judge ordered the city to pay. "Our judge really cares, and she's very smart," Smith says. "If we didn't have her, we'd have problems."

Juvenile and family courts play a critical part in decisions that affect the lives of children and families caught up in the child-protective system. The process often begins with judicial review of a social-service agency's decision to remove a child from his home. Passage of the Adoption Assistance and Child Welfare Act of 1980, in an effort to guard against unnecessary removals and foster care "drift," greatly expanded the duties of the courts. The new Adoption and Safe Families Act is also likely to have a significant impact on the nation's juvenile and family courts.

While the precise requirements vary with state laws, many juvenile courts have a number of key roles in addition to reviewing agency decisions to remove children from their home. They must oversee agencies' family-preservation and rehabilitation efforts; approve case plans to achieve permanency for children whether at home or with another family; and periodically review cases and decide whether or not to terminate parental rights when children cannot safely return home.

Clearly, the courts' ability to make such decisions efficiently weighs heavily on outcomes for children and families in the foster care system. "State agencies alone do not make permanency decisions for children," said Jess MacDonald, director of the Illinois Department of Children and Family Services. "The legal system is a partner in permanency." [1]

Yet relatively few resources are allotted to support the work of family courts, according to critics of the current system. While the number of child-abuse and neglect cases has soared in recent years, the number of judges available to handle them has remained almost constant. (*See graphs, p. 8.*) In an American Bar Association (ABA) study of six states where statistics were available on both the number of child-victim cases filed and the number of family and juvenile court judges, the number of cases increased 120 percent while the number of judges increased only 7 percent between 1984 and 1990. [2]

Compounding the demands of new responsibilities and increased caseloads is the difficulty of the cases, which often involve drug-exposed children and abused children who are also handicapped. "It is no exaggeration to refer to this situation as a crisis in many large, urban courts," concluded another ABA study. [3]

Reports on courtroom conditions on the urban frontlines paint a chaotic picture — poorly represented clients, cursory hearings and missed deadlines, inadequate facilities and overworked and underpaid workers ranging from judges and lawyers to caseworkers.

"Family Court in Brooklyn on any morning can seem more like a bazaar than like a serious courthouse," observed Joe Sexton of *The New York Times*. "Lawyers yell for clients, then race to other courtrooms. Where there ideally should be urgency, there are adjournments. Children roam everywhere. Parents cry. Deals on the future of families are made hastily, in full view of other parents." [4]

"You're expected to do incredible things with no time and no resources," says Judge Philip C. Segal of Kings County Family Court. "Ultimately, things get done, but they may not get done very quickly. The court just doesn't

parent who has worked on behalf of hard-to-place children for many years. "They suffer from many of the same problems their parents did — bipolar disorder, substance abuse problems and fetal alcohol syndrome."

As a result, Smith argues, successful adoption placements require a special kind of parent. "There really are professional skills involved if you're dealing with kids who are traumatized and have special needs," she says. For this reason, child advocates argue that additional funds for adoption support services are essential if adoption placements are in-

deed to remain "permanent."

Finally, advocates argue, some situations call for alternative placements rather than adoption. As more and more children enter foster care with serious learning disabilities and emotional problems, for instance, placement in a group-care facility with trained staff offering specialized services may be more beneficial than a family placement. Smith has seen children, she says, "for whom the intimacy of a family placement is more than they can handle." And while the specter of a return to orphan asylums remains repellent to

many, well-staffed and well-funded institutions have been shown to be a benign alternative, especially for hard-to-place older children. [16]

In recent years, child-protective agencies increasingly have turned to an alternative child-care arrangement known as "kinship care." The approach, which places children with relatives, has greatly expanded the pool of out-of-home placement possibilities for children requiring alternative care. In Illinois, for example, more than half of the children in foster care live with relatives, said Jess McDonald, director of the state Department of Children and

... Benefit From the New Adoption Law?

have sufficient resources."

Critics blame the lack of resources in part on the low status of the family court, which is viewed by many lawyers as a low-paying and unrewarding venue and by judges as a steppingstone to more prestigious appointments to criminal courts.

What's more, Segal says, "family court is a poor people's court." Often, the families involved are recent immigrants who speak little or no English and have brought with them quite different child-rearing customs.

Another part of the problem, according to Mark Hardin, director of the ABA's foster care and family preservation program, has been a simple failure to recognize that the court system is an intrinsic part of the foster care crisis. Delays in court proceedings translate into extended stays in foster care, which not only increase government costs but also lessen with each passing month a child's ultimate chance for adoption.

"People have been thinking of court budgets as separate from foster care costs," Hardin says. "It's a big piece of the problem, and there's been a pretty tiny investment."

But, he adds, the situation is gradually changing. While investments in improving juvenile and family courts remain small, he says, "there has been a growing recognition of the importance of it. A lot of chief justices [of state court systems] have been taking this under their wing and encouraging it."

On the federal level, the 1993 Family Preservation and Support Services program included funds for modest grants available to state courts to perform self-assessments and then plan and implement improvements. The 47 states and the District of Columbia that chose to participate have produced "some very impressive reports," says Howard Davidson, director of the ABA Center on Children and the

Law. The recently enacted Adoption and Safe Families Act extended the grant program for three more years to implement improvements.

Inevitably, the new act will affect the judicial process in untold other ways as well, but observers are unwilling to speculate. "It's unclear what the impact will be," Davidson says. "It's a question how Health and Human Services will interpret the law, and regulations are typically long in coming."

But while concern exists that the law's new, tighter timelines will further overburden courts, there is optimism as well that the law will help the process by defining the circumstances under which children need not be returned to their families. Under the 1980 law, agencies had to make "reasonable efforts" to reunify families. But the new law, by placing a clear priority on the health and safety of children, will prevent cases from bogging down over the question of whether or not reasonable efforts have been made to reunify families.

"A certain number of cases should move forward promptly to termination of parental rights," Hardin says. "The law will help states do triage. I hope it will be helpful, and it may well be."

[1] From testimony before the House Ways and Means Human Resources Subcommittee, April 8, 1997. McDonald testified on behalf of the American Public Welfare Association.

[2] Mark Hardin, "Judicial Implementation of Permanency Planning Reform: One Court that Works," American Bar Association Center on Children and the Law and the National Conference of Special Court Judges, 1992, p. 12. The states were Colorado, Georgia, Hawaii, Rhode Island, Massachusetts and New York.

[3] Mark Hardin, H. Ted Rubin and Debra Ratterman Baker, *A Second Court That Works: Judicial Implementation of Permanency Planning Reforms*, 1995, p. 11.

[4] *The New York Times*, June 10, 1996, p. A1.

Family Services and a spokesman for the American Public Welfare Association (APWA). [17]

Some experts worry that standards for kinship care are laxer than for licensed foster care providers, and can lead to tragedies like the case of Sabrina Green. They also say that the placements are less permanent than in legal adoptions. But kinship care also has been praised for maintaining family ties and for building on traditional extended family structures.

For black children, who are disproportionately represented in the foster care population and adopted

at a much lower rate than white children, kinship care holds the promise of increasing the number of permanent placements. [18]

Research shows that adoption is not common in kinship arrangements, often because of a reluctance on the part of the care providers to initiate termination of parental rights. As a result, some states are now experimenting with an arrangement called "subsidized guardianship," which provides relatives with an ongoing subsidy similar to adoption assistance and establishes them as permanent legal guardians. [19]

What's more, child advocates say, attempts to establish strict timetables designed to move children more quickly toward adoption, as adoption proponents have proposed, can work against the best interests of a child. Mandatory TPR hearings according to an arbitrary schedule could short-circuit efforts to heal a family, for example, or force the separation of sibling groups, when it has been shown to be in the best interests of children to keep siblings together. (*See story, p. 12.*)

To tighten the timetable for completing adoptions without also inten-

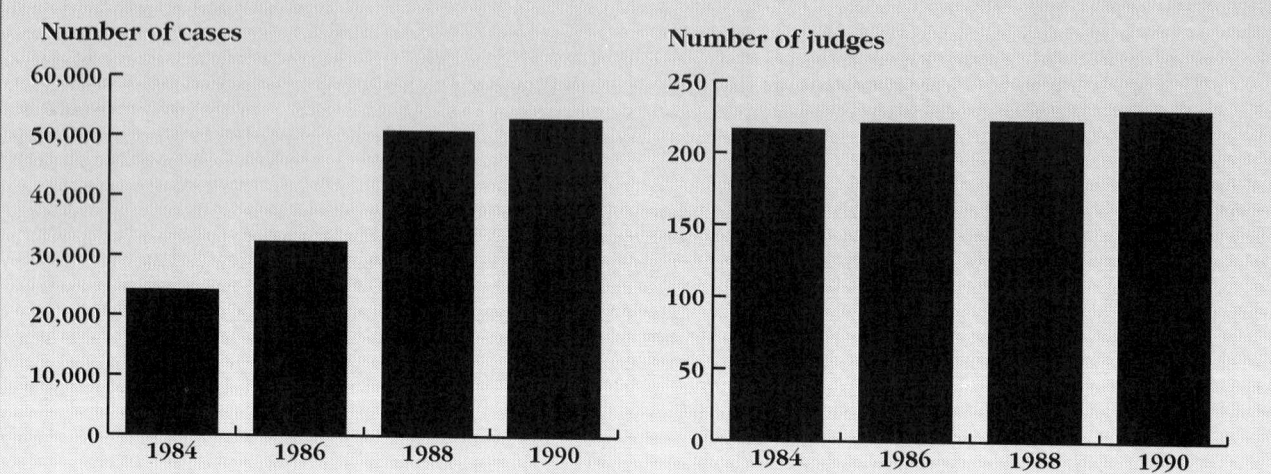

Abuse Caseload Overwhelms Courts in Six States

*While the number of child-abuse and neglect cases more than doubled from 1984 to 1990, (graph at left), the number of judges available to handle them remained almost constant (graph at right). ***

Number of cases

	1984	1986	1988	1990

Number of judges

	1984	1986	1988	1990

*** Based on a study of the six states where statistics were available for both cases and judges: Colorado, Georgia, Hawaii, Rhode Island, Massachusetts and New York.*

Sources: American Bar Association Center on Children and the Law; National Center for State Courts

sifying services "seems a prescription for disaster," Allen of the CDF told lawmakers, "especially given that the resources required to do the various components of the first could deplete even the limited staff resources currently available for the second." [20]

Do federal laws discourage the movement of children out of the foster care system?

The Adoption Assistance and Child Welfare Act responded to many of the problems that continue to plague the foster-care system. The 1980 act confronted the specter of children being snatched from their homes with scant attention paid to the family problems that precipitated removal. It asserted that children should be placed "in the most homelike setting." Rather than addressing the foster care crisis from the "back end," as the new Adoption and Safe Fami-

lies Act does, the 18-year-old law addressed it from the "front end," reducing the number of children facing extended stays in foster care by preventing, or mending, the breakup of families.

In addition to adding financial supports for adoption, the 1980 law encouraged states to "make a reasonable effort" to reunify families by providing services.

" 'Of course, state child-protective agencies will continue to have authority to remove children immediately from dangerous situations,' " Allen quoted Sen. Alan Cranston, D-Calif., one of the law's chief sponsors, as saying. " 'But where removal can be prevented through the provision of home-based services, these agencies will be required to provide such services before removing the child and turning to foster care.' " [21]

As time has passed, however, the

"reasonable efforts" requirement appears to have unleashed a host of problems. "Our current system of laws believes in family preservation at almost any and all costs," proclaimed Mink of Hear My Voice. [22] Craig, who says privatization of the child-welfare system would encourage quicker adoptions, put it even more bluntly: "The same social worker who will turn down an adoptive family because they think spanking is OK is legally required to send children back to parents who have fractured their skulls." [23]

As debate progressed on new legislation to reform the child-welfare system, a consensus emerged that in the effort to preserve families, some children were being returned to dangerous situations, and permanency decisions were being delayed while caseworkers went to extraordinary ends to reunite families.

"Although states never intended that this provision be interpreted as requiring unreasonable efforts, or returning children to unsafe families or impeding permanency, Congress has heard . . . that in practice, such action is, on occasion, an unintended consequence of an erroneous interpretation of the law," McDonald of the Illinois Department of Children and Family Services told lawmakers in April.

Other critics of federal policy have asserted that federal funding practices create an incentive for child-welfare agencies to maintain children in foster care rather than move them into adoption. "The federal government reimburses states for foster care costs on a per-day, per-child basis — even after children are legally free for adoption — rewarding growth in program size instead of effective care," Craig wrote. [24]

Hogan of Adopt a Special Kid asserts that "many children in foster care are literally being held hostage" by state agencies [that] receive funds to administer foster placements but fail to pass on the full amount to foster families. [25]

But other experts counter that while the federal government has reimbursed foster care expenses for children whose biological families are eligible for Aid to Families with Dependent Children (AFDC), most foster care costs are borne by the states. They point to statistics showing that children whose expenses are paid entirely by the state stay in foster care for the same amount of time, or less, than children whose expenses are repaid by the federal government. What's more, the Adoption Assistance and Child Welfare Act "removed the financial disincentive [for adoption] by reimbursing adoption costs as well as foster care costs," according to Elizabeth Oppenheim of the APWA. [26]

Since passage of the Adoption and Safe Families Act, the key issue has become whether the new federal law

will encourage the movement of the right children into adoption without swinging too far in the other direction. "In clarifying the 'reasonable efforts' provision, Congress must proceed cautiously so as not to create new problems by . . . widening the arc of pendulum swings in an area of policy that is already too volatile for children's well-being," said the CDF's Allen. "It is important not to . . . set off a new chain of unintended consequences — such as overzealous removals of children from parents' homes when their safety is not endangered." [27]

While consensus has emerged on the need to clarify federal policy regarding the removal of children from dangerous homes, the "reasonable efforts" requirement is only one of the factors that slow the movement of children out of the system and into permanency.

In responding to President Clinton's charge to double the number of adoptions nationally, HHS officials spoke with scores of participants in the foster care system. In addition to identifying "the varied interpretations of the reasonable efforts requirement" as a problem, they concluded that, "Delays in making timely permanency decisions result from high caseloads for judges and caseworkers; incorrect beliefs and outdated assumptions about the adoptability of children; [and] the limited pool of permanent families for children with special needs." [28]

Other analysts of the child-protective system argue that advocates of accelerated adoption are asking the wrong question, or focusing on the wrong issue. These other analysts blame the slow-down in adoptions in part on the enormously increased workloads imposed by other elements of the child protective system, such as investigating child abuse complaints and providing family-support services.

Should the foster care system be privatized?

Private adoption agencies, social-welfare agencies and group-care operators have long played a part in America's foster care system. Proponents of privatization point to their successes — and what they see as the failure of the current government-run system — to argue for expanding their share of the job.

"Private, community-based organizations are providing foster and adoptive-parent recruitment and support," wrote Craig and Derek Herbert of the Institute for Children. "Businesses are contributing time, talent and treasure to promote adoption. Individuals are spearheading efforts to assist children through mentoring programs for foster teens. Combined with needed public policy reforms, these private endeavors can create a more efficient and more humane system for America's foster children." [29]

On the other hand, evidence suggests that merely because an agency is privately run does not assure its effectiveness. In New York City, the vast majority of out-of-home placements are made through private, nonprofit agencies that have contracts with the city. In August 1997, a month after two foster parents were arrested in connection with the death of 4-year-old Clarice Reid, who had been placed in their home by a private agency, the city suspended more than a third of the agencies for unsatisfactory performance.

Kansas began serving as a statewide laboratory for privatization in January 1996, when private agencies submitted bids to provide services throughout the state. Agencies receive a fee for each child or family they handle, and must meet specific performance goals. For instance, 90 percent of the children referred for foster care cannot have more than three placements after referral.

Kansas' experiment has attracted

so much national attention that the state agency responsible for foster care held a conference in November to explain its approach to other state officials. Observers agree that it is far too soon to judge Kansas' experiment. But Gary Prunk, executive director of Kansas Action for Children, sees potential problems.

Prunk worries that the new system, by moving supervisory functions from the 13 existing state offices into five big regions, overcentralizes services. "We've gotten further centralized, further away from communities," he says. "There's been lots of lip service paid to local control, but we've really seen something else." At the same time, because the system has been divided by function, he adds, "there seems to be no incentive built into the system to increase coordination, and the result could be that family needs will go unmet."

Prunk also fears that the new system shortchanges prevention by not funding community-based family services and supports that could keep children from entering the foster care system in the first place. With a "capitated" funding system — one that places a strict lid on the amount of money available to the provider agencies to treat troubled families — and little attention given to keeping the number of families low through prevention, he feels that "the cost-containment issue becomes really big."

Prunk and others point to health maintenance organizations (HMOs) as a comparable "managed care" model. "A key characteristic of the early health maintenance organizations was to control cost by emphasizing prevention and early intervention," reports the Monitoring Project at Kansas Action for Children. "That emphasis has changed somewhat in more recent years, to one of controlling cost by reducing overutilization of services through limiting access to providers." [30]

Susan Notkin, director of the Pro-gram for Children at the Edna McConnell Clark Foundation in New York City, also is skeptical about privatization.

"You have to look at what's driving the argument for privatization," she says. "If it's a code word for managed care — meaning that you have capitated rates for services and are trying to contain costs — then I have some question whether it can respond and not sacrifice quality of care. It hasn't worked that well for health care, and now we're talking about something much more complicated."

At the recent Kansas foster care conference, the state's Republican governor, Bill Graves, said, "We have seen some improvements. They are not what I would call dramatic or significant improvements, but they are improvements statistically over the previous system." Teresa Markowitz, state commissioner of children and family services, said that early data show increases in the number of children adopted and the number of foster parents. [31]

In reporting on the first year of the program, the Kansas chapter of the National Association of Social Workers found the new system generally positive in handling adoptions, somewhat negative in family preservation and generally negative in foster care.

"We do believe that positive steps have been taken," wrote chapter President Monica Flask. "Nevertheless, the evidence suggests that there are still both immediate and long-term concerns which require attention." [32]

Outside observers have praised Kansas' willingness to change the status quo.

"This is not an end-all, be-all program, but I am impressed that they are not nibbling around the edges but really working on changing the entire system," said James Paul McComb, executive director of the Maryland Association of Resources for Families and Youth. [33] ■

BACKGROUND

Era of Indenture

Americans have always arranged for some children to be reared by adults other than their own parents," wrote Tim Hacsi, a scholar with the Chapin Hall Center for Children at the University of Chicago. "But the ways that they were cared for have changed." [34]

In Colonial America, children were regarded as miniature adults in need of training rather than innocents to be nurtured. Consequently, children were commonly indentured to other families, where they could live and learn a trade. Initially, the practice was employed at virtually all levels of society, but it was especially common for orphans and other children in need of care.

Between 1800 and 1850, societal changes shaped public attitudes toward neglected and impoverished children. As a new urban middle class emerged and new conceptions of childhood took hold, only children from low-income families were indentured, as were orphans and children whose parents were deemed unable or unfit to care for them.

At the same time, numerous religious and charitable organizations, recoiling from the cholera epidemic of 1832 and the poverty of the nation's new urban centers, founded orphan asylums. While asylums never completely supplanted family placements, they became the predominant mode of caring for dependent children between 1830 and 1860.

Yet even as asylums were gaining currency, out-of-home placements were experiencing a rebirth as well. In 1853, Charles Loring Brace founded the New York Children's Aid Society.

Continued on p. 12

Chronology

19th Century

Religious and charitable organizations found orphanages to care for indigent and parentless children. After 1860, placing children in families begins to replace institutional solutions.

1853

Charles Loring Brace founds the New York Children's Aid Society to transport children to family farms in the West.

1870s

Societies for the prevention of cruelty to children gain the power to remove children from "unfit" families.

———— • ————

1900-1930s

Child-welfare agencies begin to supervise substitute homes more closely; the development of a separate court system for minors increases the number of children who became state wards.

1935

Title IV of the Social Security Act, "Aid to Dependent Children," involves the federal government for the first time in supporting families. The act enables more poor families to stay together.

———— • ————

1940s-1950s

The number of dependent children being cared for outside their own homes stays relatively stable while the ratio of foster children to children in institutions rises.

1960s-1970s

Growing awareness of child abuse sparks legislation requiring the reporting and investigating of all potential abusers. Foster care population skyrockets.

1961

Congress passes Title IV-A of the Social Security Act, making federal matching payments available to states for foster care of children from AFDC-eligible households.

1962

Henry Kempe's identification of the "battered-child syndrome" places child protection on the national agenda.

1974

Following the lead of the states, Congress passes the Child Abuse Prevention and Treatment Act (CAPTA), mandating that teachers, doctors and other professionals report suspected child abuse.

1977

Foster care population reaches new peak of 503,000 children.

———— • ————

1980s

Reform efforts reduce the foster care population early in the decade, but drug abuse and other problems drive numbers back up.

1980

Federal Adoption Assistance and Child Welfare Act requires child-welfare agencies to make "reasonable efforts" to keep families intact before permanently removing a child.

1990s

Reform efforts focus increasingly on promoting the adoption of foster children as a way to reduce the foster care population and end foster care "limbo."

1993

President Clinton approves $1 billion for states to undertake family-reunification efforts as part of the Omnibus Budget Reconciliation Act. Budget regulations require employers to provide health insurance for adoptive children regardless of pre-existing medical conditions.

October 1994

The Multiethnic Placement Act blocks the use of race as a determining factor in adoption placements.

1996

Congress approves a $5,000 tax credit for families that adopt a child. President Clinton directs the Department of Health and Human Services (HHS) to develop recommendations to double the number of adoptions and permanent placements of foster children by 2002.

Nov. 13, 1997

Congress passes the Adoption and Safe Families Act, which makes the health and safety of children the primary consideration in determining the disposition of neglected and abused children. It offers financial incentives to states to promote permanency planning for foster children and encourage the adoption of children who cannot return to their birth families.

Keeping Brothers and Sisters Together

As director of the Illinois Department of Children and Family Services, Gordon Johnson witnessed more than his share of human tragedy. Yet in a system so fraught with inadequacy that it was recently placed in court receivership, one problem struck him as especially hurtful, and unnecessary. Children almost always wound up being separated from their siblings, making an already traumatic situation even worse.

"When we split up brothers and sisters, we are taking away the only connection they have left to people they love," Johnson says. "This pain literally drives children crazy. The child-welfare system is supposed to help troubled children and families, not make the situations worse."

Studies have shown that foster children who are placed with their siblings display fewer emotional and behavioral problems than children who have been separated from their siblings. Moreover, they are more likely to remain in their first foster home and less likely to experience multiple placements.

In 1990 Johnson left the state agency to become president of the Jane Addams Hull House Association, a private, nonprofit social-service agency in Chicago. There he began developing a new approach to foster care designed to keep siblings together. Now up and running, the Neighbor to Neighbor program places groups of four to six siblings in foster homes in the children's own communities. It is thought to be the only program of its kind in the nation.

In the past, sibling groups were split up because agencies sought to place children in foster homes on a case-by-case basis, and few foster families were equipped to handle more than one child. The key to the Hull House program's success is professionalizing the care givers, Johnson says. Hull House not only recruits foster parents specifically for large sibling groups but also hires the primary care giver in the foster family as a regular employee of the agency, complete with salary and benefits. The pay, about $16,000 annually, is enough to enable one parent to provide full-time, focused care for the children, but not enough to attract people solely for the money.

After training, the foster parents become part of a social-services team that also includes caseworkers and therapists. Part of the care giver's job is to work with the children's birth parent, providing her with a role model and mentor and keeping her in touch with the children as she struggles to get her life in order.

Locating the foster homes in the children's own neighborhoods also limits the trauma usually involved in starting new schools, such as making new friends and becoming acclimated to new settings. Like other community-based child-welfare programs, the approach aims to strengthen the network of community supports available to troubled families, which often suffer from isolation.

"This helps the children and the natural parents, too, connecting them to established community-based organizations and programs in one place," says Isabel Blanco, Hull House's planning director. Even after children leave foster care and return to their birth parents, they are able to stay in touch with the agency.

Eighty percent of the children in Neighbor to Neighbor, which is funded by the state of Illinois, qualify as special-needs children. The average cost of the program is $102 per day per child, in line with the cost of care by specially trained foster parents but less than care in an institutional setting.

Other savings are harder to itemize. Keeping brothers and sisters under one roof reduces the number of caseworkers involved with each family as well as the number of foster homes that need to be found. And any successful placement means money saved, since statistics show that additional placements for foster children are increasingly costly.

The program also facilitates monitoring the progress of the birth parents, who not only can visit all their children in one place but also develop a relationship with the foster care giver, if they choose to. By setting up effective lines of communication, Hull House can eventually make the all-important determination about final custody for a sibling group based on long-term, sound information.

Continued from p. 10

Like many late-18th-century reformers, Brace espoused a pastoral ideal that gained much of its power as the counterpoint to increasingly crowded, sooty, immigrant-filled cities. A vehement critic of asylums, Brace transported children to farms in the West on so-called "orphan trains." Typically, the younger children were cared for as family members while the older children became farmworkers. Imbued with a religious sense of mission, the society and other child-placement agencies often recruited placement families unscreened, provided no follow-up and often swept children away from parents they deemed "unfit" with little attention to legal process.

System Evolves

In the 1880s and '90s, some agencies began to pay families for boarding young children so that they would not be forced to work. The agencies also sought homes for children who were difficult to place. Thus began a practice that, with increasing government involvement and the professionalization of social work, would develop into the modern family foster care system.

By the 1920s, "boarding out" (putting children with families that received a stipend) had all but replaced "placing out" (in which substitute care families received no pay) as the standard practice in child placement. And as child-welfare agencies began to pay for out-of-home services, they also began to supervise the homes more closely.

As other agencies, both governmental and private, began to acknowledge the existence of child abuse and neglect, the fortunes of the child-protective system and its charges became inextricably linked to public perceptions about child abuse. From the beginning, institutionalized foster care has been part of the wide range of efforts to assure safety and a basic level of well-being to dependent children. Unlike their parents, they were viewed as innocent victims who could not be held responsible for their living conditions. During the 1870s, child abuse and neglect became headline news, and societies for the prevention of cruelty to children sprang up in Eastern cities. Courts granted them powers to remove children from their families.

The increasing use of boarding out, or foster care, was closely tied to the growth of a separate court system for minors in the three decades after 1900. (*See story, p. 6.*) "The creation of a court system specifically for minors greatly increased the number of children who became state wards," wrote Hacsi. "Juvenile courts spoke a great deal about maintaining families. In practice, however, they were far more prone to remove children from their parents than to try to help the family as a whole.

"The growing involvement of government in child welfare, first at the state and later at the federal level, was a central reason for the expansion of foster care in the 20th century," he

Summie and Pamela Lott of Chicago adopted four brothers and sisters through the Hull House Association, which places children only in homes that can also accept their siblings and hires the primary care giver as a regular employee. The Lotts have two biological children and another adopted child.

continues. State boards of charity, which proliferated in the late 19th century and gained increasing power during the Progressive Era, strongly favored home placements over asylums. "The best place for a child is a good home," stated the 1906 report of California's State Board of Charities and Corrections, which believed that home placements would more effectively break all ties between "bad" parents and their children.

First Federal Legislation

The first federal legislation to affect the prevalence of foster care was Aid to Dependent Children, or Title IV of the Social Security Act, passed in 1935. For the first time, federal funds could be used to keep impoverished families together. As a result, many families "that previously would have turned to an orphan asylum or child-placement agency were able to keep their children at home," according to Hacsi. "At the same time, the increasing financial involvement of state governments in the child-welfare system meant that children were more likely to be boarded in a family than in institutions, and between 1950 and 1968 the ratio of foster children to children in institutions rose from a slight majority to a factor of three times. Yet during the 1940s and '50s, the total number of dependent children being cared for outside of their own homes stayed relatively stable, between 3.5 and 4.5 per thousand children under age 18.

Ballooning Caseloads

Federal funding for foster care first became available in significant amounts in the early 1960s. When a number of states adopted policies denying cash assistance to families considered unfit by the state, Congress in 1961 passed an amendment to the Aid to Families with Dependent Children program. AFDC made federal matching payments available to states for children who were removed from AFDC-eligible households and placed in foster care. Later amendments to the Social Security Act would also make more federal

Percentage of Minority Foster Children Rose

The percentage of minority children in foster care increased from just over 50 percent of the total in 1990 to nearly two-thirds in 1995. During the same period, the gap between black and white foster children widened by almost 10 percentage points. *

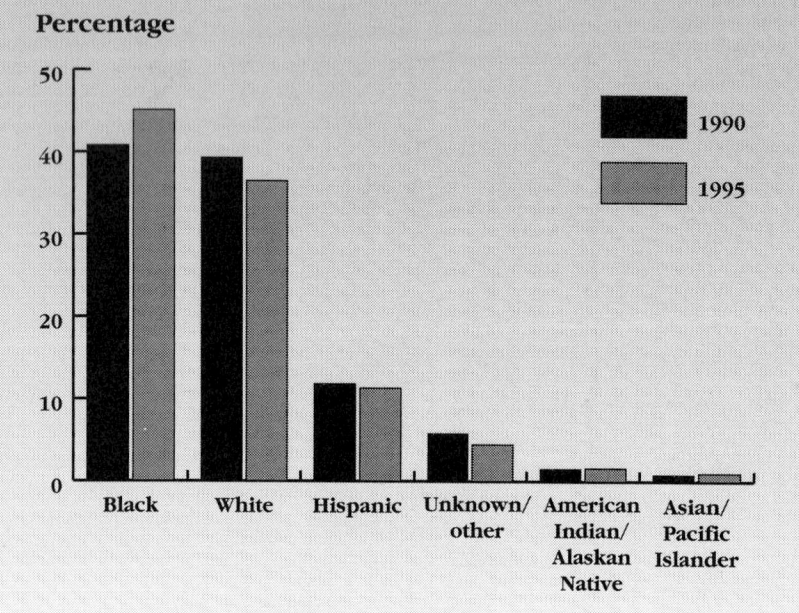

Percentage

■ 1990
■ 1995

Black   White   Hispanic   Unknown/other   American Indian/Alaskan Native   Asian/Pacific Islander

* *Based on data from 38 states representing 87.6 percent of the U.S. foster care population.*

Source: American Public Welfare Association, March 1997

money available for foster care.

In the 1960s, child abuse once again gained the public spotlight. In 1962, Henry Kempe presented a paper to the American Academy of Pediatrics in which he identified the "battered child syndrome." The American public recoiled at subsequent media images of victimized children, and by 1968 all 50 states had enacted laws that required such child-care professionals as doctors and teachers to report any suspicion of child maltreatment. [35]

Congress followed the states' lead, enacting the Child Abuse Prevention and Treatment Act (CAPTA) in 1974. In exchange for modest grants, states were required to establish the basic elements of a child-protective service system, including procedures for reporting known or suspected cases of child abuse and neglect, investigating the reports and taking immediate steps to protect children in danger. CAPTA grants have been used primarily to support child-protective service systems, although funds were authorized for community-based family resource programs as well. [36]

The availability of federal funding for foster care and the adoption of mandatory reporting laws are commonly cited as reasons for the sharp increase in the foster care population in the mid-1970s. The number of children in substitute care had averaged about 300,000 between 1962 and 1972. By 1977, it had spiked to 502,000.

As the number of children removed from their homes rose, local agencies were hard-pressed to keep up. Concerns intensified that children were being removed from their homes unnecessarily, only to languish, often in a series of foster homes, with little effort made either to reunite them with their birth families or to place them for adoption. [37] Advocates of "permanency planning" argued that foster care should be short-term and that healthy child development required a permanent home, with the child's own family, if possible, or with an adoptive family.

Action by Congress

After several years of debate, Congress in 1980 passed the Adoption Assistance and Child Welfare Act, intended to prevent unnecessary foster care placements and promote permanence for children. The bill required "reasonable efforts" to reunite children with their families and provided funding to support social services to that end.

This approach, Hacsi says, "fights against the [child-centered] ideology that has driven child placement since Charles Loring Brace's time." As a result, he says, the family preservation programs that have been implemented in many states since then have often been criticized "for keeping children with 'unfit' parents."

The 1980 act also sought to regularize state programs, requiring states to submit plans to the federal government assuring that their child-welfare and foster care programs contained certain protections for children, including requirements for specific-case plans, periodic case reviews at least every six months and a dispositional hearing within 18 months. The law transferred foster care to a new Title IV-E of the Social Security Act, which also included a new adoption assistance program to provide incentives for parents to adopt children with special needs. The law also revised an existing grant program to states for child-welfare services under Title IV-B.

Since 1980, Titles IV-B and IV-E have been amended periodically and new programs have been authorized, including grants to help states provide independent living services for older foster children, enacted in 1986, and grants to states for family preservation and family support services, enacted in 1993. But the Adoption Assistance and Child Welfare Act remained the definitive legal framework for foster care policy and planning for the next 17 years.

Deepening Crisis

After passage of the adoption assistance act, the number of children in foster care dropped precipitously. Policy and practice changes successfully reduced the number of children in out-of-home care to 262,000 in 1982, despite a continued rise in the number of reports of child abuse and neglect.[38] Yet over the last decade the number of children in foster care has surged again and is currently approaching the high of 1977, especially in urban areas.

Hacsi points to the close correlation between poverty and foster care as one cause of the increase. The purchasing power of grants to families receiving AFDC, he points out,

"has dropped dramatically since 1970. In 1990 inflation-adjusted dollars," he says, "the median monthly AFDC grant for a family of three with no other income fell from $601 in 1970 to just $364 in 1990."[39]

Other frequently cited causes are the crack epidemic and other kinds

"The child-welfare system is supposed to help troubled children and families, not make the situations worse."

— Gordon Johnson
President, Jane Addams
Hull House Association

of drug and alcohol addiction. In Los Angeles County, New York City and Philadelphia County, for example, 29 percent of preschool-age foster children in 1986 were at risk of health problems due to prenatal drug exposure; by 1991, the rate had more than doubled to 62 percent.[40] Drug abuse is associated with 80 percent of substantiated abuse and neglect cases, according to child welfare agencies.[41]

Reports of child abuse and neglect continued to rise dramatically. One study found that the number of chil-

dren reported for abuse and neglect has more than quadrupled in the last 20 years. It is generally agreed that the increase in reports of child abuse does not necessarily translate exactly into a huge increase in the actual incidence of child abuse.[42] Interestingly, as child abuse reporting has increased over time, the percentage of substantiated cases has decreased. But whether precisely true or false, the large number of reports represents a burden to child-welfare caseworkers, who must give consideration to all reports of child abuse.

Meanwhile, as the number of children in care has risen and their needs have grown more complex, data suggest that the number of foster family homes has not increased, and the capacity of these homes has grown smaller. At the same time, the states have found themselves hard-pressed to hire and retain qualified caseworkers in the face of sometimes staggering caseloads coupled with low wages.[43] The sense of crisis that pervades many child-welfare systems means that foster families often do not receive the support they need, either in money or in services, to care for troubled children.

The reason children are not moved more quickly into adoption, says Judy Meltzer, a policy analyst and senior associate with the Center for the Study of Social Policy, "is not because they're maintaining their jobs, but because they're not doing their jobs." It's very difficult to take a child into court and ask for the termination of parental rights, she explains, if no family services have been provided. "The presumption, and rightly so, always goes to the parent, and it becomes hard to prove that rights should be terminated." ∎

CURRENT SITUATION

Attempts at Reform

State and local policy-makers, goaded in part by court orders to reform, have begun to experiment with procedural changes and to propose organizational improvements to help the system function better by helping it function differently. Some agencies have attempted to promote programs of "concurrent planning," in which a child is prepared simultaneously for either family reunification or adoption or guardianship. Developing a back-up plan for a child, the thinking goes, would save time if efforts to restore the original family were unsuccessful and would help prepare the child for the transition.

In Chicago, the Jane Addams Hull House Association is attempting to improve the level of care and promote permanency by professionalizing foster parenting. (*See story, p. 12.*) A similar approach, known as "therapeutic foster care," trains foster care parents to address the mental and physical handicaps of their foster children, and pays them accordingly — still a less costly arrangement than placing children in institutional care.

Most such efforts have looked at foster care as one part of the continuum of child-welfare services — the part that kicks in when other attempts at helping a family cope have failed.

"By working with families at the front end," says Allen of the CDF, "we can preserve foster care for children who truly cannot be maintained safely at home and move them to adoption or other permanent settings in a more timely fashion." [44]

In 1993, 48 states offered some family preservation services — programs that deliver intensive services to families at risk of child abuse or neglect. Under these programs, caseworkers make frequent visits and arrange services such as training in parenting and housekeeping, transportation assistance, mental health and drug rehabilitation services and family counseling.

But federal funding for such preventive programs lags far behind the funds available for foster care. In 1981, the ratio of foster care expenditures to child-welfare services appropriations was about two to one; by 1992 the ratio was eight to one. [45]

Focus on Families

A related approach to improving the foster care system has been to examine its relationship to the communities in which troubled families live. "Community-centered responses," proponents argue, better protect children and support families as they strengthen neighborhoods.

Ultimately, they argue, family foster care services should become one part of a much-broader network of resources for children and families. That way, foster care agencies can focus on endangered children while other agencies and community services would support families struggling with temporary crises and the strains of poverty. Child welfare workers, who traditionally have been seen as figures of suspicion in many disadvantaged neighborhoods, would come to be seen more as allies.

Since 1992, the Annie E. Casey Foundation has funded pilot programs in six states to build what it calls "Family to Family foster care." According to program Director John Mattingly, the program has two key goals: identifying and working closely with foster families in the communities from which foster children are usually drawn, and training the foster families to work closely with the birth parents — family to family. When the two families are collaborators rather than antagonists, Mattingly says, more responsible decisions can be made sooner about whether or not children can return to their families, and children do not feel that they are being forced to choose.

"We felt you had to solve the placement problem first," Mattingly says. "The numbers show that a fair number of foster parents come in, but so many wash out because of the crisis the system is in. As a result, too many children are being put into institutions and with relatives who really are not suited to them, with too many left at risk because the placement system is so limited. Until there are enough good placement resources, the system will never come out of crisis."

The Edna McConnell Clark Foundation has spent the last three years working to develop programs to address problems even earlier in the child-protection process in an effort to keep children out of the foster care system. In St. Louis, Mo., Jacksonville, Fla., Louisville, Ky., and Cedar Rapids, Iowa, the goal is to reduce the incidence of child abuse and neglect by creating a network of stakeholders — parents, neighborhood residents, public and private agency staff — working together to design services and supports to keep kids safer.

Each plan, by design, is unique to its community, but all share four common themes — each a major departure from traditional child welfare agency practices:

• The activities are centered in schools or community centers within the targeted neighborhoods, so that a familiar, welcoming atmosphere encourages parents to ask for help.

• Staff are assigned to specific neighborhoods and work with other

Continued on p. 18

At Issue:

Will additional federal funding improve foster care?

JESS MCDONALD

Director, Illinois Department of Children and Family Services

FROM TESTIMONY ON BEHALF OF THE AMERICAN PUBLIC WELFARE ASSOCIATION BEFORE THE HOUSE WAYS AND MEANS HUMAN RESOURCES SUBCOMMITTEE, APRIL 8, 1997.

*t*he [proposed Adoption and Safe Families Act] appropriately asks states to do a better job of protecting child safety and providing permanency for children in the child-welfare system. It proposes a number of procedural changes to overcome some of the barriers to protecting children and providing for permanency.

We caution you not to expect that procedural changes alone will accomplish these goals. States are making administrative and policy changes, but these alone will not achieve the desired outcomes. Congress must recognize the need for resources to accomplish these goals.

State agencies alone do not make permanency decisions for children. The legal system is a partner in permanency. Congress must recognize the critical role that juvenile and family courts play in making such decisions. Parental rights are among the most sacred of rights in our country, and judges are often reluctant to terminate parental rights unless they believe that there have been efforts made and services provided to keep a family together.

We strongly support the use of Title IV-E dollars for reunification services, where safe and appropriate, for one year, in order to promote prompt permanency decisions.

These resources are critical to accomplishing the objectives of the bill to assure that states can achieve permanent and safe outcomes for children and particularly to meet any requirements for termination of parental rights. Such efforts and resources require a level of funding that currently is not adequately supported by the federal government.

States provide the bulk of such funding with their own state dollars, but such funding is not enough. Such funding should not come at the expense of other programs for vulnerable children. These proposals, in the long run, will reduce costs in the foster care system because they will result in moving children out of foster care, whether it be back safely with their families or in adoptive or other permanent placements. . . .

We recognize that . . . financing these proposals will require difficult decisions in prioritizing limited resources. However, we believe that the committee fully intends that the objectives of safety and permanency contained in this bill not just send a message but that they become a reality for vulnerable and waiting children. Thus, there must be adequate resources provided by both the states and the federal government. . . .

CONNA CRAIG AND DEREK HERBERT

President and associate director, Institute for Children

FROM "THE STATE OF THE CHILDREN: AN EXAMINATION OF GOVERNMENT-RUN FOSTER CARE," NATIONAL CENTER FOR POLICY ANALYSIS, AUGUST 1997

*f*or most of America's history, the care of parentless children was handled by private, often faith-based, entities. This was to the benefit of needy children. Privately funded organizations must prove their efficacy to stay in business; funders will cease to support a charity that is failing its constituents. By contrast, today's government-run foster care is essentially funded to fail. The system has developed into a monopoly run by state and county bureaucracies, but substantially directed through funding by the federal government. . . .

The system is expensive. In fact, Americans spend more on the foster care "industry" than we spend on Major League Baseball. This year, America will spend $12 billion on public agency (that is, government-operated) child welfare. A year in foster care costs an estimated $17,500 — not including counseling and treatment programs for biological parents or foster and adoptive-parent recruitment. . . .

The size and scope of America's public agency child-welfare system has grown exponentially in the past three decades. . . . Fewer children are leaving foster care than are coming in. For each of the years from 1983 to 1994, more children entered than exited the system. . . .

States are failing to expedite the adoption of foster children who are legally free for adoption. The federal government does not require states to finalize foster child adoptions expeditiously, and even its attempts to do so have proved impotent. For example, although the 104th Congress tried to eliminate adoption delays caused by race-matching, a social work preference for same-race adoption is still practiced in many jurisdictions. . . .

With more than 50,000 foster children legally free for adoption, a favorable attitude by a preponderance of Americans toward considering the adoption of a foster child and a large number of families seeking to adopt, why are more foster children not adopted? . . .

The system itself must bear much of the blame. . . . Both federal and state governments must reduce the barriers to adoption. . . . Further, the system must reward efforts to increase adoptions and penalize laggard performance. . . .

Child-welfare policy must shift away from reliance on government programs, toward an expanded role for the private, charitable sector. The focus should be on the well-being of children, rather than the growth of state-run programs. Since no program can ever replace the love and commitment of a caring family, the ultimate goal must be a permanent home for every one of America's children.

service providers and neighborhood residents, making it easier to refer parents to other local services.

- The partnerships draw on community members and non-traditional service providers to form a wider safety net for children. Close connections with service providers in closely related disciplines, such as substance abuse or domestic violence, enable child-protection workers to refer parents to the help they need before child abuse becomes a problem.

- Community members have prominent roles in decision-making.

"It's about trying to identify at-risk families before child abuse occurs and differentiating between those who need child-protective services and those who need some other agency," says Notkin at the Clark Foundation. "It's part of the answer. Family preservation and foster care are others."

New Adoption Law

Passage of the Adoption and Safe Families Act on Nov. 13, 1997, marked a change in federal adoption policy. As Congress adjourned for the year, the House passed the measure 406-7, and the Senate approved it by voice vote without opposition. [46]

Signed by President Clinton on Nov. 19, the bill puts more emphasis on protecting children's safety rather than uniting them with troubled families. And it would give states new financial incentives to find adoptive parents for children in foster care.

"We know that foster parents provide safe and caring families for children," Clinton said at the signing ceremony, "but the children should

not be trapped in them forever, especially when there are open arms waiting to welcome them into permanent homes.

"We have put in place here the building blocks of giving all of our children what should be their fundamental right, a chance at a decent, safe home," Clinton added.

"We know that foster parents provide safe and caring families for children, but the children should not be trapped in them forever, especially when there are open arms waiting to welcome them into permanent homes."

— President Clinton

In a similar vein, Sen. John H. Chafee, R-R.I., said, "Too often, children who cannot return to their parents wait for years in foster care before they are adopted. In today's child-welfare system, it has become a lonely and tragic wait with no end. To us, that is an unacceptable way of life for any child to have to endure."

In the House, Dave Camp, R-Mich., and Barbara B. Kennelly, D-Conn., were active in fashioning the bill. "There are tens of thousands of precious lives out there in a state of limbo," said Rep. Earl Pomeroy, D-N.D., who has two adopted children. "This legislation offers an opportunity to change that."

Rep. E. Clay Shaw Jr., R-Fla., chairman of the Ways and Means Human Resources Subcommittee, said he was

struck by the words of a 3-year-old girl in foster care when she first met her adoptive parents. "Where have you been?" she asked.

The new legislation clarifies circumstances under which states would no longer have to make "reasonable efforts" to reunite families, a requirement under the 1980 child welfare legislation. The situations include those in which a child has been subjected to "aggravated circumstances" such as abandonment, torture, chronic abuse and sexual abuse, or when the parent has killed or assaulted another child.

States would be required — unless they opted out of the provision — to run criminal records checks on any prospective foster or adoptive parents. Their application would be denied if they have had a felony conviction for child abuse or neglect, spousal abuse, crimes against children or violent crimes. In addition, states would be required to initiate actions to terminate parental rights and to begin to identify potential adoptive families once a child has been in foster care for 15 out of the last 22 months.

States would also receive a financial incentive under the act to get children out of foster care. A state would receive $4,000 for each adoption from foster care that exceeds its previous annual level. (For fiscal 1998, the amount would be the average of fiscal 1995-97.) The payment would be $6,000 for a child with disabilities. Overall federal payments for these adoption incentives would be authorized for $20 million a year for five years beginning in fiscal 1999.

The legislation also reauthorizes and revises a program designed to keep troubled families together and give early help to children at risk of being put in foster care. The Family Preservation and Support Services program — created as part of the 1993 budget-reconciliation act — would be renamed the Promoting Safe and Stable Families program. [47]

The legislation makes it clear that the program's funds can be used for activities to promote adoptions and to help reunify families for up to 15 months after a child is removed from his or her home. The program would be authorized for $875 million over three years.

"This is really the first time where federal legislation has made it clear in fact that the safety and health of children becomes the predominant national policy," said Sen. John D. Rockefeller IV, D-W.Va. ■

OUTLOOK

FOR MORE INFORMATION

American Bar Association Center on Children and the Law, 740 15th St., N.W., 9th Floor, Washington, D.C. 20005; (202) 662-1720. The center has produced numerous studies of the family- and juvenile court systems and works with states to implement improvements.

American Public Welfare Association, 810 First St., N.E., Suite 500, Washington, D.C. 20002; (202) 682-0100. The APWA develops national social policy positions on behalf of state and local human services agencies and individuals in the field.

Center for the Study of Social Policy, 1250 I St., N.W., Suite 503, Washington, D.C. 20005; (202) 371-1565. The center has been a leader in the study and promotion of child-welfare reform at all levels of government.

Children's Defense Fund, 25 E St., N.W., Washington, D.C. 20001; (202) 628-8787. CDF represents the interests of children, particularly poor and minority children, in national debates about family policy, health care, education and related issues.

Institute for Children, 18 Brattle St., Cambridge, Mass. 02123; (617) 868-4000. The IFC is dedicated to reshaping foster care and adoption policies in America and the United Kingdom.

National Council for Adoption, 1930 17th St., N.W., Washington, D.C. 20009; (202) 328-1200. In addition to assisting would-be adoptive parents, the council tracks legislation and advocates pro-adoption policies.

Sense of Optimism

With passage of the Adoption and Safe Families Act, America's foster care and child protective systems entered a new phase, if not a new era. Regulations must be written, and much will depend on the ways state and county agencies choose to implement them.

The passage in 1996 of a historic welfare reform law, which provided block grants to the states to create their own welfare programs, is also expected to place new, but as yet unclear, stresses on the foster care system. Among other things, the sweeping new law reduces entitlement payments to families and places some limits on reimbursements for foster care and adoption. [48]

Yet the very fact of the new adoption law's passage suggests a sense of optimism in the face of staggering problems. "The bipartisan congressional attention, coupled with the reforms and innovative practices being undertaken around the country, present us with an unprecedented opportunity to make a real difference in the lives of some of America's most vulnerable children," said Olivia A. Golden, acting assistant secretary for children and families at HHS. [49]

And there is some evidence that recent reform efforts are working. In Illinois, between June 1986 and June 1995, the substitute-care population expanded at an average annual rate of 15 percent, from 13,734 children to 47,862 children, McDonald said. Since July 1995, through a variety of legislative and administrative changes, the annual caseload growth has been held below 5 percent. [50]

The response to community-based care initiatives has been enthusiastic, as well. "The early experience has been very positive," says Meltzer of the Center for the Study of Social Policy. And the Family to Family initiative of the Casey Foundation, she says, "has shown really positive results."

A community-based, network approach to child welfare services has been endorsed by Nicholas Scoppetta, the head of New York City's huge child-welfare agency. A similar effort in Los Angeles has reduced the number of children being put into foster care in one of the city's poorest neighborhoods. [51]

Whether or not adoptions can be increased enough significantly to reduce the foster care population is now unanswerable, but evidence suggests that concerted efforts to promote adoption can yield results. Craig points to the Children with AIDS Project in Phoenix, Ariz., as evidence that no child is unadoptable. The organization has recruited more than 1,000 parents to adopt AIDS orphans and HIV-positive babies. [52]

Numerous states have already increased their adoption rates, according to letters from their governors to HHS Secretary Donna E. Shalala. Florida reports increasing adoption rates by more than 80 percent over the past five years. Maryland reports an increase of at least 15 percent in 1995, Michigan an 18 percent increase between fiscal 1995 and '96.[53]

Yet the challenges remain complex, and the answers require equally complex solutions. "You've got to work with the families, because the state cannot be grabbing children and deciding it likes some other family better," says Nancy Smith, the Washington foster parent and activist.

But for all the emotional and sentimental reasons that exist for trying to address the problems of troubled children effectively, there is also simple economics. "It's so much cheaper to address the problems early," Smith says, "than to have kids go down the tubes and end up in jail." ■

Rachel S. Cox is a freelance writer in Washington, D.C.

Notes

[1] For background, see "Adoption," *The CQ Researcher*, Nov. 26, 1993, pp. 1033-1056.
[2] Department of Health and Human Services, Administration for Children and Families, "Adoption 2002: A Response to the Presidential Executive Memorandum on Adoption Issued Dec. 14, 1996," February 1997, p. 5.
[3] Conna Craig and Derek Herbert, "The State of the Children: An Examination of Government-Run Foster Care," National Center for Policy Analysis, August 1997, p. 11.
[4] Department of Health and Human Services, *op. cit.*, p. 5.
[5] *Ibid.*
[6] Craig and Herbert, *op. cit.*, p. 9. Herbert is associate director of the Institute for Children.
[7] For background, see "Foster Care Crisis," *The CQ Researcher*, Sept. 27, 1991, pp. 705-

729.
[8] Karen Spar, "Adoption, Foster Care and Child Welfare: Issues for Congress," Congressional Research Service, Feb. 5, 1997, p. 2.
[9] Craig and Herbert, *op. cit.*, p. 4.
[10] *The New York Times*, Sept. 8, 1996, p. A1.
[11] Jeffrey L. Katz, "President Expected To Sign Foster Care Adoption Bill," *CQ Weekly Report*, Nov. 15, 1997, p. 2858.
[12] *The Christian Science Monitor*, Dec. 23, 1996.
[13] Testimony before House Ways and Means Human Resources Subcommittee, April 8, 1997.
[14] *Ibid.*
[15] *Ibid.*
[16] See Mary-Lou Weisman, "When Parents are not in the Best Interests of the Child," *The Atlantic Monthly*, July 1994.
[17] Testimony before House Ways and Means Human Resources Subcommittee, April 8, 1997.
[18] Richard D. Barth, "Effects of Age and Race on the Odds of Adoption versus Remaining in Long-Term Out-of-Home Care," *Child Welfare*, March/April 1997, p. 285.
[19] Mark F. Testa, et al, "Permanency Planning Options for Children in Formal Kinship Care," *Child Welfare*, September/October, 1996, p. 466.
[20] Testimony before House Ways and Means Human Resources Subcommittee, April 8, 1997.
[21] Sen. Cranston's remarks were quoted by Allen in her testimony before the House Ways and Means Human Resources Subcommittee, April 8, 1997.
[22] Testimony before House Ways and Means Human Resources Subcommittee, April 8, 1997.
[23] Quoted in *Los Angeles Times*, May 23, 1996, p. E1.
[24] Craig and Herbert, *op. cit.*, p. 6.
[25] Quoted in *The New York Times*, Oct. 6, 1996, p. D14.
[26] Elizabeth Oppenheim, "Adoption Assistance," *Public Welfare*, winter 1996, pp. 8-9. Oppenheim is project manager for the Interstate Compact on Adoption and Medical Assistance at the American Public Welfare Association.
[27] Testimony before House Ways and Means Human Resources Subcommittee, April 8, 1997.
[28] Department of Health and Human Services, *op. cit.*, p. i.
[29] Craig and Herbert, *op. cit.*, p. ii.
[30] Monitoring Project at Kansas Action for

Children, "Welfare Reform and Child Welfare Services: Changes in Public Policy and the Implications for Children and Families," October 1997, pp. 26-27.
[31] Quoted in *Lawrence Journal-World*, Nov. 8, 1997.
[32] Kansas Chapter of the National Association of Social Workers, "Kansans Talk Back: Early Responses to the Move to Privatization of Child Welfare Services," October 1997, p. 1.
[33] Quoted in in *Lawrence Journal World*, Nov. 8, 1997.
[34] Unless otherwise noted, information in this section is from Tim Hacsi, "From Indenture to Family Foster Care: A Brief History of Child Placing," *Child Welfare*, January/February 1995, pp. 162-179.
[35] Frank Farrow, with the Executive Session on Child Protection, "Child Protection: Building Community Partnerships, Getting From Here to There," John F. Kennedy School of Government, Harvard University, 1997, p. 4.
[36] Spar, *op. cit.*, p. 12.
[37] *Ibid.*, p. 11.
[38] *Ibid.*
[39] Hacsi, *op. cit.*, p. 176.
[40] U.S. General Accounting Office, "Child Welfare: Complex Needs Strain Capacity to Provide Services," September 1995.
[41] Spar, *op. cit.*, p. 6.
[42] *Ibid*, pp. 3-4.
[43] U.S. General Accounting Office, *op. cit.*, p. 19.
[44] Testimony before House Ways and Means Human Resources Subcommittee, April 8, 1997.
[45] U.S. General Accounting Office, "Foster Care: Services to Prevent Out-of-Home Placements Are Limited by Funding Barriers," June 1993.
[46] Unless otherwise noted, information in this section is from Katz, *op. cit.*
[47] For background, see the *1993 CQ Almanac*, p. 377.
[48] For background, see *1996 CQ Almanac*, p. 6-13.
[49] Testimony before House Ways and Means Human Resources Subcommittee, April 8, 1997.
[50] *Ibid.*
[51] *The New York Times*, Sept. 8, 1996, p. A1.
[52] Craig and Herbert, *op. cit.*, p. 14.
[53] Department of Health and Human Services, *op. cit.*, Appendix e.

Bibliography

Selected Sources Used

Books

Harnack, Andrew, *Adoption: Opposing Viewpoints,* Greenhaven Press, 1995.

This compendium of articles and excerpts explores a range of issues connected with adoption and foster care.

Palmer, Sally E., *Maintaining Family Ties: Inclusive Practice in Foster Care,* Child Welfare League of America, 1995.

This empirical study by a professor of social work at McMaster University in Ontario, Canada, examines how child-welfare workers help children address separation issues.

Articles

Barth, Richard D., "Effects of Age and Race on the Odds of Adoption versus Remaining in Long-Term Out-of-Home Care," *Child Welfare,* March/April 1997.

Among the many nuggets of information in this scholarly treatment of adoption rates is the finding that the likelihood of adoption is four times lower for black children than for whites.

Hacsi, Tim, "From Indenture to Family foster Care: A Brief History of Child Placing," *Child Welfare,* January/February 1995, pp. 162-179.

In tracing the history of out-of-home child placements in America, Hacsi illuminates issues and trends that have characterized treatment of the subject for two centuries.

Hardin, Mark, "Responsibilities and Effectiveness of the Juvenile Court in Handling Dependency Cases," *The Future of Children,* winter 1996.

Hardin analyzes why courts unevenly fulfill their legal mandates to monitor child-protection services and considers the prospects for improvement.

Oppenheim, Elizabeth, "Adoption Assistance," *Public Welfare,* winter 1996, pp. 8-9.

Oppenheim, an adoption project manager at the American Public Welfare Association, describes the federal and state laws that fund adoption assistance.

Weisman, Mary-Lou, "When Parents are not in the Best Interests of the Child," *The Atlantic Monthly,* July 1994, pp. 43-63.

The author surveys the group-care facilities that have replaced traditional orphanages and finds them good.

Reports and Studies

Center for the Study of Social Policy, "Community Partnerships for Protecting Children: Documentation of the First Year," Edna McConnell Clark Foundation, April 1997.

This report documents efforts to set up communitywide networks to help foster caregivers and children in St. Louis, Mo., Jacksonville, Fla., Cedar Rapids, Iowa, and Louisville, Ky.

Davis, Noy S., and Susan J. Wells, (eds.), "Justice Systems' Processing of Child Abuse and Neglect Cases: Executive Summary," American Bar Association Center on children and the Law, et al, February 1996.

In summarizing a comprehensive examination of child-abuse and neglect cases in the courts, the authors highlight the problem of coordinating law enforcement and child-protective services and the difficulty of case-tracking.

Hardin, Mark, "Judicial Implementation of Permanency Planning Reform: One Court that Works," ABA Center on Children and the Law and National Conference of Special Court Judges, 1992.

This detailed analysis of the Hamilton County Juvenile Court in Ohio shows how the role of the judiciary in foster care and child-custody planning has expanded since 1980 and how one court system has adapted effectively.

Additional Reports

Spar, Karen, "Adoption, Foster Care, and Child Welfare: Issues for Congress," Congressional Research Service, Feb. 5, 1997.

U.S. Department of Health and Human Services, Administration for Children and Families, "Adoption 2002: A Response to the Presidential Executive Memorandum on Adoption Issued Dec. 14, 1996," February 1997.

U.S. General Accounting Office, "Child Welfare: Complex Needs Strain Capacity to Provide Services," September 1995.

U.S. General Accounting Office, "Foster Care: Services to Prevent Out-of-Home Placements Are Limited by Funding Barriers," June 1993.

Waldfogel, Jane, "Toward a New Paradigm for Child Protective Services," Malcolm Wiener Center for Social Policy, John F. Kennedy School of Government, Harvard University, April 1996.

The Next Step

Additional information from UMI's Newspaper & Periodical Abstracts™ database

Children's Welfare

Bradley, Latasha J., "Neglected children to be focus of child welfare group," *Chicago Defender,* April 24, 1997, p. 4.

In an effort to support President Clinton's Summit for America's Future, 100 voluntary agencies of the Child Care Association of Illinois announced a plan to aid thousands of neglected children by finding them permanent living arrangements.

Firestone, David, "Giuliani is forming a new city agency on child welfare," *The New York Times,* Jan. 12, 1996, p. A1.

Declaring the protection of children a paramount priority for the second half of his term Mayor Rudolph W. Giuliani, R-N.Y., on Jan. 11, 1996, pulled the troubled Child Welfare Administration out of New York City's welfare bureaucracy and created a new department to be run by Nicholas Scoppetta, a close friend who will report directly to him. The newly formed agency, to be known as the Administration for Children's Services, will be responsible for the city's foster care and child-protection programs.

Pear, Robert, "Many states fail to meet mandates on child welfare," *The New York Times,* March 17, 1996, p. A1.

According to court records, at least 21 states are under court supervision for failing to take proper care of children who had been abused or neglected, and many of them have flouted their obligations even after promising in legal settlements to protect the constitutional rights of foster children.

Smith, Robert, "Managed child welfare: Kansas breaks new ground," *Behavioral Health Management,* March 1997, pp. 22-23.

A managed-care partnership to improve Medicaid-funded foster care among the state of Kansas and two major private agencies — the Salvation Army and Value Behavioral Health — is demonstrating how public and private agencies can collaborate in providing improved social services on a managed-care basis.

Swarns, Rachel L., "Child Welfare Gets Extra Aid For This Year," *The New York Times,* Sept. 2, 1997, p. B1.

New York City's child welfare system will receive an additional $22.7 million in combined city, state and federal aid this year to ease a shortage of beds in foster care that had forced more than 1,000 children to sleep on office floors since January, city officials said yesterday.

Tyson, Ann Scott, "Kansas Pioneers a Solution to Child-Welfare Woes," *The Christian Science Monitor,* Aug. 15, 1997, p. 1.

This spring, Kansas became the first state in the country to privatize its child-welfare system, contracting out all adoption, foster care and family-preservation services to private agencies. The primary goal of the reform is to cut the time abused or neglected children spend outside of permanent homes

Family Preservation

Danzy, Julia, and Sondra M. Jackson, "Family preservation and support services: A missed opportunity for kinship care," *Child Welfare,* January 1997, pp. 31-44.

The historical significance of kinship care in preserving the African-American family, the development of kinship care and family preservation programs and the importance of the natural relationship between kinship care and family preservation services are discussed.

Murphy, Patrick, "Family preservation and its victims," *The New York Times,* June 19, 1993, p. A21.

Murphy criticizes so-called family preservation programs that give aid to often abusive and drug-addicted parents in order to keep children at home instead of in foster care.

"States' progress in implementing family preservation and support services," *Spectrum: The Journal of State Government,* spring 1997, pp. 6-9.

A Government Accounting Office survey found states are using federal funds successfully to increase the availability of family preservation and family support services. Early indicators show the programs have achieved positive outcomes.

Thieman, Alice A., and Paula W. Dail, "Predictors of out-of-home placement in a family preservation program: Are welfare recipients particularly vulnerable?" *Policy Studies Journal,* spring 1997, pp. 124-139.

Thieman and Dail examined the relationship between poverty and out-of-home placements in a family preservation program, which was designed specifically to avoid such placements.

Walton, Elaine, "Enhancing investigative decisions in child welfare: An exploratory use of intensive family preservation services," *Child Welfare,* May 1997, pp. 447-461.

Investigative decisions in a child-welfare agency were enhanced by the use of brief, intensive, family preservation services. Almost from the moment of referral, personnel worked with child-protection investigators to assess the needs and resources of families in crisis and to effectuate viable management plans.

Wells, Kathleen, and Elizabeth Tracy, "Reorienting intensive family preservation services in relation to public child welfare practice," *Child Welfare,* **November 1996, pp. 667-692.**

Family preservation has been supported as a policy, an approach to service delivery and a program model, but sufficient knowledge has accumulated to warrant reconsidering the use of intensive family preservation programs in public child welfare practice. The prevention of placement should be abandoned, and a new rationale should be developed.

Shortage of Foster Homes

Anderson, Ed, "La. Might Be Forced to Send Foster Children Out of State," *Times-Picayune,* **Oct. 9, 1997, p. A25.**

Louisiana officials may have to once again resort to placing children who need foster care in out-of-state homes because the state is not providing adequate financing. The costs of placing children have escalated because 85 to 90 percent of the children placed in foster care now have special problems. Many have mental and physical handicaps; others have drug-addicted mothers.

Bivins, Larry, "Thousands languish in foster care: Michigan ranks 19th in placing children; nearly two-thirds are not adopted into permanent homes," *Detroit News,* **Aug. 8, 1997, p. A1.**

Michigan failed to find permanent homes last year for almost two-thirds of the foster care children available for adoption in the state, according to a new study released Thursday. The state's 36.6 percent adoption rate ranked 19th among the 50 states and the District of Columbia.

Kiernan, Louis, "David S. Liederman, Child-Welfare Expert," *Chicago Tribune,* **Nov. 16, 1997, Sec. 2, p. 3.**

On Thursday, Congress passed a bill to speed up adoptions for children and give states bonuses for placing them with adoptive families. Child-welfare experts have praised the bill, but they also worry that the fallout from welfare reform will push another wave of children into the already overloaded foster care system.

Swarns, Rachel L., "Foster Care System Is So Strained, Children Sleep in Agency Offices," *The New York Times,* **June 12, 1997, p. A1.**

Hundreds of New York City's most troubled children are stranded in city offices, psychiatric hospitals and private homes because the child welfare system is virtually filled to capacity.

Special Needs

Pierre, Robert E., "Maryland Seeks to Boost Adop-

tions of Black Boys; Rising Number of Foster Care Children Spurs State to Add Its Voice to National Efforts," *The Washington Post,* **June 30, 1997, p. B3.**

Alarmed by the fast-growing number of children in foster care, Maryland officials plan to begin an aggressive campaign today to encourage adoption of young black boys, who account for more than half the children statewide awaiting placement in new homes. African-American boys are so difficult to place that they are part of the "special needs" category, which also includes older children, multiple siblings and children with physical and emotional problems.

Rainey, James, "Action Urged on Homes for Troubled Youths; Shelter Advocates call on L.A. County to expedite separation of the emotionally disturbed from delinquents," *Los Angeles Times,* **Oct. 14, 1997, p. B1.**

In the aftermath of a child's death last week at MacLaren Children's Center, advocates for foster children are urging an acceleration in plans to separate juvenile delinquents, the emotionally disturbed and victims of child abuse, who are now housed together at the county children's shelter.

Teenagers

Carey, Anne R., and Suzy Parker, "Home away from home," *USA Today,* **Oct. 27, 1997, p. A1.**

About 500,000 children under 18 are in out-of-home or foster care, a rate of 6.3 per 1,000 kids (vs. 4.9 in 1990). States with the highest rate of kids in out-of-home care are depicted in a graph.

Esparza, Santiago, "Agency finds homes where teens can get help: Spectrum's youths are usually wards of juvenile court," *Detroit News,* **Aug. 20, 1997, p. A8.**

Spectrum Human Services is one of the state's largest nonprofit organizations helping troubled youths and young adults. Teens placed in Spectrum's custody usually are wards of a juvenile court, and the private agency finds group homes where they can receive counseling while waiting to rejoin their families.

"Transition, Not Abandonment; L.A. County program is a boon to ex-foster care youths," *Los Angeles Times,* **July 28, 1997, p. B4.**

Going out on one's own is tough for anyone, but especially for the 1,000 young people who annually leave the Los Angeles County foster care system. Their early years are difficult; the overburdened system often has no choice but to shift children from one foster home or foster care facility to another. So when they are emancipated at 18, many find it hard to cope with newfound freedom. Officials say almost half end up on the streets within six months.

Back Issues

Great Research on Current Issues Starts Right Here ... Recent topics covered by The CQ Researcher are listed below. Before May 1991, reports were published under the name of Editorial Research Reports.

JUNE 1996
Rethinking NAFTA
First Ladies
Teaching Values
Labor Movement's Future

JULY 1996
Recovered-Memory Debate
Native Americans' Future
Crackdown on Sexual Harassment
Attack on Public Schools

AUGUST 1996
Fighting Over Animal Rights
Privatizing Government Services
Child Labor and Sweatshops
Cleaning Up Hazardous Wastes

SEPTEMBER 1996
Gambling Under Attack
The States and Federalism
Civic Journalism
Reassessing Foreign Aid

OCTOBER 1996
Political Consultants
Insurance Fraud
Rethinking School Integration
Parental Rights

Back issues are available for $5.00 (subscribers) or $10.00 (non-subscribers). Quantity discounts apply to orders over ten. To order, call Congressional Quarterly Customer Service at (202) 887-8621.

Binders are available for $18.00. To order call 1-800-638-1710. Please refer to stock number 648.

NOVEMBER 1996
Global Warming
Clashing Over Copyright
Consumer Debt
Governing Washington, D.C.

DECEMBER 1996
Welfare, Work and the States
The New Volunteerism
Implementing the Disabilities Act
America's Pampered Pets

JANUARY 1997
Combating Scientific Misconduct
Restructuring the Electric Industry
The New Immigrants
Chemical and Biological Weapons

FEBRUARY 1997
Assisting Refugees
Alternative Medicine's Next Phase
Independent Counsels
Feminism's Future

MARCH 1997
New Air Quality Standards
Alcohol Advertising
Civic Renewal
Educating Gifted Students

APRIL 1997
Declining Crime Rates
The FBI Under Fire
Gender Equity in Sports
Space Program's Future

MAY 1997
The Stock Market
The Cloning Controversy
Expanding NATO
The Future of Libraries

JUNE 1997
FDA Reform
China After Deng
Line-Item Veto
Breast Cancer

JULY 1997
Transportation Policy
Executive Pay
School Choice Debate
Aggressive Driving

AUGUST 1997
Age Discrimination
Banning Land Mines
Children's Television
Evolution vs. Creationism

SEPTEMBER 1997
Caring for the Dying
Mental Health Policy
Mexico's Future
Youth Fitness

OCTOBER 1997
Urban Sprawl in the West
Diversity in the Workplace
Teacher Education
Contingent Work Force

NOVEMBER 1997
Renewable Energy
Artificial Intelligence
Religious Persecution
Roe v. Wade at 25

DECEMBER 1997
Whistleblowers
Castro's Next Move
Gun Control Standoff
Regulating Nonprofits

Future Topics

▶ *IRS Reform*

▶ *The Black Middle Class*

▶ *U.S.-British Relations*

THE CQ Researcher

PUBLISHED BY CONGRESSIONAL QUARTERLY INC.

IRS Reform

Is the tax-collection agency really so bad?

T
he Internal Revenue Service is under
bipartisan attack, as both political parties
prepare to exploit Americans' hostility toward
taxes to win votes in coming elections. After
taxpayers related stories of IRS abuses at congressional
hearings last September, the House overwhelmingly
passed a bill to restructure the agency and give taxpayers
more clout in dealing with it; Senate passage is expected
early this year. Despite initial reservations, the White
House endorsed the measure when House Democrats
jumped aboard the anti-IRS bandwagon. Most tax experts,
however, say the real problem is not the IRS, but the
complex tax code the agency must enforce. Tax-reform
proposals, chiefly a flat tax on income and a national
sales tax, are coming under renewed discussion.

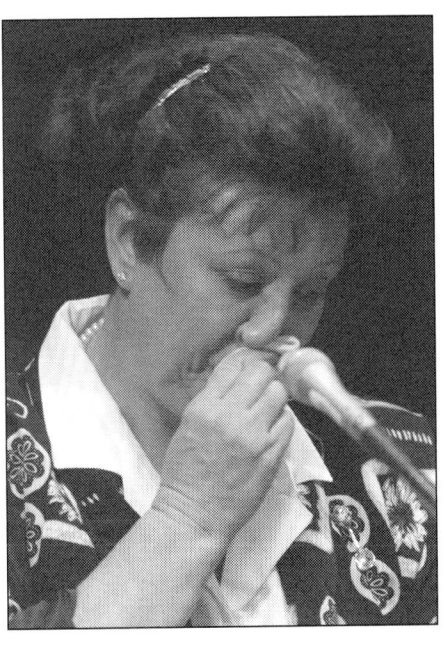

C Q   **Jan. 16, 1998** • **Volume 8, No. 2** • **Pages 25-48**

Formerly Editorial Research Reports

CQ Researcher

January 16, 1998
Volume 8, No. 2

EDITOR
Sandra Stencel

MANAGING EDITOR
Thomas J. Colin

ASSOCIATE EDITOR
Sarah M. Magner

STAFF WRITERS
Mary H. Cooper
Kenneth Jost
David Masci

PRODUCTION EDITOR
Melissa Hall

EDITORIAL ASSISTANT
Vanessa E. Furlong

PUBLISHED BY
Congressional Quarterly Inc.

CHAIRMAN
Andrew Barnes

VICE CHAIRMAN
Andrew P. Corty

PRESIDENT AND PUBLISHER
Robert W. Merry

EXECUTIVE EDITOR
David Rapp

The CQ Researcher (ISSN 1056-2036). Formerly Editorial Research Reports. Published weekly, except Jan. 2, May 29, July 3, Oct. 30, by Congressional Quarterly Inc., 1414 22nd St., N.W., Washington, D.C. 20037. Annual subscription rate for libraries, businesses and government is $340. Additional rates furnished upon request. Periodicals postage paid at Washington, D.C., and additional mailing offices. POSTMASTER: Send address changes to The CQ Researcher, 1414 22nd St., N.W., Washington, D.C. 20037.

COVER: DURING SEPTEMBER HEARINGS ON IRS ABUSES, NANCY JACOBS OF BAKERSFIELD, CALIF., TOLD THE SENATE FINANCE COMMITTEE THAT SHE AND HER HUSBAND PAID THE IRS $11,000 THEY DID NOT OWE TO END ENFORCEMENT ACTIONS THAT COULD HAVE CLOSED HER HUSBAND'S OPTOMETRY PRACTICE. (GARY CAMERON/REUTERS)

IRS Reform

BY MARY H. COOPER

THE ISSUES

For two years after her divorce, Katharine Lund was "financially destitute." But slowly, life began to turn around for her and her 12-year-old daughter, she told senators last September.

"I had just managed to get an apartment — a real home for the two of us," Lund testified. Then she learned she owed the IRS $3,500 on the last tax return she had filed with her former husband, in 1983. Lund was earning just $15,000 as a new bank employee, but she immediately sought to pay off the bill.

Her effort to settle, however, launched her on a decade-long journey through bureaucratic hell. When Lund tried to pay the bill, she was told she owed nothing, then later was assessed $8,000 and still later faced liens on her property after the IRS misplaced her check. Lund's second husband even filed for divorce to escape levies on his salary resulting from the agency's errors.

"For over 10 years the IRS has conducted itself as a legalized extortion operation willing to commit abusive acts to collect money, even that which they know is not owed," Lund told the lawmakers. "It is a disgrace to our nation that an arm of our democratic government is allowed to behave as if it were an extension of a police state. I hope that Congress can act to end this national shame." [1]

Lund was among several taxpayers who told the Senate Finance Committee about IRS abuses they had suffered.* The stories were corrobo-

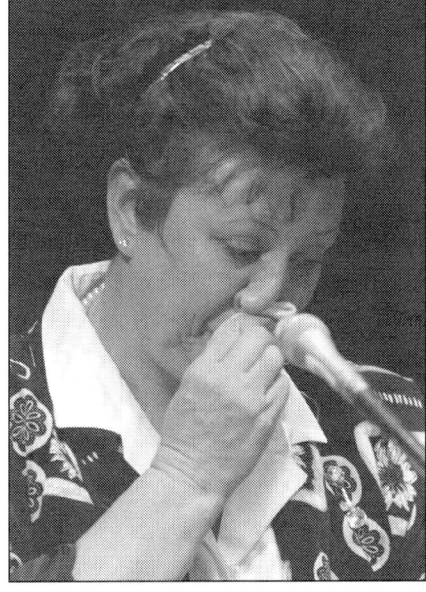

rated by several IRS employees, who testified from behind screens to protect their identity. The hearings unleashed a barrage of attacks against the tax-collection agency, fueled by intensive media coverage, including a report by CBS' "60 Minutes."

According to a *USA Today*/Gallup Poll taken a week after the hearings, 69 percent of Americans believe the IRS "frequently abuses its powers," while just 27 percent think the agency generally uses power responsibly. In addition, nearly three-quarters of the respondents said the IRS has more power than it needs, and 15 percent felt they had been treated unfairly in direct dealings with the agency. [2]

"There are two kinds of taxpayers," says Michael J. Graetz, a law professor at Yale University Law School and author of the 1997 book *The Decline (and Fall?) of the Income Tax*. "You get those who are mad at the IRS because they've been audited and are subject to heavy interest and penalties. And you get taxpayers who never hear from the IRS but are confident that everybody else is getting away with something."

In the wake of the attacks, defenders of the agency quickly backed off. The Clinton White House had initially opposed some provisions of a bill to restructure the IRS, introduced by Rep. Rob Portman, R-Ohio. Treasury Secretary Robert E. Rubin warned that the bill's creation of an oversight board composed largely of private citizens would lead to conflicts of interest. After House Minority Leader Richard A. Gephardt, D-Mo. — a likely challenger to Vice President Al Gore for the Democratic presidential nomination in 2000 — threw his support to the bill, however, the White House quickly withdrew its opposition. On Nov. 5, the House passed the Internal Revenue Service Restructuring and Reform Act on a nearly unanimous 426-4 vote. A stronger version is expected to be approved by the Senate early this year.

The House bill incorporates some of the recommendations made last summer by the bipartisan National Commission on Restructuring the Internal Revenue Service. The measure seeks to make the IRS more "customer-friendly" and features a "taxpayer's bill of rights" aimed at strengthening the taxpayer's hand when faced with an audit. Among other things, the bill would shift the burden of proof in court proceedings from the taxpayer to the IRS.

"What this is is really the Republicans and Democrats coming together to respond to the very clear signal we're getting from our constituents that it's time to fix this system," Portman said. "This is basically an attempt to make the IRS much more taxpayer-friendly. And there are a lot of things we can do in the area of taxpayer rights . . . in the area of making the IRS work better in terms of answering the phones, having the computer system work and so on to improve its service to the taxpayer. That's the foundation of this bill. It's

---

* Lund said that after Sen. William V. Roth Jr., R-Del., intervened on her behalf, the IRS released the liens against her and returned the $3,500 she had paid earlier.

A Statistical Profile of the IRS, 1996

Revenue collected: **$1,486,546,674,000**

Number of tax returns: **208,938,000***

Tax paid, per capita: **$5,586**

Refunds issued: **88,281,474**

Total amount of refunds (including interest):
   $131,056,307,000

Operating cost of agency: **$7,305,604,000**
 • *Cost of collecting $100:* **49 cents**

Percent of total returns audited: **1.38**
 • *Percent of returns audited resulting in disputed penalties:* **3.8**
 • *Average penalty and tax, per return audited (individuals):* **$3,915**
 • *Average penalty and tax, per return audited (corporations):*
    $300,155

Number of employees: **102,082**
 • *Special agents for fraud investigations:* **3,352**
 • *Revenue agents for return examinations:* **15,153**

Legal actions against employees: **58**
 • *Number found guilty:* **32**

Administrative actions against employees: **586**
 • *Number penalized:* **350**

* *Includes individual and corporate returns*

Source: 1996 IRS Data Book

really a good, common-sense approach." [3]

From a political standpoint, the controversy could hardly have come at a better time for House Speaker Newt Gingrich, R-Ga., and other Republicans. In early 1997, Republicans had won passage of a balanced-budget agreement and tax-cutting legislation — both longstanding GOP goals. As a result, they were seeking a new issue, one that would galvanize voter support not only for Republican candidates in last fall's elections but also in this year's midterm congressional contests and the presidential election of 2000.

"When you have agreements on a balanced budget and a lot of other things, you run low on issues," says Donald C. Alexander, a Washington tax attorney who served as IRS commissioner during the Nixon, Ford and Carter administrations. "But if you demonize the IRS, you've got an automatic winner. And it certainly worked that way when Mr. Gephardt folded his tent and suddenly agreed to the restructuring bill. Mr. Gore, of course, had to do the same thing. In the end, four brave souls voted against the bill."

The IRS is only one target of the Republican anti-tax strategy, however. In October, just weeks before the House vote to restructure the agency, two leading GOP legislators launched their "Scrap the Code" campaign to replace the current federal income tax system with a simpler and reputedly fairer method of collecting revenue. The campaign is built around a good-natured debate between House Majority Leader Dick Armey, R-Texas, and Rep. W.J. "Billy" Tauzin, R-La. Armey, in his trademark cowboy boots, tells audiences he supports a flat tax that would enable taxpayers to file their returns on a post card. Tauzin wants to replace the income tax with a national sales tax.

In the view of former Rep. Jack Kemp, R-N.Y., a GOP presidential hopeful in 2000, the flat tax and sales tax both address the problem of high taxes. "If you bring down the top tax rate from where it is today at 39.6 percent, imposed by the president and the Democratic Party, you'll get a bigger pie, more revenue," he said Jan. 11 on NBC's "Meet the Press." "And you will actually help the poor, because the single greatest need in America, particularly in our nation's inner cities, [is] more jobs, and jobs cannot come from people who are taxed on the formation of the capital, of the seed corn, necessary to make America more enterprising on the eve of the 21st century."

William Gale, an economist and tax expert at the Brookings Institution, takes a dim view of Tauzin and Armey's efforts. "I think it's fair to say that there's no policy area in the country where the gap between rhetoric and reality is larger than in tax policy," he says. "This Scrap the Code tour is a good example. The things that are being proposed are patently ludicrous, and the sales tax and the flat tax aren't anywhere close to the only options."

But GOP strategists are betting that anti-tax fervor runs so deep in the American psyche that the mere call for changing the status quo is enough to win votes. Nowhere did this analysis prove more accurate than in last fall's gubernatorial election in Virginia, where Republican James S. Gilmore III won in a landslide on the strength of four words — No More Car Tax!

The extent to which Virginia voters accepted Gilmore's slogan at face value became clear shortly after the election, when personal-property tax assessments began arriving in the mail. As irate callers to tax offices made clear, many voters hadn't understood that the car tax would remain in force for five more years under Gilmore's phase-out plan, or that the state General Assembly would have to approve the plan before it could take effect.

The same level of misinformation threatens to cloud meaningful debate over federal tax issues, Gale says. "Tax reform — how a society chooses to tax itself — is a really important issue, and we should talk about it," he says. "But it would be nice if the debate could get on the level of fact, or at least something close to fact, so people could start making some informed choices."

As lawmakers and taxpayers consider the drive to restructure the IRS — the first major proposal to change the federal tax system — these are some of the questions they should ask.

Does the Internal Revenue Service deserve its reputation for abusing taxpayers?

The September Senate hearings provided a highly publicized platform for some of the strongest condemnations of the agency ever heard in one forum. "I have never seen overall morale in the IRS as low as it is right now," an IRS employee testified anonymously. "It appears that management is more concerned about maintaining high statistics than with the quality of work being performed, or even whether the taxes were collected, or were just written off." [4]

In the words of former IRS historian Shelley Davis, the IRS is "an agency composed of bureaucrats, career bureaucrats who have spent their

Taxpayer Katharine Lund told lawmakers last September the IRS behaved "as if it were an extension of a police state."

Reuters

careers learning how to spin IRS arrogance and abuse into an impenetrable defensive shield, who have learned how to hide behind the privacy laws that are meant to protect taxpayers to protect only themselves." [5]

And there was this opening salvo from Senate Finance Committee Chairman William V. Roth Jr., R-Del.: "There is no other agency in this country that touches the lives of more Americans, nor strikes more fear into their hearts. The threat of an audit, the awesome power of the IRS, looms like the sword of Damocles over the heads of taxpayers." [6]

Critics also accuse IRS management for allowing, if not encouraging, abuse of taxpayers. "When I asked [former IRS Commissioner Margaret] Richardson how many people out of the agency's 110,000 employees she had fired for being rude and abusive, the answer was none," says Grover G. Norquist, a member of the bipartisan National Commission on Restructuring the Internal Revenue Service and president of Americans for Tax Reform, a conservative anti-tax group. "Now, I don't know what the proper answer is, but it ain't zero. To be told in the same conversation that their No. 1 agenda item is a customer-friendly IRS and they've never fired anybody for violating that goal tells me they don't really take the goal seriously."

Norquist, who is a leading Republican strategist, also charges that the IRS harasses individuals and groups by targeting them for audits for political reasons. When Norquist asked the IRS why it was auditing conservative groups like the National Rifle Association, the Christian Coalition and the Heritage Foundation — as well as Paula Jones, the plaintiff in a pending sexual-harassment suit against President Clinton — he says, "they made no effort at all to dissuade me from this belief."

Norquist stops short of accusing political leaders of sicking the IRS on their enemies. "I don't think Clinton called and said, 'Audit the woman,'" Norquist says. "But he didn't have to because there's a

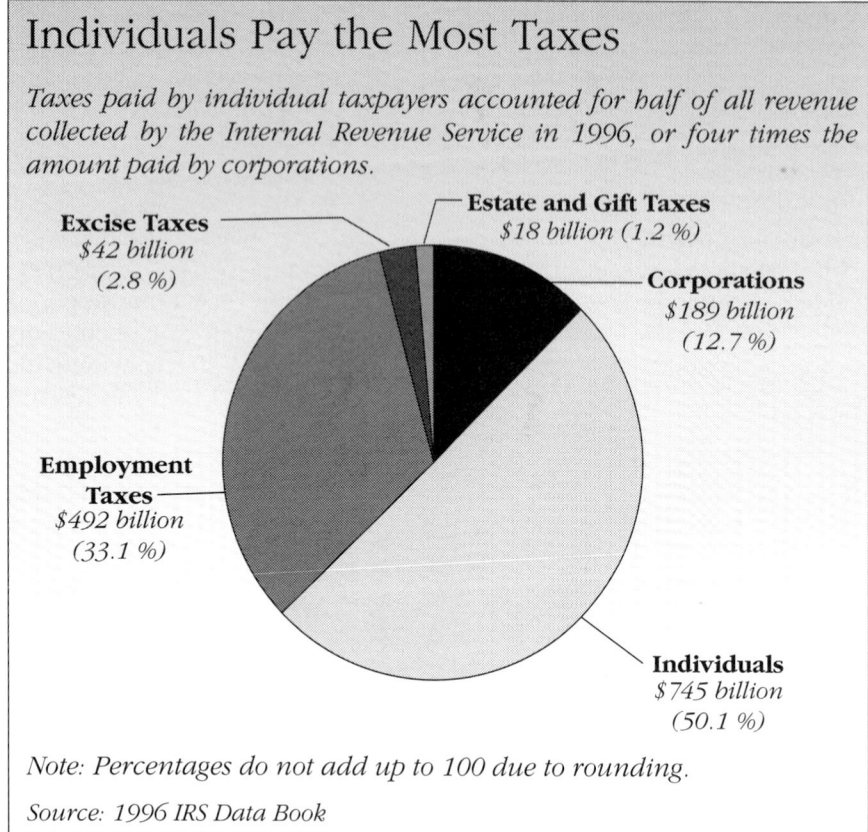

Individuals Pay the Most Taxes

Taxes paid by individual taxpayers accounted for half of all revenue collected by the Internal Revenue Service in 1996, or four times the amount paid by corporations.

Excise Taxes
$42 billion
(2.8 %)

Estate and Gift Taxes
$18 billion (1.2 %)

Corporations
$189 billion
(12.7 %)

Employment Taxes
$492 billion
(33.1 %)

Individuals
$745 billion
(50.1 %)

Note: Percentages do not add up to 100 due to rounding.

Source: 1996 IRS Data Book

prejudice in that direction. I think this is a very serious problem."

In addition to mistreating taxpayers, critics say the agency is among the most wasteful and inefficient of government entities. With some 102,000 employees and more than 200 million returns to process each year, the chances of error, understandably, are considerable. But critics say there's no excuse for the agency's archaic, 1960s-era computer system, which was largely responsible for Katherine Lund's nightmarish experience.

The computer system remains in place despite a modernization program that has cost $3.5 billion, $400,000 of which was virtually thrown away when a longstanding upgrade project was abandoned. IRS employees testified at the September hearings that managers routinely pressure them to bring in more revenue and threaten workers who

publicly criticize these practices.

"The IRS certainly deserves some of the blame for its reputation," Gale says. "If even some of the stories are true, there have been taxpayers who are mistreated. There's no excuse for that. Taxes should be enforced, but there's no reason they have to be enforced with the type of practices that were discussed."

Perhaps surprisingly, the IRS restructuring commission had few disparaging remarks about the agency. "The agency spends significant resources educating personnel to treat taxpayers fairly, and the commission found very few examples of IRS personnel abusing power," the commission's report concluded. "Nevertheless," the report continued, "with the complexity of the tax law and an agency of its size with powers to audit and collect from taxpayers, there likely will continue to be the few unfortunate examples of abuse. Many of the additional safeguards against abusive actions

enacted over the last few years are helping people deal with these systemic problems, however." [7]

Based on the commission's findings, says former IRS Commissioner Alexander, the finger-pointing at the tax-collection agency is clearly unfair. "Members of the commission, looking carefully, dispassionately and non-politically at IRS, found a far different IRS than that portrayed in those theatrical hearings," he says.

Indeed, many tax experts insist that the IRS — whose job it is to enforce federal tax laws — is only a small part of the problem. "Congress certainly deserves a chunk of the blame in that they passed these tax laws in the first place that are so complicated and difficult to enforce," Gale says.

Decades of tinkering by Congress have produced a federal tax code that now covers more than 10,000 pages of complex exclusions, deductions and other rules that require many taxpayers to hire an expert to prepare even the most straightforward returns.

"The combination of trying to eliminate tax evasion and trying to make fine distinctions between sources and uses of income requires the IRS in some cases to be intrusive," Gale says. "And there's no way they can get the right answers unless they act in ways that annoy people under some circumstances."

Of all the change to the tax code over the years, says Yale's Graetz, none are more pernicious than the burdensome penalties and interest that Congress wrote into the law in the 1980s in an attempt to eliminate tax shelters. "As a result," Graetz says, "though the IRS is auditing very few people, those people who do get audited are almost always hit with penalties and interest — very steep interest by the time the IRS gets to it — even when they did the best they could to file an accurate return."

The commission suggests that the IRS has been made a convenient scapegoat for problems taxpayers have with the system. "While the commission recognizes that much of the tax law's complexity is a product of congressional and executive attempts to tailor the law narrowly while maintaining fairness, progressivity and revenue neutrality," it concluded, "the fact remains that the law is overly complex and that this complexity is a large source of taxpayer frustration with the IRS." [8]

Gale spreads responsibility for IRS abuses beyond Congress, to the taxpayers themselves. "Somewhere along the line, we shouldn't forget to blame the American public," he says. "The core problem here is that our attitudes toward tax evasion, toward what the tax system should do and toward what the IRS should do are all mutually inconsistent.

"On the one hand, we're all outraged when we hear stories about tax evasion. But then we support and vote for members of Congress who pass laws that make incredibly fine distinctions about the sources and uses of income," facilitating legal tax evasion.

Will restructuring the IRS significantly improve most Americans' dealings with the agency?

Acting on recommendations of the IRS restructuring commission, Rep. Portman and Sen. Bob Kerrey, D-Neb., introduced House and Senate versions of the 1997 Internal Revenue Service Restructuring and Reform Act in July. But the measures attracted little attention until the September hearings exposed instances of IRS mistreatment of taxpayers. (The bill that was passed nearly unanimously by the House was actually a slightly modified version of the Portman/Kerrey legislation that was introduced by House Ways and Means Committee Chairman Bill Archer, R-Texas. [9])

Designed to enhance taxpayer rights and generally make the IRS more customer-friendly, the restruc-

Electronic Filing Appeals to Many

More than 10 percent of personal tax returns were filed electronically in 1996. Taxpayers have been able to file returns electronically since 1986 — either through professional return preparers or from personal computers. Since 1992, a file-by-phone system, TeleFile, has been available.

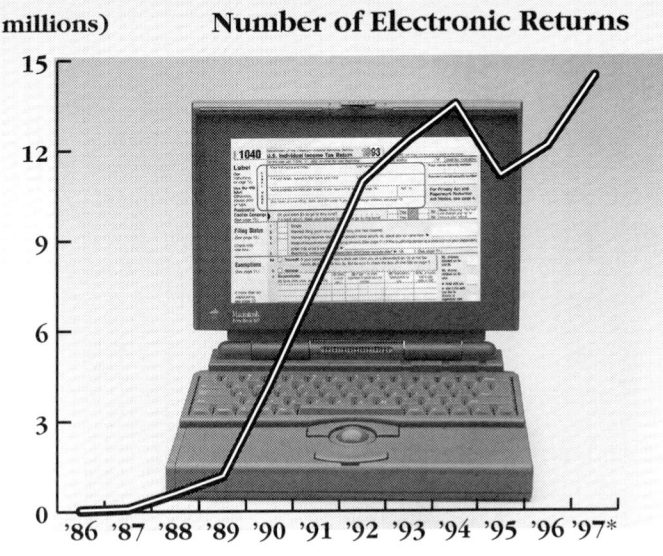

(in millions)   **Number of Electronic Returns**

'86 '87 '88 '89 '90 '91 '92 '93 '94 '95 '96 '97*

* As of Sept. 5, 1997

Source: 1996 IRS Data Book

turing bill would:

• Establish an 11-member board to oversee IRS management;

• Prohibit the IRS from conducting audits for political purposes;

• Shift the burden of proof from the taxpayer to the IRS in Tax Court proceedings;

• Make it harder for the IRS to hold an "innocent" spouse responsible for mistakes on tax returns by the other spouse;

• Allow taxpayers to sue the IRS for negligence; and,

• Require the IRS to provide taxpayers with information on their rights.

Changing the IRS is unlikely to affect the lives of most Americans, however. Of the 118 million individual income tax returns filed in 1996, only about 2 million were audited, or less than 2 percent of

the total filed. By comparison, the percentage of corporate income tax returns that are audited is somewhat larger, 2.3 percent of the total, about 60,000 returns. [10] Only about 30,000 contested returns end up in Tax Court each year, and most of those are settled before they go to trial. For the vast majority of taxpayers, dealing with the IRS is a matter of receiving, filling out and mailing in their 1040s and related forms each year.

But the bill's supporters say it promises to reduce instances of abuse such as those recounted during the September hearings. "I believe the legislation is a good step forward," Graetz says. "It improves IRS personnel practices, it improves the IRS' ability to budget for long-term events and it improves congressional oversight of the agency."

The bill's main benefits, Norquist

says, are of a subjective nature. "It is a step in the right direction, a shot across the bow," he says. "What it changes are things on the extreme, but that reverberates all the way down. 'If you don't do what I want you to do or we'll throw you into Tax Court' is less of a threat if throwing you into Tax Court does not amount to an automatic conviction."

Shifting the burden of proof from the taxpayer to the IRS is controversial, however. Unlike the criminal justice system, where the accused are presumed innocent until proven guilty, taxpayers called to appear before Tax Court are required to prove the IRS wrong by presenting documents to back up their claims. Because the federal income tax relies on voluntary compliance, the taxpayer holds all the supporting documents that determine how much tax is owed. While reversing the burden of proof to the IRS may appeal to taxpayers facing an appearance in Tax Court, the new provision may force the agency to take extraordinary steps to recover necessary documents to make its case.

"I would guess there are a lot of people out there who have been audited who are mad as hell about it and just want to get the IRS off their backs," Gale says. "This might get the IRS off many people's backs, but it might actually make the IRS more intrusive in certain cases. Since the taxpayer keeps the records, if the taxpayer is not required to bring forth the records, then the IRS will either decide it can't prove anything, or it will be forced to take a much more intrusive approach, which is to go out and interview all the family, friends and clients of the taxpayer in question."

Another controversial provision of the new bill is the oversight board. Treasury Secretary Rubin and other critics charge that a board dominated by private-sector members would face conflicts of interest.

"Having been IRS commissioner during Watergate, when nobody believed anything anybody said, I have every reason to believe that if a question is decided in favor of a particular industry that happens to have a representative on the board, the press is hardly going to take the position that that person had nothing to do with the decision," Alexander says. "This will be a particular problem if the Senate gives the board authority to look at specific cases, as it is threatening to do."

Both supporters and critics of the restructuring measure agree that its impact will be limited as long as the current tax system remains in place. "I don't believe that you can restructure the IRS until you restructure the tax law," Graetz says. "You have to get the IRS out of the lives of the everyday American family, and you're not going to get a transformation of the IRS until that happens."

Graetz is particularly skeptical of the bill's stated goal of making the agency customer-friendly. "You can't convert the American taxpayer into a 'customer' of the IRS just by saying so," he says. "For my part, I'll become a werewolf before I'll become a customer of the IRS." ∎

BACKGROUND

Blame Lincoln

Taxes and hatred of them, have been integral to the American experience since the Boston Tea Party. Even after a bitter war of independence to escape Britain's power to tax the Colonies, one of Congress' first acts was to create a new system to collect revenues needed to run the new government. [11] In 1791, Congress passed taxes on alcohol and carriages, which brought in $208,942.81. The forerunner of today's commissioner of revenue was appointed to oversee the nascent tax system in 1792. The alcohol tax, as well as subsequent taxes on houses, land and slaves, proved unpopular and were later repealed.

The first president to campaign on a platform of lower taxes and reduced government spending was Thomas Jefferson. Following his election in 1800, almost all internal taxes were repealed, leaving tariffs as the sole source of government revenue. Tariffs proved inconsistent, however, as the volume of imports fluctuated and sometimes fell dramatically, as during the War of 1812. Tariffs also raised prices on imported goods. Opposition to other forms of taxation remained high, however, and tariffs continued to provide the bulk of federal revenues almost through the rest of the 19th century.

The federal income tax was first signed into law by President Abraham Lincoln on July 1, 1862, to help pay for the Civil War. It was repealed in 1872, at a time of federal budget surplus. Tariffs, meanwhile had risen to almost 50 percent of the value of imported goods. Raising tariffs even higher would have priced goods beyond the reach of consumers, and Congress reduced them in 1894.

The same year Congress reinstated the income tax to compensate for the tariff cuts. But in 1895 the Supreme Court ruled the income tax unconstitutional because it was a direct tax and not apportioned among the states, on the basis of population, as the Constitution required. With widespread support, the 16th Amendment was adopted in 1913, allowing Congress to tax income "from whatever source derived." The same year Congress enacted a tax on income of individuals and corporations. In 1916, after the Supreme Court sustained the new tax, the federal income tax took effect.

Continued on p. 34

Chronology

1800s **Tariffs provide the bulk of federal revenues.**

1862
President Abraham Lincoln signs into law the first federal income tax, which is repealed 10 years later. The Internal Revenue Service is created to enforce the federal tax system.

1895
The Supreme Court rules that the federal income tax, reintroduced in 1894, is unconstitutional.

1910s **The Constitution is amended to allow the income tax.**

1913
The 16th Amendment is adopted, allowing Congress to tax income "from whatever source derived."

1916
The federal income tax takes effect, following Supreme Court approval.

1960s **Policy-makers begin using tax cuts to stimulate the economy.**

1963
President John F. Kennedy sets a precedent by introducing a tax cut to encourage consumers to buy more and thus increase output and employment.

1969
The Tax Court is created as an independent forum to mediate taxpayer disputes with the IRS.

———— • ————

1980s **Frustrated by high tax rates and an increasingly complex tax law, taxpayers call for reforms.**

1981
Congress passes the largest tax cut in U.S. history.

1986
The Tax Reform Act, touted as the biggest tax change since World War II, cuts tax rates, broadens the tax base and eliminates loopholes that have enabled wealthy individuals and corporations to shelter many of their assets from taxation.

———— • ————

1990s **Tax cuts give way to tax hikes as lawmakers try to eliminate the federal budget deficit. Support builds for restructuring the federal tax system.**

1992
The "tax gap," the difference between taxes owed and taxes collected, exceeds $90 billion, exacerbating a trend attributed to the tax code's growing complexity.

June 25, 1997
The National Commission on Restructuring the Internal Revenue Service releases the results of a yearlong investigation into IRS operations. Co-chaired by Sen. Bob Kerrey, D-Neb., and Rep. Rob Portman, R-Ohio, the commission finds few instances of IRS abuse of taxpayers, but recommends steps to upgrade the agency's outdated computer system, improve management training and other measures to enhance efficiency.

Sept. 24-25, 1997
The Senate Finance Committee holds widely publicized hearings at which taxpayers complain of abuses by the IRS.

October 1997
House Majority Leader Dick Armey, R-Texas, and Rep. W.J. "Billy" Tauzin, R-La., launch a "Scrap the Code" tour aimed at gaining support for abolishing the federal income tax and replacing it with a simpler and reputedly fairer system for gathering government revenue. Armey proposes a flat tax, while Tauzin wants to replace the income tax with a national sales tax.

Nov. 5, 1997
The House approves, by a 426-4 margin, the 1997 Internal Revenue Restructuring and Reform Act.

1998
Senate Finance Committee Chairman William V. Roth Jr., R-Del., will consider the House-passed IRS restructuring bill early in the year, which the Senate is expected to approve by a wide margin. Congress also is expected to consider fundamental tax reform proposals.

The Tax Gap

Each year, the Internal Revenue Service collects 83 percent of the money individual taxpayers owe through voluntary compliance, and 4 percent more through enforcement efforts. The IRS cannot collect about 13 percent of the taxes owed by individuals, mainly due to underreporting of income. The resulting "tax gap" in 1992, the most recent year for which information is available, was about $94 billion.

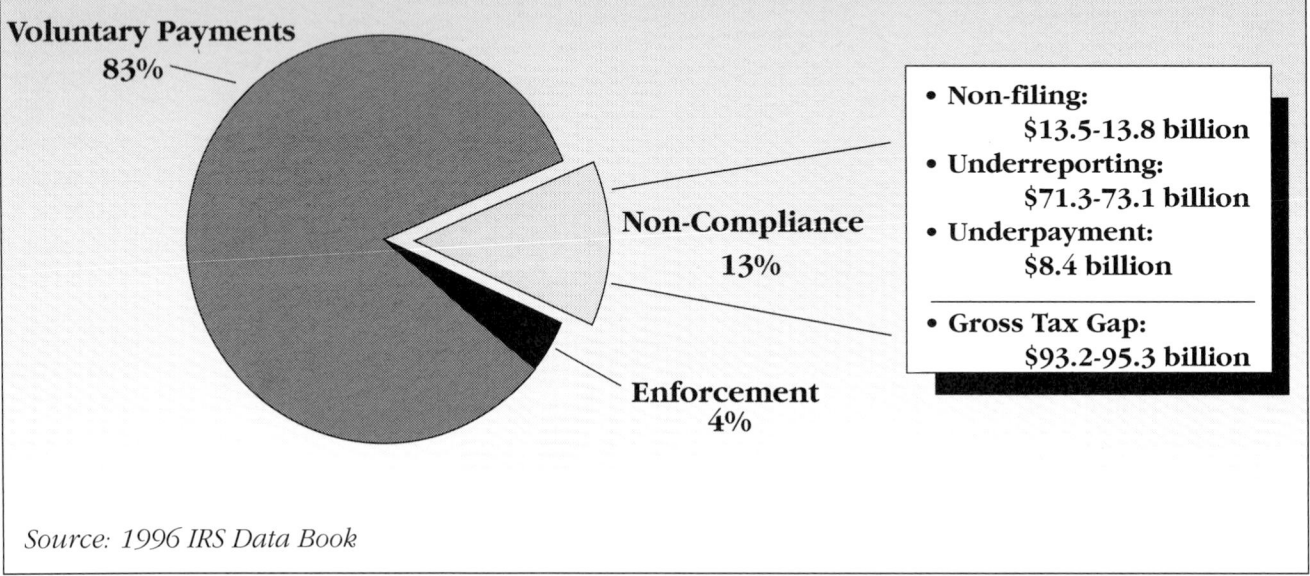

Voluntary Payments
83%

Non-Compliance
13%

Enforcement
4%

- **Non-filing:**
  $13.5-13.8 billion
- **Underreporting:**
  $71.3-73.1 billion
- **Underpayment:**
  $8.4 billion

- **Gross Tax Gap:**
  $93.2-95.3 billion

Source: 1996 IRS Data Book

Continued from p. 32

Endless Tinkering

The seeds of the current campaign against the IRS and the income tax were sown almost from the inception of income taxes. Responding to changes in economic conditions, lawmakers repeatedly raised and lowered tax rates, often with unintended consequences. They also tinkered endlessly with the law, adding deductions and other refinements that often made the tax system fairer, but nearly always made it more complex.

For almost three decades, the income tax and its growing complexity were not an issue for most Americans. Only 400,000 individuals were wealthy enough to pay the tax, and

tax rates were low. But that changed with the outbreak of World War II and the need to raise additional revenues for the war effort. For the first time, the federal income tax was applied to middle-income Americans.

After the war, the top tax rate declined from its wartime high of 94 percent. But the broadening of the tax base to include middle-income Americans was to be a permanent feature of the income tax. And changes intended to reverse some inequities created others. An example is the so-called marriage penalty, which requires many married taxpayers to pay higher taxes than they would if they were single. The marriage penalty was added in 1969 to correct a bias against single taxpayers that had been introduced into the code in 1948.

In 1964, an income tax cut that had

been championed by President John F. Kennedy was introduced in an effort to stimulate the economy. Policy-makers would use this technique frequently in subsequent years on the theory that consumers would spend the money they save in taxes, spurring production of goods and services that would in turn increase employment, raise incomes and thus generate additional tax revenues.

Acting on this notion, Congress in 1981 passed the largest tax cut in U.S. history. Tax cuts gave way to tax increases shortly thereafter, however, as successive administrations in the 1980s and early '90s tried to reduce unprecedented federal budget deficits. At the same time, high inflation during the late 1970s pushed taxpayers into higher and higher tax brackets.

By the 1980s, taxpayers were clamoring for relief, not only from high tax rates, but also from the complexities of the tax law that had spawned an entire industry of tax preparers to help bewildered taxpayers file their returns. President Ronald Reagan and Congress responded with the 1986 Tax Reform Act. Touted as the biggest tax change since World War II, the law cut tax rates, broadened the tax base and simplified some tax forms by eliminating loopholes that had enabled wealthy taxpayers and corporations to avoid taxation on many of their assets.

But the 1986 law's improvements were short-lived. Some provisions, such as the earned-income tax credit for lower-income families, were expanded and made more complex. In 1990 and 1993, tax increases were introduced in continued efforts to lower the budget deficit. In the 1980s alone, lawmakers enacted nine tax laws containing more than 8,000 pages of changes. They may surpass that record in the 1990s. [12]

vestments, self-employment and other sources under the tax system's voluntary compliance system. [13]

With the income tax's growing complexity, however, the IRS' job has gotten harder. Compliance with the law has fallen over the years, from more than 90 percent in the early 1960s to 87 percent today. The result is a "tax gap" that totaled more than $90 billion in 1992, according to the IRS' most recent estimate. [14] In order to enforce the system, the IRS

Tax-reform advocates Rep. W.J. "Billy" Tauzin, R-La., and House Majority Leader Dick Armey, R-Texas, debate their proposals.

now employs about 102,000 people at its headquarters in Washington, 33 district offices and 10 service centers around the country.

When the agency finds discrepancies between its records and a taxpayer's return, it can conduct an audit. In recent years the agency has been auditing about 1 percent to 2 percent of the more than 100 million income tax returns filed each year by individuals. Taxpayers have 90 days to pay unpaid taxes or file a protest in Tax Court, an independent forum set up in 1969 to mediate taxpayer disputes with the IRS. A judge hears the

cases which often are settled by a reduction in the amount of tax owed. [15]

Not only were IRS agents facing a growing compliance problem, but the agency's antiquated computer system was not up to the task of accurately recording the myriad income reports and payments the changing tax law required. A $4 billion program to upgrade the agency's system, known as Tax Systems Modernization, produced few improvements.

But even before the recent congressional hearings drew attention to problems at the IRS, the agency began taking steps to improve its track record. A telephone assistance system called TeleTax provides 24-hour-a-day recorded information on a number of tax issues. The agency provides volunteer income tax assistance and tax counseling at thousands of sites around the country.

In addition to ordering over the phone, taxpayers can obtain most tax forms and publications online, by Fax or from a CD-ROM issued by the Government Printing Office.

Filing returns has been made easier as well. TeleFile, the IRS telephone system, enables taxpayers to file over the phone. Returns can also be filed electronically, an option that more than 14 million taxpayers chose in 1997.

IRS Enforcement

Created in 1862 to enforce the federal tax system, the Internal Revenue Service has had to adapt to the changes lawmakers periodically make to the tax code. As recently as the 1950s, the IRS' work load was considerably lighter than it is today. Only wages were reported directly to the agency. It was up to the taxpayer to disclose income from in-

IRS Study Commission

In June 1996 a bipartisan commission began a yearlong study to ex-

Tax Info and Politicians' Pitches a Click Away

Most federal agencies have Internet Web sites, but few agencies have embraced cyberspace with as much enthusiasm as the Internal Revenue Service. The IRS has established online services that can greatly ease the burden of compiling and filing tax returns for Net-savvy taxpayers.

• In 1996, the IRS launched a new Web site (http://www.irs.ustreas.gov) that enables taxpayers with Fax machines or computers to download forms and instructions and receive highlights of the tax law, answers to frequently asked questions and an interactive guide to common tax issues.

For last-minute filers, this service can end the desperate search for forms long after post offices and libraries have run out of them. The site has been a hit with taxpayers: During its first year of operation, it logged more than 100 million hits and downloaded more than 3 million documents.

• Taxpayers also can file their returns online through another IRS service. The agency reports that more than 14 million returns were filed electronically in 1997, either through tax preparers or home computers. The service has recently been expanded to enable taxpayers to file both their federal and state returns online.

The IRS is not the only purveyor of tax-related information on the Net. House Republican leaders introduced a site last November. And champions of various tax-reform bills also have Web sites touting their proposals:

• The Republicans are soliciting taxpayer "horror stories" at http://hillsource.house.gov/irs.html.

• House Majority Leader Dick Armey, R-Texas, promotes his flat tax at http://flattax.house.gov.

• Rep. W.J. "Billy" Tauzin, R-La., promotes a national sales tax at www.house.gov/tauzin/cvr.htm.

• House Minority Leader Richard A. Gephardt, D-Mo., the Democratic Party's leading champion of tax reform, describes his 10 percent tax plan at www.house.gov/democrats/taxplan/taxplan.html.

amine ways to improve IRS efficiency. Co-chaired by Sen. Kerrey and Rep. Portman, the National Commission on Restructuring the Internal Revenue Service came up with nine recommendations it said should make it easier for citizens to interact with the IRS:

• Improve congressional oversight of the IRS through a new entity to help lawmakers make more informed decisions regarding tax policy;

• Establish a new board of directors, including members who have experience running large service organizations, to be appointed by the president and confirmed by the Senate for five-year terms; the Treasury Department would continue to be responsible for tax policy, and the board would have no say in tax law enforcement or legislation;.

• Appoint the IRS commissioner to a five-year term. (Because there is no fixed term under current law, the commissioner is vulnerable to political pressure.);

• Stabilize funding of IRS for three years to facilitate restructuring;

• Strengthen employee training,

technology and taxpayer education to improve the agency's focus on its customers;

• Update computer technology and improve access to tax information;

• Make paperless filing the preferred method of filing for most taxpayers within 10 year;

• Enable taxpayers to recover damages for wrongful actions by the IRS; and

• Simplify the tax law to relieve the burden on taxpayers. [16]

IRS Restructuring

The IRS restructuring bill that won House approval Nov. 5 replicates virtually all of the commission's recommendations. Lawmakers tacked on several additional provisions, such as shifting the burden of proof to the IRS in Tax Court proceedings, relieving "innocent" spouses of the former spouse's tax errors and allowing taxpayers to claim rebates on taxes wrongly paid by infirm relatives. The bill would also extend attorneys' right to protection against subpoena for client records to other accountants and other tax preparers, and it would make it a felony for executive branch officials to interfere with IRS audits. [17]

Even as lawmakers were drawing up radical changes to the IRS, the agency was taking steps on its own to improve efficiency and relations with taxpayers. On Saturday, Nov. 15, the IRS held the first of so-called problem-solving days in an attempt to resolve outstanding tax disputes. More than 6,000 taxpayers met with agency representative at 33 sites around the country. According to the IRS, about a third of the cases were resolved. The agency plans to continue holding Saturday problem-solving days each month in different cities.

Further changes were expected following the appointment and Senate confirmation of a new IRS commissioner. Charles O. Rossotti, who was sworn in Nov. 13, is the first person to hold the job who was not a tax lawyer or accountant. Formerly chairman of American Management Systems, a computer consulting firm in Fairfax, Va., Rossotti is expected to use his experience in management and technology to hasten the technological modernization of the IRS and improve the agency's service record.

"The IRS must do a far better job of serving taxpayers," Rossotti told lawmakers at his confirmation hearing. "I believe the long-term goal should be to provide service to taxpayers that is consistently as good as they receive from leading companies in the private sector." [18]

Rossotti's first move after taking over the agency came in early December, when he required senior managers to give advance approval before the IRS can seize taxpayers' property for unpaid taxes. [19] ■

CURRENT SITUATION

Anti-Tax Campaign

The timing of September's hearings on IRS abuse of taxpayers and the overwhelming House vote in favor of the bill to restructure the agency is hardly coincidental. In letters sent out to constituents in June, Republican leaders began soliciting potential witnesses for the hearings as well as contributions to support the anti-tax effort.

One letter, sent by the National Republican Senatorial Committee and signed by its chairman, Sen. Mitch McConnell, R-Ky., called on recipients to "abolish the IRS." "Working together, we can publicly expose the IRS' worst transgressions against honest, responsible taxpayers," McConnell wrote. The letter was accompanied by a survey that asked

such questions as, "Should the IRS be allowed to use your tax dollars to pay for special seminars that brainwash IRS employees into thinking you are a cheat and a liar?"

"The letter is very revealing," says Alexander. "The point that is made by the committee is that they planned the hearings months and months in advance and were soliciting people who actually or allegedly had been mistreated. Then, of course, they made a selection [of witnesses] from that list."

In Alexander's view, the IRS bill is just the first step in a Republican campaign to weaken the agency's enforcement ability as an indirect way to dismantle the federal income tax system altogether. "The more you demonize IRS, the more ineffective you make it," Alexander says. "And if you make everyone in IRS one great taxpayer advocate, then there's nobody left to tell the taxpayers who don't pay that they have to pay. Then, if the system doesn't work, we'll have to replace the system. The pieces all fit together."

While Republican strategists do not describe their campaign in these terms, they readily concede that the IRS restructuring bill is just the first salvo in a longer-term offensive to reduce taxes and reduce the size and power of government — goals they believe will win the GOP votes in coming elections.

"The most radical change that took place [in 1997] in the tax code started April 15, when Speaker Gingrich got up and said it is the goal of the Republican Party to abolish the estate tax and the capital gains tax," Norquist says. "Six months earlier the goal was to vaguely reduce the two, but the idea is not so radical any more. The central question is not just the shape of the tax cut, but the total size. The center-right coalition needs to work on how to reduce the total size and scope of government in order to get taxes down."

The next phase of the anti-tax campaign was launched in October, when Reps. Armey and Tauzin went on the

road to promote tax reform, a centerpiece of the 1996 presidential campaign debates. [20] Expected to hit a number of cities around the country, the "Scrap the Code" tour, sponsored by the nonprofit Citizens for a Sound Economy, takes the form of an amiable debate between the two lawmakers on the merits of their proposed alternatives to the income tax.

Displaying a giant replica of the post-card-sized tax form he says is all taxpayers would need to file under his plan, Armey claims his flat tax would radically simplify filing and be fairer to taxpayers because it would eliminate all the current system's deductions and loopholes. The Armey flat tax, similar to one proposed by Steve Forbes in his 1996 bid for the Republican presidential nomination, would impose a single tax rate of 20 percent initially, falling to 17 percent after a phase-in period of several years.

Tauzin's approach, supported by House Ways and Means Committee Chairman Archer, would replace the income tax altogether with a 15 percent national sales tax. Because the tax would be collected at the retail level, Tauzin says, its adoption would allow for the complete elimination of the IRS. If the sales tax is enacted, Tauzin promises "April 15 is just another pleasant day in your life." [21]

Republicans are hoping the "Scrap the Code" tour will spark a national debate that will spur voters to consider alternatives to the current tax code and support proposals that would further the basic GOP goals of lower taxes and a smaller government.

"What we're going to do starting this fall is ask every American taxpayer, as they go through looking at the taxes for next year, take a look at the alternatives," Gingrich said in 1997. "And, hopefully, by April 15 we can form a consensus around a major, decisive tax reform . . . that would move us to a much simpler system, a more honest system and a fairer system, and one which made it more possible to compete in the world market." [22]

New Law Complicates the Tax Code

The same Congress that is poised to endorse IRS reform and simplify the Tax Code only last summer passed a tax law that, ironically, complicates filing returns for many taxpayers. Indeed, the 1997 Taxpayer Relief Act added 285 sections and 824 amendments to the Code.

To be sure, the new law was widely hailed for providing the first major tax cut in 16 years, lowering rates on capital gains, making it less burdensome to sell a house and offering new incentives for saving. But some of the changes will force taxpayers to make difficult choices based on complex calculations.

"There's no question that lawmakers made the tax code more complicated with the 1997 tax act," says William Gale, an economist and tax expert at the Brookings Institution. "But they complicated taxes in a way that cut taxes. People may not like complexity, but they dislike complexity that cuts their taxes a lot less than they dislike complexity that raises their taxes."

Owners of long-term investments were cheered by the law's lowering of taxes owed on capital gains. Most taxpayers who sell stocks, bonds or other assets after holding them for at least 18 months and a day will owe a 20 percent capital gains tax on any profits, down from 28 percent under the old law. The tax rate for short-term capital gains, held for 12 months or less, remains the same as that for ordinary income, up to 39.6 percent. [1] But the new law also complicated the capital gains issue by setting a new five-year rate that imposes different conditions on taxpayers according to their income.

One of the most difficult decisions taxpayers will face involves saving money for retirement in a tax-favored vehicle known as the Individual Retirement Account. The traditional IRA, introduced in the late 1970s, allowed workers to set aside up to $2,000 a year, deducting the amount from their taxable income. They would not pay taxes on the money until they began withdrawing it upon retirement, when they would presumably fall into a lower tax bracket. The IRA was later restricted to a narrow range of middle- and lower-income workers.

The 1997 law adds a new type of IRA to the mix. Called the Roth IRA, after its sponsor, Sen. William V. Roth Jr., R-Del., the new IRA allows a broader category of workers to save up to $2,000 from their income. The Roth IRA also taxes retirement savings up front, but not at withdrawal. In other words, contributions are not tax-deductible, but the money is not taxed at withdrawal.

The new IRA is expected to draw many savers among higher-income workers excluded from most benefits of the traditional IRA. The rules governing early withdrawal are also more lenient than those for traditional IRAs, allowing withdrawals without penalties for first-time home purchases and several other purposes. But critics say the Roth IRA creates almost as many problems as it solves. Because of the complexity involved, most taxpayers will have to hire an accountant to decide whether it is financially advantageous to roll over their existing IRAs into Roth IRAs, whether to continue investing in traditional IRAs or whether to bother with the Roth IRA at all.

The complexities of the new tax law will not be apparent to most taxpayers facing this year's filing deadline because most of its terms did not go into effect until Jan. 1. But next year lawmakers may face a barrage of taxpayer complaints if they fail to tackle fundamental tax reform or even fail to just try to simplify the existing law. But simplification is most unlikely, in Gale's view. "We could try to clean up the income tax, which is just the boring, old, eat-your-vegetables approach to tax reform," Gale says. "But Congress has shown that it can't do that and that they shouldn't be trusted with bigger reforms. The [complicated] new law is, to me, one of the best arguments against giving them the keys to the brand new Caddy."

---

[1] For assets sold after the law went into effect on May 6 but before July 29, 1997, the assets had to be held for more than 12 months for the 20 percent long-term rate to apply. The 28 percent rate applies to assets sold after July 28, 1997, that were held between 12-18 months.

National Sales Tax

Any meaningful discussion about tax reform will have to go much deeper into the details than either lawmaker has done so far on the "Scrap the Code" tour. The more radical of the two proposals, the national sales tax, would be more regressive, or unfair to lower-income Americans, than the current income tax, with its graduated rates and myriad provisions that ensure that wealthier Americans shoulder a larger proportion of the tax burden.

An unmodified sales tax does the opposite, because poorer people must spend a greater portion of their assets on food, housing and other necessities than the rich. A sales tax also raises the price of taxed goods and services, much as tariffs did during the 19th century.

"If you shift to a national sales tax, we would raise the price of all products dramatically, and we don't know what that would do to inflation in America," said President Clinton shortly after the Scrap the Code tour began. "We don't know whether it could be done without any kind of destructive economic consequences. Also, we don't know whether that wouldn't be much more regressive for people in the middle- and lower-income working groups." [23]

Sales tax supporters say it would not necessarily hurt the poor. "It is relatively easy to construct a national sales tax that protects the poor from paying any tax and is roughly as progressive as the current income tax," contends Gilbert E. Metcalf, an economics professor at Tufts University and an economist with the National Bureau of Economic Research.

Because Tauzin's proposal would provide rebates to low-income Americans, Metcalf writes, it would be "about as progressive as the current income tax." In any case, Metcalf says, fairness is not the most important goal of tax policy. "When evaluating the merits of major tax reform . . . policy-makers should not focus unduly on distributional considerations," he writes. "Rather, Congress would be better advised to focus on the efficiency gains and the broad economic benefits of moving to a consumption tax system." [24]

But critics say regressivity is only one of several pitfalls inherent in the sales tax. Tax experts say the sales tax has other pitfalls as well. "No country has a retail sales tax at the level Tauzin is talking about because it can't be enforced," Graetz says. "The incentives for retailers to cheat are just too high."

Many European countries and Japan long ago abandoned the retail tax in favor of the value-added tax (VAT), essentially a sales tax that is collected from manufacturers and producers rather than from retailers and that has incentives built in to ensure compliance. "We know the VAT can be collected because other countries collect it fairly effectively," Graetz says. "If we're going to be serious about a sales tax, it needs to be a VAT if you want to collect the taxes."

Gale is even more emphatic in dismissing the retail sales tax. "The sales tax is essentially a non-starter, so I'm not sure why they're talking

about it at all," he says. "If you look at the rates that you would need to raise the revenues to replace the income tax, they reach absurdly high levels very quickly." Some purchases, such as financial services, cannot be taxed easily, Gale says, and taxing others, such as education and health insurance, would face public protest.

With other factors, including a 10-15 percent assumed tax evasion rate and an exemption for everyone equal to the poverty line, Gale says, a retail sales tax would have to approach 40 percent to generate the same amount of revenue as today's income tax. "There would be a huge incentive to evade," he says.

Finally, Gale says, a national retail sales tax would be unfair. "If we eliminated the corporate and personal income tax, as well as the estate tax, and replaced them all with a sales tax, there would be massive tax cuts for the households in the top 1 percent."

Despite its apparent drawbacks, a national sales tax may appeal to those who favor a reduction in government spending. "Americans would begin to demand less government because taxpayers could receive an immediate dividend from reductions in spending — via a reduction in the sales tax rate," writes Stephen Moore, director of fiscal policy studies, at the Cato Institute. "Politicians could ask the voters: Which would you rather have, a Department of Energy or a 1 percent reduction in the national sales tax?" [25]

The Flat Tax

The other "Scrap the Code" proposal, Armey's 17 percent flat tax, also draws criticism, though not as strong as the sales tax. "I have never seen a flat tax proposal that was revenue-neutral — that is, it kept the balanced budget we worked so hard for

now, that didn't impose higher taxes on people with incomes below $100,000," Clinton said. "And that's most Americans, and that's not fair." [26]

Some critics see hope for a significantly modified version of the flat tax as a promising alternative for the current tax system. "I think the flat tax could be a starting point for a restructuring of the tax code," Gale says, "but it's being vastly oversold. [Former Rep.] Jack Kemp's claim that it would double the growth rate for a decade is just wrong."

Like the sales tax, the flat tax would shift the burden of taxation from the wealthiest Americans to middle- and lower-income groups. "I don't want to sound like a class warrior, but these things aren't being said on the Scrap the Code tour," Gale says. "The single biggest feature of the flat tax is that it radically cuts taxes for the top 1 percent of households."

Without modifications, the flat tax's main asset — the absence of complex exclusions and deductions — may also turn out to be its greatest weakness. Homeowners would lose their deduction for mortgage interest payments under Armey's plan, a provision that has potentially devastating ramifications for the housing industry.

Most Americans are covered by health insurance and pension plans through their employers, largely because the current income tax provides breaks for employers to provide these benefits. "You have to be concerned about what a proposal like the flat tax does to employer-provided health insurance and pensions," Graetz says, "since it provides no tax advantage for either of these things."

Because the flat tax would apply in full to U.S.-made products but only to dealers' markups for imports, it would discriminate against domestic industry, Graetz says. "This is an issue on which American business and labor will be on exactly the same side," he says. "It's a huge political problem that either Mr. Armey and other proponents of the flat tax have not focused on, or they're just burying their heads

FOR MORE INFORMATION

Americans for Tax Reform, 1320 18th St. N.W., Suite 200, Washington, D.C. 20036; (202) 785-0266; amtxreform@aol.com or http://www.atr.org. Advocates reduction of federal and state taxes and encourages candidates for public office to pledge their opposition to income tax increases through a national pledge campaign.

Brookings Institution, 1775 Massachusetts Ave., N.W., Washington, D.C. 20036; (202) 797-6000; http://www.brook.edu. The institution sponsors economic research and publishes studies on domestic and international economics, public finance and social policy.

Cato Institute, 1000 Massachusetts Ave. N.W., Washington, D.C. 20001; (202) 842-0200; cato@cato.org or http://www.cato.org. This public policy research organization advocates low and simple taxes and reduced government spending.

Citizens for a Sound Economy, 1250 H St., N.W., Suite 700, Washington, D.C. 20005; (202) 783-3870; http://www.cse.org/cse. This citizens' advocacy group promotes reduced taxes and is a sponsor of the "Scrap the Code" tour led by House Majority Leader Dick Armey, R-Texas, and Rep. W.J. "Billy" Tauzin, R-La.

Citizens for Tax Justice, 1311 L St. N.W., Suite 400, Washington, D.C. 20005; (202) 626-3780; http://www.ctj.org. This coalition works for progressive taxes at the federal, state and local levels.

National Taxpayers Union, 108 N. Alfred St., 3rd floor, Alexandria, Va. 22314; (703) 683-5700; http://www.ntu.org. This citizens' interest group promotes tax and spending reductions and participated in the National Commission on Restructuring the Internal Revenue Service.

Tax Executives Institute, 1001 Pennsylvania Ave., N.W., Suite 320, Washington, D.C. 20004; (202) 638-5601; http://www.tei.org. This trade association of accountants, lawyers and others dealing with tax issues opposes the restructuring bill's shift of the burden of proof from the taxpayer to the IRS.

in the sand for the moment."

Flat tax supporters predict that by greatly simplifying taxation, the flat tax will benefit everyone. "Obviously, the American people are fed up with the existing tax code," Armey said. The flat tax "gives us a better chance for better jobs, more promotions, greater opportunities, greater economic growth and the simplicity, fairness and honesty that goes with it." [27]

Other Tax Plans

Even the harshest critics of Armey's and Tauzin's tax reform proposals agree that the current tax code needs to be simplified. In addition to plans that were introduced during the 1996 presidential campaign, a number of lawmakers and tax experts have recently advanced alternative tax plans aimed at correcting some of those proposals' shortcomings. [28]

Although the tax reform movement appears to be dominated by Republicans, they are not the sole participants in the debate. House Minority Leader Richard A. Gephardt, D-Mo., continues to push for a modified flat tax that would put 75 percent of taxpayers in a 10 percent tax bracket. The wealthiest 25 percent would pay a graduated tax on income of up to 34 percent. Gephardt's plan would eliminate all deductions and loopholes, except the mortgage interest deduction.

Moore of the Cato Institute offered a plan last spring that would let taxpayers choose between a 25 percent flat tax and the current system. Under his plan, called the Max Tax, taxpayers would receive two forms from the IRS: a traditional 1040 and a Max Tax post card. Moore's plan is incorporated in a bill introduced last year by Rep. Vince Snowbarger, R-Kan., and won praise in a recent *Wall Street Journal* editorial. [29]

In his recent book on the tax code, Graetz proposes a two-track tax consisting of a flat rate on individual income above $75,000 and a 50 percent corporate tax cut combined with a VAT to replace the revenue lost through the income tax cuts. The plan has generated considerable interest because it preserves some of the current system's progressivity. According to Gale, Graetz's plan would remove more than 90 percent of taxpayers from the tax rolls.

"The problem with my proposal," concedes Graetz, "is that it's not easy to explain in sound bites, unlike the flat tax or sales tax that sound OK to people and generate political support."

Some experts say the best way to reform the tax code is to eliminate a few deductions or exemptions, see what happens and then proceed to simplify the law further if the changes help. "We could take just the boring, old eat-your-vegetables approach to tax reform, which is to clean up the income tax," Gale says. "That approach would let us move unambiguously in the right direction. We could make it simpler, we could reduce some of the deductions, we could use the money to reduce some of the rates and we could see if we like moving in that direction. If we kept going, eventually we'd get to fundamental tax reform." ■

At Issue:

Is it fair to characterize Internal Revenue Service employees as abusive and poorly trained?

DAVID PATNOE

Former IRS Revenue officer, now representing taxpayers before the IRS Collections Division

FROM TESTIMONY BEFORE SENATE FINANCE COMMITTEE HEARING ON IRS TREATMENT OF EMPLOYEES AND TAXPAYERS, SEPT. 24, 1997

i have found dealing with IRS personnel to be quite disturbing in a few cases, and downright maddening in others. In particular, I have had my worst experiences with people I believe had insufficient training to be performing the jobs they were assigned. In some instances their actions were outright illegal and highly abusive . . . .

Let me give you an example that I think will demonstrate what I believe is occurring far more frequently than people may realize. I was hired to assist in a matter involving the improper use of a levy. A levy is generally the seizure of money in some form. The IRS had issued a levy on one of my client's receivables owed to his business, a sole proprietorship. But the tax that the IRS was trying to collect on the levy was not owed by my client, but was in fact owed by a company that my client had worked for at one time as an employee. . . .

The Revenue officer . . . went to my client's business with seizure papers in hand. The client, being faced with the seizure of his new business, became very afraid and paid a payment of $7,000 to forestall the seizure. Now, he paid this despite the fact that he did not owe any tax. The IRS basically scared this person or "extorted" him into paying money that he didn't owe with the threat of seizing his business for the debt of the company he had at one time worked for . . . Despite having the explanation laid out in black and white, the Revenue officer would not release the levy nor refund the $7,000 she had collected illegally by scaring the taxpayer when she first showed up at his door . . .

I informed the Revenue officer that . . . her actions were not just abusive, but blatantly illegal. Only when the Revenue officer realized that we would make every effort possible to expose this action did she come back with a release of the levy . . . When you consider that this was an experienced Revenue officer acting with her group manager's approval, and not to mention [who] also trains other Revenue officers, her actions were absolutely beyond comprehension. . . .

I would like to say that this type of action did not occur while I was a Revenue officer. Unfortunately, it did. I know of seasoned tax collectors, who were well-aware of the law, [who took] actions that were out of the realm of legal tax collection.

ROBERT TOBIAS

Member, National Commission on Restructuring the Internal Revenue Service and president, National Treasury Employees Union

FROM TESTIMONY BEFORE HOUSE WAYS AND MEANS OVERSIGHT SUBCOMMITTEE HEARING ON IRS RESTRUCTURING, JULY 24, 1997

t he [National Commission on Restructuring the Internal Revenue Service] report . . . accurately portrays IRS employees as competent, hard-working and motivated individuals . . . It provides the basis for a truce, a much needed cease-fire in the hostility against the IRS . . .

Eighty-five percent of the IRS employees interviewed by the commission requested that Congress stop bashing the IRS. They rightly stated that broadsiding the institution for difficulties and controversies surrounding federal tax policy makes their jobs more difficult. The commission wholeheartedly agreed with that assessment.

IRS bashing by public figures and some members of Congress is, unfortunately, well-documented. Quotes such as "we should kill the IRS, drive a stake through its heart," . . . are irresponsible at best and dangerous at worst.

These comments quite literally endanger the lives of the men and women of the IRS whose job it is to enforce the laws Congress creates and collect the accurate amount of taxes owed. Attacks on IRS Revenue officers attempting to perform their duties are well-documented. Carole Jones and Stephen Golder, IRS Revenue officers from Wilmington, Del., were forced to flee from an attempt to seize property when the taxpayer's daughter threatened that she was going to blow their (expletive) heads off . . .

In May of 1995, the IRS office in Denver issued an internal memorandum warning that 10 Montana individuals associated with the United Apostolic Brethren, a group with armed-militia links that believes it has sovereign immunity from federal income tax law, had sworn an oath to kill any IRS agent who attempted to arrest them . . .

The guiding principle of the commission's report was that IRS customer service and taxpayer satisfaction must become paramount. I concur. The IRS collects the taxes that run our government, and increased compliance with tax laws will only occur when Americans find the IRS to be fair and efficient.

But the employees charged with carrying out the IRS' mission must stop receiving conflicting messages from Congress, from the press and from the public that seem to indicate that the services they perform have no merit and serve only to harass the taxpaying public . . .

OUTLOOK

GOP Strategy?

Supporters of the House-passed IRS restructuring bill were disappointed when Senate Finance Committee Chairman Roth decided to postpone consideration of the measure until 1998. Roth said he wanted to strengthen two key provisions of the bill. He proposed extending the oversight board's authority by allowing it to examine individual taxpayer complaints. Roth also would like to strengthen the shift in the burden of proof to the IRS not only in Tax Court, as the House bill provides, but also during pretrial administrative proceedings. Some observers predict that the changes would reignite earlier controversies and jeopardize Senate approval of the IRS restructuring bill. [30]

But other analysts say Roth's delay is part of a Republican strategy to string out the IRS debate — and maintain public hostility to the agency — into this fall's election campaign on the theory that anti-IRS sentiment will translate into votes for GOP candidates. "The campaign this fall will undoubtedly be on demonizing the IRS," Alexander says. "This will be the prime reform proposal — if you want to call it that — of a lot of people who will say the tax is too complex, but if this evil agency weren't administering it, everything would be fine."

Anti-tax advocates also hope the push for tax reform and tax cuts will pay off in terms of GOP gains this year. Americans for Tax Reform, for example, is leading a "taxpayer protection pledge" campaign in which candidates for office are asked to sign a pledge not to raise taxes either by raising tax rates or broadening the base of the individual and corporate income tax.

According to Norquist, the group's president, 203 members of the House and 40 senators have signed the pledge. On the state level, he says, 827 state legislators and five governors have also pledged not to raise taxes. "I believe that we will double that number," he says, "and that up to 22 percent of state legislators will have signed the pledge by November."

Norquist is optimistic that Republicans stand to benefit from the mounting opposition to taxes that last fall's hearings into IRS abuses helped fan, not only this fall but in the presidential campaign in 2000.

"A conservative cannot be in favor of tax increases," he says. "This is the backbone of the success for the Republican Party. It is the one non-negotiable." ∎

Notes

[1] Lund testified Sept. 24, 1997, before the Senate Finance Committee.

[2] *USA Today*, Sept. 30, 1997, p. 1A.

[3] From an interview on ABC's "Good Morning America," Oct. 22, 1997.

[4] Testimony before the Senate Finance Committee, Sept. 25, 1997.

[5] Testimony before the Senate Finance Committee, Sept. 24, 1997.

[6] Opening statement at Senate Finance Committee hearings, Sept. 24, 1997.

[7] National Commission on Restructuring the Internal Revenue Service, "A Vision for a New IRS," June 25, 1997, p. 43.

[8] *Ibid.*, p. 35.

[9] For background, see "IRS Reform," *House Action Reports*, Nov. 3, 1997.

[10] Internal Revenue Service, "IRS by the Numbers," *Fact Sheet*, September 1997.

[11] Information in this section is based on Michael J. Graetz, *The Decline (and Fall?) of the Income Tax* (1997), pp. 13-18.

[12] *Ibid*, p. 86.

[13] See Charles Adams, *For Good and Evil* (1993), pp. 382-383.

[14] From testimony by James White, associate director for tax policy and administration issues at the General Accounting Office, before the House Ways and Means Subcommittee on Oversight, Sept. 26, 1997.

[15] See Carol Jouzaitis, "Tax Court: Controversial, Little Understood," *USA Today*, Nov. 19, 1997.

[16] National Commission on Restructuring the Internal Revenue Service, *op. cit.*, pp. v-vi.

[17] For background, see Jonathan Weisman, "IRS Overhaul Sails Through House, But Reality Check Waits in Senate," *CQ Weekly Report*, Nov. 8, 1997, pp. 2755-2756.

[18] Testimony before the Senate Finance Committee, Oct. 23, 1997.

[19] See Albert B. Crenshaw, "IRS Tightens Its Procedures for Seizing Property," *The Washington Post*, Dec. 3, 1997.

[20] For background. see "Tax Reform," *The CQ Researcher*, March 22, 1996, pp. 241-264.

[21] See Amity Shlaes, "The Great Tax Debate," *The Wall Street Journal*, Oct. 23, 1997.

[22] From a speech at the National Press Club, Sept. 30, 1997.

[23] Clinton spoke on NBC's "Meet the Press," Nov. 10, 1997.

[24] Gilbert E. Metcalf, "The National Sales Tax: Who Bears the Burden?" *Policy Analysis*, Dec. 8, 1997. *Policy Analysis* is a publication of the Cato Institute, a policy research organization that advocates limited government.

[25] Stephen Moore, "The Economic and Civil Liberties Case for a National Sales Tax," in Michael J. Boskin (ed.), *Frontiers of Tax Reform* (1996), p. 118.

[26] From the Nov. 10 interview on "Meet the Press."

[27] Interviewed on "Fox Morning News," April 15, 1997.

[28] For a description of the main alternative plans, see *The CQ Researcher, op. cit.*, p. 252.

[29] See "Max Tax Choice," *The Wall Street Journal*, Nov. 25, 1997.

[30] See Weisman, *op. cit.*

Bibliography

Selected Sources Used

Books

Adams, Charles, *For Good and Evil: The Impact of Taxes on the Course of Civilization*, Madison Books, 1993.

A tax lawyer looks at history through the lens of taxation and comes up with a mostly negative view of the myriad ways governments have supported themselves.

Boskin, Michael J., ed., *Frontiers of Tax Reform*, Hoover Institution Press, 1996.

Boskin, an economics professor at Stanford University and former economic adviser to President George Bush, presents a collection of essays in which tax experts examine the goals of tax reform and describe in detail the various reform proposals that dominated the 1996 presidential campaign debate.

Graetz, Michael J., *The Decline [and Fall?] of the Income Tax*, W.W. Norton, 1997.

The author, a Treasury official during the Bush administration, decries the tax code's growing complexity over the past two decades as the cause of Americans' anti-tax sentiment. He points out the failings of the leading tax-reform proposals and offers as an alternative a value-added tax, combined with an income tax for upper-income individuals.

Articles

"Binning the IRS," *The Economist*, Oct. 4, 1997.

Restructuring the IRS would do little, according to this editorial, to improve the U.S. tax system. A better solution would be fundamental tax reform to simplify the tax code itself. But champions of current proposals have thus far failed to dispel fears that the changes will do more harm than good.

Birnbaum, Jeffrey H., "Does Not Compute," *The Washingtonian*, December 1997.

Since 1989, the IRS has wasted millions of taxpayer dollars in a failed attempt to modernize its antiquated computer system. Most of the problems stem from the agency's reluctance to use outside experts for fear of jeopardizing taxpayer privacy.

Chait, Jonathan, "The Flat Tax Scam," *The New Republic*, Dec. 15, 1997.

Adoption of the flat tax espoused by House Majority Leader Dick Armey, R-Texas, the author writes, would jeopardize the nation's employer-based health insurance system, home ownership and charities, which depend on tax-deductible contributions.

Hirsh, Michael, "Infernal Revenue Disservice," *Newsweek*, Oct. 13, 1997.

The IRS is not so much a mere enforcer of the tax code as a malign bureaucracy that abuses taxpayers at will with little or no oversight, the author writes. While its victims are few, considering the number of taxpayers overall, they are largely helpless to defend against the agency's allegations of wrongdoing.

Kettl, Donald F., "The Battle Over Fixing the IRS," *The Brookings Review*, winter 1998.

The author takes issue with two elements of the IRS restructuring bill now before Congress. Creating a new oversight board including individuals from the private sector, he writes, would create unavoidable conflicts of interest. Shifting the burden of proof on the IRS in tax court cases also would be counterproductive because it would force the agency to adopt more aggressive tactics to collect unpaid taxes.

Reports and Studies

Congressional Budget Office, "The Economic Effects of Comprehensive Tax Reform," July 1997.

Adoption of a consumption-based tax to replace the current income tax system would likely leave younger generations better off, but older generations worse off, the CBO concludes. A final assessment of tax reform must await further refinement of the proposals under discussion.

National Commission on Restructuring the Internal Revenue Service, "A Vision for a New IRS," June 25, 1997.

A bipartisan commission co-chaired by Sen. Bob Kerrey, D-Neb., and Rep. Rob Portman, R-Ohio, reports after a yearlong investigation of the IRS that instances of taxpayer abuse are rare, but that the agency should become more efficient by improving such areas as management training and computer technology.

Willis, Lynda D., "Taxpayer Compliance: Analyzing the Nature of the Income Tax Gap," General Accounting Office, Jan. 9, 1997.

The tax policy director of the General Accounting Office reports that American taxpayers pay only about 87 percent of the taxes they owe, leading to a "tax gap" of lost revenues that amounts to billions of dollars each year. Because adopting more intrusive record-keeping requirements would be unacceptable to the public, she calls on the tax-collecting agency to find cost-effective ways to close the gap.

The Next Step

Additional information from UMI's Newspaper & Periodical Abstracts™ database

Abuse/Horror Stories

Maier, Timothy W., and Sean Paige, "A new tax revolt," *Insight on the News,* Nov. 3, 1997, pp. 8-12.

Americans are outraged about abuses and eager to replace the IRS. Some of the alleged IRS abuses against taxpayers and the national dialogue begun by House Speaker Newt Gingrich, R-Ga., about how to replace the tax code are discussed.

Millar, Jeff, "Being ticked at the IRS is nothing new," *Houston Chronicle,* Oct. 5, 1997, p. C6.

Millar discusses the recent congressional hearings into IRS taxpayer abuses, focusing on his own experience of a tax audit.

"Time to Reform the IRS," *St. Louis Post-Dispatch,* Sept. 26, 1997, p. C8.

For three days this week, the Senate Finance Committee heard taxpayers' horror stories about the Internal Revenue Service. They depicted an arrogant, uncaring and abusive agency. Deputy Treasury Secretary Lawrence Summers had it right when he said even one such case is one too many.

Topolnicki, Denise M., and Elizabeth MacDonald, "How the IRS Abuses Taxpayers," *Reader's Digest,* February 1991, pp. 83-86.

Although attempts have been made to reform the system of taxation, the methods employed by the IRS to collect taxes are often abusive to taxpayers.

Clinton Proposal

Ivanovich, David, "Clinton to unveil IRS reform plan today," *Houston Chronicle,* Oct. 10, 1997, p. C1.

The White House is expected to reveal an IRS-reform plan that would create 33 new regional advisory boards that would work in conjunction with two national boards and make recommendations to help the agency operate more efficiently and fairly. The White House proposal falls far short of the kinds of changes being called for in Congress.

"The IRS Isn't the Problem," *Detroit News,* Oct. 27, 1997, p. A10.

The Clinton administration reversed field this week and agreed to support a Republican proposal to overhaul the Internal Revenue Service. Although we like the idea of lightening the oppressive burdens of the U.S. tax system, two provisions in the proposal seem likely to do more harm than good.

Flat Tax

Armey, Dick, and Billy Tauzin, "Q: Does IRS restructuring need a flat tax more than a consumption tax?" *Insight on the News,* Nov. 3, 1997, pp. 24-27.

House Majority Leader Dick Armey, R-Texas, and Rep. W.J. ''Billy'' Tauzin, R-La., debate whether IRS restructuring needs a flat tax more than a consumption tax. Armey argues that a flat tax will close loopholes for the rich, reduce IRS bureaucracy and encourage savings, while Tauzin claims a consumption tax would abolish the IRS, now five times the size of the FBI.

Gergen, David, "The flat-tax diversion," *U.S. News & World Report,* Feb. 5, 1996, p. 80.

The debate over tax reform, specifically the flat tax proposal, is detracting from other issues that are more important. America needs tax simplification, but it also needs to keep a steadier focus on pressing problems.

Golob, John E., "How would a flat tax affect small businesses?" *Economic Review,* Third Quarter 1996, pp. 5-19.

Golob examines the effects of a flat tax on businesses in general and on small businesses in particular.

"Is a flat tax the right cure?" *U.S. News & World Report,* Jan. 15, 1996, p. 38.

Advocates of a flat tax believe it would simplify the tax system and boost savings. Opponents say a flat tax would increase the budget deficit and favor the wealthy.

"Lexington: The Steve Forbes drum-beat," *The Economist,* Sept. 20, 1997, p. 33.

While the Clinton administration and Congress are touting rival plans to reform the IRS, former presidential candidate Steve Forbes continues to push for abolishing the IRS and instituting a flat tax.

McNamee, Mike, "Commentary: A Flat Tax Might Make Apr. 15 Trickier," *Business Week,* April 8, 1996, p. 135.

A simple tax form does not necessarily mean a simple tax. A flat tax's gaping loopholes could keep IRS auditors busier than ever.

Roberts, David, and Mark Sullivan, "The flat tax: Would wealthy individuals really pay?" *Challenge,* May 1996, pp. 24-28.

Two accounting experts take a close look at the flat tax. They think the burden will fall on working men and women.

National Commission on Restructuring the IRS

Davidson, Paul, "Commission unveils plan for new, user-friendly IRS," *USA Today,* **June 26, 1997, P. B2.**

An idyllic blueprint for a new Internal Revenue Service featuring prompt, courteous phone service, a simplified tax code and a reduced emphasis on the dreaded tax audit was presented Wednesday to Congress. The National Commission to Restructure the IRS also wants to simplify tax forms and letters, and encourage most Americans to file their returns electronically by 2007. After more than a year of study and a cost of $1 million, the 17-member panel set up by Congress unveiled a 208-page plan for transforming the IRS.

"Fixing the IRS — The Wrong Way," *St. Louis Post-Dispatch,* **July 7, 1997, p. B6.**

Shocked by the Internal Revenue Service's bungling of a $3.4 billion computer modernization program, last year Congress created the National Commission on Restructuring the Internal Revenue Service. The idea was to give the IRS the tools to become a modern, well-run agency at last. The commission has just issued its report, full of sensible, if obvious recommendations — but for one. The commission suggests that while the IRS would remain under Treasury Department supervision, a seven-member outside board would run it.

Grant, Lorrie, "Panel recommends board oversee IRS operations," *USA Today,* **June 6, 1997, p. B2.**

The National Commission on Restructuring the IRS made 50 recommendations, among them, creating a board of directors to oversee the agency. But plans stop short of taking the IRS away from its parent agency, the Treasury Department. The IRS has been roundly criticized for bungling a $4 billion upgrade of its computer systems and failing to improve customer service enough. "This has to do with the Treasury, which cannot give adequate guidance," says Rep. Rob Portman, R-Ohio, who chairs the 17-member bipartisan commission with Sen. Bob Kerrey, D-Neb.

Schlesinger, Jacob M., "House Republican leadership supports commission's plan to overhaul the IRS," *The Wall Street Journal,* **June 26, 1997, p. A4.**

The House GOP leadership endorsed the final report by the congressional National Commission on Restructuring the IRS, setting the stage for a bitter fight with the White House.

"Tax report: Reaching the IRS by phone is easier but still much too tough, a report says," *The Wall Street Journal,* **July 2, 1997, p. A1.**

IRS officials, embarrassed by years of criticism about abysmal telephone service, took steps in 1997 to im-

prove access significantly. But they haven't done nearly enough, according to a recent report by the National Commission on Restructuring the IRS.

Overhaul Legislation

Goode, Stephen, "From atop his bully pulpit, the Speaker sounds off on IRS," *Insight on the News,* **Nov. 3, 1997, pp. 20-22.**

In an interview, House Speaker Newt Gingrich, R-Ga., discusses IRS harassment of law-abiding citizens and his call for a sweeping overhaul of both the tax code and the IRS.

"House OKs Bill to Revamp the IRS: Vote Is 426-4 to Create Outside Board, Give Taxpayers New Rights," *Chicago Tribune,* **Nov. 5, 1997, Sec. EVENING, p. 1.**

With strong bipartisan support, the House approved a bill Wednesday to restructure the much-maligned IRS, building on the political momentum of hearings that put the spotlight on taxpayer abuses and mismanagement.

"New IRS restructuring bill," *Journal of Accountancy,* **October 1997, pp. 28-29.**

Legislation (HR 2292 and S 1087) has been introduced to significantly change the way the IRS is governed.

Rust, Michael, and Jennifer G. Hickey, "Purging the IRS could cure or kill," *Insight on the News,* **Nov. 3, 1997, pp. 16-17.**

As New Democrats and liberals struggle with national outrage about the dictatorial administration of tax policy, the GOP is trying to catch the wave and get the credit before President Clinton does. GOP efforts to overhaul the IRS and make the tax code fairer are detailed.

Oversight Board

"Just Imagine: An IRS That Serves the Taxpayer; Creation of oversight board will be an important first step," *Los Angeles Times,* **Nov. 7, 1997, p. B8.**

Try to imagine this: The Internal Revenue Service is stripped of its bullying arrogance. It's held accountable for the costs to taxpayers of improper or faulty audits and investigations. When the agency owes you money, the situation is regarded as seriously as when you owe the agency. Honest taxpayer mistakes are treated like, well, honest mistakes. The agency acquires computer systems that function properly. Vital personal information is closely protected, and use of the word "competence" in connection with the IRS is no longer a contradiction in terms.

Kim, James, "IRS overhaul: A taxing topic," *USA Today,* **Sept. 15, 1997, p. B1.**

The future of the Internal Revenue Service will be the

issue Tuesday, when the House Ways and Means Committee begins hearings on who should govern the agency. The National Commission on Restructuring the IRS, a panel chaired by Rep. Rob Portman, R-Ohio, and Sen. Bob Kerrey, D-Neb., has argued that the agency should be run by a seven-person board including the Treasury secretary, an IRS employees' union person and five non-IRS employees. The panel charges that the current overseer, the Treasury Department, is not up to the task.

McTague, Jim, "Reforming the IRS," *Barron's,* March 24, 1997, p. 15.

Last week Deputy Treasury Secretary Lawrence Summers unveiled a five-point program to overhaul the IRS. The plan calls for making permanent the management board Treasury created last year to oversee the IRS' technology-modernization efforts.

Wiseman, Paul, "IRS reform: Effect on taxpayers," *USA Today,* Oct. 23, 1997, p. A13.

The full House is expected to pass the bill soon, putting pressure on the Senate to move on similar legislation. Its key provisions would give taxpayers more rights in their dealings with the IRS and create a new board with people from the private sector to oversee IRS operations.

IRS Response

Mintz, Bill, "Hearings spur IRS to action / Offices open Saturday to resolve problem cases," *Houston Chronicle,* Nov. 13, 1997, p. C1.

The first "problem-resolution day" will be held at the IRS office in Houston, Texas, and in 32 other cities, as the tax collection agency struggles to improve its image. The agency plans similar monthly sessions for at least the next six months.

"Taxpayers can gripe to IRS Saturday," *Detroit News,* Nov. 12, 1997, p. A5.

The Internal Revenue Service launches its most visible response to taxpayer complaints — "problem-solving days" — starting Saturday in 33 cities across the country. The tax agency hopes to handle at least some problems on the spot and send a message of a new commitment to personal attention, particularly after Senate hearings into alleged IRS abuses in September. Citizens can get the ear of IRS employees and talk about tax problems, which could range from unresolved bills to errors with payments or IRS collection tactics.

Wiseman, Paul, Dennis Cauchon and John Larrabee et al, "Helpful IRS attracts thousands; Open houses in 33 cities called successful," *USA Today,* Nov. 17, 1997, p. A3.

"Open Houses" are the first step in the IRS' effort to repair its image after Senate hearings this fall into IRS mistreatment of taxpayers and congressional calls for

wide-ranging reforms at the tax-collection agency. Treasury Secretary Robert Rubin and IRS Commissioner Charles Rossotti separately talked to taxpayers at the IRS' Baltimore, Md., office.

Scrap the Code Tour

Dart, Bob, "Republicans take IRS attack on national tour Fanning flames: House members hope anger about taxes boosts the GOP," *Atlanta Constitution,* Oct. 10, 1997, p. A3.

The "Scrap the Code Tour" opens in Columbus, Ohio, today and stops in Atlanta, Ga., next week in what House Speaker Newt Gingrich, R-Ga., predicted will be a historic early step toward replacing the nation's "impossibly complicated" income tax system. The traveling debate features House Majority Leader Dick Armey, R-Texas, and Rep. W.J. "Billy" Tauzin, R-La. Both want to replace the current progressive income tax system.

Graetz, Michael J., "Taxes: What the Children Said," *The Washington Post,* Nov. 9, 1997, p. C9.

Following up on its recent hearings on IRS abuses of certain taxpayers' rights, Congress is about to enact legislation that would restructure the governance and some operations of the Internal Revenue Service. Congressional Republicans are trying to capitalize on the current wave of anti-IRS sentiment to spark a public rebellion against the income tax. Last month, House Majority Leader Dick Armey, R-Texas, and his colleague W.J. "Billy" Tauzin, R-La., set out on their first "Scrap the Code" tour of the country, a stylized "debate" about whether the income tax should be replaced with a flat tax of 17 percent or a 15 percent national sales tax.

"GOP leaders celebrate tour to promote tax changes," *Congressional Quarterly Weekly Report,* Oct. 11, 1997, p. 2469.

House Speaker Newt Gingrich, R-Ga., Majority Leader Dick Armey, R-Texas, and Rep. W. J. "Billy" Tauzin, R-La., began their "Scrap the Code" tour on Oct. 9. The tour, which is scheduled to visit five cities, is the GOP's latest attack on the IRS .

Kuttner, Robert, "The rich can't lose in this tax 'debate,' " *The Boston Globe,* Oct. 5, 1997, p. E7.

The Republicans have just launched what House Speaker Newt Gingrich, R-Ga., calls a "national dialogue" on how to replace the progressive income tax.

Schneider, Craig, "Gingrich rouses anti-tax crowd; Large Cobb crowd cheers IRS-bashing," *Atlanta Journal Constitution,* Oct. 18, 1997, p. A10.

Sacrificing the relaxation of a Friday night, some 2,000 people crowded a Cobb County forum to verbally bash, hammer and stomp the IRS as too big, too powerful and too greedy. The evening marked the fourth stop on the "Scrap the Code Tour," during which House Majority Leader Dicky Armey, R-Texas, and Rep. W.J. "Billy" Tauzin, R-La., discuss replacing the current tax code with either a flat tax or a national sales tax.

Survey

Crenshaw, Albert B., "GOP Seeks Survey on IRS Despite Earlier Sampling; Poll Showed Tax Law as Key Source of Anger," *The Washington Post*, Nov. 7, 1997, p. D1.

Just as congressional Republicans are pressing the Internal Revenue Service to spend about $35 million to survey taxpayers' views of the agency and the federal tax system, it turns out that a congressional commission conducted a similar, though smaller, poll this summer for $20,000. That poll was not made public by the National Commission on Restructuring the Internal Revenue Service because the body viewed it as supporting material for its report on the IRS, which was released June 25.

Schlesinger, Jacob M., "Republicans, on the Offensive Again, Push Plan to Survey Public About IRS," *The Wall Street Journal*, Nov. 5, 1997, p. B13.

In the latest tussle, GOP leaders are confident of passing legislation this month that would require the IRS to take the unusual step of sending taxpayers a public opinion survey along with their tax forms next year. Privately, administration officials and Democrats have qualms about the idea. The last-minute decision could prove expensive and create a logistical headache, officials say. They add that the proposed questions and surveying method are unscientific.

Sherman, Mark, "GOP wants to poll taxpayers on IRS," *Atlanta Journal Constitution*, Nov. 1, 1997, p. A3.

Congressional Republicans want to spend nearly $60 million to find out what the public thinks about the IRS. Taxpayers would receive questionnaires with their 1997 federal income tax returns, under a proposal Speaker Newt Gingrich, R-Ga., said will come to a vote this month. They would be asked such questions as how long they need to prepare their returns, whether their tax bill is fair and if they have ever been penalized by the IRS, Gingrich said Friday.

Welch, William M., "IRS mail-in survey a waste of money, Democrats say," *USA Today*, Nov. 4, 1997, p. A8.

A Republican plan to mail a tax-reform questionnaire with income tax forms came under Democratic attack Monday as a waste of money. At the same time, GOP leaders began considering an alternative. But Rep. Robert T. Matsui, D-Calif., a leading Democrat on the tax-writing Ways and Means Committee, said he had been told by the Treasury Department that it would cost at least $20 million to include the surveys in packages mailed to taxpayers. Democrats also raised questions about whether it is too late to include any survey with 1997 tax forms, which are now being printed and will be mailed at the end of the year.

Welch, William M., "Poll: 69 percent say IRS abuses power often," *USA Today*, Sept. 30, 1997, p. A1.

Most Americans believe the Internal Revenue Service has too much power and frequently abuses it, a new *USA Today*/CNN/Gallup Poll shows. The poll confirms that Republicans in Congress have struck a chord with Americans in targeting the IRS for reform. The poll, conducted after a week of Senate hearings into IRS abuses, found 69 percent believe the IRS "frequently abuses its powers," and just 27 percent think the agency generally uses power responsibly.

Tax Code Complexities

Largent, Steve, "We Can Do Something About IRS Abuses . . . Like Wiping the Slate Clean," *Chicago Tribune*, Oct. 5, 1997, p. 23.

Confusing. Cumbersome. Complicated. Intimidating. Such words have been used to describe America's tax laws. That the preparation of tax returns is difficult shouldn't be a surprise, considering that the tax code itself — the complete listing of tax laws currently on the books — is 3,458 pages long.

"Witnesses want simpler code and better taxpayer rights," *Journal of Accountancy*, May 1997, p. 24.

The National Commission on Restructuring the IRS heard a lot of complaints that the tax code was so complex that it interfered with the fair and efficient administration of the law.

Back Issues

Great Research on Current Issues Starts Right Here . . . Recent topics covered by The CQ Researcher are listed below. Before May 1991, reports were published under the name of Editorial Research Reports.

JULY 1996
Recovered-Memory Debate
Native Americans' Future
Crackdown on Sexual Harassment
Attack on Public Schools

AUGUST 1996
Fighting Over Animal Rights
Privatizing Government Services
Child Labor and Sweatshops
Cleaning Up Hazardous Wastes

SEPTEMBER 1996
Gambling Under Attack
The States and Federalism
Civic Journalism
Reassessing Foreign Aid

OCTOBER 1996
Political Consultants
Insurance Fraud
Rethinking School Integration
Parental Rights

NOVEMBER 1996
Global Warming
Clashing Over Copyright
Consumer Debt
Governing Washington, D.C.

Back issues are available for $5.00 (subscribers) or $10.00 (non-subscribers). Quantity discounts apply to orders over ten. To order, call Congressional Quarterly Customer Service at (202) 887-8621.

Binders are available for $18.00. To order call 1-800-638-1710. Please refer to stock number 648.

DECEMBER 1996
Welfare, Work and the States
The New Volunteerism
Implementing the Disabilities Act
America's Pampered Pets

JANUARY 1997
Combating Scientific Misconduct
Restructuring the Electric Industry
The New Immigrants
Chemical and Biological Weapons

FEBRUARY 1997
Assisting Refugees
Alternative Medicine's Next Phase
Independent Counsels
Feminism's Future

MARCH 1997
New Air Quality Standards
Alcohol Advertising
Civic Renewal
Educating Gifted Students

APRIL 1997
Declining Crime Rates
The FBI Under Fire
Gender Equity in Sports
Space Program's Future

MAY 1997
The Stock Market
The Cloning Controversy
Expanding NATO
The Future of Libraries

JUNE 1997
FDA Reform
China After Deng
Line-Item Veto
Breast Cancer

JULY 1997
Transportation Policy
Executive Pay
School Choice Debate
Aggressive Driving

AUGUST 1997
Age Discrimination
Banning Land Mines
Children's Television
Evolution vs. Creationism

SEPTEMBER 1997
Caring for the Dying
Mental Health Policy
Mexico's Future
Youth Fitness

OCTOBER 1997
Urban Sprawl in the West
Diversity in the Workplace
Teacher Education
Contingent Work Force

NOVEMBER 1997
Renewable Energy
Artificial Intelligence
Religious Persecution
Roe v. Wade at 25

DECEMBER 1997
Whistleblowers
Castro's Next Move
Gun Control Standoff
Regulating Nonprofits

JANUARY 1998
Foster Care Reform

Future Topics

▶ *The Black Middle Class*

▶ *U.S.-British Relations*

▶ *Patient Rights*

T
H
E

C QResearcher

PUBLISHED BY CONGRESSIONAL QUARTERLY INC.

The Black Middle Class

Is its cup half-full or half-empty?

In spite of steady growth in the black middle-class over the past 30 years, many African-Americans still believe they face race-based obstacles. As a result, they argue that affirmative action is still necessary to give even highly qualified blacks a fair chance at getting ahead. But others dispute the notion that discrimination is a serious problem and warn that the policy will hurt rather than help blacks by giving them a disincentive to work hard. At the same time, another debate rages over black flight to the suburbs. The American dream of a house in the suburbs only recently has become reality for many African-Americans. But some members of the black community say that successful blacks should move back to the cities in order to help disadvantaged African-Americans left behind.

C
Q | **Jan. 23, 1998** • **Volume 8, No. 3** • **Pages 49-72**

Formerly Editorial Research Reports

COVER: INDEPENDENT BUSINESSWOMAN WANDA ALEXANDER OF UPPER MARLBORO, MD. (DOUGLAS GRAHAM/CONGRESSIONAL QUARTERLY)

CQ Researcher

January 23, 1998
Volume 8, No. 3

EDITOR
Sandra Stencel

MANAGING EDITOR
Thomas J. Colin

ASSOCIATE EDITOR
Sarah M. Magner

STAFF WRITERS
Mary H. Cooper
Kenneth Jost
David Masci

PRODUCTION EDITOR
Melissa Hall

EDITORIAL ASSISTANT
Vanessa E. Furlong

PUBLISHED BY
Congressional Quarterly Inc.

CHAIRMAN
Andrew Barnes

VICE CHAIRMAN
Andrew P. Corty

PRESIDENT AND PUBLISHER
Robert W. Merry

EXECUTIVE EDITOR
David Rapp

The CQ Researcher (ISSN 1056-2036). Formerly Editorial Research Reports. Published weekly, except Jan. 2, May 29, July 3, Oct. 30, by Congressional Quarterly Inc., 1414 22nd St., N.W., Washington, D.C. 20037. Annual subscription rate for libraries, businesses and government is $340. Additional rates furnished upon request. Periodicals postage paid at Washington, D.C., and additional mailing offices. POSTMASTER: Send address changes to The CQ Researcher, 1414 22nd St., N.W., Washington, D.C. 20037.

The Black Middle Class

By David Masci

The Issues

By any measure, Wanda Alexander is a success. Just 39, she has built her own real estate consulting business and lives in Upper Marlboro, Md., a comfortable suburb south of Washington.

But Alexander's journey to reach the American dream wasn't easy. As a black woman, she faced obstacles that she believes were placed in her way because of her race. Before striking out on her own, for example, she watched her less experienced white colleagues receive training and promotions ahead of her. "I got tired of people telling me in subtle and sometimes overt ways that I would never do better than I had because of my race and gender," she says.

Stories like Alexander's are common among black professionals. Many feel anger and frustration even as they achieve personal and professional success. Indeed, polls show that a solid majority of well-off African-Americans still feel that racism is an obstacle to their advancement. A 1995 poll commissioned by *The Washington Post*, the Kaiser Family Foundation and Harvard University found that 84 percent of all black Americans with an annual household income of between $30,000 and $75,000, believed that "past and present discrimination is the major reason for the economic and social ills blacks face." Perhaps surprisingly, only 66 percent of poor and working-class blacks felt the same way. [1]

The sense that discrimination is still a problem for middle-class blacks is hard for many Americans to understand. By all accounts, the post-civil rights era has been a time of great growth for the black middle class. Today, more than one-third of all Afri-

can-Americans meet the fiscal definition of middle class: They reside in households that earn the median national income of $35,000 per year or more. In the 1960s, fewer than 10 percent of black Americans fit this description. Moreover, the number of black doctors, lawyers and engineers has grown exponentially since World War II. Indeed, the percentage of African-Americans in white-collar jobs has jumped from under 6 percent in 1940 to roughly half today. [2]

Blacks also have made great strides in the business world. The number of successful black entrepreneurs is increasing every year in fields as diverse as finance, software and manufacturing. Blacks serve as the presidents of several big U.S. corporations, including American Express and Maytag, putting them just one rung below CEO.

And yet, in the minds of many well-to-do African-Americans, all is not well. "Despite its evident prosperity, much of America's black middle class is in pain," writes *Newsweek* reporter Ellis Cose in his 1993 book, *The Rage of a Privileged Class*. The reason, according to Cose,

is that white America has broken its "covenant" with blacks. The idea, he writes, "that if you work hard, get a good education and play by the rules you will be allowed to advance and achieve to the limits of your ability" has never been fully realized. [3]

For many middle-class African-Americans, the "pain" is felt most keenly in the workplace, where they say their race is still a factor in hiring and promotion. "Discrimination still exists, even if it's masked well," says Joanne Dowdell, an African-American who is vice president for new product development at Washington Business Information Inc.

Many scholars of race relations echo such sentiments, arguing that while some businesses — especially large corporations — have become more open to blacks and other minorities, racism is still a big problem. "It's still an obstacle. It just takes a more subtle form," says Bart Landry, an associate professor of sociology at the University of Maryland at College Park.

Some white managers mean well and don't know that they are discriminating, Landry and others say. But they feel that many managers still view African-Americans as lazy or less capable than whites, or both. And so, they say, even at companies that pride themselves on hiring and promoting minorities, few African-Americans ever rise to the top or even to positions of real responsibility. "People in control want to work with people who look like them," says Ronald Walters, a professor of government at Maryland. As a result, Walters and others point out, there are no black CEOs at America's largest, most powerful corporations.

But other observers argue that discrimination is no longer a great stumbling block for African-Americans. In fact, says Shelby Steele, a research fellow at the Hoover Institution, universities, companies and

How Are Blacks Doing?

African-Americans don't think they are faring as well as whites think they are, according to a comprehensive Gallup Poll in early 1997. But the poll also showed substantial improvement over time in blacks' satisfaction with their lives.

How are blacks treated in your community?

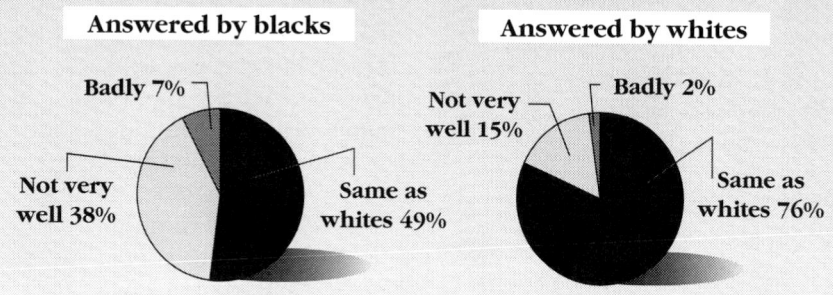

Answered by blacks

Badly 7%
Not very well 38%
Same as whites 49%

Answered by whites

Not very well 15%
Badly 2%
Same as whites 76%

How do you feel about affirmative action?

	Answered by Blacks	Answered by Whites
Increase affirmative action	53%	22%
Keep affirmative action the same	29%	29%
Decrease affirmative action	12%	37%

Blacks in your community have as good a chance as whites to:

	Answered by Blacks	Answered by Whites
Get a job	46%	79%
Get housing	58%	86%
Get an education	63%	79%

Percent who think blacks are treated the same as whites in your community:

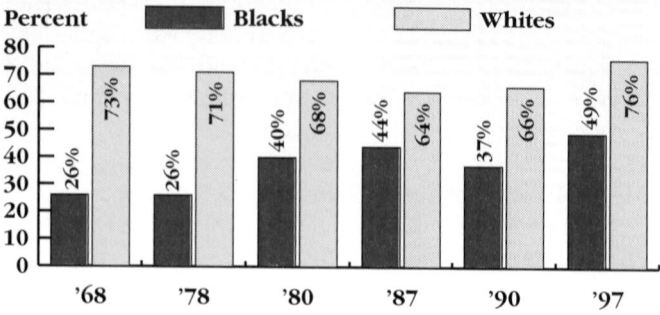

Percent   ■ Blacks   ☐ Whites

80
70
60
50
40
30
20
10
0

'68: 26%, 73%
'78: 26%, 71%
'80: 40%, 68%
'87: 44%, 64%
'90: 37%, 66%
'97: 49%, 76%

Source: The Gallup Organization conducted a telephone poll of 3,076 black and white Americans between Jan. 4 and Feb. 28, 1997.

the government are working hard to find, hire and promote blacks. "This is the new spirit of corporate America," says Steele, who is black.

Steele and others argue that the problem for African-Americans on the job isn't racism, but lack of progress in education and training. For instance, they point out, blacks — even from middle-class backgrounds — don't score as well on standardized tests and are more likely to drop out of college than whites, even poor whites. [4] "The fact is that in many [occupational] areas there is a very small pool of qualified black applicants, and that's the problem," says Gerald Reynalds, president of the Center for New Black Leadership.

According to Steele, Reynalds and others, the view that racism is still the primary obstacle to black advancement on the job and elsewhere has hurt African-Americans by shifting the emphasis from self-improvement to fighting discrimination. "People put too much stock in discrimination today," says Walter Williams, chairman of the Economics Department at George Mason University in Fairfax, Va. Blaming discrimination, says Williams, has undercut blacks' advancement by leading them to rely on racial preferences instead of their own efforts.

To begin with, Williams and other black conservatives say, preferences created by the policy known as "affirmative action" are damaging to society as a whole because it is fundamentally unfair to judge someone based on race, regardless of the reason. Such efforts lead to resentment among whites and bolster stereotypes of black inferiority.

But, Williams argues, the policy does the greatest harm to those it is intended to help because it lowers the standards by which African-Americans are judged. Giving someone a preference "doesn't do them any favor," he says, because people who don't have to work as hard to get ahead, won't. In other words, by lowering standards for African-Americans, companies, universities and others are giving them a disincentive to achieve on their own.

The net result of such assistance, Williams says, is that it produces problems when the beneficiaries of affirmative action are eventually forced to compete head to head with everyone else. It also makes blacks "passive," in Steele's view. "It makes me into someone who cannot move forward unless white people are benevolent and help me move forward," he says.

But supporters of affirmative action counter that it is necessary simply to give African-Americans a chance to succeed in the face of past and present racism. The bottom line, they say, is that there is no level playing field when it comes to competition between blacks and whites. White men have controlled all the levers of power in American society from the beginning, they say, conferring upon them an advantage that did not go away when the Civil Rights Act of 1964 was passed.

"The effects of discrimination linger," says Cecilia Conrad, a research associate at the Joint Center for Political and Economic Studies, which focuses on issues of interest to blacks. "Whites are still benefiting from Jim Crow," she adds.

But vestiges of traditional discrimination have been felt far beyond the workplace. For instance, until recently, many suburban areas were virtually off-limits to African-Americans. And while housing discrimination has not been entirely eliminated, most neighborhoods that were, in effect, reserved for whites are now open to black homeowners. Not surprisingly, the number of African-Americans living in the suburbs has risen dramatically in the last three decades. [5]

But some black thinkers argue that "black flight" from the inner cities has hurt African-Americans. As the best and the brightest have left for the suburbs,

many formerly segregated communities, usually in cities, have degenerated into neighborhoods characterized by high crime, little economic opportunity and hopelessness. "Talented individuals and stable families have left, and left a vacuum," says Roy Brooks, a law professor at San Diego State University.

Brooks is among the blacks who urge middle-class African-Americans to move into black urban areas in order to revitalize them. They argue that black professionals can serve as role models for members of the underclass. In addition, they say, by living and shopping in these areas, professionals and other residents will increase economic opportunities in the neighborhood as businesses are established to serve them.

But many black professionals reject the notion that they should feel obliged to live in a poor, crime-ridden area in order to serve the less fortunate. "I want to live where I'm most comfortable," Alexander says. Elijah Anderson, a professor of ethnography at the University of Pennsylvania, agrees. "The bottom line is that people should be able to do what they want."

Anderson and others argue that there is no sense in working hard and succeeding if you can't live where you want to. In addition, he doubts that an influx of the black middle class back to the cities would make a big difference in the lives of poor African-Americans. Instead, he argues, the underclass needs training and jobs, not role models.

Besides, they contend, one does not have to live next door to someone in order to help them. "There are other ways that you can give back to the community," Dowdell says. Alexander and Dowdell, who lives in a predominantly white part of Washington, both work to help other African-Americans get ahead. Alexander, for instance, helps to finance scholarships for young, black women.

But others are torn over the issue. "You need good role models so that

kids can see that there are legitimate alternatives to poverty," says Gavin Jackson, a human resources specialist at the Department of the Treasury, who lives in suburban Burtonsville, Md., with his wife and two children. At the same time, Jackson admits that he is not ready to move out of suburbia. "I can't sacrifice my children. I mean, we moved [to the suburbs] because the schools were better." [6]

Like many black professionals, Jackson feels the tug of group identity even as he strives to build a life for himself and his family. As Jackson and other African-Americans look toward the future, these are some of the questions they are asking:

Is racism still a big obstacle to advancement for many black professionals?

In November 1996, oil giant Texaco agreed to pay $176.1 million to settle a discrimination suit filed by 1,400 current and former black employees. Many of the workers who sued alleged that they had repeatedly lost out on promotions and raises because of their race. They also claimed that they were subjected to racial slurs and other indignities. [7]

For many black Americans, the Texaco case is simply the tip of a very large iceberg. According to recent polls, fully two-thirds of middle-class blacks think that discrimination is still a real problem in their lives. Racism, most of these professionals say, is a fact of life in corporate America, a fact that puts African-Americans at a serious disadvantage as they try to compete with whites in the workplace.

Many whites and others wonder how their black colleagues can still feel discriminated against. After all, they say, the days of Jim Crow, of overt, institutionalized racism, are over.

"It's not a nationwide problem," said Michael Losey, president and CEO of the Society for Human Resource Management. According to

Blacks in White-Collar Occupations

In stark contrast to 1940, when most blacks did manual labor, more than half the black women and a third of the men had white-collar jobs in 1990.

	1940	1970	1990
		(Percentage)	
Men			
Professionals	1.8	7.8	9.4
Proprietors, managers and officials	1.3	4.7	6.7
Clerical and sales	2.1	9.2	15.9
Total white-collar	5.2	21.7	32.0
Women			
Professionals	4.3	10.8	15.9
Proprietors, managers and officials	0.7	1.9	7.6
Clerical and sales	1.4	23.4	35.4
Total white-collar	6.4	36.1	58.9

Sources: Stephan and Abigail Thernstrom, America in Black and White: One Nation, Indivisible, *1997, based on U.S. Census Bureau, "Money Income in the U.S.: 1995."*

Losey, who is white, when a case like Texaco does occur, there is a reason people are shocked. He says that "many people recognize this as inconsistent with what they see in their community, what they see as their company policy where they work, what they see as a practice."[8]

But many black thinkers argue that discrimination encountered by minorities today is harder to recognize because it is much different from the obvious examples of past prejudice. "We are dealing not with overt racism, but a subtler form," says Professor Robert Hill, director of the Institute for Urban Research at Morgan State University in Baltimore.

Hill argues that many white managers don't know that they are discriminating against their black colleagues. "They are doing their best," he says, "but they don't realize that their best is not adequate." For instance, Hill says, whites exclude blacks from their network of close co-workers ("the buddy system"), which in effect excludes African-Americans from important decisions and promotions.

Others argue that many whites still view blacks as their intellectual inferiors. "A lot of white people have not really viewed black people close-up," says the University of Pennsylvania's Anderson, "operating instead on stereotypes."

And so, even at companies that try to hire and promote a lot of minorities, there are few black professionals in any important slots, says Sharon Collins, an associate professor of sociology at the University of Illinois in Chicago. "Black managers tend to go in the personnel or public relations departments," she add. "These don't tend to be the most career-enhancing jobs."

Moreover, says Conrad of the Joint Center for Economics and Politics, African-Americans are excluded from key posts because whites don't trust blacks to do the most important work in the corporation. "They tend not to be in the company's profit centers, like sales or product development," she says.

As a result, Collins and Conrad say, the very top of the corporate hierarchy includes very few black executives. In addition, they say, there are no black CEOs at *Fortune* 500 companies, with the exception of Beatrice Foods Inc., which is black-owned.

But other African-American thinkers reject the idea that black professionals are being held back in large numbers by discrimination. In fact, many say, large companies and government agencies are working overtime to hire and promote minorities. "Every major company is busting its ass looking for brown faces," says Reynalds of the Center for New Black Leadership.

The Hoover Institution's Steele, author of the best-selling treatise on race *The Content of Our Character*, agrees with Reynalds, pointing out that "in corporations, universities and the government, people are looking for ways to encourage and mentor blacks."

Steele, Reynalds and other thinkers are not saying that America is a color-blind society. "People have lost their minds if they think they can do away with prejudice," Reynalds says. But he believes that racism today is not a powerful enough force in our society to hold back minorities who want to succeed.

The problem, Reynalds, Steele and others say, isn't discrimination, but a lack of education and training. For instance, they point out, blacks do score significantly lower on standardized tests and are much more likely to have been involved in the criminal-justice system than whites. "If you've been convicted of a felony or don't have a proper education, that will be a much greater obstacle to job advancement than your race," Reynalds says.

Steele agrees, arguing that poverty and other social factors have "brought us to a point where we're not as competitive as other groups are."

But what about polls showing middle-class blacks' concern over discrimination and anger over the way society is treating them? Some, like Ward Connerly, the

California businessman behind Proposition 209, the ballot initiative ending affirmative action programs in California, say that African-American anger is due to outmoded attitudes about race. "I think part of our racial problem is that my fellow black Americans are so sensitive to the issue of racism that it almost becomes a self-fulfilling prophecy," he says. "You look for it, and by golly, it's there — whether it's real or not." [9]

Others are less forgiving. Steele, for instance, believes that African-Americans, either consciously or unconsciously, often cry racism because it produces results. "If I'm black and I'm angry, I'm more likely to get attention and get preferential treatment than if I'm black and not angry," he says. In short, the accusations of racism and the anger are tools that give black employees leverage over their white managers, who do not want to be accused of racism.

"This [behavior] trips white guilt and obligation and gets [blacks] preferential treatment, like a promotion or an all-black lounge at the office," Steele says. In many cases these African-American professionals convince themselves that they are victims. "We all tend to believe in what serves us, even if it's wrong," he says.

Do members of the black middle class have an obligation to other blacks to live in predominantly African-American neighborhoods, especially in poorer areas in the inner city?

Buying a home in the suburbs is the quintessential right of passage for middle-class Americans. But before the civil rights movement of the 1950s and '60s, African-Americans were not welcome in most suburban areas.

Today, the situation is different, although housing discrimination is far from eradicated. A recent study in the Washington, D.C., area, for instance, showed that many real estate agencies still "steer" minorities away from certain areas. But by and large, suburban enclaves that were once

Marchers protesting Proposition 209 cross the Golden Gate Bridge led by Jesse Jackson, San Francisco Supervisor Mabel Teng and Mayor Willie Brown.

segregated are now open to African-Americans.

Statistics bear out this new interracial reality. Polls show that since 1960 the number of African-Americans living in suburban areas has more than doubled. Today roughly 32 percent of all black Americans live in the suburbs. [10] And in some areas, blacks comprise the majority of suburbanites. For instance, Prince George's County, Md., outside Washington, is now 62 percent African-American. [11]

For a member of the black middle class, the suburbs have the same allure that they do for their white counterparts: better schools, lower crime rates and bucolic settings usually not found in cities.

But some African-Americans view the middle-class exodus with dread and call for black professionals to move back to the urban areas where they grew up.

"Integration has resulted in a depletion of human and economic resources from the black community," says San Diego State's Brooks. "We need to find a way to reintegrate the black middle class into inner-city areas," Walters adds.

The problem, Brooks, Walters and others say, is that middle-class migration to the suburbs has drained traditionally black areas of some of their most productive and valuable citizens. In the past, when segregation forced all blacks to live together regardless of class, professionals and other accomplished African-Americans served as leaders and role models in the community. Today, they say, there is a void in many areas created by the absence of successful people. "They need to reconnect with their roots and serve as role models to the rest of the community," Walters says.

Walters also argues that "the middle class leaves behind a much weaker institutional base and a citizenry denuded of resources." For example, he says, the presence of middle-class residents gives the areas greater political clout, which in turn could lead to better city services, like police and sanitation. In addition, he says, middle-class children and par-

Lou Denatteis/Reuters

Blacks Flocked to the Suburbs

Many black Americans moved to the suburbs following the civil rights movement of the 1950s and '60s. From 1960 to 1995, the number of suburban blacks tripled, and the percentage of blacks who were suburbanites doubled.

Blacks in the Suburbs

	Number (in millions)	Percent of total black population	Percent of total suburban population
1950	2.2	15	5.5
1960	2.9	15.2	4.8
1970	3.6	16.1	4.8
1980	5.9	22.3	5.9
1995	10.6	31.9	8.1

Sources: Stephan and Abigail Thernstrom, America in Black and White: One Nation, Indivisible, *1997, based on data from* Statistical Abstract of the U.S.: 1974 *and U.S. Bureau of the Census.*

ents "raise the standards at schools, which benefits everyone."

Finally, Walters and Brooks argue, the presence of a large group of people with disposable income will give blighted areas an economic shot in the arm, which in turn will create needed jobs. "Businesses will be created to serve them, and they will start businesses of their own in the community," Brooks says.

The idea that the presence of a middle class is necessary for healthy community development has prompted a number of cities, including Philadelphia and Cleveland, to offer tax and other incentives to lure professionals back to inner-city neighborhoods long abandoned by all but the poor. Cleveland, for instance, is offering lots in run-down areas for as little as $100 to anyone willing to build a house and live there. The city also offers mortgage assistance and will waive property taxes for up to 15 years. "Cities cannot survive if they are full of old and poor people," says Cleveland Mayor Michael White, an African-American. [12]

The city's plan seems to be working. Since 1990, 2,400 new homes have been built in the special areas, almost all by African-Americans. More broadly, the percentage of black households nationwide with an income of $75,000 or more that have stayed in cities has remained at 48 percent throughout the 1990s. [13]

But while many thinkers on race applaud the back-to-the-city trend, others argue that middle-class African-Americans should not feel obligated to stay in or move back to inner cities. "I like the idea that people have choices . . . and if I want to move to a certain area because it's, say, close to work, I should be able to do that," says Conrad, who grew up in a segregated neighborhood. "If you have the money and wherewithal, you should live where you want to, period," agrees George Mason's Williams.

Others say that trying to push middle-class blacks back into their old, largely African-American neighborhoods is bad for both them and the country. To begin with, they argue, more blacks and whites should be living together, not trying to stay

with their own kind. "What we're talking about here is resegregation, plain and simple," Anderson says. "We will lose the idea of making America into a universalist, egalitarian society," he says.

Anderson and others also argue that the middle-class African-Americans who move into inner-city neighborhoods are making a sacrifice in the name of racial unity. For one thing, he says, blacks are financially penalized when they go to sell their city houses because the only people who will want to purchase a home in these areas are other African-Americans. "This is a limited housing market because whites, Asians and other folks aren't interested in these neighborhoods," he says. "That's a bad way to play the capitalist game."

Finally, opponents of efforts to lure professionals back to cities argue that the presence of some middle-class African-Americans in the neighborhood isn't a solution to the real problems of the black underclass. "What inner-city blacks need is not the middle class but a real job base," Landry says. According to Landry and others, the presence of middle-class residents might improve local government and create a few new service jobs, but it won't generate the kind of employment, such as a factory work, that allows poorer residents the opportunity to make a decent living.

Landry also rejects the notion that black professionals will make a difference by serving as role models for their less fortunate brethren. "Black kids don't need these role models in that sense," he says, "because in our media age the role models and avenues to success are well-known."

Do middle-class African-Americans need affirmative action to have equal opportunities at school and work?

On Nov. 5, 1996, proponents of

affirmative action suffered a stunning blow when voters in California passed Proposition 209, a ballot measure that outlawed the use of racial or gender preferences at all state government institutions. A year later, on Nov. 3, Prop. 209 went into effect when the Supreme Court refused to review an earlier Court of Appeals decision upholding the referendum's constitutionality. [14]

The success of Proposition 209 has inspired similar efforts in other parts of the country. Voters in Colorado and Ohio, among others, will have a chance to eliminate gender and racial preferences in the upcoming 1998 elections.

Meanwhile, recent court challenges to affirmative action programs also have proven successful. For instance, in 1996 the Supreme Court refused to review (and hence effectively upheld) a 5th Circuit Court of Appeals decision prohibiting the University of Texas from using race or gender in admissions. In New Jersey, a discrimination suit brought by a white teacher was settled before it went to the Supreme Court. Settlement was prompted by the likelihood that the court would rule that the affirmative action policy that led to the teacher's dismissal was unconstitutional. She had been laid off and a black teacher retained, although both had equal tenure and qualifications, because the school system wanted to maintain racial diversity.

To many black professionals, the success of efforts to eliminate or scale back affirmative action is both disheartening and misguided. "A lot of white people say: 'We've solved racism, so just get on with [life] already,'" says the University of Pennsylvania's Anderson.

But the reality, according to Anderson and others, is that affirmative action is still needed to give African-Americans simply a fighting chance of competing in a world where the

Blacks in College Steadily Increased

Four times as many blacks had attended college for at least four years in 1995 as in 1960.

Percent with Four Years or More of College

White

Black

Year	Black	White
1960	3.1%	8.1%
1970	4.4%	11.3%
1980	8.4%	17.1%
1995	13.2%	24%

Sources: Stephan and Abigail Thernstrom, America in Black and White: One Nation, Indivisible, *1997, based on U.S. Census Bureau, "Money Income in the U.S.: 1995."*

odds are still stacked against them, even three decades after the successes of the civil rights movement.

"You cannot do in 30 years what [America has] done with great success for 300 years — that is, give affirmative action to white people," says historian John Hope Franklin, who heads the advisory panel on race relations established in June by President Clinton. [15]

Wade Henderson, executive director of the Leadership Conference on Civil Rights, agrees that whites have enjoyed such great advantages historically that attempts to rectify past injustices require more than a level playing field. He points out, for example, that African-Americans graduating from college and looking for work might not have either the financial resources or "connections" that their white counterparts may enjoy thanks to their families. "The roots of racism run deep," he says.

In fact, Henderson and others argue, it's not possible to have a level playing field, and so it's counterproductive to pretend otherwise. "Nepotism and favoritism, that's white affirmative action, and it determines a lot of hiring and promotion decisions," says the University of Maryland's Landry. "Blacks don't have those kind of connections, and so they shouldn't feel apologetic if they substitute affirmative action instead," he adds.

Finally, supporters of affirmative action say, the evidence to support the policy is in the numbers. To begin with, they point out, blacks are still woefully underrepresented, both as students in universities and as white-collar workers. For example, according to 1995 Department of Education statistics, only 44.9 percent of African-Americans had attended at least some college, compared with 55.4 percent of whites. [16] In addition, as of 1994, only 14.7 percent of black men and

20.1 percent of black women held what would be considered managerial or professional jobs. By contrast, 27.5 percent of white men and 29.9 percent of white women worked in such jobs. [17] (*See graph, p. 54.*)

The disparity between the number of African-Americans and whites in higher learning and executive-level jobs would be much higher if it were not for affirmative action, say supporters of race and gender preferences. "If you ended affirmative action, many of the people who run these businesses wouldn't give a fig about hiring black people," Anderson says.

Others point to the University of California at Berkeley as an example of what would happen in university admissions of blacks nationwide if affirmative action were totally abolished. At the university's law school, for instance, admission of African-American students dropped 81 percent the year after racial preferences were eliminated. "Imagine if we had Proposition 209 nationwide," Anderson says. "We'd have institutionalized segregation again."

But opponents of affirmative action argue that the policy — far from helping African-Americans — actually has had a detrimental impact on the black middle class. To begin with, they say, affirmative action lowers standards by which black Americans are judged, at school or on the job. This in turn creates what Reynalds calls "perverse incentives" for African-Americans to expect more for less. "If you don't have to work as hard, you won't," he says. "That's just human nature."

The problem, Reynalds argues, comes when black students or workers have to compete head to head with their white counterparts. "Once they get into the real world, they're in for a rude awakening because most folks run into the higher standard sooner or later and often don't know how to handle it." This leads to higher rates of black failure, Reynalds contends. For instance, he says, many more black than white students who get into good colleges and universities drop out before they graduate.

By accepting unqualified candidates, opponents like Reynalds say, universities, companies and other institutions help to mask the real problem in the black community: poor achievement.

"Affirmative action has suppressed the development of black America because it is a disincentive to becoming more competitive," Steele says. According to Steele and others, preferences make African-Americans much more accepting of the inferior educational system that many are subjected to because they look to white America and affirmative action for uplift, not themselves.

Lower standards also fuel false stereotypes of black inferiority, opponents say, because people will always wonder whether African-Americans owe their success to hard work and intelligence or affirmative action. "If you have a white who has graduated from an Ivy League school, you know something about that kid and the work he's had to do to get there," Steele says. But "if someone has been getting a preference since high school, you don't know much about his true worth, regardless of his credentials on paper." In the end, Steele argues, "the big tragedy is that many blacks have high SAT scores, but they're tarred with the same brush." In other words, affirmative action distorts the connection between your credentials and your ability, regardless of the reality of the situation.

Others say that preferences also create white resentment, which in turn leads to race-based anger. "In many places, they'll kick the white guy's butt if he does shoddy work, but not the black guy's," Williams says. "This, of course, creates ill will among the races."

Most important, opponents say, affirmative action is simply immoral in a society that claims to be working toward true equality. "If you believe in equality before the law, you have to be offended by an institution that uses racial preferences," Williams says. ∎

BACKGROUND

The Migration North

Until the turn of the century, most black Americans lived in rural areas of the South. Even in 1940, a majority of African-Americans were still working in agriculture below the Mason-Dixon line.

The concentration of blacks in the South retarded African-American progress. On purely economic grounds, few blacks, even after Emancipation, benefited from the industrialization and urbanization taking place in the North and other parts of the country. In the decades following the Civil War, most blacks stayed in the areas where they had been slaves, many working as sharecroppers on land owned by whites.

Meanwhile, throughout the country, but especially in the South, government institutions and businesses treated African-Americans like pariahs. From restaurants to universities to the local Woolworth's, the list of indignities was endless. In many parts of the country, African-Americans were effectively barred from voting or sitting on juries. Public facilities were often segregated, and many businesses refused to serve blacks. Well-funded state universities attended by whites didn't admit blacks.

Continued on p. 60

Chronology

1940s-1950s

World War II and its after-math presage big changes for African-Americans as the migration north intensifies and the civil rights movement takes off.

1941

U.S. entry into World War II causes an immediate shortage of industrial labor at home, increasing the migration of African-Americans from the South to Northern urban areas.

1946

President Harry S Truman orders an end to racial segregation in the armed forces.

1947

Jackie Robinson joins the Brooklyn Dodgers, becoming the first African-American to play Major League baseball.

1954

The Supreme Court's landmark *Brown v. Board of Education* ruling overturns the previous "separate but equal" policy in public education.

1955

Rosa Parks refuses to give up her seat on a city bus to a white man, sparking the Montgomery, Ala., bus boycott. The Rev. Martin Luther King Jr. emerges as a civil rights leader.

1960s
The civil rights movement becomes a national crusade. Congress enacts a raft of legislation aimed at ending discrimination.

1961

President John F. Kennedy uses the term "affirmative action" for the first time, ordering federal contractors to take affirmative action not to discriminate in hiring, but does not set numerical quotas.

1963

Martin Luther King Jr. gives his stirring "I Have a Dream" speech at the Lincoln Memorial in Washington.

1964

Congress passes the sweeping Civil Rights Act, which prohibits discrimination by employers on the basis of race, sex or national origin.

1965

In August President Lyndon B. Johnson signs the Voting Rights Act, which outlaws unreasonable barriers to voting. In September he issues Executive Order 11246 requiring federal contractors to actively recruit minorities.

1966

The Black Panthers, a group advocating "black power," is founded.

1968

Civil Rights leader Martin Luther King Jr. is assassinated, touching off race riots in many American cities.

1970s-present
In the post-civil rights era, new policies like affirmative action are adopted, sparking a backlash among whites.

1970

President Richard M. Nixon expands upon Executive Order 11246 to require contractors to set goals for minority employment.

1978

In *University of California Regents v. Bakke*, the Supreme Court rules that universities can use race as a factor in admissions, but may not impose quotas.

1980

Affirmative action foe Ronald Reagan is elected to the presidency. The Justice Department begins attacking racial quotas.

1995

Middle-class blacks are widely represented among the hundreds of thousands of people at the Million Man March in Washington, D.C.

1996

Voters in California approve Proposition 209 outlawing the use of race or gender preferences at all state government institutions.

1997

President Clinton names an advisory panel on race relations as part of a "national dialogue on race."

1998

Referendums in Colorado, Ohio, Washington and Florida will give voters a chance to strike down racial preferences in hiring and college admissions.

Continued from p. 58

Still, even in this harsh economic and social environment, a small black middle class slowly grew. The process was aided in the early part of the century by a migration of African-Americans to Northern industrial areas. The first great wave of this movement occurred during World War I. The conflict cut off the flow of immigrants from Europe, forcing American factories to look for cheap labor elsewhere. By 1920, most Northern cities had sizable black communities.

World War II also played a key role in black population shifts. While heavy industry was expanding almost exponentially to produce weapons and other war materiel to fight the Axis powers, many of the nation's white factory workers were in uniform. Blacks, on the other hand, were not inducted into the armed forces at as great a rate as whites, making them prime candidates to fill the void. As a result, African-Americans moved in large numbers to the industrial North and would continue to do so for the next three decades.

This second great migration ballooned black populations in cities from Los Angeles to New York. By the end of the war, more than one-quarter of all African-Americans lived outside the South. By 1960, the number had risen to 40 percent. [18]

As more and more black Americans shifted from agricultural to factory work, income levels began improving. More money meant more power for blacks, as consumers and voters. It also — along with the GI Bill and other factors — led to a significant increase in black educational attainment. As a result, the number of African-Americans with at least a high school diploma jumped from 12.3 percent in 1940 to 38.6 percent in 1960. During the same period, the percentage of black men doing white-collar work jumped from 10 percent to nearly one-quarter. [19]

But the Second World War altered more than income and education levels. Many blacks, and a few whites, saw the irony of more than 300,000 young, black men fighting — in segregated units — for freedom around the world. By the end of the war, black Americans felt that they had done their

---

> **"The Second World War altered more than income and education levels. Many blacks, and a few whites, saw the irony of more than 300,000 young, black men fighting — in segregated units — for freedom around the world."**

---

part and deserved to be treated accordingly by the broader society. More important, black leaders and liberal, white politicians began to forcefully and openly campaign against the nation's overtly racist policies.

Their efforts produced some startling results. The armed forces, and, more slowly, professional sports, were integrated. Some colleges and universities began accepting African-Americans, albeit in small numbers. Ten years after the war ended in 1945, however, many barriers to full integration remained.

Civil Rights Era

Still, the winds of change were blowing. In 1954, the Supreme Court's historic *Brown v. Board of Education* decision declared state-sponsored segregation in schools to be unconstitutional. At the same time, the civil rights movement was beginning to attract the attention of white America. Just a year after the *Brown* ruling, Rosa Parks was arrested on a city bus in Montgomery, Ala., for refusing to give up her seat to a white passenger.

The arrest united Montgomery's black community and led to the Montgomery bus boycott. The Parks incident also catapulted a young Atlanta clergyman into the leadership of the boycott and, eventually, the national spotlight. His name: the Rev. Martin Luther King Jr.

After almost a year, the boycott ended when a federal court ruled that segregation on the city's buses was unconstitutional. But the incident had an impact far beyond the city's boundaries. King built on the victory in Montgomery to found a national civil rights organization, the Southern Christian Leadership Conference (SCLC). Run largely by black clergymen, it was dedicated to non-violence as an agent of change. Throughout the late 1950s and early '60s, the SCLC and other civil rights groups scored a number of stunning victories in the fight against racial segregation. From the sit-in at Woolworth's in Greensboro, N.C., to the business boycott in Birmingham, Ala., blacks, sympathetic whites and civil rights groups made slow but steady gains in the struggle for equality.

Outside the South, white America had awakened to the realities of Jim Crow. Television networks regularly

Continued on p. 62

At the NAACP, a Challenge to Integration

The unthinkable occurred at the NAACP's annual meeting in Pittsburgh last July. As the nation's oldest and most respected civil rights organization gathered to chart a course for the coming year, a sizable and vocal minority of members were calling for reconsideration of the group's longstanding support for integration.

The proposal caused a fire storm both within the organization and around the country. After all, the NAACP had been founded on the principle that "separate but equal" was an unworkable fallacy and had to be ended.

Indeed, integration has been the bedrock of mainstream civil rights philosophy for decades. Black leaders ranging from Supreme Court Justice Thurgood Marshall to the Rev. Martin Luther King Jr. to Jesse Jackson have all supported the idea that blacks and whites should strive toward a society where all peoples work, learn and live together. In addition, most of the great grass-roots victories of the civil rights movement involved integrating institutions from universities to lunch counters.

The NAACP's new chairperson, Myrlie Evers-Williams, the widow of slain civil rights leader Medger Evers, led the fight to beat back the anti-integration effort. "We're doing what we have always done, and our position remains the same," she said at the time. [1]

It was not the first time that integration has come under black attack. Scientist Booker T. Washington believed that the races could work better together by working separately. Others, from black nationalist Marcus Garvey to the Nation of Islam's Louis Farrakan have called for black separatism as the only way to encourage African-American advancement.

But the fact that so strong and public a challenge occurred on such a fundamental issue was seen as telling. For a growing number of African-Americans, the question isn't whether to integrate, but how to build prosperous, stable black communities. Many of these critics are not opposed to blacks and whites living and working together. Instead, they argue, civil rights groups should end their quest for integration above and beyond all other concerns. "Integration hasn't served African-Americans well, especially poorer ones," says Roy Brooks, a law professor at San Diego State University.

Brooks and others argue that instead of trying to push people into a broader society that may not fully accept them, groups like the NAACP should work to foster black self-help. "African-Americans, like Italians, Jews and Cubans, must pull together," Brooks says. "These groups were able to succeed within their own segregated communities and used that as a springboard to the wider community."

Such sentiments are especially strong with regard to schools.

NAACP President Kweisi Mfume

Critics of integration argue that the civil rights community has focused on busing at the expense of quality education. For one thing, they argue, busing black students to white schools leads to white flight, which in turn leads to resegregated schools. In fact, two-thirds of all black students already attend schools where a majority of the pupils are from minority groups. And if integration as an ideal is sacrificed on the altar of good education, so be it, say these critics. "Our biggest concern now is whether our schools will be equal. Separate but equal would not be too bad," says Amos Quick, an African-American who is a member of a citizens' committee redrawing school boundaries in Greensboro, N.C. [2]

But civil rights leaders, including NAACP President Kweisi Mfume, argue that separating the races will not improve the quality of schools. In addition, Mfume says, "most parents want their children to have the most diverse, comprehensive educational experience they can have. And they want them to have it with different races." [3]

Mfume and other civil rights advocates say that recent talk of ending the fight for integration is a result of African-American frustration after years of trying to gain acceptance by whites. According to Theodore Shaw, associate director-counsel of the NAACP Legal Defense and Education Fund, this frustration is natural in the current environment in which most blacks live. "You're beating your head up against the wall until it's bloody. At some point you have to ask, 'Should I continue to beat up against this wall?'" [4]

But others argue that the civil rights groups are reaping what they have sown by pushing for racial preferences in hiring and education at the expense of the colorblind society. According to Shelby Steele, a research fellow at the Hoover Institution, the growing rejection of integration is "an outgrowth of the same incentive system that created affirmative action."

Black people, he says, have been encouraged to think of themselves in largely racial terms, making integration harder. "They have been rewarded for saying their black identity is their first identity," he says, "so it's not surprising" that their group identity overrides all other concerns.

---

[1] Quoted on National Public Radio, "Weekend All Things Considered," July 12, 1997.

[2] Quoted in Nat Hentoff, "The Undercutting of Thurgood Marshall — by the NAACP," *The Washington Post*, July 12, 1997.

[3] Quoted on National Public Radio, *op. cit.*

[4] Quoted in James S. Kunen, "Integration Forever?" *Time*, July 21, 1997.

Continued from p. 60

broadcast the indignities suffered by African-Americans who were jailed, beaten and abused for protesting segregation. The dramatic media coverage helped effect a tremendous shift in public opinion in favor of civil rights. By 1963, 83 percent of all whites said they favored equality in the workplace, almost double the number who responded to the same question 19 years earlier.

The campaign for equality culminated in the Civil Rights Act of 1964, which prohibited discrimination based on race. The following year, Congress passed the Voting Rights Act, which put an end to literacy tests and other tactics used by Southern states to prohibit blacks from registering to vote. These two laws, and others that followed, did not end institutional discrimination overnight. But they did reflect the federal government's commitment to rooting out the race-based policies that had long been a part of American life.

Affirmative Action

By the 1970s, most historians agree, the worst excesses of the past had been eliminated. Meanwhile, black Americans were making great strides in catching up to white America. By 1969, median income for a black family was $22,000, a far cry from the white average of almost $36,000 but a significant improvement over the previous decades. Other factors also showed that the gap was closing. For instance, by 1970, 36.1 percent of African-Americans were in white-collar jobs, up from 6.4 percent in 1940. And the percentage of blacks attending college rose by a factor of five, from 7.2 percent in 1960 to 37.5 percent in 1995. [20]

During the civil rights battles of the 1950s and '60s, the vast majority of white Americans came to believe in the justness of the struggle against discrimination. But in the post-civil rights era, this relative consensus broke down. Part of this schism grew out of the "Black Power" movement in the late 1960s and early '70s. Black power represented the repudiation of the civil rights movement. First, it explicitly rejected cooperation between races, which had been a hallmark of the struggle. It also advocated acquiring power "by any means necessary," including violence. Hence, it rejected King's strategy of non-violent action.

At the same time, America's cities experienced a sharp increase in crime and an explosion of race-related riots. All of this made white America, as well as many blacks, highly uncomfortable.

In addition, new initiatives aimed at fighting poverty and fostering black advancement in general have proven much more controversial than the original anti-discrimination laws of the early 1960s. The new initiatives, part of President Lyndon B. Johnson's "Great Society" program, did not entirely achieve their goals. Many of these programs have since been altered or eliminated.

One policy from this era that has become increasingly controversial is affirmative action. President John F. Kennedy first used the term in 1961, when he issued an executive order requiring federal contractors to take "affirmative action" to ensure that they did not discriminate. In 1965, President Johnson put teeth into the policy, issuing an executive order that required federal contractors not merely not to discriminate, but to actively recruit minorities. During the Nixon administration, the mandate was strengthened to require contractors to establish and meet specific minority-hiring goals.

By the end of the 1970s, affirmative action had spread to most sectors of society. Colleges and universities were using it in admissions. The federal government had expanded it to "set aside" a certain percentage of contracts for minority-owned businesses. [21] And corporations were voluntarily setting up minority-recruitment and other affirmative action programs.

But even as affirmative action was becoming more commonplace, it was coming under attack. During the 1970s, the Supreme Court heard a number of challenges to the policy, including the landmark 1978 case, *University of California Regents v. Bakke*. The case involved a white law school applicant, who claimed that he had been rejected in favor of less-qualified blacks under the university's affirmative action program. The justices agreed, outlawing the use of numerical racial quotas in university admissions. The court also ruled, however, that while quotas were unconstitutional, race could still be a *factor* in making admission decisions.

Attacks against affirmative action intensified in the 1980s. President Ronald Reagan and his successor, George Bush, were opposed to race-based preferences, and the Justice Department in their administrations worked to eliminate quotas and other race-based hiring programs. In addition, the six new justices chosen for the Supreme Court during this period either opposed or had serious reservations about the policy. In the 1990s, as a result, the high court has handed down several decisions striking down affirmative action programs. [22]

At the same time, the policy has been attacked at the grass-roots level. In 1996, Californians voted to approve Proposition 209, the first statewide repeal of affirmative action programs. Similar referenda are slated for votes this year in Washington, Ohio, Florida and Colorado.

Today, according to recent polls, roughly 60 percent of whites and 40 percent of blacks oppose affirmative action. [23] It has become a litmus test in most debates over race. For instance, the recent GOP opposition to Bill Lann Lee, President Clinton's nominee to head the Civil Rights Division at the Justice Department, revolved around Lee's support for preferences. And at the president's recent "town hall" meeting in Akron, Ohio, part of his national dialogue on race, affirmative action sparked the fiercest debate. [24]

For members of the black middle class, affirmative action is often a difficult issue. But, regardless of their position, many blacks worry that it will lead whites to devalue all achievement by African-Americans, be it in the workplace or the classroom.

"You know, I just want the opportunity to succeed, nothing more," says Alexander, who supports the policy. ∎

CURRENT SITUATION

Economic Gains

As the list of CEOs at the nation's 500 largest companies confirms, white men still run corporate America. But in the last 30 years African-Americans have made progress in their quest to join the country's business elite. Some gains, of course, were inevitable given the fact that until the civil rights movement, there were virtually no high-ranking black executives. "We really had nowhere to go but up," says Morgan State's Hill.

Today, the situation is somewhat different. At many of the nation's biggest corporations, African-Americans are near the very top of the

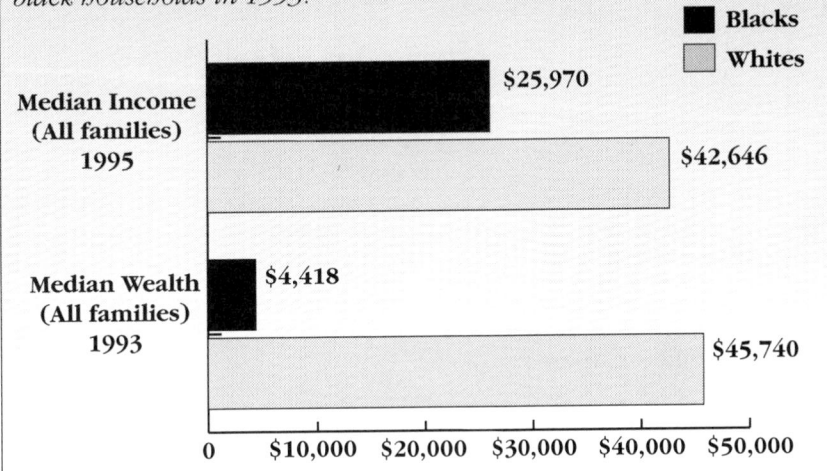

Blacks' Income and Assets Lag

The median income of white families was 65 percent more than that of blacks in 1995. White households had 10 times the material assets of black households in 1993.

■ **Blacks**
▨ **Whites**

Median Income (All families) 1995 — Blacks: $25,970; Whites: $42,646

Median Wealth (All families) 1993 — Blacks: $4,418; Whites: $45,740

0    $10,000 $20,000 $30,000 $40,000 $50,000

Sources: Stephan and Abigail Thernstrom, America in Black and White: One Nation, Indivisible, *1997, based on U.S. Census Bureau, "Money Income in the U.S.: 1995."*

corporate totem pole, including Kenneth Chenault and Lloyd Ward, the presidents of American Express and Maytag. Other corporations, among them General Motors, Walt Disney and Morgan Stanley, have African-Americans in top-level slots. According to Richard Parsons, president of entertainment giant Time Warner, "people of color are achieving corporate positions that their parents never dreamed of reaching, and in unprecedented numbers." [25]

But according to many blacks, the fact that some African-American executives have managed to climb most of the way up the corporate ladder should not be taken as a sign that racism has been eliminated from the boardroom. For one thing, none of the big corporations has ever been run by a black person. "You'd think over the last 30 years someone would have made it to the top" says Collins, author of the recent book *Black Corporate Executives*. In addition, Collins notes, since the 1970s, there have always

been a few black executives who were touted as the next CEO. "But all of them were moved to less important positions or they left," he says.

Many black executives who cut their teeth in large corporations have gone on to start their own businesses. Some just want to go it alone. Others go into business for themselves, at least in part, because of the frustration they felt in largely white corporate America. Alexander started her own business because she was tired of being mistreated and taken for granted while at the same time working diligently. "I thought: 'I've made so much money for [my white boss] over the years, why shouldn't I do it for myself?' " she says.

Alexander is far from alone. The number and size of black-owned businesses have grown significantly in the last few decades. According to *Black Enterprise* magazine, the 100 largest black-owned companies generated $14.1 billion in revenue in 1996. In 1973, the top 100 produced less than a half-million. [26]

Still, as with African-American executives, the success of black-owned businesses, while notable, is not staggering. For instance, if the top 100 black businesses today merged into one company, it would only be the 83rd-largest corporation in the United States as ranked by annual revenue. [27]

The Asset Gap

While a significant disparity in income exists between whites and blacks, the difference in total worth is even more profound. In 1993, the median net worth of the average white household was $45,740; the average black household was worth only $4,418.

Even among households with equal income levels, net worth among African-Americans is still much lower. According to the new book *America in Black and White* by scholars Stephan and Abigail Thernstrom, the asset gap, even among high-earners, largely is determined by inherited wealth. They write that "only within the past few decades have any but a handful of black people had the opportunity to acquire substantial property; few of their parents and grandparents, living under slavery and then Jim Crow, bequeathed significant estates to their descendants." [28]

The impact of the asset gap is significant, scholars say. For instance, it is not uncommon for young middle-class whites to ask their parents for financial help for everything from their education to buying their first home. This option is available to far fewer black people. "It puts you at a disadvantage

early on," Hill says. It also contributes to segregation, since many black professionals do not have the financial backing to afford as expensive a house as their white counterparts.

Not having the assets to buy a nice house, or any house, tends to make the net-worth disparity self-perpetuating. That's because a house, for most middle-class people, is the primary asset. And for those African-Americans who own a home, it is more likely to be a greater source of total wealth than having a house is for whites. According to 1991 statistics, the house makes up 63 percent of the total wealth of the

---

"In 1993, the median net worth of the average white household was $45,740; the average black household was worth only $4,418."

---

average black homeowner compared with 41 percent for the average white homeowner, who is more likely to have other financial assets. [29] (*See graph, p. 63.*) ■

OUTLOOK

Guarded Optimism

A recent CNN/*Time* magazine poll showed that only 18 percent of black teens think that the problems

faced by African-Americans today are caused by whites. Similarly, only 23 percent said that they had ever been the victim of discrimination. [30]

Some scholars say that statistics like these confirm their optimism about the future. Children, they say, are not as hobbled by America's segregated past as are their parents. "If you go to a suburban mall and look at groups of kids, you'll see a girl from India, three WASPs, a Jew and two blacks," says the University of Pennsylvania's Anderson. "That's the future."

But, Anderson and others point out, middle-class blacks are struggling with their children's willingness to mix with whites. "On one hand, they know it's good to have all different kinds of friends," he says. "But on the other, they feel their kids should know what it means to be black — so that you know where it comes from when you're kicked."

How best to raise black children in today's America is part of a larger question that middle-class African-Americans are asking: How far should I assimilate? The question is different for blacks than it has been for many other groups. Long after the Civil War and Emancipation, the idea of African-American assimilation was absurd to both blacks and whites, although for different reasons. But the advent of the civil rights movement and the rise of the black middle class make the proposition much less unrealistic.

Some, like Reynalds, say that the death of Jim Crow and the birth of economic opportunity will slowly push blacks into the mainstream. One particularly telling sign of this change, he argues, is that younger blacks have turned their backs on govern-

Continued on p. 66

At Issue:

Is affirmative action still necessary?

HILARY SHELTON
Deputy Director, Washington bureau, National Association for the Advancement of Colored People

Opponents of affirmative action have distorted the meaning of the principle, rewritten history and clearly ignored present realities in their eagerness to eliminate present programs. Since the end of slavery, African-Americans, as well as other ethnic minority groups and women, have struggled for economic justice, an equal opportunity to enter the workplace to earn equal pay and equal access to higher education.

Dr. Mary Frances Berry, U.S. Commission on Civil Rights chairperson, has stated: "Some progress in job opportunities for African-Americans was made during World War II and beyond. But it was limited. In grocery and department stores, clerks were white and janitors and elevator operators were black. Generations of African-Americans swept the floors in factories, while denied the opportunity to become higher paid operators on the machines."

The reality of life in America before affirmative action included thousands of towns and cities in which the police departments and fire departments were all white males. . . .

Detractors of affirmative action use the battle cry of "merit" over any racial or gender considerations. They seem to forget there were no merit standards for employment for white males who occupied the best jobs. . . . Men with the privilege of white skin, whether their granddaddies ever owned slaves or not, whether they were early or late immigrants, had the good-job pie all to themselves.

To be sure, women and minorities have been the major beneficiaries of affirmative action over the past three decades. Few realize, however, that white males are also beneficiaries. Before affirmative action, the "old-boys' network" way of doing things prevailed.

Because of affirmative action, fairness is now the rule, guaranteeing more opportunities for white males as well as minorities and women to compete for jobs. Indeed, the purpose of affirmative action has always been to create an environment where merit can prevail.

On July 19, 1996, President Bill Clinton delivered an address on affirmative action at the National Archives in Washington, D.C., while standing in front of the original U.S. Constitution. He said:

"If properly done, affirmative action can help us come together, go forward and grow together. It is in our moral, legal and practical interest to see that every person can make the most of his [or her] life. In the fight for the future, we need all hands on deck, and some of those hands still need a helping hand."

GERALD REYNALDS
President, Center for New Black Leadership

Race-based affirmative action policies harm many of their intended beneficiaries, as well as better-qualified white and Asian competitors. For example, data from elite public colleges clearly demonstrate that double standards in admissions policies have harmed many of the black beneficiaries of preference policies. College administrators are quick to point out any increase in minority enrollment. However, they never mention that a disproportionate number of these students never graduate. . . .

By shielding blacks from unfettered competition in college admissions, contracting and employment, proponents of preference polices have placed too many middle-class blacks in a protective cocoon. Many of these blacks have no incentive to work hard enough to meet or exceed "real world" standards since they are not penalized for a substandard performance. Preference policies also cheapen the accomplishments of those blacks who meet or exceed the same standards met by whites and Asians.

Recently President Clinton implied that Gen. Colin Powell owed his success to racial-preference policies. President Clinton is not alone. Many supporters of preference policies believe that the tremendous gains achieved by the black middle class are due, in large part, to preference policies and that these policies are still needed. They are wrong. The data do not support the assertion that preference policies were the primarily cause behind the growth of the black middle class. In fact, the data suggest that the groundwork for the growth of the black middle class was in place prior to the implementation of racial preference policies.

The confluence of black migration from the South to the North, a strong work ethic, enhanced employment opportunities, the enactment and enforcement of anti-discrimination statutes and improved educational opportunities enabled black strivers to reach the middle class. Racial preference policies merely accelerated the advancement of those blacks who possess middle-class values. These policies have never been prerequisites for advancement.

For much of our history black Americans lived under a racial caste system. Prior to the civil rights revolution, one's chances of economic, social and political advancement were not determined by talent, initiative and industry. The prospects of the majority of blacks were severely limited by state-sponsored segregation and a hard-core white racism. However, racial discrimination is no longer an insurmountable obstacle for black Americans. My grandmother use to argue that because of racism, blacks had to be twice as good their white competitors. While the level of racism has waned substantially, the need to strive for excellence has not.

Are Black Conservatives on the Rise?

Thomas Sowell once joked that if you put all African-American conservatives in one room there wouldn't be enough people for a game of pinochle.

Sowell, the much-quoted Hoover Institution scholar, would have plenty of card players to sit down with nowadays. In the last decade, the number of black conservatives in the public eye has jumped dramatically. From Supreme Court Justice Clarence Thomas and Rep. J.C. Watts, R-Okla., to talk-show host Armstrong Williams and anti-affirmative action crusader Ward Connerly, more and more black conservatives are entering the limelight.

Indeed, Alan L. Keyes, a Harvard-educated radio talk show host and former Foreign Service officer, ran for the GOP presidential nomination in 1996. Another black Republican, retired Gen. Colin Powell, is considered his party's front-runner for the 2000 presidential nomination, although he has said he's not interested.

These new faces come at a time when black support for the Democratic Party endures. Since the Great Depression of the 1930s, the vast majority of blacks have voted for Democrats in presidential and congressional elections. Today, fewer than 10 percent of all African-Americans identify themselves as Republicans. Black Republicans hold just one seat in Congress (Watts). Furthermore, as of 1997, only 11 of the 550 African-Americans in state legislatures were members of the GOP. [1]

Conservatives explain these statistics by arguing that there is a tremendous pressure within the black community to conform politically. "Black America is a one-party system," says Shelby Steele, another black research fellow at Hoover and author of the best-selling book on affirmative action *The Content of Our Character*. "Black conservatives are immediately labeled as 'Uncle Toms' and as traitors to their race," he says.

The "one-party system," as Steele labels it, is perpetuated by more than just loyalty to race. It is built, he says, on adherence to an overriding belief. "As a black man, I am judged on [my attitude about] one issue: whether victimization is black America's biggest problem. If I say 'yes,' it's OK. If I say 'no,' I'm a black conservative, period."

The reality, Steele and others say, is that African-Americans are much more conservative than their Democratic political affiliation would indicate. Gavin Jackson, a human relations specialist at the Department of the Treasury and a self-described conservative, agrees. "I think black folks are inherently conservative," he says, "especially when you look at our attitudes toward religion, family and money."

Indeed, according to a 1996 poll commissioned by the Joint Center for Political and Economic Studies, a black-oriented think tank, 30 percent of all African-Americans identified themselves as "conservative." By contrast, only 31 percent of the blacks polled said that they were "liberal." [2]

Why, then, does the GOP fare so poorly with black Americans? The answer, according to black liberals, is tied directly to the hostility the Republican Party and conservatives in general have shown toward African-Americans and their priorities. "It is not even close to think that the assault on government that [House Speaker] Newt [Gingrich] and company are leading is in the interest of the vast majority of black people in this country," says famed civil rights activist Julian Bond. [3]

In addition, many black Democrats accuse the GOP of using wedge issues like affirmative action to scare white voters into supporting them. While this tactic has helped Republicans capture the Congress, they say, it has alienated African-American voters.

But black conservatives are optimistic about the growth of their movement. "It's going to keep expanding," Steele says. He and others compare the black community today with Jewish Americans, a traditionally liberal group that has begun to diversify ideologically. "During the 1980s, we started to see Jewish Republicans," Steele says. He predicts a similar trend in black America as the old, liberal mantras begin to ring hollow. "There's no other way for us to go," he says.

Yet some black conservatives are not convinced that the expansion of conservatism is inevitable. According to Gavin Jackson, the GOP can't just wait for African-Americans to come to them. "I think more black folks will vote Republican when [the GOP] focuses some attention on black issues."

---

[1] Stephan and Abigail Thernstrom, *America in Black and White: One Nation, Indivisible* (1997), pp. 302-303.

[2] *Ibid.*, p. 303.

[3] Quoted in Eric Alterman, "The Right Brothers," *The Nation*, March 4, 1996.

ment as the prime engine of opportunity. "Young folks tend to look to themselves more than the government," he says. "The folks wedded to government solutions tend to be older ones, and that's understandable since it was government that broke the back of Jim Crow."

If there is a problem, conservative African-Americans and others say, it is the influence of many black leaders, who are pushing for greater dependency on the government. According to Thomas Sowell, a fellow at the Hoover Institution: "Too many black 'leaders' today have a vested interest in the application of old myths. They are like Moses in reverse — leading their people back into the welfare state, to a self-imposed isolation from the growing opportunities all around them." [31]

But others are less sanguine, arguing that racism is still causing a lot of middle-class African-Americans to feel ostracized and angry. And, they say, these negative feelings multiply when whites show impatience with the lack of black progress. "You know, it's like, 'After 30 years, haven't we done enough for you people,' " says Collins of the University of Illinois.

Henderson agrees, arguing that attacks on affirmative action and other programs have left many well-to-do blacks suspicious of white America's motives. "Some people feel like refugees in their own country," he says. According to Henderson and others, blacks have done all they can to integrate into American society, and now just need to be welcomed.

"African-Americans are among the most patriotic of citizens, " Henderson says. "We ascribe to core American values and see ourselves as part of the mainstream of America." ∎

Notes

[1] Kevin Merida, "Worry, Frustration Build for Many in the Black Middle Class," *The Washington Post,* Oct. 9, 1995.

[2] Cited in Stephan and Abigail Thernstrom, *America in Black and White: One Nation, Indivisible* (1997), p. 185.

[3] Ellis Cose, *The Rage of a Privileged Class* (1993), p. 1.

[4] For background, see "Intelligence Testing," *The CQ Researcher,* July 30, 1993, pp. 649-672.

[5] For background, see "Housing Discrimination," *The CQ Researcher,* Feb. 24, 1995, pp. 169-192.

[6] For background, see "Racial Tensions in Schools," *The CQ Researcher,* Jan. 7, 1994, pp. 1-24.

[7] See Connie Aitcheson, "Corporate

America's Black Eye," *Black Enterprise,* April 1997.

[8] Quoted on "The NewsHour with Jim Lehrer," Nov. 12, 1996.

[9] Quoted in Eric Pooley, "Fairness of Folly," *Time,* June 23, 1997.

[10] Thernstrom, *op. cit.,* p. 211.

[11] Lisa Frazier, "Pr. George's is 62% Black, Study Finds," *The Washington Post,* Dec. 7, 1997.

[12] Quoted in Haya El Nasser, "In Cleveland, Dream Homes Displace Decline," *USA Today,* Oct. 23, 1997.

[13] Haya El Nasser, "Growing Middle-Class Isn't Fleeing to the Suburbs," *USA Today,* Oct. 23, 1997.

[14] See Carol Morello, "Controversial Measure Proves Difficult to Enforce," *USA Today,* Nov. 17, 1997.

[15] Quoted in Susan Page, "Race Panel Head Sees Progress, Backsliding," *USA Today,* Nov. 17, 1997.

[16] Thernstrom, *op. cit.,* p. 391.

[17] Doris Warriner, Joint Center for Political

and Economic Studies, "African Americans Today: A Demographic Profile," 1996, p. 32.

[18] Thernstrom, *op. cit.* p. 80.

[19] *Ibid.,* p. 84.

[20] *Ibid.,* p. 192.

[21] For background, see, "Rethinking Affirmative Action," *The CQ Researcher,* April 26, 1995, pp. 369-392.

[22] *Ibid.*

[23] Pooley, *op.cit.*

[24] Warren P. Strobel, "Forum Finds No Consensus on Race Issues," *The Washington Times,* Dec. 4, 1997.

[25] Quoted in Roy S. Johnson, "The New Black Power," *Fortune,* Aug. 4, 1997.

[26] Cited in *Ibid.*

[27] *Ibid.*

[28] Thernstrom, *op. cit.* p. 198.

[29] Warriner, *op. cit.* p. 53.

[30] Christopher John Farley, "Kids and Race," *Time,* Nov. 24, 1997.

[31] Thomas Sowell, "Yes, Blacks Can Make It on Their Own," *Time,* Sept. 8, 1997.

FOR MORE INFORMATION

Hoover Institution, Stanford University, Stanford, Calif. 94303; (650) 723-1754; www.hoover.org.
The Hoover Institution is a public-policy think tank that has attracted a large number of conservative scholars.

Joint Center for Political and Economic Studies, 1090 Vermont Ave., N.W., Suite 1100, Washington, D.C. 20005; (202) 789-3500; www.jointctr.org.
This think tank researches issues that are of concern to black Americans.

Lincoln Institute for Research and Education, 1001 Connecticut Ave., N.W., Suite 1135, Washington, D.C. 20036; (202) 223-5112.
The Institute studies issues that impact middle class African-Americans. Topics include education, employment and health.

National Association for the Advancement of Colored People (NAACP), 1025 Vermont Ave., N.W., Suite 1120, Washington, D.C. 20005; (202) 638-2269; www.nvi.net/naacp_washington_bureau/.
The NAACP works for civil rights in all sectors of society. Efforts include lobbying, legal action and education.

National Urban League, 1111 14th St., N.W., Suite 1001, Washington, D.C. 2005-5603; (202) 898-1604; www.nul.org.
This federation of affiliates is concerned with the welfare of African-Americans and other minorities.

Bibliography

Selected Sources Used

Books

Cose, Ellis, *The Rage of a Privileged Class,* HarperCollins, 1993.
Cose, a writer at *Newsweek*, tries to answer the question: Why are successful black professionals so angry? The answer, he says, is that many African-Americans who have "made it" still do not believe they are operating in a system that will fully reward them for their intelligence, education and effort.

D'Souza, Dinesh, *The End of Racism: Principles for a Multiracial Society,* The Free Press, 1995.
D'Souza, a fellow at the American Enterprise Institute, argues that civil rights advocates are fighting against a largely non-existent enemy. One reason, he says, is that fighting racism has become an industry, one that is self-perpetuating.

Shipler, David K., *A Country of Strangers: Blacks and Whites in America,* Alfred A. Knopf, 1997.
A journalist and Pulitzer Prize-winning author, Shipler looks at how Americans are dealing with the issue of race. By combining history and statistics with literally hundreds of anecdotes and stories, Shipler paints a picture of a nation and a people that are not close to achieving any kind of racial harmony.

Thernstrom, Stephan and Abigail, *America in Black and White: One Nation, Indivisible,* Simon & Schuster, 1997.
Stephan Thernstrom, a professor of history at Harvard University, and his wife Abigail, a fellow at the Manhattan Institute, have produced a sweeping portrait of black America as it was and is. The Thernstroms argue that blacks have made much more progress during the 20th century than is generally acknowledged. They also make the case that race relations are better than many people think.

Articles

Biskupic, Joan, "On Race, a Court Transformed," *The Washington Post,* Dec. 15, 1997.
Biskupic describes the transformation of the Supreme Court from "the salvation of civil rights advocates" to "a place to be avoided." The reason, she writes, is that Presidents Ronald Reagan and George Bush appointed justices who were generally less friendly to affirmative action and some other programs favored by the civil rights community.

El Nasser, Haya, "Growing Middle Class Isn't Fleeing to Suburbs," *USA Today,* Oct. 23, 1997.
El Nasser details a growing trend among middle-class blacks: suburban flight. Many African-Americans who can afford to live in the suburbs are choosing instead to move to inner-city areas, many of which have high crime and other problems. Some are lured by cheap land, an opportunity made even sweeter in certain cities through tax breaks and cheap loans. Other blacks found the largely white suburbs "isolating" and want to live with people of their own race.

Johnson, Roy. S, "The New Black Power," *Fortune,* Aug. 4, 1997.
Johnson's piece is the lead-off to several articles on African-Americans and business. He argues that while blacks have made substantial progress in the business world, both as corporate executives and entrepreneurs, "people of color still confront huge obstacles in the workplace."

Merida, Kevin, "Worry, Frustration Build for Many in the Black Middle Class," *The Washington Post,* Oct. 9, 1995.
Merida looks at middle-class black attitudes and discovers a surprising amount of anger and fear. Black professionals are plagued by the same problems that affect their white counterparts, such as the fear of being downsized out of a job. But African-Americans also say they have problems that are unique to minorities, like feeling devalued at work by their white colleagues.

Pooley, Eric, "Fairness or Folly?" *Time,* June 23, 1997.
Pooley does a good job of describing the players and dynamics in the debate over affirmative action. In particular, he focuses on Ward Connerly, the African-American businessman who successfully led the fight for Proposition 209, the California ballot initiative that eliminated the use of preferences at all state agencies and institutions.

Reports

Doris Warriner, "African Americans Today: A Demographic Profile," Joint Center for Political and Economic Studies, 1996.
This report from the black-oriented think tank contains a wealth of statistical data on the state of black America. Topics include education, income, wealth and political participation.

The Next Step

Additional information from UMI's Newspaper & Periodical Abstracts™ database

Affirmative Action

"Connerly Blasts Feds' UC Admissions Policy Probe," *Los Angeles Sentinel*, **July 24, 1997, p. A8.**

Ward Connerly, a black Republican who has become a national critic of affirmative action, says a federal probe into plunging minority enrollment at University of California graduate schools is harassment. However, representatives of the groups that filed the complaint resulting in the investigation said they believed it would turn up violations.

Miller, Fayneese, Alicia Xae Reyes and Elizabeth Shaffer, "The contextualization of affirmative action: A historical and political analysis," *American Behavioral Scientist*, **October 1997, pp. 223-231.**

Miller et al. chronicle the progression of affirmative action and show how it has benefited all of society and not just a select few.

Rhode, Deborah L., "Affirmative action," National Forum: *Phi Kappa Phi Journal*, **spring 1997, pp. 12-16.**

Rhode suggests that affirmative action has been crucial to the advances that women have made and that dismantling it is a mistake of grand proportions.

Rodriguez, Richard, "Affirmative Action Is Dead; Let's Address the Demerits of Social Class; Discrimination: Poor whites are the last PC villains, but they and the working class in general have been the forgotten ones," *Los Angeles Times*, **Nov. 7, 1997, p. B9.**

Even now, as affirmative action is finished here in California, nobody is really saying what was wrong with affirmative action: It was unfair to poor whites.

Sherman, Mark, "Gingrich: Race talk a 'monologue' on affirmative action: Speaker says John Hope Franklin, Clinton should allow critics to contribute," *Atlanta Constitution*, **Nov. 21, 1997, p. A3.**

House Speaker Newt Gingrich, R-Ga., attacked historian John Hope Franklin and the presidential race panel he heads for excluding foes of affirmative action programs. The speaker was reacting to Franklin's widely quoted remarks Wednesday that opponents of affirmative action, such as African-American businessman Ward Connerly, would not add much to the panel's discussions on making universities more diverse.

"Yes or No, Mr. President?" *The Wall Street Journal*, **Dec. 5, 1997, p. A18.**

John Hope Franklin, chairman of the President's National Advisory Committee on Race, refused to invite a single opponent of affirmative action to participate, saying that serious people like California activist Ward Connerly had "nothing to contribute." This of course triggered a predictable response of outrage.

Job Discrimination

Baldi, Stephane, and Debra Branch McBrier, "Do the determinants of promotion differ for blacks and whites? Evidence from the U.S. labor market," *Work & Occupations*, **November 1997, pp. 478-497.**

Baldi and McBrier argue that to understand the systematic differences in black-white outcomes in the workplace, the assumption regarding the advancement of blacks and whites in the workplace needs to be re-examined.

Fletcher, Michael A., "Bias settlement approved in Corps of Engineers case," *The Washington Post*, **Jan. 25, 1997, p. A9.**

A federal judge on Jan 24, 1997, approved an $800,000 settlement of a suit alleging that African-American employees in the Army Corps of Engineers' sprawling Pittsburgh district faced an almost daily gauntlet of physical abuse, racial epithets and blatant job discrimination

Gilliam, Dorothy, "Seeking Power Through The Purse," *The Washington Post*, **Aug. 9, 1997, p. D1.**

Hugh B. Price, native son and president of the National Urban League, arrived in Washington last week stating "the gates of opportunity should be [kept] open, not shut, and all those glass ceilings that have kept us in our place must be smashed for good."

"Job discrimination hearings set for Capitol Hill," *Jet*, **Aug. 4, 1997, p. 9.**

Hearings will be held in September 1997 to discuss racial discrimination in the federal workplace.

King, Martin Luther III, "King's dream of equal rights for all mankind still unfulfilled," *USA Today*, **April 4, 1997, p. A12.**

"My father, Dr. Martin Luther King Jr., devoted his life to the struggle for equal rights for all humankind, regardless of race," writes Dr. King's son. "Today, 29 years after his assassination, the race problem remains, as he depicted it, 'America's greatest moral dilemma.' Lending institutions continue to discriminate in their lending practices along the color line, and glass ceilings have replaced 'white only' signs. Yet today there are those who question the continued need for affirmative action."

Prince George's County

Frazier, Lisa, "Curry Calls Desegregation Order 'Obsolete'; Court Urged to Release Schools in Pr. George's," *The Washington Post*, Dec. 11, 1997, p. B1.

Prince George's County Executive Wayne K. Curry, who nearly four decades ago was one of the first black children to attend a formerly all-white county school, testified yesterday that a federal court desegregation order should be lifted because it has become "obsolete" in a majority-black jurisdiction.

Frazier, Lisa, "Pr. George's Is 62 percent Black, Study Finds; White Population Declines to 31%," *The Washington Post*, Dec. 7, 1997, p. A1.

The black population in Prince George's County has increased to 62 percent, up from 51 percent in 1990, reaching its highest point yet as African-American professionals continue to relocate there in large numbers from Washington and from outside the metropolitan area.

Raspberry, William, "This Is Where I Get Off," *The Washington Post*, Dec. 19, 1997, p. A25.

I have trouble understanding why after some 25 years of court-ordered busing in suburban Prince George's County — with at best marginal academic success — the NAACP is so reluctant to let busing go.

Proposition 209

Morello, Carol, "Opponents chip away at PROP. 209; Controversial measure proves difficult to enforce," *USA Today*, Nov. 17, 1997, p. A1.

Proposition 209 is now the law of the land in California, at least in theory. But in cities and counties where the constitutional amendment to outlaw race and gender preferences was never popular, the push is not to dismantle affirmative action but to keep it alive. At turns defiant and creative, these officials are devising new programs to circumvent the law or simply refusing to abolish existing programs.

Page, Clarence, "A Timely Message from Houston on Affirmative Action," *Chicago Tribune*, Nov. 9, 1997, p. 23.

No matter how they try to spin it, opponents of affirmative action suffered a setback when Houston's voters rejected a measure to end it, not mend it, in city jobs and contracting. Foes of affirmative action have tried to explain away Houston's vote last Tuesday as the result of the city's high minority population (The voter turnout of Houston's black, Latino and Asian-American voters combined roughly equals that of white voters.) and the vigorous support of the city's outgoing mayor, Bob Lanier.

Parker, Emanuel, "High court rapped for Prop. 209 non-action," *Los Angeles Sentinel*, Nov. 6, 1997, p. A1.

Local and national black leaders were unanimous in November 1997 in condemning the U.S. Supreme Court's refusal to hear arguments against California's Proposition 209, the anti-affirmative action law. The court's action cleared the way for implementation of the initiative.

"Silent statement," *The Boston Globe*, Nov. 4, 1997, p. A16.

With courts as with political figures, a "no comment" can say much, while it leaves troubling questions unanswered. So it was yesterday as the U.S. Supreme Court upheld California's anti-affirmative action Proposition 209, by sustaining, without comment, the Appeals Court view of the case

Stewart, Jocelyn Y., "Black Colleges Woo Students Alienated by Prop. 209," *Los Angeles Times*, Nov. 25, 1997, p. A1.

With the Supreme Court signaling its approval of California's Proposition 209 and the end of affirmative action, supporters of black colleges are reaching out to California students with a new sense of urgency. The impact of the ban on black enrollment at public colleges and universities and the efforts of historically black private schools to recruit high school students are discussed.

Redlining

Browne, J. Zamgb, "Schumer cites lending disparity while Chase refutes charges," *Amsterdam News*, Nov. 6, 1997, p. 14.

Chase Manhattan Bank on Nov. 3, 1997, sharply refuted allegations contained in a recent study conducted by Rep. Charles E. Schumer, D-N.Y., that the bank has a policy of redlining blacks and Latinos for home mortgage loans. A Chase executive called the assertion "unfounded."

Dangerfield, Dalia, "Survey finds home loan bias," *Chicago Defender*, Sept. 13, 1997, p. 1.

African-Americans are facing a downward trend in getting loans in Chicago according to a national survey conducted by the Association of Community Organizations for Reform Now. According to the survey, between 1995 and 1996 blacks were rejected three times more than white applicants in the city, the highest rejection rate of 15 cities studied.

"Mortgage Rejections Stay Higher for Blacks," *The New York Times*, Aug. 5, 1997, p. A16.

Mortgage lenders rejected black applicants twice as often as whites in 1996, despite a push by regulators since the start of the Clinton administration to toughen enforcement of fair-lending rules. According to the data made public on Monday, banks, savings institutions, credit unions and mortgage companies turned down 48.8 percent of applications from blacks and 24.1 percent from whites. The denial rates were 34.4 percent for Hispanic applicants, 13.8 percent for Asians and 50.2 percent for American Indians. The data covered 14.8 million home-loan applications and were compiled from 9,300 institutions.

"Redlining won't go away," *Call & Post*, Aug. 14, 1997, p. A4.

An editorial contends that redlining — a nice way of describing racial discrimination against blacks and other minorities by financial institutions — continues to be the status quo. The editorial acknowledges that President Clinton has given fair lending a prominent place on his agenda, but notes that the discriminatory practices that pervade the financial markets were ingrained as a way of doing business long before he came on the scene.

Texaco

Bryant, Adam, "How Much Has Texaco Changed?" *The New York Times*, Nov. 2, 1997, Sec. 3, p. 1.

The story of Texaco has grown only more complex with time. The protest over the tapes last year demanded simple, concrete answers: How would the executives be punished? Would Texaco stand up to a national boycott? Or would it settle the lawsuit, which accused it of systematically denying minority employees promotions because of their race? Texaco employees who filed the original lawsuit fear that any changes will be only cosmetic.

Hamilton, Martha M., "Texaco Board Member Mary Bush Sees Opportunities for Change," *The Washington Post*, Aug. 25, 1997, Sec. WBIZ, p. 9.

For months before Texaco Inc. invited Mary K. Bush to join its board this summer, the oil giant was buffeted by accusations of racism, lawsuits, investigations and bad-news headlines. But Bush, a consultant in international finance who also is African-American, said she didn't hesitate when Chairman Peter I. Bijur called. "I had no misgivings," said Bush, who as a former managing director of the U.S. Federal Housing Board once helped to oversee the nation's 12 Federal Home Loan Banks.

Poole, Shelia M., "Texaco affiliates host minority seminar," *Atlanta Constitution*, Sept. 26, 1997, p. F2.

About 200 female and minority business owners Thursday learned the how-to's of doing business with Star Enterprise, a refiner and marketer of Texaco products, during a day-long conference in Atlanta Ga. The conference, which was cosponsored by Texaco Lubricants Co., comes almost a year after Texaco agreed to a $176 million settlement of a racial discrimination lawsuit by black employees. The highly publicized lawsuit was based on a tape in which top-level Texaco executives made racist remarks and discussed destroying documents in a discrimination case.

Reifenberg, Anne, "Texaco settlement in racial-bias case endorsed by judge," *The Wall Street Journal*, March 26, 1997, p. B15.

U.S. District Judge Charles Brieant, in a ruling issued March 21, 1997, and made public March 25, endorsed the $176 million settlement in the Texaco Inc. racial-bias case, but reserved judgment on a plan to allot $29 million in fees to the plaintiffs' legal team and $800,000 in "incentive awards" to the six African-Americans who filed the discrimination lawsuit in 1994.

Sullivan, Allanna, and Leon E. Wynter, "Recipients of Checks From Texaco Suit Chart Their Futures," *The Wall Street Journal*, Nov. 5, 1997, p. B1.

A year after Texaco reached a record settlement of charges of discrimination against its African-American employees, it's an emotional time for the 1,400 plaintiffs. This summer they collected the $115 million settlement they won last November. They've spent the past year in an uncomfortable spotlight at work. Many tell of cooling relations with colleagues outside of the suit who are resentful of the plaintiffs' complaints and extra pay.

TLC Beatrice

Barrett, Paul M., "Ex-Drexel officials battle Reginald Lewis even after his death," *The Wall Street Journal*, April 15, 1997, p. A1.

Reginald Lewis became an icon of black business success in 1987 by acquiring TLC Beatrice International Holdings Inc. in a $1 billion leveraged buyout, financed by Michael Milken's Drexel Burnham Lambert crew. A decade later and four years after Lewis' death from a brain tumor, a group of former Milken aides that holds about 22 percent of TLC Beatrice is pressing lawsuits in state courts in Delaware and New York. The suits allege that Lewis took tens of millions of dollars from the company in illegal pay and frills.

Serju, Tricia, "Prayer, tenacity keep CEO of worldwide company on track," *Detroit News*, Feb. 25, 1997, p. B3.

Every morning, Loida Nicolas Lewis takes 10 minutes to collect her thoughts. It's in those calming moments reading the Bible that Lewis, chairwoman and chief executive of TLC Beatrice International Holdings Inc., finds guidance to run one of the world's largest multinational food companies. Lewis inherited TLC Beatrice International Holdings — at the time the nation's largest African-American-owned business — in 1994, after the death of her husband, Reginald Lewis. The company reported sales of $2.1 billion in 1995 and employs about 4,500 people worldwide.

Back Issues

Great Research on Current Issues Starts Right Here ... Recent topics covered by The CQ Researcher are listed below. Before May 1991, reports were published under the name of Editorial Research Reports.

JULY 1996
Recovered-Memory Debate
Native Americans' Future
Crackdown on Sexual Harassment
Attack on Public Schools

AUGUST 1996
Fighting Over Animal Rights
Privatizing Government Services
Child Labor and Sweatshops
Cleaning Up Hazardous Wastes

SEPTEMBER 1996
Gambling Under Attack
The States and Federalism
Civic Journalism
Reassessing Foreign Aid

OCTOBER 1996
Political Consultants
Insurance Fraud
Rethinking School Integration
Parental Rights

NOVEMBER 1996
Global Warming
Clashing Over Copyright
Consumer Debt
Governing Washington, D.C.

Back issues are available for $5.00 (subscribers) or $10.00 (non-subscribers). Quantity discounts apply to orders over ten. To order, call Congressional Quarterly Customer Service at (202) 887-8621.

Binders are available for $18.00. To order call 1-800-638-1710. Please refer to stock number 648.

DECEMBER 1996
Welfare, Work and the States
The New Volunteerism
Implementing the Disabilities Act
America's Pampered Pets

JANUARY 1997
Combating Scientific Misconduct
Restructuring the Electric Industry
The New Immigrants
Chemical and Biological Weapons

FEBRUARY 1997
Assisting Refugees
Alternative Medicine's Next Phase
Independent Counsels
Feminism's Future

MARCH 1997
New Air Quality Standards
Alcohol Advertising
Civic Renewal
Educating Gifted Students

APRIL 1997
Declining Crime Rates
The FBI Under Fire
Gender Equity in Sports
Space Program's Future

MAY 1997
The Stock Market
The Cloning Controversy
Expanding NATO
The Future of Libraries

JUNE 1997
FDA Reform
China After Deng
Line-Item Veto
Breast Cancer

JULY 1997
Transportation Policy
Executive Pay
School Choice Debate
Aggressive Driving

AUGUST 1997
Age Discrimination
Banning Land Mines
Children's Television
Evolution vs. Creationism

SEPTEMBER 1997
Caring for the Dying
Mental Health Policy
Mexico's Future
Youth Fitness

OCTOBER 1997
Urban Sprawl in the West
Diversity in the Workplace
Teacher Education
Contingent Work Force

NOVEMBER 1997
Renewable Energy
Artificial Intelligence
Religious Persecution
Roe v. Wade at 25

DECEMBER 1997
Whistleblowers
Castro's Next Move
Gun Control Standoff
Regulating Nonprofits

JANUARY 1998
Foster Care Reform
IRS Reform

Future Topics

▶ *U.S.-British Relations*

▶ *Patients' Rights*

▶ *Deflation Fears*

U.S.-British Relations

Are the two allies growing apart?

P
rime Minister Tony Blair arrives in America in February at a time of transition for U.S.-British relations. During the Cold War, the two nations' solid front formed the foundation of the Western alliance. But the Soviet Union's demise has raised questions about how much the longtime allies still need each other. With Europe relatively secure, British dependence on American strength has diminished. Moreover, the rise of the European Union is changing economic priorities in Europe. For its part, the United States no longer leans so heavily on Europe for its security and trade interests. Despite having so much in common, the U.S. and Britain may decide that their "special relationship" has run its course.

Jan. 30, 1998 • Volume 8, No. 4 • Pages 73-96

Formerly Editorial Research Reports

COVER: PRESIDENT CLINTON AND PRIME MINISTER BLAIR AT 10 DOWNING STREET IN LONDON LAST MAY, WITH THEIR WIVES. (REUTERS)

CQ Researcher

January 30, 1998
Volume 8, No. 4

Editor
Sandra Stencel

Managing Editor
Thomas J. Colin

Associate Editor
Sarah M. Magner

Staff Writers
Mary H. Cooper
Kenneth Jost
David Masci

Production Editor
Melissa Hall

Editorial Assistant
Vanessa E. Furlong

Published By
Congressional Quarterly Inc.

Chairman
Andrew Barnes

Vice Chairman
Andrew P. Corty

President and Publisher
Robert W. Merry

Executive Editor
David Rapp

The CQ Researcher (ISSN 1056-2036). Formerly Editorial Research Reports. Published weekly, except Jan. 2, May 29, July 3, Oct. 30, by Con-gressional Quarterly Inc., 1414 22nd St., N.W., Washington, D.C. 20037. Annual subscription rate for libraries, businesses and government is $340. Additional rates furnished upon request. Periodicals postage paid at Washington, D.C., and additional mailing offices. POSTMASTER: Send address changes to The CQ Researcher, 1414 22nd St., N.W., Washington, D.C. 20037.

U.S.-British Relations

BY PHILIP M. SEIB

THE ISSUES

They stood together in the sun-dappled garden of 10 Downing Street, the young American president and the even younger British prime minister.

Bill Clinton at 50 was the elder statesman, a fact reinforced by his graying hair and the cane he was using after knee surgery. Tony Blair, 44, bright and eager as always, clearly relished standing as an equal beside the world's most powerful leader.

The camaraderie of the occasion — a news conference just after Blair and the Labor Party rose to power last May — reflected the remarkable similarities between the two men. Each attended Oxford; each is a lawyer married to a lawyer; and each pulled his political party away from a self-defeating liberalism and onto the middle ground.

Moreover, each is a skillful politician who understands the importance of consensus-building in domestic politics and presumably recognizes the need for the same in the international arena. At the London meeting, every indication was that theirs would be a politically and personally congenial partnership.

In a world of shifting loyalties and uncertain friendships, ties between the United States and Great Britain have remained remarkably strong. Britain's American Colonies grew up to become a superpower, but despite occasional spats, the offspring has remained on friendly terms with its parent.

The two nations' shared culture has been important, as have personal relationships between the countries' leaders. President Franklin D. Roosevelt and Prime Minister Winston Churchill worked together

closely to wage war and preserve peace, as Ronald Reagan and Margaret Thatcher did later.

As special as this relationship may have been in the past, the necessity in which it was grounded during the last half-century has narrowed. The American nuclear umbrella, on which Britain and the rest of Western Europe relied, is far less relevant today. The economic strength of North America is now well-matched by that of resurgent Europe. What is emerging is a friendship without dependence. [1]

Nevertheless, a time of transition is likely to produce some friction. On both sides of the Atlantic, debate goes on about how close the bilateral ties should now be. In the United States, there are those who argue that Germany will dominate Europe and therefore should be America's principal European partner. This tension began to emerge during the presidency of George Bush, when Thatcher detected what she considered to be a tendency "to put the relationship with Germany — rather than the 'special relationship' with Britain — at the center of U.S. policy

toward Europe." [2]

In Britain, the debate is more complicated, entangled with issues related to the European Union. Europhiles say Britain's future depends on its being a full participant in the EU, which means cultivating closer ties in Europe (particularly with Germany and France) even if at the expense of those with America. Europhobes, on the other hand, warn against surrendering sovereignty to the EU and are particularly wary of monetary union. They see Atlanticism as a safer option, with North America as a more reliable and less demanding economic partner.

Laurence Martin, former director of the Royal Institute of International Affairs, says that a key issue for the future will be the evolution of "the British identity" in light of many Britons' desire "to avoid becoming just a piece of a new European mechanism."

On security matters, similar debate is under way. America's dilatory response to the war in the former Yugoslavia disturbed many Britons and others in Western Europe who saw it as a sign that the United States will be less concerned about Europe's internal problems now that a menacing Soviet Union no longer lurks in the background. But many of these same critics of America's initial sluggishness acknowledge that only U.S. muscle — even if belatedly flexed — made possible the relative peace produced by the Dayton agreement.

In the United States, some policymakers see Britain — and, for that matter, Europe — as decreasingly significant in America's grand economic and security strategies. Also, as Michael Mandelbaum of the Johns Hopkins University School of Advanced International Studies has noted, "Europe could come to appear to Americans to be a large, wealthy, undeserving welfare case, indeed one whose own vitality has been sapped by its dependence on American protection." [3]

British analysts recognize the potential for American disaffection. Charles Powell, national security aide to prime ministers Thatcher and John Major, acknowledges the magnetism of the Pacific, saying that "the Atlantic will come to be seen as something of a backwater." He notes that it is important for Britain to keep the American worldview "focussed on Europe." Similarly, Nicholas Henderson, former British ambassador to the United States, says, "There is a widely held view that America thinks Asia is more important than Europe."

Certainly there is a substantial body of opinion among American policy-makers that Asia and even Latin America are more intriguing as trade partners because of their vast and relatively untapped potential. As for security concerns, the Middle East and East Asia present more pressing problems than Europe does. Overall, so this thinking goes, Britain is a second-level power of second-tier importance and should be treated accordingly.

But formulations that denigrate U.S.-U.K. ties may be too simplistic, ignoring the updated realities of this long-term partnership. For instance, Anglo-American economic relations are thriving. Britain has surpassed Japan to become the largest foreign investor in the United States, which in turn is the largest outside investor in the U.K. With its flourishing service industries, Britain aggressively promotes itself as the "gateway to Europe" for American companies interested in tapping into the European market. Similarly, new efforts are under way to increase British economic presence in the United States. Quintessentially "American" companies ranging from Dunkin' Donuts to Smith & Wesson now have British parents.

Andrew Fraser, director of the Invest in Britain Bureau, says "mutual investment is reinvigorating the

unique relationship" between the two countries. He cites a business executive from Boston who observed that "the U.K. is closer than California" in terms of the ease of doing business.

As a military force, Britain proved during the Persian Gulf War that, in the words of former Foreign Secretary Douglas Hurd, it still "punches above its weight" and remains America's most reliable and most effective ally.* Britain also has been the staunchest supporter of the Clinton administration's plan for NATO expansion.

Despite these strengths, the very closeness of the Anglo-American relationship sometimes breeds problems. For example, the Clinton administration waded into the Northern Ireland peace process with either remarkable insensitivity or remarkable wisdom, depending on who judges the effort. When Sinn Fein leader Gerry Adams was invited to the White House in 1995, many Britons were incensed and asked how Americans would like it if Oklahoma City bomber Timothy McVeigh had been invited to Buckingham Palace? [4]

Of course, as it turned out the Clinton effort met with some success. Since then, Adams has even visited 10 Downing Street himself as part of the Blair government's efforts to forge a peace plan. Hurd notes that although the Clinton effort "began in a rather ill-thought-out way," it has in the long run "been helpful." Nevertheless, there remain those who criticize the presumptuousness of an American president intervening without invitation in Britain's domestic political affairs.

Similarly, the Helms-Burton Act — the American law designed to punish companies doing business in Cuba — has been criticized in Britain as an attempt to impose American policy on

other countries. The British government has made clear that it will protect U.K. businesses against extraterritorial enforcement of such U.S. legislation.

These are bumps along a mostly smooth road. The relationship remains fundamentally strong as it evolves. For Britain, critical decisions now must be made about balancing relationships with the United States and Europe. Blair has said: "I do not believe we have to choose between Europe and America. No other European country would dream of doing so. In fact, the two relationships are crucially interdependent. . . . It is only if we are at the heart of decision-making in Europe that we will be taken seriously in Washington. And it is only if we have a new, strong, post-Cold War relationship with the U.S. that we will have the same degree of influence in Europe." [5]

While Britain grapples with defining its role in the new Europe, the United States remains supportive. At his London meeting with Blair last May, Clinton cited the "unique partnership" between the two countries and praised the "unbreakable alliance . . . based on shared values and common aspirations."

The upcoming meeting in Washington on Feb. 5-6 between Clinton and Blair is likely to produce similar rhetoric, but the subtext will also be important. For his audience in Britain and in other EU countries, Blair's visit will underscore the comfortable closeness the United States and Britain continue to enjoy. Clinton — despite his administration's heavy emphasis on cultivating friendships in Asia — will presumably engage Blair in discussions about general political philosophy and the particulars of European security strategy, all on the apparent footing of equal partners.

The message will be one of solidarity. But beneath the bonhomie will remain several important issues that go to the heart of the Anglo-American relationship:

---

*Britain sent air, sea and ground forces to the Gulf War, and was the second-largest contributor of troops, behind the U.S.

Is the "special relationship" between the United States and Great Britain obsolete?

As phrase-making goes, "special relationship" is neither precise nor poetic, and yet it has had great staying power over the years. When Winston Churchill used the term in his 1946 "Iron Curtain" speech in Fulton, Mo., it merely amplified his call for "the fraternal association of English-speaking peoples." This meant, he said, "a special relationship between the British Commonwealth and Empire and the United States."

Such a partnership, Churchill added, would guarantee that there would be in the world "no quivering, precarious balance of power to offer its temptation to ambition or adventure." Instead, there would exist "an overwhelming assurance of security."

This relationship was a good one — a firm strategic partnership that was instrumental in winning the Cold War. Now, the phrase and perhaps the relationship itself seem archaic to some in both Britain and the United States.

Raymond Seitz noted in a 1994 speech in London, as he ended his tenure as U.S. ambassador to Great Britain, that when first assuming the job, "I said I would eschew the phrase 'special relationship' not because I had any particular aversion to it, but because I felt its misty quality clouded what was at stake. . . . The phrase relies on unarticulated givens at a moment in history when all givens need re-examination."

Similarly, Douglas Hurd, who served as British foreign secretary in the Thatcher and Major governments, said in 1995: "I don't believe in talking about a 'special relationship' in ways that diminish other relationships. I don't think it is like children in a schoolyard rushing up and down and saying, 'My relationship is more special than yours.'"

Churchill considered Anglo-American bonding to be not merely desirable but necessary. That necessity no longer exists. The shared top priority of the United States and the U.K. during the Cold War was to ensure

British troops were part of the NATO force sent to Bosnia to help enforce the peace accord.

the West's strategic superiority vs. the Soviet Union. Today, despite still having much in common, the two nations' priorities diverge. The future of Britain has come to be tied more closely to the rest of Europe than to America. Britain's economy and to a certain extent its security will depend on the European Union, regardless of how much federal authority the EU eventually exercises and how Britain defines its participation in the union.

For its part, the United States appreciates the ease of working with Britain, but is trying to define its own role as the sole superpower. Globalism has grand allure, but it might not mesh well with American domestic politics. A mild form of isolationism, which has been called the recessive gene in the American character, may be influencing U.S. perceptions of its place in the world. Sen. Jesse Helms, R-N.C., is not alone in his footdragging when it comes to committing American resources abroad, even when it involves an alliance as historic and close as the one with Britain.

Despite there being grounds for pronouncing "the special relationship" obsolete, arguments also can be made about its renewed importance. Even with the Cold War over, defense issues remain an important aspect of Anglo-American cooperation. During the Gulf War, Britain once again proved its dependability. Appraising the British as an ally in such conflicts, former U.S. Defense Secretary Dick Cheney says, "The Brits are good." He adds, "It's easier for us to work with the Brits than just about anybody else" because of the history of the partnership, the common language and similar military doctrine.

Looking ahead, the last thing Britain wants to see is the United States relinquishing its role as the ultimate guarantor of European security. Despite occasional declarations by some Europeans (principally the French) that Europe can take care of itself quite nicely, a U.S. departure would leave a defense leadership vacuum

Reuters/Peter Andrews

The Politics of Tony Blair

The chemistry between youthful Prime Minister Tony Blair and President Clinton is undeniable. But the two politicians share much more than personal style. After their talks last May in London, Blair said that he and Clinton had agreed "that this is a new era which calls for a new generation politics and a new generation leadership. This is the generation that prefers reason to doctrine, that is strong in ideals but is indifferent to ideology, whose instinct is to judge governments not on grand designs but on practical results."

In turning his back to ideology, Blair illustrated how much had changed since the days of President Ronald Reagan and Prime Minister Margaret Thatcher, and underscored his affinity for Clinton's approach to winning a national election.

During the preceding years, Democratic Party strategists close to Clinton had served as mentors for Labor's rebuilding. Just as Clinton had targeted the political middle by running as a "New Democrat" in 1992, Blair portrayed himself as the exponent of "New Labor."

Blair's fascination with Clinton's accomplishments has been controversial in some Labor circles, fueling arguments between modernizers and traditionalists in the party. This is particularly the case whenever Blair seems to be positioning himself as a centrist. He sounded very much like Clinton when, in May 1993, for example, he said: "We play the Tory game when we say we've got to speak up for the underclass rather than the broad majority of people in this country. It's not just an electoral fact that you will lose an election if you allow yourself to be painted into that corner, though you will. ... What we have got to do is to show how, by giving those people opportunity, we actually assist the whole of society to prosper." [1]

This appeal to a broad and moderate "middle England" electorate echoed the Clinton rhetoric of 1992. Although Blair dislikes being characterized as a Clinton clone, his repositioning of Labor in preparation for the 1997 campaign was much like Clinton's strategy: Move the party rightward, exile the radicals and offer voters a non-threatening centrism. This shrewd transformation of Labor, coupled with public disenchantment with the Conservative Party (which had been in power since 1979), helped produce the Blair-led Labor landslide.

During his first months as prime minister, Blair found that the middle of the road can be treacherous terrain. For instance, in December the Blair government's proposal for welfare reform provoked a mini-revolt among his party's most liberal members. The measure, which cuts benefits to single parents by about $17 a week, produced defections in Labor's parliamentary ranks — not nearly enough to defeat the bill, but enough to signal that Blair's New Labor pragmatism will sometimes collide with the party's socialist tradition.

Reiterating his credo to Labor lawmakers, Blair said: "We ran as New Labor. We govern as New Labor. Tax and spend is not the way to run an efficient, dynamic, modern economy."

So far, no Labor version of Rep. Richard A. Gephardt, D-Mo., has emerged to challenge Blair within the party in the way the House minority leader has confronted Clinton and Vice President Al Gore. Nevertheless, dissension within Labor's ranks is certain to flare occasionally.

Since Labor's victory, relations with the Clinton administration have been close. In November, members of the Blair government met at Chequers, the prime minister's official country residence, with first lady Hillary Rodham Clinton and a number of Clinton advisers to discuss "the progressive agenda." The session was just one instance of a renewed policy-shaping partnership between political leaders of the two countries. When Chancellor of the Exchequer Gordon Brown granted independence to the Bank of England, he reportedly did so after conversations with U.S. Federal Reserve Board Chairman Alan Greenspan and Deputy Secretary of the Treasury Lawrence Summers. These connections are evidence, noted *The Economist*, that "intellectually, the British government is still a lot closer to America than to Europe." [2]

The Clinton-Blair Washington meetings in February will, presumably, reinforce that closeness.

---

[1] Quoted in John Rentoul, *Tony Blair* (1995), p. 280.

[2] "The American Connection," *The Economist*, Nov. 8, 1997, p. 63.

that would be filled initially by Britain and France (as nuclear powers), but possibly soon thereafter by Germany. Former Ambassador Seitz has said: "This vague thing called 'the American presence' is so important for Europe. It siphons off the poisons and anxieties of European history."

German military prominence would rattle nerves in numerous places, Moscow among them. Such dramatic change from the status quo could seriously destabilize the currently placid relationship among the major European states.

Another reason — more subtle, but still important — that the special ties will continue can be seen in the rapport between Clinton and Blair. In many ways, they are kindred spirits. With similar outlooks on policy and politics, they understand each other well when they discuss the ingredients of a pragmatic, new progressivism. (*See story, above.*)

Despite Clinton's penchant for pasta feasts with German Chancellor

Helmut Kohl, Blair may turn out to be the European counterpart to whom Clinton becomes closest. The traditional comfort level of American-British dialogue combined with personal political kinship should make for a solid friendship. More specifically, actions such as Blair's prompt endorsement of Clinton's NATO expansion plan and his backing of America's hard line toward Iraq, which set him apart from other European leaders, are duly noted at the White House. Blair's upcoming Washington visit should further reinforce these personal ties.

The "special" nature of the Anglo-American relationship is certain to change. But, as British journalist John Dickie observes in his 1994 book *"Special" No More*, "however much the memories fade, Britain will never be 'just another foreign country' to the Americans."

Is the European Union pulling Britain away from the United States?

The European Union's impact on the U.S.-U.K. relationship is large and growing. Predictions differ about whether that impact over the long term will be positive or negative.

James Schlesinger, a former U.S. secretary of Defense and CIA director, has voiced the pessimistic view: "Almost unavoidably, the single market will be a vehicle for joint discrimination against the United States," he wrote. "One may accept European assurances that there is no desire or intention to create a high-barrier Fortress Europe. That barriers may be no higher in absolute terms does not mean they will be no higher in relative terms. After all, the purpose of the single market is to eliminate internal barriers, which inherently means increased joint discrimination against the outside world." [6]

On the other hand, the optimistic outlook has its believers, such as

Britain Ranks Among Top U.S. Markets

Britain imported $38 billion in U.S. goods in 1996, making it America's fourth-largest export market, trailing behind Canada, Mexico and Japan. The U.K.'s 1996 exports to the United States amounted to $33 billion.

Amount of Exports

(in $billions)

Legend: ■ U.K. to U.S. □ U.S. to U.K.

Source: U.S. Department of Commerce, International Trade Center

Malcolm Rifkind, who served as foreign secretary in Major's government: "The single market has opened new opportunities not only for its members but also for the rest of the world," he said. "Imports to the EU have risen, not fallen, since its creation." [7]

Blair has been a bit more cautious, noting the complexity of the issue: "We need a framework within which we can deal with the economic disputes that are certain to arise between the two sides of the Atlantic," he wrote. "The EU is a frustrating partner for the U.S. There is no one center of power. . . . The relationship will in reality need to pass through London, Paris and Bonn as well as Brussels. Cooperation and consultation on this axis needs to be reinforced." [8]

Rules enforced by the World Trade Organization guarantee that neither the EU nor the United States can turn itself into a tariff-protected fortress. This is important because the stakes are huge: the EU and the U.S. together account for about half of world trade, the EU 37 percent and the U.S. 14 percent.

U.S.-EU trade so far has been functioning relatively smoothly. Although trade between the U.S. and the EU exceeded $250 billion in merchandise and $115 billion in services in 1995, American economic relations with the EU have a decidedly British slant. More than 40 percent of U.S. investment in the EU is in Britain. [9]

This apparent pro-U.K. tilt by the Americans has, however, provided fuel for anti-EU sentiment in some quarters in Britain. Atlanticism is seen as a safe haven by Euroskeptics who theorize that the U.S. is a more reliable and less intrusive partner than the increasingly powerful EU In other words, "Who needs the EU when we have America?"

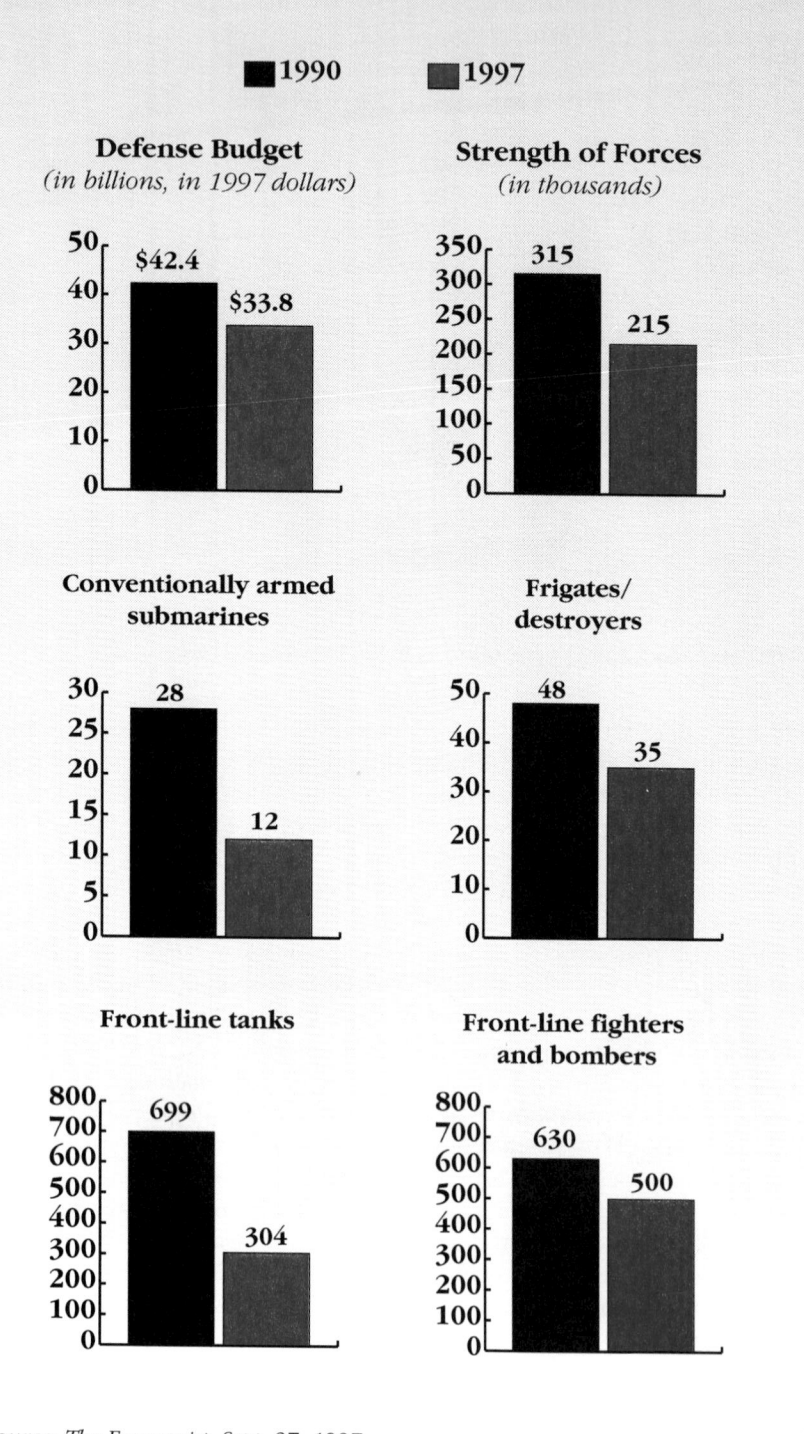

British Defense Cuts

Britain has reduced its defense budget by 20 percent since 1990, resulting in across-the-board cuts in troop strength and armaments.

■ 1990   ■ 1997

Defense Budget
(in billions, in 1997 dollars)

$42.4
$33.8

Strength of Forces
(in thousands)

315
215

Conventionally armed submarines

28
12

Frigates/ destroyers

48
35

Front-line tanks

699
304

Front-line fighters and bombers

630
500

Source: The Economist, Sept. 27, 1997.

Asian countries, while not U.K. trading partners at the level of the U.S., are also seen as alternatives to Europe.

Blair addressed this issue before the 1997 elections: "The Euroskeptics sometimes suggest that the high level of inward investment in the U.K. demonstrates that we could go it alone. But they miss the point. The Japanese, the Americans and the Koreans invest here because we are part of the European Union. If they see us slipping to a second tier, they will put their investment elsewhere." [10]

Alistair Hunter of the British-American Chamber of Commerce makes the same point. He says that "the more thoughtful U.S. businessmen say, 'At some point you have to become more involved in the EU or we'll have to transplant our investments to the continent.'" So far this kind of pressure has been relatively gentle, but it is one of the factors in the discussion about Europe that became a crucial element in Britain's 1997 elections. It will continue to be debated during the next several years.

There is no denying the growing importance not only of the EU as an international economic power but also of the European states — collectively and individually — as British trading partners. By the early 1990s, Western Europe took nearly two-thirds of Britain's exports, while trade with Commonwealth countries declined in importance. During the 1980s, the U.S. was Britain's largest single market, but it was overtaken in 1990 by Germany. Germany is also Britain's largest single supplier. In 1992, it took almost 14 percent of Britain's exports and supplied 15 percent of its imports. [11]

This shift in the relative importance to Britain of the U.S. and Europe requires readjustment of world view. British journalist Henry Brandon wrote of this in 1992: "The fact that the British have now decided they must be part of the new Europe indicates the growing gravitational pull of the Community. The British know they will have to swallow hard to overcome their island psychology and their deep-seated attachment to century-old symbols of sovereignty as well as to face the devaluation of their 'special relationship' with the United States." [12]

Passionate debate continues in Britain about one particular aspect of the EU: participation in the European Monetary Union. Journalist Martin Kettle of *The Guardian* has summed up the unease about joining the EMU: "The single currency argument is inseparable from a passionately felt argument about British history and identity, in which the sense of British independence is powerfully and offensively challenged by any attempt to assert that Britain's interests lie in a union with other European nations, especially Germany. Others believe . . . that these deep instincts are nothing less than a historic illusion. They believe that this vision of a freestanding Britain has been irrevocably shattered by the collapse of the British Empire, by the unavailing struggle to claim superpower status in a world manifestly dominated by the United States, by the rise of the Asia-Pacific powers and not least, by the destruction of the British industrial base." [13]

The Blair government has deferred final judgment about EMU membership, declining to join at the outset (January 1999), but leaving open participation beginning in 2002, when the EMU currency — the Euro — is scheduled to replace national currencies. Although the Blair decision to forgo immediate EMU membership has proved politically sound in Britain, debate continues there about whether the U.K. should ever join. (*See "At Issue," p. 89.*)

The United States will probably encourage British membership in the EMU in 2002, the next opportunity. MIT Professor Rudi Dornbusch wrote that that would benefit the U.S. "If it helps Europe grow, that is good for international prosperity," he noted in *Business Week*. "If it disarms the Bundesbank, with its deflationist tendencies, that's even better. If it creates better financial markets in Europe, U.S. investment houses and banks will be big players." [14]

As Britain becomes ever more closely tied to its EU partners, fears sometimes surface about Anglo-American relations suffering as a result. Blair is among those who say that won't happen: "Our road to maximum influence leads through Europe," he wrote. "If we are to be listened to seriously in Washington or Tokyo . . . we will often be acting with the rest of Europe. If we want to influence trade negotiations, we have to act as part of the EU, the world's largest trading bloc. If we want to attract inward investment, it must be clear we are part of Europe." [15]

Former Foreign Secretary Hurd notes that Americans need to understand the cohesiveness of the EU. "There is not a triangle" of the U.S., U.K. and EU, he says, because "Europe negotiates as one." Not only is Britain not a gatekeeper in terms of American access to EU policy-making, but also it must maintain a certain distance from the U.S. so other Europeans will not perceive Britain as a stalking horse for the Americans. How far that distance should be — the difference between "close" and "too close" — is difficult to determine but is an essential element in shaping the future of the two nations.

Can the United States and Britain still rely on each other as military allies?

Images of Americans and Britons fighting as allies in two world wars have faded, left to grainy newsreels and dusty history. But in 1991, the alliance found itself revived on the battlefields of the Gulf War.

The war against Iraq underscored Britain's status as America's most competent military ally. Martin, the former director of the Royal Institute of International Affairs, said that in this war, "all of a sudden the British counted again."

Hurd, who was foreign secretary during the war, appraises British strength this way: "We're a military power — not a great military power but a good military power. We have a global view of the world. We're willing to participate. The one superpower cannot do everything on its own. . . . We are a medium-sized nation with some very good troops. They don't make us pre-eminent, but they make us interesting."

The Gulf War is offered as proof that the U.S.-British alliance is intact and effective. But this may have been the exception rather than the rule. Iraq's behavior was so egregious and the stakes — the oil reserves — were so high that taking firm action was virtually unavoidable. That kind of clear-cut situation is rare. The more common scenario may turn out to be one such as unfolded in the Balkans, where the fighting had enough ripple effects in Europe to make it in Britain's interest to do something, but was distant enough from the United States (except when television brought gory scenes into American living rooms) to make activism problematic.

Martin asks an important question: "Will the United States really participate in peacekeeping operations on a regular basis, will it be a true partner, or will it rather pursue a course of 'erratic dominance'?" [16]

Before the United States finally asserted itself in the former Yugoslavia, Hurd says, "it was very unattractive for the Europeans to be acting on the ground while the United States was standing on the sideline. It was very irksome. We were taking the risks and getting the blame." From the American standpoint, however, the Balkans war illustrated that not all European defense issues will be viewed as "Atlantic issues" by the

U.S. Seitz notes that "there is no longer a seamless security interest" as had existed during the Cold War.

Budget as well as strategic issues will shape decisions about how much military capability is necessary today. Britain and the U.S. are reducing the size of their armed forces. Since 1989, America's armed forces have shrunk from 2.1 million personnel to about 1.5 million. In Europe, U.S. troop strength declined from 317,000 in 1989 toward the eventual target of 100,000. Britain's reductions were equally substantial. (*See graphs, p. 80.*)

As a matter of post-Cold War domestic politics, sharing costs with allies is essential. In the past, support could be found — although sometimes with difficulty — for substantial defense budget outlays to counter the Soviets, especially in Europe. Now, with so much pressure on American politicians to balance the national budget, eliminate the long-running deficit and reorder spending priorities, defense expenditures generally — and spending for the defense of Europe in particular — require different rationales.

This kind of restructuring does not mean the U.S. is looking for a way out of Europe. Former Secretary of Defense Cheney is among those who believe that a strong U.S. presence remains vital to European security. That means, he says, "military force on the ground." Noting that "the Europeans are not capable of overcoming their divisions" when it comes to forging a unified defense policy, Cheney says the U.S. role is that of "the anchor of effective security. The U.S. is the one that has to provide the leadership."

Britain and other allies must decide how much money, personnel and equipment they will provide. If they make relatively substantial contributions, they will alter the essence of the alliance, and American dominance will decrease. This will not reach the point at which the U.S. becomes a secondary player, but realignment of responsibility logically brings with it

a realignment of authority.

The Blair government has backed Clinton's 1997 NATO expansion formula and has sided with the U.S. while France and, to a lesser extent, Germany have sought an expanded and more formalized European security role within or even beyond NATO. But no one will benefit in the long run from a schism between Anglo-American and Franco-German interests. To retain its maximum influence within Europe, Britain cannot be seen as being unduly in thrall to the U.S. If American policy-makers recognize this, they will work with the British to bridge gaps in the Atlantic alliance, and the British should nudge the Americans to make sure this happens.

Despite the need for some delicacy in shaping how the two nations' closeness is perceived, there remains a fundamental collegiality, particularly among senior policy-makers. Hurd calls it "the feeling of being a bit upstream," of being ahead of what's happening; Henderson cites "the ability to discuss things noncommittally."

For the most part, Churchill's vision of a grand strategic partnership between the United States and Great Britain has been fulfilled. It will not, however, be sustained by nostalgia. Among the items on the Clinton-Blair agenda will, presumably, be an evaluation of future security responsibilities, with emphasis on determining who does what and who pays for it. ∎

BACKGROUND

The Evolving Alliance

On Aug. 26, 1814, British army Lt. George Robert Gleig wrote in his journal: "The sky was brilliantly

illumined by the different conflagrations. . . . I do not recollect to have witnessed at any period of my life a scene more striking or sublime."

The sublime scene was the city of Washington in flames, courtesy of Gleig and the rest of a British force that was marauding through mid-Atlantic America during the final months of the War of 1812.

Anglo-American relations have improved considerably since then, but it is useful to remember the tempestuous past from which today's friendship emerged. Although photo-op amicability has become the most familiar imagery of the alliance — with president and prime minister grinning at each other at the White House or 10 Downing Street — tensions sometimes surface. The problems usually do not last long, but they illustrate that even this well-established relationship should not be taken for granted.

America's military and economic clout allowed the U.S. to assert itself as the leader in the relationship with Britain by the end of World War I. At the outset of the Second World War, the British government found itself in the position of supplicant, desperately requesting aid from a United States that officially was clinging to neutrality. Fortunately for Britain, because of the Churchill-Roosevelt friendship the American president found ways, as Churchill said, to "wage war if not declare it."

After the Japanese attack on Pearl Harbor and America's formal entry into the war, U.S.-British teamwork became closer. When Roosevelt died soon before the final allied victory in 1945, Churchill noted that he and Roosevelt had exchanged more than 1,700 messages and had met nine times for a total of about 120 days. Eulogizing his American colleague, Churchill called him "the greatest champion of freedom who has ever brought help and comfort from the

Continued on p. 86

Chronology

1940s *World War II pulls the U.S. and Britain closer together, and the partnership continues as the Cold War begins.*

December 1940
President Franklin D. Roosevelt declares that America will be the "arsenal of democracy," laying the groundwork for the "Lend-Lease" plan that will supply Britain with desperately needed military equipment.

August 1941
Roosevelt and Churchill meet off the Newfoundland coast and produce the Atlantic Charter, the foundation of the formal alliance that emerges when America enters the war four months later.

March 5, 1946
Churchill delivers his "Iron Curtain" speech at Westminster College in Fulton, Mo., calling for a "special relationship" between Britain and the United States to check Soviet ambitions.

1950s-1970s *The United States leads and Britain (usually) follows during the Cold War.*

November 1956
President Dwight D. Eisenhower repudiates the Anglo-French seizure of the Suez Canal and forces Prime Minister Anthony Eden to abandon the venture.

December 1962
President John F. Kennedy agrees to provide Polaris missiles to sustain Britain's independent nuclear capability.

August 1969
The British army takes over security and police duties in Northern Ireland.

January 1973
Britain belatedly becomes a member of the European Economic Community (the Common Market).

May 1979
The Conservative Party wins a parliamentary majority in the general election; Margaret Thatcher becomes prime minister.

1980s *Ronald Reagan and Thatcher form their Cold War partnership.*

April-June 1982
With behind-the-scenes U.S. help, Britain reclaims the Falkland Islands from Argentina.

October 1983
U.S. troops invade Grenada, a member of the British Commonwealth, to oust a pro-Cuba government. Thatcher initially opposes Reagan's decision, but later calls the intervention a success.

April 1986
Thatcher approves Reagan's request to use American aircraft based in Britain to attack Libya.

1990s *With the end of the Cold War, the United States and Britain reshape their relationship.*

August 1990
Iraq invades Kuwait, and Thatcher supports a strong American response, telling President George Bush, "This is no time to go wobbly."

November 1990
Thatcher steps down as party leader and prime minister and is succeeded by John Major.

January-February 1991
During the U.S.-led liberation of Kuwait, British forces participate in the ad hoc anti-Iraq coalition.

December 1991
The Maastricht Treaty is signed, creating the European Union. Britain is allowed to opt out of the common currency provisions, a concession necessary to enable Major to win Parliament's approval of the treaty.

March 1995
Despite British government objections, President Clinton greets Sinn Fein leader Gerry Adams at the White House.

May 1, 1997
Following a Labor Party landslide victory that ends 17 years of Conservative government, Tony Blair becomes prime minister.

May 29, 1997
Clinton and Blair meet at 10 Downing Street, where Blair underscores the importance to Anglo-American relations.

Oct. 27, 1997
Chancellor of the Exchequer Gordon Brown announces the Blair government's decision not to join the European Monetary Union at present.

Clinton's Involvement in Northern Ireland . . .

Since 1820, almost 5 million Irish immigrants have come to the United States. That is roughly the combined population of today's Irish Republic and Northern Ireland, and it translates into some 39 million Americans of Irish ancestry, the nation's second-largest ethnic group, after German-Americans.

With so many millions, Irish-Americans wield considerable clout in U.S. politics, particularly when one of their number — such as John F. Kennedy or Bill Clinton (whose mother's maiden name was Cassidy) — lives in the White House. On Capitol Hill in recent years, powerful figures such as Sen. Edward M. Kennedy, D-Mass., and the late House Speaker Thomas P. "Tip" O'Neill, D-Mass., have not been bashful about championing Irish interests.

The Irish Republican Army (IRA) and its fund-raising operation, NORAID, have enjoyed substantial American political and financial backing. Depending on who is asked, the support is for widows and orphans and mainstream political activity, or for weapons and terrorism.

Former Prime Minister Margaret Thatcher subscribes to the latter theory. "The emotions of millions of decent Irish-Americans are manipulated by Irish Republican extremists, who have been able to give a romantic respectability to terrorism that its sordid reality belies," she wrote in her memoirs. [1]

She urged an end to American support of the IRA and related groups. "It is not enough to decry individual acts of terrorism but then refuse to endorse the measures required to defeat it. That applies to American Irish who supply NORAID with money to kill British citizens." [2]

Extradition of IRA members continues to produce diplomatic tension between the United States and Britain. As recently as September 1997, the Clinton administration suspended deportation action against six IRA members who had served time in British prisons for terrorist acts. The suspensions were almost certainly a payoff to Sinn Fein — the political arm of the IRA — for its recent endorsement of non-violence. Protestant leaders in Northern Ireland, however, decried the American decision, arguing that the IRA remained a terrorist organization and that the U.S. should not implicitly sanction IRA tactics.

Sometimes the pursuit of votes based on Irish issues becomes particularly heavy-handed. In New York, for example, a statute was passed by the legislature and signed by Republican Gov. George Pataki in 1996 requiring not only that study of the 19th-century Irish famine be included in school curricula but that the famine be depicted as genocide, with the British as the perpetrators. "The great Irish hunger was not the result of a massive failure of the Irish potato crop," Pataki said, "but, rather, was the result of a deliberate campaign by the British to deny the Irish people the food they needed to survive."

Several other federal and state measures have also embraced this approach to teaching public school students about the famine. British officials have little to say on the record about such matters, but privately they call them "sensational and emotive," "obstructions to constructive measures" and "pandering to an ethnic voting bloc."

Far larger issues arose during Clinton's first term, when U.S. involvement (or, some would say, meddling) in Irish affairs became particularly assertive. During the 1992 campaign, Clinton wooed Irish-American voters by promising policy changes. In a campaign letter sent to these voters several weeks before the election, Clinton said: "I believe the appointment of a special U.S. envoy to Northern Ireland could be a catalyst in the effort to secure a lasting peace. We believe that the British government must do more to oppose job discrimination that has created unemployment rates two-and-a-half times higher for Catholic workers than Protestant workers. . . .The MacBride [fair employment] principles set forth appropriate guidelines. . . . We also believe that the British government should establish more effective safeguards against the wanton use of lethal force and against further collusion between the security forces and Protestant paramilitary groups." [3]

As appealing as such rhetoric might be to some Irish-Americans, it was not well-received by British officials. They particularly objected to the notions that Britain was engaged in "wanton use of lethal force" or had been in "collusion" with Protestant paramilitary groups.

The MacBride principles cited by Clinton are another irritant. The British say their law incorporates adequate anti-discrimination rules and that another layer of guidelines is a disincentive to investment. This view is shared by many labor unions and the Social Democratic Labor Party (a relatively moderate Catholic/nationalist organization) in Northern Ireland, while support for the MacBride rules comes primarily from the more militant Sinn Fein.

The worst Ireland-related strains on U.S.-British relations came in 1994, when Clinton ordered that Gerry Adams, the leader of Sinn Fein, be granted a temporary visa (which had previously been denied) so he could make a 48-hour visit to the U.S. Clinton saw it as an opportunity to pull Sinn Fein into peace talks and push the IRA toward a cease-fire.

"We didn't come here to sit around like potted plants," Clinton told his national security adviser, Anthony Lake, who favored granting the visa. "If we have a chance to move this thing forward, we have to take it." [4]

The visa decision sparked angry reaction in the U.K. Among press comments, *The Sun* demanded that "the

... Reflects Closeness of Anglo-American Ties

Yanks keep their noses out of Ulster," and the *Daily Express* said Clinton's decision was "a coarse insult from a country we thought was our friend." [5]

Some members of the American foreign policy establishment have also been critical of Clinton's dealings with Adams. In his just published memoir, former U.S. ambassador to Britain Raymond Seitz writes, "America, which had suffered so often at the hands of terrorists around the world, should have been the last place to offer a platform to Gerry Adams, but in the end, this is what the president did."

Seitz also notes that because of British unhappiness about Clinton administration dealings with Adams, "London even stopped passing sensitive intelligence to the White House because it often seemed to find its way to the IRA." [6]

In addition to the low-key efforts at the White House, Clinton made his commitment to Irish peace a keystone of his December 1995 trip to Britain and Northern Ireland. When he visited Belfast, tens of thousands of Catholics and Protestants gathered to hear him urge reconciliation. A widely published photograph from the occasion showed Clinton and Gerry Adams shaking hands.

Through this visit and the White House-orchestrated diplomacy, Clinton was seen as not only intervening in the Anglo-Irish relationship but taking the lead. In an analysis piece for *The New York Times*, journalist James F. Clarity wrote of the Northern Ireland visit: "Mr. Clinton managed to refocus attention on the overall goal of peace by speaking eloquently and forcefully over the heads of the politicians and paramilitary leaders, whose wrangling over details had slowed the peace effort to a halt in recent months." Also, wrote Clarity, "Mr. Clinton persuaded Prime Minister John Major to change London's long-held policy that the United States should have no direct role in Northern Ireland." [7]

The process Clinton introduced was a "twin-track" approach: an international commission chaired by former Sen. George Mitchell, D-Maine, would address disarmament of the IRA, while the British government held talks with all Northern Ireland parties. Getting the major players to agree to try this was a significant accomplishment in itself. In practice, the effort predictably has had its ups and downs, particularly when violence has sporadically erupted.

Prime Minister Tony Blair, whose first official trip after taking office was to Northern Ireland, made clear that he did not expect "to see Northern Ireland as anything but a part of the United Kingdom." He also pledged to continue to work for peace and to support Mitchell's approach. Blair promptly sent his Northern Ireland secretary, Mo Mowlam, to Washington to urge the Clinton administration to keep pressure on all parties to the peace talks. Help from the White House was also requested in the effort to get an IRA cease-fire.

For his part, Clinton — during a May 1997 visit to Blair in London — made clear that the U.S. would not back away. "Again I urge the IRA to lay down their guns for good," he said, praising Blair's initial efforts to push the peace process along.

In addition to its diplomatic initiatives, the United States has provided economic support to Northern Ireland — $1.65 billion in investment since 1991. American trade missions visit Northern Ireland regularly, and assuming that a reasonable level of peace can be maintained, more investment is sure to follow.

Also, Clinton's willingness to deal with Adams has been adopted by Blair, who met with Adams in Belfast in October and at 10 Downing Street in December 1997. (The Blair-Adams meeting was the first visit of an Irish republican leader to the prime minister's official residence since Michael Collins came to see David Lloyd George in 1921.)

Despite the merging of American and British approaches to Northern Ireland issues and the apparent success of recent efforts, tensions remain. Among Britons, some unhappiness, or at least wariness, about the Clinton administration's policy is understandable, because the U.S. is involving itself in what is fundamentally a matter of domestic politics.

But the very intrusiveness of the Clinton initiative underscores the closeness and complexity of Anglo-American ties. Clinton has forged ahead in a way that would be unthinkable in other contexts, such as the longstanding dispute between the Spanish government and Basque nationalists. The invitation to Adams, in particular, directly contravened British policy at the time toward Sinn Fein. That Clinton's judgment apparently was correct and helped push negotiations forward does not wholly overcome British resentment about the interference.

And still, no lasting damage to Anglo-American ties appears to have been done.

[1] Margaret Thatcher, *The Downing Street Years* (1993), p. 58.

[2] *Ibid.*, p. 415.

[3] Conor O'Clery, *The Greening of the White House* (1996), p. 23.

[4] Martin Walker, *The President We Deserve* (1996), p. 279.

[5] O'Clery, *op. cit.*, p. 119.

[6] See Warren Hoge, "U.S. Leaked British Intelligence to IRA, Ex-Envoy Says," *The New York Times*, Jan. 19, 1998, p. A17.

[7] James F. Clarity, "Clinton's Role in Northern Ireland Talks: Restoring the Focus on the Big Picture," *The New York Times*, Dec. 5, 1995, p. A6. For background, see "Northern Ireland Cease-Fire," *The CQ Researcher*, Sept. 15, 1995, pp. 801-814.

Continued from p. 82

New World to the old."

During the war, the New World had again proved able to shape the fortunes of the old. In the peace of sorts that followed, the new world's dominance continued, and Britain and the United States grew closer than they had ever been before.

That new closeness, however, brought with it a change in the relationship that the British were slow to comprehend. In November 1956, the British and French governments sent a "peacekeeping" force to seize Egypt's Suez Canal without first consulting with the Americans. British Prime Minister Anthony Eden had apparently assumed that the United States would stand by its ally, regardless of the circumstances. He was wrong. President Dwight Eisenhower angrily used economic pressure to force Britain to back down.

The relationship was no longer one between equals. Eisenhower made clear to the British that they were out of line and should not expect automatic U.S. backing for their foreign adventures. American diplomat Robert Murphy reported that as the Suez crisis developed it was clear that Eden "had not adjusted his thoughts to the altered world status of Great Britain." [17]

Harold Macmillan succeeded Eden as prime minister and mended the rift with Eisenhower. Henry Kissinger, former secretary of State in the Nixon and Ford administrations, has observed that "it was under Macmillan that Britain completed the transition from power to influence." [18] Implicitly, both nations

had come to recognize that on matters of mutual concern the United States would lead and Britain would follow.

Reagan and Thatcher

Of all the post-World War II personal relationships between officials of the two countries, the most significant was that between President

Prime Minister Winston Churchill, President Franklin D. Roosevelt and Soviet Premier Josef Stalin meet at Yalta in February 1945 to discuss the Soviet Union's entry into the war against Japan and plans for treating Germany.

Reagan and Prime Minister Thatcher, which former Secretary of State George Shultz has said was "as close as any imaginable between two major leaders." [19]

With similar political philosophies and world outlooks, the two usually worked smoothly together. When she visited Reagan soon after he became president, Thatcher vowed that the two would "promote stability, prevent aggression and oppose tyranny," and she promised that "your problems will be our problems, and when you look for friends, we will be

there." [20] That promise was to be tested, but always — in the end, at least — it was kept.

The Falklands Crisis

Just a year after that 1981 meeting, the Anglo-American relationship endured its most severe strain since the Suez crisis. Argentina seized the Falkland (or Malvinas) Islands — 8,000 miles from England but home to 2,000 British subjects (and their many sheep). Thatcher dispatched warships and troops to reclaim the territory.

This created a dilemma for the Reagan administration. Although there may have been an inclination to stand by the long-time ally, the realities of Western Hemisphere politics posed a problem. The United States was trying to shed its image of "gringo imperialism," and to side with a European power against a Latin American state would significantly damage that effort.

Secretary of State Alexander Haig tried to mediate the dispute, but to no avail. Even after British troops had landed on the islands, Reagan attempted to convince Thatcher to stop the offensive and let diplomats take over. She would have none of it, and told the president so bluntly.

With Reagan's foreign policy team split about what course to take, the administration looked increasingly like a befuddled bystander as events proceeded. Beneath the political surface, however, the U.S. was supporting the British military effort. Haig and White House National Security Adviser William Clark privately told Henderson,

Britain's ambassador to Washington, that they and the president were firmly on Britain's side. [21]

Beyond those assurances, the most important contribution was a supply of Sidewinder air-to-air missiles, which gave the British clear superiority in the air. As British journalist Dickie has reported, the U.S. also supplied the British with 6 million gallons of aviation fuel, shoulder-held Stinger missiles, Shrike anti-radar missiles, Harpoon anti-ship missiles, mortar and artillery ammunition, air-drop containers and helicopter parts. All this was done quietly, expedited with the support of Secretary of Defense Caspar Weinberger. Also, CIA Director William Casey made his agency's gleanings available to his British counterparts. [22]

U.S. Action in Grenada

In October 1983, Reagan and Thatcher were again in disagreement about military action, this time a venture far smaller in scale than the Falklands war had been. At the request of the Organization of Eastern Caribbean States, the U.S. sent troops into Grenada to dislodge a pro-Cuban leader and protect about 1,000 American citizens on the island.

Grenada is a member of the British Commonwealth, and although Britain had indicated it would not involve itself in the country's political turmoil, the Thatcher government expected to be consulted before the U.S. took unilateral action. Communication between Washington and London about this matter was remarkably inefficient, leaving Foreign Secretary Geoffrey

Howe in the embarrassing position of telling the House of Commons that he knew of no American intervention plans, even as the military operation was about to get under way.

Thatcher wrote in her memoirs that she felt "dismayed and let down

Former British Prime Minister Margaret Thatcher and President Ronald Reagan.

by what had happened. At best, the British government had been made to look impotent; at worst we looked deceitful." She had to explain to Parliament "how it had happened that a member of the Commonwealth had been invaded by our closest ally."

In Washington, Reagan was chagrined by Thatcher's opposition. As

Secretary of State Shultz recorded in his memoirs, Reagan "had supported her in the Falklands. He felt he was absolutely right about Grenada. She didn't share his judgment at all. He was deeply disappointed." [23]

The realities of Anglo-American cooperation were underscored by this small crisis. Reagan saw the Grenada decision as a matter of U.S. policy that did not require approval from London. Granted that the British should not have been misled — as they apparently were initially — he viewed his consultation with Thatcher as a courtesy, nothing more. He was taken aback by Thatcher's presumption that she would play a substantive role in determining whether U.S. military action would be taken.

Attack on Libya

In 1986, the relationship would be tested in yet another military situation. Again, the United States was about to launch a military operation, but this time it officially requested British help. The target was Libya — an air attack in response to a series of terrorist bombings including one in Berlin that U.S. intelligence agencies had convincingly proved had been orchestrated by Muammar el- Qaddafi's government. Reagan wanted Thatcher's permission to launch the raid — to be carried out by American F-111 jets — from NATO bases in England.

Initially, Thatcher was hesitant. She

finally gave her approval, even though she knew that by doing so she would likely suffer politically at home and open Britain to reprisals in the Middle East. According to her aide Charles Powell, Thatcher's Cabinet balked, but she said: "This is what allies are for. If you're an ally, you're an ally. If one wants help, they get help." [24]

The U.S. attack proved less precise than promised. Some bombs missed their targets. Civilians were killed and wounded. Americans nevertheless supported Reagan's move; polls showed 77 percent approving. But in Britain, roughly 70 percent of those polled said Thatcher should not have cooperated.

The prime minister, however, did not second-guess herself. She agreed with Reagan's view that countries sponsoring terrorism must be shown that they could not do so without paying a price. In her memoirs, she wrote: "Whatever the cost to me, I knew that the cost to Britain of not backing American action was unthinkable. If the United States was abandoned by its closest ally, the American people and their government would feel bitterly betrayed — and reasonably so."

Thatcher's standing with the American president and the American public rose after this incident. Particularly when contrasted with France, which had refused to let the American planes fly over French airspace, Britain appeared to be the one ally on whom the United States could count.

It may turn out that personalized partnerships as close as the Reagan-Thatcher pairing are obsolete. Thatcher has noted that George Bush wasted little time in distancing himself from her. In her book *The Downing Street Years*, she recited a litany of praise for Bush, but added that "he had never had to think through his beliefs and fight for them when they were hopelessly unfashionable as

Ronald Reagan and I had had to do." Also, Reagan seemed susceptible to the sentimental allure of the "special relationship," Bush less so.

Pragmatism, more than sentiment, is also a characteristic of Clinton's presidency. So far, his relationship with Tony Blair is good, in part because both men are more oriented to the future than to the misty past. ∎

CURRENT SITUATION

Economic Realities

When Clinton and Blair met in London last May, just a few weeks after Blair had become prime minister, the dynamics of Anglo-American friendship were clearly changing. "The Americans have made it clear," Blair said, "that they want a special relationship with Europe, not with Britain alone."

The importance of establishing that balance will certainly influence the agenda of Blair's Washington visit and the two nations' foreign policies in the years ahead. Today, despite the challenges posed by the new Europe, the overall relationship between the United States and Britain remains strong.

Trade between the two countries is an example of this strength. In 1996, Britain exported $33 billion in goods to the United States, an increase of 11 percent over 1995, and imported $38 billion worth, an increase of 7 percent over 1995. (Britain is America's fourth largest export market, trailing only Canada, Mexico, and Japan.) Also, Britain's exports to

the U.S. of services (ranging from computer programming to tourism) were worth another $19 billion.

U.S.-U.K. investment also is booming. In 1979, British investments in the United States amounted to $15 billion. By 1995, that figure had reached $132 billion, which is 24 percent of the total foreign investment in the United States and a larger amount than any other country's. Flowing across the Atlantic in the other direction, American investment in Britain by 1996 exceeded $102 billion, which is 17 percent of total U.S. overseas investment and more than the U.S. has invested in Germany, France and Italy combined.

Both Britain and the United States have aggressive programs under way to promote still more economic activity. Crucial to this effort is Britain's position not just as a target market in itself, but also as a gateway to the larger EU market. Among the government agencies working on this, the Commercial Service of the U.S. Department of Commerce urges American businesses to develop a regional perspective, and Britain's Department of Trade and Industry stresses the comfort level for Americans doing business in Britain.

That comfort level is also a factor for British businesses looking at America. Hunter of the British-American Chamber of Commerce cites survey findings that "90 percent of British businessmen feel more comfortable doing business in the U.S. than in Germany." The reasons most often given, he says, are language, style of doing business and temperament.

The American presence in Britain is likely to expand. The Invest in Britain Bureau's Fraser says inward investment has been spurred by the U.K.'s recent emphasis on deregulation and privatization. American companies have taken advantage of the opportunity to invest in newly privatized British utility companies. Fraser

Continued on p. 90

At Issue:

Should Britain join the European Monetary Union?

JOHN PALMER
Former Europe Editor, **The Guardian**

FROM *THE SINGLE CURRENCY: SHOULD BRITAIN JOIN?*
(VINTAGE, 1997)

*i*n an era of sweeping economic globalization, European monetary union will provide an essential foundation for stable and sustainable growth that generates jobs. A single European currency will weaken the power of those who thrive on monetary chaos and financial speculation. It can also help ensure that the overweaning power of the global market place is better balanced and constrained by democratically decided economic and social priorities . . . .

There might be a practical alternative to monetary union if the clock could be turned back a decade or more to an era before global markets and global capital liberalization. But apart from isolationist anarchies and dictatorships, such a reversion is neither a possible nor desirable option for democracies. By reducing the disruptive powers of the financial markets, European monetary union can help governments begin to regain some control over global economic developments . . . .

In summary, European monetary union will:

• lay the basis for long-term lower interest rates;

• encourage more investment and trade, by reducing instability and currency turmoil;

• reverse economic short-termism and create the foundations for sustainable growth and job creation;

• cut financial transaction costs (which are perhaps equal to 0.4 percent of the European Union's GDP), by eliminating the need for currency transactions or 'hedging' operations, where companies try to protect themselves against sudden currency fluctuations and, as a consequence, help to bring them about. . . .

Participation in the single currency would help insulate the United Kingdom from a repetition of monetary turbulence and would thus improve Britain's long-term economic under-performance. Britain's attractiveness as a site for international investment would be enhanced. Conversely, self-exclusion from the single currency could choke off important foreign investment in the [United Kingdom].

This brings me to an absolutely critical point. Whatever the British government's eventual decision, the opponents of a single currency have not sketched out even the outlines of an alternative economic and financial policy designed to deal with the consequences of unhitching the United Kingdom from a core project of all the other EU countries. Nor have they said what Britain should do in these circumstances to keep the "confidence" of the international money markets.

LARRY ELLIOTT
Economics Editor, **The Guardian**

FROM *THE SINGLE CURRENCY: SHOULD BRITAIN JOIN?*
(VINTAGE, 1997)

*b*ritain has been a lone voice in Brussels since 1973, and there is scant evidence that that will change under the single-currency regime. Monetary union is likely to lead to a call for further harmonizations of laws and customs, crowned by a single fiscal policy, which in turn will further undermine public support for membership of the [European Union], and perhaps puts the future of even the single market at risk . . .

In America a single currency is workable not only because the U.S. has a single language and a shared cultural identity (the famed melting pot), but because it has a system of fiscal transfers that shifts resources to poor parts of the union from rich states. But to do this adequately, the U.S. has a federal tax base that amounts to around 25 percent of the GDP, 10 times the current level of the EU's budget . . . .

The United Kingdom is likely to be at odds with the rest of Europe because our economy does not move in step with those of other European countries and is structurally different. An oil-price shock, for example, would have different effects in the United Kingdom and the rest of Europe, because the U.K. is a significant oil producer and our economy is more service-oriented than that of most other European countries. Increases in European interest rates would be more damaging in the U.K., where households and companies tend to have variable-rate debt. Mortgage debt accounts for two-thirds of household income in the U.K., compared with less than a quarter in Germany. Monetary union could actually increase the policy shocks here, rather than be a factor for stability. . . .

The clincher for the single-currency enthusiasts is that Britain has suffered for being a 'Johnny-come-lately' in the past and should not risk bringing up the rear again. This is ludicrous. Just because Britain made the wrong decision [in the 1950s] does not mean that it would be a mistake to stay out of a single currency in 1999.

It is as if, out there on the tarmac, is a jet destined for an unknown location. The danger of not getting on board is that all the best seats in club class will be taken and that, when Britain does decide to take the plunge, there will only be seats in steerage left. On the other hand, the plane has been on the tarmac for some time now and, for all the attention of an army of engineers, the suspicion is that one of the engines is a bit dodgy. The question is: would you get on board? Well, would you?

Common Culture or Cultural Divide?

"In taste and learning they are woefully deficient." That was Frances Trollope's appraisal of Americans, in whose midst she had spent almost four often unhappy years. Her *Domestic Manners of the Americans*, published in 1832, won her acclaim at home in Britain as a savvy judge of the upstarts across the Atlantic.

The upstarts no longer can be dismissed with a few insults. In culture as in much else, the United States looms large, and fears of American intrusiveness are grounded in recognition of the economic giant's pervasive commercial presence. Without doubt, the United States dominates modern cultural media, such as television and film.

Nevertheless, many Americans still embrace British tradition, as evidenced by the recent surge of interest in Jane Austen. Her novels have been made into several successful films and television series, including "Pride and Prejudice," which in 1995 attracted the largest audience in the history of the Arts and Entertainment cable channel; "Clueless," a much modernized version of *Emma* that made Alicia Silverstone an overnight sensation with young moviegoers; and "Sense and Sensibility," starring Emma Thompson and Hugh Grant.

The discovery of Austen by large audiences gives new heart to those who cherish literature and literacy. Henry Grunwald, former editor in chief of *Time* Inc., wrote that "watching each of the Austen productions, I was struck by the good manners and the correct English — language representing manners of the mind. The contrast with the vulgarity of most other films and much of daily life brought me a sense of relief, of being in an oasis."

Grunwald also cited survey research that found that Americans — including young people — "deplore the lack of civility and the disappearance of respect. Those are among the things they seem to find in Jane Austen. They also find excitement and passion, courage and independence, and they may be surprised to see that these are not undermined but reinforced by manners." [1]

Pamela Anderson of TV's "Baywatch" is a big hit in Britain, while the works of Jane Austen were popular in America, including "Sense & Sensibility" starring Emma Thompson.

The cultural balance between America and Britain sometimes gets knocked askew. For instance, in exchange for Jane Austen's decorous Bennet sisters, the U.S. offers Pamela Lee Anderson and the other sexy women of TV's "Baywatch." To defenders of British culture, this may seem ample proof that the barbarians — American cultural imperialists — are at the gate.

The exploits of the female lifeguards on "Baywatch" are unlikely to be confused with "Masterpiece Theatre." Not that Britons are complaining. At its peak, the show had 10 million British viewers. One British cultural expert says only half-jokingly that in the U.K. Anderson "is one of the best-known living Americans."

In late 1996, the British "Baywatch" audience fell to 6 million and Britain's ITV network dropped the show. Six months later, series star and executive producer David Hasselhoff brought several of his comely "lifeguards" to London and announced, "We have gone overboard on the babes this season." The show was promptly returned to the network's schedule.

---

[1] Henry Grunwald, "Jane Austen's Civil Society," *The Wall Street Journal*, Oct. 2, 1996, p. 20. For background on attitudes about the royal family's survival, see "The British Monarchy," *The CQ Researcher*, March 8, 1996, pp.193-216.

Continued from p. 88

also says Britain is not resisting this globalization of its economic base; there is little detectable economic xenophobia about foreign investment. The U.K. is so focused on job creation, Fraser says, that there is minimal worry about the flood of investors from overseas.

The intense and pervasive business activity between the United States and Britain provides an important, if sometimes overlooked, foundation for summit-level dealings between presidents and prime ministers. Economic relations between the two countries do not need an overhaul, just some fine-tuning: coordinating product standards, liberalizing procurement policies (such as by curtailing "buy American" contract provisions), and generally making it easier for businesses to do business.

Global Problems

The Clinton administration's involvement in the Northern Ireland peace process has been endorsed by the Blair government, which considers the negotiating skills of former Sen. George Mitchell, D-Maine, to be an essential tool in forging a workable, lasting agreement. (*See story, p. 84.*) Blair has been more receptive to American participation than was his predecessor, Major. The U.S. effort has gone from being considered a high-risk venture to now being treated as a solid, constructive act of goodwill toward all parties involved.

Although Blair has supported Clinton's NATO expansion plan (inviting the Czech Republic, Hungary, and Poland to join), the costs of expansion and a formula for sharing them have yet to be specifically defined. The Clinton administration has consistently been optimistic about the price tag, estimating that it will be no more than $35 billion, spread over 13 years. The Congressional Budget Office, however, says the figure could be as high as $125 billion. Other sources offer in-between estimates.

Whatever the amount turns out to be, there will almost certainly be strong political pressure within the United States to get Europeans to pay more for their own security. But Blair and other European leaders are downsizing their defense budgets and have shown little willingness to cover costs that the new NATO members cannot handle themselves.

With the Senate getting ready to consider NATO's future, the White House needs help from Blair and his counterparts in other NATO countries to talk positively about taking on this burden.

While discussions about the future of NATO proceed, a more immediate security problem exists in the former

FOR MORE INFORMATION

Embassy of the United Kingdom, 3100 Massachusetts Ave., N.W., Washington, D.C. 20008; (202) 462-1340. The embassy's press and public information section provides information about British government institutions and policies.

British-American Chamber of Commerce, 52 Vanderbilt Ave., New York, N.Y. 10017; (212) 661-4060. The chamber publishes *UK&USA* (a business magazine) and provides material about U.S.-U.K. trade.

Invest in Britain Bureau, Department of Trade and Industry, 1 Victoria St., London SW1H 0ET; (44) 171-215-5615. This government department provides information about outside investment in the U.K.

Royal Institute of International Affairs, Chatham House, 10 St. James' Square, London SW1Y 4LE; (44) 171-957-5700. This organization publishes a wide range of material about world affairs, including work about Britain's relations with the United States and the rest of the world.

U.S. Department of Commerce, Trade Information Center, 14th St. and Constitution Ave., N.W., Washington, D.C. 20230; 1 (800) USA TRADE; www.ita.doc.gov

Royal Oak Foundation, 285 W. Broadway, Room 400, New York, N.Y. 10013; (212) 966-6565; www.royal_oak.org. This is the American membership affiliate of the British National Trust. It sponsors more than 100 lectures a year on the shared cultural heritage of the United States and the U.K. as well as travel and study programs in Great Britain.

Yugoslavia. President Clinton's announcement in December that he was abandoning a set timetable for the withdrawal of American troops from Bosnia was greeted with relief by Britain and other U.S. allies. The consensus among them has been that if the U.S. pulls out, so will they, which would almost certainly mean a resumption of the war. Clinton and Blair now must explore ways to keep from being stuck in the Balkans forever.

On another front, Blair has backed Clinton's hard line about maintaining sanctions against Iraq, and presumably will continue to do so, despite the more flexible stance of some other EU members. More generally, however, even Blair would not endorse the American infatuation with sanctions as a key foreign policy tool. [25] The Helms-Burton Act (which targets Cuba) is just one example; other countries also are targets of U.S. sanctions of one kind or another. Clinton is unlikely to find much support from Britain for extraterritorial

enforcement of U.S. law.

This is one of the few areas of substantive disagreement between the two governments, and even it is unlikely to provoke a visible dispute now. When Clinton and Blair meet in February, personalities rather than policies will probably attract the most attention. ∎

OUTLOOK

Follow the Money

A danger inherent in a close partnership such as that between the United States and Great Britain is the tendency to take for granted the stability of the status quo. Compared with many bilateral relationships, certainly, the U.S.-U.K. pairing is remarkably solid. It is hard to imagine any serious disruption, but complacency could foster problems.

In economic matters, the current transatlantic flow of trade and investment will probably grow if — and this is a crucial if — Britain remains a major player in the European Union. That means joining the monetary union. British failure to maintain a leadership role in the EU would put the U.K. at a competitive disadvantage in dealings with the U.S. The allure of the powerful, unified market will be irresistible to American businesses, and a certain amount of U.S.-based investment would shift from Britain to the continent.

Already, Britain is finding itself something of an outsider as 11 of the 15 EU members plan to unify their currencies on Jan. 1, 1999. The U.K. (along with Denmark, Greece and Sweden, the other EU members not now joining the EMU), has been pointedly excluded from EMU rule-making sessions. French Finance Minister Dominique Strauss-Kahn said in December, "People who are married do not want others in the bedroom."

The Clinton administration will probably gently nudge Britain toward EMU membership. Not much urging may be needed, because the Blair government is likely to join when the Euro replaces national currencies in all EMU nations in January 2002.

Regardless of what the White House does about Britain and the EMU, American business leaders will keep the pressure on, because it is in their interest to see that nothing impairs British economic strength. This in itself says something about the potency of U.S.-U.K. relations: The day-to-day ties of commerce are so pervasive that business-to-business links often supersede government-to-government dealings.

In security matters, the future is more obscure. Although the United States has abandoned its timetable for departure from Bosnia, the broader post-Cold War security role for the U.S. in Europe remains only partially defined. In a new strategic bargain that may evolve, the United States might provide high-tech communications and intelligence resources and logistical support (for example, aircraft needed for rapid troop deployment) to its European friends such as Britain while refusing to commit troops on the ground except in extraordinary circumstances.

Although the Blair government has solidly supported the Clinton administration's plan for NATO expansion, American expectations of financial burden-sharing could well cause problems in London, as in Paris and elsewhere. Britain, for example, has been critical of the U.S. failure to pay what it owes the United Nations, and Blair is unlikely to risk political problems at home by endorsing much of a contribution to Clinton's NATO plan.

None of these problems is insoluble. The reservoir of Anglo-American good will remains nearly full. According to most objective appraisals, the relationship between the United States and Great Britain will remain strong as long as it is properly valued by both parties. ∎

Philip M. Seib is a professor of journalism at Southern Methodist University. He is the author of Headline Diplomacy: How News Coverage Affects Foreign Policy *(1997) and* Taken for Granted: The Future of U.S.-British Relations *(in press).*

Notes

[1] For background, see "Expanding NATO," *The CQ Researcher*, May 16, 1997, pp. 433-456.

[2] Margaret Thatcher, *The Downing Street Years* (1993), p. 783.

[3] Michael Mandelbaum, *The Dawn of Peace in Europe* (1996), p. 159.

[4] For background, see "Northern Ireland Cease-Fire," *The CQ Researcher*, Sept. 15, 1995, pp.

[5] Tony Blair, *New Britain* (1996), pp. 266-267, a collection of Blair's speeches.

[6] James Schlesinger, "An American Assessment: 'Hands Across the Sea' Less Firmly Clasped," in Henry Brandon (ed.), *In Search of a New World Order* (1992), p. 150.

[7] Malcolm Rifkind, "The Transatlantic Partnership: The Future Economic Agenda," speech to the Transatlantic Policy Network, 1996.

[8] Blair, *op. cit.*, p. 267.

[9] U.S. Deputy Treasury Secretary Lawrence Summers, speech to *EuroMoney* Conference, April 30, 1997.

[10] Blair, *op. cit.*, p. 283.

[11] "Britain's Overseas Trade," Foreign and Commonwealth Office, 1994.

[12] Henry Brandon, "A More Promising Era Beckons at Last," in Brandon (ed.), *op. cit.*, p. 161.

[13] Martin Kettle, "Background to the Debate," in *The Single Currency: Should Britain Join?* (1997), p. 13.

[14] Rudi Dornbusch, "Monetary Union Might Just Put the Spring Back in Europe's Step," *Business Week*, Dec. 23, 1996, p. 24.

[15] Blair, *op. cit.*, 210.

[16] Laurence Martin, "Risky Rush for a Doubtful Goal," *The World Today*, February 1997, p. 51.

[17] Donald Neff, *Warriors at Suez* (1981), p. 291.

[18] Henry Kissinger, *Diplomacy* (1994), p. 598.

[19] George Shultz, *Turmoil and Triumph* (1993), p. 154.

[20] John Dickie, *"Special" No More* (1994), p. 175.

[21] Nicholas Henderson, *Channels and Tunnels* (1987), p. 101.

[22] Dickie, *op. cit.*, pp. 3-6.

[23] Shultz, *op. cit.*, p. 340.

[24] Quoted in Robin Renwick, *Fighting With Allies* (1996), p. 360.

[25] For background, see "Economic Sanctions," *The CQ Researcher*, Oct. 28, 1994, pp. 937-960.

Bibliography

Selected Sources Used

Books

Blair, Tony, *New Britain*, Fourth Estate, 1996.
This collection of speeches from pre-prime ministerial days provides useful insight into Blair's domestic and foreign priorities.

Cannadine, David (ed.), *Blood, Toil, Tears and Sweat: The Speeches of Winston Churchill*, Houghton Mifflin, 1989.
This collection includes speeches that were crucial in building the modern relationship between Britain and the U.S.

Cook, Chris, and John Stevenson, *Britain Since 1945*, Longman, 1996.
This collection of capsule biographies, chronologies and statistics is a helpful reference.

Dickie, John, *"Special" No More*, Weidenfeld & Nicolson, 1994.
A veteran British journalist appraises changes in the Anglo-American relationship, noting that both countries' diverse interests have made the notion of a "special relationship" obsolete.

Gompert, David C., and F. Stephen Larrabee (eds.), *America and Europe*, Cambridge University Press, 1997.
This thoughtful Rand Corporation study of prospects for a redefined Atlantic partnership focuses on such topics as the need for a redefinition of NATO's structure and mission and the prospects for the United States as a European Union trading partner.

Henderson, Nicholas, *Channels and Tunnels*, Weidenfeld and Nicolson, 1987.
The former British ambassador to the United States (and to France and West Germany) addresses, among other topics, U.S.-British cooperation during the Falklands war.

Heuser, Beatrice, *Transatlantic Relations*, Pinter/Royal Institute for International Affairs, 1996.
Heuser, a British academic, takes a short but still thorough look at the many ties that bind North America and Europe.

Kettle, Martin, John Palmer, Larry Elliott and Victor Keegan, *The Single Currency: Should Britain Join?* Vintage, 1997.
Journalists from *The Guardian* offer pro and con arguments about Britain's membership in the European Monetary Union, and do so in a way that even non-economists can understand.

King, Anthony (ed.), *New Labour Triumphs: Britain at the Polls*, Chatham House, 1998.
This is a thorough analysis of how Tony Blair led a revitalized Labor Party to a landslide victory in Britain's 1997 elections.

Renwick, Robin, *Fighting With Allies*, Times Books, 1996.
The former British ambassador to the United States presents a lively history of "the special relationship," illuminating the dynamic tension that has been part of the ties between the two countries and their leaders.

Thatcher, Margaret, *The Downing Street Years*, HarperCollins, 1993.
The former prime minister chronicles her tenure, including her close relationship with Ronald Reagan.

Articles

"The American Connection," *The Economist*, Nov. 8, 1997, p. 63.
An analysis of ties between the Clinton administration and the Blair government, offering examples of the ongoing exchange of ideas between the advisers to Prime Minister Tony Blair and President Clinton.

Grunwald, Henry, "Jane Austen's Civil Society," *The Wall Street Journal*, Oct. 2, 1996, p. 20.
An explanation of the revival of American interest in the mores of Jane Austen's fictive England, with applause for good manners and proper language.

"New Labour's Model Army," *The Economist*, Sept. 27, 1997, p. 61.
This report about Britain's armed forces looks at their ability to meet post-Cold War responsibilities, focusing on their self-sufficiency and capabilities in joint operations.

The Next Step

Additional information from UMI's Newspaper & Periodical Abstracts™ database

Clinton/Blair Relationship

"Bill and Tony: new best friends; The special relationship is now about things closer to home," *The Guardian,* May 30, 1997, p. 18.

Britain and America, it is often said, are two countries separated by a common language, but the two leaders who met in Downing Street yesterday seemed to understood each other uncommonly well, on and off-camera. Of course, President Clinton and Prime Minister Tony Blair discussed Northern Ireland, NATO expansion and Bosnia. Yet it was striking that the issues they talked about most enthusiastically had very little to do with the old ties that bind.

Gillan, Audrey, "Tony Blair and the 'New Special Relationship;' British Prime Minister's Bond With Clinton Reflects Personal Affinity and Changing Labor Party Image," *The Washington Post,* Aug. 11, 1997, p. A12.

The British ambassador, Sir John Kerr, told a recent luncheon that he was returning to his homeland because there was nothing left for him to do in Washington. President Clinton and British Prime Minister Tony Blair, are getting along so well, he joked, that the opportunity for diplomats to heal any political rifts seems to have gone.

"Isn't that a special relationship?" *Chicago Tribune,* April 7, 1995, p 22.

An editorial discusses the relationship between the U.S. and Britain, and questions whether their "special relationship" with Britain can survive the 20th century, when Germany is clearly the premier political and economic power of Europe.

Jenkins, Roy, "Special relationships: The postwar bequest," *Foreign Affairs,* May 1997, pp. 200-204.

Jenkins notes that aside from the direct economic effects and the free transatlantic transfer of billions of dollars, the Marshall Plan had several long-lasting political consequences. Perhaps the most important is improved relations between the U.S. and the UK.

Peterson, Jonathan, "On London Jaunt, Clinton Reaches Out to Iran; Diplomacy: After warm meeting with Britain's new leader, president calls Tehran moderate's win a 'hopeful development' but outlines conditions for repairing relations," *Los Angeles Times,* May 30, 1997, p. A18.

On Clinton's recent trip to London he and British Prime Minister Tony Blair discussed problems that have slowed the peace processes in Bosnia-Herzegovina and Northern Ireland and other shared concerns on a sunny day in which their friendship was evident. In the afternoon the two men strolled into the sun-bathed garden behind Blair's official residence at 10 Downing St. and met with members of the U.S. and British media.

"The President's news conference with Prime Minister Tony Blair of the United Kingdom in London," *Weekly Compilation of Presidential Documents,* June 2, 1997, pp. 796-807.

At a news conference, President Clinton and U.K. Prime Minister Tony Blair comment on NATO and answer questions on a variety of topics, including the Northern Ireland peace process, NATO expansion and the U.K.'s economy.

White, Michael, and Ian Black, "The new special relationship," *The Guardian,* May 30, 1997, p. 1.

Tony Blair and Bill Clinton yesterday sealed their commitment to pragmatic "new generation politics" with a lavish display of mutual admiration and an agreement to stage an ambitious employment summit of industrial countries in Britain next year.

European Union

Burgess, Michael, "Introduction: Federalism and building the European Union," *Publius,* fall 1996, pp. 1-15.

A centerpiece of the new European Union is to be the European Monetary Union, which should move the European Union in a more decidedly federal direction.

Ibrahim, Youssef M., "Britain Getting That Left-Out Feeling," *The New York Times,* Dec. 27, 1997, p. D2.

Eleven of the 15 European Union members — but not Britain, Greece, Denmark or Sweden — have chosen to unify their currencies on Jan. 1, 1999. Because Britain has decided not to join the initial marriage of currencies, it will not be allowed to take part in the monthly discussions of the so-called Euro-X council, whose meetings will formulate rules that may affect the economies of the entire European Union.

MacLeod, Alexander, "A Winner at Home, Britain's Premier Takes On Europe; Blair meets Clinton in London Today. On the agenda: a bigger role on the Continent," *The Christian Science Monitor,* May 29, 1997, p. 6.

British Prime Minister Tony Blair, with backing from President Clinton, is bidding to give his country a more influential and possibly decisive voice in the affairs of Europe. Close aides say he is determined that Britain will play a leading role in the European Union while also defending his country's interests amid attempts by other European governments to arrive at unified financial, economic and foreign policies on a high-speed timetable.

MacLeod, Alexander, "Britain Asserts Its Culture With a Language Lesson Before Taking on the EU Presidency Jan. 1; British diplomats told to use English only as a way to help define the national character,"

The Christian Science Monitor, Dec. 17, 1997, p. 8.

The British, notorious for their reluctance to attempt other people's tongues, are preparing to give their European Union (EU) partners a six-month language lesson. Ministers and officials in Prime Minister Tony Blair's government have been ordered to conduct all diplomatic transactions in English.

Foreign Investment

Atkinson, Mark, and Martin Wainwright, "Testing the Tiger's claw; What impact will the South Korean crisis have on investment in Britain? Mark Atkinson and Martin Wainwright add up the loss potential," *The Guardian,* **Nov. 22, 1997, p. 28.**

The display of power by the jurassic demolisher, distinguishable by its big black Samsung badge, should have symbolized the mutual benefits of South Korean investment in Yorkshire. Two years after the first Korean joined the county's American, European and Japanese companies, Samsung is closing its plant on Flaxby Moor.

"Interim Services Bids for British Recruiter," *The New York Times,* **March 4, 1997, p. D8.**

Continuing its expansion into global markets, Interim Services Inc. said yesterday that it had offered $574 million in cash for Michael Page Group, a British-based provider of professional recruitment and temporary employment services worldwide. Interim, of Fort Lauderdale, Fla., is a staffing and employment concern with some 1,000 offices in North America and Europe.

Salpukas, Agis, "Pacificorp in Biggest Deal Yet for a British Utility," *The New York Times,* **June 14, 1997, p. A37.**

Pacificorp became the latest American utility company to move into the British market, announcing yesterday an expected deal to acquire the Energy Group, an electricity-distribution company, for about $5.8 billion in cash. Pacificorp's acquisition of the Energy Group, if approved by British regulators, would create an electricity giant with plenty of low-cost power in Britain and the United States and the marketing muscle needed to sell that power as utilities are forced to open up their service areas to competitors.

Salpukas, Agis, "2 U.S. Utilities to Buy British Company for $2.4 Billion," *The New York Times,* **Feb. 25, 1997, p. D4.**

Two United States utilities, the American Electric Power Co. and the Public Service Co. of Colorado, announced yesterday that they had agreed to acquire Yorkshire Electricity Group P.L.C. for $2.4 billion. The deal, which was expected, would leave only one of Britain's 12 power distributors independent.

Gerry Adams

"Blair Adams at 'Moment in History;' British, Sinn Fein Chiefs Meet in Downing Street," *Chicago Tribune,* **Dec. 11, 1997, Sec. EVENING, p. 1.**

Sinn Fein leader Gerry Adams declared Thursday a "moment in history" after a Downing Street meeting with Tony Blair, the first time a British prime minister has received political allies of the IRA since negotiations 76 years ago that led to the division of Ireland. Adams, one of a seven-member Sinn Fein delegation, said his party repeated its demands to Blair that Britain leave Northern Ireland completely. Downing Street said Blair would have no comment on the one-hour meeting, Sinn Fein's first with the prime minister since an October session in Belfast.

Montalbano, William D., "Sinn Fein Leader, Blair Hold Historic Meeting; Europe: Gerry Adams tells premier Britain must leave Northern Ireland. Nation's chief says it's not on agenda," *Los Angeles Times,* **Dec. 12, 1997, p. A4.**

In a historic, high-risk meeting for both men, Sinn Fein leader Gerry Adams went to Downing Street on Thursday to tell Prime Minister Tony Blair that Britain must leave Northern Ireland. It was Adams who did most of the public talking Thursday. But it was Blair who arranged the encounter as a means of wrapping Sinn Fein, the political wing of the outlawed IRA, ever more tightly within the democratic, non-violent political process.

Persian Gulf War

"Ex-British Official Says London Sought to Press Gulf War," *The Boston Globe,* **Aug. 21, 1991, p. 68.**

Sir Charles Powell, a member of the British war cabinet during the Persian Gulf War, has said that Britain wanted to continue fighting Iraq but was overruled by the U.S.

Trueheart, Charles, "Support for strikes falls short of Gulf War consensus: France, Russia criticize U.S. action; Britain, Germany call move justified," *The Washington Post,* **Sept. 4, 1996, p. A19.**

France and Russia pointedly criticized the Sept. 3, 1996, U.S. airstrikes on Iraq, marring the Clinton administration's hopes for Gulf War-style unanimity against President Saddam Hussein.

Northern Ireland

Montalbano, William D., "Britain's Minister for Northern Ireland Visiting Los Angeles," *Los Angeles Times,* **Nov. 14, 1997, p. A19.**

A British Cabinet minister arrives in Los Angeles today to urge American support for Northern Ireland peace efforts jeopardized by internal stresses within Roman Catholic and Protestant factions in the divided province.

Smith, Geoffrey, "Luck of the Irish?" *National Review,* **July 28, 1997, pp. 25-26.**

U.K. Prime Minister Tony Blair has gone farther than any of his predecessors in trying to gain a peaceful settlement in Northern Ireland.

Back Issues

Great Research on Current Issues Starts Right Here ... Recent topics covered by The CQ Researcher are listed below. Before May 1991, reports were published under the name of Editorial Research Reports.

Back issues are available for $5.00 (subscribers) or $10.00 (non-subscribers). Quantity discounts apply to orders over ten. To order, call Congressional Quarterly Customer Service at (202) 887-8621.

Binders are available for $18.00. To order call 1-800-638-1710. Please refer to stock number 648.

Future Topics

▶ *Patients' Rights*

▶ *Deflation Fears*

▶ *Caring for the Elderly*

THE
CQ
Researcher

PUBLISHED BY CONGRESSIONAL QUARTERLY INC.

Patients' Rights

Are stronger legal protections needed?

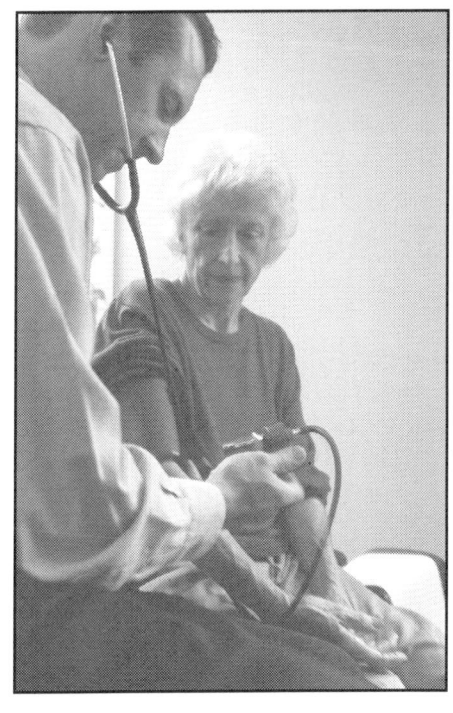

T
he continuing growth of managed-care health
plans is provoking a powerful backlash.
Many patients say managed care makes it
harder simply to see a doctor, let alone get
insurance coverage for needed treatment. Doctors are also
chafing under restrictions that limit the way they treat
patients. The managed-care industry insists, however, that
it is improving the quality of health care and slowing the
rise in costs. More than 30 states have passed laws
strengthening patients' rights in dealing with insurers.
Now Congress may consider imposing new regulations on
managed-care companies. Patient and consumer groups
are pushing for reforms this year, but insurers' and
employers' groups warn that the result may be higher
premiums and more uninsured workers.

CQ   **Feb. 6, 1998** • **Volume 8, No. 5** • **Pages 97-120**

Formerly Editorial Research Reports

PATIENTS' RIGHTS

THE ISSUES

COVER: COPYRIGHT©PHOTODISC

CQ Researcher

February 6, 1998
Volume 8, No. 5

EDITOR
Sandra Stencel

MANAGING EDITOR
Thomas J. Colin

ASSOCIATE EDITOR
Sarah M. Magner

STAFF WRITERS
Mary H. Cooper
Kenneth Jost
David Masci

PRODUCTION EDITOR
Melissa Hall

EDITORIAL ASSISTANT
Vanessa E. Furlong

PUBLISHED BY
Congressional Quarterly Inc.

CHAIRMAN
Andrew Barnes

VICE CHAIRMAN
Andrew P. Corty

PRESIDENT AND PUBLISHER
Robert W. Merry

EXECUTIVE EDITOR
David Rapp

The CQ Researcher (ISSN 1056-2036). Formerly Editorial Research Reports. Published weekly, except Jan. 2, May 29, July 3, Oct. 30, by Congressional Quarterly Inc., 1414 22nd St., N.W., Washington, D.C. 20037. Annual subscription rate for libraries, businesses and government is $340. Additional rates furnished upon request. Periodicals postage paid at Washington, D.C., and additional mailing offices. POSTMASTER: Send address changes to The CQ Researcher, 1414 22nd St., N.W., Washington, D.C. 20037.

Patients' Rights

BY KENNETH JOST

THE ISSUES

Minnesota computer executive Patrick Shea thought he should see a cardiologist. He had been experiencing shortness of breath and dizzy spells. And heart disease ran in his family.

But Shea's physician assured him a specialist wasn't necessary and refused to give him the written referral required by his health plan. Instead, he told Shea that his problems were stress-related and that he was too young to have heart problems.

Later, while on an overseas business trip, Shea suffered chest pains so severe that he was hospitalized and had to return home. But his doctor still dismissed his concerns.

Shea never saw a specialist. He died in March 1993, less than a year later, leaving his wife Dianne with two young children and troubling questions. He was 40. An autopsy disclosed that Shea had suffered from arteriosclerosis — blocked arteries — which might have been corrected with cardiac bypass surgery.

"We repeatedly asked for referral to a cardiologist," Dianne later told a Minnesota legislative committee. "Not only were our pleas ignored, we were assured time and time again that our fears were unfounded."

In the months that followed, Dianne sought to discover how a man who had always followed his doctor's advice could die of an undiagnosed disease. What she found shook her confidence not only in their own doctors but also in the health care that more than 150 million Americans receive today from so-called managed-care systems: health maintenance organizations (HMOs) and similar network health-care plans.[1]

Supporters say managed care helps

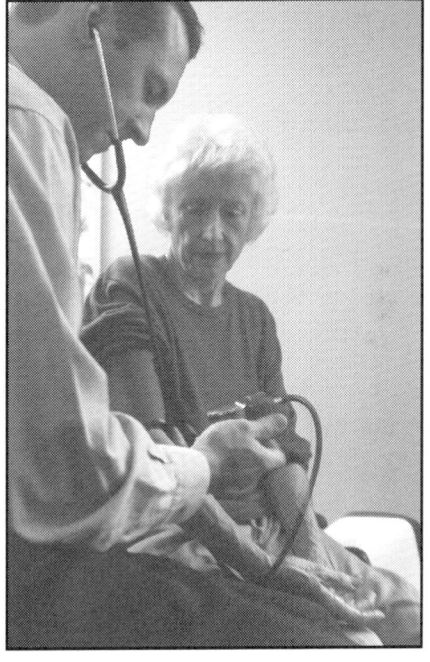

provide affordable, high-quality health care at a time when patients, health-care providers, insurers and employers are all straining to keep down costs. But Dianne became convinced from the inquiry she and her lawyers made that cost controls helped kill her husband.

She claims in a wrongful death lawsuit that Shea's doctor had an undisclosed financial conflict of interest in refusing to refer him to a cardiologist because he received extra compensation from their HMO, Medica, for not sending patients to specialists.

The defendants in the federal court suit — Shea's doctors, their HMO clinic and Medica — deny that the doctors' compensation in any way depended on rejecting Shea's request to see a specialist. "Sheer speculation," Medica's lawyers say. The defendants also deny they were negligent in failing to diagnose Shea's heart disease. A trial in the case is expected later this year.[2]

Dianne Shea, meanwhile, has begun advocating reform of managed care. She urged the Minnesota Legislature to require health insurers to disclose their "payment methodology" — information she says that might have prompted Shea to ignore his doctor's advice and see a cardiologist. "People have to understand that health care is a business," she says. "Just as we would never buy an investment blindly, we just cannot trust our doctors blindly."

The state Legislature last year passed a weakened version of Shea's proposal, requiring disclosure of the financial arrangements only on the patient's request. Minnesota thus became one of more than 30 states to pass legislation in the past three years aimed at strengthening the rights of patients enrolled in managed care — by far the dominant form of health care in the United States. *(See chart, p. 102.)*

Congress is also set to consider legislation that would impose far-reaching regulations on managed-care systems and possibly make it easier to sue health insurers for malpractice. Consumer and patient advocacy groups as well as the American Medical Association (AMA) are generally backing the proposals, which are strongly opposed by health-care insurers and employers.

The reform efforts reflect a widespread belief that patients are being harmed in the shift away from traditional "fee-for-service" health insurance, which gave consumers greater freedom in choosing their own doctors and doctors greater freedom in prescribing treatment that insurers would pay for.

"Patients feel less personally taken care of, that they have interactions with too many health-care providers, that there's too much red tape in getting access to the specialists," says Myrl Weinberg, president of the National Health Council, a coalition of more than 40 patient advocacy

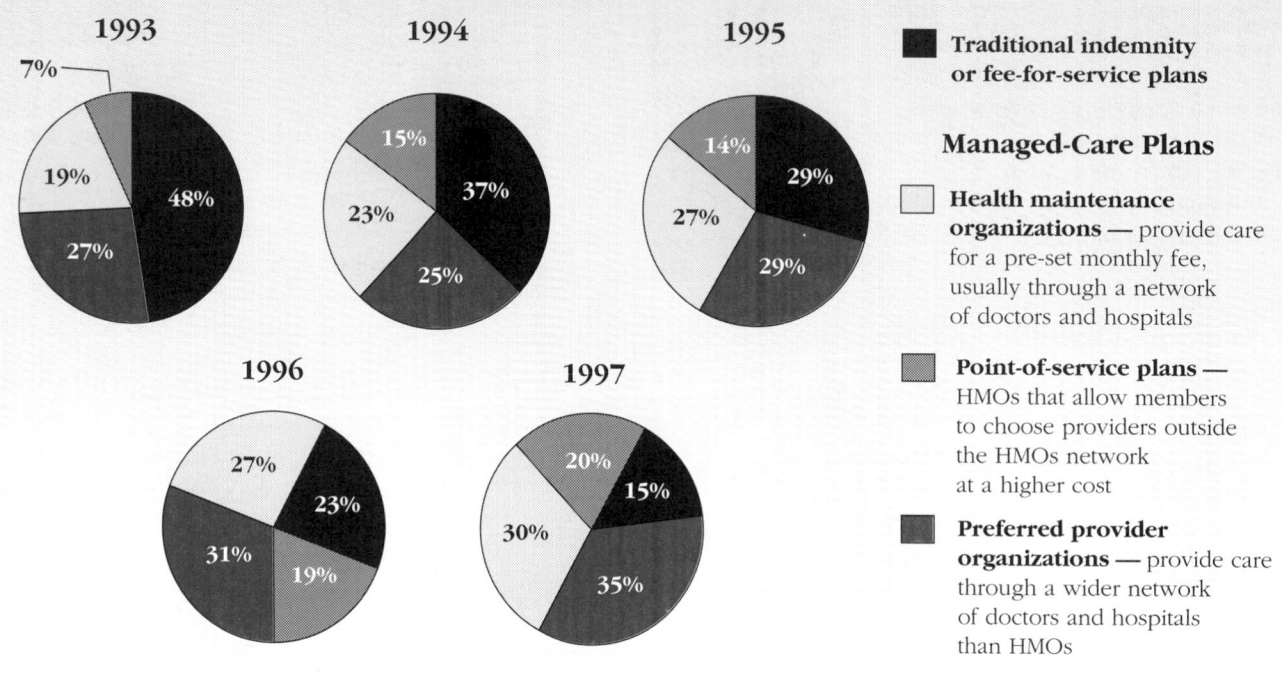

Managed-Care Plans Continue to Grow

The number of workers in managed-care health plans outnumbered those in traditional plans by nearly 6-to-1 in 1997, reflecting the continuing shift away from traditional plans in recent years.

1993
7%
19%
27%
48%

1994
15%
23%
37%
25%

1995
14%
29%
27%
29%

1996
27%
23%
31%
19%

1997
20%
15%
30%
35%

■ **Traditional indemnity or fee-for-service plans**

Managed-Care Plans

□ **Health maintenance organizations** — provide care for a pre-set monthly fee, usually through a network of doctors and hospitals

▨ **Point-of-service plans** — HMOs that allow members to choose providers outside the HMOs network at a higher cost

■ **Preferred provider organizations** — provide care through a wider network of doctors and hospitals than HMOs

Note: Percentages do not add up to 100 because of rounding. The survey includes all employers with 10 or more employees.

Source: Mercer/Foster Higgins "National Survey of Employer-Sponsored Health Plans," 1997.

groups, such as the American Cancer Society and American Heart Association, as well as major drug manufacturers and health insurers.

But health insurance industry officials insist that patients actually receive better care under managed-care plans.

"There's a tremendous possibility [with HMOs] to receive better, more integrated care," says Karen Ignagni, president of the American Association of Health Plans (AAHP). She says greater coordination among health-care providers also enhances accountability. "We've put in place

the beginnings of quality measurement so that we can ensure significant improvements," she says.

Critics of managed care generally stop short of blaming it for an overall decline in the quality of health care. "For the most part, the studies have shown that the care is relatively the same," says Thomas Reardon, an Oregon physician and chairman of the AMA's Board of Trustees.

But the critics cite cases like Shea's to argue that managed-care plans have an incentive to skimp on care at the patient's expense. "There are pluses and minuses," says Adrienne

Mitchem, legislative counsel for Consumers Union. "Some of the minuses are the overriding cost pressures. With traditional fee-for-service, you had the financial incentives to overtreat. With managed care, you have the financial incentives to undertreat."

Managed-care advocates indeed take credit for helping contain health-care cost increases — and now feel unjustly blamed for the difficulties that patients and providers face in adjusting to the changes.

"The public said to do something about health-care inflation, and we've been largely successful in doing that," says former Rep. Bill Gradison, R-Ohio, president of the Health Insurance Association of America (HIAA), which includes companies offering both managed care and fee-for-service insurance.

"Now, patients are saying, 'Hold on, we don't like the way you're doing it,' " Gradison continues. "The pace of change is bewilderingly fast and off-putting to a lot of people, and I mean not just the patients but the providers as well."

Gradison warns that new regulations "run the risk of increasing the cost of health plans and discouraging innovation." But critics say some changes are needed. "Managed care can do a lot of things well, but it needs to be regulated differently than we're now regulating it," says Lawrence Gostin, a health-law expert at Georgetown University Law Center.

The proposal with the greatest support in Congress is the Patient Access to Responsible Care Act (PARCA), sponsored in the House by Rep. Charlie Norwood, a Georgia Republican, and in the Senate by New York Republican Alfonse M. D'Amato. Norwood, a dentist, says he wants to "reverse what's going on in this country in health care."

"We've gone from patients having the right to choose their own doctors to patients being denied care and being denied the right to choose their own doctors to save money," Norwood says. "I don't oppose managed care, but I think there needs to be rules and regulations."

President Clinton also strongly endorsed managed-care reform in his State of the Union address on Jan. 27. "Medical decisions ought to be made by medical doctors, not insurance company accountants," Clinton said. The line drew bipartisan applause from lawmakers that continued as Clinton spelled out his proposal:

"I urge this Congress to reach across the aisle and write into law a consumer bill of rights that says this: 'You have the right to know all your

medical options, not just the cheapest. You have the right to choose the doctor you want for the care you need. You have the right to emergency room care, wherever and whenever you need it. You have the right to keep your medical records confidential.' Now, traditional care or managed care, every American deserves quality care."

Clinton's plea covered the main parts of a "Patients' Bill of Rights" issued in November by a 34-member commission he created last March. But he made no specific reference to one of its most contentious recommendations: a proposal to give patients greater ability to contest decisions by health plans to deny coverage for medical treatment.

Earlier, the administration also proposed separate legislation aimed at protecting patients' medical information. The privacy issue has become increasingly worrisome as computers have become more capable of accessing the most personal information. But the administration's proposals were widely criticized as too weak — in particular for giving law enforcement agencies broad discretion to obtain medical records without a patient's consent (see p. 104).

When Congress and state legislatures tackle managed-care reform this year, these are some of the questions likely to be considered:

Should managed-care health plans be required to make it easier for patients to see specialists outside the plan's network of physicians?

The most visible difference between managed-care health plans and traditional fee-for-service insurance involves choosing a doctor and deciding when to seek treatment. Traditional insurance plans leave those choices to the patient; managed-care plans limit the patient's options.

Typically, a patient who enrolls in an HMO, like Patrick Shea, selects a "primary-care provider" from its network of doctors. That doctor then functions as a "gatekeeper" — overseeing the patient's health care and deciding when the patient needs to be referred to a specialist. [3]

The earliest group-health plans, in the 1920s and '30s, centralized medical decisions both to improve health care and lower costs. But since the federal government began promoting HMOs in the '70s, and later as for-profit managed-care plans came to dominate the industry, the emphasis increasingly has been on cost.

Critics, including patients, doctors and some outside observers, say the result has been to deny patients needed care in some cases. "Obviously, you can cut costs by cutting services," says George Annas, a professor of health law at Boston University, "but that wasn't the idea."

Managed-care health plans do take credit for helping hold down costs, but they insist that the quality of care has not suffered. "I don't know of many physicians who are devoted more to controlling costs than to care delivering," says AAHP President Ignagni.

Access to specialists is the most frequent source of friction between patients and health plans. Health plans control costs by limiting the number of specialists in the plan and the number of referrals to specialists outside the plan; they may pay their primary physicians in ways that create incentives to minimize the number of referrals. For patients, those incentives may create minor burdens — for example, a woman's need to get a referral for routine obstetric care — or more serious disputes.

Critics say the industry has been making it more difficult for health-plan subscribers to see specialists. "Managed-care plans are increasingly using payment systems that discourage providers from referring patients

States Where Patients Get Special Treatment

Specialist care — *Thirty states make it easier for people in managed-care health plans to see certain specialists; all but Kentucky allow women either to designate an obstetrician-gynecologist as their primary-care provider or see an ob-gyn without a referral:*

Alabama, Arkansas*, California, Colorado, Connecticut, Delaware, Florida**, Georgia***, Idaho, Illinois, Indiana, Kentucky****, Louisiana, Maine*****, Maryland, Minnesota, Missouri, Mississippi, Montana, Nevada, New Jersey, New Mexico, New York, North Carolina, Oregon, Rhode Island, Texas, Utah, Virginia and Washington

External review — *Eleven states allow health-care patients to appeal coverage decisions to outside bodies:*

Arizona, California, Connecticut, Florida, Minnesota, Missouri, New Jersey, Rhode Island, Texas, New Mexico and Vermont

Post-mastectomy care — *Thirteen states require coverage of post-mastectomy inpatient care:*

Arkansas, Connecticut, Florida, Illinois, Maine, Montana, New Jersey, New Mexico, New York, North Carolina, Oklahoma, Rhode Island and Texas

Gag-rule ban — *Thirty-six states bar insurers from limiting doctors' communications with patients about treatment options:*

Arkansas, California, Colorado, Connecticut, Delaware, Florida, Georgia, Idaho, Illinois, Indiana, Kansas, Maine, Maryland, Massachusetts, Minnesota, Missouri, Montana, Nebraska, Nevada, New Hampshire, New Jersey, New Mexico, New York, North Carolina, Ohio, Oklahoma, Oregon, Rhode Island, South Carolina, Tennessee, Texas, Utah, Vermont, Virginia, Washington and Wyoming

* also covers optometrist or ophthalmologist; ** also covers chiropractor, podiatrist, dermatologist; *** also covers dermatologist; **** only covers chiropractor; ***** also covers nurse-practitioner, nurse-midwife

Sources: American Association of Health Plans, National Conference of State Legislatures.

you went to the phone book, now you have the ability to seek care through a network of professionals working together," Ignagni says.

Moreover, she points out that many plans in recent years have given consumers more options — for example, "point-of-service" (POS) plans that allow enrollees to see physicians outside the plan's network if they pay part of the cost through a higher deductible or a percentage of the fee. "We recognize that [a closed-plan HMO] doesn't meet the needs of all consumers," she says, "and that's why these other products have been developed."

Still, state and federal legislators are seeking ways to assure patients easier access to specialists. Some 30 states require health plans to give women the option of selecting an obstetrician as their primary-care provider. *(See table, at left.)* A number of states are considering bills to establish a procedure for a "standing referral" to a specialist for patients with chronic or life-threatening diseases or conditions. In Congress, Norwood's bill includes a similar provision.

Annas says health plans should be required to pay specialists whenever a subscriber must go outside the network. "I don't think that would happen very often," he says. "But it's not really a health plan if it doesn't offer the full range of medical services."

Norwood's bill, as well as some bills in the states, also includes a provision requiring health plans to offer a "point-of-service" option. Some critics say that would harm patients by undercutting the ability of HMOs to control costs and reduce premiums.

"The way HMOs keep costs down is by hiring physicians who practice conservatively" and don't order a lot of tests, says John Goodman, president of the National Center for Policy Analysis, a free-market think tank in Dallas. "You can lower your premiums by joining an HMO that employs doctors who practice conservative

to specialized care," John Seffrin, president of the American Cancer Society and chairman of the National Health Council, told the president's patients' rights commission last year.

"For the patient, it is difficult to know what they need to do" to see a specialist, agrees Weinberg, the council's president.

Industry officials, however, say that managed care — with its "gatekeeper" physician and network of specialists — actually simplifies decisions for patients. "Unlike the old days, where

medicine. If you take away the HMO's ability to do that, you take away one of the options that people have."

For their part, industry officials argue against any regulatory requirements, saying that market forces will drive health plans to give patients more choices for getting to a doctor of their choice. "Many plans are moving in that direction," Gradison says. "The question is whether the law should require that in every case, and my answer would be no."

But Paul Starr, a professor of sociology at Princeton University and author of a well-regarded history of the medical profession, says the industry cannot be counted on to give patients adequate choices for health care.

"We need legislation because whatever they're doing today doesn't guarantee what they'll do tomorrow," says Starr, who was an adviser for President Clinton's unsuccessful national health-care initiative in 1993 and '94. "They can just as easily withdraw access as provide it."

Should health plans be subject to medical malpractice liability?

When Ron Henderson died in a Kaiser Permanente hospital in Dallas in 1995, his family sued the HMO and several of its doctors for not diagnosing his heart disease.

Kaiser denied any wrongdoing and depicted Henderson as an overweight smoker who had ignored doctors' instructions. But the family's lawyers turned up embarrassing evidence of Kaiser's efforts to control costs by limiting hospital admissions in cardiac cases. In December 1997, Kaiser settled the case for $5.3 million. [4]

Kaiser was subject to a malpractice suit because, unlike most HMOs, it directly employs the physicians and nurses in its clinics. Courts have held that HMOs that contract with individual doctors or medical groups are shielded from malpractice suits on the theory that the doctor rather than

the health plan is actually providing the care. But a new Texas law seeks to erase that distinction. [5]

"I can see no reason why a private, very profitable enterprise ought not be held accountable for mistakes that are made when everybody else is," says Texas state Sen. David Sibley, a conservative Republican and oral surgeon.

The new Texas law, which took effect on Sept. 1, was strongly pushed by the state medical association but vigorously opposed by health insurers. Geoff Wurtzel, executive director of the Texas HMO Association, called the law "bad policy" and blamed its enactment on what he termed "medical politics."

"In 1995, the Legislature overwhelmingly agreed that the threat of being sued didn't produce a better standard of care," Wurtzel said, referring to a restrictive malpractice law passed that year. "But all of a sudden, if it was HMOs, liability was OK."

Texas is so far the only state to directly subject health plans to malpractice liability. But Missouri has opened the door to malpractice suits against HMOs by repealing a law that gave health plans a defense against malpractice. And Rhode Island and Washington last year created commissions to study the issue.

The Texas law is being challenged in federal court by the Aetna insurance company on the grounds that it is pre-empted by the federal law that governs employee benefits, including health insurance.

That law — known as ERISA, short for the Employee Retirement Income Security Act — is also now at the center of the legislative debate in Congress. Norwood's bill would provide that ERISA does not pre-empt state laws dealing with malpractice liability, as some federal courts have held. Those courts have held that health-plan subscribers who feel they were wrongly denied medical care can sue the plans only for reimbursement of the value of the care they did not receive. [6]

Norwood says there is no justification for shielding health plans from malpractice suits. "If you're a health-plan accountant or administrator and you want to make decisions about medical necessity," Norwood explains, "then you have to be responsible about those decisions in a court of law."

The AMA, a strong supporter of limiting medical malpractice suits in the past, supports the change. "When I make a decision, I as a physician accept accountability and liability," says Reardon. "When the plan makes a decision to provide or not to provide treatment, they should have the same responsibility and liability, especially when they're overriding a recommendation from the treating physician."

But the health insurance industry is adamantly opposed. "That's a perfect example of raising the costs of insurance with little, if any, discernible effect on the quality of the care," says the HIAA's Gradison. "It's a boon for the trial lawyers; I don't think it's a boon for the patients at all."

"All of the data suggest that consumers are not the beneficiaries of the current system," says AAHP President Ignagni. "We don't do families very much good if we provide them in the end with a situation that is designed to maybe provide compensation, maybe not, vs. trying to set up a situation that is built on quality improvement in which injuries don't occur in the first place."

One patients' group voices a similar interest in improving medical care without resorting to litigation. "We feel [litigation] is not necessarily the most productive way to resolve problems," says Weinberg of the National Health Council. Instead, Weinberg says her group favors strong complaint-resolution procedures, such as the use of ombudsmen.

Other consumer groups go further and call for some independent external review of treatment decisions. "When a

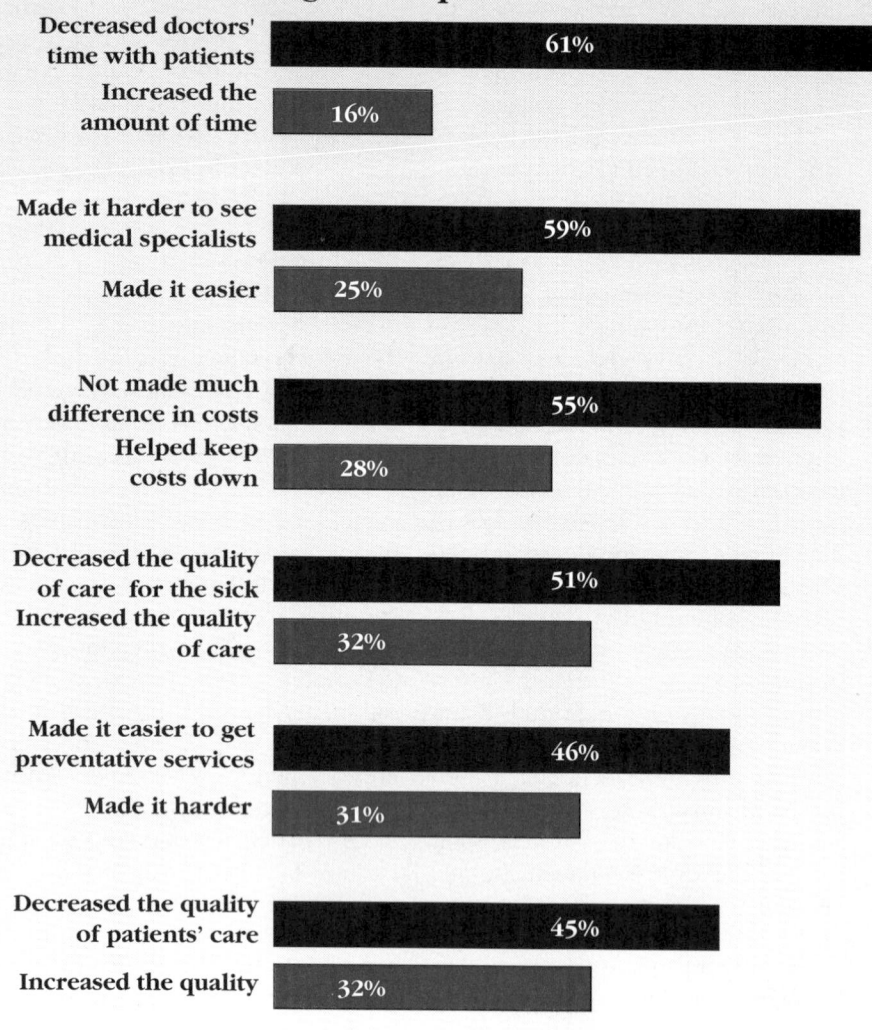

The Downside to Managed Care

A majority of Americans believe health maintenance organizations (HMOs) and other managed-care plans have had some adverse effects on health care, according to a 1997 survey. Overall, though, two-thirds of the respondents in managed care gave their plans an A or B, compared with three-fourths of the people with traditional health insurance coverage.

Percent of Americans who say HMOs and other managed-care plans have . . .

Decreased doctors' time with patients	61%
Increased the amount of time	16%
Made it harder to see medical specialists	59%
Made it easier	25%
Not made much difference in costs	55%
Helped keep costs down	28%
Decreased the quality of care for the sick	51%
Increased the quality of care	32%
Made it easier to get preventative services	46%
Made it harder	31%
Decreased the quality of patients' care	45%
Increased the quality	32%

Note: Percentages do not add up to 100 because "No effect" and "Don't know" responses are not shown.

Source: "Kaiser/Harvard National Survey of Americans' Views on Managed Care," November 1997.

patient is denied coverage, it's ludicrous to think that they can appeal to the same system that denied them," says Mitchem of Consumers Union. But her group also favors malpractice liability for health insurers. "We want to ensure that there's some type of remedy that consumers can have access to," she says.

Health insurers are balking at any requirement for outside review procedures. "Some plans are doing this," Gradison says. "The question is whether it should be required by law."

Experts differ sharply on the potential effects of subjecting HMOs to malpractice liability. "If you apply tort liability to HMOs, you'll force them to do things that are not cost-effective," Goodman says. "You'll force them to waste money."

But Barry Furrow, a professor of health law at Widener University School of Law in Wilmington, Del., says that the threat of liability would result in better medical care by forcing managed-care administrators to focus more on quality than on costs. "You want to shift the competition more away from price and toward quality," Furrow says.

Are stronger safeguards needed to protect the privacy of patients' medical records and information?

The Clinton administration unveiled its proposal to protect the privacy of patients' medical information after a media buildup that began with a speech at the National Press Club by Health and Human Services Secretary Donna E. Shalala in late July. "The way we protect the privacy of our medical records right now is erratic at best and dangerous at worst," Shalala said. When she presented the administration's proposal to the Senate Labor and Human Resources Committee on Sept. 11, Shalala declared: "With very few exceptions, health-care information about a consumer should be disclosed for health purposes and health purposes only." [7]

The administration won little praise for its proposal, however. Senators in both parties criticized the proposal at the hearing. Afterward, experts and interest groups said it left wide discretion for disclosing medical information to public-health and law enforcement officials without patients' consent.

"Would the administration proposal make things better or worse?" commented Denise Nagel, a Boston psychiatrist and executive director of the National Coalition for Patient Rights. "I think it would really make things worse." [8]

In fact, the administration's 81-page recommendation spends nearly 40 pages detailing and justifying exceptions to the general rule prohibiting disclosure of patient records without the patient's consent. The list includes exceptions to disclose information necessary for the patient's health care, for payment and for internal oversight of the patient's treatment. The recommendation also calls for permitting disclosure of individually identifiable information to public health authorities for "disease or injury reporting, public health surveillance or public health investigation or intervention."

Most controversially, the administration also said that law enforcement or intelligence agencies should be able to obtain such information, without a court order, if needed for "a legitimate law enforcement inquiry" or — in the case of intelligence agencies — if needed for "a lawful purpose."

Shalala disputed advance reports

that the proposal broadened law enforcement access to patient information. [9] She said the provision simply restated existing law. But Sen. Tim Hutchinson, an Arkansas Republican, said the proposal gave patients less privacy than existing federal law for bank records, cable television and video store rentals. Sen. Patrick J. Leahy of Vermont, the committee's ranking Democrat, was also critical. "There is divided opinion in the administration," Leahy said, "and right now the anti-privacy forces are winning on the key issue of law enforcement access to medical records." [10]

"HHS completely dropped the ball" on the issue, says Georgetown's Gostin. "They made an unforgivable mistake."

Gostin also faulted the privacy recommendations from the president's commission, issued two months after Shalala's testimony on Capitol Hill. The report called for permitting disclosure of patient information for purposes of "provision of health care, payment of services, peer review, health promotion, disease management and quality assurance." It addressed law enforcement only obliquely, saying law enforcement agencies "should examine their existing policies to ensure that they access individually identifiable information only when absolutely necessary."

"Everybody's in favor of privacy," Gostin says. "But the devil's in the details, and these don't provide any details. It basically does nothing."

For their part, however, health industry and business groups saw the administration's proposals as unduly restrictive. "The industry is very concerned about interrupting the flow of health information," said Heidi Wagner Hayduk, a consultant on privacy issues for the Healthcare Leadership Council, a coalition of major insurers, hospitals and drug companies. Medical innovation would be "stifled," she warned, if health-care providers and research-

ers were required to obtain patient authorization "every time information changes hands." [11]

Health-care industry groups also said federal legislation should pre-empt any state laws setting stricter protections for patient privacy. The administration's proposal would leave state laws unaffected, as would a stricter bill introduced by Leahy. But Sen. Robert F. Bennett, a Utah Republican, has introduced a bill that would set a single federal standard on the issue.

The administration also has endorsed a separate privacy proposal affecting the health insurance industry: a bill to bar health insurance companies and managed-care plans from discriminating against people on the basis of their genetic make-up. [12] The proposal has been pushed by a number of bioethics and privacy-advocacy groups, which point to studies documenting instances of genetic discrimination by, among others, employers and insurers.

The genetic privacy bill has languished in Congress for several years. Clinton endorsed the measure in July. Last month, Vice President Al Gore announced the administration's support for also banning genetic discrimination in the workplace. [13]

The administration's medical-records privacy proposal drew additional criticism at a second Senate Labor Committee hearing on the issue on Oct. 28. Two medical groups, the AMA and the American Psychiatric Association, both called for stronger protection than the administration supported, while witnesses representing drug manufacturers and the American Hospital Association said the proposal went too far.

Such praise as the administration received for its proposal has been typically begrudging, at best. Boston University's Annas says the administration deserved credit for proposing a federal law guaranteeing patients the right to see their own records.

And Robert Gellman, a privacy consultant who led Shalala's outside advisers on the recommendations, stressed that the package would be "stronger than any comparable state law." [14] But both men also faulted the law enforcement provisions, among other exceptions. "The administration," Annas concludes, "has a long way to go." ∎

BACKGROUND

Health Insurance

Health care became widely available to most Americans, and a financially secure profession for most doctors, only in the recent past. [15] Well into the 20th century, routine health care was a luxury available only to well-to-do Americans. And many doctors had only modest incomes, since they did not see enough patients often enough to have a lucrative practice.

Two 20th-century developments changed the face of health care in the United States: widespread private health insurance and government-funded medical programs. Together, the two developments produced the mythic image that forms the backdrop of today's debate over medical care. In that idealized vision, most Americans enjoyed the services of a family doctor, a Marcus Welby figure who gave skilled and compassionate care from birth to death with little concern about fees. And the government stepped in to provide care for those few who could not afford medical services. But the two developments also contained the germs of the cost problems that beset the health-care system today.

Private insurance entered the health field tentatively, limited at first to covering accidental injury and death. By the late 19th and early 20th centuries, however, many employers were providing limited medical care for their workers — motivated as much to reduce absenteeism caused by illnesses as to promote their employees' welfare.

The labor scarcities of World War II prompted some employers to begin offering health insurance as a benefit for workers. Labor unions, strengthened by New Deal legislation in the 1930s, included demands for health benefits in contract negotiations. And the postwar economic boom allowed major U.S. corporations to grant the demands.

Through the 1950s, more and more big corporations were including health benefits in union contracts; other employers followed suit. By the end of the decade, around two-thirds of the population at least had hospitalization insurance. [16]

The bill for these benefits was largely invisible. The expense was not a big cost item for employers, at least initially. For employees, the benefits were not taxed: In fact, the amounts did not even appear on pay stubs. As a result, many critics and observers contend, no one — neither business, labor, insurers nor health-care providers — had much incentive to watch the bottom line.

A second problem — access to care — was also somewhat obscured. With so many Americans sharing in the widened availability of health care, it was easy to overlook those who were not: the elderly, the poor and the uninsured.

Government's Role

The government's initial moves to help provide health care were also tentative and limited. Some local governments began including medical benefits for the poor in general welfare programs in the early 20th century, and a New Deal program helped bring health care to some rural areas during the Depression. Throughout the century, progressives and labor interests called for compulsory national health insurance, but the efforts were blocked by business interests and, most important, the medical profession.

The two big federal health programs, Medicare and Medicaid, were enacted over the continuing opposition of the medical profession in the brief moment of liberal triumph in the 1960s. Congress had passed a limited bill to provide health insurance for the elderly poor in 1960, but the program proved to be unpopular. President Lyndon B. Johnson put the issue of health care for the elderly at the top of his Great Society agenda and pushed legislation through the overwhelmingly Democratic Congress in 1965.

As enacted, Medicare included the original idea of a contributory insurance program to cover hospitalization for the elderly (Part A) plus a similar plan for doctors' services (Part B). In addition, the law established the framework for Medicaid, the federal-state health-care program for the poor and the disabled.

Some doctors talked of boycotting Medicare, but they quickly realized that the program was — as Starr writes — "a bonanza," guaranteeing payment for medical services that many doctors had previously provided for free or for reduced fees. [17] Medicare and Medicaid closed the biggest gaps in health-care access, but liberals still said health care was too costly and favored broader national health insurance to ensure access for all.

Under President Richard M. Nixon, however, the federal government took a different tack to deal with the intertwined issue of access and costs. It backed a free-

Continued on p. 108

Chronology

Before 1950

Earliest forms of managed care are organized; employers begin to offer hospitalization insurance to workers.

1960s *Federal government establishes free health insurance for the elderly (Medicare) and a joint state-federal program to provide health care for low-income persons (Medicaid).*

1970s *The Nixon administration backs the creation of health maintenance organizations (HMOs) to control health-care costs.*

1973
The Health Maintenance Organization Act provides funds and regulatory support for HMOs, but also includes some coverage mandates that slow their growth.

1976
Congress eases some regulations on HMOs; two years later, Congress votes increased funding.

1980s *HMOs grow rapidly, gaining support from employers and consumers worried about spiraling increases in health-care costs.*

1985
Supreme Court rules that Employee Retirement Income Security Act (ERISA) supersedes state laws regulating private employers' health plans *(Massachusetts Mutual Life Insurance Co. v. Russell)*; some lower federal courts interpret decision as barring malpractice suits against managed-care plans.

1990s *Backlash against managed care grows.*

1993
President Clinton proposes National Health Security Act, aimed at providing health insurance for all Americans; plan is assailed by business interests, medical lobby and Republicans.

1994
Clinton health-care plan dies in Congress.

1995
Many states pass laws requiring managed-care plans to allow women to designate ob-gyns as their primary-care provider.

Aug. 21, 1996
Clinton signs law making it easier for people to keep their health insurance when they lose or change jobs, start their own business or get sick; bill includes provision to facilitate sharing of patient information among health-care providers, but also requires government to develop privacy-protection guidelines by 1999.

September 1996
Congress responds to criticism of "drive-through deliveries" by requiring health insurance plans to cover at least 48 hours of hospital care for new mothers.

May 1997
Texas enacts legislation subjecting health maintenance organizations to medical malpractice liability; Aetna insurance company challenges law in federal court as pre-empted by ERISA.

July 1997
House and Senate conferees agree on provision in budget bill to bar Medicare-eligible HMOs from imposing "gag rules" on doctors by preventing them from discussing treatments or specialists that the plan would not pay for.

Sept. 11, 1997
Health and Human Services Secretary Donna E. Shalala presents medical-information privacy legislation to Congress; proposal is faulted by lawmakers, advocates and experts.

October 1997
Two House subcommittees hold hearings on Patient Access to Responsible Care Act sponsored by Rep. Charlie Norwood, R-Ga.

Nov. 19, 1997
Proposed "Patients' Bill of Rights" is issued by President Clinton's Advisory Commission on Consumer Protection and Quality in the Health Care Industry.

January 1998
Managed-care plans continued to grow in 1997 despite complaints about their services; coalition of health insurance and business lobbies announces plans for advertising campaign against managed-care reform legislation; Clinton urges Congress to pass consumer bill of rights.

Are Elderly Americans 'Trapped' by Medicare?

Lawmakers and rival interest groups are clashing over the ability of senior citizens to see the physician of their choice outside the federal Medicare system. [1]

Conservatives want to get rid of a policy that largely prevents doctors and patients from arranging for Medicare-covered services outside the system's reimbursement scheme. They view the issue as a simple question of patients' rights.

"When you're sick, the federal government should not stand in the way of your getting the medical treatment you want," says Sen. Jon Kyl, an Arizona Republican who took up the issue after a constituent's complaint last year and forced a limited amendment to the law through Congress.

But the Clinton administration, Democratic lawmakers and the nation's largest senior citizens' group all argue that totally lifting the restriction would create the risk of gouging senior citizens and threaten the viability of the federal government's 33-year-old health insurance program for the elderly.

Seniors "would lose much of the financial protection that they are currently provided under Medicare" if the policy were eliminated, according to Rep. Pete Stark, a California Democrat and veteran legislator on health-care issues.

The dispute stems from a policy adopted by the Health Care Financing Administration (HCFA), the Health and Human Services agency that administers the Medicare program. For many years, the HCFA has prohibited doctors participating in the Medicare program from letting patients pay them out of their own pockets for services covered by Medicare.

Defenders of the policy say Medicare is acting just like any other insurer by requiring participating doctors to limit their fees to its schedule for reimbursements. Medicare reimbursements are sometimes markedly lower than prevailing fees for some services.

"Private payment would undermine the whole rationale for the Medicare fee schedule," says John Rother, legislative director of the American Association of Retired Persons (AARP). The 30-million-member organization strongly opposes lifting the ban.

Critics say the ban is bad for senior citizens and also bad for the Medicare program. They say it prevents senior citizens who can afford it from picking a particular doctor, for example, or from getting treatment without going through government red tape.

As for Medicare itself, these critics say that letting well-off seniors pay for some services themselves would strengthen the financially beleaguered insurance program. Supporters counter that lifting the ban would result in a two-tiered system — with one group of doctors for well-to-do seniors and another for Medicare patients.

Kyl won Senate passage on a party-line vote of an amendment to narrow the policy last summer as part of the Medicare reform provisions of the balanced-budget bill. [2] But the Clinton administration reportedly threatened to veto the entire bill over the issue. The result was a limited compromise that allows physicians to accept private payments for Medicare-covered services if they "opt out" of the Medicare program for two years. Critics say that few doctors could afford to drop out of the Medicare program.

A conservative senior citizens' organization is challenging that law in federal court in Washington. [3] United Seniors Association, a 60,000-member group founded in 1992, claims the law violates senior citizens' constitutional rights.

United Seniors President Sandra Butler says the new law makes health care less accessible for senior citizens. "Because seniors will be barred from contracting privately, many health- and life-saving services will be difficult for them to obtain, if they could obtain them at all," Butler says.

But Rother says few seniors agree. "I don't think I have a single letter in my file asking for the privilege of paying more for the services that Medicare already covers," he says. "This is not a patient-driven concern."

Medical groups are also divided on the issue. The American Medical Association (AMA) strongly supports Kyl's effort this year to repeal the restriction on private payments. "Medicare patients deserve the same rights as other patients to purchase health care directly from their physicians — without interference from the federal government," the AMA says.

But the American College of Physicians, which represents about 100,000 internists, opposes Kyl's bill. It says the measure "could threaten the viability of Medicare as an insurance program that offers accessible, affordable high-quality care."

---

[1] For background, see *USA Today*, Nov. 26, 1997, p. A6 and "Retiree Health Benefits," *The CQ Researcher*, Dec. 6, 1991, pp. 930-953.

[2] See *Congressional Quarterly Weekly Report*, June 28, 1997, p. 1529.

[3] The case is *United Seniors Association v. Shalala*, pending before U.S. District Judge Thomas F. Hogan.

Continued from p. 106

enterprise solution to the problems: a scheme being pushed by a physician-turned-health-care reformer in Minnesota that came to be called a "health mainte-nance organization" or HMO.

Rise of Managed Care

Managed care had its origins in ideas pushed by socially con-scious health-care reformers in the early 20th century. [18] In one form — known as cooperative or prepaid group health plans — consumers paid a modest annual fee to one or more doctors to cover their families' pre-ventive and sick care. The medical profession opposed the idea, however, and succeeded in getting laws passed in many states to bar consumer-controlled cooperatives.

Then during World War II, California industrialist Henry J. Kaiser set up two prepaid group health plans for his company's employees, known as Permanente Foundations. Unlike the health-care cooperatives, Kaiser's plans flourished — and served as the forerunner for what is today the country's largest HMO, Kaiser Permanente.

The Nixon administration saw in HMOs an appealing alternative to the liberal-backed national health insurance plans. Administration officials were sold on the idea by Paul M. Ellwood, today regarded as the father of managed care. Ellwood, a Minneapolis physician, argued that the traditional fee-for-services system penalized health-care providers who returned patients to health. He met with the administration's key health policy-makers on Feb. 5, 1970, to make his case for organizations to provide members comprehensive care for prepaid amounts. At that meeting Ellwood coined the phrase "health maintenance organizations." [19]

Financial and regulatory help were needed to put the idea into effect. The administration initially found money to help launch HMOs beginning in 1970, without specific congressional authorization, even as it was asking Congress to pass a law to promote the plans. The law enacted three years later — the Health Maintenance Organization Act of 1973 — provided more money, $375 million over five years, for grants and loans to help start up HMOs. [20] More important, the law required all businesses with more than 25 employees to offer at least one HMO as an alternative to conventional insurance if one was available.

At the same time, though, the act established requirements that proved to be regulatory obstacles to the growth of HMOs. It required HMOs to offer not only basic hospitalization, physicians' services, emergency care and laboratory and diagnostic services but also mental health care, home health services and referral services for alcohol and drug abuse.

These requirements, combined with the government's delay in promulgating regulations to implement the law, stunted the growth of HMOs, according to Starr's account. At the same time, the medical profession viewed the idea with skepticism or hostility. But Congress eased some of the burdens in 1976, and then provided another shot of money in 1978: $164 million over three years. [21] By then, HMOs were starting to take off in the market. At the end of the decade, HMOs had enrolled 7.9 million members — double the figure in 1970. Still, the number represented only 4 percent of the population and — as of the early 1980s — was expected to grow only to 10 percent of the population by 1990. [22]

In fact, enrollment in HMOs more than tripled over the next decade, reaching about 25 million in 1990. Despite a decade of rapidly rising health-care costs, HMOs had to keep fees down and provide good service in order to attract customers. Most faced business losses, and some went bankrupt. But they were generally regarded as successful in containing cost increases, enough so that traditional fee-for-service health plans began copying some of their practices, such as utilization review, where insurers scrutinized doctors' fees and practices.

Meanwhile, the once comfortable relationship between patients and doctors had become badly frayed. The growth of specialized medicine had weakened the bond with the old-style family doctors — who now likely as not called themselves "internists." The rise in doctors' income created a distance between an increasingly well-to-do profession and its patient-customers. And the increase in malpractice litigation led many physicians to adopt "defensive-medicine" practices to guard against the threat.

Managed-Care Backlash

The 1990s saw managed care reach a dominant position in the health insurance market. By 1993, most workers covered by employer-provided health insurance were enrolled in some form of managed care — either an HMO, a preferred provider organization (PPO) or a "point-of-service" (POS) plan. As of 1995, industry figures estimated a total of 150 million people nationwide were in a managed-care plan. Managed care was also credited with helping to bring down the rate of increase in health-care costs. But the decade also witnessed a growing backlash against managed care as many doctors chafed under cost-cutting pressures from HMO administrators, and many patients complained of delays in receiving — or outright denials of — needed medical care.

The consumer backlash against HMOs manifested itself most dramatically in court. A small number of HMO enrollees won whopping verdicts or settlements in suits claiming that their health plans had wrongfully denied or delayed necessary medical care. In California, the family of Helene Fox, who died of breast cancer after her HMO, Health Net, refused to pay for a bone marrow transplant, collected a $5 million settlement after a jury awarded her $89 million. In Georgia, Lamona and James Adams won a $45 million jury award in a suit that blamed Kaiser Permanente for the botched handling of a bacterial infection that forced doctors to amputate their infant son's arms and legs; the company later settled for an undisclosed sum. [23]

A mid-decade survey produced statistical evidence of the consumer dissatisfaction with HMOs, at least in comparison with traditional fee-for-service health plans. The survey, conducted for the Robert Wood Johnson Foundation by researchers at Harvard University and Louis Harris and Associates, found that significantly more HMO subscribers than fee-for-service plan subscribers complained about their medical care.

The complaints came only from small minorities: For example, 12 percent of HMO subscribers said their doctors provided incorrect or inappropriate medical care, compared with 5 percent of fee-for-service plan subscribers. Still, the higher levels of dissatisfaction with HMOs prompted a cautionary note from the survey's director. "Consumers need to be aware that all health plans don't treat you the same way when you are sick," said Robert Blendon, chairman of the department of health policy management at Harvard's School of Public Health. [24]

Health-care providers were also voicing dissatisfaction with managed care. In one incident, Massachusetts internist David Himmelstein attacked the HMO that he worked for, U.S. Healthcare, in an appearance on Phil Donahue's nationally syndicated television program in November 1995. Himmelstein charged that the company rewarded doctors for denying care and forbade them from discussing treatment options with patients. The company — later acquired by Aetna — responded by terminating its contact with Himmelstein just three days after the TV show. But it reinstated him in February 1996 after a storm of criticism and also modified its contracts to permit doctors to discuss payment methods with patients.

Himmelstein's comments reflected the concerns that many doctors and hospital administrators had about managed care. "This is all about cost, not improving patient care," a doctor told *Wall Street Journal* reporter George Anders in a 1994 interview. "You survive in managed care by denying or limiting care," William Speck, chief executive of Presbyterian Hospital in New York, told Anders in June 1995. "That's how you make money." [25]

As the complaints escalated, state and federal lawmakers took up the issues. By mid-decade, hundreds of bills were being introduced in state legislatures around the country. The earliest legislation dealt with specific problems — like allowing women to select an ob-gyn physician as their primary-care provider, or prohibiting health-care plans from imposing "gag clauses" on physicians. Congress in 1996 passed a provision requiring health insurance plans to cover at least 48 hours of hospital care for new mothers — prohibiting so-called "drive-through maternity stays." [26]

By 1997, more comprehensive reform packages were being together, both in state capitals and in Washington. Health insurers opposed most of the proposals. But they also responded in the market — for example, by making access to specialists easier, though typically for an added cost. [27] In addition, managed-care administrators and advocates sought to take credit for the continuing progress in taming the health-care-cost-increase monster. In a study released last summer, the AAHP claimed that the lower costs due to managed care had allowed more than 3 million people to have health insurance than would have had coverage without managed care.

"By driving down health-care inflation, health plans have provided a safety net, assuring more families access to affordable, high-quality coverage," AAHP President Ignagni said. [28] ■

CURRENT SITUATION

Reform Efforts

The managed-care revolution that Kaiser started in California for his workers now provides health insurance for around 70 percent of the state's residents. Predictably, Californians have also led the backlash against managed care — first in the courts and, for the past three years, in the political arena. But regulatory proposals have failed at the polls or been vetoed by the state's Republican governor, Pete Wilson.

Today, the fate of efforts to rein in managed-care companies in California remains uncertain even after a special task force appointed by the governor and legislators spent eight months trying to develop a consensus package of regulatory changes for the industry.

The 30-member task force — representing health-care providers, insurers, patients' groups, consumers, business and labor — issued a report in early January recommending the creation of a new state agency to regulate HMOs and the enactment of some 60 changes in the way managed-care plans operate. [29] Among the major steps endorsed by the panel:

• An "unbiased, independent, third-party" review process for resolving HMO members' complaints involving denials of medical care.

• Mandatory, standardized procedures for resolving consumer complaints, including a member's right to appear in person at a grievance hearing.

• Collection and publication of detailed information on members' complaints.

- Standard descriptions of HMO products to facilitate comparison-shopping among plans.

Many outside observers described the task force's recommendations as fairly modest. In fact, it rejected the idea of subjecting managed-care companies to malpractice liability. Even so, a leading industry representative on the task force has stopped short of endorsing them, while a consumer representative on the panel believes enactment is not likely.

"The thing I would first ask the Legislature to do is to look at how the private sector has addressed the issue and decide whether the system is addressing the problem in a public-private partnership," says Ron Williams, president of Blue Cross of California. "In most situations," he adds, "I believe the market will suffice."

"The industry representatives have already said that this is too costly," says Jeanne Finberg, a senior attorney with Consumers Union and a task force member. As for Wilson, Finberg says, "He has an opportunity to embrace the package, but I'm not confident that he will."

Wilson, in fact, cited the task force's deliberations in deciding last summer to veto all but one of some 85 HMO reform bills passed by the Democratic-controlled Legislature during the year. Wilson called the bills "piecemeal" changes and said he wanted to wait for the task force's recommendations for comprehensive reform.

Wilson's decision — making an exception only for a bill to require 48-hour coverage for maternity stays — startled task force members and industry officials. Anthony Rodgers, a Los Angeles HMO executive, told the *Los Angeles Times* that Wilson had assured the task force it would not be used as "a graveyard" for legislation. [30]

The rejection of the legislatively approved changes marked the second defeat in two years for managed-care reform. In November 1996, Cali-

Managed-Care Reforms Get Qualified Support

Most Americans support several of the frequently mentioned proposals to make managed care more user-friendly. But their support drops when they are asked to consider potential consequences of the changes such as higher premiums.

Percentage of Americans who want health plans to . . .

	Favor	Oppose
Provide more information about how health plans operate	**92%**	**6%**
If higher premiums result	58%	34%
If the government gets too involved	55%	38%
If employers drop coverage	54%	43%
Allow appeal to an independent reviewer	**88%**	**9%**
If higher premiums result	63%	32%
If the government gets too involved	51%	41%
If employers drop coverage	49%	45%
Allow a woman to see a gynecologist without a referral	**82%**	**16%**
If higher premiums result	63%	34%
If the government gets too involved	51%	43%
If employers drop coverage	48%	47%
Allow people to see a specialist without a referral	**81%**	**18%**
If higher premiums result	58%	39%
If the government gets too involved	47%	48%
If employers drop coverage	46%	51%
Pay for an emergency room visit without prior approval	**79%**	**18%**
If higher premiums result	62%	33%
If the government gets too involved	52%	41%
If employers drop coverage	48%	47%
Allow people to sue health plan directly	**64%**	**31%**
If higher premiums result	58%	34%
If the government gets too involved	55%	38%
If employers drop coverage	54%	43%

Note: Percentages do not add up to 100 because all respondents did not answer.

Source: Kaiser/Harvard "National Survey of Americans' Views on Managed Care," January 1998.

fornia voters decisively rejected two ballot initiatives that called for a variety of new regulations on HMOs, including the right to a second opinion when medical care is denied. Proposition 214 received about 42 percent of the vote, while Proposition 216, which included new fees on managed-care companies, garnered only 39 percent. [31]

The continuing divisions among task force members indicates the difficulty of getting any changes enacted. In transmitting the report to the governor and the Legislature, task force Chairman Alain Enthoven, a professor of business management at Stanford University, emphasized that the panel had not had time to assess the cost implications of its recommendations.

But Enthoven, widely regarded as the nation's leading expert on managed care, stressed that he "fully" supports the panel's recommendations, which he said "would lead to a greatly improved managed-health-care system in California."

For his part, Williams says he expects some legislation to pass this year, but he, too, faults the task force for failing to consider costs. He warns that some changes could drive up premiums and force small businesses to drop health insurance for their employees.

"We are essentially spending other people's money," Williams says. "Every change that costs one more cent in premiums has to come out of somebody's pocket."

But Finberg minimizes the potential cost increases and says the task force did not go far enough to protect consumers. As for the fate of the recommendations, she says Wilson holds the key.

"If it's not taken seriously by the governor," she says, "then I will have wasted a lot of time, and California consumers will have a lot to be angry with the governor about."

Proposed Legislation

In his 15 years in Congress, Rep. John R. Kasich, R-Ohio, has been a leading spokesman for anti-Washington, anti-regulatory sentiment among House Republicans. But late last year, the powerful House Budget Committee chairman bluntly warned the managed-care industry that Congress will impose "comprehensive regulations" on the industry unless it takes "direct and responsible actions" to address consumers' complaints.

"Too often, cost control has been achieved at the expense of patients' legitimate interests," Kasich wrote in a Dec. 31 letter to Ignagni of the AAHP. He said the industry should "develop and implement" a code of ethics, allow doctors to be "the advocate" for the patient and make sure that health plans deliver "quality care" even while controlling costs. "Simply stated," Kasich concluded, "you must put the patient first." [32]

Kasich's letter exemplifies the surprisingly wide support that managed-care-reform proposals have attracted among conservative Republicans along with the more customary support for consumer-protection plans from Democratic lawmakers. Republicans are pushing the major reform bills in both chambers of Congress: Norwood's bill in the House and the companion measure introduced in the Senate by New York's D'Amato. Norwood's bill currently has 218 co-sponsors, including 89 Republicans, 128 Democrats and one independent.

Norwood says he introduced the bill despite his aversion to federal regulation. "It turns my stomach to turn this over to the Labor Department," he said, referring to the agency that would have principal responsibility for implementing the bill's provisions. "But it makes me even more nervous not to do anything."

Among its major provisions, Norwood's bill would require health plans to give consumers an option to buy "point-of-service" coverage — allowing them to select their own doctor for an additional cost. It would also require adequate access to specialists and emergency care, require internal grievance procedures and subject managed-care companies to medical malpractice liability for negligent treatment decisions.

Despite professed support from a majority of the House, prospects for Norwood's bill are uncertain. The House Republican leadership is divided on the issue. In November, House Majority Whip Dick Armey of Texas wrote a strongly worded letter to GOP members urging opposition to the forthcoming recommendations from President Clinton's health-care commission. Even though Armey did not refer to Norwood's bill, he called for restricting rather than expanding medical malpractice liability and recommended medical savings accounts rather than regulatory changes to give consumers more health-care choices. [33]

For its part, the health insurance industry is gearing up for an all-out lobbying campaign to defeat Norwood's bill or anything much like it. "It's our No. 1 issue," says HIAA's Gradison. "It's very bad public policy."

In a two-page lobbying flier, the AAHP warns that Norwood's bill would represent "the single, largest expansion of tort liability in memory," establish "federal price controls" and make it harder for families to get "affordable" health coverage. But Ignagni also hints at the possibility of supporting some legislative changes. "We intend to be very involved and will provide whatever information that we can," she says.

Democratic lawmakers have their own managed-care reform bills in both chambers, similar to the GOP-sponsored measures in thrust but different in detail. The main bill — introduced by Rep. John D. Dingell of Michigan and Sen. Edward M. Kennedy of Massachusetts — includes provisions aimed at ensuring access to specialists. Among its differences with

Continued on p. 114

At Issue:

Has the rise of managed care hurt patients' rights?

ADRIENNE MITCHEM

Legislative counsel, Consumers Union

*a*mericans are experiencing a true crisis in confidence in today's managed-care industry. Consumers' faith is shaken because of signs that managed care may be sacrificing quality health care to boost profits.

As managed care replaced the old fee-for-service system, the financial incentives driving the health-care industry have turned upside down. This revolution, replacing incentives to overtreat patients with incentives to undertreat, has provoked a strong backlash. Nearly three in five Americans in a recent poll believe managed-care plans make it harder for people who are sick to see a specialist.

But this revolution also creates an opportunity to reintroduce a simple and old-fashioned idea: consumer protection laws. Responding to grass-roots uprisings, states have passed laws giving consumers tools to help them be smart shoppers, ensure accountability when costly mistakes are made, provide more access to specialist and emergency care and guarantee a fair system to review patient disputes.

A presidential advisory commission has developed a "Consumer Bill of Rights," spurring a flurry of bill introductions on Capitol Hill and the promise of a healthy debate about nationwide reform. On one side is a multimillion-dollar scare campaign, funded by industry, designed to preserve the status quo. On the other, a coalition of consumer groups and individual Americans who have been burned by the current system and want change.

A scorecard of principles for reform from Consumers Union will help measure who wins:

• The linchpin for consumers is an appeals system that gives patients access to an independent entity to settle disputes over medically necessary care when benefits are denied, terminated or delayed. The current system, where the managed-care company serves as both judge and jury for every appeal, is stacked against patients.

• Another vital component is full disclosure. Plans should be required to provide consumers with information to help them understand all of their alternatives for treatment, not just the cheapest.

• Consumers also want assurance that they will not be holding the bag for medical mistakes. Families shouldn't shoulder the financial burdens of medical negligence because industry is unaccountable for its actions.

* Finally, a consumer bill of rights should set minimum standards for all managed-care plans. Voluntary provisions won't suffice. When you get sick, doctors, not accountants, should call the shots.

Congress can restore consumer confidence in the managed-care system by passing enforceable and loophole-free legislation that includes a fair review process, full disclosure and accountability. Anything less falls short of true reform.

KAREN IGNAGNI

President, American Association of Health Plans

*b*ealth plans have advanced the cause of patients' rights with important patient protections that weren't available under the old system. Health-care practices and procedures have been made far more accountable — ensuring that the great majority of patients get the right care, at the right time and in the right setting — and appeals systems are in place to make sure that any patient who disagrees with a coverage or treatment decision has effective recourse.

Discussions of patients' rights should start with the fact that, from a patient's perspective, all other rights are meaningless without access to care. Under the old system, health care was being priced beyond reach. So one of the most important victories that health plans have won for patients' rights is to make health coverage more affordable for millions of working Americans.

Once assured of coverage, you should have the right to be protected against inappropriate care. Health plans promote quality care by emphasizing prevention and early diagnosis and monitoring practice patterns in order to do away with the wide variations in quality that did so much to make the old system not just costly but often downright dangerous. This commitment to accountability represents a major advance in patient protection.

But what if a conflict arises about what's covered or whether a particular treatment is in order? Despite critics' claims, disputes are rare and are usually resolved satisfactorily. Still, there's room for improvement — and health plans are participating in a nationwide initiative to continually improve care by identifying consumer concerns and developing patient-centered solutions. This, too, represents an unprecedented commitment to patients' rights.

Consumers should be wary of much that is being touted today as "consumer protection." For example, efforts to make health plans liable for individual practitioners' actions would simply clog the courts (at taxpayer expense) and enrich trial lawyers (not patients). At the same time, such efforts would adversely affect care by forcing health plans to act defensively, causing higher costs without producing better outcomes. Does that protect patients' rights? No — it just turns back the clock.

And we can't afford that. The health-care revolution that's in progress today was a necessary answer to the costly flaws of the old system. If the revolution has imperfections, the answer is to correct them — not to roll back progress or micromanage plans. Health plans are fully committed to making sure consumers are informed and their concerns met. That way, we can protect patients' rights without smothering innovative health care under layers of inflexible regulations and unproductive litigation.

Estimated Costs of Reform Vary Widely

Two recent studies — one funded by an industry group, the other by a patient-consumer coalition — reached dramatically different conclusions about the likely cost impact of the leading managed-care reform proposal. But the industry's substantially higher estimate depends on interpretations of the bill, the Patient Access to Responsible Care Act (PARCA), that its sponsor says are wrong.

A report prepared for the insurance-business Health Benefits Coalition by the Washington consulting firm of Milliman & Robertson projected the bill would raise health insurance premiums by 23 percent. [1]

A study prepared for the Patient Access to Responsible Care Alliance — also known as PARCA — by Muse & Associates predicted a rate increase of between 0.7 to 2.6 percent. [2]

The reports made strikingly similar predictions about the effects of some provisions. Both reports, for example, predict little if any effect from provisions requiring emergency care coverage, easing referrals to specialists or giving consumers a choice between types of managed-care plans.

The industry-funded study, however, predicted substantially higher costs for three provisions in the bill:

• No payments to providers as an inducement to reduce or limit medically necessary services. Milliman & Robertson assumed the provision would prevent health plans from negotiating discount rates with providers and projected a 9.5 percent cost increase as a result. Muse & Associates noted that newly drafted report language specifically denied any intention to bar discounts; on that basis, it predicted no cost impact. Difference: 9.5 percent.

• Equal reimbursement for out-of-network providers. Milliman & Robertson say the provision could have no impact if interpreted to apply only to doctors' fees, but could raise premiums by 11 percent if it prevented point-of-service (POS) plans from requiring enrollees to pay a higher deductible for using an out-of-network provider. The firm then averaged the two figures to produce a "best estimate midpoint" of 5.5 percent. Muse & Associates says

the bill would not bar higher deductibles for using a doctor outside the network. Difference: 5.5 percent.

• No discrimination against health professionals. Milliman & Robertson says the provision could require health plans to cover services of professionals not now covered, such as chiropractors or acupuncturists. Muse & Associates said new report language stipulates the bill will not have that effect. Difference: 5.5 percent.

In addition, the industry-funded study predicted that because of its projected increases, some customers would drop their coverage — raising rates still further for consumers still in plans. The consumer-funded study predicts a much smaller effect. Difference: 4.5 percent. [3]

The Muse study predicted only a slight increase from a provision subjecting group health plans to medical malpractice liability; the Milliman-Robertson study did not analyze the provision.

Milliman & Robertson qualified its study by stating that several of its projections "depend heavily on interpretation of PARCA." For its part, Muse & Associates noted that its study took account of legislative changes made after the Milliman & Robertson study was completed.

Rep. Charlie Norwood, R-Ga., the main sponsor of PARCA, says the industry-funded study is based on a misreading of his bill. "The assumptions made are neither reasonable nor honest," he says.

But the Health Benefits Coalition, the business group that released the study, is standing by its predictions. "We have other studies that show that mandates at the state level have raised rates," a spokeswoman says, "and we expect federal regulation to be even more costly."

---

[1] Milliman & Robertson Inc., "Actuarial Analysis of the Patient Access to Responsible Care Act (PARCA)," released Jan. 21, 1998.

[2] Muse & Associates, "The Health Premium Impact of H.R. 1415/S.644, the Patient Access to Responsible Care Act (PARCA)," Jan. 29, 1998.

[3] Milliman & Robertson says its individual cost estimates total more than its "composite" prediction of 23 percent because some PARCA provisions overlap.

Norwood-D'Amato is a provision — also included in the Clinton commission's recommendations — for external grievance-review procedures.

Clinton led a White House pep rally with House and Senate leaders on Jan. 14 to drum up support for the proposals — and take partisan credit for the issue. Health industry opponents will be "surprised at how many Republicans come over and join our

side in this battle," Clinton said.

Norwood says the tone of the White House session could hurt his bill's prospects. "You need to be a little less partisan on this, a little less demagoguery," he says.

Procedurally, Norwood's bill went through the first of the legislative hurdles in October with hearings by the two subcommittees with jurisdiction over managed-care health plans

— the Commerce Subcommittee on Health and the Environment and the House Education and the Workforce Subcommittee on Employer-Employee Relations. Today, he says he is optimistic that he can get the bill out of both committees after markups.

Norwood is also working on the House leadership. He says Armey assured him that the November memo was not intended to signal opposition to his bill. As for House Speaker Newt Gingrich, R.-Ga., Norwood says the two Georgians often talk about the issue when flying back to their home districts. Gingrich "clearly understands something has to be done with this," Norwood says. ∎

OUTLOOK

Weighing the Costs

With Congress poised to start its new session, a coalition of health insurance and business lobbies unveiled plans in January for a $1 million-plus advertising campaign aimed at convincing the public that managed-care reform proposals will be bad medicine for patients. Their theme: Government mandates will drive up premiums and force some small businesses to drop health insurance coverage for their employees.

"The White House and some in Congress are proposing mandates that will drive up costs, forcing millions of Americans to lose their health insurance," one of the planned ads proclaims. The message appears alongside a picture of Dr. Frankenstein's monster: "Be careful how you play doctor," the ad warns in big type. "You might mandate a monster." [34]

The formation of the coalition by the two major health insurance groups, AAHP and HIAA, along with such big-business lobbies as the U.S. Chamber of Commerce, National Association of Manufacturers and National Federation of Independent Businesses, had been expected by opposing advocacy groups and by Norwood, the lead congressional sponsor of managed-care reform.

"This is pretty normal," he says.

FOR MORE INFORMATION

American Association of Health Plans, 1129 20th St., N.W., Suite 600, Washington, D.C. 20036; (202) 778-3200; www.aahp.org. The trade association represents health maintenance organizations (HMOs) and similar network health-care plans.

American Medical Association, 1101 Vermont Ave., N.W., 12th Floor, Washington, D.C. 20005; (202) 789-7400; www.ama-assn.org. The AMA, with 300,000 members, is the nation's largest physicians' group; it supports some managed-care reform proposals.

Consumers Union, 1666 Connecticut Ave., N.W., Suite 310, Washington, D.C. 20009; (202) 462-6262; www.consumersreport.org. Consumers Union, publisher of Consumer's Report, lobbies on health issues in Washington and in state capitals.

Health Benefits Coalition, 600 Maryland Ave., S.W., Washington, D.C. 20004; (202) 554-9000. The ad hoc coalition, comprising 31 business trade associations, opposes managed-care reform bills in Congress.

Health Insurance Association of America, 555 13th St., N.W., Suite 600E, Washington, D.C. 20004; (202) 824-1600; www.hiaa.org. This trade association represents 250 of the country's major for-profit health insurance carriers.

Patient Access to Responsible Care Alliance, 1111 14th St., N.W., Suite 1100, Washington, D.C. 20005; (202) 898-2400. The ad hoc coalition of 70 patient, provider and consumer-advocacy groups supports the major managed-care reform bill in Congress — the Patient Access to Responsible Care Act (PARCA).

"The insurance companies stay in the background and try to push the Chamber of Commerce into the front. Yes, that will be formidable opposition. The problem is that they don't have the people on their side, and we do."

The coalition's Jan. 21 news conference came on the same day that a health policy study group released the results of a new public opinion poll that indicated widespread but conditional support for many of the provisions included in managed-care bills in Congress and in state legislatures. The survey by the Kaiser Family Foundation and Harvard University found substantial majorities in favor of such proposals as allowing people to appeal to an independent reviewer, to see a specialist or to sue health plans directly.

The survey also indicated, however, that public support for those ideas drops significantly if people are asked about the consequences forecast by opponents: higher premiums

and reduced health insurance coverage. (*See poll, p. 111.*)

"Support may fall if the public comes to see [the proposals] as part of a larger government health-reform plan that could result in employers dropping coverage of higher health insurance premiums," Drew Altman, president of the Kaiser Family Foundation, told reporters.

Many of the major companies in the industry have been very profitable during the past decade, but last year some of the biggest — including Kaiser, Aetna and Oxford Health Plans Inc. — reported losses. [35] The pressure on the industry has eased somewhat because of the slowing pace of health-care inflation; the government estimates that health-care costs rose a modest 4.4 percent in 1996 — the lowest increase since the annual survey began in 1960. [36]

Even so, some insurers are starting to raise premiums now in anticipation of accelerating increases in health-care costs over the next few years. [37]

The cost debate will turn in part on which side manages to convince the public that it has "credible experts" on its side, according to Altman and Blendon. The debate has also produced the first set of dueling studies on the issue. *(See story, p. 114.)* One study prepared for the insurance-business coalition projected a 23 percent increase in health insurance premiums if the Norwood-D'Amato bill were enacted. But a rival study for the Patient Access to Responsible Care Alliance forecast a "slight increase" in managed care premiums of from 0.7 to 2.6 percent. [38]

"We're about to engage in the latest of our great wars of spin," Altman says. "The debate at this stage is very much up for grabs."

In Minnesota, however, Dianne Shea believes that the debate over patients' rights should not turn on costs. "This is the richest country in the world, and we're arguing about how to provide health care for everyone," she says. "Isn't it the right of every American to have health care?"

"We've come up with a solution to every problem in this country," Shea concludes. "I know we can come up with a way to provide good health care to people." ∎

Notes

[1] The American Association of Health Plans reported that nearly 150 million Americans belonged to managed-care plans at the end of 1995, the most recent year surveyed: 58.2 million in HMOs and 91 million in preferred provider organizations (PPOs). See "1995 AAHP HMO and PPO Trends Report." An annual survey of employer-provided health-benefit plans released last month shows that the percentage of employees enrolled in managed-care plans rose in 1996 and 1997. See Mercer/Foster Higgins "National Survey of Employer-Sponsored Health Plans." In his State of the Union address on Jan. 27, Presi-

dent Clinton said that 160 million Americans are in managed-care plans today.

[2] The 8th U.S. Circuit Court of Appeals ruled on Feb. 26, 1997, in *Shea v. Esensten* that the suit could proceed. The court ruled that Shea could sue her HMO under the federal benefits protection law known as ERISA for failing to disclose its system for reimbursing doctors.

[3] For background, see "Managed Care," *The CQ Researcher*, April 12, 1996, pp. 313-336.

[4] See *The Dallas Morning News*, Dec. 23, 1997, p. 1C and *The Washington Post*, Dec. 20, 1997, p. D1.

[5] For background on the debate over medical malpractice litigation, see "Too Many Lawsuits," *The CQ Researcher*, May 22, 1992, pp. 433-456.

[6] For background, see Barry R. Furrow, "Managed Care Organizations and Patient Injury: Rethinking Liability," *Georgia Law Review*, Vol. 31, winter 1997, pp. 419-509, and Clark C. Havighurst, "Making Health Plans Accountable for the Quality of Care," *ibid.*, pp. 587-647.

[7] For background, see *Congressional Quarterly Weekly Report*, Nov. 1, 1997, pp. 2682-2684.

[8] PBS, "The NewsHour With Jim Lehrer," Sept. 16, 1997.

[9] See *The New York Times*, Sept. 10, 1997, p. A1.

[10] See *The New York Times*, Sept. 12, 1997, p. A24.

[11] PBS, "The NewsHour With Jim Lehrer," Sept. 16, 1997.

[12] For background, see "Medical Screening Raises Privacy Concerns," *The CQ Researcher*, Nov. 19, 1993, p. 1023. For opposing views on the issue, see *USA Today*, April 19, 1996, p. 13A.

[13] See *USA Today*, Jan. 20, 1998, p. 1A.

[14] Quoted in *The Washington Post*, Sept. 12, 1997, p. A1.

[15] Some background is drawn from Paul Starr, *The Social Transformation of American Medicine: The Rise of a Sovereign Profession and the Making of a Vast Industry* (1982).

[16] See *ibid.*, p. 334.

[17] *Ibid.*, pp. 369-370.

[18] Some of this material can also be found in "Managed Care," *The CQ Researcher*, April 12, 1996, pp. 324-327.

[19] Starr, *op. cit.*, p. 395.

[20] See 1973 *Congressional Quarterly Almanac*, pp. 499-507.

[21] See 1976 *Congressional Quarterly Almanac*, pp. 544-548, and 1978 *Congressional Quarterly Almanac*, pp. 576-580.

[22] Starr, *op. cit.*, p. 415.

[23] Details of the Fox and Adams case, along

with citations to contemporaneous news accounts, can be found in George Anders, *Health Against Wealth: HMOs and the Breakdown of Medical Trust* (1996). Health Net had argued in the Fox case that the bone marrow transplant was not covered because it was an experimental procedure; Kaiser contended that it provided proper care in the Adams case.

[24] See "Sick People in Managed Care Have Difficulty Getting Services and Treatment," Robert Wood Johnson Foundation, June 28, 1995.

[25] Anders, *op. cit.*, pp. 42, 47.

[26] See 1996 *Congressional Quarterly Almanac*, pp. 10-85. The provision was included in the fiscal 1997 appropriations bill for the Veterans Administration, Department of Housing and Urban Development and other agencies. For a critical view of the impact of the law, see *Newsweek*, Aug. 4, 1997, p. 65.

[27] See *The New York Times*, Feb. 2, 1997, p. A1.

[28] Lewin Group, "Managed Care Savings for Employers and Households: 1990 through 2000," June 24, 1997.

[29] The task force's report can be found on its home page at http://www.chipp.cah-wnet.gov/mctf. For background, see *Los Angeles Times*, Dec. 31, 1997, p. A1, and *The New York Times*, Jan. 6, 1998, p. A1.

[30] See *Los Angeles Times*, Aug. 6, 1997, p. A3; Aug. 7, 1997, p. A22.

[31] For background on the initiatives, see *Los Angeles Times*, Nov. 1, 1996, p. D1; Oct. 7, 1996, p. A1.

[32] Kasich's letter was first publicized in *Congress Daily*, Jan. 6, 1998.

[33] For background, see *Congressional Quarterly Weekly Report*, Nov. 22, 1997, pp. 2909-2911.

[34] See *The New York Times*, Jan. 22, 1998, p. A18, and *The Wall Street Journal*, Jan. 22, 1998, p. A20.

[35] See *The Wall Street Journal*, Dec. 22, 1997, p. A1 (Kaiser) and *The Washington Post*, Jan. 4, 1998 (Aetna, Oxford).

[36] *The Washington Post*, Jan. 13, 1998, p. A1. The figures are from the Health Care Financing Administration's National Health Statistics Group; *The Wall Street Journal*, reporting the same study, described the increase as "an inflation-adjusted 1.9 percent."

[37] See *The New York Times*, Jan. 11, 1998, p. A1.

[38] Milliman & Robertson, Inc., "Actuarial Analysis of the Patient Access to Responsible Care Act (PARCA)," released Jan. 21, 1998; Muse & Associates, "The Health Premium Impact of H.R. 1415/S.644, the Patient Access to Responsible Care Act (PARCA)," Jan. 29, 1998.

Bibliography

Selected Sources Used

Books

Anders, George, *Health Against Wealth: HMOs and the Breakdown of Medical Trust*, Houghton Mifflin, 1996.

Anders, a reporter for *The Wall Street Journal*, provides a strongly written, critical account of the impact of health maintenance organizations on patients' rights. The book includes detailed source notes.

Annas, George J., *The Rights of Patients: The Basic ACLU Guide to Patient Rights* [2d ed.], Humana Press, 1989.

This American Civil Liberties Union handbook, updated in 1989, gives an overview of patients' rights in such areas as informed consent, medical records, privacy and confidentiality and medical malpractice. The book includes source notes and an eight-page list of organizations and other references. Annas is a professor of health law at Boston University's schools of medicine and public health.

Goodman, John C., and Gerald L. Musgrave, *Patient Power: Solving America's Health Care Crisis*, Cato Institute, 1992.

Goodman and Musgrave argue strongly that the country's health-care "crisis" calls for free-market solutions — reducing government regulation, diminishing the role of insurance and giving individual consumers and patients greater responsibility for paying for their health care. Goodman is president of the National Center for Policy Analysis, a free-market think tank in Dallas; Musgrave is president of Economics America Inc., a consulting firm in Ann Arbor, Mich.

Patel, Kent, and Mark E. Rushefsky, *Health Care Policies and Policy in America*, M.E. Sharpe, 1995.

The book gives an overview of contemporary health-care issues. It also includes a brief chronology (1798-1995) and a 23-page bibliography. Patel and Rushefsky are professors of political science at Southwest Missouri State University.

Starr, Paul, *The Social Transformation of American Medicine: The Rise of a Sovereign Profession and the Making of a Vast Industry*, Basic Books, 1982.

This widely praised study traces the history of the U.S. medical profession and health-care system from the 1700s through the birth and emerging growth of managed care in the 1970s and early '80s. Starr, a professor of sociology at Princeton University, has been an adviser to President Clinton on health-care policy. The book includes detailed source notes.

White, Joseph, *Competing Solutions: American Health Care Proposals and International Experience*, Brookings Institution, 1995.

White compares the U.S. health-care system with those in other countries, including Australia, Canada, France, Germany, Great Britain and Japan. He is a research associate in governmental studies at the Brookings Institution.

Articles:

Langdon, Steve, "Critics Want More 'Management' of Managed Care Industry," *Congressional Quarterly Weekly Report*, March 15, 1997, pp. 633-640.

The article provides an overview of legislative developments on managed care at the start of the 105th Congress, along with summaries of major bills, legislative activity in selected states and a glossary.

Reports and Studies

Advisory Commission on Consumer Protection and Quality in the Health Care Industry, *Consumer Bill of Rights and Responsibilities: Report to the President of the United States*, November 1997.

The 72-page report by the 34-member commission appointed by President Clinton contains recommendations dealing with such issues as choice of providers and health plans, complaints and appeals and confidentiality of health information. A list of references and selected reading are included.

Computer Science and Telecommunications Board, National Research Council, *For the Record: Protecting Electronic Health Information*, National Academy Press, 1997.

This book-length report details a scientific panel's findings and recommendations on protections for electronic health information. The book includes an 11-page bibliography as well as detailed source notes.

Kaiser Family Foundation/Harvard University, "National Survey of Americans' Views on Managed Care," Nov. 5, 1997; "National Survey of Americans' Views on Consumer Protections in Managed Care," Jan. 21, 1998.

The first survey found that majorities of the public are concerned about key aspects of managed health care. The second found majority support for many of the major reform proposals currently being debated, but support dropped when people were asked about potential consequences of changes, such as higher insurance premiums.

The Next Step

Additional information from UMI's Newspaper & Periodical Abstracts™ database

Genetic Testing

Gollaher, David, "The Paradox of Genetic Privacy," *The New York Times*, Jan. 7, 1998, p. A19.

Genetic testing, despite its promise, is provoking a sense of moral crisis in the United States. In the popular imagination, genes are thought to contain the code to an individual's fate, and the idea that someone might crack our personal code and use it against us is unsettling. Our fears, however, are producing a spate of ill-advised laws that will have serious unintended consequences in America's private insurance industry.

"Insurers' Use of Gene Tests: Curbs on Abuse Are Needed; Congress is right to seek safeguards for high-tech data," *Los Angeles Times*, Nov. 1, 1997, p. B7.

The practice of using genetic information to determine whether to insure people and how much to charge them is actually becoming popular among health and life insurers. There are 450 tests now available to determine people's susceptibility to diseases like Alzheimer's, Huntington's and breast cancer, and insurers are eager to employ the tests for risk assessment.

Health-Care Costs

Freudenheim, Milt, "Progress on Health Costs, But Nagging Woes Persist," *The New York Times*, Jan. 5, 1998, p. D10.

Most Americans are members of managed-care plans, often for-profit health maintenance organizations (HMOs) that try to keep profits growing to please Wall Street. But the growth of managed care has not reduced costs enough to help millions of people who feel that they cannot afford insurance.

"HMO Laws: a Middle Road," *Los Angeles Times*, Jan. 5, 1998, p. B4.

Managed care, once regarded as a sure way of controlling health-care costs, became strikingly unmanageable in 1997. Leading HMOs posted dismal earnings, and over half of the nation's 650 HMOs lost money. Forty states passed laws that guaranteed certain medical services, while competition kept a lid on premium increases.

Hilzenrath, David S., "Large Firms Paying More for Health Care; Survey Shows 4 Percent Rise This Year, Bigger in '99," *The Washington Post*, Jan. 7, 1998, p. D11.

Health-care cost increases are accelerating at big corporations, according to a study released yesterday. Corporate managers are predicting even steeper increases next year, on the order of 7 percent for managed-care plans and 9 percent for conventional health insurance, according to the survey by Towers Perrin, a consulting firm that advises businesses on employee benefits.

HMOs and Legislation

Goldstein, Amy, "Clinton Backs 'Bill of Rights' For Patients; President to Seek Law To Enforce Standards," *The Washington Post*, Nov. 20, 1997, p. A1.

Clinton will propose federal legislation to create a broad new set of government standards aimed at guaranteeing Americans better care and more clout in the nation's changing health-care system, according to White House officials. The officials said that Clinton plans to give his full endorsement to a health care "bill of rights" that would assure insured patients easier access to treatment, more information to help them select health plans and doctors and new ways to appeal if they are dissatisfied with their care.

"Health Care New Rules Would Help Consumers," *St. Louis Post-Dispatch*, Jan. 5, 1998, p. B6.

In the last legislative session, Missouri lawmakers passed a progressive managed-care reform law — HB 335 — giving patients the right to hold HMOs accountable through medical malpractice lawsuits. This law affects the 1.3 million Missourians who get care through 33 HMOs. To their credit, most HMOs already comply with many of the proposed regulations.

McGinley, Laurie, "Panel's Prescription for Quality Care Will Be Core of Health-System Overhaul," *The Wall Street Journal*, Oct. 21, 1997, p. B19.

President Clinton is poised to endorse a broad range of patient protections being developed by an advisory panel charged with improving the quality of managed health care, administration officials said. Beefed-up consumer guarantees are the next logical move in the president's step-by-step effort to alter the nation's health-care system, aides said. The panel's recommendations will become the core of a legislative proposal that will be one of the administration's top priorities next year.

Miller, Andy, "Norwood urges new standards for managed care health plans," *Atlanta Constitution*,

Oct. 23, 1997, p. A15.

U.S. Rep. Charlie Norwood, R-Ga., has sponsored the most visible of a handful of bills in Congress that would clamp new federal rules on HMOs and other network plans. To support his bill the results of a national poll were unveiled at a Washington news conference. The survey, commissioned by consumer and medical groups, found that nine out of 10 Americans support various significant reforms within managed-care health plans.

Rubin, Alissa J., "Panel to Propose 'Bill of Rights' for Health Care; Treatment: Clinton is likely to embrace patient protections as political debate over managed plans grows," *Los Angeles Times*, Nov. 19, 1997, p. A1.

A presidential commission will propose a far-reaching health care "bill of rights" that could begin to swing the balance of power away from managed-care companies and back toward patients.

Managed Care and Doctors

Krauthammer, Charles, "Driving the Best Doctors Away; Physicians are getting hammered by managed care micromanagement and malpractice insurance premiums," *The Washington Post*, Jan. 9, 1998, p. A21.

While President Clinton is blithely proposing a huge expansion of the teetering Medicare program, there is a looming health-care crisis that has yet to show up on radar. It is not reflected in statistics because it is just beginning to unfold: We are about to lose a whole generation of our most skilled and senior doctors to early retirement.

Tuft, Carolyn, "Medical Society President Attacks Managed Care Plans as Being 'Destructive of Trust.' She Calls Them 'an Immoral Force,' " *St. Louis Post-Dispatch*, Jan. 11, 1998, p. C6.

Dr. K. Lynne Moritz, president of the St. Louis Metropolitan Medical Society, began her term by declaring war against managed care — which she called "a fraud upon the American public." In her speech, Moritz said that managed care — including health maintenance organizations (HMOs) — has diverted money away from patient treatment and into the pockets of insurance stockholders and administrators.

Medical Records and Privacy

Hymowitz, Carol, "Health Care: Psychotherapy Patients Pay a Price for Privacy — To Skirt Scrutiny, Some Refuse to File Insurance Claims," *The Wall Street Journal*, Jan. 22, 1998, p. B1.

Under managed care, therapists must file reports about their patients to case managers, who review the clinician's observations and recommend a treatment plan before approving insurance benefits. Therapists also must submit frequent progress reports, and sometimes even share their notes about what patients have confided to them.

Lore, Diane, "Carter gathering focuses on privacy of mental records," *Atlanta Constitution*, Nov. 20, 1997, p. D1.

The 13th annual Rosalynn Carter Symposium on Mental Health Policy focused on the confidentiality and appropriate use of mental health records. Former first lady Rosalynn Carter, a leading mental health advocate for more than two decades, answered questions about the issue.

Parsons, Christi, "State Justices Take a Swipe at Tort Reform Law," *Chicago Tribune*, Nov. 21, 1997, p 1.

Knocking down what it deemed an unreasonable invasion of privacy, the Illinois Supreme Court on Thursday overturned provisions in a state law that give defendants access to the medical records of people filing personal injury suits against them.

"Pursuing Medical Privacy," *The Washington Post*, Nov. 3, 1997, p. A20.

Though alarm is now widespread about the erosion of privacy for medical data — especially the ever-more-prevalent swapping of electronic medical records among doctors, hospitals and insurers — it's far from obvious how to curb the erosion while restoring patients' trust in the safety of their files.

Medicare

"Changes in Medicare," *The Denver Post*, Jan. 6, 1998, p. B8.

Medicare serves 38 million people over the age of 65 and costs in excess of $200 billion in annual revenue. It is like a lumbering railroad train that can neither be stopped or turned around quickly. Now, however, thanks in part to the Clinton administration and to the Republican-controlled Congress, a series of small but important changes in the program are under way.

McGinley, Laurie, "Medicare plans to unveil rules to fight fraud," *The Wall Street Journal*, Jan. 19, 1998, p. A6.

Medicare officials are scheduled to propose rules tomorrow that would crack down on fraud and abuse by companies that supply long-lasting medical equipment such as wheelchairs. In the last few years, the Medicare agency, part of the Department of Health and Human Services, has targeted so-called durable medical equipment, along with home health care, as ripe for potential fraud and abuse.

"The Extension of Medicare," *The Boston Globe*, Jan. 9, 1998, p. A18.

President Clinton's proposal to expand Medicare coverage to people between 55 and 65 is worth supporting despite the quick dismissal offered by Republican leaders. The plan would provide an important insurance option to many on the cusp between full-time work and retirement.

Back Issues

Great Research on Current Issues Starts Right Here . . . Recent topics covered by The CQ Researcher are listed below. Before May 1991, reports were published under the name of Editorial Research Reports.

JULY 1996
Recovered-Memory Debate
Native Americans' Future
Crackdown on Sexual Harassment
Attack on Public Schools

AUGUST 1996
Fighting Over Animal Rights
Privatizing Government Services
Child Labor and Sweatshops
Cleaning Up Hazardous Wastes

SEPTEMBER 1996
Gambling Under Attack
The States and Federalism
Civic Journalism
Reassessing Foreign Aid

OCTOBER 1996
Political Consultants
Insurance Fraud
Rethinking School Integration
Parental Rights

NOVEMBER 1996
Global Warming
Clashing Over Copyright
Consumer Debt
Governing Washington, D.C.

Back issues are available for $5.00 (sub-scribers) or $10.00 (non-subscribers). Quantity discounts apply to orders over ten. To order, call Congressional Quarterly Customer Service at (202) 887-8621.

Binders are available for $18.00. To order call 1-800-638-1710. Please refer to stock number 648.

DECEMBER 1996
Welfare, Work and the States
The New Volunteerism
Implementing the Disabilities Act
America's Pampered Pets

JANUARY 1997
Combating Scientific Misconduct
Restructuring the Electric Industry
The New Immigrants
Chemical and Biological Weapons

FEBRUARY 1997
Assisting Refugees
Alternative Medicine's Next Phase
Independent Counsels
Feminism's Future

MARCH 1997
New Air Quality Standards
Alcohol Advertising
Civic Renewal
Educating Gifted Students

APRIL 1997
Declining Crime Rates
The FBI Under Fire
Gender Equity in Sports
Space Program's Future

MAY 1997
The Stock Market
The Cloning Controversy
Expanding NATO
The Future of Libraries

JUNE 1997
FDA Reform
China After Deng
Line-Item Veto
Breast Cancer

JULY 1997
Transportation Policy
Executive Pay
School Choice Debate
Aggressive Driving

AUGUST 1997
Age Discrimination
Banning Land Mines
Children's Television
Evolution vs. Creationism

SEPTEMBER 1997
Caring for the Dying
Mental Health Policy
Mexico's Future
Youth Fitness

OCTOBER 1997
Urban Sprawl in the West
Diversity in the Workplace
Teacher Education
Contingent Work Force

NOVEMBER 1997
Renewable Energy
Artificial Intelligence
Religious Persecution
Roe v. Wade at 25

DECEMBER 1997
Whistleblowers
Castro's Next Move
Gun Control Standoff
Regulating Nonprofits

JANUARY 1998
Foster Care Reform
IRS Reform
The Black Middle Class
U.S.-British Relations

Future Topics

▶ *Deflation Fears*

▶ *Caring for the Elderly*

▶ *Corporate Philanthropy*

The CQ Researcher

PUBLISHED BY CONGRESSIONAL QUARTERLY INC.

Deflation Fears

Are falling prices a bigger threat than inflation?

Just when Americans were ready to declare victory in the war against inflation, a new potential enemy has appeared: deflation. Some economists, citing both long-term changes in the global economy and the current economic crisis in Asia, warn that the U.S. faces a greater danger today that prices might fall uncontrollably than that they will start climbing again. Many economists dismiss such fears, and insist that inflation remains the greater hazard. But jitters over the continuing financial turmoil in Asia have led theoreticians and policy-makers to re-examine some basic assumptions about how the U.S. and global economies work. In particular, they wonder whether businesses and financial institutions are equipped to avert the problems that can arise from falling prices — including higher unemployment and bankruptcy.

CQ   Feb. 13, 1998 • Volume 8, No. 6 • Pages 121-144

Formerly Editorial Research Reports

THE ISSUES

BACKGROUND

CURRENT SITUATION

OUTLOOK

SIDEBARS AND GRAPHICS

FOR FURTHER RESEARCH

COVER: TRADERS AT THE PHILIPPINE STOCK EXCHANGE IN MANILA REACT TO A SELLOFF ON WALL STREET AND ASIAN MARKETS ON OCT. 28, 1997. (REUTERS)

CQ Researcher

February 13, 1998
Volume 8, No. 6

EDITOR
Sandra Stencel

MANAGING EDITOR
Thomas J. Colin

ASSOCIATE EDITOR
Sarah M. Magner

STAFF WRITERS
Mary H. Cooper
Kenneth Jost
David Masci

PRODUCTION EDITOR
Melissa Hall

EDITORIAL ASSISTANT
Vanessa E. Furlong

PUBLISHED BY
Congressional Quarterly Inc.

CHAIRMAN
Andrew Barnes

VICE CHAIRMAN
Andrew P. Corty

PRESIDENT AND PUBLISHER
Robert W. Merry

EXECUTIVE EDITOR
David Rapp

Bibliographic records and abstracts included in The Next Step section of this publication are the copyrighted material of UMI, and are used with permission.

The CQ Researcher (ISSN 1056-2036). Formerly Editorial Research Reports. Published weekly, except Jan. 2, May 29, July 3, Oct. 30, by Congressional Quarterly Inc., 1414 22nd St., N.W., Washington, D.C. 20037. Annual subscription rate for libraries, businesses and government is $340. Additional rates furnished upon request. Periodicals postage paid at Washington, D.C., and additional mailing offices. POSTMASTER: Send address changes to The CQ Researcher, 1414 22nd St., N.W., Washington, D.C. 20037.

Deflation Fears

BY CHRISTOPHER CONTE

THE ISSUES

To some economists, last year's 1.2 percent drop in wholesale prices was like a warning shot across the bow of the American economy.

"In the new era, the risk is deflation, not inflation," warns Edward C. Yardeni, chief economist for the investment banking firm Deutsche Morgan Grenfell.

For a generation of Americans who have grown accustomed to seeing prices increase year after year, it is hard to imagine that overall prices could turn downward, but a number of economists agree with Yardeni. They cite, among other things, plunging prices for manufactured goods ranging from semiconductors to toys, sharp drops in real estate and stock markets throughout Asia and falling prices for commodities like gold, which some analysts consider a good gauge of future price trends.

Many economists dismiss fears of deflation — which is defined as a general decline in the price of goods and services. In fact, they argue that the underlying economic forces still point toward renewed inflation rather than deflation. But these analysts concede that prices have been unexpectedly calm.

As a result, economists have begun to ask whether the United States could be more vulnerable than they thought to the risks associated with stagnant or falling prices — risks such as declining corporate profits, rising debt burdens, tumbling prices for stocks and real estate, faltering financial institutions and rising unemployment. If financial institutions and policy-makers don't understand these risks and prepare for them, a downturn in prices could push the economy into a recession, they say.

If overall prices do start falling in the United States, it would represent a major turn in economic history. The nation last experienced deflation in 1954, when the Consumer Price Index (CPI) dropped 0.5 percent. But there hasn't been a severe case of deflation since the Depression. At its worst point, from 1929 to 1933, prices fell, on average, 6.7 percent per year. [1]

Economists have differing explanations for why deflation could be a problem in the near future. Many note that prices are dropping around the world for a broad swath of raw materials and for manufactured goods ranging from automobiles to semiconductors. This, they argue, suggests that global supply is climbing much more rapidly than demand. "Thanks to a building binge throughout Asia, continuing economic expansion in the U.S. and the recovering economies in Europe, production everywhere is running ahead of consumption," *Business Week* magazine warned last November. [2]

The imbalance has been magnified because demand for goods and services is relatively slack in the advanced, industrial countries. "In Europe and the U.S., population growth has slowed down," says Neil Johnson, an economic consultant based in Toronto, Canada. "And with populations aging in Japan, Europe and the U.S., more people are becoming concerned about preserving

their assets," and thus are saving more and spending less.

Some economists view government policy as a more important factor. Eager to keep inflation under control, the United States, Europe, Japan and Canada all have been restraining growth in the money supply, and they may have gone too far, these analysts say. Supply-side economist Jude Wanniski is probably the most fervent advocate of this view. *(See story, p. 128.)* Wanniski contends the Federal Reserve is not providing enough money to meet the needs of the economy. He says this "shortage of liquidity" is driving down prices and could bankrupt many enterprises. "The [economy] is trying to finance sound transactions, but cannot," he says.

Whatever the cause of deflation, economists generally agree that falling prices, by themselves, do not necessarily pose a serious economic threat. If price declines are mild, companies can cope with disappointing earnings by cutting costs, improving productivity or increasing sales. But a steep decline in prices could be more troublesome because companies operating close to the margin could see their profits disappear altogether.

Deflation would be most worrisome, though, if it spreads to banks. In a serious bout of deflation, many debtors may find themselves unable to pay back their loans. At the same time, steep declines in real estate and stock prices could reduce the value of assets that banks hold as collateral. Ultimately, the losses might leave banks unable to extend new loans, even to creditworthy borrowers. That could send the economy into a tailspin.

"It is possible to imagine a vicious circle developing between falling asset prices, falling prices in the shops, rising real debt levels and downwardly spiralling expectations, reminiscent of what

Continued on p. 125

Are We There Yet?

Has the U.S. economy entered a deflationary period? Judging from the Consumer Price Index (CPI), the most commonly used measure of price changes, it appears to be close but not quite there. The CPI rose 1.7 percent in 1997, about half as much as it had climbed the previous year. This seemed to continue a long-term trend; overall price increases have been slowing since 1980. (*See graph.*)

But while most economists believe the CPI is the best gauge of inflation, they admit it isn't perfect. In fact, the evidence suggests the United States is probably much closer to an overall decline in prices than the index suggests.

In 1996, a group of experts appointed by the Senate Finance Committee concluded that the CPI overstates increases in the cost of living by about 1.1 percentage points — and possibly by as much as 1.6 percentage points. If that is true, last year's 1.7 percent increase in the CPI actually could have represented an increase of just 0.6 percent or, if the upward bias is as high as the panel believes possible, an almost invisible 0.1 percent rise.

The Boskin Commission, as it was known, cited several reasons why the CPI may overstate the actual increase in living costs.[1] First, it noted that the CPI measures changes in the price of a fixed "basket" of goods, and therefore fails to capture the common consumer practice of substituting cheaper goods for more expensive ones when prices rise.

Perhaps the most important failing of the CPI may be that it does not account for improvements in the quality of goods. A refrigerator may cost more today than it did 10 years ago, for instance, but it probably is more energy efficient. Some of the price increase, then, reflects the fact that consumers are getting something more than they did in the past. Similarly, medical care is certainly more expensive than it used to be, but a significant portion of the higher cost reflects the fact that doctors and hospitals can test for and treat afflictions they could not handle in the past.

The challenge of measuring price changes becomes even greater when one considers that new products are coming to market at an unprecedented pace. How can statisticians compare the price of a computer today with the price of one manufactured even a year or two ago that had considerably fewer capabilities?

Federal Reserve Chairman Alan Greenspan pondered these issues in a speech on Jan. 3. "For most purposes, biases of a few tenths in annual inflation rates do not matter when inflation is high," Greenspan noted. "They do matter when, as now, inflation has become so low that policy-makers need to consider at what point effective price stability has been reached."[2]

Greenspan, along with many economists, believes the economy's current condition can best be described as "disinflation," not deflation. Disinflation is defined as a situation where the overall price level is still increasing, but at a slower rate than it previously had.

The Fed chairman's interest is more than academic. If the economy slips into deflation, the central bank might find it more difficult to respond adequately. One problem is that the Fed cannot reduce interest rates below zero, so it is limited in how far it could go in combating severe deflation.

In addition, the currently happy combination of low inflation and low unemployment might become more difficult to maintain. Workers in the U.S. have accepted very modest wage increases in recent years, but it's doubtful they would acquiesce to outright wage cuts. In a deflationary situation, then, the level of real wages — wages adjusted for price changes — would rise. And that would put employers, already hit by declining prices for their goods, in a financial bind. The result could be an increase in unemployment that the Fed would be powerless to combat.

"A little deflation is worse than a little inflation," concludes James O'Sullivan, a vice president at J.P. Morgan, an international banking company.

Not so, argues Greenspan. Policy-makers should strive to achieve perfect price stability, not a little inflation or a little deflation, he said Jan. 3. Nevertheless, he added, "We central bankers need to better judge how to assess our performance in achieving and maintaining that objective in light of the uncertainties surrounding the accuracy of our measured price indexes."

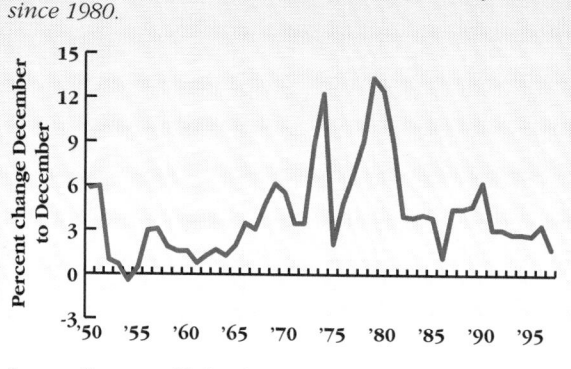

Changes in the Consumer Price Index

Although consumer prices have climbed in every year since 1954, the annual increases have generally slowed since 1980.

Percent change December to December

Source: Bureau of Labor Statistics

---

[1] The committee's chairman was former presidential economic adviser Michael J. Boskin. See *Final Report of the Advisory Commission to Study the Consumer Price Index*, December 1996.

[2] Remarks at the annual meeting of the American Economic Association and the American Finance Association, Chicago, Ill., Jan. 3, 1998; available online at http://www.bog.frb.fed.us.

Continued from p. 123

happened in the 1930s," British economist Roger Bootle writes in his 1997 book, *The Death of Inflation*. "If consumers expect prices to fall, then they defer purchases, which puts more downward pressure on prices. Falling prices raise the real value of debt and force debtors to cut back on their spending. Some debtors inevitably go under, thereby endangering financial institutions and the banking system, which depresses confidence further." [3]

Japan and several developing countries in Asia appear close to this kind of damaging deflation. Thailand, Indonesia, Malaysia and South Korea, for instance, are suffering from excess production capacity. "All the countries there tried to build capacity in the same industries at once, resulting in far too much capacity in such industries as autos and high-tech," says David Wyss, chief economist for Standard & Poor's DRI, an economic consulting and information company. "The problem has been exacerbated by a tendency to build landmark projects, such as high-rise office buildings, that have little economic justification."

Japan and Thailand also have seen speculative booms in real estate turn to busts, with devastating effects on the balance sheets of financial institutions. In Japan, real estate prices have plunged about 65 percent since the bubble burst in the early 1990s. Shares traded on the Japanese stock market have lost almost 60 percent of their value. The Japanese economy has been stagnant in the wake of this "kakadu hakai," or "price destruction," and some analysts believe the country could slip back into recession if sharply diminished investor and consumer confidence produces a very sharp slowdown among its Asian trading partners. [4]

Deflation has hit Asian financial institutions particularly hard. The International Monetary Fund estimates that problem loans at South Korean banks equaled almost 70 percent of the banks' capital at the end of 1996, even after taking account of reserves held to cover possible losses. While reliable information for 1997 isn't yet available, the situation clearly has worsened. In Japan, the 19 largest banks have bad loans totaling an estimated $400 billion, or 14 percent of all their outstanding credit. Insolvent or close to it, many lenders throughout the region are unable to extend loans. [5]

Supply-sider Wanniski likens these institutions to canaries in a mine, arguing they are just the first victims of global deflation. But many others say the Asian financial institutions brought on their own problems by lending lavishly to ventures that lacked economic merit. In South Korea, critics say, banks failed to assess lending risks objectively because they had too many close ties to their corporate borrowers. In Indonesia, loans were channeled to friends and family members of President Suharto regardless of whether the underlying projects made sense economically.

"In too many places, corruption has replaced communism as the greatest threat to world order," says Rep. Jim Leach, R-Iowa, chairman of the House Banking Committee. "In many countries, banks are particularly vulnerable to inside thievery for the same reason Willy Sutton stuck them up from outside — that's where the money is."

In contrast to Asia, the United States appears for the moment to be relatively safe from a devastating downturn in prices. The service sector, which represents about 75 percent of U.S. economic output, faces relatively little foreign competition. Perhaps as a result, prices for services are climbing about 3 percent a year. Because manufacturing represents such a small portion of the economy, prices for manufactured goods would have to drop precipi-

tously to drag down the entire Consumer Price Index, notes James O'Sullivan, a vice president at J.P. Morgan & Co., an international banking company.

Moreover, wages in the U.S. are showing signs of picking up, not declining as one would expect in a deflationary period. The Commerce Department reported that real, or inflation-adjusted, average hourly earnings rose 2.2 percent in 1997, a modest increase but still the largest in a decade.

The money supply also is growing at a healthy pace, suggesting — though not proving — that lack of liquidity may not be a serious problem. One monetary measure, M2, rose at a 5 percent rate in January, its fastest pace since the start of the 1990s, while another, M3, was increasing at an 8 percent clip, the strongest rise since the mid-1980s. * "Deflation will not occur when money supply growth is accelerating," declares Mark Zandi, chief economist for Regional Financial Associates, an economic consulting firm in West Chester, Pa.

Even if prices remain stable or start to decline, U.S. companies appear fairly well-equipped to thrive. After-tax corporate profits were rising at better than a 10 percent annual rate in the third quarter of 1997, the most recent period for which data are available. While final figures for 1997 won't be available from the Commerce Department until March, it appears that corporations chalked up their fifth consecutive year of double-digit profit increases.

In addition, corporate-debt burdens in the U.S. generally are falling. Many

---

* M2 consists of cash and balances in checking and savings accounts, certificates of deposit less than $100,000 and money-market funds. M3 is a broader measure of money, consisting of everything in M2 plus, among other things, large-denomination certificates of deposit and balances held in institutional money-market funds.

companies have taken advantage of strong earnings and the rising stock market to pay back loans, and others have aggressively refinanced their loans at today's lower interest rates. As a result, pretax profits last year totaled almost six times net interest expenses, the highest level in more than 25 years, according to John Lonski of Moody's Investors Service. "You don't see anywhere near as many leveraged buyouts as you did in the late 1980s," Lonski adds. "Today, mergers and acquisitions are much more likely to improve balance sheets."

Similarly, U.S. banks have significantly strengthened their financial position. Partly as a result of tough regulations imposed in the wake of the savings and loan crisis of the 1980s, their ratio of past-due loans and other non-performing assets dropped to less than 1 percent of their total assets in September 1997 from more than 3 percent at the end of 1991. According to the Federal Deposit Insurance Corporation, U.S. banks currently hold almost $2 in reserve for every $1 in problem loans. And while their total 1997 profits have not yet been reported, they appear likely to set a new record, exceeding the previous high mark, $52.4 billion, recorded in 1996. "The U.S. banking system is well-capitalized, and we aren't seeing much speculative activity," says Paul Kasriel, chief U.S. economist for Chicago-based Northern Trust Co.

None of the current economic indicators are conclusive, however. Economists agree that the underlying forces at work today will only show up in the official statistics after a delay of uncertain duration. Moreover, the measures themselves are inexact. Economists generally agree, for instance, that the Consumer Price Index probably overstates the real inflation rate by at least 1 percentage point. (*See story, p. 124.*) The biggest uncertainty, however, involves how

the current world situation will play out. While most economists believe the crisis in Asia will slow the U.S. economy only slightly, nobody knows for sure how long the crisis will last and how widespread its effects will be.

As the situation in Asia demonstrates, the increased integration of the global economy adds another layer of complexity to the challenges policy-makers face. What is the connection between deflationary developments in Asia and current trends in the U.S. economy? What responsibility does the U.S. have to help Asia out of its crisis? And what would be the appropriate policy stance if Asia stands on the brink of serious deflation while the United States still faces a strong threat of renewed inflation? All these issues come into play as policy-makers in the U.S. confront two major policy questions:

Should the Federal Reserve loosen the monetary reins to fight deflation, or keep them tight to prevent inflation?

Federal Reserve Chairman Alan Greenspan has signaled that the central bank stands ready, if necessary, to switch from its long-standing preoccupation with inflation to an anti-deflation stance. "A persistent deflation in the prices of currently produced goods and services — just like a persistent increase in these prices — necessarily is, at its root, a monetary phenomenon," Greenspan told the American Economic Association on Jan. 3. [6]

The Fed chairman discounted the threat of deflation, and he suggested that he would be most worried by a steep drop in real estate or stock prices, which he said might occur for any number of reasons, "some of which may be only tangentially related to the state of the economy and monetary policy." Nevertheless, his statement clearly established that if

the Fed perceives deflation to be a threat, it will ease monetary policy — that is, pump more money into the economy and reduce interest rates — just as it has long battled inflation by constraining the money supply and raising interest rates.

Economists generally agree that easier money is a solution to deflation, though there is some disagreement about how it helps. Traditionalists believe that expanding the money supply increases the level of aggregate demand by encouraging spending. Supply-siders, who say efforts to manipulate demand don't work, argue that loosening the monetary reins simply provides needed liquidity.

In his speech, Greenspan pointedly refused to abandon the view held by most central bank officials that inflation remains the primary economic danger in the United States. The Fed's policy-making arm, the Federal Open Market Committee, summarized this position at a meeting held Sept. 30, 1997. Warning that the economy could not continue growing as fast as it had been without causing prices to rise, and fretting that labor markets were so tight that employers would have to start bidding up wages to attract workers, the panel said, "The risks to the economy [appear] to be strongly tilted toward rising inflation."

Accordingly, the committee voted to maintain interest rates at their current levels but to lean toward tightening monetary policy in the event additional upward pressure on prices became evident. Some participants actually were ready to raise rates immediately, and decided to postpone action only because "a policy tightening was not anticipated at this time and such an action might therefore have unintended adverse effects on financial markets." [7]

Asia's economic troubles changed the equation by diminishing the near-term threat of inflation. "The Asia crisis will produce such a wave of cheap imports that it will have a dampening effect on goods prices," says Dan Laufenberg, chief U.S. economist for American Express Financial Advisers in Minneapolis, Minn. At the same time, economic weakness in Asia will reduce demand for U.S. exports, slowing the U.S. economy and further easing potential pressures on prices here. "Before Asia, the Fed would have had to tighten" monetary policy, suggests Wyss of Standard & Poor's DRI. "This does their job for them."

Many economists, however, believe the good news on inflation will be short-lived. At the December Fed meeting, William Broaddus, president of the Federal Reserve Bank of Atlanta, argued that the central bank should tighten the monetary reins modestly in light of "persisting strength in aggregate demand for goods and services." Broaddus "recognized the case for holding policy steady given recent developments in East Asian economies and financial markets," according to minutes of the meeting. But he argued that a "slight firming" would "provide valuable insurance" against the risk that inflation would accelerate and require "a sharper policy response" later. The majority disagreed, and in fact voted to adopt a "symmetric" policy stance — that is, to be just as ready to ease as to tighten the monetary reins — instead of leaning toward a tighter policy. [8]

Some argue that the Fed should take the threat of deflation more seriously. "The Fed should ease," declares Philip Braverman, chief economist for DKB Securities (USA) Corp. in New York. "It is no longer appropriate to operate on the assumption that just because the U.S. economy is operating at a high rate of capacity, inflation is a threat. We have become part of a global economy, and there is a lot of excess capacity globally. To

fight a rearguard action against a nonexistent enemy [inflation] creates more of a risk of deflation."

Even some economists who believe inflation remains the bigger long-term danger predict that governments may have to abandon the fight against inflation to prevent bankruptcies and financial-system failures in places like South Korea, Thailand and Indonesia from spreading to China or beyond. Stephen Roach,

The financial crisis in Asia has reduced the threat of renewed inflation in the U.S., but Federal Reserve Chairman Alan Greenspan worries that inflationary pressures may soon reappear.

chief economist for the investment banking and securities firm Morgan Stanley Dean Witter, predicts that the Fed and central banks in other advanced, industrial countries will have to reduce interest rates to increase liquidity and keep financial weaknesses from spreading.

While these steps may be necessary to shore up the world's financial system, Roach says, they will leave the global economic system awash in money. The resulting low level of

interest rates will heat up the U.S. economy at just the time restraint will be needed to prevent it from growing too fast, Roach suggests. "We are sewing the seeds of the next inflation," he concludes.

Should the International Monetary Fund rescue Asian countries that face deflation?

While the ultimate responsibility for preventing deflation or inflation may rest with the Federal Reserve and other central banks, the front-line job of fighting today's most serious deflation crisis has fallen to the International Monetary Fund. The IMF last year arranged more than $100 billion in emergency credits to help South Korea, Thailand and Indonesia stay afloat after foreign investors fled those countries amid falling prices and widespread insolvency.

Help from the IMF comes with strings attached. The international organization has exacted commitments from recipient countries to shut down insolvent institutions, to strengthen financial regulation and public disclosure laws, and to open their markets to foreign financial institutions. It also has required countries to tighten monetary policy and drive up interest rates in order to defend their currencies and attract skittish foreign investors back.

IMF programs have been attacked by some for being too lenient and by others for being too stringent. Critics who say the organization is too indulgent warn that the IMF, in effect, is letting investors and financial institutions that made bad decisions off the hook. This could encourage worse behavior in the future, these critics contend.

"A free-market economy has a very efficient way of dealing with misjudgment, excess and failure. It's called bankruptcy," argues James K. Glassman, a resident fellow at the

In Wanniski's School of Economics ...

In an era of economic uncertainty — of money that is worth one thing today and something else tomorrow, of fluctuating exchange rates, of economic theories that often fail to predict what will happen or when it will happen — is there any reliable guidepost for policy-makers?

Jude Wanniski, a former *Wall Street Journal* editor, economic consultant and leading proponent of "supply-side" economics, [1] believes he has found one, and it's as old as the hills: gold. Unfortunately, he complains, almost nobody else — not even his philosophical compatriots — fully appreciates its importance. As a result, he contends, policy-makers have been fiddling while a serious, deflationary fire has started to burn.

Though his background is in journalism, Wanniski considers himself a "classical" economist. In his world, gold is a "proxy for everything that has a price," a universal yardstick for measuring the value of things. "All you need to know about gold is that from the dawn of civilization, it has been used by ordinary people to measure other goods and services," he says. "It has been the numeraire, and it still is."

Money, on the other hand, can rise and fall in value depending on government policy. If a government prints too much money — that is, more than people actually need to carry out the myriad transactions that make up the economy — prices rise and you have inflation. In this situation, the value of money declines, since each dollar will buy less today than it did yesterday. On the other hand, if the government does not print enough money, prices fall and you have deflation. Deflation implies a rising value of money since each dollar will buy more today than it did yesterday.

Since the real value of gold does not change, Wanniski argues, fluctuations in its dollar price indicate whether policy-makers are printing too much or too little money. In his view, a rising price of gold indicates there is too much money in circulation; unless the government removes this "surplus liquidity," all prices will ratchet up. A falling price of gold, on the other hand, indicates that there is too little money in circulation; unless the government prints money to offset this "shortage of liquidity," prices will fall. [2]

Beginning in late 1996, the price of gold started falling from around $385 an ounce; by the end of 1997, the price had dropped below $300 an ounce. Wanniski had begun warning that the economy was entering a deflationary period around February 1997. As the financial crisis unfolded in Asia later in the year, he claimed vindication for his theories.

According to Wanniski, Asia's problems were made in America. In the early 1990s, he says, the dollar price of gold rose from $350 to $385, suggesting there was too much money in circulation. (Wanniski says tax increases in 1993 had reduced demand for money, [3] and that the Federal Reserve failed to mop up the resulting excess.) Asian countries that tied their currencies to the dollar had to inflate to maintain parity with the dollar, and Asian banks, in turn, "were forced" to push the resulting surplus of reserves into risky loans.

The price of gold started falling in late 1996, signaling there now was a shortage of money. (Wanniski says the shortage became more acute when Congress approved tax cuts in 1997.) Asian central banks had to withdraw money

American Enterprise Institute and a columnist for *The Washington Post*. "Lenders, investors, managers and sometimes employees and politicians all take part of the hit — and assets pass from weak hands to strong. Everyone learns important lessons and starts afresh. But by rushing to the rescue, the IMF is preventing this cleansing process." [9]

The IMF's supporters reply that the Asia crisis has swelled far beyond the lenders and borrowers who made bad investments. The sudden and massive withdrawal of investors from Asia has "the hallmarks of a classic market mania," a panic that damages well-managed companies and financial institutions along with poorly run ones, argues Laura D'Andrea Tyson, an economist at the University of California at Berkeley and former eco-

nomic adviser to President Clinton.

Only government action, Tyson adds, can correct such a problem. "Once destabilized, markets are not self-equilibrating," she says. "Government intervention is required to provide the public good of monetary stability on which normal economic transactions depend." She adds that the United States has "substantial economic, democracy and security inter-

... Gold Is The Answer

from the system to push their currencies down along with the dollar, a move that choked off those who had borrowed a few years earlier when funds were more readily available.

Why is Wanniski almost alone in this analysis? For one thing, many analysts doubt his assertion that gold is a perfectly reliable indicator of price trends. "Gold moves for a lot of reasons other than whether there's inflation or deflation," argues Frederick Mishkin, an economist at Columbia University's Graduate School of Business. "Its price is influenced by what's happening in our ability to mine it and the cost of doing so, what [non-monetary] uses it can be put to and whether central banks want to hold it or not."

The latter point may be especially important. Central banks hold huge stockpiles of gold, but they have no real use for them since governments do not back their currencies with gold anymore. As a result, central banks have been shedding their gold supplies; governments sold about 6 percent of their gold holdings between 1989 and 1996, contributing to gold's slide in value from an all-time high of $850 an ounce in 1980. [4]

Even if gold is a good gauge of whether inflationary or deflationary pressures are present in the economy, it's unclear what the optimum or equilibrium price of gold should be. Federal Reserve Chairman Alan Greenspan, who at times has said a rising price of gold can signal incipient inflation, noted at a 1997 congressional hearing that the price of gold, despite falling that year, remained nine times higher than it was a generation ago. [5]

Wanniski, for his part, suggests that $350 would be the optimal price of gold; he admits the figure is a bit subjective, but notes that gold has averaged about $350 an ounce since 1975, suggesting that debtors and creditors have become "comfortable" with that price.

Many U.S. analysts — including Wanniski's supply-side compatriots — dismiss his warnings about deflation because falling prices do not seem to be causing much trouble in the United States, at least not yet. They blame Asia's problems on unsound banking practices, not on mistakes

by the Federal Reserve. "By general agreement among practically all my supply-side colleagues, the economic wreckage around the world that [I] attribute to the Fed's deflation is being attributed to a general outbreak of stupidity among Asian and Latin bankers," Wanniski complains.

Eventually, Wanniski believes, the deflationary disease may spread to the point that Federal Reserve policy-makers cannot ignore it. At that point, they will add money to the system, he predicts. But in the meantime, a lot of deflationary dislocation could be avoided, he says, if the central bank simply would maintain a constant dollar price for gold.

Life would be simpler for central bankers, too, he maintains. They would not have to try to figure out whether aggregate supply and demand are in balance, whether labor markets are too tight to sustain stable wages, whether rising productivity is increasing the economy's growth potential or most of the other complex issues that preoccupy economists today.

"Gold gives all the power to the marketplace. It is the most democratic of all monetary policies," Wanniski says. "It takes all discretion away from the central bank, which today has too much power over the people of the world." [6]

---

[1] Supply-siders believe traditional economists put too much emphasis on the demand side of the supply-and-demand equation. They say economic policies should focus on maximizing the output of goods and services (primarily through tax policies that reward investment), rather than on increasing or reducing demand.

[2] See Jude Wanniski, "The Optimum Price of Gold," *The Wall Street Journal*, Jan. 7, 1998, p. A22.

[3] For background, see *1993 CQ Almanac*, pp. 107-139.

[4] See Richard W. Stevenson, "The Gold Standard: Spinning Gold Into Dross," *The New York Times*, Dec. 28, 1997; Section 4, p. 5.

[5] Testimony before the House Banking and Financial Services Committee, Nov. 4, 1997.

[6] Wanniski explains his views in detail on his consulting company's Web site: http://www.polyconomics.com/

---

ests in Asia, all of which would be jeopardized by a prolonged depression there." According to Tyson, these interests include preventing financial weakness in Asia from spreading to other emerging markets. [10]

The IMF, for its part, contends that the conditions it imposes on countries it assists are enough to discourage other countries from engaging in risky lending and investment behav-

ior. But another set of critics argues that at least one of those conditions — that countries maintain tight money in order to bolster their currencies — may be exactly the wrong medicine for economies on the brink of runaway deflation.

The IMF contends that loose-money policies in the early 1990s contributed to Asia's problems; it says Thailand, for instance, allowed "over-

heating pressures" to produce large trade deficits and artificial surges in stock prices, or "bubbles." Critics counter that the Asian countries were not living beyond their means. They note that the countries now in trouble all had budget surpluses and low inflation. According to these analysts, trade deficits in these countries reflected softening export prices, not overconsumption, and the run-up in stock and other prices stemmed from huge foreign investment, not from errors in monetary policy.

All this suggests that Asia does not need tight money and some of the other disciplinary actions sought by the IMF, they conclude. "The region does not need wanton budget cutting, credit tightening and emergency bank closures," says Jeffrey D. Sachs, director of the Harvard Institute for International Development. "It needs stable or even slightly expansionary monetary and fiscal policies to counterbalance the decline in foreign loans."

Sachs likens IMF-imposed tight money policies to moves by U.S. banks to tighten credit in 1933 rather than lend money to banks to help them calm frightened crowds that were lining up to withdraw their funds. At the time, close to 10,000 banks suspended operations, lending dried up and the economy spiraled downward into the Depression. If policy-makers today would take the opposite approach, moving to increase liquidity rather than restrict it with higher interest rates and emergency bank closures, Asia's underlying strengths — high savings, budget surpluses, flexible labor markets, low taxation — will reassert themselves and the region will be able quickly to resume rapid economic growth, Sachs contends. [11]

Supply-sider Wanniski agrees that easier money is the answer to Asia's crisis, but he argues that the loosening should begin in Washington at the Federal Reserve. According to Wanniski, the Fed started Asia's tailspin by letting the dollar appreciate in value against gold, and Asian countries imported the deflation because their currencies were tied to the U.S. greenback. Further tightening now will only worsen the situation, he concludes, asserting that IMF Director Michel Camdessus and his deputy, Stanley Fisher, "are a menace to the world." ■

BACKGROUND

The End of Inflation?

Even before the Asia crisis catapulted deflation into the headlines, policy-makers and analysts were debating whether profound economic changes have eliminated the danger of inflation and made declining prices the greater risk today.

The mainstream view holds that inflation may be down, but it definitely isn't out. (*See "At Issue," p. 131.*) In fact, traditionalists believe the U.S. economy is very close to the point at which inflation will be triggered by "excess" demand in the labor market.

Economists use two measures to determine whether there is excess demand. One approach is to compare the actual and "potential" growth rates of the economy. Potential growth is presumed to equal the sum of the growth in the labor force plus any gains in productivity, or output per worker. Currently, the labor force is projected to grow about 1 percent a year, and productivity is thought to be rising somewhere between 1 percent and 1.5 percent. Therefore, the potential growth rate is assumed to be somewhere between 2 percent and 2.5 percent.

The other gauge of excess demand is what economists awkwardly call NAIRU, or the "non-accelerating inflation rate of unemployment." Over time, economists have noted that inflation tends to accelerate when joblessness drops below a certain level. In the decade that ended in the early 1990s, economists generally believed NAIRU was around 6 percent. Since then, they say, it may have slipped to perhaps 5.5 percent, perhaps because of demographic changes, adjustments in government programs (welfare reform, for instance) or other factors.

By either measure, the U.S. economy currently is in the inflation danger zone. Preliminary estimates by the Commerce Department show that the gross domestic product, a standard measure of the size of the nation's economy, rose 3.8 percent last year, well ahead of its presumed long-run potential. The Bureau of Labor Statistics reports that the unemployment rate dropped to just 4.7 percent in December and January, its lowest level since 1969. Yet even though the economy crossed these thresholds, consumer price inflation slowed to 1.7 percent from 3.3 percent a year earlier, and it shows no signs of picking up.

Some economists attribute the unexpected price moderation to temporary factors. For one thing, the labor force has been growing about twice as rapidly as would be expected based on growth of the adult population, easing much of the strain in labor markets. "It is as if demand is calling forth its own supply," says Federal Reserve Governor Laurence H. Meyer. Chairman Greenspan argues, however, that the current rate of labor-force growth can't be sustained. He notes that more than half of the 2 million net new hires each year are being drawn from the ranks of the unemployed or from among those who had not been actively seeking work, two sources of labor that eventually will dry up. [12]

Many economists believe the United States has nearly reached the bottom of the well, and that labor markets are beginning to tighten significantly. As a result, they expect wage increases to start putting more pressure on prices. Still, they have expected that to happen for some time, and wages remain fairly quiescent. The 2.2 percent jump in average hourly earnings in 1997 was considered unusually mild, though it did

Continued on p. 132

At Issue:

Is the nation on the verge of a new period of inflation?

MARK ZANDI
Chief economist, Regional Financial Associates, West Chester, Pa.

WRITTEN FOR *THE CQ RESEARCHER,* JANUARY 1998.

*c*laims that the economy is on the verge of outright deflation are misplaced. Not only will there be no deflation this year, but inflation will accelerate by year's end. Much of the deceleration in inflation during the past year is the result of a number of what will prove to be temporary events.

Energy prices, for example, have been pummeled by a myriad of factors, including the financial and economic woes in Asia, resumption of Iraqi exports, the recently announced increase in OPEC production quotas and the warm winter in the Northern Hemisphere. It is unlikely world energy markets will make it through the year without another disruption of Iraqi oil exports, however. Asian oil demand may even rise somewhat in coming months since many Asian buyers probably have been holding off buying dollar-denominated oil as long as possible in the hope that their very depressed currencies make at least a partial comeback.

Falling import prices also have contributed to weaker inflation during the past year. The dollar's seemingly inexorable rise will come to an end in coming months as the Asian currency and financial crisis finally subsides. As investors deem Asian financial markets have hit bottom — and there is increasing speculation that this may soon be at hand — the dollar will lose some of its luster as a global safe haven.

Collapsing computer prices also have been a major constraint on inflation. Personal computer prices fell by 12 percent during the past year. But it is hard to expect similar declines this year. Margins in the industry have fallen enough to suggest that a significant shakeout may soon occur. That eventually will limit the rate of future price declines.

A further deceleration in the cost of health care also was an important constraint on inflation last year. Health care cost inflation is expected to accelerate this year as the process of moving over to managed care is largely over.

Inflation also will continue to get a lift from stronger growth in labor costs. Labor markets are acutely tight, and at the economy's current rate of growth they will grow tighter. Moreover, productivity will not increase enough to offset rising compensation costs, as employers will have to hire less than qualified labor in the tight labor market.

All this suggests that consumer price inflation will accelerate from just under 2 percent currently to near 3 percent a year from now. While this is still very modest inflation by nearly any standard of the past quarter-century, it is inflation nonetheless.

EDWARD YARDENI
Chief economist, Deutsche Morgan Grenfell, New York, N.Y.

WRITTEN FOR *THE CQ RESEARCHER,* JANUARY 1998.

*t*he forces of disinflation are permanent, not transitory, in my opinion.

The end of the Cold War marked the beginning of intense global competition. The U.S. economy has adapted better than the Continental European and Japanese economies to the competitive challenges, and the dollar reflects this situation. In both Europe and Japan, market structures remain too rigid, with too much government intervention in the form of excessive regulation, protection and subsidies. Consequently, the uncompetitive economies of Europe and Japan are weak.

The Europeans and Japanese are deregulating and restructuring their economies, but too slowly. Interest rates remain very low over there, especially compared with rates available in the U.S. So, the dollar is strong, and will likely remain strong. Indeed, the weak deutsche mark and yen are the only reasons that there is any growth in Europe and Japan at all. These countries need weak currencies to keep out of recessions. The Japanese financial system is still a mess. Huge loan losses have yet to be fully realized. A strong dollar should continue to be an important source of disinflation.

Why aren't wages rising at a faster pace with the unemployment rate so low? The favorite explanation is that the Federal Reserve's models didn't include variables for job insecurity, but that the models should soon be back on track once job insecurity goes away. I disagree. Job security may improve, but we all face much greater business insecurity because markets are becoming more competitive globally as a result of the end of the Cold War trade barriers, and domestically as a result of ongoing restructuring, deregulation and privatization. We can all look forward to keeping our jobs as long as our companies don't fail.

The Fed's inflation models also seem to be missing variables to capture how price security is keeping a lid on wages. Workers and consumers are becoming increasingly secure about price stability. They perceive that prices are not rising fast enough to threaten their financial well-being, so they aren't very militant about wages.

My bottom line is that the forces of disinflation remain very much intact. They are not temporary; they are permanent. Tight labor markets are not inflationary because global competition is keeping a lid on prices and lowering workers' inflationary expectations.

Continued from p. 130

represent an acceleration from the 0.5 percent gain in 1996.

Meyer and Greenspan believe that workers may have held back on wage demands because they feel unusually insecure about their jobs. In 1991, at the bottom of the last recession, a poll by International Survey Research Corp. found that 25 percent of workers feared they would be laid off. In 1996, even though the economy had been growing for five years and unemployment had dropped to 5.3 percent from 7.3 percent, the portion of workers who were worried about layoffs had grown to 46 percent, the survey firm found.

Similarly, while labor contracts in the past rarely exceeded three years, it is not uncommon today to have five-year or even six-year contracts — and many of the new contracts emphasize job security in lieu of substantial wage increases. [13]

Greenspan attributes heightened job insecurity in part to efforts by companies to reduce their work forces by farming certain functions to outside contractors. [14] Technological change also may play a role, he suggests, by leading workers to fear that unless they upgrade their skills continuously they won't remain employable. Whatever the cause, the Fed chairman questions how much longer wage demands will remain suppressed. "There is a limit to the value of additional job security people are willing to acquire in exchange for lesser increases in living standards," he says. [15]

Traditionalists also believe that sedate health-care costs have brought temporary relief from inflation, but that prices could start jumping soon. A number of economists argue, for instance, that health maintenance organizations by now have squeezed much of the fat out of doctor and hospital bills, and will have more trouble restraining cost increases in the future. [16]

Similarly, economists question how much longer the dollar can continue rising against foreign currencies, a trend that has cut the price of imports and brought additional price relief to U.S. consumers. For much of 1997, analysts were predicting the dollar would halt its rise as imports enlarged the U.S. trade deficit. With the wave of currency depreciations in Asia, they have postponed predictions of a falling dollar, but they still say the dollar cannot keep rising forever.

A New Paradigm

While many economists predict that "temporary" factors masking inflation eventually will disappear and forces pushing prices upward will reassert themselves, one group of analysts argues that inflation poses no threat for the foreseeable future.

Their theory, dubbed the "new paradigm," holds that two major new forces — increased global competition and a significant, though as yet unmeasured, rise in productivity — will prevent renewed inflation and enable the economy to expand much faster than the 2.5 percent annual growth rate commonly assumed to be its upper limit. If true, these new theories suggest that the Federal Reserve's continuing focus on inflation is, at the very least, unnecessarily restraining growth and, at worst, actually could push the economy into a deflationary downturn.

A new economic era began with the end of the Cold War, argues economist Yardeni of Deutsche Morgan Grenfell. He believes the end of the U.S.-Soviet confrontation eliminated an "unprecedented trade barrier." Now that the conflict is over, trade is flourishing — even between the West and China,

which remains communist but is eagerly pushing economic integration with the rest of the world. According to Yardeni, the sum of all nations' exports rose 70 percent between 1989 and 1995 to a record $5.1 trillion. He predicts that total will double to $10 trillion by 2000.

As a result, manufacturers who previously could raise prices easily because they were relatively sheltered, now are exposed to much more competition. That means they can't increase prices — even if tight labor markets are forcing them to raise wages. To remain profitable, Yardeni says, they instead must increase sales volume, constantly develop new products and find ways to operate more efficiently.

"The new era is inherently deflationary," he says. "To offset these deflationary pressures, companies must sell more units of their products and services. The best way to do so is to cut costs, lower prices, improve quality and innovate."

The argument, though tantalizing, is controversial. Paul Krugman, an economist at the Massachusetts Institute of Technology, disagrees that global trade is having such a decisive impact. He argues that the service sector, which now comprises the bulk of the U.S. economy, is largely insulated from foreign competition. Even many U.S. manufacturers don't compete head-to-head with foreigners, Krugman suggests. "Seen any Chinese refrigerators lately?" he asks. [17]

Van Bussman, corporate economist for Chrysler Corp., buttresses Krugman's point. Around the world, automobile manufacturers will be able to produce 80 million cars a year by 2000 — 25 percent, or 20 million cars, more than projected sales. But U.S. companies will escape much of the heightened competition. Most new foreign manufacturers produce primarily sub-compact cars, but there is no excess capacity to produce the vehicles most important to U.S. automakers — sport-utility vehicles, pickups and minivans. "We are somewhat buffered from excess capacity," Bussman says.

The other main plank of the new paradigm theory — that gains in productivity have increased the economy's growth potential — also is hotly disputed among economists. "New paradigm" theorists believe that computer technology has enormously increased the efficiency of U.S. production. The computer industry itself is their favorite example. Computer prices have been declining at double-digit rates every year, and most analysts project they will continue falling indefinitely. Yet profits remain strong, thanks to constant innovation and increasing sales. "Everybody asks how can we keep this up, but the light at the end of the tunnel keeps moving ahead with every long-range plan," notes Rich O'Brien, corporate economist for Texas Instruments.

Some analysts believe computers also may be enhancing productivity in countless other industries. "What we may be observing in the current environment is a number of key technologies, some even mature, finally interacting to create significant new opportunities for value creation," says Greenspan. For instance, advances in laser technology and fiber optics have converged to create a revolution in telecommunications, and new software innovations have made it possible to take advantage of significantly increased computer capacity to create the Internet. [18]

Greenspan notes that in high-tech industries, the lead time required to bring new production facilities on line is much shorter than in the days when manufacturing required heavy equipment such as open-hearth steel furnaces. As a result, output today can be increased quickly to meet rising demand, and the kind of bottlenecks and capacity shortages that led to rising prices and economic slowdown in the past are less likely. Greenspan notes, for instance, that the ratio of unfilled orders to shipments of non-defense capital goods has declined by 30 percent in the last six years. [19]

Dell Computers

Computer prices have been declining at double-digit rates in recent years, yet industry profits remain strong, thanks to constant innovation and increasing sales.

Many economists scoff at the notion that computers have increased productivity. They note that economic statistics have not yet detected a quantum leap in productivity. Computers have increased productivity in some respects, these analysts say, but may actually reduce it in others. "Don't forget that rapid turnover of hardware and software keeps us perpetually in the learning mode, that people spend countless hours mindlessly exploring the Internet and playing amusing computer games, and that most of us suffer more from information overload than from information shortage," says Alan Blinder, a Princeton University economist and former vice-chairman of the Federal Reserve Board. "A productivity miracle based on the computer may be just around the corner. . . . But, if so, it is around the next corner, not the last one." [20]

The bottom line is that the new paradigm remains unproven — a situation that Greenspan says justifies the central bank's reluctance to relax its vigilance concerning inflation. "Is it possible that there is something fundamentally new about this current period?" he asks. "Yes, it is possible. Markets may have become more efficient, competition is more global, and information technology has doubtless enhanced the stability of business operations. But regrettably, history is strewn with visions of such 'new eras' that, in the end, have proven to be a mirage. In short, history counsels caution." [21] ◼

CURRENT SITUATION

Japan's Bubble Bursts

While the United States ponders whether inflation is still a threat, Asia appears to be near — if not already into — a period of destructive deflation. Different countries in the region are suffering many of the ailments commonly associated with deflation — plunging asset prices, bankruptcies, badly damaged financial systems, chary consumers and stagnant or declining economies. Nobody yet knows how far the region may fall.

Just as the stock market crash of 1929 is often considered the opening event of the Depression, Asia's deflation of the 1990s began when Japan's so-called bubble economy burst in 1990-91, sending greatly overvalued real estate and stock markets plummeting. According to many economists, the decline was a classic bust following a speculative boom.

Between 1988 and 1990, Japanese land and stock prices had more than doubled in what Geoffrey P. Miller, director of the Center for the Study of Central Banks at New York University Law School, describes as "possibly the largest speculative event in the history of the world." Miller blames the speculative surge in part on an easy-money policy pursued in the late 1980s by the Bank of Japan. Japan had come under intense pressure from the U.S. to allow more American imports into its market. In response, the Japanese central bank slashed interest rates in 1986 and 1987, and then held them low through 1989 in an effort to stimulate domestic demand for imports. [22]

The resulting surge in credit sent the Japanese stock and real estate markets soaring, pushing prices well above what most analysts considered the true value of the assets. The bubble soon became self-inflating: Rising real estate prices increased the value of collateral held for loans, thus encouraging even more lending; much of the new credit helped finance purchases of stock, driving up the Japanese stock market; then, high-priced securities were used as collateral to buy more property.

By the beginning of 1989, Miller says, Japanese "share markets" accounted for more than 42 percent of the value of all markets worldwide, up from 15 percent in 1980. A year later, the Bank of Japan finally concluded the situation had gotten out of hand. It started tightening the monetary reins. Rising interest rates choked off the credit binge, and the house of cards fell. Real estate and stock prices plunged. Banks staggered under a crushing load of bad debt — a problem that persists to this day.

In January, the Japanese Finance Ministry reported that bad or questionable loans still exceed $575 billion, an amount equal to about 16 percent of Japan's gross domestic product. By comparison, the U.S. savings and loan debacle of the 1980s cost the U.S. government about $150 billion to clean up. [23]

Asset deflation has seriously damaged the Japanese economy. Bank lending has contracted. Tokyo and other cities are littered with half-finished or abandoned office buildings and hotels. New investment has dropped sharply, as many companies are burdened with inventories they can't unload. Even though interest rates have dropped about as far as they can go — the Bank of Japan's official rate is just 0.5 percent — the economy hasn't been able to muster more than 1 percent growth in any year since 1992.

Interest rates at rock bottom are one of the classic symptoms of deflation. So is moribund consumer demand; in a serious deflation, consumers stop buying, either because they have lost confidence or because they see prices falling and decide to hold off purchases in hope that prices will fall further still. In the case of Japan, however, the lack of consumer demand may reflect an even more fundamental flaw in the country's economy: Archaic laws and byzantine regulations prevent the emergence of a vibrant consumer sector.

For instance, if a Japanese bank wants to open a branch, it must obtain permission from the Ministry of Finance in Tokyo. The Ministry of Health requires 21 separate approvals if a store wishes to sell meat, fish, milk, bread or frozen foods. Regulations sought and vigorously promoted by small-retailer associations make it extremely difficult to open a large store; prospective investors must file as many as 75 applications relating to 26 different government permits to open a large, multipurpose store. [24]

Many economists in the West believe this system artificially suppresses consumption. "Japan has a world-class manufacturing sector tied to a Third World service sector," says Wyss of Standard & Poor's DRI. "Its service sector is not generating demand for manufactured goods."

Unable or unwilling to consume at a rate that matches its productive capacity, Japan has invested much of its enormous cash surplus overseas. That has produced income that helps cushion the country from the most harmful effects of deflation; unlike some of its East Asian neighbors, Japan appears unlikely for the foreseeable future to go bankrupt and require emergency financial assistance from the International Monetary Fund. But Japanese investment has contributed to deflationary pressures elsewhere, as some of the country's Asian neighbors have learned.

The Asia Crisis

The financial crisis that gripped Thailand, Indonesia and South Korea in 1997 began, ironically, with the remarkable success that those countries and their neighbors achieved in attracting foreign investment. In the early 1990s, investment prospects in the advanced economies dimmed considerably in the wake of deflation in Japan and disappointing economic growth in Europe. Looking for better returns, international investors became enthralled with East Asian nations, whose economies were growing at an astounding 9 percent annual rate after adjusting for inflation. Such growth not only was well above the rate experienced in advanced economies, it probably was higher than ever experienced before by economies of comparable size, according to the International Monetary Fund. [25]

The World Bank estimates that net capital flows into the Asia Pacific region exploded from just $25 billion in 1990 to $110 billion by 1996. In retrospect, analysts say, that was more than the countries could handle. [26]

"Financial markets were swamped," Robert Hormats, vice chairman of the investment banking and securities firm Goldman Sachs, told the House Banking Committee in November. "Pressures to lend to politically favored projects (particularly commercial real estate) that had little economic justification, lax credit standards, weak supervisory regimes and in some cases inadequate bank capital were among the problems."

Compounding the trouble, many Asian banks sought to take advantage of relatively low U.S. interest rates by borrowing dollars on international financial markets and then lending in their local currencies. That strategy paid off for a while, as the interest-rate differential favored Asian banks. But the dollar began rising in value against Asian currencies in mid-

1995, making it harder for the Asian banks to repay their loans.

Some economists trace the rise in the dollar to actions by the Federal Reserve. The Fed, concerned that inflation would soon hit the U.S., had tightened monetary policy in November 1994 and February 1995. Other analysts say the dollar started rising because international investors, impressed with the U.S. economy and

An investment boom in Thailand in the early 1990s led to many construction projects that were not economically viable.

Reuters

concerned about economic stagnation in Europe and Asia, were flocking to the dollar.

Whatever the cause, the effect was to weaken Asian banks. But the rising value of the dollar hurt the East Asian economies in other ways as well. Most had long maintained a fixed relationship between the value of their currencies and that of the dollar. When the dollar went up beginning in 1995, they therefore had to increase the value of their own currencies, which required tightening their own monetary policies and increasing domestic interest rates. This made their exports relatively more expensive in global trade.

Falling prices, especially in the glutted global electronics market, reduced their exports further. Soon, the countries were chalking up swelling trade deficits. But the East Asians were hamstrung in dealing with this situation.

Normally, a trade deficit causes a country's currency to decline in value. That reduces the price of its exports, making them more competitive internationally. Eventually, exports rise until they are closer to being in balance with imports. The East Asians, however, resisted letting their currencies depreciate because that would have meant abandoning the link to the dollar, a step that would have shaken investors' confidence. But they also were reluctant to defend the currencies because that would have required them to tighten monetary policy and raise interest rates, which would further weaken their already troubled financial institutions.

While the East Asians struggled with this quandary, international investors became alarmed that large trade deficits eventually would force them to let their currencies fall. By mid-1997, investors were heading for the exits. Suddenly, borrowers in Thailand, Indonesia and South Korea could not roll over their international loans, and widespread bankruptcy became a serious threat.

Deflation had turned to panic. By December, Sherry Cooper, chief economist for Nesbitt Burns, a Canadian investment firm, said glumly: "One-third of the global economy is near paralysis." ■

OUTLOOK

Global Uncertainty

Asian economies are expected to slow sharply in 1998, and the problems in that region will reverberate around the world. But forecasters predict the impact beyond the South Pacific will be manageable if the rescue effort led by the International Monetary Fund succeeds in restoring investor confidence so that capital starts flowing back into the troubled region soon.

The longer-term outlook, however, may depend on a number of as-yet-unknown variables — in particular, whether the United States and other advanced countries take steps to strengthen the world's financial system.

As recently as May 1997, the IMF was projecting that most Asian economies would expand at a healthy rate. But just seven months later, the outlook seemed considerably less rosy. The table below, which compares the IMF's May 1997 and December 1997 forecasts for growth in real gross domestic product for countries at the center of the Asian maelstrom, shows how prospects for 1998 have dimmed: [27]

	May **Forecast**	**December** **Forecast**
Thailand	7.0%	0.0%
Indonesia	7.5	2.0
Malaysia	7.9	2.5
Philippines	6.4	3.8
Japan	2.9	1.1
South Korea	6.3	2.5

For the world economy as a whole, the IMF said, growth will slow in 1998 to about 3 percent after adjustment for price changes, compared with 4 percent in 1996 and '97. But the U.S.

economy will be affected only slightly; the IMF projected in December that this country's GDP will rise 2.4 percent, just 0.2 percentage point less than previously projected.

While the Asian slowdown will reduce demand for U.S. exports to that region, the overall impact on the United States is expected to be modest because exports represent only 10 percent of total U.S. GDP, and only about one-third of American exports go to Asia. Moreover, some of the harm to the U.S. economy will be offset by the stimulative effect of lower interest rates. Given concerns in the U.S. about the threat of inflation, many analysts believe a modest slowdown such as the IMF projected would actually be beneficial. [28]

The situation could turn out worse, however. The IMF assumed in its forecast that the net flow of capital into Asia will drop by two-thirds, or $67 billion, in 1998. For all developing countries, the decline could be about $78 billion. But if Asian governments fail to convince investors that they have made substantial reforms, new foreign investment could fall by as much as $100 billion, according to the IMF. [29]

Moreover, Japan remains a major question mark. U.S. officials generally have been disappointed in the Tokyo government's response to its own deflationary difficulties. Prime Minister Ryutaro Hashimoto took what they considered a step in the right direction on Jan. 12 by proposing a $227 billion financial-stabilization plan to clean up the nation's banking problems, along with a $15 billion income-tax cut. That marked a significant departure for the Japanese government.

The Hashimoto administration previously had played down the nation's continuing banking difficulties. And as recently as April 1997, it actually had increased taxes, boosting the nation's sales tax to 5 percent from 3 percent

and letting some $17 billion in income-tax breaks expire. Japanese officials have resisted tax cuts because the government's budget deficit already is equal to about 3 percent of GDP, and the country faces mounting fiscal demands because the Japanese population is aging.

Despite the change of direction, some Western analysts questioned whether Hashimoto's proposals will be enough to turn the country's economy around. They noted that the Tokyo government remains reluctant to shut down failed banks, and some suggested the tax cut would be too small to spark strong growth.

China, meanwhile, remains perhaps the biggest wild card in the Asia crisis. By all appearances, it has escaped the turmoil affecting its neighbors. But analysts say its financial system may be just as shaky as theirs. Chinese banks have extended tens of billions of dollars in loans to state-owned enterprises that are given little chance of being able to make good on the credit any time soon.

"If China's citizens ever grow concerned about the stability of its banks and decided to save in shoe boxes under the bed instead of in state-sanctioned banks, China would face a full-fledged banking disaster," warns Greg Mastel, vice president of public relations for the Economic Strategy Institute in Washington. [30]

Such lingering dangers undoubtedly helped persuade the Clinton administration to seek congressional backing for plans to bolster the International Monetary Fund. The international organization says Asian rescue efforts have left it short of funds to address future crises. The White House is asking Congress to appropriate about $14.5 billion to cover the U.S. share of an international plan to replenish IMF funds, plus another $3.5 billion as part of a new $25 billion IMF program, the New Arrangements

Continued on p. 139

Chronology

1980s *The United States and other advanced, industrial countries push policies that lead to heavy investment and rapid growth throughout Asia.*

1985

The major industrial countries agree to drive down the value of the dollar against other major currencies. The Plaza Accord, as it is known, leads to a boom in exports from East Asian countries whose currencies are pegged to the dollar.

1986-1987

Under pressure from the U.S. to buy more American goods, the Bank of Japan cuts interest rates, encouraging a boom in the Japanese real estate and stock markets.

1990-96 *Japan falters, but its East Asian neighbors grow rapidly, as foreign investment more than quadruples in just six years.*

1990

Japan's stock and real estate markets plummet, as the Bank of Japan tightens monetary policy to ward off excessive speculation. The Japanese economy becomes mired in bad debt and sluggish growth.

1994

China devalues its currency, the yuan, by about 40 percent, making Chinese goods more competitive but undermining exports from countries whose currencies are tied to the dollar.

1995

The U.S. dollar starts rising in foreign exchange markets, partly as a result of steps by the Federal Reserve to raise U.S. interest rates and partly because investors decide the U.S. may be a better credit risk than countries in Asia.

1997 *Financial crisis grips Asia.*

January-June

Thailand's exports slacken as the country's currency, the baht, appreciates along with the dollar and as prices fall in the glutted electronic market. Investors, worried that Thais won't be able to repay their debt, start moving out of Thai currency and into the U.S. dollar. The Thai government uses its dollar reserves to buy baht in an effort to maintain its value, drawing them down to a dangerously low point.

July

Thailand abandons its effort to defend the baht, which promptly falls almost 20 percent in value. Shaken investors start converting their funds throughout East Asia to the dollar, putting downward pressure on other regional currencies. They also balk at rolling over loans to Asian borrowers.

August

The International Monetary Fund arranges a $17 billion emergency line of credit to keep Thailand solvent. The country agrees, in turn, to shut down insolvent financial institutions and to tighten monetary policy. On Aug. 28, stock markets plunge

all across Asia.

October

The International Monetary Fund orchestrates a $40 billion rescue package for Indonesia, again requiring financial-sector and policy reforms in return. Financial fears spread through Asia and beyond. The Hong Kong stock market loses nearly one-quarter of its value Oct. 23-28. The U.S. stock market plunges 7.2 percent on Oct. 27, although it quickly recovers.

Nov. 1-21

New financial weaknesses surface in Japan. Sanyo Securities, a major stock brokerage, declares bankruptcy on Nov. 3. Hokkaido Takushoku, the country's 10th-largest bank, fails on Nov. 16. Yamaichi, the country's largest securities firm, folds on Nov. 21.

Nov. 24-Dec. 3

Concerns mount about the financial health of South Korea. The country's currency, the won, collapses on Nov. 17, and the IMF announces a $57 billion rescue package on Dec. 3.

Dec. 17

The Japanese government, in a significant policy reversal, announces that it will propose new spending to shore up banks, as well as income tax cuts designed to help pull its economy out of the doldrums.

Dec. 31

Financier George Soros, saying that the Asia crisis is far from over, warns we are "on the verge of global deflation."

Trade Deficits and Free Trade

The last time the United States and the rest of the world encountered serious deflation, during the Depression, Congress enacted the highly protectionist Smoot-Hawley Act. Some people worry that Congress may make a similar mistake today.

Backers of the 1930 law, which increased tariffs on more than 20,000 imports, were trying to shore up failing American industries and prevent unemployment from rising. But European countries quickly retaliated with tariff increases of their own. The result was a sharp contraction in global trade, which analysts generally agreed aggravated the Depression. [1]

A turn toward protectionism today would be very worrisome to countries like Thailand, South Korea, Malaysia and Indonesia, whose hopes of economic recovery hinge in part on their ability to gain badly needed foreign cash by exporting goods to the United States and other advanced economies. But proponents of liberalized trade say the U.S. would be a big loser, too.

As yet, there are few signs of a decisive move toward protectionism in the United States. But that could change if, as expected, America's trade deficit grows as a result of the Asian crisis. American exports to the region are expected to drop this year and next, as the economic slowdown in that region reduces demand for American products. Imports from Asia, meanwhile, will increase as the depreciation of Asian currencies makes goods from the region cheaper here. As a result, says David Hale, chief global economist for Zurich Kemper Investments, the American merchandise trade gap could grow to $250 billion or even $300 billion by 1999, compared with $191.2 billion in 1996.

A larger trade deficit isn't necessarily bad news, Hale insists. With the U.S. economy already operating at a "full-employment" level, the nation does not seem to be suffering in international trade. Instead of hurting the U.S., cheaper imports could act as a potential "inflation safety valve" by reducing prices for goods consumed here, Hale says. But he concedes that many people won't see it that way. "The problem with trade deficits is political," Hale says. "Many Americans perceive the trade deficit to be a source of job losses or slower wage growth, not an inflation brake which permits a stronger and longer expansion." [2]

The biggest test of the U.S. stance on trade this year will come in congressional debates over the Clinton administration's request for "fast-track" trade negotiating authority. Under fast-track, Congress agrees to restrict itself to voting only to accept or reject a negotiated trade agreement within a specified period of time and without amendments. U.S. presidents had such authority for most years from 1974 to 1994, when it was allowed to expire. The administration wants it now to negotiate a free-trade pact with Chile, as well as to advance broader efforts to liberalize trade in the Americas and between the U.S. and East Asian countries.

Proponents say that few countries would negotiate trade pacts with the United States if they knew Congress could amend any agreement after negotiations conclude. "Access to fast-track is a critical element to the success of any negotiating strategy," argued Thomas J. Donohue, president and chief executive of the U.S. Chamber of Commerce. "As anyone in business knows, you do not waste your time making deals with negotiators who are not in a position to commit their principals . . . to an agreement." [3]

Critics of fast-track — most notably the AFL-CIO and such prominent Democrats as House Minority Leader Richard A. Gephardt, D-Mo. — say they do not oppose free trade. But they insist that any trade pact should require other countries to strengthen their labor and environmental laws before letting them compete more directly with the U.S. Otherwise, the critics say, foreign companies will have too great an advantage.

Brookings Institution scholars Robert Z. Lawrence and Robert E. Litan argue in response that free trade hasn't cost Americans any jobs. "Lower trade barriers promote faster growth in the standard of living for Americans," Lawrence and Litan argue. "Broader export markets enable U.S. companies to reap larger returns on their innovations. Lower trade barriers here, meanwhile, enhance competitive pressure on our firms to innovation. In addition, U.S. firms increasingly rely on imported high-tech capital equipment and know-how, which accelerates the growth of productivity and living standards here." [4]

Both sides agree on one point: Fast-track legislation faces tough going in Congress. The Clinton administration had hoped to win the authority last year but yanked it in the face of strong opposition, mainly from House Democrats. A bigger trade deficit arising from the Asian financial crisis won't make the task any easier. [5]

[1] Gary H. Stern, "Achieving Economic Stability: Lessons from the Crash of 1929," *Federal Reserve Bank of Minneapolis 1987 Annual Report;* available online at http://woodrow.mpls.frb.fed.us/pubs/ar/ar1987.html.

[2] Testimony before the House Banking and Financial Services Committee, Nov. 4, 1997.

[3] Testimony before the House Ways and Means Committee, Sept. 30, 1997.

[4] Robert Z. Lawrence and Robert E. Litan, "Globaphobia: The Wrong Debate Over Trade Policy," Brookings Institution Policy Brief No. 24 (1997); available online at http://www.brook.edu/ES/POLICY/Polbrf24.htm.

[5] For a compilation of news stories, background reports and position statements on fast-track legislation, see the U.S. Information Agency Web site: http://www.usia.gov/topical/econ/fasttrak/

Continued from p. 136

to Borrow, that would supplement other loan programs. [31]

President Clinton argued in his State of the Union address on Jan. 27 that IMF rescues such as the emergency Asia packages are in America's own self-interest. "First, these countries are our customers," the president said. "If they sink into recession, they won't be able to buy the goods we'd like to sell them. Second, they're also our competitors, so if their currencies lose their value and go down, then the price of their goods will drop, flooding our market and others with much cheaper goods, which makes it a lot tougher for our people to compete. And finally, they are our strategic partners. Their stability bolsters our security."

FOR MORE INFORMATION

American Enterprise Institute, 1150 Seventeenth Street N.W., Washington, D.C. 20036; (202) 862-5800; fax: (202) 862-7177; Web site: http://www.aei.org. This conservative-leaning think tank publishes studies on numerous domestic and international issues. Scholars John Makin and Lawrence Lindsey have written a number of articles on the Asian financial crisis and the threat of deflation.

Brookings Institution, 1775 Massachusetts Ave. N.W., Washington, D.C. 20036; (202) 797-6000; fax: (202) 797-6004; e-mail: brookinfo@brook.edu; Web site: http://www.brook.edu. This private, nonpartisan research organization has produced numerous studies of domestic and international economics, including a number of discussion papers on Asian countries such as South Korea, Japan and China.

Economic Policy Institute, 1660 L Street N.W., Suite 1200, Washington, D.C. 20036; 1-800-EPI-4844 [in Washington, D.C.: (202) 331-5510]; e-mail: economic@cais.com; Web site: http://www.epinet.org. This liberal leaning think-tank offers analysis of a wide range of economic issues, with particular emphasis on matters affecting the distribution of income, social policy, living standards and working conditions.

Institute for International Economics, 11 Dupont Circle N.W., Washington, D.C. 20036-1207; Phone: 202-328-9000; Fax: 202-328-5432; e-mail: bcoulton@iie.com; Web site: http://www.iie.com. This private, nonprofit, nonpartisan research institution has been analyzing international economic problems and proposing policy responses to them in speeches, books and working papers since 1981.

Fundamental Reform

No matter how the immediate crisis is resolved, the coming years are almost certain to see considerable discussion about whether the world's financial system needs fundamental reform. Financial institutions are the lifeblood of any economy, but they play an especially important role in a time of deflation, when borrowers can come under severe stress. If financial institutions scrutinize borrowers carefully and lend only to the best credit risks, the chances of serious dislocation can be minimized; but if they lend carelessly to unqualified borrowers, they can damage themselves and thereby magnify deflation.

Many analysts believe financial institutions are the weak link in today's global economy. "During the past 15 years, there has been an epidemic of banking crises in the developing world," notes C. Fred Bergsten, director of the Washington-based Institute for International Economics. Bergsten

says that in at least 57 cases during the period, banking systems lost all or almost all of their capital, and that in a dozen cases countries ended up losing 10 percent or more of their gross domestic product. Overall, he says, banking crises in the developing world have cost governments at least $250 billion to clean up. [32]

Morris Goldstein, a colleague of Bergsten, attributes these problems to a litany of financial-system deficiencies familiar to those who have watched the current Asian crisis unfold: excessive government involvement in the banking industry; weak disclosure, accounting and legal frameworks for banking; too much lending to bank owners, managers and their affiliated companies; inadequate bank capital; and official safety nets that protect bank owners and creditors from the consequences of misdeeds that render their institutions insolvent. [33]

While all of these weaknesses should be corrected, reform should

begin by requiring far more public disclosure by financial institutions, according to many economists. "The ability of financial markets to work efficiently in channeling resources to their most effective uses stands or falls by the quality of information available to market participants," explained Deputy Treasury Secretary Lawrence H. Summers in testimony to the House Banking and Financial Services Committee in November 1997. "In addition, imprudent or illegal behavior is much less likely where individuals and firms know that their actions will in time be revealed."

While Summers suggested that the international community should encourage individual countries to strengthen their own banking laws, financier George Soros suggests a bigger role for international institutions like the IMF. In December 1997, Soros proposed establishing a new sister institution to the IMF that would guarantee international loans for a "modest fee." This

International Credit Insurance Corporation would require countries that seek international credit to provide data on all borrowings from within their borders, public or private. The authority then would set a ceiling on how much it would be willing to insure, thereby preventing runaway investment.

"The private sector is ill-suited to allocate international credit," Soros explained. "It provides either too much or too little. It does not have the information with which to form a balanced judgment. Moreover, it is not concerned with maintaining macroeconomic balance in borrowing countries. Its goals are to maximize profit and minimize risk. This makes it move in a herdlike fashion." [34]

The Soros proposal hasn't attracted many backers, though that could change if deflationary pressures grow or the world experiences more financial crises. In any event, his comments underscore the blend of opportunity and danger that countries face in the evolving global economy. Financial markets can almost instantaneously move capital anywhere in the world. As a result, economic output is rising, new products are coming to market at an unprecedented rate and prices are remarkably restrained. But the gains may not seem worthwhile if institutions, public and private, fail to adjust to a new environment of flat or even declining prices.

"Around the world, we have been witnessing the emergence of a truly global economy, one in which trade, investment, capital, information and know-how can flow ever more freely," Summers told the Banking and Financial Services Committee. But, he cautioned, "being a member of a more integrated world brings risks as well as opportunities." ∎

Christopher Conte is a freelance writer in the Washington, D.C. area, and a former reporter and editor for The Wall Street Journal.

Notes

[1] *The McGraw-Hill Encyclopedia of Economics,* 2nd edition (1994), p. 531.

[2] "The Threat of Deflation," *Business Week,* Nov. 10, 1997, pp. 55-59.

[3] Roger Bootle, *The Death of Inflation* (1997), p. 10.

[4] See Martin Feldstein, "Japan's Folly Drags Asia Down," *The Wall Street Journal,* Nov. 25, 1997.

[5] The figures on Korea's banking situation are from International Monetary Fund, *World Economic Outlook, Interim Assessment,* December 1997, p. 23; figures on bad loans in Japanese banks are from Robert Edelstein and Jean-Michel Paul, "How to Get Japan Back on its Feet," *The Wall Street Journal,* Dec. 11, 1997.

[6] Alan Greenspan, remarks at the annual meeting of the American Economic Association and the American Finance Association, Chicago, Ill., Jan. 3, 1998; available online at http://www.bog.frb.fed.us.

[7] Federal Reserve Board, Federal Open Market Committee minutes, meeting of Sept. 30, 1997; available online at http://www.bog.frb.fed.us.

[8] Federal Reserve Board, Federal Open Market Committee minutes, meeting of Dec. 16, 1997; available online at http://www.bog.frb.fed.us.

[9] James K. Glassman, "Who Needs the IMF?," *The Washington Post,* Dec. 12, 1997.

[10] Laura D'Andrea Tyson, "Leadership in a Crisis," *The Washington Post,* Jan. 22, 1998, p. A21.

[11] Jeffrey D. Sachs, "The Wrong Medicine for Asia," *The New York Times,* Nov. 3, 1997.

[12] Laurence H. Meyer, remarks at the Forecasters Club of New York, April 24, 1997; Alan Greenspan, Monetary Policy Testimony and Report to the Congress, July 22, 1997; available online at http://www.bog.frb.fed.us.

[13] Alan Greenspan, Monetary Policy Testimony and Report to the Congress, Feb. 26, 1997; available online at http://www.bog.frb.fed.us. For background, see "Labor Movement's Future," *The CQ Researcher,* June 28, 1996, pp. 553-576.

[14] For background, see "Contingent Work Force," *The CQ Researcher,* Oct. 24, 1997, pp. 937-960.

[15] From Feb. 26, 1997, remarks, *op. cit.*

[16] For background, see "Patients' Rights," *The CQ Researcher,* Feb. 6, 1998, pp. 97-120.

[17] Paul Krugman, "How Fast Can the Economy Grow?" *Harvard Business Review,* July-August 1997, pp. 123-129.

[18] Alan Greenspan, Monetary Policy Testimony and Report to Congress, July 22, 1997; available online at http://www.bog.frb.fed.us.

[19] *Ibid.*

[20] Alan S. Blinder, "The Speed Limit: Fact and Fancy in the Growth Debate," *The American Prospect,* No. 34, September-October 1997, pp. 57-62.

[21] Alan Greenspan, Monetary Policy Testimony and Report to the Congress, Feb. 26, 1997; available online at http://www.bog.frb.fed.us.

[22] Geoffrey P. Miller, "The Role of a Central Bank in a Bubble Economy," to be published in the *Journal of Legal Studies* in June 1998; available online at http://www.gold-eagle.com/editorials/cscb002f.html.

[23] The estimates of problem loans in Japanese banks come from Bloomberg News and were quoted in Sandra Sugawara, "Japan's Lawmakers Get Stabilization, Tax Cut Proposals," *The Washington Post,* Jan. 13, 1998, p. D1. The estimates of the cost of the U.S. savings and loan bailout were cited in Frederick S. Mishkin, *The Economics of Money, Banking and Financial Markets,* Fifth Edition (1998), p. 318.

[24] Lucien Elington, "Government Regulation, Productivity, and Trade Tensions: Are 'Lifetime Employment' and Seniority Endangered?" May 1995; available online at http://www.indiana.edu/~japan/digest8.html.

[25] International Monetary Fund, *op. cit.,* p. 3. Much of the analysis in the section concerning the Asian financial crisis is based on this report.

[26] Figures on investment flows in Asia quoted by Alan Greenspan, remarks to the Economic Club of New York, Dec. 2, 1997; available online at http://www.bog.frb.fed.us).

[27] International Monetary Fund, *op. cit.,* p. 53.

[28] See Alan Greenspan, testimony before the Senate Budget Committee, Jan. 29, 1998; available online at http://www.bog.frb.fed.us.

[29] International Monetary Fund, *op. cit.,* pp. 54, 59.

[30] Greg Mastel, "A China the World Could Bank On," *The Washington Post,* Dec. 29, 1997, p. A17. For background, see "China After Deng," *The CQ Researcher,* June 13, 1997, pp. 505-528.

[31] See *CQ Weekly Report,* Jan. 10, 1998, pp. 64-65, and Jan. 31, 1998, pp. 232-235.

[32] C. Fred Bergsten in Morris Goldstein, ed., *The Case for an International Banking Standard* (1997), p. vii.

[33] *Ibid.*

[34] George Soros, "Avoiding a Breakdown," *Financial Times,* Dec. 31, 1997.

Bibliography

Selected Sources Used

Books and Reports

Bootle, Roger, *The Death of Inflation: Surviving and Thriving in the Zero Era*, Nicholas Brealey Publishing, 1997.

Bootle, a former lecturer at Oxford and well-known British commentator on economics, argues that the inflation-ridden era of the last 40 years was an aberration, but one so imprinted in our minds that economists and policy-makers alike can't see that fundamental changes in the global economy are making deflation a much greater threat today than inflation.

International Monetary Fund, *World Economic Outlook, Interim Assessment*, December 1997.

This report chronicles how Asia's powerhouse economies got into trouble, examines the implications of the crisis for other countries and explains the reasoning behind IMF loan packages to the region. The report, along with much more information on global economic conditions, can be obtained from the International Monetary Fund, Washington, D.C. 20431; 202-623-7300; fax: 202-623-6278; Web site: http://www.imf.org.

Mishkin, Frederic S., *The Economics of Money, Banking and Financial Markets* (Fifth Edition), Addison-Wesley, 1998.

This popular textbook by a former Federal Reserve economist provides a wealth of information on practically every important event in recent financial history. Mishkin, who is a professor of economics at Columbia University's Graduate School of Business, presents a detailed theory for why banking crises will continue to occur unless reforms are made to improve the flow of information to all participants in the financial system.

Articles

Blinder, Alan S., "The Speed Limit: Fact and Fancy in the Growth Debate," *The American Prospect*, No. 34, September-October 1997, pp. 57-62. Available online at http://epn.org/prospect/34/34blinfs.html.

Blinder, a Princeton economist, former vice chairman of the Federal Reserve Board and member of President Clinton's original Council of Economic Advisers, forcefully disputes the "new paradigm" theories that the economy now can grow much faster than previously believed without rekindling inflation. "Much as we might wish otherwise, it just ain't so," he says, offering a strong defense of the Federal Reserve's stance on monetary policy.

Mandel, Michael, Pete Engardio, Emily Thornton and Christopher Farrell, "The Threat of Deflation," *Business Week*, Nov. 10, 1997, pp. 55-59.

Much of the current debate about deflation began after *Business Week* published this article. Arguing that the world's capacity to produce goods far exceeds demand, the magazine suggests that the world has become "dangerously dependent on the U.S. as the consumer of last resort." If the U.S. economy falters, it concludes, "the world could end up with all sellers and no buyers — and on a path that leads to a devastating deflation."

"Will the World Slump?" *The Economist*, Nov. 15, 1997, pp. 15-16.

While acknowledging that Asia's "acute financial fragility" poses a serious threat to the global economy, *The Economist* says any problems associated with excess production capacity could be overcome by easing monetary policy. "Deflation, when it happens, exposes not the flaw in capitalism but the incompetence of central banks and governments," the magazine concludes.

Shephard, Stephen B., "The New Economy: What it Really Means," *Business Week*, Nov. 17, 1997, pp. 38-49.

In this commentary, *Business Week's* editor-in-chief lays out the case that global economic integration and the revolution in information technology are combining to "raise Americans' standard of living, create jobs, spur entrepreneurial effort — and do all this without boosting inflation."

On-Line Resources

Cents Financial Journal, Electronic Publishing Company, http://lp-llc.com/cents.

Until recently, a layman trying to fathom economic trends had few options between sifting through the mountain of raw statistics ground out by the government and reading journalistic analyses that often are incomplete. Now there's a useful alternative in cyberspace. The Electronic Publishing Company in California compiles analyses of current trends by leading economists and strategists.

Federal Reserve Board, http://www.bog.frb.fed.us.

Sometimes criticized as an aloof and unresponsive institution, the nation's central bank provides a wealth of information about its operations and the ideas that lie behind its conduct of monetary policy. Particularly noteworthy are its twice-annual monetary-policy reports to Congress and the minutes of its policy-making arm, the Federal Open Market Committee. Federal Reserve Chairman Alan Greenspan's speeches and congressional testimony also offer insights into the workings of the economy.

Dr. Ed Yardeni's Economics Network, http://www.yardeni.com.

The prolific chief economist for Deutsche Morgan Grenfell maintains this comprehensive Web site full of data, analysis and arguments supporting the thesis that the global economy has entered an inflation-free "new era."

The Next Step

Additional information from UMI's Newspaper & Periodical Abstracts™ database

Asian Economic Turmoil & the U.S.

Barr, Cameron, "Asia Waiting to Exhale: Why do currencies still tumble, despite IMF help? Reforming banks is not easy," *The Christian Science Monitor,* **Jan. 7, 1998, p. 1.**

East Asia's crisis could bring worldwide deflation. In order to forestall potential doom in the U.S. and elsewhere, policy-makers are struggling to understand why a region known for economic "miracles" has begun to implode.

Belton, Beth, "Too much of a good thing could mean deflation," *USA Today,* **Nov. 10, 1997, p. B3.**

Some U.S. executives and many economists worry that the Southeast Asian crisis could trigger a global chain reaction of deflation.

Butler, Steven, Philip J. Longman and Matthew Miller, "Pacific grim," *U.S. News & World Report,* **Dec. 8, 1997, pp. 26-30.**

Economic conditions are the worst since 1929 for the Far East. The authors describe how the crisis will affect America.

Forsyth, Randall W., "Current yield: As usual, bad news cheers the bond market, but not enough to push yields below 6%," *Barron's,* **Nov. 24, 1997, p. MW10.**

While the economic impact of the financial crisis in Asia has been unambiguously negative, the effect on the U.S. economy remains a matter of debate. In the markets, much talk of deflation is heard, although the term is bandied around loosely. The disinflationary impact on the U.S. economy from Asia has done part of the Federal Reserve's work in forestalling inflationary overheating.

Kahn, Joseph, and Michael Schuman, "Depression's Ghost Hovers Over Asia: Deflation," *The Wall Street Journal,* **Oct. 31, 1997, p. A16.**

The storm is deflation, or falling prices. Deflation has short-term advantages — helping keep consumer prices down, for example, or reducing Asia's real-estate and stock-market bubbles. But prolonged deflation can drag an economy to a halt, and some economists fear Asia has entered the worst deflationary period since the 1930s.

Neil, Andrew, Robert Gottliebsen and Bill Jamieson, "After the meltdown," *World Press Review,* **January 1998, pp. 13-15.**

Four reports are presented on the cascading currency crisis that has swept Southeast Asia and rocked Western markets in recent months.

Petruno, Tom, "Sorting Winners, Losers as Deflation Hits Home," *Los Angeles Times,* **Dec. 14, 1997, p. D4.**

Price deflation in the world economy was supposed to be one of the long-term side effects of Asia's economic slump. But the long-term apparently is already here. "The Asian crisis has unleashed tremendous deflationary pressures in the global economy," said Edward Yardeni, an economist at Deutsche Morgan Grenfell.

Welling, Kathryn M., "Why worry?" *Barron's,* **Nov. 10, 1997, p. 30.**

In an interview, Martin H. Barnes, managing editor of *Bank Credit Analyst,* discusses the deflationary forces at work around the globe. In Asia, he argues, all the classic background symptoms of deflation are present, such as a fragile banking system, a fragile economic system and falling equity prices of truly epic proportions. There is still a naive tendency to argue that the implications for U.S. investors can be quantified in terms of the share of U.S. exports that go to non-Japan Asia, which is about 20 percent. There is no current indication that a U.S. recession will unfold next year, but the case for a slowdown, such as GDP growth of 2 percent or less for a few quarters, in the U.S. is compelling.

Declining Prices and Deflation Fears

Brindley, David, "Going down . . . ," *U.S. News & World Report,* **Jan. 19, 1998, p. 70.**

Deflation is Wall Street's latest problem as the Labor Department announces that producer prices declined 1.2 percent in 1997, the sharpest drop since 1986. The drop is causing problems for bond markets.

Hamilton, Walter, "Deflation Talk Out in Open as Prices Fall," *Los Angeles Times,* **Jan. 6, 1998, p. A1.**

Federal Reserve Chairman Alan Greenspan stopped far short of proclaiming deflation a reality in a speech Saturday. But his mere mention of the subject indicated that even the longtime inflation hawk considers lower prices to be a possibility, and it stoked anticipation on Wall Street that the central bank will lower interest rates in coming months.

"Inflation's Evil Twin," *Detroit News,* **July 18, 1997, p. A10.**

Evidence is mounting that the Fed's enemy in the future will be deflation rather than the more familiar devil, inflation. Wholesale prices fell for the sixth straight month in June. The Consumer Price Index also has been trending down and commodities are below last year's levels. Finally, the price of gold, traditionally a key barometer of future price levels, has sunk to about $320 an ounce from last year's high of nearly $400.

Lucchetti, Aaron, "Commodities Market, Despite Gains, Will Be Remembered for Its Losses," *The Wall Street Journal*, Jan. 2, 1998, p. R34.

While disappointing to some, the downward spiral was a soothing melody to those worriedly listening for inflationary peeps. Economists and analysts say commodities prices instead showed a trend toward disinflation, an economic environment without price increases.

Ratajczak, Donald, "Upward pressure on wages takes steam out of deflation argument," *Atlanta Journal Constitution*, Dec. 7, 1997, p. H4.

Gold prices are below $300, oil prices are falling in winter, soybean prices are dropping, coffee prices are turning soft and almost anything from Asia is being ordered at lower dollar prices than a few months ago. Not surprisingly, many analysts have begun to talk about deflation, which is actual price declines throughout the economy.

Senner, Madis, "The buck should stop here," *Barron's*, Oct. 6, 1997, p. 59.

The world's economies are gripped by deflationary pressures. Global inflation is near historical lows and is falling. Some items have been declining in price, such as consumer durables in the U.S., which have fallen at a 3 percent-plus annual rate for the past two years. The potential for other prices to fall is growing, creating true deflation. Collectively and individually, governments are pursuing deflationary policies while fighting the last war of inflation.

Stevenson, Richard W., "Inflation Climbed Only 1.7 percent in 1997, Its Smallest Increase in 11 Years," *The New York Times*, Jan. 14, 1998, p. D2.

With the economic turmoil in Asia expected to drive the prices of many imported goods lower in coming months, the outlook is for inflation to remain tame. Since economists believe official statistics overstate inflation, some analysts think the economy could be on the brink of widespread decreases in the prices of commodities and manufactured goods, although prices for services are likely to go on rising.

Tanzer, Andrew, "Dr. Doom," *Forbes*, Jan. 26, 1998, p. 14.

Money manager Marc Faber is still advising investors to avoid Asian markets and to be cautious about U.S. markets. He believes the world may be moving from an inflationary environment into a deflationary recession.

Deflation Fears Overrated

Francis, David R., "Don't Worry About Deflation," *The Christian Science Monitor*, Jan. 12, 1998, p. B8.

"There is ample monetary growth to prevent systematic deflation," says economist Charles Plosser of the University of Rochester in New York. It isn't like deflation in the Depression, when the Federal Reserve let the supply of money fall 25 percent between 1929 and 1933. That pushed price levels down 22 percent in those years. Nonetheless, deflation could happen for a month or a quarter, says Plosser, dean of the university's business school.

Norton, Rob, "Why not to worry about deflation," *Fortune*, Sept. 8, 1997, p. 32.

Wall Street analysts need something to worry about and the latest concern is deflation. Sustained deflation could be scary, but there is no evidence of deflation occurring today.

Wessel, David, "Greenspan Ponders Risks Of Deflation," *The Wall Street Journal*, Jan. 5, 1998, p. A3.

Federal Reserve Chairman Alan Greenspan tiptoed up to the sensitive subject of stock prices in a weekend speech, cautioning that "very rapid asset price declines — in equity and real estate, especially — can be a virulently negative force in the economy." The Fed chairman dismissed the chances of a decline in prices of goods and services as "not . . . a significant near-term risk." An outspoken minority of economists is arguing that deflation in Japan and excess industrial capacity throughout Asia could produce a global glut of goods and commodities that leads to widespread declines in prices. But Greenspan has countered that prices of services aren't affected by Asia's woes and that the Fed's monetary policy is well-equipped to resist deflation in prices of goods and services should it arrive in the U.S.

Wysocki, Bernard Jr., "The Talk of Deflation Can Be Easily Deflated," *The Wall Street Journal*, Jan. 19, 1998, p. A1.

Talk of deflation has spiraled over the past six months. One investment house pored over a recent speech by Federal Reserve Chairman Alan Greenspan and noted that he mentioned deflation 18 times, even though Greenspan himself said he saw little likelihood that overall prices would fall anytime soon. Despite all the talk about deflation, the definition of it remains murky. Amid growing overcapacity and rising imports from Asia, many goods prices are falling. But that isn't deflation, because overall prices are still rising, especially for most services, from haircuts to school tuitions to cable-TV bills.

Back Issues

Great Research on Current Issues Starts Right Here . . . Recent topics covered by The CQ Researcher are listed below. Before May 1991, reports were published under the name of Editorial Research Reports.

AUGUST 1996
Fighting Over Animal Rights
Privatizing Government Services
Child Labor and Sweatshops
Cleaning Up Hazardous Wastes

SEPTEMBER 1996
Gambling Under Attack
The States and Federalism
Civic Journalism
Reassessing Foreign Aid

OCTOBER 1996
Political Consultants
Insurance Fraud
Rethinking School Integration
Parental Rights

NOVEMBER 1996
Global Warming
Clashing Over Copyright
Consumer Debt
Governing Washington, D.C.

DECEMBER 1996
Welfare, Work and the States
The New Volunteerism
Implementing the Disabilities Act
America's Pampered Pets

JANUARY 1997
Combating Scientific Misconduct
Restructuring the Electric Industry
The New Immigrants
Chemical and Biological Weapons

FEBRUARY 1997
Assisting Refugees
Alternative Medicine's Next Phase
Independent Counsels
Feminism's Future

MARCH 1997
New Air Quality Standards
Alcohol Advertising
Civic Renewal
Educating Gifted Students

APRIL 1997
Declining Crime Rates
The FBI Under Fire
Gender Equity in Sports
Space Program's Future

MAY 1997
The Stock Market
The Cloning Controversy
Expanding NATO
The Future of Libraries

JUNE 1997
FDA Reform
China After Deng
Line-Item Veto
Breast Cancer

JULY 1997
Transportation Policy
Executive Pay
School Choice Debate
Aggressive Driving

AUGUST 1997
Age Discrimination
Banning Land Mines
Children's Television
Evolution vs. Creationism

SEPTEMBER 1997
Caring for the Dying
Mental Health Policy
Mexico's Future
Youth Fitness

OCTOBER 1997
Urban Sprawl in the West
Diversity in the Workplace
Teacher Education
Contingent Work Force

NOVEMBER 1997
Renewable Energy
Artificial Intelligence
Religious Persecution
Roe v. Wade at 25

DECEMBER 1997
Whistleblowers
Castro's Next Move
Gun Control Standoff
Regulating Nonprofits

JANUARY 1998
Foster Care Reform
IRS Reform
The Black Middle Class
U.S.-British Relations

FEBRUARY 1998
Patients' Rights

Back issues are available for $5.00 (subscribers) or $10.00 (non-subscribers). Quantity discounts apply to orders over ten. To order, call Congressional Quarterly Customer Service at (202) 887-8621.

Binders are available for $18.00. To order call 1-800-638-1710. Please refer to stock number 648.

Future Topics

▶ *Caring for the Elderly*

▶ *The New Corporate Philanthropy*

▶ *Teenage Drinking*

THE CQ Researcher

PUBLISHED BY CONGRESSIONAL QUARTERLY INC.

Caring for the Elderly

Is adequate long-term care available?

Americans today live longer than their parents did — often two or three decades after retirement. For many, modern medicine's gift of time is a blessing. But when independent living is no longer possible, few elderly people or their families are prepared for the confusing and emotionally wrenching world of long-term care. Despite reforms passed by Congress, nursing homes remain controversial. Moreover, they are too expensive for many people, and the federal Medicare and Medicaid insurance programs provide limited benefits for nursing home care. Although innovative alternatives to nursing homes have emerged in recent years, long-term care remains a costly and complex issue. And the problems are only likely to intensify when the nation's baby boomers enter old age.

CQ | Feb. 20, 1998 • Volume 8, No. 7 • Pages 145-168

Formerly Editorial Research Reports

THE CQ Researcher

February 20, 1998
Volume 8, No. 7

EDITOR
Sandra Stencel

MANAGING EDITOR
Thomas J. Colin

ASSOCIATE EDITOR
Sarah M. Magner

STAFF WRITERS
Mary H. Cooper
Kenneth Jost
David Masci

PRODUCTION EDITOR
Melissa Hall

EDITORIAL ASSISTANT
Vanessa E. Furlong

PUBLISHED BY
Congressional Quarterly Inc.

CHAIRMAN
Andrew Barnes

VICE CHAIRMAN
Andrew P. Corty

PRESIDENT AND PUBLISHER
Robert W. Merry

EXECUTIVE EDITOR
David Rapp

Bibliographic records and abstracts included in The Next Step section of this publication are the copyrighted material of UMI, and are used with permission.

The CQ Researcher (ISSN 1056-2036). Formerly Editorial Research Reports. Published weekly, except Jan. 2, May 29, July 3, Oct. 30, by Congressional Quarterly Inc., 1414 22nd St., N.W., Washington, D.C. 20037. Annual subscription rate for libraries, businesses and government is $340. Additional rates furnished upon request. Periodicals postage paid at Washington, D.C., and additional mailing offices. POSTMASTER: Send address changes to The CQ Researcher, 1414 22nd St., N.W., Washington, D.C. 20037.

COVER PHOTO BY LINDA BARTLETT

Caring for the Elderly

BY MARY H. COOPER

THE ISSUES

Lillian Taylor had not planned on remaining in Virginia. But while visiting her daughter in a suburb outside Washington, she suffered a debilitating stroke.

When her condition stabilized, she faced not returning home to Alabama and an even grimmer prospect: living out her life in a nursing home.

But the place her daughter found did not conform to the popular stereotype of a stark, malodorous warehouse for lonely, mistreated people. Instead, Taylor discovered a cheerful, homey refuge that bustled with dogs, cats, birds and visiting schoolchildren who were as much a part of the environment as the elderly residents themselves.

"I like it here very much," Taylor says as she strokes a cat purring contentedly in her lap. "I had a beautiful yellow cat back home, but I had to farm him out to another lady. Here everybody is friendly, and I like that because I like people."

The Fairfax Nursing Center is among a small but growing number of nursing homes around the country that follow the "Eden Alternative" approach to improving the quality of life for their residents.

The Eden model, founded by a family practitioner in upstate New York, is one of many improvements in long-term care that have emerged over the last decade or so. *(See story, p. 150.)* The improvements stem in large measure from the 1987 Nursing Home Reform Act, which imposed stricter regulation and oversight of the nursing home industry. The law is widely regarded as the single most important legislation affecting long-term care for the nation's 1.6 million nursing home residents.

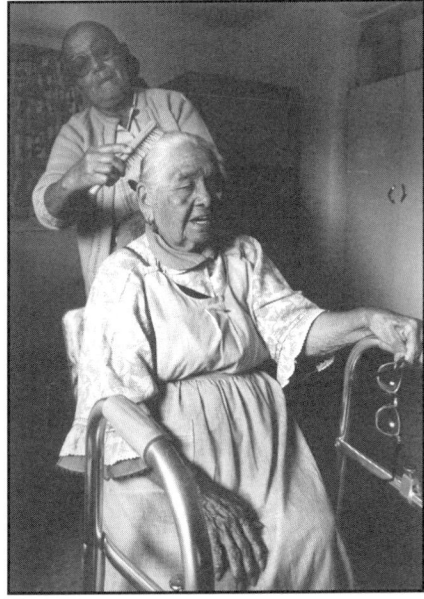

"There's no doubt that the law brought a great deal of improvement," says Sarah Burger, acting director of the National Citizens' Coalition for Nursing Home Reform. "It addressed something that had never been addressed before — the quality of life in nursing homes — which it defined as the highest practicable mental, physical and psychosocial well-being for each individual. In other words, the law said it's not OK for just some individuals to get good care. Every individual is important."

Despite the overall improvements, critics say facilities like the Fairfax Nursing Center are the exception.

"Despite regulations designed to ensure adequate nutrition, malnutrition is a common, potentially serious, yet frequently undetected and often untreated or undertreated problem in long-term care institutions," said Jeanie Kayser-Jones, a professor of physiological nursing and medical anthropology at the University of California at San Francisco who conducted a study of nutritional standards in nursing homes. "When we think of people going to bed hungry, many of us tend to think of people in developing countries, such as little children in Rwanda or people in North Korea. Most of us would probably not believe that in some American nursing homes people also go to bed hungry, not because food is unavailable, but because, among other factors, no one takes the time to feed them." [1]

Public opinion polls also reflect the concern about nursing home quality. A 1996 poll by the Alliance for Aging Research found that Americans' No. 1 worry about growing older was "living for many years in a nursing home because of physical frailty or long-term illness." A 1995 survey by the Daniel Yankelovich Group for the American Association of Retired Persons (AARP) found that the No. 1 financial concern of Americans was "getting quality long-term care." [2] And in a survey of more than 9,000 hospital patients, fully 30 percent said they would "rather die" than live permanently in a nursing home. [3]

But the rapid aging of American society is forcing more and more people to contemplate long-term care, for themselves or for others. The average life span has grown dramatically, from 33 years in Colonial times, to about 72 for men and 79 for women. About 33 million people — one in eight Americans — were 65 or older in 1994. By 2030, there will be an estimated 69 million Americans 65 and over, or one in five.

The number of Americans needing long-term care is expected to reach 9 million by 2000 and mushroom to 24 million by 2060. And while most elderly people continue to receive long-term care at home or with relatives or friends, two out of five Americans will be cared for in a nursing home for at least a short time. [4]

To meet the growing demand for long-term care, new alternatives to traditional nursing homes have proliferated over the past decade. Agencies that provide Medi-

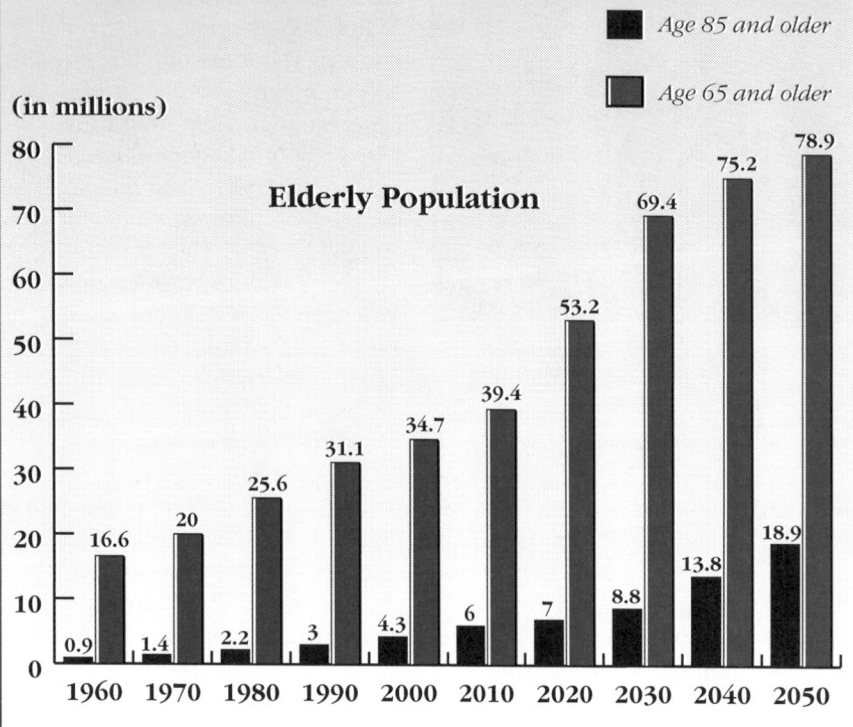

Profile of an Aging Nation

Americans 85 and older are the nation's fastest-growing age group. From 1960 to 1990, this group increased by more than 200 percent, compared with a gain of less than 100 percent for those 65 or older. By 2050, the 85-and-over population is expected to be six times its 1990 size.

(in millions)

■ Age 85 and older

▬ Age 65 and older

Elderly Population

	1960	1970	1980	1990	2000	2010	2020	2030	2040	2050
Age 85 and older	0.9	1.4	2.2	3	4.3	6	7	8.8	13.8	18.9
Age 65 and older	16.6	20	25.6	31.1	34.7	39.4	53.2	69.4	75.2	78.9

Sources: U.S. Census Bureau, August 1997; American Health Care Association, based on U.S. Census Bureau, Current Population Reports, *April 1996*

---

care-certified home health-care personnel represent the fastest-growing segment of the long-term care industry. They supply trained aides who provide limited medical assistance to stay-at-home seniors as well as help with daily activities such as bathing, dressing, going to the bathroom and eating.

In addition, some 65,000 assisted-living facilities have sprung up around the country, most over the past decade. Offering room, board and help with daily activities, these facilities fill a middle ground between living at home and in a nursing home

for an estimated 1 million residents. [5]

"Assisted living is best at giving the kind of care that relatives can provide, were they available," says Elizabeth C. Clemmer, associate director for consumer policy research at the AARP's Public Policy Institute. "But everybody works these days and can't help care for relatives. And people are living a lot longer and need more years of this kind of care. Assisted living is terrific for dressing, bathing, helping with incontinence and caring for people with dementia or people whose medical conditions are stable." [6]

"All these services have become big alternatives to nursing homes fairly recently," says Robert Greenwood, a spokesman for the American Association of Homes and Services for the Aging (AAHSA). "Home health aide was the fastest-growing occupation in the United States last year, and assisted-living facilities are growing very quickly as well."

Encompassing the full range of services for older Americans are so-called continuing-care retirement communities. These self-contained facilities provide cottages and apartments for self-sufficient residents, as well as assisted-living and nursing facilities, and offer dining rooms, social activities and health-care services.

While demographic changes are increasing the demand for quality long-term care, few elderly people or their families are prepared to make rational choices about long-term care when the need arises. Clemmer advises the elderly and their families to take the time to comparison shop among care facilities, perhaps eating a meal and chatting with residents. But this rarely happens.

"The choice of a long-term care facility is frequently made on a very short-term basis," she says. "Typically, you arrive at your parents' home and notice a crisis, or a parent is about to be discharged from the hospital after a fall or a minor stroke. People resist thinking about long-term care until they need it because they don't like the idea of leaving their own homes."

A major concern is cost. Nursing homes, for example, charge on average more than $40,000 a year. Continuing-care communities charge entry fees of up to $100,000 and monthly rents of $1,000 and up for those who don't buy their units. And that doesn't even count the cost of care in the community's assisted-living or nursing facility. [7]

Many people are unaware that long-term care for the so-called "frail elderly" is not covered by private health insurance. Long-term care policies have been available for the past decade or so, but have failed to catch on because of the high cost of coverage. *(See story, p. 162.)* Long-term care coverage is also problematic under public insurance programs. Medicare, the federal health insurance program for the elderly and disabled, only covers short stays in skilled-nursing homes following a hospital discharge. [8] And Medicaid, the federal-state health insurance program for the poor, cannot be used for nursing home care unless virtually all the resident's assets have been used up.

"Although Medicaid now pays for over half of all nursing home care, it was not designed to be a long-term care program," Greenwood says. "Medicaid was designed as a program for poor people. So basically what we're doing is making people become poor before we'll pay for their care."

The problem of finding long-term care for the elderly often falls to their baby boomer children, adults typically in their 40s and 50s who often live far from their aging relatives. Older baby boomers face the same challenges that confronted their parents: holding down jobs, raising children and paying for college. But because of rising life expectancies, they now often face the additional problem of obtaining and monitoring long-term care for their parents as well. Caught in the middle between their own kids and their parents, they have been dubbed the "sandwich generation."

Clemmer herself experienced the sandwich generation's dilemma. As a full-time AARP employee, she lived in Washington with her husband and children. But her aging parents in New Jersey needed help. "I was driving to New Jersey every other weekend," she recalls. "It was absolutely exhausting." The commute took an emotional as well as a physical toll on Clemmer's life. "Everybody was losing out because I was running back and forth between two families. I was the wife and mother in one family and the daughter of two parents who needed a lot of attention 200 miles away. If I had ever considered what the situation would have been like if I hadn't done it, I might have felt better about what I was doing. But I was so aware of how I was shortchanging everyone."

"People are just now starting to speak up because they're being squeezed," says Howard Bedlin, vice president for public policy and advocacy at the National Council on the Aging. "The burdens are not only financial but physical and emotional as well. Many of the caregivers are in their 50s, and they can't help but realize the problem is only going to get much worse. If you look at the demographics, the baby boom generation is going to increase the demand for long-term care services enormously. The sooner we deal with it, the more affordable it will be."

As the number of Americans over age 65 continues to spiral, these are some of the questions being asked:

Do nursing homes provide high-quality care for elderly Americans?

The difference between nursing homes today and facilities of 20 or 30 years ago is often apparent as soon as one enters. Posted for all to see will be a list of residents' rights as well as the name and address of the area ombudsman, to whom residents and relatives may appeal when their complaints about poor service go unheeded. [9] The atmosphere is probably cheerier, there are fewer bad odors and residents are less likely to be restrained in bed or left for long periods in hallways with nothing to do.

"Nursing homes aren't what they were in the 1950s, '60s or even the '70s," says Tom Burke, a spokesman for the American Health Care Associa-

tion (AHCA), which represents 11,000 of the nation's 17,000 nursing homes. "They continue to evolve and change, and as they do the practice of long-term care improves dramatically."

Whatever improvements have been made have resulted in large part from the Nursing Home Reform Act. Part of the 1987 Omnibus Budget Reconciliation Act (OBRA), the law was the first measure requiring sweeping improvements in the quality of care provided by nursing homes. "One really good thing about OBRA '87 is that people have begun to realize that they do have rights in a nursing home setting," says Faith Mullen, a senior analyst at the AARP specializing in nursing home issues. "That concept didn't exist in 1973, when my grandfather was in a nursing home. Then, you were just sort of grateful when the staff didn't yell at the residents so much. Things really have changed a lot."

Perhaps most important, the law required nursing homes to establish a formal patient-assessment process. Nursing home administrators must bring together their nurses, aides, social workers and therapists, as well as attending physicians and available family members, to develop a course of care for each resident. Care for patients with Alzheimer's disease, who might wander or endanger themselves, would differ from that prescribed for a mentally stable but frail resident who needs extra care for feeding and incontinence. [10]

"Since the implementation of OBRA in the nation's nursing homes, quality of care has dramatically improved," says Catherine Hawes, co-director of the program on aging and long-term care at the Research Triangle Institute, a North Carolina think tank. "Moreover," says Hawes, who led a four-year study of the law's impact, "improvements in nursing home care have significantly reduced the use of hospitals by nursing home

Cats, Dogs and Kids Add Cozy Touch . . .

In the late 1980s, several years into his career as a family practitioner and emergency room physician, William H. Thomas embarked on a new calling as a nursing home doctor.

"In four years at Harvard Medical School, I never set foot inside a nursing home," he recalls. "My new job required that I rethink my prejudices and biases about nursing homes. On the one hand, I found the possibility of a nurturing, supportive home for the frail, ill, elderly to be a warm and civilized thought. On the other hand, I knew that nursing homes, ostensibly dedicated to caring, were widely perceived as cold, sterile and uncaring. Why? Tackling this paradox led me toward a new approach to giving care in the nursing home — an approach that recognizes each resident's desire for a life worth living." [1]

Together with his wife and partner Judy, Thomas devised a new approach to caring for the elderly which he introduced in 1991 at Chase Memorial Nursing Home, an 80-bed facility in New Berlin, N.Y. By integrating animals, plants and children into the nursing home environment, the so-called Eden Alternative attempts to restore communication, interest and warmth to the everyday lives of residents.

After introducing birds, dogs, cats, rabbits, plants and children's play groups into the home, Thomas found that

Nursing home residents' interest in their environment picked up, and their use of anti-depressants dropped, when animals, plants and children were introduced, says Eden Alternative founder William H. Thomas.

residents' interest in their environment picked up. The use of psychotropic drugs to combat depression, anxiety and psychosis dropped, as did the incidence of respiratory and other infections. "While medical science wages its ultimately futile war on death, the Eden Alternative campaigns for life," Thomas writes. "Reasons to live are what living is all about." [2]

The Fairfax Nursing Center, a 200-bed, family-owned facility in Northern Virginia, is one of more than a hundred nursing homes around the country that have adopted the Eden Alternative approach. Visitors are greeted by Toodles, a small gray dog, and the song of a canary perched in a cage over the reception desk. Pots of green plants are everywhere. Diva, an overweight black Labrador retriever, ambles down the hall, weaving her way among residents in wheelchairs who are on their way to a meeting to discuss the next month's menu and vote on what will be served at the monthly "diet holiday" dinner.

Throughout the facility are touches rarely found in traditional nursing homes, from popcorn carts and candy dispensers in the hallways to the "please play me" signs on pianos and other musical instruments in the reception areas. And each new resident is greeted with a warmed blanket on arrival.

residents, with an estimated savings of more than $2 billion per year, according to the Medicare program."

According to Burger of the coalition for nursing home reform, however, the assessment process has not been uniformly embraced. "It has been a highly effective instrument for those who have been able to use it

correctly," she says. "But even now, six years after the assessment initiative took effect, there are still a lot of nursing homes that consider this something that the government makes them do rather than looking at it as something that could help them meet their residents' needs."

In fact, while consumer advocates

and industry spokesmen agree that the 1987 law has improved nursing home care, they disagree over the extent of the changes. For all the improvements in nursing home care, critics say, there are still poor-quality and even abusive facilities.

"Do they still exist? Yes, they do," Burger warns. "Are there fewer of them?

... At 'Eden Alternative' Nursing Homes

Even the section reserved for residents with Alzheimer's disease and other forms of dementia has a resident dog, as well as a cozy electric-log fireplace and music. The scent of baking bread drifting through the hallways reflects the facility's use of aroma therapy as yet another way to foster residents' interest in their environment.

Although most residents share rooms with one to three others, all the rooms at the Fairfax Nursing Center are decorated differently to give the facility a homelike atmosphere. There are plants in every room, as well as the occasional cat curled on a bed. The facility's dogs and cats roam freely throughout the building, except for one floor that is reserved for people with allergies. Visitors are encouraged to bring their leashed dogs to visit residents, and pet-therapy volunteers bring additional dogs and cats for residents to hold.

"Some assisted-living facilities may have one rabbit, but I don't know of any nursing homes like this," says Sharyn Henderson, who cares for two rabbits, five cats, five dogs, 18 canaries and fish at Fairfax Nursing Center. "Nursing-home directors are calling me now to find out how to introduce animals. It's a program that's getting more and more popular."

In addition to the animals and plants, Eden-style facilities like Fairfax also differ from traditional nursing homes in their flexible staffing policies. Registered and licensed nurses, nurse assistants and activities staff share many duties, which lends a more familylike quality to resident care. Specialized staff provide services that are absent from most institutions. In addition to Henderson, the center employs two massage nurses, who give each resident a 10-15-minute massage twice weekly, and a full-time manicurist. Activities specialists arrange numerous events, such as van rides in the country and shopping trips, as well as a full calendar of in-house events, including religious services, crafts, language classes, storytelling and other activities.

"I like playing in the bell choir," says Clara Gilmore, who moved into the center two years ago. "But what I like best are the board games like bingo." Volunteers help provide spontaneous activities, such as a young man with a guitar singing "Sweet Adeline" to a group of wheelchair-bound residents gathered around a nursing station.

Because nursing-home residents often miss interaction with other age groups, Edenized homes bring children into the environment as often as possible. At Fairfax Nursing Center a neighborhood play group of mothers and preschool children comes to the center periodically to play in the reception areas or on the play lot just outside.

"Having the children come here is the nicest part of it," says Arless Almany, who arrived three years ago. "I miss my grandchildren, and it's good to see these nice little kids in the play group."

To enable residents to interact regularly with other age groups, Eden Alternative facilities bring children into the homes as often as possible.

---

[1] William H. Thomas, *Life Worth Living* (1996), pp. xii, xiv.

[2] *Ibid*, p. 59.

I hope so. But we still get family members who call us repeatedly and tell us, for example, when they went to visit their relative in the nursing home there was one aide for 61 patients. A percentage of nursing homes give perfectly abominable care."

The Creekside Care Convalescent Hospital in Vacaville, Calif., received widespread notoriety last fall for its allegedly poor care. Residents reportedly were not permitted outside, and were left bedridden for long periods, causing life-threatening bedsores.

A statewide investigation prompted by the Vacaville case, and others, found that more than 7 percent of nursing home deaths in California were from preventable conditions, including starvation, dehydration and infections related to untreated bedsores.[11] Similar cases of neglect and abuse can be found in other states as well.

Industry representatives downplay such horror stories. "Obviously, there are always problems in any large system," Burke says. "There are pock-

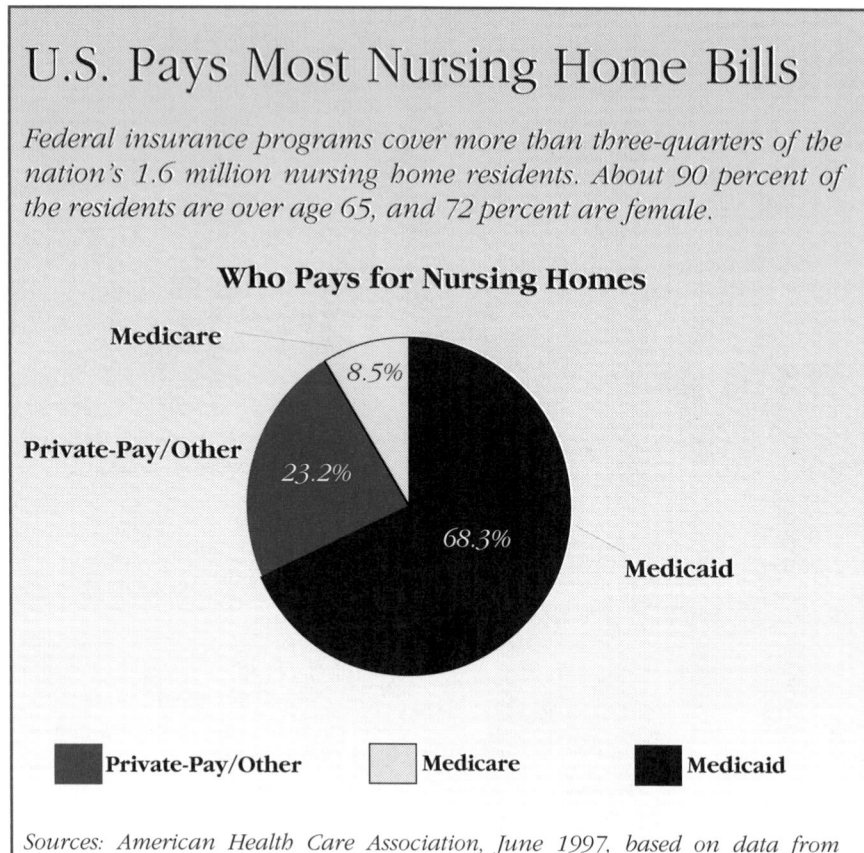

U.S. Pays Most Nursing Home Bills

Federal insurance programs cover more than three-quarters of the nation's 1.6 million nursing home residents. About 90 percent of the residents are over age 65, and 72 percent are female.

Who Pays for Nursing Homes

Medicare — 8.5%

Private-Pay/Other — 23.2%

68.3% — Medicaid

■ Private-Pay/Other   ▢ Medicare   ■ Medicaid

Sources: American Health Care Association, June 1997, based on data from National Center for Health Statistics and Health Care Financing Administration

ets where some quality isn't up to snuff, and sometimes good facilities run into problems with individual patients. But overall, quality has improved. Thanks to the 1987 law, for example, there is now a formal care plan for each resident. Also, there is a greater effort not to use restraint devices and drugs, which has greatly improved the quality of life in nursing homes."

Should facilities for the elderly be more strictly regulated?

Of all the types of facilities that provide long-term care for the elderly, only nursing homes come under federal regulation. The Nursing Home Reform Act tightened the standards used by state surveyors to assess the quality of care at nursing homes.

"Nursing homes," says AAHSA's Greenwood, "are one of the most highly regulated industries in the United States right now."

The 1987 law was mainly intended to halt the widespread abuse of "frail elderly" residents. "Historically, you have to look at how dismal the quality of such care was in nursing homes," says Mullen of the AARP. But another key reason for the heavy regulation derives from the fact that, unlike assisted-living or independent-living facilities, nursing homes receive more than half their income from Medicaid, and, to a much lesser extent, from Medicare. *(See graph, above.)* "So there is a lot of regulation as a way of controlling costs and quality," Mullen says, "because the person who is paying for these services is the taxpayer. No other long-term care environment has quite

the same funding base."

In Mullen's view, the current regulations are not only appropriate but should be strengthened to require all states to adopt consistent standards for the periodic surveys that are conducted to assess compliance with regulations governing food preparation, sanitary conditions and staffing levels.

"The law is a wonderful starting place because it offers in great detail a way to really assess care in nursing facilities," she says. "What's probably needed, though, is more money and more training of the people who actually go out and do the surveys. There are surveyors who find violations that are not probably indicative of bad care, while there are others who are not finding things that are indicative of bad care. There's just a big disparity nationally within the survey process."

The nursing home industry is less enthusiastic about the regulatory regime. "We're not opposed to regulations in general," Burke says. "We realize that they create a stable environment for the vulnerable elderly." But he claims that nursing homes are bearing an unfair share of the cost of compliance with federal regulations. "We don't believe that the [large] amount of regulations is supported by the rate paid for Medicaid patients. In other words, the federal and state governments are not paying for the regulations that they want nursing homes to enforce."

Burke also says nursing home regulations focus excessively on irrelevant details, creating red tape for administrators while ignoring the more important goal of residents' well-being. "Just about everything that goes on in a nursing facility is regulated, from food service to safety to physical plant," he says. "Sometimes those regulations attempt to micromanage too much and are too inflexible, and their application sometimes suffers from the subjective interpretation of surveyors."

More important, in Burke's view, is the clinical outcome for residents. "Often inspectors don't look at that, and really there's no good way of measuring it, so they go in and count the dust balls instead."

If a nursing home is not in compliance with the regulations, there is hell to pay, Burke says. "A facility with an excellent staff may suffer from a poor physical plant, but that doesn't necessarily make it a bad facility," he says. "Trying to comply with the plethora of duplicative regulations just becomes numbing. And of course, for a nursing facility, if you don't comply with something it always comes out [in the press] as a horror story, regardless of whether it's a patient-care issue, which obviously is very serious, or some other issue."

While complaining of regulatory overkill, Burke argues that the industry could use more help from state and federal governments in providing background checks to help them weed out former criminals among nursing home employees.

"We're dealing with a very vulnerable population," he says. "But we are hiring people at the nurse's-aide level, who tend to be people who are in and out of jobs. You're supposed to check their references, but sometimes former employers will only confirm whether or not they worked for them."

Should the government shoulder a greater burden of long-term care?

Long-term care can be one of the biggest expenses retirees face, especially if they live long enough to require the level of attention that nursing homes provide. Yet many older Americans fail to consider the costs of such care as they prepare to stop working. At $40,000 a year on average, nursing homes cost more than most workers earn in a year and are far out of reach for the vast majority of elderly Americans. [12]

Nursing home care that is paid for by patients is largely paid for out-of-pocket, rather than by private insurance. In fact, because long-term care insurance is expensive, and has only become available in recent years, less than 1 percent of nursing home residents were covered in 1995, the last year for which statistics are available. [13] Medicare, which only provides coverage for acute health care, only

This man entered a nursing home after minor surgery. He was regularly restrained and died within two months, according to University of California Professor Jeanie Kayser-Jones.

covers limited nursing home stays following hospitalization and skilled home health-care services *(see p. 157)*. And Medicaid, which largely aids the poor, only pays for nursing home care when a person's assets are almost completely exhausted.

"There is an enormous institutional bias in public funding for long-term care," says Bedlin of the NCOA. "In the Medicaid program, four out of five dollars go to institutional care. We need to provide more incentives and more options for people so they are not forced prematurely into nursing homes. That's the challenge for government — to shift resources to home- and community-based alternatives."

Some industry representatives call for expanding Medicare coverage for nursing home residents. "Medicare is a great system because it protects people 65 and over from catastrophic consequences," Burke says. "But at the point you become the most vulnerable in your life and need care, Medicare dumps you. You've got to go into a welfare program called Medicaid."

A proposal from the AHCA calls for expanding Medicare to include long-term as well as acute care. "Fundamental compassion and fairness demand shifting our nation's long-term care financing system from the Medicaid welfare program to the mainstream of our nation's health-care financing scheme," the association declares. [14]

People in assisted-living facilities and other long-term care facilities also can face an even worse financial dilemma, even though the cost of care is usually less than for nursing homes. "There's nothing wrong with saving for your old age and having enough to pay for your care," says Burger of the coalition for nursing home reform. "But people often run out of money early. What happens if you're an older person in assisted living, which is private-pay, and your money runs out before you die? What do you do? Where do you go?"

For many people, the only recourse is an older version of assisted living called a board-and-care facility, which will often accept impoverished residents' Social Security checks for payment.

"Whatever the Social Security amount is, that's what the operator of the facility gets," Burger says. "So you can imagine what the care is like in those places."

The financial dilemma faced by many residents of assisted-living facilities has become so severe that some experts say Medicaid should be extended to cover part of the cost of their care. "After a while, we will run out of people who can pay the average of $72 a day for assisted living," says Clemmer of the AARP. "That's more money than the average single person can shell out, particularly because we're talking about a population in which the average age is 84, and three-quarters are women. So we're talking about Social Security and their husbands' pensions to a large extent. Now the industry itself is really looking toward getting adequate public payment in order to maintain its reputation and standards."

But some experts say Medicare and Medicaid are too hard-pressed satisfying their current mandates to take on the added burden of long-term care for the elderly. "The government — that is, the taxpayers — can no longer pay for long-term care for middle- and upper-income families who are able to save, insure and pool resources on their own," former Commerce Secretary Peter G. Peterson wrote in a 1996 book. "These families must be encouraged to purchase private long-term care insurance — something Medicaid's de facto universal entitlement now gives them no incentive to do." [15] ■

BACKGROUND

Rising Demand

Until a few decades ago, long-term care for the elderly wasn't a matter of public policy. There was no need.

Compared with today, people died at an earlier age, and death often followed quickly after acute illness. Moreover, in years past, the vast majority of old people remained in their own communities, cared for by relatives or friends. Today, however, as more people survive serious illness to become the "frail elderly," the demand for institutional long-term care is greater.

There are now more than 33 million Americans age 65 or older, or about one in eight people. That number is expected to grow to 53 million by 2020, or one in six. By 2050, some 80 million Americans, or 20 percent of the population, will be at least 65.

But the fastest-growing portion of the population is the so-called "old old," people over 85. The 3.6 million members of this group are most likely to spend their last years with chronic debilitating conditions, such as dementia or paralysis following a stroke. They also are likely to require more hands-on care than most families or friends are equipped to provide. But even less hands-on care will be available because more women — the traditional caregivers for the elderly — are now in the work force.

As a result of these demographic and work-force trends, the long-term-care industry has boomed over the past few decades, from just over 500,000 nursing home beds in 1963 to 1.7 million today. [16]

In the 1960s, as demand for long-term care began its rapid ascent, nursing homes were typically small, converted residential houses run by a husband and wife team with additional staff, and, at least during the day, managed by a licensed nurse-practitioner. Less closely supervised facilities, called board-and-care homes, provided less disabled residents with help in daily activities. These precursors to today's assisted-living facilities generally were used as a solution of last resort for the poor

elderly, who were unable to continue living independently and had no family or friends to care for them but did not require the constant supervision a nursing home could provide.

1987 Reform Act

The rapid expansion of nursing homes and other long-term care institutions in the 1960s and '70s outpaced the states' efforts to oversee the industry. Opportunistic and illegal operators exploited the lack of oversight, resulting in numerous reports of abuse and neglect.

In an effort to improve conditions, a reform movement was launched to impose stronger regulations on the industry at both the federal and state levels. President Richard M. Nixon bolstered the movement in 1971 when he called for expanded enforcement of existing federal nursing home regulations and convened the first White House Conference on Aging.

The coalition for nursing home reform, created in 1975, spurred the tightening of regulations by the late '70s to include uniform fire-protection standards, higher staff-qualification requirements and lower staff-resident ratios. [17]

Despite the improved oversight, lapses in long-term care for the elderly persisted. Support for stiffer regulation of the industry grew following the 1986 release by the Institute of Medicine of a study denouncing the treatment of many nursing home residents as "shockingly deficient." [18] The following year Congress rewrote and strengthened the standards governing nursing homes that are eligible to participate in the Medicare and Medicaid programs.

The new standards enacted by the 1987 Nursing Home Reform Act applied equally to skilled-nursing facilities —

Continued on p. 156

Chronology

1960s-1970s
Demand for long-term care grows rapidly with the rise in the elderly population.

1960
Developer Del Webb opens the Sun City retirement community in Phoenix, Ariz., paving the way for many similar communities throughout the desert Southwest and Florida.

1965
Congress launches Medicare, the federal health insurance program for the elderly and the disabled, and Medicaid, the federal-state insurance program for the poor.

1970
The number of "old old" Americans — those 85 and older — exceeds 1 million, fueling the demand for long-term care.

1971
President Richard M. Nixon calls for expanded enforcement of federal regulations on nursing homes and convenes the first White House Conference on Aging.

1975
The National Citizens' Coalition for Nursing Home Reform is founded by 12 citizen advocacy groups to promote higher standards in long-term care.

————— • —————

1980s
Concern over the poor quality of care in nursing homes prompts Congress to tighten regulations over the industry.

1986
An Institute of Medicine study denounces the treatment of many nursing home residents as "shockingly deficient."

1987
The Nursing Home Reform Act, part of the fiscal 1987 Omnibus Budget Reconciliation Act, imposes sweeping changes in nursing home regulations and creates a "Residents' Bill of Rights" to reduce abuses.

————— • —————

1990s
As the graying of America continues, the demand for long-term care mounts.

1996
Concerned about the long-term solvency of federal health and disability programs, Congress makes it a federal crime to give away property in order to become eligible for Medicaid. The measure is later rewritten to bar lawyers and accountants from advising consumers to give away assets for this purpose. Former Commerce Secretary Peter G. Peterson writes in his book *Will America Grow Up Before It Grows Old?* that middle- and upper-income Americans "must be encouraged to purchase private long-term care insurance."

Aug. 7, 1997
Lawmakers incorporate options for managed care into Medicare in an effort to save the program money. By the end of the year, the number of Americans 85 and older reaches about 4 million. The number of nursing home beds hits 1.7 million, up from just over 500,000 beds in 1963.

Oct. 21, 1997
The Leadership Council of Aging Organizations calls for an expansion of Medicare to cover the cost of prescription drugs, preventive services and long-term care.

Jan. 8, 1998
President Clinton proposes expanding Medicare to cover younger displaced workers and retirees ages 55-64, who often are unable to obtain private health coverage.

March 1, 1999
The National Bipartisan Commission on the Future of Medicare is scheduled to release its recommendations on ways to ensure the program's solvency in the 21st century.

————— • —————

2000s
Aging baby boomers swell the ranks of consumers of long-term care.

2011
The first baby boomers reach 65, making them eligible under current law for Medicare.

2030
People 65 years and older account for one in five Americans, up from one in eight in 1994.

2050
As the last baby boomers reach 85, the number of potential consumers of long-term care approaches 19 million.

The 'Residents' Bill of Rights'

The 1987 Nursing Home Reform Act required all nursing homes to post a "Residents' Bill of Rights." It must list patients' legal rights under the act as well as the name and address of the area ombudsman, to whom residents and their relatives can appeal when they feel their complaints or problems have not been resolved. The "Bill of Rights" gives patients the right to:

• choose a personal physician and be informed in advance about treatment;

• be free from physical or chemical restraints;

• have privacy (though not a private room);

• obtain prompt resolution of grievances concerning the behavior of other residents;

• participate in social, religious and community activities that do not violate the rights of other residents;

• enjoy confidentiality of records;

• receive needed services;

• complain without reprisal;

• examine the results of the most recent survey of the facility by government inspectors; and,

• have immediate access to a state or local long-term care ombudsman.

Continued from p. 154

the only nursing homes that receive Medicare coverage — and intermediate-care facilities, where qualifying patients are covered by Medicaid.

To participate in either federal program, nursing homes were required by the new law to formally assess the medical and psychological needs of each new resident and set out a plan of care to meet those needs. The care plan had to be updated at least annually. Mentally ill or retarded patients could not be admitted unless they also required the level of nursing care provided by the facility. In addition to medical care, facilities had to offer a broad range of ancillary social and medical services, including physical therapy and dental and dietetic care. The law also set sanitation standards to prevent the spread of infections and diseases, as well as construction standards to promote health and safety.

An innovative feature of the law required all nursing homes to post a "Residents' Bill of Rights" spelling out the right, among other things, to be free from physical or chemical restraints, enjoy confidentiality of records and complain without reprisal.

The law addressed complaints about poor quality of care by requiring all facilities participating in Med-

icaid or Medicare to have at least one registered nurse on duty eight hours a day and at least one licensed practical nurse on duty at all times. Homes with more than 120 beds were required to employ at least one full-time social worker. And all nursing aides — the least-qualified caregivers — had to complete a 75-hour training course and pass a competency evaluation.

The law assigned to the states the responsibility for ensuring compliance with the new federal standards through a uniform survey and certification process. Surveyors have to assess each facility at least every 15 months for quality of care and compliance with all standards. The results of these surveys are periodically reviewed by the Department of Health and Human Services (HHS) to further ensure compliance. Non-compliant facilities face sanctions ranging from fines to closure.

Maryland officials emphasize that the difference in minimum standards does not mean that the state's elderly are necessarily forced to accept inferior accommodations. "There's nothing preventing an assisted-living provider in Maryland from offering something that looks like the Oregon model," says Ilene Rosenthal, chief of housing services for the Maryland Office on Aging. "There are choices

for consumers, based on their personal preferences and ability to pay." However, while Oregon offers Medicaid coverage for assisted living, that is a benefit Maryland cannot yet afford to offer. "We already have a significant inventory of nursing homes in the state, and while assisted living may be better and in most cases cost less than nursing home care, the state would have to appropriate huge, new sums in order to do that."

Alternative Facilities

The 1987 law covers only nursing homes that participate in the Medicare and Medicaid programs. But while nursing homes remain the predominant source of institutional long-term care for the elderly, other providers have emerged in recent years for senior citizens who are no longer willing or able to live at home but who do not need full-time nursing care.

At one end of the spectrum are facilities that provide no care at all, merely housing with fewer of the hassles that come with traditional home ownership. So-called senior-housing or retirement complexes are not unlike condominium or apartment complexes, except that they typically have a minimum-age requirement of 55 (a spouse can be as young as 45), allow pets but not children and offer a wide array of sports and entertainment facilities as well as a full program of leisure activities. Retirement complexes appeal chiefly to empty-nesters who are eager to shed possessions, downsize their living space and eliminate the grass-mowing and other concerns that go with home ownership.

"Two-story glass-enclosed aquatic center, rooftop tennis pavilion with a viewers' lounge, elegant restaurant and grill, ballroom, theatre, painting, ceramics, sculpture studios, classrooms, woodworking, billiards, convenience shopping and services," trumpets an ad for Leisure World of Virginia, a new "active community intended for older persons" outside Leesburg.

Developed by The IDI Group Companies, Leisure World is patterned after a 30-year-old facility in neighboring Maryland and several other communities, mostly in the Mid-Atlantic region. The complex features high-rise apartment houses in a gated community built around a golf course. Prices range from about $130,000 to about $260,000, and the monthly condominium fee averages $350.

The active-retirement concept took hold after 1960, when developer Del Webb opened the Sun City retirement community in Phoenix, Ariz. The concept proved such a success that Webb and other developers built similar communities throughout the Southwest, now a leading retirement alternative to Florida. As Florida, Arizona, Nevada and Southern California have become heavily developed, however, many retirees are opting to stay in or near their communities, where they can be close to children and friends. Responding to the new trend, developers are opening retirement complexes in the East and Midwest. [19]

Assisted Living

When senior citizens begin to need some form of care, but are reluctant to move from their homes, there are a growing number of agencies that provide full-time or part-time aides to help with everyday tasks. Since Medicare coverage was expanded to include home health services in the 1980s, the number of Medicare-certified home health agencies has mushroomed from 5,700 in 1989 to nearly 10,000 in 1997. [20] Such agencies also can provide nursing services such as intravenous therapy, physical and occupational therapy, mental health services and round-the-clock nursing.

Medicare is supposed to cover the cost of home nursing services for the elderly whose physicians certify are "confined to the home," and fully 10 percent of the 38 million Medicare beneficiaries now receive care at home. Coverage of home health care is a fast-growing item in the program budget, totaling $17.5 billion in 1997, up from $4 billion in 1990. But court records show that Medicare routinely denies coverage to thousands of qualified beneficiaries. The majority of elderly who contest Medicare's denial of coverage for home health care eventually receive coverage, but only after paying thousands of dollars out of pocket for the year or more it takes to complete the appeal process. [21]

The long-term care industry also offers help for family caregivers. Often targeted to people with Alzheimer's disease, "respite care" enables family caregivers to have their elderly relatives taken care of for short periods at adult day-care centers. The number of centers has increased from 2,100 in 1989 to about 4,000 today, according to the National Adult Day Services Association.

Partially disabled elderly people who do not live with family members but need help with everyday tasks

have a relatively new alternative called "assisted living." An improved and more upscale version of the older board-and-care homes, assisted-living facilities appeared about 10 years ago. With the exception of some states that allow Medicaid payments for assisted-living facilities, they are not covered by federal programs and thus cater to people who can pay their own way. Fees vary widely, ranging from about $1,000-$4,000 a month, but even the most expensive assisted-living facility costs about the same as the average nursing home.

Like board-and-care homes and other long-term care facilities that do not participate in Medicare or Medicaid, assisted-living facilities are licensed and certified by the states. They provide room and board, housekeeping, assistance with eating, bathing, dressing and walking, emergency call systems, personal laundry services and medication management, as well as social and recreational activities and transportation.

For example, Sunrise Assisted Living, which operates 12 facilities in Northern Virginia, typically offers a two- or three-story Victorian-style structure with front porches and other design features aimed at providing "a home-like quality-care alternative for seniors." Demand for assisted-living care has grown rapidly; the American Health Care Association estimates that there are up to 65,000 facilities now in operation.

A growing number of candidates for assisted living are people with various forms of dementia who require full-time assistance but not necessarily full-time nursing care. Some assisted-living facilities specialize in the care of Alzheimer's or treat these residents in separate quarters because of their often disruptive behavior. Some facilities are specially designed to meet the needs of Alzheimer's patients.

Many retirees want to stay in their homes as long as possible, but begin shopping for alternatives when illness leaves them unable to negotiate stairs, shovel snowy sidewalks or drive safely. For these older Americans, a relatively new housing alternative, the continuing-care retirement community, may be ideal.

A recent ad for a facility run by the Marriott Corp., now a major player in the continuing-care market, reflects the needs that such facilities answer. "Don't you wish you were living in a Marriott senior living community at times like these?" reads the ad, featuring a photo of a snow-covered road. "Dangerous roads. Slippery sidewalks. No milk in the fridge. Marriott residents don't have to contend with the vagaries of Mother Nature." [22]

Continuing-care communities typically contain three levels of care. One-story cottages and buildings with apartments provide "independent living" at essentially the same level found in retirement communities like Leisure World. Grounds maintenance, house-cleaning, community activities and other services are covered by a monthly fee. Residents are encouraged to eat dinner in a central dining room. For those who need help with so-called daily-living activities, there is an assisted-living section, as well as a skilled-nursing facility. ■

CURRENT SITUATION

Caveat Emptor

Older Americans today have many more choices for long-term care than in the past, when retirement communities were mainly in Florida and the Southwest, and nursing homes were the only alternative to home

health care for the frail elderly. The market now offers housing and care alternatives that enable senior citizens and their families to pick facilities according to the degree of assistance they need and the cost of care, often close to friends and family.

But problems remain in the long-term care industry, forcing the elderly and their families to be wary consumers at a time when they may be least prepared to closely examine the choices they face.

"No one says, 'Oh goody, it's time for assisted living, I think I'll go start trying them out,'" says Clemmer of the AARP. "A few plan-ahead types will do the research, but most people wait until they need it. In a classic situation, you visit your parents and discover the stove is still on, or your mother hasn't gotten dressed and it's four in the afternoon. Suddenly, you realize it isn't safe or healthy for her to be alone anymore."

Even seniors who are not forced by sudden health problems to quickly choose a long-term care facility are rarely aware of the vast differences in standards of care among continuing-care communities, assisted-living facilities and other institutions. Uniform federal standards only apply to nursing homes that are approved to participate in Medicare and Medicaid. The quality of care in all other facilities depends entirely on the degree of state oversight and the willingness of administrators to comply with voluntary standards set by industry groups.

Standards for assisted-living facilities in Oregon and Maryland illustrate the wide variations in regulating care facilities. Oregon, where some of the first assisted-living facilities appeared, set unusually high standards from the start, including a requirement that assisted-living residents have access to a private room and bath. By requiring all assisted-living operators to demonstrate that they will be able to meet the standards before they open for business, Clemmer

says, "they eliminate the bad apples, the people who would pack two to four people to a room because they want to make an extra $500."

Oregon also provides Medicaid assistance for people who cannot afford to pay out-of-pocket for assisted-living care. The result, Clemmer says, has been improved conditions throughout the long-term care industry. "Even the old board-and-care homes have had to shape up in order to keep people coming through their doors," she says. "Why would anybody go to a crummy board-and-care home for lack of money if they qualify for Medicaid and can go to a decent assisted-living home instead? Oregon is one of the few states that has had a decrease in nursing home beds because it has high enough standards that many people who would have been in nursing homes can be in assisted living."

By contrast, Maryland grouped four existing types of institutions, including homes for the mentally ill and those with developmental disabilities, into a single category now called assisted living. "That way they were stuck with all the existing facilities," Clemmer says. As a result, Clemmer says, facilities providing a level of care that barely meets Maryland's standards offer a lower quality of life than corresponding facilities in Oregon. *(See floor plans, p. 159.)*

Eliminating Abuses

Although nursing homes are the most heavily regulated long-term care facilities, consumer advocates say they remain the focus of their concern. "People living in a continuing-care retirement community or other facility who have the ability to advocate for themselves often get the care they need, because those who demand it get it," says reform advocate Burger.

"But when you enter a nursing

home," she continues, "often it's not where you are, it's the amount of energy you have left to advocate for yourself and what you need. By the time they enter nursing homes, many residents are demented and cannot advocate for themselves."

The 1987 Nursing Home Reform Act is widely viewed as having reduced the incidence of abuse, but horror stories still persist of nursing home residents being left for hours restrained in chairs or drugged into silence. And even in the absence of outright abuse, lapses in the quality of care persist. The Department of Health and Human Services recently reported, for example, that almost half of nursing home pharmacists say patients often receive inappropriate prescription drugs, sometimes with serious consequences. [23]

Burger calls understaffing a major cause of quality lapses. "Nursing homes are incredibly short-staffed," she says. "They'll tell you it's because the employment rate is so high they can't get anybody, but they gave the same story long before that happened." Most nursing homes are operated for profit, and over half are operated as part of a chain. Burger blames operators for the problem.

"Staffing is the greatest expense they face, and that's where they want to save money," she says. "They have to please their investors before they have to please anybody else."

Industry spokesman Burke downplays the staffing issue. "Often the staffing problems that people complain about on an anecdotal basis are caused by very explainable circumstances," he says. "If several people on a wing have bad occurrences at the same time, it's going to look like the place isn't staffed properly." But low wages for nurse's aides, who typically earn between $6 and $8 an hour and provide the bulk of nursing home care, also play a role. [24]

"People don't show up, people quit, the situation is very fluid," Burke concedes. "We're not dealing neces-

---

Assisted-Living Facilities Vary Widely

Standards for assisted-living facilities vary widely from state to state. In Oregon, for example, each resident must have access to a private room with a bathroom, while Maryland requires two residents to share a smaller room and eight persons to share a shower and a telephone.

State Requirements for Living Units Vary

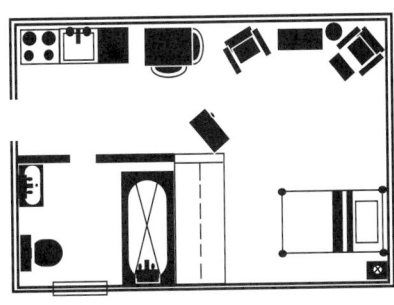

Oregon

Minimum: 220 sq. ft. in a private efficiency apartment with bathroom

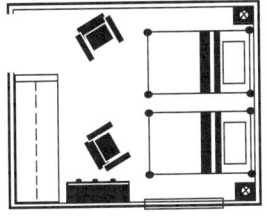

Maryland

Minimum: two persons share 120 sq. ft. room with one shared dresser
- *four persons share a toilet*
- *eight persons share a shower and a telephone*

Source: American Association of Retired Persons, April 1997

---

sarily in a professional environment." But he adds that the survey process ensures that nursing homes with chronic staff shortages will not survive. "If the staffing isn't there, it's going to show up in the survey eventually," he says. "You're going to have increased pressure sores, you're going to have increased bad outcomes."

Other analysts see hope in the fact that some nursing homes are beginning to move beyond the requirements imposed by the law and take steps on their own to improve quality of care.

"There is a real emphasis on each resident and maximizing the quality of

life and the quality of care for each resident," says Mullen of the AARP. "There have been a lot of efforts to link facilities in different regions or states so they can learn from one another."

She cites examples of simple, low-cost measures some nursing homes are taking voluntarily to improve care, including the practice, devised by a home in Mississippi, of marking the charts of residents at risk of developing bedsores so that every time they are seen by an aide they are turned. "This is an innovative approach, it's certainly low-cost and it really helps," Mullen says.

"I'm sorry, but this is not innovation,

this is basic, minimum care," Burger says. "At this stage in the development of nursing home care, any facility that doesn't do this ought to be just run out of business."

To promote widespread adoption of such voluntary measures, the Health Care Financing Administration (HCFA) is creating a Web site enabling nursing homes around the country to share their ideas for improving the quality of care.

'Sandwich' Generation

For all the interest in long-term care, many elderly people — even Alzheimer's patients needing almost constant oversight— remain in the care of family members or friends. According to the National Alliance for Caregiving, nearly one in four American households cares for an elderly relative or friend. The typical caregiver is a 46-year-old working woman who spends 18 hours a week caring for her 77-year-old, chronically ill mother who lives nearby. Most caregivers get help, usually from a son or daughter, in providing services for their relative, which usually involves transportation, grocery shopping, household chores and assistance in activities of daily living such as bathing, dressing and eating. [25]

But providing care for the elderly takes a heavy toll on family caregivers. Almost half the respondents to a survey by the alliance said that caregiving caused them to have less time for other family members and give up vacations and other activities. Forty-one percent of caregivers also care for children under 18. Coping with the stress of caring for both children and parents can be overwhelming.

"It's just really hard," says Clemmer, who helped care for her parents and whose father later lived with her and her family. "It was a

year and a half of unbelievable sandwich-generation problems," she says. "With the best will in the world you aren't necessarily doing the best thing because you don't know what that is. What worked yesterday won't work today, but how you're supposed to figure it out, I don't know." ∎

OUTLOOK

Aging Boomers

Demographic trends bode well for the long-term care industry. People 85 and older, the biggest users of long-term care, are the fastest-growing segment of the U.S. population. The number of "old old" people has risen from just over 1 million in 1970 to about 4 million today, which helps explain the boom in long-term care facilities. As surviving members of the baby boom generation begin to hit 85, however, the number of elderly people over 85 will more than double. By 2050, when the last of the boomers reach 85, there will be an estimated 18.2 million potential consumers of long-term care.

"The demographics are changing rapidly," says industry spokesman Burke. "If every family cared for their elderly relatives, there would be no concern for this trend. But people live longer than they used to, and today's families don't lend themselves to supporting the elderly at home. So the elderly have to find guardian angels in some other setting, especially when they begin to need assistance with the activities of daily living."

Some analysts are hopeful that the baby boomers, accustomed to getting what they want, will demand better long-term care than today's nursing home residents. "I'm not going to be

the same kind of consumer of long-term care that my grandparents were," says Mullen of the AARP. "If the dry cleaner shrinks my clothes, I'm gong to complain. I don't think that was the approach that people took 20 or 30 years ago, and I think it will have a positive effect on the quality of life in nursing facilities."

The boomers may indeed be able to force improvements in the quality of long-term care, but it is not at all clear how they — or tomorrow's taxpayers — will pay for it. Bolstered by the current availability of Medicare and Medicaid, few boomers are thought to be setting aside the large sums they would need to buy long-term care in the event of debilitating chronic illness.

As the ranks of the elderly swell in coming years, Medicaid and Medicare will quickly run out of money for long-term care, barring hefty tax increases and a restructuring of the programs themselves. A presidential commission is studying ways to finance Medicare in the future and is expected to release its findings in March 1999.

"What's going to happen when the elderly boomers begin qualifying for Medicaid and find that it's not available to them?" Burke asks. "We're trying to get people to pay attention to this problem, but lawmakers will have to come up with a solution."

With regard to Medicaid, which pays the bulk of nursing home care, lawmakers have focused thus far not on fraud but on limiting eligibility to the program. (See "At Issue," p. 161.) For example, a measure passed in 1996 made it a federal offense punishable by fines or imprisonment to give away property in order to become eligible for Medicaid. Dubbed the "Send granny to jail" law by critics, the measure was changed last year.

"Congress may be able to recover some funds for the program," Mullen says, but there's a limit to the amount of money that can be wrung out of people to pay for long-term care. It's

Continued on p. 162

At Issue:

Should certain therapies be curtailed in the effort to crack down on nursing home fraud?

STEPHEN K. SPAHR

Deputy attorney general, New York State Medicaid Fraud Control Unit

FROM TESTIMONY AT A HEARING ON FRAUD AND ABUSE IN NURSING HOMES, HOUSE GOVERNMENT REFORM AND OVERSIGHT SUBCOMMITTEE ON HUMAN RESOURCES, APRIL 6, 1997

*t*he New York Attorney General's Medicaid Fraud Control Unit is the largest state law enforcement agency in the country dedicated exclusively to the investigation and prosecution of health-care crime. . . .

The office was created in 1975 following the revelation of widespread and shocking abuses plaguing the state's nursing home industry. The exposure of scandals in the late 1974 by both the media and the Temporary State Commission on Living Costs and the Economy drew national attention to the problem that millions of Medicaid dollars earmarked for the care of elderly and indigent patients were instead lining the pockets of greedy and politically influential nursing home owners and operators. . . .

The [Medicaid fraud control units] have witnessed sophisticated cottage industries springing to life in response to recent legislation increasing federal requirements for certain treatment modalities. Three examples of problems, which require immediate regulatory guidance or outright legislative change in order to staunch a hemorrhage of federal and state funds, are:

1. The explosive increase in nursing home-based contract speech and rehabilitative therapy services rendered sometimes to patients who are medically incapable of benefiting from them;

2. Managed care, which presents a new and difficult area for prosecutors and oversight agencies because of the new nature of provider relationships and billing patterns; and

3. Drug diversion, which has become a black market industry paid for by the Medicaid program.

Although legislative changes in the above areas are being proposed or enacted to deal with the problem, the [Medicaid fraud control units] are facing big problems in dealing with an ever-changing health-care fraud landscape. It is clear that huge amounts of public dollars are being expended on high-profit services which have little or no value to the patients. To the frustration of both civil auditors and criminal prosecutors who are charged with policing fraud and abuse, there are far too few rules or regulations to constrain these providers' imaginations when it comes to billing ridiculously simple services at outrageous sums. . . .

SUZANNE M. WEISS

Vice president and counsel for public policy, American Association of Homes and Services for the Aging (AAHSA)

FROM TESTIMONY AT A HEARING ON FRAUD AND ABUSE IN NURSING HOMES, HOUSE GOVERNMENT REFORM AND OVERSIGHT SUBCOMMITTEE ON HUMAN RESOURCES, APRIL 16, 1997

*c*ontrol of fraud and abuse in health care has evolved considerably over the 30-plus years since the Medicare and Medicaid programs were established. . . . All the goals are admirable; however, the statutory and regulatory framework for meeting those goals achieve a level of complexity that only lawyers and accountants can love. . . .

In effect, federal regulations have established a "failure to thrive" standard for nursing home residents, most of whom are well over 80 years of age. This standard exists without the research to establish benchmarks for the "average" elderly nursing home resident. Considering the consequences under the [1987 Omnibus Budget Reconciliation Act] of not complying with the regulations . . . providers can hardly be faulted for occasionally erring on the side of somewhat more therapy than may be needed in the eyes of the inspector general. . . .

Certainly nobody wants to spend the last hours or days of his or her life on a treadmill or learning how to swallow again. But the difficulty of defining terminal illness (as evidenced by recent stories about hospice care and the debate about physician-assisted suicide) makes it risky to say that as a class, and without qualification, the "terminally ill" should not be receiving certain therapies. . . .

AAHSA also is bothered about the possibility that fraud and abuse authorities might systematically limit certain kinds of therapy for persons with Alzheimer's disease or other forms of dementia. We understand that there have been cases of inappropriate therapy for these individuals, such as having a therapist give complex instructions to an afflicted person and then expecting the individual to follow through independently with a series of exercises. This IS a waste.

But there are valuable forms of therapy for persons with dementia, including physical therapy to maintain mobility, and speech therapy to maintain swallowing ability. Keeping residents with dementia free of contractures, out of wheelchairs, and off of feeding tubes not only enhances their quality of life but dramatically cuts the cost of their care. We urge the government to consider that just because a person does not remember his or her therapy does not mean that the person cannot benefit from the therapy's effects. . . .

Buying Long-Term Care Insurance

Getting old can be frightfully expensive. Nursing homes cost an average of $40,000 a year — far beyond the resources of most elderly Americans or their families. And alternative long-term care arrangements are often not much cheaper.

Most private health insurance policies don't cover institutional care after a hospital stay. Medicare, the federal insurance program for the elderly, only covers a brief stay in a skilled-nursing facility, but only if the patient first received at least three days of treatment in a hospital. The only public insurance program that covers long-term care is Medicaid. But because it is intended to pay for the health-care needs of the poor, Medicaid will provide coverage only after patients have spent down virtually all of their personal assets.

To help the elderly provide for their long-term care without exhausting their personal savings or their children's inheritance, private insurers began offering long-term care insurance in the late 1970s. Many employers now offer it as part of their workers' benefits packages. Individuals can also buy coverage, and some insurers now offer long-term care insurance as part of their life insurance coverage. More than 3.5 million long-term care insurance policies are now in force, according to the American Association of Homes and Services for the Aging.

"I think long-term care insurance is probably worthwhile," says Sarah Burger, acting director of the National Citizens' Coalition for Nursing Home Reform. "It helps relieve the worry elderly people often have about protecting the money they saved for their children from the financial ravages of their own long-term care."

But the need for long-term care insurance is not as clear as the need for, say, health insurance. For one thing, premiums and copayments may be prohibitively expensive, especially if the policy is started at age 65 or older. The average policy purchased is for four years, costs $92 a month and provides $80 a day in nursing home benefits and $40 a day in home health benefits. [1] For people who don't expect to have many assets when they are elderly, long-term care insurance may not be worth the expense because they will probably be eligible for Medicaid. On the other hand, if a person has enough money to easily afford long-term care, buying insurance may be deemed a waste of money since it may never be needed at all.

Long-term care insurance has become more widely available in recent years because most states have required insurers to provide it. But policies vary widely among the states where they are available. For example, since 1993 California has required long-term care policies to pay for home-based care — even when provided by a friend or relative — as well as care by a nursing home or licensed caregiver. [2] But California's regulations are more consumer-friendly than those adopted by most other states. "If you find an insurance company that covers nursing home care, it doesn't cover home care, or if it covers home care, it doesn't cover nursing home care," Burger says. "It's an absolute morass."

People shopping for long-term care insurance can take hope from changes in the tax law that went into effect last year. Many — but not all — insurance-policy premiums may be deductible on tax returns as a medical expense. And people who pay for long-term care out-of-pocket can also deduct the cost as a qualified medical expense. However, the new provisions covering long-term care are so confusing that the Treasury Department plans to issue a clarification.

---

[1] Health Insurance Association of America data provided by the American Association of Homes and Services for the Aging.

[2] See Kathy M. Kristof, "Regulations, Competition Spur Changes in Care Policies," *Los Angeles Times* (Washington edition), July 19, 1993.

Continued from p. 160

wrong to create a situation where people who are otherwise eligible are too terrified even to apply for Medicaid benefits because it may bring on some criminal penalty."

Congress rewrote the law to target lawyers or accountants who advise elderly people to give away their assets in order to become eligible for Medicaid. "Now it's send granny's lawyer to jail," quips Mullen, who doubts the measure will stand up to legal scrutiny. "There's a First Amend-ment problem with the law because it makes it unlawful for someone to counsel a person to do something that is lawful. There are thoughtful ways to address the Medicaid issue, and it's important because so many people depend on the program."

Anticipating the strain on Medicare when the first wave of boomers turns 65 in 2011 and becomes eligible, Congress and the Clinton administration have been trying to reduce the cost of the health-care program. Under a measure signed Aug. 5, 1997, Medicare incorporated several managed-care options in an effort to save money. [26]

But on Jan. 6, President Clinton proposed that the program be expanded to cover younger displaced workers and retirees, ages 55 to 64, who often are unable to obtain private health coverage. [27] That change would add to Medicare's impending solvency problem. Advocates for the frail elderly want the program to be expanded to provide coverage for long-term care as well.

Some experts are hoping that the plight of the frail elderly will not be buried by concerns for the Medicare program's solvency. "We need to take a look at the entire program and the degree to which people actually need its benefits," says Bedlin of the National Council on the Aging. "As we approach the millennium, the program is not meeting the needs of many of the elderly, especially those with chronic illness." ■

Notes

[1] Testimony before the Senate Special Aging Committee, Oct. 22, 1997.

[2] Polling data provided by the National Council on the Aging.

[3] See Thomas J. Mattimore *et al.*, "Surrogate and Physician Understanding of Patients' Preferences for Living Permanently in a Nursing Home," *Journal of the American Geriatrics Society*, July 1997.

[4] Data from "Secure Care: Meeting the Needs of an Aging Nation," American Health Care Association, undated. The association is the main body representing the nursing home industry.

[5] American Health Care Association, "Assisted Living Quick Reference," August 1966.

[6] For background, see "Mental Health Policy," *The CQ Researcher*, Sept. 12, 1997, pp. 793-816, and "Mental Illness," *The CQ Researcher*, Aug. 6, 1993, pp. 673-696.

[7] See Claudia Kalb, "Caring from Afar," *Newsweek*, Sept. 22, 1997, p. 88.

[8] For background, see "Retiree Health Benefits," *The CQ Researcher*, Dec. 6, 1991, pp. 930-953.

[9] For background, see "Patients' Rights," *The CQ Researcher*, Feb. 6, 1998, pp. 97-120.

[10] For background, see "Alzheimer's Disease," *The CQ Researcher*, July 24, 1992, pp. 617-640.

[11] See Mark Thompson, "Fatal Neglect," *Time*, Oct. 27, 1997, pp. 34-38.

[12] See Richard Price, "Long-Term Care for the Elderly," *CRS Issue Brief*, Congressional Research Service, Dec. 1, 1997.

[13] *Ibid.*

[14] American Health Care Association, "Secure Care: Meeting the Needs of an Aging Nation," undated.

[15] Peter G. Peterson, *Will America Grow Up Before It Grows Old?* (1996), p. 177.

[16] William W. Lammers, *Public Policy and the Aging* (1983), p. 158.

[17] *Ibid*, p. 165.

[18] Information in this section is based on *1987 CQ Almanac* (1988), pp. 540-544.

[19] See Lyn Riddle, "Sun City Formula Moves East and North," *The New York Times*, Jan. 4, 1998.

[20] Leslie Aronovitz, "Medicare Home Health Agencies," General Accounting Office, July 28, 1997.

[21] See Robert Pear, "Home-Care Denial in Medicare Case Is Ruled Improper," *The New York Times*, Feb. 15, 1998, p. 1A.

[22] The ad ran Jan. 13, 1998, in *The Washington Post*.

[23] See Peter Eisler, "Study: Many Elderly Given Wrong Drugs," *USA Today*, Nov. 17, 1997.

[24] American Health Care Association, *Facts & Trends: The Nursing Facility Sourcebook* (1997), p. 42.

[25] National Alliance for Caregiving, "Family Caregiver Fact Sheet," undated.

[26] For background, see "Managed Care," *The CQ Researcher*, April 12, 1996, pp. 313-336.

[27] See Judith Havemann and Helen Dewar, "Medicare Expansion Proposed," *The Washington Post*, Jan. 7, 1998.

Bibliography

Selected Sources Used

Books

Burger, Sarah Greene, Virginia Fraser, Sara Hunt and Barbara Frank, *Nursing Homes: Getting Good Care There*, Impact Publishers, 1996.

This manual, issued by the National Citizens' Coalition for Nursing Home Reform, offers a wealth of information for consumers searching for nursing home care. It spells out residents' legal rights, describes warning signs indicating poor quality of care and suggests ways residents and their families can get help if problems arise.

Peterson, Peter G., *Will America Grow Up Before It Grows Old?* Random House, 1996.

A former Commerce secretary and member of President Clinton's Bipartisan Commission on Entitlement and Tax Reform warns that working-age Americans will not receive the public pension and health insurance benefits they have come to expect and must greatly increase their savings.

Thomas, William H., *Life Worth Living: How Someone You Love Can Still Enjoy Life in a Nursing Home: The Eden Alternative in Action*, VanderWyk & Burnham, 1996.

Thomas, a nursing home doctor, describes a new approach to long-term care involving the integration of animals, plants and children into the nursing home environment. He argues that it greatly improves the quality of life and health of residents.

Articles

'Will the Baby Boom Be Ready for Retirement?" *The Brookings Review*, summer 1997, pp. 4-9.

The author provides statistical data indicating that few Americans are financially prepared to retire, posing a threat to the stability of the nation's retirement system.

Gladwell, Malcolm, "The Alzheimer's Strain," *The New Yorker*, Oct. 20 & 27, 1997, pp. 125-139.

Alzheimer's patients are especially difficult to care for because they tend to wander and often display aggressive or disruptive behavior. To better meet these patients' needs, dementia experts designed a special long-term care facility in Western Pennsylvania incorporating circular paths and calming interiors that reduce the need for physical restraints.

Green, Joshua, "All the Comforts," *The Washingtonian*, October 1997, pp. 157-160.

Assisted-living facilities, which provide less hands-on care than nursing homes, have proliferated in recent years, but operate under state, not federal, regulation. Green cites organizations consumers can contact for help in choosing assisted-living facilities.

Kalb, Claudia, "Caring from Afar," *Newsweek*, Sept. 22, 1997, pp. 87-88.

Baby boomers living far from their aging parents can get help in finding high-quality care from a number of sources, including geriatric-care managers who serve as on-site family proxies to oversee the quality of long-term care.

Shapiro, Joseph P., "Comfort and Care," *U.S. News & World Report*, June 2, 1997, pp. 66-72.

Because two-thirds of nursing home residents suffer from dementia, operators are devising new ways to meet their needs, such as housing them in a "special care" wing.

Thompson, Mark, "Fatal Neglect," *Time*, Oct. 27, 1997, pp. 34-38.

Despite federal regulations aimed at ensuring high-quality care, serious cases of abuse and neglect persist in nursing homes around the country.

Reports and Studies

Congressional Budget Office, *Policy Choices for Long-Term Care*, June 1991.

This report reviews existing federal policy on nursing homes and other forms of long-term care and examines alternatives, including expanding Medicaid coverage, private financing and state coverage of the cost of care.

Price, Richard, *Long-Term Care for the Elderly, Congressional Research Service Brief for Congress*, Dec. 1, 1997.

This report, which can be obtained only from members of Congress, reviews federal policies on long-term care, examines recent congressional measures to expand federal programs and encourage private-sector support for care in nursing homes and at home.

Styring, William III, and Thomas J. Duesterberg, *The Cost Effectiveness of Home Health Care*, Hudson Institute, November 1997.

Home health care offers a promising solution to the financial problems facing Medicare and Medicaid. The authors describe Indiana's successful home-health program.

Wiener, Joshua M., and David G. Stevenson, "Long-Term Care for the Elderly and State Health Policy," *New Federalism: Issues and Options for States*, The Urban Institute, November 1997.

Payments to nursing homes by Medicaid, the main source of public financing for long-term care of the elderly, are expected to double over the next decade. Strategies for reducing these expenditures include halting construction of new homes and cutting rates of reimbursement.

The Next Step

Additional information from UMI's Newspaper & Periodical Abstracts™ database

Abuse/Neglect

Eisler, Peter, "Prosecutors join forces with nursing homes," *USA Today,* **July 3, 1997, p. A3.**

The case is all too typical: Nelson Simon, a nursing home aide awaiting trial on charges of beating and groping a 92-year-old patient, got his job in upstate New York in spite of previous convictions for everything from felony assault to killing a pet guinea pig. New York Attorney General Dennis Vacco says about one in four of his nursing home abuse cases involve caregivers with serious criminal records. New York, like 25 other states, has no law requiring criminal background checks for nursing home workers. Now, the nation's attorneys general are forging an unusual alliance with the nursing home industry to push for federal legislation to require background checks for nursing home staff.

Eisler, Peter, "Report: More drug rules needed in nursing homes," *USA Today,* **Nov. 17, 1997, p. A3.**

Ten years after Congress attacked improper drug use by nursing homes in a sweeping set of reforms, federal investigators say tougher rules are needed to combat lingering problems.

Eisler, Peter, "Study: Many elderly given wrong drugs," *USA Today,* **Nov. 17, 1997, p. A1.**

A recent federal report that surveyed nursing home pharmacists nationwide found that patients are often given improper prescription drugs, often with serious consequences. The survey is being released today as part of a report that urges reforms in the way nursing homes administer medicine and the way regulators monitor the process. Prepared by the inspector general of the Department of Health and Human Services, the report also includes audits of Texas nursing homes, where investigators found 17 percent of patients got improper drugs.

Ruane, Michael E., "U.S. Criticizes Response to Nursing Home Abuse in Montgomery," *The Washington Post,* **Nov. 29, 1997, p. B1.**

The state program charged with monitoring care in Montgomery County nursing homes responded slowly to alleged abuse of elderly residents, failed to properly investigate such reports and neglected to contact police or other officials even when warranted, according to a federal report released yesterday.

Uhlenberg, Peter, "Replacing the nursing home," *Public Interest,* **summer 1997, pp. 73-84.**

The type of care patients in nursing homes receive, and ways in which their care can be improved, are examined.

Alternatives to Nursing Homes

Barton, Linda J., "A shoulder to lean on: Assisted living in the U.S.," *American Demographics,* **July 1997, pp. 45-51.**

Assisted-living residencies offer a homelike alternative to older and disabled people who can't manage on their own.

Eicher, Diane, "Home, Sweet Home: Residences' fee structure lets seniors stay put, pay only for services they need," *The Denver Post,* **Feb. 10, 1997, p. E1.**

Assisted-living facilities may be the fastest-growing option in the housing and long-term care market in the country, says the American Association of Homes and Services for the Aging (AAHSA), a Washington, D.C., trade group. To date, there are roughly 30,000 to 40,000 assisted-living facilities in the U.S., serving an estimated 1 million older people.

Franklin, Mary Beth, "NORC, Sweet NORC; For Many Americans, Life Is Sweet in a 'Naturally Occurring Retirement Community,' " *The Washington Post,* **Jan. 13, 1998, Sec. WH, p. 7.**

NORCs — naturally occurring retirement communities — offer a comforting alternative to nursing homes. Franklin highlights the comforts of a NORC located in Washington, D.C.

Fischler, Marcelle S., "Elderly Are Turning To Assisted Living," *The New York Times,* **Aug. 24, 1997, Sec. LI, p. 1.**

Twenty years ago, Ted Peck left New York to retire to a condominium in Florida. Now his daughters, Randee and Merri, both with college-age children of their own, are looking to bring their 83-year-old father back to Long Island to live in an assisted care facility. In Great Neck Plaza, two such facilities, literally around the corner from each other, were approved simultaneously by the Village Board in July and ground is expected to be broken by the end of the summer.

Holsendolph, Ernest, "Boom in assisted living leads to greater choices: As competition heats up, baby boomers and their parents can even expect some price competition," *Atlanta Constitution,* **Dec. 22, 1997, p. E2.**

The market for assisted-living facilities in the Atlanta

area is growing steadily. A key to understanding the new boom is to realize that assisted living helps both the senior citizen residents as well as their busy baby boomer children. Some services go back 10 years or more. American ElderServe Corp., which started in Atlanta in 1987 and has since merged with another company, now operates five facilities under the name Atria.

Karuhn, Carri, "Now Booming, Adult Day Care Is under Scrutiny," *Chicago Tribune*, Aug. 8, 1997, Sec. 2MC, p. 1.

Karuhn discusses adult day-care centers as an alternative to full-time care facilities. Unlike day-care facilities for children, which are governed by state and local laws, adult day-care centers are not regulated unless they receive state or federal funding.

Murer, Matthew J., "Assisted living: The regulatory outlook," *Nursing Homes*, July 1997, pp. 24-27.

Assisted living is a booming industry and seems poised to make its mark on the long-term care industry; its future and the outlook for federal regulation are discussed.

Helping the Elderly

Carey, Anne R, and Marcia Staimer, "USA Snapshots: Long-term care takes its toll," *USA Today*, June 16, 1997, p. D1.

According to the National Council on the Aging and John Hancock Mutual Life Insurance, about one in three adults age 35-54 have provided hands-on help for friends or family needing long-term care. Of these, 79 percent have made sacrifices in personal time to do it.

Van Allen, Peter, "First Union Launches Family Trust Program To Aid Elderly Clients," *American Banker*, May 12, 1997, p. 13.

First Union Corp. unveiled a Family Trust program that offers a range of unusual services for trust clients, from setting up nursing home care and home repairs to helping with medical insurance claims and paying bills. In a similar spirit, last week, Merrill Lynch & Co. announced its Retirement Management Service, offering medical-bill management, long-term care insurance, a pharmacy discount card, a Visa Gold Card and other products and services. Merrill, which targeted middle-market clients, will charge an annual fee of $500.

Legislation/Call for Reform

"Approve long-term care bill," *Atlanta Journal*, March 21, 1997, p. A22.

An editorial urges state Sen. Steve Henson, D-Ga., to introduce a bill that would allow the state Dept. of Medical Assistance to run a Medicaid pilot program for assisted-living care for those seniors who need limited help with daily living.

Hughes, Polly Ross, "House toughens regulations on nursing homes," *Houston Chronicle*, April 22, 1997, p. A13.

Texas nursing homes would face tough new regulations and hefty penalties for abusing or neglecting residents under legislation approved by the state House on Monday. The bill, already adopted by the Senate, calls for tougher state standards than existing federal ones, new rights for nursing home residents, strict licensing procedures, extensive background checks and steeper fines for violators.

Levine, Susan, "Nursing-home reform now!" *Modern Maturity*, November 1997, pp. 89-90.

By testifying at the Texas state capitol, Elaine Brooks helped bring about a much-needed nursing home reform bill. Levine discusses the reform and the role that the American Association of Retired People (AARP) played in getting it passed.

Presecky, William, "State Panel on Aging Takes up Issue of Elder Abuse," *Chicago Tribune*, Sept. 24, 1997, Sec. 2SW, p. 5.

An Illinois House committee that has heavy representation from the south and southwest suburbs began setting the table Tuesday for a potentially heated debate next year over the issues of elder abuse and neglect and a demand for meaningful nursing home reform.

Scallan, Matt, "Ordinance on Nursing Homes Is Postponed," *Times-Picayune*, June 20, 1997, Sec. BK, p. 1.

For a second time, Harahan aldermen put off a vote on an ordinance requiring city police to be called to investigate crimes at nursing homes in the city, as Police Chief John Doyle and owners of the Harahan Guest House work toward a compromise. Doyle and Robert Rotolo, a co-owner of the home, said that under the outlined compromise, police will be called to investigate criminal allegations, but Doyle will not call the media to accompany him on investigations. State law allows nursing homes to call either local police or state authorities to investigate possible abuse of their residents. Like most nursing homes in Louisiana, the Harahan Guest House notified the state when there were problems, not city police.

Medicaid

Bullen, Bruce, "Giving the care elders need," *The Boston Globe*, Dec. 16, 1997, p. C4.

About 106,000 seniors in Massachusetts are both Medicare beneficiaries and Medicaid recipients who qualify for coverage under the Massachusetts Division of Medical Assistance because of their low-income status. While Medicare covers chiefly acute and rehabilitative care, Medicaid is both the secondary payer for those services and the primary payer for long-term care. For frail and vulnerable low-income seniors and their families, navigating between the two systems while coping with chronic illness can be a confusing and frustrating experience.

Hinden, Stan, "Taking Cover From High Nursing Home Costs; Finding the Right Long-Term Care Policy at the Right Price Involves Study, Work," *The Washington Post*, July 13, 1997, p. H1.

I don't know what scares you about growing older, but I can tell you what scares me. It's the idea that my health or the health of my wife, Sara, might deteriorate to the point where one of us would have to become a resident of a nursing home for an extended period of time. But what happens if you are so ill you have to stay in a nursing home indefinitely? It's no secret. Inevitably, you go on Medicaid, a medical program for the poor, which allows you to remain in a nursing home without paying. But to become eligible for Medicaid, you have to pay the nursing home until you virtually run out of money.

"Would They Dare Send Grandma to Jail?" *St. Louis Post-Dispatch*, Feb. 23, 1997, p. B2.

While most lawmakers apparently weren't looking, one or more of their colleagues slipped a bombshell of a clause into a bill that has made health insurance benefits available to millions of Americans who otherwise would have lost them once they changed jobs. The bombshell is this: The law makes it a federal crime for the elderly to dispose of assets in order to qualify for Medicaid-covered nursing home care. Though abuse of the Medicaid program among the elderly isn't thought to be widespread, the punishment is severe. Those found guilty could be fined $10,000 and imprisoned for one year.

Medicare

Ahmed, Kamal, "Funding crisis looms: How other nations pay for care: Kamal Ahmed on differing solutions to a problem shared by industrial nations," *The Guardian*, March 11, 1997, p. 10.

President Clinton's health-care reforms were supposed to fund long-term care, but floundered during the last administration. For those without insurance, costing upwards of $300 a month, the outlook is poor. Medicare, the state health-care provider, will pay for just 100 days of care after discharge from hospital.

"Medicare Mistake," *The Christian Science Monitor*, Dec. 9, 1997, p. 20.

President Clinton, who recently proposed to lower the Medicare eligibility age from 65 to 55, chose an odd moment to launch a bid to add some 20 million so-called "near elderly " Americans to the Medicare rolls. Unemployment, at 4.6 percent, has reached the lowest point in a quarter century. This is not the time to lure millions of the most skilled white- and blue-collar workers to take early retirement, up to 10 years sooner than they normally would.

Meyer, Harris, "Home improvement," *Hospitals & Health Networks*, April 20, 1997, pp. 40-42.

President Clinton's plan for reforming Medicare home health care practices is examined.

Norman, Al, "Moving carefully beyond Medicare," *The Boston Globe*, Oct. 14, 1997, p. D4.

The challenge at the conclusion of Alex Pham's three-part series on home health care was clearly stated by a home health nurse: "Medicare was not designed to take care of people forever. . . . Once the person gets better. . . . there needs to be something beyond Medicare." More than 20 years ago, Gov. Frank Sargent took us beyond Medicare when he signed into law a state-funded home-care program to address chronic-care needs, such as help with eating, bathing and dressing. One million clients later, the home care program is still filling the gap that Medicare could not. The second move beyond Medicare came last year when Gov. William F. Weld, R-Mass., described the long-term care system for the elderly in Massachusetts as a "pinball machine" bouncing consumers from agency to agency. The same year, he signed into law the Aging Services Access Points legislation. ASAPs are designed to create a one-stop shopping system for long-term care services. They are nonprofit and do not own services directly.

Profiting on the Elderly

Gladstone, Mark, "Quackenbush Overruled on Care Policies; Government: A judge orders the insurance commissioner to stop allowing firms to offer long-term health coverage with benefit levels below those required by state law," *Los Angeles Times*, Feb. 19, 1997, p. A3.

Insurance Commissioner Chuck Quackenbush has been ordered to rescind a controversial directive that allowed insurance companies to sell long-term health care policies with benefit levels lower than previously permitted by California law.

Gottlieb, Marilyn, "Want sales success? Try selling directly to seniors," *Direct Marketing*, August 1997, pp. 18-23.

Gottlieb discusses how companies can market to the over 68 million seniors who represent over $1.6 trillion in buying power, which is expected to increase 29 percent in the next couple of years.

Horvitz, Leslie Alan, "Aging America is big business," *Insight on the News*, Dec. 8, 1997, pp. 38-39.

While the market for senior residential communities of all kinds is expanding rapidly, the biggest trend in the senior-housing sector appears to be assisted care.

Back Issues

Great Research on Current Issues Starts Right Here . . . Recent topics covered by The CQ Researcher are listed below. Before May 1991, reports were published under the name of Editorial Research Reports.

AUGUST 1996
Fighting Over Animal Rights
Privatizing Government Services
Child Labor and Sweatshops
Cleaning Up Hazardous Wastes

SEPTEMBER 1996
Gambling Under Attack
The States and Federalism
Civic Journalism
Reassessing Foreign Aid

OCTOBER 1996
Political Consultants
Insurance Fraud
Rethinking School Integration
Parental Rights

NOVEMBER 1996
Global Warming
Clashing Over Copyright
Consumer Debt
Governing Washington, D.C.

DECEMBER 1996
Welfare, Work and the States
The New Volunteerism
Implementing the Disabilities Act
America's Pampered Pets

JANUARY 1997
Combating Scientific Misconduct
Restructuring the Electric Industry
The New Immigrants
Chemical and Biological Weapons

FEBRUARY 1997
Assisting Refugees
Alternative Medicine's Next Phase
Independent Counsels
Feminism's Future

MARCH 1997
New Air Quality Standards
Alcohol Advertising
Civic Renewal
Educating Gifted Students

APRIL 1997
Declining Crime Rates
The FBI Under Fire
Gender Equity in Sports
Space Program's Future

MAY 1997
The Stock Market
The Cloning Controversy
Expanding NATO
The Future of Libraries

JUNE 1997
FDA Reform
China After Deng
Line-Item Veto
Breast Cancer

JULY 1997
Transportation Policy
Executive Pay
School Choice Debate
Aggressive Driving

AUGUST 1997
Age Discrimination
Banning Land Mines
Children's Television
Evolution vs. Creationism

SEPTEMBER 1997
Caring for the Dying
Mental Health Policy
Mexico's Future
Youth Fitness

OCTOBER 1997
Urban Sprawl in the West
Diversity in the Workplace
Teacher Education
Contingent Work Force

NOVEMBER 1997
Renewable Energy
Artificial Intelligence
Religious Persecution
Roe v. Wade at 25

DECEMBER 1997
Whistleblowers
Castro's Next Move
Gun Control Standoff
Regulating Nonprofits

JANUARY 1998
Foster Care Reform
IRS Reform
The Black Middle Class
U.S.-British Relations

FEBRUARY 1998
Patients' Rights
Deflation Fears

Back issues are available for $5.00 (subscribers) or $10.00 (non-subscribers). Quantity discounts apply to orders over ten. To order, call Congressional Quarterly Customer Service at (202) 887-8621.

Binders are available for $18.00. To order call 1-800-638-1710. Please refer to stock number 648.

Future Topics

▶ *The New Corporate Philanthropy*

▶ *Israel at 50*

▶ *Federal Judiciary*

THE CQ Researcher

PUBLISHED BY CONGRESSIONAL QUARTERLY INC.

The New Corporate Philanthropy

Is U.S. business cutting back on charity?

As print and TV ads frequently boast, corporate America takes pride in supporting worthy causes, from fighting breast cancer to feeding the hungry. Indeed, American firms donated $8.5 billion in cash and products in 1996, making them the most charitable in the world. Yet the percentage of corporate earnings set aside for philanthropy has fallen steadily for the past 10 years, even as corporate profits have tripled. Meanwhile, government cutbacks in social services are creating new demands for emergency food and shelter. But there is hope. Experts think America is on the verge of a new golden age of philanthropy — but they expect most of the aid to come from individuals and foundations, not from corporations.

CQ **Feb. 27, 1998** • **Volume 8, No. 8** • **Pages 169-192**

Formerly Editorial Research Reports

February 27, 1998
Volume 8, No. 8

EDITOR
Sandra Stencel

MANAGING EDITOR
Thomas J. Colin

ASSOCIATE EDITOR
Sarah M. Magner

STAFF WRITERS
Mary H. Cooper
Kenneth Jost
David Masci

PRODUCTION EDITOR
Melissa Hall

EDITORIAL ASSISTANT
Vanessa E. Furlong

PUBLISHED BY
Congressional Quarterly Inc.

CHAIRMAN
Andrew Barnes

VICE CHAIRMAN
Andrew P. Corty

PRESIDENT AND PUBLISHER
Robert W. Merry

EXECUTIVE EDITOR
David Rapp

The CQ Researcher (ISSN 1056-2036). Formerly Editorial Research Reports. Published weekly, except Jan. 2, May 29, July 3, Oct. 30, by Congressional Quarterly Inc., 1414 22nd St., N.W., Washington, D.C. 20037. Annual subscription rate for libraries, businesses and government is $340. Additional rates furnished upon request. Periodicals postage paid at Washington, D.C., and additional mailing offices. POSTMASTER: Send address changes to The CQ Researcher, 1414 22nd St., N.W., Washington, D.C. 20037.

COVER: IBM AND OTHER COMPUTER COMPANIES MAINLY GIVE CHARITABLE DONATIONS IN THE FORM OF ELECTRONIC EQUIPMENT. (PHOTO COURTESY OF IBM)

The New Corporate Philanthropy

BY KATHY KOCH

THE ISSUES

As the year 2000 nears, the philanthropic spirit that ushered in the century seems about to blossom anew. Billionaires like media magnate Ted Turner and financier George Soros are leading the way.

But so are ordinary citizens like octogenarian Oseola McCarty, whom Turner credits as a role model. The retired domestic gave away her $150,000 life savings to send black students in her Mississippi hometown to college. [1]

Turner, who has exhorted his fellow billionaires to strive to top the list of the most generous in America, rather than the wealthiest, last September pledged $1 billion to the United Nations — the largest philanthropic gift in history.

"Turner stuck a real marker on the board, a real challenge for other multibillionaires to live up to," said Peter C. Goldmark, president of the Rockefeller Foundation. [2]

It apparently worked. The top 25 donors on *Fortune's* "most generous" list gave $3.3 billion last year — more than twice as much as the top 25 donors gave in 1996. [3]

Corporate America has also been challenged to do more. Retired Gen. Colin Powell urged CEOs at last April's Presidents' Summit for America's Future to encourage more employee volunteerism. And actor/philanthropist Paul Newman, who raises millions for charity through his Newman's Own foods, and *George* magazine are offering a $250,000 award for the "Most Generous Company in America" (to be donated to its favorite charity).

"Considering that last year alone American corporations earned in excess of $600 billion, yet gave away

only $8.5 billion to charities, it appears that more can be done," said a full-page announcement in the November issue of *George*.

"We're just trying to get these corporations to realize that in these times of huge earnings, it's important to give back to the community," says A.E. Hotchner, treasurer of Newman's Own.

Indeed, corporate giving has not kept pace with skyrocketing profits. American corporations made a record $676.6 billion before taxes in 1996. Yet the $8.5 billion they donated to charity was only 1.2 percent of those profits. In the past 10 years, while corporate profits have tripled, the percentage of earnings set aside for charity has declined by 50 percent from its 1986 historical peak of 2.6 percent. [4]

The downward trend has led many to conclude that newly merged and downsized corporate America has forgotten its traditional commitment to philanthropy.

Yet the public is deluged with endless advertisements and commercials portraying corporations aiding countless nonprofit groups. "Buy this cup of gourmet coffee," consumers are urged, "and help CARE"; "use our credit card, feed the hungry"; "buy our bubblebath, save world wildlife."

The cacophony of pitches reflects the

latest twists in corporate giving — strategic philanthropy and cause-related marketing.

"The major trend of the last five to 10 years has been toward ensuring that contributions not only assist community needs but also business interests," says Timothy J. McClimon, executive director of the AT&T Foundation.* "Now it's pretty much standard for corporate philanthropy."

Strategic philanthropy is a direct by-product of the downsizing, hostile takeovers and leveraged buyout fever that swept corporate America in the late 1980s and early '90s. As the competitive pressures of globalization intensified, corporations found it harder to justify giving away company money, and charity budgets and staffs were slashed — even eliminated — by hard-nosed managers.

"I don't believe in corporations giving away their money," Albert J. Dunlap, CEO of Sunbeam Corp., wrote in his autobiography, *Mean Business*. "That money is not mine to give. I have no right to give away a shareholder's money." [5] *(See "At Issue," p. 185.)* Dunlap eliminated Scott Paper Co.'s $3 million philanthropy program when he took over the ailing company in 1994.

Few CEOs are so extreme. More than 90 percent of America's largest corporations make philanthropic contributions, and most of their CEOs echo Ben Cameron, supervisor of community relations for Target stores.

"We can look our shareholders squarely in the eye and say that by

---

*About 40 percent of corporate charitable contributions are given through company-operated foundations, which can receive tax advantages by putting profits into a tax-exempt foundation during profitable years; during lean years, the corporation can continue its giving program by drawing foundation assets. The other 60 percent of corporate donations are by direct grants.

Individual Americans Give the Most

More than three-quarters of the $151 billion contributed by Americans to charity in 1996 came from individuals, compared with less than 6 percent from corporations.

1996 Sources of Contributions
(in $billions)

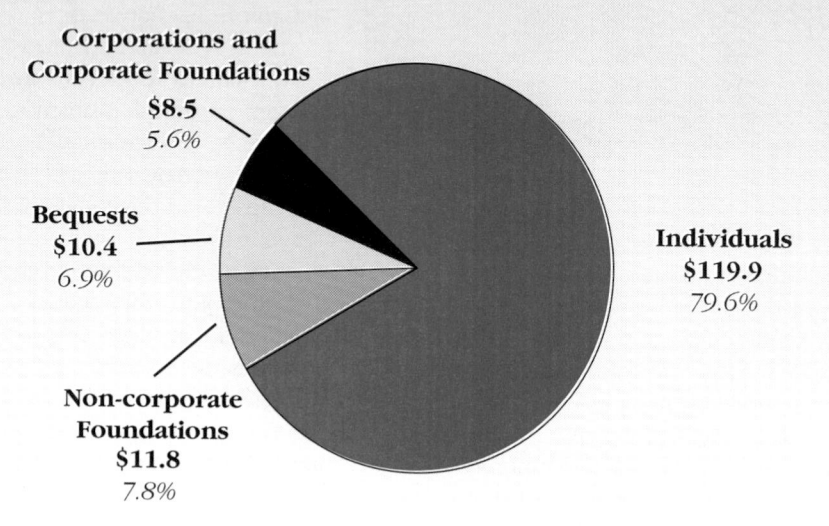

Corporations and
Corporate Foundations
$8.5
5.6%

Bequests
$10.4
6.9%

Non-corporate
Foundations
$11.8
7.8%

Individuals
$119.9
79.6%

Note: Percentages do not add to 100 percent due to rounding.

Source: The Conference Board

investing in our community we are stimulating profits," Cameron says. "It builds customer loyalty and produces more livable, viable communities and better-educated and better-skilled workers and consumers." Target donates an unusually generous 5 percent of its profits each year.

Many newly streamlined corporations, however, say that to justify continued corporate giving, their gifts must directly help the company's bottom line.

"Ten years ago, corporate philanthropy was 'doing good for the sake of doing good,'" McClimon says. "Corporations supported causes that were popular with executives, their spouses and their peers. It was 'peer philanthropy.'"

"Today corporate giving ... has become much more sophisticated, calculated and focused," wrote Conference Board analyst Myra Alperson. [6]

Companies now view contributions as "social investments" and are demanding a "reasonable return" on that investment, usually through either an enhanced corporate image, increased employee morale or improved customer loyalty.

"Chief executives are all asking, 'What kind of value are we getting for our investment?'" said Curt Weeden, vice president of corporate contributions at Johnson & Johnson. [7]

According to Alperson, companies now strategically focus their donations by:

• Supporting programs that con-

cern customers, usually based on a theme, such as protecting the environment or fighting domestic violence;

• Encouraging more employee volunteerism, especially in areas where a company is making donations;

• Giving more non-cash forms of support, such as products, services and employee expertise;

• Aggressively publicizing company donations; and

• Giving in localities where employees live and work, or to their favorite charities in order to boost morale.

For example, gifts may be targeted at literacy- or computer-training programs to prepare students for entry-level jobs. Or a company may give its higher-education grants to schools with research-and-development programs that could directly benefit the company. Grants to the arts may be restricted to locations where a company has facilities. [8]

Often areas of prime concern to customers are targeted. Whirlpool, whose primary customers are women, refocused its previously scattershot contributions program on two areas of special concern to women: day care and job training for women. Dayton Hudson Corp., the Minneapolis-based parent of Target stores, surveys customers and employees every two years to find their areas of chief concern.

Corporations now aggressively advertise their good works to increase the bang for their charitable buck, which helps explain the seemingly constant promotions about corporate charity. In earlier times, by contrast, giving was done quietly, without excessive fanfare.

"It doesn't cost much to produce press releases and publicize programs that remain, even if there are fewer of them," Alperson noted.

A natural and ubiquitous outgrowth of strategic giving is "cause-related marketing," in which companies tie sales of their products to a popular cause. It ranges from credit card purchases and new account openings to affinity credit cards and sponsorship of celebrity concerts. But the techniques all have one thing in common — extensive advertising campaigns to boost sales and corporate name recognition. For example:

• American Express, a cause-marketing pioneer, raised $22 million for Share Our Strength during its "Charge Against Hunger" promotion, in which money was donated to the organization each time customers used their credit cards.

• Ford sponsored a "Murphy Brown" episode last fall about breast cancer, and ran public service announcements linking its name to the fight against breast cancer.

• Target donates 1 percent of the amount charged on company credit cards to elementary schools that customers designate.

Fueling the move toward cause-marketing is the increasing public demand that companies be good corporate citizens. If price and quality are the same, according to a recent Cone/Roper study, 76 percent of consumers would switch to a brand or a retail store associated with a good cause. And 58 percent have a favorable opinion of companies that support charitable causes.

"Consumers in the 1990s take for granted that they can buy high-quality products and services at low prices. Marketers need to stand out from the crowd," said the study. "Offering a connection to a cause is an excellent way to do that." The study also found that Americans believe companies should take greater steps to deal with crime, education, the environment and poverty.

Meanwhile demands for corporate donations have shot up, as communities and nonprofit groups try to fill the gap left by federal, state and local cuts to nonprofits and social welfare programs. Sometimes even the government itself seeks donations. In 1996, for instance, Interior Secretary Bruce

Babbitt asked 35 major corporations to help restore the flood-damaged C&O Canal National Historical Park. [9]

As the nation adjusts to philanthropy in the downsized 1990s, these are among the questions being asked:

Should corporate giving be linked to corporate strategy?

Supporters of strategic philanthropy call it a win-win proposition that benefits a corporation's bottom line while helping needy causes.

"When this sea change in business giving is complete, companies and their communities will be the better for it," wrote Craig Smith, a consultant for The Conference Board and former editor of *Corporate Philanthropy Report*. [10]

Previously, Smith wrote, corporate grants were "scattered like crumbs to all the 'safe' causes. Corporations did their duty, but the gifts didn't make much of an impact on the companies or society." Now, with the more sophisticated and focused approach, companies hire professional grantmakers to design giving programs that fit specific needs of each company — illiteracy for publishers, hunger for food companies, AIDS for insurers.

"Once [a company] finds its focus, it is inclined to throw the full weight of its resources, not just grant dollars, behind the cause," Smith wrote. As corporate partnerships with charities strengthen, more money and support pours into the nonprofit from other departments, like marketing, recruitment and product development, forging a more holistic approach to giving.

The deepening partnership between nonprofits and corporations is perhaps the most profound societal benefit of the new-style philanthropy, Smith wrote. Strategic philanthropy is "steering corporate America into a more powerful and direct social role" and could "make corporate culture more benevolent."

Strategic philanthropy gives compa-

nies a "staggering opportunity, not only to develop sustained community relationships but also to shape the future of the community, the nation and the world," says Cameron of Target, which supports education, the arts and family-violence prevention.

Critics of strategic philanthropy, especially those from the old school of altruistic giving, say corporations have lost sight of the true meaning of philanthropy. "Don't call it philanthropy," argues Irving Warner, a fund-raising consultant from Los Angeles and author of *The Art of Fund Raising*. "If it helps sell your sneakers, your bananas or your orange juice, it is no longer philanthropy," he says. "It's like a prostitute saying she does it for love. The purpose of the new giving is not to relieve suffering, advance education or to bring art to the community. It's just good, old public relations gobbledygook."

Others question the basic premise behind strategic philanthropy — that contributions must benefit the bottom line to appease shareholders.

"That argument is based on the idea that there is a significant movement of shareholders who object to companies being philanthropic. I see no evidence that shareholders have been up in arms about corporate philanthropy," says Dwight Burlin-game, author of *Corporate Philanthropy at the Crossroads*. "Research shows clearly that consumers will buy the product of a socially responsible company over another product at the same price."

Others fear that philanthropic resources are being allocated based on what is best for companies, not necessarily what is best for communities. "Some companies will use this as an excuse to try to convert all of their philanthropic activity into self-serving business activity," wrote Robert L. Payton, a professor at Indiana University's Center on Philanthropy and a former president of the Exxon Foundation. [11] Target's Cameron says companies should deter-

Drug Companies Are Top Corporate Givers

Pharmaceutical and computer firms were the most generous corporate contributors to U.S. beneficiaries in 1996, donating more than a half-billion dollars in cash as well as drugs, equipment and software.

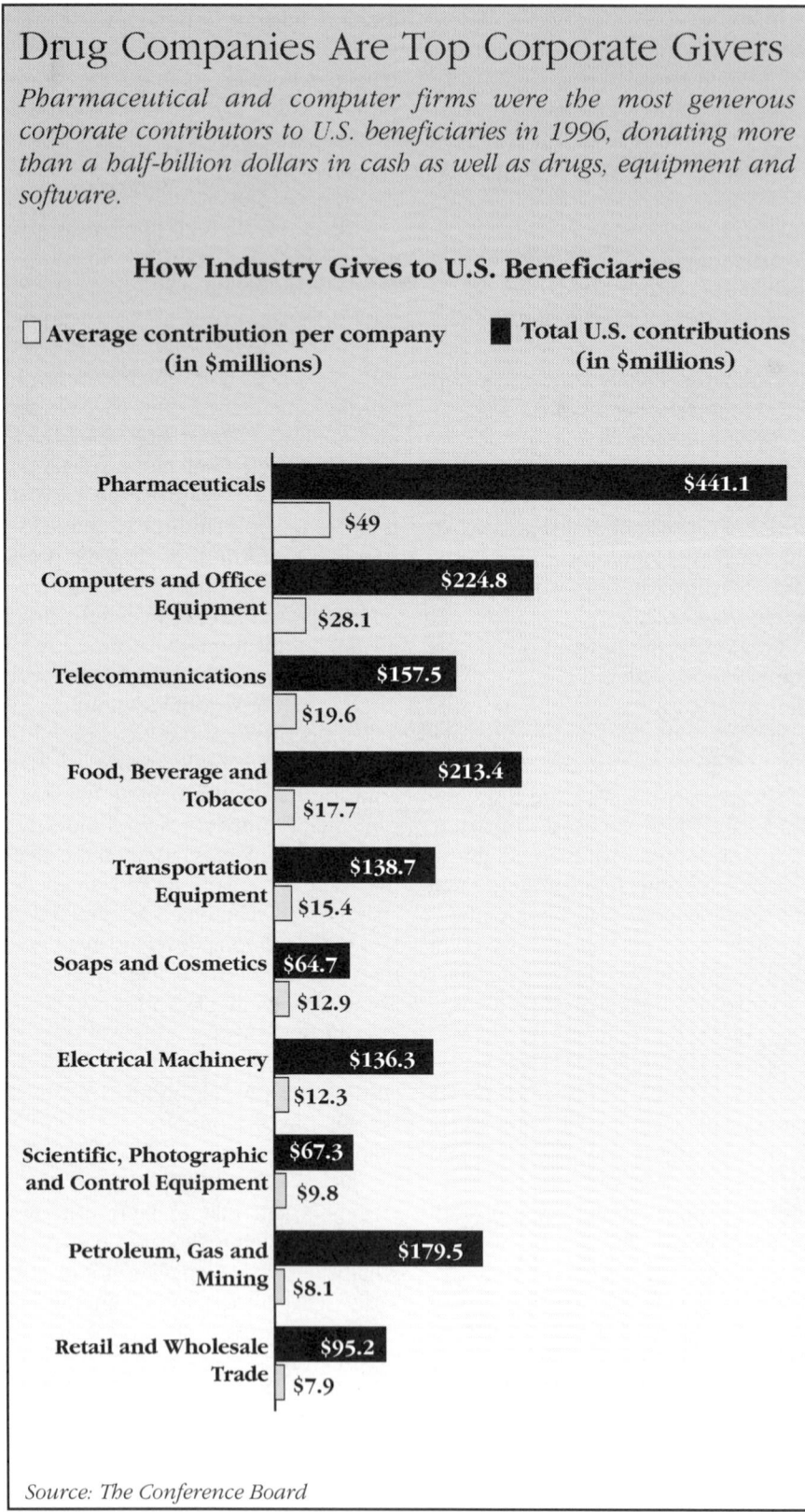

How Industry Gives to U.S. Beneficiaries

☐ **Average contribution per company (in $millions)**   ■ **Total U.S. contributions (in $millions)**

- Pharmaceuticals — $441.1 / $49
- Computers and Office Equipment — $224.8 / $28.1
- Telecommunications — $157.5 / $19.6
- Food, Beverage and Tobacco — $213.4 / $17.7
- Transportation Equipment — $138.7 / $15.4
- Soaps and Cosmetics — $64.7 / $12.9
- Electrical Machinery — $136.3 / $12.3
- Scientific, Photographic and Control Equipment — $67.3 / $9.8
- Petroleum, Gas and Mining — $179.5 / $8.1
- Retail and Wholesale Trade — $95.2 / $7.9

Source: The Conference Board

mine the community's greatest needs and see where they intersect with their shareholders' interests.

Some corporations do take a less self-centered view. "If we were a retailer or a bank, we'd be more customer-driven in our contributions policies," said Gene Wilson, president of the ARCO Foundation. "We tend to take a broader view of social issues. For example, our interest in school reform is not tied so much to workforce readiness — we don't hire that many people. To us, it's an issue of the society continuing to function." [12]

In fact, much corporate giving doesn't resemble the old-style corporate largess, which often went to a CEO's alma mater. "Compared with the 1980s, corporate support for elementary and secondary education has grown rapidly," said the *Foundation Giving Yearbook.* [13] Indeed, some corporations now support pre-college education with a passionate urgency.

"My interest in education reform is not just philanthropic," says IBM Chairman and CEO Louis V. Gerstner Jr. "It is fueled by intense anger and frustration. I am dismayed by the slowness and indifference our country brings to the crisis in public education." IBM has pledged $35 million over the next several years in computers, software and training to jumpstart what Gerstner calls "fundamental, bone-jarring" education reform in 22 school districts nationwide.

Some critics fear corporations may be taking social policy decision-making out of the public's hands.

"When marketing determines philanthropy, will only the marketable causes get help?" wrote Peter Goldberg, then-vice president for public responsibility at American Can Co. [14]

Company foundation chiefs point out, however, that because corporations only represent 5.6 percent of total U.S. giving, the public still decides where most charitable dollars are spent.

Critics also complain that local and

lesser-known charities that received funding under the old-style philanthropy now lose out to the non-controversial, nationally recognized charities favored by cause-related marketing campaigns. It's a case of the "fat cats getting fatter," said a respondent to a 1988 survey by Independent Sector.

A 1995 study by the National Committee for Responsive Philanthropy (NCRP) found that favorite causes for cause-marketing campaigns were children/teens, health, women, environment, crime, community arts, disaster relief, housing/homelessness and voter registration. Cause marketing does not help "emerging, small, non-visible and/or controversial charities — 90 percent of the charity universe," wrote NCRP Executive Director Robert Bothwell. [15]

Corporate philanthropy executives suggest that needy groups being ignored by corporate giving should focus their fund-raising efforts on corporate employees. "I tell them they've got to work on the individual employees, because then we can match their donations," says Paul M. Ostergard, president of Citicorp Foundation.

Should charities rent their names to corporations?

This year charitable organizations will receive $544 million from corporations through cause-related marketing, partnerships and sponsorships, according to the Chicago-based newsletter *IEG Sponsorship Report*. That's a big jump from the $8 million they received in 1985 for renting their names and reputations to corporations.

"Nonprofit groups were really leery about accepting corporate donations at first," says John Thomas, vice president of communications for Independent Sector. "Now a lot of groups think it's the way to go."

"These are huge amounts of money being taken by nonprofit groups," says Brent Blackwelder, executive director

of Friends of the Earth. "Any organization should think twice before taking this money. They should have guidelines governing how and when they can take such money to make sure there is no conflict of interest."

Some critics also fear nonprofits can become too dependent on assistance from corporate sponsors, leaving themselves financially vulnerable if the companies pull out. Marketing campaigns by nature are short-lived. If the campaign does not generate increased sales, it might be terminated or cut short.

Critics also fear that cause marketing will replace regular corporate contributions. "Corporate contributions could well dry up as executives come to view them as producing too modest a return compared with profit-yielding, cause-related marketing," wrote Maurice G. Gurin, former chairman of the Trust for Philanthropy at the American Association of Fund-Raising Counsel. [16]

Still others fear that if nonprofits depend too much on corporate largess they risk compromising their integrity. "The voluntary sector is being corporatized," says Michael Jacobsen, executive director of the Center for Science in the Public Interest and co-author of *Marketing Madness*. "America needs a vigorous, independent, nonprofit community with organizations that can call the shots as they see them. Links to corporations can have a muzzling effect, or they might be persuaded to say something different than they would if those links weren't there."

In the mid-1990s, Jacobsen notes, Philip Morris asked arts groups it supported in New York to oppose a proposed ban on smoking in restaurants and public places. Many of the groups sent letters to the city explaining that, while they were not taking a position on the bill, they wanted the city to know how much Philip Morris would be missed if it left New York in protest over the bill, as it was threatening. [17]

"The corporate sponsor gets a tremendous amount out of cause marketing," Jacobsen says, "far more than the nonprofit gets. Very often it's the companies that make junk food, alcohol or tobacco that are seeking innocence by association. In my mind, it taints the nonprofit."

Jacobsen is especially offended when he sees government agencies like the Smithsonian Institution "begging and pleading" corporations to sponsor exhibitions. "I think it raises questions about our society's values," he says. "Do we want industry controlling everything?"

Some nonprofits limit the percent of their budgets that can come from corporate partnerships. "We keep our revenue stream diversified," says Elizabeth McGeveran, managing director of Co-op America, which publishes the *Green Pages*, a directory of environmentally friendly companies. "That way we are never in a position where a corporation makes up even 5 percent of our income. Then a company can walk, and financially we're fine."

Proponents of cause marketing argue that government cutbacks in social programs like food stamps put more demand on charity budgets. "Many nonprofits are turning to corporations for money they might have earlier gotten from government," Thomas says.

Critics also complain that cause marketing mainly benefits advertisers. For every dollar raised for charity, $2 is spent on advertising, says the *IEG Sponsorship Report*. Others point out that the amount of money consumers actually donate to a charity through cause marketing is minuscule.

Do the math, said Tom Riley, a senior analyst at the Statistical Assessment Service in Washington. He examined several cause-marketing campaigns last fall for *Philanthropy*, including American Express' hunger-relief campaign. The company donated 3 cents per credit card purchase during November and December 1996. If cardholders used their credit cards to buy a $30 dinner

Education and Social Needs Get the Most

More than 60 percent of corporate contributions in 1995 were targeted to education and social programs. Most of the education funds aided primary and secondary schools.

1995 Distribution of Corporate Contributions

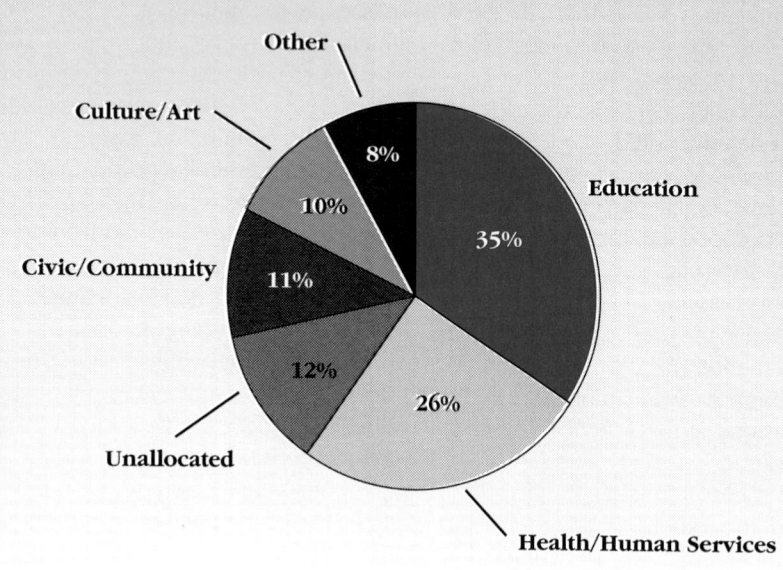

Note: *Percentages add to more than 100 due to rounding.*

Source: *The Conference Board*

half that, 0.7 percent. [19]

Average Americans, by contrast, donate about 1.9 percent of their household income to charity. If U.S. corporations gave at that rate last year, they would have donated an additional $4.7 billion — bringing total corporate donations to $13.2 billion.

Should U.S corporations give more? "Absolutely," says Dorothy S. Ridings, president and CEO of the Council on Foundations. "I don't have any doubt about it." Asking companies to match the percentage given by individuals is "modest enough as a national average," she says. "But how much a company gives depends on the industry and the profit margins of that industry."

"We would like corporations to be more generous," says Sara Melendez, president of Independent Sector. "Especially since the corporate sector traditionally advocates for smaller government budgets." Budget cuts in social services have put added strain on charities represented by Independent Sector. Meanwhile, new reports about record-breaking profits and million-dollar bonuses on Wall Street spark bitterness among those working in the trenches to serve those hit hardest by budget cuts.

"The average partner at Goldman Sachs last Christmas made $4 million in bonuses," says Lynn Shea, executive director of the Community Council for the Homeless at Friendship Place in Washington, D.C. "That's just about how much the city has budgeted this year to serve the homeless."

At Goldman Sachs, a media relations spokeswoman declined to discuss the company's charitable contributions.

"Corporate America should be giving 2.5 percent of income," says Bell Atlantic Foundation President Suzanne DuBose. "I think the nonprofit community should do a major public relations campaign exposing how little corporations are giving as a percent of pretax income. Wall Street

every night during the period, they would have spent $1,830, while raising only $1.83 each for the charity.

Further, Riley pointed out, such contributions are tax deductible for the corporate sponsor, but not for the consumer. Both the customers and the charity would be better off, he said, if the consumers bypassed the marketer, sent a $5 check directly to their favorite charity, and took the tax deduction themselves.

Should corporations give more to charity?

American companies give far more

to charity than their foreign competitors. And the $8.5 billion given by corporations in 1996 was 8 percent more than they gave the previous year. [18]

But critics point out that behind the "corporate giving is 'hot' " hype, American businesses still give only 5.6 percent of total U.S. charitable contributions. They also point to the steady decline in the percentage of profits donated to charity over the last 10 years, even as corporate profits tripled.

Indeed, while the average U.S. corporation donates about 1.2 percent of profits each year, the nation's biggest companies — those with incomes over $1 billion — donate only about

is especially dismal. They are not giving back into the community at all."

"We would like to see corporations at least double what they're giving now, or even go to 3 percent," says Hotchner of Newman's Own.

Johnson & Johnson's Weeden, a long-time student of corporate giving, says manufacturers should give 3.5 percent of pretax income, and service companies 2.5 percent. "These are realistic attainable figures, compared with what was happening 12 years ago when corporate contributions were closer to 2.1 percent a year," Weeden says. [20]

Weeden has devised a formula to standardize the way companies calculate their philanthropic contributions, providing "a more accurate accounting of what's actually going on." He spells it out in a new book, *Corporate Social Investing*, due this summer. Some companies may already be reaching the recommended goals and may not even know it, he says, because they are not counting all their charitable donations.

Proposed legislation in Congress would require corporations to report their charitable donations in a more standardized manner.

In addition, when companies practice "strategic philanthropy," many of the innovative methods they use to help nonprofits — such as in-kind gifts, loans of company personnel and use of corporate facilities or services — are not counted as charitable contributions because many of them are not considered truly philanthropic in nature.

"We do not view cause-related marketing as philanthropy," says Greg Barnard, a spokesman for the Council on Foundations. "It is an attempt to influence a point-of-sale decision. The money comes out of the consumer's pocket. He is the contributor, not the company." Yet charities are expected to receive $544 million from corporations this year through such marketing arrangements. Clearly, nonprofits are receiving more from corporations than the traditional con-

Corporate Giving Is Both Up and Down

The total value of contributions from all U.S. companies has risen steadily since 1966, but corporate giving as a percentage of pretax income began dropping after passage of the 1986 Tax Reform Act.

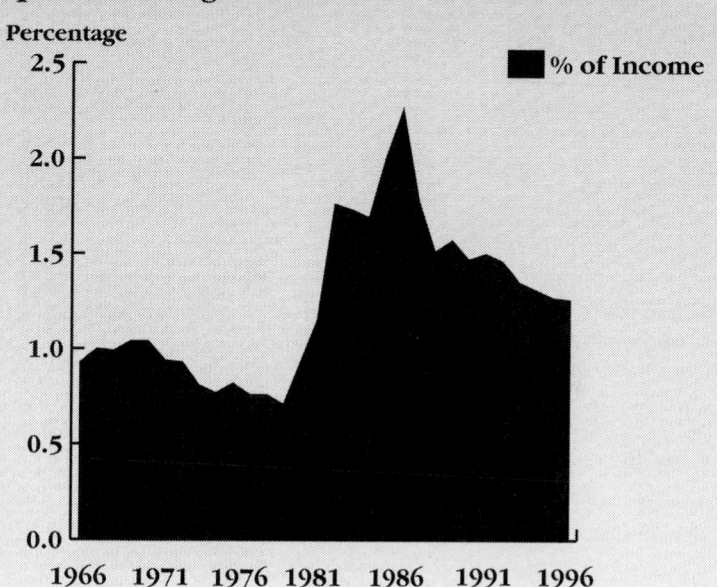

Corporate Giving as a Percent of Pretax Income

Corporate Gifts and Pretax Income
(in $billions)

	Total Corporate Income	Gifts		Total Corporate Income	Gifts
1966	$85.1	$0.79	**1982**	$176.7	$3.11
1967	81.8	0.82	**1983**	212.8	3.67
1968	90.6	0.90	**1984**	244.2	4.13
1969	89.0	0.93	**1985**	229.9	4.63
1970	78.4	0.82	**1986**	222.6	5.03
1971	90.1	0.85	**1987**	293.6	5.21
1972	104.5	0.97	**1988**	354.3	5.34
1973	130.9	1.06	**1989**	348.1	5.46
1974	142.8	1.10	**1990**	371.7	5.46
1975	140.4	1.15	**1991**	374.2	5.62
1976	173.8	1.33	**1992**	406.4	5.92
1977	203.5	1.54	**1993**	465.4	6.26
1978	238.1	1.70	**1994**	535.1	7.00
1979	261.8	2.05	**1995**	622.6	7.90
1980	241.4	2.25	**1996**	676.6	8.50
1981	229.8	2.64			

Source: The Council for Aid to Education; U.S. Department of Commerce

Calculating the Value of Corporate Charity . . .

Tracking corporate donations can be an exercise in confusion and obfuscation, not to mention controversy.

"Frankly, we don't have a clue what companies are really giving away," said Curtis Weeden, vice president of corporate contributions at Johnson & Johnson. [1]

Because there is no universal standard of comparison, companies report donations in different ways. Some value their product donations at retail prices, others at wholesale. Some include the value of sponsorships and partnerships with nonprofit groups, others call that marketing expenses. And some companies don't bother to tally charitable contributions at all.

For instance, says Citicorp Foundation President Paul Ostergard, "If we counted charitable events and dinners where we take a table, it would be another $5 million in donations. But we book those as business expenses."

"We need to be able to add up all of the apples and oranges and bananas and find out what is in this fruit salad," says Suzanne DuBose, president of the Bell Atlantic Foundation.

In an upcoming book, *Corporate Social Investing*, Weeden

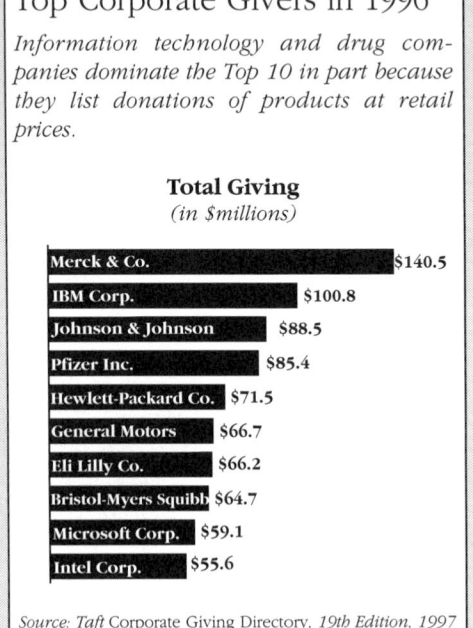

Top Corporate Givers in 1996

Information technology and drug companies dominate the Top 10 in part because they list donations of products at retail prices.

Total Giving
(in $millions)

Merck & Co.	$140.5
IBM Corp.	$100.8
Johnson & Johnson	$88.5
Pfizer Inc.	$85.4
Hewlett-Packard Co.	$71.5
General Motors	$66.7
Eli Lilly Co.	$66.2
Bristol-Myers Squibb	$64.7
Microsoft Corp.	$59.1
Intel Corp.	$55.6

Source: Taft Corporate Giving Directory, 19th Edition, 1997

lays out an elaborate formula for calculating charitable donations that would enable all corporations to "sing from the same page." He recommends that com-panies count all their charitable contributions, research, mem-berships, sponsorships and cause-marketing contributions, and that product donations be calculated at fair-market value.

Nowhere is the confusion over corporate contributions more apparent than in compiling annual lists of the top corporate donors. The 1995 list compiled by *Corporate Giving Watch* newsletter touched off a controversy over whether companies donating products to charity were inflating their value to appear more generous.

When the rankings came out, Microsoft Corp. had knocked IBM off its perennial perch as the nation's top donor. IBM, which values its product donations based on their wholesale cost, cried "Foul!" because Microsoft had listed the retail value of its in-kind gifts. IBM promptly recalculated its donations based on fair-market value and asked the newsletter to review its rankings. It did, and IBM regained its No. 1 ranking.

---

tributions figures would indicate.

Being careful not to call it "philanthropy," The Conference Board in 1995 analyzed corporate "assistance" disbursements to charities, such as cash, property and products that were not reported as charitable contributions. The board found that average cash disbursements for such non-charitable expenditures increased by 52 percent between 1992 and 1993, and average product and property disbursements increased by 74 percent — while total corporate charitable giving did not grow. [21]

"Could corporations give more? Everyone could be doing more," says AT&T's McClimon. "But whether they should depends on individual circumstances, just

as an individual's ability to give is different from one year to the next. Companies may need that capital to invest in other countries and in products and services to make their product more competitive. That money is not just sitting around collecting dust. It's being used or funneled back to the shareholders."

Corporate executives cite several reasons why contributions have dropped in relation to profits in the past 10 years:

• Most companies do not tie contributions to profits, but instead budget a dollar amount. Thus when corporate income is down, as in 1986, the contributions ratio increases, hence the 1986 peak. Conversely, when profits are high, as in 1996,

the contributions ratio drops. When viewed over a 30-year period, corporate contributions have remained fairly steady at about 1 percent of profits.

• U.S. tax cuts in 1986 made charitable contributions less attractive.

• Some companies are shifting to product donations and in-kind services in lieu of cash. These often go unreported, as does stepped-up volunteerism by employees.

• Most companies match employee charitable donations. So when individuals are laid off, their matching donations also disappear. Many companies also have been reducing their matching grants from 2-to-1 to 1-to-1 ratios.

• To remain competitive, many

... Sparks Confusion and Controversy

In the next top 10 list, published in December *(see list)*, both IBM and Microsoft used retail values for their product donations. IBM ranked second and Microsoft ninth among the top 10 corporate givers. Two other computer giants, Intel Corp. and Hewlett-Packard Co., were also ranked in the top 10, and they, too, had listed their sizable product donations at retail value. The other top donors were also manufacturers — five of them drug companies — and all had listed non-cash products as a large part of their contributions.

Now it was the service industries' turn to cry foul. They have long grumbled that manufacturers' donations of products rather than cash makes the service companies look stingy by comparison. That's because banks and insurance and telecommunications companies primarily give cash because they have relatively few products to donate.

"We don't have products, so we're always at a disadvantage when compared to companies reporting products," said Westina Matthews, director of philanthropic programs at Merrill Lynch & Co. [2]

According to The Conference Board, the service industry donated $702 million last year, 97 percent of it in cash. Of the manufacturing industry's $1.7 billion in gifts, 65 percent was cash, the rest products.

Donated software particularly raises eyebrows because it traditionally enjoys a bigger markup than most products. Some analysts say Microsoft has as much as an 85 percent gross profit margin on most software. [3]

Some software companies don't even take tax deductions for their product donations. Oracle Corp., which says it has donated software valued at more than $350 million retail since 1995, doesn't bother to take a tax deduction because under Internal Revenue Service rules it would have to be based on manufacturing costs, and the tax breaks would be negligible. "It would cost more in paperwork to do the write-off than you get back," an Oracle spokeswoman said. [4]

"Inflated software gifts are the junk bonds of the new philanthropy," said Josef Woodman, founder of the Lightworks Technology Foundation, which helps nonprofits obtain computer hardware and software. [5]

The five pharmaceutical companies rated in the top 10 also listed product donations as a large part of their charitable gifts. For instance, of the $140 million donated by top donor Merck & Co., $116 million was in donated drugs and products.

In response to the controversy, *Corporate Giving Watch* in January began listing the top 10 cash and product givers separately for 1996. As a result, the new list of top 10 cash-givers reflects a better mix of corporate America — including oil, auto and service companies — compared with the original list, dominated by drug and computer firms.

---

[1] Quoted in "Gift Rift: High-Tech Companies Battle Over the Value of Donated Software," *The Wall Street Journal*, Sept. 9, 1997, p. 1A.

[2] Quoted in *Ibid.*

[3] *Ibid.*

[4] Quoted in *Ibid.*

[5] *Ibid.*

---

companies practice "benchmarking," or basing their donations on what their competitors are giving, rather than linking donations to earnings.

For a group of companies in Minnesota known as the Keystone Club, the "benchmark" is far above the national average. Started in 1976 by 23 companies that promised to give 2-5 percent a year to charity, the club now boasts 240 firms, including 38 that are publicly held.

In the view of Citicorp's Ostergard, donations also have not kept up with rising profits because many contributions staffs have been either eliminated or cut to the bone while cutbacks to social-service budgets have caused an upsurge in requests for donations. "We are concerned about how much additional load we can handle without letting standards slip," he says.

"We've all been downsized," says Bell Atlantic's DuBose. "We're not giving out less, we just have fewer people internally to do it." To retain oversight, many firms offer fewer but larger grants, she says.

To increase corporate-giving programs to keep up with rising profits would be "logistically difficult," says Fran Eaton, director of corporate services for the Council on Foundations. "People think it's easy to give money away, but not if you do it right."

At Dayton Hudson, however, tying donations to profits is a longstanding tradition. The firm has donated 5 percent of its profits in cash each year for 50 years. "It's a defining trait of our corporate culture," Cameron says. "We would love it if other corporations emulated that and gave more."

Ostergard predicts that corporate donations may eventually rise to more closely track profits. "Corporate contributions are always a lagging indicator of the health of companies," he says. "So it will take a little more time to begin to see the big numbers. For instance, Citicorp has doubled its giving since 1992, but our earnings have taken off like a rocket. There is a lot of catch-up we have to do." ■

BACKGROUND

Roots of Responsibility

The notion that U.S. companies are responsible for the welfare of their employees and the public dates back to the Industrial Revolution. The migration of workers in the early 1800s to New England's mill towns led to the creation of the "company town," in which employers found it necessary to provide food and shelter for their employees. As the concept evolved over the years, some companies built free parks and recreational facilities for the communities at large as well as homes for their workers.

This "benevolent paternalism" spread to other parts of the country. For instance, retailer Julius Rosenwald made a great success of Sears, Roebuck & Co. by employing agricultural extension agents to bring technology to farmers to make them more productive. "Sears needed a healthy farm community if it was to prosper, and the farm agents enabled their clientele to acquire the purchasing power to buy from Sears," writes Joel Schwartz.[22] Rosenwald was clearly practicing today's so-called "strategic philanthropy," but with a more long-term view of how helping the community at large would help his company.

In fact, the idea of self-interested corporate philanthropy, far from new, has been debated in the courts for decades. In the late 1880s, corporate donations were considered legitimate only if they directly benefited the company.

This "direct-benefit" rule was first enunciated in the 1883 British case, *Hutton v. West Cork Railway Co.*, when the judge ruled that "Charity has no business at the board of directors."

Early U.S. railroad companies were abiding by the "direct-benefit" rule when they donated to local YMCAs to provide affordable temporary lodging for itinerant railroad men. Likewise, companies that donated to "community chests" during the 1920s could argue that their own well-being was tied to the communities where they existed. Then in 1934, the Supreme Court ruled in *Old Mission Portland Cement v. Helverling* that a company could not contribute to the San Francisco Community Chest because it did not directly benefit the company.

Notwithstanding the court's decision, the Internal Revenue Service consistently ruled that charitable donations were legitimate business expenses. In 1921 the IRS said donations were deductible if they served the needs of employees. Then a 1935 Tax Code amendment allowed corporations to deduct charitable donations of up to 5 percent of income.

Finally, in the landmark 1953 *Smith v. Barlow* case, the New Jersey state Supreme Court essentially eliminated the direct-benefit constraint, ruling that A.P. Smith Manufacturing Co. had legitimately donated $1,500 to Princeton University. Basing its ruling on "the widespread belief that free and vigorous non-governmental institutions of learning are vital to our democracy and the system of free enterprise," the court said charitable donations could be made if they benefited society.

"The *Smith* case ushered in an era, extending through the 1970s, in which corporate philanthropy was liberated from bottom-line considerations," writes Schwartz. During that 20 years, corporate philanthropy amounted to unfocused responses to public demand, largely motivated by executives' desires to "do good."

Companies typically spent about 40 percent for education, 30 percent for health and human services and 10 percent on the arts. By 1978, more than 20 percent of corporate giving went to "wholesalers," or federated giving programs like the United Way, which kept donors at arms length from specific charities.

In a seemingly unrelated development, between 1969 and 1972 new regulatory agencies and public interest watchdog groups suddenly sprang up in Washington, including the Big Four business regulatory agencies - the Occupational Safety and Health Administration, the Equal Employment Opportunity Commission, the Consumer Product Safety Commission and the Environmental Protection Agency. Businesses suddenly were inundated with new regulations and demands from the public for corrective action on a wide range of practices. In part to forestall further government intrusion, a shell-shocked corporate world went into a proactive mode with regard to its responsibility to society.

"We sort of lost track of the ethical roots of social responsibility and moved into social responsiveness," said Donna J. Wood, a professor at the University of Pittsburgh's Katz Graduate School of Business. "The idea was that companies had to be responsive to social demands in order to survive. That's quite different from the concept of social responsibility."[23]

The result, Wood continued, was a new emphasis on corporate political action, public affairs, lobbying and ultimately the birth of "cause-related marketing" and "strategic marketing."

Turbulent Times

In 1981, the Economic Recovery Tax Act raised the limit on charitable donations from 5 percent of profits to 10 percent. In response, companies dramatically increased their giving. By 1986, company contributions had

Continued on p. 182

Chronology

Early 1800s

The Industrial Revolution fosters company responsibility for the welfare of employees and the general public. New England mill towns become America's first "company towns."

— • —

Late 1880s

Self-interested corporate philanthropy — the precursor of "strategic philanthropy" — is debated.

1883

The principle that corporate charitable donations must "directly benefit" the corporation is first enunciated in a British case, in which the judge declares, "Charity has no business at the board of directors."

— • —

1920s-1930s

Corporate donations to community chests go legally unchallenged because companies argue that their own well-being is tied to that of the community.

1934

U.S. Supreme Court rules that a company cannot contribute to a community chest because it did not directly benefit the company.

1935

The IRS amends the Tax Code to allow corporations to deduct charitable donations of up to 5 percent of annual income.

1950s-1970s

The link between corporate donations and the "bottom line" is broken and replaced by a broader test — the collective interest of society. Corporate philanthropy expands significantly until it plateaus at about 1 percent of profits. Most corporate philanthropy is essentially unfocused responses to public demand motivated by CEOs' desire to "do good," or exercises in community relations.

1953

The New Jersey Supreme Court in *Smith v. Barlow* eliminates the direct-benefit test when it accepts the right of A.P. Smith Manufacturing Co. to donate $1,500 to Princeton University. The court opines that "corporate power to make reasonable charitable contributions exists under modern conditions."

1969-1972

The creation of four key regulatory agencies and public interest watchdog groups — the Occupational Safety and Health Administration, the Consumer Product Safety Commission, the Equal Opportunity Employment Commission and the Environmental Protection Agency — spotlights questionable corporate practices and leads to new regulations, calls for corrective action and eventually cause-related marketing and strategic marketing.

— • —

1980s

The overall level of corporate giving is affected by changes in tax laws as well as changes in America's corporate structure caused by mergers, globalization and downsizing.

1981

The Economic Recovery Tax Act raises the limit on charitable donations from 5 percent to 10 percent, spurring a significant increase in corporate giving.

1986

The Tax Reform Act of 1986 lowers the corporate tax rate from 46 percent to 34 percent, reducing the incentive for philanthropy.

— • —

1990s

A growing number of CEOs espouse corporate social responsibility, linking the well-being of the corporation and the community. Corporate contributions staffs are downsized, and companies begin practicing strategic philanthropy and cause-related marketing.

1997

Media magnate Ted Turner gives his history-making $1 billion gift to the United Nations. Assets of the nation's largest foundations increase in value by 22 percent, bringing total endowments of the nation's richest foundations to more than $126 billion — more than 12 times as much as the federal government spent last year to aid the poor. Experts predict that America is about to enter a golden age of philanthropy as graying baby boomers inherit their parents' wealth and reach their peak "giving years."

International Giving on the Increase ...

As American corporations increasingly have become global enterprises, they have stepped up their philanthropic activities overseas. "Anecdotally, we know that more U.S. companies are giving more money overseas," said Ann Kaplan, research director of the Trust for Philanthropy at the American Association of Fund Raising Counsel (AAFRC). "But it is very difficult and cumbersome to track down the numbers." [1]

The Conference Board's latest report on corporate giving — based on a study of 289 major companies — shows that gifts to U.S.-based international organizations such as CARE increased from 1.4 percent of total giving in 1992 to 5 percent in 1996. [2] However, the report does not list corporate donations to organizations overseas separately.

Since large companies now have many employees overseas, and more revenues coming from international operations, they are evaluating ways to give internationally, says Myra Alperson, a research analyst at The Conference Board. Many businesses, in fact, no longer consider the U.S. their top growth area and are focusing their expansion

This woman is blind, but drugs donated by Merck protect millions of other Africans from river blindness.

plans on South Africa, Eastern Europe and Asia.

"We expect more and more of our philanthropy budget to go overseas," says Paul M. Ostergard, president of Citicorp Foundation. "More than half our Citibank staff is located outside the U.S., and almost all of our growth is outside the United States." Citibank gave $9.9 million to overseas recipients last year — 28.3 percent of its $35 million contributions budget.

Ostergard says Citibank is expanding the two programs that it funds in the United States into its overseas markets. Banking on Education is a 10-year, $25 million program designed to help failing inner-city schools. The five-year, $10 million Banking on Enterprise initiative promotes microenterprise lending. Loans can be as small as $25, Ostergard says, but that can be enough to launch a small business in a developing country.

Lockheed Martin Corp. began giving internationally last year, says David Phillips, manager of corporate philanthropy. "But this year, for the first time, we have budgeted significant amounts of money for

Continued from p. 180

peaked at 2.26 percent of profits. Then the Tax Reform Act of 1986 lowered the corporate tax rate from 46 percent to 34 percent. The new rate is less appealing for tax deductions and helps explain why corporate donations suddenly reversed their upward trend in 1986 and headed back down to their perennial 1 percent.

But the late 1980s were also a time of dramatic change, as corporate America moved from the industrial to the information era. The decline in manufacturing's fortunes is mirrored in corporate giving statistics. In 1980, manufacturers accounted for 62 percent of all corporate giving. By 1993, manufacturers gave slightly more than half. Meanwhile the service industry's share of charitable contributions jumped from 14 percent to about 22 percent.

The steady drop in corporate donations compared with profits leads many in the philanthropic world to believe that there is little room for corporate social responsibility in the newly streamlined American corporations.

In the past decade of downsizing, Indiana's Burlingame says, the corporate philosophy espoused by CEO Dunlap and University of Chicago economist Milton Friedman — that businesses have no business giving away corporate funds — has re-emerged.

Corporate Citizenship Re-emerges

Slowly but surely, the number of CEOs who embrace a broadly defined social responsibility has been growing in the 1990s. They are the pioneers of the more activist modern-day version of corporate social responsibility called "corporate citi-

zenship." Their leaders are executives from the aggressively responsible companies like Ben & Jerry's, the Body Shop, Levi Straus and Stride Rite, who typically donate from 2-5 percent of pretax profits.

"We look at public service as an investment," said Arnold Hiatt, director of the Stride Rite Foundation. "We believe the well-being of a company cannot be separated from the well-being of the community. If we're not providing the community with access to day care and elder care, if we're not providing proper funding for education, then we're not investing properly in our business." [24] Stride Rite earmarks 5 percent of pretax earnings to the company's foundation.

In 1992 Hiatt helped found Business for Social Responsibility (BSR), a San Francisco organization that advises companies on how they can

... As U.S. Firms Go Global

international contributions."

Companies are also using contributions programs for market penetration and customer relations, said fund-raising consultant Linda B. Gornitsky. "It's amazing how linked" giving and penetration are. Companies "understand that if they want to get into a country, they had better get involved." [3]

Although international contributions budgets generally are relatively small, they are growing quickly, Gornitsky said.

In addition, when manufacturers open plants in the Third World, the living conditions surrounding their factories are often dismal, and sometimes they institute programs to improve the communities where their employees live.

"We are looking at steadily trying to increase the amount of giving to charities and other organizations in other countries, simply because that is where we do business," said J.W. "Skip" Rhodes, corporate contributions manager for Chevron, which operates in 80 countries. [4]

The growth in overseas giving is likely to continue, most analysts say.

"Over the past decade the field of international grantmaking has gone through enormous changes due to the geopolitical transformation of the world," according to a Foundation Center report. "The blooming of democracy and more open societies has opened up new geographic areas for grantmakers. At the same time, the explosive growth of indigenous non-governmental organizations in many countries has stimulated vast new opportunities for funding overseas in nearly every philanthropic field." [5]

However, Alperson points out, "There are lots of problems in giving money overseas that you don't have here," such as differences in culture, language and currency.

As overseas charities begin realizing that U.S. multinational companies are increasing their overseas giving, they have been flocking to the United States seeking donations, said Suzanne Mink, a senior consultant with Campbell and Co. "We have friends in England who are aggressively over here picking our pockets," she told a recent conference on fund-raising. "They're getting their act together very quickly." [6]

---

[1] Quoted in Bill Reinhard and Kate Muth, "Over There, Over There," *Corporate Philanthropy Report*, July 1995.

[2] *Giving USA 1997 Annual Report on Philanthropy for the Year 1996*, 1997.

[3] Linda B. Gornitsky, "Benchmarking Corporate International Contributions," The Conference Board, 1996.

[4] Quoted in Reinhard and Muth, *op. cit.*

[5] Foundation Center, "International Grantmaking: A Report on U.S. Foundation Trends," 1997.

[6] Comments at the 10th annual conference of the National Society of Fund-Raising Executives, Greater Washington, D.C., chapter, Dec. 15-16, 1997.

---

act responsibly without sacrificing profitability. President Bob Dunn says BSR's membership has increased from 45 firms in 1994 to more than 1,400 companies with total revenues of more than $900 billion.

"As companies have become profitable again, investors, customers and employees are insisting that companies act in a responsible manner," Dunn said. Studies have shown that customers and stockholders want to buy products and stocks from socially responsible companies, and business school graduates want to work for socially responsible companies, he said. "And there is considerable evidence that over the long haul socially responsible companies generate a more favorable return for their shareholders."

During the 1996 election, President Clinton hosted a day-long White House Summit on Corporate Citizenship, at which he honored 13 companies with worker-friendly policies. These companies, Clinton said, were proof that companies can "do the right thing and still make money." ■

CURRENT SITUATION

Legislative Initiatives

Given the lack of reliable data on corporate giving, Rep. Paul E. Gillmor, R-Ohio, is calling for legislation that would require publicly held companies to report what charities they support and how much they give.

"There are some companies that don't want the shareholder to know what they're doing," Gillmor says. Corporations are "taking shareholders' money and putting it into purposes that may not be in shareholders' interests."

Gillmor said his bill would not cover gifts to corporate foundations, because that information is already public, but only large gifts to charities. Gifts to educational institutions would be exempted, as would personal property gifts and gifts to local charities.

Several corporations that commented on the bill via the Securities and Exchange Commission's Web site said that if it became law, they would either discontinue donations or would give only to educational institutions or to local charities to avoid additional paperwork.

Congress has asked the SEC to study the proposed legislation; its report is expected in March. "I don't know if we will get any momentum for it this session," Gillmor says, "but I will continue to push for it."

A companion bill proposed by Gillmor would require corporations to give shareholders a voice in determining which charities receive donations.

Both bills have stimulated howls of opposition among corporate charity staffs and nonprofits who commented on the SEC Web site. The companion bill would be "a horror to deal with," said the Council on Foundation's Ridings. "Local charities would suffer, corporations themselves would go nuts."

In the view of Alan F. Senger, vice president of the Cleveland-based TRW Foundation, "Shareholders do not decide internal procedures regarding personnel, accounting, purchasing, etc., so neither should they decide how corporate dollars are invested in philanthropic projects." Such a practice would result in "extremely fractured philanthropy" and would "negate a company's efforts to strategically align its corporate giving with its business goals."

Some groups have favored the disclosure bill because it would simplify data-gathering. "Companies disclose what they want to, so you get comparisons between apples and oranges," said the Conference Board's Smith. [25]

Several large corporations have said that reporting donations would be a very burdensome requirement, especially if they have millions of shareholders. Most said they reveal the information to anyone who asks.

"We do release annually a report describing our charitable involvement," said Patricia J. Smith, corporate secretary of Coors. "It has been our experience, however, that the level of interest in this area among shareholders is, in fact, negligible." ∎

OUTLOOK

Boomers' Generosity

Predictions that the nation is about to enjoy a resurgence of philanthropy is based on three converging trends: the graying of the baby boomers, the astounding amount of new wealth created by the roaring stock market and a predicted doubling in foundation assets in the coming decade.

"America is about to enter a golden age of philanthropy," wrote Philanthropy Roundtable President John Walters. "In virtually all respects, giving by Americans, individually and institutionally, is poised to grow at an astounding rate. The question is no longer whether this will happen, but how rapidly, to what level and to what end." [26]

In a much-quoted study, Cornell University economists Robert Avery and Michael Rendall predicted that graying baby boomers will receive the "biggest inter-generational transfer of wealth in United States history" as they inherit some of the $6.8 trillion in assets their parents accumulated. [27] Conservative estimates put the actual amount they will receive between 1990 and 2005 at $2 trillion.

In turn, baby boomers themselves, who have accumulated their own significant wealth, are expected to donate about $10 trillion between 1990 and 2040, Walters wrote. When people enter their 50s, dubbed the "giving years" by fund-raisers, they generally donate more to charity as they feel more financially secure.

Not only will aging boomers probably be big donors, but they have "unparalleled potential" as volunteers. "They will live longer, healthier lives than their parents yet retire earlier, allowing for years in which to give their time to community service work." [28]

The bullish stock market also presages a philanthropic upswing. It has spawned a new generation of super-rich, including 4 million millionaires and 170 billionaires, who are deemed more likely to donate a higher percentage of their disposable income to charity than the average person. [29]

For instance, those with net worth between $1 million and $10 million donated 5.5 percent of their household income to charity in 1995, compared with the 1.9 percent given by the average American, according to *Giving USA 1996*, published by the AAFRC Trust for Philanthropy. Those with a net worth of $50 million donated 17.8 percent of their annual income.

However, fundraisers report that the wealthy baby boomers who will lead the country into its new philanthropic era are more results-oriented and hands-on than were the Carnegies, Rockefellers and Fords who led America's earlier golden age of philanthropy. The new individual givers are echoing corporate America's shift to "strategic planning."

Their role models are pragmatic businessmen like billionaires Turner and Soros — who earmark their gifts for specific purposes and demand results.

Turner's $1 billion gift to the U.N. targets women's and population issues, children's health, water purification and climate change. He said he is dishing it out over 10 years, the better to keep track of results. Currency speculator Soros, who focuses on encouraging democracy in Eastern Europe and Russia, decriminalizing drugs, reforming education and fighting poverty and crime in America, is known for cutting off inefficient charities.

The highly educated baby boomers are far more skeptical than their parents, in part because of much-publicized charity fraud scandals.

"The new generation evaluates charities on a different basis," said Betty Beene, president of the scandal-plagued

At Issue:

Is corporate philanthropy fair to shareholders?

BEN COHEN

Chairman, Ben & Jerry's Homemade, Inc.

WRITTEN FOR THE CQ RESEARCHER, JANUARY 1998.

business has a responsibility to make great products for its customers, create economic rewards for its shareholders and employees, and recognize its role in society. Ben & Jerry's mission statement declares a commitment to all three parts: high-quality products, economic reward and social commitment.

Corporate philanthropy is just one part of our social commitment. Our formula for giving creates value for shareholders because it's directly linked to our profitability. Seven and a half percent of our pretax dollars go to employee-led corporate philanthropy. The more profitable we are, the more value there is for shareholders and the more we can give back to the community.

Ben & Jerry's is a successful, growing company because we turn our deeply felt social values into financial value. We've shown that a company can do well by doing good. Our social values, combined with our high-quality products, provide a distinction in the marketplace and create brand loyalty with customers, leading them to choose our products over the competition. This creates more financial value to our shareholders.

If people who have social concerns can buy ice cream from a company that shares those concerns and puts its business power to addressing those concerns, all other things being equal, they will buy ice cream from that company. That's turning values into value.

As well, many investors purchased Ben & Jerry's shares because the company has a social mission alongside its product and economic missions. Our annual meetings draw 3,000 shareholders, who often push the company to higher social standards. They own shares in the company because they know it has a heart and soul and values.

Investors have realized good returns by investing in values-led companies. The Domini Social Index shows that stocks screened for social responsibility outperformed the Standard & Poor's 500 during seven years ending December 1997. During that incredible bull market run, that's saying something about values delivering value.

Our share value has run in up-and-down cycles, not unlike any publicly traded company. However, when we've successfully managed all three parts of our mission — product quality, economic reward and social commitment — we've realized our best growth cycles and share value. The better we perform the more we can give back. The more we give back the more we receive in return, building more value in the company.

ALBERT J. DUNLAP

CEO, Sunbeam Corp.

if you're in business, you're in business for one thing, to make money. You must do everything fiducial, legal and moral to achieve that goal. And making excellent products that are expertly marketed is the primary way of making money.

Executives who run their businesses to support social causes — such as Ben & Jerry's or The Body Shop — would never get my investment dollars. They funnel a portion of their profits into things like saving the whales or Greenpeace. That is not the essence of business. If you want to support a social cause . . . join Rotary International.

I have no problem with giving. I've left in my estate the largest gift ever to be presented to my alma mater, West Point. And my wife and I give money regularly to hospitals and animal shelters. But it's our money, we earned it.

Corporate charity exists so that CEOs can collect awards, plaques and honors, so they can sit on a dais and be adored. But that is not what the shareholder is paying them a million bucks a year — plus stock options and bonuses — to do!

Show me a chief executive who's on five boards and who lends his or her name, prestige and time to 15 community activities, and I'll show you a company that's under-performing. A chief executive is paid to run the company. That's the CEO's job. Corporations become woefully inadequate when CEOs think they are great social messiahs.

My distaste for corporate giving began as I worked my way up the ladder at American Can in the 1970s. American Can gave away scads of shareholder money. As a representative of the Connecticut-based company, an executive such as myself could have gone to a charity event every night of the week in New York City. It was totally part of the corporate culture.

One day it occurred to me how wasteful this was, and not just from a financial angle. If you went into the city midweek and had to be at work the next morning, you couldn't help but be tired and unproductive — two big fat strikes against the shareholders. . . .

I know people look at me and say, "He's against the corporations giving to charity? What a cheap SOB!" But that money is not mine to give. I have no right to give away a shareholder's money, but I have every right to give away my own money.

Whether the United Way or the Red Cross should be supported is a decision that should be made by individuals. Why should the chairman of the company make a decision about the worthiness of a charity on behalf of shareholders?

When Nonprofits Rent Their Reputations

You've probably seen the commercial. A toddler sits in his car seat next to a bag full of groceries, a jug of orange juice peeping out. Suddenly a radio announcer declares that the American Cancer Society has just determined that orange juice helps prevent cancer. As Dad glimpses in the rearview mirror, he is amazed to see Junior chugging down the gallon of juice.

The ad reflects a new and controversial fundraising trend among health groups: Allowing their logos to be displayed, usually exclusively, on companies' products in exchange for handsome royalties. The thirsty toddler ad brings the cancer society $1 million a year from the Florida Orange Growers Association, which puts the society's logo on ads and juice cartons.

Critics of such "partnerships" — the groups are very careful not to call them endorsements — say they are fraught with hazards. Perhaps the most obvious potential problem is that to many consumers the logos represent seals of approval, misleadingly suggesting that the associations have tested the products.

The American Lung Association ran into trouble when it allowed its logo to be used on carbon monoxide detectors by American Sensors Inc. *Consumer Reports* later tested the sensors and found three models "not acceptable," according to *Slate*, the online magazine.[1] Although the design flaws were later fixed, the damage had been done to the organization's reputation.

"I think [renting logos] is flat-out misleading," said Robert Lawry, director of the Center for Professional Ethics at Case Western Reserve University, because at least some consumers are misled into thinking the logos imply a product endorsement.[2]

In addition to the ALA, at least three other groups have had to back out of logo deals. Two of the contracts, one with the American Heart Association and one with the Arthritis Foundation, were challenged by the government.

In 1990 the heart association discontinued its HeartGuide Seal program after the Department of Agriculture complained it misled consumers. The Arthritis Foundation's $1 million-a-year deal with McNeil Consumer Products was challenged by 19 state attorneys general who considered ads for the company's "new" Arthritis Foundation-brand aspirin misleading. The company settled the suit for $2 million.

The American Medical Association (AMA) is the latest group to run into partnership problems. The doctors' group raised its members' temperatures when AMA officials signed an exclusive five-year contract to allow the Sunbeam Corp. to display the prestigious AMA logo on Sunbeam home health-care products such as vaporizers, heating pads and blood-pressure monitors.

No sooner was the deal announced than it plunged the 300,000-member association into a tempest of protests from consumer advocates, editorial writers and AMA board members, who feared the partnership would erode the group's reputation for objectivity and impartiality. Within a week, the AMA declared the deal a "mistake" and tried to cancel it. Since then, Sunbeam, led by CEO Albert J. Dunlap, sued the AMA for breach of contract. It must either honor its contract, the suit says, or pay damages that could exceed $20 million. The ill-fated deal led five top AMA officials to resign, including CEO P. John Seward, who had helped negotiate the deal.

In a *New York Times* op-ed piece last fall, Dunlap insisted he will pursue the suit "vigorously to its rightful conclusion."

Ironically, Dunlap is among the most vocal critics of corporate philanthropy. *(See "At Issue," p. 185)* He defended the Sunbeam/AMA partnership as a win-win proposition for both the AMA and Sunbeam's shareholders.

"Sunbeam and its shareholders were winners because this creative program provided added value to Sunbeam's customers and a point of differentiation from competing manufacturers," he wrote.

Cause-marketing arrangements like the Sunbeam/AMA partnership are not considered to be true philanthropy by most people in the philanthropic community, even though they garner more than $500 million a year for nonprofits. Instead, they are considered to be marketing mechanisms. Many nonprofits have turned to the controversial technique because they say it's getting harder and harder to solicit funds from corporations on a strictly philanthropic basis.

"Nonprofits can't count on corporations to give millions of dollars just because they want to be good citizens," said Peter Paris, formerly with the ALA. "Now everything has to be linked to a stronger benefit."[3]

---

[1] John Merline, "Selling Seals of Approval," *Slate*, May 2, 1997.

[2] *Ibid.*

[3] Quoted in Merline, *op. cit.*

United Way of America (UWA). "It's driving, candidly, one of the most profound changes in the United Way we've seen in our history." Instead of counting outputs, or how many people are served at a shelter per day, the UWA now counts outcomes, or how many families are moved from homelessness to independent living.[30]

The Robin Hood Foundation in New York, founded by a 43-year-old multimillionaire commodities trader and two Wall Street colleagues, raises money from the city's elite for charities with efficient and creative solutions to inner-city poverty and at-risk youths.

"We consider ourselves to be socially responsible venture capitalists," said Executive Director David Saltzman. "We think we can give donors the biggest bang for their charitable buck." [31]

Meanwhile, the philanthropic community is still waiting for the "cyber-rich" to start giving. Most of the fabulously wealthy young entrepreneurs who struck it rich in high technology have not yet begun donating to charity in large amounts.

Foundations' Trove

Many of the new rich are expected to start putting their appreciated assets into private foundations. "The buzz is that we are on the verge of a tidal wave," said Jan Masaoka, executive director of the Support Center for Nonprofit Management in San Francisco, the largest nonprofit consulting firm in the country. [32]

Indeed, community-based foundations are the fastest-growing element of philanthropy in the country today, with assets that increased by 28.6 percent in 1996. And private family foundations grew by 42 percent in the past decade. [33]

Ann DeBusk, executive director of the American Leadership Forum of Silicon Valley, has launched Project Involve!, designed to help the newly rich get involved in community relations and philanthropy. "It has really taken off," she said. "We plan to increase corporate giving in the valley from $56 million annually to $1 billion by the year 2000." [34]

The new wealthy are also expected to put their money into private or community foundations while they are still alive, unlike previous wealthy generations, whose fortunes were disbursed by foundations posthu-

mously. They want more control over how their money is spent, philanthropy experts say.

Microsoft founder Bill Gates, 42, the richest man in the world, has vowed to give away 90 percent of his $40 billion while he is still alive. Last June, he gave $210 million — or .005 percent of his net worth — to connect libraries to the information superhighway.

In the coming decade, big-name foundations are expected to come under increasing scrutiny when their assets double, as Hudson Institute economist Alan Reynolds predicts. Reynolds contends that foundations have been "hoarding assets" by "minimizing payouts in order to maximize asset growth" during the last decade. Since 1969, tax-exempt foundations generally have been required to distribute at least 5 percent of their assets each year. But Reynolds says that many large foundations treat the 5 percent minimum as an absolute maximum. [35]

Today foundations account for only 7.5 percent of total U.S. philanthropic giving, compared with 8.2 percent in 1969, when the 5 percent minimum was enacted. "The fact that foundations account for a smaller share of total giving than they did before 1969 is rather startling, considering the enormous growth in the number and assets of foundations," Reynolds wrote.

Indeed, the assets of the nation's wealthiest foundations grew 22 percent in 1997, according to a recent study. [36]

Reynolds predicts that if America's major foundations "continue to put assets first and charity last," their assets will swell to $5.9 trillion or more by 2035. By that time, he adds, the country will face "an unprecedented fiscal crisis," as the government tries to pay Social Security and Medicare benefits to retired baby boomers.

"What is the likelihood, under those circumstances, that Congress will fail to notice a tax-exempt hoard of $5-7 trillion?" he asks.

But before that happens, foundations

and charities will be under increasing pressure in the more immediate future as the 1996 Welfare Reform Act kicks in. Already, even before the full effects of the law have been felt, many city and charity-run emergency food shelters were not able to keep up with increased demand last year.

"For the first time, our agencies are having to turn people away — the shelves are bare — for the first time ever," said Sharon Daley of Catholic Charities USA. "That's what we find so shocking" in the midst of the booming economy, she said. [37]

In December, the U.S. Conference of Mayors reported that 19 percent of requests for emergency food went unfulfilled last year. And requests for shelter by homeless families increased by 5 percent. In addition, 88 percent of the cities surveyed say they regularly turn away homeless families because of lack of resources. Most of the increased demand for food and shelter came from families with at least one working parent and from those whose food stamps have been cut. Congress removed thousands of legal immigrants and childless adults from the food stamp program last year. [38]

What role will corporations play in this new era of philanthropy as demands from the needy escalate? Unless corporations increase their rate of giving, they will contribute an ever-decreasing portion of total giving, simply because individuals and foundations probably will be increasing their giving, experts say.

"Ironically, the government's message as it stepped back from its commitments was, 'We expect corporations to step forward,'" Cameron says. "The clear message is that this needs to be picked up by the private sector."

"There's going to be more expectation put on companies as the needs grow," predicts Chris Parks, director of the Dayton Hudson Foundation.

Gen. Powell's volunteerism summit last April thus far has had limited success at getting corporations to pledge to help 2 million needy children by 2000. Powell, who heads America's Promise: The Alliance for Youth, reported last November that 300 companies in 200 communities had joined the movement. But he did not say how much money or how many hours had been pledged. "We're just getting started," he said. [39]

However, David R. Morgan, vice president for research of the Council for Aid to Education, does not foresee significant increases in the percent of profits donated by corporations. "At some level, I think corporations believe 1 percent is about the right level of giving," he said. "There have been many efforts in the past to get them to give more, but with no appreciable effect."

Kathy Koch is a freelance writer in the Washington, D.C., area.

Notes

1 "Why Do We Donate?" *The New York Times*, Dec. 9, 1997.
[2] Quoted in "The Land of the Handout," *Newsweek*, Sept. 29, 1997.
[3] Anne Faircloth and Caroline Bollinger, "*Fortune's* 40 Most Generous Americans," *Fortune*, Feb. 2, 1998.
[4] *Giving USA: The Annual Report on Philanthropy for 1996* (1997), AAFRC Trust for Philanthropy and Department of Commerce. For background, see "Charitable Giving," *The CQ Researcher*, Nov. 12, 1993, pp. 985-1008.
[5] Quoted in the Fort Lauderdale, Fla., *Sun-Sentinel*, Aug. 25, 1996.
[6] Myra Alperson, "Corporate Giving Strategies That Add Business Value," The Conference Board, 1995.
[7] Quoted in "Corporations Adopt a Different Attitude: Show Us the Value," *The New York Times*, Dec. 9, 1997.
[8] For background, see "Arts Funding," *The CQ Researcher*, Oct. 21, 1994, pp. 913-936.
[9] For background, see "Regulating Nonprofits," *The CQ Researcher*, Dec. 26, 1997, pp. 1129-1152.
[10] "Are Corporations Less Charitable?" Op-ed article, *The New York Times*, Feb. 21, 1988.
[11] "Giving Gets Unfashionable," Op-ed article, *The New York Times*, Feb. 28, 1988.
[12] Quoted in "Changing Demographics Push Corporate Giving Boundaries," *Responsive Philanthropy*, winter 1994.
[13] *The Yearbook of the Foundation Center*, 1996.

[14] Op-ed article, *The New York Times*, March 29, 1987.
[15] "For the Public Good? Corporate Sponsorships and Their Impact on the Nonprofit Sector," National Committee for Responsive Philanthropy, August 1995. See "Helping the Homeless," *The CQ Researcher*, Jan. 26, 1996, pp. 73-96.
[16] From "Phony Philanthropy?" *Foundation News*, May/June 1989.
[17] See Paul Goldberger, "Philip Morris Calls in I.O.U.'s in the Arts," *The New York Times*, Oct. 5, 1994.
[18] Profits increased 8.7 percent that same year.
[19] The Conference Board, *op. cit.*, p. 5. The 0.7 percent figure is based on total income from worldwide operations. When only U.S. income is considered, the percent donated to charity is 0.9 percent.
[20] Weeden recommends a higher percentage for manufacturers because they often donate products as a large component of their contributions, whereas service companies usually give cash.
[21] Audris D. Tillman, *Corporate Contributions 1993*, The Conference Board, 1995.
[22] Information in this section based on Joel Schwartz, *Giving Better, Giving Smarter* (1997), p. 133. Schwartz is a research fellow at the Hudson Institute.
[23] Joel Makower, *Beyond the Bottom Line* (1994), p. 29.
[24] Quoted in "Seeing Public Service as an Investment," *Newsweek*, May 4, 1992.
[25] Quoted in Jennifer Moore and Grant Williams, "Give and Tell," *The Chronicle of Philanthropy*, Nov. 13, 1997.
[26] John Walters, "The Coming Philanthropic Explosion," *Philanthropy*, Dec. 17, 1997.
[27] "Why Do We Donate?" *The New York Times*, Dec. 9, 1997.
[28] "Charities Get Ready for the Boom," *The*

Chronicle of Philanthropy, Nov. 27, 1997. For background, see "The New Volunteerism," *The CQ Researcher*, Dec. 13, 1996, pp. 1081-1104.
[29] See Gerald E. Auten, Charles T. Clotfelter and Richard L. Schmalbeck, *Taxes and Philanthropy Among the Wealthy* (1997).
[30] Speaking on "The Diane Rehm Show," National Public Radio, Nov. 18, 1997.
[31] Quoted in Paul Geitner, "In New York, Unconventional Charity Hits the Target," *Philadelphia Inquirer*, Dec. 26, 1991.
[32] Quoted in Judith Havermann, "Philanthropy: the Next Generation," *The Washington Post*, Nov. 16, 1997. See also Judith Havermann, "More to Give Away: Wealth of Top U.S. Foundations Grew 22 Percent in 1997," *The Washington Post*, Feb. 23, 1998, p. A20.
[33] Thom Geier, "Average Americans, Not the Super-Rich Are the Real Givers," *U.S. News & World Report*, Dec. 22, 1997.
[34] Quoted in Mollie Mudd and Bill Reinhard, "High-Tech Firms Get a Nudge," *Corporate Philanthropy Report*, p. 5.
[35] Alan Reynolds, "Forswearing Foundation Frugality," *Philanthropy* magazine, winter 1998. Reynolds' comments are based on his recent study, "Death, Taxes and the Independent Sector."
[36] Debra E. Blum and Marina Dundjerski, "Foundations' Endowment Explosion," *The Chronicle of Philanthropy*, Feb. 26, 1998.
[37] Speaking on "The Diane Rehm Show," National Public Radio, Dec. 23, 1997.
[38] Linda Feldman, "Amid U.S. Prosperity, Hunger Grows," *The Christian Science Monitor*, Dec. 15, 1997.
[39] Quoted in Susan Gvozdas, "Powell: Volunteer Effort Gets Good Start," *USA Today*, Nov. 26, 1997.

FOR MORE INFORMATION

The Conference Board, 845 Third Ave., New York, N.Y. 10022-6679; (212) 759-0900; http://www.conference-board.org. This organization of senior executives from the largest 1,000 U.S. companies does research on a wide variety of corporate concerns.

Council on Foundations, 1828 L St. N.W. Suite 300, Washington, D.C. 20036; (202) 466-6512; http://www.cof.org. The council promotes effective philanthropy through educational programs, government relations and the development of standards for effective grant-making.

Foundation Center, 79 Fifth Ave., New York, N.Y. 10003; (202) 331-1400; http://www.fdncenter.org. The center publishes foundation guides and serves as a clearinghouse on foundation and corporate giving.

Independent Sector, 1828 L St. N.W. Suite 1200, Washington, D.C. 20036; (202) 223-8100; http://www.indepsec.org. This organization of corporations, foundations and voluntary and philanthropic groups encourages volunteerism, giving and not-for-profit initiatives by the private sector.

National Committee for Responsive Philanthropy, 2001 S St. N.W., Suite 602, Washington, D.C. 20009; (202) 387-9177; http://www.ncrp.org. The committee directs philanthropic giving aimed at the socially, economically and politically disenfranchised.

Bibliography

Selected Sources Used

Books

Barry, John W., and Bruno V. Manno, (eds.), *Giving Better, Giving Smarter: Working Papers of the National Commission on Philanthropy and Civic Renewal*, National Commission on Philanthropy and Civic Renewal, 1997.

This compilation looks at the moral, historical and economical aspects of philanthropy, obstacles to effective foundation philanthropy and corporate philanthropy today.

Burlingame, Dwight F., and Dennis R. Young (eds.), *Corporate Philanthropy at the Crossroads*, Indiana University Press, 1996.

Two professors at Indiana University's Center for Philanthropic Studies compiled this collection of essays on the future of corporate philanthropy in the United States. The authors examine the need for more data, the growing use of volunteerism to boost employee morale, the ethics of corporate philanthropy and how firm size affects philanthropy.

Dunlap, Albert J., *Mean Business: How I Save Bad Companies and Make Good Companies Great*, Random House, 1996.

The controversial CEO explains how he revived the ailing Scott Paper Co., outlining the "Dunlapping the Corporation" technique that he says any CEO can emulate.

Makower, Joel, and *Business for Social Responsibility, Beyond the Bottom Line: Putting Social Responsibility to Work for Your Business and the World*, Simon & Schuster, 1994.

This in-depth look at the trend toward corporate social responsibility begins by reviewing the evolution of the concept since the 1970s. It then explains the link between social responsibility and profits and gives numerous examples of successful, socially responsible companies.

Articles

Smith, Craig, The New Corporate Philanthropy, *Harvard Business Review*, June 1994.

A leading authority on corporate philanthropy contends that the new paradigm in philanthropy gives companies a powerful competitive edge and encourages them to play a leadership role in social problem-solving.

Reports and Studies

AAFRC Trust for Philanthropy, *Giving USA: The Annual Report on Philanthropy for the Year 1996*, 1997.

This compilation, published by the American Association of Fund-Raising Counsel in New York City, provides comprehensive statistics and analysis of charitable and philanthropic giving.

Alperson, Myra, *Corporate Giving Strategies That Add Business Value*, The Conference Board, 1995.

This report, which includes survey findings from 483 of the country's largest companies and a number of case studies, outlines how companies are developing "strategic philanthropy" programs that fit in with their business goals. Among other trends, it looks at employee volunteerism, partnerships with nonprofits and global giving.

Auten, Gerald, Charles T. Clotfelter and Richard L. Schmalbeck, *Taxes and Philanthropy Among the Wealthy*, presentation at a University of Michigan conference, "Does Atlas Shrug: The Economic Consequences of Taxing the Rich," October 1997.

Three analysts look at giving patterns of the wealthy and examine the prospect of a massive transfer of wealth over the next decade as the baby boomers inherit wealth from their parents.

Frumkin, Peter (ed.), *Measuring the Value of Corporate Citizenship*, Council on Foundations, 1996.

This report reviews the findings of a two-year study of how corporate citizenship can add value to a business. It examines which measurement tools are most effective and how to integrate citizenship into a corporation.

Morgan, David R., "Corporate Philanthropy: Law, Culture, Education and Politics," *New York Law School Law Review*, 1997.

The vice president of research at the Council on Aid to Education analyzes data from the Internal Revenue Service showing corporate giving patterns and trends.

Reynolds, Alan, *Death, Taxes and the Independent Sector*, The Philanthropy Roundtable, 1996.

The director of economic research at the Hudson Institute looks at the relationship between taxes and charitable giving, especially bequests and foundation grants. He predicts that if current trends continue, an increasing share of charitable giving will be done through foundations.

Tillman, Audris D., *Corporate Contributions in 1996, An Advance Report*, The Conference Board, 1996.

This annual survey looks at the largest American corporations, those with income over $1 billion. Using charts and graphs, it examines what they gave, who the beneficiaries were and the outlooks for 1997 and 1998.

The Next Step

Additional information from UMI's Newspaper & Periodical Abstracts™ database

Cause-related Marketing

Allen, Scott, "Environmental donors set tone; Activists affected by quest for funds," _The Boston Globe_, Oct. 20, 1997, p. A1.

In the 1970s, major groups such as the Environmental Defense Fund in New York were run by low-paid idealists, grass-roots groups had almost no budgets and the joke about so-called "tainted money" from corporations was that there "taint enough of it." Charitable foundations may be the most influential income source of all for environmental groups, even though they account for less than 20 percent of their income. Many new groups would never get started without foundation grants.

Cooper, Colleen, "Give and thou shall receive," _Sales & Marketing Management_, March 1997, pp. 75-76.

Strategic philanthropy is discussed. In search of more bang for their philanthropic buck, some corporations want to "own" a cause by making a long-term commitment.

Fogarty, Thomas A., "Corporations use causes for effect; Charity tie-ins show results for marketers," _USA Today_, Nov. 10, 1997, p. B7.

Cause-related marketing is winning acceptance from consumers, and companies are seeing the lucrative results of such arrangements. Peter Frumkin, an expert on nonprofit organizations at Harvard's Kennedy School of Government, says cause-related marketing has become a permanent fixture in American society.

Goozner, Merrill, " 'Strategic Philanthropy' a Hot Trend; Tie-Ins Used to Help Needy, Promote Company Images," _Chicago Tribune_, April 27, 1997, p. 1.

At first glance, a restaurant promotion would not appear likely to help meet the goals of the Presidents' Volunteer Summit, but one-fifth of the proceeds will go to Ronald McDonald House, the charity arm of the fast-food giant. Organized by the Corporation for National Service, the Points of Light Foundation and headed by retired Gen. Colin Powell, the three-day summit is designed to spur more community-based volunteer efforts to help at-risk children.

Hamlin, Jesse, "Corporate support for the arts often has marketing strings attached," _San Francisco Chronicle_, Dec. 9, 1997, p. E3.

Local arts organizations are looking to corporate America to fill part of the gap caused by shrinking National Endowment for the Arts funds. To get corporate money these days, arts groups increasingly are packaging themselves to appeal to corporate "strategic philanthropy" programs and making straight-out marketing deals.

Kadlec, Daniel, "The new world of giving," _Time_, May 5, 1997, pp. 62-64.

Socially conscious capitalism, typified by the policies of Ben & Jerry's Homemade ice cream, is becoming increasingly popular in the business world. Companies' motives aren't exactly altruistic.

Mullen, Jennifer, "Performance-based corporate philanthropy: How "giving smart" can further corporate goals," _Public Relations Quarterly_, summer 1997, pp. 42-48.

The nonprofit and corporate expectations involved in charitable giving are examined. Strategic charitable giving can bring added value to corporations.

Saporta, Maria, "Coca-Cola, other companies offer strategic philanthropy'," _Atlanta Journal Constitution_, April 26, 1997, p. E3.

"Strategic philanthropy" is the wave of the future, the late Roberto C. Goizueta, Coca-Cola's chairman and CEO, told the annual meeting of the Boys & Girls Clubs of America. Under strategic philanthropy, Goizueta said, nonprofit organizations gain access to corporate expertise in marketing, public relations, information technologies and other areas.

Charitable Donations

Chandler, Susan, "Freebies Getting Less Frivolous As Corporate America Tightens Its Ethics Codes; More and More Companies Are Making Contributions to Charities Instead of Giving Gifts to Their Clients," _Chicago Tribune_, Dec. 11, 1997, p. 3-1.

Companies big and small have stopped sending holiday gifts. And while some recipients of expensive scotch and Cuban cigars may miss the good old days, the change in corporate gift-giving practices is proving a boon to charities, many of which are receiving corporate contributions that previously would have gone to clients.

Pogrebin, Robin, "Philanthropic Magazines' Circulation Rises, Along With Interest in Giving," _The New York Times_, Dec. 15, 1997, p. D13.

Charitable giving is in. Americans are donating $150 billion a year to charity. Nonprofit organizations now number more than 1 million. People are taking an increasing interest in volunteerism. And some publications are reaping the benefits.

"Ring Out 1997 by Giving," _Los Angeles Times_, Dec. 26, 1997, p. B6.

Charitable donations nationally rose 8 percent after inflation last year, but that increase did not keep pace with the much larger increase in the nation's wealth, which was driven by a bullish stock market, low inflation, low interest rates and low unemployment rates. The rosy economic news, and the chance to take tax deductions, should persuade individuals and corporations to give more.

Corporate Philanthropy and the Arts

Hartigan, Patti, "Wanted: business dollars. Critics say corporate leadership is falling short in Boston," *The Boston Globe*, Aug. 18, 1997, p. A1.

Boston arts administrators often look to cities such as Seattle, Minneapolis and Milwaukee with longing. When it comes to funding for the arts, these cities have long histories not only of corporate largess but also of corporate leadership. That's not to say that Boston corporations ignore cultural institutions entirely. An informal Globe survey revealed that at least 807 firms contributed to one or more arts groups in the past year.

Miller, Judith, "Study Links Drop in Support To Elitist Attitude in the Arts," *The New York Times*, Oct. 13, 1997, p. A1.

The report reflects growing anxiety about the future of the arts from Jane Alexander, the outgoing chairwoman of the embattled National Endowment for the Arts, whose budget has been cut almost in half during her four-year tenure. But unlike most arts surveys, "American Canvas," as the report is titled, does not attribute the "marginalization of the arts" in American life even mainly to the loss of support from federal, state and local governments. It emphasizes factors like the increasing commercialization of American culture, the aging of audiences, the decline of corporate and private giving and the loss of arts education in public schools.

"Sagging Support for the Arts; Legislators should resist ending contributors' tax breaks," *Los Angeles Times*, March 9, 1997, p. M4.

Federal funding for the arts plunged after revelations in the early 1990s that public dollars had been used to fund art that gave new meaning to the word "risque," from postmodernist belly dancing at the Brooklyn Academy of Music to salacious photographs by Robert Mapplethorpe. Arts and humanities endowments were slashed from $334 million in fiscal 1995 to $209.5 million in fiscal 1996 and '97.

Corporate Philanthropy and Politics

Abramson, Jill, " '96 Campaign Costs Set Record at $2.2 Billion," *The New York Times*, Nov. 25, 1997, p. A18.

A study by the Center for Responsive Politics, which analyzes campaign spending, shows a significant shift in giving by corporations and other businesses away from Democrats and toward Republicans since the GOP took control of Congress in 1994. While labor unions continued to shower the Democratic Party and Democratic congressional candidates with large donations, the overwhelming support for the Republicans in the business community, which has many more individual donors and political action committees, provided Republicans with a giant financial edge.

"Corporate Campaign Giving: Money Aimed at a Bull's-Eye; The givers need something, and they know where to get it," *Los Angeles Times*, Sept. 29, 1997, p. B4.

It now seems apparent that the Senate investigation into campaign fund-raising abuses during the 1996 election is having an effect. This past week, the Senate's Republican leadership grudgingly agreed to permit a full Senate floor debate on reform, which began Friday. It is a giant step from where the Senate leadership was at the beginning of this year.

Cushman, John H. Jr., "Corporate Gifts Help Gain Access to U.S. Governors," *The New York Times*, May 17, 1997, p. A1.

In the past several years, a select group of the nation's biggest corporations has given millions of dollars to the National Governors' Association and an affiliated research arm. In return for their tax-deductible contributions, the corporations' lobbyists have gained unusual access to the governors' policy-making apparatus.

Dao, James, "Corporations Flout Limits On Donations," *The New York Times*, July 14, 1997, p. B1.

Corporations can give no more than $5,000 a year to candidates in state and local elections under a 1974 law. But officials with the state Board of Elections, the agency charged with enforcing the rule, say the law is often impossible to enforce, is routinely violated and is so full of loopholes that almost any corporation can easily circumvent it.

Hohler, Bob, "Trade-trip firms netted $5.5 Billion in aid; Donated $2.3 Million to Democrats," *The Boston Globe*, March 30, 1997, p. A1.

Twenty-seven corporations that sent executives on trade trips with the late Commerce Secretary Ronald H. Brown obtained part of a multibillion-dollar commitment in federally guaranteed assistance from the Overseas Private Investment Corp., according to a Globe analysis of fund-raising records, trip manifests and OPIC documents.

Vartabedian, Ralph, "Corporate Traffic Heavy on U.S. Political Money Trail," *Los Angeles Times*, Sept. 21, 1997, p. A1.

According to a *Los Angeles Times* analysis of political giving by every major corporation in America, the big contributors include a number of firms that have become the focus of federal investigations, or whose reputations have declined within their industries. The corporate role in political finance is further analyzed.

Back Issues

Great Research on Current Issues Starts Right Here . . . Recent topics covered by The CQ Researcher are listed below. Before May 1991, reports were published under the name of Editorial Research Reports.

AUGUST 1996
Fighting Over Animal Rights
Privatizing Government Services
Child Labor and Sweatshops
Cleaning Up Hazardous Wastes

SEPTEMBER 1996
Gambling Under Attack
The States and Federalism
Civic Journalism
Reassessing Foreign Aid

OCTOBER 1996
Political Consultants
Insurance Fraud
Rethinking School Integration
Parental Rights

NOVEMBER 1996
Global Warming
Clashing Over Copyright
Consumer Debt
Governing Washington, D.C.

DECEMBER 1996
Welfare, Work and the States
The New Volunteerism
Implementing the Disabilities Act
America's Pampered Pets

Back issues are available for $5.00 (subscribers) or $10.00 (non-subscribers). Quantity discounts apply to orders over ten. To order, call Congressional Quarterly Customer Service at (202) 887-8621.

Binders are available for $18.00. To order call 1-800-638-1710. Please refer to stock number 648.

JANUARY 1997
Combating Scientific Misconduct
Restructuring the Electric Industry
The New Immigrants
Chemical and Biological Weapons

FEBRUARY 1997
Assisting Refugees
Alternative Medicine's Next Phase
Independent Counsels
Feminism's Future

MARCH 1997
New Air Quality Standards
Alcohol Advertising
Civic Renewal
Educating Gifted Students

APRIL 1997
Declining Crime Rates
The FBI Under Fire
Gender Equity in Sports
Space Program's Future

MAY 1997
The Stock Market
The Cloning Controversy
Expanding NATO
The Future of Libraries

JUNE 1997
FDA Reform
China After Deng
Line-Item Veto
Breast Cancer

JULY 1997
Transportation Policy
Executive Pay
School Choice Debate
Aggressive Driving

AUGUST 1997
Age Discrimination
Banning Land Mines
Children's Television
Evolution vs. Creationism

SEPTEMBER 1997
Caring for the Dying
Mental Health Policy
Mexico's Future
Youth Fitness

OCTOBER 1997
Urban Sprawl in the West
Diversity in the Workplace
Teacher Education
Contingent Work Force

NOVEMBER 1997
Renewable Energy
Artificial Intelligence
Religious Persecution
Roe v. Wade at 25

DECEMBER 1997
Whistleblowers
Castro's Next Move
Gun Control Standoff
Regulating Nonprofits

JANUARY 1998
Foster Care Reform
IRS Reform
The Black Middle Class
U.S.-British Relations

FEBRUARY 1998
Patients' Rights
Deflation Fears
Caring for the Elderly

Future Topics

▶ *Israel at 50*

▶ *Federal Judiciary*

▶ *Teenage Drinking*

The CQ Researcher

PUBLISHED BY CONGRESSIONAL QUARTERLY INC.

Israel at 50

Can Benjamin Netanyahu solve Israel's problems?

The Jewish state has come a long way since its founding on May 14, 1948. But while Israel's survival is no longer in question, it nonetheless faces several difficult issues. The country is divided over how much land and sovereignty should be given to the Palestinian Arabs in the West Bank and Gaza Strip. Repeated political crises are causing many Israelis to ask if the just-reformed political system should again be changed. In addition, Israel's relations with the American Jewish community have been strained of late over the peace process and other issues. And, finally, there is growing division among Israelis themselves. In particular, the country's secular majority is becoming increasingly impatient with the agenda of Israel's more religious citizens.

C_Q **March 6, 1998 • Volume 8, No. 9 • Pages 193-216**

Formerly Editorial Research Reports

THE ISSUES

BACKGROUND

CURRENT SITUATION

OUTLOOK

SIDEBARS AND GRAPHICS

FOR FURTHER RESEARCH

COVER: A RELIGIOUS JEW AND AN ISRAELI PEACE ACTIVIST ARGUE OVER ISRAEL'S PALESTINIAN POLICY. (REUTERS)

CQ Researcher

March 6, 1998
Volume 8, No.9

EDITOR
Sandra Stencel

MANAGING EDITOR
Thomas J. Colin

ASSOCIATE EDITOR
Sarah M. Magner

STAFF WRITERS
Mary H. Cooper
Kenneth Jost
David Masci

PRODUCTION EDITOR
Melissa Hall

PUBLISHED BY
Congressional Quarterly Inc.

CHAIRMAN
Andrew Barnes

VICE CHAIRMAN
Andrew P. Corty

PRESIDENT AND PUBLISHER
Robert W. Merry

EXECUTIVE EDITOR
David Rapp

The CQ Researcher (ISSN 1056-2036). Formerly Editorial Research Reports. Published weekly, except Jan. 2, May 29, July 3, Oct. 30, by Congressional Quarterly Inc., 1414 22nd St., N.W., Washington, D.C. 20037. Annual subscription rate for libraries, businesses and government is $340. Additional rates furnished upon request. Periodicals postage paid at Washington, D.C., and additional mailing offices. POSTMASTER: Send address changes to The CQ Researcher, 1414 22nd St., N.W., Washington, D.C. 20037.

Israel at 50

BY DAVID MASCI

THE ISSUES

As Israel approaches its 50th anniversary, Benjamin Netanyahu faces an unusually large number of challenges, even for an Israeli prime minister.

A key member of Netanyahu's already shaky coalition government recently resigned, leaving the Israeli leader with a one-vote majority in the Knesset, or parliament. And Netanyahu is widely blamed for the breakdown in negotiations with the Palestinians over the fate of the West Bank. Netanyahu's perceived intransigence also has strained relations with the Jewish state's most important ally, the United States, as well as the influential American-Jewish community.

Some of these problems are of the prime minister's own making, critics say. They accuse Bibi, as the Israeli leader is known, of everything from arrogance to incompetence. *The Economist* magazine recently called him "The Serial Bungler."

But Netanyahu's troubles, in many ways, reflect the difficulties facing Israeli society as a whole. Indeed, many argue that the 48-year-old leader is making the best of a very difficult situation.

He has been applauded, for instance, for his tough stand in negotiating with Yasir Arafat, leader of the Palestinian Authority, which represents the interests of Palestinian Arabs. Far from stalling the talks, supporters say, the prime minister is simply trying to ensure that any agreement on the final status of the West Bank and the Gaza Strip — known as the occupied territories — does not compromise Israel's long-fought-for security. They support Netanyahu's opposition to the creation of a Palestinian state and his insistence that Israel keep large portions of the West Bank.*

Netanyahu's supporters point out that the Palestinian Authority already administers most West Bank areas occupied by Arabs, giving them a high degree of autonomy. They argue that the establishment of an independent Palestinian state, with the right to raise an army and conduct foreign policy, would put a potentially hostile power right next to Israel's capital, Jerusalem.

But others say that it is unrealistic to expect the estimated 2 million Palestinians in the occupied territories to accept a solution that leaves them with little power and even less land. "They see themselves as a state, and they're not going to accept anything less," says Judith Kipper, director of the Council on Foreign Relations' Middle East Forum. Kipper and others argue that thwarting Palestinian national aspirations will only spark increased tension and violence.

The recent impasse over the peace process has strained Israel's relations with the United States. *(See story, p. 202.)* American policy-makers, traditionally sympathetic to Israel, are showing increasing irritation with its Palestinian policies. Indeed, during his trip to Washington in late January, Netanyahu reportedly received a stern talking to from President Clinton, who believes the prime minister is not being flexible enough in the negotiations. [1]

Polls consistently show that while Israelis may be divided about the peace process, they are of one mind about maintaining close ties with the United States. But the nature of the friendship itself is much debated. In particular, many observers believe that a cornerstone of the relationship, America's $3 billion annual aid package to Israel, should be phased out. [2]

They argue that the assistance takes up too large a share of the overall U.S. foreign aid budget, leaving little for countries that are more important or needier. They also note that the aid doesn't seem to buy the United States much influence with the Jewish state.*

Finally, foes of aid say, Israel is a relatively rich and developed country that no longer needs financial help. "They have welfare benefits that exceed our own, and that raises legitimate questions," says Henry Siegman, a senior fellow at the Council on Foreign Relations.

The current Israeli government, in fact, has called for phasing out the economic aid, which makes up $1.2 billion of the package each year. But supporters of aid say most of it is needed because, despite Israel's

---

* Israel has already ceded control of most of the Gaza Strip, along the country's southern Mediterranean coast, to the Palestinians. Hence, negotiations over the final status of Gaza have taken a back seat to talks over the fate of the West Bank.

---

*In addition to the aid to Israel, the U.S. also gives $2.1 billion to Egypt annually as part of a deal worked out between the three countries in 1979 following the Camp David peace accords.

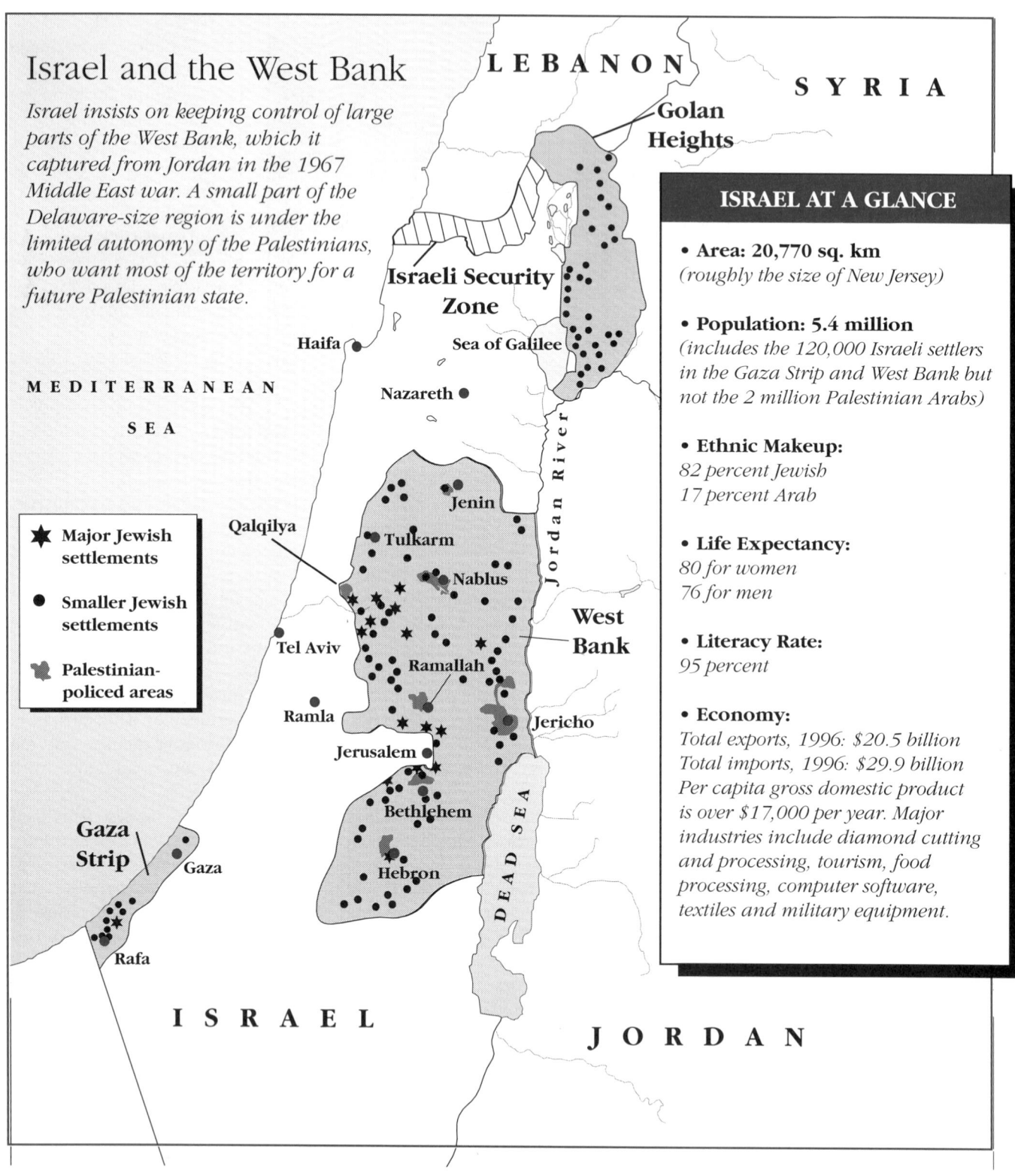

Israel and the West Bank

Israel insists on keeping control of large parts of the West Bank, which it captured from Jordan in the 1967 Middle East war. A small part of the Delaware-size region is under the limited autonomy of the Palestinians, who want most of the territory for a future Palestinian state.

LEBANON

SYRIA

Golan Heights

Israeli Security Zone

Haifa

Sea of Galilee

MEDITERRANEAN SEA

Nazareth

Jordan River

★ Major Jewish settlements

● Smaller Jewish settlements

🗺 Palestinian-policed areas

Qalqilya

Jenin

Tulkarm

Nablus

Tel Aviv

Ramallah

West Bank

Ramla

Jericho

Jerusalem

Bethlehem

DEAD SEA

Gaza Strip

Gaza

Hebron

Rafa

ISRAEL

JORDAN

ISRAEL AT A GLANCE

- **Area: 20,770 sq. km**
  (roughly the size of New Jersey)

- **Population: 5.4 million**
  (includes the 120,000 Israeli settlers in the Gaza Strip and West Bank but not the 2 million Palestinian Arabs)

- **Ethnic Makeup:**
  82 percent Jewish
  17 percent Arab

- **Life Expectancy:**
  80 for women
  76 for men

- **Literacy Rate:**
  95 percent

- **Economy:**
  Total exports, 1996: $20.5 billion
  Total imports, 1996: $29.9 billion
  Per capita gross domestic product is over $17,000 per year. Major industries include diamond cutting and processing, tourism, food processing, computer software, textiles and military equipment.

progress, it is still surrounded by hostile or potentially hostile states.

In addition, they argue, cutting off the assistance would create the impression that the United States was displeased with Israel. In the view of Dan Brumberg, a Middle East specialist at Georgetown University, that would strengthen the hand of hard-liners in Israel, who oppose the U.S.-sponsored peace process, while bolstering Arab extremists who still want to destroy the Jewish state.

But such concerns may be academic if, as many pundits predict, Netanyahu's government collapses and he is forced to call a new election. That possibility became more than idle speculation following the defection of Foreign Minister David Levy in January. Moreover, the prime minister faces the prospect of additional departures from other parties in his ruling coalition.

Israel's system of proportional representation has often produced shaky coalition governments. To bring more stability to the political system, reformers pushed though a change in the constitution before the 1996 national election that allowed for the direct election of the prime minister. But Netanyahu's continuing troubles suggest that the reform did not deal with the system's fundamental problem: the plethora of small parties in parliament. *(See graph, p. 200.)* Many experts argue that Israel can only create more stable governments by raising the percentage of the vote needed by parties to enter the Knesset.

Currently, any party can take a proportional share of seats if it receives at least 1 percent of the vote. Some Israel-watchers, like Richard N. Haass, director of foreign policy studies at the Brookings Institution, argue that the threshold should be raised to at least 5 percent. According to Haass and others, that would reduce the number of small parties in the Knesset, which in turn would lower the number of parties in the governing coalition. Fewer groups jockeying for power would increase stability, they say.

But others argue that Israel is a fractious society with a multitude of diverse groups, and that denying them a voice by marginalizing their parties would only force them to search for undemocratic alternatives to the political system. *(See story, p. 206.)* Brumberg is among those who warn that many of these groups, from Jewish settlers in the occupied territories to recent immigrants from Russia, could even resort to violence if they lose access to the decision-making process.

As Israelis prepare to celebrate the nation's golden anniversary on April 30, concern about the political system is among several important issues facing the Jewish state:

Is the establishment of a Palestinian state in the occupied territories necessary for lasting peace between Israel and the Palestinians?

On Jan. 14, Netanyahu's Cabinet announced that large parts of the West Bank would remain permanently under Israeli control. The announcement did not specify precise boundaries, but the Cabinet did say that Israel would retain strips of land along the eastern and western borders of the West Bank, as well as areas currently occupied by Jewish settlements, important historical sites, major roads, military bases and water and power installations. [3]

The Palestinians renounced the Cabinet's move, calling it another nail in the coffin of the peace process that began with the Oslo accords in 1993 *(see p. 208)*. "I say this is another signal and symptom of the very severe sickness — political sickness — of this government, saying that there is no chance with these [territorial] positions," said Ahmed Tevi, a senior adviser to Arafat. [4] The announcement was also condemned as "counterproductive" by left-wing Israeli groups.

But on the same day as the Cabinet's decision, 30,000 Jews, many of them West Bank settlers, rallied in Jerusalem in support of the government and urged it not to give up any more territory to the Palestinians. [5]

Soon afterward, however, the Cabinet eased its stand on ceding territory. One of Netanyahu's top advisers, David Bar-Illan, and other Israeli officials stated publicly that the initial policy announcement had been intentionally vague to leave latitude for future negotiations. [6] In addition, on the eve of Netanyahu's trip to Washington, the Cabinet rejected proposals by its more hard-line members to set strict limits on how much land he could give away during the next round of negotiations.

This dance of promises and threats is not new to the Middle East peace process. But it does highlight the issue that has always divided Israel and the Palestinians: land. How much can Israel still give away and feel secure? And how much will the Palestinians need to form a viable state — assuming a permanent settlement is worked out?

Currently, Palestinian authorities control about a quarter of the West Bank's territory, including most of the urban areas like Jericho, Ramallah, Nablus and Bethlehem. That makes the Palestinian Authority the governing body for 98 percent of all Arabs in the Delaware-size West Bank. But these autonomous zones are a patchwork of isolated areas, islands in a sea of Israeli-controlled land. [7]

Arafat and other Palestinian officials have demanded that any final settlement lead to the establishment of a state encompassing the Gaza Strip and all or most of the West Bank. Without such a state, they say, the legitimate aspirations of the Palestinian people will be thwarted, which in turn will lead to greater instability and violence in the region. "If Netanyahu continues with his policies, it's inevitable, it's like a powder keg," Arafat said during a visit to Washington to meet with President Clinton in late January. "There will be explosions in the area."

Many Middle East experts argue that Arafat's assessment is correct. "Short of a Palestinian state, which means Palestinian administration of the bulk of the West Bank and Gaza, this will not work," says Michael Hudson, a professor of international relations at Georgetown.

Siegman, of the Council on Foreign Relations, agrees. "There is no deal short of a viable state in most of the West Bank," he says.

Hudson and Siegman are among those who say it is not realistic to expect the 2 million Palestinians in the occupied territories to live under Israeli occupation indefinitely. "They are not prepared to live under the rule of anyone else," says Kipper of the Middle East Forum. "They want to govern themselves, and they have a right to."

Kipper notes that 85 percent of all Palestinians in the territories were born after Israel took control in 1967, and hence have lived in a sort of political limbo their entire lives. They are especially committed to Palestinian statehood and won't be satisfied with anything less. "Palestinian nationalism is a very strong force, and it's not going to go away," she says. "You can't hold back such forces," Siegman agrees, adding that Palestinians will "fight and die" for their own country.

Many of those who support an independent Palestinian state reject the suggestion put forth by some Israelis that it could not have a standing army or an independent foreign policy. "The notion in this day and age that one country could micromanage the affairs of another is ridiculous," Siegman says. Even if such conditions were agreed to by Arafat, "they would erode over time" because they would be unworkable. "It would be like the Treaty of Versailles," which unsuccessfully tried to limit German rearmament after World War I.

But others say that talk of an unfettered Palestinian state is unrealistic. To begin with, they argue, the Palestinians already control almost all of their population in the occupied territories, even though Israel still administers roughly three-quarters of the West Bank. In essence, Palestinian rights of self-determination have been honored, and a de facto Palestinian state has already been established, they say.

A new home is built for a Jewish family in the West Bank. Israel is building 300 homes in defiance of a U.S. call for a halt in Jewish settlement in the occupied territories.

"They are no longer an occupied people. They control their own destiny," says Morton Klein, national president of the Zionist Organization of America, which opposes an independent Palestinian state.

"Don't be misled by the map," agrees Peter Rodman, a fellow at the Nixon Center for Peace. "They are arguing over largely desolate land."

And yet, much of this "desolate land" has strategic importance for Israel, Rodman and others say. And, they argue, the Jewish state has every right to keep any territory it needs to ensure its security, including East Jerusalem, a buffer zone between the West Bank and its eastern border and the territory in the Jordan River valley. "Even the most dovish Labor government would not give these areas up," Rodman says. The Oslo accords were negotiated under the Labor Party, which is generally considered more sympathetic to Palestinian aspirations than Netanyahu's Likud Party.

Israel's security concerns are the inevitable outgrowth of repeated invasions by Israel's Arab neighbors, say those who oppose giving up more territory. Indeed, they point out, polls show that a sizable majority of Palestinians in the West Bank and Gaza still do not recognize Israel's right to exist.

Under such circumstances, Klein says, a Palestinian state on Israel's border "would be a mini-Iraq, with more terrorism and more violence [against Israel] than there is today. If Yasir Arafat and the Palestinian Arabs are acting so abominably now, before they have a state and all the land they want — when they have an incentive to act properly — they will be worse once they get what they want."

Ultimately, Klein and others argue, stepped-up terrorism by a new Palestinian state would force Israel to invade, which could lead to a full-scale war with her other Arab neighbors.

Other statehood opponents argue that, security concerns aside, the idea that both Israelis and the Arabs in the territories can get what they want is absurd because there simply is not enough land. "If you say that any deal must embody a secure Israel and a solid Arab state that meets the aspirations of the Palestinian people, you'll never get there," says Douglas Fiest, an attorney and Middle East expert in Washington. "You can't squeeze that much Jewish and Arab nationalism into that little territory."

But others argue that both sides may be able to walk away from the negotiations and claim they got what they wanted. "I think it's possible to have an entity that the Palestinians proclaim a state but that Israelis don't" officially recognize, says Phil Baum, executive director of the American Jewish Congress. Such a state probably would not have an army, Baum says, but "would be represented in world councils and accorded all the honors of statehood."

Should Israel try to bring more stability to its political process by altering the existing parliamentary system?

When Israelis went to the polls in 1996, for the first time in the nation's history they cast two votes: one for the party to represent them in the Knesset and a second, new, ballot to pick the prime minister.

The direct election of the prime minister represented a big change in the country's political structure. Since its founding in 1948, Israel had been a strict parliamentary democracy. Participating political parties divided up the 120 seats in the Knesset based on their percentage of the popular vote. Some of these parties in turn formed a government and chose a prime minister.

Israel is a diverse society with many different parties representing different groups and ideologies. Not surprisingly, no single party has ever won the 61 seats needed for an outright parliamentary majority. Each government has always been a coalition, usually consisting of the party that received the most votes (always Labor or Likud) and a group of smaller parties supporting one or the other of the main parties.

Initially, the system was relatively stable. Labor and its precursors dominated Israeli politics until the 1970s and were usually able to form strong coalitions. But in the late 1970s and '80s, the political landscape changed.

Israeli Prime Minister Benjamin Netanyahu and Palestinian leader Yasir Arafat

The more conservative Likud Party came to power a number of times, ending Labor's traditional dominance.

More important, since the 1970s Likud and Labor have been steadily losing support to a growing number of smaller groups. These parties often have fewer than five seats and represent interests ranging from ultraorthodox religious groups to Israeli Arabs to Russian immigrants.

Both Labor and Likud have become more dependent on these proliferating small parties to form governments and stay in power. Since these parties often have very different agendas, prime ministers have often found themselves pushed and pulled in a variety of directions in their efforts to please a host of different interests and keep their coalitions together.

Critics of the system argue that it produces governments that are not only incapable of action but also unstable. A shift in the allegiance of one of the minor parties is often enough to bring down the government and force new elections.

The system's growing instability inspired the push for the direct election of the prime minister. A leader chosen by the voters, the thinking went, would enjoy a powerful mandate and would, correspondingly, be less dependent on the smaller Knesset parties. "In a divided society, you need an anchor of stability," says Uriel Reichman, a professor of law at Tel Aviv University and one of the reformers. [8]

But most observers agree that the new system has not achieved the desired stability. Indeed, Netanyahu's majority in the Knesset melted to 61, or one vote, on Jan. 5, after Foreign Minister Levy resigned and took the five votes of his Gesher Party (which champions Sephardic Jews) with him. [9] Levy's resignation leaves Netanyahu little wiggle room and makes him even more dependent on the remaining parties in his coalition.

In fact, only 27 of the coalition's 61 votes come from Netanyahu's Likud Party. "Likud has a smaller number of seats than any previous ruling party," Rodman says. "In the past, the winning party always had a large plurality." The other 34 votes

Israel's Knesset Kaleidoscope

Israel is a diverse society with many small parties representing different groups and ideologies, from ultraorthodox Jews to Israeli-Arabs to Russian immigrants. No party has ever won the 61 seats needed for a majority in the 120-member Knesset, or parliament. The two major parties, Labor and Likud, have become increasingly dependent on these small parties to stay in power. Critics argue that the fragmented political system produces governments that are not only hamstrung but also unstable.

Seats in the Knesset

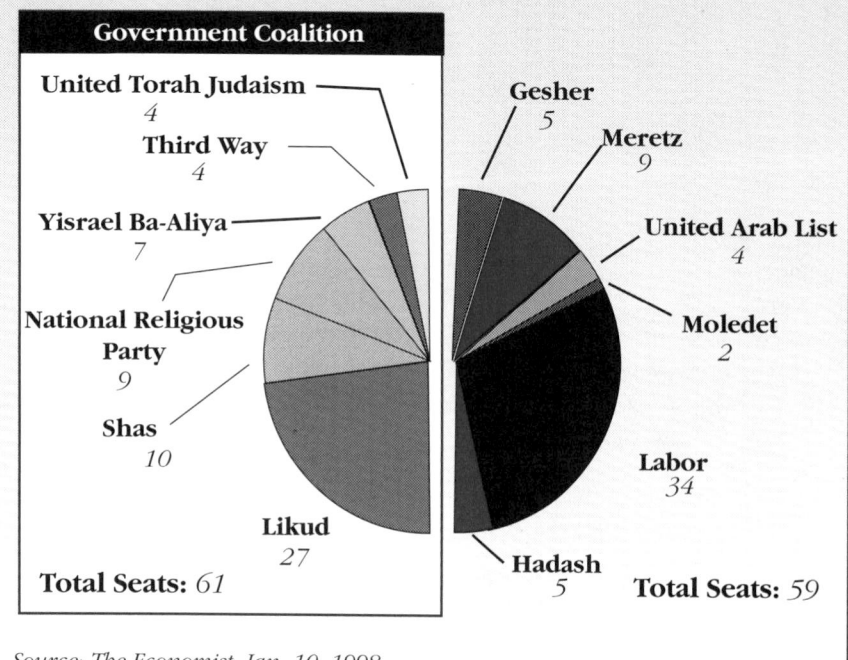

Government Coalition

United Torah Judaism — 4
Third Way — 4
Yisrael Ba-Aliya — 7
National Religious Party — 9
Shas — 10
Likud — 27
Total Seats: *61*

Gesher — 5
Meretz — 9
United Arab List — 4
Moledet — 2
Labor — 34
Hadash — 5
Total Seats: *59*

Source: The Economist, Jan. 10, 1998.

more ideological parties."

Many analysts say that to bring real stability to the political structure, Israel should raise the percentage of the vote a party needs to be represented in the Knesset. Currently, any party that receives 1 percent or more of the vote receives a share of seats.

"I would raise the base requirement for Knesset representation to 5 percent," says the Brookings Institution's Haass. Raising the threshold needed for representation would reduce the number of small parties, leaving Labor and Likud more seats and fewer potential coalition partners. For instance, under Haass' proposal, which echoes the system in Germany, four out of the 10 small parties currently in the Knesset would not have won representation in the last election.

According to Georgetown's Hudson, raising the threshold would produce more stability by significantly reducing the ability of the small parties to "blackmail" Israeli leaders who need their support to stay in power. "Right now it's a sad spectacle, with naked bargaining and crass payoffs to the leaders of small parties to buy their support," he says. Less "naked bargaining," he says, would also produce a government capable of acting decisively, since it would not be beholden to so many parties with different priorities and agendas.

Others argue that Israel needs a more constituent-based system, as in Great Britain or the United States. Currently, Knesset members are chosen from party lists. In other words, citizens vote for a party that, in turn, chooses its members of parliament.

"The problem is that these people in the Knesset don't really represent anyone, except their party," says Klein, who favors constituent-based voting. "So these members are unresponsive to the needs of their citizens."

Kipper agrees that a constituent-based system would better serve the people. In addition, she argues that requiring each member of parliament

come from five smaller, mostly religious, parties. [10]

Some of these coalition partners have threatened to pull out if Netanyahu gives more territory to the Palestinians. According to Ehud Sprinzak, a professor of political science at Hebrew University in Jerusalem, it's "a question of not whether the government will fall, but when."

Others predict that the prime minister, a tough and skillful politician, will remain in power. But most agree that direct election did not bring hoped for stability. One reason, they

say, is that voters felt less inclined to support either of the two big parties, since they could cast another vote for Likud or Labor in the prime ministerial ballot, which pitted Netanyahu against Labor's candidate, then-Prime Minister Shimon Peres. In the past, according to Rodman and others, Israelis supported the larger parties, since the result of the Knesset election determined who would be prime minister. "They didn't want to waste their vote," Rodman says. "Now, people who might have voted Labor or Likud felt freer to support smaller,

to be elected by a geographical constituency would significantly reduce the chances that a candidate from a small party could win. For instance, in the United States and Britain, only candidates from the largest parties are able to effectively compete because they must win at least a plurality in a specified voting district to be sent to the legislature.

But other political analysts say that efforts to stabilize the political situation by mitigating the power of small parties is undemocratic and could create a raft of new problems.

"If you shut some of these parties out, you won't get a more stable system because they will turn to other means and disrupt the process," Brumberg contends. For instance, he says, "if some of these groups felt that their agenda wasn't being taken into account, they could become violent.'"

The problem, Brumberg and others say, isn't the political process, but the nature of Israel's society. "There are many dangerous fault lines in Israel; some are economic and some are religious," says Siegman of the Council on Foreign Relations. "You have all of these people jockeying for power, the religious, the Russian immigrants, the Sephardic and the Arabs," he adds, naming just some of the groups that have their own parties.

The answer, Siegman and others say, is not to tinker with the political system and shut some of these groups out. "You can't deal with the grievances of these groups by changing the political system," he says.

Rodman agrees, arguing that it would be unnatural to try to fit the country's diverse political spectrum into a few parties. "Israelis are very fractious people. I don't think you can force them into [large] parties."

Many observers say that the system really doesn't need fixing, that for all its instability, direct proportional representation is the only way that all Israelis can have a voice in how their nation is governed. "If something isn't terribly broke, don't fix it," Brumberg advises.

Palestinian Arabs illegally leave the West Bank and cross into Jerusalem to attend Friday prayers. Palestinian leader Yasir Arafat had urged the action to protest Israeli settlement policies.

Reuters/Jim Hollander

Should the United States reduce or eliminate the assistance it gives to Israel?

Israel occupies a unique position among America's allies. Though other nations may have stronger bonds with the United States, or greater strategic importance, or more pressing needs, none consistently receives the attention and support given to the Jewish state over the last few decades.

There are, not surprisingly, many reasons for the special attention. In spite of its size, Israel is the greatest military power in the volatile Middle East. It is also the oil-rich region's only full democracy and its strongest pro-American voice. Moreover, the two countries have the same long-term foreign policy goals: encourage the development of moderate Arab states and keep in check regional troublemakers like Iran and Iraq.

But Israel's status in the U.S. goes far beyond its international importance. The United States is home to roughly half the world's Jews. This community has worked tirelessly on Israel's behalf, lobbying Congress and sending private donations to assist the young nation.

America's support for Israel has remained strong even when the two countries disagreed over important issues, such as the expansion of Jewish settlements in the occupied territories. And a cornerstone of this support is money.

Nothing is a sure bet on Capitol Hill, but support for Israel's annual $3 billion aid package comes close. The level of assistance has been the same since it was set in 1979, (along with an annual grant of $2.1 billion for Egypt) as part of the Camp David peace accords. Together, both countries receive roughly 40 percent of the U.S. foreign aid budget.

Israel spends more than half of the aid, $1.8 billion, on weapons, almost all of which are purchased from U.S. suppliers. The remaining $1.2 billion is earmarked for economic assistance, mainly to pay back U.S. loans.

Despite recent budgetary concerns in the U.S., there has been little effort in Congress to eliminate or even reduce aid to Israel. Still, many Middle

Continued on p. 203

Israel and American Jews: Friends Forever?

On the night of Jan. 21, 1998, more than 500 people packed into a ballroom at Washington's Mayflower Hotel to see Prime Minister Benjamin Netanyahu. As the Israeli leader arrived, the crowd greeted him with a standing ovation and shouts of support.

Israeli prime ministers usually receive rousing welcomes from American Jewish groups when they visit the United States. But that night, Netanyahu was introduced by the Rev. Jerry Falwell to a crowd mostly of evangelical Christians. Netanyahu had come seeking support for his tough negotiating stand with the Palestinians, and he got it. Falwell, along with other evangelical leaders like Christian Coalition Executive Director Randy Tate, promised to lobby Congress on the Israeli leader's behalf.

Evangelical Christians have long supported Israel as a homeland for the Jewish people. But the high-profile event was notable because Israeli leaders don't usually court Christians so openly and vigorously. Also unusual was the critical response from U.S. Jewish organizations. "These meetings, with these people, at this time, under these circumstances, were a mistake," said Phil Baum, executive director of the American Jewish Congress. [1]

To many American Jews, Netanyahu's open embrace of evangelicals is the latest in a series of troubling signs that the rock-solid relationship between Israel and its Jewish supporters in the U.S. is in trouble. "There are some serious problems between the American Jewish community and the current government of Israel," says Judith Kipper, director of the Council on Foreign Relations' Middle East Forum.

American Jews have long felt a kinship with and an obligation to their brethren in the Middle East. Over the last half-century, Jews in the United States have given billions of dollars to assist Israelis. In addition, the Jewish community has played a key role in lobbying the U.S. government to support Israel.

Nowadays, however, many American Jews are openly critical of the direction being taken by the Israeli government on a number of fronts. Many are frustrated with what they perceive as Netanyahu's unwillingness to give ground, literally, in negotiations with the Palestinians over the final status of the West Bank.

"Many American Jews are concerned that Netanyahu is not committed to an equitable peace plan," says Dan Brumberg, a Middle East specialist at Georgetown University. According to Brumberg and others, there is a fear that the prime minister's hard-line negotiations with the Palestinians stem from his dependence on ultraorthodox religious parties to maintain his coalition government.

The ultraorthodox feature even more prominently in another issue currently causing problems between the government and American Jews: the law of conversion. The prime minister is backing a bill in the Israeli Knesset that would prohibit all but Orthodox rabbis from conducting Jewish conversions and marriages in the country. In other words, only with the blessing of an Orthodox rabbi can one convert to Judaism or be married in Israel. This Orthodox monopoly already exists in practice, but it is being challenged in court by Reform and Conservative Jews. Hence the need for the bill, say the Orthodox.

The Reform and Conservative movements, while small within Israel, hold the allegiance of over 80 percent of Jewish Americans. Not surprisingly, for many Jews in the United States, the conversion bill is nothing less than an attack on the validity of their religious beliefs. "For them to say that no one in the world is Jewish if they're not Orthodox is ridiculous, insulting, alienating and narrow-minded," says Martin Ashram, a history teacher at a Reform synagogue near Cleveland. [2]

This is not the first time relations between American Jews and Israel have been strained. Many Jews in the United States opposed the 1982 Israeli invasion of Lebanon. Others were critical of Israel's tough tactics during the Palestinian uprising, or *intifada*, in the late 1980s and early '90s.

But many worry that the growing rift between the two Jewish communities will widen and become permanent. They note that some American rabbis now openly criticize the Jewish state in their sermons, especially over the conversion controversy. Many also have urged their congregants to stop giving directly to Israel and instead channel donations to Jewish charities in the U.S. In addition, they say, intermarriage and assimilation have left a growing number of American Jews, especially the young, much less connected to the idea of Israel as a homeland and center for Jewish life.

Others see recent trends from a different perspective — as a sign that Israel is maturing as a nation. They note that the country now acts with more self-confidence and less dependence on the Jewish Diaspora. "Israel is now a state with its own identity," Brumberg says. Baum agrees. "Some Israelis say [to American Jews:] 'Don't try to save us from ourselves.' "

Still, there is wide agreement that while the ties between Israel and the American Jewish community may weaken, they will not disappear. "The Israelis will remain tied to the American Jewish community," Kipper says, "but much less dependent on it."

---

[1] Quoted in Caryle Murphy, "Jewish Leaders in U.S. Assail Netanyahu," *The Washington Post*, Jan. 22, 1998.

[2] Quoted in Laurie Goodstein, "Feeling Abandoned by Israel, Many American Jews Grow Angry," *The New York Times*, Nov. 16, 1997.

Continued from p. 201

East experts question the need for continuing American assistance.

In an age of shrinking foreign-aid budgets, these opponents say, devoting so much funding to one area doesn't make sense. "From the American point of view, it's bizarre to put so much of our foreign assistance into two countries," says Georgetown's Hudson.

Hudson also wonders how much influence the United States buys with the aid, given that the strength of the pro-Israel lobby virtually guarantees that the assistance will be given, regardless of what Israel does. "Israel is in a very good position," Hudson says. "They can pretty much do what they want, and Congress won't cut them off."

For example, Hudson says, the United States is clearly unhappy with the Netanyahu government's refusal to stop building Jewish settlements in the West Bank, but "Congress has voted for the money anyway."

Hudson and others also argue that Israel no longer really needs the aid, given a modernized economy that is as developed as those of many Western European countries. "Israel's per capita GDP is $17,000," says Andrew I. Killgore, publisher of the *Washington Report on Middle East Affairs.* "Let the Israeli taxpayer pay for his country's armaments."

For all of Israel's success, many economists say its economy is still too dependent on the government, which reduces its competitiveness. American aid worsens the situation, they say, because it insulates Israel from the need to make painful but necessary economic changes.

Haass agrees that aid should be replaced with reform. "Israel is past the point where it needs American aid," he says. "If they used [an aid cutoff] as an excuse to reform their economy, they would more than generate the revenue they lost," he argues.

Indeed, the Israeli government has indicated that it is ready to accept a reduction in economic aid. During a January trip to Washington, Finance Minister Yaacov Neeman proposed eliminating the $1.2 billion in economic assistance over 10 years.

But many supporters of Israel worry that reducing aid would send the wrong signal to those states still unfriendly to Israel. "We should leave [the assistance]

Theodor Herzl (top) and Menachem Begin

as it is for the time being," Kipper says, "because reducing it now would be viewed as a punishment."

A perceived break between Israel and its primary patron could embolden Israel's enemies and increase tension in the region, she says. Rodman of the Nixon Center agrees. "If the Arabs started to think that Israel could possibly be pushed into the sea, there would be a resurgence of radicalism," he says.

Rodman and others also argue that, in spite of its advanced economy, Israel still needs American military aid because it must spend a higher proportion of its budget on its armed forces than other nations to ensure its survival. "They're in a bad neighborhood, and the situation is still tense," says Baum of the American Jewish Congress.

And, other supporters add, the aid is more pressing than ever due to the rising sophistication and cost of today's weapons. For instance, says Geoffrey Aronson, director of the Foundation for Middle East Peace, Israel "can't hope to build a front-line fighter plane, and the cost of buying such a thing has become increasingly expensive."

In addition, supporters argue, American aid does translate into American influence. "Israel is not a banana republic, but the U.S. has a lot of influence," says Klein of the Zionist Organization of America.

Finally, and most important, supporters of aid say, the United States benefits tremendously from the presence of a strong Israel in the Middle East. "It's in our interest to keep them stronger than their enemies, because their enemies are our enemies," Rodman says, referring in particular to Iran and Iraq. ■

BACKGROUND

Israel's Birth

The founding of the state of Israel has its roots in an event that occurred almost 2,000 years ago. In 70 AD, the Romans, in an effort to quell repeated Jewish revolts in Palestine

— now Israel — destroyed the Second Temple in Jerusalem and subsequently scattered most of the area's Jews throughout the empire.

In the ensuing two millennia, many Jews assimilated into the countries of the Diaspora. But others retained their religion and culture and never lost the dream of returning to the land that the Bible says God gave to the Jewish people.

But for hundreds of years, the idea of returning to the "land of milk and honey" could never be more than a dream. In the 7th century, Palestine became one of the many territories absorbed by Arab conquerors who swept through the entire Middle East spreading their new religion, Islam. By the mid-19th century, when Jews first seriously considered reclaiming Palestine, the area had been ruled for hundreds of years by the Ottoman Turks, as part of their declining but still far-reaching empire.

The movement to reclaim Palestine was prompted by a new interest in ethnic identity throughout Europe, coupled with a growing and often violent anti-Semitism in Eastern Europe, especially in Russia. The increasingly dire situation led many Jews to ask a fundamental question, as historian Paul Johnson has written: "Was it not possible to bring into existence an ideal community where Jews were not merely safe, not just suffered, or even tolerated, but welcomed . . . a place where they, and not others were masters?" [11]

The answer for many Jewish people was "no." Many of them emigrated to the United States and a host of other countries ranging from Argentina to Australia. But some embraced the idea of a Jewish nation, which sparked the Zionist movement, led eventually by a wealthy Austrian Jew named Theodor Herzl. After years of trying to assimilate into the broader culture, Herzl had come to the conclusion that Jews would never be accepted in any country except their own. [12]

By the late 19th century, small numbers of Zionists were establishing agricultural communities in Palestine. At the same time, Herzl and other Zionists in Europe were working to build support for a Jewish state.

A breakthrough came in 1917 with the Balfour Declaration, named for British Foreign Secretary Arthur Balfour. Siding with the Germans during World War I had cost the Ottomans their entire empire, including Palestine, which

David Ben-Gurion led Israel to statehood.

Embassy of Israel

was put under British control. The declaration, which came before the war ended, promised British support for a Jewish state in Palestine. [13]

Over the next two decades, immigration from Europe increased Palestine's Jewish population. The year after World War I, there were 65,000 Jews living in the territory. By 1936, there were almost 400,000, many of whom had fled the escalating Nazi persecution in Germany.

Meanwhile, Britain's ardor for a Jewish state weakened. In 1937, it shifted from support for a Jewish state to partitioning Palestine into separate Jewish and Arab countries. Two years later, with war in Europe just months away, the British

scrapped the two-state solution in favor of Arab control of the territory.

When World War II ended in 1945, the Palestine question resurfaced. The Nazi holocaust against Europe's Jews had dramatically increased support in the United States and other nations for a Jewish state. Still, Britain remained sympathetic to Arab opposition to Jewish statehood. Frustration over the British position led the Jews to mount a guerrilla war. For almost two years, a loosely organized Jewish resistance fought British occupation while clandestinely bringing in more refugees from war-torn Europe.

Finally, in April 1947, a weary United Kingdom turned over its responsibility for Palestine to the United Nations. Seven months later, on Nov. 29, the U.N. General Assembly, with American prodding, voted to partition Palestine into Jewish and Arab states. [14]

Almost immediately thereafter, the Arabs, who did not accept the partition, attacked the Jews. After some initial defeats, the Jews routed the Palestinian Arabs. On May 14, 1948, David Ben-Gurion and other Jewish leaders proclaimed the establishment of the state of Israel. Ben-Gurion immediately assumed the posts of prime minister and defense minister. But the newly minted nation had little time to celebrate.

Arab-Israeli Wars

Immediately after declaring statehood, Israel was attacked by Egypt, Syria, Jordan, Lebanon and Iraq. The coalition's stated aim was to destroy Israel and establish an Arab state in Palestine. Outnumbered and outgunned, the Israelis nonetheless inflicted stunning defeats on the coalition. By January 1949 an armistice had been signed, and Israel

Continued on p. 206

Chronology

1900s–1940s
The Zionist movement and rising Jewish immigration to Palestine culminate in the creation of the state of Israel.

1917
Great Britain issues the Balfour Declaration pledging support for a Jewish state in Palestine.

1918
After World War I, Palestine becomes a British mandate.

1937
Great Britain officially revises its policy on Palestine, calling for partition of the territory into Jewish and Arab countries.

1945
A Jewish resistance movement mounts a two-year guerrilla war against the British.

1947
The war-weary British turn over responsibility for Palestine to the United Nations, which votes to partition Palestine into two states. Palestinian Arabs attack the Jews, who recover from initial defeats and rout Arab forces.

May 14, 1948
David Ben-Gurion proclaims the state of Israel. The new country is immediately attacked by five of its Arab neighbors. Israel defeats the coalition, and an armistice is signed in January 1949.

1950s–1970s
Israel fights a series of wars that increase its territory and make it the premier military power in the Middle East.

1956
In a coordinated attack, Britain, France and Israel capture the Sinai Peninsula. U.S. pressure subsequently forces Israel to return the captured territory.

1967
During the "Six Day War," Israel captures the Gaza Strip and Sinai Peninsula from Egypt, the West Bank from Jordan and the Golan Heights from Syria.

1973
Egypt and Syria attack Israel. After some initial success, the Arab armies are defeated.

1980s–1990s
Israel and some of her former enemies make peace. The Jewish state begins to grapple with the fate of Palestinian Arabs in the occupied territories.

1977
Egyptian President Anwar el-Sadat makes a historic trip to Israel that prompts both countries to begin negotiations.

1978
Sadat and Israeli Prime Minister Menachem Begin meet with American President Jimmy Carter at Camp David in the United States. The two agree to an Israeli withdrawal from Sinai in exchange for full diplomatic relations between the two countries.

1981
Arab extremists assassinate Sadat.

1982
Israel invades Lebanon and succeeds in ousting the Palestine Liberation Organization (PLO), which was using the country as a base of operations.

1987
Palestinian youths in the occupied territories begin a grass-roots uprising known as the *intifada*. The uprising lasts more than five years and focuses world attention on the problems of the Palestinians.

February 1993
Israeli and Palestinian negotiators begin secret talks in Oslo, Norway, that lead to an agreement by Israel to withdraw from most of Gaza and the West Bank town of Jericho. The Palestinian Authority led by PLO chief Yasir Arafat is to administer these areas. The final status of the occupied territories is to be determined over the next five years.

September 1993
Arafat and Israeli Prime Minister Yitzhak Rabin meet in Washington to sign the historic deal.

1994
Israel establishes full diplomatic relations with Jordan.

1995
Rabin is assassinated by a Jewish extremist.

1996
Rabin's successor, Shimon Peres, is defeated in elections by Likud candidate Benjamin Netanyahu.

1997
Netanyahu agrees to a withdrawal from most of the West Bank town of Hebron. But subsequent negotiations stall.

January 1998
Trips to Washington by Arafat and Netanyahu fail to jump-start the peace negotiations.

Israelis See the Greatest Threats . . .

Perhaps it is a sign that Israel is enjoying a new degree of normalcy. According to a recent poll, Israelis say they do not think that the greatest threat to their country comes from outside the beleaguered nation's borders. Instead, many Israelis say, the primary challenge facing their country is the multiplying and ever-widening rifts between various segments in society. [1]

Israel may be more than 80 percent Jewish, but it is far from homogeneous — ethnically or ideologically. In the past, the need to remain united in the face of external threats helped paper over differences. But today, the threats are diminishing and the differences are becoming more of a problem.

The greatest problem, many say, is a growing division between secular and religious Israelis. "It's becoming an absolute civil war," says Judith Kipper director of the Council on Foreign Relations' Middle East Forum.

Israel was founded by largely non-religious men and women, many of whom were more committed to socialism than to Judaism or God. They tried to create a Jewish state that was at the same time a paragon of secular humanism. Today, an estimated 80 percent of all Israeli Jews are known as "secular" Jews, a term that doesn't necessarily mean that they are atheists, although some are. "Many are not interested in religion, but are not irreligious either," says Gil Kulick, communications director for the New Israel Fund, a Washington-based philanthropic organization that aids progressive groups in Israel. They may celebrate important Jewish holidays but don't attend synagogue regularly or follow dietary or other religious laws.

The remaining 20 percent of the Jewish population is intensely religious. The ultraorthodox, as they are known,

live according to the laws laid down in the Bible. As they have grown in recent decades — through immigration and high birth rates — so has their influence. Religious parties now control 23 seats in the 120-seat Knesset and are often (as is currently the case) part of the governing coalition, giving them substantial leverage.

Secular Israelis complain that the ultraorthodox are using their influence to impose their beliefs on the rest of the country. In some towns now, for example, Orthodox voters are trying to shut everything down on Saturday, the Jewish Sabbath. "There are efforts to close businesses on the Sabbath and beat up women who are 'too immodest,' " Kulick says.

Orthodox control over the nation's marriage laws also angers many Israelis. A prohibition on civil ceremonies prompts large numbers of secular Jews to look for alternatives to having their weddings in Israel, such as traveling to nearby Cyprus.

In addition, many secular Israelis complain about special treatment accorded the religious. For example, the Orthodox are exempt from military service. In addition, the state supports a series of religious schools, or Yeshivas, where many Orthodox men study.

The Orthodox counter that they are not trying to tell people how to live their lives or turn Israel into an oppressive state. "We're not going to make a second Iran," says Rabbi Abraham Ravitz, a Knesset member from the United Torah Judaism Party. [1] But, Ravitz and others say, they do want to preserve Israel's unique Jewish character. In other words, living, at least to some degree, by Jewish law and supporting the study of Judaism are ways that can distinguish Israel from the rest of the world.

While the secular are concerned about the growing power

Continued from p. 204

found itself occupying sizable new chunks of territory. [15]

A period of relative tranquility followed, only to be broken by the "Suez Crisis." In October 1956, Israel joined France and Britain in the invasion of Egypt's Sinai Peninsula. The Europeans sought to oust Egyptian President Gamal Abdel Nasser, who had recently nationalized the Suez Canal. For Israel, the Anglo-French action offered, among other things, an opportunity to thwart Palestinian Arab guerrilla attacks being launched from the Gaza Strip.

While the action was a military success for the Jewish state, Ameri-

can opposition to the entire operation forced Israel to halt its offensive and withdraw to its original borders. Suez taught the Israelis a valuable lesson: Military undertakings had to have U.S. support. [16]

The next Israeli action had a U.S. green light. On June 5, 1967, in response to repeated terrorist attacks sponsored by Syria and a threatening mobilization by Egypt, Israel launched surprise air attacks on Egyptian, Syrian and Jordanian air fields. (Jordan and Egypt had signed a mutual defense pact on May 30.) In six days Israel effectively destroyed the Egyptian army and air force and utterly defeated Syria and Jordan. "The Six-Day

War" also left Israel with significant territorial gains: the Sinai Peninsula and Gaza Strip were taken from Egypt; Jordan lost the West Bank, including East Jerusalem, which had been divided since Israeli independence; and Syria gave up the strategic Golan Heights.

The victory established Israel as the undisputed power in the region. On the domestic front, too, things were going well. A series of left-leaning governments, headed by Ben-Gurion, developed the country's social as well as physical infrastructure. By the late 1960s the economy was robust and growing.

In 1973, Israelis were forced to return

... As Coming From Within Their Society

of the Orthodox, religious Israelis worry about the more materialistic, Americanized society that is emerging, a view shared by observers of every stripe. "Just look at the place. There are American businesses on every street," Kulick says. This globalization, coupled with increased wealth, is turning Israel "into a typical bourgeois society," he says. To the Orthodox, these changes are dangerous. "In the eyes of the religious, the posters are more immodest, the legitimacy of homosexuality and lesbianism is growing and many cinemas and clubs are open on the Sabbath," says Yair Sheleg, a secular journalist with the Israeli newspaper *Ha'aretz*.

The struggle between the two groups has erupted beyond the boundaries of civil debate. While not condoned by most religious Israelis, the assassination of Prime Minister Yitzhak Rabin in 1995 by an ultraorthodox law student is seen by many as symptom of the split.

Less serious, but still troubling, are the clashes between the two groups. Last year, secular and religious Israelis fought in Jerusalem over the issue of open roads on the Sabbath. In July, secular Israelis drove through a religious neighborhood on a Saturday afternoon with signs mockingly wishing the Orthodox a "Good Sabbath." The religious responded with rocks and epithets. [2]

Other divisions also plague Israeli society. For example, while the majority of Israeli Jews are Ashkenazim, or from Europe, a sizable minority are from North Africa and the Middle East. These non-European, or Sephardic, Jews have long complained about discrimination at the hands of the Ashkenazy. As a result, the Sephardim say, they are less educated and poorer than their fellow Jews and look to the government to restore some sort of balance.

And then there are the 1 million Arabs who are Israeli citizens. They claim that they are not treated like fellow countrymen by Jews. Indeed, most Israelis agree that the nation's Arab minority, which makes up 17 percent of the population, has faced discrimination in employment, education, housing and other spheres. Like African-Americans before the civil rights movement, they hold a higher proportion of unskilled jobs and often live in segregated communities. [3]

And yet, they say, they are loyal to Israel. "These people have cast their lot with Israel," says Henry Siegman, a senior fellow at the Council on Foreign Relations in New York. "They place equal treatment in Israel ahead of solidarity with their Palestinian brothers" in the occupied territories, he adds.

But others say that it is only natural for Jews to harbor suspicions. "Given the fact that they are linked to a vast number of people who are trying to destroy Israel, the Jews have been very liberal," says Doug Fiest, a Washington attorney and Middle East expert. Indeed, others point out, Israeli Arabs should not complain. "They live better than other Arabs and have more freedoms, such as the right to vote and a free press," says Morton Klein, national president of the Zionist Organization of America.

---

[1] Quoted in John Lancaster, "Clout of Orthodoxy Worries Secular Israel," *The Washington Post*, June 6, 1996.

[2] Marjorie Miller, "Sabbath War Flares in Holy City," *Los Angeles Times*, July 26, 1997.

[3] See Serge Schmemann, "Israeli Learns Some Are More Israeli Than Others," *The New York Times*, March 1, 1988, pA1.

---

to the battlefield. On Oct. 6, Egypt and Syria sought to retake the Sinai and the Golan Heights. This time it was the Israelis who were surprised. After initially retreating, they regrouped and began pushing the Arabs back. By the following year, cease-fires had been signed and the Israelis were back in control of all the territories they had lost.

The Quest for Peace

Israel's first 25 years had been marked by animosity and war. But in the next quarter-century, the Jewish state made peace with some former enemies and began to grapple in earnest with the fate of Palestinian Arabs living in the occupied territories.

The road to peace began in November 1977, when Egyptian President Anwar el-Sadat (who replaced Nasser after his death in 1970) made a historic trip to Israel. In a speech before the Knesset, Sadat called for a return of the Sinai and all other occupied territories. In return, he said, "I declare to the whole world that we accept living with you in permanent peace and justice." [17] A month later, Israeli Prime Minister Menachem Begin went to Egypt.

Sadat's olive branch set the stage for the 1978 Camp David meetings, during which he, Begin and President Jimmy Carter negotiated a formalization of relations between the two countries. In exchange for full diplomatic relations with Egypt, Israel agreed to give up the Sinai Peninsula. In addition, both countries, along with Jordan, were to begin talks on resolving "the Palestinian question."

The euphoria over the peace agreement was soon overtaken by events. The talks concerning Palestinian Arabs quickly stalled; and Arab militants assassinated Sadat in 1981.

Israel Invades Lebanon

Then, in 1982, in an effort to destroy the Palestine Liberation Organization, Israel invaded Lebanon, a longtime PLO base of operations.

Eight days after the invasion began, the PLO had been pushed back to Beirut and surrounded. The organization was saved only after the United States pressured the Israelis to let the PLO withdraw and leave the country.

The operation was not without cost to the Israelis, however. They soon found themselves ensnared in a grinding guerrilla war with Lebanese Shi'ite Muslims. And Israel's efforts to establish a pro-Western government in Lebanon fell apart, exacerbating the destructive civil war that had been raging since the 1970s.

Perhaps most important, the invasion of Lebanon was perceived by many people in Israel and the United States as a foolhardy and even cruel military adventure. This belief was strengthened after hundreds of Palestinians in refugee camps were murdered by Lebanese soldiers allied with Israel. Israel was widely denounced for not having taken steps to prevent the massacres. Lebanon badly tarnished Israel's image in the United States and around the world. In the eyes of many observers, the once scrappy state fighting for its right to exist had turned into a neighborhood bully.

Israel finally managed to withdraw from the country in 1985, leaving a 10-mile security zone along the border. But a bigger problem for the Jewish state arose in 1987, when a grass-roots rebellion began in the West Bank and Gaza Strip. What became known as the *intifada* grew out of the Palestinians' anger at what they regarded as unfair Israeli policies in the territories. In particular, they complained of harsh treatment by Israeli soldiers and the expropriation of Palestinian land and water for Jewish settlements.

The revolt was organized and carried out primarily by young adults and children, mostly armed with rocks. Still, the Israeli army and police found it impossible to contain. To make matters worse for the Jewish state, images of well-armed Israeli soldiers firing on children were soon

Egyptian President Anwar el-Sadat, President Jimmy Carter and Israeli Prime Minister Menachem Begin sign the Camp David accords. The two former enemies established diplomatic relations, and Israel agreed to withdraw from Sinai.

beamed all over the world, garnering sympathy for the Palestinian cause.

The intifada sparked renewed interest in the Palestinian Arabs. In 1988, the U.S. opened talks with the PLO in an effort to establish a peace process. These efforts were aided by two subsequent events. In 1991 the United States drove Iraq from Kuwait, making the U.S. an indispensable ally for most of the region's Arab states, as well as Israel. And in 1992, the Labor Party defeated the more hard-line Likud Party of Yitzhak Shamir, ushering in a government more open to negotiating with the Palestinians.

The Oslo Agreement

Israelis and Palestinians had been publicly negotiating in Madrid since 1991. But real progress was not made until both sides began meeting secretly in Oslo, Norway, in February 1993. Outside the media spotlight, the two sides agreed to an Israeli withdrawal from Gaza and the city of Jericho in the West Bank. These areas would be effectively ruled by Arafat. The final status of the remaining occupied territories was to be decided in talks over the next five years. In September 1993, Arafat and Rabin signed the deal in Washington and for the first time shook hands in public. [18]

The following year, building on the success of Oslo, Israel established diplomatic relations with Jordan. But, as with the Camp David accords, violence and other factors jeopardized progress made in Norway. On Nov. 4, 1995, Rabin was assassinated by an Orthodox Jew who opposed the Oslo accords. Soon after, Palestinians unhappy with an accommodationist Arafat set off two powerful bombs in Israel, killing dozens of Jews.

The bombings undermined Rabin's successor Shimon Peres — a key architect of Oslo — and he was narrowly defeated in May 1996. Israel's new leader, Netanyahu, has taken a much harder line with the Palestinians than the previous governments. At the same time, many Israelis have renewed their distrust of the Palestinians and PLO leader Arafat because of their apparent inability to control continuing terrorist acts against Jews. ■

Continued on p. 210

At Issue:

Should U.S. military assistance to Israel be reduced or eliminated?

MICHAEL C. HUDSON

*Professor of international relations and Arab studies,
Georgetown University*

WRITTEN FOR THE CQ RESEARCHER, FEBRUARY 1998.

t here are many reasons to reduce or terminate U.S.
military assistance to Israel, the main one being
that Israel doesn't need it any more.

Military experts rate Israel's armed forces as among the
half-dozen most powerful in the world. Israel has nuclear
bombs and the means to deliver them. Among its contigu-
ous neighbors, only Syria (and Lebanon) have not signed
peace treaties, and Syria knows it is no match for the
Israelis. Furthermore, Israel is now quite a wealthy, highly
developed country with a strong economy and European-
level living standards.

Let us count some of the ways that Israel has abused
our generosity and worked against American interests:

• In the 1967 Arab-Israeli War, Israeli warplanes "accidentally" launched more than 30 sorties against a clearly marked
U.S. Navy ship, the *Liberty*, killing 34 U.S. crewmen.

• Israel has developed by far the largest weapons-of-
mass destruction capability in the Middle East, yet refuses
to join the nuclear non-proliferation treaty.

• Israel has spied on the U.S. military — former Pentagon employee Jonathan Pollard is now serving a life sentence
for passing highly sensitive U.S. Navy documents to Israel.

• Israel utilized U.S. arms, specified for defensive
purposes only, in its invasion of Lebanon in 1982 (and
regularly since then), killing thousands of Lebanese civilians.

• Thanks in part to U.S. military assistance subsidies,
the Israeli arms industry now competes against American
arms manufacturers in overseas markets.

• Last, but far from least, today Prime Minister Benjamin Netanyahu's government is sabotaging the U.S.-
sponsored peace process, rejecting the "land for peace"
formula set forth in U.N. Security Council Resolution 242,
refusing to honor the previous government's commitments
and punishing the Palestinians with closures and economic
sanctions, and continuing to expand Jewish settlements.

The bottom line is that the United States has lavished
so much military aid on Israel that the Jewish state feels no
urgency about negotiating a balanced and durable settlement with its Arab neighbors. Israel's value as a "strategic
asset" was always overrated, but with the demise of the
Soviet Union it has become plainly irrelevant. And in the
Gulf crises, it has been more of a complicating factor than
an asset for American policy. We can put the taxpayer's
money to far better use elsewhere.

MORTON A. KLEIN

National president, Zionist Organization of America

WRITTEN FOR THE CQ RESEARCHER, FEBRUARY 1998.

i srael is a tiny island of democracy and Western
values in a sea of Islamic dictatorships armed with
chemical and biological weapons. The Arabs have
invaded Israel four times, sponsored continuous terrorism
against Israel and continue to incite their people to hatred
and violence against Israel. American military aid to Israel
is an important demonstration of America's moral commitment to helping its ally Israel defend itself. But even more
than that, U.S. military aid is good for America itself.

Israel's military strength has consistently served America's
strategic interests in the Middle East. The presence of a strong
American ally deterred the Soviet Union from being able to
dominate the entire region, which would have threatened
America's access to oil. In a regional crisis, the United States
knows that the Israeli army is its only reliable military ally —
as recently demonstrated by the refusal of Saudi Arabia, Egypt
and the Palestinian Authority to cooperate in possible U.S.
military action against Iraq.

Military aid to Israel also protects American lives. It
enables Israel to defend itself without the help of American
troops — unlike many of America's allies in Europe and Asia,
who need and have tens of thousands of American soldiers
on their soil to protect them from potential enemies.

The U.S.-Israel military relationship directly benefits
America's own military. Israel purchases weapons systems
from the United States, improves them and shares the new
technology with America — saving the U.S. billions of
dollars in research and development. American soldiers are
safer because their infantry vehicles have Israeli-designed
armor on their sides; U.S. Army commanders on the
ground can locate enemy units because of high-flying
unmanned aircraft — developed by Israel; U.S. Air Force
bombers are armed with Israeli-designed missiles that can
be fired from long ranges; joint military exercises between
the two countries give the U.S. opportunities to benefit
from Israel's military experiences.

America's military aid to Israel also benefits American
industry and the American public. Israel spends 85 percent
of its U.S. aid in America, purchasing goods made in 43
different states. That means jobs for many thousands of
Americans and profits for industry.

Annual U.S. military aid to Israel is less than one-tenth
of 1 percent of the federal budget. In the case of Israel,
that means the United States is making a very small
investment and receiving a huge return.

CURRENT SITUATION

Israeli-style Socialism

Most of Israel's founders were socialists, and they put a substantial portion of the economy, including much heavy industry, transportation, agriculture, banking and defense, under state control. They also put in place generous subsidies and benefits for industry and workers as well as a raft of pro-labor laws, all designed to create a fair, equitable society.

Private enterprise was not outlawed, however. Entrepreneurs flourished in many sectors of the economy, including retailing and diamond processing, a major industry.

Throughout Israel's first 40 years, its "mixed economy" served the nation well. In spite of wars and an Arab economic blockade, the country's standard of living improved steadily.

But in the 1980s, the system began to show strains. Inflation rose dramatically — reaching over 1,000 percent at one point in 1985 — and growth slowed. Since then, Israeli governments on the left and right have cautiously worked to liberalize the economy by cutting state subsidies and freeing up trade.

As a result, many economists say, Israel has enjoyed almost a decade of high growth. From 1990 to 1996, the gross domestic product grew at an annual rate of 6 percent. Last year, however, economic growth sank to 2.5 percent, due, many say, to pessimism in the business community over the breakdown in peace talks. [19]

Still, many economists predict that Israel will enjoy high rates of growth for years to come if it fully liberalizes its economic system. The biggest problem, they say, is the state sector, which still accounts for nearly half of the nation's annual economic output. Another stumbling block is Israel's penchant for overregulation, which many say stifles innovation and hard work.

> Many economists predict that Israel will enjoy high rates of growth for years to come if it fully liberalizes its economic system. The biggest problem, they say, is the state sector, which still accounts for nearly half of the nation's economic output.

Enter Prime Minister Netanyahu. A war hero like many of his predecessors and never one to shrink from a fight, Netanyahu has initiated a far-reaching overhaul of Israel's economy aimed at reducing the role of the state. Many of the prime minister's free-market ideas come from the United States, where he lived for more than a decade. He worked as a management consultant in Boston after earning degrees in architecture and business from the Massachusetts Institute of Technology.

Economic Overhaul

At the core of the prime minister's plan is a drive to privatize many state-owned industries. Some, like the nation's biggest bank, Hapoalim, have already been sold. Others, like part of the state-owned airline, El Al, are up for sale.

Netanyahu also has retooled other aspects of the economy. Foreign-exchange controls have been lifted, and Israel's financial markets have been deregulated in an effort to increase foreign investment and make the country a regional center for financial services.

In addition, Netanyahu is trying to encourage the growth of private industry, especially in the high-technology sector. Hundreds of high-tech start-up companies have been given seed money to create new products. And established foreign firms like Intel, Motorola and Hewlett-Packard have been lured to Israel, where they have set up research and development operations. "Israel is the Silicon Valley of the Eastern Hemisphere," the prime minister said last year. [20]

Netanyahu has good reason to put a lot of hope in the high-tech sector. The country already has an estimated 2,000 technology firms. Perhaps more important, a good educational infrastructure and the recent influx of skilled Jewish immigrants from the former Soviet Union have left Israel with a work force well-suited to the information age. According to the Ministry of Industry and Trade, Israel has 130 scientists and engineers for every 10,000 workers; the United States has just 80. [21]

Economic deregulation, coupled with solid growth in technology-related industries, should allow Israel to prosper in the coming decade, many economists say. "We can double gross domestic product per capita in 10 to 12 years," Netanyahu claims. [22]

The economy also will almost certainly receive a boost if the peace process goes forward. The establishment of diplomatic relations with Arab states like Syria and Saudi Arabia likely will open new markets for Israel's goods. Also, easing tensions is always good for business and should lead to increased foreign investment. "As the peace process proceeds, our region will become a much more attractive economic entity," said Jacob Frenkel, governor of the Bank of Israel. [23]

But slow or no growth are also possibilities. The peace process has been stalled for almost a year and could remain so for some time, dampening growth. And negotiations between the Palestinians and Israelis could end and be replaced with escalating violence.

Also, several sectors of society oppose some or all of Netanyahu's changes, from the legal profession, which benefits from the high levels of regulation in the economy, to labor unions, which fear the job losses that would almost certainly follow privatization. In fact, workers at state industries staged a one-day general strike in December to protest the government's economic plan. ■

OUTLOOK

Is Peace at Hand?

While most analysts see tough days ahead for Israel, many are optimistic about the country's long-term prospects. In particular, they say, the peace process will move forward

FOR MORE INFORMATION

American Israel Public Affairs Committee (AIPAC), 440 1st St. N.W., Suite 600, Washington D.C. 20001; (202) 639-5200. http:// WWW.AIPAC.ORG. AIPAC is considered the most influential pro-Israel lobbying group in the United States.

American Jewish Congress, 15 East 84th St., New York, N.Y. 10028; (212) 879-4500; http://www.ajcongress.org. This 50,000-member organization works to advance the security and prosperity of Israel and its democratic institutions and to support its search for peaceful relations with its neighbors.

Brookings Institution, 1775 Massachusetts Ave. N.W., Washington, D.C. 20036-2188; (202) 797-6010; http://www.brook.edu. The Foreign Policy Studies division studies international trade and economic issues as they relate to foreign policy.

Embassy of Israel, 3514 International Dr. N.W., Washington, D.C. 20008; (202) 364-5500. The embassy represents the interests of Israel in the U.S.

Foundation for Middle East Peace, Council on Foreign Relations, 1763 N St. N.W., Washington D.C. 20036; (202) 835-3650; http:// www2.ari.net/fmep. The foundation promotes understanding and resolution of the Israeli-Palestinian conflict.

Institute for Palestine Studies, 3501 M St. N.W., Washington D.C. 20007; (202) 342-3990. The institute studies issues affecting Palestinian Arabs.

National Association of Arab-Americans, 1212 New York Ave. N.W., Suite 230, Washington, D.C. 20005-3987; (202) 842-1840; http:// www.steele.com/naaa
This organization of Americans of Arab descent represents its members on political issues.

New Israel Fund, 1625 K St. N.W., Suite 500, Washington D.C. 20006; (202) 223-3333; http://www.nif.org. The fund is a philanthropic organization that supports civil liberties for all Israelis as well as Jewish-Arab co-existence in Israel.

United Palestinian Appeal, 2100 M St. N.W., Suite 409, Washington, D.C. 20037; (202) 659-5007; http://www.nif.org. This charitable organization is dedicated to improving the quality of life for Palestinians in the Middle East, particularly in the occupied territories.

Washington Institute for Near East Policy, 1828 L St. N.W., Suite 1050, Washington D.C. 20036; (202)452-0650. http:// WWW.Washingtoninstitute.org. The institute conducts research on the Near East with the aim of promoting debate and improving the effectiveness of U.S. policy in the region.

Zionist Organization of America, 4 East 34th St., New York, N.Y., 10016; (212) 481-1500; http://www.zoa.org. The oldest pro-Israel organization in America, founded in 1897, works on behalf of Israel's interests in the United States.

in spite of problems and delays.

"If you look at the last 10 years, both sides have increasingly shown wisdom about what needs to be done," says Rodman of the Nixon Institute, who predicts that Arafat and Netanyahu will hammer out a

deal. "Likud and the PLO are in the ballpark, even though they get hysterical with each other."

Rodman and others argue that Netanyahu's tough stand is aimed, in part, at mollifying legitimate fears at home. "Bibi needs to show strength in order to make concessions," Rodman says.

Klein agrees that Netanyahu is not the intractable hard-liner that the media have often made him out to be. "After all, they said he would never give up Hebron and, of course, he did," he points out, referring to Israel's withdrawal from most of the West Bank city in 1997.

In addition, many argue that Netanyahu's hard-line, war-hero image might allow him to more easily honor any deal he eventually makes. "Netanyahu claims that he can sell [to the Israeli people] any agreement he makes, and there is some historical precedent for this," says Aronson of the Foundation for Middle East Peace. "When Begin made the deal with Sadat, there was some thought that a Labor government could not have or would not have given away the Sinai Peninsula." In other words, just as only President Richard M. Nixon could make the first U.S. overtures to China, only someone with similar hard-line credentials can make a final deal with Israel's longtime enemy, the PLO.

But others argue that the prime minister's tough positions have sunk, for now, any realistic hopes for a lasting peace agreement. "Arafat has no reason to believe that he can cut a good deal with Netanyahu, especially after the Cabinet removed over 60 percent of the West Bank from the negotiating table," says Siegman of the Council on Foreign Relations.

Khalil Jahshan, president of the National Association of Arab Americans, agrees. "I think the Middle East peace process, or what is known as the Oslo process, has basically been dead, for all practical purposes." According to Jahshan, by killing Oslo, Netanyahu is, in essence, asking for another violent uprising among Palestinians in the territories, similar to the intifada that plagued Israel during the late 1980s and early '90s.

"The situation is very tense, it's very explosive," Jahshan says, "and it could lead to that type of unfortunate situation, if the process remains dead or comatose, the way it is today." ■

NOTES

[1] "Loves me, Loves me not," *The Economist*, Jan. 24, 1998. For background, see "The Palestinians," *The CQ Researcher*, Aug. 30, 1991, pp. 609-632.

[2] *Ibid*. For background, see "Reassessing Foreign Aid," *The CQ Researcher*, Sept. 27, 1996, pp. 848-871.

[3] Lee Hockstader, "Israel Says Parts of West Bank Will Never Be Ceded," *The Washington Post*, Jan. 15, 1998.

[4] Quoted by Linda Gradstein, "All Things Considered," National Public Radio, Jan. 14, 1998.

[5] Hockstader, *op. cit.*

[6] Gradstein, *op. cit.*

[7] Hockstader, *op. cit.*

[8] Quoted in Gershom Gorenberg, "Bibi King," *The New Republic*, Jan. 26, 1998.

[9] Rebecca Trounson, "Israel's Foreign Minister Resigns, Deepening Crisis," *Los Angeles Times*, Jan. 5, 1998.

[10] "Bibi's Foundering Ship," *The Economist*, Jan. 10, 1998.

[11] Paul Johnson, *A History of the Jews* (1987), p. 374.

[12] *Ibid.*, p. 395.

[13] Howard M. Sachar, *A History of Israel: From the Rise of Zionism to Our Time* (1997), pp. 107-110.

[14] Daniel C. Diller (ed.), *The Middle East* (1994, 8th ed.), p. 247.

[15] Sachar, *op. cit.*, pp. 317-353.

[16] Diller, *op. cit.*

[17] Quoted in Sachar, *op. cit.*, p. 848.

[18] Diller, *op. cit.*, p. 253.

[19] Peter Passell, "Despite Welfare State Origins, Israeli Enterprise Blooms," *The New York Times*, June 5, 1997.

[20] Quoted in John Rossant and Stephen B. Shepard, "A Talk with Benjamin Netanyahu," *Business Week*, Feb. 17, 1997.

[21] Linda Himelstein, "Land of Milk and Venture Capital," *Business Week*, Feb. 3, 1997.

[22] Quoted in Rossant and Shepard, *op. cit.*

[23] Quoted in John Rossant and Stephen B. Shepard, "Remaking Israel," *Business Week*, Feb. 17, 1997.

Bibliography

Selected Sources Used

Books

Diller, Daniel (ed.), The Middle East, *Congressional Quarterly*, 1994 (8th ed.).

Diller offers a wealth of information on the Middle East. Particularly good are chapters on the Arab-Israeli conflict and detailed profiles of every state in the region. Also useful is a long, thoughtful chapter on the history of U.S. policy in the Middle East.

Sachar, Howard M., *A History of Israel: From the Rise of Zionism to Our Time*, Alfred A. Knopf, 1996.

Sachar, a professor of history at George Washington University, chronicles Israel's history from the early Zionists to the assassination of Prime Minister Yitzhak Rabin. Particularly good are chapters on peace negotiations with the Egyptians and the Palestinians.

Articles

Bethel, Alan, "Whose Country Is It?" *The American Spectator*, January 1998.

Bethel explores the culture war currently raging in Israel between secular and religious forces in society. He argues that the Orthodox have been unfairly tarred as extremists in the press. In reality, Bethel writes, it is secular Israelis who are becoming the extremists, as they use the courts, media and other levers of power to push an agenda that deeply troubles many religious Jews.

"Bibi's Foundering Ship," *The Economist*, Jan. 10, 1998.

The article details the labyrinth that is currently Israeli politics. In particular, it focuses on the fortunes of Israeli Prime Minister Benjamin Netanyahu. The Israeli leader has struggled with a slim majority in the Knesset since Foreign Minister David Levy resigned in January.

Cassata, Donna, "Disagreement Among Friends Strains U.S.-Israeli Ties," *Congressional Quarterly Weekly Report*, Jan. 10, 1998.

While frustration over the stalled peace process has strained relations between Israel and her many friends on Capitol Hill, Cassata concludes that support for $3 billion in annual aid to the Jewish state remains rock solid.

Cooperman, Alan, "America's Jews and Israel's Leader," *U.S. News & World Report*, Nov., 17, 1997.

Cooperman gives a good overview of the current strains in the relationship between Netanyahu and the American Jewish community. He concludes that the Israeli leader "faces a growing loss of confidence among a broad spectrum of American Jews.

Goodstein, Laurie, "Feeling Abandoned By Israel, Many American Jews Grow Angry," *The Washington Post*, Nov., 16, 1997.

Goodstein chronicles the growing rift between American Jews and Israel. In particular, she writes, many of the foundations of Jewish support for Israel in the United States, such as political lobbying and charitable donations, are beginning to crack.

Gorenberg, Gershom, "Bibi King," *The New Republic*, Jan. 26, 1998.

Gorenberg, the op-ed editor of *The Jerusalem Post*, examines the impact of the recent decision to directly elect the Israeli prime minister. Gorenberg writes that the reforms have produced a more fractious and unstable government, rather than a more stable one.

Miller, Marjorie, "Sabbath War Flares in Holy City," *Los Angeles Times*, July 26, 1996.

Miller describes the recent conflicts between religious and secular Jews in Jerusalem. She points out that the fight going on in Jerusalem mirrors a larger conflict unfolding throughout Israel.

Rossant, John, and Neal Sandler, "Remaking Israel," *Business Week*, Feb. 17, 1997.

Rossant and Sandler detail Netanyahu's plan's to promote economic growth by privatizing many Israeli industries and instituting other market-oriented reforms.

Rupert, James, "Arab Citizens of Israel Express Deepening Despair," *The Washington Post*, Feb. 5, 1998.

Rupert profiles Israel's Arab community, which comprises 17 percent of the country's population. He writes that while polls show most Israeli Arabs accept the right of the Jewish state to exist, they are not treated like full citizens and are subjected to discrimination in areas like education and housing. "Their disaffection is deepened by Jewish suspicions that Israel's Arabs form a disloyal fifth column in its confrontation with the Arab world," he writes.

Satloff, Robert, "Scuttle Diplomacy," *The New Republic*, Feb. 8, 1998.

Satloff, executive director of the Washington Institute for Near East Policy, chronicles America's growing role in negotiating an Israeli-Palestinian settlement.

The Next Step

Additional information from UMI's Newspaper & Periodical Abstracts™ database

Israeli Politics

Borger, Julian, "Profile: Bibi Netanyahu," *The Guardian*, Jan. 12, 1998, p. 6.

More than ever before, the fate of the contorted wreckage of Middle East peace balances in the hands of a man who has squeezed it within an inch of extinction. But Benjamin Netanyahu, Israel's prime minister, is in turn dangling by the slenderest of political threads. The grin is still there, but all else is wobbling frantically. His foreign minister resigned last week and his defense and interior ministers have threatened to follow suit if Netanyahu does not withdraw troops from a substantial slice of the West Bank.

Schmemann, Serge, "Barak, Retired Israeli Army Chief, Elected Head of Labor Party," *The New York Times*, June 4, 1997, p. A13.

Ehud Barak, a tough former commando who retired as the army chief only 28 months ago to take up politics, was overwhelmingly elected the new leader of the Labor Party on Tuesday, and thus the probable next challenger to Prime Minister Benjamin Netanyahu. The ascendancy of Barak, 55, marked a critical generational change in the Labor Party, which governed Israel through its first decades with leaders like David Ben-Gurion, Levi Eshkol, Golda Meir, Yitzhak Rabin and Peres, 73.

Sharrock, David, "Rebellious Likud plans coup to ditch Netanyahu," *The Guardian*, Nov. 18, 1997, p. 13.

Benjamin Netanyahu, Israel's right wing prime minister, is facing a rebellion in his party and could be toppled, fellow Likud members said yesterday. "There are very serious actions under way and dramatic political developments should be expected," the Likud mayor of Tel Aviv, Roni Milo, told Israel's Army Radio. The rebellion emerged as Mr Netanyahu cut short a visit to the United States last night to hold a meeting with King Hussein of Jordan in London in a fresh attempt to breathe life into the moribund peace process.

Slavin, Barbara, "Netanyahu once again on precipice Says latest crisis isn't enough to send him tumbling over," *USA Today*, Jan. 5, 1998, p. A10.

The government of Israeli Prime Minister Benjamin Netanyahu has lurched from crisis to crisis in the past 19 months. Is it finally about to fall? On Sunday, an early demise looked more plausible. Foreign Minister David Levy submitted his resignation, complaining that his Likud Party partners had been too stingy toward his low-income constituents and had failed to make progress toward peace with the Palestinians.

Trounson, Rebecca, "Middle East; The Party's Over for Netanyahu; Though he heads off a mutiny among Likud politicians, the near-rebellion underlines Israeli prime minister's increasing travails," *Los Angeles Times*, Nov. 21, 1997, p. A5.

Immediately after Netanyahu's return from Britain and the United States, where he was greeted coolly by Jewish community leaders and snubbed by the Clinton administration, the Israeli leader had to work overtime to put down a rebellion within Likud that some feared might lead to a split.

Middle East Peace Process

Crossette, Barbara, "Palestinians Confront Israel On Representation at U.N.," *The New York Times*, Oct. 24, 1997, p. A12.

Reopening a diplomatic front against Israel that has been quiet for nearly five years, Palestinians are planning to challenge the Israeli government's right to represent the people of the West Bank, Gaza and Jerusalem in the United Nations. The Palestinian observer mission at the United Nations has reintroduced an amendment to constrict Israel's legitimacy here with strong backing from developing nations, say diplomats from the Israeli and Palestinian delegations.

Jehl, Douglas, "Arafat Says the U.S. Should Do More for Peace in the Mideast," *The New York Times*, Sept. 21, 1997, p. 9.

Yasir Arafat said today that the United States should do more to rescue the quest for a broader Middle East peace, and he called on the Clinton administration to support the creation of a Palestinian state. Addressing a gathering of foreign ministers at the Arab League, Arafat said it was vital that the United States renew its efforts "to overcome obstacles" that have left peace talks between Israelis and Palestinians frozen for more than six months.

Prusher, Ilene R., "In Crossfire of Mideast Conflict," *The Christian Science Monitor*, Jan. 16, 1998, p. 7.

Samaritans welcome efforts toward Arab-Israeli reconciliation, but they fear for their future under a final peace settlement. When borders are eventually drawn between Israel and a Palestinian state , the Samaritans worry they will be separated by a border that will once again cut one half of the 611-member community off from the other.

Sennott, Charles M., and David Marcus, "Albright lashes out at Arafat, also raps Netanyahu," *The Boston Globe*, Sept. 11, 1997, p. A6.

Secretary of State Madeleine K. Albright injected the United States into the center of a crisis-torn peace process yesterday, publicly berating Palestinian leader Yasir Arafat for not doing enough to "root out terror" and privately pressing Israeli Prime Minister Benjamin Netanyahu to breathe life into negotiations by offering concessions. Albright and her aides had billed this Middle East trip as an even-handed attempt to get both sides back to the bargaining table, with reprimands for Palestinians and Israelis alike. But in her words and scheduling, Albright quickly and dramatically underscored that Washington's first priority is to support Israel in the aftermath of the renewed tension.

Teepen, Tom, "Withdrawal could advance Middle East peace process," *Atlanta Constitution*, Dec. 9, 1997, p. A19.

The Israeli-Palestinian peace process can hardly be called robust these days, but at least it is still twitching. That much, at any rate, can be said about the recent Israeli Cabinet statement offering further military withdrawal from the West Bank. And the Cabinet hinges the withdrawal on greater Palestinian effort to suppress terrorism.

Trounson, Rebecca, "Netanyahu Vows Not to Be Pressured Into Further W. Bank Withdrawal; Israel: Premier calls nation's future his overriding concern," *Los Angeles Times*, Dec. 10, 1997, p. A14.

Israeli Prime Minister Benjamin Netanyahu dug in his heels Tuesday against American calls for quick decisions in the Middle East peace process, saying Israel will not yield to external pressures on such critical issues. But Netanyahu told reporters Tuesday that the only real pressure he feels about a West Bank pullback is the heavy responsibility of making decisions affecting Israel's future. His Cabinet decided Nov. 30 to approve the withdrawal but left open the questions of its scope and timing.

Palestinian State

Deans, Bob, "Mideast diplomacy in D.C. gets off to busy start; Israel's leader says he is willing to bend on a military pullout from the West Bank, but only with security guarantees," *Atlanta Constitution*, Jan. 21, 1998, p. A3.

In an arduous effort to avert another eruption of violence in the Middle East, Israeli Prime Minister Benjamin Netanyahu and President Clinton talked into the night Tuesday, trying to devise a formula for how much of the West Bank Israel should turn over to Palestinians. Secretary of State Madeleine Albright, a dove of peace pinned on her shoulder, her voice hoarse from a desperate effort to save the Mideast peace process, emerged from the White House to say the talks were "friendly" and that Netanyahu wanted to hear more of Clinton's ideas.

Marcus, David L., "Embattled Netanyahu May Feel a Nudge from U.S. Envoy," *The Boston Globe*, Jan. 7, 1998, p. A1.

As the U.S. envoy to the Middle East landed in Israel yesterday, the Clinton administration found itself with extraordinary clout, perhaps enough to make or break Benjamin Netanyahu's fragile government. But privately, the officials conceded that they are in a tricky position: By pushing the government to cede larger swaths of the West Bank to Palestinians, the United States might prompt more resignations or shift votes in next week's confidence vote on Netanyahu at the Knesset. While the administration has made no secret of its disagreements with Netanyahu, some officials maintain that Secretary of State Madeleine K. Albright and envoy Dennis Ross have developed trust with the hard-line prime minister.

U.S. Aid to Israel

Clarke, Duncan L., "U.S. security assistance to Egypt and Israel: Politically untouchable?" *Middle East Journal*, spring 1997, pp. 200-214.

Since the 1970s, Egypt and Israel together have received the lion's share of worldwide U.S. security assistance allocations — about $100 billion. This aid has helped the U.S. achieve short-term political objectives, but several factors suggest a need to reduce or eliminate at least the economic portion of this assistance.

Morgan, Dan, "Israel Seeks U.S. Aid Shift From Economic to Military," *The Washington Post*, Jan. 29, 1998, p. A23.

The Israeli finance minister has proposed phasing out the $1.2 billion of annual U.S. economic aid to his country in return for a one-third increase in military assistance over the next 10-12 years, U.S. and Israeli officials said yesterday. The proposal was outlined this week by visiting Finance Minister Yaacov Neeman during meetings with top administration and congressional officials.

Zionism

Cohen, Roger, "100 Years Ago, a Dream of Israel: Celebration Caught in Crosswinds," *The New York Times*, Aug. 29, 1997, p. A1.

It was for its tolerance, as well as its rail connections, that Theodor Herzl chose Basel for the first Zionist Congress and then, on Sept. 3, 1897, penned the unlikely words: "In Basel, I have founded the Jewish state." The phrase was prophetic. But perhaps not even Herzl could have foreseen how the Holocaust, as belatedly refracted through the vaults of Swiss banks, would cast a shadow over a centennial commemoration of the meeting that first gave political coherence to Jewish aspirations for a homeland. Returning to his Basel home for lunch one day this week, the vice president of the Swiss Jewish Federation, Thomas Lyssy, found a letter awaiting him. It contained a photograph of an Orthodox Jew covered in written insults borrowed from Nazi propaganda.

Jones, Owen Bennett, "Basel marks centenary of political dream," *The Guardian*, Aug. 19, 1997, p. 12.

The centennial of the first Zionist Congress comes at a sensitive moment in Swiss-Jewish relations. The World Jewish Congress has led the recent criticism about Switzerland's conduct during the World War II. Many Swiss Jews are reporting an increase in anti-Semitism.

Back Issues

Great Research on Current Issues Starts Right Here . . . Recent topics covered by The CQ Researcher are listed below. Before May 1991, reports were published under the name of Editorial Research Reports.

AUGUST 1996
Fighting Over Animal Rights
Privatizing Government Services
Child Labor and Sweatshops
Cleaning Up Hazardous Wastes

SEPTEMBER 1996
Gambling Under Attack
The States and Federalism
Civic Journalism
Reassessing Foreign Aid

OCTOBER 1996
Political Consultants
Insurance Fraud
Rethinking School Integration
Parental Rights

NOVEMBER 1996
Global Warming
Clashing Over Copyright
Consumer Debt
Governing Washington, D.C.

DECEMBER 1996
Welfare, Work and the States
The New Volunteerism
Implementing the Disabilities Act
America's Pampered Pets

JANUARY 1997
Combating Scientific Misconduct
Restructuring the Electric Industry
The New Immigrants
Chemical and Biological Weapons

FEBRUARY 1997
Assisting Refugees
Alternative Medicine's Next Phase
Independent Counsels
Feminism's Future

MARCH 1997
New Air Quality Standards
Alcohol Advertising
Civic Renewal
Educating Gifted Students

APRIL 1997
Declining Crime Rates
The FBI Under Fire
Gender Equity in Sports
Space Program's Future

MAY 1997
The Stock Market
The Cloning Controversy
Expanding NATO
The Future of Libraries

JUNE 1997
FDA Reform
China After Deng
Line-Item Veto
Breast Cancer

JULY 1997
Transportation Policy
Executive Pay
School Choice Debate
Aggressive Driving

AUGUST 1997
Age Discrimination
Banning Land Mines
Children's Television
Evolution vs. Creationism

SEPTEMBER 1997
Caring for the Dying
Mental Health Policy
Mexico's Future
Youth Fitness

OCTOBER 1997
Urban Sprawl in the West
Diversity in the Workplace
Teacher Education
Contingent Work Force

NOVEMBER 1997
Renewable Energy
Artificial Intelligence
Religious Persecution
Roe v. Wade at 25

DECEMBER 1997
Whistleblowers
Castro's Next Move
Gun Control Standoff
Regulating Nonprofits

JANUARY 1998
Foster Care Reform
IRS Reform
The Black Middle Class
U.S.-British Relations

FEBRUARY 1998
Patients' Rights
Deflation Fears
Caring for the Elderly
The New Corporate Philanthropy

Back issues are available for $5.00 (subscribers) or $10.00 (non-subscribers). Quantity discounts apply to orders over ten. To order, call Congressional Quarterly Customer Service at (202) 887-8621.

Binders are available for $18.00. To order call 1-800-638-1710. Please refer to stock number 648.

Future Topics

▶ *Federal Judiciary*

▶ *Drinking on Campus*

▶ *The Economics of Recycling*

The Federal Judiciary

Are the attacks on U.S. courts justified?

C onservative groups and some Republican lawmakers charge that many federal judges are "judicial activists" who issue liberal rulings based on their personal views rather than the law. The critics also accuse President Clinton of appointing activist judges and have tried to block confirmation of some of his nominees. Most legal experts, however, say that Clinton's judicial selections have been mostly moderates. And so far, the Republican-controlled Senate has not rejected any of Clinton's choices for the federal bench. But liberal lawmakers and advocacy groups say that delays in the confirmation process are creating a "vacancy crisis" in some courts that is causing problems for litigants. And they warn that the attacks on federal judges are threatening the independence of the judiciary.

C_Q | **March 13, 1998 • Volume 8, No. 10 • Pages 217-240**

Formerly Editorial Research Reports

COVER: THE NEW ALBERT V. BRYAN U.S. DISTRICT COURTHOUSE IN ALEXANDRIA, VA. (NICK MERRICK/HEDRICH BLESSING; COURTESY OF SPILLIS CANDELA & PARTNERS, INC.)

CQ Researcher

March 13, 1998
Volume 8, No.10

EDITOR
Sandra Stencel

MANAGING EDITOR
Thomas J. Colin

ASSOCIATE EDITOR
Sarah M. Magner

STAFF WRITERS
Mary H. Cooper
Kenneth Jost
David Masci

PRODUCTION EDITOR
Melissa Hall

PUBLISHED BY
Congressional Quarterly Inc.

CHAIRMAN
Andrew Barnes

VICE CHAIRMAN
Andrew P. Corty

PRESIDENT AND PUBLISHER
Robert W. Merry

EXECUTIVE EDITOR
David Rapp

The CQ Researcher (ISSN 1056-2036). Formerly Editorial Research Reports. Published weekly, except Jan. 2, May 29, July 3, Oct. 30, by Congressional Quarterly Inc., 1414 22nd St., N.W., Washington, D.C. 20037. Annual subscription rate for libraries, businesses and government is $340. Additional rates furnished upon request. Periodicals postage paid at Washington, D.C., and additional mailing offices. POSTMASTER: Send address changes to The CQ Researcher, 1414 22nd St., N.W., Washington, D.C. 20037.

The Federal Judiciary

BY KENNETH JOST

THE ISSUES

When President Clinton nominated Margaret M. Morrow for a federal judgeship in 1996, her confirmation to the lifetime post seemed certain.

Morrow's impressive résumé includes a Harvard law degree, 20 years' experience as a litigator with a prestigious law firm and service as the first woman president of the State Bar of California.

But Morrow fell victim to election-year politics. The Republican-controlled Senate had little interest in approving judicial nominations made by the man the GOP hoped to defeat in November.

Even after Clinton's re-election, a few Republican senators tried to block Morrow's confirmation. Led by Missouri's John Ashcroft, they branded her as a "liberal activist," pointing to comments she had made years earlier, including one in which she wrote that "any real hope of intelligent voting" by citizens on ballot initiatives is "ephemeral."

Ashcroft, a would-be GOP presidential hopeful, declared during Senate floor debate in mid-February that "she believes the courts are the place where the law can be made."

Morrow's supporters decried both the accusations and the long delay in acting on the nomination. "It is time to stop holding her hostage," Sen. Patrick J. Leahy, D-Vt., said at the start of the Feb. 11 debate. Morrow's chief sponsor, Sen. Barbara Boxer, D-Calif., complained that Morrow had spent "two years twisting in the wind."

In the end, Sen. Orrin G. Hatch, R-Utah, chairman of the Senate Judiciary Committee, stood up for Morrow. "I believe she understands the proper role of the judge in our system," he

told his colleagues, "and understands the importance of the rule of law."

Hatch's endorsement helped pave the way for Morrow's confirmation by a 67-28 vote. Even so, the leader of the conservative groups that had opposed Morrow calls the vote a victory of sorts.

"Twenty-eight votes against a district court nominee is significant opposition by historical standards," says Thomas Jipping, head of the Judicial Selection Monitoring Project of the Free Congress Foundation. "I think it shows that the very quiet, patronage-oriented approach to judicial selection is over."

On the opposite side, a liberal lobbying group on judicial nominations is pressing for quicker action on Clinton's nominees to help ease a "vacancy crisis" in federal courts.

"There are still 80 vacancies that are creating problems for litigants around the country," says Stephan Kline, legislative counsel at the Alliance for Justice. "They need to be filled."

Kline's comments echo complaints that Democratic senators and Clinton himself had been making over the past year about the Republican-controlled

Senate's slow pace in acting on judicial nominees. At one point, the number of federal court vacancies topped 100 — more than 10 percent of the approximately 840 authorized lifetime federal court judgeships. But the issue gained both visibility and credibility at year's end when Chief Justice William H. Rehnquist voiced his concern, too.

"Vacancies cannot remain at such high levels indefinitely without eroding the quality of justice that has traditionally been associated with the federal judiciary," Rehnquist said in his year-end report on the federal court system. "The president should nominate candidates with reasonable promptness," Rehnquist said, "and the Senate should act within a reasonable time to confirm or reject them." [1]

Hatch and other Republican lawmakers defend their record, insisting that Clinton himself has been slow to send up nominations and that the number of nominees approved during the year — 36 — was close to normal. In any event, Hatch wrote in an op-ed article a week later, the Senate had to consider Clinton's nominees carefully to prevent the confirmation of "judicial activists."

"We should reject nominees," Hatch wrote, "who will not apply the Constitution and statutes as written and will instead substitute their own personal preferences." [2]

Legal experts divide along ideological lines in their assessment of the debate. Liberal law professors agree with the Democrats' charges that Republicans have been slow-walking Clinton's nominees. "The Republicans are on a deliberate stall," says Herman Schwartz, a law professor at American University in Washington.

But Daniel Troy, a partner in a Wash-

Civil Cases Are Majority of Federal Caseload

Four times more civil suits than criminal suits were filed in federal District courts in 1997.* Federal-prisoner petitions — mostly habeas corpus actions — comprise nearly one-fourth of the civil caseload, and torts, or personal-injury cases, about one-fifth. Nearly a third of the criminal cases involved drugs.

Civil Cases

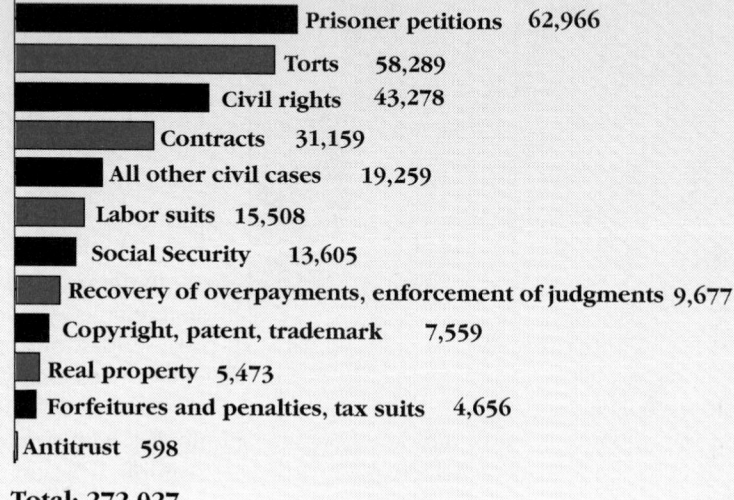

Prisoner petitions   62,966
Torts   58,289
Civil rights   43,278
Contracts   31,159
All other civil cases   19,259
Labor suits   15,508
Social Security   13,605
Recovery of overpayments, enforcement of judgments 9,677
Copyright, patent, trademark   7,559
Real property   5,473
Forfeitures and penalties, tax suits   4,656
Antitrust   598

Total: 272,027

Criminal Cases

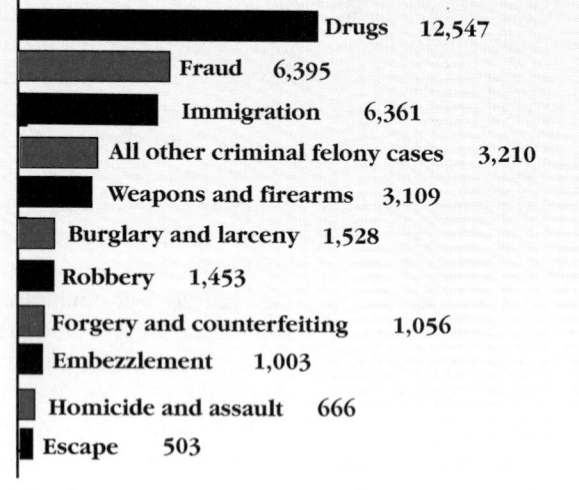

Drugs   12,547
Fraud   6,395
Immigration   6,361
All other criminal felony cases   3,210
Weapons and firearms   3,109
Burglary and larceny   1,528
Robbery   1,453
Forgery and counterfeiting   1,056
Embezzlement   1,003
Homicide and assault   666
Escape   503

Total: 37,831

* For the fiscal year ending Sept. 30, 1997

Sources: Administrative Office of U.S. Courts; Long Range Plan for the Federal Courts, *Judicial Conference of the United States, December 1995*

ington law firm and former Justice Department official under President Ronald Reagan, says any slowdown is a natural result of partisan divisions between the Senate and the White House.

"You can't expect a Senate to confirm nominees from a president of the other party as fast as they confirm nominees from a president of the same party," says Troy, who is also an associate scholar in legal studies at the American Enterprise Institute.

Whether or not the Senate had engaged in a slowdown in 1997, the pace appears to be picking up in the new year. The Senate acted on three Clinton nominees on the first business day of the new session in late January, and three more were approved by March 2.

Some of the nominations moved smoothly, but others attracted criticism. The day before approving Morrow's nomination, the Senate put off action on Frederica A. Massiah-Jackson, a state court judge nominated for a federal district court in Philadelphia. Hatch said the Judiciary Committee would examine the contention by Pennsylvania prosecutors that Massiah-Jackson was biased in favor of defendants and intemperate toward police and prosecutors.

Republicans and conservative activists have also been pushing other ways to rein in federal judges who they say exceed their legitimate judicial powers by substituting personal views for the views of elected legislators or policymakers. One GOP senator, New Hampshire's Robert C. Smith, has proposed a bill to eliminate life tenure for federal judges and instead require reconfirmation after a 10-year term. In the House, Judiciary Committee Chairman Henry J. Hyde of Illinois is pushing a bill that would require a three-judge court to hear constitutional challenges to state ballot measures approved by voters. And House Majority Whip Tom DeLay of Texas has called for the use of impeachment to restrain "judicial activism" among federal judges *(see p. 232).*

Clinton's supporters in Congress and liberal legal experts insist the complaints about judicial activism have little basis in fact. They point to studies indicating that Clinton's judicial appointees have more moderate backgrounds and more moderate records than judges appointed by previous Democratic presidents. "The judicial activist thing is, frankly, a red herring," Kline says.

Many bar leaders and legal experts go further and warn that the GOP attacks on the federal judiciary are threatening what they view as a fundamental constitutional principle: the independence of the judiciary. "What marks our nation from so many unstable or authoritarian governments is, to a substantial measure, the independence of our judges as preservers of our constitutional rights," says Jerome Shestack, president of the American Bar Association (ABA).

But the critics insist that their efforts are aimed at upholding an equally important principle: judicial restraint. "Judicial activism is a serious problem," Jipping says. "It is directly contrary to the kind of judiciary that America's founders established."

As the debate continues about the role and powers of the federal judiciary, here are some of the questions being considered:

Is "judicial activism" a problem among federal judges?

Over the past two years, the country's attention has been riveted on trials arising from gruesome terrorist episodes: the bombing of the World Trade Center, the destruction of the Oklahoma City federal building and the series of mail-bombs sent by the so-called "Unabomber." Each of the trials ended with convictions — and with general praise for the federal judges who presided over the proceedings. [3]

Federal judges are more likely to draw widespread attention not from successful criminal trials, however, but from controversial rulings on constitu-

"Vacancies cannot remain at such high levels without eroding justice," said Chief Justice William H. Rehnquist.

Bettmann — UPI

tional issues. Federal judges may strike down state laws, order new trials for defendants convicted in state courts or require state or local officials to bring schools, prisons, mental hospitals or other institutions into compliance with constitutional requirements.

Rulings in such matters prompt recurrent charges of "judicial activism." In the early 20th century, the charge came most often from liberals and progressives who objected to decisions by conservative judges striking down social welfare legislation. Today, the accusation is heard most often — though not exclusively — from conservatives.

During the past two years, for example, conservatives have complained about rulings by federal judges in California that struck down three voter-approved initiatives setting legislative term limits, eliminating racial preferences in state programs and seeking to control illegal immigration. Even though the rulings on term limits and affirmative action were later overturned, the decisions helped provoke a new round of attacks on judicial activism from conservative activists and Republican senators.

But liberal advocates see evidence of judicial activism among some conservative judges, including the Supreme Court's current conservative majority. [4] They cite as recent examples a federal judge's decision — later overturned — to strike down Oregon's initiative allowing physician-assisted suicide and a ruling by a federal judge in New York acquitting anti-abortion protesters of obstructing access to abortion clinics. *(See chart, p. 222.)*

Many liberals, however, simply discount the idea of judicial activism altogether. "It's a meaningless term the way it's been used," says Sheldon Goldman, a professor of political science at the University of Massachusetts in Amherst who has studied judicial selection for more than 30 years. "It simply means that you don't like how the judge rules."

But Ronald Rotunda, a conservative law professor at the University of Illinois in Champaign, disagrees. "There are

Judicial Activism: In the Eyes of the Beholder?

Legal experts do not agree on a definition of "judicial activism." Conservatives and liberals alike often label rulings they disagree with as examples of judicial overreaching. But some legal scholars say the question of whether judges substitute their personal views for the views of elected legislators or policy-makers simply boils down to whose ox is being gored. Here are some recent decisions by federal judges that have drawn criticism from both sides of the political spectrum:

Examples of "Liberal Activism"

Case Name	Date	Judge*	Ruling	Status
League of United Latin American Citizens v. Wilson	*Nov. 14, 1997*	*Mariana R. Pfaelzer (Los Angeles)*	*Struck down California ban on benefits for illegal immigrants*	*State expected to appeal to 9th Circuit*
Jones v. Bates	*Oct. 7, 1997*	*Stephen Reinhardt (Los Angeles)*	*Struck down term limits for California legislators*	*Overturned by 9th Circuit, Dec. 19, 1997*
Coalition for Economic Equity v. Wilson	*Dec. 24, 1996*	*Thelton Henderson (San Francisco)*	*Struck down California ban on racial preferences*	*Overturned by 9th Circuit, April 8, 1997*

Examples of "Conservative Activism"

Case Name	Date	Judge*	Ruling	Status
U.S. v. Lynch	*Jan. 13 1997*	*John E. Sprizzo (New York)*	*Acquitted anti-abortion protesters because of religious beliefs*	*On appeal to 2nd Circuit*
Lee v. Oregon	*Aug. 3 1995*	*Michael Hogan (Portland, Ore.)*	*Struck down Oregon law to allow physician-assisted suicide*	*Overturned by 9th Circuit, Feb. 19, 1997*

* All judges except Reinhardt serve on U.S. District courts; Reinhardt, a judge on the 9th U.S. Circuit Court of Appeals, authored the 2-1 opinion in the California term limits case that was later overturned in an en banc decision by a vote of 8-3.

Source: Administrative Office of U.S. Courts

[judges] who are going beyond what is a fair reading of the Constitution, statutes or regulations," says Rotunda, a leader in the conservative Federalist Society for Law and Public Policy Studies. "If they do it for liberal reasons or conservative reasons, it's still judicial activism."

Experts and advocates also disagree over whether President Clinton's federal court appointees have engaged in judicial activism, as conservative critics have charged. "With neutral court-watchers, it's been shown that his nominees are moderate," says Kline of the Alliance for Justice. "They're closer to Gerald Ford's [judicial appointees] than to Jimmy Carter's or Lyndon Johnson's."

But conservatives say that many of Clinton's appointees have "activist" records on the bench. Jipping cites votes by 20 Clinton-appointed judges on such issues as gay rights, anti-pornography laws and term limits.

Troy also says Clinton's judges have been more activist than his supporters acknowledge. "His appointments have perhaps not been as overtly activist and left-wing as some have feared," Troy says, "but that does not mean that they have not been quite activist."

For its part, the White House has denied the accusations of appointing "activist" judges — most specifically when the issue arose during the 1996 presidential campaign. "Every objective observer who has looked at the issue agrees: President Clinton has appointed moderate, mainstream judges," then-White House counsel Jack Quinn said April 23 in response to an attack from the prospective GOP presidential nominee, Senate Majority Leader Bob Dole, R-Kan.

For many observers, the debate over judicial activism has a dark side. They view the use of the term as a political pejorative deliberately aimed at reducing public respect for the judiciary and ultimately threatening judicial independence. "Labeling judges 'activists' simply because they make unpopular decisions is unjustified," a special ABA commission said last summer, "and only serves to undermine public confidence in the judiciary." [5]

But conservative advocates and experts maintain that the debate over judicial activism is both legitimate and important. "The people who use those terms are genuinely concerned about separation of powers and the rule of law," says Leonard Leo, director of the lawyers division of the Federalist Society. "To suggest that speaking of judicial activism and being critical of the federal courts somehow threatens the independence of the federal judiciary really strikes me as fanciful."

Is President Clinton or the Senate to blame for the delay in filling federal court vacancies?

For nearly a year, the country's largest federal appeals court has had about one-third of its allotted 28 judgeships vacant. The personnel shortage at the 9th U.S. Circuit Court of Appeals — which covers nine Western states — has overwhelmed the remaining judges and forced the court to drop oral arguments or formal opinions in less serious cases.

"The situation is extremely serious," the circuit's chief judge, Procter Hug Jr. said last May, when there were nine vacancies. "It is impossible

10 Percent of Judgeships Are Vacant

Of the 839 lifetime federal judgeships currently authorized by Congress, about 10 percent are vacant. Cases are also heard by the 437 retired "senior" judges. The federal judiciary also includes 314 bankruptcy judges and 491 magistrates, who mainly handle misdemeanors.

Court	Authorized Positions	Active Judges	Vacant Positions	Senior Judges	Total
U.S. Supreme Court	9	9	—	4	13
Court of Appeals	179	155	24	91	246
District Court	642	582	60	336	918
International Trade	9	6	3	6	12
Total lifetime judges	839	752	87	437	1,189
Bankruptcy judges**	326	314	12	—	314
Magistrate judges**	508	491	17	—	491

**Bankruptcy and magistrate judges are appointed by district selection committees for 14- and eight-year terms, respectively.

Source: Administrative Office of U.S. Courts

to expect 19 active judges to handle the increased caseload with the care each appeal deserves." [6]

The 9th Circuit's problems are especially pronounced, but judges and lawyers in other parts of the country also report strains and delays from unfilled court slots. [7] On Capitol Hill, however, the Republican senators who hold the key to approving judicial nominations see little evidence of a "vacancy crisis" in the federal courts.

Judiciary Committee Chairman Hatch calls the talk of a vacancy crisis "misleading." "Today, there are more sitting judges than there were throughout virtually all of the Reagan and Bush administrations," he said as the Senate took up three nominations on Jan. 28, the first business day of the new session. Hatch said the 756 "active" federal judges and the 432 retired "senior" federal judges consti-

tuted a "near record number" of 1,188 judges in the federal court system.

Democrats and liberal legal experts, however, say the vacancies — which reached 100 last May before falling to 82 at the end of the year — create severe hardships for judges, lawyers and litigants. They say that women and minority group candidates have been the most frequent victims of delays. [8] And they blame the Republican Senate for most of the problem.

"Republicans are engaged in an effort unprecedented at this point in a presidential term to deny the Clinton administration as many nominations as possible," says the University of Massachusetts' Goldman. "We haven't seen that before. It's a new ballgame."

Rehnquist himself cited statistics in his year-end report to show the Senate's

A Judge's Lie Reveals the Difficulties . . .

Judge James Ware's promotion to a federal appeals court fell victim late last year to a lie. It was a lie that went undetected when Ware was first confirmed to a federal judgeship in 1990 and that he managed to conceal almost to the end of a second set of investigations by the Justice Department, the American Bar Association and the Senate Judiciary Committee.

Ware, an African-American who grew up in Birmingham, Ala., had long claimed that he decided to become a lawyer because of the killing of his teenage brother by white racists in 1963. In fact, it was another James Ware whose younger brother Virgil was shot and killed in Birmingham on Sept. 15, 1963. And when the truth came out in November, Judge Ware had to ask President Clinton to withdraw his nomination to serve as the first black judge on the 9th U.S. Circuit Court of Appeals in California. [1]

Ware remains a federal district court judge in San Jose, a post to which President George Bush appointed him in 1990. The disclosure of his fabrication — thanks to a tip to Senate investigators from another black federal judge in Alabama — prompted puzzled questions of why Ware would make up such a story. But the episode also indicates the difficulties that confront both the president and the Senate in nominating and confirming qualified individuals for lifetime positions on the federal courts.

Most presidential nominees for federal judgeships attract little public notice or controversy as they move through their confirmation hearing in the Senate Judiciary Committee and eventual vote on the Senate floor. Typically, several nominees are heard from in the same session, only a few senators attend, and there are few, if any, outside witnesses. Roll-call votes are uncommon either in committee or on the floor.

The process galls the federal judiciary's critics. Thomas Jipping of the Free Congress Foundation's Judicial Selection Monitoring Project calls the confirmation hearings "group hugs" and accuses the Republican-controlled Senate of "rubber-stamping" Clinton's nominees.

"They haven't defeated a single one," Jipping complains. "And in Clinton's first term, there were only four roll-call votes, and two of those were for Supreme Court nominees."

For their part, though, the federal judiciary's supporters say the confirmation process is too long and too contentious. "It's unfair not to give a nominee a prompt hearing," says Jerome Shestack, president of the American Bar Association. The ABA has endorsed a proposal — first set out by a study commission at the University of Virginia — that the Judiciary Committee conduct hearings on nominees within two months after the president submits the nomination. [2]

Caught in the middle of these forces is Judiciary Committee Chairman Sen. Orrin G. Hatch. The Utah Republican has been pressured by GOP conservatives to raise the heat on Clinton's nominees; last spring, he pulled out all stops to beat back a proposal by several conservative Republicans to allow GOP senators within

slow pace. The Senate confirmed only 17 judges in 1996 — a presidential election year — and 36 in 1997. By contrast, the Senate confirmed 104 judges in 1994, Rehnquist said — without noting that was the last year the Senate was under Democratic control.

Republicans and conservative advocates, however, say the number of vacancies is not unusually high. "The number of vacancies was higher when the Democrats controlled the Senate than when the Republicans took control," Jipping says. "Two-thirds of the time since 1990, vacancies have been higher than the number is now."

Indeed, the number of federal court vacancies was above 120 in January 1991, peaked at 146 in May 1991 and remained above 80 until summer 1994. But Goldman explains that the large number of vacancies resulted from the creation of 85 new judgeships by Congress in 1990 and President George Bush's slow pace in filling those posts in 1991 and '92. "How can you complain when those positions had just been created?" Goldman asks.

Republicans also contend that the president himself bears part of the blame for any delays because of his own slow pace in making judicial nominations. They note, for example, that out of the 86 vacancies at the start of the year, Clinton had submitted nominees for 45 — just a little over half. The Senate "cannot confirm an individual who has not yet been nominated," Hatch wrote in his op-ed article.

Chief Judge Hug faulted the president in his remarks last May. He said White House officials had assured him in March that Clinton would submit 100 nominees by July, but then reduced their estimate by half. "I'm disappointed," Hug said.

The judge put most of the blame on the Senate, however. Today, leaders of national bar and court-reform groups also say the Senate bears most of the responsibility for the vacancy problem.

"I think the White House could be faster and the Senate could be much faster," says ABA President Shestack.

But conservatives continue to minimize the caseload problems facing most judges, defend the Senate's role in scrutinizing nominees and see greater risks to the judicial system in rushing the process.

"If you're concerned about public safety, it's more important not to put judges on the bench who are going to

. . .in Nominating Judicial Candidates

a federal circuit effective veto power over nominations to the regional federal appeals courts. [3]

But Hatch also prides himself on a measure of bipartisanship in heading the Judiciary Committee. Seemingly stung by the criticisms of the slow pace of judicial confirmations last year from Clinton, Senate Democrats and Chief Justice William H. Rehnquist, Hatch opened the new session this year with a spurt of activity on nominees.

Still, Hatch defends his committee's pace — and cites Ware's case as an example of the need to ensure enough time to conduct a thorough investigation. The committee had already held a hearing on Ware's nomination and was scheduled to vote on him within a week when his fabricated story was disclosed.

"Just think if we had followed the ABA's recommendation and moved even more swiftly on [the nomination]," Hatch remarked in a speech to the Federalist Society on Jan. 27. "If the committee fails to do the groundwork," he continued, "it fails the Senate and prevents that body from fulfilling its constitutional duty."

For its part, the Justice Department apparently acknowledges that it cannot completely guard against the possibility of deception by a judicial nominee. After the disclosure about Ware, an unidentified senior department official told *The New York Times* that the purpose of FBI background checks was "to search for instances of wrongdoing and lawbreaking, and not to fact-check every anecdote at a dinner party." [4]

The ABA itself has long played an important but controversial role in the nomination process. Since the 1950s, a 15-member Standing Committee on the Federal Judiciary has given the Justice Department and White House confidential evaluations of potential judicial nominees — rating the candidates "well-qualified," "qualified" or "not qualified." The ratings supposedly are limited to judging a candidate's integrity, experience and ability and judicial temperament. But conservatives have long complained that the ABA has a liberal political bias — an accusation made frequently since a minority of the ABA committee voted to give unsuccessful Supreme Court nominee Robert H. Bork a "not qualified" rating in 1987. (Bork received a "qualified" rating from the full committee.)

Hatch began the new Congress by declaring that the Judiciary Committee would no longer participate with the ABA committee in the evaluation process. But Shestack says the panel has continued to send its evaluations to the committee after the president submits a nomination.

---

[1] See *The New York Times*, Nov. 7, 1997, p. A1, and *The Washington Post*, Nov. 9, 1997, p. A3.

[2] See The Miller Center of Public Affairs, "Improving the Process of Appointing Federal Judges: A Report of the Miller Center Commission on the Selection of Federal Judges," University of Virginia, September 1996.

[3] For background, see *The New York Times*, April 27, 1997, p. 1, and April 30, 1997, p. D22.

[4] *The New York Times*, Nov. 7, 1997, p. 1.

---

turn out criminals on bogus theories than to confirm judges just to have someone on the bench," Troy says.

Should the size and caseload of the federal judiciary be limited?

Five years ago, the federal judiciary's policy-making arm started a little noticed but vastly important debate: whether to cap the number of federal judges at 1,000 or allow the federal judiciary to continue to grow with the nation's growing population and growing caseload.

"We oppose an expanded judiciary because further growth will damage the institution and ultimately undermine the need to have a federal judicial branch at all," Judge Jon O. Newman of the federal appeals court in New York wrote in an op-ed article urging the 1,000-judge limit. The result, he said, would be an "inevitable drop in quality of judges" and "the inefficiency of large appellate courts."

But Judge Stephen Reinhardt of the federal appeals court in California countered that a cap would "shut off access to federal courts for poor people, minorities, women and other disadvantaged persons." [9]

The debate between the two judges, both appointed by President Carter, came as the U.S. Judicial Conference was developing a long-range plan for the federal courts. Two years later, the process ended with a report rejecting a fixed limit on the number of federal judges but calling for limiting the growth of the federal judiciary by improved caseload management and by controls on the kinds of cases assigned to federal courts. [10]

Today, some federal judges view the Judicial Conference's stance as too lenient and are continuing to call for a fixed limit on the number of federal judges. "A numerical cap would strike a historic blow for limited government," Judge J. Harvie Wilkinson III, a Reagan appointee who heads the federal appeals court in Richmond, Va., wrote in an op-ed article last month. [11]

With 839 authorized lifetime judgeships today, the federal judiciary has doubled in size in 30 years. But, as the authors of a study of the federal judicial system note, the rate of growth is not unusual: The number of judges has approximately doubled every 30 years since the end of the Civil War. [12] The caseload has also been increasing. Federal district courts heard about 270,000 civil cases and 37,000 criminal felony cases last year. The number represented a modest 2 percent increase over the previous year's total, but there had been double-digit caseload growth in the four previous years going back to 1992. *(See chart, p. 220.)*

For many judges, lawyers and experts, the growth results naturally from the country's increasing size and economic activity. Wilkinson, however, argues that increasing the number of federal judges contributes to the number of cases brought to federal courts and to increased intrusiveness toward state court systems. "Local disputes are tossed into federal court on the assumption that there will always be plenty of federal judges to resolve them," Wilkinson wrote.

Liberal advocates and experts deride Wilkinson's argument. "I don't know what he's talking about," says American University's Schwartz. "Federal judges do not file cases. Litigants file cases, and many of them have been waiting for a long, long time for justice simply because there are no judges."

The Alliance for Justice's Kline agrees. "That's absurd," he says of Wilkinson's argument, noting that federal court caseloads have increased tenfold since 1960 while the number of judges has only tripled.

Many liberal court-watchers, however, do complain about the growth of the federal courts' criminal caseload. Those concerns are also heard from many federal judges and bar leaders. "The tendency to throw more criminal cases into the federal courts is unwise," Shestack says. "Those cases belong in the state courts."

Some conservative members of Congress echo the complaints from conservative judges and advocates about the size of the federal judiciary. But Congress

itself plays a major part in increasing the federal courts' caseload — for example, by raising the penalties in drug cases, which makes prosecuting them in federal court more attractive to prosecutors, or by creating new federal remedies, like the recent law giving domestic violence victims the right to sue in federal court.

Meanwhile, Congress is loath to cut off access to federal courts. The Judicial Conference has long favored cutting back the federal courts' responsibilities for civil cases involving citizens of different states — so-called diversity jurisdiction. But Congress has refused to make major changes in the rules. Lawmakers instead have yielded to arguments from lawyers' groups that federal courts still provide an important safeguard against the possibility of state courts' favoring their own citizens against citizens of another state.

"It's kind of a chicken-and-egg problem," says Leo of the Federalist Society. "Congress passes all these laws that federalize all these issues. Congress also creates all these judgeships. The question is which comes first." ■

BACKGROUND

Power in the Making

When the Framers of the Constitution met in Philadelphia in 1787, they disagreed about the need for lower federal court judges in the new government. [13] Delegates who supported states' rights expressed concern about the cost, as well as the risk that federal judges would encroach on the existing state court systems. The compromise embodied in Article III was to provide for "one supreme Court" and "such inferior Courts as the Congress may from time

to time ordain and establish."

Even with the compromise, supporters of the Constitution had to allay concerns about the new federal judiciary during the debate over ratification of the Constitution. Writing in *The Federalist* (No. 78), Alexander Hamilton famously described the judiciary as "the weakest" and "the least dangerous" branch of the new government. But Hamilton also stressed the safeguards in the new Constitution for the independence of federal judges: life tenure and protection against salary reductions while in office.

When the First Congress turned to putting the new Constitution into effect, it immediately exercised the authority to create lower federal courts. The Judiciary Act of 1789 provided for a federal district court judge in each of the states and the territories of Maine and Kentucky, along with six justices on the Supreme Court. The act sought to safeguard federal power by giving the Supreme Court authority to review decisions by state courts questioning federal statutes or treaties. But lower federal courts had only limited powers: They were not given the power to hear all cases arising under federal laws even though the Constitution permitted such jurisdiction.

Congress did give federal courts jurisdiction over "federal question" cases in the ill-fated Judiciary Act of 1801, passed in the final days of John Adams' presidency. But Jeffersonian Republicans viewed the law as an effort by the outgoing Federalists to entrench their control of the federal judiciary. Congress repealed the measure within a year after Thomas Jefferson became president.

For the next 70 years, the federal judiciary remained relatively weak. By 1869, the number of federal judges had quadrupled to 61, but the nation's population had increased nearly tenfold, and the country had expanded to reach the Pacific Coast. Through most of the 19th century, federal judges did not even have their own

Continued on p. 228

Chronology

Before 1900
Federal courts have limited power for most of the period.

1789
After ratification of the Constitution, the Judiciary Act of 1789 lays the basis for the federal court system.

1875
Congress passes law giving federal courts jurisdiction over any cases involving claims under the Constitution or federal statutes.

1891
Congress establishes the Circuit Courts of Appeals, the first federal intermediate-level appellate court.

———— • ————

1901-1949
Congress creates administrative apparatus for federal judicial system; President Franklin D. Roosevelt reshapes Supreme Court and federal judiciary in more liberal image.

1922
At urging of Chief Justice William Howard Taft, Congress establishes the Judicial Conference of the United States to help coordinate work of federal courts.

1939
The Administrative Office of the United States Courts is created to supervise the administration of the courts.

1950s-1960s
Supreme Court under Chief Justice Earl Warren expands the role of federal judiciary in civil rights, criminal procedure and First Amendment areas.

1952
President Harry S Truman agrees to have the American Bar Association's Standing Committee on the Federal Judiciary evaluate potential nominees for federal courts; first use of the procedure, however, occurs under President Dwight D. Eisenhower.

———— • ————

1970s
Under Chief Justice Warren E. Burger, the Supreme Court tempers its activism. President Jimmy Carter appoints record number of women and minorities to the federal bench.

1978
Omnibus Judgeships Act creates 150 new federal judgeships; Carter issues executive order requiring "affirmative efforts" to identify women and minorities for court vacancies.

———— • ————

1980s
President Ronald Reagan gives a conservative cast to the federal judiciary with more than 380 appointments during eight years in office.

1986
Reagan nominates William H. Rehnquist, the Supreme Court's most conservative member, to be chief justice.

1990s
President Clinton steers a moderate course in judicial appointments but is criticized by some Republicans and conservatives for appointing liberal activists to the bench.

1996
Republican presidential candidate Bob Dole, R-Kan., attacks Clinton for appointing liberals to Supreme Court and lower federal courts, but accusation is dismissed by many observers; Congress passes several laws to limit powers of federal judges.

Jan. 20, 1997
More than 90 federal court posts are vacant as President Clinton is sworn in for a second four-year term.

April 1997
Senate Republicans reject moves to gain greater influence over judicial appointments, but adopt resolution opposing "judicial activism."

May 1997
House Majority Whip Tom DeLay, R-Texas, suggests impeachment of federal judges at Judiciary Committee hearing.

Jan. 1, 1998
Chief Justice Rehnquist, in his annual report on the judiciary, warns that "high levels" of federal court vacancies risk "eroding the quality of justice."

Jan. 28, 1998
The Senate, in its first business day of the new session, confirms three Clinton nominees to federal courts; Judiciary Committee Chairman Orrin G. Hatch, R-Utah, says he is satisfied with pace of confirmations.

Continued from p. 226

courthouses but used state or local government public buildings instead.

The growth of the national government after the Civil War, however, brought about a parallel increase in the size and powers of the federal judiciary. In 1875, Congress gave federal courts jurisdiction over all cases arising under the Constitution or federal statutes. The law had "a profound impact," according to historian Erwin Surrency, "changing the jurisdiction from a limited one to one embracing all federal rights." [14] Sixteen years later, Congress created a system of intermediate-level appellate courts between the trial courts and the Supreme Court — the Circuit Courts of Appeals.

The federal judiciary's work increased both because Congress was adding new federal laws and because judges themselves were taking on new powers. As early as the 1870s, Congress began expanding the federal government's criminal jurisdiction with laws prohibiting, for example, interstate trafficking in lotteries and obscene literature.

Beginning with the creation of the Interstate Commerce Commission to regulate railroads in the 1880s, Congress also began to put in place the beginning of the modern regulatory state. For their part, federal courts and, in particular, the Supreme Court, disapproved of some of these developments and crafted new doctrines to invalidate some economic regulations as violations of property rights.

The period of what can be regarded as conservative activism in the federal judiciary climaxed in the 1930s. In a two-year span, the Supreme Court struck down a total of eight laws that Congress had passed as part of President Franklin D. Roosevelt's New Deal program to lift the country out of the Depression. Roosevelt railed against the court and, in 1937, tried unsuccessfully to get Congress to give him power to appoint additional justices. Vacancies over the next few years, however, gave

Roosevelt the opportunity to remake both the Supreme Court and the lower federal courts in a more liberal image.

Liberal Activism

The federal judiciary's role in Americans' day-to-day lives has increased steadily since Roosevelt's second term. Each branch of the federal government contributed to the change. The Supreme Court played a major part with rulings that gave federal judges new powers over such areas as civil rights, criminal procedure and First Amendment issues. Congress also gave federal courts more work with laws expanding federal regulation of economic affairs as well as the federal government's law enforcement responsibilities. And — until Reagan's presidency — chief executives of both parties appointed judges who either embraced or accepted the federal judiciary's enlarged responsibilities. [15]

Roosevelt's success in giving the Supreme Court a liberal majority after the failure of his "court-packing" plan in 1937 is well-known. Less attention has been given to his comparable success in filling federal trial and appellate courts with New Deal supporters. As Goldman points out in his authoritative work *Picking Federal Judges*, Roosevelt took a personal interest in judicial selection and — especially after 1937 — gave top priority to "policy-agenda" considerations instead of political or personal factors in picking candidates for the federal bench. By his death, Roosevelt had appointed 133 district court judges and 50 appeals court judges — well over half the federal judiciary and far more than any previous president. The result, Goldman says, was "a New Deal Democratic judiciary." [16]

Roosevelt's success in remaking the federal judiciary allowed the next three Democratic presidents — Harry S

Truman, John F. Kennedy and Lyndon B. Johnson — to pay less attention to policy considerations in picking federal judges. Truman, in particular, looked on judicial selection primarily as a form of political patronage, according to Goldman. But civil rights was an important issue for each of them. Truman became the first president to appoint an African-American to a regular federal court judgeship when he named William Hastie to the federal appeals court in Philadelphia; Kennedy followed by appointing the first blacks to federal district court posts; and Johnson completed the breakthroughs by elevating Thurgood Marshall to the Supreme Court in 1967.

More broadly, Kennedy and Johnson both looked on support for civil rights as a litmus test for judicial candidates. Their efforts were complicated by the role that Southern senators played in recommending candidates for district court posts. In one notorious example, Mississippi Sen. James O. Eastland, who served as Judiciary Committee chairman, strongly urged an appointment for Harold Cox, who proved to be an ardent segregationist on the bench. For the most part, though, Kennedy and Johnson were successful in staffing the federal courts with pro-civil rights judges.

Affirmative Action

For their part, the three Republican presidents before Reagan — Dwight D. Eisenhower, Richard M. Nixon and Gerald R. Ford — gave even less attention to policy considerations in lower federal court appointments. Eisenhower largely delegated judicial selection to the Justice Department; his instructions appear to have been as he expressed at the time of a Supreme Court vacancy in 1958: to look for candidates who held "a middle-of-the-road political and governmental philosophy." [17] Nixon, despite his 1968 campaign pledge to reshape the Supreme Court, gave little attention to lower federal courts, according to Goldman. And Ford's brief two-year presidency was notable chiefly for a measure of bipartisanship in judicial appointments: Out of 64 appointees, 13 were Democrats — the highest percentage of nominees from the opposing party of any modern president.

With ideology unimportant to the GOP chief executives, their judicial appointees were largely moderates who did not set themselves against the trend of Supreme Court decision-making in civil rights, civil liberties and criminal procedure. The Warren Court thrust the federal judiciary into desegregation battles in the 1950s and oversight of state criminal justice systems in the 1960s.

Under Chief Justice Warren E. Burger, the court continued to enlarge the federal courts' role in some areas, such as abortion rights and prisoner rights. Meanwhile, liberalized rules on class-action suits and "legal standing" helped draw public-interest litigation into federal courts — producing the kind of ongoing court supervision of schools, prisons, mental hospitals and other institutions that cheered public-interest advocates and dismayed political conservatives.

Carter's presidency, undistinguished in many areas, had a profound impact on the federal judiciary. Like Johnson, the Georgia native was committed to opening up opportunities for African-Americans. But Carter had a broader commitment to naming women and members of other minority groups to the federal bench as well. In November 1978 — weeks after Congress created a record 150 new federal judgeships for him to fill — Carter issued a revised executive order that directed the attorney general to make "an affirmative effort" in the case of each vacancy to identify qualified candidates, including women and members of minority groups." [18]

Carter pressed his affirmative-action efforts through special nominating committees for federal appeals court vacancies and through pressure on Democratic senators to follow suit in their recommendations for district court posts. The result: among his 258 judicial appointments, Carter named a record number of women (40), African-Americans (37) and Hispanics (16). Some of Carter's appointees had played vital roles in enlarging the federal courts' role — like Ruth Bader Ginsburg, a leading women's rights litigator before her appointment to the federal appeals court in Washington, or Nathaniel Jones, the NAACP's longtime general counsel before his appointment to the federal appeals court in Cincinnati. More broadly, Carter's judges had grown up with a powerful federal judiciary, and most had few qualms about exercising those powers once on the bench.

Reagan's Mission

Reagan came to the White House with a mission to make the federal judiciary as conservative as it was liberal under Carter. Reagan campaigned for president in 1980 on a Republican platform that called for the appointment of federal judges who believed in "protecting the rights of law-abiding citizens," "decentralization of the federal government" and "the sanctity of innocent human life" — that is, opposition to abortion rights. [19]

Once in office, Reagan centralized decision-making for judicial appointments by establishing a Federal Judicial Selection Committee that included several presidential aides, including the White House counsel and Reagan's longtime adviser, Edwin Meese III, who later served as attorney general.

Although the Justice Department was represented on the committee and continued to have responsibility for background checks, the ongoing, active role for presidential aides in the process was an innovation. The delegation-prone

Reagan did not participate himself in the decision-making in most cases, but he did adopt a new practice of personally placing the call to offer the position to prospective nominees.

Early in his presidency, Reagan began staffing federal appeals courts with prominent, outspokenly conservative legal scholars. Robert H. Bork of Yale and Antonin Scalia of the University of Chicago were named to the D.C. Circuit, Richard Posner of the University of Chicago to the 7th Circuit and Ralph Winter of Yale to the 2nd Circuit. Other conservatives received appointments later: Chicago's Frank Easterbrook to the 7th Circuit and the University of Virginia's Wilkinson to the 4th Circuit. Reagan also elevated Scalia to the Supreme Court in 1986 and tried but failed to get a Supreme Court post for Bork the next year.

Bork failed to win Senate confirmation after critics depicted him as outside the ideological mainstream. Two other high-profile conservative scholars failed to win judicial posts for similar reasons: the University of Texas' Lino Graglia and the University of San Diego's Bernard Siegan. Two Southern conservatives failed to get judicial posts because of their civil rights views: Alabama attorney Jeff Sessions, now a Republican U.S. senator, and Louisiana Gov. David C. Treen.

Within the administration, some potential nominees were either dropped or delayed because of views regarded as too liberal by the White House judge-pickers or outside conservative groups. The most prominent victim was Judith Whittaker, a corporate lawyer in Kansas City and daughter-in-law of former Supreme Court Justice Charles E. Whittaker. She had the support of many leading Missouri Republicans, including Sen. John C. Danforth, a member of the Judiciary Committee. But the administration dropped her after conservative activists accused her of being a "pro-abortionist." Whittaker and her supporters said she had never taken a position on the issue, but their pleas were unavailing.

Reagan's efforts to shift the federal

judiciary to the right bore fruit, both at the Supreme Court and in the lower courts. Reagan's four appointments to the high court, combined with Bush's appointment of Clarence Thomas in 1991, produced a conservative majority that cut back on affirmative action and defendants' rights even though it disappointed conservatives by failing to overturn the *Roe v. Wade* abortion-rights decision. In the lower courts, Reagan's judges rank among the most conservative of any president's appointees in the past 80 years, according to a study by three longtime judicial scholars.

In a study published in 1993, they found that Reagan-appointed district court judges issued "liberal" decisions in 36 percent of their cases — the lowest figure of any of the previous presidents studied, dating back to Woodrow Wilson. Although Bush's appointees ranked slightly more conservative in that study, a later compilation published in 1996 found that Reagan's district court judges were more conservative than Bush's, although Bush's appeals court judges were slightly more conservative than Reagan's. [20]

As those figures indicated, Bush continued Reagan's work in moving the federal courts toward the right. The results could be seen in more and more trial-level and appellate decisions that favored law enforcement, narrowed civil rights remedies and backed governmental interests in individual rights issues. Quantitatively, the 12 years of Republican appointments produced a federal bench that included the highest percentage of GOP appointees — 72 percent — since Herbert Hoover left the White House in 1933.

Clinton's Moderation

B ill Clinton campaigned for the White House in 1992 and again in 1996 as a "New Democrat." The label was intended to connote more moderate stances on crime and law enforcement, among other issues. After five years in office, his appointments to the federal bench are regarded by a wide range of legal experts as generally moderate, but still denounced by many Republicans and conservatives as liberal activists. There is no dispute, though, that Clinton has made history with the large number of women and minorities he has named to the bench. Indeed, as Goldman points out, a majority of the judges Clinton appointed during his first term were either women or minorities — a record unequaled by any previous president. [21]

In his first two years in office, Clinton made two appointments to the Supreme Court that somewhat typified his approach to judicial selection. Ruth Bader Ginsburg and Stephen G. Breyer were both experienced appellate judges with somewhat moderate reputations; both won confirmation relatively easily, with only a few Republican senators voting against them. His first-term appointments to district and appeals courts similarly drew relatively little controversy. Only two were brought up for roll-call votes in the Senate — Rosemary Barkett and H. Lee Sarokin — and both won confirmation with more than 60 votes.

Liberals were quietly disappointed with the moderate cast to Clinton's appointments. In one publicized episode, Clinton backed away from appointing Peter Edelman, a longtime friend serving as assistant secretary in the Department of Health and Human Services, when the liberal former law professor drew criticism from Senate Republicans. But conservatives insisted Clinton's appointees were more liberal than their reputation. As the 1996 campaign got under way, Terry Eastland, a former Reagan Justice Department official turned commentator, complained that Clinton had "managed to appoint liberal if 'no-name' judges." [22]

Republicans tried to make an issue of Clinton's judicial appointments in the 1996 campaign, but to little effect. Judge Harold Baer, a Clinton appointee to the federal district court in New York, became the target of attacks after he suppressed 80 pounds of cocaine and heroin seized as evidence from a confessed drug courier. Baer ruled police had no probable cause for the search after stopping the suspect for a traffic violation, saying in part that she ran away because residents of the predominantly African-American neighborhood had reason to view police as "corrupt, violent and abusive."

The decision, along with the provocative comment, provoked a storm of protest. Congressional Republicans used the episode as exhibit No. 1 in attacks on Clinton's appointees. Clinton himself disagreed with the ruling. Baer, in a highly unusual move, reversed himself on April 1 and then pulled out of the case.

Even after the reversal, however, Senate Republican leader and prospective presidential nominee Dole said Baer exemplified the "liberal judicial activism" of Clinton's appointees. Clinton's re-election, he said in an April 19 speech to the American Society of Newspaper Editors, would result in "an all-star team of liberal leniency." The White House called the attack "phony." "[T]he president has appointed moderate, mainstream judges," White House counsel Jack Quinn said. "That's why Bob Dole voted for 98 percent of them." [23]

The dust-up stayed in the news for a while, but observers generally agreed that the issue was not generating much support for the Republicans, and it faded before fall. Meanwhile, though, the Republican-controlled Congress was taking action on another front by enacting new restrictions on the powers of federal courts. The Illegal Immigration Reform and Immigrant Responsibility Act sharply curtailed the power of federal judges to block deportations. The Prison Litigation Reform Act limited federal judges' powers in prisoner rights cases. And the Antiterrorism and Effective Death Penalty Act established stringent new limits on the power of federal judges in habeas corpus cases to overturn state court convictions or sentences.

The voters' decision to send Clinton back to the White House with a Republican-controlled Congress set the stage for more conflict over judicial appointments in his second term. The confirmation process had slowed to a walk during the campaign: The Senate approved no appellate judges and only 17 district court judges during the year. And the Senate continued to take its time on judicial nominations during most of 1997. By September, only nine Clinton nominees had been confirmed. Clinton complained of the delays in one of his weekly radio addresses, echoing criticisms voiced earlier in the year by, among others, Vermont's Leahy, the ranking member of the Judiciary Committee.

The criticisms appeared to have some effect: The Senate confirmed 27 judges during the next two months, raising the year's total to 36. But the year ended with 82 vacancies left and 41 Clinton nominations pending. Chief Justice Rehnquist's decision to raise the issue in his year-end report on the judiciary gave Clinton and Senate Democrats a new opportunity to pressure Senate Republicans on the question. "The judicial system is more important than playing politics," the White House declared in a prepared statement. But Hatch was unapologetic. "The No. 1 problem," he told *The New York Times*, "happens to be activist judges who continue to find laws that aren't there and expand the law beyond the intent of Congress."[24] ■

CURRENT SITUATION

Unblocking the Jam

T he nomination of Ann L. Aiken to a federal judgeship in Oregon in 1995

Scott Ferrell

File Photo

Sen. Orrin G. Hatch, R-Utah, and Rep. Tom DeLay, R-Texas (bottom)

attracted little attention outside her state as it moved through the Senate. But the state trial judge finally won confirmation to the federal bench in January only after a 26-month delay and with 30 Republi-

can senators opposing her.

Aiken's opponents gave only one reason for voting against her on Jan. 28: her 1993 decision to sentence a man convicted of raping a 5-year-old girl to a 90-day jail sentence with five years' probation instead of a five-year prison term, the other option under state law.

Aiken explained at the time that the defendant could enroll in a sex-offender treatment program in jail but there was no such program in prison and that five years' probation following the jail term would allow stricter supervision than parole after a prison term. In the Senate debate, however, Republican Michael B. Enzi of Wyoming said the ruling was evidence of Aiken's "unjustified leniency toward convicted criminals."

Missouri's Ashcroft agreed. "I find this type of social engineering from the bench troubling," he said.

Aiken's supporters, including Oregon's two senators, Democrat Ron Wyden and Republican Gordon H. Smith, also faulted the decision, but they noted that Aiken herself had expressed regrets about her handling of the case. They also cited other examples of cases where Aiken had handed down sentences at the top of the permissible range. "Judge Aiken has been tough on crime throughout her career," Smith said.

Opposing interest groups draw different conclusions from the episode. Kline of the Alliance for Justice is surprised that 30 senators would vote against a nominee because of a single ruling. "That was the only thing against her in the record," Kline said. "And she was doing exactly what the legislature allowed."

But the Free Congress Foundation boasted that the 30 votes against Aiken were double the number that observers had anticipated. And it laid the groundwork for similar attacks on other Clinton nominees. In a "judicial nomination memorandum," the group cited evidence of what it described as activism on the part of seven Clinton nominees.

Meanwhile, the Senate was holding off a final decision on Clinton's nomination of Massiah-Jackson to be Philadelphia's first black federal trial court judge; she cleared the Judiciary Committee by a 12-6 vote. But Ashcroft put a hold on the nomination at the end of the 1997 session.

The Pennsylvania District Attorneys Association then launched a campaign against her, citing accounts of Massiah-Jackson's actions in some 50 or so cases as evidence that she was soft on crime and hard on police and prosecutors. The attack touched off a sharp debate in Philadelphia that included dueling press conferences, advertisements in the city's legal newspaper and a small rally of Massiah-Jackson's supporters at the state courthouse. [25]

Meanwhile, conservative groups in Washington helped turn the local controversy into a national issue, papering senators' offices with fliers repeating the prosecutors' attack on the judge. Pennsylvania's two Republican senators, Arlen Specter and Rick Santorum, responded by backing away from their previous support for Massiah-Jackson. Santorum predicted in January that she would not get the votes needed for confirmation. And when the Senate began debating the nomination on Feb. 10, Specter called for delaying a vote in order to permit the Judiciary Committee to review the cases cited by the district attorneys; a new hearing was to be held on March 11.

Limiting the Judiciary

When two Texas legislators sought to intervene in the state's long-running prison overcrowding suit two years ago, the federal judge overseeing the case turned them down. But the lawmakers filed a new motion in December, thanks to an amendment passed by Congress late last year that gives any state or local official the right to intervene in such suits under certain conditions. [26]

The little-noticed provision was added to a must-pass money bill by House Republican whip DeLay. A strong critic of so-called activist federal judges, he delights in believing that his amendment riled the judge in the case.

"He's been legislating from the bench," DeLay says of the judge, William Wayne Justice, a 30-year veteran of the federal bench who has been overseeing the prison overcrowding suit since the 1970s.

"He wouldn't allow other parties in this suit," DeLay explains. "I opened it up so that other parties like state legislators could enter. I understand it drove him crazy." [27]

DeLay's amendment was one of many legislative proposals introduced in the current Congress aimed at what the conservative Federalist Society calls "relimiting" the federal judiciary. Some of the other proposals were also responses to decisions by federal judges that angered individual lawmakers:

• The late Rep. Sonny Bono, R-Calif., introduced a bill to require the convening of a three-judge federal court to rule on the constitutionality of any voter-approved state initiative or referendum. Lower court federal judges have ruled three California initiatives invalid in the past two years, though two of those rulings were overturned on appeal.

• Sen. Specter introduced a bill to limit the ability of a federal judge reviewing a state criminal conviction on habeas corpus to bar the state from retrying the defendant. The bill came after a federal judge in Philadelphia ruled that a defendant in a highly publicized murder case was "actually innocent" and could not be tried again. [28] (That ruling was also overturned on appeal, and the case is now back in state court.)

• A House Judiciary subcommittee approved a bill last summer that includes a provision to bar federal judges from forcing a tax increase on state or local governments. The subcommittee acted after a federal judge in Kansas City forced a property tax increase to pay for improvements he ordered in a

school desegregation case.

Other proposals are aimed at more general complaints about the federal judiciary. The House Judiciary subcommittee's bill also includes a provision to allow litigants in the country's biggest federal court districts a right to one reassignment to a different judge. New Hampshire's Sen. Smith is sponsoring a proposed constitutional amendment to abolish life tenure for federal judges and instead give them 10-year terms.

So far, DeLay's measure is the only provision to make its way into law. But the proposals have drawn sharp attacks from bar leaders, court advocates and liberal advocates and experts. "They're very dangerous in terms of the precedent that they would be setting," says Kline. "I would put them in the realm of attacks on the independence of the judiciary rather than good-faith efforts to improve the system."

But Leo of the Federalist Society says the criticisms are overdrawn. Still, he acknowledges that conservatives have mixed views about some of the proposals. "Conservatives are not of one mind," he says. "There are some conservatives who want to limit the terms of federal judges. There are others who think that is a very dangerous means of dealing with this problem."

DeLay himself opposes any change in judicial tenure. "I believe in the Constitution and the way judges are appointed and serve," he says. But he also continues to defend the threat he first made last spring to use impeachment to remove judges for issuing "activist" decisions that go beyond their constitutional powers. (See story, p. 234.)

For their part, liberal advocates say most of the proposed changes are unwarranted. "We're concerned that the legislative branch is tinkering with the balance of powers between the branches based on some very extreme examples," says Ira Pilchen, associate editor of the American Judicature Society's magazine

Continued on p. 234

At Issue:

Do the current attacks on federal judges for being too "activist" threaten judicial independence?

STEPHAN O. KLINE
Legislative counsel, Alliance for Justice

WRITTEN FOR THE CQ RESEARCHER, FEBRUARY 1998.

*t*he judiciary is under attack, threatened by numerous vacancies and assaults on judicial independence. Politically driven legislation would curtail many powers exercised by federal judges, eliminate judicial seats and restructure courts for partisan results. Proposed constitutional amendments would impose term limits and elections of judges. Hearings were convened on "Judicial Misconduct and Discipline," equating judicial activism with violations of the law and serving notice that judges will be harassed for their decisions.

Criticism is levied against those judges who refute the "will of the people," but only if they issue "liberal" decisions. Oregon District Judge Michael Hogan blocked implementation of the Death with Dignity Act, a referendum permitting doctor-assisted suicide; no objections were ever raised by conservatives. However, when California District Judge Thelton Henderson temporarily stopped Proposition 209, an initiative seeking to end state affirmative action programs, he became a judicial activist.

The recent and overwhelming Senate vote confirming Margaret Morrow's nomination demonstrates the emptiness of these charges of judicial activism. Morrow, a corporate litigator and former president of the California Bar, became "judicial activist incarnate" because of her membership in California Women Lawyers and supposed challenge of the initiative process. Eventually, the Senate discovered the meritlessness of these claims, but Morrow was forced to put her life on hold for more than 21 months, and the vacancy contributed to slower justice in Los Angeles.

The Senate's first debate of 1998 revealed the unfair tactics and strategies being used in the confirmation process. Despite her excellent credentials as a state judge, the Senate delayed Ann Aiken's confirmation for 26 months, because of a single decision.

Some say that the confirmation battles are replays of the Bork and Thomas debates, but the analogies are inappropriate. The fight over those Supreme Court confirmations involved single nominees, rather than an effort to completely shut down the confirmation process; and both Judge Bork and Justice Thomas received their "day in court" and the process to which they were entitled. Collectively, the current attacks on judges and judicial nominees are unprecedented, unwise and dangerous. They amount to the most severe assault on judicial independence since President Franklin D. Roosevelt's infamous court-packing plan of 1937.

THOMAS L. JIPPING
Director, Free Congress Foundation's Judicial Selection Monitoring Project

WRITTEN FOR THE CQ RESEARCHER, FEBRUARY 1998.

*a*merica's founders separated three government branches, allowing each to check the others' power, and created self-government under a written Constitution. This naturally requires that unelected federal judges take the law as it is and not make it up.

Some of America's founders actually opposed the new Constitution because it might allow judges to change the law through "interpretation." Alexander Hamilton assured the others that judges would not dare usurp legislative power because Congress could impeach them for it. The phrase "judicial activism" today identifies this excessive judicial power.

Feigned confusion notwithstanding, judicial activism is not difficult to define. In an episode of ABC's "The Practice" last September, Ed Asner's judicial character asked: "Do you really think I should leave legislative policy to the legislature?" Even Hollywood gets it.

Those whose political agenda is unpopular also get it and turn from the statehouse to the courthouse. Because it is impossible with a straight face to defend turning judges into legislators, however, the only way to preserve their little racket is to make everyone butt out of activist judges' business. They want to turn "judicial independence" into a gimmick protecting a judge's improper excesses.

Yet what does judicial independence really mean when Congress can establish, rearrange, and even abolish all tribunals but the Supreme Court; regulate their jurisdiction; control their budgets; and confirm or impeach their members?

Real judicial independence is internal rather than external. America's founders said judges must only exercise "judgment" and not "will." Judicial independence is threatened not by Congress exercising legitimate power but by judges exercising illegitimate power.

In May 1991, with 146 judicial vacancies, Alliance for Justice President Nan Aron called for "grass-roots vigilance" pressuring senators to reject nominees she did not like. Today, with 80 judicial vacancies, the Alliance says the same strategy involving nominees they like is an "attack" on "judicial independence."

America needs independent judges who take the law as it is and won't make it up. Legitimate congressional efforts to check excessive judicial power, or involvement by grass-roots Americans simply cannot threaten judicial independence. It's time to blow away the smoke and debate the real issue.

Critics' Call to Impeach Judges . . .

T he people of Lancaster County, Pa., reacted strongly last year after a federal judge ordered the release of a young woman who had been convicted of slitting the throat of a romantic rival. An estimated 37,000 of the county's residents signed petitions demanding that the judge, Stewart B. Dalzell, be impeached and removed from office. [1]

The calls for impeachment have faded now that a federal appeals court has set aside Dalzell's order. But critics of the federal judiciary in Washington are continuing to defend the idea that a federal judge can be impeached not merely for committing a crime but also for issuing rulings that go beyond his or her authority as a judge.

"I agree with Gerald Ford, with Justice John Marshall, with Thomas Jefferson in saying that you can impeach a federal judge for anything you can get a majority of the House to vote for," says House Majority Whip Tom DeLay, R-Texas. DeLay first broached the idea of impeaching "activist" federal judges a year ago, first in interviews and then in an appearance before a House Judiciary subcommittee. [2]

Under the Constitution, the House can impeach, or accuse, a judge by a simple majority. It takes a two-thirds vote in the Senate to convict the judge and remove him or her from office.

"Obviously, it would have to be pretty serious in order to get that kind of vote," DeLay acknowledges. "But this notion that a judge has to go break the law before he can be impeached is ridiculous."

DeLay's comments attracted immediate attention and widespread — and continuing — criticism from a range of advocates and experts, including some fellow conservatives.

"We've never had impeachment on the ground of disagreeing with a judge, and I don't favor that," says Ronald Rotunda, a conservative law professor at the University of Illinois in Champaign. "It would be troubling to go down that road."

Herman Schwartz, a liberal law professor at American University in Washington, more bluntly labels DeLay's comments "evil, pernicious talk." And Leslie Ann Reis, director of the American Judicature Society's Center for Judicial Independence, calls the talk of impeachment "very scary."

"Impeachment is supposed to be the remedy for high crimes and misdemeanors committed by judges, not for unpopular decisions," Reis says.

In fact, all of the seven judges removed from office by the impeachment process were found guilty of judicial misconduct or criminal behavior. But partisan motives figured in the country's first judicial impeachment.

In 1803 President Thomas Jefferson sent to the House of Representatives evidence of drunken and profane behavior on the bench by a Federalist-appointed federal judge, John Pickering of New Hampshire. Two months later, Jefferson followed with a complaint about partisan behavior by a Supreme Court justice, the Federalist Samuel Chase.

With Jefferson's Democratic-Republicans in control of Congress, Pickering was impeached by the House and a

---

Continued from p. 232
Judicature. "The balance provides for protections that have served us well in the long run." ∎

OUTLOOK

Continued Slowdown?

W hen a federal judge in Washington last month ruled the newly enacted line-item veto law unconstitutional, there was hardly a peep about judicial activism. The Feb. 12 ruling by U.S. District Court Judge Thomas F. Hogan threw out a budget-control measure strongly pushed by President Clinton and congressional Republicans. But neither Clinton nor GOP lawmakers challenged Hogan's power to entertain the challenge to the law — or the Supreme Court's ultimate authority to settle the issue, which it is likely to do before July. [29]

The muted reaction to the line-item veto ruling is evidence of the quiet acceptance of the federal judiciary's role in settling disputes between the other two branches of the federal government. But the federal courts' role in protecting individual rights has always been more controversial, whether exercised in disputes involving the national government itself or state or local governments.

Today's critics believe that too many federal judges have gone overboard in protecting individual rights by going beyond the text of the Constitution and the Bill of Rights. "Very few judges admit that they ignore the text," says former Justice Department official Troy, "but they construe the text in such a flexible manner that they rob it of any meaning."

But the federal judiciary's defenders say the attacks threaten the ability of federal judges to protect individual rights. "This is telling judges that if in all good conscience you find an individual's constitutional rights have been violated, you are in peril," Goldman says. "If you think you are going to be promoted to the court of appeals level, forget it. And maybe we might have the muscle at some point to start impeachment proceedings."

The critics show no signs, however, of letting up. Jipping vows to keep up pressure both on the Clinton administration and Senate Republicans to try to delay or block some of the president's judicial nominees.

... Termed 'Evil' and 'Very Scary'

year later convicted by the Senate. But Chase was acquitted after a two-month Senate trial in 1805; historians view the outcome as an important milestone in establishing the independence of the judiciary in the United States.

Since that time, no Supreme Court justice has been impeached, and the six other lower court federal judges who were impeached and convicted were cited for judicial misconduct or criminal offenses. Three U.S. District Court judges were removed from office in the 1980s, all for charges arising from criminal prosecutions. [3]

As House Republican leader in 1970, however, then-Rep. Gerald R. Ford of Michigan called for the impeachment of Justice William O. Douglas based on five allegations of judicial misconduct. Ford's remark that the House was free to determine what actions would constitute "high crimes and misdemeanors" for purposes of the Constitution's impeachment clause has been quoted ever since by those who favor an expansive view of Congress' removal power.

In his remarks, DeLay has listed a number of federal judges for possible impeachment. Among his targets: Harold Baer in New York, who stirred a national debate by throwing out evidence in a major federal drug case; Fred Biery in Del Rio, Texas, who blocked local election officials from counting absentee ballots cast by members of the military who no longer lived in the area; and Thelton Henderson of San Francisco, who ruled unconstitutional the California initiative banning racial preferences in state programs.

Thomas Jipping, director of the Free Congress Foundation's Judicial Selection Project, says DeLay's views are in line with those of the Framers of the Constitution. "They believed that a pattern of activist decisions which evidences a judge's acting outside his role was impeachable," Jipping says. "The Founding Fathers thought so, and we believe so too."

But most of the reaction to DeLay's remarks has ranged from critical to incredulous. "I can't believe that any discussion of impeachment can be treated seriously," says Jerome Shestack, president of the American Bar Association.

"Of course, that's all threat and bluster," says Sheldon Goldman, a political scientist at the University of Massachusetts in Amherst and a leading liberal expert on the federal judiciary. "I don't think anyone believes that can happen here."

---

[1] See *The New York Times*, Dec. 27, 1997, p. A1. Dalzell was appointed in 1991 by President George Bush, although a conservative fundraising video described him as an example of "activist liberal judges" appointed by President Clinton. See *The New York Times*, Nov. 3, 1997, p. A23.

[2] See *The Washington Times*, March 12, 1997, p. A1.

[3] The District judges removed after conviction in impeachment trials in the 1990s were West H. Humphreys (1862, supported secession); Robert W. Archbald (1913, financial misconduct); Halsted L. Ritter (1936, bringing office into disrepute); Harry E. Claiborne (1986, tax fraud); Alcee L. Hastings (1989, conspiracy to accept a bribe) and Walter L. Nixon Jr. (1989, lying under oath). Hastings is now a Democratic representative from Florida in the House.

"The Republican Senate has not defeated a single [Clinton] nominee," Jipping complains. "I don't see the Senate Republicans yet determined to act on what they said they believed last year, when they passed a resolution opposing judicial activism." [30]

Hatch has promised to step up the pace of hearings on Clinton's nominations. But liberal lobbying groups acknowledge the conservatives' campaign will likely slow the confirmation process.

"There are going to be some conservative wedge issues; there will be an attack on some judges," Kline says. "There will be more nominees confirmed this year [than last year]," he adds, "but not as many as in 1994, for example."

The slowdown creates problems both for the courts and for the nominees themselves. "It creates delays in docketing all over the country, especially in civil cases,"

says Leslie Ann Reis, director of the American Judicature Society's Center for Judicial Independence. For nominees, Reis says, the delays "certainly can take a toll in terms of putting their professional and personal lives on hold."

Conservatives are less concerned about the courts' ability to handle current caseloads. "Appellate judges are not overwhelmed, overburdened or overworked," Troy says. "There may be some district courts where they need a few more judges, but I still don't think that merely filling those slots for the sake of filling them serves the public."

For its part, the U.S. Judicial Conference is urging Congress to create 36 additional permanent judgeships and 17 temporary slots to deal with "the continuing high caseload" in the federal courts. Sen. Leahy introduced legislation embodying the request last May; no one

expects it to be acted on this year.

As for judicial nominations, the Senate continues to move at a measured pace. On March 2, senators gave unanimous approval to the nomination of an Indiana trial judge, Richard L. Young, to the United States District Court in Indianapolis; Young became the sixth federal judge confirmed in the first three months of the session.

"The Senate is not living up to its responsibilities," Leahy declared during the brief floor debate. "We are not measuring up to the pace this very Senate attained last fall."

In fact, the number of vacancies has risen since the beginning of the year because of various retirements. As of March 1, the Administrative Office of U.S. Courts said there were a total of 87 vacancies, including 24 appellate positions, 60 district court posts and three seats on the U.S. Court of International Trade. The office said 47 nominations were pending before the Senate.

Jipping continues, however, to minimize the importance of vacancy counts. "Pulling a single figure out of the air and trying to give some significance to it is impossible," he says.

For his part, Kline says numbers are important, but they are only part of the story. "It's not just a numbers game," he says. "It's treating people fairly and treating the judiciary with respect." ■

Notes

[1] For coverage of the report and reaction, see *The New York Times*, Jan. 2, 1998, p. A1, and *The Washington Post*, Jan. 2, 1998, p. A1.

[2] Orrin Hatch, "Judicial Nominees: The Senate's Steady Progress," *The Washington Post*, Jan. 11, 1998, p. C9.

[3] Judge Richard P. Matsch in Denver conducted the trials of Timothy McVeigh and Terry Nichols for the 1995 bombing of the Oklahoma City federal building; Judge Garland E. Burrell Jr. in Sacramento presided over the trial of Theodore Kaczynski in the Unabomber case; and Judge Kevin Thomas Duffy in New York presided over the trial of Ramzi Ahmed Yousef for the 1993 World Trade Center bombing. For profiles of the judges, see *The New York Times*, Jan. 9, 1998, p. A14 (Matsch); the *Los Angeles Times*, Nov. 24, 1997, p. A1 (Burrell); *The New York Times*, Aug. 10, 1997, p. 31 (Duffy).

[4] For background, see "States and Federalism," *The CQ Researcher*, Sept. 13, 1996, pp. 793-816 and "Supreme Court Preview," *The CQ Researcher*, Sept. 17, 1993, pp. 817-840.

[5] American Bar Association, "An Independent Judiciary: Report of the Commission on Separation of Powers and Judicial Independence," July 4, 1997, p. vi.

[6] Quoted in the *Los Angeles Times*, May 30, 1997, p. A1. The number of vacancies rose to 10 last summer, then dropped back to nine with the Senate's confirmation of Judge Barry Silverman of Arizona in late January.

[7] For representative coverage, see *The Washington Post*, May 15, 1997, p. A1 (Texas); *Las Vegas Review Journal*, Aug. 13, 1997, p. 9A (Nevada); *The Chicago Tribune*, Aug. 15, 1997, p. 1 (Illinois).

[8] See Herman Schwartz, "The GOP's Judicial Delays and the Cost to Minorities," *Los Angeles Times*, Feb. 15, 1998, p. M1.

[9] "Dialogue: Are 1,000 Federal Judges Enough?"

The New York Times, May 17, 1993, p. A17. See also Federal Judicial Center, "Imposing a Moratorium on the Number of Federal Judges: Analysis of Arguments and Implications," 1993.

[10] Judicial Conference of the United States, "Long Range Plan for the Federal Courts," December 1995, p. 38.

[11] J. Harvie Wilkinson III, "We Don't Need More Federal Judges," *The Wall Street Journal*, Feb. 9, 1998, p. A16.

[12] Deborah J. Barrow, Gary Zuk and Gerard S. Gryski, *The Federal Judiciary and Institutional Change* (1996), p. 3.

[13] Some background is drawn from Erwin Surrency, *History of the Federal Courts* (1987). See also Robert A. Carp and Ronald Stidham, *The Federal Courts* [2nd ed.] (1991), pp. 1-36.

[14] Surrency, *op. cit.*, p. 49.

[15] Background and statistics on presidential nominations to the federal courts are drawn from Sheldon Goldman, *Picking Federal Judges: Lower Court Selection from Roosevelt through Reagan* (1997).

[16] *Ibid.*, p. 68.

[17] Quoted in *Ibid.*, p. 124.

[18] Quoted in *Ibid.*, p. 247.

[19] Background for this section, as well as the title, are drawn from *Ibid.*, pp. 285-345. The quote from the GOP platform is on p. 297.

[20] See Robert A. Carp, Donald Songer, C.K. Rowland, Ronald Stidham and Lisa Richey-Tracy, "The Voting Behavior of Judges Appointed by President Bush," *Judicature*, April-May 1993, pp. 298-302, and Ronald Stidham,

Robert A. Carp and Donald R. Songerm "The Voting Behavior of President Clinton's Judicial Appointees," *Judicature*, July-August 1996, pp. 16-20.

[21] See Sheldon Goldman and Elliot Slotnick, "Clinton's First Term Judiciary: Many Bridges to Cross," *Judicature*, May/June 1997, pp. 254-273; "Clinton's Nontraditional Judges: Creating a More Representative Bench," *Ibid.*, September-October 1994, pp. 68-73.

[22] Terry Eastland, "If Clinton Wins, Here's What the Courts Will Look Like," *The Wall Street Journal*, Feb. 28, 1996, p. A15.

[23] See *The New York Times*, April 20, 1998, p. 1.

[24] Quoted in *The New York Times*, Jan. 2, 1998, p. A1.

[25] See *The Philadelphia Inquirer*, Jan. 21, 1998, p. A1, and Feb. 1, 1998, p. B1.

[26] For background, see *Legal Times*, Nov. 24, 1997, p. 1.

[27] For background on the Texas prison case, see *The Fort Worth Star-Telegram*, Dec. 25, 1997, p. 1 (Metro section).

[28] Specter's bill would allow a federal judge to prohibit a retrial only for violation of a specified constitutional right, such as the right to a speedy trial or the right against double jeopardy. The defendant in the case is Lisa Michelle Lambert; for an account of the appeals court ruling, see *The New York Times*, Dec. 30, 1997, p. A13.

[29] For background, see *Congressional Quarterly Weekly Report*, Feb. 14, 1998, p. 380.

[30] For background, see *The New York Times*, April 30, 1997, p. D22.

FOR MORE INFORMATION

Alliance for Justice, 2000 P St. N.W., Suite 712, Washington, D.C. 20036; 202-822-6070; http://www.afj.org. The alliance represents some 40 liberal advocacy groups on issues affecting the judicial system.

American Bar Association, 750 North Lake Shore Dr., Chicago, Ill. 60611; 312-988-5000; http://www.abanet.org. The ABA is the country's largest voluntary bar organization, with about 390,000 members.

American Judicature Society, 180 N. Michigan Ave., Suite 600, Chicago, Ill. 60601-7401; 312-558-6900; http://www.ajs.org. The AJS is an organization of lawyers, judges and others devoted to improving the administration of justice in state and federal courts.

Federalist Society, 1015 18th St. N.W., Suite 425, Washington, D.C. 20036; 202-822-8138; http://www.fed_soc.org. The Federalist Society for Law and Public Policy Studies is a group of conservatives and libertarians interested in a variety of legal issues.

Federal Judicial Center, 1 Columbus Circle N.E., Washington, D.C. 20002; 202 273-4000; http://www.fjc.gov. The center is the research arm of the federal court system.

Free Congress Foundation, Judicial Selection Monitoring Project, 717 2nd St. N.E., Washington, D.C. 20002; (202) 546-3004; http://www.fcref.org. The project serves as a clearinghouse for some 400 conservative organizations on issues affecting the judicial system.

Bibliography

Selected Sources Used

Books

Barrow, Deborah J., Gary Zuk and Gerard S. Gryski, *The Federal Judiciary and Institutional Change*, University of Michigan Press, 1996,

The book traces the organizational development of the federal judicial system from Reconstruction through 1992. It includes statistical tables on the size and partisan composition of the federal judiciary as well as detailed source notes. Barrow is a lawyer; Zuk and Gryski are associate professors of political science at Auburn University.

Carp, Robert A., and Ronald Stidham, *The Federal Courts* [2nd ed.], Congressional Quarterly, 1991.

The book provides a compact overview of the history and current structure of the federal courts. Detailed chapter notes and an eight-page bibliography are included. Carp is a professor of political science at the University of Houston; Stidham is a professor of political science and criminal justice at Appalachian State University. They are also the authors of *Judicial Process in America* (Congressional Quarterly, 3rd ed., 1995).

Goldman, Sheldon, Picking Federal Judges: *Lower Court Selection from Roosevelt through Reagan*, Yale University Press, 1997.

Goldman, a professor of political science at the University of Massachusetts and a leading expert on selection of federal judges, provides a chapter-by-chapter analysis of the judges appointed by each of the presidents from Franklin D. Roosevelt through Ronald Reagan. The book includes statistical tables on judges appointed by each of the presidents along with detailed source notes.

***Hart and Wechsler's The Federal Courts and the Federal System* [3rd ed.], University Casebooks, 1990.**

This comprehensive law school casebook includes excerpts and commentary on major decisions by the Supreme Court and other federal court rulings affecting the powers and organization of the federal judicial system from *Marbury v. Madison* (1803) to the present. The current editors are Paul M. Bator, University of Chicago Law School; Daniel J. Meltzer and David Shapiro, Harvard Law School, and Paul J. Mishkin, University of California-Berkeley School of Law.

Katzmann, Robert, *Courts and Congress*, Brookings Institution/Governance Institute, 1997.

Katzmann, a visiting fellow at the Brookings Institution, examines the relationship between Congress and the federal judiciary in two major areas: confirmations and statutory interpretation. The book includes detailed source notes.

Surrency, Erwin, *History of the Federal Courts*,

Oceana Publications, 1987.

The book traces the history of the federal courts from the Articles of Confederation and the First Judiciary Act of 1789 through the expansion of the federal judiciary's role beginning in the late 19th century. The book includes detailed chapter notes. Surrency is a professor and director of the law library at the University of Georgia.

Volcansek, Mary L., *Judicial Impeachment: None Called for Justice*, University of Illinois, 1993.

Volcansek, a professor of political science at Florida International University, details the recent impeachment trials of three federal judges: Harry E. Claiborne, Alcee L. Hastings and Walter L. Nixon. The book includes a 10-page list of references.

Articles

"Relimiting Federal Judicial Power: Should Congress Play a Role?" *Journal of Law and Politics* (University of Virginia), summer 1997, pp. 627-668; "Term Limits for Judges?" *Ibid.*, pp. 669-703.

The journal includes presentations by speakers at a 1996 conference sponsored by the Federalist Society on proposals to limit the power of federal judges and to establish term limits for federal judges.

Reports and Studies

American Bar Association, *An Independent Judiciary: Report of the Commission on Separation of Powers and Judicial Independence*, July 4, 1997.

The ABA commission's 65-page report calls for protecting the independence of federal judges by preserving life tenure, limiting talk of impeachment, providing cost-of-living pay increases and having bar associations counter unfair criticism of the judiciary. The report also includes a historical essay on the evolution of judicial independence and a five-page bibliography.

Judicial Conference of the United States, *Long Range Plan for the Federal Courts*, December 1995.

The 205-page report was intended to serve as a framework for planning the structure and operations of the federal judiciary in the 21st century. The conference's 91 recommendations include a number of steps to control the number of cases in federal courts.

Jipping, Thomas L., *Selecting and Confirming Federal Judges: What Has Gone Wrong?*, National Legal Center for the Public Interest, October 1997.

The 51-page pamphlet calls for the White House to eliminate the ABA's role in evaluating candidates for federal judicial nominations and for the Senate to have roll-call votes on each nominee.

The Next Step

Additional information from UMI's Newspaper & Periodical Abstracts™ database

Chief Justice Rehnquist

Cushman, John H. Jr., "Senate Imperils Judicial System, Rehnquist Says," *The New York Times*, Jan. 1, 1998, p. A1.

Chief Justice William H. Rehnquist today criticized the Senate for failing to move more quickly on judicial appointments, saying that the "vacancies cannot remain at such high levels indefinitely without eroding the quality of justice."

"Depleted Courts," *The Christian Science Monitor*, Jan. 16, 1998, p. 20.

In his year-end report on the federal judiciary, Supreme Court Chief Justice William H. Rehnquist noted that nearly 1 in 10 judgeships are unfilled. The 9th Circuit, embracing several Western states, has a vacancy rate of more than one-third.

Fields, Gary, and Paul Wiseman, "Senator blames White House for concerns in Rehnquist report," *USA Today*, Jan. 2, 1998, p. A9.

Responding to a year-end report on the federal judiciary from Supreme Court Chief Justice William H. Rehnquist, Sen. Orrin G. Hatch, R-Utah, says that it is the White House and not the Senate that must change if the chief justice's concerns about confirmation delays are to be addressed.

Hatch, Orrin G. "Judicial Nominees: The Senate's Steady Progress," *The Washington Post*, Jan. 11, 1998, p. C9.

News reports have failed to acknowledge that the chief justice's cautious comments regarding judicial vacancies were but a small part of a much larger report stating that Congress has generally been responsive to issues affecting the judiciary, Sen. Orrin G. Hatch, R-Utah, wrote.

"Rehnquist Sees Threat to Judicial System," *The Washington Post*, Jan. 2, 1998, p. A21.

Chief Justice William H. Rehnquist released his annual report on the federal judiciary Wednesday, warning that the nation's quality of justice may be threatened by Senate delays in acting on scores of President Clinton's judicial nominees. Rehnquist also discussed judicial pay and growing court workloads due partly to laws expanding federal jurisdiction over drug- and firearm-related crimes.

Tumulty, Karen, "When Rehnquist talks, the fight begins," *Time*, Jan. 12, 1998, p. 22.

The response to Supreme Court Chief Justice William H. Rehnquist's comments blaming the Senate for holding up presidential nominees is discussed.

Federal Courts

"Courts Without Judges," editorial, *The Washington Post*, May 16, 1997, p. A24.

All across the country, the judiciary has been left short-handed because Washington has failed in its responsibility to fill vacancies in the courts. The workload cannot be handled by subordinates, as it might be in industry or in the executive branch. Only judges can exercise judicial power. And it cannot be postponed indefinitely without a risk of constitutional violation and real injustice.

Curtius, Mary, "Reno Blames Senate for Slow Pace in Confirming Judges; Courts: Workload is increasing, she tells lawyers' group, while 33 judgeships have remained vacant 18 months or more," *Los Angeles Times*, Aug. 6, 1997, p. A3.

Attorney General Janet Reno on Tuesday accused the U.S. Senate of damaging the judicial system by deliberately slowing the pace of judicial confirmations. Reno also spoke out against what she said are efforts to "undermine the very credibility of the judiciary" by congressional and other critics who have assailed federal judges for judicial activism.

Elsasser, Glen, "Senator Unmoved by Judges' Plight Critic of Waste Wants Cuts Despite Backlog," *Chicago Tribune*, Nov. 16, 1997, p. 4.

For more than a year, Judge J. Phil Gilbert has heard virtually only criminal cases in his southern Illinois district, postponing action on all but two matters on his crowded civil docket of Social Security, consumer and business claims. In Texas, Chief Judge George Kazen talks about "the tidal wave" of drug and illegal-immigrant cases flooding his district. Yet Sen. Charles Grassley, R-Iowa, an arch-critic of government waste, wonders if there are too many federal judges. Grassley, who chairs the Senate Judiciary Subcommittee on Administrative Oversight and the Courts, has initiated hearings to determine whether federal courts can do their job with fewer judges.

Fein, Bruce, "Judge Not," Op-ed, *The New York Times*, May 8, 1997, p. A31.

The supreme jewel of our Constitution is a fiercely independent federal judiciary. But congressional Republicans are attacking this gem. Rep. Tom DeLay, R-Texas, is pressing forward with his plan to seek impeachment of federal judges who have issued what he considers wayward opinions — opinions that offend him or his constituents. In the Senate, Republicans have vowed to reject any of President Clinton's nominees for the federal bench who show signs of "judicial activism." These efforts should be unflinchingly rebuffed.

Gest, Ted, "Making a case for judges," *U.S. News & World Report*, **Jan. 12, 1998, p. 29.**

The workload for federal trial judges has increased greatly in recent years, in part because President Clinton and Senate Republicans can't get together to fill nearly 100 judicial slots, one-tenth of the total. Chief Justice William H. Rehnquist asked them to hurry up or risk "eroding the quality of justice."

Keeva, Steven, "Coming to the judiciary's defense," *ABA Journal*, **October 1997, p. 8.**

Attorney General Janet Reno and leaders of the American Bar Association expressed concern that the relationship between the federal judiciary and Congress is becoming a crisis, with politics threatening the separation of powers.

Wickham, DeWayne, "Halt the stonewalling on judicial nominees," *USA Today*, **Jan. 5, 1998, p. A13.**

"Justice delayed is justice denied." That's the point I think Chief Justice William H. Rehnquist tried to drive home last week when he criticized the painfully slow pace of Senate confirmation of judicial appointments.

Impeachment

Lewis, Anthony, "Menacing The Courts," Op-ed, *The New York Times*, **March 28, 1997, p. A29.**

Those who framed our Constitution believe that liberty would not last unless courts were independent in making their decisions. But the House Republican whip, Tom DeLay of Texas, let it be known recently that he wants to start impeachment proceedings against a number of federal judges who have made decisions he dislikes. Now the Senate confirmation process for federal judicial nominees is being affected.

McDonald, Greg, "Conservative lawmakers propose impeachment of activist judges," *Houston Chronicle*, **March 13, 1997, p. A6.**

Conservatives led by House Majority Whip Tom DeLay, R-Texas, are planning to rid the federal judiciary of activist judges by impeaching them on grounds that their decisions often ignore existing laws and are influenced by their political ideologies.

McDonald, Greg, "Reno urges DeLay not to impeach judges/AG warns charges would hurt judiciary," *Houston Chronicle*, **March 14, 1997, p. A11.**

Attorney General Janet Reno contended Thursday that House Majority Whip Tom DeLay's plan to rein in activist federal judges by impeaching them "threatens the independence of one of the critical branches of our government."

"The Impeachment Bomb," *Detroit News*, **March 21, 1997, p. A10.**

Texas Republican Tom DeLay, majority whip in the U.S. House of Representatives, proposes that his colleagues draw up articles of impeachment against "activist" federal judges. In effect, he is seeking a political veto over the rulings of federal judges. Contrary to the howls of the legal establishment, Congress has this power. But exercising it would be extremely unwise.

Judicial Activism

Broder, David S., "Partisan Sniping on Judicial Vacancies Gets Louder; Democrats Talk of 'Constitutional Crisis' While Republicans Assert Clinton Is to Blame," *The Washington Post*, **Jan. 3, 1998, p. A7.**

Partisan finger-pointing over blame for the rising number of judicial vacancies became sharper yesterday, with Senate Democrats warning of a "constitutional crisis" and Republicans asserting that the responsibility lies with President Clinton and the judges themselves. Democrats, who have been complaining since 1996 that the Republican majority is unfairly holding Clinton judicial appointees hostage, pounced on Chief Justice William Rehnquist's words as proof of their charges. But Judiciary Chairman Orrin G. Hatch, R-Utah, responded in an interview that Clinton has submitted names for barely half of the current vacancies — 42 of 82.

Reske, Henry J., "Withholding consent," *ABA Journal*, **February 1997, pp. 8-29.**

Senate Judiciary Committee Chairman Orrin G. Hatch, R-Utah, has vowed not to approve any activist judges. At a November 1996 meeting of the conservative Federalist Society, Hatch leveled charges that President Clinton's appointees to the federal bench have started to develop a disturbing liberal track record.

Schwartz, Herman, "One man's activist..." *The Washington Monthly*, **November 1997, pp. 10-13.**

Judges who go beyond interpreting the law into the realm of what GOP lawmakers consider "making" the law are the new target of congressional Republicans. GOP efforts against "judicial activists" are discussed.

Shea, Dennis, "Impeaching abusive judges," *Policy Review*, **May 1997, pp. 62-63.**

In case after case, federal judges are expressing contempt for democracy, overturning laws passed by state legislatures or adopted directly by the people through the initiative process. Conservatives are trying to find ways to curb the activism of some federal judges, and term limits and impeachment have both been examined.

Back Issues

Great Research on Current Issues Starts Right Here . . . Recent topics covered by The CQ Researcher are listed below. Before May 1991, reports were published under the name of Editorial Research Reports.

SEPTEMBER 1996
Gambling Under Attack
The States and Federalism
Civic Journalism
Reassessing Foreign Aid

OCTOBER 1996
Political Consultants
Insurance Fraud
Rethinking School Integration
Parental Rights

NOVEMBER 1996
Global Warming
Clashing Over Copyright
Consumer Debt
Governing Washington, D.C.

DECEMBER 1996
Welfare, Work and the States
The New Volunteerism
Implementing the Disabilities Act
America's Pampered Pets

JANUARY 1997
Combating Scientific Misconduct
Restructuring the Electric Industry
The New Immigrants
Chemical and Biological Weapons

FEBRUARY 1997
Assisting Refugees
Alternative Medicine's Next Phase
Independent Counsels
Feminism's Future

MARCH 1997
New Air Quality Standards
Alcohol Advertising
Civic Renewal
Educating Gifted Students

APRIL 1997
Declining Crime Rates
The FBI Under Fire
Gender Equity in Sports
Space Program's Future

MAY 1997
The Stock Market
The Cloning Controversy
Expanding NATO
The Future of Libraries

JUNE 1997
FDA Reform
China After Deng
Line-Item Veto
Breast Cancer

JULY 1997
Transportation Policy
Executive Pay
School Choice Debate
Aggressive Driving

AUGUST 1997
Age Discrimination
Banning Land Mines
Children's Television
Evolution vs. Creationism

SEPTEMBER 1997
Caring for the Dying
Mental Health Policy
Mexico's Future
Youth Fitness

OCTOBER 1997
Urban Sprawl in the West
Diversity in the Workplace
Teacher Education
Contingent Work Force

NOVEMBER 1997
Renewable Energy
Artificial Intelligence
Religious Persecution
Roe v. Wade at 25

DECEMBER 1997
Whistleblowers
Castro's Next Move
Gun Control Standoff
Regulating Nonprofits

JANUARY 1998
Foster Care Reform
IRS Reform
The Black Middle Class
U.S.-British Relations

FEBRUARY 1998
Patients' Rights
Deflation Fears
Caring for the Elderly
The New Corporate Philanthropy

MARCH 1998
Israel at 50

Back issues are available for $5.00 (subscribers) or $10.00 (non-subscribers). Quantity discounts apply to orders over ten. To order, call Congressional Quarterly Customer Service at (202) 887-8621.

Binders are available for $18.00. To order call 1-800-638-1710. Please refer to stock number 648.

Future Topics

▶ *Drinking on Campus*

▶ *The Economics of Recycling*

▶ *Biology and Behavior*

The CQ Researcher

PUBLISHED BY CONGRESSIONAL QUARTERLY INC.

Drinking on Campus

Can colleges get it under control?

A lcohol-related deaths at several schools in recent months, including the Massachusetts Institute of Technology, have prompted many administrators to take tougher stands on student drinking. The tragedies — often involving "binge" drinking — underscore how available alcohol is, even to students under 21, and how much drinking is a part of campus life, especially among fraternity and sorority members. School administrators say the nation's minimum drinking age presents them with two equally unappealing options: banning alcohol and running the risk of out-of-control off-campus parties, or looking the other way at underage drinking while trying to teach students responsible behavior. Administrators and health officials agree, however, that alcohol abuse is a communitywide affliction, not merely a campus problem.

C_Q | **March 20, 1998 • Volume 8, No. 11 • Pages 241-264**

Formerly Editorial Research Reports

March 20, 1998
Volume 8, No.11

EDITOR
Sandra Stencel

MANAGING EDITOR
Thomas J. Colin

ASSOCIATE EDITOR
Sarah M. Magner

STAFF WRITERS
Mary H. Cooper
Kenneth Jost
David Masci

PRODUCTION EDITOR
Melissa Hall

EDITORIAL ASSISTANT
Laura S. Cavender

PUBLISHED BY
Congressional Quarterly Inc.

CHAIRMAN
Andrew Barnes

VICE CHAIRMAN
Andrew P. Corty

PRESIDENT AND PUBLISHER
Robert W. Merry

EXECUTIVE EDITOR
David Rapp

The CQ Researcher (ISSN 1056-2036). Formerly Editorial Research Reports. Published weekly, except Jan. 2, May 29, July 3, Oct. 30, by Congressional Quarterly Inc., 1414 22nd St., N.W., Washington, D.C. 20037. Annual subscription rate for libraries, businesses and government is $340. Additional rates furnished upon request. Periodicals postage paid at Washington, D.C., and additional mailing offices. POSTMASTER: Send address changes to The CQ Researcher, 1414 22nd St., N.W., Washington, D.C. 20037.

COVER: AN UNDERAGE DRINKER MIXES DRINKS AT A SPRING BREAK PARTY IN OCEAN CITY, MD. (JONATHAN SUMMERS/TIMES COMMUNITY NEWSPAPERS)

Drinking on Campus

BY KAREN LEE SCRIVO

THE ISSUES

Leslie Anne Baltz had been drinking heavily before she died last November in a fall down a flight of stairs. In fact, the 21-year-old honors student may have died after observing what some students claim is a longtime custom among University of Virginia (UVA) seniors—the "fourth-year fifth"—downing a fifth of liquor before the football team's last home game.

Baltz's friends left her sleeping on an upstairs couch and went to the game. Upon returning, they found Baltz unconscious at the foot of the stairs. She was rushed to the university medical center, where she died. Her blood-alcohol level was 0.27 percent — more than three times the state's legal limit for intoxication. [1]

Two days later, Susan J. Grossman discussed Baltz's death with her "Substance Abuse and Society" class. Some students said it changed their outlook about drinking, but few actually planned to change their own drinking habits, recalls Grossman, associate director of the university's Institute for Substance Abuse Studies.

"They felt drinking was their choice," she says. "Some said, 'These things happen once in a while.' I was astounded. There is this feeling that they're invulnerable, that it can't happen to them."

Less than a month after Baltz's death, UVA students at a popular Charlottesville bar echoed those feelings of invincibility. Some said they drank heavily once or twice a week to relieve the stress of school and their personal lives. Steve Bremer, a third-year fraternity member, said he got intoxicated six or seven times a month. "It's absolutely the norm at UVA," he said.

Like Grossman's students, few of the students at the bar planned to change their drinking habits, but many said they

would take better care of their drunken friends. "I'll never leave a friend alone in that condition again," said Dave Clark, another junior. [2]

Baltz, of Reston, Va., was the fifth Virginia college student in less than two months to die following a night of heavy drinking. A few weeks earlier, Melinda Somers, a Virginia Polytechnic Institute (VPI) freshman, apparently rolled out of bed and through an open eighth-floor dormitory window. She had been drinking heavily at a Halloween party. She died the day before her 19th birthday.

Somers' death prompted Virginia's attorney general to form a task force of college presidents, students and health experts to find ways of curbing alcohol abuse on campuses. UVA President John T. Casteen III sent out a letter after Baltz's death, calling for the community "to learn how to change a culture that too often considers alcohol abuse a normal stage of growing up."

The deaths of Somers and Baltz were the latest in a string of campus

alcohol-related tragedies. In September, an 18-year-old Massachusetts Institute of Technology (MIT) freshman honors student — Scott Krueger — died after an off-campus party at the Boston house of the Phi Gamma Delta fraternity, which he was pledging. He had an alcohol level of 0.41 — more than five times the legal limit. A month earlier, Benjamin Wynne died after a party at the Sigma Alpha Epsilon fraternity house at Louisiana State University. Wynne, a fraternity pledge, had an alcohol level of 0.58, nearly six times the state's legal limit.

It's unclear whether more students are dying from alcohol-related incidents or whether the issue has simply received more media attention recently. There certainly wasn't much media attention after a New Hampshire sophomore died from alcohol poisoning last year following a fraternity party, says William DeJong, director of The Higher Education Center for Alcohol and Other Drug Prevention. "It got a two-inch story in the back of the paper," DeJong recalls.

Health experts say they know of no long-term statistics on alcohol-related deaths specifically among college students. It is known, however, that in 1995 318 people died in the United States from alcohol poisoning, including 24 ages 15-24, according to the National Center for Health Statistics.

Just how widespread alcohol abuse is on college campuses depends on whom you ask and how you define "binge drinking."

According to a 1993 Harvard School of Public Health study of more than 17,000 students nationwide, 44 percent had engaged in binge drinking, or five drinks in a row within a short period for men, and four drinks for women.* And 19 percent said they were frequent

---

* A drink is defined as a 12-ounce beer or wine-cooler, a four-ounce glass of wine, or a shot of liquor taken straight or in a mixed drink.

Alcohol Linked to Campus Problems

Alcohol was involved in more than two-thirds of all the campus incidents last year that occurred in residence halls or involved violent behavior, according to school administrators.

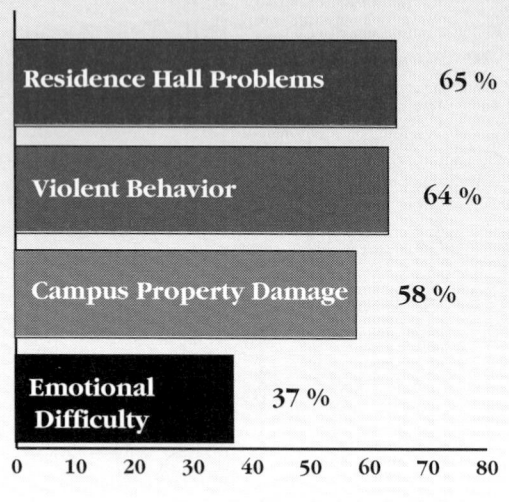

Percentage Involving Alcohol

Note: The survey involved 330 colleges and universities throughout the country and had a 74 percent response rate, or 245 colleges.

Sources: "College Alcohol Survey, 1979-1997," George Mason University and West Chester University

binge drinkers, or had binged three or more times in the past two weeks.

Some of the students taking the survey also recounted their own drunken experiences or those of friends or roommates.

"I went to a fraternity party off campus," one woman wrote. "I had at least 12 shots of liquor and two mixed drinks. That night I went home with this guy I did not know and had sex with him. The guy and his roommates carried me to my dorm, where two RA's [resident assistants] caught me. I went to the hospital for alcohol poisoning and rape. I blacked out. I never pressed charges because he used the condom in my wallet."

Another student recalled: "My roommate had a drinking contest with her boyfriend. They each had five shots of Wild Turkey, two beers and then started a 'power hour' — one shot of beer per minute for 60 minutes. My roommate began falling down and looked ill. She lay down to go to sleep and began throwing up for two hours straight. She rolled over and almost choked in her own vomit."

"While there has been an overall decline in drinking in American society as a whole, recent studies have shown no proportionate decline among college students," said Henry Wechsler, director of College Alcohol Studies at the Harvard University Department of Health and Social Behavior. [3]

According to the 1993 Harvard study directed by Wechsler:

• Residents of fraternity and sorority houses had the highest rate of campus binge drinking — 86 percent and 80 percent, respectively.

• 61 percent of the men and 50 percent of the women involved in intercollegiate sports engaged in binge drinking. [4]

• 50 percent of all the college males and 39 percent of the females were binge drinkers.

• 48 percent of white students engaged in binge drinking, compared with 38 percent of Hispanic students, 34 percent of Native Americans, 21 percent of Asians and 16 percent of African-Americans.

• More binge drinking occurs at colleges in the Northeast and North Central United States than the rest of the country.

• Half of the college binge drinkers had binged as high school seniors.

"The same student can be a healthy drinker or a binge drinker, depending on who writes the story," says Michael P. Haines, coordinator of Health Enhancement Services at Northern Illinois University, in DeKalb. He argues that the term "binge drinking" conjures up images of "the lost weekend" and being intoxicated for long periods. He defines binge drinking as taking 14-21 drinks in a 12-to-24-hour period.

Furthermore, Haines says, Wechsler's Harvard study creates the impression that binge drinking is the norm, when the reality is that most students do not harm themselves by their drinking. Indeed, he says, exaggerating the severity of the binge-drinking problem makes the problem worse because youths tend to follow what they think their peers are doing. Correcting these misperceptions, Haines says, would help reduce alcohol abuse. [5]

Wechsler defends his study's binge-drinking definition, pointing to the health, social and academic problems connected with binge drinking. Students defined as binge drinkers in the study were up to 10 times more likely to drive after drinking compared with non-binge drinkers. And they had up to a 25 percent greater chance of experiencing at least one of several alcohol-related problems, he says, such as getting behind in schoolwork, arguing with friends, unplanned and unprotected sexual activity, getting hurt, damaging property and getting in trouble with police.

Binge drinkers also cause problems for other students, Wechsler says, ranging from "date rape," assaults and unwanted sexual advances to vandalism, having their sleep interrupted or having to baby-sit a drunken friend.

In light of such problems, college administrators consider reducing alcohol abuse as one of their biggest challenges. Many find that the age-21 drinking minimum makes it difficult to teach students responsible drinking when most of them are not supposed to be drinking in the first place. Some argue that a lower drinking age would help colleges monitor student drinking and help promote more moderate drinking behavior.

Yet when Virginia's then-Attorney General Richard Cullen suggested last November that the state task force should consider looking into lowering the drinking age, outraged lawmakers quickly made it clear they strongly opposed even talking about it. Many pointed to national traffic-fatality statistics that show a sharp drop in alcohol-related fatalities for drivers ages 18-20 since the age-21 limit was adopted nationwide.

Because of the drinking-age law, colleges are often faced with one of two options, neither very appealing: trying to ban alcohol and running the risk of off-campus parties that turn tragic; or looking the other way when underage students imbibe while trying to teach them how to drink responsibly.

For many students, heavy drinking is part of the college experience. "A lot of students have no intention of having [only] two or three drinks but drink to get plastered, ploughed, blitzed — there are a thousand and one words for it," says Rich Zeolia, a 22-year-old senior at the University of Maryland at College Park. "They say, 'I want to get so drunk I get sick.' That's the culture."

While there is considerable debate about how to change the culture, many agree that schools need to do more than just set aside "alcohol-awareness week" once a year. "Schools need to stop seeing this as a campus problem and think of it as a community problem," DeJong says, "and reach out to community leaders, police, neighborhood groups, apartment owners and bar and restaurant owners."

A 1996 study of campus alcohol programs at more than 500 institutions recommended integrating alcohol-abuse prevention efforts "into the fabric of the institution." The survey, "Promising Practices: Campus Alcohol Strategies Sourcebook," called for a long-range, broad-based approach including adequate staffing and resources, a clearly defined message communicated to students and participation by everyone from the college president to members of the community. [6]

But such programs take money as well as vision, and many college administrators face tight budgets and dwindling federal funding for alcohol-awareness programs. In 1987, the Reagan administration allocated $8 million to start substance-abuse centers on 100 college campuses. By the time President George Bush left office in January 1993, funding had increased to $14 million. This year, however, the amount was cut back to $1.7 million on seven campuses. [7]

Some experts suggest the problems on campuses are part of a much larger cultural attitude toward alcohol in the United States. "In cultures where alcohol is part of the diet, there are fewer alcohol problems," says Ruth

C. Engs, a professor of applied health science at the University of Indiana. "Children start drinking with parents [in controlled situations]. They see the modeling of parents consuming alcohol in moderation."

Aileen McChesney, a junior at Washington College in Chestertown, Md., agrees. "In the United States, it is not considered a party unless there is alcohol," says McChesney, who has traveled and worked overseas. "In cultures where there is dancing and other alternatives, there is not so much alcohol. In the States, people go to a party and sit down and drink."

"And when people in our culture do have problems with alcohol, no one wants to talk about it," says David Anderson, an associate research professor at the Center for the Advancement of Public Health at George Mason University, in Fairfax, Va. "We can talk about anything else — even sex — but don't challenge a person's drinking."

As public health and school officials try to cope with drinking on campus, these are some of the questions they are facing:

Should the drinking age be lowered?

The minimum legal drinking age has been 21 in all the states since 1988, when Wyoming, faced with the loss of federal highway funds, became the last state to raise its drinking age. Supporters say the minimum is working and point to the decrease in traffic fatalities involving underage drinkers. *(See graph, p. 246.)* The National Highway Traffic Safety Administration (NHTSA) estimates that the minimum-age laws have reduced traffic fatalities involving drivers ages 18-20 by 13 percent and saved an estimated 16,513 lives since 1975. In addition, from 1986-1996 the percentage of intoxicated drivers between ages 15-20 killed or involved in fatal crashes plummeted 54 percent — the

Higher Drinking Age Saves Lives

More than 16,000 lives have been saved since states began setting the drinking age at 21 in 1975, according to the National Highway Traffic Safety Administration. Now in force across the country, minimum-age laws have reduced traffic fatalities involving drivers ages 18-20 by an estimated 13 percent.

Cumulative Estimated Number of Lives Saved

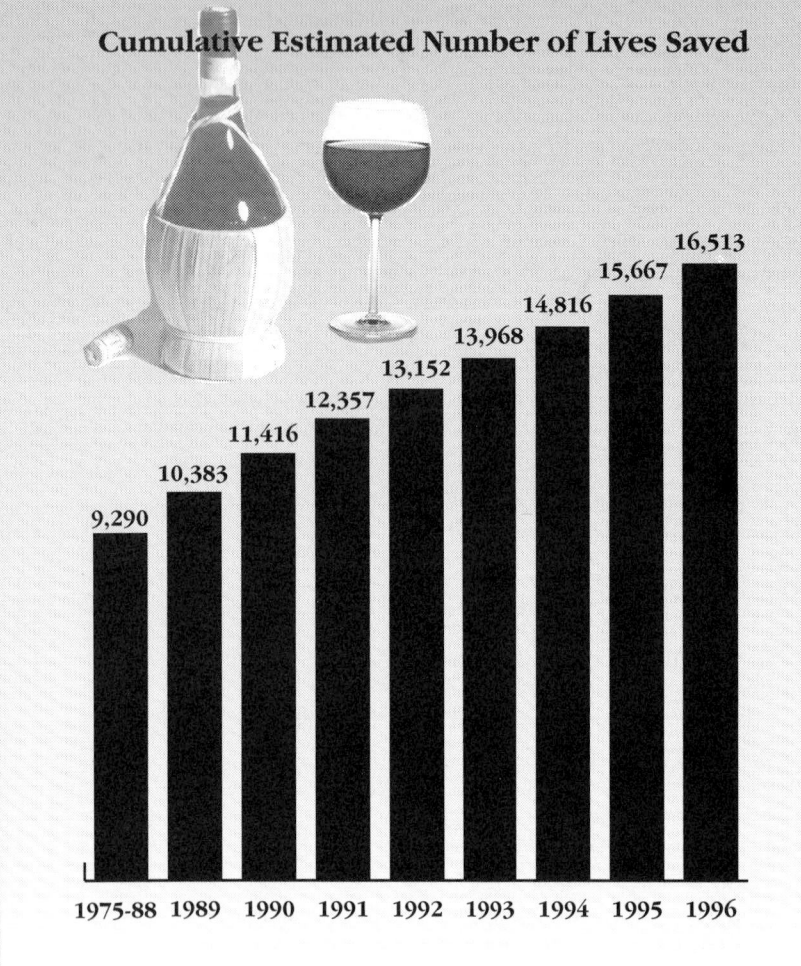

9,290	10,383	11,416	12,357	13,152	13,968	14,816	15,667	16,513
1975-88	1989	1990	1991	1992	1993	1994	1995	1996

Source: National Highway Traffic Safety Administration

largest decline of any age group.[8]

There is "overwhelming data to support" the law, says Charles A. Hurley, public affairs director of the National Safety Council. "Saving thousands of teens is a good argument. It's not a panacea, but it has been effective."

But some question whether the higher drinking age is entirely responsible for the drop in drinking-related accidents and fatalities among young people. They point to the increased use of seat belts and air bags, the effectiveness of campaigns warning against drinking and driving and safer cars. NHTSA statistics show that intoxication rates decreased for drivers of all ages involved in fatal crashes from 1986-1996.[9]

"All this happened at the same time as raising the drinking age," says Haines at Northern Illinois University. "It's hard to know if age is responsible."

In addition, Haines says the law has been ineffective in changing the fundamental drinking behavior of teenagers, considering that about 75 percent of students under 21 drink. Consequently, he and others suggest rescinding the law and finding ways to help teenagers become responsible drinkers.

"We're dealing with real hypocrisy to say that kids under 21 don't drink," said Roderic Park, former chancellor at the University of Colorado at Boulder. "What we are doing is teaching them to flout the law."[10]

Instead, Park advocates "drinking licenses" for those 18-20 who have passed courses on alcohol risks and responsibilities. A license would allow drinking in restaurants and bars but not buying alcohol in liquor stores. The license could be rescinded if the person were convicted of drunken driving.[11]

"I have always believed that the way young people become responsible is by giving them responsibility," Park said. "I am convinced that federal legislation allowing states to experiment, within certain guidelines, with careful monitoring would lead us to more civil, productive and effective citizenship for our sons and daughters."

Democratic Colorado state Rep. Ron Tupa agrees. The current law is "not fair, and it's not enforceable," he says. "It's kind of a joke. Students are drinking now."

Tupa, whose district includes the Boulder campus, proposed a drinking license similar to Park's. Under the measure, which was killed in committee in February, students 18-20 could purchase a permit allowing them to drink low-alcohol beer. Permit holders who drink and drive could lose their permit and driver's license.

"We'd give you the privilege, but

don't mess up or we whack you hard," Tupa says. "I think it's a workable solution."

Professor Engs also supports a drinking permit. She says that most problems associated with alcohol — among them fighting, damaging property and lower grades — have increased in frequency in the last decade, indicating that students are not drinking responsibly.

"We do not automatically give our young people a driving license at 16 and tell them to drive without education," she says. "Likewise, how can we expect youth to know how to drink if they are not educated about sensible consumption?"

Engs favors allowing 18- and 19-year-olds to drink in restaurants, taverns, college pubs and campus parties with adults present.

However, health professionals at the federal Centers for Disease Control and Prevention (CDC) disagree with the limited-usage approach.

"Increasing alcohol availability to young people, based on the statistics we have, will be a big mistake," said Robert Brewer, an epidemiologist at the CDC's National Center for Injury Prevention and Control. [12] The accident risk for young drivers begins to increase at very low blood-alcohol levels, according to CDC statistics. In addition, the risk of young people being involved in a crash is greater at all blood-alcohol levels than it is for older drivers.

The National Council on Alcoholism and Drug Dependence also opposes lowering the drinking age.

"Some say it will teach kids to become more responsible drinkers," says Sarah Cayson, the council's director of public policy, "but there's no science to prove that."

On the other hand, she says, a recent National Institute of Alcohol Abuse and Alcoholism (NIAAA) study linking younger drinking ages with a greater chance of long-term alcohol problems later in life is just one more reason to keep the minimum drinking age at 21. [13]

Vanderbilt University in Nashville, Tenn., tightened its alcohol policies after three students, all non-fraternity members, died last year in alcohol-related incidents.

Andrew Popoff

In fact, "Most students have their initial drink between 10 and 13," says Gail Gleason Milgram, director of education and training at Rutgers University's Center for Alcohol Studies. "It might be champagne at their sister's wedding. Or if they're Catholic, wine at Mass, or a Seder, if they're Jewish."

But such experiences are separated from adolescent drinking — treated as if they had no relation to it, Milgram says. "Add to that parents who don't talk about the use of alcohol with their children," she says, "and it can all become very confus-

ing to young people."

Should colleges ban alcohol?

The recent spate of alcohol-related student deaths has renewed calls for banning alcohol on college campuses. While most undergraduates cannot legally buy alcohol, many still drink. The clash between legality and reality sparks debate on whether banning alcohol reduces irresponsible drinking or just encourages out-of-control, off-campus parties like the one that ended tragically last August for LSU student Wynne. The 20-year-old drank himself to death with a potent mixture of 151-proof rum, whiskey and liqueur at a seven-hour off-campus fraternity party. LSU had banned alcohol at fraternities and campus events in an effort to curb campus drinking.

In view of such tragedies, some college administrators think that allowing on-campus drinking for students 21 and older would at least let the school regulate it. Salisbury State University in Maryland, for example, converted a dining hall into a bar in an effort to control how much students drink and keep them from driving after drinking. Unlike regular bars, the Crossroads Pub doesn't have a "happy hour" or reduced-price specials that encourage drinking. At Johns Hopkins University in Baltimore, a former security officer manages the school's bar. But underage drinking problems closed the Underground, a bar at Brown University. [14]

When Drinking Turns Lethal

Several college students have died in alcohol-related incidents in the past year. Health experts say there are no long-term statistics on alcohol-related deaths among college students. However, it is known that in 1995, 318 people died in the United States just from alcohol poisoning, including 24 people ages 15-24. College students involved in fatal alcohol-related incidents in the past year include:

• Leslie Anne Baltz, 21, a senior honors student at the University of Virginia in Charlottesville, died in November 1997 after falling down a flight of stairs in an off-campus house following a night of drinking. Her blood-alcohol level was 0.27 percent, more than three times the state limit for intoxication. [1]

• Melinda "Mindy" Somers, 18, a sophomore at Virginia Polytechnic University (VPI) in Blacksburg, died in November 1997 when she fell from an eighth-floor dormitory window after a night of Halloween partying. She had a blood-alcohol level of 0.21 percent, more than twice the state's intoxication level. [2]

• Three students, from VPI, Virginia Commonwealth University and Radford University, died in car accidents in October and November 1997. [3]

• Scott Krueger, 18, a sophomore at the Massachusetts Institute of Technology in Boston, went into a coma and died in September 1997 after attending an off-campus party with the fraternity he was pledging, Phi Gamma Delta. His blood-alcohol level was 0.41 percent, five times the state's legal limit. [4]

• Benjamin Wynne, 20, died in August 1997 after a party at the Sigma Alpha Epsilon fraternity house at Louisiana State University. Wynne, a fraternity pledge, had a blood-alcohol level of 0.58 percent, nearly six times the legal limit. Eleven other students at the off-campus party were treated for alcohol poisoning. [5]

• Rob Jordan, 22, of Hartwick University in Oneonta, N.Y., drowned in May 1997 after attending a party with his Alpha Delta Omega fraternity brothers beside a river near the campus. [6]

• Five students died in a May 1997 fire in a North Carolina fraternity house; four of the youths may have been too drunk to escape. [7]

---

[1] *The Washington Post*, Dec. 7, 1997, p. B1.

[2] *The Washington Post*, Nov. 12, 1997.

[3] *The New York Times*, Jan. 4, 1998, p. 30.

[4] *The New York Times*, Oct. 1, 1997, p. A12. *USA Today*, Oct. 10, 1997.

[5] *USA Today*, Aug. 28, 1997, p. 3A.

[6] *The New York Times*, Nov. 3, 1997, p. A24.

[7] *Newsweek*, Oct. 13, 1998, p. 69.

"I favor campus pubs, if they are strictly enforced," DeJong says. "Even students under 21 enjoy them. There is food and entertainment. Nothing is accomplished by pushing alcohol entirely off campus."

But Harvard's Wechsler urges universities to stop the flow of alcohol on campus. He also urges colleges to crack down on fraternities and sororities that encourage binge and underage drinking, to work with local police to keep local bars from serving underage drinkers and to avoid sending "mixed messages" about drinking.

"If you let them drink on campus, it doesn't mean they'll only drink on campus," he said. [15]

MIT announced tougher penalties for underage drinking in February following the death last fall of 18-year-old Scott Krueger, who lost consciousness after heavy drinking at an off-campus party held by a fraternity he was pledging. He never woke up. This school year, another MIT student was hospitalized for alcohol poisoning and 22 others were charged with alcohol violations. Under the school's new policy, violators face disciplinary action ranging from mandatory counseling and loss of housing to $1,500 in fines and expulsion.

"There is no question that the events of last fall highlighted this gap in our overall alcohol policy," said Rosalind Williams, MIT's dean of students and undergraduate education. The new system will "demonstrate to local governments, to the nation at large and to ourselves that we can govern ourselves responsibly." [16]

In December, not long after the alcohol-related deaths at UVA and VPI, police cracked down on underage drinking at a fraternity party at Virginia Commonwealth University in Richmond and arrested 53 people for rowdiness and underage drinking, giving new urgency to the task force on campus alcohol abuse.

While the Promising Practices study rated UVA's alcohol-abuse program as one of the 12 most comprehensive in the country, the percentage of heavy drinkers at the university jumped from 47 percent in 1996 to 51 percent in 1997, according to the school's Institute of Substance Abuse Studies.

"There is a strong drinking environment here," Grossman says. "Our goal is to change the environment."

The university has not tried to stop

drinking but rather to reduce abuse and make sure people are safe, she says. The university program includes training for resident advisers, student athlete mentors, peer prevention, a hospitality committee that holds alcohol-free events, Drug Awareness Week, education and information for fraternities and sororities and classes on substance abuse.

Vanderbilt University in Nashville, Tenn., tightened its alcohol policies after three students, all non-fraternity members, died last year in alcohol-related incidents. Students who use fake identification cards or devices for fast alcohol consumption, such as funnels, now face sanctions, and no alcohol is permitted in first-year dormitories.

But first-year students who want to drink just get fake IDs and drive to downtown bars a few blocks away, said David Burch, editor of the *Hustler*, the campus newspaper. [17]

A *U.S. News & World Report* survey of more than 1,000 college presidents found that schools that allow drinking on campus are three times more likely to have high percentages of binge drinkers. The magazine also found that when schools included their alcohol policies and penalties in recruiting material, they were half as likely to have large numbers of binge drinkers. [18]

The University of Rhode Island, once considered a party school, bans drinking anywhere on campus for students under 21. Legal-age students are limited to one six-pack at a time in dorm rooms. Students with three

violations of the restrictions are suspended. The policy has led to a reduction in alcohol-related violations such as vandalism and violence. [19]

But even if such bans work, some question whether they send the right message. "Zero tolerance sounds great on paper, but it reinforces the mystique of intoxification," said a *Wall Street Journal* editorial after the death of Wynne of LSU. [20]

Rather than banning alcohol, universities need to change student misperceptions that everyone drinks a lot, Haines says, because they lead to a self-fulfilling prophesy.

Universities need to get the message out that most students — if they drink — drink responsibly, says Haines, a consultant to more than 30 schools, including California Polytechnic University, Montana State University and the University of Arizona. [21]

At Northern Illinois, Haines' anti-alcohol abuse campaign included

eye-catching ads and prizes for students who guessed the percentage of heavy drinkers on campus. In the process, students learned that most of their classmates, in fact, were not heavy drinkers, and student drinking decreased by a third, Haines says.

"Students will be more responsible about their drinking if they understand the situation," he says.

Are fraternities and sororities to blame for binge drinking?

When it comes to heavy drinking, student fraternity leaders are at the head of the class. Nearly 74 percent said they had engaged in binge drinking, according to a 1994-1995 survey of more than 25,000 students at 61 colleges. Moreover, they reported having an average of 14 drinks each week, while non-fraternity members averaged six drinks. [22]

"In other words, the leaders are participating in setting the norms of heavy drinking and behavioral loss of control," the study notes.

The study found that college women drank less than men, but that sorority leaders and active sorority members drank more than unaffiliated women. Nearly 55 percent of sorority leaders had engaged in binge drinking compared with 26 percent of those not in sororities.

"[T]he data indicated that students see alcohol as a vehicle of friendship, social activity and sexual opportu-

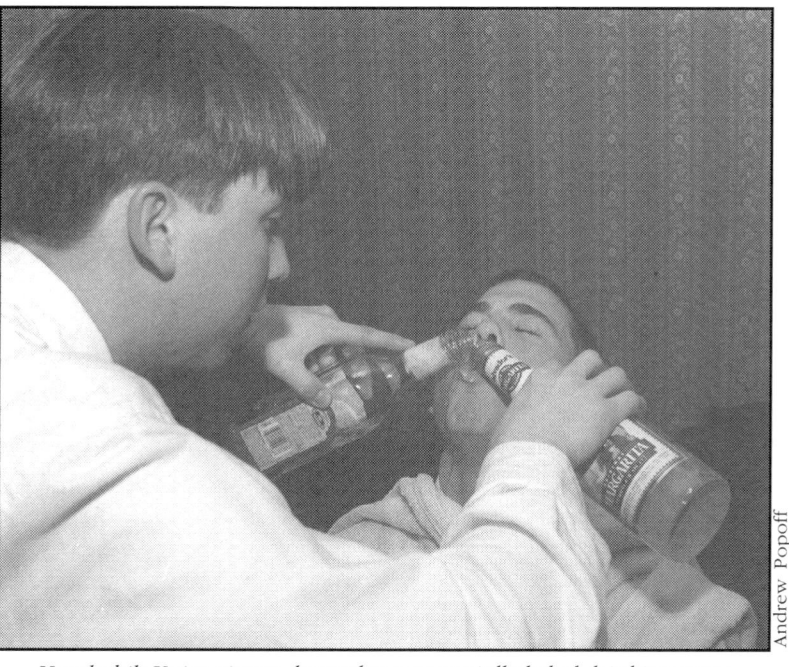

Vanderbilt University students play a potentially lethal drinking game. University of Virginia President John T. Casteen III has called for changing "a culture that too often considers alcohol abuse a normal stage of growing up."

Andrew Popoff

nity, and these beliefs occur to a greater extent among Greeks than non-Greeks," the study said.

The 1993 Harvard study found similar fraternity and sorority drinking patterns. In fact, the rate was even higher for residents of fraternity and sorority houses — 86 percent and 80 percent, respectively. [23]

"The alcohol-use pattern [by Greeks] is higher," says George Mason's Anderson, "but that's not to say they cause it. That's where the heavy drinkers are, and the other heavy drinkers join. It's a cycle."

Many people think of fraternities as "drinking clubs," says Jonathan Brant, executive vice president of the 66-member National Interfraternity Conference. "We don't want to be perceived that way," he said. "The only way we will accomplish that is to substantially change our behavior." [24] In December, the conference unanimously approved a resolution encouraging member fraternities to maintain alcohol-free chapters. [25]

About 2,000 chapters reportedly have agreed to go substance free, which means they will not host parties with alcohol, nor allow alcohol in rooms.

Last year, Phi Delta Theta and Sigma Nu became the first national fraternities to ban any drinking in fraternity houses, beginning in 2000. [26] And many sorority houses have been dry for years. Lissa Bradford, president of the National Panhellenic Conference, says the organization's nearly 3,000 chapters do not allow alcohol in their chapter houses.

Four schools — Florida Southern College, Southern Illinois University at Carbondale, the University of Northern Colorado and Villanova — are testing a program this academic year requiring all fraternity houses on campus to be "dry." But some fraternities at Southern Illinois balked at complying with the program, which was created by national fraternity leaders and college administrators. [27]

National peer networks like BACCHUS (Boost Alcohol Consciousness Concerning the Health of University Students) and GAMMA (Greeks Advocating Mature Management of Alcohol) are also working with Greek houses to promote responsible attitudes toward alcohol.

Rich Zeolia, a senior at the University of Maryland and past president of the Phi Delta Theta chapter, says fraternities at Maryland must comply with university rules or forgo parties. The rules include checking IDs, party monitoring by sober fraternity members, no hard liquor and the posting of date-rape information and emergency hotline numbers. Zeolia says he made sure the rules were followed when he was president, but that, "In my opinion, the university is not strict enough. We are just one drink away from a tragedy here, like on other campuses. When there is alcohol poisoning or hazing, universities need to send a strong message."

While some of the stories about fraternities' wild drinking are true, Zeolia adds, there are also fraternity members who are dedicated to reviving the original purpose of Greek organizations: school service and fostering friendship. ∎

BACKGROUND

Control Efforts

The move to lower the drinking age began in 1971, when 18-year-olds got the right to vote (and became eligible to be drafted for the Vietnam War). But when alcohol abuse among teens increased, states — led by Minnesota — began raising their legal drinking ages. From 1976-1984, 27 other states increased their drinking ages.

The federal government got into the act during the Reagan administration, when Congress passed the Federal Uniform Drinking Age Act of 1984, which threatened states with the loss of highway funds if they didn't raise their minimum drinking age to 21. By 1987, after attempts by some states to challenge the constitutionality of the legislation failed, all the states had raised their drinking age to 21. However, grandfather clauses in some states permitted drinking for those under 21 until mid-1989. [28]

Despite the federal legislation, irresponsible drinking, including drinking contests, beer "busts" and chugalugging, remains common on many college campuses. Students are not only drinking more but also are consuming more potent drinks, such as pure grain alcohol and powerful homemade concoctions of several alcoholic beverages — sometimes through funnels or directly from keg taps. The nation's 12 million undergraduates polish off some 4 billion cans of beer a year, averaging 55 six-packs apiece and forking over $446 on alcohol — more than they spend on textbooks and soft drinks. [29]

Studies also show that heavy drinkers face greater risks of lower grades, unprotected sex, injuries, trouble with the law and death. Bingeing at marathon parties has resulted in at least five student deaths in the past year, and drinking and driving accounted for at least three.

Alcohol abuse not only affects the drinkers themselves but also their fellow students, who complain of lost sleep, disrupted studies, having to "baby-sit" drunken students, damaged property and sexual assaults.

Tougher alcohol policies at several universities, including the University of Colorado, the University of Iowa and Ohio State, touched off "beer riots" last year. At Colorado, students threw rocks and Molotov cocktails, and police responded with rubber bullets and tear gas during the three-day standoff. When the

Continued on p. 252

Chronology

1980s *Anti-alcohol abuse movement gains momentum with formation of pressure groups against student alcohol abuse.*

1981
Inter-Association Task Force on Alcohol and Other Substance Issues is created to study campus alcohol marketing.

July 17, 1984
President Ronald Reagan signs highway bill containing National Minimum Drinking Age Act.

Sept. 25, 1986
Congress passes Higher Education Act Amendments requiring all schools receiving federal financial aid to have drug abuse prevention programs for officers, employees and students.

Nov. 18, 1988
President Reagan signs omnibus anti-drug bill requiring drug-free workplace policies and health labels on alcoholic beverage containers.

1990s *The federal government steps up its campaign against underage drinking and drunken driving.*

Sept. 15, 1990
National Commission on Drug-Free Schools calls alcohol and tobacco the most misused drugs and criticizes the alcohol and tobacco industries for targeting youth.

March 5, 1991
Surgeon General Antonia Novello urges alcohol companies to tone down spring break ads.

June 22, 1991
Novello releases a survey estimating that half of the nation's 20.7 million youths drink.

Jan. 27, 1992
White House Drug Office releases anti-drug strategy that for the first time includes a campaign against underage drinking.

1993
U.S. Department of Education creates the Higher Education Center for Alcohol and Other Drug Prevention to help schools develop substance-abuse programs.

Dec. 7, 1994
The Harvard Study of Binge Drinking on College Campuses is published in the *Journal of the American Medical Association*. It reports that 44 percent of the students responding are binge drinkers.

July 1995
A provision sponsored by Rep. Scott L. Klug, R-Wis., that would have allowed states to lower their drinking age without losing federal highway funds is defeated.

1996
The U.S. Department of Education publishes "A Social Norms Approach to Preventing Binge Drinking at Colleges and Universities."

May 1996
Rep. Klug introduces legislation that would sever the link between a state's drinking age and federal highway funds. The measure fails to make it out of committee. The Louisiana Supreme Court reverses its March decision that the state's minimum drinking age represented unconstitutional age discrimination.

November 1996
Publication of "Promising Practices: Campus Alcohol Strategies Sourcebook" recommending a campuswide approach that also involves the community.

March 1997
Two national fraternities — Phi Delta Theta and Sigma Nu — announce they will ban alcohol from their chapter houses beginning on July 1, 2000.

August-November 1997
Awareness of binge drinking increases following the alcohol-related deaths of students at several schools.

November 1997
The Presidential Leadership Group — six college and university presidents — offers its recommendations on alcohol and drug prevention in "Be Vocal, Be Visible, Be Visionary," published by the Higher Education Center for Alcohol and Other Drug Prevention.

January 1998
A 1994-95 survey published in the *Journal of Studies on Alcohol* finds that student fraternity leaders are among the heaviest drinkers on campus.

March 4, 1998
The Senate votes 62-32 to pressure states to reduce the legal blood-alcohol level to 0.08 percent; it is now 0.10 percent in most states. States that don't go along by 2001 would lose federal highway money. Stiff opposition to the measure is expected in the House.

Campus Aid Declined for Problem Drinkers

Universities reduced their alcohol-abuse counseling efforts after 1991, according to the annual "College Alcohol Survey." Schools may have cut back the programs, according to Professor David Anderson of George Mason University, because they appeared to be having little impact on student alcohol abuse.

Percentage of Schools With Counseling Programs

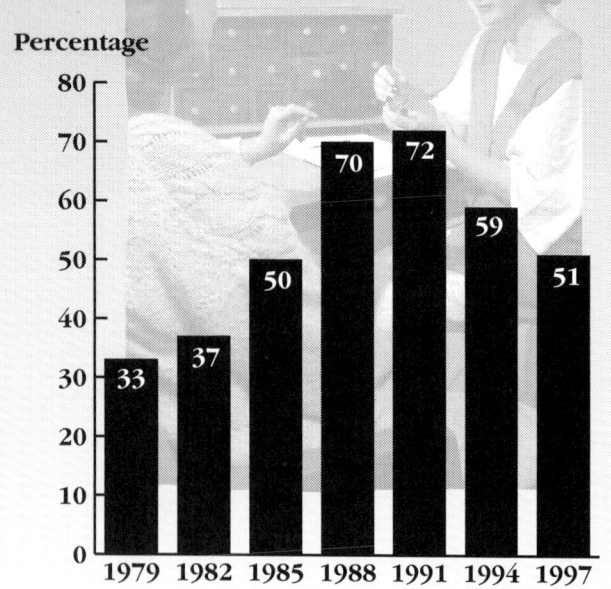

Percentage

Year	Value
1979	33
1982	37
1985	50
1988	70
1991	72
1994	59
1997	51

Sources: "College Alcohol Survey, 1979-1997," George Mason University, West Chester University

Continued from p. 250

smoke cleared, 29 people had been injured and 31 arrested. One Boulder resident said, "The only thing [the students'] actions proved is that [they're] not ready for the responsibility of being an adult." [30]

At many schools, social activities typically revolve around alcohol-saturated parties at fraternities and sororities, off-campus bars and tailgate parties before athletic events. In addition, local bars cater to students with nickel pitchers of beer, ladies'-night specials, low-priced, all-you-can-drink policies, drinking contests and even shuttle buses to round up students.

Being under the legal drinking age rarely stands in the way of underage drinking. Fake IDs are said to be ubiquitous on many campuses, and local bars can be lax about enforcing the law. Underage students drink at fraternity parties or at off-campus parties where older students buy the alcohol, or they get older students to buy beer or alcohol for them.

Pre-College Drinking

For some youths, alcohol use starts well before college. The University of Michigan's 1997 "Monitoring the Future" study of 51,000 middle- and high school students showed that nearly 15 percent of the eighth-graders reported recent binge drinking as did 25 percent of 10th-graders and 31 percent of the 12th-graders.

"Alcohol use remains very high among American young people, but has not changed much in the past few years," said Lloyd Johnston, the study's principal investigator. [31]

It now appears that young drinkers face more than just the short-term dangers of increased car accidents, risky behavior or unprotected sex. Children who start drinking regularly by age 13 are more than four times more likely to become alcoholics than those who wait until age 21 or older to drink, according to an NIAAA study released in January.

The study's findings underscore the importance of preventing underage drinking and delaying alcohol use, say health officials.

"We have known for some time that alcohol, a legal drug that many use without negative consequences, holds unique dangers for underage drinkers," Health and Human Services Secretary Donna E. Shalala said in announcing the study's findings on Jan. 14. The study also suggests that "young people are risking even more than they — and we — had known."

The study of nearly 28,000 people found that children who started drinking at 13 faced a 47 percent risk of becoming an alcoholic compared with a 25 percent risk for those who took their first drink at 17 and a 10 percent risk for those who waited until age 21. It was not clear from the study why delaying the start of drinking helps lower the risk of long-term alcoholism.

About 8 percent of American adults are thought to be alcoholics. Researchers still don't completely understand why one person becomes an alcoholic while another can drink without ever having a problem. Some suggest a genetic link since alcoholism often runs in families. [32]

Parents' Role

Parents have a critical role to play in helping their children understand the dangers of drinking and driving, according to Robert Brewer and David Sleet of the National Center for Injury Prevention and Control.

"Although young people have many other influences in their lives besides their parents," they said, "we have every reason to believe the adage, 'like father, like son' applies as much to drinking and driving as it does to other destructive health behaviors." [33]

But some parents don't think of alcohol as a drug or realize it is the "No. 1 drug of choice among young people," said Mary Dufour, deputy director of the NIAAA. "People say, 'Well at least they're not doing drugs, it's just alcohol.' But people don't know the magnitude of alcohol abuse." [34]

Others, perhaps thinking of their own youthful experiments with drinking, consider it a normal part of adolescence, or aren't sure how or when to broach the subject with their children.

The Center for Substance Abuse Prevention urges parents to tell their children that alcohol is a drug that can lead to serious and even fatal consequences, and that alcohol use by anyone under 21 is unacceptable. The center also recommends setting and communicating clear policies and consequences for alcohol use.

The National Council on Alcohol and Drug Dependence has produced a video for parents, "What Should I Tell My Child About Drinking?" Hosted by actress Meryl Streep, it shows parents how to use "teachable moments" to initiate alcohol-related

discussions with their children.

The National Commission Against Drunk Driving has published several booklets on underage drinking as part of its "Alcohol, Drunk Driving and You" program, including "Yes, you may use the car, but First."

Anheuser-Busch Co., which makes Budweiser beer, has produced a booklet — "Family Talk About Drinking" — that makes suggestions on teaching children about responsible alcohol use, including respect for the law when it comes to drinking.

Banning Alcohol Ads

Some find the Budweiser frogs as insidious as they found Joe Camel when it comes to influencing teenagers' behavior, and they want the catchy ads banned. They say that cute animals or music-video-type images are appealing to kids and teenagers and make alcohol consumption attractive. But the beer and alcohol industry says that while kids may like such commercials or recognize the characters, they don't lead to underage drinking. [35]

A 1997 *USA Today* survey of 534 teenagers in four cities found that teenagers recognized four of the six beer ads shown to them, especially those for Budweiser and Bud Light. While there didn't seem to be a connection between liking the ads and buying the products, the teens said the ads did have an influence on their decision to drink, the paper said. [36]

In addition to ads on television, beer and alcohol marketing messages reach kids through brand names emblazoned on apparel such as Budweiser and Absolut vodka T-shirts, as well as radio, magazines and billboards.

"While it's easy to say we target kids, the facts don't bear that out," says Jeffrey G. Becker, a vice president at the Beer Institute. "Our industry is trying to

prevent underage drinking."

Meanwhile, some colleges are reassessing the relationships between their athletic programs and the alcoholic beverage industry in the wake of increased awareness of college alcohol abuse.

Last December, University of Minnesota Vice President McKinley Boston recommended cutting short an agreement allowing the Minnesota Brewing Co. to install signs in the university's athletic arenas and use the school's mascot in advertising. Last fall, the University of North Carolina at Chapel Hill joined Baylor and Brigham Young universities in banning alcohol advertising in their arenas and on radio broadcasts of their games. And California State University at Fresno recently retired the inflatable silver tunnel that resembled a Coors "Silver Bullet" beer can after a basketball player left the team to deal with a substance-abuse problem. But the Big Ten and Pacific-10 conferences failed to convince the city of Pasadena not to sell beer at the Rose Bowl. [37] ■

CURRENT SITUATION

Focus on Education

The rising concern over alcohol abuse on college campuses has generated many programs but little agreement over what really works. And few studies have evaluated the effectiveness of these programs.

The "Promising Practices Sourcebook," which stresses the need for a comprehensive, campuswide pro-

Giving Kids the Facts of Life ... About Drinking

John and Beverly Gaffney of Bowie, Md., didn't talk much about drinking with their two daughters when they were young.

"They got the education from school and the example from home," Beverly Gaffney says.

The couple — he's a Unitarian Universalist minister and she's a nurse — enjoy an occasional glass of wine with dinner and drinks with friends. They say they introduced wine with meals when Juliette and Rachel were about 16 or 17, and offered them a sip, but neither liked the taste.

Juliette, a Drew University graduate who works for Sen. Paul S. Sarbanes, D-Md., and considers herself a moderate drinker, says that her parents did not talk much about drinking but she and Rachel, a junior at Elon College, saw that they drank moderately.

When it comes to drinking, studies show that many kids take their first drink in middle school between the ages of 10 and 14. Yet many parents don't even bring up the subject of alcohol until high school. And when they do, they're often not sure what to say. But experts say that just telling kids to say "No" to underage drinking isn't always enough.

In an effort to help parents cope with potential young drinkers, several organizations — including some affiliated with the alcohol industry — produce materials and videos aimed at helping parents talk about alcohol with their children.

In the 30-minute video "Ready or Not: Talking with Kids about Alcohol," middle-school students cite several reasons why they or their friends drink, such as curiosity, peer pressure, looking for excitement, stress reduction, rebellion and trying to be an adult.

The video also outlines five ways parents can prevent underage drinking:

• Giving children information about alcohol's effect on their growing bodies, including why they can get intoxicated much faster than adults and how alcohol affects judgment and reflexes.

• Being a good role model by drinking moderately and never allowing anyone to drive home after drinking.

• Disapproving of illegal underage drinking and making sure your child knows why.

• Knowing where your child is and whom they are with.

• Recognizing problem behavior and seeking help when necessary.

It's also important to set clear consequences for drinking and enforcing them as well as helping kids come up with effective ways of dealing with peer pressure to drink, according to the video.

If parents discover that a child has been drinking, they should find out how much they had and make sure they are safe, the video advises. Parents should remain calm and discuss the matter after the child's intoxication — and the parent's anger — wear off.

Juliette, who didn't drink in college, says the fact she never liked the taste of beer made it easy not to drink while she was at Drew. Being a cross-country runner, she says, also provided an easy excuse not to drink.

But the 23-year-old says there were plenty of people who did drink on the New Jersey campus, many of whom were underage. There were also weekend parties and binge drinking. As a dormitory resident assistant, she remembers having to take a student to the hospital for alcohol poisoning.

Kathy Cunningham, a religious educator and writer in Bowie who has two sons, says it is important for parents to talk with their teens about drinking.

"Telling your kids the 'facts of life' involves talking about a whole lot more than sex," she says, but a lot of parents don't. She has talked with her sons, 17-year-old Dan and his brother Kyle, 13.

Drinking and driving is one of her biggest concerns. When Dan goes to parties, she asks if alcohol is being served and tells him he can always call for a ride home. She knows Dan doesn't drink but that other teens do and might want him to get in the car with them.

"It's hard to tell a friend, 'You're too drunk to drive,'" she says. "I would even have a hard time with that."

When Dan has parties at their house, no alcohol is served, and he tells his friends not to bring any.

Thinking back to her drinking experiences in college, Cunningham admits she did drink and drive.

"I didn't think much about it. And I was a smart kid," she says. "Now I think what an idiot I was."

---

gram rather than a quick-fix approach, identifies 12 model university programs and lists 10 recommendations for improving campus alcohol programs.

One of the campuses cited was Central Michigan University. In addition to awareness and information campaigns, its program also features peer-based activities, mandatory classes on drugs for all athletic team members, 12-step programs and counseling and training for residence hall staff in identifying alcohol problems. The university and the community take a zero-tolerance approach toward alcohol abuse with police writing tickets to enforce underage drinking laws.

Project WE-CAN at Western Washington University encourages students to drink only at safe and legal levels. It features a marketing campaign to combat misperceptions about drinking on campus, alcohol-free residence halls, training for student advisers that includes the health benefits of not drinking or drinking moderately and help for those experiencing alcohol problems. The program's "Hospitality Resource Alliance" — which includes local bar owners, retailers, police, educators and health officials — promotes reducing alcohol abuse and responsible use of alcohol. [38]

The University of Maryland at College Park, which was also cited in the report, focuses on education and prevention, says Ronnie Brown, director of the campus substance-abuse program. The program includes a freshman orientation program that deals with alcohol issues; the Caring Coalition, which sponsors non-alcoholic activities; a substance-free residence hall and a publicity program emphasizing that one-third of Maryland students socialize without alcohol.

"Maryland [at College Park] used to be considered a drinking school, and now it is not," says Brown, who also runs substance-abuse treatment programs. "But there is still a problem on this campus as there is across the country. It [college alcohol abuse] is far from solved."

Allison Grad-Lynch, coordinator of the university's Terp CHOICES (Choosing Healthy Options in a College Environment Safely) sponsors educational programs and non-alcoholic parties before games and on holidays such as Valentine's Day and Fat Fridays, a dance with a live band that includes food and non-alcoholic beverages. "We try and make students enthusiastic about the alternatives," she says. "We host a spring challenge for non-alcoholic parties and give a $300 prize."

Community Outreach

The Higher Education Center for Alcohol and Other Drug Prevention recommends that university and college presidents work with their local community to change environmental factors that contribute to alcohol-related problems.

"Traditional approaches to prevention have tacitly accepted the world as it is and then tried to teach students as individuals how to resist temptations," says the group's 1997 report, "Be Vocal, Be Visible, Be

After taking on a fellow student's drinking dare at Vanderbilt University, the winner collects his prize. According to a 1993 Harvard School of Public Health study, 44 percent of U.S. college students had engaged in binge drinking.

Visionary." "In contrast with the environmental-management approach, there is a coordinated effort to change the world — that is, the campus and community environment — in order to produce a large-scale impact on the entire student body."

The report urges college presidents to push for stricter state and local laws, work with community and campus leaders to eliminate practices that encourage alcohol abuse and participate in local and national organizations to change public policy.

The American Medical Association (AMA) takes a similar approach in a seven-year, $8.6 million program aimed at eliminating factors that encourage excessive drinking such as pricing and marketing practices. The program, "Matter of Degree: The National Effort to Reduce High-Risk Drinking Among College Students," is supported by the Robert Wood Johnson Foundation. A second AMA program, "Reducing Underage Drinking Through Coalitions," seeks to reduce alcohol consumption among minors.

"We need to take a closer look at what it is about our society that is creating this problem," said Sandra Hoover, director of "A Matter of Degree," at the program's introduction last October. "Youth are bombarded with glamorous alcohol advertisements and heavy promotion of cheap alcohol. Then we expect them not to drink to excess. What we're saying is that we have to stop blaming youth and instead look at how we're setting them up for failure." [39]

In Virginia, the Task Force on Drinking by College Students is exploring ways to reduce alcohol-related problems at the state's public universities. The task force — including university presidents, students, health experts, parents and legislators — was formed in December by then-Attorney General Cullen following several drinking-related campus deaths. Cullen's successor, Mark Earley, is continuing the effort.

The task force is considering banning alcohol on campuses and imposing student curfews, said Deputy Attorney General Alton Martin, who is overseeing the effort. It is also looking at ways to effectively curb binge drinking and its effects on non-drinking students and to decrease the availability of alcohol.

Starting comprehensive prevention efforts at the middle school level may also reduce underage drinking. Project Northland significantly reduced alcohol use in 24 Minnesota school districts in its first three years. Only 15 percent of the students who participated in the program drank, compared with 21 percent of those who didn't. The program included special skills training, alcohol-free outside activities to reduce drinking, parental education, peer leadership and use of communitywide task forces. [40]

Getting the message out early is vital, says Bill Halsell, program coordinator at Mothers Against Drunk Driving (MADD). "By the time they're in junior high, they've already begun to experiment with alcohol," he says, "and we've lost an opportunity."

Drinking and Driving

When it comes to fighting drunken driving and underage drinking, a broad coalition has taken up the cause ranging from the government to special interest groups to the beer and alcohol industry. The effort includes:

• MADD stresses ending drunken driving but is also working to prevent underage drinking. It pushed for passage of the national age-21 drinking law; advocates strict enforcement of underage drinking laws; supports "zero-tolerance" laws that lower illegal blood-alcohol levels to 0.02 percent for drivers under 21; and seeks license revocation for underage

youths who buy, possess or consume alcoholic beverages. MADD has also promoted several prevention programs for youth, including Operation Prom Graduation, a national poster contest, Teen Court and TeamSpirit.

MADD's new programs include: Youth In Action Initiative, which will provide training and resource materials about drinking prevention; Motivational Media Assembly Programs that make young people aware of the dangers and consequences of underage drinking; National Youth Summits that give young people a chance to talk to policy-makers about reducing underage drinking; and Action Kits for Teachers, with lesson plans on underage drinking and impaired driving.

• Students Against Drunk Driving (SADD), with chapters in middle schools, high schools and college campuses, helps organize alcohol-free proms and parties and raise awareness of the problems of underage drinking.

• The Center for Substance Abuse and Prevention Teen Drinking Prevention Program aims to prevent underage drinking by raising public awareness about underage drinking, changing community norms that encourage underage drinking, creating community-specific prevention materials and messages and ensuring that community special events encourage healthy lifestyle choices. The center is part of the HHS department.

In addition to national groups, there are also regional efforts such as the Washington (D.C.) Regional Alcohol Program (WRAP), which works with the area Council of Governments and the Washington Area Drug Consortium of Higher Education. It has produced strategies for reducing underage alcohol purchase and consumption in the Washington area that will be implemented nationwide by the National Highway Traffic Safety Administration. Other WRAP efforts include a spring campaign to keep

proms, graduations and beach weeks safe for area high school students, an interactive college presentation about alcohol that includes the use of "Fatal Vision" goggles simulating how alcohol can impair vision, alcohol-free teen parties, information for parents about underage drinking and a Youth Resource Guide.

The alcohol industry is combating underage drinking through the Century Council, which has helped fund Alcohol 101, an interactive CD-ROM program produced by the University of Illinois at Urbana-Champaign aimed at reducing alcohol abuse on college campuses. The program allows students to attend a "virtual party" and make choices about drinking and learn about real-life campus tragedies involving alcohol abuse.

"Alcohol 101 is like a flight simulator for college students," said Geneen Wright, a senior at the University of Illinois, who participated in the program. "You make choices for students in typical social situations involving alcohol and witness the consequences of abusive behavior. It gives you ideas on how to stay safe and in control when you're really at a party." [41]

The program, being tested by about 25,000 students at 55 schools across the country, is set for national distribution this fall.

Other Century Council programs include: "Ready or Not: Talking with Kids About Alcohol," a community program with the Boys and Girls Clubs of America for middle-school students; a driver-education program; and a video and lecture program and video by a teenager who was permanently disabled after drinking and driving. The council also funded the nationwide sourcebook on effective campus alcohol awareness programs, "Promising Practices: Campus Alcohol Strategies."

Efforts by the beer industry in-

Continued on p. 258

At Issue:

Should the legal drinking age be lowered to 18 or 19?

RUTH C. ENGS

Professor, applied health science, Indiana University

WRITTEN FOR THE CQ RESEARCHER, FEBRUARY 1998.

*t*he legal drinking age should be lowered from 21 to about 18 or 19, and young people should be allowed to drink in the presence of adults in such settings as restaurants, taverns and pubs and at official school and university functions. Allowing young people to consume alcohol in such controlled environments would enable them to learn mature and sensible drinking behaviors.

The flouting of current drinking-age laws is readily apparent among university students. Those under age 21 are more likely to be heavy, or "binge," drinkers — consuming over five drinks at one sitting at least once a week; 22 percent of students under age 21 classify themselves as heavy drinkers, compared with 18 percent of students over age 21.

Research has documented a decrease in problems associated with drinking and driving that has paralleled a decrease in per capita consumption of alcohol. However, these declines started in 1980, before Congress passed the law that required states that had not already done so to raise the drinking age to 21 if they wanted to continue receiving federal highway funds. The decrease in drinking and driving problems is the result of many factors, including education programs concerning drunk driving, designated-driver programs, increased seat belt and air bag usage, safer automobiles and lower speed limits.

While drunk driving problems have declined over the past two decades, there has been an increase in other problems related to heavy and irresponsible drinking among college-age youth. These include vomiting after drinking, missing classes, getting lower grades and getting into fights.

Our current approach to controlling underage drinking is not working, and we need to try alternatives based on the experiences of other cultures that do not have these problems. Ethnic groups that have few drinking-related problems tend to share some common characteristics: They see alcohol as neither a poison nor a magic potion; there is little or no social pressure to drink; irresponsible behavior is never tolerated; young people learn from their parents and other adults how to handle alcohol in a responsible manner; there is a societal consensus on what constitutes responsible drinking.

Because the laws making 21 the legal drinking age are not working, and, in fact, are counterproductive, it behooves us as a nation to change our current policy and instead concentrate on teaching responsible drinking techniques for those who choose to consume alcoholic beverages.

CHARLES A. HURLEY

Executive director for public affairs,
National Safety Council

WRITTEN FOR THE CQ RESEARCHER, FEBRUARY 1998.

*b*inge drinking on college campuses and elsewhere is a very serious problem that recently has caused a number of highly publicized tragedies. It also has triggered several calls for consideration of lowering the drinking age from campus officials and the alcohol industry. The National Safety Council welcomes this debate for two reasons: The real causes of binge drinking must be addressed, and the case for maintaining the current drinking age is overwhelming.

There are no simple answers to campus binge drinking, but a number of promising strategies are being developed by a consortium led by the Harvard School of Public Health and others through the Higher Education Center for Alcohol and Other Drug Prevention. The consortium fosters a broad campus approach to change the underlying culture and environment that condones irresponsible behavior.

As far as lowering the drinking age, I do not believe you solve a problem by expanding it. Binge drinking did not start with the uniform drinking age of 21. In fact, we may be in danger of seeing history repeat itself. During the Vietnam War, drinking ages were lowered based on the adage "old enough to fight, old enough to drink." The results were horrific. The surgeon general of the U.S. found in the early 1980s that longevity was increasing for all age groups except one — those under 21 — and the leading cause of their deaths was drunk driving. As states individually moved to correct this by raising their drinking ages, they often were penalized severely by border states trying to attract underage drinkers to travel across state lines, then try to make it home. The enactment by the Congress of the uniform drinking age legislation in 1984 was a direct outcome of those tragedies.

What has been the outcome of the uniform age-21 drinking law? One thousand young lives are being saved every year, making it one of the more effective things that Congress has done in recent memory. Has it magically eliminated underage or binge drinking? No, but it has sharply reduced the late-night, bar-to-bar, across-state-lines patterns that had proved so fatal in the early 1980s. It has also saved nearly 1,000 families per year, some 15,000 to date, the senseless devastation that was occurring with lower drinking ages. Those who propose a return to the days when young people were being killed on our highways in record numbers must shoulder the burden of proving that lowering the drinking age would benefit anyone but the alcohol industry.

Continued from p. 256

clude programs, videos, books and curriculum supplements for high school and middle school students about the consequences of underage drinking and drunken driving and dealing with peer pressure. There are also programs to help beer retailers spot fake IDs and give high school students information on the effect of alcohol on judgment, behavior and driving. [42]

American brewers are also involved in efforts aimed at college students. They provide financial support for BACCHUS, which works with Greek houses, residence halls, education associations and government officials to promote responsible drinking. The alcohol industry also participates in National Collegiate Alcohol Awareness Week.

Legislative Initiatives

State and local governments initiate most of the laws dealing with drunken driving. Forty-five states and the District of Columbia have passed so-called "zero-tolerance" laws making it illegal for a driver under 21 to have a blood-alcohol level above 0.02 percent. Some say these laws are more effective when tied to administrative license revocation (ALR) laws, which automatically suspend the license of a driver who fails or refuses to take a blood-alcohol test. Some 39 states and the District of Columbia have ALR laws, according to the Century Council.

Some states, including Ohio and Virginia, have state task forces on college drinking. While Virginia's group is just getting organized, in

Ohio some 45 colleges and 36 agencies have been involved in the effort.

"We must work together to bring the problem out into the open, change the campus culture and improve the quality of life for all students," said then-Ohio State President E. Gordon Gee, who has worked with the project. [43]

"We must work together to bring the problem out into the open, change the campus culture and improve the quality of life for all students."

— *E. Gordon Gee*

President, Brown University

The Ohio Department of Alcohol and Drug Addiction Services and the Statewide Prevention Coalition, funded by the National Center for Substance Abuse Prevention, helped Ohio Parents for Drug Free Youth to work with 19 colleges and universities. Each school received a $2,500 grant to develop a plan to eliminate practices that promote heavy drinking. School representatives attended a training program offered by the Higher Education Center and the Ohio Department of Criminal Justice Services. A second group of 19 schools each received training and $2,500 grants to build campus-community coalitions. In addition, the state Department of Public Safety is working on a statewide binge-drinking prevention awareness campaign.

In Congress, Rep. Joseph P.

Kennedy II, D-Mass., introduced several bills in 1997 dealing with alcohol and youth. So far, none has seen any committee or floor action. Kennedy's Comprehensive Alcohol Abuse Prevention Act would establish strict limits on alcohol ads in any medium that targets young audiences; require health warnings on all alcohol advertisements; prohibit alcohol promotional campaigns on college campuses and require a report to Congress on how alcohol advertising relates to children.

Another Kennedy bill would ban hard-liquor ads from television and radio. The liquor industry had — until recently — voluntarily refrained from television and radio ads but began limited television ads last year in response to declining revenues.

Kennedy's Voluntary Alcohol Advertising Standards for Children Act would allow an antitrust exemption so that the alcohol industry could establish a new code of "kid-friendly" standards for alcohol advertising. While the legislation does not say what the final code should be, it asks the industry to look at content, frequency and timing of ads, program placement and balancing alcohol ads with informational messages about the risks of alcohol use by children. The bill gives broadcasters a year to develop the code. The Federal Communications Commission would have to approve the code before it could be implemented.

Rep. Scott L. Klug, R-Wis., who in previous years has unsuccessfully tried to sever the connection between a state's drinking age and its receipt of federal highway funds, is undecided about whether to offer similar legislation this year, according to a spokeswoman. Klug's position, however, remains that states — not the federal government — should determine drinking ages.

Although not aimed at underage drinkers, there are also bills in both the House and Senate aimed at requiring all states to make 0.08 percent the national blood-alcohol limit for drunken driving for those age 21 and above. The definition of drunken driving now varies across the country, with 35 states and the District of Columbia having a looser standard of 0.10 while 15 states use the 0.08 standard. [44]

On March 4, the Senate passed a bill to withhold highway funding for states that do not set a blood-alcohol content limit of 0.08 percent by 2001. The 62-32 vote sets up a potential confrontation with the House, where opponents hope to defeat the measure by emphasizing Republicans' promises to oppose unfunded mandates that cost the states millions to comply with federal regulations.

"It will save hundreds of lives each year," said President Clinton. But the restaurant and beer industries joined states' rights advocates in opposing the tougher standard, arguing that it would penalize social drinkers instead of the heavy drinkers who cause most car accidents.

"This proposal simply punishes behavior that is not part of the drunken-driving problem and distracts us from real solutions," said Rick Berman, general counsel of the American Beverage Institute, which represents restaurants that serve alcohol. [45]   ∎

OUTLOOK

New Approach Needed

When it comes to dealing with alcohol abuse on college cam-

FOR MORE INFORMATION

BACCHUS/GAMMA Peer Education Network, P.O. Box 100430, Denver, Colo. 80250; (303) 871-3068; http://www.bacchusgamma.org. This 800-chapter, student-based organization uses peer education to work with fraternities, sororities and residence halls to prevent alcohol abuse.

The Beer Institute, 122 C St. N.W., Suite 750, Washington, D.C. 20001; (202) 737-2337; http://www.beerinst.org. This trade organization of brewers, distributors and retailers lobbies Congress and federal agencies and works with its members to inform customers about responsible drinking.

The Century Council, 550 South Hope St., Suite 1950, Los Angeles, Calif. 90071; (213) 624-9898. Funded by beer, wine and liquor makers, the council is dedicated to reducing drunken driving and underage drinking.

The Higher Education Center for Alcohol and Other Drug Prevention, Education Development Center, 55 Chapel St., Newton, Mass. 02158; (800) 676-1730; http://www.edc.org. Created by the Department of Education, the center assists colleges and universities in developing, implementing and evaluating programs and policies for alcohol and drug education.

Mothers Against Drunk Driving, 511 E. John Carpenter Freeway, Irving, Texas 75062; (800) GET-MADD. This nationwide organization fights drunk driving through lobbying state legislatures and Congress and providing information.

The National Clearinghouse for Alcohol and Drug Information, P.O. Box 2345, Rockville, Md. 20847; (800) 729-6686; http://www.health.org. This agency of the Center for Substance Abuse Prevention provides information on the prevention and treatment of alcohol and drug abuse.

The National Council on Alcoholism and Drug Dependence, 12 West 21st St., New York, N.Y. 10010; (212) 206-6770; http://www.ncadd.org. The NCADD offers alcohol and drug abuse prevention programs for schools and organizations as well as information and referral services to children, teenagers and adults seeking help.

The National Commission Against Drunk Driving, 710 11th Ave., Suite 110, Greeley, Colo. 80631; (800) 972-4636; http://www.ncadd.com. This organization of public- and private-sector leaders provides videos and other educational resources to families, schools and community groups through its "Alcohol, Drunk Driving and You" (ADDY) program.

puses, the only thing everyone seems to agree on is that a new approach is needed.

DeJong at the Higher Education Center for Alcohol and Other Drug Prevention says that simply trying to educate students about the dangers of heavy drinking is not the answer.

"We need a community-based program," he says. "We tried the education approach with seat belts and drinking and driving. Only certain people are reached. We need to change the policy and enforcement — this is the biggest thing, along with making students aware that this behavior is not something everyone is doing."

George Mason's Anderson is concerned that universities cut back on their efforts to curb alcohol abuse after 1991. "They saw increased effort but no change in student drinking," he notes, "so they said, 'Why bother?' "

But behavior regarding alcohol is established over a long period of time and influenced by a college's culture, says Anderson, who co-directed the "Promising Practices" sourcebook. And it takes a long time and a lot of effort to change. He compares it with the thrust a spacecraft needs to escape the Earth's gravitational pull. Although there has been a lot of effort on the part of colleges to deal with the problem, it might not yet be enough to show a difference, he says.

Anderson says colleges need to "look at what drives students to drink, not just provide symptomatic relief," although he concedes that relieving the symptoms is also important. "If we deal with the underlying issues better, there will be less of a drug and alcohol problem." ■

Karen Lee Scrivo is a freelance writer in the Washington, D.C., area.

Notes

[1] *The New York Times*, Jan. 4, 1998, Education Life section, p. 29.

[2] Bremer and Clark were quoted in *The Washington Post*, Dec. 7, 1997, p. B7.

[3] Quoted in "Binge Drinking on American College Campuses: A New Look at an Old Problem," Harvard School of Public Health, August 1995.

[4] For background, see "Athletes and Drugs," *The CQ Researcher*, July 26, 1991, p. 519-542.

[5] The U.S. Department of Education has published a booklet on Haines' approach: "A Social Norms Approach to Preventing Binge Drinking at Colleges and Universities."

[6] David S. Anderson and Gail Gleason Milgram, "Promising Practices: Campus Alcohol Strategies Sourcebook" (1996). The 1996 study was funded by the Century Council, which is supported by distillers, vintners, brewers and wholesalers.

[7] *The New York Times*, Jan. 4, 1998, Education Life section, p. 31.

[8] National Highway Traffic Safety Administration, Traffic Safety Facts 1996 — Young Drivers.

[9] For background, see "Highway Safety," *The CQ Researcher*, July 14, 1995, pp. 609-632.

[10] Quoted in *Alcoholism & Drug Abuse Weekly*, Aug. 19, 1996, p. 4.

[11] See *The Washington Post*, Dec. 6, 1996, p. C1.

[12] Quoted in *Alcoholism & Drug Abuse Weekly*, *op. cit.*

[13] Bridget Grant and Deborah Dawson, "Age of Onset of Alcohol Use and Its Association with Alcohol Abuses and Dependence," *Journal of Substance Abuse*, Vol. 9, 1997, pp. 103-110.

[14] See *The Wall Street Journal*, Jan. 29, 1998, p. A1.

[15] Quoted in *U.S. News & World Report*, Jan. 26, 1998, p. 66.

[16] Quoted in *The New York Times*, Feb. 6, 1998, p. A14.

[17] Quoted in *The Washington Post*, Dec. 7, 1997, p. B1.

[18] *U.S. News & World Report*, *op. cit.*, p. 64.

[19] *Ibid.*

[20] *The Wall Street Journal*, Sept. 15, 1997, p. A12.

[21] See *The Chronicle of Higher Education*, Oct. 24, 1997, p. A62.

[22] "Alcohol Use in the Greek System: Follow the Leader?" *Journal of Studies on Alcohol*, January 1998, pp. 63-70. See also *The New York Times*, Dec. 15, 1997.

[23] Henry Wechsler, "Alcohol and the American College Campus," *Change*, July-August 1996, pp. 20-26.

[24] Quoted in *U.S. News & World Report*, Sept. 1, 1997, p. 96.

[25] *U.S. News & World Report*, Jan. 26, 1998, p. 67.

[26] *U.S. News & World Report*, Sept. 1, 1997, p. 96, and *USA Today*, March 20, 1997.

[27] *The Chronicle of Higher Education*, Oct. 24, 1997, p. A62.

[28] *Contemporary Economic Policy*, October 1996, pp. 112-113, published by the Western Economic Association International, Huntington Beach, Calif.

[29] *Time*, Sept. 8, 1997, p. 55.

[30] Quoted in *The Christian Science Monitor*, May 16, 1997, p. 20. See also *Time*, *op. cit.*

[31] University of Michigan press release, Dec. 18, 1997.

[32] *The Washington Post*, Health section, Jan. 20, 1998, p. 7. For background, see "Treating Addiction," *The CQ Researcher*, Jan. 6, 1995, pp. 14-37.

[33] Quoted in *The Washington Post*, Dec. 8, 1997, p. C7.

[34] Quoted in *The Washington Post*, Health section, Jan. 20, 1998, p. 7.

[35] For background, see "Alcohol Advertising," *The CQ Researcher*, March 14, 1997, pp. 217-240. R.J. Reynolds has agreed to drop its Joe Camel ads.

[36] *USA Today*, Jan. 31, 1997, p. 1A.

[37] *The Chronicle of Higher Education*, Jan. 1, 1998, p. A57.

[38] Other programs cited were at Western Michigan University, Colorado State University, George Mason University, Inter American University of Puerto Rico, North Central College, Southern Illinois University at Carbondale, State University of New York at New Paltz, University of Connecticut, University of Scranton, University of Texas at Austin and the University of Virginia.

[39] AMA press release, Oct. 2, 1997. Schools participating in the program with their local community include the University of Colorado, Boulder; University of Delaware, Newark; University of Iowa, Iowa City; Lehigh University, Bethlehem; University of Vermont, Burlington; and the University of Wisconsin, Madison.

[40] *The Washington Post*, Health section, Jan. 20, 1998, p. 7; *American Journal of Public Health*, Vol. 86, 1996, p. 923.

[41] Quoted in Century Council press release, Sept. 4, 1997.

[42] "Commitment to the Future, Public Service Initiatives," The Beer Institute, 1997.

[43] Quoted in *Prevention Pipeline*, Center for Substance Abuse Prevention, September/October 1997, p. 10. Gee is now president of Brown University.

[44] *The Washington Post*, editorial, Nov. 8, 1997.

[45] See "Drunken-Driving Plan Stirs Controversy," *CQ Weekly Report*, March 7, 1998, p. 555, and *USA Today*, March 5, 1998, p. 11A.

Bibliography

Selected Sources Used

Reports and Studies

Anderson, David S., and Gail Gleason Milgram, *Promising Practices: Campus Alcohol Strategies Sourcebook*, 1996.

This study highlights more than 100 campus alcohol programs and offers recommendations for achieving effective programs. A 1997-98 supplement has been added. The study was funded by the Century Council, a distillers' group.

Cashin, Jeffrey, Cheryl Presley and Philip Meilman, "Alcohol Use in the Greek System: Follow the Leader?" *Journal of Studies on Alcohol*, January 1998, pp. 63-70.

The 1994-1995 study of more than 25,000 students from 61 institutions found that fraternity and sorority members drank more frequently and consumed more alcohol than non-Greeks.

Center for Substance Abuse and Prevention, Health and Human Services Department, *Teen Drinking Prevention Program*, 1995.

This program aims to prevent underage drinking by raising public awareness about the problem, changing community norms that encourage underage drinking, creating community-specific prevention materials and messages and ensuring that community special events encourage healthy lifestyle choices. It includes a Community Action Guide, a Law Enforcement Action Guide, an Event Action Guide, a Teen Action Guide and a Community Risk Assessment Guide.

Grant, Bridget, and Deborah Dawson, "Age at Onset of Alcohol Use and Its Association with Alcohol Abuse and Dependence," *Journal of Substance Abuse*, Volume 9, 1997, pp. 103-110.

This study by the National Institute on Alcohol Abuse and Alcoholism found that the younger children were when they started drinking the greater the chance of developing alcohol problems later in life.

Haines, Michael P., *A Social Norms Approach to Preventing Binge Drinking at Colleges and Universities*, the Higher Education Center for Alcohol and Other Drug Prevention, 1996.

Funded by the U.S. Department of Education, this publication looks at efforts at Northern Illinois University to reduce binge drinking and alcohol-related problems by changing students' erroneous perceptions about the prevalence of binge drinking among classmates.

The Higher Education Center for Alcohol and Other Drug Prevention, Presidents Leadership Group, *Be Vocal, Be Visible, Be Visionary*, 1997.

This report from six college presidents offers recommendations on combating student alcohol abuse.

Mothers Against Drunk Driving, Commission on Youth, 1996.

The commission was created to examine innovative programs and propose new initiatives to reach young people with MADD's message. The report recommends eight MADD programs including Motivational Media Assemblies, Youth Leadership Training Camps and Rating the Colleges.

National Commission Against Drunk Driving, "Yes, you may use the car, but First," 1996.

This guide assists parents in talking with their teenagers about drinking and driving.

Presley, Cheryl, Philip Meilman and Jeffrey Cashin, *Alcohol and Drugs on American College Campuses*, Vol. 4, 1992-94.

Known as the Core alcohol and drug survey, this is the fourth in a series of reports that analyzes the nature, scope and consequences of alcohol and drug use on college campuses. The study surveyed more than 45,000 students at 89 institutions. It was prepared at the Core Institute at Southern Illinois University.

Wechsler, Henry, et al., "Health and Behavioral Consequences of Binge Drinking in College," *Journal of the American Medical Association* (JAMA), Dec. 7, 1994, pp. 1672-77.

Wechsler, a professor at the Harvard School of Public Health, reports on one of the seminal studies of drinking on campus.

Videos

The Century Council and Boys and Girls Clubs of America, "Ready or Not: Talking with kids about alcohol," 1995

This 30-minute guide for parents and other adults who deal with middle-school students recommends five steps to prevent underage drinking. A guide booklet is included.

National Commission Against Drunk Driving, "Driving Drunk: Your Choice?" 1997.

This 20-minute video focuses on four real-life situations in which someone decided to drive after drinking and the tragic and far-reaching consequences of those choices.

National Council on Alcoholism and Drug Dependence, "What Should I Tell My Child About Drinking?" 1996.

Hosted by actress Meryl Streep, this 45-minute video offers advice to parents about discussing alcohol with their children. It uses "teachable moments" to show parents how they can initiate alcohol-related discussions and also encourages parents to examine their own drinking habits and develop specific house rules about drinking. A guide booklet is included.

The Next Step

Additional information from UMI's Newspaper & Periodical Abstracts™ database

Bans on Alcohol

Chacon, Richard, "Views mixed on banning alcohol at state schools," *The Boston Globe*, Oct. 10, 1997, p. A1.

A proposal to ban alcohol entirely from state college campuses, initiated by Board of Higher Education Chairman James Carlin, drew mixed reactions yesterday from campus officials, with some arguing the plan would hinder rather than help current efforts to curtail alcohol use among students. Carlin's proposal came a day after UMass-Amherst officials prohibited alcohol at tailgate parties.

Gover, Tzivia, "UMass contends with a 4th R — Reveling; drinking continues, despite talk of ban," *The Boston Globe*, Oct. 12, 1997, p. B1.

Raucous parties with free-flowing beer kegs, Jell-O shots and potent punches are standard Friday night fare on Fraternity Row at the University of Massachusetts. Friday night's unusual calm was probably the result of a long holiday weekend that sent many students home more than a sign of sobering reflection after last month's death of UMass student Adam Prentice of Hyannis. Toxicology results show Prentice was legally drunk when he fell through a greenhouse roof on Sept. 27. He died on homecoming weekend, a time of rampant partying on campus.

Marklein, Mary Beth, "Colleges nudge fraternities toward restricting alcohol," *USA Today*, Oct. 22, 1997, p. D5.

Campus-based alcohol-education programs have been the norm. But with recent studies suggesting that binge drinking in college is often most likely to occur among fraternity and sorority members, some administrators are focusing new efforts on Greek Row. Four campuses have signed on to a pilot project by the National Interfraternity Conference, based in Indianapolis, to ban alcohol in fraternities by 2000. They are Southern Illinois University at Carbondale; Villanova University in Pennsylvania; Florida Southern College, Lakeland; and the University of Northern Colorado in Greeley. Fraternities at Utah State University in Logan and the University of Colorado in Boulder went dry in 1995 after too many run-ins with police.

Naughton, Jim, "Health secretary urges NCAA members to ban alcohol advertising at games," *The Chronicle of Higher Education*, Jan. 23, 1998, pp. A43-A44.

Donna Shalala called for NCAA members in Division I to adopt voluntary restrictions on beer and wine advertising at college sporting events and on television and radio broadcasts of college games. Her plea, which was proposed at the 92nd annual convention of the NCAA, drew mixed reactions.

Drinking on Campus

Arenson, Karen W., "Fraternity Leaders Appear to Be the First in Line for Alcohol," *The New York Times*, Dec. 15, 1997, p. A20.

College officials who look to fraternity leaders to help curb drinking on campus may be letting the fox guard the henhouse. "One would hope the leaders would be better," said Cheryl A. Presley, director of the CORE Institute Center for the Study of Alcohol and Other Drugs at Southern Illinois University and one of the three authors of the study, which will be published today in the *Journal of Studies on Alcohol*. In recent months, both Louisiana State University and the Massachusetts Institute of Technology have experienced drinking deaths.

Brenner, Elsa, "New Effort To Combat Student Use Of Alcohol," *The New York Times*, Dec. 7, 1997, p. WC1.

The rallying cry among young drinkers used to be a rousing "Party Hearty!" Increasingly, it is now a sobering "Party Hardly," especially after the alcohol-related death of a Port Chester college student earlier this year, the suspension of high school athletes in Harrison and Peekskill this fall and recent drinking fatalities at college campuses nationwide. In Westchester and the rest of the country, college and high school students — along with their teachers, guidance counselors and deans — are taking a fresh look at an old problem.

Hendrick, Bill, "Drinking often part of college education," *Atlanta Constitution*, Oct. 16, 1997, p. E3.

It's a crisp fall afternoon, and thousands of people clad in red are streaming toward Sanford Stadium to watch the University of Georgia Bulldogs play. Gray-haired alumni chew fried chicken and sip rum and Cokes. And hundreds of young students sit on sheets or stand around cars, swilling beer out of bottles and cans. Openly. Defiantly.

Kirn, Walter, "Call a halt to fraternities' alcoholic haze," *Houston Chronicle*, Oct. 5, 1997, p. C1.

Kirn argues that banning alcohol from college campuses is not the way to prevent more tragedies like the death of 18-year-old Scott Krueger after attending an MIT fraternity party on Oct. 4, 1997. The answer, Kirn believes, is for colleges and universities to do away with the selective campus fraternities and sororities that have bullied, insulted and hazed their students for generations.

Lloyd, Jillian, "Licensing students to drink?" *The Christian Science Monitor*, May 28, 1996, p. 3.

Chancellor Roderic Park of the University of Colorado at Boulder has proposed a controversial plan to deal with the problem of underage drinking on campus. Park's proposal would literally license students to drink by giving students under the legal drinking age of 21 drinking "learner's permits" in order to educate them to drink responsibly and better monitor who is actually drinking.

Mehren, Elizabeth, "Drinking Deaths Cast Pall on Campuses; Three Massachusetts students die after bingeing at parties. It is an age-old problem that persists nationwide," *Los Angeles Times*, **Oct. 4, 1997, p. A1.**

Three alcohol-related deaths in a week in Massachusetts are prompting government and college officials around the country to take a fresh, hard look at underage binge drinking. Authorities say the deaths last week of an 18-year-old freshman at the Massachusetts Institute of Technology, a high school student in Andover and a University of Massachusetts undergraduate who fell through the roof of a greenhouse will have repercussions at campuses nationwide. All three cases here remain under investigation, but authorities said none appears to involve hazing or initiation rituals. Rather, the students simply drank too much.

Nichols, Hank, "Students alone at fault in binge drinking," *The Boston Globe*, **Oct. 12, 1997, p. 2.**

There was a mini-brouhaha in Henniker a couple of weeks ago when a local variety store offered discounts on kegs of beer to New England college students. The discount promotion was not a great idea, and it came at a bad time — shortly after an MIT student died of alcohol poisoning after a night of fraternity binge drinking. Peter Thomson, head of the state Highway Safety Agency, sent a harsh letter to the store's owner, who apologized, and the tempest died quickly. But the issue of binge drinking on campuses will not disappear.

Thompson, J.J., "Plugging the kegs," *U.S. News & World Report*, **Jan. 26, 1998, pp. 63-67.**

A survey on college drinking suggested that schools that allow drinking on campus are much more likely to have high numbers of binge drinkers. Thompson discusses what colleges can do to limit excessive drinking and how students benefit when schools do so.

Parents and Teen Drinking

Agha, Marisa, "Lake Zurich targets adults to stop underage drinking," *Chicago Tribune*, **July 20, 1994, p. 2.**

Lake Zurich, Ill., now holds parents responsible for underage drinking in their homes, under an amendment to the municipal liquor-control ordinance approved by a unanimous Village Board. It's now illegal for an adult to permit a gathering where anyone under age 21 possesses or consumes alcohol.

Chacon, Richard, "Questioning campus drinking, Applicants, officials seek responsible alcohol rules," *The Boston Globe*, **Nov. 23, 1997, p. A1.**

This year, in the wake of three highly publicized, alcohol-related deaths on college campuses — two of them in Massachusetts — a greater number of students and parents are asking about the college-drinking scene. "I don't remember having as many parents ask questions about alcohol as I have this year," said Gail Berson, dean of admissions at Wheaton College in Norton, Mass.

Mount, Charles, "Dad convicted under new law on kids, liquor," *Chicago Tribune*, **Dec. 21, 1995, p. 1.**

Mark Rush of Holiday Hills became the first parent in McHenry County, Ill., to be convicted under a new state law that increases parental responsibility for preventing underage drinking in the home.

Teen Drinking and Driving

Marshall, Scott, "Roadblocks help police snare teenage drinkers," *Atlanta Constitution*, **Feb. 20, 1997, p. 1.**

Fulton County police are turning to roadblocks to try to catch underage drinkers behind the wheel. The roadblocks are one of several tactics police are using as they review ways to implement a commission resolution passed last month, which ordered them to use decoys and whatever else necessary to stop young people from obtaining alcohol and drinking.

Roughton, Bert Jr., "Paying the price: A few beers, a childish dare and a young man's life changes forever. But at least he still has one — his victims weren't so lucky," *Atlanta Journal Constitution*, **Jan. 5, 1997, p. E3.**

Joe Wiggins, who is serving a 12-year prison sentence after pleading guilty in January 1991 to vehicular homicide, discusses his anguish at being responsible for the deaths of three 37-year-old lawyers. Wiggins had been drag-racing down Ponce de Leon Ave outside Atlanta after drinking three beers at a June 1990 party when he was 19.

Teegardin, Carrie, "Wrecks with young drivers are on the rise," *Atlanta Journal Constitution*, **Jan. 5, 1997, p. E4.**

The equivalent of an entire Georgia high school, 1,040 teenagers ages 15-19, died in car crashes on the state's roads between 1990-1995. After years on the decline, crashes involving young drivers are on the rise again.

Whitt, Richard, "Pressure on to restrict teens behind the wheel," *Atlanta Journal Constitution*, **Jan. 5, 1997, p. E4.**

After refusing in 1996 to enact a tough law to combat teen drinking and driving, Georgia lawmakers appear ready to restrict driving privileges of young new licensees. Several tragic accidents, including two Cobb County crashes that killed seven teenagers, have moved legislators to consider tightening the screws on young drivers in Georgia.

Back Issues

Great Research on Current Issues Starts Right Here ... Recent topics covered by The CQ Researcher are listed below. Before May 1991, reports were published under the name of Editorial Research Reports.

SEPTEMBER 1996
Gambling Under Attack
The States and Federalism
Civic Journalism
Reassessing Foreign Aid

OCTOBER 1996
Political Consultants
Insurance Fraud
Rethinking School Integration
Parental Rights

NOVEMBER 1996
Global Warming
Clashing Over Copyright
Consumer Debt
Governing Washington, D.C.

DECEMBER 1996
Welfare, Work and the States
The New Volunteerism
Implementing the Disabilities Act
America's Pampered Pets

JANUARY 1997
Combating Scientific Misconduct
Restructuring the Electric Industry
The New Immigrants
Chemical and Biological Weapons

FEBRUARY 1997
Assisting Refugees
Alternative Medicine's Next Phase
Independent Counsels
Feminism's Future

MARCH 1997
New Air Quality Standards
Alcohol Advertising
Civic Renewal
Educating Gifted Students

APRIL 1997
Declining Crime Rates
The FBI Under Fire
Gender Equity in Sports
Space Program's Future

MAY 1997
The Stock Market
The Cloning Controversy
Expanding NATO
The Future of Libraries

JUNE 1997
FDA Reform
China After Deng
Line-Item Veto
Breast Cancer

JULY 1997
Transportation Policy
Executive Pay
School Choice Debate
Aggressive Driving

AUGUST 1997
Age Discrimination
Banning Land Mines
Children's Television
Evolution vs. Creationism

SEPTEMBER 1997
Caring for the Dying
Mental Health Policy
Mexico's Future
Youth Fitness

OCTOBER 1997
Urban Sprawl in the West
Diversity in the Workplace
Teacher Education
Contingent Work Force

NOVEMBER 1997
Renewable Energy
Artificial Intelligence
Religious Persecution
Roe v. Wade at 25

DECEMBER 1997
Whistleblowers
Castro's Next Move
Gun Control Standoff
Regulating Nonprofits

JANUARY 1998
Foster Care Reform
IRS Reform
The Black Middle Class
U.S.-British Relations

FEBRUARY 1998
Patients' Rights
Deflation Fears
Caring for the Elderly
The New Corporate Philanthropy

MARCH 1998
Israel at 50
The Federal Judiciary

Back issues are available for $5.00 (subscribers) or $10.00 (non-subscribers). Quantity discounts apply to orders over ten. To order, call Congressional Quarterly Customer Service at (202) 887-8621.

Binders are available for $18.00. To order call 1-800-638-1710. Please refer to stock number 648.

Future Topics

▶ *The Economics of Recycling*

▶ *Biology and Behavior*

▶ *Liberal Arts Education*

The CQ Researcher

PUBLISHED BY CONGRESSIONAL QUARTERLY INC.

The Economics of Recycling

Is it worth the effort?

I
n the late 1980s, acting on fears that landfill space
was running out, communities across the country
began curbside collection of paper, glass, metal
and plastic waste. Polls suggest that Americans
strongly support recycling, despite the fact that the United
States remains the world's leading "throwaway society."
But critics say recycling is often a wasted effort, helping
consumers' consciences more than the environment or the
economy. Markets for recycled materials are notoriously
volatile, and it often costs more to recycle waste than it
does to simply bury it in a landfill. Recycling supporters,
however, say the benefits of recycling far outweigh its
drawbacks and predict a strong market for recycled
materials in the future.

CQ **March 27, 1998 • Volume 8, No. 12 • Pages 265-288**

Formerly Editorial Research Reports

COVER: ©PHOTODISC

March 27, 1998
Volume 8, No.12

EDITOR
Sandra Stencel

MANAGING EDITOR
Thomas J. Colin

ASSOCIATE EDITOR
Sarah M. Magner

STAFF WRITERS
Adriel Bettelheim
Mary H. Cooper
Kenneth Jost
David Masci

PRODUCTION EDITOR
Melissa Hall

EDITORIAL ASSISTANT
Laura S. Cavender

PUBLISHED BY
Congressional Quarterly Inc.

CHAIRMAN
Andrew Barnes

VICE CHAIRMAN
Andrew P. Corty

PRESIDENT AND PUBLISHER
Robert W. Merry

EXECUTIVE EDITOR
David Rapp

The CQ Researcher (ISSN 1056-2036). Formerly Editorial Research Reports. Published weekly, except Jan. 2, May 29, July 3, Oct. 30, by Congressional Quarterly Inc., 1414 22nd St., N.W., Washington, D.C. 20037. Annual subscription rate for libraries, businesses and government is $340. Additional rates furnished upon request. Periodicals postage paid at Washington, D.C., and additional mailing offices. POSTMASTER: Send address changes to The CQ Researcher, 1414 22nd St., N.W., Washington, D.C. 20037.

The Economics of Recycling

By Mary H. Cooper

THE ISSUES

Reduce, reuse, recycle. Since the first Earth Day in 1970, the mantra of the environmental movement has prescribed a simple remedy for the country's growing mountain of waste: If Americans would simply reduce the volume of stuff they buy, reuse what they have and recycle the rest, the depletion of natural resources would be slowed and there would be fewer potentially toxic garbage dumps.

Nearly three decades into the war on waste, however, most Americans have proved reluctant soldiers. There is little evidence that we are reducing our consumption of goods. The U.S. economy is in its eighth year of uninterrupted growth, driven largely by domestic consumption. If Americans were heeding the call to reuse what they have, environmentalists argue, they wouldn't be buying so many new products or tossing so much out. Although the sheer volume of trash is growing more slowly today than it did in the past, the United States remains the world's leading throwaway society. [1]

"Our per-capita waste is just so out of whack," says Michele Raymond, whose firm, Raymond Communications Inc., tracks state recycling efforts. "We're just 20 percent of the people in the world, but we consume 80 percent of the world's resources. Our per-capita waste is the highest in the world and about twice the level of Germany and the United Kingdom. We're just trashing more than anyone else."

The only part of the anti-waste message that has taken hold to any noticeable degree is the call to recycle. Since 1988, when the Environmental Protection Agency (EPA) first set a recycling goal for the United States at 25 percent of total waste, communities across the

country have introduced more than 8,000 curbside recycling programs and more than 3,000 composting facilities, all aimed at reducing the amount of household trash that ends up in landfills and incinerators. Colorful recycling bins are now a familiar sight on neighborhood streets.

"When I announced the 25 percent goal, only about 12 percent of the nation's garbage was recycled," says former EPA Assistant Administrator J. Winston Porter, now president of the Waste Policy Center, a research and consulting firm in Leesburg, Va. "The recycling rate grew pretty rapidly, and our goal was reached in 1995." The nation's overall recycling rate today is 27 percent of the total municipal solid waste stream. Sixteen percent is burned, while the remaining 57 percent ends up in landfills. [2]

Communities have been recycling trash for decades. Most early programs used drop-off points where people could leave their used newspapers, glass bottles and metal cans for a re-

cycler to pick up every week or so. More than 9,000 drop-off centers are still in operation. But lackluster participation in drop-off programs prompted many communities to begin adopting curbside programs in the late 1980s as a way to boost recycling rates. For several years, the supply of recyclable materials was adequate for the infant recycling industry. Indeed, newspaper publishers created such a demand for old newsprint that "garbage rustlers" prowled neighborhood streets to collect junked papers from curbside bins.

But markets for recycled materials, much like those for pork bellies, corn and other commodities, are notoriously volatile. Prices often gyrate when unusual weather, technological advances or other events cause sudden gluts or scarcities of a given commodity. When an oversupply of paper caused the booming market for recycled paper to collapse in the mid-1990s, a number of paper-processing facilities went under, and some recycling operators simply delivered the papers to the local landfill. Since then, recycling has come under closer scrutiny.

Critics blamed the collapse on state and local government goals and mandates for recycling. "Recycling may be the most wasteful activity in modern America: a waste of time and money, a waste of human and natural resources," wrote journalist John Tierney in a scathing criticism of recycling that appeared in *The New York Time Magazine* two years ago. [3] He and other skeptics charge that recycling programs fail to appreciably help the environment while imposing an unwarranted government intrusion into people's lives and disrupting the economy.

Tierney's criticism prompted a flurry of angry responses from readers and experts alike. "If we are serious about lowering the costs of recy-

Recycling Efforts Span Wide Range

More than half the states recycled at least 20 percent of their municipal solid waste in 1995. Thirteen states require recycling, and 16 states have set recycling goals of at least 50 percent by the year 2000.

Washington

Montana*

North Dakota

Minnesota

Michigan

Maine*

Oregon

Idaho

Wyoming*

South Dakota*

Wisconsin

Vt.

New York*

N.H.

Mass.

R.I.
Conn.

Nevada*

Utah

Colorado

Nebraska

Iowa

Illinois

Indiana

Ohio

Pennsylvania

N.J.

Delaware
Maryland

California

Kansas

Missouri

Kentucky

West
Va.

Virginia

D.C.***

Arizona

New
Mexico

Oklahoma

Arkansas

Tennessee

North
Carolina

Texas**

La.

Miss.

Alabama

Georgia*

S.C.

Florida

Alaska

Hawaii

Amount of Waste Recycled

>30%

20-29%

10-19%

<10%

Data unavailable

* 1994 data

**1991 data

*** Recycling program temporarily suspended

Sources: ©Raymond Communications, 1997, State Recycling Laws Update, 1997 Year-End Edition; *Natural Resources Defense Council*

cling, the best approach is to study carefully how different communities improve efficiency and increase participation rates — not to engage in debating-club arguments with little relevance to the real-world problems these communities face," write Richard Denison and John Ruston of the Environmental Defense Fund (EDF).

"By boosting the efficiency of municipal recycling, establishing clear price incentives where we can and capitalizing on the full range of environmental and industrial benefits of recycling, we can bring recycling much closer to its full potential." [4]

Polls indicate that public opinion favors the environmentalists when it

comes to recycling. Sixty-three percent of respondents to a recent survey reported that they were "personally doing more now" to help the environment, mainly by recycling. [5]

Skeptics dismiss such statistics, however. "I don't buy them for a second," says Jerry Taylor, director of natural resource studies at the Cato

Institute, a Washington think tank that promotes free-market policies. "If you ask people if they recycle, you're basically asking them if they care about the Earth, or if they like animals. They're going to say 'sure' because they don't want to sound like cretins." Whatever the reason, however, the polls suggest a high degree of public interest in recycling.

Many experts in solid waste management say the debate over recycling has been cast in overly simplistic terms that fail to accommodate the complexities of the markets for different recyclable materials. Whether it makes economic or even environmental sense to recycle, they say, depends on the material in question. "Recycling is like a vacuum cleaner that sucks up dispersed materials and reuses them," says Lynn Scarlett, vice president for research at the Reason Foundation, a nonprofit think tank in Los Angeles, Calif. "Where the material is of uniform quality, collected in large quantities and easy to isolate from contaminants, there are net benefits to recycling."

Steel scrap is one such recycling success story. Used cars, appliances and other goods that end up in junkyards are broken apart to allow giant magnets to separate the steel from plastics and other contaminants; then crushers collapse and bale the metal. Electric arc mini-mills melt the metal down to produce high-quality recycled steel, at less cost than "virgin" steel and ready to be made into new products. Steel has been recycled profitably for years, without the benefit of government support, and now accounts for about half of all steel consumed, Scarlett says.

The economic picture for materials collected in curbside programs is mixed. "Tin" cans, which actually are largely steel, are profitably recycled like steel scrap. Recycled aluminum beverage cans also are a hot commodity because they can be processed into new cans at less cost — and with less pollution — than mining and processing bauxite into virgin sheet aluminum. And despite the market's volatility, there usually is strong demand for old newspapers and cardboard boxes.

But the case for recycled plastics is more complex. There are six major types of plastic resins found in consumer products, only two of which

are relatively easy to recycle. Containers made with these resins often have to be manually separated out of the recycling bin and carefully washed to remove contaminants before they can be reprocessed, an expensive process that is not always cost-effective.

"Environmentalists are right to say there are many opportunities for recycling," Scarlett says. "But for some products, it makes little sense to have any recycled content. Like any manufacturing process, recycling is a way of making products, an alternative to using virgin feed stocks. The question is whether you can do it and get the product you want at a cost you want. In many cases the answer is yes, in others no. Each product has its own story to tell."

Nonetheless, a growing number of Americans have incorporated recycling into their daily lives and expect curbside service as a basic amenity, like electricity and other utilities. Supporters predict that recycling will keep expanding if Americans are made more aware of the benefits of waste reduction. To that end, more than 1,000 communities participated in the first America Recycles Day last Nov. 15. Sponsored by the EPA and environmental organizations, the event was designed to encourage recycling and the use of products containing recycled materials.

"For many people across the United States, recycling is a matter of habit, something they do in the course of their daily lives, both in the office and at home," says Richard Keller, chief of recycling at the Maryland Environmental Service, a state agency that sorts and markets recycled materials. "But recycling is at a fairly critical crossroads right now. We're already recycling the materials that are easy to recycle. The next step is going to depend on whether we start dealing with materials that are hard to recycle." These include more grades of plastics, as well as organic materials such as food wastes, paper food wrapping, diapers and tissues, which could go to special composting facilities.

The success of recycling programs varies widely according to local conditions. In some highly populated regions of the Northeast and the West,

Our Throwaway Society

- *Every week more than 500,000 trees are used to produce the two-thirds of newspapers that are never recycled.*

- *Americans throw away enough office and writing paper annually to build a wall 12 feet high from Los Angeles to New York City.*

- *Every year Americans dispose of 24 million tons of leaves and grass clippings, which could be composted to conserve landfill space.*

- *Americans throw away enough glass bottles and jars to fill the 1,350-foot twin towers of New York's World Trade Center every two weeks.*

- *American consumers and industry throw away enough aluminum to rebuild our entire commercial air fleet every three months.*

- *Americans throw away enough iron and steel to continuously supply all the nation's automakers.*

- *Americans use up 2.5 million plastic bottles every hour, only a small percentage of which are now recycled.*

Source: Environmental Defense Fund

---

high fees for landfill dumping make recycling especially attractive. In rural areas of the Rocky Mountain West, the high cost of collecting materials and the low cost of land for dumping waste have hindered recycling efforts. Ultimately, it is up to consumers and their elected officials in state and local governments to decide how best to dispose of their trash. These are some of the issues that shape their decisions:

Do the environmental benefits of recycling outweigh the costs?

Some markets for recyclable materials are strong enough to pay for their collection and conversion into new products. Recycled steel from cars and appliances is one of the most profitable post-consumer materials. Recovery of steel and aluminum cans also tends to more than pay for itself.

But demand for other products is less predictable. Plastics are hard to recycle economically because there are so many types of materials, and most are costly to clean and return to a usable form for new consumer products. Paper is less difficult to recycle, but the market for recycled paper has fluctuated wildly in recent years. After peaking in 1995, prices of recycled newsprint sank so low that some recycling contractors simply dumped the paper they collected in landfills.

On average, curbside recycling programs tend to cost slightly more than they earn from the sale of collected materials. According to Franklin Associates Inc., a Prairie Village, Kan., research firm that conducts solid waste studies for the EPA, residential recycling programs cost on average $2 a month per household. "The cost varies widely from

community to community," says Bill Franklin, the firm's chairman. "But recycling costs are a very small percentage of the total cost of solid waste removal, which averages $10 a month per household." Commercial recycling, which generally is contracted out by businesses to private haulers, probably makes more money than it costs. "We don't have good numbers on commercial recycling," Franklin says. "But it must be cost-effective, or they wouldn't bother to do it."

Environmentalists say the quantifiable financial costs of collecting, sorting and processing recyclable materials are far outweighed by an array of benefits to the environment. Nobody disputes the fact that recycling reduces the amount of trash that ends up in landfills or incinerators. Of the 208 million tons of municipal solid waste generated in the U.S. in 1995, 27 percent, or more than 56 million tons, was recycled. Fifty-seven percent ended up in landfills, and the remaining 16 percent was burned. [6]

But some critics dispute the importance of saving landfill space. "It's not in the least bit true that we're running out of places to put our garbage," Taylor says. He cites a Cato Institute estimate that all the trash generated in the United States over the next 1,000 years would fit into a single, 30-square-mile landfill 1,000 feet deep. "Of course, nobody is going to build that big a landfill," Taylor says. "But this shows the idea that we're running out of places to put garbage is just silly. Anyway, most landfills, when they're retired, are sodded over and turned into golf courses or other public facilities."

Many experts say recycling does far more to help protect the environment than merely preserve land that would otherwise be needed for waste disposal. "The more important goals of recycling are to reduce environmental damage from activities such as strip mining and clear-cutting and to conserve energy, reduce pollution and minimize solid waste in manufacturing new products," write Denison and Ruston of the EDF. "[R]ecycling is an environmentally beneficial alternative to the extraction and manufacture of virgin materials, not just an alternative to landfills." [7]

But some experts say the environmental benefits of recycling depend on the material in question. "Each material has its own tale to tell," Scarlett says. "It takes about 95 percent less energy to make a new can out of recycled aluminum than to make can sheeting by mining bauxite and smelting the ore. But the energy

savings offered by recycled glass are very modest because it takes only slightly less heat to process cullet [recycled glass] than to make glass from silica. And if you have to transport the glass hundreds of miles to a reprocessing facility, those gains may be undone because glass is very heavy and consumes a lot of energy to transport."

Lackluster participation in drop-off programs prompted many communities to adopt curbside collection programs to boost recycling rates.

Even aluminum recycling can harm the environment under some circumstances. "If you have to drive trucks far out into the countryside to pick up the cans, the air pollution generated by the trucks will outweigh the pollution saved by recycling," Porter says. "If you try to get the last squeal of the pig, you end up doing more

environmental damage than good. While the environmental benefits of recycling outweigh the costs for most things, people who treat recycling as a religion haven't considered the whole picture." [8]

Some critics go further, saying the environmental benefits of recycling have been grossly exaggerated. "You'd be hard-pressed to find real environmental benefits in recycling under any circumstances," Taylor says. "If you're recycling glass, what commodity are you saving, sand? We're not running out of sand. We're also not running out of energy — energy prices are the lowest ever, adjusted for inflation. And while, as a general matter, you can argue that energy consumption is a precursor of industrial pollution, if we suddenly started recycling everything instead of using virgin materials, the reduction in energy use wouldn't be all that dramatic."

Do government recycling mandates impede the creation of efficient markets for recyclables?

Most curbside recycling programs now in effect were introduced in the wake of the "landfill crisis" of the late 1980s, when several cities in the Northeast appeared to be running out of space to bury their garbage. Although the perceived crisis never materialized, governments at all levels called for increased recycling. In 1988, when the nationwide recycling rate stood at about 12 percent, then-EPA Assistant Administrator Porter called for Americans to boost that rate to 25 percent by 1993. States followed suit by setting goals of their own, prompting local governments to create or expand curbside residential recycling programs.

Garbage Loaded With Paper, Lawn Trimmings

Cardboard boxes, newspapers and yard trimmings comprised nearly two-thirds of the nation's municipal solid waste recovered in 1995. Some recycled materials, such as batteries and aluminum cans, had high recovery rates but contributed only a small percentage of the total materials recovered.

Recovery of Products in Municipal Solid Waste, 1995

Product	Tons Recycled (in thousands)	Percent of Product Recycled	Percent of All Solid Waste Recovered
Corrugated boxes	18,480	64%	33%
Yard trimmings	9,000	30	16
Newspapers	6,960	53	12
Glass bottles and jars	3,140	27	6
High-grade office papers	3,010	44	5
Major appliances	2,070	61	4
Lead-acid batteries	1,830	96	3
Steel packaging	1,550	54	3
Aluminum beverage cans	990	63	2
Magazines	670	28	1
PET soft drink bottles	300	46	1
HDPE milk and water bottles	190	30	<1
All other products	8,000	8	14
Total recovery	**56,190**	**27%**	**100%**

Source: Environmental Protection Agency, "Characterization of Municipal Solid Waste in the United States," 1996 Update

The majority of recycling mandates are merely goals, with no enforcement provisions. "Most recycling in this country is voluntary," Raymond says. "Some states have mandatory curbside separation, and some have mandatory goals, but most of it is voluntary."

Some jurisdictions, however, including California and New York City, impose fines for non-compliance with recycling mandates. In addition to recycling goals, some governments require agencies to buy a specified percentage of recycled goods, such as office paper, plastic traffic cones or paving materials made of old tires. At the federal level, for example, President Clinton issued an executive order in 1993 requiring all federal agencies to buy printing and writing paper with at least 30 percent recycled content by the end of 1998.

There is little doubt that government mandates have spurred growth in recycling programs. About 40 states have set recycling goals, ranging from 15-70 percent of the waste stream, according to Keller. "Most programs call for 25-50 percent recycling over varying periods of time," he says. "I think that without those mandates, especially on the residential side, you'd see far lower rates of recycling than what you're seeing now."

But critics say mandates distort the markets for recycled materials, possibly impeding their development over time. "Post-consumer material is a resource just like water, energy or any other resource, and a certain amount of it is going to be reused because it makes economic sense to reuse it," Taylor says. "But there's a lot of it that it doesn't make economic sense to reuse, and that's where government mandates come in. It cannot make economic sense to mandate the use of a material that nobody would otherwise use. You can build a nice Potemkin village marketplace out of that, but it doesn't mean you're really helping the economy, because the money used to pay for recycling programs is money that would otherwise have gone to more productive uses."

Many critics blame recycling mandates for the collapse in recycled paper prices in 1995. By suddenly increasing the supply of recycled paper in the early 1990s, this argument goes, governments flooded the market with more material than reprocessors could absorb. But Keller, who finds buyers for his agency's recycled materials, says mandates do not significantly distort the market, at least over the longer term. "In Maryland, which has set recycling goals of 20 percent for large subdivisions and 15 percent for small ones, the marketplace is very resilient," he says. "There may have been some marketplace dislocations when the programs came on line, but as a matter of fact there are some industries that we're working with that are scrambling to find materials. You have to recognize that the markets fluctuate."

Most curbside programs collect recyclables from individual houses, making them most common in urban and suburban neighborhoods as well as residential areas in smaller communities. Typically, apartment houses and commercial businesses are not included in public recycling programs. Some experts charge that by focusing on households, which generate relatively small quantities of trash, governments targeted the least suitable population for efficient recycling programs. "If they had actually studied where the trash was coming from, they would have put the mandates on industrial plants first, then commercial businesses and then multifamily housing units," Raymond says. "Curbside recycling would have come last in order of priority."

Like many other experts, Raymond says mandates have a positive role to play in helping markets for recyclables get started. But in her view, the focus on curbside collection has actually stymied that effort. "Had they phased curbside collection in last, these markets might have stabilized, and they would know what makes sense to pick up and what doesn't," Raymond says. "With commercial re-

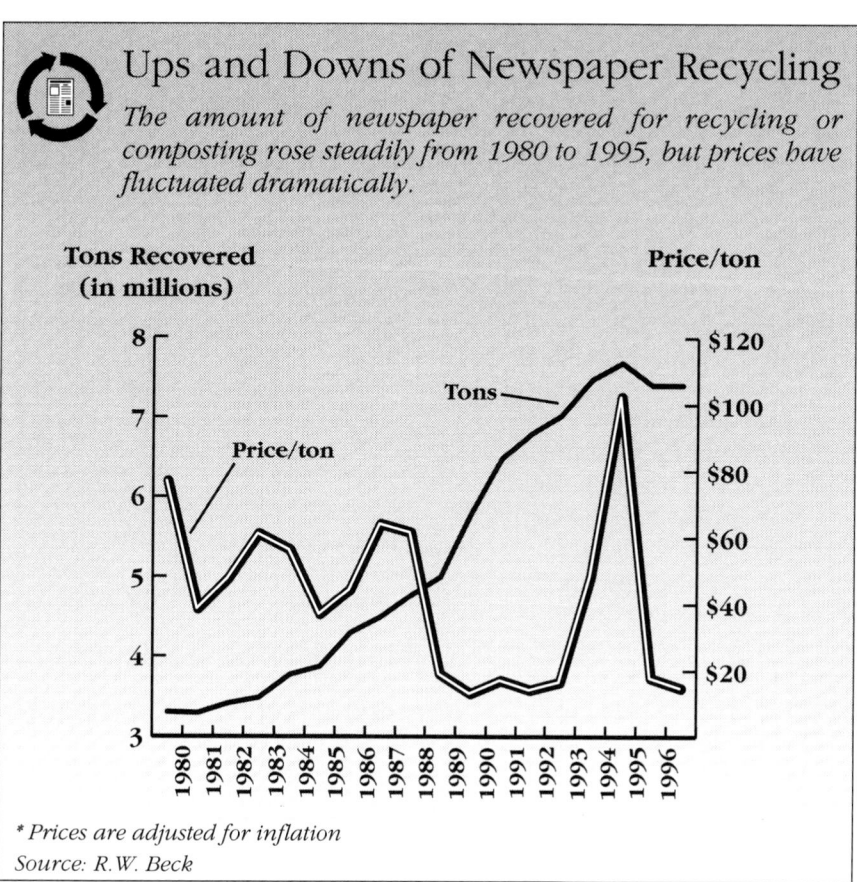

Ups and Downs of Newspaper Recycling

The amount of newspaper recovered for recycling or composting rose steadily from 1980 to 1995, but prices have fluctuated dramatically.

Tons Recovered (in millions)

Price/ton

Tons

Price/ton

* Prices are adjusted for inflation
Source: R.W. Beck

cycling, if the market goes bad for paper they simply stop recycling. But you can't do that with curbside recycling because it takes so long to educate people about what stuff to put in their bins. You can't just drop the glass and continue collecting the plastics, even though that probably would be better for the environment in the long run. With residential recycling, once you turn on that spigot you can't turn it off again."

Is a "pay-as-you-throw" system a more rational approach to waste management than other programs?

Experts agree that it is virtually impossible to educate consumers to periodically adjust the list of materials they leave for curbside pickup in

response to fluctuations in the markets for recyclables. But program operators have found other ways to make recycling more cost-effective. Costs can be trimmed by shifting pickup schedules from weekly to every other week, investing in automated trucks to reduce labor costs or simply redesigning collection routes to use fewer trucks or reduce the time needed to complete collection.

But the most promising cost-saving measure may be variable-rate waste management. Also known as pay-as-you-throw, this approach replaces the flat fee typically charged households for waste removal, including recyclables, yard trimmings and other trash, with fees that vary according to the amount of trash destined for the landfill or incinerator. "Pay-as-you-throw is an excellent program that bears consideration in most communities," says Lisa A. Skumatz, president of Skumatz Economic Research Associates in Seattle, who found the system raised recycling rates by up to 10 percent in more than 500 communities she studied. [9] "It can be extremely cost-effective, the biggest-bang item you can get to improve recycling and yard-waste diversion." She estimates that more than 5,000 communities have adopted variable-rate programs to date.

Pay-as-you-throw works by charging households for the waste they generate, and so provides an economic incentive to recycle or compost as much trash as possible. Customers usually are charged by the garbage can or by the bag for non-recyclable trash. In Seattle, for example, customers pay by the container. The program is not without glitches: Customers often jam as much as they can into one container — a practice so common it's known as the "Seattle stomp." "Some guy actually hurt his back jamming stuff into his trash barrel and sued the city," Franklin says. "But in general, the pay-as-you-throw system does seem to work. If we know there's a penalty for the second barrel of trash, the economic incentive helps us manage waste better."

Some communities have made the system more accurate by using special trucks equipped with scales to weigh the trash they collect. "The variable-rates approach works for the customer because it says you can do what you want," Skumatz says, "but you'll save real dollars if you recycle."

By placing greater responsibility on the customer, variable rates not only encourage people to recycle but also to reduce their consumption. "Recycling programs, whether they're mandatory or not, in no way encourage source reduction in the

first place," Skumatz says. "They don't encourage you to buy less, use both sides of the paper for photocopies or do other things to reduce the amount of stuff consumed. Variable rates does that — it adds something that even mandatory recycling can't accomplish."

But there is a downside to variable rate-systems. "While unit-based pricing rewards people who are more efficient, it's not a total panacea," Porter says. "People will haul their garbage to the Dumpster in the

> "Recycling programs don't encourage you to buy less, use both sides of the paper for photocopies or do other things to reduce the amount of stuff consumed. Variable rates does that — it adds something that even mandatory recycling can't accomplish."
>
> — *Lisa A. Skumatz, president, Skumatz Economic Research Associates*

McDonald's parking lot on their way to work, or they'll sort their mail in the post office and throw away the junk mail before going home. So there's a lot of trash shifting going on."

Porter also questions the ability of most people to drastically reduce the amount of stuff they consume. "What exactly are you supposed to do, stop buying milk or feeding the dog?" he asks. "You may get a 10 percent reduction in consumption with pay-as-you-throw, but not much more. People can't

change their habits that much."

Variable-rate programs also have limited impact beyond the supply side of the market for recyclables. "Pay-as-you-throw is the best idea we have now because it provides the correct signal to the consumer for wasting less," Raymond says. "The problem is, it doesn't solve the problems we have with recycling right now because it doesn't create markets. It just changes consumers' habits and improves their cooperation in putting all of their recyclables out. Now what are you going to do with them? You've got to have markets for them. Industry has to use recycled materials for the markets to operate properly."

Other critics object to pay-as-you-throw for the same reasons they object to all recycling programs. "I'm suspicious whenever governments at any level think they know exactly the right way to do things," Taylor says. "Some people will be annoyed at having to pay for each bag they throw out and would far rather pay a flat fee for trash removal. I don't think government should be involved in recycling at all. Each household should be allowed to make its own decisions about who's going to collect their garbage and under what terms." ■

BACKGROUND

Birth of a Movement

Throughout history, recycling has been the rule rather than the ex-

Continued on p. 276

Chronology

1940s *The first widespread residential recycling efforts emerge during World War II as consumers contribute scrap metals and paper to wartime industries.*

— • —

1960s *Concern builds over the nation's mounting waste stream.*

1962
Author Rachel Carson warns of the dangers of toxic chemicals left in landfills in her best-seller *Silent Spring*.

1965
The Solid Waste Disposal Act launches federal research into the technology of waste disposal and provides technical and financial assistance for state and local waste programs.

— • —

1970s *The environmental movement spurs interest in residential recycling.*

1970
The Resource Recovery Act extends federal assistance to recycling programs and waste incineration and requires states to come up with plans for managing their waste.

1975
More than 100 communities across the country have introduced curbside recycling, mostly for newspapers, in an effort to boost recycling. More than a quarter of all aluminum beverage cans, the most valuable post-consumer material, are recycled.

1976
The Resource Conservation and Recovery Act (RCRA) sets national standards for landfills and incinerators. By requiring the use of expensive landfill liners and smokestack scrubbers, the law indirectly encourages recycling.

1978
The Public Utilities Regulatory Policies Act (PURPA) encourages the development of waste-to-energy plants. Support for these alternatives to landfills later wanes, however, because of their emissions of toxic ash.

— • —

1980s *Acting on fears that landfill space is running out, communities across the country step up curbside recycling programs.*

1987
The *Mobro 4000*, a garbage barge out of Long Island, attracts national attention as it sails down the East Coast to the Caribbean in the vain search for a place to dump its cargo. The incident prompts concern, largely unfounded, that the entire country faces a landfill crisis.

1988
The Environmental Protection Agency (EPA) sets a recycling goal for the United States at 25 percent of total waste.

1990s *Recycling comes under scrutiny after a series of supply gluts causes upheaval in the markets for recycled materials.*

1991
Manufacturers' demand for recycled materials fails to keep pace with the supply following the sudden increase in curbside programs, causing the first major crash in the market for recyclables.

1993
President Clinton issues an executive order requiring all federal agencies to buy printing and writing paper with at least 30 percent recycled content by the end of 1998.

1995
The nationwide recycling rate reaches 27 percent, exceeding the EPA's 25 percent goal. Prices of recycled newsprint and some other materials reach historic peaks, prompting "garbage rustlers" to raid curbside bins for valuable materials. The Chicago Board of Trade sets up an electronic listing for recycled plastic, paper and glass that helps link buyers and sellers of these materials and thus improves the market's efficiency.

1996
Newsprint prices sink so low that some recycling contractors dump collected paper in landfills.

1997
The pace of new curbside programs begins to slow because most programs already collect the materials that are in demand by manufacturers.

How Germany Copes With Recycling Success

The United States may have launched the recycling movement, but other countries have embraced stricter recycling requirements, notably Germany. German manufacturers must take responsibility for collecting and recycling or reusing the packaging materials for the products they sell. Unlike U.S. recycling programs, which focus on consumers and for the most part rely on their cooperation, the German system embodies the "polluter-pays" principle. It holds that because industry is responsible for choosing what packaging it uses, it should bear the burden of recycling it.

The law was partly a consequence of the collapse of European communism. Before German reunification in 1990, West Germany had "solved" the problem of dwindling landfill space by exporting its trash to East Germany, where landfill regulations were minimal. [1] Meanwhile, West Germany's increasingly influential Green Party helped pass strong environmental protection regulations. With reunification, those regulations were extended to the whole country, and a new solution to Germany's waste problems had to be found.

The Ordinance on Avoidance of Packaging Waste, which took effect in June 1991, required industry to switch to reusable shipping cartons and reduce its use of non-essential "secondary" packaging, such as cardboard boxes containing bottles of aspirin or the plastic "blister" packs used to display many consumer goods. Beverage producers were able to comply with the law by using refillable bottles, a longstanding practice in much of Europe.

But problems quickly arose for essential, "primary" packaging materials, the countless pill bottles, toothpaste tubes and myriad other containers that manufacturers were required to take back and recycle or reuse under the law. Faced with a near-impossible obligation, German industries banded together and created a consortium — the Duales System Deutschland (DSD) — to provide collection and recycling services on their behalf. Manufacturers pay DSD for the right to place a green dot on their packaging, which exempts those items from the law's take-back provision. DSD then pays waste companies to collect those packaging materials from curbside bins or drop-off centers and sells the materials to industry for recycling.

The German system immediately boosted recycling rates.

By 1994, DSD had grown into a multibillion-dollar business and was recycling two-thirds of the country's packaging materials. But the system has also been the victim of its own success, especially in the collection and recycling of plastics. Overwhelmed by a glut of collected plastic packaging, DSD exported much of the excess to other countries where it was often buried or burned.

Despite its drawbacks, the German recycling system is being emulated in other countries, particularly in Europe, where high population densities make landfills less feasible than in the United States. As part of an effort to harmonize regulations throughout the 15-member European Union, the EU in 1994 adopted a Packaging Directive setting both minimum and maximum recycling goals — the latter aimed at avoiding some of the German system's problems. By 2001, all member countries are to recycle from 25-45 percent of their packaging. Germany, which already exceeds the maximum quota for all materials, must either reduce its recycling rate or demonstrate that it can recycle its own materials.

A number of countries have adopted or are considering recycling programs based on the German green dot system. For example, Austria, Belgium and France have introduced similar programs, modified to allow incineration of recyclables as a way to avoid the oversupply of materials that has hampered the German program.

The German model may have little appeal, however, in the United States, where recycling has always been a largely voluntary effort based on individual participation. Additionally, the German approach owes much of its success to the country's high population density and limited geographical area. In the United States, with its vast distances and large tracts of undeveloped land, landfilling is still an option, while transportation costs discourage recycling in many parts of the country.

"Germany's packaging law is the most stringent in the world, and they spend up to $4 billion a year enforcing it," says Michele Raymond, publisher of *State Recycling Laws Update*. "It's a totally different system there."

---

[1] Information in this section is based on Frank Ackerman, *Why Do We Recycle?* (1997), pp. 108-109.

Continued from p. 274

ception. Even after the Industrial Revolution ushered in the modern era of mass production and consumption of consumer products, many basic materials continued to be recycled. Until the late 19th century, for example, paper was made from rags, and the demand for rags upheld a robust market for used clothing and other textile scraps. [10] Scavengers picked garbage dumps for these and other materials that were routinely fed back into the production cycle. Today, the remnants of older types of recycling persist in the form of scrap dealerships where cars, appliances and other goods are broken up, sorted into their steel and other metal components and sold to mini-mills for use in new products.

Although recycling had always been a common business activity, it was not until the 1940s that people began collecting materials for reasons other than profit. During World War II, Americans voluntarily contributed metals, rubber and other materials for the war effort. More than a third of all paper and paperboard products, as well as other materials, were recovered and recycled by the war industries.

Recycling fell from view after the war, but re-emerged in the 1960s in response to a new concern — the environment. Lady Bird Johnson, the wife of President Lyndon B. Johnson, helped launch a campaign to clean up the trash strewn along the nation's roadways, and Rachel Carson, in her 1962 best-seller *Silent Spring*, warned of the dangers of toxic chemicals left in landfills. Largely unregulated at the time, landfills were frequently used as dumps for hazardous wastes, which leached into the groundwater. [11] Recycling was seen as a way to reduce the amount of trash and thus the need for more landfills.

By the early 1970s, thousands of grass-roots recycling centers had appeared where consumers could drop off newspapers, glass bottles and aluminum cans. In addition, by 1974 more than 100 communities had set up curbside collection services for recyclables, mostly newspapers. Newspaper collection fell off following a slump in the newsprint market in the mid-1970s. But the demand for recycled aluminum remained strong; by 1975, a quarter of all aluminum cans were being recycled.

Federal Role

Although recycling has always been a matter of state and local jurisdiction, the federal government has enacted several laws since the environmental movement's inception in the 1960s that have indirectly influenced the progress of recycling programs. [12] The 1965 Solid Waste Disposal Act launched federal research into the technology of

Of the 208 million tons of municipal solid waste generated in the United States in 1995, 57 percent ended up in landfills.

waste disposal and provided technical and financial assistance for state and local waste programs. The 1970 Resource Recovery Act extended the federal effort to include recycling programs and waste incineration, including waste-to-energy facilities, which generate steam or electricity from burning garbage. [13] The law stopped short, however, of setting standards, and it required states to come up with plans for managing their waste as a condition for receiving the federal aid.

The 1976 Resource Conservation and

Recovery Act (RCRA) set national standards for landfills and incinerators that were strengthened in 1984. While the law did not address recycling directly, its requirements of environmental safeguards, such as landfill liners and smokestack filters, made it more expensive to bury or burn waste and thus encouraged recycling indirectly.

Waste incineration gained support as an attractive source of energy in the wake of the energy crises of the 1970s. In 1978, Congress encouraged the development of waste-to-energy facilities with the Public Utilities Regulatory Policies Act (PURPA), which required utilities to buy power from these plants at favorable rates. Enthusiasm for waste-to-energy facilities soon cooled, however, out of concern over the toxic ash they generate, which must be disposed of in special landfills. As a result, only about 16 percent of municipal solid waste is incinerated. [14]

Landfill 'Crisis'

The administration of Ronald Reagan (1981-1989) enacted no major laws dealing with solid waste. But public perceptions that the country's mounting trash flow posed threats to the environment continued. These fears escalated in 1987, when the *Mobro 4000*, a garbage scow, sailed for days down the East Coast and into the Caribbean Sea in search of a port to dump its fetid cargo.

The widely publicized voyage came to symbolize the emergence of a landfill "crisis," in which cities, having run out of space to bury their own garbage, were desperately trying to export it to other jurisdictions.

As it turned out, the *Mobro's* problems had little to do with the lack of landfill space. The barge operator had simply set sail without signing any agreements with landfill operators to dump its garbage, and port authorities turned the scow away, not because local landfills were full but because they feared it carried hazardous wastes. [15] But the *Mobro's* wayward journey bolstered public support for recycling as a solution to the problem.

By this time, recycling operations had expanded in number and in the range of materials collected. Beginning in the early 1980s, recycling operators built "material-recovery facilities" where they could sort, bale and market the recyclable materials they collected in curbside programs. In the absence of federal standards for recycling, states set their own standards. Today, most states have passed laws aimed at reducing the total waste stream and encouraging recycling as well as composting of yard trimmings. [16] ■

CURRENT SITUATION

An Uncertain Market

C ommunity recycling programs are just the first link in the recycling process. The next role is played by markets for recyclable materials — the paper mills, steel mills, aluminum smelters, glass container makers and plastics reprocessors that transform these materials into new products.

The 1990s have seen both unprecedented growth in recycling programs and volatility in the markets for recyclable materials. A glut in the supply of recyclables that followed the sudden increase in curbside programs in the late 1980s caused a crash in prices in 1991, as new manufacturing plants failed to keep pace with the supply of raw materials. A so-called "basket" of recyclables that fetched $70 a ton in 1989 went for just $25 a ton by 1992, prompting some communities to pay haulers to cart away the materials they had collected. [17]

Barely two years later, however, prices soared. Old corrugated cardboard rose in value from $25 to $150 a ton during the first six months of 1994, while mixed paper prices skyrocketed from $5 to more than $200 a ton. Prices for old newsprint, plastic soda bottles and milk jugs and aluminum cans also soared. [18] Boom again turned to bust in mid-1995, when prices for paper and plastics plummeted.

Such extreme swings in the market come as no surprise to recycling experts. "After all, these are market commodities, and how they fare depends on what is going on in the overall economy," Keller says. "If the economy goes south and people stop making as many houses and automobiles and buy less retail goods, you'll see a drop-off in the end market for recyclables."

Today, recycling in the United States is a $30 billion industry. As the industry has grown, the market for recyclables has become somewhat more stable, and while prices for most materials are nowhere near their peaks of three years ago, they are close to historical norms. According to R.W. Beck Inc., a consulting and engineering firm that tracks the market in recyclables, the value of a basket of nine materials it measures stood at an estimated $80 a ton in 1997, much lower than the $145

reported in 1995 but higher than the $68 reported in 1996. [19] A closer look shows how different market conditions are for the most commonly recycled materials:

Paper — Almost 40 million tons of paper were recovered from the waste stream in 1996, or nearly 85 percent of all recycled materials. More than half of that was corrugated containers, the single largest item in Beck's index. These are primarily boxes used for packaging and shipping goods from factories to retailers, and most are collected through privately contracted recycling programs. Demand for this material is generally strong.

The glut of old newspapers that sent the market into a tailspin three years ago has abated, in part because growth in newspaper circulation has slowed with the advent and growth of electronic news media. Mixed paper, one of the more recent items included in curbside collection, is expected to be in greater demand as an alternative to corrugated boxes for the production of paperboard, used to make shoeboxes, cereal boxes and other items. Likewise, high-grade paper is in demand, in part because of federal and state purchasing mandates requiring public agencies to buy writing and printing paper with recycled content.

Prices for recycled paper in 1997 ranged between $5.69 per ton for mixed paper to $109 per ton for high-grade paper. With the exception of old newspapers, which fell slightly in 1997 to $15 a ton, prices for recycled paper materials rose slightly from 1996 to 1997.

Although many deinking plants were built in response to the 1995 peak in paper prices, a number of paper recycling manufacturers have been in business for years. Marcal Paper Mills Inc., for example, has been using a variety of waste papers to make 100 percent recycled-content napkins, tissues and paper towels at its Elmwood Park, N.J., plant since 1947.

New deinking technology that can reprocess coated paper, such as old magazines and catalogs, has increased demand for a broader range of paper products than was once collected for recycling. But paper mills still report problems resulting from contamination of the materials, especially from "stickies," or adhesive notes, which raise the cost of producing recycled paper. [20]

Glass — After newspapers, glass containers are the most common item by weight found in residential waste. Although they are rapidly being replaced by plastics for soft drinks, glass bottles and jars are widely used to package beer, other drinks and food products. Recovery of glass containers has fallen slightly since it peaked in 1994. Prices for clear glass — the only type measured in Beck's analysis — fell 20 percent in 1997, to $37 a ton.

Clear, green and brown glass bottles have different properties and must be processed separately. In areas where they are collected together, breakage can quickly contaminate the recovered materials. Another obstacle to reprocessing glass is its weight, which makes it costly to ship, especially in sparsely populated regions such as the Mountain West. Transportation is becoming a greater factor in the cost of reprocessing glass because of consolidation: 127 regional plants have been replaced by 62 larger plants over the past 20 years. [21]

Steel cans — Scrapped appliances as well as steel cans collected curbside account for most steel and iron recovered from municipal solid waste. Almost 60 percent of all steel cans produced in the United States, mostly food cans, are recov-

ered for recycling, and the percentage is growing steadily, thanks in part to the recent inclusion of aerosol cans in many curbside programs. Perhaps reflecting that trend, prices for baled steel cans fell to $50 a ton in 1997, the lowest level reported by Beck since 1980. However, given high demand for scrap steel by the steel industry in the United States and abroad and the recent increase in the number of electric-arc furnaces in

After peaking in 1995, prices for recycled newsprint sank so low that some contractors simply dumped the paper they collected in landfills.

operation, prices for recycled steel are expected to rise in coming months. [22]

Aluminum cans — At 64 percent, the 1997 recycling rate for aluminum beverage cans outstrips that

for steel cans, and amounts to about a million tons a year. But the price of aluminum cans is much higher — $1,090 a ton in 1997 — and has risen by more than half since 1993, making these the most valuable items collected in most curbside programs. Unlike most recyclables, aluminum is relatively unaltered by reprocessing, so it can be recycled over and over again with little sacrifice in quality. Aluminum cans are unusual also because they typically emerge from the recycling process as new aluminum cans, completing the closed loop depicted in the universal symbol designating products with recycled content. Domestic demand for aluminum cans is so high that less than 1 percent of them are exported to overseas processors.

Plastic — More than half of the nation's roughly 32,000 communities have access to programs that collect one or more types of plastic. [23] But plastic recycling has been hampered by the difficulty of separating the different types of containers and packaging materials and reprocessing them into materials suitable for remanufacture. Of the scores of plastic resins used in manufacturing, six are most commonly found in everyday consumer products. Of these, only two have been widely included in recycling programs — polyethylene terephthalate (PET), used to make beverage bottles, and high-density polyethylene (HDPE), used in milk jugs and other containers.*

———————————————

*Plastic containers are numbered from 1-7 depending on which resins they contain.

Prices for old PET bottles, much like those for recycled paper, have fluctuated in recent years, ranging from a record high of $354 per ton in 1995 to $40 per ton in 1996. The main reason for the crash in prices for PET bottles was the opening of numerous factories here and abroad producing virgin resin, which curbed demand for scrap PET. Last year, Beck reports, PET prices rebounded to $118 per ton. There is no lack of capacity to reclaim PET — 27 plants in 18 states processed more than 300,000 pounds of post-consumer PET in 1995. [24]

Both the recovery rate and prices for HDPE bottles have risen in recent years. Many recycling programs have expanded the list of eligible HDPE items to include water and juice bottles as well as pigmented bottles used for liquid detergents. Baled HDPE containers, which totaled 660 million tons, brought $421 a ton last year, almost as much as during the 1995 peak. Recycled HDPE is often used to make new containers, plastic plumbing pipes, leaf bags and plastic "lumber."

The complexity of plastics recycling makes it hard to develop stable markets for products made of resins other than PET and HDPE, however. New technologies are making it possible to break plastic materials down into their original state, so that they are virtually indistinguishable from virgin resins, but most resin producers have not invested in this technology. [25] "Remember, these producers are the Exxons of this world, large, traditional companies that are not likely to spend money for a small niche business like recycling," Raymond says. "Anyway, why should they want to use

less virgin resin? They're selling more and more of it, 40 percent more over the past six years alone. Plastics surpassed steel in the 1970s in terms of volume. Today it's bigger than just about anything."

Most of the plastic that is recycled

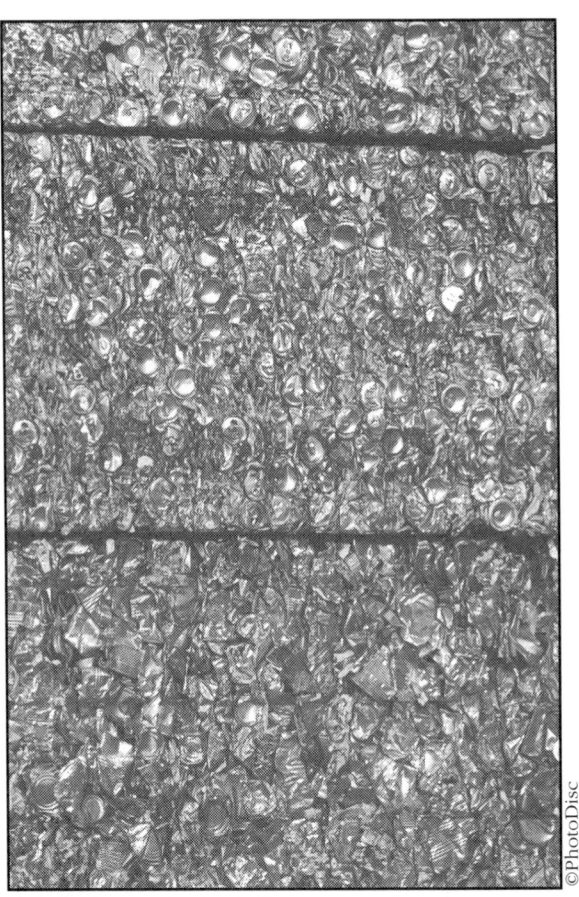

Nearly two-thirds of all aluminum beverage cans were recycled in 1997. About a million tons of aluminum cans are recycled each year.

©PhotoDisc

undergoes only partial reprocessing before it is transformed into new products, products that bear little resemblance to the bottles and packaging materials consumers tossed in the bin. In such an "open-loop" application, plastic bottles are washed, ground up and made into fiber for fleece jackets and carpets, or they are exported. Only about 16 percent is used to make new bottles. [26]

Another obstacle to further plastic

recycling is the growing popularity of single-serve PET drink bottles. Because they are often used and discarded away from home, these bottles often elude recycling programs and end up in the trash. Businesses and public agencies are beginning to install special bins to encourage recycling of these bottles.

Compost — Though it is collected separately from other recycled items, yard trimmings are commonly picked up curbside and hauled to a municipal composting facility. Once composted, leaves, grass clippings, branches and some food wastes produce a nutrient-rich soil additive that is purchased by nurseries, landscapers and residential gardeners. But because its value is so low in most parts of the country, the cost of collecting yard wastes is usually borne by consumers and embedded in the bill for solid waste removal.

Some communities provide special bins to encourage households to compost their own organic wastes and keep this material out of landfills. In the Northeast and other areas where landfill operators charge high "tipping" fees to dump trash, yard wastes are actually banned from the waste stream.

Communities Pitch In

The 1990s have seen rapid growth in recycling efforts. Today, about 27 percent of the nation's municipal solid waste is being recovered through

Continued on p. 282

At Issue:

Does recycling make economic sense?

RICHARD A. DENISON AND JOHN F. RUSTON

Denison is a senior scientist and Ruston is an economic analyst at the Environmental Defense Fund

FROM "ANTI-RECYCLING MYTHS," ENVIRONMENTAL DEFENSE FUND, JULY 18, 1996.

*r*ecycling is not just an alternative to traditional solid waste disposal, it is the foundation for large, robust manufacturing industries in the United States that use recyclable materials. These businesses are an important part of our economy and provide the market foundation for the entire recycling process. . . .

Recycling provides manufacturing industries with raw materials that are less expensive than virgin sources, a long-term economic advantage that translates into value for consumers who ultimately spend less on products and packaging. For example, in the area of paper manufacturing, new mills making paper for corrugated boxes, newsprint, commercial tissue products and folding cartons have lower capital and operating costs than new mills using virgin wood. . . . Recycling has long been the lower-cost manufacturing option for aluminum smelters, and is essential to the scrap-fired steel "mini-mills" that are part of the rebirth of a globally competitive U.S. steel industry. . . .

In a recent study examining 10 Northeastern states, recycling was found to have added $7.2 billion in value to recovered materials through processing and manufacturing activities. These activities employed approximately 103,000 people, 25 percent of them in materials processing and 75 percent in manufacturing. . . .

Market prices for materials like polystyrene are set in the near term by supply and demand forces, underpinned by a host of production cost factors, many of which have nothing to do with environmental impact. An entire sub-discipline of environmental economics has developed to address a range of environmental damages, called externalities, that are not reflected in market prices even in the most regulated industries. . . . [When] a coastal wetland in the Carolinas is converted to a pine plantation and results in damage to estuarine fish hatcheries or reduced water quality, such impacts are certainly not captured in the market price of wood taken from the site.

Nor are any of the costs of disposal included in product prices. If someone drains motor oil from a car into the gutter, it may pollute surface water or groundwater. But the price originally paid for the oil does not anticipate its proper or improper disposal. Finally, another major obstacle to incorporating environmental factors into market prices is the difficulty or impossibility of assigning a meaningful economic cost to such "goods," for example, the value of preserving a rare animal or plant species.

JERRY TAYLOR

Director of natural resource studies at the Cato Institute and senior editor of Regulation *magazine*

FROM "MINIMUM CONTENT: MINIMUM SENSE," THE CATO INSTITUTE, April 25, 1997.

*t*en years into America's holy war against garbage, the case for residential curbside recycling has run smack into the harsh realities of economics. If resources are indeed becoming more scarce, they have a funny way of showing it. Prices for energy, minerals and paper have continued to fall as they have over the course of the century. . . . Post-consumer material is less competitive with virgin material than ever before. . . .

"But," you might point out, "what about the environmental externalities of the mining, timber, paper and energy industries? If you accounted for that, wouldn't recycling be competitive?" Again, not necessarily. First, we have no reliable means by which we can "price" those externalities. Second, those industries do spend tens of billions of dollars annually to comply with federal and state environmental regulations. Are the environmental externalities they impose greater than, less than or equal to the regulatory costs they pay to do business? No one knows for sure, but a number of respected economists . . . strongly suspect the environmental externalities of those industries are more than paid for through the cost of regulatory compliance.

Nor are the externalities of recycling's alternative all that impressive. EPA regulations now ensure that solid waste landfills cause only one additional cancer risk every 13 years, and that's assuming we use such worst-case scenarios and assumptions that even that figure, according to most risk assessment specialists, probably overestimates the actual risk by 100 to 1,000 times the actual risk. Likewise, municipal waste incinerators, according to those same worst-case assumptions, pose less than a 1 in 1 million risk to neighboring communities. . . .

Finally, recycling has its own environmental externalities that must be put into the equation. After all, the actual process of extracting usable raw material from a product is an industrial activity every bit as involved as the process of combining various raw materials to make a product. Both are industrial activities. And both create waste. For example, recycling 100 tons of old newsprint generates 40 tons of toxic waste. Is this consequential? Sure. EPA has reported that 13 of the 50 worst Superfund sites are/were recycling facilities.

If recycling makes economic sense, we don't need to mandate it. And if it doesn't, we shouldn't. You can make a silk purse out of a sow's ear . . . but it's usually cheaper to use silk.

Continued from p. 280

recycling, up from just 17 percent in 1990. But because materials that are relatively easy to recycle are already being collected by many programs, the pace of new program start-ups has slowed over the past year, a trend that experts predict will continue.

Recycling often pays for itself in peak years, such as 1995, when communities earn more from selling materials than they spend to collect them. But when the value of recyclables drops, as it did in 1996, recycling often poses a financial burden on local governments, undermining support for the programs.

State and local budget cuts also are forcing many communities to reassess recycling programs. Several cities, including beleaguered Washington, D.C., dropped residential recycling altogether. Miami's City Council planned to do the same until public protests against the move. Many localities have cut back on frequency of collection and taken other steps to reduce costs. [27]

Even in Washington state, one of the leaders in recycling efforts, budget cuts are taking a toll. The Clean Washington Center is a state agency that helped Seattle and Tacoma achieve recycling rates of about half their waste by developing markets for recyclables. But last year the center, which also provides information to recycling programs throughout the country, was cut from the state budget altogether and forced to become an independent organization. ■

OUTLOOK

No End of Trash

While recycling programs are not growing as fast as they did in the early 1990s, many experts predict that they will continue to expand. "The amount of trash out there is tending to grow at a slower rate than in the past," Franklin says. "Longer-term, we expect the recycling rate to reach 30 percent of the waste stream by 2000 and 35 percent by 2020." He predicts that most of the increase will result from expanding municipal composting facilities to include more yard waste and food waste rather than new materials collected for sale to manufacturers. "We'll see more composting of paper that's too contaminated for traditional recycling, such as food packages, paper napkins, food waste and even wood."

Consumer preference is likely to be a key determinant of recycling's future in the United States. Americans — both manufacturers and consumers — may embrace recycling on the supply side by participating in recycling programs, but they have been less enthusiastic consumers of recyclable materials and recycled-content end products. "Recyclables tend to be the last hired and the first fired," Keller quips. "If the economy is good, more recyclables get used, but if the economy is not going well, people go back to things they're more comfortable with."

In the absence of pressing consumer demand for recycled products, Raymond predicts, manufacturers are unlikely to boost production of these goods. "We don't have a crisis, virgin materials are cheap, energy is cheap and tip fees are very low, so industry has no incentive to use more recycled materials," Raymond says. "That's just corporate behavior as history has always shown it to be."

Many experts say the decade since curbside recycling took off, boosting the supply of recyclable materials, is too short a time to accurately assess the recycling market's full potential. Technological advances continue to broaden the range of materials that can be recycled cost-effectively, and new processing facilities can be expected to boost demand for post-consumer materials. "We will never reach the point where industries will be dependent on recycled materials alone," Keller says. "Although steel can be recycled an infinite number of times, paper loses a little fiber every time it's recycled, so we're going to still need virgin materials. But the technology will continue to improve, and we'll find ways to recycle materials now considered non-recyclable. There's no question that as technology changes, the variety of things we can recycle will improve over time."

Anticipating such an expansion, the Chicago Board of Trade in 1995 set up an electronic listing for recycled plastic, paper and glass that helps link buyers and sellers of these materials and thus makes the market more efficient. "It's not a full-fledged commodities market," Scarlett says, "but it's growing and provides another tweaking mechanism that helps increase information flows and improve recycling markets."

Of course, industry responds to consumer demand as well as the cost of raw materials. And for the most part, Americans remain unreliable end users of products made from recycled materials, which many view as inferior in quality.

"People in the food-processing industry will tell you that as a rule putting the green seal of approval on a product indicating it is environmentally benign is going to cost them market share," Taylor says. "People avoid it because they think it's flimsy, unsanitary or not up to standard performance."

Even active participants in recycling programs overlook recycled-content products. "Sure, there are some 'greens' out there, but the vast majority of us are more sensitive to price and quality than to environmental concerns," Raymond says. "Do I have the time to read the labels on all the products that I buy in the grocery store when I have only 30 minutes to get the shopping done? Get real."

Recent trends suggest those attitudes are slowly changing, however. Environmentally concerned consumers are driving growth in retail businesses such as the Fresh Fields-Whole Foods grocery chain, which specializes in environmentally benign products, including those with recycled content. In any case, consumer demand for recycled-content products may not be necessary for further expansion of this market, which Keller says already accounts for at least $10 billion in sales each year, because so many products include recycled materials even though they don't bear the green seal.

"There is no question that there are still remnants of the population who view recycled materials as inferior," Keller says. "But lots of recycled-content products have been quietly used for decades. There is no steel in the United States that doesn't have a minimum of 25 percent recycled content. There are no paper mills being built in the United States today that depend on virgin materials alone. Even *Air Force One* flies on retread tires." ∎

Notes

[1] See Franklin Associates Ltd., *Solid Waste Management at the Crossroads* (December 1997). For background, see "Garbage Crisis," *The CQ Researcher*, March 20, 1992, pp. 241-264.

[2] Franklin Associates Ltd., *op. cit.*, p. 1-16. Franklin Associates provides the EPA with data on recycling. See also J. Winston Porter, *Trash Facts IV*, Waste Policy Center, 1997.

[3] John Tierney, "Recycling Is Garbage," *The New York Times Magazine*, June 30, 1996.

[4] Richard A. Denison and John F. Ruston, "Recycling Is Not Garbage," *Technology Review*, October 1997.

[5] The poll, conducted by American Opinion Research for the now-defunct Council on Packaging in the Environment in 1996, was cited in Bill Noone, "'Closing the Loop' Remains a Priority for Packagers," *Packaging Technology & Engineering*, November 1996.

[6] Porter, *op. cit.*

[7] Denison and Ruston, *op. cit.*

[8] For background on air pollution, see "New Air Quality Standards," *The CQ Researcher*, March 7, 1997, pp. 193-216.

[9] Lisa A. Skumatz, "Nationwide Diversion Rate Study: Quantitative Effects of Program Choices on Recycling and Green Waste Diversion: Beyond Case Studies," Skumatz Economic Research Associates Inc., July 1996.

[10] Information in this section is based on Frank Ackerman, *Why Do We Recycle?* (1997), pp. 14-19.

[11] For background, see "Cleaning Up Hazardous Wastes," *The CQ Researcher*, Aug. 23, 1996, pp. 745-768 and "Water Quality," *The CQ Researcher*, Feb. 11, 1994, pp. 121-144.

[12] For background, see "Environmental Movement at 25," *The CQ Researcher*, March 31, 1995, pp. 288-311.

[13] For background, see "Renewable Energy," *The CQ Researcher*, Nov. 7, 1997, pp. 961-984.

[14] Ackerman, *op. cit.*, p. 18.

[15] *Ibid*, pp. 11-12.

[16] *Ibid*, p. 18.

[17] See Lynn Scarlett, "Roller Coaster Recycling Markets: Down, Up, and What's Next?" *MSW Management*, January/February 1996, p. 51.

[18] *Ibid*.

[19] See Jessica Lucyshyn and Robert Craggs, "A Five-Year History of Recycling Market Prices: 1997 Update," *Resource Recycling*, February 1998, p. 16.

[20] See Franklin Associates Ltd., *op. cit.*, p. 4-8.

[21] *Ibid*., p. 4-14.

[22] *Ibid*., p. 4-12.

[23] "'America Recycles Day' to Raise Awareness of Recycling and Buying Recycled Products," *PR Newswire*, Nov. 14, 1997.

[24] Franklin Associates Ltd., *op. cit.*, p. 4-9.

[25] See Susan Warren, "Environment: Polyester Trash Is Pure Plastic after an 'Unzip,'" *The Wall Street Journal*, Nov. 6, 1997.

[26] Franklin Associates Ltd., *op. cit.*, p. 4-9.

[27] See Jim Glenn, "Year End Review of Recycling and Composting," *BioCycle*, December 1997.

Bibliography

Selected Sources Used

Books

Ackerman, Frank, *Why Do We Recycle? Markets, Values, and Public Policy*, Island Press, 1997.

The author, a professor at Tufts University's Global Development and Environment Institute, reviews the history and market development of recycling. He argues that environmental as well as economic concerns must be included in any assessment of recycling's value.

Articles

"America's Recyclers: A Funny Sort of Market," *The Economist*, Oct. 18, 1997, pp. 63-64.

Government mandates have skewed the markets for recyclable materials, according to this article, by increasing supply with no concern for demand by industry.

Denison, Richard A., and John F. Ruston, "Recycling Is Not Garbage," *Technology Review*, October 1997.

In this response to an earlier critique of recycling, two researchers at the Environmental Defense Fund point out the economic and environmental benefits of recycling and call for efforts to improve the efficiency of community programs.

Lucyshyn, Jessica, and Robert Craggs, "A Five-Year History of Recycling Market Prices: 1997 Update," *Resource Recycling*, February 1998.

Two recycling analysts with R.W. Beck Inc., a national consulting and engineering firm, point out that markets for recycled materials have become less volatile in the past two years and suggest that program managers may be better prepared to avert the oversupply that buffeted the markets in 1996.

Scarlett, Lynn, "Roller Coaster Recycling Markets: Down, Up, and What's Next?" *MSW Management*, January/February 1996, pp. 50-53.

The gyrations in the markets for recycled materials seen in the mid-1990s are likely to continue, the author writes, because numerous events that are beyond the control of governments will continue to affect demand.

Skumatz, Lisa A., Erin Truitt and John Green, "The State of Variable Rates: Economic Signals Move into the Mainstream," *Resource Recycling*, August 1997, pp. 31-35.

By charging consumers for the amount of non-recyclable waste they generate, the authors write, communities can greatly increase recycling rates. More than 4,400 communities in the United States and Canada have integrated this approach into their waste collection programs.

Reports and Studies

Franklin Associates Ltd., *Solid Waste Management at the Crossroads*, December 1997.

This research firm, which provides recycling data to the EPA, predicts that the recovery of recyclable materials will continue to grow, though more slowly than in the past, reaching 35 percent by 2010.

Raymond Communications Inc., *State Recycling Laws Update*, Year-End Edition 1997.

State lawmakers enacted a total of 70 recycling bills in 1996, out of nearly 200 bills followed by this annual study. Local governments, however, maintained their commitment to recycling.

Scarlett, Lynn, Richard McCann, Robert Anex and Alexander Volokh, *Packaging, Recycling, and Solid Waste*, Reason Public Policy Institute, July 1997.

This study from a think tank in Los Angeles, Calif., examines the economic costs and benefits of recycling and concludes that government mandates for recycling rates or levels of recycled content in finished products are unlikely to help the environment.

U.S. Environmental Protection Agency, *The Consumer's Handbook for Reducing Solid Waste*, August 1992.

This overview of recycling includes a guide to help consumers understand what types of materials are commonly included in curbside programs as well as community drop-off centers.

U.S. Environmental Protection Agency, *Manufacturing from Recyclables: 24 Case Studies of Successful Recycling Enterprises*, February 1995.

Companies specializing in products containing recycled materials are profiled. Most are small manufacturers in or near the communities generating the recyclables. They include makers of paper, plastic, glass and other products.

U.S. Environmental Protection Agency, *Recycling Works! State and Local Solutions to Solid Waste Management Problems*, January 1989.

This dated but still relevant study examines innovative approaches to recycling — including programs that didn't work — in 14 states and communities.

The Next Step

Additional information from UMI's Newspaper & Periodical Abstracts™ database

Environmental Benefits vs. Costs

Barlow, Jim, "Industry Embraces Built-In Recycling," *Houston Chronicle*, **July 20, 1997, p. E1.**

There's a gradual shift by business into something called life-cycle environmental management. Life-cycle management means companies look at the entire environmental impact of their products — starting from raw material to disposal after its useful life is over.

Fiske, John, "Americans Recycle More Paper Despite Low Demand," *Christian Science Monitor*, **Oct. 20, 1997, p. 13.**

Americans are recycling more paper than ever before. But for recycling to reduce the amount of virgin materials used and to reduce pollution, more demand is needed for recycled products. The American Forest & Paper Association reports that 63 percent of newsprint was recovered in 1996, up from 43 percent in 1990, to become an important new source of paper fibers. Recycling experts say recovered fiber is becoming as important a source of raw material as virgin fiber — or trees. Recycled fiber now represents 30 percent of the supply of new materials industrywide.

Kendall, Peter, "City Recycling as Much in the Bag as in Landfill," *Chicago Tribune*, **Dec. 16, 1997, p. 1.**

This fall, officials announced with pride that Chicago's ambitious, controversial and assuredly unique blue-bag recycling program had reached its goal of keeping 25 percent of the city's waste from going into a landfill. The problem is yard waste — and the unsortable dross it creates when mixed with other garbage. The stuff has too much garbage in it to be considered yard waste, which can be tilled into the soil. But it also has too much yard waste in it to be considered garbage, which is sent to the landfill.

Mohl, Bruce, "Wasted effort? The bottle-deposit law works: Four out of every five containers covered by the law get recycled," *The Boston Globe*, **Nov. 16, 1997, p. BGM23.**

Studies from supporters and opponents of expanding Massachusetts' successful bottle-deposit laws concur — expanding the law would be expensive and inefficient.

Scallan, Matt, "Harahan Leaders Aren't Pleased with Recycling," *New Orleans Times-Picayune*, **Oct. 10, 1997, p. BK1.**

Harahan started one of the first curbside recycling programs in the New Orleans area in 1991, but six years later several city officials are ready to dump it. City officials say the program collects about 550 tons of recyclables at a cost of about $75,000 a year.

Scallan, Matt, "Recycling Diverts Tiny Portion of Trash," *New Orleans Times-Picayune*, **Oct. 27, 1997, p. A1.**

Efforts have been made weekly in thousands of households across the New Orleans area for the past few years, yet recycling programs have made only a small dent in the stream of garbage flowing into landfills around the state. With some exceptions, most cities and parishes with curbside programs divert only 8-15 percent of the waste from landfills and into recycling, far short of the 25 percent target set by the Legislature in 1989. Even recycling supporters admit the program is an expensive, "feel-good" solution that has not gone far enough. That kind of arithmetic has some public officials wondering whether, despite its environmental benefits, curbside recycling is worth the money.

Snyder, Mike, "Brown Will Face Issue of Popular, but Costly, Curb Recycling Pickup," Dec. 15, 1997, *Houston Chronicle*, **p. A17.**

About 17 percent of Houston's residents use the city's curbside recycling operations, which is considerably lower than city officials' original goal of 100 percent. In 1997, the city estimates spending about $2 million to operate the curbside program and about $500,000 for eight drop-off recycling centers.

Volokh, Alexander; Scarlett, Lynn, "Is Recycling Good or Bad — or Both?" *Consumers' Research Magazine*, **September 1997, p. 14.**

Recycling makes economic and environmental sense in some cases and not in others, but the challenge is to know the difference.

Worthington, Rogers, "Suburban Recycling May Be Near a Peak: Northwest Surpasses 40 percent Rate, But Landfill Capacity a Concern," *Chicago Tribune*, **March 6, 1997, p. 1D1.**

A decade ago, many suburban officials fretted about brimming landfills and loaded garbage trucks with no place to unload. Then they got serious about recycling. In fact, the northwest suburbs have been so successful in recycling their residential trash that they may have maxed out, said Brooke Beal, executive director of the Solid Waste Association of Northern Cook County, which has 23 member municipalities. The northwest suburbs also are well ahead of neighboring DuPage and Lake Counties, which each recycle about 30 percent of their garbage.

Market for Recyclables

"Biking Your Way to a Recycling Company," *Biocycle:*

Journal of Waste Recycling, October 1997, p. 18.

Graham Bergh's Portland, Ore.-based Resource Revival recycles used bicycle parts into CD racks, picture frames and other household goods.

"Carpet Recycling Project Proposed," *Biocycle: Journal of Waste Recycling*, January 1998, p. 22.

Allied Signal and DSM Chemicals are planning a joint venture that should recycle more than 200 million pounds of used carpet each year. The facility will be located in Augusta, Ga.

"Have Bike, Will Recycle," *Biocycle: Journal of Waste Recycling*, August 1997, p. 20.

The Fresh Aire Delivery Service collects recyclables using bicycles. The company currently collects recyclables from 230 residents and 30 businesses in Ames, Iowa, as well as 160 locations at the Iowa State University campus.

"Institute Encourages Steel Recycling," *Workbench*, October 1997, p. 16.

North America's most recycled consumer product is the automobile, and steel recycling saves enough energy annually to power one-fifth of the homes in the United States. The Steel Recycling Institute hopes to see 25 percent of new homes framed in steel by the year 2000.

"Recycling Textbooks," *Biocycle: Journal of Waste Recycling*, November 1997, p. 18.

Textbook industry executives have formed Book Value Inc. to recycle textbook samples that might otherwise end up in landfills when a proposed curriculum is rejected.

Biddle, David, "What's Wrong with Office Paper?" *Biocycle: Journal of Waste Recycling*, November 1997, p. 75.

Deinking mills have increased the flow of office paper wastes in the recycling stream, but lower grades of paper have been a problem. Recyclers are looking for a higher-quality mix.

Brown, Warren, "Chrysler Close to Turning Plastic Recyclables Into a Car," *The Washington Post*, Sept. 9, 1997, p. C3.

Chrysler takes material from pop bottles, adds chopped glass and something to resist the effects of ultraviolet rays, and puts in impact-resistant material such as rubber. These materials are then formed into a four-piece body that is put on a frame. Such a car could help Chrysler stay well on the right side of federal fuel economy standards in the United States, which says new-car fleets must average 27.5 miles per gallon. The CCV is designed to get 50 miles per gallon.

Carrier, Jim, "U.S. Home going 'green built'," *The Denver Post*, March 9, 1997, p. H1.

Tree-hugging became a mainstream business last week when U.S. Home, a $1 billion contractor, announced that every one of its new homes in the Denver area will be "green built," with more insulation, efficient appliances and recycled materials used in construction. The Houston-based company will build 900 homes in the metro area this year, each one containing environmentally friendly features required by an industry checklist. Their key improvement will be wrapping basement walls with insulation and stuffing insulation into hard-to-reach areas near the roof. U.S. Home's announcement triples the size of the Green Builder Program of the Home Builders Association of Metropolitan Denver. Last year, about 300 homes qualified.

Cortez, Angela, "Coors 'Desperate' for Recycled Glass," *The Denver Post*, Jan. 11, 1998, p. C1.

Although one of the state's largest trash haulers prefers not to pick up curbside glass for recycling anymore, the Coors Brewing Co. says it is "desperate" for glass and is urging people to continue to recycle. Coors spokesman Jon Goldman said recycling glass may not mean big money, but it can turn a profit and it's the responsible thing to do because recycling keeps the glass out of the landfills. The company's move concerned Goldman because Coors depends on recycled glass to make new bottles. Recycling glass also burns less energy than making new glass.

Eaton, John, "At Recycled Products, Plastic Makes Perfect," *The Denver Post*, May 5, 1997, p. E1.

Its products are attracting the attention of heavy hitters such as Sears, Roebuck & Co., Gates Rubber Co. and Payless Cashways' Hugh M. Woods stores. They're looking at the company's PlastiFence and its ParkingSpot. The products, both with patents pending, are unique, says Recycled Products CEO Gene Pendery. Perhaps most significant is what the fence does for the environment. Or what it doesn't do: "Each 100 feet of our fence will save the dumping of 5,000 one-gallon plastic jugs in a landfill," he says.

Ericson, Edward Jr., "Recycling the Army Way," *E: The Environmental Magazine*, March 1997, p. 16.

The Pentagon uses Depleted Uranium (DU) for artillery shells and armor plating for tanks, and it is now being fashioned into bullets. DU is a dense radioactive waste product left over after extracting U-235 to make bombs.

Esparza, Santiago, "Program Lets Cell-Phone Users Recycle Discarded Batteries," *Detroit News*, Feb. 13, 1997, p. C8.

For years, people have thrown away cellular phone batteries that could no longer be recharged. The batteries, made of nickel and cadmium, would then sit in landfills adding to the toxicity of the dump. Now the environmentally conscious can drop the batteries off at national retail stores, or even set up their own collection site. Collected batteries are sent to a nonprofit corporation that breaks batteries down, using the nickel for stainless steel and cadmium for making new cellular phone batteries.

Grogan, Peter L., "No Miracle Markets," *Biocycle: Journal of Waste Recycling*, January 1998, p. 86.

The growth of the middle class in Asia is creating a huge market for American recyclable commodities. Grogan discusses this growing market and how the United States can make the most of it.

Pardo, Steve, "In Fraser: Duo Arrested in Recycling Scheme," *Detroit News*, Oct. 21, 1997, p. D3.

Two Pennsylvania men were arrested at a Meijer store in Fraser after they brought at least 20,000 out-of-state cans to turn in for Michigan's dime deposit. They are the second pair from outside Michigan to be arrested this month at the same store on charges they tried to take advantage of the law that pays 10 cents per used bottle or can — the highest rate in the nation. The two men bought $500 worth of scrap aluminum cans, put them into a trailer and drove the cargo to Michigan, police said.

Government's Role

"Mayor Argues Asphalt, Concrete Count Toward Recycling Goals," *Biocycle: Journal of Waste Recycling*, August 1997, p. 23.

The State Supreme Court will rule on New York City's appeal of a decision that asphalt and concrete do not count toward recycling goals. The city has fought recycling quotas in court before and lost, but the city has delayed the deadline for meeting the quota of recycling one-quarter of the city's waste, which it does not meet if asphalt and concrete are not counted.

Bukro, Casey; Young, David, "EPA Ruling on Scrap Gives Recycling a Boost," *Chicago Tribune*, May 22, 1997, p. 3.

A new EPA ruling says scrap is not waste. After years of campaigning by the scrap industry, EPA Administrator Carol Browner on April 18 signed a final rule-making decree declaring that scrap metal is not solid waste under federal law. The ruling is especially important to metropolitan Chicago and the Midwest because both are major recycling centers.

Howe, Peter J., "State Eyes a Broader 'Recycle or Pay' Policy," *The Boston Globe*, Sept. 22, 1997, p. A1.

Massachusetts state officials are proposing to offer communities cash bounties for every ton they recycle and pay for the

cost of launching "pay-as-you-throw" trash collections.

Pillsbury, Hope, "Standardizing Recycling Measurements," *Biocycle: Journal of Waste Recycling*, January 1998, p. 39.

After several years of study, experimentation and field testing, the EPA has come up with a standardized methodology for measuring recycling rates. Pillsbury discusses these new standards and what they mean.

Schroer, Bill, "Recycling Program Generates Capital Where Drivers' Rubber Meets the Road," *The Denver Post*, March 10, 1997, p. C4.

Since the late 1960s, the environmental movement has earnestly embraced recycling by connecting consumption to mining, resource depletion and groundwater pollution. In 1993, the Colorado Legislature, with an understanding of these conditions and the vast public appeal for recycling, established Renew at the Colorado Housing and Finance Authority. This agency is a state-government-created, but independent, authority that provides housing and economic-development financing. Renew offers private or nonprofit recyclers, or firms that incorporate waste-diversion activities or recycling in their operations, below-prime-rate loans for working capital, equipment or real estate. Because applicants need not be recyclers to seek these loans, thousands of Colorado businesses are eligible for this financial assistance.

Scott, Peter, "Walton to Begin Quantity-Based Garbage Fees," *Atlanta Constitution*, Jan. 15, 1998, p. XJR7.

This article describes Walton County, Ga.'s "pay-as-you-throw" system of trash hauling. If citizens don't wish to utilize one of six designated sites throughout the county, they have the option of hiring a private hauler.

Landfills

"City Exceeds Its Recycling Goal of Diverting Garbage from Landfills," *Chicago Tribune*, Sept. 29, 1997, p. 2C3.

Chicago's recycling efforts are going so well that the city says it has exceeded its goal of diverting 25 percent of all city-collected garbage from landfills.

"More Is Recycled, but There's Also More of It," *Christian Science Monitor*, July 21, 1997, p. 16.

It may be garbage to you, but it's 'municipal solid waste' to trash professionals. Here are highlights from a report on municipal solid waste prepared for the EPA and released last month: 208 million tons of municipal solid waste were generated in the United States in 1995, down 1 million tons from 1994. (In 1960, it was 88 million tons.)

Back Issues

Great Research on Current Issues Starts Right Here.
Recent topics covered by The CQ Researcher are listed below.
Now available on the Web
For information, call (800) 432-2250 ext. 279 or (202) 887-6279.

If you would like to have any of these CQ Researchers updated, or need more information
about these topics, please call CQ Custom Research. Special rates for CQ subscribers.
(202) 887-8600 or (800) 432-2250, ext. 600, or email Custom.Research@cq.com

DECEMBER 1996
Welfare, Work and the States
The New Volunteerism
Implementing the Disabilities Act
America's Pampered Pets

JANUARY 1997
Combating Scientific Misconduct
Restructuring the Electric Industry
The New Immigrants
Chemical and Biological Weapons

FEBRUARY 1997
Assisting Refugees
Alternative Medicine's Next Phase
Independent Counsels
Feminism's Future

MARCH 1997
New Air Quality Standards
Alcohol Advertising
Civic Renewal
Educating Gifted Students

APRIL 1997
Declining Crime Rates
The FBI Under Fire
Gender Equity in Sports
Space Program's Future

MAY 1997
The Stock Market
The Cloning Controversy
Expanding NATO
The Future of Libraries

JUNE 1997
FDA Reform
China After Deng
Line-Item Veto
Breast Cancer

JULY 1997
Transportation Policy
Executive Pay
School Choice Debate
Aggressive Driving

AUGUST 1997
Age Discrimination
Banning Land Mines
Children's Television
Evolution vs. Creationism

SEPTEMBER 1997
Caring for the Dying
Mental Health Policy
Mexico's Future
Youth Fitness

OCTOBER 1997
Urban Sprawl in the West
Diversity in the Workplace
Teacher Education
Contingent Work Force

NOVEMBER 1997
Renewable Energy
Artificial Intelligence
Religious Persecution
Roe v. Wade at 25

DECEMBER 1997
Whistleblowers
Castro's Next Move
Gun Control Standoff
Regulating Nonprofits

JANUARY 1998
Foster Care Reform
IRS Reform
The Black Middle Class
U.S.-British Relations

FEBRUARY 1998
Patients' Rights
Deflation Fears
Caring for the Elderly
The New Corporate Philanthropy

MARCH 1998
Israel at 50
The Federal Judiciary
Drinking on Campus

Back issues are available for $5.00 (sub-scribers) or $10.00 (non-subscribers). Quantity discounts apply to orders over 10. To order, call Congressional Quarterly Customer Service at (202) 887-8621.

Binders are available for $18.00. To order call 1-800-638-1710. Please refer to stock number 648.

Future Topics

▶ *Biology and Behavior*

▶ *Liberal Arts Education*

▶ *Income Inequality*

THE

CQ Researcher

PUBLISHED BY CONGRESSIONAL QUARTERLY INC.

Biology and Behavior

How much do our genes drive the way we act?

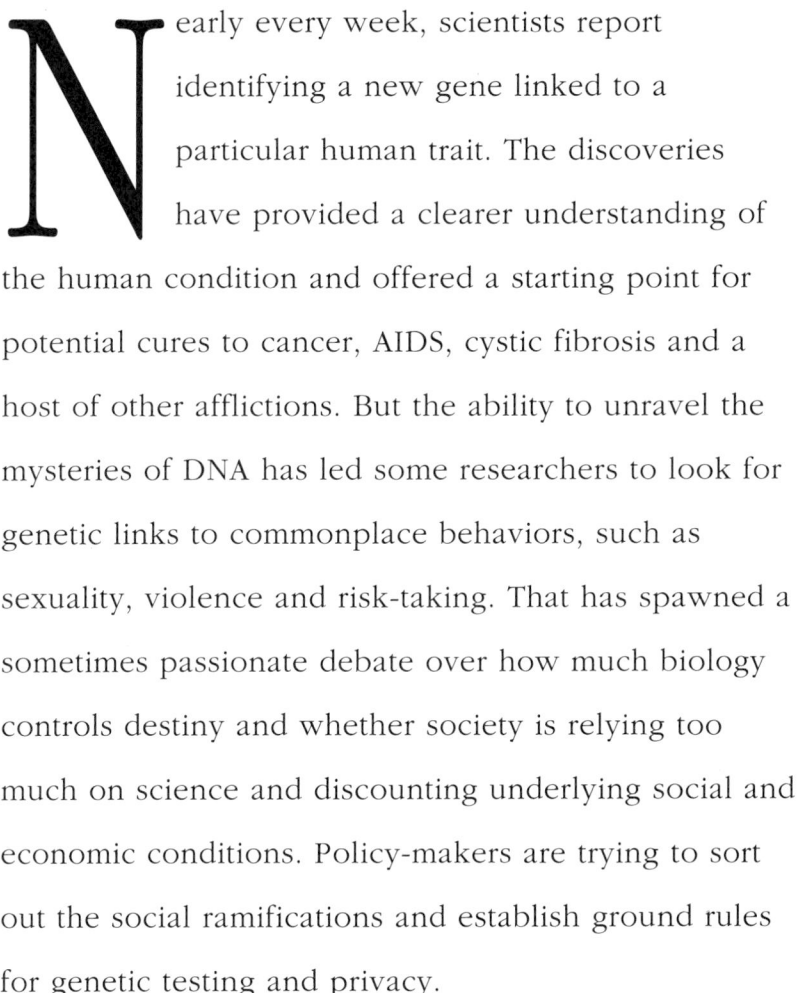

early every week, scientists report identifying a new gene linked to a particular human trait. The discoveries have provided a clearer understanding of the human condition and offered a starting point for potential cures to cancer, AIDS, cystic fibrosis and a host of other afflictions. But the ability to unravel the mysteries of DNA has led some researchers to look for genetic links to commonplace behaviors, such as sexuality, violence and risk-taking. That has spawned a sometimes passionate debate over how much biology controls destiny and whether society is relying too much on science and discounting underlying social and economic conditions. Policy-makers are trying to sort out the social ramifications and establish ground rules for genetic testing and privacy.

CQ April 3, 1998 • Volume 8, No. 13 • Pages 289-312

Formerly Editorial Research Reports ®

THE CQ Researcher

April 3, 1998
Volume 8, No.13

EDITOR
Sandra Stencel

MANAGING EDITOR
Thomas J. Colin

ASSOCIATE EDITOR
Sarah M. Magner

STAFF WRITERS
Adriel Bettelheim
Mary H. Cooper
Kenneth Jost
David Masci

PRODUCTION EDITOR
Melissa Hall

EDITORIAL ASSISTANT
Laura S. Cavender

PUBLISHED BY
Congressional Quarterly Inc.

CHAIRMAN
Andrew Barnes

VICE CHAIRMAN
Andrew P. Corty

PRESIDENT AND PUBLISHER
Robert W. Merry

EXECUTIVE EDITOR
David Rapp

Bibliographic records and abstracts included in The Next Step section of this publication are the copyrighted material of UMI, and are used with permission.

The CQ Researcher (ISSN 1056-2036). Formerly Editorial Research Reports. Published weekly, except Jan. 2, May 29, July 3, Oct. 30, by Congressional Quarterly Inc., 1414 22nd St., N.W., Washington, D.C. 20037. Annual subscription rate for libraries, businesses and government is $340. Additional rates furnished upon request. Periodicals postage paid at Washington, D.C., and additional mailing offices. POSTMASTER: Send address changes to The CQ Researcher, 1414 22nd St., N.W., Washington, D.C. 20037.

PHOTO: LAB MICE HAVE PLAYED A CRITICAL ROLE IN RECENT GENETIC DISCOVERIES.
©G. ROBERT BISHOP

Biology and Behavior

THE ISSUES

Laboratory mice usually are very attentive parents, constantly herding their pups into nests and crouching over the offspring to nurse them and keep them warm. So why would lab mice at the University of Washington start neglecting their young?

Neurobiologist Steven Thomas and molecular biologist Richard Palmiter inactivated a gene in the mice that plays a key role in preparing the brain for motherhood. The gene is responsible for creating a protein needed to manufacture the brain chemical norepinephrine, which is believed to promote nurturing. When the mice with the altered gene gave birth, they left the pups scattered around the cage, not even bothering to remove placental material. Nearly three out of four of the pups died of neglect. But when the surviving pups were given to foster mothers with the normal gene, 85 percent survived.

"It makes sense that maternal instincts would be reinforced in the brain just before they're needed," Thomas says. [1]

The researchers' work is part of a fast-growing field that is attempting to answer the age-old nature-nurture question: Does biology or the environment play a greater role in determining behavior? More than 130 years after Austrian monk Gregor Mendel formulated the laws of heredity while studying pea plants, researchers continue to disagree over how much genes control destiny and what that means for public policy.

Research in behavioral genetics is different, but no less controversial, than the burst of cloning research that has dominated news in recent months. [2] Though both come under the rubric of "barnyard biotech," the developmental research does not involve the creation of new organisms. Instead, it explores how genes in DNA carry chemical messages that may influence behavioral traits.

Scientists since the mid-1930s have known that certain mutant genes, acting alone or in combination with one another, can cause hereditary diseases. Technology has since been perfected to identify the precise genetic code for conditions such as cystic fibrosis, Huntington's chorea and Tay-Sachs disease, and, in limited cases, physicians are applying gene therapy to treat symptoms.

But over the last two decades researchers have found ways to isolate and characterize DNA sequences from individuals. With these new tools, some scientists now are searching for biological explanations to far more complex phenomena, such as sexuality, risk-taking and violence.

"There is now a perception that we are closing in on a molecular understanding of the human condition," writes Tennessee medical researcher R. Grant Steen in his 1996 book, *DNA and Destiny: Nature and Nurture in Human Behavior*. "Most people are aware that, though genes can determine good health and above-average intelligence, genes are also responsible for many undesirable traits."

Popular attention to the field was sparked by the publication of the controversial 1994 book *The Bell Curve*, in which authors Richard Herrnstein and Charles Murray asserted that IQ is largely hereditary. The authors went on to argue that, since people often marry people like themselves, the differences between intelligence of races and classes are growing wider, and efforts to help the poor are likely to fail because poverty is a function of inherited low intelligence. Many scientists disputed the conclusions, charging the authors' statistical measurements were inadequate and that IQ was not a true indicator of intelligence. [3]

Biologists, psychologists and others drawn to the field say they are concerned about drawing similar broad societal conclusions from limited studies that could have weaknesses in methodology. But their work is nonetheless presenting headline-grabbing evidence that genes may account for previously unexplainable, but commonplace, behaviors.

In 1996, a research team reported discovering a link between anxiety-related behavior and a gene that controls the brain's ability to use a neurochemical called serotonin — the same neurotransmitter targeted by Prozac and other antidepressants. Researchers at the National Institutes of Health (NIH) and the University of Würtzburg in Germany studied more than 500 people and found that individuals who have a slightly shorter version of the gene for the serotonin transporter tend to be more anxious and harbor more negative thoughts and feelings than those with a longer version of the gene. [4]

That same year, two groups working independently at NIH and in Israel reported a link between excitability, thrill-seeking and quick temper and a gene involved in the activity of the neurotrans-

Continued on p. 293

CQ on the Web: www.cq.com   **April 3, 1998   291**

Nature vs. Nurture: How the Public Views the Debate

Most Americans believe the environment and society a person grows up in has more influence on behavior than heredity or genetic makeup, according to a poll conducted last year for U.S. News & World Report. But more than two-thirds of those polled said heredity does play a role in determining behavior.

Which has more influence in shaping how people behave?

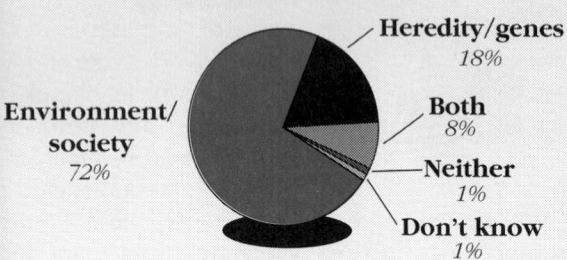

Heredity/genes
18%

Environment/
society
72%

Both
8%

Neither
1%

Don't know
1%

Overall, how much is an individual's behavior determined by heredity and genes?

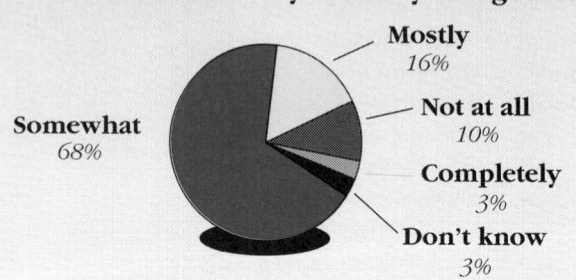

Mostly
16%

Not at all
10%

Somewhat
68%

Completely
3%

Don't know
3%

Has scientific research into genes improved people's lives?

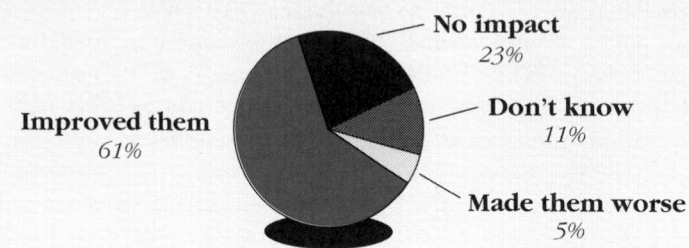

No impact
23%

Don't know
11%

Improved them
61%

Made them worse
5%

How much are the following behaviors determined by heredity and genetic makeup?

	Completely	Mostly	Somewhat	Not at all	Don't know
Alcoholism	9	24	44	20	2
Drug addiction	4	11	44	38	4
Mental illness	10	24	52	11	4
Violent behavior	5	14	54	24	3
Homosexuality	7	13	29	40	11
Intelligence	11	39	40	9	2
Happiness	5	14	41	36	3
Neurotic behavior	5	18	56	17	4
Criminal behavior	3	8	47	39	3
Religious behavior	6	12	25	54	2
Shyness	5	13	50	29	3
Dependability	5	13	39	41	2

Is homosexuality something a person is born with or is it due to other factors?

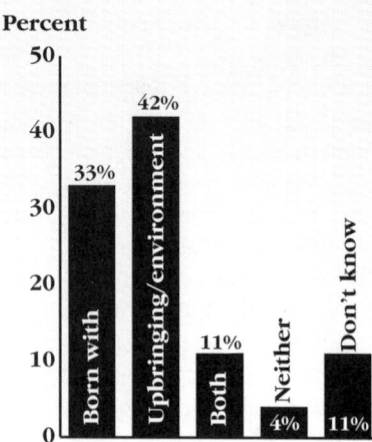

Percent

Born with 33%
Upbringing/environment 42%
Both 11%
Neither 4%
Don't know 11%

Note: Numbers may not add to 100 because of rounding.

Source: The survey of 1,000 adults was conducted by KRC Research, Feb. 6-9, 1997, for U.S. News & World Report and Bozell Worldwide, an international marketing organization. The margin of error is plus or minus 3.1 percent.

Continued from p. 291

mitter dopamine, which, among other things, transmits sensations of pleasure. The studies focused on a segment of the gene's molecular code that is repeated either four or seven times in a row. Novelty-seeking seemed more common in people with the sevenfold repetition. [5]

Since then, there have been near monthly announcements of newly discovered suspect genes, often with the caveat that they act in tandem with other genes and the environment to express a trait. Last year, researchers at NIH reported finding that an abnormally long variant of the gene tied to risk-taking could also account for drug addiction. The type of behavior expressed depends on whether the suspect sequence acts in tandem with up to 10 other genes that also might determine novelty-seeking. Someone with two or three active genes might be somewhat impulsive in nature, or maybe drive race cars for a hobby. Someone with all 10 might thrive on risks like taking heroin. [6]

Extensive research has also been done on genes believed to be linked to schizophrenia, manic depression and alcoholism. The specific cause of each condition remains unknown, and most serious researchers acknowledge that environment may play as important a factor as genetic inheritance. Indeed, the biological connections are murky enough that scientists in some cases can identify a gene sequence linked to a condition but not be able to explain how it works.

Arguably the most controversial connection between genes and behavior concerns suspected links to crime and violence. Researchers studying a dysfunctional Dutch family announced in 1993 that aggressive behavior may be linked to a single faulty gene that causes a shortage of enzymes needed to break down serotonin molecules that transmit signals in the brain. Since then, scientists and policymakers have engaged in an often stormy debate over the roots of crime and possible solutions for society. [7]

Proponents of continued research say that while the concept of a single "criminal gene" may be the stuff of science fiction, biological markers exist that could make a person more likely to commit crimes or provide clues about populations that are more at risk. Gene therapy to correct any inborn problems could also make an attractive and humane alternative to incarceration, they argue.

"Nobody suddenly becomes a homicidal maniac at 18," says Diana Fishbein, a psychobiologist and criminologist at the U.S. Department of Justice who designs crime-prevention programs. "There is a history, and we can intervene early." [8]

But critics say labeling a group as predisposed to violence recalls the eugenics movement of the early 20th century, which led to the sterilization of convicts and some mental patients in the hope of reducing crime among future generations. Many social scientists say researchers, in a rush to "biologize" behavior, are ignoring environmental influences, such as poverty, broken families and racism.

"We tend to seek quick and easy technological conclusions that aren't always for the public good," says Dorothy Nelkin, a New York University sociologist. "Clearly, there are some genetic factors that contribute to behavior. But if you read the media, it's all in the genes. It's easier to blame the individual than take up what's wrong with the social system."

"A lot of biologists are chasing genes. I tell them, why don't you clone the gene for poverty?" says Craig Ferris, a professor of psychology at the University of Massachusetts Medical Center in Worcester. "Things are more complex, and behavior is acted out in a social context. The chemical coding for some molecules isn't going to influence how you get through the day."

Many researchers in the pro-gene camp are uncomfortable with such criticisms and take pains to note they are only branching out to study specific biological systems, not prescribing broad solutions.

"When you study how a biological pathway works, you know the details,

but you're not always able to see the forest from the trees," says Judith Greenberg, director of the division of genetics and development biology at the National Institute of General Medical Sciences. "You're seeing researchers trying system approaches to more fully understand the complexities of how cells work."

University of Colorado psychologist Gregory Carey, who has studied the biological roots of crime, says talk about genetic advances is oversimplified and contributes to a misunderstanding of DNA's power, especially when it comes to predicting individual traits.

"We may be able to say a certain percentage of the population is predisposed to a condition, but I doubt we'll ever be able to identify whether Joe Smith will have it or not," Carey says. "Genes influence differences in behavior, to some degree. But our knowledge is embryonic, and any big headlines have to be taken with a lot of caution."

The whole concept of discovering a "gene for" a particular condition is somewhat misleading. When researchers identify a gene linked to a trait, they mean they have targeted an "allele," or a stretch of DNA that has been changed by mutation, that will code for a physical or behavioral trait under normal conditions. But conditions vary, and having a certain allele does not necessarily mean the trait will be expressed. Studies on identical twins, who have the same sequences of DNA, show that one may be predisposed to a condition like schizophrenia while the other isn't, meaning that environment also plays a role. [9]

As researchers continue to study and debate the basis for behavior, these are some of the questions they are asking:

Is criminal behavior more a product of our genes than our environment?

University of Maryland legal scholar David Wasserman endured three years of criticism while trying to organize a conference on genetic links to violence and

No Mickey Mouse Research for these Rodents . . .

They're cheap, easy to breed and have genes that can be easily manipulated at the molecular level. Is it any wonder laboratory mice have become the test animals of choice in the current explosion of genetic research?

Over the last decade, researchers have used millions of the rodents to study the detailed function of individual genes. Because scientists can pinpoint the DNA code of many genes — and because researchers have a complete genetic map of the mouse — they are able to chemically alter the code and inactivate, or "knockout," specific genes in the rodents. The resulting "knockout" mice are providing important clues about the development of cancer, sickle-cell anemia and myriad other conditions.

In addition to switching genes on and off, scientists are cloning genes from other animals and introducing them in mice. The mice then transmit the genes to offspring. Because mouse and human genomes are similar, these "transgenic" rodents provide useful models of human tendencies to certain conditions. [1]

Mice have gradually replaced primates, cats and dogs as the pre-eminent test animals in university, government and corporate labs. Part of this is due to practical considerations — a typical lab mouse costs between $2 and $2.50 and can produce offspring in three weeks. Also, public sympathy tends to be lower for rodents than for cats, dogs or monkeys, reducing the likelihood of emotional protests against animal research. [2]

One important use of transgenic mice is in cancer research. Researchers have found cancer is partly caused by damage to genes that regulate cell growth. Harvard University geneticist Philip Leder introduced active damaged genes, called oncogenes, into special strains of mice, then watched them pass on the genes to offspring. The results indicate that conditions such as leukemia and lymphoma are often caused by two or more oncogenes, meaning cancer likely requires several activating events.

Lab mice have played a critical role in recent genetic discoveries.

©Tom Levy

"Our work has been considerably advanced by introducing active oncogenes into the hereditary makeup of special strains of lab mice," Leder says. "In many ways, [the] mice become useful models of human malignancy." [3]

Last year, researchers at the University of Alabama at

---

crime. When 70 biologists, criminologists and social scientists finally gathered at a conference center in Queenstown, Md., in the fall of 1995, some moments resembled a street brawl.

After one panel discussion, a participant accused Wasserman of using pseudoscience to legitimize racism. Soon after, a group of 30 bullhorn-wielding protesters from mental health and civil rights groups disrupted the proceedings, chanting "Maryland conference you can't hide, we know you're pushing genocide." Wasserman tried to shout down the group, while two other conference participants engaged in a brief scuffle. [10]

The scene illustrated the passions surrounding a debate tinged with racial and political implications. Wasserman, himself skeptical about claims of a biological root for violence, says continued research, if handled appropriately, could make society more compassionate toward criminals. "As a society, we make intermittent efforts to understand and identify with those who engage in conduct that frightens and repels us," Wasserman says. "It is possible to imagine a society fairer and more humane than our own where findings of individual differences in behavioral predispositions could be used in an appropriate fashion." [11]

People have pondered links between biology and crime for more than a century. In the 1800s, Italian physicist Cesare Lombroso asserted that anatomical signs of "primitiveness" — sloping foreheads and prominent chins, among others — were indications of criminals because crime amounts to primitive behavior. Similar connections are found throughout popular American culture in the first half of the 20th century; the Dick Tracy comic strips, for example, featured villains with physical deformities.

The best scientific work on the subject to date explores the connection between violent behavior and the neurotransmitter serotonin. Groundbreaking research on the Dutch family and subsequent work concluded that low levels of serotonin can contribute to aggressive, impulsive and sometimes violent behavior, including suicide. Many factors influ-

... Mice Are the Test Animals of Choice

Birmingham, Lawrence Berkeley National Laboratory and the University of California at Berkeley used knockout mice to develop the first animal model for sickle-cell disease. The scientists successfully transplanted human genes with defective hemoglobin into the rodents, capping a long-running research effort. [4]

"This is a major advancement a lot of labs have been trying to achieve for more than a decade," says Alan Schechter, a sickle-cell expert at the National Institutes of Health. "It's probably as good a mouse model as you could ever have for sickle-cell disease."

Knockout mice also provide insights into behavior and the nature-nurture debate. Researchers at the National Human Genome Research Institute last year reported using knockouts to isolate what they termed the first gene affecting social behavior in mammals. The gene was the mouse version of the so-called "disheveled" gene, first found in fruit flies, that controls cell-to-cell signal pathways. [5]

Mice that had the gene inactivated appeared to have normal learning and memory patterns. But they consistently exhibited odd anti-social behavior, interacting less, failing to fluff up suitable beds for nesting material and, most notably, not engaging in a characteristic pattern of trimming each other's whiskers. Researchers hope finding a genetic link will provide clues about the development of autism, schizophrenia and Tourette's syndrome in humans.

Designing the mice has become something of a specialty. The Jackson Laboratory, founded in 1929 in Bar Harbor, Maine, is among the largest suppliers, shipping 2 million mice a year from more than 1,700 stocks and strains. The lab has the world's largest frozen mouse embryo repository so particular genetic strains can be thawed and carried to full term with no damage in foster mothers.

But animal-rights groups, while praising legitimate scientific findings, say the genetic tinkering has many unintended consequences. Some transgenic mice bred to develop eye tumors also suffered cancer throughout their bodies. There are other published examples of animals being born with loss of limbs, facial clefts and massive brain defects.

Animal Aid, the largest British animal rights group, urges scientists to do more work on human cells in test tubes, noting some diseases like cystic fibrosis are expressed differently in mice and men. The group advocates removing human cells from patients, incorporating healthy genes into the cells in a test tube, then returning them to the patient.

"Ultimately, it is clinical, patient-oriented studies that give the most valid results," the group says.

---

[1] See Holly Ahern, "It's A Knockout: Mice Advancing Research as Lab Animals of Choice," *The Scientist*, Vol. 9 No. 14, July 10, 1995, p. 18.

[2] For background, see "Fighting Over Animal Rights," *The CQ Researcher*, Aug. 2, 1996, pp. 673-696.

[3] Quoted in Howard Hughes Medical Institute, *1995 Annual Report, Biomedical Research*, p. 53.

[4] See Warren Leary, "Gene-Altered Mice Are Called First True Sickle Cell Model," *The New York Times*, Oct. 31, 1997, p. A20.

[5] See Nicholas Wade, "First Gene for Social Behavior Identified in Whiskery Mice," *The New York Times*, Sept. 9, 1997, p. C4.

---

ence serotonin production. Males tend to have 20-30 percent less of the chemical than females, and levels tend to fall as one enters adolescence, then rise again as one gets older. Certain diets and consumption of alcohol also can lower serotonin levels.

Scientists have expanded on the work in recent years by looking for similarities in the criminal records of identical twins raised separately and studying chemical changes in the brains of children with attention-deficit hyperactivity disorder *(see p. 307)*. The National Research Council in 1994 reported substantial evidence of genetic links to anti-social behavior but cautioned that the connection "is likely to involve many genes and substantial environmental variation." [12]

A furious debate continues over how to interpret the findings. At one extreme is J. Phillipe Rushton, a psychologist at the University of Western Ontario at London, who asserts that criminality and violence are significantly linked to genes. He argues that blacks worldwide show a higher incidence of criminal behavior because of genetic factors, such as higher testosterone levels and differences in brain size. "If race were an arbitrary, socially constructed concept, devoid of all biological meaning, such consistent relationships would not exist," Rushton says. "Facts remain facts, and require appropriate scientific, not political, explanation." [13]

Others insist any exploration of the biology of violence is perilous precisely because it will be exploited to stigmatize groups. Peter Breggin, a Bethesda, Md., psychiatrist and author of the 1991 book *Toxic Psychiatry*, says the quest is driven by scientists more interested in research dollars than in looking at the society around them. "There's a vast research community hungering for money, and the government and pharmaceutical industry are ready to spend huge amounts of money to convince the public there's something there," Breggin says. "They don't want to talk to black kids in inner cities or find out why people are shooting each other."

Breggin helped derail Wasserman's first effort at organizing a conference on genetics and crime in 1992 by organizing protests and charging the meeting was part of a government effort to screen black children and treat them with drugs. That same year, charges of racism prompted the resignation of Frederick Goodwin, then director of NIH's Alcohol, Drug Abuse and Mental Health Administration, after he compared aggressive young blacks to primates in the jungle. [14]

James Gilligan, director of the Center for the Study of Violence at Harvard University, rejects notions that violence is instinctual or hereditary, arguing socially determined gender roles are partly to blame. He says theories of criminal genes are promoted to push a conservative political agenda. "If violence is innate and instinctual, then clearly there is no point in trying to change our social and economic system," Gilligan writes in his 1996 book, *Violence: Our Deadliest Epidemic and Its Causes.* "If the assumption is violence is an inextricable part of our inborn 'human nature,' then clearly the only way to keep the problem under control is to emphasize just that: control."

Several recent and notable findings suggest a complicated comingling of nature and environment may be responsible for aggressive, delinquent behavior. A study of 301 inner-city boys in Pittsburgh found exposure to lead in the environment may be a factor. The study by the University of Pittsburgh School of Medicine builds on previous research showing lead in paints and contaminated soils commonly found in inner cities reduces IQ by damaging brain cells in children. [15]

University of Southern California criminologist Adrian Raine also reports a significant link between birth complications and early maternal rejection and violent crime at age 18. His conclusion: a chain of events begins before conception and continues through one's lifespan that can trigger violent behavior. "There is no single gene capable of producing criminal behavior per se," Raine says. "But despite strong criticisms from social scientists, empirical data from several sources provide strong converging lines of evidence indicating some degree of genetic predisposition for crime."

Proposals to screen for specific genes that influence anti-social behavior — and using gene therapy to treat some conditions — have caught on with some clinicians. David Comings, director of the department of medical genetics at City of Hope National Medical Center in Duarte, Calif., reports success treating children with nervous tics, hyperactivity and disruptive behavior. The work involves manipulating genes in the frontal lobes of the brain. Left unchecked, such conditions would lead many of the children to drop out of school and turn to alcohol and drugs, Comings maintains. [16]

But the thought of taking matters a step further by screening children at high risk for adult violence and treating them with gene therapy concerns critics. They note predicting violence, even in adults with a history of anti-social behavior, is an uncertain exercise. And pre-emptive strikes by administering drugs to children is regarded by many as both intrusive and expensive.

"Effective education and decent material support are far more important to violence prevention than drug therapy," says Franklin Zimring, professor of law at the University of California at Berkeley. "We should not be forced to choose only between governmental neglect and ineffectual therapeutic interventions." [17]

Does society benefit when genetics is used to identify certain traits?

Neurobiologist Evan Balaban has a unique distinction: Last year he made a chicken behave like a Japanese quail. The senior fellow at the Neurosciences Institute in San Diego, Calif., painstakingly isolated brain cells that control sounds and head motions in quail and transplanted them into chicken embryos. When the chicks hatched, they wobbled their heads and crowed like quails, ignored calls from their mother hen but responded to warning cries from quails.

Balaban says his experiments may help stroke victims and others suffering from brain damage. By studying how brain cells come to control inborn behavior, Balaban hopes researchers may eventually train certain healthy cells to take over the functions of cells damaged by disease or injury.

"The first thing you do when you find a gene linked to a condition isn't to call a news conference," Balaban says. "It's not until much later that you find out whether there's a real link or it's spurious. Researchers who've done work on this for a long time recognize that. The guys who jump from gene to gene to gene don't."

It's a message frequently repeated by scientists: Developmental biology yields real results that can improve the human condition. But, they caution, it also raises false hopes with sometimes simplistic explanations to complex phenomena, and may provide a new means to intrude on privacy and stigmatize groups.

"People like simple stories, but we're complex creatures," says National Institute of Mental Health Director Steven Hyman. "For human behavior, there's no single gene that's the equivalent of fate. Genes are critical tools for discovery that are beginning to open real doors to understanding what we are."

As an example, Hyman points to recent research on autism, a neurological disorder that affects about one in 1,000 children and limits the ability to form relationships. The condition was once thought to be caused by maternal rejection. But in recent years, biologists have zeroed in on a gene that codes for a protein that reabsorbs serotonin into the nerve cell after it has been released. NIH is in the midst of a five-year, $27-million research effort to explore a shorter-than-normal strand of DNA believed to play a significant role in the disorder.

Isolating genes for traits is the first step in the broader process of gene therapy, in which scientists can clone healthy genes to take over for defective ones that cause diseases. [18] The process is expected to set the standard for medical care in the 21st century.

Gene therapy has been sanctioned by NIH for patients suffering from cystic fibrosis, a previously untreatable hereditary disease that causes mucous buildup and infections in tissues, especially the lungs. Seventy percent of cystic fibrosis patients have one identified faulty gene. Scientists are participating in a $40-million research program to spray a solution of virus containing a healthy gene into the nose or lungs of a patient. The hope is the virus will enter the cells of the patient and deliver the healthy gene to compete with the protein made by the faulty gene.

The societal benefits from genetic research extend beyond the treatment of diseases. Police and the FBI increasingly are using DNA extracted from blood, saliva and semen left at crime scenes with DNA profiles in databases. The FBI and state labs recently agreed on technical standards and began pooling data in what some believe is the first step toward establishing an American DNA database. [19] Such a database already exists in Brit-

ain and has helped identify repeat sex offenders and other felons. However, big questions remain over who must submit to testing, who can have access to the data and how the DNA samples will be handled.

Despite the advances, many social scientists are concerned that increased reliance on DNA and genes will prompt an Orwellian assault on privacy. Insurers already use family histories to deny coverage or charge higher premiums. If a person's entire DNA map became available in several years, as many researchers predict, insurers, prospective employers

Studies of identical and fraternal twins are giving scientists clues to the relative importance of biology and the environment.

Photo Courtesy of Twins Day Festival

and others could use computers to quickly scan for predispositions to certain diseases or personality traits, even an individual's life expectancy.

"Everyone wants to minimize unpredictability," says Jeremy Rifkin, president of the Washington-based Foundation on Economic Trends and a critic of most new biotechnology research. "A company will want to know if a 38-year-old on the fast track has a predisposition to breast cancer. It has the potential to be a new and virulent form of discrimination."

The Clinton administration in January said it would send a bill to

Congress to prevent U.S. companies from requiring genetic tests in hiring or obtaining genetic information about employees. Several states, including Maryland and Virginia, have passed laws banning genetic discrimination. State lawmakers around the country introduced 153 bills related to genetic privacy last year — many to prevent employers from using DNA information to deny benefits, according to the National Conference of State Legislatures.

Beyond privacy concerns is the cost to society of overstating the results of DNA research. Near weekly news reports of breakthrough discoveries create false expectations and make society too reliant on science to cure all ills, according to the University of Colorado's Carey. "The average person should walk away with the knowledge that genes contribute to individual differences in behavior; they influence things to some degree, but don't necessarily determine things," Carey says. "Any big headlines have to be taken with a lot of caution."

The public was captivated, for instance, by the 1995 discovery of a gene linked to breast cancer. The identification of the defective tumor suppressor gene known as BRCA1 led to optimistic predictions of gene tests that could prolong lives through early detection. But lost in some news reports was the fact that only 5-10 percent of all breast cancer is inherited, and not everyone who has the suspect gene develops cancer.

Researchers worry that such information will be misinterpreted by a mass media intent on harvesting catchy sound bites and quick explanations.

Is Sexual Orientation Genetically Determined? ...

Much of the conflict between homosexual activists and their foes springs from disagreements over the nature of homosexuality. Most gays and lesbians contend their sexual orientation is either an inborn trait or an immutable and healthy psychological condition developed in the early years of life. In contrast, opponents of gay rights insist homosexuality is a consciously acquired mode of behavior that can be changed or acquired at will.

The debate over the basis of homosexuality took a new turn in 1993, when National Cancer Institute scientist Dean Hamer reported in the journal *Science* that he had linked male homosexuality to a small region of one human chromosome. Hamer emphasized that he had not isolated a single gene, and had no way of knowing how the DNA in question contributes to sexual orientation or how often people were likely to become gay as a result of carrying it. [1] But the notion that homosexuality could somehow be partly inborn, or that there could even be something as simplistic as a "gay gene," unleashed an intense discussion over the scientific and political ramifications.

Hamer's work was built around a study of 40 pairs of gay brothers. In 33 of the pairs, the brothers were found to have identical pieces of the end of the sausage-shaped X chromosome. Normally, only half of the pairs of brothers should have shared the common region. The odds of Hamer's results turning up randomly were less than half a percent.

The timing was dramatic, coming as the nation was in the midst of a debate over gay rights in the military. In addition, several states were considering measures barring laws that protect gays and lesbians from discrimination. Legal experts speculated that if homosexuality could be demonstrated to be inborn, discriminatory laws against gays and lesbians would probably be invalidated by courts. [2]

Yet in succeeding years Hamer's results were never duplicated. Moreover, his work was investigated by the Office of Research Integrity, a branch of the U.S. Public Health Service, after a colleague accused him of cooking the results. Hamer eventually moved on to other research, including studying whether there is a gene for nicotine addiction.

"I'm convinced that in the end the positives [of linking genes to behavior] will outweigh the negatives," he says. "We'll learn more about ourselves and others. Understanding your genetic makeup is the key to figuring out who you are. This is a tool for liberation, a scientific window into the soul." [3]

Hamer's work has sparked intense criticism and division in the scientific and gay-rights communities. Some homosexual leaders fear that any legitimate link between genes and sexuality will spark calls for therapy to correct the condition. Indeed, the Rev. Louis Sheldon, president of the Traditional Values Coalition in Anaheim, Calif., has asserted that if the findings are confirmed, society should develop gene therapy "to correct that genetic defect." [4]

Conservative groups, who tend to depict homosexuality as a behavioral choice, also have attacked the research, citing it as an example of how federal funding is being used to advance gay political activism. Hamer's work is part of the Clinton administration "methodically unleashing an avalanche of pro-homosexual policies and advocacy," according to Robert Maginnis, policy analyst for the Family Research Council. [5]

But others see positive results from such work. Simon LeVay, a former Harvard University researcher and founder of the Institute of Gay and Lesbian Studies in West

Parents in a few years may face the dilemma of subjecting their children to a battery of new genetic tests for a variety of conditions. That could pose troubling dilemmas: If a teenage daughter is found to have the breast cancer gene, should she do nothing, or should she follow the example of some women and have her breasts removed?

"If we have nothing new to offer once the gene has been identified—well, then what?" asks Malcolm Paterson, a Canadian molecular biologist and cancer researcher. "The serious problem is we have to say to these women, 'We do not know the underlying causes for 70 percent of all breast cancer. We don't know why other

women—those who are not predisposed genetically in ways we are aware of—develop breast cancer.' " [20]

Concerns deepen when society uses genetics to make inferences about specific types of behavior. In 1993, NIH researcher Dean Hamer reported a genetic marker for homosexuality — an aberration on the X chromosome found in 75 percent of gay brothers. The findings, which researchers have not been able to duplicate, caused a tempest and thrust Hamer into a heated gay-rights debate. Some homosexuals felt a biological explanation in the form of a "gay gene" would make society more tolerant of their lifestyles. Others said Hamer

was providing ammunition for groups eager to stigmatize gays and lesbians even more.

While many remain divided on the wisdom of studying how biology influences behavior, the federal government firmly backs the work with huge sums of money. President Clinton's fiscal 1999 budget request asked for $13.1 billion for NIH, a 2.6 percent increase over 1998 levels. Of that amount, $12.5 billion is earmarked for research on sequencing DNA and isolating more genes.

The funding priorities are in marked contrast with those in the 1960s and early '70s. In sync with the social psychiatry of the times, NIH in

... Researchers Are Looking for a 'Gay Gene'

Hollywood, Calif., says the perception that gays are a distinct biological group, rather than heterosexuals behaving inappropriately, helps the gay political agenda.

LeVay points to polls showing people who think homosexuality is a choice are more likely to be homophobic. One such poll taken last year for *U.S. News & World Report* found that while only 45 percent of 1,000 adults surveyed favor gay rights, 69 percent of those who believe homosexuality is completely or mostly controlled by heredity and genes favor gay rights.

"We think it's important there be sound scientific research into sexuality," says Kim Mills, director of education for the Human Rights Campaign, a Washington-based gay-rights group. "While the basic issue is equal rights for us, it's important that the public understand whatever the basis is for sexual orientation."

Many still believe there is some genetic component to gayness, though the connections — like so many others between biology and behavior — are murky at best.

"There is a consensus that none of the possible factors for establishing orientation are ones ordinarily considered to be under an individual's control," says Georgetown University Law Center Professor Chai Feldblum. "Sexual orientation is not a characteristic which an individual can be said to easily change through simple choice." [6]

Researchers continue to explore the subject. LeVay has concluded that the hypothalamus, a region of the brain that controls hormonal functions, is much larger in straight men than in gay men or in women.

A team at the University of Texas at Austin reported in March that, compared with heterosexual women, the hearing of homosexual and bisexual women tends to be more like that of men. The findings suggest that homosexual and bisexual women develop in slightly different ways than heterosexual women, and that their brains may also form differently, accounting for their sexuality. [7]

"It's an indication that other brain sites have also been masculinized," says Dennis McFadden, a professor of experimental psychology at the University of Texas who led the study. He says he and his colleagues are doing follow-up research to see if they can identify specific differences in the brains between heterosexual, homosexual and bisexual women. [8]

---

[1] See Natalie Angier, "Report Suggests Homosexuality is Linked to Genes," *The New York Times*, July 16, 1993, p. A1.

[2] For background, see "Gay Rights," *The CQ Researcher*, March 5, 1993, pp. 193-216; and "New Military Culture," *The CQ Researcher*, April 26, 1996, pp. 361-384.

[3] Quoted in Robert Pool, "Portrait of a Gene Guy," *Discover*, October 1997.

[4] Quoted in Larry Thompson, "A Search for a Gay Gene," *Science*, June 12, 1995.

[5] Robert Maginnis, "Insight: Federal Government Promotes Homosexuality Using 'Diversity' Cover," Family Research Council, December 1994.

[6] Testimony before the House Small Business Subcommittee on Government Programs and Oversight, July 17, 1996.

[7] See Rob Stein, "Study Suggests Biological Basis for Lesbianism," *The Washington Post*, March 3, 1998, p. A9.

[8] *Ibid.*

---

those days spent heavily on finding the roots of behavioral illnesses in conditions such as racism and poverty. "Even 15 years ago, it was common to have purely psychological explanations" for conditions like autism, says Hyman of the National Institute of Mental Health. "Now, we've discovered genes make us vulnerable to serious illnesses. Our challenge is to translate basic discoveries to treatment."

But New York University's Nelkin predicts that emphasis will gradually eat away at the social welfare system, with policy-makers more willing to accept science-based conclusions and dis-

mantle federal programs to deal with crime and poverty. "Clearly, there are genetic factors that contribute to behavior, but all the talk deals with data," Nelkin says. "The technical focus masks having to make serious political and moral choices and deal with the real source of things like crime."

Should the government regulate genetic research?

Unlike telecommunications and the Internet, Washington policy-makers have been wary about regulating genetic research. Many are reluctant to appear to be standing in the way of science and

appear more interested in protecting patents of U.S. drugs and technologies that are produced as a result of the work.

Congress in 1996 began to address genetic privacy issues by passing the Health Insurance Portability and Accountability Act, which bars group health insurance plans from denying enrollment based on an individual's pre-existing genetic condition. Insurers are still able to price policies depending on what they know about an applicant's genetic profile.

The Equal Employment Opportunity Commission also has considered whether genetic handicaps are protected by the law. The commission in

1995 ruled genetic susceptibility to a disease is a disability protected by the Americans with Disabilities Act of 1990. Commission members reasoned that rules must allow a level playing field so people born with a disadvantage don't remain at one forever. [21]

It's still unclear what these rulings mean for people with traits suspected of having genetic causes. But many agree that the ability to completely map a body's DNA — expected to be a reality within five years — will make it possible to show that virtually everyone has a gene that may contribute to some undesirable trait. Lawmakers will likely face questions about whether to make testing for some conditions compulsory, and what to do if a person tests positive for highly undesirable traits.

Vice President Al Gore began to address this dilemma in January when he announced the administration's bill limiting what genetic information American companies can collect about their employees. "It is clear that cracking the genetic code would be of significantly less benefit if we allow our moral code to become cracked as well," Gore said in a speech to members of the Genome Action Coalition, which promotes public support of genetic research.

But Heidi Wagner, spokeswoman for the Washington-based Healthcare Leadership Council, which represents concerned employers, said the law proposed by the Clinton administration was too far-reaching because many applications of the research are still unknown. "Genetic testing is so new. My concern is that when the federal government decides to get involved, though well intended, there might be some unintended effects," Wagner says, adding that existing laws preventing workplace discrimination may suffice.

Gore said the use of genetic testing to predict diseases is already causing prejudice. "The fear of genetic discrimination is prompting Americans to avoid those genetic tests that are now available that could literally save their lives." [22]

In Congress, lawmakers' attention to genetic research intensified after Chicago physicist Richard Seed announced his determination to clone human beings. At least three bills were introduced in the Senate expressing the belief that cloning a living or dead person was morally indefensible. But the efforts ran into sharp criticism from the biotechnology industry, which said the proposals would block legitimate medical research.

The Senate in February succumbed to pressure from groups such as the American Heart Association and Cystic Fibrosis Foundation and blocked floor debate on an anti-cloning bill backed by Sens. Christopher S. Bond, R-Mo., and Bill Frist, R-Tenn. The bill would have blocked a procedure that allows the nucleus of a human egg cell to be replaced with another cell component, which theoretically could allow an organism to develop in the womb as a human being. Bond and Frist's language thus considered an embryo worthy of the same protection abortion opponents give embryos conceived through fertilization. [23]

Medical groups argued such language could cut off research aimed at cloning cells to treat cancer, heart disease and other maladies. "I don't think Dr. Seed's announcement brought any closer the reality of a human clone," observes Sean Tipton, spokesman for the American Society for Reproductive Medicine, echoing the sentiments of many biotech groups. "But he may have brought closer to reality the passage of dangerous legislation."

Anti-cloning lawmakers say their bills are specifically targeted at the cell transfer procedure but allow other types of cloning, such as recombinant DNA technology. "I am extremely reluctant to place any limits on scientific research," says Rep. Vernon J. Ehlers, R-Mich., a physicist and a member of the House Science Committee, who has authored two anti-cloning bills. "However, while the possibilities of scientific experimentation may seem limitless, there are times when society — through the governmental process — can and should place limits." [24]

As lawmakers grapple with the complex debate, scientists also are trying to establish some ground rules. This year the National Research Council convened a study committee of 10 pre-eminent researchers to define "appropriate uses of new [genetic] discoveries and to clarify ways of thinking about such information." Committee members, consisting of biologists and social scientists, are expected to make recommendations on the use and misuse of scientific information on human health and behavior and transmit their findings to politicians, the press and public policy analysts, according to council spokesman Dan Quinn.

Ferris at the University of Massachusetts Medical Center says he hopes such efforts will lead biologists and social scientists to collaborate on preventing harmful conditions instead of frequently talking past one another and disagreeing on the root causes. "Part of our American culture is we see a problem, and we want to correct it," Ferris says. "We're a bright, dynamic society with some of the best science in the world. We should focus on the preventive side, and create more resilient, healthier minds and bodies." ∎

BACKGROUND

Unlocking the Code

The recent burst of developmental research revolves around DNA, or deoxyribonucleic acid, a huge, incredibly complex molecule that contains all of the genetic information needed to create a being. First discovered in the

Continued on p. 302

Chronology

1860s-1940s
Scientists begin to understand the principles of heredity, hastening medical advances — but also the birth of the eugenics movement.

1865
Austrian monk Gregor Mendel develops the laws of heredity while studying the patterns and relationships of pea plants. The units of inheritance later become known as genes.

1869
British explorer and anthropologist Sir Francis Galton, a cousin of Charles Darwin, founds the modern eugenics movement, presenting evidence that intelligence runs in certain families.

1927
In *Buck v. Bell*, the U.S. Supreme Court upholds the constitutionality of a Virginia sterilization law. Sterilization laws were passed in 32 states between 1907 and 1937, reflecting public acceptance of using science to improve the quality of the gene pool.

1934
Norwegian chemist Asjborn Folling discovers phenylketonuria, a disorder of body chemistry that, if untreated, causes mental retardation. He subsequently determines the disease is inherited.

1950s-1960s
Researchers unravel the genetic code while a school of psychology asserts human behavior is a response to the environment.

Feb. 28, 1953
James Watson and Francis Crick unveil the structure of deoxyribonucleic acid, or DNA, the material from which genes are made.

1950s
American psychologists Clark Hull and B.F. Skinner modify laboratory animal behavior and develop the concept of reinforcement, or reward, to explain the response to certain stimuli.

1970s
As molecular biologists develop the tools for splicing genes, public-policy groups begin to debate the social and ethical implications.

1974
The Recombinant DNA Advisory Committee is established at the National Institutes of Health to develop guidelines for the safe conduct of gene research.

1978
U.S. geneticists J.C. DeFries and Robert Plomin report there exists a genetic component in lab animals affecting diverse behaviors like learning, sexual activity and aggression.

1980s-1990s
New laboratory advances usher in an era of experimentation.

1980
Religious leaders send a letter to President Jimmy Carter expressing concern about the potential consequences of genetic engineering.

May 22, 1989
The first human gene-transfer experiment takes place at NIH, on a cancer patient.

October 1990
NIH launches the Human Genome Project, a $3 billion, 15-year effort to map and sequence the human body's genes.

1993
Researchers identify genes linked to a half-dozen major illnesses, including Huntington's disease and colon cancer. Human embryos cloned by two U.S. scientists survive for several days in a Petri dish. New findings suggest homosexuality may be inherited.

1994
Richard Herrnstein and Charles Murray draw popular attention to DNA research with their controversial book, *The Bell Curve*, which asserts IQ is largely hereditary.

October 1995
First human gene therapy trial shows success treating two girls with a rare immunodeficiency disease.

October 1996
Scientists working on the Human Genome Project unveil a map of more than 16,000 genes in human DNA, about one-fifth of the total DNA packaged in chromosomes.

1998
The Clinton administration proposes legislation limiting what genetic information companies can collect from their employees. Congress' attention to genetic research increases in the wake of the cloning controversy.

Continued from p. 300

1860s, DNA's function was not fully revealed until American bacteriologist Oswald Avery and his colleagues at Rockefeller University in New York demonstrated in the 1940s that it contains genes that trigger the production of proteins. The proteins are key ingredients in chemical reactions that govern form and function in the body.

The modern research era was ushered in by biologist James Watson and physicist Francis Crick, who in 1953 proposed their now famous model showing DNA composed of two spirally wound chains. The "double-helix" structure demonstrated that a gene carries information written in a kind of chemical code that can be copied and passed on from generation to generation. The genes are packed into sausage-shaped chromosomes that reside in the nucleus of a cell. In the simplest sense, the chemical code dictates the creation of a protein, and the protein controls the expression of a particular trait, such as eye color or blood type.

Gregor Mendel believed all traits can be inherited. He was only partly correct. Scientists have found mutations in individual genes that give rise to specific physical conditions. One is sickle-cell anemia, which is caused by a mutation affecting one blood protein that reduces the ability of hemoglobin to bind to oxygen and distorts the shapes of the cells. Its ability to restrict the flow of oxygen can be fatal.

Most traits aren't as clear-cut, however, and involve complex interactions between a number of genes and the environment. Here, science has its limits. Researchers do not know yet how many genes come together to express specific conditions, or exactly how the genes interact. Moreover, there are myriad environmental factors from radiation to diet that can play important roles.

Separated at Birth

To assess the relative importance of biology and environment, researchers over the last two decades have turned to so-called "split twin" studies of identical and fraternal twins reared apart. Because identical twins come from the same egg and have identical genes, their biological traits should be more similar than fraternal twins, which come from separate eggs. But fraternal twins raised in the same environment sometimes show uncanny similarities — a convincing argument, some say, that genes aren't everything.

The problem is finding enough separated twins to make a study statistically valid. Some universities have set up "twin registries," quizzing siblings on a regular basis about everything from religious beliefs to drug abuse and mental illness. Researchers then measure the degree of similarity in the answers. [25]

One study by the University of Minnesota of more than 100 sets of twins reared apart found that identical twins score much more closely than fraternal twins for IQ and psychological traits like extroversion and neuroticism. Researchers also found identical twins raised apart did not score much differently from identical twins raised together. "In the current environments of the broad middle-class, in industrialized societies, two-thirds of the observed variance in IQ can be traced to genetics," writes David Lykken, a professor of psychology at the University of Minnesota. [26]

Skepticism remains high over twin studies, in part because they describe behavioral variations in a group and cannot be used to predict how an individual acts. Nor do they consistently account for the full and complex influence of the environment, in particular, personality traits from shared experiences, like a war or economic depression.

"These studies are flawed from beginning to end because there are all kinds of suppositions," says Rifkin of the Foundation on Economic Trends. "There were a lot of legitimate breakthroughs when we began to isolate genes in the laboratory. Now, we've probably shifted too far to the extreme."

Nature vs. Nurture

The concern about "extremes" is due in part to the connection between the behavioral studies and the eugenics movement of the early 20th century. The movement was founded by Sir Francis Galton, a cousin of Charles Darwin, who asserted in his 1869 book *Hereditary Genius* that individuals should not get credit for their virtues or blame for their vices because both are beyond their control. Galton also first paired the terms "nature" and "nurture" in trying to explain development.

Galton had the lofty goal of trying to advance aristocratic British civilization. But by the beginning of the 20th century, his followers were subdividing society and singling out certain groups as degenerates, unworthy of reproduction. Many leading psychologists of the time believed that while normal people could control their behavior, the feeble-minded and insane could not.

This led to alarming public policies aimed at cleaning up the gene pool. From 1907 to 1937, 32 American states passed laws permitting the sterilization of the mentally ill, handicapped and those convicted of sexual, drug or alcohol-related crimes. Congress also passed, and President Calvin Coolidge signed, the Immigration Restriction Act of 1924, designed to restrict the entry of persons from Eastern Europe and other areas referred to as "biologically inferior."

Genome Project Makes Progress

The Human Genome Project is the most ambitious single effort under way to understand how genes influence functions in the human body. The $3 billion international research project aims to completely map the body's approximately 80,000 genes by 2005. The knowledge will help researchers understand how genes work together, and is expected to provide important clues about the treatment of diseases.[1] Following are some noteworthy recent developments:

February 1998: Researchers at the National Institutes of Health (NIH) and Johns Hopkins School of Medicine demonstrate for the first time in a non-human primate that gene therapy works against viruses that destroy the immune system. The work may eventually benefit patients infected with HIV, the virus that causes AIDS.

January 1998: NIH researchers find a mutated gene that causes Hirschsprung's disease in lab mice. The rare genetic malady leaves the colon with no nerve cells, meaning it can't relax. Scientists are looking for the equivalent mutated gene in humans.

November 1996: Teams at NIH, Johns Hopkins and the University of Umea in Sweden identify the location of the first major gene that predisposes men to prostate cancer. The so-called HPC-1 gene is situated on the long arm of chromosome 1.

November 1996: For the first time, scientists pinpoint the location of a gene they believe is responsible for some cases of Parkinson's disease, a degenerative neurological disorder. They hope to learn why nerve cells die in Parkinson's and how to stop them from dying.

October 1996: A team of 100 scientists from government, university and commercial labs reveal a map that details the locations of more than 16,000 genes in human DNA — about one-fifth of the total DNA packaged in human chromosomes. The results mean the number of mapped human genes has tripled in less than two years.

July 1996: Technology is perfected to translate computer-generated light waves into a full-color palette and assign each of the body's 23 pairs of chromosomes its own distinct hue. The development is expected to help researchers examine for missing or extra pieces of genetic material and other alterations.

April 1996: An international consortium finishes spelling out the entire genetic code of a common species of yeast, among the most advanced organisms to be entirely sequenced. Sequences in the 12,057,500 chemical subunits of its nuclear DNA will help researchers understand the function of individual human genes in medical problems.

March 1996: The Human Genome Project completes a five-year effort to develop a genetic map of DNA from a common lab mouse. The mouse's genetic information is about 75 percent similar to a human's. Spelling out the entire sequence takes 500 journal pages.

October 1995: Results from the first human gene therapy trial show success treating two girls with adenosine deaminase deficiency, a very rare form of immunodeficiency disease. Both received copies of a replacement gene that codes for the enzyme ADA.

June 1995: A gene is isolated for the childhood disease ataxia-telangiectasia, a rare hereditary neurological disorder. Researchers believe it could provide a marker for predisposition to certain cancers and people sensitive to radiation.

---

1 For background, see "Gene Therapy," *The CQ Researcher*, Oct. 18, 1991, pp. 777-800, and "Gene Therapy's Future," *The CQ Researcher*, Dec. 8, 1995, pp. 1089-1112.

The eugenics movement reached grotesque extremes in the Holocaust, when the Nazis exterminated millions of Jews, Gypsies and psychological patients and set up forced sterilization and selective breeding programs in an effort to purify their gene pool. Revelation of the wartime horrors disgraced the movement and led many researchers to embrace an "environmentalist" school that reached its peak in the 1950s. Adherents argued that human nature was malleable and that all differences among people were related to environment and upbringing. Evolution had little influence, except, perhaps, in making people's brains better at making associations between things.

The pendulum began to swing back to more evolutionary explanations in the 1960s, when psychologists and sociologists began to question whether certain "modules" in the brain aided cognitive ability and the way people learn languages. A school of evolutionary psychologists argued the real question about human society is not why it varies but why it stays the same. Their conclusion: We inherited a common set of psychological mechanisms from our evolutionary past.[27]

Human Genome Project

Advances in laboratory research in the 1970s and '80s — particularly the ability to insert genes from one species into another, giving the "transgenic" organism a new trait or enhancing an existing one — finally pushed the debate firmly in the DNA camp and triggered lengthy and expensive explorations of the very essence of biology.

The most noteworthy is the Human Genome Project, a $3 billion, 15-year international research effort to map all of the human body's approximately 80,000 genes. The goal of the project, due to be completed by 2005, is to understand how different genes are linked together and to identify previously unrecognized genes that govern diseases like cancer. The outcome could yield strategies to diagnose, prevent and, possibly, treat the diseases.

The research so far illustrates both the promise and uncertainties of molecular genetics. Last year, project scientists discovered a new gene linked to the growth and progression of human breast cancer. The gene is found in unusually high levels in tumor cells of most cancer patients. Researchers expect it will help reveal the basic biology of not just breast cancer, but also ovarian and prostate cancer.

Another recent development was the identification of a gene abnormality believed to cause Parkinson's disease, a progressive neurological disorder. The mutation involves one "incorrect" letter in a 400-letter sequence of a normal gene that plays a role in the function of nerve cells.

But eight years after the project began, despite huge costs and the participation of a global team of scientists, it still has not found a single cure for a genetic disease. Project officials defend the scope of the work, saying it will be remembered as a landmark of science.

"Although there is still debate about the need to sequence the entire genome, it is now more widely recognized that DNA sequences will reveal a wealth of biological information that could not be obtained in other ways," says Francis Collins, director of the National Human Genome Research Institute. "The technology and data ... will provide a strong stimulus to broad areas of biological research and biotechnology." [28]

Steen, in his book *DNA and Destiny*, worries that the current research signals a "reductionist" approach, in which all behaviors are gradually being explained in terms of chemistry and biology. He says that may yet lead to another round of eugenics. Steen points to trends that, taken together, are cause for concern: the ability to screen for medical conditions in the unborn, laws that allow women to abort fetuses with undesirable traits and the ability to use information from genetic tests to discriminate.

"The door is now open to a resurgence of the eugenic ideas that led to such gross excesses in the past," Steen says. "When people speak of relieving the burden of suffering of the sick, one must ask whose burden is actually being lifted? Any answer other than 'the individual' potentially comes from tainted motives." ■

CURRENT SITUATION

'Fountain of Youth' Gene

Scientists have sliced, spliced and transplanted genes to better understand the human condition. Now, they are manipulating them to try to make human cells live indefinitely.

Researchers at Menlo Park, Calif.-based Geron Corp. and the University of Texas Southwestern Medical Center surprised the science world in January when they announced they had altered cells grown in a test tube so that they divide up to 90 times without an abnormality. Conventional human cells divide about 50 times, then die of old age. [29]

The findings capped a 30-year effort to understand a mechanism in living cells

that is critical both to the aging process and cancer. The "fountain of youth" is believed to be a rarely expressed gene that creates telomerase, an enzyme responsible for lengthening the ends of DNA that are packaged in chromosomes.

The enzyme is critical because of the way DNA is copied when cells divide. The device that copies the double-helix can't transcribe the last few units of DNA at the tip of the chromosome, so each time a cell divides, a little part of the chromosome is lost. The end section, known as a telomere, effectively serves as a molecular clock, ticking off units until it runs out, and the cell is incapable of dividing again.

Geron scientists inserted the telomerase gene into human cells, then sent a chemical signal that activated the cells. They found the cells began to build their telomeres back up, effectively rewinding the molecular clock to a more youthful state and creating many more chances to divide.

The discovery only applies to cells that continually divide in adulthood, such as those for blood, skin and other tissues and body fluids. Other cells, such as those for neurons in the brain, do not divide in adulthood. The way they age is still largely unknown.

The scientists referred to the re-engineered cells as "rejuvenated." But they noted that does not mean one will be able to rejuvenate human tissues. Rather it could lead to therapies that revive telomeres on specific cells — perhaps growing new skin for burn victims or manufacturing blood vessels for elderly patients suffering from macular degeneration, a disease of the retina.

"If everything turns out to be safe and we can turn telomerase on in many different tissues, that might be where this research leads," says Calvin Harley, Geron's vice president and chief scientific officer.

It's still unclear how the research will affect cancer treatment. Telomerase is dormant in most cells but is active in about

Continued on p. 306

At Issue:

Does biology play a dominant role in determining human behavior?

FRANS B. M. DE WAAL

Professor of psychology and research professor at the Yerkes Regional Primate Research Center at Emory University

FROM "THE BIOLOGICAL BASIS OF BEHAVIOR," THE CHRONICLE OF HIGHER EDUCATION, JUNE 14, 1996.

i would argue that the source of universal human traits, such as the capacity for language, attraction between the sexes, the mother-child bond, facial expressions and male cooperation in warfare, cannot be investigated without reference to biology. Many academics, though, still appear to believe that biology's role in human behavior was miraculously reduced to zero after our descent from animals.

This view came in handy in the post-Vietnam era, when people of my generation clung to the ideal of unlimited social malleability. Those were the days of flower power: Given the right cultural and educational environment, we could be anything we wanted to be. Led by wishful thinking, and misled by informants whose language they had not bothered to learn, anthropologists of that period described societies without violence, sexual jealously or status hierarchies. Their romantic fiction was capped by what was then known about our closest animal relatives: Like them, our ancestors probably had been peaceable vegetarians.

One cannot keep biology at a distance, however, while at the same time embracing the anthropoid apes as models of the human primogenitor. When discoveries of lethal violence, power politics and infanticide began to taint the apes' image, the scientists who had used ape behavior to argue that human beings are inherently peaceful could not hide from the implications. . . .

Almost every week, the science pages of our newspapers report on a new human gene involved in such diseases as schizophrenia, epilepsy or Alzheimer's, or even in traits such as thrill-seeking behavior. Soon we may be able to treat certain physical disorders with "gene therapy." We are also learning more about genetic and neurological differences between men and women, as well as between gay and straight men. For example, scientists found that a region of the brain in transsexual men, who dress and behave like women, resembles the same region of the brain in women.

The list of such scientific advances is getting longer by the day, resulting in a critical mass of evidence that is impossible to ignore. Understandably, academics who have spent years condemning the idea that genes influence human behavior are reluctant to change course, but the general public is ready to accept that genes are involved in just about everything we do and are. The pendulum in the eternal debate about nature *versus* nurture is swinging back toward nature, even though a growing number of scientists believe that choosing between the two is simplistic.

STANTON PEELE AND RICHARD DEGRANDPRE

Peele is a fellow at The Lindesmith Center, New York, N.Y., and DeGrandpre is the author of Ritalin Nation: Rapid Fire Culture and the Transformation of Human Consciousness

FROM "MY GENES MADE ME DO IT," PSYCHOLOGY TODAY, JULY/AUGUST 1995.

j ust about every week now, we read new headlines about the genetic basis for breast cancer, homosexuality, intelligence or obesity. In previous years, these stories were about the genes for alcoholism, schizophrenia and manic depression. Such news stories may lead us to believe our lives are being revolutionized by genetic discoveries. . . . In addition, many believe we can identify the causes of criminality, personality and other basic human foibles and traits.

But these hopes, it turns out, are based on faulty assumptions about genes and behavior. Although genetic research wears the mantle of science, most of the headlines are more hype than reality. Many discoveries loudly touted to the public have been quietly refuted by further research. Other scientifically valid discoveries — like the gene for breast cancer — have nonetheless fallen short of initial claims. . . .

The public is hard pressed to evaluate which traits are genetically inspired based on the validity of scientific research. In many cases, people are motivated to accept research claims by the hope of finding solutions for frightening problems, like breast cancer, that our society has failed to solve. At a personal level, people wonder about how much actual choice they have in their lives. Accepting genetic causes for their traits can relieve guilt about behavior they want to change, but can't.

These psychological forces influence how we view mental illnesses, social problems like criminality and personal maladies like obesity and bulimia. . . . The public wants to hear that science can help, while scientists want to prove that they have remedies for problems that eat away at our individual and social well-being. . . .

If who we are is determined from conception, then our efforts to change or to influence our children may be futile. There may also be no basis for insisting that people behave themselves and conform to laws. Thus, the revolution in thinking about genes has monumental consequences for how we view ourselves as human beings. . . .

When a distinct gene is not involved, linking genes to traits may well be an absurdity. Any possible link between genes and traits is exponentially more complex with elaborate behavior patterns like overdrinking, personality characteristics like shyness or aggressiveness, or social attitudes such as political conservatism and religiousness. Many genes might be involved in all such traits. More importantly, it is impossible to separate the contributions environment and DNA make to attitudes and behaviors.

Continued from p. 304

85 percent of cancer cells. Thomas Cech, a University of Colorado biochemist and 1989 Nobel laureate, speculates it may be possible to develop a drug to turn off telomerase production in cancer cells, causing them to revert to normal activity.

Others believe the mechanism by which cells divide, age and die is the body's evolutionary response to the spread of dangerous cells like cancer. Using rejuvenated cells to override the division limit could weaken the body's defenses against tumors.

"Geron would have us believe that telomerase is the key to immortal life, and I have no idea if there is any wisp of truth in that," says Robert Weinberg, an expert on cancer genetics at the Whitehead Institute in Boston.

The 'Gene Chip'

Besides manipulating genes in test tubes, researchers are blending semiconductor technology with biology to find quick, low-cost ways of exploring the variations in DNA.

Scientists at the Palo Alto, Calif., technology firm Affymetrix last year perfected a "gene chip" that is similar to the silicon wafers found in electronics but contains molecules of DNA instead of transistors. Researchers at pharmaceutical companies and universities use the chips to measure gene expression and detect mutations that may trigger dispositions to cancer, AIDS and other conditions. [30]

The dime-sized glass chips are encased in a small cartridge and contain molecules of DNA programmed for the sequence of whatever gene researchers want to target. The DNA chemically recognizes a real gene and can highlight the mutations it carries and offer clues about how well the gene is working.

The technology means a researcher can download the DNA sequence of an organism from a computer data bank, then have a programmer design a chip to study the activity of all of its genes. The genes to be tested are cut into fragments, tagged with a fluorescent chemical, then injected into the gene chip cartridge. By scanning with a laser, the researcher can see portions light up where the chip's DNA probes match fragments. The brightness indicates the order of DNA in the targeted gene.

The cutting-edge technology enables researchers to probe the mysteries of life without touching lab animals or human tissue. Many scientists rave about the process, saying it's faster and cheaper than creating mutant cells and subjecting them to a host of conditions, hoping for clues about its function.

"This technology is a rapid and accurate way of obtaining information about genomes," says Joseph Hacia, a researcher at the National Human Genome Research Institute, who used the chips to detect sequences of primate genes. "You have to make a big investment to get [the initial] sequences, but then you can use that investment to get sequences of close relatives at a relatively cheap price."

Hacia and his colleagues hope to compare chimpanzee and human genes, which only differ in about 1.5 percent of all DNA sequences. The differences may explain why humans have bigger brains and are capable of more complex thoughts.

Affymetrix expects to perfect a new chip that can monitor 50,000 human genes at once. Longer-term, the company is working under a $31-million grant with Stanford University and the U.S. Commerce Department to develop automated miniature genetic diagnostic systems that can be used in doctors' offices.

Enal Ravzi, biotechnology analyst for Frost & Sullivan, a market research firm in Mountain View, Calif., predicts that within five years, pending Food and Drug Administration approval, clinical diagnostics firms will routinely use the equipment to test for life-threatening conditions at a much lower cost than what is currently available on the market.

But the rapid developments concern many bioethicists, who predict insurance companies and employers also will quickly turn to the devices as a low-cost way to screen for high-risk applicants and prospective employees. They note the companies now are reluctant to use genetic tests because they are too expensive.

"This is a social disaster waiting to happen," says Curtis Naser, a bioethics expert at Fairfield University in Connecticut. "We presently have little or no public policy to deal with these problems, yet the development of genetic testing proceeds apace. It would be naive to expect those contributing to the 'progress' of the human genome project . . . to slow down their efforts. There simply is too much money at stake." [31]

Even scientists using the technology have concerns. Last year, a federal task force on genetic testing completed a two-year study concluding the rapid pace of test development, combined with the rush to market them, may create an environment in which genetic tests are available to health-care consumers before they have been adequately validated. [32]

Neil Holtzman, professor of pediatrics at Johns Hopkins Medical Institutions and chairman of the panel, says members were particularly concerned about tests predicting the risk of future disease in people who are currently healthy when no other tests are available to confirm the diagnosis. "We want to set up principles for the development of genetic tests, assure lab quality for these tests and see that [test-takers] are educated and counseled," Holtzman says. "A lot of people are concerned about these issues."

■

OUTLOOK

Race for the Cure

Now that researchers have spelled out large parts of the human genome and identified individual genes linked to many afflictions, they are rushing to develop a new generation of blockbuster drugs to treat diseases.

Pharmaceutical firms are scrambling to find biotechnology partners to underwrite the cost of developing new agents and sell them around the world. The big drug companies hope combining research and development will drive down the cost of bringing a drug to market, which industry analysts say can total $300 million or more.

Even government and university labs that once concerned themselves with fundamental questions such as how cells divide and how genes are regulated are trying to direct their research toward increasingly practical applications. "We're trying to translate more discoveries into actual treatments, and I think five years from now you'll see a lot of basic science turned into targeted therapies," says Hyman at the National Institute of Mental Health.

"Most of the research focus has been on improving diagnoses and treating straightforward diseases," says Greenberg of the National Institute of General Medical Science. "I think we're beginning to enter a new era that tries to get at the complexity of things, understand how genes interact with the environment and deal with the roots of common afflictions like high blood pressure and diabetes."

One recent example was the development of a new generation of drugs to treat HIV, the virus that causes AIDS. Virologist David Ho of the Aaron Diamond AIDS Research Center in New York studied how the virus manifests itself in the body's biochemical pathways and gradually overwhelms the immune system by killing lymphocyte cells. He found a key agent was protease, an enzyme that catalyzes the breakdown of proteins. Ho and others developed a new group of highly specific drugs that enter the active site of the enzyme, slow down the action of protease and suppress viral replication.

The new drugs, called protease inhibitors, have proved to be effective in treating very ill AIDS patients, with few dangerous side effects. But large doses are required and the cost of the so-called "cocktails" can reach $20,000 a year, making them beyond the reach of all but the best-insured patients. The ideal remedy would be a vaccine that inoculates against HIV infection. But because the virus is so deadly, scientists can't inject a weakened virus for immunization, as they did for polio. [33]

Scientists like Greenberg and Hyman note that the social and economic costs of behavior fuel the quest for better remedies. Drug and alcohol addiction, which are both believed to be heritable, cost the United States billions of dollars each year in medical services and counseling and lower worker productivity. Similarly, learning disabilities are estimated to cost taxpayers $5.8 billion a year because of special education needs.

However, skeptics remain concerned that the push to develop wonder drugs for some conditions may raise public expectations to sometimes unreasonable levels. To many, the stimulant drug Ritalin illustrates the inherent dangers.

The drug is prescribed to children suffering from attention-deficit/hyperactivity disorder, or ADHD, which is sometimes associated with learning disabilities, delinquency, substance abuse and academic problems. Advocates say it efficiently pinpoints and stimulates the area of the brain that secretes chemicals that tell a person to pay attention to specific stimuli and ignore others.

But many have grown suspicious of the drug, saying it amounts to a quick fix but does not address underlying behavioral problems. Skepticism intensified after a recent surge in the number of children diagnosed with ADHD. Some estimates show as many as 5-6 percent of all school-age boys in the United States now take Ritalin for the condition. The United Nations International Narcotics Control Board has questioned whether the drug is being overprescribed. [34]

Biotech critic Rifkin says the rapid pace of research goes deeper than merely promising cures and revises fundamental notions of evolution. Gradually people perceive living things as bundles of information, without individual characteristics or souls, he says.

"All living beings are drained of their substance and turned into abstract messages," Rifkin writes in his new book, *The Biotech Century*. "Life becomes a code to be deciphered. There is no longer any question of sacredness or specialness. How could there be when there are no longer any recognizable boundaries to respect? . . . Everything is pure activity, pure process."

Rifkin sees a "bio-industrial world" emerging, in which animal and human cloning will become commonplace. And people will be able to obtain precise genetic readouts of themselves and offspring, even allowing them to make genetic changes to fetuses to correct diseases, enhance mood and change appearance and intelligence. "The biotech revolution will force each of us to put a mirror to our most deeply held values," Rifkin writes.

Neuroscientist Evan Balaban hopes the hubub over genes determining complex behavior will slowly subside, to be replaced by a more empirical focus on the basic roots of human development. But he predicts society will continue to rely on science to provide easily digestible explanations.

"It's a particularly American thing to view the individual as somehow no longer responsible — we look to explain away something as pathological," Balaban says. "The focus isn't so much on the attribute as on how you got it. I find that curious." ■

Notes

[1] Quoted in Philip Cohen, "The Right Chemistry," *New Scientist*, Dec. 13, 1997. Thomas is now at the University of Pennsylvania.

[2] For background, see "The Cloning Controversy," *The CQ Researcher*, May 9, 1997, pp. 409-432.

[3] For background, see "Intelligence Testing," *The CQ Researcher*, July 30, 1993, pp. 649-672.

[4] See Natalie Angier, "Grumpy, Fearful Neurotics Appear to Be Short on a Gene," *The New York Times*, Nov. 19, 1996, p. A1. For background, see "Prozac Controversy," *The CQ Researcher*, Aug. 19, 1994, pp. 721-744.

[5] See Curt Suplee, "Personality Type Tied to DNA Sequence," *The Washington Post*, Jan. 2, 1996, p. A3.

[6] See Sharon Begley, "Is Everybody Crazy?" *Newsweek*, Jan. 26, 1998, pp. 51-55.

[7] See Virginia Morell, "Evidence Found for a Possible 'Aggression Gene,'" *Science*, June 18, 1993, pp. 1722-1723.

[8] Quoted in Peter Maass, "Crime, Genetics Forum Erupts in Controversy," *The Washington Post*, Sept. 24, 1995, p. B1.

[9] See "Behavioral Genetics '97: American Society of Human Genetics Statement: Past Accomplishments and Future Directions," *American Journal of Human Genetics*, 60: pp. 1265-1275, 1997.

[10] See David L. Wheeler, "The Biology of Crime: Protesters disrupt meeting on possible genetic basis of criminal behavior," *The Chronicle of Higher Education*, Oct. 6, 1995, p. A10.

[11] Wasserman's comments were included in a collection of perspectives on the conference that was published in *Politics and the Life Sciences*, March 1996, pp. 83-109.

[12] See Albert J. Reiss Jr., Klaus A. Miczek and Jeffrey A. Roth, eds., *Understanding and Preventing Violence, Vol. 2, Biobehavioral Influences* (1994). The National Research Council is the operating arm of the National Academy of Sciences and the National Academy of Engineering.

[13] Statement responding to critics, issued Nov. 4, 1996, from "Stalking the Wild Taboo" Web site, www.groupz.net~lrand/jpr01.html.

[14] See John Horgan, "Genes and Crime: A U.S. plan to reduce violence rekindles an old controversy," *Scientific American*, February 1993, p. 24.

[15] See Thomas H. Maugh II, "Lead Exposure May Contribute to Crime," *Los Angeles Times*, Feb. 7, 1996. For background, see "Lead Poisoning," *The CQ Researcher*, June 19, 1992, pp. 525-548.

[16] Politics and Life Sciences, *op. cit.*, p. 84.

[17] *Ibid.*, p. 105.

[18] For background, see "Gene Therapy's Future," *The CQ Researcher*, Dec. 8, 1995, pp. 1089-1112.

[19] See Carey Goldberg, "DNA Databanks Giving Police Powerful Weapon: The Instant Hit," *The New York Times*, Feb. 19, 1998, p. A1. For background, see "Science in the Courtroom," *The CQ Researcher*, Oct. 22, 1993, pp. 924-925.

[20] Quoted in *Alberta Heritage Foundation for Medical Research Newsletter*, March/April 1995. For background, see "Breast Cancer," *The CQ Researcher*, June 27, 1997, pp. 553-576.

[21] See R. Grant Steen, *DNA and Destiny: Nature and Nurture in Human Behavior* (1996), pp. 273-274.

[22] Quoted in "Gore Urges Curbs on Genetic Testing," The Associated Press, Jan. 21, 1998.

[23] See Dan Carney, "Senate Vote Blocks Debate On Bill To Ban Cloning," *CQ Weekly Report*, Feb. 14, 1998, p. 395.

[24] Opinion piece, *Roll Call Health Care Policy Briefing*, Feb. 23, 1998, p. 14.

[25] See Arthur Allen, "The Mysteries of Twins," *The Washington Post Magazine*, Jan. 11, 1998.

[26] See Thomas J. Bouchard, David T. Lykken, Matthew McGue, Nancy L. Segal and Auke Tellegen, "Minnesota Study of Twins Reared Apart," *Science*, Oct. 12, 1990.

[27] See "Biology Isn't Destiny," *The Economist*, Feb. 14, 1998, pp. 83-85.

[28] Quoted in "A New Five-Year Plan for the U.S. Human Genome Program," National Human Genome Research Institute Web site, http://www.nhgri.nih.gov/HGP/HGP — goals/plan.html.

[29] See Nicholas Wade, "Cells' Life Stretched in Lab," *The New York Times*, Jan. 14, 1998, p. A1.

[30] See Sandeep Junnarkar, "'GeneChip' Encodes DNA on Silicon," *The New York Times*, March 15, 1997.

[31] From Loyola University, Chicago, Department of Mathematical and Computer Sciences, 1997 ethics papers. Available on the Web at www.math.luc.edu/ethics1997/papers/naser.html.

[32] National Institutes of Health and U.S. Department of Energy Task Force on Genetic Testing, October 1997.

[33] For background, see "Combating AIDS," *The CQ Researcher*, April 21, 1995, pp. 345-368.

[34] See Kristin Leutwyler "Paying Attention," *Scientific American*, August 1996. For background, see "Learning Disabilities," *The CQ Researcher*, Dec. 10, 1993, pp. 1081-1104.

FOR MORE INFORMATION

If you would like to have this CQ Researcher updated, or need more information about this topic, please call CQ Custom Research. Special rates for CQ subscribers. (202) 887-8600 or (800) 432-2250, ext. 600, or email Custom.Research@cq.com

National Human Genome Research Institute, 31 Center Dr., Bldg. 31, Room 4B09, Bethesda, Md. 20892; (301) 402-0911; http://www.nhgri.nig.gov. Founded in 1989, this agency within the National Institutes of Health oversees the research effort to map all of the human body's approximately 80,000 genes and identify genes for specific characteristics.

National Research Council, 2101 Constitution Ave., N.W., Washington, D.C. 20418; (202) 334-2000; http://www.nas.edu. Part of the National Academy of Sciences, the council advises the nation's leaders on scientific issues that pervade policy decisions, including the ramifications of linking genetics to behavior.

Foundation on Economic Trends, 1660 L St., N.W., Washington, D.C. 20036; (202) 466-2823. Headed by Jeremy Rifkin, the foundation examines the environmental, economic and social consequences of genetic research and pursues public-policy initiatives.

Biotechnology Industry Organization, 1625 K St., N.W., Suite 1100, Washington, D.C. 20006; (202) 857-0244. Representing more than 500 biotech companies, this trade association monitors government activities at all levels, promotes educational activities and organizes workshops.

Bibliography

Selected Sources Used

Books

Ridley, Matt, *The Origins of Virtue*, Viking, 1996.

A science writer and zoologist discusses the biological basis for human behavior and how the individual gene has replaced the species as the basic unit of evolution. He focuses on how social values can evolve when evolutionary biology teaches that people are driven by "selfish" genes.

Gallagher, Winifred, *I.D.: How Heredity and Experience Make You Who You Are*, Random House, 1996.

A journalist examines the nature-nurture debate through a 40-year case study of a woman named Monica. Born with a serious birth defect and neglected by her mother, the child nonetheless had a cheerful disposition and was nurtured by the hospital staff. Her transformation into a happy productive wife and grandmother is intended to illustrate the argument that biology and environment work in tandem to influence behavior.

Hamer, Dean and Peter Copeland, *Living With Our Genes: Why They Matter More Than You Think*, Doubleday, 1998.

Hamer is the National Cancer Institute biologist who caused a stir when he claimed to have discovered a so-called "gay gene." In this recently published book, he asserts that genes influence myriad human behaviors and conditions, including sex, anxiety and anger. The authors explain the biochemistry underlying the conditions and examine how much of it is under genetic control.

Herrnstein, Richard J., and Charles Murray, *The Bell Curve*, Free Press, 1994.

In this controversial book, the authors argue that IQ is substantially inherited and that efforts to help the poor are likely to fail because poverty is a function of inherited low intelligence.

Steen, R. Grant, *DNA and Destiny: Nature and Nurture in Human Behavior*, Plenum, 1996.

A researcher in brain physiology argues human behavior is roughly half the result of genes and half the result of the environment. He explores the interplay between the two forces by discussing possible genetic links to alcoholism, homosexuality and intelligence.

Articles:

Begley, Sharon, "Is Everybody Crazy?" *Newsweek*, Jan. 26, 1998, pp. 50-56.

This special report provides a cleverly written look at how researchers are providing biological explanations to previously unexplained behavioral quirks.

Allen, Arthur, "The Mysteries of Twins: Why Genes Aren't Everything," *The Washington Post Magazine*, Jan. 11, 1998, pp. 6-11, 21-25.

Behavioral studies on similarities between twins pose difficult questions about whether biology or environment play a bigger factor.

Herbert, Wray, "Politics of Biology: How the nature vs. nurture debate shapes public policy — and our view of ourselves," *U.S. News & World Report*, April 21, 1997, pp. 72-80.

An overview of the uneasy questions posed by advances in development biology and the difficulties of establishing root causes of behavioral traits.

Garelik, Glenn, "Born Bad? New Research Points to a Biological Role in Criminality," *American Health*, November 1993, pp. 66-71.

An even-handed view of the growing body of research suggesting some people are biologically predisposed to violence.

Reports and Studies:

Reiss, Albert J. Jr., Klaus A. Miczek and Jeffrey A. Roth, eds., *Understanding and Preventing Violence, Vol. 2, Biobehavioral Influences*, National Academy Press, 1994.

A National Research Council overview of influences on violence concludes there is substantial evidence of genetic links to antisocial behavior. It concludes there are diverse and subtle biological influences that work in tandem with environmental factors.

The Next Step

*Additional information from UMI's Newspaper
& Periodical Abstracts™ database*

The Gene Factor

Gould, Stephen Jay, "The Internal Brand of the Scarlet W," *Natural History*, March 1998, pp. 22-25.

Gould discusses the eugenics movement and its use in the early 20th century to identify those immigrants to the United States who were undesirable. He also considers the continuing desire of society to find genetic causes for every behavior or personality trait.

Kiernan, Vincent, "Genetic Mutation Tied to Mental Illnesses," *The Chronicle of Higher Education*, Jan. 16, 1998, p. A18.

Researchers say that a mutation in a single gene appears to predispose people to mental illnesses severe enough for hospitalization. The conclusion came after analyzing the DNA of 11 blood relatives of individuals previously diagnosed with mental illness.

Kong, Dolores, "Obesity Study Cites Nature and Nurture," *Boston Globe*, Sept. 25, 1997, p. A20.

Many surmise that children of obese parents are more likely to grow up overweight, but until this study, published this week in the *New England Journal of Medicine*, there had been no major research on how parents' weight affects their offspring's prospects. The study finds that chubby babies with obese parents have a 40 to 79 percent chance of becoming obese young adults, as much as 15 times the risk for plump babies with slim parents.

Maugh, Thomas H. II, "Scientists Identify Gene That May Raise Schizophrenia Risk," *Los Angeles Times*, Oct. 31, 1997, p. A3.

University of California-Irvine scientists have identified a gene they believe increases the risk of both schizophrenia and manic-depressive illness — mental disorders that, combined, affect as many as 5 million Americans. Although the history of attempts to associate genes with mental illness is littered with claimed links that could not be verified, the new finding seems credible, some experts said. They noted that the mutated gene falls into the same class of mutations as recently discovered genes linked to Huntington's disease, fragile X syndrome and several other disorders of the brain.

Saltus, Richard, "British Scientists Hint at Genetic Link to Social Behavior," *Boston Globe*, June 12, 1997, p. A5.

British scientists say they have found evidence of a gene that makes girls superior to boys at winning friends and knowing how to behave in social situations. The research team, led by Dr. David H. Skuse, a child psychiatrist at University College, London, inferred the gene's existence by studying girls with a rare genetic disorder called Turner's syndrome.

Saltus, Richard, "Study Finds Gene Defect Can Cause Overeating," *Boston Globe*, June 24, 1997, p. A3.

Providing the first concrete proof that a genetic mutation alone — not simply a lack of willpower — can cause humans to overeat, scientists have discovered flawed genes that apparently caused massive obesity in two cousins and an unrelated woman.

Violence and Aggression

Brody, Jane E., "Genetic Ties May Be Factor In Violence in Stepfamilies," *The New York Times*, Feb. 10, 1998, p. F1.

Dr. Martin Daly and Dr. Margo Wilson, evolutionary psychologists at McMaster University in Hamilton, Ontario, found that the rate of infanticide was 60 times as high and sexual abuse was about eight times as high in stepfamilies as in biologically related families.

Maass, Peter, "Crime, Genetics Forum Erupts in Controversy," *The Washington Post*, Sept. 24, 1995, p. B1.

A University of Maryland conference on links between genes and criminal behavior is facing criticism, with protesters saying scientists are trying to find a gene that links minority groups, especially African Americans, to violent behavior.

Rose, Steven, "A Pizza Killer's Defense: Steven Rose Thinks That Genetic Science May be Used to Try and Explain Away the Causes of Crime and Violence," *The Guardian*, Jan. 22, 1998, p. 19.

The author discusses whether all human activities can be blamed on genes. Using genes as an explanation for violent, criminal or socially deviant activities is simplification, he says, and fallacious.

Roush, Wade, "Conflict Marks Crime Conference," *Science*, Sept. 29, 1995, p. 232.

Charges of racism and eugenics exploded at a controversial University of Maryland meeting exploring the genetic basis of crime. Common ground found by the conference participants is discussed.

'Gay Gene' Controversy

Gallagher, John, "Gay for the Thrill of It," *Advocate: The National Gay & Lesbian Magazine*, Feb. 17, 1998, p. 32-39.

Geneticist Dean Hamer has written a new book entitled *Living With Our Genes: Why They Matter More Than You Think*. Hamer doesn't think there is a "gay gene," but rather a variety of genetic markers that shape a person's tendency to be gay or straight. Brief excerpts from the book are offered.

Pool, Robert, "Portrait of a Gene Guy," *Discover*, October 1997, p. 50-55.

Part molecular biologist and part psychologist, Dean Hamer is one of a small but growing group of researchers who look for the genes that shape our individual personalities. Hamer, who believes that something important about human behavior can be learned by studying its genetic basis, is profiled.

Schuklenk, Udo, Edward Stein, Jacinta Kerin and William Byne, "The Ethics of Genetic Research on Sexual Orientation," *Hastings Center Report*, July 1997, pp. 6-13.

Research into sexual orientation provokes intense controversy for a number of reasons. The very motivation for seeking an "origin" of homosexuality reveals homophobia, the authors maintain, and such research may lead to prenatal tests that claim to predict homosexuality.

Human Genome Project

Allen, William, "Scientists See Perils in Unraveling the Mysteries of Human Genetics," *St. Louis Post-Dispatch*, Feb. 15, 1998, p. A16.

The hype surrounding the Human Genome Project could lead to the return of an abusive social movement known as eugenics, warns Garland Allen, a Washington University historian. Allen traced the links between the genome project and the eugenics movement of the early 20th century in a lecture during the annual meeting of the American Association for the Advancement of Science in Philadelphia.

Saltus, Richard, "Top Scientist Urges Shortcut on Gene-Mapping Research," *Boston Globe*, Sept. 7, 1997, p. A8.

The government's top genetic scientist is calling for an urgent shortcut in the human genome project , saying researchers should quickly hunt down common genetic differences that make some people more susceptible to diseases rather than continuing to decipher genes randomly. If the genome scientists don't change course and hone in on the variations, private biotech companies may locate and patent the disease-related sequences, potentially inhibiting research, Dr. Francis S. Collins warned at a medical symposium last week.

Lab Mice

Mihill, Chris, "Scientists Breed Mice with Full Human Chromosomes," *The Guardian*, June 4, 1997, p. 12.

Scientists are today claiming a new milestone in genetic engineering with the transfer to mice of entire human chromosomes — long strands of DNA containing thousands of genes — rather than just the implantation of single genes. For years it has been possible to insert isolated human genes into mice and other animals.

Petit, Charles, "Firefly Genes Light Up Stanford Research Mice," *San Francisco Chronicle*, Oct. 11, 1997, p. A1.

Scientists at Stanford University are using mice and rats that glow faintly in the dark — thanks to firefly genes inserted into their cells — as potent new tools for medical science. By using genes that give cells the power to glow, researchers can more easily tell whether transplanted DNA is functioning in living cells selected for therapy or study.

Trafford, Abigail, "A World of Research on the Shoulders of a Mouse," *The Washington Post*, July 29, 1997, p. WH6.

Mickey and Minnie would be stunned by all the new members of the mouse family: inbred mice, hybrid mice, mice made to carry human genes, mice with a particular gene deleted — the so-called knockout mouse — so that scientists can see what that gene really does. The mouse is also a living test tube for new drugs.

Genetic Discrimination

Armour, Stephanie, "Workers Fear Genetic Discrimination," *USA Today*, Feb. 25, 1998, p. B4.

The surge in genetic research has employees worried bosses will use DNA tests in hiring and firing. Research advances are making it possible to identify a host of health risks related to genetic traits. Just this month, a federal appeals court ruled secret testing of employees is unconstitutional. The ruling stemmed from a lawsuit by workers who say Lawrence Berkeley National Laboratory covertly tested them for syphilis, pregnancy and the sickle-cell trait. The action sends the lawsuit to a lower court for trial.

Page, Susan, "White House: Ban Gene Bias in Workplace," *USA Today*, Jan. 20, 1998, p. A1.

The White House today will endorse a federal ban on discrimination against workers in hiring or promotion because of their genetic makeup. "In the next five to 10 years, there will be tens if not hundreds of genetic predisposition tests available," says Francis Collins, director of the Human Genome Project, a federal research effort to map human DNA. "If no protections are in place, it could be used to deny us a job, and that seems patently unfair. One thing you don't have much choice about is your DNA sequence."

"The New Discrimination," *Los Angeles Times*, July 20, 1997, p. M4.

Simple blood tests have been developed in recent years that use genetic markers to identify hereditary leanings toward certain diseases. The tests give valuable early warnings but also are a potential source of discrimination, providing reasons for denial of employment or insurance coverage. Proposed federal legislation would go far toward blocking that threat. While new genetic tests are swiftly coming on the market, however, studies show that many Americans avoid them out of a justified fear of discrimination.

Back Issues

Great Research on Current Issues Starts Right Here.
Recent topics covered by The CQ Researcher are listed below.
Now available on the Web
For information, call (800) 432-2250 ext. 279 or (202) 887-6279.

If you would like to have any of these CQ Researchers updated, or need more information
about these topics, please call CQ Custom Research. Special rates for CQ subscribers.
(202) 887-8600 or (800) 432-2250, ext. 600, or email Custom.Research@cq.com

DECEMBER 1996
Welfare, Work and the States
The New Volunteerism
Implementing the Disabilities Act
America's Pampered Pets

JANUARY 1997
Combating Scientific Misconduct
Restructuring the Electric Industry
The New Immigrants
Chemical and Biological Weapons

FEBRUARY 1997
Assisting Refugees
Alternative Medicine's Next Phase
Independent Counsels
Feminism's Future

MARCH 1997
New Air Quality Standards
Alcohol Advertising
Civic Renewal
Educating Gifted Students

APRIL 1997
Declining Crime Rates
The FBI Under Fire
Gender Equity in Sports
Space Program's Future

MAY 1997
The Stock Market
The Cloning Controversy
Expanding NATO
The Future of Libraries

JUNE 1997
FDA Reform
China After Deng
Line-Item Veto
Breast Cancer

JULY 1997
Transportation Policy
Executive Pay
School Choice Debate
Aggressive Driving

AUGUST 1997
Age Discrimination
Banning Land Mines
Children's Television
Evolution vs. Creationism

SEPTEMBER 1997
Caring for the Dying
Mental Health Policy
Mexico's Future
Youth Fitness

OCTOBER 1997
Urban Sprawl in the West
Diversity in the Workplace
Teacher Education
Contingent Work Force

NOVEMBER 1997
Renewable Energy
Artificial Intelligence
Religious Persecution
Roe v. Wade at 25

DECEMBER 1997
Whistleblowers
Castro's Next Move
Gun Control Standoff
Regulating Nonprofits

JANUARY 1998
Foster Care Reform
IRS Reform
The Black Middle Class
U.S.-British Relations

FEBRUARY 1998
Patients' Rights
Deflation Fears
Caring for the Elderly
The New Corporate Philanthropy

MARCH 1998
Israel at 50
The Federal Judiciary
Drinking on Campus
The Economics of Recycling

Back issues are available for $5.00 (sub-scribers) or $10.00 (non-subscribers).
Quantity discounts apply to orders over 10. To order, call Congressional Quarterly Customer Service at (202) 887-8621.

Binders are available for $18.00. To order call 1-800-638-1710. Please refer to stock number 648.

Future Topics

▶ *Liberal Arts Education*

▶ *Income Inequality*

▶ *High-Tech Labor Shortages*

T H E
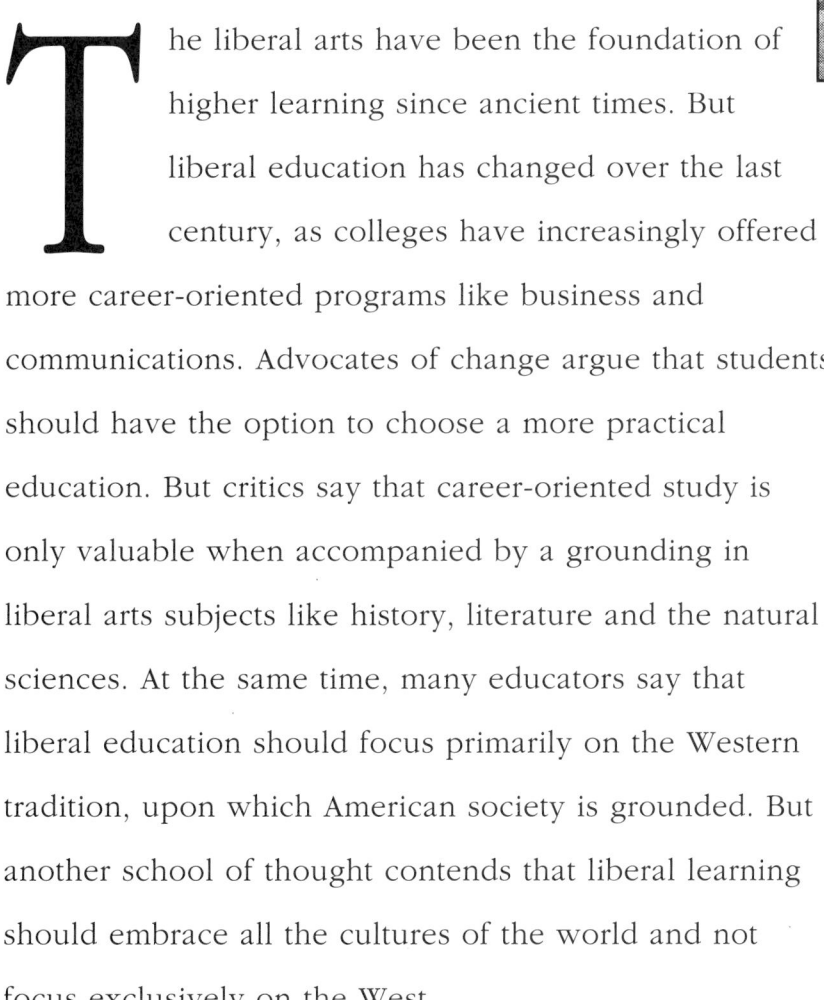
CQ Researcher

PUBLISHED BY CONGRESSIONAL QUARTERLY INC.

Liberal Arts Education

Should colleges get back to basics?

The liberal arts have been the foundation of higher learning since ancient times. But liberal education has changed over the last century, as colleges have increasingly offered more career-oriented programs like business and communications. Advocates of change argue that students should have the option to choose a more practical education. But critics say that career-oriented study is only valuable when accompanied by a grounding in liberal arts subjects like history, literature and the natural sciences. At the same time, many educators say that liberal education should focus primarily on the Western tradition, upon which American society is grounded. But another school of thought contends that liberal learning should embrace all the cultures of the world and not focus exclusively on the West.

C
Q | **April 10, 1998 • Volume 8, No. 14 • Pages 313-336**

Formerly Editorial Research Reports ®

Liberal Arts Education

COVER: PHOTO COURTESY OF DAVIDSON COLLEGE

CQ Researcher

April 10, 1998
Volume 8, No.14

EDITOR
Sandra Stencel

MANAGING EDITOR
Thomas J. Colin

ASSOCIATE EDITOR
Sarah M. Magner

STAFF WRITERS
Adriel Bettelheim
Mary H. Cooper
Kenneth Jost
David Masci

PRODUCTION EDITOR
Melissa Hall

EDITORIAL ASSISTANT
Laura S. Cavender

PUBLISHED BY
Congressional Quarterly Inc.

CHAIRMAN
Andrew Barnes

VICE CHAIRMAN
Andrew P. Corty

PRESIDENT AND PUBLISHER
Robert W. Merry

EXECUTIVE EDITOR
David Rapp

Bibliographic records and abstracts included in The Next Step section of this publication are the copyrighted material of UMI, and are used with permission.

The CQ Researcher (ISSN 1056-2036). Formerly Editorial Research Reports. Published weekly, except Jan. 2, May 29, July 3, Oct. 30, by Congressional Quarterly Inc., 1414 22nd St., N.W., Washington, D.C. 20037. Annual subscription rate for libraries, businesses and government is $340. Additional rates furnished upon request. Periodicals postage paid at Washington, D.C., and additional mailing offices. POSTMASTER: Send address changes to The CQ Researcher, 1414 22nd St., N.W., Washington, D.C. 20037.

Liberal Arts Education

BY DAVID MASCI

THE ISSUES

Michael J. Collins maneuvers between two students in the first row of his Shakespeare class at Georgetown University and stops abruptly. He is all energy and enthusiasm.

In his left hand Collins holds aloft the bard's epic tragedy, "Hamlet." His right is raised above his head, motionless, almost as if he were using it to balance himself.

Two students have just performed the pivotal scene in which the play's troubled heroine, Ophelia, and her father, Polonius, argue about her relationship with Hamlet. Now Collins is looking for feedback.

"Why is Polonius angry?" he asks.

Silence. No one wants to be the first to speak up. Finally, a young woman begins, slowly, to explain the source of Polonius' anger. Another offers her impressions of Ophelia's predicament.

Similar discussions take place daily in college classrooms around the country. The liberal arts tradition, embracing not only Shakespeare, but the Civil War, biology, Langston Hughes and myriad other topics, lives on, sustained by teachers like Collins.

The liberal arts have been taught since ancient times. In fact, until the 20th century, liberal arts was just about the only form of higher education available in the United States, or anyplace else. Today, the humanities, social sciences and natural sciences — the three foundations of a contemporary liberal arts education — still form the core of most college and university programs.

But much has changed in the last century. A large number of students no longer focus on the liberal arts. At many colleges and universities, business, communications, education and engineering programs are much more popular than, say, history or English. According to the U.S. Department of Education, 234,323 undergraduates earned bachelor's degrees in business-oriented subjects in 1995. By comparison, only 128,154 students earned bachelor's degrees in the social sciences, and only 51,901 received English degrees. [1]

Many liberal arts professors and others involved in education argue that colleges and universities are doing students a great disservice by allowing them to devote most of their time to the study of career-oriented subjects like business. Some go so far as to say that non-vocational schools should largely or wholly eliminate professionally oriented programs for undergraduates. "If a student wants to study business, let him do it at the graduate level," says Kenneth Pennington, a professor of medieval history at Syracuse University.

Pennington and others say that a real undergraduate education should entail immersion in liberal arts subjects like history, literature, philosophy and the natural sciences. They believe that students should spend their undergraduate years reading, talking and thinking about ideas, not the finer points of marketing or journalism. *(See story, p. 322.)*

Others agree in part, arguing that career-oriented programs for undergraduates are acceptable so long as they are accompanied by a solid grounding in the liberal arts. "I don't begrudge someone the opportunity of getting a more vocational education," says Glenn Ricketts, public affairs director at the National Association of Scholars (NAS), in Princeton, N.J. which favors tougher academic standards. "But you need to know something about things like our political system, about history, philosophy and how to express yourself."

But many say that Pennington and even Ricketts are elitists, as well as unrealistic. "They believe they know what's best for the individual, and they simply don't," says Omer Waddles, president of the Career College Association, representing schools with career-oriented programs.

Waddles and others argue that students, not faculty, should decide what kind of education they will receive. After all, he says, students and their families are paying for their schooling, and the choice should be theirs, not some academic's.

But if students choose liberal arts or something in-between, what should they be required to study? What books should they read, and what history should they learn? A century ago, those questions would have been easy to answer. Students immersed themselves in the culture of the West, including the great classical civilizations of Greece and Rome, the Judeo-Christian tradition and the artists and thinkers of the Middle Ages, the Renaissance, the Enlightenment and the early modern period.

For many scholars, the Western tradition is still the foundation of any good education. Americans, regardless of their

Mandatory Courses Plummeted

The portion of graduation requirements devoted to "core" curriculum courses like science, math and literature dropped below 10 percent from 1964 to 1993 at the nation's 50 most selective colleges.

Average Percentage of Mandatory Courses Needed for Graduation

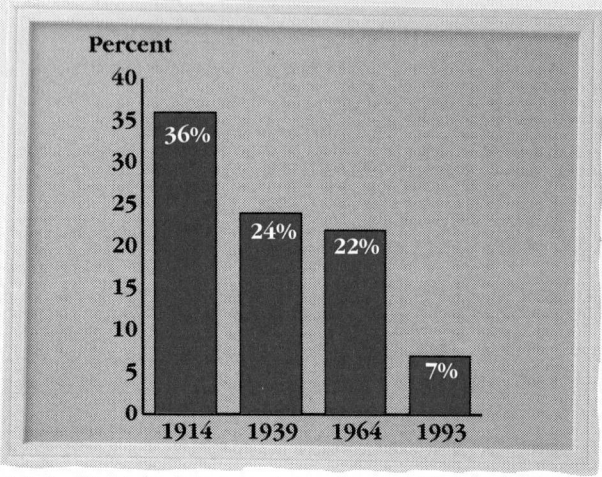

Source: The Dissolution of General Education 1914-1993, *National Association of Scholars, 1996*

States from a nation peopled largely by the descendants of Western Europeans into a multiethnic society.

"We need to prepare students for living in a diverse democracy," says Carol Schneider, president of the Association of American Colleges and Universities. Focusing only on the West won't accomplish that, she says.

The debates over the primacy of the Western tradition or the utility of a liberal arts education are not new. Indeed, academics have argued and deliberated over the question, in one form or another, for decades.

A more recent controversy has involved the growing concern among some educators about how colleges and universities treat their students. The problem stems from student attitudes. "Students want to be entertained," Ricketts says, largely blaming television and computers.

But the bigger problem, many say, is that administrations and faculty are laboring to comply. They point out that in the last decade more and more universities have squandered precious resources on plush dorms, fitness centers and other amenities in an effort to keep students happy.

Even more disturbing, they say, many professors spend their time trying to be diverting and entertaining instead of instructive. "Affability and the one-liners often seem to be all that land with students," wrote Mark Edmundson, a professor of literature at the University of Virginia. [2] Edmundson also charges that many professors don't openly challenge or vigorously question students for fear of offending them or being seen as insensitive.

Others disagree and applaud new attempts on the part of many institutions to be more accountable to undergraduates' needs. "We need to take students much more seriously," says Caryn McTighe Musil, a senior research associate at the Association of American Colleges and Universities.

The real problem, Musil says, isn't

ethnic origin, live in a Western country, governed by Western ideas in politics, economics and the world of science and technology, they say. Hence, they cannot understand their society without a grounding in the Western culture, these scholars maintain.

In addition, many argue, the intellectual achievements of the West far surpass those of all other cultures. For instance, they say, almost all scientific and political advances have taken place in the West. Even in less quantifiable disciplines, like literature or philosophy, the size and historical impact of the Western canon far outweigh those of, say, Asia or Africa. "There just isn't much in the other traditions," says Alvin Schmidt, a professor of sociology at Illinois College in Jacksonville, Ill.

But other scholars say that focusing on the primacy of Western tradi-

tion is misguided. Non-Western cultures also have rich traditions that any student could and should benefit from, they claim. In fact, people steeped only in the art and ideas of Europe cannot consider themselves well-educated, they say.

Just as important, these scholars argue, the curriculum needs to reflect trends in our world and our country. Revolutions in transportation and communications have brought the planet much closer together. In this new global society, they say, students need some understanding of all traditions, not just that of the West.

"In today's global environment, learning about other cultures is vital for everyone," says Yolanda Moses, president of the City College of New York.

In addition, immigration and other factors are transforming the United

oversensitive or spoiled students but arrogant professors who themselves are pampered and inattentive to the needs of those in their classes. Pennington agrees, but adds that the biggest reason students are neglected is that universities require professors to devote most of their time to research and not teaching. "It's a big problem," he says.

The needs of students — what they should learn and how they should learn it — have long concerned educators. But the arguments over the liberal arts have never been more insistent. Indeed, many educators predict a resurgence in liberal education as liberal arts degrees become more, not less, important in the coming decades *(see p. 330)*. These educators believe that as people try to prepare for living and working in an increasingly fast-paced and mobile society, they will need basic skills like writing and analytical thinking, more than specific professional training.

As professors and others look to the future of liberal education, these are some of the questions they are asking:

Should a liberal arts education primarily entail the study of Western civilization?

If the so-called "culture wars" have a Lexington and Concord, it is the 1987 publication of Allan Bloom's *The Closing of the American Mind: How Higher Education Has Failed Democracy and Impoverished the Souls of Today's Students.* The surprise best-seller was literally a shot

heard 'round the world of academia.

Within months of publication, it had sold more than 1 million copies. A year later it was still on the best-seller list. And Bloom, until then a respected but little known philosophy professor, had became a media superstar.

Bloom traced what he deemed to be the precipitous decline of higher learning. He concluded that students, even at the nation's best universities, were being fed a diet devoid of intellectual and spiritual nourishment. To restore proper university education, Bloom recommended, among

The term liberal arts comes from the Latin phrase "liberales artes" (that which should be known by a free man).

other things, a return to key texts and ideas of the Western tradition. [3]

Bloom brought the debate on the primacy of Western civilization — previously confined to campuses — into the open. A few months after his book appeared, civil rights leader Jesse Jackson and a group of students at Stanford University made headlines by marching against the school's core curriculum, which focused on the Western tradition. "Hey, hey, ho, ho, Western culture's got to go," they chanted. [4] Later that year, Stanford's

Western-oriented core curriculum was replaced with a new program titled "Cultures, Ideas and Values," which offered students more choice and included non-Western authors.

Similar headlines were made at other universities. And everyone from professors to pundits weighed in on the debate with a barrage of books and articles that continues to this day.

On one side of the divide are the many who say that it is undemocratic and just plain narrow-minded to expose students solely or largely to Western culture and a Western point of view. Those who focus only on the traditions of the West, they argue, are missing out on the tremendous richness offered by cultures in Asia, Africa and Latin America. "These other traditions are also important," Moses says, "and we need to make sure students are taught them, too."

Moses further argues that it is hubris to presume that all or most of "the answers" are contained in the Western canon, a view shared by Musil. "This notion that the West did it all alone is a fallacy," she says. "Take the Greeks, for instance. They were influenced by the rich cultures of the Mediterranean and Africa."

In fact, Martha Nussbaum, a professor of law and ethics at the University of Chicago, argues that the ancient Greeks — the very pillars of Western tradition — rejected the idea that people should focus on one tradition. In her 1997 book *Cultivating Humanity: A Classical Defense of Reform in Liberal Education*, she writes, "Plato . . . alludes frequently to the study of other cultures, especially

Few Schools Require Core Courses

Courses in math, history and literature were required by fewer than 15 percent of the nation's top colleges and universities in 1993. The requirements for natural science and a foreign language dropped significantly from 1964-1993.

Percentages of Schools That Require At Least One Course in the Listed Subject

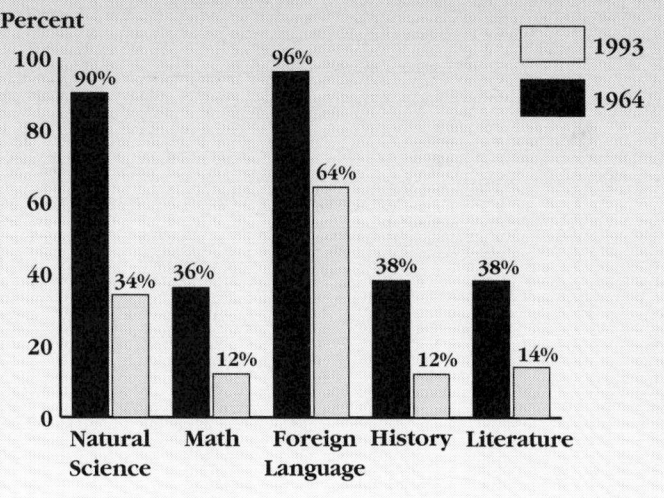

Legend: 1993, 1964

Natural Science: 90%, 34%
Math: 36%, 12%
Foreign Language: 96%, 64%
History: 38%, 12%
Literature: 38%, 14%

Note: Data were taken from college catalogs and focused on the bachelor of arts degree; the top 50 schools were rated by U.S. News & World Report *in fall 1989.*

Source: The Dissolution of General Education: 1914-1993, *National Association of Scholars, 1996*

those of Sparta, Crete and Egypt." [5]

Advocates of a broader curriculum also argue that a change away from the West makes sense in light of the growing diversity of American students. "The demographics today are very different," says Robert Orrill, executive director of The College Board, a New York City-based association of colleges and universities. "Until recently, a large number of students were of Western European origin, and that is no longer true."

As a result, Orrill and others say, the curriculum should be broadened to reflect other "points of view." Such inclusion — known today as multiculturalism — is among the

foundations of an open and free society, they argue. "With greater [student] diversity there needs to be greater cultural diversity," Orrill says. "That's how it is in a democracy."

And, Orrill and others say, broadening the curricula to include non-Western cultures should not be limited to non-white students. "We are interconnected to the rest of the world, economically and in other ways," Musil says. She and others argue that students, regardless of their color or ethnicity, cannot properly prepare to live in an increasingly global society without having at least some understanding of a broad range of cultures. "We are in a transnational world, and we need to be

exposed to these other cultures, period," says Peter Magrath, president of the Association of State Universities and Land Grant Colleges.

But proponents of the Western tradition argue that while they favor teaching students about other cultures, the core of any required curriculum should still focus primarily on the writers, ideas and achievements of the West.

To begin with, they say, Americans, regardless of their heritage, live in the West, with Western traditions, institutions and culture. "We live in a Western society, whether we know it or not," says the NAS' Ricketts.

As a result, Ricketts says, students in the United States need a grounding in the Western tradition in order to understand their own society. For example, he and others point out, the Founding Fathers were heavily influenced by Greek and Roman culture as well as by Enlightenment philosophers like Rousseau and Locke. "Notions like equality before the law and democratic institutions come out of the Western tradition," he says.

But this tradition is more than just the foundation of American government. It encompasses every aspect of American life, Ricketts and others argue. "The Western tradition is our shared culture," says George Douglas, a professor of English at the University of Illinois, Champaign-Urbana. Douglas argues that it is important for all Americans to have "common cultural connections" to preserve national unity and cohesiveness. "There's something to be said for all of us reading the same things."

On the other hand, Douglas argues, multiculturalism destroys the idea of shared culture. "When you add a lot of different pieces without any connections, you lose that cohesiveness and the benefits that accrue to society with a shared tradition," he says.

Finally, some opponents of multiculturalism argue that the

achievements of the West far surpass those of any other cultural tradition. "The world is governed by Western models in science, government and other areas," says Schmidt of Illinois College. As a result, he says, the Western tradition is, to a large extent, a global tradition and not just important to Europeans and Americans.

Another problem with broadening the core curriculum, Schmidt and others say, is that many peoples, including American Indians and most sub-Saharan Africans, have not had a written tradition until recently. "What do we have from the American Indians that matches Shakespeare, Dante, Goethe or Sophocles?" he asks, adding: "People say I'm prejudiced, but I say, 'Show me the works.' They can't because [the other groups] don't have the literature available."

But opponents argue that multiculturalism is not an attempt to push Western ideas and history aside. "There is no either-or choice here," Magrath says. "I see no inconsistency in exposing a student to Plato and Aristotle and Confucius and Lao-tse at the same time."

sors who were tardy or did not teach what their young charges wanted could be fined or even fired by them. In a very real sense, the university, founded in the 11th century, was a business whose students were its customers.

Today's universities are different, of course. The faculty, overseen by an administration, sets academic policy on behalf of the students. But some professors and education-watchers are begin-

critics is the University of Virginia's Edmundson. In an article published in *Harper's* magazine in September 1997, Edmundson details what he sees as a transformation of the student body and the academy over the last few decades. Today, he writes, the "university culture, like American culture writ large, is, to put it crudely, ever more devoted to consumption and entertainment, to the using and using up of goods and images." [6] As a result, he and others say, learning and real critical thinking take a back seat to enjoyment.

The biggest impact of this trend, according to Edmundson, is that students now want to be entertained continually. Institutions meet some of these needs by spending ever-increasing sums on building plush new dorms, gyms, student centers and other facilities designed to make university life comfortable.

But even more disturbing, Edmundson and others say, is the pressure to please in the classroom. With a clientele that has grown up on television and the Internet, they argue, professors today feel compelled to use a variety of "tricks" to keep their students engaged. "I'm disturbed by the serene belief that my function — and, more important, Freud's or Shakespeare's or Blake's — is to divert, entertain and interest," Edmundson writes. [7]

Schmidt agrees. "We're teaching the "Sesame Street" kids, who have been taught to expect instant gratification —

Since the turn of the century, colleges have offered more career-oriented programs like business and communications.

Courtesy of Davidson College

Have universities become too consumer-driven, focusing on what students want as opposed to what they need in pursuing a liberal education?

The first modern university, in Bologna, Italy, was funded and largely administered by its students. Profes-

ning to complain that many institutions are pandering to their students and giving them too much control. What they call a growing "consumerism" on campus is degrading the quality of education that students receive because they are increasingly getting what they want instead of what they need.

One of the most outspoken of these

What Is a Liberal Education?

The term "liberal arts" is taken from the Latin phrase "liberales artes" (that which should be known by a free man). But the definition of liberal education has never been static.

The Greek philosopher Plato believed that education should focus primarily on civics and social responsibility in order to prepare the best and brightest for their role as leaders in society. Enlightenment thinker Jean Jacques Rousseau, on the other hand, argued that learning should protect a child from civilization's corrupting influences and seek to bring out his natural instincts.

Today, views on the purpose of a liberal arts education still range wide and far. For some educators, a good liberal education teaches how to see the world from a variety of viewpoints. "We need to give students the capacity to grapple with several competing versions of the truth," says Caryn McTighe Musil, a senior research associate at the Association of American Colleges and Universities. The purpose is not to turn students into relativists, or those who see all truth as variable, she argues. Instead, she says, it's about giving students the tools they need "to come to their own conclusions."

To Alvin Schmidt, a professor of sociology at Illinois College in Jacksonville, Ill., the aim of a good liberal education should be knowledge. "Education is about freeing and liberating the human mind from the shackles of ignorance," he says.

Schmidt is troubled by the thought that students can graduate without knowing a foreign language or acquiring a grounding in "core" subjects like philosophy, history and literature.

On the other hand, many educators are more focused on skills. "Students should be able to write and communicate in English," says Yolanda Moses, president of City College of New York. In addition, she says, "it is important that they are able to think analytically." Many educators share Moses' concern that too many students leave college unable to draft a proper letter or give a short speech.

Others, echoing Thomas Jefferson, argue that while knowledge and skills are important, liberal education should also concern itself with turning students into good citizens. "Education should prepare us to live in a democratic society," says Robert Orrill, executive director of The College Board, by focusing on citizenship and social responsibility.

Above all, says Kenneth Pennington, a professor of medieval history at Syracuse University, a liberal arts education must give students the tools they need to spend the rest of their lives learning and thinking. "Most of the time," he says, "teachers don't convey well enough to students that college is only the beginning."

---

and that learning is fun," he says. But, he says, a lot of learning is sometimes very painful. "For instance, many people don't like conjugating Latin verbs, but you have to do it if you want to learn Latin."

To Edmundson, working with students in the age of instant gratification pressures professors in a variety of ways. In his own case, it has resulted in a change in his style of teaching. For instance, he says, he often finds himself trying to be more funny and affable with students, all in an effort to engage them.

At the same time, Edmundson claims, he and many of his colleagues in the liberal arts are afraid to confront students or challenge them in class for fear of offending them. "Students frequently come to my office to tell me how intimidated they feel in

class; the thought of being embarrassed in front of the group fills them with dread," he writes. [8] But, he and others argue, how can you learn if your views and opinions are always affirmed and never questioned?

Teachers also say they are pressured to give students high grades, whether they deserve them or not. "Many students today feel that they are entitled to good grades," says Joseph Scimecca, chairman of the department of sociology and anthropology at George Mason University in Fairfax, Va.

Some of these "offended" students get teachers in trouble by complaining to a receptive administration that believes faculty members must be sensitive to student needs. "Colleges have brought in hordes of counselors and deans to make sure that every-

thing is smooth, serene, unflustered and everyone has a good time," Edmundson writes. [9]

Tougher teachers are also kept in line with evaluations that students fill out at the end of a semester rating their professors' performance. "The bottom line is that if you're rigorous and demand a lot, you get a poor teacher evaluation and don't get tenure," Douglas says. "So you're always pressured to keep [students] happy."

But many other faculty members and education experts argue that most university faculty are not mindlessly pandering to every student whim. In fact, many say, the new consumerism is long overdue because the real problem is that professors and administrators don't listen enough to their students.

"At some point we lost sight of the

students because schools became too professor-oriented," says Musil of the Association of American Colleges and Universities. "There was this feeling that the students were just supposed to sit at the professors' feet and learn."

Syracuse's Pennington agrees. "The real problem is the teachers, who have spent too much time worrying about research," he says. As a result, Pennington and others say, undergraduates have often been ignored by their professors, even at good universities.

Indeed, they argue, teachers who complain about students are often the problem themselves. "In studies that we've done, we've found that faculty members who are effective as teachers are often perceived as effective in their teaching by their students," says Schneider of the Association of American Colleges and Universities. "Those who are not effective often do not like their students."

Hence, many educators argue, universities should spend more time listening to students. "To me, the whole purpose of universities is to focus on students," Magrath says. "We need to put students first."

In addition, he says, there is nothing wrong with treating students, to a certain extent, like customers. "I don't think consumer or customer is a dirty word," he says. The reason, Magrath and others argue, is simple: Students are investing a lot of money and time in their education, and it is unrealistic to think that they won't see universities as they do other businesses. "We are a consumer-driven, marketplace society," he says, "and universities have to keep that in mind when they provide services to students."

And if part of those services include changing long-held teaching methods in order to better relate to the students, then so be it, supporters of consumerism say. "I think the job of a teacher is to convey the information in as interesting and in as compelling a way as is possible," Pennington says. "We need to present material in a way that will arouse students."

Moses of City College agrees that professors shouldn't assume they are pandering when they try to connect with their students. "Learning is multi-

More undergraduates earned degrees in business-related fields in 1995 than in English or the social sciences.

dimensional, encompassing a lot of things," she says, "and you need to be flexible when you're teaching."

Is a liberal arts education the best way to prepare for the workplace?

A recent poll commissioned by Hobart and William Smith Colleges in Geneva, N.Y., found that 75 percent of all parents and 85 percent of their college-bound high-schoolers believe that the goal of higher education is to prepare students for a career. By contrast, only 37 percent of business executives questioned in the same survey felt that career should be the primary focus of education. They were much more supportive of "learning for learning's sake" than were parents or high-schoolers. [10]

Why the disparity between those who are preparing (or helping someone to prepare) for a career and those who will hire them? According to Richard Hersh, president of Hobart and William Smith, the high cost of higher education as well as the perception that the job market is extremely competitive have made parents and children very pragmatic when choosing schools and fields of study. "The smart choice, they say, is a professional program tailored to specific jobs in business, computer technology, engineering, law or medicine," he writes. [11]

By contrast, he says, business executives value employees who are prepared for a long-term career, not just their first job. "But to them [this] means the ability of higher education to produce people of strong character with generalized intellectual and social skills and capacity for lifelong learning." [12]

A century ago there was little argument over how to best take advantage of higher education. To begin with, few people — fewer than 3 percent of the population — actually attended college or university. In addition, 70 percent of those who did go attended liberal arts colleges

Aristotle and Plato Still Reign ...

What is "natural?" Is something unnatural if it is the product of human labor or invention? Is a wooden table more a part of nature than a jumbo jet?

On a balmy evening recently in Annapolis, Md., 14 college students, sat around a large table and wrestled with such weighty questions, having just read selections from Aristotle's *Physics*.

As is the practice at St. John's College, the students did almost all of the talking. The two professors guiding the session, known as tutors, broke in only occasionally to pose a new question or nudge the inquiry in a new direction.

Such seminars reflect the approach to education at St. John's, "Where great books are the teachers." The college is dedicated to providing "a true liberal arts education" to 850 undergraduates on campuses in Annapolis and Santa Fe, N.M. In the process, it breaks many of the rules by which most institutions of higher education operate today.

The traditional class lecture — common at most colleges and universities in the United States — has largely been discarded at St. John's. Instead, students attend a series of seminars and tutorials each week, where

---

On the Great Books Shelf

St. John's College students study more than 100 works of literature, science and music, including the following:

First Year
Homer: *Illiad, Odyssey*
Sophocles: *Oedipus Rex, Antigone*
Plato: *Meno, The Republic, Apology, Phaedo, Symposium*
Aristotle: *Poetics, Metaphysics, Nicomachean Ethics*
Lucretius: *On the Nature of Things*
Lavoisier: *Elements of Chemistry*

Second Year
The Bible
Virgil : *Aeneid*
Tacitus : *Annals*
St. Augustine: *City of God, Confessions*
Dante: *Divine Comedy*
Machiavelli: *The Prince* **Shakespeare:** *Richard II, Henry IV, The Tempest, As You Like It* **Montaigne:** *Essays*
Bach: *St. Matthew Passion, Inventions*

---

their participation is emphasized, from discussing ideas to demonstrating mathematical principles. Moreover, the usual complement of midterm and final exams does not exist. Grades are given, but they are not shown to students unless they ask for them. And students are encouraged not to ask.

But the most unique thing about St. John's is its curriculum: a four-year tour of the great books and great ideas of the West. There are no majors or minors. And except for two nine-week elective seminars, everyone studies the same subjects.

The great-books curriculum is based on the idea that the issues addressed in the classics of literature, philosophy and science are just as important today as they were when they were written. "The heart of a liberal education is reading very good books, thinking very hard about them and talking about it," says Harvey Flaumenhaft, dean of the Annapolis campus.

Freshmen start with Homer, Plato, Sophocles and other Greek writers and work their way through the great authors of ancient Rome to James Joyce and Virginia Wolff in the 20th century — more than 100 novelists, philosophers and scientists in all. Many are still

where courses in subjects like business or journalism did not exist. [13]

Today, the situation could not be more different. Such factors as the expanding middle class and the GI Bill and other government-assistance programs have dramatically increased the number of people going to college. Currently, more than one-third of all high school graduates go on to college (although not all graduate) at one of the more than 3,500 institutions of higher learning around the country.

At the same time, the percentage of students who choose liberal arts has declined dramatically. In 1968, more than 21 percent of all bachelor's degrees were awarded in the hu-

manities. A quarter-century later the figure had dropped to 13 percent. [14]

Today, all but a few four-year colleges offer a wide range of career-oriented majors, from accounting to education to nursing. And the number of occupations that can be quantified and studied increases every year. Today, students can major in fields as diverse as advertising and theater design.

But many liberal arts faculty and some in the business world question whether colleges and universities are doing their students a service by allowing them to study pragmatic fields such as business, with often little or no exposure to the humani-

ties or sciences. Some, like Syracuse's Pennington, go so far as to say that universities should eliminate or largely eliminate professional schools at the undergraduate level and focus solely on the liberal arts.

"Many universities have rejected the idea that there's a core body of knowledge that every student should have, and that's wrong," he says. "When you graduate, you should know something about history, art, music and the great philosophical and religious traditions."

Pennington sees the modern emphasis on more practical fields of study as part of a movement toward what he calls "experiential" learning.

... At St. John's College

widely read like St. Thomas Aquinas, Montaigne, Goethe and Darwin. Others, like the Italian mathematician Evangelista Torricelli and the French statesman Lazare Carnot, are important, although no longer household names.

The great books are not just used to teach literature and philosophy. In the mathematics tutorial, for instance, students learn from Euclid, Ptolemy, Descartes and other giants in the field. The science readings combine the writings of great scientists like Newton and Niels Bohr with work in the laboratory. Rounding out the curriculum are languages (ancient Greek and French) and music.

Some have criticized St. John's for its focus on great books to the exclusion of everything else. "The kind of education you get there is very tight and structured, and the real world isn't like that," says Robert Orrill, executive director of The College Board.

But St. John's students don't feel constricted by the lack of choice. "I needed the structure they offer here," says sophomore Eowyn Levene. Classmate Buck Cooper agrees, adding that many students pursue outside intellectual interests by forming clubs and informal study groups. Indeed, extra groups tackle

> ### On the Great Books Shelf
>
> #### Third Year
> **Cervantes:** *Don Quixote*
> **Galileo:** *Two New Sciences*
> **Pascal:** *Pensees*
> **Swift:** *Gulliver's Travels*
> **Newton:** *Principia Mathematica*
> **Rousseau:** *Social Contract*
> **Mozart:** *Don Giovanni*
> **Austen:** *Pride and Prejudice, Emma*
> **Melville:** *Billy Budd, Benito Cereno*
>
> #### Fourth Year
> **Moliere:** *The Misanthrope, Tartuffe*
> **Darwin:** *Origin of Species*
> **Lincoln:** *Selected Speeches*
> **Thoreau:** *Walden*
> **Nietzsche:** *Thus Spoke Zarathustra, Beyond Good and Evil*
> **Dostoevski:** *Brothers Karamazov, The Possessed*
> **Jung:** *Two Essays in Analytic Psychology*
> **Woolf:** *To the Lighthouse*
> **Conrad:** *Heart of Darkness*

everything from the Bible to the Chinese language.

The students also are not put off by the school's focus on the Western tradition. "There isn't some kind of belief that what we're reading is the only thing worth reading," says Cooper, who spent much of his free time last summer reading the classic texts of the East. And yet, Cooper and others argue, it's important to have an understanding of the works that shape our culture. "We live in the West, and there's no getting around that," says sophomore Marshall Hevrone.

In any event, the process seems to work. The college says that almost 75 percent of its graduates go on to graduate or professional school.

More important, the school generates great enthusiasm for learning. "You don't have to work to get them interested," Flaumenhaft says. Indeed, five minutes after it had begun, more than half the students at the seminar on Aristotle's *Physics* had spoken at least once. There were no pregnant pauses or silent moments as every comment elicited at least one response and usually a question. All the while, the tutors listened, saying almost nothing.

"This is the bane of education because it does not involve reading books or thinking about ideas."

Schmidt largely agrees with Pennington that undergraduate education should focus almost entirely on the liberal arts. "I might let them have a few [career-oriented] courses to whet their appetite," he says, but "the whole purpose of education is to stretch the mind, not train for a job."

In addition, Schmidt argues, narrowly focused training in a career-oriented major will probably give a student little practical knowledge because fields like business and technology change so rapidly. "By the time you finished, it would probably

be out of date," he says. By contrast, "the liberal arts are eternal. The *Odyssey, Crime and Punishment* and *The Aeneid* address concerns that never change."

George Mason's Scimecca sees another practical reason to favor liberal arts. "Look at business leaders: They feel like all their new hires with business degrees are not prepared," he says. "They want people who are literate and can think analytically, and that's what you get with a good liberal arts education."

But others say that the emphasis on liberal arts to the exclusion of everything else is both elitist and unrealistic. Those who favor solely

liberal arts "assume that the same shoe will fit everyone," says the Career College Association's Waddles. "That's a narrow-minded way of looking at things because many kids and their families choose a career-oriented form of study because they have to," he says, referring to students who are less well-off financially and must maximize career opportunities.

Waddles and others argue that some liberal arts supporters are longing for the days when an institution of higher learning "was like some great castle on a hill" guiding students through the halls of rarefied learning. "In the past, you went to college, and they told you what to take and when to take it," he says.

But today, students have much more influence over the direction of their course of study, "And that's a good thing," Waddles says. "People should have as many choices as they can." In other words, if a student wants an all-liberal arts education or one with only career-oriented courses, that's fine.

Colleges and universities embrace this philosophy and have restructured accordingly. "Colleges are simply responding to the demands of parents and students, who want to make sure that when they get a degree they are employable," says Sheldon Steinback, general counsel of the Business-Higher Education Forum.

And, Waddles and Steinback contend, being employable, especially in certain fields, often entails a professional degree. "Talk to employers today," Waddles says, "and they say the first thing they want is specific skills to do a specific job." After that, they look for other skills, like effective communication and analytical thinking, he adds.

Other observers take a more middle-of-the-road view. They favor choice in education, but with some conditions. "I think the best kind of education is one that combines liberal arts and professional study," says Magrath of the Association of State Universities and Land Grant Colleges. He and others argue that it is fine to study business or computer science so long as it offers exposure to the liberal arts as well. The two are not "as inconsistent or incompatible as many people think," Magrath says. ∎

BACKGROUND

Higher Ed Evolves

Although Harvard University and the College of William and Mary were founded before 1700, higher education in the American Colonies did not develop in earnest until the 18th century. Even then, progress was slow. By the time the United States declared independence, the 13 Colonies still had only 10 collegiate institutions.

Most early colleges, like Harvard and Yale, were founded to train ministers. Not surprisingly, their students spent the bulk of their time mastering theology and classical languages.

But there were a few exceptions, most notably the University of Pennsylvania. Founded in 1740, the university (under its first president, Benjamin Franklin) emphasized the natural and social sciences.

Through the 19th century, the number of institutions of higher learning grew at a rapid rate, keeping pace with an America expanding in both area and population. Like earlier colleges, many of the new institutions were founded by Christian denominations with an eye toward training clergy. But as the century progressed, more and more colleges and universities were created with a secular mission, often by state governments.

Before the Civil War, Maryland, Iowa and other states had already established public universities. But in 1862, efforts to create state institutions of higher learning were given a huge boost by congressional passage of the Morrill Act. The law made every state eligible to receive a grant of 30,000 acres of federal land for every senator and representative it had serving in Congress. The land, if accepted by the state, was to be used for the creation of vocational schools known as industrial colleges. [15]

The Morrill Act led to the founding of many so-called land-grant colleges and universities. Many states also allowed existing institutions, including Rutgers, the Massachusetts Institute of Technology and the University of Missouri, to use public property to expand.

The new schools quickly changed the U.S. higher-education landscape.

In 1870, fewer than 15,000 Americans were enrolled in institutions of higher learning. By 1895, nearly 25,000 students were attending land-grant colleges and universities alone. [16]

The second half of the 19th century also produced great changes in curriculum. Until the Civil War, most institutions of higher education had no electives. Students followed a set course of study — emphasizing Greek and Latin, rhetoric, theology and mathematics — designed to give them a thorough grounding in the liberal arts.

But after the war, more colleges began deviating from the set curriculum to one that included a choice of disciplines and elective courses. The trend was spearheaded by Charles W. Eliot, president of Harvard from 1869-1909. Eliot believed that in the new, freer and more mobile society taking shape in America students should have greater freedom to choose what they wanted to learn than their more class-conscious counterparts in the Old World. [17]

By 1900, most liberal arts colleges were allowing students to meet the requirements for a bachelor's degree by focusing on one of a variety of disciplines ranging from history to chemistry. In addition, the number and types of courses offered had grown tremendously.

While Eliot was pushing for more choice within the liberal arts, others, particularly at institutions in less-settled parts of the country, began teaching more pragmatic subjects, like agriculture and engineering. At Kansas State University in 1875, for instance, students could take wagon-making, blacksmithing and carving. [18]

New Age, New Mission

During the 20th century, the role of colleges and universities

Continued on p. 326

Chronology

1600s-1700s
American higher education develops slowly and is largely religiously based.

1636
Harvard College is founded near Boston to train ministers. It is the first institution of higher learning in America.

1693
The College of William and Mary is founded in Williamsburg, Va.

1740
The University of Pennsylvania is founded with an emphasis on the natural and social sciences rather than theology.

1795
The University of North Carolina is founded, becoming the first state university.

— • —

1800s
Growth in the number of colleges and universities accelerates, especially after the Civil War.

1862
Congress passes the Morrill Act, which grants property or money to states for the purpose of higher education and leads to the founding of scores of so-called land-grant colleges and universities.

1869
Charles W. Eliot becomes president of Harvard University and begins instituting reforms, such as elective courses, aimed at giving students more educational choice.

1870
Fewer than 15,000 Americans are enrolled in institutions of higher learning.

— • —

1900s
New debates over the purpose of liberal education emerge as the number of students entering college skyrockets, fed by the growth of the middle class and government aid programs.

1900
Institutions of higher education are attended by 238,000 people in the United States.

1915
The Association of American Colleges and Universities is founded to promote liberal education.

1930
The number of Americans enrolled in colleges and universities hits 1 million.

1936
The Higher Learning in America by University of Chicago President Robert Maynard Hutchins calls for education to be a search for great truths.

1937
Educator John Dewey criticizes Hutchins' ideas, sparking a debate between the "pragmatists" and the "idealists" over the purpose of liberal education.

1944
Congress passes the GI Bill of Rights, which provides returning soldiers with financial support for higher education.

1987
University of Chicago Professor Allan Bloom attacks relativism and other trends in higher education in his best-selling book *The Closing of the American Mind*.

1988
After heated debate, Stanford University replaces its "Great Books" requirement with "Cultures, Ideas and Values," a program designed to broaden the required curriculum by including non-Western works.

1995
The Department of Education grants the American Academy for Liberal Education the power to accredit liberal arts colleges.

1996
Brooklyn College announces that it will reorient its core curriculum, prompting a well-publicized debate over the role of general education.

1997
Martha Nussbaum publishes *Cultivating Humanity*, which argues that the concept of multiculturalism is supported by the great writers and thinkers of the classical world.

1998
The Virginia Association of Scholars accuses that state's colleges and universities of "dumbing down" core curricula and urges a back-to-basics approach.

Life at Medieval U. Was No Picnic

The Middle Ages may have been chaotic and violent at times, but they were anything but intellectually bleak. Many of the ideas, inventions and institutions that are fixtures of modern life came into existence then, including the modern university.

Higher learning did not begin in medieval Europe. Sophisticated centers of education had flourished in ancient Greek cities like Athens and Alexandria more than 1,500 years before the first university was founded. But the systematic approach to higher education that characterizes the modern college or university, hinging on formal curricula and exams, only came into being in the late 11th century.

The medieval university has its roots in Italy. For centuries, Italy's many independent or semi-independent towns and cities had grown rich through trade and industry. With economic success came a growing political sophistication that required the new city governments to establish an increasingly complicated legal structure. To seek guidance, administrators turned to the law of ancient Rome.

But few knew or understood Rome's ancient codes, leading to a chronic shortage of capable administrators. The first school, in Bologna, arose to fill that need. By the early 12th century, students from around Europe were flocking to the northern Italian city to study the Code of Justinian and other key Roman laws. By century's end, the school had expanded its curriculum to include rhetoric, canon law and medicine.

During the second half of the 12th century, two of Europe's other important universities were founded. The first, in Paris, was formed by scholars who had congregated around a school affiliated with the city's famed cathedral, Notre Dame. The second, at Oxford, was created by English scholars who had been studying in Paris and were forced to flee when one of the many wars between England and France began in 1167. [1]

These early universities were often loosely organized affairs with little physical or institutional structure. Typically, there were no lecture halls or dormitories. Instead, classes were held in rented rooms, and students were required to provide their own room and board.

Over the next three centuries, universities were founded in Cambridge, Padua, Naples, Heidelberg, Prague and other cities. By 1500, Europe boasted 80 universities, including many where the faculty and administration had become more permanent and structured.

The life of a medieval university student was in many ways harder than that of today's typical undergraduate. Students rose with the sun, often after spending the night in cold, cramped quarters. Each day was devoted largely to class attendance and study.

Lectures were not as free-wheeling as they often are today. Professors spoke *ex cathedra* (from the chair) about a specific text. Often, the teacher simply read the book to the students, who were expected to take copious notes on wax tablets, which were cheaper than parchment. Afterwards, they would neatly recopy their notes on paper. [2]

The language of students and professors (and literature) was Latin, and not only in class. Students were expected to speak only Latin to each other. Those caught conversing in Italian, French or some other vernacular tongue could be penalized.

Unlike today's students, undergraduates in the Middle Ages did not declare majors or take electives. All generally studied the same subjects, which allowed them to change universities (a common practice) without having to begin their studies again. [3]

A liberal arts education was comprised of seven subjects. The first three, known as the trivium, were rhetoric, grammar and logic. When a student had mastered the trivium, he became a bachelor of arts. Next, he moved onto the quadrivium: arithmetic, geometry, music and astronomy. Study of the last four subjects usually lasted five years or more, after which the student became a master of arts. [4]

Students who finished the liberal arts course of study had several options: They could teach at a university or go on to the medieval equivalent of graduate school to study law, medicine or theology. Those who pursued an advanced degree usually faced another four or more years of hard study.

Still, all was not books, writer's cramp and damp rooms. Contemporary accounts indicate that gambling, drunkenness and rowdiness were not uncommon among university students. *Plus ça change.*

---

[1] Brian Tierney and Sidney Painter, *Western Europe in the Middle Ages: 300-1475* (1983), pp. 405-406.

[2] James Powell, *The Civilization of the West* (1967), p. 177.

[3] *Ibid.* p. 178.

[4] Tierney and Painter, *op. cit.*, p. 408.

Continued from p. 324

changed dramatically, as the trends that had begun after the Civil War accelerated greatly. The shift toward more practical fields of study continued as professions that had once been learned through apprenticeship were increasingly offered as courses of study.

Some American educators and philosophers, known as the pragmatists, applauded efforts to give higher learning more real-world applications. Led by philosopher and educator John Dewey, they argued that there were no universal truths and that knowledge should focus less on the abstract and more on solving real problems.

Others, who came to be known as the idealists, disagreed. Led by University of Chicago President Robert Maynard Hutchins and, later, philosopher Mortimer Adler, the idealists argued that a traditional liberal arts education based on the great ideas of Western thought was still important. [19] In 1936, Hutchins published *The Higher Learning in America*, which sparked a heated debate between the two schools that continues, in various forms, to this day.

After World War II, colleges and universities again changed. The GI Bill of Rights offered generous government assistance to any ex-serviceman who wanted to go to college. It was followed by student loans and other government programs designed to make higher education affordable to any American who qualified.

The resulting explosion of students seeking a higher education in the 1940s and '50s prompted the expansion of existing schools and the creation of many new ones. The GI Bill generation was followed by the maturing of the baby boomers in the 1960s and '70s. Many of the boomers, born just after World War II, were from newly minted middle-class families that could, for the first time, afford to send their sons and daughters to college.

As the number of students increased, the trend toward more prac-

tical fields of study continued, with schools of business, engineering, nursing, journalism and other professions cropping up on campuses all over America.

Within the liberal arts, big changes came as well, especially after 1960. The number of fields of study expanded tremendously to include so-called interdisciplinary studies, which knitted together a number of different academic areas. [20] For instance, American studies, an especially popular discipline, encompassed history, political science, lit-

Many educators want liberal education to focus on the Western tradition, but others say it should embrace all cultures.

Courtesy of Davidson College

erature and other fields.

Another trend in liberal education has been the movement to focus more on non-Western cultures. Before World War II, courses on Asia or Africa were rare, even at the best universities. By the 1970s, many schools were forming new departments to study the language, history and culture of non-Western peoples. ∎

CURRENT SITUATION

Curriculum Battles

In late 1996, Brooklyn College announced that it was going to "reorient" the institution's famed core curriculum. Instead of the existing 10 required courses — among them "The Classical Origins of Western Culture," "Knowledge, Existence and Values" and "Landmarks of Literature" — future students would fulfill graduation requirements by taking classes offered in a broad, new program called "Brooklyn Connections." The new, less rigid core curriculum would be organized around four "themes": Community Studies, Communications, Environmental Studies and Science Studies. [21]

By summer 1997, a growing number of faculty and alumni were demanding that the traditional curriculum not be replaced. Calling "Connections" a radical departure from the college's liberal arts mission, they argued it would give students only "skills and tactics, not bodies of knowledge." [22]

A letter released by a group of prominent alumni, including scholars Gertrude Himmelfarb and Eugene D.

Genovese, said implementation of the new scheme would be a "tragic mistake." [23] And a number of local newspaper articles portrayed the new plan in an unfavorable light.

But "Connections" had supporters as well. Many faculty members and administration officials argued that it was intended to expand the core curriculum to include issues — like environmental and community studies — that were closer to the real world and the everyday lives of Brooklyn's students.

Still, within months of the alumni letter, Brooklyn College President Vernon E. Lattin announced that "Connections" would in no way replace the core curriculum and that any impression to the contrary was due to confusion and misunderstanding.

Cuts to the 'Core'

Similar curriculum battles have taken place all over the country. And, according to a recent study of the nation's top 50 colleges and universities by the NAS, the advocates of change appear to be winning. It concluded that "during the last 30 years the general-education programs of most of our best institutions have ceased to demand that students become familiar with the basic facts of their country's history, political and economic systems, philosophic traditions and literary and artistic legacies that were once conveyed through mandated and preferred survey courses." [24]

For instance, the NAS report states, the average number of required courses at the 50 schools surveyed dropped from 9.9 in 1914 to 6.9 in 1964 to 2.5 in 1993. More specifically,

90 percent of the institutions required students to take at least one course in the natural sciences in 1964, compared with 34 percent in 1993. The percentage of institutions with history requirements dropped during the same period from 38 percent to 12 percent. [25]

The NAS and other critics say that many universities have replaced general survey courses with no requirements at all or a broad range of often-unrelated classes that the student can

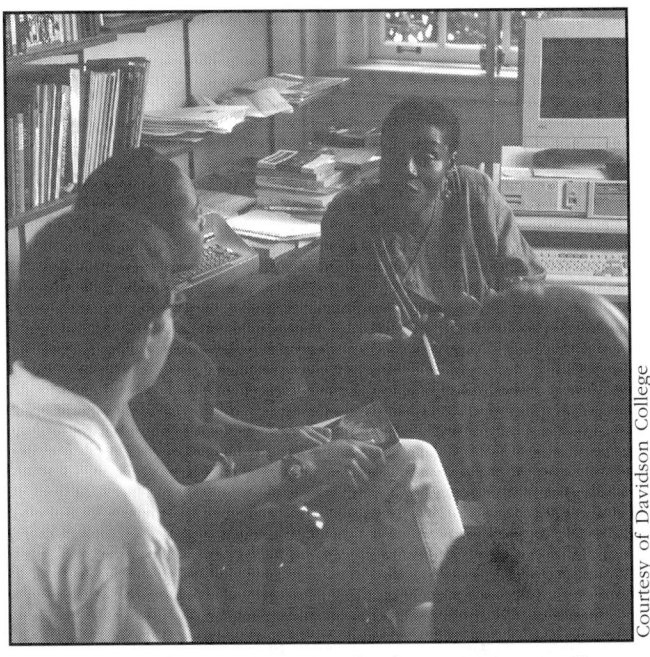

Courtesy of Davidson College

Liberal arts education is expected to become more popular in the future because it enhances career flexibility.

choose from. "A [selective] college like Dartmouth — or Harvard, Princeton, etc. — has requirements so broadly defined that almost anything goes," wrote Jeffrey Hart, who teaches English at Dartmouth. [26] At George Mason, for example, students can choose from 419 different classes to fulfill their four core requirements. [27]

Moreover, critics of the anti-core curricula trend argue, many of the classes students can choose to fulfill requirements are very specialized and of questionable value. A member of the Vir-

ginia Council on Higher Education recently noted that parents would be "flabbergasted" to learn that students at Virginia Polytechnic Institute could take a course in basic floral design to satisfy an art history requirement. [28]

Leaving basic curriculum choices to students is dangerous, the critics argue, because many are not qualified enough or mature enough to understand what their educational needs are. "Many students don't think a great deal about what they study," says the NAS' Ricketts, "which is why requirements are so important."

Without educational requirements, Ricketts and others say, students end up with few of the cultural reference points they need to be well-informed, well-educated people. "Educators always talk about concepts instead of facts today," says Schmidt of Illinois College. "But you can't understand the concept unless you know the facts behind it." For instance, he says, many students don't have even a rudimentary knowledge of the key players, places and dates of the American Revolution or the Civil War. "How can you truly know about the Civil War when you don't know when it occurred?" he asks.

But many educators say that people with Schmidt's point of view are alarmists who are clinging to an old way of learning by focusing too much on imprinting certain kinds of knowledge on students. They argue that schools can't just assume that if they've provided students with a broad survey of the humanities and sciences they will be educated.

"I don't want 'bingo' education,

Continued on p. 330

At Issue:

Should a liberal arts education primarily entail the study of Western civilization?

ALVIN J. SCHMIDT
Professor of sociology, Illinois College

WRITTEN FOR THE CQ RESEARCHER, APRIL 1998

*t*o be well-educated, students need to know and understand the underlying foundations of Western civilization. They also need to know the noteworthy contributions it has made to their nation and to much of the world. Here are a few key examples:

• From the Bible's portrayal of a rational God, Western thinkers concluded that human beings — the crown of creation — also were rational beings, capable of critical thinking, of discovering objective knowledge and truth, deductively and inductively. Without these premises, the world would still be in the pre-Industrial Age.

• In the Middle Ages, the monasteries of the Christian church created universities. Here knowledge was discovered and disseminated, giving rise to the seven liberal arts: grammar, rhetoric, logic, arithmetic, geometry, astronomy and music. All enriched human life.

• The brilliant Greek philosophers theorized, but because of their low view of manual labor they never tested their theories. With Christianity dignifying manual work, the West linked theory to practice, making it possible for modern science to appear.

• The Greco-Romans had no hospitals for their people. Hospitals were first built in the fourth century as Christians, moved by Christ's compassion, cared for the sick.

• The Athenians introduced a limited democracy. But England's Magna Carta and America's Declaration of Independence and Constitution made government by the people a reality. These documents often inspire nascent democracies today.

• At times, the West mimicked some of the evil practices of other cultures, such as its treatment of women and slavery. But it was the first to repent of these sins. It has elevated the rights of women, whereas in some non-Western societies women still have very few rights. Inspired by Christian leaders, the British were the first to outlaw slavery in the 1830s. Thirty years later America followed suit. In India, slavery existed until 1976, and African Sudan still has slavery.

We cannot afford to dilute or cut the lifeline of a liberal arts education — the study of Western civilization — because of a self-imposed guilt complex, prompted by the propaganda of anti-Western multiculturalists. Students have the right to see and understand how the knowledge, insights and contributions of Western civilization, unlike those of any other civilization, have benefited billions of people.

CAROL GEARY SCHNEIDER
President, Association of American Colleges and Universities

WRITTEN FOR THE CQ RESEARCHER, APRIL 1998

*o*ur current debates about societal diversity and multiculturalism are part of a continuing negotiation over the meaning and application of this nation's fundamental democratic principles. The Founders espoused equal dignity, liberty and justice for all. They laid a foundation for pluralism by accepting religious diversity and by a constitutional design that allowed states with disparate histories and cultures to live together in a federated republic. They challenged earlier views that a republic must be small and homogeneous to succeed. Instead, Americans with a vision for a new society opted for diversity.

Today, similar debates about the small, homogeneous republic vs. the diverse, democratic society are being waged in higher education. The college curriculum, which underwent revolutionary changes at the turn of the century, is changing again to provide students with the skills needed to lead this diverse American democracy in the future. Simultaneously, the curriculum is also changing in order to foster knowledge of global cultures, and of the connections between distant regions and new American communities sprouting up in all parts of the United States.

The question, then, is not whether we should address diversity and multiculturalism in the curriculum, but how to do it in ways that strengthen our democratic commitments. Drawing from myriad traditions, we must keep in mind always the founding commitments to liberty, equality, justice and voice, not only for individuals but for all the communities and cultures that are the nursery of our democracy.

In this spirit, the Association of American Colleges and Universities has released a set of recommendations for addressing diversity in the college curriculum. Economic realities have already answered the question whether students "ought" to learn about global cultures. We have warned that it would be a mistake to view courses on world cultures and United States diversity as interchangeable, or that giving attention to U.S. diversity can be optional. "Education for United States democratic and cultural pluralism," we observed in a recent report titled "American Pluralism and the College Curriculum," "is just as important as global study and deserves its own space and time in the curriculum." This study should include knowledge of diverse cultural traditions and histories, including one's own. The goal is to graduate students who are both prepared and inspired to take responsibility for the future of our diverse democracy.

Continued from p. 328

where you pick one course from Column A and another from Column B and then shout: 'Bingo! I'm educated,'" says Robert Zeminsky, director of the Institute for Research on Higher Education. Instead, Zeminsky says, schools need to help students grow other skills as well. "We're focused on the question of whether the student develops a real capacity to learn and to apply his knowledge to the world," he says.

Applying knowledge to the here and now is important, argues Schneider of the Association of American Colleges and Universities: "There is and there should be a determination in the world of higher education to engage learning with important contemporary issues, to make it more relevant to the present." For instance, she says, students should be able to learn about the creation of the American republic more than 200 years ago and, at the same time, compare it with the fight by Nelson Mandela and others to create democratic institutions in South Africa today.

Efforts to make knowledge more relevant are vital, says City College's Moses, because they offer students more opportunities to learn and connect what they've learned to other knowledge. "We must provide multiple points of entry for students to give them what they want," she says. ■

OUTLOOK

Liberal Arts Revival

Educators may argue about the direction liberal arts education should take, but most involved in the debate agree on one thing: In the

FOR MORE INFORMATION

If you would like to have this CQ Researcher updated, or need more information about this topic, please call CQ Custom Research. Special rates for CQ subscribers. (202) 887-8600 or (800) 432-2250, ext. 600, or email Custom.Research@cq.com

American Academy for Liberal Education, 1015 18th St. N.W., Suite 204, Washington, D.C. 20036; (202) 452-8611. The academy accredits colleges and universities that meet its standards in the liberal arts.

American Council on Education, 1 Dupont Circle N.W., Suite 800, Washington D.C. 20036; (202) 939-9300; www.acebet.edu. The council, which represents a large number of colleges and universities, conducts research on a variety of issues concerning higher education.

Association of American Colleges and Universities, 1818 R St. N.W., Washington, D.C. 20009; (202) 387-3760; www.aacu-edu.org. The association works to strengthen and promote liberal education.

Career College Association, 750 1st St. N.E., Suite 900, Washington D.C. 20002; (202) 336-6700; www.career.org. The association works to expand accessibility to career-oriented education at the university level.

National Association of Scholars, 575 Ewing St., Princeton, N.J. 08540; (609) 683-7878; www.nas.org. Representing college and university faculty, administrators and graduate students, the NAS seeks to raise academic standards at institutions of higher education.

National Association of State Universities and Land Grant Colleges, 1 Dupont Circle N.W., Suite 710, Washington D.C. 20036; (202) 778-0818. The association serves as a clearinghouse for issues involving public higher education.

The College Board, 45 Columbus Ave., New York, N.Y. 10023; (212) 713-8000; www.collegeboard.org. The board provides information and other support for college faculty and students.

future, liberal educations will become more, not less, important.

Ironically, it is the changing nature of work that is brightening the future for liberal arts education, the experts say. Vocational study, while still valued, does not have the flexibility to effectively prepare many of the people who are entering the new world of shifting careers.

"Most of us will have four or five careers in our lifetime," Moses says. "So training you in one area or field won't get you another job."

But a liberal arts education, with its broad fields of study and emphasis on communication and analytical thinking, will give graduates the ability to move from one job to another. "In a way, liberal arts education prepares you for all careers," Moses says.

The question then becomes: How will liberal arts education change, if at all, in the coming decades? Many conservatives see a rollback of multiculturalism and other educational "fads," like interdisciplinary studies. "You can already see some kids rebelling against this stuff," Ricketts says. "They want a more traditional education."

The University of Illinois' Douglas agrees. "In a generation or two, this ideological and politically correct stuff will be overturned. People will become disenchanted and demand a return to more traditional methods."

And yet, Ricketts and others say, the change will not come overnight. "The people who hold such views are outfunded and outgunned right now," he says.

Schmidt goes a step further, arguing that things will get much worse for traditionalists before they get better. "This kind of thing is hard to fight because we have lost our moral foundations, and in the postmodern era truth is relative and a lie is not a lie."

But many say that the proponents of traditionalism are screaming into the wind. "They've lost the war even if they are very strategic in their arguments," says Musil at the Association of American Colleges and Universities. While the conservatives are still arguing "about what you can read," everyone else has gotten on with teaching and learning. "They don't realize how much excitement there is on campus today between students and professors."

Magrath of the Association of State Universities and Land Grant Colleges agrees. "This whole idea that we've gone to hell in a handbasket is nonsense," he says. "We have more educated and more cultured people today than we've ever had before." ∎

Notes

[1] Cited in *The Chronicle of Higher Education, 1997-1998 Almanac Issue*, Aug. 29, 1997.

[2] Mark Edmundson, "On the Uses of a Liberal Education: As Lite Entertainment for Bored College Students," *Harper's*, September 1997.

[3] Allan Bloom, *The Closing of the American Mind: How Higher Education Has Failed Democracy and Impoverished the Souls of Today's Students* (1987), pp. 62-67.

[4] See Dinesh D'Souza, *Illiberal Education: The Politics of Race and Sex on Campus* (1991), p. 59. For background, see "Academic Politics," *The CQ Researcher*, Feb. 16, 1996, pp. 145-168.

[5] Martha Nussbaum, *Cultivating Humanity: A Classical Defense of Reform in Liberal Education* (1997), p. 55.

[6] Quoted in Edmundson, *op. cit.*

[7] *Ibid.*

[8] *Ibid.*

[9] *Ibid.*

[10] For background see Richard Hersh, "Intentions and Perceptions: A National Survey of Public Attitudes Toward Liberal Arts Education," *Change*, March/April, 1997.

[11] *Ibid.* For background, see "Getting Into College," *The CQ Researcher*, Feb. 23, 1996, pp. 169-192, and "Paying for College," *The CQ Researcher*, Nov. 20, 1992, pp. 1001-1022.

[12] *Ibid.*

[13] *Ibid.*

[14] Edmundson, *op. cit.*

[15] George Roche, *The Fall of the Ivory Tower* (1994), pp. 28-29.

[16] Daniel J. Boorstin, *The Americans: The Democratic Experience* (1973), p. 486.

[17] *Ibid.* pp. 493-494.

[18] *Ibid*, p. 485.

[19] George M. Marsden, *The Soul of the American University* (1994), p. 376.

[20] Robert Orrill (ed.), *Education and Democracy: Re-imagining Liberal Learning in America* (1997), pp. 141-142.

[21] Denise K. Magner, "Professors and Influential Alumni Join Forces to Protect Brooklyn College's Core Curriculum," *The Chronicle of Higher Education*, Oct. 17, 1997.

[22] Quoted in *Ibid.* For background, see "What Should College Students Be Taught?" *Editorial Research Reports*, Jan. 5, 1990, pp. 1-16.

[23] Quoted in *Ibid.*

[24] The National Academy of Scholars, *The Dissolution of General Education: 1914-1993*, 1996.

[25] *Ibid.*

[26] Jeffrey Hart, "How to Get a College Education," *The National Review*, Sept. 30, 1996.

[27] Victoria Benning, "Va. Colleges Are Goofing Off, Group Says," *The Washington Post*, Feb. 14, 1998.

[28] Quoted in *Ibid.*

Bibliography

Selected Sources Used

Books

Bloom, Allan, *The Closing of the American Mind*, Simon & Schuster, 1987.

The late University of Chicago professor traced what he deemed to be the precipitous decline of higher learning. He concluded in the runaway best-seller that students, even at the nation's best universities, were being fed a diet devoid of intellectual and spiritual nourishment. To revive university educational fare, Bloom recommended, among other things, a return to key texts and ideas of the Western tradition.

D'Souza, Dinesh, *Illiberal Education: The Politics of Race and Sex on Campus*, The Free Press, 1991.

D'Souza, a fellow at the American Enterprise Institute, chronicles what he sees as absurd and damaging trends in the academy, from multiculturalism and Afrocentrism to affirmative action. He concludes that "the current revolution of minority victims threatens to destroy the highest ideals of liberal education, and with them enlightenment and understanding, which hold out the only prospects for racial harmony, social justice and minority advancement."

Marsden, George M., *The Soul of the American University: From Protestant Establishment to Established Nonbelief*, Oxford University Press, 1994.

Marsden chronicles the declining role of religion at colleges and universities and the impact on higher education.

Nussbaum, Martha C., *Cultivating Humanity: A Classical Defense of Reform in Liberal Education*, Harvard University Press, 1997.

Nussbaum, a professor of law and ethics at the University of Chicago, argues that multiculturalism and other educational trends attacked by conservatives are supported by the great writers and thinkers of the classical world. For instance, she notes, Plato encouraged the study of other cultures.

Orrill, Robert (ed.), *Education and Democracy: Reimagining Liberal Learning in America*, The College Board, 1997.

Orrill, executive director of The College Board, has put together a collection essays by various scholars on the future of liberal education and its role in preparing students as citizens.

Schmidt, Alvin, *The Menace of Multiculturalism: Trojan Horse In America*, Praeger, 1997.

Schmidt, a professor of sociology at Illinois College, argues against multiculturalism as an ideology. In the end, he writes, it will lead to a nation fragmented along ethnic lines.

Articles

Edmundson, Mark, "On the Uses of a Liberal Education: As Lite Entertainment for the Bored College Students," *Harpers*, September 1997.

Edmundson, a professor at the University of Virginia, examines the attitudes of the current crop of college students and finds them wanting. Instead of looking to be challenged and changed by courses, undergraduates today want to be entertained, he writes. Edmundson blames their attitude on the prevailing consumer culture — TV and computers in particular — which has created a generation of students that seeks instant gratification, even in education.

Hart, Jeffrey, "How to Get a College Education," *National Review*, Sept. 30, 1996.

Hart, a professor at Dartmouth College, bemoans the lack of basic knowledge that so-called educated people have. At Dartmouth, he writes, freshmen arrive with little or no understanding of their culture, and many leave the same way, since the school has few liberal arts requirements.

Leatherman, Courtney, "10 Years After Bloom's Jeremiad Scholars Weigh Its Significance," *The Chronicle of Higher Education*, Jan. 17, 1997.

Leatherman examines the debate sparked by *The Closing of the American Mind* 10 years after its publication. She finds that the book and the issues it raised are still being debated.

Magner, Denise K., "Professors and Influential Alumni Join Force to Protect Brooklyn College's Core Curriculum," *The Chronicle of Higher Education*, Oct.. 17, 1997.

Magner details the recent battle over the fate of the core curriculum at Brooklyn College and the thus-far unsuccessful attempt to "reorient" it away from the 10 broad survey courses.

Reports

American Association of Colleges and Universities, *The Academy in Transition: Contemporary Understandings of Liberal Education*, 1998.

The report examines the changes that are taking place in American higher education, from new methods of instruction to the role of technology.

National Association of Scholars, The Dissolution of General Education: 1914-1993, 1996.

The association, which favors more liberal arts requirements, traces the decline of mandatory courses at 50 top universities.

The Next Step

Additional information from UMI's Newspaper & Periodical Abstracts™ database

Computers

Ames, Oakes, "A Program for Technological Literacy in the Liberal Arts: Does Technology Have a Place in the Liberal Arts Curriculum?" *Journal of College Science Teaching*, **March 1994, pp. 286-288.**

An overview is presented of proposals — submitted at the invitation of the Alfred P. Sloan Foundation — for improving liberal arts students' quantitative reasoning skills and understanding of technology. The proposed courses introduce the science underlying one or more technologies and help students understand the basic concepts of technology.

Walker, Henry M., and G. Michael Schneider, "A Revised Model Curriculum for a Liberal Arts Degree in Computer Science," *Communications of the ACM*, **December 1996, pp. 85-95.**

Combining the strengths of a liberal arts environment with those of computer science education, Walker and Schneider present recommendations for a high-quality undergraduate computer science major within a liberal arts setting. They build upon the traditional strengths of a liberal arts education while ensuring reasonable depth in the fundamental areas of computer science.

Watts, Lisa, "Technology and the Liberal Arts," *Education Digest*, **January 1997, pp. 56-59.**

New technology is taking college faculty and students beyond routine E-mail correspondence and word processing. The creation of a single locus for technology at one liberal arts college is discussed.

Consumerism in Education

Benning, Victoria, "Liberal Arts at GMU Targeted by Degrees; Proposed Cuts Draw Immediate Protests," *The Washington Post*, **March 15, 1998, p. B3.**

The dean of George Mason University's College of Arts and Sciences has proposed eliminating more than a dozen degree programs, prompting an outcry from faculty members who say the cuts will decimate their departments and hurt the university's stature. The cuts, outlined by Dean Daniele C. Struppa last week, are in response to GMU President Alan G. Merten's call for the university to narrow its mission and abolish or consolidate programs with low student enrollment.

Gilbert, Joan, "The Liberal Arts College — Is It Really an Endangered Species?" *Change*, **September 1995, pp. 36-43.**

Many believe that higher education is losing sight of its historic mission of offering a broad liberal arts education, and many institutions are moving toward curricula that focus increasingly on specialized and professional preparation. Data from the past and present are examined to determine whether these beliefs reflect reality.

Magner, Denise K., "Many Colleges have Survived by Moving Away from the Liberal Arts," *The Chronicle of Higher Education*, **March 2, 1994, p. A18.**

Dozens of liberal arts colleges survived the 1980s by changing their curricula to attract students and moving away from liberal arts to focus on career training and professional education.

Core Curriculum

"Liberal Arts: Universities Do Need to Question Their Curricula," *Detroit News and Free Press*, **Nov. 10, 1996, p. F2.**

A *Free Press* editorial says that there is good reason to hear out arguments by the Mackinac Center for Public Policy that undergraduate education in Michigan has become far too liberal academically.

Boot, Max, "The Vast Emptiness at the Core of Today's Liberal Arts Education," *Los Angeles Times*, **June 16, 1991, p. M3.**

University of California-Berkeley alumnus Boot argues that his alma mater has not fashioned its humanities and liberal arts curriculum into a coherent whole, but instead has developed too many overly specialized courses.

Davis, Brenda M., "A Case for the Small Liberal Arts Colleges and the Preparation of Teachers," *Journal of Teacher Education*, **May 1994, pp. 229-235.**

Private liberal arts colleges have presented strong cases for preserving the options of integrating teacher preparation as part of the undergraduate liberal arts curriculum.

Klein, Ilona, "Teaching in a Liberal Arts College: How Foreign Language Courses Contribute to 'Writing Across the Curriculum' Programs," *Modern Language Journal*, **spring 1990, pp. 28-35.**

Interaction between foreign-language instructors and English teachers helps provide a solid liberal arts core. In this area, "Writing Across the Curriculum" has become the most widely accepted liberal arts core program.

Light, Kathleen M., "Wellness and the Liberal Arts: A New Dimension in the Core Curriculum," *Wellness*

Perspectives: Research, Theory & Practice, spring 1995, pp. 28-35.

A two-semester sequence of wellness courses was developed at the University of Wisconsin and taught by an interdisciplinary faculty team. An evaluation of the program reveals that the goals of wellness and liberal arts are compatible.

Levy, Dan, "Yale Chief, in San Francisco, Stands up for Liberal Arts Schooling," *San Francisco Chronicle*, May 11, 1995, p. A28.

Yale University President Richard Levin says that a liberal arts education is the best kind of background to have in an era increasingly influenced by computers.

Job Market

Chesler, Herbert A., "Tell Them That a 'Pure' Liberal Arts Degree is Marketable," *Journal of Career Planning & Employment*, spring 1994, pp. 50-53.

The results of a survey that investigated how college graduates with a dual major in liberal arts and business performed in the job market compared with those with traditional liberal arts degrees are discussed. The findings demonstrate that liberal arts students may gain significantly in starting salaries and number of job offers.

Kleiman, Carol, "Liberal Arts Majors are Getting Down to Specifics," *Chicago Tribune*, June 30, 1993, p. 5.

Kleiman offers advice for liberal arts majors who want to make sure their "generalist" education fits into a tight labor market.

Kleiman, Carol, "Outlook Bright for College Seniors: Survey Indicates Students Are in a Strong Position with Hiring and Salaries up, Especially for Liberal Arts Graduates," *Chicago Tribune*, Jan. 29, 1998, p. 5.

An annual survey of employers' plans to hire new graduates showed plenty of job opportunities and respectable starting-salary offers, largely due to the strong economy, a labor shortage and low inflation. Members of the National Association of Colleges and Employers, which conducted the survey, say college seniors are in a strong position.

Lutz, Robert A. "The Higher Education System: Liberal Arts and the Business World," *Vital Speeches of the Day*, Aug. 15, 1996, pp. 649-652.

Liberal arts education has an important impact on the business world, and vice versa. Liberal arts graduates must ask themselves some questions before entering the business world.

Maguire, Mary, "Liberal Arts Earns an 'A'," *Chicago Tribune*, March 28, 1993, Sec. 19, p. 4.

The liberal arts degree, whose wide-ranging curriculum is seen by many as the shelter of artists, writers and other fanciful thinkers, often seems the subject of professional

ridicule and scorn. But though the standard liberal arts graduate may not be first in line for a loan officer position, banks and other professional institutions nevertheless have some jobs that are best-filled by the liberal arts grad.

Scheetz, L. Patrick, and Susan Stein-Roggenbuck, "Learn to Market Your Liberal Arts Degree for a Lifetime Career," *Black Collegian*, October 1994, pp. 111-118.

The career outlook for college students with a liberal arts degree is discussed. A liberal arts degree does not preclude graduates from finding meaningful employment.

Short, Joseph, "Yes, a Liberal Arts Education can be Productive," *Boston Globe*, Nov. 28, 1997, p. A27.

The author, who is president of a liberal arts college and the father of an English-literature grad, believes liberal arts is the best choice for an undergraduate education, one that prepares students to make a good living.

Weinstein, Bob, "Networking for Jobs: Small Liberal Arts Colleges Pool Resources to Share Job Information," *Boston Globe*, Oct. 5, 1997, p. C5.

Small schools are being short-changed when it comes to helping their students get jobs and persuading recruiters from high-profile corporations to visit their campuses. Phil Jones, director of the career resource center at Mount Holyoke College in South Hadley, Mass., and his colleagues at 24 other small colleges were so incensed by the problem that they helped create the NetWORK, a consortium of small schools around the country.

Liberal Arts vs. Career Training

"Wanted: Liberal Arts Grads," *Fortune*, May 12, 1997, p. 151.

While college students and parents believe that college is a place to obtain work skills, corporate CEOs value the liberal arts, where critical thinking and problem-solving skills are developed.

Ahmed, Zafar V., and Franklin B. Krohn, "The Symbiosis of Liberal Arts and International Business," *Journal of Education for Business*, March 1994, pp. 199-203.

The article suggests a way for U.S. liberal arts institutions to develop international business programs by employing existing resources. That would allow institutions to compete more effectively for the growing global market of students seeking international business programs.

Bebow, John, "U-M Plans to Shift Journalism Classes From Liberal Arts Program," *Detroit News and Free Press*, Jan. 15, 1995, p. C8.

The University of Michigan plans to remove journalism from its College of Literature, Science and the Arts, leaving journalism faculty wondering whether the change means the end of their program or a new beginning.

Delucchi, Michael, " 'Liberal Arts Colleges and the Myth of Uniqueness," *Journal of Higher Education*, July 1997, pp. 414-426.

Statistics reveal that 68 percent of colleges promoting a liberal arts mission are dominated by professional disciplines.

Goodman, Walter, "The Liberal Arts: No Match for Career Training," *The New York Times*, July 7, 1993, p. C18.

Goodman reviews three PBS TV shows about liberal education, including "Firing Line: What Is Liberal Education?"

Kirtz, Bill, "Good Journalists Have a Good Grasp of the Liberal Arts," *The Chronicle of Higher Education*, Feb. 7, 1997, p. B6.

Across the United States, journalism departments are being closed or merged into communications programs. Kirtz argues that journalism education should continue to be housed in traditional liberal arts schools or colleges rather than being submerged in communications schools or eliminated from university curricula as not being "scholarly" enough.

Kleiman, Carol, "Best 'Liberal Arts' Program: Engineering," *Chicago Tribune*, Aug. 27, 1995, p. 1.

The best liberal arts degree to receive, according to longtime engineer Eugene E. Lunger, is an engineering degree.

Kleiman, Carol, "This Question Is Not Just an Academic One — It Seems to Be a Toss-Up Whether Business or Liberal Arts Graduates Are More in Demand," *Chicago Tribune*, March 13, 1997, p. 5.

Though there's much debate on the subject, one expert says, "Liberal arts majors are finding liberal opportunities in the job market . . . even for jobs of a technical nature."

Wireman, Billy O., "Promoting Professional Education at the Small Liberal Arts College," *Vital Speeches of the Day*, Dec. 15, 1996, pp. 136-139.

The importance of designing liberal arts programs that help people achieve noble lives as well as productive careers is addressed.

What Colleges Are Teaching

Biemiller, Lawrence, "A Senior's Handmade Book and

Five Englemann Oaks: A Lesson in the Liberal Arts," *The Chronicle of Higher Education*, May 5, 1995, p. A51.

In his senior thesis, Pitzer College student James Lippincott explored the parallels between music and architecture. Lippincott's interest in music, architecture and plants is discussed.

Biemiller, Lawrence, "Where Students Still Study Ptolemy's Cosmology in Pursuit of the Liberal Arts," *The Chronicle of Higher Education*, Oct. 17, 1997, p. B2.

St. John's College in Annapolis, Md., is profiled as a liberal arts school attempting to right the failure of traditional liberal arts, which makes it impossible for people in different disciplines to communicate with each other. The school's extensive reading list and discussion-style classes are discussed.

Mura, Karen E., and Linda A. McMillin, "Not a Damsel in Distress: Feminist Medieval Studies at a Small Liberal Arts University," *Feminist Teacher*, winter 1996, pp. 49-58.

Susquehanna University, in central Pennsylvania, offers an interdisciplinary course on women's roles in medieval society.

Other Issues

Gose, Ben, "Liberal Arts Colleges Ask: Where Have the Men Gone?" *The Chronicle of Higher Education*, June 6, 1997, pp. A35-A36.

As female enrollment grows at liberal arts colleges, some institutions are considering a new form of affirmative action.

Oppenheimer, Gerald M., "Comment: Epidemiology and the Liberal Arts — Toward a New Paradigm?" *American Journal of Public Health*, July 1995, pp. 918-920.

Epidemiology has developed into an academic discipline that is technology-bound and depersonalized. Education in the humanities can broaden and deepen the concerns and questions that epidemiologists bring to their work.

Shields, George C., "The Physical Chemistry Sequence at Liberal Arts Colleges," *Journal of Chemical Education*, November 1994, pp. 951-953.

The revamping of the physical chemistry course at Lake Forest College is described. The restructuring included reordering the curriculum, modernizing the laboratories and reducing the lab write-up requirements.

Back Issues

Great Research on Current Issues Starts Right Here.
Recent topics covered by The CQ Researcher are listed below.
Now available on the Web
For information, call (800) 432-2250 ext. 279 or (202) 887-6279.

If you would like to have any of these CQ Researchers updated, or need more information
about these topics, please call CQ Custom Research. Special rates for CQ subscribers.
(202) 887-8600 or (800) 432-2250, ext. 600, or email Custom.Research@cq.com

DECEMBER 1996
Welfare, Work and the States
The New Volunteerism
Implementing the Disabilities Act
America's Pampered Pets

JANUARY 1997
Combating Scientific Misconduct
Restructuring the Electric Industry
The New Immigrants
Chemical and Biological Weapons

FEBRUARY 1997
Assisting Refugees
Alternative Medicine's Next Phase
Independent Counsels
Feminism's Future

MARCH 1997
New Air Quality Standards
Alcohol Advertising
Civic Renewal
Educating Gifted Students

APRIL 1997
Declining Crime Rates
The FBI Under Fire
Gender Equity in Sports
Space Program's Future

MAY 1997
The Stock Market
The Cloning Controversy
Expanding NATO
The Future of Libraries

JUNE 1997
FDA Reform
China After Deng
Line-Item Veto
Breast Cancer

JULY 1997
Transportation Policy
Executive Pay
School Choice Debate
Aggressive Driving

AUGUST 1997
Age Discrimination
Banning Land Mines
Children's Television
Evolution vs. Creationism

SEPTEMBER 1997
Caring for the Dying
Mental Health Policy
Mexico's Future
Youth Fitness

OCTOBER 1997
Urban Sprawl in the West
Diversity in the Workplace
Teacher Education
Contingent Work Force

NOVEMBER 1997
Renewable Energy
Artificial Intelligence
Religious Persecution
Roe v. Wade at 25

DECEMBER 1997
Whistleblowers
Castro's Next Move
Gun Control Standoff
Regulating Nonprofits

JANUARY 1998
Foster Care Reform
IRS Reform
The Black Middle Class
U.S.-British Relations

FEBRUARY 1998
Patients' Rights
Deflation Fears
Caring for the Elderly
The New Corporate Philanthropy

MARCH 1998
Israel at 50
The Federal Judiciary
Drinking on Campus
The Economics of Recycling

APRIL 1998
Biology and Behavior

Back issues are available for $5.00 (subscribers) or $10.00 (non-subscribers). Quantity discounts apply to orders over 10. To order, call Congressional Quarterly Customer Service at (202) 887-8621.

Binders are available for $18.00. To order call 1-800-638-1710. Please refer to stock number 648.

Future Topics

▶ *Income Inequality*

▶ *High-Tech Labor Shortages*

▶ *Census Controversy*

Income Inequality

Are poor Americans falling further behind?

T
he gap between the incomes of poor and
wealthy citizens is larger in the United States
than in any other industrialized country. Last
year, for the first time in almost two decades,
low unemployment and increases in the minimum wage
helped boost the earnings of Americans at the bottom of
the pay scale. But tax policies and the use of stock
options as part of corporate executives' compensation
packages are helping to divert a growing portion of the
nation's wealth to the richest Americans and away from
the poor and the middle class. If the current economic
boom continues, unskilled workers and those at the low
end of the compensation pool will continue to benefit,
experts say. But the disparity in Americans' incomes is not
likely to disappear.

April 17, 1998 • Volume 8, No. 15 • Pages 337-360

Formerly Editorial Research Reports®

CQ Researcher

April 17, 1998
Volume 8, No.15

EDITOR
Sandra Stencel

MANAGING EDITOR
Thomas J. Colin

ASSOCIATE EDITOR
Sarah M. Magner

STAFF WRITERS
Adriel Bettelheim
Mary H. Cooper
Kenneth Jost
David Masci

PRODUCTION EDITOR
Melissa Hall

EDITORIAL ASSISTANT
Laura S. Cavender

PUBLISHED BY
Congressional Quarterly Inc.

CHAIRMAN
Andrew Barnes

VICE CHAIRMAN
Andrew P. Corty

PRESIDENT AND PUBLISHER
Robert W. Merry

EXECUTIVE EDITOR
David Rapp

Bibliographic records and abstracts included in The Next Step section of this publication are the copyrighted material of UMI, and are used with permission.

The CQ Researcher (ISSN 1056-2036). Formerly Editorial Research Reports. Published weekly, except Jan. 2, May 29, July 3, Oct. 30, by Congressional Quarterly Inc., 1414 22nd St., N.W., Washington, D.C. 20037. Annual subscription rate for libraries, businesses and government is $340. Additional rates furnished upon request. Periodicals postage paid at Washington, D.C., and additional mailing offices. POSTMASTER: Send address changes to The CQ Researcher, 1414 22nd St., N.W., Washington, D.C. 20037.

COVER: WALT DISNEY CO. CEO MICHAEL EISNER TOOK HOME $575 MILLION LAST YEAR. (REUTERS/PETER MORGAN)

Income Inequality

BY MARY H. COOPER

THE ISSUES

By most people's standards, a salary of $750,000 is almost beyond comprehension. But last year that was just the appetizer for Walt Disney Co. CEO Michael Eisner. By exercising his stock options, Eisner boosted his take to an astounding $575 million — more than a million dollars a day. And while Eisner's case is extreme, it is hardly unique. Earnings for top executives in 1997 rose by as much as 21 percent. [1]

But rank-and-file workers didn't fare as well. They only received 3 percent raises, on average.

The U.S. economy has rarely been in better shape. The current recovery, now entering its eighth year, has created so many new jobs that unemployment fell to 4.6 percent in February, its lowest level in 24 years. [2]

A tight labor market usually fuels a round of inflation, as workers demand higher wages and manufacturers pass on the labor costs to the consumer. But not this time. Inflation stands at a mere 1.6 percent. Interest rates also are low, enabling businesses and consumers to borrow cheaply. And the stock market continues to set new records, bringing unexpectedly high returns to investors.

There's just one flaw in this glowing picture. While Eisner and other Americans are reaping benefits from the long period of prosperity, many others are falling behind. Moreover, it's the least well-off who are losing out, while those who are already prosperous are benefiting the most. As a result, the income gap — the difference in income between the richest and the poorest Americans — is widening. At the same time, the number of people in the middle class — the traditional objective of working Americans — is actually shrinking.

The picture was not always so bleak for the nation's have-nots.

"Looking at income growth over the postwar period, we saw income rising at all levels," says Elizabeth McNichol, a director at the Center on Budget and Policy Priorities. "But that's not what is happening now. Income at the low end is falling, while it's increasing a lot at the high end, and the middle is flat or dropping. It's not like one group is doing just a little better than the other."

In analyzing Census Bureau data, the center found that the income of the richest Americans increased by 30 percent from the late 1970s to the mid-'90s, while the poorest saw their incomes shrink by 21 percent. Americans occupying the middle range experienced a paltry 2 percent gain in income. Because the inflation-adjusted data do not include annual incomes over $100,000, the figures actually understate the breadth of the income gap. [3]

There are a number of reasons for the growing disparity in income. The decline in manufacturing during the 1980s eliminated thousands of high-wage, blue-collar jobs, which were replaced with largely low-paid jobs in the expanding service sector. Labor unions, which had won high wages for industrial workers throughout the postwar

era, lost their clout as factories closed and unions were kept out of many service workplaces. At the same time that the earning potential of low-skilled workers waned, rapid technological advances increased demand for better-skilled workers. This trend also widened the income gap between high school and college graduates.

Black Americans are disproportionately represented at the bottom of the income distribution, as they always have been. Thirty years ago, when the Kerner Commission submitted its landmark report on the roots of civil disorders in the United States, it concluded, "Our nation is moving toward two societies, one black, one white — separate and unequal." A recent update of that report found that black Americans are still locked out of economic prosperity. [4]

"The main problem is that poverty has increased since the Kerner report," says Fred R. Harris, a former Democratic U.S. senator from Oklahoma and Kerner Commission member, who co-authored the update. "We have more poverty and a greater percentage of poor people than we did 30 years ago, while the wealth and income gaps have widened."

Like other low- to middle-income workers, black Americans have suffered from the disappearance of industrial jobs. But poor black residents of the country's central cities have been especially disadvantaged by the migration of businesses to the suburbs. "The new jobs are out in the suburbs, where it's hard for central-city people to get to, and the ones in the city are low-paying service jobs," Harris says.

Technological changes also have left many black Americans particularly ill-prepared for today's high-wage jobs. "These jobs have high requirements for skills and education," Harris says. "So we've seen another kind of gap emerge between people with high school or college edu-

CQ on the Web: www.cq.com

April 17, 1998   339

Income Equality Depends on Location

The Southeast and Southwest had the greatest family income inequality in the mid-1990s, while the Midwest Plains and New England had the least. In seven states, the richest fifth of families earned more than 14 times the bottom fifth. In five states, the richest fifth had less than eight times the average income of the bottom fifth.

Family Income Inequality, 1994-1996

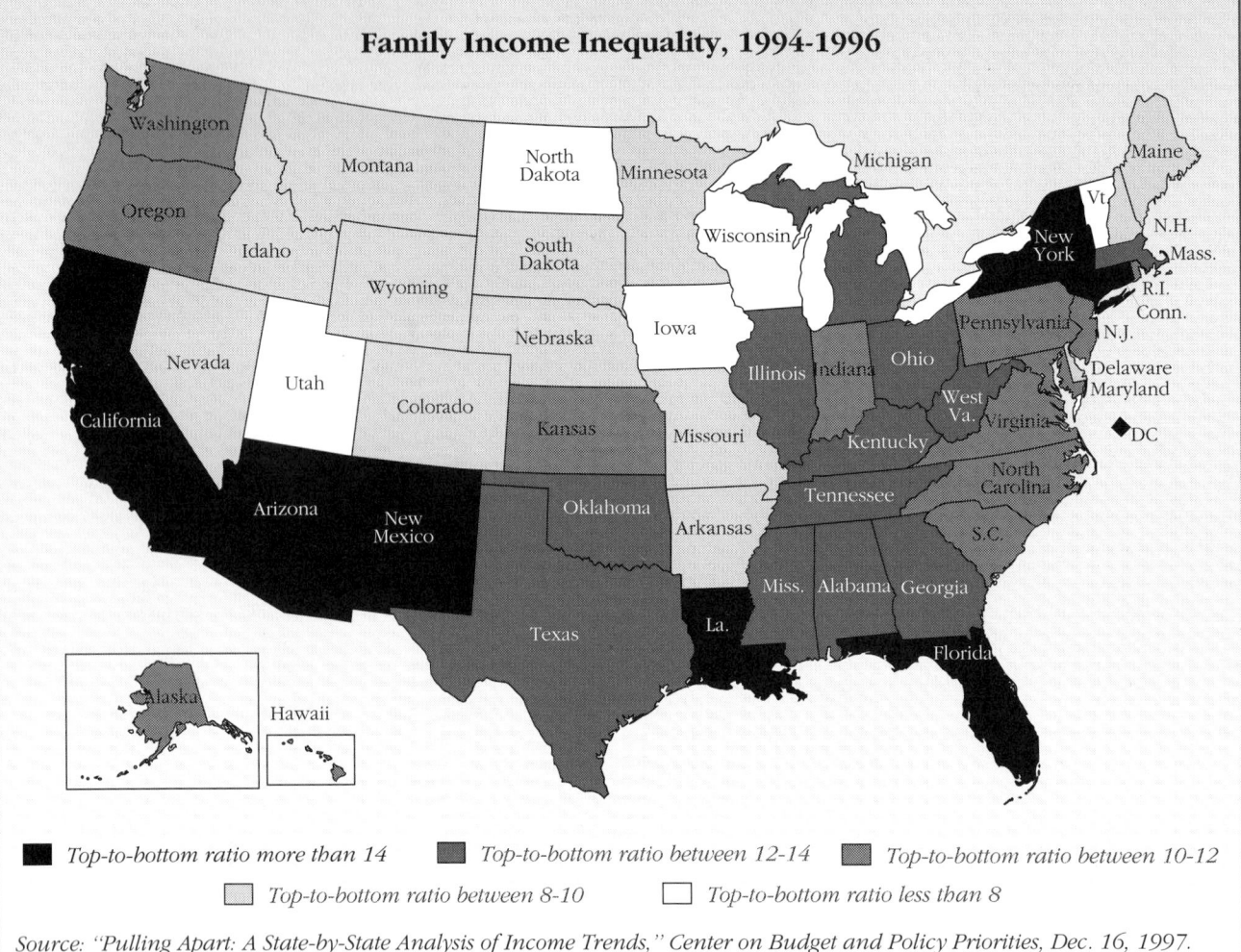

■ *Top-to-bottom ratio more than 14*　■ *Top-to-bottom ratio between 12-14*　■ *Top-to-bottom ratio between 10-12*
▨ *Top-to-bottom ratio between 8-10*　□ *Top-to-bottom ratio less than 8*

Source: "Pulling Apart: A State-by-State Analysis of Income Trends," Center on Budget and Policy Priorities, Dec. 16, 1997.

cations and those without, and this is a huge and growing gap."

At the other extreme of the income spectrum, rising stock prices have boosted the investment income of shareholders, who are mostly higher-income Americans. According to the center's analysis, average investment income received by the wealthiest 5 percent of families rose 56 percent, adjusted for inflation,

between 1979 and 1994, averaging more than $51,000 per household in 1996 alone. Here too, because the Census data do not include capital gains, the actual total-income figures are probably considerably higher.

Further skewing income distribution toward the wealthiest Americans is the widespread corporate practice of rewarding top executives with stock options, which enable recipi-

ents to buy shares at a set price for a specified period. As the stock market has boomed, so too has the value of the options available for executive compensation.

"CEOs are cashing in on the bull market," says William Patterson, director of the AFL-CIO's office of investment. "And that's based less on their good works or their own particular merits than on the enormous amount of capital that has entered the stock market in the last five years."

Some analysts say the gap in living standards is more accurately measured by including not just household income but net worth — a household's accumulated wealth minus outstanding debts. "The distribution of wealth is even more skewed than the distribution of earnings," says Alan B. Krueger, a labor economist at Princeton University and former chief economist at the Labor Department. For example, Bill Gates, the 41-year-old chief executive of Microsoft, who topped last year's *Forbes* 400 list of the richest Americans, is worth an estimated $40 billion. "That's equivalent to the combined net worth of the bottom 40 percent of U.S. households," Krueger says. "Even when you account for the fact that the bottom 18 percent have no net worth, 40 percent is a lot of people. In a democracy, one needs to be worried about that kind of concentration of wealth."

The Clinton administration points to signs that the ever-widening income gap may recently have reversed course. According to *The 1998 Economic Report of the President*, household income has grown across the income spectrum since 1993, with the greatest improvement going to the poorest households. The report points optimistically at a reduction in the poverty rate from 15.1 percent in 1993 to 13.7 percent in 1997, a development that has been especially beneficial to black Americans, whose poverty rate is at the lowest level ever. [5]

Some economists agree that today's strong economy may have stopped the income gap from widening. "The income gap is still there, in fact it's worse than it was as recently as 1980," says Richard Freeman, an economist at Harvard University. "But it hasn't widened all that much in recent years, and now it's leveled off. There's even some evidence that the

very bottom is coming up as well. So it's safe to say that income inequality may have gotten better."

The latest economic data seem to confirm the optimists' views. The Labor Department reported in March that wages for the lowest-paid workers reversed their downward course last year and rose by 1.6 percent to $260 a week, the biggest increase since the government began collecting such data in 1979. [6]

But any narrowing of the income gap seems unlikely to bite into the fortunes of Gates and other tycoons. "The momentum of prosperity in the United States suggests that the income gap will start to narrow, but not at the expense of the very, very rich, the 1 percent of the income distribution who are raking in megamillions on this incredible stock market," says Allen Sinai, chief economist at Primark Decision Economics in Boston. "But, on average, the lower end of the income distribution is picking up speed."

If the optimists are right, low unemployment is finally helping workers who have not shared in the current recovery. "The economy is dipping into unskilled workers and the lowest end of the compensation pool in a significant way because there's a shortage of workers everywhere," Sinai says. "General prosperity is doing its thing, raising the pay of ordinary workers."

Just how long the current recovery will last is, of course, a matter of speculation. Economic turmoil in Asia may yet slash demand for U.S. goods and services and tip the economic balance once again into recession. But even if the recovery continues to boost average incomes, the wide disparity in Americans' incomes is likely to persist.

As economists watch the impact of burgeoning economic growth on the income gap, these are some of the questions being asked:

Does the income gap matter?

Income inequality in the United States is at an all-time high. But because of advances in health care, agriculture and other factors that contribute to the overall standard of living, some experts say the United States is now enjoying a period of prosperity that has a far greater impact on all Americans' living standards than the persistent income gap.

"[I]t is true that, by some measures, there has been a recent increase in income inequality in the United States," writes Christopher C. DeMuth, president of the American Enterprise Institute for Public Policy Research, a conservative think tank. "But it is a very small tick in the massive and unprecedented leveling of material circumstances that has been proceeding now for almost three centuries and in this century has accelerated dramatically. In fact, the much-noticed increase in [income] inequality is in part a result of the increase in real social equality." [7]

DeMuth cites the general availability of food, shelter and clothing, medical advances, the replacement of social class with intellectual ability as the key to success and the reduction of workplace discrimination against women as trends that have contributed to our society's unprecedented prosperity. "One implication of these trends is that in very wealthy societies, income has become a less useful gauge of economic welfare and hence of economic equality," he writes. [8]

This view reflects the economic adage "a rising tide lifts all boats," which suggests that economic growth makes life better for everyone in society by making the kinds of advances DeMuth describes available throughout society. But other experts maintain that the income gap is clear evidence that the benefits of today's booming economy are not being enjoyed by all.

"It is correct to look at a lot of

Continued on p. 343

Today's Rich Are Really Rich

Income inequality is hardly a secret in American society. Poor workers who are struggling to get by on the minimum wage, currently $5.15 an hour by federal law, are bombarded by television advertisements hawking luxury cars, cruise vacations and other amenities that only the wealthy can afford. They root for athletes who take home millions of dollars a year and are entertained by actors and musicians whose annual incomes are hundreds of times higher than their own meager wages. Adding insult to injury, the rich are getting a lot richer. It took a net worth of $475 million to get on the annual *Forbes* 400 list of the wealthiest Americans last year, up from $415 million in 1996. [1]

But the truly rich Americans — the megamillionaires — are less visible than the mere millionaires who populate Hollywood and the sports arenas. As one might expect, they are typically old white men, such as William Hewlett, 84, co-founder of Hewlett Packard (net worth $4.1 billion) and Metromedia founder John Kluge, 83 ($7.8 billion). Talk-show hostess Oprah Winfrey was the only black person in *Forbes'* rankings last year, and she placed a lowly 343rd, with a net worth of only $550 million.

But the technology boom has added younger blood, and a lot more money, to the top of the heap. The richest man in America is Microsoft co-founder William Henry Gates III, who at 41 has already amassed a fortune of about $40 billion — more than the gross national product of many countries. Another Microsoft founder, Paul Gardner Allen, 44, ranks third at $17 billion. Of the richest 25 Americans, seven made their fortunes in high technology.

But there are other roads to riches. Many who made the list were simply in the right place at the right time and inherited their wealth, such as the widow and four children of Wal-Mart founder Sam Walton, who share the family fortune of $32 billion. William Wrigley ($2.5 billion) got rich from the family chewing gum empire, while liquor magnate Edgar Bronfman Sr. ($3 billion) took over Joseph E. Seagram & Sons from his father. John Richard Simplot amassed his $3.3 billion growing potatoes — and later producing microchips. [2]

Microsoft co-founder Bill Gates is worth an estimated $40 billion.

Reuters/Ian Hodgson

What do they do with all their wealth? Most, of course, make more by investing their fortunes. And if the stock market continues its current upward spiral, the multibillionaire club can only multiply. Others buy land — lots of it. Media mogul Ted Turner (net worth $3.5 billion) has acquired hundreds of thousands of acres of pristine forest and prairie throughout the Mountain West.

The super-rich also give some of their money away, if for no other reason than the fact that the Internal Revenue Service rewards philanthropy by excluding donated funds from taxation. But wealth and generosity do not always go hand in hand.

Bill Gates may be the richest man in America, but he has given away a relatively paltry $100-$500 million to date, according to a recent listing of America's 100 leading philanthropists. [3] Compare that with the generosity of retired publisher Walter Annenberg, who has donated more than $1 billion, nearly a third of his $3.8 billion fortune, or Paul Mellon, who has given away almost all of his $1.2 billion oil and banking inheritance. (Turner's pledge last year of $1 billion to the United Nations isn't included in the listing because it only considered disbursed contributions.)

Granted, Annenberg and Mellon are in their 90s, while Gates has a wife and child to support. In fact, Gates is not alone among tycoons who, to date, have not distinguished themselves as great philanthropists. Only 61 of the people who made the *Forbes* 400 list also made the *American Benefactor* 100 list.

[1] See "The 400: The Average Net Worth of the Forbes Four Hundred is $1.6 billion," *Forbes*, Oct. 13, 1997, pp. 181-250.

[2] "The Top 25," *Forbes*, Oct. 13, 1997, pp. 152-166.

[3] Dan Rottenberg, "100 Most Generous Americans," *The American Benefactor*, fall 1997, pp. 42-68. For background, see "The New Corporate Philanthropy," *The CQ Researcher*, Feb. 27, 1998, pp. 169-197.

Continued from p. 341

things, such as medical advances, but clearly a very important determinant of well-being is the wage rate people command," Krueger says. "And a large income gap is cause for concern."

Some critics also dispute DeMuth's assertion that the non-wage benefits of industrial development help everyone. "The whole point of the surge in inequality is that the benefits are far from equally enjoyed," says Jared Bernstein, an economist at the liberal Economic Policy Institute. "It's pretty meaningless to say don't worry about it if the gains themselves are unequally distributed." A wealthy American, for example, can buy the latest medical treatment, even if it isn't covered by health insurance, while many poor workers cannot afford even the most basic health coverage. "With medical care, the further you are down on the income scale, the less access you have to the system, especially to quality health care," Bernstein says.

Even the recent narrowing of the income gap fails to convince some economists that the boom is having a significant impact on the poorest Americans. "The gap grew considerably during the 1980s, stabilized in the 1990s and last year incomes at the bottom grew a bit more than they did in the middle," Krueger says. "But the gap that opened in the 1980s was only slightly reduced. So to the extent that one was concerned about the income gap before, one should still be."

Supply-side economists, who support the notion that the benefits of economic growth "trickle down" to the lowest income levels, say the income gap is not the most important measure of well-being. "A capitalist economy over time produces an affluent society, a society with a high level of average income," writes Irving Kristol, an American Enterprise Institute fellow and co-editor of *The Public Interest*, a conservative magazine. "In such a society, income inequality tends to be swamped by even greater social equal-

Prosperity Boosts CEOs, Not Workers

The booming economy boosted corporate profits by 50 percent from 1990 to 1995 and added more than $1 million to the average CEO's pay, but layoffs of workers increased by more than a third and their pay decreased slightly.

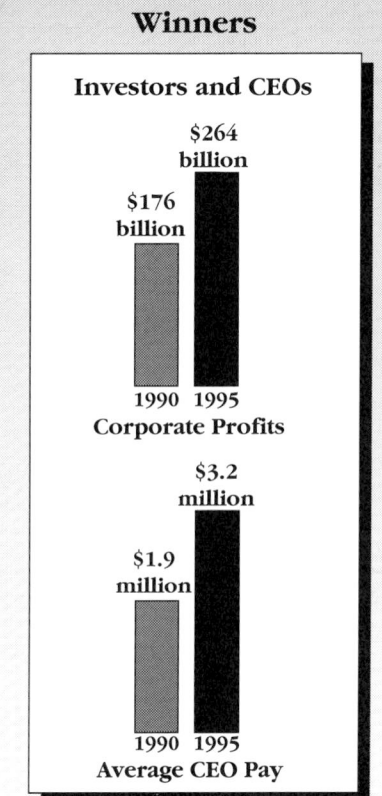

Winners

Investors and CEOs

Corporate Profits: $176 billion (1990), $264 billion (1995)

Average CEO Pay: $1.9 million (1990), $3.2 million (1995)

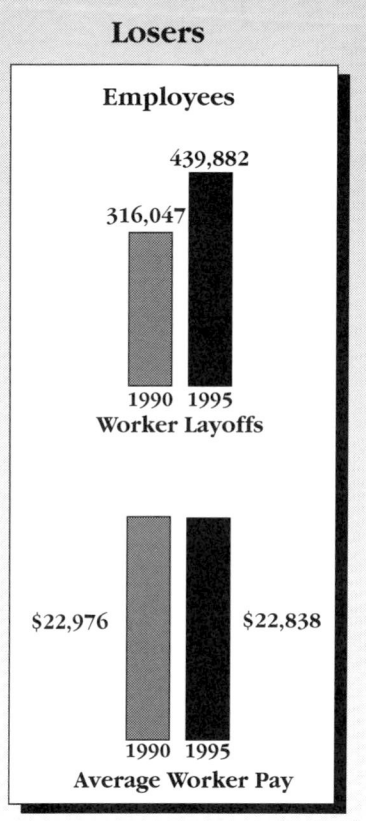

Losers

Employees

Worker Layoffs: 316,047 (1990), 439,882 (1995)

Average Worker Pay: $22,976 (1990), $22,838 (1995)

Note: Dollar amounts are in constant 1990 dollars.

Sources: United for a Fair Economy, from Business Week, *April 22, 1996; Bureau of Labor Statistics and Challenger, Gray and Christmas*

ity." Kristol observes that all Americans wear blue jeans and buy expensive cars on installment. "In all of our major cities, there is not a single restaurant where a CEO can lunch or dine with the absolute assurance that he will not run into his secretary," he writes. "If you fly first class, who will be your traveling companions? You never know." [9]

But this view does not take into account the persistent failure of some groups in the population to benefit from the general prosperity. "It's just

not so for a lot of people, especially people who are locked in the poorhouse in the central city," Harris says. "Today 14.4 million Americans have incomes at less than half the poverty threshold, which is an increase over 1995. So there are more poor people today, and people who are poor are poorer, so it's much harder for them to get out of it. And poverty is more concentrated in the central cities, and thus among African-Americans and Hispanic-Americans."

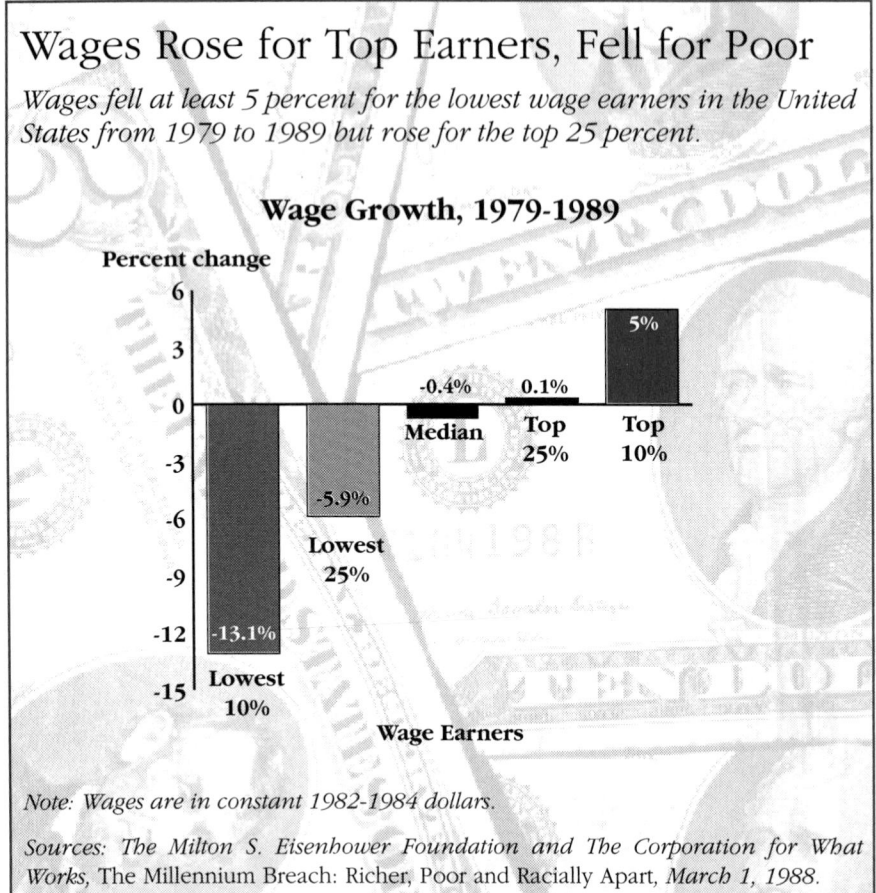

Wages Rose for Top Earners, Fell for Poor

Wages fell at least 5 percent for the lowest wage earners in the United States from 1979 to 1989 but rose for the top 25 percent.

Wage Growth, 1979-1989

Percent change

Note: Wages are in constant 1982-1984 dollars.

Sources: The Milton S. Eisenhower Foundation and The Corporation for What Works, The Millennium Breach: Richer, Poor and Racially Apart, March 1, 1988.

Is racism a leading cause of income disparity in the United States?

The civil rights movement of the 1960s and early '70s led to changes in public policy that have greatly improved the lot of black Americans over the past 30 years. The number of African-Americans who have been elected to public office has risen dramatically, as has the number of black business owners, white-collar employees and high school graduates. Laws barring racial discrimination and affirmative-action policies in college admissions and hiring have helped more and more black Americans to join the middle class.

But beginning in the 1980s, efforts to combat racial discrimination came under attack, culminating in the recent bans on affirmative-action rules

in the California and Texas state-university systems. As a result, admissions offers to black and Hispanic students for next fall's freshman class at the University of California at Berkeley, the First class chosen without affirmative-action rules, fell by more than half over last year. [10]

Supporters of affirmative action say its erosion has resulted in a worsening of living standards among black and Hispanic-Americans that is closely linked to the deepening income gap. The Eisenhower Foundation's recent update of the Kerner Commission report, for example, points out that while overall unemployment in the United States fell to 4.6 percent in February, it still stands at 9.9 percent for African-Americans. While 11.2 percent of white teenagers are unable to find jobs, teen unemployment is more than

three times higher among black teens. The median income of black and Hispanic-Americans is still just over half that of non-Hispanic, white Americans. And more than three-quarters of poor people live in central cities today, up from about half in the late 1960s. [11]

"This concentrated poverty certainly involves race, because of segregation of housing and schools, which is happening once again," Harris says. "Families in the inner city, where poverty is concentrated, have a really difficult time breaking out. Shut off from contact with people in the middle class, those who are left behind don't have contact with the institutions or people to help them get out of poverty."

Harris stops short of blaming income inequality on racial discrimination alone. But, he says, "it has been very much involved with it. We've knocked down the legal and political barriers of discrimination, but we still have a great deal of institutional discrimination. There's no question that we've made enormous progress with regard to race — many African-Americans are middle-class people and officials," he says. "But that does not mean that we should give up on affirmative action."

Not all black commentators agree that racial discrimination plays a significant role in income inequality. "If race were at the bottom of it, then why aren't all blacks suffering equally?" asks Robert L. Woodson Sr., chairman of the National Center for Neighborhood Enterprises. "The biggest income gap today is not between black and white people," he says, "but between upper-income blacks and low-income blacks."

Woodson says most black teachers in the Washington, D.C., public school system send their children to schools outside the system, but oppose adoption of a voucher program that would allow other black parents to do the same. "So poor black kids are being disadvantaged in a system controlled by other blacks. They are suffering at the hands of their own people."

Even Woodson concedes that institutional discrimination still contributes to inequality in America. Citing a recent survey finding that two out of five blacks applying for mortgage loans from 75 institutions faced stiffer requirements to qualify than did whites, he says, "institutional discrimination plays some role in income disparity. But it's not the dominant role."

Income is not the sole measure of racial inequality, however. "When you talk about racial disparities, it's really important to move beyond income and look at wealth, because that is where the disparity is the greatest," Bernstein says. In 1993, he notes, the median net worth of white families was $45,740, more than 10 times the $4,418 net worth of African-American families. "Regardless of where you think racial discrimination is today, the cumulative history of discrimination has resulted in huge disparities in wealth between minorities and whites."

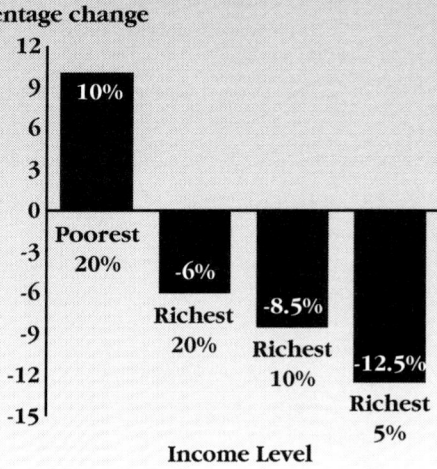

Tax Cuts Benefited Rich, Not Poor

Taxes for the poorest 20 percent of the population rose 10 percent from 1980 to 1990, while taxes for the richest 5 percent were reduced by about 13 percent.

Changes in Tax Rates

Sources: *The Milton S. Eisenhower Foundation and The Corporation for What Works,* The Millennium Breach: Richer, Poor and Racially Apart, *March 1, 1998; Congressional Budget Office*

Should the government do more to reduce income disparity?

Through policies ranging from the progressive income tax to the minimum wage, the federal government has long interfered in the free market in an attempt to reduce the extremes of wealth and poverty. Tax rates that increase with income ensure that the rich pay the greatest percentage of their income in taxes, while laws guaranteeing workers a minimum wage and the earned-income tax credit are attempts to buoy the disposable incomes of the poorest workers.

But some of these safeguards were eroded during the 1980s as the Republican administration of Ronald Reagan adopted a supply-side approach toward managing the economy. By reducing tax burdens, especially those of investors and business owners, policy-makers reasoned, the economy would grow faster, producing more jobs and raising incomes

at the middle- and lower-income levels as well.

The 1986 Tax Reform Act and other changes in the 1980s did, in fact, lower the burden of taxation on the wealthy. But other initiatives eroded the "safety net" of social programs designed in the wake of the Great Depression to raise the living standards of the poorest Americans. At the same time, low-wage workers saw their incomes actually fall as inflation reduced the value of the minimum wage, which was left unchanged from 1981 to 1990.

Policies adopted since 1990 have reversed some of the economic policies of the '80s. The minimum wage, for example, has been increased four times, twice during the Bush administration and twice during the Clinton administration. But the overriding concern of balancing the federal budget has meant that gov-

ernment programs designed to aid the poor have not been strengthened. Some programs, notably Aid to Families with Dependent Children (AFDC), have been cut back even further under the 1996 Welfare Reform Act. [12]

Supporters of the law say it will help boost earnings at the low end of the income spectrum by forcing current welfare recipients to work and eventually go off the welfare rolls. "Along with family disintegration," says Woodson of the National Center for Neighborhood Enterprises, "policies that discourage work, such as welfare, are among the leading factors contributing to income inequality."

Although the most recent data show a slight reversal in the trend toward greater income disparity, many analysts say the federal government should do more to reduce the wage gap. "The minimum

Gender Gap Adds to Income Inequality

The gender gap — the difference in earnings between men and women — is a persistent contributor to income inequality in the United States. American women make only 74 cents for every dollar earned by men, although the gap has narrowed by five cents over the past two decades, according to the AFL-CIO. [1]

For years, wage discrimination against female workers was attributed to lack of education and training. Because many women went directly from high school or college to marriage and life as full-time homemakers and mothers, they tended to have less formal job training than men. When they finally entered the work force, often in their late 30s or 40s, women also lacked the years of service — and annual raises — their male counterparts had built up.

The 1970s and '80s saw a rapid increase in the number of women in the work force. The loss of high-paying manufacturing jobs, the decline in union representation and rampant inflation had all reduced men's earnings in this period, forcing many married women to seek employment. At the same time, young women began entering graduate schools in increasing numbers, preparing them for high-paying jobs in law, medicine and business.

But even after women began entering the work force in large numbers, the gender gap remained stubbornly high. Female business-school graduates, many now in their 30s and 40s, complain repeatedly of a corporate "glass ceiling" preventing them from ever attaining top management jobs. Today women hold only 3 percent of the top six executive positions at the country's biggest companies, and only a few have become chief executive officers. [2]

Most workers, male or female, lack the education and training that would enable them to aspire to top positions. But women throughout the work force claim that men routinely receive higher pay for similar work. According to the Census Bureau, the average income of college-educated, white, female managers is $38,800, or $17,100 less than that of white males of the same category. The gender gap is less conspicuous among African-Americans: Black female managers earn $31,000, which is $10,000 less than African-American males. But the racial divide is clear, even at this highly skilled level. [3]

Perhaps reflecting wage inequality, a recent survey found that 56 percent of working women were unable to save part of their paychecks or even keep up with their bills. The vast majority of women polled — 91 percent — said

laws should be strengthened to ensure equal pay for equal work. [4]

"There is still a glass ceiling preventing women from gaining access to leadership positions in both corporate and government jobs," writes Kate Bronfenbrenner, director of labor education research at Cornell University's New York School of Industrial and Labor Relations. "Even more damaging, however, is the pervasiveness of the 'sticky floor,' the combination of forces which confine the majority of women to low-wage occupations." [5]

Working women are beginning to strike back at sexual discrimination that still pervades the workplace. According to polling data and a new study by the AFL-CIO, women in unprecedented numbers are taking an active role in bringing unions to their job sites to achieve wage parity as well as pension and health-insurance coverage and such family-related benefits as day care and elder care. While unions have weakened in male-dominated manufacturing industries as a result of downsizing and outsourcing over the past two decades, union representation has begun to pick up again with health-care and social-service providers, hotels and other service establishments where women make up the majority of employees. [6]

As part of a campaign to boost the numbers further, the AFL-CIO recently named April 3 Equal Pay Day, estimating that it takes until April of the following year for women to catch up with the earnings received by their male counterparts the year before.

---

[1] "Today's Working Women Are Organizing Unions in Escalating Numbers," press release of the American Federation of Labor and Congress of Industrial Organizations, March 19, 1998.

[2] See Kirstin Downey Grimsley, "MBA No Ticket to Top for Women," *The Washington Post*, March 24, 1998. For background, see "The Glass Ceiling," *The CQ Researcher*, Oct. 29, 1993, pp. 973-960.

[3] See Julianne Malveaux, "Women, Blacks See Between the Bottom Lines," *Los Angeles Times*, July 6, 1997.

[4] Peter D. Hart Research Associates, Inc., conducted the survey from Jan. 31-Feb 4, 1997 for the AFL-CIO.

[5] Kate Bronfenbrenner, *Lifting as They Climb: The Promise and Potential of Organizing Women Workers*, AFL-CIO, March 18, 1998.

[6] For background, see "Labor Movement's Future," *The CQ Researcher*, June 28, 1996, pp. 553-576.

wage should be increased again," says Bernstein of the Economic Policy Institute. "For nine years we allowed inflation to erode the value of the minimum wage, and those years correspond quite neatly to the time when the bottom was beginning to really fall out. Raising it again would help lift the fortunes of those at the bottom, who've lost the most."

Opponents to further increases in the minimum wage argue that they would spark inflation and harm small-business owners. "Small-business owners were just hit with a minimum-wage increase last year, and they can't afford another one," said Jack Faris, president of the National Federation of Independent Business. "Every time there's a minimum-wage hike, more small-business owners are forced to lay off employees, pass costs on to consumers or not hire new employees." [13]

Faris also argues that the minimum wage does not keep low-wage workers out of poverty. "In reality, 84 percent of employees whose wages would be hiked either live with their parents or another relative, live alone or have a working spouse," he said. "By increasing the minimum wage, low-skilled employees are priced out of the market, denying them an opportunity to get a job and gain valuable experience."

Tax policy is another tool that could be used to narrow the income gap. Tax reform proposals now before Congress, such as the flat tax and the national sales tax, would fall more heavily on the poor than the current income tax. [14]

In a book soon to be published, author Steve Brouwer argues that the most effective step the federal government could take to reduce income inequality would be to institute a new tax on wealth. "If we had a Congress and a president who were willing to promote the interests of the vast majority of Americans," he writes, "we could recapture some of the accumulated wealth that has been transferred to the rich over the last two decades." [15] An annual wealth tax of 3 percent on the richest 1 percent of Americans, he estimates, would add $250 billion a year to the Treasury's coffers.

Labor economist Krueger focuses on education, not fiscal policies, as the ultimate solution to income in-

equality. "The reason the income gap expanded in the 1980s was the demand for more skilled workers," he says. "And the best way to narrow the gap would be to increase the skills of workers." In his view, training programs should be targeted to women coming off welfare, displaced workers and other people who are most likely to benefit from them. "The group that is most difficult to help is out-of-school youth," he says. "We also need to develop new initiatives to help these disadvantaged people."

While emphasizing the need for gov-

> "The reason the income gap expanded in the 1980s was the demand for more skilled workers. And the best way to narrow the gap would be to increase the skills of workers."
>
> — *Alan B. Krueger*
> *Labor economist*
> *Princeton University*

ernment intervention to boost the incomes of the poor, Freeman suggests that middle-income workers would benefit the most from corporate decisions to make stock options and other investment opportunities available to all workers, not just executives.

"Making profit-sharing schemes and stock options more widely available throughout the work force would take care of most workers," he says. "If it's good for executives, it's good for workers. This is an extraordinarily positive

thing that can happen without government intervention." ∎

BACKGROUND

Postwar Prosperity

The Great Depression still serves as the bench mark for measuring economic misery in the United States. By the mid-1930s, average incomes had dropped by almost a third, and unemployment approached 25 percent. [16] New Deal legislation funneled large amounts of federal dollars into employment and welfare initiatives. By 1940, the U.S. economy was well into recovery, and incomes, at least for whites, had returned to their pre-Depression levels.

Unemployment was all but wiped out when the United States entered World War II. Workers who were not in the armed services were employed in wartime industrial production. Black workers, however, were largely excluded from all but low-wage, menial jobs.

The United States emerged from World War II as the only industrial power that had been left relatively unscathed from the war and was thus in the best position to profit from demand for manufactured goods both at home and abroad. This circumstance produced an economic boom that boosted the incomes of Americans of all earning levels. High-paying manufacturing jobs enabled men with high school educations to buy a car, a house and the myriad other accoutrements that went with membership in the growing middle class. High manufacturing wages also meant that two-income families were a rarity, as most married women stayed at home.

In 1949, as the postwar boom gathered steam, only a fifth of families were in the lowest earnings quintile, or lowest 20 percent. Almost half of these were comprised of the elderly and the small number of families headed by women, whose incomes were limited by the lack of widespread retirement or welfare benefits. The lowest quintile also included a quarter of all white families and half of all black families, who lived in the mainly rural Southeast, the poorest region of the country at the time. Children actually fared better than families: Only 15 percent were in the lowest quintile, though these included almost half of all black children.

Not surprisingly, the typical family in the top income quintile was headed by a middle-aged man in a professional job somewhere other than the Southeast. But in pre-suburban America of 1949, fully 30 percent of the families living in central cities belonged in the top quintile.

By the end of the 1950s, the "Ozzie and Harriet" economy had produced further improvements in income distribution. Despite three recessions, the Korean War and three periods of inflation, the decade also was marked by a fall in poverty from 32 percent to 22 percent of the population and a 43 percent rise in median family income. The portion of total income going to the lowest quintile even rose slightly during the 1950s, from

4.5 percent to 4.9 percent. Greater access to higher education, technological developments and increased efficiency all contributed to greater productivity, the main engine of income growth over the decade. Incomes also rose as farmworkers left the countryside for higher-paying jobs in city factories and offices.

The 1960s saw an even more dramatic narrowing of the income gap, in part as a result of the civil rights movement, President Lyndon B. Johnson's "War on Poverty" and other efforts to

---

By the end of the 1950s, the "Ozzie and Harriet" economy had produced further improvements in income distribution. Despite three recessions, the Korean War and three periods of inflation, the decade also was marked by a fall in poverty from 32 percent to 22 percent of the population and a 43 percent rise in median family income.

---

end racial discrimination — a major contributor to income disparity. Helped by favorable economic conditions — mainly continued rising productivity and low inflation — these policies helped reduce unemployment to as low as 4.4 percent in 1963 and raise incomes by 38 percent over the decade. Unemployment among black men fell twice as fast as among white men, providing

a strong boost to black family incomes. The share of total income going to the bottom quintile again grew, to 5.6 percent, while the percentage of people in poverty fell by almost half; by the end of the 1960s, it stood at 12 percent.

The end of the '60s also marked the end of the steady gains in income growth and income distribution, however. The economic boom and low unemployment had begun to fuel inflation, which President Richard M. Nixon — following the Keynesian model — tried to brake in 1971 by introducing wage and price controls.

Inflation failed to drop, however, even in the face of a recession, resulting in the first of a series of bouts of stagflation — inflation accompanied by sluggish economic growth. This development was to help reverse the postwar narrowing of the income gap.

Energy Crises

But even more damaging to income disparity were the energy crises of the 1970s. Caused by a cutback in crude oil exports by the Organization of Petroleum Exporting Countries (OPEC) following the 1973 Arab-Israeli War, the first oil shortage resulted in a tripling of oil prices. As the price increase rolled through the economy, prices for all other goods rose, causing consumers to curtail purchases.

As businesses cut back on production, unemployment rose as well, and income growth came to a halt. From 1973 to 1975, median family income fell below the 1969 level.

Worsening the slowdown in income levels was an abrupt fall in productivity growth. Although it had slowed in the late 1960s, it was not until the energy crisis struck that pro-

Continued on p. 350

Chronology

1950s *A postwar economic boom lifts the incomes of all Americans.*

1950
Only a fifth of American families — a quarter of all whites and half of all blacks — are in the lowest earnings quintile. Almost half of the poor are elderly and families headed by women.

1959
Twenty-two percent of Americans live in poverty, down from 32 percent at the beginning of the decade, and median family incomes are 43 percent higher than they were in 1950.

1960s *Racial discrimination continues to exclude many African-Americans from enjoying the fruits of a booming economy, but the income gap overall continues to narrow.*

1968
The Kerner Commission's landmark report on the roots of civil disorders describes a growing income gap between black and white Americans.

1969
The burgeoning economy and President Lyndon B. Johnson's "War on Poverty" help raise the median family income by 38 percent over 1959 and cut unemployment, especially among black men. The share of the nation's total income going to the bottom quintile of families grows to 5.6 percent of the total.

1970s *The energy crisis brings America's post-war boom to a halt, widening the gap between rich and poor.*

1973
Following the Arab-Israeli War, the Organization of Petroleum Exporting Countries (OPEC) imposes an oil embargo, resulting in a tripling of oil prices.

1975
Inflation and business closures stall family income growth.

1979
Median family income remains below the level of 1973, while inflation continues to rise.

1980s *The decline in manufacturing eliminates thousands of high-paying, blue-collar jobs.*

1980
A second energy crisis raises oil prices fourfold. Unemployment stands at 7.5 percent.

1981
Republican President Ronald Reagan begins his eight years in the White House, marked by cuts in benefits for the poor and tax breaks for the wealthy.

1984
The Reagan administration's anti-inflation drive pushes unemployment up to more than 9 percent. Median family income is 6 percent below the 1973 level and poverty has risen to 14.4 percent of the population.

1990s *A prolonged recovery begins to slow the gap in incomes.*

1990
The first of two increases in the minimum wage during the administration of Republican President George Bush takes effect, marking the first increase since 1981.

1993
Democratic President Bill Clinton takes office. A tax increase on the wealthy results in a slight decrease in the share of income going to the richest Americans, but this group continues to receive a higher share than in 1973.

1996
The Welfare Reform Act forces welfare recipients to find work. The minimum wage is increased from $4.25 to $4.75 an hour.

Sept. 1, 1997
The minimum wage is increased again, to $5.15 an hour. Walt Disney Co. CEO Michael D. Eisner receives $575 million in compensation for the year, mostly from stock options.

Feb. 10, 1998
The 1998 Economic Report of the President declares that "since 1993, living standards for all Americans are on the rise, especially for those at the bottom of the income distribution."

March 1, 1998
An update of the Kerner Commission report finds that income and wealth inequality is greater than it was three decades ago.

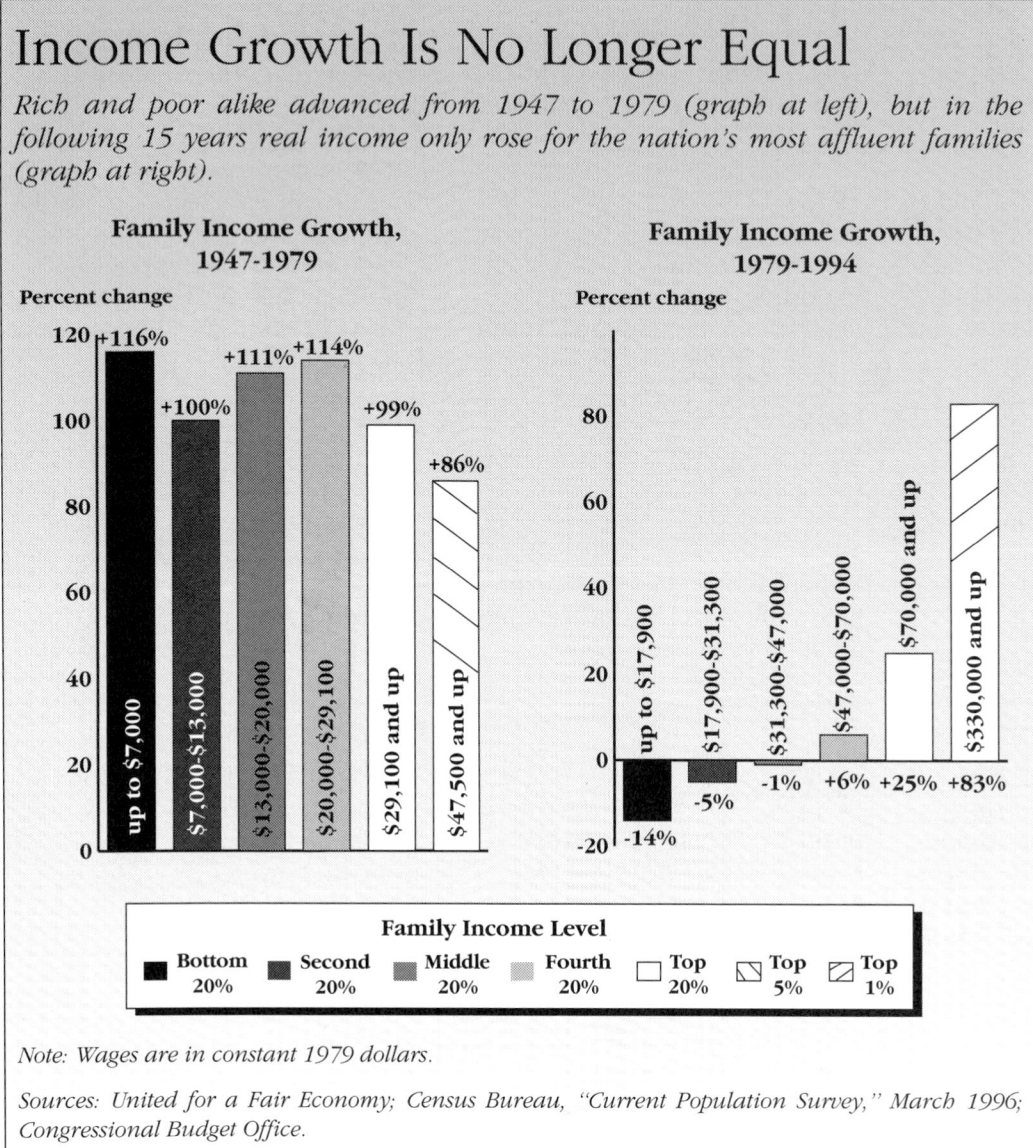

Income Growth Is No Longer Equal

Rich and poor alike advanced from 1947 to 1979 (graph at left), but in the following 15 years real income only rose for the nation's most affluent families (graph at right).

Family Income Growth, 1947-1979

Percent change

+116% (up to $7,000)
+100% ($7,000-$13,000)
+111% ($13,000-$20,000)
+114% ($20,000-$29,100)
+99% ($29,100 and up)
+86% ($47,500 and up)

Family Income Growth, 1979-1994

Percent change

-14% (up to $17,900)
-5% ($17,900-$31,300)
-1% ($31,300-$47,000)
+6% ($47,000-$70,000)
+25% ($70,000 and up)
+83% ($330,000 and up)

Family Income Level

- Bottom 20%
- Second 20%
- Middle 20%
- Fourth 20%
- Top 20%
- Top 5%
- Top 1%

Note: Wages are in constant 1979 dollars.

Sources: United for a Fair Economy; Census Bureau, "Current Population Survey," March 1996; Congressional Budget Office.

ductivity growth fell below 1 percent a year, a level it would not exceed for the next eight years. Meanwhile, growing competition from other industrial countries that had rebuilt their war-torn economies into export-driven powers depressed demand for U.S.-made products, further eroding income growth in the United States.

Stagnant productivity proved so entrenched that efforts by Presidents Gerald R. Ford and Jimmy Carter to reduce unemployment failed to result in significant income gains. By 1979, unemployment had fallen more than two percentage points to 4.2 percent, but median family income remained below the level of 1973, before the first energy crisis began to take its toll. Inflation, meanwhile continued to rise, as wage and price increases outpaced productivity growth.

Incomes suffered further with a second energy crisis, in 1980. This time OPEC raised crude prices fourfold, following the halt of oil production by Iran after the 1979 overthrow of the shah. By late 1980, inflation exceeded 11 percent, while unemployment stood at 7.5 percent, producing an economic debacle that helped scuttle Carter's re-election bid and usher in the free-market policies of President Reagan.

Upon taking office in 1981, the Reagan administration launched a tough monetary policy aimed at bringing down inflation. Though the policy quickly paid off, it also helped raise unemployment to more than 9 percent. By 1984, a decade after the first energy crisis unfolded, median family income had fallen by 6 percent. The progressive narrowing of the income gap of earlier decades reversed course. The trend intensified with the Reagan administration's cuts in welfare programs, such as AFDC, which increased the portion of the population living in poverty.

A clear sign of the growing income inequality was the fall in the portion of total income going to the lowest quintile of families. In 1984, this group received 4.7 percent of total income, down almost a full percentage point from the 1973 level. At the same time, the percentage of people in poverty rose from 11.1 percent to 14.4 percent. A leading culprit in the spread in poverty was, of course, unemployment, which reduced the income of low-skilled workers and also contributed to a rise in the number of families headed by women.

Manufacturing industries, the source of much of the rise in blue-collar income levels throughout the postwar period, were especially hard hit in the early 1980s, eroding the earlier gains made by this group of workers.

The Shrinking Middle

Another phenomenon that appeared in the wake of the energy crises was the shrinking of middle-class incomes. While earlier periods had seen a rise in the middle class, the years 1973 to 1984 brought a reversal in that trend. The percentage of families with incomes over $50,000 rose slightly, from 14.9 percent to 15.6 percent, while the proportion of families earning less than $20,000 rose from 32.1 percent to 36.4 percent. As a result, the percentage of families in the middle of the income spectrum, which had represented just over half the population, declined from 53 percent to 47.9 percent.

Middle-income jobs became scarcer for several reasons. Squeezed by higher energy costs and growing competition from abroad, many large U.S. companies shut down factories in the heavily unionized industrial centers of the Midwest and shifted production to lower-wage, non-union areas of the South, or overseas. As a result of this "outsourcing," the portion of the work force employed by the 500 largest U.S. corporations has fallen from 20 percent to just 10 percent since the 1950s. [17] Many of the lost jobs were highly paid union positions, and many of the workers who were displaced from them had to work for lower wages.

Another way U.S. businesses tried to maintain their competitive advantage during the 1980s and '90s was by paring back operations, keeping only the most profitable enterprises, and hiring fewer workers to do the job. Corporate "downsizing" has been accompanied by a fall in union representation. "A harsh new world of work has emerged: Average workers are accustomed to declining wages, while the top managers who instituted the new 'lean and mean' production standards expect extraordinary growth in their compensation," Brouwer writes. While workers' wages rose just 16 percent from 1989 to 1995, he calculates, corporate profits rose 23.3 percent and CEO salaries jumped 54 percent in 1996 alone. "Once again," he writes, "millions of employees had nothing to show for their efforts: Wages went up 3 percent, lagging just behind inflation." [18]

Demand for more highly skilled workers widened the income gap still further. The decline of manufacturing industries over the past two decades has been accompanied by a shift toward service industries, many of which require highly skilled workers, and toward low-wage retail businesses. College graduates with specific training in such areas as computer technology, engineering and management have continued to experience real income gains in the 1990s. But low-skilled workers, especially those who have not completed high school, have seen their wages drop. [19] ■

CURRENT SITUATION

Clinton's Policies

President Clinton came to office in 1993 promising to reverse many of the policies introduced during the previous 12 years, when Republican Presidents Reagan and George Bush occupied the White House. Clinton launched his presidency with a campaign to make health insurance available to all Americans, restore greater progressivity to the income tax code and raise the minimum wage — all steps aimed at improving living standards for middle- and lower-income Americans and narrowing the income gap.

But Clinton's policy agenda has become less ambitious over the past five years. Buoyed by a Republican majority in both houses of Congress since 1995, opponents eviscerated some of his more ambitious proposals, such as universal health insurance. Others, notably welfare reform and last year's budget agreement that promised to balance the budget, became law because they matched longstanding Republican goals.

The 1993 budget law, which barely won passage by Congress, imposed a tax increase on the wealthy, including upper-income beneficiaries of Social Security, and provided tax credits for the working poor. This law attacked the income gap at the upper end and resulted in a slight decrease in the share of after-tax income going to the top 20 percent of families from 49.9 percent in 1992 to 49.3 percent in 1994. The share of after-tax income received by the wealthiest 1 percent of families fell from 12.1 percent to 11.4 percent over the same period, even as their share of pretax income rose. But even after these changes, the share of after-tax income going to the top 20 percent of the population in 1994 was much higher than in 1974. [20]

The administration's tax policies have done much less to reduce income inequality since the Republican Party took control of Congress in 1995. The budget agreement signed on Aug. 5, 1997, provided far less tax relief to low- and middle-income families than it did to the wealthiest taxpayers. According to Citizens for Tax Justice, the richest 1 percent of Americans will receive a third of the benefits from the law's tax cuts once they go into effect, more than the benefits that will be received by the bottom 80 percent of the population.

"The tax provisions of the budget agreement consequently will accentuate the already-large disparities in the distribution of income," concludes an analysis of the law by the Center on Budget and Policy Priorities. "High-income families — the one group whose average after-tax income has risen sharply since the 1970s — will ultimately be the principal beneficiaries." [21]

Some analysts see risk in the Clinton administration's emphasis on economic growth over investments in social welfare, as reflected in the budget agreement. "The United States has taken a big gamble that full employment will continue," says Freeman, who sees this as the biggest difference between the United States and Europe, where generous social welfare programs help compensate for the region's high unemployment. "The United States' answer to problems at this point is to put all our hope in jobs. We have tremendously reduced the safety net, so that the fraction of out-of-work people actually getting unemployment compensation today is really small. We're counting on full employment," he says, "and we're betting that we can get former welfare recipients jobs. The problem is, they'll lose them in the next recession."

Impact of NAFTA

Another policy area that many analysts say affects income distribution is trade. The North American Free Trade Agreement (NAFTA), signed by President Bush on Dec. 17, 1992, was strongly supported by President Clinton, who won congressional ap-

proval of the agreement in 1993. [22] By removing barriers to trade among the United States, Canada and Mexico, he and other supporters promised, the agreement would spur demand for American goods and stimulate job creation for American workers.

But free trade also has negative effects. By facilitating the sale of cheap

Superstars like Michael Jordan have raised incomes for athletes to the stratosphere.

Reuters/Steve Grayson

imports to U.S. consumers, free trade can hurt U.S. manufacturers and strengthen their hand in holding down wages for American workers. "Trade policy has a big impact on jobs in the United States as well as wages," Bernstein says. "But the benefits of free trade — and there are some — have been the exclusive focus in the policy debate. Only recently has Clinton started to acknowledge that there are losers, too. Free-trade policy

has resulted in non-college-educated workers who have lost jobs in industries that compete with imports. We should pursue a trade policy that's mindful of those who are hurt."

Minimum Wage Increases

Perhaps the most effective policy change supported by the Clinton administration has been a series of increases in the minimum wage. Following two increases in 1990 and 1991 during the Bush administration — the first since 1981 — the federal minimum wage was increased from $4.25 to $4.75 an hour on Oct. 1, 1996, and again, to $5.15, on Sept. 1, 1997. "Even with the increases, the minimum wage hasn't kept pace," says Harris of the Eisenhower Foundation. "The increases have helped a little, but we're still way behind in terms of purchasing power compared with earlier times because the minimum wage hasn't kept up with inflation."

Clinton supports a further increase in the minimum wage introduced March 19 by Sen. Edward M. Kennedy, D-Mass., and Rep. David E. Bonior, D-Mich. The Fair Minimum Wage Act would raise the minimum wage to $5.65 an hour in 1999, and then to $6.15 in 2000. Conservatives and business representatives oppose the legislation as a threat to the current economic recovery.

"Although wage differences have widened over the past 20 years, such bad economic policy as a mandated minimum wage for workers serves only to exacerbate this problem," writes D. Mark Wilson, labor economist at the Heritage Foundation, a conservative think tank. "President Clinton's proposal to raise the minimum wage, moreover, works against the efforts of Congress to address the problem of moving unskilled Americans from

Continued on p. 354

At Issue:

Do American workers lack the necessary skills to qualify for better-paying jobs?

RICHARD W. JUDY AND CAROL D'AMICO
Senior research fellow and senior fellow, Hudson Institute

FROM WORKFORCE 2020: WORK AND WORKERS IN THE 21ST CENTURY, *A 1997 UPDATE OF* WORKFORCE 2000 *(1987), THE HUDSON INSTITUTE.*

One of *Workforce 2000's* important contributions was to identify an emerging shortage of skilled workers in the American economy. The book foresaw a gap between the qualifications of workers and the changing job mix of the American economy.

Can a "skills gap" exist? In one sense, no: A free labor market tends to equilibrate the supply and demand of various kinds of labor. But in a second, perhaps more important sense, there can be a skills gap. *Workforce 2000* argued presciently that America's productivity (and hence its standard of living) would rise significantly only if its work force came to be much better educated and much more highly skilled. *Workforce 2000* also stated that major public and private efforts would be needed to bring about those improvements. In other words, *Workforce 2000* raised a normative concern about a mismatch between the skills that might be available and those that would be most desirable; it did not predict imbalance in the labor market.

Is the American economy changing so rapidly that the skills of today's work force will be obsolete early in the 21st century? Must new entrants into the work force require vocational skills that are much more sophisticated than those of today's jobholders? To answer these questions, we compare the Bureau of Labor Statistics projections for future employment (by occupational category) with information contained in the Department of Labor's *Dictionary of Occupational Titles*, which describes skills needed to work in various occupations. . . .

Whether we look at language, mathematics or reasoning, [the data] tell essentially the same story: 99 percent of the jobs in decline require skills at Level 3 or lower [with Level 6 the highest skill level]. By contrast, much job growth will be in occupations requiring skills rated at Level 4 or higher; for example, over 30 percent of expanding jobs will require reasoning skills at Level 4 or above. In short, shrinking occupations overwhelmingly require modest skills, but high skills are called for by a significant component of the expanding occupations. The words of *Workforce 2000* still ring true: "The fastest-growing jobs require much higher math, language and reasoning capabilities . . . while slowly growing jobs require less." If anything, the case is stronger today than when those words were written in 1987.

JARED BERNSTEIN
Economist, Economic Policy Institute

FROM TESTIMONY BEFORE THE HOUSE EDUCATION AND THE WORKFORCE SUBCOMMITTEE ON OVERSIGHT AND INVESTIGATIONS, OCT. 29, 1997.

Like its predecessor, *Workforce 2020* paints an unrealistically rosy scenario of the future of work.

The analysis overestimates the acceleration in technology and its impact on the economy, the increase in the demand for skilled workers and the quality of the current labor market conditions. This last point is central because [the authors'] overly optimistic view of the present generates an unrealistic view of the future. . . .

My view is that we have less a skill deficit in our present and future economy than a wage deficit, caused by the unleashing of market forces and the erosion of worker protections. Strengthening labor market institutions that have been allowed to erode is the way forward. . . .

Workforce 2020 argues that there has been (and will continue to be) a growing mismatch between workers' skills and employers' skill demands. This story leaves the impression that the U.S. work force has been growing less well-educated over time. Of course, the opposite is the case. . . . Yet this fact by itself does not prove *Workforce 2020* to be incorrect. The book argues that while the work force's skills are growing, they are not growing fast enough.

This is a testable hypothesis. If [the authors] are correct, then the wages of high-skilled workers should be rising, as they are bid up by employers who seek this scarce resource. . . . Instead of having their wages bid up, the real hourly wages of both male and female young college graduates fell by about 10 percent [from 1989 to 1996]. . . . [T]he wage offers to new college graduates with engineering and computer degrees have also been falling. . . .

Workforce 2020 correctly points out that with increased deregulation and expanded trade, an increasing share of the work force will be fighting an uphill battle in the face of unleashed market forces. Historically, labor market institutions such as labor unions, minimum wages, anti-discrimination enforcement and workplace-safety protocols have protected those workers whose bargaining power has been severely diminished.

Strengthening these vital labor market institutions is the best way to address the wage deficit, so that future growth can be shared by all workers.

Continued from p. 352

welfare to work. It is an uncompassionate mandate that gives some low-wage workers an increase in their earnings while depriving others of the opportunity to earn anything at all." [23]

The Strong Economy

For the first two years of the Clinton administration, the income gap continued to widen, one of the few blemishes on an otherwise rosy economic record. Finally, last year came the statistics the policy-makers were waiting for.

"Since 1993, living standards for all Americans are on the rise, especially for those at the bottom of the income distribution," proclaimed the Council of Economic Advisers' *1998 Economic Report of the President.* "The poverty rate fell to 13.7 percent in 1996, from 15.1 percent in 1993; the poverty rate for black Americans is at a historical low, and in 1997 unemployment among blacks fell to its lowest rate since 1973. Since 1993, household income has grown in each quintile of the income distribution, with the largest percentage increase going to the poorest members of our society. Maintaining a full-employment economy is essential if this progress is to continue." [24]

But to some analysts, finding good news in the Census statistics is merely grasping for straws. Indeed, considered over the longer term, last year's improvements in income inequality pale in comparison to the devastating trends of the past several decades. "Since the Kerner Commission's report 30 years ago, actual poverty, in numbers and as a percentage of the population, is up," Harris says. "Thirty years ago, 12.8 percent of the population, or 25.4 million people, were in poverty. Today it's 13.7 percent, or 36.5 million people."

Poverty also is worsening among the most vulnerable members of society, children. "In 1994, half the kids under 6 years of age were living at or below the lower half of the poverty line, and that is twice what it was 20 years earlier, in 1974," Harris says. "In addition to more poverty today, poor people are poorer now than they were before."

If income inequality is the main focus of concern about the economy, the latest statistics are actually more alarming than in the earlier years. For while the widening of the income gap halted in 1993 at the lower end of the income spectrum, it proceeded even faster at the high end. According to one survey, average compensation of the top executives at the biggest U.S. companies was $8.7 million last year, an increase of 37.8 percent over 1996. Salaries and bonuses accounted for $2.1 million of the total, making for a hefty 12.3 percent pay increase — compared with the 3.5 percent average increase for workers. But the bulk of executive compensation came from stock options. [25]

In light of the huge pay increases granted executives, some economists point with irony to recent attempts by U.S. corporations to gain special exemptions from immigration rules so that they can hire foreign skilled workers for jobs they claim Americans are unqualified to perform. [26] "There's no scarcity of skilled American workers," says Freeman of Harvard. "They just don't want to give skilled workers wage increases. What if we turned that around and said that because top executives are pulling in these huge pay increases we should declare an executive shortage? I don't hear anyone saying we should be importing business leaders. It's just incredible chutzpah on the part of executives."

Other economists are less concerned about the rise in incomes at the top, even the use of stock options as a principal source of compensation. "This is one of the reasons the market has done so well," says economist Sinai, who sees stock options and other stock plans as useful incentives for workers as well as executives. "They keep down costs and foster an ownership mentality among workers. More and more publicly listed companies are selling company stock at discount to employees because they're a very big incentive to be more productive."

Despite the recent evidence of improvement on the income front, labor economist Krueger is concerned about the long-term stagnation of earnings among middle-income workers. "The strong economic growth is starting to reach the bottom, which is a very good development, though it doesn't reverse the fall of the 1980s," he says. "Meanwhile, the middle has experienced falling real wages, which is one reason average wage growth has been so subdued in the 1990s. In the last year or so, that has come to a halt, which is a good sign. But one year does not an era make." ∎

OUTLOOK

Fear of a Downturn

With compensation at the top of the income spectrum based so heavily on the stock market and wage growth dependent on continued low unemployment, the prospects for further narrowing of the income gap are clearly tied to the business cycle. As long as the current economic boom continues apace, creating jobs and spurring confidence in the stock market, the income gap could well continue to narrow.

But recovery has always been followed by recession, and many experts predict that the next downturn will erase last year's progress toward income equality. "The only things helping narrow the income gap a little is today's tight labor markets, recent increases in the minimum wage and low inflation," says Bernstein of the Economic Policy Institute.

In his view, underlying trends in the workplace and the economy at large make it unlikely that all income groups will benefit equally as they did before the 1980s. "The structural problems are still very much in place, and if and when labor markets loosen up a bit, I'm afraid we'll be back where we were a couple of years ago."

With inflation and unemployment at bay, there have been few public complaints about the income gap. But because welfare programs have been eliminated or cut back in recent years, some analysts predict the next downturn will unleash a torrent of criticism of the political leadership's handling of the economy. "Full employment makes everybody feel good," Freeman says. "The trouble will surface when and if we run into a recession, and then it will hit with a vengeance because the safety net will have vanished. Then we'll see a big movement to deal with the problem of income inequality."

But optimists believe that changes in the global economy may help break the traditional cycle of boom and bust in the U.S. economy, or at least mitigate its impact on incomes. "I believe that the general prosperity we're enjoying today will go on, fed by technological breakthroughs and a global economy that buys more and more from the United States," Sinai predicts. "The conditions for ordinary Americans are the best in decades and will stay that way. And while I don't really think the wealth gap will change, the income gap definitely has turned, so the situation is no longer so negative for ordinary working Americans and the working poor." ∎

Notes

[1] See Tim Smart, "An Eye-Popping Year for Executive Pay," *The Washington Post*, March 22, 1998. For background, see "Executive Pay," *The CQ Researcher*, July 11, 1997, pp. 601-624, and "Fairness in Salaries," *The CQ Researcher*, May 29, 1992, pp. 457-480.

[2] The unemployment rate crept back up to 4.7 percent in March. For background, see "Jobs in the '90s," *The CQ Researcher*, Feb. 28, 1992, pp. 169-192.

[3] Kathryn Larin and Elizabeth C. McNichol,

FOR MORE INFORMATION

If you would like to have this CQ Researcher updated, or need more information about this topic, please call CQ Custom Research. Special rates for CQ subscribers. (202) 887-8600 or (800) 432-2250, ext. 600, or E-mail Custom.Research@cq.com

American Enterprise Institute for Public Policy Research, 1150 17th St. N.W., Washington, D.C. 20036; (202) 862-5846; www.aei.org. The institute's Economic Policy Studies division examines trends in employment, earnings and income in the United States. Published materials tend to minimize the impact of income inequality in the face of rising overall living standards.

Census Bureau, Housing and Household Economic Statistics, Washington, D.C. 20233; (301) 763-08550; www.census.gov. This division collects and analyzes income data and other economic, social and demographic statistics and publishes a periodic survey of incomes.

Center on Budget and Policy Priorities, 820 1st St. N.E., Suite 510, Washington, D.C. 20002; (202) 408-1080; www.cbpp.org. This research group analyzes federal, state and local government policies affecting low- and moderate-income Americans.

Economic Policy Institute, 1660 L St. N.W., Suite 1200, Washington, D.C. 20036; (202) 775-8810; www.epinet.org. This research organization analyzes income distribution and other economic data. Its published materials emphasize the negative impact of the income gap on American workers' living standards.

Pulling Apart: A State-by-State Analysis of Income Trends, Center on Budget and Policy Priorities, Dec. 16, 1997.

[4] The Milton S. Eisenhower Foundation and The Corporation for What Works, *The Millennium Breach: Richer, Poorer and Racially Apart*, March 1, 1998. For background, see "The Black Middle Class," *The CQ Researcher*, Jan. 23, 1998, pp. 49-72.

[5] *The 1998 Economic Report of the President*, Council of Economic Advisers, Feb. 10, 1998.

[6] See Jacob M. Schlesinger, "Wages for Low-Paid Workers Rose in 1997," *The Wall Street Journal*, March 23, 1998.

[7] Christopher C. DeMuth, "The New Wealth of Nations," *Commentary*, October 1997, pp. 23-24.

[8] *Ibid.*, p. 25.

[9] Irving Kristol, "Income Inequality without Class Conflict," *The Wall Street Journal*, Dec. 18, 1997.

[10] See Rene Sanchez, "Black, Hispanic Admissions Plunge at 2 Calif. Campuses," *The Washington Post*, April 1, 1998. For background, see "Rethinking Affirmative Action," *The CQ Researcher*, April 28, 1995, pp. 369-392.

[11] Eisenhower Foundation, *op. cit.*, p. 10.

[12] For background, see "The Working Poor," Nov. 3, 1995, pp. 969-992, and "Welfare Reform," *The CQ Researcher*, April 10, 1992, pp. 327-350.

[13] From a March 19, 1998, NFIB press release.

[14] For background, see "IRS Reform," *The CQ Researcher*, Jan. 16, 1998, pp. 25-48, and "Tax

Reform," *The CQ Researcher*, March 22, 1996, pp. 241-264.

[15] Steve Brouwer, *Sharing the Pie* (1998), p. 157.

[16] Unless otherwise noted, information in this section is based on Frank Levy, *Dollars and Dreams* (1987), pp. 45-61.

[17] Brouwer, *op. cit.*, p. 48.

[18] *Ibid.*

[19] See Daniel H. Weinberg, "A Brief Look at Postwar U.S. Income Inequality," U.S. Census Bureau, June 20, 1996, available on the Census Web page at www.census.gov.

[20] See Isaac Shapiro and Robert Greenstein, "Trends in the Distribution of After-Tax Income: An Analysis of Congressional Budget Office Data," Center on Budget and Policy Priorities, Aug. 14, 1997.

[21] *Ibid.*, p. 8.

[22] For background, see "Rethinking NAFTA," *The CQ Researcher*, June 7, 1996, pp. 481-504.

[23] D. Mark Wilson, "Increasing the Mandated Minimum Wage: Who Pays the Price?" *Backgrounder*, The Heritage Foundation, March 5, 1998.

[24] Council of Economic Advisers, *op. cit.*, available on the White House Web page at www.whitehouse.gov.

[25] See Adam Bryant, "Flying High on the Option Express," *The New York Times*, April 5, 1998.

[26] See "High-Tech Labor Shortages," *The CQ Researcher*, April 24, 1998.

Bibliography

Selected Sources Used

Books

Brouwer, Steve, *Sharing the Pie: A Citizen's Guide to Wealth and Power in America*, **Henry Holt, 1998.**

This soon-to-be-published volume blames a rightward shift in American politics since 1980 for what the author describes as a steady decline in the living standards of most Americans.

Judy, Richard W., and Carol D'Amico, *Workforce 2020: Work and Workers in the 21st Century*, **Hudson Institute, 1997.**

The sequel to an earlier Hudson study on workplace trends warns that technological advances will continue to create demand for skilled workers and recommends bigger investments in primary and secondary education as well as job training.

Levy, Frank, *Dollars and Dreams: The Changing American Income Distribution*, **Russell Sage Foundation, 1987.**

This analysis of Census data shows how social and economic changes, as well as public policies, have affected the distribution of income and wealth in the United States during the postwar period.

Wolff, Edward N., *Top Heavy: The Increasing Inequality of Wealth in America and What Can Be Done about It*, **Twentieth Century Fund, 1995.**

The author, an economics professor at New York University, describes the unprecedented shift in income from lower- and middle-income Americans to the wealthy over the past decade and a half.

Articles

Burtless, Gary, "Worsening American Income Inequality: Is World Trade to Blame?" *Brookings Review*, **spring 1996, pp. 26-31.**

While liberal trade with developing countries undoubtedly hurts the job prospects of low-skilled American workers, writes the Brookings economist, the widening income gap is more closely related to other changes, such as deregulation, increased immigration, a low minimum wage and the weakening of unions.

DeMuth, Christopher C., "The New Wealth of Nations," *Commentary*, **October 1997, pp. 23-28.**

Social and economic advances have produced the highest standards of living in history throughout the developed world, writes the president of the American Enterprise Institute. These advances benefit everyone, all but erasing the significance of remaining disparities in income and wealth.

"The 400: The Average Net Worth of the Forbes Four Hundred is $1.6 Billion," *Forbes*, **Oct. 13, 1997, pp. 181-250.**

As evidence that the rich are getting richer, it took a net worth of $475 million to get on the list of the 400 richest Americans last year, up from $415 million in 1996.

Fox, Justin, "Manage Your Stock Options," *Fortune*, **Dec. 29, 1997, pp. 167-173.**

Stock options have thus far been used mainly to boost compensation to top executives, but more and more companies are beginning to offer stock option plans to other workers as well.

Mishel, Lawrence, Jared Bernstein and John Schmitt, "The State of American Workers," *Challenge*, **Nov. 21, 1996, p. 33.**

Despite the fall in unemployment and the steady growth of full-time jobs in the 1990s, most workers' real wages have fallen during the current recovery. As a result, income inequality between the richest Americans and the rest of the population continues to grow.

Rottenberg, Dan, "100 Most Generous Americans," *The American Benefactor*, **fall 1997, pp. 42-68.**

Each of the 100 biggest contributors to charity has given away $20 million or more over their lifetimes, about half of it during the past 10 years. But the list does not mirror the *Forbes* 400 list of the richest Americans, as some of the wealthiest people prefer to hang on their riches.

Reports and Studies

Larin, Kathryn, and Elizabeth C. McNichol, *Pulling Apart: A State-by-State Analysis of Income Trends*, **Center on Budget and Policy Priorities, Dec. 16, 1997.**

According to this analysis of Census data, since the late 1970s the average, inflation-adjusted incomes of the poorest families with children fell more than 20 percent. At the same time, the average incomes of rich families grew by almost 30 percent. As a result, the income gap between the richest and poorest American families has widened significantly.

The Milton S. Eisenhower Foundation and The Corporation for What Works, *The Millennium Breach: Richer, Poorer and Racially Apart: A Thirty-Year Update of the National Advisory Commission on Civil Disorders*, **March 1, 1998.**

This update of the 1968 Kerner Commission report on civil disorders finds that income and wealth inequality is even greater than it was three decades ago, especially for African-American residents of the nation's inner cities.

The Next Step

Additional information from UMI's Newspaper & Periodical Abstracts™ database

Executive Compensation

Behr, Peter, "It Pays to Be a Top Executive; Compensation Not Always Tied to Performance," *The Washington Post*, June 16, 1997, p. W12.

Throughout corporate America, executive compensation has been accelerating in the past few years despite efforts by Congress and regulators to curb mega-awards of stock and cash to the nation's highest-paid chief executives. Nationwide, the average salary and bonus for CEOs rose 39 percent last year to $2.3 million, well above the 11 percent gain in corporate profits.

Bosco, Pearl, "Executive Compensation: Offering the Brass Ring, and Paying For It," *American Banker*, May 19, 1997, p. 8A.

Senior-level pay in corporate America rose some 30 percent in 1996. Industry experts conservatively estimate that bank CEO pay has quintupled in the last 10 years. "If you were the CEO of a top-50 bank 10 years ago, you couldn't get rich," says Alan Johnson, managing director of Johnson Associates Inc. "After taxes, you could have a huge home, a few million dollars. But by most standards you could not become rich. If you were one of the top five executives in one of the 50 banks today, by any standard you could become rich. America at the senior level now is obsessed with money."

Carlton, Jim, "Apple to Set Aside 17 Million Shares for Top-Executive Compensation Plan," *The Wall Street Journal*, March 17, 1996, p. B6.

Apple Computer plans to set aside 13 percent of its shares outstanding for top executives and key employees in a move to tie pay to performance. The allotment — one of the largest that executive-compensation experts can remember — is aimed at attracting and keeping managerial talent as the computer-maker struggles to recover from a downward spiral. Approved by the board and subject to a shareholders' vote at the company's annual meeting April 22, the plan reverses Apple's longstanding policy of rewarding its executives primarily with salaries and bonuses.

Income Trends

Bass, Alison, "Income Inequality, Mortality Linked," *The Boston Globe*, April 19, 1996, p. 14.

Two surveys show that the widening income gap between rich and poor in the United States is hurting more than the poorest of the poor. The surveys found that wide disparities are accompanied by health repercussions affecting middle-income families as well.

Bishop, John A., John P. Formby and W. James Smith, "Demographic Change and Income Inequality in the United States," *Southern Economic Journal*, July 1997, pp. 34-44.

The authors investigate the effects of demographic factors on income inequality in the United States between 1976 and 1989.

Chakravorty, Sanjoy, "A Measurement of Spatial Disparity: The Case of Income Inequality," *Urban Studies*, November 1996.

Chakravorty presents an approach to understanding urban inequality in terms of the spatial distribution of population and income. A group of spatial disparity measures is proposed in the article.

Chu, C. Y. Cyrus, Jiang, Lily, "Demographic Transition, Family Structure and Income Inequality," *Review of Economics & Statistics*, November 1997, pp. 665-669.

The authors study the impact of the population's changing age structure on family income inequality.

Deininger, Klaus, and Lyn Squire, "Economic Growth and Income Inequality: Re-examining the Links," *Finance & Development*, March 1997, pp. 38-41.

Many economists have long believed that income disparities increase in the early stages of economic development, making the poor relatively worse off. The authors examine recent research suggesting that an unequal distribution of income can hamper growth.

Freeman, Scott, "Equilibrium Income Inequality Among Identical Agents," *Journal of Political Economy*, October 1996.

A theory of income differences is offered in which income inequality exists and persists despite identical tastes and talents. The article shows three equilibrium phenomena.

Lerman, Robert I., "The Impact of the Changing U.S. Family Structure on Child Poverty and Income Inequality," *Economica*, 1996 Supplement, p. S119-S139.

Lerman analyzes links among rising income inequality, child poverty and one-parent families in the United States from 1971 to 1989.

Murray, Alan, "The Outlook: Income Inequality Grows Amid Recovery," *The Wall Street Journal*, July 1, 1996, p. A1.

The author discusses the politics of income inequality. He points to economic data showing that the rich are getting richer and examines the difficulty either political party will have taking advantage of the issue.

Overberg, Paul, "Taking a World View for Keys to Income Inequality," *USA Today*, Sept. 23, 1996, p. B3.

Keys to the puzzle of growing income inequality may lie outside of the United States, in a diverse group of industrial nations like Britain and Sweden undergoing the same trend. Economists figure the gap between rich and poor in the United States is the widest of any industrial nation except possibly Russia.

Partridge, Mark D., Dan S. Rickman and William Levernier, "Trends in U.S. Income Inequality: Evidence from a Panel of States," *Quarterly Review of Economics & Finance*, spring 1996, pp. 17-37.

Data from the lower 48 states are used to explore trends in U.S. income inequality. Increasing inequality is blamed on increasing international migration, a denser urban population and more female-headed households.

Smeeding, Timothy, "America's Income Inequality: Where Do We Stand," *Challenge*, September 1996, pp. 45-53.

The article presents evidence indicating that America's income distribution is now the most unequal among advanced countries.

Stein, Herbert, "The Income Inequality Debate," *The Wall Street Journal*, May 1, 1996, p. A14.

The author discusses some problems inherent in the debate over income inequality.

Thompson, J.J. "A Tool for Measuring Income Inequality," *Nieman Reports*, Spring 1997, pp. 42-43.

Income inequality is a hot topic for reporters, but since the gap between the haves and have-nots grows slowly, perception becomes the problem. The Gini coefficient of inequality makes figuring the gap easier.

Visgaitis, Gary, Jerding, Grant, "Mapping Income Inequality," *USA Today*, Sept. 20, 1996, p. B3.

Income distribution in the United States for 1980 and 1990 is compared in two sets of data.

Wilkinson, Richard G., "Comment: Income, Inequality, and Social Cohesion," *American Journal of Public Health*, September 1997.

Wilkinson argues that no single study on how income and mortality are related can remove all grounds for doubt. Instead, scientific progress depends on putting together a coherent picture from wider research.

African-Americans

Aubry, Larry, "Income Inequality Still Persists for Blacks," *Los Angeles Sentinel*, Jan. 30, 1997, p. A7.

The author says that the average household income of African-Americans continues to be substantially lower than that of whites. He also notes that this trend is evident at the upper and lower ends of the income spectrum.

Caputo, Richard K., "Income Inequality and Family Poverty," *Families in Society: The Journal of Contemporary Human Services*, December 1995, pp. 604-615.

Research results comparing black and white family income inequality and poverty for the periods 1969-80 and 1981-92 call into question the legitimacy of economic and social policies in the past two decades.

LaFree, Gary, and Kriss A. Drass, "The Effect of Changes in Intraracial Income Inequality and Educational Attainment on Changes in Arrest Rates for African Americans and Whites, 1957 to 1990," *American Sociological Review*, August 1996, pp. 614-634.

The authors argue that crime increases may be more understandable in a historical context. Their analysis indicates that the relationship between education and crime for African-Americans and whites is contingent on levels of intraracial income inequality.

Nielsen, Francois, and Arthur S. Alderson, "The Kuznets Curve and the Great U-Turn: Income Inequality in U.S. Counties, 1970 to 1990," *American Sociological Review*, February 1997, pp. 12-33.

In addition to studying global trends in social inequality from 1970 to 1990, the authors study the effect of changes in intraracial income inequality and educational attainment on changes in arrest rates for African-Americans and whites from 1957 to 1990.

Minimum Wage

Clark, Charles M.A., Kavanagh, Catherine, "Basic Income, Inequality and Unemployment: Rethinking the Linkage Between Work and Welfare," *Journal of Economic Issues*, June 1996, pp. 399-406.

The authors discuss a basic income policy, which is a response to the economic maladies the developed world currently faces. The goal of the basic income policy would be to reduce poverty and unemployment.

Crenshaw, Albert B., "Inside Minimum Wage Bill, Big Changes for 401(k)s," *The Washington Post*, July 28, 1996, p. H1.

The author comments that the bill pending before Congress to increase the federal minimum wage also contains provisions that could have a profound impact on the retirement savings of middle- and upper-income Americans.

Durbin, Richard, "Americans Deserve More — Let's Hike the Minimum Wage," *Chicago Defender*, April 20, 1996, p. 12.

Rep. Richard J. Durbin, D-Ill., calls for an increase in the minimum wage, saying that millions of working families are facing stagnant wages and declining incomes and that responsible Americans who go to work every day deserve more.

Georges, Christopher, "GOP Leaders in House Won't Support Measure to Boost the Minimum Wage," *The Wall Street Journal*, April 25, 1996, p. A2.

House Republican leaders said they would not support a vote on raising the minimum wage and instead would propose another package aimed at increasing low-income workers' take-home pay.

Glassman, James K., "A Better Way to Raise the Minimum Wage," *The Washington Post*, April 30, 1996, p. A13.

The author believes that rather than raising the minimum wage by government decree, a tax change could be a solution. He comments that instead of raising the price of labor, it could be lowered if the payroll tax was eliminated for anyone who makes less than $6 an hour.

Greenhouse, Steven, "Minimum Wage, Maximum Debate," *The New York Times*, March 31, 1996, p. 3.

In an election year, President Clinton and the Democratic Party see raising the minimum wage as a way to score political points and to address the problem of the growing income gap between Americans on the bottom rungs and those on the top.

Healy, Melissa, "GOP Picks a Budget Fight With Welfare Legislation," *Los Angeles Times*, June 5, 1997, p. A14.

House Republicans embarked on a collision course Wednesday with the White House over welfare policy, deciding that terms under which legal immigrants could receive public assistance should be changed and asserting that "workfare" participants are not subject to federal wage and workplace protections.

Marshall, Jonathan, "Higher Minimum Wage May Not Help the Poor," *San Francisco Chronicle*, Oct. 21, 1996, p. D1.

The author discusses the implications of Proposition 210, which would raise the wages of more than 2 million low-wage Californians. Marshall suggests that the initiative may, in fact, hurt workers in a variety of ways, including fewer jobs and higher food prices.

"Minimum Wage vs. Supply and Demand," *The Wall Street Journal*, April 24, 1996, p. A14.

Several economists respond to the proposed increase in the minimum wage and predict the impact on employment opportunities for low-wage earners.

Shogren, Elizabeth, "Clinton Weighing Minimum Wage Hike; But White House Officials Say No Firm Conclusion was Reached on Advantages, Drawbacks of Revisiting this Highly Contentious Issue," *Los Angeles Times*, Jan. 13, 1998, p. A12.

President Clinton is considering proposing another increase in the minimum wage to give the working poor a bigger stake in the vibrant economy, White House officials said Monday. But the administration wants to analyze the potential impact of a wage hike on the economy before deciding whether to proceed.

"The Minimum Wage Trade-Offs," *Chicago Tribune*, April 24, 1996, p. 14.

An editorial says that although an increase in the minimum wage is popular with the American public, it's not necessarily economically sensible. The editorial discusses the advantanges of improving the Earned Income Tax Credit.

Young, J.T., "Workers Need Tax Cuts, Not a Minimum Wage Hike," *The Wall Street Journal*, Feb. 23, 1998, p. A22.

The author argues that contrary to the push by President Clinton and Sen. Edward M. Kennedy, D-Mass., to increase the minimum wage again, workers need to have their personal income taxes cut.

Back Issues

Great Research on Current Issues Starts Right Here.
Recent topics covered by The CQ Researcher are listed below.
Now available on the Web
For information, call (800) 432-2250 ext. 279 or (202) 887-6279.

If you would like to have any of these CQ Researchers updated, or need more information about these topics, please call CQ Custom Research. Special rates for CQ subscribers. (202) 887-8600 or (800) 432-2250, ext. 600, or E-mail Custom.Research@cq.com

DECEMBER 1996
Welfare, Work and the States
The New Volunteerism
Implementing the Disabilities Act
America's Pampered Pets

JANUARY 1997
Combating Scientific Misconduct
Restructuring the Electric Industry
The New Immigrants
Chemical and Biological Weapons

FEBRUARY 1997
Assisting Refugees
Alternative Medicine's Next Phase
Independent Counsels
Feminism's Future

MARCH 1997
New Air Quality Standards
Alcohol Advertising
Civic Renewal
Educating Gifted Students

APRIL 1997
Declining Crime Rates
The FBI Under Fire
Gender Equity in Sports
Space Program's Future

MAY 1997
The Stock Market
The Cloning Controversy
Expanding NATO
The Future of Libraries

JUNE 1997
FDA Reform
China After Deng
Line-Item Veto
Breast Cancer

JULY 1997
Transportation Policy
Executive Pay
School Choice Debate
Aggressive Driving

AUGUST 1997
Age Discrimination
Banning Land Mines
Children's Television
Evolution vs. Creationism

SEPTEMBER 1997
Caring for the Dying
Mental Health Policy
Mexico's Future
Youth Fitness

OCTOBER 1997
Urban Sprawl in the West
Diversity in the Workplace
Teacher Education
Contingent Work Force

NOVEMBER 1997
Renewable Energy
Artificial Intelligence
Religious Persecution
Roe v. Wade at 25

DECEMBER 1997
Whistleblowers
Castro's Next Move
Gun Control Standoff
Regulating Nonprofits

JANUARY 1998
Foster Care Reform
IRS Reform
The Black Middle Class
U.S.-British Relations

FEBRUARY 1998
Patients' Rights
Deflation Fears
Caring for the Elderly
The New Corporate Philanthropy

MARCH 1998
Israel at 50
The Federal Judiciary
Drinking on Campus
The Economics of Recycling

APRIL 1998
Biology and Behavior
Liberal Arts Education

Future Topics

► *High-Tech Labor Shortages*

► *Census Controversy*

► *Child-Care Options*

CQ Researcher

PUBLISHED BY CONGRESSIONAL QUARTERLY INC.

High-Tech Labor Shortage

Should more foreign workers be admitted?

A merican employers say that a severe shortage of skilled high-tech workers is delaying projects and reducing expansion plans. To avoid economic disaster, they want Congress to admit more foreign workers. But critics, including the Clinton administration, say employers are simply seeking more foreign workers because they are cheaper. The critics say the answer to a shortage of skilled workers is training or retraining American workers and hiring more women, minorities and unemployed or underemployed technical workers. As Congress debates the issue, many employers say that the globalization of high-tech jobs is inevitable, and that U.S. borders eventually should be opened to any skilled workers.

CQ April 24, 1998 • Volume 8, No. 16 • Pages 361-384

Formerly Editorial Research Reports ®

CQ Researcher

April 24, 1998
Volume 8, No.16

EDITOR
Sandra Stencel

MANAGING EDITOR
Thomas J. Colin

ASSOCIATE EDITOR
Sarah M. Magner

STAFF WRITERS
Adriel Bettelheim
Mary H. Cooper
Kenneth Jost
David Masci

PRODUCTION EDITOR
Melissa Hall

EDITORIAL ASSISTANT
Laura S. Cavender

PUBLISHED BY
Congressional Quarterly Inc.

CHAIRMAN
Andrew Barnes

VICE CHAIRMAN
Andrew P. Corty

PRESIDENT AND PUBLISHER
Robert W. Merry

EXECUTIVE EDITOR
David Rapp

The CQ Researcher (ISSN 1056-2036). Formerly Editorial Research Reports. Published weekly, except Jan. 2, May 29, July 3, Oct. 30, by Congressional Quarterly Inc., 1414 22nd St., N.W., Washington, D.C. 20037. Annual subscription rate for libraries, businesses and government is $340. Additional rates furnished upon request. Periodicals postage paid at Washington, D.C., and additional mailing offices. POSTMASTER: Send address changes to The CQ Researcher, 1414 22nd St., N.W., Washington, D.C. 20037.

COVER: NORTHERN VIRGINIA COMMUNITY COLLEGE'S COMPUTER SCIENCE DEPARTMENT IS POPULAR WITH FOREIGN STUDENTS. (COURTESY OF NORTHERN VIRGINIA COMMUNITY COLLEGE)

High-Tech Labor Shortage

BY KATHY KOCH

THE ISSUES

Recruiters flew Andrew F. Stark to the West Coast three times last month. Since September he has been wined and dined by firms around the country. One suitor even gave him a bird's eye tour of their city — via helicopter.

After considering a dozen offers, some with hefty signing and performance bonuses, Stark made his choice — a Wall Street financial services firm. He won't say how much he's getting, but salaries in his league typically top out at $75,000 per year. Not bad for a 23-year-old engineering and computer science graduate student fresh out of MIT.

It's a sellers' market for talented techies, as the information revolution seems to gobble up all the brain power in sight. America's transformation from an industrial to a knowledge-based economy has created robust demand for computer workers, especially in California's Silicon Valley.

"A year and a half ago, we had a Ph.D. who was making $95,000," says John Rohde, president of FirsTel Co., a Silicon Valley firm that develops operating systems for telephone companies. "He went to work for somebody else for $115,000 and we just got him back by offering him an additional $10,000, plus stock options."

FirsTel expects to double its labor force every year for the next five years, but not with Americans. "It'll be done in India and in Northern Ireland," Rohde says. "We can't get the computer engineers we need quickly enough in this country." Indeed, his small company can hardly compete with titans like Microsoft, which has more full-time recruiters (80) than he has employees.

To woo prospective systems analysts, computer scientists, Internet specialists and other high-tech wizards, some companies are offering $20,000 signing bonuses and $5,000-$15,000 finders' fees to employees for referrals. Some recruiters are even signing up teenage techies still in high school. *(See story, p. 370.)*

And to retain existing employees, companies are offering enticements ranging from stock options and flextime to subsidized laundry service and day care. One company arranges white-water rafting trips for workers.

The computer industry's voracious labor needs have been intensified by the emergence of hundreds of new software companies in recent years, plus the explosive growth of the Internet. Last year, $10 billion in goods and services were traded online, according to the Commerce Department. In five years, the amount could exceed $400 billion. In fact, in less than 15 years, a fifth of the world's population — more than a billion people — will be linked by the Internet, said Secretary of Commerce William M. Daley.

"We are in the midst of the most far-reaching technology revolution we have ever known," Daley said. "There is a very real threat that technology could overwhelm us — that it could move faster than our ability to train our people to manage it." [1]

The problem, many government and business leaders say, is that America isn't producing enough information technology (IT) workers to fight the revolution. The shortage of IT professionals "threatens the growth of the entire U.S. economy, our global competitiveness and the wage stability that is the bedrock of this country's low inflation," says Harris N. Miller, president of the Information Technology Association of America (ITAA).

But skeptics like Rep. Ron Klink, D-Pa., charge that industry allegations of a labor shortage "have no credibility in the world of labor statistics" and amount to a "conspiracy" to convince Congress that "the doors to foreign workers must immediately be flung wide open." [2]

In response, 14 high-tech CEOs told the Senate Judiciary Committee in a letter dated March 31, "We are not interested in academic or theoretical disputes about the methodology of surveys. We live and work in the real world. Failure to address current and future worker shortages could mean a loss of America's high-technology leadership in the world."

In fact, the CEOs added, shortages of qualified American workers could force U.S. firms to locate future factories abroad, taking thousands of U.S. jobs with them.

Such grave predictions catch Washington's attention. "In this new economy, technology is our engine of growth," Daley said. High-tech accounts for 40 percent of America's annual gross domestic product growth, and Silicon Valley is "as vital to our economy as Detroit or New York." [3]

The Hudson Institute predicts that if left unaddressed, the labor shortage could result in a 5 percent drop in economic growth — $200 billion in lost output.

The Commerce Department pre-

Slow Growth Expected for Programmers

The number of jobs in three major software job categories are expected to double in the next few years, becoming the nation's fastest-growing occupations. Jobs for computer programmers, however, are only expected to grow by a relatively modest 23 percent.

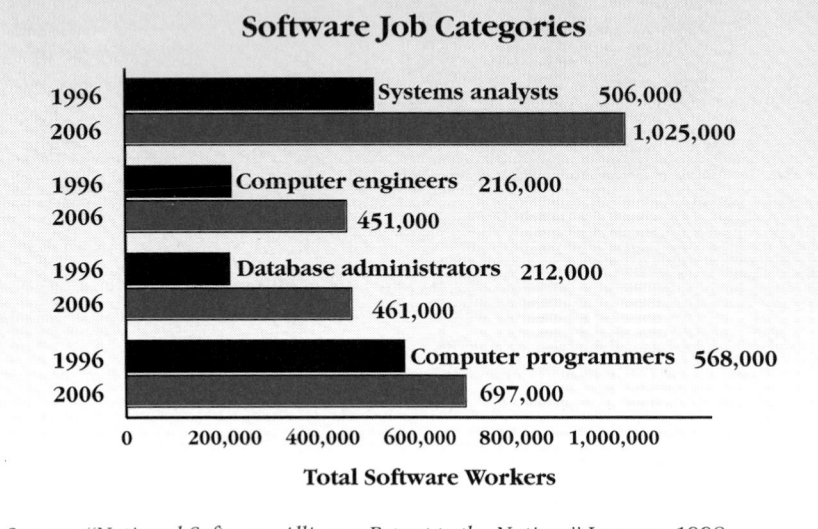

Software Job Categories

Systems analysts — 1996: 506,000; 2006: 1,025,000
Computer engineers — 1996: 216,000; 2006: 451,000
Database administrators — 1996: 212,000; 2006: 461,000
Computer programmers — 1996: 568,000; 2006: 697,000

Total Software Workers

Source: "National Software Alliance Report to the Nation," January 1998

dicts that the U.S. will need 1.3 million new computer workers in the next 10 years — or about 138,000 a year. Sen. Spencer Abraham, R-Mich., says part of the solution is to loosen immigration laws to admit up to 115,000 additional temporary workers each year. Abraham's proposal is awaiting Senate action; a House subcommittee held hearings on a similar proposal on April 21.

In Abraham's home state, meanwhile, computer science classes are swamped at Michigan State University, and lab space and graduate teaching assistants are in short supply. "All our classes are full to capacity," says department Chairman Anil K. Jain, adding that since 1994, enrollments have skyrocketed 58 percent.

"It's a nationwide problem," Jain says. "Every major university in the country is looking for computer science professors." And it's not just computer majors packing the classes. Of

the more than 6,600 students taking computer classes at Michigan State last year, only 584 were computer science and engineering majors.

Computer science and engineering enrollments nationwide rose about 40 percent in 1996 and '97, following a decade in which they declined or stagnated. University officials predict a significant rise in the number of computer science graduates, starting in 1999. [4]

Community colleges and private computer-training schools report a similar upsurge in enrollments. However, most experts predict the supply of home-grown computer workers won't catch up with demand anytime soon.

Exacerbating the talent crunch is the so-called "Year 2000" (Y2K) problem posed by the impending end of the millennium. Thousands of programmers with knowledge of older computer languages like COBOL are needed to painstakingly rewrite billions

of lines of code so the nation's older mainframe computers can seamlessly switch from the 1900s to the 2000s. To find them, recruiters are beating the bushes from Sun Belt golf courses to Russia and Asia. *(See story, p. 374.)*

American recruiters in talent-rich countries like India, Ireland and the Philippines are beginning to stumble over European recruiters competing for the same programmers, not only for their own Y2K problems but also to convert Europe's computers to the Euro monetary system.

With U.S. unemployment at 4.7 percent and the economy increasingly relying on computers, the skills gap goes beyond high-tech industries.

"We're not just talking about a shortage of qualified engineers and scientists for our top software [and] semiconductor firms," Daley added. "Every nook of our economy now depends on technology." [5]

In past periods of low unemployment, U.S. companies typically responded by raising wages. But in today's global economy, business executives say they cannot hike prices and stay competitive with foreign companies paying lower wages.

For computer workers, real wages remained essentially flat from 1988 until 1996, when they began rising, according to the Bureau of Labor Statistics (BLS). But the high-tech industry says the BLS statistics are low because they don't include benefits like stock options.

The introduction of cheaper computers — they are now available for under $1,000 — has also helped to keep high-tech wages down.

Since 1990, American high-tech firms have increasingly tapped overseas talent and outsourced lower-end programming work overseas to keep costs down. Partly as a result, the number of programming jobs in America remained constant from 1988-1996, while jobs for all other professionals expanded by nearly 30 percent, according to Robert I. Lerman, director of the Urban Institute Human Resources Policy Center. [6]

But now the tight labor market is apparently ratcheting high-tech wages upward. A variety of studies indicate that since 1996 wages have risen from an average of 7 percent to as much as 20 percent for some skills, especially computer scientists and systems analysts. Wages for programmers — the high-tech equivalent to assembly-line jobs — aren't rising as fast.

Similarly, jobs for computer scientists and engineers are expected to grow by 114 percent in the coming decade, but programming jobs by only about 23 percent. Unless significant numbers of new workers are produced, however, the national skills gap may widen.

"By the turn of the century, 60 percent of our nation's jobs will demand skills currently held by only 20 percent of the population," Daley said.

As the high-tech debate continues, these are among the most frequently asked questions:

Is the labor shortage a myth?

"An enormous amount of anecdotal evidence from the business community" indicates there is a tight labor market, said Kelly Carnes, deputy assistant Commerce secretary for technology policy. "No one disputes the BLS estimate that we will need more than a million new information-technology workers in the next 10 years. But there are not a lot of good statistics on the supply" of workers. [7]

Skeptics charge that the high-tech industry has exaggerated the severity of the problem to frighten Congress into loosening restrictions on foreign workers.

Industry claims of a "desperate software labor shortage" are a myth, according to Norman Matloff, a computer science professor at the University of California, Davis. "Access to cheap labor is the 'hidden agenda' behind ITAA's campaign to develop an image of a software labor shortage in the public consciousness," he charges in an online report on the controversy. [8]

Those claiming that there is a labor crisis base their arguments on two controversial studies, one by ITAA, the other by Commerce.

"Nothing I've read from either the Commerce Department or the ITAA has any credibility whatsoever," says Lawrence Mishel, director of research for the Economic Policy Institute.

The American Engineering Association (AEA) charged in February that both reports were "grossly unscientific and very biased toward the conclusion that there is a critical shortage of IT workers."

But, ITAA's Miller responds, "The only people calling this shortage a myth are unions and think tanks — the same people who run around saying the Earth is flat. The reality is that this economy is red hot, and jobs are very hard to fill."

In its initial report in January 1997, the ITAA said there were 190,000 high-tech job openings in the United States in 1996. In a January update, the group estimated that computer and non-computer companies actually had 346,000 vacancies for programmers, systems analysts, computer engineers and scientists. [9]

ITAA's findings are based on an "unacceptably low" response rate and thus cannot be generalized to the national level, said the General Accounting Office (GAO) in a March 23 report. [10]

"We would never equate the number of vacancies in any occupation with saying that means there's a shortage of X number of people," Carnes said.

Miller says his group's vacancy figure is actually "undercounted" because it only estimated job openings in companies with more than 100 employees, and small businesses create most of the nation's new jobs.

The report also narrowly defined high-tech workers as those in only four categories, he added. "We could have included lots of other types of computer workers, like those who work on technology 'help' desks, those who install systems, routers and wires, etc," he says. The study also did not count job vacancies in the nonprofit sector, or in federal, state and local governments, he points out.

Indeed, 90 percent of the nation's software workers are employed in non-software companies and by government agencies, says the National Software Alliance (NSA). "These jobs . . . pay less and [thus] are often more difficult to fill," said the NSA. [11]

The Commerce Department stopped short of calling the situation a "shortage," labeling it a "skilled-worker deficit." Drawing on BLS figures, Commerce said last September that between 1994 and 2005 the United States would need 95,000 new workers each year to fill a million newly created computer jobs. [12]

In January, however, the department updated its figures and said 137,800 new workers a year would be needed to fill a total of 1.3 million new high-tech jobs. [13] In making its case for a worker deficit, the department noted that only 24,553 students had graduated with a bachelor's degree in computer and information science in 1994.

The GAO cited "serious analytical and methodological weaknesses" in Commerce's findings, chiefly that it understated the number of technically skilled Americans available for high-tech jobs. Focusing only on the number of bachelor's degrees awarded in computer science and engineering does not prove a worker shortage, the GAO said, because computer workers traditionally come from a variety of educational backgrounds. In reality, only 29 percent of computer scientists, programmers and systems analysts have computer science degrees, according to the National Science Foundation.

"Some of the most high-tech jobs

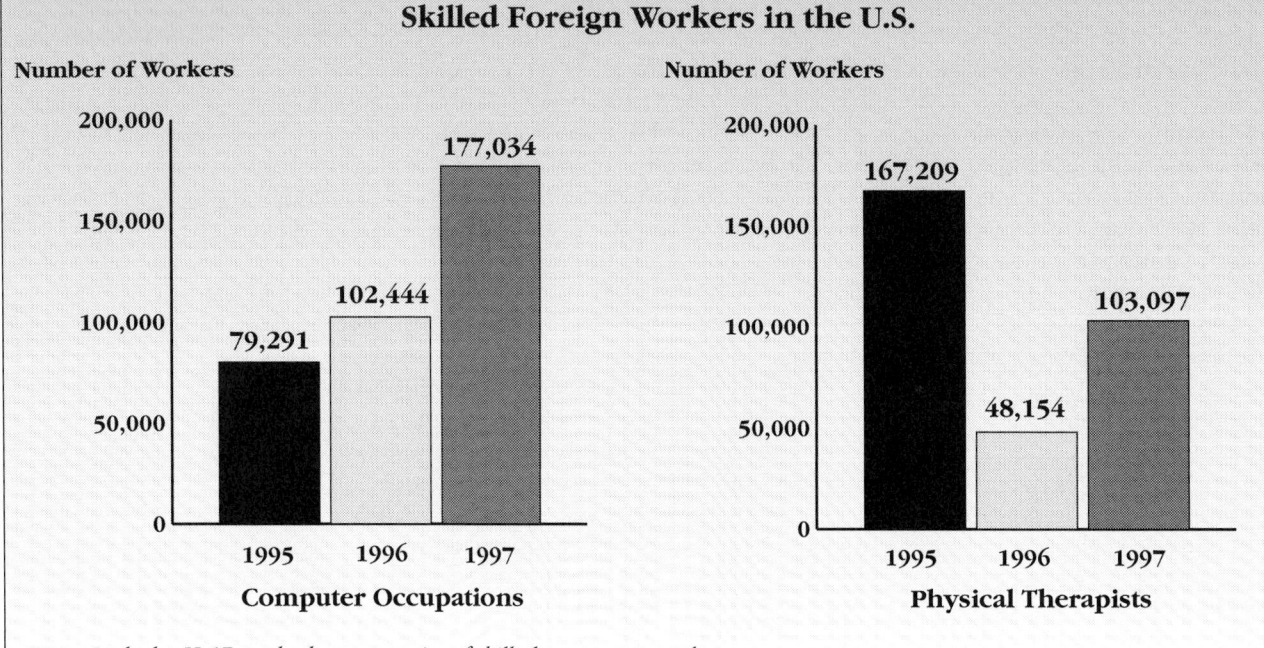

Computer Jobs Attracted Most Foreign Skilled Workers

Computer workers comprised only a quarter of the 312,563 temporary foreign workers in the United States in 1995, but by 1997 the percentage had grown to nearly half the total.* At the same time, physical therapists, the biggest group of skilled foreign workers in 1995, dropped to a quarter of the total in 1997.

Skilled Foreign Workers in the U.S.

Number of Workers

Computer Occupations

- 1995: 79,291
- 1996: 102,444
- 1997: 177,034

Number of Workers

Physical Therapists

- 1995: 167,209
- 1996: 48,154
- 1997: 103,097

Note: Includes H-1B and other categories of skilled temporary workers.

Source: Department of Labor, 1998

out there just don't require college degrees," says Gordon Brace, network engineer at the American Geological Institute (AGI).

The NSA study pointed to an obviously much larger pool of qualified employees available than just those with computer-science degrees. "Since 1993, the number of [computer-science] graduates has remained flat. However, over this same period, the number of software workers increased 62 percent," the NSA added.

"Workers from many fields, with a variety of degrees, are pouring into software jobs," the NSA said.

Klink contends that the United States produces 810,000 bachelor's, master's and Ph.D. degrees in all categories of engineers and in all the hard and soft

sciences. "Any one of these degrees could be used to develop a career in information technology," he says.

Brace, a 14-year computer-industry veteran, recently took a six-month, $8,000 course to become a Microsoft-certified systems engineer.

"Out of the 20 people in my class, only one or two had a computer-science or engineering degree," he says. "And the database manager here at AGI has a music degree."

Focusing only on four-year computer-science degrees also ignores the more than 15,000 high-tech graduates turned out each year by community colleges, as well as thousands of others coming from vocational and technical schools.

"There's not been enough atten-

tion paid to that group," Miller acknowledges. "We need to look more at short-term educational programs as a way of dealing with the work force problem."

A complete picture of the available high-tech labor pool should also include unemployed or underemployed skilled workers, the NSA said.

Skeptics also charge that if there were a true shortage, wages would be going up disproportionately in the computer field. "We have not been able to discern a shortage in our review of the wage data," said EPI's Mishel.

But BLS statistics do not reflect the lucrative benefit packages being offered, such as signing bonuses, say proponents of higher quotas for foreign computer workers.

"That's absurd," Matloff says. "The vast majority of new workers do not get signing bonuses" nor benefit packages like those being offered to graduates of schools like MIT and Stanford. "And of course employees who are already working don't get them either."

Matloff also notes that if companies were desperate, they would not be rejecting 98 percent of their applicants. "The fact that employers can be so picky demonstrates an oversupply of labor," he says.

Employers, on the other hand, say that many of those who send in résumés do not have the skills they need. It's a "skill shortage" rather than a shortage of warm bodies, they say.

So is there a true shortage?

"Markets are tight," Carnes concluded. "Whether or not there's a shortage, and you can say it's 190,000 or 350,000 [jobs], we don't think is really the relevant question," she said. "The relevant question is, 'How can we prepare Americans to have the skills needed to go out and get those 1.3 million new jobs?'"

Should the United States import more temporary foreign computer workers?

The supercharged debate over foreign workers boils down to two key questions: How will they affect American jobs and wages? And will they discourage more Americans from entering the computer field?

The computer industry wants Congress to increase the number of skilled temporary workers who can enter the country using H-1B visas, now capped at 65,000 workers. The controversial visas were designed to allow employers to quickly fill urgent vacancies on a temporary basis. Last August, for the first time since the cap was established in 1990, all the H-1B visas were issued just before the Sept. 30 end of the fiscal year.

This year all the visas are expected to be gone by June, just before the graduation hiring crunch.

Businesses say they must be able to hire the "best and brightest" from American universities. About a third of the new engineering graduates Microsoft hires each year are foreign students, Microsoft Vice President Michael Murray told the Senate Immigration Subcommittee in February. Nearly 40 percent of the electrical and computer engineering master's and Ph.D. students at American universities are foreign-born, he pointed out.

Denying U.S. industry a crack at the brightest foreign graduates is like "sending the first-round draft choices of the high-tech world to play on other countries' teams," writes T.J. Rodgers, president of Cypress Semiconductor Corp. [14]

No one objects to U.S. companies hiring creative geniuses, regardless of their nationality. But as immigration experts have been telling Congress since 1993, that's not the majority of H-1B workers.

"The geniuses are only a tiny fraction of the H-1Bs," says Michael Teitlebaum, a demographer at the Alfred P. Sloan Foundation and former vice chairman of the National Commission on Immigration Reform. "Most H-1Bs are programmers being brought in several hundred at a time. They are code writers [and] they are doing the kind of things any well-educated American with the proper training can do."

Following a series of well-publicized abuses of the H-1B system in 1993 and 1994, then-Labor Secretary Robert B. Reich told the Senate Judiciary Committee in 1995 that some employers bring in hundreds of foreign workers at a time to work in relatively low-level computer-related and health-care occupations.

"These employers include job contractors — some of which have a work force composed predominantly, and even entirely, of H-1B workers

— [who] then lease these employees to other U.S. companies or use them to provide services previously provided by laid-off U.S. workers," Reich told the committee.

The H-1B law does not prohibit employers from replacing American workers with foreign temporary workers. Nor does it require an H-1B employer to show that he first recruited domestically or that there is a shortage in the United States of the type of workers being imported. The Labor Department has been asking Congress since 1993 to close these loopholes; industry has opposed such moves.

The latest Immigration and Naturalization Service (INS) figures show that the 11 companies that imported the most H-1B workers last year each brought in more than a hundred workers. The top importer was Mastech, a Pittsburgh, Pa., labor contractor who imported 672 workers and whose clients include AT&T and Citibank as well as the Department of Defense and the Federal Aviation Administration.

Matloff contends that huge numbers of American employees have been displaced by foreign workers. Pointing out that while the number of foreign computer professionals arriving on H-1B visas increased more than 450 percent from 1988 to 1995, new programming jobs increased by only 35 percent during roughly the same period, according to the NSA.

But Cypress' Rodgers told the Senate Immigration Subcommittee in 1996 that it is "preposterous" to worry that foreign workers will displace American workers. "Each Cypress engineer creates jobs for six additional people who make or administer or sell the products developed" by those engineers.

Not raising the cap will cost Americans jobs, he said. When the cap was reached last August, Cypress had to lay off workers awaiting final visa approval, "delaying the sale of millions of new chips and the cre-

High-Tech Wages Rank Near Top

The average American high-tech worker earned nearly $50,000 in 1996, or 73 percent more than the average private-sector wage earner (top). Salaries for workers in software services led the high-tech field (bottom).

Wage Comparisons

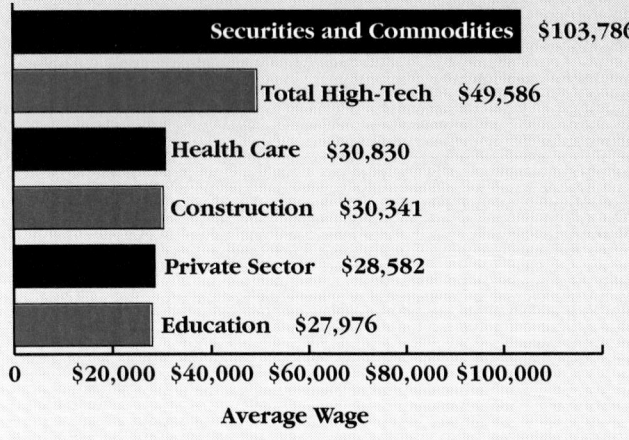

Securities and Commodities	$103,786
Total High-Tech	$49,586
Health Care	$30,830
Construction	$30,341
Private Sector	$28,582
Education	$27,976

0   $20,000 $40,000 $60,000 $80,000 $100,000

Average Wage

Leading High-Tech Industries

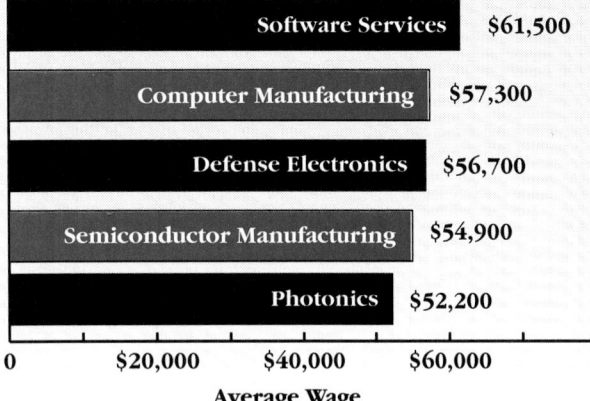

Software Services	$61,500
Computer Manufacturing	$57,300
Defense Electronics	$56,700
Semiconductor Manufacturing	$54,900
Photonics	$52,200

0        $20,000 $40,000 $60,000

Average Wage

Source: "Cybernation," The American Electronics Association and NASDAQ; U.S. Bureau of Labor Statistics

ation of hundreds of manufacturing jobs." Many H-1B applicants are already working for U.S. companies — usually on student visas — as they await their H-1B visas.

Rodgers said that because he has been unable to find as many American computer engineers as he needs, his company has opened offices in Ireland and India, where he employs 60 engineers. "We are being forced by government policy to fill the jobs offshore that we cannot fill here," he said.

Several executives have told the Senate subcommittee that not being able to import foreign workers forces them to cut back on programming projects, delay new products and trim expansion plans. Two-thirds of the companies surveyed by the ITAA said that the labor shortage was the biggest barrier to growth for their companies.

Rohde explains that he often needs to hire someone quickly or he will lose out on a contract. "Let's say I get a big project, and it needs to be done in six months, but I'll need 10 more engineers. I know it will take me six months just to find the engineers in the U.S. But in India I can find them in 10 days."

A major concern of American labor unions is that the H-1B program depresses American wages. "It is imperative that the H-1B visa program be reformed to eliminate employer abuse, which has resulted in the displacement of U.S. workers and depression of wages," AFL-CIO President John J. Sweeney said in a March 26 statement.

To prevent undercutting of Americans' salaries, the law requires employers of foreigners to pay at least 95 percent of the "average prevailing wage" in a region. But unions say that the law in effect provides a 5 percent "discount" for employers who rely on foreign labor. Further, they say, the law allows employers to simply lay off higher-paid, mid-career American workers and bring in foreign workers at entry-level "prevailing" wages.

Proponents of raising the cap say such abuses are a thing of the past that wouldn't happen in a tight labor market. "A company today that doesn't pay prevailing wages won't get employees," says Chuck Rudisill, director of investor relations for Mastech. "We always pay by the book."

Besides, says ITAA's Miller, competitors would complain. "They watch each other like a hawk. If a company saw a competitor paying less than prevailing wage, it would go ballistic."

"We have one pay scale, no matter whether a person's name is Sanjay or Jack," says William Bold, director of government affairs for Qualcomm, a major San Diego, Calif., wireless phone manufacturer.

A Labor Department official who asked

not to be quoted by name says that despite the current tight labor market, "We're still receiving complaints at about the same steady rate as always." About 90 percent of the H-1B employers that the department investigates are paying less than the prevailing wage, he says.

The official noted that complaints come from competitors more than from the H-1B employees because the employee is usually being sponsored for permanent resident status by his boss. "They have a lot of incentive not to complain," he notes. About half of the immigrants approved for permanent status entered the country as H-1B workers, he says.

While some critics say dependency on employees makes H-1B workers "indentured servants," Rohde disagrees. "People on H-1B visas come and go all the time. The days of slavery in this country are long past. We've even had people in the middle of the green card process who have been hired away." In order to keep his foreign engineers from jumping ship, he says, he is constantly upgrading their benefits.

The Labor official says it's not quite that simple, however, because if the worker leaves his job he loses his visa. "These folks are not free to move in the labor market," he says, "because they have to first find another employer willing to start the H-1B process all over again."

But Matloff argues that being able to constantly increase the labor pool with temporary workers depresses Americans' wages. "Even if employers pay the foreign workers the prevailing wage," he says, "the temporary nature of the H-1B visa means they can continually replace workers as they rise in the salary scale."

Immigration experts Demetrios G. Papademetriou and Stephen Yale-Loehr agree that immigrants depress wages but say that in the long run they end up creating other jobs. "It is true that immigrant labor has prob-

ably moderated wage inflation among U.S. engineers, scientists and other highly qualified professionals," they write. "This has provided U.S. business with a key competitive advantage internationally, thus helping them to prosper and, in the long run, to create more and better jobs." [15]

Critics of raising the cap fear that admitting more foreign computer workers will discourage America's own "best and brightest" from going into the field.

"People thinking about going into the computer industry are not stupid," Teitlebaum says. "If they see this is how government responds to rising salaries in the computer industry, they will go into law or medicine."

The critics also claim that raising the cap would relieve the pressure for companies to retrain existing employees in "hot" new skills. "Too many employers are using the H-1B program to avoid their responsibility to train U.S. workers for high-tech jobs," Reich told the Senate committee in 1995.

Raising the cap will also interfere with the natural workings of the labor market, which is already adjusting, critics point out. "What you have is an industry that has been boom and bust," Teitlebaum says. "It was bust five years ago. It's been booming since. It takes time for the market to adjust. But they don't want to wait."

Indeed, industry says that the high-tech world moves too fast to wait. In the fast-paced high-tech industry, "this deficit of skilled workers will lead to lost business opportunities, slower innovation and an erosion of the dominance of U.S. high-tech companies in the world market," Kenneth M. Alvares, a Sun Microsystems vice president, told lawmakers in February.

Are industry recruitment and labor practices to blame for the tight labor market?

Much of the high-tech industry's tight labor situation is "self-inflicted," the AFL-CIO charges, "created by shortsighted human-resource practices" and insufficient training and education programs. Lifting the cap removes any pressure for the industry to alter its labor practices, the group said. Its executive council said in a March 26 statement that rather than raising the cap the high-tech industry should do more to:

- Retain and retrain experienced workers;
- Recruit more women and people of color;
- Hire and retrain older, downsized workers who are unemployed or underemployed;
- Pay higher salaries; and
- Improve working conditions.

The labor group's complaints were echoed in six government-sponsored ITAA task force reports released in January, which explored ways the industry can increase the pool of available workers.

One task force found that high-tech companies subtly discriminate against older men and women with families because they are perceived as "less available for the overtime, night and weekend work."

As one Silicon Valley manager said: "The top management in our company has directed us to focus our hiring on new or recent graduates only. These are people who have no family and can work long hours. Yes, salary is a major factor. . . . You work the young ones for five years and then replace them." [16]

"I call it the vampire industry," says a congressional staffer who works on the H-1B issue. "Every day they need fresh, new blood."

Software management consultant Edward Yourdon noted the trend toward the disappearance of mid-career software professionals in his 1996 book: "I've visited organizations that used to have 100 software people [and] then returned two years later to

Teenage Techies Win Praise ...

Can't find a programmer? Desperate software companies are advertising in high school newspapers these days — and they're hitting pay dirt. Teenage techies win praise for their passion, time and energy — things many older workers don't have.

"Passion is the key," says Grady Ogburn, a manager at Datametrics Systems Corp., in Fairfax, Va. "You have to be passionate about the new things the technology is capable of doing. You have to be a techno-geek, because it's easy for people who love the technology to stay on top of it."

Two summers ago, Ogburn hired Brent Metz, then 15, as an intern. He turned out to be an extremely valuable Unix programmer for Datametrics, which develops software to help clients manage mainframe performance. Brent joined 15,000 other American youths 16-19 who worked as either programmers or systems analysts last year — up from 4,000 in 1994, according to the Bureau of Labor Statistics.

Teens have time to surf the Worldwide Web and keep up with what's happening in technology, Ogburn points out.

"Older workers have jobs — they're working to put bread on the table," Ogburn says. "They can't surf the Web all day, and they certainly don't go home at night and play on the Web, which is what these kids do."

While kids are surfing, they're also learning, says Travis Riggs, president of Creative Edge Software, in Sterling, Va., who hired 16-year-old Seth Berger to help develop video games.

"Kids have time to try new things, like learning how to do all the graphics," Riggs says. "Most of what Seth knows he learned on his own. Somebody in their mid-20s doesn't have that kind of free time to learn new things." In fact, said Riggs, some of his older graphic artists sometimes turn to Seth for help.

Teenagers also have the energy needed to work the "crazy hours" required to get a new company off the ground, says Elliott Frutkin, president of four-year-old Ideal Computer Strategies, of Washington, D.C. Last summer, Frutkin hired Josh Foer to help develop Web pages for clients. He was astonished at what the 14-year-old could do — like integrating a database to a Web site using the new "Cold Fusion" program.

"That's one of the really big skills people are looking for right now," he says. Josh had learned it while playing around on the Web.

"He had also surfed enough Web sites to know the difference between a professionally done Web page and a homemade one," Frutkin says, unlike most of the applicants who come to him when he advertises in the regular classified ads.

"Ninety-nine percent of the people who answer classified ads are not qualified," he says. They are mostly "old

---

find that the staff had been reduced to a dozen younger and less expensive people." [17]

But computer-firm executives say their highly competitive industry requires long hours. "If you want to succeed, that's what you have to do," Rohde said. "Are you telling me doctors and lawyers work less hours?"

The industry's reputation for working young employees grueling hours and then nudging them out after a few years to make room for entry-level or foreign workers discourages prospective employees interested in a career with longevity, the task force said.

"The half-life of a programmer is six years," says AEA President Bill E. Reed. "That's a hell of a waste of an education. What about the other 30 years of their lives? The companies should be retraining them, at their own expense."

Rohde says he pays for his employees to keep their skills current. "We have people in school all the time," he says. "We pay 100 percent of their education costs if they want to go to night school."

Miller denies that the industry discriminates against older workers or women. "If companies are practicing all this age and sex discrimination, where are all the lawsuits?" he asks.

"It's not an age-discrimination thing," says an industry lobbyist. "It's a skills thing. We need people right away with the latest skills."

Many industry critics complain that recruiters often can't find workers because they focus too narrowly on finding someone with the "hot" skill-of-the-month, rather than searching for those with talent and aptitude.

"You could train a person who is

literate in computer programming but doesn't know a particular language, and he can become proficient in about a month," Teitlebaum says. "But when you say you'll only take people with two years' experience in Java, when Java is such a new language, you're not going to find them."

For instance, he suggests, there is a "gold mine" out there of technically oriented Ph.D.s in related fields — such as unemployed mathematicians and physicists — who could become systems designers with minimal retraining.

Rohde says he would hire any Ph.D. who walked into his office as long as he had some computer experience. "Why should I train a new employee?" he said. "If people want to find a job they have to re-educate themselves and then come to you for a job."

The AFL-CIO claims that because

. . . And Big Bucks for Their Passion

school Cobol programmers" trying to pick up new skills. "They're definitely not as on top of the technology as Josh was," he says.

Does he feel that employers discriminate against older programmers, as some industry critics have alleged?

"I don't care if someone is 15 or 50, if they have one of the hot skills I need," he says. He advises anyone looking for a job in Web site development to teach themselves one of the new database-to-Web integration programs.

Both Ogburn and Frutkin said they do not understand why industry executives are complaining that the country is not producing enough graduates with four-year computer science degrees to fill all the country's high-tech job vacancies.

"You don't need a four-year degree to do a lot of this stuff," Ogburn says. "You can't get a degree in passion for technology."

He concedes that a four-year degree shows that a person has perseverance and diligence, and can prioritize and use time wisely. "But when I see a 4.0 [grade-point average] from Carnegie Mellon [University]," he says, "all that means is I have to pay them more."

"Sure, we have people who learned their skills in the classroom," Frutkin says. "But we also need tons of people who didn't get them that way."

Frutkin has concluded that the best way to develop a long-term staff is to recruit college interns and give them on-the-job training. "We're trying to work with people who are less developed in their skills, less set in their ways. It takes new ways of thinking to be able to market effectively on the Internet."

Some teens find their summer or part-time jobs so appealing they drop out of high school or decide not to go to college at all. Seth is seriously considering skipping college because he fears he will fall behind on his skills, and says he can gain more experience working.

Besides, the next video project he's scheduled to do for Riggs could net him a six-figure check. If he gives all that up and then shells out for college tuition, "That's over a quarter of a million dollars it would cost me to learn stuff I already know," he says.

Computer-science teacher Donald Hyatt gets calls all the time from recruiters looking for summer interns or prospective employees among his students at prestigious Thomas Jefferson High School of Science and Technology in suburban Washington. He advises all his students to stay in school and go on to college.

"Most students realize that they need a long-term education, not just a few skills," Hyatt says. "These kids could leave school right now and make $70,000 a year. It's hard to tell them not to do it. After all, after 29 years of teaching, I'm not making that much myself."

the industry is beginning to rely more and more on temporaries, part-timers and contractors, it lacks incentives "to make crucial investments" in training its work force.

On the contrary, ITAA says, high-tech companies spend $210 billion a year on employee training of all kinds.

The biggest problem is that the technology changes faster than either schools or employers can train workers in the new skills. To stay competitive, companies say they need employees already trained in the newest technology who can hit the ground running.

With technology changing every 15-18 months, companies say they cannot afford to train somebody in the latest program. Besides, employers fear that as soon as they train someone, they'll be hired away. Some companies ask employees to sign a contract promising to repay the company for training costs if they accept another job within two years.

The Clinton administration is urging the industry to spend more on training. "You should be as active as we are in the development of a well-trained work force," Daley told a group of business leaders. "Invest time and resources in [your employees], and it will pay off." [18]

Finally, critics say, if the industry really wanted to retain good employees, it would upgrade salaries across the board, rather than giving employees a patchwork of stock options and benefits.

"If high-tech workers are so important to the development of the economy over the next 20 years, then you would expect their salaries to reflect that," says Paul Kostek, president of the U.S. branch of the Insti-

tute of Electrical and Electronics Engineers.

Microsoft's Murray pointed out in his Senate testimony that the average software job pays $60,000, more than double the $28,000 paid to the average private-sector employee. *(See graph, p. 368.)*

Rohde scoffed at complaints that salaries aren't high enough. "The average [experienced] engineer's salary in Silicon Valley is $75,000-$80,000, and going up $10,000 a year," he said. "That's not enough?"

According to the annual salary survey by *Computerworld* magazine, however, the salaries of new computer science graduates with a bachelor's degree had increased to an average of $36,666 in 1997, while experienced programmers received from $45,000-$75,000. ∎

BACKGROUND

Skills Gap or Glut?

The roots of the current skills gap lie partly in the high-tech industry's boom-bust cycles over the past two decades. The resultant periodic gluts of scientists and engineers kept salaries low, encouraging America's own "best and brightest" to choose more lucrative fields, like law or medicine, some analysts say. Science and engineering wages also have been depressed in part because immigration policies enacted by Congress in 1990 resulted in a huge influx of overseas scientists and engineers, according to engineers' unions.

"This is the third 'crisis-level shortage' of high-tech professionals in the last two decades we have heard about from corporate America," says the AEA's Reed. "In each of the first two instances, the shortage never materialized. We do not believe this one will either."

Reed notes that in the early 1980s predictions by the high-tech industry of a coming shortage of skilled workers were followed by an oversupply of computer engineers and scientists, after a record number of degrees were awarded in 1986.

Then in the late 1980s — in an unpublished report that was nonetheless widely circulated and roundly criticized — the National Science Foundation (NSF) predicted imminent shortages of scientists and engineers. The 1990 Hudson Institute's "Workforce 2000" report seemed to bolster the NSF prediction.

Congress cited the two studies when it amended immigration law in 1990, substantially increasing the number of skilled workers allowed to immigrate to the United States each year. The Immigration Act of 1990 increased the number of permanent, work-based admissions allowed each year from 54,000 to 140,000 and created tens of thousands of slots for various types of temporary skilled workers, including 65,000 under the controversial H-1B program.

Immediately thereafter, the Soviet Union broke up, defense spending was slashed and the aerospace and other industries were aggressively downsized. Not surprisingly, the job market for scientists and engineers once again collapsed. Still, from 1990-1993, the United States produced 50 percent more bachelors' degrees in computer science, math and engineering than it needed. The unemployment rate reached 12 percent for Ph.D.s in mathematics and physics, forcing many into low-paid, "post doctoral" positions, Lawrence Richards, then executive director of the Software Professionals' Political Action Committee, told lawmakers in 1995. [19] Growth in wages stagnated.

Despite the oversupply of domestic engineers and scientists, more than 314,000 foreign scientists and engineers entered the country on a variety of temporary visas between 1991 and 1995, said immigration researcher and former Labor Department official David S. North. And another 100,000 became permanent residents, he said.

"Government and industry may be reducing their investments in science and engineering; unemployment may be growing in both fields; but the government keeps admitting more and more non-immigrants in science and engineering," North told the Senate Judiciary Committee in 1995.

In a book outlining his research, North concluded that the presence of numerous highly skilled and hard-working foreign scientists and engineers had "soothed the establishment" in government, industry and academia. However, he concluded, they also had depressed wages, led indirectly to more unemployment, hastened the retirement of middle-aged, native-born scientists and engineers and reduced incentives to increase the number of female, black, Hispanic and Native American scientists and engineers. He also concluded that the low number of Americans choosing science and engineering careers was due to lower salaries. [20]

In a lengthy 1996 report for Empower America, author Stuart Anderson challenged North's findings. "No evidence exists that foreign-born engineers in the high-technology field have lowered the earnings or harmed the employment prospects of native-born American engineers as a group," he wrote." [21]

Indeed, Anderson found that median earnings for engineers in electronics, electrical machinery and computers, seven years after they obtained their bachelor's degrees, increased by 43.4 percent from 1975-1995, compared with 12.6 percent for the average American worker.

H-1B Controversy

In 1993 and 1994 the TV news shows "60 Minutes" and "48 Hours" revealed that labor contractors had brought in hundreds of programmers on H-1B visas to replace Americans being laid off. In one infamous case, the workers being fired had to retrain their replacements. One of the contractors bringing in guest workers told "48 Hours" that he had been unable to find enough Americans to do the jobs.

"What he did not mention was that his guest workers were earning $10,000-$20,000 a year less than the laid-off Americans," Richards told lawmakers. The Labor Department said that because of loopholes in the H-1B law, companies were increasingly using it to bring in lower-end programmers en masse and as a quick first step for importing skilled foreign workers on the way to

Continued on p. 374

Chronology

1970s *Revolutions in microchip technology, including the invention of the microprocessor, drastically reduce the cost of the thousands of electronic components required in a computer.*

1971
American engineer Marcian E. Hoff combines the basic elements of a computer on one tiny silicon chip, which he calls a microprocessor.

1974
The first affordable desktop computer designed specifically for personal use, the Altair 8800, is sold by Micro Instrumentation Telemetry Systems.

1977
Tandy Corp. becomes the first major electronics firm to produce a personal computer. Soon afterward, a small company named Apple Computer, founded by engineer Stephen Wozniak and entrepreneur Steven Jobs, begins producing a superior model.

1980s *The high-tech industry predicts a shortage of skilled workers, followed by an oversupply of computer engineers and scientists, after a record number of degrees are awarded in 1986. Later in the decade, the National Science Foundation (NSF) predicts imminent shortages of scientists and engineers.*

1981
IBM introduces the "Personal Computer," or PC. Competition from the makers of "clones" (computers modeled after IBM PCs), drives down the price of PCs.

1990s *The job market for scientists and engineers collapses following the collapse of the Soviet Union and widespread defense and aerospace downsizing in response to global competition. The unemployment rate for engineers more than doubles by 1994. Yet more than 314,000 foreign scientists and engineers enter the country on a variety of temporary work visas between 1991 and 1995. Another 100,000 become permanent immigrants during the same period.*

1990
The Hudson Institute's "Workforce 2000" report seems to bolster the NSF prediction of an impending skilled-labor shortage. Congress cites the two studies when it amends immigration law, increasing from 54,000 to 140,000 the number of permanent, work-based admissions allowed each year and creating myriad other skill- and profession-based visas for foreign nationals coming to study, work and conduct business on a temporary basis. The controversial H-1B program, allowing up to 65,000 skilled workers to enter the country each year, is born.

April 8, 1992
The House Committee on Science, Space and Technology holds a hearing blasting the earlier NSF study as seriously flawed.

1993 and 1994
Several high-profile cases reveal that companies are using H-1B visas to bring in hundreds of workers to replace American programmers being laid off.

January 1995
The Labor Department tries to implement new regulations to plug some H-1B loopholes. The department is sued by the National Association of Manufacturers. Congress convenes hearings partly because of the negative publicity about the H-1B program.

1996
In May, the Labor Department's inspector general finds that the H-1B program "is broken and needs to be fixed." Bills are introduced slashing some of the entry slots for skilled workers, but after intense lobbying by a coalition of industry, university administrators and immigration lawyers' associations, no reforms are enacted. In July, a court strikes down the new Labor Department rules.

1997
The Commerce Department and Information Technology Association of America (ITAA) declare a severe shortage of skilled high-tech workers and set up six task forces to study the problem.

1998
In January, the task force reports are released and the administration announces a $28 million program to boost skilled-worker training. In April the Senate Judiciary Committee agrees to increase the H-1B cap to 95,000 this year and up to 115,000 in subsequent years.

The 'Year 2000 Problem' ...

Predictions about the impact of the so-called "Year 2000 Problem" range from apocalyptic havoc to a mere blip on the computer screen. Doomsayers say it could resemble a Hollywood disaster film: chaotic international money markets, inaccessible bank vaults, blank air-traffic control screens, blacked-out power grids, crippled missile defense systems. Not to mention non-functioning telephones, ATMs and elevators.

Others say it will be the biggest non-event in history. To show how safe the skies will be, Federal Aviation Administrator Jane F. Garvey plans to board a plane at midnight on December 31, 1999, and fly from Washington, D.C., across three time zones to California.

Whether one subscribes to the big bang or the big yawn theory, the cost of fixing the problem, nicknamed Y2K, will be steep — from $200 billion to $600 billion at last count, says the Gartner Group, a Stamford, Conn., computer consulting firm. But that doesn't include hundreds of billions more in potential litigation costs if calendar-challenged computer systems aren't brought up to date.

All because of two little digits. The Y2K millennium bug was born in the early days of programming, when mainframe memory was precious. To save memory space, dates were abbreviated to two digits, without the 19; thus 1999 would appear as 99. But computers weren't programmed to deal with the year 2000. So on Jan. 1, 2000, it is feared that computers may go haywire. Some could shut down; some might just hiccup; some might roll back the date to 1900, invalidating much of the date-sensitive data they store.

It's a digital nightmare with a grindingly boring and time-consuming solution. Literally billions of lines of computer code must be painstakingly scanned for any dates, then rewritten to recognize the new century. A lengthy testing phase then follows. One estimate says the problem will take 700,000 person years to fix. Because the bug lurks mostly in mainframes, it requires knowledge of old computer languages, like COBOL, which today's young PC programmers never learned.

But the bug also lives in millions of embedded chips found in just about every electronic device — from elevators to coffee makers — with time- or date-sensitive mechanisms. Repairing these is particularly maddening for manufacturers, many of whom were late in waking up to the Year 2000 problem. They must find millions of these computerized devices hidden among their production

equipment, such as machine tools, measuring instruments and computerized valves. General Motors is already encountering "catastrophic problems" in every one of its plants, said chief information officer Ralph J. Szygenda.[1]

Most experts think it could take months or even years to work out all the bugs in repaired systems. Moreover, many companies and governments targeted only their most critical systems to repair first, leaving the others until later. Some fear that when a repaired system interacts with an unrepaired system, it could transmit the problem back to the bug-free system — much like a computer virus — wiping out years of repairs.

Many companies are already feeling the bug's effects. In a survey released in March, the Information Technology Association of America (ITAA) found 44 percent of member companies had experienced failures under actual operating conditions, and 67 percent reported failures under test conditions.

The ITAA and industry executives blame the nationwide shortage of high-tech workers, at least in part, on the Y2K problem, saying that thousands of key personnel have been diverted to sort out Year 2000 problems. But companies that supply commercial clients with Y2K workers say business is slow. The ITAA surveyed its members last July and found that only 4 percent had all the business they could handle. More than 80 percent said they could easily provide more Year 2000 workers if needed.

Edward E. Yardeni, chief economist at Deutsche Morgan Grenfell, a New York investment bank, says the low demand for Y2K workers means "there isn't enough alarm about it." Yardeni sees as much as a 60 percent chance that the lack of Y2K preparedness could trigger a severe global recession. European countries have not focused on the problem to a large extent because they have been busy trying to convert to the Euro by next year, and Japanese companies have been distracted by their own economic problems.

"The time has come to act as though we are preparing for a war," Yardeni told representatives of the global banking community on April 7 at a "Year 2000" symposium organized by the Bank for International Settlements (BIS) in Basle, Switzerland. He recommends establishment of a multinational Year 2000 Alliance, with a commander in chief to organize a global militarylike campaign to increase public awareness, develop fail-safe systems to prevent an accidental nuclear missile launch and make sure vital utilities and

---

Continued from p. 372
becoming permanent residents.

As written, the law "amounts to nothing more than a way for employers to obtain cheap labor and to drive down the

wages of native workers," Richards said.

The industry not only brings in large numbers of foreigners to do code-writing but also exports a lot of it, particularly to India. New developments in satellite tech-

nology allow companies here to work closely with employees abroad.

The trend toward foreign workers was predicted by Yourdon in his 1992 book, *Decline and Fall of the American*

... Titanic Disaster or Big Yawn?

telecommunications are secure. "Measures must be taken to thwart terrorists, hackers and other malevolent opportunists from taking advantage of any Y2K chaos," he told the group.

Meanwhile in the U.S., Yardeni says, although larger U.S. companies have been working on Y2K for years, the government and smaller companies are not panicked enough. Many computer labor market experts echo the same sentiment.

"Companies aren't desperate enough yet," says Bill Payson, who runs Senior Staff 2000, a job clearinghouse aimed at linking retired COBOL programmers with companies needing Y2K repair work. Payson says he has plenty of experienced programmers willing to work on Year 2000 problems, but they want to telecommute.

Most of them live in Sun Belt states. "They say to me, 'I'm damned if I'm going to leave this golf-course community and come live in a hotel in Chicago to pull their chestnuts out of the fire, when I told them 20 years ago that this was going to be a problem,'" Payson says.

"But most employers won't even consider letting them telecommute," he says. "They're not quite panicky enough to be innovative. But when they realize they have to choose between letting a critical program literally collapse or use these folks living near the golf course, they'll see the light."

Yet other companies are willing to outsource at least some of their Year 2000 work — via satellite — to job shops in India and other nations.

"We get solicitations from Indian firms at least two or three times a week," says Dave Ehlke, of Y2K Plus, which provides Y2K swat teams for a dozen companies and government agencies around the country. "Their general pitch is that they can get us people 20 percent cheaper than Americans," he says. "But I'm not going to hire somebody just because they are cheaper. You really have to know the people you hire."

Industry lobbyists deny that labor contractors are bringing in computer workers who are being paid less than Americans. In the current tight labor market, they say, such lower-paid workers would immediately be hired away by another firm offering them more.

Even the Russians are coming to the rescue of American companies. Russia is a rich source of COBOL and mainframe programmers, although they are not as familiar with business applications as programmers from more capitalistic economies. "A tremendous number of Y2K remediation shops in New York City are staffed by Russians," says Bruce Grant, president of Resource Solutions International, in Herndon, Va.

Grant's company recruits at industries in the Midwest, and among downsized and retired military personnel, especially those in the Washington, D.C., area.

"The military is about a quarter the size it was during Desert Storm," he says. "There's a large amount of talent still out there."

Many experts say that most firms won't be ready on Dec. 31, 1999, because of the "industrial chain reaction" effect.

Large companies and governments depend on independent suppliers for critical goods and services, notes Stephanie Moore, senior analyst for Giga Information Group, a Stamford, Conn., consulting firm. "Even if you fix all your systems internally, if somebody you rely on for supplies hasn't fixed all theirs, it can cause a domino effect — breaking the supply chain and putting people out of business."

Even if all the banks and financial institutions around the world have debugged their own computers, it could all crash if the hundreds of telecommunications and electrical power systems they rely on haven't been repaired, the BIS warned on April 9.

The domino effect also could affect government agencies that depend on each other. Rep. Steve Horn, R-Calif., chairman of the House Oversight Subcommittee on Government Management, Information and Technology, recently reported that only nine out of 24 federal agencies are expected to finish all their critical Year 2000 conversion work on time. In fact, the Defense Department has converted only 24 percent of its 2,915 critical systems and is not expected to finish until 2009, he said, calling the situation "intolerable."

John Koskinen, who was appointed by President Clinton on Feb. 4 to spearhead the government's conversion program, is convinced that all 7,850 critical systems within the government will be completed on time. "There is not an agency in the government that is not devoted to solving this problem," he says.

Koskinen says his team must perform the "delicate balancing act" of increasing worldwide awareness of how urgent the problem is while not "creating panic and precipitous, counterproductive activity."

---

[1] Gene Bylinsky, "Industry Wakes Up to the Year 2000 Menace," Fortune, April 27, 1998.

Programmer. "During the 1990s," Yourdan wrote, "software development may well move out of the U.S. into software factories in a dozen countries whose people are well-educated, less expensive and more passionately devoted to quality and productivity."

Those in favor of raising the cap say it makes more economic sense for those jobs to be done by foreigners here. "The work's got to be done. It will either be done here or overseas. Why not bring the foreigners here to do it?" asks a Senate staffer who works on the legislation. "Then we get the economic benefit of those jobs being done here — and all the support jobs they create."

In addition, executives argue, having the drudge work done wherever it is cheapest frees up money for higher-paid programmers and systems designers who do the more creative work.

If you look at labor strictly as a commodity, says Cato Institute economist Stephen Moore, bringing in foreign engineers is a "great deal" for America. "It costs about $150,000 to educate an engineer. If we let the Indian government pay for the education, then we get that benefit for free. In a sense, we're really robbing that country of its investment. The Indians are the ones who should be upset about this, not the Americans."

During 1995 and 1996, Congress worked on several reform proposals. Reich had asked for more effective investigatory and enforcement authority to prevent employers from abusing the program. Bills were introduced slashing some of the entry slots for skilled workers, and hearings were held on Capitol Hill. However following intense lobbying by a coalition of industry, university administrators and immigration lawyers' associations, none of the reforms was enacted.

In 1995, the Labor Department tried to implement new regulations to plug some of the H-1B loopholes. The new rules would have allowed the department to launch an investigation without first having to receive a complaint; reduced from six years to three the maximum time an employee could remain under an H-1B visa; and required companies to provide more evidence that they were paying the going rate in their region. The department was sued by the National Association of Manufacturers, which said the department had not given sufficient public notice, and that the new regulations were "onerous and anticompetitive."

In July 1996 the court struck down the new rules as having been insufficiently advertised. Also that year, the Labor Department's inspector general found that the H-1B program "is broken and needs

to be fixed." It does not protect U.S. workers' jobs and salaries, largely because the department's role is limited by law to no more than "rubber stamping" employers' applications, said the report. [22]

To illustrate this weakness in the law, Richards had told the Senate committee, he applied to the Labor Department for permission to hire 40 foreign programmers at $4.50 an hour. "This application was approved and sent back to me in nine days," he said. [23]

Focus on Education

Annual caps on enrollment in university computer science departments also add to the current shortage of home-grown computer experts. "Competing for a finite number of dollars, enrollment is limited in computer science and other popular fields to force enrollment in less popular ones," said the NSA report. "Because private and public research dollars are often awarded to less popular fields (e.g., physics, chemistry, biosciences), these departments hold a financial advantage over other fields. This gives them a political edge in faculty employment and in holding enrollment down in other fields in favor of theirs."

The Michigan State experience reflects that dilemma. "The department budget doesn't get influenced by how many students are in the classes," says Chairman Jain, who had to impose grade-point cutoff criteria in order to limit the number of students entering junior-year computer science programs. "That's one way we are handling the increased demand for classes."

Other computer department heads noted that because of tenure limitations, universities are not free to hire and fire professors as demand fluctuates from year to year.

Besides, says Jain, there aren't a lot of Ph.D.s in computer science hanging

around looking for jobs. "We have to compete with major research labs like Lucent Technologies and IBM, which are hiring a large number of Ph.D.s," he says. "Private industry can offer much larger salaries than we can."

Even graduate assistants are hard to find, he said, because the private job market is so good. "It's so easy for graduate students to go out and get a good-paying job right now in private industry."

Industry says the roots of the current problem lie in the failure of America's education system. American high schools don't provide world-class math and science curricula and universities teach too much theory and not enough applied technology, they say.

"When we are looking for engineers we turn a lot of people away because they don't have the right skills," says FirsTel's Rohde. But when he recruits in India or China, he finds qualified people "in droves," he adds. "The engineers we get out of Ireland, Scotland, China and India are more disciplined, they work harder, they are more dedicated and they are better trained."

"Why don't American educators go over there and find out what they're doing right?" he asks. Many companies, resigned to the apparent inability of the education system to provide capable workers, have established training centers to bring new graduates up to speed, not only in technology but also in basic skills and literacy.

In the latest international rankings in math and science, U.S. high school seniors were nearly last among students from 21 participating nations. Even America's academically elite students — who take physics or advanced math courses in high school — scored last in physics and second from the bottom in high-level math.

The rankings were from the Third International Mathematics and Science Study (TIMSS), which periodically tests fourth-, eighth- and 12th-

Continued on p. 378

At Issue:

Should more foreign high-tech workers be allowed into the United States?

WILLIAM T. ARCHEY

President and CEO, American Electronics Association

WRITTEN FOR THE CQ RESEARCHER, APRIL 1998.

i speak on behalf of the entire high-technology industry when I say legal immigrants play a critical role in the high-technology industry. A cap on the number of temporary, employment-based visas, or H-1B visas, is a cap on our industry's growth.

The high-tech industry is experiencing tremendous growth and is a driving force in this nation's economy. From 1995 to 1996 alone, the high-tech industry created more than 240,000 jobs. We are the single largest exporter of manufactured goods in the country, exporting $150 billion worth of goods last year.

However, to continue this level of growth, we need to ensure there are enough qualified workers in the United States. In other words, we need to ensure that the supply satisfies the demand. Our companies, therefore, invest millions of dollars per year retraining our U.S. work force.

Unfortunately, after exhaustive searches in the United States, native workers are sometimes not available. And sometimes the position requires a culturally diverse background. Despite popular opinion, there is no financial advantage to hiring highly skilled legal immigrants. Relocation fees, visa processing costs, legal bills and the much-in-demand talents of individuals being recruited frequently make the process more expensive than hiring a U.S. worker.

Legal immigrants play a small but critical role in addressing the short-term needs of the industry. Although constituting an infinitesimally small percentage of the overall high-tech work force, their innovative expertise creates intellectual property and products in the United States, which in turn creates jobs for U.S. workers. Without legal immigrants, the world leadership position the U.S. high-tech industry enjoys today would be undermined.

Opponents of increasing the cap on H-1B visas call on industry to train, retrain and recruit existing U.S. workers. We are doing that, and then some. Many of the problems in producing qualified U.S. workers are also a function of the inadequacies of the U.S. educational system, particularly grades K-12. Our companies are very involved in educational reform, but that reform is a long-term proposition. Our companies cannot cease hiring highly skilled legal immigrants while waiting for these reforms to take hold. Indeed, many of those legal immigrants will make the kind of contributions that will help assure future generations of American workers opportunities for high-skilled, high-paying jobs.

NORMAN MATLOFF

Professor of computer science, University of California at Davis, and former software developer in Silicon Valley

WRITTEN FOR THE CQ RESEARCHER, APRIL 1998.

t he information technology (IT) industry is using the H-1B work visa program far in excess of its intended function, which is to deal with temporary, spot shortages. The number of visas requested by employers for computer specialists increased by 352 percent from 1990-1995, during which time the number of jobs in the field increased by only 35 percent.

An audit conducted by the Department of Labor found rampant abuse in the visa program. Several independent studies have confirmed that the foreign-national computer programmers and engineers are paid on average 15-30 percent less than comparable U.S. workers.

IT employers claim a desperate labor shortage, yet wages for computer programmers went up by only 7 percent last year. If you were an employer who was desperate to hire, wouldn't you be willing to pay a salary premium of more than 7 percent?

Industry lobbyists claim that H-1Bs are needed because few of our nation's young people have the interest and ability to go into computer science and related fields. That claim is false; computer science enrollment has doubled in the last two years. Yet one wonders why the industry wants more graduates when it is not even bothering to recruit many of them. Even the Information Technology Association of America, which is leading the lobbying effort to increase the H-1B cap, concedes that most IT employers recruit new graduates at only a small number of colleges.

The IT industry is not making good use of the labor pool of experienced workers either. Most firms in the industry, large and small, hire only about 2 percent of their applicants for IT positions. Age discrimination is widespread, with an unemployment rate of 17 percent among computer programmers over age 50. Most don't make it that far. Only 19 percent of those with a computer science degree are still in the field 20 years after graduation, compared with 52 percent for civil engineering. Sun Microsystems, a firm vociferously demanding a higher H-1B quota, classifies as "senior" anyone with six years of experience, say at age 28.

The sky won't fall if the H-1B program is not expanded. On the contrary, without this pool of imported labor to rely on, the industry would be forced to take a closer look at the workers who are already here.

Continued from p. 376
graders from 40 nations.

An education task force set up by the ITAA and the Commerce Department has recommended a wide range of improvements, including:

• Requiring all middle and high school math and science teachers to have at least a bachelor's degree in math or science;

• Requiring four years of physics for all high school students and more advanced mathematics in grades four through eight; and

• Increasing corporate donations for public K-12 education; boosting teacher salaries and having teachers take extra math, science and computer courses.

Educators who have compared the United States with high-performing countries have found that American schools cover too many subjects on a superficial level. For instance, American textbooks are encyclopedic in size, compared with small paperback textbooks used in high-performing countries. Other countries also encourage more independent thinking and group problem-solving, researchers say.

Meanwhile, a plethora of public and private efforts are under way across the country to bring technology to the nation's elementary and secondary schools, many of which don't have the hardware, software or teacher training to make wide use of high-tech. ■

CURRENT SITUATION

Action in Congress

The congressional debate over the cap on foreign temporary workers pits a powerful coalition of computer companies, immigration lawyers and university administrators against labor unions and engineers' groups.

The measure ran into only token opposition in the Senate Judiciary Committee earlier this month, unlike two years ago when former Sen. Alan K. Simpson, R-Wyo., tried to make it harder for employers to import foreign workers. After industry complaints that it would cripple their global competitiveness, Simpson abandoned his efforts, calling the claims "hype and hysteria." [24]

At the time, Simpson was joined by Sen. Edward M. Kennedy, D-Mass., with strong support from then-Labor Secretary Reich. Now Simpson and Reich are out of the picture, and Kennedy's once strong attempts to reform the H-1B program appear tempered.

Caught between his usual labor constituency and strong new pressure from high-tech companies back home, Kennedy offered an alternative measure jointly with Sen. Dianne Feinstein, D-Calif., whose constituency includes Silicon Valley. Their measure was supported by the Clinton administration, which said it "strongly opposes" Abraham's measure to raise the cap.

The Kennedy-Feinstein alternative, which was rejected on an 8-10 vote along party lines, would have raised the cap to 90,000 but limited the visas to three years. It included most of the enforcement enhancements the administration has sought for five years, including requiring employers to first try to recruit Americans and making it illegal to lay off Americans to hire foreigners.

Sen. Abraham at the last minute presented an amended version of his original bill, raising the cap to 95,000 this year and 105,000 each year from 1999 through 2002. In 2003, the number would drop back down to 65,000. Up to 10,000 additional workers could be admitted each year after 1999, if those slots were not used up by physical therapists the previous year. [25]

In an effort to garner bipartisan support, Abraham added provisions sought by both Kennedy and the administration. One would make it illegal to lay off Americans within six months before hiring foreign workers or 90 days afterward. In addition, the Labor Department would be allowed to conduct spot inspections — without waiting for a complaint — but only of employers who had previously violated the law.

The measure was approved 12-6 on April 2, with Democrats Feinstein and Herb Kohl, Wis., joining the panel's 10 Republicans.

The bill provides $50 million in federal matching grants for 20,000 scholarships a year for low-income students studying mathematics, engineering or computer science. Another $10 million would be authorized to train unemployed Americans in new high-tech skills, and $8 million would be used to set up a job bank on the Internet. The money for scholarships, training and the job bank were designed to appease the White House, which had already proposed similar initiatives.

Nonetheless, the administration still opposes Abraham's bill, says Sally Katzen, deputy director of the National Economic Council.

"They made a modest step," she says. "But there's a lot of work that needs to be done. We've been very clear that having employers both recruit and retain U.S. workers is very important."

One of the alternatives suggested by the administration is to require employers to "simply check off a box" attesting that they had tried to hire Americans before recruiting foreign workers, she says. "We believe that request is not unreasonable." The industry staunchly opposes such a requirement because it fears it could delay hiring for years while the Labor Department defines what kind of a recruitment effort employers would have to make.

Katzen points out that the Abraham bill only authorizes money for scholarships and training, without specifying where the money would come from. The

Kennedy-Feinstein bill would have required employers to pay a $250 application fee, raising $100 million, of which $90 million would be used for loans to workers needing training. The other $10 million would be used to develop "regional skills alliances" between government and industry to identify local labor market needs and develop regional strategies for meeting them.

As the Abraham bill awaits full Senate action, the House Immigration Subcommittee was scheduled to hold hearings on the issue April 21. Subcommittee Chairman Rep. Lamar Smith, R-Texas, has promised to propose legislation to raise the cap, but "with safeguards."

Meanwhile the administration recently announced $28 million in new initiatives to bring technology to underserved communities, retrain laid-off workers from other industries and create a Web site listing high-tech job vacancies. ■

OUTLOOK

More Foreign Workers?

Even if Congress raises the cap on foreign workers, it will probably only be the latest round in the eventual globalization of high-tech industry jobs.

"The foreign technical worker has become the drug of choice for American industry," says AEA's Reed. "Make no mistake about it, they are addicted. Within the next four years, they will be back asking for more."

"I don't understand why we should have a quota at all on very high-skilled talent," FirsTel's Rohde says.

"It's an international world now, and this is an international industry. Eighty percent of my revenues come from outside the U.S. If we couldn't hire internationally and if we couldn't sell internationally, we couldn't sur-

vive. This is the wave of the future," says Rohde. "Having an insular mentality about jobs in the U.S. is crazy."

But hiring foreign workers may get harder and costlier, as international competition for foreign workers intensifies, say industry analysts.

"The rest of the world is waking up to the same demand and the same shortages," Gale Fitzgerald, CEO of Computer Task Group, of Buffalo, N.Y., told National Public Radio in February. "I think we should attract as many qualified people [from overseas] as we possibly can to help U.S. industry, but that's a short-term fix. That's not the long-term answer to the U.S.'s problem."

Barring any catastrophic fallout from either the Asia crisis or the Year 2000 computer glitch, most expect the industry's explosive growth to continue for the foreseeable future. Thus most see the current robust job market for high-tech workers continuing unabated.

"I think the demand will be this way for a number of years," said Harvey Shrednick, professor at Ari-

zona State University's College of Business. "Because technology is a continuously changing, continuously competitive environment." [26]

Others are more cautious. They point to skyrocketing computer enrollments at universities, community colleges, technical and vocational schools, as well as increasing internships and computer vocational classes at the high school level. Industry is constantly striving to invent labor-saving software, they say, and if Asia's economic troubles worsen it could spur an exodus of Asian high-tech talent to the United States.

"On top of those pressures, you're going to have all those people who have been diverted to fix the Year 2000 problem out on the labor market in a couple of years," says a Labor Department official. "I worry that when all these kids studying computer science come out on the other end, there isn't going to be anyplace for them to go."

ITAA's Miller dismisses such fears. "The administration needs to get those Neanderthals over at the Labor Department on board."

Model Programs

As the tight labor market becomes a worldwide problem, U.S. companies are investing more in the nation's education infrastructure, and partnerships between industry and educational institutions are proliferating. A number of model programs around the country, including several highlighted in the ITAA task force report, show how industry, academia and government can work together to solve the problem:

• Cisco Systems Inc., of San Jose, Calif., has launched an $18 million program to train more than 1,000 students for entry-level networking positions via a rigorous two-year academic and hands-on training program in 57 high schools and junior colleges.

• Syntel Inc., a Michigan-based computer labor contractor has launched an eight-week "technology boot camp" to provide metropolitan Detroit with well-trained junior software programmers.

• The Tech Corps, a national organization with chapters in 40 states, recruits IT professionals to volunteer in their local schools to help install and integrate new technologies into the curriculum.

• Microsoft has teamed up with the nonprofit Green Thumb organization in a pilot program to provide IT training to low-income older workers in three cities. Microsoft has also committed $7 million plus software and technical assistance to 25 community colleges over a five-year period to train unemployed or underemployed workers, welfare recipients, single parents, legal immigrants and the disabled in IT skills.

• Omaha's Applied Information Management Institute is perhaps the most comprehensive example of regional coordination. The institute is a consortium of 34 businesses, 10 colleges and universities, the chamber of commerce and the state government. It helps develop IT curriculums, sponsors publicity campaigns encouraging students to consider computer careers and offers paid internships at local businesses.

The institute also established an on-line mentoring project pairing students with professional advisers, sponsors an on-line Virtual Career Fair and holds a one-week summer Cyber Camp for middle and high school students. The group also gave scholarships to 22 elementary and secondary teachers to develop technology-oriented curricula to share with other Nebraska teachers.

"The good news is that there's a lot of stuff going on," Miller says "The marketplace is responding. I see a lot of good old-fashioned American ingenuity trying to solve the problem."

It will also take a collaborative effort, says Secretary Daley. "We are at an economic crossroads, and we have to work harder until education catches up with innovation. That will require a strong partnership between government, the private sector, labor groups, high schools, trade schools, community colleges and academia." [27]

Kathy Koch is a freelance writer in the Washington, D.C., area.

Notes

[1] From a speech to the Third Annual Technology for Learning Summit, Los Angeles, Calif., June 25, 1997.

[2] Testimony before Senate Judiciary Immigration Subcommittee, Feb. 25, 1998.

[3] Speech to the Commonwealth Club and San Jose, Calif., Chamber of Commerce, June 26, 1997.

[4] Dexter Kozen and Stu Zweben, "Undergrad Enrollments Keep Booming, Grad Enrollments Holding Their Own," *Computing Research News*, March 1998.

[5] Technology for Learning Summit, *op. cit.*

[6] Testimony before Senate Judiciary Immigration Subcommittee, Feb. 25, 1998.

[7] Carnes spoke on National Public Radio's "Science Friday," Feb. 27, 1998.

[8] Norman Matloff, "Debunking the Myth of a Desperate Software Labor Shortage," University of California, Davis, 1998.

[9] "Help Wanted: A Call for Collaborative Action for the New Millennium," Information Technology Association of America and Virginia Polytechnic Institute and State University, 1998.

[10] "Information Technology: Assessment of The Department of Commerce's Report on Workforce Demand and Supply," General Accounting Office, March 23, 1998.

[11] Jack A. Bobo and Susan Tinch Johnson, "Software Workers for the New Millennium: Global Competitiveness Hangs in the Balance," National Software Alliance, 1998.

[12] "America's New Deficit: The Shortage of Information Technology Workers," Department of Commerce, September 1997.

[13] "Update: America's New Deficit," Department of Commerce, Office of Technology Policy, January 1998.

[14] T.J. Rodgers, "Give Us Your Tired, Your Poor — and Your Engineers," *The Wall Street Journal*, March 9, 1998.

[15] Demetrios G. Papademetriou and Stephen Yale-Loehr, *Balancing Interests: Rethinking U.S. Selection of Skilled Immigrants*, Carnegie Endowment for International Peace, 1996.

[16] Quoted in Matloff, *op. cit.*

[17] Edward Yourdon, *The Rise and Resurrection of the American Programmer*, 1996.

[18] From remarks to the Chicago Economic Club, Dec. 18, 1997.

[19] Testimony before Senate Judiciary Committee, Sept. 28, 1995.

[20] David S. North, *Soothing the Establishment: The Impact of Foreign-Born Scientists and Engineers on America* (1995).

[21] Stuart Anderson, "Employment-Based Immigration and High Technology," *Empower America*, 1996.

[22] "The Department of Labor's Foreign Labor Certification Programs: The System Is Broken and Needs to Be Fixed," Office of Inspector General, Department of Labor, May 1996.

[23] Quoted in the *Los Angeles Times*, July 15, 1996.

[24] Quoted in *CQ Weekly Report*, March 30, 1996.

[25] Until last year, the largest users of H-1B visas were hospitals importing physical therapists. Last year, for the first time, computer companies became the largest user of H-1B visas.

[26] Quoted in Rochelle Garner, "Pressure Gap: Transforming the IT Workforce," *Computerworld*, Feb. 2, 1998.

[27] Technology for Learning Summit, *op. cit.*

Bibliography

Selected Sources Used

Books

North, David S., *Soothing the Establishment: The Impact of Foreign-Born Scientists and Engineers on America*, University Press of America, 1995.

A former Labor Department official studies the economic impact of the steady growth in the number of foreign-born scientists and engineers on graduate schools, university faculties and industry. He concludes that they have depressed wages and thus discouraged native-born students from pursuing engineering and science careers.

Papademetriou, Demetrios G., and Stephen Yale-Loehr, *Balancing Interests: Rethinking U.S. Selection of Skilled Immigrants*, Carnegie Endowment for International Peace, 1996.

Two analysts with the International Migration Policy Program of the Carnegie Endowment for International Peace examine U.S. policy regarding both permanent and temporary immigration of skilled workers.

Yourdon, Edward, *Decline and Fall of the American Programmer*, Yourdon Press, 1992.

Software industry expert Yourdon warns that American programmers may be replaced by talented and much cheaper programmers in India, Russia, Brazil, Singapore and Manila. To survive, the American software industry must restructure and re-engineer itself, increasing productivity and quality at the same time.

Yourdon, Edward, *Rise and Resurrection of the American Programmer*, Prentice Hall, 1996.

Software industry expert Yourdon revisits his previous dire predictions about the decline of the American software industry, and says that higher-paid American programmers have been "saved" from competition from cheaper overseas programmers by the introduction of visually oriented software development tools, which helped boost productivity.

Reports and Studies

Anderson, Stuart, "Employment-Based Immigration and High Technology," *Empower America*, 1996.

The author, who wrote this report before becoming director of immigration research and analysis for the Senate Judiciary Subcommittee on Immigration, argues that immigrants are a catalyst for economic growth and do not displace American workers or depress American wages. Instead, immigrants create jobs, the author argues.

Bobo, Jack A., and Susan Tinch Johnson, "Software Workers for the New Millennium: Global Competitiveness Hangs in the Balance," *National Software Alliance*, Arlington, Va., January 1998.

This in-depth look at the computer industry contends that America can't produce enough computer workers to fill the current shortfall without importing more workers. The authors argue that more effort should be made to recruit and train/retrain American workers.

Department of Commerce, Office of Technology Policy, "America's New Deficit: The Shortage of Information Technology Workers," September 1997.

The Department of Commerce concluded that the growth of high-tech jobs exceeds America's ability to produce enough skilled workers to fill those jobs. To boost that argument, it says the country will need 95,000 new high tech workers a year in each of the next ten years, but that U.S. universities only awarded 24,553 bachelors' degrees in computer and information science in 1994.

Department of Commerce, Office of Technology Policy, "Update: America's New Deficit," January 1998.

This study, which updates the department's September study (above), finds that the country will need 137,800 new computer workers a year between 1996 and 2006.

Information Technology Association of America and Virginia Polytechnic Institute and State University, "Help Wanted: A Call for Collaborative Action for the New Millennium," 1998

This study by the information technology industry trade association contends there are 346,000 vacant IT jobs in the United States, representing a "severe shortage" of skilled workers.

Matloff, Norman, "A Critical Look at Immigration's Role in the U.S. Computer Industry," University of California at Davis, August 1997.

The industry critic and computer science professor examines computer hiring and employment practices. Matloff says the industry casts aside mid-career professionals in order to hire foreign nationals because they will work for less in order to get the employer to sponsor them for permanent immigrant status.

Matloff, Norman, "Debunking the Myth of a Desperate Software Labor Shortage," University of California at Davis, 1998.

The computer professor who has become a thorn in the side of the computer industry argues that there is no shortage of software workers, but that the computer industry is trying to scare Congress into allowing more foreign nationals into the country.

The Next Step

Additional information from UMI's Newspaper & Periodical Abstracts™ database

Age Discrimination

DeBare, Ilana, and Tom Abate, "Tech Help Scarce — Or Not? Older Workers Finding Doors Closed to Them," *San Francisco Chronicle*, **March 9, 1998, p. B1.**

Silicon Valley executives have focused national attention on the high-tech labor market in recent weeks by lobbying for more temporary-work visas for foreign engineers. But some older high-tech workers say it's hard for them to find jobs. "High-tech companies want the right person with the right skills, who can go from 0 to 60 miles per hour in 0 seconds flat," said Chris Benner of Working Partnerships, a nonprofit group affiliated with the South Bay Labor Council in San Jose.

Johnson, Maryfran, "Silicon Shame," *Computerworld*, **Oct. 20, 1997, p. 36.**

Age discrimination seems to be a nasty fact of life among the high-tech enterprises of California's Silicon Valley.

King, Julia, "Are Hiring Managers Just Being Too Picky?" *Computerworld*, **Jan. 19, 1998, p. 16.**

It is argued that there is no high-tech labor shortage — it's all a myth, perpetuated by picky employers who refuse to hire the vast number of workers with experience in older technologies.

Matloff, Norman, "Now Hiring! If You're Young," *The New York Times*, **Jan. 26, 1998, p. A19.**

Readers of recent reports about a shortage of computer programmers would be baffled if they also knew that careers in computer programming tend to be short-lived. According to a survey conducted by the National Science Foundation and the Census Bureau, six years after finishing college, 57 percent of computer science graduates are working as programmers, at 15 years the figure drops to 34 percent, and at 20 years — when most are still only in their early 40's — it is down to 19 percent.

Labor Shortages

Abate, Tom, "New Bill on Tech Workers Is More Like a Legislative Gun," *San Francisco Chronicle*, **March 18, 1998, p. C3.**

Three weeks ago, Rep. James P. Moran, D-Va., introduced a bill to make it easier to import at least 15,000 permanent foreign engineers yearly. The affected workers don't need Department of Labor approval to take permanent jobs with U.S. firms, speeding the entry of permanent tech workers. Otherwise, the DOL can take six months or more to certify new permanent foreign workers.

Behr, Peter, "A Program for Producing Techies; Area Pilot Project Training Workers From Other Fields," *The Washington Post*, **Jan. 29, 1998, p. E1.**

This information-technology project offers a solution for employees and employers. If students pay their own way through three months of computer-technology training, they will be offered paid internships at companies, including several big information-technology firms. The project rests on a unique compact between the students and Washington-area employers in dire need of technicians.

Bronson, Po, "Manager's Journal: Silicon Valley, the Workers' Paradise," *The Wall Street Journal*, **Aug. 25, 1997, p. A18.**

The author comments on the problems Silicon Valley high-tech companies are having recruiting qualified employees.

Chandrasekara, Rajiv, "U.S. Cites Shortage of High-Tech Workers," *The Washington Post*, **Sept. 30, 1997, p. C3.**

The Commerce Department, joining a chorus of technology industry leaders, yesterday issued its first warning that a growing shortage of workers with cutting-edge computer skills could hinder the nation's economic growth. In delivering that message, officials said the Commerce and Education departments would take the unusual step of working with the technology industry to jointly propose solutions to the labor shortage through a series of task forces and a nationwide summit.

Chandrasekara, Rajiv, "U.S. to Train Workers for Tech Jobs; Initiative Seeks to Increase Ranks of Skilled Employees; 1 in 10 Positions Now Unfilled," *The Washington Post*, **Jan. 12, 1998, p. A1.**

The Clinton administration will announce today a broad and unique federal effort to help train more computer programmers, responding to concerns from economists and business leaders that U.S. companies have a critical shortage of skilled technology workers.

DeBare, Ilana, "High-Tech Careers for Low-Tech Workers," *San Francisco Chronicle*, **Jan. 26, 1998, p. E1.**

The trend of high-tech firms recruiting professionals with backgrounds weak in computer technology is featured.

DeBare, Ilana, "Job Boom Goes Beyond High-Tech: Bay Firms Scramble to Find Workers," *San Francisco Chronicle*, **Oct. 6, 1997, p. B1.**

Garner Gremillion received five separate job offers within two weeks of moving to the Bay Area early this year. Most paid more than $70,000 yearly. All were at least 20 percent higher than what he'd been earning before. And his multiple job offers are a sign of how heated parts of the Bay Area job market have become this year — not just the market for computer professionals, but for everyone from construction workers to cappuccino servers.

Estrada, Richard, "Matching High-Tech Jobs with Ill-Prepared Workers," *Chicago Tribune*, Jan. 20, 1998, p. 13.

If idle hands make work for the devil, much of the industrialized world today is Beelzebub bait. As the United Nations and an army of labor economists have long argued, the globalization of the marketplace figures to make joblessness and underemployment two major challenges of the 21st century.

Gomes, Lee, "Filling High-Tech Jobs Is Getting Very Tough," *The Wall Street Journal*, Dec. 1, 1997, p. A1.

The much-discussed shortage of skilled information-technology workers is entering a new phase. A recent Commerce Department study shows there are 100,000 new computer jobs each year, but only 25,000 computer-related bachelor's degrees. This year, an estimated three out of every 10 computer-related vacancies will take six months or longer to fill, up from two in 10 a year ago. Because of those empty desks, companies are cutting back programming projects, delaying new products and trimming expansion plans.

Rosenberg, Ronald, "Help Wanted: Desperately Seeking . . . For Start-Ups, Hiring High-Tech Workers is a Daunting Task," *The Boston Globe*, Sept. 14, 1997, p. E4.

Entrepreneurs say they have distinct challenges when recruiting high-tech workers. With relatively little money for recruiting, they often rely on friends or an informal network of peers and university sources to find people, bypassing traditional job recruiters, newspaper advertising and job fairs.

Simons, John, "GAO Questions Studies Showing U.S. Is Short on Skilled High-Tech Workers" *The Wall Street Journal*, March 24, 1998, p. B6.

Government analysts are questioning the methodology of two oft-quoted studies showing the United States suffers a shortage of skilled high-tech workers. The General Accounting Office said it doesn't dispute the existence of a shortage; it does question how large the shortage really is, however, and the logic and methodology used to quantify it.

Immigration Quotas

Kaufman, Jonathan, "Foreign Legions: A U.S. Recruiter Goes Far Afield to Bring In High-Tech Workers — On the Coastline of Brazil, John Nyhan Interviews Dozens Eager to Leave — 'But My Mother Is So Upset'," *The Wall Street Journal*, Jan. 8, 1998, p. A1.

Even with salaries starting at $55,000, recruiting foreign talent is cheaper than hiring Americans. Companies are going farther afield to find workers. Indeed, many are setting up off-shore computer-programming facilities to take advantage of lower labor costs abroad and recruiting programmers overseas to work in the United States.

Pear, Robert, "Higher Quota Urged for Immigrant Technology Workers," *The New York Times*, Feb. 23, 1998, p. A13.

Under pressure from Congress and the computer industry, the White House is seriously considering proposals to increase the immigration quota for computer scientists and other information technology workers, so that foreigners can fill thousands of U.S. job openings.

Van Slambrouck, Paul, "Key Import: Keen Minds Shortage of High-Tech Workers Drives Debate About Visas and the Direction of America's 21st-Century Workplace," *The Christian Science Monitor*, March 23, 1998, p. 1.

Filling high-tech vacancies, in the short term, is pitting the growing political strength of the technology sector against the traditional muscle of big labor, as well as groups opposed to increased immigration. And filling them in the long term is spurring new thinking among government, schools and industry. The immediate flash point is a legislative effort to fill the top-end jobs by expanding a program that permits 65,000 immigrants each year under H-1B visas.

Wilgoren, Jodi, "California: News and Insight on Business in the Golden State; Industry Pleads for More High-Tech Visas," *Los Angeles Times*, Feb. 26, 1998, p. D2.

Leaders of the burgeoning information-technology industry — including several from Silicon Valley — told a key U.S. Senate committee Wednesday that an acute labor shortage threatens their global competitiveness unless a cap on the number of skilled foreign workers allowed into the country is lifted.

Zitner, Aaron, "More Visas for Workers Are Sought: U.S. Firms Say Foreigners Needed to Fill Jobs," *The Boston Globe*, March 8, 1998, p. A1.

Massachusetts software and computer companies say business is so strong that their biggest problem is an acute shortage of engineers and scientists. Keane Inc. of Boston has hired 100 recruiters to keep the 8,600-worker company staffed. The chairman of EMC Corp. of Hopkinton has taken to trolling the halls at local colleges for recruits.

"High-Tech Firms Seek Quick Fix," *San Francisco Chronicle*, March 2, 1998, p. A20.

The leaders of some of the nation's leading high-tech companies described to Congress the national shortage of highly skilled workers in dire terms. Microsoft, for example, said it could not fill half of the 2,500 technical positions it had available last year. The Senate Judiciary Committee heard similar tales of desperation from other big-name players.

Back Issues

Great Research on Current Issues Starts Right Here.
Recent topics covered by The CQ Researcher are listed below.

Now available on the Web

For information, call (800) 432-2250 ext. 279 or (202) 887-6279.

If you would like to have any of these CQ Researchers updated, or need more information about these topics, please call CQ Custom Research. Special rates for CQ subscribers. (202) 887-8600 or (800) 432-2250, ext. 600, or E-mail Custom.Research@cq.com

Back issues are available for $5.00 (subscribers) or $10.00 (non-subscribers). Quantity discounts apply to orders over 10. To order, call Congressional Quarterly Customer Service at (202) 887-8621.

Binders are available for $18.00. To order call 1-800-638-1710. Please refer to stock number 648.

Future Topics

▶ *Census Controversy*

▶ *Child-Care Options*

▶ *Alzheimer's Disease*

The CQ Researcher

PUBLISHED BY CONGRESSIONAL QUARTERLY INC.

Census 2000

What is the best way to get an accurate count?

The next national census is two years away, but it is already the subject of a fierce, partisan battle in Washington. The Census Bureau wants to use statistical sampling techniques to try to reduce the "undercount" — the difference between the number of people missed by the census and the number who were counted twice. Scientific experts generally favor this method. So do many big-city mayors and civil rights leaders, who believe that the people most likely to be missed are minorities and the poor, especially in urban centers. But Republicans in Congress say that sampling violates the Constitution's call for an "actual enumeration" of the population and invites political manipulation by the Clinton administration. The debate is expected to continue right up to Census Day — April 1, 2000 — and beyond.

C_Q | May 1, 1998 • Volume 8, No. 17 • Pages 385-408

Formerly Editorial Research Reports

COVER: PHOTO COURTESY OF U.S. BUREAU OF THE CENSUS

CQ Researcher

May 1, 1998
Volume 8, No.17

EDITOR
Sandra Stencel

MANAGING EDITOR
Thomas J. Colin

ASSOCIATE EDITOR
Sarah M. Magner

STAFF WRITERS
Adriel Bettelheim
Mary H. Cooper
Kenneth Jost
Kathy Koch
David Masci

PRODUCTION EDITOR
Melissa Hall

EDITORIAL ASSISTANT
Laura S. Cavender

PUBLISHED BY
Congressional Quarterly Inc.

CHAIRMAN
Andrew Barnes

VICE CHAIRMAN
Andrew P. Corty

PRESIDENT AND PUBLISHER
Robert W. Merry

EXECUTIVE EDITOR
David Rapp

The CQ Researcher (ISSN 1056-2036). Formerly Editorial Research Reports. Published weekly, except Jan. 2, May 29, July 3, Oct. 30, by Congressional Quarterly Inc., 1414 22nd St., N.W., Washington, D.C. 20037. Annual subscription rate for libraries, businesses and government is $340. Additional rates furnished upon request. Periodicals postage paid at Washington, D.C., and additional mailing offices. POSTMASTER: Send address changes to The CQ Researcher, 1414 22nd St., N.W., Washington, D.C. 20037.

Census 2000

BY KENNETH JOST

THE ISSUES

Katherine Trimnal has been a cheerleader for the census since she was a teenager. In 1960, Trimnal prevailed on her Greek-American parents to complete the census questionnaire that was mailed to their South Carolina home. "They didn't understand what it was all about," Trimnal recalls. "A lot of times people are suspicious when they get something from the government."

Today, Trimnal is a member of a citizens advisory group that is working with the U.S. Bureau of the Census to encourage people in her home state to participate in a "dress rehearsal" for the 2000 census — one of three trial runs now being conducted across the country.

Trimnal, a 51-year-old author living in the state capital of Columbia, still views it as a civic duty to fill out the census questionnaire. But she also tells her fellow South Carolinians that a complete count will mean more federal money for the state and their communities.

"When you figure out the dollars that come back to the states, you see that it's really important," Trimnal says. "It all depends on the data that comes back from the census. This has been a real eye-opener for me."

The Constitution requires that a census be conducted every 10 years to determine how many seats each state gets in the House of Representatives. In addition, the population figures from the decennial census — the most comprehensive of the many "censuses" conducted by the Census Bureau — are used to allocate funds to state and local governments for various federal assistance programs, including community development and law enforcement block grants.

Despite the political and financial stakes, the Census Bureau, part of the U.S. Department of Commerce, faces a

massive challenge in counting all Americans — first in trying to find everyone and then in getting them to return the census form without the labor-intensive, and expensive, process of sending census "enumerators" on door-to-door visits.

Now a fierce, partisan battle is raging in Washington over the bureau's plans to change its methods to try to get the most accurate count possible two years from now. At issue is the use of "statistical sampling" to make an estimate rather than an actual count of the country's population.

President Clinton and Democratic lawmakers support the change in methodology as the best, most cost-effective way to correct, or at least reduce, the acknowledged "undercount" of Americans from previous censuses. Civil rights organizations and many big-city mayors agree, believing that the people most likely to be missed are minorities and the poor, especially in urban centers.

But Republican lawmakers, including House Speaker Newt Gingrich of Georgia and Senate Majority Leader Trent Lott of Mississippi, are bitterly opposed to the use of sampling and are pulling out all the stops to try to block the plan. They say the method amounts to nothing more than guesswork and invites Democratic administration to manipulate the numbers for partisan gain. They also say sampling would not meet the constitutional requirement that the government conduct "an actual enumeration" of the popula-

tion every 10 years.

"The Republicans are convinced that this is just a big Democratic plot," says Margo Anderson, a professor of history at the University of Wisconsin in Milwaukee and author of a history of the census. "And the Democrats are convinced the Republicans are out to lower the population counts in areas that vote Democratic."

The census has become increasingly contentious since the 1960s. The political and legal controversies peaked 10 years ago when the Bush administration rejected the Census Bureau's recommendation to make a statistical adjustment to correct for the undercount in the 1990 census. Today, the bureau estimates that the "net undercount" — the difference between the number of people missed and the number counted twice — was 1.6-1.8 percent in 1990, or 4.0-4.7 million people. *(See chart, p. 388.)*

Most troubling to critics of the current methodology, the undercount was higher in 1990 than it was in 1980, making it the first population count in recent history to be less accurate than the one before. And the undercounts of African-Americans and other minorities were the largest ever recorded, both in absolute terms and relative to the white population.

The problems prompted Congress and the Census Bureau to re-examine the process to try to figure out how to reduce the undercount. The result was a plan to adopt estimating techniques widely used in other contexts — from public opinion polls and market research to the several specialized social and economic censuses conducted by the Census Bureau itself. [1] The plan was endorsed by scientific groups and a range of other experts, including the Bush administration's census director, Barbara Everitt Bryant, who had unsuccessfully urged use of a statistical adjustment to correct for the undercount in 1990.

Census Undercount Has Fallen Since 1940, but It Rose in 1990

The net undercount — the difference between the number of people missed and the number who were counted twice — was higher in 1990 than it was in 1980, making it the first population count in recent history to be less accurate than the one before. The undercount of African-Americans was the largest ever recorded, both in absolute terms and relative to the white population.

Net Population Undercount by Demographic Analysis*

Undercount Rates and Numbers	1940	1950	1960	1970	1980	1990
Total						
Population (millions)	131.7	150.7	179.3	203.3	226.6	248.7
Undercount rate (%)	5.4	4.1	3.1	2.7	1.2	1.8
Net Undercount (millions)	7.0	6.3	5.6	5.5	2.8	4.7
Non-blacks						
Population (millions)	118.8	135.7	160.5	180.7	199.9	218.2
Undercount rate (%)	5.0	3.8	2.7	2.2	0.8	1.3
Net Undercount (millions)	5.9	5.2	4.3	4.0	1.6	2.9
Blacks						
Population (millions)	12.9	15.0	18.9	22.6	26.7	30.5
Undercount rate (%)	8.4	7.5	6.6	6.5	4.5	5.7
Net Undercount (millions)	1.1	1.1	1.3	1.5	1.2	1.8
Difference: black-non-black						
Net undercount rate	3.4	3.6	3.9	4.3	3.7	4.4

* *Demographic analysis uses birth and death records to estimate the undercount. A second technique — the post-enumeration survey — estimates the net undercount on the basis of a survey of randomly selected households after the official census. The post-enumeration survey for 1990 indicated a net undercount of 1.6 percent, slightly lower than the figure derived from demographic analysis.*

Note: Alaska and Hawaii became states in 1959. For 1950 and earlier, the population data and undercount estimates are for the 48 coterminous states. For 1960 and after, the data include Alaska and Hawaii.

Source: Bureau of the Census, cited in Barry Edmonston and Charles Schultze (eds.), Modernizing the U.S. Census, *National Academy of Sciences, 1995.*

As Census 2000 neared, however, Republicans came to view the use of statistical sampling as a political threat, one that could even endanger their control of the House of Representatives. Clark Bensen, a political consultant to Republicans on redistricting issues, circulated a memo saying that the use of sampling could have shifted the results in 24 House races in 1990 — a large enough number to wipe out the GOP's current 227-205 edge in the House. [2]

Last year, Republicans in Congress tried to prohibit the Census Bureau from using sampling altogether. A presidential veto blocked the move, but the Republicans later succeeded in inserting into the Commerce Department's annual spending bill a provision forcing the Census Bureau to use its traditional enumeration methods in one of the three dress rehearsals being conducted this year. In addition, the law sought to provide a mechanism for an early court ruling on the Republicans' constitutional challenge to the use of sampling.

Census Bureau officials insist that sampling is the only way to correct the net undercount. "We've been trying to improve the accuracy without sampling, and we haven't been able to get rid of the differential," says John Thompson, the bureau's associate director and director of the decennial census management division.

Census Bureau officials and Democratic lawmakers emphasize the support for sampling from scientific groups and accuse Republicans of purely partisan motivations in opposing it. "I thought the census was for the country, not for a particular party but for the country," says

Rep. Carolyn B. Maloney, a New York Democrat and ranking minority member on the House Government Reform and Oversight Subcommittee on the Census.

But GOP lawmakers argue that the Census Bureau's sampling plan is flawed both in theory and — in the bureau's work so far — in practice. Instead of sampling, congressional Republicans and other critics argue that the Census Bureau should work harder to find and count everyone.

"We need to do the best we can," says Census Subcommittee Chairman Rep. Dan Miller, a Florida Republican. "But to say we can adjust the population to get the population that we think is correct, you just can't do that."

Meanwhile, Census Bureau officials are hard at work on the three dress rehearsals being conducted in an 11-county area of South Carolina, on the Menominee Indian Reservation in northern Wisconsin and in Sacramento, Calif. In all three sites, bureau personnel are trying out many of the steps recommended to improve coverage, such as compiling more complete address files, making more extensive use of community "partnerships" with local governments and private groups and — for the first time ever — using paid advertising to encourage people to return questionnaires. (See story, p. 396.)

Census 2000 will also provide the first use of a new method of asking Americans about their racial and ethnic backgrounds. Under a directive issued by the Office of Management and Budget (OMB) last fall, census forms will allow individuals to check more than one box to indicate their racial background — for example, white and African-American. The change represents a compromise to the demands from advocacy groups representing people of mixed racial and ethnic backgrounds for a new "multiracial" category in the census.

As Census Bureau officials prepare to tally the results of their dress rehearsals, and lawmakers on Capitol Hill continue to spar over the prepa-

rations for Census 2000, here are some of the questions being debated:

Would the use of statistical sampling produce a more accurate count for the decennial census?

The accuracy of the decennial census has been disputed ever since the first nationwide count in 1790. President George Washington believed the final count — 3,929,214 — was low. Thomas Jefferson, who directed the census, agreed. But Jefferson himself was double-counted: once at his home in Monticello and once in the then capital city of Philadelphia.

Today, nearly all census experts acknowledge that there has been a significant undercount for decades. There is also widespread agreement among statistical experts that some use of sampling to estimate the number and characteristics of people who do not return the mailed questionnaires represents the most practicable way to improve the accuracy of the count.

A few statisticians, however, doubt the potential for improving accuracy through sampling. Political critics echo those doubts and add their own accusations that sampling is both unconstitutional and rife with the potential for political manipulation.

Sampling advocates point out that such techniques are used in all sorts of statistical work — from public opinion polling and economic data to medicine and public health. They also point out that three panels appointed by the National Academy of Sciences have endorsed the use of sampling. "We're very confident that it will be more accurate," says Keith Rust, chairman of one of the panels and a vice president of Westat Inc., a research company based in Rockville, Md.

A blue-ribbon panel of the American Statistical Association also has endorsed sampling. In a report issued in 1996, the panel said sampling potentially can in-

crease the accuracy of the count while reducing costs, and "is consistent with the best statistical practice." [3]

Census Bureau officials themselves say sampling is a necessary response to the fact that fewer and fewer people — only about 65 percent in the 1990 census — are returning the mailed questionnaires. "We'd be happy if everybody mailed back their forms, but they don't," says Thompson, the bureau's associate director.

Under the plan for Census 2000, bureau enumerators will make door-to-door visits to "a scientifically selected sample" of non-responding households. The visits will continue until the enumerators reach about 90 percent of all households in each census tract (about 4,000 people or 1,700 housing units). Information gathered from the visits will be used to estimate the characteristics of the households not included in the sample.

Census enumerators will then go back to 750,000 randomly selected households nationwide to determine whether they were included in the initial count. By comparing the results of the first and second counts, the bureau will determine the number of people who were missed, the number of people who were counted twice or counted in the wrong place and the net undercount. [4]

Skeptics question whether these steps will actually improve the accuracy of the count. "I just don't think this thing is going to work," says David A. Freedman, a professor of statistics at the University of California at Berkeley, adding there are "ample opportunities for error" in the bureau's sampling plan. Among the potential problems, he says, are people who are counted twice, or in the wrong place; people who move between census day and the follow-up day; a baby born after census day, who should not be counted, or someone who dies between census day and the follow-up, who should be. "None of these [errors] will be large," Freedman says. "But the aggregate of these small errors can easily add up." [5]

Another critic, Peter Skerry, a political

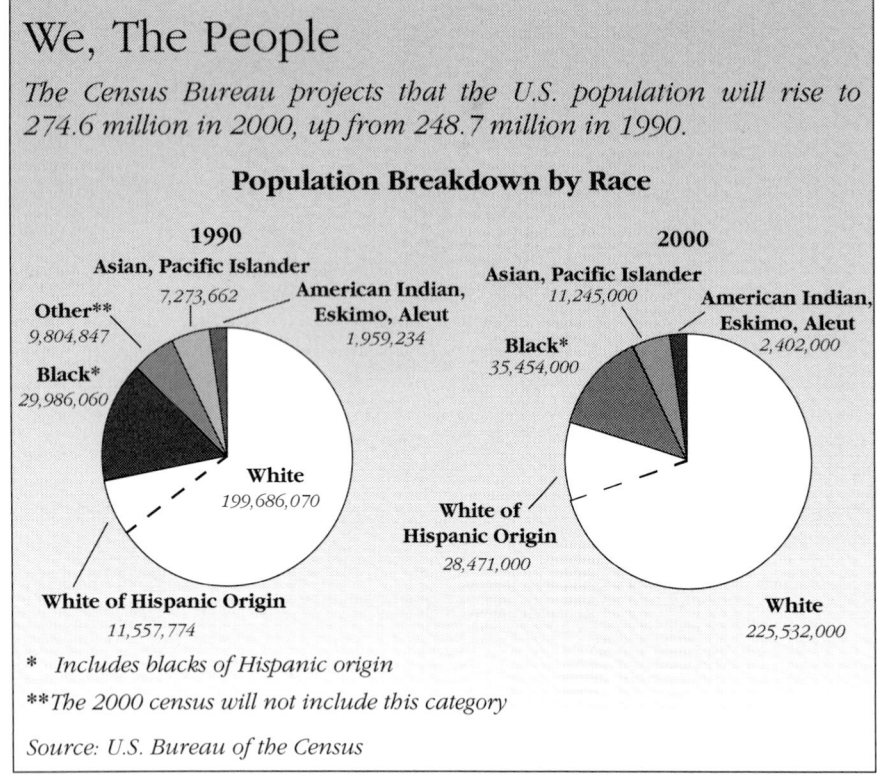

We, The People

The Census Bureau projects that the U.S. population will rise to 274.6 million in 2000, up from 248.7 million in 1990.

Population Breakdown by Race

1990

Asian, Pacific Islander
7,273,662

American Indian, Eskimo, Aleut
1,959,234

Other**
9,804,847

Black*
29,986,060

White
199,686,070

White of Hispanic Origin
11,557,774

2000

Asian, Pacific Islander
11,245,000

American Indian, Eskimo, Aleut
2,402,000

Black*
35,454,000

White of Hispanic Origin
28,471,000

White
225,532,000

* *Includes blacks of Hispanic origin*

***The 2000 census will not include this category*

Source: U.S. Bureau of the Census

scientist at Claremont McKenna College in Claremont, Calif., says that even if sampling produces better data at the national and state levels, it will not ensure the accuracy of information for smaller geographical or political divisions. "The problem is at the substate levels, down to the block levels, where the variance due to sampling is very large," Skerry says. "And I don't know anybody who argues at that level that the numbers will be more accurate across the board."

Republican lawmakers and political figures attack sampling more pointedly by insisting that it opens the door to manipulation of the figures by the Census Bureau to benefit the Democratic administration. "Whereas you know that the numbers coming out of the full head count are not correct, you at least know that they're objective," says political consultant Bensen.

Democratic lawmakers and political figures dismiss the Republicans' concerns. They insist that the Census Bureau has a proven record of professionalism, but

they also say that manipulation is simply not possible. "Once the numbers come in, you can't manipulate them for partisan gain," says Jeffrey Wice, an attorney who has worked for Democratic party organizations on redistricting issues.

James Holmes, the acting director of the Census Bureau, goes further, saying that sampling actually reduces the opportunity for any manipulation. "In an environment where you use statistical methods, there are fewer opportunities for playing with the numbers than in an environment where you do an actual count," Holmes says. "In a sampling environment, you don't really know exactly which units have been targeted for follow-up until the sampling has been drawn up."

Outside Washington, the business community has followed the sampling debate with interest but generally without taking sides. Kenneth Hodges, a director of demography at Claritas Corp., which sells population data research to businesses, says he personally supports sampling even though there may be

some risk of tinkering with the numbers. "Maybe the one thing that scares me more than a census with sampling is a census without sampling," Hodges says. "We pretty well know what that's going to result in: a less accurate census than possible."

Will the option to list multiple racial backgrounds on the decennial census hurt civil rights enforcement or affirmative action?

The United States has been counting, or not counting, by race ever since the first census in 1790. The Constitution specified that the census add to "the whole number of free persons," including indentured servants, three-fifths of the number of slaves ("all other persons"). The tally was to exclude "untaxed Indians."

The abolition of slavery after the Civil War ended the fractionation of African-Americans. All Native Americans have been counted since the 1940 census. And over the years racial and ethnic categories have been added to the census in order to count Asians and Pacific Islanders and persons of Hispanic origin.

Over the past two decades, persons of mixed racial backgrounds have been lobbying for their own "multiracial" category in the census. Established civil rights groups — those representing African-Americans, Asian-Americans and Pacific Islanders, Hispanics and Native Americans — have opposed the idea, fearing that a multiracial category would dilute their own numbers and political influence. Last year, the Office of Management and Budget approved a compromise. It rejected a separate multiracial category, but directed all federal agencies, including the Census Bureau, to allow individuals to check more than one racial category to indicate a multiracial background.

The compromise has not ended the

debate, however. Many people of multi-racial backgrounds say they still want a separate category, while traditional civil rights groups continue to worry that the tabulation of the data could weaken the enforcement of anti-discrimination laws and the implementation of already embattled affirmative action policies. [6]

"The 'more than one box' option still poses serious risks to the appropriate use of data in a way that protects the interests of minority populations in this country," says Wade Henderson, executive director of the Leadership Conference on Civil Rights, an umbrella organization representing some 185 civil rights groups.

But the head of one of the multiracial advocacy groups that still wants a separate category says other civil rights groups are insensitive to the need for people of multiple racial backgrounds to have a way of affirming their identities. "This is no different from the people who have been fighting for the right to determine what they are called," says Susan Graham, executive director of the Georgia-based organization Project Race, referring to the continuing debate over nomenclature for the major racial and ethnic minority groups. "If appropriate names are important for those communities, I should think that they should understand why an appropriate name is important for the multiracial community."

But the Association of Multiethnic Americans supports the compromise. Ramona Douglass, head of the California-based organization, says she is "satisfied" with the more-than-one-box option because it serves to weaken the so-called "one-drop" rule. "It dispels the myth that if you have one drop of minority blood, you're that person," says Douglass, daughter of an Italian-American mother and a father of mixed Native American and African-American ancestry. "Prior to [the OMB directive], it was not acknowledged that a person was the sum total of all his heritages."

In announcing its decision last fall, OMB said the multiple-box option allowed the collection of "more detailed information" while emphasizing that racial or ethnic categories were to reflect "self-identification" rather than governmental definition. [7] An administration official, interviewed on a not-for-attribution basis, said the separate multiracial category was rejected in part because it "wouldn't yield information about specific racial backgrounds."

Civil rights groups accepted the OMB compromise, but they still worry that the tabulation of the data will make it harder for so-called protected minority groups to use racial statistics to prove discrimination, to increase minority groups' voting power through redistricting or to design affirmative action programs. "We are concerned that people who identify in protected classes right now won't be counted, or we won't be able to derive that information from the data they're presenting," says Eric Rodriguez, a policy analyst working on census issues for the National Council of La Raza, a Hispanic advocacy group.

Native American groups were especially concerned about a possible reduction in their numbers because of the high rate of intermarriage among their population. "For Indian people, it is a little more important to have higher numbers, because some of the money we get from the federal government is based on our numbers," says Jack Jackson Jr., director of government affairs for the National Congress of American Indians.

In its order, OMB said agencies should provide "as much detailed information on race and ethnicity as possible." But it acknowledged that some combinations of racial backgrounds might yield small numbers and have to be "collapsed" with other combinations. The administration official stressed that the tabulation issues are still being worked on by an interagency committee. But the

official said that Justice Department lawyers have described the directive as "a reasonable solution in terms of the data that will be available for work that's carried out by the enforcement agencies."

"There's no perfect way to tabulate this," concludes Karen Narasaki, executive director of the national Asian Pacific American Legal Consortium in Washington. "There's no way that's going to satisfy everybody or anybody. We think in the civil rights context that there's going to be litigation over this for years to come."

Is there a less expensive way to take the census?

The cost of the decennial census has skyrocketed over the past several decades. The projected cost of Census 2000 is $4 billion, more than $14.50 per person, compared with about $222 million in 1970, or $1.09 per person. *(See chart, p. 392.)* The increase has prompted some members of Congress and others to look for ways to control costs. Some of the proposals viewed as potential cost-savers have been rejected, however, either as impractical or ineffective. Meanwhile, the Census Bureau says that without the use of sampling the cost will be even higher — as much as $5 billion.

Many countries — including Belgium, the Netherlands, Switzerland and the Scandinavian nations — are spared the expense of a national census because they maintain "population registers" that record all births and deaths in one central national registry. But creating a population registry for a country the size of the United States would be both difficult and expensive, according to a National Academy of Sciences panel that examined the idea as part of a two-year study commissioned after the 1990 census. [8]

More important, the panel said, the idea would likely provoke "strong political and cultural opposition" from people who resented the burden of having to report every change of

Census Costs Outstrip Population Gains

The cost of the decennial census has skyrocketed over the past several decades. For 2000, the projected cost in $4 billion, or more than $14.50 per person. That's up from about $222 million in 1970, or $1.09 per person.

	Total U.S. Population	Total Census Costs*	Cost Per Capita
2000	*274,634,000*	*$4 billion*	*$14.56*
1990	*248,718,301*	*$2.5 billion*	*$10.16*
1980	*226,542,199*	*$1.1 billion*	*$4.76*
1970	*203,302,031*	*$221.6 million*	*$1.09*
1960	*179,323,175*	*$104.9 million*	*$.59*
1950	*151,325,798*	*$68 million*	*$.45*
1940	*131,669,275*	*$67.5 million*	*$.51*
1930	*122,755,046*	*$40.2 million*	*$.33*
1920	*105,710,620*	*$25.1 million*	*$.24*
1910	*91,972,266*	*$16 million*	*$.17*
1900	*75,994,575*	*$11.8 million*	*$.16*
1890	*62,947,714*	*$11.5 million*	*$.18*
1880	*50,155,783*	*$5.8 million*	*$.12*
1870	*39,818,449*	*$3.4 million*	*$.09*
1860	*31,443,321*	*$2 million*	*$.06*
1850	*23,191,876*	*$1.4 million*	*$.06*
1840	*17,069,453*	*$833,000*	*$.05*
1830	*12,866,020*	*$379,000*	*$.03*
1820	*9,638,453*	*$209,000*	*$.02*
1810	*7,239,881*	*$178,000*	*$.03*
1800	*5,308,483*	*$66,000*	*$.01*
1790	*3,929,214*	*$44,000*	*$.01*

*Note: Cost figures are not adjusted for inflation. 1950 population figure includes Alaska and Hawaii, which did not become states until 1959.

Source: U.S. Bureau of the Census

address to the government as well as from privacy advocates concerned about the potential abuses of such a nationwide data bank.

The panel also rejected the idea of a so-called administrative records census that would gather names from other agencies — notably, the Internal Revenue Service and the Social Security Administration — to try to get a universal count. The panel noted that neither of those agencies has universal coverage or gathers the kind of information — in particular, racial and ethnic backgrounds — that the current census provides. Two other ideas — having the U.S. Postal Service conduct the census or conducting a "rolling" census over several years — were also discounted as unlikely to produce either greater accuracy or reduced costs. [9]

Some lawmakers — notably Rep. Harold Rogers, a Kentucky Republican who now heads the House Appropriations subcommittee that handles the Commerce Department spending bill — have suggested that some cost-savings could be achieved by dropping the so-called long form. This detailed questionnaire is sent to one-sixth of U.S. households along with the "short form" that everyone receives as part of the decennial census.

Business groups and other data users, however, strongly objected to the potential loss of information that companies use for such purposes as identifying markets, siting stores or factories and the like. "It's a gold mine of information not available elsewhere," says Joan Naymark, director of research and planning for Dayton Hudson Corp., the Minneapolis-based retailer.

In any event, Census Bureau officials and outside panels studied the idea and concluded that dropping the long form would not save much money or have much effect on the response rate for the short form. The idea now appears dormant, at least for the 2000 census. The Census Bureau, however, did re-examine and slightly trim the questions on the long form to assure skeptical lawmakers that all the information was being gathered for governmental purposes not just to benefit business groups.

As a result, the only active cost debate centers on sampling — and it puts fiscally conservative Republicans in the unaccustomed position of opposing a plan that the administration and Democratic lawmakers say will save money. Census Bureau officials maintain — and the GOP lawmakers do not deny — that without sampling the cost of the 2000 census will rise as the bureau is forced to hire extra enumerators

Democrats chide the GOP on the issue. "In most Republicans' minds, they're usually cost-conscious," Maloney says. "They ought to be cost-conscious on this, too."

Miller counters that the risks of using sampling have to be considered. "The worst thing you could do is to spend $4 billion and have a failed census," he says. But he also says that cost should not be the deciding factor on how to conduct

the census. "Most people acknowledge there would be an additional cost" without sampling, he says. "But that should not be the driving factor for something that is so critical to our system of government." ∎

BACKGROUND

Counting Controversies

The practice of counting the population every 10 years to apportion seats in the House of Representatives has been established for so long to be regarded as commonplace and noncontroversial. But the United States was actually the first country to use regular population counts to determine representation in a legislative body. And the manner of counting, or the results, have generated sharp controversies through much of U.S. history. [10]

Censuses had been used since biblical times to levy taxes. The Constitutional Framers' innovation of requiring an "enumeration" every 10 years to apportion seats among the states in one chamber of the new, bicameral Congress was not an especially contentious issue at the Constitutional Convention in 1787, according to historian Margo Anderson. The delegates worried about what was termed "the biblical curse" as well as the mechanics of the census. But they also saw what Alexander Hamilton later described as "a very salutary effect" in linking the use of population for both representation and taxation.

Writing in *The Federalist No. 54*, Hamilton noted that states would have an interest in exaggerating their population to increase representation but an incentive to minimize their count to reduce taxation. The opposite interests, he concluded, "will

control and balance each other, and produce the requisite impartiality."

Hamilton devoted the bulk of his essay to defending the Constitution's infamous compromise to count three-fifths of a state's slave population for purposes of apportionment. Phrasing the argument as "one of our Southern brethren" might have put it, Hamilton explained that slaves were both persons and property and that it would have been "inconsistent" to count the slaves for taxation but to exclude them for purposes of apportionment. He conceded the argument was "a little strained in some points," but concluded that "on the whole, it fully reconciles me to the scale of representation which the convention has established."

The census helped feed controversy over slavery in the final decade before the Civil War. As Anderson points out, the census never collected detailed data about the slave population, but the 1850 census gathered somewhat more information about slaves as well as expanded information about agricultural and industrial production. In his book *The Impending Crisis of the South*, the anti-slavery author Hinton Helper used the statistics to show the North's economic domination over the South and to attribute the South's shortcomings to one factor: slavery. Southerners responded by using the same data to show what they regarded as the North's maltreatment of wage laborers — what one Southerner called the North's "white slavery system." [11]

In victory, the North changed the constitutional incentives for counting the now-freed African-American population. The 14th Amendment included a provision that a state's apportionment was to be reduced by the proportion of the adult male population that was denied the right to vote in federal or state elections. The provision — adopted before the voting rights amendment, the 15th — was viewed as a politically acceptable way to punish Southern states without guaranteeing suffrage for blacks and without hurting Northern states, where the population of freed slaves was expected to be low. After the 15th Amendment, the provision might have been expected to give all the states incentives to ensure voting rights for blacks. As Anderson points out, however, interest in the issue faded quickly and the clause became "a dead letter." [12]

Population counts again became controversial in the late 19th and early 20th centuries because of the great waves of immigration into the United States from Southern and Eastern Europe. Concerns about the effects of immigration merged with worries about urbanization after the 1920 census, which showed for the first time that a majority of Americans lived in cities rather than on farms.

The count had an unacceptable political implication for the Republicans in power in Congress and the White House. It called for taking away 11 House seats from 10, predominantly Republican rural states and giving them to eight urbanizing states, where the Democratic Party was stronger. The prescription was too strong for the GOP. Congress refused to carry out the constitutionally mandated apportionment for the decade — the only such default in U.S. history.

In the meantime, Congress also sought to close the door to the "new" immigrants by enacting a national quota system that reduced overall annual immigration and set quotas tied to the national origins of the population as of 1890, before the influx of Southern and Eastern Europeans.

Modernizing the Census

By the end of the 19th century, the census had grown from a primitive if daunting undertaking into a more sophisticated — and even more daunting — enterprise. The project grew not only in size, but in scope. It counted not only people, but agricultural and industrial production, work force information and what came to be called "social statistics." The census became, as Anderson writes, "a full-fledged instrument to monitor the overall state of American society." [13]

Until after the Civil War, the census was conducted by U.S. marshals, who appointed assistants to take the enumeration. The enumerators had months to prepare the tallies, which — before the current laws guaranteeing the confidentiality of census information — listed heads of household by name. The tallies were then posted in two public places in each community so they could be checked for accuracy.

Initially, the census asked only for limited information: the name of the head of the household and the numbers but not the names of other free white adult males, free white males under 16, free white females and slaves. James Madison urged that the 1790 enumeration also collect information about manufacturing. The idea was rejected then, but adopted in 1810, when the first census of manufactures was taken.

Four decades later, the census took its first major step toward modernization with the creation of a Census Board — consisting of the secretaries of State and the Interior and the postmaster general — and the appointment of Joseph Kennedy as its secretary. Kennedy was a well-to-do Pennsylvania farmer whose only qualification for the post, Anderson writes, was the "ardent effort" he made for the election of President Zachary Taylor in 1848. Despite his limited qualifications, Kennedy enlisted the help of the newly formed American Statistical Association (1849) in drawing up the questions for the 1850 census. The expanded list of questions included basic information — such as name, address, age, sex, color, occupation, place of birth — as well as school attendance, marital status, literacy and real estate holdings. On a separate schedule, assistant marshals were asked to provide a description of their subdivision, including taxes collected, wages, "pauperism," crime, schools, libraries and religion.

The central tallying operation expanded with the increased statistics-gathering, but the counting was still done by hand until the 1890 census. Mechanization arrived thanks to the work of Herman Hollerith, a Columbia University graduate who worked on the 1880 mining census and was then employed to devise a mechanical method of tabulating population returns. Hollerith invented an electrical tabulating machine, patented in 1887, that allowed for tabulation and cross-tabulation of data by the use of punch cards. Primitive by today's standards, the machine nonetheless provided more detailed statistics than in previous censuses and allowed most tabulations to be completed within three years, compared with eight years for the 1880 census. [14]

Organization, however, lagged behind the technological progress. Responsibility for the census had been transferred from the secretary of State to the secretary of the Interior in 1850, and a census office was established within the Interior Department in 1880. Through 1900, however, there was no permanent census organization; the process began anew with each decennial count. Census officials had been lobbying since mid-century for a permanent office. In 1900 they gained valuable support for the idea by taking over the gathering of cotton production statistics from the Department of Agriculture, which had been providing crop estimates that were both unreliable and late. The census office's work proved to be sufficiently valuable that Congress voted in 1902 to make the office permanent and, one year later, to place the office in the newly established Department of Commerce and Labor. It stayed in Commerce when the Labor Department was created 10 years later, in 1913.

Even with a permanent status, personnel policies at the census of-

Continued on p. 396

Chronology

Before 1890

The federal government uses labor-intensive methods to locate and count U.S. population every 10 years as required by the Constitution.

1787
New Constitution provides for census every 10 years to apportion seats in the House of Representatives and direct taxes among the states; slaves are counted as three-fifths of a person, untaxed Indians are not counted at all; population in first census, in 1790, is 3.9 million.

1870
With end of slavery, the three-fifths count for African Americans is discontinued.

---•---

1890-1950

Census methods advance from mechanized tabulation to computerization; Bureau of the Census is established.

1890
The 1890 census is the first to use Herman Hollerith's electrical punch-card tabulating machine; population: 63 million.

1902
Congress votes to establish permanent Census Office, later renamed the Bureau of the Census; the office is housed one year later in the Department of Commerce and Labor and stays in Commerce when the two departments are split in 1913.

1920
Census for first time finds a majority of Americans live in cities, not on farms; to avoid transfer of power from rural to urban states, Congress fails to reapportion House seats for a decade; population: 106 million.

1941
First concrete evidence of undercount emerges when number of men reporting for wartime draft significantly exceeds number projected by 1940 census figures; undercount is put at 5.0 percent for whites, 8.4 percent for blacks.

1951
The newly invented computer known as Univac is put into service in final stages of 1950 census.

---•---

1960-1990s

Concern about the undercount grows among big cities and states, racial and ethnic minority groups and civil rights organizations.

1970
Civil rights coalition mobilizes to encourage blacks to be counted; undercount is reduced; population: 203 million.

1980
Undercount is reduced again in 1980 census, but some cities and states fight long legal battle to try to force Census Bureau to adjust figures; fight ends with 1987 court ruling that adjustment is not "feasible or warranted."

1990
For first time since 1940, the Census Bureau fails to reduce undercount in its tally; population: 249 million.

1991
Commerce Secretary Robert A. Mosbacher rejects Census Bureau's recommendation to adjust census figures for undercount; several states and cities sue to force adjustment.

March 1994
Bureau of the Census first puts census data on the Internet.

March 20, 1996
Supreme Court rejects cities' effort to force undercount (*Wisconsin vs. City of New York*).

June 9, 1997
President Clinton vetoes flood-relief appropriations bill because of provision prohibiting Census Bureau from using statistical sampling in 2000 census; compromise spending bill in November requires Census Bureau to develop separate plans with and without sampling and seeks early court test to determine whether sampling satisfies Constitution's requirement of "actual enumeration."

Oct. 30, 1997
Office of Management and Budget adopts new rules for listing racial and ethnic makeup on federal forms, allowing people to identify themselves as members of more than one race; separate "multiracial" category is rejected.

April 18, 1998
Census Day for the dress rehearsals for Census 2000.

April 1, 2000
Census Day for the nation's 22nd decennial population count; national population projected to be about 275 million people.

Bureau Gears Up for Census 2000

The Census Bureau is taking steps to try to reduce the undercount in the 2000 census. "The experience of the 1990 census made clear the need for innovative changes in the way the decennial census is taken," the bureau noted. "[We've] responded to this challenge with a redesign of the process that improves accuracy, promotes inclusion, saves money and produces one set of numbers that is right the first time." A summary of the bureau's plan follows:

1. Create the best possible address list — with the help of the U.S. Postal Service and state, local and tribal partners.

2. Create a "responsive" environment — use advertising, outreach and promotion to ensure that everyone knows the census is coming and how it will benefit their community.

3. Use a questionnaire delivery strategy that contacts every address many times (notice letter, questionnaire, reminder postcard and replacement questionnaire).

4. Make other response opportunities widely available (leave blank forms for people to pick up, set up toll-free telephone numbers and provide forms in many languages).

5. Check responses against the address list.

6. Use new technology to convert responses from paper forms to computer files.

7. Remove duplicate responses.

8. Determine the list of non-responding addresses.

9. Use the telephone to call as many non-responding addresses as possible.

10. Make personal visits to remaining non-responding addresses until reaching at least 90 percent completion by census tract [about 4,000 people or 1,700 housing units].

11. Develop estimates for the remaining non-responding households.

12. Check all responses.

13. Fill in missing answers based on responses already received.

14. Select the sample of households for the quality check.

15. Load census responses for "quality check" sample address into laptop computers.

16. Conduct intensive interviews at quality-check addresses.

17. Match quality-check responses with census responses to determine differences.

18. Reconcile differences.

19. Bring together mail responses, telephone responses, field interviews, non-respondent estimates and quality-check results to compute the one-number census total for each state and the nation before issuing apportionment totals by Dec. 31, 2000.

20. Develop totals for all population groups and all geographic levels before issuing redistricting totals by April 1, 2001.

21. Develop data files for users to do their own tabulations.

Source: "Creating a Census for the 21st Century: The Plan for Census 2000," Bureau of the Census, February 1997.

Continued from p. 394

fice continued to reflect political patronage more than professional skills into the 1930s.[15] In 1934, for example, the bureau employed only five professional statisticians. Under President Franklin D. Roosevelt, however, the bureau began to develop into a more professional agency. The professionalization of the bureau, Anderson notes, was stimulated in part by the administration's need for better information to implement the various New Deal programs for economic revitalization and social assistance.

One more critical step forward came after World War II: computer-ization. The government had sponsored the development of the first electronic computers during the war for military purposes; but the work came to the attention of Census Bureau officials, who immediately saw the potential for improvements in efficiency and accuracy for the bureau's work. The bureau placed its order for the first Univac — the Universal Automatic Computer — in 1948, and the machine was delivered in March 1951, too late for most of the data processing for the 1950 census but in time to demonstrate the feasibility of using electronic computing to tabulate and analyze large amounts of information.

Undercounting Disputes

After conducting the nation's first census, Thomas Jefferson is believed to have prepared a tally sheet showing the official population count for the 13 states as well as Jefferson's own, higher estimate of the number of people in each. This first evidence of an undercount — referred to in one of Jefferson's letters but never located — was based only on Jefferson's intuition rather than hard evidence. But in the early 1940s the Census Bureau developed statistical proof that it was failing to count many Americans, in particular young, black men.

When the government instituted a military draft in the fall of 1940, the bureau provided estimates of the number of men who would report for registration based on the just-completed decennial census. The estimates proved to be low: "Many, many more men — and many, many more black men — showed up than the Bureau of the Census expected," Anderson explains. Statisticians pored over the numbers and came up with this estimate: the 1940 census failed to count 5.0 percent of white men and 8.4 percent of black men.

For each succeeding decennial census, the bureau has prepared its estimate of the "differential undercount" — the difference between the "gross undercount," the number of people missed, and the "gross overcount," the number of people counted twice. Through the 1980 census, the bureau was improving on its record from the previous count. But even as the census was becoming more accurate, the political and fiscal stakes were increasing, along with the criticisms from state and city governments and population groups who believed they were adversely affected.

The undercount became a more significant political issue because of three developments beginning in the 1960s. First, the reapportionment and redistricting revolution required by the Supreme Court's "one person, one vote" rulings forced state legislatures to draw congressional and legislative districts with equal populations — limiting their ability to manipulate district boundaries for political gain. Second, President Lyndon B. Johnson's "Great Society" programs expanded the importance of federal aid to state and local governments, and many assistance programs used funding formulas based at least in part on population. Third, the civil rights revolution led to the government's first affirmative action programs, with federal mandates to reach employment goals tied to minority-group populations.

As the 1970 census approached, a coalition of civil rights groups led by the National Urban League tried to reduce the undercount with a "Make Black Count" campaign. "We were the first group to look over the shoulders of the Census Bureau," recalls Morgan State Professor Robert Hill, who was the Urban League's director for the project. "We uncovered a lot of mistakes, and we had some ideas on how they could get more minorities counted." The most concrete recommendation: creation of separate racial and ethnic advisory groups to help the bureau's outreach efforts with African-Americans, Asian-Americans, Hispanics and Native Americans.

By the time of the 1980 census, concern about the undercount had spread to other groups, including local officials, academics and members of Congress. [16] Many urged that the bureau plan to adjust the actual count in 1980 to correct for the undercount. At the same time, the bureau faced increasing criticism about the escalating cost of the census — criticisms that helped force the resignation of Manuel Plotkin as director in 1979.

As the 1980 numbers were being tallied, New York City filed a federal court suit in August to try to force an adjustment. It won a lower court ruling, but the decision was reversed on appeal and the Supreme Court refused to intervene. At that point, Census Director Vincent Barabba, who had been brought back to the post that he had held during the Nixon and Ford administrations, said the bureau would not adjust the figures "unless directed by the courts." The litigation continued for more than seven years, with some 50 suits filed in various courts by big cities, the states of New York and California and civil rights groups. But in December 1987 a federal judge in New York settled the issue with a decisive ruling that a statistical adjustment was "not technically feasible or warranted." [17]

Even as the litigation was nearing its end, the Census Bureau itself was moving toward a recommendation for an adjustment in the 1990 census. Barbara Bailar, the associate director for statistical standards and methodology who had supported the decision not to adjust in 1980, had set in motion research and planning that led in 1987 to an internal recommendation to prepare for an adjustment. But Commerce Department officials rejected the recommendation; Bailar resigned in protest. Once the census had been completed, the bureau again recommended an adjustment; but Commerce Secretary Robert A. Mosbacher rejected the recommendation in 1991. [18]

Again, litigation ensued, with suits brought by the city and state of New York, Los Angeles and Texas. A federal judge in 1993 upheld Mosbacher's decision, saying in legal terminology that it was not "arbitrary or capricious." But the federal appeals court for New York ruled a year later that because of the conceded undercount of minorities, the government should have been required to prove a legitimate government objective to justify the decision. The case then went to the Supreme Court, which unanimously ruled in March 1996 that Mosbacher's decision "was not subject to heightened scrutiny." Mosbacher's decision, Chief Justice William H. Rehnquist wrote in *Wisconsin v. City of New York*, was "entirely reasonable." [19]

The Sampling Debate

After officials in two Republican administrations had rejected statistical adjustments for the 1990 census, the election of a Democratic president in 1992 changed the politics on the undercount issue. Meanwhile, two independent reviews of census procedures were heading toward recommendations that the use of statistical sampling techniques to adjust the initial census would produce a more accurate census.

The two studies by separate panels

established by the National Academy of Sciences-National Research Council stemmed from a law passed by Congress in 1992, the Decennial Census Improvement Act. The Panel on Census Requirements in the Year 2000 and Beyond was directed to study "means by which the government could achieve the most accurate population count possible." A second Panel to Evaluate Alternative Census Methods was established at the request of the Commerce Department and Census Bureau to conduct a complementary study on the possibility of devising other ways to conduct the decennial count.

Both panels issued interim reports in 1993 and then published their final reports in 1995 and 1994, respectively. In the first of the final reports to appear, the panel on alternative methods complimented the Census Bureau for its work on "response and coverage improvements" since the 1990 census and endorsed a number of other steps to get better results — from hiring more "community-based enumerators" and creating an 800 telephone number for assistance in filling out census forms to the more radical step of testing the feasibility of an administrative records census. But the panel also said that statistical sampling was essential to improve accuracy. "The differential undercount cannot be reduced to acceptable levels at acceptable costs," the panel stated, "without the use of integrated coverage measurement and the statistical methods associated with it." [20]

The other panel rejected what it called "radical alternatives" to the current census methods, including a national population register or an administrative records census. It also starkly proclaimed that it was "fruitless to continue trying to count every last person with traditional census methods of physical enumeration." On that basis, the panel concluded that follow-up efforts for households that fail to return the mailed questionnaire should be "simplified and truncated" and "statistical sampling should be used to estimate the number and characteristics of the non-respondent households that remain." [21]

By the time both final reports had appeared, however, the politics of the issue had changed. By capturing control of both houses of Congress in the 1994 elections, Republicans gained a forum to press their case in opposition to tinkering with the basic census methodology. At the same time, Republican lawmakers working on the issue complained about the escalating cost of the census and warned the bureau not to repeat what was often termed a "1990-style census." In addition, some GOP lawmakers — in particular, Rogers — called for reconsidering the use of the census long form, which Rogers said was both expensive and unnecessary.

The issue came to a head in 1997 as Republicans tried to attach an amendment to a must-pass money bill to prohibit the Census Bureau from going forward with statistical sampling. With strong backing from House Speaker Gingrich and Senate Majority Leader Lott, Republicans inserted the rider last May on a supplemental appropriations bill that included $8.6 billion in emergency flood relief. Clinton administration officials warned the bill would be vetoed, but GOP leaders doubted the president would risk delaying the flood assistance over the issue. Clinton proved them wrong, vetoing the bill on June 9. "Without sampling," the president said, "the cost of the decennial census will increase as its accuracy, especially with regard to minorities and groups that are traditionally undercounted, decreases substantially." [22]

Republicans, however, refused to give up. They added provisions over the summer to the regular Commerce Department spending bill to restrict the Census Bureau's ability to use sampling in 2000. The bill, as passed by the House on Sept. 30, provided $382 million for the bureau for planning on the 2000 census but included language to allow an expedited review of sampling and barred any spending on census preparations until the courts had settled the issue. The White House labeled the provision "an unprecedented and unacceptable attempt to micromanage the decennial census." GOP leaders dug in their heels, forcing a showdown on the issue in the final House-Senate conference on the bill.

The compromise that emerged retained the Republicans' idea of forcing a court test and provided that both traditional enumeration and statistical sampling would be tested in the 1998 dress rehearsals. The bill also established an eight-member oversight board — with an equal number of members to be appointed by the White House and congressional GOP leaders — to evaluate the dress rehearsals and to return the issue to Congress for a final decision in early 1999. ■

CURRENT SITUATION

'Dress Rehearsals'

The city of Sacramento celebrated its participation in the Census 2000 dress rehearsals on April 18 with a six-hour festival featuring multicultural entertainment ranging from jazz to salsa to Native American dancing. Census workers speaking a variety of languages were on hand to help anyone who had not met that day's deadline for returning the census questionnaires that had been mailed to 170,000 households in late March.

Census Bureau officials say Sacramento, with a 1990 population of 370,000, has been enthusiastic about its role as one of three sites picked for the dress rehearsals for the official count two years from now. "It's going extremely well," says Michael Burns, who oversaw the dress rehearsal as the director of the bureau's Seattle region. [23]

Still, the response rate leaves something to be desired: only 47.1 percent of the questionnaires had been mailed back as of April 24. Burns stresses that dress rehearsals do not attract as much interest as the official census. Even so, the figures leave census workers with a huge job of "non-response follow-up" and appear to give little encouragement for the hope of boosting the response rate in the official census in 2000.

The response rates at the other two dress rehearsal sites were roughly comparable: slightly better in South Carolina (48.9 percent) and somewhat lower at the Menominee Reservation in Wisconsin (37.1 percent).

The Census Bureau is using the dress rehearsals to test some of the techniques it hopes to use in 2000 to get a better response rate. It formed partnerships in each location with local governments, businesses and private organizations to try to maximize outreach. For the first time, paid advertising was used as a supplement to news coverage and public-service announcements to tell people about the census and encourage people to return their forms. Earlier, Census Bureau personnel in all three sites had worked to improve the address lists used to mail the questionnaires, supplementing lists from the U.S. Postal Service with additional addresses picked up by census workers scouring back-country roads and inner-city apartment buildings for households that had been missed.

Census Bureau officials say the techniques are proving to be effective. But investigators for the General Accounting Office (GAO), the auditing and oversight arm of Congress, were less confident. In a report released in late March, the GAO said the dress rehearsals would "leave a number of design and operational issues unresolved" and repeated its

warning from a 1997 report about "the high risk of a failed census in 2000." [24]

The GAO report cited four primary concerns. First, it said that the Census Bureau had not been able to test revised procedures aimed at developing address lists that are 99 percent complete. The auditors noted the increased outreach and promotional efforts, but said that participation in the local partnerships was "in-

consistent." Third, the GAO said that there were "uncertainties" surrounding the bureau's ability to staff the 295,000 mostly temporary jobs needed to conduct the official count in 2000. Finally, the GAO report noted that the proposed use of statistical estimation procedures faces "methodological, technological and quality control challenges."

Census Bureau officials acknowledge the difficulties. Recruitment was especially difficult in South Carolina, where the low unemployment rate forced the agency to raise the basic pay rate for census field workers to $10.50 from $9.50 an hour. As of mid-April, the Census Bureau had a pool of 4,600 qualified applicants in South Carolina — well shy of its goal of 11,600.

Sacramento and the Menominee Reservation will provide the only tests for statistical sampling among the three dress rehearsal sites since Congress specifically required the Census Bureau to conduct one trial run with traditional enumeration techniques. Burns stresses the efforts to ensure quality control for the sampling, noting that the enumerators used in the so-called integrated coverage measurement will work independently of the field workers assigned to get questionnaires from the non-responding households.

Still, critics of sampling insist that the dress rehearsal will provide no useful test of the validity of the technique. "It will not tell you whether the yardstick is accurate or not," says UC-Berkeley statistician Freedman. "There is no external truth against which to measure it."

For its part, the GAO said statistical sampling "could reduce costs and improve accuracy if properly implemented." But it also noted that the dispute between Congress and the administration about what method to use in Census 2000 could frustrate the goal of getting an accurate count. "The longer this impasse continues," the GAO report concluded, "the greater the likelihood of a failed census."

Sparring in Washington

The political and legal skirmishes over the census continued in Washington even as the Census Bureau worked to make the dress rehearsals a success. Republican lawmakers sharply attacked the bureau's preparations for the trial runs at a House Census Subcommittee hearing. Meanwhile, lawyers in two suits aimed at blocking the Cen-

sus Bureau from using sampling asked federal court panels for an early ruling on the issue, while the Clinton administration, civil rights groups and more than a dozen municipalities argued that the legal challenges should be thrown out.

Miller opened the subcommittee's March 26 hearing by citing the GAO's critical report and adding his own blunt warning of the consequences. "What they are finding scares me," Miller declared. "All indications are that we may be headed directly to a failed census."

The GOP lawmaker went on to issue an anticipatory caution against using the dress rehearsals to compare the sampling methodology with traditional enumeration techniques. He stressed that there were many demographic differences between Sacramento, where sampling was to be used, and South Carolina, where traditional techniques were planned. "If some process works in the dress rehearsal setting," Miller said, "it is not guaranteed to work in the actual census setting."

Maloney countered Miller's criticisms by drawing supportive comments about sampling from the GAO witnesses and from Acting Director Holmes. Any census is "high-risk," L. Nye Stevens, the main author of the GAO report, told Maloney. But without the use of sampling, he said, "we have no confidence that [the 2000 census] will be any better" than the 1990 count.

Holmes also insisted that efforts to improve accuracy through traditional enumeration techniques were futile. "Traditional census methods alone will not" correct the undercount, Holmes said. "It doesn't matter how much money you throw at the problem."

Under questioning, Holmes sought to assure Miller that the bureau was faithfully complying with the directive in the Commerce Department spending bill to prepare alternative plans, one with sampling and one without. But in his testimony and his questioning, he stressed that the requirement was taking a toll on bureau personnel. "The staff would obviously be less concerned

if they were focusing on a single plan rather than two plans," Holmes said.

A week after the hearing, lawyers moved into action in the two anti-sampling lawsuits: one filed in the name of the House of Representatives before a three-judge federal court in Washington and a second filed with a three-judge panel in Northern Virginia on behalf of a group of individual plaintiffs led by Matthew Glavin, president of the Southeastern Legal Foundation, a conservative public interest law firm based in Atlanta. Lawyers for the plaintiffs argued that sampling would violate both the constitutional requirement for an "actual enumeration" and a statutory provision mandating the use of sampling by the Census Bureau to the extent feasible "except for the determination of population for purposes of apportionment of Representatives in Congress."

Maureen Mahoney, the private Washington attorney representing the House, said statistical sampling would be inconsistent with the dictionary definition of "enumeration," historical tradition and the Framers' purpose of guarding against political manipulation of the population count. As for the federal statute, she contended the proviso "plainly prohibits the use of sampling for purposes of apportionment."

For its part, the Justice Department argued that sampling would comply with both the Constitution and the statute, which it said delegated the decision on how to conduct the census to the secretary of Commerce. In addition, the administration asked both courts to dismiss the suits on grounds that the plaintiffs had no legal standing to sue or that the suits were premature — in legal terms, not "ripe" for adjudication. "With the results of Census 2000 unknown until the census process is concluded and its results certified to Congress, this case is not ripe," the Justice Department lawyers wrote.

Miller questions the administration's legal strategy of seeking to dismiss the suits without a ruling on the merits after

Continued on p. 402

At Issue:

Should statistical sampling be used for Census 2000?

REP. CAROLYN B. MALONEY, D-N.Y.
Ranking minority member, House Government Reform and Oversight Subcommittee on the Census

WRITTEN FOR THE CQ RESEARCHER, APRIL 1998.

*t*he 2000 census could be the best since 1790, when Thomas Jefferson's U.S. marshals fanned out across the country on horseback for the first population count . . . or it could be the worst. The outcome is largely in the hands of Congress, and there's reason to believe the House leadership will choose to spend more money than ever before for a census that intentionally misses millions of Americans. The heart of the matter is politics. Because census numbers are used to allocate seats in the House of Representatives and draw congressional boundaries, some decisions about the census are colored by partisan concerns, rather than sound, scientific, operational and cost considerations.

The census controversy centers on the use of modern statistical methods to complete the count. To make the census more accurate and keep costs under control, the Census Bureau has developed a plan for 2000 that incorporates modern sampling and statistical methods as part of the massive counting effort. The use of sampling to improve upon direct counting in the census is not new. The General Accounting Office, the Commerce Department's Inspector General and two panels convened by the National Academy of Sciences have all said that the Census Bureau's plan to use sampling techniques to account for the hardest-to-reach 10 percent is the only way to make the census more accurate and keep costs down.

Ironically, the plan to use sampling to complete the head count was a direct response to a congressional mandate. The cost of the 1990 census was up 250 percent over 1970, but it was the first population count in modern history to be less accurate than the one before it. The final figures were found to be off by 4 million: 10 million people were missed; 6 million were counted twice. Worse yet, the undercounts of African-Americans and other minority populations were the largest ever recorded, both in absolute terms and relative to the white population. The 2000 census is truly the civil rights issue of the 1990s.

The bureau is already making an unprecedented effort to count most Americans directly, either through the mail, by telephone or by going door-to-door to find those people who didn't respond. Only then will it use widely accepted scientific sampling procedures to estimate those who are hardest to find, and include them in the final numbers.

The importance of an accurate census can't be overstated. The census is the basis of our democracy. By including everyone, even those who are difficult to count, we ensure that all Americans are represented fairly in Congress and in state and local legislatures.

REP. DAN MILLER, R-FLA.
Chairman, House Government Reform and Oversight Subcommittee on the Census

WRITTEN FOR THE CQ RESEARCHER, APRIL 1998.

*a*t census time, most Americans carefully fill out their census form, answering every question as best they can, knowing that the information they provide will determine how much federal money their community receives for its roads and schools or how many elected representatives their state will send to Congress.

The last census, in 1990, was the second most accurate in history. However, follow-up surveys suggested that it may have missed as many as 4.8 million Americans. How did this happen? A study by the National Academy of Sciences found that half of these people never got a census form in the mail because the government's address list was so bad. About a third didn't fill out the form correctly, and thus were not counted. The remainder simply avoided the census-takers.

Taken together, common sense tells us the way to address these problems is to get back to basics. Unfortunately, the Census Bureau, under the direction of the Clinton administration, has other ideas — and their cure is worse than the disease.

The Census Bureau wants to give up the head count after they think they've reached 90 percent of the population, and then juggle a bunch of statistical equations to finish the job. Then they'll use this untested theory to add "virtual people" to some areas and subtract real people from others. That means the Census Bureau will take the form you so carefully filled out and throw it in the trash if they think there are "too many of you." Since only the very largest cities in America will have virtually all of the "found" people added to their counts, most other communities in the country will be losers, meaning their share of federal and state funds received will be reduced, and consequently, their taxes will be raised to make up the shortfall. Is that fair?

This is simply a bad idea. Its constitutionality and legality are suspect. It sends the wrong message about civic participation. We want every American to be counted – not created or deleted by some statistical theory. The "sampling" method failed when it was tried in the last census, and would have made the 1990 census less accurate. Now, we see the administration's solution is to try to pull off a sampling scheme five times larger in half the time as the one that didn't work before. Does anyone believe that this is a reasonable approach to solving this problem?

As chairman of the Subcommittee on the Census, I am working hard to prevent a failed 2000 census. I have urged the Census Bureau to get back to basics and do the job right.

Census Bureau Chief: 'We Collect the Data'

When Martha Farnsworth Riche resigned as director of the Bureau of the Census in January, in frustration with the controversy over the use of statistical sampling for the 2000 census, the Clinton administration turned to a career civil servant, James Holmes, to serve as acting director until a permanent successor could be chosen. In his 30 years with the Census Bureau, Holmes had served in half a dozen cities, including stints as the bureau's regional director in Philadelphia and, most recently, Atlanta. *CQ Researcher* staff writer Kenneth Jost interviewed Holmes on April 7 in the director's office at the bureau's headquarters in Suitland, Md., outside Washington.

Why has the Census Bureau been involved in political and legal controversies almost continuously for the past 20 years? Has the bureau been doing a bad job?

No, I don't think that has anything to do with it at all. My sense would be that most of the attention that the Census Bureau gets is a direct result of the importance that the Congress, the general public, the business community and the data-users place on the products that the Census Bureau produces.

The General Accounting Office says we are at "high risk" of a "failed census." Do you agree with the GAO's warning?

Absolutely not. [GAO] goes on to say that there are some risks associated with any type of census. [GAO has] some concerns. We have the same set of concerns.

The 1990 census was less accurate than the 1980 census. What is the Census Bureau doing to try to correct the problem?

First and foremost, the plan that we've developed, the one that includes statistical methods, allows us to account for those populations that we've had the most difficulty counting.

Acting Director James Holmes

Courtesy of U.S. Bureau of the Census

Why should the public have any confidence in the statistical sampling methods that the bureau is considering for use in the 2000 census?

Why would the public or the critics not have confidence? The use of statistical methods is not something new. The process that we're planning to use is not something that we've developed in secrecy.

Why is it important to count the population by racial and ethnic category?

There are legislative requirements — obviously, the first and foremost is the Voting Rights Act [of 1965]. There are a number of other federal programs that require data by race or Spanish origin.

If it's important, why shouldn't there be a separate category for people of multiple racial backgrounds?

That's a decision that the Office of Management and Budget dealt with. That's really not the Census Bureau's call. We're the ones that collect the data.

Will the option to check more than one racial category hurt the enforcement of anti-discrimination laws or implementation of affirmative action programs?

I don't have any idea.

Are you concerned about it?

No. Our responsibility is to collect the best data we can collect. If we do our job, [the government agencies concerned with such issues] have a much better chance or opportunity to do their jobs.

Does the census cost too much?

I'm not in a position to say whether or not it costs too much. The cost figure that we've put together is somewhere in the neighborhood of $4 billion. That's a cost associated with the most cost-effective, accurate and fair census.

Would the census cost more if sampling is not used?

Absolutely [because we'd have to hire more enumerators].

Continued from p. 400

having agreed to the provisions for a legal test in the Commerce Department spending bill. "Obviously, there's some inconsistency in that," Miller says. But White House officials defend the strat-

egy, noting that President Clinton voiced doubts about the propriety of an early legal test of sampling when he signed the appropriations measure on Nov. 26. "We are not reneging on our agreement," a spokesman for the White

House legal counsel's office said.

Other groups sought to intervene on the administration's side in the cases. They included a group of six Democratic lawmakers led by House Minority Leader Richard A. Gephardt of Missouri. The city of Los Angeles also filed a motion to intervene that was joined by the state of New Mexico; 13 other cities or counties, including Chicago, Denver, Miami/Dade County, Fla., San Francisco, and San Jose; and 19 members of Congress, all Democrats except for Connecticut's Christopher Shays.

In one other development, GOP congressional leaders and the White House appointed their representatives to the eight-member oversight board called for in the Commerce Department spending bill. The four Republican appointees included Ohio's state treasurer, Kenneth Blackwell, whom Gingrich designated as co-chairman. The White House picked former Rep. Tony Coelho of California to be the other co-chairman. [25] ■

OUTLOOK

Picturing America

For more than a century, the Census Bureau has helped Americans visualize their country by pinpointing on a map the population center of the United States — the point on which the country could theoretically balance if it were a flat plane and all people weighed the same. The population center, calculated to have been in Maryland in 1790, over time moved steadily to the west and has lain in Missouri for the last two censuses.

Political and economic power has followed the population center across the country, slowly moving from the North and the East in the country's first few decades to the Midwest and then toward the West. Today, the so-called Sun Belt states — stretching along the country's southern tier from Florida to California — have surpassed the old Rust Belt states in economic and political clout.

Census 2000 is expected to show a continuation of these trends. The popula-

tion center is likely to move a bit farther to the southwest in Missouri. Sun Belt and Western states are projected to make a net gain of nine House seats, while seven Northeastern and Rust Belt states are expected to lose a total of nine seats:

State	Seats Gained/Lost
Arizona	(+2)
Connecticut	(-1)
Colorado	(+1)
Illinois	(-1)
Florida	(+1)
Michigan	(-1)
Georgia	(+2)
Mississippi	(-1)
Montana	(+1)
New York	(-2)
Nevada	(+1)
Ohio	(-1)
Texas	(+2)
Oklahoma	(-1)
Utah	(+1)
Pennsylvania	(-2)
Wisconsin	(-1)

This 22nd decennial census will also confirm another changing picture of America: increased racial and ethnic diversity. The 1990 census showed that African-Americans comprised 12 percent of the population, Hispanics about 9 percent and Asian-Americans and Pacific Islanders about 3 percent. The Census Bureau now projects that African-Americans will increase to nearly 13 percent of the population, Hispanics to 11 percent and Asian-Americans and Pacific Islanders to about 4 percent. "We will have a much better understanding that the country is more diverse than it was in the 1990 census," says Acting Director Holmes.

The shifts in power revealed by the Census Bureau numbers — from East to West, from rural and small-town America to the cities and suburbs — have stirred controversy and conflict throughout U.S. history. The latest example is the debate over how to conduct the census and, in particular, how to reduce the undercount of the country's racial and ethnic minorities. "Whenever a political dispute be-

comes congruent with a demographic issue," historian Anderson says, "you get what I call a politics of population."

The Census Bureau's dress rehearsals will provide some evidence about the two opposing methodologies — traditional enumeration or statistical estimation — when the results are released at the end of the year. But opponents of sampling are already contending that the results from the Sacramento and South Carolina test sites cannot be used to compare the validity of the two methods.

Whatever the experts say about the results, politics rather than science will determine the final decision on sampling. Congress has the power to block sampling even if the courts refuse to bar the method, as most legal experts expect. One point of leverage for Republican opponents of sampling will be the administration's selection of a permanent Census Bureau director — a post subject to confirmation in the Republican-controlled Senate.

The Washington Post reported late last month that there are three finalists for the position: Barbara Everitt Bryant, who held the post in the Bush administration; Norman Bradburn, senior vice president for research at the National Opinion Research Center; and Ken Prewitt, president of the Social Science Research Center in New York City. [26] Bryant has been a vocal proponent of sampling; Bradburn endorsed sampling in the 1995 National Academy of Sciences report as chair of its Committee on National Statistics. Prewitt has not been involved in census issues in the past.

Some supporters of sampling fear that the administration will decide that it can win a showdown fight with congressional Republicans on the issue, if at all, only at too great a cost to other items on its legislative agenda. That fear helps explain why supporters of sampling are stoking the rhetoric. Rep. Maloney describes sampling as "the civil rights issue of our time." Meanwhile, outside groups are urging the administration not to give in. "I would hope that the administration remains strong on this and insists that the Census Bureau do whatever it needs to do to get an accurate count," says Larry Jones, assistant executive director of the U.S. Conference of Mayors.

For their part, critics of sampling also are sharpening the political rhetoric. Bensen, the GOP political consultant, calls the plan to use sampling "the California Financial Assistance Act." He says California would get a substantial share — 40 percent — of the financial aid shifted as a result of the new census method. "This would take money from the many and give to the few — and the few is California," Bensen says.

Despite the controversies, the census continues to hold a special place in the American political system. The decennial census provides not only an orderly method for reapportioning political power in legislative bodies from Congress down to the smallest city hall, but also a symbolic gathering of the country's people — the closest equivalent to a national town hall meeting. And the data produced by the Census Bureau — in the decennial census, its periodic population surveys and its other specialized censuses — are the taken-for-granted raw material for news reports, articles and books that help Americans understand their country and their fellow countrymen and women.

"The creation of this instrument was both a real innovation in government and has become a kind of decennial national ritual of stock-taking," says Anderson. "We use it for governmental functions, to go through a periodic reallocation of political power and economic resources. And we have a kind of mirror held up to ourselves collectively once every 10 years which then allows us to evaluate and think about ourselves — and even primp a little bit — and come to understand ourselves better." ∎

Notes

[1] In addition to the decennial census, the Census Bureau conducts a number of specialized economic censuses: agriculture; business (retail, wholesale, services); construction industries; foreign trade; governments; housing; manufactures; mineral industries; and transportation. It also conducts or assists in conducting surveys published by other government agencies — for example, the Bureau of Labor Statistics' monthly employment and unemployment reports.

[2] As of April 24, there were two vacancies in the House and one Independent member.

[3] American Statistical Association, "Report of the Census Blue Ribbon Panel," September 1996.

[4] See "Creating a Census for the 21st Century: The Plan for Census 2000," Bureau of the Census, February 1997.

[5] For an earlier exposition of his thesis, see David A. Freedman and Kenneth W. Wachter, "Planning for the Census in the Year 2000," *Evaluation Review*, Vol. 20, No. 4, August 1996, pp. 355-377.

[6] For background, see "Rethinking Affirmative Action," *The CQ Researcher*, April 28, 1995, pp. 369-392.

[7] See *Federal Register*, Vol. 62, No. 210, Oct. 30, 1997, pp. 58782-58790.

[8] See Barry Edmonston and Charles Schultze (eds.), *Modernizing the U.S. Census, Panel on Census Requirements in the Year 2000 and Beyond*, National Academy of Sciences, 1995, pp. 60-63.

[9] *Ibid.*, pp. 63-68 (administrative records census), pp. 68-71 (Postal Service census), pp. 71-73 (rolling census).

[10] Background is drawn from various Bureau of the Census publications, interviews with Census Bureau historians and from Margo J. Anderson, *The American Census: A Social History* (1988).

[11] See Anderson, *op. cit.*, pp. 53-57.

[12] *Ibid.*, pp. 74-76.

[13] *Ibid.*, p. 85.

[14] *Ibid.*, pp. 102, 106-107; Bureau of the Census, "100 Years of Data Processing: The Punchcard Century," January 1991.

[15] Anderson, *op.cit*, pp. 173-175.

[16] For background, see "1990 Census: Undercounting Minorities," *Editorial Research Reports*, March 10, 1989, pp. 117-132; Margo A. Conk, "The 1980 Census in Historical Perspective," in William Alonso and Paul Starr, *The Politics of Numbers* (1987).

[17] The case is *Cuomo v. Baldrige*, 674 F.Supp. 1089 (S.D.N.Y. 1987).

[18] U.S. Dept. of Commerce, Office of the Secretary, "Decision of the Secretary of Commerce on Whether a Statistical Adjustment of the 1990 Census of Population and Housing should Be Made for Coverage Deficiencies Resulting in an Overcount or Undercount of the Population," *Federal Register* 56 (140): 33582 (1991).

[19] The case was originally known as *City of New York v. U.S. Dept. of Commerce;* the decision by the 2nd U.S. Circuit Court of Appeals was issued on Aug. 8, 1994; Wisconsin, which stood to lose a House seat under an adjusted count, intervened on the side of the federal government in opposition to an adjustment.

[20] See Duane L. Steffey and Norman M. Bradburn (eds.), *Counting People in the Information Age: Report of the Panel to Evaluate Alternative Census Methods* (1994), pp. 1-14 [summary].

[21] See *Modernizing the U.S. Census, op. cit.*, pp. 3-5 [summary].

[22] For text of veto message, see *Congressional Quarterly Weekly Report*, June 14, 1997, p. 1393.

[23] The Seattle region covers Alaska, Washington, Oregon, Idaho and Northern California.

[24] U.S. General Accounting Office, "Decennial Census: Preparations for Dress Rehearsal Underscore the Challenges for 2000," March 26, 1998.

[25] Other panel members are David Murray, a statistical researcher, appointed by Gingrich; Atlanta attorney Joseph Whitley and former Commerce Department official Mark Neuman, appointed by Senate Majority Leader Lott; and White House appointees Everett Ehrlich, a former under secretary of Commerce; Gilbert Casellas, a former chairman of the Equal Employment Opportunity Commission; and Lorraine Green, an Amtrak executive.

[26] *The Washington Post*, April 24, 1998, p. A25.

Bibliography

Selected Sources Used

Books

Anderson, Margo J., *The American Census: A Social History*, Yale University Press, 1988.

Anderson, a professor of urban studies at the University of Wisconsin in Milwaukee, provides a thorough and insightful history of American censuses from 1790 through 1980. Each chapter has detailed source notes; the book also includes historical tables and a three-page bibliographic essay. For a good account of the increasing controversy over the undercount issue in the 1960s and '70s and the decision not to adjust the 1980 census figures, see her article "The 1980 Census in Historical Perspective," in William Alonso and Paul Starr (eds.), *The Politics of Numbers*, Russell Sage Foundation, 1987 [published under the name Margo A. Conk].

Bryant, Barbara Everitt and William Dunn, *Moving Power & Money: The Politics of Census Taking*, New Strategist Publications, 1995.

Bryant gives a lively account of her three years as director of the Bureau of the Census, which included the debate and start of litigation over statistically adjusting the 1990 census figures. The book includes reference notes for each chapter. Bryant is now a research professor at the University of Michigan.

Choldin, Harvey, *Looking for the Last Percent: The Controversy Over Census Undercounts*, Rutgers University Press, 1994.

Choldin, a professor emeritus of sociology at the University of Illinois in Urbana, provides a balanced account of the undercount controversies of the 1980 and 1990 censuses. The book includes five pages of source notes and a 13-page bibliography.

Eckler, A. Ross, *The Bureau of the Census*, Praeger, 1972.

Eckler, who served in the Census Bureau for nearly three decades, including four years as director (1965-1969), gives an informative overview of the bureau's history from its founding in 1902 through 1970. The book includes the population and housing questions asked on each of the decennial censuses from 1790 through 1970, a list of Census Bureau directors from 1902-1972 and a four-page bibliography.

Articles

"A Look at . . . Racial Identity," *The Washington Post*, June 8, 1997, p. C3.

In two opposing opinion pieces, Joseph E. Lowery and Amitai Etzioni discuss the potential impact of adding a multiracial category to Census Bureau forms. Lowery, president of the Southern Christian Leadership Conference and chairman of the National Black Leadership Forum, argued against the proposal; Etzioni, a professor at George Washington University, argued in favor.

Holmes, Steven A., "Two Communities Illustrate Debate Over Census," *The New York Times*, Aug. 30, 1997, sec. 1, p. 1.

The article uses two communities — an inner-city neighborhood in Harrisburg, Pa., and an adjacent suburb — to illustrate the difficulties of getting accurate population counts and to examine the Census Bureau's plan to use sampling to try to get more accurate tallies in Census 2000.

Reports and Studies

Edmonston, Barry and Charles Schultze (eds.), *Modernizing the U.S. Census*, Panel on Census Requirements in the Year 2000 and Beyond, Committee on National Statistics, Commission on Behavioral and Social Sciences and Education, National Research Council, National Academy Press, 1995.

This 460-page final report by a 15-member panel of scientists concluded that physical enumeration could not be used to produce a complete census and endorsed the use of statistical sampling to improve the accuracy of the population count. Schultze, chair of the panel, is a senior fellow at the Brookings Institution; Edmonston, study director, is a staff member at the National Academy of Sciences' Commission for Behavioral and Social Sciences and Education.

Steffey, Duane L. and Norman M. Bradburn (eds.), *Counting People in the Information Age: Report of the Panel to Evaluate Alternative Census Methods*, Committee on National Statistics, Commission on Behavioral and Social Sciences and Education, and National Research Council, National Academy Press, 1994.

This 226-page final report by a 13-member panel of scientists called for steps to improve response and coverage of traditional census methods as well as use of statistical sampling to produce a final count. Bradburn, chair of the panel, is with the National Opinion Research Center at the University of Chicago; Steffey, the study director, is a professor of mathematical sciences at San Diego State University.

White, Andrew A., and Keith F. Rust [eds.], "Preparing for the 2000 Census: Interim Report II," Panel to Evaluate Alternative Census Methodologies, Committee on National Statistics, Commission on Behavioral and Social Sciences and Education, National Research Council, 1997.

The panel concluded last year that the Census Bureau's research and planning were "going in the right direction to ensure an efficient and accurate census." It also said that sampling was "likely to increase confidence" in the accuracy of the census unless there was "an organized negative publicity campaign."

The Next Step

Additional information from UMI's Newspaper & Periodical Abstracts™ database

Sampling Controversy

"Census Counts a Loss," *The Denver Post*, Jan. 15, 1998, p. B6.

An editorial examines the resignation of Census Director Martha Farnsworth Riche, blaming it on disagreements between President Clinton and Republican members of Congress over using computerized sampling for the 2000 census.

El Nasser, Haya, "Census Director Resigning after Sampling is Tested," *USA Today*, Jan. 13, 1998, p. A2.

U.S. Census Bureau Director Martha Farnsworth Riche, who's been fighting Republican lawmakers over how the 2000 census should be conducted, said Monday that she's quitting at the end of the month. Riche, census director since January 1994, has pushed for the use of statistical sampling, a way of estimating people missed by a traditional headcount. The 1990 census missed 4 million people, a disproportionate number of them minorities.

Fiore, Faye, "Gingrich Files Suit to Block Sampling Method in Census," *Los Angeles Times*, Feb. 21, 1998, p. A16.

Moving to block a counting method that Republican leaders fear could threaten their political power, House Speaker Newt Gingrich filed a lawsuit Friday to prohibit statistical sampling in the 2000 census. The lawsuit is the second filed this month that would thwart the Clinton administration's plan to use sampling to compensate for the undercount in the 1990 census, when an estimated 1.6 percent of the nation's population was missed. Although the legal arguments are purely constitutional, Democrats accuse the GOP of putting politics before an accurate census. The undercounted are largely minorities and urban poor, who tend to be Democratic, and counting them could jeopardize the GOP voting base when congressional districts — as well as state legislative districts — are redrawn using the 2000 census results.

James, Frank, "Census Director Resigns as Disputed Count Nears," *Chicago Tribune*, Jan. 13, 1998, p. 5.

The Census Bureau's director unexpectedly resigned Monday, adding more uncertainty to preparations for the 2000 census, already clouded by a partisan fight between congressional Republicans and the White House. Martha Farnsworth Riche said she decided to leave because she accomplished her goals, among them redirecting the bureau's approach to conducting the census. She did not cite the partisan feuding as a reason for her departure.

Pianin, Eric, and Helen Dewar, "Compromise Found on Census Sampling; Congress Also Clears FDA Changes," *The Washington Post*, Nov. 10, 1997, p. A4.

The White House and Republican congressional leaders yesterday put the finishing touches on a politically sensitive compromise for conducting the 2000 census that would allow the administration to experiment with statistical sampling to achieve a more accurate count but give Republicans ample time and resources to challenge the technique in court.

Shuster, Beth, "City to Join Those Trying for Census Sampling," *Los Angeles Times*, March 4, 1998, p. B1.

City Attorney James K. Hahn announced that his office will intervene in two federal lawsuits seeking to prohibit statistical sampling in the 2000 census. When the census was last taken eight years ago, Hahn said, Los Angeles residents were significantly undercounted, which resulted in the loss of at least $12 million in federal and state funds and deprived the city of at least one, and possibly two, congressional seats to which it is entitled. With the aid of a Los Angeles law firm, Hahn said his office will intervene to oppose recent lawsuits filed by House Speaker Newt Gingrich on behalf of the House of Representatives, and by the Southeastern Legal Foundation of Atlanta, a conservative, public-interest law firm.

Vobejda, Barbara, "Scientific Consensus Backs Sampling for 2000 Census; Statistical Approach Still Dividing Lawmakers," *The Washington Post*, June 11, 1997, p. A4.

Republicans on Capitol Hill are so determined to count every head for the 2000 census that they have held up a politically popular bill giving relief funds to flood victims in the Midwest. But in the scientific community, the question of how best to conduct the census has drawn a clear answer: Trying to count every person is the wrong way to go. Yesterday, a National Academy of Sciences panel endorsed statistical sampling, adding to a list of many other academic groups concluding that this technique is the most accurate and cost-efficient way to count the nation's population.

Racial Backgrounds

"Our Racial Complexity," *Boston Globe*, July 10, 1997, p. A12.

A special commission's proposal to allow persons in the 2000 census to select more than one racial box is a step forward. If approved by the Clinton administration and Congress, it will relieve those of mixed racial ancestry of the current obligation either to deny part of their heritage or choose the catchall "other" category. The commission left one foot in mid-air, however, when it failed to detail how the information should be used. This is crucial, because if someone of mixed parentage checks both "black" and "white" boxes, how is he or she counted for purposes of affirmative action or congressional redistricting?

Barr, Stephen, and Michael A. Fletcher, "U.S. Proposes Multiple Racial Identification for 2000 Census," *The Washington Post*, July 9, 1997, p. A1.

The Clinton administration yesterday proposed that Americans for the first time be allowed to choose more than one racial category when identifying themselves for the census and other government programs. The long-awaited proposal, coming after numerous studies and congressional hearings, is an attempt to resolve how the federal government should describe a population comprising an increasingly complex blend of racial and ethnic groups. The proposal represents the unanimous recommendation of 30 federal agencies that have studied the issue for three years.

Dickerson, Jeff, "The Time has Come for 'Mixed Race' Category," *Atlanta Journal Constitution*, May 20, 1997, p. A12

The author says it's time for a "mixed-race" or "multiracial" category on the 2000 census.

Fulwood, Sam III, "Little Effect Seen by Adding Multiracial Listing to Census," *Los Angeles Times*, May 16, 1997, p. A12.

Adding a multiracial category to the 2000 census is unlikely to affect the way most black or white Americans identify themselves, but it could reduce the number of respondents who choose other racial categories. The creation of a mixed-race category has been proposed by multiracial advocacy groups who contend that existing classifications force them to make a choice between the racial identities of their parents. Critics, however, argue that a mixed-race category could reduce minority head counts and weaken enforcement of civil rights laws.

Malone, Julia, "2000 Census Will Offer More Racial Categories, But Multiple Choices Could be a Statistical Nightmare for Officials to Tabulate," *Atlanta Journal Constitution*, Oct. 30, 1997, p. A3.

Americans will be given a new option of identifying with more than one race when U.S. census-takers come calling in the year 2000. Franklin M. Raines, director of the Office of Management and Budget, released new guidelines that will offer five racial categories and permit respondents to check off as many as they choose. As widely expected, Raines rejected calls from some groups for a new "multiracial" category to accommodate the growing number of Americans with mixed-race backgrounds.

McLeod, Ramon G., "Mixed-Race People Cheer Census Proposal," *San Francisco Chronicle*, July 9, 1997, p. A3.

Americans could choose more than one racial category on the 2000 census, under federal rules proposed today and applauded by advocates for mixed-race people. The federal task force representing 30 agencies made the recommendations to the Office of Management and Budget, which sets the reporting guidelines for the census and other forms. The proposed rules were pub-

lished in a report in today's *Federal Register*.

Shepard, Scott, "Moving from 'Other' to 'Multiracial' Melting Pot: Many Pushing to Establish New Race Category in Census," *Atlanta Journal Constitution*, July 5, 1997, p. A9.

With the federal government nearing a decision on a multiracial census category, Americans on both sides of the issue are bracing for a long, hot summer of rancorous debate.

Shogren, Elizabeth, "Panel Rejects 'Mixed-Race' Census Category," *Los Angeles Times*, July 9, 1997, p. A1.

A Clinton administration task force on Tuesday rejected a campaign to add a "multiracial" classification to the 2000 census but recommended allowing mixed-race Americans for the first time to check off more than one racial category. Plunging into a contentious cultural debate, the 30-agency task force unanimously opposed a change sought by Americans of mixed racial heritage who object to identifying themselves as members of a single race. Although studies have indicated that fewer than 2 percent of Americans would identify themselves as mixed-race, their ranks are growing as interracial marriages become more common.

Census Forms

Cohn, D. Vera, "Brevity as Soul of Writ: Census Shrinks Short Form, 7-Question Survey Aims for Bigger Response," *The Washington Post*, April 1, 1997, p. A15.

The short questionnaire for the 2000 census — the one that most U.S. households will receive — will be the briefest one this century. It will include seven questions, down from 12 in the 1990 census. Under pressure from Congress to slim down, the Census Bureau also will drop five subjects from the longer questionnaire that about 20 percent of U.S. households will receive. No longer will people be asked the year they last worked, their home's water source and type of sewage system, whether they live in a condominium and — if female — how many children they have had.

Duff, Christina, "Census Bureau Plans to Trim its 'Long Form'," *The Wall Street Journal*, March 21, 1997, p. 9B.

With Census 2000 just three years away, the U.S. Census Bureau plans to present Congress in April 1997 with a tighter version of its most comprehensive data-gathering questionnaire.

Stout, David, "Census Plans Shorter Forms For Year 2000," *The New York Times*, April 1, 1997, p. A21.

Trying to balance the need for information against demands for efficiency, the Census Bureau today proposed using the shortest questionnaire in almost two centuries for the 2000 census, plus a more concise long form. Seven subjects, the fewest since the 1820 census, were proposed for the short form: name, age, sex, relationship to others in the household, race, whether one is of Hispanic origin and whether the respondent rents or owns a home.

Back Issues

Great Research on Current Issues Starts Right Here.
Recent topics covered by The CQ Researcher are listed below.
Now available on the Web
For information, call (800) 432-2250 ext. 279 or (202) 887-6279.

If you would like to have any of these CQ Researchers updated, or need more information about these topics, please call CQ Custom Research. Special rates for CQ subscribers.
(202) 887-8600 or (800) 432-2250, ext. 600, or E-mail Custom.Research@cq.com

Back issues are available for $5.00 (subscribers) or $10.00 (non-subscribers). Quantity discounts apply to orders over 10. To order, call Congressional Quarterly Customer Service at (202) 887-8621.

Binders are available for $18.00. To order call 1-800-638-1710. Please refer to stock number 648.

Future Topics

▶ *Child-Care Options*

▶ *Alzheimer's Disease*

▶ *U.S.-Russian Relations*

THE
CQ Researcher
PUBLISHED BY CONGRESSIONAL QUARTERLY INC.

Child-Care Options

Are there enough good facilities?

A bout 13 million children under age 6 get daily care from someone other than their parents. For many working families, finding child-care that stimulates their children's physical, emotional and intellectual development is a continuing problem. For others, simply finding an affordable facility is the challenge. Full-day care for one child can often cost more than the tuition at a public university. Still, child-care workers rank among the lowest paid in the country, which contributes to high staff turnover and high child-staff ratios. Several studies say U.S. child care is so poor it threatens children's health and development. But conservatives challenge the findings and urge Congress not to increase subsidies for child-care or set federal standards for providers.

C_Q **May 8, 1998** • **Volume 8, No. 18** • **Pages 409-432**

Formerly Editorial Research Reports

May 8, 1998
Volume 8, No.18

EDITOR
Sandra Stencel

MANAGING EDITOR
Thomas J. Colin

ASSOCIATE EDITOR
Sarah M. Magner

STAFF WRITERS
Adriel Bettelheim
Mary H. Cooper
Kenneth Jost
Kathy Koch
David Masci

PRODUCTION EDITOR
Melissa Hall

EDITORIAL ASSISTANT
Laura S. Cavender

PUBLISHED BY
Congressional Quarterly Inc.

CHAIRMAN
Andrew Barnes

VICE CHAIRMAN
Andrew P. Corty

PRESIDENT AND PUBLISHER
Robert W. Merry

EXECUTIVE EDITOR
David Rapp

Bibliographic records and abstracts included in The Next Step section of this publication are the copyrighted material of UMI, and are used with permission.

The CQ Researcher (ISSN 1056-2036). Formerly Editorial Research Reports. Published weekly, except Jan. 2, May 29, July 3, Oct. 30, by Congressional Quarterly Inc., 1414 22nd St., N.W., Washington, D.C. 20037. Annual subscription rate for libraries, businesses and government is $340. Additional rates furnished upon request. Periodicals postage paid at Washington, D.C., and additional mailing offices. POSTMASTER: Send address changes to The CQ Researcher, 1414 22nd St., N.W., Washington, D.C. 20037.

COVER: PHOTO COURTESY OF FRIENDSHIP HOUSE

Child-Care Options

BY KAREN LEE SCRIVO

THE ISSUES

Lisa Fajardo was frantic. When she arrived at her daughter's day-care center, the building was locked and dark. But through a window, she saw 14-month-old Savannah crying in the shadows. She had been overlooked at closing time.

"I thought, 'No, it can't be,' " recalled Fajardo, a 21-year-old psychology student from Centreville, Va. "She was sobbing, and I was pounding on the door, saying 'See, Mom is here. You'll be OK.' "

In desperation, Fajardo smashed a window and crawled into the building.

"I got Savannah out of the crib and wiped her tears, because she was hysterical, as you might imagine," Fajardo said. [1]

Unbeknown to Fajardo, other disquieting incidents had occurred at the ABC Children's Learning Center in Fairfax City, which was being allowed to operate while it appealed a license suspension. The incidents included allowing a 4-year-old boy to get into an unlocked car that rolled down a hill; failing to call 911 after a child had a seizure; and letting young children play "Mortal Kombat," a violent video game for teenagers.

For most parents, horror stories like Fajardo's are the exception. The biggest problem is finding good-quality care or simply finding child care at all.*

Writer Patricia Elam remembers looking for day care for her three children when they were younger. "There are so many things to balance," she recalls, such as affordability, convenience, the needs of the children, the staff-child ratio and the patience level of the staff. Elam was fortunate in finding a wise and wonderful grandmother in her Washington, D.C., neighborhood to care for her young children.

"Yes, someone is spending more time with your child than you are," she says, "but I don't go as far as to say that person is raising the child. That's why I didn't want someone in my home. I didn't want someone else raising my kids."

Decisions about working and child care are individual choices, says Elam, whose own mother stayed home and baked cookies, in a family she characterizes as "an African-American Ozzie and Harriet."

By any standard, child care is a major expense, costing up to $10,000 a year per child, or more than the cost of tuition at many public universities. About half of all American families with young children earn less than $35,000 a year. A family with both parents working full time at minimum wage earns only $21,400 a year. [2]

An estimated 13 million children under age 6 whose mothers are employed outside the home — including 6 million infants and toddlers — spend part of their day being cared for by someone other than their parents. Fifty-one percent of those children are cared for by day-care centers, preschools or other providers, according to the Census Bureau. The rest are cared for by the father or by relatives.

Recent changes in the welfare law require all parents on welfare to work, even those with a child as young as three months. (States can exempt a parent from the work requirements until a child's first birthday, but many, including New Jersey and Michigan, are not doing so.)

Many child-care experts say the supply of licensed caregivers has not kept up with the demand, especially for infants and toddlers and school-age children. Parents who work nights and weekends often have additional trouble finding caregivers, as do those with special-needs children, those whose regular caregiver is unavailable or whose child is sick and those in rural and inner-city areas.

In California, for example, a recent study found that just 4 percent of the child-care centers are licensed to serve toddlers and infants under age 2. And only 2 percent of the state's centers were open weekends, evenings or overnight. [3]

Those who can find care often worry about whether their child is getting enough attention, eating well, learning and adjusting well to the environment, according to a 1997 *Parents* magazine survey. Sixty percent of those using out-of-home care and 50 percent of those using an in-home provider reported having a bad experience that prompted them to discontinue that arrangement. [4]

But conservative groups like the Cato Institute challenge the warnings about a child-care crisis, saying that most parents are satisfied with their children's care and that high-quality care is available and affordable for all, including low-income parents. "Congress should resist any attempt to increase funding for child care and to impose federal standards on providers and parents," says a recent institute report. [5]

The institute points to nationwide surveys showing, it says, that 96 percent of parents are satisfied with their child-care arrangements; child-care ex-

---

*Child-care experts generally agree that high-quality care offers more teachers caring for fewer children, better educated and better trained staff, relatively high wages and low staff-turnover rates.

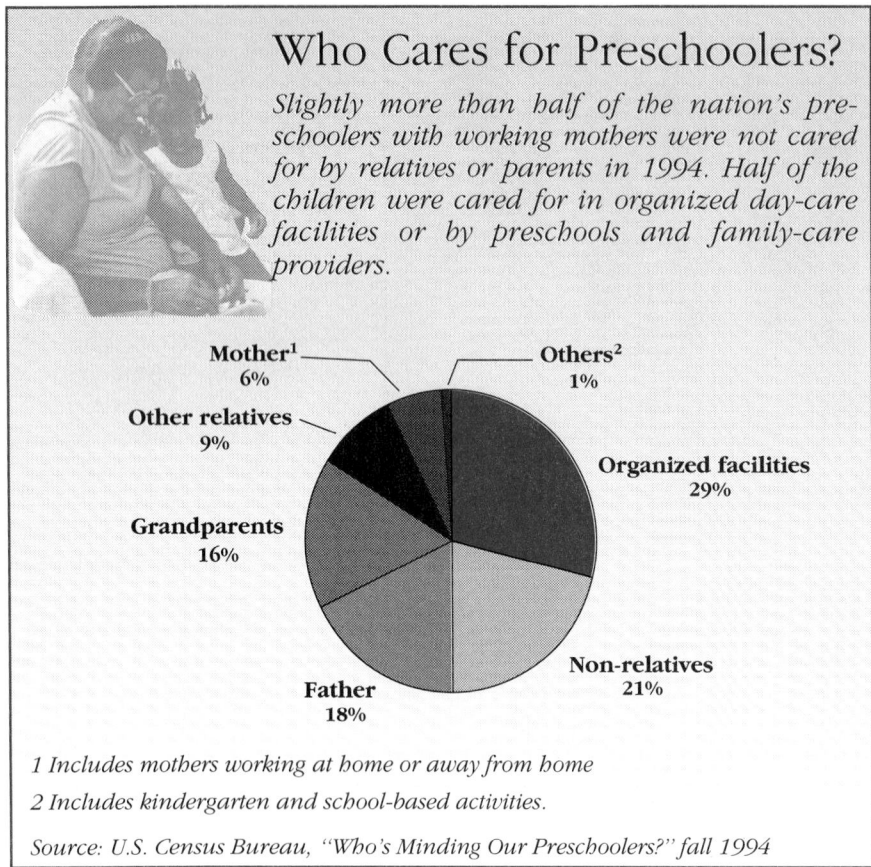

Who Cares for Preschoolers?

Slightly more than half of the nation's preschoolers with working mothers were not cared for by relatives or parents in 1994. Half of the children were cared for in organized day-care facilities or by preschools and family-care providers.

Mother[1]
6%

Other relatives
9%

Grandparents
16%

Father
18%

Others[2]
1%

Organized facilities
29%

Non-relatives
21%

1 Includes mothers working at home or away from home

2 Includes kindergarten and school-based activities.

Source: U.S. Census Bureau, "Who's Minding Our Preschoolers?" fall 1994

penditures by parents have risen less than 5 percent since the 1970s; and the supply of child care has kept up with the demand. [6]

But the Carnegie Foundation says child care and early-education services have been neglected for so long in this country that they are among "the worst services for children in Western society" and the care that most children receive can not only "threaten their immediate health and safety but can also compromise their long-term development." [7]

A 1995 University of Colorado at Denver study concluded that the quality of child care at centers in the United States is "poor to mediocre." The study found that 12 percent provided less than minimal-quality care, which can jeopardize children's health, safety and development. Only 14 percent ranked as having good-

quality care for children overall. [8]

"Babies in poor-quality rooms are vulnerable to more illnesses because basic sanitary conditions are not met for diapering and feeding; are endangered because of safety problems that exist in the room; miss warm, supportive relationships with adults; and lose out on learning because they lack books and toys required for physical and intellectual growth," the study noted.

A 1994 study of children cared for in providers' homes, known as family-care providers, painted an equally grim picture. The study rated more than one-third of the programs as inadequate, or capable of harming a child's development. Only 9 percent of the homes studied were deemed as enhancing the growth and development of children. In addition, low-income and minority children in family-based care received lower-quality care than other children. [9]

These studies are particularly worrisome in light of recent research on the development of the brain, which shows the importance of infants' early learning experiences.

Tragically, poor-quality care occasionally is fatal. Three-month-old Jeremy Fiedelholtz died last year in a licensed family child-care home in Plantation, Fla., after being put to sleep on his stomach, which doctors say increases the chance of sudden infant death syndrome (SIDS). When his mother, Julie Fiedelholtz, stopped by to visit during his first day, she found him in a crib not breathing; he had choked in his own vomit. An aide, who was watching 12 other children in different rooms, called 911. The center's owner — who was out grocery shopping — was later fined $200 for violating the state's minimum child-adult ratio and for leaving the children with an aide who lacked certification in cardio-pulmonary resuscitation (CPR). [10]

Cases like Jeremy and 8-month-old Matthew Eappen, who died in the care of 19-year-old British au pair Louise Woodward, account for less than 2 percent of infant and child deaths, according to the National Child Care Information Center. A 1996 *U.S. News & World Report* investigation found that 76 children and infants died in child-care facilities from drownings, falls, being hit by cars and SIDS. [11]

Minimum child-care requirements vary from state to state, even in health and safety basics such as requiring all children to be immunized and providers to know CPR and first aid.

There are also wide differences among states on the number of caregivers needed per child. In Texas, for example, one adult can care for up to 10 year-and-a-half-year-olds. In Maryland, the ratio is one adult for every three children up to 18 months. [12]

Most states do not license or inspect small family-care providers, such as those serving three to six children in their homes. In addition, 39 states and the District of Columbia do not require training before providers can care for children in their homes. [13]

Recent battles over states' rights have led most child-care experts to stop pressing for passage of federal child-care standards. Some experts still argue, however, that national standards — perhaps set by a private, nonprofit organization — are essential.

The quality of child care is directly affected by low pay, high staff turnover and lack of training, says Helen Blank, director of the Child Care and Development Division at the Children's Defense Fund (CDF). The average care worker only earns about $12,000 a year, she says, and in 32 states workers in child-care centers do not need a background in early-childhood education or training before starting to work with children.

"We pay less for the care of our children per hour than we pay for someone to park our car," says Philadelphia pediatrician Susan Aronson, a board member of the American Academy of Pediatrics (AAP). "We're not parking children. Our youngest need the stimulation of a warm and close relationship with their caregivers."

Some suggest that government should play a larger role in subsidizing child care for all parents, regardless of income, and point to Western Europe and Scandinavia.

"There is the belief [in Europe] that quality child care is too expensive, so the whole society helps" pay for it, says Faith Wohl, president of the New York-based Child Care Action Campaign. "Here [in America] the argument is that child care is too expensive, and that people should have thought about that before they had kids."

But conservatives want to pare down government's role in child care. "What families desperately need is a decreased role of government so that the role of parents and loved ones can increase," said Gary Bauer, president of the Family Research Council. "Taxpayer-funded day care does nothing to expand opportunities for families to spend time with their children." [14]

Following last October's White House Conference on Child Care, the issue became part of the nation's agenda. Two months later, on Jan. 7, President Clinton proposed $21.7 billion in spending measures and tax breaks aimed at helping working families pay for child care over the next five years. But the plan depends

---

"We pay less for the care of our children per hour than we pay for someone to park our car."

— Dr. Susan Aronson
American Academy of Pediatrics

---

in part on getting money from the increasingly unlikely tobacco-company settlement, and many members of Congress have other ideas on how to spend the windfall.

Meanwhile, Republicans and some Democrats have introduced legislation that includes a tax credit for stay-at-home mothers, which is reopening the so-called "mommy war" pitting stay-at-home mothers against working mothers. But some observers question the fairness of providing tax credits for middle-income, stay-at-home mothers while requiring welfare mothers to work. [15]

When Clinton unveiled his proposal, he talked about his mother's experience as a single parent. "I've often wondered how my mother, when she was widowed, would have been able to go back to school if I hadn't been able to move in with my grandparents," the president said. "I was lucky, and it turned out reasonably well for me. How many children are out there with exactly the same potential who never got the same break?" [16]

As the child-care debate continues, these are some of the issues facing parents and policy-makers:

Does day care help or hurt a child's intellectual or emotional development?

Liberals and conservatives often draw very different conclusions from the same studies of the impact day care has on children's emotional and intellectual development.

In April, a major nationwide study found that children cared for with several other children had fewer behavior problems than those watched alone by a nanny or in a very small group. It also found that children in poor-quality day care are more likely to have behavior problems than those in care environments where well-trained staff interact with the children frequently, according to researchers at the National Institute of Child Health and Human Development (NICHD). [17]

To Ginny Holloway, who cares for four preschoolers in her Franconia, Va., home, the study is right on target. Group care "promotes sharing, patience, learning to take your turn," says Holloway, who teaches her charges to follow rules at mealtime and share toys. "One-on-one attention is good for children, but children learn in a group," she says. [18]

But in the view of Joseph Adelson, a professor emeritus of psychology at the University of Michigan, child care is fraught with problems. "The typical child in day care simply does not

Several States Set Tougher Staff Rules

Eight states lowered the child-staff ratios for infants in child-care centers from 1986 to 1997, including three states that now prohibit the care of infants in facilities where the ratio is 7:1 or 8:1.

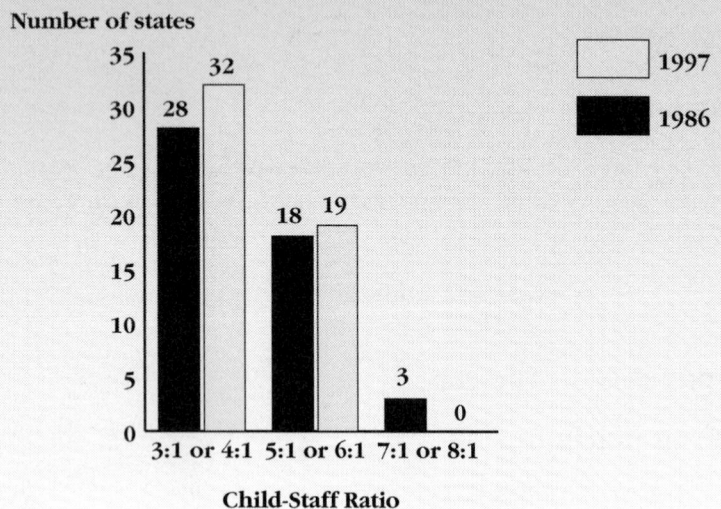

Child-Staff Ratios for Infants

Number of states

	1997
	1986

3:1 or 4:1 — 28 (1986), 32 (1997)
5:1 or 6:1 — 18 (1986), 19 (1997)
7:1 or 8:1 — 3 (1986), 0 (1997)

Child-Staff Ratio

Note: In 1986, the total of the states and the District of Columbia adds to 49 because two states are not included, one that was unregulated and one in which day care was prohibited for infants.

Source: The Center for Career Development in Early Care and Education, Wheelock College, 1997

receive the same amount of individual attention, or the same degree of focused intensity, he would receive from a parent," he said. "There is rarely the same degree of continuity in the relationship between child and adult. Nor is there a family history or sense of lineage to help a child establish his identity." [19]

The NICHD findings were the third installment in a seven-year research project that is considered the most comprehensive look at the effects of day care on children's development.

Launched in 1991, the nationwide study is tracking 1,364 socially and racially diverse children in a variety of care arrangements. [20]

Earlier reports focused on children's emotional and cognitive development.

Last year's report concluded that children in day care learned to talk and think as well as those cared for by their mothers. The 1996 report found that child care — if of good quality — does not affect an infant's attachment to his or her mother. [21]

"The characteristics of the family are a better predictor of a child's overall development than whether he or she is in day care," says Kathleen McCartney, an NICHD investigator.

Generally, the reports have found that children's development depends more on coming from a loving, stable home than on whether they are in day care. Low-quality care, more than 10 hours a week in care and multiple child-care arrangements during the first 15 months of life hurt infants' attachment to their mothers when combined with maternal insensi-

tivity to infant needs, the study said. In addition, boys who spent more than 30 hours a week in child care were somewhat more likely to have an insecure attachment to their mothers compared with other boys, according to the study. And several NICHD findings stress the importance of quality care.

But not everyone is reassured by the NICHD findings or other recent studies supporting the benefits of quality child care.

Patrick Fagan, former deputy secretary for family policy in the Health and Human Services Department in the Bush administration, remains concerned about how well infants in day care bond with their mothers. In his opinion, the NICHD study does not invalidate findings from the 1980s that infants who spent more than 20 hours in day care were less attached to their mothers.

"The national consensus is that the best care for children is by their mother," says Fagan, now a fellow at the Heritage Foundation.

Maggie Gallagher, a scholar affiliated with the Institute for American Values, sees a disturbing pattern in the NICHD findings. "Day care has the worst immediate effects on children with less sensitive mothers," she wrote recently. "And over time, women who put their children in day care become somewhat less sensitive." [22]

Recent discoveries about the critical role infancy plays in brain development have also renewed concerns about the effects of child care on very young children. A 1996 Families and Work Institute conference on children's brain development stressed that early care plays a decisive role in developing the child's ability to learn and to control emotions. The conference report called for "intensive efforts to improve the quality of child care." [23]

Research has shown that children in good child care and early-education programs have stronger language, pre-math and social skills as well as better relationships with teachers and a more positive self-image than those in poor centers and programs. Moreover, quality care has an even greater impact on the language skills and self-perception of "at-risk" children. [24]

"For African-American children in poverty, education is the greatest determiner of success," says Carla Taylor, a senior policy analyst at the National Black Child Development Institute.

The research is also rekindling the debate on whether mothers should stay at home with infants and young children.

But for many women, economic realities eliminate any choice about working, even during their child's first year. And for welfare recipients, new requirements mean going back to work soon after their child's birth.

What is clear is that when mothers feel they are doing the wrong thing — either by working or staying at home — the anxiety hurts the children as well as the mothers.

"Ultimately, what is best for families is to have real choices, and that requires policies and societal attitudes that support parents whether or not they work outside the home," the Families and Work Institute report says. "In particular, families need access to affordable, high-quality child care and early education." [25]

Do national standards, subsidies and tax credits improve the quality of child care?

A recent four-year study takes a comprehensive look at improving child care in the United States. The effort involved hundreds of early-childhood experts. [26] Among the report's recommendations:

• expect high quality in all child-care programs;

Children in good-quality child care and early-education programs have stronger language, pre-math and social skills than kids in poor centers.

Courtesy of Friendship House

• develop age-appropriate goals for children;

• focus on measurable results;

• involve parents and the community;

• license all staff and establish clear training requirements;

• expand early-childhood educa-tion training;

• license all child-care programs;

• create local and state early-care and education boards responsible for the infrastructure and governance of programs.

Georgetown University Professor William T. Gormley Jr., who has written a book about child care as a public-policy problem, says there are many ways to improve child-care quality, such as lowering staff-child ratios and requiring better training for teachers. But some measures can lower the supply of good child care. [27]

"States have found that lower [staff-child] ratios mean fewer licensed centers," Gormley says. "When licensed centers decline, parents use unregulated facilities, and that's the worst possible situation. [You] can't enhance quality if child care is not available."

Improving education and training, however, does not undermine the supply of good child care, says Gormley, who recommends states have stronger education standards for child-care providers such as early-childhood education training at community colleges and universities or through seminars. Studies also show that college-educated people make better caregivers, regardless of their major, he says.

Florida recently tried both improving the child-to-teacher ratio and increasing teacher-education requirements. The state changed staff ratios

Teacher Requirements Vary Widely

Thirty states do not require teachers at child-care centers to have specialized training or experience in early-childhood education (ECE) when they are hired, although they do require ongoing training. Only 20 states require pre-service training, and two states, Michigan and Louisiana, have no ECE requirements.

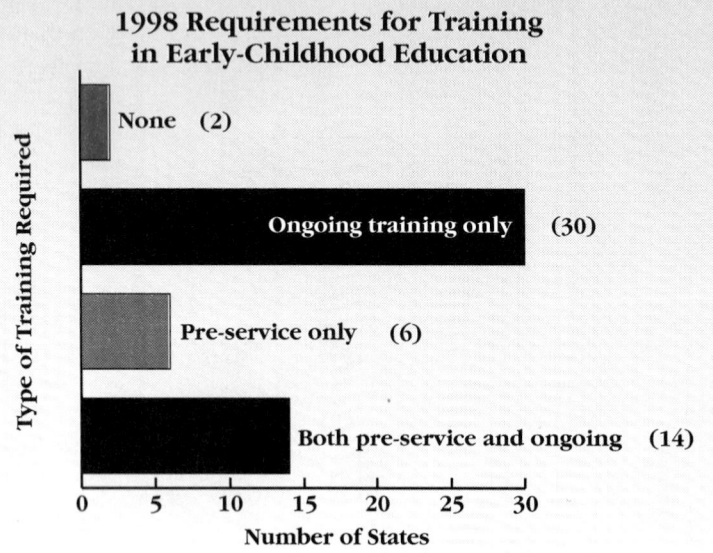

1998 Requirements for Training in Early-Childhood Education

Note: The number of states totals 52 because New York City and the District of Columbia are included.

Source: Center for Career Development in Early Care and Education, Wheelock College, 1998.

for infants from one adult to every six infants to 1-to-4 and for toddlers from 1-to-8 to 1-to-6. It also required at least one staff member for every 20 children to have early-childhood training or education. A study of the state's efforts concluded that "regulatory improvements have a powerful capacity to affect children's outcomes and improve the quality of their early education and care." The higher standards did not affect the cost or availability of care, according to the study.

The study also found an improvement in children's cognitive and emotional development and language skills, a decrease in behavior problems, more time spent on learning activities and teachers being more responsive to children. [28]

While most child-care experts have abandoned hope of federal child-care standards, many hope that minimal national guidelines based on research and professional practice will be accepted for setting staff ratios, group size, caregiver education and training and health and safety issues. Several groups have standards that could be used.

"There need to be incentives for states to use national standards," says Aronson of the AAP, which encourages child-care providers to follow national guidelines like its "Caring for Our Children" health and safety standards. "Government can enable the standards by providing incentives" such as loans to remove hazardous playground surfaces or install additional sinks, Aronson says. "That

works better than requirements."

In addition to the AAP's standards, the National Association for the Education of Young Children (NAEYC) accredits child-care centers that meet its standards on such factors as teacher-child ratios, staff qualifications and health and safety issues. Centers must have been in operation for at least a year and complete an extensive evaluation that includes an on-site inspection. There are about 6,000 NAEYC-accredited centers in the United States. Home child-care operations are accredited through the National Association of Family Child Care.

NAEYC-accredited child-care centers generally offer higher-quality care than non-accredited centers, but accreditation does not guarantee excellence, according to a 1997 study by the Center for the Child Care Work Force. The study says the main problem is that accreditation alone doesn't address high teacher turnover and its effect on quality. But accreditation coupled with stability of teachers, higher pay and non-profit status is a good predictor of high-quality care, noted the study, which looked at 92 care programs in three Northern California communities. [29]

"Accreditation is a good thing. It's an indicator [of quality]," says Rosemarie Vardell, the center's director of leadership. "But without good wages and better teaching staff, it is not as good an indicator."

Indeed, many observers blame the limited quality of care on the high cost of child care and the fact that most of the money for care comes out of parents' pockets, rather than from government. In the United States, for every dollar spent on child care, parents pay 60 cents, government pays 39 cents and the private sector spends a penny, says Wohl of the Child Care Action Campaign.

"You hear parents moaning about paying for college, but they pay a much smaller percentage of the total [than the government] compared with child care," she says, noting that parents pay just 23 cents of every dollar for public colleges and universities and 27 cents for private schools.

The economics of child care needs to be changed, Wohl says. More money needs to come from private corporations and foundations, she says, adding that government can provide incentives for private-sector funding through tax credits.

Some major corporations are investing in child-care initiatives (see p. 424). In fact, one estimate put the figure at $350 million from 1990-1995. Much of that money has gone toward starting new child-care centers, recruiting new family child-care homes and improving the quality of child-care services. [30]

Aletha Huston, a professor of human development at the University of Texas at Austin, sees a larger role for government.

"All of us are better off if government subsidizes quality care," she says, especially poor families. "Many spend 20-25 percent of their income on child care. That's a huge chunk if you're poor."

But, she says, child-care tax credits don't help those who earn so little they don't pay taxes. Instead, she recommends a subsidy for parents seeking quality care. Putting a limit on the amount of the subsidy can make it harder for parents to use standard child-care centers, which are generally better for a child's development — assuming they are of high quality — than other forms of care, such as a nanny or family child care.

"The United States has a lot to learn from other countries that have a strong commitment to family policies and support families," says Valerie Polakow, an education professor at Eastern Michigan University in Ypsilanti. Those countries accept collective responsibility to members of society, which "requires government to redistribute resources and create sensible conditions."

In Denmark, government-subsidized child care is available for children from 6 months to age 7 regardless of the parents' income or marital status, and the quality of care is uniformly high, says Polakow, who studied child care in Denmark as a Fulbright scholar. There are trained professional teachers in each classroom, and low child-teacher ratios, she adds.

"Denmark has had a support base [for working parents] for several decades, and it has been supported across the political spectrum," Polakow says, noting that the country has paid maternity and paternity leave, universal child and family allowances, a single-parent allowance and a monthly assistance stipend as well as housing subsidies, generous unemployment benefits and universal health care.

But the Cato Institute argues against "government intrusion" in child care that takes away parental choices and responsibility. "Advocates of child care should not propose policies that will ultimately render child care less affordable," policy analyst Darcy Olsen writes in a recent report on child care. "The fact is that high-quality child care is available and affordable even for low-income parents. Misguided policies that would increase regulations and subsidies would increase the costs of child care, pricing it out of the reach of those they are intended to help." [31]

Moreover, Bauer of the Family Research Council argues that the demand for more government involvement in child care is exaggerated. He points to 1993 Census Bureau statistics showing that only 29.9 percent of all children under age 5 with working moms are in day-care centers.

"While not all mothers can stay home with their children, child-care policy must preserve and promote as many choices as possible for these families, including at-home care, church-based care and other informal arrangements," Bauer said. "Any expansion of federal oversight, by definition, will limit options and pose regulatory nightmares." [32]

Is a shortage of affordable child care hurting the effort to move people from welfare to work?

The 1996 welfare reform act, or the Personal Responsibility and Work Opportunity Reconciliation Act, requires families to work and imposes a five-year time limit on benefits for most participants. The act consolidated four child-care programs into the Child Care and Development Block Grant. The block grant money goes to the states, which distribute it to low-income families to help pay for child care. Parents can choose child-care centers, family child-care homes, neighbors or relatives to care for their children.

"We have an opportunity to reduce poverty only if there is sufficient child care and health care," says retired economics Professor Barbara R. Bergmann, who is writing a book on child care and welfare reform. "If universal child care is not available, we will not be able to move dependent people off welfare."

States can allow those with children age 6 or younger to work only 20 hours a week, and exempt mothers with children under age 1 from the work requirements. But some states send mothers back to work sooner. A state can also exempt a single parent with children under 6 who cannot find appropriate and affordable child care. However, families are not exempt from the time limits. By 2002, 50 percent of welfare recipients in each state must be working or the state could lose part of its money and face penalties. [33]

Earlier this year, the General Accounting Office found that seven states it studied were using the additional federal funds as well as their own money to expand child-care programs in response to the increased demand brought on by the work requirement. Six of the seven states reported an increase in the number of children served under these programs. Even though the states are expanding their programs, they are still unable to provide child-care subsidies for all the eligible families, the report said.

(The seven states were California, Connecticut, Louisiana, Maryland, Oregon, Texas and Wisconsin.)

The report concluded, however, that it was too early to tell how effective the states' efforts will be in meeting the child-care needs of low-income families. The states' initial efforts came at a time of declining caseloads, which provided some states with additional money to invest in child care. But uncertainty about the economic future and the number of welfare families needing child-care help could easily change the picture and affect states' ability to fund programs over the long haul. [34]

But even if states find ways to meet the increasing demand for child care by welfare recipients, they may not be able to help low-income families who don't qualify for the welfare benefits.

The Congressional Budget Office projects that by 2002 there could be a $1.4 billion shortfall in funds needed to meet welfare work requirements and maintain current levels of assistance for the working poor who don't receive benefits. [35]

Many states already have long waiting lists of families eligible for child-care assistance. As of January, about half the states had to turn away eligible working families, according to the CDF. In California, the waiting list exceeds 200,000 families, mostly low-income workers not on welfare. But waiting-list numbers often underestimate the real need since administrators say many families don't bother adding themselves once they hear how long it is. [36]

And then there are the working poor who don't even qualify for assistance. A family of three with two parents working full time at minimum wage ($21,400) would be ineligible in 15 states according to a 1998 CDF survey. These families face what the report calls a "series of locked doors," such as low state-eligibility cutoffs for child-care assistance, long

waiting lists or inadequate funding for additional child care or lack of information that they qualify for assistance.

"This leaves millions of American working families 'locked out' and unable to get the help they need to succeed," the report said. "Those fortunate enough to actually qualify for child-care assistance face additional locked doors: In some cases, the amount the state will pay for care is so low that parents cannot find quality providers, or they have to pay so much in fees or copayments that child-care expenses are still a staggering burden." [37]

The CDF recommends $20 billion over the next five years in new, mandatory funding for the Child Care and Development Block Grants to the states to be paid for by increasing the tobacco tax or through a budget surplus. It also calls for tax credits for families who need child care because they work outside the home as well as families where one parent stays home to care for the children.

Finding affordable child care can also be particularly difficult for mothers who work at nights, weekends or rotating shifts such as nurses, waitresses, cooks, child-care workers and hairdressers. Women with limited education are more likely to work these hours, according to a study by Harriet B. Presser, director of the Center on Population, Gender and Social Equality at the University of Maryland in College Park. And these occupations are among those the Bureau of Labor Statistics projects will grow in the next 10 years, she says, adding that there could be serious implications for welfare reform.

"Accordingly, to achieve the primary objective of welfare reform — moving mothers permanently from welfare to employment — child care will need to be expanded markedly during non-standard times, including evenings and weekends," Presser wrote. [38]

BACKGROUND

U.S. Gets Involved

The debate over government involvement in child care goes back to at least the 1930s and early '40s, when men marched off to war and millions of women entered the work force. First lady Eleanor Roosevelt, going against tradition, fought to create child-care centers.

In 1933, the Roosevelt administration's New Deal legislation created the Works Progress Administration, which included a child-care component. Seven years later, in 1940, Congress passed the Lanham Act and later amendments that provided child-care assistance for women workers during World War II. By 1950, the Census Bureau was reporting that there were 2 million children under age 6 with working mothers. And in 1954, changes in the Tax Code included a child-care deduction of up to $600.

In 1965, the federal government created the Head Start program to help low-income children get ready for school. [39] In the 1970s, the federal government substantially increased its support of child care. It not only began requiring the states to spend some of their federal social-services money on child care but also allowed welfare families to disregard some of their child-care expenses before calculating their cash-assistance levels. The government also gave families a tax credit for a part of their child-care expenses. [40]

But in 1971, President Richard M. Nixon vetoed an Office of Economic Opportunity bill because it included a $2 billion child-development pro-

Continued on p. 420

Chronology

1970s
Government figures show there are 6 million children under age 6 with working mothers. White House conference on Youth emphasizes need for federal help with child care.

December 1971
President Richard M. Nixon vetoes federal child-care bill introduced by Sen. Walter F. Mondale, D-Minn., and Rep. John Brademas, D-Ind., saying it would "Sovietize" American child care.

1976
Tax Code amended to create Child and Dependent Care Credit of up to $2,000 for one child per year; funds are consolidated for child-care services under Title XX of Social Security Act.

1980s
President Ronald Reagan reduces the federal role in child-care regulation; "mommy wars" break out between working and stay-at-home mothers; many employers set up tax-deductible "flexible-spending" accounts and other child-care benefits.

1981
Congress passes Economic Recovery Act, making child care a non-taxable benefit, and cuts federal child-care aid and regulations.

1987
The first Act for Better Child Care is introduced in Congress.

1988
Republican and Democratic presidential candidates come out in favor of child-care legislation.

1988
Congress passes the Family Support Act, with provisions requiring welfare parents to meet work requirements.

1990s
President Clinton supports increased aid for child care but also welfare reforms requiring mothers to work.

1993
President Clinton signs the Family and Medical Leave Act, which allows companies to grant employees up to 12 weeks of unpaid leave a year to care for a newborn or newly adopted child. The law applies to private companies with more than 50 employees and to federal, state and local governments.

1996
President Clinton signs the welfare reform bill, which eliminates Aid to Families with Dependent Children and requires most mothers with children age 1 and older to work.

October 1997
President Clinton hosts a White House conference on child care that highlights the need for affordable and quality care. The president also unveils several proposals, including a scholarship program for child-care training and a call for better background checks on child-care workers.

November 1997
A Massachusetts jury finds British au pair Louise Woodward guilty of second-degree murder in the death of an 8-month-old infant in her care. Eleven days later, the judge in the case reduces the charge to involuntary manslaughter and sets her free, saying the 279 days she had served in prison was a sufficient sentence.

January 1998
President Clinton proposes a $21.7 billion plan to help working families with child care, including giving states more money to subsidize child care for low-income parents, increasing child-care tax credits, boosting funding for Head Start programs, adding money for after-school programs, giving tax credits to businesses that provide child care and adding money to enforce health and safety standards. Republicans offer a child-care bill that includes some of the president's proposals but also includes a tax credit for stay-at-home parents.

April 1998
One of the longest-running nationwide studies on child care, conducted by the National Institute of Child Health and Human Development finds that children cared for with several other children had fewer behavior problems than those watched alone by a nanny or in a very small group. An earlier part of the study found that quality child care did not affect an infant's attachment to his or her mother.

What's a Kid to Do After School?

What's a kid to do after school or during summer vacation when Mom and Dad have to work?

There are plenty of answers for those participating in the DCKids program at Friendship House in Washington, D.C., one of Washington's oldest social-service agencies. They can take guitar lessons, learn how to resolve conflicts peacefully, talk about African-American history, write a play about drug abuse and violence, or visit one of the Smithsonian Institution museums.

The program for children ages 7-14 operates from 3:30-6:30 p.m. weekdays when school is in session and all day during the summer. It seeks to develop leadership and learning through education, adventure, exploration and teamwork, says Rhonda Muse, youth services director at Friendship House. During the school year, about 27 students attend the program, and last summer it attracted 144 students.

"Our city is a city of contrasts," Muse says. "For some children, time outside the classroom offers exploration, adventure, learning and structured recreation. For others, free time offers very little opportunity, outside of what they experience hanging out in the streets."

A recent Department of Education survey found that more than 70 percent of parents — regardless of income level or race — want their children to attend an after-school program. [1]

The demand for after-school programs is expected to grow as women on welfare enter work programs as a result of the 1996 welfare reform law. While women with children under age 6 cannot be required to work if they can't find child care, there is no such exemption for those whose children are over 6 and need care.

Students need a safe place to go after school and access to enriching activities, homework help and a chance to make friends with peers and caring adults, says Michelle Seligson, executive director of the National Institute on Out-of-School Time at Wellesley College's Center for Research on Women.

But many children whose parents work come home to an empty house or apartment. It's hard to verify the number of "latchkey children," but the Census Bureau and other analysts estimate that close to 5 million young school-age children take care of themselves after school and do not have access to quality after-school programs.

Studies show that latchkey children are more likely to engage in risky behavior such as substance abuse and early sexual encounters and are more likely to miss school and receive poor grades. Conversely, children who attended good after-school programs had better peer relations and grades and were emotionally better adjusted. They also had more learning opportunities, academic and enrichment activities and spent less time watching television. [2]

In an effort to meet the growing need for such programs, Sen. Edward M. Kennedy, D-Mass., and Rep. Rosa DeLauro, D-Conn., are sponsoring bills that would give states an estimated $1 billion a year to expand before- and after-school care and summer and weekend activities for schoolchildren up to age 15. "Across the country today, crime survivors, law enforcement representatives and prosecutors have joined together in calling for a substantial federal investment in after-school programs," Kennedy said. "Clearly, financial assistance is needed to help parents and entire communities.

"Too often, parents cannot afford the thousands of dollars a year required to pay for after-school care — if it exists at all."

---

[1] Department of Education, "Family Involvement in Education: A Snapshot of Out-of-School Time," 1997.

[2] Fact Sheet on school-age children, National Institute on Out-of-School Time, October 1997, and *ChildCare ActioNews*, Child Care Action Campaign, January-February 1997.

Continued from p. 418

gram that he said had "family-weakening implications." [41]

In the early 1980s, the requirement that states spend some of their federal social-services money on child care was eliminated, with the result that some states all but eliminated their public child-care funding.

In 1988, Congress passed the Family Support Act, which recognized child-care assistance as an important part of any welfare-reform efforts.

This led to the JOBS program, the first child-care guarantee for working welfare recipients or those attending school or a job-training program. In addition, a program known as transitional child care (TCC) provided child care for up to a year after a person moved from welfare to work. [42]

In 1990, after a three-year battle, President George Bush signed a budget-reduction bill that included $22.5 billion in subsidies for child care and tax credits for working families over five years. The plan expanded the earned-income credit for the working poor and created grant programs for state-sponsored programs. Among the programs created were the Child Care and Development Block Grant (CCDBG) and the At-Risk Child Care Program, which provided subsidies to low-income working families. The block grant earmarked money for improving the quality and the supply of child care.

By 1994, the federal government was helping to cover the child-care costs of 1.4 million low-income children whose parents needed assistance to work or become self-sufficient.

In 1993, President Clinton signed the Family and Medical Leave Act allowing companies to grant employees up to 12 weeks of unpaid leave each year to care for a newborn or newly adopted child as well as care for family members with health problems. The law applies to private companies with more than 50 employees and the federal, state and local governments.

Additional child-care provisions were put in place in 1996, when President Clinton signed a broad welfare-reform bill. It eliminated Aid to Families with Dependent Children, the federal welfare program that guaranteed cash assistance to low-income families and replaced it with a new, limited program called Temporary Assistance for Needy Families. The law also scrapped several other federal child-care subsidy programs including JOBs child care, transitional child care and At-Risk Grants to the states, folding them into the existing CCDBG.

In October 1997, a White House conference on child care focused national attention on the need for high-quality and affordable child care, bringing together experts and advocates from across the country. During the conference, the president unveiled several proposals, including a five-year, $300 million scholarship fund to encourage child-care workers to get training and stay in the field, and a crime-prevention plan that would make it easier for states to conduct background checks on child-care providers and share the information with other states. [43]

"No parent should ever have to choose between work and family, between earning a decent wage and caring for a child," Clinton told conferencegoers.

The DC Kids Program at Friendship House offers a vitally needed all-day education and exploration program during the summer for children ages 7-14 in Washington, D.C.

Courtesy of Friendship House

Major Programs

The main federal program dealing with child care remains the CCDBG. It now provides block grants the states can use to subsidize child-care costs for families with children under age 13 if the parents are working or in school and the family income is at or below 85 percent of the state's median income. Parents receive vouchers or certificates that can generally be used to pay a child-care provider of their choice, including relatives.

States can also use the money to help families who need child care to get off and stay off welfare as well as to provide protective child care for children at risk of abuse and neglect.

Some of the CCDBG money requires state matching funds, and all states receiving grants must have child-care licensing standards for at least some providers. In addition, all providers receiving CCDBG subsidies must meet minimal state health and safety standards that address prevention and control of infectious diseases, building safety and health and safety training for caregivers.

The Head Start program provides comprehensive early-childhood education and family-support services for preschool children ages 3-5 whose families are below the poverty line. The new work requirements for welfare recipients have expanded existing efforts by Head Start programs to provide full-day services. The federal government provides money directly to Head Start programs, which must comply with detailed federal performance standards. In fiscal 1998, $4.35 billion has been appropriated for Head Start, with $279 million earmarked for infants and toddlers.

Several other federal programs also deal with child care. The Child and Adult Care Food Program provides subsidies for meals to low-income children in licensed child-care cen-

Welcoming Special-Needs Children

A child with multiple disabilities changed things at the Resurrection Children's Center in Alexandria, Va. At first, the child spent part of the day with other handicapped children and the rest of the day in a regular class. But during the preschool center's summer camp, all the children were together, and everyone benefited, says Program Director Kim Messinger.

That was more than 25 years ago. Now 20-30 percent of the children at the center have Down's syndrome, cerebral palsy, hearing problems, language difficulties, autism and other problems.

"For kids with special needs, [being with non-handicapped children] provides role models for language and behavior and helps their families become part of the community instead of being on the fringes," Messinger says. "For typical kids, the interaction provides growth with coping and dealing with imperfections better."

Preschoolers are generally self-centered and often don't notice the differences of special needs children unless it is something obvious such as a child wearing a brace, and then they are more direct than adults about asking about it, Messinger says.

But often parents of non-handicapped children worry that the special-needs children will take away time from their child, Messinger says, adding that it's actually the children with behaviorial problems who are the problem.

To address such concerns, classes are held for all parents on the benefits of including children with special needs.

The center, which is housed in an Episcopal church but is non-sectarian, accommodates 45 children ages 2 ½ to 5 in four classes, each with a teacher, an assistant and a parent volunteer. Teachers and assistants have backgrounds in early-childhood education or special education.

"Every child is welcome," Messinger says, but she stresses that the staff meets with parents first to make sure that the center is right for their child.

Unfortunately for parents with special-needs children, there aren't enough child-care centers like Resurrection, according to child-care experts. While there are laws to ensure that children are placed in the least restrictive education environment, many day-care centers do not accept children with special needs, says Dalice Hertzberg, project coordinator for First Start, an organization at the University of Colorado that teaches child-care providers how to accommodate special-needs children.

The 45-hour program focuses on human development and how conditions such as cerebral palsy, mental retardation or spina bifida affect children. The course also covers behavior-management techniques and the procedures that special-needs children undergo at home.

Above all, says Hertzberg, "The philosophy is one of inclusion of those with disabilities, not segregating them."

ters and family and group day-care homes and Head Start centers. Social Services Block Grants (Title XX) can be used by the states for child-care services, and several Education Department programs provide support for early-childhood and special-needs programs as well as after-school activities.

For parents paying taxes, there is also a tax credit for child-care expenses for working parents. The maximum credit is 30 percent of expenses up to $2,400 for one child and $4,800 for two or more children. This means a $720 credit for one child and $1,440 for two or more children. The credit rate is gradually reduced for taxpayers with adjusted gross incomes of over $10,000 until it reaches 20 percent for taxpayers with incomes above $28,000. [44] The credit does not benefit low-income parents.   ■

CURRENT SITUATION

Role of the States

States call most of the shots when it comes to federal and state child-care subsidy programs. First, states are responsible for administering federal funds as well as determining how much they will contribute of their own resources; state contributions vary considerably from state to state. While the federal government provides some guidelines for subsidy programs, states decide who qualifies based on income levels and activities. States also establish sliding-fee scales, set the amount they will reimburse for child-care providers and determine health and safety regulations for child-care providers who are exempt from state licensing regulations but receive public money. [45]

States also can decide how to spend money on improving or expanding the supply of care, through funding training, resource and referral agencies, grants and loans, or by picking up start-up costs for programs in underserved areas. Before 1990, states had to invest their own money for these efforts, but now they can also use federal funds.

Licensing of child-care facilities — whether or not they receive federal funds — also falls within the states' domain, and as a result requirements vary widely.

Many states exempt smaller providers from any regulations, including those serving up to 12 children in some states. Other states do not regulate programs run by religious schools and organizations or part-time and drop-in programs such as those in shopping centers or health clubs.

There also are differences among the states on basic health and safety standards, including staff first aid and CPR training and the frequency of inspections. [46]

Legislative Initiatives

President Clinton's $21.7 billion plan to help working families with child care started the legislative debate on the issue. His plan would, among other things:

• provide $7.5 billion more in state block grants to subsidize child care for low-income parents over five years;

• increase child-care tax credits for families earning less than $60,000;

• boost funding for the Head Start preschool program and Early Head Start;

• create an "early learning fund" for local programs to improve training and safety at child-care centers and homes;

• provide more money for after-school programs; and

• offer tax credits for businesses that provide child care for employees. [47]

Republicans, while supporting parts of the president's proposal, wanted to include benefits for parents who stay at home to care for their children.

A bill introduced by Sen. John H. Chafee, R-R.I., would provide such credits as well as expand the existing tax credits to low- and middle-income families, create a new tax credit

for businesses that build or operate child-care centers for employees and provide money to improve training for child-care providers and supply child-care information to parents. [48]

Part of the president's plan is incorporated in a bill proposed by Sen. Christopher J. Dodd, D-Conn., which would also give monetary rewards to states for efforts to improve child-care quality such as fewer children per caregiver, enforcement of standards, background checks on providers and parent education.

Dodd's bill would also expand the Family and Medical Leave Act to

---

"We're facing a child-care crisis in this country. It's time we give parents a greater choice and peace of mind as they juggle the responsibilities of work and home."

*— Sen. Christopher J. Dodd
D-Conn.*

---

include more families.

"We're facing a child-care crisis in this country," Dodd said in February when he introduced the measure. "It's time we give parents a greater choice and peace of mind as they juggle the responsibilities of work and home. Unless we take necessary and dramatic steps to address this problem, our children and our nation will approach the 21st century at an extraordinary disadvantage."

At least 40 other child-care proposals pending in Congress address basic child care issues such as availability, affordability and quality. Some call for tax incentives or grants for employers to provide child-care for their employees; others expand the existing tax credits or target them more to lower-income families; still others fund after-school programs or provide grants for states to improve care quality. Several proposals also focus on better training and education for child-care workers.

Legislation is also pending that would require child-care centers at federal agencies to meet local and state health and safety standards. These 1,024 facilities serving 215,000 children of federal workers are currently exempt. The Defense Department, which operates 788 centers for military families, would remain exempt. President Clinton has also directed all government child-care centers to obtain independent accreditation based on safety and quality standards. [49] Agency and military child-care facilities are generally excellent.

Welfare to Child Care

Under the 1996 welfare-reform regulations, women with children over age 1 must find work as well as child care for their children. Some states are trying to solve both problems by training welfare mothers to be child-care providers.

Child-care experts and advocates alike caution that it is important to recruit only those welfare recipients who truly want to become child-care workers and to provide adequate support and training. In addition, others argue it may not be the best route to self-sufficiency since the work is demanding and often low-paying and without benefits.

In California, welfare recipients interested in becoming child-care workers are participating in a two-year program that includes attending classes at a community college, meeting with a mentor teacher and working up to 32 hours a week during the second year. The goal is to complete 24 units of early-childhood education classes and 16 units in general education and receive a child-development teacher permit at the end of the program.

David Houtrouw, an Education Department consultant, says the program is going well. Nearly 250 California women with basic language skills and an interest in child care are participating in and around San Francisco, Fresno and Los Angeles.

The program is not aimed at having the graduates turn their homes into child-care centers but making them eligible to teach in the state's preschool program, which pays about $10 an hour, or in child-care centers and Head Start programs.

After graduating, the women can also take advantage of the state's tuition-reimbursement program for teachers and work toward a bachelor's degree, climbing what Houtrouw calls the "first solid rung of the ladder" to careers as child-care leaders and administrators.

The state's Department of Social Services is also funding county welfare projects to train welfare recipients as in-home or family child-care providers. A special effort is being made to recruit providers for infants and mildly sick children as well as for child care during non-tradi-

tional hours. [50]

In Pennsylvania, the YMCA of Philadelphia and Vicinity helps low-income and unemployed people to become child-care workers. The YMCA assists with licensing and insurance fees, ongoing training through local universities and $1,000 in start-up costs for furniture, equipment and toys. It also conducts unannounced monitoring visits and offers technical assistance to

Children cared for with several other children had fewer behavior problems than those watched alone by an au pair or in a very small group, according to a recent study by the National Institute of Child Health and Human Development.

the providers. The program includes 36 homes; 13 are already accredited, and several more are in the process of achieving accreditation. Several Latino providers are in training, and there are plans for training Vietnamese, Cambodian and Korean caregivers. [51]

Colorado's Neighbor-to-Neighbor Child Care Training and Education Pilot Program funds 10 sites throughout the

state to train welfare recipients to become child-care workers or providers. The program helps new providers with training, obtaining necessary state and local licenses and start-up costs. [52]

Although such efforts are relatively new, there have been some success stories, such as that of 26-year-old Diana Insula, who cares for up to seven children in her Columbia, Md., townhouse. The former welfare recipient received her license as a family child-care provider in 1995. Insula, who had spent time in a homeless shelter with her daughter, credits her success to a state official who took an interest in her case.

"I wanted to follow my dreams to take care of kids," said Insula, who worked a second job to get enough money to buy her townhouse. [53]

And almost all of the 43 family child-care providers connected to the Acre Family Day Care center in Lowell, Mass., were once on welfare. The center provides training and economic aid and has a social worker on call. "I believe a welfare recipient has to be part of a network," said Anita Moeller, Acre's executive director. "Being a family child-care provider is just too isolating to make it on your own." [54]

Helping Hands

Some businesses and communities consider it good business to invest in child care.

Continued on p. 426

At Issue:

Do government regulations improve the quality of child care?

GINA ADAMS

Assistant Director, Child Care and Development Division, Children's Defense Fund

WRITTEN FOR THE CQ RESEARCHER, APRIL 1998.

i t is common sense that state regulation of child care protects children from harm and improves the quality of care. Parents know this and want basic consumer protections to help keep their children safe. A recent survey, for example, found that about 90 percent of parents support regulation of child care. Parents understand that requiring programs to follow basic health and safety practices (such as washing hands after diapering, covering electrical outlets and securing poisonous substances) and monitoring their compliance with these requirements help protect their children.

Regulation prevents countless tragedies every day. The whole country watched as preschooler Jessica McClure was pulled from an open well in Texas a few years ago. She was in an unregulated family child-care home, which if regulated would never have been allowed to care for children without putting fencing around the well. Regulation also protects children by screening out providers who have histories of child abuse, helping providers address safety and health hazards and closing down illegally operating family child-care homes caring for too many children. (For example, licensing inspectors in Maryland and Illinois discovered — and closed down — family child-care homes illegally caring for as many as 50 young children with only one adult.)

Research has shown that regulations improve the quality of care and children's well-being. Recent studies have shown that states with stronger licensing standards have fewer poor-quality programs, that regulated, home-based child care provides better quality care than unregulated care and that the quality of care improves when regulations are improved. For example, a recent study examined the impact of improving staff-to-child ratios and staff training requirements in Florida, and found significant improvements in children's intellectual and emotional development, children's attachment to caregivers, teacher responsiveness and sensitivity and the overall quality of care — all without significantly increasing fees. Similarly, a study of the impact of licensing inspections found that even good programs deteriorate when inspected less frequently, and poor programs improve when visited more frequently.

Despite this evidence, far too many children in child care are inadequately protected. Many states allow a significant number of programs to be exempt from licensing altogether, have inadequate protections for those programs that are licensed and fail to adequately inspect and enforce their laws. Additional resources and stronger laws would better protect children.

DARCY OLSEN

Entitlements Policy Analyst, Cato Institute

FROM "THE ADVANCING NANNY STATE: WHY THE GOVERNMENT SHOULD STAY OUT OF CHILD CARE," OCT. 23, 1997.

a dvocates of national child-care standards generally argue that (1) parents are unable to distinguish between low- and high-quality care, (2) the government has the information to determine what constitutes high-quality care and therefore (3) the government should set standards to guarantee high-quality care for all children. That line of reasoning assumes that parents are ignorant of the quality of care their children receive. It further assumes that there is one universal definition of "high-quality care." On the basis of those assumptions, advocates of national standards would abrogate parental care-taking responsibility and limit care only to what meets government standards. . . .

Of course, standards and regulations do not guarantee excellence. A recent special report in *U.S. News & World Report* opened, "Too many parents have learned that day-care licensing and regulation, even when they exist, do not guarantee quality." Advocates of standards typically argue that this is because current regulations are too lax, but that is unlikely. Consider, for example, the record of unregulated family day care. The National Day Care Home Study conducted for the Department of Health and Human Services found no indication that unregulated family day care was either harmful or dangerous to children; in fact, it caters successfully to the needs of the children in care. . . .

A recent investigative report in *The Washington Post* also provides evidence that regulations do not guarantee excellence. The regulated but poorly maintained child-care centers uncovered by the *Post's* reporter are a casebook example of the unintended results of government-selected, government-subsidized care. The centers in question, which include the city's largest providers of taxpayer-subsidized child care, continue to receive government funds regardless of the conditions of the facilities. The Department of Human Services chooses the centers that get public money for poor children and then continues to subsidize those centers despite the fact that they have failed to meet safety and health standards. . . .

One thing is clear: there is no consensus, scientific or political, on what is best for every child. That makes sense to parents who know firsthand that every family and every child have unique needs. Congress and the administration should acknowledge those facts — that is, they should recognize that the push for national standards is politically driven and scientifically unfounded. They should further respect the fact that 96 percent of parents are satisfied or very satisfied with their current child-care arrangements.

How to Find Good Child Care

Parents can take several steps to ensure that their child's day care or preschool is of high quality, according to child-care experts.

First, check to see if the program is licensed and complies with state regulations. All states license child-care centers, and some regulate family child-care homes, which care for children in the provider's home. Standards vary from state to state but generally focus on health precautions, building and fire safety, staff-to-child ratios, class size and teacher qualifications. Part-time child-care centers and church-based centers may be exempt from licensing.

The National Association for the Education of Young Children (NAEYC) recommends that parents visit different programs in their area to determine the kind of care available.

NAEYC's Web site (www. naeyc.org) provides access to lists of child-care centers and preschools accredited by the National Academy of Early Childhood, organized by city or ZIP code. The academy is a division of NAEYC, and programs it accredits have been in operation for at least a year and complete an extensive evaluation that includes an on-site visit. Reports are reviewed by nationally recognized early-childhood experts.

Child-care centers and preschools that meet the academy's standards for staff-child ratios, training and health and safety standards are accredited for three years and can display the academy's insignia — a torch — on their literature.

Family child-care facilities are accredited through the National Association of Family Child Care.

NAEYC suggests several questions to ask child-care providers and what to look for when visiting to ensure finding good-quality care:

• Who will care for your child? Do staff members enjoy and understand how young children grow? Are there enough staff members to care for the individual needs of the children? How well does the staff work together? NAEYC recommends that all groups of children have at least two adults with them at all times. Staff-to-child ratios should be three infants under 6 months per adult, four infants between 7 months and 11 months per adult; three to five toddlers ages 12 months to 24 months per adult; four to seven 2- and 3-year-olds per adult and eight to 10 4- to-5-year-olds per adult. Infants should be in groups of no more than six to eight babies; 2- to-3-year-olds in groups of 10 to 14 children; 4- and 5-year-olds can be in groups of up to 20 children.

• What program activities and equipment are available? Observe the daily routine of the staff and the center or preschool. Does the school or center nurture young children's growth and development as they work and play together? Do children have ample amounts of active learning such as playing outside and games as well as quiet learning such as reading stories or doing puzzles? Are sufficient and age-appropriate materials available to all children — blocks, books, paints and play clothes?

• Are the children encouraged to increase their language skills as well as expand their understanding of the world?

• Is the equipment up-to-date and safe?

* Is the facility spacious and designed to meet the various needs of young children, their families and the community? Do programs support and consider the needs of the whole family? Strong programs contribute to the needs of the community and promote the health of all children, parents and staff. Talk to the staff and neighbors.

Continued from p. 424

The American Business Collaboration for Quality Dependent Care (ABC) — which includes 21 major U.S. companies [55] as well as regional and local businesses — concentrates on expanding and improving the supply of child care. Since its inception in 1992, the ABC has funded child-care centers and worked on developing back-up care and after-school programs and improving the quality of centers through staff-training programs.

ABC initiatives are targeted to the needs of employees in a particular geographic area. During the first phase, 45 communities in 25 states and the District of Columbia were involved in ABC projects.

"We believe that supporting the diverse dependent-care needs of our employees is critical to our success as it enables our companies to attract and retain a competitive, committed and motivated work force," the 21 companies said. [56]

Some companies also help employees to pay for child care by reducing their tax burden or setting up flexible work arrangements such as flextime, part-time, job-sharing or telecommuting.

Few companies, however, go as far as Arkansas-based Con Agra Refrigerated Foods, which pays part of its employees' child-care costs. The company also works with Head Start, child-care agencies and a nonprofit organization to expand early-childhood programs to accommodate its workers, many of whom make $6 and $7 an hour, do shift work and live in rural areas where regulated child care is scarce. [57]

In some communities, private and public partnerships have been formed to fund child-care initiatives. In New York state, the American Express and Travelers foundations and the state government formed the Early Childhood Investment Fund (ECIF) in 1992 to improve the availability and quality of child care for working parents. No longer in operation, the ECIF funded grants to find solutions to community child-care problems, to start new programs and to pay for program equipment, professional development and public-awareness campaigns. Priority was given to low-income communities. [58]

Another community-based effort is the T.E.A.C.H. Early Childhood Project, which began in North Carolina and has been replicated in Georgia, Florida and Illinois; several other states are also considering it. The program, funded by public and private dollars, provides scholarships for child-care teachers and family-care providers. Salary increases and bonuses are paid upon completion of the program. Established in 1990, the program is seen as a way of increasing child-care quality without significantly raising parent fees or adding more regulations and providing incentives for providers to upgrade their education. [59] ∎

OUTLOOK

Political Problems?

The current child-care debate sounds surprisingly similar to the debate a decade ago. What are the effects of child care? How do parents find care that's affordable, accessible and of high quality? What role should government play in helping make good child care available to all? What, if any, standards should be applied to child care, and at what level — local, state or national?

"The frustrating thing is that this is not a problem where we don't know what to do," says Gina Adams, assistant director of the Child Care and Development Division at the Children's Defense Fund. "We know what children need. But without resources we can't do it."

The national child-care debate started with a full head of steam after President Clinton's October White House Conference and his budget proposal two months later. Now some are suggesting that it's sputtering, in a large measure due to the president's political problems.

"Without President Clinton's political and legal problems, the world for children would look different," says Georgetown's Gormley. "Children's needs have taken a back seat to the political and legal battles between Clinton and [Independent Counsel Kenneth] Starr."

Still, some experts remain optimistic. "We're encouraged by what's going on in Congress," says Taylor of the National Black Child Development Institute. "There's recognition of the need to provide quality child care."

But other observers see the need for deeper changes.

"We need to mobilize society to make an investment in kids," says Aronson of the American Academy of Pediatrics. "It pays off immediately in the productivity of their parents, and in the future in the kind of people children become."

Barbara Willer, public affairs director of the National Association for the Education of Young Children, says the debate has to move beyond rhetoric and into action.

"We need to get to the point of recognizing the importance of an infrastructure for child care like the infrastructure for highways," she says. "The frustrating part is that childhood is a fleeting period, and when we lose another year, we've lost another group of children who could benefit from high-quality care." ∎

Karen Lee Scrivo is a freelance writer in the Washington, D.C., area.

Notes

[1] Quoted in *The Washington Post*, Jan. 13, 1998, p. A1.

[2] Children's Defense Fund, "Child Care Basics," Nov. 7, 1997, p. 2.

[3] For additional studies of child-care needs, see "Child Care Prices: A Profile of Six Communities — Final Report," The Urban Institute, 1995, p. 72, and "Kinder-Care Report: Perspectives on Child Care in America," *Research and Forecasts*, Montgomery, Ala., 1989.

[4] Children's Defense Fund, "Common Myths about Child Care," Jan. 26, 1998, pp. 1-2.

[5] Darcy Olsen, "The Advancing Nanny State," *Cato Institute*, Oct. 23, 1997, p. 1.

[6] "Is There a 'Crisis' in Child Care in America?" *Cato Institute Fact Sheet*, Jan. 9, 1998.

[7] Carnegie Corporation of New York, "Year of Promise: A Comprehensive Learning Strategy for American Children," 1996, cited in Gina Adams and Nicole Oxendine Poersch, "Key Facts about Child Care and Early Education," Children's Defense Fund, 1997.

[8] Suzanne Helburn, et al, "Cost, Quality and Child Outcomes in Child Care Centers," *Executive Summary*, 1995, p. 2.

[9] Ellen Galinsky, et al, "The Study of Children in Family Child Care and Relative Care: Highlights of Findings, Families and Work Institute," 1994, p. 4.

[10] Reported in Senate Labor and Human Resources Committee hearing report, "Improving the Quality of Child Care," July 17, 1997.

[11] *U.S. News & World Report*, Aug. 4, 1997, p. 34. Precise figures are unavailable because some states do not track child-care deaths, and many facilities throughout the country are unregistered.

[12] Center for Career Development in Early Care and Education, Wheelock College, Boston, Mass.

[13] Children's Defense Fund, "Child Care Basics," *op. cit.*

[14] Press release in response to President Clinton's $21.7 billion child-care proposal, Jan. 8, 1998.

[15] For background, see "Welfare, Work and the States," *The CQ Researcher*, Dec. 6, 1996, pp. 1057-1080.

[16] Quoted in *The Washington Post*, Jan. 8, 1998, p. A14.

[17] *The Washington Post*, April 3, 1998, p. A1.

FOR MORE INFORMATION

If you would like to have this CQ Researcher updated, or need more information about this topic, please call CQ Custom Research. Special rates for CQ subscribers. (202) 887-8600 or (800) 432-2250, ext. 600, or E-mail Custom.Research@cq.com

Child Care Action Campaign, 330 Seventh Ave., 17th Floor, New York, N.Y. 10001; (212) 239-0138. A national nonprofit advocacy group that addresses child-care trends, research and legislation.

Children's Defense Fund, 25 E St. N.W., Washington, D.C. 20001; (202)-662-8787; http://www.childrensdefense.org. This advocacy group gathers data and distributes information on children's issues, lobbies Congress and state legislatures and tracks the development of federal and state policies.

National Association for the Education of Young Children, 1509 16th St. N.W., Washington, D.C. 20036; (800) 424-2460; http://www.naeyc.org. The association represents early-childhood professionals and others who work to improve the quality of early-education programs. The association also administers the National Academy of Early Childhood Programs — a voluntary, national accreditation system. Its Web site provides lists of accredited centers by location.

National Child Care Information Center, 301 Maple Ave. West, Suite 602, Vienna, Va. 22180; (800) 616-2242; http://nccic.org. This information clearinghouse on various aspects of child-care is sponsored by the Child Care Bureau of the U.S. Health and Human Services Department.

National Black Child Development Institute, 1023 15th St., N.W., Suite 600, Washington, D.C. 20005,; (202) 234-1738; www.nbcdi.org. This advocacy group focuses on the care, education and health of African-American children.

[18] Quoted in *ibid.*

[19] Joseph Adelson, "What We Know About Day Care," *Commentary*, November 1997, p. 53.

[20] NIH News Alert, "Results of NICHD Study of Early Child Care," April 3, 1997.

[21] *Ibid.*

[22] Maggie Gallagher, "Day Careless," *National Review*, Jan. 26, 1998, p. 39.

[23] Families and Work Institute, "Rethinking the Brain: New Insights into Early Development," 1997, p. 23.

[24] Helburn, *op. cit.*, p. 4.

[25] Families and Work Institute, *op. cit.*, p. 28.

[26] Sharon Lynn Kagan, "Not By Chance: Creating an Early Care and Education System for America's Children," Bush Center in Child Development and Social Policy, Yale University.

[27] William T. Gormley Jr., *Everybody's Chil-dren: Child Care as a Public Problem,* 1995.

[28] Families and Work Institute, "The Florida Child Care Quality Improvement Study," 1997, pp. 1-5.

[29] *Education Week,* April 4, 1997, p. 1.

[30] Anne Mitchell, *Financing Child Care in the United States,* The Ewing Marion Kauffman Foundation and The Pew Charitable Trusts, 1997, p. 67.

[31] Olsen, *op. cit.*, p. 23.

[32] Press release, Jan. 8, 1998.

[33] See Helen Blank, "Helping Parents Work and Children Succeed: A Guide to Child Care and the 1996 Welfare Act," Children's Defense Fund, 1997, and "Welfare Block Grant Basics," a Child Care Action Campaign Issue Brief, September 1996.

[34] General Accounting Office, "Welfare Reform: States' Efforts to Expand Child Care

Programs," January 1998.

[35] "The New Welfare Law," Center on Budget and Policy Priorities, Aug. 14, 1996.

[36] Gina Adam, et al, "Locked Doors: States Struggling to Meet the Child Care Needs of Low-Income Working Families," Children's Defense Fund, 1998.

[37] *Ibid.*, p. 2.

[38] Harriet B. Presser and Amy Cox, "The Work Schedules of Low-educated American Women and Welfare Reform," *Monthly Labor Review*, April 1997, p. 33.

[39] Adams and Poersch, *op. cit.,* pp, J-1-2.

[40] For background, see "Head Start," *The CQ Researcher*, April 9, 1993, pp. 297-320.

[41] *CQ Weekly Report,* Jan. 17, 1998, p. 130.

[42] Adams and Poersch, *op. cit.*, p. J-2.

[43] *Child Care Bulletin*, Health and Human Services Department, September/October 1997, p. 3.

[44] For information on federal programs dealing with child care, see "Child Care Legislation in the 105th Congress," *CRS Issue Brief*, Feb. 26, 1998.

[45] Adams and Poersch, *op. cit.*, pp. J-2-3.

[46] *Ibid*, p. J-7.

[47] *The Washington Post*, Jan. 8, 1998, p. A1.

[48] Summary of bill from Chafee's Web site and *The New York Times*, Jan. 24, 1998, p. 22.

[49] See *The Washington Post*, March 6, 1998, p. A23, and the *Los Angeles Times*, March 11, 1998, p. A5.

[50] Health and Human Services Department, *op. cit.*, p. 6.

[51] *Ibid.*

[52] *Ibid.*, p. 6.

[53] Quoted in *U.S. News & World Report*, Nov. 3, 1997, p. 37.

[54] *Ibid.*

[55] The companies are AT&T, IBM, Mobil and Xerox, Aetna Life and Casualty, Allstate Insurance Co., Amoco, Bank of America, Chevron, Citibank, Deloitte & Touche, Eastman Kodak, Exxon, GE Capital Services, Hewlett-Packard, Mobil, NYNEX, Price Waterhouse, Texaco and Texas Instruments.

[56] Quoted in Mitchell, *op. cit.*, p. 73.

[57] For more examples of corporate child-care subsidies, see *ibid*, pp. 67-86.

[58] Mitchell, *op. cit.*, pp. 88-90.

[59] *Ibid.*, pp. 93-94.

Bibliography

Selected Sources Used

Reports and Studies

Adams, Gina, Karen Schulman and Nancy Ebb, *Locked Doors: States Struggling to Meet the Child Care Needs of Low-Income Working Families*, **Children's Defense Fund, 1998.**

The report surveys all 50 states, looking at the enormous gaps that remain in efforts to help low-income parents work and take care of their children.

Adams, Gina, and Nicole Oxendine Poersch, *Key Facts About Child Care and Early Education*, **Children's Defense Fund, 1997.**

This briefing book includes facts about child care, the importance of quality care, the inadequacy of supply, the effects of welfare reform, programs and policies that help families with child care and state-by-state data on regulated child care, extended-day programs and child-care funding.

Blank, Helen, *Helping Parents Work and Children Succeed: A Guide to Child Care and the 1996 Welfare Act*, **Children's Defense Fund, 1997.**

Blank identifies some of the key child-care issues related to implementing the 1996 Welfare Act, which imposes new work requirements for mothers receiving benefits.

General Accounting Office, *Welfare Reform: States' Efforts to Expand Child Care Programs*, **1998.**

The report looks at efforts by California, Connecticut, Louisiana, Maryland, Oregon, Texas and Wisconsin to expand child-care programs to meet the increased demand brought on by welfare reform.

Kagan, Sharon L., and Nancy E. Cohen, *Not By Chance: Creating an Early Care and Education System for America's Children*, **1997.**

Based on the work of the Quality 2000 Initiative, the authors document the quality crisis in early-childhood care and education. They offer eight recommendations for improving quality and care and coming up with new ways of thinking about young children and the care they receive.

Beth Miller, et al., "I Wish the Kids Didn't Watch So Much TV: Out-of-School Time in Three Low Income Communities," School-Age Child Care Project, Wellesley College Center for Research on Women, 1996.

A look at how children in three communities spend their daytime hours after school.

Beth Miller, "Out-of-School Time: Effects on Learning in the Primary Grades," School-Age Child Care Project, Wellesley College Center for Research on Women, 1995.

This paper reviews the research on the effects of out-of-school time on children's learning and makes several recommendations to help enhance opportunities for making the most of after-school time.

Mitchell, Anne, Louise Stoney and Harriet Dichter, *Financing Child Care in the United States*, **Ewing Marion Kauffman Foundation and Pew Charitable Trusts, 1997.**

This report highlights state and community strategies for financing child care using public, private and mixed sources of funding. It highlights those that generate new revenue or expand the current share of money allocated to child care.

Senate Labor and Human Resources Committee, "Improving the Quality of Child Care," July 17, 1997.

The report on hearings held by the committee examines proposals to improve the quality of child care in the United States.

Shelly L. Smith et al, "Early Childhood Care and Education: An Investment That Works," National Conference of State Legislatures, Washington, D.C., 1997.

This publication highlights how states are applying the lessons of early-childhood education in areas ranging from education, health and welfare to economic development, regulation and juvenile justice. It provides specific state examples throughout.

U.S. Department of Education, "Extending Learning Time for Disadvantaged Students," Vol. 1: Summary of Promising Practices, 1995.

This idea book suggests numerous ways to extend learning time using available community resources.

Marcy Whitebrook, et al, "NAEYC Accreditation as a Strategy for Improving Child Care Quality," National Center for the Early Childhood Work Force, Washington, D.C., 1997.

This study assesses the National Association for the Education of Young Children (NAEYC) child-care center accreditation process and the link between accreditation and the quality of care.

The Next Step

Additional information from UMI's Newspaper & Periodical Abstracts™ database

Clinton Proposal

Hall, Mimi, "$22 Billion Child Care Package Proposed," *USA Today*, Jan. 8, 1998, p. A1.

President Clinton Wednesday proposed a $21.7 billion package of grants and tax breaks to help working families pay for child care. He will submit the plan to Congress in his budget proposal on Feb. 2. The number of children whose families get subsidies would double to 2 million, the White House estimates.

Healy, Melissa, "GOP Lawmakers Take Aim at Clinton Child-Care Initiative," *Los Angeles Times*, Jan. 26, 1998, p. A14.

For many Republican lawmakers, a battle against President Clinton's child-care initiative is a no-win proposition that could mean election-time disaster. But the way Sen. Daniel R. Coats, R-Ind., figures it, Clinton's package has a fatal flaw, and Republicans should not shy from pointing it out. For starters, Republicans plan to lambaste Clinton's approach for offering an unfair break to American families with two working parents and children in day care.

Mathis, Nancy, "Clinton Pushes for Child-Care Reforms," *Houston Chronicle*, March 11, 1998, p. A5.

President Clinton prodded Congress on Tuesday to pass his five-year, $22 billion child-care initiative as the administration sets the stage to make legislative inaction a possible issue. Barry Toiv, a White House spokesman, said the president was prodding Congress because legislation could easily become stalled. "If the Congress does not begin working soon, we're going to lose the opportunity to pass major legislation," Toiv said.

Neikirk, William, "Clinton Asks $21 Billion for Child-Care Package; Plan Raises Stakes, Puts GOP in Bind," *Chicago Tribune*, Jan. 8, 1998, p. 1.

President Clinton offered another major prize Wednesday to baby boomers with a proposed $21.7 billion expansion in federal child-care programs over five years that will put political pressure on Republicans. A day after announcing his plan to allow 55-to-65-year-old Americans to join Medicare, the president disclosed a series of child-care subsidies, tax credits and grants designed to help families struggling with the demands of work and the growing cost of child care.

Government's Role

"Kerry's Child-Care Compromise," *The Boston Globe*, Jan. 11, 1998, p. C6.

After years of frustration with partisan squabbling while solutions to social crises are deferred, Sen. John Kerry, D-Mass., has arrived at a kind of post-ideological maturity that

could benefit millions of needy children. Kerry has proposed a carefully targeted Early Childhood Development Act to create "a solution to the stalemate" that pits so-called "nanny-state liberalism" against laissez-faire conservatism.

Altbach, Philip G., and Constance Gresser, "Child Care is a Right; The State Should Support Two Views of Who Should Rock the Cradle," *The Christian Science Monitor*, Nov. 25, 1997, p. 19.

Society needs to provide quality child-care alternatives for families. But sadly, every few decades the crisis in child-care becomes a topic in the news media — whether in a political candidate's platform or the latest study. Good child care is hardly a revolutionary idea, but it seems beyond us. Organized child care has many advantages for children, caregivers and families. Children can interact with other children, learn from their peers and from adults and benefit from an educational environment.

Logue, Trinita, "Child-Care Plans Need Local Focus," *Chicago Tribune*, Feb. 23, 1998, p. 14.

Pledges of support for more child-care funding resound at the federal, state and local levels, particularly now that President Clinton has announced a $21 billion child-care package. Affordable, quality child-care is a crucial issue for working families at any income level, and the first step in expanding child-care options requires strategic, thorough planning to assess a community's child-care options.

Pear, Robert, "Republicans Draft Child-Care Legislation That Would Also Help Stay-at-Home Parents," *The New York Times*, Jan. 25, 1998, p. 22.

As an alternative to President Clinton's child-care initiative, Republican members of Congress are developing proposals of their own that would help not only parents who work outside the home but also those who stay home to care for their children. The package is being put together by an influential group of Republican senators led by John H. Chafee of Rhode Island, with encouragement from Republican leaders in the Senate.

Impact of Care on Child's Development

Iveson, Candice J., "Quality Child-Care Starts Kids on Right Path to Adulthood," *St. Louis Post-Dispatch*, Oct. 23, 1997, p. C15.

Recent research shows the critical nature of a child's first three years: Brain cells proliferate and, when stimulated, synapses link at a rapid rate. Those early connections shape brain function for life. Inadequate or inappropriate stimulation can result in children with brains 20 percent to 30 percent smaller than normal. About 49 percent of children in care are in some type of licensed or regulated child care, leaving more than half, or almost 150,000 children, in unlicensed, unregulated settings.

Shellenbarger, Sue, "Impact of Child Care is Mixed, Study Says," *The Wall Street Journal*, April 4, 1997, p. A5.

The most comprehensive study yet of the effects of child care on children shows mixed results, revealing neutral or positive effects on some important fronts, while raising new questions about whether heavy child-care use hurts the mother-child relationship. The 10-site, federally sponsored study shows that using child care doesn't hurt the cognitive and language development of children, when compared with kids at home with their mothers.

Quality of Care

Brooks, Nancy Rivera, "Work and Careers; New Child-Care Coalition Planning Modest — but Innovative — Programs," *Los Angeles Times*, Nov. 16, 1997, p. D5.

Eight major corporations announced plans Thursday to sprinkle $600,000 among several projects to improve the quality of child care and elder-care services in Los Angeles. This is the work of a nationwide coalition of 22 corporations that two years ago pledged to invest more than $100 million in dependent-care programs around the country. The business collaboration also includes about 100 companies that participate in a limited way.

Dennis, Diane, "Experiences Raising Chelsea Attuned Clintons to Need for Quality Child Care," *USA Today*, Jan. 16, 1998, p. A10.

It can be career suicide for a rising corporate executive to admit he or she has a child-care problem. While a breakdown in a working couple's child-care arrangements dominates cocktail-party conversation, even a hint of the problem around the office water cooler is to confess you can't give your employer the expected 100 percent of your time. So, when a parent's school has yet another teachers' conference — after all those snow days — the solution is to call in sick. On average, employees with children miss eight days of work a year due to a disruption in normal child-care arrangements.

Jackson, Derrick Z., "The Universal Struggle for Quality Child Care," *The Boston Globe*, Nov. 12, 1997, p. A23.

The trial of British au pair Louise Woodward provoked considerable pomposity from the people who should display it the least: parents. In the nine months after baby Matthew Eappen died in Woodward's care, many of them carried on in the Globe as if they had total control over their children's lives. "I cannot imagine meeting for the first time — at Logan Airport — the person who is going to be taking care of my child," said one parent. This suburban self-absorption — a loss of grip promoted by the media since we heard only from suburban, relatively well-off parents for most of the trial — muffled discussion of the universal struggle by all Americans for good child care.

Mann, Judy, "Help Wanted for Child-Care System," *The Washington Post*, Nov. 14, 1997, p. E3.

The vast majority of people to whom we entrust our children have no more training in child care than British au pair Louise Woodward. Yet a lot of working parents, desperate to find supervision for their children, gamble that their child-care workers will be saints. The miracle is that we are not hearing more horror stories out of day care than we are.

West, Debra, "When the Quest for Child Care Leads Home," *The New York Times*, Aug. 17, 1997, p. 13.

Diana Rothenberg gave up a career and established a day-care center in her Tudor home in Yonkers because she refused to leave her children in someone else's care. With more than a decade of teaching experience, Rothenberg did not doubt her knowledge of curriculum or teaching methods. But she wasn't sure she could make a living as an in-home provider of family day care.

Subsidies and Tax Credits

Barr, Stephen, "GSA Plans to Raise Money for Child Care; $10 Million Needed to Make Service Affordable for Government Workers," *The Washington Post*, May 22, 1997, p. A23.

The government's child-care system needs an additional $10 million per year to make day care more affordable for low-income federal employees, the General Services Administration said yesterday. "This amount of money could, for example, reduce the cost of care by about a third for between 5,000 and 6,000 children," GSA said in a letter to the Office of Management and Budget. "Also, some of the new money could be used to help fill the more than 1,000 vacant slots in federal child-care centers with children of low-income families."

Feldmann, Linda, "Quest for Good Child Care Intensifies; Sagging Quality and an Influx of Kids from Welfare-Reform Incite Action by Lawmakers," *The Christian Science Monitor*, July 25, 1997, p. 1.

For many Americans, high-quality child care is an unaffordable luxury. Full-time day care for a 1-year-old can easily cost $4,000-$8,000 a year, and in some cities matches the tuition for a top private school. Washington has taken notice. The dual issues of quantity and quality in day care have roared back onto the agenda. In Congress, legislators from both parties have introduced some two dozen bills this year focusing on child care. And at least five states are looking at — or have already approved — funding to subsidize day care for qualified low-income families.

Winter, Christine, "Child-Care Costs Clog Worker Pool," *Chicago Tribune*, Dec. 9, 1997, p. N1.

The Rolling Meadows Chamber of Commerce is surveying employers and employees around town to gauge the interest in supporting an affordable, 24-hour child-care center for employees of Rolling Meadows businesses.

Back Issues

Great Research on Current Issues Starts Right Here.
Recent topics covered by The CQ Researcher are listed below.
Now available on the Web
For information, call (800) 432-2250 ext. 279 or (202) 887-6279.

If you would like to have any of these CQ Researchers updated, or need more information about these topics, please call CQ Custom Research. Special rates for CQ subscribers. (202) 887-8600 or (800) 432-2250, ext. 600, or E-mail Custom.Research@cq.com

JANUARY 1997
Combating Scientific Misconduct
Restructuring the Electric Industry
The New Immigrants
Chemical and Biological Weapons

FEBRUARY 1997
Assisting Refugees
Alternative Medicine's Next Phase
Independent Counsels
Feminism's Future

MARCH 1997
New Air Quality Standards
Alcohol Advertising
Civic Renewal
Educating Gifted Students

APRIL 1997
Declining Crime Rates
The FBI Under Fire
Gender Equity in Sports
Space Program's Future

MAY 1997
The Stock Market
The Cloning Controversy
Expanding NATO
The Future of Libraries

JUNE 1997
FDA Reform
China After Deng
Line-Item Veto
Breast Cancer

JULY 1997
Transportation Policy
Executive Pay
School Choice Debate
Aggressive Driving

AUGUST 1997
Age Discrimination
Banning Land Mines
Children's Television
Evolution vs. Creationism

SEPTEMBER 1997
Caring for the Dying
Mental Health Policy
Mexico's Future
Youth Fitness

OCTOBER 1997
Urban Sprawl in the West
Diversity in the Workplace
Teacher Education
Contingent Work Force

NOVEMBER 1997
Renewable Energy
Artificial Intelligence
Religious Persecution
Roe v. Wade at 25

DECEMBER 1997
Whistleblowers
Castro's Next Move
Gun Control Standoff
Regulating Nonprofits

JANUARY 1998
Foster Care Reform
IRS Reform
The Black Middle Class
U.S.-British Relations

FEBRUARY 1998
Patients' Rights
Deflation Fears
Caring for the Elderly
The New Corporate Philanthropy

MARCH 1998
Israel at 50
The Federal Judiciary
Drinking on Campus
The Economics of Recycling

APRIL 1998
Biology and Behavior
Liberal Arts Education
Income Inequality
High-Tech Labor Shortage

MAY 1998
Census 2000

Back issues are available for $5.00 (subscribers) or $10.00 (non-subscribers). Quantity discounts apply to orders over 10. To order, call Congressional Quarterly Customer Service at (202) 887-8621.

Binders are available for $18.00. To order call 1-800-638-1710. Please refer to stock number 648.

Future Topics

▶ *Alzheimer's Disease*

▶ *U.S.-Russian Relations*

▶ *Student Press*

THE

CQ Researcher

PUBLISHED BY CONGRESSIONAL QUARTERLY INC.

Alzheimer's Disease

Could it bankrupt the health-care system?

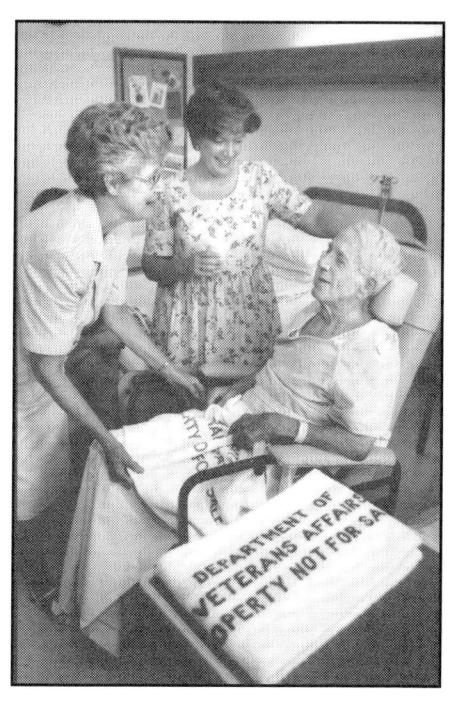

A lzheimer's disease has been described as health care's "ticking time bomb." The degenerative disease slowly destroys the brain's ability to remember, reason or control simple bodily functions like swallowing food. While scientists have found compelling evidence suggesting possible causes, they still don't have a cure or a generally accepted way to screen for the disease. With the number of Americans age 65 and over expected to more than double by 2030, health-care experts are bracing for a surge of new cases that could devastate families psychologically and economically and strain the nation's health-care system. Researchers are hoping a series of new treatments may delay the onset of symptoms. But some experts say progress hinges on Congress providing more research funding.

C Q | **May 15, 1998 • Volume 8, No. 19 • Pages 433-456**

Formerly Editorial Research Reports

COVER: ALZHEIMER'S ASSOCIATION

CQ Researcher

May 15, 1998
Volume 8, No.19

EDITOR
Sandra Stencel

MANAGING EDITOR
Thomas J. Colin

ASSOCIATE EDITOR
Sarah M. Magner

STAFF WRITERS
Adriel Bettelheim
Mary H. Cooper
Kenneth Jost
Kathy Koch
David Masci

PRODUCTION EDITOR
Melissa Hall

EDITORIAL ASSISTANT
Laura S. Cavender

PUBLISHED BY
Congressional Quarterly Inc.

CHAIRMAN
Andrew Barnes

VICE CHAIRMAN
Andrew P. Corty

PRESIDENT AND PUBLISHER
Robert W. Merry

EXECUTIVE EDITOR
David Rapp

The CQ Researcher (ISSN 1056-2036). Formerly Editorial Research Reports. Published weekly, except Jan. 2, May 29, July 3, Oct. 30, by Congressional Quarterly Inc., 1414 22nd St., N.W., Washington, D.C. 20037. Annual subscription rate for libraries, businesses and government is $340. Additional rates furnished upon request. Periodicals postage paid at Washington, D.C., and additional mailing offices. POSTMASTER: Send address changes to The CQ Researcher, 1414 22nd St., N.W., Washington, D.C. 20037.

Alzheimer's Disease

BY ADRIEL BETTELHEIM

THE ISSUES

Day after day, Cary Henderson felt Alzheimer's disease slowly stripping away his memory and intellect. So in the first years after he was diagnosed, the former history professor took special pleasure in doing the simple things he had once taken for granted: watching Duke University basketball on television, listening to his favorite symphonies, walking his beloved Yorkshire terrier.

But Henderson's inability to do simple day-to-day tasks frequently brought on panic and despair, like the time he couldn't remember how to use a can opener.

"My dog, precious little dog, of course, has to eat once in awhile and my wife was sleeping and I don't know how to open the can of dog food," Henderson recalled in a tape-recorded journal he kept at the beginning of his illness. *(See story, p. 438.)* "So the best I could do was to try to dig a hole, make a little perforation and see if I could extend the side of it — and it was something like a panic. . . . I had to find some way to get the doggie some food, but this was one of those things that you get into if you're going to have a life with Alzheimer's. . . . Maybe my wife, one of these hours, will be feeling better and she can really open the can. Right now the doggie seems to be in fairly good shape. I'm not too sure I am."

Experiences like the ones Henderson described are only the beginning of an irreversible slide into helplessness that ultimately robs Alzheimer's patients of the ability to walk, speak, eat solid food and even control their bladders.

It's a slide scientists and policymakers say could become increasingly commonplace in the next century. With aging baby boomers expected to more than double the

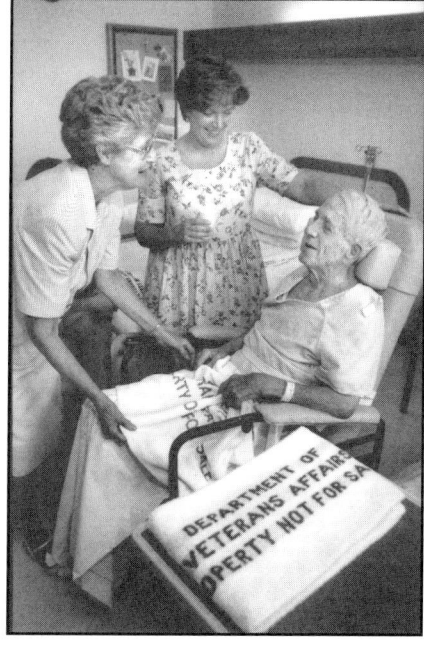

population of Americans 65 and older by 2030, many experts are predicting a surge of new Alzheimer's cases that could psychologically and economically devastate families and strain the nation's health-care system.

An estimated 4 million Americans now suffer from some form of Alzheimer's. The General Accounting Office (GAO) estimates that after age 65, the prevalence of the disease in men and women doubles every five years. The Alzheimer's Association, a Chicago-based advocacy group for victims of the disease and their families, projects the total number of cases will reach 14 million by 2050 unless a cure is found.

Such an increase could bring about a significant financial squeeze for health care in the new millennium. The average annual cost of caring for Alzheimer's patients at home now stands at about $12,500. The annual bill for nursing-home care ranges from $42,000 to $70,000 in urban and suburban areas. With many Alzheimer's patients living 10 or more years after the initial diagnosis, families frequently exhaust most of their savings on medical care, even if they get

home-care benefits and other aid from Medicare, the federal-state health-care program for the elderly. Taxpayers then must step in and pay their future bills through Medicaid, the health-care program for the poor. [1]

"The only way we are truly going to save Medicare from bankruptcy when the baby boomers retire is to reduce the length and incidence of expensive illnesses like Alzheimer's," says Sen. Tom Harkin, D-Iowa, who contends Congress should head off what he calls "a ticking time bomb" by spending more to find a cure for the disease.

The Alzheimer's Association is lobbying Congress to spend $100 million more on Alzheimer's research next year to fund clinical trials on new treatments. The federal government has earmarked $349.2 million on preventing the disease this year, making Alzheimer's the fourth-most-funded affliction after cancer, HIV/AIDS and heart disease. *(See graph, p. 440.)*

However, many observers say Alzheimer's is only a small piece of a much larger health-care riddle and dismiss predictions it will single-handedly bankrupt entitlement programs. They say rising general health-care costs and the growing number of retirees in the coming decades are a far greater threat to the solvency of Medicare and Medicaid than any single disease.

"Projections of the frequency of a disease 30 years from now should be taken with a grain of salt," says Gail Wilensky, chairman of the federal Physician Payment Review Commission and a former deputy assistant to the president for policy development in the Bush administration. "We don't know how the frequency of other diseases will rise or fall, and how that will affect longevity. And even though medical research has brought increased longevity and quality-of-life improvements, it's difficult to prove it has saved us a lot of money."

The new concerns about Alzheimer's

Alzheimer's Cases Could Skyrocket

The number of Alzheimer's victims in the United States could skyrocket after 2030, when the first baby boomers hit age 85. People over 85 face the greatest risk of being incapacitated by Alzheimer's and needing long-term nursing care. About 4 million Americans are now afflicted with the disease.

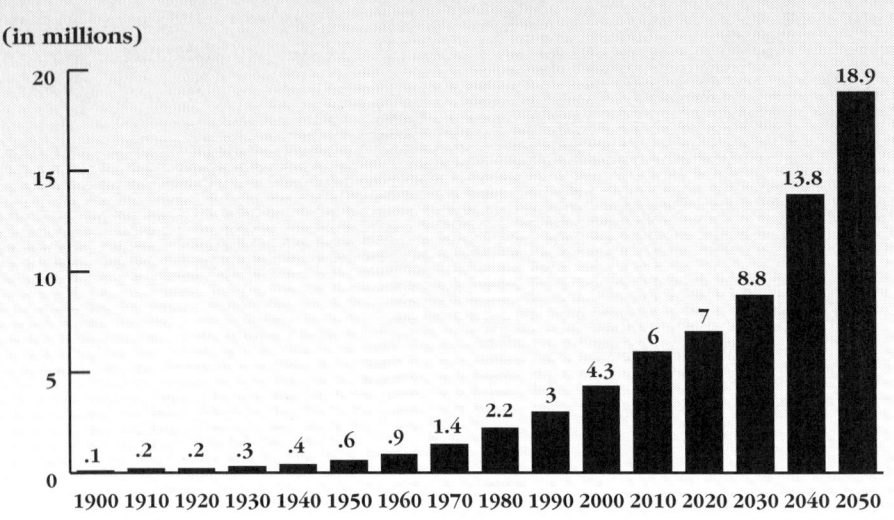

Americans age 85 and over

Source: "Report to Congress on the Scientific Opportunities for Developing Treatments for Alzheimer's Disease," June 1995; U.S. Census Bureau

breakdown of the brain chemical acetylcholine observed in Alzheimer's patients, though neither can restore memory or reverse the disease's pattern of killing brain cells.

There are no tests that can reliably predict who among the general population has Alzheimer's. Even the apparently straightforward act of estimating how many people have the condition has proven dicey because there's no single definition of Alzheimer's and the disease sometimes occurs in tandem with strokes and other neurological disorders.

Perhaps most ominously, Alzheimer's still suffers from the image of being an old person's disease. The commonly held, if rarely expressed, view is that devoting more money and effort to curing the disease will only prolong the life of very elderly people a few more years. Put another way: if you don't die of complications from Alzheimer's, you'll still die of something else. Even former President Ronald Reagan's 1994 announcement that he had the early stages of the disease didn't prompt a flood of new money for finding a cure.

"There's definitely some ageism at work," says John Morris, professor of neurology and co-director of the Alzheimer's disease research center at Washington University School of Medicine in St. Louis. "We kind of anticipate people are going to slip a bit in their older years, and we tolerate it until we

come at a time when significant advances in aging research are offering new hopes of finding a cure, or at least of forestalling symptoms. Scientists over the last decade have identified genetic mutations on four human chromosomes that can make a person more predisposed to Alzheimer's, providing important clues for how to detect the illness in its earliest stages.

Several promising therapies are also being tested, including administering megadoses of the anti-oxidant vitamin E to slow the progression of the disease. Other potential treatments include the use of estrogen replacement in postmenopausal women and administering anti-inflammatory drugs. [2]

"I'm very optimistic that in 10 years

we will be able to significantly alter the course of the disease," says Zaven Khachaturian, a Maryland neurobiologist and former director of Alzheimer's research at the National Institutes of Health. "It's more of a technical problem than a conceptual one; the key is finding a way to detect it early, years before the first symptoms are seen."

But such optimism is tempered by the vexing nature of the disease, which researchers admit they still aren't close to fully understanding. Despite federal expenditures of more than $3 billion on Alzheimer's research since 1976 scientists only have been able to develop two drugs approved by the Food and Drug Administration to treat the disease. Both have been found to temporarily delay the fast

have to provide care or there are behavioral complications. As more baby boomers get older, we ought to find a way to indicate where the normal aging process differs from early dementia and build more interest."

Alzheimer's slowly robs memory and judgment through a still-unexplained process that kills neurons in the brain. The disease gets its name from Alois Alzheimer, a German neuropathologist who first observed severe memory lapses, paranoia and anxiety in a 51-year-old female patient. When she died in 1906, Alzheimer examined her brain and found lesions and abnormal deposits of a sticky plaque outside and around the nerve cells. Masses of tangled fibers lined the inside of the cells. Even today, doctors rarely can make a definite diagnosis of Alzheimer's until an autopsy turns up those hallmarks of the disease. However, they believe the disease can eat away at the brain for 20 years or longer before the first symptoms of memory loss are noticed.

Despite the way it physically ravages the brain, Alzheimer's doesn't actually kill its victims. Patients can live 20 years or longer after an initial diagnosis, slowly losing the ability to carry out everyday tasks like reading a book or eating a meal. Sometimes they undergo significant personality changes, wander aimlessly and can turn violent. The patients often die of pneumonia or other complications from their weakened condition.

The effects of the disease are nearly as devastating on the families of victims, who frequently move in with ailing loved ones only to watch their personalities and cognitive abilities slip away. Donna Lyttle, a Queens, N.Y., health-care program manager, moved in with her 76-year-old widowed mother, who has suffered from Alzheimer's for 11 years, instead of sending her to a nursing home. She spends evenings trying to make some contact.

"To look at her you'd think she's the picture of health, but there's just no response," says Lyttle, who estimates her mother's care costs $25,000 to $30,000 annually. "I talk to her and say, 'This is Donna,' and she looks at you like somewhere in the back of her mind she's seen the face before.

Alzheimer's slowly robs memory and judgment through a still-unexplained process that kills neurons in the brain.

Courtesy of Alzheimer's Association

But it's a distant look."

As scientists try to better understand the disease, and public policy experts debate how it will affect health-care in the 21st century, here are some questions they are asking:

Could a surge of new Alzheimer's cases bankrupt the Medicare and Medicaid programs?

What happened to Lynda Gormus of Richmond, Va., illustrates what some say is a looming crisis in long-term health care.

Gormus' 85-year-old father died in 1992 after an 11-year battle with Alzheimer's that exhausted most of the middle-class family's savings. Her 80-year-old mother now suffers from Parkinson's disease, seizures and a brain tumor. Gormus is trying to sell her parents' house to pay her mother's medical bills, which she says total about $2,100 a month. In the meantime, she's negotiated a reduced-payment schedule with the assisted-living center where her mother resides.

"Just dealing with the emotional part of it is tough, but it's real scary how quickly the funds go down," says Gormus, who works part time. "You think that you're not going to have problems, that old age is a way down the road. Then something like this happens, and the funds just aren't there."

The Gormus' story illustrates a perilous cycle in which millions of Americans outlive their ability to take care of themselves. Those with chronic conditions like Alzheimer's have to pay the majority of their long-term care costs out of pocket before they become poor enough to qualify for Medicaid. Their grown children often help pay the bills but, in the process, deplete their own savings. [3]

Medical care for Alzheimer's patients typically is more expensive than for the elderly without cognitive problems. Alzheimer's patients have trouble following directions for taking medication, requiring nurses or other specialized care. Those who suffer from acute illnesses like heart

An Alzheimer's Journal

Familiar places like one's own home become foreign and difficult to navigate. A family get-together turns into a confusing jumble of sounds. There's a nagging fear of being belittled or cheated. Everyday items like eyeglasses are always being misplaced.

Alzheimer's patients experience such frustrations as the disease begins to eat away at their cognitive skills.

To help others understand their frustration and despair, social workers at the Duke University Center for Aging in Durham, N.C., asked some patients to keep journals during the early stages of the disease.

Cary Henderson, a former American history professor at James Madison University in Harrisonburg, Va., was diagnosed with Alzheimer's when he was 55. His physician first thought he had a rare disorder that can cause Alzheimer's-related symptoms but can be surgically corrected. Henderson's wife, Ruth, feared otherwise. At her urging, the neurologist removed a tiny amount of his brain tissue and performed a biopsy, confirming her suspicions. Henderson, thus, is one of the few living patients with an absolutely confirmed case of the disease.

Henderson kept his tape-recorded journal in 1991 and 1992, when he was in his early 60s. Portions of the journal were transcribed by Ruth and published in "The Caregiver," the newsletter of the Duke Family Support Program, in 1994. Henderson today is in the late stages of Alzheimer's and lives in an assisted-living facility. His complete journal will appear as a book, *Partial View*, to be published this fall by Southern Methodist University Press. Following are excerpts:

"Being dense is a very big part of Alzheimer's. And forgetting things. Although I'm not as bad as I sometimes am, it comes and goes. It's a very come-and-go disease. When I make a real blunder, I tend to get defensive about it — a sense of shame for not knowing what I should have known and for not being able to think things and see things that I saw several years ago when I was a normal person. But everybody by this time knows I'm not a normal person, and I'm quite aware of that.

"Whenever there's a gathering of people, it seems, at least in my mind, to be a lot of confusion. I just feel the need for quiet. I have to acknowledge the fact that for somebody like me, and I assume it's true of a lot of people with Alzheimer's, I can only think of one thing at a time. And large gatherings, whatever they may be, are very hard to understand. I really never quite know what is going on. As I've said before, I have not the vaguest idea about time, and after being a professor of history for 31 years, it's kind of weird to think I no longer have a sense of time and sense of change.

"With Alzheimer's you just know you're going to forget things, and it's impossible to put things where you can't forget them because people like me can always find a place to lose things, and we have to flurry all over the house to figure where in the heck I left whatever it was . . . It's usually my glasses. No matter where I put my glasses, they don't seem to be in the right place at the right time. You've got to have a sense of humor in this kind of business, and I think it's interesting how many places I can find to lose things.

"With Alzheimer's people, there's no such thing as having a day which is like another day. Every day is separate, and you don't know what's going to happen in any one day or any other thing like that. It's as if every day you have never seen anything before like what you're seeing right now. It just never will be the same again. But you can't beat Mother Nature.

"One of the things, I guess, people like myself with Alzheimer's put up with is the fact that other people have to put up with us. I think this disease does make us kind of irrational — and sometimes it's out of fear and sometimes it's being left out of things . . . I do think it's bad that we sometimes become almost afraid of ourselves and almost afraid of our caregivers and family . . . I think for a lot of us the feeling of being cheated or belittled and somehow made jokes of, I think that's the one thing that is among the worst things about Alzheimer's.

"We have some music to start off with today. This is Mahler's 'Resurrection Symphony,' which I dearly love. It's a little bit loud, but sometimes, I actually feel that way. I want to shout. I want to raise some hell. I want to be somebody I'm not."

---

disease frequently are unable to detail their full medical histories to doctors, creating the need for expensive batteries of tests. The federal Health Care Financing Administration (HCFA) estimates per capita Medicare expenditures for Alzheimer's patients stand at $7,682, compared with $4,524 for non-Alzheimer's recipients. [4]

But Medicare and private insurance only cover a fraction of health-care costs for Alzheimer's sufferers. The federal program, created in 1965 to provide medical care for the aged, is heavily weighted to providing acute care. It doesn't pay for the long-term care that many Alzheimer's patients require unless there is a coexisting medical condi-

tion. Medicaid comes to the rescue if a patient is at least 65, blind or disabled and meets strict income and asset limitations. But that means the patient first must turn over a significant part of his life savings to the nursing home or other qualified care facility.

Demographics suggest the problem will only get worse in the next century. The U.S. Census Bureau estimates the number of Americans 85 and over, who are at the greatest risk of needing long-term care for Alzheimer's, will rise from 3 million in 1990 to 4.3 million by the turn of the century. By 2030, the number of the nation's "oldest old" citizens will total 8.8 million, and by 2050 the number will rise to 18.9 million.

"We're confronting this [flood of new cases] for the first time," says Stephen McConnell, vice president for public policy at the Alzheimer's Association. "At the turn of the century, life expectancy was in the mid-40s. One of the benefits of the advances in health-care and modern technology is people are living longer. The downside is we have diseases like Alzheimer's to contend with."

Congress spent much of 1995 and 1996 debating how to solve the problems with Medicaid and Medicare spending to head off a financial squeeze, proposing a series of measures that would affect long-term care for the elderly. One controversial proposal passed in 1996 and since changed would have made it a federal crime for the elderly to give away assets or personal property in order to become eligible for Medicaid—a proposal derided by critics as the "Send grandma to jail" law. [5]

More recently, Congress made sweeping changes to Medicare, encouraging the elderly to enroll in health maintenance organizations and other health plans like those offered by employers. Policy-makers also considered reducing payments to doctors and hospitals, increasing beneficiary cost-sharing and offering new alternatives to financing health-care, such as private medical savings accounts.

Joshua Wiener, a long-term care specialist with the Urban Institute's Health Policy Center in Washington, is skeptical of claims that more Alzheimer's cases will cripple the health-care system. He estimates inflation-adjusted spending on long-term care will roughly double from 1993 and 2018, from $75.5 billion to $168.2 billion, adjusted for inflation. But assuming modest economic growth, that will only account for about 2.2 percent of the gross domestic product.

"It's a sizable increase, but I don't know if it's the end of civilization as we know it," Wiener says. "Long-term care for the Alzheimer's caseload would be easily manageable. The problem really is that Social Security and Medicare are also looking for additional revenues to help the same population—the elderly. Long-term care may be the last straw that breaks the camel's back."

Guy King, former chief actuary for HCFA, which administers Medicare and Medicaid, agrees. King says the Medicare program has already factored in rapidly aging baby boomers and projections of future Alzheimer's cases. The far bigger threat to the program's solvency is rising health-care costs and the growing number of retirees by the end of the next decade, King and others say.

King says Medicaid will be under more pressure from future Alzheimer's cases, though current projections only predict the state of the program five years ahead. "One of the problems with baby boomers is they have very low savings rates, in comparison to previous generations," King says. "It's going to be a problem, and the burden will fall on the program and their relatives."

Buying private long-term care insurance may be an option. The policies are expensive and aren't suited for everyone. But proponents say they can protect one's life savings if an Alzheimer's patient needs expensive care at home or in a nursing home. Employers have traditionally been reluctant to offer new long-term insurance because they already face millions of dollars of unfunded pension benefits.

Terms and prices of the private policies vary widely, and more than 100 companies sell them. The terms range from one year to as long as the patient needs. Coverage usually specifies nursing home-care, home care or assisted living facilities, with comprehensive coverage, offering a choice of care arrangements, costing more. They also have significant deductible payments, meaning the policyholder will have to pay for a certain number of days of long-term care before the insurance kicks in.

Stephen Moses, spokesman for LTC Inc., a Seattle company that markets long-term care insurance, offers an example of a typical policy that costs $2,376 a year. A healthy 69-year-old man would get $96 a day for assisted living or $120 a day for nursing home care for four years (on average, people die 2 $1/2$ years after entering nursing homes). The plan has 5 percent inflation protection but the policyholder has to pay the cost of the first 100 days of long-term care himself, or $12,000 to $15,000 out of pocket. [6]

Health economist Wilensky says it's worthwhile for people to save their money or buy long-term care insurance in a society where personal savings are low. However, she notes, "It's tricky to get people to focus on something 10 to 20 years down the road, unless they're already focused on the problem because they have a relative with Alzheimer's."

Are researchers close to finding an effective treatment for Alzheimer's disease?

Until the 1960s, scientists viewed Alzheimer's disease as one of those unexplained byproducts of aging — if they thought about the disease at all. There was understandably little cause for concern. At the time Alzheimer made his first diagnosis, only one in 25 Americans lived beyond 65.

But increasing life expectancy and rapid advances in molecular biology in the 1970s allowed scientists to begin to understand the biological underpinnings of the disease. Research is now progressing in several directions: un-

Research Funding a Recent Phenomenon

Scientific breakthroughs and increased public awareness led the federal government to begin funding Alzheimer's research in the 1970s. Today it is the fourth most funded affliction, after cancer, HIV/AIDS and heart disease.

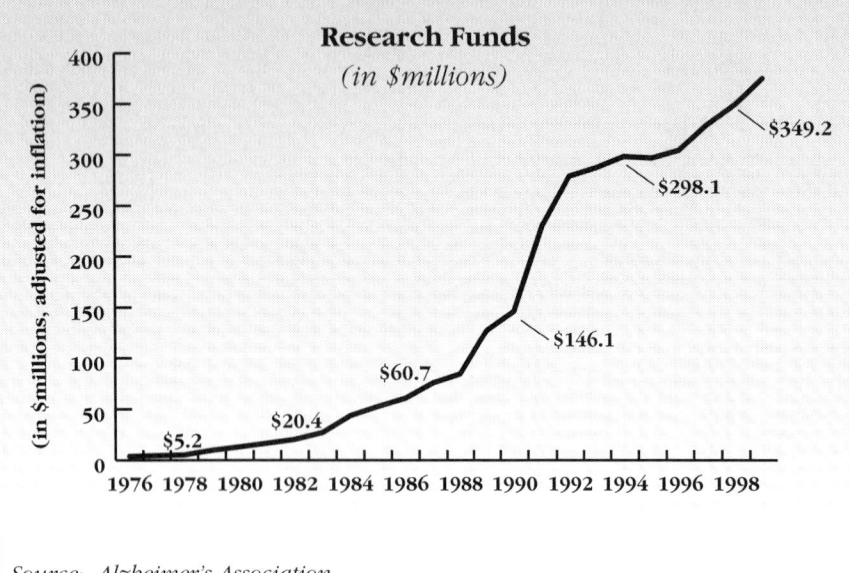

Research Funds
(in $millions)

$349.2

$298.1

$146.1

$60.7

$20.4

$5.2

Source: Alzheimer's Association

derstanding how mutant genes make some people predisposed to the disease; finding ways to slow the progression of its symptoms; and trying to identify precisely when Alzheimer's first begins in the brain.

"We have to work on all these different avenues at once because we don't know which will lead fastest to a cure," says Marcelle Morrison-Bogorad, associate director of the neuroscience of aging program at the National Institute on Aging in Bethesda, Md. "We understand how the liver and heart work, but the brain is so incredibly complex that if we waited to know every little bit before we tried to slow the progression of the disease, the public wouldn't thank us."

On the genetics front, researchers over the last six years have identified a series of mutations on genes that are believed to make a person more susceptible to the disease, though the presence of one doesn't always give rise to the condition. The presence of a num-

ber of biological markers has led some to speculate Alzheimer's actually may not be a single disease but a group of closely related disorders.

One important development came in 1992 when biologists at Duke University in Durham, N.C., identified a variant of the gene responsible for creating the chemical apolipoprotein in patients who developed the most common form of "late-onset" Alzheimer's. Apolipoprotein normally carries blood cholesterol throughout the body. But researchers believe the suspect gene, known as apoE4, may contribute to the buildup of the abnormal protein plaques that strangle brain cells in Alzheimer's patients. The gene also may lower the age at which patients begin to suffer the onset of the disease. ApoE4 is found in about 40 percent of all late-onset Alzheimer's cases. [7]

Genetic screening for the mutation could someday help scientists find people with markers for the disease

to include in clinical trials of new drugs. Indeed, a simple blood test can turn up the presence of apoE4 or two other common Alzheimer's-related mutations. But some researchers say there's little point to screening until a preventive treatment for Alzheimer's is available. Moreover, testing could cause unintended harm, exposing those who test positive to discrimination in obtaining insurance or healthcare and causing unnecessary anxiety in people who have the gene but don't develop the disease. The American Association for Geriatric Psychiatry, the Alzheimer's Association and the American Geriatrics Society issued a consensus statement last year, declaring testing may not prove useful in diagnosing dementia patients. [8]

The difficulty of linking the disease with a single gene was illustrated in March, when researchers at Columbia University in New York examined different ethnic and racial groups' chances of getting the disease. The team reported blacks and Hispanics who carry the apoE4 gene are about as likely as whites to get the disease by the time they reach age 90. But blacks without the suspect gene are at four times the risk of contracting Alzheimer's, and Hispanics who lack the gene variation are at more than twice the risk. The findings suggest other genes or environmental circumstances are at work in minority populations. [9]

While researchers sort out various risk factors, they also are looking for new ways to forestall symptoms of the disease. Most involve shoring up brain cells by boosting their energy or blood supply with commonly used substances. Most of the agents have already been approved by the FDA for use in humans, making the treatment much cheaper than developing completely new drugs.

The most battle-tested regimen so far may be the anti-oxidant vitamin E, given alone in 2,000-unit megadoses

Mystery of 'Hexed' Russian Villagers Solved

Most Alzheimer's patients develop the so-called "late-onset" form of the disease, which strikes at random in people age 65 and over. But there are scattered cases of a faster-spreading version that can develop in individuals as young as their mid-30s and appears to run in families.

Scientists over the last six years have pinpointed mutations on any one of three genes that, if present in an individual, almost always result in familial, or early-onset, Alzheimer's. The high predictability gives researchers an unusual opportunity to explore how the disease manifests itself in the brain and how genes may affect when a person develops symptoms.

"The reason we focus on it is because [the high predictability makes it] the path of least resistance," says Gerard Schellenberg, a geneticist at the Veterans Affairs Medical Center in Seattle, who helped discover the genetic links. "People get it early in life and usually die before there are complications from other chronic diseases; the mechanism for the disease is basically the same as late-onset Alzheimer's."

Researchers at the University of Washington began to explore the condition in the mid-1980s after discovering it in five families that all traced their ancestry to ethnic Germans who settled in Russia's Volga Valley in the 18th century. Some of the families emigrated to the United States between 1870 and 1920.

Descendents told researchers that residents in the Volga villages of Walter and Frank were said to be bewitched, hexed or possessed. Follow-up studies on four more families with identical ties led the Washington researchers to conclude the "hexing" was evidence of Alzheimer's-like dementia. The geneticists said the villages likely experienced a "founder effect" — essentially all of the residents were distant blood relatives who inherited an Alzheimer's gene from some unknown common ancestor who lived centuries ago.

"Germans from Russia as a group aren't any more predisposed to Alzheimer's than anyone else," says University of Washington neurologist Tom Bird. "But people from these two villages were essentially all distant cousins with a predisposition for the trait."

Similar cases have turned up elsewhere, such as the small farming community of Harvey, in New Brunswick, Canada. Barb Hatfield, 42, grew up in the town and lost her mother to Alzheimer's-related symptoms when she was 56. Hatfield's maternal grandmother, three maternal aunts and an uncle also died from the disease. Some of her mother's first cousins now suffer from Alzheimer's.

"My mom would never talk about it. She literally would only say, 'She lost her mind' and that was the end of the conversation," Hatfield recalled. [1] "I can remember many times wishing it was some normal disease like cancer or something. This was something nobody understood."

The suspect mutations linked to the condition arise in the genes that code for the proteins presinilin 1 and 2 and amyloid precursor protein. Carriers of the mutation for presinilin 1 and amyloid precursor protein are practically guaranteed to get Alzheimer's before they turn 60, Schellenberg says.

People carrying the mutation for presinilin 2 tend to develop Alzheimer's at middle age but sometimes don't develop the condition until well into their 70s. Scientists want to study the gene more to understand how chemical changes may influence when the disease strikes.

Early-onset Alzheimer's is a particularly cruel version of the disease that strikes in the prime of life and moves quickly, destroying brain cells and leading to patient deaths in six to eight years, compared with 10 or more years in late-onset Alzheimer's.

Some researchers have used gene coding for the amyloid precursor protein to breed laboratory mice with the mutation causing early-onset symptoms. The animals have provided convenient models for observing when the characteristic Alzheimer's plaques form in brains and how they kill neurons.

"We're much closer to finding a cure," said Linda Nee, a geneticist at the National Institutes of Health, who has studied the New Brunswick villagers. "We've come light years from where we started because the technology has improved so much." [2]

---

[1] Quoted in Chris Morris, "Family Curse Key to Medical Mystery? Village's High Incidence of Alzheimer's Leads to Major Study," *Toronto Star*, March 27, 1998, p. F6.

[2] *Ibid.*

---

or in combination with selegiline, a prescription drug used to treat Parkinson's disease. A research team led by Mary Sano, a biologist at Columbia University's College of Physicians and Surgeons in New York, conducted clinical trials on 341 patients and reported last year that memory loss and cognitive problems were slowed by about seven months in test groups of patients who took the drugs compared with those who received no medicine. [10]

The results could explain how antioxidants like vitamin E and selegiline eradicate toxic substances known as "free radicals" that contribute to the breakdown of brain cells. However, the drugs didn't improve patients' scores on cognitive tests as compared with untreated patients. Skeptics said the treatment may only have affected patients' behavior but not the underlying disease.

Another prospective treatment is estrogen, a hormone credited with helping prevent heart disease and osteoporosis that also can influence the levels and function of several brain chemicals—seratonin, dopamine and acetylcholine—linked to Alzheimer's.

Scientists at Johns Hopkins University in Baltimore and the National Institute on Aging reported last year that estrogen-replacement therapy halved the risk of Alzheimer's in a control group of 472 menopausal and post-menopausal women that was observed over 16 years. But researchers still don't know how the hormone affects memory or what effect decades of missing estrogen has on the female body, let alone the brain.

The therapy also can present dangerous side effects, such as increased risk of stroke. Richard Mayeux, professor of neurology, psychiatry and public health at Columbia University, regards the hormone as an "effective primary or secondary treatment" that, taken in conjunction with other drugs, acts as a kind of nerve-growth factor that makes neurons survive better and longer. [11]

Clinicians have also reported success administering regular doses of ibuprofen and other anti-inflammatory drugs on Alzheimer's patients to improve blood flow in the brain. Even the plant extract Ginkgo biloba has been shown to have some therapeutic effects in limited clinical trials and has been approved for the treatment of dementia in Germany.

Scientists acknowledge that knowing Alzheimer's symptoms without knowing the true cause of the disease makes their efforts look somewhat scattershot and uncoordinated. But neurobiologist Khachaturian draws comparisons to early efforts to treat polio in the 1940s and '50s. The first treatments for the disabling disease centered around providing care and easing pain. Only later did research lead to a vaccine that finally eliminated the disease.

"As scientists develop new drugs, they pursue leads that will shed light on the causes of the disease," he says. "You can always look at the empty portion of the glass, but I prefer to look at the current situation more positively. It's half full."

Should Congress and the White House earmark more money for Alzheimer's research?

"I cannot bear to see anyone I love go through this ever again," David Hyde Pierce, who stars as Dr. Niles Crane in the television show "Frasier," told a House Appropriations subcommittee in January, as he recalled how his grandfather succumbed to Alzheimer's. "If we do not find a way to prevent it soon, Alzheimer's will be the epidemic of the 21st century." [12]

Pierce was one of 20 witnesses to come before the panel, seeking more money for various scientific research and education programs. In what has become a familiar Washington scene, celebrities with personal connections to diseases join forces with advocacy groups to lobby Congress to earmark funds for certain afflictions in annual spending bills.

Pierce and the Alzheimer's Association are pressing for $100 million more in research money in fiscal 1999. It would mark the first significant increase in Alzheimer's funding since 1991, when annual spending jumped 57 percent, to $229.8 million. That increase was largely due to the efforts of a lawmaker with a personal connection to the disease — former Sen. Mark O. Hatfield, R-Ore., then ranking Republican on the powerful Senate Appropriations Committee, whose father died of Alzheimer's-related complications.

Alzheimer's research funding has increased modestly since then, despite wider public awareness of the disease after former President Reagan's announcement that he had the condition. The current $349.2 million funding level lags well behind the approximately $1 billion spent annually on heart disease and $1.5 billion a year spent on HIV/AIDS. Cancer research receives by far the largest targeted spending — approximately $3.1 billion a year. [13]

Congress in recent years has been reluctant to target certain diseases over others, preferring to let NIH make the choices. Most lawmakers, aware there isn't enough money to please everyone, don't want to risk appearing insensitive to certain groups of chronic disease sufferers.

"Congress' role has been one of appropriation and oversight, not micromanagement of disease research," says Rep. John Edward Porter, R-Ill., chairman of the House Appropriations Subcommittee on Labor, Health and Human Services and Education to which Pierce delivered his testimony.

Porter and others opposing earmarks for specific diseases argue that NIH administrators closest to the labs are in the best position to decide how money should be spent. Targeting more money toward a specific disease also ignores the interdisciplinary nature of research, they say. For instance, research on infectious particles called prions that have been linked to so-called "mad cow" disease also are shedding new light on brain damage in Alzheimer's and may provide a foundation for new drugs.

But other lawmakers say Congress should play a greater role in dictating basic research priorities. A few like Rep. Ernest Istook, R-Okla., have openly criticized NIH for playing politics and spending heavily on HIV/AIDS research while not devoting more resources to conditions with higher incidence, including cancer, Alzheimer's and heart disease.

"Whether you analyze it by the number of patients, a per death basis, a cost-per-patient basis or any other common-sense way, our research dollars are not being spent where they could do the most good," Istook says. [14]

Harkin, whose home state of Iowa

has one of the largest percentages of residents 85 and over, takes a different tack, saying spending more on new Alzheimer's treatments like vitamin E will save money decades later. Harkin cites studies by the American Federation for Aging Research showing that delaying the onset of Alzheimer's even five years could save as much as $260 billion in healthcare costs each year. In contrast, a clinical trial on a promising drug costs $1-$2 million.

"For years, the focus of research has been to identify a cure or a way to prevent [Alzheimer's]. Delaying the onset holds great hope and could bring more immediate results than traditional means," Harkin says.

But the notion of bigger research budgets and targeted spending doesn't sit well with everyone. Daniel Callahan, director of international programs at the Hastings Center, a bioethics think tank in Garrison, N.Y., argues American society and the medical industry are on an endless quest to conquer all diseases and should recognize the finiteness of the human condition. The more pro-gress that is made against disorders that strike earlier in life, the harder it will be to tackle those that emerge at later ages, he says.

"We can shuffle the causes of death, and we can live longer in the process. But death is still waiting in hiding for all of us, eventually to make its appearance," Callahan writes in his new book, *False Hopes: Why America's Quest for Perfect Health Is a Recipe for Failure*. Chronic diseases, such as cancer, heart disease, Alzheimer's and kidney failure, "will continue to take thousands of lives. In the diseases of aging, we seem to be up against some formidable biological barriers." ∎

BACKGROUND

An Ancient Evil

Alzheimer's disease is hardly a new condition. The ancient Greeks and Romans occasionally described symptoms resembling Alzheimer's and other forms of dementia. Among the chroniclers was the Greek playwright Sophocles, who in the fifth century B.C. observed: "All evils are ingrained in long old age, with vanished, useless actions, empty thoughts."

Centuries later, William Shakespeare wrote about very old age as a time of

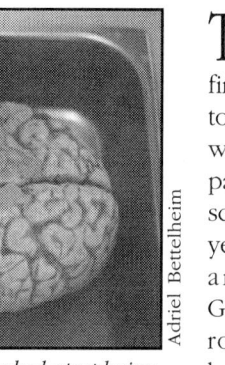

The brain of an Alzheimer's victim, left, shows marked atrophying compared with a normal brain. (Oregon Brain Bank, Oregon Health Sciences University; National Museum of Health and Medicine, Armed Forces Institute of Pathology)

Adriel Bettelheim

"second childishness and mere oblivion." Toward the end of the play, Shakespeare's King Lear laments to his daughter Cordelia: "I am a very foolish fond old man/Fourscore and upward, not an hour more or less/And, to deal plainly/I fear I am not in my perfect mind."

Though symptoms were easily noticed, few people bothered to explore the causes of dementia, often assuming it was an irreversible consequence of aging and "hardening of the arteries." Additionally, so few people lived to the age at which dementia of the Alzheimer's type

usually strikes that the disorder rated scant public attention.

That began to change in the mid-1800s, when British psychiatrist James Pritchard outlined stages in the progression of dementia, from memory impairment to the loss of reason, incomprehension and the loss of instinctive action. French psychiatrist Jean Etienne Dominique Esquirol coined the term "senile dementia" in 1838, writing in his book *Des Maladies Mentales* that the disease progresses slowly, weakening sensations and slowly robbing sufferers of their impulses and will.

Alzheimer's Discovery

The disease finally received a name and a firm definition of the symptoms in November 1906, when German neuropathologist Alzheimer described the case of a 51-year-old female patient to a meeting of the South West Germany Society of Neurologists. The woman, known as Auguste D., suffered from fits of paranoid jealousy, anxiety and disturbing memory lapses. Alzheimer tracked her condition for four years and, upon her death, autopsied her brain tissue, finding the distinctive lesions that are now a telltale sign of the disease.

Some of Alzheimer's contemporaries suspected he misdiagnosed Auguste D., and that she instead suffered from a rare metabolic disorder called metachromatic leukodystrophy. Earlier this year, scientists uncovered slides containing long-lost samples of her brain tissue in a basement at the University of Munich and retested them. They confirmed she, indeed, suffered from classic Alzheimer's. [15]

Because Alzheimer's patient was relatively young, most of the scientific community dismissed his report on Auguste D. as a rare case of pre-senile dementia and forgot about it. Interest was rekindled only after British researchers in the 1960s compared autopsied brain tissues from relatively young and elderly dementia sufferers and found in both the classic pathologic signs of the disease: plaques (the dense protein deposits that surround brain cells) and neurofibrillary tangles (the twisted strands inside the cells). The presence of the same abnormalities in two types of patients suggested the disease was more widespread than previously thought.

The physical scars come from the way the disease destroys neurons in parts of the brain that control memory. The damage occurs when neurons congregate and form protein masses called amyloids that are water-soluble in normal brains but undergo structural changes and can't be dissolved in Alzheimer's patients. The masses disrupt nerve cell functions and begin to cause symptoms such as the loss of short-term memory. Gradually the damage spreads to the cerebral cortex, which controls language and reasoning. As more nerve cells die, patients begin to lose their language skills and judgment and sometimes become easily agitated.

The deterioration of the brain is accompanied by a drop-off in the production of the neurotransmitter acetylcholine, which plays a key role in cognitive functioning. The two FDA-approved drugs that have been developed to combat Alzheimer's — tacrine (Cognex) and donepezil hydrochloride (Aricept) — can temporarily boost acetylcholine levels in mild to moderate cases, though they can't reverse the progression of the disease.

It's unclear whether the amyloid plaques actually cause Alzheimer's disease or result from some process in the development of the disease. Other possible causes, or contributing factors, include head injuries and abnormally high concentrations of calcium brought on by metabolic imbalances. Recent research in Britain and Norway found groups of Alzheimer's patients had higher blood levels of the amino acid homocysteine — a condition that can be treated with a dietary supplement of folic acid and vitamin B12.

U.S. Launches Program

As the long-term implications of the disease became clear in the 1970s, federal officials realized that finding an effective treatment or cure should be made a priority. The National Institute on Aging launched an Alzheimer's program in 1978 and now devotes approximately half of its budget to improving screening for the disease and developing therapies.

Prompted by the federal effort, seven private caregiver organizations combined in 1980 to form the Alzheimer's Disease and Related Disorders Association, since renamed the Alzheimer's Association. The Chicago-based nonprofit has grown from a fledgling organization with an $85,000 annual budget into a prominent health-care lobbying group, with 200 chapters and a budget of nearly $100 million. It promotes scientific research and lobbies Congress for long-term health care, nursing home reform and respite care for family members of Alzheimer's victims.

Former President Ronald Reagan greets a visitor to the Ronald Reagan Presidential Library in July 1997, three years after he announced he had Alzheimer's.

Reuters/Mike Guastella

Reagan's Dramatic Disclosure

The steadily building interest in Alzheimer's reached new heights on Nov. 5, 1994, when former President Ronald Reagan disclosed he had been diagnosed as suffering from early stages of the disease. Reagan, then 83, said the diagnosis indicated he had begun "the journey that will lead me into the sunset of my life."

In a handwritten letter released by his Los Angeles office, Reagan said he had experienced acute memory loss and other Alzheimer's symptoms for about a year. He said he decided to make his condition public to increase awareness of the disease. Reagan joined a list of high-profile

Continued on p. 446

Chronology

1900s *The pathological signs of Alzheimer's disease in the human brain are described for the first time.*

November 1906

German neuropathologist Alois Alzheimer details his findings about the disease that now bears his name.

———— • ————

1970s *New research makes the American public aware that Alzheimer's is a disorder, not simply a natural part of the aging process.*

1976

British researchers report that levels of the neurotransmitter acetylcholine fall sharply in people with Alzheimer's disease. The National Institutes of Health (NIH) and other federal agencies with interest in the aging brain subsequently stress the importance of distinguishing between Alzheimer's and other forms of dementia.

———— • ————

1980s *Government funding of Alzheimer's research increases while various studies report progress establishing causes of the disease.*

1980

Families, physicians and healthcare professionals across the country meet at NIH and form the Alzheimer's Disease and Related Disorders Association. The group, since renamed the Alzheimer's Association, is now based in Chicago.

October 1984

The National Institute on Aging (NIA) announces the establishment of five Alzheimer's disease research centers.

1986

President Ronald Reagan signs into law the Alzheimer's Disease and Related Dementias Services Research Act, which establishes a council on Alzheimer's disease in the U.S. Department of Health and Human Services.

November 1989

On the basis of a study of elderly people living in East Boston, Mass., the NIA estimates that 4 million Americans have some form of Alzheimer's — nearly twice the previous estimate.

———— • ————

1990s *New studies reveal Alzheimer's has multiple causes as public interest and research efforts intensify.*

1990

Congress approves a 57 percent funding increase for Alzheimer's research for fiscal 1991, to $229.8 million, as Sens. Mark O. Hatfield, R-Ore., and Tom Harkin, D-Iowa, argue the disease represents a looming public health crisis.

1992

Researchers at Duke University find an increased risk for the common "late-onset" Alzheimer's in patients over age 65 who inherit the apoE4 gene on chromosome 19. NIA-affiliated scientists also uncover evidence of a defective gene on chromosome 14 that leads to a rarer inherited form of Alzheimer's.

1993

The Food and Drug Administration approves the sale of tacrine (Cognex), the first prescription drug to treat early and middle stages of Alzheimer's. Congress creates the "Safe Return" program, a public-private effort to locate Alzheimer's patients who wander and become lost.

Nov. 5, 1994

Former President Ronald Reagan, 83, announces he has been diagnosed with Alzheimer's disease after suffering acute memory loss and other symptoms for about a year.

1996

The FDA approves donepezil hydrochloride (Aricept), another drug to treat Alzheimer's symptoms. An international panel of neuroscientists develops new guidelines for definitively diagnosing Alzheimer's at autopsy.

1997

Alzheimer's researchers report commonly available substances may delay the onset of Alzheimer's. Columbia University-led clinical trials show megadoses of vitamin E and the prescription drug seligiline can delay symptoms of Alzheimer's by about seven months. Johns Hopkins University researchers report a 16-year study shows estrogen may slow the disease in post-menopausal women.

1998

The Alzheimer's Association presses for a $100-million increase in funding for Alzheimer's research. NIA researchers focus on identifying people at risk of Alzheimer's before they develop any signs of the disease.

Sometimes It Isn't Alzheimer's

Alzheimer's disease is often confused with other neurological conditions that also cause memory loss and behavioral changes and impair reasoning. Doctors must administer a battery of physical and mental tests and consult with family members before making a diagnosis. Conditions that cause Alzheimer's-like symptoms include:

Depression — A common affliction among the elderly, especially those with physical problems. Symptoms include sadness, inactivity, difficulty thinking and concentrating and feelings of despair. Depressed persons often have trouble sleeping, experience changes in appetite, fatigue and agitation. Depression can often be treated with drugs such as Prozac that affect concentrations of brain chemicals known as neurotransmitters.

Delirium — A state of temporary but acute mental confusion that comes on suddenly. Symptoms may include anxiety, disorientation, tremors, hallucinations, delusions and incoherence. Delirium can occur in older persons who have short-term illnesses, heart or lung disease, long-term infections, poor nutrition or hormone disorders. Alcohol or drugs, including medications, also may cause confusion.

Parkinson's disease — A degenerative nerve disease that causes rhythmic tremors of the hands and other parts of the body, spastic motion of the eyelids and a bent-over posture. Patients have trouble walking and take slow, shuffling footsteps. More than a half-million Americans suffer from the condition, which is caused by a deficit of a chemical messenger in the brain called dopamine. Doses of the medication L-dopa can help, but they often lose their effectiveness over time.

Huntington's disease — An inherited brain disorder that leads to progressive deterioration of physical and mental capabilities. Symptoms include uncontrollable nervous movements of parts of the body, an abnormal gait, slurred speech, difficulty swallowing, cognitive difficulties and personality changes. The condition has been linked to a gene on chromosome 4.

Pick's disease — A relatively rare, hard-to-diagnose neurological disorder usually confined to the frontal lobes of the brain. Unlike Alzheimer's, the disease usually strikes people between ages 40 and 60, and death follows after five to six years. Another difference from Alzheimer's is that personality changes are observed before memory loss. New cases of Pick's are rare after 60.

Creutzfeldt-Jacob disease — A rare disorder caused by a viral-type organism called a prion. Onset typically takes place around age 50, with symptoms including personality changes, loss of coordination, dementia, muscle tremors and rigid posture. The loss of brain function with the telltale presence of lesions in cerebral tissue is similar to Alzheimer's but progresses faster. The disease can be caused by tissue transplants and also is believed to be heritable in some families.

Multi-infarct dementia — The second most common form of dementia in older persons, after Alzheimer's. Multi-infarct dementia is caused by a series of strokes that damage or destroy brain tissue. The strokes may be so tiny that the first few produce no observable symptoms. Gradually, victims may exhibit forgetfulness, incontinence and emotional problems and get lost in familiar places. Those most at-risk are between ages 60 and 75. Men are slightly more likely to develop the condition than women. High blood pressure, diabetes and high blood cholesterol are important risk factors.

Sources: National Institute on Aging, Alzheimer's Association.

Continued from p. 444

victims that includes actress Rita Hayworth, humorist E.B. White, illustrator Norman Rockwell, former middleweight and welterweight boxing champion Sugar Ray Robinson and former Metropolitan Opera General Manager Sir Rudolf Bing.

"Unfortunately, as Alzheimer's disease progresses, the family often bears a heavy burden," Reagan wrote. "I only wish there was some way I could spare Nancy from this painful experience. When the time comes I am confident that with your help she will face it with faith and courage."

Dueling Statistics

Establishing reliable estimates of just how many people suffer from Alzheimer's has been problematic. Researchers in the 1970s and '80s relied on surveys of specialized-care facilities, psychiatric hospitals and nursing homes to arrive at a generally accepted population of 2 million to 2.5 million sufferers nationwide.

In 1989, a group of Boston-area researchers took a different approach, administering simple memory tests to 3,811 residents age 65 and over in the working-class community of East Boston. More elaborate clinical tests were then administered as a follow-up to 467 of the individuals to rule out other causes of mental impairment. After calculating the data, the researchers concluded that 10.3 percent of elderly East Boston residents probably had Alzheimer's disease.

By extrapolating the numbers to the entire United States, the researchers concluded the current Alzheimer's population stands at approximately 4 million patients, effectively doubling the accepted estimate. They further projected the number of Alzheimer's patients would rise to as high as 14.3 million by 2050, with the most significant increases coming in people age 85 and over. From 1980 to 2050, the researchers said the number of Alzheimer's patients in that age group would rise almost sevenfold, from 1.02 million to 7.07 million. [16]

The researchers cautioned that their numbers could be low because they only surveyed non-institutionalized people. But many public policy analysts and medical researchers embraced the study in succeeding years, crediting it with sounding the alarm about rising Alzheimer's caseloads. The National Institute on Aging, among others, began using the group's 4 million estimate of current patients.

"[The study is] likely to be disturbing to the general public, given the widespread fear of Alzheimer's disease, and should receive the careful attention of health planners and physicians: the fastest growing segment of our population is this same group of persons more than 85 years old," the *Journal of the American Medical Association* said in an editorial. [17]

Early this year, the U.S. General Accounting Office threw some cold water on the estimates after analyzing 18 published studies of Alzheimer's prevalence. Using a statistical analysis, the GAO concluded only 1.9 million Americans 65 and older suffered from some level of the disease. The agency said the population would likely rise to 2.1 million if one counted cases of Alzheimer's combined with other dementia and instances where some patients slipped through the screening process.

The National Institute on Aging disputed the numbers, saying the GAO relied on 15 studies of Alzheimer's patients outside of the United States that may have used different diagnostic criteria. Institute director Richard Hodes said NIH was trying to arrive at accurate estimates of its own, including studies of various racial and ethnic minority populations that have largely been left out of earlier surveys.

"An accurate estimate of Alzheimer's prevalence in the U.S. is important, but it is even more important that policymakers and public health officials improve their understanding of the differences in prevalence among populations in the U.S.," Hodes says. ∎

Researchers in Boston estimate there are now 4 million Alzheimer's sufferers in the United States and could be 14 million by 2050.

Courtesy of Alzheimer's Association

CURRENT SITUATION

Diagnosing Dementia

How does one establish whether a person has Alzheimer's disease? Short of directly obtaining a sample of brain tissue, clinicians have to rely on memory tests, physical evaluations and personal accounts from patients' relatives. There is no widely accepted screening test in use for the general population.

A group of Vermont psychologists is trying to change that with a seven-minute word-and-picture test they claim is 90 percent accurate in identifying patients with early Alzheimer's. The results of a study of the test given to 120 people were published in March in the *Archives of Neurology*. [18]

"The judgment we can make is that someone is performing in a way that is entirely normal or that they have a dementia characteristic of Alzheimer's disease," says Paul Solomon, co-director of the Southwestern Vermont Medical Center memory clinic and a psychologist at Williams College in Williamstown, Mass.

The study involved 60 patients who had been referred to the Vermont clinic because of a suspected problem and 60 people with no known memory problems. Examiners who administered the test — consisting of four short quizzes and a clock test — did not know which patients had memory problems. The test correctly identified 13 of 13 patients known to have early Alzheimer's. A follow-up study on another 800 people has shown similarly encouraging results but has yet to be published, according to Solomon.

The quizzes examine a patient's ability to recall sets of flash cards in 16 different categories just moments after they are displayed. Patients who can't recall everything are provided with reminder words as prompts. The reminders help non-Alzheimer's patients but don't help people with the disease. Patients are also asked to draw a clock face with all 12 numbers in the proper place, and to arrange the hands to show the time of 20 minutes to four. Patients with memory problems will leave out numbers or arrange the hands incorrectly.

Researchers say such tests could be useful diagnostic tools if they can be proven to work consistently on very large populations. But they note the new test can't distinguish between Alzheimer's patients and people who suffer memory lapses from other diseases — and have to be tested on much larger populations to be validated. "None of the existing tests, to my mind, can reliably predict who has Alzheimer's," says Washington University neurologist Morris.

The difficulty of assessing who has the disease can also be compounded by cultural attitudes toward mental illness in some ethnic groups. Sue Levkoff, associate professor in the department of social medicine at Harvard University Medical School, spent four years studying how African-American, Latino and Asian communities in Boston dealt with Alzheimer's-like dementia. Many resisted seeking medical care for ailing relatives, regarding Alzheimer's and similar diseases as a normal product of aging.

"There's a certain inability to admit there's a problem that could require someone to go to a nursing home," Levkoff says. "There are communities [particularly Asian and His-

panic] where not directly caring for family is viewed as a stigma."

Ethnic Differences in Seeking Treatment

Levkoff says she found different rationalizations for not seeking medical help. Some Chinese families she studied believe the body is something akin to a machine, and parts naturally begin to break down. Latinos were more apt to view the condition as the outcome of failings, such as the family not treating the

There is no widely accepted screening test for Alzheimer's in use for the general population. Clinicians have to rely on memory tests, physical evaluations and personal accounts from patients' relatives.

Courtesy of Alzheimer's Association

mother well. African-Americans tended to turn to the Bible, though they didn't necessarily seek out support from their church. Most of the time, a doctor's visit was only considered after patients began to display disturbing behavioral problems.

Science is gradually providing more precise ways to diagnose the disease, even though the most advanced imaging techniques still can't turn up the characteristic plaques and tangles that reside deep in the brain.

Investigators at the General Clinical Research Center at the New England Medical Center in Boston have used magnetic-resonance imaging to diagnose older patients with Alzheimer's by looking for lower blood volume in parts of their brains.

Other physicians are focusing on brain structures that can be damaged by the disease in its early stages. Johns Hopkins University researchers have used CT scans to show a relationship between a decline in cognitive functions in Alzheimer's patients and enlargement of the suprasellar cistern, a fluid-filled area in the base of the brain.

A study at the National Institute on Aging is using another radiological technique, positron emission tomography, to assess how early plaques and tangles can be detected in the brain. Researchers have used a small group of Down's syndrome patients, ages 32 to 61, because their affliction often leads to Alzheimer's-like symptoms after middle age.

The aging institute's Morrison-Bogorad says such work may eventually pinpoint exactly when Alzheimer's begins to physically manifest itself. Because the disease can go undetected for decades, finding a precise biological starting point could allow doctors to begin administering drugs to delay symptoms.

"If you want to have healthy aging, we have to understand where unhealthy aging begins," Morrison-Bogorad says. "It's like digging the first dike as the waves start lapping over the wall, you try to slow the progression." ∎

Continued on p. 450

At Issue:

Should Congress earmark research funds for specific diseases like Alzheimer's?

M. Marsel Mesulam

Director, Alzheimer's Disease Program, Northwestern University School of Medicine

TESTIMONY BEFORE APPROPRIATIONS SUBCOMMITTEE ON LABOR, HEALTH AND HUMAN SERVICES AND EDUCATION, APRIL 17, 1997.

*a*s you have heard in previous testimony from [National Institutes of Health Director Harold] Varmus and others. Alzheimer's disease is very common and very costly, both in terms of human suffering and in health-care spending. Its annual cost, borne primarily by families, is already a staggering $100 billion. Each year an effective treatment is delayed, another 400,000 Americans are stricken. The only hope for reversing this trend lies in research.

Basic research supported by this subcommittee in the past has opened the door to several promising developments. We now have two drugs to aid in treating the symptoms of Alzheimer's disease, and at least eight others are undergoing clinical trials. The real breakthroughs will come when science comes up with drugs that can disarm the trigger that kills nerve cells in the brain of patients with Alzheimer's disease.

Alzheimer's can last 15 years, yet we still do not have tests that can definitively diagnose the disease in a living patient. The development of a diagnostic test remains a high priority.

The changes in the brain that lead up to Alzheimer's may begin 10 to 20 years before they cause observable changes in memory and behavior. If we could detect the disease at the very beginning and then find a way to slow its progression by as little as five years, the number of people who show the symptoms of Alzheimer's disease would be cut in half and society would save $50 billion annually. . . .

Lastly, we still know very little about this disease in African-American and Hispanic populations. We must fund research and outreach programs that examine any special features that may need specific interventions.

Clearly, Mr. Chairman, how quickly we overcome these challenges depends in large measure on how much this subcommittee invests in Alzheimer's research. . . . We have the know-how. We have the research infrastructure. We have shown a willingness to make the most of scarce resources by collaborating with one another. And we have momentum on our side. . . .

We urge this subcommittee to appropriate a minimum of $355 million for Alzheimer's research at NIH and $10 million to [the Health Resources and Services Administration] to enable more states to reach underserved populations.

Rep. John Edward Porter, R-Ill.

Chairman, Appropriations Subcommittee on Labor, Health and Human Services and Education

*t*here is a serious and growing threat to biomedical research within Congress: a well-intended but extremely ill-advised effort to allocate specific amounts within the federal budget for research into specific diseases. This practice, commonly known as "earmarking," substitutes political decisions for scientific judgment.

In my view, this would be a tragic mistake. To understand why, we must examine the history and methods of [National Institutes of Health]-funded research.

From the inception of NIH 50 years ago to the present, Congress' role has been one of appropriation and oversight, not micro-management of disease research. We in Congress are responsible for the bottom line and for determining how much we can allocate to NIH and its 18 separate institutes in any given year. We do not — and neither does NIH — fund by disease. Once funds have been allocated by institute, proposals seeking funding for research are considered by professional peer-review groups composed of accomplished investigators who evaluate applications for scientific merit. In determining research priorities, NIH also consults with a broad range of advisory groups, including health advocacy and research organizations. The result is a wide range of research conducted not at NIH's Bethesda campus but principally at academic research institutions throughout the United States.

In June, I invited Dr. Harold Varmus, director of NIH, to testify before my subcommittee and explain in greater detail how these funding decisions are made. His presentation and responses to members' questions were enlightening, and he outlined important reasons why funding is not allocated on a disease-specific basis. . . .

Varmus noted that "no disease is confined to one institute, and no institute is confined to a specific disease . . . hence distribution of funds is usually an inadequate measure of support for research on a specific disease. We know from repeated experience that research aimed in one direction frequently provides benefits in an unexpected direction."

In other words, biomedical research is serendipitous. Research on a cancer-related issue may yield a breakthrough on Parkinson's disease; an AIDS research project may lead to new ways to treat diabetes. As Varmus put it, "It is therefore crucial that the system for allocating NIH funds be sufficiently flexible to accommodate a new proposal with an important, imaginative idea, regardless of the category to which it might be assigned."

FOR MORE INFORMATION

If you would like to have this CQ Researcher updated, or need more information about this topic, please call CQ Custom Research. Special rates for CQ subscribers. (202) 887-8600 or (800) 432-2250, ext. 600, or E-mail Custom.Research@cq.com

Alzheimer's Association, 919 N. Michigan Ave., Suite 1000, Chicago, Ill. 60611-1676; (800) 272-3900; www.alz.org. A nationwide advocacy group for Alzheimer's patients and their families that lobbies Congress and provides information on types of care available.

Alzheimer's Disease Educational and Referral Center, P.O. Box 8250, Silver Spring, Md. 20907-8250; (800) 438-4380; www.alzheimer's.org. The center is the National Institute on Aging's clearinghouse for information on Alzheimer's and related disorders.

American Association of Retired Persons, 601 E. St. N.W., Washington, D.C. 20049; (202) 434-6030; www.aarp.org. The AARP offers consultation and information to consumers on long-term care and provides extensive references on specific caregiving and housing needs.

Health Care Financing Administration, 200 Independence Ave. S.W., Suite 314G, Washington, D.C. 20201; (202) 690-6113; www.hcfa.gov. This agency of the Department of Health and Human Services administers the Medicare and Medicaid programs and operates a center for long-term care that monitors compliance of nursing homes with federal standards.

National Council on Aging, 409 Third St. N.W., 2nd floor, Washington, D.C. 20024; (202) 479-1200; www.ncoa.org. This advocacy group for the elderly monitors legislation and regulations governing long-term care.

OUTLOOK

Focus on Benefits

Policy-makers in March began to explore how chronic diseases like Alzheimer's will affect baby boomers when a bipartisan commission on the future of Medicare held the first of a yearlong series of meetings. The commission, authorized by the 1997 balanced-budget act and appointed by Congress and President Clinton, has until March 1, 1999, to recommend how to keep the health-care system solvent and meet the projected increase in elderly patients.

Few expect the panel to order radical changes. But the commission — consisting of members of Congress, public-policy experts and health-care professionals—is expected to modify the Medicare benefit package and try to coordinate the program with Medicaid and long-term service providers.

"Millions more Medicare recipients will depend on long-term care (in the next century) than today," says Sen. John B. Breaux, D-La., chairman of the commission. "It is necessary to look at and evaluate the effects these strains on our health-care system will have on individuals' and families' pocketbooks." [19]

One key issue for Alzheimer's patients is whether the panel tightens eligibility for home health benefits. Many early and middle-stage Alzheimer's patients get subsidized care at home but still attend adult day-care programs at nearby hospitals. However, some Alzheimer's advocates report patients are being denied home care if they leave their house for periods of time. "The explosive growth in home care is making this a big focus of proposed changes," says health economist Wilensky.

Meanwhile, some members of Congress are taking up the Alzheimer's Association's call for more money for research. Sens. Arlen Specter, R-Pa., and Harkin have introduced a resolution calling on the Senate Budget Committee to make room in the fiscal 1999 budget resolution for a $2 billion increase in funding for NIH — $860 million more than the increase proposed by President Clinton. Sixty-four senators and House members — including House Speaker Newt Gingrich, R-Ga. — separately have endorsed the call to increase Alzheimer's research funding by $100 million.

If more money does come, it will likely help fund additional clinical trials on vitamin E and its ability to delay the onset of Alzheimer's symptoms. The National Institute on Aging wants to test the agent on people with mild cognitive impairment — a common precursor to Alzheimer's — to see whether it can reduce the number of people who would otherwise progress to more advanced stages of the disease.

Ultimately, researchers hope to identify people at risk before they show any signs of the disease and treat them with drugs that can halt development of clinical Alzheimer's. The search for more Alzheimer's genes continues, as well, providing new opportunities for studying cellular events that may lead to the disease. A team of University of Pittsburgh geneticists reported in March that people with a particular variant of the gene that controls production of the enzyme bleomycin hydrolase appear to have twice the risk of developing the disease. [20]

Research isn't confined to Alzheimer's victims. Recent studies have documented the mental and physical toll the disease has left on family members of Alzheimer's patients. Ohio State University biologists have documented how caregivers under stress are more vulnerable to diseases like influenza. This year, Stanford University psychologists reported a greater incidence of high blood pressure and racing hearts in women, rather then men, caring for parents with Alzheimer's, Parkinson's disease and strokes. Daughters tended to show more resentment, anger and a sense of being trapped, while wives tended to have a greater sense of duty about caring for their husbands. [21]

The National Institutes of Health is in the midst of a five-year study to develop and test new ways for families and friends to manage daily activities and stresses of caring for Alzheimer's victims. That's some comfort to Donna Lyttle, the Queens, N.Y. woman who cares for her ailing mother at home and often ponders the ravages of the disease.

"It's almost as if you can't understand it unless you're actually experiencing it," she says. "You think how this person had so much life and was always on the go, and now you realize this just isn't a quality life." ∎

Notes

[1] Many of the national cost estimates of caring for Alzheimer's patients are derived from a 1993 study of patient care in Northern California and adjusted for inflation and regional differences. See Dorothy P. Rice et al., "The Economic Burden Of Alzheimer's Disease Care," *Health Affairs*, summer 1993, pp. 164-176.

[2] See Richard Hodes, "Meeting the Challenges of an Aging Population," *Academic Medicine*, October 1997, pp. 892-893.

[3] For background, see "Caring for the Elderly," *The CQ Researcher*, Feb. 20, 1998, pp. 145-168.

[4] See Franklin Eppig and John Poisal, "Mental Health of Medicare Beneficiaries: 1995," *Health Care Financing Review*, spring 1997, pp. 207-210.

[5] Congress rewrote the law to target lawyers or accountants who advise the elderly to give away their assets to become eligible for Medicaid.

[6] Quoted in Michael Vitez, "The High Cost of Living Longer," *Philadelphia Inquirer*, March 16, 1998, p. A1.

[7] See National Institute on Aging, "Progress Report on Alzheimer's Disease, 1997," National Institutes of Health Publication No. 97-4014, pp. 7-28.

[8] See Gary Small et al., "Diagnosis and Treatment of Alzheimer's Disease and Related Disorders," *Journal of the American Medical Association*, Oct. 22/29, 1997, pp. 1363-1371.

[9] See Brigid Schulte, "African-Americans, Hispanics At Greater Risk of Alzheimer's," *Knight-Ridder Tribune News Service*, March 11, 1998.

[10] See Mary Sano et al., "A Controlled Trial of Selegiline, Alpha-Tocopherol or Both as Treatment for Alzheimer's Disease," with accompanying editorial, *The New England Journal of Medicine*, April 24, 1997, pp. 1216-1245.

[11] See Jamie Talan, "The Memory Molecule? Studies of Estrogen Intensify, Look Encouraging," *Newsday*, Oct. 21, 1997, p. C5.

[12] See Ruth Larson, " 'Boomer' Numbers Fuel Plea for Funds; Alzheimer's Gets Attention on Hill," *Washington Times*, Jan. 30, 1998, p. A6.

[13] A separate category of Alzheimer's spending is the "Safe Return" program, created by Congress in 1993 to assist in the timely return of Alzheimer's patients who wander and become lost. The program — operated by the Alzheimer's Association with money from the U.S. Justice Department and Janssen Research Foundation — provides identification tags for patients and training for police and emergency personnel to recognize and assist them. President Clinton requested $900,000 for the program in his fiscal 1999 budget, the same amount as 1998. Congress will take up the request later this spring.

[14] Weekly column to constituents, June 9, 1997.

[15] See Martin Enserink "First Alzheimer's Diagnosis Confirmed," *Science*, March 27, 1998, p. 2037.

[16] See Denis A. Evans et al. "Estimated Prevalence of Alzheimer's Disease in the United States," *Milbank Quarterly*, Vol. 68, No. 2, 1990.

[17] Quoted from "Alzheimer's Disease in the Community," *Journal of the American Medical Association*, Nov. 10, 1989, p. 2591.

[18] See "Quick Screening Test Developed for Alzheimer's," The Associated Press, March 13, 1998.

[19] Testimony before the Senate Special Committee on Aging, March 9, 1998.

[20] See Charles Henderson, "Another Gene Discovered To Be Associated With Alzheimer's," *Gene Therapy Weekly*, March 16, 1998.

[21] See "Stress on Caregivers Measured," *UPI Science News*, March 27, 1998.

Bibliography

Selected Sources Used

Books

Mace, Nancy, and Peter Rabins, *The 36-Hour Day*, The Johns Hopkins University Press, 1991 (revised edition).

Two psychiatrists explain in exhaustive detail what it's like to live with an Alzheimer's patient and what steps prospective caregivers should be prepared to take when the disease strikes a loved one.

Field, Marilyn, and Christine Cassel, eds., *Approaching Death: Improving Care at the End of Life*, National Academy Press, 1997.

A National Academy of Sciences committee of health, legal and public-policy experts offers perspectives on how Americans die and the dimensions of caring at, the end of life.

Rowe, John, and Robert Kahn, *Successful Aging*, Pantheon, 1998.

The president of Mount Sinai Hospital and School of Medicine in New York and a former psychology professor at the University of Michigan assert that far too many assumptions about the elderly are based on people who were sick or in institutions. They note that in many people ages 74-81, short-term memory loss doesn't lead to mental decline or Alzheimer's.

Articles

Wilcock, Gordon, "Current Approaches to the Treatment of Alzheimer's Disease," *Neurodegeneration*, Vol. 5, 1996, pp. 505-509.

A British neurologist provides a well-organized overview of current strategies for forestalling the symptoms of Alzheimer's.

Gladwell, Malcolm, "The Alzheimer's Strain: How to Accommodate Too Many Patients," *The New Yorker*, Oct. 20 & 27, 1997, pp. 125-139.

Gladwell describes how dementia specialists at a Pennsylvania long-term care group designed a safe, familiar facility in which Alzheimer's patients could freely wander around without being a threat to themselves.

Rovner, Sandy, "An Alzheimer's Journal," *Washington Post health section*, March 29, 1994, pp. 1-15.

Rovner profiles Cary Henderson, a former American history professor at James Madison University, who kept a journal during the early stages of Alzheimer's disease.

Vitez, Michael, "Life's Last Chapter: How Well Will We Care?" *Philadelphia Inquirer*, March 15-18, 1998.

A Pulitzer Prize-winning reporter examines the economic and societal issues surrounding care for the frail elderly, including Alzheimer's patients, in a four-part series.

Reports and Studies

Alzheimer's Disease: Estimates of Prevalence in the United States, U.S. General Accounting Office, GAO/HEHS-98-16, January 1998.

The GAO, the investigative arm of Congress, reviewed 18 studies of the prevalence of Alzheimer's disease and arrived at a conservative estimate that the disease affects at least 1.9 million Americans.

Evans, Denis, et al., "Estimated Prevalence of Alzheimer's Disease in the United States, *The Milbank Quarterly*, Vol. 68, No. 2, 1990, pp. 267-287.

The authors detail a Harvard Medical School study of elderly residents in East Boston, Mass., that prompted the National Institutes of Health and others to revise upward the estimate of the number of Alzheimer's cases in the United States.

National Institute on Aging, *Alzheimer's Disease: Unraveling the Mystery*, 1995, National Institutes of Health Publication No. 95-3782, U.S. Government Printing Office.

This booklet for people interested in Alzheimer's research includes basic definitions, the search for causes, research on diagnosis and possible treatments.

Advisory Panel on Alzheimer's Disease, *Alzheimer's Disease and Related Dementias: Acute and Long-Term Care Services*, 1996, National Institutes of Health Publication No. 96-4136, U.S. Government Printing Office.

An advisory panel to the U.S. Department of Health and Human Services delivers a sometimes critical assessment of the health-care system's ability to provide long-term care to Alzheimer's patients.

The Next Step

Additional information from UMI's Newspaper & Periodical Abstracts™ database

Blacks and Hispanics

"Blacks and Hispanic Americans Face Greater Risk of Alzheimer's," *The New York Times*, March 11, 1998, p. A14.

Blacks and some Hispanic-Americans have a risk factor that makes them much more susceptible than whites to Alzheimer's disease, researchers say. It has been known since 1992 that people with a certain gene have a greatly elevated risk for developing Alzheimer's, but now researchers say that even without that suspect gene, blacks and a group of Hispanic-Americans have been found to be at greater risk than whites for the disease. The survey of 1,079 elderly men and women found that blacks who lacked the gene were four times more likely than whites to get the disease. Hispanic-Americans had double the risk.

"Blacks, Hispanics More Prone to Alzheimer's," *USA Today*, March 11, 1998, p. D6.

Researchers say blacks and Hispanics have a puzzling, additional risk factor that makes them much more susceptible than non-Hispanic whites to Alzheimer's disease.

Brownlee, Shannon, "Alzheimer's and Odd Genes," *U.S. News & World Report*, March 23, 1998, p. 28.

Research into the gene variation apoE4 continues to result in questions about its role in Alzheimer's disease. Blacks and Hispanics with this variation are as likely as whites to get Alzheimer's by age 90, but without the variation blacks have four times the risk and Hispanics have twice the risk.

Colburn, Don, "Blacks, Hispanics Have More Alzheimer's," *The Washington Post*, March 17, 1998, p. W5.

African-Americans and Hispanics appear much more likely than whites to develop Alzheimer's disease in old age, according to a five-year study of Medicare patients. Researchers interviewed more than 1,000 healthy Medicare recipients from the Washington Heights neighborhood of New York and followed them with annual checkups for five years. The group was fairly evenly divided among Hispanics, African-Americans and whites.

Diagnostic Breakthroughs

"Brain Lesion Is Seen as Clue In Diagnosing Alzheimer's," *The New York Times*, June 29, 1997, p. 21.

Lesions made of a previously unidentified protein have been found in the brains of Alzheimer's patients, a discovery that could shed light on the cause of the disease and offer a means of early diagnosis and perhaps even treatment. "This is a spectacular lesion, never before seen, that tracks closely with the disease state," said John Q. Trojanowski, director of the Alzheimer's Disease Center at the University of Pennsylvania

and senior author of the study detailing the findings. The report was published in the July issue of *The American Journal of Pathology*.

Friend, Tim, "First Alzheimer's Blood Test Speeds Diagnosis," *USA Today*, Feb. 19, 1998, p. A1.

The first blood test to help diagnose Alzheimer's disease may help those with dementia get earlier treatment and should be used routinely, scientists report today. The blood test is for the gene apoE4 and could be given on the first or second doctor's visit by a person with symptoms of dementia, said Duke University's Ann Saunders, co-author of the 26-center study recommending use of the new test.

Mihill, Chris, "Alzheimer's Drug Hopes Hit by Cost," *The Guardian*, March 28, 1997, p. 10.

A new drug, Aricept, is said to slow progression of Alzheimer's disease, but it is not known how long its benefits last. It is being hailed as an advance in treating first symptoms of the illness. Aricept is similar to a drug called Tacrine, which received considerable publicity for its apparent ability to slow the progress of Alzheimer's in its early stages. Tacrine failed to win a license in Britain because of fears of side effects.

Genetic Links

Baird, Rachel, "Alzheimer's Fear as Gene is Found," *The Guardian*, Nov. 8, 1997, p. J6.

The discovery of a gene that seems to contribute to the development of Alzheimer's disease has raised fresh questions about the limitations of long-term care insurance just as insurers are trying to win support for their new code of practice on genetics.

Elias, Marilyn, "Knowing Alzheimer's Chance Carries Risk," *USA Today*, Oct. 30, 1997, p. D6.

Recent advances in finding the genetic links to Alzheimer's disease have kicked up a storm of questions about whether this "progress" will be used to help or hurt people. Peace of mind may be one casualty of the genetic breakthroughs as people are increasingly able to find out their risk of getting the brain-destroying disease, experts say. "The problem is, you can be falsely reassured if you don't have it and live your life terrified if you're at higher risk — but you may wind up never getting it," says Gary Small, geriatric psychiatrist at the University of California, Los Angeles.

Schreuder, Cindy, "Alzheimer's Researchers Zero in on Second Gene," *Chicago Tribune*, Oct. 15, 1997, p. 10.

Researchers say they are closing in on a second gene linked to late-onset Alzheimer's disease, a gene that could account for 10-15 percent of the cases of the ailment, which causes cognitive impairment and memory loss. They said Tuesday that the gene functions independently of a gene found in 1993 that also was linked to late onset of the disease, defined as occurring in people age 60 or over. Several additional genes previously have been associated with Alzheimer's but only with rare, early-onset forms. In a separate genetics study announced Tuesday, scientists said they also may be better able to determine who is most likely to carry a genetic mutation linked to breast and ovarian cancer.

Ginko Biloba

"Gingko Biloba and Alzheimer's; Scientists Unsure how Plant Extract Helps Block Mental Deterioration," *USA Today*, **Oct. 22, 1997, p. D5.**

A new study showing that the plant extract gingko biloba slowed the progression of Alzheimer's disease and vascular dementia raises hope — and questions — for millions of people with the disorders and their families.

"Ginkgo Shows Some Benefit In Alzheimer's," *The New York Times*, **Oct. 22, 1997, p. A18.**

Ginkgo biloba extract, a herbal medicine used for thousands of years by the Chinese, has been shown to slow the progression of Alzheimer's disease slightly in some patients. In a study to be published on Wednesday in *The Journal of the American Medical Association*, researchers say about a third of the dementia patients treated with ginkgo extract showed some improvement after 52 weeks when compared with a similar group of patients who took a placebo. Pierre L. LeBars of the New York Institute for Medical Research, chief author of the study, said benefits from the treatment were modest and were apparent only after about six months of taking the extract.

Brown, David, "Ginkgo Extract Shows Benefit In Slowing Alzheimer's Disease; Herbal Remedy's Effect Most Apparent to Family Members," *The Washington Post*, **Oct. 22, 1997, p. A2.**

A popular herbal medicine derived from ginkgo leaves has a small but measurable effect on slowing the progression of Alzheimer's disease over the course of a year, according to a new study. The effect of the drug on Alzheimer's patients is more noticeable to family members than to doctors. Overall, it may delay a worsening of the disease by about six months. However, even the modest benefits were seen in only about one-third of patients.

Knox, Richard A., "Ginkgo Extract May Help Some with Alzheimer's, Study Finds," *The Boston Globe*, **Oct. 22, 1997, p. A6.**

An extract of ginkgo tree leaves, nuts and bark used in traditional Chinese medicine has modestly reversed mental decline in some Alzheimer's disease patients, according to a study published today. Although the effect was mild, and fewer than one-third of the patients benefited, the ginkgo extract was about as effective as the only two anti-Alzheimer's

drugs approved in this country, the study's author said in an interview. The news provides hope that more effective measures may yet be found against Alzheimer's disease, which afflicts 4 million Americans and is by far the most common type of dementia.

Maugh, Thomas, H. II, "Ginkgo Extract Appears to Slow Alzheimer's," *Los Angeles Times*, **Oct. 22, 1997, p. A1.**

Scientists may now have one more weapon in their continuing war against Alzheimer's disease, an herbal medicine called ginkgo biloba, researchers said Tuesday. They found that 27 percent of patients who took the herbal extract for six months or longer showed improvements in mental functioning — including reasoning, memory and ability to learn — compared with only 14 percent of those who took a placebo. The results were "modest," in the words of study author Pierre L. LeBars, and the team has no idea which of the many chemicals present in the extract were responsible for the effect. Ginkgo is extracted from the bark, nuts and leaves of the Ginkgo biloba or maidenhair tree, which grows mainly in temperate climates. It is a complex mixture of as many as 300 chemicals that has been used medicinally for more than 5,000 years because of its antioxidant and anti-inflammatory properties and a perceived ability to increase blood flow.

Sternberg, Steve, "Gingko Extract Stalls Alzheimer's Effects, Study Suggests," *USA Today*, **Oct. 22, 1997, p. D1.**

An extract from leaves of the Ginkgo biloba tree, used in Chinese medicines for 5,000 years, appears to slow the mental decline of some people with Alzheimer's disease for at least six months, doctors reported Tuesday. Known as ginkgo biloba extract, the substance is generally regarded as safe and sold as a nutritional supplement in the USA. It is used widely in Europe to relieve asthma, to improve circulation and to halt or delay the loss of "mental capacity, memory and vigilance" in the elderly and people with Alzheimer's disease, researchers say.

New Drugs

"Swiss Approve Alzheimer's Drug," *The New York Times*, **Aug. 5, 1997, p. D4.**

Novartis says its Exelon drug was approved by Swiss authorities for treatment of mild to moderately severe Alzheimer's, based on a clinical study conducted among more than 3,330 patients in Europe and North America.

Gillis, Justin, "Breakthrough Or Backfire on Alzheimer's; Firm Draws Criticism For Claims of Progress," *The Washington Post*, **April 9, 1998, p. C1.**

Maryland-based Nymox Pharmaceutical Corp., which is reportedly close to a potential treatment for Alzheimer's, has drawn sharp criticism from some neurologists and from the national Alzheimer's Association. The critics contend that the company is prematurely marketing a test that it says can accurately detect the disease. Some experts do not believe there's enough evidence yet that

Nymox's test is useful, and are even more skeptical of the company's recent claims that it may have found a major cause of Alzheimer's.

Hall, Carl T., "New Alzheimer Hopes; Experimental Brain Drain May Slow Dementia," *San Francisco Chronicle*, **March 3, 1998, p. C3.**

Gerald Silverberg, a veteran Stanford neurologist, is beginning tests in patients of what would be the first Alzheimer's implant — a newly designed version of the same shunts used for years to drain excess cerebrospinal fluid in hydrocephalus patients. Estrogen hormone supplements, for example, may help in Alzheimer's if dosages can be adjusted properly. New anti-inflammatory drugs are in the works that may benefit both arthritis and Alzheimer's patients without damaging the stomach and intestinal tract.

Saltus, Richard, "New Drugs Aim to Halt Alzheimer's Progress," *The Boston Globe*, **Feb. 25, 1998, p. A14.**

Scientists say a new generation of drugs to combat Alzheimer's disease is showing promise in animal tests, and some of these compounds could move into human testing in a year or two. At a meeting in Boston of top Alzheimer's disease researchers, a company reported that it has developed a drug that can curb by 90 percent the brain's production of beta-amyloid, a starchy substance that forms nerve-killing plaques in the brains of Alzheimer's patients.

Vitamin E

"Alzheimer's Progression May Be Eased By Vitamin E," *The New York Times*, **April 24, 1997, p. A2.**

Researchers have found that high doses of vitamin E may modestly slow the progression of Alzheimer's disease. Patients with Alzheimer's who took high doses of the vitamin in a two-year study delayed major milestones — such as going into a nursing home — by about seven months. The study, the largest ever involving Alzheimer's, also found that selegiline, or Eldepryl, a standard prescription drug for Parkinson's disease, does the same thing and seems to work about as well as vitamin E.

Boodman, Sandra G., "Alzheimer's Study 'Not a Major Breakthrough'; Some Experts See a Clue in the Results, Others Call Them Insignificant," *The Washington Post*, **April 29, 1997, p. 9.**

When Deirdre Pollock heard reports last week that large doses of vitamin E might temporarily postpone the onset of severe dementia in patients with Alzheimer's disease, she experienced a different reaction than the general public. Pollock, who cares for her 91-year-old grandmother who has Alzheimer's, feared that the stopgap remedy might not provide much relief and might instead extend the suffering of Alzheimer's patients and their families.

Brown, David, "Alzheimer's Patients in Study Benefit Slightly From High-Dosage, Daily Vitamin E," *The*

Washington Post, **April 24, 1997, p. A10.**

Daily high doses of Vitamin E can prolong slightly the length of time people with moderate Alzheimer's disease are able to function at home before their illness becomes so severe they need to be placed in a nursing home or other protective institution. That is the main finding of a study published today that tested the effects of Vitamin E, and an unrelated drug called selegiline, on the downward course of Alzheimer's, which affects about 4 million Americans. "The research is very encouraging, but it is premature to actually recommend Vitamin E or selegiline as a specific treatment for Alzheimer's disease without additional, confirming research," said Edward Truschke, president of the Alzheimer's Association.

Friend, Tim, "Alzheimer's Slowed by Vitamin E or Parkinson's Drug, Study Shows," *USA Today*, **April 24, 1997, p. A1.**

The progression of Alzheimer's disease can be delayed by about seven months with vitamin E or a drug normally prescribed for Parkinson's, a study out today says. The drug is the first to slow progression in those with moderately advanced symptoms, allowing patients to dress and feed themselves and live at home longer, experts say. The 23-site Alzheimer's Disease Cooperative Study, funded by the National Institute on Aging, is the longest-running drug study on Alzheimer's.

Maugh, Thomas H. II, "Alzheimer's Slowed by Vitamin E, Study Finds," *Los Angeles Times*, **April 24, 1997, p. A1.**

In the latest of a remarkable string of new findings about the prevention or slowing of Alzheimer's disease, researchers report today that either vitamin E or a common anti-Parkinson's drug can significantly delay the deterioration of daily functioning caused by the disease. Recent reports have shown that both estrogen replacement therapy and ibuprofen can delay the onset of Alzheimer's in people with no symptoms. Today's results "are very exciting findings because . . . they show for the first time that drugs are effective for people with the moderately severe stages of the disease," said Edward Truschke, the president of the Alzheimer's Association.

Paul, Annie Murphy, "A Vitamin that Slows Alzheimer's," *Psychology Today*, **September 1997, p. 16.**

A long-term study of patients moderately afflicted with Alzheimer's disease has found that high doses of vitamin E delayed patients' entry into nursing homes by about seven months.

Schieszer, John, "New Therapies for Alzheimer's; Vitamin E, Common Drug Slow Down Disease," *St. Louis Post-Dispatch*, **April 24, 1997, p. A1.**

Physicians in St. Louis who helped test two new drug therapies for Alzheimer's patients say vitamin E and another common drug can slow the ravages of the brain disease — and may mark the beginning of a new era in treating it.

Back Issues

Great Research on Current Issues Starts Right Here.
Recent topics covered by The CQ Researcher are listed below.
Now available on the Web
For information, call (800) 432-2250 ext. 279 or (202) 887-6279.

If you would like to have any of these CQ Researchers updated, or need more information
about these topics, please call CQ Custom Research. Special rates for CQ subscribers.
(202) 887-8600 or (800) 432-2250, ext. 600, or E-mail Custom.Research@cq.com

FEBRUARY 1997
Assisting Refugees
Alternative Medicine's Next Phase
Independent Counsels
Feminism's Future

MARCH 1997
New Air Quality Standards
Alcohol Advertising
Civic Renewal
Educating Gifted Students

APRIL 1997
Declining Crime Rates
The FBI Under Fire
Gender Equity in Sports
Space Program's Future

MAY 1997
The Stock Market
The Cloning Controversy
Expanding NATO
The Future of Libraries

JUNE 1997
FDA Reform
China After Deng
Line-Item Veto
Breast Cancer

JULY 1997
Transportation Policy
Executive Pay
School Choice Debate
Aggressive Driving

AUGUST 1997
Age Discrimination
Banning Land Mines
Children's Television
Evolution vs. Creationism

SEPTEMBER 1997
Caring for the Dying
Mental Health Policy
Mexico's Future
Youth Fitness

OCTOBER 1997
Urban Sprawl in the West
Diversity in the Workplace
Teacher Education
Contingent Work Force

NOVEMBER 1997
Renewable Energy
Artificial Intelligence
Religious Persecution
Roe v. Wade at 25

DECEMBER 1997
Whistleblowers
Castro's Next Move
Gun Control Standoff
Regulating Nonprofits

JANUARY 1998
Foster Care Reform
IRS Reform
The Black Middle Class
U.S.-British Relations

FEBRUARY 1998
Patients' Rights
Deflation Fears
Caring for the Elderly
The New Corporate Philanthropy

MARCH 1998
Israel at 50
The Federal Judiciary
Drinking on Campus
The Economics of Recycling

APRIL 1998
Biology and Behavior
Liberal Arts Education
Income Inequality
High-Tech Labor Shortage

MAY 1998
Census 2000
Child-Care Options

Back issues are available for $5.00 (subscribers) or $10.00 (non-subscribers). Quantity discounts apply to orders over 10. To order, call Congressional Quarterly Customer Service at (202) 887-8621.

Binders are available for $18.00. To order call 1-800-638-1710. Please refer to stock number 648.

Future Topics

▶ *U.S.-Russian Relations*

▶ *Student Press*

▶ *Environmental Justice*

The CQ Researcher

PUBLISHED BY CONGRESSIONAL QUARTERLY INC.

U.S.-Russian Relations

Is the post-Cold War friendship in trouble?

After the breakup of the Soviet Union, friendship blossomed between Russia and the United States. But relations have cooled in recent years, and now the decision to admit Poland, Hungary and the Czech Republic into NATO over Russian objections has added new tensions to the relationship. While enlargement is seen by many as a step toward permanent peace in post-Cold War Europe, others argue that including old Soviet allies in the alliance will only antagonize Russia. Moreover, many enlargement opponents say the days of antagonism between Russia and the U.S. are over, making NATO unnecessary. But NATO boosters argue that Russia is growing increasingly hostile to U.S. interests and that other dangers, including Moscow's lack of control over her nuclear arsenal, make NATO enlargement vital to U.S. and European safety.

CQ May 22, 1998 • Volume 8, No. 20 • Pages 457-480

Formerly Editorial Research Reports

CQ Researcher

May 22, 1998
Volume 8, No.20

EDITOR
Sandra Stencel

MANAGING EDITOR
Thomas J. Colin

ASSOCIATE EDITOR
Sarah M. Magner

STAFF WRITERS
Adriel Bettelheim
Mary H. Cooper
Kenneth Jost
Kathy Koch
David Masci

PRODUCTION EDITOR
Melissa Hall

EDITORIAL ASSISTANT
Laura S. Cavender

PUBLISHED BY
Congressional Quarterly Inc.

CHAIRMAN
Andrew Barnes

VICE CHAIRMAN
Andrew P. Corty

PRESIDENT AND PUBLISHER
Robert W. Merry

EXECUTIVE EDITOR
David Rapp

The CQ Researcher (ISSN 1056-2036). Formerly Editorial Research Reports. Published weekly, except Jan. 2, May 29, July 3, Oct. 30, by Congressional Quarterly Inc., 1414 22nd St., N.W., Washington, D.C. 20037. Annual subscription rate for libraries, businesses and government is $340. Additional rates furnished upon request. Periodicals postage paid at Washington, D.C., and additional mailing offices. POSTMASTER: Send address changes to The CQ Researcher, 1414 22nd St., N.W., Washington, D.C. 20037.

COVER: U.S.-RUSSIAN RELATIONS WERE MORE CORDIAL IN OCTOBER 1995, WHEN RUSSIAN PRESIDENT BORIS N. YELTSIN AND U.S. PRESIDENT CLINTON SHARED A LAUGH DURING A JOINT WHITE HOUSE PRESS CONFERENCE. (REUTERS/RICK T. WILKING)

U.S.-Russian Relations

BY DAVID MASCI

THE ISSUES

On April 30, the Senate did something that would have been unthinkable just 10 years ago: It voted to admit three former Soviet-bloc nations into the North Atlantic Treaty Organization (NATO), the very alliance created to rebuff Soviet aggression.

In an age that has seen the Berlin Wall fall and a McDonald's open in Moscow, admitting Poland, Hungary and the Czech Republic to NATO may seem anticlimactic. After all, the countries of Eastern Europe, once locked in a forced alliance with the Soviet Union, have been free for almost a decade. The Soviet Union itself deconstructed more than six years ago into Russia and 14 other independent countries. Moreover, Russia, once the epicenter of world communism, is now struggling to become a capitalistic democracy.

Indeed, by most reckonings Russia is no longer a mighty superpower but a basket case — weak economically, militarily and politically.

Hoping to help, the United States and its Western allies have provided advice and billions of dollars in aid since Russia became an independent state in December 1991. [1] For its part, Russia has tried to reform its economic and political systems along Western lines. It has also supported some key American foreign-policy initiatives, notably in Bosnia.

At the same time, Russia has shown that old, totalitarian habits sometimes die hard, as in President Boris N. Yeltsin's forcefully shutting down the Duma, or legislature, in 1993, and supporting pugnacious former Soviet clients, like Iraq.

Such Soviet-era behavior reflects the paradoxical nature of U.S.-Russian relations. While the two countries have grown closer since the Soviet Union's dissolution, they are still not

the allies that some had predicted they would become. "There was this assumption after the Cold War that Russia and the U.S. would be pals, and that hasn't always panned out," says Anne Phillips, an assistant professor at American University's School of International Service. In fact, in the last few years relations between Russia and the United States increasingly have been characterized by friction.

Only time will tell whether the tension will increase or fade. The issue certainly was at the heart of the debate on the Thursday night that 80 senators voted to enlarge NATO. Indeed, to many Americans the enlargement debate boils down to one question: How far can the United States trust Russia?

Many supporters of NATO enlargement argue that the alliance must be maintained and strengthened to guard against the very real possibility that Russia not only will become powerful again but also aggressive. As columnist Charles Krauthammer recently wrote: "[J]ust because Russia is no longer an ideological rival doesn't mean that it has ceased to be a Great Power rival." Moreover, he added, "a country that expanded at the rate of one Belgium every two years [for] 300 years does not easily learn the virtues of self-containment." [2]

Others argue that it's not just a question of trusting Russia but of giving

countries formerly dominated by the Soviet Union the freedom to choose whether or not to ally with the West.

"After all those years of living in effective slavery, [the Russians have] turned to us and said, 'We have the opportunity to express our national will, to be free,' " said Sen. Joseph I. Lieberman, D-Conn., during the Senate debate.

And, Lieberman and others say, bringing the new democracies of Eastern Europe into the world's largest and most powerful military alliance will promote stability in an unstable region. "We're not just collecting new countries here," says Sen. Richard G. Lugar, R-Ind., the second-ranking Republican on the Senate Foreign Relations Committee and a staunch NATO expansionist. "It's in our interest to create a larger sphere of security and stability, and that's what NATO expansion will do."

Finally, Lugar and others say, expanding NATO's zone of stability eastward is in Russia's interest too, since it will reduce the possibility of conflict in the region. There are even those who predict that Russia itself will join NATO someday.

But others say that NATO expansion will do little more than exacerbate already-existing tensions between Russia and the West, increasing rather than reducing the prospect for conflict. To begin with, they claim, Russia's weakness makes the need for an expanded NATO almost laughable. And yet, anti-expansionists say, the United States and its allies are sacrificing good future relations with Russia for an unnecessary alliance. "We're poisoning our relations with Russia for nothing," says Ted Galen Carpenter, senior vice president for defense and foreign policy at the Cato Institute.

At the same time, Carpenter and others argue, expanding NATO into Eastern Europe only loads more security commitments onto a U.S. military

NATO's New Look

The 16-member North Atlantic Treaty Organization will be expanded for the first time in 15 years when Poland, Hungary and the Czech Republic are formally admitted in 1999. Nine other countries in Eastern Europe are seeking admittance to the alliance.

Iceland

Finland

- NATO members
- Invited to join NATO
- Former Warsaw Pact nations
- Former Soviet republics
- Other NATO applicants

Norway

Sweden

Estonia

Russia

United Kingdom

Latvia

Denmark

North Sea

Lithuania

Netherlands

Belarus

Germany

Poland

Atlantic Ocean

Luxembourg

Belgium

Czech Republic

France

Slovak Rep.

Ukraine

Switzerland

Austria

Hungary

Slovenia

Croatia

Romania

Moldova

Portugal

Spain

Bosnia Herzegovina

Black Sea

Italy

Yugoslavia

Bulgaria

Albania

Macedonia

Greece

Turkey

Mediterranean Sea

Source: Congressional Budget Office, "The Costs of Expanding the NATO Alliance," CBO Papers, March 1996.

that is already overextended. And, they add, the new countries are militarily weak and able to contribute little to collective security, requiring the Western European allies to shoulder more burdens for almost no benefit.

Expansion opponents also point out that Russia, its conventional forces cash-starved and virtually disintegrating, will rely more heavily on nuclear weapons to counter the greater NATO presence. Concern about nuclear weapons, already re-

alized to some degree, is especially intense because of questions about Russia's control over its nuclear arsenal.

Some worried experts view the accidental launch of a Russian missile or some other nuclear catastrophe as highly possible, even likely. "It's the greatest national security threat the United States faces today," says Bruce Blair, a senior fellow at the Brookings Institution.

Blair and others claim that Russia's nuclear weapons are on "hair-trigger"

alert, or ready to be fired the instant a possible attack is detected. Even more frightening, they say, parts of the old Soviet early-warning system are either off-line or improperly maintained.

But others are less concerned about accidental firing, noting that, unlike regular soldiers, the troops who guard and operate Russia's nuclear arms are still a disciplined, coherent force.

In addition, they say, if Russia's early-warning system were no longer adequate, the Americans who help maintain the Russians' nuclear arsenal would undoubtedly voice concern. "[American] specialists have confidence that there is no danger," says Vladimir Petrov, a professor emeritus of international affairs at The George Washington University.

Experts may debate the effectiveness of Russia's command and control over its nuclear arsenal, but there is wide agreement that the nuclear brinkmanship that once characterized the Cold War has subsided, at least for now. Still, some Russia-watchers say that competition between the two countries in the international arena remains intense. Some argue that Russia still views its relations with the United States as a zero-sum game — that they win each time the Americans lose, and vice versa.

According to proponents of this view, a number of recent events prove Moscow's ill intentions. For instance, it is noted that Russia worked diligently to thwart U.S. efforts to punish Iraq for not cooperating with United Nations weapons inspectors. According to Jeff Gedmin, a research fellow at the American Enterprise Institute (AEI), Russia's behavior in the case of Iraq was designed to obstruct what the Russians saw as another example of U.S. global hegemony. "They look for ways to block us as a way to increase their own stature," he says.

But others argue that Moscow is simply pursuing its own interests, as any country would. "Russia's resistance to some U.S. moves around the world is no longer a balance of power or ideological contest but is driven by national prestige and national interest," says Leon Aron, a senior fellow at the AEI. For instance, in Iraq, Russia has very important interests, Aron and others point out. For starters, they say, the Iraqis, as a former client state of the Soviet Union, borrowed billions for weapons purchases that they have never repaid.

Differences over Iraq, or NATO for that matter, illustrate the complexity of relations between the U.S. and Russia. As policy-makers and academics try to understand and improve this all-important relationship, here are some of the questions they are asking:

Does Russia's firm opposition to NATO expansion justify slowing or stopping new members from joining?

Since its founding in 1949, NATO has been the world's premier military alliance. Anchored in Western Europe and held together by American military might and leadership, NATO was the West's primary bulwark against Soviet aggression. And for more than 40 years, millions of NATO troops (including, at one time, 500,000 Americans) guarded the frontiers of Western Europe, from the frozen fields of Norway above the Arctic Circle to the warm Mediterranean waters off Turkey.

Still, although the borders of the alliance stretched across Europe, its hub and the focus of most of its activity was in the heart of the continent, in West Germany. The great war that never came between the forces of East and West, capitalism and communism, would have been fought there, in the heart of Europe. Hence it is not surprising that the first new members admitted to NATO were Poland, Hungary and the Czech Republic.* Not only are they the most politically and economically advanced of the former Soviet-bloc countries, but they also are just to the east of Germany, right in Europe's center. More specifically, they give the alliance another layer of protection against its old (and perhaps future) foe: Russia. Or, as columnist Krauthammer wrote recently in *The Washington Post*: "NATO . . . is expanding in the service of its historic and continuing mission: containing Russia." [3]

Not surprisingly, Russia has objected to this first round of NATO expansion. But it has accepted the entry of its three former allies as a fait accompli. For one thing, there was little it could do about the expansion, except scream from the sidelines. Russia, with its economy and military in ruins, is largely powerless to oppose the West these days.

Now other countries — from the Baltic states in the north to Ukraine in the center to Romania and Bulgaria in the south — are trying to enter the NATO alliance, a prospect that makes political and military planners in Moscow furious (*see p. 470*).

Many say that NATO should welcome new members, regardless of Russia's objections. To start with, they say, after decades and, in many cases, centuries under Russia's yoke, the states of Central and Eastern Europe should be free to build economic, political or military links with the West and, in particular, the United States. "These are newly free states, and they should be able to decide on their own whether they want to apply for NATO membership without being dictated to by the Russians," says Gedmin of the AEI.

And, Gedmin and others argue, by bringing these states into NATO, the West is helping to promote much-needed stability in the region. In particular, they say, NATO brings American influence and prestige to the new member countries, which can be a force for resolving local disputes and coaxing them closer together. "NATO offers Central and Eastern Europe America as an umpire or fair broker, a role that Russia, Germany and other powers of Europe cannot play for reasons of history," Gedmin says.

Supporters also argue that NATO is a defensive alliance and not, in any way, threatening to Russia. "No one, anywhere, honestly believes that NATO is going to attack Russia," says John Tedstrom, a research leader in Russian, Ukrainian and Eurasian affairs at the Rand Corp. The problem, Tedstrom and others say, is one of Russian perceptions, not any credible threat from the West.

---

*Poland, Hungary and the Czech Republic are expected to be formally admitted into NATO at the alliance's 50th anniversary meeting on April 4, 1999.

What Is Boris Yeltsin Up to?

Boris Yeltsin's behavior has often confounded his allies and adversaries alike. Over the years, the Russian president has sometimes appeared confused and, at times, even inebriated in public. Coupled with his heart problem and other ailments, Yeltsin's strange comportment has prompted regular speculation about his mental and physical health.

But Yeltsin-watchers were working overtime recently when the Russian leader fired his prime minister of five years and the entire Cabinet without warning or obvious reason. Yeltsin further stunned observers by naming a relatively unknown 35-year-old politician, Sergei Kiriyenko, to replace Victor Chernomyrdin.

Even though Yeltsin's March 24 move does not seem to have backfired — Kiriyenko was confirmed by the usually hostile Duma — many speculate that the Cabinet shakeup is a sign that after years of erratic behavior, the president has finally come totally unhinged.

This is not the first time Yeltsin has been written off. In addition to his repeated erratic behavior, the president has faced several serious health scares — including a quintuple coronary-artery by-pass in 1996 — only to re-emerge from convalescence with his hands still firmly holding the reins of power.

Still, many question how much longer Yeltsin will be able to carry on. "There's a lot of evidence that he is increasingly in his dotage, in a general state of incipient senility with moments of lucidity and energy," says Frank Gaffney, director of the Center for Security Policy. As a result, he says, "we're increasingly seeing a stage-managed presidency with more scripted events."

Gaffney and others point to a number of recent incidents that, in addition to the Cabinet firing, leave one wondering about Yeltsin's overall condition. For example, during the most recent standoff between the United States and Iraq, Yeltsin warned President Clinton that military action against Saddam Hussein's regime would lead to a "world war." Others talk of his now famous offer (subsequently withdrawn) during a December trip to Sweden, to reduce Russia's nuclear forces by one-third.

One of the president's closest confidants, business tycoon Boris Berezovsky, has publicly worried about Yeltsin's alleged incapacity. Berezovsky, who virtually bankrolled Yeltsin's 1996 presidential campaign, admitted that "the president's health prevents him from doing practical, political work every day." [1]

Many wonder how Yeltsin has lasted this long — politically and otherwise. At 67, he has already exceeded the average life expectancy for a Russian male by a decade. Add to this a lifetime of rumored heavy drinking and political intrigue, and Yeltsin's condition might not seem so surprising.

But other observers note that many, including the president's predecessor, Mikhail Gorbachev, have underestimated Boris Yeltsin, only to be surprised later by his resiliency and determination. In fact, some say, far from being a sign of mental instability, the recent Cabinet firing was a bold stroke.

"It seems it wasn't the irrational move we all thought it was at first," says Leon Aron, a resident scholar at the American Enterprise Institute. Bringing in a new team may actually help to jump-start the now moribund economic-reform process, he says.

Blake Marshall, executive vice president of the U.S. Russia Business Council, agrees, arguing that Chernomyrdin, a centrist with presidential ambitions, was too afraid of offending business interests and other powerful elites to make bold and necessary moves on the economy. Kiriyenko, on the other hand, is a liberal reformer who doesn't have the same ties to the powers that be in Russia. Consequently, he has a lot less to lose if he steps on toes to get things done, Marshall says.

Others perceive another, more political motive in Yeltsin's recent actions. By denying Chernomyrdin the high-profile post of prime minister, Yeltsin is dampening his former colleague's chances in the presidential election of 2000.

Does that mean that the Russian leader is contemplating another run for the presidency? In spite of Yeltsin's health problems and Russia's constitutional two-term limit, many feel that he wants to keep his job when his second term ends in 2000. "Like most revolutionary politicians," Aron says, "he feels that his staying in power is what is needed for the country and what the people really want."

[1] Fred Coleman, "Who's Running Russia?" *USA Today*, April 6, 1998.

Moreover, Tedstrom and others contend, NATO is good for Russia, even if it doesn't yet know it. "If we want Russia to complete its transformation into a modern European power, the last thing we should do is to act as if Central Europe is still a Russian sphere of influence," Secretary of State Madeleine K. Albright wrote recently in *The New York Times*. [4]

On the other hand, supporters of expansion say, enlarging and strengthening NATO is a good way to ensure that Europe and the United States will be ready for any unforeseen threats that may arise in the future if Russia doesn't remain a friendly state. "Russia isn't a threat today, but it's possible that a new Russia — a hard-line communist state or nationalistic state — could emerge," says Gedmin.

But others argue that NATO has lost it's raison d'être since the breakup of the Soviet Union and should, at the very least, not be expanded. Opponents of broadening NATO membership point out that the new Russia is smaller in both area and population than the Soviet Union was. Moreover, its economy is in a weak, almost anemic, state. In addition, they say, the country is no longer the communist state that once sought to spread its influence — and Marxist revolution — around the globe.

And, opponents of expansion point out, Russia's conventional forces have shrunk and decayed dramatically. No longer the fearsome steamroller of the Cold War, the country's military could not even pacify the small, breakaway province of Chechnya, let alone threaten a big country like Poland.

More important, these opponents say, expanding the alliance now is like taunting an injured animal, a stupid and dangerous act that could lead to a backlash. "It's very unwise to crowd a great power, especially one that's in distress," argues the CATO Institute's Carpenter. Not surprisingly, Carpenter and others say, NATO expansion has only made the Russians more paranoid and jumpy, at a time when their nation is in chaos and their military is falling apart.

Petrov of The George Washington University, agrees, adding that Russia's paranoia is not entirely unfounded. "These arguments from the West about building stability and the other things are hypocrisy," he says. "NATO is directed against Russia, period."

As a result, Petrov and others say, a new, stronger alliance may well create a more unstable and aggressive Russia — just the result the West wants to avoid. According to Grigory Yavlinsky, leader of the reformist Yabloko party, NATO expansion is a vote of no-confidence in Russia that could well become a self-fulfilling prophecy. "The most important message of NATO expansion for Russians . . . is that the political leaders of Western Europe and the United States do not believe that Russia can become a real Western-style democracy within the next decade or so," he writes in a recent issue of *Foreign Affairs*. [5]

Indeed, opponents argue, Russia's anxiety over NATO has already produced undesirable results. Most notably, in 1997, the Russians moved more of their tactical nuclear weapons closer to their western border in an effort to beef up their sagging conventional forces close to Europe. "Since they can't match NATO conventionally, they're relying more and more on nuclear weapons," Carpenter says. "No one really wants that," he adds, referring to the greater likelihood that a catastrophic accident or mistake will occur.

In addition, Carpenter and others claim, expansion has pushed Russia closer to non-Western powers like China and Iran. "By forcing them to accept this, we're pushing them into the arms of others instead of building closer and better relations with them," Carpenter says.

Finally, opponents argue, NATO expansion isn't going to make the alliance stronger, because the nations of Central and Eastern Europe are not militarily powerful. "Having small powers as allies doesn't strengthen but weakens you because you incur obligations to defend these countries and get nothing for it in return," Petrov says.

Russian soldiers in Belarus guard the last Soviet-era nuclear missile outside Russia in December 1996, just before it was shipped to Russia.

Reuters/Gleb Garanich

Does Russia currently have adequate control over its nuclear arsenal?

On Jan. 25, 1995, a scientific rocket launched from Norway threw Russia's nuclear forces into a state of high alert. Early-warning stations had reported that the projectile was heading for Russian territory and was probably an American nuclear missile fired from a Trident submarine. Within minutes, President Yeltsin had opened the briefcase containing the launch codes for Russia's nuclear weapons. Twelve minutes after first detecting it, the military informed the president that the rocket was now heading out to sea and ended the alert. [6]

The false alarm sent shivers through many in the arms-control and military communities and, for some, highlighted the potential weaknesses in Russia's command and control over its nuclear weapons. Many analysts, like the Brookings Institution's Blair, say that Russia's lack of control over

Russia's Economy on the Rise

After shrinking for six years, Russia's gross domestic product (GDP) is growing again, albeit slowly.

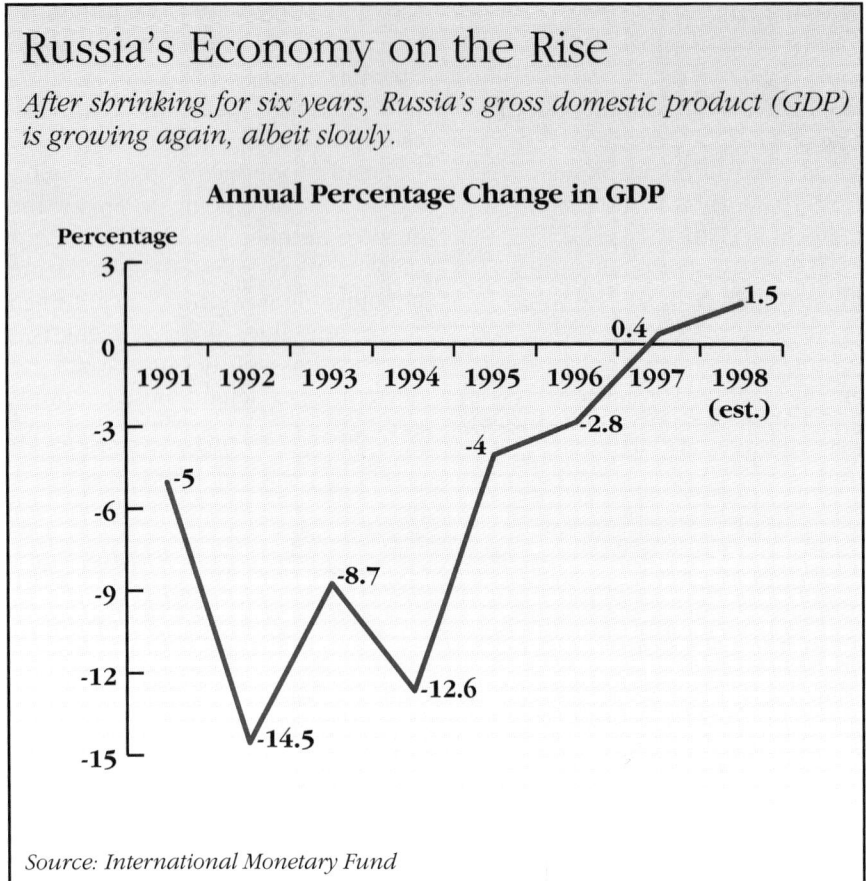

Annual Percentage Change in GDP

Source: International Monetary Fund

its nuclear arsenal is America's No. 1 national-security problem.

Even though nuclear forces in Russia have been reduced significantly since the heyday of the Cold War in the 1970s and '80s, the country still maintains about 6,000 warheads mounted on 1,300 missiles. And while the START II treaty (ratified by the U.S. Senate but not the Russian Duma) would bring the numbers of missiles and warheads down much further, many say Russia's control over these weapons is inadequate to ensure that an accidental or unauthorized launch will not occur. *(See story, p. 470.)*

To begin with, Blair argues, Russia maintains its nuclear forces on "high alert," meaning that it will fire its missiles if there is evidence that an enemy nuclear attack is in progress. This "hair-trigger" setting makes the prospect of an accidental launch much more likely.

Pessimists like Blair maintain that

having nuclear forces on high alert is even more troubling when one considers that the country's early-warning system (which detects incoming attacks) has degraded significantly since the 1980s, making it more likely that Russia will mistake non-military missile launches (like the one from Norway) as aggressive actions.

The reasons for the degradation of the warning system are twofold. First, due to a lack of funds, Russia's spy satellites are not being replaced when they stop operating. Hence the country no longer has as many "eyes" in space as it once did. Second, many of the early-warning radar stations are located in former Soviet republics that are now independent countries. Some of these new states, like Ukraine and Latvia, no longer allow the Russians to use the facilities on their territory. "This has left some gaping holes in the system," says Sherman Garnett, a senior associate

at the Carnegie Endowment for International Peace. And, Garnett says, those facilities still controlled by the Russians (both in and out of their country) are not operating at peak performance levels. "The system is breaking down, and there simply is no money to fix it," he says.

In addition, the pessimists say, more than machinery is deteriorating. The Strategic Rocket Forces, those personnel charged with guarding and operating the land-based nuclear arsenal, have suffered from the same decline in money, training and moral that has affected the rest of the military. "They're still better than the average military units," Blair says. But, he adds, due to a decline in proper training, "they are less proficient than they once were in handling nuclear weapons." In addition, he says, "they are much less motivated to adhere to safety standards than they used to be because their housing and food are less than adequate."

But others argue that Russia's control over its nuclear forces, while far from perfect, is not the catastrophe waiting to happen that many claim it to be. "The command and control system is reliable," says Dmitri Simes, a former adviser on Russia to President Richard M. Nixon and president of the Nixon Center for Peace.

Simes and others point out that Russia has put great value in its nuclear forces in the last decade as its conventional capability has declined. "It's the one area where there is still parity with the United States and so, even with the deterioration of the rest of their military, the nuclear weapons are still relatively well-maintained," Petrov says.

As for the Strategic Rocket Forces, optimists say, there is still adequate unit cohesion and acceptable moral. "They've deteriorated less [than other Russian units] because they've gotten special budgetary treatment, in part because the Russians are relying on nuclear weapons more and more," says Bruce Parrott, director of Russia Area and East European Studies at the Brookings Institution.

Optimists also point out that American officials who have unprecedented access to Russia's nuclear forces have not expressed deep concern about command and control. "We have hundreds of people over there, and they are not screaming that the sky is falling," Petrov says. And, optimists like Petrov point out, the situation is going to get better as overall conditions in Russia improve. "The worst is over because the economy is going to begin improving, and they will have more money to put into things like this," Simes says.

Does Russia, in the spirit of past Cold War rivalry, often oppose American foreign-policy initiatives to prevent the United States from growing too strong internationally?

Late last year, Saddam Hussein expelled United Nations weapons inspectors from his country, prompting the United States to prepare an aerial barrage against Iraq that would have rivaled the firepower used in the Persian Gulf War. Into this tense standoff stepped Russian Foreign Minister Yevgeni Primakov.

Near the end of November, Primakov met with the Iraqis and convinced them to allow weapons inspectors back into the country. The deal was grudgingly accepted by the United States, and the conflict, at least for a short while, was avoided.

Many view Primakov's efforts as a triumph of diplomacy over force. But others argue that the Russian's actions allowed Saddam to thwart the United Nations for a time without ultimately paying any price. "[The Russians] were running interference for a bad guy," says Frank Gaffney, president of the Center for Security Policy.

More important, Gaffney and others say, Primakov's actions in Iraq are part of a broader foreign-policy strategy whose primary goal is to obstruct American initiatives wherever possible. For example, they point to Russia's continued sales of nuclear reactors to Iran in spite of vociferous U.S. objections. In addition, they say, Russia has blocked or has tried to block other American initiatives, from NATO expansion to U.S. efforts to build oil pipelines in the former Soviet republics of the Transcaucasus, such as Azerbaijan, Armenia and Turkmenistan.

Indeed, these analysts say, Russia largely views its relations with the United States as a zero-sum game. In others words, according to AEI's Gedmin, Russian policy-makers "think that whenever America loses, Russia wins."

Gedmin and others argue that Russia's view of the United States is driven by a number of factors, including a desire to restrain what they see as America's immense and unique global power. "They are keen on ensuring that the United States doesn't have a free hand to do whatever it wants," Gedmin says.

Much of the sentiment against the United States is left over from the days of superpower competition. "There's a continuity between the foreign policy of the communists and the current government's position," says Chandler Rosenberger, a research fellow at the Institute for the Study of Conflict, Ideology and Policy in Boston. "The U.S. is still the enemy."

Anti-American sentiment is also viewed as a product of the effort to restore Russia to the status of a great power. "They think that Russian greatness can only be restored at our expense," Gaffney argues. And since Russia currently cannot project power in the same way that the old Soviet Union once did, "thwarting the United States is the only way at this stage of the game to put Russia back on the map," he says.

Indeed, defying the United States is a popular course of action in many parts of the world today. Many countries, from regional powers like France and China to developing nations like Malaysia, regularly question Washington's wisdom on a variety of issues.

But, those suspicious of Moscow argue, Russia is perhaps the most active player in this drive to curtail what is seen as American hegemony. "Primakov looks at the map and finds

Secretary of State Madeleine K. Albright and Russian Foreign Minister Yevgeni Primakov met for talks in Spain in January in an effort to resolve the conflict over U.N. weapons inspections in Iraq.

Reuters/Desmond Boylan

countries that are in trouble and tells them that they're not going to be pushed around any more," Rosenberger says. He points to a recent speech the foreign minister gave before a summit of East Asian nations in which he criticized the United States for pressuring them to make painful economic reforms. "Of course, he's a hit when he does this."

But other scholars say that it is unnecessarily alarmist to view Russia as an enemy or even with unusual suspicion. "There isn't a zero-sum game anymore," George Washington University's Petrov says. "That's ridiculous."

Petrov and others point out that the country, while no longer a super power, is still a great power, with legitimate interests outside their borders. "As the Russians have gotten back on their feet a little, they have begun to define their interests," says the Nixon Center's Simes. "And of course, there are genuine differences in interests and perspectives."

And yet, Simes says, these "differences" are not a sign of some plot or strategy to undermine the United States. "They are not driven by some ideology or desire to oppose the U.S. like they were in the old [Soviet] days," he says, noting that France and other traditional U.S. allies often have serious policy disputes with Washington. "It is natural."

Simes and others point out that in Iraq, for instance, the Russians have their own interests, which, when examined, make their recent actions understandable. For one thing, Iraq is much closer geographically to Russia than it is to America and was, for many years, a close ally of the Soviet Union. In addition, the country still owes the Russian government close to $8 billion for past purchases of weapons and other items, which largely explains Primakov's desire to diffuse the crisis and restore a more "business as usual" atmosphere.

And, George Washington's Petrov points out, Russia was joined by most of the rest of the world in its Iraq policy. "We shouldn't view Iraq as some sort of betrayal [by the Russians]," he says. "Except for the British, we were alone in our policy."

Petrov, Simes and others argue that Washington needs to understand that Russia will not blindly follow the United States simply because it won the Cold War, nor should it. Such unrealistic expectations stem, in part, from Moscow's behavior in the year or so just before and after the fall of the Soviet Union, Parrott contends. "We got into a situation where they gave us everything we wanted," he says, referring to Russian support for the Persian Gulf War and other American initiatives. "That sort of spoiled us."

In addition, he argues, the United States still often approaches Russia as a vanquished foe instead of a potential ally. "There is a certain triumphalism at work here on our part," he says. "The Russians are tired of hearing that we won the Cold War."

Finally, Petrov and others point out, Russia has played ball with the United States on the big issues that are important to Washington. For instance, they say, Moscow has cooperated with the United States in Bosnia, where Russian troops currently work alongside NATO peacekeepers. Even on the first round of NATO expansion, they say, Russia bowed to the inevitable without kicking up too much of a fuss.

"When we are firm with the Russians and let them know that it's something important, like NATO expansion or Bosnia, they come around," says AEI's Aron. ∎

BACKGROUND

'Honeymoon' Days

The United States greeted the collapse of the Soviet Union and the birth of the new Russian Republic in 1991 with a burst of goodwill and optimism. Almost overnight, the focus of nearly 50 years of American fears was replaced by a seemingly friendly, pro-democratic government. In a Christmas Day speech to the American people that year, President George Bush reflected the upbeat mood, welcoming "the emergence of a free, independent and democratic Russia led by its courageous president, Boris Yeltsin." [7]

Of course, Soviet-American relations had improved dramatically under Yeltsin's predecessor, Mikhail S. Gorbachev. Indeed, roughly a year before Bush's speech, the Soviets had supported the United States and its allies against Iraq, which would have been inconceivable just a few years earlier. Still, the emergence of the dozen-plus independent, former Soviet republics signaled definitively that the Cold War was officially over.

Almost immediately after the Soviet breakup, the Bush administration began working with Russia and other new states on a plan to safeguard the USSR's nuclear weapons. In particular, the Americans wanted Russia to retain control over not only its own warheads but also over those deployed in other former republics. Bush did not want to create a host of new nuclear powers.

By May 1992, the three new states that also had nuclear weapons — Ukraine, Belarus and Kazakhstan — all agreed to give them to Russia. (Ukraine delayed transferring its nuclear weapons in an apparent effort to extract more American aid, but it eventually abided by the agreement.)

The following month, Bush and Yeltsin agreed to reduce their strategic nuclear forces by 50 percent more than the cuts called for in the original START treaty that had been negotiated during the Soviet era. The new agreement became the basis for

Continued on p. 468

Chronology

1990-1991 The Soviet Union dissolves, leaving Russia and 14 other independent countries in its place.

1990
Boris Yeltsin wins a seat in the Russian Duma, or parliament, returning to the political arena three years after being forced out of the ruling Politburo.

August 1991
As the new president of the Russian Federation, Yeltsin successfully leads the resistance to a hard-line coup against Soviet President Mikhail Gorbachev. Although Gorbachev is returned to power, Yeltsin's role in resisting the coup leaves him as the most powerful man in Russia.

December 1991
Gorbachev resigns, and the Soviet Union dissolves. Congress passes the Nunn-Lugar Cooperative Threat Reduction Act, which aims to help the Russians and others dismantle nuclear weapons.

— • —

1992-1994
Russia and the United States work closely on arms control and other issues.

April 1992
The Group of Seven (G7) industrial democracies announce a $24 billion aid package for Russia and other former Soviet republics.

May 1992
Under pressure from the United States, Ukraine, Belarus and Kazakhstan give up their nuclear weapons, leaving Russia as the only former Soviet republic with a nuclear arsenal.

January 1993
President Clinton and Yeltsin sign the START II (Strategic Arms Reduction Talks) agreement in Moscow.

October 1993
Yeltsin orders an artillery attack on the White House, site of the Congress of People's Deputies, after members refuse his order to leave. He earlier had disbanded the legislature after it voted to end economic reforms.

January 1994
Russia agrees to join the Partnership for Peace, a group of former Soviet-bloc countries affiliated with NATO.

Dec. 11, 1994
Yeltsin orders Russian troops to attack separatist rebels in Chechnya.

— • —

1995-1999
Relations between Russia and the United States are strained over NATO expansion and other issues.

January 1996
Senate ratifies the START II treaty.

July 1996
Yeltsin is re-elected for a second four-year term.

March 1997
Clinton and Yeltsin meet in Helsinki to discuss Russia's concerns over NATO expansion.

May 1997
Clinton and Yeltsin sign the NATO-Russian Founding Act in Paris, which gives Russia an advisory role in NATO decision-making.

July 1997
Hungary, Poland and the Czech Republic are invited to join NATO.

December 1997
Foreign Minister Yevgeni Primakov brokers a last-minute deal with Iraq over United Nations arms inspections, delaying U.S. military action against Iraq.

March 1998
Yeltsin sacks his entire Cabinet, including Prime Minister Victor Chernomyrdin. His new choice for premier, Sergei Kiriyenko, is approved by the Duma in April.

April 1998
Senate ratifies the resolution adding Hungary, Poland and the Czech Republic to NATO.

Summer 1998
Duma is expected to vote on START II.

April 1999
NATO is expected to formally admit Poland, Hungary and the Czech Republic.

Race for Space Now a Team Effort . . .

Many people think that cooperation in space between Russia and the United States began only after the Soviet Union collapsed in 1991. But the famous link-up between America's *Apollo* and Russia's *Soyuz* capsules occurred in 1975, more than a decade before the Cold War ended.

Still, today the two countries are working together in space in a way that previously would have been unimaginable, even during the height of detente in the 1970s. The focus of U.S.-Russian efforts is a new International Space Station (ISS), which is scheduled to begin operation in 2004. The project is being headed by the United States, which has been the world's premier power in space since it landed a man on the moon in 1969. But the Russians are playing a crucial role in the development and construction of the new station.

Russia now has the only permanent space station in orbit. *Mir* (which means "peace" in Russian) may be 12 years old and over the hill. But it is still flying and has been used by a string of American astronauts in the last few years to prepare them for the long stays in space that will come when ISS is aloft.

In addition, Russia is helping to build parts of the station, including a crucial service module. The cylindrical, 43-foot-long component will contain some of the station's living quarters and its life-support system.

Space exploration was one of the hottest areas of competition between the United States and the then-Soviet Union during the Cold War. The launching of *Sputnik* in 1957 began the "space race." And until the mid-1960s, Russia seemed to be winning, racking up one triumph after another. In 1960, it became the first nation to send a human, Yuri Gagarin, into orbit. Over the next few years, the Russians passed a number of other milestones, including the first woman in space and the first space walk.

But in May 1961, President John F. Kennedy, in a now famous speech before Congress, committed the United States to putting the first man on the moon before the end of the decade. During the next eight years, the United States poured tens of billions of dollars into developing the technology needed to achieve Kennedy's dream. America's deep pockets and ingenuity paid off in July 1969, when Neil Armstrong and Buzz Aldrin landed on the moon. A similar Russian effort had become mired in problems and was abandoned.

The 1970s saw a warming in relations between the two countries. And just as intense Cold War competition had led to the space race, detente brought a new spirit of cooperation, culminating with the *Apollo-Soyuz* link-up. The Soviet invasion of Afghanistan in 1979 and the election of cold warrior Ronald Reagan the following year sidelined any future plans for cooperation in space.

Things are different now. Russia's space program, suffering from low budgets and low moral, is dependent on the United States, which provides much-needed funding. In fact, the U.S. provides about one-sixth of the $600 million budgeted by Russia for its work in space in exchange for permission to put American astronauts aboard *Mir*.

But some American analysts question whether the United

Continued from p. 466
START II, which was signed in Moscow in January 1993. *(See story, p. 470.)*

In addition to helping the former Soviet republics sort out their nuclear weapons, the United States and its Western allies also attempted to aid Russia and the other members of the new Commonwealth of Independent States (CIS) in jump-starting their moribund, statist economies. On April 1, 1992, the U.S. and its primary allies, the largest industrial nations known as the Group of Seven (G7)*, announced a $24 billion aid package to

---

* Members of the G7 are France, Germany, Italy, Great Britain, Canada, Japan and the United States. The group has since been expanded to include Russia.

help Russia and the other CIS states.

As it turned out, much of the announced aid was in the form of previously pledged assistance; other chunks of it came in the form of loans. In short, the $24 billion figure was greatly inflated, leading the Russians to refer to it as "The April Fool's Day Gift." [8]

Still, U.S. assistance was not insignificant. From 1991-1995, America gave about $4 billion to Russia and another $4.7 billion to other former Soviet republics. Much of the aid came in 1992 and '93, when U.S. goodwill toward its former enemy was running high. By 1996, however, aid to all former Soviet republics had dropped to $640 million, or a quarter of what it had been just a few years before. [9]

Clinton's Initiatives

The early summit meetings between Bush and Yeltsin were more than just politically productive. In addition to hammering out agreements on arms control and other matters, the two leaders had established, in three summits spread over a year, a publicly warm relationship. But in November 1992, Bush lost the presidency, leaving Yeltsin to face a new American chief executive the following year.

Like Bush, Bill Clinton believes in the need to establish close personal ties with other world leaders. At his first meeting with Yeltsin in Vancouver, Canada, in 1993, the new

... But Uncle Sam Is at the Helm

States is getting its money's worth by investing in and relying on Russia's space program. They say that sending American astronauts to *Mir* for long stays has largely been a waste of time and money because it is so old and poorly maintained that the astronauts spend most of their time keeping it operational instead of engaging in learning and experimentation. Indeed, last year, *Mir* suffered a number almost devastating accidents and problems, including a collision with another Russian space vehicle that almost forced two cosmonauts and an astronaut on board to abandon ship.

Others argue that America's investment in Mir has been worthwhile. "The training and knowledge we've gotten from *Mir* will prove useful," says Henry Hertzfeld, a senior research scientist at The George Washington University's Space Policy Institute. In particular, Hertzfeld says, the station's problems may have provided invaluable lessons for the Americans. "You learn when things go wrong," he says. "Even if the problems on ISS turn out to be different, we will have learned a lot about managing problems from our experience on *Mir*."

Another criticism of U.S-Russian cooperation revolves around the service module that Russia is building for ISS. In late April, NASA announced that the launch date for the first part of the station, originally set for June, would be pushed back into the fall. The reason, the space agency said, is that its Russian counterpart is behind schedule in the delivery of the service module. The Russian space agency in turn blames Moscow for the delay, pointing out that the central government has not put up all of the

funding promised for the project. A similar delay occurred a year before for the same reasons. [1]

Many analysts say that including Russia in the ISS project was a mistake because the country lacks the financial wherewithal and political stability to honor commitments. Indeed, the Russian government currently owes its space agency $45 million in funding for the module. Moreover, the recent change in cabinets has left everyone wondering whether the new prime minister, Sergei Kiriyenko, will be more or less effective at finding money to fulfill Russia's ISS obligations. [2]

But Hertzfeld and others say that Russia's problems are not atypical, pointing out that lack of funding and indecision on the part of the United States has delayed the space station numerous times. "No project of this magnitude comes in on time and at cost," he says.

In addition, Hertzfeld argues, giving space-station work to Russia serves another important purpose: keeping its scientists from working on missiles and other weapons for unfriendly regimes, such as those in Iran and Iraq. "They have a highly trained labor force with a lot of experience and no money," he says. "If we can benefit from that experience and, at the same time, ensure that it isn't used by the wrong kind of country, then everyone wins."

---

[1] "The Space Station: No Business, as Usual," *The Economist*, May 2, 1998.

[2] *Ibid.*

president succeeded in establishing a good rapport with his counterpart. A few months later, a joint commission was established by their seconds, Vice President Al Gore and Russian Prime Minister Viktor Chernomyrden. The new body was to meet every six months in an effort to maintain a continuous dialogue on important issues.

The close relationship between Clinton and Yeltsin has paid handsome dividends for the Russian leader. Clinton refused to criticize Yeltsin when he disbanded and then bombed the Duma in 1993. And, the American president remained silent the following year, when Russia invaded Chechnya, causing the deaths of tens of thousands of civilians.

In Clinton's first term, a variety of

agreements were signed. At the Moscow summit in January 1994, the two leaders agreed to de-target their nuclear missiles, previously aimed at each other. Moreover, several arms-control treaties were extended or enacted, including the Chemical Weapons Convention in 1993, the non-proliferation treaty in 1995 and the 1996 Comprehensive Nuclear Test Ban.

Progress was also made with regard to conventional forces. The process had begun in 1990 (just before the Soviet Union's breakup) with the Conventional Forces in Europe Treaty, which required both sides to significantly reduce their military presence in Europe. Further progress was made in 1994, when Russia joined the "Partnership for Peace," an

organization created by NATO to foster military cooperation among NATO members and former Soviet-bloc states.

Under the partnership's auspices, Russia and the United States held joint military exercises in 1994 for the first time. Repeated in 1995, the exercise culminated in Russia's participation in peacekeeping operations in Bosnia at year's end. Even more surprising, the Russians agreed to place their forces in Bosnia under overall U.S. command.

The relationship between the two countries was growing in other ways, as well. In 1992, Russia agreed to participate in the American-led effort to build a space station. And by 1996, American astronauts were training

Progress Predicted on Nuclear Weapons

The second Strategic Arms Reduction Treaty (START II) has yet to be ratified. But officials in both the United States and Russia are already thinking about START III and even IV.

START II, which would radically cut nuclear warheads in both countries, was agreed to in early 1993 at the last summit meeting between Presidents George Bush and Boris Yeltsin. The U.S. Senate ratified the treaty in 1996. But Russia's counterpart, the Duma, has yet to consider the agreement, a political hot potato in Russia.

Currently, both countries have roughly 8,000 deliverable strategic warheads. Many are mounted on ground- and submarine-based missiles. Others would be delivered aboard strategic bombers.

If ratified by the Duma, START II would reduce each country's nuclear arsenal to about 3,000 warheads. The proposals put forth for START III would bring that number down to about 2,000 or just 20 percent of the arsenal each nation had during the height of the Cold War.

President Yeltsin resubmitted an amended version of Start II to the Duma on April 13. The change, approved by the United States, would extend the deadline for destroying all warheads covered under the agreement from Jan. 1, 2003, to the end of 2007. Russia requested the extra time, claiming that it needed to allow them to spread out the cost of dismantling and destroying the weapons.

Guessing political outcomes in Russia is a difficult proposition. But many predict that the president, who just scored a victory in the Duma by getting his new prime minister, Sergei Kiriyenko, approved, will win on the START treaties as well. "There's a sense in Moscow right now that they will grudgingly get done," says Sherman Garnett, a senior associate at the Carnegie Endowment for International Peace.

"Grudgingly," because powerful, nationalistic politicians in Russia see START II as another step in the country's long slide into obscurity on the world stage. They point out that Russia's nuclear forces are the only vestige remaining of its former superpower status. According to Victor Ilyukhin, the Communist chairman of the Duma's Security Committee, START II is "beneficial only for the United States and NATO, but not for Russia, which may lose its last defense shield if this document is ratified."

But many experts, including the top brass of Russia's armed forces, argue that the treaty will be good for the country, even from a chauvinist's viewpoint. Almost all agree that the country's nuclear arsenal is deteriorating at an alarming rate. Some argue that many of Russia's existing missiles may not even work anymore, due to age or lack of maintenance. That number is expected to grow dramatically in the coming decade, they say. "These weapons are expensive to maintain and upgrade, and Russia simply doesn't have the money to do that anymore," says John Tedstrom, a researcher at the RAND Corp.

Bruce Blair, a research fellow at the Brookings Institution, agrees. "The whole system is in a tailspin," he says. And so, Blair, Tedstrom and others say, Russia's nuclear arsenal will be reduced through attrition, regardless of whether they ratify the treaty or not. "STARTs II and III are the only chance they have to maintain some sort of nuclear parity with the United States," Tedstrom says.

Supporters of the treaty have something else working in their favor: The Americans have let it be known that final negotiations on START III cannot begin until START II is ratified. "We think it would be better for me to go to Russia after the Duma ratifies START II, because then we can work on START III," President Clinton said last December. [1]

Still, the two countries have already worked out a broad outline for START III. And officials in both countries, including Duma Foreign Affairs Committee Chairman Vladimir Lukin, predict that, at this stage, the details could be ironed out quickly if the presidents were to meet. [2]

Some are even looking beyond START III. According to a recent report in Jane's Defense Weekly, Clinton administration officials have raised the prospect of a fourth START agreement that would reduce warhead levels among all declared nuclear powers, not just Russia and the U.S. [3]

Of course, thinking two treaties ahead may be premature when the fate of START II has yet to be resolved. Still, anxious arms-control officials may not have to wait much longer. The Duma is expected to take up START II before the summer ends.

[1] Quoted in "Clinton Ready to Go to Russia After Duma Ratifies START II," Agence France Press, Dec. 16, 1997.

[2] David Hoffman, "START II Approval Imperiled, Russian Says," The Washington Post, Dec. 7, 1997.

[3] Barbara Starr, "New U.S.-Russian Arms Control Talks Imminent," Jane's Defense Weekly, March 11, 1998.

aboard *Mir.* [10] *(See story, p. 468)* In addition, a barrage of American products — from movies and music to Coke and McDonald's — opened a window into life in the United States.

NATO Expansion

During the first few years of the U.S.-Russian "honeymoon," Moscow desperately sought guidance and help, and Washington eagerly obliged. In recent years, however, the relationship often has been strained.

NATO enlargement has been a particular sore point. In 1994, the United States and its Western European partners began their campaign to include some former Warsaw Pact nations in the alliance. While Yeltsin had previously expressed little concern over the prospect of expansion, he and Primakov began a campaign to stop former Soviet allies from joining. Many analysts say that Yeltsin's change of heart grew out of his perceived need to insulate himself from more nationalist politicians like Vladimir Zhirinovski, who view an expanded alliance as a threat. [11]

Still, Yeltsin undoubtedly knew that he was ultimately powerless to stop at least the first round of enlargement — adding Hungary, Poland and the Czech Republic. In spite of their loud protests, Russian officials knew the West was far more powerful than Russia and that a larger NATO was, in Clinton's view, a question of "not if, but when." [12]

In March 1997, Yeltsin met Clinton in Helsinki, Finland, to discuss, among other things, accommodating Russia's concerns before the new members joined in July. The talks led to a new agreement signed by the two leaders in Paris in June, along with other NATO officials. The so-called "Founding Act" gave Russia assurances — if not airtight promises — that NATO would not place nuclear weapons or large numbers of troops on the territory of its new members. In addition, the act established a joint council to give Moscow an advisory role in all NATO decisions. The new council would allow the Russians to be heard, but not to vote, at alliance meetings. [13]

Friction over NATO enlargement is unlikely to end. President Clinton and other Western leaders have stated publicly that the alliance plans to take in more members in the future. Some of these candidates, such as the Baltic republics and Ukraine, were

once part of the Soviet Union, and Russia has called NATO membership for them unacceptable. "If they took in the Baltics, that would be different for the Russians, since it was once theirs," Simes says. He warns that admitting former Soviet republics into NATO could make Russia less friendly and more obstructionist to the West.

But NATO has not been the only sore point between the two countries. The United States has been troubled by Russia's apparent indifference to arms proliferation. American policy-makers have often chided Moscow for its willingness to sell weapons or nuclear technology — from ballistic-missile technology for India to nuclear materials for Iran — with little seeming regard for the potential consequences.

For its part, Russia has been angered by what it considers excessive U.S. unilateralism. Lately, Moscow has been exercised over America's unwillingness even to consult with Russia when planning to use force against a former Soviet ally or client. "Thus, United States air strikes against Libya in 1993, Serbs in Bosnia in 1994 and Iraq in 1995 and 1996 brought Russian protests," writes Raymond L. Garthoff, a retired senior fellow at the Brookings Institution. [14] ■

'Connections' Called Key to Success

A recent survey in Russia shows that citizens are deeply cynical about how to get ahead in the new capitalistic economy.

What are the reasons for:

Poverty		Wealth	
Economic system	82%*	Connections	88%*
Laziness and drinking	77	Economic system	78
Unequal possibilities	65	Dishonesty	76
Discrimination	47	Good possibilities	62
Lack of effort	44	Talents	50
No talents	33	Luck	42
Bad luck	31	Hard work	39

* Percentage of respondents agreeing to each reason

Source: The Economist, Nov. 22, 1997; Interfax-AIF

CURRENT SITUATION

Troubled Economy

Even as he was firing the entire Cabinet on March 24 in an effort to stimulate efforts at economic reform, President Yeltsin was declaring those selfsame reforms to be "irreversible." But many economists are uncertain that Russia will continue on the reformist or, as some cynics say, the quasi-reformist, path toward a free market.

Of one thing there is no doubt: The average Russian has been through tremendous economic pain in the last decade. Moreover, many economists assert, most Russians are worse off today than when they were Soviet citizens. Indeed, real income has fallen by one-third over the last decade, leaving almost one-quarter of all Russians living below the poverty line. Not surprisingly, 41 percent of the Russians polled recently chose former Soviet President Leonid Brezhnev as their favorite leader. Yeltsin, by contrast, received top votes from only 14 percent. [15]

Hardships were expected when the Soviet Union collapsed and newly independent Russia began to transform its state-run economy. But Yeltsin has been in power for nearly a decade, some economists argue, and the near future looks no better than the recent past. "The problem is not only that the majority of Russians remain worse off than before the economic transition but that they cannot become better off," writes economist and Duma member Grigory Yavlinsky. [16] Yavlinsky and others argue that improvements in the nation's standard of living will not come until certain structural impediments to the economy are removed, notably a small but powerful group of wealthy businessmen who run much of Russia's economy. Much like America's 19th-century "Robber Barons," they own vast conglomerates engaged in a variety of enterprises. [17]

Most of Russia's tycoons are believed to be profoundly corrupt, having benefited more from insider connections and bribery than business acumen. Predictably, many influential businessmen exercise tremendous influence within the government and oppose reforms to the system which has benefited them so handsomely. [18] According to Yavlinski, "their market of insider deals and political connections stands in the way of an open economy that would benefit all Russian citizens." [19]

Another impediment to market-oriented reforms is the broader, more general corruption that pervades the country. "Everything in Russia is for sale. Everything can be bought," Potter says. Yavlinsky agrees. "Graft per-

meates the country, from street crime to Mafia hits to . . . rigged bids for stakes in privatized companies." [20] As a result, contracts and the rule of law in general are often not enforced, making it much harder to conduct legitimate business.

Understandably, the rampant corruption has made Russians cynical. According to a November 1997 poll taken by Russia's Interfax-AIF news agency, 88 percent of those surveyed said that a person needs "connections" to get ahead. Almost as many respondents, 78 percent, said that

Russian Foreign Minister Yevgeni Primakov, left, meets with his Iranian counterpart, Kamal Kharrazi, in Moscow in February. Critics point to such encounters as evidence of Russia's increasing belligerence toward the U.S.

Reuters/Sergei Karpukhin

"dishonesty" is also crucial to success. "Hard work" was deemed an important factor for only 39 percent of those polled. [21]

At the same time, millions of government pensioners and employees, as well as those from state-owned enterprises, are owed months of back pay. The arrearage has largely been caused by the failure of the government to enforce the tax laws. Some experts estimate that Russians owe an astounding $100 billion in back taxes

— roughly one-quarter of the nation's gross domestic product (GDP). [22]

Helping Hands

Still, the economic news is not all bad. The GDP, after shrinking for nearly a decade, has slowly begun to grow. Many economists say that the economy has "bottomed out," pointing to last year's 0.4 percent increase and a projected growth rate of 1.5 percent in 1998. Other key economic indices also leave some room for cautious optimism. Industrial production grew 1.4 percent last year. And inflation, the bane of many developing economies, was only 11 percent in 1997. [23]

Much of the good news comes on the heels of success in reforming the economy. A cornerstone of the reform program is the effort to privatize state-owned businesses. So far, tens of thousands of state companies and small businesses — about 75 percent of the economy — are now in private hands. In addition, the country has a small, but growing, stock market. And soon it is likely to also have a new, streamlined tax code that experts think will create a fair and effective tax-collection system.

Many economists and others argue that the United States and other advanced countries can best help Russia along the path to economic reform by encouraging the continued development of the institutions needed to

Continued on p. 474

At Issue:

Should the United States be more sensitive to Russia's concerns about NATO expansion?

SEN. BYRON L. DORGAN, D-N.D.

WRITTEN FOR THE CQ RESEARCHER

*r*ussia's opposition to NATO expansion does not itself justify slowing down or stopping other countries from joining the alliance. Russia should not have a veto over this policy.

However, America's relationship with Russia is among the most important in the world, and we need to manage it in a way that makes America more secure. No matter how well-intentioned NATO expansion may be, I believe it will harm our relationship with Russia and jeopardize some of our highest diplomatic priorities.

Only Russia can destroy its nuclear weapons in accordance with arms-control agreements. Only Russia can control the thousands of tactical nuclear warheads that it retains. Only the Russian Duma can ratify START II and lock in new strategic nuclear weapons reductions. And only Russia can negotiate further reductions with the United States, to culminate in a possible START III accord.

NATO expansion — particularly expansion to include the Baltic states — will likely cause Russia to rely more, not less, on nuclear weapons. Russia's military planners will have to plan for defense the same way NATO's planners always have — by judging a potential adversary's capabilities, not its intentions. With NATO tanks on Russia's borders, Russian planners will be less likely to want further reductions in their stockpile of nuclear weapons.

NATO enlargement also threatens the cooperation with Russia in other areas, including crisis management in the former Yugoslavia, control of weapons technology and responses to rogue regimes. Since the administration's policy to expand NATO became clear, Russia has opposed military action against Iraq, has sought to block sanctions against Serbia over the crisis in Kosovo and has boosted its weapons sales to Iran. Further expansion of NATO will likely lead to further examples of Russia countering American diplomatic efforts.

This is frustrating because the end of the Cold War presented us with an historic opportunity to draw Russia to the West, to integrate it into the family of democratic and capitalistic nations. Rather than repeating the mistakes of the World War I peace settlement, which humiliated a defeated Germany and alienated it from the international community, we should repeat the successes of the World War II peace settlement, in which we aided Germany and Japan following the war and won their lasting friendship by welcoming them into international institutions.

SEN. RICHARD G. LUGAR, R-IND.

WRITTEN FOR THE CQ RESEARCHER

*c*entral and Eastern European stability is as much in Russia's interest as America's. NATO enlargement provides an opportunity for the alliance to be proactive in shaping peace and stability, and lessens the chances of U.S. involvement in a regional conflict.

NATO enlargement neither punishes nor isolates Russia. There is nothing inconsistent between a healthy U.S.-Russian relationship and an expanding NATO. Russia has accepted, in the NATO-Russia Founding Act, the rights of neighbors to choose their security arrangements.

NATO members will continue to have both common and divergent interests with Russia, whether NATO enlarges or not. There will be areas of collaboration and discord in the relationship. Distinctions will be determined by differences in geography, history and economic standing, not by Cold War ideology or NATO enlargement. Managing coincidental and conflicting interests will be done by building bridges where possible and drawing lines where necessary.

Some critics believe that NATO enlargement somehow condemns the START II Treaty and cooperative U.S.-Russian nuclear dismantlement activities to the dustbin of history. But Russia's recent ratification of the Chemical Weapons Convention would indicate that the linkage between NATO enlargement and arms control is more political than strategic.

Russian tardiness in arms-control matters has more to do with internal Russian politics surrounding the Russian budget than defense policy planning. Although the Russian Duma continues to drag its heels in deliberations on the START II Treaty, it should be remembered that they began this practice long before NATO enlargement. Recently, Duma Speaker [Gennady] Seleznev has said that START II would be ratified by the Duma before it adjourns this summer because it "meets Russia's interests." NATO enlargement does not change the fact that START II, and a potential START III, is in their security interests.

In my recent trips to Russia it has been clear that NATO enlargement is unlikely to affect our cooperation with Russia to reduce the threat from weapons of mass destruction.

NATO enlargement and deeper NATO-Russian relations both have immense value for the United States and Europe. They are complementary and reinforcing objectives. The best outcome for the United States and Europe is success for both tracks.

Continued from p. 472

establish a market economy. "We ought to be emphasizing the kinds of things that allow the economy to grow fairly, like the rule of law, effective regulation and standardized practices," Rosenberger says.

According to Blake Marshall, executive vice president of the U.S.-Russia Business Council, "We need to be there to offer advice and answer questions when these reforms are taken up by the Duma." In addition, Marshall says, U.S. officials and business people need to "rally public support [for reform] by explaining that these changes will bring benefits."

Another way to encourage change would be to facilitate meetings, both in Russia and the United States, between business people and government officials. "We need to foster more human-to-human contact so that [the Russians] can see how we do things," says Herman Pirchner Jr., president of the American Foreign Policy Council.

Very few Russia-watchers think that U.S. aid is having much of an impact on Russia's economy. "It's basically a drop in the bucket," Pirchner says, referring to the roughly $250 million Russia received last year.

Moreover, Pirchner and others argue, large dollops of assistance, such as the International Monetary Fund's (IMF) current $10 billion loan to Russia, often can do more harm than good. "The payments they're receiving from the IMF often have the effect of postponing needed structural reforms," he says, "because they give the Russians enough cash to get by."

In the end, Pirchner and others say, the IMF, the United States and other would-be friends of Russia can only have so much impact because the drive for reform must come from the Russian people. "Whatever we do will be on the margins because 150 million Russians are going to have a far greater impact on their economy than will the rest of the world," Pirchner says. ∎

OUTLOOK

Rising Nationalism

Winston Churchill once called Russia "a riddle wrapped in a mystery inside an enigma." The country has become more open and arguably less Byzantine since Britain's wartime leader used the evocative description in a 1939 BBC radio address. But Russia nonetheless remains difficult to fathom even today, making attempts to predict the future particularly daunting.

And yet, divining the future in Russia is important, experts say, because the nature of its relations with the United States will depend more on what happens in Moscow than in Washington. So much hinges on Russia, they say, because it, unlike the United States, is in the midst of a profound transformation.

Most scholars agree that if Russia moves toward market reforms and democracy, it will forge closer ties to the West and the United States. But if it drifts back toward authoritarian and nationalistic policies, it will probably have more troubled relations with Washington.

For some, the future looks bright. "Russia is heading toward greater democracy, even if it isn't quite what we think of as democracy in the West," says American University's Phillips, who notes that Japan and other Asian countries have unique democratic institutions that work well for them.

Phillips offers two reasons for her optimism. First, she argues, the IMF and other Western institutions and countries are using the promise of loans and other benefits to nudge Russia toward becoming a more market-oriented, democratic society. "We're using carrots and sticks to push Russia in the right direction," she says.

In addition, Phillips says, Russia is naturally moving toward democracy. "There's been a real decentralization of authority there," she says, referring to the growing independence of the country's many regions and states. "This is a democratic movement in a sense."

Sen. Lugar, who shares Phillips' optimism, sees another hopeful sign. "When you look at the young people, who are the future, you realize that they don't want to go back to the old ways," he says. "That's one reason why, with all the back and fill, I think the trend in Russia is positive."

But Gaffney and others see a more ominous trend. "When democracy tries to exist with quasi-authoritarianism, as is the case there now, one always prevails over the other," he says. "Given Russia's tradition of the strong hand and ruthless repression, it seems quite likely that authoritarianism will prevail."

Rosenberger agrees, comparing Russia's post-Soviet history with that of Yugoslavia over the last decade. "In both countries you see a shift from the nationalism of communism to plain nationalism," he says. Indeed, he argues, the nationalist card is a good one for people like Yeltsin and Serbian leader Slobodan Milosevic to play, since it is very appealing in countries (like Serbia and Russia) where the people feel frustrated and resentful over their nation's reduced economic and political power. "A lot of [Westerners] have a hard time believing this, but many people in both countries are supportive of the strong nationalist position," Rosenberger says.

And "nudging" from the IMF and others is only going to make things worse, he warns. "This well of resentment will grow even bigger as long as we push our own free-market determinism on Russia," he says.

If a stronger and more nationalistic Russia emerges, the United States could have a much harder time getting Moscow to cooperate. "If you look at their aggressive foreign policy now, when they're so weakened," Gaffney says, "you realize that it will get much worse as they become more armed and powerful in coming years."

Can the United States prevent the emergence of an aggressive, nationalistic Russia? Many argue that the West, and the United States in particular, must be firm with Russia's leaders when they begin acting like their Soviet predecessors.

"It doesn't help the cause for reform in Russia when we roll over and don't do anything when they do something wrong . . . like invade Chechnya and kill tens of thousands of civilians," Rosenberger says. "Out of fear of not offending the Russians, we go soft, which of course only encourages the nationalists, who think their room to maneuver against the West has expanded."

Reformer and Duma member Yavlinsky agrees. "[T]he West should hold those in power in Russia accountable for undemocratic deeds, in much the same way it is willing to criticize its allies," he writes. "Western leaders should apply to Russia the same criteria for evaluating the health of its democracy and the strength of its market economy that they apply to themselves." [24] ▓

Notes

[1] For background, see "Aid to Russia," *The CQ Researcher*, March 12, 1993, pp. 217-240, and "Russia's Political Future," *The CQ Researcher*, May 3, 1996, pp. 385-408.

[2] Charles Krauthammer, "Good Geopolitics," *The Washington Post*, April 17, 1998. For background, see "Expanding NATO," *The CQ Researcher*, May 16, 1997, pp. 433-457.

[3] Krauthammer, *op. cit.*

FOR MORE INFORMATION

If you would like to have this CQ Researcher updated, or need more information about this topic, please call CQ Custom Research. Special rates for CQ subscribers. (202) 887-8600 or (800) 432-2250, ext. 600, or

American Enterprise Institute, 1150 17th St. N.W., Washington, D.C. 20036; (202) 862-5846; www.aei.org. This research and educational organization studies a wide range of policy issues.

Brookings Institution, 1775 Massachusetts Ave. N.W., Washington, D.C. 20036; (202) 797-6111; www.brook.edu. This think tank sponsors research on domestic and international economics and other areas.

Carnegie Endowment for International Peace, 2400 N St. N.W., Washington, D.C. 20037; (202) 483-7600; www.ceip.org. The endowment is an international-affairs research organization with an affiliate office in Moscow.

Center for Security Policy, 1250 24th St. N.W., Suite 350, Washington D.C. 20037; (202) 466-0515; www.security-policy.org. The center is an educational institution that focuses on defense and arms-control policy.

Council on Foreign Relations, 58 East 68th St., New York, N.Y. 10021; (212) 434-9400; www.foreignaffairs.org. This foreign policy think tank has several Russia scholars.

[4] Madeleine K. Albright, "Stop Worrying About Russia," *The New York Times*, April 29, 1998.

[5] Gregory Yavlinsky, "Russia's Phony Capitalism," *Foreign Affairs*, May/June 1998.

[6] Bruce W. Nelan, "Nuclear Disarray," *Time*, May 19, 1997.

[7] Quoted in Raymond L. Garthoff, "U.S. Relations with Russia: The First Five Years," *Current History*, October 1997.

[8] *Ibid.*

[9] *Ibid.*

[10] "The Space Station. No Business as Usual," *The Economist*, May 2, 1998. For background, see "Space Program's Future," *The CQ Researcher*, April 25, 1997, pp. 361-384.

[11] Robert Service, *A History of Russia in the Twentieth Century* (1998), pp. 533-534.

[12] Quoted in Melinda Liu, "Eastward Expansion," *Newsweek*, May 26, 1997.

[13] *Ibid.*

[14] Garthoff, *op. cit.*

[15] Cited in "Russia's Part-Time President," *The Economist*, Feb. 14, 1998.

[16] Yavlinsky, *op. cit.*

[17] David Hoffman, "Russia's 'People's Capitalism Benefiting Only the Elite," *The Washington Post*, Dec. 28, 1997.

[18] *Ibid.*

[19] Yavlinsky, *op. cit.*

[20] *Ibid.*

[21] "Russia's Reforms in Trouble," *The Economist*, Nov. 22, 1997.

[22] Daniel Williams, "Russia's Ever Mounting Back Taxes," *The Washington Post*, Dec. 26, 1997.

[23] Statistics from the World Bank's Web site.

[24] Yavlinski, *op. cit.*

Bibliography

Selected Sources Used

Books

Mandelbaum, Michael, *The Dawn of Peace in Europe*, Twentieth Century Fund, 1996.

Mandelbaum, a professor at Johns Hopkins University's School of Advanced International Studies, argues that NATO is still necessary for Europe's security, even in a post-Soviet world. At the same time, he says, Russia's interests must be constantly considered if new security arrangements are to be lasting.

Service, Robert, *A History of Twentieth-Century Russia*, Harvard University Press, 1998.

Service, a professor of Russian history and politics at the University of London, chronicles Russia's history from the days of the czars to President Boris Yeltsin's re-election in 1996. His analysis of communism and the Communist Party in post-Soviet Russia is particularly insightful.

Articles

Albright, Madeleine, K., "Stop Worrying About Russia," *The New York Times*, April 29, 1998.

The secretary of State argues that NATO enlargement will not produce an aggressive and hostile Russia as many predict. In fact, she says, expanding the alliance is the best way to encourage democracy in Russia. "If we want Russia to complete its transformation into a modern European power, the last thing we should do is to act as if Central Europe is still a Russian sphere of influence," she writes.

Cooper, Mary, "Expanding NATO," *The CQ Researcher*, May 16. 1997.

Cooper's excellent overview of the NATO enlargement debate looks at the issue from a number of important angles, including NATO's continued usefulness to the validity of Russia's concerns.

Garthoff, Raymond, "U.S. Relations with Russia: The First Five Years," *Current History*, October 1997.

Garthoff details the ups and downs of relations between the United States and Russia. In particular, he chronicles the many summits and agreements that make up the brief history of the relationship.

Hoffman, David, "Russia's 'People's Capitalism' Benefiting the Elite," *The Washington Post*, Dec. 28, 1997.

Hoffman documents the rise of Russia's "tycoons," a small group of wealthy, well-connected businessmen who are squeezing out smaller, more legitimate businesses in their quest for complete control of the country's economy.

Bruce W. Nelan, "Nuclear Disaster," *Time*, May 19, 1997.

Nelan describes the sorry state of Russia's still enormous nuclear arsenal. He argues that a number of scenarios, from a political crisis to the misidentification of a non-threatening, foreign rocket, could lead to the use of nuclear weapons.

Rosenberger, Chandler, "Russian Roulette," *National Review*, Jan. 26, 1998.

Rosenberger, a research fellow at the Institute for the Study of Conflict, Ideology and Policy, argues that Russia's foreign policy is guided by a desire to block the United States at every turn. He notes that Russian Foreign Minister Yevgeni Primakov has spent the last few years whipping up anti-American sentiment among Russia's allies in Europe and Asia while at the same time opposing U.S. actions against rogue regimes like Iraq and Iran.

Yavlinsky, Grigory, "Russia's Phony Capitalism," *Foreign Affairs*, May/June 1998.

Yavlinsky, a reformist member of the Duma, claims that Russia is at a crossroads, both politically and economically. To make sure the country moves in the right direction, he writes, Western nations "should apply to Russia the same criteria for evaluating the health of its democracy and the strength of its market economy that they apply to themselves."

Zakaria, Fareed, "Can't Russia Join the Club Too?" *Newsweek*, May 4, 1998.

Zakaria presents a number of arguments in favor of admitting Russia to NATO, including this one: "If one of NATO's new goals is to strengthen democracy, then surely its place lies with the most important democratic experiment taking place on the European continent — in Russia."

Reports and Studies

Kober, Stanley, "NATO Expansion and the Danger of a Second Cold War," The Cato Institute, Jan. 31, 1996.

Kober, a research fellow at the Cato Institute, presents a host of arguments against expanding NATO. He predicts, among other things, that enlarging NATO will create a more nationalist Russia that is suspicious of the West.

The Next Step

Additional information from UMI's Newspaper & Periodical Abstracts™ database

Economic Reform

Clinton, William J., "Joint Statement on United States — Russia Economic Initiative," *Weekly Compilation of Presidential Documents*, **March 24, 1997, pp. 393-395.**

The March 21, 1997, joint statement on a U.S.-Russia joint initiative to stimulate investment and growth in Russia and deepen the two nations' economic ties is presented.

Liesman, Steve, "Russia's Chubais Faces High-Stakes Test," *The Wall Street Journal*, **March 10, 1997, p. A15.**

On March 7, 1997, Russian President Boris Yeltsin appointed Anatoly Chubais as first deputy prime minister in charge of the economy. Chubais also will be in charge of completing Russia's half-finished transition to a market economy.

Thomas, Scott, "Tales from Two Privatizations: Russia and the Former East Germany," *Journal of International Affairs*, **winter 1997, pp. 505-518.**

Thomas compares the privatization efforts in Russia and the former East Germany by analyzing the experiences of several firms. He also offers some lessons to be learned from the East German process.

Foreign Policy

Gordon, Michael R., "An Ex-Spymaster Revives Russia's Mideast Influence," *The New York Times*, **Nov. 21, 1997, p. A17.**

Seven years ago, when Yevgeni M. Primakov was racing around the Middle East in a futile bid to stop the Persian Gulf War, the Americans regarded him as a meddlesome nuisance, and the Iraqis were not eager to listen. But now Primakov is finally where he has always thought Russian diplomats should be: at the center of world attention. Primakov is a bureaucratic survivor. As foreign minister, his professionalism and lack of ideology have earned him the grudging respect of American diplomats. But he also has his critics, who note that these have not been the best years for Russian foreign policy.

Holmes, Charles, and Julia Malone, "Iraq-Russia Talks Raise Hopes of Ending Impasse in Gulf," *Atlanta Constitution*, **Nov. 19, 1997, p. A12.**

Russian President Boris Yeltsin met Tuesday with a senior Iraqi official in urgent talks that produced a plan to resolve the crisis between Iraq and the United Nations, Russian officials said. Tariq Aziz, Iraq's deputy prime minister, brought Yeltsin a letter from President Saddam Hussein seeking a "balanced political solution." Russian Foreign Minister Yevgeni Primakov said the meeting produced a plan to avoid military force and to require Iraq to comply with "the corresponding U.N. Security Council resolutions" for allowing arms inspections by U.N. observers, including Americans.

Massie, Suzanne, and Priscilla McMillan, "We Need a Policy on Russia," *The Boston Globe*, **Oct. 9, 1997, p. A29.**

The authors postulate that the Clinton administration's insistence on making NATO expansion the cornerstone of its policy in Europe is merely the latest symptom of a much deeper problem — the absence of a real American policy toward Russia. Before the United States can fashion a policy toward the new Russia, Americans must first appreciate the pain and extent of Russia's post-imperial collapse. During its three-quarters of a century of Soviet rule, Russia lost a third of its population and suffered unspeakable deformation. In an encompassing effort to control every corner of society, the regime demolished the social fabric to the point where Russians now are left without a single strong institution. The government is feeble. The nation has been environmentally ravished. The people have been humiliated. Yet the West refuses to grasp this, only paying lip service to Russia's suffering. The U.S. expects Russians to pick up where they left off in 1917, as if Soviet rule had never happened, attempting to thrust upon Russians solutions that have worked in the U.S. — economic solutions. The U.S. preaches "marketization" as if it were a cure-all, ignoring the reality that Russia's most deep-seated problems lie outside the realm of economics.

Williams, Carol J., "Russia Says Iraq Approves Its Plan to Defuse Standoff; Diplomacy: No Details of Proposal are Revealed, and U.S. Knows Little About It," *Los Angeles Times*, **Nov. 19, 1997, p. A1.**

Tariq Aziz, Iraq's deputy prime minister and President Saddam Hussein's chief envoy in the U.N.-Iraqi stand-off, flew to Moscow after Russian President Boris Yeltsin sent a message to the Iraqi president earlier this week that "the Iraqi leadership couldn't help but react to," Russian Foreign Minister Yevgeni Primakov told reporters. "The negotiations resulted in working out a certain program that we believe allows avoidance of a clash of forces and resolving the crisis by Iraq's implementing relevant resolutions of the U.N. Security Council," Primakov said after his talks with Aziz, who also met with Prime Minister Viktor Chernomyrdin at the Russian White House and with Yeltsin at a country dacha 60 miles north of Moscow.

NATO Expansion

Apple, R.W. Jr., "On NATO Coup, Russia's Shadow," *The New York Times*, **July 9, 1997, p. A8.**

"We bridged a chasm in Europe," President Clinton said after

NATO leaders had agreed to admit three Eastern European countries as members by 1999. Secretary of State Madeleine K. Albright spoke of an "irreversible process" of alliance-building. American diplomacy succeeded, where many thought it would fail, in achieving a common front supporting NATO expansion, in limiting it in the first instance to three countries and in persuading the Russians to go along. In that sense, today was a great day for President Clinton and the alliance, as he said. After World War II, the West's bet — "the bluff," as a senior American official called it recently — was that the promise to use nuclear weapons to resist Soviet expansion would obviate the need actually to use them. Today's bet is that the promise of sending British or German or American troops to defend Warsaw or Prague against an unnamed enemy will not only make that unnecessary but will also help to entrench democracy and a free-market system in Eastern Europe.

Eisenhower, Susan, "Price for Super-NATO Is Too High; Europe: The Quiet U.S. Commitment to Back the Baltics' Membership Needlessly Angers Russia," *Los Angeles Times*, Feb. 1, 1998, p. M5.

The author comments that during President Clinton's State of the Union address, he spent less than a minute of his hour-plus speech explaining his position on NATO expansion. Yet, she claims, expansion will create what has been dubbed a "geostrategic revolution. There is no consensus on a range of related unknowns concerning the Baltic states' future, such as what the new mission of the post-Cold War NATO will be, how many countries will eventually join, what Russia's rightful place in the new Europe is, what the costs of expansion will be and who will pay those costs.

Hart, Gary, and Gordon Humphrey, "Perspectives on NATO Expansion; Con: Russia Will Reject Cold Peace; The Prospect of the Western Allies Camped on the Republic's Border has Stalled Reduction of its Nuclear Arsenal," *Los Angeles Times*, March 12, 1998, p. B9.

The authors say the Senate vote on NATO expansion will set the tone of U.S.-Russian relations for the next generation. If membership is approved for Poland, Hungary and the Czech Republic, NATO will move right up to Russia's border, seriously endangering the once-in-a-century opportunity for the United States to build a constructive relationship with the vast and important country.

Krauthammer, Charles, "Good Geopolitics; Is NATO Expansion Directed Against Russia? Of Course It Is," *The Washington Post*, April 17, 1998, p. A23.

The author debates admitting Poland, Hungary and the Czech Republic to NATO, which he says would not extend the borders of peace, as proponents claim, but instead exclude and contain Russia.

Shalikashvili, John, "Perspectives on NATO Expansion; Pro: Seal the Victory of Cold War; The Inclusion of Three Former Soviet Satellites Won't Alienate

Russia, Which Stands to Benefit from the New Stability," *Los Angeles Times*, March 12, 1998, p. B9.

The former chairman of the Joint Chiefs says the Senate should demonstrate overwhelming bipartisan support for including Poland, Hungary and the Czech Republic in NATO. He says America's belief in democracy and individual freedoms helped us win the Cold War, and to cease to defend these principles weakens the nation.

Nuclear Weapons

Ellis, Jason D., and Todd Perry, "Nunn-Lugar's Unfinished Agenda," *Arms Control Today*, October 1997, pp. 14-22.

In 1991, the United States established a wide-ranging security-assistance initiative to help alleviate the adverse risks associated with many of the newly independent states' nuclear-related problems. The question of whether the U.S. will marshal the "Nunn-Lugar" political will and devote the resources necessary to sustain the program is examined.

Goshko, John M., "U.S., Russia Reaffirm Nuclear Pact; Leaders Sign Accords to Preserve ABM Treaty and Boost START II," *The Washington Post*, Sept. 27, 1997, p. A16.

The United States and Russia added some new links to their post-Cold War relationship today by signing agreements aimed at clearing the way for new radical reductions in strategic nuclear weapons and by launching a new NATO-Moscow partnership designed to dispel Russian fears of Western military power. Secretary of State Madeleine K. Albright and her Russian counterpart, Yevgeni Primakov, were at the center of day-long activities culminating with the signing of accords to preserve the viability of the 1972 Anti-Ballistic Missile (ABM) Treaty and to boost the chances that the Russian parliament will ratify the START II Treaty reducing long-range nuclear weapons.

Hoffman, David, "Downsizing A Mighty Arsenal; Moscow Rethinks Role As Its Weapons Rust," *The Washington Post*, March 16, 1998, p. A1.

Russia's strategic forces are suffering a dramatic decline because of arms-control treaties, the Soviet breakup, looming obsolescence and Russia's economic depression. Regardless of whether the United States and Russia move ahead on bilateral arms-control treaties, a decade from now Russia's military forces will be less than one-tenth their size at the peak of Soviet power, according to estimates prepared in Russia and in the West. At the same time, if current economic trends continue, Russia may have a strategic nuclear force only larger than that of one other country, China, and somewhat larger than Britain's and France's combined. In the West, too, the decline of Russia's strategic forces could have serious repercussions, raising questions about the size and posture of U.S. forces.

Isaacs, John, "Cold Warriors Target Arms Control," *Arms Control Today*, September 1995, pp. 3-7.

If Republican lawmakers are successful in making

current arms-control legislation into law, a series of arms-control agreements could be consigned to the trash heap. Republicans are targeting arms-control legislation.

Pincus, Walter, "Russia Considering Increased Nuclear Dependence; Move Would Allow Moscow to Cut Armed Forces, CIA Tells Congress," *The Washington Post*, Dec. 7, 1997, p. A11.

Russia's military and civilian leaders are debating whether to increase reliance on nuclear weapons to deter attacks from neighboring nations, enabling Russia to make further cuts in its large and costly standing army, navy and air force, according to the CIA. "At present, a number of Russian observers advocate placing greater reliance on nuclear weapons to compensate for the deficiencies of [Moscow's] conventional forces," the CIA told Congress. Some Russian officials, the agency added, even "have called for developing first-use and limited-use nuclear options to prevent a regional conflict from expanding into a broader war." And in a reference to the former Warsaw Pact countries now in line to join NATO, State Department analysts said: "The 1993 doctrine also stated that Russia reserved the right to initiate the use of nuclear weapons if it is attacked by a non-nuclear weapons state allied with or supported by a nuclear weapons state," a change that brought Russian policy in line with longstanding U.S. policy.

"Russia's Nuclear Temptation," *The New York Times*, Jan. 12, 1998, p. A20.

The end of the Cold War has produced an alarming nuclear irony. Russia is becoming more dependent on its nuclear weapons as those weapons become more vulnerable, increasing the chances that in a severe crisis Moscow might consider using them. It is imperative for Washington to help reverse that trend, and President Clinton has the tools to do so, if he is willing to use them. When the Cold War ended, the Soviet Union had one of the largest land armies in the world, an abundance of conventional weapons and a nuclear strike force nearly equal to that of the United States. Since then, domestic politics, economic problems and general neglect of the military have left Russia with a hollow conventional force. As that force has deteriorated, Russian military planners have placed increased emphasis on nuclear weapons, which are less expensive to maintain.

Organized Crime

DiConsilglio, John, "From Russia with Guns," *Scholastic Update*, Feb. 7, 1997, pp. 7-8.

Since the USSR was dismantled, organized crime has exploded in Russia, and the country's violent-crime rate has doubled. Russian expert Howard Schmalling of Harvard University believes the mob is running Russia.

Varese, Federico, "The Transition to the Market and Corruption in Post-Socialist Russia," *Political Studies*, 1997, pp. 579-596.

In its transition to a market economy, Russia has had

corruption problems, which are discussed.

Space Station

Carreau, Mark, "Foale Blames Russia's Economy; Astronaut Says Effort to Save Money Led to Accident Aboard Mir," *Houston Chronicle*, Oct. 25, 1997, p. A4.

Russia's economic problems, rather than its cosmonauts or mission-control personnel, are to blame for the near-disastrous collision between the *Mir* space station and the unmanned *Progress* cargo capsule, U.S. astronaut Mike Foale said Friday. Foale, who returned to Earth earlier this month after a 145-day trip to *Mir*, witnessed the June 25 collision and the events leading up to it. The *Progress* careened into the station's Spektr science module as now-departed cosmonauts Vasily Tsibliev and Alexander Lazutkin attempted to berth it using a new, manual docking system installed aboard the cargo capsule.

Gessen, Masha, "Scary Fires, Crashes, and Glitches — Isn't That Just Life in Russia? The Mir Dilemma: Would You Go Up There?" *The Christian Science Monitor*, Sept. 26, 1997, p. 18.

Considering the dire reports from the aging *Mir* space station, the author wonders why a Russian, let alone an American, would choose to blast off into space just to spend months fixing one mechanical problem after another. Contemplating what kind of nerve it takes to risk a visit to *Mir*, she says there are fundamental differences in approach between an American astronaut and a Russian cosmonaut.

Radford, Tim, "Russia and U.S. Congress at Odds on Mir Safety," *The Guardian*, Sept. 20, 1997, p. 17.

Russia and the United States could be heading for a collision over the hapless space station *Mir*. A congressional committee has recommended that no more Americans be sent to work with cosmonauts in the 11-year-old Russian orbiting laboratory. "There has been sufficient evidence put before this hearing to raise doubts about the safety of continued American long-term presence on *Mir*," said Rep. James F. Sensenbrenner Jr., R-Wis., chairman of the House Science Committee. As he spoke, astronaut David Wolf was preparing to be launched next week in the shuttle *Atlantis*. He is due to replace Michael Foale, who has survived computer shutdowns, a collision, power failures and oxygen-generator shutdowns.

"Shuttle Leaves Russia Outpost for a Return Sunday Night," *The New York Times*, Oct. 4, 1997, p. A10.

The space shuttle *Atlantis* pulled away from the Russian space station *Mir* today for the flight home, leaving behind an American physician and a new computer that should make his four-and-a-half-month stay safer and more productive. David A. Wolf watched quietly as *Atlantis* backed away in darkness 250 miles above Russia. Wolf replaced Dr. Michael Foale, who headed home after four and a half months aboard the run-down Russian space station.

Back Issues

Great Research on Current Issues Starts Right Here.
Recent topics covered by The CQ Researcher are listed below.
Now available on the Web
For information, call (800) 432-2250 ext. 279 or (202) 887-6279.

If you would like to have any of these CQ Researchers updated, or need more information about these topics, please call CQ Custom Research. Special rates for CQ subscribers. (202) 887-8600 or (800) 432-2250, ext. 600, or E-mail Custom.Research@cq.com

FEBRUARY 1997
Assisting Refugees
Alternative Medicine's Next Phase
Independent Counsels
Feminism's Future

MARCH 1997
New Air Quality Standards
Alcohol Advertising
Civic Renewal
Educating Gifted Students

APRIL 1997
Declining Crime Rates
The FBI Under Fire
Gender Equity in Sports
Space Program's Future

MAY 1997
The Stock Market
The Cloning Controversy
Expanding NATO
The Future of Libraries

JUNE 1997
FDA Reform
China After Deng
Line-Item Veto
Breast Cancer

JULY 1997
Transportation Policy
Executive Pay
School Choice Debate
Aggressive Driving

AUGUST 1997
Age Discrimination
Banning Land Mines
Children's Television
Evolution vs. Creationism

SEPTEMBER 1997
Caring for the Dying
Mental Health Policy
Mexico's Future
Youth Fitness

OCTOBER 1997
Urban Sprawl in the West
Diversity in the Workplace
Teacher Education
Contingent Work Force

NOVEMBER 1997
Renewable Energy
Artificial Intelligence
Religious Persecution
Roe v. Wade at 25

DECEMBER 1997
Whistleblowers
Castro's Next Move
Gun Control Standoff
Regulating Nonprofits

JANUARY 1998
Foster Care Reform
IRS Reform
The Black Middle Class
U.S.-British Relations

FEBRUARY 1998
Patients' Rights
Deflation Fears
Caring for the Elderly
The New Corporate Philanthropy

MARCH 1998
Israel at 50
The Federal Judiciary
Drinking on Campus
The Economics of Recycling

APRIL 1998
Biology and Behavior
Liberal Arts Education
Income Inequality
High-Tech Labor Shortage

MAY 1998
Census 2000
Child-Care Options
Alzheimer's Disease

Back issues are available for $5.00 (subscribers) or $10.00 (non-subscribers). Quantity discounts apply to orders over 10. To order, call Congressional Quarterly Customer Service at (202) 887-8621.

Binders are available for $18.00. To order call 1-800-638-1710. Please refer to stock number 648.

Future Topics

▶ *Student Press*

▶ *Environmental Justice*

▶ *Antitrust Policy*

ⒸＲesearcher

PUBLISHED BY CONGRESSIONAL QUARTERLY INC.

Student Journalism

Are First Amendment rights in danger?

Ten years after the Supreme Court gave school administrators broad powers to censor student journalists, high school papers are still publishing unflinching stories about AIDS, drug abuse and other teen problems. But would-be journalists face an uncertain future. College journalism programs turn out far more graduates than the nation's newsrooms can hire. Public trust in the news media is at a shockingly low level, and for those who labor within the industry, long hours and low pay are the usual rewards. Moreover, campus protests of editorial content have become commmonplace. On the plus side, the rise of the Internet offers new job possibilities, and career prospects for minority journalists are better than ever. And while high school journalism has nearly disappeared from America's inner-city schools, it thrives elsewhere.

CQ   **June 5, 1998** • **Volume 8, No. 21** • **Pages 481-504**

Formerly Editorial Research Reports

THE ISSUES

BACKGROUND

CURRENT SITUATION

OUTLOOK

SIDEBARS AND GRAPHICS

FOR FURTHER RESEARCH

COVER: STUDENTS IN RURAL ALABAMA ARE SERVING THEIR COMMUNITIES WHILE LEARNING TO BE JOURNALISTS. (PACERS PHOTOGRAPHY)

CQ Researcher

June 5, 1998
Volume 8, No.21

EDITOR
Sandra Stencel

MANAGING EDITOR
Thomas J. Colin

ASSOCIATE EDITOR
Sarah M. Magner

STAFF WRITERS
Adriel Bettelheim
Mary H. Cooper
Kenneth Jost
Kathy Koch
David Masci

PRODUCTION EDITOR
Melissa Hall

EDITORIAL ASSISTANT
Laura S. Cavender

PUBLISHED BY
Congressional Quarterly Inc.

CHAIRMAN
Andrew Barnes

VICE CHAIRMAN
Andrew P. Corty

PRESIDENT AND PUBLISHER
Robert W. Merry

EXECUTIVE EDITOR
David Rapp

Bibliographic records and abstracts included in The Next Step section of this publication are the copyrighted material of UMI, and are used with permission.

The CQ Researcher (ISSN 1056-2036). Formerly Editorial Research Reports. Published weekly, except Jan. 2, May 29, July 3, Oct. 30, by Congressional Quarterly Inc., 1414 22nd St., N.W., Washington, D.C. 20037. Annual subscription rate for libraries, businesses and government is $340. Additional rates furnished upon request. Periodicals postage paid at Washington, D.C., and additional mailing offices. POSTMASTER: Send address changes to The CQ Researcher, 1414 22nd St., N.W., Washington, D.C. 20037.

Student Journalism

BY SUSAN PHILIPS

THE ISSUES

At 14, Dan Vagasky didn't have much experience as a journalist. But as the editor of his middle school paper in Otsego, Mich., he had no doubt that the arrest of a student shoplifter during a school trip last year should be reported, as long as the student's name wasn't used. So did the *Bulldog Express'* faculty adviser.

When school administrators heard about the story, however, they killed it. And soon afterward, they shut down the paper.

"I view any piece of information that comes out of our schools as our opportunity to put our best foot forward," said Otsego School Superintendent James Leyndyke. "We would not pay to show what we do poorly." [1]

But in the view of the Newseum, a museum devoted to journalism, in Roslyn, Va., Vagasky's effort, as he put it, to "just tell the truth," warranted a Courage in Student Journalism Award, accompanied by a $5,000 college scholarship. "It made me feel [the experience] was a little worthwhile," he says.

The *Bulldog Express* is not the only paper to be affected by a 1988 Supreme Court decision giving school officials wide latitude to censor public school student publications:

• In Texas, a high school principal last year refused to let the student paper report students' plans to hold an "alternative prom," sparked by the school's warning that it would give Breathalyzer tests to those attending the official prom. [2]

• In Alaska, administrators at Chugiak High School removed newspapers from students' mailboxes last year when teachers objected to a column criticizing cheerleading as an

official sport. [3]

• In Chicago, a student was suspended in 1993 for writing an editorial criticizing a rule against students wearing shorts. [4]

"Educators do not offend the First Amendment by exercising editorial control over the style and content of student speech in school-sponsored expressive activities so long as their actions are reasonably related to legitimate pedagogical concerns," Justice Byron White wrote for the majority in *Hazelwood School District v. Kuhlmeier.*

Now college journalists are also facing new limitations on their First Amendment rights. Earlier this year, a Kentucky District judge cited the *Hazelwood* decision in upholding the right of Kentucky State University officials to confiscate student yearbooks deemed to be of too poor quality. The decision by Judge Joseph M. Hood marks the first time *Hazelwood* has been applied to a college publication.

"If this decision stands, I think we are opening a huge can of worms," says Mark Goodman, executive director of the Student Press Law Center in Arlington, Va. "The lesson the world has learned is that if you give those in power the authority to censor, they will use it."

Most efforts to silence the college media, however, come from students, not administrators. While college populations

have become more racially and ethnically diverse, the campus media, like their real-world counterparts, have not reflected those changes. "On so many campuses, student newspaper staffs have continued to be almost entirely Caucasian," Goodman says. "That alone perpetuates the impression that sometimes they don't understand the perspective of minority students." [5]

Protests against objectionable editorial content have become almost commonplace on college campuses in recent years, particularly the theft and destruction of offending newspapers. Last year, papers were stolen from at least seven issues of the University of California at Berkeley paper. And school papers have fueled critics' bonfires at the University of Texas in Austin, the University of North Carolina, the University of Kentucky and Cornell University.

One of the thefts at Berkeley, for example, was prompted by a column supporting legislation to end affirmative action in university admissions. And a parody of "ebonics," or black syntax, sparked one of the many attacks on the conservative *Cornell Review.*

Censorship is not the only problem student journalism faces in the post-*Hazelwood* era. There are deep divisions at the high school and college level over how journalism should be taught. And the near total disappearance of meaningful journalism instruction in many inner-city high schools suggests that for administrators under pressure to cut spending and increase test scores, student newspapers are often considered expendable.

"In some places, high school journalism isn't just dying, it's dead. In inner-city and poor, rural areas, it doesn't exist, and where it does exist it is a joke," says former reporter and journalism Professor Mary Arnold-

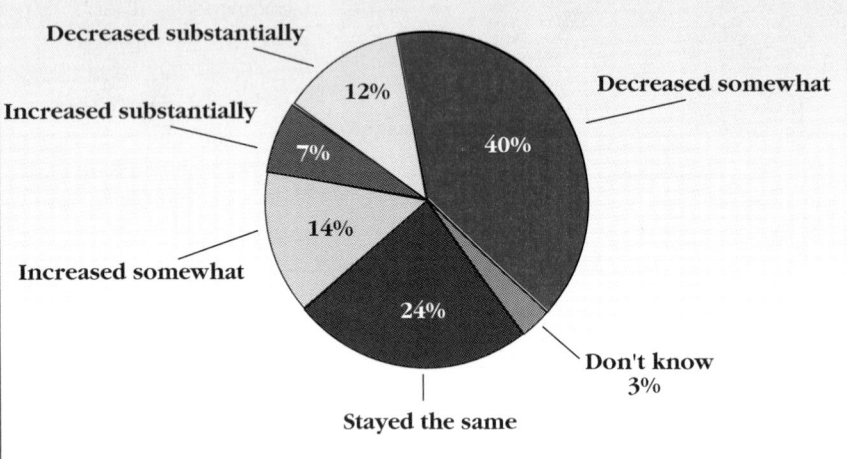

Interest in Journalism Decreased

Twice as many journalism students decided not to become journalists in the past 10 years as decided to join the profession, according to university instructors surveyed in 1995.

Did the number of would-be journalists increase or decrease?

Decreased substantially — 12%

Increased substantially — 7%

Increased somewhat — 14%

Stayed the same — 24%

Decreased somewhat — 40%

Don't know — 3%

Source: Betty Medsger, Winds of Change, *Freedom Forum, 1996*

Hemlinger, who now develops minority journalism programs for the Newspaper Association of America. In Washington, only one high school in the entire city has published more than one issue of its newspaper this year. *(See story, p. 498.)*

At the other end of the spectrum are schools like Carmel High School in Indiana. Students turn out the *Carmel HiLite* — a hard-hitting, full-color tabloid — every week, along with a sophisticated online version. The paper's adviser, Tony Willis, has a degree in journalism and experience as a reporter, rare in a field where fewer than one-third of high school journalism teachers and advisers are certified to teach the subject.

For college students interested in journalism, there are hundreds of programs to choose from, and almost as many ideas about what should be taught, and how. For decades, college-level journalism education has been undergoing a profound and controversial transformation. Many journalism programs no longer stress a broad, liberal arts education backed up with core skills courses such as reporting and news writing. Instead, many programs focus on mass-communications theory, examining how mass media work in society. Such programs prepare students not only for traditional journalism but also for careers in advertising, marketing and public relations, as well as academia.

The rapid emergence of new communications technologies has pushed journalism education in an unexpected direction. New alliances between journalism/mass communications programs and engineering/computer-science departments reflect the powerful interest in preparing students for work in cyberspace. Columbia University's School of Journalism, for example, has linked up with Columbia's engineering department to develop technologies for its new-media courses.

"High-technology is where the students see the exciting jobs," says Bill Dickinson, resident professional at the University of Kansas' William Allen White School of Journalism and Mass Communication. "The kids feel the future is on the Web." [6]

Some journalists and educators worry that the new interest in technology will deflect attention away from teaching traditional journalism techniques. Others believe the new technologies will force journalism schools to return to the basics, as journalists become conduits for ever-increasing floods of information.

"The pendulum has begun to swing back, to recognize that at the heart of all the new communication industries is journalism: how to gather, organize and prepare information," says Robert H. Giles, executive director of the Freedom Forum's Media Studies Center.

Not surprisingly, many working journalists deride much journalism education as inadequate and irrelevant. "Many of the people we get are lacking the basics," said Linda Green, city editor at *The Californian*, in Salinas. "They don't know a lead from a nut graph." [7]

As journalists and journalism educators face the challenges of the new millennium, these are some of the questions they are asking:

Are students and administrators becoming less tolerant of free speech in the student press?

In a 1997 survey of attitudes toward the First Amendment, 54 percent of Americans disagreed with the following statement: "High school students should be allowed to report controversial issues in their student newspaper without approval of school authorities." [8]

School administrators in Frederick, Md., relied on the *Hazelwood* decision when they established a review board for the newspaper at Governor Thomas

Johnson High School. The board reviews articles and advertisements that "may be offensive to the school community," and was established after Principal Joseph Heidel barred distribution of the 1997 year-end edition of the newspaper because he feared a headline might be libelous.

Before *Hazelwood*, students' First Amendment rights were protected in the Supreme Court's *Tinker v. Des Moines Independent Community School District* decision, which overturned the suspensions of several students for wearing black armbands to protest the Vietnam War. The 1969 ruling was subsequently interpreted to give broad free-speech rights to student journalists. As a result, journalism advisers used it to encourage students to cover more controversial areas of concern to young people.

"I think when I was working on my high school paper, the most controversial story I wrote was about whether Madras plaid will bleed when you wash it," Arnold-Hemlinger quips. High school newspapers now tackle edgy topics such as racial prejudice, AIDS, drug abuse, teen pregnancy, body piercing and youth violence.

Student journalists and their advisers say that censorship today often seems more a matter of whim than policy, with lines drawn in unpredictable places. Journalism adviser Cindy Dixon says she had her principal's full support when students

at Alabama's Greensboro East High School asked for permission to survey other students for a story on safe-sex practices. But when the School Board learned of a planned story criticizing the cafeteria's food, "They axed it," Dixon says. "We are getting to be very quiet, hoping they won't get wind of things ahead of time."

To stay out of trouble, advisers advise: "Don't criticize coaches or cafeteria food, and don't try to be funny."

"Humor is hard to do," says Rebecca Sipos, the journalism adviser at McLean High School in Northern Virginia. "We don't all find the same things funny, and these students are just finding their voices as writers."

Humor presents pitfalls for college journalists as well, as they negotiate the tricky political terrain of campuses where students often align

themselves with groups based on race, ethnicity, gender, religion and sexual orientation. Students at The George Washington University in Washington, D.C., have asked the student association to stop funding *Protest THIS!*, a newspaper of student humor that has "satirized domestic violence and rape and lampooned such events as the schoolyard shootings in Jonesboro, Ark." [9]

The paper sparked a protest rally attended by about 80 students when it ran mock advertisements for "Masta-Card" ("Helping Whitey Keep Us Down") and the "Asian Student Alliance," including five photos of the same young Asian man, each with a different name. ("We all look the same," said the caption.)

"I don't think the university should fund it," says James Allen Jr., head of the university's Black People's Union, "and if they keep publishing what they're publishing, I don't think it should exist."

Humorous or serious, campus coverage of race provokes intense reactions. In the mid-1990s, Eric Stern, then-editor of the *Daily Northwestern* at Northwestern University, Evanston, Ill., described the tense relations between the campus paper and minority students. Matters came to a head in October 1996, when a black student organization attempted to bar the newspaper from covering an appearance by black advocate Sister Souljah. The group had been angered by the *Daily's* coverage of her appear-

Dan Vagasky, former editor of the Bulldog Express *in Otsego, Mich., and Phillip F. Gainous, principal of Montgomery Blair High School, Silver Spring, Md., received* Courage in Student Journalism Awards *in April from the Newseum for their efforts on behalf of student-press freedom.*

The Freedom Forum/Judy G. Rolfe

Majority of Teachers Favor Press Restrictions

Among public high school teachers, more than twice as many teachers of non-journalism courses as teachers of journalism favored the Supreme Court's 1988 Hazelwood *ruling increasing principals' authority to censor student publications. The general public was much more likely than journalism teachers to agree with the decision.*

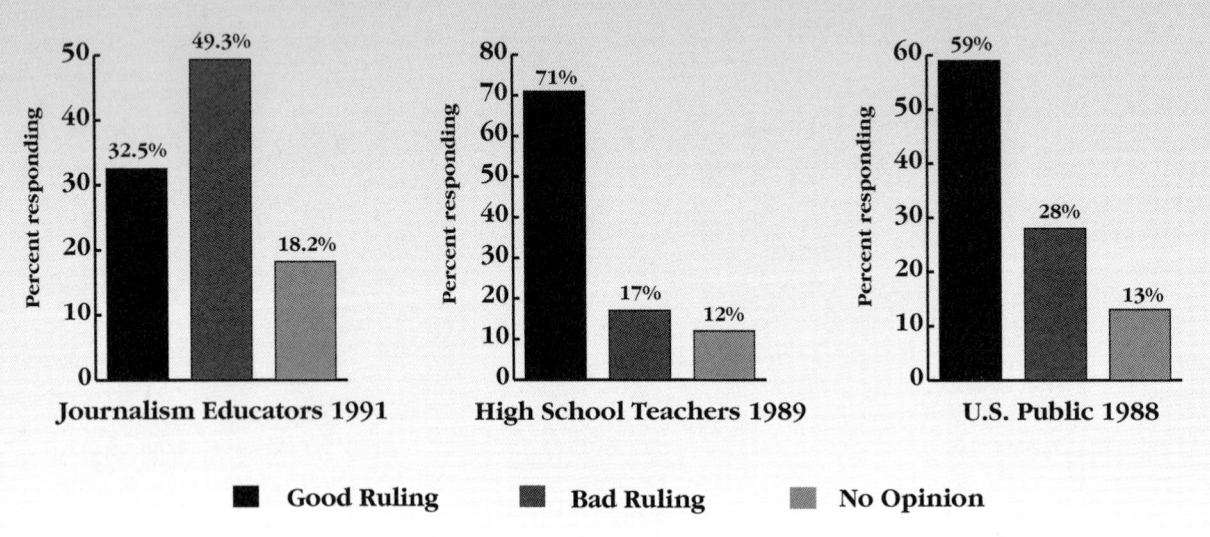

Was *Hazlewood v. Kuhlmeier* a good or bad ruling?

Journalism Educators 1991: Good Ruling 32.5%, Bad Ruling 49.3%, No Opinion 18.2%

High School Teachers 1989: Good Ruling 71%, Bad Ruling 17%, No Opinion 12%

U.S. Public 1988: Good Ruling 59%, Bad Ruling 28%, No Opinion 13%

■ Good Ruling   ■ Bad Ruling   ■ No Opinion

Source: Journalism Kids Do Better, *1994*

ance on campus three years earlier, when her anti-Semitic comments sparked several negative editorials. A reporter who managed to get into the event was denounced to the crowd as "another example of white supremacism." [10]

"Taking newspapers hostage is intended as a statement to the campus media that coverage needs to reach beyond white perspectives," Stern wrote. "It's also meant to raise awareness of legitimate complaints by black student groups about biased coverage and careless mistakes."

Administrators vary in their response to attacks on campus newspapers. At Cornell, university officials have argued that because the Review is distributed free, and because an entire press run was never burned, there is nothing to punish. "We support the right of news-papers to publish and the right for people to protest what newspapers publish," said Jacqueline Powers, a Cornell spokeswoman. [11]

First Amendment advocate Nat Hentoff blasted Cornell, arguing that "so prestigious a university might have been expected to tell the revengeful students that the best antidote to bad speech is more speech — not a match." [12]

Other institutions have responded more forcefully. Last year, for example, a student suspected of burning 1,000 copies of the *Tiger Weekly*, a conservative student paper at Louisiana State University, was charged with suspicion of theft and criminal mischief.

Student governments, frequently critical of students' coverage of their activities, occasionally cut off funding for campus publications. Last October, the student government at the State University of New York, Plattsburg, abruptly stopped payments to the local newspaper that prints the student paper in an attempt to block the distribution of a story that named a student suspected of setting fire to a campus dormitory. The local newspaper printed the edition for free.

Administrative censorship of college newspapers is relatively uncommon, however. "In general, there is very little oversight of college papers," says Kansas' Dickinson. "Universities in many cases have washed their hands of student newspapers."

And courts often have been willing to give college media considerable leeway. In February, the Virginia Supreme Court upheld the dismissal of an $850,000 defamation lawsuit filed against the *Collegiate Times* of Virginia Polytechnic University by Sharon Yeagle, a school administrator.

She had sued the newspaper in 1996 over a picture of her accompanied by a derisive, mock title. The court acknowledged that the title was "disgusting, offensive and in extremely bad taste," but said it could not be considered defamatory because no reader would believe it to be accurate. [13]

The Internet has opened up a new field for student journalism — and censorship. Hundreds of college and high school newspapers are now available online to a worldwide audience. Many observers worry that such access places school districts on shaky legal ground. "My sense is school officials are more inclined to censor online publications than traditional print publications," Goodman says. "Students are facing a lot more headaches and burdens online."

Wheeling High School in Illinois began publishing its *Spokesman On-Line* about three years ago. But administrators worry that the use of names and photos could expose students to hate mail for expressing unpopular views, or even to sexual predators who see their picture on the Internet. They are considering a proposal that would allow the full names of students to be used in reports about organized activities, such as athletic events or student competitions, because parents already know that their students are involved. But quotes from students on any other topic would require parental permission before they could be included on the Web site. And no students would be identified in photo cutlines. "I would

be devastated if a student at Wheeling was harmed by something on our site, but I do think we're being overly cautious," said newspaper adviser Susan Hathaway Tantillo. [14]

In addition to giving student journalism worldwide reach, Internet publishing quickly blurs the lines between school and non-school publications. "I think the move online may open up a whole new realm in *Hazelwood* we haven't thought through," says *Carmel HiLite* adviser Willis. "The Web site is not actually a publication of the school, so it isn't

Student newspapers are published at 79 percent of the nation's 22,785 high schools, including, clockwise from lower left, Carmel (Indiana) H.S.; Suitland H.S., Forestville, Md.; H.D. Woodson H.S., Washington, D.C.; Montgomery Blair H.S., Silver Spring, Md.; McLean (Virginia) H.S.; and Gaylesville (Alabama) H.S., which serves as a community newspaper.

clear if *Hazelwood* applies."

Candace Perkins Bowen, coordinator of the Scholastic Media Program at Kent State University, advises school administrators not to worry too much over the perceived dangers of Internet publishing. "Part of the U.S. Supreme Court's 1997 ruling on the Communications Decency Act indicated that content on the Internet is legally equivalent to the printed word, and ought to be protected in a similar way," Bowen writes. "If the

student newspaper serves as an open forum for exploring problems and issues in a responsible manner, students should be entitled to reach the wider audience that's available through the Internet." [15]

Should high schools teach journalism, and if so how?

English teacher Carol Lange holds a Kit Kat bar in one hand and a chocolate Easter bunny in the other. "What are the similarities?" Lange asks. "They're both made of chocolate," a student offers. "Right, and how might we characterize that?" Lange asks. "Are we talking about style or content?"

The students are in Lange's intensive journalistic writing (IJW) course at Thomas Jefferson High School for Science and Technology in Alexandria, Va. The candy exercise serves as a mental warm-up for comparing style and content in passages from Jane Austen and Charles Dickens. Lange's students make the leap from Kit Kat to *Pride and Prejudice* effortlessly, near the end of an academic year that ranged through literature, advertising and newspaper and magazine writing.

With no newspaper to put out, there is no scramble to meet production deadlines, no worry about offending sensitive administrators. Lange uses a tightly focused, academic approach to journalistic writing to prepare her students for the advanced placement (AP) exam in English language and composition.

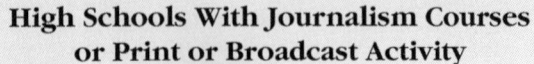

Most High Schools Offer Journalism

An overwhelming majority of the nation's 22,785 high schools offer a journalism curriculum or activity (graph at left). More than 90 percent publish yearbooks, but more than 20 percent do not have student newspapers (graph at right).

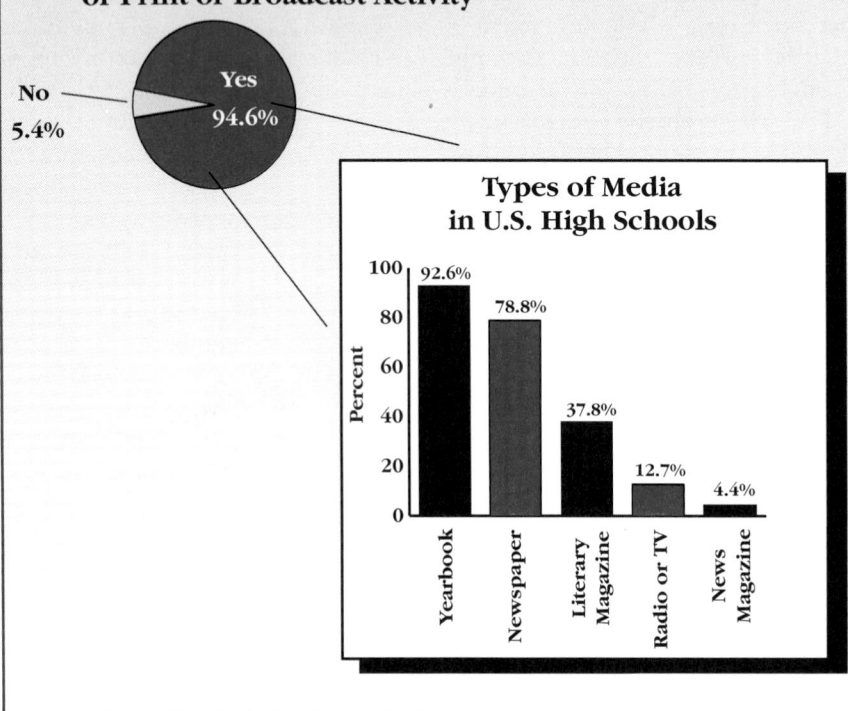

High Schools With Journalism Courses or Print or Broadcast Activity

No 5.4%
Yes 94.6%

Types of Media in U.S. High Schools

Percent

- Yearbook 92.6%
- Newspaper 78.8%
- Literary Magazine 37.8%
- Radio or TV 12.7%
- News Magazine 4.4%

Source: Journalism Kids Do Better, *1994*

---

something that newspaper production classes often have difficulty doing.

Still, there are many who feel that newspapers are the heart of high school journalism. "Putting out a high school newspaper raises First Amendment issues in a kind of in-your-face way that teaches students a lot," says former newspaper publisher Loren Ghiglione, chairman of the fledgling journalism program at Emory University in Atlanta. "It involves teamwork, it involves assuming responsibility, often for a budget, certainly for ideas and language. It's a real-world experience."

But there is little evidence that this view is widely shared by the public, by high school teachers or by school administrators.

"I have had peers, my fellow English teachers, pass the newspaper out to their classes and say, 'Your assignment is to find 50 mistakes in here.' That is really not very supportive," says Pat Graff, a longtime newspaper adviser in New Mexico who serves as the liaison between the JEA and the National Council of Teachers of English.

While few school administrators are openly hostile to journalism classes or school newspapers, current trends in curriculum development have tended to push journalism to the edge of the high school universe. Increasing the number of required English, foreign language, science and math courses leaves little room for other courses.

Even when English credit is given for a journalism course, many colleges will not accept it. The National Collegiate Athletic Association (NCAA) has been keeping journalism advisers up nights with its refusal to recognize even highly academic journalism classes as contributing toward its requirement that college athletes complete four years of high school English. "I have a very academic program," says journalism adviser Sipos. "I think my students learn how to write better than they do in English

---

The approach has been growing, although slowly, since the Dow Jones Newspaper Fund first pioneered the IJW curriculum a decade ago. It is a key way that high school journalism has moved to align itself more closely with English and language arts.

"We have a lot of journalism teachers who are not certified to teach English," says Homer Hall, president of the Journalism Education Association (JEA). "That's been a problem. We don't want to offend those teachers, many of whom are doing a great job. Still, I believe it would be best if we could all agree that journalism is English." Hall believes lack of training is a major fac-

tor in the short lifespan of most journalism advisers. "The turnover is incredible, something like three years," he says. "The best programs are the ones with advisers who have had time to build a program."

By using journalism to teach writing and analytical skills, IJW serves the needs and interests of Lange's technology-oriented students at the nationally recognized magnet school. She estimates that less than 10 of her students are considering careers in journalism. By successfully preparing them for the AP exam, Lange proves conclusively, year after year, that her course meets its academic goals,

classes. The NCAA doesn't agree; it seems to think that it's a blow-off course."*

Ten years ago, New Mexico began requiring high school students to take at least a year of communications skills. "We went and said to the state Board of Education, 'Journalism should count as communication skills,' " Graff recalls. "They said 'No, the students write, but they don't talk.' I said, 'Well, how do you suppose they know what to write about? They interview people.' I didn't get anywhere."

In poor urban districts, there isn't anything to debate, journalism is so far down on the wish-list. "I haven't even tried to get money from the school system," says Dorothy Gilliam, a former *Washington Post* columnist who heads the paper's effort to cultivate minority student journalists in the District of Columbia. *(See story, p. 498.)* "My understanding is this would not be a priority."

Students in Charmaine Turner's journalism class at H.D. Woodson High School in Washington, D.C., receive elective English credit, one credit per semester, with a maximum of two credits over their high school careers. "My students this year won't get credit if they want to do the paper next year," Turner says. "They'll have to work during lunch or after school. For them to get credit, we'd need to have an advanced journalism class. There is no such class in the system — there's no money."

Academic credit is certainly not the only, or even the best, motivator of high school journalists. Some simply seek the feeling described by Brian Yolles, editor-in-chief of the *Carmel HiLite.* "When the paper comes out, I stand in the hallway and watch people picking it up. I look to see what they read first, what they

react to — that's the dream for print journalists." Others find working on the school paper a way to establish an identity among their peers. "It's how I got my name around the school; I'm always taking pictures," says Woodson student Patrick Scott. "People say, 'Hey, take my picture, take my picture.' "

Still, the wide differences in how high schools make room for journalism reflects what journalism researcher Jack Dvorak calls "the fragility" of journalism programs. "A program is going to be just as good as its teacher/adviser," says Dvorak, a former journalism teacher. "For journalism, that's usually just one person. When you have a great person, everything is great. Then something happens, and the program falls apart."

Co-author of the 1994 book *Journalism Kids Do Better,* Dvorak has researched how well-designed journalism courses can mesh with a language-arts curriculum.

In a 1994 study, Dvorak found that at-risk Native Alaskan high school students who studied journalism and produced a newspaper as part of their English instruction showed significant gains in standardized vocabulary tests and writing skills. Early this year, Dvorak published research examining how students who took IJW courses fared on the AP English Language and Composition Examination. In May 1997, fewer than 900 IJW students took the exam, compared with about 66,500 students who had taken traditional English composition courses. The journalism students had a 72.7 percent pass rate, compared with just over 65 percent for the students who took traditional composition courses.

Supporters argue that journalism is particularly well-suited to meeting the goals of high school reform, as identified in a series of reports over the past decade. "We say we want schools that teach children to be problem-solvers, to be critical thinkers, help-

ing them to gain insight into the world," Dvorak says. "All the things we give lip service to are happening in high school journalism."

High school reform "should prepare students to succeed in a fast-paced, technologically sophisticated setting," wrote Rima Shore in a Carnegie Foundation report. "At the same time, it should foster the kind of work habits, including the ability to sustain focus and to approach new challenges, that will hold students in good stead as they move through many different work settings in their lifetimes. High school should nurture in students the habit of engagement in a broader community, preparing them for active, thoughtful participation in the democratic process, and helping them to think through ethical standards for themselves and society." [16]

But many advisers say that to meet its potential, journalism must raise the standard of teaching and advising, which will require support from school administrators. "I often say to principals, 'You would never hire a football coach who had never played the game,' " says New Mexico's Graff. " 'You would never hire a chemistry teacher who had never studied chemistry. But you're always handing over the single, most high-profile products of your school, the newspaper and the yearbook to someone who doesn't know anything about it. And then you wonder why you have problems.' "

Indeed, all too often the job of school newspaper adviser is handed to a newly hired English teacher without the clout to refuse. Sometimes, the result is serendipity. Woodson's Turner has logged 11 years as the journalism adviser, keeping her program alive in one of the most demoralized school districts in the nation. "The principal wanted a newspaper, and I didn't know how to say no," is how she got into the job. Dixon of Alabama's Greenboro East had the same experience, and found herself

Continued on p. 491

---

*The NCAA says it is planning to change its procedures, and accept English credit for journalism courses if the high school gives it.

Spreading the Word in Rural Alabama

Not surprisingly, when the First Baptist Church welcomed a new pastor in January, the story was front-page news in the *Notasulga Times*. And in another rural Alabama community, when local students fared poorly on the SAT and ACT tests, the *South Barbour News* also carried the story on page one.

What is surprising is that both papers are staffed and run by high school students. They are among 25 community monthlies serving small towns in Alabama, all started within the last five years with help from the University of Alabama's Program for Rural Services and Research. Most turn modest profits, which are reinvested in technology to improve the papers. And most are the only newspapers offering regular coverage of their communities.

"I think Notasulga had the *Universalist Herald*, back in the 1800s," says Notasulga High School Principal Robert Anderson. "The newspaper has really brought the community together, and closed a gap between the school and some people in the town, especially older people."

"The idea from the beginning was to become a real newspaper, to publish on schedule, on newsprint," says the university's Jim Rye, one of the originators of the project. "The papers cover the Town Council, the police. And they've had an impact."

It was coverage by the *Gaylesville Enterprise*, for example, which led the Town Council to adopt street names and house numbers, so the community could have 911 emergency service. "For 14- and 15-year-olds to be able to effect positive change in their communities through the newspaper, that's really something," Rye says. "That's what newspapers are all about."

The papers are not polished, especially those established within the past year. They have their share of typos and awkward sentences.

Still, Rye contends that the newspapers "have become the best writing labs you can imagine. Student work becomes public work, and it really raises the bar for the students. Having an audience has a tremendous impact on how students perceive the importance of their work."

According to a spring 1997 survey of the participating schools, the newspaper staffs represent 7 percent of the schools' enrollment, with 341 students involved overall. The newspaper staffs are 58 percent female and 53 percent African-American. Staffers report that participation in the newspaper project improved their computer skills and made them more likely to consider going on to college.

Brandon Tubbs, a freshman journalism major at the University of Alabama, is the former editor-in-chief of *The Oakman Times*, one of the first papers produced by the project. The Times "was the one thing I learned the most from, and that includes the classes I'm taking now at the university," he says. "I'm taking stuff now, and I think, I've been there and done that."

Tubbs, whose career plans in high school originally had him heading to veterinary school, now plans to graduate from Alabama "with the best grades possible, go on out in the real world and work my way up the ranks in the profession, and be an editor and publisher of a newspaper in the South."

Like several graduates of the newspaper project, Tubbs now works at the rural services office at the University of Alabama while pursuing his journalism studies. One of his jobs is to help new high schools joining the project get their newspapers up and running.

At first, Rye says, administrators at the various high schools needed some convincing to sign on to the project. "Alabama is really looking to the standardized tests, to the Stanford 9, that's what schools are judged by," Rye says. "In that climate, when you tell a principal, 'You're going to publish a community newspaper,' they tend to say, 'No, our test scores are down, we have to hit the books.' "

But now, he says, most administrators are supportive. When the English teacher in Notasulga retired, Rye says, "The principal told me, 'I'm not hiring an English teacher, I'm hiring a newspaper teacher who also is going to teach English.' Kind of a twist on the old Alabama joke, 'I'm hiring a football coach who also teaches social studies.' "

"What it has done for writing skills in the school is beautiful," Anderson says.

Rye is hoping the Alabama project can be expanded to other areas of the rural South. "The newspapers have blurred the boundaries between the schools and their communities. They have become powerful demonstrations of the capacities of the students — they are economically viable, they are incredibly important for the town and they've had tremendous impact on the schools."

The University of Alabama's Program for Rural Services and Research brings journalism to small communities.

Pacers Photography

Continued from p. 489

"bitten by the journalism bug."

But for every Dixon or Turner, there are uncounted other advisers who never get "bitten." "There are some teachers who just don't want to cause trouble, and they produce boring things," Arnold-Hemlinger says. "And then there are the ones who are too hands-off, and that's dangerous, like handing the kids the keys to the car without giving them a driving lesson."

Several states, notably Indiana and Ohio, have fairly stiff requirements for journalism teachers — and turn out some of the best high school journalism in the country. But in Ohio, the certification requirements are being eliminated. The new system will allow teachers holding language-arts licenses to teach journalism, speech, theater or traditional English. Education students seeking the license will have to take a course in press law, but no other journalism courses will be required. Hall of the JEA believes broad language-arts licensure will eventually become a nationwide standard. "We need to make sure we don't get left behind," he says.

Is journalism education keeping pace with new technologies?

Five years ago, American University integrated computer skills into every level of journalism instruction. A state-of-the-art computer lab was constructed, with Internet access at every terminal. That was the easy part.

"Suddenly, the faculty had to learn computer skills, and use them. It created a real division," says Wendy Williams, an assistant journalism professor. "When I came to AU nine years ago, I was the first faculty member to come from a newspaper with a computer system. Some of the older members decided they'd rather not make that change, and they went into retirement a little earlier."

Even those who embraced new technology have struggled to keep up, Williams says. Sometimes, they must even ask their students for help. "I had to tell my students, 'I'm not very adept with Quark,' " Williams says. "Two or three of the students in the class are adept, and I pulled them aside, and said, 'For this part of the course, you are the teachers.' Most students feel empowered. But some faculty have trouble with it."

Williams sees AU's emphasis on computer skills — from how to dig in a database to designing a home page — as crucial to students, especially given the tight journalism job market. "A lot of our graduates are getting jobs because they have higher-level computer skills than people inside the news organizations," Williams says. "We give them the basic journalistic skills, but the computer skills are often what gets them in the door."

According to a 1996 survey by the Roper Center at the University of Connecticut, 75 percent of newsroom recruiters and supervisors rated computer-research skills as "somewhat" or "very important." Among journalists hired within the last 10 years, 86 percent said it was "very important" for journalism-education programs to teach students how to use computers for communication and research. Yet highlighting the conflicting attitudes toward new technologies, 56 percent of the journalists surveyed described themselves as "enthusiastic" about the technological changes in the industry, while 54 percent described themselves as feeling "threatened" by them. [17]

Journalism educators at the college level share the combination of enthusiasm and fear. "We're in a trap," says Professor Maurine Beasley of the University of Maryland, College Park. "We want to teach students to think critically, to gather information, to analyze it, to write well. But employers say they want people who know software, who can design a Web page, who can use databases. Most journalism programs are not set up to do that."

The number of online daily newspapers has tripled in the past year, to about 175. Just two years ago, researchers Gerald M. Kosicki of Ohio State University and Lee Becker of the University of Georgia found that among 1996 graduates of journalism and mass-communications programs, 20 students, or just under 1 percent, took jobs in online publishing. Kosicki and Becker note that the number, while small, represents a fourfold increase over the five graduates who reported taking such jobs in 1995. [18] By now, given the explosion of Web-related journalism products, high-tech jobs are probably grabbing a much bigger share of freshly minted J-school grads.

"The kids feel the future is on the Web, that news isn't going to be written the same way," says Dickinson of the University of Kansas. "The inverted pyramid, objectivity — these things are all being discredited by cyberspace geeks."

But many educators worry that poor and minority students may find themselves handicapped at the college level by lack of computer experience. According to a recent report in *Science* magazine, 73 percent of white students in the United States have home computers, compared with 32 percent of black students. The study also found that white students without a home computer are more likely than black students to go elsewhere to access the Internet. [19]

Barbara Hines, a journalism professor at predominantly black Howard University, says that many entering students, including those from the inner city, have considerable computer skills. "We're seeing kids who have had access in high school, middle school even elementary school," Howard says. "Some people are saying that particularly in the inner-city communities, young people don't have the access to new technology. But we are also seeing all kinds of programs to address that."

"I think a lot of people in journalism education are worried about technology, but I see it as an opportunity," says John Pavlik, director of the Center for New Media at Columbia. "Journalism education has an opportunity to take a leadership role. After all, the Web got its start in academia. We led the way, but a lot of us were asleep at the wheel when it came to seeing how it might be used by everybody else."

Pavlik argues that students, unhampered by the one-medium-at-a-time mentality that divides journalism into print, radio and broadcast, are the perfect guides to take the industry into the era of "convergence," when technology allows reporters to tell stories using text, graphics, still photos and video all at once, while providing links to related stories and information, giving consumers the freedom to explore just the aspects of a story that interest them.

"We don't need to be hamstrung by the constraints of the old technologies," Pavlik says. "We can go back to the basics of good storytelling." ∎

BACKGROUND

Educating Journalists

Three men are generally considered the "fathers" of journalism education: Willard G. Bleyer, who launched journalism education at the University of Wisconsin; Walter Williams, who established the University of Missouri School of Journalism; and Joseph Pulitzer, who endowed the School of Journalism at Columbia University in New York City. [20]

All three "looked beyond the immediate goal of educating journalists and improving newspapers. The larger goal to which they aspired was to produce a more-informed citizenry through better journalism," writes journalism educator Betty Medsger. [21]

But improving the image of journalists, then considered an unruly, poorly educated lot, was also part of the program. Pulitzer initially had wanted to start his program at Harvard University, but college officials felt it would attract too many undesirables.

The first college-level program for aspiring journalists was established in 1869 at Washington College, now Washington and Lee University, in Lexington, Va. "We look upon this action as a very important step toward raising American journalism from the slough of venality, corruption and party subserviency into which it has too notoriously fallen to the high position it should occupy," wrote John Plaxton, a member of the Nashville Typographical Union, at the time.

Bleyer was an early supporter of accreditation for journalism programs and the guiding force behind what is now the Accrediting Council on Education in Journalism and Mass Communications. To many observers, its birth in 1947 marked the rise of journalism as an academic discipline.

Mass-Communications Studies

In the 1950s, the emergence of mass-communications studies created another new turning point for journalism education. Wilbur Schramm, who headed the journalism program at the University of Iowa shortly after World War II, went on to establish institutes of communication research at the University of Illinois and Stanford University. It was Schramm who brokered what Medsger terms "an institutional marriage" between journalism and mass-communications studies, a develop-

ment seen by some as terribly misguided, and by others as inevitable.

Schramm and his followers, seeking the academic respectability bestowed by a doctoral degree, pushed journalism education away from the practical aspects of the craft and toward a social-science view of mass communications. Writing in 1943, Schramm described the traditional journalism school as "a group of teachers and students, sitting on the periphery of the university, playing with their toys, putting together the picture of who, what, where and when in the first paragraph." Schramm's goal, in contrast, was to study how mass-media institutions function in society, and how they affect people.

Gradually, the requirement that doctoral students in communication studies have journalism experience, preferably in newspapers, was dropped. As a result, such experience is no longer a prerequisite for teaching in journalism programs. Some 17 percent of faculty members in journalism programs today do not have professional journalism experience.

Working journalists tend to dismiss doctorate-holding professors who have never scrambled to nail down a late-breaking story. That attitude can create skepticism on the part of hiring editors and recruiters as to how well-trained J-school graduates really are. Journalism graduates are "absolutely not" better prepared than other recent college graduates, says Sheila Rule, senior manager of reporter recruiting for *The New York Times*.

Stanley Allison, hiring editor and internship director at the *Los Angeles Times,* says of recent interns from journalism programs, "I don't know if these kids always know how to handle a quote. Some of them think if it has slang, or might embarrass a person, then you need to clean that up. Or you can just say what you think they meant, as a quote."

Despite the doubts, journalism

Continued on p. 494

Chronology

1700s *The student press debuts early in the new nation's history.*

1777
The first student newspaper in the United States, Students' Gazette, is published on June 11 at the William Penn Charter School in Philadelphia.

1860s *Journalism joins academia.*

1869
The first college-level program for would-be journalists is established at Washington College, now Washington and Lee University, in Lexington, Va. The move is hailed as a step toward "raising American journalism from the slough of venality, corruption and party subserviency."

1920s *Scholastic journalism gets organized.*

1921
National Scholastic Press Association established in Minneapolis, Minn.

1924
The Journalism Education Association is founded to represent journalism teachers and advisers nationwide, while the Columbia Scholastic Press Association is launched in the New York metropolitan area.

1926
The Quill and Scroll Society is established by Gallup Poll founder George H. Gallup to recognize individual student achievement in scholastic journalism.

1960s-1970s *The Supreme Court recognizes free-speech rights for public school students, and student journalists respond with coverage of controversial issues.*

1969
The Supreme Court rules in *Tinker v. Des Moines Independent Community School District* that the constitutional rights of students in Des Moines, Iowa, had been violated when they were suspended for wearing black armbands to protest the Vietnam War.

1974
The Commission of Inquiry into High School Journalism finds that despite the protections of the *Tinker* decision, student journalists still face high levels of censorship. In the same year, the Student Press Law Center is founded to educate high school and college students about their First Amendment rights.

1978
The American Society of Newspaper Editors (ASNE) finds that only 4 percent of the journalists at daily papers are members of ethnic minorities and pledges to increase minority newsroom staffing to equal the U.S. minority population level by the year 2000.

1980s *Student free-speech rights are sharply limited by the Supreme Court. High school journalism struggles to move beyond its trade-school image.*

1984
The National Council of Teachers of English passes a resolution in favor of schools granting English credit for appropriately ???designed journalism classes.

Jan. 13, 1988
The Supreme Court rules in *Hazelwood School District v. Kuhlmeier* that school officials can censor student expression when such censorship is "reasonably related to legitimate pedagogical concerns."

1990s *The impact of the Hazelwood decision begins to be debated.*

Nov. 14, 1997
Kentucky District Judge Joseph M. Hood relies heavily on the Supreme Court's 1988 *Hazelwood* ruling in upholding Kentucky State University administrators who refused to release the school's 1994 yearbook.

February 1998
Virginia Supreme Court upholds the dismissal of an $850,000 defamation suit against Virginia Polytechnic University's *Collegiate Times* by a school administrator.

October 1998
The ASNE is expected to discuss adopting a new, scaled-down diversity goal of 20 percent minority representation by 2010.

The Long Road to Newsroom Diversity

Twenty years ago, the American Society of Newspaper Editors (ASNE) looked out into the nation's newsrooms and saw a sea of white faces: Only 4 percent of the journalists at daily newspapers were members of ethnic minorities — just 1,700 out of 43,000 newsroom employees.

Following that first-ever annual newsroom employment census, the ASNE in 1978 adopted what then seemed an ambitious but reachable goal: to increase minority staffing in newsrooms to a level equivalent to the U.S. minority population by the year 2000.

But as the self-imposed deadline approaches, ASNE is preparing to acknowledge that the goal is unattainable. The organization's 1998 census found that the minority newsroom work force is only 11.5 percent. While that's an improvement over 1978, it is less than half the minority population of the U.S., which is estimated at about 26 percent. About 6,300 U.S. journalists at daily newspapers are members of ethnic minorities, out of a total newsroom work force of 54,700.

Not only has progress been slower than the organization had hoped, but the nation's ethnic makeup has been changing more rapidly than the ASNE expected. In 1978, ASNE estimated that minorities would make up 15 percent of the nation's population by the year 2000, not 26 percent.

So in October, when ASNE's board members meet in Miami, they will discuss adopting a new, scaled-down diversity goal of 20 percent minority representation by 2010, with a secondary goal of achieving "parity with local communities as soon as possible."

The proposal will certainly encounter opposition. A. Stephen Monteil, president of the Maynard Institute for Journalism Education, is part of a group of ASNE members who will push for a more ambitious set of goals. "There's a widespread sense of diversity fatigue," Monteil said. "The need is for the passion or the will to be reignited." But Rick Rodriguez, managing editor of the *Sacramento Bee* and a member of ASNE's board, warned that "an unrealistic goal is a disincentive to editors and publishers."[1]

Here is the ASNE's draft statement on diversity:

"Newsroom diversity is essential to the newspaper's responsibility in a democratic society and success in the marketplace. To accurately and sensitively cover the community, newsroom staffs must reflect society as a whole. The newsroom should be a place in which all employees contribute their full potential, regardless of their race, ethnicity, color, age, gender, sexual orientation, physical disability or other defining characteristic.

"To drive the quest for diversity and inclusion in the workplace, the American Society of Newspaper Editors will:

• Commit a significant portion of the Society's energy and resources to fostering newsroom diversity.

• Advocate diversity in content as a journalistic core value.

• Encourage and assist all newspapers to have minority journalists representation, to increase representation of journalists of color to reach 20 percent industrywide by 2010, and to achieve parity with local communities as soon as possible.

Monitor year by year the employment of Asian Americans, blacks, Native Americans and Hispanics in the newsroom.

Encourage collaboration on diversity among various groups."

---

[1] Quoted in *The New York Times*, April 6, 1998

Continued from p. 492
seems safely ensconced in academia. The number of journalism and mass-communications programs grew from 394 in 1988 to 449 in 1996, when total enrollment was almost 150,000 students, the highest number since 1991.

High School Struggles

At the high school level, however, journalism often struggles at the margins. "High school journalism started in the vocational programs," notes the NAA's Arnold-Hemlinger. "The kids learned how to set type. Then it became the typing teacher's job. Because it has always been tied to a technology, high school journalism has always had that dual mission, and that dual identity, to overcome."

When Arnold-Hemlinger first taught high school journalism, "I was all fired up," she says. "I thought I'd get the best and the brightest. I was teaching at a small high school in Minnesota, and the kids I was getting were barely literate. I asked the principal, and he told me, 'We always put the kids who flunked out of English into journalism.'"

The uneven quality of journalism programs makes it harder for even the best programs to win academic respectability. "In a nationwide survey, we found only 28 percent of teachers had state certification to teach journalism," Dvorak says. "If the situation were the same in math or science, we'd have an uproar from parents and communities." What exactly that 28 percent of certified teachers knows about journalism is also far from clear, since almost half of the states do not require journalism educators to take any journalism courses.

High school journalism teachers find different ways to meet the dual burden of teaching and producing a publication. At Carmel High School, students must take a two-semester introductory journalism class before they can work on the newspaper. That means that adviser Tony Willis is not teaching the basics of the inverted pyramid while trying to get the paper out. With 21 news staffers out of a student body of 3,000, he can be sure that his staff is interested in journalism. "The school is very academically oriented," says Willis. "There are a lot of excellent programs here across the board, a real culture of excellence. No newspaper staff wants to do less than the previous year."

But for poor inner-city schools, just getting the paper out can become overwhelming. Carol Merrill, an English teacher at West Philadelphia High School, struggled for five years to help her students put out *Quest*, a student-produced community newspaper.

Merrill still believes in the project. "For one student in particular, this was his saving grace. He learned to speak to people, to develop an idea, to write. It changed how he viewed himself." But Merrill is tired, and this year she took a break.

"When we started, most of the students were college-bound, and they were interested in the paper," Merrill says. Then the school was reorganized in small learning communities, and Merrill had to draw her staff from a population of students not necessarily inclined toward journalism. "The last three years, my students had problems with reading and writing," she says. "It was good exposure for them, but it was harder." The number of annual issues dropped from four to three, and now, with a new adviser, to one.

"It's a Catch-22," says Bowen of the struggle to strengthen journalism programs. "We need good, viable programs, so we can convince state departments of education that it's important. Then we have to convince the universities to train the teachers, so we can have good viable programs."

Few Minorities Attracted to Journalism

Most high school journalism students and advisers are white. Only about 12 percent of the nation's Hispanic and African-American students participate in journalism.

Percentage of:	All Students	Journalists	Advisers
White	72.6%	80.6%	90%
Hispanic	10	6.5	2.1
African-American	10	5.6	1.2
Asian-American	4.6	5.3	1.5
Native American	1.6	1	1

Note: Numbers do not total 100 percent due to rounding or no answer given.

Source: Death By Cheeseburger: High School Journalism in the 1990s and Beyond, *1994; Journalism Education Association, 1992*

Supreme Court Action

The idea that the free-speech protections embodied by the Bill of Rights should be extended, within limits, to high school students did not become case law until 1969, when the Supreme Court ruled in *Tinker v. Des Moines Independent Community School District*. The court held that school officials could only censor student expression when "material and substantial disruption of school activities or invasion of the rights of other students" could be proven. "Neither students nor teachers shed their constitutional rights to freedom of speech or expression at the schoolhouse gate," wrote Justice Abe Fortas.

From 1969-88, Tinker factored into several lower-court decisions involving high school publications. But in 1988, a reconstituted court gave public school administrators greater censorship power in *Hazelwood School District v. Kuhlmeier.* In May 1983, Principal Robert Reynolds decided that a story about three Hazelwood East High School students who became pregnant was inappropriate, and that the girls' identities had not been adequately protected. Reynolds also felt that a story on the impact of divorce on students was unfair because it quoted a student's criticism of her father but failed to include a response from the father. To eliminate the offending articles, Reynolds excised two full pages of the newspaper, eliminating four other articles on the pages along with the censored articles.

It took the case five years to reach the Supreme Court. In its 5-3 decision, the high court cited Fortas' "schoolhouse gate" comment but modified it with reference to a 1986 case, *Bethel School District No. 403 v. Fraser*, in which the court upheld the district's right to suspend a student for making a lewd campaign speech. The court ruled in *Bethel* that "A school need not tolerate student speech that is inconsistent with its basic educational mission."

The *Hazelwood* decision empowered schools to censor any forms of expression deemed "ungrammatical, poorly written, inadequately researched, biased or prejudiced, vulgar or profane, or unsuitable for immature audiences," or any expression that advocated "conduct otherwise inconsistent with the shared values of a civilized social order."

High school advisers today, while generally professing a preference for the good, old, *Tinker* days, often report that when *Hazelwood* is applied in the context of a consistent policy rather than at an administrator's whim, it does not interfere with the development of a strong newspaper.

Meanwhile, college media are wondering if the strictures of *Hazelwood* are about to "trickle up" to campus newspapers and radio stations, which have long operated within the free-speech culture enjoyed by the mainstream press. On Nov. 14, 1997, Judge Hood upheld the university officials who had confiscated the 1994 KSU yearbook.

The yearbook editor and another student sued, claiming the administration had abridged their First Amendment right to free speech. Hood's decision quoted from *Hazelwood*: "A school must be able to set high standards for the student speech that is disseminated under its auspices, and may refuse to disseminate student speech that does not meet those standards." ∎

CURRENT SITUATION

State, Local Efforts

Five states give student journalists press freedoms modeled on the earlier *Tinker* decision: California, Massachusetts, Iowa, Colorado and Kansas. California's law predates *Hazelwood*; the others were passed following the 1988 decision. A number of local school districts also have adopted policies that are more liberal than the standard set by *Hazelwood*.

However, a recent effort to pass such a law in Illinois failed late last year after last-minute lobbying by the School Management Alliance, a coalition of school boards and school administrators. The bill had passed both houses of the Illinois General Assembly, and a veto by Republican Gov. Jim Edgar had been overridden by the House. But a Senate override vote was canceled at the last minute, after polling indicated the override would fail as senators' support wavered under an avalanche of alliance faxes and phone calls.

In Kansas, no action was taken this session on a bill in the Senate to amend the state's Freedom of Student Expression law to give school officials new censorship power. "It wouldn't be *Hazelwood*, but it would be a trimming back from what they have now," says JEA President Hall, a newspaper adviser at Kirkwood High School in Missouri.

At the school-district level, strong support of student free-speech rights can collapse in the face of controversy. In Montgomery County, Md., an 18-month-old battle over a student-produced television program that included a panel discussion of same-sex marriage resulted in a new county policy that makes it easier for administrators to censor student TV productions and publications.

After *Hazelwood*, says the Student Press Law Center's Goodman, the momentum to strengthen student press rights at the state level "was very strong, but it has diminished somewhat." Still, he believes that student journalists soon may benefit from a broader political alliance working in their favor.

"This was initially perceived as a lib-eral-conservative issue," Goodman says. "That's ludicrous. As conservatives see their perspectives being silenced in the scholastic press, this is slowly becoming something more bipartisan."

Meanwhile in Missouri, home of the *Hazelwood* case, Hall of the JEA takes part in an annual ritual: drumming up support for a long-shot bill to give back to Missouri students the rights they lost in 1988. "I think we're making some headway," Hall says. "*The Post-Dispatch* and the *Kansas City Star* have come out editorially in favor — at least there's progress there."

Dismal Economics

The fundamental issues facing college journalism programs are clearly evident in the dismal economics facing journalism graduates. In 1995, the average starting salary for journalists was $20,154, making new journalists the lowest-paid college-educated people entering the work force. More than 20 percent of all new journalists under age 25 earned below $15,000. Perhaps most disturbing, at least for journalism educators, is the finding that holders of undergraduate journalism degrees are more likely than other new newsroom employees to earn less than $20,000 a year. [22]

"There are so many small dailies and weeklies in this country that are still paying just above the minimum wage," says Howard University's Hines. "These kids want to know where the dollars are. They hear the number $20,000, and they laugh, especially when they have classmates in advertising who are hearing the number $33,000, plus $3,000 hiring bonus, plus we'll pay you to move.'"

"For reporters, part of the pay is supposed to be the psychic reward of the byline," Gilliam says. "So there's an additional issue for minori-

Continued on p. 499

At Issue:

Should would-be journalists pursue undergraduate degrees in journalism?

DEAN MILLS

Dean, University of Missouri School of Journalism

WRITTEN FOR THE CQ RESEARCHER, MAY 1998

d*o you need a journalism education to become a journalist? No, as thousands of successful journalists have shown. Will a good journalism education help you become a good journalist? Of course, as thousands of other journalists have shown — many of whom might not have entered the field without the encouragement and support they got from dedicated journalism faculty.

Some of the sillier, but alas persistent, critics of journalism education cherish a false dichotomy. They argue that students should get a "good liberal arts education" instead of taking a journalism degree. They are wrong, whether the degree in question is a bachelor's degree or a professional master's degree.

A bachelor's degree in journalism at all accredited schools is not something chosen instead of a liberal arts degree. It is a liberal arts degree, and one of the best. Journalism students take 75 percent of their course work outside the journalism school. And that non-journalism course work is often more coherently structured and more rigorous than that required of students in other liberal arts fields. What's more, most journalism courses require students to find, analyze, organize and communicate information and ideas.

Journalism students in a rigorous program spend more time on core, liberal learning activities than students in any other major. Other journalism courses, whether about the history, law or institutions of journalism, deepen students' understanding of one of the most powerful forces in the modern world, an understanding that could benefit any citizen.

Journalism education serves the cause of democracy as well as the students it educates, attracting a wide range of students into the field. The world's democracies need skilled, thoughtful journalists from a wide spectrum of economic, ethnic and social backgrounds. Good journalism schools recruit and educate just such people.

The master's degree in journalism has also never prevented a student from getting "a good liberal arts education." The master's adds work in journalism to an educational portfolio that already includes four years of liberal arts and sciences. It is an efficient way for the degree holder to learn the skills, traditions and ethics of the craft.

Bachelor's and master's programs are also beneficial when graduates apply for jobs. Smaller news organizations — where most recent graduates get their first jobs — hire people who can do the job. Journalism graduates can, and do.

DOUG RAMSEY

Senior Vice President, Foundation for American Communications; former newspaper and broadcast journalist

WRITTEN FOR THE CQ RESEARCHER, MAY 1998

u*ndergraduates should major in substantive fields that will equip them with analytical minds they can employ to help people understand issues that affect their lives. It does not take four years to obtain the craft skills of journalism.

Journalism schools respond to what they think their market demands. They see their market as editors and news directors who want a steady supply of young people trained in the processes of newspapers or broadcasting. Their true market is the consumer of news, the reader, viewer and listener who wants to understand the issues that influence his life. The training in craft and process that fills the curricula of most undergraduate schools of journalism or communications does little to prepare a student to analyze, understand and report on those issues.

Undergraduate journalism schools should be abolished or absorbed into institutions teaching bodies of academic knowledge that shape minds into critical instruments able to handle complex problems. The rigors of education in history, philosophy, science or economics shape a mind for analytical thinking. An understanding of page layout or videotape editing does not. If students learn to think, writing well for publication or air will follow with a reasonable amount of guidance.

Technology is delivering floods of information at increasing rates. A journalist must be able to examine a mass of information, absorb it, analyze it, subject it to critical examination and ask himself and his sources the right questions. He may then be able to tell with clarity what it means, making the information useful to his audience. Too often, journalists do not ask the right questions because, apart from how intelligent they may be, they do not have the intellectual tools to understand the story they are reporting.

If schools teach production and process techniques, they should keep them at a minimum. The basic principles of accuracy, fairness and balance do not require a four-year curriculum. A reasonably intelligent person can learn the nuts and bolts of journalism in about six weeks. Among the best reporters I ever hired were a lawyer, a medical doctor and a historian. None had journalism experience, but each had a keen, critical intelligence and a passion for issues and public affairs. After a few weeks of on-the-job training and a certain amount of fumbling around, each became a superb reporter.

The Washington Post Lends a Hand

Patrick Scott ponders a blackboard crammed with story and photo assignments for *The Insider*, the school newspaper at Washington's H.D. Woodson High School. "We're not shooting baseball because they're not sure they're going to have a season," Scott says. It's a familiar problem at Woodson. A few months ago, the paper ran a front-page story about the school's struggling swim team, which hopes to survive despite having no pool, no funds and no meets.

Scott and other Woodson journalism students are familiar with the problem: Last year, *The Insider* didn't publish a single issue, for similar reasons: no funds, no camera, no film, not enough computers. "We wrote stories, but they didn't get published," says Mirena Heigh, 17. But this year, the newspaper is having a fine season: With substantial financial and volunteer assistance from *The Washington Post, The Insider* is publishing five issues — four more than any other high school in the financially strapped city.

The Insider is one beneficiary of a high-profile new commitment by the Post to finding and nurturing local journalism talent among minority teenagers in the region. Nationally, newspapers offer varying levels of assistance to high school journalists. Many run regular youth pages, made up of articles written by local teens. Youth editors sometimes work closely with the writers. Some papers, like the Post, offer free or reduced-price printing to high school publications, and some welcome high school advisers into their newsrooms for training. But there is general agreement that the industry doesn't do enough. "Newspapers are starting to pay attention, but it may be too little too late," says Mary Arnold-Hemlinger, who helps the Newspaper Association of American set up scholastic journalism projects for minorities.

Dorothy Gilliam, a reporter and columnist at the Post for more than 20 years, is now working full time to direct its new Young Journalists' Development Project. At Woodson, the Post has donated photographic equipment, computers, a fax machine and other materials to *The Insider*. The newspaper also matched a $2,500 grant from the American Society of Newspaper Editors (ASNE) and the Freedom Forum to purchase printers and software. And 60 newsroom employees have volunteered to work with the students on putting out the newspaper.

"We're keeping an eye out for six to eight bright kids to put into the University of Maryland 'boot camp' this summer," Gilliam says. The two-week session for high school students is sponsored by the university and the National Association of Black Journalists. "Some will go on to college, some will go back to their high school newspaper," she says. "We're hoping it will give us a way to keep in touch with bright, local students." The long-term goal is to help a few of those students eventually make it to the Post.

Woodson was selected for the project in large part because of Charmaine Turner, Woodson's veteran journalism adviser. For Turner, the newspaper is both a way for her to find and nurture special students, and an important voice for the school community. "Every year, there's always at least one talented student who gets motivated by the paper," Turner says.

But if Gilliam and the Post are looking for future interns, Turner has more modest goals. Almost 60 percent of Woodson students tested below average in reading on the spring 1997 Stanford 9 Achievement Test, and more than 98 percent tested below basic in math. "Yes, journalism is a way to teach writing," Turner says. "But first you need advanced grammar and experience with other kinds of writing. Our kids don't get that. I have kids who can't write a sentence come to me and want to be on the paper, and I take them. Because I won't close my door on anybody."

The Insider has published stories on a student father who is raising his young daughter, a recent shooting outside the school and persistent problems with broken escalators, bathrooms and lockers. But it has also celebrated school life with front-page spreads on homecoming week, athletic victories and a 25th reunion for alumni.

The Post is printing *The Insider* and papers at two other suburban Maryland schools free this academic year. Students from all three newspapers attended a four-hour workshop at the newspaper in January.

Gilliam says the transition from columnist to director of the development project was made easier by her own strong feelings about the sorry state of high school journalism in the nation's capital. "As we were beginning to put this together, I was continuing to write my column, and doing the research for this project with my left hand — and I was getting more and more outraged. So when the time came to switch full time to this, I was ready."

The Young Journalists Development Project has other facets. The Post is providing primary financial aid for two-dozen high school journalists who have been attending Saturday workshops sponsored by the Washington Association of Black Journalists. At the college level, *The Washington Post* Semester will be offered in fall 1998 at the University of Maryland, and then in spring 1999 at Howard University. Post reporters, editors, photographers and others will team-teach a for-credit course for upper-level undergraduate and graduate students.

"Newspapers are not doing enough to bring in and retain minorities," Gilliam says. "Having a full-time director represents a substantial commitment by the Post. It's the first time they have done something like this."

Continued from p. 496

ties, in that given the coverage of their communities, the reality is that in many minority communities journalism has a negative value, so that psychic payoff isn't there."

However, the Roper survey found that minorities entering journalism are faring better in some regards than whites. For example, 29 percent of the new ethnic-minority journalists, defined as those entering the profession within the past 10 years, work at large dailies, which offer the highest-paying entry-level jobs in the industry. Among new journalists at large dailies, 37 percent are ethnic minorities. And a larger percentage of new minority journalists are making more money than whites: 7 percent of whites make less than $15,000 a year, but only 1 percent of minorities earn at that level; and while 9 percent of whites make more than $50,000, 21 percent of ethnic minorities earn above that amount. [23]

Despite the generally low pay, the number of journalism programs is growing. Giles of the Media Studies Center says that the current roster of 105 accredited journalism programs has grown by 20 in the past few years. "There is a real unevenness in the quality of schools," says Giles, who is also president of the accrediting council. "In my view, some of the accredited schools don't represent a quality program. We should be able to guarantee quality."

In 1997, journalism programs awarded 32,150 undergraduate degrees and 3,600 graduate degrees. But only 20 percent of the new grads wound up at newspapers, magazines, radio or television stations; about 12 percent landed in public relations and advertising. [24]

At many J-schools, including highly regarded Medill at Northwestern, courses in marketing, public relations and advertising now draw more students than journalism. "The question

is whether you will see [only] a few traditional schools, like Columbia, Missouri and, I trust, Maryland, that stand alone from the trend toward consolidation with the communication department," Beasley says. ■

OUTLOOK

Impact of Internet

The rise of the Internet is opening the door to a creative explosion among high school and college newspapers, with the best online student papers exceeding professional standards.

Some observers are hoping that as computers with Internet links become universally available in schools one of the constant killers of publications in poor schools — the high cost of printing — will gradually be eliminated. In a 1993 survey of 19 schools where newspapers ceased production, 10 cited a lack of funds for production as a primary reason. Printing expenses often eat up about 50 percent of the annual budget for high school papers. [25]

By fall 1997, 78 percent of U.S. public schools were connected to the Internet. Among schools in low-income areas or with more than 50 percent minority enrollment, 63 percent had Internet access, according to the Department of Education. The agency projects that by 2000 fully 95 percent of all schools — including 91 percent of poor and minority schools — will be, hooked up to the Web. [26]

But according to Richard Holden of the Dow Jones Newspaper Fund, these figures are misleading. "You go to some high schools, in Newark or Camden [N.J.], and they may be wired," he says, "but it's all in a locked room open one

hour a day. The students aren't getting the same exposure as the ones who have computers at home."

Nevertheless, computers are already luring students to newspaper staffs who ordinarily wouldn't be interested. Terrance Dennis, a sophomore at Woodson, has learned to use Quark Express, a popular publishing program, as part of the newspaper project at Woodson. "That's why I like it. I like computers," says Dennis. "I don't have one at home. I have two or three years here to really get good at it." "One wonderful thing about a computer is, it doesn't see what color you are," says Howard's Hines. "Kids can go out on the Web and develop their voice." The opportunity may exist to make the newspaper a truly interdisciplinary, community-building project, bringing together the computer geeks and the campus newshounds, the shutter-bugs and the writerly recluses.

But such an optimistic vision will require a much deeper commitment from the news industry toward supporting the student press. "The industry really hasn't done enough," Hines says. "It's a relatively recent phenomenon that they are starting to do stuff for kids, particularly minorities."

If there is a bright spot for minority students, it's that talented, young, minority journalists are targeted early and have no trouble landing internships at top newspapers, Holden says. The problem comes in the second tier of newspapers, and the second tier of students. "A lot of editors are eager to have minority interns," he says. "So they hire one, and the intern winds up in some small town with no other minorities, and they might have a great experience and learn a lot, but they're not going to go back there to work. It's a difficult issue to resolve."

The newspaper fund is trying to deepen the pool of available minority talent. "Out of 117 [historically black colleges and universities], 105 offer journalism programs," Holden says. Below the top tier of schools like Howard and Grambling, "There's an issue of quality. Even if they have good students, quite honestly, they don't have the faculty. The students might have more talent than the professors. We've had an increase in applications, but the test scores are so low."

Holden says the news industry needs to do more to improve the journalism programs at historically black institutions. "A lot of people in the industry seem to think they can send someone to a campus for a week to teach a little seminar, and that's going to make a difference. That's unrealistic," Holden says. "You need at least a semester to raise the level of language skills. But no [newspaper] wants to let someone go for that long." ■

Susan Phillips is a freelance writer in Washington, D.C.

Notes

[1] Quoted in *The Kalamazoo Gazette*, Jan. 19, 1998.

[2] *Student Press Law Center Report*, fall 1997.

[3] *SPLC News Flash*, June 27, 1997.

[4] *SPLC Report*, op. cit.

[5] Quoted in Eric Stern, "Black Students vs. Campus Newspapers," *American Journalism Review*, May 1997, p. 14.

[6] For background, see "High-Tech Labor Shortage," *The CQ Researcher*, April 24, 1998, pp. 361-384, and "Jobs in the '90s," *The CQ Researcher*, Feb. 28, 1992, pp. 181-204.

[7] Quoted in Betty Medsger, *Winds of Change: Challenges Confronting Journalism Education* (1996), p. 160.

[8] Student Press Law Center Web site, "Support for a Free Press," Jan. 19, 1998.

[9] *The Washington Post*, May 17, 1998.

[10] Stern, op. cit., p. 14.

[11] Quoted in Nat Hentoff, "Students Burning Newspapers (Again)," *The Washington Post*, March 7, 1998.

[12] *Ibid.*

[13] Larry O'Dell, "Va. Court Clears Student Newspaper," The Associated Press, Feb. 28, 1998.

FOR MORE INFORMATION

If you would like to have this CQ Researcher updated, or need more information about this topic, please call CQ Custom Research. Special rates for CQ subscribers. (202) 887-8600 or (800) 432-2250, ext. 600, or E-mail Custom.Research@cq.com

Journalism Education Association, Kansas State University, 103 Kedzie Hall, Manhattan, Kan. 66506-1505; (785) 532-5532; jea@spub.ksu.edu The 1,800-member JEA is the only independent national scholastic journalism organization for teachers and advisers.

The Freedom Forum, 1101 Wilson Blvd., Arlington, Va. 22209; (703) 284-2876; news@freedomforum.org. An international foundation dedicated to "free press, free speech and free spirit."

Columbia Scholastic Press Association, 2960 Broadway, CMR 11, New York, N.Y. 10027-6902; (212) 854-9400 cspa@columbia.edu. The CSPA publishes the monthly *Student Press Review* and holds an annual convention for high school journalists in New York City. It also offers critiques of student publications and gives awards.

National Scholastic Press Association/Associated Collegiate Press, 2221 Univ Ave SE Suite 121, Minneapolis, Minn. 55414; (612) 625-8335; info@studentpress.journ.umn.edu. These two nonprofit organizations devoted to high school and college journalism provide a critique service for publications and hold national contests and workshops.

Association for Education in Journalism and Mass Communication, Room 121, LeConte College, University of South Carolina, Columbia, S.C. 29208-0251; (803) 777-2005; aejmc@sc.edu. The AEJMC is the primary organization for faculty and administrators of college journalism and mass-communications programs. It publishes the *Journalism & Mass Communication Educator* and the *AEJMC News*.

Student Press Law Center, 1101 Wilson Blvd., Suite 1910, Arlington, Va 22209-2248; (703) 807-1904; splc@splc.org The SPLC offers free educational materials and legal advice to high school and college journalists facing problems with access to information or censorship. Mark Goodman is the executive director.

---

[14] Quoted in Candace Perkins Bowen, "What Are Your Students Publishing on the Web," *The School Administrator*, April 1998.

[15] *Ibid.*

[16] Rima Shore, "The Current State of High School Reform," A Report to the Carnegie Corporation of New York, 1996, p. 7.

[17] Medsger, *op. cit.*

[18] Lee B. Becker and Gerald M. Kosicki, "Annual Survey of Enrollment and Degrees Awarded," *Journalism and Mass Communication Educator*, autumn 1997, pp. 63-74.

[19] D.L. Hoffman and T.P. Novak, "Information Access: Bridging the Racial Divide on the Internet," *Science*, April 17, 1998.

[20] Unless otherwise noted, information in this section is from Medsger, *op. cit.*

[21] Medsger, *ibid.*, p. 54. Medsger is a former newspaper reporter and former journalism

professor at San Francisco State University.

[22] Medsger, *op. cit.*, p. 29.

[23] Medsger, *op. cit.*, pp. 111-112.

[24] James Ledbetter, "The Slow, Sad Sellout of Journalism School," *Rolling Stone*, Oct. 16, 1997, p. 78.

[25] *Death by Cheeseburger: High School Journalism in the 1990s and Beyond* (1994), p. 68.

[26] Adam Clayton Powell III, "78 percent of public schools Net-connected, new study shows," *The Freedom Forum On-Line*, March 9, 1998. For background, see "Networking the Classroom," *The CQ Researcher*, Oct. 20, 1995, pp. 921-944.

Bibliography

Selected Sources Used

Books

Dvorak, Jack, Larry Lain and Tom Dickson, *Journalism Kids Do Better: What Research Tells Us about High School Journalism*, Eric Clearinghouse on Reading, English, and Communication, 1994.

The authors provide a comprehensive report for and about high school journalism editors, including innumerable charts and graphs.

Articles

Bowen, Candace Perkins, "What Are Your Students Publishing on the Web?" *The School Administrator*, April 1998.

Bowen, a former high school journalism teacher who now coordinates the Scholastic Media Program at Kent State University, reviews some of the concerns of high school administrators worried about liability and other issues connected with giving students access to the World Wide Web.

Hentoff, Nat, "Students Learning to Burn Newspapers," *The Washington Post*, Aug. 16, 1997.

Hentoff takes Cornell University administrators to task for failing to condemn black students who burned copies of the *Cornell Review* to protest offensive articles.

Kushner, David, "Young Editors Speak Up and Out," *The New York Times*, Feb. 26, 1998.

Kushner looks at the founding of *Bolt Reporter*, an online site for teenagers that features a regular section on stories that have been banned from high school papers.

Ledbetter, James, "The Slow, Sad Sellout of Journalism School," *Rolling Stone*, Oct. 16, 1997.

Ledbetter looks at the journalism/mass-communications model of journalism education, and doesn't find much to like. The impact of marketing and public relations courses on journalism programs, the low pay and tight job market faced by graduates and the lack of consensus on what students need to know are all reviewed here.

Parker, Rosemare, "In Otsego: Student keeps up fight for press rights; Administrators take editorial control of formerly award-winning school paper." *The Detroit News*, Jan. 19, 1998.

Parker looks at the chain of events surrounding the shutdown of the award-winning middle school newspaper, *The Bulldog Express,* following the editor's efforts to publish a story about a shoplifting incident.

Powell, Adam Clayton III, "78% of public schools Net-connected, new study shows," *Free! — The Freedom Forum Online*, March 3, 1998.

Powell reviews findings of a fall, 1997 study conducted by the U.S. Department of Education and released by the National Center for Statistics. The study found that most public schools have Internet access, with small-town schools leading the way, and urban schools trailing.

Stepp, Carl Sessions, "The New Journalist," *American Journalism Review,* March 10, 1998.

Stepp looks at the skills and qualities online publishers are looking for in the people they hire and suggests ways in which the new technologies may change journalism.

Reports

Dvorak, Jack, "High School Journalism Student Performance on the Advanced Placement English Language and Composition Examination," Jan. 17, 1998. A research paper presented at the midwinter meeting of the Association for Education in Journalism and Mass Communication.

Dvorak presents evidence that students in Intensive Journalism Writing courses fare better on the Advanced Placement exam in English Language and Composition than students who prepare for the test by taking a traditional AP English class.

The Freedom Forum, *Death By Cheeseburger: High School Journalism in the 1990s and Beyond,* February 1994.

This report, drawing on hundreds of interviews and an analysis of hundreds of high school newspapers, presents a clear picture of the the situation facing high school journalists and their teachers. The report finishes with 12 recommendations, including a call for every high school to publish a newspaper at least once a month.

Betty Medsger, *Winds of Change: Challenges Confronting Journalism Education,* The Freedom Forum, 1996.

Based on surveys and interviews with industry professionals, recent journalism school graduates and journalism educators, Medsger's report paints a bleak picture of journalism education as deeply divided and unsure of its mission. Medsger recommends the development of graduate programs focussed more clearly on journalism as opposed to communications; and stronger relationships between journalism education and the news industry.

Rima Shore, *The Current State of High School Reform,* a Report to the Carnegie Foundation of New York, 1996.

Shore summarizes current thinking on the goals of high school reform efforts, and the barriers to achieving them, such as the low percentage of high school students graduating with proficient writing skills.

The Next Step

Additional information from UMI's Newspaper & Periodical Abstracts™ database

Censorship

Ackerman, Todd, "UH Group Rips Campus Paper," *Houston Chronicle,* **Oct. 9, 1996, p. A17.**

The University of Houston's College Republicans are outraged over a political cartoon in the student newspaper depicting them in front of a swastika. Leaders of the student group said they will sue the *Daily Cougar,* flood it with calls and letters of protest and take their story to national talk-radio outlets like Rush Limbaugh to protest the cartoon.

"Free Speech has Limits", *Atlanta Journal-Constitution,* **June 7, 1997, p. A10.**

An editorial says that Brookwood High School administrators acted swiftly and appropriately after two students slipped anti-Semitic statements and racial slurs into the school's literary magazine. The officials were right to immediately suspend the students responsible and to ask that magazines already distributed with the offensive material be destroyed, to be replaced later with uncontaminated copies.

"Near Miami, Arrests Test Free Speech For Students," *The New York Times,* **March 4, 1998, p. B9.**

The high school students say it was a prank. But a pamphlet titled "First Amendment," with racist comments, obscene cartoons and a cover drawing of their black principal shot through the head with a dart has earned nine suburban Miami teenagers a trip to jail and possible expulsion from school. School officials say there are limits to students' free-speech rights when the comments are so inflammatory.

"Respect the Shield Law," *San Francisco Chronicle,* **Oct. 15, 1996, p. A20.**

An editorial argues that the shield law, which protects journalists from having to reveal confidential sources or give up unpublished information, should be respected in the case of Soren Hemmila, a photographer for Contra Costa College's newspaper. The editorial supports Hemmila's refusal to give police unpublished photos of a gang-related shooting.

"Students Censored, But Issue Lives On," *The New York Times,* **Sept. 7, 1997, p. 35.**

When student reporters for the *Naperville Central Times,* a suburban high school newspaper, learned that district administrators spent taxpayers' money on travel at the time of a budget crisis, they did what any responsible journalist might do — they investigated. But the information never made it into the paper. Tom Paulsen, principal of Naperville Central High School, directed the students to remove the administrators' names before publication. His action three years ago thrust Naperville Central, a school of 2,700 in an affluent community west of Chicago, into rekindling a longstanding journalistic debate: Do high school newspapers have the same constitutional rights as the rest of the press?

Bower, Carolyn, "School Chief in Hazelwood Court Case Will Retire," *St. Louis Post-Dispatch,* **Jan. 25, 1997, p. 11.**

Robert E. "Gene" Reynolds, a school administrator in Hazelwood, Mo., who gained national attention because of a journalism case that reached the Supreme Court, will retire in June. The case focused on his censorship of Hazelwood East High School's newspaper in 1983, which the court upheld.

DeGette, Cara, "Gay Article in School Paper Causes Stir," *The Denver Post,* **Oct. 31, 1996, p. B1.**

An article in the Oct. 24, 1996, issue of Palmer High School's monthly student newspaper describing the difficulties of being a gay or lesbian teenager, and an unrelated editorial supporting same-sex marriages, has rankled the president of the Colorado Springs, Colo., School Board and Will Perkins, chairman of Colorado for Family Values.

Ganey, Terry, "Principal Backs Student Press Bill," *St. Louis Post-Dispatch,* **Mar. 26, 1997, p. B2.**

Kirkwood High School Principal Franklin McCallie spoke in favor of a Student Freedom of the Press bill in the Missouri House of Representatives, which would give high school students the right to write, publish and disseminate news and opinions in student publications. The bill would prevent school administrators from reviewing material before publication, making it up to the student adviser to make sure that no obscene, libelous or private information gets published.

McDermott, Kevin, "Student Free-Press Bill Gets Its Last Chance," *St. Louis Post-Dispatch,* **Nov. 14, 1997, p. C8.**

A measure to extend more rights to high school journalists faces a last-chance vote in the Illinois Senate today, amid a growing campaign by school officials to stop it. The measure, initially passed by the legislature last spring, would guarantee basic free-press rights to high school newspapers, preventing school administrators from censoring the papers except in certain circumstances.

Naylor, Janet, "In Macomb County: Roseville Students Say Newspaper was Censored: Former Editors Say

Principal Pulled Stories Before Publication," *Detroit News,* July 7, 1997, p. D5.

The problem of teenagers and sexually transmitted diseases struck home for Ann Marie Stanley of Roseville when an 18-year-old friend told her she had AIDS. Stanley was an editor at Roseville High School's student newspaper at the time, and wanted to write an article about what she called the deadliest of diseases: ignorance. But the story never ran. Before she could pen one word, Stanley said, "I was told it was never going to be published." Stanley and other former student editors at the school say their efforts to cover anything but the fluffiest of news stories at the monthly publication were stymied last year by the principal.

High School Journalism

"A Journalism Class Act," *The Denver Post,* June 16, 1997, p. B11.

Denver school officials have given notice that starting with next fall's school term, smut and other coarse or abusive material will no longer be allowed in the district's high school newspapers. The clean-up ultimatum aims primarily at year-end editions, which often contain prurient stories and attacks on teachers and students.

Helm, Jane, "Are High School Newspapers Dying Out?" *Minneapolis Star Tribune,* Jan. 22, 1998, p. 2E.

At some high schools, new technology has overtaken old-fashioned newsprint in getting information to students. There is no school newspaper at Kennedy High School in Bloomington, Minn., and the situation is the same at Eagan High School, where students get school news from Web sites and by watching TV monitors. Getting school news through the announcements is different from reading stories written by students in a school newspaper, because although announcements cover the basics, they may not include elements that make student newspapers unique, including editorials, feature stories and photographs.

Nakamura, David, "At Broad Run, Students Giving School Air Time; Televised News Program Debuts This Week," *The Washington Post,* Oct. 26, 1997, p. L6.

Like Virginia's other high schools, Broad Run has a newspaper, literary magazine and yearbook. But the school's latest venture into the news media world is a weekly, 10- to 15-minute television news broadcast in the cafeteria produced by students.

Pearson, Rick, "Edgar Vetoes Student Newspaper Bill," *Chicago Tribune,* Aug. 11, 1997, p. C4.

Gov. Jim Edgar vetoed legislation Sunday that would have given broad powers to students to decide the content of high school newspapers and publish the papers without the total oversight of school boards and administrators. Under the measure, school officials could only edit the content of newspapers produced by students to catch libel, obscenity, material harmful to minors, invasion of privacy or statements that could lead students to commit unlawful acts. The measure would have allowed students to sue local school boards if they believed the actions of administrators to make changes in newspaper content didn't fall into those categories.

Wishart, Nicholas C., and Lee Khorll, "School Newspaper Focuses on Fashion, Splits Student Body," *St. Louis Post-Dispatch,* Nov. 21, 1996, p. S1.

The Northwest School Board in House Springs, Mo., is considering how best to handle a situation that threatens to split the high school and perhaps the community. The Northwest High School's October 1996 issue of the student newspaper, which listed fashion "do's" and "don'ts" and characterized groups of students by their clothing, has offended a group of students who fell into the "don't" category.

Newspaper Circulation

"Don't Write Off Newspapers," *Printing World,* Oct. 6, 1997, p. 8.

Newspapers have been written off almost as much as they have been written about over the last 20 years. Declining circulations, aging readership and competition from television and radio would conspire to drive newspapers out of business — or so it has been claimed. It had, of course, nothing to do with the fact that newspapers had scarcely changed in the previous 30 years. All that has now changed. The last decade has seen the daily press galvanized into action. Changing formats, changing typographic treatment and quality color printing have breathed new life into newspapers all over the country. Indeed, one problem that many face is that color is not available in all the slots that the advertisers and editorial teams want. This has sparked investment in printing machinery on an unprecedented scale.

Rieder, Rem, "Betting on the Future of Newspapers," *American Journalism Review,* May 1997, p. 6.

The buzz that newspapers are relics may not be so true, if Knight-Ridder's actions are any indication. Last month, Knight-Ridder proved its commitment to newspapers when it bought the *Kansas City Star,* the *Fort Worth Star-Telegram* and two other papers from the Walt Disney Co. Not only is Knight-Ridder beefing up its roster of dailies, it's also shedding its non-newspaper interests, abandoning online information services and cable as it did its television unit a while back.

Back Issues

Great Research on Current Issues Starts Right Here.
Recent topics covered by The CQ Researcher are listed below.
Now available on the Web
For information, call (800) 432-2250 ext. 279 or (202) 887-6279.

If you would like to have any of these CQ Researchers updated, or need more information about these topics, please call CQ Custom Research. Special rates for CQ subscribers.
(202) 887-8600 or (800) 432-2250, ext. 600, or E-mail Custom.Research@cq.com

FEBRUARY 1997
Assisting Refugees
Alternative Medicine's Next Phase
Independent Counsels
Feminism's Future

MARCH 1997
New Air Quality Standards
Alcohol Advertising
Civic Renewal
Educating Gifted Students

APRIL 1997
Declining Crime Rates
The FBI Under Fire
Gender Equity in Sports
Space Program's Future

MAY 1997
The Stock Market
The Cloning Controversy
Expanding NATO
The Future of Libraries

JUNE 1997
FDA Reform
China After Deng
Line-Item Veto
Breast Cancer

JULY 1997
Transportation Policy
Executive Pay
School Choice Debate
Aggressive Driving

AUGUST 1997
Age Discrimination
Banning Land Mines
Children's Television
Evolution vs. Creationism

SEPTEMBER 1997
Caring for the Dying
Mental Health Policy
Mexico's Future
Youth Fitness

OCTOBER 1997
Urban Sprawl in the West
Diversity in the Workplace
Teacher Education
Contingent Work Force

NOVEMBER 1997
Renewable Energy
Artificial Intelligence
Religious Persecution
Roe v. Wade at 25

DECEMBER 1997
Whistleblowers
Castro's Next Move
Gun Control Standoff
Regulating Nonprofits

JANUARY 1998
Foster Care Reform
IRS Reform
The Black Middle Class
U.S.-British Relations

FEBRUARY 1998
Patients' Rights
Deflation Fears
Caring for the Elderly
The New Corporate Philanthropy

MARCH 1998
Israel at 50
The Federal Judiciary
Drinking on Campus
The Economics of Recycling

APRIL 1998
Biology and Behavior
Liberal Arts Education
Income Inequality
High-Tech Labor Shortage

MAY 1998
Census 2000
Child-Care Options
Alzheimer's Disease
U.S.-Russian Relations

Back issues are available for $5.00 (subscribers) or $10.00 (non-subscribers). Quantity discounts apply to orders over 10. To order, call Congressional Quarterly Customer Service at (202) 887-8621.

Binders are available for $18.00. To order call 1-800-638-1710. Please refer to stock number 648.

Future Topics

▶ *Antitrust Policy*

▶ *Environmental Justice*

▶ *Sleep Deprivation*

The CQ Researcher

PUBLISHED BY CONGRESSIONAL QUARTERLY INC.

Antitrust Policy

Should more be done to promote competition?

For more than a century, federal law has sought to encourage competition by prohibiting monopoly behavior and other anticompetitive business practices. Now the government is accusing giant Microsoft Corp. of illegally trying to stifle competition in computer software markets. Microsoft says it has done nothing wrong and argues that the parallel suits by the federal government and a coalition of 20 states will stifle innovation and hurt consumers. The high-stakes court action comes as the Justice Department and the Federal Trade Commission are also more closely scrutinizing corporate mergers that may restrict competition. With a record wave of mergers, some people are cheering the more aggressive policy and some want the government to do even more, but others say the government should let the marketplace alone.

C_Q | **June 12, 1998** • **Volume 8, No. 22** • **Pages 505-528**

Formerly Editorial Research Reports

CQ Researcher

June 12, 1998
Volume 8, No.22

EDITOR
Sandra Stencel

MANAGING EDITOR
Thomas J. Colin

ASSOCIATE EDITOR
Sarah M. Magner

STAFF WRITERS
Adriel Bettelheim
Mary H. Cooper
Kenneth Jost
Kathy Koch
David Masci

PRODUCTION EDITOR
Melissa Hall

EDITORIAL ASSISTANT
Laura S. Cavender

PUBLISHED BY
Congressional Quarterly Inc.

CHAIRMAN
Andrew Barnes

VICE CHAIRMAN
Andrew P. Corty

PRESIDENT AND PUBLISHER
Robert W. Merry

EXECUTIVE EDITOR
David Rapp

The CQ Researcher (ISSN 1056-2036). Formerly Editorial Research Reports. Published weekly, except Jan. 2, May 29, July 3, Oct. 30, by Congressional Quarterly Inc., 1414 22nd St., N.W., Washington, D.C. 20037. Annual subscription rate for libraries, businesses and government is $340. Additional rates furnished upon request. Periodicals postage paid at Washington, D.C., and additional mailing offices. POSTMASTER: Send address changes to The CQ Researcher, 1414 22nd St., N.W., Washington, D.C. 20037.

COVER: ATTORNEY GENERAL JANET RENO ANNOUNCES THE GOVERNMENT'S SUIT AGAINST MICROSOFT CORP. ON MAY 18, FLANKED BY, FROM LEFT, ASSISTANT A. G. JOEL I. KLEIN, NEW YORK A. G. DENNIS VACCO, IOWA A. G. TOM MILLER AND CONNECTICUT A. G. RICHARD BLUMENTHAL. (REUTERS/LARRY DOWLING)

Antitrust Policy

BY KENNETH JOST

THE ISSUES

It has been called the most valuable square foot of real estate in the world, and it's at the center of a bitter fight between the world's richest man and most powerful nation.

The fight heated up last month when the U.S. government and 20 states launched antitrust suits against Bill Gates' giant Microsoft Corp. At issue is control of that little piece of "real estate" — the first screen that personal computer users see when they boot up machines powered by Microsoft's ubiquitous Windows operating system.

Microsoft chairman and co-founder Gates says the icon-filled screen opens the door for computer users to vast storehouses of information and countless opportunities for enhanced productivity. But Microsoft, he says, should hold the key to that door: His company designed it, sells it and can best be relied on to continue improving it.

Government lawyers say that Windows — used in 90 percent of the world's personal computers — is essentially "the on-ramp to the information superhighway," and no single company should control it. Moreover, they say, Microsoft has abused its power through a host of allegedly anti-competitive practices to boost its business at the expense of rival firms.

The Justice Department's lawsuit, Assistant U.S. Attorney General Joel I. Klein declared on May 18, "seeks to put an end to Microsoft's unlawful campaign to eliminate competition, deter innovation and restrict consumer choice."

Two hours later, an amiable but unyielding Gates answered the charges in a news conference at the company's Redmond, Wash., headquarters. "Federal and state regulators have taken the unprecedented step of trying to intervene in America's most successful and

growing industry," Gates said. "This is a step backwards for America, for consumers and for the personal computer industry that is leading our nation's economy into the 21st century." [1]

The lawsuits came in the week that Microsoft was scheduled to ship the latest upgrade of its PC operating system, Windows 98, to computer manufacturers in advance of a scheduled release to customers this month.

The suits stop short of seeking to block the release of Windows 98. But they ask a federal judge in Washington, D.C., to order a major change in Microsoft's operating system. The Justice Department and the states are seeking a preliminary injunction to require all future versions of Windows that include Microsoft's Internet Explorer software for browsing the Internet also to include a competing software developed by a rival firm, the Netscape Navigator. [2]

Allowing Microsoft to "bundle" its browser with its monopoly operating system without including Netscape's, Klein told reporters, "could well cause irreversible harm to competition by letting Microsoft unlawfully achieve a second monopoly, this time in Internet browsers."

To back up its charges, the Justice Department included in its 53-page complaint seemingly damaging quotes from internal Microsoft messages and documents suggesting a conscious plan to use

its Windows monopoly to "leverage" its new browser and displace Netscape's earlier — and market-leading — product.

"Pitting browser against browser is hard since Netscape has 80 percent market share, and we have [less than] 20 percent," Microsoft Senior Vice President James Allchin was quoted as telling a colleague in January 1997. "I am convinced we have to use Windows — this is the one thing they don't have."

But Gates and other Microsoft executives depicted the proposed remedy as a punishment for the company's success and a disservice to customers. "Forcing Microsoft to include Netscape's competing software in our operating system is like requiring Coca-Cola to include three cans of Pepsi in every six-pack it sells," Gates said.

As for the internal communications quoted in the Justice Department complaints, Gates and others insisted they were taken out of context. Gates also branded as "absolutely false" the most damning allegation — that he had personally met with Netscape executives in May 1995 to divide up the market, offering to keep Microsoft out of the browser market if Netscape promised not to try to produce a rival operating system. [3]

The lawsuit immediately conjured up images of some of the country's most historic antitrust actions — from the early 20th-century suit that broke up John D. Rockefeller's Standard Oil trust to the more recent litigation that split up AT&T in the 1980s. Microsoft executives offered a less flattering comparison. They likened the suit to the Justice Department's failed antitrust suit against IBM, which lasted for 13 years before the government dropped the case in 1982 for lack of evidence.

The suit against Microsoft comes at a time of increased antitrust activity both at the Justice Department and the Federal Trade Commission (FTC).

Antitrust Activity Has Increased

In the past 10 years, the number of planned corporate mergers rose 35 percent while antitrust investigations quadrupled and cases filed more than doubled.

Premerger Notifications

	1988	1997
Received	*2,747*	*3,702*
Investigations initiated	*56*	*220*
Cases filed	*6*	*14*

Source: Justice Department, Antitrust Division

Antitrust enforcement peaked in the 1960s and early '70s, when many policy-makers viewed corporate size as an inherent economic and political problem. But antitrust laws went out of favor in Washington under President Ronald Reagan, who filled key antitrust posts with avowed advocates of big business and determined skeptics of antitrust laws except in limited circumstances.

President Clinton has not been especially vocal on antitrust issues, but his appointees — Klein and his predecessor at the Justice Department, Anne Bingaman, and Robert Pitofsky as FTC chairman — view antitrust enforcement more positively than their counterparts from the Reagan-Bush era. "It seems to be far more robust than what we had seen earlier," says E. Thomas Sullivan, dean of the University of Minnesota Law School.

"There's a revived interest," says Irwin Stelzer, director of regulatory policy studies at the American Enterprise Institute in Washington. "You've got two good people — Klein and Pitofsky — and they're doing a very good job. They're not crazy like some of the old 'big is bad' people."

The increased interest in antitrust action stems in part from a wave of corporate mergers in the United States and around the world over the past few years. The consolidations — last year's were valued at more than $1 trillion in assets — affect everything from banking and telecommunications to pharmaceuticals and office supplies. [4] *(See chart, p. 522.)*

The Justice Department and FTC have approved some of the mergers while blocking others. "It's hard to accuse the Clinton administration of being either a pushover for transactions or relentlessly hostile," says William E. Kovacic, who teaches antitrust law at George Mason University School of Law in Fairfax, Va.

Some of the biggest deals are still awaiting review, in some cases by other independent agencies. The proposed merger of Citicorp and Travelers is being reviewed by the Federal Reserve Board, while the Federal Communications Commission will study the planned acquisition of MCI Communications by British-based WorldCom Inc. Meanwhile, the Justice Department already had one major antitrust case in court before the Microsoft suit: an effort to block the merger of two giant defense contractors, Lockheed Martin and Northrup Grumman *(see p. 520.)*

As Microsoft's Sept. 18 trial date approaches, here are some of the major issues being debated:

Have antitrust laws been good or bad for the economy overall?

The Supreme Court once called the nation's first antitrust law, the 1890 Sherman Act, the "Magna Carta of the free enterprise system" — in effect, a fundamental guarantee for the right of all businesses to fair competition in the marketplace. [5] In the 108 years since then, Congress has periodically reaffirmed that commitment by expanding antitrust laws to cover other business practices besides classic monopolies and cartels. *(See chart, p. 510.)* And the federal government has repeatedly invoked those laws to break up or control business monopolies — generally to public approval.

Some experts and advocates say the laws have served the country well by promoting and preserving competition. Others maintain that antitrust laws and antitrust enforcers have proved to be too weak to prevent anti-competitive abuses and the growth of giant corporations that wield undue economic power. But still others say that the antitrust laws have been bad for the U.S. economy, even bad for competition — punishing successful companies, protecting inefficient ones and in the end hurting rather than helping consumers.

"It's been an uneven 100 years," says Rudolph Peritz, a professor at New York Law School and author of a recent history of antitrust policy. "Antitrust enforcers and policy-makers have done better at some times and worse at others."

Peritz says the early focus of antitrust laws in breaking up monopolies like the Standard Oil and tobacco trusts established a pattern of generally preventing the creation of single-company industries. But he says the laws have been less effective in dealing with "oligopolies" — industries in which a small number of producers control the market and, according to antitrust advocates, provide less than complete competition.

The more centrist Kovacic says antitrust laws have served an important purpose by committing the federal government to free markets rather than central planning as a central economic principle. "The [Justice Department] antitrust divisions have historically been a voice for promoting private enterprise and rivalry," he says.

More concretely, Kovacic says the laws have discouraged the formation of "producer cartels" — agreements between rival firms to set prices or divide the market. But he notes that price-fixing agreements persist — citing, for example, the recent prosecution of Archer Daniels Midland Inc. that last fall cost the agriprocessing firm a then record $100 million fine for fixing prices on two products. (A price-fixing case against Ucar International, the nation's leading manufacturer of graphite electrodes, a key component in electric arc furnaces, produced a new record fine of $110 million in April.) [6]

Some conservative and libertarian antitrust experts, however, see little but negative effects from the government's use of antitrust laws. In his influential book, *The Antitrust Paradox*, published in 1978, Robert Bork complained that the antitrust laws had evolved into "rules that significantly impair both competition and the ability of the economy to produce goods and services efficiently." [7] Bork, a Yale law professor at the time and later a federal judge and unsuccessful Supreme Court nominee, was one of the leading members of the so-called "Chicago school" that advocated a more strictly economic approach to antitrust issues (*see p. 517*).

Robert Levy, a senior fellow in constitutional studies at the libertarian Cato Institute, says the overall effect of the antitrust laws has been "deleterious."

"I don't think that antitrust laws ever had any legitimate functions," Levy says, "and I don't think they have any legitimate function now given the dynamism of today's markets."

Unlike Levy, most conservatives accept the idea that antitrust laws should prohibit what one of Bork's disciples — federal Judge Frank Easterbrook Jr.— once labeled "plain-vanilla cartels and mergers to monopoly." [8] But they criticize the expansion of antitrust to two other business practices.

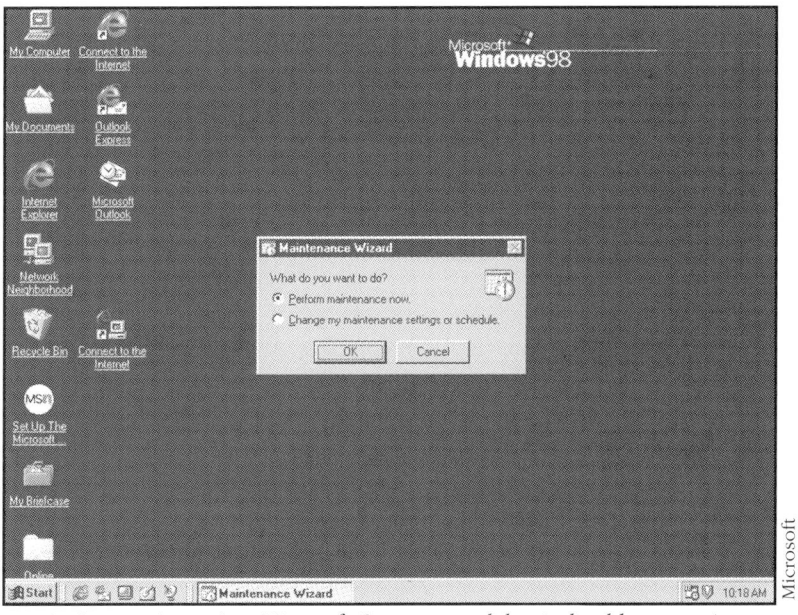

Antitrust suits against Microsoft Corp. contend that it should not require computer makers to include Internet Explorer, Microsoft's browser software, as a condition of using its Windows 98 operating system. Microsoft says Explorer is an integrated feature of Windows that can't be lopped off.

First, they say that antitrust laws should generally not apply to so-called vertical mergers between, for instance, a manufacturer and a retailer, or to vertical "restraints" — such as a restriction by a manufacturer on a dealer's ability to set prices or expand outside a specified territory. Second, they generally defend the legality of so-called "tying" arrangements that condition the sale of one product on the buyer's agreement to purchase a second product. And they believe that the antitrust laws were of-

ten enforced too rigorously, particularly in the 1950s and '60s, against so-called horizontal mergers — combinations between firms producing the same product or service. Conservatives viewed many of these mergers as likely to produce greater efficiencies without adverse effects on competition.

Some more liberal-leaning experts today agree that the Supreme Court under Chief Justice Earl Warren was too strict in disallowing any mergers that would result in increased concentration in the industry. "In retrospect, the antitrust policies of the Earl Warren era were excessive in the way they defined markets," Sullivan says.

For their part, conservatives say that the Supreme Court and lower federal courts have become more sophisticated in handling antitrust issues because of the growing influence of the Chicago school since the late 1970s.

"If the federal government wants to challenge a merger, it has to define a relevant market and then show how the concentration in that market rises to a troublesome level and show why there are barriers to entry," says John Lopatka, a professor at the University of South Carolina Law School. "And if the defendants raise the issue, the government is going to have to explain that the mergers do not generate efficiencies — that is, cost savings — all of which is a proper analysis."

But the emphasis on so-called microeconomics — the study of firm behavior — discomforts liberal antitrust experts. "Microeconomics is a

---

Major Federal Antitrust Laws

Sherman Act (1890) — *Prohibits any "contract, combination or conspiracy . . . in restraint of trade" (section 1) or monopolizing or attempting to monopolize interstate or foreign trade or commerce (section 2); Justice Department authorized to bring criminal cases or civil suits; criminal violations punishable by up to a year in prison and $5,000 fine; individuals may bring civil suits, with triple damages allowed.*

Clayton Antitrust Act (1914) — *Prohibits price discrimination (section 2), exclusive dealing and "tying" contracts (section 3), and stock acquisitions of other companies (section 7) where effect "may be to substantially lessen competition or tend to create a monopoly in any line of commerce."*

Federal Trade Commission Act (1914) — *Prohibits "unfair methods of competition" and "unfair or deceptive acts or practices" (section 5); creates FTC as independent agency with authority to issue cease-and-desist orders to enforce law.*

Robinson-Patman Act (1936) — *Outlaws "unjustified" price discounts that result in injury to competition (section 2(a)); buyers seeking unjustified price discounts also subject to liability (section 2(f)).*

Celler-Kefauver Act (1950) — *Strengthens Clayton Act's provision against anti-competitive mergers to cover acquisition of assets as well as stock of another company and to cover merger with firms in different line of commerce.*

Antitrust Procedures and Penalties Act (1974) — *Changes price-fixing and other violations from misdemeanors to felonies; raises maximum fines to $1 million for companies and $500,000 for individuals; increases maximum prison sentence to three years. Also requires public disclosure and judicial review of case settlements negotiated by Justice Department.*

Hart-Scott-Rodino Antitrust Improvements Act (1976) — *Requires merging companies above specified size to notify Justice Dept. and FTC before completing transaction; establishes mandatory waiting period for completing transaction or beginning joint operations.*

Source: Ernest Gellhorn and William E. Kovacic, Antitrust Law and Economics in a Nutshell *(1994).*

---

narrow lens that can tell us at best about one particular kind of economic power: market power," Peritz says. "But firm size reflects another kind of economic power. You can have a merger between two multibillion-dollar companies, like Nynex and Bell Atlantic, that will fly through antitrust scrutiny because they are in different 'markets,' but we all know from our experience that there [was] an increase in economic power of all sorts when those two companies merged."

Is the current wave of mergers good or bad for consumers?

When the government divided AT&T into seven regional telephone companies and a separate long-distance carrier, it hoped to be ushering in an era of wide-open competition that would improve service and lower rates. Long-distance service has become a heartily competitive market, but local telephone service remains a monopoly. Now, some of the so-called Baby Bells are getting back together and promising —

in the face of consumer-group skepticism — that the mergers will enhance competition and bring customers better service and lower prices.

The developments in the telephone industry encapsulate a debate that has raged since the beginning of U.S. antitrust policy: whether corporate mergers help consumers by lowering costs and thereby prices or hurt consumers by reducing competition and thereby the incentives to keep prices low. Despite 100 years of argument and reams of academic research, the issue continues to sharply divide policy-makers, interest groups and experts.

Chicago school experts stoutly insist that most mergers do benefit the economy. "The presumption is that the merger is going to be beneficial," Lopatka says. "If one wants to interfere with the market, one has to prove that interference with the market is going to produce greater benefits than allowing the market to work."

"You can't stop every merger, and it would be bad if you did," says Stelzer, a conservative who does not count himself in the Chicago school.

But Peritz maintains that the view that large firms will be more efficient is overstated. "Efficiency and large size do not correlate so simply," Peritz says. "Large firms are much, much bigger than they need to be to take advantage of economies of scale in production."

The Clinton administration's record on mergers draws mixed reviews. Critics on the right say the administration has been too aggressive. "There's a long list of anti-merger activity," says the Cato Institute's Levy. As one example, he describes the opposition to the planned merger between the two giant office-supply chains, Staples and Office Depot, as "plain silliness."

"There was no evidence at all that there was any monopoly power being exercised by those two companies," Levy says. "There were plenty of competitors in the office-supply market."

Critics on the left, however, say the administration has been too timid in challenging corporate combinations. "The antitrust officials have not been as aggressive in challenging transactions until it gets to an extreme level of concentration," says Gene Kimmelman, co-director of the Washington office of Consumers Union. "I would not call that aggressive enforcement."

A number of experts, however, including several self-described conservatives, give the administration generally good marks in merger cases.

"My impression is that they're applying the law pretty consistently," says Thomas Kauper, a professor at the University of Michigan Law School.

Stelzer agrees. "I think they've got it about right," he says. But Stelzer does fault Klein for not opposing the merger last year of two Baby Bells serving the Eastern and Mid-Atlantic states: Bell Atlantic Corp. and Nynex Corp.

Lopatka also declines to criticize the administration's stance on mergers. He specifically notes that he came to agree with the FTC's opposition to the Staples-Office Depot merger despite his initial skepticism. "They had pretty strong empirical evidence that when the two firms were not competing with each other, the price went up," Lopatka says.

For his part, though, Peritz regrets the reduced concern about corporate growth that dates from the Reagan-Bush presidencies and continues today. One reason for the changed attitude, he says, is that policy-makers have come to focus more on increasing shareholder value than on protecting consumers.

"What's not happening is a sufficient concern for what's happening to consumers, suppliers, and others who deal with these now even more enormous firms," Peritz says.

Should the federal government and the states have filed antitrust suits against Microsoft?

From the moment the suits were filed — indeed, in the several weeks leading up to the filing — the antitrust case against Microsoft was being played out in the political and public relations arenas as much as in court. Members of Congress and newspaper editorials weighed in on opposite sides of the dispute. So did other computer executives.

The suit also drew sharply divided reactions among antitrust experts. Supporters of the suits maintain that they are well-grounded in established antitrust doctrines and that the requested remedies were both appropriate and modest. Critics see the allegations against Microsoft as weak, both factually and legally, and predict either a defeat for the government or at most a fairly weak settlement.

"It was important that the suit was filed," Peritz says. "The remedies that the Justice Department and the state attorneys general are asking for are reasonable, and consistent with the kind of anti-competitive behavior they're claiming Microsoft is engaged in."

"This is an old-time antitrust case in which Bill Gates is trying to establish that high-tech industries are so different from the rest of the world that antitrust laws shouldn't apply," Stelzer says in agreement. "It's a pretty straightforward tying case, a straightforward abuse of monopoly-position case."

But in Lopatka's view, "It's not a very strong complaint, not a very strong theory." Each of the government's theories, he says, presents difficult problems of proof under existing antitrust precedents. "I think the government is going to lose," he concludes.

The Justice Department has already battled Microsoft in court twice, with limited results. It ended its first investigation in July 1994, when Microsoft agreed to a consent decree requiring it to change some of the restrictions in its contracts with PC manufacturers and other software makers. Today, the decree — formally issued in August 1995 after one judge balked at approving it — is widely regarded as weak. "They proposed solutions that became obsolete in a hurry," George Mason's Kovacic says.

Then, last October, the Justice Department returned to court, claiming that Microsoft was violating the 1995 decree by forcing computer makers to include its Internet Explorer browser as a condition of selling Windows 95. U.S. District Judge Thomas Penfield Jackson granted an injunction in December requiring Microsoft to allow computer makers to unbundle the browser. But

United States v. Microsoft ... The Main Event

1990
- *Microsoft introduces Windows 3.0 on May 22, using point-and-click system first developed by Apple Computer*
- *Federal Trade Commission (FTC) opens investigation of Microsoft, without public announcement*

1991
- *Microsoft confirms FTC investigation on March 11; depicts probe as "technical"*

1992
- *FTC investigation continues*

1993
- *FTC on Feb. 5 deadlocks, 2-2, on seeking court order to force Microsoft to cease manufacturing software incompatible with rivals' operating systems*
- *FTC deadlocks again July 21; closes probe, but turns file over to Justice Department*
- *Justice Department opens antitrust investigation in August*

1994
- *Microsoft reaches settlement July 16 with Justice Department and European authorities, agreeing to change contracts with computer makers and eliminate some restrictions on other software makers*

1995
- *Federal Judge Stanley Sporkin on Feb. 14 rejects settlement as "not in the public interest"*
- *Federal appeals court in Washington on June 16 overturns Sporkin's decision; assigns case to new judge, to be picked at random*
- *Federal Judge Thomas Penfield Jackson approves settlement on Aug. 21*
- *Windows 95 launches retail sales Aug. 24*

1996
- *Microsoft discloses on Sept. 19 that Justice Department had opened new antitrust probe*

1997
- *Bill Gates listed in Forbes (July 28 issue) as world's richest private individual, with estimated net worth of $36.4 billion*
- *Justice Department files petition on Oct. 20 charging Microsoft with illegally coercing computer makers to equip PCs with Internet Explorer browser software*
- *Judge Jackson issues order on Dec. 11 requiring Microsoft to allow PC makers to offer Windows 95 with or without Internet Explorer*

1998
- *Federal appeals court hears Microsoft's appeal of Jackson's order, on April 21*
- *Justice Department and the states put off plans to file broad antitrust suit on May 14 as Microsoft asks for talks aimed at settlement; talks collapse on May 16*
- *U.S., states file suit May 18, seeking preliminary injunction to force Microsoft to change restrictive contracts and to include Netscape Navigator, competing browser software, in Windows 98*
- *Judge Jackson on May 22 schedules trial for Sept. 18 on U.S., states' motion for preliminary injunction*
- *Windows 98 to be made available to customers on June 15*

when the federal appeals court in Washington heard Microsoft's appeal of the injunction in April, the government conceded that no computer maker had exercised that option up to then. [9]

The appellate judges appeared skeptical of the government's case in the April 24 arguments. In any event, the case concerned only Windows 95

U.S. v. Microsoft: The Lines Are Drawn

U.S. Assistant Attorney General Joel I. Klein
Comments accompanying filing of antitrust suit against Microsoft by the Justice Department, May 18, 1998

In essence, what Microsoft has been doing, through a wide variety of illegal business practices, is leveraging its Windows operating system monopoly to force its other software products on consumers. This is like having someone with a monopoly in CD players forcing consumers to take its CDs in order to get the machine. We believe most Americans would prefer to choose their own CDs and, for their matter, their own software products as well. . . .

Microsoft is unwilling to compete fairly and on the merits; rather, it prefers to leverage its Windows monopoly 'to make people use' its browser. The antitrust laws take a very different view of the way the marketplace should work: those laws are premised on the belief that . . . people should be able to choose for themselves what products they use.

. . . [N]othing we are doing here will or should prevent Microsoft from innovating or competing on the merits. What cannot be tolerated — and what the antitrust laws forbid — is the barrage of illegal, anti-competitive practices that Microsoft uses to destroy its rivals and to avoid competition on the merits. That, and that alone, is what this lawsuit is all about.

Bill Gates
Chairman, Microsoft
Comments following filing of federal antitrust suit, May 18, 1998

Forcing Microsoft to include Netscape's competing software in our operating system is like requiring Coca-Cola to include three cans of Pepsi in every six-pack it sells. The changes the government is demanding on the boot-up screen is like telling Coca-Cola that it must remove its name from every can of soda. And saying that we must remove Internet technology from Windows is like telling Coca-Cola that it must take something out of its formula. . . .

Computer users today have more choices than ever before. PC users can already choose between Microsoft's Internet Explorer and any other Web browser, and computer manufacturers are free to install Netscape browsers on any computers they sell. . . . Computer manufacturers choose to configure the first scren differently. They choose to add any browsers. They choose to market whatever productivity software they want. . . .

We believe an antitrust lawsuit is counterproductive, costly to the taxpayers, and ultimately will be unsuccessful in the courts. . . . I am confident that in the end, America's judicial system will uphold our right to innovate on behalf of consumers. I look forward to presenting our case in court and continuing to create great software for our consumers.

and was already being overshadowed by the broadening investigations of Microsoft.

The government's lawsuit includes four allegations that also appear in the states' complaint. The first charges that Gates and other Microsoft executives unsuccessfully tried to persuade Netscape to divide up the browser and operating-system markets. The government quotes Netscape Executive Vice President Marc Andreesen as describing the no-compete proposal in a meeting between executives of the two companies in June 1995. Gates has vehemently denied the allegation.

The three other claims involve ongoing Microsoft activities: the bundling of Internet Explorer with Windows; restrictions on computer manufacturers' discretion to alter the initial Windows boot-up screen; and Microsoft's agreements with Internet service and content providers that the government says are aimed at promoting Microsoft services and excluding those of competing firms. The states add one other claim in their lawsuit: a contention that Microsoft is also trying to monopolize the market for office-services software through similar tying arrangements and exclusionary contracts.

Peritz says the evidence of antitrust violations is strong. "Microsoft has tried to achieve a monopoly in applications," Peritz says. "They've done that by taking applications and integrating them into the operating system." As for the remedy, he agrees with the government's effort to force Microsoft to include the Netscape browser in its Windows programs — but prefers the states' request that a third browser be included as well. "Just as we don't want Microsoft to dominate that field," he says, "we don't want Microsoft and Netscape to dominate it either."

Lopatka, however, doubts the government's evidence is strong enough to prevail in court. And, if so, he believes the suits are a mistake.

"We have a market that's certainly functioning well, in terms of generating lots of benefits for consumers," The University of South Carolina's Lopatka says. "I don't think you want to interfere with the market on a hunch." ∎

BACKGROUND

Trust Busting

Congress passed the first of the federal antitrust laws in 1890 with bipartisan support at a time of rapid industrial consolidation and rapacious business practices. Four times since then — in 1914, 1950, 1974 and 1976 — Congress approved major revisions of the law aimed at tightening the prohibitions against monopoly power and adding new curbs on unfair business practices. But the executive branch and the federal courts have followed an uneven course in enforcing and interpreting the laws, alternating between periods of somewhat stricter and laxer antitrust enforcement. [10]

The Sherman Act bears the name of Sen. John Sherman, a Republican from Ohio — home of the biggest industrial trust of the late 19th century, John D. Rockefeller's Standard Oil of Ohio. Actually, though, Sherman's original proposal to ban any practices that restrained "full and fair competition" was amended in favor of narrower language prohibiting any contracts or combinations "in restraint of trade." The amended bill passed Congress overwhelmingly in July 1890 and was signed into law by a Republican president, Benjamin Harrison.

Today, Congress' intent in passing the law is one of the major points of disagreement. Bork and others in the so-called Chicago school argue that Sherman himself and Congress as a whole had one goal in mind: "consumer welfare," by which they mean lower prices. "The touchstone of illegality is raising prices to consumers," Bork wrote in an influential law review article in 1966. [11]

Most experts, however, say Bork's thesis ignores the substantial evidence that Congress also wanted to preserve and promote smaller businesses for social and political as well as economic purposes. "His view is far too narrow," says Thomas Sullivan. [12]

Supreme Court Rulings

Whatever Congress' intent, the Sherman Act had a mixed initial reception in the courts. The Supreme Court took a literalist approach in some of its earliest cases — for example, breaking up a rate-fixing agreement in 1897 among 18 freight railroads that lower courts had ruled legal. This literalist approach also led the court to cite antitrust law in curbing the powers of labor unions — an interpretation that Congress eventually put to rest by declaring that labor was not a "commodity" for purposes of antitrust law. At the same time, though, the high court narrowed the scope of the law by ruling in the 1895 "sugar trust" case that the act applied only to "commerce" and not to manufacturing — a doctrine that the court itself repudiated in the late 1930s.

The court created a more durable limitation on the law in 1911 in two decisions that nonetheless broke up Rockefeller's Standard Oil trust and James Duke's American Tobacco trust. Viewing the law as a limitation on constitutionally protected freedom of contract, the court's conservative majority declared that those trusts were illegal only because they were created through "unnatural and wrongful" acts. [13] This so-called Rule of Reason approach to the law prevailed for the next two decades. It then yielded to a more literal "per se" interpretation of the law, but re-emerged in the mid-1970s to become

what is now the accepted method for applying the law.

Congress responded to the decisions three years later with a new law expressly aimed at reversing what one senator called the court's "deadly blow to trust litigation." [14] The Clayton Antitrust Act added a laundry list of specifically prohibited business practices, including price discrimination, tying agreements and stock acquisitions, where the effect might be "to substantially lessen competition or tend to create a monopoly." A separate law created a new regulatory agency, the Federal Trade Commission (FTC), with broad power to identify and enjoin unfair commercial conduct.

Despite the Clayton Act's broad language, the Supreme Court again weakened the law through judicial interpretation. By 1950, antitrust-minded lawmakers determined the law needed revision if it was to prevent anti-competitive mergers. The Celler-Kefauver Act strengthened the law in two ways: first, by extending the act's prohibition against mergers achieved through stock acquisitions to the purchase of a competitor's assets as well; and second, by extending the law not only to mergers between competitors but to all corporate mergers with anti-competitive effects.

The law has blocked relatively few of these so-called conglomerate mergers. But the provision is nonetheless very controversial between liberals, who applaud Congress' effort to restrict corporate growth, and conservatives, who see no benefit in restraining mergers between non-competing companies.

A quarter-century later, Congress acted again to stiffen antitrust laws. In 1974, it substantially raised penalties for antitrust violations. Then in 1976 it passed a law, the Hart-Scott-Rodino Antitrust Improvements Act, requiring any company with more than $100 million in assets or sales to

Continued on p. 516

Chronology

1890-1950
Congress passes antitrust laws aimed at preventing anti-competitive business practices.

1890
Sherman Act prohibits any "contract, combination or conspiracy . . . in restraint of trade" or monopolizing or attempting to monopolize interstate or foreign trade or commerce.

1911
Supreme Court upholds government's effort to break up Standard Oil trust, but ruling softens Sherman Act by allowing "reasonable" restraints of trade.

1914
Clayton Antitrust Act prohibits a number of anti-competitive practices, including exclusive dealing and "tying" contracts. In the same year, Congress creates Federal Trade Commission (FTC) with power to bar "unfair" competition.

1936
Robinson-Patman Act outlaws "unjustified" price discounts that result in injury to competition.

1941
Report by Temporary National Economic Committee questions economic benefits of mergers.

1945
Appeals court upholds government's antitrust suit against Aluminum Co. of America (ALCOA).

1950
Celler-Kefauver Act strengthens Clayton Act's provision against anti-competitive mergers.

1950s-1960s
Supreme Court adopts strict stance against mergers.

1962
Supreme Court, in *Brown Shoe Co.*, bars manufacturer from acquiring Kinney Shoe Co.; acquisition would have given firm 5 percent of retail market.

1968
Justice Department guidelines call for challenging mergers if four firms would have more than 75 percent of market.

1970s
Antitrust laws are strengthened by Congress but sharply challenged by members of "Chicago school."

1974
Antitrust Procedures and Penalties Act raises penalties for price-fixing and other violations.

1976
Hart-Scott-Rodino Act requires large companies to report planned mergers.

1978
Robert Bork's *The Antitrust Paradox* sharply criticizes antitrust laws.

1980s
Reagan administration severely restricts antitrust enforcement.

1982
Assistant Attorney General William Baxter announces settlement of seven-year-old antitrust suit against AT&T, with agreement for divestiture of local telephone companies; divestiture is completed in 1984. On same day, Baxter announces government is dropping 13-year-old suit against IBM; action is "without merit," Baxter says. Later in year, Justice Department adopts new merger guidelines, raising standard for challenging corporate combinations.

1990s
The Clinton administration adopts stricter antitrust policies; wave of domestic and global mergers begins in mid-decade.

1993
Anne Bingaman appointed assistant attorney general for antitrust; doubles number of mergers challenged by division in two years in office.

1995
Robert Pitofsky appointed FTC chairman; leads commission in challenging mergers or forcing concessions before mergers are approved.

1997
Joel I. Klein named to head Justice Department Antitrust Division; wins Senate confirmation despite criticism for approving Bell Atlantic-Nynex merger.

1998
Justice Department and 20 states file antitrust suits against Microsoft Corp.; FTC launches major antitrust action against Intel Corp. on June 8; both agencies have other major antitrust cases ready for trial.

Private Antitrust Suits Allow Big Awards

Pepsi vs. Coke may sound like a consumer taste test, but it's actually a court case: a high-stakes effort by second-ranked Pepsi Cola to use federal antitrust laws to gain on the long-time industry leader, Coca-Cola Co.

Pepsico Inc. filed suit in federal court in New York last month claiming that Coke was illegally monopolizing the soft-drink market in violation of the Sherman Antitrust Act. The 16-page suit claimed that Coke improperly bars food-service distributors — the companies that supply products for restaurants, theater chains, stadiums and the like — from providing Pepsi products to their customers if they already handle Coke.

A Coca-Cola spokeswoman immediately branded the May 7 suit as "totally without merit." But in a motion to dismiss the complaint, filed on May 28, Coca-Cola acknowledged the heart of the complaint while maintaining that it was perfectly legal to insist that distributors handle only Coke products. Pepsi, the motion said, was "seeking to force Coca-Cola to allow its distributors also to carry the brands of its main competitor."

The court fight between the two soft-drink giants rests on Congress' decision in passing the 1890 Sherman Act to provide for enforcement of the law both by the government and by private individuals and companies. In the century since then, private antitrust suits have allowed consumers and companies injured by anti-competitive conduct to recover big damage awards: Successful plaintiffs can collect three times the amount they lost because of the antitrust violations plus punitive damages and attorney's fees.

In addition, private suits have sometimes pushed the government into taking action on its own. Most notably perhaps, an antitrust suit filed in March 1974 by an upstart long-distance carrier, MCI, against AT&T helped pave the way for the government suit eight months later that eventually forced the breakup of the telephone monopoly.

More recently, competitors of Microsoft Corp. were first to bring unfair competition claims against the computer giant while the Justice Department was still investigating. And the Federal Trade Commission's June 8 complaint against Intel Corp. stems in part from an antitrust claim against the microprocessor manufacturer by a manufacturer of computer work stations.

Private antitrust suits "have had a big impact," says William E. Kovacic, a professor at George Mason University Law School in Fairfax, Va. But he notes that since the mid-1970s the Supreme Court has issued a number of rulings creating substantive or procedural obstacles for antitrust plaintiffs. The trend continues. In October the high court issued a unanimous ruling making it harder for a dealer to challenge a maximum-price requirement imposed by a manufacturer or supplier.

Thomas Kauper, a professor at the University of Michigan Law School, agrees that Supreme Court rulings helped curb private antitrust suits after the boom period of the 1960s and early '70s. But he thinks litigation is now picking up. "My impression is that over the last seven or eight years, we're seeing a good deal more private litigation," Kauper says.

Joe Sims, a private antitrust lawyer in Washington, D.C., agrees, but he also sees a change in the kinds of suits being filed. In the past, Sims says, the most common kinds of suits were class actions brought on behalf of consumers injured by price-fixing or other anti-competitive conduct, or suits by dealers challenging restrictions imposed by manufacturers or suppliers. But Supreme Court rulings have made distribution suits more difficult, Sims says, while class actions have become too expensive to justify the risk.

Instead, Sims says there is an increase in what he calls "strategic litigation" — like the Pepsi-Coke suit. "It's big company vs. big company," Sims explains. "One big company is trying to deal with a business problem by invoking the antitrust laws. That's becoming reasonably common."

Whether brought by the government or by a private company or individual, antitrust litigation is expensive, time-consuming and dicey. But the payoff can be well worth the expense — as MCI's success in the telecommunications industry since 1974 shows. As for Pepsi, Sims says the cost of its antitrust suit is "not very relevant."

"Say it costs you $2-$3 million in legal fees to generate one of these cases," Sims says. "Two or three million dollars in the context of an important business issue is peanuts. If the result of what they do is they gain one or two or three market-share points, that completely overwhelms that expense."

Continued from p. 514

give the Justice Department and FTC advance notice of any merger valued at more than $15 million. The law also gives state attorneys general power to file civil antitrust suits on behalf of consumers — the provision being used in the states' antitrust suit against Microsoft. [15]

The Politics of Antitrust

The first great "trust-busting" president was a Republican: Theodore Roosevelt, who led the fight to break up Frank Harriman's Northern Pacific trust in 1904 and later bolted from the GOP because of what he saw as weakness on the issue on the part of his successor, William Howard Taft. Since then, support for antitrust enforcement has tended to be stronger in Democratic than in Republican administrations. That partisan split deepened with the conservative shift on antitrust issues during the Reagan and Bush administrations.

The Supreme Court continued to slow antitrust enforcement for a quarter-century after its Standard Oil decision. In 1918 and 1920, for example, the court rejected efforts to break up two giant companies, United Shoe Corp. and U.S. Steel Corp., despite evidence that each controlled more than 80 percent of its industry and had been guilty of questionable business practices. In the 1920s, the court also gave its blessing to the creation of industry trade associations despite concerns among some antitrust advocates that the groups could facilitate price-setting and market divisions among competitors.

President Franklin D. Roosevelt reinvigorated antitrust policy after a failed effort in his first term to link government, business and labor in the National Recovery Administration as a means of lifting the country out of the Great Depression. In his second term, he appointed Yale law Professor Thurman Arnold to head the Justice Department's antitrust division. Arnold viewed antitrust as a tool to eliminate "bottlenecks" that prevented full competition and increased prices to consumers.

His pragmatic approach disappointed some business critics, but it bore fruit in a number of consent decrees reshaping industry practices and some significant court victories after his departure from government — such as a celebrated 1945 decision curbing the Alcoa Co.'s monopoly power in unprocessed aluminum.

Roosevelt also had a lasting impact on antitrust policy through his appointment of liberal justices to the Supreme Court, two of whom — William O. Douglas and Hugo L. Black — each served for more than 30 years. The court's more favorable attitude toward government regulation did not produce an immediate change in antitrust doctrine. In 1947, for example, it issued an important decision rejecting the government's effort to prove a conspiracy to monopolize because of parallel-pricing policies followed by major film studios vis-a-vis independent theater owners. And in 1956 it rejected an effort to break the duPont chemical company's monopoly on cellophane, reasoning that other wrapping materials competed with duPont's product.

By the 1960s, however, Black and Douglas, along with Chief Justice Earl Warren and others, provided a somewhat reliable liberal majority that produced some of the court's furthest extensions of antitrust law. In the most controversial ruling, the court in 1962 upheld the government's effort to block the merger of Brown Shoe Co., the country's largest shoe manufacturer and third-largest retailer, with another major retailer, Kinney Shoe Co. Together, the two companies would have controlled only 5 percent of the retail market, but the court agreed with the government that the merger would violate the Celler-Kefauver Act by hastening concentration. Most controversially, Warren's opinion declared that the law called for the protection of small businesses even if it meant higher prices for consumers. [16]

The pro-small-business philosophy — derided by critics as "big is bad" — was seen in other court rulings in the decade that broke up mergers in industries that by today's standards would not have been viewed as concentrated. For its part, the Justice Department in 1968 adopted somewhat more lenient merger guidelines that nonetheless promised to oppose combinations even of relatively small firms in industries that were already "highly concentrated" — defined as four or more firms controlling 75 percent of market share.

Outside Washington, however, antitrust doctrine was shifting out from under the government's control. A band of scholars at the University of Chicago was shaping a new view of antitrust law that would displace the Jeffersonian rhetoric of protecting small businesses with a single-minded focus on economics and a predisposition to permit all but the most evidently anti-competitive mergers and business practices. By the 1980s, this so-called "New Learning" would come to dominate not only academic debate about antitrust issues but also policy decisions by the government and in the courts.

The Chicago School

The so-called Chicago school of antitrust traces its origins to works in the 1950s and '60s by University of Chicago law Professor Aaron Director and economists George Stigler and Ronald Coase. But the two Chicago scholars best known for propagating its tenets are Bork and Richard Posner. [17]

Posner, now a federal appeals court judge, set out what he regarded as a "scientific" theory of economic efficiency — one based on empirical study, not ideology — in two books: *Economic Analysis of Law* (1973) and *Antitrust Law: An Economic Perspective* (1976). [18] In Posner's view, competition was a means to an end — efficiency — rather than an end in itself. On that basis, he argued that "whenever monopoly would increase efficiency, it should be tolerated, indeed encouraged." In addition, as Peritz points out in his critical analysis, Posner focuses solely on maximizing production — "productive efficiency" — and dismisses any concerns about distribution of wealth as "political" or "social" rather than economic.

Bork's *The Antitrust Paradox* followed in 1978 with an even stronger denunciation of antitrust laws and the Supreme Court's decisions interpreting the laws. Antitrust law, he declared, was a "policy at war with itself" because of "mutually incompatible goals." Instead of focusing on the "only legitimate goal . . . the maximization of consumer welfare," antitrust law, he said, was primarily used to protect "the survival or comfort of small business." [19]

With surprising speed, the Chicago school displaced the previously dominant Harvard school of antitrust analysis, which had viewed the growth of large industrial organizations as a problem rather than a natural or even salutary feature of the economy. [20] Bork's book is acknowledged today even by its many critics as perhaps the most influential work on antitrust ever. Chicago school adherents take credit for ushering in an antitrust "revolution" with their emphasis on free-market economics. And, in fact, the Harvard school has all but disappeared, at least in name: The competing intellectual camp today is called the "post-Chicago school."

The Chicago school's anti-regulatory views matched the philosophy that Ronald Reagan brought to the White House after his election as president in 1980. Reagan appointed Chicago school disciples to key policy-making posts: William Baxter to head the antitrust division, James Miller to chair the FTC. Baxter took office saying that he would not consider "industry concentration" as a factor in decision-making. The Justice Department issued new merger guidelines in 1982, significantly relaxing the test for objecting to a combination; through the 1980s, the department challenged only 28 out of the 10,000 merger notifications filed. [21] Reagan also named Bork, Posner and many other Chicago school disciples to the federal bench, where they helped reorient the courts' interpretation of antitrust statutes. [22]

New Court Philosophy

For its part, the Supreme Court had already begun to take a more re-

laxed stance on antitrust issues by the mid-1970s. In one important decision, the court in 1974 approved a merger of two coal producers that resulted in a company with 50 percent market share; the opinion was written by Justice Potter Stewart, a dissenter from the court's stricter merger rulings in the 1960s. Three years later, the court in 1977 gave manufacturers leeway to impose restrictions on dealers, such as territorial franchises, even if the result was reduced competition among retailers. In the same year, the court made it somewhat harder for private companies to prove injury in antitrust suits. [23] The high court's conservative trend continued through the 1980s, especially after the Reagan-appointed justices forged a somewhat solid conservative majority under Chief Justice William H. Rehnquist.

The conservative trend did not completely supplant stricter antitrust views. Despite his general orientation, for example, Baxter presided over the completion of the breakup of AT&T in 1984 — and proudly took credit for his role. [24] The Supreme Court in 1985 issued a ruling, little noticed outside the antitrust bar, adopting the view that firms with monopoly power may violate antitrust law by refusing to let competitors use "essential facilities" — a doctrine with potential application to the Microsoft case. [25] Still, by decade's end, conservative antitrust perspectives had clearly come to dominate both the executive branch and, perhaps more significantly, the federal judiciary as well.

Antitrust Revival?

President Clinton gave encouraging signals to antitrust advocates by picking liberals for the government's

two top antitrust posts at the FTC and Justice Department. But as a self-styled New Democrat, Clinton was also interested in reassuring both Wall Street and Main Street that the administration was not reflexively pro-regulation or anti-business. In addition, the administration inherited the Reaganized federal judiciary, skeptical of expansive antitrust enforcement, as well as an increasingly globalized economy in which antitrust barriers were widely viewed as anachronistic and counterproductive.

To head the Justice Department's antitrust division, Clinton in 1993 appointed Bingaman, a former law professor and antitrust litigator with a Washington law firm. In her first two years in the antitrust post, Bingaman, the wife of New Mexico's Democratic senator, doubled the number of division cases challenging, restructuring or blocking proposed mergers. [26] But she also presided over one of the division's most embarrassing courtroom defeats when a federal judge in fall 1994 threw out a high-profile criminal price-fixing case against General Electric Co. on grounds the evidence was too weak.

When the term of holdover FTC Chair Janet Steiger expired in 1995, Clinton nominated Robert Pitofsky, a staunch liberal who had served two tours of duty at the agency and gone on to be a professor and dean of Georgetown University Law Center in Washington. Like Bingaman, Pitofsky brought to his post a more skeptical attitude toward mergers that helped thwart a number of proposed combinations submitted to the agency for review in his first year — for example, a $1.8 billion merger between two big drugstore chains, Rite Aid Corp. and Revco D.S. Inc. [27] But some mergers went through even after a hard look from the agency, most notably the 1996 telecommunications marriage of Time Warner Inc. and Turner Broadcasting System Inc. [28]

Klein won Senate confirmation to the Justice Department post last summer, but only after weathering some congressional criticism for approving the Bell Atlantic-Nynex merger while holding the position in an acting capacity. [29] While he continues to say he has no ideological predisposition against mergers, his more activist stand in recent cases has won over some skeptics. "Klein is underrated," Peritz says. "I certainly underrated him until recently." Sen. Ernest F. Hollings, a South Carolina Democrat who criticized Klein over the Bell Atlantic merger, said he "has done a fine job" so far. [30]

The antitrust division's statistics reflect an increase both in corporate marriages and in the Justice Department's scrutiny of the deals. In 1997 the division received 3,702 pre-merger notifications — more than double the number in the early years of the decade and one-third more than in 1988, the last full year of Reagan's presidency. The department initiated investigations in 220 of the cases in 1997 — nearly four times the 56 investigations begun in 1988. *(See graph, p. 508.)*

So far this year, the Justice Department has moved in court against two big deals: the Lockheed-Northrup Grumman merger and the plan by a satellite TV company jointly owned by MCI and Rupert Murdoch's News Corp. to merge with one owned by major cable TV companies. In announcing the satellite TV suit on May 12, Klein said, "unless this acquisition is blocked, consumers will be denied the benefits of competition — lower prices, more innovation and better services and quality."

In the same week, Justice Department attorneys and state attorneys general were putting the final touches on their lawsuits against Microsoft. Plans were set for a news conference to announce the suit on Thursday, May 14. But Gates, who had met with Klein privately the week before, made an eleventh-hour bid to try to settle the case without litigation. The suits were put on hold while lawyers on both sides met on Friday and Saturday. But the sessions ended with nothing but recriminations.

Software executives testify during a March 3, 1998 Senate Judiciary Committee hearing on competition and antitrust issues; from left: Bill Gates, Microsoft; Scott McNealy, Sun Microsystems; and Jim Barksdale, Netscape Communications.

Congressional Quarterly/Douglas Graham

After the suit was filed, Gates said he had tried to settle the case, but the government had presented Microsoft with "non-negotiable demands" that were designed to benefit its competitor, Netscape, at consumers' expense. For his part, Klein told reporters that Microsoft had not gone far enough to respond to the antitrust issues in the case. "What they put on the table would not by any means have benefited consumers or eliminated the anti-competitive practices that are alleged in the complaint," Klein said. ∎

CURRENT SITUATION

'Aggressive Competitor'

U ntil recently, Microsoft has enjoyed the kind of reputation that cannot be bought. In much of the public's mind, the company went from start-up to multibillion-dollar giant in less than two decades on the basis of nothing more than American-style work, smarts and entrepreneurship. "Microsoft should be celebrated as a hero," says James K. Glassman, a senior fellow at the American Enterprise Institute and columnist for *The Washington Post*.

Within the computer industry, however, another image of Microsoft formed in the past few years: that of a greedy monopolist that grew by imitating innovations by other companies and maintained its dominance through hardball negotiations with its partners and ruthless business practices toward its rivals.

"Microsoft is a very aggressive competitor," says James Love, director of the Consumer Project on Technology at the Center for the Study of Responsive Law, founded by Ralph Nader. "They use every conceivable weapon at their disposal to destroy their competitors."

The federal and state suits filed May 18 will give the government and Microsoft an opportunity to air those opposing views of the company in a federal court this fall. Microsoft asked for a seven-month delay before a hearing on the motions for a preliminary injunction, saying it needed time to study the allegations in the suits and the evidence already gathered by the Justice Department and the states. But federal Judge Thomas Penfield Jackson gave Microsoft a first-round defeat by cutting the requested delay nearly in half.

Jackson said he was concerned that a longer delay would allow Microsoft too much time to market Windows 98 without a ruling on the government's effort to force inclusion of Netscape's competing browser software. "By the time you propose to be ready," Jackson said at a May 22 hearing, "16-18 million horses will already be out of the barn, and that's too late."

Heading the Justice Department's team of lawyers at the hearing was David Boies, until recently a star litigator on Wall Street who years earlier led IBM's successful defense of the government's antitrust suit. [31] "This will be resolved very expeditiously," Boies said outside the courtroom.

For his part, Microsoft lead attorney William Neukom told reporters, "We will use the time the court has provided to . . . present a very powerful case."

The dueling press conferences on the day of the suits' filing, along with the complaints themselves and the Justice Department's accompanying 71-page legal memorandum, hint at the arguments both sides will make in the fall.

The most damning accusation — that Gates offered to divide the operating-system and applications markets with Netscape executives in 1995 — was backed up by depositions from Netscape officials. But Gates called the allegation "absolutely false." And Lopatka at the University of South Carolina says that even if the accusation is proved, the government may be entitled to nothing more than an injunction against any collusion in the future. "That

doesn't amount to much," he says.

Lopatka says Microsoft will be able to convince the judge that Microsoft's bundling of the browser software, limits on changing the Windows boot-up screen and restrictive agreements with Internet service and content providers all have sufficient business reasons or consumer benefits to offset any adverse effects on competition.

Other experts view the government's chances more positively, but still hedge their bets. "This is a pretty powerful complaint as complaints go," says AEI's Stelzer. "It's got a lot of good documentary evidence, but you can't say who's going to win."

Meanwhile, the FTC is preparing its own antitrust action against another computer industry giant: Intel Corp., which manufactures the Pentium microprocessing chip used in an estimated 80 percent of PCs. In a complaint filed with an FTC administrative law judge on June 8, the commission charged Intel with abusing its monopoly power by refusing to share technical information with three other computer companies that were both customers and potential competitors: Compaq Computer Corp., Digital Equipment Corp. and Intergraph Corp. The complaint charged that Intel was retaliating against the three companies for their actions in connection with patent-related disputes with Intel. In a statement, Intel denied that it had violated any laws, but executives reportedly acknowledged in interviews many of the facts alleged in the FTC complaint. [32]

The Urge to Merge

Supporters and critics of big business have sharply divergent views of the reasons for the current wave of corporate mergers and their likely effects. Supporters say the combinations stem from a desire to increase efficien-

cies in production and enhance opportunities, all to the ultimate benefit of consumers. Critics, however, say the mergers typically stem from an effort to reduce competition or take advantage of undervalued stock, benefiting corporate managers and shareholders but rarely producing the claimed benefits for consumers.

Many disinterested observers doubt the claims for consumer benefits. "There is scant hard evidence that mergers, hostile or friendly, have in fact generated the promised efficiencies," writes Peter Passell, an economics columnist for *The New York Times* generally sympathetic to business. [33]

Nonetheless, supporters of mergers appear to be dominating the current debate over the issue both in Washington and among the public at large. When Chrysler Corp. and the German automaker Daimler-Benz AG made the stunning announcement of their planned merger on May 6, hardly anyone was heard raising concerns about the effects on competition or consumers. *The Wall Street Journal*, the first newspaper to disclose the planned merger, reported after the announcement that antitrust lawyers in Europe and the United States — not specifically identified — expect the deal to be approved "because it wouldn't create a dominant player in the industry." [34]

Critics and observers did raise some concerns a month earlier when two giants in the financial-services industry, Citicorp and Travelers Group Inc., announced their planned merger on April 6. Still, most observers expect the deal to be approved. And the House of Representatives narrowly voted a few weeks later, on May 13, to repeal the federal Glass-Stegall Act, which limits the ability of banks to merge with securities firms. [35]

There is some evidence, however, of an increased willingness in Washington to question or challenge some mergers. The Justice Department's lawsuit filed March 23 to block the Lockheed Martin-Northrup Grumman

Continued on p. 523

At Issue:

Are antitrust enforcers right to be going after Microsoft?

THE NEW YORK TIMES

FROM AN EDITORIAL, MAY 19, 1998.

*i*n their sweeping antitrust suit against Microsoft, the Justice Department and 20 state attorneys general have made reasonable demands to preserve competition in the world of computers and the Internet. Bill Gates needs to respond with something better than disingenuous countercharges that his company is being punished for its success. Instead of forcing a protracted court battle over remedies, Microsoft should work with federal and state lawyers to reshape the marketplace to help consumers obtain the products they may want. . . .

Much will now depend on whether the Justice Department and attorneys general can prove their charges of illegal anti-competitive conduct. One of the most explosive charges disclosed yesterday was that Microsoft first tried to cut a deal with Netscape, makers of the main rival to its Web browser, to carve up the browser market. Only when that approach failed, said the department, did Microsoft shift tactics and try to muscle Netscape out of the market, fearing that its success on the Internet would supplant Microsoft's dominance in the operating system business. In response, Microsoft says that its conversations with Netscape were innocent and that every one of its decisions was a legal effort to serve its customers.

For all its heated language, the Justice Department stepped back from trying to block the shipment of Microsoft's Windows 98 operating system. . . . Instead, the government wants Microsoft to unbundle its own browser, Internet Explorer, from Windows 98 or to include the rival Netscape browser along with it. The government also wants Microsoft to stop giving preference to its own software products on the screen that first comes up when customers turn on their computers.

Microsoft maintains that everything it is being asked to do is impractical. That is for the courts to decide. But Mr. Gates must know better than to assert that the government's demands are the equivalent of asking Coca Cola to include cans of Pepsi in all its six-packs. Coca Cola is not a monopoly, but Microsoft's operating system is. It would be better if Mr. Gates recognized that reality and stopped behaving as if his company were still a struggling upstart. As he said yesterday, the world awaits an era of accelerating change in computers, with undreamed-of products in voice recognition, artificial intelligence and Internet commerce. The Justice Department and the attorneys general are right that the inventors of products in these areas must be allowed to market them to consumers free of a stranglehold by Microsoft.

THE ROCKY MOUNTAIN NEWS

FROM AN EDITORIAL, MAY 20, 1998.

*i*f the Justice Department's antitrust action against Microsoft is justified — and we emphasis if — it is because the law, as interpreted by the U.S. Supreme Court, prohibits a dominant company in any industry from engaging in ruthless restraint of trade and anti-competitive acts. And while it has yet to be ruled on in court, Microsoft at least appears to have taken occasional unfair advantage of the fact that it's the producer of 90 percent of all computer operating systems in place in this country. . . .

The difficulty for anyone inclined to support the government's lawsuit on those limited grounds is that the Justice Department has much broader and more dubious motives for its lawsuit. While government lawyers apparently don't envision breaking Microsoft up, in the manner of Standard Oil and AT&T, they are intent on regulating the content of Microsoft's products. This is bad business, bad economics and utterly perverse public policy. Federal and state prosecutors must recognize that Microsoft became as dominant as it is through business savvy and ingenuity and because consumers want its products. It is nothing short of alarming that prosecutors should insist that Microsoft either exclude its own browser from its new Windows 98 software or include Netscape's. . . .

The government has no business prescribing what such a product might be like, and becomes something as bad as anti-competitive when it does. It becomes anti-innovative. There are many other extraordinary software features that could soon be coming around the bend, and Microsoft technicians should have an incentive to develop them and stick them in Windows. In what other instance has a firm been told it must diminish what it sells or promote and sell a competitive product? An equally disturbing aspect of the government's case is its focus: the most dynamic sector of the U.S. economy. After all, it is hard to identify the victims of Microsoft's alleged predatory activities. Netscape? Perhaps, although it retains a healthy share of the browser market. Consumers? Hardly. The price of software and other computer products has continued their 20-year plunge. If Microsoft were exploiting consumers and stifling innovation — the classic profile of a monopolist — then a government lawsuit might be more understandable. Instead, Microsoft leads a sector of the economy that is the envy of the world. The truth is that Microsoft represents just a small fraction of all software business and is far from immune to a competitor who has better ideas.

U.S. Mergers Add Up to $Billions

Here are some of the major corporate mergers proposed recently involving U.S. firms:

	Companies	Date Proposed	Value	Status
PENDING	American Home Products Corp., Monsanto Co.	June 1, 1998	$35 billion	Likely to be reviewed by the Federal Trade Commission(FTC)
	Citicorp, Travelers Group Inc.	April 6 , 1998	$70 billion	Pending review by Federal Reserve Board, Comptroller of the Currency
	Daimler-Benz AG, Chrysler Corp.	May 7, 1998	$38 billion	Being reviewed by U.S., European authorities
	Lockheed Martin Corp. Northrup Grumman Corp.	July 3, 1997	$2.9 billion	Justice Dept. opposing merger in court
	McKesson Corp., AmeriSource Health Corp.	Sept. 23, 1997	$1.7 billion	FTC opposing merger in court, as well as merger of two other wholesalers: Cardinal Health, Inc., and Bergen Brunswig Corp.
	NationsBank Corp. BankAmerica Corp.	April 13, 1998	$30 billion	Pending review by banking regulators
	SBC Communications Inc., Ameritech Corp.	May 11, 1998	$56.2 billion	Pending review by Federal Communications Commission (FCC), Justice Dept., state regulators
	WorldCom Inc., MCI Communications Corp.	Nov. 10, 1997	$37 billion	Pending review by Justice Dept., European Union (EU) Commission
APPROVED	Bell Atlantic Corp., Nynex Corp.	April 21, 1996	$23 billion	Approved by FCC in August 1997, with some pro-competitive conditions; Justice Dept. decided in April 1997 not to oppose deal
	Bertlesmann AG, Random House Inc.	March 23, 1998	$1.5 billion	Approved by FTC May 29; FTC initiated "second request" review
	Boeing Co., McDonnell Douglas Corp.	Dec. 15, 1996	$13 billion	Completed July 1997 after FTC decision not to oppose deal; some concessions to win approval of European Union
	Thomson Corp., West Publishing Co.	Feb. 26, 1996	$ 3.4 billion	Justice Dept. approved merger, June 1996, after firms agreed to license products, sell some publications
FAILED	SBC Communications Inc., AT&T Corp.	May 1997 (talks disclosed)	$50 billion	Merger talks called off June 27 because of business disagreements, likely opposition from FCC
	SmithKline Beecham PLC, American Home Products Corp.	Jan. 20, 1998 (talks disclosed)	$60 billion (estimate)	British firm called off talks to pursue merger with Glaxo Wellcome PLC; those talks also failed
	Staples Inc., Office Depot Inc.	Sept. 4, 1995	$3.4 billion	Merger blocked after federal judge upheld FTC bid to enjoin deal, June 30, 1997

Source: Facts on File

Continued from p. 520

merger surprised many observers because it had failed to move against previous mergers among defense contractors in the past several years, including the $13.4 billion merger between Boeing and McDonnell Douglas last August. [36]

FCC Chairman William Kennard similarly took a tougher line than the agency's previous stance on mergers when SBC and Ameritech announced their planned merger on May 11. The two companies will have "a high burden" to prove that the merger is in consumers' best interest, Kennard told the *Chicago Tribune* the day after the announcement. He said that in approving the Bell Atlantic-Nynex merger and SBC's earlier acquisition of Pacific Telesis, the commission "didn't contemplate further mergers" between the so-called Baby Bells. [37]

Some lawmakers also were raising questions about reduced competition in other industries. The day after American Airlines and US Airways announced plans for a so-called marketing alliance on April 23, Senate Commerce Committee Chairman John McCain, an Arizona Republican, criticized the move and called for legislation to remove what he called "institutional impediments to competition" in the airline industry.

Still, most industry observers appear to expect most of the proposed mergers to win approval either in whole or in part. One recent trend has been for companies to announce merger plans and then gain regulatory approval by making concessions — for example, selling off some parts of one or the other company or agreeing to certain conditions aimed at promoting competition. [38] MCI Communications was following that strategy when it announced plans on May 28 to sell off its Internet facilities in order to win approval from European regulators of its merger with the British-based telecommunications giant, WorldCom. ■

OUTLOOK

'Hundred Years' War'

When it recently surveyed the history of the U.S. market system in the 20th century, *The Wall Street Journal* prepared a chart with major events characterized either as "promoting" or "restricting" markets. Most of the economic regulatory statutes on the list — like the Food and Drug Act of 1907 or the National Labor Relations Act of 1937 — were shown as restricting markets. But as the century's first important event promoting markets, the newspaper listed, "[Theodore] Roosevelt begins 'trust-busting' campaign." [39]

The view of antitrust laws as an important, even essential, element of a free-market system has lasted for more than a century and still has a powerful hold on the views of policymakers and the public at large. "In the long run, the enormous productivity and wealth of the American economy depends on keeping competitive forces powerful," says the AEI's Stelzer.

But that favorable assessment of antitrust policy has never gone unchallenged. Today, the criticism of antitrust enforcement is gaining strength in some quarters even as the federal government shows greater interest in flexing its muscles to promote competition in the marketplace. "Given innovation, technology and dynamic markets, it's hard to imagine that there is such a thing as a sustainable monopoly absent governmental barriers" to competition, says Levy at the Cato Institute.

The spurt of antitrust enforcement by the Justice Department and the FTC over the past year has been depicted — sometimes positively, sometimes not — as an antitrust "revival." "The temperature is rising," Stelzer says.

But some consumer advocates say that even with the increased activity and interest, both the administration and Congress are too weak in promoting and protecting competition.

"This administration has been in the last few years extremely modest and timid to the point of endangering the emergence of competition in key industries," says Kimmelman of Consumers Union. "And Congress and state and federal regulators have eliminated a lot of ownership restrictions and permitted a lot of consolidations to take place."

Federal courts are also less receptive toward antitrust cases than they had been in the past, chiefly from the late 1930s through the mid-'70s. "In the modern era, when the government has been forced to litigate, their track record has not been particularly good," George Mason's Kovacic says.

The likely outcome of the administration's current major antitrust cases is very much uncertain. The Supreme Court precedents on illegal tying arrangements that the administration cites in its suit against Microsoft are viewed by some legal observers as inconclusive. As for the mergers, the high court has not issued a ruling in the area for 25 years. And Kovacic believes one reason for the gap is that the Justice Department has been loath to appeal merger cases to the court for fear of getting a ruling that would raise the standard for blocking corporate combinations.

In his history of "competition policy," Peritz characterizes the period since passage of the Sherman Act as a "hundred years' war" between two competing visions of freedom: freedom from private economic power or freedom from government power. "Because we dread domination — both political and economic — we have called for policy that limits both kinds of power, policy that satisfies commitments to both individual liberty and rough equality," he writes. [40]

"Antitrust policy has been almost a Rorschach test" for social and political values, Peritz adds today. "Has it been successful in serving the dominant interests at the time? Yes. Has there been historical consistency? No, but I don't know that historical consistency is something that we should demand." ∎

Notes

[1] The cases filed in U.S. District Court in Washington, D.C., are *U.S. v. Microsoft Corp.*, 98-1232, and *New York v. Microsoft Corp.*, 98-1233.

[2] The states filing suit were California, Connecticut, Florida, Illinois, Iowa, Kansas, Kentucky, Louisiana, Maryland, Massachusetts, Michigan, Minnesota, New Mexico, New York, North Carolina Ohio, South Carolina, Utah, West Virginia, and Wisconsin. The District of Columbia also joined the suit. See *The Wall Street Journal*, May 28, 1998, p. A24. For background on the Internet, see "Regulating the Internet," *The CQ Researcher*, June 30, 1995, pp. 561-584.

[3] For background on Microsoft and Gates, see Stephen Manes and Paul Andrews, *Gates: How Microsoft's Mogul Reinvented an Industry — And Made Himself the Richest Man in America* (1993), James Wallace and Jim Erickson, *Hard Drive: Bill Gates and the Making of the Microsoft Empire* (1992), and, for a sharply critical account, Jennifer Edstrom and Marlin Eller, *Barbarians Led by Bill Gates: Microsoft from the Inside* (1998).

[4] For background on antitrust policy and professional sports, see "The Business of Sports," *The CQ Researcher*, Feb. 10, 1995, pp. 121-144.

[5] The quote comes from the decision in *United States v. Topco Associates Inc.* (1973).

[6] For background on Archer Daniels Midland, see *The Wall Street Journal*, Oct. 16, 1996, p. A4. The Decatur, Ill.- based company pleaded guilty to two criminal counts for fixing prices with foreign producers of lysine, a livestock-feed additive, and citric acid, an ingredient in numerous foods and beverages. For background on Ucar International, see *The Washington Post*, April 8, 1998, p. C13. Ucar alleg-

edly conspired with unnamed co-conspirators to set prices and production levels in the world market.

[7] Robert H. Bork, *The Antitrust Paradox: A Policy at War With Itself* (1978), p. 4.

[8] Frank H. Easterbrook, "Workable Antitrust Policy," *Michigan Law Review*, Vol. 84, p. 1701 (1986).

[9] Packard Bell NEC Inc. became the first PC maker to take advantage of the option when it announced on May 29 that it would block access to Microsoft's browser in a new line of notebook computers about to be unveiled.

[10] Much of the background is drawn from Rudolph J.R. Peritz, *Competition Policy in America, 1888-1992: History, Rhetoric, Law* (1994).

[11] Robert H. Bork, "Legislative Intent and the Policy of the Sherman Act," *Journal of Law and Economics*, Vol. 9, pp. 7-48 (1966). See also Bork, *The Antitrust Paradox*, op. cit., pp. 50-71. Bork, now a fellow at the American Enterprise Institute, emerged in spring 1998 as a supporter of the government's antitrust actions against Microsoft. Bork said his stance was consistent with his previous views but also acknowledged that he was working as a paid consultant to Microsoft's rival, Netscape. See Robert H. Bork, "What Antitrust Is All About," *The New York Times*, May 4, 1998, p. A19.

[12] For differing interpretations of Congress' intent in passing the Sherman Act, see Robert H. Lande, "Wealth Transfers as the Original and Primary Concern of Antitrust: The Efficiency Interpretation Challenged," *Hastings Law Journal*, Vol. 34 pp. 68-151 (1982), excerpted in Sullivan, op. cit., pp. 71-84; and David Million, "The Sherman Act and the Balance of Power," *Southern California Law Review*, Vol. 61, pp. 1219-92 (1988), excerpted in Sullivan, op. cit., pp. 85-115.

[13] The decisions are *Standard Oil v. United States* and *United States v. American Tobacco Co.* See Peritz, op. cit., pp. 50-52.

[14] The speaker was Sen. James Reed, a Missouri Democrat; quoted in ibid., p. 65.

[15] See *1976 Congressional Quarterly Almanac*, p. 431-438, and *1974 Congressional Quarterly Almanac*, pp. 291-292. For assessments of the impact of the premerger notification rule and other provisions of the law, see "Symposium: Twenty Years of Hart-Scott-Rodino Merger Enforcement," *Antitrust Law Journal*, Vol. 65, spring 1997, pp. 813-927.

[16] The decision is *Brown Shoe Co. v. United States*.

[17] For background, and a critical interpretation, see Peritz, op. cit., pp. 236-245. Peritz cites as a seminal article Ronald Coase, "The

Theory of Social Cost," *Journal of Law & Economics*, Vol. 3, 1960, pp. 1-44.

[18] For a summary of Posner's views, contrasted with those of the "Harvard school," see Richard A. Posner, "The Chicago School of Antitrust Analysis," *University of Pennsylvania Law Review*, Vol. 127, pp. 925-948 (1979), excerpted in Sullivan, op. cit., pp. 193-209.

[19] Bork, op. cit., pp. 3-11.

[20] The classic Harvard school text is Carl Kaysen and Donald Turner, *Antitrust Policy: An Economic and Legal Analysis* (1959). For an excerpt, see Sullivan, op. cit., pp. 181-192.

[21] See Peritz, op. cit., p. 278.

[22] See William E. Kovacic, "Reagan's Judicial Appointees and Antitrust in the 1990s," *Fordham Law Review*, Vol. 60, 1991, pp. 49-124.

[23] The cases, in order, are *United States v. General Dynamics* (1974); *Continental T.V., Inc. v. GTE Sylvania, Inc.* (1977); and *Brunswick Corp. v. Pueblo Bowl-O-Mat, Inc.* (1977). See ibid., pp. 97-98.

[24] For an account of the AT&T case, see Steve Coll, *The Deal of the Century: The Breakup of AT&T* (1986).

[25] The case is *Aspen Skiing Co. v. Aspen Highlands Skiing Corp.* (1985).

[26] For background, see *The New York Times*, Oct. 22, 1995, sec. 3, p. 1.

[27] See *The New York Times*, April 25, 1996, p. D1. For biographical background, see *The Washington Post*, April 13, 1995, p. D12.

[28] See *The New York Times*, Sept. 13, 1996, p. D1.

[29] For a profile, see *The Wall Street Journal*, May 18, 1998, p. A1.

[30] *The Washington Post*, March 24, 1998, p. C5.

[31] For a profile of David Boies, see Amy Singer, "A Firm Of His Own," *The American Lawyer*, May 1998, p. 62.

[32] See *The New York Times*, June 9, 1998, p. A1; *The Wall Street Journal*, June 9, 1998, p. A3.

[33] Peter Passell, "Do Mergers Really Yield Big Benefits?", *The New York Times*, May 14, 1998, p. D1. See also Peter Passell, "When Mega-Mergers Are Mega-Busts," *The New York Times*, May 17, 1998, p. E18.

[34] *The Wall Street Journal*, May 7, 1998, A10.

[35] See *CQ Weekly*, May 16, 1998, p. 1301. Senate action is regarded as less likely.

[36] See *The Washington Post*, April 7, 1998, p. C2.

[37] *The Chicago Tribune*, May 13, 1998, p. A1.

[38] See *The Wall Street Journal*, March 4, 1997, p. A1.

[39] *The Wall Street Journal*, May 14, 1998, p. A10.

[40] Peritz, op. cit., p. 3.

Bibliography

Selected Sources Used

Books

Bork, Robert H., *The Antitrust Paradox: A Policy at War With Itself,* Basic Books, 1978.

Bork, a Yale law professor at the time, helped provoke a thorough re-examination of antitrust doctrine with his controversial thesis that antitrust laws have no justification except to promote "consumer welfare" — defined in terms of productive efficiency. The book includes detailed source notes.

Gellhorn, Ernest, and William E. Kovacic, *Antitrust Law and Economics in a Nutshell,* West Publishing, 1994.

This primer, written for a legal audience, covers the major topics in antitrust law, including horizontal and vertical restraints, mergers, price discrimination and so forth. It includes the text of the key parts of the Sherman and Clayton acts as well as a table of cases. Gellhorn, a former law school professor and dean, is an attorney in Washington; Kovacic is a professor at George Mason University School of Law.

High, Jack C., and Wayne E. Gable (eds.), *A Century of the Sherman Act: American Economic Opinion, 1890-1990,* George Mason University Press, 1992.

The book includes 17 articles — most of them critical of antitrust policy — written by leading economists dating from the early 20th century through the mid-1980s. High and Gable are professors at George Mason University.

Peritz, Rudolph J.R., *Competition Policy in America, 1888-1992: History, Rhetoric, Law,* Oxford University Press, 1996.

Peritz, a professor at New York Law School, synthesizes the history of antitrust law with other political, economic and intellectual trends from the adoption of the Sherman Act in 1890 through the Reagan and Bush presidencies. The book includes detailed source notes. For a number of articles discussing and critiquing the book, see "Symposium: Provocations and Reflections Upon Competition Policy in America," *The Antitrust Bullet,* Vol. 42, No. 2 (summer 1997), pp. 239-456.

Shenefield, John H., and Irwin M. Stelzer, *The Antitrust Laws: A Primer* [3d ed.], American Enterprise Institute Press, 1998 [forthcoming].

This 142-page primer, written for a business audience, provides a compact overview of antitrust laws, agencies and concepts. It includes a two-page suggested list of further readings. Shenefield, a former assistant attorney general for antitrust, is now a Washington lawyer; Stelzer, an economist, is director of regulatory policy studies at the American Enterprise Institute in Washington.

Sullivan, E. Thomas [ed.], *The Political Economy of the Sherman Act: The First One Hundred Years,* Oxford University Press, 1992.

This anthology includes 15 excerpted articles by leading scholars and policy-makers representing major developments in the political, economic and intellectual debates about antitrust policy. Sullivan is dean of the University of Minnesota law school. He is also co-author with Herbert Hovenkamp of the University of Iowa law school of an antitrust casebook, *Antitrust Law, Policy, and Procedure* (Michie Publishing, 3d ed., 1994).

Articles

Lowenstein, Roger, "Trust in Markets: Antitrust Enforcers Drop the Ideology, Focus on Economics," *The Wall Street Journal,* Feb. 27, 1997.

The 3,350-word article gives an excellent overview of the development of antitrust policy from passage of the Sherman Act in 1890 through President Clinton's first term. The article was part of a series entitled "Amalgamated America." A later article analyzed enforcement policies by antitrust agencies. See John R. Wilke and Bryan Gruley, "Merger Monitors: Acquisitions Can Mean Long-Lasting Scrutiny by Antitrust Agencies," *The Wall Street Journal,* March 4, 1997, p. A1.

FOR MORE INFORMATION

If you would like to have this CQ Researcher updated, or need more information about this topic, please call CQ Custom Research. Special rates for CQ subscribers. (202) 887-8600 or (800) 432-2250, ext. 600, or E-mail Custom.Research@cq.com

Information and documents about the antitrust suit against Microsoft Corp. and the company's response can be found at the following world wide web sites: **Justice Department**, www.usdoj.gov/atr; **states** [National Association of Attorneys General], www.naag.org; **Microsoft**, www.microsoft.com.

Cato Institute, 1000 Massachusetts Ave., N.W., Washington, D.C. 20001; (202) 842-0200; www.cato.org. The libertarian think tank has published a number of monographs critical of government regulation of the marketplace.

Center for Responsive Law, P.O. Box 19367, Washington, D.C. 20036; (202) 387-8030; www.essential.org. The center's Consumer Project on Technology studies competition issues in the computer industry.

Consumers Union, 1666 Connecticut Ave., N.W., Suite 310, Washington, D.C. 20009; (202) 462-6262; www.consunion.org. Consumers Union, publisher of *Consumer Reports,* lobbies on a range of consumer issues.

The Next Step

Additional information from UMI's Newspaper & Periodical Abstracts™ database

Mergers

Barrie, Chris, and Stephen Moss, "Analysis: Publishing Mergers: Meet Some German Literary Types; At Least They are All Published by Random House, Which is Being Taken Over by the German Giant Bertelsmann; Can the Book World Survive Such Mergers," *The Guardian*, March 25, 1998, p. 17.

When Random House bought Reed Consumer Books last year, it was labeled the publishing merger of the decade. Some threw up their hands in horror at the concentration of so much publishing muscle in one firm, so many of Britain's finest literary imprints in one corporate headquarters. Yet that merger has now been dwarfed by the news that last year's predator has become the prey, and that Random House is now to be bought by the giant German media conglomerate Bertelsmann AG.

Block, Sandra, "Mergers Creating Windfall; Financial Services Stock Funds Surge," *USA Today*, April 20, 1998, p. B1.

The bank mega-mergers of the last two weeks have created a windfall for investors in bank stocks and financial services mutual funds. Often, that kind of explosive growth is followed by a sharp decline. But with more consolidation expected among the USA's 9,000 banks, fund managers say there's plenty of fuel left in financial-services stocks. "Buying funds from the hottest sector usually blows up on you," says Russ Kinnel, analyst for fund-tracker Morningstar. "This is the one exception. It just keeps going and going."

Heightchew, Alison, "Antitrust and Affiliations Among Healthcare Providers: The Need for a Level Playing Field," *Hospital & Health Services Administration* (HHS), winter 1997, pp. 559-565.

Under pressure to remain competitive in the rapidly changing health-care industry, policy leaders and health-care administrators face the challenge of resolving antitrust matters arising from the creation of innovative health-care provider affiliations. Softening antitrust laws in favor of provider-sponsored health-care affiliations will provide the flexibility necessary for effective health-care reform.

Herman, Edward, "The Threat from Mergers: Can Antitrust Make a Difference," *Dollars & Sense*, May 1998, pp. 10-15.

Ever since President Ronald Reagan took office, there has been a more relaxed attitude towards giant mergers. Some of the dangers posed by these mergers are discussed.

"House Panel Is Told Huge Bank Mergers Raise Customers' Fees," *The Wall Street Journal*, April 30, 1998, p. C20.

On the heels of several huge financial-services mergers, a House Banking Committee hearing yesterday turned into a forum on why bigger isn't necessarily better. Lawmakers and consumer advocates complained that big mergers often result in higher fees for individual customers and fewer loans for small businesses.

Pae, Peter, "Bank Executives Defend Mergers; Rep. Kennedy Calls for Moratorium on Deals Until Effects on Consumers Are Probed," *The Washington Post*, April 30, 1998, p. D4.

Huge bank mergers will benefit consumers, bank executives insisted yesterday at a House panel exploring the impact of the recent shake-up in the financial services industry. But one panel member, Rep. Joseph P. Kennedy II, D-Mass., said he was not convinced by the bankers' assurances at the day-long House Banking Committee hearing, and he called for a moratorium on the mergers until their effects are fully investigated.

Strazewski, Len, "Silicon Prairie Begins to Flourish But Labor Shortages, Mergers Spark Fears," *Chicago Tribune*, April 20, 1998, p. 16.

Andrew "Flip" Filipowski, chief executive officer of Platinum Technology Inc. in Oakbrook Terrace, sees a lot more than highways and housing developments in the suburbs surrounding Chicago. He sees a fertile Silicon Prairie, a natural habitat for thriving high-tech companies, cutting-edge research and new business development that is slowly starting to compete with California's famed Silicon Valley.

Truell, Peter, "Buoyant Stock Market Keeps Mergers in Pipeline," *The New York Times*, Jan. 5, 1998, p. D3.

Telephone companies, regional banks, Wall Street firms, hotels and casinos, oil and gas ventures, radio and television stations — the list is almost endless as a growing procession of industries is caught up in the enthusiasm for takeovers. After yet another record year for mergers and acquisitions, the trend shows little sign of abating, experts say. With just the deals that are now in the pipeline, they say, 1998 will be another very active year for the merger mavens, particularly those who specialize in telecommunications, financial, high-technology and health-care companies. The total value of mergers and acquisitions announced in the United States last year was $919 billion, according to the Securities Data Company.

Microsoft Suit

Cortese, Amy, Mike France, Susan Garland, Steve Hamm and Michael Mandel, "Epilogue: Weighing the Risks

and Rewards," *Business Week*, April 20, 1998, p. 126.

The Microsoft case will test whether antitrust still matters. The Justice Department must ultimately decide what antitrust policy will best promote competition and innovation in the software industry.

Telephone Companies

Gruley, Bryan, John Simons and John Wilke, "Alarm Bells: Is This Really What Congress Had in Mind With the Telecom Act? SBC-Ameritech Deal Sparks Debate Over Big Mergers Fostered by Deregulation — 'Nobody's Got a Clear Vision'," *The Wall Street Journal*, May 12, 1998, p. A1.

In a statement yesterday, William Kennard, chairman of the Federal Communications Commission, issued a challenge to SBC and Ameritech, in the midst of a mega-merger: "The bottom-line question is: Is this merger going to create competition, or will it be a non-aggression pact? The Telecom Act was all about opening markets for competition. SBC and Ameritech must show us that this merger will serve the public interest and enhance competition." The political reaction is crucial, and not just to the two companies. If the merger is flatly rejected, it sends the message that the Baby Bells' forays into other businesses — especially the lucrative long-distance market — won't be tolerated until and unless they open their local markets to competition.

Price-Fixing

Fairclough, Gordon, "Ucar to Pay Record $110 Million In Federal Probe of Price Fixing," *The Wall Street Journal*, April 8, 1998, p. B21.

Ucar International Inc., one of the world's largest makers of graphite electrodes, said it agreed to plead guilty to criminal price-fixing and pay the largest antitrust fine in U.S. history, $110 million. Federal prosecutors say Ucar, based in Danbury, Conn., conspired with other, unidentified, companies to rig prices and squelch competition in the international market for graphite electrodes, an essential component in electric-arc furnaces used to produce steel.

Felsenthal, Edward, "Court Clears Way for Price-Fixing Case," *The Wall Street Journal*, March 24, 1998, p. B12.

The justices, without comment, let stand a ruling by the federal appeals court in Chicago that exposed the companies to potentially significant liability. The massive litigation, filed by 40,000 independent drugstores around the country, challenges a two-tiered pricing system in

which pharmaceutical concerns offer discounts to health-maintenance organizations.

Goodyear, Charlie, "Ex-Paper Boy Throws Suit at Newspaper; Contra Costa Times Accused of Price- Fixing," *San Francisco Chronicle*, April 23, 1998, p. D2.

A 16-year-old former paper boy and his stepfather are suing the *Contra Costa Times* on behalf of more than 1,000 newspaper carriers, accusing the daily of antitrust violations and price-fixing. The suit seeks $33 million in damages and claims that the Times forced carriers to deliver newspapers to deadbeat subscribers and never told them that they could choose the price at which to sell the papers.

Millman, Nancy, "ADM Will Pay $36 Million to Settle Citric-Acid Price-Fixing Suit," *Chicago Tribune*, March 5, 1998, p. 1.

Archer Daniels Midland Co. agreed Wednesday to pay $36 million to four food companies to settle a civil lawsuit that claimed the companies were overcharged for a food additive because ADM and its competitors had fixed prices. Along with this payment, ADM has paid nearly $200 million to resolve federal criminal charges and civil complaints. And the company may have to pay more because it still faces a class-action suit alleging price-fixing in its biggest market, high-fructose corn syrup.

O'Donnell, Jayne, "Price-Fixing Charged in Laser Eye Surgery," *USA Today*, March 25, 1998, p. A1.

The Federal Trade Commission voted Tuesday to charge the two companies that sell the laser used for corrective eye surgery with price-fixing. Consumers should pay $500 less for the procedure to correct nearsightedness if a judge upholds the action. The agency wants to dissolve a partnership formed by VISX of Santa Clara, Calif., and Summit Technology of Waltham, Mass., because the companies agreed to charge ophthalmologists a $250 royalty fee per eye for each procedure.

O'Donnell, Jayne, "Stiffer Fines Sought in Price-Fixing Cases," *USA Today*, Feb. 26, 1998, p. B1.

The Justice Department will ask Congress today to increase from $10 million to $100 million the maximum fines the government can seek from price-fixers and other antitrust violators. Antitrust chief Joel I. Klein says bigger penalties will deter the growing threat of international cartels — multinational conspirators who get together to fix prices, rig bids and divvy up customers. Officials say many antitrust conspiracies — some involving more than $1 billion in commerce annually — can make back the cost of a $10 million fine within months.

Back Issues

Great Research on Current Issues Starts Right Here.
Recent topics covered by The CQ Researcher are listed below.
Now available on the Web
For information, call (800) 432-2250 ext. 279 or (202) 887-6279.

If you would like to have any of these CQ Researchers updated, or need more information about these topics, please call CQ Custom Research. Special rates for CQ subscribers. (202) 887-8600 or (800) 432-2250, ext. 600, or E-mail Custom.Research@cq.com

Back issues are available for $5.00 (subscribers) or $10.00 (non-subscribers). Quantity discounts apply to orders over 10. To order, call Congressional Quarterly Customer Service at (202) 887-8621.

Binders are available for $18.00. To order call 1-800-638-1710. Please refer to stock number 648.

Future Topics

▶ *Environmental Justice*

▶ *Sleep Deprivation*

▶ *Encouraging Teen Abstinence*

Environmental Justice

Does the movement help poor communities?

oxic-waste dumps, sewage-treatment plants and other pollution sources rarely are found near middle-class or affluent communities. Inner-city neighborhoods, rural Hispanic villages and Indian reservations are far more likely to suffer. But a burgeoning new movement is helping poor communities across the country to close the door on unwelcome dumps and factories. Charging that they are victims of environmental racism, activists are winning court battles on the ground that siting polluting facilities among disadvantaged people violates Title VI of the 1964 Civil Rights Act. But business representatives and residents of some affected minority communities say that the movement is stifling their opportunities for economic development and growth.

CQ | **June 19, 1998** • **Volume 8, No. 23** • **Pages 529-552**

Formerly Editorial Research Reports

Environmental Justice

CQ Researcher

June 19, 1998
Volume 8, No.23

EDITOR
Sandra Stencel

MANAGING EDITOR
Thomas J. Colin

ASSOCIATE EDITOR
Sarah M. Magner

STAFF WRITERS
Adriel Bettelheim
Mary H. Cooper
Kenneth Jost
Kathy Koch
David Masci

PRODUCTION EDITOR
Melissa Hall

EDITORIAL ASSISTANT
Laura S. Cavender

PUBLISHED BY
Congressional Quarterly Inc.

CHAIRMAN
Andrew Barnes

VICE CHAIRMAN
Andrew P. Corty

PRESIDENT AND PUBLISHER
Robert W. Merry

EXECUTIVE EDITOR
David Rapp

Bibliographic records and abstracts included in The Next Step section of this publication are the copyrighted material of UMI, and are used with permission.

The CQ Researcher (ISSN 1056-2036). Formerly Editorial Research Reports. Published weekly, except Jan. 2, May 29, July 3, Oct. 30, by Congressional Quarterly Inc., 1414 22nd St., N.W., Washington, D.C. 20037. Annual subscription rate for libraries, businesses and government is $340. Additional rates furnished upon request. Periodicals postage paid at Washington, D.C., and additional mailing offices. POSTMASTER: Send address changes to The CQ Researcher, 1414 22nd St., N.W., Washington, D.C. 20037.

COVER: CONTAMINATED DRAINAGE DITCHES RUN THROUGH THE LARGELY AFRICAN-AMERICAN HYDE PARK NEIGHBORHOOD IN AUGUSTA, GA. (ENVIRONMENTAL JUSTICE RESOURCE CENTER)

Environmental Justice

BY MARY H. COOPER

THE ISSUES

An impoverished area of southern Louisiana has become the latest battleground in the struggle for civil rights. Only this time the goal is not desegregation or affirmative action but the right to a clean environment.

The controversy in rural St. James Parish focuses on 3,000 acres of sugar cane and a $700 million plastics plant planned by a Japanese manufacturer. The fight pits Shintech Inc. and a cadre of local supporters against environmental activists and other residents who want no part of it.

"This is our *Brown v. Board of Education*, our line in the dirt," says Robert D. Bullard, executive director of the Environmental Justice Resource Center at Clark Atlanta University. "This community is already overburdened with toxic plants."

Indeed, the parish lies along a stretch of the Mississippi River between Baton Rouge and New Orleans that is so heavily industrialized it's known as "cancer alley." More than 120 chemical plants line the 120-mile river corridor, many of which have spewed thousands of tons of dioxin and other carcinogens into the air, water and soil for decades. The parish itself is already home to 11 fertilizer and chemical plants.

Bullard and other activists argue that it is no accident that so many toxic polluters have zeroed in on the region. Throughout the country, they say, poor and minority communities are disproportionately exposed to noxious industry byproducts. Siting the Shintech plant in St. James Parish, they contend, would amount to yet another instance of environmental racism, another ex-

ample of a poor community not benefiting from the nationwide improvements in environmental quality over the past three decades.

Since Bullard helped lead the call for environmental justice in the early 1980s, the movement has won high-level support. In 1994, President Clinton issued an executive order directing all federal agencies with a public health or environmental mission to make environmental justice an integral part of their policies and activities. "All communities and persons across this nation should live in a safe and healthful environment," the president's order declared. [1]

Since then, 19 federal departments, agencies and executive branch offices, from the Environmental Protection Agency (EPA) to the Federal Highway Administration, have been required to ensure that their policies do not have a disparate impact on poor and minority communities.

In February, EPA Administrator Carol M. Browner lent an even stronger endorsement to the environmental justice argument by issuing "interim guidance," or guidelines, for processing a rash of claims of environmental injustice, based on the 1964 Civil Rights Act. Title VI of the act, the country's basic civil rights law, prohibits discrimination based on race, color or national origin in

programs or activities that are supported by federal funds.

Among the agencies covered by the law are state environmental commissions, which issue permits to factories and other potential polluters. According to regulations issued under Title VI, an agency violates the law if its policies or activities have a discriminatory effect, even if there was no intent to discriminate. An agency found guilty of such civil rights violations would face the loss of federal funds and be required to implement costly mitigation programs.

When Shintech proposed building the plant in St. James Parish, residents opposed to the move, together with Bullard, the Tulane University Environmental Law Clinic, Greenpeace and other environmental justice advocates lodged a formal complaint against the project. Although the state Department of Environmental Quality had already cleared Shintech to begin construction, last September Browner ordered the agency to rescind one of the project's permits and launched an investigation into charges that the choice of the site amounted to environmental racism.

Shintech joins a growing list of companies whose expansion plans have run afoul of the environmental justice movement in recent years. Since the first lawsuit of this type was filed in 1979 against a waste-dump operator in Houston, activists have turned increasingly to the courts on behalf of poor and minority communities seeking protection from pollution. [2]

Although environmental justice advocates have successfully lobbied companies to change their siting plans in a number of U.S. communities, they finally won their first legal victory in April. A Nuclear Regulatory Commission (NRC) hearing board rejected plans to build a uranium-enrichment plant in a poor, minority community in northwestern Louisiana (*see p. 540*).

Residents of Sierra Blanca, Texas, are fighting a plan, recently approved by Congress, that would allow Vermont, Maine and Texas to dump their low-level nuclear waste at a facility to be built near their largely Hispanic community. And the EPA has agreed to study a claim of environmental racism brought by the Coeur d'Alene Indians in Idaho, who have asked the agency to designate a 1,500-square-mile area polluted by decades-old mine tailings as a vast Superfund site.

Another case has made it to the U.S. Supreme Court. Residents of Chester, Pa., a majority-black town in overwhelmingly white Delaware County, went to court to block construction of a waste facility in their community. Because there are already five such facilities in the town, and only two in the rest of the county, residents charged the decision to build yet another dump in their midst amounted to environmental racism. The court announced June 8 that it would decide whether activists can bring suits in federal court alleging environmental racism. The state claims such charges can only be filed with the EPA.

But Shintech has become what the company's controller, Richard Mason, calls the "poster child" of the environmental justice movement. He rejects the claims of environmental racism made against his company. "We did not choose that site because there were African-Americans there,"

he says. "We chose it because there was nobody there."

Not only is the planned location a mile and a half from the nearest residential areas, Mason says, but the company's other U.S. plant, in Freeport, Texas, has a good environmental record. "In the 24 years we have produced polyvinyl chloride (PVC) resin at the Texas plant, we have had three or four incidents, in

Residents of Chester, Pa., went to court to block construction of a waste facility in their community. The Supreme Court agreed on June 8 to decide whether the activists can bring suit in federal court alleging environmental racism.

which no one was injured and no remediation was required."

Shintech has promised to provide jobs and training, including opportunities for management positions, to local residents. "We've worked very hard to get to know the people there and understand their concerns," he says. "And a lot of those concerns are economic in nature."

Indeed, not all local residents are opposed to Shintech's plan. The St. James and Louisiana chapters of the National Association for the Advancement of Colored People (NAACP) are vocal supporters of the new plant, which they hope will bring jobs and

economic development to a region that suffers 12 percent unemployment and where 44 percent of residents live in poverty. [3] "Poverty has been the No. 1 crippler of poor people, not chemical plants," Ernest L. Johnson, president of the Louisiana State Conference NAACP, said in a statement. "Also, the present mortality rate for African-Americans in St. James is less than the Louisiana state rate, despite the 11 previously existing petrochemical plants in the area." Johnson says an NAACP survey shows broad local support for the new plant. "Unequivocally, the residents of the 'affected community' want Shintech!"

But environmental justice advocates say jobs and other investments are inadequate tradeoffs for the health risks, noxious odors and sheer ugliness that many industrial and waste facilities impose on poor communities. "Citizens want control of their environment rather than money," says Robert Knox, acting director of EPA's Office of Environmental Justice. "The time is past when companies could come in and pay for new school buses or other amenities in exchange for locating in poor, minority communities. Everyone understands about environmental pollution now, and they are not going to accept that any more."

The Shintech case and the shift in policy that gave rise to it have created a growing backlash against the environmental justice movement. In March the Environmental Council of the States (ECOS), made up of the top appointed environmental regulators from the states, denounced the EPA's interim guidelines, claiming they were vague, detrimental to economic development and poorly devised because the state commissioners, who are EPA's partners in administering federal environmental laws, had no say in the guidelines. Furthermore, the state commissioners say the policy undermines the democratic process.

"Most decisions to locate industrial facilities are not made by bureaucrats but by locally elected officials," says ECOS member Russell J. Harding, director of the Michigan Department of Environmental Quality. "That is absolutely the way these decisions should be made in an elected democracy. The EPA guidance turns the process upside down by calling for us — the regulators who are unaccountable to local voters — to make those decisions. This is not right."

As this latest chapter in the struggle for civil rights unfolds, these are some of the questions being asked:

Do poor and minority populations suffer disproportionately from exposure to toxic materials?

"Poor and minority communities are where you find children with lead poisoning living near polluting industries, garbage dumps, incinerators, petrochemical plants, freeways and highways — all the stuff that other communities reject," says Bullard of the Environmental Justice Resource Center. "And the fact that the problem has existed for so many years seems to be still a matter of denial for a lot of people."

Statistics seem to confirm Bullard's view. A widely cited study of U.S. Census data by the NAACP and the United Church of Christ Commission for Racial Justice found that people of color were 47 percent more likely than whites to live near a commercial hazardous-waste facility. The study also found that the percentage of minorities was three times higher in areas with high concentrations of

Children play in a park across from a Shell Oil refinery in Norco, La.

such facilities than in areas without them. Moreover, the study suggested that minorities' exposure to environmental toxins was getting worse. [4]

The EPA found similar disparities in exposure to toxins depending on income and race. Ninety percent of the nation's 2 million farmworkers, the agency estimates, are people of color, including Chicanos, Puerto Ricans, Caribbean blacks and African-Americans. Of these, more than 300,000 are thought to suffer from pesticide-related illnesses each year. Even air pollution affects minorities disproportionately, according to EPA. The 437 counties and independent cities that failed to meet air-quality standards in

1990, for example, are home to 80 percent of the nation's Hispanics and 65 percent of African-Americans but just 57 percent of all whites. [5]

Some critics of the environmental justice movement say the stunning improvements in environmental quality brought by 30 years of anti-pollution legislation benefit everyone in the United States. They also claim that the remaining environmental threats do not necessarily impact poor or non-white Americans more than anyone else.

"Since toxic air emissions, pesticide runoffs and groundwater contamination cannot neatly select their victims by race or income, the inequities visited upon minorities afflict a great many others as well," writes Christopher H. Foreman Jr., a senior fellow at the Brookings Institution. "Indeed, the range of arguably significant environmental-equity comparisons is so broad that some doubtless cut the other way: Many Native Americans, for example, breathe cleaner air than urban Yuppies and live further from hazardous waste than New Jersey's white ethnics." [6]

Activists reject this reasoning out of hand. "Sure, everyone is exposed to some level of toxins," says the EPA's Knox, "but exposure is disproportionate in poor and minority communities. He points to a black neighborhood in Gainesville, Ga., that accounts for just 20 percent of the town's population but handles 80 percent of its waste. The predominantly black town of Chester, Pa.,

An Indian Leader Speaks Out for the Land ...

Most instances of environmental racism that come to public attention involve black or Hispanic communities trying to keep polluting factories, sewage plants or toxic-waste dumps out of their communities. But an older and much less visible struggle is being fought by remote Indian tribes that are trying to clean up water supplies contaminated by mine tailings. Since the mid-19th century, miners and mining company executives have scoured the West for gold, silver and other minerals. They have left behind vast deposits of waste rock, or tailings, containing toxic materials. Cyanide and other chemicals used to separate some ores from rock also are left behind, usually in holding ponds. Over the years, rainwater carries these pollutants into streams and rivers, where they can be carried for miles, killing fish and contaminating drinking water.

Native Americans' pleas for environmental protection were ignored for decades, but now Indians are gaining a voice in the environmental justice movement. In what could turn out to be the most sweeping federal cleanup of pollution from mining activities ever undertaken, the Environmental Protection Agency (EPA) in February agreed to study the feasibility of designating the entire Coeur d'Alene River basin in Idaho as a Superfund site. The decision came largely as a result of the efforts of Henry SiJohn, environmental leader of the 1,600-member Coeur d'Alene tribe, whose reservation lies along the southern banks of Lake Coeur d'Alene. Staff writer Mary Cooper interviewed SiJohn by phone from his home in Plummer, Idaho.

How long has pollution in the Coeur d'Alene River basin been a problem?

In the 1920s and '30s, we noticed that the water potatoes, which grow along the lake, began to have a strange, metallic taste. We used to drink water from the lake, but we haven't since then.

How did government authorities react to your complaints about the water pollution?

The situation was different then because we were Indians, and everything was done by the superintendents of the Bureau of Indian Affairs. They had charge of us on our reservation. They said we didn't have any voice, that we couldn't buck the state or the federal government. They wouldn't do anything for us.

Do you think minority communities like yours are exposed to more pollution than white Americans?

I'm afraid that's true. It seems we have embedded an undercurrent of racism here in America. The Indian people have been for the longest time put into a situation whereby they were considered people who were unfamiliar with things. They couldn't participate in politics until 1924, when Congress allowed American Indians to have the vote. But even that didn't help for a long time because we

accounts for 11 percent of Delaware County's population but has 70 percent of the county's waste facilities. "That's clearly disproportionate," Knox says. "And it's not atypical for the country as a whole."

Some business representatives reject the notion that factory owners even look for communities of any kind to site their facilities. They say that when petrochemical companies flocked to southern Louisiana early in the century, for example, they were drawn primarily by the fact that such a long segment of the Mississippi River was deep enough to enable oceangoing barges to transport large shipments of raw materials and finished products.

"No one lived near the Baton Rouge Exxon refinery, the oldest in Louisiana, when it was built in the early 1900s," says Dan S. Borné, president of the Louisiana Chemical Association in Baton Rouge. "It and other chemical plants were built in agricultural areas, and communities literally grew toward them because that's where the jobs were. What's inferred in this debate — that people of color are targeted for chemical plants simply because they're people of color — is repugnant and ridiculous."

Does President Clinton's 1994 executive order provide sufficient guarantees of environmental justice?

When President Clinton issued his 1994 environmental justice executive order, more than 10 years had passed since the first complaints of environ-

mental racism gained public attention. In November 1992, in response to growing pressure to address the concerns of communities exposed to toxins, President George Bush created the Office of Environmental Equity within EPA to study the problem.

But it was not until Clinton's 1994 policy statement that the goal of environmental justice gained formal recognition at the federal level. "[E]ach federal agency shall make achieving environmental justice part of its mission by identifying and addressing, as appropriate, disproportionately high and adverse human health or environmental effects of its programs, policies and activities on minority populations and low-income populations," Clinton declared.

The agencies were not only re-

... An Interview with Idaho's Henry SiJohn

had to establish our tribal government as an entity in itself and prove to people we knew what we were doing. Then we had to do assessment screenings to determine the pollution in the river basin.

Is the government responding adequately to your requests now?

I wish the EPA would protect the environment, especially of Indian people, through the enforcement arm of their agency. I feel they have been neglectful of punishing people that are the perpetrators of this pollution. If the Indians were the polluters, the public would have gotten up in arms and demanded that the Indians pay. However, this isn't the case. And the federal government has not protected the Indian people or the environment to the point where they enforce the law.

Has President Clinton's support of environmental justice affected your dealings with EPA?

By good fortune, I feel optimistic, in that someone is getting to the president of the United States with this issue. I have a lot of faith in Vice President Al Gore and his staff. I feel they truly have the interests of the environment at heart. But they can't move without the Congress of the United States. Congress is for corporate America, and corporate America is the segment of society that has dug this hole for us, and I don't know if we can escape.

Has the environmental justice movement helped your cause?

Environmental justice advocates are trying to help, but they don't have any idea how to go about it. I feel they and the Clinton administration could do more if they would only take a stand and tell the perpetrators they're the guilty ones.

Industry is polluting the rivers of America. People need to understand the Indian philosophy of the cycle of life. Fish have to spawn, and the spawning beds have to be protected, so they can complete the cycle of life. Because people don't understand this, they jeopardize the species to the point where they're endangered, and then we have this big to-do with the Endangered Species Act. So we have a political response rather than a natural response. Things would be different if people let animals complete the cycle of life.

Do you think EPA will accept your request to clean up the Coeur d'Alene River basin?

I'm very optimistic. If America doesn't wake up and take hold of things, it's going to put us all in jeopardy. People need to realize they can't survive without the environment. That's where the Indian philosophical view comes in. It perpetuates the purity of the environment. Without the natural resources of fish, animals, birds and the like we can't live. We will starve.

---

quired to correct existing problems but also had to take steps to prevent environmental injustice from occurring in the first place. Clinton gave each federal agency a year to develop and submit its strategy for achieving environmental justice and another year to report on progress in implementing the strategy.

Even though the new policy directive does not change laws currently in force, environmental justice advocates say it strengthens both the 1964 Civil Rights Act and the 1969 National Environmental Policy Act, which calls for environmental information to be made available to citizens. "We have two important pieces of legislation on the books which, if used in tandem, can be very potent weapons against environmental racism," says

Bullard, pointing to several instances in which plans to build polluting facilities in communities of color were rejected after Clinton issued his executive order.

"These decisions make a lot of states nervous because they haven't really enforced equal protection when it comes to permitting," he says. "They could even lose transportation dollars because environmental justice is not just incinerators and landfills. It's also construction of highways, which have definite impacts on low-income communities and communities of color."

According to Knox of the EPA, the president's executive order has already changed the way states are dealing with the issue. At least three states — Louisiana, Maryland and Oregon

— have passed executive orders on environmental justice that mirror the president's policy in order to pre-empt possible complaints of environmental racism and the loss of federal funds for highway building and other state operations. "They did this as a result of the executive order," Knox says. "They want to look at problem areas in the states so they can get ahead of the problem and make recommendations to their governors."

But some civil rights activists fear the policy may tip the scales in favor of those who want to keep industry out of poor areas at all costs, even when vital job opportunities are at stake. "In light of the executive order, environmental justice requires balancing economic benefit with environmental risks," writes Johnson of the Louisiana NAACP. "It is critical that we not succumb to outside pressure by those who have otherwise failed to promote their ideologies and now use the 'environmental race card' for their own agendas."

Does the focus on environmental justice distract attention from bigger health problems in poor and minority communities?

Some observers suggest that by single-mindedly opposing industrial development in poor communities, environmental justice activists may be hurting the very people they purport to represent. "It's very common to meet people in St. James, both black and white, who say their great-great-grandfather lived here," says Mason of Shintech. "They also say they want to continue living here with their families but that there are no job opportunities that will allow them to stay. Because the base of employment there now is the parish government and the existing chemical plants, the only way to find a job is if someone quits, retires or dies."

Not only are poverty and joblessness more serious problems for most minority communities than pollution, critics say, but so are a whole range of health and social ills. "Hypertension, obesity, low birthweights, inadequate prenatal care, substance abuse and violence are only some of the forces that arguably deserve pride of place in the struggle to improve the lives

and health of communities of color," writes Foreman of Brookings. "That such forces are more intractable and harder to mobilize around than a Superfund site or a proposed landfill must not deter communities from asking . . . hard questions about overall health priorities." [7]

Activists say it's false logic to draw distinctions between their quest for environmental equity and these other goals of poor, minority communities.

Riverbank State Park was built on top of the North River Sewage Treatment Plant in West Harlem, N.Y.

"Environmental justice is also about health," Bullard says. "The No. 1 reason why children in these communities are hospitalized is not because of drive-by shootings. It's because of asthma." The incidence of respiratory diseases has increased, especially among children and the elderly, in areas of high concentrations of ozone and particulate matter, notably urban neighborhoods close to major roadways. [8]

Bullard also points to lead poisoning as an environmental threat to health in minority communities. "The No. 1 threat to kids is lead poisoning,

and this, too, is an environmental justice issue because African-American children are three to five times more likely to be poisoned by lead than are low-income white children," he says. "That's the direct result of residential segregation, so housing is another environmental justice issue."

Even crime and illiteracy can be traced to environmental racism, in Bullard's view. "There is a direct correlation between lead poisoning and learning disabilities, aggressive behavior and kids dropping out of school," he says. "So if you look at the root of many of the problems facing minority communities, both physical and environmental, you'll see they are all about health. It's no longer just a matter of a chemical plant."

Knox of the EPA agrees that environmental pollution has far-reaching effects on the quality of life in poor and minority neighborhoods. "Some people say the fight against crime should take precedence over other issues in these neighborhoods," he says. "But environmental problems only exacerbate such problems as crime and asthma in minority communities. Just because a community is poor doesn't mean the people there should not breathe clean air, drink clean water and be able to eat fruit from their gardens. You would not expect to find the same environmental quality in South Central Los Angeles that you find in Beverly Hills, but that doesn't mean that the people in South Central L.A. should not have clean air, clean water and clean soil." ∎

Environmental Justice Resource Center

BACKGROUND

Plight of the Poor

The poor have always suffered the health effects of inferior living conditions. Even before the Industrial Revolution unleashed the toxic byproducts of the manufacturing process in Europe and North America, serfs, slaves and farm laborers often lived amid farm animals in crowded, drafty hovels under unsanitary conditions that took a disproportionately heavy toll in the form of infant mortality and premature death among adults.

Industrialization added numerous new environmental threats to health and well-being that were borne overwhelmingly by the poor. As factories sprang up along the railroads and rivers in the center of towns and cities, wealthy families moved out of range of the smoke and foul odors they emitted. Lacking transportation or the money to move away from the industrial centers, poor factory workers had little choice but to live close to their places of work. Where factories sprang up in rural areas along rivers and other transportation corridors, new communities of workers and job-seekers grew up around them.

In the United States, race compounded poverty as a factor in determining exposure to industrial toxins. Beginning in the 1950s, when many black farmworkers moved to cities in the East and Midwest in search of better-paying jobs, they were drawn to downtown neighborhoods where housing was affordable and close to work. Hispanic immigrants also gravitated to low-cost, inner-city neighborhoods where manufacturing jobs could be found, or to farming communities in remote agricultural areas of the West — frequent sites of toxic-waste dumps and pesticide contamination.

Native Americans were exposed to inordinate levels of toxic waste by virtue of another historical phenomenon — the relegation of Indians to remote reservations, many of which were later found to harbor vast deposits of uranium, gold, silver and other minerals. Mine tailings exposed many tribes to toxic runoff that contaminated their water supplies.

Birth of a Movement

The environmental plight of poor and minority communities was not an immediate priority of the modern environmental movement, which took shape in the late 1960s. [9] The first Earth Day, held April 22, 1970, marked the start of a national campaign whose main legislative victories were the 1970 Clean Air Act, the 1972 Clean Water Act, the 1973 Endangered Species Act and the 1980 Superfund legislation (the Comprehensive Environmental Response, Compensation and Liability Act).

These basic environmental laws focused on reducing the sources of pollution but basically ignored the varying impact of pollution on different income or racial groups. The first official acknowledgement that poor, non-white Americans were disproportionately impacted by environmental degradation was a statement in the Council on Environmental Quality's 1971 annual report that racial discrimination adversely affects the urban poor and the quality of their environment. [10]

That discrete communities could be disparately affected by environmental degradation became clear in 1978, when 900 families living in the Love Canal neighborhood of Niagara Falls, N.Y., discovered that their homes had been built near 20,000 tons of toxic waste. Initially rebuffed in their calls for reparations, residents demanded, and eventually won, relocation benefits. Their struggle also helped galvanize public support for federal legislation to clean up hazardous waste — the 1980 Superfund law.

Race and income were not the main issues at Love Canal. Working-class and mostly white, the neighborhood nonetheless served as a model for communities trying to ward off environmental threats. The first largely minority community to take up the challenge was in Warren County, N.C., where residents in 1982 demonstrated against a state plan to dump 6,000 truckloads of soil laden with polychlorinated biphenyls (PCBs), a highly toxic compound similar to dioxin. More than 500 protesters were arrested, calling national attention to the issue. Although the landfill was completed as planned, the protesters won agreement from the state that no more landfills would be put in their county, the state's poorest. [11]

A series of reports on environmental threats to poor and minority communities followed the Warren County protest, helping galvanize the nascent movement for environmental justice. The General Accounting Office found in a 1983 study that three of four hazardous-waste facilities in the Southeast were in African-American communities. In 1987, the United Church of Christ issued a widely cited study showing that landfills, incinerators and other waste facilities were found disproportionately in or near poor or minority communities across the country. [12]

In 1990, Bullard published the first of his four books on the subject. Like most other early works on environmental justice, *Dumping In Dixie* focused on toxic wastes and their close association with black communities in the Southeast. Bullard also called attention to the fact that black Americans are far more likely to be exposed to lead than whites, and that Hispanics are more likely to live in areas with high soot pollution. In his efforts to help impacted communities, Bullard was joined by Benjamin Chavis Jr., former executive director of the NAACP, other civil rights groups as well as mainstream environmental organizations such as Greenpeace and the Sierra Club, whose Earthjustice Legal Defense Fund works with poor communities.

The Bush administration recognized the environmental justice movement's growing clout in 1990, when then-EPA Administrator William K. Reilly established the Environmental Equity Workgroup to study the issue. Two years later, the movement gained permanent federal status with the creation of EPA's Office of Environmental Equity.

Office of Environmental Justice.

"Many people of color, low-income and Native-American communities have raised concerns that they suffer a disproportionate burden of health consequences due to the siting of industrial plants and waste dumps, and from exposure to pesticides or other toxic chemicals at home and on the job, and that environmental programs do not adequately address these disproportionate exposures," she said shortly after taking office.

"EPA is committed to addressing these concerns and is assuming a leadership role in environmental justice to enhance environmental quality for all residents of the United States. Incorporating environmental justice into everyday agency activities and decisions will be a major undertaking. Fundamental reform will be needed in agency operations." [13]

On Sept. 30, 1993, Browner established the National Environmental Justice Advisory Council (NEJAC), a 23-member group of representatives of environmental organizations, state and local agencies, communities,

tribes, businesses and other interested parties to increase public awareness of the issue and help EPA develop strategies to ensure environmental equity. By rotating membership in NEJAC (pronounced "knee-jack," or "knee-jerk" by its critics) every three years, the agency is trying to involve as many interested parties as possible in the ongoing policy debate.

President Clinton elevated environmental justice to yet a higher plane with Executive Order 12898, which required each federal agency involved in public health or environmental matters to "make achieving environmental justice part of its mission," particularly as minority and low-income populations were affected. The order also directed Browner to create and chair an interagency working group on environmental justice to coordinate federal policies aimed at furthering environmental equity. ∎

Residents claim that Fort Lauderdale's Wingate Incinerator, now contaminated and a Superfund cleanup site, spewed ash and soot for over 25 years on the mostly African-American Bass Dillard neighborhood.

Environmental Justice Resource Center

Clinton's Policies

President Clinton took office in January 1993 promising to restore federal environmental protections that he said had eroded during the previous 12 years of Republican administrations. His newly appointed EPA administrator, Browner, declared that environmental justice would be a priority for the agency and renamed the Office of Environmental Equity the

CURRENT SITUATION

Recent Cases

The cause of environmental justice has been advanced on several fronts since President Clinton's 1994

Continued on p. 540

Chronology

1960s *Job opportunities draw black workers to cities in the industrial East and Midwest and Hispanic farmworkers to agricultural areas of the West.*

1964

Congress enacts the Civil Rights Act, establishing the country's basic law to protect the rights of minority groups. Title VI of the law prohibits discrimination based on race, color or national origin under programs or activities supported by federal funds.

1969

The National Environmental Policy Act calls for information on pollutants to be made public.

1970s *The environmental movement produces major laws to curb pollution.*

April 22, 1970

The first Earth Day marks the start of a national campaign to improve environmental protection, starting with the Clean Air Act, passed the same year.

1971

The Council on Environmental Quality acknowledges that racial discrimination adversely affects the urban poor and the quality of their environment.

1972

Congress passes the Clean Water Act, requiring reductions in polluting runoff into the nation's waterways.

1978

Residents of the Love Canal neighborhood of Niagara Falls, N.Y., discover that their homes sit atop a toxic-waste dump. They demand, and eventually win, relocation benefits, establishing a model for later action by poor, minority communities.

1979

The first lawsuit claiming environmental racism is filed against a waste-dump operator on behalf of a poor community in Houston.

1980s *Environmental justice movement takes off.*

1980

The Comprehensive Environmental Response, Compensation and Liability Act creates the Superfund to pay for the identification and cleanup of severely polluted sites.

October 1982

More than 500 protesters are arrested after trying to block a landfill being created for soil laced with polychlorinated biphenyls (PCBs) in Warren County, N.C., the poorest county in the state. The landfill project goes ahead, but the state agrees to build no more landfills there.

1983

The General Accounting Office finds that three of four hazardous-waste facilities in the Southeast are in black communities.

1987

The United Church of Christ issues a study showing that landfills, incinerators and other waste facilities are sited disproportionately in or near poor or minority communities.

1990s *Environmental justice gains federal support.*

November 1992

President George Bush creates the Office of Environmental Equity within the Environmental Protection Agency (EPA).

1993

Newly appointed EPA Administrator Carol M. Browner renames the Office of Environmental Equity the Office of Environmental Justice and promises to promote environmental protection for all Americans.

Feb. 11, 1994

President Clinton issues Executive Order 12898 directing all federal agencies with a public health or environmental mission to make environmental justice an integral part of their policies.

Sept. 10, 1997

The EPA delays permission for Shintech Inc. to build a new plastics plant in St. James Parish, La., a highly industrialized, largely African-American area.

Feb. 5, 1998

Browner issues "interim guidance" to provide a framework for processing claims of environmental injustice, based on Title VI of the Civil Rights Act.

June 8, 1998

The U.S. Supreme Court agrees to decide whether lawsuits alleging environmental racism can be brought in federal court.

Fighting for Environmental Justice . . .

The ongoing controversy over plans by Shintech Inc. to open a new plastics plant in St. James Parish, La., is among the most visible environmental justice cases. The following are some of the other notable battles being waged around of the country:

Sierra Blanca, Texas — Residents of this West Texas community, located in the 10th poorest county in the nation, fought construction of a low-level nuclear-waste facility outside the town. The facility would be the final repository for radioactive wastes from hospitals and research facilities in Texas, Maine and Vermont. Opponents complained that Sierra Blanca already is home to a large sewage sludge dump and said its selection as a dumping ground for nuclear waste amounted to environmental racism against the area's predominantly Hispanic population. Residents called on Congress to reject the three-state compact authorizing the facility. *(See "At Issue," p. 545.)* They lost their battle April 1, when the Senate approved the House-passed plan after adding amendments requiring an environmental review of the proposed site and barring other states from dumping radioactive wastes there as well.

Brunswick, Ga. — Contamination from lead, mercury, polychlorinated biphenyls (PCBs) and other toxins around an inactive LCP Chemicals-Georgia Inc. plant led to a $40-million, EPA-directed cleanup of this industrial area several years ago. Afterwards, the agency led a detailed area study, called the Brunswick Initiative, which failed to turn up other pollution threats to neighboring communities. But an environmental justice group called Save the People rejected the study's findings. The group and many residents of a mostly black community adjacent to another chemical plant, owned by Hercules Inc., claim that their yards are contaminated by toxaphene, an insecticide that Hercules manufactured until it was banned two decades ago.

Oak Ridge, Tenn. — Residents of the predominantly black neighborhood of Scarboro attribute a range of diseases in their community to the nearby Department of Energy (DOE) Y-12 nuclear weapons plant. The federal Centers for

Disease Control and Prevention is investigating a possible link between the plant and respiratory illnesses in Scarboro. The DOE has offered to pay for health assessments but has not yet taken responsibility for any illnesses reported, some of which are the subject of pending litigation.

Houston, Texas — Three decades ago, the Kennedy Heights neighborhood was built over abandoned oil pits once owned by Gulf Oil. Today residents of this African-American community claim that leakage of oil sludge into their water supply is responsible for at least 60 cases of serious diseases found there, such as cancer and lupus, as well as hundreds of other lesser health complaints. In a lawsuit brought against Chevron, which bought out Gulf Oil, plaintiffs claim a corporate document slating the contaminated site for "Negro residential and commercial development" proves that environmental racism is at the root of their medical problems. Chevron denies that the incidence of disease in Kennedy Heights is high enough to prove a link with oil contamination. [1]

Huntington Park, Calif. — After four years of community opposition, the operator of a concrete recycling plant was forced to close it. Similarly, black and Hispanic residents of South East Los Angeles are organizing to get rid of the growing number of recycling facilities in their part of the city. Glass-recycling ventures spew ground glass into the air, residents say, aggravating asthma and other respiratory diseases and killing trees. Metal crushers at car- and appliance-recycling plants cause walls of neighboring houses to crack and release tiny fragments of oil and metal that contaminate the soil. [2]

Pensacola, Fla. — The Escambia Treating Co. ran a wood-treating facility here for 40 years, depositing highly toxic dioxin into the soil and prompting a $4 million Superfund cleanup of the site. Residents of the primarily low-income, black neighborhood adjacent to the site objected to the cleanup, saying it exposed them to an even greater health threat by bringing toxins to the surface. A local activist group, Citizens Against Toxic Exposure,

Continued from p. 538

executive order. Activists cite three cases that they say set legal precedents that will help reduce the incidence of environmental racism.

In northwest Louisiana in May 1997, a citizens' group blocked plans by a German-owned firm, Louisiana

Energy Services, to build the first private uranium-enrichment plant in the United States. After nearly seven years of opposition, Citizens Against Nuclear Trash persuaded the Nuclear Regulatory Commission (NRC) to deny the company the required license based on evidence that race

had played a part in site selection.

"The communities around that site are 97 percent black," says Bullard, who drafted a social and economic analysis of the area for the NRC. "The company didn't consider the fact that these people live off the land as subsistence hunters, fishermen and

... From New Jersey to California

convinced the Environmental Protection Agency (EPA) to test the soil and, as the results proved compelling, pay for the relocation of all 358 households around the site, which is expected to cost $18 million.[3]

Newark, N.J. — A section of the city's East End, known as Ironbound, lies in one of the most polluted areas of the country. It is home to a garbage incinerator that serves all of Essex County and a sewage-treatment plant serving 33 municipalities and 1.5 million people. The area also contains the now-closed Diamond Alkali plant, which once produced Agent Orange, the defoliant used in the Vietnam War. The area is thought to have among the highest concentrations of dioxin in the world. When Wheelabrator Technologies tried to build a $63 million sewage sludge treatment facility there, Ironbound's residents claimed that the placement of yet another waste plant in their community, home to many poor Portuguese immigrants, blacks and Hispanics, would constitute environmental racism. The Ironbound Committee Against Toxic Waste persuaded the state Department of Environmental Protection to deny the plant's final permits.[4]

Anniston, Ala. — In the low-lying industrial and residential neighborhood of Sweet Water, production of toxic PCBs had been going on since the 1930s. In 1996, the Alabama Department of Public Health declared Sweet Water and the adjacent community of Cobb Town a public health hazard. Monsanto stopped producing PCBs at the facility in 1971, eight years before EPA banned the chemical, a known carcinogen in laboratory animals. The company also began buying out residents and relocating them, even before agreeing with the state to do so and clean up the polluted areas. But

the Sweet Valley-Cobb Town Environmental Justice Task Force charges Monsanto with environmental racism against the black communities by knowingly releasing PCBs from the plant after the environmental threat became apparent in the late 1960s. About 1,000 residents have sued the company.

Coeur d'Alene, Idaho — Silver mining came to the pristine area around Lake Coeur d'Alene in the 1880s. By the 1920s, members of the Coeur d'Alene Indian tribe began noticing that the water and root vegetables had taken on a metallic taste. Ignored by the mining companies and governmental officials for decades, the 1,600-member tribe finally convinced the EPA in February to consider declaring the entire Coeur d'Alene River basin a Superfund site. If the agency adds the site to its list — which is strongly opposed by local businesses in this recreational area — it will become the largest federal cleanup ever undertaken, covering an area of 1,500 square miles including the Idaho Panhandle and part of western Washington, where mine tailings have also polluted the Spokane River.[5] *(See story, p. 534.)*

Responding to public health concerns in a black neighborhood in Anniston, Ala., Monsanto has begun buying out residents and relocating them.

Environmental Justice Resource Center

---

[1] See Sam Howe Verhovek, "Racial Tensions in Suit Slowing Drive for 'Environmental Justice,'" *The New York Times,* Sept. 7, 1997.

[2] See David Bacon, "Recycling — Not So Green to Its Neighbors," posted on EcoJustice's Web page, www.igc.org, July 28, 1997.

[3] See Joel S. Hirschhorn, "Two Superfund Environmental Justice Case Studies," posted on Ecojustice's Web page, *op. cit.*

[4] See Ronald Smothers, "Ironbound Draws Its Line at the Dump," *The New York Times,* March 29, 1997.

[5] See Michael Satchell, "Taking Back the Land That Once Was So Pure," *U.S. News & World Report,* May 4, 1998, pp. 61-63.

---

farmers whose water comes from wells. That plant would have been slam-dunk, in-your-face racism."

The company appealed the ruling, but a three-judge NRC panel rejected the appeal. Not only was there evidence that racial discrimination had played a role in the siting process,

the judges ruled, but also that the NRC staff had failed to consider the plant's environmental and social impact on the surrounding community, as required by the executive order as well as by the 1969 National Environmental Policy Act.

"This was the first environmental

justice case that we actually won in court outright," Bullard says. It was also the first time a federal agency had used President Clinton's executive order to deny a license or permit.

In Flint, Mich., last year, environmental justice activists succeeded in delaying the issuance of a permit for a power plant sited in a mostly black neighborhood. The case began after the Michigan Department of Environmental Quality issued a permit to Genesee County to build a cogeneration electric power plant fueled in part by wood scraps from building construction and demolition, which might have been contaminated with lead-based paint. The permit allowed lead emissions from the plant of 2.4 tons a year. The Flint chapter of the NAACP and other plaintiffs sued the department, charging that the surrounding community was already overburdened by lead contamination and that by issuing the permit the state had violated its mandate to protect the health of all citizens.

In response, the department reduced the allowable level of lead emissions, but the plaintiffs proceeded with the suit, charging the department with practicing racial discrimination in issuing the permit in the first place. According to Director Harding, the department agreed to comply with additional demands but refused to settle the case because the plaintiffs would not drop their charges of racial discrimination.

Both sides claimed a victory of sorts from the judgment, handed down on May 29, 1997, by Circuit Judge Archie Hayman. Plaintiffs won an injunction against future permits, pending the state's performance of risk assessments to be paid for by applicants and the holding of broader public hearings when applications for toxic facilities are made. They also won recognition that compliance with air-quality standards under the Clean Air Act does not necessarily mean that a community is not adversely affected by air pollution.

For its part, the state claimed vindication on the racial discrimination charges. "The judge said there was no racial discrimination," Harding says. "In fact, he complimented my agency, saying our overall environmental regulatory system

The Southwest Network for Environmental and Economic Justice staged a protest in Phoenix, Ariz., in 1995.

was sufficiently protective, though he directed the agency to do more initial determinations of environmental impact."

In Chester, Pa., residents complained that their predominantly African-American city had become the main waste dump for all of largely white Delaware County. In 1996, after the Pennsylvania Department of Environmental Protection issued a permit to Soil Remediation Services Inc. to build yet another waste facility in the city, Chester Residents Concerned for Quality Living sued the agency for racial discrimination in its permitting process.

Their suit, *Chester Residents Concerned for Quality Living v. Seif,* was the first filed against a state agency

under Title VI of the 1964 Civil Rights Act, which prohibits agencies that receive federal funds from practicing racial discrimination, either deliberately or by effecting "policies or practices [that] cause a discriminatory effect."

On Nov. 6, 1996, U.S. District Judge Stewart Dalzell dismissed the suit for technical reasons. On Dec. 30, 1997, however, the 3rd Circuit Court overturned the lower court, allowing the citizens' group's suit to proceed. The ruling also set an important legal precedent by enabling a low-income and minority community to pursue a charge of environmental racism regardless of whether the discrimination was deliberate. The Supreme Court has agreed to hear the case, addressing the question of whether lawsuits alleging environmental racism can be brought in federal court.

Pressure on EPA

The Circuit Court's ruling in the Chester case did not, however, elaborate on the question of evidence needed to mount a successful environmental justice suit against a state agency.[14] With the proliferation of charges of environmental racism in the 1990s, the EPA has come under increasing pressure to clarify the procedures for dealing with such cases. According to Knox of EPA's Office of Environmental Justice, the agency has received 49 complaints based on Title VI alone, about 20 of which are now under investigation. "EPA had to respond to a backlog of complaints," he says. "The agency had to do something to respond to this, so we issued guidelines to help identify who could bring claims and what constitutes a disparate impact on a community."

The backlogged complaints include the one in Louisiana brought against Shintech, which proposed in September 1997 to build a state-of-the-art plant to produce PVC, used to make a range of consumer products, such as plumbing pipes and shrink-wrap food wrapping. On May 23, 1997, the Louisiana Department of Environmental Quality issued three air permits for the facility. But on Sept. 10, in response to a citizens' petition, EPA Administrator Browner took the agency's first formal action on the environmental justice issue.

She canceled one of the firm's permits and directed the state agency to take environmental justice into greater consideration when reissuing the permit. In addition, she ordered further investigation of charges that the choice of St. James Parish for the plant site amounted to environmental racism. "It is essential the minority and low-income communities not be disproportionately subjected to environmental hazards," Browner wrote in her decision. [15]

The Shintech case is also the test case for the EPA's interim guidance, or guidelines. Browner issued the guidance on Feb. 5, 1998, in the wake of the Chester ruling, seeking to clarify the conditions under which a decision to issue a permit violates Title VI. The guidance describes a five-step process by which EPA must identify the affected population, primarily on the basis of proximity to the site in question, determine the race or ethnicity of the affected population and decide whether the permitted activity will impose an "undue burden" on the community. The agency will then identify any other

Residents of Wagner's Point, a working-class enclave in South Baltimore, link the abnormally high cancer rates in their neighborhood to emissions from a nearby wastewater treatment plant, an oil refinery and other industrial sites.

permitted facilities in the vicinity that may compound the community's environmental threat.

If EPA determines that the community is impacted at a "disparate rate," the permit recipient may mitigate the environmental impact by offering other benefits to the community. Shintech, for example, has promised to spend about $500,000 for job training and small-business development in St. James Parish.

State environmental officials quickly identified what they saw as numerous flaws in the EPA's guidance, however, and asked the agency to rescind the guidance and draft a new policy together with the states. Fourteen state attorneys general and the U.S. Chamber of Commerce endorsed the environmental officials' request. "We believe the guidance is vague," says Robert E. Roberts, executive director of ECOS. "It speaks of mitigating or justifying 'disparate impacts' but doesn't make clear what such an impact is. So for those of us who have to carry out the policy, it's very difficult to know what the policy is."

Knox defends the guidance language and suggests that the state environmental officials are mainly concerned because they were left out of the drafting process. "The states are upset because they thought they should be sitting at the table," he says. "We think the guidance should work out pretty well."

Roberts says the state officials' exclusion is more than a matter of pique. "The fact that the states weren't included is important," he says, "because the state environmental departments will be making decisions that will be the basis for any environmental justice complaints that arise. Because we weren't involved in helping to craft the approach to this issue, chances are we won't do it the way EPA wants it done. At some point, we're bound to make decisions improperly because we don't know what their perspective is."

Since ECOS voiced its objections to

S.C. Delaney/Environmental Protection Agency

the new guidance, EPA has set up a special committee responsible for implementing Title VI, which also includes several state environmental officials.

Aid for 'Brownfields'

The EPA's latest attempt to promote environmental justice may prove to be a double-edged sword. For while the interim guidance is intended to make it easier for minority and low-income communities to protect themselves from environmental threats to their health, it may also weaken economic development in these communities by discouraging companies from building new, non-polluting facilities in their midst that could provide needed employment. EPA has led an effort to convert abandoned commercial and industrial sites into productive use.

Many of these so-called "brownfield" sites scare off investors, fearful of being held liable for potential lawsuits by users of the site. While the sites are polluted, they are not polluted enough to qualify for federally funded cleanup under the Superfund program. On Jan. 25, 1995, EPA launched a program to encourage investors to build non-polluting businesses on brownfield sites, which tend to be in urban areas in or near poor or minority communities. By the end of fiscal 1997, EPA had awarded $200,000 seed-money grants to 121 brownfield restoration projects. [16]

"A lot of brownfields are in environmental justice communities," says Knox of EPA. "These communities

see brownfields as providing an opportunity to get involved in the siting process and address problems in the city, an opportunity for jobs and a chance to reverse the fiscal deterioration that has drained resources from their neighborhoods. Most of all, brownfields allow communities to get their vision involved in development because they have a seat at the table."

In Knox's view, furthering environmental justice goes hand in hand with brownfield development. "The

Residents of this African-American neighborhood built on top of the Agriculture Street Landfill in New Orleans are petitioning the EPA to relocate them from the area, now a Superfund site. Activists call this the "black Love Canal."

interim guidance actually helps," he says. "By ensuring that environmental justice has to be considered in the permitting process and bringing affected communities to the table, we are educating residents so they can take over their own communities and bring in clean industries."

But state environmental officials predict the new guidance will be a killer for brownfield development. "The guidance enables anyone with a typewriter to stop a permit from being issued," says Harding, Michigan's environmental commissioner. "We're not opposed to environmental justice, but the guidance

goes against getting brownfields going, especially in places like Detroit." Hit by widespread plant closings in the 1970s and '80s, Detroit and other Midwestern cities have many lightly polluted sites that qualify for brownfield development.

"Under the interim guidance, anybody who files an objection in an urban area can show a disparate impact," he says. "It makes it easy to make that showing and turns permitting into a nebulous process that can drag on for years."

Business representatives agree. "We're not saying there aren't concerns that need to be dealt with," says Borné of the Louisiana Chemical Association. "We are saying that with this interim guidance EPA is forever changing the landscape of development in this country. And you can forget about brownfield development because most brown-field sites are in minority communities." ■

OUTLOOK

Impact on Business

Industry representatives predict that EPA's policy to promote environmental justice will harm more than just brownfield development. Mason says that charging Shintech with environmental racism sends a message to industry that may not be what the

Continued on p. 546

At Issue:

Would constructing a low-level radioactive nuclear-waste dump near Sierra Blanca, Texas, constitute "environmental injustice"?

BILL ADDINGTON
Rancher, farmer and merchant, Hudspeth County, Texas

FROM TESTIMONY BEFORE THE HOUSE COMMERCE SUBCOMMITTEE ON ENERGY AND POWER, MAY 13, 1997.

i speak today on behalf of Save Sierra Blanca, our citizens group, and many people in West Texas who feel run over by the state and federal governments. These people are opposed to the forced placement of this risky radioactive-waste cemetery at Sierra Blanca near the Rio Grande River. . . .

Most of the people in Hudspeth County and Sierra Blanca are poor — the median annual income is $8,000. Seventy percent of the people are of Hispanic origin, like myself. This is the reason Texas "leaders" have focused on our county for the dump site since 1983. This appeared to be the political path of least resistance. But there is strong resistance locally, regionally and internationally. There are about 3,000 people and 1,300 registered voters in the county, and every one of them who was asked signed the petition against the dump. . . .

The siting of the Sierra Blanca dump by the state legislature was a violation of environmental justice and our civil rights. . . .

If the radioactive-waste dump is approved in Sierra Blanca, it is likely that additional radioactive and hazardous facilities will follow. Westinghouse Scientific Ecology Group has entered into an option agreement to lease 1,280 acres of land adjoining the proposed Sierra Blanca site for radioactive waste processing and storage, possibly including incineration. There is also a proposal for an additional sludge dump in the community. This concentrating of hazardous facilities in communities is a characteristic of environmental injustice.

The proposed radioactive dump site is geologically fatally flawed. It is in an earthquake zone, and there is a buried fault underneath the proposed trenches. . . .

The real reason for the compact is economic — to make it cheaper for nuclear power generators to bury their waste and shift their liability. It does not "protect Texas," as has been touted. . . .

Texas began negotiations with . . . Maine in 1988, and in 1992 passed the compact. Maine's and Vermont's legislatures have approved the compact. They failed to develop their own waste sites because of heavy opposition. Maine voters approved the compact by referendum, yet people in my home are not even heard or considered. We do not get to vote on the measure or placement of the dump like Mainers, who chose to dump on us, did.

SEN. OLYMPIA J. SNOWE, R-MAINE

FROM A SENATE FLOOR SPEECH, APRIL 1, 1998.

a s the law requires, Texas, Vermont and Maine have negotiated an agreement that was approved by each state. . . . So, we have before us a compact that has been carefully crafted and thoroughly examined by the state governments and people of all three states involved. Now all that is required is the approval of Congress, so that the state of Texas and the other Texas Compact members will be able to exercise appropriate control over the waste that will come into the Texas facility. . . .

Opponents of the Texas Compact would have you believe that should we ratify this compact it will open the doors for other states to dump nuclear waste at a site, in the desert, located five miles from the town of Sierra Blanca, exposing a predominantly low-income, minority community to health and environmental threats.

The truth is that Texas has been planning to build a facility for its own waste since 1981, long before Maine first proposed a compact with Texas. That is because whether or not this compact passes, Texas still must somehow take care of the waste it produces. . . .

The opponents of the compact would have you believe this issue is about politics. It is not about politics, it is about science: sound science. It is very dry in the Southwest Texas area, where the small amount of rainfall it receives mostly evaporates before it hits the ground. The aquifer that supplies water to the area and to nearby Mexico is over 600 feet below the desert floor and is encased in rock.

The proposed site has been designed to withstand any earthquake equaling the most severe that has ever occurred in Texas history. Strong seismic activity in the area is non-existent. All these factors mean that the siting of this facility is on strong scientific grounds.

Our opponents say we will be bad neighbors if we pass this compact because the proposed site is near the Mexican border. In fact, the U.S. and Mexico have an agreement, the La Paz Agreement, to cooperate in the environmental protection of the border region. The La Paz Agreement simply encourages cooperative efforts to protect the environment of the region.

Any proposed facility will be protective of the environment because it will be constructed in accordance with the strictest U.S. environmental safeguards.

FOR MORE INFORMATION

If you would like to have this CQ Researcher updated, or need more information about this topic, please call CQ Custom Research. Special rates for CQ subscribers. (202) 887-8600 or (800) 432-2250, ext. 600, or E-mail Custom.Research@cq.com

Center for Health, Environment and Justice, P.O. Box 6806, Falls Church, Va. 22040; (703) 237-2249; www.essential.org/cchw. The center helps community-based groups fend off environmental hazards. It was founded by a former resident of Love Canal, N.Y., the community built near a toxic-waste dump.

Earthjustice Legal Defense Fund, 180 Montgomery St., Suite 1400, San Francisco, Calif. 94014; (800) 584-6460; www.earthjustice.org. Formerly known as the Sierra Club Legal Defense Fund, this nonprofit law firm is active in cases involving environmental justice.

Environmental Justice Resource Center, Clark Atlanta University, 223 James P. Brawley Dr. S.W., Atlanta, Ga. 30314; (404) 880-6911. www.ejrc.cau.edu. Directed by Robert D. Bullard, a longtime environmental justice leader, the center helps communities protect themselves from pollution sources.

Environmental Council of the States, 444 N. Capitol St. N.W., Suite 305, Washington, D.C. 20001; (202) 624-3660; www.sso.org/ecos/. A membership group representing environmental officials of the states and the District of Columbia, ECOS opposes the EPA's new rules for handling environmental justice complaints.

Greenpeace, 1436 U St. N.W., Washington, D.C. 20009; (202) 462-1177; www.greenpeace.org. This research and activist group has recently become involved in several cases involving complaints of environmental racism.

Office of Environmental Justice, U.S. Environmental Protection Agency, 401 M St. S.W., Washington, D.C. 20460; (202) 564-2515 or (800) 962-6215; es.epa.gov/environsense/oeca/oej.html. The OEJ coordinates EPA activities and provides technical assistance to communities threatened by environmental hazards.

Continued from p. 544

activists intended.

"The message is, 'You're stupid if you try to move into a community with a significant number of African-Americans, or any other racial minority,' " Mason says. "We don't want to be in a community that doesn't want us there. But this policy will deprive many people of economic opportunity, and it's bad news for economic development in general."

Some critics predict that the EPA's policy is such a deterrent to industrial development and job creation that many companies will shift production overseas.

"In the long run, this is the best economic-development program for Mexico that's ever come down the pike," Borné says. "If EPA really wants to chase our industry over the border, then this is a first-class ticket. I already see how detrimental this policy is to economic development in my state."

EPA is still investigating the Shintech case. However it is resolved, supporters of the environmental justice movement are optimistic that more aggressive steps to combat environmental racism will pay off,

not only for poor and non-white Americans but also in the development of cleaner manufacturing and waste technologies.

"The movement has moved beyond the siting of facilities," Bullard says. "It's bigger than that. It embraces the full question of prevention, health and employment. We're now asking if we really need more chemicals entering the waste stream, as opposed to changing production processes to protect health and the environment. A company that produces waste is a wasteful company. So it makes sense to reduce waste so we won't need as many facilities to dispose of this stuff."

Knox agrees with Bullard's assessment and argues that the struggle for environmental justice need not be adversarial because it will benefit everyone. "If this is to be the greatest industrial society of all time, industry has to be clean," he says. "But we all have to work together to make that happen. There's a role for everybody, including business and communities. We all have to sit at the table."

Bullard says pressure from low-income and minority communities that have lodged environmental racism complaints has already spurred manufacturers to develop and adopt cleaner production processes and products, including soy-based ink for newspapers, recycled paper for packaging and pesticide-free fruits and vegetables.

"But I think the biggest impact of the environmental justice movement has not come yet," Bullard says. "That is consumers who are selective and educated about what they will buy and what they won't buy. Creating educated consumers who will start punishing companies that hurt the environment and rewarding those that adopt environmentally sound business practices will be the last civil rights battle." ∎

Notes

[1] Executive Order 12898, "Federal Actions to Address Environmental Justice in Minority Populations and Low-Income Populations," Feb. 11, 1994. For background, see "Cleaning Up Hazardous Wastes," *The CQ Researcher*, Aug. 23, 1996, pp. 752-776.

[2] In *Bean v. Southwestern Waste Management*, residents of a predominantly black subdivision in Houston charged that Browning-Ferris Industries had practiced environmental discrimination by choosing their community to site a municipal solid-waste landfill. They lost the case.

[3] For background, see "Jobs vs. Environment," *The CQ Researcher*, May 15, 1992, pp. 409-432.

[4] Benjamin A. Goldman and Laura Fitton, *Toxic Wastes and Race Revisited*, Center for Policy Alternatives, National Association for the Advancement of Colored People and United Church of Christ Commission for Racial Justice, 1994.

[5] U.S. Environmental Protection Agency, Office of Environmental Justice, *Serving a Diverse Society*, November 1997. For background, see "New Air Quality Standards," *The CQ Researcher*, March 7, 1997, pp. 193-217.

[6] Christopher H. Foreman Jr., "A Winning Hand? The Uncertain Future of Environmental Justice," *The Brookings Review*, spring 1996, p. 24. Foreman's new book, *The Promise and Peril of Environmental Justice*, is due to be published by the Brookings Institution in the fall.

[7] *Ibid.*, p. 25.

[8] See American Lung Association, "Health Effects of Outdoor Air Pollution," 1996.

[9] For background, see "Environmental Movement at 25," *The CQ Researcher*, March 31, 1995, pp. 283-307.

[10] See Environmental Protection Agency, Office of Environmental Justice, *Environmental Justice 1994 Annual Report: Focusing on Environmental Protection for All People*, April 1995.

[11] See Robert D. Bullard, *Unequal Protection* (1994), pp. 43-52.

[12] General Accounting Office, *Siting of Hazardous Waste Landfills and Their Correlation with Racial and Economic Status of Surrounding Communities* (1983); United Church of Christ Commission for Racial Justice, *Toxic Wastes and Race in the United States* (1987).

[13] Quoted in EPA, *Environmental Justice 1994 Annual Report, op. cit.*, p. 3.

[14] See Andrew S. Levine, Jonathan E. Rinde and Kenneth J. Warren, "In Response to Chester Residents, EPA Releases Environmental Justice Rules," *The Legal Intelligencer*, Feb. 18, 1998.

[15] See Paul Hoverten, "EPA Puts Plant on Hold in Racism Case," *USA Today*, Sept. 11, 1998.

[16] See "New EPA Report Lists Positive Effects of Agency Superfund Reform Efforts," *Hazardous Waste News*, Feb. 16, 1998.

Bibliography

Selected Sources Used

Books

Bullard, Robert D., *Dumping in Dixie: Race, Class and Environmental Quality,* Harper Collins, 1996.

A leading activist in the environmental justice movement examines the enforcement of environmental-protection laws in the Southern United States, where poor, mostly black communities are commonly chosen as sites for waste dumps and incinerators.

Bullard, Robert D., ed., *Unequal Protection: Environmental Justice and Communities of Color,* Sierra Club Books, 1994.

This collection of essays describes how communities of poor and non-white Americans are disproportionately exposed to toxic wastes and other environmental hazards.

Szasz, Andrew, *EcoPopulism: Toxic Waste and the Movement for Environmental Justice,* University of Minnesota Press, 1994.

The author describes the environmental justice movement's evolution from grass-roots activism to federal policy. By focusing on pollution prevention rather than cleaning up polluted sites, the movement is changing the focus of environmental policy.

Articles

Arrandale, Tom, "Regulation and Racism," *Governing,* March 1998, p. 63.

The Environmental Protection Agency's decision to overturn a state-issued permit to build a plastics plant near a poor, minority community in Louisiana last fall does not further the goal of environmental justice, the author writes, because it will discourage industry from bringing jobs to the very communities that are hardest hit by unemployment.

Hampson, Fen Osler, and Judith Reppy, "Environmental Change and Social Justice," *Environment,* April 1997, pp. 12-20.

The authors apply the tenets of environmental justice to global environmental issues, including global warming. Developed nations, which have contributed the most to this problem, should help devise solutions that reduce economic inequality between rich and developing nations, the authors contend.

Northridge, Mary E., and Peggy M. Shepard, "Comment: Environmental Racism and Public Health," *American Journal of Public Health,* May 1997, pp. 730-732.

The authors call for further study of the disparate impact of environmental hazards on poor, non-white communities and a broad public health initiative, similar in scope to the anti-smoking campaign, to prevent and remove toxins from these communities.

Parris, Thomas M., "Spinning the Web of Environmental Justice," *Environment,* May 1997, pp. 44-45.

This collection of Internet addresses provides a wealth of sources, including Environmental Protection Agency (EPA) reports and non-governmental studies, on efforts to combat pollution that affects poor and minority communities.

Sachs, Aaron, "Upholding Human Rights and Environmental Justice," *The Humanist,* March-April 1996, pp. 5-8.

The author reviews the international movement for environmental justice that took off after the 1988 murder of Chico Mendes, a Brazilian rubber tapper who fought for the rights of rain forest inhabitants against cattle barons who were clearing the forests for grazing land.

Schoeplfle, Mark, "Due Process and Dialogue: Consulting with Native Americans under the National Environmental Policy Act," *Common Ground,* summer/fall 1997, pp. 40-45.

The 1969 National Environmental Policy Act provides standards for informing Indian tribes of environmental hazards and taking steps to protect themselves from pollutants.

Reports and Studies

Goldman, Benjamin A., and Laura Fitton, *Toxic Wastes and Race Revisited,* Center for Policy Alternatives, 1994.

This update of a 1987 report on the racial and socioeconomic characteristics of communities with hazardous-waste sites finds that poor and minority communities are even more disproportionately exposed to toxins than before, despite the growth of the environmental justice movement.

National Environmental Justice Advisory Council, *Environmental Justice, Urban Revitalization and Brownfields: The Search for Authentic Signs of Hope,* December 1996.

An EPA advisory committee finds that the development of brownfields — abandoned industrial sites that are not polluted enough to warrant federal cleanup under the Superfund program — is an important contribution to the goal of environmental justice.

U.S. Environmental Protection Agency, Office of Environmental Justice, *Serving a Diverse Society,* November 1997.

This pamphlet summarizes the adverse impact of air pollution, pesticides, agricultural runoff and other environmental hazards on communities of color and suggests steps communities can take to minimize exposure.

The Next Step

Additional information from UMI's Newspaper & Periodical Abstracts™ database

Environmental Racism

Brook, Daniel, "Environmental Genocide: Native Americans and Toxic Waste," *American Journal of Economics & Sociology (AES),* **January 1998, pp. 105-113.**

Environmental genocide is perpetrated by the U.S. government and by private corporations alike; some of the methods are legal, while others are not. Against this backdrop, Native Americans are more unified and are becoming better organized than ever, and they are fighting back for their very survival.

Elie, Lolis Eric, "Let Them Eat Toxic Waste," *New Orleans Times-Picayune,* **Sept. 12, 1997, p. B1.**

A Japanese company, Shintech, wants to build a plastics factory in Convent, La., despite opposition from those who live near the proposed site. A lawyer on public television in July contended that Shintech was winning support for the proposed plant, not on its merits, but because the poor residents of St. James Parish couldn't afford to buy as many experts as Shintech could.

Friedman, David, "A Tale of Two Worlds; Globalization is Reigniting Class Conflicts in America and Around the World," *Los Angeles Times,* **Oct. 26, 1997, p. M1.**

More than liberals versus conservatives, the nation's politics are evolving toward a future first imagined in the 1950s by science fiction author Isaac Asimov. He wrote of two increasingly polarized societies battling to control space exploration. One was a technologically sophisticated, rabidly isolationist, sparsely populated community whose most refined citizens, the Solarians, abhorred "filthy" human contact and lived alone on vast, ecologically balanced estates maintained by thousands of robots. The other was a decidedly low-brow, overcrowded, urbanized Earth populated by short-lived, disease-ridden, but far more dynamic people than the pampered Solarians. The global-warming controversy, for example, is incomprehensible except as a struggle between America's new Solarians and the country's poorer classes. It's an open secret that the proposed treaty will not reduce greenhouse emissions. By exempting 130 "developing" countries, including China, all of Latin America, India and Indonesia from any proposed controls, however, it will shift polluting industries from the heavily regulated First World, and particularly the United States, to the utterly unregulated Third World.

Kendall, Peter, "Report Calls 'Environmental Racism' Garbage; University of Chicago Study Finds Yuppies by Toxic Sites," *Chicago Tribune,* **April 4, 1997, p. 1.**

In the 10 years since the term "environmental racism" was coined, the idea that minorities are more likely to live near dumps and toxic-waste sites has become as deeply embedded as an old oil tank beneath a vacant lot. On Thursday, researchers released a paper concluding that there is no good evidence that African-Americans of any income class are more likely to live in areas with more concentrated waste sites in the city of Chicago. Offering the most detailed look yet at the question of environmental racism in Chicago, the study sets out to explain the relationship between race and waste in terms of a panoply of social forces that have shaped the city.

Reitman, Janet, "The Battle for Convent," *Scholastic Update* **(Teacher's Edition), April 13, 1998, pp. 4-6.**

Brenda Huget and her neighbors are determined to prevent a proposed plastics factory from being built in Convent, La. Huget's battle against the Japanese company Shintech is discussed.

Sapolsky, Robert, "How the Other Half Heals," *Discover,* **April 1998, pp. 46-52.**

People have long known about the socioeconomic status (SES) gradient in health. Studies have demonstrated that whatever the gradient's causes, low SES leaves a persistent health scar.

Environmental Activism

Bergman, B.J., "Club's EPEC Sweep," *Sierra,* **May 1998, pp. 73-74.**

The Sierra Club's Environmental Public Education Campaign (EPEC) was designed to allow the club's thousands of volunteer activists to tailor a broad message — "Protect America's Environment: For Our Families, For Our Future" — to local and regional needs. EPEC efforts are described.

Brandt, Barbara, "Can We Build a New American Dream," *Dollars & Sense,* **May 1998, pp. 28-29.**

Ellen Furnari, director of the Center for a New American Dream, is interviewed about the nonprofit organization, reducing American consumption and waste, and economic policy.

Duncan, David James, "The War for Norman's River," *Sierra,* **May 1998, pp. 44-55.**

The Blackfoot River in Montana is the incredible river of Norman Maclean's book, *A River Runs Through It,* and the Robert Redford film of the same name. An army of river lovers is fighting to keep its waters pure from a proposed cyanide heap-leach gold mine site just upstream of Missoula.

Howe, Peter J., "Environment Group Tracks Toxic Waste with Web Page," *Boston Globe,* **April 17, 1998, p. E12.**

Massachusetts residents can track down the locations

of industrial toxic waste emitters near their homes through a new Web page launched in 1998.

Kriz, Margaret, "Fish and Foul," *National Journal*, Feb. 28, 1998, pp. 450-453.

Public outrage over fish kills is spurring demands for a crackdown on toxic runoff from farms, streets and mines. The contamination — such as the organism Pfiesteria piscicida — is the most urgent water pollution problem facing the nation.

Knickerbocker, Brad, "Fighting for a Cleaner Environment; Two Decades After Love Canal Put Toxic Waste on the Map, Industry Tries to Keep Clean," *Christian Science Monitor*, April 30, 1998, p. 4.

Twenty years ago this spring, Lois Marie Gibbs suspected that her son's chronic health problems might be tied to a chemical dump next to the 99th Street School where he was a kindergartner. Thus began the story of Love Canal, the Niagara Falls neighborhood in western New York that became synonymous with toxic waste. By the time it was over, 239 homes had been demolished, an additional 564 were evacuated and Ms. Gibbs had become a nationally known community organizer and activist fighting industrial pollution around the country. Last summer, Pennsylvania began posting environmental inspection results on the Internet. The EPA also provides such data online, and last week the Environmental Defense Fund (EDF) fired up its new website where anybody with access to the Internet can mouse-click to maps, charts and other federal government data on potential chemical dangers in small communities as well as in large, industrial cities. The EDF site covers every state in the country.

Rodriguez, Cindy, "State Vows Probe into Nyanza Site, But Cleanup Stalled 'Til 1999," *Boston Globe*, March 8, 1998, p. W1.

Kevin Kane remembers the shortcuts he took to the Tasty Treat from Ashland High School through Nyanza Inc., a dye and chemical manufacturer. He played football and baseball on adjoining fields, an area where residents complained of billowing purple smoke and technicolor puddles. When two of his schoolmates died of cancer several years ago and another four developed the disease, Kane didn't suspect Nyanza — even after the state documented a high number of kidney and bladder cancer diagnoses near the site. Kane's family recently asked the Local Emergency Planning Committee to convene to answer questions about the multi-million-dollar cleanup of the toxic-waste site.

Simon, Stephanie, "Tourism With a Message; 'Reality Tours' Acquaint Vacationers with Sweatshops, Slums and Toxic Waste; Guilt is For Sale, as Well as Inspiration and, Perhaps, Redemption," *Los Angeles Times*, Feb. 15, 1998, p. A1.

Global Exchange is a San Francisco nonprofit organization that has made a $1 million-a-year business of carting tourists to some of the world's most woeful places. For the last decade, reality tours focused on overseas heartache in countries such as Cuba, Haiti, Guatemala and Vietnam. Then, last year, co-director Medea Benjamin realized that Americans could use a reality check in their own backyard. "We decided," she said, "to start looking at ourselves." Tourists pay to see oil drums oozing poison slime in a beat-up San Francisco neighborhood. To meet garment workers sewing at all hours in miserable conditions. To tour apartments with flaking lead paint and strawberry fields that are soaking in pesticides.

Superfund Cleanups

"Back New Waste Strategy," *The Denver Post*, April 3, 1998, p. B10.

An editorial endorses a proposal for a "good Samaritan" Superfund provision exempting organizations that attempt to clean up toxic-waste sites. Presently, such organizations can become liable for attempting to clean up Superfund sites even if they aren't to blame for creating the mess.

"EPA Rules Let Heavy Industries Sell Toxic Wastes to Fertilizer Companies," *The Wall Street Journal*, March 27, 1998, p. B7.

The Superfund program run by the Environmental Protection Agency (EPA) coordinates the cleanup of abandoned toxic-waste sites. EPA rules allow industries to send toxic ash from smokestacks to fertilizer plants without testing it or recording where it is being shipped. The ash is a valuable source of zinc, an important ingredient for plant growth. Furthermore, regulations let companies sell other by-product toxic waste, such as sulfuric acid or ammonium, to be recycled in fertilizer if it meets the EPA's Land Disposal Rule, a standard that measures how safe a product is when it is put in regulated, lined landfills.

"Occidental Chemical Settles Cleanup Suits Over Love Canal Site," *The Wall Street Journal*, April 29, 1998, p. B2.

Occidental Chemical Corp. has agreed to drop its multi-million-dollar claims against the city of Niagara Falls to settle 19-year-old lawsuits stemming from the evacuation of the neighborhood over the Love Canal toxic-waste site.

Howe, Peter J., "A Personal Link in Pittsfield; Pollution Woes Face City GE Chief Once Called Home," *Boston Globe*, **May 14, 1998, p. B1.**

General Electric has kept up its consistently aggressive resistance as the government brings Superfund suits at more than 80 U.S. toxic-waste sites linked to the company. The company is now wrestling with a PCB pollution mess in Pittsfield that could become a $3 billion fiasco involving cleanup of the Hudson River as well. Critics say the company is using familiar tactics: bombard the government with records requests, play up credible scientific doubts about the severity of the pollution and keep its lawyers on the attack.

Revkin, Andrew C., "Ex-Toxic Dump Is Linked To Rise in Birth Problems," *The New York Times*, **Sept. 11, 1997, p. B2.**

Medical investigators poring over thousands of birth records from households near a former toxic-waste dump in southwestern New Jersey have found unusually clear evidence of a link between industrial chemicals in the environment and their impact on human health. Federal and New Jersey health officials reported yesterday that they had found a significant drop in birthweight and a doubled incidence of pre-term births in infants born to women who, in the early 1970s, lived near the Lipari landfill in Gloucester County, which went on to hold the No. 1 spot on the Federal Superfund list of hazardous waste sites around the country. The birthweight reduction of about four ounces from households closest to the dump was about the same as in mothers who smoke during pregnancy, according to the study, which is being published in the latest issue of *Environmental Health Perspectives*, a monthly journal of the National Institute of Environmental Health Sciences, a federal agency in Atlanta.

Rosenfeld, Dave, "Superfund Tax Should Be Restored," *St. Louis Post-Dispatch*, **March 16, 1998, p. B7.**

Suppose there is a tax on the oil and chemical industries that raises $4 million a day to clean up the worst hazardous-waste sites across the country. Suppose the tax expired two years ago, and every day, $4 million is lost. Suppose that some members of Congress and major polluting industries argue that the tax should not be renewed until we let many polluters off the hook for cleaning up the sites and weaken cleanup standards at those sites. Approximately 85,000 known or suspected hazardous-waste sites are scattered across the United States, exposing the public to highly toxic chemicals such as lead, mercury, benzene and arsenic. These dump sites are poisoning the soil, water and air in neighborhoods throughout Missouri and the nation. They are the legacy of the past use and disposal of toxic chemicals by polluters. Chemicals found at these sites are known to cause cancer, birth defects and numerous other illnesses. The worst of these sites are called "Superfund sites." One in four Americans lives within four miles of a Superfund site.

Environmental Enforcement

Bruno, Kenny, "Philly Waste Go Home," *Multinational Monitor*, **January 1998, pp. 7-8.**

For the first time in 10 years, there is a chance that the 4,000 tons of toxic incinerator ash dumped by Philadelphia in Gonaives Bay, Haiti, may actually be going back to Philadelphia.

Johnston, David Cay, "Companies Would Be Given Rewards for Retirement and Education Plans," *The New York Times*, **Feb. 3, 1998, p. A18.**

The Clinton administration supports a plan that would make permanent a provision of the 1997 Taxpayer Relief Act that allows companies to treat the costs of cleaning up toxic-waste sites as expenses that can be immediately deducted, instead of capital investments that must be amortized over many years.

Reilly, Sean E., "Down the Drain," *The Environmental Magazine*, **March 1998, pp. 26-27.**

The "pre-treatment" program developed by the Environmental Protection Agency in the 1970s and '80s is currently in place at some 1,500 public sewage treatment plants across the nation. It calls for industrial plants to set up their own treatment operations to remove the most dangerous toxic waste before dumping the remainder into sewers running to the public plant. The program has made a significant dent in decreasing water pollution but still has recurring problems.

Zinko, Carolyne, "Three-Year Prison Term Over East Palo Alto Toxic Waste Case; City Wants Bayfront Area Cleaned Up," *San Francisco Chronicle*, **April 8, 1998, p. A18.**

When an East Palo Alto autoyard owner was sentenced to prison for failing to clean up toxic waste, it was a signal that the city has had enough of renegade business owners blocking the development of prime bayfront land. Melvin Curtaccio, who ran Pick & Save Auto Wrecking for more than two decades, was sentenced to 3 years, 8 months in prison on Friday by a San Mateo County judge. The bayfront community — long a dumping ground for junked autos from San Francisco and other parts of the Bay Area — has unsuccessfully tried to get rid of the wrecking yards and other businesses that might be contaminating the groundwater and soil.

Back Issues

MARCH 1997
New Air Quality Standards
Alcohol Advertising
Civic Renewal
Educating Gifted Students

APRIL 1997
Declining Crime Rates
The FBI Under Fire
Gender Equity in Sports
Space Program's Future

MAY 1997
The Stock Market
The Cloning Controversy
Expanding NATO
The Future of Libraries

JUNE 1997
FDA Reform
China After Deng
Line-Item Veto
Breast Cancer

JULY 1997
Transportation Policy
Executive Pay
School Choice Debate
Aggressive Driving

AUGUST 1997
Age Discrimination
Banning Land Mines
Children's Television
Evolution vs. Creationism

SEPTEMBER 1997
Caring for the Dying
Mental Health Policy
Mexico's Future
Youth Fitness

OCTOBER 1997
Urban Sprawl in the West
Diversity in the Workplace
Teacher Education
Contingent Work Force

NOVEMBER 1997
Renewable Energy
Artificial Intelligence
Religious Persecution
Roe v. Wade at 25

DECEMBER 1997
Whistleblowers
Castro's Next Move
Gun Control Standoff
Regulating Nonprofits

JANUARY 1998
Foster Care Reform
IRS Reform
The Black Middle Class
U.S.-British Relations

FEBRUARY 1998
Patients' Rights
Deflation Fears
Caring for the Elderly
The New Corporate Philanthropy

MARCH 1998
Israel at 50
The Federal Judiciary
Drinking on Campus
The Economics of Recycling

APRIL 1998
Biology and Behavior
Liberal Arts Education
Income Inequality
High-Tech Labor Shortage

MAY 1998
Census 2000
Child-Care Options
Alzheimer's Disease
U.S.-Russian Relations

JUNE 1998
Student Journalism
Antitrust Policy

Future Topics

▶ *Sleep Deprivation*

▶ *Encouraging Teen Abstinence*

▶ *Population and the Environment*

THE

T
H
E

CQ Researcher

PUBLISHED BY CONGRESSIONAL QUARTERLY INC.

Sleep Deprivation

What's keeping Americans up at night?

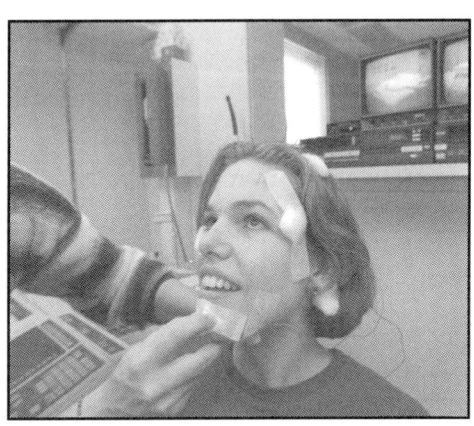

Tens of millions of Americans trudge through the day feeling tired and lethargic because they don't get enough sleep. Studies show that while the average person needs eight to nine hours of sleep each night, most only get seven. The effects are felt in lost worker productivity, fatigue-related transportation accidents, health problems and lower grades and behavioral difficulties in schools. But society is reluctant to deal with its "sleep deficit," viewing sleep as a luxury and inconsistent with the Information Age's round-the-clock environment. Scientists are trying to raise awareness by publicizing the consequences of sleep deprivation and learning how to treat sleep disorders like insomnia, narcolepsy and sleep apnea.

C_Q | **June 26, 1998 • Volume 8, No. 24 • Pages 553-576**

Formerly Editorial Research Reports

CQ Researcher

June 26, 1998
Volume 8, No.24

EDITOR
Sandra Stencel

MANAGING EDITOR
Thomas J. Colin

ASSOCIATE EDITOR
Sarah M. Magner

STAFF WRITERS
Adriel Bettelheim
Mary H. Cooper
Kenneth Jost
Kathy Koch
David Masci

PRODUCTION EDITOR
Melissa Hall

EDITORIAL ASSISTANT
Laura S. Cavender

PUBLISHED BY
Congressional Quarterly Inc.

CHAIRMAN
Andrew Barnes

VICE CHAIRMAN
Andrew P. Corty

PRESIDENT AND PUBLISHER
Robert W. Merry

EXECUTIVE EDITOR
David Rapp

The CQ Researcher (ISSN 1056-2036). Formerly Editorial Research Reports. Published weekly, except Jan. 2, May 29, July 3, Oct. 30, by Congressional Quarterly Inc., 1414 22nd St., N.W., Washington, D.C. 20037. Annual subscription rate for libraries, businesses and government is $340. Additional rates furnished upon request. Periodicals postage paid at Washington, D.C., and additional mailing offices. POSTMASTER: Send address changes to The CQ Researcher, 1414 22nd St., N.W., Washington, D.C. 20037.

COVER: ELECTRODES TO MONITOR BRAIN ACTIVITY ARE CHECKED BEFORE A SLEEP TEST AT NEBRASKA WESLEYAN UNIVERSITY (AP/LINCOLN JOURNAL-STAR, IAN DOREMUS)

Sleep Deprivation

BY ADRIEL BETTELHEIM

THE ISSUES

It's 5:45 a.m., and Scott McCann is struggling to get out of bed — as he does every weekday. The 10th-grader has just enough time to shower, gather his homework and dash out the door to catch the bus to Winston Churchill High School in Potomac, Md.

At 7:25 a.m., McCann is tuning his saxophone for a 50-minute jazz band class. But drowsiness often makes his fingers feel leaden, making it difficult to play all the notes and keep pace with the quick rhythms. The fatigue carries over to mid-morning English and French classes, where, he admits, he occasionally dozes off.

"Sometimes I really drag my feet in the morning and have to tell myself to wake up," he explains. "I try to be in bed by 10 or 10:15 but usually can't fall asleep for another hour. My friends have the same problem and keep complaining about how tired they are."

McCann is one of the tens of millions of Americans suffering from sleep deprivation. In the Information Age, when life seems to run on a 24-hour-a-day, seven-day-a-week basis, many people are struggling to find the time to work, play, run errands and care for their families. As a result, experts say, the nation is amassing an alarming "sleep deficit" that can lead to accidents, depression and a general loss of productivity. But sleep problems are so common they have bred complacency.

"Sleep disorders aren't being recognized in America," says pioneering sleep researcher William Dement, now a professor of medicine at Stanford University in Palo Alto, Calif. "People are skeptical, just like they used to be about tobacco."

The average adult needs eight to nine

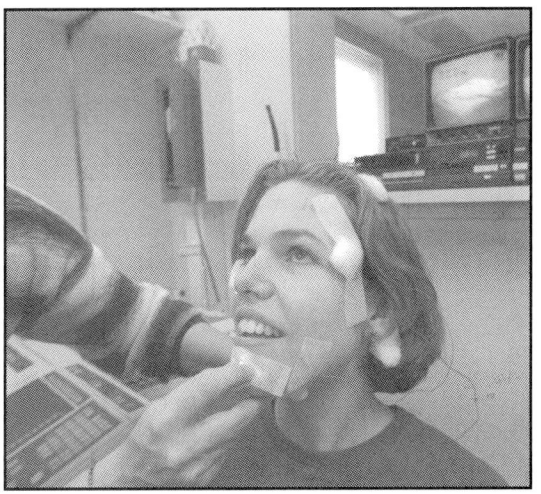

hours of sleep a night. However, studies show most of us get less than seven. Nearly 32 percent of adults surveyed recently for the National Sleep Foundation said they sleep less than six and a half hours a night in a typical workweek. More than half said they suffer from a serious sleep-related disorder, such as insomnia. [1]

Such findings are hardly new. A congressionally appointed commission on sleep disorders reported in 1993 that some 40 million Americans suffer from some type of chronic sleep problem — a situation the panel said cost the United States at least $15.9 billion in health-care costs each year. Accidents and lost worker productivity would likely add to that amount, though actual costs have never been calculated. [2]

"There's no question that sleep loss in the average person is getting worse," says Thomas Roth, director of the division of sleep medicine at the Henry Ford Health Sciences Center in Detroit, Mich. "Sleep is a biological drive that's no different than hunger or thirst. But while every sixth-grader gets lectures on nutrition, most people don't think about how long they sleep. And under-sleeping is [considered] macho."

The effects of sleeplessness are

found everywhere. Worker errors linked to lack of sleep were identified as contributing factors in incidents such as the 1979 explosion at the Three Mile Island nuclear reactor near Harrisburg, Pa., and the 1989 grounding of the supertanker *Exxon Valdez* in Alaska's Prince William Sound. The National Highway Traffic Safety Administration estimates that 1,500 deaths each year are caused by drivers who fall asleep at the wheel. And educators and psychologists point to research showing that lack of sleep is linked to lower grades, inattention and behavioral problems in schools.

But because sleep disorders are not a distinct medical condition, such as heart disease or cancer, efforts to find solutions have been fragmented and slow. The American Medical Association only designated sleep medicine as a specialty in 1996. Surveys show that until recently medical students only received two to six hours of instruction in sleep disorders during their four years of basic training. Calls to take more naps and improve sleep habits, moreover, are still widely regarded as frivolous in a fast-paced culture where people brag about 14-hour workdays.

"It's an area of study that's a bit new and a bit orphaned," admits James Kiley, director of the National Center on Sleep Disorders Research, a division of the National Institutes of Health that oversaw $84.7 million in federally supported sleep research last year. "We sleep one-third of our lives, but it doesn't have a real natural home in the health-care system because it touches on everything from psychiatric conditions to heart and lung problems to aging."

Gradually the problem is getting more attention. Recent research suggesting that teens' body clocks un-

America's Sleep Deficit

The average adult needs eight to nine hours of sleep per night, but most adults get less than seven. Nearly a third of the adults responding to a recent survey conducted for the National Sleep Foundation said they sleep as little as six hours or less per night during the workweek. Most people compensate for sleep lost during the week by sleeping more on the weekends. While there is little difference between the sexes, age affects sleep patterns. Adults 24-64 get significantly less sleep than either younger or older adults.

Average Number of Hours Slept on Weekdays

		Sex			Age	
	Total	Men	Women	18-29	30-64	65+
Less than 6 hours	12.1%	10.8%	13.3%	13.6%	12.5%	7.3%
6 - 6 hours 29 min.	19.3	17.5	20.9	15.0	22.6	12.7
6 hours 30 min. - 59 min.	3.7	4.6	2.9	2.1	4.3	2.6
7 - 7 hours 29 min.	23.5	27.6	19.8	22.7	23.8	22.7
7 hours 30 min. - 59 min.	4.5	5.1	3.8	3.7	5.0	3.7
8 hours or more	35.2	33.5	36.7	41.6	30.2	46.8
Don't know/not applicable	1.8	0.9	2.6	1.3	1.6	4.1
Mean (in hours)	6.9	7.0	6.9	7.0	6.8	7.4

Average Number of Hours Slept on Weekends

		Sex			Age	
	Total	Men	Women	18-29	30-64	65+
Less than 6 hours	8.4%	8.1%	8.8%	9.1%	8.5%	7.2%
6 - 6 hours 29 min.	12.3	11.2	13.2	10.9	13.6	7.4
6 hours 30 min. - 59 min.	1.8	1.9	1.7	0.5	2.3	2.3
7 - 7 hours 29 min.	19.2	22.2	16.6	20.6	17.6	25.7
7 hours 30 min. - 59 min.	3.3	3.9	2.8	1.9	3.6	5.3
8 hours or more	53.4	51.6	55.0	55.4	53.5	46.8
Don't know/not applicable	1.5	1.1	1.9	1.5	0.8	5.2
Mean (in hours)	7.5	7.5	7.5	7.7	7.5	7.4

Source: Telephone survey of 1,027 adults conducted by DataStat for the National Sleep Foundation, published March 1998. Estimates have an error range of plus or minus 3 percentage points.

dergo fundamental changes at puberty is prompting McCann's Maryland school district and others around the nation to study adjusting starting times to better accommodate adolescents' sleep clocks.

Spurred by mounting public safety concerns, the U.S. Department of Transportation is considering new rules limiting the number of hours commercial truckers can drive, and the agency has looked at rewriting similar regulations for airlines and railroads. Some unregulated businesses have set up "sleep friendly" workplaces with nap rooms, allowing shift workers and employees pulling all-nighters to doze without guilt.

"People are beginning to realize it doesn't make sense to pay heavy school taxes when the audience you're teaching is asleep," says James Maas, a psychologist at Cornell University in Ithaca, N.Y., and author of the new book *Power Sleep.* "Similarly, government is realizing that drowsy driving can have the same effects as drunken driving. And companies also have to address this because it's affecting their bottom lines."

Scientists don't exactly understand why people need to sleep, but they know it's driven by the so-called biological clock — a cluster of nerve cells deep in the center of the brain known as the suprachiasmatic nucleus. The cells respond to light and control alertness, body temperature and hormone production.

When the sun goes down, the pineal gland at the base of the brain gets a signal to begin producing the hormone melatonin, which induces sleepiness and sets the body's circadian rhythms. The body is programmed for a period of wakefulness typically lasting about 16 hours and a sleep state that lasts about eight hours. It can easily accommodate swings of an hour or so in either direction.

The problems begin when people go to sleep at vastly different times during the workweek and on weekends, or if they are shift workers who frequently rotate between day and night schedules. With their body clocks chronically out of sync, many go to bed wide awake and alert but slog through the day feeling foggy and lethargic. The same goes for jet-lagged business travelers who fly across multiple time zones and all-night Internet surfers, who log on to their message systems hours before dawn.

Going to bed at the same time every day, taking strategically timed naps or, in some cases, prescription drugs can help most people catch up on their sleep deficits. But many others suffer from physical sleep disorders. An estimated 30 million Americans have some form of sleep apnea, a condition in which the airway narrows or collapses during sleep, restricting or preventing breathing. At least 250,000 others suffer from narcolepsy, a disorder of the central nervous system that brings on an uncontrolled attack of deep sleep during the day. Doctors can treat the conditions but say most sufferers are unaware they have a problem until their loved ones point it out.

Researchers are trying to understand the differences between brain cells in the sleeping and waking state and answer riddles such as whether certain sleep-inducing substances in the body influence how long and how deeply people sleep. Maas says finding answers may reinforce the notion that sleep is healthy and restorative, not just a nuisance for busy people.

As Americans continue to get by on less sleep, and scientists try to understand the biological roots of sleep, here are some of the questions they are asking:

Should high schools adjust their schedules to allow students to sleep later?

Aarthi Belani recalls occasionally looking around in her 7:20 a.m. class during junior year of high school in Edina, Minn., and noticing the majority of her classmates were barely awake. "It was an ungodly hour to be studying chemistry or something," says Belani, then 17 and now a student at Stanford University. "In the first period, 75 percent of the kids would have their heads down on their desk at one time or another." [3]

The school district in Edina, like many others across the country, staggered starting times for high schools and middle schools to save money and maximize the number of runs each school bus could make. But in doing so, researchers say administrators shortchanged teenagers, who actually need more sleep than their younger siblings.

"The original hypothesis was, 'The older you get, the less sleep you need,'" says Mary Carskadon, director of the E.P. Bradley Hospital Sleep Research Lab in Providence, R.I., and a professor of psychiatry at Brown University. "But with teens, we now know changes happen that create a biological need to sleep later in the morning."

Over the last decade, Carskadon and her colleagues discovered that as adolescents go through puberty, their biological clocks undergo a fundamental shift that pushes their preprogrammed period of wakefulness about an hour later than it was in their early teens. The hormonal changes lead the pineal gland to release melatonin after 10:30 at night, instead of around 9:30 in younger teens.

The changes not only delay when teens go to sleep but push back all subsequent stages of sleep. Carskadon's research on children ages 10 to 17 showed that, given the opportunity to sleep as long as they want, older teens slept an average of 9.25 hours. Most younger teens could easily get by on seven to eight hours. The clock resets itself as teens pass into adulthood, establishing the approximately eight-hour sleep cycle.

The research countered the widespread perception that adolescents stay up later mainly to assert their independence from parents or participate in new social pursuits like evening sports or late-night outings with friends. It also suggested that parents who order teens to go to bed earlier might not be helping the situation.

Follow-up research showed sleep deprivation was directly connected to scholastic performance. Psychologists at the College of the Holy Cross in Worcester, Mass., working with Carskadon, surveyed more than 3,120 Providence-area high school students and found students who got A's and B's averaged about 35 minutes more sleep on both weeknights and weekends than students who received D's and F's. [4]

Carskadon isn't the only researcher drawn to teen sleep habits. David Dinges, chief of the division of sleep and chronobiology * at the University of Pennsylvania Medical School in

---

*Chronobiology is the study of biological rhythms.

Are You Getting Enough Sleep?

Cornell University psychologist James Maas has devised this 15-question test to gauge whether someone is sleep deprived. Maas says answering "true" to three or more of the items means the person probably is not getting enough sleep.

Please indicate true or false for the following statements:

T   F

☐   ☐   *I need an alarm clock in order to wake up at the appropriate time.*

☐   ☐   *It's a struggle for me to get out of bed in the morning. Weekday mornings I hit the snooze button several times to get more sleep.*

☐   ☐   *I feel tired, irritable and stressed-out during the week.*

☐   ☐   *I have trouble concentrating and remembering.*

☐   ☐   *I feel slow with critical thinking, problem solving and being creative.*

☐   ☐   *I often fall asleep watching TV.*

☐   ☐   *I often fall asleep in boring meetings or lectures or in warm rooms.*

☐   ☐   *I often fall asleep after heavy meals or after a low dose of alcohol.*

☐   ☐   *I often fall asleep while relaxing after dinner.*

☐   ☐   *I often fall asleep within five minutes of getting into bed.*

☐   ☐   *I often feel drowsy while driving.*

☐   ☐   *I often sleep extra hours on weekend mornings.*

☐   ☐   *I often need a nap to get through the day.*

☐   ☐   *I have dark circles around my eyes.*

Source: Reprinted from James Maas, Power Sleep *(Villard, 1998).*

Philadelphia, found teens who stay up late on weekends remain sleepy during the week, even if they go to sleep at more reasonable hours on weeknights. His conclusion: consistent sleep habits are as important as the hours of sleep one gets.

The assorted findings have caught the notice of educators and physicians. In 1994, the Minnesota Medical Association urged public school districts in the state to let high school students get more sleep before class, reasoning that they would be more alert during the day and also have less time to get into trouble during afternoon hours.

The Edina school district was the first to make changes, moving up the start time for its 1,350 high school students one hour, to 8:30 a.m. from 7:30 a.m., in 1996. Administrators report the later schedule has led to better grades, fewer behavioral prob-

lems and a better-rested student body, according to Kyla Wahlstrom, associate director of the Center for Applied Research in Educational Improvement at the University of Minnesota, who studies the effects of changing high school starting times. [5]

School officials in other localities — including Seattle, Arlington County, Va., and Montgomery County, Md., where Scott McCann attends classes — are now studying teenagers' sleep needs and contemplating later start times. Montgomery County School Superintendent Paul Vance calls the issue "a quality of life issue, as much or more than it is a strictly academic concern."

But school districts are learning that solving one scheduling problem can create new ones. Because most districts don't have enough buses to transport all of their students at the same time, changes in high school start times have meant changes in middle school and elementary school scheduling.

In Minnesota, some school officials noticed increased tardiness in seventh- and eighth-graders after their school starting times were moved up to 9:30 a.m. Wahlstrom speculates the later hour was well after many parents left for work, giving the kids less incentive to leave their houses on time.

Later start times also put a squeeze on high school students' afternoon and evening activities. Earl Rainey, 16, who attends South High School in Minneapolis, was one of the students who noticed a change when the city school system moved up its high school start time for an estimated 17,000 students to 8:40 a.m. last year. Rainey says he now feels more alert in the mornings and ready to learn. But Rainey says the later school starting time means his basketball practices sometimes conclude at 8 p.m., leaving little time for homework. "I wouldn't have enough time [in the evening] to do my homework. Then I'd have to get up early in the morning to do it, so I wouldn't get the extra hour of sleep," he says. [6]

In Montgomery County, Md., school officials estimate it would cost $31 million to buy enough buses to accommodate later starting times for high school students without inconveniencing other students, and they are looking at less expensive scheduling options. In Prince William County, Va., administrators considered later starting times but dropped the idea last year after parents complained they depend on their high school children to return early in the afternoon to care for younger children. [7]

Carskadon says high-schoolers still have options if districts don't change starting times. They include opting for quiet activities like reading and avoiding bright lights or loud music before bedtime. She also urged school districts to teach students about sleep deprivation and encourage good sleep habits.

"Many need to learn how to manage their schedules and understand that less sleep doesn't necessarily mean they'll have more time to do things during the day," she says.

Should the government mandate rest and sleep for transportation workers in the name of public safety?

The tanker truck carrying 9,200 gallons of flammable propane traveled along Interstate 287 in White Plains, N.Y., on July 27, 1994, operated by a driver who had slept only two and a half hours in his previous 65 hours on duty. Then disaster struck. The weary driver, Peter Conway, dozed off at the wheel, causing the truck to veer into a bridge support. The force of the crash sent the giant propane tank hurtling more than 100 yards into a house across the highway. Fuel gushed from the ruptured tank and ignited, sending up a huge fireball that torched the residential neighborhood, injuring 23 people and destroying seven homes.

Conway, who investigators found had falsified log books in violation of

An 18-wheel truck crashed into the office of an Econo Lodge motel in Brunswick, Maine, after the driver claimed he fell asleep at the wheel. The driver was charged with falsifying his driver's logbook.

AP/Portland Newspapers, David A. Rogers

federal hours-of-service rules that mandate no more than 10 hours of consecutive driving, died in the crash. [8]

Safety advocates say the incident was dramatic evidence of the need for tougher government regulations limiting the number of hours commercial truckers can drive. It's a debate that has since extended to other modes of transportation.

Federal rules governing how long operators of trucks, trains and airplanes can work continuously without breaks haven't changed since the 1930s, despite dramatic changes to those industries and a new under-standing of the need to sleep. In the case of trucks, the National Transportation Safety Board notes many companies still pay drivers by the load delivered instead of by the hour, encouraging drivers to squeeze in extra runs instead of rest. [9]

But businesses and the safety advocates are sharply divided over whether the government should mandate specific rest periods or let businesses work them out with employees. *(See "At Issue," p. 545.)* Transportation industries have strenuously opposed proposed rule changes limiting hours of consecutive service, saying they are counter-productive, don't take into account what time of day work is scheduled or individuals' different sleep needs.

"Hours of work, while a factor, are in no way the sole — or even primary — determinant of fatigue," American Trucking Associations President and Chief Executive Officer Walter Mc-Cormick Jr. told the American Bar Association's transportation law section in March. "We want rules that are safety based. Does that mean truck drivers should be able to work more hours? If they can do so safely, why not?"

Safety advocates point to statistics showing crashes involving trucks have on average killed 5,000 people and injured 100,000 every year since 1984, though not all have involved sleepy drivers. The advocates claim industry leaders are asking for flexibility to craft their own operating rules as a way of getting out from under even the outdated — and, in the advocates' opinion, lax — federal regulations.

"President Clinton had a special presidential commission working night and day on airline safety, but deaths caused by commercial trucking are 28 times higher," says Joan Claybrook, president of the Washington advocacy group Public Citizen. "If the airline industry were killing and maiming people at that rate, all planes would be grounded." [10]

Truckers have come under increased scrutiny since a U.S. Department of Transportation-sponsored study last year found 56 percent of 80 drivers surveyed over the course of one week had at least one six-minute interval of drowsiness while their driving was studied. Notably, all of the drivers followed existing rules that mandate no more than 10 hours of consecutive driving, after which they had to rest for eight hours. [11]

The Transportation Department, which often blames truck safety problems on drivers who falsify logs and break rules, is using the results to draft new rules that would replace existing regulations that were drafted in 1937. Transportation Secretary Rodney Slater has appealed for more enforcement powers, including expanded latitude to take some carriers off the road.

But the government has had mixed success implementing such policies. In 1996, the Federal Aviation Administration (FAA) proposed limiting commercial pilots' duty hours and lengthening minimum rest periods from eight to 10 consecutive hours per day. Regulators were particularly concerned about fatigue on marathon international flights and the growing use of new wide-body jets designed to be flown by two crew members instead of three.

However, major airlines argued they would have to hire 5,000 additional pilots and absorb $10 billion in extra costs over 15 years to meet the new requirements. The FAA put an indefinite hold on the rule changes after they prompted an outcry from large air carriers and some members of Congress.

While regulators, industry leaders and pilot unions remain at odds over what to do, many international carriers now are allowing their pilots to nap during long flights. British Airways, Qantas, Swissair, Finnair and Lufthansa, among others, encourage pilots to doze for as long as 40 minutes during the less demanding portions of long flights, though the carriers avoid publicizing the practice.

FAA officials say it's common knowledge that U.S. pilots also nap on long-haul flights. But regulations sanctioning naps face long odds in Congress because lawmakers are worried about scaring the flying public, according to Gary Davis, deputy manager of the FAA's air transportation division. Regulators like Davis also fear a possible backlash if a crash or near-accident involved an aircraft with a napping pilot. [12]

The dilemma over regulation also extends to the rail industry, where crews often battle fatigue in the middle of the night waiting to load and unload freight trains. The Clinton administration has proposed a 1998 Federal Railroad Safety Authorization Act that would guarantee a minimum number of consecutive days off for freight crews that have to deal with significant down time between arrivals.

Some railroads are trying their own solutions. Conrail, Canadian National and Canadian Pacific, among others, have tinkered with new scheduling systems that allow crews to know the days and hours they will be on duty months in advance. Martin Moore-Ede, a professor of physiology at Harvard University Medical School and a consultant to railroads, says such regularly timed schedules are more important than simply giving employees more hours off because they promote consistent sleep patterns.

The attention to operator fatigue has prompted more research into how to physically monitor alertness in a trucker's cab or airplane cockpit. Scientists are developing a series of dashboard-mounted devices and motion sensors that emit signals like red lights, beeping alarms or vibrations when an operator shows signs of drowsiness, or when a driver's steering and lane-changing becomes suspect. The devices are similar to those that currently alert pilots when their planes encounter wind shear or suddenly lose altitude.

University of Pennsylvania sleep researcher Dinges says perhaps the most reliable device is a monitor developed at Virginia Polytechnic Institute in Blacksburg, and Carnegie-Mellon Research Institute in Pittsburgh, Pa., that uses a small camera to count how frequently a driver's eyelids close — a common precursor to nodding off. In trials, the monitor proved even more effective than encephalograms, which directly measure brain activity through electrodes attached to the scalp but can't always pinpoint drowsiness. [13]

Dinges says it's too early to tell how such devices may be used by regulators or transportation industries or to predict their effectiveness on many subjects. "There are a lot of concerns, like if warning a driver would encourage him to speed and get somewhere before he falls asleep," Dinges says. "It will probably end up being used as a kind of personal monitor that the individual can turn on and off. Industries may adopt them and ask their operators to use them as safeguards to warn if they're impaired."

Meanwhile, doctors are urging police to be more aware of sleep-related problems. The American Medical Association's Council on Scientific Affairs warned this month that motorists who nod off cause up to 3 percent of the motor vehicle crashes in the United

States, and tens of millions more Americans are short of sleep when they are behind the wheel.

Should businesses establish more "sleep friendly" work environments?

Craig Yarde has added an unusual touch to his new round-the-clock metals distribution plant in Bristol, Conn.: a "napping room" that allows his 220 employees to catch some sleep without recriminations when they feel fatigued. "We're trying to see how we can give them a break or a perk, a napping area where they can unwind," says Yarde. He freely admits some workers were shocked when he first disclosed his plans. "They thought I was crazy," he laughs. [14]

Yarde's company is one of dozens that are trying to redefine the concept of working in shifts while giving employees the opportunity to reset their body clocks at odd hours. The trend extends beyond traditional manufacturing, which has operated around the clock since the late 1800s, to banks and brokerages, health-care firms and service industries.

The changes stem partly from the growth of computers and the Internet, which created a virtual environment in which work and clients can be found around-the-clock. Stock and currency brokers now execute trades around-the-clock while many business executives wake up before dawn to fire off E-mail messages to clients or staff. Forty-six percent of respondents to the National Sleep Foundation's survey said they would get to bed earlier if they didn't have a television or access to the Internet.

Society's rising affluence is also increasing the demand for goods and services beyond the standard workday and weekends. Malls and department stores now stay open as late as 10 p.m. on weeknights to accommodate working women and dual-career couples after work. Mail-order businesses and investment firms maintain 24-hour customer service lines, while express delivery services tout their ability to deliver packages by sunrise the next morning.

University of Maryland sociologist Harriet Presser estimates that one in five full-time American workers now works outside conventional 9-to-5 hours, and that one in three are part of so-called "split shift" couples, where one partner works primarily outside normal daytime hours. [15]

But sleep researchers say the 24-hour focus conflicts with the body's natural tendency to shut down at night. It also increases the reliance on caffeine and promotes bad nutritional habits and other health problems. Studies of all-night workers in Italy and Germany showed that disturbed sleep, poor eating habits, excessive coffee consumption, smoking and psychological stress put them at significantly higher risk of developing stomach ulcers, heart disease and women's reproductive health problems. [16]

In Japan, as many as 10,000 workers each year succumb to *karoshi* — literally translated, "death from overwork" — a blend of fatigue, high blood pressure and hardening of the arteries that the government now officially recognizes as an industrial disease.

"Most companies have the tendency to say, 'This is a job, take it or leave it,'" says Steve Mardon, editor of *ShiftWork Alert*, a Cambridge, Mass.,

ENGLEMAN

"He's back from his power lunch, now he's taking his power nap."

From *The Wall Street Journal*. Permission, Cartoon Features Syndicate.

monthly newsletter that examines workplace fatigue and related safety issues. "Big accidents that result from lack of sleep tend to change those attitudes, but only a few companies are trying to get ahead of the curve."

Some manufacturing companies are tackling the problem by tweaking work schedules. Mardon says a growing number are embracing the concept of a "compressed workweek" and converting from standard eight-hour shifts to 12-hour shifts. The longer shifts allow workers to squeeze the total hours of a regular workweek into fewer days, giving them more weekends and days off between shifts.

So far, there have been anecdotal successes. A James River Paper Co. plant in Ashland, Wis., offered employees eight- and 12-hour options and found workers on 12-hour shifts had more leisure time and reported a positive effect on personal, social and family lives. Similar results were reported at sites as diverse as an Amax Coal mine in Gillette, Wyo., and high-tech manufacturer Advanced Micro Devices in Sunnyvale, Calif. [17]

However, unions and European governments have generally opposed longer shifts, saying they lead to accidents and greater fatigue. Concern is particularly great in the electric power industry, where slow worker response to emergencies can be costly and disastrous. The Three Mile Island explosion was partly attributed to an overnight crew's slow response to malfunctions in the reactor's cooling system. A similar sluggish response in the early morning hours was linked to the 1986 fire at the Chernobyl nuclear power station in Ukraine.

Short of changing schedules, com-

panies are catering to sleepy workers by encouraging healthy diets and lifestyles. Some are stocking cafeterias with fruits, vegetables and other healthy snacks and keeping them open 24 hours to discourage late-night consumption of spicy or fried foods that cause heartburn and keep people awake. The National Sleep Foundation also urges companies to install light boxes next to work stations to reset the circadian cycle and help workers adjust to new shift

Most people slept an average of 10 hours a night before Thomas A. Edison, shown here in 1933, invented the light bulb in 1879.

AP/J. Walter Thompson

schedules (see p. 561).

Nap rooms and less formal rest areas are another recent innovation and have been especially embraced by West Coast computer businesses that require employees to work long hours to meet deadlines. Officials at Berkeley, Calif.-based 42 IS Consulting, a computer consulting firm, recently set up a queen-size bed in an upstairs loft for employees, who of-

ten work 10 to 12 hours a day. The company says it's a response to the bad eating habits, lack of exercise and sleep they've noticed when employees work long periods nonstop. The bed has proven so popular that users now have to reserve it on a sign-up list.

Microtek Lab Inc., a computer scanner company in Redondo Beach, Calif., has an area in its library with a couch and soft lighting for workers who need to catch naps. But President S.C. Lee says the room is rarely used, a possible sign of workers' reluctance to publicly acknowledge sleepiness. "People use it if they're feeling ill or if they had a really bad night," he says, adding taking naps seems "kind of odd in this culture." [18]

Yarde says he was prompted to install a nap room by a 1997 paperback book by Boston University sleep researcher William Anthony, *The Art of Napping*, which concluded that sneaking naps was nothing to be ashamed of. "We're a pretty lean and mean operation, and our people work hard. It seemed like the right thing to do," Yarde says.

An informal survey of employees confirmed some of his suspicions. Despite stares of disbelief, Yarde says, "It turned out we had a lot of closet nappers." [19] ∎

BACKGROUND

Edison's Light Idea

"Everything comes to him who hustles while he waits," said Tho-

Continued on p. 564

Chronology

1870s-1930s
Technological advances change society's work-sleep schedule while scientists begin to explore the mechanisms of sleep.

1879
Thomas A. Edison invents the electric light, eliminating the need to limit activity to the day's natural light. Until now, most people sleep nine to 10 hours each night.

1914
Henry Ford uses a chain-drive conveyor and stationary locations for workers to perfect the modern assembly line, institutionalizing the concept of "shift work" and 24-hour-a-day manufacturing.

1929
German psychiatrist Hans Berger attaches small electrodes to patients' scalps and makes brain-wave recordings showing distinct changes in the brain's activity between sleep and wakefulness.

1930s-1960s
Congress begins to regulate the length of the workday as researchers gain a greater understanding of sleep patterns and the body's natural clock.

1938
After decades of debate, Congress passes the Wages and Hours Act, mandating the eight-hour workday and 40-hour workweek. The legislation is credited with creating the so-called "eight-eight-eight lifestyle" — eight hours of work, eight hours of sleep, eight hours of play — that became an emblem of the growing middle class.

1951-1952
University of Chicago graduate students Eugene Aserinsky and William Dement, under the direction of physiologist Nathaniel Kleitman, discover periods of sleep characterized by rapid eye movements, known as REM, during which dreaming takes place. For the first time, sleep is regarded as an "active" process.

January 1964
San Diego high school senior Randy Gardner sets a world record for documented time without sleep by staying awake for 264 hours (11 days) as part of a science project. He then goes home and sleeps for 14 and three-quarters hours.

1970s-1980s
A series of tragedies and disturbing incidents draw national attention to worker fatigue.

March 28, 1979
A malfunctioning cooling system leads to an explosion and near meltdown late at night at the Three Mile Island nuclear power plant near Harrisburg, Pa. Investigators later cite a series of human and mechanical failures, including inadequate training and response of the night shift.

1987
Congress passes legislation requiring the National Institutes of Health to develop a plan for coordinating sleep research within the U.S. Public Health Service.

March 24, 1989
The supertanker *Exxon Valdez* crashes into a reef in Alaska's Prince William Sound, spilling 258,000 barrels of crude oil and triggering a $2 billion cleanup. The third mate at the helm is later described as being too sleepy to perform his duties. The captain had been drinking and was asleep in his cabin.

1990s
The federal government becomes more involved in sleep research.

1992
A national commission on sleep disorders research estimates 40 million Americans suffer from chronic lack of sleep — a situation the panel estimates costs society at least $15.9 billion a year. The findings spur creation of the National Center on Sleep Disorders Research at the National Institutes of Health (NIH).

June 1993
President Clinton signs a bill establishing the National Center on Sleep Disorders Research.

July 1996
The Federal Aviation Administration proposes rules limiting the number of consecutive hours pilots can fly commercial airliners. Protests from airlines and lawmakers eventually squelch the effort.

March 1998
A National Sleep Foundation poll reveals that nearly 32 percent of Americans get less than six and a half hours of sleep per night during the workweek.

Is Melatonin the Answer ...

It eases jet lag, improves alertness and helps shift workers adjust to rotating work schedules. Some claim it even reverses aging and enhances sexual performance.

Since the early 1990s, the hormone melatonin has emerged as one of the nation's hottest sleep aids and become a mainstay of health-food and nutrition stores. The substance's promise of sound sleep and renewed vigor appears irresistible in a society where working long hours is considered a virtue and many people complain of chronic fatigue.

Melatonin is naturally produced in the body by the pineal gland at the base of the brain. Secreted into the bloodstream at night, it causes people to become drowsy and plays a role in setting their biological clocks. But production drops in half by age 45, making supplements an attractive option.

Unlike most other hormones, melatonin isn't classified as a drug, meaning it doesn't require Food and Drug Administration approval or a doctor's prescription. The small doses sold in stores as "nutritional supplements" provide 10 to 100 times higher concentrations than the body's natural nighttime production. The most common variety is a 3-

milligram pill that is about 10 times the dose produced naturally.

Despite its appeal, many physicians advise patients not to take melatonin because there isn't enough scientific proof that it helps people with chronic sleep problems.

The National Institute on Aging also urges caution, saying overuse of hormone supplements can pose dangerous health risks, including cancer and depression.

But demand for the substance continues to rise due to favorable news reports and the growing use of prescription hormones like estrogen for a variety of ailments. Source Naturals, a Scotts Valley, Calif., supplier of melatonin pills, reported that demand quadrupled after a favorable article appeared in *Newsweek* magazine in 1995. [1]

"A large number of Americans are participating in a large-scale, uncontrolled clinical trial of the toxicity of this hormone," the National Sleep Foundation concluded in a 1997 white paper on the substance. [2]

Melatonin's popularity in large part stems from the research

Continued from p. 562

mas A. Edison, inventor of the light bulb, notorious workaholic and, to many, creator of the sleep deficit. Edison regarded a good night's sleep as a sign of slothfulness, preferring to catch frequent naps in his laboratory. Fittingly, his best-known creation ensured that generations of others could work at all hours, no longer constrained by the day's natural light.

Before Edison's 1879 discovery, most people slept an average of 10 hours a night. But within a few years, Gilded Age industrialists, particularly in the steel industry, used lightbulbs to turn their plants into 24-hour enterprises, rotating employees to work 12-hour shifts, seven days a week. Employees typically switched between day and night shifts every two weeks.

"To accomplish this changeover, one employee had to work 24 consecutive hours at the end of every 28-day cycle, while his co-worker got

those 24 hours off," Stanford University sleep researcher Richard Coleman wrote in his 1986 book, *Wide Awake at 3:00 a.m.: By Choice or By Chance?* "That happened on Sunday and represented the only time off each month."

Church, civic and labor leaders protested that such schedules were inhuman, deprived workers of rest and social time with their families and generally shortened life expectancies. But despite passionate debates in legislatures — and dozens of violent turn-of-the-century strikes — Congress did little to change working conditions until the 1930s.

The 1938 Wages and Hours Act finally mandated an eight-hour workday and 40-hour workweek. It is widely credited with establishing the so-called "eight-eight-eight" lifestyle — eight hours of work, eight hours of sleep, eight hours of play — that became an emblem of the nation's rising middle class.

Sleep Research

While rest was generally regarded to be a healthy thing, few early 20th-century scientists bothered to study exactly how and why people sleep. Early brain-wave recordings by German psychiatrist Hans Berger in the 1920s revealed distinct changes in the brain's activity between sleep and waking hours. But it was widely assumed that once brain activity slowed, it continued like that throughout the night.

In 1935, Harvard University researchers monitoring brain activity established that sleep was divided into several different levels, from drowsiness to shallow sleep to deep sleep. But scientists were content to turn off their brain-wave recorders after an hour or so instead of tracking a full night's sleep, missing the distinct changes the body undergoes as it goes from phase to phase.

Those secrets were finally unlocked in 1951 when University of Chicago physi-

... Or a Dangerous Health Risk?

of Italian endocrinologist Walter Pierpaoli and Medical College of Virginia physician William Regelson. Their 1995 book, *The Melatonin Miracle*, detailed experiments in which they claimed doses of the hormone added six months to the two-year lifespan of laboratory mice, strengthened the rodents' immune systems and made them more sexually active. The researchers also transplanted pineal glands from younger mice into older ones and reported the older mice were rejuvenated and had extended lifespans. [3]

Other scientists have questioned the work. Harvard University pediatrician Steven Reppert wrote in *Cell* magazine that the pineal gland transplant proved nothing because the strain of mice used in the experiment were genetically incapable of producing melatonin. He also warned that large doses of melatonin in other strains of mice caused tumors in reproductive organs. [4]

The Canadian government last year halted over-the-counter sales of melatonin over such concerns until scientists can prove its safety in human clinical trials.

Wallace Mendelson, a neurologist at the Cleveland Clinic Foundation, says it's difficult to assess melatonin's effectiveness because timing, dosage, individuals' sensitivities to the substance and purity of the hormone vary greatly. In addition,

most studies have been done with healthy, young people instead of insomniacs, who presumably would show the greatest change in sleep habits. Only two studies took up whether melatonin helped insomniacs under age 65, and they showed conflicting results.

The National Sleep Foundation, which promotes healthy sleep habits, urges caution, saying users often complain of side effects including headaches and grogginess the next day and mild depression.

"Melatonin is underresearched," says Thomas Roth of the Henry Ford Health Sciences Center in Detroit. "The lack of data on adverse effects fails to ensure none exist."

---

[1] See Marilyn Elias, "Melatonin May Be Blessing, Curse," *USA Today*, Sept. 4, 1997; and Geoffrey Cowley, "Melatonin Mania," *Newsweek*, Nov. 6, 1995, p. 62.

[2] See Charles Czeisler and Fred Tureck, "Is Melatonin a Treatment for Insomnia and Jet Lag?" White paper of the National Sleep Foundation, 1997.

[3] See Susan Okie, "Can Hormones Stop Aging?" *The Washington Post*, Feb. 24, 1998, page Z12.

[4] See Steven M. Reppert and D.R. Weaver, "Melatonin Madness," *Cell*, Vol. 83, 1995, pp. 1059-1062.

---

ologist Nathaniel Kleitman and two graduate students, Eugene Aserinsky and William Dement, studied a full night's sleep and discovered periods of sleep characterized by darting, rapid eye movements, during which dreaming is most likely to take place. This so-called REM phase was distinct from the slow eye movements that accompany sleep onset and confirmed that sleep was an "active" process. The discovery kicked off a new era of research exploring how the sleeping brain affects daytime functioning.

Researchers now know there are five distinct phases of sleep. As people get drowsy and nod off they enter an introductory phase of light sleep known as Stage 1 lasting up to 10 minutes in which the heart beats slower and breathing is shallower. Skeletal muscles relax, sometimes giving the sleeper a sense he or she is falling.

Stage 2 is the actual beginning of sleep, lasting 10 to 20 minutes. At this point, the lack of movement reduces activity of muscle nerves that stimu-

late the brain stem when one is awake. Sleepers at this point stop sensing most ambient noise or movement.

Stages 3 and 4 are phases of progressively deeper sleep characterized by low frequency, high-voltage brain waves. The sleeper's blood pressure drops and the breathing and pulse rates slow. After 30 to 40 minutes, one enters the first stage of REM sleep, in which neurons in the brain are randomly stimulated and the first dreams of the night are likely to occur.

Healthy sleepers go through four or five progressively longer REM cycles in a given night, passing back and forth between REM sleep and Stages 2 and 3. Sleep-deprived people, alternatively, miss several stages of REM sleep and are more likely to feel the effects in diminished learning, memory and thinking the next day.

Scientists don't completely understand dreaming but think it represents the brain's way of filing away ideas and memory accumulated during the waking hours. Kiley of the National

Institute on Sleep Disorders Research says some new learning may be lumped with older information already in the brain to make storage more efficient. The theory may explain why some people report they have solved problems in their sleep, or recalled some essential but long forgotten fact. It also would imply that the brain prioritizes memories, retaining important ideas and images but forgetting non-essential information.

Sleep Disorders

Many things cause sleep deprivation. Job-related stress or anxiety linked to personal problems can cause insomnia. Sufferers are often referred to psychologists or psychiatrists to treat the underlying problems.

The most common physiological
Continued on p. 567

No Wake-Up Call Required at This 'Hotel'

The guest room boasts a comfortable bed, a television set, a private bathroom and pleasant wall hangings. Not unlike a typical hotel — until you notice the panel of knobs, dials and protruding electrodes mounted on the bed's headboard.

This is where the sleepless check in. The six-bed Sleep Disorders Center at Johns Hopkins University in Baltimore, Md., is a sanctuary for the sleep-deprived — a place where chronic snorers, people who kick in their sleep and individuals who wake up in the middle of the night gasping for breath learn what ails them.

"It usually takes the patient — or, more precisely, the patient's bed partner — to sense something's wrong in the first place," says Philip Smith, a pulmonologist and the center's medical director. "When you're asleep, it's hard to know you have a problem. Once they get here, it usually takes just one night's sleep for us to figure out the problem."

The sleep lab is one of about 300 across the country accredited by the American Sleep Disorders Association, a Rochester, Minn.-based professional medical association for sleep researchers. Staffed by neurologists, psychologists and respiratory specialists, the Johns Hopkins facility is designed as a kind of one-stop center to diagnose an individual's sleep disorder by simultaneously monitoring the brain, heart and lungs and assorted muscle actions.

New patients arrive complaining of sleeplessness, fatigue and, often, accompanying depression. Virtually none know what is causing the problems. Some clues come from bed partners' descriptions and the patient's physical appearance. Smith says many patients weigh 210 pounds or more and have breathing difficulties that are telltale signs of sleep apnea. The obvious solution would be to tell them to lose weight, but Smith says most can't do it. "Most of them have been obese for years. It's very difficult for them to lose weight and keep it off," he says.

After patients are grilled on their medical histories, they are checked into one of the rooms around 9:30 p.m. and wired to an assortment of medical equipment. Doctors attach five electrodes running from the headboard of the bed to the patient's face and scalp to track the brain's electrical activity and follow the individual's passage

Philip Smith, director of the Sleep Disorders Center at John Hopkins University.

Adriel Bettelheim

through each phase of sleep. The patient also is connected to an electrocardiogram that monitors heart function. Other devices in the room measure breathing effort in the chest and abdomen, and the amount of oxygen in the blood.

Smith says most patients have little trouble falling asleep with all of the equipment running. And while they slumber, the medical gadgetry churns out reams of data in an adjacent room staffed by technicians. One night's sleep can yield up to 1,000 pages of brain wave readings. The data also reveal the severity of the problem — for instance, whether an apnea sufferer needs to be outfitted with an oxygen mask or, in the most serious cases, requires surgery to open the airway.

Tony Mercandante, who manages an insurance office and owns two Little Caesar's pizza stores in Baltimore, ignored his sleeping problem for two years until his wife insisted he see a specialist about his loud snoring. Tests showed the portly businessman was experiencing about 101 episodes of apena each hour. Mercandante was outfitted with a mask and says the improvement has been so noticeable he referred four friends to the center for help. [1]

About 50 patients pass through the lab each week for diagnostic tests or follow-up visits. Because a one-night test can cost $1,500, some managed-care organizations are reluctant to refer patients without a preliminary doctor's approval. The total annual cost of outfitting an apnea patient with a mask is an additional $1,500. Narcolepsy patients typically pay several hundred dollars a year for stimulant medications.

Smith says he's noticed increasing numbers of over-stressed business executives have checked themselves in and paid their bills out-of-pocket, a sign that society may be taking sleep problems more seriously.

"There's been a disturbing spin about sleep disorders," he says. "You think of all the jokes that have been made about snoring, and kind of wonder, 'Would they be making jokes about symptoms of cystic fibrosis or heart disease?' Maybe it's changing."

---

[1] See Janet Farrar Worthington, "Rest For The Weary," *Hopkins Medical News*, fall 1991, pp. 35-43.

When Counting Sheep Does Not Help

Snoring and insomnia are the most common sleep problems. Forty-three percent of the adults responding to a recent survey said they are affected, a few nights of the week or more, by at least one symptom of insomnia: They woke up and could not go back to sleep, woke up a lot during the night or woke up too early.

How Often Do You Experience These Sleep Problems?

	Every or almost every night	Few nights a week	Few nights a month	Rarely or never	DK/NA
	%	%	%	%	%
Snoring	25.5	15.4	10.5	44.6	4.0
Insomnia	21.8	21.3	27.2	29.7	0
Pauses in Breathing	6.8	5.4	4.2	71.3	12.3
Tingling in legs	7.9	6.8	10.5	74.4	0.4

Source: Telephone survey of 1,027 adults conducted by DataStat for the National Sleep Foundation, published March 1998. Estimates have an error range of plus or minus 3 percentage points.

Continued from p. 565

problems are breathing disorders that block the airway in the throat during sleep. Snoring, long the subject of jokes and marital discord, occurs when throat muscles relax too much or throat structures like the tonsils, uvula or palate are too large. As air passes around the blockage, the structures vibrate and rattle against each other, causing the familiar rumble.

A more serious disorder is sleep apnea, which occurs when the throat structures completely block the airway. The brain tells the body to wake up just long enough to tighten the muscles and unblock the air passage. Sufferers emit a loud gasp, then go back to sleep unaware that anything happened. The blocking and unblocking can occur dozens of times in a night and is especially pronounced in obese people.

Pulmonary specialists treat sleep apnea with an air pressure device called continuous positive airway pressure (CPAP) that consists of a small plastic face mask attached to an air blower. The blower sends a steady stream of air into the throat, keeping the throat structures from collapsing and blocking. Surgery can also be performed in serious cases to clear the airway. The cost of diagnosis and treatment with CPAP is about $3,000 annually.

"People are dying from this condition," says Philip Smith, professor of medicine and director of the Johns Hopkins University Sleep Disorders Center in Baltimore, Md. "We don't know how many, but clearly there are cases where sufferers just don't start breathing again. They often have other conditions like heart disease or hypertension, and those are assumed to be the cause."

Neurological conditions also rob people of sleep. Narcolepsy is caused by an unexplained disruption of the brain's sleep-wake system that runs in families and immediately plunges sufferers into a state of REM sleep during the day. Contrary to popular perceptions, narcoleptics rarely have "sleep attacks" in the middle of conversations or while they're driving, but are more likely to fall asleep during passive activities, such as sitting at a desk. The condition can strike individuals as young as 10 years old.

Doctors treat narcolepsy with stimulants such as Ritalin or Dexedrine, combined with antidepressants that prevent the loss of muscle control and hallucinations that often come with the condition. Another sleep disorder treated by drugs is so-called restless leg syndrome, in which patients feel "creepy-crawly" sensations in their legs when they lie in bed and try to sleep. Doctors list possible causes as too much caffeine, kidney disease, pregnancy or anemia and prescribe opiates and drugs commonly used to treat Parkinson's disease, a neurological disorder.

Despite the widespread recognition of sleep problems, federal support for sleep research has lagged far behind funding for better-defined chronic and infectious diseases. Congress established the National Institute on Sleep Disorders Research in 1993 on the recommendation of the same national commission that reported tens of millions of Americans had chronic sleep problems. But the three-person office operates as a small division of the National Heart, Lung and Blood Institute and had a fiscal 1997 budget of $84.7 million—a pittance compared with more than $1 billion spent each year for research on better-defined conditions such as HIV/AIDS and heart disease.

The situation angers pioneering sleep researcher Dement. "I'm almost ready to get a lawyer to sue NIH for defrauding the public," he says. "There's a warehouse of life-saving cures and information for people who don't know they have a disorder, but it just isn't getting out."

Center Director Kiley says he understands Dement's frustration but says more recognition may come as sleep disorders are linked to other chronic conditions like hypertension, obesity and aging. "We need to keep pointing out why it's important to recognize sleep disorders. Slowly, this field is growing in terms of respect," he says. ∎

CURRENT SITUATION

Let There Be Light

A jet-lagged air traveler needs to freshen up for an appointment at his next destination. Instead of hot towels or a caffeinated drink, he reaches for a knee brace outfitted with a small light. By shining the light on his leg as he dozes, the traveler resets his biological clock and can fast-forward his body rhythms by several time zones.

It seems like a strange plot from a science fiction movie. But recent research suggests strategically timed doses of light can alter people's master biological clocks, helping them overcome fatigue from long trips or insomnia. Curiously, the light doesn't have to be shined through the eyes. [20]

Researchers at Cornell University Medical College in White Plains, N.Y,. proved this in January by shining a bright light on the back of 15 subjects' knees and advancing their state of alertness by up to three hours. The subjects were tested over four days and nights and placed in reclining chairs outfitted with small tables designed so they didn't know when they were getting light treatments. Researchers administered the treatments for three hours at a time and measured subjects' body temperatures and concentrations in the sleep-inducing hormone melatonin.

Previous experiments with lights delivered to the eyes showed it's possible to manipulate the body clock. But the new findings suggest the biological mechanisms governing sleep are far more complex than previously thought — possibly involving light-sensitive skin or blood cells that transmit information to the biological clock in the brain.

"No one ever imagined we had light sensitive cells on any part of our bodies" outside of the eye, says chronobiologist Scott Campbell, a lead investigator on the Cornell team.

Cat Naps Offer Clues

Similar explorations into the biology of sleep have captivated scientists for decades. At the turn of the century, French physiologists Rene Legendre and Henri Pieron tapped cerebrospinal fluid from sleep-deprived dogs and injected it into well-rested canines, making them fall into a deep slumber. However, they were never able to isolate the sleep inducing substance.

Researchers now believe that sleep is regulated by two distinct systems: the circadian rhythms that are somehow linked to the light-dark cycle and a separate chemical process that influences the amount and depth of sleep a person gets.

Much of the current attention surrounding the chemical process is focused on adenosine, a compound that binds to brain cells, reducing alertness and arousal after long periods awake. Certain substances like caffeine prevent adenosine from binding to the brain cells, explaining the temporary jolt one gets from a cup of coffee.

Robert McCarley, a professor of psychiatry at the Brockton (Mass.) Veterans Affairs Medical Center, last year demonstrated the compound's behavior by keeping cats awake for six hours — more than three times longer than felines normally stay awake — by playing with them and petting them. His measurements showed the amount of adenosine outside the cats' brain cells surged over the six hours, corresponding with a decrease in wakefulness and an increase in slow-wave, or deep, sleep. When the cats were allowed to go to sleep for three hours, the adenosine levels dropped significantly. [21]

The results support prevailing theories that the body sleeps to replenish its energy stores. Adenosine forms the core of adenosine triphosphate, or ATP, an important molecule that stores energy and powers many of the biochemical reactions in cells.

While research continues on Earth, NASA intends to make sleep research a focus of this fall's mission of the space

Continued on p. 570

At Issue:

Should the government limit how many hours truckers can drive consecutively and prescribe specified rest periods?

CITIZENS FOR RELIABLE AND SAFE HIGHWAYS

A grass-roots, activist group based in San Francisco, Calif.

FROM A POSITION PAPER DATED JUNE 30, 1997.

*t*here is no question that fatigue dangerously impairs truck driver performance. Two-thirds of long-haul truck drivers surveyed by the Regular Common Carrier Conference in 1989 agreed that fatigue is a safety problem. . . . [T]wo researchers under contract to the Department of Transportation combined an accident study, field experiments and a truck driver survey and reported that drivers on irregular schedules had an increased risk of accidents after five to six hours of driving. Even drivers on regular daytime schedules experienced adverse affects after 8.5 hours of driving. The researchers also reported increased risks between midnight and 6 a.m. and earlier fatigue occurring among drivers using sleeper berths. . . .

Today, approximately 93 percent of long-haul truck drivers are paid either by the miles traveled or by the load. Less than 5 percent of truck drivers work for companies with union contracts. Because compensation per mile or per load is low, drivers feel pressured to drive as many miles as possible in as short a time as possible in order to survive economically. The 1989 . . . survey found that of the two-thirds of drivers who felt fatigue was a safety problem, 58 percent of them believe tight schedules are major contributors to fatigue. . . .

While law enforcement may threaten truck drivers with fines, employers can cut off or jeopardize a truck driver's means of making a living. Companies are the source of incentives to drivers to operate their large trucks responsibly or irresponsibly. Trucking companies, not truck drivers, are the origin of operating practices [that] put the motoring public at risk. . . .

[C]arriers should pay drivers from the time the truck driver is on duty until he or she is off-duty. To remove economic incentives to truck drivers to speed, forgo safety checks and drive fatigued, all of a truck driver's encumbered time must be paid for. The encumbered time must be paid for from the moment he or she is put on standby until released from duty at a location of his or her choosing. The purpose of this provision is straightforward: to eliminate the incentive that drivers now have to lie about the amount of time they drive, and allow them to be paid for the time they actually work. If drivers are fully compensated for all of their encumbered time, there will be no need to cheat on their log books or drive beyond their capacities.

GREG LEBEDEV

Managing director, American Trucking Associations Foundation

FROM A SPEECH TO THE "MANAGING FATIGUE IN TRANSPORTATION" CONFERENCE, APRIL 29, 1997.

*t*he real problem associated with operator fatigue is not a lack of knowledge — although there is always much to learn. The real problem is the lack of implementation of what we know, and [that] suggests we must do something now — both in an operational as well as a regulatory context. For example, research has shown that the current hours of service regulations are based on faulty intuition: Time on task is not the best predictor of fatigue; night does not equal day; and sleep is pivotal to the whole equation.

We've learned from our friends in Australia and Canada, as well as our colleagues in the railroads, that prescriptive regulations don't have to be the only option; that programs can be devised to manage fatigue and manage it effectively, but not without effort. Any new performance-oriented fatigue-management regime will require cultural, attitudinal and operational changes. . . . But if we in transportation . . . ask the government for more flexibility, we must be willing to make the changes in our own environment to do the job right. . . .

Convincing evidence shows that by timing the amount of sleep, human performance can remain at 100 percent. These win/win findings will have the potential to enhance the productivity as well as the safety of all transportation operations. I was particularly struck by the work of our distinguished Australian guest, Lawrence Hartley, who found fatigue to be more of an issue for the "regulated" truck drivers of eastern Australia than the unregulated drivers of western Australia. . . . [D]o prescriptive regulations diminish fatigue, or can they create fatigue?

Let's also pause for a moment to consider where we are with respect to new technologies to monitor operator alertness. Some promising areas relate to changes in eye activity consistent with the effects of fatigue. Interesting work is also under way in developing predictive tools — such as actigraphy — as an aid to facilitate work and rest scheduling. And the ATA Foundation, in partnership with the Federal Highway Administration, is currently conducting over-the-road tests of a continuous fitness-for-duty monitor, a concept that could revolutionize on-the-job real time recognition and management of fatigue.

It is clear that fatigue can be responsibly managed, and the task at hand is to create an operational and regulatory environment to do it.

Asleep at the Wheel

More than half of the adults in the United States have driven when feeling drowsy, but only a few have had an accident that they attribute to drowsy driving, according to a recent survey.

Driving Drowsy

No Response

Adults who say they had an accident because they dozed off or were too tired
1.4%

19%

22.6%

57%

Adults who say they dozed off while at the wheel

Adults who say they drove a car or other vehicle while feeling drowsy

Source: Results of a telephone survey of 1,027 adults conducted by DataStat for the National Sleep Foundation, published March 1998. Estimates have an error range of plus or minus 3 percentage points.

Continued from p. 568

shuttle *Discovery.* The space agency is installing special monitoring equipment on board, allowing crew members — including Sen. John Glenn, D-Ohio, the first American to orbit the Earth — to gauge how well they sleep before and after taking melatonin as a sleep aid.

A shuttle flight provides an intriguing laboratory. Astronauts experience a unique form of jet lag when they circle the globe, as their day-night cycle is compressed from 24 hours to about 90 minutes. Most only sleep six hours a night, though it's unclear whether lack of gravity also plays a part.

Because the elderly often complain of insomnia, the 77-year-old Glenn's experiences may shed light on the problem. It also may settle a long-running debate on whether

melatonin is an effective treatment for insomnia and whether the hormone should be considered a drug. (*See story, p. 564.*) ∎

OUTLOOK

Fatigue-Related Lawsuits

As Americans learn more about sleep deprivation, they are confronting thorny legal and ethical questions about exactly who is responsible.

A series of lawsuits has called into question whether individuals or the companies they work for are liable for the consequences of fatigue-related accidents. Separately, courts are

being asked for the first time to consider whether sleep disorders are distinct medical conditions that qualify for protections under the federal Americans with Disabilities Act. [22]

Attention to the debate increased after a 1991 Oregon case in which a jury awarded $400,000 in damages to a motorist injured in a collision caused by a McDonald's employee who fell asleep in his car after working an overnight shift. The verdict, later affirmed by a state appellate court, concluded the restaurant chain should have known that allowing the youth to work so many hours would impair his ability to drive home safely. The youth was killed in the head-on crash. [23]

Harvard Medical School Professor Moore-Ede says as sleep research advances, lawyers are becoming more adept at applying knowledge about the biological clock in litigation. Until the mid-1980s, he notes fatigue-related lawsuits were typically characterized by weak claims and unsupportable defenses. "Ironically, it was evolving strategies in the litigation of driving under the influence [of alcohol] that eventually led to greater acceptance of the concept of employer liability for actions of an employee suffering from fatigue," he says.

Sleep disorders have also been used as a defense against manslaughter charges. In a 1995 Maryland case, a tractor-trailer driver who plowed into the back of a van stopped at a light in Upper Marlboro, Md., killing four people, escaped charges after doctors at the University of Pittsburgh diagnosed him as having sleep apnea. The physicians said the condition led to sleep deprivation that caused him to fall asleep at the wheel of his rig. [24]

A pending case in Connecticut is testing whether the biological clock can impede a worker's abilities. A Glastonbury, Conn., school custodian identified only as John Doe sued the Board of Education and the town this year in federal court on the ground that a disability identified as shift-maladaption syndrome restricts his ability to rotate day and night shifts. [25]

The custodian, who agreed to work the overnight shift when he accepted the job in 1993, argues the board and town violated his rights under the Americans with Disabilities Act when it refused his request to be transferred to another shift. Officials at the Equal Employment Opportunity Commission say they are not aware of any similar claim that has been affirmed.

Though sleep deprivation increasingly is cropping up as a medical defense, it appears juries aren't yet ready to ignore personal responsibility. Last year, an Indianapolis jury took up the case of English teacher David McClain, who was accused of hitting a police officer with a beer bottle in 1993 and breaking his jaw. McClain's lawyers said the incident took place after McClain had taken a 25-hour flight from Japan and was too jet-lagged to know what he was doing. [26]

The jury rejected the novel defense and found him guilty of battery and resisting arrest. ∎

How to Get a Good Night's Sleep

Certain lifestyle changes promote better sleep. But what works for some people doesn't necessarily work for others. The National Sleep Foundation says the following general recommendations tend to help most people:

 Avoid caffeine, nicotine and alcohol in the late afternoon and evening. Caffeine and nicotine can delay sleep, while alcohol may interrupt sleep later in the night.

 Exercise regularly, but do so at least three hours before bedtime. A workout after that time may actually keep you awake because the body doesn't have a chance to unwind.

 Establish a regular and relaxing bedtime routine that allows you to unwind and send a signal to the brain that it's time to sleep.

 Try to adjust your schedule to allow seven to eight hours of sleep and follow the routine as regularly as possible, even on weekends.

 Don't use your bed for anything other than sleep or sex. The bed should be associated with sleep, not reading or television watching.

 If you can't go to sleep after 30 minutes, don't stay in bed tossing and turning. Get up and find a relaxing activity, such as listening to soothing music or reading. Try to clear your mind; don't use this time to solve your daily problems.

 If problems persist, see a doctor.

Notes

[1] The telephone survey of 1,027 adults was conducted by DataStat. See "1998 Omnibus Sleep in America Poll," National Sleep Foundation, March 1998.

[2] See "Wake Up America: A National Sleep Alert," Executive Summary and Volume One Overview of the "Report of the National Commission on Sleep Disorders Research," U.S. Government Printing Office, Doc. No. 1993-342-299/30631, January 1993.

[3] Quoted in Rick Weiss, "Wake Up, Sleepy Teens," *The Washington Post*, Health Section, Sept. 9, 1997, p. Z7.

[4] See Lynne Lamberg, "Some Schools Agree to Let Sleeping Teens Lie," *Journal of the American Medical Association*, Sept. 18, 1996, p. 859.

[5] See Kyla Wahlstrom, "Accommodating The Sleep Patterns of Adolescents Within Current Educational Structures: An Uncharted Path," paper presented at "Contemporary Perspectives on Adolescent Sleep," an international conference organized by the Youth Enhancement Service at the University of California at Los Angeles, Marina del Rey, Calif., April 17-20, 1997.

[6] Quoted in Norman Draper, "Later School Starting Times Produce Worrisome Problems for Many Parents," *Minneapolis Star-Tribune*, March 15, 1998, p. 1B.

[7] See Jay Mathews, "Students Want to Deliver a Wake-Up Call," *The Washington Post Virginia Weekly*, Nov. 6, 1997, p. V1.

[8] See Thomas Strah, "Propane Carrier Admits Falsifying Driver Logs," *Transport Topics*, Jan. 6, 1997.

[9] See National Transportation Safety Board Report No. HAR-95-02, adopted Nov. 14, 1995.

[10] Statement from a May 20, 1997, press conference at the U.S. Capitol sponsored by Citizens for Reliable and Safe Highways.

[11] See Matthew Wald, "A Study of Truckers' Need for Sleep Raises New Alarms," *The New York Times*, Oct. 10, 1997.

[12] See Charles Goldsmith, "Nap Time: More Pilots Are Catching Some Winks on Long Flights," *Chicago Tribune*, April 19, 1998, p. 21A.

[13] An overview of safety measures under development can be found in proceedings from "Managing Fatigue in Transportation,"

a conference held April 20-30, 1997, in Tampa, Fla., sponsored by the trucking and rail industries and the U.S. Department of Transportation and National Transportation Safety Board.

[14] Quoted in Maggie Jackson, "A Daily Nap on the Job: Sleep On It, Says Author," The Associated Press, May 18, 1997.

[15] See Jane Katz, "Working At Odd Hours," *Regional Review of the Federal Reserve Bank of Boston*, Vol. 8, No. 1 (1998), pp. 8-13.

[16] See "Growing Body of Research Shows Shift Work Presents Range of Risks to Overall Health," *ShiftWork Alert*, April 1998.

[17] See Connie Maiwald et al., "Working 8 p.m. to 8 a.m. and Loving Every Minute of It!" *Workforce*, No. 7, Vol. 76, July 1997, p. 30.

[18] See Stuart Silverstein, "On The Job, Work and Careers: A Little More Shut-Eye Would Work Better For Most, Sleep Expert Says," *Los Angeles Times*, Feb. 1, 1998, p. D5.

[19] Quoted in "Napping Coming Out Of the Closet," *ShiftWork Alert*, Vol. 3, No. 3, March 1998, p. 1.

[20] See Scott Campbell and Patricia Murphy, "Extraocular Circadian Phototransduction in Humans," *Science*, Jan. 16, 1998, p. 396.

[21] See Tarja Porkka-Heiskanen et al., "Adenosine: A mediator of the sleep inducing effects of prolonged wakefulness," *Science*, May 23, 1997, p. 1265.

[22] For background, see "Implementing the Disabilities Act," *The CQ Researcher*, Dec. 20, 1996, pp. 1105-1128.

[23] See "Employer's Liability Upheld in Accident Caused by Overworked, Tired Employee," *Employment Liability*, Vol. 9, No. 8, June 21, 1995.

[24] See David Montgomery, "Charges Dropped in Fatal P.G. Crash: Trucker's Sleep Disorder Made Case Hard to Prove," *The Washington Post*, Jan. 31, 1996, p. A1.

[25] See Stephanie Reitz, "Can Inability to Work Nights Be Judged a Disability?" *Hartford Courant*, April 22, 1998, p. A1.

[26] See "Jury Rejects Jet Lag As Assault Defense," The Associated Press, July 20, 1997.

FOR MORE INFORMATION

If you would like to have this CQ Researcher updated, or need more information about this topic, please call CQ Custom Research. Special rates for CQ subscribers. (202) 887-8600 or (800) 432-2250, ext. 600, or E-mail Custom.Research@cq.com

American Medical Association, 515 N. State St., Chicago, Ill. 60610, (312) 464-5000, www.ama.assn.org. Promotes ethical, educational and clinical standards for the medical profession. Now recognizes sleep medicine as a distinct specialty.

American Sleep Disorders Association, 6301 Bandel Road, Suite 101, Rochester, Minn. 55901, (507) 287-6006, www.asda.org. A professional medical association representing 3,400 sleep researchers and 300 institutions nationwide.

National Center on Sleep Disorders Research, Two Rockledge Center, 6701 Rockledge Drive, Suite 10018, Bethesda, Md. 20892, (301) 435-0199, www.nhlbi.nih.gov/nhlbi/nhlbi.html. A branch of the National Heart, Lung and Blood Institute at the National Institutes of Health that oversees federally funded sleep research and develops educational programs.

National Highway Traffic Safety Administration, 400 7th Street, S.W., #5220, Washington, D.C. 20590, (202) 366-9550, www.nhtsa.dot.gov. This branch of the U.S. Department of Transportation implements motor vehicle safety programs and conducts research into drowsy driving.

National Sleep Foundation, 729 15th St., N.W., Washington, D.C. 20005, (202) 347-3471, www.sleepfoundation.org. An independent, nonprofit organization that promotes healthy sleep habits, commissions polls on sleeplessness and publishes guides to sleep disorders and medications.

Bibliography

Selected Sources Used

Books

Anthony, William, *The Art of Napping*, Larson Publications, 1997.

A Boston University psychiatrist tries to change the negative view of napping as a sign of laziness by promoting what he says are its restorative powers. He includes a chapter on famous people who napped on the job.

Carskadon, Mary, ed. *The Encyclopedia of Sleep and Dreaming*, Macmillan, 1993.

An all-purpose guide to the biology of sleep and dreams, edited by a respected Brown University sleep researcher.

Coren, Stanley, *Sleep Thieves*, Free Press, 1996.

A University of British Columbia neuropsychologist offers dozens of tidbits about sleep, gives advice for insomniacs and argues that people should sleep nine to 10 hours a night.

Maas, James, *Power Sleep*, Villard, 1998.

A Cornell University psychologist offers advice on determining the amount of sleep necessary to operate at peak performance levels and asserts that American society has become seriously sleep-deprived.

Schor, Juliet, *The Overworked American: The Unexpected Decline of Leisure*, BasicBooks/Harper Collins, 1992.

Schor, a lecturer in economics at Harvard University, details how the average American came to spend more than 55 hours each week working just to keep up with the working-spending cycle.

Articles

Dement, William, and M.M. Mitler, "It's Time to Wake Up to the Importance of Sleep Disorders," *Journal of the American Medical Association*, No. 261, 1993, pp. 1548-1550.

Two Stanford University sleep researchers raise concerns about the dangerous consequences of sleepiness in highway crashes.

Lyznicki, James et al. "Sleepiness, Driving and Motor Vehicle Crashes," *Journal of the American Medical Association*, No. 279, 1998, pp. 1908-1913.

The American Medical Association's council on scientific affairs warns that police and doctors need to be more aware of potentially drowsy drivers who could cause accidents by falling asleep at the wheel.

Mack, Alison, "Genetic and Molecular Mysteries of Sleep Are Keeping Researchers Alert," *The Scientist*, Vol. 10, No. 21, Oct. 28, 1996, pp. 13-16.

A look at how scientists are trying to understand what purpose sleep serves and how molecular biology is providing clues about how the body regulates sleeping and waking.

Pasztor, Andy, "An Air Safety Battle Brews Over The Issue of Pilots' Rest Time," *The Wall Street Journal*, July 1, 1996, p. A1.

The Federal Aviation Administration's effort to limit airline pilots' consecutive duty hours spawned a battle between federal regulators and the transportation industry.

Weiss, Rick, "Wake Up Sleepy Teens," *The Washington Post*, Sept. 9, 1997, p. Z7.

An overview of efforts across the country to adjust high school starting times to accommodate teens' biological clocks. Weiss explains social and biological factors that keep many high school students from getting enough sleep.

Reports and Studies

Government Institutes Inc., *International Proceedings: Managing Fatigue in Transportation*, American Trucking Associations, April 29-30, 1997.

Proceedings from a two-day conference in Tampa, Fla., during which representatives of the railroad and trucking industries, sleep researchers and government regulators discussed ways of increasing operator alertness and reducing fatigue on the job.

National Commission on Sleep Disorders Research, *Report of the National Commission on Sleep Disorders Research, Executive Summary and Volume One Overview*, U.S. Government Printing Office, Doc. No. 1993-342-299/30631, 1993.

A federally commissioned study on sleep disorders concludes that approximately 40 million Americans suffer from chronic sleep disorders, and that 20 million to 30 million experience intermittent sleep-related problems. It urges more research and federal funding.

National Sleep Foundation, *1998 Omnibus Sleep in America Poll*, March 1998.

A national survey of 1,027 adults found nearly one-third get six hours or less of sleep during a typical work week. A total of 67 percent said they had some sleep-related disorder or problem, such as insomnia or snoring.

The Next Step

Additional information from UMI's Newspaper & Periodical Abstracts™ database

Biology of Sleep

Acebo, Christine, Mary Carskadon, Gary Richardson, Ronald Seifer and Barbara Tate, "An Approach to Studying Circadian Rhythms of Adolescent Humans," *Journal of Biological Rhythms*, June 1997, pp. 278-289.

The article illustrates that the "long nights" protocol is a feasible way in which to assess circadian parameters in young people, as well as to examine intrinsic sleep processes.

Giles, Donna E., David Kupfer, Howard Roffwarg, and A. John Rush, "Controlled Comparison of Electrophysiological Sleep in Families of Probands with Unipolar Depression," *American Journal of Psychiatry*, February 1998, pp. 192-199.

Giles et al present polysomnographic data and psychiatric history for parents and siblings of probands with unipolar depression and short REM latency, probands with unipolar depression and normal REM latency and normal-comparison probands.

Oren, Dan A., and Michael Terman, "Tweaking the Human Circadian Clock with Light," *Science*, Jan. 16, 1998, pp. 333-334.

Scientists show that the endogenous clock of humans can be trained by light application to an unexpected spot on the back of the knee. Results show that illuminating the spot can shift human circadian rhythms without any transduction of light through the eye.

Deprivation Problems

Goldsmith, Charles, "Airlines: More Carriers Sanction Their Pilots' Cockpit Snoozes," *The Wall Street Journal*, Jan. 21, 1998, p. B1.

Armed with sleep research conducted by the National Aeronautics and Space Administration (NASA), among others, airlines ranging from British Airways to Australia's Qantas encourage exhausted pilots — even in two-man cockpits — to doze off in their seats for as long as 40 minutes during less-demanding parts of long-haul flights.

Greenwood, Tom, "Sleepy Drivers Cause 100,000 Crashes a Year," *Detroit News*, April 2, 1998, p. C8.

When it comes to sleep, Americans are in big trouble, especially when driving, according to the American National Sleep Foundation and the National Highway Safety Administration.

Hellmich, Nanci, "British Researcher Says Seven Hours Can be Enough," *USA Today*, Feb. 3, 1998, p. D6.

Many busy people argue that with demanding jobs, commuting and family obligations, there simply isn't time to sleep eight hours a night. Are they doomed? It depends on whom you ask. Some experts argue that eight hours of sleep a night may not really be necessary. Jim Horne, of the sleep research laboratory at Loughborough University in England, says many people do very well on just seven hours a night.

John-Hall, Annette, "Getting Those ZZZs," *Chicago Tribune*, Nov. 28, 1997, p. E7.

Everybody, it seems, knows someone who is suffering from some form of sleep deprivation — whether it be from daily stresses or from medical problems. Authors write about it, sleep clinics research it, sitcoms poke fun at it. Tryptophan and melatonin have been suggested for it. "Insomnia gets worse with age. We don't really understand the reason, but something goes wrong with the sleep drive," Dinges said. "As we age, we produce less melatonin, which is believed by some to be the sleep hormone." Environmental changes disturb sleep, too, and Dinges said it's important to have a pre-sleep ritual and a restful sleep setting.

Lombardi, Kate Stone, "Scientist Says Sleepy Teen-Agers Aren't Just Tired," *The New York Times*, Nov. 23, 1997, p. W1.

By 6:45 a.m., Lizzy staggers onto the school bus, where she joins dozens of other sleepy teen-agers on their way to Horace Greeley High School in Chappaqua, N.Y., which begins at 7:45 a.m.. There, as in other high schools starting from 7:15 to 7:50 a.m., teachers, students and administrators describe early morning classes where teen-agers sit bleary eyed, trying to focus on biology, math and other first-period subjects. It's not startling news that teen-agers often are not their best in the early hours. But now sleep researchers are discovering that adolescent sleepiness in the morning has a physiological basis. And educators are beginning to take notice of the research and questioning whether the school schedule is optimal for teaching today's teen-agers.

Reiss, Tammy, "Wake-Up Call on Kids' Biological Clocks," *NEA Today*, February 1998, p. 19.

New research has shown that teenagers' biological clocks are at odds with most high school schedules, which affects their ability to learn. Reiss discusses the problems this creates and what can be done.

Wald, Matthew L., "Truckers Are Driving With Too Little Sleep, Research Shows," *The New York Times*, Sept. 11, 1997, p. A22.

A week-long, moment-by-moment study of 80 truck drivers found that they got too little sleep to stay alert, less than five hours a night, and that two drivers had had repeated episodes of a sleeplike state while driving. Part of the study, which was sponsored by the Department of Transportation, is described in an article that appears in the current *New England Journal of Medicine*.

Insomnia

"Questions to Ask Patients With Insomnia," *Patient Care*, Feb. 28, 1997, p. 89.

The article presents questions that physicians should ask patients who complain of insomnia.

Epperson, Michael T., Kenneth Lichstein, Britt Ann Peterson, Brant Riedel, et al, "A Comparison of the Efficacy of Stimulus Control for Medicated and Non-Medicated Insomniacs," *Behavior Modification*, January 1998, pp. 3-28.

Twenty-one medicated and 20 non-medicated insomniacs participated in a sleep-medication-withdrawal program that provided education about sleep medication and a gradual withdrawal schedule.

McGhan, William F., and Marilyn Dix Smith, "Insomnia: Costs to Lose Sleep Over," *Business & Health*, June 1997, pp. 57-60.

Insomnia problems among workers cost companies an estimated $92.5-$107.5 billion each year. The article discusses causes of insomnia and treatment options.

Talarico, Lori D., "How to Prescribe a Good Night's Sleep," *Patient Care*, Feb. 28, 1997, pp. 87-100.

Medication can only go so far in helping people with insomnia, and it may not be appropriate for everyone. Early detection and treatment are important in preventing long-term insomnia.

Other Sleep Disorders

Begany, Tim, "Be on the Alert for Sleep Apnea," *Patient Care*, Oct. 30, 1997, pp. 41-54.

Despite the high prevalence of sleep apnea, the condition is seriously underdiagnosed. The article discusses identifying apnea and some of its many treatments.

Berga, Sarah L., et al, "Blunted Phase-Shift Responses to Morning Bright Light in Premenstrual Dysphoric Disorder," *Journal of Biological Rhythms*, October 1997, pp. 443-456.

Patients with premenstrual dysphoric disorder respond therapeutically to sleep deprivation and light therapy. The authors sought to test the hypothesis that these distur-bances are a reflection of a disturbance in the underlying circadian pacemaker or, alternatively, that they reflect a disturbance in the input pathways to the clock.

Burkhart, Ford, "Silent Night Therapy," *The New York Times*, May 19, 1998, p. F7.

People with severe snoring problems sleep better and feel more rested after radio-wave energy is used to shrink their soft palate tissue, doctors report. In the treatments, a doctor inserts a probe into the back of the roof of the mouth and aims energy into the palate. That generates molecular action — as in a microwave — that causes heat and shrinks the tissues obstructing the air passage. Such blockage is one cause of snoring. Nelson Powell, co-director of the Sleep Disorders Research Center at Stanford University Medical Center, said the technique might one day offer hope for those who suffer from sleep apnea.

Dickinson, Ben, "Spring Forward, Crash Car," *Esquire*, April 1997, p. 112.

Motor vehicle accidents jump 8 percent the day after the United States "springs forward," losing an hour of sleep to daylight savings time; not surprisingly, in the fall, when the U.S. "falls back" to standard time, there is a commensurate decrease in such accidents.

Martin, Paul, "Sleep Tight All Night," *American Legion Magazine*, February 1998, pp. 40-41.

Sleep deprivation affects nearly half of all adult Americans, causing many to experience a nightmare of maladies. Information about various sleep disorders and steps that can be taken to treat them is offered.

Stevens, Darlene Gavron, "Midday Naps Get the Nod from Researchers, Workers," *Chicago Tribune*, May 8, 1996, p. 1.

Sleep scientists and trend researchers are predicting that in the not-too-distant future, forward-thinking employers will encourage naps and even provide special rooms or sleep-friendly office furniture. Napping is the next rung up the ladder of the nation's health craze and a crucial part of what one trend predictor calls "full spectrum fitness."

Tutt, Bob, "Fast Asleep; Houston Doctor Studying Sleep Attacks and New Medication," *Houston Chronicle*, Feb. 10, 1997, p. D6.

Connie Moore is studying narcolepsy as part of her work as director of sleep research laboratories at the Veterans Affairs Medical Center and Baylor College of Medicine. People with narcolepsy — five in every 10,000 — don't go through the normal sleep cycle, Moore explains, which is "two stages of light sleep, then two stages of deeper sleep into REM (rapid eye movement) or dreaming sleep."

Back Issues

MARCH 1997
New Air Quality Standards
Alcohol Advertising
Civic Renewal
Educating Gifted Students

APRIL 1997
Declining Crime Rates
The FBI Under Fire
Gender Equity in Sports
Space Program's Future

MAY 1997
The Stock Market
The Cloning Controversy
Expanding NATO
The Future of Libraries

JUNE 1997
FDA Reform
China After Deng
Line-Item Veto
Breast Cancer

JULY 1997
Transportation Policy
Executive Pay
School Choice Debate
Aggressive Driving

AUGUST 1997
Age Discrimination
Banning Land Mines
Children's Television
Evolution vs. Creationism

SEPTEMBER 1997
Caring for the Dying
Mental Health Policy
Mexico's Future
Youth Fitness

OCTOBER 1997
Urban Sprawl in the West
Diversity in the Workplace
Teacher Education
Contingent Work Force

NOVEMBER 1997
Renewable Energy
Artificial Intelligence
Religious Persecution
Roe v. Wade at 25

DECEMBER 1997
Whistleblowers
Castro's Next Move
Gun Control Standoff
Regulating Nonprofits

JANUARY 1998
Foster Care Reform
IRS Reform
The Black Middle Class
U.S.-British Relations

FEBRUARY 1998
Patients' Rights
Deflation Fears
Caring for the Elderly
The New Corporate Philanthropy

MARCH 1998
Israel at 50
The Federal Judiciary
Drinking on Campus
The Economics of Recycling

APRIL 1998
Biology and Behavior
Liberal Arts Education
Income Inequality
High-Tech Labor Shortage

MAY 1998
Census 2000
Child-Care Options
Alzheimer's Disease
U.S.-Russian Relations

JUNE 1998
Student Journalism
Antitrust Policy
Environmental Justice

Future Topics

▶ *Encouraging Teen
Abstinence*

▶ *Population and the
Environment*

▶ *Democracy in Asia*

The CQ Researcher

PUBLISHED BY CONGRESSIONAL QUARTERLY INC.

Encouraging Teen Abstinence

Should birth control information be taboo?

U

p to nine times as many teenagers give birth in the United States as in other industrialized countries. Moreover, more American youths under age 15 are becoming sexually active. Although overall U.S. teen birthrates are declining, out-of-wedlock births are skyrocketing in the United States and throughout the industrialized world. To reverse these trends, Congress and the states are spending $837.5 million over the next five years to encourage teenagers and unmarried adults to abstain from sexual intercourse, without teaching them about contraception or disease prevention. But critics say that withholding such information leaves youths "defenseless."

C_Q **July 10, 1998 • Volume 8, No. 25 • Pages 577-600**

Formerly Editorial Research Reports

CQ Researcher

July 10, 1998
Volume 8, No.25

EDITOR
Sandra Stencel

MANAGING EDITOR
Thomas J. Colin

ASSOCIATE EDITOR
Sarah M. Magner

STAFF WRITERS
Adriel Bettelheim
Mary H. Cooper
Kenneth Jost
Kathy Koch
David Masci

PRODUCTION EDITOR
Melissa Hall

EDITORIAL ASSISTANT
Laura S. Cavender

PUBLISHED BY
Congressional Quarterly Inc.

CHAIRMAN
Andrew Barnes

VICE CHAIRMAN
Andrew P. Corty

PRESIDENT AND PUBLISHER
Robert W. Merry

EXECUTIVE EDITOR
David Rapp

Bibliographic records and abstracts included in The Next Step section of this publication are the copyrighted material of UMI, and are used with permission.

The CQ Researcher (ISSN 1056-2036). Formerly Editorial Research Reports. Published weekly, except Jan. 2, May 29, July 3, Oct. 30, by Con-gressional Quarterly Inc., 1414 22nd St., N.W., Washington, D.C. 20037. Annual subscription rate for libraries, businesses and government is $340. Additional rates furnished upon request. Periodicals postage paid at Washington, D.C., and additional mailing offices. POSTMASTER: Send address changes to The CQ Researcher, 1414 22nd St., N.W., Washington, D.C. 20037.

COVER: THE BEST FRIENDS JAZZ CHOIR, COMPRISED OF HIGH SCHOOL GIRLS FROM WASHINGTON, D.C., SALUTES THE ORGANIZATION'S 10TH ANNIVERSARY LAST YEAR AT THE JOHN F. KENNEDY CENTER FOR THE PERFORMING ARTS. (COURTESY BEST FRIENDS)

Encouraging Teen Abstinence

BY KATHY KOCH

THE ISSUES

Saying "no" to sex, drugs and alcohol has been easy for 18-year-old Latasha Lewis. The secret of her success: She had Best Friends by her side.

"Best Friends taught me to stand up for what I believe in," says the Ohio Wesleyan University sophomore. "It gave me the extra support I needed to stand up to peer pressure. And it's an extra shoulder to lean on when you're not at home."

Lewis and 800 other students from across the country gathered recently at the group's annual rally in Washington, D.C., to salute the program, whose adult mentors help girls from the fifth to eighth grade avoid premarital sex and finish high school.

In doing so, participants are clearly going against the national grain. Girls of all races are experimenting with sex at younger and younger ages, experts say. The percentage of girls who have had sex before age 15 jumped from 11 percent in 1988 to 19 percent in 1995. The number of boys who had sex before 15, meanwhile, remained stable at 21 percent. [1]

Yet 84 percent of young girls say they want to know "how to say 'no' without hurting the other person's feelings." [2]

Best Friends is one of thousands of groups teaching both girls and boys to say no, and now there is federal money to help. Under a controversial "abstinence-only" block grant program — a dividend of the 1996 welfare reform law — grant recipients must teach teens to remain chaste until marriage. To send teens an unambiguous message, Congress said the money could not be used to teach teens about contraception or how to protect themselves from sexu-

ally transmitted diseases.

Because of the restrictions, many governors hesitated at applying for the grants. But eventually all 50 governors applied, alarmed that America has the highest teen birth rate in the industrialized world and faces increasing numbers of illegitimate babies, who often end up on welfare.

The grants account for about half of the $837.5 million the welfare reform bill obligated state and federal agencies to spend over five years to discourage childbearing among teens and unmarried adults.

The federal funding gave a big boost to the growing abstinence movement, which seeks to reinsert "values" and personal responsibility into teens' sexual behavior. [3] The conservative-led movement picked up steam in the 1990s, and now thousands of American youths are joining chastity clubs, signing abstinence pledge cards and proudly declaring their virginity.

"Ten years ago, abstinence was almost something you couldn't mention," says Peter Brandt, executive director of the National Coalition for Abstinence Education, an ad hoc group monitoring implementation of the block grants. "Now the culture is embracing it."

National statistics appear to confirm the trend toward abstinence, but only among older teens from the suburbs. From 1990 to 1995, the

percentage of all teens ages 15-19 who had ever had intercourse declined from 55 percent to 50 percent, reversing steady increases since the 1970s. Most of the decrease was among black and white suburban teens. And only 38 percent said they had had sex in the last three months, compared with 42 percent in 1988, suggesting some teens are having sex less frequently. [4]

"Abstinence is unquestionably in vogue," says Rebekah Saul, a policy analyst for the Alan Guttmacher Institute, which conducts research and policy analysis in reproductive health issues.

Abstinence may be gaining in the suburbs, but the number of sexually active, inner-city black teenagers remains about the same as in 1988. Hispanic teenagers, on the other hand, are having sex at significantly higher levels today than in 1988, according to the National Center for Health Statistics.

But while their older siblings may be cooling their jets, younger teens apparently aren't getting the message. "[Teachers] talk about not having sex before marriage, but no one listens," says 13-year-old Shana, from Denver. "I use that class for study hall." [5]

The jury is still out, however, on whether teaching abstinence results in fewer pregnancies, especially when taught without birth-control information.

In 1992, with broad bipartisan support and an extensive media campaign, California launched the largest statewide abstinence-only effort ever initiated. Some 187,000 middle-schoolers in 31 counties attended fairs, rallies and assemblies urging them to postpone sex. They received five hours of instruction on how to resist peer pressure to have sex. Three years and $15 million later, participants were no less likely to avoid sex, pregnancy or sexually transmit-

Teen Sexual Activity Varies Widely

Fewer than 30 percent of U.S. 15-year-olds had had intercourse in 1995. But more than half of the 17-year-olds and three-quarters of the 19-year-olds were not virgins.

Teens 15-19 Who Have Had Sexual Intercourse, 1995

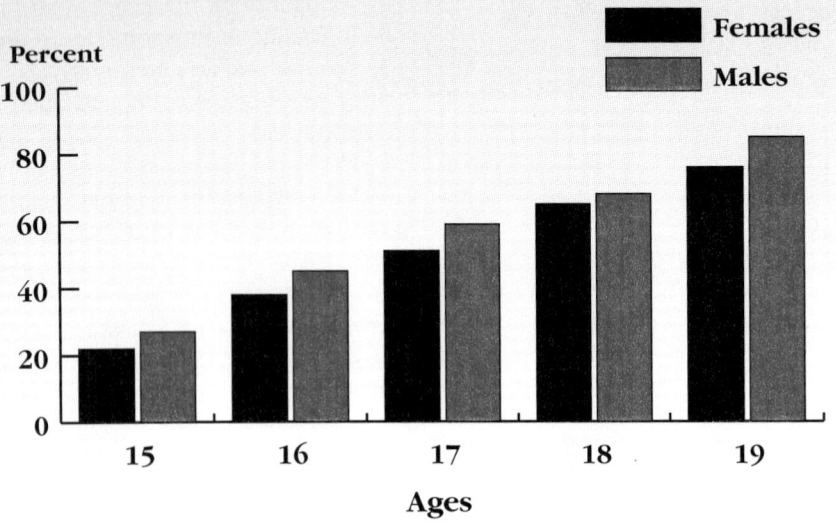

Sources: Alan Guttmacher Institute, Henry J. Kaiser Family Foundation and National Press Foundation; "1995 National Survey of Family Growth"; "1995 National Survey of Adolescent Males."

ted diseases (STDs) than teens in a control group. [6]

In December 1995, Republican Gov. Pete Wilson scrapped the much-heralded program, saying, "We need a much more comprehensive strategy to deal with out-of-wedlock pregnancy."

Yet eight months later, while putting final touches on the welfare reform bill, Congress quietly voted to spend $250 million over five years for abstinence-only programs. Since the states will chip in $187.5 million in matching funds, the total being spent for abstinence education is $437.5 million. Congress also promised an additional $400 million bonus over four years to the five states showing the greatest drop in unwed motherhood without increasing abor-

tion rates.

Americans have been arguing about what to teach kids about sex for decades. As a result, sex education has always been a strictly local affair — a patchwork of curricula based on the widely divergent sensibilities of the nation's different communities. Nonetheless, 93 percent of U.S. high schools today offer some kind of sexuality or HIV-AIDS education.

Congress' new abstinence-only law added a few caveats to the perennial chastity vs. birth control debate. The law not only prohibits teaching about contraception but also requires teenagers to be taught that adults in America are expected to refrain from extramarital sex because it "is likely to have harm-

ful psychological and physical effects."

Reflecting the new wrinkle in the controversy, more than 600 sex-ed battles are now being fought in school districts throughout the country, according to the nonprofit Sexuality Information and Education Council of the U.S. (SIECUS). In 1994, by comparison, only 200 local sex-ed battles were being fought.

Polls show that while most parents want their teenagers to abstain from sex at least until they finish high school, the majority also want schools to teach about contraception. [7]

Refusing to provide contraceptive information leaves teenagers "defenseless," says Henry Foster, an obstetrician who is special adviser to President Clinton on reducing teen pregnancy. "They don't have the facts on how to protect themselves, yet they are bombarded with media messages" telling them to "just do it."

"You're turning your back on those kids who choose not to abstain," Foster says, abandoning them to cope with raging hormones in a sexually saturated culture that "titillates and stimulates kids in dress, song, dance and images."

Abstinence advocates argue just as vehemently that teaching about "safe sex" is fundamentally dishonest because condoms are not 100 percent effective. Moreover, they say, teaching about birth control gives teenagers tacit approval to have sex. Decades of "safe-sex" education and easier teenage access to confidential services offering contraceptives and abortions have produced a generation of teens who treat sex casually and irresponsibly, they say. As evidence, they cite alarming news reports about sexual behavior among children, from fourth-graders found having oral sex in an empty Washington, D.C., classroom to a syphilis outbreak among 22 affluent Atlanta girls who gave public health officials 450 names as potential past sex partners.

By giving teens "non-directive" sex

education, wrote Patricia Funderburk Ware, former director of the Bush administration's adolescent pregnancy program, society has "abdicated its responsibility to instill values in this generation of young people. We've left childrearing to the TV executives and video producers." [8]

A California gang member seemed to echo Funderburk's concerns. Then 17-year-old Eric Richardson, whose gang was accused of raping hundreds of girls, some only 10, told a reporter in 1993: "They pass out condoms, teach sex education and pregnancy-this and pregnancy-that. But they don't teach us any rules." [9]

Birth-control proponents, meanwhile, say that the declines in teen sexual activity, births and abortions prove that their efforts are working. (See graph, p. 580.) Indeed, they say, the rates are down because teens use birth control more than ever before: From 1975-1995, the percentage of teenagers who used condoms the first time they had sex tripled, increasing from 18 percent to 54 percent.

But abstinence groups say birthrates are down because teens are abstaining. "It's due to less sex, not more protected sex," Brandt says.

Family planners warn, however, that switching to abstinence-only education could reverse the positive trends. "We'd be taking the reverse path from the Europeans, who have the lowest rates of STDs, teen pregnancy and abortions" even though their teens are just as sexually active as Americans, says Gloria Feldt, president of the Planned Parenthood Federation of America.

Sex education is universally taught and contraception easily accessible in many European countries, Feldt notes. In addition, sexually active European teens generally use condoms and birth control pills simultaneously, while American teenagers in recent years primarily have used condoms and dramatically re-

duced their use of "the pill." (See sidebar, p. 590.)

To move the debate forward, the bipartisan National Campaign to Prevent Teen Pregnancy persuaded the perennially warring camps — both represented on its board — to adopt the goal of reducing adolescent pregnancies by one-third by 2005. Both sides agreed, moreover, that a clear message should be sent: Teenage pregnancy — especially if you're not married — is not OK.

"It's a breakthrough, really," says Kristin A. Moore, president of Child Trends, a Washington-based research firm, and a member of the campaign's Board of Trustees. "It's a very pragmatic approach that basically tries to get the adults to stop arguing and concentrate on solving the problem." The campaign left it up to the opposing sides to "do what they do best" to bring the pregnancy rate down.

But lowering the pregnancy rate faces big obstacles:

• Although teen birthrates have dropped in recent years, a million American teenagers — 76 percent of them unwed — still get pregnant every year, according to the Alan Guttmacher Institute. And U.S. teens have twice as many pregnancies per capita as their counterparts in England, Wales or Canada and nine times more than in the Netherlands or Japan.

• Although U.S. teens are having less sex, younger kids are becoming sexually active earlier and earlier, especially in urban areas.

• STDs are rampant among U.S. teens, with 3 million new cases reported each year. STD rates are 50-100 times higher in the U.S. than in other industrialized countries, according to the Centers for Disease Control and Prevention (CDC).

• The percentage of American girls ages 15-17 who were unmarried when they gave birth has more than tripled, from 23 percent in 1950 to 84

percent in 1996. [10]

As educators and health officials grapple with the nation's high teen birthrate, these are some of the questions they are asking:

Is abstinence-only education good for teenagers?

Today's teenagers face a much more dangerous sexual landscape than their baby boom parents did during the sexual revolution. In the 1960s, syphilis and gonorrhea — both easily treatable with penicillin — were the most common STDs. Today, there is HIV-AIDS as well as more than 20 other newly discovered sexually transmitted diseases. And one in five Americans are infected with a penicillin-resistant viral STD. [11]

But the new abstinence-only grants stipulate that grant recipients can only teach students to abstain from sex. They are not permitted to discuss birth control.

"Sex is a serious business, and it's for adults only," says Elayne Bennett, founder of Best Friends and wife of former Education Secretary William J. Bennett. "When one spends a lot of time instructing teens on all the various paraphernalia for protecting themselves, the message is that it's perfectly safe to do this as long as you protect yourself. But we know that [using protection] does not protect against many STDs."

"The public debate on this whole issue has centered around condoms," Brandt says. "That was a mistake. The reality of the situation is that sexual abstinence is the only way for kids to avoid out-of-wedlock pregnancies and STDs."

Obstetrician Joe S. McIlhaney Jr. of Austin, Texas, agrees so strongly with the abstinence approach that he quit his medical practice and founded the Medical Institute for Sexual Health to counteract what he calls the government's "dishonest" message that condoms can make sex "safe."

What You Should Know About Teen Sex

■ Although teen birthrates have dropped in recent years, a million American teenagers ages 15-19 still get pregnant every year — 76 percent of them unwed. [1]

■ Although teens overall are having less sex, younger kids are becoming sexually active earlier, especially in urban areas. For example, in 1995, 17 percent of 15-year-old girls were sexually active, compared with 3 percent in the 1950s. More black youths (24 percent) initiate intercourse before age 13 than Hispanic (8.8 percent) or white students (5.7 percent). [2]

■ Sexually transmitted diseases (STDs) are rampant among U.S. teens, with 3 million new cases reported each year. STD rates are 50-100 times higher in the United States than in other industrialized countries. [3]

■ Only 70 percent of adolescent mothers finish high school. Teen mothers and their children have more health problems than adult mothers and their children. The federal government spends $39 billion a year to support families begun by teen mothers. [4]

■ Children of teenagers have more social and behavioral problems than other children, and they are more likely to become teen parents later.

■ Children raised by unwed mothers are more likely to end up in prison. Some 70 percent of long-term prison inmates grew up without fathers, as did 60 percent of rapists and 75 percent of teens charged with murder. [5]

■ Fatherless children are 40 times more likely to experience child abuse and three times more likely to fail at school and commit suicide. [6]

[1] Fact Sheet, Alan Guttmacher Institute, 1996.
[2] "Sex and America's Teenagers," Alan Guttmacher Institute, 1994, and "Youth Risk Behavior Surveillance, 1995," Centers for Disease Control and Prevention.
[3] "Facts in Brief," Alan Guttmacher Institute, 1993.
[4] Advocates for Youth.
[5] The Hudson Institute.
[6] Ibid.

McIlhaney says condoms fail to prevent pregnancy up to 13 percent of the time and don't protect against AIDS 31 percent of the time. Such failure rates are "unacceptable when compounded over five to 10 years" of premarital sexual activity, he says, since most teens don't use condoms consistently and correctly, especially when alcohol or drugs are involved.

But the CDC says the 31 percent AIDS failure rate cited by McIlhaney is from an outdated and "flawed" 1993 study by researcher Susan C. Weller. [12] In fact, two newer, larger

studies show that condoms are "highly effective" against AIDS, according to the CDC. The new studies show condoms fail less than 2 percent of the time, when used correctly and consistently. [13]

McIlhaney also points out that condoms don't protect against the human papilloma virus (HPV), an STD raging among today's teens. The virus causes venereal warts and is suspected as a major cause of cervical cancers and precancerous cervical changes, both increasing among young women in recent years, he says.

Condoms do not protect against chlamydia, the nation's most rampant STD, which can cause sterility if left untreated, he argues. The CDC says there is little research as to whether condoms protect against chlamydia. McIlhaney also says that condoms are not very effective against genital herpes, which is increasing among teenagers faster than among the general population.

McIlhaney points out that sexually active younger teens are up to 10 times more susceptible to pelvic inflammatory disease (PID) than adult women because teen reproductive systems are undeveloped. "PID is the most rapidly increasing cause of infertility in the U.S. and is a primary reason for the 600 percent increase in ectopic pregnancies since 1970," McIlhaney writes. [14]

Given all this evidence, promoting condom use among teenagers is dangerous, McIlhaney says. "The best that 'safer-sex' approaches can offer is some risk reduction. Abstinence, on the other hand, offers risk elimination," he writes.

Critics say McIlhaney's anti-condom approach is dangerous, especially for the 50 percent of teens already sexually active. "Young people may get the impression that condoms are not effective" and stop using them, warns SIECUS President Debra Haffner.

Presidential adviser Foster agrees that a strong abstinence message is wise for younger teens, but he says it's dangerous to let teens enter high school uninformed about how to protect themselves. "We should tell kids to abstain, but they also need to know how to protect themselves from diseases," Foster says. "They aren't going to stay middle school kids forever."

Because teens often do the opposite of what adults advise, keeping them ignorant about protecting themselves is irresponsible, he says, especially in the AIDS era.

Telling kids to "just say no" leads to what public health experts call the "swept away" syndrome, in which teens know they are supposed to abstain so they don't carry condoms. Then they end up having sex in the heat of the moment, without protection.

Even though polls show most Americans want contraception taught in schools, abstinence advocates say parents should be the ones to tell kids about birth control.

"It's nice to say that the parents should be the ones to educate their kids about sex," Foster says, "But what if the parents never learned all the facts themselves?"

"When you've got a 12-year-old girl whose mother is a drug addict and her daddy's in prison, who teaches her?" asked Gilbert Burnett, a retired judge who runs a pregnancy-prevention program in North Carolina. "What do we do? Forget about her?" [15]

Sex educators also object strenuously to Congress' requirement that educators teach that marriage is the standard for human sexual activity in the United States, and that extramarital sex is psychologically and physically harmful. It's "unrealistic, irresponsible and hypocritical" to tell kids that "when more than 90 percent of the marriages in this country are not virginal," says Barbara Huberman, director of training for Advocates for Youth, which seeks to reduce teenage pregnancy and AIDS. A 1994 study found that fewer than 7 percent of men and 20 percent of women ages 18-59 were virgins when they married, and 77 percent of America's 74 million single adults had had sex within the last year. [16]

"The concept of chastity until marriage may have made more sense 100 years ago when teenagers reached puberty in their middle teens and marriage closely followed," Haffner says. Today, the average American girl hits puberty at 12 $\frac{1}{2}$ and marries at 25.

"They're asking young people to deny powerful hormonal urges for more than 12 years," Huberman says. "We set kids up for failure by telling them to remain chaste all that time."

But expecting a young person to practice birth control 100 percent effectively and remain disease-free for 12 years is also unrealistic in today's world, says Family Research Council analyst Gracie Hsu. "Isn't that setting them up for failure?" she asks.

Do abstinence-only programs work?

Several eighth-graders used to be pregnant each year at Nathan Hale Middle School in suburban Chicago. But after three years of the abstinence-only program Project Taking Charge, the school graduated three pregnancy-free classes in a row.

Among Best Friends participants in Washington, D.C., only 5 percent of the 15-year-olds in the program had had sex, compared with 63 percent of the youths throughout the city, according to an independent researcher. By the time they graduated, only 14 percent of participants had engaged in sexual intercourse, compared with 73 percent citywide. [17]

Abstinence advocates have dozens of similar success stories. The problem, social scientists say, is that none of the abstinence studies have been conducted scientifically. Even though the federal government has funded abstinence-only programs since 1981 through the Adolescent and Family Life Act (AFLA) program, proponents have not published "a single peer-reviewed study showing that they work," Haffner points out (see p. 585).

The abstinence coalition points to findings from the National Longitudinal Study on Adolescent Health, published last September in the *Journal of the American Medical Association* (*JAMA*). Known as the "Add Health" study, it found that teens who had taken abstinence pledges were "sig-

nificantly" less likely to engage in early sexual activity than teens who had not.

"The Add Health study now places scientific research soundly on the side of the abstinence message," said a coalition letter last December to state officials who administer abstinence-only grants. The study "raises serious questions" about sex-education programs that teach both abstinence and contraception, the letter said.

When authors of the Add Health survey heard about the coalition's letter, however, they sent out a clarification of the coalition's "erroneous" interpretation of their findings.

"They have . . . imputed causality where there is no causality," says Robert W. Blum, one of the authors. "You cannot look at the data and say that an abstinence pledge leads to virginity. This is not a random population of kids in America who make abstinence pledges. There's a religious and ethnic skew to it. The abstinence pledge is just one piece of a constellation of factors we see in kids who are less likely to have intercourse."

To determine which sex-education programs work best, the Campaign to Prevent Teen Pregnancy last year published an extensive evaluation of 33 sex-ed studies. After examining six abstinence-only studies, the evaluation found that the abstinence-only programs do not delay sexual activity. But the evidence is inconclusive, the evaluation said, because all of the studies were methodologically flawed except one — the one showing that California's much-touted program didn't work. [18]

"The jury is still out," says Douglas Kirby, author of the campaign's evaluation.

Abstinence opponents also cite a study published in *JAMA* in May — the first-ever comparing the chastity-vs.-condoms approaches. It found that over several years, abstinence-only was not as effective as a safer-

Most Teenage Mothers Are Unmarried

The percentage of teenage mothers ages 15-19 who were unmarried in 1996 was nearly six times the percentage in 1950. The increase reflects sharply rising birthrates among unmarried teenagers and a decline in teenage marriages since the mid-1970s.

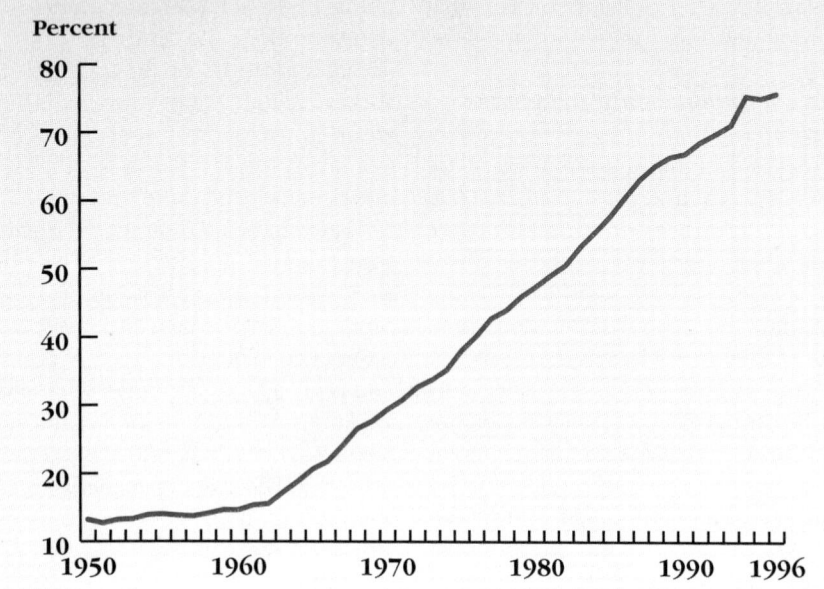

Births to Unmarried U.S. Teenagers Ages 15-19

Percent

Source: National Center for Health Statistics, Centers for Disease Control and Prevention, April 1998

sex program at preventing inner-city African-American teens from having sex. The safer-sex program had stressed abstinence as the safest way to avoid STDs and pregnancy but also taught about condoms. [19]

Given the lack of "clear and compelling data" showing significant and consistent benefits from abstinence-only programs, said a *JAMA* editorial, "it is difficult to understand the logic behind the decision to earmark funds specifically for abstinence programs. "Unfortunately," it continued, debate over the issue appears "ideologically motivated rather than empirically driven."

But the Family Research Council's Hsu says the results of the *JAMA* study cannot be generalized, because it was conducted among African-American youths living in a "sex-saturated" community. You cannot expect a message that is so "counter-cultural" to have an impact after only two four-hour Saturday morning sessions, she says.

Do contraception-education programs encourage teen sex?

Abstinence advocates argue that youths receive a mixed message when adult authority figures explain how to obtain and use contraceptives, even if they tell them chastity is best. "It's talking out of both sides of your mouth," and it undermines parental directives to abstain from

sex, Brandt says.

"Giving kids contraception information gives them permission to have sex," Hsu says.

"By now," Moore counters, "there are at least 16 studies showing that sex-ed does not increase sexual activity among kids. But it remains a very widely held belief."

"That's like saying that driver's ed increases traffic accidents," says Gloria Feldt, president of the Planned Parenthood Federation of America. "It's silly."

Yet abstinence proponents turn the driver's education analogy on its head, especially when describing programs like those in more than 400 U.S. high schools, which provide students with free condoms. "Just because you give a kid driver's education doesn't mean you give him a car," Brandt says.

Giving teens condoms, they argue, takes away one of their excuses for avoiding sex, leaving them with one less weapon in their anti-peer-pressure arsenal.

The Family Research Council cites two studies that it says show that either pregnancy or sexual activity increased at San Francisco and Dallas schools after they began distributing condoms. [20]

Yet Kirby, who authored both studies, says that the council selectively chose anomalies in each study, though they both concluded that there was no overall impact from making condoms available. "For instance, out of 36 measures of sexual activity, 33 showed that there was no impact, two showed that the program actually delayed sexual activity and one showed that it hastened the onset of intercourse," he says. "They highlighted the one statistic that showed sexual activity increased. I looked at all 36 factors and concluded that there was no impact on sexual activity."

In addition, he said, numerous

studies since then show "absolutely overwhelming" evidence that sex-education programs that teach contraception do not increase sexual activity. The most comprehensive was Kirby's own massive evaluation of studies of 33 sex education and HIV-prevention programs, *No Easy Answers,* for the National Campaign to Prevent Teen Pregnancy.

"Sexuality- and HIV-education curricula do not increase sexual intercourse, either by hastening the onset of intercourse, increasing the frequency of intercourse or increasing the number of sexual partners," Kirby says. "We have more data supporting that than anything else." Some of the programs, however, did the opposite: They either delayed sexual activity, reduced the frequency or reduced the number of sexual partners, he notes.

In 1993, the World Health Organization published an extensive review of 35 studies of sex-education programs, some dating back to the 1970s. "The overwhelming majority of studies over time, despite various methodologies and countries of study, found no evidence that sex-education encourages sexual experimentation or increases activity," said a CDC fact sheet. One study did vary from the trend — an abstinence-only program that actually increased the level of sexual activity in young people, according to the CDC.

On the other hand, the recent *JAMA* study comparing safe-sex programs with abstinence-only programs among inner-city youths (*see above*) found that teens in the safe-sex program were having sex less than either the abstinence-only or the control group participants when interviewed six and 12 months later. Similarly, a recent study of condom availability in school-based health centers in Philadelphia showed a marked decline in the number of students engaging in sexual activity — from 75 percent to 66 percent — and increased condom

use among sexually active teens who used the health centers. [21]

Most experts now agree overwhelmingly that the best sex-education programs teach both abstinence and how to reduce the risk of pregnancy and STDs.

Apparently, most Americans agree. While 95 percent of Americans believe that teens should receive strong messages to abstain from sex — at least until they are out of high school — 60 percent want kids to have access to contraceptives if they are sexually active. Less than 25 percent believe teenagers should never be able to obtain contraceptives. [22]

"The concern is how do you present the risk-reduction message without unduly encouraging sexual activity?" says former Bush official Ware.

Kirby's evaluation found that the most effective programs focused on clear, directive messages aimed at encouraging specific behaviors, like delaying intercourse or using contraception. "These programs gave a clear message by continually reinforcing a clear stance on these behaviors," he says. "They did not simply lay out the pros and cons of different sexual choices and implicitly let the students decide which was right for them. Rather, most of the facts, activities, values and skills were directed toward convincing the students that abstaining from sex, using condoms or using other forms of contraception was the right choice."

Kirby's comments would appear to bolster the conservatives' claim that the "non-directive," values-free method of teaching sex education is not effective.

Ware sees the abstinence-only movement as a backlash to the values vacuum that resulted from the moral relativism of earlier eras: "It was the idea that nothing was wrong unless you personally decided it was wrong," she says. "In the last few years, we've seen the consequences of that.

"Our young people are killing each

other, doing drugs, having babies out-of-wedlock and generally exhibiting behavior that is frightening adults. The adults are now saying, 'Wait a minute. Maybe it's asking too much for young people to make decisions about things that we as adults even have trouble making.' " ■

BACKGROUND

'Chastity Act' Passed

Congress has actually been funding community-based abstinence-only education programs since 1981, when it passed the Adolescent Family Life Act (AFLA), commonly known as the "chastity act."

Conceived during the first year of the Reagan administration as the conservative "alternative" to family planning, AFLA was the result of a quiet political deal — conservatives agreed not to block federal funds for family planning clinics if liberals supported AFLA. [23]

Sponsored by Republican Sens. Jeremiah Denton, R-Ala., (1981-87), and Orrin G. Hatch, R-Utah — who believed family planning programs encourage teen sexual activity and abortion — the bill was inserted into a budget bill without hearings or floor votes in either house.

Partly to win liberals' support, the original bill stipulated that two-thirds of AFLA funds would be used to support already-pregnant teens and one-third to promote abstinence. That ratio was reversed in 1997 and '98.

Like the current abstinence-only program, AFLA sprang from social conservatives' deep conviction that too much emphasis and money have been given to "comprehensive" sex-education and contraception-based pregnancy-prevention efforts. Both programs were "consciously constructed to steer funds toward conservative 'pro-family' groups and away from family planning and sexuality education providers," wrote Saul of the Guttmacher Institute. [24]

Conservatives say the Clinton administration has weakened the program, turning it into "AFLA lite" through liberal interpretations of agency rules. For instance, they note, in 1997 a Planned Parenthood affiliate in northern Michigan received AFLA money to teach seventh-graders to resist sex. Conservatives have pinned their hopes on the "purer" version of abstinence education, as defined in the welfare reform law.

Critics of the statute said its eight-point definition of abstinence was a bold attempt to legislate morality — particularly its call for all adults to abstain from sex unless married. In a statement clarifying congressional intent, the authors admitted, "This standard was intended to put Congress on the side of social tradition — never mind that some observers now think the tradition outdated. That both the practices and standards in many communities across the country clash with the standard required by the law is precisely the point." [25]

Although the federal government has disbursed $186 million in AFLA grants over the past 16 years — including about $50 million for abstinence programs — no long-term scientifically rigorous evaluations of the programs were conducted.

Initially, the 1996 welfare reform law did not earmark funds to evaluate the $250 million in abstinence-education grants it was mandating either. After a barrage of criticism, however, Congress set aside $6 million for evaluations.

Welfare Reform Debate

In the mid-1990s, teenagers and their babies were swept up into the highly politicized debate over how to overhaul the welfare system. The debate quickly centered on reasons for the decline of the American family, as evidenced, in part, by skyrocketing rates of illegitimacy among both teens and adults. Conservatives blamed a welfare system that rewarded illegitimacy and penalized marriage among poor parents.

"Preventing teen pregnancy and out-of-wedlock births is a critical part of welfare reform," said President Clinton in sending his welfare-overhaul proposal to Congress in June 1994. "To prevent welfare dependency, teenagers must get the message that staying in school, postponing pregnancy and preparing to work are the right things to do."

His proposal put less emphasis on the Reagan-Bush era's abstinence-only approach and more reliance on sex education, contraception and abortion. The president's proposal was ignored in 1995 by the new Republican-led Congress as it debated welfare reform.

In his 1995 State of the Union address, Clinton challenged the nation to fight "our most serious social problem, the epidemic of teen pregnancies" and out-of-wedlock births.

The "epidemic" of out-of-wedlock births became a major rallying point for conservatives seeking to overhaul welfare in 1995 and '96, partly because of an influential 1993 *Wall Street Journal* column by the late Charles Murray. Titled "The Coming White Underclass," it predicted that the problems generally attributed to the demise of the black inner-city family — violence, crime and poverty — would rapidly spread to white neighborhoods because of rising illegitimacy rates among white teenagers.

The number of illegitimate babies born to white teenagers more than tripled from 1970 to 1995, from 10.9 per 1,000 to 35.5 per 1,000. Meanwhile, the percent of black babies born out of wedlock — while three times as high as the rate among whites — actually declined modestly, from 96.9 per 1,000 to 92.8 per 1,000. [26]

When viewed from a historical perspective, fewer teenagers are giving birth today than in 1957, at the height of the baby boom. But the baby boomers' teenagers are not getting married first, like their moms did. (*See chart, p. 584.*)

Today, for a variety of reasons, women are postponing marriage until much later, and skyrocketing illegitimacy is common throughout the industrialized world. More out-of-wedlock births occur in Great Britain and France than in the U.S. And most involve adult women, not teenagers.

Douglas Besharov, a resident scholar at the American Enterprise Institute, sees the drop in marriage rates as a function of women's political and social emancipation. "In the post-industrial age, when the earning power of men and women becomes quite equal, that creates a very different relationship between men and women and makes it easier for women to leave unhappy relationships." [27]

But declining marriage rates alarm other conservatives. They see premarital and extramarital sex, as well as the increasing acceptance of out-of-wedlock childbirth by both teens and adults, as major threats to the institution of marriage. Hence, a primary goal in the welfare reform bill was not just preventing teen pregnancy but stamping out premarital and extramarital sex among all teens and adults.

In the end, Congress imposed a five-year lifetime limit on eligibility for welfare. It also required parenting teens under 18 to live at home and finish high school to receive benefits.

Conservatives argued that the abstinence grants merely "level the playing field" between the amount of federal funds spent on family planning and the amount spent promoting abstinence. "This amount simply brings federal financing for absti-

Continued on p. 588

Chronology

1950s *Teen birthrates hit an all-time high, but most baby boom mothers are married when they give birth.*

1957
The teen birthrate peaks at 96 births per 1,000, then begins a steady decline.

- • -

1960s *Out-of-wedlock births rise as women begin marrying later.*

1965
Sen. Daniel P. Moynihan, D-N.Y., warns that out-of-wedlock childbearing is threatening the black family and causing social disruption in the black community.

- • -

1970s *As the baby boom generation enters adolescence, teen births surge, and out-of-wedlock births among teens continue to rise.*

1970
President Richard M. Nixon creates a comprehensive family-planning program for poor women at federally subsidized clinics, through Title X of the Public Health Service Act.

1972
The Social Security Act is amended to require that states provide family planning services to "minors who are sexually active." Changes to Title IX of the 1972 Education Amendments prohibit public schools from barring pregnant and parenting students from class.

1973
The Supreme Court's *Roe v. Wade* decision legalizes abortion, which spurs publication of statistics that make it possible to calculate reliable teen pregnancy rates.

1976
The Alan Guttmacher Institute declares adolescent pregnancy an "epidemic" in the U.S.

- • -

1980s *Out-of-wedlock births become the norm for teen childbearing; battles over sex education ensue between advocates of abstinence and birth control.*

1981
Congress passes the so-called "chastity bill" — the Adolescent Family Life Act — providing grants for community-based, abstinence-only education programs. The programs not only encourage teens to delay sexual activity but also to consider adoption (instead of abortion) if they are already pregnant.

1985
The Guttmacher Institute notes that the United States has the highest teen pregnancy, abortion and birthrates in the industrialized world.

1987
After two decades of decline and then a 10-year leveling-off period, the teen birthrate begins a four-year climb.

1989
In *Webster v. Reproductive Health Services,* the Supreme Court makes it more difficult for teens to obtain abortions.

1990s *Teen birthrates decline as contraception use increases and community-based abstinence programs gain in popularity. Chastity-vs.-condoms battles proliferate as some parents oppose "comprehensive" sex-education curricula taught in some schools.*

1993
New York City schools chief Joseph Fernandez is fired amid criticism of his program to give away condoms in schools.

1994
President Clinton declares that preventing teen pregnancy and out-of-wedlock births is a critical part of his welfare reform plan.

1995
In his State of the Union address, Clinton challenges "parents and leaders all across this country to . . . make a difference" against "our most serious social problem, the epidemic of teen pregnancies" and out-of-wedlock births.

1996
The privately funded, bipartisan National Campaign to Prevent Teen Pregnancy is created in February with the goal of reducing teen pregnancy by one-third by 2005. In August a welfare-reform bill is signed into law providing $250 million over five years for abstinence-only education.

1997
All 50 states apply for abstinence-education grants, which must be matched with 75 percent state funding. An estimated 600 local battles are being fought over sex education.

Asking Hollywood Writers ...

One childlike face after another flashed onto the television screen. The pubescent, pimply complexions, sometimes with braces flashing, belied the adult pain in their eyes. One by one, with wrenching simplicity, the teenagers spoke of dashed dreams.

They were just a few of the 1 million teenagers who get pregnant every year in America.

When the four-minute video ended and the lights came on, several of the 40 veteran television writers and executives in the room "were dabbing at their eyes," says Marisa Nightingale, media programs manager for the National Campaign to Prevent Teen Pregnancy.

Nightingale uses the powerful video, which was donated by Ogilvy and Mather public relations, to brief magazine and television writers and executives. As part of the campaign's goal to reduce teen pregnancy by one-third by 2005, she's asking Hollywood to help get the message across to teens that adolescence and pregnancy don't mix.

"We cannot hope to reduce the high rates of teen pregnancy in this country without engaging the vast power of the media," says campaign Director Sarah Brown. "The media can be just as persuasive in convincing young people that parenting is not child's play as they are in informing them that the ZIP Code for Beverly Hills is 90210."

Contrary to popular belief, Nightingale says, Hollywood executives are not deaf to public opinion. "They're all enthusiastic to help," she says. "Every time I go to L.A., I'm overwhelmed by how positive the response is. They're tired of getting beat up" by the public and politicians.

"The media [are] speeding the moral breakdown of our society," said Sen. Joseph I. Lieberman, D-Conn., in a speech last September at the University of Notre Dame. He and former Education Secretary William J. Bennett, a Republican, have been leading what they call the "Revolt of the Revolted," giving voice to the "disgust millions of Americans feel toward the growing culture of violence, perversity and promiscuity" in the media.

Congress responded to complaints about TV sex and violence in 1996 by passing legislation requiring a "V-chip" to be installed in all new American-made TV sets beginning this fall. The technology will allow parents to screen out shows carrying certain ratings. [1]

Nightingale's friendly reception in Hollywood may reflect her efforts to build bridges and form a partnership with film and TV executives, rather than attack them. Realizing that screen and magazine writers "are allergic to being told what to write," she is careful not to sound directive in her approach. "They are hungry for ideas. But the minute you act like you know what a good story line is, you're out of there."

Instead, she offers 10 messages about teen pregnancy, any one of which writers can use "at their own pace and in their own way" to develop their own story lines, she says. One message says that, contrary to what parents think, teens want to know what adults think about sex, love and relationships.

"Our surveys show that kids are looking for guidance from their parents," she says. That message particularly resonated with a group of daytime soap opera writers Nightingale briefed recently, since their audiences are adult women, most of whom are parents.

The Henry J. Kaiser Family Foundation, in Palo Alto, Calif., has worked for years to get Hollywood to stop portraying teenage sex as not having consequences.

"Now, when a couple hops into bed, there are no consequences. We'd like to change that," says Vicky Rideout, director of Kaiser's entertainment, media and public health programs. "Our purpose isn't to get sex off

Continued from p. 586

nence up to parity with annual Title X financing to promote teenage use of contraceptives," Richard A. Panzer, author of a book on teenage sex education, wrote in a letter to *The New York Times.* [28]

Title X of the Public Health Service Act, signed into law in 1970 by President Richard M. Nixon, created a comprehensive family planning program for poor women through federally subsidized clinics. For the past two decades, conservatives have attacked the program, primarily because many of the clinics provide abortions. About 13 percent of the Title X clinics are affiliates of the Planned Parenthood Federation of America.

But conservatives also argue that by allowing teenagers to obtain birth control pills — and sometimes abortions — without parental notification or consent, the clinics encourage teen sexual activity and undermine parental authority. The Title X program has been a dismal failure, they say, because sexual activity, STDs and out-of-wedlock birthrates have skyrocketed among teens over the 30-year life of the program, notwithstanding the recent drop in teen sexual activity.

Family planning proponents bristle at any effort to equate funds spent on family planning clinics with the amounts now being spent on abstinence education.

"It's absolutely ludicrous to say that this levels the playing field," Feldt says. Title X clinics provide health care like Pap smears, medical exams and testing for STDs for adult women, she points out, and fewer than 10 percent of the clients are under 18. "That's totally different from providing sex education in the schools.

"Furthermore," she adds, "any birth control counseling done in the

... To Cut Down on Irresponsible Sex

TV, but to get the entertainment community to think more about the impact of what they are doing."

But she also sees a potential "sex educator" role for television. "TV can be a very important source of information for kids about sex," she says. The Media Project, a partnership between Kaiser and Advocates for Youth, periodically briefs television writers to inform them about teen pregnancy, sexually transmitted diseases (STDs) and other health issues and operates a hotline writers can call if they have a question about rates of STDs or pregnancies.

In February, the Media Project briefed television writers and producers in Los Angeles about the results of a Kaiser survey showing where teens learn about sex. About 54 percent said they learned about sex and birth control from television. A third said some teens have sex because television and movies make it seem "normal" for teens to be sexually active.

"We've also measured the impact when information is included in a show," Rideout says. "We survey people before and after the show, and we find that it's an incredibly effective way to get a message across. When we explain this to the writers, they are surprised and a little frightened. It's not a responsibility that they asked for."

Yet, Rideout says, she agrees with Nightingale that "a lot of writers care about what they do." She points to several examples of responsible TV programming that have resulted from the groups' efforts:

• MTV did a series of humorous, attention-grabbing public service ads offering 25 different ways to say "Put on a condom."

• The NBC drama "ER"" has done several segments focusing on teen pregnancy, including one dealing with the "emergency" contraception pill, which can be taken within the first 72 hours of unprotected sex.

• Two ABC soap operas are weaving a message about teen pregnancy prevention into their story lines over the next two years.

Kaiser has found that parental concern about sex on TV has escalated in the past two years. In a 1996 Kaiser survey about "family hour" shows, 43 percent of parents said they were concerned about sexual content (compared with only 40 percent who were worried about violence). Last April, a new Kaiser survey found that 67 percent of parents were "greatly concerned" about sex, compared with 62 percent who were worried about violence.

"There's been a lot of brouhaha about violence on TV," Rideout says, "but almost no studies of the impact of sexual content on kids."

The WB network's titillating, new teen soap opera, "Dawson's Creek," may be the last straw. The controversial and highly popular show featured a 15-year-old having an affair with his 30-something English teacher.

"It raised a lot of hackles for parents," Nightingale says.

"That show alone could counteract our entire program," says Peter Brandt, executive director of the National Coalition for Abstinence Education, which has lobbied for years to get $50 million a year in federal grants for community-based programs that teach kids to abstain from sex. "We should have used the $50 million to buy out 'Dawson's Creek' and pay them not to produce."

But Nightingale isn't giving up. This summer she will try to get WB network shows, including "Dawson's Creek," to put in a word for responsible sex.

---

[1] For background, see "Children's Television," *The CQ Researcher,* Aug. 15, 1997, pp. 721-744.

---

clinics includes encouraging abstinence and encouraging young people to talk to their parents."

Furthermore, Haffner points out, "The federal government does not spend a penny for comprehensive sex education in the schools, and it never has."

"The welfare reform law created a dedicated funding stream for abstinence education," Feldt says, noting that the abstinence funds are "entitlements" and do not have to get annual appropriations. "There is no federal funding stream dedicated specifically to providing responsible, balanced sex education. There ought to be, but there isn't." ■

CURRENT SITUATION

Sex-Ed Battles

Although Clinton signed the welfare reform law, he does not see it as an effort to force states to replace existing sex education programs with abstinence-only programs.

"The policy of the administration is that we should encourage abstinence among our young people," Clinton said. "The question of contraception is one that should be resolved at the local level involving all sectors of the local community. There is no national policy on that, and there will not be." [29]

Meanwhile, sex education and illegitimacy issues continue to clog legal and legislative agendas at the local, state and federal levels.

Now that all states have received block grants for abstinence-only programs, some legislatures and school

Heartland Honor Societies Face a Dilemma . . .

In America's heartland, communities are facing a problem that inner cities have long wrestled with — skyrocketing rates of unwed teen parenthood. To send a clear message that it is not OK, some communities have drawn a line in the sand at the National Honor Society's front door.

This spring, two small towns in Ohio and Kentucky blocked three academically qualified high school girls from membership in the prestigious society. All were either unwed teen mothers or pregnant at the time.

Elsewhere, however, pregnant teens are quietly inducted. Last year in Tipton, Ind., for instance, the high school salutatorian was an unwed mother as well as an honor society member. "We don't believe in shaming kids," says Tipton school Superintendent Tom Fletcher.

But in Xenia, Ohio, and Williamstown, Ky., the faculty selection committees said that the three pregnant or parenting girls in their communities did not qualify for society membership because they did not meet its "character" criterion. The girls failed the character standard not because they were unwed mothers — federal law prohibits schools from discriminating against pregnant or parenting teens — but because they had obviously engaged in premarital sex, school officials said.

Xenia school Superintendent James Smith said that his school's standard has been on the books since 1952, and that it has been equally applied to exclude boys who were known to be unwed fathers. But Amanda Lemon, the 18-year-old teen mother who was excluded in Xenia, asked, "What about the people who have had sex, and then had abortions? I was told by one of the people [at school] that

they do know people on the National Honor Society that had had abortions, but that I have visual evidence."

"What do you think that makes people think?" she continued. "You can have sex and use protection and you can be in the National Honor Society. You can have sex and have an abortion, and you can be in the National Honor Society. But if you have sex and make the choice to keep your baby and do the morally right thing, then you cannot be in the National Honor Society." [1]

The exclusions set off a firestorm of controversy that erupted onto editorial pages and on television and radio talk shows across the country, opening up what some say is a much-needed national debate about what is acceptable sexual behavior for teenagers.

Given the reactions to the honor society moms — opinions were split about 50-50 on whether they should be inducted — clearly America hasn't reached a consensus on the issue.

The controversy raised numerous thorny questions that honor society selection committees have been grappling with in recent years: Should only virgins be allowed to join the honor society? If so, how will the society prove their chastity? Is it legal (or fair) to exclude sexually active girls, whose "mistakes" cannot easily be hidden, but not the boys? Should students be asked to swear they have never had sex before they can join?

How many honor society male members have secretly fathered a child? If a local council hears a rumor that a boy has fathered a child, should they demand a paternity test? How many of the society's female members have had an abortion? Do they have more "character" than someone

---

boards are overhauling their existing sex education curricula to qualify for the abstinence-only grants.

Florida, for instance, now requires public school health education to teach "an awareness of the benefits of sexual abstinence as the expected standard." In Arizona, the Legislature funded an abstinence-only program despite a recent public opinion poll showing 80 percent opposition to the program.

"We are gravely concerned that these abstinence-only-until-marriage guidelines are changing the landscape of sexuality education in America," Haffner says. "Good programs that are effective are being replaced by fear-based education programs."

In South Carolina, where a recent

poll found that 84 percent of citizens want sex education instruction time increased, a bill has been introduced in the state Senate limiting class time spent on sex education and refocusing instruction on abstinence. [30]

Despite Haffner's fears, only a handful of states have mandated that schools revise their sex-education courses to fall in line with Congress' abstinence curriculum. Most are using the money for programs that supplement — rather than replace — existing sex-education curricula. Most are targeting younger youths, 9-14 years of age, for the abstinence message. There is widespread agreement that abstinence is especially appropriate for younger teens, although

some conservatives want the message sent to all teens.

According to the Maternal and Child Health Bureau, which administers the grants, only 29 out of the 155 groups receiving grants this year are school-based, and only half will teach classes during school hours. The rest of the abstinence courses are being offered by city or county health departments, community groups, church-affiliated groups and universities.

The National Coalition for Abstinence Education says it is quite pleased with the "excellent and very creative" abstinence programs that most states have developed. Initially, however, about 30 proposals did not abide by the legislative intent of the law, Brandt says.

... Over Admission of Unwed Teen Mothers

who chooses to keep her child?

"I respect what [Amanda] has done," in keeping her baby and staying in school, Smith says. "But is she a good role model for teen mothers, or is she a good role model for the National Honor Society? Therein lies the debate."

The messages teens are receiving from Washington are equally confusing. On the one hand, the government urges pregnant teens to finish high school and forbids schools from kicking them out. Yet, those who "do the right thing" by finishing school and excelling at the same time are told they are not exhibiting character worthy of the National Honor Society.

The National Campaign to Prevent Teen Pregnancy trumpets what it calls a "clear message" to America's teens: that teen pregnancy is not OK. But the group is silent on whether that means kids should remain chaste or just be very prudent in choosing and using birth control.

Congress voted in 1996 to send its own "clear message" to teens: Do not have sex until you get married. It pledged $437.5 million in state and federal funds over the next five years to send that message, as well as $400 million to discourage unwed motherhood. In the same legislation, Congress said that all Americans are expected to refrain from sex unless married. But in a country where 77 percent of the single adults had had sex within the last year and a president accused of multiple sexual indiscretions receives consistently high approval ratings, some editorialists question which "clear message" teenagers are getting about non-marital sex?

The National Association of Secondary School Principals, which administers the National Honor Society, says the society is not just an academic organization. To qualify for membership a student must exhibit four qualities: scholarship, community service, leadership and character.

"Membership is an honor," says Pat Scanlan, spokeswoman for the association. "It is not a right." The association allows each local faculty selection council to decide, based on local sensibilities, how they define the four criteria. "It's impossible for us to decide on individual cases. That's up to the local chapters."

When cases have arisen in the past, the association has advised local chapters that pregnancy, whether within or out of wedlock, "cannot be the basis for automatic rejection." It could be construed as discriminating against someone based on gender, since boys don't get pregnant, she says.

William Galston, a University of Maryland professor and chairman of the campaign's task force on religion and values, says the current debate is a perfect chance for local communities to clarify their values and the messages they want to send kids about sex among teens.

"If I were in a position of authority at one of these schools, I would convene a school or town meeting and say, 'Here are the four general criteria for induction into the honor society. I intend to interpret the character criterion in such-and-such a way as the definition of honorable behavior in handling one's sexuality. If you disagree with me, let's have that discussion right now.'"

"You can't have a person in authority suddenly jumping up and saying, 'Surprise!'"

---

[1] Quoted on CNN "Talkback Live," April 28, 1998.

"Overall, we think it's going quite well," Brandt says. "We're seeing a much broader approach to the problem. States are addressing the kids almost holistically." Many of the programs take a communitywide approach, involving the medical profession, service organizations, the business community, peer groups and after-school as well as in-school programs, he says.

Meanwhile, states are also scrambling to compete for the $20 million "illegitimacy bonuses" the federal government will award to the five states that achieve the greatest reduction in out-of-wedlock births. Some states, like Georgia, Mississippi and Oklahoma, are incorporating the federal abstinence-only criteria into their welfare programs in hope they will help bring down illegitimacy rates. Other states are looking for ways to expand family planning services for low-income women.

Federal Initiatives

At the federal level, congressional conservatives are seeking restrictions on birth control and abortion services for teenagers. They have introduced bills requiring parents of teenagers to be notified before their children can obtain contraceptive services from a federally funded Title X clinic. Since Republicans took majority control in Congress, there have been three efforts to require parental consent for teen birth-control counseling at such clinics. The last attempt, in September, failed by only 19 votes, so proponents have vowed to try again this year. Illinois Republican Rep. Donald Manzullo has also introduced a similar bill, which has been referred to the House Commerce Committee.

Congressional action is also expected this session on highly controversial legislation making it illegal for an adult to take a minor across state lines to evade laws requiring parental notification before an abortion can be performed. Emotional hearings were held in May on measures pending in both houses, foreshadowing what is likely to be an intense debate when the bills come to the House and Senate floors. Sen. Hatch has vowed to send Clinton such a bill before Congress adjourns.

Targeting Unwed Dads

Alarmed at both skyrocketing STD rates and out-of-wedlock births, legislators, prosecutors, social workers and public health providers are increasingly focusing the spotlight on unwed fathers.

"Changing the reproductive behavior of males is a crucial element of strategies to prevent the transmission of STDs," said a 1997 Urban Institute study. Most STDs can be prevented through consistent condom use, the study said. [31]

But it's the increasing fatherlessness of America's children that most worries policy-makers.

"All of the problems tearing apart the fabric of our society have deep roots in this exploding epidemic of out-of-wedlock births," said California Gov. Wilson in 1996 in his sixth State of the State address.

The lack of a father in the home can have a devastating impact not only on the child but also on the community, said a 1997 Hudson Institute study. For instance, 70 percent of long-term prison inmates grew up without fathers, as did 60 percent of rapists and 75 percent of teenagers charged with murder. Compared with children raised in two-parent homes, fatherless children are 40 times more likely to experience child abuse and three times more likely to fail at school, require psychiatric treatment and commit suicide, the study said. [32]

Forty states have enacted strategies to encourage male reproductive responsibility. They range from beefing up statutory rape laws to increased efforts to establish paternity.

Some states are vigorously enforcing child-support laws and excluding school-age unwed fathers from extracurricular activities.

As welfare reform goes into effect and states begin moving millions of single welfare mothers into the work force, attention is also being focused on how to get unwed fathers involved in their children's lives.

"Providing jobs to single mothers is not enough," said the Hudson Institute. "Welfare stands at the center of a larger social crisis: the demise of marriage and the increasing disappearance of fathers from families."

The study recommended a number of measures state welfare officials can take to entice the fathers to either marry the mother of their child or become more involved in their children's lives. For instance, welfare offices can give preferential treatment to married parents in distributing discretionary benefits, like Head Start and public housing slots. States could require mothers to cooperate with visitation orders as a condition for receiving welfare benefits, or let fathers satisfy the work requirement for families on aid.

Growing concern about the impact of children growing up in fatherless households has led to the fatherhood movement, exemplified by the recent Million Man and Promise Keepers marches on Washington.

In addition, pioneering fatherhood programs have been established across the country, ranging from education/outreach programs at health clinics to school- or church-based peer-mentor programs.

Even at Operation Fatherhood in Trenton, N.J., where an evaluation of the program has been less than glowing, officials say participants have gotten more involved in their children's lives. "We may not have made the biggest strides," says Director Dolores Bryant, "but we are definitely working small miracles one at a time." [33] ■

OUTLOOK

Parents' Influence

As the last of the baby boomers' teenagers reach puberty, the total U.S. teen population is expected to surge by 13 percent, or 2.5 million additional youths ages 15-19, by 2008. In addition, as Hispanic immigration continues climbing, the absolute number of teen births will jump, demographers say, even if the birthrate doesn't. [34]

Eyeing that coming increase, most experts now agree that prevention is not just about chastity or condoms. It requires a holistic approach addressing the psychological, behavioral, moral, social and cultural variables that predispose teenagers to get pregnant.

Many veterans of the sex-education wars say that youth-development programs have been the most successful at preventing teen pregnancy. "A lot of people think youth development is the way to go," says Brian L. Wilcox, director of the Center on Children, Families and the Law at the University of Nebraska and a board member of the Campaign to Prevent Teen Pregnancy.

"This is an area that shows great promise that everybody can agree on," says William Albert, a spokesman for the campaign. Youth-development programs are comprehensive approaches, offering everything from dropout prevention to supervised after-school recreational activities. They usually offer adult mentoring and encourage kids to establish career goals and help them develop skills to achieve them. Most also involve teens in community service work, he says.

"I'm optimistic about these sorts of

Continued on p. 594

At Issue:

Are "abstinence-only" sex-education programs good for teenagers?

JOE S. MCILHANEY JR.

President, Medical Institute for Sexual Health, Austin, Texas

FROM THE WASHINGTON TIMES, SEPT. 29, 1997

*W*e have had at least 20 years of an educational message that says, basically, "If you can't say no, act responsibly." Yet these safe/safer/protected sex curricula have been tried and found wanting in terms of preventing the skyrocketing damage to our teens and their long-term physical, emotional, social, spiritual and economic health. It is time for an honest and open-minded look at a new sexual revolution: abstinence until . . . marriage. . . .

Non-marital teen pregnancy all too often has a devastating impact on teen parents and their children. Indeed, teen pregnancy has received much analysis because of the long-term effects not only to the mother and child but to the father, to extended families and ultimately to society. . . . [O]nly 30 percent of girls who become pregnant before age 18 will earn a high-school diploma by the age of 30, compared with 76 percent of women who delay child bearing until after age 20. And 80 percent of those young, single mothers will live below the poverty line, receive welfare and raise children who are at risk for many difficulties as they grow to adulthood. . . .

In addition to pregnancy, adolescents and young adults are in the age group at highest risk for contracting STDs [sexually transmitted diseases]. . . .

The statistics for disease and pregnancy are not in dispute. The concern is in what we should do about preventing these problems from occurring and devastating young lives. This is where the controversy starts.

The prevailing opinion for the last two or three decades has been that kids will do it anyway, so we have to give them condoms and contraceptives so they can be protected. Education programs have given a nod to abstinence as the only 100 percent safe choice outside of marriage but then have gone on to spend much time and emphasis on the "how to's" of safer sex. . . .

The bottom line is that although studies show that "safer sex" approaches do not increase sexual activity among students, none of these programs has dramatically lowered the number of teens who choose to be sexually active, who have to deal with pregnancy or who acquire STDs. Nor have they dramatically increased contraceptive use among those who are sexually active.

Why should abstinence be emphasized in schools? The best that "safer sex" approaches can offer is some risk reduction. Abstinence, on the other hand, offers risk elimination. When the risks of pregnancy and disease are so great, even with contraception, how can we advocate anything less?

DEBRA HAFFNER

President, The Sexuality Information and Education Council of the United States (SIECUS)

FROM THE WASHINGTON TIMES, SEPT. 29, 1997

*W*e believe young people should receive comprehensive sexuality education that will serve as a foundation for a lifetime of sexual health. This education is designed to assist people to develop a positive view of sexuality, provide them with information about taking care of their sexual health and help them acquire the skills to make decisions. . . . Abstinence education is an important part of this program. A goal of comprehensive sexuality education is to help young people exercise responsibility and resist pressure to become prematurely involved in sexual relationships. SIECUS believes, however, that it also is important to teach young people about a full range of issues related to sexual health and behavior. . . .

By contrast, there is no evidence that abstinence-only programs work. No published evaluations are available to show that these programs truly help young people postpone sexual relationships. And, in fact, an analysis of a recent $5 million abstinence-only program in California found that it not only did not increase the number of young people who abstained but, in one school, actually resulted in more students engaging in sexual intercourse after participating in the course. . . .

Unfortunately, proponents of these abstinence-only programs scored a huge victory last year. They convinced Congress to create a new federal entitlement program for abstinence-only education as part of welfare reform. It provides nearly $88 million [a year] in federal and state funding for programs that must have as their "exclusive purpose teach social, psychological and health gains to be realized by abstaining from sexual activity." . . .

The program requires adults to teach young people that "abstinence from sexual activity is the only certain way to avoid out-of-wedlock pregnancy, sexually transmitted diseases and other associated health problems." This may give them the dangerous impression that contraception and condoms aren't worth using. Many fear-based, abstinence-only programs discuss contraception only in negative terms. This message threatens to reverse significant strides American youth have made during the last two decades to delay sexual activity or else protect themselves. . . .

There is no question that young people want help saying no. Too many young people still are having sexual intercourse too early. Too many of them report that they regret their experiences. Too many are pressured by their friends, the media and older partners. We must teach teens the skills to handle the challenges of dating, intimacy and sexual limit-setting.

Why Did Black Teens' Birthrate Decline?

Social scientists have theories, but no firm answers, as to why the birthrate for black teenagers is declining faster than for any other ethnic group.

Some say it's probably due to more effective birth control. Others say it represents a dramatic shift in sexual mores. Still others contend it heralds the beginning of a rebirth of conservative values among black teenagers.

From 1991 to 1996, birthrates declined 5-12 percent for all teenagers. But among African-Americans the rate dropped a dramatic 21 percent, to 91.7 births per 1,000 — the lowest rate ever recorded. For younger black teenagers 15-17, the drop was even more dramatic, 23 percent, while the rate for blacks 18-19 fell by 16 percent. [1]

Hispanic teenagers now have the highest birthrate in the country, at 101.6 births per 1,000. Their birthrate declined only 5 percent.

In explaining the drops, statisticians point to the growing popularity of the contraceptives Depo-Provera, which is injected once every three months, and Norplant, an implant that lasts up to five years. By contrast, birth control pills, which are becoming less popular among American teens, must be taken daily.

"Two principle changes in contraceptive use among black teenagers occurred between 1988 and 1995," says statistician William D. Mosher of the National Center for Health Statistics (NCHS). "There were big decreases in the use of the [birth control] pill (down from 75 percent to 38 percent), and sizable increases (24 percent) in the use of implants and injectibles."

Overall, 8.4 percent of all black teenagers use implants or injectibles, compared with 2.6 percent of all white teenagers, he says.

Henry Foster, the teen pregnancy adviser to President Clinton, sees a different reason for the decline of teen births among blacks. Foster, an obstetrician, says that the growing black middle class has taken an aggressive stance against teen pregnancy. Affluent black women and their influential sororities have begun mentoring young black girls and accessing private and government funds to fight teen pregnancy, sexually transmitted diseases and substance abuse, he adds.

Patricia Funderburk Ware, former Bush administration director of the Office of Adolescent Programs, sees the decline as the first wave of a much bigger cultural revolution in the black community. But she says it's coming primarily from the inner cities, not the suburbs.

"We see what happens when these kids don't have a father," Ware says. "They're in the streets killing each other. We aren't telling our kids anymore that [casual sex] is OK.

"I don't think the white community is telling their kids that yet. They haven't suffered as much. Their daughters haven't had so many abortions that they can't have another one. They haven't become infertile from the sexually transmitted diseases or haven't been traumatized enough by going from one broken sexual relationship to another."

Ware notes that a majority of youths 14-18 rated declines in the family as the No. 1 problem facing the nation, according to a recent poll. [2] Moreover, she says, NCHS statistics show that 44 percent of teen girls who identified themselves as virgins said it was against their religious or moral values to have premarital sex.

Led by inner-city teenagers, she says, "We are beginning to see a real possibility for a swing in the proverbial pendulum toward a more drastic and long-lasting decrease in sexual activity rates among teens."

But if inner-city teens are in the vanguard of change, it has not yet shown up in national statistics. According to preliminary findings by the NCHS, even though the number of teens 15-19 who are sexually active dropped 42 percent from 1988 to 1995, most of the decline occurred among black and white teens in the suburbs.

"Suburban youth were much more likely than central city or rural youth to have lower levels of sexual activity in 1995 compared with 1988," according to Joyce Abma, an NCHS statistician. And, she notes, among black and white inner-city youths, there was no difference in levels of current sexual activity between 1988 and 1995. [3]

---

[1] "Teenage Births in the United States; National and State Trends, 1990-96," National Center for Health Statistics, April 1998.

[2] "The State of the Nation's Youth," Horatio Alger Association of Distinguished Americans Inc., 1996.

[3] Joyce Abma and Freya L. Sonenstein, "Teenage Sexual Behavior and Contraceptive Use: An Update," National Center for Health Statistics, April 28, 1998.

Continued from p. 592

programs, especially if combined with family life education," Wilcox says. But, he warns, "They take enormous investment. I'm worried that we'll try to replicate some of the more successful programs on the cheap, and then they won't work."

And as most who work on the problem agree, it can't be solved by Washington alone but through the commitment of the entire society.

"The federal government can only provide guidance and information," says Clinton adviser Foster. "It's too big and too divisive for a one-size-fits-all solution."

As a Phoenix grandmother and guardian of two teenagers told a Campaign to Prevent Teen Pregnancy focus group last year: "Let's face it.

The media, entertainment, news, sports, the society in general, politicians, everybody needs to get more responsible. How can we expect teenagers to be responsible for themselves when we're showing grownups on TV not being responsible and getting away with it?"

Studies increasingly show that, contrary to popular belief, parents have more influence over whether their teens will get pregnant than any other factors. Not only is communication needed but also a strong sense of connectedness between parent and child, says Blum, the "Add Health" study co-author.

"Our data shows screamingly loudly that far more overriding than whether there is parental sex education is the sense of connection between parent and child," he said.

Perhaps more surprisingly, teenagers want to know what their parents have to say about whether or not they should engage in sex. "Our most recent survey shows that teenagers really want to hear from their parents about sex and sexuality," says campaign spokesman Albert. "Not just one talk about the birds and the bees. It needs to be an ongoing conversation over a lifetime."

The campaign recommends that parents first clarify in their own minds how they feel about teenage sexuality in today's world, and then clearly relay those values and attitudes to their children. That might be difficult for baby boomer parents who might be conflicted about their own teenage sexual histories or fearful that their kids will ask them about their own sexual past.

"Somehow, over time, we have lost a cultural consensus on what is acceptable teen sexual behavior," Brandt says. Perhaps a benefit of the abstinence legislation is that it has opened up a national debate and is getting society to focus on the issue, he says.

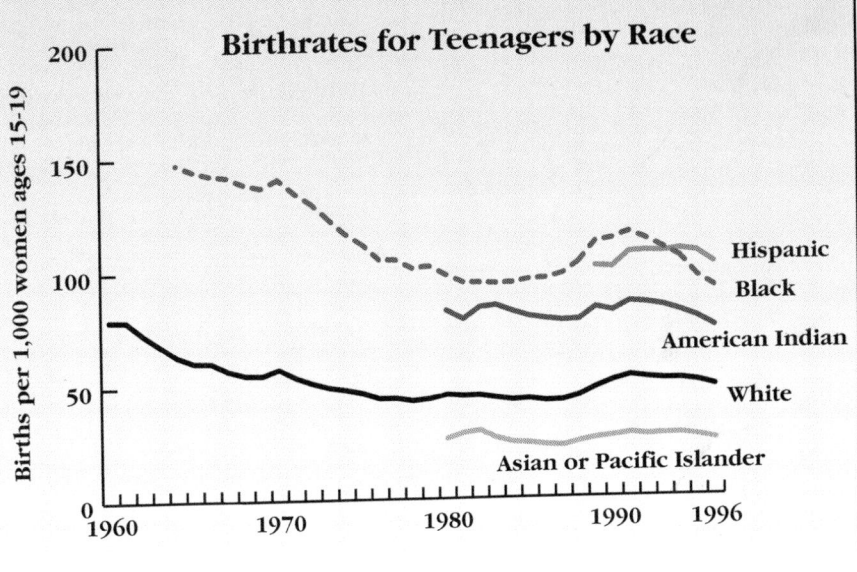

Birthrate for Black Teens at Record Low

The birthrate for black teenagers ages 15-19 fell 21 percent from 1991 to 1996 to the lowest rate ever: 91.7 births per 1,000. Birthrates for other teens dropped from 5-12 percent during the same period. Despite the sharp decline for blacks, their birthrates and those for Hispanic teens are higher than for other groups.

Birthrates for Teenagers by Race

Births per 1,000 women ages 15-19

- Hispanic
- Black
- American Indian
- White
- Asian or Pacific Islander

Note: Complete data are not available for some groups.

Source: National Center for Health Statistics, April 1998

The Family Research Council would like to focus that debate less on teen sexual activity and more on all non-marital sex. "We believe the real problem is out-of-wedlock sexual behavior," Hsu says.

"We're uneasy as a society about the social and cultural balance that we've struck in the last generation," says William Galston, a University of Maryland professor and chairman of the campaign's task force on religion and values. "We're searching for adjustments that are tolerable. I doubt very much that we will return to the sexual mores of the 1950s. I do think we are fumbling our way toward a new balance, and not just a simple repetition of the distant past." ■

Notes

[1] Preliminary figures in a National Center for Health Statistics study due in August.
[2] Marion Howard and Judith Blamey McCabe, "Helping Teenagers Postpone Sexual Involvement," *Family Planning Perspectives*, January/February 1990.
[3] For background, see "Teaching Values," *The CQ Researcher*, June 21, 1996, pp. 534-557.
[4] "National Survey of Family Growth," August 1997.
[5] Quoted in Ron Stodghill II, "Where'd You Learn That?" *Time*, June 15, 1998.
[6] Douglas Kirby et. al., "The Impact of the Postponing Sexual Involvement Curriculum Among Youths in California," *Family Planning Perspectives*, May/June 1997.
[7] For background, see "Parental Rights," *The CQ Researcher*, Oct. 25, 1996, pp. 946-969.

[8] Patricia Funderburk, "None, Not Safer, Is the Real Answer," *Insight,* May 9, 1994. For background, see "Children's Television," *The CQ Researcher,* Aug. 15, 1997, pp. 721-744 and "Sex, Violence and the Media," *The CQ Researcher,* Nov. 17, 1995, pp. 1017-1040.

[9] Jane Gross, "Where Boys Will be Boys and Adults Are Befuddled," *The New York Times,* March 29, 1993.

[10] National Center for Health Statistics, April 1998.

[11] "Facts in Brief," Alan Guttmacher Institute, 1993.

[12] See Susan Weller, "A Meta-Analysis of Condom Effectiveness in Reducing Sexually Transmitted HIV," *Social Science and Medicine,* June 1993.

[13] I. DeVincenzi et al, "A Longitudinal Study of Human Immunodeficiency Virus Transmission by Heterosexual Partners," *The New England Journal of Medicine,* No. 6, 1994, pp. 341-346 and A. Saracco et al, "Man to Woman Sexual Transmission of HIV: Longitudinal Study of 343 Steady Partners of Infected Men," *Journal of Acquired Immune Deficiency Syndromes,* Vol. 6, 1993, pp. 497-502.

[14] "The Sexually Transmitted Disease Epidemic," published by the Medical Institute of Sexual Health.

[15] Quoted in Christina Nifong, "Paying Cash for Good Behavior," *The Christian Science Monitor,* March 25, 1998.

[16] E. Laumann et al, *The Social Organization of Sexuality* (1994).

[17] Study data were provided by Best Friends.

[18] Douglas Kirby, *No Easy Answers: Research Findings on Programs to Reduce Teen Pregnancy,* National Campaign to Prevent Teen Pregnancy (1997).

[19] John B. Jemmott III, et al., "Abstinence and Safer Sex HIV Risk-Reduction Interventions for African American Adolescents," *Journal of the American Medical Association,* May 1998.

[20] Douglas Kirby, et al, "An Assessment of Six School-Based Clinics," Center for Population Options, 1989, and "Six School-Based Clinics: Their Reproductive Health Services and Impact on Sexual Behavior," *Family Planning Perspectives,* January/February 1991.

[21] F. Furstenberg et al, "Does Condom Availability Make a Difference?" *Family Planning Perspectives,* May/June 1997.

[22] "A Summary of the Findings from National Omnibus Survey Questions About Teen Pregnancy," National Campaign to Prevent Teen Pregnancy, May 1997.

[23] See "Preventing Teen Pregnancy," *The CQ Researcher,* May 14, 1993, pp. 409-432.

[24] Rebekah Saul, "Whatever Happened to the Adolescent Family Life Act?" *The Guttmacher Report,* April 1998.

[25] Ron Haskins and Carol Statuto Bevan, "Abstinence Education Under Welfare Reform," University of Maryland, 1998.

[26] National Center for Health Statistics, *op. cit.*

[27] Quoted in Tamar Lewin, "Family Decay Global, Study Says," *The New York Times,* May 30, 1995.

[28] Letter to *The New York Times,* May 16, 1997.

[29] Remarks upon nominating Henry Foster as surgeon general, Feb. 2, 1995.

[30] The South Carolina Council on Adolescent Pregnancy Prevention conducted the poll.

[31] "Involving Males in Preventing Teen Pregnancy," Urban Institute, 1997.

[32] Wade Horn and Andrew Bush, "Fathers, Marriage and Welfare Reform," Hudson Institute, 1997.

[33] Quoted in *The Washington Post,* June 8, 1998, p. A1.

[34] Hispanics, at 38 percent of all immigrants, account for the largest share of U.S immigration. Most Hispanic immigrants are Mexican-Americans, who traditionally have more babies in their teen years than whites, blacks or even other Latinos.

FOR MORE INFORMATION

If you would like to have this CQ Researcher updated, or need more information about this topic, please call CQ Custom Research. Special rates for CQ subscribers. (202) 887-8600 or (800) 432-2250, ext. 600, or E-mail Custom.Research@cq.com

Alan Guttmacher Institute, 120 Wall St., New York, N.Y. 10005; (212) 248-1111; www.agi-usa.org. The institute promotes the prevention of unintended pregnancies as well as a woman's freedom to terminate unwanted pregnancies.

Henry J. Kaiser Family Foundation, 2400 Sand Hill Road, Menlo Park, Calif. 94025; (415) 854-9400; www.kff.org. Devoted exclusively to health, the foundation focuses on U.S. health policy, reproductive health, HIV and health and development in South Africa.

Medical Institute for Sexual Health, P.O. Box 4919, Austin, Texas, 78765-4919; (512) 451-7599; www.mish.org. MISH is a non-profit medical education organization that espouses abstinence as the only safe way to avoid disease and pregnancy before marriage.

National Campaign to Prevent Teen Pregnancy, 2100 M St. N.W., Suite 300, Washington, D.C. 20037; (202) 857-8655; www. teenpregnancy.org. This bipartisan, nonprofit organization aims to reduce teen pregnancy by one-third by 2005. It doesn't take a position on abstinence or sex education.

National Coalition for Abstinence Education, P.O. Box 536, Colorado Springs, Colo. 80901-0536; (719) 531-3388. This group of community-based abstinence-only education programs monitors implementation of the $50 million per year in abstinence grants under the Welfare Reform Act of 1996.

Sexuality Information and Education Council of the United States, 130 West 42nd St., Suite 350, New York, N.Y. 10036-7802; (212) 819-9770; www.siecus.org. SIECUS promotes comprehensive education about sexuality and advocates the right of individuals to make responsible sexual choices.

Bibliography

Selected Sources Used

Books

Lichter, S. Robert, Linda S. Lichter and Stanley Rothman, *Prime Time: How TV Portrays American Culture,* **Regnery Publishing, 1994.**
This comprehensive study focuses on how prime-time entertainment has portrayed American society from the 1950s to the '90s. In a lengthy chapter on TV, it notes, for instance, that during the 1976-77 season there were seven references to casual extramarital sex for every one time marital sex was mentioned.

Lind, Michael, *Up From Conservatism,* **The Free Press, 1996.**
Lind, a conservative-turned-moderate, argues that conservative intellectualism is dead as a result of the rise of the radical right of Pat Robertson, Patrick Buchanan and anti-government militias. He contends that the epidemic of illegitimacy is a myth, knowingly perpetrated on the public by conservatives manipulating statistics in order to dismantle the welfare system.

Luker, Kristin, *Dubious Conceptions: The Politics of Teenage Pregnancy,* **Harvard University Press, 1996.**
Luker argues that both liberals and conservatives have "constructed" an epidemic of teenage pregnancy. She traces the way popular attitudes came to demonize young mothers and examines the social and economic changes that have influenced debate on the issue.

Teenage Pregnancy: Opposing Viewpoints, **Greenhaven Press, 1997.**
This collection of essays offers opposing viewpoints on the most controversial issues surrounding teenage pregnancy, including whether it really is a problem.

Articles

Funderburk, Patricia, "None, Not Safer, Is the Real Answer," *Insight, The Washington Times,* **May 9, 1994.**
The former Bush administration official argues that teaching youngsters to abstain from sex is better than teaching them how to protect themselves from pregnancy and sexually transmitted disease. She says that by not giving teenagers clear messages in sex-education classes, adults have failed to give today's teenagers any values.

McIlhaney, Joe S., "Are abstinence-only sex-education programs good for teenagers?" *Insight, The Washington Times,* **Sept. 29, 1997.**
An obstetrician-turned-activist writes that given the enormous health risks from rampant sexually transmitted diseases, it is irresponsible to teach teenagers that "safe" sex is possible.

Reports and Studies

Horn, Wade, and Andrew Bush, "Fathers, Marriage and Welfare Reform," Hudson Institute, 1997.
The authors argue that welfare helped cause the demise of marriage and the increasing disappearance of fathers from families and outline ways states can promote marriage-friendly welfare policies.

"Into a New World," Alan Guttmacher Institute, 1998.
This comprehensive study looks at sexual relationships, marriage and childbearing among the world's adolescents and young women. Numerous charts and graphs compare data on education levels, ages of first sexual experiences, age of first marriage and childbearing in 46 developing and developed countries.

Jemmott, John B. III, et al., "Abstinence and Safer Sex HIV Risk-Reduction Interventions for African American Adolescents," *Journal of the American Medical Association,* **May 20, 1998.**
This first-ever study comparing chastity vs. condoms found that abstinence-only was not as effective as a safer-sex program at preventing inner-city teens from having sex. The safer-sex program had stressed abstinence as the safest way to avoid STDs and pregnancy but also taught about using condoms.

Kirby, Douglas, "No Easy Answers: Research Findings on Programs to Reduce Teen Pregnancy," National Campaign to Prevent Teen Pregnancy, March 1997.
Kirby, a respected teenage sexuality researcher, evaluated 33 sex-ed studies and found that abstinence-only programs do not delay sexual activity.

Kirby, Douglas, et al, "The Impact of the Postponing Sexual Involvement Curriculum Among Youths in California," *Family Planning Perspectives,* **May/June 1997.**
This massive study of the Education Now and Babies Later (ENABL) program in California, the largest statewide abstinence-only effort ever initiated, found that participants were no less likely to avoid sex, pregnancy or STDs than teens in a control group.

Sonenstein, Freya L., et al, *Involving Males in Preventing Teen Pregnancy,* **Urban Institute, 1997.**
Researchers examine the crucial role that males play in teen pregnancy and STD prevention, and evaluate 23 programs around the country that focus on male behavior as a means of preventing pregnancy.

The Next Step

Additional information from UMI's Newspaper & Periodical Abstracts™ database

Abstinence

"Birth Control and the Schools," *San Francisco Chronicle,* Aug. 25, 1991, p. A14.

An editorial supports the dispensing of birth control pills, diaphragms and condoms in schools to prevent teen-age pregnancy, saying that many students are past the point of listening to advice about abstinence and don't have enough parental guidance.

"Editorials Speak Out Today for Teen Plus," *The Atlanta Constitution,* April 15, 1998, p. A12.

State Rep. Steven Cash, R-Stockbridge, says Georgia's Teen Plus pregnancy prevention program "sickens my stomach." But will Cash be able to stand the sight of a pregnant 13-year-old? That's the likely consequence of his holy war to forgo $150,000 in state funding for a clinic in Henry County, ranked 26th among Georgia's 159 counties in number of teen pregnancies.

Goodman, Ellen, "Just Say No to Abstinence-Only Sex Education Funds," *The Boston Globe,* May 29, 1997, p. A15.

Goodman agrees that teens need help saying no to premarital sex, but she questions the government's offer to spend $50 million a year for educational programs that teach only abstinence.

Henry, Jacqueline, "Advocate of Abstinence, not Condoms," *The New York Times,* April 24, 1994, p. L10.

The pro-abstinence Life Center of Long Island refers pregnant teenagers to group homes or the homes of volunteer families and helps arrange for prenatal care.

"Keeping Kids Ignorant, Concerned Adults Shouldn't 'Protect' Teenagers from Pregnancy Prevention Information," *The Atlanta Constitution,* April 1, 1998, p. A12.

To live up to its name, Citizens for Protecting Our Children should cease its dangerous and ideological crusade against pregnancy-prevention efforts aimed at teenagers, according to this editorial. With 26,000 teen pregnancies annually in Georgia, communities cannot allow an extremist agenda to dictate social policy. Twenty-seven Teen Plus clinics operate throughout Georgia. The state wants to spend $6 million to set up more clinics, which stress sexual abstinence but may offer contraception. Small bands of parents are pressuring several counties to reject the clinics and state money.

Mann, Judy, "Talk About Attitudes, Not Just AIDS," *The Washington Post,* Jan. 22, 1992, p. C22.

The author discusses nurse Crystal Groth's belief that the AIDS epidemic may reduce the pressure on teenagers to be sexually active by providing them a way of saying no that is accepted by their peers. She also discusses her belief that sex education is not just about using condoms properly, it's also about abstinence.

Mirsky, Howard, "Teen Talks," *Chicago Tribune,* Jan. 9, 1993, p. 20.

In a letter to the editor, Mirsky says abstinence should be the primary focus in sex education, but when that fails, condoms should be available to students.

Nadler, Richard, "Abstaining from Sex Education," *The National Review,* Sept. 15, 1997, pp. 50-51.

Conservatives want sex education in the public schools changed to "abstinence education." Recent studies show the value of inculcating fear and resistance in teens in reducing teenage sex and pregnancy.

Napier, Kristine, "Chastity Programs Shatter Sex-Ed Myths," *Policy Review,* May 1997, pp. 12-15.

New curricula in place across the U.S. are proving they can cut teenage sex and pregnancy rates. Five programs that are teaching chastity rather than sex education are discussed.

Olinger, David, "Nine Groups Win 'Abstinence' Grants, Funds Aim to Deter Teens from Sex," *The Denver Post,* Jan. 6, 1998, p. B5.

Nearly $500,000 in federal money will go to nine Colorado programs that espouse premarital abstinence. Most of the money, which comes from a 1996 "abstinence only" program created by Congress, will go to Colorado public-health agencies. Advocates say the federal abstinence-education program will give children a needed message that avoiding extramarital sex is the only sure way to avoid unwanted pregnancies and sexually transmitted diseases.

Shogren, Elizabeth, "Clinton Airs Plan to Curb Teen Births; Health: Strategy Based on Abstinence Will Bolster Existing Programs," *Los Angeles Times,* Jan. 5, 1997, p. A13.

President Clinton announced a new national strategy to reduce teen pregnancies through federal programs built around the unifying theme of encouraging adolescents to abstain from sex. Clinton cited new figures pointing to a drop of more than 10 percent in teenage birth rates in 10 states.

Sullivan, Kathleen M., "Sexual Abstinence: The Healthiest Lifestyle," *St. Louis Post-Dispatch,* June 22, 1997, p. B3.

The author says that abstinence until marriage is not a

moral judgment but a prescription for physical and emotional health.

Weiss, Joanna, "Abstinence Program Hits Delays," *Times-Picayune*, April 29, 1998, p. A3.

Amid much ballyhoo in November, Gov. Mike Foster, R-La., announced a statewide sexual-abstinence program with access to $3 million per year to help keep teens chaste. On Tuesday, Foster questioned why some of that money hasn't been spent. Foster spoke as he signed a proclamation declaring May "Teen Pregnancy Awareness Month" in Louisiana, and as some activists complained about a dearth of spending to stop teen pregnancies.

Wetzstein, Cheryl, "Congressmen Want States to Use Federal Grant to Urge Abstinence," *Insight on the News*, Feb. 9, 1998, p. 44.

House GOP leaders want to know if states are misusing government funds intended to promote abstinence and marriage. All 50 states applied for their portions of the $50 million grant program this year.

Williams, Leslie, "Campaign Targets Teen Pregnancies," *New Orleans Times-Picayune*, April 22, 1998, p. B3.

A nonprofit group has joined forces with Baptists and businesses to battle teen-age pregnancy — an $876 million-a-year problem in Louisiana. Paulette Irons, a state senator from New Orleans and president of the Louisiana Initiative on Teen Pregnancy Prevention, formally launched a billboard campaign encouraging parents to communicate the importance of sexual abstinence. Sex Education in School

Carman, Diane, "Abstinence — and Not Just From Sex — a Great Idea," *The Denver Post*, Nov. 30, 1991, p. E1.

Abstinence from sex, alcohol, tobacco, high-fat foods and red meat would solve many problems, Carmen says, but it's just not realistic. For this reason, she advocates sex education that includes condoms for teenagers.

Daubenmier, Judy, "Is Sex Education Program Too Explicit for Children?" *The Detroit News*, Nov. 20, 1991, p. B6.

A former Haslett, Mich., teacher testified against Michigan's health program for its alleged failure to emphasize sexual abstinence as a way to prevent AIDS and other sexually transmitted diseases. He also blamed it for the state's social ills, ranging from drug use to teen pregnancies.

Etzioni, Amitai, "Education for Intimacy," *Tikkun*, March 1997, pp. 38-42.

The author argues that a public school program for sex education should be folded into an encompassing treatment of interpersonal relations, family life and intimacy.

Samenfink, J. Anthony, "It's Time to Take a 'Correct' Approach to Sex Education," *Chicago Tribune*, April 5, 1998, p. 9.

To prevent teen pregnancies, it is time to take a new approach: Orthosexuality is a method of sex education focusing on correctly channeling the sexual drive while emphasizing the importance of preventing pregnancy, AIDS and other sexual diseases.

Volland, Victor, "Black Teens Discuss Responsible Sex," *St. Louis Post-Dispatch*, Aug. 6, 1995, p. D10.

A workshop presented by the Teen Health Clinic at People's Health Centers, part of a Youth Educational and Leadership Development Conference at the Union Avenue Christian Church in St. Louis, encouraged abstinence as the only sure way of preventing pregnancy and sexually transmitted diseases (STDs) for black teens.

Sexually Transmitted Diseases

Beck, Donna T., Alan R. Fleischman, Lynne M. Mofenson and Catherine Wilfert, "Human Immunodeficiency Virus/ Acquired Immunodeficiency Syndrome Education in Schools," *Pediatrics*, May 1998, pp. 933-935.

Education remains critical in the fight to prevent HIV infection and AIDS, particularly in schools. Accurate teaching of prevention needs to be included in K-12 health education curriculum.

Rabin, D.L., "Adapting an Effective Primary Care Provider STD/HIV Prevention Training Programme," *AIDS Care*, April 1998, p. 5-S82.

Preventing sexual transmission of HIV can be accomplished through patient behavior change. The author discusses the findings of a program developed to improve primary-care physicians' prevention practice.

Schoofs, Mark, "Aids Ed in the 'Hood," *The Village Voice*, May 26, 1998, p. 59.

The Young Adults Against Drugs & Alcohol (YAADA) agency is sponsoring a group of teenage outreach workers who try to educate their peers about AIDS prevention. The teenagers, based in the Bronx, are targeting black and Latino youths, the most common victims of AIDS.

Tilles, Mark C., "Groups Fight Teen Pregnancy, STD's," *Michigan Chronicle*, April 5, 1995, p. B3.

The Michigan Abstinence Partnership, a broad-based group of health professionals, parents, teens and educators, helps youths 9-14 avoid risky behaviors such as sexual activity.

Back Issues

Great Research on Current Issues Starts Right Here.
Recent topics covered by The CQ Researcher are listed below.
Now available on the Web
For information, call (800) 432-2250 ext. 279 or (202) 887-6279.

If you would like to have any of these CQ Researchers updated, or need more information about these topics, please call CQ Custom Research. Special rates for CQ subscribers. (202) 887-8600 or (800) 432-2250, ext. 600, or E-mail Custom.Research@cq.com

MARCH 1997
New Air Quality Standards
Alcohol Advertising
Civic Renewal
Educating Gifted Students

APRIL 1997
Declining Crime Rates
The FBI Under Fire
Gender Equity in Sports
Space Program's Future

MAY 1997
The Stock Market
The Cloning Controversy
Expanding NATO
The Future of Libraries

JUNE 1997
FDA Reform
China After Deng
Line-Item Veto
Breast Cancer

JULY 1997
Transportation Policy
Executive Pay
School Choice Debate
Aggressive Driving

AUGUST 1997
Age Discrimination
Banning Land Mines
Children's Television
Evolution vs. Creationism

SEPTEMBER 1997
Caring for the Dying
Mental Health Policy
Mexico's Future
Youth Fitness

OCTOBER 1997
Urban Sprawl in the West
Diversity in the Workplace
Teacher Education
Contingent Work Force

NOVEMBER 1997
Renewable Energy
Artificial Intelligence
Religious Persecution
Roe v. Wade at 25

DECEMBER 1997
Whistleblowers
Castro's Next Move
Gun Control Standoff
Regulating Nonprofits

JANUARY 1998
Foster Care Reform
IRS Reform
The Black Middle Class
U.S.-British Relations

FEBRUARY 1998
Patients' Rights
Deflation Fears
Caring for the Elderly
The New Corporate Philanthropy

MARCH 1998
Israel at 50
The Federal Judiciary
Drinking on Campus
The Economics of Recycling

APRIL 1998
Biology and Behavior
Liberal Arts Education
Income Inequality
High-Tech Labor Shortage

MAY 1998
Census 2000
Child-Care Options
Alzheimer's Disease
U.S.-Russian Relations

JUNE 1998
Student Journalism
Antitrust Policy
Environmental Justice
Sleep Deprivation

Back issues are available for $5.00 (subscribers) or $10.00 (non-subscribers). Quantity discounts apply to orders over 10. To order, call Congressional Quarterly Customer Service at (202) 887-8621.

Binders are available for $18.00. To order call 1-800-638-1710. Please refer to stock number 648.

Future Topics

▶ *Population and the Environment*

▶ *Democracy in Asia*

▶ *Forever Young: Baby Boomers at Mid-Life*

T H E

CQ Researcher

PUBLISHED BY CONGRESSIONAL QUARTERLY INC.

Population and the Environment

Is Earth getting too crowded to sustain life?

A t the dawning of the 20th century, there were 1.6 billion people on Earth. Now, at century's end, there are nearly 6 billion. The phenomenal population growth has renewed a longstanding debate about how many people Earth can support. Thomas Robert Malthus launched the debate 200 years ago, predicting that global population would eventually overwhelm food supplies. Technological advances thus far have enabled agricultural productivity to outpace population growth. But the rekindled debate over mankind's survival is about more than food supplies: Population growth causes environmental problems from water shortages to global climate change.

CQ **July 17, 1998** • **Volume 8, No. 26** • **Pages 601-624**

Formerly Editorial Research Reports

CQ Researcher

July 17, 1998
Volume 8, No.26

EDITOR
Sandra Stencel

MANAGING EDITOR
Thomas J. Colin

ASSOCIATE EDITOR
Sarah M. Magner

STAFF WRITERS
Adriel Bettelheim
Mary H. Cooper
Kenneth Jost
Kathy Koch
David Masci

PRODUCTION EDITOR
Melissa Hall

EDITORIAL ASSISTANT
Laura S. Cavender

PUBLISHED BY
Congressional Quarterly Inc.

CHAIRMAN
Andrew Barnes

VICE CHAIRMAN
Andrew P. Corty

PRESIDENT AND PUBLISHER
Robert W. Merry

EXECUTIVE EDITOR
David Rapp

The CQ Researcher (ISSN 1056-2036). Formerly Editorial Research Reports. Published weekly, except Jan. 2, May 29, July 3, Oct. 30, by Congressional Quarterly Inc., 1414 22nd St., N.W., Washington, D.C. 20037. Annual subscription rate for libraries, businesses and government is $340. Additional rates furnished upon request. Periodicals postage paid at Washington, D.C., and additional mailing offices. POSTMASTER: Send address changes to The CQ Researcher, 1414 22nd St., N.W., Washington, D.C. 20037.

COVER: A MOTHER IN SOUTHERN SUDAN WAITS FOR AID AT A FEEDING CENTER LAST APRIL. (REUTERS/CORINNE DUFKA)

Population and the Environment

BY MARY H. COOPER

THE ISSUES

Two hundred years ago, an English cleric named Thomas Robert Malthus wrote an essay that would forever change the secure view people had of their place on Earth. Like other animal species, Malthus wrote, humans can reproduce faster than the natural resources they require to survive. As a result, he postulated, humans eventually would overwhelm the environment, possibly resulting in their extinction.

"Famine seems to be the last, the most dreadful resource of nature," Malthus wrote. "The power of population is so superior to the power in the Earth to produce subsistence for man, that premature death must in some shape or other visit the human race." [1]

Malthus wrote his treatise in response to the prevailing optimism of the time, which saw population growth as an unqualified boon to mankind. The Marquis de Condorcet, a French mathematician and pioneering social scientist, and William Godwin, an English social philosopher, held that man was perfectible, headed toward a future free of all evil, discomfort and disease. As mankind approached immortality, Godwin predicted, population growth would cease altogether because sexual desire would be extinguished.

Two hundred years later, the debate continues — but amid profound changes. In Malthus' day, there were fewer than 1 billion people on Earth. More recently, global population has mushroomed, growing from 1.6 billion to almost 6 billion in the 20th century alone, numbers that surely would have been taken by 18th-century thinkers as confirmation of the Malthusian nightmare. But technological changes, equally unimaginable to observers at the dawn of the Indus-

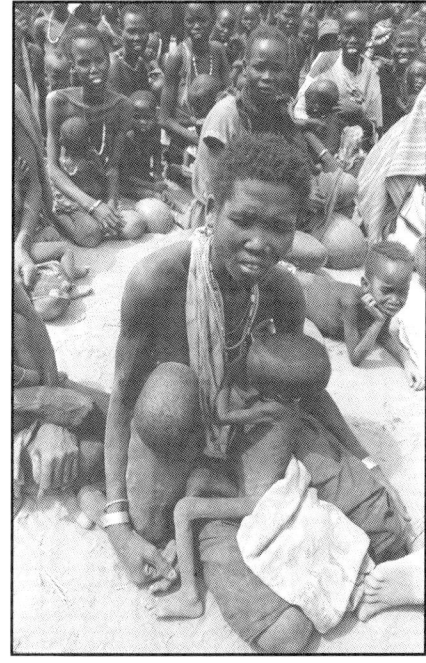

trial Revolution, have vastly increased global food supplies, giving credence to Malthus' optimistic critics. [2]

What hasn't changed over the past two centuries is the distance separating the two sides in the ongoing debate over human population. On the one side are Malthus' intellectual heirs, dubbed doomers or Cassandras. They see the continuing rise in global population as a recipe for disaster. The crash will come not only because of food shortages, they say, but because of myriad insults to the environment humans exact by their sheer numbers. *(See graph, p. 618.)*

"I certainly think we face an environmental crisis, whether it amounts to a Malthusian outcome or not," says Leon Kolankiewicz, coordinator of the Carrying Capacity Network, which promotes sustainable development. Rather than the global collapse of food supplies that Malthus envisioned, Kolankiewicz foresees any number of localized crises, similar to that which may have struck Easter Island in the Pacific Ocean, whose inhabitants are believed to have died out after exhausting the island's natural resources.

"For a time, people can exceed the long-term carrying capacity for an area, but this eventually leads to collapse," he says. "In a given region, if not the world, not only will the population collapse, but there also will be such damage to the natural capital — the resources that sustain life — that for a long time to come the environment will no longer be able to support human life."

On the other side of the debate are Godwin's successors — the boomers or Pollyannas — who say more people mean a larger pool of human ingenuity to discover new ways to thrive on planet Earth. They point to the successes of the Green Revolution, an international drive to increase crop yields in the 1950s and '60s, as evidence that humans will always come up with a technological fix to accommodate their growing numbers.

Several new developments have colored the population debate in recent years. One is the discovery that human activities — especially in the developed world — affect the atmosphere, long considered a relatively inexhaustible asset of Earth's environment. When scientists demonstrated that the release of chlorofluorocarbons from man-made coolants and aerosols had eroded Earth's protective ozone layer, world leaders agreed in 1992 to ban the chemicals.

More recently, scientists have concluded that burning fossil fuels may cause a gradual but potentially catastrophic warming of the atmosphere. Fear of so-called global warming resulted in last December's agreement in Kyoto, Japan, to curb the burning of oil, coal and natural gas.

Malthus' supporters point to these and other strains on the environment as signs that human population has exceeded Earth's "carrying capacity," its ability to sustain life indefinitely.

Continued on p. 605

Childbearing Is Greatest in Africa and Asia

The fertility rate — the average number of children that women in a country have — is generally higher in Africa and Western Asia and lower in North America, Europe and Eastern Asia. In the future, according to United Nations projections, small differences in childbearing levels will result in large differences in global population. If women average a moderate two children, population would rise to 11 billion in the 21st century and level off. If women average 2.5 children, population would pass 27 billion by 2150. But if the fertility rate fell to 1.6 children, population would peak at 7.7 billion in 2050 and drop to 3.6 billion by 2150.

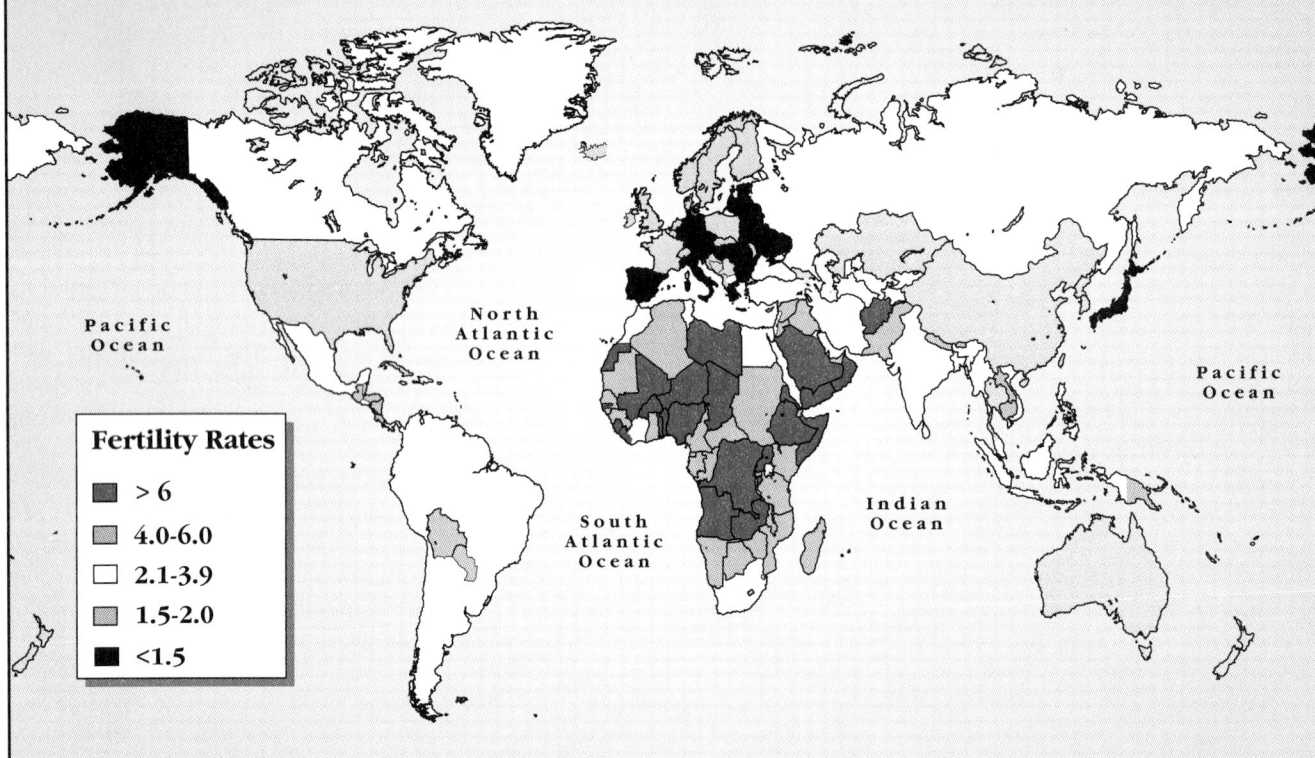

Fertility Rates
- > 6
- 4.0-6.0
- 2.1-3.9
- 1.5-2.0
- <1.5

The 10 Highest Fertility Rates	
Gaza	7.4
Yemen	7.3
Angola	7.2
Oman	7.1
Ethiopia	7.0
Somalia	7.0
Uganda	6.9
Western Sahara	6.9
Burkina Faso	6.9
Togo	6.8

The 10 Lowest Fertility Rates	
Hong Kong	1.1
Latvia	1.2
Bulgaria	1.2
Czech Republic	1.2
Russia	1.2
Italy	1.2
Spain	1.2
Greece	1.3
Slovenia	1.3
Estonia	1.3

Source: "1998 World Population Data Sheet," Population Reference Sheet

Continued from p. 603
Other signs include the rapid disappearance of plant and animal species as humans settle in once-remote parts of the world, a sharp decline in certain fish from overfishing, water shortages as agriculture and industry outpace existing water reserves and land degradation resulting from the relentless spread of agriculture onto land that is ill-suited to cultivation.

Although these strains have not yet precipitated a global environmental collapse, ecologists say we are living on borrowed time. "There is tremendous momentum in population growth," says Brian Halweil, a research fellow at the Worldwatch Institute, which studies global environmental problems. "Even if the total fertility rate were now at replacement level, world population growth would still be a problem." *(See map, p. 604.)* Halweil points to regions that are fast approaching a food crisis, such as the Nile River basin, whose current population of 110 million is expected to more than triple to 380 million by 2050. "With so many people being added," he says, "the per capita availability of resources will zoom down."

It's not that women are having more babies than their grandmothers. In fact, fertility rates have fallen in much of the world, especially where women have gained access to education and economic opportunities that make bearing large numbers of children less attractive. What has happened is that more children now survive to adulthood, thanks to vaccines, improved hygiene and more reliable food supplies.

Optimists in the population debate point to other statistics to refute Malthusian predictions of impending doom. While population growth continues, the rate of growth has slowed considerably in recent years as births in a growing number of countries are falling below 2.1 children per couple — the "replacement level," below which population begins to decline. This trend has forced the United Nations Population Division to lower its projections of future population growth. Under the "low" variant of its most recent projection, the U.N. agency expects human population to peak at 7.7 billion around the middle of the next century before starting a slow decline. Under its "high" variant, however, there would be 27 billion people on Earth by 2150, with no end of growth in sight.

But some optimists in the debate focus on the low numbers and conclude that the real threat today is the prospect that there will be too few people in coming decades — a virtual birth dearth.

"Predictions of a Malthusian collapse have been vastly exaggerated over the last few decades and continue in the face of new evidence that fertility rates are falling worldwide," says Steven W. Mosher, president of the Population Research Institute, in Falls Church, Va. "This is happening not only in the developed world but also in many developing countries, such as Thailand and Sri Lanka, which are already below replacement level, so that their populations will shortly be declining. The world's population will never double again."

Indeed, say optimists in the population debate, the real problem humanity faces is the coming loss of population, especially in Europe, where births have fallen far below replacement level. *(See story, p. 612.)* Ironically, Italy — homeland of the Vatican, contraception's archenemy — has the lowest fertility rate in the world: Each woman has an average of just 1.2 children in her lifetime. "If you built a fence around Europe, which has an average fertility rate of 1.35, the last European would turn out the lights in 300 years," Mosher says. "If current trends continue, the continent's population would go from 860 million today to zero."

But the Cassandras say it's too soon to start mourning the loss of European civilization. For one thing, they say, no one can predict with any certainty how many children future generations of people will choose to have. Moreover, because of high birthrates in earlier decades, the large number of women entering their child-bearing years will ensure that population continues to grow despite falling fertility rates. The fastest growth will come in the very countries that are least able to support more people — poor countries of sub-Saharan Africa and South Asia. "Population dynamics are like a supertanker," says Robert Engelman, director of the program on population and the environment at Population Action International. "They don't go from zero to 60 in 30 seconds, and they don't stop so fast either. So while total population growth has slowed more than demographers had expected, it's wrong to say the trend is irrevocable or permanent."

For 200 years, worldwide food production defied Malthusian predictions of global starvation. But now there are ominous signs that worldwide grain production will be unable to keep up with the population growth that is expected to continue for at least the next several decades. According to Worldwatch President Lester R. Brown, impending water shortages will soon force China to begin importing vast quantities of grain to feed its 1.2 billion people. This will drive up grain prices, Brown predicts, leaving developing countries in Africa and elsewhere unable to import enough to meet their food needs. The result: Malthus' nightmare.

"The jury's still out on Malthus," said Robert Kaplan, author of numerous articles on population and environmental issues. "But 200 years later, some people still agree with him. I think that's his ultimate success." [3]

In this bicentennial of Malthus' essay, these are some of the key questions being asked about population growth and the environment:

Will World Population Keep Climbing?

The world's population reached nearly 6 billion in 1997, more than double the 1950 level.

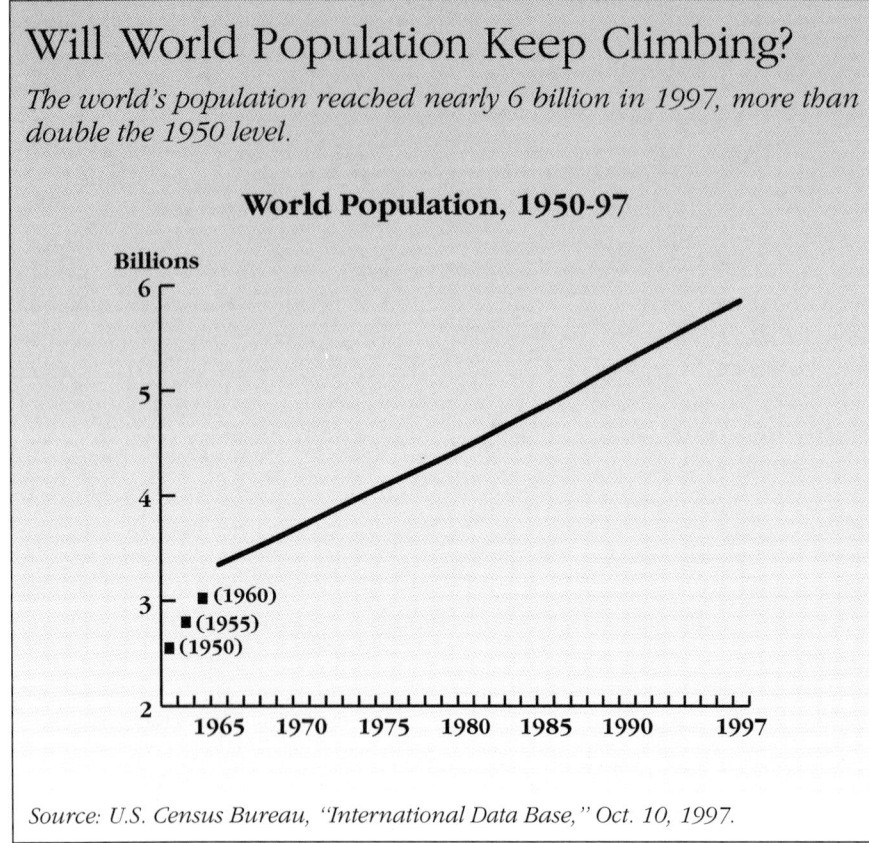

World Population, 1950-97

Source: U.S. Census Bureau, "International Data Base," Oct. 10, 1997.

Can agricultural productivity increase without causing irreversible damage to the environment?

In the 1950s and early '60s, a time of unprecedented high population growth in the developing world, demographers and policy-makers in the industrial countries realized that global food supplies — much provided by exports from developed nations — would soon fall short of demand. Agricultural researchers embarked on an urgent project to develop better-yielding grains in an attempt to avert widespread famine.

The results of this effort, later dubbed the Green Revolution, were stunning. Hybrid strains of rice, wheat and other grains were developed that produced more food per plant and shortened maturation periods so that more than one crop could be cultivated each growing season. In some instances, crop yields tripled.

The Green Revolution's success leads some experts to conclude that further advances in agronomy will suffice to feed the world's growing population. According to Mosher of the Population Research Institute, researchers at the United Nations' Food and Agriculture Organization (FAO) are confident that, even using current technology, enough food could be produced to feed as many as 14 billion people — well above most projections of Earth's population at its peak.

"There is a curious dichotomy between the world's political leaders, who are talking famine, and the researchers who are running the numbers," Mosher says. "The experts aren't being listened to by their own political bosses." In his view, the reason no one is listening to scientists who are confident in the world's ability to feed so many more people comes down to self-interest. "Popu-

lation programs have been generously funded for the past 30 years, and there are a lot of researchers who have benefited from these programs and don't want to see them ended," he says. "As the Chinese would say, they don't want to see their own rice bowls broken."

While other experts agree that further improvements in food production are possible, they worry about the environmental effects of intensifying agriculture much beyond current levels. "I suspect that there is more the Green Revolution can do, that there are more opportunities to increase the yield of a set unit of land," says Engelman of Population Action International. "The important point is that almost all agricultural experts agree that the vast majority of all food will be produced on land we're now cultivating. There just isn't a whole lot of new farmland out there."

Intensifying output on existing farmland can only continue so long before the land is seriously degraded, Engelman warns. "I worry that we may not be able to increase output generation after generation without irrevocably damaging the resources we depend on for food." These include the soil, fresh water and the whole complex of systems that produce food, including organisms in the soil that facilitate the uptake of nutrients in plants.

Each year, an estimated 25 billion metric tons of nutrient-rich topsoil are blown or washed away, largely as a result of intensive agriculture. The soil that is left is denser, making it less able to retain water and allow root penetration. Irrigation produces another problem, salinization, or the buildup of salt and other waterborne minerals in the soil, which can destroy the land's productivity over time.[4] According to David Pimentel, an agricultural expert at Cornell University, soil degradation poses an even more serious threat to the environment than global warming. "It takes 500 years to produce one inch of soil," he said. "Erosion is a slow, gradual problem, but considering that 99 percent of our food comes from the land, it's one that's basic to the survival of the food system." [5]

Besides depleting the soil, irrigation and other modern agricultural techniques pose additional environmental hazards. "Inherent in Green Revolution technologies is the dependence on greater quantities of water, pesticides and fertilizers," says Kolankiewicz of the Carry Capacity Network. "The environmental effects of this kind of agriculture are numerous and far-reaching, including pesticides that can be bioaccumulated and affect whole species and the drawdown of aquifers and depletion of stream flows by irrigation. So we're already robbing Peter to pay Paul."

Drawing on his experience as a Peace Corps volunteer in Latin America during the 1980s, Kolankiewicz also points to the damage caused as more and more marginal lands are brought into cultivation. "Very steep land is being stripped of trees because of the desperate need for food, population growth and inequitable land distribution," he says. "In many countries the best land for sustainable agriculture is owned by just a few people, who hold it idle, raise cattle on it or grow grain for export."

Some experts see a way out of this quandary through a more efficient global economy. "In an ideal, future world, there would be a number of places where people farming today would trade their labor for food produced elsewhere," says Nicholas Eberstadt, a Harvard University demographer and scholar at the American Enterprise Institute for Public Policy Research. "The environmental implications of such specialization are positive, however, because marginal lands would be under less pressure" from cultivation.

But a key condition for this outcome, Eberstadt says, is broader access to property rights. Environmental degradation occurs "when nobody feels they

own a common resource, and everyone feels they can plunder it," he says, citing desertification in the Sahel in southern Sahara — caused by trying to turn marginally productive land into farmland — and severe industrial pollution in China, where property rights are severely limited. "Both a clear and rational framework of property rights and a more relaxed regimen of international trade could be facilitating mechanisms for ensuring sustainable food supplies in the future."

Should the U.S. government support international efforts to curb population growth?

The United States has led the industrialized nations in funding programs that provide family-planning services to developing countries since the late 1960s. At that time, the U.N. Population Fund was set up to coordinate programs aimed at slowing rapid population growth. The federal government provides funding through the U.N. fund as well as through the U.S. Agency for International Development (AID), which helps other governments and non-governmental organizations (NGOs) in voluntary family-planning projects that provide information, services and supplies to communities throughout the world.

U.S. population assistance has been controversial, however. Anti-abortion activists charge that many overseas programs are coercive, forcing women to be sterilized or undergo abortions against their will. China's one-child policy — the toughest population-control policy in the world — has been especially criticized for allegedly forcing pregnant women who already have a child to have abortions, even late in pregnancy.

In response to the critics, President Ronald Reagan initiated the so-called Mexico City policy — named for the 1984 international population conference. Federal law already barred the use of U.S. funds to pay for abortions performed under international family-planning programs. Reagan took the

ban a step further, issuing an executive order that prohibited federal funding of any NGO involved in abortion activities, even if U.S. funds were not used specifically to pay for abortions. [6]

As one of his first acts after taking office, President Clinton reversed the Mexico City policy, sparking a renewed debate over funding of international population programs. Supporters of these programs say they are largely responsible for the fall in fertility rates over the past three decades. "These programs are absolutely effective," says Carl Haub, senior demographer at the Population Reference Bureau. "A lot of countries can't get started [on cutting population growth] without outside help."

While many countries with high population growth can afford to pay for family-planning clinics, medical personnel and supplies such as birth control pills and condoms, U.S.-funded AID personnel help governments coordinate their programs, Haub says. "AID personnel provide continuity in countries with unstable local governments," he says. "They basically keep the ball rolling by providing the social marketing needed, especially in illiterate societies where it's hard to educate people on how to use birth-control methods like the pill."

Critics say that despite the existing ban on funding programs that provide abortion services or abortion-related lobbying or research, part of the $385 million AID budget earmarked for family-planning services inevitably finds its way into such programs. "Population-control programs in Third World countries involve various forms of coercion," says Mosher, who spent a year studying life in a commune in China in 1979, as the one-child policy there began to be enforced. "China is the worst case in terms of the sheer number of women who are brutalized, but it's not alone," he says. His institute has documented instances of abuse in 38 countries, including sterilizations performed

High Fertility Means Low Development

Regions with high fertility rates like Africa and Latin America have a lower per capita gross national product (GNP) and greater annual population increases than more developed areas, such as North America and Europe. Indeed, Europe's 1.4 fertility rate is below the replacement level, and its population is declining by 0.1 percent a year.

Major Regions of the World

	Population mid-1998 (millions)	Natural Population Increase (Annual %)	Projected Population (millions) 2010	2025	Total Fertility Rate	1996 GNP Per Capita
World	5,926	1.4%	6,903	8,082	2.9	$5,180
More Developed Nations	1,178	0.1	1,217	1,240	1.6	20,240
Less Developed Nations	4,748	1.7	5,687	6,842	3.3	1,230
Africa	763	2.5	979	1,288	5.6	650
North America	301	0.6	333	376	2.0	27,100
Latin America & the Caribbean	500	1.8	591	697	3.0	3,710
Oceania	30	1.1	34	40	2.4	15,430
Asia	3,604	1.5	4,235	4,965	2.8	2,490
Europe	728	-0.1	731	715	1.4	13,710

Source: "1998 World Population Data Sheet," Population Reference Bureau, 1998

without informed consent, coerced abortions and unhygienic conditions in clinics.

"In countries like Mexico, Peru, Bangladesh and Indonesia, agents of the state are going to people's homes and telling women what they should do," Mosher says. "Imagine U.S. Health and Human Services agents coming to your home and telling you to take contraceptives. You would be outraged, yet this is the nature of population-control campaigns overseas."

But supporters of continued U.S. funding of international family-planning programs point instead to the gradual fall in fertility rates as evidence that women are voluntarily embracing the opportunity to

have fewer children. "There's almost nothing rational about the debate over whether the United States is somehow contributing to abortions overseas," Engelman says. "We see the fall in fertility rates in developing countries as great news. It shows that population assistance is having the impact it was designed to have — more women are wanting fewer children."

Haub fears that the recent warnings about the dangers of population decline in the industrialized world will further erode support for U.S. funding of population programs. "This trend most definitely can have an effect on people's opinions about these programs," he says. "But fertility trends in Europe have

absolutely nothing to do with trends in developing countries, which have very young populations and account for 80 percent of world population and 98 percent of the population growth."

Haub points to Mali, where the fertility rate has remained unchanged from around 7 children per woman for the past decade or more. "It's ridiculous to say that fertility rates in Africa are plummeting." Indeed, AID surveys suggest that more than 100 million married women in developing countries have an unmet need for family-planning information and contraceptives. [7]

But support for population programs remains weak in Congress, where the abortion controversy remains the primary focus of the debate on population. In April, for example, Congress added a stipulation to a State Department authorization bill (HR 1757) to pay nearly $1 billion in back dues to the U.N. that would bar U.S. aid to any international groups that lobby for abortion rights. President Clinton threatened to veto the measure. [8]

Some experts say the abortion debate in Washington undermines the progress made by family-planning efforts to date. "The U.N. estimates that if there isn't an immediate stepping up of international family planning there will be 3 billion more people in 50 years," says Halweil of Worldwatch. "That's 9.5 billion people by 2050. But reports that the population explosion is over, combined with pressure from groups that oppose abortion, are eroding domestic support for international family-planning efforts."

Should immigration be limited to protect the U.S. environment from overpopulation?

Like most industrialized countries, the United States has experienced a decline in fertility rates in recent decades, as the postwar baby boom was replaced with the baby bust of the 1970s and '80s. Today, American women have, on average, 2 children. That's slightly below the 2.1 level demographers identify as replacement level fertility, since it allows for the replacement of both parents, with a small allowance for children who die before reaching adulthood.

But the U.S. population, now 270 million, is expected to grow almost 50 percent by 2050, to 387 million. [9] With fertility rates steady among native-born American women, experts say the increase is largely due to immigration. More than 800,000 immigrants legally enter the United States each year (1.1 million, if illegal immigrants are included). That level

is almost triple the average annual immigration of 255,000 from World War II until 1970.

Almost as controversial as using abortion to control population growth is cutting immigration levels to slow environmental degradation. Indeed, although many environmental groups identify population growth as a threat to the environment, and most population growth in the United States today is a result of immigration, few of these organizations actually advocate capping immigration levels.

Earlier this year, the Sierra Club, one of the oldest and most respected environmental groups in the United States, ignited controversy among its members: It asked whether the group should abandon its neutrality on immigration or advocate caps on the number of people admitted each year in the interest of protecting the environment from the effects of overpopulation. When the votes were counted in April, the membership chose by a 3-to-2 margin to continue to stay out of the immigration quagmire altogether.

"This is a resounding defeat for a misguided policy," said Carl Pope, the Sierra Club executive director and a strong proponent of the group's neutral position on immigration. "Through this vote, our members have shown they understand that restricting immigration in the United States will not solve the environmental problems caused by global overpopulation. The common-sense solution to overpopulation is birth control, not border patrols." [10]

But supporters of immigration caps say the vote was little more than a politically correct cop-out encouraged by the group's leaders, who fear alienating the Hispanic and Asian immigrant population of California, its main political base. "There's no way we can stabilize population without reducing immigration," says Kolankiewicz, a Sierra Club member who was involved

in the effort to bring the issue to the vote. "The Sierra Club tried to step very delicately around a very controversial domestic issue. But it's duplicitous to suggest that with continued international family-planning measures we'll be able to stabilize our population."

Over the past 45 years, Kolankiewicz says, U.S. immigration levels have quadrupled at the same time global fertility has declined by 40 percent. "We have the right and the responsibility to control our own population," he says.

While acknowledging the link between population growth and environmental degradation, some experts dispute the value of capping immigration levels in the United States. Of the 800,000 foreigners who legally enter the United States each year, all but about 120,000 gain entry because they are related to current residents or citizens. A significant reduction in immigration levels, says Haub, "would mean we'd have to tell the people who are already legal residents they can't bring over their immediate relatives. That's a political impossibility."

For its part, the Clinton administration has not taken a clear position on the issue of immigration's impact on the environment. A 1996 report by a White House task force concluded that "reducing immigration levels is a necessary part of population stabilization and the drive toward sustainability." [11] But the president recently defended immigration, calling immigrants "the most restless, the most adventurous, the most innovative and the most industrious of people."

Clinton condemned "policies and ballot propositions that exclude immigrants from our civic life" and praised the United States' tradition as an immigrant nation. "Let me state my view unequivocally," Clinton said. "I believe new immigrants are good for America." But he sidestepped the question of whether current immigration levels are appropriate. ■

BACKGROUND

A Radical Idea

When Malthus launched the on-going debate over population growth in 1798, Europe was on the threshold of a radically new era. The Industrial Revolution was just getting under way, opening the way for dramatic shifts in Europe and North America from an agricultural to a modern industrial economy.

Malthus graduated from Cambridge University and later became an Anglican priest. In 1805 he became what is considered the world's first professor of political economy, a position he held at the college of the East India Company until his death in 1834.

The essay that made him famous arose from a friendly argument with his father over man's place in the world. Daniel Malthus espoused the optimistic view that prevailed at the time — no doubt inspired by the rise of democracy and technological progress — that man's ability to improve his lot is unlimited.

Two philosophers were the main purveyors of this view. In France, the Marquis de Condorcet welcomed the revolution in his country as evidence of mankind's ceaseless progress toward perfection. Even after he was imprisoned for criticizing the new Jacobin constitution, Condorcet never lost his optimism. Before starving to death in prison, he completed his writings, which were published posthumously in 1795. [12]

In England, social philosopher William Godwin shared Condorcet's views. In "An Enquiry Concerning Political Justice, and Its Influence on General Virtue and Happiness" (1793), Godwin took Condorcet's utopian thinking even further, calling for the abolition of all governmental and social institutions, including religion, school and family. All such associations, Godwin wrote, were oppressive and would no longer be needed when mankind reached its inevitable goal of perfection. At that point, he predicted, population growth would cease to be a concern. "The men who exist when the earth shall refuse itself to a more extended population will cease to propagate, for they will no longer have any motive, either of error or duty, to induce them. In addition to this they will perhaps be immortal." [13]

In refuting Condorcet and Godwin, Malthus argued that the notion that all people can live in ease and comfort defies laws of nature. Because population will always tend to grow faster than food supplies and other natural resources required for human survival, he wrote, humankind will always be afflicted with "misery and vice," such as war, famine, disease and abortion. "Famine seems to be the last, the most dreadful resource of nature," Malthus wrote. "The power of population is so superior to the power in the earth to produce subsistence for man, that premature death must in some shape or other visit the human race." [14]

Godwin's prediction that population growth will cease as people stop reproducing, Malthus wrote, defies another of the "fixed laws of our nature." "[T]owards the extinction of the passion between the sexes, no progress whatever has hitherto been made," he wrote. "It appears to exist in as much force at present as it did two thousand or four thousand years ago. . . . Assuming, then, my postulata as granted, I say that the power of population is indefinitely greater than the power in the earth to produce subsistence for man." [15]

Malthus modified his views slightly in later essays on the subject, suggesting that population growth could be slowed somewhat by delaying marriage and childbirth. But his basic thesis that there are natural limits to population growth was to greatly influence thinkers of his time and later. Charles Darwin acknowledged a debt to Malthus in devising his theory of evolution, published in 1859. Karl Marx, who published *Principles of Political Economy* the same year, denounced Malthus as a pawn of conservatives because his theory ruled out the Marxist ideal of the classless society. [16]

20th-Century Concerns

Record population growth in the 1960s and '70s sparked renewed interest in Malthus. The burgeoning environmental movement also raised concern about the effect of population growth on fossil fuel supplies and other natural resources. As in Malthus' time, optimists dismissed such worries, arguing that technological advances would provide for virtually limitless numbers of people.

Throughout this century, no voice has been more influential in rebutting Malthus than the Roman Catholic Church. In 1968, Pope Paul VI declared in an encyclical, "Humanae Vitae," that "each and every marriage act must remain open to the transmission of life," effectively banning all forms of birth control short of abstention. Population growth is not the problem among poor nations, the pope implied, but poor government and a lack of social justice. He called for humanity to undertake "the efforts and the sacrifices necessary to insure the raising of living standards of a people and of all its sons."

The same year the encyclical was

Continued on p. 612

Chronology

1700s *The debate over the impact of population growth begins.*

1793
English social philosopher William Godwin calls for the abolition of all governmental and social institutions as oppressive obstacles to human perfection. He predicts that population growth will eventually cease.

1795
Posthumously published writings by the Marquis de Condorcet, a French philosopher, argue that mankind is evolving toward perfection.

1798
Thomas Robert Malthus, an English cleric, warns in *An Essay on the Principle of Population* that unlimited population growth will overwhelm food supplies.

1950s-1960s
The Green Revolution greatly increases crop yields, quelling fears that famine will halt Earth's rapid population growth.

1960
The International Rice Research Institute (IRRI) is created to increase rice yields. Research eventually leads to a doubling and tripling of yields, averting famine in Asian countries with high population growth.

1968
Pope Paul VI issues an encyclical entitled "Humanae Vitae," banning all artificial methods of birth control and ensuring the Roman Catholic Church's position as the most influential opponent of international population-control efforts.

1970s *Record population growth renews Malthusian fears, while China launches its controversial one-child policy.*

1971
The Consultative Group on International Agricultural Research (CGIAR) is set up to coordinate the improvement of food production worldwide. Its 16-member research organization helps boost crop and fish yields.

1980s *U.S. support for overseas family-planning programs wanes amid anti-abortion sentiment.*

1980
Stanford University biologist Paul Ehrlich bets University of Maryland Professor Julian Simon that commodity prices will rise as a result of population growth. Ten years later, Ehrlich loses the bet to Simon, who argues that technological progress will increase commodity supplies and lower prices.

1984
President Ronald Reagan initiates the so-called Mexico City policy — named for the population conference held there — prohibiting federal funding of any non-governmental organization involved in abortion activities.

1990s *Forecasters alter their future projections in the wake of an unexpected slowing of population growth.*

January 1993
Shortly after taking office, President Clinton overturns the Mexico City policy.

1996
A White House task force calls for curbs on immigration to stabilize the U.S. population and protect the environment.

November 1996
The World Food Summit sets a goal of cutting in half the number of undernourished people on Earth from 800 million to 400 million by 2015.

2000s *Population growth is expected to continue, albeit at a slower pace.*

2000
After a century of rapid growth, Earth's population is expected to reach 6 billion, up from 1.6 billion in 1900.

2050
The population of the United States is expected to reach 387 million, up from 270 million in 1998. According to the United Nations Population Division's "middle" variant, world population is expected to peak at 7.7 billion before starting a slow decline.

Falling Fertility Rates Threaten ...

The population debate usually focuses on the impact of overpopulation on food supplies, health and the environment in developing countries. But scores of developed nations face an equally ominous threat: dwindling populations caused by low fertility.

Falling fertility rates have helped slow population growth throughout the world in recent years, but in some 50 countries the average number of children born to each woman has fallen below 2.1, the number required to maintain a stable population. Nearly all of these countries are in the developed world, where couples have been discouraged from having large families by improved education and health care, widespread female employment and rising costs of raising and educating children.

Conservative commentator Ben Wattenberg and others who question the value of family-planning programs have seized on this emerging trend to shift the terms of the population debate. "Never before have birthrates fallen so far, so fast, so low, for so long all around the world," Wattenberg writes. "The potential implications — environmental, economic, geopolitical and personal — are both unclear and clearly monumental, for good and for ill." [1]

According to Wattenberg, the implications are particularly dire for Europe, where the average fertility rate has fallen to 1.4 children per woman. *(See map, p. 604.)* Even if the trend reversed itself and the fertility rate returned to 2.1, the continent would have lost a quarter of its current population before it stabilized around the middle of the next century. With fewer children being born, the ratio of older people to younger people already is growing. "Europe may become an ever smaller picture-postcard continent of pretty old castles and old churches tended by old people with old ideas," Wattenberg writes. "Or it may become a much more pluralist place with ever greater proportions of Africans and Muslims — a prospect regarded with horror by a large majority of European voters." [2]

Some European governments are clearly concerned about the "birth dearth" in their midst. With fewer children being born, they face the prospect of shrinking work forces and growing retiree populations, along with slower economic growth and domestic consumption. Italy, whose fertility rate of 1.2 children per woman is among the lowest in the world, stands to suffer the most immediate consequences of shrinking birthrates. "Italy's population will fall by half over the next half-century, from 66 million now to 36 million," says Steven W. Mosher, president of the Population Research Institute. "The Italian government warns that the current birthrate, if it continues, will amount to collective suicide."

Like Italy, France and Germany have introduced generous child subsidies, in the form of tax credits for every child born, extended maternal leave with full pay, guaranteed employment upon resumption of work and free child care. Mosher predicts that the European Union will likely extend these and other policies to raise birthrates throughout the 15-nation organization in the next couple of years because all members are below replacement level.

"Humanity's long-term problem is not too many children being born but too few," Mosher says. "The one-child family is being chosen voluntarily in many European countries like Italy, Greece, Spain and Russia, which are already filling more coffins than cradles each year. Over time, the demographic collapse will extinguish entire cultures."

Although it is most pronounced in Europe, the birth dearth affects a few countries in other parts of the world as well. Mosher calculates that Japan's population will fall from 126 million today to 55 million over the next century if its 1.4 fertility rate remains unchanged. The trend is already having a social and cultural impact on the country.

"In Japan, which boasts the longest lifespans of any country in the world, it's now common for an elderly

Continued from p. 610

issued, Stanford University biologist Paul Ehrlich issued an equally impassioned plea for expanded access to birth-control services in *The Population Bomb*. In this and other warnings about the dangers of population growth, Ehrlich and his wife, Anne, also a Stanford researcher, predicted that the resources on which human survival depends would soon run out. "Population control is absolutely essential if the problems now facing mankind are to be solved," they wrote. [17]

At the same time, Worldwatch's Brown began warning of an impending food crisis. "As of the mid-1970s, it has become apparent that the soaring demand for food, spurred by both population growth and rising affluence, has begun to outrun the productive capacity of the world's farmers and fishermen," he wrote. "The result is declining food reserves, skyrocketing food prices and increasingly intense international competition for exportable food supplies." [18]

The voices of alarm were dismissed by some free-market economists, who,

echoing Godwin's view of man's perfectibility, asserted that human ingenuity would resolve the problems of population growth. The late Julian Simon, a professor at the University of Maryland, declared that Earth's natural resources will never be completely exhausted because human intellect, which is required to exploit them, is infinite. [19] To prove his point, Simon bet Paul Ehrlich that between 1980 and '90 the prices of several minerals would fall as technological progress raised their supply. Ehrlich bet that growing resource scarcity, stemming in part from population growth,

... Dire Consequences for Europe

person to hire a family for a day or a weekend to experience family life and enjoy interaction with young people," Mosher says. "It's sad to have to rent a family for a weekend, but this is a way of life that is no longer available to the Japanese because the country is dying."

The birth dearth has geopolitical implications, as well. "As the population plummets, you can say goodbye to Japan as a world power," Mosher says. "And this trend is very hard to reverse. Every young couple would have to have three or four kids to stop the momentum, and that's not going to happen."

Apart from encouraging childbirth, the only way governments can halt population loss is to open the doors to immigrants. In the United States, where the 2.0 fertility rate is just below replacement level, the population is growing by 160,000 people a year, thanks to immigration.

While immigration has always played a prominent, if controversial, role in the United States and Canada, it is a far more contentious issue in the rest of the developed world. Most European countries have more homogeneous societies than those of North America, and deeply entrenched resistance to immigration, especially by people from non-European countries, has fueled support for right-wing politicians like France's Jean-Marie Le Pen. Anti-immigrant sentiment has occasionally escalated into violence, such as the firebombings of housing for Turkish "guest workers" in Germany during the 1980s.

Still, immigration has become more acceptable throughout much of Europe in the past decade, and many of the "guest workers" who come from North Africa, Turkey and other places in search of jobs have stayed and even gained citizenship. "Immigrants are continuing to move to Europe, bringing their cultures and their religions with them," Mosher says. "Intermarriage also is increasing." Japan has been much less hospitable to foreigners.

"Immigration is a very sensitive subject in Japan," Mosher says, "and it is unlikely to be used in the short term to address the growing shortfall of workers there."

Advocates of population-control programs dismiss the concern over shrinking birthrates. "We are delighted to see falling birthrates in our lifetimes, and will continue to encourage the trend," says Robert Engelman, director of Population Action International's program on population and the environment. "I don't want to minimize the problems associated with aging populations. But because this is a slow process, societies will have plenty of time to adjust to the economic and political stresses by increasing immigration from parts of the world where population will continue to rise for some time."

Of course, immigration will be a viable solution to depopulation only as long as humanity continues to grow in number in other parts of the world. Those who worry about falling population point to the United Nations' most conservative projections, which suggest that global population could begin to shrink as early as 2040. But others see little cause for concern.

"If world population starts to fall in 2040, so what?" Engelman asks. "Please identify the danger of population decline that starts at a level much higher than today's and at worst may bring population down to levels seen earlier in the 20th century. There's only so much fresh water, so much atmosphere to absorb the waste greenhouse gases we inject into it every day, so much forest, so much land that can be cultivated. When you consider the enormity of these problems, there's nothing to be afraid of with gradual population decline."

---

[1] Ben J. Wattenberg, "The Population Explosion Is Over," *The New York Times Magazine*, Nov. 23, 1997, p. 60.

[2] *Ibid.*

---

would drive prices up. Simon won the bet.

Green Revolution

A cting on concerns that rising populations in developing countries were outstripping the world's capacity to produce enough food, leaders of NGOs, foundations and national governments launched an international agricultural-research

effort to avert famine. In 1960, the International Rice Research Institute (IRRI) was created to increase the yield of rice, the basic food for more than half the world's population. Within a few years, IRRI developed the first of several dwarf breeds that enabled farmers to grow more rice on limited land, using less water and fewer chemicals.

Under the leadership of the Consultative Group on International Agricultural Research (CGIAR), set up in 1971, biologists and agronomists from 16 research centers around the world have

since produced hundreds of hybrid strains of staple grains, such as rice, wheat and corn. They have recently extended their efforts to improve yields of potatoes, fish and other basic foods.

These efforts have been so successful that they are known as the Green Revolution. Indeed, although world population has almost doubled since 1961, per-capita food production has more than doubled. The FAO estimates that people in the developing world consume almost a third more calories a day than in the early 1960s. As a result, experts say, there are fewer deaths from

Population Programs Depend ...

The International Conference on Population and Development, held in Cairo, Egypt, in 1994, laid out a formula for stabilizing the world's growing population. Adopted by 180 nations, the plan called for improvements in women's health and job opportunities and greater access to high-quality reproductive health care, including family planning.

As the following examples show, countries that embraced the Cairo conference's "program of action" are at varying stages in population planning, due to varying levels of development, status of women and religious beliefs:

China — In 1971 Mao Zedong acknowledged the threat posed by China's more than 850 million people and launched a family-planning policy urging later marriage, increased spacing between children and a limit of two children per couple. The policy was later intensified into the radical "one-child" policy, which attracted international condemnation for its practice of forced abortions. The policy has since been relaxed, however. According to firsthand reports, it never covered most of rural China, where many families have three or more children. Still, the fertility rate has plummeted, from 5.8 children per woman in 1970 to 2 today. China's 1.2 billion people makes it the most highly populated country in the world. [1]

India — In 1951 India launched the world's first national family-planning policy. Although almost half of the nation's married women use family planning, and birthrates have come down, most of the slowdown has come in the more developed southern part of the country. "The real story in the past 20 years has been in the large illiterate states of the north known as the Hindi belt," says Carl Haub, senior demographer at the Population Reference Bureau. "In Uttar Pradesh, with a population of 150 million people, women still have an average of five children." That compares with 3.9 children for the country as a whole. With 989 million people, India today is the second most populous country in the world. With an annual growth rate of almost 2 percent — twice that of China — India may surpass China by 2050. [2]

Pakistan — Just across India's northwestern border, Pakistan has been much less aggressive in its population program. The fertility rate has fallen only slightly, from 6.6 children per woman in 1984-85 to 5.6 children today. A number of factors have contributed to the slow fall in fertility, including official indifference, inadequate funding of population programs and the country's Islamic traditions, which grant women little status, give men the leading role in family decisions and place a high value on sons. [3]

Bangladesh — When Bangladesh won independence from Pakistan in 1971, it had roughly the same population — 66 million people — and the same population growth rate — 3 percent a year — as Pakistan. But the new leaders of Bangladesh, unlike Pakistan, made family planning a top priority. As a result of a sweeping education program and widespread distribution of contraceptives, the fertility rate has dropped from more than 6 children per woman to three. Today, the population of Bangladesh is 120 million, compared with 140 million in Pakistan. [4]

Thailand — Population-control advocates consider Thailand a major success story. Its strong government program is credited with raising contraceptive use from 8 percent to 75 percent of couples over the past 30 years. As a result, the fertility rate has plummeted from 6.2 to 2 births per woman, slightly below the replacement level of 2.1. The relatively high status of Thai women, an extensive road network facilitating access to health clinics and low child mortality are cited as reasons for the program's success. [5]

Rwanda — Since the bloody civil war in 1994, when as many as 750,000 Tutsis were slaughtered by rival Hutus, members of both tribes have set about what one doctor calls "revenge fertility" — a competition to procreate in

famine and malnutrition than ever before. [20] The famines that have occurred in the past 35 years, such as those in Ethiopia and Somalia in the 1980s, and now in Sudan, have been largely the result of war and civil unrest rather than scarcity of global food supplies.

A little-mentioned side effect of the Green Revolution, however, was the environmental damage that accompanied the astonishing increase in crop yields. Some of the new strains were more sus-ceptible to insect infestation than traditional breeds. Pesticide use in rice production, for example, increased sevenfold, threatening the safety of water supplies. Some insects have developed resistance to the chemicals, resulting in yet heavier pesticide use. Green Revolution crops also require fertilizer, in some cases up to 30 times the amount used on traditional crops. With prolonged use, fertilizers can damage the soil. Finally, because many new plant strains require irrigation, the Green Revolution has been accompanied by increased erosion and water run-off, further harming land productivity.

"The reduced productivity requires added fertilizer, irrigation and pesticides to offset soil and water degradation," write David Pimentel and Marcia Pimentel of Cornell University. " This starts a cycle of more agricultural chemical usage and further increases the production costs the farmer must bear." [21] ∎

... On Wide Range of Factors

what is among Africa's most densely populated countries. With fertility at about 7 children per woman and population growth of 3.5 percent, the population of this impoverished country roughly the size Maryland is expected to grow from 7.2 million people today to 25 million by 2030. [6]

Kenya — Although it was one of the first African countries to introduce family-planning services, Kenya saw its fertility rate continue to grow for some time, from 5.3 children per woman in 1962 to 8 children per woman by 1977. In 1982, however, the government strengthened the program, providing community-based services in isolated areas that have increased the use of contraceptives among rural populations. As a result, the fertility rate has fallen to 4.5 children per woman — a rate that ensures continued population growth for decades but one that places Kenya well below the average rate of 6 children per woman in all of sub-Saharan Africa. Kenya's success in lowering fertility rates is now being mirrored in several other countries in the region, including Zimbabwe, Ghana, Nigeria and Senegal. [7]

Tunisia — Since 1957, Tunisia's population has doubled from 4 million to 8 million. While that's a huge increase, it pales in comparison with neighboring Algeria, which also started out in 1957 with 4 million inhabitants but now is home to 57 million. The difference, according to journalist Georgie Ann Geyer, is culture. "Thirty percent of the budget in Tunisia goes to education," she said. "Also, population control is part of the culture." [8] The government population program provides free family-planning services in most parts of the country, and mobile units serve rural areas. The program also is sensitive to religious customs: Rather than urging new mothers to use birth control methods right after delivery, for example, health personnel schedule a return visit to hospital 40 days later — the day new mothers return to society from seclusion, according to Islamic custom. [9]

Iran — Since the 1979 Islamic revolution, Iran's

population has jumped from 35 million to 60 million, fueled in part by official encouragement for large families. In 1993, the government adopted a strict family-planning program that encourages vasectomy and other means of birth control — though abortion remains illegal in most cases — and denies subsidized health insurance and food coupons to couples with more than three children. As a result of these efforts, the population growth rate has dropped from 4 percent a year in the 1980s — among the highest in the world — to about 2.5 percent in 1996. [10]

Peru — To stem its 2.2 percent annual increase in population, the government of Peru in 1995 stepped up its population-control program, with the additional goal of raising the status of women in the country. Since then, the program has come under fire, as health workers are accused of offering gifts to illiterate women to undergo sterilization in often unhygienic conditions. [11]

---

[1] See Mark Hertsgaard, "Our Real China Problem," *The Atlantic*, November 1997, pp. 96-114.

[2] See "India's Growing Pains," *The Economist*, Feb. 22, 1997, p. 41.

[3] Population Reference Bureau, "Pakistan: Family Planning with Male Involvement Project of Mardan," November 1993.

[4] See Jennifer D. Mitchell, "Before the Next Doubling," *World Watch*, January/February 1998, pp. 20-27.

[5] Population Reference Bureau, "Thailand: National Family Planning Program," August 1993.

[6] See "Be Fruitful," *The Economist*, Feb. 1, 1997, p. 43.

[7] See Stephen Buckley, "Birthrates Declining in Much of Africa," *The Washington Post*, April 27, 1998.

[8] Geyer spoke at "Malthus Revisited," a conference held May 8-9, 1998, by the Warrenton, Va.-based Biocentric Institute, which studies ways to enhance the quality of life for all peoples.

[9] See Population Reference Bureau, "Tunisia: Sfax Postpartum Program," March 1993.

[10] See Neil MacFarquhar, "With Iran Population Boom, Vasectomy Receives Blessing," *The New York Times*, Sept. 8, 1996.

[11] See Calvin Sims, "Using Gifts as Bait, Peru Sterilizes Poor Women," *The New York Times*, Feb. 15, 1998.

CURRENT SITUATION

Population Explosion

The 20th century has seen by far the fastest population growth in human history. For the first million years or so of man's existence on Earth, global population probably did not exceed 6 million — fewer than New York City's current population. With the beginning of agriculture some 10,000 years ago, population expanded gradually until it approached 1 billion by 1700 and 1.6 billion by 1900. Population growth never exceeded 0.5 percent a year over that 200-year period. [22]

By 2000, global population is expected to reach 6 billion. The unprecedented population explosion of the 20th century peaked in the 1970s, when the growth rate reached 2 percent a year. It has since slowed, thanks to improved access to family-planning information and contraceptives and expanded educational and employment opportunities for women in developing countries.

As couples become less dependent

on children to help in the fields and take care of them in old age, the value of large families decreases. The same medical advances that helped fuel the population explosion by reducing infant mortality also enable couples to have fewer children in the knowledge that they will survive to adulthood.

As a result of these changes, fertility rates of most developing countries are following those in industrialized countries, where fertility rates have fallen dramatically in recent decades. As more people move to the cities, the cost of raising children — housing, food, clothing and schooling — is a powerful inducement to reducing family size. "Birthrates in a large number of countries in the developing world, except for Africa, Pakistan and some countries in the Persian Gulf, have come down to a degree," says Haub of the Population Reference Bureau. "The big question is whether they will come down to the 2.1 level seen in developed countries. That would bring the population growth rate to zero."

But while fertility rates are slowly falling in many developing nations, the population momentum of the earlier boom ensures that population growth will continue in these countries for years to come. While population growth rates have dropped in industrial nations, in the developing world more than 2 billion young people under age 20 are entering or will soon enter their childbearing years, according to the Population Reference Bureau. This trend is especially significant in sub-Saharan Africa, the region with the highest fertility rate in the world — an average of 6 births per woman. With 45 percent of the inhabitants of sub-Saharan Africa age 15 or younger, population growth will likely continue, no matter what the birthrate may be in the next few decades. [23]

The difference in fertility rates between industrialized and developing countries

has implications for the future. Today, there are four times as many people in developing countries as in industrial countries. Because 98 percent of global population growth is taking place in developing countries, that gap is likely to widen. If current trends continue, many industrial nations will soon begin to lose population, especially young, working-age people. [24] As developing countries struggle to support and employ their growing number of youth, many more young people from the developing world may migrate to other regions, including the developed countries.

Norman Myers of Oxford University, in England, puts the number of "environmental refugees" at 25 million, primarily in sub-Saharan Africa, China, the Indian subcontinent, Mexico and Central America, who are fleeing drought, erosion, desertification, deforestation and other environmental problems.

"The issue of environmental refugees is fast becoming prominent in the global arena," Myers writes. "Indeed it promises to rank as one of the foremost human crises of our times." Myers foresees increased resistance to immigration in industrial nations. "Already migrant aliens prove unwelcome in certain host countries, as witness the cases of Haitians in the United States and North Africans in Europe. No fewer than nine developed countries, almost one in three, are taking steps to further restrict immigration flows from developing countries." [25]

Environmental Impact

As global population continues to mount, so does the strain on the environment, as people move into previously uninhabited areas and consume ever-increasing amounts of natural resources. In recent times, the first signs of population's impact on the environment were regional food shortages in

the 1960s and '70s. Initially, the Green Revolution resolved the shortages by introducing high-yield grains and innovative farming techniques. But the more intensive methods of agriculture required to boost food production in many parts of the world have since produced environmental damage of their own. "You can't fertilize crops without fresh water," says Halweil. "If you increase fertilizer use, you have to increase water use. As a result, large areas of Latin America, Africa and China are now suffering water shortages."

Another result of intensified irrigation and fertilizer use is the buildup of salt and other minerals that are left in the soil after the water evaporates. After prolonged irrigation, land also tends to become waterlogged and no longer suitable for growing plants. Even before land degradation sets in, there are limits to the benefits of fertilizers. "You can't just keep putting fertilizer on the land indefinitely," Halweil says. "Eventually the yield increases cease."

With economic development, more people around the world are consuming poultry, beef, pork and other meat products. As demand for such foods rises, cattle ranches are occupying land once used for agriculture, pushing farmers onto marginal lands such as steep hillsides and virgin forests. The deforestation that results, most evident recently in tropical South America and Africa, promotes erosion and has been implicated in global warming.

Biologists recently warned that a "mass extinction" of plant and animal species is now taking place, the result of human destruction of natural habitats. [26] Even the oceans are showing signs of strain from population growth. Overfishing and pollution have caused sudden decreases in fish catches, prompting temporary bans in many fisheries that only a few decades ago seemed limitless. [27]

Population growth has also been accompanied by air and water pollution. While developed countries have made

Continued on p. 618

At Issue:

Has economic development proved Malthus wrong?

JAMES P. PINKERTON
Lecturer, Graduate School of Political Management, The George Washington University

JOHN F. ROHE
Attorney and author of A Bicentennial Malthusian Essay *(1997)*

*i*n 1798, a 32-year-old minister from England published, anonymously, a 54,000-word "Essay on the Principle of Population." In it, he argued that "the power of population is indefinitely greater than the power in the Earth to produce subsistence for man." And so, he concluded in his famous formulation, "Population, when unchecked, increases in a geometrical ratio. Subsistence increases only in an arithmetical ratio." Neither the author nor his essay stayed obscure for long. Yet for all the renown of Thomas Robert Malthus, it is hard to think of an idea that has been simultaneously more influential and more wrong.

On the bicentennial of his famous treatise, Malthus lives on as adjective; a Nexis database search for the word "Malthusian" just in the last year found 138 "hits." Indeed, Malthusianism has become an intellectual prism for explaining the world, like Marxism or Freudianism — even for those who have read little or nothing of the original texts. Just as Marxists explain everything as a consequence of class structure or Freudians interpret behavior by identifying underlying sexual impulses, so Malthusians start with an inherent presumption of scarcity and impending doom. And so Malthus stands as the patron saint of pessimists, those who see the glass as half-empty, not half-full. As he wrote then, his view of the world had "a melancholy hue."

Interestingly, the first Malthusians were on the political right. The landed gentry from which Malthus sprang looked upon the swelling population of the big cities with fear and even loathing . . . .

Today's Malthusians, of course, are on the environmental left. Once again, the dynamic is that many among the elite look upon their fellow humans as liabilities. And once again, they have been mostly wrong.

The leading Malthusian today — if you don't count Vice President Al Gore — is Stanford Professor Paul Ehrlich. His landmark book, *The Population Bomb*, published in 1968, began with an alarm. "The battle to feed all humanity is over," he declared, predicting worldwide famine. A more recent book, *The Population Explosion* (1990), co-written with his wife Anne, carries on the same doom-gloom argument. Praising, of course, the memory of Malthus, the Ehrlichs prescribe a long list of control on virtually every aspect of human activity . . . .

Ironically, toward the end of his life, Malthus altered his views. In "Principles of Political Economy" (1820) he acknowledged that economic growth would improve the prospects of the populace. But as so often happens, the original outrageous assertion is remembered forever, while the subsequent revision, even if it is closer to the truth, fades away quickly.

*p*hilosophers at the dawn of the Industrial Revolution . . . suggested that prosperity and wealth were dependent on more people. In his essay, "Of Avarice and Profusion" in 1797, William Godwin states, "There is no wealth in the world except this, the labor of man . . . ." While serving as an ordained priest in the Church of England, Thomas Robert Malthus questioned these findings. He pondered basic mathematical principles. If parents had four children, and if the population continued to double every generation, the exponential progression would be as follows: 2, 4, 8, 16, 32, 64, 128, 256, 512, 1024, 2048. The numerical surge becomes explosive. Malthus determined a finite planet could not accommodate perpetual growth . . . .

Thomas Robert Malthus unlocked the door to one of nature's best-kept and most formidable secrets. He discovered a universal law of biology. For every plant and animal, there are more offspring than the ecosystem can sustain. And we are just beginning to grapple with the ethical dilemma resulting from his humbling conclusion: This universal law even applies to us.

The view from a seemingly lofty perch on nature's food chain can be deceptive. We enjoy but a brief reprieve from universal biological principles. The prescient message of a pre-scientific era has not been rendered obsolete by modern technology.

Our planet now experiences a daily net population gain of 250,000 people (total births minus deaths), and approximately 1.3 billion go to bed hungry every night. Several hundred thousand slip beyond the brink of malnutrition every year.

While the Earth's natural capital is systematically dismantled, efforts to discredit Malthus persist. For example, Julian Simon claims the world's resources can continue to accommodate human growth for 7 billion years! By then, the unchecked human biomass would fill the universe.

Efforts to discredit Malthus do not always plummet to such overt absurdities. Subtle efforts to refute him are exhibited every time a politician promises to add more exponential growth to the GNP. Proponents of growth are implicitly found in every financial report, business forecast and economic news publication. An abiding faith in growth has become the unexamined conviction of our age. Notions of sustainability are not on the table. The talismanic affinity for growth is an implicit rejection of Malthus . . . .

We were not exempt from the laws of biology unveiled by Thomas Robert Malthus in 1798. And we are not exempt now. At the bicentennial anniversary of his essay, Malthus deserves recognition for predicting the cause of today's most pressing concerns and most challenging ethical challenges. We discredit him at our peril.

such as Germany, which is cleaning up the Rhine River and has greatly improved air quality. Mankind is capable of creative solutions."

Even more controversial is the link between population growth and global warming. Consumption of coal, oil and natural gas has been implicated in the gradual heating of the atmosphere that scientists fear will cause melting of polar ice caps, rising water levels and flooding of crowded coastal areas. Warming may also speed desertification and the spread of malaria and other insect-borne diseases. Although carbon-fuel consumption can be expected to continue to rise with economic development, many scientists predict that the growth in human population alone will increase demand for these fuels until cheap alternatives are developed.

But optimists in the population debate firmly reject this argument. "The odd suggestion that babies are somehow responsible for pollution tends to be the mindset of people who blame problems on the sheer number of people who exist," says Mosher, reflecting the view of many critics of the Kyoto Protocol, which was endorsed last December by the United States and 167 other countries. "But this view is wrong and was also rejected at Kyoto.

When the developed countries asked developing countries to further decrease their total fertility rates as part of the treaty, they were rejected outright, and rightly so. There is no necessary connection between the number of children being born and the level of carbon dioxide in the air."

Critics also charge that the global-warming theory rests on shaky scientific evidence. Consequently, they oppose U.S. participation in the treaty, which they say would cost more than 3 million jobs as businesses curb production to comply with its requirement to cut carbon emissions. The Clinton administration, which strongly supports the treaty, faces an uphill battle in the

Developed Nations Use the Most Resources

The United States accounts for only 5 percent of the world's population but uses a third of its paper and dumps three-quarters of the hazardous waste. Similarly, other developed countries account for a small fraction of Earth's population but use the largest percentage of its metals and paper.

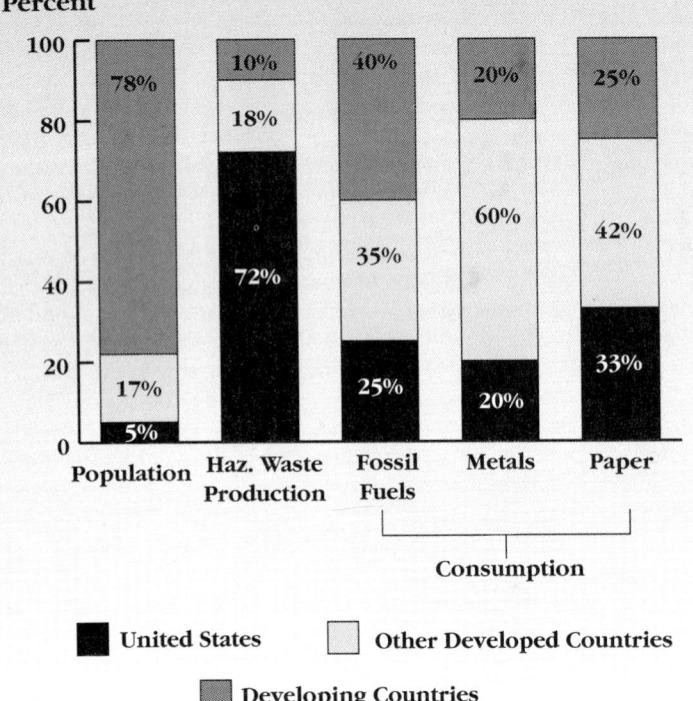

Share of Population, Waste Production and Resource Consumption

Sources: "New Perspectives on Population: Lessons from Cairo," Population Bulletin, March 1995; Natural Resources Defense Council

Continued from p. 616

strides in these areas, industrializing countries are facing mounting problems. China, for example, which uses coal for industry, as well as for heating and cooking, has among the worst air pollution in the world. Taiyuan, in northern China, has seven times as much particulate matter as Los Angeles, by far the most polluted city in the United States. Beijing and other Chinese cities are also blanketed by pollutants. [28]

Optimists in the population debate reject the notion that population growth by itself causes environmental damage. "I don't think there is a direct link between population and the environment," says the Population Research Institute's Mosher, who blames misguided government policies. "You can create environmental problems in a lightly populated country by failing to control pollution, just as you can have a very clean environment in a densely populated country,

OUTLOOK

Grain Crunch?

For the past several decades, the Green Revolution has largely discredited the Malthusian prediction of imminent collapse of the global food supplies needed to feed a rapidly expanding population. But the environmental degradation that has continued apace during that time may have laid the groundwork for just such a calamity in the not too distant future. According to Worldwatch, rapid industrialization in China is reducing the supply of water farmers use to irrigate their grain crops. Because 70 percent of the grain consumed by China's 1.2 billion inhabitants comes from irrigated land, the diversion of water for industrial use may soon force the country, now largely self-sufficient, to start importing grain.

Because of its sheer size, China would quickly overwhelm the global supply of grain, driving up prices and forcing less affluent grain-importing countries, such as those of sub-Saharan Africa, out of the market. The result, Worldwatch warns, would be widespread famine. "For the 1.3 billion of the world's people who live on $1 a day or less, higher grain prices could quickly become life threatening," write Brown and Halweil. [30]

Brown has made similarly dire predictions in the past that have proved wrong, drawing the scorn of optimists in the Malthusian debate. But now, the situation he describes is sufficiently alarming to have drawn the attention of the U.S. National Intelligence Council, which calls for greater U.S.-China cooperation in agricultural production and technology. Brown and Halweil endorse the idea.

"If the world's two leading food producers can work closely together to protect their agricultural resource bases, while the world works to stabilize population," they write, "it will benefit not only each of those countries, but the rest of the world as well." [31]

Although the implications of China's water shortage are especially alarming, it is hardly the only country faced with competing demands on dwindling water supplies. According to Population Action International, some 80 percent of the world's population lives in countries facing problems with fresh water supplies. Population growth will lead to more widespread water shortages, the group predicts, heightening the risk of conflict over water supplies in areas such as the Tigris-Euphrates basin, where water rights are already a source of tension among Iraq, Syria and Turkey. [32]

Meanwhile, the CGIAR continues trying to ward off famine with further improvements in crop yields as well as fish and meat production. In an effort to halve the number of undernourished people on Earth to 400 million by 2015 — the goal set by the World Food Summit in November 1996 — the international research organization is studying the potential of bioengineering as the next weapon in its arsenal to continue the Green Revolution into the next century. [33]

Consumption to Blame?

Today's consumer society has added a new twist to the warning issued by Malthus about inadequate food supplies. Latter-day Malthusians warn that the economic systems prevalent in most of the world today can only accelerate that end by encouraging consumption of resources without regard to its impact on the environment. In the United States, advertisements promise consumers that buying an endless array of products will bring greater happiness. With the end of the Cold War and the demise of the Soviet Union, the Western model of economic life is being pursued throughout most of the world.

Some experts say the combination of population growth and rising consumption do not threaten Earth's carrying capacity. "The long-term trend for inflation-adjusted prices of commodities has been going down, not up," Eberstadt says. "This suggests to me that natural resources are less scarce today than they were when there was less demand. In any case, we're heading toward a knowledge-and-service economy, so the direction of our development is less resource-intensive and more reliant on human skills. That gives me hope that we may be able to manage our resource demands in the future."

But many environmentalists say Malthus' nightmare will become reality that much sooner if the rest of the world adopts the consumption-based model developed in North America and Western Europe. In their view, economic growth has become a fundamental, but flawed, barometer of well-being. "Every news report, every business forecast assumes that growth is good and that more growth is better," says attorney John F. Rohe, author of the 1997 book *A Bicentennial Malthusian Essay.* "But the issue is not how we grow. It's how we can develop sustainably." *(See At Issue, p. 617)*

In this view, current efforts to protect the environment fall far short of the changes that are required to ensure sustainability. "People wonder whether the economy can continue to grow if we stop excessive consumption of oil and polluting goods," Halweil says. "They say we can shift to solar energy, fuel cells and biodegradable plastics. But the answer isn't having a hybrid-fuel car in everyone's garage. It's having fewer people driving and more taking public transportation."

The only answer to having more people on the planet, Halweil says, is to drastically cut consumption. "We are addicted to consumption, and we have to be slowly weaned off it," he says. "I don't know what it will look like, but the economic system will have to be different if the environment is to be protected." ■

Notes

[1] Thomas Robert Malthus, *An Essay on the Principle of Population* (1798), cited in Philip Appleman, ed., *An Essay on the Principle of Population* (1976), p. 56. For background, see "World Hunger," *The CQ Researcher*, Oct. 25, 1991, pp. 801-824.

[2] See "Population Growth," *The CQ Researcher*, July 16, 1993, pp. 601-624.

[3] Kaplan spoke at "Malthus Revisited," a conference held May 8-9, 1998, by the Warrenton, Va.-based Biocentric Institute, which studies ways to enhance the quality of life for all peoples.

[4] See Population Action International, *Conserving Land: Population and Sustainable Food Production*, April 1995.

[5] Pimentel spoke at the May conference on Malthus (see above).

[6] See "International Population Assistance," *Congressional Digest*, April 1997.

[7] See "What Birth Dearth? Why World Population Is Still Growing," *Population Action International Fact Sheet*, 1998.

[8] See "Clinton Uncaps Veto Pen As State Department Bill Clears," *CQ Weekly*, May 2, 1998, pp. 1167-1168.

[9] See James P. Smith and Barry Edmonston, eds., *The New Americans* (1997), p. 95.

[10] Quoted in William Branigin, "Sierra Club Votes for Neutrality on Immigration," *The Washington Post*, April 26, 1997.

[11] President's Council on Sustainable Development, "Task Force Report on Population and Consumption," 1996, p. iv.

[12] Condorcet's last work was *Esquisse d'un tableau historique des progrès de l'esprit humain*.

[13] Quoted in Gertrude Himmelfarb, "The Ghost of Parson Malthus," *Times Literary Supplement* (London), Jan. 23, 1998.

[14] Malthus, *op. cit.*, p. 56.

[15] *Ibid*, p. 19-20.

[16] For more information on Malthus and his

time, see David Price, "Of Population and False Hopes: Malthus and His Legacy," *Population and Environment*, January 1998, pp. 205-219. See also Keith Stewart Thomson, "1798: Darwin and Malthus," *American Scientist*, May-June 1998, pp. 226-229.

[17] Paul R. and Anne H. Ehrlich, *Population Resources Environment* (1972), quoted in Appleman, *op. cit.*, p. 240.

[18] Lester R. Brown, *In the Human Interest* (1974), quoted in Appleman, *op. cit.*, p. 243.

[19] See Julian Simon, *The Ultimate Resource* (1981).

[20] See "Environmental Scares: Plenty of Gloom," *The Economist*, Dec. 20, 1997, p. 20.

[21] David Pimentel and Marcia Pimentel, "The Demographic and Environmental Consequences of the Green Revolution," *The Carrying Capacity Briefing Book* (1996), p. XII-101.

[22] *Ibid*., p. XII-97.

[23] Population Reference Bureau, *1998 World Population Data Sheet*, May 1998.

[24] See Michael Specter, "Population Implosion Worries a Graying Europe," *The New York Times*, July 10, 1998, p. A1.

[25] Norman Myers, "Environmental Refugees,"

Population and Environment, November 1997, pp. 175-176.

[26] See William K. Stevens, "One in Every 8 Plant Species Is Imperiled, a Survey Finds," *The New York Times*, April 9, 1998.

[27] See "The Sea," *The Economist*, May 23, 1998, Survey section, pp. 1-18.

[28] See Elisabeth Rosenthal, "China Officially Lifts Filter on Staggering Pollution Data," *The New York Times*, June 14, 1998.

[29] See "Fresh Focus on Global Warming Does Not Dispel Doubts About Kyoto Treaty's Future," *CQ Weekly*, June 6, 1998, pp. 1537-1538.

[30] Lester Brown and Brian Halweil, "China's Water Shortage Could Shake World Food Security," *Worldwatch*, July/August 1998, p. 10.

[31] *Ibid*., p. 18.

[32] See Tom Gardner-Outlaw and Robert Engelman, "Sustaining Water, Easing Scarcity: A Second Update," *Population Action International*, Dec. 15, 1997.

[33] See Consultative Group on International Agricultural Research, "Nourishing the Future through Scientific Excellence," Annual Report 1997.

Bibliography

Selected Sources Used

Books

Appleman, Philip, ed., *An Essay on the Principle of Population: Thomas Robert Malthus*, W.W. Norton, 1976.

This volume contains not only the writings of Malthus and his contemporaries but also those of 20th-century thinkers who joined the debate over Earth's ability to support a rapidly growing population in the 1970s.

Brown, Lester R., Michael Renner and Christopher Flavin, *Vital Signs 1998: The Environmental Trends That Are Shaping Our Future*, W.W. Norton, 1998.

Among the trends featured are population growth and grain yields, two essential ingredients in the Malthusian prediction of famine. Though population growth has slowed, it continues, and further increases in grain yields may be hampered by dwindling water supplies.

Easterbrook, Gregg, *A Moment on the Earth: The Coming Age of Environmental Optimism*, Penguin Books, 1995.

The author claims that prevailing concerns over a number of environmental issues are overstated. The recent slowing of population growth, he writes, marks the beginning of an era when man's impact on the environment will be insignificant: "Human overpopulation, which environmental orthodoxy today depicts as a menace of unimaginable horror, will be seen by nature as a minor passing fad."

Rohe, John F., *A Bicentennial Malthusian Essay: Conservation, Population and the Indifference to Limits*, Rhodes & Easton, 1997.

The author attributes many of today's problems, from famine to road rage, to the same overpopulation that concerned Malthus 200 years ago. Compounding the problem, he writes, is the quest for economic growth regardless of its impact on natural resources.

Articles

Ashford, Lori S., "New Perspectives on Population: Lessons from Cairo," *Population Bulletin*, March 1995.

The International Conference on Population and Development, held in September 1994 in Cairo, Egypt, produced a list of goals for family-planning programs. This article presents an overview of these programs around the world and identifies policies that have had the most success in reducing population growth.

Brown, Lester R., and Brian Halweil, "China's Water Shortage Could Shake World Food Security," *Worldwatch*, July/August 1998, pp. 10-18.

Rapid industrialization and population growth are depleting China's water supplies so fast that the country's farmers may soon be unable to meet domestic food needs. If China is forced to buy its grain, global grain prices will rise, perhaps beyond the means of poorer developing countries that depend on imports to meet their food needs.

Hertsgaard, Mark, "Our Real China Problem," *The Atlantic*, November 1997, pp. 97-114.

During a trip through rural China, the author found that the country's infamous one-child policy has been largely abandoned and that continuing population growth is compounding China's serious environmental pollution.

Mann, Charles C., "Reseeding the Green Revolution," *Science*, Aug. 22, 1997, pp. 1038-1043.

The Green Revolution prevented widespread famine in recent decades, but many scientists worry that the potential for increasing crop yields is reaching its limit. Bioengineering and other breakthroughs may provide the tools to achieve another major leap in agricultural productivity.

Price, David, "Of Population and False Hopes: Malthus and His Legacy," *Population and Environment*, January 1998, pp. 205-219.

The author, an anthropologist at Cornell University, presents an excellent overview of the life and times of Thomas Robert Malthus on the bicentennial of his essay on population and the relevance of his ideas to modern concerns about Earth's carrying capacity.

Smail, J. Kenneth, "Beyond Population Stablization: The Case for Dramatically Reducing Global Human Numbers," *Politics and the Life Sciences*, September 1997.

A Kenyon College anthropology professor opens a roundtable presentation by 17 population experts who support greater efforts to curb population growth.

Reports and Studies

Gardner-Outlaw, Tom, and Robert Engelman, Sustaining Water, Easing Scarcity: A Second Update, Population Action International, 1997.

Water supplies are threatened in many parts of the world by rising population. By 2050, the authors report, at least one person in four is likely to live in countries that suffer chronic or recurring water shortages.

Population Reference Bureau, *World Population Data Sheet: Demographic Data and Estimates for the Countries and Regions of the World*, 1998.

This pamphlet presents a country-by-country assessment of population, fertility rates, life expectancy and other statistics that help demographers forecast future population growth trends.

The Next Step

Additional information from UMI's Newspaper & Periodical Abstracts™ database

Agricultural Issues

Albrecht, Don E., "The Industrial Transformation of Farm Communities: Implications for Family Structure and Socioeconomic Conditions," *Rural Sociology*, March 1998, pp. 51-64.

The industrialization of agriculture has resulted in extensive declines in the number of farms and in the number of people employed in agriculture. Albrecht analyzes family structure and socioeconomic conditions in 281 Great Plains counties that were economically dependent on agriculture at one time.

Bradshaw, Ted K., and Brian Muller, "Impacts of Rapid Urban Growth on Farmland Conversion: Application of New Regional Land Use Policy Models and Geographical Information Systems," *Rural Sociology*, March 1998, pp. 1-25.

Geographical Information Systems (GIS) computer mapping programs and new land-use policy models are useful in understanding the dynamics of rural land conversion to urban uses. The authors discuss how new land-use models and GIS programs enable rural sociologists to better understand how rural communities and their spatial environments interact.

Duncan, Marvin, and Won W. Koo, "Can Developing Countries Afford the New Food System? A Case Study of the Chinese Agricultural Sector," *American Journal of Agricultural Economics* (AAE), May 1997, pp. 605-612.

A study analyzes the relationship between agricultural and industrial sectors of high-performance developing economies important as trade partners to the U.S., answering the question of whether these developing countries can afford the new food system. It is based on a quantitative analysis for the Chinese agricultural sector

Food Production

Avery, Dennis T., "Saving Nature's Legacy Through Better Farming," *Issues in Science & Technology*, fall 1997, pp. 59-64.

Unless growing world food demand is met with improved farm productivity, much undeveloped land with its biodiversity will be lost to agriculture. The need to develop and perfect better farming techniques is addressed.

Carter, Colin A., "The Urban-Rural Income Gap in China: Implications for Global Food Markets," *American Journal of Agricultural Economics* (AAE), 1997.

As long as the Chinese government forces farmers to produce grain and restricts labor mobility, farm incomes will be kept low. The current challenge of the government is to adopt a practical agricultural development policy that is based on the existence of abundant farm labor.

"Laboratory Launches Agriculture and Food Processing Initiative," *Resource*, March 1998, p. 5.

A research project that will explore food-processing alternatives for the rapid increase in world population is discussed. The Pacific Northwest National Laboratory study will focus on biotechnology and information technology.

Mydans, Seth, "Scientists Developing 'Super Rice' To Feed Asia," *The New York Times*, April 6, 1997, p. 9.

The rice plant that has fed Asia for thousands of years needs an overhaul: such weak and slender stems, so many unproductive stalks, such vulnerability to insects and disease, such sensitivity to sunlight. At the International Rice Research Institute, the delicate green plant is being thoroughly redesigned into a more efficient grain-producing engine. It is an urgent task as Asia's population expands and its farmland shrinks. Three decades ago, the scientists here at the International Rice Research Institute gave the world "miracle rice," helping to begin the Green Revolution and avert what appeared to be an imminent famine in Asia.

Rosegrant, Mark W., and A. Sombilla, "Critical Issues Suggested by Trends in Food, Population, and the Environment to the Year 2020," *American Journal of Agricultural Economics* (AAE), 1997.

The authors discuss the emerging trends in global food supply and demand up to 2020. They highlight policy challenges and possible environment constraints to meeting the projected future food demand.

Tran, Mark, "Africa's Poverty Trap Gapes as Lending Slumps; Sub-Saharan Region Unlikely to Meet Targets, says World Bank," *The Guardian*, April 17, 1998, p. 25.

If you thought that an Asian tiger enjoyed the world's fastest-growing economy in the past three decades, you'd be wrong. Botswana's per capita income grew 9.2 percent between 1965 and 1996, compared with 7.3 percent for the second-fastest performer, South Korea. China was third, achieving 6.7 percent. "There is a common perception that there is no good news to report on development," said World Bank chief economist Joseph Stiglitz, "but the WDI is full of data to the contrary."

Green Revolution

Combs, Gerald F., John M. Duxbury and Ross M. Welch, "Toward a 'Greener' Revolution," *Issues in Science & Technology*, fall 1997, pp. 50-58.

Two billion people suffer from terrible nutrition. The need to start producing not just more food, but more nutritious food is addressed, focusing on four methods that will make this goal a reality.

Conway, Gordon, "Green-green: Feed the World," *New Statesman*, Dec. 5, 1997, pp. 10-11.

The first Green Revolution transformed the nature of crop yields. Its successor needs to do the same on a sustainable basis if the world is to cope with its rising population.

Immigration

Branigin, William, "Sierra Club Votes for Neutrality on Immigration; Population Issue 'Intensely Debated'," *The Washington Post*, April 26, 1998, p. A16.

Members of one of the nation's leading environmental organizations have voted to maintain neutrality on U.S. immigration policy, turning back a call for reduced immigration as a means of limiting U.S. population growth to preserve natural resources. In a referendum that generated intense debate, Sierra Club members voted 60 percent to 40 percent to "take no position" on immigration levels but to work toward solving global population problems."

Foner, Nancy, "The Immigrant Family: Cultural Legacies and Cultural Changes," *International Migration Review: IMR*, winter 1997, pp. 961-974.

The author examines the way family and kinship patterns change in the process of immigration and why these changes occur.

Glazer, Nathan, "Coming and Going," *The New Republic*, Nov. 17, 1997, pp. 13-14.

Americans remain divided over immigration because they are divided over the moral issues behind the question of how many people we should admit into the country.

Levine, Candice S., " Reorienting for Sustainable Development: Support for a National Science and Technology Policy," *Journal of International Affairs*, spring 1998, pp. 675-688.

The national science community does not receive consistent or adequate political support, despite public enthusiasm for environmentally friendly growth. Levine offers a critical look at the effect of some of these political dynamics on the scientific community, which reveals the need for a national policy that is consistent and directed.

Population Growth

Cloud, David S., "Developed Nations Assailed Over Population Control," *Chicago Tribune*, May 29, 1997, p. 7.

United Nations officials on Wednesday castigated the United States and other developed countries for not paying their share of international aid programs aimed at expanding women's access to family planning.

Hastings, Marilu, "Viewpoints," *Houston Chronicle*, March 21, 1997, p. A41.

The author discusses Roland M. Howard's questioning of the source of a projection that anticipates a doubling of the Earth's population in the 21st century. For almost two decades, the United Nations, the World Bank and individual demographers have projected a likely world population between 8 billion and 12 billion that stabilizes sometime within the next century (compared with today's 5.7 billion).

"India's Exploding Population," *USA Today*, Sept. 26, 1997, p. A1.

India is expected to pass China as the world's most populous nation within 50 years.

Kuper, Alan, and Dick Schneider, "Why We Need a Comprehensive U.S. Population Policy," *Sierra*, January 1998, pp. 105-107.

A commentary discusses why stabilizing population is essential to protecting the environment. Kuper and Schneider urge the Sierra Club to develop and advocate a comprehensive policy for solutions to problems of excess immigration.

McHugh, James T., "Overpopulation and What to Do About It," *National Catholic Reporter*, Oct. 31, 1997, p. 19.

Father Robert Drinan recently told Catholics that they must stop their silence on the world overpopulation crisis.

Petersen, William, "Parents vs. State," *American Scholar*, winter 1997, pp. 121-127.

Petersen examines what reduces actual family size below its potential in virtually all societies. The standard that a marriage should be founded on the ability to care for the resultant family is contradicted by the usual inverse relation between social class and fertility.

Rogers, David, "Senate's Vote on Population Planning Pushes GOP Toward Veto Confrontation," *The Wall Street Journal*, April 29, 1998, p. B11.

Republicans pushed toward a veto confrontation with President Clinton, as the Senate gave final approval to a State Department bill reasserting Reagan-era curbs on population-planning programs overseas. The narrow 51-49 vote underscores the continued divisiveness of the abortion issue. As approved, the bill authorizes an estimated $819 million to pay U.S. back debts to the U.N.

Swanson, Stevenson, "U.N. Analysts Trim Global Population Forecasts," *Chicago Tribune*, Feb. 17, 1998, p. 1.

Using calculators and computers rather than smoke and mirrors, the United Nations' population forecasting unit said this month that global population will peak at about 11 billion, probably around the year 2200. Recent reports showing a slowdown in population growth have ignited a furious debate among demographic experts and population-program advocates over whether the population bomb has turned out to be a dud.

Back Issues

Great Research on Current Issues Starts Right Here.
Recent topics covered by The CQ Researcher are listed below.
Now available on the Web
For information, call (800) 432-2250 ext. 279 or (202) 887-6279.

If you would like to have any of these CQ Researchers updated, or need more information about these topics, please call CQ Custom Research. Special rates for CQ subscribers. (202) 887-8600 or (800) 432-2250, ext. 600, or E-mail Custom.Research@cq.com

APRIL 1997
Declining Crime Rates
The FBI Under Fire
Gender Equity in Sports
Space Program's Future

MAY 1997
The Stock Market
The Cloning Controversy
Expanding NATO
The Future of Libraries

JUNE 1997
FDA Reform
China After Deng
Line-Item Veto
Breast Cancer

JULY 1997
Transportation Policy
Executive Pay
School Choice Debate
Aggressive Driving

AUGUST 1997
Age Discrimination
Banning Land Mines
Children's Television
Evolution vs. Creationism

SEPTEMBER 1997
Caring for the Dying
Mental Health Policy
Mexico's Future
Youth Fitness

OCTOBER 1997
Urban Sprawl in the West
Diversity in the Workplace
Teacher Education
Contingent Work Force

NOVEMBER 1997
Renewable Energy
Artificial Intelligence
Religious Persecution
Roe v. Wade at 25

DECEMBER 1997
Whistleblowers
Castro's Next Move
Gun Control Standoff
Regulating Nonprofits

JANUARY 1998
Foster Care Reform
IRS Reform
The Black Middle Class
U.S.-British Relations

FEBRUARY 1998
Patients' Rights
Deflation Fears
Caring for the Elderly
The New Corporate Philanthropy

MARCH 1998
Israel at 50
The Federal Judiciary
Drinking on Campus
The Economics of Recycling

APRIL 1998
Biology and Behavior
Liberal Arts Education
Income Inequality
High-Tech Labor Shortage

MAY 1998
Census 2000
Child-Care Options
Alzheimer's Disease
U.S.-Russian Relations

JUNE 1998
Student Journalism
Antitrust Policy
Environmental Justice
Sleep Deprivation

JULY 1998
Encouraging Teen Abstinence

Back issues are available for $5.00 (subscribers) or $10.00 (non-subscribers). Quantity discounts apply to orders over 10. To order, call Congressional Quarterly Customer Service at (202) 887-8621.

Binders are available for $18.00. To order call 1-800-638-1710. Please refer to stock number 648.

Future Topics

▶ *Democracy in Asia*

▶ *Forever Young: Baby Boomers at Mid-Life*

▶ *Oil Production in the 21st Century*

CQ Researcher

PUBLISHED BY CONGRESSIONAL QUARTERLY INC.

Democracy in Asia

Is democracy making gains in Asia?

D
emocracy has not fared well in Asia,
through history or in recent times. Today,
most Asians live under communist
governments, military regimes or virtual
one-party states. But Asia also includes two big, long-
established democracies: India and Japan. And with the
fall of Indonesia's autocratic longtime president,
Suharto, the world's fourth most populous country
could be joining the ranks of democratic nations. But
the country's new president, B.J. Habibie, faces a dire
economic crisis, and some reformers doubt his
commitment to political change. In addition, some
Asians continue to debate whether democracy conflicts
with Asian values, and U.S. policy-makers are often at
odds with interest groups on how best to promote
democracy in Asia.

CQ **July 24, 1998** • **Volume 8, No. 27** • **Pages 625-648**

Formerly Editorial Research Reports

CQ Researcher

July 24, 1998
Volume 8, No.27

EDITOR
Sandra Stencel

MANAGING EDITOR
Thomas J. Colin

ASSOCIATE EDITOR
Sarah M. Magner

STAFF WRITERS
Adriel Bettelheim
Mary H. Cooper
Kenneth Jost
Kathy Koch
David Masci

PRODUCTION EDITOR
Melissa Hall

EDITORIAL ASSISTANT
Laura S. Cavender

PUBLISHED BY
Congressional Quarterly Inc.

CHAIRMAN
Andrew Barnes

VICE CHAIRMAN
Andrew P. Corty

PRESIDENT AND PUBLISHER
Robert W. Merry

EXECUTIVE EDITOR
David Rapp

Bibliographic records and abstracts included in The Next Step section of this publication are the copyrighted material of UMI, and are used with permission.

The CQ Researcher (ISSN 1056-2036). Formerly Editorial Research Reports. Published weekly, except Jan. 2, May 29, July 3, Oct. 30, by Congressional Quarterly Inc., 1414 22nd St., N.W., Washington, D.C. 20037. Annual subscription rate for libraries, businesses and government is $340. Additional rates furnished upon request. Periodicals postage paid at Washington, D.C., and additional mailing offices. POSTMASTER: Send address changes to The CQ Researcher, 1414 22nd St., N.W., Washington, D.C. 20037.

COVER: STUDENTS PROTEST IN JAKARTA, INDONESIA, ON MAY 13, 1998, AFTER THE DEATHS OF SIX STUDENTS IN CLASHES WITH SECURITY POLICE. (REUTERS)

Democracy in Asia

BY KENNETH JOST

THE ISSUES

When political change came to the world's fourth most populous nation this spring, it arrived with stunning speed.

On May 20, an estimated 1 million Indonesians, mostly youths, rallied in the central square of Yogyakarta, a large university city on the south Javan coast. They listened to speaker after speaker call for the resignation of President Suharto, the country's autocratic, longtime leader.

"We expected that the struggle could linger on for several months before we could push Suharto," recalls Mohtar Mas'oed, an activist and senior lecturer at Gadjah Mada University, who attended the rally.

Less than 20 hours later, however, the former general went on television and abruptly ended his 32-year rule over the sprawling chain of islands.

"It was very surprising for us when he decided to step down by himself," Mas'oed says.

In truth, Suharto had little choice. He had amassed billions of dollars for himself, his family and his political cronies after taking power in a 1965 coup. But as he hunkered down in the presidential palace in Jakarta, the capital, members of parliament and his Cabinet deserted him, along with the leader of Indonesia's powerful military.

A turbulent year of economic collapse and political turmoil — climaxed by the killing of six students at Jakarta's Trisakti University eight days earlier — had left Suharto, at age 76, with virtually no support.

The killing of the students sealed Suharto's fate, says Nasir Tamimi, deputy chief editor of the newspaper *Republika*. "People were very angry," he recalls. Five hundred people were killed in rioting in Jakarta over the

next three days — forcing Suharto to cut short a trip to Egypt in a fruitless effort to calm the country and keep his office.

But William Liddle, a professor at Ohio State University and an expert on Indonesia, says that Suharto's demise was due more broadly to public discontent over the collapse of the economy in the wake of the financial crisis that swept Asia beginning last July. [1] The economic woes also heightened public resentment about the system of corruption and cronyism that had allowed Suharto and his family to amass a fortune estimated at $30 billion to $40 billion in a country with an annual state budget in 1997 of about $30 billion.

"It's the economy, stupid," Liddle says, recalling the slogan from President Clinton's 1992 campaign. Suharto "really did depend on that economic base. And there was the family favoritism: He just let [his children] do whatever they wanted."

Suharto yielded the presidency to his vice president, B.J. Habibie, a Western-educated aeronautical engineer, who removed some of Suharto's close associates from the Cabinet and promised to institute political reforms. But he also disappointed the country's unseasoned reform movement by announcing an election schedule that called for parliamentary balloting in mid-1999 and the election of a new president at the end of the year.

"Some observers think he's not going fast enough," says Donald Emmerson, a professor of political science at the University of Wisconsin in Madison who visited Indonesia in June. Even so, Emmerson says that Habibie is "comfortable with the ideology of democracy" and has been "extremely adroit" in managing a delicate political situation.

But Emmerson and other experts stress that Indonesia's path of political reform depends most on Habibie's ability to manage a dire economic situation. Poverty and unemployment have soared in the year since Indonesia's rupiah first plunged in value last July. Last year, the International Monetary Fund (IMF) put together a $43 billion bailout package only to see Suharto balk at its terms. Now the IMF estimates that Indonesia's gross national product will decline 10 percent this year — in stark contrast to the 6.6 percent average annual growth between 1985 and 1994.

Political reform in Indonesia would represent a major gain for advocates of democracy in Asia. But the uncertainty about the outcome matches the mixed assessments that human rights advocates in the United States make about the path of democratization in the region.

"There have been major gains in the past year, but I wouldn't say this is an overall trend," says Mike Jendrzejczyk, Washington director for the Asia division of Human Rights Watch.

Charles Graybow, an Asia specialist at the conservative-leaning human rights group Freedom House, sees both "bright spots" and "setbacks" in Asia

Democracy in Asia

Basic political rights and civil liberties are limited for most Asians, according to the human rights group Freedom House.

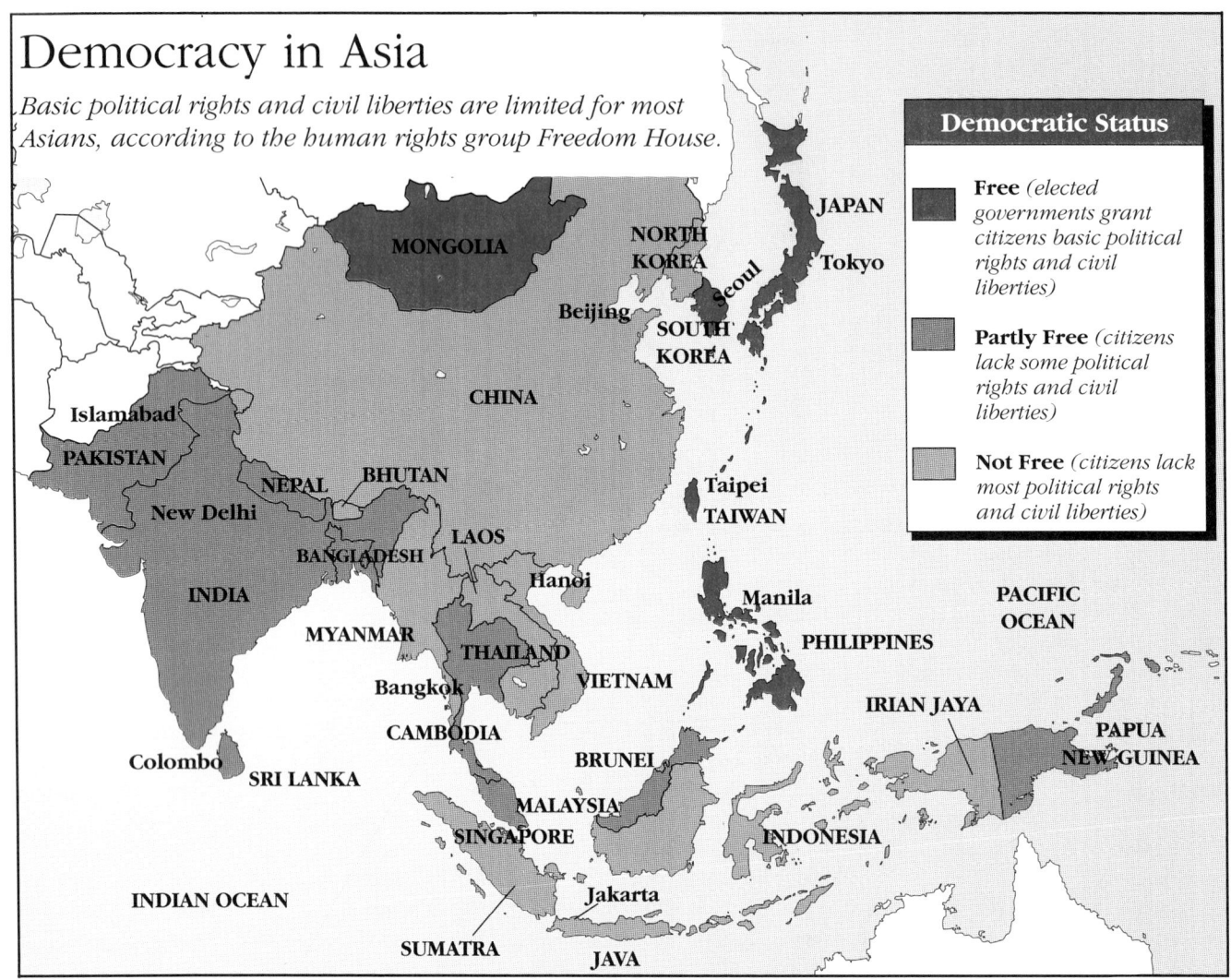

Democratic Status

Free *(elected governments grant citizens basic political rights and civil liberties)*

Partly Free *(citizens lack some political rights and civil liberties)*

Not Free *(citizens lack most political rights and civil liberties)*

over the past decade. Many countries with formal democratic processes, he says, still have "weak" institutions, such as political parties, labor unions, business groups and so forth.

On the plus side, advocates of democracy point to moves toward freer political systems in such countries as South Korea, Taiwan and Thailand in East and Southeast Asia and in Bangladesh, Nepal and Pakistan in South Asia. *(See chart, p. 630.)* But the military regime in Myanmar, the former Burma, remains intractable; the elections being held in Cambodia on July 26 are widely viewed as rigged by the country's dictator, Hun Sen; the "dominant party" democracies in such coun-

tries as Malaysia and Singapore show few signs of welcoming free political competition; and political change is expected to be slow, at best, in China, much less in the region's other communist countries. [2]

Still, one former Clinton administration official is optimistic about the long-term prospects for reforming Asia's undemocratic political systems. "Political liberalization is definitely spreading in Asia," says Catharin E. Dalpino, a guest scholar at the Brookings Institution who served as deputy assistant secretary of State for human rights in President Clinton's first administration.

On the other hand, Larry Diamond,

editor of the *Journal of Democracy* and a senior research fellow at the Hoover Institute at Stanford University, is less optimistic. "I see, frankly, a region where there's maybe growing popular aspirations but not a rising tide that would be likely to lead to new democratic transitions," says Diamond, who spent the last year as a visiting scholar at the Academia Sinica in Taiwan.

The goal of democracy — pushed by human rights groups and the United States — is not universally shared. Over the past two decades, a few Asian leaders and Western scholars have contended that democratic government may be incompatible with Asian culture and economic growth.

Human rights advocates scoff at this so-called "Asia-values" debate. "It's said that ordinary Asian citizens prefer order and stability and that they're not really interested in participating in politics," Graybow says. "But what we've seen is that when Asian citizens have the opportunity to participate, they do. The voter turnout, when citizens feel that there is a choice, tends to be very high."

Amartya Sen, an Indian economist, also debunks the claimed linkage between economic growth and closed political systems. "If you look merely to economic growth, there's nothing to indicate in general that authoritarian governments do better than non-authoritarian countries," says Sen, a former professor at Harvard University and now master of Trinity College, Cambridge University, in England.

As experts debate the impact of President Clinton's recent trip to China, and the chances for political reform in Indonesia, these are some of the questions being asked:

Does "Western-style" democracy conflict with "Asian values"?

Since gaining independence from British colonial rule, Malaysia and Singapore have had governments that were democratic in form but widely viewed as undemocratic in practice. Both countries have been ruled continuously by a single political party or coalition, and both governments place what the U.S. State Department calls in Singapore's case "formidable obstacles" in the path of political opponents. [3]

Despite the criticism — or perhaps because of it — the longtime leaders of the two countries have helped spark an international debate over the role of democracy in Asia. In speeches, writings and interviews, Malaysia's prime minister, Mahathir bin Mohamad, and Singapore's Lee Kuan Yew, who served as prime

minister for 31 years and since 1990 has continued to wield influence as "senior minister," have defended their countries' political system as better suited for "Asian values" than so-called Western-style democracy.

"Asian societies are unlike Western ones," Lee remarked in one widely noted interview. In Lee's view, Western societies exalt individual interests over the collective good while Asian culture looks more to the best interests of society as a whole. A free-for-all-democracy, he told *The Wall Street Journal*, would produce a "tinderbox kind of society" for Singapore. Malaysia's Mahathir has similarly warned against the risk of allowing "pedantic notions of democracy" to result in "an excess of freedom." "To Asians," Mahathir says, "democracy does not confer a license for citizens to go wild." [4]

Human rights advocates in and outside Asia insist that the supposed tension between democracy and Asian values reflects a misunderstanding of both concepts. Asian cultures are not as hostile to democracy as the theory assumes, they say, and Asian peoples have demonstrated in many countries that they are willing to work and sacrifice for popular self-government.

"It would be a mistake to think that in Asia people haven't been willing to sacrifice a great deal to have democracy established and guaranteed," Professor Sen says.

Sen says that ancient Hindu and Buddhist writers emphasized the importance of individual freedom and tolerance and that the common depiction of Confucianism as valuing administrative efficiency over individual freedom is oversimplified. In recent history, he says, Asians in many countries have demonstrated "a strong commitment" to democracy — despite resistance first from colonial powers and then from home-grown authoritarian governments.

Still, some political scientists do see a distinctive Asian model of

democratic government — a so-called dominant party system that minimizes political competition for the sake of social order and economic growth. In his influential book, *The Third Wave*, Harvard political scientist Samuel Huntington called it "democracy without turnover" and said it represented "an adaptation of Western democratic practices, to serve not Western values of competition and change, but Asian values of consensus and stability." [5]

Lucian Pye, a political scientist at the Massachusetts Institute of Technology, likens the current dominant-party systems in Asia to China's Nationalist Party in the early 20th century, which envisioned a "tutelary role" for itself in creating democratic government. Today, Pye says at least some of the dominant-party systems — including South Korea's and Taiwan's — deserve credit for promoting both economic growth and democratic development. [6]

Asia's economic growth during the past two decades, in fact, created a receptive climate for the "Asia-values" theory. Growth was particularly strong in countries that limited political rights, like Indonesia, Singapore, South Korea and Taiwan. With an economic crisis sweeping through Asia over the past year, however, advocates of democracy are arguing that semiauthoritarian governments actually threaten economic development.

"This has really spelled the death knell for the Asia-values argument," says Freedom House's Graybow, "because it shows that authoritarian governments may have brought some illusion of stability, but in the long run you need openness and accountability to have sustainable economic growth."

Singaporean leaders defend their political system as democratic and bristle at the recurrent criticisms from the State Department in its annual human rights report, and from human rights groups. "What Asians object to

Continued on p. 631

Democracy Eludes Many Nations in Asia

Country and Population	Type of Government	Political Conditions
East Asia		
China 1.2 billion	*Communist one-party*	*Chinese Communist Party "holds absolute power, has imprisoned nearly all active dissidents, uses the judiciary as a tool of state control and severely restricts freedoms of speech, press, association and religion."*
Japan 125.8 million	*Parliamentary democracy*	*Liberal Democratic Party government weakened by economic crisis, but no credible opposition party.*
Mongolia 2.3 million	*Presidential-parliamentary democracy*	*Formerly communist Mongolian People's Revolutionary Party recaptured presidency in June 1997 because of discontent with economic "shock therapy" program enacted by reformist coalition elected in 1996.*
North Korea 23.9 million	*Communist one-party*	*"Most tightly controlled country in world"; Kim Jong Il, son of the late longtime leader Kim Il Sung, formally assumed leadership in October 1997*
South Korea 45.3 million	*Presidential-parliamentary democracy*	*Election of opposition leader Kim Dae Jung as president in December 1997 caps decade-long political liberalization; National Security Law still used to curb contacts with North Korea.*
Taiwan 21.4 million	*Presidential-legislative democracy*	*Democratic transition consolidated by 1996 elections, but ruling Kuomintang Party maintains political advantages through control of media, business interests.*
South Asia		
Bangladesh 119.8 million	*Parliamentary democracy*	*June 1996 elections were freest in country's history, despite violence and irregularities; but parliamentary boycotts and other confrontational political tactics make normal legislative operations impossible.*
Bhutan 0.8 million	*Traditional monarchy*	*King wields absolute power; government arrested monks and civilians in 1997 to curb support for pro-democracy movement*
India 942 million	*Parliamentary democracy*	*Fairest elections in country's history in 1996 produced fractured parliament with no consensus on major issues; weak rule of law and social tensions contribute to widespread violations of civil liberties.*
Nepal 23.2 million	*Parliamentary democracy*	*Parliamentary government in place since end of absolute monarchy in 1991 is fragmented, but human rights conditions have improved*
Pakistan 133.5 million	*Presidential-parliamentary democracy*	*Nawaz Sharif led Pakistan Muslim League to victory in February 1997 election, then consolidated power in showdown in December with president, supreme court; democratic institutions weak, corruption widespread.*
Sri Lanka 18.7 million	*Presidential-parliamentary democracy*	*Political institutions "severely tested" by civil war, ethnic tensions, partisan violence; government put forth proposal in 1997 to end ongoing civil war with Tamil separatists.*
Southeast Asia		
Brunei 0.3 million	*Traditional monarchy*	*Sultan serves as prime minister and, along with inner circle of relatives, holds "absolute power."*
Cambodia 10.9 million	*Monarchy, constituent assembly*	*Co-premier Hun Sen regained total power after 1997 coup; "bleak" prospects for fair vote in 1998 elections*
Indonesia 207.4 million	*Dominant party (military-dominated)*	*"Turbulent year" in 1997 included violent parliamentary election campaign, crackdown on dissidents and student leaders, ethnic and sectarian violence due to frustration over corruption, and financial crisis; [President Suharto was forced out of office in 1998 and was replaced by Vice President B.J. Habibie].*

Country and Population	Type of Government	Political Conditions
Laos 5 million	*Communist one-party*	*One-party state controlled by Lao People's Revolutionary Party; some elements of state control relaxed in recent years.*
Malaysia 20.6 million	*Dominant party*	*Government has "significant control" over media, uses security laws to limit freedom of expression and chill political activity; judiciary subject to government influence in sensitive cases.*
Myanmar 46 million	*Military*	*"Effectively a garrison state ruled by one of the most repressive military regimes in the world."*
Papua New Guinea 4.3 million	*Parliamentary democracy*	*Elections marred by irregularities and violence; democratic institutions tested by fiscal pressures, corruption and challenge of nation-building in diverse country.*
Philippines 72 million	*Presidential-legislative democracy*	*Free elections marred by vote-buying and fraud; official corruption rampant; populist Vice President Joseph Estrada was front-runner in presidential race [elected, May 1998]*
Singapore 3 million	*Dominant party*	*Authoritarian People's Action Party crushed opposition in January 1997 election; government chills dissent through civil defamation suits, security laws and other harassment of opponents and journalists.*
Thailand 60.7 million	*Parliamentary democracy (military-influenced)*	*New constitution adopted in September 1997 aimed at rooting out corruption and establishing greater accountability in wake of public protests over economic crisis; new prime minister in office since November heads eight-party coalition.*
Vietnam 76.6 million	*Communist one-party*	*Vietnamese Communist Party rules nation as Leninist state with "tight control of all political, economic, religious and social affairs"*

Source: Freedom in the World: the Annual Survey of Political Rights and Civil Liberties, 1997-98, *Freedom House; updates from news accounts are bracketed*

Continued from p. 629
is U.S. arrogance and self-righteousness," says Tommy Koh, an ambassador-at-large in Singapore's Ministry of Foreign Affairs and executive director of the Asia-Europe Foundation.

Sen acknowledges that the Asia-values debate reflects anti-Western, anti-imperialist feelings among some Asians. "There was a tendency," he says, "to reject your rule, reject your authority and reject your values, too." But he says the persistent efforts by democracy movements throughout Asia show that democracy has universal appeal.

"The fact that people continue to agitate for political rights and individual freedom indicates that people do have an intrinsic interest in freedom without regard to economic development," Sen says. "That applies as much to Asia as to anywhere else."

Should the United States do more to encourage democracy in Asian countries?

When Secretary of State Madeleine K. Albright attended last year's meeting of the Association of Southeast Asian Nations (ASEAN), she urged Asian leaders to join the United States in pressuring Myanmar's military government to allow political reforms. "We must insist that we work together to promote conditions that will lead toward true democracy," Albright told the nine-nation group on July 27.

The response was polite but noncommittal. "It is for ASEAN to decide what we will do," said Malaysia's foreign minister, Abdullah Ahmad Badawi, "and we will bear in mind the views of Ms. Albright and others." [7]

The tepid reaction to the call for pressuring an evidently authoritarian regime in a relatively small country gives one measure of the difficulties the United States faces in trying to encourage democratization in Asia. The United States' professed commitment to democratic change is simply not shared by countries in the region — not by the communist regimes of China, North Korea and Vietnam; not by countries that themselves have less than completely democratic political systems; and not even by the big democracy that is the United States' major ally in the region, Japan. [8]

Meanwhile, human rights advocates and Republican lawmakers give the Clinton administration no more than middling grades for its efforts to promote democracy in the region. The administration, in the view of these critics, was slow and half-hearted in adopting economic sanc-

Indonesia: A Country Profile

• INDONESIA

At a Glance

- **Area:** 735,510 sq. mi.
- **Population:** 207.4 million
- **Religion:** *86.9% Muslim, 9.6% Christian, 1.9% Hindu, 1% Buddhist, 0.6% traditional*
- **Major Ethnic Groups:** *Javanese (45%), Sudanese (14%), Madurese (8%), Coastal Malay (8%), Chinese (3%)*
- **Literacy Rate:** *83.8% (1995)*
- **Life Expectancy:** *62.7 years*
- **Labor Force:** *81,446 million*

With the exception of Jendrzejczyk, most observers say the U.S. sanctions on Myanmar — which no U.S. allies have supported — are having little, if any, effect. "We either have to persuade our European allies to go along and isolate the Burmese regime," Diamond says, "or else we need to pursue other means of pressuring for change in Burma."

The United States can take some credit for helping bring democracy to Asian countries in the past. The U.S. put the Philippines on a slow path toward self-government after seizing the islands as a colony from Spain at the turn of the century. It introduced democracy into occupied Japan after World War II and pressured European powers to yield up their colonies — for example, in Indonesia.

Today, however, the impetus for democratization comes from Asian peoples themselves. "It's inaccurate to imply that we jump-started any of these transitions," Dalpino says. "The Asians jump-started them themselves, which is the way it ought to be."

tions against the Myanmar regime, has given little emphasis to human rights in other countries and has simply abandoned any pretense of pressuring China to grant political and human rights to its 1.2 billion people.

"The administration's track record in Asia on human rights and democracy is very mixed," says Jendrzejczyk of Human Rights Watch. "In some ways, the administration has positioned itself to keep human rights and democracy issues very much in the background while focusing very much on economic and security concerns."

Clinton's policy of "engagement" with China has drawn criticism from human rights groups on the left and the right. "The administration hasn't made a powerful push for the rule of law in China," Graybow says. "It's

possible to promote human rights and commercial interests at the same time," he says.

Elsewhere in the region, the administration manages to draw flak alternately for being too timid in pushing human rights issues or for being too assertive. Jendrzejczyk, for example, criticizes the administration's belated decision to impose economic sanctions on Myanmar. "They waited until the very last minute when pressure from Congress became almost unbearable," he says.

Some Indonesia experts, however, say Albright made a mistake by publicly calling on Suharto to step down prior to his resignation. "Indonesians are very nationalistic," Liddle says. "It's a very delicate situation."

In any event, the U.S. influence on events in Asia is easy to exaggerate.

Is Indonesia on the road to a successful transition to democracy?

On May 23, in his first speech to Indonesians after assuming the presidency, Habibie sent ambivalent signals about his commitment to political change by promising to undertake "gradual and constitutional reforms." [9] Habibie's background was itself ambivalent. He was an engineer who had attended school and worked in Europe but also advanced politically and prospered financially under Suharto.

Since taking office, Habibie has instituted some significant changes — for example, permitting new political parties and freeing some political prisoners. But Indonesians and outside observers are divided about Habibie's commitment to thoroughgoing changes — and about his own prospects for holding on to power.

"He is now perceived as going with the reformists," Tamimi says. "He has established a style where a president is just like any other citizen."

But Muhammed Hikam, a political scientist at the Indonesian Institute of Sciences, is less impressed. "Unfortunately, Habibie can do only so much," Hikam remarked during a visit to the United States last month with other members of the International NGO [non-governmental organizations] Forum on Indonesian Development.

Hikam says Habibie and his family are still linked to the corruption and favoritism of the Suharto regime. "He is not talking about reform within himself," Hikam says, "so he's still lacking moral credibility."

U.S. experts on Indonesia have similarly mixed views about Habibie. Emmerson calls him "extremely cosmopolitan" and "able to bridge gaps." Liddle is more critical. "He is a very arrogant person," he says.

Even so, Liddle credits Habibie with a real commitment to reform. "I think he's serious," Liddle says, "because without it he simply can't govern. He has to get some kind of political legitimacy."

The prospects for change are also clouded by weaknesses within Indonesia's reform movement, which has only limited political experience and no unifying platform or individual leader. "The problem of the

reform movement is basically structural," Hikam says. "It has had no real political platform that is shared by all reform groups in Indonesia, including the students."

Liddle also fears that pro-democracy sentiment might fade if the government is unable to right the economy and restore political order. "These people are not used to the typical to-and-froing of democracy," he says. "If it looks to most of the middle class that the new government is not able to control the forces erupting in society, people will turn to the military very quickly again."

Other observers fear the military may unilaterally intervene to slow or prevent political changes. "The fragmented pro-reform forces and the economic disaster will bring new temptation for the military to step in," says Goenawan Mohamad, an editor of the pro-democracy newspaper *Tempo*.

For his part, though, Tamimia believes both the government and pro-democracy groups are on a path toward reform. "People and the government are starting to talk with each other," he says. "That didn't happen for 40 years."

As for Habibie, the economy may hold the key to his political fortunes. "The economy is bad and unlikely to get better," Emmerson says. "Whoever is president is likely to suffer, and that is going to hurt Habibie."

On the other hand, Tamimi says, "If Habibie's successful in making democracy a reality, and if he's successful in establishing the economic situation, people will follow him."

Despite the problems and uncertainties, observers and advocates in Indonesia and the United States voice a measure of cautious optimism about the prospects for democracy there.

"Now people are starting to make a program, to talk with each other," Tamimi says. "It will take time, but I think we are on the right track."

"There's a golden moment of opportunity here," Liddle says. "Indonesia could create a democracy here if it just seizes the moment." ∎

BACKGROUND

East Meets West

Asians had relatively little experience with democracy before the arrival of European explorers, traders and colonizers in the 15th century. Asian societies — from sophisticated China and Japan to the less developed kingdoms and sultanates of the Indian subcontinent, the Malay Peninsula and the East Indies — were mostly hierarchically organized and governed. Asia has been late to develop the kind of representative assemblies, popular elections and written constitutions that comprise what is sometimes called "Western-style" democracy.

Hierarchical tendencies were reinforced by the region's dominant religions: Buddhism and Hinduism, both of which predated Christianity, and Islam, which spread through much of Asia beginning in the seventh century. Some scholars find democratic strains in Buddhism and Hinduism by focusing on the rulers' obligation in both religions to govern wisely and with the consent of his subjects. But historically, both Buddhism and Hinduism have been associated with elitist, authoritarian ruling systems. Similarly, Confucianism, the Chinese school of political thought that dates from the sixth century before Christ, contains some germs of democratic theory — for example, the right of the people to depose an unjust ruler. In practice, however, it, too, came to be associated with authoritarian rulers. [10]

The European powers also did little to prepare their Asian colonies for self-government until the very end of the colonial period. Spanish and Portuguese sailors were the first Europeans to explore the region, followed by Dutch traders in the 17th century, the British in the 18th and the French in the 19th. Developing trade was the first and most important objective; ruling colonies was an afterthought and nation-building did not make the agenda until the 20th century, if then. [11]

Of the major European colonies, only India had begun to take shape as a nation by 1900. France ruled what is now Vietnam as two disconnected colonies: Tonkin in the north, Cochin-China in the south. Britain had "organized" the Malay Peninsula into federated states, unfederated states and the "Straits Settlements." The Dutch East Indies was a geographic location, not a political entity. The 20th century saw some moves toward education and self-government in Asia — so-called enlightened policies — but they were typically limited. In Indonesia, for example, only 230 native-born Indonesians had college educations in 1942. [12]

Asia's largest countries that escaped colonization — China and Japan — did make some early moves toward democracy. In 1890 Japan adopted a constitution modeled on the Prussian charter, with a bicameral Diet including an elected lower house and a Cabinet of advisers to make decisions to be issued in the emperor's name. Competitive political parties developed by the 1920s, and the prime minister and Cabinet became responsible to the Diet. But in the 1930s the military took power, repressed democratic processes and led the nation into war first in China and then throughout East Asia.

In China, Western-trained Sun Yat-sen led a revolutionary movement that sought to unify China under a federal republic. But democratic impulses proved weaker than warlordism and communism. The Nationalist Party — the Kuomintang or KMT — emerged as the leading power in the elections of 1912 but came to be dominated by local warlords more interested in protecting their power bases than in establishing democracy. The Chinese Communist Party split from the KMT in the 1920s, joined in unsteady alliance during the war with Japan but then gained power after a four-year civil war following the Japanese surrender in 1945.

It was the Japanese who ousted the European powers from most of their Asian colonies, embarrassing the white rulers with their easy conquests of the East Indies, Indochina and the British-ruled territories, including the supposedly impregnable Fortress Singapore. The Japanese occupiers encouraged anti-imperialist and pan-Asian sentiment even while subjugating the native peoples. At war's end, the colonial rulers expected to return. As author John Keay writes, however, the colonies were "reoccupied" but "never retaken." [13]

Paths of Independence

Nationalist movements gained strength in Asia before and during World War II and immediately challenged the European powers' attempt to return after the war's end. Over the next two decades, the British, Dutch and French were ousted and independence won in India (1947), Burma (1948), Vietnam (1954) and Malaya (1957, renamed Malaysia in 1963). Meanwhile, the United States had imposed a U.S.-style constitution on the defeated Japanese. Democratic government took hold in Japan, but elsewhere in Asia ethnic, religious, economic and ideological divisions stunted the growth of democracy and helped bring authoritarian regimes to power. [14]

India's democratic movement began with the formation of the National Congress Party in 1875, which first advocated self-government, then independence from Britain. The movement came to be led by Mohandas K. Gandhi, an Indian lawyer whose masterful political organizing and strategy of civil disobedience forced Britain to cede independence after the end of World War II. The movement toward independence, however, unleashed violence between the majority Hindus and minority Muslims, resulting in partition and the establishment of Pakistan as a Muslim homeland. Burma, ruled by Britain as part of India, had been moving toward separation before the war and gained its own independence in 1948.

In Indonesia, a nationalist movement also had been forming under Sukarno, who founded the Indonesian National Party (PNI). He encouraged strikes and non-cooperation with Dutch authorities and was imprisoned or exiled for most of the 1930s. During the war, he collaborated with the Japanese while other nationalists opposed the occupiers. As the war was ending, Sukarno and his colleagues declared Indonesia's independence. [15]

During four years of fighting and diplomatic maneuvering, the Dutch sought to preserve their rule by decentralizing power through a federal structure. The nationalists rejected the idea and fought a guerrilla war that, combined with diplomatic pressure from the United States and the United Nations, forced the Dutch to yield. Queen Juliana gave her formal assent to independence in December 1949. The new constitution called for a parliamentary democracy, with the first post-independence national elections to be held in 1955. In defiance of nationalist sentiments, the Dutch remained on the eastern half of New Guinea while Portugal still ruled the eastern half of the smaller island of Timor.

In Indochina, the nationalist movement was led by Ho Chi Minh, who (under the name Nguyen Ai Quoc) had presided over the founding meeting of the

Continued on p. 636

Chronology

Before 1945

Asia has limited experience with democratic forms before colonialism; European powers do little to prepare their colonies for self-government.

1890
Japan establishes democratic constitution, the first in Asia.

1935
Britain provides limited self-government for India, but move does not satisfy independence movement.

●

1945-1965

Era of European colonialism ends; most of the newly independent nations adopt some form of parliamentary democracy, but many come to be dominated by one party or yield to military rule.

1947
Japan adopts U.S.-style constitution, providing for parliamentary democracy under constitutional monarch; India gains independence from Britain; Pakistan is established as Muslim homeland.

1949
Indonesia gains independence from the Netherlands; Communists come to power in China.

1954
France is ousted from Indo-China; Vietnam is partitioned between communist and pro-West governments.

1963
Malaysian Federation is established as independent nation, ending British colonial era in Southeast Asia; Singapore is ousted from federation two years later.

●

1965-1989

U.S. fights protracted war in Vietnam but fails to prevent communist victory; Cold War politics shapes U.S. ties with authoritarian regime.

1965
Sukarno is ousted in Indonesia; Suharto comes to power.

1979
U.S. recognizes People's Republic of China, downgrades relations with Taiwan.

1986
Philippines President Ferdinand E. Marcos ousted, succeeded by human rights activist Corazon Aquino.

1989
Chinese military suppresses pro-democracy rally at Tiananmen Square, killing hundreds.

●

1990s

With end of Cold War, democratization gains prominence in U.S. diplomatic agenda; democracy activists step up efforts in Asia, with uneven results.

1990
Burmese military government nullifies election won by National League for Democracy.

1991
Burmese pro-democracy leader Aung San Suu Kyi awarded Nobel Peace Prize; military coup in Thailand; king forces coup leader to resign in 1992, paving way for return of democracy.

1993
Cambodia holds first election under 1991 Paris peace agreement, resulting in coalition government; Japan's Liberal Democratic Party yields power after losing parliamentary election.

1995
U.S. and Vietnam re-establish diplomatic relations; Malaysia's ruling coalition wins electoral landslide, with opposition party reduced to nine seats in parliament.

1996
Congress Party defeated at polls in India, but Hindu nationalist party falls short of majority; Taiwan holds first popular election for president; Bishop Carlos Belo and Jose Ramos-Horta, activists for East Timorese self-determination, are awarded Nobel Peace Prize.

1997
Singaporean opposition parties reduced to two seats after parliamentary elections; Hong Kong reverts to China; opposition leader Kim Dae Jung elected president of South Korea.

1998
Hindu nationalist party again leads coalition government, but wins only one-fourth of seats in Indian parliament; Suharto is ousted in Indonesia; his successor as president, B.J. Habibie, promises reforms, elections in 1999; President Clinton visits China; Cambodian elections, scheduled for July 26, are widely criticized as weighted in government's favor.

Indonesia's Year of Living Turbulently

May 1997 Ruling Golkar party wins sixth consecutive victory in parliamentary elections on May 29; more than 200 people die in riots before balloting.

July 1997 Rupiah closes down 5 percent on July 21 (about 2,500 to the dollar) in the wake of the July 2 devaluation of the Thai bhat.

October 1997 International Monetary Fund (IMF) announces three-year, $33 billion loan package to stabilize Indonesia's economy; accord follows President Suharto's agreement to institute reforms in banking and elsewhere.

January 1998 Rupiah plunges to more than 9,000 to the dollar, prompting panic-buying for food and staples; Suharto, in new accord with IMF, promises Jan. 15 to end system of patronage favoring his children and friends.

Suharto

March 1998 IMF delays first $3 billion installment of aid package on March 6 as Suharto balks at reforms; Suharto re-elected president March 11 by People's Consultative Assembly; after swearing-in, as many as 10,000 students protest at Gadjah Mada University in Yogyakarta, burning an effigy of the president.

May 1-10, 1998 Suharto is quoted May 1 as ruling out reform before end of five-year term in 2003; student protests held throughout Indonesia next day; rioting follows on May 5 as fuel and energy prices rise after government cuts subsidies.

May 11-20, 1998 Six students killed May 12 after police open fire on protesters at Jakarta's Trisakti University; 500 people die in rioting over next three days concentrated in Jakarta's wealthy ethnic Chinese neighborhoods; Suharto, after returning from Egypt May 15, announces May 19 he will hold new elections and not run for president again; behind the scenes, military chief Gen. Wiranto pressures Suharto to step down immediately.

May 21-31, 1998 Suharto announces immediate resignation May 21; Vice President B.J. Habibie is sworn in as successor; Gen. Wiranto removes Suharto's son-in-law from military command May 22; Habibie drops key Suharto associates in new cabinet named May 23 and promises "gradual and constitutional reforms," but says on May 25 that elections may not be held before mid-1999.

Habibie

June 1998 IMF commits additional $4-$6 billion to aid package June 24; Habibie announces five-year action plan on human rights on June 25; the next day he proposes to release East Timorese rebel leader Jose Xanana Gusamo in exchange for recognition of Indonesian sovereignty; Gusamo says no deal.

July 1998 National Golkar party conference July 9-11 elects Habibie-backed candidate Akbar Tanjung as party leader in secret ballot; rupiah drops to more than 14,000 to the dollar.

Continued from p. 634

Vietnamese Communist Party in Hong Kong in 1930. The French responded to a campaign of hunger marches and commandeering of local estates with an air and ground offensive; many party activists were arrested, and Ho himself was later held by British authorities in Hong Kong. He was reported to have died in detention, but in fact escaped, eventually to Moscow, and returned to lead the nationalist movement during World War II. The French, like the Dutch, had expected to resume their colonial rule, but — despite fitful U.S. support — left Indochina after the 1954 defeat at Dien Bien Phu. Two decades later, Vietnam was unified under communist rule after the U.S. failed in its efforts to preserve a pro-American regime in the south.

The nationalist movement was weaker in what became Malaysia, in part because of the mix of native Malays and ethnic Chinese Malayans. Britain also proved more adroit in countering a communist-dominated insurgency with a mixture of military and political responses. With the insurgency deemed defeated, Britain granted independence to Malaya in 1957 while continuing to hold Singapore and its possessions on the island of Borneo: the sultanates of Sabah and Sarawak. Singapore, with its majority-Chinese population, was added to what became the Malaysian Federation in 1963 — balanced by the addition of the predominantly Malay populations of Sabah and Sarawak. But the Malay-dominated government ousted Singapore two years later out of concern that its Chinese population would threaten the ethnic Malays' political control.

Asian-Style 'Democracy'

Democratic forms, including regular elections and representative assemblies, took hold in most of the non-communist Asian countries after the colonial period ended. But from India to Japan and in most of the smaller countries in between, the political systems were dominated by single parties. Political rights were generally protected in some of the countries, including India and Japan, but less so in many others, including Indonesia, Malaysia, Singapore, South Korea and Taiwan.

Indonesia, according to Huntington, was the most authoritarian of these supposedly democratic countries. [16] The only free election in the nation's history, in 1955, gave four parties roughly comparable power in the parliament: Nationalists, Communists and two Muslim parties. Four years later, Sukarno, who served in the largely ceremonial role of president, joined in a coup with the military, which also chafed under the political fragmentation and its own limited role. The coup returned Indonesia to the strong presidential system of the short-lived 1945 constitution. "Guided democracy," Sukarno called his new system. "Far more guided than democratic," Emmerson says.

Sukarno, according to Liddle, sought to reduce his dependence on the military by aligning himself domestically with the communists as he also took on a leading role internationally as spokesman for the non-aligned nations. Communist-instigated unrest climaxed in the assassination of six Indonesian generals in 1965, most likely by leftist officers. The coup enabled Maj. Gen. Suharto to assume control of the military and lead a crackdown on the communists, depicted later by the film "The Year of Living Dangerously."

Suharto began his 32-year rule by restating the five principles that Sukarno had proclaimed in 1945 — monotheism, humanitarianism, unity, democracy and justice. He also eventually reduced the number of recognized parties to just three: the governing Golkar party and two opposition parties. Suharto was assured of re-election by the People's Consultative Assembly, since he effectively controlled 500 of its 1,000 seats. And the army buttressed Suharto's power by suppressing any signs of political opposition.

Elsewhere in East and Southeast Asia, one-party rule proved almost as durable despite somewhat greater political freedom. In Malaysia, the ruling National Front has dominated every election since 1971. In Singapore, Lee's People's Action Party has held even greater sway.

Meanwhile, South Korea and Taiwan also were effectively ruled by single parties, thanks in part to periods of martial law justified by the threats posed by their communist neighbors, North Korea and mainland China. In Thailand, a period of relative democracy in the 1970s produced a degree of political disorder that a military-dominated government sought to control in the 1980s with authoritarian measures. In neighboring Burma, on the other hand, the military strongman Gen. Ne Win crafted a new constitution in 1974 that made his Burma Socialist Program Party the only recognized party.

Of the former European colonies, India was the most auspicious in its early years of democracy. Its first prime minister, Jawaharal Nehru, an ally of Gandhi's in the independence struggle, also proved skillful in the practical politics of democracy. But his daughter, Indira Gandhi, who succeeded to the post in 1966, stirred harsh criticism when she assumed virtually dictatorial powers from 1975 to 1977 and was widely blamed for politicizing the judiciary and civil service and permitting corruption to flourish at the local level. Her son, Rajiv, showed even less political talent in his years as prime minister after his mother's assassination in 1984. Throughout, however, India continued to hold regular national elections, and the Congress Party peacefully yielded power when it failed to maintain its majority position in 1977 and 1989.

'People's Power'?

Over time, Asia's authoritarian and semiauthoritarian governments bred domestic pro-democracy and human rights movements. In some countries they gained sufficient strength to challenge the regimes at the polls; elsewhere, they had to focus on mass protests, court challenges and pleas for international support. Meanwhile, the collapse of the Soviet Union and the end of the Cold War freed both the United States government and conservative U.S.-based groups to give greater emphasis to human rights and democracy as a diplomatic and political goal abroad.

The first demonstration of the potential impact of these Asian pro-democracy movements came in the Philippines, where longtime President Ferdinand E. Marcos was forced from office in 1986. Marcos, elected in 1965, imposed martial law in 1971 and ruled with an iron hand for the next 15 years. The assassination of opposition leader Benigno Aquino in 1982 helped galvanize the "People's Power Movement," which rallied behind his widow, Corazon. By 1985, when Marcos had all but lost his grip on power, President Ronald Reagan passed the word that there would be no U.S. intervention for its longtime ally. Marcos went into exile in Hawaii, and Corazon Aquino was installed as president and later elected in her own right. [17]

Events in the Philippines may have inspired challenges to the military regime in Burma, too, but the effort backfired. The military in 1988 installed a new ruling body, the State Law and Order Restoration Council, which proceeded simultaneously to suppress popular dissent and set elections for 1990. When the opposition National League for Democracy emerged as the winner — despite the house arrest of its leader, Nobel Peace Prize-winner Aung San Suu Kyi — the government ignored the results. [18]

Other military-dominated regimes

Indonesia's Troubled Rule Over East Timor

Indonesia invaded and then annexed East Timor 22 years ago to eliminate a potential threat to its stability. Instead, Indonesia's often violent rule over the tiny former Portuguese colony fueled an independence movement and eventually became a major diplomatic embarrassment for President Suharto.

Now, with Suharto's resignation, some observers see the possibility of resolving the issue. "The political transition in Indonesia has opened up the political middle ground," says Donald Emmerson, a political scientist at the University of Wisconsin in Madison.

Indonesia's new president, B. J. Habibie, is willing to discuss some measure of autonomy for East Timor, whose 600,000 residents occupy the eastern half of an island about the size of Maryland.

East Timorese independence advocate Jose Ramos-Horta, who shared the 1996 Nobel Peace Prize, has suggested that a referendum on East Timor's status could be held not immediately — as the movement has demanded — but five years from now.

Emmerson, a longtime student of Indonesian politics, thinks that a delayed vote offers something to both sides in the dispute. "The independence movement is realizing that it makes no sense politically to insist on a referendum tomorrow," he says. As for the Indonesian government, he continues, "the longer the time before the referendum, the more time Indonesia has to build a sense among the East Timorese that they belong in Indonesia."

The current-day dispute is a legacy of arbitrary boundaries drawn by European colonial powers centuries ago.[1] Portugal and the Dutch East India Trading Company established trading posts on opposite ends of the island, which lies near the coast of Australia at the southern end of the major chain of Indonesian islands.

The Indonesian national revolution after World War II brought the Dutch-ruled western half of the island into the new nation, but Portugal retained control of its colony — which, unlike Muslim-dominated Indonesia, was predominantly Roman Catholic. Portugal began to decolonize only decades later, in the 1970s, when a long-ruling dictatorship fell to a socialist-led opposition.

By then, the East Timorese people were themselves divided between three forces: an avowedly leftist independence movement, Fretilin (the Revolutionary Front for Independence of East Timor); the more elitist Timorese Democratic Union (UDT), which favored gradual independence and some continuing ties to Portugal; and a group favoring incorporation within Indonesia: the Timorese Popular Democratic Association, known by the acronym Apodeti.

Fretilin, with the largest amount of support, stirred fears in Jakarta and in Washington of a communist stronghold in the Indonesian archipelago. When a civil war broke out in August 1975, Portugal sided with Fretilin, Indonesia with Apodeti. On Dec. 7, Indonesia invaded East Timor. Historian M.C. Ricklefs says the invasion — supported by the U.S. — may have resulted in as many as 60,000 civilian casualties.

Indonesia formally annexed East Timor in July 1976, as Fretilin retreated to the hills. William Liddle, a political scientist at Ohio State University who visited East Timor in January, says the Suharto government brought "a lot of material progress" to the island — roads, schools, health centers and so forth. But the military presence remained — and continued to exact a heavy toll in deaths and injuries. "There was an awful lot of random, wanton killing," Liddle says.

In the worst such incident, Indonesian troops killed up to 200 East Timorese at the funeral of a separatist sympathizer in 1991. Subsequently, Fretilin rebel leader Xanana Gusma was sentenced to 20 years in prison.

Awarding the Nobel Peace Prize to Ramos-Horta and Bishop Carlos Belo in 1996 helped gain international support for East Timor. U.S. policy, however, continued to recognize East Timor as part of Indonesia.

Liddle thinks Habibie's offer to talk about autonomy may only embolden the independence movement. Emmerson, however, thinks the East Timorese may be cautioned by the current economic crisis in Indonesia and the region.

The political calculations in Jakarta are also multisided. Resolving the issue may appeal to Habibie, Emmerson says, but he also has bigger political problems.

Catharin E. Dalpino, former deputy assistant secretary of State for human rights, notes that any change in East Timor could encourage anti-Jakarta sentiment in other areas, notably Irian Jaya. Indonesia incorporated Irian Jaya, which occupies the western half of the former New Guinea, in 1969 after administering the former Dutch colony for the United Nations for seven years.

For now, Dalpino thinks Habibie's willingness will encourage more pro-independence demonstrations on East Timor. "It will kick up more dust," she says. But, she adds, "there's probably more hope for a mid-term to long-term solution."

---

[1] For background, see M.C. Ricklefs, *A History of Modern Indonesia since c. 1300* (2d ed., 1993); *The Washington Post*, July 10, 1998, p. A27.

in East Asia, however, did yield to domestic pressure or outside events during the 1980s and '90s.

In South Korea, the government, on the eve of hosting the Olympic Games, agreed to a new constitution and popular elections in 1988; the balloting left the governing Democratic Justice Party in shaky control and boosted the opposition Party for Peace and Democracy. Today, the longtime opposition leader Kim Dae Jung — imprisoned or exiled for years by the military government — serves as the country's president after a narrow election victory in December.

Taiwan began a decade-long path toward democracy in 1986 when its president, Chiang Ching-kuo decided to lift martial law, ease press censorship and permit political parties. After his death in 1988, constitutional reforms were carried forward by his successor, Lee Teng-hui, who went on to win Taiwan's first popular election for president in 1996.

In Thailand, the military upset a fragile balance between democracy and authoritarianism by seizing power from the elected government in 1991. After parties aligned with the military won a narrow victory in elections in March 1992, the leader of the coup, Gen. Suchinda Krapayoon, tried to put the prime minister's post under military control. Public protests followed, and eventually King Bhumibol Adulyadej forced Suchinda's resignation and a new beginning of democratization.

Suharto's Final Days

There were few signs of democratization in Indonesia, however, as late as last year. Suharto's hold on power appeared secure, thanks to a rigged electoral system, the military's support and impressive economic growth. Leading up to the May 1997 parliamentary election, Suharto had engineered the ouster of the head of the Indonesian Democratic Party (PDI) and banned any discussion of a possible alliance with the other recognized party, the Muslim United Development Party. The result: The governing Golkar political bloc secured its largest majority ever — about 73 percent of the vote. [19]

When the rupiah fell last July, however, Asia's economic crisis caught up with Indonesia — and Suharto. The IMF eventually pledged up to $43 billion in bailout aid but insisted on stringent fiscal conditions that included eliminating subsidies on critical consumer goods. When the rupiah fell further in January, Indonesians took to the streets to protest rising prices; by spring, pro-democracy students were calling for Suharto's ouster.

Suharto might have survived, nonetheless, but for the deaths of six students at Jakarta's Trisakti University on May 12. The shootings fueled more unrest and destroyed any remnant of Suharto's credibility with key military and political leaders. Publicly, armed forces chief Gen. Wiranto criticized the calls for Suharto's resignation, but privately he was scripting his removal. Suharto on May 19 promised to hold new elections and step down at some unspecified future date. But two days later, deserted by the military and by his Cabinet, Suharto announced his resignation on television "as of the reading of this statement." He named Habibie as his successor. [20] ∎

CURRENT SITUATION

Building Democracy

Four days after taking office, Habibie announced a "national action plan" on human rights. The plan called for the government to ratify international human rights accords, publicize human rights policies and give "top priority" to implementing human rights provisions.

The initiative was "very big news" to journalist Tamimi, who attended the session. "I'm satisfied because he has signed all these international agreements on human rights," Tamimi says. "So now Indonesia has joined the rest of the world."

But in the two months since Habibie's accession, both the government and its opponents have found that the path to political change is treacherous.

Habibie has drawn criticism both within and without Indonesia for the new election schedule. "The longer you have Habibie in power without democracy, the Indonesian crisis will be worse and worse," says political scientist Hikam.

"International confidence will be increased by holding an election for the Indonesian people to choose both a president and a representative assembly — and much sooner than the schedule" outlined by Habibie, says Human Rights Watch's Jendrzejczyk.

For its part, the reform movement appears unprepared to offer the country a unified platform or a strong alternative to Habibie. "It's been 40 days now, and we still don't know what to do with this," Mas'oed, the Gadjah Mada lecturer and activist, remarked recently.

Habibie scored a significant political victory earlier this month with the election of his executive secretary, Akbar Tanjung, to head the ruling Golkar party. Akbar was elected by secret ballot, 17-10, at the end of the party's special three-day conference July 9-11 in Jakarta; he defeated a Suharto-backed candidate, Edy Sudrajat, a former armed services chief. After winning, Akbar told reporters he would reform Golkar and "rid it of nepotism, corruption, and collusion." [21]

Tamimi says the party gathering was a "big victory for democracy" because of the first-ever direct election of the chairman. He also believes that Akbar himself rather than Habibie may prove to be the long-run winner from the meeting. "It pushes him toward being a prominent political figure," Tamimi says. "If Indonesia is becoming a real democracy, he will be in the best position to put himself forward as a candidate for president."

Habibie continues to gain generally positive reviews from Indonesian and U.S. observers. "Habibie has without a doubt surprised his critics," Emmerson said after the Golkar meeting. Tamimi, however, is more cautious about Akbar. "He was a part of the Suharto system," Tamimi says. Asked if he doubts Akbar's commitment to reform, Tamimi pauses before answering: "We should give him the benefit of the doubt."

Among the government's opponents, the prevailing picture is disarray. More than 30 political parties had registered as of mid-July, stirring fears of electoral fragmentation. Tamimi, however, expects the opponents to sort themselves out by next year's elections. He sees five major opposition parties: two predominantly Muslim parties, one modernist, the other traditional; a nationalist party; a party for Christians and other religious minorities; and a social democratic party. None of the parties is likely to win a majority, Tamimi says, and the opponents could gain enough strength to put together a coalition to deny Golkar a role in a new government.

Meanwhile, the economy remains the dominant issue for Habibie. In his speech to Golkar, Habibie conceded that the government's economic reforms had yet to yield "concrete results." [22] But even after acknowledging the country's lackluster financial markets and other problems, Habibie was optimistic. "In reality, the country has huge natural resources, manpower, experience, institutions and strong determination to come out of the crisis," he said.

Democracy in India

Fifty years after India became the world's most populous democracy, President K.R. Narayanan called the anniversary "a golden moment in the history of India and the world." But Narayanan also acknowledged that democracy's record in India has been mixed. [23]

"I am painfully aware of the deterioration that has taken place in our country ... in recent times," Narayanan said on Aug. 15, 1997. He pointed to the ill treatment of women and low-caste Indians; the lack of adequate education, health care and clean water; and the "criminalization of politics."

Throughout India, the anniversary turned into "a very somber celebration," recalls Sumit Ganguly, an Indian political scientist at Hunter College of the City University of New York. "People focused more on India's shortcomings. There was a great deal of soul-searching."

Political events have also raised concerns about India's democracy outside the country. The rise of Hindu nationalism as a political force has rekindled worries about the sectarian divisions in Indian society. The Hindu nationalist Bharatiya Janata Party (BJP) emerged as the leading vote-getter in parliamentary elections in 1996 and early this year but fell short of a majority. Today, the BJP's leader, Atal Behavi Vajpayee, leads a shaky coalition government. Some observers fear that the government decided to test nuclear weapons in May in part to strengthen its domestic political support.

Ganguly acknowledges concerns about the commitment to democracy among some BJP members. "There are some people who have some fascist orientation, and I don't use that term loosely," he says. But he also says that "countervailing forces" limit the influence of the party's more extreme elements. Freedom House's Graybow agrees. "Hopefully, [the party] will be moderated by having to form a coalition with others," he says.

India's commitment to democracy has also been tested by the secessionist movement in predominantly Muslim Kashmir. Ganguly, author of a new book on the problem, says the Indian government has practiced "calibrated but ruthless" repression

against the insurgents; the U.S. State Department similarly cites what it calls "serious human rights abuses" by government forces in Kashmir and neighboring Jammu. [24]

Despite those shortcomings, Sunil Khilnani, an Indian who teaches politics at Birkbeck College, University of London, says democracy has taken root in the Indian consciousness. "As an idea, it's been an enormous success," says Khilnani, author of a new book assessing Indian democracy. "There's no one in India today who questions democratic politics, whether they're on the right or left, rich or poor. There's a general feeling that democracy is the only way for India." [25]

Conflicted Democracies

India's neighbors, however, have had less success with democracy. Pakistan has had military rule for more than half its half-century of independence. [26] Democracy was restored in 1988, but the military still wields great influence. In addition, Islamic fundamentalists pressure the government on religious issues, ethnic and regional divisions run deep and political and economic corruption persist. The country's president resigned in December after complaining that Prime Minister Nawaz Sharif had politicized the judiciary while defending himself against corruption charges.

Bangladesh, the former East Pakistan, also has had frequent periods of military rule since independence in 1971. But Graybow lists Bangladesh among emerging democracies in the 1990s, and the State Department credits the country with a relatively free multiparty system.

Sri Lanka, on the other hand, had a strong tradition of democratic practice predating its independence from

Continued on p. 642

At Issue:

Has the Clinton administration done a good job of promoting democracy in Asia?

CATHARIN E. DALPINO
Guest Scholar, The Brookings Institution, former deputy assistant secretary of State for human rights

WRITTEN FOR THE CQ RESEARCHER, JULY 21, 1998.

yes

Crafting effective U.S. strategies to promote democracy in Asia is difficult in today's policy environment. The lingering sense of triumph over the collapse of Soviet communism has encouraged a Eurocentric approach to political change and an exaggerated estimate of the power of external actors, even superpowers, to direct democratic transitions. Moreover, some politicians and the press recall only the moments of dramatic resolution — the fall of the Berlin Wall — and therefore view democratization as a sprint. In reality, it is a marathon.

The strength of the Clinton administration's approach to Asia is its willingness to play a strong supporting role in helping Asians find their own democratic solutions to political problems, despite domestic pressure at times for more dirigiste or high-decibel policies.

U.S. assistance programs in the Philippines to decentralize power and strengthen civil society have helped that country stay the democratic course. In Mongolia, democracy-assistance programs paid off in 1996 when parliamentary elections turned the communists out of power. Equally important, the defeated party took its place on the back bench without protest.

Clinton administration support to Indonesia's struggling non-governmental sector and to the National Human Rights Commission has helped to build the foundation for a democratic transition with Suharto's departure.

The administration's response to democratic backsliding in Cambodia last July was firm, but appropriately nuanced. Support was increased to Cambodian human rights organizations while aid to the government itself was suspended. U.S. pressure has kept the Cambodian seat vacant at the United Nations, pending a democratic resolution to the conflict. With U.S. urging, the Association of Southeast Asian Nations (ASEAN) pressed Hun Sen to agree to elections.

The success of the most important Clinton administration policy in Asia — to promote political liberalization in the Leninist states — can't be measured for years. Requests in the fiscal year 1999 budget, for programs such as the president's Rule of Law Initiative for China, are realistic first steps that will help to change the relationship between state and society in these countries. Paradoxically, our ability to encourage eventual democratization in China and its Leninist neighbors will depend upon our willingness to leave Cold War models and methods behind.

MIKE JENDRZEJCZYK
Washington Director, Human Rights Watch, Asia Division

WRITTEN FOR THE CQ RESEARCHER, JULY 21, 1998

no

The Clinton administration has tried to balance competing agendas in Asia, generally placing the highest priority on economic and security interests rather than on human rights and democratization. The results are decidedly mixed.

While enthusiastically promoting an agenda of free trade and open markets, the administration has been slow to see the linkage between the meltdown of Asian economies and growing aspirations in many countries for more open, accountable governance, the rule of law and an end to corruption. And in countries like China and Vietnam, it has been willing to abandon potentially effective policies and sources of leverage, relying instead on the market to eventually produce political change.

Indonesians trying to jettison repressive institutions and a political culture created over more than 30 years are now eager for change. They are clearly looking for U.S. support that goes beyond aid to non-governmental organizations or humanitarian assistance, as vital as that may be. They want U.S. support for a speedier transition and creative help in solving longstanding human rights problems such as East Timor.

Citizens of Burma and Cambodia, struggling under military rule or trying to restore democracy, believe that by withholding legitimacy — and funding by international financial institutions — the U.S. can create the political space they urgently need. They've already waited years to peacefully exercise their basic rights and feel they can ill afford to wait much longer.

Next week's meeting of the Association for Southeast Asian Nations (ASEAN) in Manila will provide an interesting window on the shifts under way in the region. Thailand and the Philippines have publicly called for the abandonment of "constructive engagement" (i.e. not interfering in the internal affairs of other nations) as an outmoded approach. They propose instead a policy of "flexible engagement" in order to deal with destabilizing problems, including the lack of progress in democratization.

In this rapidly evolving environment, the United States should not place its major emphasis on long-term rule-of-law programs alone, or on the instincts of "visionary" leaders such as Jiang Zemin, as Clinton called the Chinese president. And while being careful not to impose "American values" or solutions, the Clinton administration should clearly articulate more effective bilateral and multilateral policies that can aid Asia's crucial transitions.

Putting Myanmar on the Political Map

When U Zarni came to the United States 10 years ago, he expected to get a degree in education and return to his native Burma. But today he leads a coalition of other Burmese expatriates working within the United States for economic sanctions against his country. Their goal is to pressure the military government to permit the restoration of democracy.

"We put Burma on the map of international politics," Zarni says of the Free Burma Coalition, which he founded in 1995. "We as a grass-roots campaign brought Burma to American and international households."

The effect of the coalition's work, however, is sharply disputed. In 1997, Congress passed and President Clinton signed into law an economic-sanctions bill prohibiting U.S. companies from making new investments in Myanmar, as the military government renamed the country. Zarni says one state — Massachusetts — and 20 municipalities have passed broader sanctions measures that cut off trade with any companies operating in Myanmar. [1]

Zarni and other human rights advocates believe the sanctions are having an effect. "The junta itself admitted that they are reeling from the effects of American sanctions," says Zarni, now a graduate student at the University of Wisconsin in Madison.

As evidence, Zarni cites recent comments by a member of the ruling council, Brig. Gen. D.O. Abel, to *Leaders* magazine, an international business-oriented publication. Abel said that American companies are "holding off" investing in Myanmar because of the sanctions and that the sanctions are having an effect on other multinational companies. "Any Japanese companies that are operating here in Myanmar cannot operate in the state of Massachusetts," Abel said. "They and other multinational companies don't want to invest here because they are afraid of retaliation from the United States."

Zarni says the sanctions have led some 25 multinational companies — including Pepsico, Texaco, Heineken, Levi Strauss, Liz Claiborne and Eddie Bauer — to pull out of Myanmar. Two big U.S.-based oil companies — Arco and Unocal — are still there, however. Unocal is joint-venturing with a French and a Thai company on a $1.2 billion gas pipeline.

Policy-makers and foreign policy experts generally dismiss the effects of the sanctions as minimal. "We don't have sufficient leverage on Myanmar to force change from the outside," says Catharin E. Dalpino, a guest scholar at the Brookings Institution and former deputy assistant secretary of State for human rights in the Clinton administration. "And we haven't been able to get our allies, both Asian and European, to join with us."

Clearly, though, Zarni's group has raised awareness of Myanmar's military government inside the United States. The coalition operates an Internet site (www.freeburma.org) with up-to-date news and pro-democracy information. The coalition also used its boycott of Pepsi Cola to good effect. "Third-graders were boycotting Pepsi because their teachers were teaching them about human rights," Zarni says. [2]

Some other Asian expatriate groups also have lobbied within the United States to try to influence U.S. policy toward their native countries — most notably Chinese groups, such as the Independent Federation of Chinese Students and Scholars. The Washington-based group has helped organize protests in the United States against the Chinese government.

Generally, though, the groups' impact on policy appears to be relatively minimal. Until recently, at least, Asian-Americans have tended to shy away from domestic U.S. politics, and their numbers have been too small to have much influence except in a few areas. The influence of expatriate groups is inherently limited by their divided attention between the United States and their home country. An earlier Burmese group, for example, the Committee for Restoration of Democracy in Burma, is less visible in the United States because it concentrates on helping students and others inside Burma. And, as U.S. policy toward China illustrates, partisan politics and broad economic interests usually carry more weight in government decision-making than pro-democracy lobbying from ethnic or expatriate groups.

Zarni cut off ties with his family still in Myanmar — parents and seven siblings — to protect them from repercussions from his work in the United States. He has been granted political asylum in the United States, but he still hopes to return. "When the country is free," he says, "I intend to go back."

---

[1] For background, see *The Christian Science Monitor*, Jan. 29, 1998, p. 6.

[2] For further background, see *The New York Times*, April 8, 1997, p. A18, and *The Chronicle of Higher Education*, Feb. 14, 1997, p. A43.

Continued from p. 640

Britain in 1948 that has been tarnished by protracted ethnic violence between the Sinhalese majority, mostly Hindu, and the predominantly Buddhist Tamil minority. The government's refusal to grant Tamil demands for more autonomy sparked a civil war that has raged since 1983. A measure of political order returned in the 1990s, but the government has yet to craft a political settlement acceptable to the separatist Tamils.

Meanwhile, Japan — arguably the region's most successful democracy — is in turmoil. "The Japanese political leadership is floundering," says Ellis Krauss, an expert on Japan at the University of California-San Diego. The Liberal Democratic Party (LDP) fell from power in 1993, regained control of the government in 1996, but — in the midst of an economic recession — suffered a stinging rejection at the polls in elections earlier this month. Prime Minister Ryutaro Hashimoto immediately resigned.

Even before Japan's economic problems surfaced, however, the government gave the United States only scant encouragement in efforts to promote democracy in Asia. "Japanese foreign policy is far more pragmatic" than U.S. policy, Krauss says. "It tends to be based on a more narrowly defined self-interest." ■

OUTLOOK

Change and Resistance

When he ended his nine-day trip to China earlier this month, President Clinton emphatically predicted the eventual rise of democracy in Asia's largest country. But Clinton also acknowledged "powerful forces resisting change" in China. And he dodged a reporter's question asking whether he expected to see democracy in China in his lifetime. [27]

Similarly, in most of Asia's nondemocratic countries. There are stirrings of democracy, but the democratic forces face strong resistance from well-entrenched governments — whether they be communist, military or one-party regimes.

"We see growing pressure for democratic change" in Asia, says the Hoover Institute's Diamond. In most of the region, though, "it's hard to discern movement" toward democracy, he says.

Other U.S. observers and advocates are somewhat more optimistic. Brookings' Dalpino predicts "a series of quiet watersheds" in several Asian

countries over the next few years. Daniel Steinberg, director of the Asia studies program at Georgetown University, even sees gradual political liberalization in Asia's most authoritarian countries.

"We're talking about the rise of alternative centers of power, which means the state is less centralized than it once was," Steinberg says. "That's happening even in China. And on the economic side, you're getting people making economic decisions without reference to the state."

The likelihood of democratic change in China remains sharply disputed. The government is encouraging villages to hold elections for local offices, but there is no movement toward electing leaders at the national level. When the *Journal of Democracy* gathered 10 experts earlier this year to offer predictions about the potential for democratization in China over the next decade, the optimists outnumbered the pessimists, but they all hedged their bets. [28]

Among Asia's other communist regimes, Vietnam and Laos have both adopted some market-oriented reforms, and both countries held national elections last year. But the State Department reports little progress toward political liberalization. In North Korea, the government has ruled out any political or economic liberalization.

Myanmar's military regime similarly shows no easing up. "Nothing's changed there," says Steinberg, who visited Myanmar earlier this summer. "They will have a civilian government at some point in the indefinite future, but it will be militarily controlled." Malaysia's and Singapore's dominant-party governments also show no signs of liberalizing political rights or, for now at least, losing popular support.

On the subcontinent, Pakistan continues to have elements of repression and arbitrary rule despite democratic forms. Bangladesh witnessed a peaceful change of government after elec-

tions two years ago, but political violence and electoral fraud persist. And Sri Lanka's civil war continues to mar its record in democratic government.

The bright spots for advocates of democratization are relatively few, but significant. "We've seen some nice consolidation of democracy in Thailand, in the Philippines, in South Korea," Dalpino says. Nepal has held four relatively free elections since political parties were legalized in 1990. Mongolia is making what the State Department calls good progress toward democracy in its transition from a communist regime. And India and Japan remain relatively secure in their democracies despite domestic political turmoil.

The U.S. role in encouraging democratic developments, most observers say, is limited but still significant. Diamond, for example, credits the Clinton administration with standing behind the Thai government as it instituted political reforms. He and others also stress the importance of the less visible U.S. support, including financial assistance, for associations, labor unions, human rights organizations and other elements of so-called civil society. "These are micro-type linkages," Diamond says, "part of the ongoing, more prosaic process of building democracy."

Many of these organizations are funded through the National Endowment for Democracy, which Diamond notes has a difficult time getting funding every year on Capitol Hill. "It's been one of the great success stories of U.S. foreign policy," he says, "but it has to fight for its existence every year."

Meanwhile, the biggest question mark for the moment is Indonesia, which must institute political reform and economic revival simultaneously. Mas'oed fears the economic problems may temper popular support for reform. "The common people tend to think more about food than about the reform movement now," he says.

"That's a problem."

After watching the Golkar conference, however, Tamimi was optimistic about the prospects for democracy. "This is very good for democracy," he says. "If the ruling party gives this good example, others will follow. When you disagree, there is no other way but through voting — no more manipulation." ∎

Notes

[1] For background, see Christopher Conte, "Deflation Fears," *The CQ Researcher*, Feb. 13, 1998, pp. 121-144.

[2] For background, see David Masci, "China After Deng," *The CQ Researcher*, June 13, 1997, pp. 505-528, and Patrick G. Marshall, "New Era in Asia," *The CQ Researcher*, Feb. 14, 1992, pp. 121-144.

[3] U.S. Department of State, *Country Reports on Human Rights Practices for 1997*, March 1998, p. 900.

[4] Fareed Zakaria, "Culture Is Destiny: A Conversation with Lee Kuan Yew," *Foreign Affairs*, March/April 1994, pp. 109-126; *The Wall Street Journal*, June 25, 1996, p. A1; Mahathir Mohamad and Shintaro Ishihara, *The Voice of Asia: Two Leaders Discuss the Coming Century* (1995), pp. 82-83.

[5] Samuel P. Huntington, *The Third Wave:*

Democratization in the Late 20th Century (1991), p. 306.

[6] Lucian Pye, "Dominant Party Democracies in Asia," in *Democracy in Asia and Africa* (1998), pp. 69-72. For background, see Kenneth Jost, "Taiwan, China and the U.S.," *The CQ Researcher*, May 24, 1996, pp. 457-480.

[7] See *The New York Times*, July 28, 1997, p. A3; *The Washington Post*, July 30, 1997, pp. A1, A19. ASEAN includes Brunei, Indonesia, Laos, Malaysia, Myanmar, the Philippines, Singapore, Thailand and Vietnam.

[8] For background, see Mary H. Cooper, "U.S.-Vietnam Relations," *The CQ Researcher*, Dec. 3, 1993, pp. 1057-1080.

[9] For excerpts, see *The New York Times*, May 23, 1998, p. A8.

[10] See Yoneo Ishii, "Buddhism"; Werner Menski, "Hinduism"; and Winberg Chai and May-klee Chai, "Confucianism," in *Encyclopedia of Democracy* (1995).

[11] Some background is drawn from John Keay, *Empire's End: A History of the Far East from High Colonialism to Hong Kong* (1997).

[12] Donald K. Emmerson, "Indonesia," in *Democracy in Asia and Africa* (1998), p. 86.

[13] Keay, *op. cit.*, p. 212.

[14] Background drawn in part from individual country articles in *Democracy in Asia and Africa* and Keay, *op. cit.*.

[15] For background, see Emmerson, *op. cit.*; Keay, *op. cit.*, pp. 32-35, 247-269.

[16] Huntington, *op. cit.* For background, see Emmerson, *op. cit.*; William Liddle, "Indonesia," in *Comparative Governance* (1992);

M.C. Ricklefs, A *History of Modern Indonesia Since c. 1300* (1993).

[17] For a detailed account, see Raymond Bonner, *Waltzing with a Dictator: The Marcoses and the Making of American Policy* (1987).

[18] See Aung Cin Win Aung, *Burma: From Monarchy to Dictatorship* (1994).

[19] See State Department, *op. cit.*, pp. 784-785.

[20] For accounts of Suharto's fall, see *Far Eastern Economic Review*, June 4, 1998, pp. 21-26; *Newsweek*, June 1, 1998, pp. 34-43; *Time*, June 1, 1998, pp. 60-63.

[21] Quoted in *The New York Times*, July 12, 1998, p. A8.

[22] Quoted in *The Washington Post*, July 10, 1998, p. A31.

[23] See *The New York Times*, Aug. 15, 1997, p. A13. For a retrospective on India's 50 years of independence, see John F. Burns, "India's Five Decades of Progress and Pain," *The New York Times*, Aug. 14, 1997, p. A1.

[24] State Department, *op. cit.*, p. 1637. See Sumit Ganguly, *The Crisis in Kashmir: Portents of War, Hopes of Peace* (1998).

[25] See Sunil Khilnani, *The Idea of India* (1998).

[26] For background, see John F. Burns, "Pakistan's Bitter Roots, and Modest Hopes," *The New York Times*, Aug. 15, 1997, p. A1.

[27] For edited transcript of the Clinton news conference, see *The Washington Post*, July 4, 1998, pp. A20-21.

[28] "Will China Democratize?" *Journal of Democracy*, January 1998, pp. 3-64.

Bibliography

Selected Sources Used

Books

Democracy in Asia and Africa, CQ Books, 1998.

This reference work includes articles by leading Asia scholars assessing the status of democracy in Asia and Africa. Each article includes a short bibliography. Additional articles on Buddhism, Hinduism and Confucianism can be found in *The Encyclopedia of Democracy* (CQ Books, 1995).

Ishida, Takeshi, and Ellis S. Krauss (eds.), *Democracy in Japan*, University of Pittsburgh Press, 1989.

Essays by 13 experts evaluate political, social and economic democracy in Japan as of the end of the 1980s.

Keay, John, *Empire's End: A History of the Far East from High Colonialism to Hong Kong*, Scribner, 1997.

Keay, a British scholar, provides a readable survey of Dutch, English, French and American colonialism in East Asia beginning in the 17th century but focusing on the period 1930-1975.

Khilnani, Sunil, *The Idea of India*, Farrar Straus Giroux, 1998.

Khilnani, a political scientist at the University of London's Birkbeck College, provides an evocative picture of Indian political culture since independence. The book includes a 25-page bibliographic essay.

Liddle, William, "Indonesia," in Philip Shiveley (ed.), *Comparative Governance*, McGraw-Hill, 1992.

Liddle, a professor of political science at Ohio State University, contributes an overview of Indonesian politics and government to this political science text.

Ricklefs, M.C., *A History of Modern Indonesia Since 1300* (2d ed.), Stanford University Press, 1993.

This authoritative history traces events in Indonesia from the arrival of Islam in the 14th century and colonization by the Dutch in the 17th century through independence and the Sukarno and Suharto eras. The book includes detailed source notes, maps and a 25-page bibliography. Ricklefs is a history professor at the Australian National University in Canberra.

Steinberg, David I., *The Future of Burma: Crisis and Choice in Myanmar*, University Press of America, 1990.

Steinberg, now a professor at Georgetown University, wrote this account of the 1988 military coup and its aftermath immediately before the national elections in 1990, which were nullified by the military regime. The book includes a short list of suggested reading, including Steinberg's *Burma: A Socialist Nation of Southeast Asia* (Westview Press, 1982). For more recent books by a prodemocracy Burmese journalist now living in the United States, see Aung Chin Win Aung, *Burma: From Monarchy to Dictatorship*, Eastern Press, 1994; *Burma and the Last Days of General Ne Win*, Yoma Publishing, 1996.

Tharoor, Shashi, *India: From Midnight to the Millennium*, Arcade Publishing, 1997.

Tharoor, a United Nations official who has lived outside India for most of his life, writes what he describes as a "paean" to India that nonetheless sharply criticizes the country's political system for producing corruption and instability. The book includes a four-page chronology covering 1947 through April 1997 and a seven-page glossary.

Reports and Studies

Freedom House, *Freedom in the World, 1997-1998*, 1998.

The 610-page volume includes country-by-country assessments of political and economic freedoms covering events through Jan. 1, 1998. The volume includes a global overview essay and regional essays on East Asia and South Asia.

Human Rights Watch World Report 1998: Events of 1997, December 1997.

Human Rights Watch's most recent annual report, covering events through 1997, includes featured essays on 10 Asian countries.

U.S. Department of State, *Country Reports on Human Rights Practices for 1997*, March 1998.

The State Department's most recent annual report provides detailed country-by-country assessments of human rights, civil liberties, political rights, protections against discrimination and workers' rights.

FOR MORE INFORMATION

If you would like to have this CQ Researcher updated, or need more information about this topic, please call CQ Custom Research. Special rates for CQ subscribers. (202) 887-8600 or (800) 432-2250, ext. 600, or E-mail Custom.Research@cq.com

The **U.S. State Department's** annual *Country Report on Human Rights Practices* can be found online at www.state.gov.; (202) 647-2492.

Here are private organizations that follow human rights issues in Asia:

Freedom House, 1319 18th St., N.W., Washington, D.C. 20036; (202) 296 5101; 120 Wall St., 26th floor, New York, N.Y. 10005; (212) 514-8040; www.freedomhouse.org. The human rights organization publishes a biennial volume, *Freedom in the World*, with country-by-country assessments of political and economic freedoms.

Human Rights Watch, 350 5th Ave., 34th floor, New York, N.Y. 10018; (212) 290-4700; 1522 K St. N.W., Suite 910, Washington, D.C. 20005; (202) 371-6592; www.hrw.org. The human rights organization publishes periodic reports and an annual volume, *Human Rights Watch World Report*.

The Next Step

Additional information from UMI's Newspaper & Periodical Abstracts™ database

China

Mann, Jim, "Clinton Urges Full China Trade Ties; Asia: Permanent Most-Favored-Nation Designation Would Abolish Stormy Annual Congressional Reviews," *Los Angeles Times*, June 20, 1998, p. A1.

President Clinton said Friday that he supports granting most-favored-nation (MFN) trade status to China on a permanent basis, abolishing the decades-old requirement that Beijing's trade benefits be submitted to Congress for approval each year. Human rights officials said this was the first time Clinton has called for granting permanent MFN status to China. "The administration knows that the [congressional] debate this year will be about the summit and whether Clinton achieved anything," said Mike Jendrzejczyk, Washington director of Human Rights Watch Asia. He said the required annual renewal of China's trade benefits "is one of the few levers remaining [in dealing with China] that the administration hasn't jettisoned." A move to extend China's trade privileges indefinitely would mark the final step in the transformation of Clinton's policy on this topic. During his 1992 presidential campaign, he attacked the Bush administration for routinely extending China's trade benefits each year. Clinton said then that the United States should refuse to renew China's trade benefits unless it made progress on human rights.

Shenon, Philip, "Annual U.N. Ritual Condemning China Loses U.S. Support," *The New York Times*, March 14, 1998, p. A1.

Only days after deciding to move up a presidential trip to Beijing, the administration has given China another important boost by dropping American sponsorship of an annual United Nations resolution condemning China's record on human rights. The move, which effectively kills a resolution before the United Nations Human Rights Commission in Geneva, was described by senior officials as a response to Beijing's recent efforts to improve its rights record, including its decision this week to sign an important international human rights treaty. "If the president visits China without clear human rights preconditions and also drops any resolution at the United Nations Human Rights Commission in Geneva, what leverage will the United States use to press for concrete progress?" asked Mike Jendrzejczyk, Washington director of Human Rights Watch Asia. "They've caved."

Indonesia

Cloud, David S., "Mindful of Stakes, U.S. Warily Backs Reform Push in Indonesia," *Chicago Tribune*, May 23, 1998, p. 4.

As the crisis in Indonesia continues, the Clinton administra-tion confronts a basic problem: How openly should it side with protesters demanding political reform and a decisive break with the authoritarian practices enshrined under former President Suharto? The United States has longstanding strategic and economic interests in a stable Indonesia, a major oil producer astride sea lanes between the Indian and Pacific oceans. Until the Asian financial crisis struck last year, Indonesia was a magnet for U.S. trade and investment, lured by cheap labor and the emerging ranks of educated, middle-class consumers. In recent days, President Clinton and his advisers have escalated their calls for a transition to democracy in Indonesia. But Washington has not spelled out in detail who should lead the effort or what those reforms should be, beyond adherence to the terms of the International Monetary Fund's bailout plan for the Indonesian economy.

Lewis, Anthony, "Their Suharto And Ours," *The New York Times*, May 25, 1998, p. A15.

In December 1975, President Gerald Ford and Secretary of State Henry Kissinger visited President Suharto in Indonesia. They reacted with a nod and a wink to his plans to seize East Timor. The day after they left, Indonesian forces invaded the distant island, using American arms. In the invasion and ensuing occupation, tens of thousands of East Timorese people died. When it was pointed out that using American arms aid for aggression violated U.S. law, Kissinger reportedly told his staff: "Can't we construe [stopping] a communist government in the middle of Indonesia as self-defense?" (East Timor was, in fact, remote from Indonesia, and its mostly Roman Catholic people wanted independence, not communism.) Kissinger was closely identified with the policy that the United States should support authoritarian rulers because they could assure stability.

South Korea

Barr, Cameron W., "Koreans Bring a Dissident in From Cold as Leader; Election Victory for Opposition Candidate Yesterday is Evidence of a Maturing Democracy," *The Christian Science Monitor*, Dec. 19, 1997, p. 1.

Yesterday's presidential election in South Korea may well be a triumph of democracy in Asia. It may also help relieve tension with North Korea and further restore a battered economy. But for Kim Dae Jung, the man leading the vote count at press time, the election demonstrates the power of perseverance. Once one of Asia's leading dissidents against dictatorship, Kim has endured exile, assassination attempts and three failed bids to become president. His victory is the first time Koreans have chosen a president from an opposition party. That's notable in a young democracy that rose to become the world's 11th biggest economy mainly under military rule.

Deans, Bob, "Authoritarianism Blamed for South Korea's Economic Troubles," *Atlanta Journal-Constitution*, **Dec. 14, 1997, p. B3.**

Ten years after students and workers braved tear gas and riot troops to topple a dictator and spark a democratic revolution in South Korea, the nation goes to the polls this week amid its worst economic crisis in a generation. "The problems in Asia generally, in large part, are due to incomplete democracy . . . insufficient opening in the banking system, cronyism and corruption," said Winston Lord, former assistant secretary of State for East Asian and Pacific affairs. The current crisis may focus the Koreans "on the practical needs of developing an economy in the information age." The country's 32 million eligible voters know the economy is the only issue in Thursday's presidential election. And whichever candidate wins — career opposition leader Kim Dae Jung, majority party candidate Lee Hoi Chang or Rhee In Je, running as a second opposition choice — will have less to say about the country's economic policies over his five-year term than will the Washington-based International Monetary Fund. Just a week ago, the IMF knitted together a $57 billion international bailout package — the largest in history — for South Korea.

Kristof, Nicholas D., "A New Kind of Leader for Korea, and Asia Too," *The New York Times*, **Feb. 23, 1998, p. A1.**

Often described as "Asia's Mandela," Kim Dae Jung becomes president with the same kind of moral authority as Nelson Mandela of South Africa and similar stature as an international figure. At a time when much of Asia has lost its footing and is groping for a more solid political and economic structure, Kim proclaims a vision for a new Korea and a new Asia: political democracy, market-oriented economics and policies that emphasize social justice. He says he is willing to speak out against human rights abuses in Myanmar or even China, and he clearly intends to transform South Korea so it can be an example for the world. "I want Kim Dae Jung to be a model that is successful in Asia , proving that democracy and the economy can go together well," he said. "This is my ambition."

Kristof, Nicholas D., "South Koreans Vote, Seeking Rescue From Economic Crisis," *The New York Times*, **Dec. 18, 1997, p. A16.**

South Korea's two leading candidates, Kim Dae Jung and Lee Hoi Chang, were neck-and-neck in opinion polls, but they come from very different backgrounds. Mr. Lee is a former judge and the epitome of the establishment, while Mr. Kim is a legendary democracy campaigner in Asia whom past South Korean presidents repeatedly tried to kill. If Mr. Kim wins, it will be the first peaceful transfer of the presidency to the opposition party in modern Korean history.

Lev, Michael A., "Asia Embraces Democratic Air Despite Economies in Turmoil, Home-Grown Styles of Democracy Are Putting Down Deeper Roots," *Chicago Tribune*, **Dec. 18, 1997, p. 1.**

As South Koreans vote in Thursday's presidential election,

the front-runner is 72-year-old Kim Dae Jung, a former political prisoner and perennial opposition candidate who survived several assassination attempts over the years - including a bizarre government kidnapping - and at one point was sentenced to death on trumped-up charges by South Korea's military ruler. Even if Kim loses, the fact that he ran a neck-and-neck race with the establishment candidate, Lee Hoi Chang, represents a remarkable coming-of-age for South Korean democracy and, in a way, for much of Asia .

U.S. Policy Toward Asia

Albright, Madeleine K., "1998: A Year of Decision in American Foreign Policy," *U.S. Department of State Dispatch*, **January 1998, pp. 5-8.**

Albright outlines U.S. foreign policy objectives in 1998, focusing on international and national security, economic growth through increased trade opportunities and continued international peace promotion.

Atwood, J. Brian, "World's Stability Requires U.S. Aid," **Forum for Applied Research & Public Policy, winter 1997, pp. 60-64.**

Most Americans have misconceptions and doubts about foreign aid, a program that makes the world safer and more stable and creates a more competitive arena for American exports.

Calleo, David P., "A New Era of Overstretch? American Policy in Europe and Asia," *World Policy Journal*, **spring 1998, pp. 11-25.**

In the wake of the Cold War, the United States has been slow in developing coherent policies toward Europe and Asia. The Clinton administration has tended toward geopolitical overconfidence and carelessness.

Kissinger, Henry A., "Continuity and Change in American Foreign Policy," *Society*, **January 1998, pp. 184-192.**

The former secretary of State traces patterns of continuity and change in U.S. foreign policy up to the late 1970s, focusing on the philosophical underpinnings of tactical decisions.

Ruttan, Vernon W., "Rapidly Changing World Challenges U.S. Policy," Forum for Applied Research & Public Policy, winter 1997, pp. 53-59.

The U.S. economic assistance program to foreign countries has declined in the years following the end of the Cold War. Changes under way in the political environment suggest the U.S. program is no longer viable.

Zhang, Ming, "The Emerging Asia-Pacific Triangle," *Australian Journal of International Affairs* (AJA), **April 1998, pp. 47-61.**

The author examines the pattern of behavioral interaction among China, Japan and the United States to determine whether these countries have become a new hostile triad in the Asia-Pacific region.

Back Issues

Great Research on Current Issues Starts Right Here.
Recent topics covered by The CQ Researcher are listed below.
Now available on the Web
For information, call (800) 432-2250 ext. 279 or (202) 887-6279.

If you would like to have any of these CQ Researchers updated, or need more information about these topics, please call CQ Custom Research. Special rates for CQ subscribers. (202) 887-8600 or (800) 432-2250, ext. 600, or E-mail Custom.Research@cq.com

APRIL 1997
Declining Crime Rates
The FBI Under Fire
Gender Equity in Sports
Space Program's Future

MAY 1997
The Stock Market
The Cloning Controversy
Expanding NATO
The Future of Libraries

JUNE 1997
FDA Reform
China After Deng
Line-Item Veto
Breast Cancer

JULY 1997
Transportation Policy
Executive Pay
School Choice Debate
Aggressive Driving

AUGUST 1997
Age Discrimination
Banning Land Mines
Children's Television
Evolution vs. Creationism

SEPTEMBER 1997
Caring for the Dying
Mental Health Policy
Mexico's Future
Youth Fitness

OCTOBER 1997
Urban Sprawl in the West
Diversity in the Workplace
Teacher Education
Contingent Work Force

NOVEMBER 1997
Renewable Energy
Artificial Intelligence
Religious Persecution
Roe v. Wade at 25

DECEMBER 1997
Whistleblowers
Castro's Next Move
Gun Control Standoff
Regulating Nonprofits

JANUARY 1998
Foster Care Reform
IRS Reform
The Black Middle Class
U.S.-British Relations

FEBRUARY 1998
Patients' Rights
Deflation Fears
Caring for the Elderly
The New Corporate Philanthropy

MARCH 1998
Israel at 50
The Federal Judiciary
Drinking on Campus
The Economics of Recycling

APRIL 1998
Biology and Behavior
Liberal Arts Education
Income Inequality
High-Tech Labor Shortage

MAY 1998
Census 2000
Child-Care Options
Alzheimer's Disease
U.S.-Russian Relations

JUNE 1998
Student Journalism
Antitrust Policy
Environmental Justice
Sleep Deprivation

JULY 1998
Encouraging Teen Abstinence
Population and the Environment

Back issues are available for $5.00 (subscribers) or $10.00 (non-subscribers). Quantity discounts apply to orders over 10. To order, call Congressional Quarterly Customer Service at (202) 887-8621.

Binders are available for $18.00. To order call 1-800-638-1710. Please refer to stock number 648.

Future Topics

▶ *Forever Young: Baby Boomers at Mid-Life*

▶ *Oil Production in the 21st Century*

▶ *Flexible Work Arrangements*

Baby Boomers
at Midlife

Are they trying too hard to stay young?

I n 1996, the first members of the baby boom
generation turned 50. But unlike their parents
and grandparents, the 78 million Americans born
from 1946 to 1964 are not accepting aging as a
time of inevitable decline. Growing numbers of
boomers are trying to stop the clock with remedies
ranging from rigorous exercise and dieting to "anti-
aging" hormones. Many experts say that fighting Father
Time will lead millions of people to longer, healthier
and happier lives and, in the long run, reduce the
nation's health-care costs. But other observers argue
that efforts to stay young will lead to inevitable
disappointment and self-delusion.

CQ   **July 31, 1998** • **Volume 8, No. 28** • **Pages 649-672**

Formerly Editorial Research Reports

CQResearcher
THE

PUBLISHED BY CONGRESSIONAL QUARTERLY INC.

COVER: AP PHOTO/SAURABH DAS

July 31, 1998
Volume 8, No.28

EDITOR
Sandra Stencel

MANAGING EDITOR
Thomas J. Colin

ASSOCIATE EDITOR
Sarah M. Magner

STAFF WRITERS
Adriel Bettelheim
Mary H. Cooper
Kenneth Jost
Kathy Koch
David Masci

PRODUCTION EDITOR
Melissa Hall

EDITORIAL ASSISTANT
Laura S. Cavender

PUBLISHED BY
Congressional Quarterly Inc.

CHAIRMAN
Andrew Barnes

VICE CHAIRMAN
Andrew P. Corty

PRESIDENT AND PUBLISHER
Robert W. Merry

EXECUTIVE EDITOR
David Rapp

The CQ Researcher (ISSN 1056-2036). Formerly Editorial Research Reports. Published weekly, except Jan. 2, May 29, July 3, Oct. 30, by Congressional Quarterly Inc., 1414 22nd St., N.W., Washington, D.C. 20037. Annual subscription rate for libraries, businesses and government is $340. Additional rates furnished upon request. Periodicals postage paid at Washington, D.C., and additional mailing offices. POSTMASTER: Send address changes to The CQ Researcher, 1414 22nd St., N.W., Washington, D.C. 20037.

Baby Boomers at Midlife

BY DAVID MASCI

THE ISSUES

Last September, 47-year-old Jim Valentine of Gaithersburg, Md., set about changing his life. "I realized that if I kept up with my current lifestyle, I'd start to really deteriorate," he says.

Valentine, a media buyer for publisher NRI McGraw-Hill, rarely exercised and compounded the damage with bad eating habits. "I was eating like I was still 16," he says. "I'd go to McDonalds and get two Big Macs — stuff like that."

Valentine kicked off his transformation campaign by replacing McDonalds and other junk foods with Weight Watchers.

"It was not so much a question of eating less as of eating the right kinds of food," he says. "Even at restaurants, I just started ordering things like salad or fish — without salt or butter."

He also started an exercise regimen that included daily workouts on a cross-country skiing machine and walks during his lunch hour or after dinner.

Since he began his new regimen, Valentine has lost 60 pounds. "I look and feel like a new person," he says.

Valentine's efforts involved more than just looking and feeling better. In retrospect, he realizes that his commitment to a healthier lifestyle came at around the same time he began to seriously ponder his upcoming 50th birthday. "For the first time, I began to think about my mortality," he says.

Millions of other baby boomers over age 50 also are collectively beginning to consider the dual implications of reaching middle age and growing older. *

---

*There are 78 million Americans in the baby boom generation, usually defined as Americans born between 1946 and 1964.

But many experts, including sociologists, demographers, psychotherapists and gerontologists, worry that many boomers are fighting the aging process, rather than accepting its inevitability with grace and dignity.

"They're so self-absorbed that the concept of mortality might shock them and lead them to go to terrible lengths to avoid it," says Cheryl Russell, a consultant on aging and author of *The Master Trend*, which profiles the baby boom generation. Or, as Gail Sheehy, the best-selling author of *Passages*, puts it: Boomers, "having indulged [themselves] in the longest adolescence in history, betray a collective terror and disgust of aging." [1]

It was the boomers, after all, who virtually created the "youth movement" in the 1960s and the "me" generation the following decade. Indeed, as Sheehy and others point out, the culture that shaped Valentine and his fellow baby boomers deplored the very idea of getting older.

While their parents listened to Frank Sinatra tell them to cope with old age by staying "young at heart," the generation that matured in the 1960s and '70s could not imagine getting old. Popular music of the day constantly reflected this attitude. In "My Generation," The Who's classic anthem to youth, Peter Townsend wrote, "I hope I die before I get old." Another '60s rock icon, Neil Young, sang, "It's better to burn out than to fade away."

Today, however, boomers like Valentine don't want to "die" or "burn out." They want to live, and live well. Indeed, aging to them represents a challenge, not inevitable decline. "I want to confront the aging process, make it a positive experience," Valentine says. "I want people to say: 'Turning 50 isn't so bad; look at Jim. I didn't know that 50 could be so cool.'"

The parents of boomers viewed aging differently, however. "I look at my parents and can see that they were middle-aged at my age," Valentine says. "But middle age is a concept I can't relate to."

Dan Perry, executive director of the Alliance for Aging Research, points out that Valentine's attitude is typical of people his age. "This is not a generation that says, 'It's God's will,' when they look at aging," he says.

Maddy Kent Dychtwald, a corporate consultant on the baby boom generation, agrees. "They are trying to bring their youth with them," she says, "and that's reflected in their attitudes as well as their behavior."

As proof of that proposition, Dychtwald notes recent polls indicating that boomers view old age as beginning roughly at 80. "For their parents, it's 51," she says.

But some observers say that for all their positive attitudes and concern about their health, baby boomers are trying too hard to stay young. "These are people who don't think they're going to die," says Alan Ehrenhalt, executive editor of *Governing* magazine and author of a 1995 book about Chicago in the 1950s, *The Lost City: The Forgotten Virtues of Community in America*. "And so, as they begin to age they become fanatical in their attempt to hang on to their youth."

According to this view, Americans who grew up in the 1960s and '70s

Continued on p. 653

How Americans Feel About Aging

1. If it were possible, would you like to live to be 100 years old?

	1996	1992	1991
YES	**61%**	**61%**	**66%**
NO	32	34	29

2. At what age do you think someone becomes middle-aged?

Less than 40	5%
40	12
41-44	1
45	15
46-49	2
50	30
51-54	1
55	12
56-59	1
60	12
61 or older	7

3. At what age do you consider someone to be elderly?

Less than 60	4%
60	9
61-64	1
65	15
66-69	2
70	26
71-74	1
75	12
76-79	1
80	17
81 or older	8

4. As you grow older, how concerned are you about the following:

	Very worried	Somewhat worried	Not worried
• *Becoming a financial burden on your children or other people*	18%	29%	53%
• *Developing Alzheimer's, a disease that destroys a person's mental capabilities*	24	32	43
• *The loss of physical attractiveness*	8	26	66
• *Living for many years in a nursing home because of physical frailty or long-term illness*	33	31	36
• *Being lonely*	10	26	63
• *Having nothing to do*	10	16	74
• *Death*	6	22	71

5. Which age group tends to be more . . . those under 50 years old or those over 50?

	Under 50	Over 50
• Generous	16%	75%
• Self-centered	75	17
• Greedy	76	15
• Stressed	79	16
• Fun to be with	55	28
• Complainers	51	40

Source: Alliance for Aging Research; poll conducted by Belden & Russonello Research and Communications, July 1996

Continued from p. 651
are not facing the natural process of getting older in a mature way. "This is a case of arrested development," says author Jeremy Rifkin, president of the Foundation on Economic Trends and a noted social commentator. "They've never, really, fully grown up."

Rifkin and others say that boomers who are feverishly fighting old age will miss the benefits and pleasures that should be enjoyed in life's later years, among them maturity and wisdom. "They will be doing themselves a disservice," he says, "because middle age and old age are different from youth, but just as rewarding."

In addition, some say that efforts to remain young will ultimately prove disappointing because they will ultimately fail. "These people are going to get hysterical," Russell says.

But others argue that attempting to stay young is healthy and should be encouraged. They say that concerns about diet and exercise, coupled with a youthful attitude, will ensure that millions of boomers will remain vigorous and self-sufficient well into old age.

"Sure, some narcissists will take it too far," Perry says. "But it's better to have a generation that tries to put off the indignities of old age than one that prematurely accepts them." He notes cultures where women wear black long after their husbands die, even if they are young. "That's the other side of this coin," Perry says, "and we don't want that."

Actually, Perry and others argue, boomers are not so much trying to stay young as to stay healthy. "This is really about maintaining a good quality of life throughout life," says Judy Ernest, executive director of the Boomer Institute, a think tank in Cleveland, Ohio.

But why should boomers stop at just trying to have a healthy retirement and a few more years than their parents? Some observers say that available anti-aging therapies, when coupled with treatments yet to be

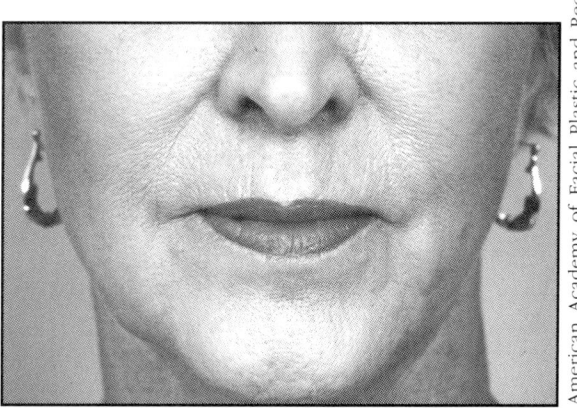

Laser plastic surgery was used to remove this woman's wrinkles. (Before, top; after, bottom)

developed, will double boomers' life spans. Already, the relatively new field of anti-aging medicine is using human growth hormone (hGH), melatonin and other natural hormones to try to stop and even reverse the aging process (*see p. 663*).

"I've met many people in their 60s and 70s who are taking hGH and other things, and they're amazing in their youth and vitality," says Ronald Klatz, founder of the American Academy of Anti-Aging Medicine and co-author of *Stopping the Clock: Why Many of Us Will Live Past 100 and Enjoy Every Minute.*

According to Klatz and others, hormones can help prolong not only the quantity but also the quality of life by increasing everything from muscle and bone mass to the thickness of skin.

But the National Institute on Aging (NIA) opposes the use of hormones as an anti-aging treatment, contending that their effectiveness and, more important, long-term side effects are not yet known.

"Frankly, we just don't know enough about any of these treatments to recommend their use," says Huber Warner, acting associate director of the NIA. Indeed, Warner says, some studies point to potentially serious side effects. For instance, Warner and others say, hGH use has been shown to lead to diabetes, high blood pressure and a number of other maladies.

Klatz and others counter that the NIA is behind the curve on hormone treatments, and that in the proper doses they are both effective and safe.

But even if anti-aging proponents are right about hormones and other treatments, who is going to pay for them? Many anti-aging treatments are expensive (hGH costs up to $15,000 per year) and generally are not covered by health insurers.

In recent months, the new anti-impotency drug Viagra has forced insurance companies to grapple with

American Academy of Facial Plastic and Reconstructive Surgery

The Boom in Aging Boomers

More than twice as many Americans 65 and older will be alive in 2050 as there were in 1996. The anticipated increase reflects the unprecedented size of the baby boom generation — people born from 1946-1964 — and likely advances in hygiene, nutrition and medical technology.

U.S. Population to 2050
(in thousands)

	1996	2010	2030	2050
All ages	265,253	297,716	346,899	393,931
Under age 5	19,403	20,012	23,066	27,106
5-13	34,809	65,605	41,588	47,805
14-17	15,167	16,894	18,788	21,207
18-24	24,616	30,138	31,826	36,333
25-34	40,374	38,292	42,744	49,366
35-44	43,311	38,521	44,263	47,393
45-54	32,341	43,564	38,897	43,494
55-64	21,360	35,283	36,348	42,368
65 and older	**33,872**	**39,408**	**69,379**	**78,859**
85 and older	3,747	5,671	8,455	18,223

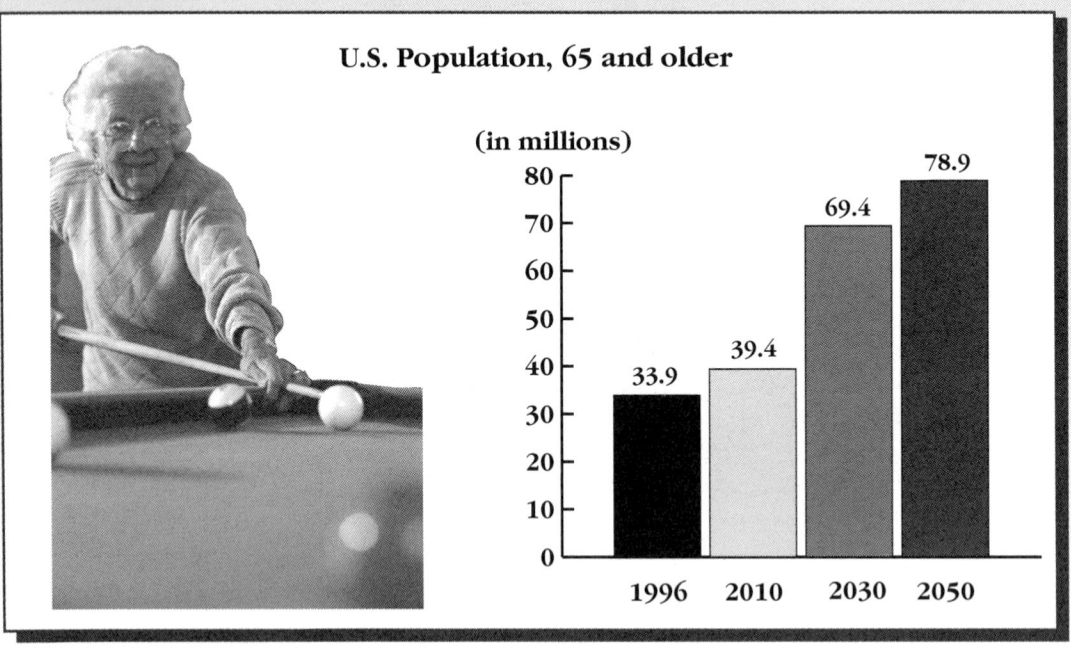

U.S. Population, 65 and older

(in millions)

1996	2010	2030	2050
33.9	39.4	69.4	78.9

Source: U.S. Census Bureau

the question of cost. While treating impotency is not the same as battling the effects of aging, both Viagra and hormones currently come under the heading of "lifestyle" drugs. To put it another way, Viagra is seen as helping people lead better lives, but it is not necessary in the same way that insulin is for a diabetic.

Many insurers are offering limited or no coverage for Viagra users, a policy that has, not surprisingly, sparked a number of lawsuits. But insurers argue that covering "lifestyle" drugs would lead to much higher rates for everyone, especially if, as expected, new anti-aging therapies become more popular.

Jane Galvin, managed-care policy director at the American Health Insurance Association, is among those who argue that insurance coverage for anti-aging therapies will drive health-care costs into the stratosphere. "There seems to be a disconnect in our society between wanting benefits and being willing to pay the cost," she says.

But others say that many lifestyle drugs, such as anti-aging therapies, will pay off for insurers in the long term as people become healthier and spend less time in doctors' offices and hospitals. Similarly, physicians argue that maintaining a healthy lifestyle during adulthood will mean less likelihood of chronic diseases or disabilities in old age.

Insurers may continue to balk at paying for lifestyle drugs, but the baby boomers are not likely to stop looking for new ways to look and feel young. As the generation enters its sixth decade, here are some of the questions observers are asking:

Are baby boomers trying too hard to stay young?

According to a new survey, roughly half of all baby boomers are "somewhat" or "very" concerned about aging. The same poll found that six out of 10 boomers have taken or are considering taking steps to fight Father Time. [2]

Indeed, baby boomers are fueling the enormous growth of industries that cater to helping people look and feel younger, from cosmetic surgeons to the makers of fitness machines to producers of anti-aging drugs and treatments. "True to the boomer ethos of having it all, this demographic bulge wants to enjoy the benefits of growing older while still retaining the vigor and vitality of youth," said Edward Keller, president of Roper Starch Worldwide, which

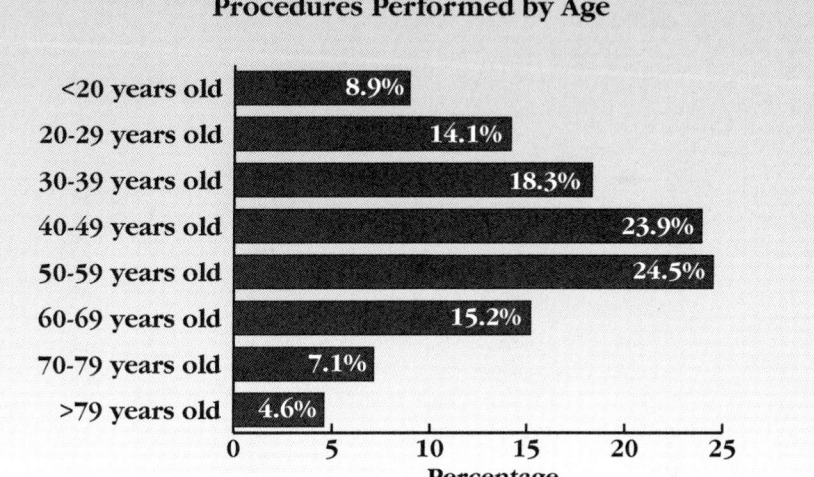

Facial Plastic Surgery Appeals to Middle-Aged

People ages 40-69 have more than 60 percent of all cosmetic facial plastic surgery performed in the United States.

Procedures Performed by Age

Age	Percentage
<20 years old	8.9%
20-29 years old	14.1%
30-39 years old	18.3%
40-49 years old	23.9%
50-59 years old	24.5%
60-69 years old	15.2%
70-79 years old	7.1%
>79 years old	4.6%

Note: Percentages do not add to 100 due to rounding and a ±7.5 % margin of error.

Source: American Academy of Facial Plastic and Reconstructive Surgery; poll by Wirthlin Worldwide, August 1997

conducted the poll. [3]

And "having it all" is growing much more likely, at least for a time. Many health experts are now saying that a lifetime of proper diet and exercise, coupled with continuing advances in medical technology, should give the average boomer a chance of living to 100, relatively free of pain and disability. Others claim anti-aging drugs will extend the average human life far beyond 100.

But some observers say that for all its concern about health, the baby boom generation is too obsessed with staying young. While there is nothing wrong with "clean living," the boomers are "definitely trying too hard to be young, to be youthful," says Rifkin of the Foundation on Economic Trends.

Rifkin finds attitudes toward youth evident in all spheres of boomer life. "Look at the way they dress, the way they act," he says. "It's like they're college kids."

Rifkin argues that such efforts to stay young are driven by Americans' collective desire to update themselves. "We now live in a culture that has replaced historical consciousness with therapeutic consciousness," he says. "The idea of time passing in your life has been replaced by a continual quest for self-improvement." In short, instead of accepting life's differing phases, boomers view their existence as a constant quest for self-betterment.

To *Governing's* Ehrenhalt, the boomers' obsession with youth suggests that, "It has never occurred to them that they are getting older. Their parents understood that you get old and die, but they don't think the normal rules apply to them. They're like a whole generation of Kennedies."

Regardless of what motivates boomers, many observers argue that their efforts to remain ever youthful will have a devastating psychological effect on their generation as their bodies and minds betray them in old

Cosmetic Surgery Is Just Another Weapon . . .

Every 7.7 seconds, a baby boomer in the United States turns 50. The generation that gave us Woodstock and disco music is getting on, and it's starting to show. Smooth faces and taut bodies are increasingly giving way to sagging chins, bulging thighs and baldness.

Polls indicate that a majority of boomers — contrary to their image as narcissistic children desperately clinging to their youth — accept the wrinkles, bulges and thinning hair as an inevitable part of aging. But a growing number are increasingly turning to cosmetic surgeons and others to restore at least some of their youthful appearance.

Plastic surgery was once reserved for movie stars and millionaires. But today cosmetic procedures are well within reach for most middle-class Americans. Average costs range from $691 for a chemical peel to $2,900 for a forehead lift and $5,439 for a rytidectomy or face lift to remove wrinkles.

Indeed, the nation may be at the beginning of a plastic surgery boom, fueled by shifts in demographics, attitudes and technology. And, like so many other past trends, boomers will lead the way.

Some would say that the boom has already begun. According to the American Society for Aesthetic Plastic Surgery, 2 million cosmetic procedures were performed in the United States last year, an increase of 75 percent over the last four years. Significantly, nearly half of the procedures were performed on people between the ages of 35 and 50. [1]

"The largest number of consultations we do are with people ages 35 to 50," confirms Stephen W. Perkins, a facial plastic surgeon in Indianapolis, Ind., and president-elect of the American Academy of Facial Plastic and Reconstructive Surgery. "They look in the mirror one day and realize that they look more like their mom or dad and say, 'Wait a minute, that's not how I perceive myself.' "

Denise Thomas, a New York-based cosmetic-surgery consultant who helps people choose the right doctor, puts it a bit more bluntly: "A lot of the baby boomers have the money, and they are fighting like hell to stay young." [2]

Indeed, according to a 1997 Gallup Poll, one-third of all female baby boomers said they would "do whatever it takes to stay looking young." And men, who made up a tiny percentage of cosmetic-surgery patients a decade ago, are now warming to the idea of liposuction, eye lifts and other procedures. [3]

Many experts say that these trends reflect a fundamental change in public attitudes about cosmetic surgery. For one thing, plastic surgery is no longer considered as strange or vain as it once was. "Cosmetic surgery had a stigma in their parents' generation, but baby boomers have grown up with it . . . they consider it an investment in themselves," said Timothy Marten, a plastic surgeon in San Francisco. [4]

In addition, a lot of people get the surgery because they expect to live and work longer and don't want to be "old" for decades. Boomers "expect and want to be more active whether they choose to continue working or to 'reinvent' themselves during retirement," says Fritz E. Barton Jr., a clinical professor of plastic surgery at Texas Southwestern University.

age. "Ultimately, everybody is going to be very disappointed," says *Master Trend* author Russell.

Instead, Russell and others argue, boomers should approach aging as a natural part of living, not an enemy that needs to be combated at every turn.

"Aging, which is to say decline and decay, is natural," writes Jonathan Yardley, a columnist and Pulitzer Prize-winning book critic at *The Washington Post*. "It is not, as all these Hefner clones lining up for their jolts of Viagra would have us believe, an ailment, but an unavoidable process that has far more to it than loss and regret." To Yardley, acting one's age offers "riches and pleasures . . . most connected in one way or another with the lessons that experience teaches." [4]

Rifkin agrees, adding that boomers who seek the fountain of youth will "become arrested in their development" because they're going to be continually trying to live at the same unrealistic age. "And so they'll miss the valuable passages in life that come with aging normally and won't have the wisdom to appreciate things in a different light when they get older."

But Yardley and Rifkin are criticized for taking a superficial view of the desire to look and feel younger.

"They're referring to the Hollywood stereotype of starlets who are trying to be 30 when they're really 60, and that's just not the way it is," Klatz says.

Trying to stay young is more about "optimal living" than anything else, he argues. People who try to stay and feel young will be more mature than others because a longer and healthier life will allow them to learn and grow more. "This is about giving yourself the time to achieve mastery of your life, to explore and do all the things you want to do," he says.

"I see this trend as a positive thing," adds the Boomer Institute's Ernest. "If people really want to maintain a good quality of life and push the boundaries of aging, so what?"

Consultant Dychtwald also sees benefits in trying to remain young even if such efforts produce little more than a youthful outlook. "That's as important as everything else," she says. Even purely appearance-oriented treatments, like cosmetic surgery and hair replacement, are good, many say. "If it boosts your self-esteem, makes you feel good about

... In the Battle to Stay Youthful

Others point out that many people think they need to look good in order to get ahead. And, in our youth-obsessed society, looking good usually means looking young. Older boomers "come in and say, 'I need to look young and fresh to compete these younger men and women at work,'" Perkins says.

In addition, boomers are being encouraged by plastic surgeons to have procedures done while they're in their 40s or even 30s. "They're saying, 'If you do it before you really need it, then it will look more natural and last much longer,'" says Maddy Kent Dychtwald, a San Francisco consultant who specializes in the baby boom generation.

Growth in cosmetic procedures is also being fueled by new developments in technology. Plastic surgery no longer just means the traditional face lift — a procedure that can be very painful and not cheap. "They're coming out with more techniques that are non-invasive and can be done in the office, cheaply and quickly," says Vicki Joy, a spokeswoman for the American Academy of Anti-Aging Medicine in Chicago.

Less intrusive ways to fight aging include removing wrinkles with lasers and shoring up sagging skin with collagen injections.

Even the more involved procedures have become safer and easier. Liposuction, in which fat is literally sucked from inside the body, has been made less difficult through the use of ultrasound, which melts the fat and makes it easier to remove.

Another technique that has gained in popularity in recent years is hair transplantation, which until recently produced mixed results and could be very painful. "It used to have the tendency not to look natural," says Perkins, who does hair transplants as well as traditional cosmetic surgery. The problem, he says, was that clumps of implanted hair follicles had to be spaced apart in order to grow properly. "We called them corn rows."

Today, Perkins says, "it looks much more natural because we've made huge advances in the procedure by figuring out ways to place hair closer together." In addition, doctors use a combination of local anaesthesia and sedatives to better control the pain associated with hair transplants.

Cosmetic procedures are likely to become more and more common as affluent boomers enter middle age. "As long as there isn't some sort of big economic downturn, I think the desire for these things will continue to grow," Perkins says.

"You know," he adds, "we spend an awful lot of time, effort and money on clothes, make-up and other things to make ourselves look good, and plastic surgery is just and extension of that."

[1] Sharon Walsh, "Cosmetic Surgeons Are Getting a Lift From the Baby Boomers," *The Washington Post*, April 3, 1998.

[2] Quoted in *ibid.*

[3] Poll cited in Kim Lamb Gregory, "Price of Beauty: Look Within Before Going Under the Knife," *Ventura County Star*, March 29, 1998.

[4] Quoted in Lorna Fernandes, "Surgeons Help Boomers Look as Young as They Feel," *San Francisco Business Times*, Feb. 6, 1998.

yourself, then it is helpful," argues Ernest. *(See graph, p. 655.)*

And feeling good about yourself is vital, Dychtwald and Ernest say. "When you feel old and think of yourself as old, then you are old," Ernest says. "Ultimately all of these efforts are about energy, vitality and behavior rather than wrinkles," Dychtwald says.

Boomers don't want to be something they're not, goes this reasoning, but the best of what they already are. "Boomers don't want to look 20, they want to look and feel good for their age," Ernest says.

Should insurers pay for some or all of the cost of Viagra and other "lifestyle-enhancing" drugs?

Paul Sibley-Schreiber, a 51-year-old psychotherapist from New York City, recently sued his medical insurance company, challenging its decision not to fully pay for Viagra prescriptions. "The first pill I took had a miraculous effect," he said, shortly after filing the suit in federal court. [5]

Like other Viagra users, Sibley-Schreiber believes that insurers and medical providers have an obligation to help impotent men. But some insurers and managed-care providers, including Aetna/U.S. Healthcare, have refused to pay for any Viagra use. In fact, only half of all insurers have said that they will cover the new drug. And many of these companies are offering only limited coverage. Cigna Healthcare, for instance, is paying for only six Viagra pills per month. [6]

Among insurers, there is a general consensus that most purely cosmetic treatments, like hair replacement or a face lift, should not be covered by medical insurance. "If plastic surgery were covered, we'd all go out and have it done," says Vicki Joy, a spokeswoman for the American Academy of Anti-Aging Medicine.

But other so-called "lifestyle" drugs, like Viagra, have posed a new and difficult question for insurance companies: When is something necessary enough and important enough to warrant insurance coverage?

This fundamental question is likely to become much more important in the near future, as pharmaceutical companies bring out a plethora of new drugs designed to restore youth (or at least the appearance of it) and vigor to millions. For instance, a number of hormones are being tested to determine if they reverse the aging process. Other drugs are being developed that aim to do everything from improve memory to promoting healthy sleep patterns.

Some anti-aging experts say that insurance companies should pay for many of these new "lifestyle" drugs. To begin with, they argue, many of the new treatments will keep people from getting sick, thus bringing the overall cost of health care down. "It's a lot cheaper to keep them healthy now than to wait until they're sick later," Joy points out. For example, she says, suppose a new growth hormone treatment could keep a 40-year-old at age 30 physically. "This means that person will, on average, be healthier, which is much cheaper for insurance companies.

Joy and others also argue that in the near future, new drugs that restore vitality will be deemed essential for healthy people. In a sense, she argues, they will be like vaccines or cholesterol tests: not absolutely necessary but an accepted part of what the medical profession believes is desirable for good health.

Proponents of insuring lifestyle drugs, like Joy, argue that if these life-enhancing therapies are not covered, only the rich will be able to afford them. This in turn will lead to two health-care systems, or even three: for people without insurance; for those with insurance; and for those with the financial wherewithal to afford anti-aging and other lifestyle drugs.

But many insurance companies contend that covering Viagra and the flood of lifestyle drugs that will be released in the coming decades will have dire consequences for the majority of Americans with private health insurance. "Unless people are willing to accept additional insurance costs, they can't have everything they want," says Galvin of the American Health Insurance Association. "People seem to think they deserve it and someone else will pay the cost."

Galvin argues that if the cost of health insurance increases due to coverage of lifestyle drugs, the burden could be shared by everyone. And that means that insurance could become prohibitively expensive for working- and lower-middle-class people who already having trouble keeping themselves and their families covered. "It's quite simple, really: The higher the cost of medical insurance, the fewer insured people there will be," Galvin says.

Others argue that covering non-necessary treatments, like anti-aging drugs, would lead to unfathomable increases in health-care spending. "Imagine if insurance companies and managed-care providers were to pay for lifestyle drugs," Russell says. "Everyone would want them, and spending would become out of control."

But many think that regardless of what the insurance companies want, they eventually will have to pay for a host of what are considered lifestyle drugs, especially those that halt or reverse aging. "They'll be forced to because the public clamor for these things is going to be overwhelming," claims Klatz. "I mean, look at how they're demanding [coverage for] Viagra. Imagine what it's going to be like when they learn all about stuff that can make you look and feel younger."

Galvin agrees that like any business, insurers and health-care organizations will provide for those lifestyle drugs that are demanded by the majority of the public. "If it becomes the standard, if it's embraced by society, then we'll cover it," she says. ∎

BACKGROUND

Birth of the Boomers

Traditionally, demographers define the so-called baby-boom generation as those born between 1946 and 1964. During these 18 years, the United States experienced unparalleled population growth.

The boom in births was precipitated by two factors. First, World War II had ended in triumph in 1945, allowing an entire generation of men to return home. Overwhelmingly, they returned after years of service with a yearning to settle down and start a family. As a result, the number of marriages in the United States doubled from 1945 to 1946, to more than 2.2 million. This boom in matrimony was given a boost by the economic prosperity that characterized the years following the war. The flourishing economy meant that jobs were plentiful and wages were rising, allowing people who wanted children to afford to have them.

In 1946, 3.4 million babies were born in the United States, or 20 percent more than the previous year. By 1952 the number of births had risen to more than 3.9 million. Two years later, the annual total topped 4 million for the first time in U.S. history and stayed above that number for the next decade. At the peak of the boom in the late 1950s and early '60s, the number of births exceeded 4.3 million. [7]

Growing up in the prosperous America of the 1950s and '60s had a profound impact on the boomer generation. For the first time, a majority of the nation's children were being raised in comfortable households. The nation's new, widespread affluence allowed parents to provide things for their children — cars, trips and higher education — that previously had been reserved largely for a privileged few.

Parents also indulged their children psychologically and emotionally in a new way. These were the "Spock" babies, raised on Dr. Benjamin Spock's child-rearing methods, which encouraged parents to be affectionate with their sons and daughters, and have fun with them. No longer to be seen and not heard, children were increasingly perceived as individuals and encouraged to think and speak for themselves.

Continued on p. 660

Chronology

1945-1964

Post-war optimism coupled with economic prosperity leads to a birth explosion in the United States.

1945
World War II ends, and millions of servicemen return home.

1946
The number of couples marrying doubles, to 2.2 million. The number of births in the Untied States also increases by 20 percent, to 3.4 million. Dr. Benjamin Spock publishes *The Common Sense Book of Baby and Child Care.*

1954
For the first time in U.S. history, more than 4 million babies are born.

1956
Elvis Presley appears on the Ed Sullivan Show.

1964-1972

The first members of the baby boom generation go to college, leading to the Youth Movement.

1964
The Beatles arrive in the United States. Congress passes the Tonkin Gulf resolution in August, authorizing a de facto escalation of the war in Vietnam.

1967
James Bedford becomes the first person to be cryonically frozen.

1968
Anti-war protests erupt at campuses across the United States.

1969
An estimated 400,000 people arrive at a farm in Woodstock, N.Y., for a three-day rock concert.

1970
Four students protesting the Vietnam War are shot and killed by National Guardsmen at Kent State University, setting off a new round of campus protests.

1972
U.S. troops pull out of Vietnam.

1973-1989

The Youth Movement fades. Boomers become more focused on having fun and making money.

1973
The Arab oil embargo throws the country into a recession.

1978
Disco music reaches its peak.

1980
Conservative standard-bearer Ronald Reagan is elected president.

1986
The Alliance for Aging Research is founded.

1990-2011

The first baby boomers begin to enter middle age.

1993
The American Academy of Anti-Aging Medicine is founded.

1995
A study commissioned by the American Association of Retired Persons (AARP) finds that people in their fifties — far from resting on their laurels and planning on retirement — consider the decade a challenging and even turbulent period in their lives.

1996
The first baby boomers, including President Clinton, turn 50.

1997
More than 700,000 Americans have some sort of cosmetic surgery procedure done, almost twice as many as were performed in 1992.

1998
The anti-impotency drug Viagra becomes one of the nation's best-selling prescription medications.

2000
Life expectancy in the United States is expected to approach 80.

2011
The first members of the baby boom generation will turn 65.

A Primer on 'Anti-Aging' Hormones

Hormones are substances produced by the body that help to regulate bodily functions. As humans age, levels of some of these substances — like estrogen — begin to decrease. Now a number of doctors and others are claiming that the aging process can be slowed or even reversed by replacing hormones that are lost through aging. These anti-aging proponents point to the thousands of middle-aged and elderly people who have restored one or more of these hormones and now look and feel years younger.

But the National Institute on Aging (NIA) and many mainstream groups warn that there is no conclusive research showing that hormone supplements can affect the aging process. In addition, they say, artificial hormones are powerful chemicals that can cause damaging side effects.

Here are some of the most widely used laboratory-produced hormones and the possible benefits and side effects of taking them:

DHEA — Naturally produced by the adrenal glands, perched atop the kidneys, DHEA may not actually be a hormone. But when broken down by the body it becomes estrogen and testosterone. After about age 30, the body begins producing less DHEA, and some anti-aging proponents claim that replacing it will improve vitality and natural immunity. But according to the NIA, DHEA may cause liver damage.

Estrogen — Millions of women take estrogen to relieve symptoms associated with menopause, a treatment widely accepted by the mainstream medical community. Studies have found that estrogen replacement significantly lowered risk for menopausal women of heart disease, osteoporosis and possibly Alzheimer's disease, while making many look and feel younger. The same studies also found an increased risk for breast and uterine cancers among those taking the hormone.

Human Growth Hormone (hGH) — Many anti-aging specialists consider hGH to be the best hormone supplement currently available in the fight against aging. Some small studies have shown that taking hGH can increase muscle mass and bring everything from increased energy to renewed sexual potency to those who take it. The hormone, which is made in the pituitary gland just below the brain, regulates human growth. It also is crucial in organ and tissue development. Very short children are often given hGH, with positive results. But the NIA argues that healthy adults should not take the hormone because it has been shown to cause problems ranging from diabetes to heart failure.

Melatonin — Many people take extra melatonin, which is naturally produced in the brain's pineal gland, to help them sleep regularly. Others claim it boosts the immune system and can slow the aging process. But the NIA says that there is no solid evidence to support these claims. In addition, the institute says, melatonin supplements, which are widely available in drug stores, can lead to drowsiness, confusion and headaches.

Sources: National Institute on Aging, American Academy of Anti-Aging Medicine

---

Continued from p. 658

Many see this period in American social history as a "great awakening," when outmoded taboos were thrown off, and a more rational approach to child-rearing was adopted. But others argue that these new methods did not have entirely positive results. "The boomers have an 'I deserve' mentality that their parents instilled in them by telling them they were special all the time," Dychtwald says.

The Youth Movement

But the baby boom generation was influenced by more than just its home life. All of American culture was adjusting to meet the needs of this huge new group of young people. In the movies, actors like James Dean ("Rebel Without a Cause," 1955) and Marlon Brando ("On the Waterfront," 1954) portrayed young men fighting against the stifling world of their elders.

Around the same time, music began to radically change. While kids growing up in the 1940s and early '50s were dancing to the likes of Sinatra and Doris Day, those who started listening to music in the mid-'50s began with Elvis Presley, who was considered so controversial that when he appeared on Ed Sullivan's popular variety TV show, the camera didn't show his sensual gyrations. Presley, though in many ways respectful of religion and his country, owed at least some of his immense popularity to his bad-boy image, his willingness to defy sexual conventions.

Adolescents and their younger brothers and sisters would move from Elvis to the "Beatles" and "Rolling Stones" and finally to the psychedelic rock of the late 1960s, popularized by Jimi Hendrix and groups like "The Doors" and "Jefferson Airplane." With each new musical phase, societal norms that had been commonplace in the 1940s and '50s, like unquestioning patriotism and the evils of illegal narcotics, were further challenged.

In 1964, the first generation born

after World War II entered college. In August of that year, Congress passed the Tonkin Gulf resolution, escalating the nation's involvement in Vietnam. In short, just as the first baby boomers were becoming eligible for college, and the draft, the government was gearing up for a new war.

Contrary to modern impressions, polls show that most Americans — including youths — supported U.S. involvement in Vietnam throughout most of the 1960s. Still, student activism against the war played an important role in turning around public opinion and political support for the war. By 1968, boomers were taking over college campuses across the country to protest the war and other issues. That same year, President Lyndon B. Johnson decided not to run for re-election, largely because of the war opposition he had fomented.

The anti-war movement reached its peak in 1969, when hundreds of thousands of boomers congregated in Washington at a massive rally for peace, and then at Woodstock, N.Y., for the outdoor rock concert that became the quintessential "'60s" event.

The following year, still more people were galvanized by the shooting deaths of four students by National Guardsmen at an anti-Vietnam War protest at Kent State University in Ohio. But the aftermath of Kent State was the movement's last hurrah. After the war in Vietnam was over, the country, worn out by the upheaval of the past decade, looked for some sort of return to normalcy.

But the impact of the student move-ment on the baby boom generation was profound. For even though only a small percentage of boomers actually participated in the rallies, the sit-ins and concerts, they nonetheless had changed the nation. The generation had tasted a kind of power that their less rebellious parents and grandparents had never known.

In addition, many of the kids who had sat on the sidelines felt at least a certain kinship with those in the trenches. As journalist Landon Y. Jones writes: "The actual attendance

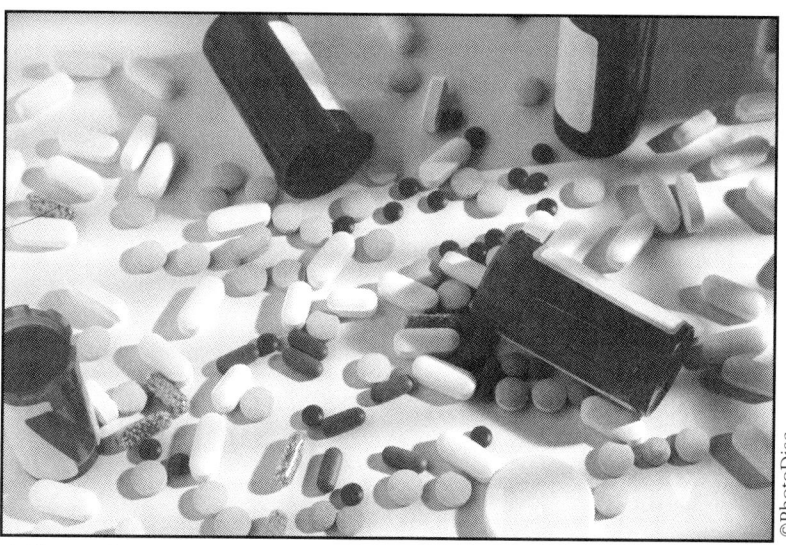

Millions of Americans take anti-aging hormones, but the National Institute on Aging cautions that their long-term effects are unknown.

at Woodstock was less than half a million, but twice as many would later claim they'd been there. And many millions more felt as if they'd been there." [8] In other words, Woodstock and the other events surrounding the student movement were for boomers what World War II had been for their parents: a defining experience.

That experience was created by more than just political activism and music. Boomers also broke new ground on a more personal level by casting aside their parents' rules on dating and mating, embracing the nascent sexual revolution. And the use of illegal drugs, heretofore confined to the fringes of society, went mainstream.

Redefining Middle Age

The student protest movement of the 1960s established boomers as generational trend-setters. Since then, they've largely been lauded (or blamed) for the "'60s," the "me" decade and the yuppie years of the '80s.

Indeed, many boomers pursued having fun during the disco years and money-making '80s with the same single-minded gusto that they exhibited during their attempts to "save the world" in the 1960s. Some see this self-absorbing energy as the key to understanding the generation and its attitudes.

"Boomers always grab hold of every phase of life they're in and assume that everyone else realizes that it's the best phase of life to be in," says demographics consultant Bill Strauss, co-author of *Generations* and *The Fourth Turning*, which explore the interplay of age groups in American society.

Now boomers are entering a new life phase and many, like Strauss, say that the generation that redefined what it meant to be young will do the same for our perception of middle and old age. In fact, Dychtwald says, "The baby boomers have already redefined what it means to be young today. The youth culture now ex-

©PhotoDisc

Cryonics: Promising Life After Death

It sounds like science fiction: Freeze people immediately after they have died and then revive them when medical science has discovered the cure for whatever killed them. Until 1964, cryonics was indeed squarely in the realm of sci-fi. Then physics Professor Robert Ettinger argued in *The Prospect of Immortality* that cryonics was possible. Three years later, 73-year-old James H. Bedford, a 73-year-old psychology professor who had died of kidney cancer, became the first human being to be frozen.

There are now four known cryonics facilities, all in the United States. So far, 73 Americans — including Ettinger's first wife and mother — have been frozen. Another estimated 500 people in the U.S. and another 300 from abroad have signed up to be cryogenically preserved after death.[1]

With so few customers, cryonics isn't quite a booming business yet. But supporters say that widespread acceptance is on the horizon. "There's a huge market there," says physician Art Quaife, president of Trans Time, a California-based cryonics company. "All we have to do is convince people that this is desirable."[2]

But it may be a hard sell. According to a January 1997 ABC News poll, only 7 percent of Americans would consider cryonics.

There are also some technical problems to overcome. Bodies may be easy to freeze, but none have been thawed. And, most biologists say, there little to suggest that they can be.

Scientists have succeeded in freezing single cells, like sperm, and bringing them back to life. Even small clusters of cells, like embryos, can be frozen and reanimated. "The problem comes when you start freezing large blocks of tissue," says Ken Hobbs, a physician at the Royal Free Hospital in London, England.

The "problem," Hobbs and others say, is that when a lot of cells are frozen together, water between them expands into ice crystals, rupturing their membranes. While some studies with frozen rat hearts have shown promise, most evidence suggests that organs, not to mention complete bodies, are unrevivable, at least for the time being.

Still, cryonics proponents are optimistic that science will overcome the problems with reanimation and other hurdles. "If the present pace of science keeps up, we might understand the whole thing over the next couple of centuries," said artificial intelligence pioneer and cryonics booster Marvin Minsky.[3]

Preparing a body for cryonic storage is a time-consuming and complicated process. First, the blood must be flushed out and replaced with fluids that aid in the freezing process. Then, the body is slowly frozen over a 20-day period before being placed in a container filled with liquid nitrogen, which keeps it at a constant temperature of -320 degrees F.

Some who opt for cryonic storage have only their heads frozen, the assumption being that in the far future science will be able to replicate everything but the brain — hence the need only for the head. With less to freeze and store, a head is cheaper than a whole body.

Still, freezing even a head can be an expensive proposition. CryoSpan, a California firm, charges about $60,000. Complete bodies cost twice as much.[4]

---

[1] Clint O'Connor, "Putting Death on Ice," *Cleveland Plain Dealer*, June 15, 1997.

[2] *Ibid.*

[3] Quoted in Gerry Byrne, "Connected: Immortality," *The Daily Telegraph*, Jan. 22, 1998.

[4] Ed Brown, "Would You Pay $125,000 to Get Frozen?" *Fortune*, Nov. 24, 1997.

---

tends into the 40s."

The Alliance for Aging Research's Perry agrees. "Middle age will never be thought of as middle age again after the baby boomers have passed through this period," he says. "People used to think of middle age as a prelude to climbing into the rocking chair. No more."

Many are actually climbing mountains. And many think that they, not the youth, are living in the best of times. "I think there are as many young people who envy us as we who envy them," Valentine says.

But others argue that boomers are fooling themselves if they think they're going to remain young and hip or that the culture will change drastically to suit their new image of themselves. "Youth is beauty, and that will never change," Russell says. "The image of what we perceive as good-looking or hip people will expand to include some people who are older than 20, but not that much."

William Dinges, a professor of religious studies at The Catholic University of America, agrees. "Youth is a powerful current in our society," he says, "and that won't change."

But others, while agreeing that wrinkles will never be "in," say that advertisers and other bellwethers of the national psyche have expanded their use of well-preserved middle-aged and older people.

"Look at all the major modeling agencies," Klatz says. "They all have senior models who have that Lauren Bacall look." The reason, Klatz and others say, is that the nearly 80 million members of the baby boom generation are too big a market to ignore, and they don't want to look at anorexic 18-year-olds all the time. ∎

CURRENT SITUATION

Fighting to Stay Young

Like many other trends in the United States, baby boomers helped to create the diet and exercise craze that first appeared in the 1970s. Today, more and more boomers see proper nutrition and fitness as a way not only to live longer but also better.

In fact, gerontologists John W. Rowe and Robert Kahn argue in their book *Successful Aging* that lifestyle choices — particularly exercise and a good diet — more than genetics or chance will determine how well and how long we live.

And boomers are being told by everyone from their doctors to the media that good eating and exercise habits cannot be put off until retirement. Regular exercise, for instance, helps to stave off the natural degenerative effects of aging. This decline begins after about age 30, when the metabolism starts to slow down and muscle and bone mass begin decreasing. At about age 40, these changes start to take their toll, with both men and women becoming more susceptible to gaining weight — especially around the waist and thighs. More important, if unchecked, this natural degeneration can lead to frailty later in life. [9]

Good eating habits are also crucial, health experts say. Indeed, a mountain of research suggests that a diet low in fat and heavy on fruits, vegetables and grains can help prevent killers like cancer and heart disease.

Hence the new interest in nutrition and fitness is not surprising. And it is reflected in dramatic increases in the sales of products and services that aim to keep people fit and trim. Health clubs and health-oriented food and nutrition outlets, like Fresh Fields and General Nutrition Centers (GNC), are proliferating at an unprecedented rate. And, sales of health-related products are soaring. For instance, since 1992, sales of fitness equipment in the United States have nearly doubled from $1.6 billion to an estimated $3.1 billion in 1998. Much of this increase is due to boomers, according to a report issued earlier this year by the Sporting Goods Manufacturers Association. [10]

At the same time, sales of vitamin and mineral supplements are increasing even more rapidly. In the last year alone, food, drug and discount stores have reported a 21.8 percent increase in vitamin sales and a 44.1 percent rise in purchases of mineral supplements. Much of the growth is coming from boomers, experts say. [11] In addition, mainstream supermarket chains like Safeway and A&P are stocking more organic (grown without pesticides) produce and all-natural, low-fat products. According to Mike Rourke, a spokesman for A&P, boomers are the impetus behind the new trend as well. [12]

And boomers will become even more interested in better diet and nutrition as they care for aging parents with chronic and debilitating diseases. "Absolutely, it has an impact on the way you think, in the sense that you want to take better care of yourself," said John Sumner, a 52-year-old factory manager from Wilmington, Del., whose mother died in 1994 after years in failing health. [13]

"Boomers know they're going to die," says Joy of the American Academy of Anti-Aging Medicine. "But they want to look and feel good while they're alive instead of spending their final years in a nursing home like so many people do today."

Still, all the news about boomers is not good. While an unprecedented number of them are trying to eat right and exercise, the majority are not. For instance, the average person between the ages of 35 and 49 consumes nearly 40 percent of his or her calories in fat, almost twice the necessary level. In addition, the desire for convenience, whether it be fast food, frozen dinners or takeout food, leaves eight out of 10 boomers without the essential minerals, vitamins and other substances needed for a balanced diet, says Udo Erasmus, author of *Fats That Heal; Fats That Kill.* [14] Finally, according to surveys conducted by the federal Centers for Disease Control and Prevention and other organizations, only about one-third of all boomers engage in regular exercise.

'Anti-Aging' Drugs

"A 50-year-old college instructor regains the face and figure of her modeling days. A 43-year-old, balding, enervated man finds both his hair and energy restored. A senior citizen recovers his interest in sex — and reports that his penis size has grown by 20 percent." [15] These are just some of the amazing claims made by those who have taken human growth hormone (hGH), a substance that many say stops and even reverses the effects of aging.

Indeed, hGH has been hailed by some, among them Klatz, as a fountain of youth waiting to be exploited. "It is only one of hundreds of therapies in the anti-aging arsenal, but it's the most dramatic one we have," says Klatz, co-author of the 1997 book *Grow Young with hGH.*

Among other things, Klatz says, hGH increases the body's muscle mass, while decreasing levels of fat.

In addition, he says, the hormone improves one's level of energy and generally gives those who take it a more youthful appearance. And, Klatz claims, "these long-term positive results are holding up."

Klatz and other proponents of hGH point to a 1994-96 study of 202 people, mostly men, between 39 and 74 conducted by L. Cass Terry and Edmund Chein of the Medical College of Wisconsin and Palm Springs' Life Extension Institute, respectively. They found that 88 percent of those who took hGH reported an increase in muscle strength. In the same group, 72 percent said they experienced a decrease in body fat; 61 percent claimed a reduction in wrinkles; and 75 percent had an increase in sexual potency. [16]

HGH is just one of a number of hormonal and other treatments that anti-aging doctors like Klatz are excited about. Others include DHEA, a substance produced by the adrenal glands, melatonin, a hormone made in the brain's pineal gland and what are known as the male and female hormones, testosterone and estrogen.

"We find these treatments work best when taken together," Klatz says, adding that the combined therapy can greatly enhance both quality and quantity of life. "These therapies are just short of a miracle," he contends.

Some of these treatments, like hGH, melatonin and estrogen, have been hailed by some experts as promising wonder drugs. But the National Institute on Aging's Warner and others worry that knowledge of these new "anti-aging therapies" is too limited to even consider their use at this time. "Our feeling is that there might be some validity to some of the claims about hGH and other [hormone therapies], but we don't know enough yet to recommend them to the public," he says.

In the case of hGH, Warner says, there is some indication that it makes patients "feel better and improves

muscle mass." But, he says, there are also side effects associated with the hormone, like diabetes, high blood pressure and possibly even heart failure. "We think this is very risky, that it can possibly do more harm than good," he says.

Warner and others argue that the scientific community needs more time to study the long-term effects of hGH and the other anti-aging hormones in order to determine both their effectiveness and safety. "We're funding a number of studies on hGH right now," he says.

In the meantime, the NIA recommends that people looking for anti-aging treatments stay away from hGH and other hormones. "The terrible thing about some of these things, like DHEA and melatonin, is that you can buy them at your local supermarket and start taking it," Warner says. That's because hormones are naturally occurring substances and hence not subject to the same regulation as would a new drug. "People, in essence, can become their own test subjects," he adds. And, he points out, with hGH the situation is even more ominous due to the great expense associated with the therapy. "People pay up to $15,000 a year for these treatments," he says.

But Klatz counters that NIA is "too conservative" in its assessment of these hormones. "NIA is creating an unnecessary hysteria because when hGH is given in [proper] doses, there have been virtually no side effects."

Of course, he says, like anything else, hGH can be dangerous if not administered properly. "Aspirin can cause you to bleed to death [internally] if you take too much of it," he says. But, Klatz says, doctors have known for a long time what a safe dosage is. And, when taken properly, hGH and the other hormones are fine.

For example, Klatz says, in the Terry/Chein hGH study, the subjects have suffered no unusual side ef-

fects. "There have been a few cases of prostate cancer in the group, but that's to be expected with men this age," he says. In addition, he claims, people have been taking hGH for a long time without trouble. "Strength athletes have been taking hGH precursors for 20 years," he says. "If this were so dangerous, the streets would be littered with the bodies of young people."

But, Warner says, Klatz's enthusiasm for anti-aging therapies is causing him to lose sight of the bigger picture. "He loves to beat on the government for being stodgy and too conservative and keeping this wonderful stuff from the people for no good reason," he says. But those who administer hGH, DHEA and other hormones to their patients "ought to be more cautious, because whatever they think, they can't know for sure that they are safe and effective." ∎

OUTLOOK

150 Years Young?

The life expectancy for an average American today is about 76. But it is widely thought that life expectancy will rise for the baby boomers and those generations that follow. Some experts predict a dramatic increase.

If recent history is any guide, average ages should soar. In 1900, the average American lived to be 47. Then came better hygiene, nutrition and medical advances (especially the development of antibiotics).

Still, some say that the greatest strides in life expectancy have already been made, and that while things will get better for boomers,

Continued on p. 666

At Issue:

Are baby boomers trying too hard to stay young?

ROBERTSON DAVIES
Canadian author who died in 1995

FROM THE MERRY HEART (1997).

*w*e live in an age when the care of physical health has attained almost to the stature of a religion.

People eat extraordinary and disagreeable foods and dose themselves with pills and supplements to ensure the uttermost perfection of healthy diet. They flog themselves to the most distressing exertions, hoping thereby to bully their bodies into some sort of exaggerated well-being. Creature comforts hallowed by centuries of acceptance as friends to man are now condemned as vile indulgences, harmful to the standers-by, harmful to the unborn, noxious and disgusting as well as ruinously expensive. It appears as though everybody under the age of 50 were convinced that by making their lives unbearable, they might extend their existence forever. Yes, it really seems as if they hoped that they might never die.

But what kind of lives are they thus preserving? Are they happy? Are they fun to be with? Are they wise? Do their contemporaries and their children hold them in high respect? Very often these questions must be answered with a resounding No! As Henry Thoreau said a century and a half ago, the mass of men lead lives of quiet desperation. If he were living today, he would have to amend that statement to include women, who can be every bit as desperate as their brothers. As they jog and diet their way among us, the faces of such people are masks of despair. Do you want to join them?

RONALD KLATZ, M.D.
President, American Academy of Anti-Aging Medicine

WRITTEN FOR THE CQ RESEARCHER, JULY 1998.

*s*ure Robertson, let's forget about diet, exercise, leading a healthy lifestyle. Instead, let's embrace the hedonistic Emperor Nero-style philosophy of live fast, die young and leave a pretty corpse behind. It is easy to cavalierly rail against the anti-aging lifestyle. But it only takes your first heart attack, stroke or tumor to change that tune.

Who ever said anti-aging medicine was for ascetics, monks or masochists? Our goal is maximum quality as well as maximum quality of life. Anti-aging medicine is about freedom — to choose our destiny, our paths in life in a society free from the fear of a slow, lingering disease or premature death, the freedom to choose just how long and well we wish to live. Anti-aging medicine is helping to create a new paradigm of health care for the next millennium, from today's disease-oriented model to an aggressive, preventative one.

We do not yet "live in an age when the care of physical health has attained almost to the stature of a religion." Statistics show that more people than ever lead sedentary lifestyles, reflected in the mortality statistics of the top killers: heart disease, obesity and diabetes. Perhaps if we did live in a time where everybody were obsessed with maintaining optimum health, our nation would be filled with wise, happy, fun-to-be-with healthy people.

Mastery in this world is simply an equation of ability/ time. With enough time and effort all of us can accomplish fantastic and beautiful things. Unfortunately, most people are cut down prematurely in life by the diseases of aging. Imagine an ageless society where it is perfectly OK to spend your first 30 years as a world traveler before even starting to consider what you would actually do for a living. One would be easily able to slip back and forth between leisure time and the working world because even at age 105 one would look, feel and think as well as any typically ahtletic healthy 55-year-old.

Such a future is within our grasp, and 50 percent of the baby boomers alive today will live to see it.

If 20 minutes per day of exercise, driving a car of at least 2,900 pounds, wearing a seat belt, avoiding cigarettes and fatty foods and HIV-positive sexual partners, and downing 10 to 20 vitamin tablets with meals two times per day is too much for you wild and crazy guys to stomach . . . in the immortal words of Steve Martin, "Well, excuse me!" I choose to live *long,* and well.

Continued from p. 664

they will not get that much better. "Oh, most of them will make it into their 80s, but they'll still begin to go downhill at that time, just like people do today," says Jurg Siegenthaler, a professor of sociology at American University.

Boomer expert Russell tends to agree. "I don't think life expectancy will rise much more," she says, "but quality of life will improve." But while boomers will have a more active and fun retirement than their parents, "most of them will still be dead in 50 years," she says.

A majority of experts on aging, however, are more optimistic about boomers' chances to live substantially longer than their parents. "I think it will be common for people to live into their 90s or to 100," NIA's Warner says.

That trend may already be beginning. Indeed, as of last year, there were about 61,000 people who are 100 years or older, according to the U.S. Census Bureau. In addition, 4 million Americans are currently over 85, almost twice the number in 1980. And the numbers are expected to increase dramatically. In fact, according to the bureau, centenarians are the fastest-growing segment of the U.S. population and will number 214,000 by the year 2020. [17]

Still, for all their optimism, Warner and others say that significant increases past the age of 90 or 100 are unlikely, at least in the foreseeable future. "I don't see a lot of people living to be 120 any time soon," he says.

Warner's choice of 120 is not a random or even half-educated guess. It turns out that 120 is something of a magic number in the aging community. For one thing, there are no records of human beings living much past 120 years. In fact, the oldest confirmed life span is 122 years.*

---

*Some people have claimed to be over 130, but no birth records exist to prove their claims.

More important, aging scientists have long believed that the human body is not genetically programmed to function much past 120 years, even under optimum conditions. "Living beyond 120 years is going to involve overriding the genetic program, and we currently aren't even close to knowing how to do that," says Perry of the Alliance for Aging Research.

But an increasing number of scientists and others are arguing that reaching or surpassing 120 may not be the near impossible hurdle that many say it is. "I think it's a reasonable expectation that we'll be able to live 150 years or more," Klatz says.

Klatz and others believe that in the coming decades medical science will make scourges like heart disease, cancer and Alzheimer's disease little more than bad memories — much as influenza and smallpox are today. [18] In addition, they say, our understanding of aging will increase enough to allow researchers to stop and even reverse the aging process.

"You have to remember, our medical knowledge doubles every three and a half years, which means that in 20 years we'll know 64 times more than we do today," Klatz says.

Others also are optimistic. "We're getting to the takeoff point where these technologies are going to start bearing fruit," says Ken Manton, a professor of demographics at Duke University. [19]

Indeed, in recent years researchers have learned how to bypass a built-in limit on the number of times each human cell can divide. In addition, scientists are learning more and more about the genes that affect and control human longevity. Some speculate that some day genetic tinkering will allow doctors to "turn off" or "reinstruct" those genes that direct aging.

This prospect was reinforced last month, when researchers at the University of Guelph in Canada trans-

planted a human gene that helps protect cells into fruit flies and extended their natural lives by 40 percent. The experiment "speaks very optimistically for our ability to directly intervene into the aging process in other higher animals, including humans," says Tom Johnson, a professor at the Institute for Behavioral Genetics at the University of Colorado in Boulder. [20]

Scientists are also looking into other means to slow the aging process. In the technique known as caloric restriction, normal caloric intake is reduced by about 30 percent. In laboratory experiments, mice subjected to reduced-calorie diets lived about one-third longer than those on regular diets.

While humans aren't expected to make such sacrifices willingly, researchers are hopeful that once they discover why caloric restriction works, they will be able to simulate it in humans, possibly prolonging boomers' lives by an extra 30 or even 50 years.

But for all the potential scientific miracles on the horizon, many experts argue that efforts to expand the quantity of life must be accompanied by corresponding improvements in life's quality. As Catholic University's Dinges and other researchers point out, people today live longer than their parents, but "there's also a longer period of misery" before many people die.

They warn that keeping people alive by using miraculous, life-extending technology can be a double-edged sword.

"We assume it will be all right," he says, "because no one ever thinks of it as happening to themselves."

Perry agrees that the focus needs to be on the health and self-sufficiency of boomers when they reach old age, not simply extending their life span no matter the impact on quality of life. "Our efforts should be at keeping people healthy through their 70s, 80s and 90s," he says, not just keeping them alive. ∎

Notes

[1] Quoted in Pat Bruce, "Forever Young: Baby Boomers Growing Old With Health and Grace," *Minneapolis-St. Paul Magazine*, October 1997.

[2] "Aging Boomers Refuse to Age, New Roper Survey Shows," *Business Wire*, May 8, 1998; Roper Starch Worldwide conducted the poll.

[3] Quoted in *ibid*.

[4] Jonathan Yardley, "From the Pharmacy, Faux Fountains of Youth," *The Washington Post*, May 4, 1998.

[5] Quoted in Helen Peterson, "Man File Suit vs. Insurers on Viagra," *Daily News*, May 19, 1998.

[6] "Insurers Urged to Cover Birth Control; Paying for Viagra Shows Double Standard, Planned Parenthood Says," *The Dallas Morning News*, May 20, 1998; "Is Sex a Necessity?" *Time*, May 11, 1998.

[7] U.S. Census Bureau, *Current Population Reports*.

[8] Jones, Landon Y., *Great Expectations: America and the Baby Boom Generation* (1980), p. 115.

[9] Bill Hendrick, "Fighting Middle-Aged Spread," *The Atlanta Constitution*, May 13, 1997. For background, see "Dieting and Health," *The CQ Researcher*, April 14, 1995, pp. 321-344.

[10] Figures cited in "Older Americans Still Active; Big Business for Fitness Industry," *The Maturing Marketplace*, April 1, 1998. For background, see "Physical Fitness," *The CQ Researcher*, Nov. 6, 1992, pp. 953-976.

[11] Laura Liebeck, "Welcoming the Wellness Generation," *Discount Store News*, May 11, 1998. For background, see "Dietary Supplements," *The CQ Researcher*, July 8, 1994, pp. 577-600.

FOR MORE INFORMATION

If you would like to have this CQ Researcher updated, or need more information about this topic, please call CQ Custom Research. Special rates for CQ subscribers. (202) 887-8600 or (800) 432-2250, ext. 600, or E-mail Custom.Research@cq.com

Alliance for Aging Research, 2021 K St. N.W., Suite 305, Washington, D.C. 20006; (202) 293-2856; www.agingresearch.org
The alliance promotes medical and social research in an effort to improve the quality of life for the elderly.

American Academy of Anti-Aging Medicine, 1341 W. Fullerton, Suite 111, Chicago, Ill. 60614; (773) 528-4333; www.worldhealth.net.
Founded in 1993, the academy includes doctors, scientists and others dedicated to slowing, stopping or even reversing the aging process.

American Academy of Facial Plastic and Reconstructive Surgery, 310 S. Henry St., Alexandria, Va. 22314; (703) 299-9291; The academy promotes research and public education on facial plastic and reconstructive surgery.

National Institute on Aging, 31 Center Dr., MSC-2292, #5C35, Bethesda, Md. 20892; (301) 496-9265; www.nih.gov/nia. NIA, part of the National Institutes of Health, conducts and funds research on many aspects of the aging process.

The Boomer Institute, One Erieview Plaza, 7th Floor, Cleveland, Ohio 44114; (330) 468-0536. The institute conducts research into the impact that aging baby boomers are having on American society.

[12] Mary Ellen LoBosco, "More Bang from Boomers," *Supermarket News*, May 11, 1998.

[13] Quoted in Irene Sege, "The Aging of Aquarius," *The Boston Globe*, May 12, 1998. For background, see Mary H. Cooper, "Caring for the Elderly," *The CQ Researcher*, Feb. 20, 1998, pp. 145-168.

[14] Quoted in Alison Ashton, "The Winners and Losers of Exercise," *Copley News Service*, March 2, 1998.

[15] Ronald Klatz and Robert Goldman, *Stopping the Clock: Why Many of Us Will Live Past 100 — And Enjoy Every Minute* (1996).

[16] Ronald Klatz and Carol Kahn, *Grow Young with HGH* (1997), p. 36.

[17] Statistics cited in Bob LaMendola, "Stretching the Limit," *The Orange County Register*, Dec. 3, 1997.

[18] For background, see Adriel Bettelheim, "Alzheimer's Disease," *The CQ Researcher*, May 15, 1998, pp. 433-456.

[19] Quoted in *Ibid*.

[20] Quoted in "Extra Gene Lets Fly Live Longer," *The Washington Post*, June 2, 1998.

Bibliography

Selected Sources Used

Books

Jones, Landon Y., *Great Expectations: America and the Baby Boom Generation*, Coward, McCann & Geoghegan, 1980.

Jones provides an engaging and well-written chronicle of the baby boom generation. While the book is dated, it contains wonderful insights on how the events of post-war America shaped and molded those born during the boom. Particularly good are Jones' chapters on the student movement during the late 1960s and early '70s.

Klatz, Ronald, and Robert Goldman, *Stopping the Clock: Why Many of Us Will Live Past 100 — And Enjoy Every Minute of It*, Keats Publishing, 1996.

Klatz and Goldman, founders of the American Academy of Anti-Aging Medicine, describe the various anti-aging therapies, ranging from proper diet and exercise to hormone treatments.

Russell, Cheryl, *The Master Trend: How the Baby Boom is Remaking America*, Plenum Press, 1993.

Russell, a consultant who specializes in the baby boom generation, explores the impact, both good and bad, that boomers have had on American society. For example, she finds that while baby boomers have helped to erode ethical and civil standards, they have spearheaded the drive toward increasing tolerance in America.

Articles

"Age Cannot Wither Them," *The Economist*, April 18, 1998.

This piece argues that boomers' desire to stay young is a natural outgrowth of their life experience. Since they avoided the difficult years of the Great Depression and World War II, most of them have never come face to face with real adversity or privation. "They have always wanted to 'have it all,' and they see no reason why they should not go on doing so," the article concludes.

Cowley, Geoffrey, "How to Live to 100," *Newsweek*, June 30, 1997.

Cowley explores the host of factors that scientists say will allow many people to live for 100 years, from better nutrition to anti-aging therapies like caloric restriction.

Cowley, Geoffrey, "Is Sex a Necessity?" *Newsweek*, May 11, 1998.

Cowley describes the debate surrounding the new anti-impotency drug Viagra and who should pay for it.

Fernandes, Lorna, "Surgeons Help Boomers Look as Young as They Feel," *San Francisco Business Times*, Feb. 6, 1998.

Fernandes looks at baby boomers' increasing use of cosmetic surgery and explores how technology and changing attitudes have made many of these procedures much more acceptable and common.

Librach, Phyllis Brasch, "Forever Young: Baby Boomers are Riding Out the Onslaught of Age with Laser Treatments, Vitamins, Exercise and Now — Viagra," *St. Louis Post Dispatch*, May 28, 1998.

Librach describes how businesses — from drug makers to car companies — have geared up to meet baby boomers' desire to look and feel young.

O'Conner, Clint, "Putting Death on Ice: Cryonicists Preserving Bodies for a Possible Thaw, Second Chance at Life," *The Cleveland Plain Dealer*, June 15, 1997.

O'Conner describes the small but dedicated group of devotees of cryonics, the science of freezing and reanimating human beings. While cryonics is the butt of jokes in the mainstream scientific community, many proponents predict that cryonics will gain in popularity as baby boomers begin to face their mortality in the coming decades.

Sege, Irene, "The Aging of Aquarius," *The Boston Globe*, May 12, 1998.

Sege gives a good overview of boomer attitudes about growing older. She predicts that this energetic cohort will live middle age to the fullest, with second careers, second families and a renewed interest in religion and spirituality.

Yardley, Jonathan, "From the Pharmacy, Faux Fountains of Youth," *The Washington Post*, May 4, 1998.

Yardley, a book critic and social commentator, argues that using drugs and other technologies to try to stay young is foolhardy and misguided. He writes that "the losses that age entails seem to me of vastly less import than the riches and pleasures it provides."

Reports

In Search of the Secrets of Aging, National Institute on Aging, 1996.

The institute, which is part of the National Institutes of Health, gives a good overview of what researchers have discovered about why and how we age, from the role of hormones to genetic factors.

The Next Step

Additional information from UMI's Newspaper & Periodical Abstracts™ database

Careers

Dodge, Robert, "Longer Careers for Boomers?" *Chicago Tribune*, **Dec. 28, 1997, p. 50.**
Many experts say boomers must continue working to help pay for the high costs of their government retirement and health-care benefits. Demands by the baby boomers after the turn of the century are expected to eventually bankrupt Social Security and Medicare. But Alan Reynolds, director of economic research at the Hudson Institute, points out that there are plenty of public policies that discourage seniors from working longer or even taking part-time jobs. Reynolds said current laws impose heavy taxes and penalties on seniors who try to work while collecting Social Security.

Knox, Richard A., "Boomers See Work Coloring Golden Years," *The Boston Globe*, **June 3, 1998, p. A3.**
Baby boomers plan to retire the very notion of retirement, judging from a national survey released yesterday. Eight out of 10 Americans in the pace-setting generation born between 1946 and 1964 say they expect to keep working at least part-time after the conventional retirement age of 65. By contrast, only one in eight elders currently stays in the work force.

Nelson, Sandy, "Scrambling for Security: How Four Americans Spend and Save — 'We'll Probably Work Until We Die'," *The Wall Street Journal*, **Dec. 12, 1997, p. R4.**
Anita and Thom LoPiccolo would seem to be living the American Dream. They run a prosperous media-production business out of their historic home. Their children attended private schools and are about to embark on their own careers. Now, as these leading-edge baby boomers head into their 50s, their biggest concern is hanging on to the good life once they eventually retire. Asked when she and her husband began saving for retirement, Mrs. LoPiccolo, 49, laughs: "Which time? It's like asking, 'How many times did you try to quit smoking?'" Actually they started when they were in their late 30s, but they don't expect to be able to save their goal — 20 percent of their annual income — until their daughter graduates from college in 2000.

Seebacher, Noreen, "Businesses Urged to Hire Older Workers: They Bring Patience, Maturity and Unrivaled Work Ethic to the Job, One Expert Contends," *Detroit News*, **May 6, 1998, p. B4.**
As the population ages, older workers are the one resource employers in Michigan and nationwide can least afford to squander, says the director of an organization that provides training and employment for older workers. "We

need to educate the business community that the myths about older workers are just that: myths," said Cathy Robinson, state director of Green Thumb, a national non-profit group. "The reality is that older workers bring so much talent and stability to the workplace that it's a big mistake not to hire them or [to] let them go." It's a lesson many employers may learn sooner than they think. The aging of America's 83 million baby boomers will have a significant impact on the nation's work force and work force development programs, according to a recent Urban Institute study sponsored by the U.S. Labor Department.

Health

"Estrogen an Aid Against Diabetes," *USA Today*, **June 15, 1998, p. D1.**
Older women who take estrogen are less likely to develop diabetes, and if they do have the disease, it's easier to manage and less likely to lead to heart disease.

"Study Finds Some Promise in Alternative to Estrogen," *The New York Times*, **May 13, 1998, p. A21.**
A new alternative to estrogen may offer older women many of the hormone's healthful effects on hearts and bones without one of its most worrisome side effects, an increased risk of breast cancer. Raloxifene has already been approved by the Food and Drug Administration to prevent osteoporosis in post-menopausal women. Now a study has found that raloxifene, like estrogen, might also protect the heart, researchers reported in Wednesday's *Journal of the American Medical Association*. The study found that raloxifene lowered levels of low-density lipoprotein, or LDL, the so-called "bad" cholesterol, by 12 percent in post-menopausal women, compared with 14 percent for estrogen.

Chase, Marilyn, "Health Journal: Getting a Bit Thick in the Middle? It's Not Hopeless After All," *The Wall Street Journal*, **June 16, 1997, p. B1.**
Two central truths about an aging body — the ease of gaining weight and the difficulty of losing it — preoccupy baby boomers and their elders alike. Research suggests that combining aerobic exercise with strength training not only promotes fitness but also helps reverse time's drag on the metabolism.

Dolby, Victoria, "Anti-Aging Strategies to Add Years of Health to Our Lives," *Better Nutrition*, **March 1997, pp. 20-22.**
There is growing consensus that aging changes are produced by free-radical reactions. Anti-aging compounds found in green tea, multivitamin supplements, DHEA and garlic are discussed.

Gonyea, Judith G., "Mid-Life and Menopause: Uncharted Territories for Baby Boomer Women," *Generations*, **spring 1998, pp. 87-89.**

Baby boomer women are exploring their options as they make the transition to menopause. A major decision facing post-menopausal women is whether or not to take hormone-replacement therapy.

Hill, Daniel, "Take a Pill!" *Brandweek*, **Dec. 1, 1997, pp. 22-25.**

Sales of natural remedies and herbs have exploded in the last several years, with many companies that sell vitamins and other nutritional supplements reporting huge sales increases.

Knox, Richard, "Osteoporosis Drugs Create Hope — and Confusion," *The Boston Globe*, **May 18, 1998, p. D1.**

Nita Goldstein was on estrogen for a decade, ever since doctors discovered osteoporosis in her spine when she was 62. But last month the Cambridge woman switched to raloxifene, a new "designer estrogen" being touted as the safer hormone for women worried about brittle bones. Studies indicate that post-menopausal women like Goldstein who take estrogen long-term — five to 10 years — have as much as a 50 percent greater risk of developing breast cancer. If new data being presented this afternoon in Los Angeles can be believed, raloxifene (marketed as Evista) actually lowers a woman's breast cancer risk as much as 74 percent in the first two years or so of taking it, compared with women who take no hormones.

Leonard, Mary, "Out of the Shadows; Women's Mid-Life Health Concerns Were Long Ignored; Now the Pendulum has Swung to the Other Extreme," *The Boston Globe*, **Aug. 10, 1997, p. D1.**

If more evidence is required that this is a menopause moment, consider this sign of the times: A top female policy-maker in the Clinton administration was recently approached by publishers of those yellow-and-black, wise-cracking guidebooks to write *Women's Health Care for Dummies*. Women already outlive men by more than seven years, on average. Now the health concerns of middle-aged females are in the spotlight and consuming more federal research dollars than many diseases that claim far more lives — male and female — each year. For example, it's estimated that far more Americans will die of lung cancer (160,400) this year than breast cancer (44,200), yet lung cancer research will get a fraction of breast cancer's funding. Because women spend two of every three health-care dollars nationally, this sudden interest in their well-being is being driven as much by economics as compassion.

Pipp, Tracy L., "Lowering the Boom: An Entire Generation May Soon Find Itself in Hot Water With a Variety of Health Problems and Diseases," *Detroit News*, **Jan. 27, 1997, p. B1.**

Health problems loom for the baby boom generation. The causes are diverse and unique, say doctors and scientists. Boomers lead a sedentary lifestyle, especially as compared with the previous generation. They're stressed, and they don't eat right. They rely on antibiotics to make them feel better when they are sick. When the boomers will most need more health care, "there will be a shrinkage of students coming into the health professions," predicts Cynthia Zane, dean of the College of Health Professions at the University of Detroit-Mercy. "Gaining even 10 pounds puts you at a greater risk for diabetes, coronary heart disease, high blood pressure, joint problems, sleep apnea and gallbladder disease," says registered dietitian Betsey Kurleto, co-author of *Nutrition Secrets for Optimum Health*. Some physicians are even expecting a near epidemic of Type II diabetes due to poor eating habits as the boomers enter their mid-50s and 60s.

Sege, Irene, "The Aging of Aquarius; Boomers Look Beyond the Old Boundaries as Doors Open for Increased Longevity, Second Careers, and Spiritual Well-Being," *The Boston Globe*, **May 12, 1998, p. C1.**

Well, get ready for the glory days of the menopausal and the bald. The baby boomers are at it again, moving into a new phase of life and, as always, taking the rest of the culture with them. Around 2006, the median age of the nation's 78 million boomers will be 50, old enough to join the American Association of Retired Persons. By the year 2000, a full third of American grandparents will be boomers. In the next millennium, the biggest generation in American history — those born between 1946 and 1964 — will be blessed with longevity and a determination to maintain their vigor. They'll manage the ongoing repercussions of their complex history of marriage and relationships. They'll shun the label "mature" and ponder the meaning of life. They'll remake themselves and then maybe do it again. As author Gail Sheehy says, "They'll make being 50-something the glamorous and newly sexy age to be." What with children leaving home and parents dying and grandchildren arriving, the path through the 50s is strewn with as many major life changes as any decade since the 20s. Some will suffer early illness, even death, and all will know someone who does. The boomers' journeys will continue to shape the public psyche, not only because of their numbers but also because a talk-about-it generation — particularly its women — that rewrote the rules of sex and rewrote the rules of work and family, and now is rewriting the rules of menopause, won't go quietly through their 50s.

Thompson, Stephanie, "Boomers Come Runnin'..." *Brandweek*, **Feb. 2, 1998, p. 1.**

Kellogg is launching Smart Start, a sweetened multigrain cereal targeted specifically at the boomer generation. The company is said to have an aggressive marketing plan ready.

Cosmetic Surgery

Gallo, Nick, "The New Face of Cosmetic Surgery," *Better Homes & Gardens*, February 1998, pp. 52-60.

The baby boom generation is a big part of the current surge in cosmetic surgery. Some of the most common surgical procedures are discussed.

Lore, Diane, "Injections of a Deadly Poison are Giving Wrinkle-Weary Baby Boomers a Shot at Beauty," *Atlanta Constitution*, June 3, 1998, p. C1.

Call it botulism for beauty. Originally harnessed to relax muscles associated with serious medical conditions such as swallowing disorders and crossed eyes, Botox — a diluted, purified form of the toxin — is one of the hottest, new weapons against wrinkles. In New York, health clubs are offering injections of Botox for clients who want other ways to enhance their appearance besides exercise. And it's become a verb in some places, as in, "I'm getting Botoxed today." Botox has, however, retained one trait of its evil twin. Like botulism, it still has the ability to slightly paralyze muscle — which allows it to eliminate wrinkles by essentially smoothing them out. The facial muscles are not frozen, but temporarily softened. Botox works best on crow's feet around the eyes, the frown lines between the brows and "surprise" lines in the forehead.

Seligson, Susan V., "The Changing Face of Cosmetic Surgery," *Health*, March 1997, pp. 84-86.

Better techniques and more choices in cosmetic surgery have many more women deciding to go under the knife. Seligson discusses some women's experiences with cosmetic surgery and the different types of cosmetic surgery.

Solomon, Judith H., "Men Turn Back the Clock — Nips, Tucks and Facial Peels Cross Over the Gender Line," *Detroit News*, April 16, 1998, p. E1.

Cosmetic surgery is just one of the beauty presents men are giving themselves today. "Look good/feel good" procedures and treatments — running the gamut from surgical nips, tucks and hair transplants to non-surgical hair dying, facial smoothing and body massages — are increasing all over Detroit. Theodore Golden, a plastic surgeon, says today's active seniors feel young, they want to live like they're young and they want to look young, too.

Impotence

'Boom in Boomer Impotence," *USA Today*, May 6, 1998, p. A1.

Before the drug Viagra, aging baby boomer men led a boom in seeking treatment for sexual dysfunction. In 1997, 1.8 million made 2.8 million doctor visits, 17 percent more than in 1996, and 628,000 were new customers.

Hoppe, Arthur, "The Bottle Of Youth," *San Francisco Chronicle*, May 6, 1998, p. A23.

No more intrepid adventurer exists than Buck Ace. Buck has swum the Alimentary Canal, trekked the Alacarte Desert and climbed the towering Peaks of Ecstasy. But today Buck faces the greatest challenge of them all — the conquest of the dread aging process. Buck was sure he had achieved his goal the other evening in the Asparagus Fern Bar and Chat Room. Daphne B., a curvaceous young woman half his age, succumbed in nothing flat to his sophisticated blandishments. He had hardly murmured, "You come here often?" and, "What's your sign?" when he felt it was time to add, "Excuse me while I swallow this little blue pill."

Librach, Phyllis Brasch, "Forever Young; Baby Boomers Are Riding Out the Onslaught of Age with Laser Treatments, Vitamins, Exercise and Now — Viagra," *St. Louis Post-Dispatch*, May 28, 1998, p. G1.

After months of hearing middle-aged men crave Viagra, William Catalona, chief urologist at Washington University, wanted to be ready to write prescriptions the day the long-awaited pill for impotence won federal approval. "It's like the Fountain of Youth," said Catalona. "Viagra is analogous to anti-wrinkle cream. This is something that will turn back the clock and make men the way they were when they were young." Even as Viagra is making its big splash, baby boomers are crowding around the Fountain of Youth for any spritz that gives hopes of erasing, or at least fading, tell-tale signs of aging — from crow's feet to varicose veins.

Lore, Diane, "Science Watch; Overcoming Impotence; In Addition to Viagra, a Variety of New Treatments are Expected Soon — But With Them Come Tough Issues for Insurers," *Atlanta Journal Constitution*, May 17, 1998, p. C6.

Although men are rushing by the thousands to get their hands on Viagra, it is only the first of a host of new medications designed to ease sexual dysfunction. From penile creams to spring-loaded injections, drug manufacturers are attempting to tap into a market of more than 30 million men who suffer from erectile problems and perhaps millions more drawn by ego and a promise of renewed youth. "It's a very satisfying time to be a urologist," said Atlanta urologist Lawrence Goldstone. "We finally have something to offer that is not invasive, that works. It's truly exciting." But the push is also testing the boundaries of insurance coverage. In less than a month, many managed-care companies are questioning whether drugs that enhance a patient's quality of life — such as Viagra — should be covered with the same consistency as pills that treat life-threatening conditions, such as heart disease or cancer. "I think there's a lot of concern about the cost of drugs in general — they are having a significant impact on the price of health insurance," said Chris Martin, spokesman for the Blue Cross and Blue Shield Association in Chicago. "Viagra and other drugs like it just point to that growing problem."

Back Issues

Great Research on Current Issues Starts Right Here.
Recent topics covered by The CQ Researcher are listed below.
Now available on the Web
For information, call (800) 432-2250 ext. 279 or (202) 887-6279.

If you would like to have any of these CQ Researchers updated, or need more information about these topics, please call CQ Custom Research. Special rates for CQ subscribers. (202) 887-8600 or (800) 432-2250, ext. 600, or E-mail Custom.Research@cq.com

APRIL 1997
Declining Crime Rates
The FBI Under Fire
Gender Equity in Sports
Space Program's Future

MAY 1997
The Stock Market
The Cloning Controversy
Expanding NATO
The Future of Libraries

JUNE 1997
FDA Reform
China After Deng
Line-Item Veto
Breast Cancer

JULY 1997
Transportation Policy
Executive Pay
School Choice Debate
Aggressive Driving

AUGUST 1997
Age Discrimination
Banning Land Mines
Children's Television
Evolution vs. Creationism

SEPTEMBER 1997
Caring for the Dying
Mental Health Policy
Mexico's Future
Youth Fitness

OCTOBER 1997
Urban Sprawl in the West
Diversity in the Workplace
Teacher Education
Contingent Work Force

NOVEMBER 1997
Renewable Energy
Artificial Intelligence
Religious Persecution
Roe v. Wade at 25

DECEMBER 1997
Whistleblowers
Castro's Next Move
Gun Control Standoff
Regulating Nonprofits

JANUARY 1998
Foster Care Reform
IRS Reform
The Black Middle Class
U.S.-British Relations

FEBRUARY 1998
Patients' Rights
Deflation Fears
Caring for the Elderly
The New Corporate Philanthropy

MARCH 1998
Israel at 50
The Federal Judiciary
Drinking on Campus
The Economics of Recycling

APRIL 1998
Biology and Behavior
Liberal Arts Education
Income Inequality
High-Tech Labor Shortage

MAY 1998
Census 2000
Child-Care Options
Alzheimer's Disease
U.S.-Russian Relations

JUNE 1998
Student Journalism
Antitrust Policy
Environmental Justice
Sleep Deprivation

JULY 1998
Encouraging Teen Abstinence
Population and the Environment
Democracy in Asia

Future Topics

▶ *Oil Production in the 21st Century*

▶ *Flexible Work Arrangements*

▶ *Coastal Development*

Back issues are available for $5.00 (subscribers) or $10.00 (non-subscribers). Quantity discounts apply to orders over 10. To order, call Congressional Quarterly Customer Service at (202) 887-8621.

Binders are available for $18.00. To order call 1-800-638-1710. Please refer to stock number 648.

The CQ Researcher

PUBLISHED BY CONGRESSIONAL QUARTERLY INC.

Oil Production in the 21st Century

When will the world run out of oil?

Twenty-five years ago, the Organization of Petroleum Exporting Countries struck at the heart of the American economy with an embargo on oil exports to the United States. The resulting rise in energy prices sparked a round of inflation and stagnant economic growth that lasted more than a decade. A quarter-century later, gasoline prices are at an all-time low, new oil deposits have been discovered in the Caspian Sea region and OPEC appears to have lost its grip on global energy prices and production. But the good times for consumers will not last forever. In a matter of time the world's oil will run out, and it's far from certain there will be sufficient alternative energy sources.

CQ — **August 7, 1998 • Volume 8, No. 29 • Pages 673-696**

Formerly Editorial Research Reports

THE ISSUES

SIDEBARS AND GRAPHICS

FOR FURTHER RESEARCH

COVER: NORTH SEA OIL-DRILLING PLATFORM (PUBLIC BROADCASTING SERVICE)

CQ Researcher

August 7, 1998
Volume 8, No.29

EDITOR
Sandra Stencel

MANAGING EDITOR
Thomas J. Colin

ASSOCIATE EDITOR
Sarah M. Magner

STAFF WRITERS
Adriel Bettelheim
Mary H. Cooper
Kenneth Jost
Kathy Koch
David Masci

PRODUCTION EDITOR
Melissa Hall

EDITORIAL ASSISTANT
Laura S. Cavender

PUBLISHED BY
Congressional Quarterly Inc.

CHAIRMAN
Andrew Barnes

VICE CHAIRMAN
Andrew P. Corty

PRESIDENT AND PUBLISHER
Robert W. Merry

EXECUTIVE EDITOR
David Rapp

The CQ Researcher (ISSN 1056-2036). Formerly Editorial Research Reports. Published weekly, except Jan. 2, May 29, July 3, Oct. 30, by Congressional Quarterly Inc., 1414 22nd St., N.W., Washington, D.C. 20037. Annual subscription rate for libraries, businesses and government is $340. Additional rates furnished upon request. Periodicals postage paid at Washington, D.C., and additional mailing offices. POSTMASTER: Send address changes to The CQ Researcher, 1414 22nd St., N.W., Washington, D.C. 20037.

Oil Production in the 21st Century

BY MARY H. COOPER

THE ISSUES

Vacationing Americans have an extra reason to celebrate this summer: At less than $1 a gallon in some areas, gasoline prices are at their lowest level in 30 years.

Several factors produced this happy turn of events. An unusually warm winter in the Northern Hemisphere, caused in part by El Niño's disruption of normal weather patterns, dampened demand for heating oil. At the same time, a severe economic crisis in East Asia forced Japan and other countries in the region to curtail industrial production, thus reducing energy consumption.

Faced with falling demand for oil, the Organization of Petroleum Exporting Countries (OPEC) and other oil producers tried to prop up global oil prices by limiting production. But with oil prices falling, many producers ignored calls to slow production in a desperate attempt to protect oil revenues. *

Just a quarter-century ago, however, OPEC had the United States and the rest of the industrialized world by the throat, and Saudi Arabian oil minister Sheik Zaki Yamani was as familiar to many Americans as their representatives in Congress. Saudi Arabia and the four other major Middle East members dominated OPEC, controlling more than a third of world oil production.

In October 1973, the cartel imposed a total embargo on its exports to the United States and the Netherlands for their support of Israel in the Yom Kippur War. Oil prices skyrocketed. The ensuing inflation and stagnant industrial output spilled over from the U.S. and Dutch economies

to infect the entire industrial world. Stagflation became even more deeply entrenched after 1978-79, when the Iranian revolution sparked a second energy crisis and rise in oil prices.

The industrial world responded to OPEC's grip on world oil supplies by searching for alternative sources. By the 1990s, non-OPEC producers such as Britain, Mexico and Norway had enabled importers to reduce their oil dependence on the volatile Persian Gulf. They also launched campaigns to reduce their consumption of oil by raising energy taxes and encouraging energy conservation through improved efficiency of automobiles and appliances. And they sought to develop alternatives to oil such as solar, wind and geothermal energy.

These efforts paid off in the next two decades. Largely by diversifying their sources of foreign oil, the United States and other major consumers have significantly reduced their vulnerability to oil price manipulations by OPEC. Technological advances in exploration and drilling equipment have enabled producers to discover new oil deposits, further relaxing pressure on oil prices posed by growing global demand for oil.

Worries about future energy crises

diminished still further when oil reserves under and around the Caspian Sea were opened to outside development after the Soviet Union's collapse in 1991. The former Soviet republics of Azerbaijan, Kazakhstan and Turkmenistan that border the Caspian — and, to a lesser extent, their Central Asia neighbors Tajikistan and Uzbekistan — stand to reap enough earnings from oil and natural gas exports alone to launch them into the modern industrial era in the space of a few years.

"The Caspian is potentially one of the world's most important, new, energy-producing regions," said former Energy Secretary Federico Peña earlier this year. "Although the Caspian may never rival the Persian Gulf, Caspian production can have important implications for world energy supplies by increasing world supply and diversifying sources of supply among producing regions of the world." [1]

The oil glut that began early this year provided the icing on the cake for oil consumers. But Americans would be foolish to gloat over their current bounty. Even counting Alaska's prolific North Slope oil fields, domestic reserves are falling. The United States now imports more than half of its oil, placing the country at added risk from future disruptions of foreign supplies. [2]

For all its promise, the Caspian Sea region is far from coming on line as a major source of non-OPEC oil. The region's remoteness and legendary political turmoil threaten to postpone or even scuttle the flow of oil before production is fully under way.

Meanwhile, low gasoline prices have lulled American motorists into trading in their energy-efficient subcompact cars for gas-guzzling sport utility vehicles, which now account for almost half of American new car sales. Programs to develop alternatives to oil are losing support in

---

* OPEC members are Algeria, Indonesia, Iran, Iraq, Kuwait, Libya, Nigeria, Qatar, Saudi Arabia, the United Arab Emirates and Venezuela.

Getting Oil Out of the Caspian

Several new pipelines have been proposed to move oil from the landlocked Caspian republics to maritime ports for export. The U.S. favors lines running from Baku, Azerbaijan, to Ceyhan, Turkey, or from Baku to Georgia. Russia prefers a northern pipeline connecting to its own system or to its Black Sea port of Novorossisk. The pipeline sought by the Caspian republics, runnning south to the Persian Gulf, is opposed by the U.S. because it crosses Iran. The route planned by China across Kazakhstan is not controversial.

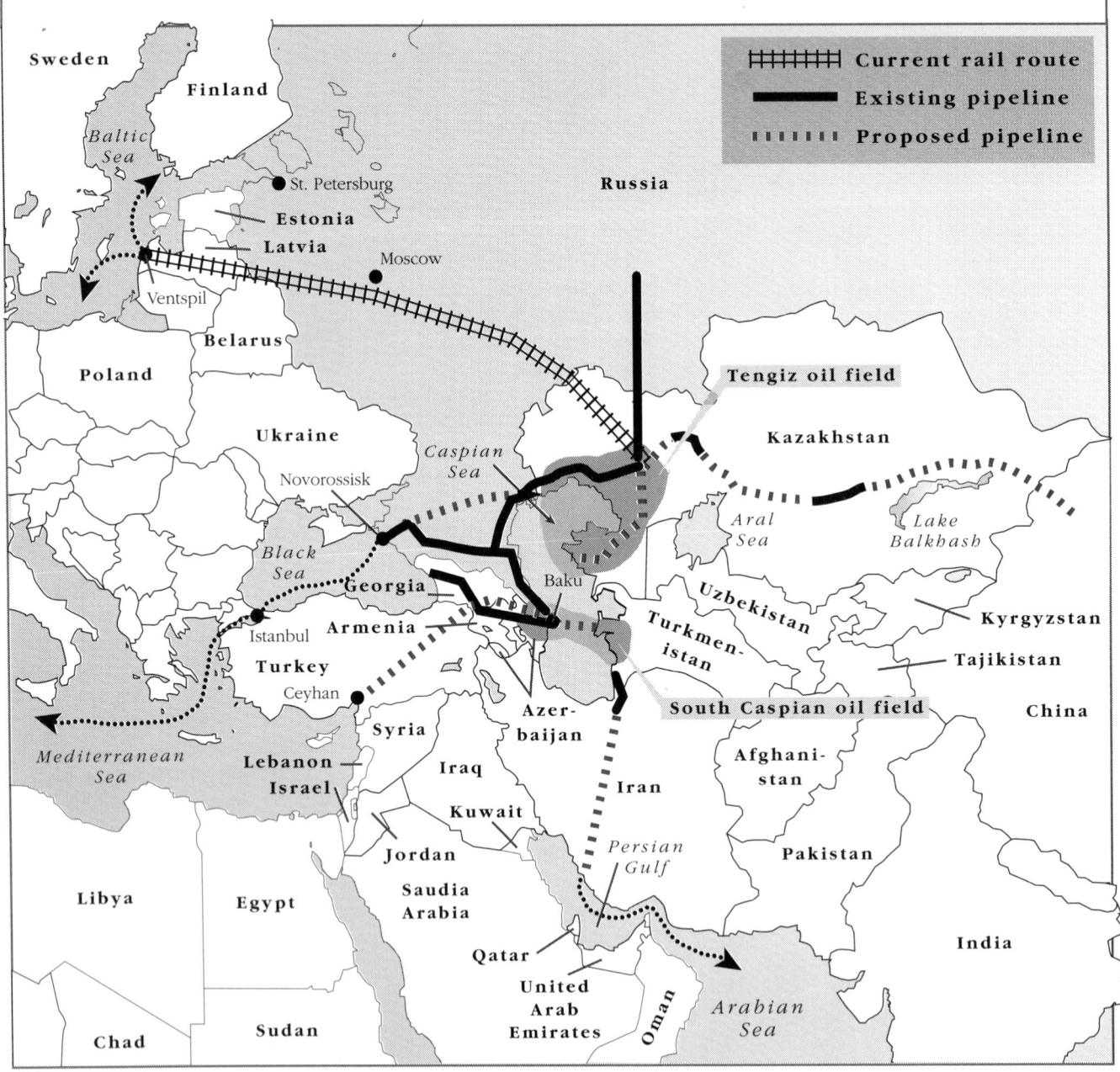

Sources: Energy Information Agency, Fortune Magazine, Parade Magazine

Congress, which has cut the Energy Department's research budget.

America's growing oil consumption also flies in the face of concern that using oil and other fossil fuels is causing a gradual but potentially catastrophic warming of Earth's atmosphere. The United States joined 167 other countries last December in agreeing to reduce fossil fuel consumption. But in the current climate of energy abundance, support for the Kyoto Protocol is flagging, and the Senate appears highly unlikely to ratify the measure anytime soon.

Although consumers may rejoice in OPEC's recent inability to curtail output and raise prices, it may be too soon to write the organization's obituary. OPEC has begun seeking agreement from non-member producers to go along with its efforts to buoy sagging prices. In March, Mexico agreed to join OPEC in cutting production, prompting some oil experts to predict that other countries soon would join in. [3]

Even absent a strengthening of OPEC's ability to manipulate oil prices over the short term, some experts contend that the recent break in oil prices will prove to be temporary. Colin J. Campbell, an oil-industry consultant in Geneva, Switzerland, and author of *The Coming Oil Crisis*, predicts that prices will rise when global oil production reaches its peak, "within the first few years of the next century." After that, he predicts, demand for oil will outpace its supply. "This will be a fundamental turning point, because until now we've always had growing oil production," he says.

As global oil deposits are depleted, OPEC's Middle East producers could be left in control of an increasing portion of world reserves. "We can expect another major price shock around 2000," Campbell says, "when the Middle East's share of world reserves will be much greater than it is

Crude Oil Prices Have Been Dropping

World crude oil prices have dropped in recent years as members of the Organization of Petroleum Exporting Countries have resisted OPEC efforts to limit their oil production. Discoveries of new oil sources in non-OPEC nations also have kept prices down.

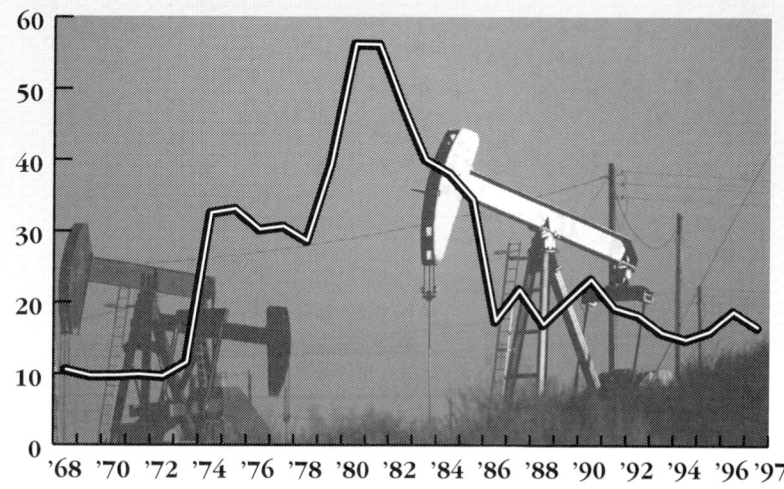

(Dollars per barrel)

Source: *Energy Information Administration,* Annual Energy Review, *1997*

now."

As Americans fire up their gas guzzlers for summer outings, these are some of the questions oil experts are asking:

Has OPEC lost its control over global oil prices?

Through new discoveries and an expanded membership, OPEC's oil reserves have grown over the years. The organization has reached beyond its stronghold in the Persian Gulf — still the main source of the world's oil — to include far-flung producers such as Indonesia and Nigeria. And OPEC's undisputed leader, Saudi Arabia, retains its clout as the world's largest oil producer.

But OPEC's grip over world oil production has slipped in the past 20 years, largely as a result of its own actions. When it set strict quotas in the 1970s that quadrupled oil prices, the cartel sparked a frantic search for alternative

sources of oil by the industrial world, which depends on petroleum products for its economic survival.

With the exception of the United States, most industrial countries imported the bulk of their energy supplies. Using sophisticated technology, Britain and Norway soon located and began working oil deposits under the North Sea. *(See story, p. 685.)* The United States and other countries shifted much of their oil demand to these and other non-OPEC producers, which now account for 45 percent of the oil export market. Norway now is the world's second-largest exporter, after Saudi Arabia.

Just how much has OPEC lost its ability to set production quotas among its membership as a way to buoy prices? That became apparent last fall, when a global oil glut began depressing prices. As usual, Saudi Arabia took the lead, calling in March for a cut in oil production of 1.2

Getting Oil Out of the Caspian . . .

Although some parts of the Caspian region and Central Asia do not hold promise as oil and gas producers, virtually every country in the vast area is likely to play a role in the industry's development. Some will serve as routes for pipelines or railroads and some, because of the threats they pose to the region's political stability, will retard progress. Here are the likely key players:

Armenia — In 1988, the largely Armenian population of Nagorno Karabakh, a province of Azerbaijan, began a six-year rebellion in an effort to become a part of neighboring Armenia. With support from Armenia, the rebels emerged victorious in 1994. Under the truce, Armenia was left in control of the province and other territory comprising 20 percent of Azerbaijan. Peace talks led by the United States, France and Russia, under the aegis of the Organization for Security and Cooperation in Europe, produced a compromise by which Nagorno Karabakh would be an autonomous province of Azerbaijan. After agreeing to these terms, rejected by the province's rebels, Armenian President Levon Ter-Petrossian was forced from office and replaced in March 1998 by Robert Kocharian, a Karabakh native who opposed the compromise. The U.S.-backed proposal to build a pipeline from Baku, Azerbaijan, to the Mediterranean port of Ceyhan, Turkey, would pass through Armenia.

Azerbaijan — Foreign oil companies have already invested heavily in the oil fields centered around the city of Baku. American companies Amoco, Exxon, Pennzoil and Unocal lead a consortium of 11 companies from eight countries — the Azerbaijan International Operating Company — that are drilling for oil for the first time in the country since it gained independence with the Soviet Union's collapse in 1991. President Heidar Aliev, a former KGB general and member of the Soviet Politburo, took power in a 1993 coup against democratically elected Abullaz Elchibey. Aliyev has survived two attempted coups since then but remains a popular leader who has brought political stability despite the destabilizing effect of the war with Armenia, which ended with the occupation of a fifth of Azerbaijan's territory, including Nagorno Karabakh. [1] Azerbaijan subsequently imposed a trade embargo against Armenia. Under pressure from the Armenian Assembly of America, Congress passed a measure in 1992 barring economic aid to the Azeri government until it takes steps to lift the embargo. An amendment to the Freedom Support Act that provides aid to the former Soviet republics, Section 907, remains in effect despite growing opposition from the Clinton administration and many lawmakers who see it as an obstacle to ensuring U.S. access to Azeri oil.

Georgia — This former Soviet republic has been torn by fighting among several distinct ethnic communities after gaining independence in 1991. President Eduard Shevernadze, a former Soviet foreign minister, has survived two assassination attempts since assuming power in 1992. An oil pipeline links the Azeri oil fields at Baku and the Georgian Black Sea port of Supsa.

Iran — A longstanding oil producer of the Persian Gulf region, Iran also borders the Caspian's southern coast. Because the region's main oil and natural gas deposits lie north of the Iranian coast, Iran's main potential role in the Caspian Sea's oil industry is as a transport link. The Caspian oil producers back construction of a pipeline that would carry the region's oil through Iran to the Persian Gulf for shipment through the Strait of Hormuz to market. The United States, which maintains a unilateral embargo against Iran for its role in supporting international terrorism, adamantly opposes this route. For

---

million barrels a day. But with prices falling — and with them precious oil revenues — many members ignored their quotas and pumped as much oil as the market would bear.

Desperate to reduce output, OPEC has appealed to other producers, which are also feeling the pinch of falling oil revenues. Russia, which has the largest oil reserves of any non-OPEC country and badly needs oil revenues to stave off its deepening financial crisis, attended OPEC's June 24 meeting in Geneva and may soon join the organization. [4] On June 4, the oil ministers of Saudi Arabia and Venezuela reached an agreement

with Mexico to cut production by 450,000 barrels a day, beginning July 1. This agreement has had some effect on prices, leading some observers to predict that OPEC will turn more often to informal agreements of this kind in an effort to regain leverage over the market and stabilize prices around the historical norm of about $20 a barrel.

"OPEC is a major factor in determining world oil prices," says Edward H. Murphy, director of finance, accounting and statistics for the American Petroleum Institute (API), which represents U.S. oil companies. "They have succeeded in reducing

production by about 2.1 million barrels a day, or 6 percent, since February. That is a significant factor that has prevented oil prices from falling even further. They're not back up to $20 a barrel, but they'd be a lot lower today in the absence of OPEC's production cuts."

Does U.S. foreign policy enhance Americans' access to foreign oil?

A fundamental, though infrequently recognized, goal of U.S. foreign policy has been to ensure the access of American businesses and consumers to foreign oil supplies,

... Involves Many Actors, Many Ifs

now, some Caspian Sea oil is making its way indirectly through Iran via a swap arrangement by which oil is shipped to refineries in northern Iran, and an equivalent amount of Iranian oil is loaded onto tankers in the Persian Gulf for transport to market.

Kazakhstan — Though only a fraction of this vast and sparsely populated country's territory lies near the Caspian, it holds one of the region's most promising oil and gas deposits — the Tengiz Basin now under development by Chevron and other companies. China plans to build a 1,900-mile pipeline from the basin across Kazakhstan to Xinjiang, China. President Nursultan Nazarbaev, a former first secretary of the Kazakhstan Community Party, was elected after the country declared its independence from the Soviet Union in December 1991. Since then he has consolidated his power by eroding the country's limited representative government.

Kyrgyzstan — Considered to be the most democratic country in Central Asia, Kyrgyzstan is led by Askar Akaev, a former physicist who often quotes Thomas Jefferson. Elected president by the Supreme Soviet in 1990, Akaev won re-election in 1995. The country's oil potential is uncertain.

Russia — Like Iran, Russia stands to play a marginal role in the Caspian's oil production, but a crucial one in transporting the region's oil and gas to market. The first developer of the region's oil a century ago, Russia — and later the Soviet Union — largely abandoned the Caspian fields in favor of other domestic reserves to build its considerable oil industry. Today Russia transports Caspian oil by rail to the Baltic Sea and maintains other oil and gas pipelines, including one from Baku to its Black Sea port of Novorossisk. A proposed pipeline would also link the Tengiz oil field and Novorossisk.

Tajikistan — Last summer, Tajik President Imomali Rakhmonov and opposition forces signed a peace agreement ending a five-year civil war waged among the country's four regional tribes and between the secular government and Islamic militants. One of the poorest of the former Soviet republics, Tajikistan supports a thriving drug trade that has hampered efforts to improve the economy. [2]

Turkmenistan — Saparmurat Niyazov, a former Communist Party leader who became president in 1990, heads an oppressive regime based on a cult of personality. Known as Turkmenbashi — "head of the Turkmen" — Niyazov has banned opposition parties and presides over the legislature. Despite considerable reserves of natural gas and oil under and around the Caspian Sea, mismanagement of the economy has impoverished the country, which borders Afghanistan and Iran. The only existing export outlets for Turkmen gas is through Russian pipelines.

Uzbekistan — With almost 24 million inhabitants, Uzbekistan is the most populous country in the region. Cotton is the country's main product, but the government has announced plans to search for oil and gas under the polluted Aral Sea, drained of much of its water for irrigation. President Islam Karimov, a former communist leader, has introduced limited democratic reforms but faces the growing influence of Islamic militants.

---

[1] See Richard C. Longworth, "Boomtown Baku," *The Bulletin of the Atomic Scientists,* May/June 1998, pp. 34-38.

[2] See Martha Brill Olcott, "The Caspian's False Promise," *Foreign Policy,* summer 1998, pp. 94-113.

especially since 1971, when domestic oil production peaked and began its gradual decline. By 1996, the United States — once a leading exporter of crude — was for the first time forced to import half of its oil. Today, imports account for 52 percent of U.S. consumption. *(See graph, p. 680.)* As demand for oil continues to rise, the United States will likely depend on imports for an ever-growing portion of its oil supply.

Like other industrialized countries, the United States has diversified its sources of foreign oil away from the Middle East since the energy crises of the 1970s. Today, Venezuela is the leading source of U.S. oil imports, followed by Canada. Although U.S. dependence on Persian Gulf oil has fallen from 28 percent of oil imports in 1991 to just over 19 percent today, the region will remain a vital oil supplier for years to come. But it is also one of the most politically unstable regions, the focus of 50 years of hostilities between Israel and its Arab neighbors and, for the past two decades, of militant Islamic fundamentalism.

Access to oil has figured prominently in the United States' activities in the Middle East throughout this period, most recently in the 1991 Persian Gulf War, when the United States led a United Nations military coalition that forced Iraq to withdraw from neighboring Kuwait. [5]

Of course, access to oil is not the sole U.S. strategic interest in the region. Even during the gulf war, the Bush administration stressed the need to repel Iraq's invasion of Kuwait to maintain the international rule of law. Because Iraq's leader, Saddam Hussein, was suspected of producing nuclear and biological weapons, the United States also sought and obtained Security Council support for a U.N. embargo against Iraq pending the completion of U.N. inspections of Iraqi arsenals. But the Clinton administration's "dual containment"

U.S. Dependence on Imported Oil Growing

U.S. oil imports have been increasing while domestic production has been falling, reflecting decreasing U.S. oil reserves.

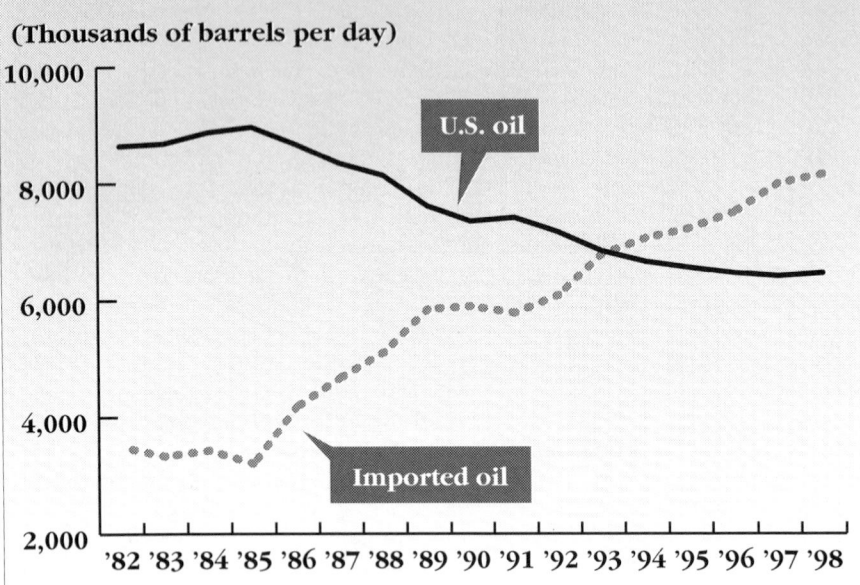

(Thousands of barrels per day)

U.S. oil

Imported oil

'82 '83 '84 '85 '86 '87 '88 '89 '90 '91 '92 '93 '94 '95 '96 '97 '98

Source: Energy Information Administration, Monthly Energy Review, *June 1998*

policy toward Iraq and Iran — which together control 20 percent of the world's proven reserves — has implications for U.S. access to the region's oil exports. [6]

Iraq, with 112 billion barrels of proven oil reserves, is second only to Saudi Arabia, with 262 billion barrels. The embargo has exacted a heavy toll on Iraq, depriving it of oil revenues and leaving many Iraqis without adequate food and medical supplies. In December 1996, the embargo was eased to allow Iraq to export just enough oil to pay for food and other essential supplies. This "oil-for-food" provision is to remain in place until the Iraqi government allows U.N. arms inspectors full access to weapons sites.

But some oil-importing countries, notably France, Russia and China, oppose continuing the embargo against Iraq indefinitely. Critics of the embargo welcomed U.N. Secretary General Kofi Annan's role in prod-

ding Saddam Hussein to allow U.N. inspectors greater access to the country last February. Annan signaled a softening of international attitudes toward Iraq by calling the Iraqi leader "a man you can do business with." For his part, Saddam has threatened to take unspecified action to break the embargo if it is not lifted this year. [7]

Indeed, Iraq is already expanding oil exports in defiance of the U.N. embargo. "The fact that Iraq continues to export sizable amounts of petroleum products illegally — and that the Iraqi government refuses to permit the U.N. to oversee or monitor these sales — strongly suggests that the proceeds from these sales are intended for non-humanitarian purposes," said Under Secretary of State Thomas R. Pickering. "We are currently seeking ways to make the Iraqi government accountable for this illegal traffic — or to end it through tougher enforcement measures." [8]

Critics say the U.S. efforts are

doomed. "American policy [toward Iraq] is nothing more than the desperate embrace of sanctions of diminishing effectiveness punctuated by occasional whining, frequent bluster, political retreat and military paralysis," said Richard Perle, assistant secretary of Defense for international security during the Reagan administration. "The pressure to relax the sanctions, which has already pushed to more than $10 billion per year the amount of revenue Iraq is allowed from the sale of oil, will not subside and will almost certainly increase. The French, Russians and others will continue to agitate for the further relaxation of sanctions, and the United States will almost certainly make further concessions in this regard." [9]

U.S. policy toward Iran, whose 93 billion barrels of proven oil reserves place it fifth in the global ranking of oil powers, elicits similar concerns. Since the 1979 Islamic revolution, the United States has identified Iran as one of the world's leading supporters of international terrorism. With the Iran-Libya Sanctions Act, the United States unilaterally barred American and foreign companies from investing more than $20 million in Iran's energy sector.

But Iran is an important source of Persian Gulf oil, and several foreign companies have defied the ban. Under pressure from Europe, Clinton announced in May that he would not impose sanctions on three French, Russian and Malaysian companies that invested $2 billion in a natural gas field in Iran.

Meanwhile, U.S. oil companies are losing lucrative oil contracts to overseas competitors. "There's no question that unilateral sanctions against Iran are hurting U.S. companies," says Murphy of the API. "By preventing them from competing in those markets, the sanctions provide a relative advantage to foreign oil companies. That's a real concern of our members. Whether or not there's a fair

Varied Sources Provide U.S. Oil Imports

U.S. oil imports come from a wide range of sources. Four of the top five providers are not Arab nations, and two of the five are not members of the Organization of Petroleum Exporting Countries (list at left). More than half the oil imported by the United States comes from non-OPEC members (list at right).

Top Five U.S. Suppliers	
(thousands of barrels per day)	
Venezuela*	1,657
Saudi Arabia*	1,508
Canada	1,460
Mexico	1,235
Nigeria*	812

OPEC vs. Non-OPEC Production	
(thousands of barrels per day)	
Arab OPEC	2,199
Other OPEC	2,519
Non-OPEC	4,976
Total	9,694

* *OPEC members*

Source: Energy Information Administration, Monthly Energy Review, *June 1998*

foreign policy tradeoff, I can't say."

Some critics see a clear clash of interests between U.S. foreign policy in the region and U.S. energy security. "The United States' vilification of Iran, Iraq and Libya makes for strange policy," Campbell says, "especially when you understand we'll be dependent on these three places for oil before long."

The Clinton administration continues to defend its policy of containment toward Iran. "Unilateral sanctions have proven costly to U.S. business," conceded Assistant Secretary of State for Near Eastern Affairs Martin S. Indyk. "However, we believe that Iran poses threats so significant that we have no choice but accept these costs. Economic pressure has an important role in our efforts to convince Iran to cease its efforts to acquire weapons of mass destruction and missiles and to support terrorism." [10]

The U.S. position toward Iran has shown signs of softening since the election last August of President Mohammad Khatami, who has loosened somewhat the strict regime set in place by his militant predecessors by expanding press freedoms and establishing more cordial relations with countries in the Persian Gulf and Europe.

But, citing evidence that Iran's support of terrorism is unchanged, the United States officially has not changed its position on sanctions. On June 17, however, Secretary of State Madeleine K. Albright held out the possibility of a future improvement in bilateral relations. Although she refrained from proposing specific steps to normalize relations, Albright said, "Obviously, two decades of mistrust cannot be erased overnight. The gap between us remains wide. But it is time to test the possibilities for bridging this gap." [11]

The Caspian Sea region is another area where foreign policy goals may clash with those of energy security. "Our interest in the Caspian is not defined simply by the region's energy resources, but no one doubts their significance," said Stephen Sestanovich, special adviser to the secretary of State for the new independent states. "Energy could become a source of conflict, a lever of control or an obstacle to progress. Or it could become a ticket to prosperity and peace, a secure link to the outside world." [12]

The United States is playing an active role in brokering peace talks in some of the region's simmering

ethnic battles, such as those between the government of Azerbaijan and leaders of Armenian rebels who occupy the region of Nagorno Karabakh. It also has funneled economic and technical assistance — totaling $372 million in fiscal 1998 — to the newly independent countries of the region, which own potentially huge deposits of oil.

But an existing measure, Section 907 of the 1992 Freedom Support Act, bars the United States from extending this assistance to Azerbaijan. Enacted at the behest of the U.S. Armenian lobby, which claimed that the government of Azerbaijan subjected ethnic Armenians to human rights abuses, the measure has attracted widespread opposition since the extent of Azerbaijan's oil wealth has become more apparent. The Clinton administration also supports the measure's repeal.

Caspian Sea oil cannot reach consumers until a pipeline network is built linking the remote, landlocked region to seaports far away. *(See map, p. 676.)* The most direct route, and possibly the least expensive to construct, would pass through Iran to the Persian Gulf. But U.S. sanctions against Iran stand in the way of that option. Instead, the United States backs a multiple pipeline network that includes the so-called main export pipeline, which would pass through Georgia and NATO ally Turkey to the Turkish port of Ceyhan on the Black Sea, where the oil would be loaded onto tankers and shipped to markets via the Mediterranean Sea.

Some experts say the United States should ease its current opposition to the Iran pipeline option. "If the international oil companies working in Central Asia do not need to start construction of new pipeline routes immediately, the U.S. government should not lock the door prematurely against the prospect of a new pipeline transiting Iran," said Richard W. Murphy, senior fellow for the Middle East at the Council on Foreign Relations. "The routing of new pipelines will have profound political and economic implications for years to come." [13]

Will the United States be ready with alternative energy sources when the oil runs out?

As a finite resource, petroleum will not last forever. Estimates of how long the world has before the oil runs out vary widely. The United States is likely to run out far sooner than many major producers, however. Using 6.8 billion barrels of oil products a year, the United States is the world's most voracious oil consumer. And it shows no sign of changing its energy habits. U.S. demand for oil is expected to grow by 20 percent by 2015. [14]

But the crunch is likely to come long before the world exhausts its oil supplies. "The idea of running out of oil, of when the last barrel comes out of the ground, is a red herring," Campbell says. "It misses the point. What's much more relevant is when world production will peak, and that will occur within the first few years of the next century." When that happens, Campbell predicts, oil consumers will be in for a major price shock as production slows.

Campbell says the United States may be especially ill-prepared for the next energy crisis. Even though U.S. oil production started declining in 1971, the United States was never seriously affected because it was able to import its oil from other countries. "This chapter is coming to an end because the other places, too, are getting close to peak production," he says. "There's monumental ignorance in the government and among the public at large on this subject."

Other critics charge that the United States, by holding oil taxes below those of other consuming nations, has encouraged oil consumption with little concern for the consequences. [15] "Part of our energy policy seems to be to keep prices low," says George Yates, chairman of the Independent Petroleum Association of America, whose 8,000 members produce almost half of the nation's domestic crude. "But we have only about 3 million barrels a day worldwide of excess capacity, and that includes Iraq, which is officially out of production because of the embargo. That's a pretty slim margin. It's like operating a factory at 100 percent capacity — you can't go on forever like this."

The development of alternatives to oil has proceeded slowly in the United States. After the energy crises of the 1970s, the federal government funded research and development of renewable energy sources such as solar, wind, geothermal and biomass energy. [16] But as oil prices subsequently fell and Congress turned its attention to reducing the federal budget deficit, support for these efforts dwindled.

According to Energy Under Secretary Ernest Moniz, his department's budgets for energy research and development fell fivefold from 1978 to 1997; privately funded research has also declined. [17] Today, much of the U.S.-developed technology for renewable energy sources is being used more intensively in Europe and Asia — where oil products are heavily taxed — than in the United States.

"The effects of world dependence on Middle Eastern oil means that while the quoted market price per barrel is about $20, the costs associated with keeping shipping lanes open, rogue states in check and terrorists at bay may more than quadruple the price per barrel," said Sen. Richard G. Lugar, R-Ind. "Given these costs, the United States may pay more than $100 billion this year for oil from the unstable Middle East. By contrast, the United States will spend less than $1 billion this year on energy research." [18]

Some analysts find little reason for concern about the United States' energy future. In their view, the technology that has enabled oil producers to discover new deposits and remove more oil from existing wells will continue to advance. "We've made tremendous advances that have made it cheaper to find and produce oil," says Murphy of the API. "If those continue, we're probably looking at oil availability for the indefinite future at today's prices or less."

When the oil crunch does come, Murphy predicts, the technology to provide cheap alternatives will be ready to take up the slack. "My feeling is that long before the use of petroleum is diminished, other sources will be there. In 10 years, all cars may be run with fuel cells instead of gasoline." ∎

BACKGROUND

OPEC's Power Play

The United States was the world's dominant oil producer for the first half of this century. [19] Outside the United States, world production fell under the control of the world's major oil companies, known as the "Seven Sisters," which acquired the right to extract oil from countries where they operated in exchange for royalties

Continued on p. 684

Chronology

1960s *Oil production comes under the growing control of Middle Eastern producers.*

Sept. 14, 1960
Iran, Iraq, Kuwait, Saudi Arabia and Venezuela form the Organization of Petroleum Exporting Countries (OPEC).

1969
Libyan strongman Muammar el-Qadaffi forces Occidental Petroleum, a U.S. company, to curtail production of Libyan oil, producing a shortage in world oil supplies and prompting OPEC to raise oil prices.

1970s *An Arab embargo leads to oil crises that quadruple the price of oil.*

1970
Domestic oil production peaks at 11.3 million barrels a day in the United States, forcing it to gradually increase its dependence on imports.

October 1973
After OPEC raises oil prices by 70 percent, to $5.11 a barrel, Arab producers impose an embargo on oil exports to the United States and the Netherlands for their support of Israel in the Yom Kippur War. Oil prices soar above $17 a barrel.

1975
The Strategic Petroleum Reserve is created to protect the United States from interruptions in oil supplies. Congress sets fuel-efficiency standards for cars.

December 1978
The Iranian revolution disrupts Persian Gulf oil supplies, causing a second oil shock and deepening inflation in oil-consuming countries.

June 1979
OPEC raises the price of crude from $14.50 to as high as $23.50 a barrel. Gas lines form in the United States.

1980s *As oil production spreads outside OPEC, prices begin to fall.*

1980
The eight-year Iran-Iraq War begins, compounding the disruption in Gulf oil. By the following January, OPEC's oil price reaches $34 a barrel, more than 10 times the price in 1972.

1986
Oil prices fall to their lowest level since the first oil crisis in 1973.

1990s *OPEC's inability to control output leads to a global oil glut.*

Aug. 2, 1990
Iraq occupies Kuwait, cutting off 1.6 million barrels of oil a day from the world market. The U.N. imposes an embargo on Iraqi oil exports as well. Panic buying pushes oil prices up from $13 a barrel to $40.

1991
The United States leads a coalition of forces in the Persian Gulf War to drive Iraqi occupying forces out of Kuwait.

December 1991
The Soviet Union dissolves, and the newly independent countries of the Caspian Sea begin opening their oil reserves to exploitation.

1992
Congress passes the Freedom Support Act providing economic assistance to the former Soviet republics. Section 907 of the law prohibits the aid from going to Azerbaijan — a major oil producer — for abuses against ethnic Armenians.

1993
Chevron Corp. invests in Kazakhstan's vast Tengiz oil field, beginning the oil rush in the Caspian Sea region.

1996
The U.S. begins to import more than half the oil it consumes.

December 1996
An "oil-for-food" provision is added to the U.N. embargo against Iraq, allowing the country to export just enough oil to pay for food and other essential supplies. The same year, energy conservation pushes oil consumption in the industrial world below the peak level of 1978.

October 1997
The financial crisis in Asia curbs oil consumption in that part of the world, leading to a glut in world oil supplies.

March 1998
As oil prices plummet to their lowest levels in decades, OPEC reaches an unprecedented agreement with a non-OPEC oil producer — Mexico — to curtail production in an effort to keep oil prices from falling further.

Continued from p. 682
paid to the host governments. So great was their power over the markets that they were able to manipulate the price of crude from their extensive holdings in the Middle East. [20] By the late 1950s, however, they faced growing competition from independent companies and cut their prices.

Because they collected taxes based on oil prices, Persian Gulf countries where the Seven Sisters extracted oil were faced with falling revenues. On Sept. 14, 1960, representatives of Iran, Iraq, Kuwait, Saudi Arabia and Venezuela met in Baghdad, Iraq, and founded OPEC. The fledgling cartel froze oil prices to prevent further erosion in oil revenues. Other producer nations joined OPEC, including Qatar, the United Arab Emirates in the Persian Gulf region, as well as Algeria, Indonesia, Libya and Nigeria. Membership in the organization enabled these countries to set a minimum royalty to be paid by companies for the privilege of extracting oil from their territories. The organization's expansion also helped the Seven Sisters by making it harder for independent companies to undercut them in the host countries.

The new order in oil development began to unravel in 1969, when Libyan strongman Muammar el-Qadaffi forced Occidental Petroleum, an independent American operator in Libya, to cut production. Because Libyan oil was of high quality, it was in high demand, and the cutback created an oil shortage. OPEC decided to profit from the change by raising oil prices. In an effort to stabilize the market, OPEC and the oil companies agreed in 1971 to a new pricing system that allowed for prices to be negotiated every five years.

Energy Crises of the 1970s

OPEC's new pricing system quickly fell apart, however. Oil was bought from companies in the open market for more than the established price, and OPEC members wanted to share in the profits. After the companies balked at their request, OPEC unilaterally raised the official price by 70 percent in October 1973, to $5.11 a barrel. The same month, the Arab producing countries imposed an oil embargo on the United States and the Netherlands for their support of Israel in the Yom Kippur War. The embargo was later replaced with a cutback in production by all Arab members except Iraq.

"Using oil supply as a political weapon was a new development in the industry and one that did great damage to OPEC's commercial credibility as a reliable supplier," writes Fadhil J. Chalabi, director of the Center for Global Energy Studies in London and acting secretary of OPEC from 1983-88. [21]

The production cutback reduced availability to all oil importers and led to a quadrupling of prices and the decade's first oil shock. The second shock came in the winter of 1978-79 following the Iranian revolution, which led to the ouster of Shah Mohammed Riza Pahlavi and his replacement by the Ayatollah Ruhollah Khomeini's militant Islamic regime. The revolution caused a disrup-

Continued on p. 686

A replica of the world's first oil well, drilled by "Colonel" Edwin L. Drake in Titusville, Pa., in 1859.

Public Broadcasting Service

As Oil Runs Out, Technology Buys Time

The world's supply of "conventional" oil — oil that is easily recovered — is running short of demand. In little more than a decade, some experts predict, global demand will so far exceed supplies of conventional oil that price shocks will occur that may lead to recession or political turmoil.

Faced with this impending shortfall, oil companies are investing heavily in research to improve existing technologies and develop new ones. Some of the work is already paying off. According to Roger N. Anderson, director of petroleum technology research at Columbia University, recent advances in finding and extracting oil may raise world oil production by more than 20 percent by 2010. [1]

Recent advances in oil exploration and extraction include:

4-D Seismic Analysis — As oil and natural gas are extracted from underground deposits, the remaining oil and gas seeps into the layers of rock. Three-dimensional monitoring with seismic instruments helps identify the location of oil deposits but cannot follow the shifting of oil that occurs as the well's contents run down. Anderson and others have developed a "4-D" system that incorporates the added dimension of time and helps drillers determine where the rest of the oil is likely to settle. Recovering this otherwise lost oil can increase the output of a given field by as much as 15 percent. The new technology has been applied at about 60 oil fields worldwide over the past four years.

Steam and Gas Injection — Drillers traditionally abandon wells when the flow of oil slows to a trickle. But scientists now know that this often leaves behind more than half the oil in a given deposit. Pumping steam, natural gas or liquid carbon dioxide into seemingly dry wells can force the remaining oil through porous rock toward a neighboring well, where it can be extracted. Another technique involves pumping water below the deposit, which increases the pressure under the oil, forcing it to the surface. Although steam or gas injection increases oil recovery by up to 15 percent, the high cost of this technique often outweighs the oil's value.

Directional Drilling — Oil wells typically are drilled straight down into the ground. But new technology allows drillers to change direction thousands of meters below ground and bore horizontally through rock in search of deposits a mile or more away from the wellhead. Sensors near the drill bit can detect oil, water and gas by measuring the density of surrounding rock or by measuring minute changes in electrical resistance. Engineers at the surface monitor the drill's progress by computer.

Deep-Water Drilling — Most offshore rigs, such as those along the coasts of Texas and Louisiana, operate at relatively shallow depths. But new technology is enabling drillers to tap into oil deposits under deeper water — currently down to 1,700 meters. Unmanned submarines install equipment on the ocean floor to regulate the flow of oil at high pressure and prevent environmentally devastating blowouts. The oil is then loaded onto tankers at sea or piped ashore or to shallow-water platforms through underwater pipelines. Recently declassified U.S. Navy technology enables geophysicists to detect underwater oil deposits through the sheets of salt and basalt that often hide them from conventional seismic surveys. While deep offshore drilling is very expensive, it is expected to become more widely pursued as conventional oil deposits dry up. Deep-water platforms are already in use off the coast of Newfoundland, Canada, and more are planned for the Gulf of Mexico, the North Sea and the Atlantic Ocean off Brazil and West Africa.

Just how much impact technological advances can have on global oil supplies is a matter of heated debate. Oil companies are optimistic about technology's ability to extend the petroleum era for decades to come. "If you look at the available proved reserves, there are about 1 trillion barrels of oil still in the ground," says Edward H. Murphy, an economist at the American Petroleum Institute. "If we continue to produce 27 billion barrels a year as we do now, that means we have 37 years left." That deadline can be extended, Murphy says, by technological advances. "We only recover 40 percent of production out of a given field today," he says. "So there's substantial room for enhanced recovery."

There's a downside to technology's impact on oil production, however, especially for small domestic producers who depend on the slow but steady flow of oil from marginal wells. "Some technologies mean that the same reserves are depleted more quickly instead of maintaining production over a long period," says George Yates, chairman of the Independent Petroleum Association of America. "So while technology has had a very positive impact on this industry, it's also put more oil on the market, which exacerbates our problems."

Still other experts say technology can only delay for a short time the inevitable demise of our oil-based economy. "Deep-water drilling is capable of producing 100 billion barrels, or about five years of world demand," says Colin J. Campbell, a consultant in Geneva, Switzerland. "It's expensive, and it's viable only in giant fields." He foresees further development of oil deposits under polar ice in Alaska, Russia and Canada, as well as the large deposits of heavy oil in Canada and Venezuela. "But even that won't make a lot of difference," Campbell says. "Whatever the accumulated advances of technology can deliver ought to be incorporated into our estimates of existing oil reserves. It's not something you can keep adding to."

---

[1] Information in this section is largely based on Roger N. Anderson, "Oil Production in the 21st Century," *Scientific American*, March 1998, pp. 86-91.

Continued from p. 684

tion of oil from the Persian Gulf that was compounded by the outbreak in 1980 of the Iran-Iraq War. By January 1981, OPEC's oil price had reached $34 a barrel, more than 10 times the price in 1972, before the first oil shock. Taken together, the shocks produced a windfall for OPEC members, whose oil revenues skyrocketed from less than $23 billion in 1972 to more than $280 billion by the end of the decade.

Oil Consumers React

But OPEC's bonanza days were numbered. The United States and other industrial countries reacted strongly to the gasoline rationing, long lines at the pump and double-digit inflation produced by the production cutbacks and price increases. They launched a frantic search for alternative sources of oil and set about trying to reduce their dependence on oil imports by making more fuel-efficient cars, improving energy conservation and developing renewable energy sources.

Over time, the growth in demand for oil slowed. By 1995, industrial nations were consuming only 2 million barrels a day more than they had in 1975. "Put another way," writes Chalabi, "oil consumption by OECD countries in 1996 was less than at its peak level in 1978, even though their [gross domestic product] had grown by 42 percent during the same period."[22]

The oil consumers' efforts to reduce their reliance on Middle East oil paid off most successfully in the development of new oil fields. Companies shifted their investments to non-OPEC countries such as Mexico and Canada, as well as Britain and Norway, where they developed new platform-drilling technology to exploit the vast deposits under the North Sea. High oil prices also made it feasible to tap the enormous reserves on Alaska's North Slope.

As a result of these efforts, OPEC's share of the global oil market fell by half, from 56 percent in 1975 to just 26 percent in 1995. Although non-OPEC countries possess only a quarter of the world's oil reserves, they now account for 60 percent of global production. ■

Part of the Caspian Sea oil-drilling installation built by Soviet leader Josef Stalin in 1949, about 40 miles east of Baku, Azerbaijan.

CURRENT SITUATION

OPEC's Dilemma

Despite the industrial nations' success in reducing their dependence on Middle East oil, OPEC has continued to reap enormous profits from oil exports. The revenues from oil sales have enabled many member countries to invest in other industries to help diversify their economies in preparation for the day when they will no longer be able to rely on petroleum exports.

But the glut in oil supplies that began last fall has dealt a serious blow to countries that still depend heavily on oil exports, both within and outside OPEC. Even Saudi Arabia is feeling the pinch of falling oil revenues.

The economic crisis has encouraged cheating on the part of some OPEC members, further undermining the organization's clout. Venezuela is said to be the most flagrant offender, and has called on fellow OPEC members to abandon quotas altogether in favor of other strategies to win market share. Algeria, Iran, Libya and Nigeria also routinely ignore the production quotas to prevent further erosion of the oil revenues they depend on for economic survival.[23]

In a desperate effort to slow production, OPEC for the first time called on non-member producer countries to cooperate with its quota system. In March, Mexico agreed to cut oil output, and Norway later agreed to curb production as well. Russia has expressed interest in joining OPEC and attended the organization's June meeting in Geneva as an observer. The March agreement sent oil prices up by 13 percent, to almost $17 a barrel. But prices have since dropped back to around $14, suggesting that the market is not confident that OPEC can hold production down for long.

Some U.S. oil-company representatives support OPEC's campaign to hold the line on output and prices. "I'm hoping that by including non-members, OPEC can exercise some restraint on oil production," says Yates of the Independent Petroleum Association. "Restraint, coupled with higher prices, will mean fewer oil wells being abandoned in the United States. It also means new wells will be drilled to find additional oil, which will make us better able to meet demand in the future. OPEC's really the American consumer's friend right now."

But many analysts question OPEC's ability over the long term to control the global market, which has changed in fundamental ways over the past two decades. "What's dominating the market today is the advance of technology, which is having a significant impact on the industry's ability to explore and produce oil in areas they were forbidden from exploring before," says Murphy of the API. Another change is the willingness of countries such as Venezuela, where the oil business was once run by state-owned companies, to have foreign, private companies come in and produce their oil. Finally, the former Soviet republics in the Caspian may have a major impact on world markets when the region's oil starts to flow. "OPEC is a bystander in this region," Murphy says.

OPEC's difficulties lead some ex-perts to predict its eventual demise. "OPEC, as such, is disintegrating," Campbell says. Indeed, OPEC members know that drastically raising prices to solve their current dilemma will backfire on them in the end. "They remember what happened

Oil companies are investing heavily in research to improve exploration and drilling technology, because conventional methods may be unable to meet demand in the near future.

©Digital Stock

after the last shock," he says, "and they fear that if they put up the price they will lose their market share, and if that happens that they will lose everything."

In Campbell's view, however, the

five leading Middle Eastern producers — Iran, Iraq, Kuwait, Saudi Arabia and Abu Dhabi (one of seven emirates comprising the United Arab Emirates) — have nothing to worry about. "They don't realize that the situation is very different today," he says. In about four years, by his calculation, world production of conventional oil — that which is easily recoverable — will peak, sending prices upward once again.

"Unlike the 1970s, when a flood of new oil production followed the price shocks," he says, "there are very few new oil deposits being found, with the exception of the Caspian." Campbell predicts that Middle Eastern producers, with about half the world's remaining conventional oil reserves, will see their share of recoverable oil rise substantially by 2000.

At that point, he says, "the Middle Eastern countries will recognize their control."

Cheap Oil

For now, however, oil-producing countries, including the petroleum-rich kingdoms of the Middle East, are suffering as a result of low oil prices. Most depend on oil exports for the bulk of their revenue. Saudi Arabia has seen its oil revenues drop from $43 billion last year to an estimated $29 billion in 1998. As a result, King Fahd's government has been forced to borrow $2 billion from Saudi banks to fund public programs and has cut its budget by at least 10 percent. [24]

The bad news for oil producers may have a silver lining over the longer term. As autocratic regimes in the Middle East are forced to reduce their generous health, education and welfare programs, social unrest may quicken the pace of economic and political reforms. Pressure for reform has surfaced in a number of the region's oil states, including Saudi Arabia and the other gulf states, as well as Syria and Iran. [25]

Oil producers outside the Middle East are suffering as well. Mexico, a major source of U.S. oil imports, announced its third budget cut in six months in early July, citing unexpectedly low oil revenues. Nigeria, in the midst of political turmoil in the wake of the sudden death of popular opposition leader Mashood Abiola, faces an even graver plight. In this poor West African country, earnings from oil exports provide a vital buffer against widespread poverty. For Russia, the price drop has only added to the country's serious economic crisis. Only Britain and Norway, with the most diversified industrial economies among the major foreign exporters, can absorb the loss of oil revenues without major disruption.

In the United States, which now imports more than half its oil, the fall in prices is a mixed bag. American motorists are benefiting from cheap gasoline, and low prices are helping keep inflation in check. But the U.S. oil industry is facing the same problems as the major producing nations. Occidental Petroleum reported a 66 percent drop in net income for the second quarter of 1998, and other major companies are expected to issues similarly bad news. [26]

Lower crude oil prices have dampened the incentive for oil companies to look for new domestic deposits and to maintain production in exist-

ing fields with marginal output. According to the API's Murphy, the number of drilling rigs used to search for oil and gas has fallen by 31 percent over the average used for that purpose over the past decade. "This drilling data should, we believe, be of major concern to those interested in this country's energy future," he said. "Oil drilling at these rates is inadequate to maintain U.S. crude oil production levels, particularly in the lower 48 states." [27]

Many smaller American oil companies are in especially bad shape. As a group, the 8,000 independent oil companies suffered a 25 percent drop in revenues over the past year. These include many companies that extract natural gas as well as oil. Natural gas prices have been largely unaffected by the oil glut. "But some of our members produce only oil," explains Yates of the Independent Petroleum Association. "For them, the impact of low oil prices is extremely dramatic. You have to go back to the 1930s for corresponding prices, and then they had to call out the Texas Rangers to bring order to the market." *

Many small companies face bankruptcy. "The worst off are those with marginal production," Yates says. "There are thousands of these mom-and-pop operations." As large oil fields have run dry in the United States, many of the 500,000 wells operated by the association's members produce just two or three barrels of crude a day. "Most of these marginal wells could go on producing forever, but not at a loss, so they are being abandoned," Yates says. "This is a very serious issue, because the oil we don't produce domestically we have to import. And it's not just the oil producers who are affected,

---

* In 1931, an oil glut in Texas and Oklahoma drove down oil prices, prompting Texas Gov. Ross Sterling to send the Texas Rangers into the East Texas oil fields to enforce a production cutback.

because as imports grow, so does the trade deficit." In May, the U.S. trade deficit hit a record $15.7 billion as imports grew and exports fell, especially to the economically troubled Asian countries. [28]

Caspian Treasure

As petroleum deposits are depleted in coming years, prices are likely to rise, ending the era of cheap oil. With few major new fields expected to be found, oil companies are in hot competition to develop the potentially huge reserves under and around the landlocked Caspian Sea, which lies between southern Russia and northern Iran. Estimates of the volume of crude oil in the region range up to 200 billion barrels — more than a quarter of the Middle East's reserves.

The region's oil has been known about for centuries. Marco Polo remarked on the seepage of oil around the Caspian Sea during his travels along the Silk Road, the ancient trade route between Europe and the Far East. Swedish businessmen Ludwig and Robert Nobel began developing oil fields in Baku, on the western coast of the Caspian Sea, more than 120 years ago. [29] The Soviet Union, with large oil reserves in other parts of the country, did little to develop the Caspian fields because most of the oil was trapped under water or salt formations and too hard to extract.

Modern technology now places the Caspian's oil within reach, and oil companies have descended on the sparsely populated region since 1991 to gain a foothold in what may be the world's last oil boom. One of the first Western companies in the region was Chevron Corp., which in 1993 began investing in Kazakhstan's Tengiz oil field in and around the northeastern

Continued on p. 690

At Issue:

Should the United States ease its sanctions against Iran to improve international access to Caspian Sea oil?

S. FREDERICK STARR

Chairman, Central Asia Institute, Nitze School of Advanced International Studies, Johns Hopkins University

FROM TESTIMONY BEFORE THE HOUSE INTERNATIONAL RELATIONS SUBCOMMITTEE ON ASIA AND THE PACIFIC, FEB. 12, 1998.

*t*wo presidential directives in 1995 and the Iran-Libya Sanctions Act of 1996 cut off all significant American and foreign investment in Iran's petroleum industry, including pipelines. The purpose was to pressure Iran into dropping its support for terrorism, abandoning programs to develop atomic weapons and [stopping its] meddling in the Middle East peace process. However laudable the aims, the burden of these measures falls disproportionately on Azerbaijan, Kazakhstan and Turkmenistan, for it prevents them from exporting their gas and oil by one of the obvious alternative routes to Russia, namely, Iran. The U.S. position has been to argue that this would not be in the Central Asians' own interest, but none of our friends there agree.

Now, let us suppose that the U.S. sanctions [remained] in place for a long time and [were] truly effective. Over time, so we have argued, planners and financial markets would adjust to this reality. They would construct the east-west pipeline and thus give Central Asians access to secure export routes bypassing both Iran and Russia.

But this is not happening. French, Indonesian and Russian firms are already investing in the construction of oil facilities and pipelines in Iran, and the U.S. seems disinclined to intervene against them. Iran itself is busy constructing a line linking Turkmenistan and Turkey. Turkmenistan and Kazakhstan have worked out swap deals with Tehran, by which Central Asia ships its crude oil to Iran's north and Iran then exports the same quantity of its own oil from the south. In short, the American quarantine of 1995-6 is not holding. . . .

[The United States could] adopt a "wait and see" posture toward Iran, one that would be cautious but less categorical than our current policy. It would replace an "all or nothing" approach with one that recognizes the existence of a large number of finely calibrated positions between these two extremes. . . . On balance, it seems to me that [this alternative] holds the most promise for achieving a balance between U.S. objectives in Central Asia, in the Caspian basin and in Iran. . . .

[I]t is no longer possible to treat U.S. policy toward Central Asia and toward Iran as totally separate from one another. Our Iranian policy, however just its goals, has a powerful and, for the most part, negative impact on our ability to achieve our stated objectives in Central Asia and the Caspian basin.

SEN. SAM BROWNBACK, R-KAN.

FROM TESTIMONY BEFORE THE SENATE FOREIGN RELATIONS SUBCOMMITTEE ON INTERNATIONAL ECONOMIC POLICY, EXPORT AND TRADE PROMOTION, OCT. 23, 1997.

*t*he countries of the South Caucasus and Central Asia — Armenia, Azerbaijan, Georgia, Kazakhstan, Kyrgyzstan, Tajikistan, Turkmenistan and Uzbekistan — are at a historic crossroads in their history: They are independent, they are at the juncture of many of today's major world forces, they are rich in natural resources and they are looking to the United States for support. . . .

First of all, these countries are a major force in containing the spread northward of anti-Western Iranian extremism. Though Iranian activity in the region has been less blatant than elsewhere in the world, they are working very hard to bring the region into their sphere of influence and economic control.

Secondly, the Caspian Sea basin contains proven oil and gas reserves which, potentially, could rank third in the world after the Middle East and Russia and exceed $4 trillion in value. Investment in this region could ultimately reduce U.S. dependence on oil imports from the volatile Persian Gulf and could provide regional supplies as an alternative to Iranian sources. . . .

The independence of the region could indeed well depend on the successful construction of pipelines on an east-west axis through non-Russian as well as non-Iranian territory. Both Russian and Iranian rhetoric on this issue shows clearly that these countries see the connection between pipelines free of Russian and Iranian control and their domination over the region. And it is no coincidence that we are seeing an intense rapprochement between these two countries.

Time is of an essence here. We have the opportunity to help these countries rebuild themselves from the ground up and to encourage them to continue their strong independent stances, especially in relation to Iran and the spread of extremist, anti-Western fundamentalism, which is one of the most clear and present dangers facing the United States today.

The window of opportunity has been closed even further by the recent investment by the French company Total . . . in the Iranian South Pars offshore gas field. It is vital that the [Clinton] administration hold strong on implementing existing sanctions and on discouraging our allies from following the despicable example of Total. If the floodgates open through Iran, the eastern Caspian will certainly fall into the Eastern sphere of dominance, and the South Caucasus will lose out on its opportunity to prosper as producer of oil and as a pivotal transit point from East to West.

Continued from p. 688

Caspian. Numerous other companies have since invested in the region as well, though Chevron has spent more than all of them put together. [30]

The main obstacle to the development of Caspian oil is the volatile political situation throughout the region. The Soviet Union's dissolution in 1991 transformed the former Soviet republics of Azerbaijan, Kazakhstan and Turkmenistan, which also border the Caspian, into independent countries. With no democratic tradition, ethnic divisions that rival those of the former Yugoslavia and virtually undeveloped economies, the Caspian is a region that journalist Richard C. Longworth describes as "Bosnia with oil."

"In this oil-soaked cockpit, the prospects for both wealth and trouble are simply stupendous," he writes. "The Caucasus is a land of ancient vendettas and warring tribes that makes the Balkans look straightforward by comparison, and the Caspian is where this bloody region meets Central Asia and the Middle East. It's where Orthodox Christianity meets both Sunni and Shi'ite Islam, where Iranians traveling north have met Russians coming south. It's an area once ruled by Iran, then by Russia, now contested by Turkey, whose language and civilization dominate the region." [31]

Pipelines and Politics

The Caspian region's political turmoil exacerbates another significant obstacle to developing Caspian oil: transportation problems. Once the crude is extracted, it must travel thou-

New pipelines are needed to move crude oil from the landlocked Caspian Sea region to deep-water ports where it can be loaded onto tankers and shipped to markets.

©Digital Stock

sands of miles to reach ports where it can be loaded onto tankers and shipped to markets. Some oil from the Tengiz field already reaches the Baltic

Sea by rail. But rail shipment is expensive and increases the risk of oil spills. [32] The only alternative under consideration is to build pipelines. Three are already being developed. The problem is where to build the next ones.

China plans a 1,900-mile pipeline from Tengiz across Kazakhstan into China. But all the other routes from the Caspian to Western markets have political drawbacks. The most direct route to open sea, and the one desired by the Caspian countries, is through Iran to the Persian Gulf. But the United States opposes that route because it would defy U.S. sanctions against Iran and make Caspian oil hostage to political instability in the gulf.

Although Secretary Albright waived the sanctions against three foreign companies that invested in Iranian oil fields in May, the move apparently did not signal an immediate change in policy. "We continue to oppose trans-Iran pipelines for Caspian energy exports in the strongest terms," said Sestanovich of the State Department. [33]

Russia has proposed a route that would carry oil from the eastern Caspian to the Russian port of Novorossisk on the Black Sea, which already serves as the terminus for an existing pipeline from Baku. Turkey opposes this and other new pipelines that would terminate at the Black Sea because the oil must then be shipped through the narrow Bosporus strait, which passes through Istanbul, to reach the Mediterranean. Some 4,000 tankers already pass through the 17-mile-long passage each year, negotiating four 45-degree turns on their way and posing the risk of disastrous oil spills. Another planned pipeline, linking Turkmenistan to Pakistan, is on hold pending resolution of Afghanistan's protracted civil war.

The Clinton administration supports a network of multiple oil and gas pipelines to make it less likely that a supply interruption in one would cut off the entire region's oil flow. It is pushing strongly for a pipeline stretching from the Caspian port of Baku, Azerbaijan, through Georgia to the Mediterranean port of Ceyhan in Turkey, a NATO ally.

The region's political turmoil leads some observers to question the ability of the Caspian region to meet the growing global demand for oil. "The Caspian states are not necessarily plunging into a maelstrom in which corrupt regimes will be challenged either by secret drug lords or social unrest," writes Martha Brill Olcott, a senior associate at the Carnegie Endowment for International Peace and professor of political science at Colgate University. "But the possibility of such chaos cannot be precluded. Each of these states faces difficult political transitions in the next five to 10 years, while peak oil production and the economic benefits that it promises are unlikely to be realized in the region until 2010." [34]

Other obstacles to the region's ascendance as a leading oil provider spring from its geological limitations. "The Caspian is the only place in the world right now with significant promise," Campbell says. "But there's been some exaggerated talk about its real potential." He estimates that the region may contain only 50 billion barrels. "Even that is stretching credibility a little bit," he says. "And that's if it comes in, which as of today is not something to count on."

FOR MORE INFORMATION

If you would like to have this CQ Researcher updated, or need more information about this topic, please call CQ Custom Research. Special rates for CQ subscribers. (202) 887-8600 or (800) 432-2250, ext. 600, or E-mail Custom.Research@cq.com

Energy Information Administration, U.S. Department of Energy, 1000 Independence Ave. S.W., #2G051, Washington, D.C. 20585; (202) 586-5214; www.eia.doe.gov. The EIA collects and publishes data on domestic production, imports, distribution and prices of crude oil and refined petroleum products.

American Petroleum Institute, 1220 L St. N.W., Washington, D.C. 20005; (202) 682-8042; www.api.org. This membership organization of U.S. producers, refiners, marketers and transporters of oil and related products provides information on the industry.

Independent Petroleum Association of America, 1101 16th St. N.W., 2nd Floor, Washington, D.C. 20036; (202) 857-4722; www.ipaa.org. Members are independent oil and gas producers and others involved in domestic oil and gas production.

International Energy Agency, 9, rue de la Federation, 75739 Paris Cedex 15, France; (33-1) 40.57.65.54; www.iea.org. Created in the wake of the energy crises of the 1970s, the IEA monitors global oil production and helps consumer countries coordinate strategies to avoid supply disruptions.

With Caspian deposits perhaps equivalent in volume to those under the North Sea, Campbell says, offshore production could total up to 4 million barrels a day by 2025. "Although that's valuable and not to be dismissed," he says, "it's unlikely to make much of an impact on the peak of global oil production," which he says will occur within the next few years. ■

OUTLOOK

Will Prices Rise?

Despite OPEC's recent efforts to curb production, it may be some time before the current oil glut subsides enough to push prices back up. But simply stopping the current over-

production may not be enough to return global supply and demand to balance, according to the Paris-based International Energy Agency. Oil importers will first have to absorb the excess oil that is already in the supply chain. They also will have to reduce their record high levels of oil stocks, the result of a warm winter in North America and of stagnant industrial production in Japan and other East Asian countries. [35]

Some economists predict that oil prices will remain low, even after the current glut has vanished, because the world has already begun to wean itself from petroleum products.

"The industrial world uses 42 percent less oil to produce an extra unit of [gross domestic product] than it needed in 1973," writes Lester C. Thurow, an economics professor at the Massachusetts Institute of Technology. "Transportation still depends upon oil, but fuel cells look as if they are about to arrive. When they do, early in the next century, oil demand will begin to fall even in this, its primary market." As a result, Thurow predicts, oil "prices will be low for the foreseeable future."[36]

Other experts are equally convinced that oil prices are headed in the opposite direction. In Campbell's view, the world is in for an oil shock that will make the energy crises of the 1970s pale in comparison. "There will be an initial price shock around 2000, with a doubling or perhaps a tripling of prices," he predicts. "Although the roof won't fall in overnight, long-term shortages will force a change in attitude about energy consumption."

The price rise will spur development of renewable energy sources, Campbell predicts. "But it's hard to picture this being done at a rate and a scale to enable renewables to act as substitutes for the way we've used cheap oil up to now."

In Campbell's view, the United States will play a crucial role in determining the global response to what he sees as the coming oil crisis. "There is an enormous danger that the United States, with its peculiar Middle East policies, may misunderstand this situation and perceive the price hikes to be a politically hostile act by Iran or Iraq," he says.

"But at the heart of the matter, the coming oil crisis isn't about politics; its simply about the distribution of a resource that events during the Jurassic Period dictated." ■

Notes

[1] Peña testified April 30, 1998, before the House International Relations Committee. Peña announced on April 6 he would resign this summer, and President Clinton nominated U.N. Representative Bill Richardson as the next Energy secretary. The Senate Energy and Natural Resources Committee voted 18-0 on July 29 to approve Richardson's nomination. The Senate approved Richardson on July 31.

[2] For background, see Mary H. Cooper, "Oil Imports," *The CQ Researcher,* Aug. 23, 1991,

pp. 585-608.

[3] For background, see Rodman D. Griffin, "Mexico's Emergence," *The CQ Researcher,* July 19, 1991, pp. 497-520.

[4] For background, see David Masci, "U.S.-Russian Relations," *The CQ Researcher,* May 22, 1998, pp. 457-480, and Mary H. Cooper, "Russia's Political Future, *The CQ Researcher,* May 3, 1996, pp. 385-408.

[5] For background, see Patrick G. Marshall, "Calculating the Costs of the Gulf War," *Editorial Research Reports,* March 15, 1991, pp. 145-156.

[6] See James Kim and Chris Woodyard, "Glut Knocks Oil Costs Down, but It Won't Last," *USA Today,* Feb. 26, 1998.

[7] See "Saddam Seeks End to U.N. Embargo This Year," *The Washington Post,* July 18, 1998.

[8] Pickering testified May 21, 1998, before a joint hearing of the Senate Energy and Natural Resources and Foreign Relations committees.

[9] Perle testified at the May 21 hearing before the Senate Energy and Foreign Relations committees.

[10] Indyk testified May 14, 1998, before the Senate Foreign Relations Subcommittee on Near Eastern and South Asian Affairs.

[11] Albright spoke before the Asia Society in New York City. See Thomas W. Lippman, "Albright Offers Iran Possibility of Normal Ties," *The Washington Post,* June 18, 1998.

[12] Sestanovich testified July 8, 1998, before the Senate Foreign Relations Subcommittee on International Economic Policy, Export and Trade Promotion.

[13] Murphy testified May 14, 1998, before the Senate Foreign Relations Subcommittee on Near Eastern and South Asian Affairs.

[14] See Tad Szulc, "Will We Run Out of Gas?" *Parade Magazine,* July 19, 1998, pp. 4-6.

[15] For background, see Mary H. Cooper, "Transportation Policy," *The CQ Researcher,* July 4, 1997, pp. 577-600.

[16] For background, see Mary H. Cooper, "Renewable Energy," *The CQ Researcher,* Nov. 7, 1997, pp. 961-984.

[17] Moniz testified Feb. 5, 1998, before the House Commerce Subcommittee on Energy and Power.

[18] Lugar, chairman of the Senate Agriculture, Nutrition and Forestry Committee, spoke before the committee on Nov. 13, 1997.

[19] For background, see Cooper, *ibid.*

[20] Unless otherwise noted, information in this section is based on Fadhil J. Chalabi, "OPEC: An Obituary," *Foreign Policy,* winter 1997-98, pp. 126-140.

[21] Chalabi, *op. cit.,* p. 130.

[22] *Ibid,* p. 133. The Organization for Economic Cooperation and Development represents the leading industrial nations.

[23] *Ibid,* p. 136.

[24] See Youssef M. Ibrahim, "Falling Oil Prices Pinch Several Producing Nations," *The New York Times,* June 23, 1998.

[25] See "When Gulf States Tighten Their Belts," *The Economist,* March 14, 1998, pp. 49-50.

[26] See Bill Meyers, "As Oil Prices Slip, So Do Earnings: 'It's a Real Mess Out There' for Now," *USA Today,* July 21, 1998.

[27] Murphy spoke July 15, 1998, at an American Petroleum Institute press conference in Washington.

[28] See John M. Berry, "Trade Deficit Soared in May," *The Washington Post,* July 18, 1998.

[29] For background on early oil development in the Caspian region, see Daniel Yergin, *The Prize* (1991), pp. 56-65. Another Nobel brother, Alfred, invented dynamite. Their father, Immanuel, invented the underwater mine.

[30] See Craig Mellow, "Big Oil's Pipe Dream," *Fortune,* March 2, 1998, pp. 158-164.

[31] See Richard C. Longworth, "Boomtown Baku," *The Bulletin of the Atomic Scientists,* May/June 1998, p. 35.

[32] For background, see Mary H. Cooper, "Oil Spills," *The CQ Researcher,* Jan. 17, 1992, pp. 25-48.

[33] From July 8, 1998, testimony before the Senate Foreign Relations Subcommittee on International Economic Policy, Export and Trade Promotion.

[34] Martha Brill Olcott, "The Caspian's False Promise," *Foreign Policy,* summer 1998, p. 110.

[35] International Energy Agency, *Oil Market Report,* July 9, 1998. The agency was set up in the wake of the 1970s' energy crises to monitor the oil market and help correct balances in supply and demand.

[36] Lester C. Thurow, "Oil Prices No longer Hold Us Hostage," *USA Today,* May 26, 1998.

Bibliography

Selected Sources Used

Books

Adelman, M. A., *The Genie Out of the Bottle: World Oil Since 1970*, MIT Press, 1995.

The author, a leading petroleum economist, builds on his earlier analyses of the global oil trade with this review of events encompassing OPEC's rise to power over oil production and its more recent decline.

Campbell, Colin J., *The Coming Oil Crisis*, Multi-Science Publishing and Petroconsultants, 1997.

A former geologist for Texaco and Amoco predicts that global oil production will peak within the next few years. It is at this point, he writes, not when supplies are close to exhaustion, that oil prices will rise significantly.

Yergin, Daniel, *The Prize: The Epic Quest for Oil, Money & Power*, Simon & Schuster, 1991,

This sweeping history of the oil industry takes the reader from the first oil well in 1859 in Titusville, Pa., through the rise of OPEC and the West's reaction to the energy crises of the 1970s.

Articles

"Asia: The Cloning of America," *Energy Investor*, June/July 1998, pp. 2-3.

Despite its current economic crisis, Asia remains a leading consumer of oil. With rapid industrialization in much of the continent, Asia already uses 70 percent of all newly discovered oil, and its demand for oil can only be expected to grow in coming decades.

Chalabi, Fadhil J., "OPEC: An Obituary," *Foreign Policy*, winter 1997-98, pp. 126-140.

A former OPEC official writes that the formerly omnipotent cartel will continue to lose its control over global oil production and prices because oil-consuming countries have found alternative sources of oil. To survive, the organization's members must introduce economic reforms and change its quota system to reflect changes in the global oil market.

Coy, Peter, Gary McWilliams and John Rossant, "The New Economics of Oil," *Business Week*, Nov. 3, 1997, pp. 140-144.

The authors conclude that today's low oil prices may continue for decades as technological advances make it easier than ever to produce oil.

Longworth, Richard C., "Boomtown Baku," *The Bulletin of the Atomic Scientists*, May/June 1998, pp. 34-38.

Political turmoil in the oil-rich countries bordering the Caspian Sea makes the region the equivalent of "Bosnia with oil," writes journalist Longworth. U.S. policies, especially those favoring Armenian separatists in Azerbaijan, work against U.S. oil companies' efforts to develop the region's oil.

Olcott, Martha Brill, "The Caspian's False Promise," *Foreign Policy*, summer 1998, pp. 94-113.

A Colgate University professor of political science describes the obstacles to oil development in the Caspian Sea region, the most promising new source of oil today. Poverty, ethnic rivalries and economic mismanagement since the region gained independence with the Soviet Union's collapse in 1991 may derail plans for large-scale oil exports.

"Preventing the Next Oil Crunch," *Scientific American*, March 1998, pp. 77-95.

Four articles describe the problems associated with falling oil reserves. Technological advances will stretch out the petroleum age, but price hikes are likely as oil reserves drop and extraction becomes increasingly costly.

"When Gulf States Tighten Their Belts," *The Economist*, March 14, 1998, pp. 49-50.

The collapse in oil prices since early this year has drastically curtailed revenues in the rich kingdoms of the Persian Gulf. Because they depend so heavily on income from oil exports, these countries are having to reduce spending on social programs and hasten economic reforms.

Reports and Studies

Energy Information Administration, Petroleum Supply Monthly, May 1998.

This publication of the U.S. Department of Energy provides updated statistics on global oil supplies and imports and exports, as well as prices and a breakdown of oil products. Historical tables show changes in supplies and prices since the early 1980s.

International Energy Agency, *Oil Market Report*, July 9, 1998.

The Paris-based IEA, created in response to the 1970s' energy crises, monitors the global oil market and helps consuming countries overcome supply disruptions. The latest report concludes that the current oil glut and low prices are likely to continue until consumer nations draw down their record high oil stocks.

The Next Step

Additional information from UMI's Newspaper & Periodical Abstracts™ database

Caspian Sea

"Union Texas Expands its Caspian-Area Position," *Oil & Gas Journal*, **April 27, 1998, p. 25.**

Union Texas Lok Batan Ltd. has purchased 75 percent of New Jersey-based BMB Oil Inc.'s 100 percent interest in a production-sharing agreement with the State Oil Co. of Azerbaijan. Union Texas's plans for the Caspian region are discussed.

Smith, Pamela Ann, "Gulf States Expand Caspian Activities," *Middle East*, **June 1998, pp. 22-23.**

The involvement of Saudi Arabia and other gulf states in the oil and gas industries of the former Soviet republic of Kazakhstan is discussed. The oil and gas reserves of Central Asia potentially rival those of the Arab states.

Environmental Issues

"Act Now to Help Reverse Climate Change and Endorse Energy Efficiency," *Amicus Journal*, **spring 1998, p. 8.**

The American Society of Heating, Refrigerating and Air Conditioning Engineers (ASHRAE) sets energy-efficiency standards for all commercial buildings in the United States. Because many companies complained that the new 1996 standards were too strict, ASHRAE watered them down, and the Natural Resources Defense Council is asking environmentalists to work together to have them raised again.

Dietz, Francis, " Clearing the Way for Emissions Reductions," *Mechanical Engineering*, **February 1998, p. 36.**

European Union and other delegates prodded, scorned and shamed the U.S. delegation at the U.N. climate talks in Kyoto, Japan, to reduce U.S. emissions of greenhouse gases below 1990 levels.

"Offshore Environmental Concerns Mitigated by Onshore-Based, Extended-Reach Drilling," *Oil & Gas Journal* (OGJ), **May 4, 1998, pp. 118-120.**

An extended-reach well operated by Benton Oil & Gas Co., in partnership with Molino Energy Co., will be closely watched by politicians, environmentalists and industry observers. If the well is successful, it may set a precedent for offshore development without the use of new offshore platforms and reduce the risk of offshore spills.

Rowe, Duncan Graham, "Resources: Energy: Better Ways Than Burning Turn a Mix of Wood, Straw and Dung Into Gas and You Have an Efficient, Eco-Friendly Fuel," *The Guardian*, **May 5, 1998, p. E8.**

The forest fires blazing a trail through the Indonesian rain forests and seemingly unstoppable global deforestation should make wood an unlikely contender for renewable energy. In fact, wood, straw, and animal waste, commonly known as biomass, are considered a highly desirable alternative to fossil fuels such as coal, natural gas and oil. However, the fuel must come from renewable sources, like forestry residue or short-rotation coppices (trees planted for this purpose). Unlike fossil fuels, biomass produces a neutral amount of carbon dioxide, one of the gases blamed for global warming. This means that carbon dioxide produced by burning wood is equal to the amount absorbed by the trees when they were growing.

Sharp, Linda, "Alternative-Fuel Vehicles Need Help to Clean Our Air," *Atlanta Constitution*, **March 20, 1998, p. S2.**

The author comments on the contributions that alternative-fuel vehicles could make to cleaning up air pollution, saying that to have a major impact on the air quality of major metro areas, mass transit will have to be the major source of transportation.

Swanson, Ken, "Rebuttal: America Benefits from Ethanol Subsidies," *Detroit News*, **April 28, 1998, p. A8.**

Instead of being chastised for their support of ethanol, Michigan Sens. Carl Levin (D) and Spencer Abraham (R) and House Speaker Newt Gingrich, R-Ga., should be commended. It's fortunate that these elected officials understand the facts about this renewable fuel and its benefits to the economy, the environment and U.S. energy security. The ethanol tax exemption is claimed by gasoline marketers, many of whom are independent, small-business owners who blend their product with ethanol. Ethanol producers benefit as well. There are 48 ethanol production plants operating in 20 states, and an increasing number of these are farmer-owned and operated co-ops that help support small towns and small businesses.

"The Wild, Wild East," *Amicus Journal*, **spring 1997, p. 8.**

China could save more than one-third of its energy through cost-effective, energy-efficient technologies. The Natural Resources Defense Council is working with American and Chinese officials to promote this and other environmental-protection issues.

Organization of Petroleum Exporting Countries (OPEC)

Bahree, Bhushan, "Saudis Lead Plan to Form New OPEC to Boost Price of Oil by Ending Glut," The Wall Street Journal, **June 29, 1998, p. A3.**

Saudi Arabia, Mexico and Venezuela are negotiating at the highest government levels to create an ad hoc group of major petroleum-producing countries that would cooperate to raise oil prices by reducing the current oil glut. The campaign, far from being a mere trial balloon, already has won converts. If successful, the new alliance would mark the most significant realignment among oil-producing nations since the formation of Organization of Petroleum Exporting Countries in 1960.

Durgin, Hillary, "OPEC Cuts Production in 'Do or Die' Situation," *Houston Chronicle*, June 26, 1998, p. C1.

Despite political entanglements at home and market-share rivalries within the Organization of Petroleum Exporting Countries, oil ministers could not overlook the economic pressures and potential chaos brought on by the lowest oil prices since 1986. For many OPEC countries, oil is the chief source of revenue. The slide in prices has meant billions of dollars in lost income, prompting budget cuts and project delays and inviting social and political unrest. The recent free-fall in the price of oil to less than $12, compared with 1997's average price of $17.64 per barrel, has prompted government officials scrambling for a solution.

Hamilton, Martha M., "Oil Powers Consider Broader Group Than OPEC," *The Washington Post*, June 30, 1998, p. E3.

Major oil-producing nations are eyeing the prospect of creating a broader group than the Organization of Petroleum Exporting Countries in an effort to curtail production and keep oil prices from falling — but the plan may be destined to fail, according to some oil-industry watchers. The idea of an expanded group of producing nations that could prop up prices has been bubbling up since March. At that time, Mexico, which is not a member of OPEC, agreed with Saudi Arabia, Venezuela and other OPEC members to reduce oil production in order to boost prices. And this week Saudi Arabia's oil minister, Ali Nuaimi, was quoted in the "Middle East Economic Survey" predicting the development of an informal group of oil producers to intervene in the market, as needed. That set off a scramble by countries that depend heavily on income from oil exports to try to strengthen prices, including last week's agreement by OPEC to cut production by about 1.4 million barrels a day. But because nations outside OPEC, including Russia and Norway, are producing increasing amounts of oil, it may take more than efforts by the fading OPEC cartel to do the job.

Ibrahim, Youssef M., "OPEC Reaches New Deal to Cut Oil Production," *The New York Times*, June 25, 1998, p. D1.

Overcoming a serious political dispute that split the Iranian delegation and threatened the final agreement, OPEC announced late today that it planned to reduce its oil production by more than 1.3 million barrels a day, or nearly 5 percent, in the latest attempt to push up prices. The much-anticipated agreement was announced here at the meeting of OPEC oil ministers near the close of the commodity markets in New York today. The dispute among the Iranians had sent oil prices dropping during the day, wiping out an early rally in European markets after reports that a deal was imminent. But prices ended little changed, with crude oil for August delivery settling up 8 cents, at $14.60 a barrel, on the New York Mercantile Exchange. The Iranian split, as well as OPEC's reputation for being unable to maintain production cutbacks, left some experts questioning how long the agreement would

hold. "It is a fragile agreement by its very nature, as it depends on the pledge of each country to cut its production," said Fadhil al-Chalabi, a former OPEC under secretary. He added that some countries might again be tempted to increase production if prices rise.

"Price Retreat Sends Message to Oil Producers, Analysts Say," *Houston Chronicle*, June 26, 1998, p. C3.

Crude oil futures prices retreated Thursday on the New York Mercantile Exchange, sending a message to world oil producers that pledges of deep output cuts must be fulfilled to end a supply glut and boost prices. Crude oil resumed its recent slide one day after members of the Organization of Petroleum Exporting Countries agreed in Vienna, Austria, to the third round of production cuts this year in an effort to combat falling prices. Analysts have said world oil producers must slash at least 3 million barrels a day from exports to see prices rise significantly, and the new agreement brings the total from all producers — OPEC and non-OPEC — to 3.1 million barrels, or 4.4 percent of daily consumption.

Rynecki, David, "Price of Oil up 13 Percent; OPEC May Trim Output," *USA Today*, June 23, 1998, p. B1.

Speculation that major oil exporters will agree this week to slice production lifted crude oil prices more than 13 percent Monday, the steepest gain since the Persian Gulf War in 1991. Crude oil prices rose $1.59, or 13.4 percent, to $13.43 a barrel on the New York Mercantile Exchange. The move came as ministers of the 11-member Organization of Petroleum Exporting Countries prepare to meet in Vienna Wednesday. Analysts largely expect OPEC to cut daily production, now about 28 million barrels, by 700,000 barrels to offset weak demand.

U.S. Oil Policy

Mossavar-Rahmani, Bijan, "Time Ripe to End U.S.-Iran Impasse," *Oil & Gas Journal*, Jan. 26, 1998, pp. 33-36.

The author discusses the importance of oil in U.S.-Iranian relations. He believes ignoring the importance of Iran's oil is a mistake and discusses what needs to be done to probe and challenge the existing political, legal and institutional constraints in order to put oil on the front burner.

Yardeni, Edward, "A Race Against the Calendar," *The New York Times*, Dec. 7, 1997, p. 13.

The year 2000 problem poses a serious threat that could disrupt the U.S. economy and bring about a yearlong global recession, beginning in January 2000. Such a recession could be as severe as the 1973-74 global downturn caused by the OPEC oil embargo. The 2000 problem is both trivial and overwhelming. Unless fixed, most computers, including many PC's, will produce nonsensical results or crash because "00" in the widely used two-digit year field on the computer screen will be recognized as 1900 rather than 2000. Assessing the likelihood that the year 2000 problem will set off a recession — as well as measuring its depth and duration — requires answers from government and business managers around the world.

Back Issues

Great Research on Current Issues Starts Right Here.
Recent topics covered by The CQ Researcher are listed below.
Now available on the Web
For information, call (800) 432-2250 ext. 279 or (202) 887-6279.

If you would like to have any of these CQ Researchers updated, or need more information about these topics, please call CQ Custom Research. Special rates for CQ subscribers. (202) 887-8600 or (800) 432-2250, ext. 600, or E-mail Custom.Research@cq.com

APRIL 1997
Declining Crime Rates
The FBI Under Fire
Gender Equity in Sports
Space Program's Future

MAY 1997
The Stock Market
The Cloning Controversy
Expanding NATO
The Future of Libraries

JUNE 1997
FDA Reform
China After Deng
Line-Item Veto
Breast Cancer

JULY 1997
Transportation Policy
Executive Pay
School Choice Debate
Aggressive Driving

AUGUST 1997
Age Discrimination
Banning Land Mines
Children's Television
Evolution vs. Creationism

SEPTEMBER 1997
Caring for the Dying
Mental Health Policy
Mexico's Future
Youth Fitness

OCTOBER 1997
Urban Sprawl in the West
Diversity in the Workplace
Teacher Education
Contingent Work Force

NOVEMBER 1997
Renewable Energy
Artificial Intelligence
Religious Persecution
Roe v. Wade at 25

DECEMBER 1997
Whistleblowers
Castro's Next Move
Gun Control Standoff
Regulating Nonprofits

JANUARY 1998
Foster Care Reform
IRS Reform
The Black Middle Class
U.S.-British Relations

FEBRUARY 1998
Patients' Rights
Deflation Fears
Caring for the Elderly
The New Corporate Philanthropy

MARCH 1998
Israel at 50
The Federal Judiciary
Drinking on Campus
The Economics of Recycling

APRIL 1998
Biology and Behavior
Liberal Arts Education
Income Inequality
High-Tech Labor Shortage

MAY 1998
Census 2000
Child-Care Options
Alzheimer's Disease
U.S.-Russian Relations

JUNE 1998
Student Journalism
Antitrust Policy
Environmental Justice
Sleep Deprivation

JULY 1998
Encouraging Teen Abstinence
Population and the Environment
Democracy in Asia
Baby Boomers at Midlife

Back issues are available for $5.00 (subscribers) or $10.00 (non-subscribers). Quantity discounts apply to orders over 10. To order, call Congressional Quarterly Customer Service at (202) 887-8621.

Binders are available for $18.00. To order call 1-800-638-1710. Please refer to stock number 648.

Future Topics

▶ *Flexible Work Arrangements*

▶ *Coastal Development*

▶ *Student Activism*

The CQ Researcher

PUBLISHED BY CONGRESSIONAL QUARTERLY INC.

Flexible Work Arrangements

Do they really improve productivity?

T housands of employers are launching flexibility programs as stressed workers — squeezed between work and child- and elder-care responsibilities — demand more family-friendly work arrangements. In addition, many employers say that flexibility reduces absenteeism, improves employee retention and reduces costs for recruitment, real estate and overhead. Yet many old-style managers resist workplace flexibility, especially telecommuting, because of apparently unfounded fears it will hurt productivity. Meanwhile, flexibility proponents charge that flexible work arrangements are still out of reach for those who need it the most — workers at the bottom end of the income scale.

C$_Q$ **August 14, 1998 • Volume 8, No. 30 • Pages 697-720**

Formerly Editorial Research Reports

FLEXIBLE WORK ARRANGEMENTS

August 14, 1998
Volume 8, No.30

EDITOR
Sandra Stencel

MANAGING EDITOR
Thomas J. Colin

STAFF WRITERS
Adriel Bettelheim
Mary H. Cooper
Kenneth Jost
Kathy Koch
David Masci

PRODUCTION EDITOR
Melissa Hall

EDITORIAL ASSISTANT
Laura S. Cavender

PUBLISHED BY
Congressional Quarterly Inc.

CHAIRMAN
Andrew Barnes

VICE CHAIRMAN
Andrew P. Corty

PRESIDENT AND PUBLISHER
Robert W. Merry

EXECUTIVE EDITOR
David Rapp

The CQ Researcher (ISSN 1056-2036). Formerly Editorial Research Reports. Published weekly, except Jan. 2, May 29, July 3, Oct. 30, by Congressional Quarterly Inc., 1414 22nd St., N.W., Washington, D.C. 20037. Annual subscription rate for libraries, businesses and government is $340. Additional rates furnished upon request. Periodicals postage paid at Washington, D.C., and additional mailing offices. POSTMASTER: Send address changes to The CQ Researcher, 1414 22nd St., N.W., Washington, D.C. 20037.

COVER: BOB BENDA WORKS FROM HOME FULL TIME AS A SENIOR SUPPORT ENGINEER FOR NORTEL—NORTHERN TELECOM LTD., IN RICHARDSON, TEXAS. THE FIRM LAUNCHED A TELECOMMUTING PROGRAM THREE YEARS AGO AS A COST-SAVING MEASURE AND NOW HAS 2,500 TELECOMMUTERS OUT OF SOME 22,000 EMPLOYEES IN NORTH AMERICA. (NORTEL)

Flexible Work Arrangements

BY KATHY KOCH

THE ISSUES

On her farm 2,000 feet above the Eel River in Northern California, Shelley Comes helps her mother tend pear, apple and plum orchards and a large vegetable garden. She mends fences and deals with the occasional bobcat or mountain lion. Recently she dispatched a 4-foot-long rattlesnake and shooed away a marauding bear.

But the real work for Comes, 48, starts when she goes into her farmhouse office. Using the Internet, E-mail and lots of phone calls, Comes works as a quality consultant for Hewlett-Packard Co. — located five hours away in the heart of Silicon Valley. She visits the home office one week every month, staying at a motel.

"When my father passed away in 1991," she says, "it soon became apparent that I would either have to move here to help my mother, who has a heart condition, or we would have to give up the farm."

Fortunately for Comes, Hewlett-Packard is a pioneer in offering employees alternative work arrangements. About 6-10 percent of the company's 67,000 U.S. employees telecommute — most not as far as Comes, of course. Fully 85 percent arrange flexible work hours, and many take advantage of job-sharing, in which two part-time employees share one job.

"When we create a desirable work/ life balance, we'll attract and we'll retain the best people," said Hewlett Chairman and CEO Lew Platt. "And that's our competitive advantage." [1]

Thousands of other companies are being pulled onto the flexibility bandwagon as stressed employees — squeezed between office work and child- and elder-care responsibilities — demand more family friendliness at work. Employ-

ers say that to attract good workers in today's tight labor market they must offer a smorgasbord of work arrangements. [2]

"It's not a question of whether you agree with some of these benefits," says Gary Bitner, a public relations executive in Fort Lauderdale, Fla. "Employees today totally expect to have such options."

"Many people we recruit today ask specifically about flexible work arrangements," says Burke Stinson, senior public relations manager for AT&T. "If AT&T didn't offer telecommuting, for instance, it would have a negative impact on our ability to recruit and retain top workers, especially in the research and development community."

Anne Chamberlain, a management consultant for The Buck Co. in New York, said that the demands for flexibility "are something I wouldn't have seen even a couple of years ago." Buck recently surveyed 1,085 employers in the insurance industry and found that 52 percent offer flextime, 22 percent offer compressed workweeks and 16 percent offer telecommuting. In addition, three-quarters of the firms without special work arrangements said they are considering allowing telecommuting, and 35 percent are thinking about flextime. [3]

Demographics are driving the changes. As the baby boomers age, they need more flexibility because many are caring for aging parents. Having more women in the work force and more

dual-career households increases the demand for flexibility to accommodate child-care problems. [4]

The percentage of married employees with working spouses increased from 66 percent to 78 percent over the past 20 years. [5] Such dual-career couples say that what they want most from employers is flexible working hours to better handle personal needs.

Finally, Generation Xers and other younger workers who grew up with computers are more likely to want options like telecommuting because of their commitment to sharing child-rearing responsibilities. According to a recent survey of college graduates, their No. 1 goal is to "achieve a balanced lifestyle and rewarding life outside of work." [6] Similar surveys have shown that having an "interesting job" surpasses "salary" as a consideration in choosing a job.

"Today's college graduates saw their parents spend a lot of time commuting and being away from the family, sometimes only to be downsized," says David Mead, president of Telecommuting Success Inc., a Colorado firm that helps companies establish telecommuting programs. "These kids want none of that."

In addition, many employers are realizing that flexible work arrangements are good for the bottom line, says Ellen Galinsky, president of the Families and Work Institute in New York City. "The attitude about flexibility used to be, 'Give them an inch and they'll take a mile,'" she says. "But now it's, 'Give them an inch, they'll give you back a mile.'"

Flexibility reduces absenteeism and improves retention, because employees are usually more loyal to a flexible company, say experts on workplace flexibility. In fact, employees who telecommute are 30-40 percent more likely to stay with a company than those who do not, says

11 Million Workers Telecommuted in 1997

The number of American workers who telecommuted grew 30 percent from 1995 to 1997, to more than 11 million. More than two-thirds of the telecommuters were conventional, or full-time workers. The rest were contract workers averaging about 19 hours per week.

	1995	1996	1997
Total telecommuters (in millions)	8.5	9.7	11.1
• **Conventional employees**	5.4	6.5	7.7
• **Contract workers**	3.1	3.2	3.4

Source: Find/SVP, a New York research firm, June 8, 1998

Jack M. Nilles, a former NASA scientist known as the "father of telecommuting."*

In turn, flexibility slices the escalating costs of recruitment, turnover and training. "It used to cost 50 percent of a person's salary to replace them," says Nilles, author of one of the first books on telecommuting. "These days, with the tight labor market, it's up to 100 percent."

Companies often find that more flexible working arrangements save money by increasing productivity. Galinsky's group found that 82 percent of employers said the cost of flexible programs was either neutral or resulted in a positive return on investment. [7]

"The good news is that we now have enough evidence to say that flexibility is good for business as well as for families," says Ellen Bravo, co-director of 9to5, the National Association of Working Women. "It doesn't cost money to help people rearrange their schedules, but it brings in benefits to the employer."

---

*Nilles, now a telecommuting consultant in California, became an early proponent of telecommuting in the 1970s after being asked to help the Los Angeles area deal with smog caused by heavy commuter traffic.

Flexible options like telecommuting can also lend diversity to the workplace. "It's easier for some disabled persons to work if they only have to commute once or twice a month," Stinson says.

But Helena Berger, executive director of the American Association of People with Disabilities, warns against using telecommuting to avoid making workplaces accessible for disabled persons. The disabled "don't want telecommuting to become another type of segregation," she says. [8]

Finance, insurance and real estate services offer the most generous flexible work arrangements, according to a recent study by the Families and Work Institute, "while wholesale and retail trades emerge as least generous time and again." [9]

On-line financial services and telephone call centers that use high-tech workers are most likely to embrace telecommuting, primarily as a recruiting and retention tool, Mead says. "The momentum has picked up tremendously" among such companies in recent months, he says. "In the first six months of this year we have done more [consulting] business than in the preceding two years combined."

Such firms can get a competitive edge in recruiting skilled workers by offering optional telecommuting to today's college grads, many of whom worked on laptop computers throughout their college years, according to Mead.

"Telecommuting and alternative work arrangements are definitely a significant part of our staffing strategy," says Janice Miholics, vice president and manager of alternative work arrangements at stock broker Merrill Lynch & Co., in Somerset, N.J. Any employee wishing to telecommute must spend two weeks working in the firm's unique telecommuting "simulation lab" to practice working from a remote environment.

Allowing personnel in creative or research and development positions to have flexible hours is particularly important, Stinson says, because most experience their most creative moments at night.

Also driving companies to offer more flexibility is the fact that more women are managers. Companies with more women in top leadership are more likely to provide such options as traditional flextime, daily flextime, a gradual return to work after childbirth and regular work-at-home options, Galinsky says. Her group found that fully 82 percent of companies with large numbers of female executives offer flexible work hours, compared with 56 percent in companies without many women in top positions. Moreover, the more female executives a company has, the more likely the firm is to provide on- or near-site child care, dependent-care assistance plans and elder-care resource and referral programs, the report found. [10]

Technological advances are also spurring the move to more flexibility, especially telecommuting, because they make it easier and cheaper to work from remote locations. "Telecommuting has come of age as some of the [electronic] connectivity hurdles have been conquered," Mead says.

Some workers initially turn to flexible arrangements during adverse conditions. During the Northeast blizzard of 1996, for instance, telephone companies reported an upsurge in telephone use. They attributed it to increased Internet use by snowbound employees trying their hand at telecommuting. And during both the Los Angeles and Atlanta Olympics, thousands of residents telecommuted to avoid traffic congestion.

The biggest obstacle to more telecommuting and workplace flexibility is manager resistance, flexibility advocates say. "There's no real incentive for most managers, on their long list of priorities, to manage flexibility," said Richard Federico, a work/life consultant for The Segal Co., a benefits consultant in Boston, Mass. [11]

Managers are often reluctant to supervise telecommuters and other employees who are out of sight. "It's especially difficult for managers with a 'command and control' personality," says AT&T's Stinson. To reduce managers' discomfort levels, some companies have gone the "halfway house" route, establishing satellite telework centers closer to employees' homes.

"It's going to take a generational shift," Nilles says. "You've got to get the old guys out of there and bring in a new generation of managers who've been brought up on computers."

As employers consider flexible work arrangements, these are some of the questions being asked:

Does telecommuting improve employee productivity?

Since telecommuting became an option for workers about 25 years ago,

the number of telecommuters in the U.S. had risen to more than 11 million, according to the New York research firm Find/SVP. *(See graph, p. 700.)*

Until recently, however, most companies viewed telecommuting as "experimental," and most still don't consider it mainstream. Telecommuting remains employers' least popular flexible work option, with only 20 percent of companies actively embrac-

---

"We've spent a lot of time since 1973 calibrating the changes in productivity among telecommuters. We find over a wide range of jobs and people, average productivity increases range from 5 percent to 20 percent. In some departments it was two to three times that."

— Jack M. Nilles
President, JALA
International Inc.

---

ing it, according to a 1997 survey by Hewitt Associates, a benefits consulting firm in Lincolnshire, Ill. Among Fortune 1000 firms, only 7 percent of the employees telecommute.

Telecommuting advocates say that the technology exists to support telecommuting, but managers' resistance prevents more employees from taking advantage of the option, de-

spite proven benefits for both workers and companies. Teleworkers report enjoying greater work/life balance, resulting in less stress and higher productivity. Some employers report higher productivity and morale, and reduced overhead, rent, absenteeism and turnover.

"Just the fact that you can work without the interruptions and distractions of the workplace increases both the quantity and quality of work," says Joanne Pratt, a Dallas-based corporate telecommuting consultant.

"We've spent a lot of time since 1973 calibrating the changes in productivity among tele-commuters," Nilles says. "We find over a wide range of jobs and people, average productivity increases range from 5 percent to 20 percent. In some departments it was two to three times that."

AT&T's productivity increased up to 40 percent in some departments after the company began its telecommuting program, Stinson says. To overcome middle managers' fears, AT&T held a companywide Telecommute Day on Sept. 22, 1994, led by none other than CEO Robert E. Allen, who worked from home that day.

"The only way to tackle the problem was to do it frontally, and to do it from the very top," Stinson says. "An emotional barrier was broken. Our telecommuting grew from 37 percent of the management staff to 55 percent who telecommute at least a couple of days a week."

In fact, Stinson notes, "About one-sixth of our management work force doesn't have an office to go to anymore."

The state of California saved $3,800 per telecommuting employee due to increased productivity, according to

Benefits vs. Drawbacks

One in four Americans says that the ability to work uninterrupted in a quiet setting is the primary benefit of working at home (top graph). But roughly the same percentage say the inability to work without interruption is the key drawback to working at home. About a quarter of the at-home workers say they like everything about working at home (bottom graph).

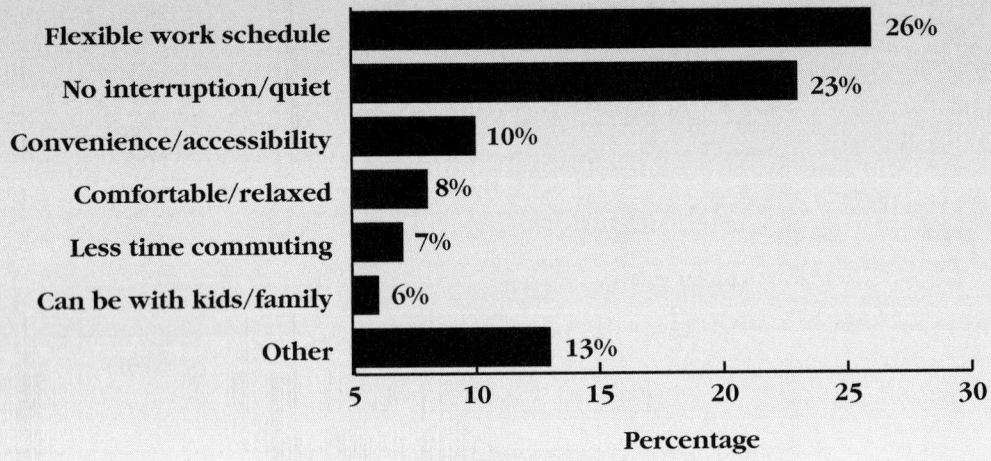

Benefits of Working at Home

Flexible work schedule	26%
No interruption/quiet	23%
Convenience/accessibility	10%
Comfortable/relaxed	8%
Less time commuting	7%
Can be with kids/family	6%
Other	13%

Percentage

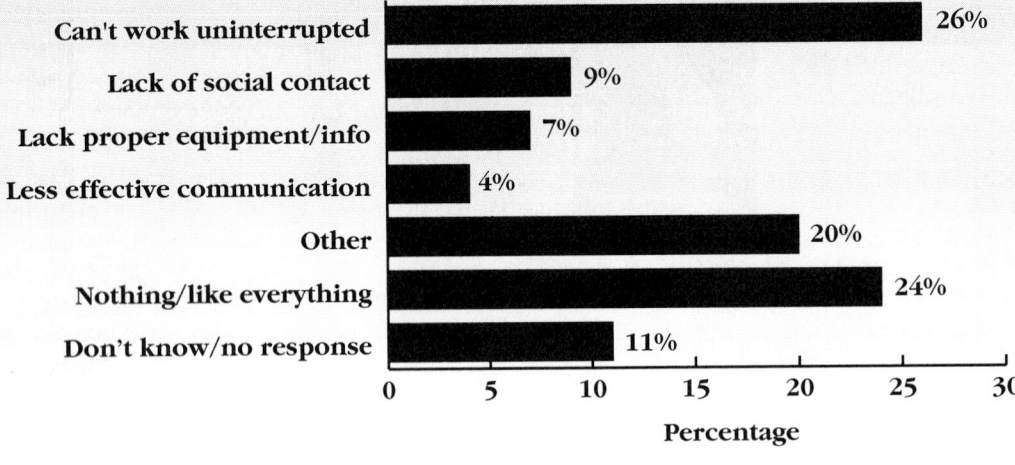

Drawbacks of Working at Home

Can't work uninterrupted	26%
Lack of social contact	9%
Lack proper equipment/info	7%
Less effective communication	4%
Other	20%
Nothing/like everything	24%
Don't know/no response	11%

Percentage

Source: The Wirthlin Report, *Wirthlin Worldwide, February 1997*

Nilles. And the city of Los Angeles saw average productivity jump 12.5 percent across 20 departments — ranging from architects to police detectives — with telecommuting, he says. Further, he says, the productivity gains are not just short-term but were still measurable three years after the programs began.

"Some employees have told me that they wanted to telecommute in order to get promoted," Nilles says, "because they were working at organizations that make promotions based on performance more than politics."

Redefining the Workplace

Many employers — including such giants as IBM and AT&T — allow workers to substitute the traditional 9 to 5 workday with flexible working arrangements that allow work to be done "anywhere/anytime." Popular arrangements include:

Compressed workweek — allows employees to condense their work week into fewer days, typically in a "4-10" configuration, or four 10-hour days each week. Another common compression scheme is nine 9-hour days over the course of 10 workdays).

Flextime or flexitime — allows employees to take advantage of a range of starting and ending times for the workday. For example, a company that had previously required all workers to work from 9 a.m. to 5:30 p.m. might allow its employees to start between 7 and 10 a.m., and leave 8 hours later. That way all workers are present during the "core" hours from 10 a.m. to 3:30 p.m.

Hot-desking — sharing the same desk with other workers, but at different times.

Hoteling — using limited office space on a reserved, as-needed basis.

Job-sharing — two workers sharing the responsibilities of one full-time position. This option often comes into play when a company wishes to keep a valued full-time employee who seeks reduced hours.

Leave time — an authorized period away from work without loss of employment rights. This option encompasses leave under the Family Leave and Medical Act (FLMA), as well as leave for education, travel, health care, etc. Sabbaticals also fall into this category.

Permanent part-time — steady part-time employment, usually for a set number of hours at a particular time each week. A variation is on-call part-time employment, in which the employee works when needed.

Personal harbor — a small work station with a work surface, storage space and a door.

Phone booth — a small workspace along a wall for use between meetings.

Satellite office — an office center typically used full time by employees who don't want to commute to the main office.

Telecommuting (flexiplace) — allows employees to work part or full time at home or at a satellite location.

Teleworking — working in a location away from the main office; may consist of telecommuting, hoteling, working in a satellite office or remote work center, or a virtual office.

Touch-down space — a work area shared by others.

Virtual office — any workplace that the employee takes advantage of by using portable technology.

Sources: Michael J. Dziak, "Surprisingly Common and It Works! The Home Office Explosion," CompetitiveEdge, *May/June 1998; Society for Human Resource Management.*

Hewlett-Packard's Comes says telecommuting definitely increased her productivity. "As part of my initial agreement to telecommute, I took on a new piece of business in addition to my existing assignments," she says. "The fact that I could usually do it all proved that I was being more productive.

"I can pay attention to medical and family issues real-time and do my HP work at night or in the early morning, when I am most creative, rather than having to be creative on demand while in the office. I also know from three years' experience that time in the office is far less productive than the same number of hours away from the office."

But John Girard, vice president and research director at the Gartner Group, a high-tech research and consulting firm in Stamford, Conn., is skeptical about the claimed productivity increases. "You can't really determine whether a person is more productive or not," he says. "You would need a very well-measured base line for current productivity, and most companies don't have that. If we don't measure productivity inside the office, then you can't measure productivity outside the office."

Moreover, he says, if employees telecommute only occasionally, productivity inevitably goes down, rather than up, because it costs more to maintain computer equipment both at home and at the office. "In the office, I share one printer with 50 people. At home, you have one printer per person," he notes. Telecommuting increases technology costs anywhere from 63 percent to 157 percent, he says.

If enough workers telecommute to make traditional offices unnecessary, companies can recoup the added technology costs in reduced overhead, he says. In addition, productivity will in-

Fastest-Growing Home-Based Fields

Three out of the 10 fastest-growing fields for home-based workers involve work with computers.

- **Cleaning services**
- **Computer consulting**
- **Computer programming**
- **Computer repair**
- **Executive search**
- **Management consulting**
- **Medical transcription**
- **Public relations**
- **Technical writing**
- **Temporary clerical work**

Sources: Competitive Edge *magazine, May/June 1998; Paul and Sarah Edwards,* Working From Home

crease at least partially as a result of workers not having to commute. "I can be closing a deal while my competitors are stuck in traffic," he says.

If not handled carefully, however, telecommuting can negatively affect productivity, Girard says. For instance, if an employee uses his own home computer, "A child could come in and install a game and blow the system," he says. Or an employee could inadvertently bring a virus to work on a disk he was using at home and infect the company computer system. Or the telecommuter could run into so many technical problems he could tie up the office help desk.

"I know one company that had an employee working at home who insisted on using his own computer, but he had so many problems interfacing the company software that the help desk had to send people to his house three times," Girard says.

In addition, without the social stimulation of the office environment, some employees become depressed, leading to dissatisfaction and a loss of productivity, he says.

Even telecommuting's staunchest advocates acknowledge that productivity will suffer if the program doesn't properly train both the employee and

the manager, as well as provide appropriate equipment, furniture and technical support. Productivity gains will not be as significant, they say, if managers who depend heavily on "face time" are not retrained to measure output rather than "desk time."

"We've got 12 to 18 years of accumulated experience of what works and what doesn't," says Gil Gordon, a telecommuting consultant in Monmouth Junction, N.J. "There is enough information out there so that any organization that really wants to succeed can do so if they follow the correct path."

For telecommuting to work, employees need good work skills and self-motivation. "If we pick the wrong people, or don't train them properly, or if they are trying to do child-care while working at home, it will fail," Gordon says. In the worst-case scenario, he argues, productivity stays the same.

Mead expects productivity to increase with new technological advances. He says the emerging asymmetric digital subscriber line (ADSL) service, which offers high-speed computer service capable of accommodating video-conferencing, will be a major boon to telecommuting. Other

technological advancements include products allowing office calls to be forwarded to home numbers and long-life batteries for cellular phones.

Mead thinks that training will reduce much of managers' resistance. "You really have to learn how to manage differently," he says. "You must set expectations and monitor the results. That's a fundamental change from managing by walking around."

But with a properly managed program, productivity typically goes up from 15 percent to 30 percent, Mead says. "Most managers don't believe that until they look at the numbers. Then they say, 'This is unbelievable.'"

Does telecommuting result in less traffic congestion?

Promoters of telecommuting say it eases traffic congestion, lessening air pollution and helping cities meet federal clean air standards.

But Nilles notes that a 50 percent reduction in congestion doesn't necessarily require a similar reduction in the number of vehicles. During the 1984 Los Angeles Olympics, he says, a 4 percent reduction in commuter automobiles, coupled with a 14 percent reduction in rush-hour truck traffic, converted the city's fabled gridlock to free-flow conditions, he says.

"Congestion virtually disappeared," Nilles says, "only to return with a vengeance once the games were over."

Nilles says his studies of telecommuting in California showed a marked decrease in automobile use among telecommuters, despite initial fears that cars would be used more to run errands.

Remarkably, in half the cases, total family car use dropped 30-40 percent, he says, in addition to the reduction due to the worker not commuting. "The telecommuter becomes better organized," he says. "People start making lists and plan their [errand] itineraries," he says.

Nilles estimates that for 1998 alone,

U.S. telecommuters will drive 82 billion fewer miles, burn 2.6 billion fewer gallons of gasoline and spew 1,411 fewer kilotons of pollutants into the air.

John S. Niles, a Seattle telecommuting consultant, disagrees. "In the traffic world, there's a fill-in phenomenon," he says. "Once roads clear up, other drivers stop taking the Metro and start driving again. So it's basically a losing battle."

That happened at the end of the 1996 Atlanta Olympics, says Atlanta telecommuting consultant Michael Dziak. When people saw that traffic congestion had diminished, largely due to telecommuting, they started driving back to the office to work.

"The good news is that telecommuting takes cars off the road," Gordon says. "The bad news is that we can't be sure they're not replaced by other cars."

Patricia Mokhtarian, a professor of civil and environmental engineering at the University of California, Davis, argues that telecommuting doesn't make much difference in traffic congestion. At any one time, only about 2 percent of the population is telecommuting, she wrote, reducing the number of miles driven by 1-2 percent, "an amount swamped by the increasing number of miles traveled by Americans in general." [12]

Nilles concedes that telecommuting may not reduce overall traffic, at least in the short term, because road-building is not keeping up with population increases. "Telecommuting will reduce the rate of growth of traffic congestion over the next few years," he says. And in 10 or 15 years, he says, enough people may be telecommuting to reduce the overall level of traffic congestion.

Does telecommuting reduce employees' stress?

Proponents of telecommuting tout its ability to reduce the stress caused by traffic and trying to balance family and work obligations.

"Employees save money on gasoline, dry cleaning and meals and have more flexibility to blend work and family life," Gordon says.

And companies save money, too. AT&T saved $3,000 per part-time telecommuter on office overhead and $8,000 a year for those who telecommute exclusively. "Not only are sales going up," Stinson says, "but costs are going down, and we are helping people balance their personal and work lives."

In addition, the company found that telecommuters actually work more at home than at the office. "They work according to their own natural schedules, without having to cram everything into the hours of 9 to 5," Stinson says. "I think that is energizing."

Many take their laptops on vacation and keep in touch with the office by regularly checking their E-mail, he says. "There wasn't that dreaded Sunday night anxiety at the end of vacation about all the work that had piled up in their absence. Nothing was gnawing at them."

Others argue that blurring the line between work and home can be even more stressful for many workers because they feel they are never able to leave work behind.

"Sometimes you work late into the night and then early in the morning," Girard says. "Then you suddenly realize you've spent a double day at work, and you wonder, 'Where did my life go?'"

"Teleworking does lead to flexibility," said Jeff Hill, a home-based human resources researcher for IBM. "So you'd think that teleworking would lead to better work-life balance. But what happens, on average, is that people work so many more hours that on the whole, they're not any better off." [13]

"I think the workaholism question is serious," says Seattle consultant Niles. "For the real striver, it's an unlimited opportunity to work 24 hours a day and be bad to your kids and your family, all in the name of productivity. A lot of the crusaders for telecommuting only give the good side. But they don't mention this very real danger."

Gordon says that when his firm helps set up a telecommuting program, he spends a lot of time telling employees how to avoid workaholism. "We suggest they set up a special workplace with specific work hours," he explains. "Just as it's possible to become a workaholic at the office, it's possible at home. But it's not inevitable."

Stinson finds the workaholic danger overblown and calls it "kind of an old notion, dating back to the idea that work is servile. If work is something that you enjoy, then working seven days a week at your own pace and pleasure is probably good, not bad. Michael Jordan practices basketball every day harder than everybody else, but no one calls him a workaholic."

Others fear that as companies go global and have 24-hour schedules, the potential exists for employees to be "on call" around the clock. Workers also fear that as their productivity increases due to telecommuting, managers will push them to be even more productive, shooting their stress levels back up.

"Teleworkers tell us over and over again that they feel trusted," Pratt says. "But if employers start demanding ever-increasing levels of productivity, the employee may start to feel that they are in a new kind of prison. The program will self-destruct."

Others worry that telecommuting will hurt their careers because it takes them "out of the loop."

Stinson says that while telecommuting does not seem to be a barrier for lower-level employees, "face-time" becomes increasingly important higher up the corporate ladder. "Under today's circumstances, yes, it's a problem," he says. "In the next century, it won't be. People who are close-minded about telecommuting will be out of the work force."

"Lots of managers have said [telecommuters] are more promotable," Gordon says. "They are working more independently, making their own decisions, becoming almost entrepreneurial. They are demonstrating skills we look for in promotable people."

Niles agrees. "If someone is watching out for their own self-interest and wants to be promoted," he says, they can stay in the loop through E-mail and office visits. "The average telecommuter typically only works at home two or three days a week," he says. "People go on vacation for two weeks at a time, and people don't forget them."

Gordon cautions, however, that both the employer and the manager need to work at keeping the employee's career on track. "If the employee does not continue to take the same interest in his career, and if the manager does not keep it in the spotlight, the person could begin to fall off people's radar screens." ∎

BACKGROUND

Forgotten Women

Early in the century, working mothers faced challenges even more difficult than those faced by working parents today.

According to Bravo, of 9to5, mothers working in factories often preferred the night shift so they could take care of their children during the day. On a typical day at a factory in Albany, N.Y., in 1914, she writes, "They worked from 7 p.m. until midnight, took half an hour for supper, then continued for another five hours, five nights a week." Each day, they averaged four and a half hours of sleep, usually in one- or two-hour naps sprinkled throughout the day. [14]

When a factory worker's child got sick, the night shift often proved untenable. Ella Mae Wiggins, who worked in textile mills in Gastonia, N.C., became a union organizer after four of her nine children died of whooping cough. "I was working nights and [had] nobody to do for them," she recalled. "I asked the 'super' to put me on day shift, so I could tend 'em, but he refused. So I had to quit my job. Then there wasn't any money for medicine, so they just died." [15]

The earliest child-care programs in America were nurseries to serve "the deserving poor," set up in 1854 by urban welfare groups. Some child-care centers were developed during World War I to serve the influx of mothers going into the work force. During the Great Depression, the Federal Emergency Relief Administration funded some nursery schools.

Women were encouraged to enter the work force in large numbers during World War II, but only about half the mothers had relatives who could care for their children. So many women left their youngsters home alone that the number of accidents involving "latchkey kids" became a national scandal, according to Bravo. As a result, emergency day-care centers were started, mostly near war plants.

Finally in 1943, the Lanham Act authorized federally funded childcare programs for employed mothers. When the federal money for the centers ran out in 1946, some of the centers were kept open with state funding.

By 1955, women were pressing for community resources to help working mothers — such as housekeeping services, meals on wheels and licensed day-care facilities. Unions were not much help, however, because they were basically seen as being the domain of men, Bravo writes. In an oral history, CIO organizer Stella Novicki recalls, "The union had so many things they had to work for — the shorter work day, improved conditions — that they couldn't worry about these things in relation to women." [16]

Workplace Changes

As the United States has shifted from manufacturing to a global services and information economy over the past 25 years, more women than ever before — and especially single parents — have joined the work force.

Women make up more than 46 percent of the work force today, compared with 29 percent in 1950. Mothers with children under age 6 make up 47 percent of workers, compared with 11 percent in 1950. In 1995, almost 70 percent of single women and 55 percent of single men had children. [17]

The demand for more flexibility has escalated. Polls show that 65 percent of Americans favor changes in labor laws that would allow more flexibility, and 58 percent would choose paid time off more often than overtime wages. [18]

The concept of flexible work schedules was first introduced in Munich, Germany, in 1967 to relieve commuting problems. "A manufacturing company on the edge of town wasn't easy to get to," says Stanley Nollen, a professor of business administration at Georgetown University and author of the 1982 book *New Work Schedules in Practice*. "The company started offering flexible working hours to help employees work out a variety of commuting arrangements."

Shortly after that, Swiss employers who needed to attract women with families back into the work force began offering flexible schedules.

In the U.S, Hewlett-Packard pioneered flexible working arrangements in Waltham, Mass., in 1972, Nollen says, by allowing workers to set their own hours. "We've always had a philosophy that employees should be able to balance work and private lives because we felt it made for happier, more productive employees," says company spokeswoman Amy Flores.

Continued on p. 708

Chronology

1800s
Urban welfare groups set up first childcare programs in America. Two-tiered care system develops for poor and rich children.

1854
Nation's first organized child-care program is established in New York City.

1900-1949
Child-care centers are developed during World War I, the Great Depression and World War II to serve the influx of mothers going to work.

1933
Federal Emergency Relief Administration funds some nursery schools. By 1938, they care for more than 200,000 children of working mothers.

1938
Fair Labor Standards Act mandates a 40-hour workweek.

1941
Lanham Act authorizes a federally funded child-care program for employed mothers during World War II.

1950s
The U.S. becomes suburbanized, leading to long commutes for working fathers.

1950
Census Bureau reports 2 million children under age 6 have working mothers.

1960s-1970s
Federal government starts Head Start program. As the U.S. economy shifts from manufacturing to service and information, more women than ever enter work force.

1963
Betty Friedan's *The Feminine Mystique* encourages women to work outside the home.

1971
President Richard M. Nixon vetoes a $2 billion child-care bill saying it would "Sovietize" American child care.

1972
Hewlett-Packard Co. pioneers flextime in Waltham, Mass.

1973
Former NASA scientist Jack Nilles coins the term "telecommuting," initially viewing it as a means of solving traffic congestion rather than work/family dilemmas.

1978
Congress enacts Federal Employees Flexible and Compressed Work Schedules Act.

1980s
Backlash against women's liberation creates conflict among American women over child-care pressures and work demands.

1982
Congress reauthorizes flextime.

1985
Congress makes federal workers' flextime law permanent, extends it to state and local workers.

1990s
Pressure for more flexibility escalates as the number of dual-career families increases, and traffic and air pollution concerns make telecommuting and flextime more attractive.

1990
Amendments to the Clean Air Act require employers in pollution-plagued cities to reduce the number of single-occupancy commuting trips made by employees. President George Bush signs the Child Care Act.

1991
House and Senate pass separate versions of the Family and Medical Leave Act.

1993
President Clinton sends Family and Medical Leave bill to Congress, which clears it Feb. 4, just nine days after it was introduced.

July 11, 1994
Clinton urges federal managers to make more family-friendly workplace arrangements.

1995
Republican-led Congress repeals the mandatory portion of the 1990 Clean Air Act amendments.

June 21, 1996
Clinton sets a goal of 60,000 federal workers tele-commuting by the end of 1998.

March 19, 1997
House passes legislation allowing employers to offer paid time off instead of wages for overtime work. With strong union opposition, the bill is blocked in the Senate.

Continued from p. 706

AT&T began offering staggered work schedules in the 1970s, Stinson notes. "It took 20 years for corporate America to open its heart to family issues such as child and elder care," he says. All of those issues were being openly discussed in the 1968-1978 era, he says. "Only in 1988 [after the breakup of AT&T] did it start changing, when the same people who were asking the questions in 1968 became the people in charge."

Most companies began embracing flexible work arrangements only six or eight years ago, Nollen says. Between 1985 and 1997, use of flextime by employers more than doubled, from 12 percent to 27.6 percent, according to the Bureau of Labor Statistics.

Some business leaders and conservatives argue that "rigid overtime provisions" of the Fair Labor Standards Act of 1938 have hampered the expansion of flexible work arrangements among private employers. They particularly bristle at the fact that government workers are not bound by the same law and enjoy more flextime options. In recent years they have lobbied for legislation allowing private companies to offer some of the same flexibility options that federal, state and local workers have enjoyed for years.

Congress Gets Family Friendly

In 1978, in response to rush-hour traffic congestion in and around Washington, D.C., Congress enacted the Federal Employees Flexible and Compressed Work Schedules Act. The trial program allowed federal workers to arrange alternative work schedules to meet family needs and reduce commuting time. It also allowed them the choice of taking overtime pay as either cash or paid time off.

The trial was so successful — reducing absenteeism and increasing productivity — that Congress reauthorized it in 1982. In 1985, they made it permanent and extended it to state and local workers.

Both President Clinton and Vice President Al Gore have urged executive branch managers to expand the use of family-friendly work arrangements in federal agencies, including telecommuting and flextime. In June 1996, Clinton set a goal of 60,000

The 1978 Federal Employees Flexible and Compressed Work Schedules Act was enacted to alleviate rush hour traffic congestion in Washington, D.C.

Courtesy of AT&T

federal workers telecommuting, either from home or satellite telework centers, by the end of 1998.

David Bibb, a deputy associate administrator at the General Services Administration (GSA), estimates that there are close to that many federal employees who telecommute either full time or part time. The Office of Personnel Management is currently surveying federal workers to determine how many are telecommuting.

In 1993, in his first legislative initiatives, newly elected President Clinton sent Congress the Family and Medical Leave bill, which cleared Congress on Feb. 4, just nine days after it was introduced. Clinton signed it into law on Feb. 5. [19]

Similar to legislation vetoed twice by former President George Bush, the law guarantees workers 12 weeks of unpaid leave to care for newborns, newly adopted or seriously ill children or sick family members. Critics complain that the law leaves out 95 percent of all businesses and more than half of all workers because it applies only to companies with 50 or more employees and only to those who work at least 25 hours a week and have been working for at least a year.

Labor Unions Resist Flexibility

Over the years, unions have played a role in whether flexible-work arrangements have been adopted, both in the government and private sectors. [20]

"Ten years ago, the unions distrusted telecommuting," Niles says. "They thought it was a trick to make people work longer hours and be paid less."

Unions also feared that telecommuting would make labor organizing more difficult, because it would be harder to contact members. Ironically, some employers feared the opposite. One large insurance company actually found that telecommuting increased productivity during a pilot project, but it nonetheless refused to broaden the program. The CEO feared it would make his employees more accessible to union organizers.

But in recent years, union leaders have dropped much of their opposition, as fears have subsided that telecommuting would result in "electronic sweatshops."

"These workers are not easily exploited because they tend to be very highly skilled," so employers are anxious to retain them and keep them happy, Nilles says.

Unions insist, however, that telecommuters not be forced to become independent contractors without benefits, and that the unions be involved in negotiating the telecommuting agreements.

Clean Air Act

The Clean Air Act has increased interest in telecommuting, but more as a means of reducing air pollution than as a family-friendly policy. The 1990 amendments required employers in pollution-plagued cities to reduce the number of single-occupancy commuting trips made by employees. Telecommuting was an option employers could use to encourage employees to reduce their driving, especially on days when there is heavy ozone, a pollutant created when warm summer air heats automobile emissions.

However, when the Republican majority took over both houses of Congress in 1995, it immediately amended the pollution reduction requirements, making them optional for employers. "The pressure was off," Gordon says, "except in certain areas like Atlanta, Phoenix and Los Angeles, where there is still a lot of effort going on to increase carpooling and telecommuting."

Comp Time or Overtime?

When it comes to business attempts to allow private-sector workers to take compensatory time off in lieu of overtime pay — the same privilege enjoyed by federal

workers — unions have resisted strongly.

The House of Representatives has passed such legislation twice, once in the 104th Congress and then again in the 105th on March 19, 1997, by a vote of 222-210. The first bill died in the Senate, and the second was blocked after Democrats threatened a filibuster, which Republicans did not have the votes to break.

Unions and women's groups have lobbied intensely against the Senate bill, called the Family-Friendly Workplace Act, introduced by Sen. John Ashcroft, R-Mo.

"We are in favor of flextime. We like flexibility," says Karen Nussbaum, director of the Working Woman's Department of the AFL-CIO. "What we don't like about this bill is that it doesn't give workers anything they don't already have. But it takes away the 40-hour workweek and pay for any work over 40 hours."

She said the bills give the employer control over when an employee works, allowing workers to work 80 hours over two weeks. A manager could require employees to work overtime any time during that two-week period, without first giving them notice.

"It's a huge boon for employees who prefer a variable work schedule," she says, "but would wreak havoc for people who rely on regular work schedules because of child-care needs."

For instance, working mothers often must pick their children up from day care by 6 p.m. or face $1-per-minute late fees. "It's knowing that you can be where you need to be that's important," she says. "These bills give workers no greater control or guarantee over their lives."

Proponents say the bills would simply extend to private-sector employees the same privileges enjoyed by federal workers — taking compensatory time off instead of pay for overtime hours worked.

"The Ashcroft bill merely removes

the federal barrier to workers negotiating flextime policies with their employees," says the Family Research Council, which supports the bill. [21]

"Congress should strongly consider extending the same opportunity to all American workers that federal employees have enjoyed for nearly 20 years," says The Heritage Foundation.

Private-sector employers argue that they cannot compete with the federal government when it comes to offering flexibility options.

"In this labor market, when I interview potential employees, it's a negative that I cannot provide comp time off in lieu of overtime pay," says Edward E. Potter, president of the Employment Policy Foundation. "I've lost candidates because I couldn't offer it."

The Senate bill is not expected to move anytime soon, but a Republican Senate staffer said highlighting Democratic opposition to the bill could make "nice sound bites" in upcoming election ads this fall. ■

CURRENT SITUATION

Two-Tiered Policies

Despite the current tight labor market, workplace stress is thought to be escalating as global competition continues to force some companies to downsize and restructure, producing greater job insecurity and heavier individual work loads. So-called work-saving electronic devices like fax machines, pagers and modems often create more tension as they induce employ-

Continued on p. 712

'Virtual Offices' May Have Vast Impact . . .

The office of the future has arrived, and it's not your father's Oldsmobile — nor his cozy corner office. Instead, today's workers are "hot-desking" and "hoteling."

"Today's workplace . . . is undergoing a profound transformation that will continue well into the 21st century," wrote New York communications consultants Kenneth Shulman and John Reiser. [1]

During the last decade, America's work force has become increasingly mobile as global competition has spurred technological advances, employee demands for flexible work arrangements, business downsizing and corporate cost-cutting pressures.

An estimated 11.1 million people now work in "virtual offices" — somewhere other than their firm's main office — at least one day a week, usually connected by computers and high-speed modems. [2]

The dispersal of America's work force into the hinterlands has triggered numerous ripple effects — impacting everything from downtown real estate prices to suburban coffee shop sales.

"The virtual office is changing the corporate landscape," wrote Michael Takagawa, executive vice president and chief operating officer of HQ Network Systems, a San Francisco high-tech firm. "As it does, it signals both challenges and opportunities for the real estate industry." [3]

With more employees working at home or on the road, companies are slashing the number of private offices they maintain in expensive downtown locations, replacing executive and prestige space with cheaper alternative office strategies. The new, modular configurations include "hoteling" — using office space at the company office on a reserved, as-needed basis — and "hot-desking" — sharing the same desk with others, but using it at different times.

The trend toward sharing and smaller spaces signals the "end of the edifice complex," wrote Gail M. Smith, president of the Northern California Chapter of the National Association of Corporate Real Estate Executives. "Status symbols such as lavish corner offices, huge boardrooms, floor after floor of exterior offices and interior cubicles filled with full-time workers are vanishing." [4]

Indeed, within 18 months after IBM pioneered "hoteling" and "hot-desking" during drastic downsizing in the early 1990s, it canceled leases on 22 million square feet of space — an amount equivalent to nine Empire State Buildings. Meanwhile, productivity quadrupled.

About 10,000 IBM employees now share offices with an average of four other persons. [5]

Likewise, AT&T reduced overhead costs and freed up about $550 million in cash flow by eliminating superfluous offices and consolidating others. "We're imploding," said AT&T spokesman Burke Stinson. "We saved $80 million in 1994 by having employees telecommute. We don't pay taxes, rent, heat, air-conditioning or any of the other expenses that go with running offices for those workers." [6]

Hoteling has already reduced fixed office costs by an average of about 15 percent, according to Smith, and industry experts predict it could cut space requirements in half. [7]

The resulting reductions in downtown corporate space could profoundly affect urban real estate prices and future city landscapes, said Edward K. Robertson, CEO of Neurosystems, a Maryland planning firm that helped IBM with its hoteling project. "Imagine the huge impact this may have on both city and company planning," he said, suggesting that plans for new buildings may be scrapped as old ones go vacant. [8]

"The effect will be most profound on the central city, because the technology revolution means that companies, as well as employees, won't be tied down to a specific spot," said John M. Peckham III, president of the Peckham Boston Advisory Co. [9]

City planners and real estate executives have begun thinking about alternative uses for vacant downtown office space, such as gyms, condominiums, shops and clinics. Some predict that traditional offices could evolve into dual-purpose commercial/residential locations.

Meanwhile, a new breed of office has been born on the suburban outskirts for use by telecommuters. Business centers, sometimes called executive office suites, offer all the comforts of a downtown office, from conference rooms and day offices to reception and administrative services and E-mail and video conferencing. Sometimes they serve as "halfway houses" for telecommuters who feel isolated at home or need the discipline of an office to be productive. Companies and government agencies are also setting up satellite offices for teleworkers.

"If I had to guess, I'd say satellite offices closer to where people live will be the growth item of the future," Peckham said. [10]

The mobile work force is also having ripple effects in the suburban communities where telecommuters live.

"The home, the local copy shop, diners where workers may meet with one another or with clients and customers over lunch will become de facto workplaces," said architect Michael Brill, president of the Buffalo Organization for Social and Technical Innovation, a think tank in Buffalo, N.Y. [11]

Jack Nilles, a Los Angeles telecommuting consultant known as the "father of telecommuting," predicts that suburban coffee hangouts will replace the office water cooler as the venue for mid-morning gossip sessions. "Local businesses, restaurants, coffee shops will benefit, possibly to the detriment of downtown shops," he says.

"I see former bedroom communities becoming more like old-time communities again," Nilles says. "People will pay more attention to what's happening in their towns. Neighbors will talk to each other more."

Nilles also predicts other family-centered changes.

... On the Future of Cities and Suburbs

"Daytime home burglary rates will probably go down," he says, and teenagers may get into less trouble with parents home during the critical 3-6 p.m. after-school hours, when youths often experiment with sex, alcohol and drugs.

Almost a third of all Americans already have a home office, according to the latest Wirthlin Home Office Trends study. That number had grown significantly from 24 percent just six months earlier. Meanwhile the National Association of Home Builders reports that 66 percent of people shopping for a new home now consider a home office "desirable" or "essential." [12]

Each new home worker spends about $3,000 to $5,000 outfitting his home office initially and about $1,000 in upgrades and supplies each year. [13]

Local home office supply stores, like Kinkos and Staples, have ridden the growth trend. Kinkos, for instance, has installed video-conferencing capabilities in some of its outlets.

Christina Erridge, media specialist for Staples, says that as home offices have become more popular, lots of new products have been introduced, and demand has skyrocketed for certain old products. For instance, laser printer paper and mailing labels have become hot items, as have storage systems for documents and supplies.

"This year, we added wooden filing cabinets and a number of other wooden accessories in a variety of finishes," Erridge says. "We're also seeing much more interest in corner desks and L- or U-shaped desks," she says. "The large executive-type desk that sits in the middle of a room is not as functional for the home office."

Staples has also established "technical centers" at some stores, offering computer help, such as loading new software or upgrading memory. "You can just bring in your computer in the trunk of your car, and we'll load it for you," she says.

The market for computer-security software has also burgeoned, Nilles says, as more and more employees are communicating with their office via the Internet. Many companies have turned to private networks, and others are using encryption programs.

Armed with fiber-optic cables and satellite dishes, thousands of virtual office converts are moving not just to the suburbs but into rural communities and popular vacation towns like Telluride, Colo.

From 1990 to 1994, migration from the cities to rural counties jumped 2.2 percent, outpacing the 1.2 percent migration to urban areas, according to the Census Bureau. In 1992, the rural unemployment rate was lower than urban unemployment for the first time since before 1980, and the trend has continued. [14]

"There's a growing strand of anti-urbanism in a fairly significant part of the population," said Kenneth M. Johnson, a Loyola University of Chicago sociologist. "People want to live and work outside the cities." [15]

Some predict that telecommuting will eventually lead the way for mass migrations out of the major cities back to the countryside, possibly equaling the mass migrations into the cities during the Industrial Revolution.

"The coming information superhighway portends an environmental disaster of the first magnitude," Northwestern University Professor James H. Snyder told the World Future Society. It will allow a massive, ecologically harmful migration of teleworkers to rural areas that do not have the infrastructure to handle it, he said. [16]

But others say any negative environmental impact is likely to be outweighed by the decline in air pollution and gasoline consumption. Besides, everyone won't be moving to the countryside, says Cherry-Rose Anderson, a research analyst for the Gartner Group, a Boston high-tech research firm. "There are still lots of reasons for people to stay in cities," she says.

However, she concedes, "There is the potential for a long-term impact on the physical, geographical shape of our society." If an employer is concerned about the environmental impact of telecommuting, she says, they should limit their employees' telecommuting to part time. "That will prevent mass migrations into the mountains."

---

[1] Kenneth Shulman and John Reiser, "Technology, Telecommuting: Genesis for Change," *Managing Office Technology*, December 1996, p. 32.

[2] FIND/SVP, a New York research and consulting firm, June 8, 1998.

[3] Michael Takagawa, "Virtual Office Brings Challenges and Opportunities to the Real Estate Industry," *National Relocation and Real Estate*, Vol. 10, No. 6, 1995.

[4] From "Focus on Telecommuting: Locating the Virtual Office," by Gail M. Smith, published on the Web at www.hqnet.com/smith.htm.

[5] Melanie Warner, "Working at Home — the Right Way to Be a Star in Your Bunny Slippers," *Fortune*, March 3, 1997, p. 165.

[6] Quoted in Kathleen Howley, "Office Workers Today, Teleworkers Tomorrow," *Today's Realtor*, June 1996. p. 48.

[7] Smith, *op. cit.*

[8] Quoted by Charles A. Cerami, "Road Warriors Alter Workplace," *Insight on the News*, Sept. 11, 1995.

[9] Quoted in Howley, *op. cit.*

[10] *Ibid.*

[11] Quoted in Leon Whiteson, "Workers of the World Disperse," *Los Angeles Times*, Dec. 13, 1995.

[12] "Home Offices on the Rise," Wirthlin Worldwide Home Office Trends Study, February 1997.

[13] Kim Clark, "Home is Where the Work Is," *Fortune*, Nov. 24, 1997.

[14] "The Boonies are Booming," *Business Week*, Oct. 9, 1995, p. 105.

[15] *Ibid.*

[16] "Information Superhighway an Environmental Menace," *USA Today Magazine*, September 1995.

Continued from p. 709

ers to demand things quicker and make it harder to escape the office.

"Jobs have become less secure . . . more demanding, more time-consuming and more hectic, making it increasingly difficult to achieve a balance between work and personal life," says a 1997 Families and Work Institute study of the changing work force. [22]

And it's not just working women who feel conflicted. At Texas Instruments recently, 120 male employees attended a seminar about juggling work and home. Both single parents and dual-career couples are stressed, especially members of the "sandwich generation" who have to care for both children and aging parents. [23]

A 1997 retention-practices survey by the Society for Human Resource Management (SHRM) found that difficulty balancing work and family life was among the top five employee complaints.

"Workplaces appear to have become a bit more supportive over the past five years," says the Families and Work Institute study. "There is, however, plenty of room for improvement."

The recent institute survey of businesses found that 68 percent of companies allow flextime, while only 24 percent allow employees to set their own hours on a daily basis, called daily flextime. More than half allow workers to switch back and forth from full-time to part-time work or to work at home occasionally, while 38 percent allow job-sharing and 33 percent let workers telecommute full time. [24]

"Some companies are doing great things," Bravo says. "Some are not doing enough and some aren't doing anything at all." Smaller companies particularly don't know that offering flexibility improves job satisfaction, productivity and retention, she says.

"We look at whether a company offers flexibility on a permanent, equitable basis to all employees in a consistent manner," she says, point-

ing out that many companies offer flexible work arrangements, but only to managers.

"Just as is the case with health insurance, pensions and retirement," Bravo says, "there is a two-tier policy, and it is inequitable." For instance, she says, a phone company may allow its managers to have flexible work arrangements but not its word processors. Lawyers may have flexibility but not their secretaries or paralegal assistants, she says.

"Companies are not doing enough for employees who might need flexibility the most," Galinsky says. "Over and over and over again, we find that low-wage, low-income workers — those who cannot afford nannies or standby child-care — have the least flexibility."

SHRM spokesman Barry Lawrence says allowing low-wage assembly line or retail workers to have flexible working hours is difficult. "When the widgets are coming across the conveyor belt and you have to put your widget on top, you can't say, 'I'll be back in an hour.' Or if customers are coming to the mall to buy shoes from you between 9 and 5, it's hard to be flexible," he says.

Galinsky argues that assembly-line workers "typically can come up with all sorts of ways" to be flexible, "because they are already doing it informally."

Erecting Barriers

Some companies have flexible programs in place but erect barriers to using them, Bravo says. "So you get desperate cases like the one related to me last winter," she says. "At 5:30 one morning, the radio announced that schools were closing because of snow. A stranger knocked on another woman's apartment door and said, 'You look like a nice person. Could I leave my kids with you?

I'll be fired if I don't go to work.' "

Half of all working parents cannot take time off for mildly sick children, according to the Families and Work Institute.

Bravo says that sometimes a company may offer on-site child care and then impose mandatory overtime for workers, arguing that they now have no excuse not to work overtime because child care is available.

One of the biggest obstacles, say most flexibility advocates, is when companies offer flexibility on paper but individual supervisors don't support the policy. One large computer company was recognized nationally for its excellent flexibility programs, Bravo says. But when an employee used family leave to care for her dying mother, her supervisor asked at one point, "When is this thing with your mother going to end?"

Employees frequently fear reprisals if they take advantage of flextime or telecommuting options. The top non-technical reason telecommuting fails, according to a March 26 Gartner Group report, is because telecommuters fear management reprisal.

"Employees get messages from managers that they don't really want people to use these policies," says Arlene Johnson, senior consultant for WFD, a Boston-based work/family consulting firm. "Or if people do use them, they lose credibility as committed workers."

Often there is a disconnect between what employees think about potential reprisals for using flexible arrangements and what employers say is likely to happen. The Families and Work Institute found that while only 10 percent of employers felt that using flextime or leave policies would jeopardize an employee's career, 40 percent of employees felt it would.

"Sometimes a company says it offers flexibility but compensates it less or in an inequitable way," says

Continued on p. 714

At Issue:

Will encouraging telecommuting decrease traffic congestion?

JACK M. NILLES
President, JALA International Inc.

WRITTEN FOR THE CQ RESEARCHER, *JULY 1998.*

*a*bsolutely. But you might not notice it. Here's why. We tested the travel patterns of telecommuters and their families in two public-sector programs: telecommuting employees of the state of California and the city of Los Angeles. In both cases we gave the employees travel logs to complete for themselves and for every other driving-age member of their families. . . . The participants were required to fill out a log entry for each trip they made. In both cases, more than 85 percent of the participants drove alone to work when they were not telecommuting; that is, they were a part of the congestion problem. The results were as we hoped: Three-quarters of the telecommuters do not use their cars at all on the days they are telecommuting. More surprisingly, we found that the automobile use of the families of the telecommuters also was reduced in one-quarter of the cases. Even in many of the cases where the telecommuters used their cars, it was to replace trips (such as ferrying the kids to/from school) that otherwise would have been made by other family members. . . .

But there is larger systemic problem: The population is increasing and road capacity isn't — more cars, but the same amount of space in which to drive them. Therefore, traffic congestion is bound to increase. What telecommuting does is to ease the pressure by taking some of the potential congesters off the road. Whether this results in an absolute decrease in the levels of congestion depends on the number of telecommuters and their rates of telecommuting. In 1998, I expect that telecommuting will reduce automobile traffic by about 70 billion vehicle miles, most of that during peak congestion hours. By 2010 that number will increase to about 200 billion vehicle miles. To put it another way, telecommuting will take about 3.5 million cars off the road every workday in 1998 and about 21 million per workday in 2010, according to my forecast. And the numbers will increase with time.

Whether this will result in an absolute decrease in congestion depends on a number of other factors, such as an (unlikely) increase in the use of mass transit and the reduction of incentives for automobile use. The latter includes tax relief for employers who provide free parking for their employees and low fuel tax rates, compared with the rest of the world. The European Commission has funded a large number of telecommuting demonstration projects in recent years, the U.S. federal government none. Perhaps a more proactive stance would help.

PATRICIA L. MOKHTARIAN
Professor of civil and environmental engineering, University of California, Davis

WRITTEN FOR THE CQ RESEARCHER, *JULY 1998.*

*p*romotion of telecommuting for public policy reasons has doubtless played an important role in raising awareness of this form of working. However, organizations will generally adopt telecommuting because they view it as good for business, not to help the environment.

Most people who telecommute do so only part time, slightly more than one day a week on average. The number of telecommuters appears to be rising each year, but not as fast as some enthusiasts predicted. There are several possible reasons for this. One is that telecommuting is not well-suited to everyone. One study estimates that no more than 16 percent of the work force is currently able to telecommute, given the constraints of management resistance, job unsuitability, technology, cost and others.

Further, not everyone who is able to telecommute (on the basis of external circumstances) and wants to do so will actually choose to do it. Some people have "psychological constraints" such as a desire for the social and professional interaction of the regular workplace, concern about career advancement if they telecommute, distractions at home, and so on. Even though they see the benefits of telecommuting and want to do it, these internal constraints are strong enough to prevent them from adopting the practice.

A final important reason for why telecommuting has not increased as fast as some expected is that most people don't telecommute forever. Several studies suggest that about half of those who start telecommuting stop within 9-18 months.

Thus, for many workers, telecommuting is likely to occur in multiple "off-and-on" cycles over a career, rather than occurring continuously. The implication is that at any given time, only a subset (possible a small one) of all possible telecommuters will be in a period of active telecommuting. Failure to account for that would highly exaggerate the forecasts of adoption and of the corresponding impacts (for example on transportation).

From my perspective, it appears that telecommuting as such will not radically transform the way we work and the amount we travel. I do believe that telecommuting will ultimately become commonplace as an alternative way of working, but that sizable proportions of the work force will not be doing it on any given day. Similarly, I believe that the transportation impacts can be modestly beneficial, but will not be dramatic, or eliminate the need to add new capacity to meet growing demand. In short: evolution, not revolution.

Continued from p. 712

Bravo. "That tells the employee they don't value it."

Another company sent out a memo telling workers that they now have the option of working part time, but warned they would lose their health benefits if they choose that option.

"Too many employers have the attitude of 'Yes, you can take leave, but, boy, will you be sorry,' " Bravo says.

One way to change that, flexibility advocates say, is to reward managers for supporting flexibility. "You have to base performance on reasonable output expectations," Hardman says, "rather than on how many hours employees sit at their desks." The Families and Work Institute study found that about 44 percent of employers train supervisors in how to respond to work/family conflicts, and evaluate how well they manage such issues when making job-performance appraisals.

Perhaps one of the biggest problems in the workplace today, she said, is the work culture that says in order to advance in one's career a person must be available to work long hours, including nights and weekends. "Most people can't do that unless they have a wife at home full time," she says. "It's like the glass ceiling, but it never gets talked about."

"You can't just have flexible work arrangements," agrees Robin Hardman, director of communications for the Families and Work Institute. "You have to have a culture where

the work can't take 12 hours a day. People with children are not the ones who are unproductive. It is people with children who are working in unreasonably demanding jobs."

Excessive job demands will offset any benefit from good work policies, she says.

"You can have all kinds of flexible policies, but it doesn't get to the

Pacific Gas & Electric Co. workers telecommute last September during a strike of the Bay Area Rapid Transit system, which they normally ride from the suburbs to PG&E's San Francisco office.

AP Photo/Thor Swift

essential issue of how work gets done," Bravo says. One thing employers could change, she notes, is how meetings are scheduled and run. "What time of day are they held? How necessary are they? How well-

planned are they? If you make meetings more efficient, it will cut down on how much time people have to spend at the office. That's one way you can change the work process to support flexible work arrangements, rather than undermining them."

Galinsky says that she is seeing a change in attitude among employers. "There is certainly a greater consciousness about this issue," she says. Even lower-wage employees are beginning to benefit from the change, partly as a result of the difficulty of finding good workers, and keeping them, she says. "Employers of lower-wage workers are increasingly becoming aware that there is a cost for high turnover," she says.

"As the market gets tighter, employers are more open to employees' needs," says Teresa Knight, another SHRM spokesperson. "Employers are really trying to hold on to the employees that they do have."

According to a "quickie benefits survey" by her group, just in the last year the percentage of employees using flextime has risen from 46 percent in 1997 to 55 percent in 1998. However, use of compressed workweeks, telecommuting and job-sharing has risen only slightly, according to the survey.

SHRM's Lawrence agrees. "This is becoming a very big competitive issue," he says. "People aren't going to come, and they aren't going to stay, if you don't offer these options." ∎

OUTLOOK

Elver Care

With the labor market expected to remain tight for the foreseeable future, employees are likely to continue pushing for more flexible benefits. The biggest obstacles standing in the way are management resistance and the rigidity that pervades the work culture, Johnson says.

In addition, managers accustomed to managing by "presence" rather than by "results" will have to change their management styles, she says, if workers are to be given more freedom.

"These cultural and management issues are the next frontier to make flexibility policies come alive," Johnson says. In addition to learning new management styles, she says, employers need to get beyond the notion that "flexibility is a favor," and view it as a new option for effectively utilizing people that increases productivity and retention.

Meanwhile, as more people live longer, more companies will be pressured to offer elder-care family leave.

"With today's smaller families, single-parent families and two-career couples, the pool of able-bodied, non-employed adults available to provide elder care is shrinking just as demand for care is rising," says the 1997 work force study by the Families and Work Institute.

Already, Stinson says, employee inquiries about elder-care referrals are rising faster than those about child care.

"We have found that 25 percent of employees are caring for elderly parents, and 42 percent expect to," Galinsky says. "I don't think we are ready for this at all. I don't think we've really begun to think about the

impact on the labor force if you've got almost half the people in five years needing to take care of an elderly parent."

Employers who do not anticipate the potential disruptions to their work force brought on by this "demographic tidal wave" will likely be taken aback by its consequences, says the institute's report.

"You can't predict the need for elder care," Galinsky explained. "You can't plan for it and it can last a very long time." Further, she noted, while employees can decide whether or not to have children, they have no choice on whether to have parents.

Johnson predicted that because the need for elder care is "gender blind," more men will be pushing for flexibility.

Pollution Concerns

Telecommuting advocates predict that as technology makes it more affordable and management mindsets slowly become more amenable, telecommuting will continue its steady growth. Moreover, environmental concerns are likely to increase pressure on governments to encourage telecommuting, says the Gartner Group.

"By 2008, strict global treaties limiting greenhouse gas emissions will force national, regional and local governments to mandate reductions in the number of vehicle miles traveled," says a recent Gartner study. [25]

The report cited the as-yet-unratified treaty that resulted from the 1997 United Nations summit on global warming in Kyoto, Japan — known as "the Kyoto Protocol" — which calls for emission-reduction targets of between 6 percent and 8 percent below 1990 levels by 2012 for most industrialized nations.

Although the treaty may never be

ratified by the United States, its existence is evidence that global attention is increasingly focusing on environmental concerns, the report said. "The question now becomes when, not if, strict greenhouse gas reductions will be mandated by local, regional and national governments — and whether enterprises will be prepared to compete in a 'green' environment," it continued. "Enterprises that begin to plan and budget for telecommuting now will be at a competitive advantage over those that do not."

As a result, Gartner predicts, by 2003 more than 137 million workers worldwide — including one-third of the U.S. work force — will engage in at least occasional remote access as a function of their employment contracts. [26]

Nilles projects that 18 million Americans will be telecommuting by the end of 1998, if recent growth rates of 15 percent a year persist.

Niles, in Seattle, is a bit more skeptical. "Don't expect downtown offices to empty out, he says. "There is a continuing need for face-to-face contact. And it's fundamentally more difficult to manage telecommuters, and that will keep telecommuting slowed down."

AT&T's Stinson is also cautious, because he loathes what he calls the "breathless gushing" that surrounds telecommuting projections. He predicts it will "inch its way along until a critical mass of about 30 percent of the U.S. work force is telecommuting. Then it will become a 'given,' " he says. "By 2008 the nature of telecommuting will shift from being something that is uncommon to being common. There will be a generation and a half of managers for whom it's no big deal."

Pratt agrees. As the price of notebook computers goes down, "it's a no-brainer that employees will start telecommuting more."

Moreover, she says, the baby boomers are just now hitting their 50s, and entering upper management. "They are much more likely to encourage it than the old, white males currently running U.S. industry," she says.

Dziak, the Atlanta consultant, focuses his telecommuting sales efforts only on top managers because the only way to overcome middle-management resistance is for top executives to say, "We will do this, and you will be a part of it."

Things are slowly beginning to change, he says. "Many organizations are now asking themselves not 'should we start a telecommuting program?' but, 'When should we start?' "

Dziak used to try to sell managers on telecommuting based on its ability to help Atlanta meet Environmental Protection Agency air quality goals. "There are a lot of problems it can solve. We're reaching a threshold of pain in air quality and traffic congestion. Economic development is going to come to a screeching halt because we can't build bigger roads. And the community wants to have a better quality of life."

But now it's not air pollution that is motivating managers to take a closer look at telecommuting, he says. "It's for specific, selfish business reasons," he says. "Generation Xers are coming out of college as mobile workers, after having spent their entire college years attached to a notebook computer."

Regardless of the motivation, he says, "The planets are in alignment to accelerate teleworking exponentially." ∎

Notes

[1] From a speech to the National Technology Fast 500 CEO Summit, March 7, 1996.

[2] For background, see Karen Lee Scrivo, "Child-Care Options," *The CQ Researcher*, May 8, 1998, pp. 409-432, Charles S. Clark, "Job Stress," *The CQ Researcher*, Aug. 4, 1995, pp. 696-719, Charles S. Clark, "Work Family and Stress," *The CQ Researcher*, Aug. 14, 1992, pp. 689-702 and Kathy Koch, "High-Tech Labor Shortage," *The CQ Researcher*, April 24, 1998, pp. 361-384.

[3] Quoted in Judy Greenwald, "Employers Warming up to Flexible Schedules," *Business Insurance*, June 15, 1998.

[4] For background, see David Masci, "Baby Boomers at Midlife," *The CQ Researcher*, July 31, 1998, pp. 649-672 and Mary H. Cooper, "Caring for the Elderly," *The CQ Researcher*, Feb. 20, 1998, pp. 145-168.

[5] James T. Bond, et. al., *1997 National Study of the Changing Workforce*, Families and Work Institute, 1998.

[6] Cited in *The Orange County Register*, June 2, 1997, p. D10.

[7] Ellen Galinsky and James T. Bond, "The 1998 Business Work-Life Study," Families and Work Institute, July 14, 1998.

[8] For background, see Kenneth Jost, "Diversity in the Workplace," *The CQ Researcher*, Oct. 10, 1997, pp. 889-912 and Richard L. Worsnop, "Implementing the Disabilities Act," *The CQ Researcher*, Dec. 20, 1996, pp. 1105-1128.

[9] Galinsky and Bond, *op. cit.*

[10] *Ibid.*

[11] Quoted in Greenwald, *op. cit.*

[12] Patricia L. Mokhtarian, "Now That Travel Can Be Virtual, Will Congestion Virtually Disappear?" *Scientific American*, October 1997, p. 93.

[13] Quoted by Sue Shellenbarger, "Families, Communities Can Benefit From Rise in Home-Based Work," *The Wall Street Journal*, May 13, 1998.

[14] Ellen Bravo, *The Job/Family Challenge: Not for Women Only* (1995).

[15] Quoted in Bravo, *ibid*, from Rosalyn Baxandall, et al, *America's Working Women: A Documentary* (1976), p. 263.

[16] Alice and Staunton Lynd, eds., *Rank and File, Personal Histories by Working Class Organizers* (1979).

[17] Mark Wilson, "Flextime for Families: What Works for the Government Can Work for the Private Sector," The Heritage Foundation, Feb. 26, 1997.

[18] Princeton Survey Research Associates, "Worker Representation and Participation Survey," October 1994; Penn & Schoen Associates Inc., "Flexible Scheduling and Compensatory Time Poll," conducted for the Employment Policy Foundation, Oct. 27, 1995, cited in Wilson, *ibid*.

[19] See *1993 CQ Almanac*, p. 389.

[20] For background, see Kenneth Jost, "Labor Movement's Future," *The CQ Researcher*, June 28, 1996, pp. 553-576.

[21] Position paper, Family Research Council.

[22] Bond, et al., *op. cit.*

[23] *Ibid.*

[24] Galinsky and Bond, *op. cit.*

[25] Cherry-Rose Anderson, "What the Kyoto Protocol Will Mean for Telecommuting," The Gartner Group, Jan. 26, 1998.

[26] Cherry-Rose Anderson, "Key Issues in Remote Access Policy and Procedures" The Gartner Group, April 10, 1998.

Bibliography

Selected Sources Used

Books

Bravo, Ellen, *The Job/Family Challenge*, John Wiley & Sons, 1995.

The executive director of 9to5, the National Association of Working Women, offers practical advice on managing work and family — including how to convince your boss that flexible work arrangements help the bottom line.

Nilles, Jack M., *Making Telecommuting Happen*, Van Nostrand Reinhold, 1994.

The "father of telecommuting" explains what every prospective manager or telecommuter needs to know to either set up and manage a successful program or be an effective telecommuter.

Perlow, Leslie A., *Finding Time*, ILR Press, 1997.

This collection of case studies examines the culture of long work hours, primarily among software engineers, and asks the troubling question: Does requiring employees to work long hours really make a company more successful?

Articles

Anderson, Cherry-Rose, "What the Kyoto Protocol Will Mean for Telecommuting," The Gartner Group, Jan. 26, 1998.

The Kyoto Protocol has focused attention on ways to reduce greenhouse gas emissions. The author argues that this could lead to telecommuting mandates.

Apgar, Mahlon, IV, "The Alternative Workplace: Changing Where and How People Work," *Harvard Business Review*, May-June 1998.

The author, a counselor on real estate and infrastructure to major corporations, writes about the various alternative workplace options that companies are adopting.

Cerami, Charles A., "Road Warriors Alter Workplace," *Insight on the News*, Sept. 11, 1995.

The author looks at the ripple effects of more and more workers being sent home by their employers.

Dziak, Michael J., "Surprisingly Common and It Works!" *Women in Business*, May/June 1998.

The author discusses how the surge in the number of home offices is changing both the retail and real estate markets, as well as the suburban landscape.

Mokhtarian, Patricia L., "Now That Travel Can Be Virtual, Will Congestion Virtually Disappear?" *Scientific American*, October 1997, p. 93.

The author, a professor of civil and environmental engineering, argues that telecommuting is not yet widespread enough to cause demonstrable decreases in traffic congestion.

Warner, Melanie, "Working at Home — the Right Way to Be a Star in Your Bunny Slippers," *Fortune*, March 3, 1997, p. 165.

The author suggests ways to avoid telecommuting pitfalls.

Whiteson, Leon, "Workers of the World, Disperse," *Los Angeles Times*, Dec. 13, 1995.

Telecommuting is not always a voluntary option, but for some downsizing and cost-cutting companies, it is seen as a way to save money. These companies are sending employees home to work and are cutting down on the amount of office space they maintain.

Reports and Studies

Becker, Franklin, et al., *Managing the Reinvented Workplace*, International Development Research Council and the International Facility Management Association, 1996.

Compiled by researchers at Cornell University and the Massachusetts Institute of Technology, this 140-page report outlines "best practices" of 30 companies that are pioneering alternative workplaces as a way to cut real estate costs and boost productivity.

Bond, James T., Ellen Galinsky and Jennifer E. Swanberg, *The 1997 National Study of the Changing Workforce*, Families and Work Institute, 1997.

Based on lengthy interviews with 2,877 employees, this study looks at how work, family and personal life affect each other. It finds that the quality of workers' jobs and the supportiveness of their workplaces are the most powerful predictors of productivity, job satisfaction, commitment to employers and employee retention.

Bureau of Labor Statistics, "Work at Home in 1997," March 11, 1998.

Based on a special supplement to the May 1997 "Current Population Survey," this survey of 50,000 households provides a snapshot of the work-at-home scene during May 1997. It finds that 21 million persons did some work at home as part of their primary job, but only half of them were being paid expressly for that work, either as employees or as self-employed workers.

Galinsky, Ellen, and James T. Bond, The 1998 Business Work-Life Study, Families and Work Institute, 1998.

This is the first and most comprehensive study of how U.S. companies are responding to the work-life needs of the nation's changing work force. Based on surveys of 1,057 companies, it is meant to complement the "1997 National Study of the Changing Workforce," (see above). It finds that the more women and minorities a company has in managerial positions the more likely that company is to offer flexible work options.

The Next Step

Additional information from UMI's Newspaper & Periodical Abstracts™ database

Family Leave

"Family Flex-Time," *The Boston Globe*, April 21, 1997, p. A14.

First parent Bill Clinton believes he has come to the rescue by extending the Family and Medical Leave Act. President Clinton supports giving workers 24 more hours of unpaid time a year, to manage routine medical needs, care for elderly relatives and participate in school and early childhood activities. But without a law, Clinton can only squeeze out extra hours for his own federal employees. And opponents insist government shouldn't be telling businesses how to manage their employees.

Doherty, William J., Martha F. Erickson and Edward F. Kouneski, "Responsible Fathering: An Overview and Conceptual Framework," *Journal of Marriage & the Family*, May 1998, pp. 277-292.

This article defines responsible fathering, summarizes the relevant research and presents a systemic, ecological framework to organize research and programmatic work in this area. A principal finding is that fathering is influenced, even more than mothering, by contextual factors in the family and community.

Flextime

"Tread Softly on the Path to Flexible Working," *Management Today*, November 1997, p. 12.

Manufacturers who are turning to flexible working practices must overcome the insecurity, uncertainty, and entrenched attitudes of the work force and some levels of management.

"Work Week: Holiday Flex Time," *The Wall Street Journal*, Jan. 28, 1997, p. A1.

Holiday flextime is catching on with employers. Beginning in 1997, Marquardt & Roche won't tell its employees which 11 holidays they must take. And ICG Communications is considering allowing employees to schedule 25 paid days off yearly as they see fit, covering holidays, vacation, sick days and personal days.

Carre, Francoise, and Chris Tilly, "Part-Time and Temporary Work: Flexibility for Whom?" *Dollars & Sense*, January 1998, pp. 22-25.

The "flexible" work arrangement has become common as part-time and temporary employment has risen in the 1990s. Unfortunately, "flexible" means quite different things to employers and employees.

Dine, Philip, "Ashcroft's Flex-Time Bill Languishes," *St. Louis Post-Dispatch*, Oct. 3, 1997, p. C7.

Sen. John Ashcroft, R.-Mo., wants to be president. He also wants to overhaul workplace rules and allow employees more flexible schedules to juggle family and job. Early this year, Ashcroft pushed his flextime bill, which alters the 40-hour work week and the way overtime is compensated to allow individual tailoring of schedules. In effect, the bill rewrites industrial relations law dating to the New Deal. With many women handling home and work chores, Ashcroft also is hoping to reduce the political gender gap.

Lewis, Diane E., "Study: Flexible Schedules Aid Workers, Employers," *The Boston Globe*, Feb. 24, 1998, p. D5.

Allowing employees to rearrange their schedules not only helps them balance the demands of work and their private lives but also helps employers. Researchers from the Cambridge Institute met with 55 workers to determine whether reorganizing work schedules and responsibilities and introducing flextime and telecommuting would enhance the quality of employees' lives and improve productivity.

McQuaid, John, "Senate Looks at Workers' Hours Comp, Flex Time May Replace Cash," *New Orleans Times-Picayune*, June 4, 1997, p. A15.

Republicans and Democrats are headed for a showdown in the Senate over a controversial measure that would let employees take time off in lieu of overtime pay. Senate Majority Leader Trent Lott, R-Miss., said Tuesday he would try to bring up the bill for a vote today, but Minority Leader Tom Daschle, D-S.D., said he still has a unified block of 45 Democrats, including Louisiana Sens. John Breaux and Mary Landrieu, who can filibuster the measure. The bill has two main components: It would let employers grant comp time to employees instead of overtime pay; in other words, a worker would get 1.5 hours of comp time for every hour of overtime worked. The bill would also allow "flex time," in which an employee could work more hours one week and fewer the following week, as long as the employees averaged a 40-hour week.

Wilson, Mark, "All Workers Deserve A Flexible-Hours Law," *The New York Times*, March 9, 1997, p. A17.

A House bill sponsored by Rep. Cass Ballenger, R-N.C., would enable employers to offer workers the choice of taking overtime pay as cash or as time off (at 1 1/2 hours for each overtime hour worked). Workers could accrue 240 hours a year in such compensatory time. But a much more comprehensive Senate bill would provide the broad flexibility now needed in the American workplace. Sponsored by Sen. John Ashcroft, R- Mo., the Family-Friendly Workplace Act would give workers the same comp-time right as the House bill, but would also authorize employers to offer both full- and part-time workers the same flexible work privileges available to federal workers.

Management Concerns

Back, Brian J., "Home Report: More People Opting to Work Where they Live; Home Offices Preferred to a Grueling Commute," *Atlanta Constitution*, June 18, 1998, p. X7.

Many people don't like to bring their work home, but new data suggest that people are finding ways to bring their homes to work. And it's a short commute from the bed to the computer. The U.S. Census Bureau released previously unpublished data showing a 56 percent increase in the last decade in the number of people who work at home in their primary jobs. These workers numbered 2.2 million in 1980 and 3.4 million in 1990.

Coolidge, Shelley Donald, "Corporations Flex for the Family; But Critics Say They Still Falter on Work-Life Issues; Key is Changing Culture at Work," *Christian Science Monitor*, Sept. 2, 1997, p. 8.

Fortune will soon join *Business Week* and *Working Mother* magazines in ranking family-friendly companies — those that offer benefits from child care to flexible hours to dry-cleaning pickup. Yet even as companies scramble to implement such programs, management experts say most miss the key issue: creating a corporate culture that encourages employees to find the balance of work and family.

Davy, Jo Ann, "Managing Manpower in the New Millennium," *Managing Office Technology*, March 1998, pp. 18-31.

The author examines the role staffing services will play in helping meet the manpower needs of the next millennium. Human resource managers will face shortages and administrative burdens in hiring new workers.

Furore, Kathleen, "Keeping in Touch and on Track; Telecommuting Doesn't Have to Be an Obstacle on a Career Path," *Chicago Tribune*, June 28, 1998, p. 1.

According to a survey released in April by the Kensington Technology Group, a San Mateo, Calif.-based company that's a leader in the design and sales of computer accessories, about 8.2 million people telecommute on a regular basis. The study identified telecommuters as "those who work from home more than three days a month or from the road more than seven days a month."

Steen, Margaret, "Balancing Work and Life," *InfoWorld*, June 8, 1998, pp. 105-106.

The author discusses ways to satisfy career expectations while keeping the home fires burning. Information professionals relate their solutions to common career problems, including part-time employment and flexible hours.

Telecommuting

"Who Works from Home?" *Detroit News*, May 4, 1998, p. F9.

More than 21 million people did some work at home as part of their primary job last May, according to a recently released report from the Bureau of Labor Statistics. Nearly nine of 10 workers doing paid work at home were in "white-collar" occupations and about six in 10 used a computer for the work they did at home.

Barlow, Jim, "What It Takes to Telecommute," *Houston Chronicle*, April 14, 1998, p. E1.

Telecommuting makes sense for many people. It's considerably cheaper for both employees and employer. The employee does not have to pay for commuting or dressing for work. The employer isn't out money for buying or renting office space and maintaining it.

Oldham, Jennifer, "Careers/Leadership; Remote Control; With so Many People Telecommuting, Managers Face a Dual Challenge: Setting Parameters for Off-Site Workers While Also Fostering their Development," *Los Angeles Times*, June 8, 1998, p. S10.

The number of telecommuters in the United States more than tripled from 3.6 million in 1990 to 11.1 million in 1997, according to New York-based market research firm Cyber Dialogue. As this number increases, so do the number of managers who are trying to manage and mentor employees who work remotely. Although telecommuting is maturing as a concept, managers confront the same issues today that they did a decade or so ago when the work style burst onto the national scene as an effective way to retain employees and save money.

Shellenbarger, Sue, "Families, Communities Can Benefit From Rise In Home-Based Work," *The Wall Street Journal*, May 13, 1998, p. B1.

The fastest-growing segment of home-based workers, full-time corporate telecommuters, will rise by 14 percent a year through 2020, according to Jack Nilles, a former government spacecraft designer who coined the term "telecommuting." Visionaries like Nilles have long hoped that more home-based work would strengthen families and neighborhoods weakened by long commutes and the expanding work day. And interviews with pioneers on this workplace frontier — longtime telecommuters at three trend-setting companies, Hewlett-Packard, IBM and AT&T — suggest it can make a difference.

Wells, Susan J., "For Stay-Home Workers, Speed Bumps on the Telecommute," *The New York Times*, Aug. 17, 1997, p. A1.

After telecommuting for years for two publishing companies in New Jersey and California, a job candidate thought twice when Sage Publishing, based in Los Angeles, wanted to hire her as acquisitions editor on the East Coast — which required telecommuting from her home in Mamaroneck, N.Y. The woman isn't alone in her rejection of telecommuting. Those who study telecommuting say it is still growing, but they acknowledge that it may have hit a turning point — some say a coming of age — for some of the same reasons the woman and others have discovered.

Back Issues

Great Research on Current Issues Starts Right Here.
Recent topics covered by The CQ Researcher are listed below.
Now available on the Web
For information, call (800) 432-2250 ext. 279 or (202) 887-6279.

If you would like to have any of these CQ Researchers updated, or need more information about these topics, please call CQ Custom Research. Special rates for CQ subscribers. (202) 887-8600 or (800) 432-2250, ext. 600, or E-mail Custom.Research@cq.com

MAY 1997
The Stock Market
The Cloning Controversy
Expanding NATO
The Future of Libraries

JUNE 1997
FDA Reform
China After Deng
Line-Item Veto
Breast Cancer

JULY 1997
Transportation Policy
Executive Pay
School Choice Debate
Aggressive Driving

AUGUST 1997
Age Discrimination
Banning Land Mines
Children's Television
Evolution vs. Creationism

SEPTEMBER 1997
Caring for the Dying
Mental Health Policy
Mexico's Future
Youth Fitness

OCTOBER 1997
Urban Sprawl in the West
Diversity in the Workplace
Teacher Education
Contingent Work Force

NOVEMBER 1997
Renewable Energy
Artificial Intelligence
Religious Persecution
Roe v. Wade at 25

DECEMBER 1997
Whistleblowers
Castro's Next Move
Gun Control Standoff
Regulating Nonprofits

JANUARY 1998
Foster Care Reform
IRS Reform
The Black Middle Class
U.S.-British Relations

FEBRUARY 1998
Patients' Rights
Deflation Fears
Caring for the Elderly
The New Corporate Philanthropy

MARCH 1998
Israel at 50
The Federal Judiciary
Drinking on Campus
The Economics of Recycling

APRIL 1998
Biology and Behavior
Liberal Arts Education
Income Inequality
High-Tech Labor Shortage

MAY 1998
Census 2000
Child-Care Options
Alzheimer's Disease
U.S.-Russian Relations

JUNE 1998
Student Journalism
Antitrust Policy
Environmental Justice
Sleep Deprivation

JULY 1998
Encouraging Teen Abstinence
Population and the Environment
Democracy in Asia
Baby Boomers at Midlife

AUGUST 1998
Oil Production in the 21st Century

Back issues are available for $5.00 (subscribers) or $10.00 (non-subscribers). Quantity discounts apply to orders over 10. To order, call Congressional Quarterly Customer Service at (202) 887-8621.

Binders are available for $18.00. To order call 1-800-638-1710. Please refer to stock number 648.

Future Topics

▶ *Coastal Development*

▶ *Student Activism*

▶ *Organic Farming*

THE

Coastal Development

Does it put precious lands at risk?

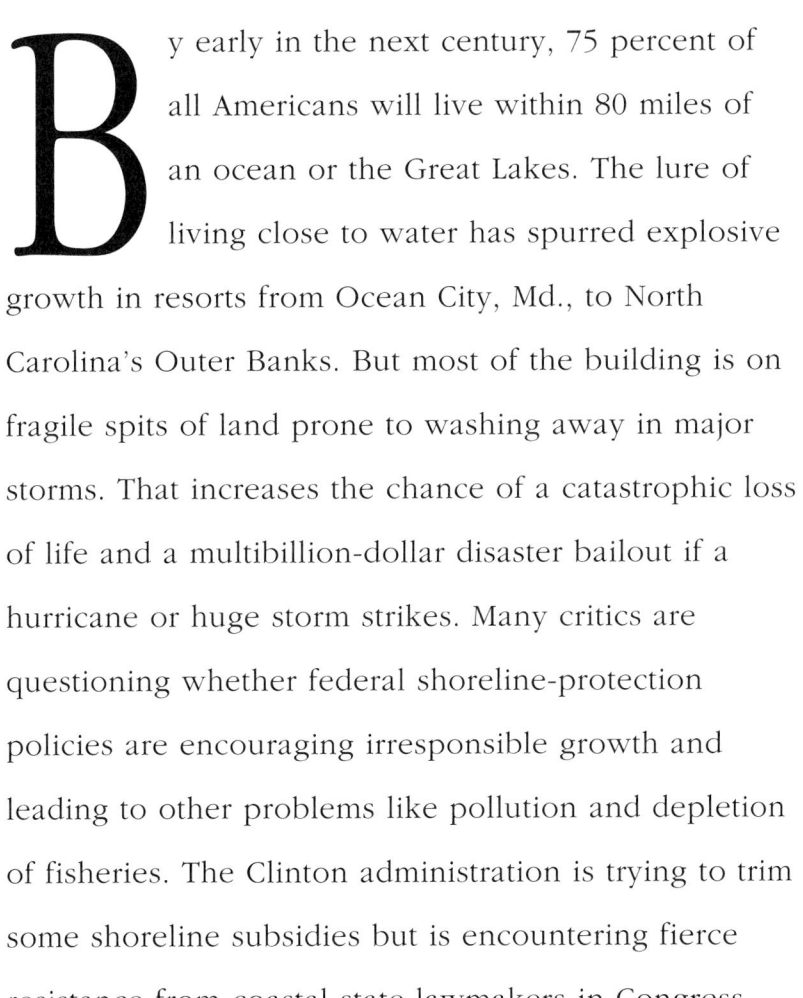

B y early in the next century, 75 percent of all Americans will live within 80 miles of an ocean or the Great Lakes. The lure of living close to water has spurred explosive growth in resorts from Ocean City, Md., to North Carolina's Outer Banks. But most of the building is on fragile spits of land prone to washing away in major storms. That increases the chance of a catastrophic loss of life and a multibillion-dollar disaster bailout if a hurricane or huge storm strikes. Many critics are questioning whether federal shoreline-protection policies are encouraging irresponsible growth and leading to other problems like pollution and depletion of fisheries. The Clinton administration is trying to trim some shoreline subsidies but is encountering fierce resistance from coastal state lawmakers in Congress.

C_Q **August 21, 1998 • Volume 8, No. 31 • Pages 721-744**

Formerly Editorial Research Reports

THE ISSUES

SIDEBARS AND GRAPHICS

CQ Researcher

August 21, 1998
Volume 8, No.31

EDITOR
Sandra Stencel

MANAGING EDITOR
Thomas J. Colin

STAFF WRITERS
Adriel Bettelheim
Mary H. Cooper
Kenneth Jost
Kathy Koch
David Masci

PRODUCTION EDITOR
Melissa Hall

EDITORIAL ASSISTANT
Laura S. Cavender

PUBLISHED BY
Congressional Quarterly Inc.

CHAIRMAN
Andrew Barnes

VICE CHAIRMAN
Andrew P. Corty

PRESIDENT AND PUBLISHER
Robert W. Merry

EXECUTIVE EDITOR
David Rapp

The CQ Researcher (ISSN 1056-2036). Formerly Editorial Research Reports. Published weekly, except Jan. 2, May 29, July 3, Oct. 30, by Congressional Quarterly Inc., 1414 22nd St., N.W., Washington, D.C. 20037. Annual subscription rate for libraries, businesses and government is $340. Additional rates furnished upon request. Periodicals postage paid at Washington, D.C., and additional mailing offices. POSTMASTER: Send address changes to The CQ Researcher, 1414 22nd St., N.W., Washington, D.C. 20037.

COVER: HURRICANE OPAL SHEARED OFF A DUNE IN 1995, LEAVING THIS BEACHFRONT HOUSE IN FLORIDA PERILOUSLY CLOSE TO THE WATER. (AP/BILL KACZOR)

Coastal Development

BY ADRIEL BETTELHEIM

THE ISSUES

O ff the coast of Ocean City, Md., engineers are making yet another attempt at reversing the forces of nature. Operators of a large dredge suck sand from the ocean floor and shoot it through a pipeline onto beaches that have been eaten away by storms and rising seas.

Two northeasters last winter washed away portions of the popular resort's beach, which had been replenished over a decade at a cost to state and federal taxpayers of $80 million.* But like many storm-battered coastal communities, Ocean City is optimistic about saving its famous strand. The federal government plans to keep pumping sand onto Ocean City's 10 miles of shoreline over the next 50 years at an estimated cost of $500 million — or $1 million a mile per year.

Local officials defend the project, saying the beach protects shoreline properties from erosion and storm damage and attracts tourism that generates some $67 million in federal tax revenues each year. "I hear the beach replenishment being referred to as a subsidy. If it's delivering a 600 percent return, exactly who's subsidizing whom?" asks City Engineer Terry McGean.

But others wonder whether beach projects like Ocean City's are really damaging fragile coastlines rather than helping them. Critics say long-term federal commitments to rebuild beaches, erect erosion barriers and pay flood insurance encourage developers and wealthy individuals to build more properties on fragile spits of land that are at the greatest risk of washing away in

major storms. That increases the chance of a catastrophic loss of life and a multibillion-dollar disaster bailout if a hurricane or major storm strikes.

"This kind of an arrangement doesn't exactly force a beach community to make wise long-term decisions," says Stephen Leatherman, a coastal geologist at Florida International University (FIU) in Miami. "These folks build and build, and are capable of forgetting they're putting static structures in the way of a dynamic landscape."

The debate is getting increased attention during this year's series of events marking the United Nations' "Year of the Ocean." At the National Ocean Conference in Monterey, Calif., in June, conferees discussed developing a national plan to deal with development along America's approximately 95,000 miles of shoreline, as well as pollution and other growth-related issues. In 1967, the last time such a plan was discussed, a White House conference known as the Stratton Commission led to the creation of the National Oceanic and Atmospheric Administration (NOAA), the ocean research and weather-forecasting branch of the U.S. Department of Commerce.

The current concerns are driven by Americans' continued attraction to the shore. Approximately 55 percent of the U.S. population — about 145 million people — now live within 80 miles of an ocean coast or one of the Great Lakes. By the year 2025, NOAA estimates close to 75 percent of the

population will live in coastal areas. [1]

Many of the most popular tourist beaches and developments from Maine to Texas sit on low-lying barrier islands that constantly migrate, change shape and even fold over on themselves due to tides, storms and sand flow. Anxious property and business owners constantly clamor for more beach fill and breakwaters to maintain a buffer zone between themselves and the sea.

The situation isn't confined to the Atlantic and Gulf coasts: In California and the Pacific Northwest, beach communities are seeking federal aid to stop erosion that reached rates of 10 feet a year during this year's El Niño-driven storms. Generally the problem has not been as widespread on the West Coast because the shoreline is characterized by sheer bluffs, not extensive sandy beaches, and there is less private ownership of coastal land.

Environmentalists argue that continued development — not erosion or bad weather — is the greatest threat to coastlines. They say construction of sea walls, breakwaters and jetties to maintain navigation inlets and protect properties creates obstacles that block the natural flow of sand. That keeps adjacent beaches from being replenished, leaving thin buffer zones that can be easily breached in major storms. [2]

In addition, coastal developments annually discharge approximately 2.3 trillion gallons of partially treated sewage into nearby waters. Nutrients and pathogens in the effluent can foul ecosystems, forcing closure of shellfish beds and swimming areas. Runoff from city streets and parking lots, along with pesticides and fertilizers that leach off farmlands, further threaten water quality. (See story, p. 739.)

"It's as if the powers that be develop the shoreline, draw a line in the sand and

---

* Northeasters, known to mariners as nor'easters, are major storms that occur along the Mid-Atlantic coast in the fall, winter and spring. They are so named because their heavy winds usually originate from the Northeast.

The Trouble With Sea Walls

Structures built too close to the shoreline typically require sea-wall construction to prevent erosion (1). But walls create a barrier to natural beach replenishment, leading to a narrowing of the beach and a steepening of the offshore slope (2). Eventually, the beach disappears, and the increased wave power due to the steepened slope causes the bulkhead to fail (3). Construction of a higher wall leads to more powerful waves and further erosion (4).

1. Before the wall

Scarped dune is evidence of eroding shoreline

Gentle foreshore

2. Wall constructed; development proceeds as buyers believe property is protected by the wall

Narrowing of beach

Steepening of offshore slope

3. Two to 40 years later

There is no beach. The bulkhead has failed. Offshore slope has steepened.

4. Ten to 60 years later

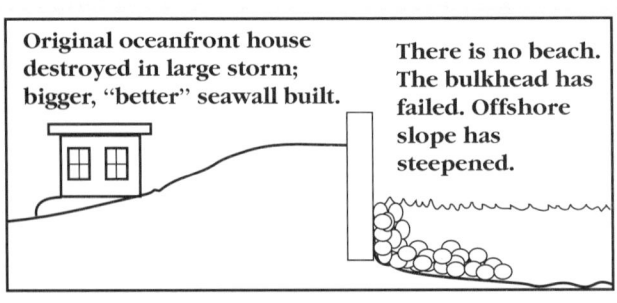

Original oceanfront house destroyed in large storm; bigger, "better" seawall built.

There is no beach. The bulkhead has failed. Offshore slope has steepened.

Source: David Bush, Orrin Pilkey and William Neal, Living By the Rules of the Sea, *Duke University Press, 1996*

challenge the sea not to cross it. They want to maintain the line at any cost," says D.W. Bennett, president of the American Littoral Society, an environmental advocacy group in Sandy Hook, N.J. "Towns, counties and states won't seriously think about alternatives to building as long as the federal government assures it's going to be a free lunch."

Charting a course to address all the concerns is proving difficult. U.S. coastal policy is a patchwork of regulations administered by more than a dozen federal agencies that sometimes have conflicting agendas. Since Congress established the Beach Erosion Board in 1930 to study deteriorating coastlines, legislation has increasingly made the federal government responsible for protecting private shorefront property, preventing floods, preserving critical coastline habitats and working with states to define hazard zones. Such a broad agenda has led to bureaucratic wrangling and lawsuits.

In one oft-cited example, local fishermen, the U.S. Army Corps of Engineers and environmentalists have skirmished since 1970 over a plan to build twin, mile-long jetties at Oregon Inlet, N.C., north of Cape Hatteras. Fishing interests say channels within the inlet are migrating with tides and storms, hindering navigation. Congress authorized construction of the jetties but never funded the project. The U.S. Department of the Interior, which owns land adjacent to the inlet, opposes the project, saying construction will endanger wildlife refuges and possibly exacerbate erosion. The corps, which designs the nation's shore protection and flood control projects, maintains the jetties will at last stabilize the inlet and eliminate the need for continually dredging navigational channels.

Scientists estimate 80-90 percent of the U.S. coastline is going the way of Oregon Inlet, eroding at rates varying from one to two feet a year to upward of 14 feet a year. They question whether the government should restrict development, move the most endangered properties away from beaches and allow coastlines to re-form naturally over time.

The Clinton administration is taking a more measured approach, attempting for the past four years to selectively reduce shoreline subsidies. In its 1999 budget proposal, the White House called for trimming the federal government's share of long-term beach replenishment and slashing the corps' shore-protection budget by 79 percent from the 1998 level of $108.9 million.

That isn't sitting well with coastal state lawmakers, who have ignored the administration's recommendations and voted to keep funding many of the beach projects. The lawmakers say cuts would threaten beaches that generate hundreds of millions of dollars in annual revenues for coastal communities and regional economies.

"Beachfront communities represent one of the most thriving sectors of the nation's economy," says Sen. Frank R. Lautenberg, D-N.J. "Stop coastal protection, and you're letting a lot of money wash out to sea."

Adds Rep. E. Clay Shaw Jr., R-Fla., "It's much more than saving some rich person's front yard."

As coastal interests and development critics grapple, here are some of the questions they are asking:

Are taxpayers subsidizing high-risk coastline development?

When Hurricanes Bertha and Fran slammed into North Carolina's Outer Banks within two months of each other in 1996, the federal government responded with speed and zeal.

On Topsail Island, Shara and Ronald Sullivan of Newton Falls, Ohio, found their $260,000 ocean-front vacation home destroyed. Federal flood insurance covered $121,000 in combined losses from the two storms. But because the couple's lot was too eroded to rebuild, the Small Business Administration (SBA) also chipped in with a $115,000 loan to buy another house one block away. The couple acknowledges the risk of living on the erosion-prone island.

"I don't think I'd take the risk if I couldn't get some kind of insurance," said Shara Sullivan. "I'm too chicken for that." [3]

The Sullivans' payments were part of $1 billion in grants, loans and insurance claims the federal government paid out to North Carolinians within a year of the hurricanes. To many, the payments symbolized Washington's increased sensitivity to the perils of living along the coast — and an attempt to avoid the criticism for slow response that occurred after Hurricane Andrew hit South Florida and Louisiana in 1992.

But scientists and government officials have increasingly questioned why the government is paying to rebuild beach homes, condominiums and other developments in high-risk areas that private insurers are reluctant to cover. And they are more closely scrutinizing the way billions of dollars in disaster relief are spent.

Much of the criticism is directed at the National Flood Insurance Program, established in 1968 to cover flood-prone shore and inland communities. Skeptics say the program's subsidized insurance discourages property owners from exercising personal responsibility and building in safer areas. Premiums average about $300 nationwide for $100,000 in coverage. The maximum coverage available for a single-family home, not including contents, is $250,000.

"The program has become a blank check signed by the federal taxpayer: a check whose total, when erosion, rising sea levels, storms and hurricanes take their toll, will be in the billions," environmentalist Beth Millemann wrote in a scathing critique of the program. [4]

The Federal Emergency Management Agency (FEMA), which administers the program, says it actually discourages risky development because flood insurance is a condition for any federally insured mortgage or construction loan in a flood-hazard area. Without such requirements, communities could be as careless with new development as they wished, according to FEMA Director James Lee Witt.

"As more people buy flood insurance, fewer flood victims must be bailed out with tax-funded federal disaster aid," Witt wrote. [5]

Since the late 1970s, FEMA has required coastal policyholders who rebuild after floods to adhere to tougher standards, such as elevating structures to above the 100-year flood level. In 1995, FEMA also embarked on a campaign to sign up homeowners in flood-prone areas who don't currently have insurance — an effort to discourage those who think they would automatically qualify for aid when a flood strikes.

David Conrad, water-resources specialist for the National Wildlife Federation, says the program still has fundamental flaws. He notes FEMA doesn't consider whether a coastline is eroding when it offers insurance in a shore community, instead relying

Win Some, Lose Some

Shorefront communities have had mixed success dealing with development and beach erosion. Here are some examples:

Presque Isle, Pa.— The Army Corps of Engineers spent millions of dollars trying to stabilize this scenic sandspit in Lake Erie, but flooding and erosion persist. The latest plan calls for installing 58 segmented breakwaters at a cost of $30 million.

Southampton and West-hampton, Long Island — Dozens of exclusive houses built along eroding beaches have been swept into the sea by storms since the 1960s. Southampton officials are debating whether to allow owners to build sea walls to protect their residences.

Sandy Hook, N.J. — The Corps of Engineers plans to spend $15 million next year to replenish about 10 miles of beaches stretching to Manasquan. It's part of a large-scale proposal to rebuild 33 miles of the state's coastline.

Ocean City, Md. — The resort community lost portions of its $80 million replenished beach during last winter's storms. The corps estimates that maintaining the town's 10 miles of beach will cost $500 million over the next 50 years.

Oregon Inlet, N.C. — Watermen and environmentalists are at odds over a plan to build twin jetties to keep the passage open to the Atlantic Ocean. Congress authorized the $100 million project in 1970 but never funded it.

Cape Hatteras, N.C. — Scientists expect the sea to swallow the area's landmark 200-foot-tall lighthouse within two decades. The National Park Service wants to move the 2,800-ton structure away from the eroding coastline.

Broward and Dade counties, Fla. — Storms over the last two years have swept hundreds of thousands of cubic yards of sand from South Florida's palm-lined coast. Concerned about the effects on tourism, state officials are pressing for federal beach-restoration help.

Sargent Beach, Texas — Federal officials recently completed an $80 million, 8-mile-long sea wall to prevent the Gulf of Mexico from breaching the Gulf Intracoastal Waterway. Dredging and jetty construction over the course of a century increased erosion rates.

Erosion-Control Projects

(Map with labels: Southampton and Westhampton, Presque Isle, Sandy Hook, Ocean City, Oregon Inlet, Cape Hatteras, Broward and Dade counties, Sargent Beach; states: Maine, Vt., N.H., Mass., R.I., Conn., N.Y., Pa., N.J., Del., Md., Va., N.C., S.C., Ga., Fla., Ala., Miss., La., Texas)

Sources: Orrin Pilkey and Katherine Dixon, The Corps and the Shore, *International Hurricane Center, Florida International University; news reports*

on the more vague historical likelihood of flooding in an area. Also, Conrad says, properties built before FEMA issued flood insurance rate maps in the early 1970s are "grandfathered" into the program, even though they often were built to weaker construction standards and are at greatest risk of being damaged.

The result, critics say, is that the flood-insurance program isn't financially stable or self-sufficient. A series of major disasters — from Hurricane Andrew to the Midwest floods of 1993 to the twin hurricanes of 1996 to last year's Red River floods that devastated Grand Forks, N.D. — triggered massive claims that dwarfed the premiums taken in. The program has had to borrow funds from the U.S. Treasury and pay back the loans with interest out of future premiums. Currently, it owes the Treasury more than $720 million.

Meanwhile, FEMA continues to pay to rebuild structures in high-risk areas. On Topsail Island, owners of 217 properties that have been flooded two or more times have collected $10.9 million from FEMA in national flood insurance payments. Ironically, some properties were in a zone designated off-limits to new coastal development by federal legislation passed in 1982 to preserve fragile coastlines.* But FEMA was still able to send aid by using a loophole that allowed payments when lives or existing properties are threatened.

*The legislation is the Coastal Barrier Resource Act, also known as COBRA.

In California, the agency is paying $1.5 million to rebuild a sea wall to protect a row of at-risk homes in Pacifica, south of San Francisco. The affluent neighborhood's previous sea wall was destroyed by coastal erosion, and El Niño-inspired storms ate away at seaside bluffs under nine homes early this year.

FEMA's inspector general and the U.S. General Accounting Office (GAO), the watchdog arm of Congress, have each recommended that FEMA improve its ability to identify applicants who should purchase flood insurance and develop a database to track compliance.

Witt, who has generally earned high marks for turning around FEMA's relief efforts, says the agency plans to "reengineer" its public-assistance program to avoid encouraging more risky development.

"If we're going to keep people out of harm's way, and if we're going to cut costs from disasters, we're going to have to change the way we do business," Witt said late last year. [6]

FEMA isn't the only agency to draw criticism. After Hurricane Fran, the corps built a 15-mile-long, $4.6 million sand dune to protect Topsail Island property that drew criticism from other federal agencies after it quickly started blowing away. The corps maintains the dune stopped further property damage.

On nearby Wrightsville Beach, the SBA provided more than $1 million in grants to build a temporary sea wall and make improvements at the $22 million Shell Island Resort, a high-rise condominium complex on an eroded spit of land that soon is expected to fall into the sea. North Carolina officials have denied permission to the buildings' owner to erect a permanent sea wall and ordered that the temporary one come down next year. The case is now in court.

Critics say the actions of the individual agencies reflect the broader political realities of disaster relief. Ever since the sluggish bureaucratic response to Hurricane Andrew embarrassed the Bush administration in the 1992 election year, the Clinton administration has taken pains to show compassion and speed assistance to stricken communities. Clinton and Vice President Al Gore have visited some of the harder-hit communities and frequently waived cost-sharing requirements with states and local governments, meaning the federal government pays 100 percent of some costs.

White House officials say the practice harks back to Clinton's experience as governor of Arkansas and his sensitivity to the effects disasters have on individuals and communities. Others say guarantees of disaster aid score big points and can secure votes in key states.

"The Clinton administration, more so than any of their predecessors, has realized the political value of disaster spending and being there to hand out the checks," says David DeSanti, executive director of the Natural Disaster Coalition, an insurers' group concerned with rising disaster costs.

Some coastal interests see it as more of a contractual obligation, viewing the aid as part of an unwritten covenant the government entered into when it began building more roads and bridges to the shore as part of the post-World War II construction boom.

"We spend billions of dollars constructing transportation corridors to enable people to get to the beach. Yet, to spend several million on ensuring that the beach exists and to protect the natural and economic resources which justify the transit projects is characterized as extravagant," says Tony MacDonald, executive director of the Coastal States Organization, a Washington lobbying group representing coastal states, commonwealths and territories. "The shortsightedness of such views should be plain."

The Morris Island (S.C.) lighthouse now stands about 2,000 feet at sea. Nearby jetties disrupted sand flow and increased erosion, causing the shoreline to retreat from under the tower in the mid-1940s.

Program for the Study of Developed Shorelines

Does beach replenishment work?

In the late 1970s, Miami Beach was hardly a beach at all. Sea walls built by hotel owners in the 1960s to halt the advancing waves interrupted the natural flow of sand. At high tide, waves lapped up against the concrete barriers, engulfing the famous strand where James Bond first met Goldfinger.

In 1982, the corps completed a massive beach replenishment, pumping 13 million cubic yards of sand that created a 300-foot-wide beach at a cost of about $64 million. Tourist

Corps of Engineers Beach Projects Cost More Than $3 Billion

Since the end of World War II, the Army Corps of Engineers has undertaken more than 1,300 federally funded beach-replenishment projects costing more than $3 billion. Areas with the most projects are listed below.

	Number of projects	Sand volume (million cubic yards)	Total cost (in $millions)
Florida (East Coast)	144	86.3	$443.2
New Jersey	124	57.4	312.7
Florida (West Coast)	113	46.4	224.8
North Carolina	108	43.5	146.2
Massachusetts	81	3.7	56.4
New York	73	98.2	523.1
Virginia	48	13.6	78.8
Connecticut	44	5.3	48.3
Lake Michigan	280	13	100.8
Lake Erie	54	9.4	77.9
Lake Superior	53	1.4	9.6

Note: Total costs are adjusted for inflation to 1996 dollars and include both known costs and estimates for projects with unknown costs.

Source: Duke University, Center for the Study of Developed Shorelines, June 9, 1998

visits soon surged, reviving the moribund city economy. Nearly two decades later, most of the beach remains and officials estimate federal tax revenues from foreign visitors alone exceed $130 million a year.

"It basically rejuvenated the place. Without the beach, it wasn't a place you'd want to visit," says James Houston, a physicist at the corps' waterways experiment station in Vicksburg, Miss., which designs beach-replenishment projects.

The Miami Beach experience is often cited by coastal-development interests as justification for authorizing large beach-fill projects to combat erosion and create tourism. However, scientists say it may be more of an exception to the rule. The unique shape of Miami Beach's sand grains, made from coral shell fragments, made the beach tightly packed and more resistant to wave erosion. The presence

of offshore reefs near the Florida coast also lessened wave action.

More typical, the scientists say, may be Mid-Atlantic beach projects that need to be replenished every three to five years because rising seas and wave action wash away most of the sand. Critics contend this leads to long-term financial commitments — such as the one in Ocean City, Md. — and a continuous cycle of federal beach subsidies.

Understanding how beaches wash away requires looking beyond the visible beach. Wave action constantly scours sand off a beach, depositing it in offshore bars and later redistributing it to the beach. Erosion takes place when storms and winds create waves that remove more sand than they give back, or when people build objects that block the flow of sand.

States and local communities typi-

cally seek out the corps for advice when they have erosion problems. The corps conducts feasibility studies and cost analyses that have to meet the approval of Congress. But critics contend this process amounts to writing a blank check; the longer the recommended life of a project, the more money the corps stands to receive in its construction budget. And coastal lawmakers have an incentive to deliver beach-fill projects in much the same way that other lawmakers vie for federal highway aid for their districts.

"Beach nourishment has been oversold by the Army Corps of Engineers," says FIU geologist Leatherman. "They need projects to work on, and the local communities see this constant flow of federal money. It's no surprise it's billed as a panacea for the erosion problem."

"If you lift up the flap, there's

more to predicting how the beach will behave than meets the eye," says Orrin Pilkey, a coastal geologist at Duke University in Durham, N.C., and a vocal critic of beach fill. "But the communities just assume it's going to last and increase the density of shorefront buildings, which means there will be much more damage if there's a big storm."

Pilkey estimates the corps has spent $3.5 billion over the past 30 years on 1,305 beach replenishments. He notes, however, that the corps uses unreliable mathematical models to calculate the useful life of beach fill. Among the notable failures: the $12 million replenishment of Folly Beach, S.C., in 1993, most of which disappeared within two years without the passage of a significant storm. [7]

Pilkey and other critics also say that the corps' cost estimates are overly optimistic. Northeasters that struck Ocean City, Md., in 1991 and 1992 were calculated to be the type of storms that occur once every 15 years. However, they added about $12 million more to the sand pumping cost than the Corps of Engineers had estimated. [8]

Corps officials defend their work, saying replenished beaches are never guaranteed to stay in place but protect billions of dollars' worth of coastline property that otherwise would get swallowed by the sea. They dispute Pilkey's 30-year cost estimates for beach replenishment, saying expenditures are much lower and now total about $150 million a year. As for the general wisdom of building at water's edge, corps officials say they don't control development,

they just save it.

"We get blamed for encouraging development, but people are going to the coast anyway, and they don't even know where the corps' projects are," says Harry Shoudy, a senior policy analyst with the corps in Washington. "It boils down to whether you want to protect them, or not."

Despite the Clinton administration's pleas for less sand pumping, the corps is studying or is in the midst of several mega-projects that continue to stir debate. The largest is designed to maintain a 100-foot-wide beach for 50 years on a 33-mile stretch between Sandy Hook and Barnegat Inlet, N.J., primarily to protect beachfront homeowners from coastal

Development on narrow barrier islands has property and business owners in communities like Ocean City, Md. clamoring for more beach fill to maintain a buffer zone between themselves and the sea.

storms. Nearly $100 million in federal funds have been spent so far, and the agency estimates the total cost of the first 21 miles to be $1.1 billion. [9]

On Fire Island, off New York's Long Island, the corps is studying a long-term plan to pump sand to protect 4,000 property owners from storms and erosion. Environmentalists oppose the plan because it may upset the barrier island's delicate ecosystem and disrupt the natural east-west sand drift.

"The biblical adage that one should

not build a house on sand is given ultimate demonstration at Fire Island," says New York state Assemblyman Steven Englebright, D-Setauket, who is also a geologist.

But property owners say a "naturalist" approach of letting beaches reform themselves doesn't correspond with reality. "This is between purists in the environmental movement and those who live in the real world," Fire Island homeowner Ken Entler said at a public hearing last December. [10]

Should there be a national coastal-management plan?

To some, the story of erosion control at Long Island's Westhampton Beach illustrates the need for better coordination among federal, state and local officials on coastal-development problems.

The Corps of Engineers built a series of groins (sea walls built perpendicular to the beach) in the 1960s to halt erosion near the exclusive resort community. The structures cut off the natural flow of sand westward, starving some beaches. When a giant winter storm hit in 1992, the ocean surged through the narrow, starved barrier, destroying 190 of 246 homes in the town. Property owners sued and won a state permit to rebuild the lost homes.

The corps spent $32 million on an emergency project to fill and widen the damaged beach. But then the U.S. Fish and Wildlife Service determined the area was a known habitat of the piping plover, an endangered shore bird, and ruled any construction may violate the Endangered Species Act. The dispute remains tied up in courts. [11]

No single governmental agency is responsible for coastal development. The corps has perhaps the greatest responsibility, charged with keeping waterways navigable and protecting vulnerable shorelines. But states ultimately approve most of the construction on coastlines — usually with the caveat that property owners are building homes and businesses at their own risk.

"The general situation seems to be that everyone should be able to use their property as they wish, as long as they build to established standards," says Rutherford Platt, professor of geography and planning law at the University of Massachusetts, Amherst. "That seems to have gotten away from the original intent of applying land-use planning to steer development away from recognized hazards."

The Coastal Zone Management Act of 1972 was supposed to help states coordinate their policies based on federal guidelines. To date, 32 out of 35 coastal states have approved programs to protect coastal resources. Conservation groups give the act mixed reviews, saying it has encouraged more responsible development away from the water's edge. However, they note the program is voluntary and doesn't require states to consider factors such as how new coastal developments affect water quality.

Some states have enacted tough restrictions, banning certain types of erosion control. North Carolina, South Carolina, Maine, Rhode Island, Texas and Oregon prohibit construction of new sea walls, jetties and other "hard structures" on beaches, citing evidence that they disrupt sand flow. The states continue to support beach replenishment where necessary.

Local officials complain it's difficult to formulate a beach policy because federal agencies with responsibility for coastal management often don't talk to each other. Tony Pratt, beach manager for the Delaware Natural Resources and Environmen-

tal Control Department, notes FEMA doesn't get involved when the corps plans an erosion-control project, even though the agency will have to step in if the beach gets stripped away by tides. "It seems to me that it's time that two sister agencies like this [work together]," he says.

Duke geologist Pilkey notes the problem is exacerbated by conflicting philosophies about coastal development. NOAA, through the Coastal Zone Management Act, advocates building away from eroding shores. Similarly, the National Park Service (NPS) has adopted a broad ban on any coastal engineering at its national seashores. But Pilkey says the corps continues to recommend sea walls, groins and jetties be built to fight the sea.

Congress has made several attempts to make sense of the bureaucratic tangles. The latest is legislation sponsored by Reps. H. James Saxton, R-N.J., Don Young, R-Alaska, and Sam Farr, D-Calif., that would create a commission appointed by the White House and Congress to draft a federal ocean policy. "We have a regulatory process dealing with marine environments that generally doesn't work well," says Saxton, chairman of the House Resources Subcommittee on Fisheries Conservation, Wildlife and Oceans.

But Saxton and others acknowledge that any changes the commission recommends will be difficult to implement because of overlapping congressional jurisdictions. In the House alone, flood insurance comes under the purview of the Banking Committee; coastal zone management is left to the Resources Committee while water quality is handled by Transportation and Infrastructure.

"There's little concerted effort anticipating long-term coastal problems," says the National Wildlife Federation's Conrad. "Getting rational decision-making will be difficult because decisions are mostly based on politics, not long-term consequences." ■

BACKGROUND

Vacation Boom

America's rush to the shore may have begun in 1802, when promoters from Cape May, N.J., took out an advertisement in the *Philadelphia Aurora*, extolling the beauty of their oceanfront and the spacious lodging available in the town.

The accommodations actually consisted of a large room with a curtain down the center separating men and women. But it was enough to start a phenomenon. By the middle of the 19th century, well-to-do residents of Philadelphia and New York were escaping the sweltering cities in the summertime to promenade on the boardwalks of Atlantic City and Ocean City, N.J. Several presidents visited Long Branch, N.J., and Winslow Homer depicted parasol-toting Victorian ladies looking down on rows of the resort's small, frame bathhouses in one of his famous oil paintings.

Even then, man was battling the advancing sea, with relocation being the only option. In 1888, the owners of the Brighton Beach Hotel in Coney Island, N.Y., jacked up the 6,000-ton landmark, deposited it on 120 rail cars and had six locomotives slowly pull it 2,000 feet inland from the rapidly eroding shoreline. All of the houses in South Seaside, N.J., were built on wooden runners so they could be moved back with the beach. [12]

By the early 20th century, working-class Americans were placing more value on vacation travel to the shore. Developers responded by building more resorts on narrow

Continued on p. 732

Chronology

1900s-1950s
Coastal communities grow with few land-use regulations.

Sept. 8, 1900
A hurricane ravages Galveston, Texas, killing 6,000 people in the worst natural disaster in U.S. history in terms of lives lost. The city responds by building a 3-mile-long sea wall.

1922
New York's Coney Island launches the first recorded beach-replenishment program in the United States in order to protect its well-known amusement park.

1930
Congress establishes the Beach Erosion Board as part of the River and Harbor Act of 1930 to study beach erosion problems at the request of localities. The federal government pays up to half of the cost of studies but doesn't pay any construction costs unless federal property is involved.

1956
Congress expands shoreline protection to authorize federal subsidies for private property if the improvements help protect publicly owned shores, or if there are other public benefits.

———— • ————

1960s-1970s
Government officials become aware of the risks of rapid coastal development and propose measures to regulate growth.

March 5-8, 1962
A northeaster known as the "Ash Wednesday storm" hammers beachfront communities from Massachusetts to Florida, causing an estimated $300 million in damages. The loss of beaches is so severe that the U.S. Army Corps of Engineers is cast in a permanent, new role as the nation's key beach-replenishment agency.

1967
The Stratton Commission leads to creation of the National Oceanic and Atmospheric Administration (NOAA), the ocean research and weather forecasting branch of the U.S. Department of Commerce.

1968
Congress enacts the National Flood Insurance Act to limit increasing expenditures for flood control and disaster relief.

April 1979
North Carolina passes oceanfront setback regulations, setting the standard for other states.

———— • ————

1980s-1990s
As major storms batter the heavily developed East Coast, federal officials try to coordinate programs and deal with land-use and environmental disputes.

1982
Congress passes the Coastal Barrier Resources Act banning federal subsidies for development of 186 undeveloped shoreline tracts on the Atlantic and Gulf coasts.

1986
Congress passes the Water Resources Development Act, mandating that erosion-control projects primarily be used to mitigate storm damage and improve recreational facilities. The federal government eventually agrees to pick up 65 percent of initial construction work.

1987
A National Academy of Sciences report predicts the sea level in the United States will rise at an unprecedented rate, endangering many low-lying coastal areas.

Sept. 22, 1989
Hurricane Hugo rips apart the South Carolina coast, causing 21 deaths and $7 billion in damage.

Aug. 24-26, 1992
Hurricane Andrew slashes across South Florida and Louisiana, killing 14 people and causing more than $20 billion in damage, making it the costliest storm in U.S. history.

June 1994
A White House task force calls for reforming the federal flood insurance program, saying the first priority should be eliminating flood risk.

1995
President Clinton recommends federal participation in termination of new shore-protection projects. Congress rejects the proposal and adds money for new projects.

Sept. 6, 1996
Hurricane Fran hits the Carolina coast, killing 22 people and inflicting $6.5 billion in damage.

June 11-12, 1998
President Clinton and conferees at the National Ocean Conference in Monterey, Calif., discuss developing a national coastal policy. Clinton unveils a series of measures to protect oceans.

The Dreaded Northeaster

When it comes to coastal weather, hurricanes get most of the headlines. Slow to form and easy to track with radar, they threaten Atlantic and Gulf coast shore communities in late summer with such frequency that weather forecasters use names to distinguish them.

Less recognizable, but arguably more destructive, are northeasters. These giant wintertime storms form quickly and behave unpredictably, born of clashing air masses and strong jet streams. The strong winds, heavy snowfall and flooding they bring inflict some of the most serious weather-related damage to coastlines, stripping away tons of sand and damaging shorefront homes and businesses.

The storms typically begin when a cold-air mass circling clockwise around a high-pressure center moves over the Atlantic coast, meeting a low-pressure system circling counterclockwise. The spinning air masses mesh, picking up warm, moist air from the Gulf coast that rises, cools and condenses into rain or snow. The turbulence sometimes is exacerbated by a second high-altitude, low-pressure system that sucks more air upward, increasing precipitation and winds. [1] The result is a huge storm with a counterclockwise rotating air mass that resembles a hurricane, packing winds from the northeast. The storms typically travel 30-50 miles per hour but don't follow a predictable direction like most hurricanes because the hot and cold air masses clash in different ways.

Such a weather system caused what meteorologists and coastal geologists regard as the worst single storm of the 20th century, the "Ash Wednesday storm" of March 1962. The storm hit the Mid-Atlantic coast on March 5, just as spring tides were peaking, then stalled south of Long Island for three days, killing 34 people and causing an estimated $300 million in damage. Disaster officials estimate damage from a similar storm today would be many times greater due to the surge of coastal development over the last four decades and the fact that about 37 million people, 15 percent of the population, now live between Boston and Washington.

Scenes from the 1962 storm linger today in coastal communities that were hit. In Virginia Beach, Va., 340 homes were destroyed or damaged and 1,000 automobiles ruined by waves that reached 40-feet high. At Long Beach, N.J., a Navy destroyer being towed to port for repairs was flung onto the shore after its towing cable broke. Damage to beaches from Massachusetts to Florida was so great the Army Corps of Engineers began sand pumping on a regular basis to rebuild beaches and provide a buffer against future shoreline damage. [2]

While such extensive damage hasn't been duplicated, a similar northeaster brought about the great New England blizzard of 1978, which dumped 36 inches of snow on the region. Last winter, two giant northeasters within a week of one another hit the Mid-Atlantic coast, eating away large portions of erosion-plagued Assateague Island, Md. and the nearby beach at Ocean City.

Weather patterns spare the West Coast from the storms, though last winter's El Niño-inspired weather brought storm swells that caused comparable damage. Storms resembling northeasters are, however, found off Australia and New Zealand. A southeasterly variant called the *suestado* is often observed off the east coast of South America. Hawaii also experiences storms with strong southerly winds, called *kona*, or leeward, storms.

---

[1] See H. Michael Mogil, "Nor'easters: Ill Winds of the Atlantic Seaboard," *The Washington Post*, Feb. 12, 1997, p. H1.

[2] See Mary Reid Barrow, "Last Week? No Comparison, Say Residents Who Lived Through the Terrifying Floods of March 1962," *The Virginian-Pilot* (Norfolk, Va.), Feb. 8, 1998, p. A1.

Continued from p. 730

barrier islands to accommodate the increasing crowds. The construction of a wooden bridge linking Miami Beach to the mainland in 1918 set off a development boom that replaced much of the island's natural dune system with hotels and vacation homes. Even a 1926 hurricane that hit the city and killed 243 people didn't deter further growth.

During the Great Depression, the federal government viewed coastal management as a means of creating large public works projects to prevent beaches from washing away. The Civilian Conservation Corps (CCC) in the 1930s constructed a huge dune system on North Carolina's Outer Banks, stretching 115 miles with nearly 142 million square feet of dune grasses and more than 600 miles of sand fencing.

But continued shorefront building led to inevitable encounters with the sea. Those who could afford vacation cottages or larger estates asked for sea walls, revetments (walls of boulders built on the slope of a dune or on an eroding bluff) and groins to protect their properties. Increasingly, local communities turned to the Army Corps of Engineers.

The corps traces its roots to 1775, when George Washington and the Second Continental Congress established a branch of engineers to build fortifications. The elite unit primarily dealt with military matters until an 1824 Supreme Court decision in *Gibbons v. Ogden* gave the federal government authority over interstate navigation. The corps was assigned to dredge the Mississippi and Ohio rivers of obstacles to navigation. Soon, it also was building jetties to protect harbors.

The corps' mission expanded as a series of coastal-protection laws passed from 1930 to 1956 increasingly made the federal government responsible for controlling coastal erosion and protecting private property from floods.

Activity intensified after World War II, when a burst of federally supported road and bridge construction spurred an exodus to destinations like Atlantic City, Virginia Beach, Va., and Hilton Head, S.C., swelling the coastal population by more than 30 million people between 1950 and 1980.

Along the Atlantic Coast, dozens of walls were constructed to halt crashing waves and keep oceanfront property owners safe. Ironically, the massive structures often cut off public access to the beach and began eroding themselves, requiring more fortifications. The result in locales like Asbury Park, N.J., was an unsightly collection of wood, steel, stone and concrete walls and thin strips of beach that Duke University geologist Pilkey refers to as the "Newjerseyization" of the coastline.

In the 1950s, the corps began embracing the alternative concept of "renourishing" heavily developed beaches, piping in sand from offshore bars to build up the buffer zones that tides had washed away. The process gained popularity after a giant northeaster known as the "Ash Wednesday storm" battered the Atlantic Coast from Massachusetts to Florida in March 1962. Tides washed over barrier islands, created new inlets and destroyed $300 million worth of property and some of the most popular beaches. The corps pumped millions of cubic

yards of sand to rebuild the strands, restoring the shore's allure.

"We're proud of the projects we've produced for the nation," says Charles Chesnutt, a coastal engineer with the corps in Washington. "If you look at the [dozens of] major projects and the accuracy we've had in cost projections, the report card is very good."

Beach erosion threatens seaside homes in Plymouth, Mass., and all along the Massachusetts coast.

Action by Congress

Congress traditionally treated beach replenishment and sea wall construction the way it did highway projects, authorizing dozens of tax-payer-supported projects in annual spending bills. The process began to come into question during the administration of President Jimmy Carter, who had grown leery of large-scale water-development projects as governor of Georgia and wanted more executive branch control over the more than $3 billion of annual federal spending on water development.

Carter implemented water-reform policies so that only those projects that were environmentally sound and economically justifiable would be funded. This irked many members of Congress, who tried to authorize some disputed projects by bundling them in annual spending bills and dared Carter to veto them. [13]

After Carter left office, various sides in the debate struck a compromise of sorts in 1982, when Congress passed the Coastal Barrier Resources Act (COBRA) to discourage construction on 186 undeveloped islands, spits and beaches along the Atlantic and Gulf coasts. The law doesn't prevent landowners from building on their land but shifts the risk to the private sector by barring federal spending for roads, bridges and flood insurance.

The question of who should fund long-term shoreline protection was sorted out in 1986, when Congress passed the Water Resources and Development Act (WRDA) and set cost-sharing requirements for shore-protection projects. The federal government agreed to pay 65 percent of the

Continued on p. 735

To Save a Lighthouse

For 128 years, the lighthouse at Cape Hatteras, N.C., has guided mariners through the dangerous shoals known as the "graveyard of the Atlantic." But if nature has its way, the landmark tower with the black and white barber pole stripes may soon join hundreds of sunken ships off the Outer Banks.

Erosion and rising seas have eaten away at land around the lighthouse, which was built in 1870 on a site that at the time was 1,500 feet from the shoreline. Today, waves lap just 120 feet from its brick and mortar base, and scientists estimate that even a moderate-strength hurricane could trigger winds and tidal surges that could topple the structure.

The National Park Service, which owns the lighthouse, wants to move it 2,900 feet away from its present location to a new spot 1,600 feet from the water. The agency recently awarded a $1.4 million contract to International Chimney Co. of Buffalo, N.Y., to begin planning the move. But local residents worry that moving the tower will cause structural damage and instead are backing an alternative plan to build an 800-foot-long steel sea wall and other fortifications around the present site.

In many ways, the debate is a microcosm of the nationwide debate over whether to continue armoring the coastline or retreat from advancing waters. The deliberations gained additional momentum in June, when the Senate Appropriations Committee, at the urging of Sen. Lauch Faircloth, R-N.C., approved $9.8 million in the fiscal 1999 budget to help pay for the move. Advocates of the sea wall — including Rep. Walter B. Jones Jr., R-N.C., whose district includes Cape Hatteras — are trying to obtain $4 million for their project in the House of Representatives.

The 208-foot lighthouse is the tallest in the United States and attracts 250,000 visitors annually. It is the biggest attraction in Dare County, which competes with Nags Head, 50 miles to the north, for summertime tourist dollars. But the lighthouse's precarious future has caused headaches for federal and local officials for nearly three decades.

In 1970, the U.S. Navy built three groins in front of the lighthouse to protect monitoring equipment that tracked Soviet submarines. The groins slowed erosion but disrupted sand flow, flattening nearby dunes and forming a bay south of the lighthouse. In 1982, a committee of local residents and business interests headed by environmentalist Hugh Morton raised $500,000 and spent $165,000 of it to buy a synthetic bed of seaweed that traps sand running toward the beach and helps rebuild dunes. Morton now wants to spend the remainder of the money to install more artificial seaweed. [1]

The Army Corps of Engineers in the mid-1980s explored building a massive stone wall around the lighthouse but decided the eroding coast would eventually move out from under the structure, leaving it stranded at sea on its own little island.

The push to move the lighthouse began in earnest in 1988, when a National Academy of Sciences committee recommended relocation of the 2,800-ton tower. The panel estimated the shoreline in front of the lighthouse would retreat 157-407 feet by the year 2018 as sea levels rise up to 6.1 inches. The conclusions were affirmed last year in a study by North Carolina State University.

It wasn't the first time relocation of a lighthouse was considered. South-west Light on Block Island, R.I., was moved from an eroding cliff in 1994, and the Cape Cod-Highland Light was transported to a safe spot on a nearby bluff in Massachusetts in 1996. Neither structure suffered any damage. But those structures were considerably smaller than the 21-story Hatteras tower. Preliminary plans call for engineers to mount the structure and two attached keepers' houses on a track and move them five feet at a time with hydraulic equipment. The entire process would take about a month.

The Cape Hatteras, N.C., lighthouse

Department of Interior

Local residents fear one wrong move would destroy the landmark and leave its 1.25 million bricks scattered along the beach. The prospect of relocating the structure even a half-mile also stirs strong emotions among local residents, who grew up in the lighthouse's shadow and derive their identity from it.

"You tell them there's another option, and nobody wants to move it. I think we can go out and put in a sea wall," says John Hooper, owner of the Lighthouse View Motel in Buxton, which is immediately next to the present site. [2]

Park Service ranger Richard Schneider says he understands the sentimental attachment but that engineering studies show the move can be pulled off without any damage. He adds that disputes delaying the move could make it difficult to obtain restoration money.

"Our feeling is we have the technology to do this and if we wait, as coastal management becomes a bigger issue, Cape Hatteras may fall to the bottom of the list," he says.

[1] See Gerrie Ferris Finger, "Fighting for the Light," *Atlanta Constitution*, June 28, 1998, p. 1D.

[2] Quoted in Brian Hicks, "Embattled Beacons: Hatteras Islanders Fight for Their Light," *The Post and Courier* (Charleston, S.C.), June 28, 1998, p. A1.

Continued from p. 733
cost of beach rebuilding, covering both initial sand pumping and, after storms eroded beaches, follow-up rounds of pumping every several years over 50 years. States and local governments typically split the remaining 35 percent.

Rising Sea Levels

As lawmakers tried to establish new ground rules for the coast, scientists were issuing a series of reports warning that sea levels were rising at unprecedented levels because of global warming, further threatening new and existing coastal development.

Scientists say sea-level fluctuations are part of a natural cycle, triggered by events like the melting of the great glaciers, which began 20,000 years ago. But many believe the phenomenon has intensified since the Industrial Revolution due to the consumption of more fossil fuels, which release carbon dioxide as a byproduct. The gas traps excess heat that would otherwise radiate into space. As a result, the atmosphere is growing warmer, melting polar ice caps, increasing the volume of the oceans and speeding up erosion. [14]

Geologists blame rising sea levels for the unique tendency of barrier islands to migrate. As storms and normal tidal action pummel dunes on the islands' ocean beaches, sand is pushed to the backside of the is-

lands, or even the lagoons or bays behind them. Over time, the backside becomes the beach and the islands literally fold over on themselves, slowly retreating up the coastal plain.

The action explains how some barrier islands in the Gulf of Mexico have retreated 80 miles over the last century and a half. It also explains how fragile, Mid-Atlantic sites like Assateague Island, Md., are in danger of being "overwashed" in a major storm, making mainland communities more vulnerable to tidal surges. [15]

Federal officials acknowledge that

A storm-damaged sea wall in Sandbridge, Va. The Army Corps of Engineers has backed off from using such "hard structures" because they tend to narrow recreational beaches.

rising sea levels eventually are likely to force a rethinking of coastal development rules. Many coastal structures are designed with the worst flooding theoretically possible over a 100-year period as their basis. But higher sea levels mean a 50-year flood may become as severe as a 100-year flood. Furthermore, FEMA estimates that with a sea-level rise of one meter, the number of households in the coastal floodplain will rise from the present 2.7 million to 6.6 million by 2100.

In such a dynamic landscape,

defining what is responsible development can be challenging. A pair of U.S. Supreme Court rulings in the 1990s tried to strike a balance between regulation and property rights by asserting that shoreline property owners still have rights to build in certain areas, even if states try to place them off-limits.

In 1992, the court ruled in *Lucas v. South Carolina Coastal Council* that South Carolina officials violated the takings clause of the Constitution by forbidding developer David Lucas from building on two beachfront lots in an "inlet erosion zone."

Lucas paid $975,000 for the lots on the Isle of Palms in 1986. Before he could put up houses, the state passed a beach management law aimed at preserving the coastline and preventing "unwise development." The high court, by a 6-3 vote, said state regulations that deny a landowner full value of his land constitute a "taking" under the Fifth Amendment and require compensation. [16]

The Supreme Court broadened the definition of property rights two years later, ruling 5-4 in *Dolan v. City of Tigard* that an Oregon landowner didn't have to turn over a portion of his property for a municipal floodplain. The University of Massachusetts' Platt says the cases continue to influence coastal states and municipalities. he says governments may refuse to regulate coastal land because they fear they will have to make large compensatory payments to a landowner. ∎

CURRENT SITUATION

Budget Battle

If coastal communities benefit the most from shorefront protection, why shouldn't they pay more to protect their homes and businesses?

That's a question the Clinton administration is posing as Congress takes up a biennial reauthorization of the Water Resources and Development Act. The legislation authorizes the Army Corps of Engineers' dredging, navigation and coastal protection projects. After four years of unsuccessful efforts to eliminate some shoreline subsidies, White House officials are taking a softer approach, trying to alter language in the law that would change the federal-local split of costs for sand-pumping on beaches, the most expensive work.

The Clinton administration says it will continue to pay two-thirds of the cost of the initial pumping but wants to reverse the ratio and have states and localities pay 65 percent of the follow-up work, with the federal government picking up the other 35 percent. The administration argues that the constraints of the 1997 balanced-budget agreement it struck with Congress prevent more expensive, open-ended commitments, such as the beach fill at Ocean City, Md.

"The reality is we have to find ways of making the most with all the resources we have," White House Deputy Budget Director T.J. Glauthier told a recent conference of the American Coastal Coalition in Washington.

The administration says it could support total annual expenditures of $80-$100 million on national shore protection out of a total corps construction budget of $1 billion. But Congress appears headed for another fight over budget levels, counting on political support for local water projects during an election year. The Senate in June earmarked $1.2 billion for corps construction — still 15 percent less than 1998 levels but more generous than the Clinton plan.

"It is significantly better than the program proposed by the administration and will allow [construction] to

---

FEMA this year launched "Project Impact," a voluntary effort designed to urge communities to reduce life and property damage by studying local zoning and building codes and consulting existing flood maps. It hopes to sign up one community per state by September.

---

move forward," says Sen. Pete V. Domenici, R-N.M., chairman of the Senate Appropriations Energy and Water Development Subcommittee. [17]

Coastal communities are banding together to cheer on lawmakers like Domenici after years of piecemeal lobbying efforts. The American Coastal Coalition was formed by Washington lobbyist Howard Marlowe in 1995 and now has a membership of 140 local governments and property owners associations. In June, the organization convened a "coastal summit" in Washington to pressure House and Senate members to continue supporting shoreline protection as they crafted 1999 spending bills.

The Army corps isn't taking a position on the battle, simply saying it will do the work Congress authorizes.

Pressure on Congress

The lobbying on coastal issues isn't restricted to states and localities. The Pentagon and business groups are pressuring the Senate to hold hearings and ratify the Law of the Sea treaty, a global pact signed by 125 countries that regulates commerce, navigation and exploration on and beneath oceans. The treaty was rejected by then-President Ronald Reagan in 1982 because it required industrialized nations to share revenues from deep-sea mining with developing nations. It has since been amended to satisfy U.S. concerns. President Clinton signed it in 1994 and sent it to the Senate, which has until Nov. 16 to act. [18]

Clinton told the National Ocean Conference in June that approving the treaty is essential for the United States to be a global leader on coastal issues. The U.S. Navy supports the pact because it guarantees passage of surface warships and submarines through strategic waterways without prior notice. The oil industry likes it because it protects offshore drilling rights and similarly guarantees rights of maritime passage for tankers.

Continued on p. 738

At Issue:

Should the federal government continue to subsidize beach-replenishment efforts?

HOWARD MARLOWE
President, American Coastal Coalition

FROM TESTIMONY BEFORE HOUSE SUBCOMMITTEE ON WATER RESOURCES AND ENVIRONMENT, MARCH 31, 1998.

*w*e believe that federal, state and local investments in beach erosion control and in the proper management of beaches, inlets and shorelines are returned many times over in revenues generated by tourism and commerce, by tax increases inspired by higher property values and incomes, by mitigation of storm wave damage to property and infrastructure and by the elevation of the quality of life for coastal residents and visitors.

Recent studies and surveys have documented the economic value of beaches to specific local communities, regions and states, and while such studies are just beginning to be undertaken on a national level, it is intuitively obvious that thriving local, regional and state coastal economies are necessary factors in a healthy national economy.

We firmly believe that beach nourishment is an effective method of shore protection based on engineering and fiscal criteria. By beach nourishment, we refer to sand placement or sand replenishment. The American Coastal Coalition believes that the federal role in shore protection and beach erosion control is clearly prescribed by current law, including the Shore Protection Act of 1996 (Section 227 of the Water Resources Development Act of 1996). Efforts to substantially reduce and eventually eliminate this role are clearly counterproductive. . . .

Furthermore, we believe the federal government must participate in the management of the nation's sandy shoreline. This includes a strong fiscal commitment to sharing the costs of construction and periodic maintenance of beach nourishment projects with states and/or local governments. . . .

Not every sandy beach is an appropriate candidate for beach nourishment. For the large number which are, there must be an understanding and acceptance of the fact that beach nourishment has as its objective the reconstruction of a beach so that the net loss of sand caused by wave action and storms — and in many cases exacerbated by the existence of inlets and other forms of human intervention — is slowed to a minimum. . . .

Withdrawing from our coastlines is an unacceptable alternative to beach nourishment. The history of mankind is replete with evidence that people are drawn to coastlines for both economic and recreational reasons. Unless the coasts are cordoned off with barbed wire, that attraction will continue.

BETH MILLEMANN
Former executive director, Coast Alliance

FROM AND TWO IF BY SEA, 1986

*f*ew areas are less suited to heavy development than the beaches, dunes and islands of the coastal zone, and accordingly in few areas is development more costly in both national and natural resource dollars. Particularly vulnerable to erosion and susceptible to routine flooding and storm damage, the nation's coasts are receding by the foot and yard every year. . . .

Since 1938, more than two dozen hurricanes have cost state and federal governments and taxpayers between $50 million to $2.3 billion in damage per hurricane by flattening homes and businesses on the vulnerable Gulf and Atlantic coasts. In addition, coastal erosion, exacerbated by profligate beach and shore development on all four U.S. coasts, has taken a huge toll on private, state and federal coffers. Add to this the cost of lost coastal wildlife and fisheries from habitat destruction and development, and the total price tag of beachfront homes and those "week-end getaways" becomes very substantial. . . .

The fact that beaches "are not stable entities, but rather, are dynamic landforms constantly subjected to forces that promote erosion and/or deposition" is often overlooked by Realtors and homeowners. Instead, they erect "defense structures" like groins and jetties. . . .

As "protective" structures, these "hard" stabilizing devices generally "benefit only a few and seriously degrade or destroy the natural beach and the value it holds for the majority." Because of the accelerated erosion often caused by hard stabilizers . . . some coastal geologists consider them to be most harmful to the beach.

Renourishment, while somewhat of an improvement over hard stabilizers, is "temporary and too costly a solution except for selected communities." Furthermore, "replenishment is often used as an excuse to intensify development," perpetuating the cycle of shore degradation and destruction.

What is often disregarded is the value of the beach itself. Although it "appears to be sterile and devoid of significant life," a large number of plant and animal species depend upon the beach. Dunes abutting the beach shelter a diverse range of life and the upland area as well, acting as "storage areas for sand to replace that eroded by waves" and storms. In turn, the beach supplies sand to renourish dunes.

In this area of constant flux, intensive development is an invitation to disaster — an invitation, unfortunately, too often accepted.

Continued from p. 736

However, Senate Foreign Relations Committee Chairman Jesse Helms, R-N.C., has yet to schedule hearings and is said to have concerns that changes to treaty language didn't go far enough. Fueling those suspicions is the fact that the treaty was negotiated under the auspices of the United Nations, a frequent target of Helms' criticism.

On a separate front, environmentalists, developers and their allies are battling over efforts to exclude certain parcels of land from protected status under the Coastal Barrier Resources Act. The 1982 legislation now forbids federal subsidies for coastal protection and post-storm disaster relief on approximately 1.2 million acres of coastal tracts on the Atlantic and Gulf coasts and the Great Lakes.

The dispute was triggered last year when Rep. Tillie Fowler, R-Fla., included language in omnibus parks legislation to lift a ban on federal flood insurance for eight flood-prone areas of Florida, including beachfront property at New Smyrna Beach that was targeted for high-rise condominiums.

The Coast Alliance, a Washington-based environmental group, and several other conservation organizations blocked the changes by filing a lawsuit, contending the move was a backdoor attempt by developers to grab more land for high-density development. But officials hardly think the chapter is closed. "They obviously want to free up some of the more attractive parcels and use argu-

ments like there was a policy mistake or technical mistake in the way the law was applied," says Jacqueline Savitz, executive director of the Coast Alliance.

Fowler says developers already had installed roads, sewers and water lines on the New Smyrna property by the time the law was passed in 1982 and insists the exemption wouldn't open up more pristine coastal property for development. She adds the exemptions she sought covered land that only totaled 36.4 acres. [19]   ■

The federal government plans to keep replenishing the 10 miles of shoreline in Ocean City, Md., over the next 50 years at an estimated cost of $500 million.

OUTLOOK

Ending the Cycle

In Louisiana, officials spend as much as $40 million a year trying to replenish some of the 35 square miles of coastal wetlands that are lost each year to erosion and rising seas. However, figuring out precisely where to shore up the marshy coast is difficult because few accurate maps exist

showing where the water's edge was even a decade ago. [20]

Critics say the situation shows that government planners have only vague ideas about how coastal flooding occurs and how extensively it leads to land loss. Climate records that NOAA and FEMA use to calculate hypothetical "storms of the century" and establish 100-year flood plains are often only 50-100 years old. Yet they define the parameters for development in the nation's fastest-growing regions; federal flood-plain maps are consulted for 15 million mortgage transactions a year.

Slowly, some agencies are launching flood mitigation efforts in an attempt to end the disaster-rebuild-disaster cycle the government long has been accused of promoting. FEMA this year launched "Project Impact," a voluntary effort designed to urge communities to reduce life and property damage by studying local zoning and building codes and consulting existing flood maps. It hopes to sign up one community per state by September.

The agency also is responding to a 1994 mandate from Congress to better evaluate coastal erosion hazards. FEMA and the H. John Heinz III Center for Science, Economics and the Environment in Washington are exploring how dynamic coastline changes can be factored into the sale of national flood insurance policies.

Longtime observers say such scattered efforts probably won't discourage the continued development at

Continued on p. 740

Mystery of the 'Cell From Hell'

The small fish began washing up by the thousands on the banks of Chesapeake Bay tributaries last summer bearing distinct red sores and lesions. Swimmers and watermen who came in contact with them soon reported nausea, headaches and, in some cases, memory loss. Within weeks, Maryland authorities declared a health advisory and closed three affected waterways. State and federal scientists began looking for a cause.

The culprit turned out to be the so-called "cell from hell," *Pfiesteria piscicida*, a microorganism that feeds off excessive amounts of nitrogen and phosphorus entering rivers in fertilizers, including manure. The bizarre microbe appears in up to two-dozen biological forms, at least three of them toxic, and symbolizes a new kind of pollution plaguing coastal waterways.

For decades, water pollution was something people could easily see or smell. In 1987, numerous East Coast beaches were closed after raw sewage, hypodermic needles and toxic waste washed ashore. But scientists say those obvious forms of pollution are perhaps less of a threat than increasing amounts of runoff from farms and cities that can foul the wide, shallow estuaries where rivers meet oceans. The new phenomenon is termed non-point-source pollution because contaminants usually end up long distances from their original source.

The U.S. Environmental Protection Agency (EPA) estimates that 32 billion gallons a day of runoff from farms, factories and urban streets and parking lots send nutrients into the water, creating algae blooms that suck oxygen from water and suffocate fish. The nutrients also feed periodic outbreaks of *Pfiesteria*, which was discovered after a series of massive fishkills in North Carolina's Neuse River in the 1980s.

Runoff also contaminates sediment in brackish waterways. A three-volume EPA report released to Congress in January estimated that the sediment in 7 percent of U.S. watersheds, including bays and estuaries, is so seriously tainted that eating fish from those waters would threaten human and animal health. Sites of greatest contamination were clustered around big cities and low-lying regions affected by discharges from farms.[1]

The findings are putting new pressure on agriculture. Farmers spreading fertilizer in Iowa and other Midwestern states are being blamed for disrupting the fishing industry in the Gulf of Mexico, a thousand miles away. Runoff washes down the Mississippi River and creates dead zones, killing slow-moving creatures like crabs while sending more mobile fish and shrimp off for cleaner waters hundreds of miles away.[2]

Some states are tightening regulations. In the wake of last summer's *Pfiesteria* scare, Maryland in January unveiled a multimillion-dollar plan to control nutrient runoff from agriculture, including large poultry-processing operations on the state's Eastern Shore. The state was particularly stung because the microbe wasn't previously known to exist in the Chesapeake Bay watershed. Publicity surrounding the outbreak sparked consumer reluctance to buy fish, resulting in $40 million in lost sales to Maryland's seafood industry. Ironically, the outbreak was largely confined to menhaden, an oily, herringlike fish that travels in very large schools but is not typically consumed by humans.

North Carolina for the first time this summer will close waterways hit by fish kills. Virginia state environmental workers this spring began a $7.7. million water-monitoring program to spot signs of *Pfiesteria* and other toxic microbes.

Pfisteria is showing signs of reappearing this summer. An estimated half-million menhaden had died along the Neuse River as of early August, and Maryland officials reported finding lesions on a small number of fish in Chesapeake tributaries.

The Clinton administration has responded by proposing a new clean-water initiative; calling for improved monitoring of non-point-source pollutants like nitrogen and phosphorous; and the placement of buffer zones along 2 million miles of streams to trap fertilizer and manure. White House Chief of Staff Erskine Bowles, a North Carolinian, in August arranged a $365,000 grant to officials in his home state to help rapid-response teams respond to the latest fish kill and is trying to speed up the awarding of $221 million in U.S. Department of Agriculture funds to help pay the state's farmers for field buffers and other pollution controls.[3]

Agriculture interests say they will comply with tougher regulations but suspect they're being unfairly singled out. Some note urban runoff does as much harm to coastal ecosystems, clogging basins with partially treated sewage and silt that kills vital organisms.

"The science with *Pfiesteria* is still catching up. You can't make a quick decision on the fate of agriculture based on *Pfisteria*," says James Perdue, chief executive officer of Salisbury, Md.-based Perdue Farms, Inc., the nation's second-largest poultry producer.[4]

Rep. Wayne T. Gilchrest, R-Md., who represents the largely agricultural Eastern Shore, where the outbreak occurred, says the problem is serious and "speeded up by at least two years" the move to control farm runoff.

"I believe [Perdue] understands that this problem is real and that we are going to have to deal with it, with the industry's cooperation or without it," Gilchrest says.

---

[1] See "The Incidence and Severity of Sediment Contamination in Surface Waters of the United States," U.S. Environmental Protection Agency.

[2] See Perry Beeman, "Engulfed by Deadly Chemicals Farm Runoff Blamed for Pollution off Gulf Coast," *The Des Moines Register*, May 24, 1998, p. 1.

[3] See Joby Warrick, "States Brace for Fish Kills After 'Cell From Hell' Returns in N.C.," *The Washington Post*, Aug. 6, 1998, p. A2.

[4] Quoted in Tom Horton, "Issue of Agricultural Runoff Isn't Going Away, Perdue says," *The Baltimore Sun*, Oct. 20, 1997, p. 1A.

Continued from p. 738

the shore, though they may encourage tougher local building restrictions. But they note the era of balanced budgets and greater concern for the coast is at least making some communities reconsider federal handouts for coastal protection. Avalon, N.J., has spent $8.6 million in local tax dollars to rebuild its five-mile beach after storms. Residents of Dewey Beach, Del., voted to tax themselves to pay for a $1 million beach protection program.

In Massachusetts, Cape Cod voters this November will be asked to endorse a 3 percent property-tax increase to raise money to buy undeveloped land and protect the coast from overbuilding. Similar measures are being proposed in New Jersey, Connecticut, Georgia and the eastern end of Long Island. [21]

"Since World War II, people have marched to the beach, and we've used the greatest technological capabilities we can harness to control nature," says geologist Leatherman. "We're on a collision course. The sea keeps on coming, and properties and buildings are going to be lost." ∎

Notes

[1] For a more comprehensive overview, see National Oceanic and Atmospheric Administration, "Year of the Ocean: Discussion Papers," a series of background issue papers published by various federal agencies in March 1998 for the National Ocean Conference in Monterey, Calif., U.S. Government Printing Office Document 1998/432-031.

[2] For background, see Rodman D. Griffin, "Threatened Coastlines," *The CQ Researcher*, Feb. 7, 1992, pp. 97-120.

[3] Quoted in Craig Whitlock, "Flooded With Generosity," *Raleigh* (N.C.) *News and Observer*, Nov. 9, 1997, p. A20.

[4] Beth Millemann, "Storm on the Horizon," Coast Alliance and National Wildlife Federation, September 1989.

FOR MORE INFORMATION

If you would like to have this CQ Researcher updated, or need more information about this topic, please call CQ Custom Research. Special rates for CQ subscribers. (202) 887-8600 or (800) 432-2250, ext. 600, or

Federal Emergency Management Agency, 500 C St., S.W., Washington, D.C. 20472; (202) 646-4600; www.fema.gov. FEMA assists state and local governments in preparing for and responding to emergencies, including hurricanes and major coastal storms. Oversees the national flood insurance program.

Coast Alliance, 215 Pennsylvania Ave., S.E., Washington, D.C. 20003 (202); 546-9554; www.coastalliance.org. A nonprofit environmental group founded in 1979 to combat development pressure and pollution on American coastlines.

American Littoral Society, Sandy Hook, Highlands, N.J. 07732; (732) 291-0055. Encourages the study and conservation of marine life and habitat, with a special emphasis on coastal zones.

Coastal States Organization, 444 N. Capitol St., N.W., Suite 322, Washington, D.C. 20001; (202) 508-3860. Represents governors of U.S. coastal states, territories and commonwealths on management of coastal, Great Lakes and marine resources.

American Coastal Coalition, 1667 K St., N.W., Suite 480, Washington, D.C. 20006; (202) 775-1796; www.coastalcoalition.org. Founded in 1996 to fight President Clinton's proposed cuts to beach nourishment programs, this organization lobbies for more federal aid for beachfront communities and property owners.

[5] Op-Ed piece circulated by FEMA to newspapers in July 1997, responding to criticisms of the program by environmental journalist James Bovard.

[6] Quoted in Craig Whitlock, "FEMA to Review its Aid to Risky Coastal Areas," *Raleigh* (N.C.) *News and Observer*, Dec. 10, 1997, p. A1.

[7] See David Bush, Orrin Pilkey and William Neal, *Living by the Rules of the Sea* (1996).

[8] See Tom Horton, "Nourishing Beaches Ad Infinitum," *The Baltimore Sun*, Feb. 13, 1998, p. 2B.

[9] See Laurence Arnold, "White House Tries Again to Halt Sand-Pumping Programs," *The Associated Press*, March 7, 1998.

[10] Quoted in Niraj Warikoo, "Debate Pumped Up Over Sand Fill Plans," *Newsday*, Dec. 12, 1997, p. A57.

[11] See Robert Hanley, "As Beaches Erode, a Debate On Who'll Pay For Repairs," *The New York Times*, April 20, 1998, p. A1.

[12] See Orrin Pilkey and Katherine Dixon, *The Corps and the Shore* (1996).

[13] For background, see *Congress and the Nation*, Vol. V, 1977-1980, Congressional Quarterly (1981), pp. 565-566.

[14] For background see Mary H. Cooper, "Global Warming Update," *The CQ Researcher*, Nov. 1, 1996, pp. 961-984.

[15] For background, see Stephen Leatherman, *Barrier Island Handbook* (1988).

[16] See Kenneth Jost, "Property Rights," *The CQ Researcher*, June 16, 1995, pp. 513-536.

[17] See Allan Freedman, "Defying Administration, Panel Boosts Water Spending, Criticizes Nuclear Regulation," *CQ Weekly*, June 6, 1998, p. 1534.

[18] See Thomas Lippman, "For Sea Treaty, It's Helms or High Water," *The Washington Post*, July 13, 1998, p. A4.

[19] See Krys Fluker, "Lawsuit Brought Against Amendment That Excludes Coastal Development from Environmental Legislation," *News-Journal* (Daytona Beach, Fla.), June 17, 1997.

[20] See Mike Dunne, "Disappearing Louisiana: Computers Aid State in Battle Against its Receding Coastline," *The Advocate* (Baton Rouge, La.), March 8, 1998, p. 1B.

[21] Fred Bayles, "Cape Cod Fighting for Its Soul," *USA Today*, Aug. 18, 1998, p. A6.

Bibliography

Selected Sources Used

Books

Pilkey, Orrin, and Katharine Dixon, *The Corps and the Shore*, Island Press, 1996.
Two Duke University coastal geologists offer a critical history of the U.S. Army Corps of Engineers and shoreline development in the United States and advocate a strategy of retreat from the advancing ocean.

Millemann, Beth, *And Two If By Sea*, Coast Alliance Inc., 1988.
A guide to coastal management, including numerous facts and figures on coastal pollution and the dangers of overdevelopment. The book highlights states with model legislation in specific areas, such as ocean dumping.

Lencek, Lena, and Gideon Bosker, *The Beach: The History of Paradise on Earth*, Viking Penguin, 1998.
Two scholars of popular culture explore how the allure of the ocean transformed 19th-century American society and grew into a commercial and recreational phenomenon.

Safina, Carl, *Song for the Blue Ocean*, Henry Holt, 1997.
A biologist-writer takes readers on a global tour of the world's oceans, arguing that the unregulated global economy is placing enormous pressures on the sea.

Hinrichsen, Don, *Coastal Waters of the World: Trends, Threats and Strategies*, Island Press, 1998.
A journalist-environmental consultant surveys 13 coastal areas around the world and projects future conflicts between development and nature.

Articles

Nash, Betty Joyce, "Shrinking Beaches, Swelling Problems," *Cross Sections* (quarterly of the Federal Reserve Bank of Richmond), Vol. 13, No. 2 (summer 1996).
An overview of questions arising from erosion along the Atlantic coast, including what prevention strategies can work, and who should pay.

Whitlock, Craig, "Flooded With Generosity," *Raleigh* (N.C.) *News and Observer*, Nov. 9, 1997.
Lavish amounts of federal disaster aid helped rebuild North Carolina's coast after Hurricane Fran smashed into the state in 1996. But critics say the subsidies were a waste of money and send the wrong message to developers.

Garland, Greg, "Down The Drain," *The Advocate* (Baton Rouge, La.), Oct. 19-21, 1997.
A three-part series examines how the federal flood insurance program spends more than homes are worth to repair flood damage.

Carr, Edward, "The Sea: A Second Fall," *The Economist*, May 23-29, 1998.
A survey article argues that while the sea once seemed infinite in its bounty, it now is suffering from overfishing and pollution and needs care and maintenance.

Haggerty, Maryann, "A Gathering Storm Over Assateague: The Forces of Beach Erosion, Tourist Trade at Odds on Island," *The Washington Post*, May 9, 1998.
Two winter storms that battered Assateague Island, Md., last winter raise questions about how to deal with the relationship of man and nature at the edge of the sea.

Weber, Peter, "It Comes Down to the Coasts," *World Watch*, Vol. 7, No. 2 (March/April 1994).
A Worldwatch Institute research associate argues that society will have to begin altering patterns of settlement and development to avoid overstressing coastlines.

Reports

Houston, James, "Beachfill Performance," *Shore and Beach*, July 1991, pp. 15-24.
A U.S. Army Corps of Engineers coastal engineer outlines reasons periodic beach renourishment is a successful way to protect shores with few accompanying environmental problems.

Pilkey, Orrin, "The Engineering of Sand," *Journal of Geological Education*, 1989, Vol. 37, pp. 308-311.
Duke University geologist Pilkey presents a study of East Coast barrier islands demonstrating that parameters used to design beach-replenishment projects don't work and that predictions of durability are incorrect.

Leatherman, Stephen, "Barrier Island Handbook," University of Maryland Coastal Publications Series, 1988.
Geologist Leatherman presents a thorough overview of how barrier islands behave in response to development and natural erosion, as well as recreational impacts and development potential.

The Next Step

Additional information from UMI's Newspaper & Periodical Abstracts™ database

Beach Replenishment

"Sand Subsidies Costly, Futile," *USA Today*, June 2, 1998, p. A12.

Waterfront communities across the nation increasingly are looking to Washington to shore up disappearing beaches. Since 1965, the federal government has pumped out more than $1 billion to replenish more than 1,300 eroding beaches — often to see them wash back into the sea. Local communities and states typically chip in only 35 percent of the cost of any project.

"Sandy Hook Seeks Pipeline To Help Fight Beach Erosion," *The New York Times*, Jan. 3, 1998, p. B5.

The federal government has been asked to approve a proposal for the first major replenishment of Sandy Hook's beaches since 1989. Securing federal funds to combat beach erosion is a tough sell, because the Gateway National Recreation Area at Sandy Hook is only one of 365 units in the federal system. The cost of replenishment can range from $12 million to $20 million, a major chunk of the Department of the Interior's $60 million annual budget for the National Park Service.

Hanley, Robert, "As Beaches Erode, a Debate On Who'll Pay For Repairs," *The New York Times*, April 20, 1998, p. A1.

The federal government, which shorefront residents have always considered their savior, now is balking at playing a major financial role in the restoration of beaches. For the federal fiscal year starting Oct. 1, the Office of Management and Budget has earmarked $3.7 million for the Army Corps of Engineers to rebuild beaches in New Jersey and on Long Island. Coastal business owners and local officials and their allies on Capitol Hill want $50.6 million to continue existing beach projects and to study the need for new ones.

Luoma, Jon R., "Oceanfront Battlefront," *Audubon*, July 1998, pp. 50-56.

Extraordinary measures are being taken to keep beaches and coastal towns from being swallowed up by the sea. The author examines how far people should go to protect the land and who should foot the bill for the work.

McLaughlin, Jeff, "Coastline Ebb, Flow Mapped in Study," *The Boston Globe*, June 15, 1997, p. W1.

Massachusetts' Coastal Zone Management office published a landmark study in June 1997 of the changes that have occurred over the past 150 years along the state's tidal shorelines.

Flood Insurance

"A Bargain in Flood Insurance; Federal Discount Could Benefit Many Residents of Region," *Los Angeles Times*, Nov. 17, 1997, p. B4.

It's well-known that certain Southern California areas are at higher risk of flooding. In Los Angeles County, for example, parts of Long Beach, Lynwood and Montebello have been on the federal government's special flood hazard area maps since the early 1980s. In Orange County, the vital but unfinished Santa Ana River Flood Control Project is designed to protect what has long been considered one of the most vulnerable flood plains west of the Mississippi River.

Edwards, Brian, and Don Hunt, "High and Dry; The Right Flood Insurance Can Help You Keep Your Head Above Water," *Chicago Tribune*, May 8, 1998, p. 1.

Available through most home or auto insurance agents, flood insurance is underwritten by the National Flood Insurance Program, a part of the Federal Emergency Management Agency. Traditional homeowners' and renters' insurance will not cover damage caused by overland flooding — a fact that is learned too late by hundreds of people each year. By federal law, homes in designated flood plains must have federal flood insurance as part of their mortgage loan. A flood plain is any area that has experienced flooding in the past, or any area that may not have flooded before but could in the future due to certain changes in the land structure, such as new property development.

Hilmes, Marsha, "Girding for Floods," *The Denver Post*, Sept. 7, 1997, p. F1.

Communities across the country have been participating in mitigation activities for years to try to prevent damages from flooding and other natural disasters. Mitigation entails actions or activities designed to help protect the citizens of a community. For example, since 1990 Fort Collins has had an education and outreach program focusing on flooding. Activities associated with this program include: Flood Awareness Week with informational displays at the Public Library and City Hall, sending special mailers to all floodplain residents and to members of the Board of Realtors and publishing flood-related articles in a newsletter that goes to all utility customers.

Tharpe, Gene, "Flood Defense Needs More Than Umbrella," *Atlanta Journal-Constitution*, March 29, 1998, p. R8.

When creeks and rivers start rising and cause millions of dollars in flood damage, as they did this month in Georgia, some homeowners start wondering about buying flood insurance to protect their homes. Those who rely on their regular homeowners insurance policy to cover flood damages normally will be disappointed. "A homeowners insurance policy for traditional site-built homes does not provide coverage for flood damage, although it does cover several other types of water damage," said David Colmans of the Georgia Insurance Information Institute.

Government Involvement

"U.S. Coastline Calamities Under Scrutiny," *New Orleans Times-Picayune*, Feb. 14, 1998, p. A2.

The National Oceanic and Atmospheric Administration, troubled by declining fisheries and rampant coastal development, is beginning an effort to identify the problems that afflict America's shoreline and marine ecosystems. "There is an urgent need to nail down the causes and extent of the problems that plague our coastal areas so solutions can be found," NOAA Administrator D. James Baker said Friday in announcing plans for the "State of the Coast" study.

Barnum, Alex, "Legislature to Consider Flood of Coastal Protection Bills; Effort Called Strongest in 25 Years," *San Francisco Chronicle*, March 24, 1997, p. A17.

A bipartisan coalition of coastal state legislators has introduced a wave of bills that is the most ambitious effort to reform California's coastal and marine laws since voters created the Coastal Commission in 1972. That commission regulates development and ensures public access to the coastline. The package includes bills that would strip regulatory control over fishing from the Department of Fish and Game and give it to a newly created commission, create a comprehensive monitoring program of coastal water pollution and establish marine sanctuaries to protect marine life.

Leitner, Peter M., "A Bad Treaty Returns: The Case of the Law of the Sea Treaty," *World Affairs,* winter 1998, pp. 134-150.

In 1982, President Reagan announced that the United States would not become a signatory to the United Nations Convention on the Law of the Sea (UNC-LOS). The author discusses how U.S. participation in the UNC-LOS was a giant step forward in the continuing delegation of U.S. foreign policy to the U.N.

Sea Walls

"Our Sandy Sentinels," *New Orleans Times-Picayune*, April 16, 1998, p. B6.

There are many avenues to trying to counter Louisiana's serious problem of coastal erosion and wetlands loss, but perhaps the most direct method is to improve and maintain the "sea wall." The sea wall in this instance is not man-made, but nature's line of barrier islands. A new federal-state project will rebuild the losses over the rest of this year under the Breaux Act, named for Sen. John Breaux, D - La., which provides money for anti-erosion projects. With the feds paying 85 percent and the state 15 percent of the $28.5 million cost, the project will pump more than 11 million

cubic yards of sand from Terrebonne Bay to bolster three of the islands: Trinity, Whiskey and East.

Reid, Alexander, "As Waves Lash, the Seawalls Crumble; Towns Tossed by Rising Costs of Repairs," *The Boston Globe*, Feb. 15, 1998, p. W1.

The wave-battered sea wall along Oceanside Drive, near Sand Hills in Scituate, collapsed last month, opening a breach wide enough to drive several trucks through. Oceanside Drive's sea wall is one of several decrepit barriers along Scituate's 20 miles of coast, and all are a serious worry, said the public works director, Anthony Antoniello. In Hull, where the town is trying to pressure the state to fund repairs to the Point Allerton sea wall, Town Manager Philip Lemnios said, "Most of these walls are of the same vintage, and they're falling apart at the same time. They're at the end of their useful lives."

Storms

Argetsinger, Amy, "After Another Ocean Storm, a New Wave of Expense," *The Washington Post*, Feb. 22, 1998, p. B1.

Even in a stormless season, coastal officials spend millions in public funds annually trying to hang onto the beachfront that the ocean washes away. By the mid-1980s, years of erosion had sent the waters of the Atlantic rushing within 20 feet of Ocean City, Md., homes and hotels at high tide. In Bethany Beach, Del., two hurricanes left a gray, pitted beach so narrow that tourists had to squeeze between boardwalk pilings to find a sandy spot to sit. The most ambitious fortification project was undertaken in Ocean City. In 1988 engineers spent $14 million in state and local funds pumping 2.5 million cubic yards of sand from the ocean bottom to the beach.

Mogil, H. Michael, "Nor'easters; Ill Winds of the Atlantic Seaboard," *The Washington Post*, Feb. 12, 1997, p. H1.

The last week of December brought record-breaking winter storms to the Pacific Northwest. They are Nor'easters, known for their strong winds that blow from the northeast. As these winds blow ashore from the North Atlantic, they often bring high tides and violent waves, causing significant coastal flooding and beach erosion. Just ask the folks in Ocean City, Md. Almost every year there, nor'easters keep the Army Corps of Engineers and local officials busy dredging sand from offshore to replenish the beach.

Vigue, Doreen Iudica, "With Seas Cresting 16 Feet Above Normal, Breakers, Sand Dunes, and Seawalls Were No Match for the Swollen, Raging Atlantic," *The Boston Globe*, Feb. 6, 1998, p. B4.

For residents of Revere, Winthrop, Scituate and Hull, the record-breaking snowfall from the Blizzard of '78 was almost an afterthought. The wind and the waves were their greatest tormentors, combining to decimate 340 houses, damage 6,000 others and take the lives of the five-man crew of a Gloucester pilot boat, a 5-year-old girl and a 62-year-old man.

Back Issues

Great Research on Current Issues Starts Right Here.
Recent topics covered by The CQ Researcher are listed below.
Now available on the Web
For information, call (800) 432-2250 ext. 279 or (202) 887-6279.

If you would like to have any of these CQ Researchers updated, or need more information about these topics, please call CQ Custom Research. Special rates for CQ subscribers. (202) 887-8600 or (800) 432-2250, ext. 600, or E-mail Custom.Research@cq.com

APRIL 1997
Declining Crime Rates
The FBI Under Fire
Gender Equity in Sports
Space Program's Future

MAY 1997
The Stock Market
The Cloning Controversy
Expanding NATO
The Future of Libraries

JUNE 1997
FDA Reform
China After Deng
Line-Item Veto
Breast Cancer

JULY 1997
Transportation Policy
Executive Pay
School Choice Debate
Aggressive Driving

AUGUST 1997
Age Discrimination
Banning Land Mines
Children's Television
Evolution vs. Creationism

SEPTEMBER 1997
Caring for the Dying
Mental Health Policy
Mexico's Future
Youth Fitness

OCTOBER 1997
Urban Sprawl in the West
Diversity in the Workplace
Teacher Education
Contingent Work Force

NOVEMBER 1997
Renewable Energy
Artificial Intelligence
Religious Persecution
Roe v. Wade at 25

DECEMBER 1997
Whistleblowers
Castro's Next Move
Gun Control Standoff
Regulating Nonprofits

JANUARY 1998
Foster Care Reform
IRS Reform
The Black Middle Class
U.S.-British Relations

FEBRUARY 1998
Patients' Rights
Deflation Fears
Caring for the Elderly
The New Corporate Philanthropy

MARCH 1998
Israel at 50
The Federal Judiciary
Drinking on Campus
The Economics of Recycling

APRIL 1998
Biology and Behavior
Liberal Arts Education
Income Inequality
High-Tech Labor Shortage

MAY 1998
Census 2000
Child-Care Options
Alzheimer's Disease
U.S.-Russian Relations

JUNE 1998
Student Journalism
Antitrust Policy
Environmental Justice
Sleep Deprivation

JULY 1998
Encouraging Teen Abstinence
Population and the Environment
Democracy in Asia
Baby Boomers at Midlife

AUGUST 1998
Oil Production in the 21st Century
Flexible Work Arrangements

Back issues are available for $5.00 (subscribers) or $10.00 (non-subscribers). Quantity discounts apply to orders over 10. To order, call Congressional Quarterly Customer Service at (202) 887-8621.

Binders are available for $18.00. To order call 1-800-638-1710. Please refer to stock number 648.

Future Topics

▶ *Student Activism*

▶ *Organic Farming*

▶ *Cancer Treatments*

THE

![CQ logo] Researcher

PUBLISHED BY CONGRESSIONAL QUARTERLY INC.

Student Activism

Are student protests still alive?

T
hree decades ago, student protesters by the hundreds of thousands marched for civil rights and an end to the Vietnam War. Today's activists say they are just as passionate about change as their predecessors, fighting for causes ranging from gay rights and environmental protection to affirmative action and workers' rights. But they complain that they do not get the media attention they deserve, leaving the impression that students today are apathetic. Many of today's activists say they have been inspired to activism by their professors and that teachers should encourage students to care about and press for social and political change. But others say that such behavior is inherently coercive, since professors grade students and thus have power over them.

| ^C_Q | **August 28, 1998 • Volume 8, No. 32 • Pages 745-760** |

Formerly Editorial Research Reports

CQ Researcher

August 28, 1998
Volume 8, No.32

EDITOR
Sandra Stencel

MANAGING EDITOR
Thomas J. Colin

STAFF WRITERS
Adriel Bettelheim
Mary H. Cooper
Kenneth Jost
Kathy Koch
David Masci

PRODUCTION EDITOR
Melissa Hall

EDITORIAL ASSISTANT
Laura S. Cavender

PUBLISHED BY
Congressional Quarterly Inc.

CHAIRMAN
Andrew Barnes

VICE CHAIRMAN
Andrew P. Corty

PRESIDENT AND PUBLISHER
Robert W. Merry

EXECUTIVE EDITOR
David Rapp

Bibliographic records and abstracts included in The Next Step section of this publication are the copyrighted material of UMI, and are used with permission.

The CQ Researcher (ISSN 1056-2036). Formerly Editorial Research Reports. Published weekly, except Jan. 2, May 29, July 3, Oct. 30, by Congressional Quarterly Inc., 1414 22nd St., N.W., Washington, D.C. 20037. Annual subscription rate for libraries, businesses and government is $340. Additional rates furnished upon request. Periodicals postage paid at Washington, D.C., and additional mailing offices. POSTMASTER: Send address changes to The CQ Researcher, 1414 22nd St., N.W., Washington, D.C. 20037.

COVER: STUDENT PROTESTERS FROM THE UNIVERSITY OF CALIFORNIA SIT IN FRONT OF THE FEDERAL BUILDING IN LOS ANGELES ON OCT. 23, 1996, TO PROTEST PROPOSITION 209, ENDING AFFIRMATIVE ACTION IN CALIFORNIA COLLEGE ADMISSIONS. (AP PHOTO/BEN MARGOT)

Student Activism

BY DAVID MASCI

THE ISSUES

To student activist John Kim, this is not the time for complacency. The Hunter College junior says students have as much, if not more, to be concerned about today than they did during the Vietnam protests of the 1960s.

"There are so many things happening that we need to be aware of," he says, pointing to income inequality, racial discrimination and police brutality, to name a few. "The work we're doing today is just as or more important than it ever was."

Kim's current crusade is against efforts to eliminate remedial courses at Hunter and other City University of New York (CUNY) campuses.* Kim and other students say that the plan is elitist and will disproportionately affect minority and other working-class students. [1]

"They are already on an uneven playing field, and this would just make it even worse," he says.

Kim and other Hunter undergrads have been fighting the plan since it was announced in February. As a leading member of the Student Liberation Action Movement (SLAM!), Kim has helped organize protest marches and education campaigns and worked to form alliances with other groups on and off campus.

"We've held a march and rally outside every meeting of the CUNY Board [of Trustees] since this began in February," he says. One such event, in April, attracted 800 protesters. And at the May board meeting, 23 activists were arrested for acts of civil disobedience. "I wasn't there," Kim says, almost apologetically, "because I had to work that day."

Today's undergraduates were not

even born when their parents marched and occupied buildings in protests that erupted all over the nation during the late 1960s. And for most Americans, young or old, "student protest" is still synonymous with the '60s and issues like civil rights and opposition to the Vietnam War. But Kim and thousands like him are keeping activism alive on college campuses across the country. *(See story, p. 752.)*

Activists complain that the media give scant attention to their activities, leaving the impression that students today are apathetic. "The media in the 1960s were much more [interested in student activism] than they are today," Kim says. "I mean, they basically ignore us now."

Yet many activists say they are addressing a host of issues ranging from environmental protection and gay rights to affirmative action and workers' rights. [2]

"There are many more pockets of activism today than there were back then," says Bill Capowski, executive director of the Center for Campus Organizing, in Cambridge, Mass. Capowski and others say that the diversity of causes makes it harder to focus the nation's attention on one or two important struggles, as students did decades ago over issues like civil rights and Vietnam.

Another reason students are generally perceived as apathetic, Kim and others say, is that many people assume that someone has to work within the traditional two-party system in order to effect change. "[Students] are cynical about tra-

ditional politics, and everyone equates that cynicism with apathy," says Anthony Samu, president of the U.S. Student Association. Instead, Samu says, students today are often very involved, but on single issues like human rights in Myanmar (formerly Burma), rather than Republican or Democratic politics.

But others argue that students today really are much less politically active than were their predecessors 30 years ago. "The level of student interest in politics and political and social activism is much less [today] than it was in the '60s," says Steven Kelman, a professor of public management at Harvard University's Kennedy School of Government. This assessment is backed by polls that show a significant decrease in political interest among students.

One reason for student apathy, Kelman and others argue, is that today's issues are narrower and not as clear-cut as, say, Vietnam was. Hence today's causes do not attract broad support among members of the student body. "Things were clearer and more well thought through back then," says Carolyn Alessio, a former university professor who has written about student activism.

Finally, observers note, there is a certain chic associated with being cool and detached that seems to pervade much of student life on campus. "People want to avoid being perceived as boring and having passion — about politics or anything," says Michael Kazin, a professor of history at American University.

But if students today are apathetic, should the university inspire them to be more passionate and committed about issues? In particular, should professors try to encourage activism on campus? *(See "At Issue," p. 755)*

Many students and teachers say "Yes," arguing that professors should reveal their convictions in the classroom as long as there is no attempt to coerce students into action. "Students should be encouraged to take a look at non-

---

*The proposal, supported by New York Mayor Rudolph W. Giuliani and approved by CUNY's Board of Trustees, aims to raise academic standards by barring students who do not meet English and math requirements, instead of admitting them and requiring them to do remedial catch-up work.

A World of Student Activism

On May 21, President Suharto, who had ruled — largely as a dictator — for 32 years, was forced to hand over power to his vice president, B.J. Habibie. Thousands of students from all over the country had been occupying the parliament building in Jakarta for three days, demanding Suharto's resignation. The size and ferocity of the protests finally convinced the military and other powers that the president had to go before order could be restored to the world's fourth most populous country. "They were really the vanguard of this movement for political reform," says John Dori, a research associate at the Heritage Foundation's Center for Asian Studies. [1] Ironically, it also was students who helped put Suharto in power in 1966.

Indonesia's influential student activism is not unique. In 1968, students all over Europe (including some Eastern-bloc countries) demonstrated against the post-war conservatism and traditionalism that was then the norm. And while they did not succeed in toppling any governments (they came close in France) they did lead to a general relaxation of sexual and other mores.

Students have had even more success in the developing world. For instance, in 1979, students in Iran played an important part in forcing Shah Reza al Pahlevi from power. Likewise, they helped to bring down the leaders of the Philippines and South Korea in the mid-1980s, setting those countries on the road to democracy. And near the end of the decade, students helped topple the Communist regimes of Eastern Europe.

Even student failures have often been significant. The 1989 massacre of Chinese pro-democracy activists in Tienanmen Square has remained a potent symbol for dissidents around the world.

Today, in addition to Indonesia, university students have recently rallied in Myanmar, the Congo, Russia, France and Kenya, where they clashed with police after protesting higher university fees. In neighboring Congo (formerly Zaire), students have been protesting the rule of Laurent Kabila, the guerrilla leader who ousted long-time president Mobutu Sese-Seko in 1996.

Students in poor nations are an elite group and are often taken more seriously than their counterparts in richer nations in the West. "Many countries, especially in Asia, accord a high amount of respect to students," Dori says.

According to Dori and others, students will continue to be an engine for change throughout the world. "If change occurs in China or Vietnam," he says. "It is likely to be led by students and young professionals."

---

[1] For background, see Kenneth Jost, "Democracy in Asia," *The CQ Researcher*, July 24, 1998, pp. 625-648.

---

violent activism," says Marv Davidov, a human relations and history professor at St. Cloud State University in Minnesota, who takes his students to rallies.

Indeed, many students say that professors like Davidov have "inspired" them to think and take action when they might otherwise have remained apolitical. "As long as there is a light touch and no heavy-handed coercion, students will appreciate it," Capowski says.

In addition, Davidov and others say, professors should stop pretending to be objective and let students know how they think and feel about important issues. In fact, he argues, teachers who keep their opinions to themselves are deceiving students because "everyone has their own world view and that's going to filter into their lecture." Better to have things out in the open, he argues.

But others say that professors who encourage activism are abusing their authority. "Because students are de-pendent on you [for grades], they may not be acting of their free will when they follow you," says Kelman, who adds that such circumstances make a professor's urgings inherently coercive regardless of their intent.

Kelman and others also say that professors should strive to be objective even though it may not always be possible. "Professors need to maintain a certain detachment — explore a variety of points of view, but let the students make up their own minds," Alessio says. "It's ridiculous to say that because you can never be completely objective, you're giving up," Kelman adds.

Regardless of what teachers do, some undergraduates will inevitably find their way to one cause or another. "Because part of being young involves questioning, there will always be a natural constituency for activism on campus," Kelman says.

But while no one doubts that stu-dent activism did not end with Woodstock, there is disagreement over the size and role of campus activism today. As students, professors and others ponder the level and impact of student activism, here are some of the questions they are asking:

Are college students in the United States less politically active today than they were 30 years ago?

Every year, the Higher Education Research Institute at the University of California, Los Angeles (UCLA), surveys college freshmen around the country on a host of issues. In addition to questions about sex, marijuana and study habits, they are asked about their level of interest and involvement in politics.

In 1966, when the poll was first conducted, 58 percent of those who responded agreed that "keeping up to date with political affairs" was an important goal. [3] But since then there has been a decrease in levels of political interest. In 1997, only 27 percent of the freshmen surveyed put a high value on political awareness. [4]

Many academics and other observers say the survey bears out what they see happening on campus. "It's obvious to anyone who spends any time on a campus that there is a lot less student activism today than there was in the '60s," says American University's Kazin.

The Kennedy School's Kelman agrees. "[Student activism] is much more of a fringe phenomenon today, like tennis club or something like that," he says.

Kazin, Kelman and others say that there are a number of reasons for the apparent decline in student activism. To begin with, they say, in the 1960s, unlike today, there were only a few, big, unambiguous issues to rally around. "Issues like civil rights and the Vietnam War were morally uncomplicated," Kelman says.

In addition, Vietnam and civil rights also were appealing because they were national, affecting people throughout the country. "There was a greater sense of urgency about all of this back then," Kazin says. "I mean, people were dying in Vietnam."

By contrast, Kazin and others say, student activists today have latched onto a huge number of different and disparate causes, ranging from gay rights to human rights in Myanmar. As a result, those students who are active are spread very thin, making it that much harder to create a groundswell of support on campuses, as occurred in the 1960s (*see p. 753*).

Kelman agrees, adding that the narrowness of today's issues, makes them less appealing to broad sectors of the student body. And he says, there no longer is the sense of certitude about causes as there once was. "Today issues are more morally muddied," he says.

But the absence of powerful, unifying causes to rally around isn't the only reason that Kelman and other observers say campuses are no longer hotbeds of activism. Many students are simply not interested in the world around them, regardless of what is happening.

"Students today don't feel like political issues are relevant to their lives," says Linda Sax, a visiting professor of education at UCLA and director of the freshman survey last year.

Polls have charted declines in political participation and increased cynicism among Americans of all ages. But some say that the young are more disengaged than other sectors of society. Mark Edmundson, professor of English at the University of Virginia, has observed that today's youth culture discourages students from speaking out or caring too passionately about something. "That would be getting too loud or brash," he wrote recently. "For the pervading view is the cool, consumer perspective, where passion and strong admiration are forbidden." [5]

Kazin agrees that many students perceive politics and political involvement as boring. "There's this attitude typified by [comedian Jerry] Seinfeld: If it ain't hip, if it ain't clever, it's bull s—," he says.

But others argue that the current crop of students aren't apathetic or nihilistic. "Students today are as active as ever, just not in the way they were before," says Samu of the U.S. Student Association.

Samu blames the myth of student apathy on several misperceptions. To begin with, he argues, many people mistakenly see students as apathetic because they are much more cynical about traditional politics than they used to be. "There isn't the same focus on partisan politics the way there was in '68 or '72," he says, referring to student support for the presidential campaigns of anti-war candidates Eugene McCarthy and George McGovern.

Today, he says, there is a feeling among many in college that the Republican and Democratic parties don't stand for anything meaningful any more. "The two parties look the same to most students," Samu says. In addition, he says, the young don't see a place for themselves in the traditional political system. "Students don't see that they can effect lasting change working through the parties because they are both so tightly controlled by very wealthy special interests," he says.

Instead, Samu and others say, students often work on single issues — ranging from campus tuition hikes to human rights in Tibet — outside the mainstream political arena. Such matters may be less attention-getting, but it's just as meaningful as the activism of the past, they say. "There's still a lot of passion and commitment out there, but no focus," says Gwen Dungy, executive director of the National Association of Student Personnel Administrators. "It's much more diffuse."

As a result, society at large tends not to notice student activists. "You know, we don't have millions of people marching on big issues like Vietnam or civil rights anymore," Capowski says, "so people just assume we're not there."

And even issues that do attract a lot of student activists, such as the elimination of affirmative action in California, are generally ignored, especially by the press. "The mainstream press doesn't cover us well at all," Capowski says. "Even the progressive press doesn't do very much on it."

Indeed, according to Peter Drier, a politics professor at Occidental College, in Los Angeles, the press is more interested in student apathy than activism. In a recent article in *The Nation*, he notes that the *Los Angeles Times* readily reported about the UCLA freshman survey showing a lack of student interest in politics. "But a few weeks earlier," he writes, "the paper had failed to report on a successful protest campaign at Occidental, located about three miles from the Times building, in which students persuaded the college president, John Slaughter, who sits on the Atlantic Richfield [Corp.] board, to issue a public statement criticizing the oil giant's support for the military dictatorship in Myanmar." [6]

In addition to getting little or no press coverage, today's young activists say they must constantly fight what they see as the "myth of the '60s." They complain that millions of baby boomers have perpetuated the view that they were agents of sweeping societal change three decades ago and, moreover, unfairly compare their nostalgic, exaggerated memories of student activism with what their children are doing.

"We have this aging group that looks back at the '60s and '70s and thinks they changed the world," Samu says. "We look back and say, 'There wasn't as much change as you think.' "

Capowski agrees, arguing that every generation looks at succeeding ones and sees something wrong. "In the past, people thought the new generation of kids was less respectful," he says. "Today, boomers think kids are less idealistic or politically active." [7]

Comparisons with the 1960s are unfair on a number of levels, Copowski and others say. Not only are the memories of that era overly rosy, they contend, but the lives of many '60s-era students were easier. For one thing, Copowski says, fewer students had to work or worry about money, since college was significantly less expensive. But today, Dungy says, "Money is [a major] issue, and so students are under tremendous stress. There are great expectations, from themselves and their parents because they need to justify the cost."

As a result, Dungy and others say, students who might otherwise be more involved in activism barely have enough time to work and keep up with their classes. [8]

Should teachers encourage students to engage in political activism?

In spring 1997, Professor Davidov took a dozen students on a far-from-typical field trip. They traveled to Hopkins, Minn., to join a protest rally against Alliant, a division of the Honeywell Corp. that manufactures munitions for the military.

For Davidov, a self-described "lifetime activist," the event was one in a long string of non-violent protests. "I was with the Freedom Riders in 1961 in Mississippi,"

he says proudly. But for the students who accompanied him to Hopkins that day, it was a new experience. "Most of them have never been exposed to anything like this before, or even thought about [weapons] issues," he says.

Davidov points out that while his students are encouraged to attend rallies, no one is penalized for not going. "I tell them that if they want to disagree with me, that's fine: Let's hear what you have to say," he says.

Some students argue that professors like Davidov are performing a valuable service. "I've been inspired to action by a number of my teachers, and I'm grateful," says Samu of the U.S. Student Association. Capowski agrees, adding that "teachers should share their convictions . . . as long as there's not coercion involved."

But many others say that professors who encourage activism are stepping way out of line, even if they don't intend to coerce students. "For a teacher in a classroom to urge students to take a position on one side of a political issue is an abuse of authority, plain and simple," Harvard's Kelman says.

He points out that teachers have tremendous influence in the classroom, and not just because they're older, wiser and better educated than their students. "Because you're grading them, students are dependent on you," he says. Hence students who are "encouraged" by professors to do something may feel obligated to comply to earn a good grade. "This may be a bit of a stretch, but it's something akin to sexual harassment," he adds.

Dan Flynn, executive director of Accuracy in Academia, a conservative campus-watchdog group, agrees. "People are always talking about the potential for abuse when someone brings religion into the classroom," he says. "With politics, it's the same thing."

That doesn't mean that Kelman and Flynn don't see a place for political discussion in the classroom. There is a difference between balanced political discussion and "indoctrination," Flynn says. "It's one thing to talk about politics,"

Kelman adds, "but the role of education isn't to effect profound social change."

And, say opponents of teacher-inspired activism, the whole point of a university education is to teach people to think for themselves. "Teachers should raise important questions," Alessio says, "but never answer them."

But Davidov and others argue that professors, like journalists, cannot be objective and so should stop pretending that they are. "I've got a particular world view," he says. "Don't you think it's better to be up front about it, tell them where you're coming from?" he asks.

Davidov agrees with Kelman that teachers have a lot of power over their students. But, he argues, "If you don't identify where you are politically, then it's indoctrination."

"That's a real cop-out," Kelman replies. "To say that you can never achieve complete objectivity doesn't mean that you shouldn't strive for it. That's like saying that because I can't be Michaelangelo, I won't be an artist." ∎

BACKGROUND

Relighting the Spark

Decades before American independence, students at Harvard and Yale organized protests against disciplinary measures and other school policies not to their liking. [9]

Still, the first mass protest associated with university students did not arise until the 1930s. Economic deprivation caused by the Great Depression, coupled with the increasing likelihood of war in Europe, spawned socialist and peace movements on many campuses. In 1935, an estimated 185,000 students marched in anti-war rallies around the country. [10]

Continued on p. 751

Chronology

1930s-1950s
The first great wave of activism hits American campuses.

1935
An estimated 185,000 U.S. students march in anti-war rallies.

1941
The United States enters World War II, ending activism.

1952
The election of President Dwight D. Eisenhower ushers in an era of great prosperity and conformity.

• ———

1960-1972
The Civil Rights Movement and then the Vietnam War spark a new wave of campus activism.

1960
The first civil rights protests occur at black universities.

1963
President John F. Kennedy is assassinated.

August 1964
Gulf of Tonkin Resolution leads to an escalation of American involvement in Vietnam.

December 1964
Mario Savio, a leader of the Free Speech Movement at the University of California, Berkeley, makes his now famous speech, outlining the movement's goals.

1967
Draft law reforms end deferments for graduate students; campus protests follow.

January-May 1968
Anti-war demonstrations are held on campuses throughout the United States; students riot in Paris and other cities in Europe.

April 1970
President Richard M. Nixon orders the invasion of Cambodia, sparking campus protests.

May 1970
National Guardsmen at Kent State University in Ohio shoot and kill four student anti-war protesters.

1972
U.S. troops begin their withdrawal from Vietnam.

1973-Today
The end of the Vietnam War and an economic recession lead to a decline in student activism.

1973
The Arab oil embargo leads to a recession.

1975
South Vietnam falls to North Vietnam and the VietCong.

1980
Conservative icon Ronald Reagan is elected president.

1981
Protesters urge colleges to stop investing in South Africa.

1985
U.S. divestiture movement peaks.

1994
Rutgers University President Francis Laurence describes African-Americans as genetically disadvantaged, setting off a firestorm of student protests.

1998
Efforts to raise standards in New York City's City University system lead to student protests.

World War II virtually ended campus activism. Troop mobilization settled economic and political questions of the day and set the nation on a clear path. When the war ended in 1945, the student movement of the 1930s did not return. The prosperity and conformity of the late 1940s and '50s kept campuses relatively quiet.

It took the Civil Rights Movement of the late 1950s and early '60s to light the spark of student protest again. The first student protests took place in 1960 at a number of Southern universities and largely involved African-Americans, usually engaging in non-violent civil disobedience. But within a year, white students began joining the Freedom Rides, sit-ins and other activities aimed at fostering civil rights for black Americans.

By the mid-1960s, the focus of the Civil Rights Movement, both on and off campus, had shifted from integration to "black power." While many African-American students remained supportive, their white counterparts began to shift to other concerns. The first of the post-civil rights student causes to gain significant support on campus was the so-called Free Speech Movement.

It was launched in 1964 at the University of California, Berkeley, where students started protesting the university's policy prohibiting political organizing on campus. Small rallies against the ban quickly grew, culminating in a campus sit-in on

Where the Action Is

The following examples "prove activism and community service are alive and well on campus," according to *Mother Jones* magazine's fifth annual roundup of activism on campus:

❶ Duke University, Durham, N.C. In March, Duke announced it would no longer license its logo to manufacturers who operate sweatshops. The policy was proposed by the Duke chapter of Students Against Sweatshops.

❷ Spelman College, Atlanta, Ga. Spelman's longstanding tradition of activism includes a student-mentoring program that pairs first-graders from an Atlanta housing project with Spelman freshmen. Students remain mentors until graduation.

❸ University of Texas, Austin. Last fall, when a law professor told reporters that black and Mexican-American students couldn't compete academically with whites at "selective institutions," almost 5,000 UT students attended a protest rally, and hundreds occupied the law school.

❹ University of Wisconsin, Madison. When Republican Gov. Tommy Thompson appointed a new member to the university's Board of Regents who had contributed $10,000 to his campaign, students collected quarters from UW students to try to "buy" a seat for their own candidate.

❺ Roxbury Community College, Boston, Mass. Last May, students at this inner-city college presented Roxbury President Grace Brown with a list of 18 demands, including

such basic supplies as library books. Unconvinced by her assurances of help, eight members of the group took over an administrative office for 30 hours.

❻ College of the Atlantic, Bar Harbor, Maine. Last fall, students developed a proposal prohibiting the school from doing business with companies that trade with Myanmar.

❼ James Madison University, Harrisonburg, Va. Last year, instead of relaxing during holiday breaks, students conducted a health survey in Appalachia, worked at an AIDS hospice in New Orleans and even built houses in Uganda.

❽ University of North Carolina, Chapel Hill. UNC's Nike Awareness Campaign, started by a junior in response to the university's proposed $7 million deal with Nike, brought Nike CEO Phil Knight to the campus to listen to student recommendations regarding Nike's overseas labor record.

❾ Marquette University, Milwaukee, Wis. More than 2,400 students last year did everything from repainting homeless shelters to taking senior citizens to the zoo.

❿ Little Big Horn College, Crow Agency, Mont. Students at this two-year tribal college volunteer on the Crow Reservation: Education majors tutor schoolchildren, and bilingual business majors file tax returns for the non-English-speaking tribe members.

From "Top 10 Activist Schools," Mother Jones, *September/October 1998. Reprinted with permission.*

Dec. 2. Before a huge crowd, Mario Savio, a 21-year-old philosophy student, gave eloquent voice to the feelings of many. "There is a time," Savio said, "when the operation of the machine becomes so odious, makes you so sick at heart, that you can't take part; and you've got to put your bodies upon the gears and upon the wheels, upon the levers, upon all the apparatus, and you've got to make it stop." [11]

Savio and fellow members of the Free Speech Movement forced the university to back down. But more important, they inspired students around the country to begin similar actions. In addition, wrote Reginald E. Zelnik, a professor of history at Berkeley, the movement "helped ignite the anti-Vietnam War protests." [12]

Anti-War Movement

When America's involvement in Vietnam escalated significantly following the 1964 Gulf of Tonkin Resolution, students began actively organizing against the war and the draft. But mass protests didn't become commonplace until the 1967-68 school year, when rules governing student draft deferments were tightened.

In the first five months of 1968, anti-war rallies erupted at more than 100 universities, including Columbia, Harvard, Oberlin and Stanford. [13] On many campuses, students targeted the Central Intelligence Agency (CIA) and Reserve Officers Training Corps (ROTC), which used universities as recruiting sites. Some of the protests

became violent, as students took over buildings and destroyed property.

In Europe, too, 1968 was the year the student movement reached critical mass. But the impetus to take to the streets came not from opposition to the Vietnam War but from a desire to overturn traditional mores and reorder society. In Paris, Rome, London and other cities, youths called for new thinking on everything from sex to the economy while fighting pitched and often violent battles with police.

The movement was fueled by a "conviction that another social order was possible, an alternative to capitalism," said Henri Weber, a leader of the protests in Paris and now a member of the French Senate. [14]

But the campus upheavals, both in the United States and Europe, began losing steam almost as soon as they started. On some U.S. campuses, student demands were met, in whole or in part. Often administrations would agree to prohibit ROTC recruiters from operating at the university. With the exception of a brief upswing in 1970 over the American invasion of Cambodia and the killing of four students at Kent State University in Ohio, the anti-war movement never reached the 1968 level of activity.

Quiet Time

The 1970s brought a number of changes that significantly reduced student activism. The Vietnam War, which had galvanized so many students, was over, and new battles were being fought on the domestic front — mainly to find jobs.

"The 1973 oil embargo ushered in an era of slower economic growth that led to a deterioration of the job market," Kelman says. As a result, "students had to look inward and study harder so that they could compete for the now scarce jobs."

By the early 1980s, the economy was on the mend, and people were once again optimistic about long-term employment prospects. Activism on campus did not return to anywhere near previous levels. One reason involved the political climate, which had shifted decidedly to the right. Indeed, in the 1980 presidential race Americans chose conservative icon Ronald Reagan, who proved wildly popular among all age groups. In addition, says Kelman, student priorities were changing, becoming more focused on attaining wealth. "The Yuppie boom of the 1980s gave students a new role model," he says.

But the decade did produce one major wave of student protest: demands for divestiture of school funds invested in South Africa, with its harsh apartheid system of segregation. The movement came to a head in the mid-1980s, when protests hit scores of campuses. [15]

During the 1980s, other movements that would become more important in the following decade began gaining ground at campuses. Gay and lesbian students began organizing, driven in part by the emergence of AIDS. Ethnically based movements also grew dramatically during these years. For example, on many campuses, groups of Asian, Latino and African-American students convinced college administrators to create ethnic-studies departments. ■

CURRENT SITUATION

Diversity of Causes

"In many ways," Capowski says, "it was easier to be a student activist" back in the late 1960s and early '70s, the so-called golden age of student protest. "You had these big issues like civil rights and the Vietnam War," he says.

Vietnam, especially, galvanized students as no other issue before or since. But there was more to the student movement of the 1960s than the presence of an overriding cause. The youth culture of the day, in film, music and fashion, spoke to the need for rebellion.

"The establishment was the enemy, and you defined yourself in opposition to that," says Sanford Pinsker, a professor of humanities at Franklin and Marshall College, in Lancaster, Pa.

And, says American University's Kazin, there was a sense of unity among activists everywhere. "It was a real student movement," he says. "It was even called 'the movement.' "

Today, most observers agree, there is no overriding issue or sense of

unity among students. Instead, there are dozens of causes of varying size, many focused on the needs of ethnic or other minority groups. "There's a lot of identity politics, so you tend to get student activism in little clusters like ethnic minorities or vegetarians or gays and lesbians," Kazin says.

Indeed, identity-based groups seem to drive much of the activism at many colleges and universities. Some campuses often have more than one small but vocal group of gay and lesbian activists as well as a plethora of advocacy groups for women and for Latinos, Asian-Americans, African-Americans and other minorities.

And the issues that prompt these groups to act tend to be narrow. "Students these days are more local in their concerns and their protests," says Arthur Levine, president of Columbia University's Teachers College. [16] For instance, a gay advocacy group will often be pressuring the university to establish a gay-studies department while at the same time Asian-American students may be working for an Asian-studies program.

In addition, some passionate advocacy today revolves around consumer or lifestyle issues, such as tuition hikes or limits on alcohol on campus. At the University of Washington, for example, two-dozen police officers were injured in a recent student riot over a policy prohibiting alcohol at fraternity parties. [17]

Such incidents have become more common in recent years, leading to a loss of support for student activism and criticism of student attitudes. "There is this feeling among many students that the right to party is an entitlement," Pinsker says, "that inside the university, normal laws do not apply to you."

Others are even critical of those students who are working on behalf of more traditional causes, arguing that activists today seem to have less commitment and staying power than they used to.

"There's a certain 'flavor of the month' phenomenon at work," Alessio says. "There are too many causes floating around today, and as a result there's less

Are Conservative Activists on the Rise?

Conservative students generally don't march, sing songs or engage in sit-ins. "We don't take over buildings and things like that," says Michael Capel, a recent graduate of Cornell University. Instead, Capel says, conservative students are more likely to publish a newspaper or bring a speaker like Oliver North to campus.

Student activism is widely regarded as synonymous with liberal politics, if not the far left. While activist groups on campus tend to be liberal, student bodies at most colleges and universities, surprisingly, reflect more balance. According to a 1997 survey of college freshmen, only 24.4 percent identified themselves as liberal; nearly 21 percent labeled themselves conservatives. [1]

Since the election of Ronald Reagan in 1980, conservatives have become more visible on campus. "It's much more in the mainstream than it used to be," says Peter LaBarbera, editor of the *Lambda Report*, a bimonthly conservative newspaper that monitors the gay and lesbian rights movements at universities. "The nation is more conservative, and that's reflected on campus."

But while they may be more prevalent than they used to be, conservatives claim they're still often treated like lepers on campus. "The people who used to say 'question authority' are now the authority themselves [at universities], and many of them are not very tolerant of different views," LaBarbera says.

Indeed, conservatives accuse some universities of trying to stifle the conservative viewpoint in the name of not offending other groups, such as racial minorities or women. "The fact is they don't recognize activism that they don't agree with," says Dan Flynn, executive director of Accuracy in Academia, a conservative campus-watchdog group.

A case in point, Flynn says, is *The Northwestern Chronicle*, a privately funded conservative newspaper at Northwestern University. According to Chronicle Editor Chi Ng, the staff was "constantly under pressure from the

administration and the student government." The school did almost everything — including declaring copies of the paper left at students' doors to be fire hazards — to shut the Chronicle down, Ng says. In another case, hundreds of copies of the conservative *Cornell Review* were burned by students last year at two rallies. [2]

Efforts like those at Northwestern and Cornell to stifle conservatives have made them adept at courting public opinion, especially off campus. "You really have to try to be creative and take your fight to the outside world, because if you try to work within the [university] system as a conservative today, you're fighting a losing battle," Flynn says. "Because these universities are so liberal, you have to appeal to the media and alumni, people who can empathize with you because they live in the real world."

But some conservatives say that many students are accepting or even supportive of their efforts. "You know, when you get four or five people together and really talk to them about things, you find that there's this silent majority out there," Capel says.

Many conservatives predict that they will win over more and more of that silent support largely because of their status as pariahs on many campuses, not in spite of it. "Conservative activism is succeeding because it's much more vibrant than liberal activism," Flynn says. "It's a form of rebellion to be a conservative on a liberal campus."

LaBarbera agrees, pointing out that "the intellectual excesses" of liberal faculty will continue to fuel growth of conservative activism on campuses. "Students are becoming increasingly offended by the Left, with their speech codes and intolerant political correctness."

---

[1] *The American Freshman: Thirty Year Trends*, February 1997, Higher Education Research Institute, University of California, Los Angeles.

[2] Nat Hentoff, "Setting Fire to Ideas at Cornell," *The Pittsburgh Post-Gazette*, March 11, 1998, p. A19.

---

focus and less commitment."

But Samu notes that while there are more issues and less unity, students, nonetheless, "are very committed today."

And, Samu and others argue, they are often working on broad issues that have national importance and appeal, not just fighting for the right to drink beer. For example, he says, environmental activism is a common focus on every campus. "College students have a great impact on the nation by raising environmental awareness," he claims.

For instance, last December, students

at Notre Dame University rallied at the campus power plant to protest global warming and university violations of Environmental Protection Agency smokestack emissions standards.

Another issue of import is affirmative action, especially in California, where Proposition 209 prohibited race-based preferences on state campuses.

"This issue has galvanized students all over the state," Samu says, pointing to a May protest at UCLA at which 88 demonstrators were arrested. [18] ■

OUTLOOK

Calm Before the Storm?

Many observers of student life argue that the level of campus activism always has been dictated by forces off campus. "Student activism is

Continued on p. 756

At Issue:

Should teachers encourage students to engage in political activism?

BILL CAPOWSKI AND KEVIN PRANIS
Capowski is executive director of the Center for Campus Organizing; Pranis is Youth Section Organizer of the Democratic Socialists of America.

Written for **The CQ Researcher**, *August 1998*

*W*e believe that, in a democracy, the primary purpose of education is not to turn people into automatons who know only how to perform tasks and follow orders, but to help them realize their full potential as individuals, as active citizens and as informed community members. Political engagement is crucial to active citizenship, and we believe it's not only the right, but also the responsibility, of teachers to encourage students to become politically active.

Not only do student activists contribute to a vibrant campus life, but as they get older, most go on to make small and large contributions to their communities and the country at large. They rebuild neighborhoods, found non-profits, start small businesses, vote and demand that elected representatives be accountable to their constituents.

Our experience has taught us that engaging in student activism has tremendous educational value. For example, we have watched students active in the struggle against sweatshops who learn more in the course of their organizing work about economics, policy and history than they ever could have learned in the classroom. Furthermore, the insights and skills gained in the course of activism are not the ivory-tower abstractions often criticized by conservatives, but concrete lessons about the way real people live their lives.

Some conservatives have argued that teachers should avoid expressing political viewpoints and perspectives, because they fear that students will be unwilling or unable to hold and express alternative views and because they fear that teachers will be unwilling to treat students objectively.

But this argument vastly underestimates the abilities of both teachers and students. Those who see students as empty vessels to be filled by teachers and textbooks fail to see that students constantly evaluate what they're taught based on their life experiences.

It is also better to have politics out in the open, because politics are ever-present. Even a professor or teacher who never mentions current events and issues of the day is expressing a set of politics to her or his students. In this instance, that disengagement from political life is legitimate. We find this troubling in a society where we bemoan low voter turnout and apathy, especially among young people.

Teachers can and should contribute to the learning of their students by encouraging their students to engage in political activism.

DANIEL J. FLYNN
Executive director, Accuracy in Academia and editor of **Campus Report**

Written for **The CQ Researcher**, *August 1998*

*l*ook through the course selection catalog of just about any major school and you're bound to find classes like Williams College's "Practicing Feminism: A Study of Political Activism," a course in which students do "fieldwork at community agencies" to "raise awareness of feminist issues in the community."

It used to be that college was a place for educators to enrich minds and prepare undergraduates for the job market. Today, many professors seek not to teach students but to conscript them as workhorses for the Left's latest cause of the moment.

A professor "asking" her students to engage in activism is something akin to a corporation "encouraging" its executives to contribute to political candidates or a mayor "urging" city employees to volunteer on his re-election campaign. Many faculty members may view appeals from the lectern as only encouragement. Students, however with grades and futures on the line read their actions as coercion.

And the record shows that what many professors are doing amounts to much more than tacit encouragement of student activism:

• Marv Davidov, a professor at St. Cloud State University in Minnesota, frequently assigns his students to protest a local defense plant. Davidov was arrested last year on a "class assignment" and several of his students received citations from the police.

• Berkeley's June Jordan led her "Poetry for the People" class on a demonstration outside of CNN studios in San Francisco to protest California's decision to end racial preferences. Her 19 students fulfilled course requirements by fasting and demanding one hour of airtime to address the nation.

• During the election cycle of 1996, students in an environmental studies course at the University of Montana heard lectures by officials from the Sierra Club, Green Corps, Common Cause and Ralph Nader's PIRG, among other groups. During the last three weeks of the class, students were required to collect signatures so that an environmentalist-sponsored initiative would be placed on the ballot in Montana.

Imagine the outrage if it were not "peace" advocates gaining college credit for getting arrested outside of a munitions factory, but pro-lifers outside of an abortion clinic.

Professors would be wise to heed President Clinton's advice from last year's State of the Union address: "Politics must stop at the schoolhouse door." Teaching, not preaching, is the mission of higher education.

Continued from p. 754

and will be dependent on larger events," Kelman says, but he sees none looming on the horizon.

Many agree that nothing like Vietnam is likely to come along and galvanize students any time soon. But some argue that today's relative inactivity on campus could be the calm before the storm. "Things change in unpredictable ways," Kazin says. "I mean, look at the 1950s: People predicted that student activism [prevalent in the 1930s] was over for good."

For starters, some say, the next presidential election in 2000 will create the impetus for more activism on campus. "This is the first [presidential] race since 1988 that will be open, with no clear sense of who is going to win," Samu says. "This will galvanize students to action."

Still others say that issues — most notably the growing gap between rich and poor in the United States [19] — will filter down to the university and inspire huge numbers of students to act. "In the next 10 years, there's going to be a mass movement again [on campus] concerning the income gap and the increasing power of the ruling class in this country," St. Cloud State's Davidov says.

Hunter College's Kim agrees. "It's going to be more like the 1930s than the 1960s," he predicts. "Today we're involved in a growing class struggle that's only going to get worse."

But if the issues hark back to a bygone era, the means by which students fight for their cause will be firmly grounded in the 21st century. In fact, some say, it may be technology, not any particular cause, that makes the biggest difference in future attempts to mobilize students. "Students will form networks on-line where they'll exchange information and organize," says Dungy of the National Association of Student and Personnel Administrators. "This will make a powerful difference."

Hundreds of student activist groups already have Web pages, from the Student Takeover Page at the University of Massachusetts to the New Abolitionist Students at the University of Texas, Austin.

A glimpse of the future of student activism could be seen in the World Wide Web petition created last year by a group of student-led organizations urging the Clinton administration and members of Congress not to cut education spending. About 10,000 on-line signatures were gathered from students and others around the country. [20]

Despite such efforts, Kim warns that student activists will never accomplish their goals unless they become more attuned to the world beyond the campus. "We need to get out there, in the community and connect with other organizations," he says. "Student activism must be linked to larger societal issues or else we're never going to get anywhere." ∎

Notes

[1] For background, see Richard L. Worsnop, "Getting Into College," *The CQ Researcher*, Feb. 23, 1996, pp. 289-312.

[2] For background, see Kenneth Jost, "Rethinking Affirmative Action," *The CQ Researcher*, April, 28, 1995, pp. 375-398, and Richard L. Worsnop, "Gay Rights," *The CQ Researcher*, March 5, 1993, pp. 193-216.

[3] Alexander W. Astin, Sarah A. Parrott, William S. Korn and Linda J. Sax, *The American Freshman: Thirty Year Trends* (1997), p. 28.

[4] Linda J. Sax, Alexander W. Astin, William S. Korn and Kathryn M. Mahoney, *The American Freshman: National Norms for Fall 1997* (1997), p. 3.

[5] Mark Edmundson, "On the Uses of a Liberal Education: As Lite Entertainment," *Harpers*, September 1997.

[6] Peter Dreier, "The Myth of Student Apathy," *The Nation*, April 13, 1998.

[7] For background, see David Masci, "Baby Boomers at Midlife," *The CQ Researcher*, July 31, 1998, pp. 649-672.

[8] For background, see Mary H. Cooper, "Paying for College," *The CQ Researcher*, Nov. 20, 1992, pp. 1001-1024.

[9] Robert A. Rhoads, *Freedom's Web: Student Activism in an Age of Cultural Diversity* (1998), p. 31.

[10] *Ibid*, p. 34.

[11] Quoted in Eric Pace, "Mario Savio, Protest Leader Who Set a Style, Dies at 53," *The New York Times*, Nov. 8, 1996.

[12] Reginald E. Zelnik, "The Lives They Lived: Mario Savio; The Avatar of Free Speech," *The New York Times*, Dec. 29, 1996.

[13] Landon Y. Jones, *Great Expectations: America and the Baby Boom Generation* (1980), p. 96.

[14] Quoted in Christopher Dickey and Judith Warner, "You Said You Wanted a Revolution," *Newsweek*, June 1, 1998.

[15] Rhoads, op. cit., p. 56.

[16] Quoted in Richard Chacon, "Individual Issues Spark Campus Unrest," *The Boston Globe*, May 20, 1998.

[17] *Ibid*. For background, see Karen Lee Scrivo, "Drinking on Campus," *The CQ Researcher*, March 20, 1998, pp. 241-264.

[18] Julianne Basinger, "88 Students Arrested at UCLA in Protest Over Ban on Racial Preferences," *The Chronicle of Higher Education*, May 29, 1998.

[19] For background, see Mary H. Cooper, "Income Inequality," *The CQ Researcher*, April 17, 1998, pp. 337-360.

[20] "On-Line Petition Drive Aims to Sway Congress on Student Aid," *The Chronicle of Higher Education*, April 25, 1997.

Bibliography

Selected Sources Used

Books

Jones, Landon Y., *Great Expectations: America and the Baby Boom Generation*, Coward, McCann and Georhegan, 1980.

Dated but classic account of the history of the baby boom generation, including its battles against "the establishment."

Loeb, Paul Rogat, *Generation at the Crossroads: Apathy and Action on the American Campus*, Rutgers University Press, 1994.

Loeb argues that students are not apathetic souls without ideals, as branded by the media and others. Instead, he argues, students today are working more than ever to effect change in a variety of ways.

Rhoads, Robert A., *Freedom's Web: Student Activism in an Age of Cultural Diversity*, Johns Hopkins University Press, 1998.

Rhoads, a professor of education at Michigan State University, assesses the impact of the rise of identity politics on student activism.

Articles

Alessio, Carolyn, "The Right to Party and the Limit of Riots," *The Chicago Tribune*, Nov. 3, 1996.

Alessio, now an editor at the Tribune, bemoans the fact that students are putting their energy and zeal for change into causes like "the right to party," as they did at Southern Illinois University, where Alessio used to teach.

Dickey, Christopher, and Judith Warner, "You Said You Wanted a Revolution," *Newsweek*, June 1, 1998.

The authors examine the long-term impact of the student revolts in Europe in 1968, particularly in Paris. Many of the radicals who led the protests are now in power and, the writers conclude, just as hidebound as the "establishment" was 30 years ago.

Edmundson, Mark, "On the Uses of a Liberal Education: As Lite Entertainment for Bored College Students," *Harper's*, September 1997.

Edmundson, a professor at the University of Virginia, examines the current crop of University of Virginia students and finds them wanting. In particular, he writes, they are governed by "the cool consumer perspective, where passion and strong admiration are forbidden."

Gruzen, Tara, "Student Activism Takes on a New Face; It's Not a Single Issue Crusade Like in 60s," *Chicago Tribune*, July 7, 1996.

The diversity of causes on campus has led many student groups to work at cross-purposes, Gruzen writes. The days when activists were united by a single issue are largely over, she adds.

Jones, Patrice M., "E-Mail Replaces Flower Power for Peace Activists," *Chicago Tribune*, March 1, 1998.

Jones examines how activists are using the Internet to organize and coordinate their activities.

Schultz, Corina, "Media Seek Stereotype, Ignore Student Activism," *Capital Times*, Oct. 15, 1997.

Schultz argues that the media advances false stereotypes of students as know-nothing partygoers. The unreported reality, she writes, is that more students than ever are working for social change.

Reports and Studies

Astin, Alexander W., Sarah A. Parrott, William S. Korn and Linda J. Sax, *The American Freshman: Thirty Year Trends*, Higher Education Research Institute, UCLA, (1997).

This report is a compilation of the first 30 years (1966-1996) of freshman surveys conducted at universities around the country. Among other things, the results show a steady decline in student interest in politics.

FOR MORE INFORMATION

If you would like to have this CQ Researcher updated, or need more information about this topic, please call CQ Custom Research. Special rates for CQ subscribers. (202) 887-8600 or (800) 432-2250, ext. 600, or E-mail Custom.Research@cq.com

Accuracy in Academia, 4455 Connecticut Ave., N.W., Suite 330, Washington, D.C. 20008; (202) 364-3085; www.aim.org. A conservative campus watchdog group that reports on harassment suffered by conservative student activists.

Center for Campus Organizing, P.O. Box 748, Cambridge, Mass. 02142; (617) 354-9363; www.cco.org. The center, founded in 1991, is a clearinghouse that supports student activists on campuses around the country.

U.S. Student Association, 1413 K St., N.W., 9th Floor, Washington, D.C. 20005; (202) 347-8772; www.essential.org/ussa. The association works to protect the civil rights of students on campus.

National Association of Student Personnel Administrators, 1875 Connecticut Ave., N.W., Suite 418, Washington, D.C. 20036; (202) 265-7500; www.naspa.org. The association aims to develop leadership and improve practices in student-affairs administration.

The Next Step

Additional information from UMI's Newspaper & Periodical Abstracts™ database

African-Americans

Shepard, Scott, "Meeting Focuses on Police Brutality; NAACP Conventioneers, Protesters Target Law Enforcement's Alleged Racial Discrimination," *Atlanta Journal-Constitution*, July 15, 1997, p. A8.

On the eve of a demonstration to protest police brutality in Pittsburgh, NAACP convention leaders and delegates complained that police departments around the country target African-Americans without legal justification. The complaints were aired at a workshop held on day four of the seven-day convention as preparations were being made for a march Tuesday to protest the 1995 death of black motorist Jonny Gammage.

Negri, Gloria, "A Child of Student Activism; Still Going and Growing, African-American Institute at Northeastern Got its Start in Turbulent '60s," *The Boston Globe*, April 26, 1998, p. L5.

The African-American Institute at Northeastern University, which was founded as a result of student activism in 1968, is discussed, focusing on its mission to tutor minority students who lack basic reading, writing and study skills but who show academic potential.

Environmental Activism

Gray, Chris, "Environmental Leader Focuses on Youth, Success," *New Orleans Times-Picayune*, April 15, 1997, p. A14.

"I am sick of environmentalists who say the sky is falling," Adam Werbach, 24, the national president of the Sierra Club, told students and activists at Tulane University. He pointed to cleaner rivers and better-quality air produced during the past decade, because of community activism. But that doesn't mean the Brown University graduate plans to sit still. Dubbed by many the environmental movement's Renaissance man, Werbach is determined to change the Generation X stereotype and motivate young people to get involved.

Sneider, Daniel, "Where Meetings on Recycling Can Last Until 3 a.m.; Once a Conservative Mill Town, then a Haven for Hippies, Arcata, Calif., Now Boasts the Only City Council in America Run by the Green Party," *The Christian Science Monitor*, Feb. 12, 1997, p. 4.

Since November, Arcata's City Council offers an added attraction: the only government in the United States controlled by the fledgling Green Party. If there is a struggle for power here, it is between graying liberals and a new generation of 20-something activists.

Feminist

"Women and Human Rights," *WIN News*, spring 1998, pp. 6-36.

Reports on women's issues and human rights are presented. In Kenya, violence against women is a serious and widespread problem, and educated men outnumber educated women 2 to 1. Reports from other countries are discussed.

Mayer, Ann Elizabeth, "Comments on Majid's 'The Politics of Feminism in Islam,'" *Signs: Journal of Women in Culture & Society*, winter 1998, pp. 369-377.

The author comments on Majid's discussion of women's status and human rights in Islamic countries. Majid employs a pseudofeminism to defend the mandates of Islamic governments regarding the dress code for women, saying that mandatory veiling is only opposed by upper-class women trying to copy Western fashions.

Human Rights

Spar, Debora L., "The Spotlight and the Bottom Line," *Foreign Affairs*, March 1998, pp. 7-12.

U.S. manufacturers of consumer products have been targeted for human rights violations committed abroad by the subcontractors who produced their products in overseas facilities, and the corporate response has been that these companies cannot be held responsible for the labor practices of their foreign suppliers. Changes in this hands-off policy and an acceptance of responsibility are discussed.

Useem, Andrea, "A Human-Rights Center in Uganda Combines Academics with Activism," *The Chronicle of Higher Education*, July 3, 1998, pp. A33-34.

The Human Rights and Peace Center at Makerere University in Uganda seeks to overcome tyranny through enlightenment.

International Activism

"Suharto Finally Takes the Cue," *Chicago Tribune*, May 21, 1998, p. 30.

Finally, with his resignation, Suharto has realized what had been apparent to the rest of the world. The protests in Indonesia have the look of a movement whose time has come. No one would have dreamed a year ago that a wave of demonstrations and riots could shake Suharto's grip on power. But with startling speed, students occupied the parliament building, the leadership of his own party called on the president to resign and Suharto was forced out.

Mydans, Seth, "Military Says It Will Allow Civil Protests In Indonesia," *The New York Times*, June 12, 1998, p. A11.

At a news conference, the defense minister and armed forces chief, Gen. Wiranto, also asserted their support for the new administration of Indonesian President B. J. Habibie and urged people to be patient and allow it to pursue reforms. Many of the student demonstrators are calling on Habibie, who was Suharto's hand-picked vice president, to step down and allow a new breed of leaders to take over. They are backed by opponents of the government who air their views almost daily on television round tables.

Shiner, Cindy, "Independence Drive Revives in E. Timor; Students Rally, but Some Urge Delay," *The Washington Post*, July 10, 1998, p. A27.

"The international community has to take the Timor problem more seriously," said Domingos de Sousa, a professor at the University of East Timor. "Sometimes East Timor is almost a forgotten case — a forgotten case because no one talked. Things were very closed under Suharto. Suharto is gone, and now we are talking." Some people in the territory, which covers the eastern part of Timor Island, are not eager to slam the door on the Indonesians. Most of these people are members of an elite who have benefited from Indonesian rule, through government service for example, or academics who believe it is unrealistic to go it alone too quickly.

Internet Activism

Buie, Jim, "Neighborhood Watch Meets World Wide Web Over the Back Yard Fence," *The Washington Post*, Sept. 28, 1997, p. C2.

The Internet and E-mail have enabled at least eight local neighborhoods to create "electronic villages," where they discuss local problems such as how to combat crime or organize cleanups. It's anybody's guess as to whether these informal initiatives will grow into powerful social forces and spawn a more participatory democracy. Some people still think that communication over the computer is too impersonal. To them, the notion of a "virtual community" is simply further proof that their physical community is vanishing.

Kealy, John, "World on the Web," *Sierra*, May 1998, pp. 80-81.

To live up to its reputation, the World Wide Web needs to deliver tailored information to people who would rather be reading than surfing. The Sierra Club's Internet activism site and its hosting of more than 150 electronic discussion lists are discussed.

Police Brutality

Hanson, Eric, " 'A war' declared on police; Black Muslim Alleges Abuse in Third Ward," *Houston Chronicle*, May 30, 1998, p. A31.

Saying police are corrupt and have been harassing people at a Third Ward-area park, a local Black Muslim declared war Friday on the Houston Police Department. "Police officers have been terrorizing this neighborhood and terrorizing this park, especially on Sunday," he said. Quanell X, former Nation of Islam youth minister, said police stop and search people indiscriminately, steal cash and jewelry and subject the park-goers to constant verbal abuse.

Hawkinson, Olivia, "Brutality Protesters Blocked Demonstration by Police," *Chicago Tribune*, July 1, 1998, p. C6.

About 150 protesters were locked out of City Hall when they tried to march in for a demonstration against police brutality. Led by the Rev. Paul Jakes and an estimated 40 community activist and religious organizations, the group demanded that Mayor Richard Daley address allegations of police brutality by implementing a civilian review board. "We're concerned that cronyism has creeped into the Police Board," Jakes said, referring to the Chicago Police Department's current system for handling complaints through the Office of Professional Standards.

Student Protests

Chacon, Richard, "Individual Issues Spark Campus Unrest," *The Boston Globe*, May 20, 1998, p. B1.

Disturbances on college campuses, complete with cars burning, students hurling stones and police wielding pepper gas, have turned more than a half-dozen universities across the nation into battlegrounds over the last few weeks. "Thirty years ago, students were protesting on national issues," said Arthur Levine, who specializes in tracking attitudes of college students. "Students these days are more local in their concerns and their protests."

Dreier, Peter, "The Myth of Student Apathy," *The Nation*, April 13, 1998, pp. 19-22.

The author discusses how frequently the media does not report on campus activism. One example of this is that the *Los Angeles Times* did not report on a successful campaign at Occidental College to persuade President John Slaughter to issue a public statement criticizing Atlantic Richfield despite the fact that Slaughter is an Arco board member.

Back Issues

Great Research on Current Issues Starts Right Here.
Recent topics covered by The CQ Researcher are listed below.
Now available on the Web
For information, call (800) 432-2250 ext. 279 or (202) 887-6279.

If you would like to have any of these CQ Researchers updated, or need more information about these topics, please call CQ Custom Research. Special rates for CQ subscribers. (202) 887-8600 or (800) 432-2250, ext. 600, or E-mail Custom.Research@cq.com

Back issues are available for $5.00 (subscribers) or $10.00 (non-subscribers). Quantity discounts apply to orders over 10. To order, call Congressional Quarterly Customer Service at (202) 887-8621.

Binders are available for $18.00. To order call 1-800-638-1710. Please refer to stock number 648.

Future Topics

▶ *Organic Farming*

▶ *Cancer Treatments*

▶ *Hispanic Americans' New Clout*

The CQ Researcher

PUBLISHED BY CONGRESSIONAL QUARTERLY INC.

Food Safety Battle: Organic vs. Biotech

Will organic farming survive?

A tidal wave of genetically engineered foods is heading for grocery shelves. Within 10 years, experts predict, an estimated 95 percent of America's plant-derived foods will be genetically engineered. Moreover, they say, organic farmers eventually will decide to grow transgenic crops. Organic activists vow that organic foods will remain a haven for consumers who want to avoid genetically modified foods. But as biotech companies gobble up the world's seed companies and re-engineer traditional organic pesticides, the unaltered seeds and pesticides needed by organic farmers may become scarce. Many observers say a nationwide debate on the biotech revolution is long overdue.

 Sept. 4, 1998 • Volume 8, No. 33 • Pages 761-784

Formerly Editorial Research Reports

FOOD SAFETY BATTLE: ORGANIC VS. BIOTECH

September 4, 1998
Volume 8, No.33

EDITOR
Sandra Stencel

MANAGING EDITOR
Thomas J. Colin

STAFF WRITERS
Adriel Bettelheim
Mary H. Cooper
Kenneth Jost
Kathy Koch
David Masci

PRODUCTION EDITOR
Melissa Hall

EDITORIAL ASSISTANT
Laura S. Cavender

PUBLISHED BY
Congressional Quarterly Inc.

CHAIRMAN
Andrew Barnes

VICE CHAIRMAN
Andrew P. Corty

PRESIDENT AND PUBLISHER
Robert W. Merry

EXECUTIVE EDITOR
David Rapp

Bibliographic records and abstracts included in The Next Step section of this publication are the copyrighted material of UMI, and are used with permission.

The CQ Researcher (ISSN 1056-2036). Formerly Editorial Research Reports. Published weekly, except Jan. 2, May 29, July 3, Oct. 30, by Congressional Quarterly Inc., 1414 22nd St., N.W., Washington, D.C. 20037. Annual subscription rate for libraries, businesses and government is $340. Additional rates furnished upon request. Periodicals postage paid at Washington, D.C., and additional mailing offices. POSTMASTER: Send address changes to The CQ Researcher, 1414 22nd St., N.W., Washington, D.C. 20037.

COVER: GENE KAHN WENT FROM VIETNAM WAR PROTESTOR TO ORGANIC FARMING HONCHO. (THE FRESH IDEAS GROUP)

Food Safety Battle: Organic vs. Biotech

By Kathy Koch

The Issues

Meet corporate CEO Gene Kahn: In the 1960s, the self-described hippie was so "disillusioned about where society was going" that he dropped out — literally. Kahn retreated to the forests of Washington state, where he took up organic farming.

Today the former Vietnam protester has turned his roadside produce stand into the nation's largest organic food company.

Kahn's metamorphosis from anti-establishment outsider to honcho of $90-million-a-year Small Planet Foods parallels the transformation of the organic food industry. Once synonymous with sad-looking produce and no-frills grocery co-ops, organic food now occupies one of the hottest — and most controversial — niches in retailing.

Gourmet grocery chains and fully half the nation's supermarkets offer everything from organic dairy products to snack foods and frozen dinners. Pricey restaurants offer organic haute cuisine, and conventional small farmers are turning to organics for the higher prices they bring. *(See story, p. 766.)*

"Our growth is led by consumer concern about pesticides and their impact on human health and the environment," Kahn says.*

"Many people have blind faith that the government will protect them," says Margaret Wittenberg, a public relations executive at Whole Foods supermarkets. "Our customers don't generally feel that way."

Indeed, when the U.S. Department of Agriculture (USDA) released proposed labeling standards for organic foods in December, 280,000 angry cards, letters and E-mails flooded the

agency — including letters from 255 members of Congress.

Although organic food proponents found more than 60 weaknesses in the proposed standards, concern focused on whether the coveted "certified organic" label should include genetically engineered foods or those irradiated or fertilized with sewage sludge. [1]

Many organic food advocates say the furor over organic labeling is small potatoes compared with the changes in global food production being fostered by giant agricultural biotechnology firms.

The impact of genetically engineered foods*, or genetically modified organisms (GMOs), on world agriculture "will make the Industrial Revolution pale by comparison," said Austen Cargill, the top scientist at Minneapolis-based Cargill Inc., the giant grain and processing company. [2]

The question is whether the resulting changes will be good or bad for farmers, consumers and global biodiversity — and how they will affect organic farming.

"This technology will help farmers increase productivity, control costs and improve quality, while protecting the environment and contributing to sustain-

able agriculture," said Robert Fraley, president of Ceregen, Monsantos Co.'s plant products business unit. [3]

The U.S. government has declared that genetically engineered foods are as safe as foods developed through hybridization, but critics have doubts about the safety and need for transgenic, or genetically altered, crops. In fact, 36 transgenic crops already have been approved for sale in the United States, including staples such as soy, corn, potatoes and canola oil.

Conventional American farming has embraced the new technology. Three years ago, not a single genetically engineered crop was planted for commercial use. This year, an estimated 65 million acres worldwide were planted with transgenic seeds, including about a third of this year's U.S. corn and soy crops, according to Monsanto Vice President Robert Horsch. [4]

Because bulk shipments of commodities like soy often commingle GMOs and conventional crops, up to 8,000 processed (packaged) foods in U.S. supermarkets could contain genetically altered soy-based ingredients like textured vegetable protein or lecithin, organic proponents say. But Americans do not know which of these foods are genetically altered because they aren't so labeled.

And more transgenic foods are on the way. Scientists are rapidly "inventing" other new foods, including at least 21 modified fish varieties. They are also studying inserting animal and human genes into plants and animals.

As genetically altered foods begin to dominate the conventional food chain, a growing market is developing for verifiable non-GMO foods — both organic and non-organic. "The more anyone tinkers with the natural processes in food production, the more the public will turn to organic products," says Bob Anderson, an organic farmer in Penns Creek, Pa., and chairman of the National Organic Standards Board (NOSB). "We are already seeing it with double-digit growth."

---

*Certified organic farming uses crop rotation, mulching, beneficial pests and plant-based rather than chemical pesticides to control weeds and harmful pests.

---

*Genetically engineered foods are crops or animals modified with genes from viruses, bacteria, pesticides or other plants or animals.

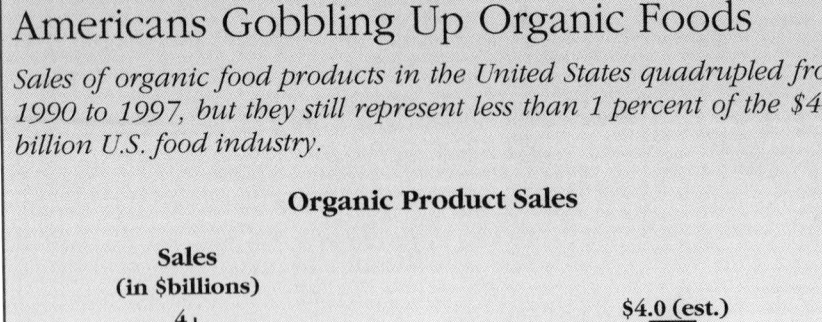

Americans Gobbling Up Organic Foods

Sales of organic food products in the United States quadrupled from 1990 to 1997, but they still represent less than 1 percent of the $440 billion U.S. food industry.

Organic Product Sales

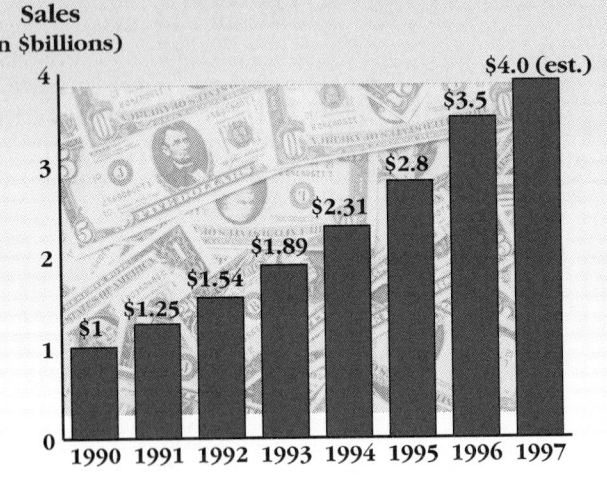

Sales (in $billions)

- 1990: $1
- 1991: $1.25
- 1992: $1.54
- 1993: $1.89
- 1994: $2.31
- 1995: $2.8
- 1996: $3.5
- 1997: $4.0 (est.)

Source: Organic Trade Association

While organic growers are enjoying the spurt in demand for organic foods, there is widespread fear that the biotech revolution eventually will:

• Make it difficult to locate non-GMO ingredients, causing customers to lose confidence in the integrity of packaged organic foods.

• Contaminate organic crops through cross-pollination with genetically engineered plants growing nearby.

• Enable plants with herbicide resistance engineered into their genes to cross-breed with wild relatives and create "monster weeds" resistant to organic farmers' natural pesticides.

• Hasten the rate at which pests become resistant to Bacillis thuringiensis (Bt). Bioengineers have created more than two-dozen varieties of transgenic crops containing genes from Bt, a bacteria long used to produce one of organic growers' favorite and safest biological pesticides.

• Endanger future non-GMO seed supplies due to the growing control of the international seed market by biotech companies like Monsanto and DuPont.

• Reduce the biodiversity of the world's seed supply through the use of so-called "terminator" seeds, which produce plants without viable seeds. *(See story, p. 774.)*

"Organic farmers need seeds specifically developed for particular ecological neighborhoods," says Fred Kirschenmann, an organic farmer in North Dakota. "One size doesn't fit all. Monsanto is clearly not interested in developing a diverse set of seeds for diverse farming operations."

Monsanto President Hendrik Verfaillie disputes the idea that control of the seed industry by giant firms will reduce biodiversity. "We would be insane to pay for these [seed] businesses and then eliminate the varieties that are useful. We want to have a broad range of varieties." [5]

But what the organic food industry fears most is being overwhelmed by genetically engineered crops. "Within five years — and certainly within 10 — some 90-95 percent of plant-derived food ma-

terial in the United States will come from genetically engineered techniques," predicts Val Giddings, vice president for food and agriculture for the 800-member Biotechnology Industry Organization (BIO). "It'll take a little bit longer for these technologies to penetrate into the organic market, but it will. As the benefits become clearer, you'll see that opposition will be replaced by understanding, and adoption will follow."

"I understand that this is their grand plan," responds Laura Ticciati, executive director of Mothers for Natural Law, a clearinghouse for information about sources of non-GMO seeds and ingredients in Fairfield, Iowa. "But genetic engineering has no place in organic agriculture, and it never will."

As the growers and government officials grapple with regulating organic farming, here are some of the questions being asked:

Are organic foods safer than conventionally grown foods?

"Shoppers with a high food-safety consciousness are looking for alternatives," says Katharine DiMatteo, executive director of the Organic Trade Association (OTA). "If they are concerned about pesticide risk, they are more likely to choose organic."

Organic farmers use crop rotation, cover crops and beneficial insects to fight pests, and composting to fertilize. They focus on keeping the soil nutrient-rich because healthy plants develop resistance to pests more readily. Occasionally, as a last resort, they will use botanical, or plant-based pesticides, which typically break down within 48 hours.

But Janet Anderson, director of biopesticides at the Environmental Protection Agency (EPA), says that some organic pesticides can be extremely toxic, even if they degrade rapidly.

And according to Christine Bruhn, director of the Center for Consumer Research at the University of California, Davis, "There is no evidence that organic food is safer from a pesticide-residue viewpoint."

According to tests by Consumers Union, however, "organic foods had consistently minimal or non-existent pesticide residue. Most green-labeled produce also had less pesticide residue than conventional foods." [6]

Carl Winter, a food toxicologist at UC-Davis, argues that it doesn't matter if organic foods have less pesticide residue because the amount typically found on conventionally grown American foods is too low to be harmful.

"If you fed laboratory animals 10,000 times what we're typically exposed to in the diet," he says, "it is not sufficient to show any adverse affects in the animals."

On the other hand, a scathing report in May by the nonprofit Environmental Working Group (EWG) challenges the safety of U.S. produce. Despite promises by the Clinton administration in 1993 that children's exposure to pesticides would be significantly reduced, "levels of carcinogenic pesticides found in fruits and vegetables heavily consumed by children" have increased significantly, the report said. [7]

Furthermore, the EWG report said, more than 1 million children a day age 5 and under ingest unsafe amounts of organophosphate (OP) insecticides, which "have the potential to cause long-term damage to the brain and the nervous system (of children)."

In August, the EPA began distributing pamphlets in grocery stores warning that "some pesticides have been shown to cause . . . birth defects . . . in laboratory animals [and] children may be more vulnerable to pesticides because their bodies are not fully mature." The pamphlet was an outgrowth of the 1996 Food Quality Protection Act, which directed the EPA to review all pesticide tolerance rules to see if they adequately protect children. The law was passed after a 1993 National Research Council report concluded that children may be at greater risk than adults from exposure to allowable pesticide residue levels. [8]

EPA's new pamphlet advises parents to wash, peel, boil and skin food to get rid of pesticide residues — or buy organic produce.

Dennis T. Avery, director of global food issues for the Indianapolis-based Hudson Institute, says the EPA misleadingly implies that organic foods are safer than conventional foods.

"People who eat organic foods are about eight times more likely to be attacked by the deadly new E. coli bacteria than are people who eat mainstream foods," Avery wrote in a recent, widely published Op-Ed article. "Organic and natural foods made up about only 1 percent of the U.S. food supply, but they were implicated in at least 8 percent of the confirmed cases" of E.coli. [9]

Organic farmer Kirschenmann calls Avery's claims "outrageous and undocumented. I don't know of a single case to date where food coming from a certified organic farm has been contaminated by a food-borne illness. All of the cases have been traced back to either imported foods or food from large industrial operations."

Avery says his figures came from the Centers for Disease Control and Prevention (CDC) in Atlanta. But Larry Slutsker, a medical epidemiologist in the CDC's food-borne and diarrheal diseases branch, says, "I cannot confirm [his] numbers. We don't have routine data collection on whether things are organic or not."

The OTA's DiMatteo says Avery's article carelessly lumps "natural" foods (those without additives or preservatives) with organic foods. Unlike natural food producers, she says, organic farms undergo strenuous certification procedures. These ensure — among other things — that strict rules are followed for using animal manure compost, which Avery says causes most of the E.coli risk in organic farming.

DiMatteo says the USDA's proposed national organic standards prohibit using composted manure on plants that will be harvested within 60 days.

Kirschenmann argues that, "The major problem [with manure] is not likely to be with organic agriculture, which uses it quite judiciously, but with the large factory farms." A large hog farm can produce enough manure to fill three to four football-field-sized lagoons, he says, and "it gets spread on fields, too."

Trevor Suslow, a UC-Davis extension specialist in microbial food safety, says, "Nobody really knows whether [organics] are safer, really, as far as bacterial contamination is concerned. The studies haven't been done to document it."

Avery also claimed in his article that the Food and Drug Administration (FDA) says organic crops have higher rates of infestation by natural toxins, including the cancer agent aflatoxin. "Organic foods suffer more damage from insects and rodents, which let toxin-causing fungi get into organic crops," Avery wrote.

But Robert L. Lake, director of policy planning at the FDA's Center for Food Safety and Applied Nutrition, says, "I'm not aware that there's a particular problem with organics and aflatoxins."

Are organic foods safer than genetically engineered foods?

Although there have been no mass protests in the United States against bioengineered foods, as in Europe, the GMO safety question nonetheless stirs high-voltage debate.

"By failing to require testing and labeling of genetically engineered foods, the FDA has made millions of American consumers unknowing guinea pigs for potentially harmful, unregulated food substances," Andrew Kimbrell, executive director of the International Center for Technology Assessment, said on May 27. Kimbrell's comments came after the center, along with other groups, health professionals and scientists, sued to force the FDA to more rigorously test and label GMOs.

But according to press releases handed out at Kimbrell's press conference by Stephen Ziller, vice president of the Grocery Manufacturers of America, "There is no scientifically val-

Watermelon Gazpacho, Anyone?

Once, organic food meant tofu, veggie burgers and funky, alternative eateries. Now celebrated, institute-trained chefs are serving up organic haute cuisine in trendy, elegant — and pricey — establishments from San Francisco to Bar Harbor.

These latter-day pioneers are perking up the public's palate with organic delights such as sea scallops in black sesame crust and watermelon gazpacho with lime and mint.

The trend was pioneered by Alice Waters, who opened famed Chez Panisse in Berkeley, Calif., in 1971, offering a daily five-course fixed-price menu that focused on seasonal produce. Organic chefs insist on seasonal, local products not only to ensure superior flavor but also to support sustainable agriculture and avoid dangerous pesticides often found on imported produce.

"Making the right choices about food can create living, caring communities," Waters told a June 6 meeting of Chef's Collaborative 2000, a group dedicated to promoting sustainable agriculture. "We have to reverse the terrible things happening to our water, dirt and air."

Waters believes so strongly in the food-community connection that she teaches youths and prison groups the pleasures of planting, harvesting and cooking their own food.

On the East Coast, Nora Pouillon has been serving only organic food at equally popular Restaurant Nora in Washington, D.C., since 1979. Also a food activist, Pouillon leads area restaurateurs to Pennsylvania Dutch country each year to visit a co-op of Amish organic farmers.

The definitive study has yet to determine whether organic or conventional produce is more nutritious. Organic chefs say organic produce wins because organic fertilizers contain more nutrients than synthetic fertilizers. Conventional farmers say their produce is more nutritious because vitamins are lost when produce is exposed to air, light and heat, and conventional produce gets to the supermarket sooner in refrigerated trucks owned by big distributors.

Rick Moonen, owner of Oceana restaurant in Manhattan, cooks organic "for flavor and safety," he says, "and I like supporting the organic effort."

Given the speed with which the food supply is being genetically engineered, Moonen says, organic will soon be the only non-engineered food available. He is among several plaintiffs who have sued the Food and Drug Administration to force it to label genetically engineered foods. "As a professional, I need to know what I'm serving my customers," he says. *(See story, p. 768)*

---

ued distinction between the safety of genetically enhanced food and food grown by traditional methods."

The EPA, FDA and USDA — all of which play a role in approving genetically engineered foods — maintain that GMOs are as safe as the original plants and organisms from which the genes are taken. The FDA requires a label or premarket testing on a genetically engineered food only if there's a significant change in the food's composition or nutritional content, or if it contains a known food allergen. Basically, the agency says, genetically engineered foods are as safe as foods produced through traditional hybridization. [10]

"Virtually every food you buy has been altered by traditional breeding and is not as nature intended it," said Eric Flamm, a senior policy adviser at the FDA. "We have no evidence that any genetically engineered foods on the market contain unapproved food additives or are adulterated." [11]

The government is engaging in "a

major disinformation campaign" when it says transgenic crops are "substantially equivalent" to crops produced through hybridization, says Steven Druker, president of the Campaign for Bio-Diversity, another plaintiff in the FDA suit. "There are a lot of scientists who take great exception to the assumption that the haphazard insertion of foreign genetic material is the same as cross-breeding through sexual reproduction."

Liebe Cavalieri, a molecular biologist at the State University of New York, Purchase, says it's "simplistic, if not downright simple-minded," to say that genetic engineering is as safe as classical hybridization. Inserting virus, bacteria and animal genes into plants "can raise the level of bioactivators in the plants to a point where they're not safe to eat," he says.

"On the one hand, you have a system that is more precise [than hybridization]," says Sheldon Krimsky, a professor of urban and environmental policy at Tufts University. "But you're passing DNA through species barriers that would never

occur in nature. Some people make the mistake that more precision means more predictability. It might disable or enhance the operation of other genetic components. Those are the things that are not being tested."

"They don't really know what they are talking about," says BIO's Giddings. "It's true that many of the techniques involve inserting genes into chromosomes in an essentially random way. But once you transform some cells, they are analyzed to see where the insertion took place, and to see if any genes were disrupted."

In fact, genetic engineering is "a thousand times more predictable and controllable" than classical plant breeding, Giddings says. Hybridization involves pairing two sets of chromosomes — one from each parent — with at least 50,000 variables on each. "With genetic engineering, you are taking only one chromosome, with 50,000 variables that you've studied, and adding one or two new variables."

Some skeptics bitterly complain that no one really knows whether GMOs are safe because the three-pronged regulatory system for reviewing their safety is severely flawed.

"With respect to genetically engineered foods, we have a weak regulatory system — put in place during the Reagan/Bush years — that the government claims to be rigorous, and it is not," says Jane Rissler, a Union of Concerned Scientists (UCS) expert and former EPA special assistant for biotechnology. "The risk-assessment scheme in this country [for genetically engineered foods] is not rigorous enough."

Lynn Goldman, the EPA's assistant administrator for prevention, pesticides and toxic substances, strongly disagrees. "We would not approve these foods if we didn't feel comfortable eating them ourselves or feeding them to our children," she says. "I am a pediatrician, and I have no qualms about feeding Bt corn to my 2-year-old daughter."

But EPA toxicologist Suzanne Wuerthele warns that genetic engineering "is so powerful that scientists are going to discover all kinds of novel hazards that we can't even imagine today. We are much like scientists in the 1940s when they first looked at DDT. They didn't even know the word for ecosystem, much less that it would harm eagles' eggs."

Margaret Mellon, a UCS molecular biologist and attorney, concedes that, "There is some chance that everything we find out [about GMOs] will be manageable and benign. But we don't know. No one is looking at whether there are any long-term chronic effects of inserting pesticides into food."

"We don't know what will happen over 30 years," concedes James Maryanski, biotech coordinator in the FDA's Center for Food Safety and Applied Technology. "We can never say that there won't be a surprise. Even if we did [long-term] studies, something could happen that won't show up in the study.

"So far, the companies haven't modified anything enough to warrant [FDA to require] long-term toxic studies," he says. "But even for food additives, we don't

usually do lifetime animal feeding studies. If the new substance is a protein and we know its functions, then there's no reason to do long-term studies."

The FDA insists that if a bio-food contains genes from a known human allergen, it must be labeled as such. But skeptics ask how a company can know whether a GMO is a potential allergen if the genes being spliced into the plant come from something humans have never eaten before?

For instance, to make Monsanto's Roundup Ready soybeans resistant to the company's Roundup herbicide, scientists injected the plants with genes from a virus, two bacteria — and petunias. "We don't know if people are going to be allergic to petunias," Wuerthele says, because petunias have never been part of the human food supply.

"What we have done is work with scientists who are experts in food allergies," Maryanski says. "We ask them to look at whether [a new substance] has similarities to known food allergens."

Some scientists and consumer groups worry that bioengineered foods contain antibiotic-resistant genes, used by scientists as "markers" to verify where the genes landed when they were inserted. They fear humans who consume those foods over a long period of time may develop resistance to important antibiotics. Scientists in Scotland have pointed out that the antibiotic gene most often used comes from the same family as ampicillin, which treats E. coli infections. [12]

Giddings calls the antibiotic-resistance a "red herring" because "there is no known mechanism by which a gene can move from a plant into a bacterium in the human gut.

"The biotech industry should be embarrassed at the extent to which they have not anticipated these fears," Giddings says. "It's really unfortunate, because there are good answers to all these concerns. Using this technology for food is not only imminently sensible but also highly desirable." For instance, he says, using Bt foods will reduce the need for topical pesticides

and thus reduce pesticide residues.

Is organic farming better for the environment?

Conventional U.S. farmers annually use about 800 million pounds of synthetic pesticides, herbicides and insecticides. Farm runoff containing such chemicals is blamed for much of America's river and groundwater pollution, as well as lake fishkills. Some experts also fear that insects and other pests are becoming resistant to many commonly used pesticides and herbicides, some of which stay in the environment for years.

Organic farmers eschew "formula pesticides," in which "at certain times of the year you apply herbicide and fungicide, whether or not there is a problem," DiMatteo says.

"The environmental benefits of organic farming are indisputable," Kahn says, "including reduced pesticide use. And the pesticides are much safer because they are plant-derived and have a much shorter life span.

Marvin Mangus, of Yale, Ill., switched from conventional farming to organics. "It got to where if you saw a weed you'd spray the whole field. Now we've reduced or eliminated pesticide usage."

Yet biotech companies argue that their products cause less environmental damage than either conventional or organic farming. "In the future, as we bring more products to market, our vision is that there will be plants resistant to all pests, and you wouldn't have to use any insecticides," says Robert L. Harness, director of government affairs at Monsanto.

"I am a passionate environmentalist," adds BIO's Giddings. "And I think biotech offers a robust suite of techniques to help us achieve sustainable agriculture. Biotech can help farmers tread more gently on the land. There is no necessary conflict between biotech and the principles on which organic farming is based."

Incorporating Bt into plants, for instance, will allow conventional farmers to reduce or eliminate chemical sprays, he

Continued on p. 770

Europe Now Labels Genetically Altered Food . . .

As Agriculture Secretary Dan Glickman approached the microphone to begin his press conference, three women in the audience suddenly stood up and began taking their clothes off. Written across their naked bodies were the words "Ban the Gene Beans!"

The November 1996 incident at the World Food Summit in Rome exposed U.S. officials to the in-your-face tactics of European environmental activists opposed to "Frankenstein foods" being exported by U.S. corporations. The women were opposing shipments of genetically engineered soybeans by American biotech giant Monsanto.

Glickman had come to convince delegates that genetic engineering can help feed the world's exploding population without plowing up marginal land and rain forests. But, he later acknowledged, convincing Europeans that biotech foods are safe "is going to be much more difficult than I thought." [1]

Europeans are indeed skittish after government scientists failed to protect them from "mad-cow" disease. They also resent the heavy-handed way that genetically modified organisms (GMOs) have been forced down their throats by exporters, who commingle them in bulk shipments with traditionally grown crops.

Since Glickman's revealing press conference, activists have vandalized test crops in the United Kingdom. Already, Norway, Austria and Luxembourg have banned GMOs. Consumer complaints have been especially strident in Germany, where Thalidomide babies and Hitlerian genetic research haunt the collective memory. British frozen-food processor Iceland has vowed to keep GMOs out of its house brand.

Europeans felt Monsanto flooded the market with commingled soybeans, depriving consumers of a choice, says American microbiologist John Fagan, who developed a method for testing whether commodities have been genetically altered. "I've heard over and over in every country I visited in Europe: 'Our customers want choice,' " says the former National Institutes of Health scientist, who now sells his Genetic ID testing services to European retailers and food processors.

After years of debate, the European Union (EU) voted on May 26 to require exporters to label shipments containing GMOs, beginning in September. Monsanto dropped its opposition to EU labeling, but still opposes labeling in the United States.

Many Europeans also argue that unless non-GMOs are kept separate throughout shipping and processing, eventually all products will have been commingled, and consumers will have no choice but to buy GMO foods. Glickman and U.S. biotech corporations insist GMOs are as safe as conventional food, and argue that labeling them, banning them or segregating them from conventional foods are violations of free-trade agreements.

Meanwhile, some European and Japanese retailers are buying non-GMO products direct from organic and small farmers in the U.S. and South America.

So far, GMO crops are not being grown on a large scale in Europe, leading some farmers to worry that they'll be left behind in the global race to jump onto the GMO bandwagon, a race led by U.S. farmers. Worldwide acreage of biotech crops is expected to triple by the year 2000, and South American farmers, especially in Brazil and Argentina, are planting biotech crops at a phenomenal rate, says Dennis Stolte, director of the Washington office of the American Farm Bureau.

In June Monsanto launched a $1.6 million ad campaign to assuage European fears about GMO safety. "I wish Monsanto had been more perceptive" and quicker to "prompt more public dialogue," Monsanto's president for Europe and Africa, Bernard Auxenfans, confessed on the company's Web site.

Prince Charles immediately responded with a lengthy essay in the *Daily Telegraph*, charging that genetic engineering "takes mankind into realms that belong to God, and to God alone." [2]

Like Prince Charles, a growing number of Americans want a public debate on biotechnology. Others are pushing for mandatory labeling of GMOs in this country.

"I was very pleased to see that Prince Charles was raising this issue in the UK," says EPA toxicologist Suzanne Wuerthele. "He was participating in something we have not had in this country — a nationwide debate on biotech foods."

Because of the profound changes biotech foods are likely to have on rural societies, many say such a debate is long overdue. "It's going to bring big changes to our lives," says Ron Roller, president of American Soy Products of Saline, Mich., "and it's unstoppable."

For example, scientists are discussing "growing" orange juice in vats and producing vanilla in the laboratory — corporate decisions that could severely impact rural societies producing such commodities — yet no one is debating these long-range consequences, he says.

Stolte agrees the United States needs a biotech debate, as long as it is not dominated by those "who would like U.S. agriculture to go back to subsistence production with shovels and rakes." But, he warns, if the United States gets bogged down in debate like Europe, American farmers could be left behind in the biotech revolution.

Stolte thinks Americans are not upset about GMOs because they are better educated and have more trust in regulators than the Europeans. "The credibility of the health claims against biotech products has not been substantiated. The number of people who accept the safety of biotech crops is growing."

But other Americans echo Prince Charles' doubts about the ethics of mixing completely unrelated species, such as animals and plants, or putting human genes into edible foods. "Mixing species is a big problem for people who

... But Debate in U.S. Just Heating Up

shop in our stores," says Margaret Wittenberg, communications manager for Whole Foods grocery chain. "That goes way too far."

"When you start adding human genes to food," asks EPA's Wuerthele, "how many genes does it take before it becomes cannibalism to eat that food?"

James Maryanski, biotech coordinator at the Food and Drug Administration (FDA), does not think any companies are considering commercializing foods with human genes at this point, although it has been done in the laboratory. But Margaret Mellon, a molecular biologist at the Union of Concerned Scientists, argues that no one can be sure because information about what genes are in GMOs is proprietary.

Some organic advocates want a public debate because they agree with Prince Charles, who fears "genetic pollution" could destroy organic farming. "It's a very real risk," says Laura Ticciati, executive director of Mothers for Natural Law, in Fairfield, Iowa, which is trying to collect a million signatures by Thanksgiving demanding that the FDA label GMOs.

"It is the stated objective of the biotech industry that the global food supply should be a genetically engineered food supply," Ticciati continues. "Consumers have to act now if we are going to get some checks and balances on this artificially produced food. This is not a back-burner issue."

Mellon thinks the biotech industry has wrongly tried to narrow the debate to only scientific questions about safety. "If people feel the 'yuck' factor, they have a right to feel it, and they have a fundamental right not to choose these foods," she says.

Because GMOs aren't labeled, "Americans don't have any idea how much genetically modified food they are eating," which is why there is no debate here like in Europe, says Marion Nestle, chairman of nutrition and food studies at New York University. "But this silence cannot continue. People will learn about this and say, "Wait a minute. This is too bizarre for me.' "

A legal battle over GMO labeling is looming. A coalition of consumers, scientists, environmentalists, chefs and religious groups sued the FDA on May 27 in U.S. District Court for the District of Columbia, demanding mandatory labeling and adequate safety testing of GMOs.

The Alliance for Biodiversity and the International Center for Technology Assessment charge in the suit that by not treating genetically modified organisms as food additives — which requires premarket testing — the agency is violating the Food, Drug and Cosmetics Act. And by not labeling GMOs, the FDA is also violating the religious freedom of those who do not want to eat them, the suit says.

Representing himself and eight other scientist plaintiffs, molecular biologist Liebe Cavalieri of the State University of New York said at a press conference just after the suit

was filed, "The claim of the FDA that genetic engineering is substantially equivalent to traditional breeding is a disgraceful sham."

Stephen Ziller, vice president for scientific and regulatory affairs for the Grocery Manufacturers of America (GMA), said in a prepared statement that "opponents of progress and science-based research" should not be allowed to "turn back the clock on the extraordinary advancements we have made to feed the world and reduce farmers' dependence on pesticides and fertilizers."

The plaintiffs contend that without labels a Moslem or Jew could unknowingly eat pork genes that have been engineered into a vegetable or other animal product. Similarly, a vegetarian would not know whether he was eating animal genes in his vegetables.

"I don't understand their thinking," says Val Giddings, vice president for food and agriculture for the Biotechnology Industry Organization. "About 70 percent of the human body is made up of genes that are identical to pork genes."

Requiring labeling for those with religious convictions is unfair to others, he says, because it would raise food costs. "If someone holds a religious point of view that requires mandated labels, then they want the rest of the population to bear the cost of their religious prejudice. That's not right," Giddings says.

"There clearly is no legitimate health or safety-related reason for requiring labels that would distinguish GMOs from other foods," he contends. Yet he would support labeling if the public is willing to pay the extra costs. (See "At Issue," p. 777.)

Currently the FDA only requires labels on a GMO if it contains a known allergen or differs in composition or nutritional value.

GMA communications manager Brian Sansoni says it won't be cheap to label GMOs. Because much of America's processed food contains soy-derived ingredients, and a third of the country's soybeans are genetically engineered and commingled with non-GMO soybeans, "it would cost consumers millions of dollars to label every type of food that contains genetically engineered soybeans." It would cost even more if consumers wanted GMO foods to be kept totally separate, or segregated, during processing, he says.

Ronnie Cummins, executive director of the Pure Food Campaign and a labeling proponent, argues, "Whatever happens in Europe on labeling and segregation will have a major impact in the U.S. It will be more difficult for companies to say they can't label in the U.S. if they're doing it overseas."

---

[1] Quoted in *National Journal's Congress Daily*, Nov. 18, 1996.

[2] HRH The Prince of Wales, "Seeds of Disaster," *The Daily Telegraph*, June 8, 1998.

Continued from p. 767
says. Modifying crops with genetic engineering is more environmentally friendly than organic farming, says Monsanto's Carlos Joly, director of sustainability, because it provides greater yields, reducing the need in the Third World for "slash and burn" agriculture. Thus it will save rain forests and prevent soil erosion throughout the world, he said. [13]

Avery agrees, noting that a global commitment to organic farming would require a doubling of the current 5.8 million square miles of the Earth's surface under cultivation just to equal today's food supply. "Biotechnology may be the only compassionate answer to the world food challenge in the 21st century — for poor people, for children and for billions of wild creatures on the planet," Avery said. [14]

In addition, using RoundUp Ready plants will reduce the number of times a farmer must enter his fields to till or apply herbicide, thereby reducing gasoline usage, soil erosion and runoff, because the soil will not be repeatedly stirred up by heavy equipment.

"The folks at Monsanto make these statements without ever having visited a real organic farm," Kirschenmann responds. "When you manage the soil organically, you are constantly improving the quality. There may be as many as 2 billion microbes in a spoonful of soil. It becomes more dense, retains more water and is not subject to wind and water erosion."

Anderson agrees. "We've had Penn State [University] folks here, and they were absolutely astounded" at the condition of the soil, he says. "The deans from the College of Agriculture said, 'Oh, my God. There's more organic matter here than we've seen in a long time.' "

In the early 1990s, researchers at North Dakota State University found little difference in soil erosion between organic and no-till methods, he says, while conventional farms were subject to more wind erosion.

Kirshenmann argues that no-till farming and genetically engineered crops that eliminate the need for tilling may cause the soil to be too compacted. "If you never disturb the soil you get pathogens in the soil, which can increase the chemicals required over the long term," he says.

Organic farmers worry about herbicide-resistant crops, like RoundUp Ready soybeans, which resist Monsanto's RoundUp herbicide and allow farmers to spray entire fields with the weed killer without killing the soybean plants. Organic farmers and environmentalists fear that growing these crops commercially on millions of acres throughout the world could create herbicide-resistant "monster weeds" that could then spread to organic fields.

They point to a 1996 Danish study showing that genetically modified herbicide-resistant canola plants had bred with a wild, weedy relative. Biologists had said if GMO plants do cross-breed, the wild relative would inherit vulnerabilities of the hybrid parent plant, and probably would not reproduce. However, on Aug. 6, an Ohio State University scientist released a new study showing that not only do genetically engineered canola plants pass on their herbicide resistance to wild relatives but after three generations the wild relative is just as healthy and prolific as its ordinary relative. [15]

"Resistance management is a legitimate concern," says Dennis Stolte, deputy director of the Washington office of the American Farm Bureau, "but the potential benefits of biotech far outweigh those concerns." Bioengineered crops have allowed farmers to reduce their per-acre pesticide use significantly, he says. "We ought to be hearing cheers from the environmental community about this stuff."

But organic advocates say such studies indicate that biotechnology could create unpredictable, potentially irreversible environmental dangers. "If there's a mistake, it can't be contained or cleaned up —ever," Ticciati says. "Pesticides can generally be cleaned up, maybe in 50 years. Nuclear wastes can be cleaned up in 10,000 years. But with genetic pollution, you cannot just come back in 20 years and say, 'Oops.' "

"There is no scientific basis for concern," says Roger Beachy, a plant geneticist at the Scripps Research Institute in California. "After 15 years of field study," he says, "there have been no surprises, no unexpected results." [16]

Anti-GMO activists, however, point to several unexpected results when genetically engineered crops have been introduced into commercial production.

"For example, Monsanto just had to pay $1.8 million in damages to three Mississippi farmers who planted RoundUp Ready cotton last year and sat by and watched as malformed bolls fell off prematurely," says UCS's Mellon.

Organic farmers and environmentalists also point to a recent study at the Scottish Crop Research Institute, which found that female ladybugs feeding on aphids that had eaten genetically engineered potatoes produced fewer eggs and had shorter lifespans than control bugs.

But Monsanto's Harness notes that if it weren't for the "environmentally benign" bioengineered potato crop, the entire field would have been sprayed with more toxic pesticides that would have killed both the aphids and the ladybugs.

"It's entirely appropriate that we have a heightened level of concern about health and the safety of our food and the environmental impact of producing that food," Giddings says. "The irony would be if this heightened concern ends up causing safer technologies and products to be unduly delayed." ∎

BACKGROUND

Organic Backlash

After Sir Albert Howard observed organic farming in India in the 1930s,

Continued on p. 772

Chronology

1800s *The first fertilizers and insecticides are developed.*

1840-45
German chemist Jules Liebig patents the first fertilizer.

1867
Arsenic-based Paris Green, the first insecticide, is used against the Colorado potato beetle.

1873
DDT is synthesized by a German scientist.

•

Early 1900s
Organic farming emerges as an alternative to conventional farming as the dangers of pesticides are recognized.

1933
The best-selling book *100,000,000 Guinea Pigs* discusses the hazards from spray insecticides.

1938
The Agriculture Department (USDA) yearbook, *Soils and Men*, describes organic farming.

1945-50
U.S agriculture becomes highly industrialized, using chemicals, mechanization and monoculture farming to feed war-torn Europe.

1946
Walnut Acres, one of the nation's first commercial organic farms, begins operations.

1950
The Food and Drug Administration (FDA) warns it is "extremely likely the potential hazard of DDT has been underestimated."

1962
Rachel Carson's chilling book, *Silent Spring*, warns of severe damage to the environment from pesticides. Chemical companies attack Carson.

1963
The President's Science Advisory Committee vindicates Carson.

1968
Science magazine links declining bird populations with reproductive failures due to pesticide accumulations in their tissues.

1970
The first Earth Day is held, prompting some Americans to adopt pesticide-free farming methods and non-chemical food preservation.

1972
DDT is banned in the United States. The International Federation of Organic Agriculture Movements (IFOAM) publishes the first standards for organic agriculture.

1980
The first state-run organic-certification program is implemented in Washington.

1986
The first national guidelines for organic production are published by the Organic Foods Production Association of North America (now the Organic Trade Association).

1988
Environmental Protection Agency (EPA) says that 74 different pesticides are found in groundwater in 38 states.

1990s *As evidence that pesticides can be dangerous piles up, the government moves to develop standards for "organic" labeling.*

1990
The Organic Foods Production Act establishes a framework to create national standards for certifying organic food products.

1993
A National Research Council report calls for greater regulation of pesticides.

1994
The government approves the genetically engineered Flavr Saver tomato and bovine growth hormone, an engineered veterinary drug that increases milk production.

1996
Congress passes Food Quality Protection Act, forcing EPA to evaluate the combined toxic effects of all pesticides.

1997
FDA approves food irradiation to kill bacteria such as E. coli in beef. Food safety activists say that the process destroys nutrients and creates chemicals that may be mutagenic and carcinogenic. In December, USDA issues proposed organic labeling regulations.

1998
The USDA receives 280,000 mostly negative responses from the public about its proposed organic standards and promises to rewrite the regulations.

Are Media Food Reports Too Bland?

Two award-winning Florida TV reporters were fired last December after Monsanto Corp. lawyers threatened "dire consequences" for Fox News if it ran their report about the dangers of bovine growth hormone (BGH).

Reporters Jane Akre and Steve Wilson have sued WTVT in Tampa, alleging it violated Federal Communications Commission rules by broadcasting a "false and misleading" re-written version of their story. (The reporters have posted their original scripts and court documents on the Internet at www.foxBGHsuit.com.)

Anti-biotech activists say the case reflects the way corporate pressure has bullied the American media into not aggressively covering the rapidly changing food industry.

"There hasn't been the outrage in the U.S. that there has been in Europe, where the media spread the message" about GMOs. Thus Americans don't know how much genetically modified foods they are actually eating, says Ronnie Cummins, director of the anti-biotech Pure Food Campaign.

Biotechnology advocates claim, on the other hand, that Americans are less upset than the Europeans because they understand and accept government and scientific assertions that genetically engineered foods are as safe as conventional crops.

Yet anti-biotech activists cite efforts by the Dairy Coalition to pressure editors not to run stories about allegations that BGH is unsafe. Questions about the safety of BGH, which boosts cows' milk production, have persisted since its introduction in 1993, even though a host of health organizations have declared it safe.

The July issue of *The Progressive* cites documents allegedly from the coalition indicating that the group had tried to pressure *The Boston Globe, The Wall Street Journal, The New York Times, The Washington Post* and *USA Today* not to run anti-BGH stories by attacking the credibility of BGH critics.[1]

U.S. debate over genetically modified foods also has been muted by the spectre of so-called state "veggie libel" laws, says Laura Ticciati, executive director of Mothers for Natural Law, which opposes transgenic foods. "We are very careful what we say around here," she says.

At least 13 states have "food disparagement" laws penalizing "false and damaging" statements about perishable foods. Supporters say the laws protect producers from unsubstantiated negative claims; critics say the laws muzzle free speech about food safety.

In the first major court test of such laws, Texas cattlemen sued television talk-show host Oprah Winfrey for $10 million, claiming her negative comments about beef during a show about "mad cow" disease caused a sharp fall in beef prices. Although Winfrey eventually won, the case left unresolved the question of whether food-disparagement statutes are constitutional.

Food-disparagement bills have been introduced in at least a dozen states. A disparagement provision introduced in the federal 1996 farm bill was rejected.

But Oprah's muzzle hasn't been removed yet. The ranchers are appealing the decision, and filed a separate suit in Texas state court.

[1] Sheldon Rampton and John Stauber, "The Gag Reflex," *The Progressive*, July 1998.

Continued from p. 770

he enthusiastically described what he had seen in a 1940 book, *An Agricultural Testament*. American publisher J.I. Rodale was so inspired by Howard's work that he published a special issue of his magazine, *Fact Digest*, on the subject. It later became the popular *Organic Gardening* magazine.

At the end of World War II, many of America's 6 million farms organically fertilized with manure and relied on crop rotation to control pests.

Then scientists experimenting with surplus war chemicals discovered how to improve crop yields and quality. From 1964-1982, chemical pesticide use soared 170 percent, with similar increases in herbicide and fer-

tilizer use. Today, sales of chemical pesticides top $5 billion a year.[17]

Meanwhile, American agriculture was shifting to large-scale, mechanized farming. The goal was to increase the volume of food production, reduce costs and expand exports. As Earl Butz, President Richard M. Nixon's Agriculture secretary put it, "Adapt or die, resist and perish . . . agriculture is now big business."[18]

Butz advised farmers to plow from fencerow-to-fencerow, enlarge their herds and buy more and bigger machines because, "You can't ever grow too much crop."[19]

Farmers succeeded too well. Overproduction lowered farm prices, and farmers found themselves on a chemically dependent treadmill of producing more and

earning less. The more that conventional farmers produced, the more they needed to produce to maintain a livable income, and thus the more dependent they became on yield-boosting chemicals.

The cheap-food part of the policy paid off in spades, however. Americans spend about 12 percent of their disposable income on food, less than consumers in any other industrialized nation.[20]

Today's organic movement largely developed as a backlash to agribusiness and increased environmental concerns about the pesticide DDT.

After the first Earth Day in 1970, small groups of Americans — often on "hippie communes" — returned to pesticide-free farming. Although they first produced just enough for themselves, others developed an appreciation for organic food, and the demand grew. Health-food stores sprouted up, often in college towns. As environmental consciousness grew, health food and other natural products trickled into mainstream outlets.

The guiding principle for organic farmers was, "If you take care of the soil, it will take care of you," says Illinois farmer Mangus.

Ironically, says Steven Pavich, research director for Pavich Family Farms, the world's largest organic grower of table grapes, "contrary to its counterculture beginnings, the organic industry evolved based strictly on free-market principles. And they've done it without the subsidies that conventional agriculture has gotten." Moreover, many small farmers have converted to organics because they could not compete with large, industrial farms.

Now, say organic advocates, the advent of bioengineered crops places American agriculture at another crossroads, similar to where it was at the advent of industrialized farming. Many in government and the biotech industry see bioengineered crops as a way to get off the pesticide treadmill.

But biotech, by its very nature, requires huge corporate investments in research and development and major gene-to-shelf consolidation of the industry, agricultural economists say. To succeed with biotech crops, most farmers will have to grow under contract to biotech companies, which small and organic farmers see as just another input-dependent treadmill.

As Mellon says, biotech seeds and pesticides "are much more compatible with monoculture and industrial agriculture."

New Regulations

The seeds for the regulation of nationwide organic standards were planted by organic farmers themselves.

The industry had asked for "field-to-fork" standards to clear up confusion caused by the current patchwork of 44 state and private certification agencies across the country, which often operate with little or no enforcement. In addition, they wanted to protect consumers from unscrupulous food distributors mislabeling conventional produce as organic.

In 1990, as part of the Omnibus Farm Bill, the federal government passed the Organic Foods Production Act (OFPA), which called for national standards for the production and handling of foods labeled "organic."

The OFPA created the National Organic Program within the USDA's Agricultural Marketing Service to oversee enforcement of the standards by monitoring the state and private organizations that will continue to certify organic producers and handlers.

To advise USDA in setting the standards, the act authorized establishment of the NOSB — including farmers, processors, retailers, environmental advocates and a scientist. The NOSB met with industry representatives for three years and developed a proposal that represented a broad consensus within the industry.

When the USDA finally published proposed regulations last December, there were 66 areas objectionable to the organic industry that had not been in the original NOSB recommendations. These included the controversial suggestion that "organic" labels apply to irradiated, genetically engineered and sludge-fertilized foods.

Some speculated that the USDA had included the three controversial provisions for economic and political reasons. According to this view, USDA officials were apparently more concerned about how excluding GMOs would impact U.S. biotech exports to Europe than about how including them would threaten organic exports. Europeans are in an uproar over U.S. exports of transgenic corn and soybeans — "Frankenstein foods" to European environmentalists. *(See story, p. 768.)*

An internal USDA memorandum, published on the Internet by *Mother Jones* magazine, outlined the dilemma: "Few if any existing [worldwide organic] standards permit GMOs, and their inclusion [by the U.S.] could affect the export of U.S.-grown organic product," the May 1, 1997, memo said. "However, the [USDA's] Animal and Plant Health Inspection Service and the Foreign Agricultural Service are concerned that our trading partners will point to a USDA organic standard that excludes GMOs as evidence of the department's concern about the safety of bioengineered commodities."

"We were just naive neophytes," says Pavich, a member of the NOSB. "We were completely unprepared for the shock of dealing with the bureaucracy. Many in the organic community were caught off guard because they assumed they had allies in [President] Clinton and [Vice President Al] Gore."

Organic farmers are also concerned that the proposed regulations would prohibit private certifiers from labeling products as adhering to organic standards that are more stringent than the USDA's standards. Advocates argue that the policy essentially gives the USDA a monopoly over the word "organic."

Finally, the proposed regulations would have allowed the secretary of Agriculture to add items to the list of substances allowed in organic farming. Organic industry activists vehemently argue that the 1990 law specifically states that only the NOSB may decide whether an ingredient may be allowed on the list.

Members of Congress who helped write the 1990 law agree. "We ask that you return to the recommendations of the National Organic Standards Board, as a model for your overhaul of the Proposed Rules," said a bipartisan April 30 letter from 31 senators to Agriculture Secretary Dan Glickman. "The Proposed Rules disregard the authority Congress granted to the NOSB to determine the narrow list of allowable synthetics." ■

Can Family Farms and Global Biodiversity Survive...

For thousands of years farmers have saved seed from one harvest to the next. Yet in the brave new world of agricultural biotechnology, Pinkerton detectives are now sent to make sure farmers are not saving seeds.

The detectives are hired by biotechnology firms like Monsanto to enforce agreements farmers sign when they buy the firm's patented, genetically modified seeds. "We investigate all reports of suspected piracy of our biotech traits," said Monsanto's Karen Marshall. [1]

Now those detectives may no longer be needed. A new biotech discovery, developed in part with U.S. taxpayer dollars, prevents saved seeds from germinating.

Dubbed "terminator" technology by critics, it is one of two startling recent biotech developments that have alarmed conventional and organic farmers around the world. The second is the rapid consolidation of much of the worldwide seed industry into the hands of three multinational biotechnology companies.

In the past year, Monsanto, DuPont and Novartis, a European firm, have acquired or merged with dozens of companies that produce much of the world's soy, corn and wheat seeds. Since the three also produce most of the world's insecticides and herbicides, they now are poised to exercise major control over what gets planted, how it's grown and how much it costs.

How these developments will affect farmers, consumers and worldwide biodiversity is the subject of passionate debate. "People are just dumbfounded by this," says Bill Heffernan, a rural sociologist at the University of Missouri. "It all happened so quickly. Nobody was paying much attention."

Heffernan and others fear it's just a matter of time before the consolidated seed/chemical companies buy or merge with major food processors, enabling them to control food production from the genes to the grocery shelves. "Three or four firms control all the genetic material that our food and feed grain comes from," Heffernan says. Add "terminator technology" to the mix, and "they really do have control."

"This country is in the final stages of sorting out who is going to produce its food," says Bill Christison, president of the National Family Farm Coalition. "The family farm is really under the gun."

"We're headed toward enveloping the food system in enormous industrial conglomerates," predicts Harold F. Breimyer, a 30-year veteran of the Agriculture Department. "In my nastier moments I call it industrial feudalism."

Because of the proprietary nature of the new crops, the biotech firms will basically contract with the farmer to produce crops according to their specifications.

Farmers will become "glorified tractor drivers" for the multinational companies, Heffernan warns, with the companies "telling farmers what to plant and which pesticides to use."

"We will have to dance to the tune of whoever owns those seed patents," complains Christison.

But others see corporate, biotech farming as a lifeline helping farmers stay afloat in the rocky shoals of global agriculture. Purdue University agricultural economist Mike Boehlje says being a contract farmer "does not automatically imply serfdom. McDonalds tells franchisees what to do, but most people wouldn't call them serfs."

Others argue that contract growing reduces the risks in farming by guaranteeing a buyer before the farmer puts seed into the ground. "Biotech is the future of agriculture," says Dennis Stolte, deputy director of the Washington office of the American Farm Bureau Federation. "Now that the government is no longer supporting commodity farm prices, this is how we'll increase income to the family farmer.

"It's a global market for agricultural commodities now," he continues. "Biotech will allow family farmers to produce more and do it smarter."

Nicolas Kalaitzandonakes, a University of Missouri associate professor of agricultural economics, agrees. Consolidation is the only way biotech companies can compete in a global economy and recoup the enormous R&D costs of genetically engineered products, he says.

"The opening of global markets is driving much of this consolidation," he says. "The underlying force is not, 'Oh, big, bad Monsanto is trying to corner the market.' It's that with information technology and biotechnology, you can reach many more markets. The economies of scale are so large that you've got to be a global player or you will be driven out of the market."

He likens the consolidation to banking, which is "probably the fastest consolidating industry in the world."

Stolte agrees. "It's more a sign of the times than something that can be blamed on biotech," he says.

Nevertheless, Iowa State University agricultural economist Neil Harl says the recent wave of seed/chemical company mergers and acquisitions has tremendous anti-competitive consequences. "The FTC and the Anti-trust Division of the Department of Justice need to watch with unusual scrutiny what is happening here," says Harl, who is also a lawyer.

What makes the consolidation worrisome, Harl says, is that a biotech company that acquires a patent on a particular part of a plant cell's structure "keeps competitors away from that area of research." Biotech consolidation is different from auto-industry concentration, others point out, because the auto companies don't own patents on the genetic makeup of the steel they use.

Spokesmen for Monsanto, Dupont and Novartis declined to comment, in part because of pending acquisitions.

Organic and small farmers who don't want to grow genetically engineered foods say the consolidations jeopardize their future supply of non-genetically modified seeds. Harl says that even though there are still many regional seed companies left that sell conventional seeds,

... 'Terminator' Seeds and Huge Biotech Firms?

many could go out of business if farmers turn heavily to biotech seeds.

Katherine DiMatteo, executive director of the Organic Trade Association, predicts tight seed supplies if the newly consolidated seed firms decide the organic market is too small to bother with their customized needs.

Kalaitzandonakes dismisses such fears. "If there is a market for organic foods, there will be seeds, producers and distributors" who will jump in to fill the demand, he says.

Others fear the consolidation could reduce biodiversity and spur more worldwide monoculture, exposing global food supplies to vulnerability from unknown pests. "The biggest threat to consumers and growers is the crunching down of diversity, so there's less variety and more power concentrated in fewer hands," says Ron Roller, president of American Soy Products of Saline, Mich.

"Just because biotech companies are connecting with the seed companies does not mean we are making the germplasm pool any shallower," Kalaitzandonakes argues. [2]

"To say that [concentrated] ownership necessarily means that we are all going to be cultivating the same hybrid is naive. There will be consolidation of the germplasm, and they'll look for better hybrids."

In fact, he says, it could increase biodiversity. "If you are global, then you can prospect globally for your germplasm," he notes.

Kelly Shea, whose Northland Organic Foods provides non-genetically modified seed, worries that multinational seed/biotech companies are on the rise just as the federal government is reducing seed research. "It's very important that we continue supporting our public seed research institutions around the world," Shea says. "No one should be able to control seed."

Concern about control was heightened on March 3, when a patent for the "Control of Plant Gene Expression" was granted to the "terminator" technique's co-creators — the USDA's Agricultural Research Service (ARS) and Delta and Pine Land Co., a Mississippi cotton seed company being acquired by Monsanto.

Critics say that by producing seeds that will not germinate, "terminator technology" forces farmers using those seeds to buy more seeds every year.

"This is not just a debate about a particular technology," says Michael Sligh, program director of the Rural Advancement Foundation International (RAFI). "It's about the future of world food supplies."

"The astonishing thing to me is that they actually used public research dollars to develop this technology," says Fred Kirschenmann, an organic farmer in North Dakota.

"The lust after this technology really gives the lie to the [companies'] mantra that biotechnology is going to feed the world," says Jane Rissler, a microbiologist at the Union of Concerned Scientists. "They're not going to allow poor farmers in the developing world [who use their seeds] to save seeds from one year to the next."

On the other hand, Delta and Pine Land President Murray Robinson said the technology opens up countries like China, India and Pakistan to genetically engineered crops because it enables such patented seeds to be protected. "Farmers in those countries have extremely serious pest problems," Robinson said, "which could be dramatically helped by new herbicide- and insect-resistance technology." [3]

Moreover, ARS officials say, terminator technology will increase biodiversity by spurring biotech companies to develop endless varieties of seeds for marginal cropland.

"There are huge numbers of genes out there," says Michael Ruff, deputy assistant administrator for ARS's Office of Technology Transfer, which can provide plants with resistance to drought, cold or pests. "But companies were very reluctant to develop those genes because there was no way to protect their [investment]," he says.

And, says Sandy Miller Hays, director of information at ARS, "No one is going to force [Third World farmers] to buy these seeds. They can continue to use their ancestral seeds if they choose.

Activists are already pushing for a ban on terminator seeds in India, fearing that uncontrolled cross-pollination could destroy ancient varieties such as long-grained aromatic Basmati rice. [4]

Organic farmers, who rely on rotating crops and a wide variety of specialty seeds, also fear that if terminator plants cross-pollinate with wild relatives it could deplete worldwide seed diversity, especially heirloom seeds handed down from generation to generation.

Ruff says such fears about widespread cross-pollination are unfounded because a single grain of pollen only fertilizes a single flower, not an entire plant. Only the seeds from that flower would fail to germinate.

Besides, the technology can be turned "on and off, like a light switch," Hays says, so unforeseen consequences can be controlled.

"We will see that all the appropriate safeguards are in place," Ruff says, especially if it is applied to crops that are major wind-borne pollinators.

"It's good that the ARS is involved," Hays adds. "We have an interest in protecting the interests of the public."

---

[1] Quoted in "Conflicts Flare Over Sales, Planting," *Omaha World-Herald*, April 9, 1998.

[2] Germplasm is the hereditary material, or the genes, that make up germ cells.

[3] Quoted in Bill Freiberg, "Is Delta and Pine Land's 'Terminator Gene' a Billion-Dollar Discovery," *Seed & Crops Digest*, March/April 1998.

[4] "Biotech Firms Sow Seeds of Discord," *Inter Press Service*, July 15, 1998.

Continued from p. 773

CURRENT SITUATION

Revised Regs Due

While the USDA goes back to the drawing board with the benefit of 280,000 suggestions from the public, the organic community nervously awaits the outcome. Revised regulations are expected to be published for public comment by year's end.

Some organic advocates were encouraged in July when Glickman told the NOSB he would not put anything on the list of substances allowed in organic farming that had not been first recommended by the board.

But Ronnie Cummins, director of the Washington-based Pure Food Campaign, fears the final rule will be a compromise. "Too many factory farm-style producers want an 'organic' label on their products," he says.

"Clinton and Gore know they are sitting on a political minefield," he continues. "If they put out a compromise rule, the people who buy organic are going to go wild when they hear that the U.S. government has come up with the lowest organic standards in the world."

Worse, he says, will be the public reaction if the final rule contains the original language prohibiting private and state certifiers from labeling according to standards higher than the federal government's. "Any final rule that gives Washington bureaucrats a monopoly on the word 'organic' is totally unacceptable," he says, "and represents a violation of our constitutional rights of free speech."

"As the proposed USDA rules read now," warns Cummins, "Monsanto, Tyson, Perdue, Cargill, Kroger, Safeway,

McDonald's will have the legal option to sue any farmer, co-op, retailer, processor or handler if we certify, label or even imply in our advertising that our products are actually 'real organic' products that might exceed . . . those of the USDA." [21]

The $430 billion food-processing industry has a lot of money to give away in a presidential campaign, he notes. "But Clinton and Gore got a lot of votes from people who buy organic foods for their kids. So I don't expect to see a national standard finalized until after the 2000 election."

Not willing to wait that long for standards he feels will be below par, Cummins' group is working with others in the industry to come up with an alternative nationwide standard that conforms to the original NOSB recommendations and the requirements of the International Federation of Organic Agriculture Movements (IFOAM). They already have 27 private and state organic certifiers signed on, as well as leading domestic and international retail and consumer organizations.

The Pure Food Campaign, along with other groups that helped organize the response to the USDA regulations last spring, is organizing a nationwide Organic Consumers Association, hoping to establish chapters in every state and congressional district to monitor the organic regulations.

Resistance to Bt

Meanwhile, even biotech industry officials admit that the widespread commercialization of transgenic Bt crops will set back the organic industry.

"The biggest threat that biotechnology presents to organic agriculture is from taking some of the most powerful techniques from organic farming and incorporating them into

sustainable, mainstream agriculture," Giddings says.

Companies promoting Bt plants are "waging an undeclared war against sustainable farming practices," charged Benedikt Haerlin, genetic engineering coordinator of Greenpeace International. Haerlin spoke at a press conference in Washington on Sept. 16, 1997, after Greenpeace, the Sierra Club, IFOAM and farmers and environmentalists filed a legal petition against the EPA. The agency's approval of transgenic Bt plants would "seriously threaten the future of organic agriculture" because it would cause "the wanton destruction of one of the world's safest, most effective and widely used biological pesticides," he charged.

"They are planting millions and millions of acres of Bt products in the U.S. and around the world," Mellon says. "It has been one of the biggest sales blitzes the seed industry has ever seen. Rather than being concerned about managing and saving this very important protein, they want to sell as much as they can to as many farmers as they can as quickly as they can."

"It very clearly is a tool that we're going to lose," Kirschenmann says. "I suspect we'll see resistance develop within three to five years."

Giddings responds that biotech companies have a vested interest in making sure that pests do not develop Bt resistance, because their products would then be obsolete.

Nevertheless, he asks, "Is it appropriate to deprive the vast acreage on which crops are grown from using the most environmentally compatible pest control technique, just to preserve a monopoly on the use of that product by a small group of farmers who produce only a minor fraction of our total consumption?"

Initially, Bt corn won't threaten organic farmers, he says, because most are located on the West Coast,

Continued on p. 778

At Issue:

Should all genetically engineered foods be labeled?

STEVEN M. DRUKER, J.D.
Executive Director, Alliance for Bio-Integrity
www.bio-integrity.org

FROM A POSITION PAPER DATED AUGUST 1998.

genetically engineered foods must be labeled because federal law and basic morality require it. The Food and Drug Administration's refusal to institute such labeling violates two statutes: the Constitution, and essential ethical principles. The Food, Drug and Cosmetic Act mandates that all "material facts" about food be labeled. The fact that one or more foreign genes have been spliced into an organism's DNA is clearly "material," since it entails new risks and adds new ingredients.

Many eminent scientists warn that gene-splicing introduces a unique set of risks not associated with traditionally produced foods: (a) Because the foreign genes enter the host DNA haphazardly and disrupt the region into which they wedge, they can broadly and adversely alter cellular function. (b) The powerful promoters artificially attached to the foreign genes can induce imbalanced expression of adjacent native genes. (c) The inserted genes produce proteins foreign to the host cells that could disturb complex biochemical feedback loops. Each type of disruption can generate toxins and carcinogens — or cause other harmful effects — in unpredictable ways, and the minimal, unsupervised testing currently performed cannot adequately screen for the potential problems.

Nine leading scientists are so concerned about these risks they are plaintiffs in the lawsuit our organization has filed against the FDA (i) challenging its unfounded assumption that gene-spliced foods are as safe as natural ones and (ii) demanding that adequate safety testing and labeling be required.

Added risks aside, the presence of novel, unexpected substances in a food is itself a "material" fact. If the same quantity of foreign substance created within a transgenic vegetable were instead added to it by conventional means, it would surely qualify as an ingredient that requires labeling.

Labeling is also required by the First Amendment of the Constitution and the Religious Freedom Restoration Act, which guarantee free exercise of religion. As a matter of religious principle, millions of Americans need to avoid foods with genes from either some or all animals, and millions of others reject all gene-spliced foods as irresponsible disruptions of the integrity of God's creation.

Citizens have a right to know when material alterations are made to their food. They have a right to choose whether they will consume foods that are inherently riskier than conventional products. They have a right to know when the genetic structure and chemical composition of food organisms are distorted in a way that broadly offends religious beliefs. The FDA's agenda to promote the biotech industry should not be allowed to override these rights.

L. VAL GIDDINGS, PH.D.
Vice president for food and agriculture, Biotechnology Industry Organization; www.bio.org

WRITTEN FOR THE CQ RESEARCHER, AUGUST 1998.

consumers have a right to accurate and informative information about the health and safety implications of food products. Whenever there is a legitimate health or safety interest involved, food labels should accurately and concisely make this clear to consumers. But labels that seek surreptitiously to stigmatize foods derived from genetically modified crops serve only to frighten consumers, not to improve their health and safety. The policy of the U.S. Food and Drug Administration is to require labeling of foods based on safety and nutritional characteristics, not the process used to produce the food.

Whenever an allergen might be introduced into a food where it was not previously found, labels should convey this information. When a food has been modified — by whatever technique — so that its nutritional content is substantially different from that in the unmodified forms with which we are most familiar, labels should convey this information. Current FDA food labeling policy already imposes these requirements under the federal Food, Drug and Cosmetic Act.

However, when the "modified" food has been derived from crops that are nutritionally indistinguishable from traditional forms, where there are absolutely no scientifically credible health or nutrition issues at stake, food producers and manufacturers should not be compelled by law to provide labels that may mislead consumers into thinking there is a material difference when there is not.

In the United States we have worked long and hard to reach the present situation, where our food labels convey a wealth of credible information related to nutrition and safety, supported by sound science. These labels help us derive the maximum benefit from the most abundant and safest food supply in the world.

The concerns of those who express moral or ethical reservations about biotechnology or genetic engineering command respect. They must be taken seriously. No one should be compelled to buy something they do not want. But in the absence of any compelling health or safety-based justification, it would be no more legitimate to have a federal mandate to label biotechnology-derived foods than for those produced under kosher or halal conditions.

On the other hand, if the marketplace produces sufficient demand, and consumers are willing to bear the additional costs of special labeling for whatever reason, there is no reason not to let this come to pass as a result of choices freely exercised in the marketplace, provided consumers are not misled in the process.

Continued from p. 775

Florida and in the Northeast — far from the Corn Belt. But biotech firms have already announced that they plan to use Bt in other major crops.

Giddings pointed out that there are 200-300 varieties of Bt, and that other configurations can be developed if resistance develops to one strain. However, Mellon and Kirschenmann note that studies have shown that once pests develop resistance to one class of pesticides, they quickly develop resistance to other products in the same class.

To prevent resistance, the UCS is urging EPA to require farmers using Bt crops to plant 30-40 percent of their land with non-Bt crops as refuges for pests. That way, even if some develop resistance, the entire pest population will not become resistant immediately. The EPA has begun asking biotech companies to have farmers do that, but the UCS wants it made mandatory.

Kirschenmann is doubtful it will work, however. "To assume that all farmers will cooperate and plant these refuges is just very naive," he says. "Farmers never follow plans that others come up with for them."

Scrambling for Seeds

As more and more genetically engineered commodities flood the markets, organic farmers and food processors are scrambling for non-GMO seeds, soybeans and ingredients for processed foods.

"Manufacturers are banding together and trying to figure out how to get these supplies," says Wittenberg of Whole Foods.

For the moment, certified organic products are the main source for non-GMO foods, since organic farmers do not use genetically engineered seeds. Thus the demand for organic soybeans and soybean-based ingredients and processing aids has skyrocketed, largely in response to increased overseas demand for non-GMO foods, especially soybeans.

"The demand for non-genetically altered foods is probably one of the things that has driven the growth of the organic industry worldwide," says Mangus, who exports non-GMO soybeans and popcorn to the Japanese. "The demand for organic soybeans has mushroomed 20-30 percent in Japan alone in the last couple of years" despite tight economic times there, he says.

To meet the increased demand, "People from the Midwest are coming into Pennsylvania, which has never been a big soybean market, and contracting with farmers to grow soybeans," says Walnut Acres' Anderson. "The price for organic soybeans in the last two years has gone up to $18 a bushel, triple that of conventional soybeans."

Observers expect the demand for organics to continue, which they hope will lead even more small farmers to switch over to organic methods.

"If the organic industry comes out of all this with the prohibition on labeling genetically engineered foods as organic, the Japanese and Europeans will be much more interested in U.S. organic foods," Commins says.

A parallel niche market is emerging for non-organic, non-GMO foods, which will cost about 40 percent over conventional prices because they have to be kept segregated from bioengineered products throughout production. For instance, many of the soybeans Mangus exports to Japan are not certified organic, but are coming from what he calls "transitional" farms — conventional farms converting to organic methods, partly to take advantage of the higher organic prices.

But the lack of organic certification does not bother Japanese and European buyers, who are more concerned that the product is GMO-free and was segregated throughout production, he says.

"My view is that within two years market demand in Europe and Japan will be such that the seed and grain industry in the U.S. will be segregated, regardless of what the laws are," says John Fagan, owner of Genetic ID, of Fairfield, Iowa. In 1996 Fagan developed a test for determining whether something has been genetically altered.

Other entrepreneurs, recognizing the growth potential for non-GMO foods and seeds, are stepping in to fill the need. "The speed at which [GMO] stuff is coming into the food supply is very quick," says Ron Roller, president of American Soy Products, Saline, Mich. "It will take a while to create a parallel food-supply system outside of the conventional system. But the seed situation is changing now. My goal is to supply 100 percent of the non-GMO seeds needed by my growers," he says. "Right now, I'm supplying about one-third."

He encourages farmers to grow their own seed. "Given what's coming with genetics, it's the only way we can know what we're growing," he says. "U.S. consumers are not yet demanding GMO-free food, so the issue is not as hot as it could be. But we feel we want to have this capability if it does heat up."

Kahn is less alarmed than some about future non-GMO seed supplies. "I think there's a bit of a panic that's really inappropriate," he says, predicting that entrepreneurs will fill the demand.

Northland Organic Foods, for example, has been exporting organic grains overseas for years. "We got into the seed business through the back door," says Kelly Shea, a grain buyer for the St. Paul, Minn., company. Shea, who tracks seed company buyouts and mergers and surfs the Internet seeking sources of non-GMO seeds, anticipated the organic seed shortage.

Because Northland was already providing segregated non-GMO soybeans to buyers from Europe and Japan, it was easy for them to begin supplying segregated non-GMO seeds.

Finding non-GMO ingredients for processed foods is much more difficult than finding non-engineered seeds. Because GMO foods are not segregated or labeled in bulk commodity shipments, it is impossible for a non-organic processor to know whether his ingredients have been genetically engineered or not.

"If a processor has to find certified GMO-free flour, there is no such thing except in the organic industry," Commins says.

Annie Kirschenmann, of Farm Certified Organics in Medina, N.D., has studied the difficulties of producing 100 percent non-GMO processed foods. "It's not possible at this time to certify a [multi-ingredient] food as being 100 percent GMO-free," she said, because it's impossible to know whether the processing aids and ingredients like lecithin or citric acid have been engineered. "So it's more accurate to say that a product is produced 'without genetically engineered organisms.' "

Ticciati's nonprofit group has become a clearinghouse for organic and natural food processors seeking information on where to find GMO-free ingredients. "Given the speed with which these things were getting into our food supply, we were very concerned about keeping GMOs out of the organic market," she says.

"We were particularly concerned about finding a commercial infant-formula company willing to produce an infant formula without GMOs," she continues. "By 1999 there will be a GMO-free formula on the market."

Mainstream Interest

Meanwhile, the organic industry's 20-25 percent annual growth (compared with conventional farming's 3 percent rate) is expected to continue for the foreseeable future. At $4 billion in annual sales, the industry now makes up only about 1 percent of the $440-billion food business. But it is expected to grow to at least $10 billion in the next decade.

Analysts point to Austin-based Whole Foods, which has recently acquired dozens of successful independents, like Fresh Fields. Fast approaching $1 billion in annual sales, Whole Foods now has 86 stores nationwide.

To harvest some of the organic profits, mainstream grocers are putting more and more organic products on their shelves. Last year, four food retailing executives founded the New Organics Co., based in Burlingame, Calif., promising to produce the nation's first line of competitively priced organic products aimed strictly at major supermarkets.

Meanwhile, big food processors like Gerber, Welches and even the candy giant Mars have been buying into the organic market. A year ago, investor Roy E. Disney bought Kahn's Cascadian Farms. And H.J. Heinz Co. bought Earth's Best organic baby food company.

Some long-time customers fear the bigness threatens the integrity of organic. For instance, when Whole Foods took over the purist California chain Mrs. Gooch's in 1996, many Gooch's customers complained that Whole Foods was offering beer, wine, coffee and ice creams and other snacks containing such no-nos as white flour and refined sugar.

"Unfounded paranoia," says Kahn, about fears that bigness means a weakening of standards. "Anybody with a lick of sense knows that what differentiates us is our adherence to standards." Besides, he says, "If organic food is going to get beyond being a yuppie food, it has to cost less and a larger population has to know its advantages." [22]

OUTLOOK

Many Questions

If the revised USDA organic regulations are accepted by the industry, they could boost consumer confidence in organic products, spurring even more growth.

"It will keep fraud to a minimum," says the OTA's DiMatteo, "and it's going to create a level playing field for the marketplace, especially for farmers and manufacturers who have been sitting on the fence, not knowing what would be required to be certified. That could lead to greater production, lower prices and a greater consumer appetite for organics." [23]

The new standards could also entice more struggling small farmers to switch to organic farming because overseas markets will open up. "If we get these standards right, there is a tremendous opportunity for small family farmers to stay on the farm," says Anderson.

The longer-term outlook for organics is still clouded by questions about what impact the biotech juggernaut will have on small farmers in general and organic farmers in particular. Worldwide acreage planted with genetically engineered crops is expected to triple by 2000. [24]

Unanswerable questions remain about the short-term: Will organic farmers continue to be able to find the kinds of non-GMO seeds they need? Will consumers worldwide learn to accept GMO foods, or turn in large numbers to organics? Or will a segregated, non-GMO food chain emerge to siphon some of that demand away from organics?

A lot will depend on whether the FDA and other governments require companies to label genetically engineered foods. Without labeling, organic food now is the only alternative for consumers wishing to avoid GMOs.

As more and more transgenic foods reach grocery stores, shortages of certain non-GMO foods are likely to arise as they have for soybeans, at least in the short-term, say organic farmers.

"I think there will be short-term supply issues in areas that we haven't even begun to know yet," Anderson says. "But we are a very resourceful group, so I'm confident we'll come up with a solution."

But the big test for the industry will occur when the second wave of biotech foods hits supermarket shelves — foods that are nutritionally or medicinally enhanced through gene-splicing.

The first generation of biotech foods focused on benefits for the farmer, such as reducing their need for insecticides and making it easier to apply herbicides. The second generation — due to hit the market in two to three years — will be "super foods" with disease-fighting, fat-eliminating qualities, such as meat that tastes, looks and smells like beef but lacks cholesterol. Oils with less fat and wheat with more protein are also coming, say biotech companies. Other foods will ease menopausal symptoms or inhibit osteoporosis, among other things. [25]

"If the consumer wants these products then the organic industry is going to be challenged to decide what to do about it," Roller says. "If you have a genetic predisposition to cancer and there is a genetically altered food that reduces your chances of acquiring that disease, then that's a pretty powerful lure to try some of that product."

If, as Giddings predicts, some of the resistance to GMOs begins to evaporate, some predict that organic farmers may be forced to revisit the whole idea of allowing genetically engineered seeds to be grown in organic farming.

"They may have proven or discovered something by then — like nutritionally enhanced food — that will swing public opinion," Anderson says.

Others agree with the world's best-known organic farmer, the Prince of

Wales, who wrote recently that biotech scientists are straying into "realms that belong to God and God alone." Prince Charles vowed never to eat genetically modified food, and never to "knowingly offer this sort of produce to my family and guests."

Still others remain deeply committed to supporting local, small farmers, firmly rejecting the industrialized agricultural model promoted by the giant biotech firms. "I've got a lot of growers who are going through transition from the conventional way of farming to the organic method," Mangus says. "They're sick and tired of the low prices they get for their products and the [high] fees the chemical companies are charging them. As organic farmers you can eliminate a lot of the pesticide costs."

He says sustainable agriculture groups are organizing all around the Illinois countryside, practicing integrated pest management, which includes some of the same methods used by organic farmers.

In the Midwest, a group of environmentalists and consumer groups have recently formed the Kansas City Food Circle, which has vowed to reconnect local consumers to local family farmers. Their mantra is to "eat locally, seasonally and know your farmer personally," says Bill Heffernan, a rural sociologist at the University of Missouri.

"They are going in exactly the opposite direction of industrial agriculture," he says, "and they strongly promote organic farmers."

Perhaps, just as it once was for the young Gene Kahn, organics may again be an anti-establishment refuge, this time for those who don't like the direction America's brave new biotech world is headed. ∎

Notes

[1] For background, see Richard L. Worsnop, "Food Irradiation," *The CQ Researcher*, June 12, 1992, pp. 505-528, Mary H. Cooper, "Food Safety," *The CQ Researcher*, June 4, 1993, pp. 481-504, and Susan C. Phillips, "Genetically

Engineered Foods," *The CQ Researcher*, Aug. 5, 1994, pp. 673-696.

[2] Scott Kilman, "Green Genes," *The Wall Street Journal*, Jan. 29, 1998.

[3] Press release dated Oct. 31, 1995, on Monsanto's Web site.

[4] Quoted in *Pest and Toxic Chemical News*, May 14, 1998.

[5] Robert Steyer, "Seed Business Becomes a Land of Giants," *St. Louis Post-Dispatch*, May 17, 1998, p. E1.

[6] "Greener greens?" *Consumer Reports*, January 1998.

[7] Richard Wiles, et. al., "Same As It Ever Was," *Environmental Working Group*, May 1998.

[8] "Pesticides in the Diets of Infants and Children," National Research Council, 1993.

[9] Dennis T. Avery, "EPA Leaflet Only Fuels Myth that Organic Foods Are Safe Foods," *Wisconsin State Journal*, Aug. 3, 1998.

[10] For a detailed explanation of how the three agencies review GMOs, see Phillips, *op. cit.*, p. 684.

[11] Quoted in Julie Vorman, "Coalition Files Lawsuit Against U.S. to Force Labels on Genetically Engineered Food," Reuters, May 27, 1998.

[12] Christopher Cairns, "E-Coli Warning on New Crops Gene," *The Scotsman*, April 13, 1998.

[13] Jonathon Riley, "GM Crops Greener than Organic Ones, Says Chem Maker," *Farmers Weekly*, May 29, 1998.

[14] Quoted in Vic Robertson, "Expert speaks his mind at lecture," *The Herald (Glasgow)*, Dec. 20, 1996.

[15] The study was announced on Aug. 6, 1998, before the Ecological Society of America meeting in Baltimore by Ohio State University Professor Allison Snow.

[16] Quoted in Richard Ernsberger Jr., "High-Tech Harvests," *Newsweek*, July 13, 1998.

[17] Lucy Warren, "Natural Wisdom," *The San Diego Union-Tribune*, March 3, 1997.

[18] Quoted in Steve Lustgarden, "The high price of cheap food," *Vegetarian Times*, September 1994.

[19] *Ibid.*

[20] *Ibid.*

[21] Quoted in *Food Bytes*, the Pure Food Campaign newsletter, June 5, 1998.

[22] Kate Murphy, "Organic Food Makers Reap Green Yields of Revenue," *The New York Times*, Oct. 26, 1996.

[23] Scott Warner, "Growing What Comes Naturally," *The Chicago Tribune*, Oct. 29, 1997.

[24] Ernsberger, *op. cit.*

[25] Kilman, *op. cit.*

Bibliography

Selected Sources Used

Books

Rissler, Jane, and Margaret Mellon, *The Ecological Risks of Engineered Crops*, The MIT Press, 1996.

Two scientists from the Union of Concerned Scientists examine the possible adverse effects when transgenic crops cross-pollinate with wild weedy relatives, and create, for instance, herbicide resistant weeds.

Articles

Ernsberger, Richard Jr., "High-Tech Harvests," *Newsweek*, July 13, 1998.

The author examines the corporate stampede into the biotech-food industry and how high-tech food has met with little consumer or political resistance in the United States but deep resistance in Europe.

Groves, Martha, "Organic Foods, a Growth Industry," *Los Angeles Times*, Oct. 2, 1997.

Groves traces the mergers, buyouts and investments made by large food processors and venture capitalists.

Lustgarden, Steve, "The high price of cheap food," *Vegetarian Times*, September 1994.

Lustgarden takes an in-depth look at the impact of the government's decision to pursue a "cheap food" policy, which enabled farmers to increase efficiency but left the country awash in surplus commodities.

Murphy, Kate, "Organic Food Makers Reap Green Yields Of Revenue," *The New York Times*, Oct. 26, 1996.

The author looks at the growth of the organic industry and discusses how some die-hard advocates worry that as the industry gets bigger and is taken over by large corporations organic standards will be weakened.

Warner, Scott, "Growing What Comes Naturally," *Chicago Tribune*, Oct. 29, 1997.

Warner discusses the proposed national organic standards and how they will lead to greater production, lower prices and a greater consumer demand for organics.

Reports

"Greener greens?" *Consumer Reports*, January 1998.

The authoritative magazine published by Consumers Union tested conventionally and organically grown produce and found that organic fruits and vegetables consistently had less pesticide residue.

***Overexposed: Organophosphate Insecticides in Children's Food*, Environmental Working Group, Jan. 28, 1997.**

The environmental research organization looks at the amount of potent insecticide residues found on foods that children eat regularly.

***Pesticides in the Diets of Infants and Children*, National Research Council, 1993.**

This study looked at the federal government's one-size-fits-all approach to pesticide regulation and recommended that it be changed to accommodate infants and children, who are smaller than adults and have different growth rates. The report was cited as one reason for passing the 1996 Food Quality Protection Act, which overhauled pesticide regulations.

Wiles, Richard, et. al., "Same as it ever was," *Environmental Working Group*, May 1998.

The environmental research group criticizes the Clinton administration's record on reducing children's exposure to pesticide residues.

FOR MORE INFORMATION

If you would like to have this CQ Researcher updated, or need more information about this topic, please call CQ Custom Research. Special rates for CQ subscribers. (202) 887-8600 or (800) 432-2250, ext. 600, or E-mail Custom.Research@cq.com

American Farm Bureau Federation, 225 Touhy Ave., Park Ridge, Ill. 60068; (847) 685-8600; www.fb.com. The federation promotes agricultural research and monitors domestic production, foreign assistance programs and rural development.

Biotechnology Industry Organization, 1625 K St. N.W., Suite 1100, Washington, D.C. 20006-1604; (202) 857-0244; www.bio.org. The 700-member trade organization monitors government activity and conducts workshops on biotech issues.

Friends of the Earth, 1025 Vermont Ave., N.W., Suite 300, Washington, D.C. 20005-6303; (202) 783-7400; www.foe.org. FOE monitors legislation and issues related to seed industry consolidation and agricultural biotechnology and their effect on food production and the environment.

International Food Information Council, 1100 Connecticut Ave. N.W., Suite 430, Washington, D.C. 20036; (202) 296-6540; http://ificinfo.health.org. This group of food and beverage companies provides scientific information about food safety and nutrition.

Mothers for Natural Law, P.O. Box 1177, Fairfield, Iowa 52556; (515) 472-2809; www.safe-food.org. Founded in 1996 to fight crime and other social problems, the group now focuses on opposing genetic engineering of foods, deeming it the nation's most serious issue.

Organic Trade Association, P.O. Box 1078, 50 Miles St., Greenfield, Mass. 01302; (413) 774-7511; www.ota.com. This 600-member group seeks to protect the integrity of organic standards and encourages sustainability.

The Next Step

Additional information from UMI's Newspaper & Periodical Abstracts™ database

Bovine Growth Hormone

Daley, Yvonne, "Hormone Breeding Hostility on Farms," *The Boston Globe*, Jan. 1, 1995, p. 32.

The author discusses the use of FDA-approved bovine growth hormone, widely called BGH, to increase milk production in Vermont.

Polston, Pamela, "The Milk Way," *The Boston Globe*, Aug. 9, 1995, p. 41.

Thanks to support for organic dairy products, and fear of bovine growth hormones, the Flint family's Organic Cow dairy farm in Vermont is thriving.

Environmental Concerns

Altieri, Miguel A., "Ecological Impacts of Industrial Agriculture and the Possibilities for Truly Sustainable Farming," *Monthly Review*, July 1998, pp. 60-71.

Until about four decades ago, the link between agriculture and ecology was quite strong. The present technology-intensive farming systems have been extremely productive but have also brought a variety of environmental problems.

Broydo, Leora, "Organic Engineering," *Mother Jones*, May 1998, p. 25.

The author discusses how the Department of Agriculture is sacrificing the organic food industry for biotechnology special interests.

Hudson, Repps, "Resistant Plants Are Threatened; Environmental Groups Plan Suits Against EPA," *St. Louis Post-Dispatch*, Sept. 18, 1997, p. C1.

Greenpeace, the International Center for Technology Assessment, the Sierra Club and organic farmers say that widespread use of Bt by large companies like Monsanto will threaten the future of organic farming . They contend that Bt use will result in insects resistant to the natural pesticide, which organic farmers worldwide use to kill insects. The organizations have petitioned the EPA to, among other things, cancel the registration of all plants engineered with the Bt pesticide and halt registration of new Bt-induced plants. The environmentalists and organic farmers say they will sue the EPA if it does not act within 90 days.

Imhoff, Daniel, "Organic Incorporated: Monocrops, Labeling, Biotechnology, and Watershed Activists Challenge the Pioneer Farmer," *Whole Earth*, spring 1998, pp. 4-9.

Warren Weber's Star Route Farm is a series of organically certified fields. With 50 acres of production, it is the largest vegetable farm in Marin County, Calif.

Genetic Engineering

Balu, Rekha, "Monsanto Asks USDA to Delay Decision On Whether Genetic Crops Are Organic," *The Wall Street Journal*, April 17, 1998, p. A6.

Monsanto Co., in a move likely to please consumer groups, is asking the U.S. Department of Agriculture to delay for at least three years a decision on whether genetically engineered crops could qualify as organic. Many consumer and organic-farming advocates contend that organic means that the crop and the growing conditions should be naturally occurring, and thus genetically altered crops shouldn't be considered organic.

"Battle Brews Over Organics," *Animals' Agenda*, March 1998, pp. 8-9.

The USDA is proposing changes to the current standards defining what is considered organically produced food. Critics of the USDA proposals charge that the agency is trying to cater to conventional agribusiness interests.

Brown, Paul, and Geoffrey Gibbs, "Organic Grower Seeks Ban on 'Mutant' Maize," *The Guardian*, May 7, 1998, p. 9.

Britain's leading organic vegetable grower is seeking a High Court order to prevent his crops being contaminated by a company planting genetically engineered maize next to his fields in Devon. Guy Watson has been warned by the Soil Association that he may lose his organic status if cross-fertilization occurs.

Masood, Ehsan, "Organic Farmer Takes Gene Battle to Court," *Nature*, July 2, 1998, p. 8.

The issue of the distance pollen can travel while still able to cross-pollinate effectively with other plants has become central to a court challenge being mounted by a farmer who is trying to stop an experimental crop of genetically modified maize from being planted next to his Devon, England, farm. The farmer fears the maize will pollinate a field of organic sweetcorn.

Masood, Ehsan, "UK Court Gives Green Light to Trial of Modified Maize," *Nature*, July 16, 1998, p. 212.

London's High Court has allowed genetically modified maize to be planted next to a farmer's crop of organically grown sweetcorn. The farmer, Guy Watson, will appeal the ruling. He is backed by Friends of the Earth and the Soil Association, which certifies his organic produce.

Steyer, Robert, "Organic Farmers Worry About Resistance," *St. Louis Post-Dispatch*, April 8, 1996, p. B10.

Critics say heavy planting of Monsanto's genetically

engineered, insect-fighting cotton could cause insects to rapidly resist its built-in toxins, ruin a popular source of insect control and harm organic farmers.

Labeling

Algeo, David, "Organic Label in Dispute; USDA Proposes Wider Definition," *Denver Post*, April 17, 1998, p. C1.

Pro-organic groups have been burying the U.S. Department of Agriculture with telegrams, letters and postcards demanding that the agency be particular about what it allows farmers and grocers to call "organic." Jim Lee, president and chief operating officer of Wild Oats, a Boulder-based natural-foods retailer, wants to make the pile of correspondence as deep as possible.

Burros, Marian, "Shoppers Unaware of Gene Changes," *The New York Times*, July 20, 1998, p. A8.

American shoppers would be surprised to know that much of the food that they buy has genetically engineered ingredients. But they cannot tell just how much because the United States, unlike many other countries, does not require the labeling of gene-modified food.

Karaim, Reed, "What's In a Label? Organic Hash From The USDA Kitchen," *The Washington Post*, March 22, 1998, p. C1.

After seven years of study, the U.S. Department of Agriculture issued proposed rules in 1997 to define what can be labeled "organic" among the fruits, vegetables, meat, poultry and even processed foods on supermarket shelves. Organic farmers, whose business is growing by 20 percent a year, had been awaiting rules they hoped would protect their industry. Instead, they got preliminary rulings with loopholes large enough to accommodate a factory farm, an irradiation plant and a biotech lab.

Lambrecht, Bill, "Growers Want to Stem Use of 'Organic' Label; They Oppose U.S. Plan to Allow It on Genetically Modified Foods," *St. Louis Post-Dispatch*, March 26, 1998, p. A10.

Last December, Agriculture Secretary Dan Glickman proposed allowing genetically engineered foods to be labeled "organic" in new agricultural standards. Since then, his department has received a record number of comments — overwhelmingly negative — on the prospect of allowing certified organic foods to be genetically modified, irradiated or fertilized with sewage sludge.

Leonard, Mary, "Grass-Roots Effort Prompts U.S. to Redefine Organic Label," *The Boston Globe*, May 9, 1998, p. A1.

Stunned by an unprecedented backlash, the Department of Agriculture announced that it would overhaul its proposed rules on what foods can be called organic. Agriculture Secretary Dan Glickman promised that because of the overwhelmingly negative reaction, a new set of rules will be drafted that "will contain fundamental changes" from the organic-labeling standards proposed in December. Specifically, the rules will not allow foods labeled organic to be irradiated, genetically engineered or grown with sewage-sludge fertilizer.

"Organic/USDA Moved in Right Direction, but not Far Enough," *Houston Chronicle*, May 5, 1998, p. A22.

An outcry of unprecedented ferocity during the four-month comment period on U.S. Department of Agriculture standards for organic foods apparently has helped Agriculture Secretary Dan Glickman to see reason in proposed new labeling rules. Around 150,000 advocates for meats, vegetables and dairy products that are free of chemicals and other synthetics are relieved that Glickman retreated from plans to allow genetically engineered and irradiated food, and crops fertilized with sewage sludge, to be labeled "organic."

Steyer, Robert, "Maine Allows No-BST Label," *St. Louis Post-Dispatch*, April 15, 1994, p. E8.

Maine Gov. John McKernan has signed a law letting dairy farmers put labels on their milk assuring that their herds have not been injected with the genetically engineered copy of a cow protein known as rBST (recombinant bovine somatotropin) or bovine growth hormone (BGH)).

Weiss, Rick, " 'Organic' Label Ruled Out For Biotech, Irradiated Food," *The Washington Post*, May 1, 1998, p. A2.

Intense pressure from tens of thousands of citizens has pushed Agriculture Secretary Dan Glickman to decide that genetically engineered and irradiated food, and crops fertilized with sewage sludge, should not be allowed to be labeled "organic." The proposed rule had left open the question of whether such foods could be deemed organic. The vast majority of comments opposed those ideas. Moreover, most were personal and passionate, as opposed to mass-produced form letters from interest groups — an indication of the American public's increasingly fervent hunger for "natural" foods.

Back Issues

Great Research on Current Issues Starts Right Here.
Recent topics covered by The CQ Researcher are listed below.
Now available on the Web
For information, call (800) 432-2250 ext. 279 or (202) 887-6279.

If you would like to have any of these CQ Researchers updated, or need more information about these topics, please call CQ Custom Research. Special rates for CQ subscribers. (202) 887-8600 or (800) 432-2250, ext. 600, or E-mail Custom.Research@cq.com

MAY 1997
The Stock Market
The Cloning Controversy
Expanding NATO
The Future of Libraries

JUNE 1997
FDA Reform
China After Deng
Line-Item Veto
Breast Cancer

JULY 1997
Transportation Policy
Executive Pay
School Choice Debate
Aggressive Driving

AUGUST 1997
Age Discrimination
Banning Land Mines
Children's Television
Evolution vs. Creationism

SEPTEMBER 1997
Caring for the Dying
Mental Health Policy
Mexico's Future
Youth Fitness

OCTOBER 1997
Urban Sprawl in the West
Diversity in the Workplace
Teacher Education
Contingent Work Force

NOVEMBER 1997
Renewable Energy
Artificial Intelligence
Religious Persecution
Roe v. Wade at 25

DECEMBER 1997
Whistleblowers
Castro's Next Move
Gun Control Standoff
Regulating Nonprofits

JANUARY 1998
Foster Care Reform
IRS Reform
The Black Middle Class
U.S.-British Relations

FEBRUARY 1998
Patients' Rights
Deflation Fears
Caring for the Elderly
The New Corporate Philanthropy

MARCH 1998
Israel at 50
The Federal Judiciary
Drinking on Campus
The Economics of Recycling

APRIL 1998
Biology and Behavior
Liberal Arts Education
Income Inequality
High-Tech Labor Shortage

MAY 1998
Census 2000
Child-Care Options
Alzheimer's Disease
U.S.-Russian Relations

JUNE 1998
Student Journalism
Antitrust Policy
Environmental Justice
Sleep Deprivation

JULY 1998
Encouraging Teen Abstinence
Population and the Environment
Democracy in Asia
Baby Boomers at Midlife

AUGUST 1998
Oil Production in the 21st Century
Flexible Work Arrangements
Coastal Development
Student Activism

Future Topics

▶ *Cancer Treatments*

▶ *Hispanic Americans' New Clout*

▶ *The Future of Baseball*

Back issues are available for $5.00 (subscribers) or $10.00 (non-subscribers). Quantity discounts apply to orders over 10. To order, call Congressional Quarterly Customer Service at (202) 887-8621.

Binders are available for $18.00. To order call 1-800-638-1710. Please refer to stock number 648.

THE CQ Researcher

PUBLISHED BY CONGRESSIONAL QUARTERLY INC.

Cancer Treatments

Should researchers try a new approach?

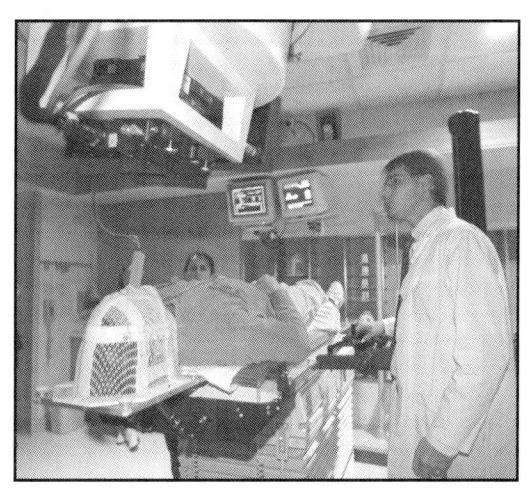

T his year 565,000 Americans are expected to die of cancer, while 1.2 million will be newly diagnosed with the disease. The National Cancer Institute projects that, within five years, cancer will pass heart disease as the nation's No. 1 killer. Yet usually cautious researchers are optimistic they finally may be able to delay, if not always prevent, the spread of malignant cells. Encouraging lab results stemming from $30 billion of publicly funded research carried out since the early 1970s are yielding new insights into the biological underpinnings of the disease. That isn't enough for critics, who say the war on cancer has produced many treatments that looked promising but fizzled. They support spending more money on cancer prevention instead of cures.

C_Q **Sept. 11, 1998 • Volume 8, No. 34 • Pages 785-808**

Formerly Editorial Research Reports

CQ Researcher

September 11, 1998
Volume 8, No.34

EDITOR
Sandra Stencel

MANAGING EDITOR
Thomas J. Colin

STAFF WRITERS
Adriel Bettelheim
Mary H. Cooper
Kenneth Jost
Kathy Koch
David Masci

PRODUCTION EDITOR
Melissa Hall

EDITORIAL ASSISTANT
Laura S. Cavender

PUBLISHED BY
Congressional Quarterly Inc.

CHAIRMAN
Andrew Barnes

VICE CHAIRMAN
Andrew P. Corty

PRESIDENT AND PUBLISHER
Robert W. Merry

EXECUTIVE EDITOR
David Rapp

The CQ Researcher (ISSN 1056-2036). Formerly Editorial Research Reports. Published weekly, except Jan. 2, May 29, July 3, Oct. 30, by Congressional Quarterly Inc., 1414 22nd St., N.W., Washington, D.C. 20037. Annual subscription rate for libraries, businesses and government is $340. Additional rates furnished upon request. Periodicals postage paid at Washington, D.C., and additional mailing offices. POSTMASTER: Send address changes to The CQ Researcher, 1414 22nd St., N.W., Washington, D.C. 20037.

COVER: A PATIENT WITH AN INOPERABLE BRAIN TUMOR UNDERGOES CONFORMAL RADIATION TREATMENT AT WESTERN PENNSYLVANIA HOSPITAL IN PITTSBURGH. NEUROSURGEONS SAY THE TECHNIQUE WILL SOON BECOME THE STANDARD. (GENE J. PUSKAR/THE ASSOCIATED PRESS)

Cancer Treatments

BY ADRIEL BETTELHEIM

THE ISSUES

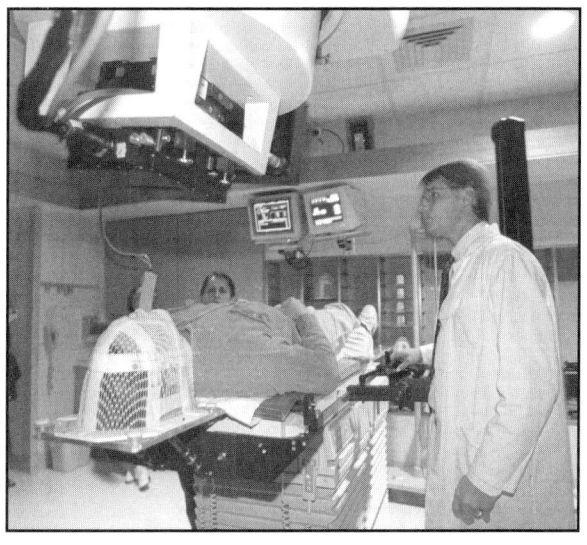

When Ellen Stovall was diagnosed with Hodgkin's disease late in 1971, doctors didn't yet understand how cancer cells formed and spread throughout the body. Many promising chemotherapies were still in development. The physicians decided their best strategy was to expose the 24-year-old Maryland writer to high doses of radiation and hope they would kill more cancer cells than healthy ones.

Six months of daily treatments left Stovall sterile and suffering from severe post-radiation sickness and heart and lung ailments. One doctor estimated she had less than a 10 percent chance of living two years. When Stovall tried to find some cancer survivors for support, those who had beaten the disease didn't want to talk about it.

"It was as if I was separated from everything that was normal and familiar and thrust into this unknown world," she recalls. "I thought I had a blessed life and could be a writer and have babies. The thought of dying was inconceivable."

Stovall was lucky. The grapefruit-sized tumor in her chest disappeared, though she suffered a relapse in 1984. In the succeeding years, researchers gained a new understanding of the biological and genetic basis for cancer, enabling them to dramatically reduce death rates for Hodgkin's disease, childhood leukemia and certain other malignancies.

But for all the scientific advances, cancer remains a death sentence for many people. This year, approximately 565,000 Americans are expected to die of cancer — 225,000 more than in 1971, when President Richard M. Nixon proclaimed war on

the disease. An additional 1.2 million new cases are expected to be diagnosed. The National Cancer Institute predicts that cancer, within five years, will pass heart disease as the nation's No. 1 killer. [1]

While the picture seems grim, a recent series of encouraging laboratory developments have made usually cautious researchers optimistic that they finally may be able to delay, if not always prevent, the spread of malignant cells.

Some new drugs now in clinical trials can home in on cancer cells and interrupt the molecular processes that allow them to divide wildly. Other agents have been shown to jump-start the body's immune system and prompt attacks on cancer cells. Another class of drugs halts the growth of blood vessels that feed growing tumors, though they may be years away from being approved for use in humans. Federal research officials believe the advances are enabling them to turn the corner on the disease — the National Cancer Institute (NCI) in March reported the first sustained decline in new cancer cases since the Great Depression.

Cancer patient advocates and survivors like Stovall are using the en-

couraging news to press the federal government to make cancer the nation's No. 1 public-health priority. Public figures including Gen. Norman Schwarzkopf and financier Michael Milken are discussing their personal battles with the disease and lobbying for more research money. This month, Stovall will lead a march on Washington and other cities to raise cancer awareness.

Scientists say the promising developments reflect $30 billion of publicly funded research carried out since the early 1970s that began to explain a complex, insidious disease for which no single cure exists. Researchers now know cancer actually comprises dozens of distinct diseases that share the feature of uncontrolled cell growth and require a combination of therapies.

"I wish we could get up one day, summon everyone and say we've cured the disease, but it's just not going to happen," says Allen Lichter, a radiation oncologist at the University of Michigan and president of the American Society of Clinical Oncology. "What we know is, if we persist long enough and make small advances, death rates will begin to decline."

Much of the current effort is aimed at reducing the risk of developing the four biggest killers — lung, colon, breast and prostate cancer. This spring, NCI officials reported that the drug tamoxifen was found in a study of high-risk women to delay the risk of developing breast cancer by 45 percent. A related drug called raloxifene has been shown to have similar effects and, unlike tamoxifen, doesn't raise older women's risk of uterine cancer. In August, an advisory committee of the Food and Drug Administration (FDA) recommended approving tamoxifen to cut women's

1.2 Million New Cases Expected in 1998

More than half of the estimated 1.2 million cases of cancer that will be diagnosed in the United States in 1998 will strike the prostate, breast, lung or colon/rectum

Leading Cancer Types	Number of New Cases	Percentage of New Cases
Prostate	184,500	15%
Breast	180,300	14.7
Lung	171,500	14.0
Colon and Rectum	131,600	10.7
Other Reproductive Cancers[1]	89,500	7.3
Non-Hodgkin's Lymphoma	55,400	4.5
Other Blood-Related Cancers[2]	49,600	4.0
Melanoma	41,600	3.4
Other Gastrointestinal Cancers[3]	39,400	3.2
Other	285,200	23.2

[1] *Other reproductive cancers (besides prostate) include cervix, endometrium, ovary, vulva, vagina and female genital, testis, penis and male genital.*
[2] *Other blood-related cancers (besides non-Hodgkin's lymphoma) include Hodgkin's disease, leukemia and multiple myeloma.*
[3] *Other gastrointestinal cancers (besides colon and rectum) include esophagus, stomach and small intestine.*

Source: American Society of Clinical Oncology

risk of developing the disease. If the FDA follows through, as expected, it will mean health insurers will be likely to pay for the drug for women who have never had cancer. Tamoxifen is now often used to prevent recurrence of breast cancer.[2]

On a more basic level, scientists are applying new molecular knowledge of the cancer cell to develop novel treatments. A once maligned class of bioengineered drugs known as monoclonal antibodies is being used to target cancer cells with a high degree of accuracy, killing tumors without damaging healthy tissue.

One such experimental drug, herceptin, is designed for patients with breast cancer that has spread to other parts of the body because their tumors overexpress a gene called HER2 that governs cell multiplica-

tion. The drug essentially turns off the signal that tells the cell to divide and may also be effective for treating ovarian cancer and cancer of the peritoneum, or the lining of the abdominal cavity. Scientists for 20 years used monoclonal antibodies with great success in lab mice but until recently couldn't replicate the effects in humans. The same FDA advisory committee that recommended approving tamoxifen also recommended approving herceptin, either alone or used in conjunction with the cancer drug taxol.[3]

John Mendelsohn, president of the University of Texas' M.D. Anderson Cancer Center in Houston, says advances in manipulating and disabling tumors may eventually allow oncologists to keep a person's cancer in check for decades, similar to the

way doctors treat diabetics with insulin without curing the disease.

"If you can stop a tumor from growing and damaging healthy tissue, the body may be able to tolerate it sitting there indefinitely," Mendelsohn says.

Not everyone is impressed, however. Critics say the war on cancer has produced many treatments that looked promising in early clinical trials but fell flat when applied to large patient populations. Interferon, inter-leukin-2 and tumor necrosis factor, to name just three, were touted as cure-alls because they worked well in experimental trials. They have found only limited usefulness in humans.[4]

John Bailar, an authority on epidemiology and biostatistics at the University of Chicago, says the federal cancer effort places too much of an emphasis on finding treatments for a disease that is hardly more curable now than it was 30 years ago. He supports spending more money studying at-risk populations, occupational hazards and environmental factors that contribute to cancer, such as chemicals in the water supply.

"We've spent an immense amount of money and scientific talent looking for broader cures that are supposed to be just down the road," Bailar says. "I don't see anything that suggests the present situation is any different."

Skeptics like Bailar are unmoved by recently released statistics showing that cancer deaths fell 2.6 percent between 1991 and 1995 and that new cases declined 0.5 percent per year during the same period — the first such declines since the 1930s. He notes most of the decline was attributed to preventive measures, such as a decline in smoking among white males. Meanwhile, lung cancer in females, prostate cancer in men and the overall incidence of non-Hodgkin's lymphoma, melanoma and bladder cancer continue to rise. At least some of the detected increases may be attributed to improved screening, particularly in the case of prostate cancer.

Remarks from skeptics like Bailar rankle federal cancer officials, who point to the lower mortality rates and other encouraging news as justification for spending more on research. NCI Director Richard D. Klausner, a noted researcher in cellular and molecular biology, publicly rebutted Bailar in *The New England Journal of Medicine* last year, accusing the University of Chicago scholar of "defeatism" and urging the cancer institute to take a broad-based approach to treatment, patient care and basic research. "We will probably not learn to prevent cancer if we do not identify its many causes and test preventive interventions carefully," Klausner wrote. [5]

This year, institute officials are asking Congress for $2.58 billion in fiscal 1999 to sustain existing research — a 5.7 percent increase over 1998 levels — and $611 million for new programs. But with federal budgets tight, the cancer researchers must compete for funding with colleagues studying other afflictions, particularly HIV/AIDS, heart disease and Alzheimer's disease. [6]

"It's easy to interpret [new developments in cancer treatment] as significant medical achievements, and as the precursor to the eventual eradication of this disease in our generation," says Rep. David R. Obey, D-Wis., ranking Democrat on the House Appropriations Committee. " I wish that they were." Obey questions whether the cancer institute shouldn't spend more on risk prevention. "The fact remains that the overall incidence of cancer is much higher than it was 25 years ago, and survival rates for most common cancers remain unchanged," he says.

Even if some of the new treatments prove to be a scientific success, questions remain over how soon — and, indeed, whether — patients will have access to them. Despite a general speedup in government approval of new drugs, cancer thera-

---

> ## "We will probably not learn to prevent cancer if we do not identify its many causes and test preventive interventions carefully."
>
> — *Richard D. Klausner, Director, National Cancer Institute*

---

pies typically require at least five years of testing to be approved by the FDA for sale. Part of the FDA's regulatory process requires large-scale clinical trials on patients at two or more hospitals. But without FDA approval, the federal Medicare program and managed-care organizations refuse to pay for such costs as hospitalization and lab fees for patients in experimental programs. Expenses can total $20,000-$50,000 over the course of a treatment.

Several pending legislative proposals would begin loosening the requirements. One, by Sens. Edward M. Kennedy, D-Mass., and Tom Daschle, D-S.D., would force health insurers to cover patients in clinical trials. A second proposal by Sens. Connie Mack, R-Fla., and John D. Rockefeller IV, D-W.Va., would do the same for Medicare patients. But the insurance industry opposes both bills, and prospects for passage in the current Congress appear unlikely. [7]

As researchers learn more about treating cancer and federal officials and policy-makers debate how to apply the findings, here are some of the questions they are asking:

Are we on the verge of curing cancer?

When President Nixon signed the National Cancer Act on Dec. 23, 1971, marking the official declaration of war on the disease, scientists had many theories about what caused cancer. Some pegged it to a disruption in the way the body breaks down carbohydrates. Others believed that viruses were the primary culprit. Few had any idea how to stop the disease on a molecular level.

The burst of molecular-genetics research in the 1980s and '90s changed that. Scientists learned how to isolate and characterize DNA from individuals and link genetic defects to specific cancers. This didn't explain every case of cancer — external factors like smoking and sun exposure still trigger the disease and the body's gene-influenced responses — but it gave the scientists a wealth of knowledge about how malignant cells behave, allowing them to target treatments at specific molecules. If cancer can't exactly be "cured," scientists say they now at least can identify cases sooner and increasingly disrupt tumor

From Scared Victim to Dedicated Activist

For more than a month after giving birth to her son in 1971, Ellen Stovall suffered from chest pains, low-grade fevers and general malaise. Doctors suspected the 24-year-old Maryland woman had allergies or an imbalanced immune system arising from her pregnancy.

During a visit to her Pennsylvania hometown, Stovall decided to visit the family doctor. He suggested an X-ray that revealed a grapefruit-sized tumor in her chest, evidence of an advanced case of Hodgkin's disease.

Stovall's options were limited. Her recent pregnancy prevented her from participating in clinical trials on a then promising experimental chemotherapy called MOPP, a combination of several chemotherapy drugs. Doctors also lacked high-tech imaging equipment to gauge the contours of the tumor and had to rely on the crude, flat image provided by the X-ray.

Ellen Stovall

The physicians decided to give Stovall the maximum dosage of radiation they calculated her body could stand and hope the tumor would go into remission. When Stovall asked if she would survive long enough to need reading glasses, the doctors, reluctant to give her much hope, changed the subject.

Six weeks after giving birth — and on the very day, Dec. 23, 1971, that President Richard M. Nixon signed into law the National Cancer Act — Stovall underwent her first radiation treatment at Georgetown University in Washington, D.C.

"I took a vow that if I survived, I would devote my life to the cancer cause," recalls Stovall, now 51. "I was young and thought cancer was an old person's disease. This was such a shock that I really lost my innocence and became an adult overnight."

Stovall survived six months of grueling chemotherapy that shrank the tumor in her chest but left her sterile and suffering from post-radiation sickness and various heart and lung ailments. A year later, she had to undergo emergency surgery for a strangulated bowel that resulted from adhesions from the radiation. The cancer returned in 1984. Ironically, Stovall was treated with MOPP, which by that time had been approved by the Food and Drug Administration for general use and become a standard treatment. Those treatments left her with peripheral neuritis, a disorder of the nervous system that results in little feeling in her hands and feet.

Stovall's unique perspective as a two-time survivor prompted her to help found the National Coalition for Cancer Survivorship, a network of individuals, organizations and research institutions that lobbies on behalf of patients suffering from all the various forms of cancer.

On Sept. 25 and 26, Stovall will take on an even more visible role as a cancer advocate, serving as president of The March, a series of gatherings in Washington and other cities designed to make cancer the nation's No. 1 public health concern. The idea for the gathering came during an appearance Stovall made on CNN's "Larry King Live" in April 1997 with fellow cancer survivors, including ABC newsman Sam Donaldson and financier Michael Milken.

Stovall's passion for advocacy began during her first cancer treatment, when she had trouble finding other cancer patients and survivors to speak with for support. She finally located four similarly young patients, all of whom had died from various ailments by the fifth anniversary of her diagnosis.

"I was very lucky to have a wonderful husband and family, but I was almost desperate to speak with another person with the disease, just to tell them how scared I was," she recalls. "I think a movement of survivors fosters a whole generation of people with a consciousness of the disease that just wasn't there before."

Stovall still faces challenges drawing together various factions in the cancer community. Some breast cancer advocates, traditionally the most vocal and successful in drawing attention to their cause, resent the presence of defrocked financier Milken, who has become a passionate advocate for prostate cancer research and screening since being diagnosed with the disease in 1993.

Milken says the cancer movement should use AIDS research spending as a successful model. In 1997, $72,000 per death was spent on HIV/AIDS research. Breast cancer research totaled $9,730 per death and prostate cancer $2,631 per death. [1]

While reluctant to take sides, Stovall says she hopes marchers will let their lawmakers know that current funding levels for research are unacceptable.

"For every $10 collected in taxes, our government spends only one penny on cancer research," she says. "People with AIDS and women with breast cancer have shown that their persistence, passion and perseverance are here to stay. We have to show there are 8 million cancer survivors, and we make a big voting block."

---

[1] See Julie Schmit, "Marching for a Cancer Cure," *USA Today*, July 21, 1998, p. 5B.

cells' biological mechanisms for growth.

"We now understand that cancer is a genetic disease, not necessarily one that's passed from father to son, but in the way that genetic material in cells gets mutated and then can multiply," says Edison Liu, director of the division of clinical sciences of the intra-mural program at the National Cancer

Institute. "This allows us to focus on a single medium that dictates the entire repertoire of cell behavior."

Cancer begins when a molecular process in a cell fails. A gene that controls cell division may go awry, leading to uncontrolled duplication that creates a tumorous mass. Sometimes a gene that is supposed to repair other damaged genes fails, causing multiple errors in a cell's genetic makeup.

Colon cancer offers one example. Many of the most aggressive cases arise because of an inherited defect in a gene called APC that was first identified in 1991 and is supposed to slow down cell division. The genetic glitch allows cells to divide wildly, resulting in the appearance of thousands of polyps in the colon that tend to become cancerous over time. Almost everyone with the condition develops colon cancer by age 40, and more than half die from the disease. [8] Scientists now can screen for the faulty gene, monitor the people carrying it for early signs of polyps and surgically remove them before they become cancerous.

Similarly, women who come from families with a strong history of ovarian and breast cancer have up to an 85 percent chance of developing breast tumors and a 50 percent chance of developing ovarian tumors if they carry a defective version of a gene called BRCA-1. And defects in three genes that produce a cancer-prevention enzyme called glutathione S-transferase have recently been linked to breast, lung, colon, bladder and testicular cancer. [9]

Knowledge of how cancer cells behave has also allowed researchers to develop vaccines with antibodies that can speed therapeutic agents to

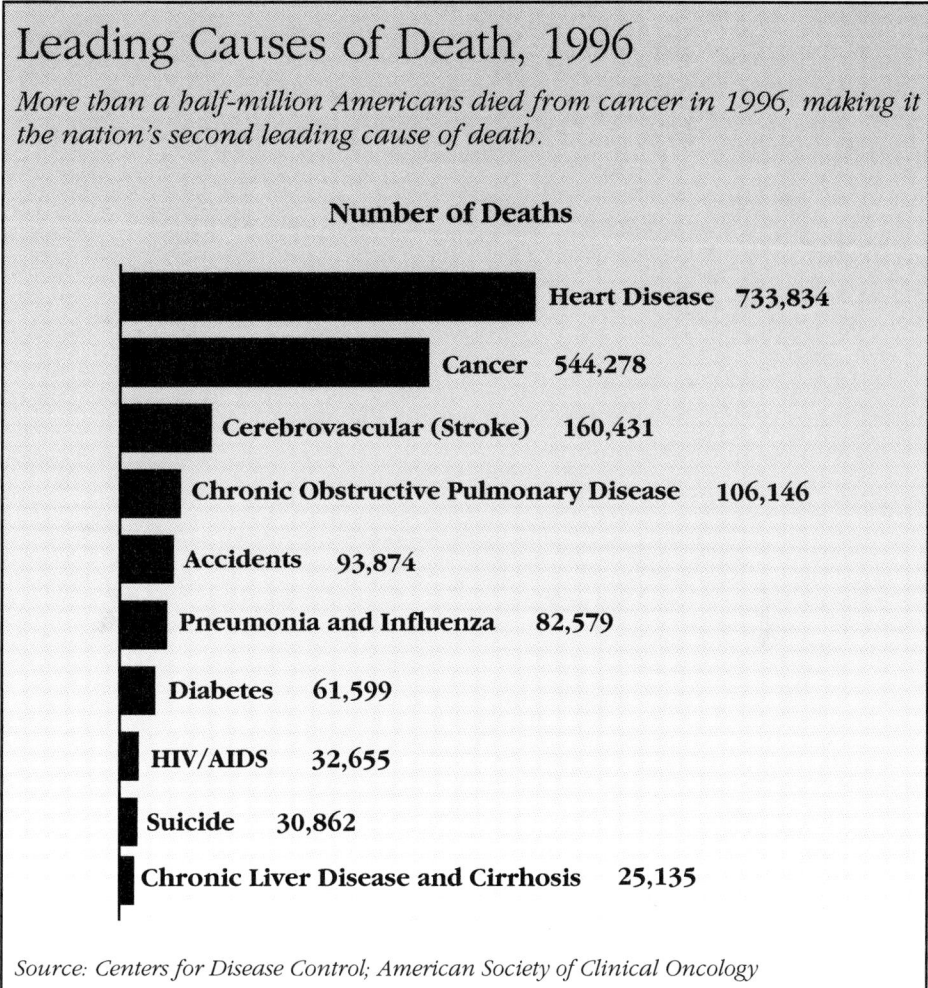

Leading Causes of Death, 1996

More than a half-million Americans died from cancer in 1996, making it the nation's second leading cause of death.

Number of Deaths

Heart Disease 733,834

Cancer 544,278

Cerebrovascular (Stroke) 160,431

Chronic Obstructive Pulmonary Disease 106,146

Accidents 93,874

Pneumonia and Influenza 82,579

Diabetes 61,599

HIV/AIDS 32,655

Suicide 30,862

Chronic Liver Disease and Cirrhosis 25,135

Source: Centers for Disease Control; American Society of Clinical Oncology

cancer cells. The agents help the body recognize distinctive proteins on tumor cells called antigens and signal the immune system to attack the cells as an invader. The word "vaccine" is something of a misnomer because the treatments don't prevent cancer in the way the Salk vaccine prevents polio. But the treatments, also known as "immunotherapies," are critical because cancer cells mutate and mask their identities, making it difficult for the body to fight back on its own. Indeed, one almost never hears of a cancer patient whose disease disappears without treatment.

One such treatment, rituxan, a recently approved drug made by the California biotech firm Genentech Inc., is used to treat non-Hodgkin's

lymphoma, a slow-growing but incurable cancer of the immune system. The drug attaches itself to a protein known as the CD20 antigen that is found on the surface of malignant immune cells. The action jump-starts the immune system and enables it to kill the cells before they can divide further. When combined with radiation treatments, the drug has been shown to shrink tumors for prolonged periods of time. [10]

Looking ahead, researchers are using their new knowledge of cancer cells to devise gene therapies they hope will fix damaged DNA or add new DNA — either to mend faulty genes or introduce genes that make cancer cells sensitive to drug therapy. [11] Of the 244 gene-therapy

The 10 Deadliest Cancers in the U.S., 1998

Lung cancer is by far the leading cause of death from cancer in the United States. Lung cancer will claim more lives in 1998 than the next three most prevalent types of cancer.

Type of Cancer	Projected Number of Deaths
•Lung	160,100
•Colon/Rectum	56,500
•Breast	43,900
•Prostate	39,200
•Pancreas	28,900
•Non-Hodgkin's Lymphoma	24,900
•Leukemia (all types)	21,600
•Ovary	14,500
•Stomach	13,700
•Brain/Central Nervous System	13,300

Source: American Cancer Society

trials registered since 1989 with the National Institutes of Health (NIH), about 150 are for cancer.

Researchers at the M.D. Anderson Cancer Center in Houston recently offered one of the first demonstrations of how gene therapy can repair damaged genes and suppress tumors. The scientists used the virus that causes the common cold to carry a gene known as p53 into cancer cells. The gene slowed growth of the cells and programmed them to kill themselves if their DNA was damaged by smoking or sun exposure. The treatment is being tested on patients with lung and prostate cancer and is expected to go into clinical trials by 2000. [12]

But researchers warn that even though cancer has a genetic basis, it is such a complex disease that it can't possibly be stopped with a single "magic bullet." At best, gene therapy would achieve partial results and have to be used in conjunction with established treatments, such as surgery, radiation and chemotherapy.

"The most effective therapy is a combination of therapies," the University of Michigan's Lichter says. "If a cancer can change forms and disguise itself to avoid several therapies, it just stands to reason you have a better chance attacking it with as many weapons as you can."

Will everyone have access to the new treatments?

Taxol is regarded as one of the most successful cancer drugs ever developed. Extracted from the bark of the Pacific yew tree, the drug takes a unique approach to fighting the disease by attaching to rodlike microtubules in cancer cells and disrupting the way they divide. It is regarded as a standard treatment for breast and ovarian cancer and is increasingly being used for other types of cancer.

However, taxol treatments on average cost $10,000-$20,000 — too much for financially strapped public hospitals like D.C. General Hospital in Washington, D.C., to use on every patient. Officials there typically opt for less expensive therapies like mastectomies so they can treat more people.

The situation illustrates what critics contend is a major problem in developing new cancer treatments. The NCI and other federally funded research institutions discover and develop new agents like taxol but lack the resources and commercial motivation to manufacture them. Instead, they turn the promising drugs over to pharmaceutical companies, which then bring them to market and reap large sums from their sale. Bristol-Myers Squibb has made an estimated $2.8 billion in sales from taxol under the arrangement since the FDA approved the extract in 1992. Indeed, 14 of the 15 cancer drugs the company sells today were developed either by the cancer institute or by clinicians working on contract for it. [13]

This uneasy trade-off between public and private-sector collaboration made sense in the 1970s, when treating cancer wasn't very appealing to drug companies. There were comparatively few patients for each cancer, and they faced long odds of surviving for many years. Drug companies believed it was far more attractive to develop compounds for people with less-fatal conditions like ulcers.

To spur development of more so-called "orphan" drugs for rare diseases, federal officials began offering drug companies exclusive marketing rights for five years if the FDA approved the agents. The companies, in return, agreed to collaborate on further research and provide free quantities of the drug to federal researchers for continued human testing. Bristol-Myers Squibb and the NCI signed their pact in 1991, and the FDA approved the drug late in the following year. But critics say the arrangement has since given the company a blank check and led to overpricing and manipulation.

James Packard Love, director of economic research for the Ralph Nader-affiliated Center for the Study of Responsive Law, says when the

FDA first approved taxol in 1992, Bristol-Myers Squibb charged $4.87 per milligram. Since then, it has raised the price to $6 per milligram — 24 times the company's initial cost of manufacturing the agent — despite promises it would price the agent reasonably. Love argues the U.S. government should impose price caps to protect consumers from gouging. [14]

Samuel Epstein, a professor of occupational and environmental medicine at the University of Illinois Medical Center in Chicago, says the relationship between Bristol-Myers Squibb and the cancer institute is symptomatic of broader conflicts of interest between the cancer research establishment and the drug industry. In his new book, *The Politics of Cancer Revisited*, Epstein charges that senior officials at the cancer institute have tailored its focus on gene-based cures to match that of drug companies, instead of devoting more energy to preventing the disease.

"For decades, the war on cancer has been dominated by powerful groups of interlocking professional and financial interests, with the highly profitable drug development system at its hub," Epstein writes. "Cancer care is a big business" with prime beneficiaries including the cancer institute, advocacy groups like the American Cancer Society, drug companies and comprehensive cancer centers, he says.

Similar criticisms spurred 1993 congressional hearings on drug pricing, during which Bristol-Myers Squibb officials and other pharmaceutical executives argued their drug prices were justified by the high level of risk associated with completing research and development. Bristol-Myers Squibb claims it has spent about $1 billion to date on taxol and says that proposed price caps on the drug and other formulations would prevent it from reinvesting some profits into developing new, even better agents. The company also points out it has operated an oncol-

---

Death Rates Fell for Some Cancers

Many cancer death rates in the United States changed dramatically from the early 1970s to the early '90s, though researchers aren't always sure why. Stomach cancer deaths plummeted for men and women, probably because diets were healthier. Lung cancer deaths among women skyrocketed, largely because more women smoke today. Prostate cancer deaths may have decreased because of increased and improved screening procedures.

20-Year Trends in Cancer Death Rates
(1972-74) — (1992-94)

| | Percentage Change | |
	Men	Women
Lung	15%	147%
Colon/Rectum	-13	-25
Breast	0	-4
Prostate	23	—
Pancreas	-9	9
Non-Hodgkin's lymphoma	41	35
Leukemia	-5	-6
Ovary	—	-9
Stomach	-38	-40
Brain/Central Nervous System	9	9

Source: American Cancer Society

---

ogy drug-access program since the 1970s to help provide cancer drugs to people who can't afford them. [15]

Some believe the price of new drugs will fall dramatically when drug companies lose their five-year exclusivity agreements, and other firms enter the cancer market with equivalent medications. But companies sometimes can fight off competition by patenting the way drugs are administered to patients. Bristol-Myers Squibb developed several FDA-approved regimens for giving taxol to patients over the course of several hours. Just before its five-year exclusivity agreement expired last Dec. 29, the company received 17- and 20-year patent protections for use of the drug. [16]

Sometimes limited supplies of drugs, not pricing, prevent patients from receiving new treatments. Many biotechnology companies that make

cancer drugs haven't been able to perfect their technologies to produce the agents in large enough quantities to be tested in people. If a promising drug gets good word-of-mouth, companies sometimes must resort to rationing their experimental batches.

San Francisco-based Genentech says it can't produce enough herceptin to give it to the more than 40,000 women who might benefit from it. The company has applied to the FDA for expedited approval, and the agency is expected to decide by this fall whether to approve herceptin for sale. In the meantime, women who aren't part of Genentech's clinical trials must put their names in a lottery. The company is accepting about 100 women per month for the special program.

"Manufacturing [herceptin] is a

complex and lengthy process that involves hundreds of complicated and, in many cases, unique procedures such as cell production, large-scale fermentation, purification, filling, freeze-drying and testing," Genentech says in a statement. It hopes to have adequate supplies by this fall.

Should the government mandate that new treatments be made available faster?

In 1991, doctors told Rhonda Best her only chance of surviving breast cancer was to undergo a new procedure called an autologous bone marrow transplant, in which a patient's bone marrow is removed, cleaned, then returned to the body after heavy doses of chemotherapy.

When the Seattle woman sought pre-authorization for the procedure, her insurance company denied coverage, saying it was experimental. Months later, when the insurer reversed itself, the cancer had spread to her brain, and the procedure could no longer be performed. Best died in 1993 at age 40. [17]

To many in the cancer field, Best's story and dozens of others like it raise a troubling question: Should the government require insurers and health-maintenance organizations to cover potentially life-saving procedures, even if the treatment is new and unproven?

Researchers complain they generally have difficulty recruiting people for studies on new cancer treatments because insurers refuse to pay medical costs associated with the therapy. Indeed, only 3 percent of the 7 mil-

lion Americans who have been diagnosed with cancer in the last five years participated in clinical trials. In most cases, drug companies and research grants paid for the experimental treatments, but patients were billed for hospital stays, lab fees and expenses stemming from complications. Even the federal Medicare program refuses to cover such costs.

"There's a real concern for the future of clinical research because of this," says Mary McCabe, director of the NCI's Office of Clinical Trials Promotion. She and other health professionals question why insurers deny coverage for promising drugs, noting health plans must pay for hospital stays and testing if cancer patients seek FDA-approved treatments.

Maryland this year enacted a law requiring insurers to pay the costs in clinical trials, and Rhode Island, Georgia, Pennsylvania and New York either have or are considering similar measures. However, David Golde, physician-in-chief of Memorial Sloan-Kettering Cancer Center in New York City, remains skeptical, saying many patients are misled into believing experimental treatments are always

Only 3 percent of the 7 million Americans who have been diagnosed with cancer in the last five years participated in clinical trials.

better. In fact, Golde says, the trials amount to borderline experiments, and many treatments fail.

"What we need are better trials, and, maybe, fewer of them," Golde says. "Every disease at some point has a big drug that comes along and is supposed to do wonders. But many of the drugs being tested are toxic, unproven and don't work."

Policy-makers are divided over whether to give patients more access to experimental agents. The effort by Mack and Rockefeller to give Medicare patients access to trials was included in the wide-ranging tobacco legislation authored by Sen. John McCain, R-Ariz., that was defeated in the Senate in June. However, Medicare early this year began paying for some experimental cancer treatments for seniors under a three-year pilot program announced by the Clinton administration. Seniors will initially be restricted to trials sponsored by NIH — about 25 percent of the total number of tests on new cancer drugs. [18]

The measure by Kennedy and Daschle forcing managed-care providers to provide access to trials also faces an uncertain fate. Republicans and Democrats in Congress have included provisions in rival managed-care bills allowing external reviews and appeals if experimental procedures, such as cancer treatments, are denied.

But the Kennedy-Daschle measure is unacceptable to some because it would likely drive up costs for HMOs and put them in a position of deciding the merits of various clinical trials. [19]

Managed-care companies argue they shouldn't have to cover experimental treatments because some of the therapies may be harmful or of no value to the patient and almost always are more expensive than standard treatments. They add the higher costs ultimately will be borne by patients in the form of more expensive premiums or lost coverage. Some suggest that the drug companies running the trials cover the disputed costs.

"Managed care has brought affordable health coverage to millions of consumers," Charles Kahn, president-designate of the Health Insurance Association of America told the Congressional Cancer Coalition in July. "We must be careful not to undermine this success by looking to private plans as a primary means for funding many of the costs associated with clinical trials. It is not appropriate to ask employers and their employees to pay higher premiums in order to fund clinical trials."

However, oncologists and cancer-research advocates argue health insurers increasingly are denying coverage for high-quality therapy in clinical studies.

"When Americans purchase insurance, whether indemnity or managed-care, they expect the patient-care costs will be the responsibility of the insurer," a coalition of cancer groups led by the National Coalition for Cancer Survivorship wrote in a letter to Kennedy in July. "There is no reason this expectation should be undermined merely because a person with cancer or another life-threatening disease seeks access to care in a well-designed clinical trial." ∎

BACKGROUND

Ancient Techniques

For more than 3,000 years, surgery was the only viable treatment for cancer. An Egyptian papyrus dated

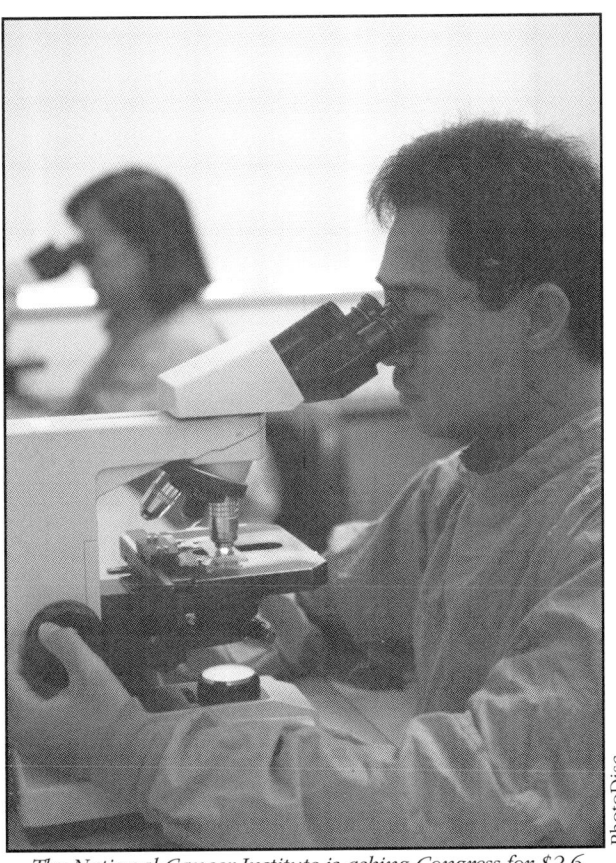

The National Cancer Institute is asking Congress for $2.6 billion in fiscal 1999 to sustain existing research and an additional $611 million for new programs.

about 1550 B.C. contains references to encounters with fatal tumors in human beings. Physicians attempted to remove easily accessible growths or swellings with knives and red-hot irons but left hard-to-reach tumors untouched because the patient would live longer if the disease was left alone.

Over the centuries, early doctors

observed how cancer spreads and refined their techniques, applying poisons like arsenic pastes and devising more localized surgeries. By 450 B.C., Hippocrates was using the word *karcinos*, Greek for crablike, to identify cancerous growths. Tumors were thought to result from an accumulation of black bile, or "melancholic humor."

In the second century A.D., the Roman physician Galen postulated that cancerous growths occurred when humors flowed to a particular part of the body, causing swollen and inflamed tissue. The theory held up until the invention of the microscope nearly 1,500 years later, when scientists concluded tumors were really an overgrowth of cellular tissue.

It wasn't until the late 18th century that physicians began having regular success curing some cancers. In 1775, British physician Percival Pott devised a surgical cure for scrotal cancer, then commonly contracted by chimney sweeps, and lobbied for changes in labor laws that helped eliminate the disease within two generations. By the 1830s, doctors concluded that cells were the fundamental unit in tumor tissue and began studying their wild, uncontrolled division.

At the beginning of the 20th century, doctors were trying to prevent recurrence of cancers and reduce the high death rate from postoperative infections. In the 1890s, New York physician William Coley tried injecting a variety of bacteria known as "Coley's cocktail" into cancer patients, who then went into feverish recoveries. The injections effectively kick-started the

Will the Sea Horse Cure Cancer?

The war on cancer isn't just fought with bioengineered drugs and souped-up genes. Scientists also utilize ornamental shrubs, tree bark, sea horses and thousands of other natural products that serve as the basis for new cancer drugs.

Each year, the National Cancer Institute's research center at Fort Detrick in Frederick, Md., screens more than 6,000 extracts from plant and marine organisms for signs of activity against cancer or HIV/AIDS. Researchers say the Earth's environment provides a promising assortment of raw materials for new medicines, though it's technically challenging to extract them in large enough quantities to be used for mass production. Additionally, extracts that work well in lab trials don't necessarily show the same anti-cancer properties in human patients. [1]

The use of natural extracts in medicine is centuries old. Hundreds of years ago, sufferers of congestive heart failure, or dropsy, chewed on foxglove leaves because they relieved the buildup of fluid. Penicillin, first derived from bread mold in the 1940s, has shown great success fighting infections, while poppy flower derivatives such as morphine and opium are potent pain killers.

The cancer institute contracts with three institutions to collect extracts from around the world. The University of Illinois at Chicago obtains samples from Southeast Asia, the Missouri Botanical Garden collects them in Asia and the Morton Arboretum in Lisle, Ill., collects samples in the continental United States.

The samples are shipped to Maryland, where they are stored at 20 degrees below zero, Celsius, until they are ready for extraction.

Taxol, the No. 1 selling cancer drug, was developed in Fort Detrick in the early 1960s after the U.S. government dispatched technicians around the world to gather exotic plants and send them back to federal labs as part of early efforts to treat cancer. The compound, derived from Pacific yew tree bark, showed some cancer-killing properties but didn't initially excite researchers. The trees were rare and died after they were stripped. Moreover, it took years for scientists to understand precisely how the complex Taxol molecule inactivates dividing tumor cells.

Taxol's eventual success — and the general push to find new cancer treatments — is fueling more research, even though just six plant-derived anti-cancer drugs have won Food and Drug Administration (FDA) approval since 1960. They include topotecan, a drug derived from a tree native to China known as camptotheca acuminata. Topotecan has been approved by the FDA for treatment of ovarian cancer and may also fight lung cancer and acute leukemia. Three other extracts of the tree are being tested in clinical trials on a variety of cancers.

The rosy periwinkle has yielded the drugs vincristine and vinblastine, both of which help fight some lymphomas and childhood leukemias. Scientists also are focusing on marine derivatives, including dolastatin-10, a drug isolated from sea horses found in the Comoro Islands off southeast Africa, that is in preclinical development. Halichondrin B, extracted from a sponge that lives off New Zealand, has also shown some early cancer-fighting qualities.

Some extracts are being combined with cancer vaccines to create more potent treatments. Progenics Pharmaceuticals of Tarrytown, N.Y., has begun testing a carbohydrate antigen and an extract derived from the bark of the South American soap tree on 800 melanoma patients. Scientists believe potent natural adjuvants will further awaken the body's immune system to the fact the cancer doesn't belong there. [2]

---

[1] For background, see Gordon Cragg, David Newman and Raymond Weiss, "Coral Reefs, Forests and Thermal Vents: The Worldwide Exploration of Nature for Novel Antitumor Agents," *Seminars in Oncology*, Vol. 24, No. 2 (April 1997), pp. 156-163. See also, Richard L. Worsnop, "Alternative Medicine's Next Phase," *The CQ Researcher*, Feb. 14, 1997, pp. 121-144.

[2] See W. Wayt Gibbs, "Healing Cancer: Vaccines That Prod the Body to Cure Itself are Finally Being Readied for Market," *Scientific American*, September 1998, pp. 40-41.

---

body's immune system, helping destroy tumors and providing the crude basis of today's immunotherapies.

In 1894, American physician William Stewart Halsted set about devising a surgical technique for preventing the common reappearance of tumors after a cancer had been removed. Halsted devised a radical surgical procedure involving the removal of healthy neighboring tissue as well as the tumors. The procedure led to introduction of the radical mastectomy in 1902, which remained the paradigm of breast cancer treatments for most of this century. [20]

Rise of Radiation Treatments

Radiation joined surgery as a viable treatment for cancer with German physicist Wilhelm Roentgen's 1895 discovery of X-rays and French chemist Marie Curie's discovery of radium a year later. The new technology allowed doctors to destroy unwanted tissue with ionizing radiation that disrupts the DNA of targeted cells. Doctors achieved early success treating basal cell carcinoma of the skin. But equipment was so crude it often destroyed many healthy cells and caused dangerous mutations.

Society at this time still regarded cancer as taboo — a social disease that somehow threatened the modern world, in the words of historian

Continued on p. 798

Chronology

1890s-1930s

Doctors pioneer new cancer treatments while organizations are formed to fight cancer.

1894
William Stewart Halsted devises a surgical technique to prevent the recurrence of cancer after a tumor is removed. It results in the first radical mastectomy.

1895
Wilhelm Roentgen's discovery of X-rays paves the way for early radiation treatments.

1913
The American Society for the Control of Cancer (now the American Cancer Society) is organized in New York City.

1937
Congress establishes the National Cancer Institute.

1940s-1960s

Scientists make progress treating cancer with radiation and chemotherapy. Evidence accumulates linking tobacco use to cancer.

1941
George Papanicolaou successfully demonstrates a method for detecting early cancer of the uterus and cervix, now known as the Pap test. Yale University researchers prove mustard gas can be used to treat malignant lymphomas.

1952
The radioactive isotope cobalt 60 is first used for radiation treatment of cancer.

1954
The American Medical Association publishes findings from a large-scale study that links smoking and lung cancer.

1964
The U.S. surgeon general states unequivocally that smoking causes lung cancer. The next year, Congress orders health warnings on cigarette labels.

1970s

The government for the first time commits large amounts of money to the war on cancer.

1971
President Richard M. Nixon signs the National Cancer Act, setting the stage for a quadrupling of funds for the National Cancer Institute by 1977. Cigarette ads are banned from radio and television.

1973
The National Cancer Institute establishes the nation's first eight comprehensive cancer centers.

1974
First lady Betty Ford undergoes a radical mastectomy after a lump is found in her right breast.

1980s-1990s

Advances are made in understanding the genetic underpinnings of cancer. Overall cancer incidence continues to rise.

1985
Doctors remove a cancerous growth from President Ronald Reagan's large intestine.

1988
Taxol, a drug made from the Pacific yew tree, is shown to be effective in treating ovarian cancer.

1991
National Cancer Institute scientists implant genetically altered cells in two melanoma patients. The cells contain an extra copy of a gene that produces a tumor-fighting substance.

1993
Researchers at Johns Hopkins University in Baltimore discover the gene for human non-polyposis colon cancer.

1994
Government and academic scientists led by University of Utah researchers discover BRCA-1, a gene for inherited breast and uterine cancer. Researchers at Children's Hospital in Boston discover anti-angiogenesis drugs that cut off the blood supply to tumors.

1995
The first patients are injected with a monoclonal antibody developed at New York's Memorial Sloan-Kettering Cancer Center that treats colon cancer.

1998
The National Cancer Institute reports a sustained drop in the cancer death rate between 1991 and 1995, the first decline of its kind since the 1930s. Several promising new drugs are shown to interrupt the molecular processes by which cancer spreads.

Thalidomide to the Rescue?

The push to develop new cancer treatments is reviving scientific interest in thalidomide, the sedative prescribed for pregnancy-related morning sickness that produced thousands of grotesque birth defects in the 1960s and was banned by the Food and Drug Administration (FDA).

Thalidomide belongs to the class of drugs known as anti-angiogenics because it disrupts the body's construction of blood vessels. Just a teaspoonful taken during the first trimester of pregnancy could prevent the fetus from developing a complete vascular system, causing babies to be born with flipper-like limbs, instead of arms and legs.

Today, thalidomide is getting a second chance and being investigated as a possible therapy for diseases including brain and breast cancer, HIV/AIDS, blindness and various autoimmune diseases. In July, the FDA approved it for treatment of a complication of leprosy. Though only a few hundred Americans suffer from the disease, the FDA approval means it is legal for U.S. doctors to prescribe thalidomide in any way they see fit. [1]

Cancer researchers are interested in thalidomide for two reasons. Like other anti-angiogenics, it could be used to cut off the blood supply to hungry tumors and shrink or eradicate malignancies. Researchers believe it also lowers levels of an inflammatory protein called tumor necrosis factor alpha that's produced by an overstimulated immune system and debilitates cancer patients.

Thalidomide could prove useful in other medical applications as well. Its angiogenic properties could fight macular degeneration, an overgrowth of new blood vessels in the central portion of the retina that causes blindness. It also could have a role treating AIDS because it appears to clear up the painful mouth ulcers some patients develop.

The drug was banned in 1962 after it was linked to approximately 12,000 birth defects in Europe and Canada. But it never completely disappeared from the world pharmaceutical market. Israeli researchers in the mid-1960s found it cleared up skin lesions associated with leprosy. In 1991, scientists at Rockefeller University in New York began investigating how the drug regulates immune responses to AIDS. Three years ago, the FDA invited biotechnology companies to apply to manufacture the substance after the agency became aware of a healthy black market for the product, then being made in Brazil.

EntreMed Inc. of Rockville, Md., has acquired a patent on the use of thalidomide as a cancer drug and is testing the compound on a group of breast, prostate and brain cancer patients under the FDA's orphan drug program. Thalidomide is currently manufactured by Celgene Corp. a small biotechnology firm in Warren, N.J.

Mindful of the nightmarish history of the compound, the FDA has attached unprecedented restrictions on its use. Women can't get it without submitting to a pregnancy test and must undergo additional tests throughout treatment. Both women and male patients also must agree to use contraception and watch a video message from a thalidomide victim.

However, researchers acknowledge drugs aren't always used for what they're approved for — and that patients sometimes don't heed warnings. Michael Gruber, a cancer researcher at New York University Medical Center who has used thalidomide and chemotherapy to shrink brain tumors, says patients shouldn't race to the risky drug.

"My fear is everybody with cancer is going to want to take this drug,' he says, noting that cancer patients have stable periods when they can get pregnant. "Wouldn't that be a tragedy, to have the same thing that happened 40 years ago happen again?" [2]

---

[1] See Lauren Neergaard, "FDA Approved Thalidomide," The Associated Press, July 16, 1998.

[2] Ibid.

Continued from p. 796

David Cantor. In 1893, President Grover Cleveland underwent a secret operation on the yacht Oneida to remove part of his upper jaw after doctors diagnosed a swelling on the roof of his mouth as cancer. After word leaked out, Cleveland's doctors insisted the president had been treated for a dental condition and was suffering from rheumatism. Public sensitivities to the word cancer were so delicate that in 1899 New York Cancer Hospital was renamed Memorial Hospital (now part of Memorial Sloan-Kettering Cancer Center) to appease patients. [21]

Various theories of the day held that cancer may be contagious or possibly inherited. Historian Cantor says such thoughts were chilling at a time when American society was shifting away from its rural roots and undergoing great upheaval. "If cancer were both a product of and a danger to industrial and urban society . . . then individuals who had the disease may themselves somehow be responsible for the social disorder," Cantor writes. [22]

Improving the Odds

Few cancer patients had any chance for long-term survival at the turn of the century. However, the combination of surgery and radiation therapy gradually improved the odds. By the 1930s, about one in four patients lived five years. Over the next two decades, doctors fined-tuned radiation therapy by switching to radioactive cobalt and designing machines that delivered more precise treatments. Even before the advent of new molecular technology in the

1980s, four in 10 cancer patients were likely to survive five years after initial diagnosis.

Research into poison gases during World Wars I and II gave rise to the third major cancer treatment, chemotherapy. Yale University pharmacologists studying mustard gas on a government project during World War II observed the poison heavily damaged bone marrow and lymphatic tissue. Subsequent injections of the compound into mice with lymphomas produced a remission of the cancers. In 1943, the scientists discovered mustard gas had similar effects on Hodgkin's disease. Four years later, Boston oncologist Sidney Farber used a related chemical called aminopterin to produce the first remissions in childhood acute leukemia, which then was nearly always fatal.

By the 1970s, more than 50 chemotherapies were available. Doctors began combining two or more in cancer "cocktails" to cure rare diseases, including lymphomas and choriocarcenomas. However, many other cancers developed resistance to chemotherapy, much as bacteria can mutate to escape some antibiotics. Tumors that shrink initially soon recur and resist other so-called "second line" chemotherapy agents.

More than half of the 1.2 million new cases of cancer expected this year will be localized cases of the disease that can be treated with surgery or radiation. Chemotherapy is a standard regimen for patients whose cancer has spread. But doctors note the majority of patients with cancer of the lung, breast, colon and central nervous system will receive only palliative benefit from chemotherapy. Most of the new treatments being developed are directed at this population. [23]

War on Cancer Declared

In his later years, former President Nixon regarded passage

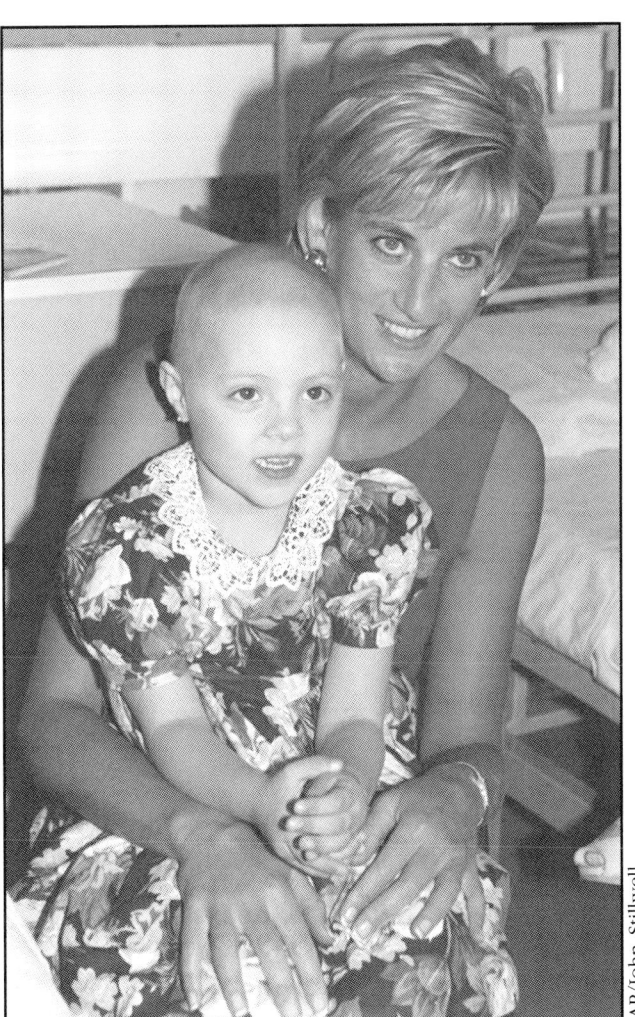

AP/John Stillwell

In July 1997, not long before her death in a car crash in Paris, Princess Diana visited with a youngster undergoing chemotherapy treatments at a London hospital.

of the National Cancer Act as one of his greatest domestic policy achievements. But the emergence of cancer as a political issue was largely thanks to the persistent efforts of Greenwich, Conn., philanthropist Mary Woodard Lasker, who had a wide range of contacts in government and business and for a half-century lobbied for increased federal funding of biomedical research.

Lasker referred to herself simply as a health-care lobbyist. Ironically, her wealth was partly thanks to her advertising executive husband, who made a fortune encouraging women to smoke Lucky Strike cigarettes. But with a cadre of fellow socialites and doctors, Lasker spent the 1960s arguing that the government should spend more money to discover cures for cancer and heart disease because they were the major causes of death.

Lasker made inroads with the Kennedy administration, in part by donating $10,000 to Jacqueline Kennedy's effort to redecorate the White House. But she had less influence with the Nixon administration, which considered cutting the National Institutes of Health budget in the name of fiscal prudence. Some biomedical researchers fought Lasker's call for targeted spending on cancer cures, saying it would come at the expense of basic science. A number of academics also believed increased funding of the NCI would divert money from universities.

Lasker fought on, lobbying influential Democrats in Congress, such as Sen. Ralph W. Yarborough, D-Texas (1957-71), chairman of the Senate Labor and Public Welfare Committee. She also enlisted pharmaceutical executive and Nixon friend Elmer Bobst to try to sway the president. To punctuate her campaign, Lasker took out a $22,000 full-page ad in *The New York Times* that declared, "President Nixon, You Can Cure Cancer" that elicited as many as 8,000 letters to the White House.

Yarborough in 1970 called for a study on the status of cancer research that became the genesis for the cancer act. Nixon, partly worried that Sen. Kennedy would run for president in 1972 and use cancer research as a campaign theme, embraced the issue. In his State of the Union address, on Jan. 22, 1971, Nixon pledged $100 million to launch a campaign to find a cure for cancer.

The cancer institute at NIH has since been the focal point of the federal research effort, though critics have regularly questioned its mission and structure. The institute experienced an exodus of key personnel from 1993-1995 amid reports of sagging morale and micro-management from Congress. [24] Critics also contended its management structure was too top-heavy and that institute directors spent excessive amounts of money on sometimes duplicative intramural research.

In 1994, a National Cancer Advisory Board panel detailed barriers to progress in the fight against cancer, blaming an absence of national coordination for research and critical service gaps.

For example, the panel said at least 23 different federal agencies were involved in cancer research, in addition to scores of private and state-sponsored programs. The panel added that many poor, elderly and uninsured Americans receive inadequate cancer care, and that not enough money is spent translating laboratory successes into treatments.

Klausner, who took over as director in July 1995, has won positive reviews for eliminating some organizational re-

dundancies and succeeded in winning bigger budgets from Congress. Researchers say he and other institute directors now must focus on developing strategies to exploit the deeper knowledge base of the disease.

"There always are lots of constituencies lobbying for their disease, whether it's breast cancer, prostate cancer or something else," says Golde at Memorial Sloan-Kettering. "A lot of the advances are coming out of less-targeted research, and [the current NCI system favoring a broad-based approach] is better than having some feudal lords presiding over the landscape." ■

The University of Michigan's Lichter says the intense focus on Judah Folkman's work was premature and inappropriately raised hopes about a treatment that may never translate to people.

CURRENT SITUATION

False Hopes?

S ome viewed it as a major scientific breakthrough, others as un-

necessary hype. On May 3, 1998, *The New York Times* featured a front-page profile of Judah Folkman, a cancer researcher at Children's Hospital in Boston and Harvard University Medical School, who for 30 years tried to prove that cancerous tumors need their own blood supply to grow. Folkman meticulously isolated protein fragments from tumors in mice that both spurred and stymied blood vessel growth, then used them with startling success to cure cancer in the rodents with no side effects.

The article quoted Nobel laureate James Watson confidently predicting Folkman would cure cancer in humans within two years. NCI Director Klausner was quoted as saying his agency had made development of Folkman's drugs its top priority. The comments sparked an intense response; Folkman's office was bombarded with thousands of calls from media outlets and severely ill patients who wanted to volunteer for clinical trials. The stocks of a dozen biotechnology companies involved in developing the drugs soared.

To many, the cure for cancer appeared just around the corner.

The agents Folkman discovered, angiostatin and endostatin, are part of a family of at least 20 compounds known as anti-angiogenesis drugs that have become the most closely watched new cancer treatments. By cutting off the blood supply of tumors instead of attacking cancer cells directly, the agents can eradicate all tumors in mice, even giant ones that would correspond to a two-pound growth in a person. Other cancer drugs can only slow the growth of tumors.

However, the experimental agents

Continued on p. 802

At Issue:

Are we losing the war against cancer?

SAMUEL EPSTEIN, M.D.

Professor of Occupational and Environmental Medicine at the School of Public Health, University of Illinois Medical Center

FROM THE POLITICS OF CANCER REVISITED

Over recent decades, the incidence of cancer has escalated to epidemic proportions while our ability to treat and cure most cancers remains virtually unchanged. Apart from the important role of tobacco, there is substantial and longstanding evidence relating this epidemic to involuntary and avoidable exposures to industrial carcinogens in air, water, the workplace and consumer products. Nevertheless, the priorities of the cancer establishment, the NCI [National Cancer Institute] and ACS [American Cancer Society], remain narrowly fixated on damage control — diagnosis and treatment — and on basic molecular research, with relative indifference to, if not always benign neglect of, prevention. Concerns over this imbalance are further compounded by serious questions of interlocking interest, particularly with the multibillion-dollar cancer-drug industry.

In spite of overwhelming resources at its disposal, the cancer establishment has failed to allocate minimal priorities to research on cancer prevention. It has also failed to provide Congress and the executive with well-documented scientific evidence on avoidable causes of cancer that would enable development of corrective legislative and regulatory action. Nor have U.S. citizens been advised of such information, which remains buried in confidential government and industry files or is relatively inaccessible in the scientific literature, to enable them to protect themselves. Even more seriously, both government and the public have been misled by repeated claims that we are "winning the war against cancer" and that we have "turned the tide against cancer." These claims are based on extravagant and unfounded announcements of dramatic advances in conventional treatment, coupled with highly prejudicial and unfounded attacks on alternative therapies.

With this background, there has been little if any pressure on industry or incentive to phase out the manufacture, use and disposal of carcinogenic chemicals and products and to replace them with safer alternatives. In short, the NCI and ACS bear major responsibility for losing the winnable war against cancer. This failure is belatedly forcing realization that right-to-know citizen initiatives, on both personal and political levels, are the basis for the most practical and effective strategies for winning the losing cancer war. In addition to these initiatives, the National Cancer Act should be explicitly amended to reorient the mission and priorities of the NCI to cancer cause and prevention.

COPYRIGHT © EAST RIDGE PRESS, 1998

RICHARD D. KLAUSNER, M.D.

Director, National Cancer Institute

FROM TESTIMONY BEFORE THE SENATE APPROPRIATIONS SUBCOMMITTEE ON LABOR, HEALTH AND HUMAN SERVICES, EDUCATION AND RELATED AGENCIES, JUNE 19, 1997.

there is one overarching message that we all agree on: Overall cancer mortality rates, which had been rising all century, have finally begun to fall. The 1-3 percent drop in age-adjusted mortality rates is, we hope, just a beginning — representing thousands of lives saved per year that would have been lost. . . .

Currently, we do have a large investment in prevention. This does and must include research into the causes of cancer, identifying who is at risk for which cancer, conducting prevention research and prevention interventions, and amounts to $911 million, or 38 percent of our budget.

Research into detection of cancer crosses the line between prevention and treatment. Early detection is of no benefit without effective treatment. Our investment in treatment-oriented research amounts to $845 million, or 35 percent of our budget. The remaining 27 percent of our budget is targeted to cancer biology, training and education, which I consider to be part of the necessary foundation for prevention, detection or treatment. . . .

Progress is dependent upon knowledge. Our investment in understanding the causes and characteristics of cancer is essential if we are to develop effective interventions, regardless of whether they are aimed at prevention or treatment.

Painstaking molecular, genetic and epidemiological studies in colorectal cancer are revealing real targets for preventing the development of polyps, the precursors of colon cancer, and preventing their progression to cancer. Cellular and molecular studies of the hormone-dependent growth of breast and prostate cancer are allowing the design of specific antagonists that are providing the first preventives now being tested for these cancers.

Progress takes time. The pace of progress against cancer frustrates all of us. Whether we like it or not, to move from an insight or an observation to a tested successful human intervention takes time, and this is why there will always be a lag between our investment, the development of the critical knowledge base and the payoff that we are finally seeing. . . .

[E]ven if all tobacco use stopped today, even if all of us instantly adopted a "perfect" diet . . . we would still be confronted with an enormous number of people who will be diagnosed with cancer. These people cannot and will not be written off because we have chosen one fork in the road and decided that if you slip past prevention, you're out of luck. Our broad-based approach is working. It would be foolish to abandon it.

Continued from p. 800

are only beginning to be tested in humans and so far have shown inconclusive results. The drugs shrank tumors in some sick patients but had no effect on others. Folkman's drugs are at least a year away from trials to evaluate whether they are safe enough for people. Even the reclusive researcher, who endured years of criticism before the burst of publicity vindicated him, is loath to claim victory.

"It's hard to work under the spotlight," Folkman recently said in a rare interview. "We know there are failures [in the early development of drugs], and the failures are magnified by critics to mean the whole field won't work." [25]

The University of Michigan's Lichter says the intense focus on Folkman's work was premature and inappropriately raised hopes about a treatment that may never translate to people. "It builds cynicism that what people read about cancer research cannot be relied upon. That will accrue to our detriment over time," Lichter told *Nature* magazine shortly after the news broke. Watson and Klausner have backed off from their initial, highly optimistic comments, though they say Folkman's work still holds much promise.

But many other researchers say Folkman's work represents a genuine watershed. If his preliminary findings can be translated into useful therapies, physicians will effectively be able to freeze lethal tumors in place and make them little more than harmless bundles of cells. Choking off the blood supply also would reduce the risk of metastases, the small tumors that often arise after a large tumor is removed.

"I'd give it to patients tomorrow [if it were available]," says Ralph Weichselbaum, a radiation oncologist at the University of Chicago. Weichselbaum recently performed a sequel, of sorts, to Folkman's experiments, showing that a combination of angiostatin and conventional radiation therapy could shrink human tumors implanted in mice.

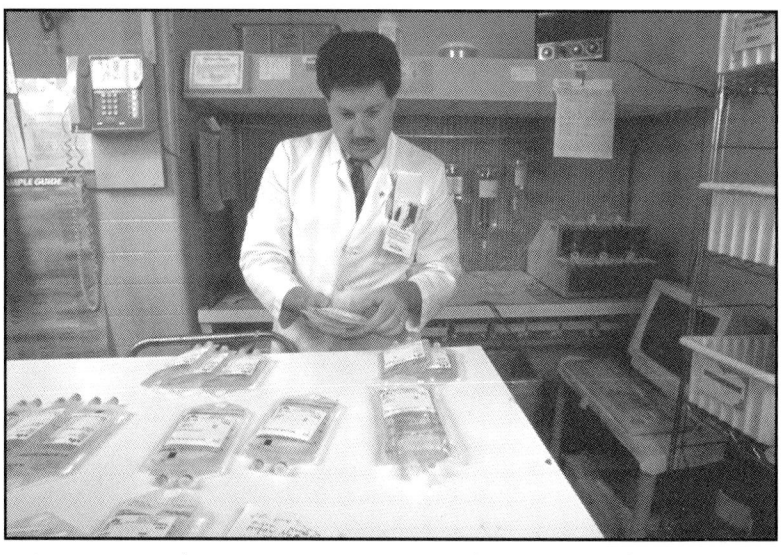

Scientists say that promising anti-cancer drugs now in clinical trials reflect the $30 billion of publicly funded research carried out since the early 1970s.

Biotechnology and pharmaceutical companies already are reaping rewards from the encouraging news. EntreMed Inc., a small Rockville, Md., company founded to create Folkman's drugs, saw its stock soar from $12.06 per share to $80 per share the day after *The New York Times* article before settling at $51.81. Since then, the stock has settled to trade at around $20.

The stocks of two companies working on compounds already being tested on humans — Redwood City, Calif.-based Sugen Inc. and Plymouth Meeting, Pa.-based Magainin Pharmaceuticals Inc. — also rose.

The focus on anti-angiogenesis drugs has even revived interest in thalidomide, the sedative that produced flipperlike limbs and other grotesque birth defects in the 1960s but earlier this year was approved by the FDA for treating leprosy. *(See story, p. 798.)*

However, isolating the tumor-starving compounds remains a difficult task. Folkman and his post-doctoral students had to collect 10 quarts of mouse urine to obtain 30-thousandths of an ounce of angiostatin. Klausner of the National Cancer Institute estimates it will probably take 18 months to collect enough of the material to begin testing in a small number of patients. The institute says it is working with EntreMed to speed up production.

"NCI has made it a high priority to move research forward on these compounds," Klausner says.

OUTLOOK

Critical Gaps in Care

Though scientists are learning more about what causes cancer, their recent discoveries are coming too late for the hundreds of thousands of people expected to die of the disease this year. Several surveys suggest there are critical gaps in providing end-of-life care for these patients and cautioning them against having false hopes.

One survey of 3,200 oncologists in the United States, Canada and England by the University of Massachusetts Center for Survey Research found most of the doctors never had formal training in how to care for dying patients. While 95 percent said they feel competent to manage pain, more than half reported that at least one in five of their patients dies in pain. About 25 percent said caring for the dying was the worst part of their work. [26]

Another recent study by the Dana-Farber Cancer Institute in Boston of 917 terminally ill adults hospitalized with lung or colon cancer that had spread to the liver found many didn't have a good understanding of their prognosis. The majority of patients said they had a 90 percent chance or better of living another six months, though only 45 percent actually lived that long.

The survey found the most optimistic patients typically were inclined to seek the most aggressive anti-cancer treatments, though those who received them generally did not live longer. Instead, they endured grueling treatments that sometimes left them debilitated and even on life support. Jane Weeks, lead author of the study, suspects part of the optimism stems from doctors not giving patients enough information about their conditions. A correct, if pessimistic, prognosis could allow patients to spend their final days at home with loved ones, or in other more comfortable surroundings. [27]

Physicians say the surveys point to the need for better medical training to provide end-of-life care, including tending to psychosocial issues, such as home care, depression and family and spiritual issues.

One particularly troubling area for doctors is care for the elderly. While half

of all new cancer cases occur in people 65 and older, experts say older patients are generally underrepresented in clinical trials. The Southwest Oncology Group in San Antonio, Texas, recently found patients 65 and older accounted for 25 percent of trial participants, even though they comprise 63 percent of the NCI's national cancer registry.

It is often assumed that older patients can't handle treatments like aggressive chemotherapy as well as younger patients because they have other health problems, such as failing kidneys that can make it more difficult to excrete toxic drugs. But several studies suggest elderly breast cancer patients respond better than their younger counterparts to aggressive chemotherapy. Without more thorough study, doctors say they will continue to make critical decisions about patient care based on gut instinct.

Some oncologists are urging elderly cancer patients to enroll in clinical trials. The American Society of Clinical Oncology also has joined with the American Geriatrics Society to develop pilot programs at a handful of health centers giving doctors instruction in caring for the elderly.

Health professionals say the situation demonstrates that cancer specialists will have to keep honing their skills and dealing with death because the day all cancer is cured is still far away.

"It's the natural tendency of people to want to do everything possible to fight the disease if they're otherwise functional," says Dallas oncologist Joseph Bailes. "It's the responsibility of the physician to counsel appropriately, to know when to go to the last resort, and also to know when to tell patients they shouldn't." ■

Notes

[1] For background, see Phyllis Wingo, et al., "Cancer Incidence and Mortality, 1973-1995: A Report Card for the U.S.," *Cancer*, March 15, 1998.

[2] See "Breast Cancer Prevention Trial Shows Major Benefit, Some Risk," National Cancer Institute press release and background documents, April 6, 1998. For background, see Sarah Glazer, "Breast Cancer," *The CQ Researcher*, June 27, 1997, pp. 553-576.

[3] For background, see Catherine Arnst, "After 25 Years, A Big Payoff," *Business Week*, June 1, 1998, p. 147.

[4] For background, see Barbara Mantel, "Advances in Cancer Research," *The CQ Researcher*, Aug. 25, 1995, pp. 753-776.

[5] Richard Klausner and Barnett Kramer, "Grappling With Cancer — Defeatism Versus the Reality of Progress," *The New England Journal of Medicine*, Sept. 25, 1997.

[6] For background, see Adriel Bettelheim, "Alzheimer's Disease," *The CQ Researcher*, May 15, 1998, pp. 433-456 and Mary H. Cooper, "Combating AIDS," *The CQ Researcher*, April 21, 1995, pp. 345-368.

[7] For background, see Richard L. Worsnop, "Reforming the FDA," *The CQ Researcher*, June 6, 1997, pp. 481-504.

[8] For background, see Rick Weiss, "Genetic Testing Is Not As Simple As It Sounds," *The Washington Post*, Feb. 10, 1998, p. Z6.

[9] See Nathan Seppa, "Genetic Flaw Linked to Breast Cancer," *Science News*, April 25, 1998, p. 271.

[10] See Lawrence Fisher, "Non-Hodgkin's Lymphoma Is Treatable by a New Drug," *The New York Times*, Nov. 27, 1997, p. A28.

[11] For background, see Craig Donegan, "Gene Therapy's Future" *The CQ Researcher*, Dec. 8, 1995, pp. 1089-1112.

[12] See "Progress Is Reported on Therapies That Target Only Malignant Cells," *Medical Tribune* (Family Physician Edition), 38(12):1997.

[13] For background, see Li Fellers, "The Price of Hope: Public Funding, Private Profits and the Cancer Drug Taxol," *The Washington Post Magazine*, May 31, 1998, p. W10.

[14] See "Pharmaceutical Drugs, Intellectual Property Rights and Public Health: A Consumer Perspective from the United States," Center for the Study of Responsive Law, 1994.

[15] See U.S. House of Representatives, Hearings of the House of Representatives, Committee on Small Business, Subcommittee on Regulation, Business Opportunities and Technology, "Pricing of Drugs Codeveloped by Federal Laboratories and Private Companies," Jan. 25, 1993.

[16] Fellers, *op. cit.*, p. W26.

[17] For background, see "9th Circuit: ERISA Preempts Claims by Kin of Cancer Victim Denied Coverage," *Mealey's Managed Care Liability Report*, Vol. 2, No. 11 (June 10, 1998).

[18] See Steven Findlay, "Proposal: Seniors Get Access to New Cancer Drugs," *USA Today*, Jan. 29, 1998, p. 1A.

[19] For background, see Mary Agnes Carey, "Patients' Rights Bill May Die Aborning," *CQ Weekly*, Aug. 1, 1998, pp. 2074-2082.

[20] For background, see Barrie Cassileth, "The Evolution of Oncology," *Perspectives in Biology and Medicine*, spring 1983.

[21] See Wendy Schlessel Harpham and Donna Hoel, "Raising The Curtain on Cancer: Is the Puzzle Finally Becoming Clear?" *Postgraduate Medicine*, Vol. 102, No. 3 (September 1997).

[22] See David Cantor, "Cancer," in W.F. Bynum, *Companion Encyclopedia of the History of Medicine* (1993), pp. 537-560.

[23] For background, see Emil Freireich, "Treatment of Malignancies Past and Present," *Hospital Practice*, March 15, 1993.

[24] For background, see Eliot Marshal, "A New Phase in the War on Cancer," *Science*, March 10, 1995, p. 1413, and Mantel, *op. cit.*

[25] Quoted in Richard Saltus, "Pioneer's Progress: As Frenzy Fades, Dr. Judah Folkman Presses On With Promising Research on Blocking the Disease's Blood Supply," *The Boston Globe*, Aug. 5, 1998, p. A1.

[26] See "Largest Survey of Cancer Specialists Finds Physician Education, Access to Services, Patient Depression Remaining Challenges to Providing Quality End-Of-Life Care," American Society of Clinical Oncology press release and background materials, May 16, 1998. For background, see Richard L. Worsnop, "Caring for the Dying," *The CQ Researcher*, Sept. 5, 1997, pp. 769-792.

[27] See Susan Gilbert, "For Cancer Patients, Hope Can Add to Pain," *The New York Times*, June 9, 1998, p. C7.

Bibliography

Selected Sources Used

Books

Waldholz, Michael, *Curing Cancer: The Story of the Men and Women Unlocking the Secrets of Our Deadliest Illness*, Simon & Schuster, 1997.

The Wall Street Journal's chief medical and science writer provides a colorful account of the competition among scientists to find the genetic causes of cancer and how the research is transforming the lives of many patients.

Davies, Kevin, and Michael White, *Breakthrough: The Race to Find the Breast Cancer Gene*, John Wiley & Sons, 1996.

The editor of *Nature Genetics* and a science journalist chronicle the search for BRCA-1, the gene for "heritable" breast cancer, and demonstrate how genetic mutations can form the basis for the disease. They caution against presuming a "quick fix" will be found.

Murphy, Gerald (ed.), *Informed Decisions: The Complete Book of Cancer Diagnosis, Treatment and Recovery*, Viking, 1997.

This American Cancer Society-endorsed book covers such topics as cancer risks, screening and diagnostic tests and treatment strategies and is regarded as one of the best reference books on the disease.

Proctor, Robert, "Cancer Wars: How Politics Shapes What We Know and Don't Know About Cancer," Basic Books, 1995.

Proctor argues that government regulatory agencies, scientists, environmentalists and trade associations have obscured the issues surrounding cancer, hindering the war on the disease.

Articles

Kolata, Gina, "Two Drugs Eradicate Tumors in Mice," *The New York Times*, May 3, 1998, p. A1.

This is the article on experimental anti-angiogenesis cancer drugs that prompted a burst of publicity and speculation over the promise of new cancer treatments.

Brownlee, Shannon, and Nancy Shute, "Killing Cancer: New Drugs Can Cure Mice, Thanks to Advances in Understanding the Disease's Basic Biology. But Cures for People Are Still Years Away," *U.S. News and World Report*, May 18, 1998.

A well-written cover story on the hubbub over the promise of anti-angiogenesis in fighting cancer that also outlines other promising therapies.

Altman, Lawrence, "Good News From the Front in the War Against Cancer," *The New York Times*, May 26, 1998, p. C3.

Altman summarizes encouraging news from cancer laboratories around the country and outlines new trends in treatments based on an increased understanding of the biological basis for the disease.

Fellers, Li, "The Price of Hope: Public Funding, Private Profits and the Cancer Drug Taxol," *The Washington Post Magazine*, May 31, 1998, p. W10.

An excellent case study of how the government discovered and helped develop the best-selling cancer drug in the world, then turned it over to pharmaceutical giant Bristol-Myers Squibb, which made billions of dollars in sales from the medication.

Altman, Lawrence, "Treating Cancer in Elderly Baffles Experts," *The New York Times*, May 20, 1998, p. A15.

With more older Americans needing cancer therapy, oncologists are having difficulty determining the safest and most effective drug treatments for them, according to experts.

Weiss, Rick, "Genetic Testing Is Not as Simple as It Sounds," *The Washington Post*, Feb. 10, 1998, p. Z6.

The generally accepted belief that cancer has a genetic component creates new dilemmas for people worried about whether they carry a potentially deadly gene.

Beardsley, Tim, "A War Not Won," *Scientific American*, January 1994.

Beardsley assesses progress in the then 25-year war on cancer and concludes that progress has been spotty.

Reports

***The Nation's Investment in Cancer Research: A Budget Proposal for Fiscal Year 1999*, National Cancer Institute, National Institutes of Health, September 1997.**

The institute's 1999 budget request, which outlines areas of high-priority research, describes clinical trials of experimental drugs and discusses new approaches to therapy.

***Cancer Facts & Figures — 1998*, American Cancer Society, 1998.**

Features detailed estimates of new cancer cases and death rates, 20-year trends in mortality and state-by-state breakdowns of cancer incidence.

***1998 Annual Meeting Abstracts*, American Society of Clinical Oncologists, May 1998.**

A series of technical reports summarizing 2,000 presentations given at the society's annual meeting in May in Los Angeles that cover virtually every aspect of current cancer research. Also available on the Web at www.asco.org.

The Next Step

Additional information from UMI's Newspaper & Periodical Abstracts™ database

Alternative Treatments

Dolby, Victoria, "More Good News About Garlic and Cancer," *Better Nutrition*, October 1997, p. 14.

Modern medicine is confirming what ancient cultures have long known: garlic is a powerful healer.

Hainer, Cathy, "Today's Patients Seek Balance, Alternatives," *USA Today*, July 21, 1998, p. D6.

Until a cure is found, chemotherapy and radiation are likely to remain the standards in cancer treatment. But more patients are turning to alternative therapies to alleviate the side effects of chemo and to aid in cancer care. Like many other healing systems, energy healing is about re-establishing balance.

Spaulding-Albright, Nancy, "A Review of Some Herbal and Related Products Commonly Used in Cancer Patients," *American Dietetic Association Journal*, October 1997, pp. S208-215.

In light of current research on the benefits of various phytochemicals in foods, it appears feasible that the chemical compounds from herbs also could be helpful in prevention or treatment of cancer and other diseases.

Tamura, Yasuaki, Ping Peng, Kang Liu, Maria Daou and Pramod K. Srivastava, "Immunotherapy of Tumors with Autologous Tumor-Derived Heat Shock Protein Preparations," *Science*, Oct. 3, 1997, pp. 117-120.

Immunotherapy of mice with pre-existing cancers using heat shock protein preparations derived from autologous cancer resulted in retarded progression of the primary cancer, a reduced metastatic load and prolongation of life span.

Funding

Dresser, Rebecca, "Setting Priorities for Science Support," *Hastings Center Report*, May 1998, pp. 21-23.

Ethical and political considerations relevant to allocation of federal research dollars to the National Institutes of Health (NIH) are examined. Testimony presented at Senate and House hearings on research priority-setting highlights the political nature of federal support for science projects.

Gerstenzang, James, "Clinton Under Fire; Gore Touts Hike in Science Spending," *Los Angeles Times*, Jan. 30, 1998, p. A17.

Putting the width of the country between himself and the furor that has enveloped the White House, Vice President Gore delved Thursday into his signature high-tech agenda and said the Clinton administration was proposing a $31 billion increase — the largest ever — in funding for three key federal science agencies. The vice president spoke at the headquarters of Genentech Inc., where he toured a facility that makes synthetic proteins used in cancer drugs and growth hormones. Before leaving Washington for California, Gore announced two cancer-related proposals: an additional $4.7 billion — a 65 percent increase — over five years in funding for cancer research at the National Institutes of Health, and the expansion of Medicare benefits for cancer patients.

Pear, Robert, "Medical Research to Get More Money from Government," *The New York Times*, Jan. 3, 1998, p. A1.

In his new budget, President Clinton plans to seek a substantial increase in federal spending on biomedical research, and members of Congress from both parties say they are virtually certain to approve an even bigger increase. Science and politics point to the same conclusion. When Congress reconvenes this month, lawmakers will be seeking more money for the NIH because they believe that researchers can exploit promising scientific opportunities like new advances in cancer treatment. They also believe that such investments will be popular with voters in an election year.

Sternberg, Steve, "$30 Billion 'War on Cancer' a Bust? Researchers Suggest Putting Emphasis on Prevention," *USA Today*, May 29, 1997, p. A1.

"The effect of new treatments for cancer on mortality has been largely disappointing," John Bailar and Heather Gornick of the University of Chicago assert in *The New England Journal of Medicine*. "The most promising approach to the control of cancer is a national commitment to prevention, with a rebalancing of the focus and funding of research." Their analysis follows two recent studies showing that the nation's cancer death rates began to decline slightly in 1991 after decades of steady increases. But researchers disagree over how much of this change is due to novel cancer treatments and how much to the fading popularity of smoking or early detection of tumors while they are small enough to remove.

Genetic Research

Brody, Jane E., "Disclosure of How a Gene Causes Breast Cancer," *The New York Times*, Aug. 14, 1998, p. A14.

Scientists at the University of North Carolina have made an important discovery about how defects in one of the two breast cancer genes, BRCA1, raise the risk of the disease, leaving cells without the normal ability to correct certain mistakes that commonly occur in their genetic machinery. The scientists and researchers say the finding has potentially important clinical implications for people known to carry the defective gene.

Haney, Daniel Q., "New Cancer Fighting Treatment Targets Genes," *Los Angeles Sentinel*, June 11, 1998, p. A10.

Attacking cancer at its genetic roots has been a goal of science for two decades. Researchers say they now have the first evidence that they can actually do it, pointing to success in an entirely new approach to fighting cancer.

Weichselbaum, Ralph R., and Donald Kufe, "Gene Therapy of Cancer," *Lancet*, Oncology Supplement, May 1997, pp. SII10-SII12.

Cancer-gene therapy — the transfer of nucleic acids into tumor or normal cells to eliminate or reduce tumor burden by direct cell-killing, immunomodulation or correcting genetic errors to reverse the malignant state — is discussed.

Medicinal Treatments

Huber, Peter, "FDA Caution Can Be Deadly, Too," *The Wall Street Journal*, July 24, 1998, p. A14.

William S. Merrell Co. of Cincinnati first applied for U.S. approval of Thalidomide in September 1960. Last week the FDA approved it. New Jersey-based Celgene Corp. may now market Thalidomide, under strict controls, to treat a rare condition associated with Hansen's disease (leprosy). Since 1960 the FDA has very quietly contrived to make Thalidomide available for "compassionate use" and "experimental programs." And for years the FDA has quietly tolerated clubs that bought Thalidomide in Brazil for underground distribution in the U.S. There is, however, much tragedy on the other side of the Thalidomide ledger, too. Rapidly dividing cells also create cancerous tumors. It is thought that Thalidomide injures fetuses by halting the proliferation of blood vessels, an effect that also shows enormous promise for starving malignant tumors.

Langreth, Robert, "Bone-Disease Drug Appears to Reduce Death Rate for Breast-Cancer Patients," *The Wall Street Journal*, Aug. 6, 1998, p. B7.

A popular class of drugs for bone disease might also help prevent complications and deaths from breast cancer, a new study indicates. The three-year study of about 300 women found that patients who took the osteoporosis drug clodronate — one of a new class of osteoporosis and bone-loss drugs called bisphosphonates — in addition to standard therapy, had a dramatically reduced risk of having the cancer recur and kill them. Overall, the drug reduced the death rate by two-thirds in patients at a high risk of recurrence, according to the

study published in this week's *New England Journal of Medicine*.

New Treatments

"Conquering Cancer," *Los Angeles Times*, May 26, 1998, p. B4.

At a Los Angeles convention last week, world cancer specialists unveiled dazzling new cancer drugs that promise to take treatment far beyond the scattershot chemotherapies that kill good cells and bad ones alike. The drugs range from herceptin, which attacks the genetic defects that cause many breast cancers, to angiostatin, which deprives tumor cells of the nutrients they need to survive.

"FDA Panel Endorses Rhone-Poulenc Drug For Cancer Treatment," *The Wall Street Journal*, June 2, 1998, p. B6.

A federal advisory panel endorsed Rhone-Poulenc Rorer Inc.'s Taxotere as a second-line treatment for locally advanced or metastatic breast cancer.

Gillis, Justin, "Wall Street's Race for the Cure; Gains in Breast Cancer Research Lifting Stocks," *The Washington Post*, May 19, 1998, p. C1.

First came the news that a drug called tamoxifen seemed to prevent breast cancer in women at high risk. Then came preliminary reports about another drug, raloxifene, that seemed to have an even stronger prophylactic effect. And at a medical conference this week, the biotechnology company Genentech Inc. reported hopeful results with a novel treatment designed to attack a virulent form of breast cancer. "We are at a very exciting point where what we have learned in the laboratory about the molecular basis for cancer can be translated into clinical trials, and eventually used in patients," breast cancer researcher Lori J. Goldstein said in a statement released by the American Society of Clinical Oncology, sponsor of the Los Angeles conference.

Guthrie, Patricia, "Medicine Cornering a Killer? 'Absolutely Convincing Proof,' Researchers Say Chemoprevention is the Long-Awaited Breast Cancer Weapon," *Atlanta Journal Constitution*, May 24, 1998, p. C4.

Data released this month point toward medical intervention known as chemoprevention. Whether such a wonder drug will be called tamoxifen, raloxifene or another name, remains unclear. But what is known is that breast cancer may be headed the way of heart disease, where high-risk patients pop a daily pill to ward off illness. Another advance was hailed in the use of taxol, a cancer medicine already approved for use against ovarian cancer and advanced breast cancer. This study showed that survival rates dramatically rose for women with early breast cancer. Taxol interferes with cancer cell division by tangling up those cells' molecular "skeletons."

Back Issues

Great Research on Current Issues Starts Right Here.
Recent topics covered by The CQ Researcher are listed below.
Now available on the Web
For information, call (800) 432-2250 ext. 279 or (202) 887-6279.

If you would like to have any of these CQ Researchers updated, or need more information about these topics, please call CQ Custom Research. Special rates for CQ subscribers. (202) 887-8600 or (800) 432-2250, ext. 600, or E-mail Custom.Research@cq.com

JUNE 1997
FDA Reform
China After Deng
Line-Item Veto
Breast Cancer

JULY 1997
Transportation Policy
Executive Pay
School Choice Debate
Aggressive Driving

AUGUST 1997
Age Discrimination
Banning Land Mines
Children's Television
Evolution vs. Creationism

SEPTEMBER 1997
Caring for the Dying
Mental Health Policy
Mexico's Future
Youth Fitness

OCTOBER 1997
Urban Sprawl in the West
Diversity in the Workplace
Teacher Education
Contingent Work Force

NOVEMBER 1997
Renewable Energy
Artificial Intelligence
Religious Persecution
Roe v. Wade at 25

DECEMBER 1997
Whistleblowers
Castro's Next Move
Gun Control Standoff
Regulating Nonprofits

JANUARY 1998
Foster Care Reform
IRS Reform
The Black Middle Class
U.S.-British Relations

FEBRUARY 1998
Patients' Rights
Deflation Fears
Caring for the Elderly
The New Corporate Philanthropy

MARCH 1998
Israel at 50
The Federal Judiciary
Drinking on Campus
The Economics of Recycling

APRIL 1998
Biology and Behavior
Liberal Arts Education
Income Inequality
High-Tech Labor Shortage

MAY 1998
Census 2000
Child-Care Options
Alzheimer's Disease
U.S.-Russian Relations

JUNE 1998
Student Journalism
Antitrust Policy
Environmental Justice
Sleep Deprivation

JULY 1998
Encouraging Teen Abstinence
Population and the Environment
Democracy in Asia
Baby Boomers at Midlife

AUGUST 1998
Oil Production in the 21st Century
Flexible Work Arrangements
Coastal Development
Student Activism

SEPTEMBER 1998
Organic Farming

Back issues are available for $5.00 (subscribers) or $10.00 (non-subscribers). Quantity discounts apply to orders over 10. To order, call Congressional Quarterly Customer Service at (202) 887-8621.

Binders are available for $18.00. To order call 1-800-638-1710. Please refer to stock number 648.

Future Topics

▶ *Hispanic Americans' New Clout*

▶ *The Future of Baseball*

▶ *School Violence*

T H E CQResearcher

PUBLISHED BY CONGRESSIONAL QUARTERLY INC.

Hispanic-Americans' New Clout

Will Hispanics desert the Democratic Party?

I
n just a few years, Latinos will become the nation's largest minority, surpassing African-Americans. As their political clout grows, Latinos are making their presence felt. Democrats have corralled a large share of the Latino vote. But Republicans say that Latinos are beginning to embrace GOP positions, such as opposition to bilingual learning, because it is not effectively teaching children to speak English. Others argue that bilingual education does lead to English proficiency and that any opposition to it among Latinos is probably misplaced anger over the poor state of public education in general.

| C_Q | **Sept. 18, 1998 • Volume 8, No. 35 • Pages 809-832** |

Formerly Editorial Research Reports

September 18, 1998
Volume 8, No.35

EDITOR
Sandra Stencel

MANAGING EDITOR
Thomas J. Colin

STAFF WRITERS
Adriel Bettelheim
Mary H. Cooper
Kenneth Jost
Kathy Koch
David Masci

PRODUCTION EDITOR
Melissa Hall

EDITORIAL ASSISTANT
Laura S. Cavender

PUBLISHED BY
Congressional Quarterly Inc.

CHAIRMAN
Andrew Barnes

VICE CHAIRMAN
Andrew P. Corty

PRESIDENT AND PUBLISHER
Robert W. Merry

EXECUTIVE EDITOR
David Rapp

The CQ Researcher (ISSN 1056-2036). Formerly Editorial Research Reports. Published weekly, except Jan. 2, May 29, July 3, Oct. 30, by Congressional Quarterly Inc., 1414 22nd St., N.W., Washington, D.C. 20037. Annual subscription rate for libraries, businesses and government is $340. Additional rates furnished upon request. Periodicals postage paid at Washington, D.C., and additional mailing offices. POSTMASTER: Send address changes to The CQ Researcher, 1414 22nd St., N.W., Washington, D.C. 20037.

COVER: THE CURRENT AND FORMER SPEAKERS OF THE CALIFORNIA ASSEMBLY, ANTONIO VILLARAIGOSA, LEFT, AND CRUZ BUSTAMONTE, ARE BOTH LATINOS. (AP PHOTO/RICH PEDRONCELLI)

Hispanic-Americans' New Clout

BY DAVID MASCI

THE ISSUES

It was a real fiesta, complete with a mariachi band and spicy Mexican food.

But the festive mood in Sacramento, Calif., last Feb. 26 belied the momentousness of the occasion. The state Assembly was swearing in its newest Speaker, Antonio Villaraigosa, and the atmosphere crackled with excitement. Not only was a Latino ascending to the state's top legislative post, but he was taking the reins from Cruz Bustamonte, the first Latino ever to hold the office.

To many analysts, Villaraigosa's rise reflects Hispanic-Americans' growing political clout. "It was clearly a watershed, to see one Latino pass the torch to another," says Rep. Xavier Becerra, D-Calif., the outgoing head of the House Hispanic Caucus. "We're graduating from the minor leagues to the big leagues."

A growing number of Hispanic-Americans are making political names for themselves these days — regionally, like Villaraigosa and Bustamonte (who is running for California lieutenant governor), and even nationally like Becerra and newly confirmed Energy Secretary Bill Richardson. At the same time, the number of Latino officials around the country has jumped dramatically, from 3,128 in 1984 to 5,191 today. [1]

The new political clout mirrors the rise in the nation's Latino population — up from just over 12 million in 1984 to nearly 30 million today. In California, the nation's most populous state, Latinos are poised to become the largest ethnic group, outnumbering both whites and blacks, in the next few years. [2] Other major states, like Texas, Florida and New York, also have large Hispanic populations.

Moreover, Hispanics are also rap-

idly moving into the nation's suburbs and its middle class; for the first time, there are now more than 1 million Latino-owned businesses nationwide. [3]

Until recently, however, demographic and even economic clout hasn't always translated into commensurate political power for Latinos. Many were not citizens or even legal residents and hence were ineligible to vote. Even among Hispanic citizens, voter turnout traditionally has been low.

But lately things have been changing. Efforts to cut health and other benefits to Latinos who are legal residents of the United States have led millions to apply for citizenship, making them eligible to vote. In California, for instance, the number of Hispanics registered to vote has jumped from 1.3 million in 1994 to 2 million today. [4]

In addition, the efforts to deny benefits to immigrants as well as bruising debates over affirmative action and bilingual education have politically galvanized many Latinos who might otherwise have stayed home on Election Day. "We're starting to see more and more Latinos turn up at the polls and seeing them

better educated about the issues," says Ingrid Duran, assistant director of the National Association of Latino Elected and Appointed Officials.

So far, the increased political participation has translated into gains for the Democratic Party. Indeed, in the last presidential election, GOP candidate Bob Dole got just over 20 percent of the Hispanic vote, less than half of what President Ronald Reagan received in 1984.

Democrats and some political analysts predict that Latinos will largely stick with the Democrats in the future. To begin with, they say, Republicans have alienated Hispanics by pushing an anti-immigrant agenda that includes cutting benefits to illegal and legal immigrants and supporting efforts to do away with affirmative action and bilingual education. "The GOP have been immigrant bashers, and they've driven Latinos into the arms of the Democratic Party," Becerra says.

In addition, Democrats say, their party is much more in tune with the aspirations and needs of most Latinos, especially on issues like education, health care and immigration. Democrats are even confident that they can win over Latino voters on issues traditionally thought to be GOP strengths, like business development and crime. "Those stereotypes that we are hostile to small business or soft on crime don't wash anymore," says Ed Kilgore, political director of the Democratic Leadership Council (DLC).

But Republicans say that they are on the verge of winning a sizable share, if not a majority, of the Latino vote. GOP strategists point to a host of Republican candidates, from Los Angeles Mayor Richard Reardon to Texas Gov. George W. Bush, who are successfully wooing Latino voters. Reardon received 60 percent of the Hispanic vote in the 1997 mayoral election. And a recent poll by Univision, the Spanish-language TV

Latino Population Is Growing Rapidly

The nation's Hispanic population increased 29.6 percent from 1990-97 — four times as fast as the overall U.S. population — due to high birth rates and rising immigration levels. The number of Hispanics is expected to increase 23.6 percent from 1997-2005. There were 29.2 million Hispanics in the United States in 1997, or 11 percent of the population.

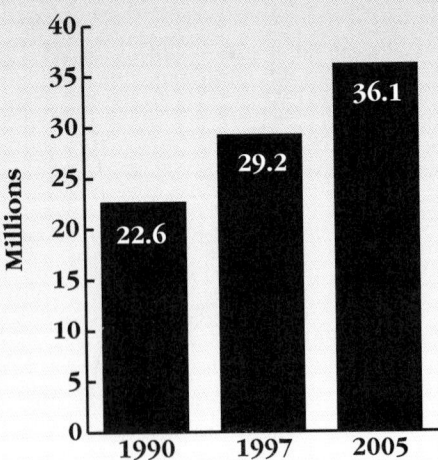

Number of Hispanic-Americans

Total does not include the estimated 3.8 million residents of Puerto Rico.

Source: "Latino Education: Status and Prospects," National Council of La Raza, July 1998, U.S. Census Bureau

network, gave Bush (who is up for re-election this year and is a top contender for his party's presidential nomination in 2000) an 80 percent approval rating among Latinos in his state.

GOP strategists argue that Reardon, Bush and other Republicans have succeeded in communicating the party's pro-family, pro-economic-opportunity message to a growing number of Hispanics, who are traditionally very conservative, especially on social issues. "You look at family issues, crime, business development — we have the message that is most in line with their thinking," says Lorenzo Lopez, a special assistant on Hispanic affairs at the Republican National Committee (RNC).

Whether Republicans draw more Latino votes in future elections or not, it is clear that the party is more focused on winning over Hispanics than it was even two years ago. Indeed, many in the GOP, including Gov. Bush, recently distanced themselves from a ballot initiative in California significantly scaling back bilingual education. But the measure, known as Proposition 227, was not perceived by many Latinos as earlier proposals had been, especially Proposition 187, a 1994 ballot initiative that denied basic benefits to illegal immigrants. In fact, Prop. 227, which was approved by voters in June, received about 40 percent of the Hispanic vote.

Opponents of bilingual education see Latino support for Prop. 227 as a sign that Hispanics, especially those with children in school, are turning away from bilingual programs because they are failing. "Many parents with children in bilingual programs are frustrated, not because they're being taught in Spanish, but because they are not learning English," says Eric Stone, director of research for U.S. English, an organization that advocates making English the nation's official language.

Indeed, say Stone and others, many children with limited or no English proficiency are kept in bilingual programs for six or more years, leaving them woefully unprepared for life in an English-speaking country. "Immigrant parents understand that English is necessary for advancement in this country," he says.

But supporters of bilingual education say that most Latinos still favor Spanish in the classroom until children are proficient in English. They claim that many Hispanics voted for Prop. 227 because they are angry with the poor overall performance of California's schools, not bilingual education per se.

In addition, supporters argue, most Latinos know that bilingual education is not a substitute for learning English but a tool that helps students while they're being taught their new nation's tongue. "The truth is that bilingual education is working for most kids," says Oscar Sanchez, executive director of the Labor Council for Latin American Advancement, a Hispanic trade union group. Sanchez points out that before the widespread introduction of bilingual learning in the late 1960s, Latino kids had a much higher dropout rate than they do today.

According to Sanchez and others, the battle against bilingual education is part of a larger war against Latinos retaining any of their culture. Indeed, he argues, many Americans expect Latinos to completely assimilate and forget about where they came from.

Advocates of cultural retention, like Sanchez, argue that it is good for

Latinos to keep not only their language but also their cultural heritage. Latinos are different from European immigrants, they argue, in that they are not crossing an ocean to come to America and, in many cases, are returning to lands once ruled by Mexico or Spain. In addition, they say, Hispanic children need to be taught the history and traditions of their ancestors in order to give them an identity and greater sense of self-worth.

But others disagree, arguing that Hispanics, like all other immigrants past and present, need to work to adopt the language, culture and traditions of their new country. Any other road will lead to ethnic separatism, they say. "Immigration is a compact between the host country and the newcomer: We welcome you into our home and you, in turn, learn our language, mores and begin identifying with your new family," says Linda Chavez, president of the Center for Equal Opportunity.

By the middle of the next century, Hispanics are likely to make up a quarter of the nation's population, and the extent to which they feel welcomed in their new country could significantly affect the country's future.

As scholars, politicians and others look at this growing community, here are some of the questions they are asking:

Will Latino Democrats remain loyal to the Democratic Party?

When Speaker of the House Newt Gingrich, R-Ga., rose to address a July meeting of the League of United Latin American Citizens (LULAC), the nation's largest Hispanic group, he was greeted with polite but muted applause. In spite of his recent support for Puerto Rican self-determination and restoration of some public benefits denied to legal immigrants, many Latinos still regard the Speaker with suspicion. [5]

But the tepid welcome was not just directed at Gingrich. Latinos generally have not been happy with Republican support for measures to

A police line separates demonstrators for and against Proposition 187 in Los Angeles, Calif., in August 1996.

deny benefits to immigrants as well as GOP opposition to bilingual education and continued high levels of immigration. In California, home to more than half of all U.S. Hispanics, Republican Gov. Pete Wilson's support for Prop. 187 has cost the GOP tremendously with the Latino community, both in and out of state. For example, since 1984, the GOP's share of the Latino vote in presidential elections has fallen from over 40 percent that year, to under 20 percent in 1996.

At the same time, the number of registered Hispanic voters has increased dramatically. For instance,

from 1992-1996, the number of Latinos registered to vote rose 30 percent, to 6.6 million, and 75 percent of the new voters registered as Democrats. [6]

In addition, Latinos are concentrated in almost all of the key electoral vote-rich states needed to win the presidency, including California, Texas, Florida and New York. "In California, which is a keystone in any presidential strategy, Latinos are not just the swing vote, they are a big part of the vote," says Roberto Suro, a reporter at *The Washington Post* and author of a recent book on Latinos, *Strangers Among Us.* Indeed, President Clinton won California, Florida and New York in his successful 1992 and 1996 races, in part due to Latino support.

The current disconnect between many Latino voters and the GOP represents a great threat to Republicans. Unless they begin to regain Latino support, the GOP could be severely handicapped in future national elections.

Indeed, Democrats know that solid Latino support in the near future could help keep a Democrat in the White House and even allow the Democrats eventually to retake control of Congress. "We recognize the importance of this community," says the DLC's Kilgore, "and we're not going to take a single vote for granted."

Kilgore and other Democrats see several reasons why Latino voters generally feel more comfortable with their party than with the GOP. Above all, they say, many Hispanics believe that Republican initiatives to limit immigration, bilingual education and benefits for recent arrivals have un-

Most U.S. Hispanics Are Mexican-Americans

Nearly two-thirds of the nation's Hispanics were Mexican-Americans in 1996. Two-thirds were American citizens, and 62 percent were U.S.-born.

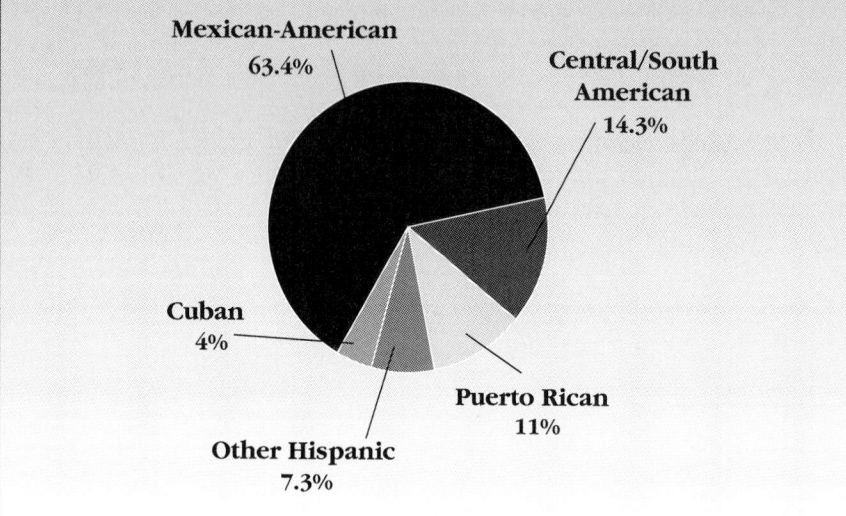

Mexican-American
63.4%

Central/South American
14.3%

Cuban
4%

Puerto Rican
11%

Other Hispanic
7.3%

Sources: *Latino Education: Status and Prospects, National Council of La Raza, July 1998, U.S. Census Bureau*

fairly targeted Latinos and are inherently racist. "Republicans in general have really been anti-Latino," says Sanchez of the Labor Council for Latin American Advancement. "There's no other way for us to look at what they've done."

Sanchez acknowledges that some Republicans, like Gingrich, have begun reaching out to Latino voters in recent months. But so far, they argue, kind GOP words have not been matched by much action. "Republicans need to go beyond the rhetoric," says Duran of the Latino officials' association. "It's nice of them to welcome us to their party, but they need to change their anti-Latino policies."

In addition to the perceived Republican hostility, Democrats say their party's message and agenda is more in line with Latino aspirations. "When you look at the profile of the Hispanic voter — very upwardly mobile, obsessed with education, concerned about crime and a belief in an active

government — you are increasingly looking at the profile of the Democratic Party," Kilgore says.

But Republicans counter that Latino aspirations are actually more in line with the GOP. "Hispanics are in tune with our pro-family, pro-business message," says the RNC's Lopez. Chavez of the Center for Equal Opportunity agrees. "There is a confluence of interests between them," she says.

The real problem, Republicans say, is not the message but the way it is being conveyed. "In the past, we failed with Latino voters because we didn't explain our positions well on things like Proposition 187, and the Democrats were able to demagogue us on that," Lopez says. The GOP needs to become more effective at showing Latinos that they have much more in common with the Republicans than with Democrats, he says.

For instance, Lopez and Chavez point out, the GOP's positions on moral and family issues are generally

in line with the Latino community. "Hispanics are very family-oriented," Chavez points out. "So on issues like homosexuality or handing out birth control in schools, they feel the same way that most Republicans do."

And, Lopez says, when it comes to family policy, the GOP puts its money where its mouth is. For example, he says, Republicans in Congress recently pushed through a $500 per child tax cut. "This really helps Latinos, who generally have larger families than others," he says.

At the same time, Republicans say, the rapid increase in the number of Latino entrepreneurs means that more and more Hispanics will embrace the party's opposition to what it considers excessive regulation and high taxes. "Latinos are bothered by red tape and an intrusive government just like other small-business men are," Chavez says.

Such predictions make the DLC's Kilgore chuckle. "If they still think they're the party of small business, they're living in the past," he says. Sanchez agrees, adding that "everyone knows that under Clinton businesses in this country have done very well."

Even on family values, where Kilgore admits there may be some differences of opinion, Democrats consider their agenda much better suited to Hispanics due to the party's emphasis on tolerance. "Given a choice between a [Republican] ideology that's intolerant and one that's tolerant, [Latinos] will choose tolerance, even if they're not always comfortable with everything we stand for, like gay rights."

According to Kilgore and others, the Democrats should be able to keep a very high percentage of the Hispanic vote in coming elections. "If we stick to our message of economic optimism and an emphasis on families, education and equal opportunity, they should stay a solidly Democratic voting group."

Sanchez agrees. "Hispanics are a natural constituency for the Democratic

Thanks to Latinos, Spicier English

Spanish has been a part of American English for centuries. Early settlers began picking up Spanish words and phrases almost from the start of the nation's long expansion. In the South, for instance, areas like Florida and Louisiana were, at times, under Spanish rule. And the American Southwest and West were part of Mexico until the Mexican-American War changed the boundaries in 1848.

Today, the huge influx of Hispanic immigrants into the United States is once again adding to the country's language. Much of this change reflects the immense popularity of Latino food, music and other cultural offerings. Anglos — the name given to non-Hispanic whites — find themselves ordering *fajitas* and listening to *Tejano* music with increasing frequency.

New and old Spanish words and phrases that have spiced up American English include:

bronco — a Mexican-Spanish word for wild or rough.

enchilada — popular filled and baked tortilla; also slang for "everything," as in "The whole enchilada."

gringo — derogatory word to refer to an outsider, usually an American. Word may be a derivative of "green grows," a song American troops supposedly sang during the war with Mexico.

guerrilla — unorthodox style of fighting developed by Latin Americans.

incommunicado — increasingly popular way to say "not available."

loco — a 19th-century Mexican word originally used to describe a weed that made horses "crazy."

macho — derived from a Mexican-Indian word that originally meant "to be known."

maquiladora — a foreign-owned factory in Mexico near the U.S. border.

mañana — Spanish for "tomorrow."

salsa — Spanish for sauce made of tomatoes (a Mexican word), onions and chilis (a Mexican-Indian word); also refers to a style of Latin American music.

tobacco — 16th-century Spanish word.

tornado — from the Spanish word *tronada*, for thunderstorm.

Sources: Merriam Webster's Collegiate Dictionary, *Earl Shorris,* Latinos: A Biography of the People.

Party," he says. "So as long as they continue to cultivate us and not take us for granted, they should reap enormous benefits come Election Day."

But, Republicans point out, they are already eroding that support. For instance, on the same day that Gingrich received a lukewarm reception before LULAC, another party leader, Gov. Bush, received a rousing ovation from the group. Bush is likely to be re-elected in November with half or more of the Hispanic vote. His brother Jeb, who is married to a Mexican-American, is running for the governor's mansion in Florida. He, too, is expected to win the election, thanks in no small part to his popularity with Florida Hispanics. Other Republicans who have recently gotten or are expected to get a sizable portion of the Latino vote include New York City Mayor Rudolph Giuliani, Michigan Gov. John Engler

and Sens. Pete V. Domenici, R-N.M., and John McCain, R-Ariz.

According to Lopez, the Bush brothers, Giuliani and McCain prove that the GOP can do well among Latinos if they reach out to them. "A lot of Latinos, especially the young, are becoming disenchanted with the Democrats because they haven't really done much for them," he says.

As a result, Lopez argues, the Latino community won't automatically be wedded to the Democratic Party in the future. "You know, Latino voters are much more savvy than most people think. Democrats just can't show up anymore, say a few words in Spanish, eat a taco and expect to automatically get their vote."

Is bilingual education losing support in the Latino community?

It was only a matter of time before

California, the state that has already held controversial referenda on everything from property taxes to affirmative action, finally got around to asking its voters to pass judgment on bilingual education. The initiative, sponsored by Silicon Valley millionaire Ron Unz, gives a preference to English-language teaching, allows bilingual programs only in schools where parents actually request them and strictly limits the amount of time a student can spend in a non-English class. [7]

When Unz first began campaigning for what would become Proposition 227, many analysts predicted that the debate would degenerate into the kind of racially charged slugfest that had characterized earlier statewide initiatives limiting affirmative action and benefits to illegal immigrants. And indeed, many Latinos and others in the education and civil rights communities charac-

One Name, Many Communities

When author Earl Shorris asked a Mexican-American woman named Margarita Avila how he should write about her ethnic community, she replied: "Just tell them who we are, and that we are not alike."

Shorris assumed that Avila was referring to Hispanics when she said "we," but she surprised him and explained that she meant "Mejicanos." [1]

Shorris' anecdote speaks volumes about Latinos. Not only did Avila distinguish between Mexicans and other Hispanics, but she saw differences within the Mexican-American community itself. Indeed, Mexican-Americans from Texas refer to themselves as Tejanos. In California and elsewhere, most Americans of Mexican descent call themselves Chicanos.

All of this goes to show that Latinos are not a homogeneous group. They come in every shade of skin color, from pale white to black. And they can trace their ancestry all over the globe. Some have largely European or African blood in their veins. Many others are at least partly from indigenous Indian stock. A few even hail from Asia. The majority are a mixture of different ethnicities.

Nor do they come from one country or even one part of Latin America. Many, like Avila, are originally from Mexico. Others come from Cuba, Puerto Rico and the Dominican Republic in the Caribbean. Still others are from Central or South America. All have different traditions, history and culture that they are proud of and think unique.

What they do largely share is a language, Spanish, although dialects abound. To a lesser extent, Latinos also share the same faith, Roman Catholicism. But that is changing. A large and growing number of Latinos have become Protestants, converted by missionaries in Latin America or after their arrival in the U.S. Most of these Protestant Latinos are Evangelical Christians. A small number of Hispanics also are Jewish.

Like Asian-Americans (another heterogeneous community) Latinos have been grouped together due to misunderstanding and convenience. Many whites (called "Anglos" by Latinos) and blacks just assumed that all immigrants from Latin America were the same, regardless of where they came from. "There's been this tendency to lump us all together into one big group," says Felix Gutierrez, senior vice president of the Freedom Forum Pacific Coast Center, in San Francisco.

Pressure to identify Latinos as a single, definable group has also come as voting-rights remedies, affirmative action and other programs designed to aid minorities have become commonplace. In fact, the word "Hispanic" was chosen by the U.S. Census Bureau in 1980 in order to classify all Spanish speakers and their descendants. "Latino" has come into widespread use more recently as an alternative that is more acceptable to the community itself.

But most Latinos do not prefer either word. Instead, they tend to refer to themselves by their country of origin: They are Bolivian, Salvadoran or Cuban.

The majority of Latinos in the United States, about 63 percent, are from Mexico. Mexican-Americans have settled predominantly in those states that were once part of Mexico: California, Texas, New Mexico, Colorado, Nevada and Arizona. Indeed, some Americans of Mexican descent can trace their family history in the United States back many generations, having lived in Texas, New Mexico or California before Mexico was forced to hand over the northern half of its territory to America in 1848.

The second-largest group of U.S. Latinos, about 12 percent, is from Puerto Rico. Puerto Ricans have largely settled in the New York City area. Because Puerto Rico has been a U.S. territory for 100 years, all people born in Puerto Rico are American citizens, giving them a unique status among Latino arrivals.

Cuban-Americans are another unique community, but for a different reason. Many were well-educated, middle-class professionals when they came to the United States in the early 1960s, not the usual "tired" and "hungry" immigrants that often seek refuge on America's shores. These Cubans, who now comprise 8 percent of the nation's Latino population, left their homes to escape Fidel Castro's communist revolution. Some (though not their children) still dream of returning to the land of their birth. But since Castro remains in power, they must be content to wait in their communities in southern Florida and, to a lesser extent, New Jersey.

Immigrants from the Dominican Republic are relatively recent arrivals in the United States. Most have come in the last two decades and have settled in the Northeast, especially New York.

About 12 percent of America's Hispanics come from Central and South America. Many of the Central Americans, from El Salvador, Honduras and Nicaragua, arrived in the 1980s fleeing terrible civil wars. A large number have settled in southern Florida. Others have moved north to Eastern cities like New York and Washington, D.C. There are fewer South Americans, although growing communities of Colombians, Bolivians and Brazilians have sprung up in the last decade.

---

[1] Earl Shorris, *Latinos: Biography of the People* (1992), p. XV.

terized Unz and his allies as everything from anti-immigrant to racist.

But the debate over Prop. 227 didn't entirely mirror those earlier battles. Throughout the campaign, polls often showed a majority of Latinos in favor of the initiative. And a number of prominent Hispanic leaders in California — notably Jaime Escalante, the high school math teacher profiled in the film "Stand and Deliver" — supported the proposition.

On June 2, 1998, Prop. 227 passed by a comfortable margin. And although a majority of Latinos voted against it, a sizable minority, about 40 percent, supported the initiative.

Why are Hispanics in California split over a program that was designed to help their children?

No one denies that California's bilingual education program, and those in other states as well, were established with good intentions. Bilingual education, which aims to help English-deficient children keep up in other subjects while they learn their new nation's language, was first instituted in California by then Gov. Ronald Reagan (R) in 1967. At that time, educators were grappling with high dropout rates among Hispanic students, and it was thought that the program might help acclimate them to the educational system and keep them in school.

Today, the question of what to do with limited-English-proficiency students is more pressing than ever. For example, California has about 1.4 million students with limited or no English ability — about one-quarter of all children enrolled in its schools. About 70 percent of them are Latinos, most Mexican-American. [8]

Few people advocate the "sink or swim" method employed with many immigrant children earlier in our history. But those who oppose all or most bilingual education argue that a growing number of Latinos, especially those with children in school, are realizing that teaching their children in Spanish — especially for lengthy periods — can jeopardize their ability to master English.

"Look, the reason there has been this backlash in California is that parents are noticing that their kids are not learning English as quickly as they should be," says Nina Shokraii, an education policy analyst at the Heritage Foundation. "You're seeing parents in other states like New Mexico and Colorado saying the same thing: 'We want our children taught in English, not their native tongue.'"

Part of the problem with bilingual education, Shokraii says, is that students are often kept in Spanish classes for years while receiving little or no English instruction. "In some places, students spend six or seven years in Spanish-only classes," says Stone of U.S. English. Indeed, in California, only 6 percent of students in bilingual classes are deemed ready each year to make the leap to English-only education.

At the same time, Shokraii, Stone and others argue, Latino parents desperately want their children to be fluent in English and as quickly as possible. "A lot of immigrants who come here want to live the American dream, and they know that that's impossible without English," Shokraii says.

And yet, Shokraii and others claim, the educational establishment as well as Latino advocacy groups in places like California are wedded to the notion that bilingual education is what Hispanic children need. "There is a real disconnect between the ethnic leadership and the rank-and-file on this," says Charles Glenn, a professor of education policy at Boston University and the author of *Educating Immigrant Children*.

Opponents of bilingual education claim that many Latino parents are beginning to take matters into their own hands. For instance, 70 mostly Mexican-American families in Los Angeles removed their children from a city elementary school in 1996 after administrators refused to place them in English instruction.

Two weeks after the boycott began, the school changed its policy. [9] "The notion of parents publicly boycotting a school for weeks because the school was refusing to teach their children English just seemed very extreme," says Unz, who claims that the incident inspired him to begin the campaign for Prop. 227. [10] Similar boycotts have taken place in a number of other cities in the Southwest.

But supporters of bilingual education argue that opponents are unfairly trying to paint Spanish instruction as a replacement for learning English. They point out that bilingual education is not meant to keep children in a linguistic ghetto. "Who is against children learning English fluently?" asks Sanchez of the Labor Council for Latin American Advancement. "No one. This is not an either/or thing."

"The whole point of bilingual education is for children to learn [other subjects] at their current level while also learning English," Duran says. "The idea that the 'English-only' people have — that you can learn it in a year — is ridiculous." Without bilingual education, Duran and others say, children will fall years behind in other subjects.

While Sanchez concedes that there may be isolated cases where bilingual learning "goes on too long," leading parents to become upset, in most cases children benefit from having some instruction in Spanish. "You look at most kids in bilingual programs, and they are able to easily shift between the two languages," he says.

Supporters also point out that many Latino parents are frustrated with poor, underfunded schools and may be taking their legitimate anger out on bilingual education. Indeed, nationwide, Latinos underperform students in other groups, including African-Americans. "When people are angry, they tend to blame the easiest thing," Sanchez says, "and in this case that's often bilingual education."

Lisa Navarette, a spokeswoman for La Raza, agrees. "I look at the Prop. 227 vote as a referendum on the California school system," she says. "So it's no wonder so many Latinos voted for it."

Finally, supporters of bilingual education point out that before Spanish-language instruction was available for Hispanic students, the dropout rate

Spanish-Language TV Taps $350 Billion Market . . .

Every morning, millions of Latinos across the country start their day with "Despierta America" ("Wake Up, America"). Like "Good Morning America" or "Today," "Despierta America" offers viewers news, weather, sports, celebrity interviews and features on everything from cooking to doing your taxes.

But there are differences. First, of course, the show is in Spanish. Indeed, it is one of the most popular offerings on Univision, the nation's largest, most-watched Spanish-language network. But the program's Latin flavor extends beyond the language. For instance, the set is decorated more like a Mexican hacienda — with earth-colored walls and bright Latin American murals — than the staid, book-lined sets of traditional morning shows. In addition, the program's hosts are much more lively, exuberant and spontaneous than, say, "Today's" Matt Lauer or "Good Morning America's" Lisa McRee. Often, they will break into loud fits of laughter or an unrehearsed dance routine.

"Despierta America," with its American format and Latino flavor, has been a tremendous success. On some days in Los Angeles, only "Today" gets higher ratings. The popularity of shows like "Despierta America" has led to predictions that Spanish-language

The Univision soap opera "Esmeralda" gets higher ratings than "Seinfeld" and "ER" in Miami, Fla.

AP/Univision

television has a bright future in the United States.

While the three biggest English-language networks in the United States (ABC, CBS and NBC) have been losing viewers since the 1970s, Univision has experienced strong growth. Since 1992, the network's audience has increased at an annual rate of 14 percent. Today, Univision is the fifth-largest network in the United States, behind the Big Three and Fox but ahead of Viacom's UPN and Time Warner's WB.

Los Angeles-based Univision is the 800-pound gorilla of Spanish-language broadcasting in the United States, with over 80 percent of the U.S. Spanish television market. During prime time, Univision often has more than 2 million viewers. Univision's only real competitor to date is Miami-based Telemundo, which has about 18 percent of the American Spanish-language television market.

In many ways, the soap operas, news and talk shows seen on Univision and Telemundo are similar to those on English-language networks — but they are not carbon copies of American television. For instance, the soaps (or *telenovelas*) tend to have moral messages intertwined with the usual steamy plots. In addition,

---

was astronomically high. "People forget that the Latino dropout rate used to be 80 percent before bilingual ed.," Navarette says. "Today it's 30 percent — not good, but a lot better."

Will encouraging Latinos to retain their language and culture hamper their ability to integrate into American society?

During a soccer match in Los Angeles last February between the U.S and Mexican national teams, something happened that many would have thought unthinkable in the United States. As the U.S. national anthem began to play, most of the more than 91,000 fans in the L.A. Coliseum started to boo or blow

horns, drowning out the song entirely. After the game, a barrage of bottles, cans and Spanish epithets rained down on the U.S. team. [11]

Speaking of the largely Mexican-American crowd after the game, U.S. player Alexi Lalas said: "I'm all for roots and understanding where you come from and having respect for your homeland, but tomorrow morning all those people are going to get up and work in the United States and live in the United States and have all the benefits of living in the United States." [12]

Lalas was asking, in essence: These immigrants and their children may live here, but do they think of themselves as Americans? Some observers worry that at least for some Latinos,

the answer is "no." The reason, they say, is that the idea of the melting pot — a place where all peoples slowly adopt a common culture — is being replaced by a new ideal, the mosaic, where everyone keeps their native culture and adopts some American values.

Most Latino-watchers agree that Hispanics behave much like other newcomers to the United States. "They want to learn English, to succeed, to become American," Chavez says. The problem, as she sees it, is that there are forces in U.S. society, especially in our educational institutions, that are encouraging Latinos to cling to their native culture, almost to the exclusion of their new one.

... But Its Future Remains Uncertain

much of the programming, including the *telenovelas*, comes from Latin America, especially Mexico.

Recently, Univision has begun replacing its imported shows with home-grown fare, including "Despierta America," which replaced a Mexican spinoff of "Sesame Street." And Telemundo has announced that it will soon begin airing newly produced Spanish-language versions of hit American TV shows like "Jeopardy" and "Mad About You." [1]

The consensus on Wall Street and elsewhere is that Spanish-language television is an industry with tremendous untapped potential. According to Jessica Reif, a stock analyst for Merrill Lynch Global Securities, networks like Univision are "tapping into the fastest-growing segment of the population that is incredibly attractive to advertisers and who are becoming bigger and better consumers." [2]

The statistics seem to back up Reif's assessment. After all, there are already some 30 million Latinos in the United States with more than $350 billion in buying power. Moreover, high birth rates and continued immigration will greatly expand the number of Spanish-speakers in the country. Indeed, the number of U.S. Hispanics will likely double in the next 20-25 years. Moreover, Latinos tend to be fiercely loyal to brands they like, making them model consumers.

And the business community has noticed. Recently Sony, cable giant Telecommunications Inc. (TCI) and a number of other investors ponied up more than $500 million to purchase Telemundo. The new owners plan to invest heavily in buying and developing new shows for the network, which is generally thought to have had a lackluster programming schedule as compared with Univision. [3]

Meanwhile, CBS recently began an all-Spanish-language news station on cable. In addition, Univision and The Home Shopping Network are starting a home-shopping channel for Spanish-speakers. And, TV Azteca, a Mexican company, plans to create another Spanish-language network to compete with Univision and Telemundo.

But there may be clouds on the horizon. Some analysts, among them Pepperdine University research fellow Gregory Rodriguez, say that within two generations Latinos will have largely assimilated into American culture, making them just as comfortable in English as in Spanish, if not more so. "People who watch Spanish-language TV are new immigrants," says Linda Chavez, president of the Center for Equal Opportunity. "If you know English, you'll watch mainstream media because it's better."

For Univision and Telemundo, the challenge is to keep English-speaking viewers who could switch to English-language media. Given the cost of mounting a whole roster of first-rate programs, that will not be easy. Already, some of Univision's key audience — young men and women — is slipping away from the network. According to a recent study from Nielsen Media Research, Univision recently lost 6 percent of its young female viewers and a whopping 26 percent of its young males. [4]

---

[1] Andrew Pollock, "The Fight for Hispanic Viewers; Univision's Success Story Attracts New Competition," *Broadcasting and Cable*, Jan. 19, 1998.

[2] Quoted in David Tobenkin, "Univision vs. Telemundo," *Broadcasting and Cable*, Oct. 6, 1997.

[3] Marla Matzer, "Telemundo Agrees to be Acquired by Sony, Liberty," *Los Angeles Times*, Nov. 25, 1997.

[4] Robert La Franco, "All in la Familia," *Forbes*, March 23, 1998.

"There is an aggressive ethnic promotion going on in the Mexican-American and other communities," she says.

For example, Chavez and others say, in California, Texas and the other Southwestern states, many Mexican-American students are taught primarily about the history of Mexico, not the United States. "You are more likely to hear about a famous Mexican leader than about Washington or Lincoln," she says.

This is not the way immigrant children were once taught. "Our public schools were the melting pot, where students learned to be Americans, where they learned to think of U.S. culture as their culture," she says.

These methods, Chavez says, need to be brought back into the classroom.

Stone of U.S. English agrees. "We have to focus on what unites us as Americans, rather than on ethnic identity and [Latinos'] status as oppressed minorities."

Opponents of this new multicultural model cite several reasons why much of the educational establishment has adopted it as the best way to educate immigrant children. "The education blob has gotten it into their heads that what is essential for immigrant children is that they feel good about themselves," says Boston University's Glenn. "Of course, there's no evidence that any of this actually works. And it goes

against what most immigrant parents want: teach my child English, to be an American and to read and write."

But Chavez thinks the problem is greater than just some misguided educational theory. "Many of the cultural elites in this country are anti-American," Chavez says. "They don't appreciate American values and culture and don't think they should be transmitted to newcomers." In other words, many who run educational and other institutions do not believe that most American traditions are worth imparting to immigrants.

But many argue that Chavez and others wrongly assume that Latino immigrants will be just like their European predecessors when it comes to assimilation. "You can't compare the Hispanic experience in this country with that of Europeans," argues the Post's Suro, "because Latinos have been here all along."

Felix Gutierrez, executive director of the Freedom Forum's Pacific Coast Center in San Francisco, agrees that the European immigrant model doesn't hold up for Latinos when it comes to assimilation. "We live in conquered territories, not a land we crossed an ocean to get to," he says, referring to the fact that much of the American Southwest and West were once part of Mexico. As a result, Gutierrez and others say, Latino immigrants in places like Texas, California and New Mexico are, in a sense, returning to places that were once their own. Moreover, other Hispanics were there when Americans arrived and never left. "In the case of my family, we didn't come to the U.S., the U.S. came to us," Gutierrez says.

Hence, Gutierrez and others argue, it is more understandable that Latinos would cling to their native culture and traditions. "We are a proud people with a rich history, a history that has always existed here," says Raul Yzaguirre, president of La Raza.

Another reason Latinos might cling to their roots a little more than others before them is that in today's interconnected world, it's easier to keep in touch and to visit the "old country" than it was for Europeans 100 or 150 years ago. "Ultimately, we will not lose our culture or Anglicize our names because we have closer contact with Cuba, Mexico, Puerto Rico or wherever we came from," Yzaguirre says. [13]

Advocates of deep cultural retention also argue that Hispanic children have a greater need to keep connected to their native traditions than other young people because of the discrimination and rejection they face. "It gives a child an identity, something they need because [Latinos] are

not fully accepted here," Sanchez says.

But retaining your native language and a sense of where you came from, does not preclude you from being an American, Sanchez and others argue. "We think of ourselves as Americans first and then Mexicans or whatever second," Yzaguirre says. He and others say that so long as Latinos are welcomed in the United States, cultural retention will not stand in the way of love of their new country. "People are afraid of these things leading to separatism," says Elizabeth Salett, president of the National Multicultural Institute. "But as long as people are included in our system, there'll be no separatism."

So what happened at the Los Angeles soccer match? "I don't condone it, but maybe when you are harassed by immigration authorities, even if you're a citizen or a legal immigrant, you get frustrated and angry," Sanchez says.

And, he points out, it was not the first time Americans showed disrespect for one of their nation's symbols. "Look at the kids who burned the American flag or spit on American soldiers during the Vietnam War," he says. ■

BACKGROUND

Spanish Heritage

People were speaking Spanish in the territory that would become the United States long before the English language was ever heard on these shores. In the 16th century, the Spanish built settlements throughout the Southwest, a legacy that lives on in the names of many American cities in the region, from San Francisco

to Santa Fe.

For centuries, the cultures of English- and Spanish-speaking America existed largely apart, separated by huge tracts of wilderness. But westward expansion from the English-speaking United States, beginning in the late 18th century, brought the two cultures increasingly into contact and conflict. In 1848, the United States defeated Mexico in a brief, bloody war. Mexico was forced to give up the territory that would become California, Texas and the rest of the American Southwest.

For Mexicans living in the conquered land, life was not easy. Although the United States offered them citizenship (an offer many refused), anti-Latino discrimination was widespread and often harsh. Still, the expansion of the railroads westward and the need for workers brought more Mexicans into what had been their country during the second half of the 19th century. By 1900, 500,000 Mexicans were living in the United States. [14]

Immigration from Mexico continued at a steady pace until World War II, when a severe labor shortage led the United States to establish a guest worker program for Mexicans. From 1942 until the program finally expired in 1964 more than 4.8 million Mexicans came to the United States, many temporarily. [15]

Mexicans were not the only Latinos coming to the United States after World War II. During the 1950s and '60s, a wave of Puerto Rican migration to the Northeast, particularly New York City, occurred. Unlike Mexicans and others in Latin America, Puerto Ricans were already citizens, since the island had been acquired by the United States following the Spanish-American War of 1898.

In the early 1960s, other groups of Latinos migrated to the United States. Cuban refugees fleeing the communist regime of Fidel Castro settled

Continued on p. 822

Chronology

1800s **English- and
Spanish-speaking America
collide, leading to war and
conquest.**

1848
The United States acquires
California and the Southwest
from Mexico after the Mexican-
American War.

1898
Puerto Rico becomes an American
territory following the
Spanish-American War.

━━━━ • ━━━━

1900-1930s
**Hard economic times and new
laws slow immigration from
Mexico.**

1900
There are 500,000 people of
Mexican descent living in the
United States.

1928
The U.S. Border Patrol is formed
to stem illegal immigration from
Mexico.

1929
The Great Depression begins.

━━━━ • ━━━━

1940s-1960s
**Economic expansion after
World War II leads to an
influx of Latino immigrants,
first from Mexico and then
from elsewhere in Latin
America.**

1941
The United States enters World
War II.

1942
In an effort to alleviate a wartime labor shortage, the U.S.
initiates a guest-worker program,
which allows Mexicans to work
in the country.

1959
Fidel Castro seizes power in
Cuba, prompting many on the
island to flee to the United States.

1965
President Lyndon B. Johnson
signs the Immigration and
Nationality Act, opening the
door to more legal immigrants
from Latin America.

1968
Congress passes the Bilingual
Education Act, providing funds
for bilingual programs around
the country.

━━━━ • ━━━━

1970s-1980s
**The size of the Latino commu-
nity in the United States grows
dramatically through immigration and high birth rates.**

1975
The Voting Rights Act is extended to include Latinos.

1980
The U.S. Census Bureau reports
that there are 12 million Hispanics in the United States.

1984
President Ronald Reagan wins
more than 40 percent of the
Latino vote.

1986
Congress passes the Immigration
Control and Reform Act, which
allows millions of illegal immi-

grants to apply for legal resi-
dency.

━━━━ • ━━━━

1990s-2000s
**Latinos begin to gain political
and economic power.**

1990
The U.S. Census Bureau reports
that there are 22.6 million
Hispanics living in the United
States.

1994
California voters approve Proposition 187, which denies basic
services to illegal immigrants.

1996
Republican presidential candidate Bob Dole wins about 20
percent of the Latino vote.

February 1998
Antonio Villaraigosa becomes
the second Latino Speaker of the
California state Assembly, replacing Cruz Bustamonte.

June 1998
California approves Proposition
227, dramatically scaling back
bilingual education.

2006
Latinos are projected to become
the nation's largest minority.

2050
Hispanics are expected to
comprise a quarter of the U.S.
population.

Continued from p. 820

primarily in the Miami area. By the end of the decade, people from the Dominican Republic began arriving in New York City, a migration that continues to this day.

Latino Influx

Since the mid-1960s, the overall rate of Latino immigration to the United States has grown rapidly. The impetus for these increases has come in part from a 1965 change in immigration law. Under the Immigration and Nationality Act, the longstanding preference for newcomers from Europe was replaced with a racially neutral policy. As a result, the door was opened to Latinos not only from Mexico but also from the Caribbean and South and Central America.

Today, according to the latest estimates from the Census Bureau, 29.7 million Latinos reside in the United States, or 11 percent of the nation's population. If the present rate of growth continues, Hispanics will become the nation's largest minority by 2006, surpassing African-Americans, who make up 12.8 percent of the population. [16]

Already, there are more Hispanics than blacks in U.S. public schools. Indeed, the 10.5 million Latinos under age 18 outnumber African-Americans in the same age group by 35,000. [17]

Demographic projections even further into the future show that Latinos will comprise nearly a quarter of the nation's population by 2050. The growth will be fed in part by continuing immigration from Latin America and the Caribbean. In addition, high birth rates among Latinos already in the United States will also add greatly to these numbers. Indeed, between 1990-1996, Latina women had 106.3 births per thousand compared with 65.6 births per thousand for whites and 79.6 for blacks. [18]

"This is clearly a huge demographic undertaking for our nation," says Suro of The Washington Post. He and others predict that absorbing this new population will cause a certain amount of collective tension. "I don't see how it can be avoided," he says.

Of course, the dramatic demographic projections could be altered by a change in the nation's immigration policy, which fuels much of the growth of the Latino population, both legal and illegal. In fact, almost half of the nation's 12 million Latinos are foreign-born. Reducing the level of legal immigration and cracking down on illegal entry into the United States would significantly slow Hispanic population growth.

Polls show that a majority of Americans currently favor reducing levels of legal and illegal immigration. "There is a feeling among some people that this is going too far," Chavez says. Nowhere is this attitude better reflected than in Rogers. Ark., a town that has seen its Hispanic population grow dramatically in the last decade. "I'm not a racist," says Rogers resident Jason Riggins. "I just don't want to be outnumbered in my own country." [19]

According to Suro, such attitudes will spread once the current economic expansion comes to an end. "The issue will really come to a head when the unemployment rate hits 6 percent nationwide," he says.

But many observers, Suro included, say it would be a mistake to stop or reduce immigration. Indeed, they argue, immigrants helped the United States reach its eighth consecutive year of economic growth. "This large expansion of immigration has come at the same time we had this unprecedented economic expansion," he says.

CURRENT SITUATION

Climbing the Ladder

The nation's growing Latino population has embraced the American dream. Like immigrant groups before them, Hispanics are striving to "make it" in America with a drive and ambition that seems especially prevalent in newcomers.

Even the poorest new arrivals from Mexico and elsewhere in Latin America aspire to the middle class. Since 1980, for example, the number of Latino middle-class households in Los Angeles has tripled, to 450,000. [20]

Indeed, more than half of all native-born Hispanic families in the United States own their own home, according to Gregory Rodriguez, a research fellow at Pepperdine University. Among foreign-born Latinos, the percentage of home ownership was lower — about one-third — but still impressive. Not surprisingly, the most common surname of new home buyers in Los Angeles County is Garcia. [21]

More broadly, recent data from the Center for the Study of Latino Health at the University of California, Los Angeles, show that Hispanics have a higher rate of male participation in the labor force than whites and blacks. At the same time, Latinos were the least likely group to use public assistance. [22]

Another important and positive indicator is the phenomenal growth in the number of Latino businesses. Nationwide, the number of Hispanic enterprises has nearly doubled in the last five years. In states like California and Texas, where Hispanics make up a sizable minority, Latino business

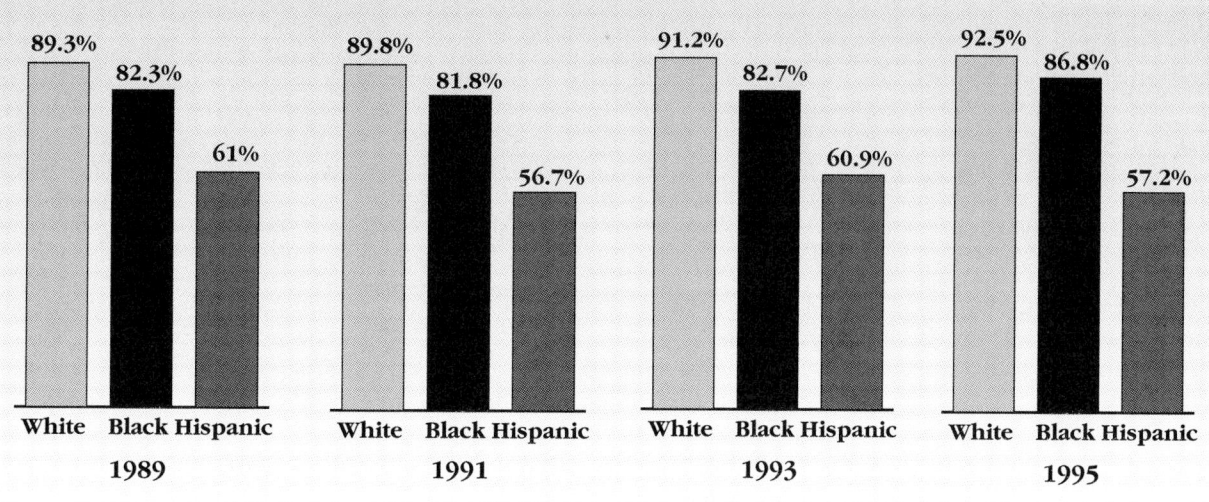

Latinos Lagged in High School Completion

Less than 60 percent of U.S. Latinos completed high school in 1995. Latinos' completion rate decreased about 6 percent from 1989-1995, while the rates for whites and African-Americans increased slightly.

High School Completion Rates, 1989-1995

1989: White 89.3%, Black 82.3%, Hispanic 61%
1991: White 89.8%, Black 81.8%, Hispanic 56.7%
1993: White 91.2%, Black 82.7%, Hispanic 60.9%
1995: White 92.5%, Black 86.8%, Hispanic 57.2%

Sources: "Latino Education: Status and Prospects," National Council of La Raza, July 1998; National Center for Education Statistics, June 1996; "Educational Attainment in the United States," Census Bureau, March 1995.

start-ups are responsible for a substantial share of economic growth.

Latino buying power also is growing and becoming an increasingly important part of the national economy. Currently, Hispanics spend over $350 billion annually, up 65 percent since 1990. This number is increasing by about $2 billion per month. [23] As a result, more and more businesses are paying attention to Latinos and marketing products and services directly to the community through Spanish-language TV and other media. *(See story, p. 818.)*

Dropout Dilemma

In spite of their impressive economic gains, Latinos are lagging behind in the classroom. According to the Department of Education, the overall dropout rate for Latino children is 30 percent, four times higher than the 7.7 percent dropout rate for whites and nearly three times the 12.6 percent dropout rate of blacks. [24]

Moreover, in 1996 only 61 percent of Latino youth completed high school, compared with 92.6 percent for whites and 86 percent for blacks. [25] Even among Hispanic students who do receive a high school diploma, only 34.9 percent go on to college; by comparison, 43.7 percent of white high school graduates enroll in an institution of higher learning. [26]

Perhaps even more troubling than the current statistics themselves are recent trends.

"It's disheartening to see that while whites and blacks have made improvements in dropout rates, for Hispanics it has been getting worse," Suro says.

Many Latino observers believe these statistics bolster an unfair stereotype of

Hispanics as largely unconcerned about learning. "There is belief in the broader culture that Latinos don't care about education, but that's not true," says La Raza's Navarette.

Much of the real problem, Navarette and others argue, lies with outside forces. In addition to the language barrier that many face, Latino children are often forced to make do with woefully underfunded and substandard schools. "There's a history of neglect when it comes to educating the Latino community," she says, adding that the "most schools are failing us."

Sanchez agrees. "Unfortunately, most education policies in this country have been geared to whites and, to a lesser extent, blacks," he says. "Meanwhile, Latinos have been left out in the cold."

Another problem is that many Latino young people may have to drop out of school, even if they are

Bilingual Education: An Old Debate

The controversy surrounding bilingual education is as old as the Republic. Throughout American history, pockets of students in different parts of the country have received instruction in tongues other than English. Beginning in the 18th century, children were taught in a variety of foreign languages, including German, French, Greek, Dutch and Swedish. Often these bilingual schools were located in isolated rural areas where members of a particular ethnic group had clustered together.

Then, as now, many English-speaking Americans opposed bilingualism as a threat to national cohesion. Benjamin Franklin, for one, complained bitterly that German immigrants threatened the culture of English-speaking America. More than a century later, President Theodore Roosevelt, pushed for schools around the country to adopt an English-only policy to ensure, as he put it, that we did not become a nation of "hyphenated Americans."

Moreover, the patriotic fervor that accompanied World War I led to a drive to remove foreign languages, especially German, from any classrooms that were still teaching them. Still, bilingual education was never as widespread as it is today. Most immigrant children arriving in the United States were taught in English.

Rapid urbanization in the 19th and 20th centuries guaranteed that a majority of newcomers would live with or near native-born people as well as immigrants from other lands. And English was often seen as the glue that would hold these new Americans together.

performing well. "Often, there is an economic necessity to work to support the family, and so people are forced out of school," Sanchez says.

Whatever the reason, Latinos know they must dramatically improve their level of educational attainment if they hope to ultimately succeed in the United States. "In an economy that values education as much as ours does, it's troubling where we are now," Suro says.

And the problem won't just be for Latinos, Gutierrez says. "When you think about the number of Latino students today and the greater number there will be tomorrow and the percentage of workers who will be Latino, you realize that this isn't just a Latino problem, it's an American problem." ■

OUTLOOK

In or Out?

For the most part, observers are at least cautiously optimistic about Hispanics becoming an accepted and integral part of the American social fabric, as immigrant groups did before them.

Some say that Latinos will succeed, in part, due to their willingness to work harder than almost anyone else, be it in the fields, the restaurant, or the board room. "The Latino work ethic has helped and will continue to help us survive," Navarette says. Indeed, Latinos are showing an uncanny ability to move from low-skill, low-wage jobs to business ownership.

But while few observers question Latinos' willingness to work and their drive to succeed, some Americans do wonder whether this fast-growing community will fully integrate into the national society or remain apart.

Part of the answer to this question may already be found in the substantial rate of intermarriage between Latinos and other Americans. Currently, roughly one-third of all Hispanics marry non-Latinos, usually whites. By contrast, only 6 percent of African-Americans wed someone outside their race. [27]

Significantly, the intermarriage rate is higher now than it was a decade ago, indicating that in the future, a majority of Hispanics will marry non-Latinos. "The rate of intermarriage is a very important, very healthy thing because it shows that this idea that we'll be a separate community is not supported by the facts," says La Raza's Yzaguirre. "When you see us marrying [non-Hispanics], supporting the military and all other American institutions or cheering at Dallas Cowboys games, you realize that there is no danger of balkanization."

At the same time, Yzaguirre and others say, while Latinos are and will be as American as anyone else, they will be different than Irish, Italians or other Europeans who have come before. "We will keep more of our language and traditions than they did," he says.

Gutierrez of the Pacific Coast Center agrees, adding that the pressures for cultural retention will come not just from the Latinos themselves but from the broader society. "[Hispanics] will be coming of age a multicultural, multilinguistic America that is very different from the Anglo-dominated country of the past," he says. "We will be the model for the new American, one who is comfortable in more than one culture."

But others, while not disagreeing that Latinos will hang on to more of their native culture longer than previous groups of immigrants, argue that it will be impossible to keep as much as they want and at the same time be American. Rep. Becerra sees Latinos only retaining what is truly important to them, like their language or cuisine. "The tent is only so big, and so we'll have to leave

Continued on p. 826

At Issue:

Is bilingual education losing support in the Hispanic community?

JORGE AMSELLE
Vice President for Education, Center for Equal Opportunity, Washington, D.C.

WRITTEN FOR THE CQ RESEARCHER, SEPTEMBER 1998.

Support for bilingual education has long been a litmus test for the Hispanic left. For three decades politicians and ethnic activists have taken the concerns of Hispanic parents for granted and assumed their unwavering support for these bilingual programs. Any doubts raised about the effectiveness of bilingual education was repeatedly met with dismissive statements like: "They used to hit us for speaking Spanish in school," and "We just need to spend more money on these programs."

Initially, the Latino community embraced bilingual education, which promised to save Hispanic children from scholastic failure. This early support was largely based on the lack of alternatives. Even today, too many Hispanic parents face a choice between bilingual education or no help at all for children who lack English proficiency.

However, as bilingual education programs are increasingly exposed as the fraud they truly are, Latino support for them is decreasing rapidly. In 1998 nearly 40 percent of California Latinos voted to eliminate their bilingual programs, despite a multimillion-dollar advertising effort against the proposal. My organization conducted its own polling of Hispanic parents in 1996, and over 80 percent wanted their children taught in English, not Spanish.

There are several reasons why it has taken nearly three decades for Hispanic opposition to bilingual education to finally reach the national spotlight. The primary cause is that all of the national Hispanic advocacy organizations wholeheartedly support bilingual education as the only acceptable method of educating Hispanic children. Parents who approach these groups for help in fighting bilingual programs are rebuffed.

Also, for many Hispanic parents the only source of information about their children's education is their school's bilingual education teacher — often more interested in preserving his or her job than in providing accurate, non-biased information to parents. But these trends are changing as parents are looking elsewhere for help. Parents in New York City turned to the Catholic Church in their fight against bilingual programs while parents in Los Angeles were aided by a local Episcopal priest and community activist.

Latino communities are breaking away from the molds their traditional advocates have forced them into and forging their own grass-roots coalitions with religious and sometimes even conservative organizations. This is leaving groups like the Mexican American Legal Defense and Educational Fund and the National Council of La Raza increasingly on the fringes of the Hispanic community.

LAURA FERREIRO
Communications Associate, Mexican American Legal Defense and Educational Fund (MALDEF)

WRITTEN FOR THE CQ RESEARCHER, SEPTEMBER 1998.

the country focused its gaze on California last June, as voters decided on an initiative that proposed to replace bilingual education programs in the state with English immersion. The initiative received a tremendous amount of media coverage, but little was learned about what bilingual education offers to students.

Before the election, inaccurate polls showed that a majority of Latinos supported the initiative. But when Election Day came around, two out of three Latinos voted against it. Despite this fact, the passage of the initiative led to the misperception that the Latino community no longer supported bilingual education. Conservative groups jumped on this bandwagon and seized the opportunity to announce that Latino political leaders and advocates who supported bilingual education were self-serving and out of touch.

But those who work directly with parents and children in the Latino community have a different story to tell. They can tell you about Latino parents who appear before school boards, pleading with them not to end their bilingual education programs. They can tell you about high school students who reaped the benefits of bilingual education programs, speak and write both English and Spanish fluently and are worried that recent immigrant students will not receive the same benefits if bilingual education were to end. They can tell you about the flood of calls Latino civil rights organizations received after the election from concerned parents wanting to know how to keep their children in bilingual education programs. And educational experts, Latino and otherwise, will tell you that bilingual education, when implemented properly, is the most effective way of teaching limited-English-proficient students.

Although the media spotlight has recently been on California, there are many flourishing, successful bilingual education programs throughout the country. In Dade County, Fla., home of the nation's fourth-largest school district, parents showed overwhelming support for the school board's plan to increase bilingual teaching for all students earlier this year. Miami residents view the ability to speak more than one language as a great business asset. And the same holds true in many states throughout the country.

Latino parents realize the importance of learning English, but also of learning other core academic subjects during the English-learning process that is done best through bilingual education teaching methods. They want their children to receive a solid education and excel in both English and Spanish.

Continued from p. 824
some stuff behind," he says.

Still others argue that the European model, in which Latinos would lose much of their original culture and take on more American traits, is the only way Hispanics will truly be accepted in the United States. "If we don't fully commit ourselves to assimilation, we'll be in trouble," Chavez says. She is "cautiously optimistic" that Latinos will follow the assimilationist path because they will recognize that it is in their best interest. "I think we are seeing the error of our ways, when we followed those who preached ethnic separatism," she says, referring to academic and Latino advocacy communities, which encourage cultural retention.

But *The Washington Post's* Suro believes that Latinos will forge a new ethnic path in the United States. "Latinos will not follow the straight line of assimilation that characterized the European experience," he says. "Neither will they hold onto the sense of permanent aggrievement that characterizes the black experience."

Still, Suro worries that a portion of America's Latinos may find themselves in the situation now faced by the black underclass. "We have 30 percent of our community living below the poverty line," he says. "If this kind of poverty persists, we will pay a terrible social price." ■

Notes

¹ Martin Kasindorf, "Latinos Tap into Expanding Political Power," *USA Today*, March 19, 1998. For background, see Nadine Cohodas, "Electing Minorities," *The CQ Researcher*, Aug. 12, 1994, pp. 697-720.

² "Enter the Garcias' Own Party," *The Economist*, Aug. 15, 1998.

³ *Ibid*.

⁴ Kasindorf, *op. cit.*

FOR MORE INFORMATION

If you would like to have this CQ Researcher updated, or need more information about this topic, please call CQ Custom Research. Special rates for CQ subscribers. (202) 887-8600 or (800) 432-2250, ext. 600, or E-mail Custom.Research@cq.com

Center for Equal Opportunity, 815 15th St. N.W., Suite 928, Washington, D.C. 20005; (202) 639-0827; www.ceousa.org. This research organization focuses on issues of race, ethnicity and assimilation and opposes bilingual education and affirmative action.

League of United Latin American Citizens, 1133 20th St. N.W. Suite 750, Washington, D.C. 20036; (202) 408-0064; www.lulac.org. The league works for political, economic and educational rights for Hispanics.

Mexican American Legal Defense Fund, 1518 K St. N.W. Suite 410, Washington, D.C. 20005; (202) 628-4074; www.maldef.org. The fund provides assistance to Mexican-Americans and other Latinos in areas ranging from voting rights to immigration and supports affirmative action and bilingual education.

National Council of La Raza, 1111 19th St. N.W. Suite 1000, Washington, D.C. 20036; (202) 785-1670; www.nclr.org. La Raza studies issues of interest to Latinos and offers technical assistance to Hispanic community organizations.

---

⁵ Dan Balz, "Gingrich Pitches GOP to Latinos, Hoping to Heal Divisions," *The Washington Post*, July 2, 1998.

⁶ Guy Gugliotta, "Democrats Hope to Translate Latino Distrust of GOP into Votes," *The Washington Post*, Jan. 5, 1998.

⁷ Rosalie Pedalino Porter, "The Case Against Bilingual Education," *The Atlantic Monthly*, May 1998. For background, see Craig Donegan, "Debate Over Bilingualism," *The CQ Researcher*, Jan. 19, 1996, pp. 49-72.

⁸ Betsy Streisand, "Is it Hasta la Vista for Bilingual Ed?" *U.S. News & World Report*, Nov. 24, 1997.

⁹ *Ibid*.

¹⁰ Quoted on National Public Radio's "Morning Edition," Jan. 5, 1998.

¹¹ Bill Plaschke, "Star Spangled Banter," *Los Angeles Times*, Feb. 17, 1998.

¹² Quoted in Grahame L. Jones, "This is Much Worse than Trash Talking," *Los Angeles Times*, Feb. 16, 1998.

¹³ For background, see David Masci, "Castro's Next Move," *The CQ Researcher*, Dec. 12, 1997, pp. 1093-1116.

¹⁴ For background, see Rodman D. Griffin, "Hispanic Americans," *The CQ Researcher*, Oct. 30, 1992, pp. 929-952.

¹⁵ *Ibid*.

¹⁶ Steven A. Holmes, "Hispanic Population Moves Closer to Surpassing That of Blacks," *The Washington Post*, Aug. 7, 1998.

¹⁷ Barbara Vobejda, "Hispanic Youths Outnumber Blacks," *The Washington Post*, July 15, 1998. For background, see Kenneth Jost, "Rethinking School Integration," *The CQ Researcher*, Oct. 18, 1996, pp. 918-941, and Susan Phillips, "Racial Tensions in Schools," *The CQ Researcher*, Jan. 7, 1994, pp. 1-24.

¹⁸ Figures cited in National Council of La Raza, *Latino Education: Status and Prospects* (1998), pp. 6-7.

¹⁹ Quoted in "Immigrant Influx," *The NewsHour with Jim Lehrer*, Feb. 16, 1998.

²⁰ Figures cited in "The Keenest Recruits to the Dream," *The Economist*, April 25, 1998.

²¹ Figures cited in "Enter the Garcias' Own Party," *op. cit.*

²² "The Keenest Recruits to the Dream," *op. cit.*

²³ *Ibid*.

²⁴ National Council of La Raza, *op. cit.*, p. 48.

²⁵ *Ibid*, p. 49.

²⁶ *Ibid*, p. 73.

²⁷ "The Keenest recruits to the Dream," *op. cit.*

Bibliography

Selected Sources Used

Books

Jones-Correa, Michael, "Between Two Nations: The Political Predicament of Latinos in New York City, Cornell University Press (1998).

Jones-Correa, an associate professor of government at Harvard University, examines the political life of Latinos in the New York City area. He finds that political participation among these communities is low, in part because of fear that they will lose touch with their homelands if they become too involved in their new country's affairs.

Shorris, Earl, *Latinos: A Biography of the People*, W.W. Norton (1992).

Shorris takes an exhaustive look at the Latino community in the United States, from Mexican-Americans in Texas to Puerto Ricans in New York. Hispanics defy categorization, he argues, because they are not really one community, but many.

Suro, Roberto, *Strangers Among Us: How Latino Immigration is Transforming America*, Knopf (1998).

Suro, a staff writer at *The Washington Post*, argues that it is misguided to compare Latino immigration with the waves of largely European newcomers who arrived in the United States in the past. Hispanics, Suro says, come from nearby and no longer have the economic opportunities in agriculture and, especially, manufacturing enjoyed by their immigrant predecessors.

Articles

Bronner, Ethan, "Bilingual Education is Facing Push Toward Abandonment," *The New York Times*, May 30, 1998.

Bronner chronicles the shift in attitude concerning bilingual education. No longer hailed as a "humane and sound" way to teach immigrant children, bilingual learning is increasingly being rejected by recent arrivals as well as native-born citizens.

Chavez, Linda, "Our Hispanic Predicament: Lack of U.S. Assimilation Despite Economic Progress," *Commentary*, June 1998.

Chavez, president of the Center for Equal Opportunity, argues that the United States will become a balkanized country if it continues to encourage Hispanics to retain their culture and language.

Donegan, Craig, "Debate Over Bilingualism," *The CQ Researcher*, Jan. 19, 1996.

A slightly dated but thorough examination of the various arguments for and against bilingualism in the United States.

"Enter the Garcias' Own Party," *The Economist*, Aug. 15, 1998.

The article argues that Latinos and the GOP have more in common (like family values) than past election results would suggest. It argues that Republicans who work for the Latino vote should be able to reap substantial benefits come Election Day.

Gugliotta, Guy, "Democrats Hope to Translate Latino Distrust of GOP into Votes," *The Washington Post*, Jan. 5, 1998.

Gugliotta details Democratic plans to solidify their already strong support within the Latino community.

"The Keenest Recruits to the Dream," *The Economist*, April 25, 1998.

This piece examines the economic, political and cultural status of Latinos and concludes that this rapidly growing minority has tremendous potential to succeed on all levels in the United States.

Kasindorf, Martin, "Latinos Tap into Expanding Political Power," *USA Today*, March 19, 1998.

The article gives a good overview of growing Latino electoral power and argues that the community's political strength is finally beginning to match its demographic size.

Porter, Rosalie Pedalino, "The Case Against Bilingual Education," *The Atlantic Monthly*, May 1998.

Porter, director of the Institute for Research in English Acquisition and Development, makes a strong case against the continuation of bilingual learning, arguing that teaching children in Spanish retards their educational development and segregates them from the rest of the school.

Streisand, Betsy, "Is it Hasta la Vista for Bilingual Ed?" *U.S. News & World Report*, Nov. 24, 1997.

Streisand gives a good overview of the debate over bilingual education that preceded the vote on Proposition 227 in California this year.

Reports and Studies

Fisher, Maria, Sonia M. Perez, Bryant Gonzalez and Jonathan Njus, *Latino Education: Status and Prospects*, The National Council of La Raza, July 1998.

This report, issued by the nation's premier Latino-advocacy group, examines all aspects of Hispanic educational achievement. The results are not encouraging. Latino children have lower test scores and higher dropout rates than their black and white peers.

The Next Step

Additional information from UMI's Newspaper & Periodical Abstracts™ database

Assimilation

Barone, Michael, "How Hispanics Are Americanizing," *The Wall Street Journal*, Feb. 6, 1998, p. A22.

Hispanics are America's fastest-growing voting bloc and are about to become its largest minority group. They have influenced America's popular culture and its culinary tastes; salsa has replaced ketchup as the nation's favorite condiment. They have created hundreds of thousands of businesses and thousands of new churches. Their large numbers in America's four largest states — California, Texas, New York and Florida — mean that they may hold the balance in the next several presidential elections. Yet they are little known to most Americans and widely misunderstood. Who are America's Hispanics, and how are they likely to affect American life and American politics?

Dominguez, Jorge I., "The Promised Land Among America's Diverse Latino Immigrants, the Second Generation Often Faces as Big a Challenge as the First," *The Boston Globe*, April 19, 1998, p. N1.

In *Strangers Among Us*, journalist Roberto Suro discusses the differences between long-settled Mexican-Americans in Houston and newly arrived immigrants. In Suro's intelligent, richly textured, well-written book, the great variation within that loose category of people known as Latinos or Hispanics in the United States comes alive. They can claim the names they would call themselves: Puerto Ricans, Mexican-Americans, Chicanos, Cuban-Americans, Mayas. They often become Latinos or Hispanics only in the eyes of the beholder.

McConnell, Scott, "Americans No More?" *National Review*, Dec. 31, 1997, pp. 30-35.

The current generation of Mexican immigrants continues to embrace its Mexican heritage. The author examines the question of whether cultural assimilation can operate today as it did a century ago — or is it going into reverse?

Rumbaut, Ruben G., "Assimilation and its Discontents: Between Rhetoric and Reality," *International Migration Review: IMR*, winter 1997, pp. 923-960.

The author examines various paradoxes of immigrant adaptation that emerge in the conceptual interstices between rhetoric and reality and advances fruitful reformulations of a seminal sociological concept.

Zhou, Min, "Segmented Assimilation: Issues, Controversies, and Recent Research on the New Second Generation," *International Migration Review: IMR*, winter 1997, pp. 975-1008.

The author examines the issues and controversies surrounding the development of the segmented assimilation theory and reviews the state of recent empirical research relevant to this theoretical approach.

Discrimination

Darity, William A. Jr., and Patrick L. Mason, "Evidence on Discrimination in Employment: Codes of Color, Codes of Gender," *Journal of Economic Perspectives*, spring 1998, pp. 63-90.

The authors examine evidence of racial and gender discrimination in employment as well as various theories that attempt to explain this discrimination.

Mauro, Tony, "Report: Minorities Not Reaching Top Legal Levels," *USA Today*, Aug. 5, 1998, p. A3.

Minorities still face "significant obstacles" in reaching the top levels of the legal profession and often drop out before they get there, the American Bar Association (ABA) reported Tuesday. Minorities represent about 7 percent of America's lawyers, up from 5 percent in 1980, according to an ABA report issued at the association's annual meeting here. But only about 3 percent of partners at law firms are minorities. That represents just a slight increase over the last dozen years. Three percent of judges at all levels are black, and Hispanics and Asian-Americans represent only about 2 percent of law school faculty, the report said. Those statistics contrast starkly with public perception, said José Gaitan, a Seattle lawyer who chairs an ABA commission on minority lawyers.

Niemann, Yolanda Flores, Kathryn I. Pollak, Stephanie Rogers and Elizabeth O'Connor, "Effects of Physical Context on Stereotyping of Mexican American Males," *Hispanic Journal of Behavioral Sciences*, August 1998, pp. 349-362.

The effects of physical context on stereotyping and willingness to affiliate with Mexican-American males is examined. In this two-part study, the effect of context alone was explored by showing a stilled video frame of a library room and a crime scene without people in them.

Noue, George R., and John C. Sullivan, "Deconstructing the Affirmative Action Categories," *American Behavioral Scientist*, April 1998, pp. 913-926.

Affirmative action preferences have benefited four racial and ethnic group categories: African-Americans, Hispanics, Asian-Americans and Native Americans. The problem of overinclusiveness is examined.

Economics

Zambrana, Ruth E., and Claudia Dorrington, "Eco-

nomic and Social Vulnerability of Latino Children and Families by Subgroup: Implications for Child Welfare," *Child Welfare*, January 1998, pp. 5-27.

The authors describe the social, economic and family structure variables that place specific Latino subgroups at risk, synthesize available data on Latino children in the child welfare system and discuss a direction for developing ethnic-specific child welfare policy for vulnerable Latino groups.

Gomel, Jessica N., Barbara J. Tinsley, Ross D. Parkes and Kathleen M. Clark, "The Effects of Economic Hardship on Family Relationships Among African American, Latino, and Euro-American Families," *Journal of Family Issues*, July 1998, pp. 436-467.

The relations between economic hardship, coping and family relationships in African-American, Latino and Euro-American families are investigated. Survey data regarding the effects of economic hardship on individuals' lifestyles were collected from parents in the three ethnic groups.

Education

Headden, Susan, "The Hispanic Dropout Mystery," *U.S. News & World Report*, Oct. 20, 1997, pp. 64-65.

The dropout rate for Hispanic students nationwide is 30 percent, nearly three times the rate for whites and twice the rate for blacks. The authors evaluate this trend and what can be done about it.

Rumberger, Russell W., and Katherine A. Larson, "Toward Explaining Differences in Educational Achievement Among Mexican-American Language-Minority Students," *Sociology of Education*, January 1998, pp. 68-92.

Results of a study of different educational achievement among Mexican-American language-minority students support a sociocultural perspective of educational achievement.

Immigration

Graham, Hugh Davis, "Unintended Consequences: The Convergence of Affirmative Action and Immigration Policy," *American Behavioral Scientist*, April 1998, pp. 898-912.

Reforms in immigration and affirmative actions brought along the unintended consequences of hard affirmative-action programs involving minority preferences and mass immigration. The consequences of reform are examined.

Johnson, James H., Walter C. Farrell Jr. and Chandra Guinn, "Immigration Reform and the Browning of America: Tensions, Conflicts and Community Instability in Metropolitan Los Angeles," *International Migration Review: IMR*, winter 1997.

The authors highlight the root causes of the growing

opposition to both immigrants and U.S. immigration policy and outline the conditions under which diversity can be brought to the forefront as one of society's strengths.

Palmaffy, Tyce, "El Millonario Next Door," *Policy Review*, July 1998, pp. 30-35.

A penchant for risk-taking and a willingness to sacrifice and work hard in pursuit of a better life are typically strong among immigrants, and those traits help to explain why a vibrant entrepreneurial culture is developing within the Hispanic community. Hispanic-Americans represent the United States' fastest-growing pool of business owners.

Perlmann, Joel, and Roger Waldinger, "Are the Children of Today's Immigrants Making It?" *Public Interest*, summer 1998, pp. 73-96.

The authors examine how successful second-generation Americans are. Findings suggest that, while the children of post-1965 immigrants begin with disadvantages no greater than those encountered by immigrant children before, their class composition is more heavily weighted toward the middle-class today, and they have moved far up the totem pole.

Radelat, Ana, "Banned at the Border," *Hispanic*, January 1998, pp. 40-46.

Hispanics are the focus for the newest twists in immigration policies. One of the newest policies expands the list of crimes that immigrants can be deported for. This rule has unfairly affected many immigrants to the United States.

Sanchez, George J., "Face the Nation: Race, Immigration and the Rise of Nativism in Late Twentieth Century America," *International Migration Review: IMR*, winter 1997.

The author examines the rise of nativism directed at Asian and Latino immigrants to the United States in contemporary American society.

Language and Bilingualism

"Encouraging Debut for Prop. 227," *Los Angeles Times*, Aug. 5, 1998, p. B6.

The first test of Proposition 227 was nothing like Armageddon, despite the predictions of opponents of the English-only measure. Teachers, often tackling the change without a new curriculum or appropriate textbooks, deserve credit for the quietly encouraging start. Now it's up to the state and the local school districts to carry through with new curriculum guides (promised in Los Angeles by Aug. 20), lesson plans and books (promised next month).

"In Plain English," *National Review*, July 6, 1998, pp. 14-16.

For fear of losing Hispanic support, Republicans have

been silent regarding the passage of Proposition 227 in California, which effectively ends bilingual education. However, since 227 won by a wide majority, which included a substantial number of Hispanics, such timidity is misplaced.

Booth, William, "In California Classrooms, A Troubled Transition; Students, Teachers Struggle to Adjust On First Day of English-Only Education," *The Washington Post*, Aug. 4, 1998, p. A3.

The sweeping social experiment known as bilingual education officially ended today in the state where it began. Confusion reigned in many California school districts and defiance in others as teachers struggled to switch from Korean, Armenian and Spanish to all-English, all the time, often without the help of textbooks or lesson plans. In Oakland and San Francisco, where schools do not open for another few weeks, officials were still holding out against implementation of Proposition 227, the voter initiative that passed with overwhelming support on June 2.

Boxall, Bettina, "With Gestures, But Not Chaos, Prop. 227 Begins; Education: L.A. Teachers Improvise on First Day of English-Only Instruction, and Students Seem to Catch On," *Los Angeles Times*, Aug. 4, 1998, p. A1.

At Van Nuys Elementary, one could hear only a sprinkling of Spanish among the students who returned Monday, as the language all but disappeared from many classrooms. Youngsters who once spent their days reading and writing Spanish were instead reciting the alphabet and greeting one another in English. The majority of Van Nuys classes offered virtually no help in Spanish except for bilingual aides who gave occasional tips to students.

Anderson, Nick, and Doug Smith, "State Board Gets Crash Course on Implementing Prop. 227; Education: Group Gives Advice on Creating English Immersion Programs to Replace Bilingual Classes, as Courts Turn Back Last-Minute Challenges," *Los Angeles Times*, Aug. 1, 1998, p. A16.

Although the initiative approved by voters in June was a loud statement against teaching children in two languages, the program it required instead — "structured English immersion" — remains suspect to many California educators. So on Friday a group of principals, teachers and researchers came here to give the state Board of Education some real-world tips on how to build an "immersion" program. Most drew on the premise that good teaching of basic skills works just as well for students with limited English abilities as for those who grew up with the language.

Ritter, John, "English Only, Ready or Not," *USA Today*, July 31, 1998, p. A3.

Proposition 227, the landmark citizens' initiative to dismantle bilingual education, becomes law in California on Sunday. By fall, all students are supposed to be taught only in English. Bill Habermehl, Orange County's associate superintendent for educational services, says the timing of Proposition 227 — it was passed June 2 and takes effect while most schools are on summer vacation — couldn't have been worse. "Principals will come back next month, look at the state guidelines and say 'OK, what do I do now? How do I order materials? How quickly can I get them?' " Habermehl says.

Sahagun, Louis, "'Gag Order' on Prop. 227 Appears to Be Softening," *Los Angeles Times*, Aug. 8, 1998, p. B1.

A dozen teachers opposed to the state's new anti-bilingual education law gathered at a downtown elementary school Friday to protest a so-called gag order barring them from advising parents to seek exemptions from English-immersion classes created under Proposition 227 guidelines. As it stands, the district offers parents four options for their children: mainstream classes, two English immersion programs known as Model A and Model B or a waiver seeking to have them enrolled in traditional bilingual education.

Latinos

"Diverse Hispanic Population to Become Largest U.S. Minority," *Population Today*, November 1997, pp. 1-2.

Hispanic-Americans will become the United States' largest ethnic minority by the early 21st century. The growing numbers of Hispanic-Americans and demographic information about them are discussed.

"Sanctuary Movement Lives On," *Migration World Magazine*, 1998, p. 14.

Many faith-based groups work in the United States with refugees from Central America and also battle for immigrants' rights. Hispanics are the United States' fastest-growing voting bloc and are about to become the largest minority group.

Blank, Susan, and Ramon S. Torrecilha, "Understanding the Living Arrangements of Latino Immigrants: A Life Course Approach," *International Migration Review: IMR*, spring 1998, pp. 3-19.

The authors examine three competing hypotheses for understanding extended-family living among Mexican, Puerto Rican and Cuban immigrants. They found no significant relationship between living with extended kin and cultural indicators or economic factors.

Chavez, Linda, "Our Hispanic Predicament," *Commentary*, **June 1998, pp. 47-50.**

The difficulty the United States is having assimilating its huge Hispanic population is discussed. If this failure continues, it will represent the United States' own failure of national self-respect.

De la Garza, Rodolfo O., and Louis Desipio, "Interests not Passions: Mexican-American Attitudes Toward Mexico, Immigration from Mexico, and Other Issues Shaping U.S.-Mexico Relations," *International Migration Review: IMR*, **summer 1998, pp. 401-422.**

The authors discuss a study conducted to determine Mexican-American attitudes toward Mexico and toward the public policy issues that shape U.S.-Mexico relations.

Kettle, Martin, "Hispanics Outstripping Blacks as Largest American Minority," *The Guardian*, **July 16, 1998, p. 18.**

A report, "America's Children: Key Indicators," published by a group of U.S. government agencies this week says there are now 35,000 more Hispanic-American children than African-American children. Fifteen percent of the United States' under-18 population are already Hispanics, a slightly greater proportion than blacks. By 2020, the Hispanic share is expected to rise to 22 percent, with African-Americans at 16 percent.

Myers, Dowell, and Cynthia J. Cranford, "Temporal Differentiation in the Occupational Mobility of Immigrant and Native-Born Latina Workers," *Sociological Review*, **February 1998, pp. 68-93.**

The authors estimate changes over time in the occupational participation of Latino workers. Results show sharp temporal differentiation among the Latina workers, even after controlling for human capital.

Robinson, Linda, "Hispanics Don't Exist," *U.S. News & World Report*, **May 11, 1998, pp. 26-32.**

Many Americans don't realize that the term Hispanic covers a diverse group of people that constitutes the fastest-growing demographic in America. Seventeen subcultures of Hispanic or Latino origin are profiled, including Miami's Cubans, Chicago's Puerto Ricans and New York City's Dominicans.

Multiculturalism

Carlisle, Chip, "Diversity Training, Recruiting Pay Off for Companies," *Houston Chronicle*, **Aug. 31, 1998, p. A19.**

According to the U.S. Department of Labor, almost one-third of the 25 million individuals entering the work force during the next several years will be minorities. By the year 2000, members of minority groups — especially Hispanics and African-Americans — will be less of a "minority" than ever before. Acknowledging diversity is about facing reality, arguably the first responsibility of any business manager. Unfortunately, many managers seem unwilling to embrace these demographic trends, which clearly foreshadow a whole new mix of employee recruits, customers and shareholders.

Coen, Jeff, "Firm Cultivating Cultural Diversity: While Some Companies Struggle to Integrate Their Workforces, Lucent Technologies Has Embraced the Diverse Nature of Its International Employees; The Naperville Communications Company Has Groups That Help Promote Cultural Awareness," *Chicago Tribune*, **June 18, 1998, p. 2D1.**

Many employees have joined one or more of the company's seven employee business partner groups, known as EBPs, and some 50 cultural clubs. Members of the employee affinity organizations claim they promote cultural awareness, improve the profile of the company's work force, help attract top recruits from other countries and offer those employees assistance when they arrive in the United States. In return, Lucent offers coaching to group members on business issues, provides meeting space and allows EBP leaders time off to attend conferences. Lucent's seven diversity organizations represent Asians, blacks, Hispanics, the disabled, Native Americans, women and gay employees.

Etzioni, Amitai, "Some Diversity," *Society*, **July 1998, pp. 59-61.**

The author argues that people's race and racial attributes do not determine their visions, values and votes as is often assumed, and examines the state of multiculturalism in America.

Politics

Beinart, Peter, "New Bedfellows," *The New Republic*, **Aug. 11, 1997, pp. 22-26.**

For decades, Jews and Latinos joined blacks under the banner of left-liberalism, but a new Jewish-Latino alliance has shattered that coalition, and it may redefine American politics. Jews and Latinos are doing together what neither group is doing with blacks: constructing a vibrant politics based on their common interests.

Cohen, Richard E., "Hispanic Democrats Strike Back," *National Journal*, **Nov. 1, 1997, p. 2202.**

Hispanics and their political leaders believe they're under attack by Republicans. This trend threatens the inroads that the GOP made among Hispanics during the 1980s.

Back Issues

Great Research on Current Issues Starts Right Here.
Recent topics covered by The CQ Researcher are listed below.
Now available on the Web
For information, call (800) 432-2250 ext. 279 or (202) 887-6279.

If you would like to have any of these CQ Researchers updated, or need more information about these topics, please call CQ Custom Research. Special rates for CQ subscribers.
(202) 887-8600 or (800) 432-2250, ext. 600, or E-mail Custom.Research@cq.com

JUNE 1997
FDA Reform
China After Deng
Line-Item Veto
Breast Cancer

JULY 1997
Transportation Policy
Executive Pay
School Choice Debate
Aggressive Driving

AUGUST 1997
Age Discrimination
Banning Land Mines
Children's Television
Evolution vs. Creationism

SEPTEMBER 1997
Caring for the Dying
Mental Health Policy
Mexico's Future
Youth Fitness

OCTOBER 1997
Urban Sprawl in the West
Diversity in the Workplace
Teacher Education
Contingent Work Force

NOVEMBER 1997
Renewable Energy
Artificial Intelligence
Religious Persecution
Roe v. Wade at 25

DECEMBER 1997
Whistleblowers
Castro's Next Move
Gun Control Standoff
Regulating Nonprofits

JANUARY 1998
Foster Care Reform
IRS Reform
The Black Middle Class
U.S.-British Relations

FEBRUARY 1998
Patients' Rights
Deflation Fears
Caring for the Elderly
The New Corporate Philanthropy

MARCH 1998
Israel at 50
The Federal Judiciary
Drinking on Campus
The Economics of Recycling

APRIL 1998
Biology and Behavior
Liberal Arts Education
Income Inequality
High-Tech Labor Shortage

MAY 1998
Census 2000
Child-Care Options
Alzheimer's Disease
U.S.-Russian Relations

JUNE 1998
Student Journalism
Antitrust Policy
Environmental Justice
Sleep Deprivation

JULY 1998
Encouraging Teen Abstinence
Population and the Environment
Democracy in Asia
Baby Boomers at Midlife

AUGUST 1998
Oil Production in the 21st Century
Flexible Work Arrangements
Coastal Development
Student Activism

SEPTEMBER 1998
Organic Farming
Cancer Treatments

Back issues are available for $5.00 (subscribers) or $10.00 (non-subscribers). Quantity discounts apply to orders over 10. To order, call Congressional Quarterly Customer Service at (202) 887-8621.

Binders are available for $18.00. To order call 1-800-638-1710. Please refer to stock number 648.

Future Topics

▶ *The Future of Baseball*

▶ *Social Security*

▶ *School Violence*

The Future of Baseball

Can it regain its old popularity?

A s the World Series approaches, baseball shines in its archaic glory. But even the home run exploits of Mark McGwire and Sammy Sosa cannot hide the fact that other sports now rival the popularity of America's "national pastime." Baseball's problems — most of them rooted in the economics of modern sports — have diminished the quality of the game and the loyalty of its fans. As baseball executives ponder further expansion, as players' salaries continue to soar and as minorities turn to other sports, big league baseball seems increasingly distant from its sandlot roots. Before it is too late, critics say, baseball owners must stop diluting the quality of play and reduce costs so that the game doesn't become too expensive for its fans.

C
Q **September 25, 1998 • Volume 8, No. 36 • Pages 833-856**

Formerly Editorial Research Reports

CQ Researcher

September 25, 1998
Volume 8, No.36

EDITOR
Sandra Stencel

MANAGING EDITOR
Thomas J. Colin

STAFF WRITERS
Adriel Bettelheim
Mary H. Cooper
Kenneth Jost
Kathy Koch
David Masci

PRODUCTION EDITOR
Melissa Hall

EDITORIAL ASSISTANT
Laura S. Cavender

PUBLISHED BY
Congressional Quarterly Inc.

CHAIRMAN
Andrew Barnes

VICE CHAIRMAN
Andrew P. Corty

PRESIDENT AND PUBLISHER
Robert W. Merry

EXECUTIVE EDITOR
David Rapp

The CQ Researcher (ISSN 1056-2036). Formerly Editorial Research Reports. Published weekly, except Jan. 2, May 29, July 3, Oct. 30, by Congressional Quarterly Inc., 1414 22nd St., N.W., Washington, D.C. 20037. Annual subscription rate for libraries, businesses and government is $340. Additional rates furnished upon request. Periodicals postage paid at Washington, D.C., and additional mailing offices. POSTMASTER: Send address changes to The CQ Researcher, 1414 22nd St., N.W., Washington, D.C. 20037.

COVER: THE CAMARADERIE AND GOOD SPORTSMANSHIP DISPLAYED BY MARK MCGWIRE OF THE ST. LOUIS CARDINALS AND SAMMY SOSA OF THE CHICAGO CUBS DURING THEIR DRAMATIC HOME RUN 'WAR' HAS BEEN A HIGHLIGHT OF THE 1998 SEASON. (REUTERS/ SUE OGROCKI)

The Future of Baseball

By Philip Seib

The Issues

Baseball has its own niche in our memories: The thwack and sting of ball in glove; the faded photograph of an ancient hero; the World Series exploits of a Mickey Mantle or Bill Maseroski.

The first embrace of baseball often comes early. When did columnist George Will first come upon the game? "I do not know," he writes, "because I have no memory of life before baseball." [1]

As well as fueling personal reminiscence, baseball has a place in the national consciousness. There is something quintessentially American about this sport, more than any other. The game belongs as much to the small-town playground as to the big-city stadium. Baseball has matured with the country, and endured many of the same growing pains. Racial discrimination and labor battles in baseball have been microcosmic versions of societywide struggles around the same issues.

Grand achievements in baseball can capture the nation's attention, overriding the dismal news that normally dominates headlines. This year's good-natured home run race between Sammy Sosa and Mark McGwire, with its smiles and hugs, provided much-needed relief from the stream of reports about the scandal engulfing the White House. When McGwire hit home run No. 62 on Sept. 8, and was matched by Sosa on the 14th, the benign ghosts of Babe Ruth and Roger Maris were much in evidence, fueling a gentle nostalgia that seemed to soften the nation's mood.[*]

But despite the allure of home runs

and the residual power of the game's mythic history, baseball's standing as "America's pastime" has changed. Football and basketball have become increasingly dominant as spectator sports, and many children today would rather kick a soccer ball than swing a baseball bat. [2] Within baseball itself, the nature of the game and its relationship with its fans have been reshaped by the unforgiving economics of professional sports.

Baseball, however, is by no means moribund. With its array of superstar players, gorgeous new ballparks and lucrative television contracts, the game's future appears promising. But underneath its glossy surface are troubling questions.

Money, not surprisingly, is at the root of baseball's biggest problems. Players' salaries continue to rise, putting pressure on teams' and fans' wallets. In 1969, when St. Louis Cardinal outfielder Curt Flood refused to accept a trade and began a legal battle that led to free agency, the players' average salary was $24,909. In 1998, the average salary is $1.4 million. Of roughly 800 major league players in 1998, 317 have salaries of $1 million or more. As the 1998 season began, team payrolls varied widely, from the Baltimore Orioles' $69 million to the Montreal Expos' $9 million. The average salary on the Orioles is more than $2.5 million; on the Expos it is $352,000. [3]

As a general proposition, the dis-

parity in spending affects play on the field. Big money is necessary to pay for the players who presumably can take a team to a championship. Tom Schieffer, president of the Texas Rangers, sees a have and have-not hierarchy among the 30 major league teams. "I think you have a Big 10, Little 20, scenario," he says. "What worries almost everybody in baseball is how do you make the teams competitive."

In the view of diehard fan George Will, "In the long run, large and chronic differences in teams' resources will destroy in many cities that which draws fans through the turnstiles — the hope that springs each spring." [4] "The key word is 'hope,'" says National League President Leonard Coleman. "We have a number of teams whose fans don't have hope."

The absence of hope drives fans away, and so do inflated ticket prices. Although teams derive income from a number of sources, individual fans remain the foundation of baseball's economic structure. As Schieffer puts it, "Player contracts come out of revenues and revenues come out of the fans."

The process, of course, is a bit more complicated than that. In addition to the money that fans spend at the ballpark on tickets and concessions, major league teams also receive broadcast and licensing revenues. As Smith College economics Professor Andrew Zimbalist points out, 76 percent of team revenues in 1950 came from ticket sales, and another 14 percent from concessions, parking and other stadium activity. By 1990, broadcast revenues accounted for more than 50 percent of teams' income.

Ticket sales, however, remain crucial. "Although the share of ticket sales in total revenue has been falling," Zimbalist writes, "gate revenue has grown handsomely in absolute terms. This increase owes to rising attendance, higher ticket prices and new income from luxury boxes." [5]

---

[*]As of Sept. 22, there were seven games left in the regular season and McGwire had 65 homers and Sosa had 63.

Regardless of teams' enhanced revenue flow, free agency drives up salaries and exacerbates the cost-containment problems that affect ticket prices. In simple terms, free agency means that a team no longer has open-ended rights to a player's future. Until the 1970s, a player remained a team's property until he was traded or sold (or retired). Now, when a contract expires, veteran players (those with six or more years in the major leagues) become "free agents" and can sign with any team they choose. For some stars, this leads to bidding wars that have driven salaries to as much as $10 million a year, and they are certain to go higher.

No single player can make or break a team, but when a team makes wholesale purchases of free agents, an also-ran can become a contender.

The Florida Marlins, for example, had not even existed until 1993 and had little success on the field and at the ticket office during their first three years. Then, before the 1997 season began, the Marlins spent $83 million on multiyear contracts for three stars and another $6 million for three more free agents. With a late-season surge, the Marlins won the National League pennant and defeated the Cleveland Indians in the World Series.

Despite their success, the Marlins attracted only 600,000 more fans than they had the previous year, averaging less than 30,000 spectators a game and losing more money than any other team. The morning after their Series victory, owner Wayne Huizenga announced, "We are pleased and excited that we won. But we lost $34 million." He then proceeded to unload many of his high-priced players, cutting his payroll almost in half.

Huizenga's move may have made good business sense, but it certainly tested the patience of Marlins' fans. In effect, the Marlins rented the players they needed to win, and then — when the financial returns were judged unsatisfactory — decided to return to mediocrity. It is not surprising that

fans may withhold their loyalty from such a transient version of a "team." [6]

Another economics-based change in baseball has been expansion. With the addition in 1998 of the Tampa Bay Devil Rays and the Arizona Diamondbacks, the major leagues now comprise 30 teams. That makes the talent pool shallower. Schieffer contends that "you still have fantastic plays made in every ballpark," but he admits that "the pitching seems to be diluted." Hall of Fame member Stan Musial is more pointed in his comments about the effects of expansion on the current quality of play compared with his time in the big leagues (1941-1963): "So many of today's players — 300-400 players — wouldn't be playing in our day."

There are, however, enough new-generation stars to overshadow the less skilled players on some of today's big league rosters — Yankee shortstop Derek Jeter, Rangers catcher Ivan "Pudge" Rodriguez, Braves third-baseman Chipper Jones, Seattle centerfielder Ken Griffey Jr. and many others. But fan interest depends on more than just high-quality play in the major leagues. Baseball's great strength is that it is more than just another spectator sport. For many fans, passion for the game is rooted in participation, whether it is stickball in the street, Little League or office softball. "If you play baseball as a child," Coleman says, "you'll love the game when you grow up." Conversely, if people have no interest in playing, they soon may have no interest in watching.

Conventional wisdom has it that playing baseball is being abandoned by young people in favor of basketball, soccer and other sports. George Will warns: "The demographics of baseball fandom are becoming increasingly ominous. Put bluntly, baseball's fan base is too old and too white. Anyone who regularly consorts with young people — say, those between 12 and 25 — knows that

interest in sports has never been higher and that interest in baseball runs a distant third to interest in the National Basketball Association and the National Football League." [7]

There is, however, evidence to the contrary. A 1996 study commissioned by the Sporting Goods Manufacturers Association found that from 1985-1995, the number of children playing in organized baseball leagues had doubled. This was due partly to the expansion of leagues to include additional age and skills groups. T-ball, for example, reaches children as young as 5. And the number of Little League players rose from just over a million in 1985 to 2.6 million in 1995. Overall, according to the study, 17 million people participated in some version of organized baseball in 1994.

Another concern about baseball's future is that minorities are turning to other sports. The sporting goods manufacturers report, however, cites strong African-American and Hispanic involvement in baseball. Of the 17 million participants in 1994, it says 72 percent were Anglo, 14 percent African-American and 11 percent Hispanic. [8]

Despite such statistics, the strength of public allegiance to baseball remains questionable. The angry public reaction to the 1994-95 major league players' strike seemed to shake, if not shatter, complacency about the game's future (see p. 848). Most team owners apparently recognized, belatedly, that they cannot take fan support for granted. Players also understand the impact of the strike. Earlier this year, Mark McGwire said, "What we did in '94 scarred the game."

As the World Series — and the new millennium — draw near, these are some of the questions being asked about baseball's future:

Is baseball's financial structure making the game too costly for teams and fans?

Forget about the timelessness of a

lazy Saturday afternoon at the ballpark, the sheer physical poetry of a deftly executed double play. Baseball is a business.

That may be crass, even sacrilegious, but for those who run baseball, financial statistics are as much a part of the game as earned run averages or slugging percentages. This is nothing new; owners have always tried to squeeze as much profit as possible out of their teams. In an editorial earlier this year, *The New York Times* observed that "baseball has always been a business run, with rare exceptions, by proprietors with an aversion to red ink far stronger than their professed loyalty to the traditions, rhythms and solidifying virtues of the game." [9]

Baseball history is filled with stories of tightwad owners who delighted in tormenting their players. When Lefty O'Doul batted .398 in 1929, the Philadelphia Phillies rewarded him with a $500 raise. When he "slumped" to .368 the next season, his salary was reduced by $1,000. [10] Today, teams pay millions to sore-armed pitchers who are lucky to win 10 games and utility infielders who might hit .270.

Aside from the many anecdotes about today's huge rewards for mediocre performance, there are systemic traits in baseball's salary structure that threaten the economic viability of the sport. At any given time, some teams always will be much better than others, but when one team has a payroll roughly seven times larger than another's (as is the

case this year with the Baltimore Orioles and the Montreal Expos), the integrity of competition can be undermined.

Certainly, a high-priced team can prove to be a dud. A few key injuries,

Home-run slugging by Sammy Sosa (top) and Mark McGwire (bottom) made the 1998 season memorable.

some players suddenly past their prime, plus a dose of bad luck can wreck a season. At midseason this year, for example, the Orioles found

themselves swept by the impoverished Expos in an interleague series.

Baseball officials recognize they must do something about baseball's economics, but they have yet to determine precisely what that "something" should be. In an effort to curb spending by the wealthiest teams, a "luxury tax" is imposed on the five teams with the biggest payrolls, but deep-pocketed owners find it more annoyance than deterrent. This form of revenue-sharing delivers about $8 million annually to the lowest-revenue teams, not enough to pull them much closer to their prosperous brethren.

Paul Beeston, president and chief operating officer of Major League Baseball (MLB), points out that teams' gross incomes range from $35 million to $150 million. "All teams need to have a chance to win," he says. "We're examining our revenue sharing, trying to get more structure." Beeston asks, however, "Why should teams apologize for being more successful?"

Coleman says that the quest for greater parity among teams "is largely a TV issue." Schieffer observes that "virtually every major league team can draw at least 2 million people," but fans buying tickets cannot sustain a team. He points to New York's built-in income advantage by virtue of being the nation's No.1 media market. (Baseball, with its 162-game season, depends heavily on local rather than just national television deals.) The New York Yankees, for instance, can reap about $50 million in local broadcasting income, while the Denver-based Colorado Rockies pull in about $5 million.

"A professional sport can achieve something akin to marketing nirvana in one of two ways," writes Pulitzer Prize-winning *Washington Post* columnist Thomas Boswell. "You can have parity. Or you can have powerhouses. Parity sounds so fair, even though, in reality, it often can be dull. Few, however, like to admit (perhaps because it sounds politically incorrect) that a sport can thrive if it's built around a core of truly glamorous teams: the haves. The situation works far better, however, if the have-nots are nonetheless respectable." [11]

Fears about maintaining respectability drive the debate about the imbalance of wealth. Musial says of the disparity among teams: "The rich clubs are getting richer, the poor clubs are getting poorer. They've got to change the system." Most team owners, however, are cautious when talking about changing the system — their system. Peter Angelos, owner of the Baltimore Orioles, is an exception. He has suggested a revenue-sharing program that would help fund new stadium construction, which he thinks would be the best way to help struggling teams. He has also said that it may become necessary to create a revenue-sharing fund that can be used to buy out the weakest franchises, shrinking the major leagues from their current 30 teams.

This, he says, might be the only way to bring payrolls under control because, "there are more teams going after players, which is driving up the cost of players and, in turn, driving up the cost of tickets and concessions. It benefits no one in the long run." [12] The players, however, certainly would resist any move to reduce the number of teams and thus the number of roster spots available.

Baseball's economic issues are not just an internal matter for the owners. Many baseball fans believe that the game belongs to them and to the country as a whole, and that the owners are merely trustees. The palpable anger of fans during and after the 1994-95 strike surprised owners, and at least some of them seem to have learned a lesson from the debacle. Baseball "has almost a religious following," Schieffer says. "It's tampering with right and wrong when you tamper with baseball."

That has not stopped some owners from just the kind of economics-driven tampering that so exasperates fans. When the Florida Marlins held their fire sale of high-salaried stars, fans were far from passive. Early in the 1998 season, with only two starting position players remaining from the championship team, attendance dropped by about 20 percent, and several season ticket holders filed lawsuits accusing the team's owners of violating Florida's Deceptive and Unfair Trade Practices Act.

Most major league franchises are far more stable than the Marlins. Their fans generally accept the realities of major league finance as long as a decent team takes the field. Baseball is still the most affordable sport, another function of its long schedule. Buying a ticket for less than $5 remains possible, but that inevitably will be jeopardized if player salaries keep climbing.

"Baseball is the last sport that the blue-collar family can afford to attend," Schieffer says, but the teams "have to be very, very careful not to price the fan out of the marketplace." Angelos agrees, saying, "Baseball is absolutely a bargain," but, he adds, he fears that it is unlikely to remain that way. He says, "If the other sports can charge three to four times what we charge for tickets and they can prosper doing that, that's their business. But that's not what I want to see happen in baseball." [13]

The Florida Marlins celebrate after defeating the Cleveland Indians in the 1997 World Series.

Baseball Hall of Fame Library

Have changes such as free agency and expansion damaged the character and quality of the game?

One of the most significant turning points in the history of baseball was the creation of free agency. It emerged in less-than-dramatic fashion, the eventual outcome of out-

Integrating Baseball — Chapter 2

Although baseball was for much of its history one of America's most segregated institutions, it also was the sport of Jackie Robinson. Robinson integrated the big leagues in 1947, opening the doors to African-Americans and some of the game's greatest — and most beloved — stars, Willie Mays, Hank Aaron and Roy Campanella among them.

But in many urban areas, the sport of Jackie Robinson is in eclipse among those for whom the trail was blazed. "There just are not that many black kids playing baseball," says Don Newcombe, Robinson's teammate, "and not that many blacks coming to games regularly."

John Young, a major league player and scout who grew up in South-Central Los Angeles, realized in the late 1980s that his old neighborhood was no longer producing many good athletes. With little community support or funding for sports programs, many young people were doing nothing or joining street gangs.

In 1989, with backing from Major League Baseball, Young started RBI — Reviving Baseball in Inner Cities. He was gradually able to pull teenagers away from gangs and stir up some enthusiasm for baseball. In RBI's first season, 180 youngsters participated. Working with a local college, Young added an academic component to the program, providing tutoring and help in preparing for standardized tests. Since then, a drug, alcohol and sex-education program has become part of RBI.

Major League Baseball has run RBI since 1991, committing more than $3 million to the effort and enlisting the Boys & Girls Clubs of America to provide the academic and life-skills components of the program. RBI serves boys ages 13-18 and also has a girls' softball program. This year, RBI has teams in 96 cities, with more than 100,000 teenagers participating. After a series of regional tournaments, RBI has its own World Series.

Thomas Brasuell, RBI's national program manager, says that the effort is producing encouraging results. "Without this program," he says, "many of these kids wouldn't have a chance to play the game. And without it, the erosion of baseball in the inner city would be even greater."

Fifty-nine percent of the participants are African-American, with Latinos constituting 25 percent and Anglos 13 percent. For African-Americans, there are some links to the black baseball of the past. In several cities, the RBI teams use the names of old Negro Leagues teams. But for the most part, says Brasuell, the educational emphasis of RBI is less on baseball history than it is on present-day life skills.

Several major league teams provide free tickets to RBI participants and on-field recognition to RBI players, and some host RBI tournaments in their stadiums. Sometimes the involvement is even more substantial. In Philadelphia, Brasuell says, the Phillies run the RBI program, and in Chicago the Cubs players pay for the local RBI uniforms.

Some RBI players have been drafted by major league organizations, but only a tiny number will reach those heights. Rather, RBI's greatest value is its ability to help rebuild a fan base that had so badly disintegrated. This means getting minorities — especially African-Americans — back into the ranks of baseball fans and into the ballparks.

The Reviving Baseball in Inner Cities (RBI) program pulls youngsters from gangs to baseball.

Major League Baseball

fielder Flood's failed lawsuit. In January 1970, reluctant to be traded, he challenged baseball's reserve clause, which basically made a player the permanent property of the team with which he had signed. If a player didn't like his contract, he could do nothing other than retire. The team could unilaterally renew the contract even if the player failed to sign it.

In April 1972, the Supreme Court, in *Curt Flood v. Commissioner of Baseball Bowie Kuhn*, upheld a lower court's dismissal of Flood's case. In doing so, the court endorsed baseball's exemption from federal antitrust laws.

Despite Flood's defeat, challenges to the reserve clause continued. The Major League Baseball Players Association negotiated the creation of an arbitration panel to handle grievances such as salary disputes. The panel changed baseball forever when it ruled in 1975 that pitchers Dave McNally and Andy Messersmith, who had played for a season without a

New Stadiums Recall Bygone Era . . .

To walk into the Baltimore Orioles new downtown stadium is to walk into a bygone era — and fans are flocking in for the experience.

In addition to the Orioles, the Cleveland Indians and Texas Rangers have seen attendance soar since moving into new homes. Rangers President Tom Schieffer says that the club's Ballpark in Arlington "is the most important thing in our franchise." Assessing its appeal, he cites "the family atmosphere, the nostalgia, the seats close to the field and people feeling safe."

Major League Baseball President Paul Beeston calls baseball's newest stadiums "fun to go to" because they offer "amenities plus charm." He says it is important that baseball teams not settle for "cookie-cutter, all-purpose stadiums." The proper way to go, he says, is "baseball only, real grass."

New stadiums can also affect the quality of play because, as Coleman says, they "change the revenue base so you

can afford to compete." There is clearly a connection between the improved performance of the Orioles, Indians and Rangers and their having moved into beautiful ballparks that have attracted significantly more fans (and thus significantly more dollars) than in the past.

Fans love the new Orioles Park at Camden Yards.

Jerry Wachter

New stadiums are on the way in Seattle, Houston, San Francisco, Milwaukee, Detroit and Cincinnati. The new generation of ballparks represents a collective investment of more than $3 billion.

Enjoying a new stadium and wanting to pay for it are, however, very different matters. In the majority of recent local elections called to approve tax measures for funding new stadiums, voters have said "No." For example, the proposed move of the Minnesota Twins to North Carolina was derailed by local voters last May. In New York City, when Mayor Rudolph W. Giuliani allied himself with New York Yankees owner George Steinbrenner, who wants to build a new Yankee Stadium in Manhattan at a cost of about $1 billion, public

contract, were no longer within the control of their respective teams. They were free agents.

The next season 24 players opted to become free agents. Outfielder Reggie Jackson reaped the biggest reward, signing a five-year, $3 million deal with the Yankees. Although a paltry sum by today's standards, it helped launch today's free agent bidding wars.

The argument against free agency has always been that it would allow the richest teams to corner the market of the best players and permanently damage the competitive balance among baseball's teams. That has not happened, at least not to the disastrous extent some had predicted. During the first 15 years of free agency, for instance, 12 different teams won the World Series. Compare that with 1927-1939, long before

free agency, when the Yankees showed what imbalance really meant, winning the World Series seven times.

As Zimbalist notes, "it can also be argued persuasively that free agency has undermined the pattern of team dynasties by making it more difficult to keep winning teams together and more possible for losing teams to rise rapidly. In sum, the era of free agency has coincided with an increase in competitive balance." [14]

On this season's Opening Day, 60 percent of major league players were not with their original teams. Only half the players were on the same teams they had played with in 1997, and only 13 percent were playing for the same teams they were with four years ago. [15]

Nevertheless, the quality of competition is somewhat segmented, with baseball's haves and have-nots oper-

ating on different planes. Occasionally a have-not will make a surprising breakthrough when certain players' performance and team chemistry produce an unexpectedly strong season. But for the most part, the teams that cannot reach an imprecise but still important threshold in terms of spending to acquire free agents are unlikely to win a championship. Even if free agency works against long-lasting dynasties, in any single season a team with deep enough pockets can acquire the free agents likely to produce a winner. The success of the 1997 Marlins is a good example of what can happen.

Ultimately, it's about money, Musial says. "You can't blame the players," he says. "It's part of the system. Like any industry, guys go where the money is." That is perfectly logical as a matter of business,

... And Bring Back the Fans, Too

reaction was strongly against the idea of using tax dollars to pay for most of the project.

Such opposition is grounded in voters' belief that their tax dollars would subsidize wealthy team owners. Opponents of tax-backed stadiums point out that there are other ways to finance ballparks. In San Francisco, after four defeats in referendums seeking public tax support for a new stadium for the Giants, team owners were able to proceed with minimal public funding. They sold stadium naming rights for $50 million, charter seat rights for $55 million and corporate sponsorships worth almost another $50 million. With those commitments in hand, the owners secured $170 million in private loans, which will be paid back from stadium revenues. The public contribution will be just a $15 million loan. The total cost of the stadium will be slightly more than $300 million. [1]

One of the main arguments used by proponents of new sports stadiums and arenas is the need for lots of high-priced luxury suites, which can provide a substantial income stream to the teams. This money can then be used to pay the salaries of the expensive free agents a winning team presumably must have. The problem that is beginning to arise is saturation of markets. In Seattle, for instance, when several new or renovated sports facilities are open for business in about two years, 194 luxury suites will be available — at prices up to $125,000 a year — in a market with only 146 companies with 500 or more employees.

Perhaps economic growth will generate more tenants, but in several markets the number of suites is greater than the number of large companies in the area. [2]

Another issue concerns the economic impact of sports facilities. In New York, for example, advocates of a Manhattan Yankee Stadium claim that it would produce $1 billion a year in economic benefits for the city, but a 1996 study conducted by KPMG Peat Marwick projected that the benefits would only be about one-tenth that much. [3]

The economic debate will certainly continue, but there is far more consensus about what fans want in their ballparks: modern comfort thoroughly laced with nostalgia; plenty of rest rooms, but a hand-operated scoreboard; lots of parking, but some old-fashioned bleachers in the outfield. With the stadiums as with much else about baseball, nostalgia is crucial. The present and future must be infused with the past.

---

[1] "Financing New Stadiums," *The New York Times*, May 7, 1998, p. A30.

[2] Tom Farrey, "Too Much of a Good Thing?" *Business Week*, May 211, 1998, p. 69.

[3] Charles V. Bagli, "'96 Stadium Study Found Fewer Benefits," *The New York Times*, April 23, 1998, p. B3.

---

but left out of the equation are the fans who cheer for their favorite players one year, only to find them gone when the next season begins.

"It undercuts fan loyalty when a team loses players and doesn't get into the playoffs," Beeston says. But, he adds, "there's fan loyalty when the team wins" with newly purchased talent, although "ties to the community suffer" when players are so transient. In any event, he says, "that's the way professional sports is."

Don Newcombe, the major leagues' first African-American pitching star and now director of community relations for the Los Angeles Dodgers, says of players who choose to move from team to team: "I worry about the impact on the fan, especially the young kid who wants somebody to emulate." He adds, "Agents have taken over the game."

Occasionally, loyalty to team and fans still prevails. In 1997, "Pudge" Rodriguez signed a five-year, $42 million contract with the Rangers despite the likelihood that he could have commanded many millions more if he had entered the free agent market. "The Rangers, they are my family," Rodriguez said. "I grew up in this organization. They gave me the opportunity to play in the major leagues. I will never forget them for that." [16]

Rangers fans were delighted with Rodriguez's loyalty, and somewhat surprised. Few players resist the allure of free agency and millions in extra dollars (even though most would, presumably, be hard-pressed to explain what they could do with $10 million that they couldn't do with $8 million).

In addition to free agency, expansion of the major leagues has raised

questions about the quality of play. Four new teams have been born during the 1990s: the Rockies and Marlins in 1993 and the Diamondbacks and Devil Rays in 1998. A big issue concerning expansion is whether baseball's talent pool is large enough to support major league-level play for 30 teams.

On the positive side, fans in more cities now have home teams to root for, and young players have the opportunity to rise more rapidly to the majors. "Players used to learn in the minor leagues," recalls Buck O'Neil, a player and manager in the Negro Leagues and the first African-American to coach on a major league team. "Now, players are learning to play Major League Baseball in the major leagues." But O'Neil does not see a serious problem, predicting that "the players will catch up."

Newcombe, however, says that expansion is "affecting the game very deeply, especially the pitching, once you get past most teams' first few starters." He contends that many of today's players could not have made his 1950s Dodgers. Newcombe notes, for example, that while he led National League pitchers with 164 strikeouts in 1951, it's a low number by today's standards. The reason, he says, is that the hitters were better then: "They put the ball in play."

Expansion is likely to continue, at least to 32 teams, with four four-team divisions in each league. Schieffer foresees more international play, with major league franchises eventually coming to cities such as San Juan, Puerto Rico, Mexico City and Monterrey, Mexico, and someday — depending on politics — Havana.

When further expansion occurs, it may be accompanied by radical realignment of the leagues. *(See "At Issue," p. 849.)* The desire to reduce travel costs and foster natural rivalries (for example, between St. Louis and Kansas City) would lead to divisions based on geography. ESPN broadcaster Jon Miller argues that realignment would wreck the concept of interleague play, which was launched, to widespread fan approval, in 1997. Geography-based realignment would mean that the interleague games would feature teams playing against their pre-realignment opponents. Miller says this approach "truly makes no sense" because it would "obliterate the two leagues, change the entire organization of the game and in

so doing destroy the exact thing that made those [interleague] games so special." [17]

Interleague play has underscored the importance of true rivalries and the insignificance of concocted ones. For instance, when the Philadelphia Phillies visited Yankee Stadium in June, attendance was poor. But when the Yankees went from the Bronx to Queens to play the New York Mets, more than 160,000 fans attended, a record for a

Ken Griffey Jr. of the Seattle Mariners was the American League's home-run champion in 1997 and is a Gold Glove center fielder.

Baseball Hall of Fame Library

three-game series at Shea Stadium.

The owners and baseball officials, recognizing that relations with fans have remained tenuous since the 1994-95 strike, are approaching realignment carefully, trying to gauge public reaction before committing themselves to such a sweeping change. Coleman sees realignment as "very controversial" and says that major shifts are unlikely to happen soon. Beeston likes the scheduling benefits that a 32-team, time zone-aligned system would provide, but "not right now."

In short, there is awareness of baseball's fundamental conservatism, and fans who don't expect it to change too much. Undercutting that strength might undercut the future of the game. "By forfeiting the century of tradition that is baseball's singular strength," Will warns, "realignment risks alienating the sport's base of support, the few million repeat customers who are buying a substantial portion of the approximately 63 million tickets that will be sold this season [1997] — 10 million more than the NFL, NBA and NHL combined." [18]

Is baseball cultivating a fan base that can sustain the game during the years ahead?

To say that baseball belongs to its fans may seem to fly in the face of economic reality. Baseball, so the realists and accountants argue, belongs to the big-bucks team owners and their highly paid star players. But without fans buying tickets and watching games on television, those big bucks will quickly shrivel.

Baseball needs its fans, but some observers of the game worry that fans are being taken for granted. They are particularly concerned that crucial parts of the fan base, such as young people and minority group members, prefer other sports to baseball.

Coleman admits that "baseball got fat and happy," and that "We have to grow" the fan base by focussing on the next generation. "Baseball has to compete effectively for kids' attention," he says. "With boys and girls — and I emphasize women — we have to be a sport that can reach every child." [19] Similarly, Musial says: "Baseball is just starting to realize the need to promote itself more among younger people." The problem, he explains, involves recruiting participants, not merely spectators. "Years ago, all the kids played baseball," he says. "Now they're playing other sports."

O'Neil sees the problem as partly a class issue. "Baseball has been sold to the suburbs," he says. "It's no longer a blue-collar game. Many people can't afford to go to baseball games like they once did." Angelos echoes this concern, saying that even though his team, the Baltimore Orioles, and others are being run as just break-even enterprises, ticket prices keep rising along with players' salaries. That, he says, inevitably will chase fans away. [20]

Beeston says the key to winning and holding fans is "to focus on the field, not on antitrust law or collective bargaining." He has been encouraged this year, he says, by fans talking "not about how much Mark McGwire is getting paid, but how many home runs he's hitting."

Recapturing the interest of minority group members is seen as one of baseball's fundamental challenges. "When Jackie Robinson broke the color barrier in 1947, baseball became the sport for African-Americans," Schieffer says. "Then in the 1960s and '70s, they drifted away." Coleman notes that "now for African-American children there is more competition" from other sports. O'Neil says the problem of finding black fans is rooted in what games African-American youngsters play. "It's so much easier to play basketball," he says.

"You just set up a hoop." He adds, "Many black high schools don't have baseball teams, but they have football and basketball." Noting major league training efforts in South and Central America, Newcombe asks, "Why isn't there a Dodgers baseball academy in Watts?" *(See story, p. 839.)*

The scarcity of black fans at games can be striking. St. Louis, for instance, is 47 percent African-American, but only 3.5 percent of the fans at 1997 Cardinals games were black. To try to level the racial playing field, the Cardinals enlisted a black-owned advertising agency to launch a campaign for black fans based on the premise that, in the words of an agency partner, "a black guy who loves baseball loves it the same way a white guy loves it." [21]

Other teams also are reaching out to the disparate populations in their communities for fans. The Los Angeles Dodgers in 1990 were the first team to broadcast a game in Korean, and in 1993 they had their first Chinese broadcast. A 1994 game between the Dodgers and the Expos was broadcast in five languages: English, Spanish, Korean, Chinese and French. The Dodgers' newsletter is published in English, Japanese, Korean, and Spanish.

Along with changes in the fan base, the player pool is evolving, becoming more international. When the 1998 season opened, 20 percent of major leaguers were foreign-born. Most were from Latin America — the Dominican Republic is the largest contributor with 62 players — but there is also an influx of Asians.

Another issue related to fan loyalty has nothing to do with economics or ethnicity. It is the nature of the game itself. Ask a non-fan why he or she doesn't like baseball, and the answer is likely to be, "BORING." Hard-core fans may dismiss such critics as too shallow to appreciate the nuances of the game, but baseball's

relaxed pace has, in fact, become even slower. In the past 20 years, the average game has gone from two-and-a-half hours often to more than three. "Our opinion polls showed that the length of our games was discouraging a growing number of parents from bringing children to the ball park," says American League President Gene Budig. [22]

In 1995 and again this year, Major League Baseball has issued guidelines to reverse the trend toward longer games. The point is not, officials insist, to "speed up" baseball, which would constitute sabotage to many fans. Instead, it is "a crackdown on unnecessary dead time." Between-inning breaks have been cut, the time a pitcher may take between pitches has been shortened and batters are limited from straying too far out of the batter's box.

Miller has his own suggestions, including one that would probably prove too expensive for owners' tastes: "Go back to the norm of the early 1980s and reduce [TV] commercial breaks between innings from two minutes back to one minute." He also suggests tighter controls on visits to the mound. "No one," he says, "comes to the park to watch the pitcher and catcher confer." He also recommends an allotment of time-outs, much as other sports have. [23]

Players and umpires have never shown much enthusiasm about such reforms, but when trying to court sports enthusiasts who have grown used to games played against the clock, some concessions may have to be made.

Not too many, though. "Within the ballpark, time moves differently, marked by no clock except the events of the game," wrote *The New Yorker's* Roger Angell. "This is the unique, unchangeable feature of baseball. . . . Baseball's time is seamless and invisible, a bubble within which players move at exactly the same pace and rhythms as all their predecessors." [24] Tampering with that is risky. ∎

BACKGROUND

Mysterious Beginning

Where baseball came from remains something of a mystery. Despite the long-prevailing myth, it is now generally accepted that Abner Doubleday did not draw up the game's rules on a summer day in 1839 in idyllic Cooperstown, N.Y. The Doubleday story owes its existence primarily to a commission of baseball executives and politicians that was created in 1905 to discover the true origins of the game. Determined to divorce baseball from any non-American — i.e., British — ancestors, the commission accepted unsubstantiated testimony about Doubleday's paternity of the game. Doubleday, who had been a Union general in the Civil War, was a convenient hero, and the commission's official judgment was that he and Cooperstown should be revered.

But some problems exist. For one thing, Doubleday was not in Cooperstown in the summer of 1839, and no solid evidence exists that he had any connection with baseball. He may not have ever seen the game played. [25]

Nevertheless, little fuss is made about Cooperstown's claim to being the birthplace of baseball. That story is more convenient than the truth about the game's origin, which is probably to be found in the unexceptional evolution of a stick-and-ball game descended from Britain's cricket and rounders. During the game's early days, rules varied depending on where it was played. How many players on a side, what constituted a score, how many outs were allowed and so on were left to local tastes.

Baseball history begins to take shape with the advent of the New York Knickerbocker Base Ball Club in 1845. Members of the Knickerbockers, particularly Alexander Cartwright and Daniel Adams, are credited with designing the diamond-shaped infield, allowing the batter three strikes and calling for players to be retired by tagging them with the ball. [26] During the next century and a half, those early rules have been refined — for good or ill, depending on the eye of the beholder.

The game and its evolving uniformity quickly took root throughout the country, in back yards, open fields and more formal settings. Profession-alism soon arrived, and by the early 1860s cash rewards were quietly being offered to good players who would desert one team for another. It hadn't taken long for the first version of free agency to appear.

As the 19th century drew to a close, many aspects of the game were dominated by one man, Albert Goodwill Spalding. He had been a star pitcher for the 1875 Boston Red Stockings, then manager and owner of the Chicago White Stockings. He also owned a sporting goods business that manufactured balls, gloves and uniforms and still bears his name.

Spalding's imperiousness might be envied by some of today's owners. His box at the Chicago ballpark had a telephone for passing instructions to his manager and a gong for summoning servants. Spalding was a tireless promoter of baseball. He preached that it was "American in its spirit, its character and its achievements" and was truly "America's national game." He also was a principal proponent of the Doubleday-as-founder story.

Despite Spalding's boosterism, not all went smoothly for the national game. In 1885, New York Giants shortstop John Montgomery Ward (a graduate of Columbia Law School) challenged the reserve clause, alleging that players were being treated like slaves. The resulting players' union that was formed gave birth to the Players' League, which briefly competed effectively against the American and National leagues before losing its financial backing and folding. Baseball's long history of fractious labor relations had begun.

Continued on p. 846

George Herman "Babe" Ruth was baseball's first great slugger.

Baseball Hall of Fame Library

Chronology

1840-1920
Baseball quickly grows into a big — and problem-plagued — industry.

1846
The first game is played in Hoboken, N.J., using rules designed primarily by Alexander Cartwright, a shipping clerk.

1869
The first admittedly all-professional team is formed, the Cincinnati Red Stockings.

1885
Led by New York Giants shortstop John Montgomery Ward, the Brotherhood of Professional Base Ball Players is formed. The union demands an end to salary caps and sales of players between teams.

1899
Ban Johnson forms the American League, challenging the National League's dominance.

1904
John McGraw manages the Giants to the National League pennant and refuses to play the American League champions in the World Series, calling AL President Johnson a crook.

1919
Members of the Chicago White Sox conspire with gamblers to throw the World Series. New baseball Commissioner Judge Kenesaw Mountain Landis bans eight members of the so-called Black Sox for life.

1920
In one of baseball's worst moves, the Boston Red Sox sell Babe Ruth to the New York Yankees.

1921-1950
Baseball is integrated, and the era of the Yankees begins.

1922
The Supreme Court declares that baseball is not subject to antitrust laws.

1927
Babe Ruth hits 60 home runs.

1935
The first major league night game is played in Cincinnati.

1947
Jackie Robinson integrates the major leagues, joining the Brooklyn Dodgers.

1948
Negro Leagues star Satchel Paige joins the Cleveland Indians at age 40-something and compiles a 6-1 record.

1949
Casey Stengel becomes manager of the Yankees. In the next 12 years, they win 10 pennants and seven world championships.

---•---

1951-1998
Players finally get the right to free agency.

1952
The Supreme Court reaffirms that baseball is not subject to antitrust laws.

1958
The former Brooklyn Dodgers and New York Giants begin their first seasons in Los Angeles and San Francisco, respectively.

1961
Roger Maris hits 61 home runs, breaking Babe Ruth's record.

1966
Dodgers pitchers Sandy Koufax and Don Drysdale stage a holdout until they receive substantial salary increases.

1970
Not wanting to accept a trade, Curt Flood sues Major League Baseball, demanding damages and free agency.

1972
The Supreme Court rules against Flood. The first full players' strike is called to protest the players' pension plan.

1974
Hank Aaron hits his 715th home run, surpassing Ruth as the greatest home run hitter.

1976
A new basic agreement between players and owners grants free agency to major leaguers with six years' experience. From 1976-1980, the players' average salary triples.

1987
An arbitrator finds owners guilty of collusion on player salaries.

1994
Players strike in midseason, canceling the World Series and delaying the 1995 season.

September 1998
Mark McGwire of the St. Louis Cardinals and Sammy Sosa of the Chicago Cubs both break Roger Maris' record of 61 homers in a single season. As of Sept. 22, McGwire had 65 homers and Sosa had 63. The regular season ends Sept. 27.

On a Field of Dreams in Montana . . .

It's a long way from Dodger Stadium in Los Angeles to Legion Field in Great Falls, Mont.. Instead of the L.A. Freeway, the Missouri River runs beyond the outfield fence. Instead of Hollywood stars, explorers Lewis and Clark — who passed through here on their famed expedition of discovery — are the local heroes. But the two communities do have one thing in common: In both cities, professional baseball players wear white uniforms with "Dodgers" emblazoned across the front.

The Great Falls Dodgers belong to the eight-team, Class A Pioneer League. The players, many still in their teens, dream of someday taking the field in Los Angeles or another big league city, reaping big league glory and big league salary.

But for now, most of them are paid $850 a month, travel by bus and live either in cheap apartments or with local families. Some of them play well and are watched carefully by the parent club. Many others are likely to be out of professional baseball by the time they turn 21.

Like Major League Baseball, the minor leagues — formally the National Association of Professional Baseball Leagues — have endured a sometimes rocky past and face a challenging future. Formed in 1901, the association reached its high point in 1949, when it included 59 leagues with 448 teams and attracted nearly 40 million fans. Shortly thereafter, television and major league expansion hit the minors hard. By 1963, there were just 20 leagues with 132 teams, and attendance had dropped to 10 million.

Today, the minor leagues comprise 21 leagues with 237 teams, and attendance has surpassed 33 million during each of the past three seasons. This year's attendance will probably hit that level again, but smaller-market teams, such as those in the Pioneer League, remain financially fragile.

They shoulder the often conflicting responsibilities of operating as successful businesses and developing young ballplayers. "We're in the mining business," says league President Jim McCurdy. "We've got the raw ore that we're sifting through. Then we send it up to double-A ball to refine it further." McCurdy adds that "the farm system is the cheapest way for a major league team to acquire players." Without the flow of young talent from the minors, the big league teams would be forced to engage even more frequently in bidding wars for established, expensive free agents.

Despite the symbiosis between major and minor leagues, major league economics are indirectly taking their toll on minor league operations. According to Stephanie Taylor, general manager of the Helena (Montana) Brewers, "A lot of the money is being taken away from the minor leagues because of the major league salaries."

Faced with their own enormous payrolls, many major league teams want to limit the financial help they provide to their subsidiaries. Although the parent clubs still pay the salaries of all the players, a new agreement between the majors and the minors shifts some other responsibilities — such as part of the cost of uniforms and balls — to the farm teams.

The minor league teams take the field with whatever players the parent clubs assign to them. The best players don't stay long in Class A ball, so a primary task for the Pioneer League teams is to give fans reasons to come to the ballpark. "We really don't have a say about the product," says Pat O'Conner, vice president of the national association. "We depend on the major league team. But we do control how we present the team

Minor league players in Helena, Mont., hold baseball clinics for local youths.

Philip Seib

Continued from p. 844

'All-American' It Wasn't

As the new century began with players and owners continuing to eye each other warily, the game itself was changing. Combative John McGraw became manager of the New York Giants in 1902, leading the team to 10 pennants and establishing the dominant role of the manager.

Even more important to the game was the career of McGraw's greatest star, Christy Mathewson. Among the most dominating pitchers in baseball history, Mathewson was one of the first professional athletes to be viewed as a role model. He had been an all-American football hero at Bucknell College and began his major

... They Play the Game for Love

to the fans."

Running a minor league team is partly a test of showmanship. Almost every game features a giveaway, contest or other promotion. The emphasis is on providing the best possible entertainment value. Team mascots frolic, and children run around the bases between innings. A recent Great Falls Dodgers promotion offered four tickets, four hot dogs and four soft drinks to a family of four — all for $10.

"Our motto is, 'Fun is good,' " says Ted Tornow, general manager of the Butte (Montana) Copper Kings. Great Falls General Manager Jim Keough (the team's batboy 29 years ago) stresses the importance of having the fans sitting close to the players. Keough, a former insurance broker, works the business community hard, and his ballpark's 685 reserved seats (out of 3,800 total) are sold out for the entire season.

The general managers spend considerable time promoting their teams as symbols of community spirit. The players have a crucial role because they are far more accessible to their fans than their big league counterparts. On a recent Sunday afternoon in Helena, the entire Brewers team turned out for a clinic attended by about 40 local youngsters. For more than an hour, the players worked on the basics — hitting, fielding and pitching — with both boys and girls, and clearly enjoyed doing so. Taylor says this is part of promoting Brewers' games "as a safe, fun place for families to be."

For the players, the lack of glamour in the Pioneer League does not deter dreams. Copper Kings pitcher Cody Salter, 22, was passed over by the major league draft during his senior year at the University of Illinois. He kept playing, though, and while pitching in a semi-pro league near Chicago he was spotted by a scout for the Anaheim Angels, the Copper Kings' parent. He signed a contract and was on a plane to Montana the next day. Salter knows he is constantly being tested and appraised, but, he says: "When I take the mound, I don't think about getting to the big leagues. I'm getting paid to play baseball, which is every kid's dream. I love it."

Pioneer League players are young and diverse. The roster of the Great Falls team has no one older than 21 and includes players from South Africa, Venezuela, Australia, Curaçao, Nicaragua and other countries. The Butte team even has a Russian infielder.

Many of the small-market teams play in ballparks that have room for only a few thousand fans. The Copper Kings, for example, play in Montana Tech University's 35-year-old football stadium, which seats only 1,500 for baseball. With ticket prices averaging about $4, making money — or just breaking even — is a constant challenge.

Linda Gach Ray, a Los Angeles attorney who is co-owner of the Helena franchise, says the finances of minor league ball "definitely can work. It's highly dependent on the support of the community, how fond the residents are of baseball and how much they value having the uniqueness of baseball's traditions here." Ray translates her own love of the game into her work with the team. No absentee owner, she visits Helena frequently and during games is often on the field recruiting fans to participate in the between-innings contests.

As with major league teams, minor league executives increasingly cite the importance of the ballpark itself as an essential part of the team's appeal to fans. In Great Falls and Butte, the teams are looking for money to renovate their existing facilities or build new ones. A formula cited by minor league executives is a cost of roughly $1 million for every thousand seats, so a small-market team would be happy with a $3 million ballpark. In the wealthy world of professional sports, that might not seem like much, but in small cities like Great Falls and Butte (population 60,000 and 34,000, respectively) finding that kind of money is not easy.

Despite the questions about facilities and the emphasis on promotions, the heart of minor league baseball remains the game on the field. "The players have the tools, but their talent is crude," says Great Falls Manager Dino Ebel. "We put them out here and have them play as many games as they can."

Team boosters know their favorite players won't be around for more than a year or two. But when these players move to other teams, they are not viewed as deserting their teammates and fans in pursuit of free-agent dollars. Rather, they are climbing one more rung up the ladder toward the majors, and that earns them the good wishes of the fans.

Indeed, many fans of minor league games have become disenchanted with what they see as the greed-driven major leagues. For them, baseball's future is right here.

---

league career when only amateurs were regarded as socially acceptable.

Refusing to play on Sundays and billed as a "fine Christian gentleman," Mathewson brought a touch of class to a sport that had been notably lacking it. He was the model for the Frank Merriwell schoolboy stories and was sought after as an endorser of commercial products, the precursor of today's sports stars who have merged their on-field accomplishments with commercial success.

As popular as Mathewson was, his appeal was later dwarfed by that of Babe Ruth. Everything about Ruth was outsize, from his prodigious home run hitting to his dominance as a cultural (and commercial) icon. By the time he hit 60 home runs in 1927, he had established himself as the first great slugger, a tradition carried on by the McGwires and Sosas of today, not to mention heroes like Joe DiMaggio, Hank Aaron and Roberto Clemente. Ruth became a celebrity of the same rank as Hollywood's biggest stars and a prolific endorser of breakfast cereal, candy, soap and even Girl Scout cookies.

Fueled by the feats of Ruth and other stars of his era, baseball's popularity continued to grow. But just as the game became "all-American" in its best respects, so too did it reflect the country's worst flaws. Baseball was a wonderful showcase for great athletes, just as long as those great athletes were white. Sadly, professional baseball was a striking example of American apartheid, with African-American players restricted to the Negro Leagues, including such superb players as Josh Gibson, Satchel Paige, Cool Papa Bell and Oscar Charleston. Except for exhibition games, Negro Leagues teams never had the chance to face the best white players. The segregation of baseball lasted until 1947, when Branch Rickey brought a shy, young man named Jackie Robinson to the Brooklyn Dodgers.

Today, O'Neil notes, "a lot of black players don't realize what they owe us. They never knew the kind of segregation we faced, but if they could turn their thoughts away from the money they make, they might identify with us old-timers, because apart from the salaries, they still face the problem of racism in our society." [27]

Robinson was soon followed by other black players — Roy Campanella, Willie Mays, Ernie Banks, Hank Aaron — and along with white superstars like Ted Williams, Mickey Mantle, Duke Snider and Yogi Berra they shaped the baseball of the 1950s. At the same time, television began supplanting radio for fans who wanted to follow their favorite teams from their living rooms.

Westward Ho!

In the early 1950s, New York was the center of the baseball universe, home to three of the best teams, the Yankees, the Dodgers and the Gi-

Jackie Robinson, sliding into third base, integrated baseball in 1947.

ants. That ended, and the geography of baseball changed forever, in 1958, when the economic allure of the West Coast overcame the power of tradition. Despite fans' anguished protests, the Dodgers took up residence in Los Angeles, and the Giants established themselves in San Francisco.

The moves to California once again underscored that baseball is a business, with only limited room for sentiment. In 1964, CBS bought the New York Yankees, the first time a major, non-baseball corporation had taken over a team.

There still were heroes: Sandy Koufax, Bob Gibson, Carl Yastrzemski, Frank Robinson. And there still were storybook teams like the New York Mets, who rose from their hideous beginning in 1962 and ninth place in 1968 to the world championship in 1969. But running just below the game's glories was an undertow of bitterness that would pull baseball more frequently into labor disputes and other money-based contentiousness.

In 1966, star Dodger pitcher Koufax and Don Drysdale threatened to retire unless they received the salaries they thought they were entitled to. They settled for less than they had demanded, but the fact that the Dodger management had responded at all was progress from the players' standpoint. That same year, the Major League Baseball Players Association tapped hard-nosed Marvin Miller, a former negotiator for the Steelworkers Union, as executive director. Miller quickly raised the players' minimum salary and improved their pension plan.

The Supreme Court's decision in the *Flood* case was handed down in 1972, which also marked the first of a series of player strikes and owner lockouts.

The 1994 Strike

To many observers, the 1994-95 players' strike launched the mod-

Continued on p. 850

At Issue:

Would realignment hurt the game of baseball?

SHIRLEY POVICH

The longtime Washington Post *columnist died on June 4, 1998*

FROM "REALIGNMENT OUT OF LINE, OUT OF BOUNDS," THE WASHINGTON POST, SEPT. 2, 1997

*t*he word now is realignment. In baseball, that is a synonym for what-a-mess. [Baseball Commissioner] Bud Selig . . . has come out of his cocoon with a cockeyed plan for solving the most painful of baseball's problems — too many franchises are losing money.

His prescription is to realign the two major leagues via wholesale franchise shifts from one league to the other, based on geographic proximity that would downsize travel costs. His major plan recommended that 15 teams switch leagues, thus cutting travel expenses, which would make everything hunky-dory in the floundering baseball business.

On the contrary, the only guarantees the Selig scheme promises are a mishmash of new and unnatural rivalries, a confounding jumble of history-bashing schedules, an imbalance of the standards by which achievements were measured for the past 97 years and the loss of fan interest, with so much of it pegged to comparing modern players with feats of the past. In short, a mess.

What realignment is trumpeting loud and clear is baseball's new and bewildering credo: "To hell with tradition." The old rules and the precise record-keeping that offered a comparison of the two leagues, teams and individuals promoted a fan interest that made baseball truly the nation's game. Realignment on Selig's scale is a wipeout of so much that the game had to offer its eager, history-loving fans. Future baseball history would be a cloud of asterisks. . . .

Realigning the leagues to cut down on travel costs can be equated with wielding a sledgehammer to knock a fly off the baby's nose. There are other available tactics. . . .

It is significant that the lords of baseball always overlook revenue sharing, the shortcut that would suckle those failing franchises in small-market towns such as Minneapolis, Milwaukee, Pittsburgh, et al. Oh, George Steinbrenner does donate a part of the $50 million he gets yearly from local radio and TV interests, but it's not a large part. And smaller towns suffer along with radio and TV fees that are trifling.

They didn't have the guts to follow the National Football League strategy of sharing all TV revenue — a strategy that enables little Green Bay to compete with the biggest cities in the league, and win Super Bowls, too. Instead, they're trying to save money by cutting travel expenses via a senseless interleague shift of franchises that will serve mainly to dilute and disrupt the game that Americans were once pleased to call their national pastime.

JIM LITKE

Reporter, The Associated Press, Chicago

FROM "WHAT'S ALL THE FUSS? IT WOULD WORK," LOS ANGELES TIMES, SEPT. 14, 1997

*f*ew ideas arouse so much passion that opponents would enlist their own kids in the campaign against it. And realignment, frankly, didn't figure to be one of them. . . . But already the forces of tradition-for-its-own-sake are lining up against it.

Never mind that any plan would be an improvement over what baseball has in place at the moment. And never mind that most versions of realignment would help nearly every team cut costs, reduce travel times and — most important — snag more and better time slots in their local broadcast markets. The anti-realignment people are doing what the powers-that-be did centuries ago when Galileo said he could prove the Earth revolved around the sun, instead of the other way around: They are dismissing the whole thing as heresy.

How shortsighted. The world has changed and, more important, the economics that shape baseball's world have changed even more. The game has been super-sized, from eight teams a few generations ago to 30 and more by the time the next generation tunes in. The bills are sizable, too. Baseball needs to get its revenue stream flowing faster.

In a perfect world, realignment would restore the cozy version of baseball that existed before expansion, before free agency, before endless schedule permutations made it impossible to keep track of who was in contention and which games mattered in which race. . . .

Naturally, traditionalists will grouse that trying to recapture only some pieces of the game's grand past is not enough. Left to their own devices, they would go back to 154-game schedules, pull up all the carpets, have the designated hitters thrown into deep wells and the players back in wool uniforms, speaking in homilies and spitting up tobacco juice after every other word. The whole nation would be traveling once more by train.

Some of those things would definitely be an improvement. The pace of daily life, for instance. But there is no going back on some things.

Baseball, as enduring as it has proven itself to be, has to think about going forward instead of back. Traditionalists are always crying about the game turning its back on its history-loving fans. But it's not like those history-loving fans have been making the turnstiles spin in recent years, either. Otherwise the owners, by and large traditionalists themselves, would not be messing with the game. And, at least as it applies to the game on the field, realignment leaves everything intact.

Continued from p. 848

ern baseball era. Although it was not the first time a season had been interrupted by a labor dispute, it was notable for the damage it wreaked, not only to the 1994 season but also to the linkage between fans and the game.

Even after the 1995 season finally got under way, fans' anger toward owners and players was reflected in sagging attendance. Many owners were viewed as money-grubbing villains, and some players who were labeled as pro-union activists were booed when they returned to the field.

The strike cost the owners $700 million in revenues and the players $230 million in salaries. Most of the owners had appeared ready to begin the 1995 season with ragtag teams of replacement players, a patently ridiculous plan that would have caused legal and public relations chaos had it been implemented.

After a federal judge sided with the players, the strike ended and the season began, although several weeks late. U.S. District Judge Sonia Sotomayor issued an injunction, requested by the National Labor Relations Board, restoring salary arbitration and anti-collusion protections for free agents, which the owners had unilaterally eliminated.

As memories of the strike recede, a slight hangover remains, although Beeston says, "It's getting so that it's not painful." Trust between owners and players remains tenuous, although civility generally prevails in formal relations between the two groups. Overall fan attendance is on the rise, but baseball officials apparently understand that the strike did

more damage than they had anticipated would occur. Beeston admits, "We broke trust with our fans," and Schieffer says, "Both owners and players recognize that a terrible thing happened, and both recognize that we just can't do that again."

Baseball is, however, fundamentally resilient. University of Virginia professor G. Edward White, who has written about baseball's legal and economic history, observed that "Americans may forgive baseball its current transgressions and restore it to its privileged place among professional sports because they find it so compelling a link to history." [28] ■

The Baltimore Orioles' Cal Ripken Jr. greets fans on Sept. 6, 1996, after he set the record of 2,131 consecutive games played. On Sept. 20, 1998, he ended his streak at 2,632 games.

Reuters/Gary Hershorn

CURRENT SITUATION

Beyond Economics

The fans have largely returned, and so has baseball's economic vitality. In 1997, paid attendance was the

second highest ever (exceeded only by 1993). Also, players' salaries totaled more than $1 billion for the first time while baseball's gross revenues exceeded $2 billion.

As the 1998 season winds up, attendance, TV ratings and merchandise sales all are heading for records. The money is not, however, spread evenly through the big leagues. The gap between baseball's haves and have-nots keeps growing.

The mix of strength and weakness does not provide the firmest possible foundation for baseball's future. For some teams, economic uncertainty has contributed to uncertainty about their future. Although the last time a franchise moved was in 1972 (when the Washington Senators became the Texas Rangers), some owners today look longingly at potential hometowns that promise new stadiums and enthusiastic fans.

The Minnesota Twins considered moving to North Carolina's "Triad" region (Winston-Salem, Greensboro, High Point), but in May voters there rejected a tax proposal that would have helped fund a new stadium. The Twins might try another North Carolina location, but that is not likely soon.

Unless a deal can be struck for a new downtown ballpark, the Expos may be sold and moved, perhaps to Northern Virginia. The Oakland Athletics may be contemplating a move to Sacramento, Las Vegas or New Orleans.

Healthy franchises remain valuable commodities. The most recent team sale was the Texas Rangers, purchased last January for $250 million by Dallas financier Tom Hicks. (The sale was approved by major league owners in June.) The price represents an almost tripling in value since the team was last sold, in 1989, for $86 million. The highest price for a team remains the reported $311 million paid by Rupert Murdoch's Fox Group for the Los Angeles Dodgers. That sale also was approved earlier this year.

Beyond economics, baseball faces other distractions that require attention. This season games occasionally looked more like hockey, as players poured out of their dugouts for fierce brawls, sometimes more than once in a game. "Current fines and suspensions — which do not include loss of pay — should be revised or reformed to deter behavior which is not in keeping with the integrity of the game," said then Acting Commissioner Bud Selig after wild fights in May and June. He urged league officials and players' union representatives to "immediately devise new and more effective penalties for those players and their managers who leave the dugout or their on-field positions to incite or inflame violence of any sort." [29]

But baseball's not-insignificant problems pale in the glow of the game's ultimate asset: its array of established and prospective superstars. For many fans, the exploits of a Juan Gonzalez or an Albert Belle offset concerns about the shallowness of the reservoir of big league talent, and let them forget, if only for a moment, the "business" side of the game. ■

OUTLOOK

Quiet Evolution

F or baseball's owners and players, the 1998 season has been pros-

FOR MORE INFORMATION

If you would like to have this CQ Researcher updated, or need more information about this topic, please call CQ Custom Research. Special rates for CQ subscribers. (202) 887-8600 or (800) 432-2250, ext. 600, or E-mail Custom.Research@cq.com

Major League Baseball, 350 Park Ave., New York, N.Y. 10022; (212) 339-7800; www.majorleaguebaseball.com.

American League of Professional Baseball Clubs, 350 Park Ave., New York, N.Y. 10022; (212) 339-7600; www.majorleaguebaseball.com.

National League of Professional Baseball Clubs, 350 Park Ave., New York, N.Y. 10022; (212) 339-7700; www.majorleaguebaseball.com.

National Association of Professional Baseball Leagues (the Minor Leagues), P.O. Box A, St. Petersburg, Fla. (813) 822-6937; www.minorleaguebaseball.com.

National Baseball Hall of Fame and Museum, P.O. Box 590, Cooperstown, N.Y. 13326; (888) 425-5633; www.baseballhalloffame.org.

Negro Leagues Baseball Museum, 1616 E. 18th St., Kansas City, Mo. 64108; (816) 221-1920; www.nlbm.com

perous and productive. Strong attendance is one good indicator that bitterness grounded in the 1994-95 strike is dissipating. "The strength of baseball this year," Coleman says, "is that the focus is on the field."

Looking ahead, baseball anticipates continued stability. With Selig finally confirmed as commissioner — the first to formally hold that position since Fay Vincent's 1992 resignation — and Beeston continuing as president and chief operating officer, baseball's leadership is more clearly defined. Perhaps more thought will now be given to the future of revenue-sharing and player salaries.

On the legal front, the Senate in July passed a bill that would alter baseball's antitrust exemption, which has shielded the game since 1922. Known as the Curt Flood Act and sponsored by Sen. Orrin G. Hatch, R-Utah, it would allow major league players — like other professional athletes — to challenge owners' policies by filing antitrust lawsuits. The measure does not cover franchise expansion or relocation, ac-

tions affecting the minor leagues or the amateur player draft.

Perhaps the biggest change will be baseball's continued, quiet evolution into a more centralized business. Until recently, Beeston says, "Baseball has been more a state system than a federal system." As a result, Coleman explains, baseball's marketing was mostly handled by individual franchises, far more so than in, say, professional football and basketball. Now, however, MLB will be exercising more control over licensing and marketing, he says, much like the NFL and NBA.

The international aspects of baseball also will be stressed more. Festivals to increase interest in the sport have been held recently by MLB in the United Kingdom, Venezuela and elsewhere. The Pitch, Hit and Run program that teaches basic baseball skills, which began in 1994, will reach more than 700,000 youngsters in Germany, Australia, South Africa and other countries in 1998. The MLB Envoy Program sent baseball coaches to 32 countries this summer. In

Canada, MLB launched its first international clinics for girls.

These efforts to stimulate new interest in the game are expected to pay off with new television deals. In South Korea, for example, MLB's 1997 package with Inchon TV was worth $350,000 for 30 games. A new agreement has provided 100 games during 1998 and raises the fee to $3 million for the 2000 season. Other international networks also are adding MLB games to their schedules. This year, overseas fans were able to help choose members of the All-Star teams by voting on the Internet via the MLB Web site.

Looking even farther ahead, Coleman advocates "a World Cup approach" every few years. A national team showcasing the best American players, including those whose teams didn't make it to the World Series, would compete against the best players of other countries for a true world title.

For many baseball fans, such innovation is interesting but unnecessary. They want tomorrow to be not too different from yesterday. As the character played by James Earl Jones says in the baseball movie "Field of Dreams," "The one constant through all the years has been baseball. . . . This field, this game, is a part of our past. It reminds us of all that once was good, and that could be again."

Baseball's future is tied to our past and our memory. In his 1998 book about the game, the late A. Bartlett Giamatti, who stepped down as president of Yale University to become commissioner of baseball, wrote that what Americans love about baseball "is what it recalls to us about ourselves at our earliest. . . . They are memories of our best hopes. They are memories of a time when all that would be better was before us, as a hope, and the hope was fastened to a game." [30]

Even during this home-run-charged season, attendance has not reached pre-strike levels. More omi-nous is the disparity in this year's attendance figures: While eight teams have drawn more than 35,000 fans a game, seven franchises have attracted fewer than 20,000 a game.

The unique power of baseball is its ability to draw strength from collective history and individual memory. For the sport and for its fans, the secret was defined by the philosopher and Yankee manager Casey Stengel: "The trick is growing up without growing old." ■

Philip Seib is a professor of journalism at Southern Methodist University in Dallas.

Notes

[1] George Will, *Bunts* (1998), p. 18.

[2] For background, see Richard L. Worsnop, "Soccer in America," *The CQ Researcher*, April 22, 1994, pp. 337-360.

[3] Ken Daley, "Salary Distance Grows Between Haves and Have-Nots," *Dallas Morning News*, April 24, 1998, p. 14B. Salary figures were obtained by The Associated Press from management and player sources and include prorated shares of signing bonuses and other guaranteed income.

[4] Will, *op. cit.*, p. 329.

[5] Andrew Zimbalist, *Baseball and Billions* (1992), pp. 48-51.

[6] For background, see Richard L. Worsnop, "The Business of Sports," *The CQ Researcher*, Feb. 10, 1995, pp. 121-144.

[7] Will, *op. cit.*, p. 327.

[8] Sporting Goods Manufacturers Association, "America's National Pastime: A Report on Participation in 1996."

[9] "Baseball's Real Tradition," *The New York Times*, March 22, 1998, Sec. 4, p. 14.

[10] Will, *op. cit.*, p. 129.

[11] Thomas Boswell, "If the Rich Get Richer, That Can Be Fun," *The Washington Post*, March 27, 1998, p. F3.

[12] Quoted in Peter Schmuck, "Angelos: Troubled Teams Need Aid," *The Baltimore Sun*, April 25, 1998, p. C1.

[13] *Ibid.*

[14] Zimbalist, *op. cit.*, pp. 98-99.

[15] Erik Brady and Mel Antonen, "Big Money, Big Trades Changing Face of the Game," *USA Today*, July 2, 1998, p. 1.

[16] Quoted in Michael P. Geffner, "Diamond in the Rough," *Texas Monthly*, June 1998, p. 166.

[17] Jon Miller, *Confessions of a Baseball Purist* (1998), p. 18.

[18] Will, *op. cit.*, p. 290.

[19] For background, see Richard L. Worsnop, "Gender Equity in Sports," *The CQ Researcher*, April 18, 1997, pp. 337-360.

[20] Quoted in Schmuck, *op. cit.*

[21] "The Red and the Black," *Sports Illustrated*, June 29, 1998, p. 23.

[22] Quoted in Dave Anderson, "Time for Crackdown: Enforce Dead Time," *The New York Times*, March 29, 1998, p. 30.

[23] Miller, *op. cit.*, pp. 99, 26.

[24] Roger Angell, *The Summer Game* (1972), p. 303.

[25] Geoffrey C. Ward and Ken Burns, *Baseball* (1994), p. 3.

[26] *Ibid*, p. 4.

[27] Buck O'Neil, *I Was Right On Time* (1996), p. 238.

[28] G. Edward White, *Creating the National Pastime* (1996), p. xii.

[29] Murray Chass, "Selig Wants to Toughen Penalties to Limit Fighting," *The New York Times*, June 9, 1998, p. C24.

[30] A. Bartlett Giamatti, *A Great and Glorious Game* (1998), p. 88.

Bibliography

Selected Sources Used

Books

Angell, Roger, *The Summer Game*, Viking, 1972.
Probably the best writer about baseball, Angell combines an understanding of fine technical points and an appreciation of the game's beauty and rhythms. This is one of his collections of pieces that originally appeared in *The New Yorker*.

Chadwick, Bruce, *When the Game Was Black and White*, Abbeville, 1992.
Sportswriter Chadwick recalls that the Negro Leagues were both a wonderful showcase for great athletes and shameful evidence of American racism. This illustrated history depicts the players' devotion to the game and the hardships they endured.

Edelman, Rob, *Baseball on the Web*, MIS:Press, 1998.
The Internet is home to hundreds of baseball-related Web sites. This directory lists some elaborate ones, such as Major League Baseball's site, and some homemade versions, such as fans' tributes to individual players. Sites exist for the minor leagues, amateur baseball, memorabilia and many more aspects of the game.

Feinstein, John, *Play Ball*, Villard, 1993.
A good reporter as well as an accomplished student of the game, Feinstein presents a detailed, inside look at the 1992 season, explaining what the players and managers did and why they did it.

Giamatti, A. Bartlett, *A Great and Glorious Game*, Algonquin, 1998.
This posthumous collection of writings by the onetime baseball commissioner and president of Yale University includes lyrical tributes to the game and lawyerly pronouncements about cheating and the banishment of Pete Rose.

Lamb, David, *Stolen Season*, Warner, 1992.
A reporter who has spent many years covering the Middle East returns home to take an RV journey through the backroads of the minor leagues. This is a beautifully written tribute to those who play and enjoy the game absent the major league glitz.

Miller, Jon, *Confessions of a Baseball Purist*, Simon & Schuster, 1998.
The longtime baseball broadcaster offers his colorful comments about his own career and the state of the game. He is mostly optimistic about baseball's prospects and is eloquent in his praise of heroes such as Cal Ripken Jr.

Ward, Geoffrey C., and Ken Burns, *Baseball*, Knopf, 1994.
The companion volume to the PBS television series is a treasury of the game's history in words and pictures. Particularly valuable are sections about the Negro Leagues and about players such as Babe Ruth who helped make the game a national preoccupation.

White, G. Edward, *Creating the National Pastime*, Princeton, 1996.
This professorial view of baseball's transformation during the first half of this century puts particular emphasis on team owners' shrewd decisions about turning a game into a business.

Will, George F., *Bunts*, Scribner, 1998.
Will is at least as articulate and passionate about baseball as he is about politics. Most of this collection consists of previously published pieces. It provides a good sense of how the game has evolved during the past two decades.

Zimbalist, Andrew, *Baseball and Billions*, BasicBooks, 1992.
An economics professor at Smith College offers a hardnosed but still affectionate look at baseball as big business, examining such issues as franchises, labor relations and antitrust.

The Next Step

Additional information from UMI's Newspaper & Periodical Abstracts™ database

Bud Selig

Armstrong, Jim, "Bud Selig: Human Dartboard, 'Small-Town Schlepper' or Baseball's White Knight? No One has Suffered More Slings and Arrows Doing a Thankless Job he Never Wanted in the First Place," *Denver Post*, May 11, 1998, p. D1.

During Bud Selig's regime as baseball's interim commissioner, he has accomplished the equivalent of splitting a double-header in the court of public opinion. To some people, he's the embodiment of hope for small-market franchises that barely can afford the ante in a rigged game. To others, he gets blamed for everything from El Niño to the national debt.

Heath, Thomas, "The Commissioner Who Wears Two Caps; Selig Serves Brewers and Baseball, and Tries to Avoid Conflicts of Interest," *The Washington Post*, June 19, 1998, p. C1.

For the past six years, the acting commissioner of Major League Baseball, Allan H. "Bud" Selig, has been the driving force behind many of the major changes in the national pastime. But now, as it appears most of his fellow owners want to name Selig the permanent commissioner, perhaps even before the All-Star break in early July, Selig's dual role as owner of the Milwaukee Brewers has become an issue bound to generate debate.

Maske, Mark, "Selig Discounts Expansion in '99; Decision Could Stifle Washington Area's Chance of Acquiring Club," *The Washington Post*, June 27, 1998, p. D6.

In what could be a crippling blow to the Washington area's chances of acquiring a major league baseball team, Acting Commissioner Bud Selig said today the sport will not award two expansion franchises next year. The labor agreement between baseball's team owners and players authorizes the owners to award two expansion clubs by Dec. 31, 1999, and have them playing by the 2002 season. Northern Virginia was among the contenders to receive one of those franchises. But Selig, the owner of the Milwaukee Brewers, said that baseball will concentrate on helping its financially troubled franchises and won't expand again in the foreseeable future.

Rogers, Phil, "Baseball, Union Headed for a Brawl Over Belle," *Chicago Tribune*, Feb. 19, 1997, p. 1.

A conflict between Bud Selig and the players' union involving Albert Belle could spoil baseball's spring of healing. With a labor contract in place for the first time since 1993, owners and players have pledged to work together to market their game. But they are poised on the verge of an ugly dispute on one issue: Is it major league baseball's business if Belle, or any other player, bets on sports other than baseball?

Decrease in Popularity

Bradley, Mark, "Baseball Past its Prime; Game's a Bore," *Atlanta Journal-Constitution*, May 25, 1997, p. E11.

Say Ken Griffey Jr. hits 62 home runs. Will that save baseball? Nope. If Griffey, who has 21 homers already, enters September with a chance to catch Maris, it will bring attention to Griffey. By way of contrast, baseball at-large will seem as it does every other month of every other year — tedious and outdated.

Kulfan, Ted, "Forgotten Legend? Knowledge of Robinson no Longer Important to Many Kids as Baseball's Popularity Drops," *Detroit News*, April 16, 1997, p. F8.

The impact of baseball legend Jackie Robinson is drifting away; mentioning his name might even bring a blank stare from some kids. "That's unfortunate because while sports was Jackie's calling card, it certainly wasn't his place in history," said Michael Bernacchi, a professor of marketing at the University of Detroit. "Unfortunately, Jackie never made a Nike commercial. He was a low-profile guy who deserves high-profile treatment."

Long, Tom, "Chat Room: Is Baseball Getting Knocked out of the Park by Hockey?" *Detroit News*, July 10, 1997, p. E1.

The hockey finals are over, Detroit is victorious. The pro football season-preview magazines are on stands right now, Detroit is hopeful. But baseball is a different story. I have yet to see Detroit Tigers flags flying from anybody's window, even though the local team apparently has improved markedly. A friendly cop directing traffic outside the stadium told me to enjoy the game; I'm used to cops asking me for some ID, not being nice. The usher who I asked to direct me to our seats just said, "Sit anywhere, doesn't matter." When I walked into the stadium I could see why: The place was maybe one-fifth full.

Shaughnessy, Dan, "Baseball Getting Cold Shoulder, and Selig is Concerned," *The Boston Globe*, Oct. 23, 1997, p. C6.

It was just a few minutes before 5 p.m. when the first snow flurries swirled in the empty stands at the ballpark yesterday. Welcome to the 1997 World Series, the Fall-Down Classic. It's the Series with no Hall of Famers, horrible weather, interminable games, absence of drama, walks, errors and faceless teams.

Wilbon, Michael, "Baseball's Fatal Detraction," *The Washington Post*, Oct. 22, 1997, p. C1.

For three years now, the baseball lobbyists have promised

us everything was going to be fine with the national pastime. Just wait and see, the apologists said after the Great Strike of 1994, people will flock back to the ballparks. Did you see the TV ratings for the first two games of the World Series between the Marlins and Indians? Lowest ever — by a lot. The TV numbers show conclusively that more people stay home on a warm June evening with the days growing longer to watch an NBA Finals contest than tune in on a cool, already-dark autumn evening to watch the World Series. Twenty years ago that was unthinkable.

Resurgence of Popularity

Heath, Thomas, "McGwire's Heroics Driving Up Profits; Griffey Jr., Sosa, Gonzalez Also Helping Boost Baseball's Popularity, Finances," *The Washington Post*, July 8, 1998, p. C7.

Streaking behind Mark McGwire's 37 home runs is a revenue stream that is having a huge financial impact on Major League Baseball. From Houston to Minnesota to Arizona, the St. Louis Cardinals and their powerful first baseman, on pace to smash Roger Maris' record of 61 set in 1961, are packing ballparks, boosting television ratings, selling food and merchandise and even jump-starting the wheezing baseball card industry.

Kiszla, Mark, "Baseball's Got Game; the Fans Want to Cheer," *Denver Post*, July 12, 1998, p. C4.

Baseball is on a major league roll that makes the NFL, NBA and NHL look poor by comparison. A fan could get blinded by the light of baseball's rising stars. Pro football has become too much point-spread frenzy and Jerry Jones schlock for the sport's own good.

Liebenson, Donald, "A New Pitch; Baseball Videos are Being Drafted to Lure Fans, Build on Excitement," *Chicago Tribune*, Aug. 20, 1998, p. 5.

Two-thirds of the baseball season is over. But America's pastime seems to be, to mix sports metaphors, on the rebound. Young phenoms such as Chicago Cubs rookie pitcher Kerry Wood and the relentless assault on Roger Maris' home run record have been key in capturing the imagination of fans, particularly those who may have been embittered by the 1994 strike. Taking a page from the NFL and NBA marketing playbooks, Major League Baseball is employing home video to build on this revitalized excitement and to scout for a new generation of fans.

Mitchell, Fred, "Baseball Has Plenty to Be Happy About," *Chicago Tribune*, Aug. 12, 1998, p. 3.

Attendance at major league baseball games is up more than 3 percent this season. Seven teams have drawn more than 2 million fans and five more (including the Cubs) are on pace to join them. With a quarter of the season remaining, every team in the majors has drawn more than 1 million fans on the road and only four of the 30 franchises have drawn less than 1 million at home.

Paige, Woody, "Baseball, the Rockies and Denver Can be Proud," *Denver Post*, July 8, 1998, p. AA2.

Four years ago, major league baseball was deader than the ball used pre-1920s. There was a nasty strike, the World Series was canceled and the fans were turned off by rising ticket prices, greedy owners and the players' haughty attitude. "Great game of baseball," said Mark McGwire in 1998, the true-life Casey at the Bat. He didn't clobber a home run to Greeley, but thoroughly enjoyed himself along with the Coors Field record crowd of 51,267. "We the players thank the fans for coming back. What we did in '94 stunted the game."

Yerak, Becky, "Home Run Derby is a Winner for Major League Baseball: Contest Lures Fans, Despite League's Cautious Marketing," *Detroit News*, Aug. 12, 1998, p. A1.

This summer, baseball's traditional marketing playbook is getting thrown out as the St. Louis Cardinals' Mark McGwire, Sammy Sosa of the Chicago Cubs and Ken Griffey Jr. of the Seattle Mariners chase one of the game's most sacred records: the most homers in a season.

Salaries

Bodley, Hal, "1998 Major League Baseball Salaries," *USA Today*, April 2, 1998, p. C6.

The 1998 salaries of all major league players on the 25-man rosters, plus those on the disabled list, are listed.

Bodley, Hal, "Baseball Puts 317 Millionaires to Work," *USA Today*, April 2, 1998, p. C1.

As the financially strapped Montreal Expos pray for a new stadium, three players — Gary Sheffield, Albert Belle and Greg Maddux — each will earn more this year than the Expos' entire team. Montreal has the lowest payroll ($9.2 million) based on *USA Today's* survey of opening-day salaries, while Baltimore became the first team to crack the $70 million plateau.

Maske, Mark, "O's Have Largest Payroll; $74.3 Million Is Baseball Record," *The Washington Post*, March 25, 1998, p. C1.

The Baltimore Orioles will begin the upcoming baseball season with the largest player payroll in major league history: just over $74.3 million. Three other major league clubs — the Atlanta Braves, Boston Red Sox and New York Yankees — also have surpassed $70 million.

Wharton, David, "Not Everyone Is Quick to Board Gravy Train; Some Players are Ruled by Free Agency and Avarice, Others, Like Angels' Finley and Brewers' Yount, are Governed More by a Sense of Loyalty," *Los Angeles Times*, March 25, 1998, p. C10.

Chuck Finley looks like any other baseball millionaire, slumped in front of his locker after a morning workout, eating a sandwich off a paper plate. Meanwhile, guys like Finley, the Minnesota Twins' Terry Steinbach and the Texas Rangers' Ivan Rodriguez have accepted less money to stay with their teams or, in some cases, return to their native cities.

Back Issues

Great Research on Current Issues Starts Right Here.
Recent topics covered by The CQ Researcher are listed below.
Now available on the Web
For information, call (800) 432-2250 ext. 279 or (202) 887-6279.

If you would like to have any of these CQ Researchers updated, or need more information about these topics, please call CQ Custom Research. Special rates for CQ subscribers. (202) 887-8600 or (800) 432-2250, ext. 600, or E-mail Custom.Research@cq.com

JUNE 1997
FDA Reform
China After Deng
Line-Item Veto
Breast Cancer

JULY 1997
Transportation Policy
Executive Pay
School Choice Debate
Aggressive Driving

AUGUST 1997
Age Discrimination
Banning Land Mines
Children's Television
Evolution vs. Creationism

SEPTEMBER 1997
Caring for the Dying
Mental Health Policy
Mexico's Future
Youth Fitness

OCTOBER 1997
Urban Sprawl in the West
Diversity in the Workplace
Teacher Education
Contingent Work Force

NOVEMBER 1997
Renewable Energy
Artificial Intelligence
Religious Persecution
Roe v. Wade at 25

DECEMBER 1997
Whistleblowers
Castro's Next Move
Gun Control Standoff
Regulating Nonprofits

JANUARY 1998
Foster Care Reform
IRS Reform
The Black Middle Class
U.S.-British Relations

FEBRUARY 1998
Patients' Rights
Deflation Fears
Caring for the Elderly
The New Corporate Philanthropy

MARCH 1998
Israel at 50
The Federal Judiciary
Drinking on Campus
The Economics of Recycling

APRIL 1998
Biology and Behavior
Liberal Arts Education
Income Inequality
High-Tech Labor Shortage

MAY 1998
Census 2000
Child-Care Options
Alzheimer's Disease
U.S.-Russian Relations

JUNE 1998
Student Journalism
Antitrust Policy
Environmental Justice
Sleep Deprivation

JULY 1998
Encouraging Teen Abstinence
Population and the Environment
Democracy in Asia
Baby Boomers at Midlife

AUGUST 1998
Oil Production in the 21st Century
Flexible Work Arrangements
Coastal Development
Student Activism

SEPTEMBER 1998
Organic Farming
Cancer Treatments
Hispanic-Americans' New Clout

Back issues are available for $5.00 (subscribers) or $10.00 (non-subscribers). Quantity discounts apply to orders over 10. To order, call Congressional Quarterly Customer Service at (202) 887-8621.

Binders are available for $18.00. To order call 1-800-638-1710. Please refer to stock number 648.

Future Topics

▶ *Social Security*

▶ *School Violence*

▶ *National Forests*

THE CQ Researcher

PUBLISHED BY CONGRESSIONAL QUARTERLY INC.

Saving Social Security

Will the system go broke?

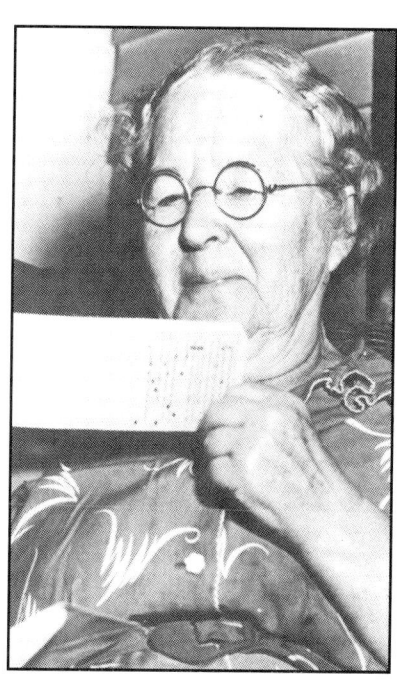

A
merica's 76 million baby boomers pose a catastrophic threat to the nation's social safety net. Simply put, the Social Security system won't take in enough money to pay all of the boomers' guaranteed benefits as they retire over the next 30 years. To meet these obligations, the government will either have to raise workers' payroll taxes, cut benefits or take more drastic steps, such as raising the retirement age. A growing number of policy-makers are embracing calls to "privatize" the system and shift some payroll taxes to private retirement accounts. But a consensus is proving elusive, particularly as President Clinton struggles with his legal problems and financial markets fluctuate due to problems in Russia and Asia.

C_Q **October 2, 1998 • Volume 8, No. 37 • Pages 857-880**

Formerly Editorial Research Reports

CQ Researcher

October 2, 1998
Volume 8, No.37

———

EDITOR
Sandra Stencel

MANAGING EDITOR
Thomas J. Colin

STAFF WRITERS
Adriel Bettelheim
Mary H. Cooper
Kenneth Jost
Kathy Koch
David Masci

PRODUCTION EDITOR
Melissa Hall

EDITORIAL ASSISTANT
Laura S. Cavender

———

PUBLISHED BY
Congressional Quarterly Inc.

CHAIRMAN
Andrew Barnes

VICE CHAIRMAN
Andrew P. Corty

PRESIDENT AND PUBLISHER
Robert W. Merry

EXECUTIVE EDITOR
David Rapp

———

Bibliographic records and abstracts included in The Next Step section of this publication are the copyrighted material of UMI, and are used with permission.

The CQ Researcher (ISSN 1056-2036). Formerly Editorial Research Reports. Published weekly, except Jan. 2, May 29, July 3, Oct. 30, by Congressional Quarterly Inc., 1414 22nd St., N.W., Washington, D.C. 20037. Annual subscription rate for libraries, businesses and government is $340. Additional rates furnished upon request. Periodicals postage paid at Washington, D.C., and additional mailing offices. POSTMASTER: Send address changes to The CQ Researcher, 1414 22nd St., N.W., Washington, D.C. 20037.

COVER: RETIRED LAW CLERK IDA MAE FULLER OF LUDLOW, VT., RECEIVED THE FIRST MONTHLY SOCIAL SECURITY CHECK IN 1940. (SOCIAL SECURITY ADMINISTRATION)

Saving Social Security

By Adriel Bettelheim

The Issues

Like many people of her generation, Claire McGrath is a loyal defender of Social Security. The 73-year-old retired state employee from Syracuse, N.Y., relies on her $916 monthly benefit check to pay her bills and views the program as a vital safety net for the elderly. But she worries it may not be around for her grandson after politicians get through tinkering with it.

"I think we need to leave it the way it is because Social Security at least guarantees you'll receive something," McGrath says. "I know there are a lot of strains on the system, and I don't blame younger people for griping about how much they have to pay into it. But I'd hate to see them monkey with it and put us at more risk."

For decades, lawmakers who considered changing the Social Security system risked incurring the wrath of seniors like McGrath and being accused of dismantling one of America's great domestic-policy programs. So few tried that the program became known as the "third rail" of American politics; touching it meant instant death.

Lately, however, Social Security could more accurately be described as a lightning rod for far-reaching reform proposals.

Since President Clinton proposed a national dialogue on Social Security in his State of the Union address in January, Congress and Washington think tanks have been abuzz with proposals to overhaul the 63-year-old retirement system. Many plans envision "privatizing" the system by redirecting some payroll taxes from retiree benefits to individual savings plans tied to stocks and bonds. Others call for gradually raising the retirement age or even allowing the government to invest the Social Security trust fund in the stocsk market.

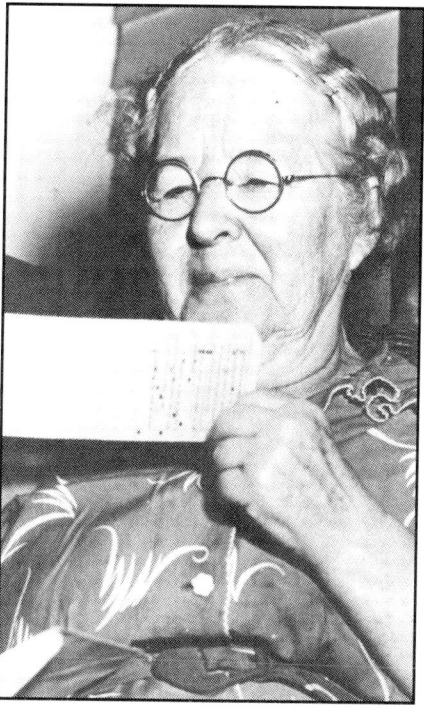

The shift in thinking is vindication for conservative and libertarian think tanks and politicians, who have long argued the present system operates like a Ponzi scheme because it relies on current workers to pay retirees more than they paid into the system. With an unprecedented 76 million baby boomers born from 1946-1964 expected to retire over the next 30 years, even some liberal Democrats concede the so-called pay-as-you-go system can't survive in its present form.

"The energy in social policy right now is to privatize," says Sen. Daniel Patrick Moynihan, D-N.Y., one of Social Security's staunchest defenders, who stunned many in March by proposing a reform plan that featured personal retirement accounts. "Any effort to keep Social Security will have to acknowledge the people who want to get rid of it, the people who are saying that government is taking your money and cheating you." [1]

Clinton and a bipartisan group of congressional lawmakers have discussed the future of the program at three town hall meetings held around the country this year. The White House, which hasn't endorsed a plan, is positioning itself to broker a compromise after the November elections and plans to host a bipartisan summit on Social Security in December.

However, recent volatility in the stock market is dampening enthusiasm for quick legislative solutions. The recent stock market gyrations tied to financial turmoil in Russia and Asia led former Labor Secretary Robert B. Reich, among others, to predict the privatization movement will stall. "Social Security was supposed to be an insurance system," he says. "The stock market is anything but an insurance system. It's more like a casino."

The calls for change are largely driven by predictions that the Social Security trust fund will face a severe financial squeeze early in the next century. According to actuarial projections, the trust fund will go broke by 2032, when benefits paid to retirees exceed revenues the system collects. The incoming money — from payroll taxes paid by current workers and their employers and the self-employed plus the interest Social Security earns on the government bonds it buys — will only be enough to pay 75 percent of all old-age, disability and survivors' benefits due. To pay the remainder, the government will have to increase taxes, cut benefits, restrict Social Security eligibility or make more drastic changes. [2]

But the reform movement is driven by more than just accounting projections. Changing public attitudes about pensions and investments have made many baby boomers and younger workers receptive to the idea of a retirement system based on accumulated wealth. The popularity of employer-sponsored 401(k) retirement plans, fueled by the bull market of the 1990s, has already tied thousands of current workers' retirement savings with personal investments. Sur-

The Graying of America

In 1900 only one in 25 Americans was 65 or older, but by 2040 the number will be one in four, putting a severe strain on the Social Security system.

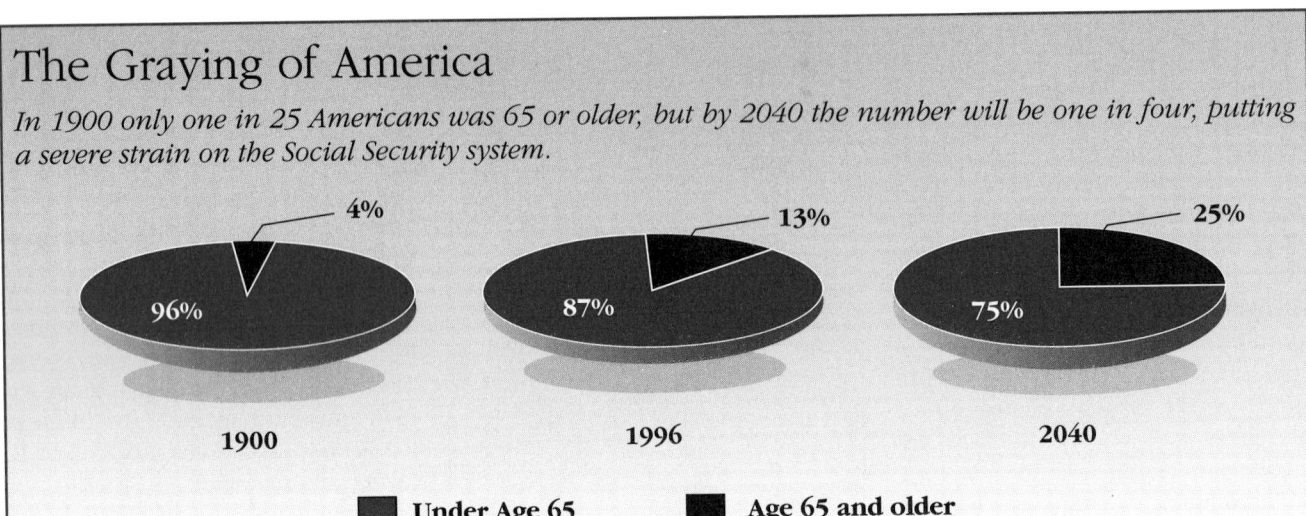

1900 4% 96%

1996 13% 87%

2040 25% 75%

■ **Under Age 65** ■ **Age 65 and older**

Source: National Commission on Retirement Policy, "Can America Afford to Retire: The Retirement Security Challenge Facing You and The Nation," January 1998

veys also suggest younger workers are so disillusioned with government that many don't expect Social Security to even exist by the time they retire. A 1994 poll by the youth advocacy group Third Millennium found more respondents ages 18-34 believe UFOs exist than believe they will ever receive Social Security.

"To maintain anything approximating today's opportunities for seniors in the future — and to do so without doing a massive injustice to younger people — we must make major changes in a system of public entitlements that now passes out huge windfalls regardless of need," says Peter Peterson, a former secretary of Commerce under President Richard M. Nixon and a member of the Clinton administration's Bipartisan Commission on Entitlement and Tax Reform.

Privatization advocates like Peterson argue that setting up personal retirement accounts would raise money to finance Social Security without raising taxes. The Concord Coalition, a Washington interest group that advocates policies to eliminate the federal budget deficit, estimates workers could earn 7 percent returns by investing the money they

now pay into Social Security taxes in stocks instead. Currently, the Social Security taxes that aren't immediately applied to paying retirees' benefits are invested in safe but low-yielding U.S. Treasury bonds that only pay 1 or 2 percentage points above inflation. The Concord Coalition analysis assumes stocks will perform at their 75-year historical averages. [3]

However, skeptics respond there's no guarantee the stock market will continue to perform at record highs and note workers' retirement savings could be threatened by market downturns lasting several years. Additionally, placing a portion of payroll taxes into private accounts reduces the amount of money available for traditional, guaranteed monthly Social Security benefits. Privatization foes such as John Sweeney, president of the AFL-CIO, say cutting guaranteed payments would be especially harmful to low-wage workers, who have less to invest and now count on a Social Security benefit formula that is weighted in favor of people with low career earnings.

Several other proposals would attempt to reduce the strain on Social Security by raising the retirement age, which is already scheduled to in-

crease to 67 from 65 by 2022. Raising the age further to 70, as has been proposed in several plans, means Social Security wouldn't have to start paying recipients as soon and, presumably, won't have to pay them for as long. Supporters of the idea say a higher retirement age additionally corresponds to Americans' increased longevity. In 1935, when Social Security was created, the average 65-year-old was expected to live about 12.6 more years. Today, that person is expected to live 17 additional years; by 2040 he will be expected to live at least 19 more years. [4]

Yet another reform plan would allow the Social Security system to invest its trust fund in common stocks, instead of the low-yielding government bonds. Advocates say the plan could boost the system's investment returns while preserving the core elements of the government's social safety net. However, polls show many current workers and senior citizens are skeptical about the government's ability to make the right investment decisions and worry about whether the proposal would leave Washington with too much influence on private capital markets.

Understanding Social Security

- Social Security, created in 1935, is the most costly item in the federal budget. The program provides old age, survivors' and disability insurance to approximately 44 million Americans. Workers and their employers fund the system by each paying payroll taxes equivalent to 6.2 percent of covered wages. Self-employed individuals pay 12.4 percent of taxable self-employment income. The Internal Revenue Service collects the taxes and deposits the money in government-administered accounts known as the Old Age and Survivors and Disability Insurance Trust Funds (OASDI).

- The payroll tax revenues are used to pay benefits to those people currently collecting Social Security pensions, a system known as pay-as-you-go. Any excess of taxes over benefit payments is invested in U.S. Treasury bonds, which earn the average rate of return on publicly traded government debt. Social Security taxes also pay for Medicare, the national health program for the elderly. The services that are funded come under Medicare Part A and include inpatient hospital care and skilled nursing care.

- Workers who accumulate enough earnings credits become eligible to receive a Social Security pension when they reach the early retirement age of 62 or become too disabled to continue working, regardless of age. A workers' dependent spouse and non-adult children can draw monthly survivors' pensions when the worker dies.

Social Security is a defined-benefit pension program, meaning each pension is based on the worker's average career earnings and on the age when the worker or worker's dependents first obtain the pension. The exact amount of the payout is determined by a formula that is codified in law and updated annually to reflect changes in wages and consumer prices.

The Social Security benefit formula is deliberately tilted in favor of workers with low career earnings, those who face an unusually high risk of becoming totally disabled and married couples with only one wage earner. It's possible to make generous payments to these groups because high-wage workers, unmarried and childless workers and dual-income married couples receive less favorable treatment under the system.

- In 1997 the Social Security system took in $457.7 billion from payroll taxes and bond interest and paid out $362 billion in benefits to retired and disabled workers and their families. Administrative costs totaled $3.4 billion. The system's assets increased $88.6 billion, to $655.5 billion, and the trust funds earned $43.8 billion on bond interest.

- The trust funds are expected to be able to cover benefits for the next 34 years. However, the 1998 Social Security trustees' report states that benefit payments will begin to exceed income in 2013, and that interest income on the Treasury bonds will be able to keep total income ahead of benefit payments only until 2021. After that, the trust funds will begin to decline until they are exhausted by 2032. At that point, tax revenue will only be able to pay three-quarters of benefit obligations.

Sources: Social Security Administration, Brookings Institution

Predicting whether any substantive reforms will be passed is difficult, given the timing of the debate and the ongoing legal problems surrounding President Clinton. Observers say a Democratic president who doesn't have to run for re-election and a Republican-led Congress have a brief window of opportunity next spring to enact substantial bipartisan reforms. Clinton, according to some advisers, views Social Security reform as a way of leaving a lasting legacy. But beyond next summer, the anticipated posturing in advance of the 2000 presidential and congressional elections threatens to turn Social Security into a purely political issue.

Federal officials and those close to the Social Security debate also have serious doubts about Clinton's ability to push an ambitious domestic agenda as he simultaneously deals with legal troubles stemming from his relationship with Monica Lewinsky. Should Clinton have to step down and be succeeded by Vice President Al Gore, it's unlikely that Gore would embrace a complicated, potentially divisive issue for Democrats that could threaten his chances of winning a full four-year term in 2000. Gore has already expressed serious doubts about privatizing the system.

If Clinton survives the scandal, his personal credibility with Congress may be too damaged to allow a grueling fight over a landmark social-policy program. And with financial markets around the world shaken by crises, Republicans and Democrats alike may have second thoughts about replacing the present system with individual accounts that rely on the compounded earnings power of stocks and bonds.

"Clearly there are a lot of risks to achieving reforms next year," says Social Security Commissioner Kenneth Apfel. "But the best thing for the American people is the long-term security of the Social Security system, and continuing to talk about the need for reform . . . is centrally important."

"Nobody really knows what will happen until the president weighs in," says Henry Aaron, senior fellow

Elderly Are Fastest-Growing Group

Due to the large number of aging baby boomers, Americans 65 and older are the fastest-growing segment of the population.

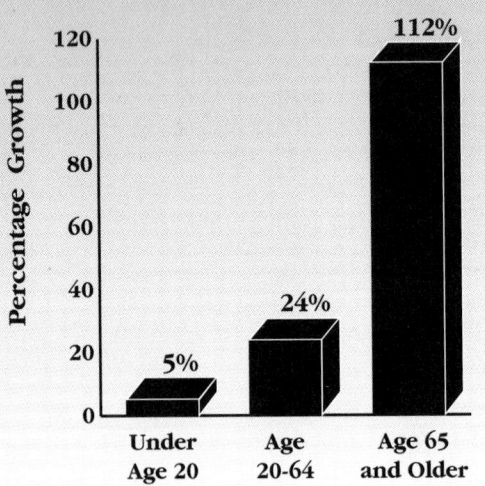

**Population Growth by Age Group
(1995-2040)**

Percentage Growth

Under Age 20: 5%
Age 20-64: 24%
Age 65 and Older: 112%

Source: National Commission on Retirement Policy, "Can America Afford to Retire: The Retirement Security Challenge Facing You and The Nation," January 1998

in economic studies at the Brookings Institution. "Everyone is putting [reform proposals] on the table. But it's up to the administration to really start the debate by coming up with its own plan. And making large-scale changes to social programs is often fraught with peril."

As policy-makers mull further changes to the system and debate its long-term viability, here are some questions they are asking:

Can the existing system survive without major reforms?

The early architects of Social Security and many liberal Democrats shake their heads at all of the recent proposals to change the system. Most believe Social Security can continue to provide a safety net for retirees and their survivors if Congress simply makes minor adjustments, occasionally raising payroll taxes or recal-

culating the way benefits are paid. Doing so would address concerns about the system's solvency while still guaranteeing that benefits will stay about where they are.*

"The key point is that we do not need to panic," says Rep. Jerrold Nadler, D-N.Y., who disputes the view that the system is in a financial crisis. "Social Security's status as a risk-free, guaranteed benefit program is, for millions of Americans, the sole protection against economic misfortune. That rock-solid dependability must be preserved."

Liberals like Nadler accuse reform advocates of manufacturing a crisis that pits generation against generation. They note Social Security has worked well for more than 60 years by providing a steady stream of

_____

* The average monthly benefit for a retired worker is $765.

monthly payments that beneficiaries can rely on. It also has helped lift millions of seniors out of poverty.

Robert Myers, who served as chief actuary of the Social Security Administration from 1947-1970 and deputy commissioner in 1981 and 1982, says the existing system was never intended to be an unchangeable or contractual program. Rather, its founders envisioned Congress stepping in to make gradual adjustments when demographic or accounting factors necessitated change.

"Fixing the system is easy, but finding the fix that fits both politically and socially is trickier," Myers says. "Some 80 million retirees and survivors will be drawing benefits from Social Security the year it is supposed to go broke. Having them go from a check one month to nothing the next is unthinkable. The country wouldn't stand for it."

Defenders of the system say the projected financial squeeze isn't as severe as it's being depicted. They note Social Security actuaries project the program's deficit will amount to only 2.19 percent of taxable payroll over the next 75 years. While that's a cause for some concern, program advocates argue a small tax increase could solve the problem without having to take more dramatic steps like raising the retirement age or making steep reductions in benefits.

One remedy being discussed among liberal House Democrats would increase the wage base for Social Security taxes by lifting the cap on income subject to the payroll tax. The current payroll tax is 12.4 percent (with 6.2 percent each paid by workers and employers) on salaries up to $68,400 a year. About 6 percent of all workers make more than that ceiling. Other options include extending the program to many federal government workers who are now excluded from participating in it, or means-testing the program to

Would Women Lose Under Privatization?

The image of an elderly widow living off her monthly Social Security check is frequently evoked in debates over the retirement program. However, the push to overhaul the program is raising questions over whether older women would gain or lose under a privatized system.

Some backers of the current system contend privatization could unfairly penalize professional women and dependent spouses for a variety of reasons. First, working women typically earn less than men (71 cents for every $1, on average), and therefore have fewer funds to invest in individual savings accounts. Dependent spouses, who now are automatically entitled to 50 percent of their husband's benefits, would lose the subsidy in a system based on private accounts. Some private savings plans may also be set up to expire at death, leaving the survivor without benefits.

Women also tend to be more averse to risk when making investment decisions. A recent U.S. General Accounting Office study of women in their prime earning and saving years shows they are less likely than men to invest in potentially higher yielding but risky assets like stocks, meaning they would be at risk of having accumulated less in their private accounts at retirement. [1]

"Difficult as Social Security reform will be, our most serious challenge may be ensuring fair treatment for women," says Rep. Barbara B. Kennelly, D-Conn., ranking Democrat on the House Ways and Means Subcommittee on Social Security.

However, privatization proponents say the current system needs to be changed precisely because it cheats working women by using an outdated "model family" with a stay-at-home mom. When the program was designed, few married women worked outside the home. If benefits were to be calculated based on one's own work history, millions of widows would be left with nothing when their husbands died.

In 1939, lawmakers introduced spousal benefits that automatically entitled a woman to half of her husband's benefits, regardless of whether she had paid payroll taxes. Thus a woman who worked all of her life and paid a significant amount of taxes into the system could receive a smaller retirement benefit than a woman who never worked, even if their household incomes are identical.

The American Society of Actuaries estimates that for a family making $68,400 in pre-retirement income, a stay-at-home spouse would be entitled to a Social Security widow's benefit of $1,354 per month, compared with $1,082 for a widow who brought home half of the household income.

The disparity becomes even larger for couples who make a combined $34,200 in annual pay. The actuaries project the stay-at-home spouse would receive a monthly check of $1,082 on being widowed, while a wife who brought home half of the income draws a monthly benefit of only $674. .

Cato Institute analyst Darcy Ann Olsen adds that working women typically qualify for smaller payouts under the present system because they frequently leave the work force for extended periods of time during their peak earning years to raise children. [2]

The Cato Institute endorses a system that consists entirely of individual investment accounts, in which a husband and wife split contributions and ownership of the accounts 50-50. If both spouses contributed 10 percent of earnings to the accounts, the think tank calculates all categories of women would be better off than under Social Security or hybrid plans that provide guaranteed minimum benefits and individual accounts.

Gender equity will continue to receive attention as the privatization debate pushes forward, particularly because two-thirds of working women have no other pension plan. "Too many women, minority women in particular, will find themselves about to enter a financial prison when they retire," says Jeffery Lewis, executive director of the Teresa & H. John Heinz III Foundation, a Washington public policy think tank.

---

[1] See U.S. General Accounting Office, "Social Security Reform: Implications for Women's Retirement," Dec. 31, 1997. For background, see Sue Kirchhoff, "Proposed Fixes Could Widen Social Security Gender Gap," CQ Weekly, April 25, 1998, pp. 1038-1044.

[2] See Darcy Ann Olsen, "Greater Financial Security for Women with Personal Retirement Accounts," Cato Institute Briefing Paper No. 38, July 20, 1998.

avoid paying benefits to rich retirees.

Another proposal to save the present system comes from Robert Ball, who served as commissioner of Social Security from 1962-1973. Ball believes the government can leave benefits roughly at current levels without significant new taxes as long as it finds a way to earn higher returns on its reserves. His solution would allow Social Security to invest about 40 percent of its trust funds in stocks, 30 percent in corporate bonds and the rest, as now, in government debt. A similar proposal is being prepared for House Democrats by Rep. Earl Pomeroy, D-N.D.

"There is no financial crisis in Social Security. But it does need adjustment," Ball says. He notes other federal retirement systems such as the Federal Employees Thrift Plan place their reserves in stocks without placing participants at significant risk. [5]

However, critics say such proposals ignore the fact that the program's fiscal situation is only expected to get worse as more baby boomers begin to collect benefits. Adding to the concerns are worrisome demographic

Low-Income Retirees Depend on Social Security

Social Security accounted for nearly 90 percent of the retirement income received by low-income Americans in 1995.

Sources of Income for Americans, 1995

■ **Social Security** ■ **Pensions** ■ **Assets**
■ **Earnings** ■ **Other**

Low Income

2.3%
6.1%
1.7%
1%
88.8%

Mid-Income

3.7%
8.3%
11.6%
1.7%
74.7%

High Income

24.3%
2.4%
28.8%
21.1%
23.3%

Percentages do not add to 100% due to rounding

Source: National Commission on Retirement Policy, "Can America Afford to Retire: The Retirement Security Challenge Facing You and The Nation," January 1998

taxes into the system. [6]

Daniel Mitchell, a senior fellow at the conservative Heritage Foundation, says the combined effect will be staggering liabilities for the Social Security trust funds. By 2075, the last year for which the Social Security Administration projects numbers, Mitchell calculates the trust funds will have a total shortfall of $20 trillion, adjusted for inflation. Eliminating the future deficit would require a 54 percent increase in payroll taxes, a 33 percent reduction in benefits or a combination of those approaches. Mitchell argues it would be far easier to scrap the current system of promised benefits in favor of a privatized system based on accumulated wealth.

"The important question to ask is whether the price tag for moving to a private system is smaller or larger than the amount of money lawmakers would have to find to fulfill the promises of the current system," Mitchell says.

Another important question is whether young workers are willing to pay higher payroll taxes to maintain the government's promise to retirees. Supporters of higher taxes say even a 2 percent hike will leave American workers paying less for social insurance than many Western Europeans.

However, Third Millennium Executive Director Richard Thau is alarmed by the prospect of ad infinitum payroll tax increases to keep the Social Security trust fund in balance. "The idea of raising taxes further just to fund the existing system isn't going to fly," he says. "The majority of young people believe the real challenge is to pre-fund the system and avoid the demographic tsunami that will come when the baby boomers retire."

Clinton, without endorsing a plan, has voiced concerns about raising payroll taxes. And Moynihan says long-time supporters should face up to reality and enact more forward-thinking reforms now, while the government has a balanced budget and before Social

trends. Medical advances are making people live longer, meaning they will collect benefits longer. People also are retiring earlier. And the tendency toward smaller families is moving the nation closer to zero population growth, meaning there will be fewer workers in coming generations to pay

Security's woes become overwhelming. "If we continue to treat this program as the untouchable 'third rail' of American politics, we could find one day in the not very distant future that the system has vanished," he says. [7]

Should individual savings accounts be included in any reforms?

In 1981, the government of Chile decided to replace its financially strapped pay-as-you-go national pension system with a program based on individually owned, privately invested accounts. The results dramatically exceeded expectations.

By requiring all covered or dependent workers who entered the work force after 1981 to place 10 percent of their monthly earnings in a savings account, government leaders boosted the national savings rate nearly threefold and solidified the developing nation's capital and labor markets. Old-age, disability and survivors' pensions in the privatized system paid 50-100 percent more than under the old system.

The bigger payouts, combined with other free-market reforms, have more than doubled economic growth in the developing nation from its historical 3 percent annual pace to an average of 7 percent per year over the past 12 years, according to Jose Pinera, the former minister of labor and now an international consultant on pension reform. [8] Argentina, Australia, Bolivia, Colombia, Mexico, Peru, the United Kingdom and Uruguay, among others, have since shifted to pension systems that rely on private accounts. *(See story, p. 871.)*

Privatization advocates say a similar move by the United States would be economically advantageous, delivering bigger pensions to workers and helping the economy grow faster. Some believe the emphasis on personal savings would have the added feature of encouraging more individual responsibility at a time when the nation prepares for a surge in its

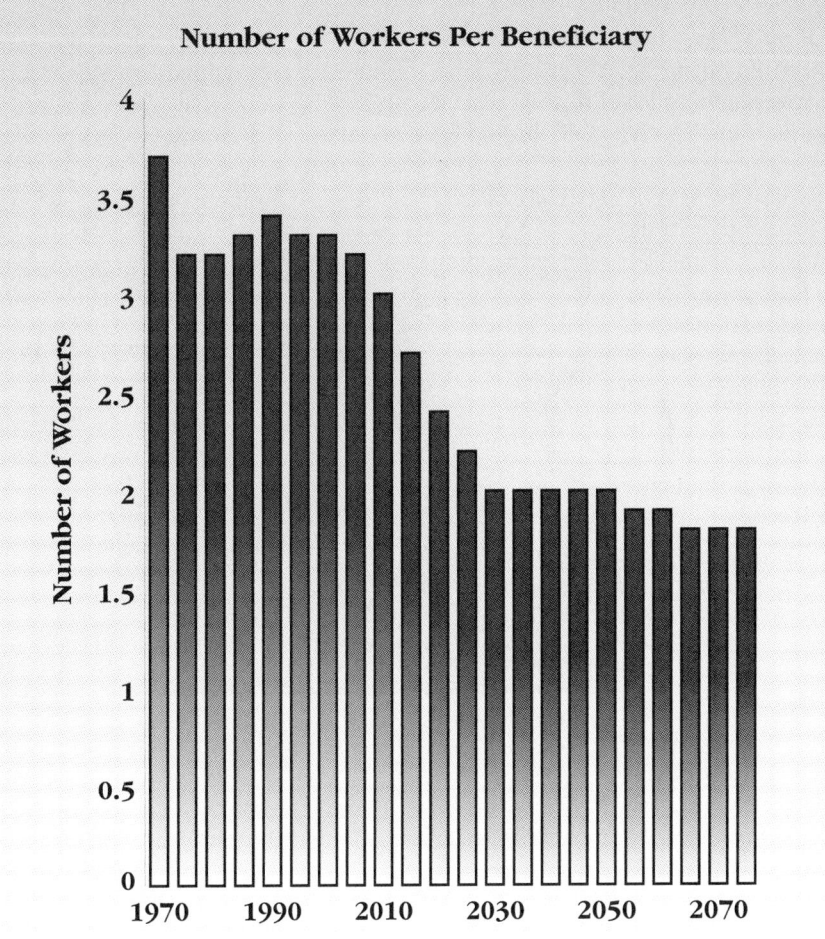

Impact of Shrinking Work Force

There were 3.7 workers per beneficiary in the Social Security system in 1970, but by 2075 the number of workers is expected to have dropped to 1.8, providing less income for the system.

Number of Workers Per Beneficiary

Source: National Commission on Retirement Policy, "Can America Afford to Retire: The Retirement Security Challenge Facing You and The Nation," January 1998

elderly population.

"Individual Americans should have a stake in the economy and more control over their own retirement benefits and the timing of when they retire," says Rep. Jim Kolbe, R-Ariz. "When you talk about security of the current system, it's illusory in the sense that you either have the political insecurity that exists today, or you have some kind of an economic risk that exists [in future years]."

Privatization would differ from So-

cial Security in two important ways. First, the amount a worker receives at retirement depends entirely on how much one contributes to the savings plan and how well the investments perform. Put another way, those who set aside more and invest wisely enjoy more comfortable retirements. Secondly, pensions are paid out of an individual's accumulated savings instead of financed by taxes on active workers.

With some 44 million Americans

currently collecting Social Security, it would be impossible to immediately switch to a private system. At least a half-dozen pending proposals envision a gradual transformation that would offer young workers the chance to voluntarily invest a portion of their wages into a private system while ensuring that retirees and people planning to retire soon would continue to receive the traditional benefits.

One of the most detailed plans offered so far comes from the National Commission on Retirement Policy, a bipartisan group of lawmakers, economists, actuaries and business executives assembled by the Washington-based Center for Strategic and International Studies. The plan would divert 2 percent of the current 12.4 percent payroll tax into individual savings accounts. Workers could choose among several investment options, including mutual funds tied to stocks. The plan also would increase the retirement age to 70 by 2029. The early retirement age, when people can stop working and receive reduced benefits, would increase to 65 from 62 by 2017. [9]

The presumed higher rate of return from private accounts would be offset in reduced guaranteed monthly Social Security payments. But the plan would design the cutbacks to hit the wealthy more than people with lower incomes. It also calls for a minimum benefit — 60 percent of the poverty line for people who have worked at least 20 years, rising to 100 percent for people who have worked at least 40 years — and would allow Social Security recipients to continue working without losing their benefits.

The bipartisan plan is expected to carry weight on Capitol Hill and is cosponsored by Sens. Judd Gregg, R-N.H., John B. Breaux, D-La., and Reps. Kolbe and Charles W. Stenholm, D-Texas. Another well-received centrist proposal is the plan offered by Moynihan and Sen. Bob Kerrey, D-Neb., that leaves the traditional Social Security system more or less intact but would allow workers to set up voluntary personal savings

President Clinton discusses the Social Security system at a recent forum sponsored by the American Association of Retired Persons (AARP) and the Concord Coalition.

accounts funded by a 2 percent cut in the payroll tax. Workers would be given a number of investment options, all tax-deferred. While details remain to be worked out, employers would likely collect the money and send it to the Social Security Administration, which would oversee the investments. [10]

A 2 percent tax cut isn't enough for some lawmakers and public-policy experts. Rep. Mark Sanford, R-S.C., has offered the most far-reaching reform proposal, suggesting that two-thirds of payroll taxes be diverted to personal investment accounts. The plan is backed by the Cato Institute, a libertarian think tank that has been one of the prime movers behind Social Security reform.

Most budget experts agree that the economic arguments for privatization are valid but say the plans still raise troubling practical questions. One concerns "transition costs." Because money has to be found for existing pension payments at the same time workers will be asked to contribute to new private accounts, Congress would probably have to raise taxes or borrow money to keep both systems financially sound for several decades. The higher taxes would effectively replace the lost payroll taxes that were shifted into the private accounts, according to Brookings Institution senior fellows Gary Burtless and Barry Bosworth. [11]

Privatization critics add that the new system's reliance on market performance creates winners and losers — a radical departure from Social Security's New Deal pledge to guarantee the elderly well-defined benefits. Moreover, it could subject workers' savings to stock market volatility and high fees charged by administrators who run the investment plans.

"With all the turmoil in Asia and Russia right now, we might want to think twice about betting on go-go financial markets," says Sen. Paul Wellstone, D-Minn. "There will always be millions and millions of Americans who depend solely on Social Security for their retirement security." *(See graph, p. 864.)*

Warren B. Rudman, the former Republican U.S. senator from New Hampshire who now chairs the Concord Coalition, acknowledges the debate could be affected by recent stock market volatility. But he says steps could be taken to minimize risks to older workers, perhaps by closing any privatization plan to workers 50 years old and over.

Oddly silent in the current debate are Wall Street investment firms, which stand to gain billions of dollars in management fees if private investment accounts are adopted. Some investment firms that provide both administrative services and investment advice quietly support diverting payroll taxes into personal investments but don't want to visibly lobby and risk being accused of acting out of self-interest. [12]

Other financial service firms are equally worried about the cost of administering thousands of small new retirement accounts, fearing lawmakers will draft new regulations to lessen recipients' investment risk. The concerns have intensified as August's stock market tumble wiped out many investors' recent gains and threatened to give the high-flying mutual fund industry a black eye.

Matthew Fink, president of the Investment Company Institute, the trade group for the mutual fund industry, says investors aren't well-served by extreme proposals on either side of the Social Security debate. Investment firms support a "targeted, moderate approach" that would allow, but not require, workers to invest some portion of their Social Security tax in individual accounts, he says.

Should the retirement age be raised?

It took a generous buyout offer to convince Carrie Cusano to retire before age 70 from her job as a purchasing agent at Southern Connecticut State University in New Haven.

"A lot of us are just old enough to retire but young enough to work, and are quite capable of staying on," says Cusano, now 74. "Raising the retirement age is a good idea because more and more people are working longer."

Many of the plans to overhaul Social Security propose allowing workers like Cusano to remain on the job longer in order to strengthen

> "The best thing for the American people is the long-term security of the Social Security system, and continuing to talk about the need for reform ...
> is centrally important."

> — Kenneth Apfel, commissioner, Social Security Administration

Social Security's financial solvency. The plans assume that delaying the time when workers collect benefits means the government won't have to pay retirees for as long and can invest some of the money to build up Social Security's reserves. Brookings economist Burtless estimates even a one-year increase in the retirement

age will result in approximately a 7 percent reduction in an average worker's total lifetime benefits.

Raising the retirement age is nothing new. In 1983, the National Commission on Social Security Reform, headed by current Federal Reserve Board Chairman Alan Greenspan, raised the retirement age as part of a package of reforms designed to save the system. The retirement age will increase in stages from 65 to 67 by 2022, while the early retirement age remains at 62. However, workers who opt out early will get only 70 percent of the full Social Security benefit.

The new bipartisan plan from the National Commission on Retirement Policy proposes taking the Greenspan commission's concept further by raising the early retirement age to 65 by 2017 and increasing the normal retirement age to 70 by 2029. The Moynihan-Kerrey plan would make similar adjustment to the normal retirement age, but not until 2073.

Such plans would reverse an early 1990s trend in which older workers like Cusano were targeted in downsizings and early retirement programs. Indeed, some companies now facing labor shortages are hiring back on a part-time basis the same workers who left several years ago. Last year, the labor force participation rate for men ages 55 to 64 was 67.5 percent, up from 65.5 percent in 1994. The participation rate for women in the same age bracket has risen steadily since the 1970s and was 50.5 percent last year. [13]

However, allowing workers to stay on the job longer could still pose problems. The U.S. General Accounting Office in July released an analysis saying millions of Americans, primarily in lower-paying blue-collar jobs, are more likely to suffer health problems well into their 60s than contemporaries in white-collar jobs. A delayed retirement age could force them to work in pain or with debilitating conditions, such as arthritis, lung disease or emotional disorders. Some might have to apply for disability benefits, increasing the cost of that program to the government. [14]

Raising the retirement age could also weigh heavily against certain ethnic groups. African-American males, for example, live nearly eight fewer years on average than white males. Raising the retirement age to 70 could prevent large numbers from drawing a pension.

There also is ample evidence that many Americans simply count on retiring early. A majority of workers, 53 percent, now start drawing Social Security benefits at 62. According to one recent analysis, America's post-World War II affluence, more generous Social Security benefits and private pension accumulations have led most workers to expect to spend, on average, one-third of their adult lives in retirement. [15]

University of Minnesota political scientist Lawrence Jacobs has analyzed public opinion polls dating to the 1970s and finds consistent opposition to raising the retirement age, sometimes exceeding 60 percent. Jacobs finds greater support for raising payroll taxes, though few are enthusiastic about that prospect. [16]

"When Americans have been asked to set spending priorities in the federal budget, they have expressed overwhelming support for maintaining or expanding the [Social Security] program," Jacobs says.

Yet Americans, perhaps paradoxically, seem receptive to working at least part of the time they are retired. Eighty percent of 2,001 baby boomers polled in June for the American Association of Retired Persons plan to work at least part time after they formally retire. Thirty-five percent said they would do it mainly for the interest or the enjoyment work provides, 23 percent wanted

the money and 22 percent envisioned starting their own business or working full time at a new job or career.

Public-policy experts are trying to accommodate this desire to stay active by focusing on the earnings limits Social Security now places on its recipients. The limits — included in the original 1935 Social Security legislation as a way of making room in the work force for young, unemployed workers — penalize workers ages 65-69 by taking away $1 in Social Security benefits for every $3 they earn in excess of $14,500 in 1998. Those 62-64 lose $1 in benefits for every $2 they earn in excess of $9,120.

Legislation sponsored by Rep. Sam Johnson, R-Texas, scrapping the earnings limits has been adopted by the House GOP leadership as one of its top tax-cut ideas. Pete DuPont, the former Republican governor of Delaware and now president of the Washington-based National Center for Policy Analysis, says removing the limits would allow the United States to better tap the experience and input of its older workers.

"At a time when the country has a labor shortage and Congress is considering expanding immigration limits so more foreign workers can come to the country to fill empty jobs, doesn't it make sense to open up opportunities for the most experienced segment of the U.S. work force?" DuPont asks. "Employers need workers, and many seniors would like to work more." [17] ■

BACKGROUND

Belated Action

Germany's "Iron Chancellor," Otto von Bismarck, established the

first social security system in 1889 to ease the financial pain of unemployment in his increasingly industrialized nation. Many historians suggest the move was less out of compassion for displaced workers than an effort to blunt Social Democratic critics of his military buildup.

Britain, Russia, France, Uruguay, Chile and Japan soon had similar versions of government-run old-age pension programs. Each provided elderly citizens with defined benefits based on strict eligibility rules. The programs were financed by current workers, their employers, or both.

However, retirement plans remained relatively rare in the United States during the first decades of the 20th century. Many in the country viewed social security as a socialistic European import that was out of sync with the Jeffersonian philosophy of self-reliance and minimal government. There were other more practical reasons: Most of the economy was still agricultural, and people could live off the riches of the land. In 1930, only about 15 percent of all workers were covered by any type of retirement plan. [18]

The Great Depression changed the equation. The financial crash wiped out industrial and trade union plans, leaving workers without pensions. Most seniors' savings disappeared in bank collapses. With few other means of support and a dearth of available jobs, many elderly people flocked to New York, Massachusetts and other states with old-age pension programs. Some hard-pressed state governments were forced to cut benefits or refused to accept new pensioners.

Facing mounting political pressure, Congress in 1935 passed the Social Security Act proposed by President Franklin D. Roosevelt, putting millions of retirees under a retirement plan for the first time. Originally, the program only aided retired workers age 65 and above — not their dependents — and was financed by a 2 percent payroll tax that was shared

Continued on p. 870

Chronology

1930s-1940s

As part of the New Deal, President Franklin D. Roosevelt launches the Social Security system.

1935
Roosevelt signs the Social Security Act, putting millions of workers under a retirement plan.

1937
The Federal Insurance Contribution Act (FICA) requires workers to pay taxes to support the Social Security system.

1939
Congress adds benefits for dependents of retired workers and surviving dependents of deceased workers.

1940
The first monthly benefit check is paid to Ida Mae Fuller, a retired law clerk in Ludlow, Vt.

— • —

1950s-1960s

Congress increases Social Security benefits and expands the number of workers covered.

1954
Coverage is extended to farm operators and most farm and domestic workers.

1956
Congress adds disabled workers over age 50 to the program. Women become eligible for benefits at age 62, rather than 65.

1961
Men become eligible to receive early retirement benefits at 62.

1965
Concern about the elderly leads to enactment of Medicare.

— • —

1970s
Congress passes Social Security increases immediately before the U.S. economy falters.

1975
Annual cost-of-living adjustments passed by Congress take effect, indexing benefits to inflation. The formula overstates the inflation rate by 25 percent, forcing the program to make larger payouts than necessary.

1977
Congress corrects the mistake and increases the payroll tax rate. Social Security is now thought to be actuarially sound.

— • —

1980s
Social Security enters another financial crisis.

1982
Inflation grows faster than wages, contrary to government projections. For the five years ending in 1982, inflation is more than 50 percent while real wages decline 7 percent. This forces the program to pay out far more than it takes in.

1983
Acting on the recommendations of the Greenspan commission appointed by President Ronald Reagan, Congress cuts benefits, delaying annual cost-of-living increases and gradually increasing the retirement age.

1985
Social Security trust funds are moved "off budget" so that the funds earmarked for the Social Security system can be tracked separately from the rest of the federal budget.

— • —

1990s
Government actuaries predict current taxes are insufficient to cover Social Security benefits when baby boomers retire.

1994
Social Security trustees predict the trust funds will run out of money by about 2030, seven years earlier than they projected in 1993.

1996
The trustees report the system will begin to run deficits in 2012. All members of a trustees' advisory panel recommend investing some or all of Social Security funds in the private sector.

1998
Congress and the White House continue to grapple with ways to shore up Social Security.

— • —

2000s
Social Security runs out of money.

2011
The first baby boomers collect benefits.

2032
Social Security system will no longer be able to pay all the benefits promised to retirees.

Continued from p. 868

equally by employer and employee on the first $3,000 of wages.

Opposition to the payroll tax at first was intense, leading Roosevelt to shrewdly depict the system as a kind of insurance program that was financed out of "premiums" workers paid for coverage in their old age. In fact, there were no individual accounts where workers' contributions were stashed for their own retirements. Instead, the existing work force was taxed to subsidize the benefits to current retirees. Asked about this discrepancy by an aide, Roosevelt responded, "That account is there so that those sons of bitches up on the Hill [Congress] can't ever abandon this system after I'm gone." [19]

At the time of Social Security's passage, American society was very different from today. There were many more workers than retired people, and the average American was only expected to live to 61, meaning many would never receive a single Social Security check. The result was a windfall for the very first retirees. Ida Mae Fuller, a retired law clerk from Ludlow, Vt., received the first Social Security check — for $22.54 — on Jan. 31, 1940. She had contributed only $22 to the system. At the time of her death 35 years later, her benefits totaled $22,000.

Signs of Trouble

Between 1935-1980, Congress gradually expanded the scope of Social Security, covering more people and paying out progressively larger benefits. In 1939, Congress added benefits for dependents and survivors of a deceased worker. In 1950, the program was extended to agricultural workers, the self-employed, members of the armed forces and disabled people age 50 and above. In 1961, President John F. Kennedy pushed through Congress a 20 percent increase in benefits and an early retirement provision that offered payouts and survivor benefits to men at age 62.

The 1970s brought the first signs of trouble, as it became apparent Social Security couldn't finance all the ben-

President Franklin D. Roosevelt signs the Social Security Act in 1935.

Bettmann/UPI

efits it promised. After decades of robust economic growth and low inflation, growth slowed and prices rose. Demographics also shifted; there had been 16 workers for every retiree in 1950, but by 1970 the figure had fallen to about 3.7. Adding to the problem were automatic cost-of-living increases, introduced in 1972, which indexed Social Security benefits to inflation.

By 1977, Social Security was facing a crisis. President Jimmy Carter and Con-

gress responded by nearly doubling taxes — passing a then-record $227 billion tax increase — and slowing down the growth of future benefits. The changes were billed as long-term solutions. But when the U.S. economy took another downturn in the early 1980s, workers' wages fell and the system faced a second financial squeeze.

In 1982, President Ronald Reagan convened a bipartisan commission to discuss Social Security reforms chaired by economist Greenspan. The commission recommended delaying cost-of-living increases, taxing the benefits of higher-income retirees and gradually increasing the retirement age from 65 to 67 by 2027 — changes that were adopted by Congress in 1983.

Greenspan predicted the reforms would keep Social Security solvent until at least 2068. However, Social Security's trustees now think the trust fund surplus will run out some 30 years sooner — by 2032. The trustees assume wages will grow more slowly than the Greenspan-led commission believed in 1983. Additionally, there are fewer workers and more retirees than when the commission did its work in the early 1980s.

The Greenspan commission also didn't fully recognize that surpluses would temporarily build up in the years before the first baby boomers retire, according to the Congressional Research Service. As a consequence, the opportunity to capture and invest Social Security surpluses to anticipate later deficits didn't even come up for discussion in 1983. [20]

In the late 1980s, it became evident that surpluses were indeed occurring and

Many Nations Trying Pension Reform

At least a dozen countries have attempted to overhaul their social security systems in recent years. Here are some of the approaches that have been taken:

• **CHILE** — Gen. Augusto Pinochet installed the world's first privatized national pension system in 1981. It requires those who enter the work force after 1981 to automatically invest 10 percent or more of their wages in an individual retirement account, which isn't taxed until withdrawal. Older workers have the option of remaining in the traditional social security system.

The retirement funds had accumulated $30 billion by last year and were widely credited with solidifying the emerging nation's capital markets. However, in the past year Chile's stock market has lost more than 25 percent in dollar terms due to declining exports to Asia and falling copper prices tied to Japan's economic slowdown. The average retirement fund has declined about 5 percent over the past 12 months, and some economists fear a recession could end years of steady growth.

• **BRAZIL** — In an attempt to streamline the economy and reduce debt, President Fernando Henrique Cardoso tried to reform social security this year by offering a constitutional amendment to raise the retirement age. The Brazilian Congress rejected the proposal in May as labor unions and rivals charged the changes would have penalized manual and unskilled laborers, who tend to enter the work force at younger ages and would therefore be required to work more years.

Officials are pledging to revisit minimum-age requirements for social security after the October elections. Under Cardoso's plan, men had to work until they turned 60 and had been employed for 35 years to qualify for pensions. Women had to be at least 55 and to have worked for 30 years.

• **POLAND** — Legislation is being considered that allows creation of private pension funds with tax-deductible contributions. The criteria for granting disability allowances have also been tightened. The reform plan, similar to Chile's, is making its way through the Polish parliament.

• **GREAT BRITAIN** — A privatization plan begun by Prime Minister Margaret Thatcher in 1988 features two tiers. All workers pay into the basic government pension plan, which provides a defined benefit. But higher-income workers can leave a supplementary government plan or their employers' pension plan and invest their contributions elsewhere, presumably for higher returns.

The restructuring has allowed the British to amass more than $1 trillion in retirement savings while controlling entitlement spending. The system is credited with helping Britain remain more vibrant and economically competitive than many other European countries by providing plentiful capital for British companies through the financial markets. However, individuals have lost billions of dollars by succumbing to high-pressure sales tactics from some financial firms. Some companies are compensating them for losses, but the actions of others have sparked criminal investigations.

• **AUSTRALIA** — The Labor government in 1986 began implementing a retirement system based on mandatory private savings. By 2002, when the system is fully in place, workers will have to set aside 9 percent of their income in designated investment funds. Contributions are now taxed before they are invested in the funds. The coalition government is reviewing its tax code and studying whether it should convert to a tax-deferred system.

Sources: Heritage Foundation, The New York Times, *news reports.*

---

being used to finance the government's annual operating budget. Sen. Moynihan tried to correct this by proposing to temporarily roll back payroll taxes, then raise them again after 2015 to meet rising costs, reaching a combined employer-employee Social Security tax of 16.2 percent by 2050. However, Congress never adopted the proposal.

More recently, Social Security actuaries have predicted the payroll tax would have to be even higher than Moynihan suggested to meet costs by the middle of the next century — perhaps in the range of 18-19 percent, according to American Enterprise Institute economist Carolyn Weaver. [21] ■

CURRENT SITUATION

Political Football

In his 1998 State of the Union address, President Clinton urged Congress to deal with Social Security's problems before spending any projected federal budget surpluses. But most observers say the issue is far more complicated than the White House depicts.

Social Security now takes in about $100 billion a year more from payroll taxes and interest income than it pays out in retiree benefits. The big surplus is factored into federal budget forecasts and tends to obscure the deficit that actually is incurred running government programs. The Congressional Budget Office (CBO), for instance, projects an overall federal surplus of $80 billion in fiscal 1999, rising to $251 billion in fiscal 2008.

Congressional Republicans, mainly in the House of Representatives, question the wisdom of keeping such a large reserve and think a portion of the surplus ought to be used to finance tax cuts for working couples, investors and heirs to large estates. But House Democrats and a bipartisan majority in the more cautious Senate believe cutting taxes would ignore the challenge of fixing Social Security before the first baby boomers retire and the program begins to operate in the red. [22]

In reality, the surplus is part of a larger game of accounting sleight-of-hand surrounding the Social Security program. The money from payroll taxes and interest income technically is invested in Social Security's trust funds. But the government really borrows it to cover year-to-year operations. In exchange, it issues the retirement system special Treasury IOU's. When it comes time for Social Security to redeem the claims plus interest, the U.S. Treasury will have to borrow from the public or levy taxes.

As a result, some economists say there is virtually no difference between applying budget surpluses to pay down the overall national debt or using it specifically for Social Security. Many suspect Clinton was really using the Social Security message in the State of the Union to appear fiscally prudent and pressure Republicans not to pass election-year tax cuts.

White House officials disagree with the assessment, saying it is possible to strengthen Social Security's financial position by applying the surplus to it. Gene Sperling, assistant to the president for economic policy and Clinton's point man on Social Security, says the president wasn't seeking a commitment that the surplus be spent in a particular way, just

that it be reserved until lawmakers have a better idea of how much is needed to save the system. [23]

"If the surpluses are drained away in the short term [via tax cuts], we're just digging ourselves in a deeper hole," adds Social Security Commissioner Apfel.

Opinion polls suggest the public would rather see the government deal with the national debt and maintain entitlements. In a recent *Wall Street Journal*/NBC News poll, 43 percent

---

"**The energy in social policy right now is to privatize. Any effort to keep Social Security will have to acknowledge the people who want to get rid of it, the people who are saying that government is taking your money and cheating you.**"

— *Sen. Daniel Patrick Moynihan, D-N.Y.*

---

of respondents said strengthening Social Security and Medicare would be a major factor in how they vote this year, compared with 28 percent whose votes would hinge on tax cuts.

Republicans nonetheless appear intent on defying Clinton, passing

some tax cuts and using them as a marquee issue in November's elections. The GOP believes tax cuts have special appeal with its core voters, whom the party is hoping to lure to the polls for what is expected to be a low-turnout election.

House Speaker Newt Gingrich, R-Ga., says it is possible to save every penny of payroll taxes to address Social Security's problems but still apply other portions of the surplus to finance tax cuts. Gingrich has promoted legislation cutting taxes by a maximum of $70 billion to $80 billion over five years. [24]

Democrats expect to hammer the Republicans, using the argument that the GOP is endangering the Social Security system so it can pass tax cuts for the rich. But perhaps the greater danger to Republicans is relying on long-term economic forecasts to make decisions about Social Security and tax policy. Even a slightly incorrect assumption about economic growth could mean the real surplus is off by billions of dollars. And global economic instability could lead to more undesirable side effects. The CBO recently revised economic projections in light of financial turmoil in Asia and Russia, forecasting U.S. economic growth would slow from a robust 3.3 percent this year to 1.8 percent in 2000.

OUTLOOK

Impact on Saving

M any experts say the most enduring legacy of the Social Secu-

Continued on p. 874

At Issue:

Will privately invested retirement accounts relieve the financial squeeze facing the Social Security system?

EDWARD H. CRANE

President and CEO, Cato Institute, Washington, D.C.

FROM AN ADDRESS DELIVERED IN PARIS, DEC. 10, 1997, REPRINTED IN VITAL SPEECHES OF THE DAY, *APRIL 15, 1998.*

i believe there is no economic issue facing the world today that is more important than converting public pension programs from pay-as-you-go government-run systems into individually capitalized, privately owned retirement systems. . . .

One of the reasons for the growing popularity of replacing a pay-as-you-go plan with an individually capped, fully funded plan is that Americans seem to intuitively know what is demonstratively true. Namely, that the returns from a privately invested retirement account will be significantly greater than the return one receives on one's alleged "investment" in Social Security. To repeat, in the United States the payroll tax is not invested, just as it's not invested in most social security systems around the world. It goes directly into payouts to current retirees, with whatever excess there may be going to help finance the federal government's deficit spending. The government leaves "Special Treasury Notes" in a so-called trust fund when it purloins these excess funds, but to see that the trust fund is a fraud, one need only consider the options facing the government whether these "bonds" are in the trust fund or not.

In the year 2010 or sooner, by our estimates, the cash flow from payroll taxes will be insufficient to meet the benefits due current retirees. Assuming the government will live up to its obligations (there is good reason to believe it will not, but for the sake of argument we will give it the benefit of the doubt), once the system's cash flow turns negative and the Social Security Administration turns to the national government for help, the government can come up with the necessary funds by: 1) increasing taxes 2) increasing borrowing 3) reducing benefits or 4) reducing other government spending. Now suppose the Special Treasury Notes are presented to the national government by the Social Security Administration for redemption to make up for the shortfall. The government, in order to raise the funds to redeem the bonds is faced with precisely the same four options as if there were no trust fund at all.

Thus, when the American government officials smugly point to the approximately $2 trillion in accumulated special Treasury Bonds that are expected to be in the trust fund by 2010 and tell us that this will help finance the system until 2029 and that therefore there is no crisis, they are being disingenuous, to put it kindly. There is no trust fund in the United States and the crisis is at hand, particularly for younger workers who face the prospect of negative rates of return on their payroll taxes over their entire working lives.

HENRY AARON

Senior Fellow, The Brookings Institution

FROM TESTIMONY BEFORE THE SENATE BUDGET COMMITTEE, JULY 23, 1998.

a dvocates of private accounts have claimed that the returns to pensioners will be higher under a privatized system than under Social Security. This claim is the exact opposite of the truth for reasons that have been developed cogently in scholarly research and can be expressed simply in non-academic terms. Furthermore, private accounts would expose individual workers to risks that are now broadly shared among workers and across generations.

The logic is straightforward. Payments to support Social Security (or Social Security and private accounts) go for two purposes: to pay Social Security benefits for current or future beneficiaries that exceed reserves (the so-called unfunded liability); and to build reserves [for] future retirees.

Whether to curtail Social Security benefits for the current elderly and those soon to retire is an important issue, but it is entirely independent of the issue of privatization. Whatever decision Congress makes on this divisive issue, current workers will have to pay the same amount for those benefits, whether we retain Social Security in its current form or gradually shift to some alternative. Current workers who support benefits for the current beneficiaries derive no personal financial gain whatsoever from paying those taxes. This situation is the inescapable consequence of decisions made over the past half-century to pay larger benefits to retirees than the payroll taxes paid on their behalf could justify. Paying out those taxes as current benefits rather than retaining them as reserves produced what policy analysts call the "unfunded liability," the obligation to pay benefits to current retirees and to currently active workers in excess of accumulated reserves. We can debate whether or not it was wise to pay those benefits and build up this unfunded liability, but we cannot avoid paying it except by reneging on commitments to current beneficiaries and older workers. On this score, there is no difference at all between the return to workers under a gradual transition to privatized accounts of any kind and retention of Social Security.

Any difference between the returns workers receive under a privatized system and under Social Security must come from the taxes paid above those necessary to support current benefits and go to accumulate reserves. The average returns from similarly invested assets would be lower under private accounts than they would be under Social Security because private accounts would be more costly to administer, and these extra costs would reduce the amounts available to support pensions

FOR MORE INFORMATION

If you would like to have this CQ Researcher updated, or need more information about this topic, please call CQ Custom Research. Special rates for CQ subscribers. (202) 887-8600 or (800) 432-2250, ext. 600, or E-mail Custom.Research@cq.com

American Association of Retired Persons, 601 E St., N.W., Washington, D.C. 20049; (202) 434-2277; www. aarp.org. This national membership organization for persons age 50 and over monitors legislation and issues affecting older Americans and provides members with training, employment information and volunteer programs.

Brookings Institution, 1775 Massachusetts Ave., N.W., Washington, D.C. 20036; (202) 797-6000; www.brookings.org. This centrist-to-left-of-center think tank assesses the effectiveness of public-policy programs and is generally skeptical of sweeping plans to overhaul Social Security.

Cato Institute, 1000 Massachusetts Ave., N.W., Washington, D.C. 20001; (202) 842-0200; www.cato.org. This libertarian think tank advocates private-sector solutions to public-policy issues and is sponsoring a $3 million program to study privatization of Social Security.

Heritage Foundation, 214 Massachusetts Ave., N.E., Washington, D.C. 20002; (202) 546-4400; www.heritage.org. This conservative think tank studies Social Security privatization around the world and advocates a similar strategy for the United States.

National Commission on Retirement Policy, 1800 K St., N.W., Washington, D.C. 20006; (202) 775-3242; www.csis.org. This arm of the Center for Strategic and International Studies tries to foster bipartisan solutions to problems with federal entitlement programs and has crafted a centrist proposal to reform Social Security.

Social Security Administration, 6401 Security Blvd., Baltimore, Md. 21235; (410) 965-3120; www.ssa.gov. This federal agency administers the national Social Security and Supplemental Security Income programs.

Continued from p. 872

rity debate may be a shift in the way Americans view personal savings. For decades, retirement income was likened to a three-legged stool — a leg for pension, a leg for savings and a leg for Social Security. But with the Social Security system under stress and employer-guaranteed pensions being replaced with 401(k) plans whose size depends on individuals' investment skills, more emphasis is beginning to be placed on personal savings habits.

"There seems to be a certain irrationality at work," says Stanford University economist John Shoven. "If you ask younger Americans, 'Do you think you're going to get any-thing from Social Security?' they answer, 'I don't think I'm going to get very much.' And if you ask them, 'Are you saving enough?' they answer, 'No. I should be saving 10 percent. I'm only saving 2 percent.' But then if you ask them, 'How well off do you think you'll be when you retire?' The answer is, 'I'll be fine.' " [25]

Indeed, studies show many Generation Xers save very little because they are busy paying off student loans and starting families. But the problem extends to other generational groups. The U.S. Department of Labor estimates that more than 50 million workers lack any kind of pension. Various academic studies show the current Social Security system ac-

tually may reduce private saving by as much as 50 percent because it promises retirement income. The studies note retirement typically is one of the main reasons people save.

Privatization advocates say the various plans to set up IRAs will change saving habits because workers will be setting aside a percentage of their wages in private accounts, instead of sending in contributions that are immediately spent on paying benefits.

But some doubt that privatization would automatically increase savings. Brookings economists Burtless and Bosworth believe setting up new accounts will probably result in workers cutting their contributions to IRAs, 401(k)s and their other existing voluntary retirement plans. Also, they note Social Security is caught in an accounting Catch 22: lowering payroll taxes to divert money to the new accounts will force the government to borrow more money from individual investors to meet its current obligations. Thus, money that would have been saved by the investors is being used to pay benefits.

"In order to boost national saving, a privatization plan must reduce someone's consumption," Burtless and Bosworth argue. They say this could only be accomplished by a privatization plan that cuts benefits to existing and soon-to-be retirees.

Clinton and other lawmakers have urged workers to save more by making a conscious decision to join 401(k) plans and other savings programs while the Social Security dilemma is worked out. Experts say that kind of forward thinking could effectively sidestep what promises to be a drawn-out debate over a volatile political issue.

Joining the plans on one's own to boost savings "is really important," says Alicia Munnell, a management professor at Boston College and former member of the president's

Council of Economic Advisers. "Life is complicated, and people have children and other immediate demands, and thinking about sitting down and saving for retirement at 30 is hard." [26] ∎

Notes

[1] See James Glassman, "Moynihan's Social Security Plan," *The Washington Post*, March 24, 1998, p. A19. For background, see Sarah Glazer, "Overhauling Social Security," *The CQ Researcher*, May 12, 1995, pp. 417-440 and Richard L. Worsnop, "Age Discrimination," *The CQ Researcher*, Aug. 1, 1997, pp. 682-705.

[2] For background, see "1998 Annual Report of the Board of Trustees of the Federal Old-Age and Survivors Insurance and Disability Insurance Trust Funds," Office of the Chief Actuary, Social Security Administration, April 28, 1998.

[3] On average, large-company stocks registered returns of 10.5 percent while smaller companies' stocks returned 12.5 percent annually.

[4] See Peter Peterson, *Will American Grow Up Before It Grows Old* (1996), pp. 21-27.

[5] For background, see Robert Ball, "A Secure System," *The American Prospect*, No. 29, November-December 1996, pp. 34-35.

[6] See Martynas Ycas, "The Challenge of the 21st Century," *Social Security Bulletin*, winter 1994, pp. 3-9.

[7] From Sen. Daniel Patrick Moynihan, "How to Preserve the Safety Net," *U.S. News & World Report*, April 20, 1998, p. 25.

[8] See testimony before the House Ways and Means Subcommittee on Social Security, Sept. 18, 1997.

[9] See Richard Stevenson, "Bipartisan Group Urged Big Changes in Social Security," *The New York Times*, May 19, 1998, p. A1.

[10] See Ronald Powers, "Moynihan Backs Social Security Privatization," The Associated Press, April 6, 1998.

[11] See Gary Burtless and Barry Bosworth, "Privatizing Social Security: The Troubling Trade-Offs," *Brookings Institution Policy Brief*, No. 14, March 1997.

[12] For background, see Brett Fromson, "A Safety Net Whets Wall St. Appetites; Social Security Proposals Could Mean Billions in Fees," *The Washington Post*, Jan. 7, 1997, p. C1.

[13] See Robert Samuelson, "Older Workers, New Patterns," *The Washington Post*, Nov. 12, 1997.

[14] For background, see U.S. General Accounting Office, "Social Security Reform: Raising Retirement Ages Improves Program Solvency but May Cause Hardship for Some," July 15, 1998.

[15] C. Eugene Steuerle, Edward Gramlich, Hugh Heclo and Demetra Smith Nightingale, *The Government We Deserve: Responsive Democracy and Changing Expectations* (1998).

[16] See Lawrence Jacobs and Robert Shapiro, "Myths and Misunderstandings About Public Opinion Toward Social Security: Knowledge, Support and Reformism," a paper prepared for the 10th Annual Conference of the National Academy of Social Insurance, Jan. 29-30, 1998, Washington, D.C.

[17] See Pete DuPont, "Punish Productive Seniors?" *The Washington Times*, Aug. 14, 1998.

[18] For background, see Peter Ferrara and Michael Tanner, "A New Deal for Social Security," Cato Institute, 1998, pp. 13-32.

[19] See Dorcas Hardy and C. Colburn Hardy, *Social Insecurity* (1991), pp. 7-12.

[20] See Congressional Research Service, "The Social Security Surplus," Nov. 21, 1988, pp. 28-31.

[21] See Carolyn Weaver, "Social Security Reform after the 1983 Amendments," paper delivered at the annual meeting of the Eastern Economic Association, Boston, Mass., March 18-20, 1994.

[22] For background, see Andrew Taylor, "Social Security Surplus Shaping Up As an Election Year Battleground," *CQ Weekly*, July 25, 1998, pp. 1999-2000.

[23] Interview in *Roll Call*, June 22, 1998, p. 3.

[24] See Robert Pear, "Wait 'Til Next Year, Gingrich Admits on Big Tax Cuts," *The New York Times*, Aug. 7, 1998.

[25] For background, see "Geezer Boom," *Hoover Digest Selections*, summer 1997, No. 3, pp. 20-23.

[26] See Jerry Morgan, "Americans Retiring Without a Stool or a Nest Egg to Sit On," *Newsday*, June 14, 1998, p. F6.

Bibliography

Selected Sources Used

Books

Steuerle, C. Eugene, Edward Gramlich, Hugh Heclo and Demetra Smith Nightingale, *The Government We Deserve: Responsive Democracy and Changing Expectations,* **Urban Institute Press, 1998.**

Four respected academics illustrate how federal spending commitments made years ago are conditioning the United States' economic future. Explores how many Americans now expect to spend a significant share of adulthood in retirement.

Peterson, Peter, *Will America Grow Up Before It Grows Old?,* **Random House, 1996.**

The former Commerce secretary under President Richard M. Nixon and chief executive officer of Lehman Brothers argues that economic disaster lies ahead if the United States continues to ignore its low savings rate and unsustainable commitments to retirees.

Carter, Marshall, and William Shipman, *Promises To Keep: Saving Social Security's Dream,* **Regnery, 1996.**

Two executives at State Street Bank and Trust Co. outline a privatization plan they say will guarantee full benefits to retirees, reduce workers' taxes and cut the Social Security system's unfunded liability by 60 percent.

Ferrara, Peter, and Michael Tanner, *A New Deal for Social Security,* **Cato Institute, 1998.**

An economist and a public-policy expert trace Social Security from its inception, contending the program's problems are the result of a fundamental flaw: Social Security taxes aren't saved or invested in any way.

Articles

Miller, Matthew, "Rebuilding Retirement: A Dramatic Shift in Generational Politics Sets the Stage for Major Social Security Changes," *U.S. News & World Report,* **April 20, 1998, pp. 20-26.**

A well-written analysis of how politicians who previously tiptoed around Social Security's problems are now offering sweeping plans to overhaul the system.

Rankin, Robert, "Privatizing Social Security has Pitfalls, Promise," Knight-Ridder News Service, July 27, 1998.

A good overview of rival plans to privatize Social Security and how the debate is being shaped in three White House-sponsored forums around the country.

Wildavsky, Ben, "Working Solutions," *National Journal,* **July 4, 1998, pp. 1560-1564.**

Explores how the concept of raising the retirement age has gained currency in the Social Security debate.

Krauss, Clifford, "Social Security, Chilean Style," *The New York Times,* **Aug. 16, 1998.**

Chile kicked off the push to privatize Social Security with a set of sweeping reforms in 1981. But the author says it has proven no panacea for the insecurities people feel when thinking about retirement.

Reports

Burtless, Gary, and Barry Bosworth, "Privatizing Social Security: The Troubling Trade-Offs," *Brookings Institution Policy Brief,* **March 1997, No. 14.**

Two Brookings senior fellows argue that the supposed economic advantages of Social Security privatization require short-term economic sacrifices.

Mitchell, Daniel, "Creating a Better Social Security System for America," *Heritage Foundation Backgrounder,* **April 23, 1997.**

A senior fellow at the conservative Heritage Foundation details why Social Security is in trouble and is a bad deal for today's workers.

Baby Boomers Look Toward Retirement, **American Association of Retired Persons, June 2, 1998.**

A Roper Starch Worldwide survey of 2,001 people born between 1946 and 1964 finds the vast majority expect to continue to work during retirement and are largely optimistic about their retirement years.

Social Security: Why Action Should Be Taken Soon, **Social Security Advisory Board, July 1998.**

An independent, bipartisan board created by Congress and appointed by the president and Congress outlines reasons that prompt action is required to fix the retirement system.

The Next Step

Additional information from UMI's Newspaper & Periodical Abstracts™ database

Al Gore on Social Security

Goldstein, Amy, "Gore Joins Social Security Dialogue, in Cautious Teaching Role," *The Washington Post,* July 2, 1998, p. A4.

More and more citizens believe the government should convert all or part of the government-run Social Security system into personal savings accounts. This idea has been bolstered by several prominent conservative think tanks and is gaining the support of Republicans and a few Democrats. Though the degree varies, the underlying theme of privatization is to reduce government benefits while allowing people to put some portion of the money into higher-earning stocks. And while the White House is sponsoring a year-long public dialogue on Social Security as a prelude to a full-scale political debate next year, many other Democrats are beginning to worry they already have lost ground in molding public opinion. As a result, they are beginning a counteroffensive, stepping up efforts to advance their own ideas for revamping the program, and becoming more vocal in warning of the potential risks of entrusting too much retirement income to the unpredictable stock market.

Stevenson, Richard W., "Social Security's Fix And Al Gore's Future," *The New York Times,* July 1, 1998, p. A18.

If the prospect of trying to fix Social Security gives heartburn to nearly all politicians, it could be downright ulcerating for Vice President Al Gore. His role in any solution to the retirement system's looming financial problems could prove either a tremendous accomplishment or a heavy burden going into the 2000 presidential race. For President Clinton, insuring Social Security's viability for the 21st century is an overriding goal, but one for the history books. With no elections in his future, he can afford to cut benefits, raise taxes or tinker with the basic structure of what is arguably the most successful of government programs. It is tougher for Gore, who has to keep his eye on crucial constituencies like organized labor, the elderly and other groups that want to keep Social Security more or less intact, while at the same time recognizing that many Americans are eager for a chance to invest some of their Social Security payroll taxes in the stock market.

Privatization

"Proposal to Privatize Retirement Long Overdue," *Atlanta Journal-Constitution,* June 2, 1998, p. A8.

The National Commission on Retirement Policy, after spending 15 months studying Social Security reforms, has hatched a plan it says would keep Social Security solvent for 75 years. But the plan includes a new element: It takes a step toward privatizing Social Security by allowing Americans to divert a portion of their payroll taxes into personal savings accounts. That one change, critical to changing the fundamental nature of Social Security, requires budget surpluses to work.

"True Social Security," *Detroit News,* Aug. 2, 1998, p. B8.

It is clear that Social Security, once considered the third rail of American politics, is now in play. A leading Democrat, Sen. Daniel Patrick Moynihan of New York, has joined Republicans in urging privatization of at least part of the system. President Clinton even devoted a recent "town meeting" to the possibility of such reforms. But Republican leaders are proposing to turn the projected Social Security surpluses of $1.3 trillion during the next 10 years over to the Federal Reserve for investment in short-term securities. This would supposedly raise enough of a return to avoid the deficits expected in subsequent years.

Georges, Christopher, "Social Security 'Privatization' Effort Makes Headway," *The Wall Street Journal,* June 22, 1998, p. A24.

Just a few years ago, the notion of privatizing all or part of Social Security was such a remote possibility that traditional defenders of the system paid it little heed. Now the landscape has been reshaped, catching supporters of the traditional system off-guard. Participants in the debate over fixing Social Security basically split into three camps. The first, call it the tinkerers, would save the New Deal program by trimming benefits, raising the retirement age, lifting taxes and, in some versions, allowing the government to invest trust fund assets in the stock market. (All the payroll taxes collected now go into Treasury bonds.) Hard-core privatizers would let workers invest most of their payroll taxes themselves, substantially diminishing the tax-financed government benefit program. A third group would create individual accounts to exist alongside traditional Social Security.

Rosenblatt, Robert A., "Democrats to Back Using Stocks for Social Security; Benefits: House Lawmakers Look to Wall Street to Close Gaps in Financing Before Baby Boomers Start Retiring," *Los Angeles Times,* July 17, 1998, p. A1.

House Democrats will embrace the idea of stock market investments by the Social Security system to assure its financial solvency and avoid more sweeping changes offered by Republicans, the architect of the Democratic plan said. The Democratic proposal, outlined in a speech by Rep. Earl Pomeroy of North Dakota, demonstrates the consensus that has developed around using stock market investments to assure the solvency of Social Security as the baby-boom generation retires in the early part of the next century. That the Democrats would embrace the stock market option represents a major break from the party's past positions, which viewed the workings of the retirement system as inviolate.

Welch, William M., and Susan Page, "System is Face-to-Face with Change," *USA Today*, July 27, 1998, p. A7.

President Clinton and congressional leaders from both parties gather in Albuquerque this morning to discuss what was politically unthinkable only a year ago: whether Americans should be permitted to invest a portion of their Social Security contributions in private savings accounts. Although Social Security has been a sacrosanct political institution and Democratic Party touchstone since 1935, a *USA Today* survey conducted this month by the Gallup Organization shows that two-thirds say Social Security faces serious problems that Congress should deal with in the next year.

Savings and Pensions

Alpert, Bruce, "U.S. Saving Too Little, Polls Find, Employer Plans Seen as Crucial," *New Orleans Times-Picayune*, June 3, 1998, p. C1.

A two-day White House summit on retirement savings will begin soon, and a joint Senate-House committee heard last week about new surveys showing that a minority of workers have not even begun calculating how much savings they'll need to supplement Social Security benefits. "Today, fewer than one-third of all Americans have even tried to calculate how much they need to save by the time they retire," said Sen. John Breaux, D-La.

Crenshaw, Albert B., "Social Security Overhaul Could Jar Private Plans," *The Washington Post*, Aug. 16, 1998, p. H1.

Corporations use different formulas to relate pensions and Social Security. Some promise a total benefit that includes Social Security, so that a decline in Social Security would mean higher costs for the company. Others promise a separate benefit that is meant to be added to Social Security, so that a decline in Social Security would mean less income for retirees.

Marron, Donald B., "Comment: Retirement Accounts Can Save Social Security," *American Banker*, June 18, 1998, p. 7.

The fiscal surplus piling up in the U.S. Treasury, courtesy of the robust economy and great bull market, will not go unspent for long. No better use could be found for this windfall than to address one of America's most pressing domestic issues: the long-term insolvency of Social Security. Of course, a key reason for anemic savings is that workers pay a huge 6.2 percent of their wages into Social Security, which is matched by employers. But Social Security is already a bad deal for young families, offering them a far lower rate of return than they could get by investing their payroll taxes in financial assets. It is tough for voters to support a system that taxes them heavily, offers them a poor return, but still appears headed for default.

Quinn, Jane Bryant, "Getting Realistic About Social Security," *The Washington Post*, May 31, 1998, p. H2.

Memo to baby boomers and 20-somethings: It's time to grow up and accept the truth about Social Security: The system won't fail. It will be around when you retire. Unlike many other proposals, this one makes some creative compromises among the many views on how Social Security should be changed, and it's currently being translated into legislation to be introduced next year.

Ryan, Richard A., "Clinton Focuses on 401(k): Workers Should be Automatically Included in Retirement Savings Plan, President Says," *Detroit News*, June 5, 1998, p. B3.

President Clinton called on companies offering 401(k) retirement savings plans to automatically include all workers in the programs unless the employees specifically ask to be exempted. Named after a section of federal law that created them, 401(k) programs allow workers to save a portion of their salaries for retirement without paying taxes until the money is actually withdrawn. Companies traditionally match a portion of the employees' contribution. Personal savings, along with company pension plans and Social Security, are the three basic sources of retirement income. But surveys show that more than one-third of working Americans are not putting anything away for retirement, planning to rely solely on pensions and Social Security.

Ryan, Richard A., "Workers Ill-Prepared for Retirement: Most Feel Social Security, Pensions Will be Enough; Only 23 Percent Have Savings Plans," *Detroit News*, June 3, 1998, p. B1.

More than one-third of all working people in the United States are not saving for their retirement, figuring Social Security or company pension plans will take care of them in their later years, according to the annual National Retirement Confidence Survey. Only 23 percent of Americans have a systematic savings plan in which they regularly put money away for their retirement, according to another national survey taken by Princeton Survey Research Associates for Americans Discuss Social Security.

Social Security Reforms

"Advisory Group Offers Plan to Save Social Security," *Chicago Tribune*, May 19, 1998, p. E1.

A group of lawmakers, business leaders and scholars is proposing a rescue plan for Social Security that would include raising the retirement age to 70 and shifting some taxes into personal accounts that workers could invest in the stock market. Besides reaching consensus on how best to solve the cash shortfall expected when 77 million baby boomers become eligible for Social Security benefits, the group suggested changes to make it easier for Americans to take retirement benefits with them when they change jobs and save on their own tax-free.

"Detoxifying Social Security," *The Washington Post*, Aug. 4, 1998, p. A14.

The Social Security forums in which the president is taking part continue to be useful. The invited politicians, from both parties, have checked their six-shooters at the door. Part of the purpose of the discussions is to detoxify the subject politically, in hope that next year — after the elections — it may then be easier to agree on a way to finance the baby boomers' retirement.

"What to Do With a Trillion; 'Fixing Social Security' is Necessary; Tax Cuts Would be Nice, But There's a Better Way to Handle Budget Surpluses," *The Christian Science Monitor*, Aug. 3, 1998, p. 12.

Even hermits at the beach know by now that both President Clinton and congressional Republicans have plans for a budget surplus. Clinton warns Congress to keep its hands off surpluses until the impending Social Security crunch is solved. But, he adds, it would be nice to spend some of the first year's surplus on worthy projects. House GOP leaders want to split the trillion. They would cut the federal taxes citizens pay by $600 billion over the decade and reserve the rest to rescue Social Security after 2012. That's when the Social Security system will start to pay out more in benefits than it takes in from payroll taxes, as baby boomers start to retire.

Browning, Lynnley, "A Social Security Hybrid Plan; Moynihan Suggests Tax Cuts, Pay-as-You-Go System," *The Boston Globe*, March 17, 1998, p. A3.

Firing a new shot in the nation's growing debate over how to remake Social Security, Sen. Daniel Patrick Moynihan, D-N.Y., outlined yesterday a hybrid proposal to trim payroll taxes, shrink cost-of-living adjustments and spur workers to set up individual retirement-savings accounts. Moynihan, the ranking Democrat on the Senate Finance Committee, which writes tax and Social Security legislation, said he would propose a wide-ranging bill this week calling for a return to a pay-as-you-go system, with provisions for workers to establish voluntary personal savings accounts. His proposal is a response to President Clinton, who urged debate on how to reshape Social Security.

Pear, Robert, "Moynihan Offers Proposal To Preserve Social Security," *The New York Times*, March 15, 1998, p. A26.

Sen. Daniel Patrick Moynihan, D-N.Y., moved today to reshape the national debate on Social Security by offering a comprehensive proposal to cut payroll taxes, reduce the annual cost-of-living adjustment and encourage workers to establish personal savings accounts for retirement. Moynihan, who is respected by members of both parties as an expert on social policy, said it was imperative that defenders of

Social Security propose changes in the program, rather than just resist the proposals of conservatives who want to turn it into a vehicle for investing in stocks and bonds.

Quinn, Jane Bryant, "How Social Security May Change for You," *The Washington Post*, June 21, 1998, p. H2.

With Social Security reform drawing ever nearer, you need to give some thought to how it might change your life. The principal trade-off is between benefits and taxes. If you don't want payroll taxes to rise, Social Security benefits have to shrink. If you want benefits to stay about where they are, payroll taxes have to rise. How those costs should be distributed is the heart of the debate.

Sherman, Mark, "Clinton, Gingrich Join in Urging Social Security Overhaul; Retirement Savings Also Raise Concern," *Atlanta Journal-Constitution*, June 5, 1998, p. A13.

In a rare bipartisan display that brought together Clinton and House Speaker Newt Gingrich, R-Ga., for the first time since Gingrich began his most recent round of attacks on the White House, top Democrats and Republicans agreed that Social Security must be put on a firm financial footing, although they did not necessarily agree on how to do it.

Stevenson, Richard W., "Democratic Allies Mount Counteroffensive on Social Security," *The New York Times*, June 17, 1998, p. A20.

Concerned that conservatives and Wall Street are winning the ideological battle over Social Security's future, liberal Democrats, unions and left-leaning interest groups are scrambling to reverse the momentum toward the adoption of private investment accounts and come up with politically appealing proposals of their own. No longer able to assume that Social Security is so sacrosanct that to fiddle with it would be political suicide, Democrats and liberal advocacy groups said they intended to offer detailed alternatives and become more aggressive in pointing out the risks and drawbacks of moving from a collective to a more individualized system.

Welch, William M., "Dem Plan Would Start Retirement Accounts for Babies," *USA Today*, June 18, 1998, p. A8.

In an attempt to expand the debate over Social Security, moderate Democrats introduced a bill Wednesday that would tap future budget surpluses to open a $1,000 personal retirement account for every newborn child. The plan is intended to be a way to establish retirement security outside of Social Security for future generations. The program is on a path to insolvency by 2031 as the number of beneficiaries balloons with the retirement of the baby boom generation. Any Social Security reform is likely to reduce future benefits to some degree, increase taxes or a combination.

Back Issues

Great Research on Current Issues Starts Right Here.
Recent topics covered by The CQ Researcher are listed below.
Now available on the Web
For information, call (800) 432-2250 ext. 279 or (202) 887-6279.

If you would like to have any of these CQ Researchers updated, or need more information
about these topics, please call CQ Custom Research. Special rates for CQ subscribers.
(202) 887-8600 or (800) 432-2250, ext. 600, or E-mail Custom.Research@cq.com

JUNE 1997
FDA Reform
China After Deng
Line-Item Veto
Breast Cancer

JULY 1997
Transportation Policy
Executive Pay
School Choice Debate
Aggressive Driving

AUGUST 1997
Age Discrimination
Banning Land Mines
Children's Television
Evolution vs. Creationism

SEPTEMBER 1997
Caring for the Dying
Mental Health Policy
Mexico's Future
Youth Fitness

OCTOBER 1997
Urban Sprawl in the West
Diversity in the Workplace
Teacher Education
Contingent Work Force

NOVEMBER 1997
Renewable Energy
Artificial Intelligence
Religious Persecution
Roe v. Wade at 25

DECEMBER 1997
Whistleblowers
Castro's Next Move
Gun Control Standoff
Regulating Nonprofits

JANUARY 1998
Foster Care Reform
IRS Reform
The Black Middle Class
U.S.-British Relations

FEBRUARY 1998
Patients' Rights
Deflation Fears
Caring for the Elderly
The New Corporate Philanthropy

MARCH 1998
Israel at 50
The Federal Judiciary
Drinking on Campus
The Economics of Recycling

APRIL 1998
Biology and Behavior
Liberal Arts Education
Income Inequality
High-Tech Labor Shortage

MAY 1998
Census 2000
Child-Care Options
Alzheimer's Disease
U.S.-Russian Relations

JUNE 1998
Student Journalism
Antitrust Policy
Environmental Justice
Sleep Deprivation

JULY 1998
Encouraging Teen Abstinence
Population and the Environment
Democracy in Asia
Baby Boomers at Midlife

AUGUST 1998
Oil Production in the 21st Century
Flexible Work Arrangements
Coastal Development
Student Activism

SEPTEMBER 1998
Organic Farming
Cancer Treatments
Hispanic-Americans' New Clout
The Future of Baseball

Back issues are available for $5.00 (subscribers) or $10.00 (non-subscribers). Quantity discounts apply to orders over 10. To order, call Congressional Quarterly Customer Service at (202) 887-8621.

Binders are available for $18.00. To order call 1-800-638-1710. Please refer to stock number 648.

Future Topics

▶ *School Violence*

▶ *National Forests*

▶ *Puerto Rico's Status*

The CQ Researcher

PUBLISHED BY CONGRESSIONAL QUARTERLY INC.

School Violence

Are American schools safe?

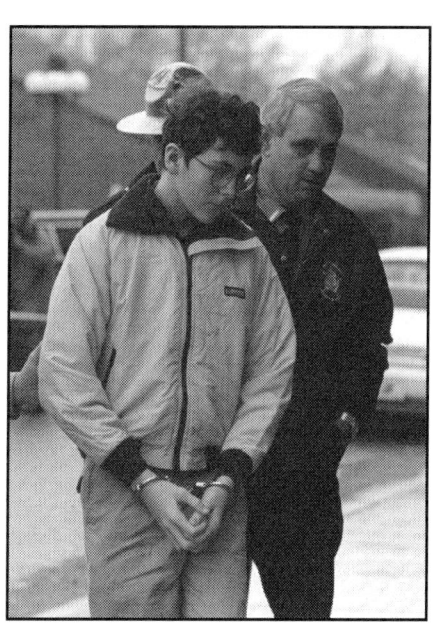

A White House conference next week will grapple with violence at public schools, including the shooting rampages last year that left 13 students and teachers dead and 47 wounded. While it was not the bloodiest year in U.S. school history, it will be remembered as the year teens turned to mass murder to solve adolescent problems. Since then, schools have adopted zero-tolerance policies on threats, established hot lines for threat tips, installed metal detectors and instituted dress codes. Many states lowered the age at which youths who murder can be tried as adults, but lawmakers refused to close gun-law loopholes that allow teens access to guns. Many parents and school officials, meanwhile, blame the deaths on society's steadily increasing glorification of violence.

C_Q October 9, 1998 • Volume 8, No. 38 • Pages 881-904

Formerly Editorial Research Reports

SCHOOL VIOLENCE

CQ Researcher

October 9, 1998
Volume 8, No. 38

EDITOR
Sandra Stencel

MANAGING EDITOR
Thomas J. Colin

STAFF WRITERS
Adriel Bettelheim
Mary H. Cooper
Kenneth Jost
Kathy Koch
David Masci

PRODUCTION EDITOR
Melissa Hall

EDITORIAL ASSISTANT
Laura S. Cavender

PUBLISHED BY
Congressional Quarterly Inc.

CHAIRMAN
Andrew Barnes

VICE CHAIRMAN
Andrew P. Corty

PRESIDENT AND PUBLISHER
Robert W. Merry

EXECUTIVE EDITOR
David Rapp

The CQ Researcher (ISSN 1056-2036). Formerly Editorial Research Reports. Published weekly, except Jan. 2, May 29, July 3, Oct. 30, by Congressional Quarterly Inc., 1414 22nd St., N.W., Washington, D.C. 20037. Annual subscription rate for libraries, businesses and government is $340. Additional rates furnished upon request. Periodicals postage paid at Washington, D.C., and additional mailing offices. POSTMASTER: Send address changes to The CQ Researcher, 1414 22nd St., N.W., Washington, D.C. 20037.

COVER: MICHAEL CARNEAL PLEADED GUILTY DUE TO MENTAL ILLNESS ON OCT. 5, 1998, IN THE DEC. 1, 1997, SHOOTING AT HEATH HIGH SCHOOL IN WEST PADUCAH, KY., IN WHICH THREE STUDENTS WERE KILLED AND FIVE INJURED. CARNEAL, NOW 15, WILL RECEIVE THE MAXIMUM PENALTY: LIFE IN PRISON WITHOUT THE POSSIBILITY OF PAROLE FOR 25 YEARS. (REUTERS/JOHN SOMMERS)

School Violence

BY KATHY KOCH

THE ISSUES

When 11-year-old Logan Hamm of Seattle went to a weekend sleepover party recently, he stuffed his water pistol into his backpack along with his pajamas.

But in the school cafeteria the next Monday, when he reached into his bag for his lunch, out tumbled the gun, which he had painted black to look more realistic. Classmates alerted school authorities, who promptly expelled the middle-schooler. [1]

Seattle schools spokesman Trevor Neilson said the district's zero-tolerance weapons policy applies to toy guns as well as real ones. "In the wake of what happened in Jonesboro, Springfield and West Paducah," he said, "we take these things very, very seriously." [2]

Five times within eight months last year, troubled boys — some as young as 11 — brought guns to school and fired on their classmates. Eleven students and two teachers were killed, and 47 were wounded in the high-profile, small-town mass murders in Pearl, Miss., West Paducah, Ky., Jonesboro, Ark., Edinboro, Pa., and Springfield, Ore.*

When experts gather at the White House on Oct. 15 to discuss school safety, they will be haunted by the riveting television images of schoolyards cordoned off by yellow police tape, paramedics rushing gurneys to waiting ambulances and police leading adolescent boys away in handcuffs and leg irons.

President Clinton called for the meeting after the massacres left a stunned nation asking how such incidents could have occurred.

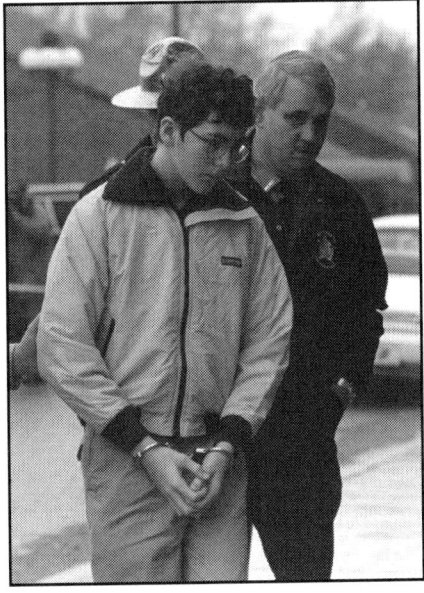

"The recent series of killings in our schools has seared the heart of America about as much as anything I can remember in a long, long time," Clinton said on July 7.

At the daylong meeting, conferees will devise ways to prevent recurrences and contingency plans for the grim possibility that it might happen again. They will also grapple with the many questions prompted by the shootings. How did the boys get access to firearms? Did they give off signals indicating that they had reached the breaking point? Who is ultimately responsible for these tragedies?

In the wake of the shootings, school officials have been tightening up on security, stringently enforcing their weapons policies and trying to ensure that such horrific incidents don't happen again. Although 1997-98 was not the bloodiest year in school history — more violent school deaths occurred in 1992-93 — it will be remembered as the year that youngsters in America's heartland turned to mass murder to solve adolescent problems.

The most reliable statistics on school deaths come from the National School Safety Center (NSSC), which surveys press accounts of incidents each year. [3] The center counted 42 "school-associated vio-

lent deaths" in the last academic year — a 68 percent jump from the previous year's total of only 25. But that was still fewer than the 55 deaths in 1992-93, the same year that juvenile crime peaked nationwide. *(See graph, p. 890.)* In the past, most violent school deaths occurred in urban secondary schools, involved firearms and both the victims and offenders tended to be male, according to the NSSC. The motives most commonly cited were interpersonal disputes. The victims last year were predominantly female.

But as many experts point out, despite the intense media attention surrounding the recent shootings, schools are the safest places for children — safer even than their own homes. "Kids are safer in schools than they are anywhere else in America," says William Modzeleski, director of the Education Department's Safe and Drug-Free Schools Program.

Shootings at schools account for less than 1 percent of the more than 5,000 firearms-related deaths of children under 19 in the U.S. each year. Juveniles are murdered outside of schools — and overwhelmingly by adults in or around the home — 40 times more often than they are killed in school, according to a study by the Justice Policy Institute (JPI), a Washington think tank. Indeed, American children are twice as likely to be struck by lightning as they are to be shot in school, the report said. [4]

Nevertheless, nearly a million students — some as young as 10 — packed guns into their backpacks along with their homework last year, according to an annual survey released June 18 by the anti-drug advocacy group PRIDE. The good news, says PRIDE, is that the number of students bringing guns to school has dropped 36 percent over the last five years.

Under federally mandated zero-tolerance policies instituted in 1994, some 6,100 students were expelled for bringing a gun to school in 1996-97, says a Department of Education report released last May 8. "Our nation's public schools are

---

*Four other multiple murders occurred at schools last year, but they involved murder/suicides by jealous boyfriends, including two by adults and a dispute between rival "party crews" at a school in California. In a separate incident at a high school in Stamps, Ark., 14-year-old Joseph Colt Todd randomly shot and wounded two students, claiming he was tired of being bullied.

Crime in Public Schools, 1996-97

Only 10 percent of the nation's public schools reported at least one serious, violent crime in the 1996-97 school year, based on a survey of 1,200 school principals. Almost half reported at least one less serious or non-violent incident.

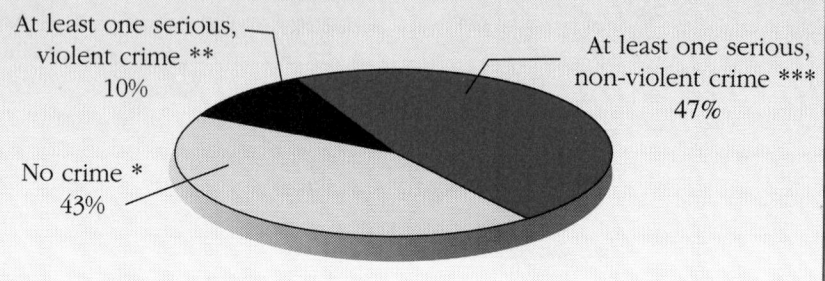

Violence in Schools

At least one serious, violent crime ** 10%

At least one serious, non-violent crime *** 47%

No crime * 43%

* *Did not report any crimes listed in the questionnaire to the police. Other crimes could have occurred or crimes that occurred were not reported.*

** *Includes murder, rape/sexual battery, suicide, attack or fight with weapon, robbery.*

*** *Includes attack or fight without weapon, theft/larceny, vandalism.*

Source: U.S. Department of Education, National Center for Education Statistics, "Violence and Discipline Problems in U.S. Public Schools: 1996-97," February 1998

cracking down on students who bring guns to school," said U.S. Secretary of Education Richard W. Riley. [5]

But while students might be less likely to be murdered at school compared with the outside world, they can also be robbed, assaulted or raped at school. It is difficult to ascertain whether non-homicidal school violence has increased or decreased over the years, because no one has kept comprehensive statistics in a consistent manner. Existing studies portray different snapshots of the problem.

According to the *1996 Sourcebook of Criminal Justice Statistics*, the number of high school seniors who reported being injured or threatened by someone with a weapon was actually lower in 1996 than 20 years ago. For example, 3.4 percent of seniors in 1976 said they had been injured by someone with a weapon, compared with 2.8 percent in 1996. Such assaults apparently peaked in 1991 at 3.9 percent and have been declining since.

Yet, another study released last April by the Education and Justice departments found that the number of students physically attacked or robbed at school increased 23.5 percent between 1989 and 1995, from 3.4 percent to 4.2 percent. The increase occurred even as overall school crime rates remained steady, at about 14 percent, during the six-year period. [6]

Gang presence in schools nearly doubled during the same period, according to the report released last April 12 by the Bureau of Justice Statistics and the National Center for Education Statistics. While almost none of the 10,000 students interviewed admitted taking a gun to school, 12.7 percent said they knew of another student carrying a gun to school.

President Clinton called the trend unacceptable. "Gangs and the guns, drugs and violence that go with them must be stopped from ever reaching the schoolhouse door," Clinton said

in a statement released with the report. He urged Congress to approve initiatives against gangs and youth violence that he proposed last year.

Although the NSSC's review of news reports found that 25 violent deaths occurred in schools during the 1996-97 school year, more than 1,200 public school principals surveyed in a nationally representative sampling by the Education Department found that no murders occurred in their schools during that year, and only four had any suicides on campus. [7]

Ninety percent of public schools had no "serious, violent crime" that year, but those that did reported 4,170 rapes, 7,150 robberies and 10,950 physical attacks or fights with weapons, according to the Education Department report. Only 4 percent of those incidents occurred in elementary schools. By far, most school crime was of a less violent nature, including 190,000 physical attacks or fights without a weapon, 116,000 thefts or larcenies and 98,000 cases of vandalism.

The report also found that most schools have a zero-tolerance policy toward weapons on campus, and 78 percent have a violence-prevention or reduction program in place. Further, violent crimes occur most often in schools with classroom discipline problems and in large schools in central cities.

Indeed, last year's high-profile shootings received overblown press coverage because of the "man-bites-dog" nature of the story: They occurred in rural schools and were perpetrated by white adolescent boys "as opposed to urban kids of color," contends JPI Diretor Vincent Schiraldi. As a result, public officials "from the school house to the state house to the White House" have overreacted to the shootings, he says. [8]

"We are witnessing a tragic misdirection of attention and resources . . . even though the real threat may lie elsewhere," the report said. To remedy the so-called "crisis of classroom violence," politicians have put extra police in schools, eliminated minimum ages at which children can be tried as adults and proposed expanding the death penalty to juveniles and eliminating after-school programs, the JPI report said. "If we want to reduce the overall number of childhood gun deaths we should be expanding after-school programs and restricting gun sales," Schiraldi said.

Since the shootings, many schools have adopted a no-nonsense, zero-tolerance policy on threats, similar to the attitude taken at airports if passengers make even joking references to highjacking. Teachers now report any mention of violence, even references in short stories, journal entries, notes passed between students and drawings of violent acts.

The new measures acknowledge the fact that in nearly all of last year's rampages, the shooters had made numerous threats or dropped hints that they were contemplating violent action. The perpetrators also had a history of violence or anti-social behavior.

"The major challenge for schools is how to react without overreacting," says Ronald D. Stephens, executive director of the California-based NSSC. He says most schools are developing comprehensive "safe school" plans, beefing up their security operations, and training their staff to recognize early warning signs of potential troublemakers. To help them do that the Education Department issued a checklist for school officials trying to sort out which threats are youthful pranks and which are coming from students likely to erupt into violence. *(See story, p. 886.)*

"Schools want to find these kids and defuse the anger before the time bomb goes off," says Barbara Wheeler, president of the National School Boards Association.

Other schools have set up hot lines for tips about threats by students so that friends worried about "ratting" on their buddies can report threats

anonymously. Others have installed metal detectors, instituted uniform dress codes and hired additional school psychologists.

Yet what has profoundly shaken most parents, policy-makers, scholars, ethicists and clergy, was the detached, premeditated, cold-blooded nature of the recent incidents.

"These attacks were planned," said Gary Goldman, author of *Books and Bullets: Violence in the Public Schools*. "This wasn't a spur-of-the-moment thing. These boys had a chance to think things over. Calmly, coolly, they decided to take care of matters with pistols and rifles." [9]

"You could spend the next five years trying to figure out if big schools or single parents or a violent movie drove these kids to this," he continues. "But the only real common thread is that they saw the way to get rid of their problem was to get rid of other people. I'm not sure there is a simple way to explain a tragedy like that." [10]

As citizens and lawmakers try to make sense of recent school shootings, these are some of the questions they are asking:

Would tighter gun control reduce school violence?

In the Jonesboro shooting, when Andrew Golden and Mitchell Johnson couldn't break into Andrew's father's steel gun vault with a blow torch, they found three guns he had left unsecured, including a .357 Magnum. Then they broke into Andrew's grandfather's house and stole four more handguns and three rifles, which were kept in unlocked storage cases.

Gun control advocates say the case clearly demonstrates the need for nationwide safe-storage laws requiring gun owners to keep their weapons locked and unloaded.

"The boys were unable to blow-torch their way into the father's gun safe," notes Nancy Hwa, a spokeswoman for the Center to Prevent

Handgun Violence. But they were able to get their hands on 10 other guns that had not been locked up, she points out.

Her group advocates child access prevention (CAP) laws, requiring gun-owners to store their firearms so they are inaccessible to kids. Sixteen states already have such laws, which also hold gun owners criminally liable if they fail to store their guns properly and those guns are then used by a juvenile committing a crime. The Clinton administration has urged Congress and the states to pass CAP laws. [11] The five states where the recent school mass murders occurred — Mississippi, Arkansas, Oregon, Kentucky and Pennsylvania — do not have CAP laws.

Supporters say such laws also prevent accidental shootings by children, a claim backed up by a recently published study. It found that accidental deaths of children dropped an average of 23 percent in states with CAP laws. [12]

In June, after the fifth mass shooting, Education Secretary Riley challenged the 2.8 million-member National Rifle Association (NRA) to help keep guns out of the hands of unsupervised children.

"Unsupervised gun use and children do not mix," Riley told 450 school officials attending a Safe and Drug-Free Schools conference June 9 in Washington, D.C. The NRA needs to "help keep our children from becoming the victims of gun violence in our schools, in our homes and in our streets. I challenge the NRA to direct its attention to getting guns out of the hands of unsupervised children," he continued.

Partly in response to the school shootings, Sen. Richard J. Durbin, D-Ill., tried to attach federal CAP language to the Justice appropriations bill. "It's time for the adults who own the guns to act responsibly, to store them safely and to take responsibility for the guns in their possession," Durbin said as he

How to Spot a Potential Killer

Most of the boys who went on school shooting rampages last year fit profiles of what kind of youngster is likely to erupt into violence. Most had been picked on and bullied. Luke Woodham, the Pearl, Miss., shooter, said, "I'm not insane. I am angry. I killed because people like me are mistreated every day."[1] Many came from troubled homes, and most had given clear warnings and threats to friends.

The National School Safety Center in Westlake Village, Calif., has developed a checklist of characteristics common among youths who have committed murders at schools. School staff should alert the parents and guidance counselors, or law enforcement agencies in some cases, if a child exhibits these characteristics:

- Has a tantrums and angry outbursts.
- Resorts to name calling, cursing or abusive language.
- Makes violent threats when angry.
- Has previously brought a weapon to school.
- Has serious disciplinary problems at school and in the community.
- Has drug, alcohol or other substance abuse or dependency.
- Is on the fringe of his/her peer group with few or no close friends.
- Is preoccupied with weapons, explosives or other incendiary devices.
- Has previously been truant, suspended or expelled.
- Is cruel to animals.
- Has little or no supervision and support from parents or a caring adult.
- Has witnessed or been a victim of abuse or neglect in the home.
- Has been bullied and/or bullies or intimidates peers or younger children.
- Tends to blame others for difficulties and problems he causes himself.
- Prefers TV shows, movies or music expressing violent themes and acts.
- Prefers reading materials dealing with violent themes, rituals and abuse.
- Reflects anger, frustration and the dark side of life in school essays or writing projects.
- Is involved with a gang or an anti-social group on the fringe of peer acceptance.

- Is often depressed and/or has significant mood swings.
- Has threatened or attempted suicide.

The American Academy of Child and Adolescent Psychiatry's (AACAP) Web-site fact sheet lists many of the same characteristics in describing violent behaviors that bear watching.[2] Its list also includes fire-setting and intentional destruction of property and vandalism. Factors cited by the AACAP as increasing the risk of violent behavior include brain damage from a head injury, firearms being present in the home and stressful family socioeconomic factors, such as poverty, marital breakup, single parenting or unemployment.

The U.S. Department of Education's "Guide to Safe Schools" also lists many of the same warning signs. In addition, it lists: excessive feelings of rejection, feelings of being picked on and persecuted, poor academic achievement and intolerance and prejudicial attitudes.

The guide warns school officials to avoid "labeling" or stereotyping children as troublemakers, and to use the list judiciously. "Know what is developmentally typical behavior, so that behaviors are not misinterpreted," it says.

The Education Department also recommends that school authorities intervene immediately if a child has a weapon or has presented a detailed plan to harm or kill others.

Many experts advise against simply expelling a troubled youth from school because such children already feel that no one cares about them. Keeping the child engaged in school activities is more likely to avert disaster, some psychologists say. For instance, Northwestern University has a program that offers suspended local high school students the option of going to a therapist instead of being expelled.

If a child exhibits troubling behaviors, says the AACAP, the parents should seek a comprehensive psychological evaluation. "Most important, efforts should be made to dramatically decrease the exposure of children and adolescents to violence in the home, community and through the media," says the AACAP's Web site. "Clearly, violence leads to violence."

---

[1] Scott Bowles, "Armed, alienated and adolescent," *USA Today*, March 31, 1998.

[2] American Academy of Child and Adolescent Psychiatry Web site, "Understanding Violent Behavior in Children and Adolescents."

---

introduced the amendment.[13] The Senate resoundingly rejected the provision (69-31), along with three other gun-control measures on July 22 — two days before Russell E. Weston Jr. entered the Capitol building and shot two Capitol Hill policemen.

Curt Lavarello, executive director of the National Association of School Resource Officers, says tightening up gun laws and requiring parents to keep guns locked up would help prevent the proliferation of guns among teens that he has witnessed during 12 years as a po-

lice officer working in schools.

"A lot of the issues that kids get into fights over are the same as they were 25 years ago," he says. "What's changed drastically is the availability and accessibility of weapons and firearms, and the desire to turn to weapons to end a dispute."

Rep. Carolyn McCarthy, D-N.Y., whose husband was killed by a gunman on a Long Island commuter train, recently introduced sweeping legislation requiring that guns be stored safely, that child safety locks be sold with all new guns and that manufacturers produce guns with improved childproof safety features.

"We lose 14 children a day to gun violence in this country," McCarthy says. "That's a classroom full of kids every two days. We need comprehensive federal legislation that will keep guns out of the hands of children who are unsupervised." Congress was not expected to consider her legislation this session, which is scheduled to end Oct. 9. *(See At Issue, p. 897)*

In 1995 about 5,300 American children under 19 were killed with firearms. Of those, about 4,700 were suicides and homicides (most committed by adults) and 440 were accidental shootings. [14] The Children's Defense Fund says that children under 15 in the United States die from gunfire 12 times more often than in 25 other industrialized countries — combined.

Further, between 1985 and 1994, the number of juveniles murdering with a gun quadrupled, while the number killing with all other types of weapons remained constant. [15]

Although it is illegal for anyone under 18 to possess a handgun, guns are easily accessible for juveniles in America, says Dennis Henigan, director of legal affairs for Handgun Control Inc. The primary route by which juveniles buy illegal guns is through high-volume gun sales, he says.

"In most states it's perfectly legal for a licensed dealer to sell 15 to 20 handguns to a single purchaser," he says. "Then the purchaser sells those guns in the black market." He noted the "spectacular suc-cess" of Virginia's new one-gun-a-month law, which has already resulted in a 61 percent decline in guns traced back to Virginia from crimes committed in New York City. Besides Virginia, Maryland and South Carolina are the only other states that limit gun sales to 12 a year.

But John Velleco, a spokesman for the Gun Owners of America, says, "It's not access to guns that is the driving force behind juvenile violence." Because the Ten Commandments have been "ordered off the walls of our schools . . . our children are growing up in an ethical never-never land, and don't know the difference between

The four students and a teacher slain March 24 at a school in Jonesboro, Ark., are (top, from left) Shannon Wright, 32; Brittany Varner, 11; Paige Ann Herring, 12; (bottom, from left) Natalie Brooks, 12, and Stephanie Johnson, 12.

right and wrong," he says.

If more gun laws would solve the problem, then juvenile gun-related crimes should have plummeted after the 1968 passage of the Gun Control Act, which made it illegal for juveniles to possess guns, he says. "If the gun control theory had any merit, we should have had more shootings by juveniles before 1968 and then it should have declined. But that didn't happen."

Alan Gottlieb, chairman of the 650,000-member Citizens Committee for the Right to Keep and Bear Arms, argues that "the knee-jerk reaction to impose more gun controls in the wake of these incidents fails to address the underlying problem. Gun control is a Band-Aid approach to a potentially serious hemorrhage." [16] Instead of gun control, the Congress should boost intervention and psychological counseling for anyone caught carrying a gun to school, he said.

Chief NRA lobbyist Tanya Metaksa says that additional laws are not needed because under the Gun-Free Schools Act of 1994 it is already illegal for anyone to bring a firearm to school. Pointing out that the Jonesboro shooters tried to blow-torch their way into a gun safe, she says, "No amount of laws are going to stop a juvenile or adult from illegally procuring a gun or knife or anything else."

Laws making gun owners responsible for crimes committed by a juvenile who breaks into their homes and steals their gun are akin to prosecuting a legitimate automobile owner whose car is stolen and used by criminals in a crime, she says.

The NRA opposes "one-size-fits-all" federal gun storage laws. "We think responsible gun storage comes from each gun owner looking at their environment and making an educated, informed decision," Metaksa says. That decision would be different for an elderly woman living in a high-crime area and a household where there are young children, she says.

Regarding mandatory purchase and use of trigger locks, Metaksa says, "The recent shootings in schools have troubled and saddened us all, but it is unsound and ultimately unsafe to prescribe a single federal gun storage standard." She also stated, "When fatal firearms accidents are at an all-time low and violent crime is on

Continued on p. 890

Society's Glorification of Violence . . .

Even after the verdicts were handed down last summer in the Jonesboro, Ark., school shootings, many of the survivors were still asking, "Why?" For many observers, the trial of 11-year-old Andrew Golden and 13-year-old Mitchell Johnson did not answer the question perhaps most often asked since the five deadly shooting sprees at American schools last year: Why would teenagers murder classmates in such a pre-meditated, seemingly remorseless, random fashion?

"These are cold-blooded, evil children," said Lloyd Brooks, the uncle of slain Jonesboro schoolgirl Natalie Brooks.[1]

But experts say it's not quite that simple. There are plenty of theories and plenty of adult blame to go around, according to most child-behavior experts.

Many say adults who create today's envelope-pushing violent culture and then allow guns to easily fall into underage hands are to blame. "The violence in the media and the easy availability of guns are what's driving the slaughter of innocents," said Barry Krisberg, president of the National Council on Crime and Delinquency in San Francisco.[2]

"There are now four privately owned guns in the U.S. for every child," notes Kevin Dwyer, president-elect of the National Association of School Psychologists. "At the same time, kids are being trained by video games to be more impulsive, less prone to think things through."

"These [school shootings] are symptoms of a changing culture that desensitizes our children to violence," President Clinton said after the incidents last spring.[3]

"Schools are being asked to pick up the pieces" from an excessively violent society, Education Secretary Richard W. Riley said. "I visit 60-70 schools a year. The message I hear again and again is that schools are being asked to 'detox' young people from the glorification of violence and to sensitize children about the value of life itself."

Many educators, psychologists and parents complain that movies and TV give kids the message that violence is an acceptable solution to complex problems, and that violence is normal behavior. They complain that children today are being taught "acceptable behavior" from the likes of shock-rocker Marilyn Manson, talk-show host Jerry Springer and the young, male techies who create the increasingly realistic, ultra-violent video games.

"We've redefined deviancy," says Ronald D. Stephens, executive director of the National School Safety Center.

"Raise your kids better or I'll raise them for you," warned Manson, the self-described anti-Christ, who simulates sado-masochistic sex acts on stage and whose songs deal with occultism, suicide, torture and murder.[4]

But parents aren't the only ones who need to more closely monitor what kids are watching and hearing. After public outcry this past summer, the controversial school-based commercial television network Channel One apologized for playing Manson's music on its news shows, which often run

during homeroom in 12,000 schools nationwide.

Some Manson fans are Goths, members of a suburban youth cult who wear black garb and like his death-rock music. In 1997 two Goths charged with committing a "thrill" murder in Washington state cited a passion for Manson's music.

Another group listed on school-sponsored Channel One's Web site is Bone Thugs-N-Harmony, whose rap lyrics explicitly refer to rapes, murder, sex and reproductive organs. Critics of Channel One say kids who learn about a musical group through TV at school probably think their music is appropriate. Jonesboro assailant Johnson was reportedly obsessed with the group's songs about gun massacres.

Some now fear that violent music lyrics may be more harmful than TV or movies. "It's not like watching a movie, which they might view once or twice," says Barbara Wyatt, president of the Parents Music Resource Center. "They listen to music over and over. It's like listening to a foreign language over and over until it becomes part of your subconscious."

Youths listen to about 10,500 hours of music during their teen years, she says. Parents complain that even if they monitor all the CDs their kids buy, they cannot control what kids hear on the radio.

Cable and broadcast TV representatives say parents are responsible for what their kids watch. "You can't put everything on the backs of broadcasters," says John Earnhardt, director of media relations for the National Association of Broadcasters. "Parents definitely have a role."

Parents should use the new TV ratings system to monitor what kids watch, he says. But the National Institute on Media and the Family says most parents find the new standards too weak. In a recent survey, the institute found that only 12 percent of parents agreed that TV-14 programs (unsuitable for those under 14) were appropriate for teenagers over 14.

"The people doing the rating seem to be out of touch with America's parents," institute President David Walsh said.[5]

Parents complain it is a full-time job filtering out all the violence inundating kids in today's music, videos, movies, advertisements and television. Many overworked parents rue the lack of quality after-school programs, causing thousands of "latchkey" kids to be left without supervision from 3-7 p.m., often with only the TV for company.

Earnhardt contends that broadcast television is not as violent as cable television. "Compared with cable, there isn't a lot of violence on broadcast television," he says.

Tell that to Topeka, Kan., teacher and mother of two Deborah Parker. She is furious that her local broadcast station has recently scheduled the fist-fighting, hair-pulling, chair-swinging "Jerry Springer Show" at 4 p.m., the time when working parents cannot supervise their adolescent kids' TV watching. She has collected 500 signatures in three weeks asking the station to schedule the show at least an hour later, when more parents are home. So far

... Gets Blame for Children's School Shootings

the broadcaster has refused, saying that to compete with cable TV's kid-friendly after-school lineup he must run the show, which is the highest-rated syndicated talk show in the country.

The aggressively tasteless program — which has dealt with such subjects as bestiality and cross-dressing and often erupts into on-stage violence between guests — is irresistible to many adolescents, who make up much of the audience. In May, a New York teacher was beaten, scratched and spat upon by 11- and 12-year-old girls when she tried to prevent them from watching the show on a classroom TV.

"Such shows contribute to the mean-spiritedness we see in so many different contexts today," says Charles P. Ewing, forensic psychologist at the State University of New York and author of *Kids Who Kill*. "There's much less civility in our society, much less empathy for people. It teaches kids that it's OK not to have respect for other human beings."

Just a few years ago "The Simpsons" was considered outrageous, he points out. "But it seems mainstream now," he says. "That's how quickly our social values are changing."

The Rev. Michael Pfleger of Chicago's St. Sabina Catholic Church worries that "when vulgar language and fistfights are portrayed as the natural response to settle disagreements, children begin to think such bizarre behavior is appropriate. This is particularly dangerous when the producers admit that young people are the primary group they seek to attract." [6]

Rev. Pfleger has picketed Springer's Chicago headquarters for months and threatened to lead a national boycott of his advertisers. Springer claims that for every advertiser who might pull its ad, "There are 20 more dying to get on — and probably willing to pay more." [7]

Politicians, psychologists and child experts are becoming increasingly worried about the long-term impact of excessively violent video games. In recent Senate hearings experts suggested that "murderous video games — more than television and movies — may do the most harm in desensitizing children to the consequences of violence," said Sen. Joseph I. Lieberman, D-Conn., who has sought a rating system for video games. [8]

"I'm not one to blame all juvenile violence on the media," psychologist Ewing says. "But I think video games are maybe the worst offenders. You win by counting the number of people you kill, and that's considered enjoyable entertainment."

Others say the fast-paced, kill-or-be-killed mentality of violent video games, which rewards those quickest on the trigger, teaches kids to be impulsive. "When a kid is watching violence on TV, he is an observer," Walsh says. "With video games he is a participant." He likens such games to the video techniques used by the military to desensitize soldiers.

A core group of video companies "keeps pushing the envelope" using cutting-edge graphics and digital technology to make the violence increasingly realistic,

Walsh says. "The games are moving closer and closer to virtual reality. Unfortunately, the most violent games — like Duke Nukem, Primal Rage and Postal — are the most popular with 8- to 13-year-old boys."

Lieberman announced July 22 that he and Sen. Herb Kohl, D-Wis., had persuaded coin-operated video game-makers and amusement arcade owners to voluntarily reduce the amount of violence in new games. The companies have also devised a voluntary, industrywide rating system allowing individual owners to limit access by younger patrons to the most violent games.

"Without some kind of access policy," Lieberman said, "these ratings may amount to little more than mayhem magnets for kids." He asked cartridge and computer game makers to also "take a hard look at some of the worst stuff they are marketing to kids and to stop making violent games that violate our values and put our children at risk."

But most kids who play video games do not go around shooting classmates. "Just because they are not taking out guns and killing people doesn't mean they're not affected by these games," Ewing says. "It normalizes violence. It gives kids the idea that violence is a normal part of everyday life."

Ewing noted that even older youths exhibit an increasing level of meanness and cruelty, citing recent deaths at fraternity and military hazings. "Hazing used to be things like paddling or humiliating pledges," he says. "Now people are actually dying."

Laws lowering the age at which adolescents can be tried as adults are "a way of appearing to do something about a social problem that adults have created," he says. "It's easier to pass a bill like that or build a new prison than to finance programs that we know work," like after-school or youth development programs.

"We've got to sit down as a community and acknowledge that our society has a problem,'" says Barbara Wheeler, president of the National School Boards Association. "We need to figure out where we lost touch with civility. Maybe we need to take the train back to that fork in the road, and take the other path."

---

[1] Nadya Labi, "The Hunter And The Choirboy," *Time*, April 6, 1998.

[2] Richard Lacayo, "Toward the Root of the Evil," *Time*, April 6, 1998.

[3] "Clinton Says School Shooting Incidents Reflect 'Changing Culture,' " *The Washington Post*, May 24, 1998.

[4] Quoted in "This Man Wants to Raise Your Children," *Entertainment Monitor*, May/June 1996, p. 19.

[5] Press release, April 23, 1998, issued with the release of the survey.

[6] Steve Brennan, "Chicago priest out to collar 'Springer,' " BPI Entertainment News Wire, Aug. 26, 1998.

[7] Leslie Ryan, "Springer not worried about ads," *Electronic Media*, Sept. 21, 1998.

[8] Press conference, July 22, 1998.

Violent Deaths in Schools

The number of school-associated deaths dropped by nearly 25 percent from 1992-93 to 1997-98. *

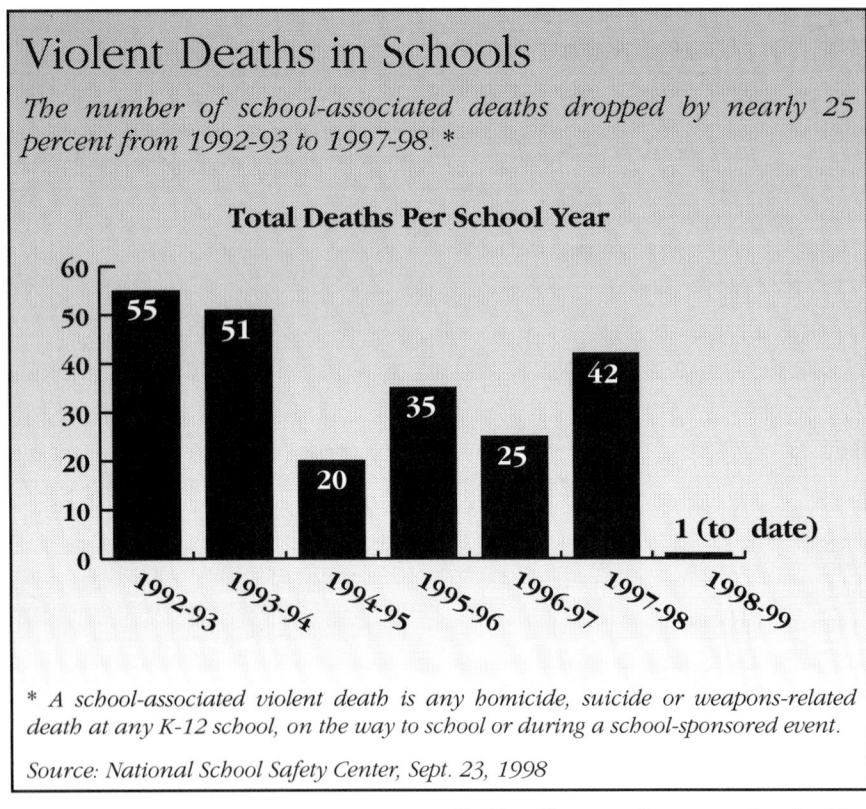

Total Deaths Per School Year

55	51	20	35	25	42	1 (to date)
1992-93	1993-94	1994-95	1995-96	1996-97	1997-98	1998-99

* *A school-associated violent death is any homicide, suicide or weapons-related death at any K-12 school, on the way to school or during a school-sponsored event.*

Source: National School Safety Center, Sept. 23, 1998

Continued from p. 887

the decline, it is senseless to propose ineffective laws that will only restrict the freedoms of law-abiding citizens and the fundamental right of self-defense."

One way to prevent kids from murdering at school, she says, is to "take threats more seriously. The kids involved last year gave lots of warning signs that nobody took seriously."

Should youths who commit adult crimes be tried as adults?

Shortly after the Jonesboro shootings, an elderly man sipping coffee at a Waffle House in a nearby town said, "I don't care how old they are; if they kill somebody, they ought to die. I don't care if they're 5 years old. The Bible says an eye for an eye and a tooth for a tooth. They need to change the law." [17]

He was referring to an Arkansas law under which the Jonesboro shooters, who were 11 and 13 when they were arrested, could not be tried as adults. Even though they have since been convicted, they can only be held until age 18 in a juvenile

facility. The state has vowed to build a special facility to hold them until they reach 21, when they must be released.

Yet in Pearl, Miss., Luke Woodham, 17, was tried as an adult for killing his mother the same day that he opened fire on classmates. He won't be eligible for parole until he is 65.

The two cases show how state laws differ in the way they treat violent juveniles. In recent years many states have lowered the age at which violent youths can be tried as adults, and Arkansas legislators say they'll do the same.

For much of this century, the juvenile justice system subscribed to the notion that children committing crimes should be treated rather than punished. That attitude began changing in the late 1980s as crack cocaine entered the American scene, and the nature of juvenile crime changed from truancy, vandalism and joy-riding in stolen cars to assault, rape and murder.

Juveniles under 18 accounted for 13 percent of all violent crimes "cleared" by arrest in 1996, according to the FBI,

and juvenile violent crime increased much faster than adult violent crime. Further, juvenile lawbreakers are getting younger and younger. Since 1965, the number of 12-year-olds arrested for violent crimes has doubled, and the number of 13- and 14-year-olds has tripled, according to the FBI. [18]

"Those statistics are a major reason why we need to revamp our antiquated juvenile justice system," wrote Linda J. Collier, a Pennsylvania juvenile court lawyer, who teaches on juvenile justice at Cabrini College in Radnor, Pa. "Too many states still treat violent offenders under 16 as juveniles who belong in the juvenile system."

Since 1994, the laws in 43 states have been changed to make it easier to prosecute juveniles as adults.

Proponents of the "adult-crime, adult-time" philosophy blame much of today's juvenile crime rate on an overly permissive juvenile justice system at which too many teenagers thumb their noses. The NRA says, "The young criminal's closest accomplice is a juvenile justice system that fails to mete out adult time for adult crime." [19]

School resource officer Lavarello says that when he warns kids about possible jail terms if they commit a crime, they don't believe him. "They tell me, 'That's not true, because I have a friend who did that, and he's not in jail,'" says Lavarello.

Under the current system, 40 percent of juveniles age 15 and older do not serve any time when they commit crimes, Rep. Mark Souder, R-Ind., said on Sept. 15, encouraging the House to pass a bill that would allow juveniles as young as 14 to be tried as adults for violent or drug crimes.

"There should be a price to pay if someone shoots somebody, if they rape somebody or if they use a gun in an armed robbery," he said. "We have spent too much time worrying about these juveniles without thinking about the people, who are terrorized by these young people."

Lavarello agrees. "Kids as young

as 12 know the dangers of shooting a gun," he says. "They need to know that there will be consequences."

Opponents of trying youths as adults say teens do not really understand the long-range implications of their actions. Sending them to an adult prison, where they are more likely to be beaten or raped, only transforms them into even harder criminals, creating more and worse crime in the long run, they argue.

"Juveniles who come from dysfunctional families need more than being locked up," said Texas Democratic Rep. Sheila Jackson-Lee, arguing against the bill. The legislation eventually passed the House, 280-126, and is awaiting conference action.

"It's just another step towards dismantling the juvenile justice system," says Charles P. Ewing, a forensic psychologist at the State University of New York at Buffalo and author of *Kids Who Kill*. "Children don't have the cognitive capacity of adults," he continues. "That's why we limit their rights to marry, drive, drink and buy cigarettes. But yet we're saying, 'Oh, but, by the way, if you commit a crime, you're suddenly an adult.'

"It's a way of appearing to do something about a problem that adults created," he adds, namely a society that inundates youths with violence in music, movies, video games and television, and allows them easy access to guns. "It's a social problem that we've all created."

It is more politically popular to try kids as adults and build more prisons than to fund programs known to work, like after-school recreational programs, youth development programs and crime prevention and intervention programs, he says.

Criminologist Jeffrey Fagan, of the Center for Violence Research and Prevention at Columbia University's School of Public Health, agrees. "These laws are about symbolism, not about substance," he says, noting that juveniles retained in adult jails have higher recidivism rates than those kept in juvenile court.

Ironically, he points out, Congress and the states are lowering the minimum ages just as juvenile crime is declining, after peaking in 1994. "The laws are targeting a problem that is far less of a problem than it was five years ago," Fagan says. "So the public is being sold a bill of goods."

Some states are successfully fighting juvenile crime by taking an innovative approach that combines heavy-duty early intervention for at-risk youths, while making sure juveniles are held accountable for even minor first-offenses. Then if juveniles become violent offenders despite the early interventions, they are tried as adults.

"If the attempt to rehabilitate juvenile delinquents is unsuccessful," said Harry L. Shorstein, state attorney for Florida's 4th Judicial Circuit in Jacksonville, "then it is my firm belief that we should treat habitual and violent juvenile criminals like adults." [20]

Shorstein's innovative program, however, does not just toss juveniles into adult jails, where they are more likely to be beaten and raped. Juveniles are tried as adults but are then segregated into juvenile jail facilities, where they must attend school and meet with an adult mentor. The program has resulted in a 78 percent drop in juvenile homicide, a 53 percent reduction in rapes committed by juveniles and a 58 percent drop in juvenile auto theft. [21]

"Prevention efforts cannot succeed if those not abiding by the law do not believe there is a consequence to criminal behavior," Shorstein told a Senate subcommittee hearing on Sept. 10. ∎

BACKGROUND

Unruly Students

School violence is not new. School-children in 17th-century France were often armed, and dueled, brawled, mutinied and beat teachers, according to Alexander Volokh, author of "Making Schools Safe," a study of school violence conducted for the Reason Public Policy Institute (RPPI).

"Schoolmasters were afraid for their lives, and other people wouldn't walk past schools because they were afraid of being attacked," said Volokh. [22]

Student mutinies, strikes and violence were also common in English public schools between 1775 and 1836, forcing schoolmasters to seek help from the military, he said. In 1797 when one group of British boys was ordered to pay for damages they had done to a tradesman, they blew up their headmaster's office door, set fire to his office and withdrew to an island in a nearby lake. "British constables finally took the island by force," said Volokh.

Early American schools had their share of unruly students. In Colonial times, students mutinied at more than 300 schools each year, often chasing off or locking out the teacher. In 1837, nearly 400 schools in Massachusetts were vandalized.

Yet in modern times, standards for classroom discipline and the definition of what is acceptable student behavior have changed dramatically in America. Corporal punishment doled out by ruler- and rod-wielding pioneer teachers is much less common today, having been replaced by judicial due process, concern for students' rights and efforts to build self-esteem.*

The classroom began changing in the early 1900s with the advent of the "progressive" education movement, which eschewed authoritarian methods of discipline and encouraged teachers to recognize students as individuals. Progressive education, although criticized as too permissive,

---

*Corporal punishment is still allowed in 23 states, but it has been outlawed in more than half of the individual school districts in those states.

was first embraced by experimental private schools and eventually gained wide acceptance during the first 50 years of this century. [23]

Students' Rights

In the 1960s, the anti-war, anti-establishment rebellion of college students spilled over into the high schools, leading students to question authority and the status quo. Then in 1967, the Supreme Court held in *Gault v. Arizona* that juveniles in court must be given the same rights and protections as adults. [24] The decision made schools and law enforcement officials more reluctant to send kids away to training schools, especially for offenses like truancy or misbehavior, which would not be crimes if committed by an adult.

In 1975, two precedent-setting developments made it extremely difficult for teachers to kick violent or disruptive students out of class. The first was a landmark ruling in *Goss v. Lopez*, in which the Supreme Court said students could not be suspended without due process of law.

"Many central-city schools have tended to abandon expulsion as the ultimate enforcer of discipline," wrote Jackson Toby, director of Rutgers University's Institute for Criminological Research. [25]

Secondly, Congress passed the Education for All Handicapped Children Act, which mandated that all children be educated in the "least restrictive environment" possible. That law required that handicapped students be "mainstreamed" into regular classrooms, along with emotionally disturbed students with severe behavioral and disciplinary problems.

"Youngsters who in the past would not have gone to regular school because of their negative behavior

are now attending mainstream schools," writes Connecticut school counselor Carl Bosch, in his book *Schools Under Seige, Guns, Gangs and Hidden Dangers.* [26]

At the same time, school officials became skittish about sending kids to alternative schools, designed for students with severe discipline problems and those expelled for carrying weapons. The schools were criticized as "dumping grounds" for minorities.

"Schools in most big cities have given up and keep kids in school who are sufficiently troublesome that it's very difficult to maintain an educational program," wrote Toby.

Over time, lack of discipline in the classroom translates into violence in the hallways, according to several studies. "In most schools it's not the sensational acts of violence, but the smaller acts of aggression, threats, scuffles, constant back talk that take a terrible toll on the atmosphere of learning, on the morale of teachers on the attitudes of students," said Clinton, in a July 20 speech before the American Federation of Teachers.

Guns and Gangs

In 1990 Congress created "gun-free school zones," making it a felony to bring guns within 1,000 feet of any school. Then in 1994, Congress passed the Gun-Free Schools Act, requiring mandatory one-year expulsion for any student caught with a firearm at school.

Nonetheless, of the nearly 1 million kids who carried a gun to school last year, almost half of them attended school armed on six or more occasions, according to PRIDE. More than half those who carried guns to school said they had threatened to harm a teacher, and two-thirds said they had threatened to harm another student. Of the students who carried

a gun to school, 59 percent were white, 18 percent were black and 12 percent were Hispanic. [27]

"These chilling numbers suggest that for every classroom of 30 students, in every school in America, on average one student has attended school with a gun in grades six through 12," said Thomas J. Gleaton, one of the authors of the nationwide survey of 154,350 students. [28]

Experts say that most students who carry guns to school do so for protection.

The presence of gangs in schools contributes to the violence. In 1989 only 15.3 percent of students nationwide reported gangs in their schools, compared with 28.4 percent in 1995. Thirty-one percent of the public school students questioned had gangs in their schools, compared with 7 percent in private schools. [29]

Gangs were most prevalent in urban schools, where 40.7 percent of students in 1995 reported gangs in their schools, compared with 24.8 percent in 1989. In suburban schools the percent of students reporting gangs almost doubled, from 14 percent to 26.3 percent, during the same period. The largest growth in gangs occurred in rural schools, where the percent of students reporting gangs jumped from 7.8 percent to 19.9 percent.

Criminologists warn that statistics on gangs should be viewed skeptically. "What we used to call peer groups are now called gangs," said Jack Levin, director of the Program for the Study of Violence at Northeastern University in Boston. [30]

Declining Violence

JPI's Schiraldi says that even though the schoolhouse shootings last year occurred in rural schools, country towns and their schools are still relatively safe places. Three rural towns where school shootings occurred last year — West Paducah, Pearl and

Continued on p. 894

Chronology

1800s *Concept of juvenile justice emerges, with "training" schools and separate courts established to keep youths out of adult jails.*

1847
The first publicly funded schools for delinquents are founded in Massachusetts.

1899
Illinois establishes the first statewide court for children.

— • —

1900s *Progressive education movement challenges emphasis on strict discipline in public schools.*

1918
National Education Association issues an influential report promoting the command of fundamental processes and the worthwhile use of leisure as educational goals and repudiating academic mastery as a goal for secondary education. The report has a pervasive influence on American public schools through the 1950s.

1919
Progressive Education Association is established.

— • —

1940s-1950s *Educators still embrace progressive education, but a rise in juvenile delinquency after World War II spurs public support school discipline.*

1955
Progressive Education Association disbands.

1957
The Soviet Union's launch of Sputnik I ignites a public uproar over concern that the United States lost the space race because of lagging educational standards.

— • —

1960s-1970s *Vietnam War protests trickle down to high schools. Courts begin extending human-rights and due-process protections to students. Schools hire security forces as vandalism, burglary and assault increase.*

1967
In *Gault v. Arizona*, the Supreme Court rules that children in juvenile court must be accorded the same procedural protections as adults on trial.

1975
In *Goss v. Lopez*, the Supreme Court rules that students cannot be suspended without due process. The Education for All Handicapped Children Act mandates that all children be educated in the "least restrictive environment" possible.

1978
National Institute of Education publishes "Violent Schools — Safe Schools," showing that school violence is national in scope.

— • —

1980s *Juvenile crime becomes more violent as crack cocaine hits the streets*

and homicide among young, black males reaches epidemic proportions.

1988
On Sept. 26, a 19-year-old gunman opens fire on a Greenwood, S.C., schoolyard, killing two and wounding nine.

1989
On Jan. 17, a man with an AK-47 assault rifle fires on a Stockton, Calif., school playground. Six die and 30 are wounded.

— • —

1990s *Violent juvenile crime rises to a peak in 1995 and then decreases.*

1990
Congress creates "gun-free school zones," making it a felony to bring guns within 1,000 feet of any school.

1992-93
Fifty-five violent deaths occur on school property and at school functions.

1994
Congress passes the Gun-Free Schools Act, requiring one-year expulsion for any student caught with a firearm at school.

1997-98
Students commit mass murder five times within eight months by firing on classmates in school settings, all in rural towns. Thirteen are killed and 47 wounded.

1998
On July 22 the Senate kills an amendment making it a felony if gun owners do not keep their guns locked away from children.

Continued from p. 892

Jonesboro — had no juvenile homicide arrests in the year before these highly publicized cases, "strongly suggesting that they are idiosyncratic events rather than evidence of a trend," said a JPI press release. In Jonesboro, for example, the number of juveniles arrested for violent offenses dropped 39 percent between 1993 and 1996.

Noting that some states have reacted to the shootings by lowering the age at which juveniles who commit violent crimes can be tried as adults, Schiraldi said, "We continue to let the tail of a few isolated cases wag the dog of the juvenile justice system. Despite these tragic cases, the fact remains that citizens in rural communities are still very safe from violent juvenile crime."

However, FBI statistics show that violent juvenile crime has increased in the nation's rural communities, even as juvenile crime nationwide is declining. For instance, rural juveniles were arrested for murder and manslaughter 14.9 percent more often in 1996 than in 1990, while juvenile homicide/manslaughter arrests declined 14.8 percent in the cities and a dramatic 26 percent in the suburbs during that same time period.

But only 100 murders were committed by juveniles in rural areas in 1996, compared with 1,868 in the cities, notes JPI researcher Jason Ziedenberg. "There is definitely a juvenile crime problem in this country," he says, "but it is not concentrated in rural areas. It is still most predominant in the cities."

Schools all over the country must cope with the same negative influences that society as a whole grapples with, writes Bosch. "Schools cannot shut their doors and expect a safe 'castle' where outside influences don't enter," he continues. "Violence in schools . . . is brought into classrooms because it exists in society, in the home and in entertainment." [31]

Ironically, even as these bizarre school shootings were shocking the nation the overall juvenile murder rate was dropping. Federal Bureau of Investigation

(FBI) 1996 statistics show that youth violence peaked in 1994 and has declined since then. Between 1994 and 1996, the number of juveniles arrested for murder declined 30 percent, and juvenile arrests for all violent crimes dropped 12 percent.

Schiraldi attributes the drop to diminished access to handguns — such as one-gun-a-month laws enacted in three states — and improving economic conditions for teenagers. For example, between 1995 and 1997, as juvenile homicide rates were falling the unemployment rate for adolescents dropped 10 percent, he points out.

Contrary to the impression that murderers are getting younger and younger, FBI statistics show that in 1965 — 33 years ago — 25 children under the age of 13 were arrested for homicide compared with only 16 in 1996. Further, 93 percent of America's counties had either one or no juvenile homicides in 1995, up from 92 percent in 1994. [32]

Noting those encouraging statistics, JPI's Schiraldi said that while incidents like the Jonesboro shootings are "so tragic as to defy description," parents should remember that "cases like this are still very much the aberration, and not the norm." ∎

CURRENT SITUATION

Clinton's Initiatives

Citing the Education/Justice Department report on school violence last April, Clinton called the increase in violence and gangs in schools unacceptable and urged Congress to approve anti-violence initiatives he proposed in his January budget. Those initiatives focus on "what we know

works: tough, targeted deterrence and better anti-gang prevention," he said in a written statement

Among other things, Clinton has promoted greater use of school uniforms and curfews, cracking down on truancy and zero-tolerance for guns in schools. In addition, the Department of Education has issued its "early warning" handbook for identifying violence-prone students.

In a meeting with school security officers in June, Education Secretary Riley asked what single change would help end school violence. The officers unanimously said that reducing overcrowding would help the most.

In its budget proposal for fiscal 1999, the administration asked Congress to provide $12.4 billion over seven years to help school districts hire and train 100,000 new teachers, in order to reduce class size in grades one through three to an average of 18 students. Neither the House nor the Senate agreed to the request, but it was expected to be offered as an amendment before the bill is finalized.

The administration's 1999 budget also asked Congress to:

• Provide $50 million for 1,300 drug and violence prevention coordinators for 6,500 middle schools with drug and violence problems. Both the House and the Senate rejected the request.

• Dramatically increase federal funding for after-school programs, from the current $80 million level to $200 million a year. Last year the administration received 2,000 requests for after-school funds, but could only fund 300. The pending House version of the Education appropriations bill would provide only $60 million, while the Senate would provide $75 million.

• Provide $5 billion in tax credits over five years to help school districts pay for modernizing crumbling school buildings. This tax legislation is still pending, but the Senate has included $100 million in school construction funds in its Education bill.

• Boost computer-literacy among students by providing $550 million for software and teacher training initia-

Safe Schools Hotline to the Rescue

The father of a teenage girl in Ohio was worried when his daughter told him recently that she and her friends were being followed and harassed at school by a 10th-grade boy. Since August the boy had been threatening to kill her and burn down her house.

Fed up, the father finally called the Safe Schools Hotline, a privately run 800 number for reporting threats and crimes in schools. The next day the information was anonymously forwarded to his daughter's school, where authorities intervened.

The hot line is the brainchild of Pat Sullivan, president of Security Voice Inc. of Columbus, Ohio. He's offered the same service to corporate clients for years, helping them uncover embezzlement, sexual harassment or inventory theft, among other things. Four years ago he decided it might help rid schools of drugs. But since last year's school shootings more and more districts are signing up to forestall school violence as well.

"It's just taken off like crazy," Sullivan says. "We're getting a significant increase in the number of reports about guns in backpacks."

"The best defense is the kids themselves," says Paul Kitchen, assistant superintendent of Sikeston Public Schools in Missouri. "In every shooting incident last year, kids knew what was going to happen before it happened. If they had had a really good way of contacting somebody anonymously, things might have turned out differently."

His school district recently joined 800 other school systems in nine states that have signed up for the hot line service. "It's a fantastic concept. I've never seen a better program for the money," Kitchen says. "You can't get enough police officers and metal detectors to solve this problem."

The beauty of the service, which costs $1.80 per student per year, is that callers talk to a machine located in Columbus, he says. The information is then transcribed verbatim and faxed to local school authorities. If the threat is imminent, transcribers call local school officials at home — even in the middle of the night.

Students feel "very, very comfortable talking to a computer" because they feel no one will recognize their voice and they won't be identified as a snitch, Kitchen says.

Administrators also prefer Sullivan's system over traditional hot lines because it enables them to ask the tipster questions. Each caller is given a four-digit case number and is asked to call back within three days in case officials need more details.

"We can communicate back and forth to infinity to get more information if we need it," Kitchen says. The call-back feature also allows the tipster to learn the outcome of the investigation, so they know their tip was taken seriously, Sullivan says.

"It's better than metal detectors and all that junk," Kitchen says. "I don't believe any of that stuff works." Someone intent on bringing a weapon to school can sidestep metal detectors, the screening takes too long and they are too expensive, he points out.

But the hotline is "very, very inexpensive," says Kitchen, whose annual bill for the 24-hour, 365-day-per-year service comes to $3,500. "I'll write a check for $3,500 to avoid one stabbing. It's sensible, functional and practical. We could hire 50 additional security people and not get the same results."

Besides, it's good public relations, he adds. "We've had lots of unsolicited letters from parents and churches praising us for joining the program."

Richard Ross, superintendent of the Reynoldsburg, Ohio, city schools, which piloted the program, says it also teaches kids to be good citizens. "It allows students to be responsible for the safety of themselves, their friends and their school," Ross says. "It's a way to break down that don't-squeal-on-your-buddy barrier. I think that's real important."

It also empowers students and parents who may have felt victimized by bullying and threats. Half of the calls are from parents, and even some grandparents, Sullivan says.

Besides nipping violence in the bud, the service has helped schools get rid of drug-dealing. "This is snitch-proof," Kitchen says. "Pushers don't know which wallflower girl over in the corner is going to go home and call the hot line. Or a dealer's best friend could tell on him if he thinks his buddy is heading down the wrong path."

---

tives. The Senate agreed to full funding for the initiatives in its Education appropriations bill, but the House bill would fund it at lower levels.

• Provide $100 million to help support charter schools, which are public schools given "charters" allowing them flexibility in decision-making in exchange for accountability of results. The charter school movement has grown from a single school in 1992 to 1,130 today. The Senate bill contains $80 million for charter schools.

• Provide $260 million for the America Reads literacy program, which would train 30,000 reading specialists to mobilize a million volunteer reading tutors over the next five years. The program was not funded by either the Senate or the House.

"Our prisons are full of high school dropouts who cannot read. That is one reason why funding the America Reads Challenge is so important," Secretary Riley said. "Yet Congress continues to dillydally and dawdle." [33]

Aid for Worst Districts

The president also asked that $125 million of the annual $531 million in

Safe and Drug-Free Schools block grants be specifically targeted at the 100 school districts with the worst drug and crime problems. Currently the program — which is the nation's premier program for reducing school violence — distributes block grant money to school districts based on a per capita formula rather than an as-needed basis, spreading the money across all the nation's 15,000 school districts. As a result, six out of 10 school districts receive $10,000 a year or less. One district received only $53, according to the *Los Angeles Times*. [34]

"The funds are so spread out that some school districts really don't get enough money to make a difference, and that's a problem," Riley told the Times. [35] The administration felt that the program would be more effective if at least some of the money were specifically earmarked for school districts with the most serious violence and drug problems.

The program has been criticized recently because there is little oversight over how the money is spent. In addition, the Times investigation found that the money has been spent on things such as motivational speakers, tickets to Disneyland, fishing trips, resort weekends for educators and a $6,500 remote-controlled toy car. A total of $5.7 billion has been spent on the program since its inception in 1987.

"We are wasting money on programs that have been demonstrated not to work," said Delbert S. Elliott, director of the University of Colorado Center for the Study and Prevention of Violence. [36]

Nevertheless, the House refused to earmark a portion of the funds for high-crime districts, preferring to continue spreading the money over all school districts on a per-student basis. But it urged the administration to develop "specific measurable standards" to show exactly how a proposed program would reduce either drug abuse or violence before receiving funding. Secretary Riley announced such guidelines in July.

The Senate bill would set aside $150 million for a new program to combat school violence through communitywide prevention programs, such as providing alternative schools for students expelled for disciplinary problems or for bringing a gun to school, mental health counseling and other services.

Clinton also asked Congress for $95 million for juvenile crime prevention programs among "at risk" populations. The money would be earmarked for communitywide programs made up of educators, police, mental health professionals and community organizations working together to prevent juvenile crime. It could be used for mentoring, after-school programs, tutoring, teaching conflict-resolution skills and reducing truancy.

The Senate version of the Justice Department appropriations bill included funds for the prevention program, but the House version did not. Instead the House created a block grant program that would coincide with programs outlined in the House's just-passed Juvenile Justice Prevention Act.

In response to last year's shootings the Senate bill also earmarked $210 million from other programs for a new Safe Schools Initiative. The funds could be used to increase community policing in and around schools, beef up crime prevention programs, weapons detection, surveillance equipment and information systems for identifying potentially violent youths. The bill is awaiting conference action.

Testing Strategies

After a comprehensive study of school violence-prevention strategies, the Reason Public Policy Institute (RPPI) found that there is no "one-size-fits-all silver bullet" approach to school violence prevention. [37]

"What works in Queens, [N.Y.] is often going to be a waste of resources in Oklahoma," said Richard Seder, RPPI director of education. "Policy-makers should recognize the diversity of our schools, and rather than saddle school boards with restrictions and mandates, promote community-oriented innovation." [38]

Authors Alexander Volokh and Lisa Snell found that "The ideal violence prevention policy will likely be different for each school." Thus each school should experiment with different approaches to find out what works best in their circumstances, the authors said. [39]

Beefing up security with metal detectors, security guards or surveillance cameras has worked at some schools, the authors noted. But such strategies are expensive and can be ineffective if only random checks are made with a metal detector "wand," or if surveillance cameras are not constantly monitored.

Other schools have reduced violence by requiring school uniforms. Uniforms decrease the likelihood of fights over clothing jealousy, students carrying concealed weapons, and the wearing of gang colors. It also fosters school pride and improves the learning atmosphere.

Long Beach, Calif., for instance, saw crime decrease 36 percent the year after a dress code was adopted; fights dropped 51 percent, sex offenses 74 percent, and weapons offenses 50 percent. Many other schools have reported similar results. [40]

"However, most dress codes have been at the elementary level, which isn't exactly where the violence is," the report said.

Violence is lowest in schools with effective discipline systems that mete out punishment swiftly and consistently, the researchers found. For instance, Catholic schools have been able to avoid much of the violence that exists in public schools, even among those parochial schools that cater to the difficult-to-educate, the report said. That's because public schools are "hamstrung by procedural burdens, such as hearing and notice requirements" before disciplinary action can be taken, mandated after the civil rights revolution of the 1960s.

Continued on p. 898

At Issue:

Would tighter gun control reduce school violence?

REP. CAROLYN MCCARTHY, D-N.Y.

WRITTEN FOR THE CQ RESEARCHER, SEPTEMBER 1998.

*t*he school shootings we experienced last year are examples of a disturbing trend — more and more of America's children are getting their hands on guns and shooting other children. In fact, every single day, we lose 12 of our children to gun violence, either from homicides, suicides or accidental shootings. Think about that: As a country, every two days we lose a classroom of our kids to gun violence. That's a national tragedy. And it doesn't have to happen. The common strand in all gun-related deaths involving children is the child's access to a firearm. We need comprehensive federal legislation that will keep guns out of the hands of children who are unsupervised.

Last June, I, along with a coalition of Republicans and Democrats, introduced the Children's Gun Violence Protection Act, legislation designed to prevent children from gaining access to guns by increasing our commitment to responsibility, education and safety.

Responsibility: The guns children use to shoot other children all start out in the hands of adults. The Children's Gun Violence Prevention Act of 1998 shuts down the sources of guns for kids by placing increased responsibility on parents and gun dealers. Parents whose children gain access to improperly stored guns in the home will risk facing criminal penalties. Gun dealers will also have to take greater responsibility for keeping weapons out of the hands of children or risk losing their federal firearms licenses.

Education: The best way to keep our schools safe is to utilize the hands-on experience of teachers, parents and law enforcement. The legislation provides funding for grants to assist successful anti-gun violence programs designed by schools that work with local law enforcement, parent-teacher organizations and community-based organizations.

Safety: When it comes to children, the safest gun is one that a kid cannot use. This bill will require gun manufacturers to produce guns with improved safety features, such as increased trigger-resistance standards, child safety locks, manual safeties and magazine-disconnect safeties.

The bill also expands the Youth Crime Gun Interdiction Initiative. This local/state/federal gun-tracing program has already helped identify and eliminate illegal sources of guns used in juvenile crime in 27 communities. Finally, the bill establishes a youth firearms injury surveillance program at the Centers for Disease Control and Prevention. The program will provide law enforcement with strategic information on the type of weapons used to shoot children and the relationship of the victim and perpetrator.

The time has come for Congress to take responsibility for stopping gun violence involving our children.

TANYA K. METAKSA
Executive director, NRA Institute for Legislative Action; chair, NRA Political Victory Fund

WRITTEN FOR THE CQ RESEARCHER, SEPTEMBER 1998.

*i*n May 1998, three men strolled up to Candace McLallen's front door and kicked it down. *The Corpus Christi Caller-Times* reported that Mrs. McLallen immediately "grabbed her husband's .38-caliber revolver in one hand and her 1-year-old daughter in the other [then] opened fire." Called "kick burglars" for the way they enter occupied homes, the three scattered, police said, because Mrs. McLallen defended herself and her infant: "They were so scared, they left their car behind."

Criminals invade occupied American homes 500,000 times annually. That's why choices about safety and security for the American family are best made by parents, not politicians eager to prescribe a one-size-fits-all gun storage mandate. The nation's declining fatal gun accident rate — now at an all-time low — and our declining violent crime rate prove American parents make wise choices.

There's a growing consensus in America on common-sense approaches to combating youth violence. A simple call to treat threats in schools as seriously as threats at airports would make a difference. The Clinton administration's "Guide to Safe Schools" suggests no new gun restrictions. According to the Department of Education report "Violence and Discipline Problems in U.S. Public Schools," school violence is more than 23 times more likely to be unrelated to guns.

This summer on a strong bipartisan vote, the U.S. Senate rejected new gun restrictions by a 2-1 margin, opting instead for common-sense approaches like federal grants to police for gun-safety education. Tens of thousands of NRA-certified instructors are ready to help law enforcement implement that sound policy.

When people say there ought to be a gun law, chances are there already is one. "[N]early everything juveniles do with their guns is already against the law," observed sociologists Joseph Sheley and James Wright in research on youth violence commissioned by the National Institute of Justice in the early days of the Clinton administration. "The problem, it seems, is not that the appropriate laws do not exist."

The problem, say the researchers, is moral bankruptcy. The August 1998 Battleground Research poll finds "moral and religious issues" now tied with "drugs and crime" as America's top concern. Truth be told, crime and moral bankruptcy are the same disorder. Both respond to the same treatment: a bold infusion of strong, principled leadership in the family, the community and the nation.

Communities Can Avoid Chaos . . .

Without warning, newscasters break into radio and TV shows to report that a student has gone on a shooting rampage at your daughter's middle school. You try to phone the school, but the lines are jammed.

In a panic, you race to the school, but all the roads are blocked by other parents with the same idea. Even the four-lane highway nearest the school has become a parking lot, as panicked parents abandon their cars and sprint the rest of the way.

At the school, chaos reigns. Emergency crews tend the wounded; teachers scream for everyone to calm down, while frantic parents search for their children. Television reporters swarm all over the campus interviewing dazed youngsters, as police try to rope off the crime scene. Eventually, you find your child and take her home.

Some of the schools where shootings occurred last year actually experienced such scenes, says school safety expert William Reisman, but with advance planning communities can avoid such chaos. "Unfortunately, a lot of mistakes occurred after the shootings last year," he says. "Fortunately, we learned from their mistakes."

Reisman convened a one-day conference last June in Memphis, Tenn., to review what happened with school and emergency personnel from the towns involved. He has written a handbook for schools and emergency personnel to use in tailoring crisis-management plans. [1]

"You can't have a one-size-fits-all plan because each school is different," he says.

Drawing on the experiences of those involved in the shootings last year, he outlines what to do and not do in similar school crises. The book lays out a one-day, two-step process through which a town can put a crisis-management plan in place within 24 hours. Reisman speaks at statewide meetings of school superintendents and principals around the country, many of whom are adopting his recommendations, including:

• Parents should not call the school or go to the hospital in an emergency. Because phone lines will be jammed

Continued from p. 896

On the other hand, private schools can require certain behavioral norms and establish certain disciplinary procedures through contract as a condition of attendance. For that reason, the authors recommend charter schools and educational choice for parents. [41]

Other schools are teaching violence-prevention through conflict resolution or peer-group mediation. The Washington-based nonprofit research institute Drug Strategies "graded" dozens of such school violence-prevention programs, and only 10 out of 84 got A's. The researchers questioned violence-prevention strategies that use scare tactics, segregate aggressive students into a separate group or focus exclusively on boosting self-esteem.

Programs that work best are those that reinforce the idea that aggression and violence are not normal behavior, teach conflict-resolution skills through role-playing and involve parents, peers, media and community organizations.

"Preventing violence requires changing norms," said the report. "This is not impossible. In the past few decades, there have been dramatic changes in social norms concerning smoking, drinking and driving, and wearing seat belts." [42]

Adding School Counselors

Many school districts are also increasing the number of school counselors, psychologists and social workers, says NSSC's Stephens. In a 1997 study on student health the National Institute of Medicine recommended that there should be one school counselor — considered the first line of defense in identifying troubled youths — for every 250 students, one social worker per 800 students and a psychologist for each 1,000 students.

However, nationwide, the actual ratios are generally well below those recommended levels, and vary widely from district to district, says Kevin Dwyer, president-elect of the National Association of School Psychologists.

For instance, Connecticut schools have one psychologist for every 750 students, while Missouri only has one per 22,000, Dwyer says. Nationwide, the average is one for each 2,200 students, well below the recommended 1/1,000 ratio. Likewise, he says, the national average for counselors is one for every 500-750 youths, instead of the recommended 1-to-250 ratio.

Since some of the shooters last year had come back onto school grounds after being expelled for weapons offenses, some schools have begun requiring detention and psychological evaluations for anyone caught with a gun at school. Others are trying to ensure that kids caught with guns at school are not simply expelled, but are referred to alternative schools.

"I urge schools to do everything possible to make sure that expelled students are sent to alternative schools," said Secretary Riley. "A student who gets expelled for bringing a gun to school should not be allowed to just hang out on the street." ∎

OUTLOOK

More Violence?

"There will be more killings," predicts Reisman, the Iowa-based

... With Crisis-Management Plan

and police will cordon off the entire school area, parents should instead go to a pre-designated location, such as a church or movie theater, where emergency personnel will keep them informed.

- All school first-aid kits should be equipped with hospital wristbands and indelible ink pens to tag wounded or dead students at the scene. A teacher with a school yearbook should be dispatched to each hospital to help identify those who were not identified at the scene.
- Principals and vice principals should have separate offices, located at opposite ends of the school building in the event hostages are taken.
- Two sets of keys and schematic drawings of the school should be stored in two separate offices, along with orange vests to be worn by those in charge of the keys and drawings.

"When the SWAT team arrives, the first person they want to see is usually the janitor, because he is the one with all the keys and knows the layout of the school," Reisman says. School and police personnel need to decide in advance who is responsible for the plans and keys, and those two people should wear the orange vests so police can quickly identify them.

- If necessary, students should be evacuated in small groups to separate areas outside, preferably behind solid objects, so as not to make an easy target for snipers.
- The press should be given a set of rules drawn up in advance. For instance, the school grounds are an official crime scene and therefore are off-limits. Press conferences will be held twice a day at 10 a.m. and 3 p.m. in a designated place away from the school. No minors are to be interviewed without the parents' permission.

"The press should stop putting the pictures of the perpetrators on the front page," Reisman says. "They should show the suffering of the victims instead."

---

[1] Reisman's book, *The Memphis Conference: Suggestions for Preventing and Dealing with Student-Initiated Violence*, can be ordered by calling (515) 961-4814.

---

independent criminal consultant who specializes in youth violence. Reisman, who was called in as a consultant on several of the recent shootings, said future incidents may be different. Based on the "escalation, the changes and the adaptations" that occurred from one incident to the next last year, he thinks student killers may shift to bombings on school grounds, or may try to take hostages.

Reisman has already heard about at least three telephoned threats from students this school year. "One caller said he was going to make Paducah and Jonesboro look like kindergarten," Reisman says.

Reisman has written a handbook for law enforcement officials and school and hospital administrators outlining how to devise a communitywide crisis management plan, based on the findings of a conference he organized last June, attended by about 60 emergency and school personnel involved in last year's shootings.

Reisman is not the only one who thinks school violence may increase. Within the next decade, America is expected to experience a 15 percent increase in its teen population as the last of the baby boom generation's kids reach puberty. That could mean an unprecedented surge in youth crime as those youths reach key at-risk ages of 14-17.

Without major increases in after-school activities and child care, say others, the situation is likely to worsen as new welfare reform legislation goes into effect. The law forces single mothers to find jobs after they have been on welfare for five years. Some say that will leave more kids home alone during the dangerous 3 p.m. to 7 p.m. hours when most teenage crime occurs.

"When the school bell rings, leaving millions of young people without responsible adult supervision or constructive activities, juvenile crime suddenly triples and prime time for juvenile crime begins," said a report to Attorney General Janet Reno by James Alan Fox, dean of the College of Criminal Justice, Northeastern University. [43]

Quality after-school programs reduce crime, says Fox, not only by providing a safe haven for youngsters, but by helping them develop values and skills as a result of the positive role models and constructive activities such programs provide.

"Until the nation makes investments in after-school and other programs for children and youth, we are likely to continue to pay a heavy price in crime and violence," said the report.

Dwyer agrees that more money needs to be put into after-school programs, as well as more school counselors, remedial support and conflict resolution programs. With almost full employment in America, "Our society uses all the adults to run the economy, but we're not taking care of the kids," says Dwyer.

Others say it is time to make gratuitous violence politically incorrect, just as smoking, drinking and driving, and not wearing seat belts have become.

"We seem to have a love affair with violence and it will take a sea change in our culture to move away from this thinking," Secretary Riley said shortly after the Springfield shooting. "As long as this society continues to glorify violence, continues to make it easy for young people to get guns — and as long as we continue to hide our heads in the sand or fail to reach out when a young person is truly troubled — we will have to confront tragedies like Springfield and Jonesboro." ■

Notes

[1] "11-year-old expelled when squirt gun falls out of bag," The Associated Press, Sept. 22, 1998.

[2] Quoted on NBC's "Today" show, Sept. 23, 1998.

[3] The Department of Education has been preparing the "First Annual Report on School Safety," to be released at the White House conference.

[4] Elizabeth Donohue, Vincent Schiraldi and Jason Ziedenberg, "School House Hype: School shootings and the real risks kids face in America," Justice Policy Institute, July 29, 1998.

[5] Quoted in a press release accompanying the "Report on State Implementation of the Gun-Free Schools Act — School Year 1996-1997," U.S. Department of Education, 1998.

[6] "Students' Reports of School Crime: 1989 and 1995," National Center for Education Statistics and the Bureau of Justice Statistics, March 1998.

[7] The report, "Violence and Discipline Problems in U.S. Public Schools: 1996-97," was conducted by the National Center for Education Statistics, a division of the Department of Education.

[8] Quoted in a July 29 JPI press release.

[9] Scott Bowles, "Armed, alienated and adolescent," USA Today, March 31, 1998.

[10] Ibid.

[11] States with CAP laws are California, Connecticut, Delaware, Florida, Hawaii, Iowa, Nevada, New Jersey, North Carolina, Maryland, Massachusetts, Minnesota, Rhode Island, Texas, Virginia and Wisconsin.

[12] Peter Cummings, et. al., "State Gun-Safe Storage Laws and Child Mortality Due to Firearms," Journal of the American Medical Association, Oct. 1, 1997.

[13] Charlotte Faltermayer, "What is Justice for a Sixth-Grade Killer?" Time, April 6, 1998.

[14] National Center for Health Statistics.

[15] James A. Fox, 1996: Trends in Juvenile Violence: A Report to the United States Attorney General on Current and Future Rates of Juvenile Offending, U.S. Department of Justice.

[16] Quoted in a June 17 press release.

[17] Faltermayer, op. cit.

[18] Linda J. Collier, "Adult Crime, Adult Time," The Washington Post, March 29, 1998.

[19] From an NRA fact sheet on proposed CAP laws.

[20] Testimony before the Senate Judiciary Subcommittee on Youth Violence, Sept. 10, 1997.

[21] "An Evaluation of Juvenile Justice Innovations in Duval County, Fla.," was conducted by Florida State University economist David W. Rasmussen and released Aug. 21, 1996.

[22] Speech to Santa Barbara educators March 4, 1998.

[23] For background, see Sarah Glazer, "Violence in Schools," The CQ Researcher, Sept. 11, 1992, pp. 796-819.

[24] In Gault v. Arizona, the Supreme Court ruled that a youth in juvenile court is entitled to due process and representation by a lawyer. The case involved a 15-year-old who was sentenced to nearly six years in reform school for allegedly making an obscene phone call to a female neighbor, an offense for which an adult would have been sentenced to 30 days in jail.

[25] Jackson Toby, "Crime in the Schools," in James Q. Wilson, ed., Crime and Public Policy (1983), p. 79.

[26] Carl Bosch, Schools Under Seige, Guns, Gangs and Hidden Dangers (1997).

[27] According to the 1997-98 USA-PRIDE Summary Report, released June 18, 1998.

[28] Quoted in a press statement released with the report.

[29] "Report on State Implementation of the Gun-Free Schools Act — School Year 1996-1997," op. cit.

[30] Shannon Tangonan, "Surveys find increases in gangs, youth violence," USA Today, April 13, 1998.

[31] Bosch, op. cit., p. 6.

[32] "Crime in the United States," Federal Bureau of Investigation, 1996.

[33] In a June 9 speech to school safety officials gathered in Washington.

[34] Ralph Frammolino, "Failing Grade for Safe Schools Plan, Los Angeles Times, Sept. 8, 1998.

[35] Quoted in Frammolino, ibid.

[36] Frammolino, ibid.

[37] Alexander Volokh and Lisa Snell, "School Violence Prevention: Strategies to Keep Schools Safe," Oct. 20, 1997.

[38] Quoted in a press statement released with the report.

[39] Volokh, ibid.

[40] Volokh, ibid.

[41] For background, see Charles S. Clark, "Attack on Public Schools," The CQ Researcher, July 26, 1996, pp. 656-679 and Kenneth Jost, "Private Management of Public Schools," The CQ Researcher, March 25, 1994, pp. 282-305.

[42] "Safe Schools, Safe Students, A Guide to Violence Prevention Strategies," Drug Strategies, 1998.

[43] James Alan Fox and Sanford A. Newman, "After-School Crime or After-School Programs."

FOR MORE INFORMATION

National Institute on Media and the Family, 606 24th Ave. South, Suite 606, Minneapolis, Minn. 55454; (616) 672-5437; www.mediaandthefamily.org. The institute is a nonprofit, national resource center for research, information and education about the impact of the media on children and families. The institute's Web site rates music, television programs, movies and video games for sexual and violent content.

National School Boards Association, 1680 Duke St., Alexandria, Va. 22314; (703) 838-6722; www.nsba.org. This federation of state school board associations monitors legislation and regulations affecting the funding and quality of public education.

Office of Juvenile Justice and Delinquency Prevention, Justice Department, 810 Seventh St., N.W., 8th floor, Washington, D.C. 20531; (202) 307-5911; www.ncjs.org/ojjhome.htm. The office administers most federal programs related to prevention and treatment of juvenile delinquency and research and evaluation of the juvenile justice system.

Justice Policy Institute, 2208 Martin Luther King Jr. Ave., S.E., Washington, D.C. 20020; (202) 678-2843; www.cjcj.org. This policy research group, a project of the nonprofit Center on Juvenile and Criminal Justice, seeks to reduce society's reliance on incarceration as a solution to social problems.

National School Safety Center, 4165 Thousand Oaks Blvd., Suite 290, Westlake Village, Calif. 91362; (805) 373-9977; www.nssc1.org. Affiliated with Pepperdine University, the NSSC is a nonprofit training organization created by presidential directive in 1984 to promote safe schools and to help ensure quality education for all America's children.

Bibliography

Selected Sources Used

Books

Bosch, Carl, *Schools Under Seige, Guns, Gangs and Hidden Dangers*, Enslow Publishers, 1997.

Bosch, who has worked in public schools for 23 years, points out that violence is no longer just an urban school problem and looks at the reasons violence has increased in recent years. Schools are not immune from what is happening in the broader context of society, where a violent culture has desensitized youths, he says.

Articles

Bowles, Scott, "Armed, alienated and adolescent," *USA Today*, March 31, 1998.

Bowles examines the similarities among the boys who rampaged in schools last spring. One major similarity was the fact that they all hinted or warned others that they were considering violent action. Schools must teach students to take seriously any such threats, and adults must intervene immediately.

Collier, Linda J., "Adult Crime, Adult Time," *The Washington Post*, March 29, 1998.

The Pennsylvania juvenile court lawyer and professor says that outdated juvenile justice laws have not kept up with the increasingly violent nature of juvenile crime. Instead of truancy and petty thievery, juveniles are now raping and murdering. Too many states prohibit trying juveniles under 16 as adults, she argues.

Faltermayer, Charlotte, "What is Justice for a Sixth-Grade Killer?" *Time*, April 6, 1998.

In the immediate aftermath of the Jonesboro shooting, the author surveys how many states now allow juveniles to be tried as adults and how many states have enacted Child Access Prevention laws, which require adults to store their guns so they are inaccessible to children.

Frammolino, Ralph, "Failing Grade for Safe Schools Plan," *Los Angeles Times*, Sept. 8, 1998.

Frammolino shines the spotlight on the federal Safe and Drug-Free Schools block-grant program, the government's premier vehicle for fighting school crime. He gives the program a failing grade because of the way it is administered — the money is allotted on a per-capita rather than an as-needed basis, and has not been governed by strict performance guidelines. As a result, the program has been used, among other things, to pay for fishing trips, resort weekends for school personnel, a $6,500 remote-controlled toy police car and a clown act promoting bicycle safety.

Reports

Donohue, Elizabeth, Vincent Schiraldi and Jason Ziedenberg, "School House Hype: School shootings and the real risks kids face in America," Justice Policy Institute, July 29, 1998.

The authors argue that schools are the safest places for youngsters, safer even than their own homes. Rather than overreacting to the over-blown press reports about the recent schoolyard shootings, they argue, the government should fund after-school programs and pass laws to keep guns out of underage hands.

Report on State Implementation of the Gun-Free Schools Act — School Year 1996-1997, U.S. Department of Education, 1998.

This annual Department of Education report issued under the Gun-Free Schools Act reveals that some 6,100 students were expelled for bringing a gun to school in 1996-97.

Safe Schools, Safe Students, A Guide to Violence Prevention Strategies, Drug Strategies, 1998.

The Washington-based nonprofit research institute graded dozens of such school violence-prevention programs, and only 10 out of 84 received A's. Programs that work best are those that reinforce the idea that aggression and violence are not normal behavior, teach conflict-resolution skills through role-playing and involve parents, peers, media and community organizations.

Students' Reports of School Crime: 1989 and 1995, National Center for Education Statistics and the Bureau of Justice Statistics, March 1998.

This study, based on interviews with 10,000 students, by the Education and Justice departments finds that the number of students physically attacked or robbed at school increased 23.5 percent between 1989 and 1995. The increase occurred even as overall school crime rates remained steady, at about 14 percent, during the six-year period. Gang presence in schools nearly doubled during the same period.

Violence and Discipline Problems in U.S. Public Schools: 1996-97, National Center for Education Statistics, Department of Education.

This study surveyed more than 1,200 public school principals in a nationally representative sampling and found that 90 percent of public schools had no "serious, violent crime," but those that did reported 4,170 rapes, 7,150 robberies and 10,950 physical attacks or fights with weapons. By far, most school crime was less violent in nature, including 190,000 physical attacks or fights without a weapon, 116,000 thefts or larcenies and 98,000 cases of vandalism. Violence occurs most often in schools with classroom discipline problems and in large schools in central cities.

The Next Step

Additional information from UMI's Newspaper & Periodical Abstracts™ database

Causes of Violence

Hunt, Albert R., "Politics & People: Teen Violence Spawned by Guns and Cultural Rot," *The Wall Street Journal*, June 11, 1998, p. A23.

There is no agreement on what causes children to become violent. Conservatives place much of the blame on popular culture — Hollywood and television are overwhelmingly violence-oriented, the argument goes, and the music industry is a villain for pandering to the worst instincts of kids by glorifying sexual obscenities and brutality. Both arguments are exaggerations. Some teenage perpetrators don't fit the stereotypes. Other teen killers are simply mentally unbalanced kids.

Hurt, Charles, "Metro Detroit Kids Ask: 'Why?' Classrooms Erupt into Discussions of School Violence," *Detroit News*, March 26, 1998, p. A1.

Teachers across Metro Detroit fielded life's toughest questions from middle-school students after two snipers their own age lured classmates out of an Arkansas middle school and inexplicably began shooting. Some students — almost all clad in baggy, bell-bottomed jeans and sneakers that rockers wear in music videos — blamed easy access to guns, violent video games and daytime TV like "The Jerry Springer Show."

Discipline

"Arming for School Violence," *New Orleans Times-Picayune*, June 20, 1998, p. B6.

Another drill might be added to the fire and severe-weather drills that Louisiana schoolchildren already know well: the bullet drill. It may be chilling to think about children practicing for the day when they are threatened with a gun at their schools. But it's not nearly as chilling as the alternative: being caught unprepared.

"Spotlight on School Violence," *The Boston Globe*, Aug. 28, 1998, p. A26.

What can be done about violent students? The question echoes through hearts, minds and school hallways. And yesterday in Worcester, Mass., President Clinton shook off the glaring cloak of his Monica Lewinsky problems to talk about a precious but rarely discussed freedom — the freedom to be safe at school. After the school shooting in May that shattered Springfield, Ore., Clinton tried to determine what, if anything, government can do.

Freeman, Gregory, "Beaumont High School's Turnaround Is Largely Based on a Creative Principal," *St. Louis Post-Dispatch*, April 23, 1998, p. B1.

Principal Floyd Crues has turned his school around with a "zero-tolerance" policy on gangs and gang-related clothing, an insistence on discipline and an increased focus on education. Standardized test scores have gone up. Having improved the atmosphere, Crues this year has taken another step: 50 freshmen are now part of a newly established Beaumont High School Academy of Finance. The school within a school lets the students participate in a four-year program about the world of finance.

Henry, Tamara, "Attorneys General, Schools Attack Violence with Web Site," *USA Today*, Sept. 3, 1998, p. D6.

The National Association of Attorneys General and the National School Boards Association announced several joint efforts this week to reduce the toll of violence in American schools. As a first step, the groups launched a school-safety Web site — www.keepschoolssafe.org — that features what they consider the best available resources for educators, community leaders and parents.

Repsher, Gail, "Strengthening Schools' Anti-Violence Programs," *USA Today*, June 25, 1998, p. D10.

Only 10 of 84 nationally available school violence-prevention programs got A's in a study released by the nonprofit research institute Drug Strategies. The study will help school administrators choose violence-prevention programs, says institute President Mathea Falco.

Weizel, Richard, "Connecticut Task Force Seeks to Combat School Violence," *The Boston Globe*, Aug. 16, 1998, p. E5.

School shootings by disturbed students around the country last year are motivating educators to find ways of preventing deadly violence in their own school districts. In Connecticut, a special task force of the state's top school and social services administrators has been appointed by the governor and is working throughout the summer to come up with proposals on combating school violence.

Gun Control

Bendavid, Naftali, "Gun-Safety Bill Targets Kids, Incumbents," *Chicago Tribune*, June 18, 1998, p. 20.

Gun-control activists, seizing on a recent spate of horrific schoolyard killings, introduced a child gun-safety bill designed to throw gun supporters on the defensive. Appearing on the U.S. Capitol grounds featuring the mother of a school shooting victim, Sen. Edward M. Kennedy, D-Mass., declared, "We do more today to regulate the safety of toy guns than real guns, and that's a national disgrace."

Cummings, Jeanne, "NRA Convention Kicks Off Amid Push For Gun Control After School Shootings," *The

Wall Street Journal, June 5, 1998, p. A4.

As the National Rifle Association gathers for its annual convention this weekend in Philadelphia, its adversaries are organizing in Washington to revive the debate over gun control after the recent spate of school shootings. Rep. Carolyn McCarthy, D.-N.Y., whose husband was killed and son wounded in the 1993 shooting spree on a Long Island Railroad commuter train, is drafting legislation to prosecute parents who do not properly store their guns, and to require manufacturers to put child safety locks on handguns. It also would raise the legal age for handgun possession to 21, from 18.

Lott, John R. Jr., "The Real Lesson of the School Shootings," *The Wall Street Journal*, March 27, 1998, p. A14.

This week's horrific shootings in Arkansas have, predictably, spurred calls for more gun control. But it's worth noting that the shootings occurred in one of the few places in Arkansas where possessing a gun is illegal. Arkansas, Kentucky and Mississippi — the three states that have had deadly shootings in public schools over the past half-year — all allow law-abiding adults to carry a concealed handgun for self-protection, except in public schools. Indeed, federal law generally prohibits guns within 1,000 feet of a school. Gun prohibitionists concede that banning guns around schools has not quite worked as intended — but their response has been to call for more regulations of guns. Yet what might appear to be the most obvious policy may actually cost lives. When gun-control laws are passed, it is law-abiding citizens, not would-be criminals, who adhere to them.

Williams, Armstrong, "Jonesboro and Gun Control," *The Amsterdam News*, May 28, 1998, p. 8.

The author argues that the Clinton administration's executive order banning the importation of dozens of assault weapons will not stop tragedies such as the Jonesboro school shootings.

Teacher Protection

Henley, Jon, "Staff Sue to End School Violence," *Guardian*, April 8, 1998, p. 15.

With the level of violence rising in French schools, teachers at a lycee in the depressed northern suburbs of Paris began legal proceedings against the government yesterday for failing to provide them with a safe working environment. The 55 staff members at the 1,300-pupil Lycee Romain-Rolland — the scene last week of a pitched two-hour battle between rival gangs with iron bars, baseball bats and knives — invoked a law that allows civil servants to stop work when they consider their lives are in danger.

Loupe, Diane, "DeKalb Teachers Learn to Fend off Potential Crises; Cool tools: Educators are Studying How to Prevent, Defuse School Violence," *Atlanta Journal-Constitution*, July 26, 1998, p. D1.

More than 200 DeKalb County teachers and administrators this summer are practicing hair-pulling, choking and restraining one another. Two teachers from every DeKalb school will learn non-violent techniques of defusing or restraining unruly students.

Violence

"New Report on Gangs, Youth Violence is Disturbing," *Chicago Defender*, April 14, 1998, p. 9.

An editorial discusses the problem of violent crime in public schools, mostly caused by gang activity.

"Youth Violence in Black and White," *Chicago Tribune*, June 7, 1998, p. 22.

The public has become so accustomed to reports of violence committed by children in the nation's big cities that even folks who have never set foot in the ghetto feel comfortable making a diagnosis. Poor schools, bad parents, gangs, poverty — the list of causes is as familiar as the television news image of yet another black or Latino child killed by a peer. But the recent spate of horrifying violence committed by white teenagers in suburban and rural areas has forced a search for new explanations.

Grace, Stephanie, "Face of Violence Has Changed, Lee Tells Student Mediators," *New Orleans Times-Picayune*, Aug. 24, 1997, p. B4.

A conference at a New Orleans high school acknowledged drugs, guns, gangs and violence as part of everyday life for teens. The students taking part in the conference are the first to be trained to help reduce violent conflict in schools as part of a peer mediation program.

Tangonan, Shannon, "Surveys Find Increases in Gangs, Youth Violence," *USA Today*, April 13, 1998, p. A2.

The number of teens reporting gangs in their schools nearly doubled from 1989 to 1995, while the number of students victimized by violent crime increased nearly 25 percent during that period, a federal report said. Based on surveys of students ages 12-19, street gangs were reported in schools by 28.4 percent of those questioned in 1995, compared with only 15.3 percent in 1989, the Bureau of Justice Statistics and the National Center for Education Statistics reported. The Department of Education reported that the gang increase was not confined to cities. In central cities, students reporting street gangs rose from 24.8 to 40.7 percent; in suburbs, from 14 to 26.3 percent; and in non-metropolitan areas, from 7.8 to 19.9 percent.

Back Issues

Great Research on Current Issues Starts Right Here.
Recent topics covered by The CQ Researcher are listed below.
Now available on the Web
For information, call (800) 432-2250 ext. 279 or (202) 887-6279.

If you would like to have any of these CQ Researchers updated, or need more information about these topics, please call CQ Custom Research. Special rates for CQ subscribers.
(202) 887-8600 or (800) 432-2250, ext. 600, or E-mail Custom.Research@cq.com

JUNE 1997
FDA Reform
China After Deng
Line-Item Veto
Breast Cancer

JULY 1997
Transportation Policy
Executive Pay
School Choice Debate
Aggressive Driving

AUGUST 1997
Age Discrimination
Banning Land Mines
Children's Television
Evolution vs. Creationism

SEPTEMBER 1997
Caring for the Dying
Mental Health Policy
Mexico's Future
Youth Fitness

OCTOBER 1997
Urban Sprawl in the West
Diversity in the Workplace
Teacher Education
Contingent Work Force

NOVEMBER 1997
Renewable Energy
Artificial Intelligence
Religious Persecution
Roe v. Wade at 25

DECEMBER 1997
Whistleblowers
Castro's Next Move
Gun Control Standoff
Regulating Nonprofits

JANUARY 1998
Foster Care Reform
IRS Reform
The Black Middle Class
U.S.-British Relations

FEBRUARY 1998
Patients' Rights
Deflation Fears
Caring for the Elderly
The New Corporate Philanthropy

MARCH 1998
Israel at 50
The Federal Judiciary
Drinking on Campus
The Economics of Recycling

APRIL 1998
Biology and Behavior
Liberal Arts Education
Income Inequality
High-Tech Labor Shortage

MAY 1998
Census 2000
Child-Care Options
Alzheimer's Disease
U.S.-Russian Relations

JUNE 1998
Student Journalism
Antitrust Policy
Environmental Justice
Sleep Deprivation

JULY 1998
Encouraging Teen Abstinence
Population and the Environment
Democracy in Asia
Baby Boomers at Midlife

AUGUST 1998
Oil Production in the 21st Century
Flexible Work Arrangements
Coastal Development
Student Activism

SEPTEMBER 1998
Organic Farming
Cancer Treatments
Hispanic-Americans' New Clout
The Future of Baseball

OCTOBER 1998
Social Security

Back issues are available for $5.00 (subscribers) or $10.00 (non-subscribers). Quantity discounts apply to orders over 10. To order, call Congressional Quarterly Customer Service at (202) 887-8621.

Binders are available for $18.00. To order call 1-800-638-1710. Please refer to stock number 648.

Future Topics

▶ *National Forests*

▶ *Puerto Rico's Status*

▶ *Internet Privacy*

National Forests

Should recreation take priority over logging?

he fees timber companies pay to cut
trees in national forests are supposed
to help the Forest Service manage the
nation's vast network of public forests
and logging roads. But growing concern over the loss
of forest habitat and its impact on endangered species,
water quality and recreational usage has raised
questions about the timber-sales program, which now
costs taxpayers more than it collects. The new chief of
the Forest Service, Michael P. Dombeck, wants to shift
the agency's priorities away from logging and toward
conservation and recreation. Timber interests blame
Forest Service mismanagement for the sales program's
shortfalls and, along with their allies in Congress, are
fighting Dombeck's initiative.

PUBLISHED BY CONGRESSIONAL QUARTERLY INC.

C_Q **October 16, 1998 • Volume 8, No. 39 • Pages 905-928**

Formerly Editorial Research Reports

THE CQ Researcher

October 16, 1998
Volume 8, No. 39

EDITOR
Sandra Stencel

MANAGING EDITOR
Thomas J. Colin

STAFF WRITERS
Adriel Bettelheim
Mary H. Cooper
Kenneth Jost
Kathy Koch
David Masci

PRODUCTION EDITOR
Melissa Hall

EDITORIAL ASSISTANT
Laura S. Cavender

PUBLISHED BY
Congressional Quarterly Inc.

CHAIRMAN
Andrew Barnes

VICE CHAIRMAN
Andrew P. Corty

PRESIDENT AND PUBLISHER
Robert W. Merry

EXECUTIVE EDITOR
David Rapp

Bibliographic records and abstracts included in The Next Step section of this publication are the copyrighted material of UMI, and are used with permission.

The CQ Researcher (ISSN 1056-2036). Formerly Editorial Research Reports. Published weekly, except Jan. 2, May 29, July 3, Oct. 30, by Congressional Quarterly Inc., 1414 22nd St., N.W., Washington, D.C. 20037. Annual subscription rate for libraries, businesses and government is $340. Additional rates furnished upon request. Periodicals postage paid at Washington, D.C., and additional mailing offices. POSTMASTER: Send address changes to The CQ Researcher, 1414 22nd St., N.W., Washington, D.C. 20037.

COVER: THE FOREST SERVICE HAS REDUCED CLEARCUTTING BY 84 PERCENT SINCE THESE MOUNTAINSIDES WERE STRIPPED IN THE WILLAMETTE NATIONAL FOREST IN OREGON. (WILDERNESS SOCIETY)

National Forests

BY MARY H. COOPER

THE ISSUES

On a crisp, clear day last August, several hikers picked their way up a steep, rocky trail in the White River National Forest, a remote area in Colorado's Rocky Mountains. As they savored the sweeping vistas that were their reward for hours of walking, the unmistakable rumble of engines shattered the tranquility — another off-road-vehicle club outing. Reluctantly, the hikers moved aside as, one by one, 14 Land Rovers lurched by, enveloping them in exhaust fumes.

The encounter between vehicles and hikers only hints at the pressures that threaten the national forests — some of the last wild places in the United States.

Environmentalists have long charged that logging and road-building in the vast system of national forests destroy wildlife habitat and muddy the streams that provide drinking water for nearly 1,000 communities and spawning grounds for endangered salmon and other creatures. Moreover, they say, clearcutting — the controversial practice of leveling every tree on a tract — not only despoils the landscape but also threatens the Northern spotted owl and other species requiring large swathes of undisturbed forest to survive.

But today the concern is beginning to shift from logging to crowding — not from logging trucks but tourists. As the nation's urban population grows, many experts say that recreationists — from members of Land Rover clubs to rock climbers — should be a major concern of the Forest Service.

The National Forest System encompasses 192 million acres of public forests and grasslands in 44 states

— more than 8 percent of the entire nation and more than twice as much land as all the national parks. *(See map, p. 908.)* Indeed, while overcrowding in Yellowstone and other national parks seems to get the headlines, the national forests get the visitors — some 800 million every year, or three times as many as the national parks. [1] Moreover, 379,000 miles of logging roads snake through the national forests. [2]

While the number of visitors has been steadily rising, logging in national forests has plummeted. Today, recreational use of national forests provides 74 percent of the jobs that depend on the forest system, compared with just 3 percent involved in logging. [3] The Forest Service's timber-sales program, once a revenue source, now loses money — more than $88 million last year alone. [4] The red ink prompts charges from critics that the logging industry gets cheap timber at taxpayers' expense.

"The timber industry and some legislators from the Western states still have the mindset that any vertical tree is not a good tree," says Michael A. Francis, director of the national forest program at the Wilderness Society. "The industry can't seem to come to grips with the fact that as we move into the 21st century Americans expect and demand more for their national forests, which are the crown jewels of the era of Teddy

Roosevelt" *(see p. 914).*

Under the Clinton administration, the Forest Service is beginning to reflect this attitudinal shift. Michael P. Dombeck, who heads the Department of Agriculture agency, has repeatedly emphasized the need to conserve forest resources over logging interests. Last January, a year after taking office, Dombeck imposed an 18-month moratorium on new-road construction in most roadless areas of the forest system. The agency will spend the time formulating a new policy on road building — in effect, a new policy on logging. "If we are to redeem our role as conservation leaders, it is not enough to be loyal to the Forest Service organization," Dombeck wrote in a July 1 letter to the agency's 30,000 employees. "First and foremost, we must be loyal to our land ethic. In 50 years, we will not be remembered for the resources we developed; we will be thanked for those we maintained and restored for future generations."

Timber industry officials are fighting back. They blame Forest Service mismanagement for the fall in timber revenues. And they insist that "disturbance" — the timber industry's term for logging — removes trees that would otherwise fuel devastating wildfires, opens up "edge" habitat favored by deer and elk and provides the roads vital to forest tourism.

"I grew up recreating on national forests, and I firmly believe that maintaining healthy forests is compatible with most recreational opportunities," says Chris West, vice president of the Northwest Forestry Association, in Portland, Ore. "Not just motorized users, but campers, mountain bikers and cross-country skiers all rely on roads put in by the timber harvesters. Big-game hunting is even more closely dependent on timber

The National Forest System

The U.S. Forest Service manages 192 million acres of public forests and grasslands in 44 states — more than 8 percent of all the land in the United States and more than twice as much land as the National Park Service.

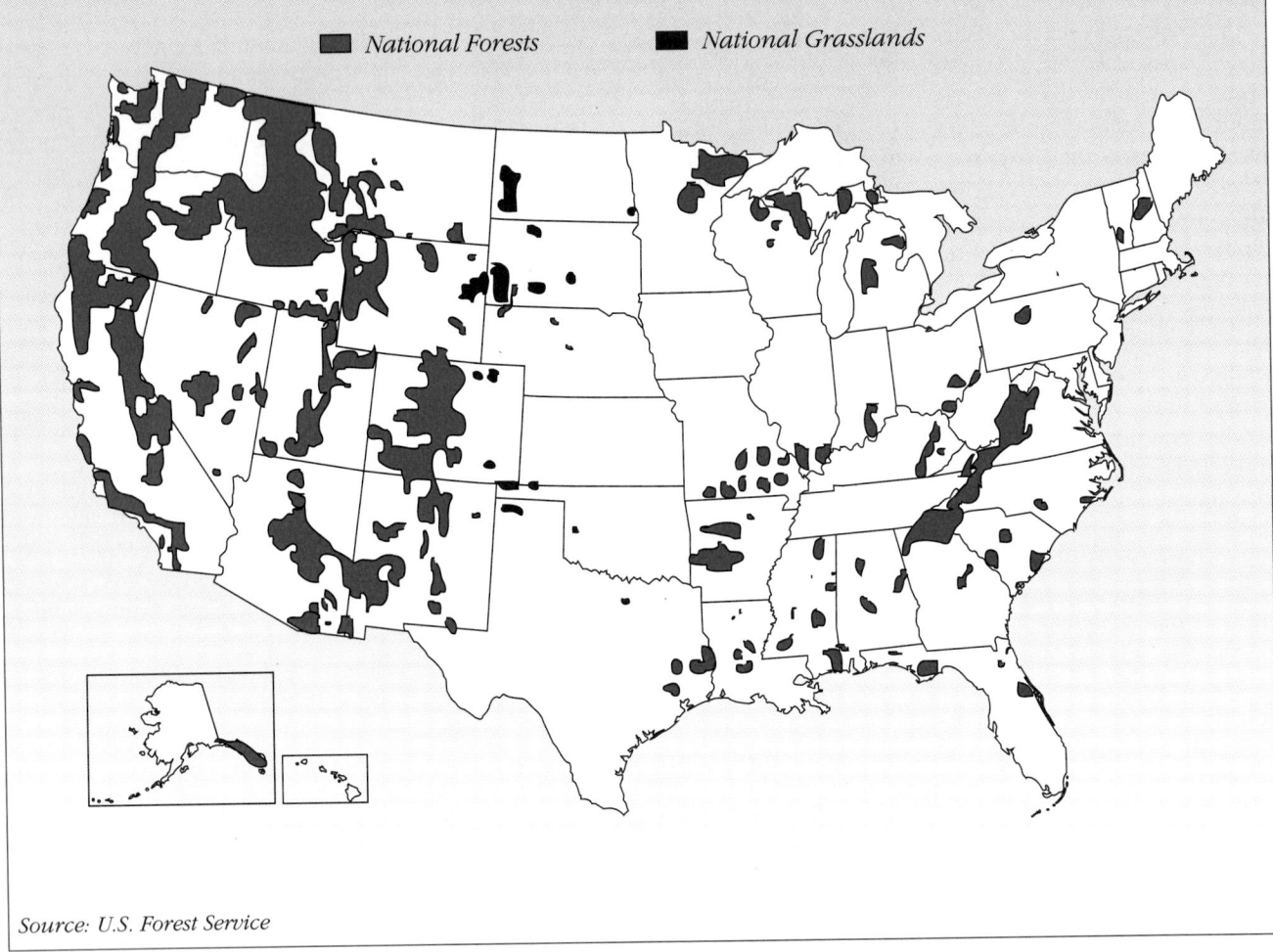

■ *National Forests*   ■ *National Grasslands*

Source: U.S. Forest Service

management because deer and elk require the grasses and brush that only grow after disturbance."

The industry has the strong support of four key Western Republicans who chair congressional committees that hold the purse strings for Dombeck's agency. Sens. Frank H. Murkowski (Alaska) and Larry E. Craig (Idaho) and Reps. Don Young (Alaska) and Helen Chenoweth (Idaho) have all held hearings recently that aired criticism of the Forest Service, and each lawmaker has threatened to slash Dombeck's bud-

get if he continues to cut timber sales.

"Judging from the more than 100 different reports done by the [General Accounting Office], the management of the Forest Service is in severe need of repair," said Chenoweth, chairman of the House Resources Subcommittee on Forests and Forest Health. "The Forest Service has nothing to offer but empty promises to improve if simply given more time. I hate to say that we have heard that before, but the simple answer is that time is up." [5]

Republican lawmakers have added a number of riders to the Interior Department's fiscal 1999 appropriations

bill that would increase logging in national forests. Forty percent more logging, for example, would be allowed in Alaska's unique Tongass National Forest, a temperate rain forest that has already undergone extensive clearcutting. The Clinton administration denounced the riders as Republican "stealth" attacks on the environment and threatened to veto the appropriations measure unless they were dropped. [6]

Meanwhile, recreationists are embroiled in a fight among themselves over access to the forests that threatens to overshadow the logging vs. tourism clash. Hikers, skiers and other "quiet" visitors to national forests charge that all-terrain vehicles (ATVs) and snowmobiles are chewing up the trails, polluting the air and destroying the forests' wild character. Many observers predict that the struggle over recreation access to national forests will plague the Forest Service for years to come.

As the fighting over the national forests continues, these are some of the questions being asked:

Should logging be banned in the national forests?

Some environmentalists doubt the Forest Service's ability or willingness to "manage" its forests in a sustainable fashion. The only sure way to preserve the nation's public forests, they say, is to completely ban logging. In 1996, members of the Sierra Club voted by a 2-to-1 margin to end commercial logging on all federally owned public lands. [7]

The 500,000-member conservation group had previously called for an end to clearcutting, logging in old-growth or roadless areas and replacing diverse native forests with single-species plantings. The group embraced a total ban only after it said the Forest Service failed to support the three policies or to follow its own legal mandate to foster multiple uses of national forests. "Multiple use has failed," said Sierra Club Executive Director Carl Pope, "not because it was a flawed concept in principle, but because the federal government lacked the integrity to carry it out." [8]

Some lawmakers support the Sierra Club's call to end commercial logging, arguing that the timber-sales program actually costs taxpayers money rather than bringing in revenues as originally intended. Reps. Cynthia A. McKinney, D-Ga., and Jim Leach, R-Iowa, have introduced a measure (HR 2789) that would prohibit all new timber sales and phase out existing timber sales within two years.

"This bill would get the taxpayers out of the timber business altogether," says Melanie Griffin, director of the Sierra Club's public lands program. The national forests provide just 4 percent of total U.S. timber consumption, she says, the rest coming from private lands. "Inside the Beltway, people like to call the notion of ending commercial logging on national forests an extreme proposal,

The number of visitors to national forests has been steadily rising while logging has plummeted. Some 800 million people visit national forests annually — three times the visitors to national parks.

but outside Washington there has been a huge response and support from the public."

A recent nationwide opinion poll suggests broad public support for a logging ban. Sixty-nine percent of 800 registered voters surveyed in June wanted to end the logging. [9]

In Griffin's view, the shift in public opinion was sparked by the increasing number of visitors to national forests who have been appalled at the conditions. "People go to see the pretty green trees and they find clearcuts," she says. "Anglers see the damage done to streams from the runoff from logging roads, and people in cities are reacting to polluted water supplies caused by logging on steep terrain."

Other environmental organizations and supporters of forest conservation, however, stop short of advocating the "zero-cut" option. The Wilderness Society, for example, a vocal critic of the Forest Service's timber program, says logging is not necessarily inappropriate. "We think the forests should be managed to protect and sustain the forested ecosystems," Francis says. "That type of management goal does not preclude the extraction of timber, water or other resources, so long as it does not harm the forest's ability to keep regenerating itself."

What the Wilderness Society strongly objects to is the way the Forest Service currently handles commercial logging. "The Forest Service talks about ecosystem management, but on the ground there are still clearcuts and extensive logging," Francis says. "We advocate a much more gentle look at the land, with a lot more restoration of damaged lands and protection of undamaged lands as the primary focus."

The timber industry insists that logging causes no harm to national forests and actually helps foresters keep forests healthy. "We have to remember that when the national forests were designated, they were identified to provide clean water and a sustainable flow of timber," says West of the Northwest Forestry Association. "Wood is the only renewable

'If We Take Care of the Land . . .

From the start of his tenure in January 1997, U.S. Forest Service chief Michael P. Dombeck broke with tradition. Unlike his predecessors, Dombeck came from outside the Agriculture Department agency. Dombeck was plucked from the federal Bureau of Land Management (BLM), where he served as acting director. Above all, Dombeck's training as a fisheries biologist indicated a likely change in the agency's long support for commercial logging. His "Natural Resources Agenda" outlines reform measures aimed at strengthening the agency's conservation efforts. In an interview with staff writer Mary H. Cooper, Dombeck discusses his efforts to free the agency from the control of the timber industry and its allies in Congress, which have set the agency's course to date.

How does your vision of the Forest Service's mandate differ from that of your predecessors?

Dombeck: The Natural Resources Agenda sets out an evolutionary process that began with the concept of ecosystem management that the Forest Service began to develop in the 1980s. Although they didn't call it that at the time, [former chief] Dale Robertson limited clearcutting. Then Jack Ward Thomas came in as chief and really talked about ecosystem management. When I was at BLM, I decided that we needed to articulate what ecosystem management was with more clarity. At a national leadership meeting that we had in St. Paul with all the executives of the Forest Service, we held a poll to define the major things we needed to address. Watershed health and restoration came out of that as the core elements of the Natural Resources Agenda.

The next thing we focused on in the agenda was sustainable forestry and ecosystem management. We knew we [also] had to deal with roads, which have been a big issue [and] with the increased recreational use [of] national

forests. The objective is really to try to bring a sharper focus to where we're going, to articulate it in a way that is more easily understood by both employees and the public, and to focus on the need to live within the limits of the land. ... As the country gets more and more developed, I think the real values are in our large, unfragmented landscapes, the scenic beauty and the water that runs off the national forests. The cleanest water in the United States flows from forested land, and 80 percent of the streams originate on national forests. Think 50 years from now. That's my focus.

What is the biggest obstacle to achieving this vision?

Dombeck: We have to continue to ... make sure that people understand and appreciate the value of public lands and where we're going. Let me put on my technical hat as an aquatic ecologist, one who has taught and worked in research. I think we communicate to the public in far too technical terms. This business of natural resource management is about recharging aquifers, it's about hunting and fishing, it's about open space, it's about healthy forests, it's about vibrant local economies, it's about preserving our cultural heritage, its about having an opportunity for any citizen of any means to be able to take their kids hunting, fishing, hiking, biking and not worrying about no-trespassing signs, not having to pay a large lease fee. The national forests are, in part, the playground of the little guy.

Is the timber industry standing in your way?

Dombeck: There are elements of the timber industry that are actually ahead of us. The direction that I've given the forest-management staff is that we need to work in partnership with industry, just as we're working in

Michael P. Dombeck, chief of the U.S. Forest Service

U.S. Forest Service

resource to build homes here and around the world, and the national forests provide half of the softwood timber in the United States."

The problem, as West sees it, is that there is too little logging in national forests. He blames part of the problem on the Forest Service's almost too-successful fire-suppression campaign, long personified by Smokey Bear. "We now

have too many trees on millions of acres of national forest land," he says. "On 40 million acres, forest health is so bad that forests are at risk for insect infestation and fire. A proactive and science-based management plan to control the stocking of our forests would help return them to health. Instead of letting the trees burn up, we should utilize some of that wood, employ hard-work-

ing Americans and return some of the money to the U.S. Treasury."

Should recreational use of the national forests be more strictly limited?

Although timber production has long been the focus of the debate, recreation and tourism have recently surpassed logging as the main profit-

... It Will Take Care of Us'

partnership with the fish and wildlife community and parts of the recreation community. We need to build partnerships because I believe the timber industry is an important element of what we do.

Should logging be phased out in national forests, as some lawmakers propose?

Dombeck: We have to determine what we want on the landscape and what we want our watersheds to look like. Then we can use science and technology and all the tools available to get there. We have tremendous problems with noxious, invasive weeds and species, both plants and animals, including Dutch elm disease, white pine blister rust, kudzu weed, star thistle in the West, leafy spurge — the list goes on and on. We've got urban wildlife interface issues, we've got tremendous fire risk in some places and we've got insect infestations in some parts of the country. We need to apply the best science and technology to get there, and that involves many tools. One is prescribed burning, but yet we can only prescribe burn about 10 percent of the Intermountain West without doing something else first. Thinning, fuel reduction and timber harvest are all tools that we need to consider.

But I've also got to say that if timber harvest is the perceived driver of what we do, we're going to stay in a sea of controversy. If we have objectives, use the best tools and work within the limits of the land, the water will flow, the wildlife and fish habitats will be there, the riparian zones will function and some wood fiber will be produced.

That's what ecosystem management is to me; it's a science-based approach, and then we apply all the tools. If the board-foot is the driver, or if recreational use is the driver, we're going to have controversy.

Should any national forest users receive subsidies?

Dombeck: It's been the position of the administration all along that we get fair market value for our resources, and we're moving in that direction by raising summer

home permits and a variety of other things. Some things are determined either by legislation or other mandates, such as the grazing fee. ... With the objective of fair market value, the other driver is the desired future condition that we want. What do we want on the land? What do we want the forest to look like? It was on the Deschutes National Forest in Oregon that someone said to me, "Mike, we want our forests to look like forests. We don't want to see mountainsides that are clearcut, we don't want to see mountainsides that are brown from insect infestations and we don't want to see mountainsides that are black from catastrophic fire."

The American public is getting less and less tolerant of soil-disturbing activities on the land — hence the roads debate. We need to develop and use light-on-the-land technology and do more selective cutting. If we use the best science, I believe this is a debate that, if we build trust, we can work through.

Does the public support your agenda for the national forests?

Dombeck: Managing public lands today is as challenging as it's ever been. One of the reasons that we have the level of complexity that we have is that people care more than ever and they want to be involved in the process. That's the way a democracy works, it works on information and the exchange of ideas and differences of opinion. I'm asking employees to become accustomed to working in this kind of inclusive environment, even though it's messier that way. People want to be involved in the goal-setting process, and they want to be able to appeal decisions.

When asked what they expected of the Forest Service, the public basically said three things. They expect us to be educators, developers of science and technology and facilitators for bringing people together in local communities to set long-term goals for managing the land. ... But the one thing that I believe has to be sacrosanct is that in order to preserve options for future generations, we've got to work within the limits of the land. If we take care of the land, it will take care of us. Everyone benefits from that.

making activity in the national forests. Campers, hikers, hunters and recreational-vehicle drivers spend almost $100 billion a year in national forests. "We have 1.7 million vehicles a day on national forest roads associated with recreation and tourism," Dombeck says. "At the Mount Baker-Snoqualamie National Forest near Seattle or the four national forests in the Los Angeles basin, there are literally thousands and thousands of people every weekend and in some cases every evening who go out and recreate on these lands. We've got to make sure that the same principles apply to recreation as apply to mining or logging, that we work within the limits of the land, because these are our options for the future."

Some environmentalists say the logging debate has overshadowed the impact of tourism on forest ecosystems. "With population projected to increase by 50 percent over the next 50 years, demand for the high-quality outdoor recreation provided by these places will increase markedly," writes William H. Meadows, president of the Wilderness Society. "In contrast, these forests pro-

Recreation Traffic Increased in Forests

Recreation traffic in national forests has grown steadily and significantly since 1950 while the use of timber vehicles has remained flat, reflecting the decline in timbering.*

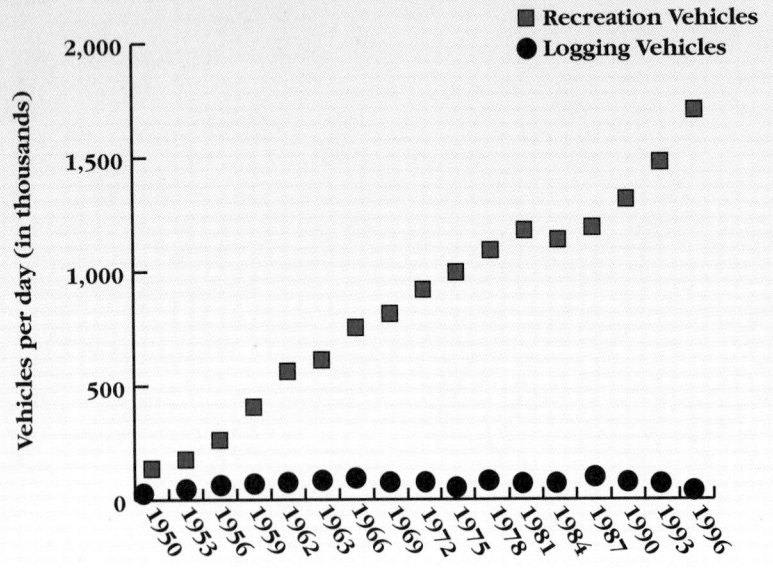

Timber Harvest and Recreation Vehicles Per Day, 1950-96

■ **Recreation Vehicles**
● **Logging Vehicles**

* The largest, single recreation activity is mechanized travel and viewing scenery, or "driving for pleasure," which accounted for 36 percent of all Forest Service recreation use in fiscal 1996.

Source: Department of Agriculture, Forest Service, "National Forest Road System and Use," Jan. 30, 1998.

vide just 4 percent of the U.S. wood fiber supply. Any reduction in logging will have no significant impact on the availability or price of lumber and paper. In other words, the trees in our national forests are worth much more when they are vertical than when they are horizontal." [10]

So many people are visiting national forests that they are exacting a heavy toll on forest habitats, polluting the air with vehicle exhausts, trampling on plants and polluting streams. One way to restrict access to environmentally sensitive areas is to designate them as wilderness areas. Under the 1964 Wilderness Act, designated lands are off-limits to all motorized vehicles and bicycles. Trail-maintenance crews are even barred from using chain saws to clear brush and fallen trees. Open

only to hikers and horseback riders, wilderness areas now account for 18 percent of the National Forest System. Expanding the wilderness system requires congressional approval, however, and since logging is banned in wilderness areas, the timber industry often prevails upon lawmakers to reject proposals for wilderness designation.

To raise revenue needed to maintain trails, restrooms, picnic areas and other amenities, the Forest Service has begun charging fees in some of the most heavily visited forests. Approved by Congress in 1996, an Adventure Pass costs $5 for a day's access to all National Parks and some national forests, or $30 for a year's access. Although the fees have been protested in some

places, particularly the Los Angeles area, they generally have been accepted.

"Congress doesn't appropriate enough money to maintain the level of recreation we need," says Dennis Tighe, president of the Montana Wilderness Association in Great Falls. "A reasonable user fee isn't inappropriate because the public needs to understand that it takes money and time and commitment to keep up public lands."

But fees may not be enough to protect some heavily visited areas. And some environmentalists say fees are unfair because they may prevent lower-income Americans from enjoying public lands. A fairer way to protect the forests, they say, would be to distribute a limited number of free permits, which would restrict the number of visitors to certain areas.

"It is the philosophy of the Wilderness Society that use of the forests should occur as long as it doesn't cause damage," Francis says. "But some areas are very sensitive, so a permit system may be needed to prevent damage to sensitive areas. Permits are more equitable than fees, which are a hidden tax on those who have already paid to protect the national forests."

Should the federal government continue to subsidize the use of national forest resources?

Since its creation in 1905, the Forest Service has been charged not only with protecting the land and resources under its care but also ensuring the production of timber for America's construction needs. That mandate was fixed as early as 1897, when the Organic Administration Act declared, "No national forest shall be established, except to improve and protect the forest within the boundaries, or for the purpose of securing favorable conditions of water flows, and to furnish a continuous supply of timber for the use and necessities of citizens of the United States."

The timber program allows logging companies to bid for tracts opened up to logging and extends them credit to help defray the cost of building roads. After the loggers leave, the Forest Service is responsible for maintaining the roads. For decades, the system profited the timber companies and the Forest Service.

But in recent years the timber program has operated at a net loss. In less than a decade, the Wilderness Society reports, the value of timber on national forests has plummeted, from $1.3 billion to $126 million. [11]

Environmentalists and some conservative lawmakers say that by allowing the program to lose money, the government, in effect, gives a massive subsidy to the logging industry, much as ranchers are subsidized by below-market fees for grazing their herds on public lands.

But timber industry representatives deny that they receive favorable treatment for logging in national forests. "When my members bid for timber sales, they bid the price up," says West. "The Forest Service gets top dollar. So there's no subsidy here. They're getting the fair market value for the trees."

Why is the Forest Service losing money from its timber program? "Mismanagement," West says. "Small mom-and-pop tree farmers, private forest landowners and the states can all manage forests, protect the environment and return money to their own pockets or to the public. It's only the Forest Service and the Clinton administration that can't get a financial return out of the forests. The standing trees that we bid on are only worth so much, and the prices are the same whether it's state or private land. If the costs are exceedingly high, it isn't the industry's fault."

But many forestry experts call that

explanation disingenuous. "Somebody is providing the companies with the infrastructure to get those logs out, and we taxpayers are the ones who are doing it," says Char Miller, an expert on the Forest Service at Trinity University in San Antonio, Texas. "From the beginning, the federal government has ineffectively applied its regulatory powers to protecting those resources so the public gets the fair market value for what those people are extracting. There is no effective accounting."

"If we ended the timber-sales program and redirected logging subsides,"

U.S. Forest Service

Many "quiet" forest recreationists like hikers and skiers want motorized vehicles — already banned in wilderness areas — restricted in other parts of the national forests as well.

writes Chad Hanson, executive director of the John Muir Project in Pasadena, Calif., which "we could provide more than $25,000 for each public lands timber worker for retraining or eco-logical-restoration work — and still have more than $200 million left over to reduce the federal deficit in the first year alone." [12] ∎

BACKGROUND

'Appalling' Destruction

When European settlers first arrived in North America, the Atlantic seaboard was thickly forested. As their numbers grew, the colonists and early Americans cleared vast tracts of land for farming, using much of the timber to build the growing cities of the Northeast, South and Midwest. As they pushed the frontier westward, Americans felled the trees before them until they reached the grasslands of the Great Plains.

By the mid-1800s, the same deforestation that had decimated the Eastern forests was hitting the West Coast as well. The California Gold Rush helped speed the construction of San Francisco and other Pacific Coast cities and build the railroad network that soon spanned the continent.

Until the late 19th century, there was little concern about the impact of unlimited logging. Trees were viewed as a limitless resource. "Outside the tropics, American forests were the richest and most productive on earth, and the best able to repay good management," wrote Gifford Pinchot, the Forest Service's far-sighted first director. "But nobody had begun to manage any part of them with an eye to the future. On the contrary, the greatest, the swiftest, the most efficient and the most appalling wave of forest destruction in human history was then swelling to its climax in the United States; and the American people were glad of it. . . . Public opinion held the forests in particular to be inexhaustible and in the way. What to do with the timber? Get rid of it, of course." [13]

Forestry — the study of forests and their scientific management through limited logging — was not even taught in American universities. So after graduating from Yale University, Pinchot enrolled in the French Forest School in Nancy to learn his trade. On his return he became the forester at Biltmore, George W. Vanderbilt's vast estate in western North Carolina.

Forest Service Born

I n response to growing concern about the rapid destruction of U.S. forests and other natural resources, the Bureau of Forestry was created in 1880 to provide information on timber harvesting and other management techniques to private woodlot owners. In 1891, Congress authorized the president to set aside public lands as "forest reserves." [14] But these reserves were not destined for conservation. The 1897 Organic Administration Act specified that one of the aims of the reserves was "to furnish a continuous supply of timber."

Theodore Roosevelt, who became president in 1901, greatly expanded the role of conservation in the United States, acquiring vast tracts and placing them under federal management. In Pinchot, who had become chief of the Forestry Bureau in 1898, Roosevelt found an enthusiastic ally for the conservation ideal,

and he transferred the forest reserves from the Interior Department to Pinchot's agency. As one of his first actions in office, Pinchot in 1905 renamed the bureau the U.S. Forest Service. Although the service remained part of the Agriculture Department, Pinchot and later chief foresters maintained considerable independence for the service.

In addition to the forest reserves already set aside for federal management, the Forest Service began purchasing previously deforested land in the East by authority of the 1911 Weeks Law, which led to the creation of national forests east of the Mississippi. Most of the National Forest System, however, lies in the West, which had undergone less intensive logging at the time the Forest Service was created. Initially, the

Critics say the Forest Service's timber-sales program is not economical, but forestry interests say the agency mismanages the program.

service focused on conservation and management of non-logging activities, such as recreation and leasing land to cattle ranchers and mining companies. But even then, conservationists such as Aldo Leopold and Robert Marshall convinced the Forest Service to set aside more than 5 million acres of public forest as wilderness or primitive areas, off-limits to disruptive human activities.

The conservation bias of the Forest

Service was short-lived, however. William Howard Taft, who succeeded Roosevelt in 1909, departed decisively from the land-management policies of Roosevelt and Pinchot, who described the new president as "the accomplice and the refuge of land grabbers, water-power grabbers, grabbers of timber and oil — all the swarm of big and little thieves and near-thieves, who, inside or outside of the law, were doing everything they knew to get possession of natural resources which . . . should have been conserved in the public interest." [15] Taft dismissed Pinchot in 1910.

Logging Boom

D espite the erosion of Roosevelt's conservation policies, the national forests were for several decades overlooked as major sources of commercial timber. That changed after World War II, when the demand f or new housing quickly overwhelmed the supply of privately held timber in the United States. As the chief remaining source of timber, the Forest Service began allowing the building of logging access roads in the national forests. By 1968, the amount of timber sold by the service had more than doubled from its early postwar level, to 12.8 billion board feet.

Intensive logging in national forests was hotly debated from the start. During the 1950s, Leopold and Marshall, cofounders of the Wilderness Society, lobbied for legal protection from logging of

Continued on p. 916

Chronology

1890s Widespread deforestation leads to early conservation efforts.

1880
The Bureau of Forestry is created in the Department of Agriculture to provide information on timber management.

1891
Congress authorizes the president to set aside public lands as "forest reserves."

1897
The Organic Administration Act opens forest reserves to commercial logging.

1900s The debate begins between loggers and conservationists over forest management.

1905
Gifford Pinchot, picked by conservationist President Theodore Roosevelt as the Forestry Bureau's first chief, changes the agency's name to the U.S. Forest Service.

1910
A year after taking office and shifting Forest Service priorities away from conservation, President William Howard Taft dismisses Pinchot, a vocal critic of the new policy.

1911
The Weeks Law authorizes the Forest Service to begin buying deforested land in the East, resulting in the creation of national forests east of the Mississippi River.

1950s-1970s The postwar housing boom spurs demand for timber; criticism of clearcutting builds.

1960
The Multiple-Use Sustained-Yield Act expands the Forest Service's mandate to encompass management of the national forests for outdoor recreation, timber, watershed conservation and other purposes.

1964
The Wilderness Act provides for designated lands to be off-limits to all motorized vehicles and bicycles. By 1998, 18 percent of national forest lands will be declared wilderness areas.

1968
Timber sales by the Forest Service reach 12.8 billion board feet, more than twice the level in the late 1940s.

1974
The Resources Planning Act requires the Forest Service to estimate every five years how much timber can be harvested from national forests with available funding.

1976
The National Forest Management Act limits clearcutting in national forests and requires the Forest Service to set more detailed plans for logging, cattle grazing, mineral extraction and other industrial activities in national forests.

1980s Logging in national forests intensifies during the Reagan administration.

1985
Fewer than half the national forests meet the deadline for completion of forest plans after the Reagan administration orders the Forest Service to "streamline" the agency's planning process.

1990s The Clinton administration tries to boost the role of conservation in national forest management.

1993
President Clinton holds a forest summit in Portland, Ore., and issues the Pacific Northwest Plan, an effort to resolve the ongoing conflict between loggers and environmentalists over protection of the Northern spotted owl's forest habitat.

1995
President Clinton signs a law enabling timber companies to perform so-called salvage logging to remove fallen or diseased trees, but environmentalists charge that the law simply enables loggers to remove more healthy trees than ever.

1996
Sierra Club members call for a ban on all commercial logging in national forests.

Jan. 6, 1997
New Forest Service chief Michael P. Dombeck takes office, calling for a major shift of the agency's priorities away from logging in favor of conservation.

Jan. 22, 1998
Dombeck proposes halt in road building in backcountry forests for 18 months.

Do Taxpayers Get Cheated . . .

America's 155 national forests cover 192 million acres, or about 8 percent of all the land in the United States. But because of 19th-century land policies, small pieces of these holdings have been nibbled away, much like a moth-eaten wool blanket.

To encourage the construction of railroads across the country, for example, the federal government in the mid-1800s gave railroad companies every other square-mile section on either side of the tracks they built, leaving a checkerboard pattern of public and private land. Civil War veterans were given parcels of public land for their service instead of pensions. Homesteading grants further ate into the fabric of public land holdings.

Today, as a result, many national forests are dotted with pockets of private and state inholdings. "The land patterns of the United States are a mishmash, a quilt work resulting from a variety of policies, some of which were appropriate and some misguided," says Forest Service chief Michael P. Dombeck. "That is what we're left with. Any landowner will tell you that this is a nightmare to manage."

In addition to making it harder to oversee the forests, the fragmentation of forested land threatens the survival of many animal species, such as grizzly bears, spotted owls and wolves, which require large, uninterrupted tracts of undeveloped land to live.

In recent years, because of limited funding for land purchases, the Forest Service has sought to consolidate its holdings by trading less ecologically fragile lands at the edge of forests for private property in the forest interior or other areas that are deemed to be environmentally sensitive. In 1997, the agency exchanged 134,000 acres of public land for 244,000 non-federal acres.[1] "The objective of our lands program." Dombeck explains, "is to achieve a land-tenure pattern that makes the most sense, that's the most efficient to manage."

But critics charge that land swaps often change the character of nearby communities, and that the Forest Service is short-changing the public through sloppy appraisals. As a result, they say, profiteers are able to turn once pristine woodlands accessible to everyone into private developments.

Criticism mounted in 1994, when the Forest Service gave Colorado developer Thomas Chapman 105 acres of national forest near the ski resort of Telluride in exchange for a 270-acre parcel he owned deep inside the West Elk Wilderness. An appraiser working for the Forest Service valued each property at $640,000. But just eight months after the swap, Chapman sold 70 acres of the land near Telluride for $2.7 million.

The public outcry was swift. "This is a rip-off, pure and simple, of a public resource for private profiteering," charged then Democratic Colorado Sen. Ben Nighthorse Campbell (who later became a Republican), "and is just one more example of the loss of control that local officials suffer when dealing with the tremendous growth occurring in ski resort towns all across Colorado."[2]

A similar controversy arose last summer in Crested Butte, another small town on the western slope of the Colorado Rockies. In that case, the land trade involved the Forest Service, the Colorado State Land Board and Crested Butte Mountain Resort (CBMR), which owns a ski resort. The town of Crested Butte and other critics of the deal appealed the Forest Service's decision to go ahead with the deal, arguing that the Forest Service land being traded to CBMR had been undervalued by as much as $15 million, or four times its

---

wilderness areas, but to no avail. The Forest Service, embracing its expanded role in the logging business, responded with an alternative legislative proposal. Under the Multiple-Use Sustained-Yield (MUSY) Act, passed in 1960, the agency's mandate was defined as management of the national forests "for outdoor recreation, range, timber, watershed and wildlife and fish purposes." The law failed to nail down the details of the new mandate, however, giving forest managers broad discretion in carrying it out.

Because the timber-sales program was designed in part to enhance agency revenues, managers were encouraged to fill their annual quotas of timber harvested on land under their care. The develop-ment of more efficient logging equipment made it possible to increase the total acreage of timber harvested in national forests. It also enabled loggers to replace selection cutting, or harvesting only those trees destined for the sawmill, with clearcutting, which also eliminated trees with little or no value as cut logs.

These techniques boosted timber-company profits but offended other national forest users. Finally, in 1964, opponents of large-scale logging in national forests gained passage of the Wilderness Act, which barred logging and other activities likely to disturb the natural habitat of wilderness areas. But clearcutting remained the method of choice for logging on national forest lands.

In response to continued public criticism of its aggressive sales of publicly owned trees to logging companies, the Forest Service devised a system of timber and land-use plans for each national forest, each involving public participation and subject to revision every 10 years. The agency was also required by court order to refrain from building roads or selling timber in any roadless area until it completed an environmental-impact statement to determine whether the tract in question would be more suitably treated under the Wilderness Act.

As logging on national forests continued to intensify in the 1960s and '70s, the timber industry challenged the For-

... By Forest Service Land Swaps?

potential market price. The Forest Service has acknowledged that the appraiser did not take into account the possibility that the 550 acres would be incorporated into the ski resort and intensively developed, increasing the land's value. The critics also charged that the Forest Service had failed to adequately assess the trade's environmental impact.

In September, after the ski resort agreed to increase the amount of open space in the area that will be closed to future development, the appeals were withdrawn and the land swap went forward.

But the Forest Service was harshly criticized for its role in this and other land swaps. "While we are content with the agreement we reached with CBMR, we are extremely disappointed with the Forest Service land-exchange program," said Sandy Shea, public lands coordinator of the High Country Citizens' Alliance, a local grass-roots organization that seeks to preserve open space. "The land trade program within the Forest Service is scandalous. No communities facing public land trades should have to [hire its own appraisers to] do the work of the Forest Service ever again. We intend to push for agency reform to ensure that land trades truly benefit the owners of the land — the American public."

Dombeck acknowledges some of the criticism of land swaps. "Americans are less willing to give up public lands because they've grown accustomed to hunting, fishing and hiking on these lands," he says. "So when the Forest Service does propose land swaps, a new piece of the equation is that local communities often oppose them because they want to continue to have access to the land."

Meanwhile, Dombeck says his agency is reviewing its handling of land trades. "I've asked my staff to very aggressively and quickly review our policies to make sure that we're getting fair market value," he says, "and to make sure that our employees have the tools they need to work through something that's very complex and changing very rapidly because of the rapidly escalating increase in land values in various areas of the country."

Some of these complexities could be eliminated if the Forest Service were simply to buy the private inholdings it covets on the open market instead of negotiating land trades. Indeed, Congress in 1964 established the Land and Water Conservation Fund for that purpose, but the program has not been used widely. 'The purchase is certainly a clean way to do it," Dombeck says. "But [little money] is being allocated."

President Clinton supports new purchases, especially in light of the first federal budget surplus in 29 years in fiscal 1998. "The money is there, the economy is in good shape, the budget is going to be balanced," Clinton said on April 22 in calling on Congress to release hundreds of millions of dollars that have been earmarked for enlarging national parks and wilderness areas. "We've made this commitment to our future, and I'd like to see us get it done." [3]

---

[1] See Matt Rasmussen, "Federal Report: Forest Service Land Swaps Cost Millions," *Inner Voice*, July 1998. *Inner Voice* is published by Forest Service Employees for Environmental Ethics, a membership group.

[2] Quoted by Laura Anderson, "Chapman Cashes in on Land: $2.7 Million and Counting," *Crested Butte* [Colo.] *Chronicle & Pilot*, Feb. 3, 1995.

[3] See Joby Warrick, "Clinton Urges Release of Wilderness Money," *The Washington Post*, April 23, 1998.

---

est Service's traditional goal of limiting timber harvests to a level that could be continued indefinitely without depleting the overall supply. Congress upheld this sustainability principle in 1974 with the Resources Planning Act, which required the Forest Service to estimate every five years how much timber could be harvested from national forests with available funding.

Widespread clearcutting in the Monongahela National Forest in West Virginia prompted a legal challenge to this practice spearheaded by oil heir Lawrence Rockefeller and the Natural Resources Defense Council (NRDC). Citing a provision of the 1897 Organic Administration Act, they forced the Forest

Service to bar clearcutting in the Monongahela. As the debate over clearcutting spread, Congress passed the 1976 National Forest Management Act. Although it fell short of banning clearcutting, the law placed certain limits on the practice. The law also refined the Forest Service's planning process, setting specific objectives for timber, cattle grazing, mineral extraction and other activities in each of the agency's nine regions.

But the new planning process ran into repeated delays stemming initially from a decision by the Reagan administration to "streamline" the rules. By the 1985 deadline for completion of plans for all the national forests, fewer than half had been drawn up.

Crackdown in the '90s

Though clearcutting was not completely eliminated in national forests, more recent rules have greatly reduced its use. As part of a new policy emphasizing an ecological approach to forest management, the Forest Service announced restrictions on clearcutting by commercial loggers that have reduced clearcutting by 84 percent, according to Dombeck.

In addition to the restrictions on clearcutting, the 1990s have seen a fundamental shift in past practices by the Forest Service. Part of the change can be explained by court decisions arising from the Endangered Species Act. Listing of the Northern spotted owl, an elusive bird that depends on large tracts of uninterrupted old-growth forest for its survival, prompted a flurry of lawsuits by logging companies and rancorous demonstrations pitting jobless loggers against environmentalists. [16] Resulting cutbacks in logging permits caused harvest levels to drop drastically.

In 1993, President Clinton held a forest summit in Portland, Ore., in an effort to resolve the seemingly irreconcilable conflict between environmentalists and the timber industry. In 1995, however, the president signed a bill that enabled loggers to perform so-called salvage logging in the name of forest health without fear of lawsuits. The measure was ostensibly aimed at facilitating the removal of fallen or diseased trees, which provide fuel for wildfires, but timber companies also removed many healthy trees as well. ∎

sources. One of the administration's first steps was aimed at breaking the so-called Iron Triangle — the informal understanding among timber companies, lawmakers and Forest Service officials that timber harvesting was the agency's first priority. Toward that end, Clinton replaced agency chief F. Dale Robertson with Jack Ward Thomas, a biologist who helped devise the plan to protect spotted owl habitat in the Pacific Northwest. Thomas came under savage attack from Republican lawmakers fighting reductions in timber harvests as well as environmentalists seeking the cuts. Thomas resigned in 1996 after serving only three years.

Dombeck, who has a doctorate in fisheries biology, was chosen from outside the Forest Service ranks. A former acting director of the Bureau of Land Management, he served notice soon after taking office on Jan. 6, 1997, that timber harvesting would no longer dominate the forest-management agenda. "The health of the land must be our first priority," he testified shortly after taking office. "Failing this, nothing else we do really matters." [17] Dombeck has outlined a

"natural resource agenda" that shifts the agency's emphasis from commodity production to watershed health and restoration and sustainable forest ecosystem management.

Because national forest lands account for only about 30 percent of U.S. woodlands, conservation of forest resources must include efforts by private landowners and state and local governments, as well as the Forest Service. In an effort to foster forest conservation outside the National Forest System, Dombeck announced in 1997 a new program to help forest owners and managers outside the federal system maintain their holdings. An obstacle to this effort, however, is the continuing fragmentation of forest properties. "Ownership of non-federal forests is in increasingly smaller units, as they are divided for family inheritance and other reasons," says Dan Smith of American Forests, a nonprofit group that encourages forest conservation. "The number of people owning forests is increasing dramatically while the total number of acres is decreasing due to development. So it's more difficult to manage forests in ways that protect the larger ecosystem."

Like his predecessor, Dombeck is walking a fine line between satisfying environmental organizations, which say he is not doing enough to protect the forests, and placating the timber industry, which charges he is caving in to radical "enviros" and destroying jobs in the process. [18]

"Dombeck's job is like asking a

Older logging roads that cause erosion into streams may be destroyed under new policies being developed by the Forest Service.

Wilderness Society

CURRENT SITUATION

Chief Dombeck

Vice President Al Gore's strong support for environmental protection has helped steer the Clinton administration's public lands policy toward conservation of natural re-

person to herd a bunch of Tyranosaurus Rex into a vegetable patch and convince them to become vegetarians," says Francis of the Wilderness Society. "They ate Jack Ward Thomas when he tried to do that, and they wouldn't mind eating Dombeck, too."

Alleged Mismanagement

Many critics agree that the Forest Service suffers from general mismanagement. The General Accounting Office has reported numerous flaws in the agency's accounting practices. [19] And the Forest Service itself has admitted that its timber-sales program is actually losing money.

But critics disagree sharply over the reasons for the Forest Service's spotty record. "The American taxpayer has been paying for irresponsible Forest Service management schemes for decades, through subsidized road-building, off-budget slush funds that support excessive logging and below-cost timber sales that cost the government more money to administer than it collects from the timber companies for the timber," writes Jim Jontz, director of the Western Ancient Forest Campaign. [20]

Timber industry supporters say blame for the Forest Service's problems lies elsewhere. "Especially in the Clinton administration, there are layers of bureaucracy and political interference that second-guess on-the-ground programs, turning what should be scientific decisions into political ones," West says. As an example, he points to the recent sale of timber salvaged from a devastating fire that swept through northern Colorado's Routt National Forest in 1996. "The value of the burned timber was $100 million just after the fire, but by the time the Forest Ser-

vice sold it in August the value was just $2 million," West says. "Because of the deterioration over two years from insects, stains, fungus and checking [cracking], only a small portion of the timber can now be salvaged."

But environmentalists denounce so-called salvage timber sales as little more than ploys to enable timber companies to harvest vast tracts of healthy trees as well as damaged timber.

The Forest Service also is under fire from whistleblowers who charge the agency is not aggressively pursuing the widespread theft of trees from national forests, often by timber companies. They contend that "wood rustlers" steal an estimated $100 million worth of trees annually by moving timber harvest boundaries, stealing paint used to mark trees approved for cutting and cutting unmarked trees while leaving less valuable trees standing. The problem has grown worse, critics say, since the service disbanded a special timber-theft task force in 1995. [21]

Advocates of a conservationist approach to public land management also take the Forest Service to task for failing to get a fair deal on land trades. *(See story, p. 916.)*

One of the biggest obstacles to Dombeck's conservationist agenda is the agency's long-standing culture favoring extraction of timber, minerals and other resources. "Management varies according to the regional foresters, and so does understanding of ecosystem protection," says Griffin of the Sierra Club. "Nationwide, the Forest Service has been dominated by timber industry interests for many years, and people know that."

If anything, the bias of extraction over conservation intensified until Clinton took office. "The Republicans during the Reagan administration demanded higher and higher cuts from people who were trained

as biologists, so in a sense the agency is fighting itself," says Miller of Trinity University. "If you don't get the cut out, you don't get promoted."

There are signs that the agency's culture is changing. Gloria Flora, supervisor of the 1.8-million-acre Lewis and Clark National Forest in Montana, broke ranks with past policy last September by denying drilling permits on forest land for the next two decades. Although the forest is believed to be rich in natural gas deposits, it also is a unique ecosystem embracing plains and mountain habitats and is home to grizzly bears and other threatened wildlife.

"I believe very strongly in what Gifford Pinchot said: that when a conflict of interest arises it should be resolved for the greatest good of the greatest number of people in the long run," Flora said in explaining her decision. "The gas will still be there in 20 years, and maybe then, if we absolutely have to have it, we can get it. But what if, by then, wild lands are so diminished that the most precious resource on public lands is these last wild places?" [22]

But for now, Flora is still in the minority. "As an eternal optimist, I hope that Flora represents a change, but I think she's still a fluke right now," Miller says. "Even now, as Forest Service officials mouth the need for change, the internal memos to field personnel still read, 'Hey, you didn't get your cut out.'"

Logging Moratorium

Of all Dombeck's initiatives, none has attracted more controversy than his Jan. 22 proposal to halt road construction in all national forest roadless areas for 18 months. With 373,000 miles of authorized roads and an additional 60,000 miles of unmanaged "ghost roads," the Forest Service faces a growing maintenance and repair backlog. Only about 40 percent of forest roads meet the safety and environmental standards to which they were designed, and the price tag just to catch up is estimated at $10 billion. [23]

The moratorium was designed to give the agency time to catch up on repairs as well as to craft a new transportation policy governing future road construction. That policy is expected to require fewer and better-built roads, the destruction of older roads that have caused erosion into nearby streams and safety improvements to existing roads that get the most public use. The announcement sparked a new round of controversy.

Environmentalists hailed the moratorium as a step toward halting one of the worst effects of forest roads, pollution of precious watersheds. But many say the proposed moratorium fails to go far enough because it does not bar logging in roadless areas, which cover some 60 million acres of national forests. "The weakness in the proposal is that it makes no mention of whether or not logging will be allowed in these areas," says Francis of the Wilderness Society. "Helicopters are still allowed to go into roadless areas and haul out timber."

In addition, the moratorium exempts forests in Alaska as well as those covered by the Northwest Forest Plan, Clinton's 1993 initiative to resolve the ongoing legal dispute over protection of spotted owl habitat. The moratorium also will not apply to 12 national forests where land management plans — which are updated every 10 years — have been completed. As a result of these loopholes, according to a report by 27 environmental groups, some 25 million acres of roadless areas

will not be protected from logging by the moratorium. [24]

Critics Call for Tougher Action

Some critics of the moratorium say it should ban logging altogether in roadless areas, a proposal that appears to find growing public support. A recent poll commissioned by the Wilderness Society found that 65 percent of all voters support a proposal

---

A recent poll commissioned by the Wilderness Society found that 65 percent of all voters support a proposal to halt timber cutting in roadless forest areas and to protect those areas from development.

---

to halt timber cutting in roadless forest areas and to protect those areas from development. [25] "When we told people that in Idaho alone 1 million acres had been lost to logging over the past decade, the percentage jumped to 74 percent," Francis says. "The idea of protecting forests is pretty universal across the country. Forests are part of our legacy, and there is a deep-seated support for protecting them, whether you're talking about forests in the Appalachians, the Rockies, the Pacific Northwest or

Alaska. This flies in the face of what the Forest Service is doing and what the industry and Western lawmakers want."

Timber Industry Responds

Timber industry representatives — and their congressional allies — decried the moratorium as yet another assault on jobs in the West, where most of the roadless areas are found, and a violation of the Forest Service's mandate to provide timber for U.S. consumption. "The environmentalists are using roads as a back door to eliminate the timber program," says West of the Northwest Forestry Association. He also says the moratorium would actually delay remediation of water courses that have been damaged by older roads. "Everybody recognizes that there are better ways to build roads to protect the environment, and many timber sales include plans for new road construction to obliterate and replace old and badly built roads," he says. "But with the moratorium, we're stuck with the old roads. We support a new transportation plan, but we just feel that we don't need to stop the world to get it done."

The industry's leading allies in Congress — Sens. Murkowski and Craig and Reps. Young and Chenoweth — have threatened to cut the Forest Service's budget unless Dombeck increases timber production. They have addressed rallies in their home districts warning constituents of impending job losses if the moratorium goes through and have conducted numerous hearings in Washington on allegations of the agency's mismanagement. "Today's proposal is more about politics than environmental protection, designed to reignite interest group conflicts over forest management rather than to address a serious problem,"

Continued on p. 922

At Issue:

Should road building in the national forests be halted temporarily?

MICHAEL P. DOMBECK

Chief, U.S. Forest Service

From testimony before House Resources Subcommittee on Forests and Forest Health, Feb. 25, 1998.

*w*hat I have proposed is essentially a "time out" on road building in roadless areas during which Congress, the administration and the American people can engage in a dialogue about when and where roads will be built in our national forests. We are going to develop a science-based forest transportation system that meets the needs of local people while minimizing and reversing the adverse environmental effects . . . roads often cause. . . .

This policy review is critical so we can focus our limited resources on the roads most in need. Finally, we intend to develop a road policy that allows us to "catch up" on our enormous backlog in road maintenance and reconstruction while meeting management objectives and access needs.

The road network on the national forest system is extensive and diverse. Many roads are essential for the active management of national forest resources and provide many and varied benefits. They are critical to timber harvest, mineral extraction, livestock grazing and recreation access. They provide important access for fire control, law enforcement, search and rescue, wildlife habitat improvement and research and monitoring. There is no question that the road network on our national forest system serves, and will continue to serve, as a fundamental component for delivery of multiple-use programs. . . .

While forest roads provide many benefits, they can also cause serious environmental damage. While new developments in road-building technology result in fewer negative environmental effects, the environmental effects from existing roads are more extensive than previously thought. Road construction may cause increased frequency of flooding and landslides, and increased stream sedimentation, with associated reductions in aquatic habitat productivity and water quality. Roads may also fragment and degrade habitat for some wildlife species. Research indicates that roading may begin or accelerate the invasion of exotic plant species that ultimately displace native species and diminish the productivity of the land.

Public use of and demands on national forest resources have shifted considerably during the past 10 years. While there has been a decrease in timber harvesting and other commodity uses, we have seen steadily increasing growth in the amount and type of recreation uses. Currently, more than 90 percent of the traffic using Forest Service roads is recreation-related. With this shift in public use has come changes in user expectations and access needs, requiring new approaches to decide which roads to close or leave open.

REP. HELEN CHENOWETH, R-IDAHO

From a statement before the House Resources Subcommittee on Forests and Forest Health, Feb. 25, 1998.

*f*orests don't take a "time-out" for Washington bureaucrats. So why is the Clinton-Gore administration taking a "time-out" from sound forest-health management practices? The administration claims that its moratorium on roadless area entry is a "time-out" on timber harvesting. But this is much larger than just timber harvesting. The ripple effect of the "time-out" affects the health of the national forests, the families and surrounding communities who rely on the forest for their livelihoods.

This "time-out" on the national forests is exceedingly harmful. While the country waits for the Clinton-Gore administration to get its act together and unchain our forests, a wide range of wildlife, hunting, fishing, conservation and recreation groups have expressed their concern about the administration's "time-out." Under this moratorium, everyone loses, except maybe some of the most extreme environmental groups who care little about people.

Recreationists have expressed their concern that they will lose access to the lands they hunt on. Conservationists have expressed their concern with the damage this poorly thought-out policy will have on the land. . . .

Why, then, is the Clinton-Gore administration moving forward with a policy that violates current law and will do nothing to improve the forest environment? The answer is clear. This is nothing more than a politically motivated decision in order to appease the most radical elements of a single interest group. In developing their policy they completely shut out Congress, the on-the-ground forest managers and the American people. . . .

[B]y starting the debate on road maintenance with a surprise moratorium on access and by raising public concerns among those who depend upon access to the public lands for their economic well-being and recreation opportunities, the Forest Service has made it less, rather than more, likely that maintenance problems can be addressed. Their approach so far is akin to starting an Olympic speed-skating event by shooting themselves in both feet.

The Clinton-Gore moratorium violates the two most important things that the Forest Service is charged to do — the first is to protect our forest resources and manage them in a sustainable manner in order to pass them on to our next generations; the second is to make wise use of taxpayer funding.

This policy, made in the back rooms of Washington, is nothing more than a political payoff to a core constituency. It is both bad for the environment and bad for people.

Continued from p. 920

Murkowski said in a prepared statement on Jan. 22. "It's as if 'the gang that couldn't shoot straight' redeclared the War on the West that it started in 1993."

Not all lawmakers support the timber industry's interests. Reps. McKinney and Leach are among a small but growing number of members who have called for cuts in timber harvests on national forests. Even some timber industry representatives support the moratorium as an essential step to protect the national forests from overcutting. The Southern Utah Forest Products Association, which represents small-scale loggers in five counties, wrote Dombeck a letter of support for more sustainable forest management, stating that current timber-cutting levels would destroy the forests, "with all the profits going to large out-of-state companies." [26]

Although the public comment period for the road-building moratorium ended in March, the final decision has been deferred until "sometime in midfall," according to Dombeck. "We had 65,000 comments on the proposal, so we have learned some things and we need to make sure those things are integrated into the policy," he says. "Then we can go on to the long-term policy, which really is the most important part of this process."

Battle Over Recreation

As tourism grows and logging declines on national forests, the For-

est Service is studying the impact of recreation on forest habitats. "One of the reasons that we've got to relook at our policies that underpin the roads program is that the policies we're working from today are based upon forest management," Dombeck says, "not upon recreation and the thousands of station wagons, kids and families that are on the national forests. We need to preserve the quality setting and experiences that people expect."

In some forests, the crush of tourists has grown so intense that Forest

The crush of tourists has grown so intense in some forests that the Forest Service has imposed fees or limits on the number of visitors admitted.

Service officials have imposed fees or limits on the number of people admitted, similar to those already in effect in such popular National Parks as Yosemite and Yellowstone. For the most part, agency officials say the fees are supported by visitors because the revenues are used to improve picnic areas and toilets and maintain trails. But this attitude is not universal. In Southern California, residents of Ojai and other California communities located near the Los Padres National Forest have organized protests against the fees. [27]

While many environmentalists ap-

plaud fees and restrictions to forests where overuse is causing damage to sensitive habitats, others fear the fees may provide an excuse for loggers and other industrial users to continue receiving government subsidies. "American taxpayers pay to maintain the national forests, but now they're also being asked to subsidize industries that are using the forests," says Francis of the Wilderness Society. "We don't oppose recreational fees for developed facilities [such as picnic areas and heavily used trails], but we are adamantly opposed to them as long as the timber, mining and cattle industries get subsidies."

Even where fees are not an issue, tensions are building between two groups of recreational forest users: hikers, cross-country skiers, hunters and campers on one side and motorcyclists, snowmobilers and all-terrain vehicle (ATV) drivers on the other. Many non-motorized, or "quiet," forest recreationists want motor vehicles — already banned in wilderness areas — restricted in other parts of the national forests as well.

"The Forest Service has abused its discretion in allowing different types of off-road vehicles into national forests without doing an analysis on their impact," says Tighe of the Montana Wilderness Association, who singles out ATVs as the most damaging vehicles. "These four-wheel-drive vehicles are wide and very stable, and they can go just about anywhere if they can squeeze through the trees." Because they are so easy to drive, Tighe says, ATVs have proliferated in the forests. "Motorcycle drivers dress up like they're going to do battle in an arena, with the shin guards, helmets and body suits. But anyone, even a young person without a driver's license, can jump on an ATV in his shorts and go up steep slopes and other places where vehicles have never gone before."

Tighe blames the Forest Service for caving in to pressure from groups representing drivers of off-road vehicles. "The Forest Service is very intimidated in some ways by off-highway vehicle groups, which are well-organized and well-funded," he says. Tighe's group has filed suit against the Forest Service in federal district court, charging the agency with mismanagement for allowing off-road vehicles in areas that are currently under study for possible designation as wilderness areas.

Meanwhile, ATV use continues to grow. The number of registered ATVs and off-road motorcycles mushroomed from 277,000 in 1977 to 2.5 million in 1993. [28] Representatives of "mechanized recreationists" say they have just as much right to enjoy the national forests as anyone else. "People choose to enjoy the outdoors in many different ways, and one of these is mechanized access to our national forests," says Ed Moreland, Washington representative of the American Motorcyclists Association, which counts 228,000 members. Unlike their critics who are trying to bar vehicular traffic in national forests, Moreland says, "Mechanized recreationists are not seeking to hinder anyone else's use of the trails they ride." For him, the debate comes down to an issue of basic fairness.

"For some people, who because of disabilities or age may not be able to hike into the woods, off-highway vehicles offer the only reasonable way to enjoy the outdoors," Moreland says. "Others just choose to recreate by means of off-highway vehicles. We all enjoy the outdoors, and we should all work together to benefit from it." ■

OUTLOOK

Shifting Priorities

As more and more urban dwellers flock to the national forests, the controversy over recreational use seems likely to intensify. "The Wilderness Act launched a whole new discourse about trees and the landscape and forced the Forest Service to think about new ways to manage the land," Miller says. "Recreation will be the next phase of the discourse."

Ironically, all parties to the emerging debate want the same thing from the forests — to find respite from daily stress in a natural setting. "We are all going there for space," Miller says. "Whether it's by foot, helicopter, bike or car, we're all doing it because we want nature to restore us in some fashion. Whether you backpack off into a wilderness area or park your RV on a roadside with the TV going, it's the same thing. But these people will fight with one another faster than the environmentalists and the loggers."

In Miller's view, the debate over recreational use of national forests will continue to escalate until lawmakers are forced to settle the issue. "Confronted with a population that is outstripping the capacity of the national forests to sustain our recreational needs, we're going to have to come up with a new set of purchases of land. Alternatively, and I think this is more likely, there will be new pressures to restrain logging even more and open the forests up to recreational uses."

No matter how lawmakers and Forest Service officials seek to resolve these issues, the debate points to a fundamental shift in attitudes toward natural resources. "The public's expectations of what it really wants from the forests has changed, especially in the past 20 years," Francis says. "A non-declining flow of timber is not at the top of their list of priorities any more. For many, it's not there at all." ■

Notes

[1] House Resources Subcommittee on Forests and Forest Health, June 23, 1998.

[2] See U.S. Forest Service, "Report of the Forest Service," 1997.

[3] See "The Forest's Future," *The Christian Science Monitor*, Feb. 23, 1998.

[4] See "Timber Sales Lose $88 Million," *The Washington Post*, June 11, 1998.

[5] Chenoweth addressed a joint hearing of the House Resources and Budget committees and the Interior Appropriations Subcommittee on March 26, 1998.

[6] See James Gerstenzang, "GOP Accused of Conducting 'Stealth' Attacks on Environment," *Los Angeles Times* (Washington edition), July 7, 1998.

[7] For background, see Tom Arrandale, "Public Land Policy," *The CQ Researcher*, June 17, 1994, pp. 529-552.

[8] Quoted in "Sierra Club Members Choose New Directors, New Forestry Policy," *The Planet*, June 1996. *The Planet* is a publication of the Sierra Club.

[9] The telephone poll was conducted June 29-July 1, 1998, by Lake Snell Perry & Associates.

[10] William H. Meadows, "National Forests Turn the Bulldozers Around," *The Christian Science Monitor*, Feb. 24, 1998.

[11] The Wilderness Society, "America's Forest Heritage at Risk," Sept. 3, 1998, p. 5.

[12] Letter to the editor, *The New York Times*, April 11, 1998.

[13] Gifford Pinchot, *Breaking New Ground* (1947), p. 1.

[14] Unless otherwise indicated, information in this section is based on Randal O'Toole, *Reforming the Forest Service* (1988), pp. 20-24.

[15] Pinchot, *op. cit.*, pp. 392-393.

[16] For background, see Kenneth Jost, "Protecting Endangered Species," *The CQ Researcher*, April 19, 1996, pp. 337-360.

[17] Testimony before the Senate Committee on Energy and Natural Resources, Feb. 25, 1997.

[18] For background, see Mary H. Cooper, "Jobs vs. Environment," *The CQ Researcher*, May 15, 1992, pp. 409-432.

[19] U.S. General Accounting Office, "Forest Service: Status of Progress Toward Financial Accountability," Feb. 27, 1998.

[20] Jim Jontz, "Forest Servicer Indictment: A Mountain of Evidence: Stewardship or Stumps?" Sierra Club, 1997.

[21] See Brad Knickerbocker, "U.S. Fight Against Timber Thieves," *The Christian Science Monitor*, March 23, 1998.

[22] Quoted by Fen Montaigne, "All's Quiet on the Rocky Mountain Front," *Audubon*, January-February 1998, p. 75.

[23] U.S. Forest Service, "Forest Service Protects Roadless Areas and Announces Development of New Transportation Policies," news release, Jan. 22, 1998.

[24] "America's Forest Heritage at Risk," The Wilderness Society in cooperation with 26 other groups, Sept. 3, 1998.

[25] The nationwide telephone poll was conducted June 29-July 1, 1998, by Lake Snell Perry & Associates.

[26] Quoted in "UT Timber Group Backs Road Moratorium," *Greenwire*, April 2, 1998.

[27] See Marcia Mieir, "Protests Heating Up Against Forest Fees," *Los Angeles Times* (Washington edition), Aug. 17, 1998.

[28] See Scott McMillion, "Man, Machine Wage Battle over Usage of Forest Lands," *The World* (Coos Bay, Ore.), July 24, 1998.

Bibliography

Selected Sources Used

Books

Barney, Daniel R., *The Last Stand: Ralph Nader's Study Group Report on the National Forests*, Grossman Publishers, 1974.
Published at a time of heightened public criticism of clearcutting techniques, this volume charges that the Forest Service has bowed to the timber industry by encouraging logging while ignoring its mandate to preserve the national forests.

Devall, Bill, ed., *Clearcut: The Tragedy of Industrial Forestry*, Sierra Club Books/Earth Island Press, 1993.
This collection of photographs of clearcut woodlands and a series of essays on the industrial exploitation of forests proposes alternative methods of forest management that promote sustainable forestry, resulting in no net loss of trees over time.

Miller, Char, *American Forests: Nature, Culture, and Politics*, University Press of Kansas, 1997.
Edited by a history professor at Trinity University who has published extensively on U.S. forestry, this collection of essays by environmental scholars reviews the history of American forestry and efforts to reform the Forest Service's mission.

O'Toole, Randal, *Reforming the Forest Service*, Island Press, 1988.
The author, an economist for a nonprofit forestry consulting firm, would replace congressional appropriations with recreational and other user fees to pay for managing the national forests. In this way, he writes, some forests would be more heavily harvested for timber while others would be reserved for recreation.

Pinchot, Gifford, *Breaking New Ground*, Island Press, 1947 (commemorative edition, 1998).
The founder and first chief of the Forest Service recounts his training as a one of the first foresters in the United States and his tenure during the administration of President Theodore Roosevelt.

Articles

John J. Berger, "9 Ways to Save Our National Forests," *Sierra*, July-August 1997, pp. 38-39.
In addition to halting commercial logging, the author calls for expanding the wilderness system; ending road building; helping logging communities that would suffer unemployment as a result of a logging ban; and mounting a public-education campaign to teach recreationists how to minimize damage of forest ecosystems.

B. J. Bergman, "Reclaiming the Public's Forests,"

Sierra, **March/April 1998, pp. 34-35.**
The Sierra Club broke ranks with most environmental groups in 1996 when members voted in favor of a ballot initiative calling for a ban on commercial logging in national forests.

"Cabins in the Wilderness: The Market Growls," *The Economist*, Sept. 26, 1998, pp. 29-30.
In an effort to collect more revenue from users of national forests, the Forest Service is raising the fees charged to holders of cabins on federally owned forest land. Renters and their representatives in Congress charge that by raising fees, the agency will shut out all but the wealthy from public land that is owned by all Americans.

Glick, Daniel, "Disturbing the Peace," *Wilderness*, 1998.
Even as an 18-month moratorium on new-road construction in national forests awaits final approval, logging companies continue to build access roads to reach remote timber stands, with what the author describes as dire consequences for water quality and wildlife habitat.

"How Subsidies Destroy the Land," *The Economist*, Dec. 13, 1997, pp. 21-22.
Timber companies are only one of several groups — including cattle ranchers and miners — that benefit from federal subsidies for their use of public land. When the price of exploiting these natural resources falls too low, however, the result is overuse and habitat destruction.

Montaigne, Fen, "All's Quiet on the Rocky Mountain Front," *Audubon*, January/February 1998, pp. 74-76.
By rejecting oil company requests for oil and gas drilling rights in the Lewis and Clark National Forest, Supervisor Gloria Flora broke with Forest Service tradition and handed the industry a surprising defeat.

Satchell, Michael, "Mountain Bikers over Corporate Loggers," *U.S. News & World Report*, May 18, 1997, p. 36.
The new chief of the Forest Service supports fundamental reforms in his agency's organization and mission, but the timber industry's allies in Congress are threatening funding cuts if timber harvests are curtailed. Environmentalists, meanwhile, are calling for a ban on all commercial logging in national forests.

Reports and Studies

The Wilderness Society, *America's Forest Heritage at Risk*, Sept. 3, 1998.
The Wilderness Society and 26 other conservation groups identify 24 wilderness forest areas they say face irreparable damage unless they are protected from timbering, road construction and other development.

The Next Step

Additional information from UMI's Newspaper & Periodical Abstracts™ database

Clearcutting

"National Forests for Sale," *St. Louis Post-Dispatch*, May 9, 1997, p. C12.

The Act to Save America's Forests, a bill introduced in the House by Reps. Anna Eshoo, D-Calif., and Carolyn Maloney, D-N.Y., is "the first federal legislation in history that would halt and reverse deforestation in the United States," says Carl Ross, director of Save America's Forests. The bill would essentially end clearcutting on all federal land while more restrictive "selection management" would be the only form of logging allowed on those federal lands still open to logging.

Michael P. Dombeck

"Showdown on the National Forests," *The New York Times*, April 4, 1998, p. A12.

The timber interests and their political patrons have reacted in fury to lessened timber production. By letter and in public hearings, Republican committee chairmen with jurisdiction over the Forest Service have threatened to slash the Forest Service budget unless agency chief Michael P. Dombeck allows logging companies to produce more timber.

Wester, Dave, "Pursuing Collaborative Stewardship," *American Forests, Summer* 1997, p. 30.

Michael P. Dombeck, who recently became the 14th chief of the Forest Service, visited Aldo Leopold's Sand Country cabin to stress what he calls "collaborative stewardship."

Wilkinson, Todd, "New Plan for America's National Forests; In Announcement Yesterday, U.S. Forest Service Chief Sets New Agenda for Agency," *The Christian Science Monitor, March 3,* 1998, p. 4.

Yesterday, in a message beamed via satellite to some 30,000 workers nationwide, Forest Service Chief Michael P. Dombeck said the agency intends to shift away from being synonymous with the timber industry and toward a focus on providing recreation and clean water. Once a storied institution defined by its woodsman-ranger hats, the Forest Service today is embattled and under attack from all sides.

Road Building

"A Positive Shift in Forest Policy," *The New York Times*, Jan. 14, 1998, p. A16.

Michael P. Dombeck, chief of the Forest Service, will soon announce a moratorium on construction of new logging roads in remote sections of most of the national forests. That will be a courageous change in policy for an agency long-regarded as a willing captive of the timber industry it is supposed to regulate.

"National Forests; Moratorium on Road Building Should be Systemwide," *Houston Chronicle*, Jan. 19, 1998, p. A18.

The Clinton administration is on the verge of signing a moratorium on road building in the national forests to give time for a panel of experts to review current policy and propose a more sensible and less destructive approach to logging, particularly in areas where there are no roads now.

"Timber Wars in Congress," *San Francisco Chronicle*, April 26, 1998, p. S6.

The United States Forest Service's philosophy is changing. A sure sign was Forest Service Chief Michael P. Dombeck's recent order for an 18-month moratorium on road building in the national forests. The decision to reassess heavy federal subsidies for logging roads — the United States already has 440,000 miles of them in national forests — made sense from both a fiscal and conservation standpoint. However, as with any major institutional change, this one is not without pain or resistance.

"U.S. to Halt Construction of Remote Logging Roads; Protecting National Forest Backcountry," *San Francisco Chronicle*, Jan. 12, 1998, p. A8.

The Clinton administration plans to suspend construction of logging roads in the backcountry of most national forests, a major environmental step that would effectively preclude logging on some of the nation's most rugged and pristine public land. To avoid starting a new round of timber wars with powerful logging proponents in Congress and further litigation with the timber industry, the administration is considering exempting two huge timber zones from the road-building moratorium.

Baker, Beth, "Rethinking Roads in the Nation's Forests," *Bioscience*, March 1998, p. 156.

Years of road construction in national forests may be coming to an end as Congress moves closer to doing away with the U.S. Forest Service's roads program. The roads take up 380,000 miles of forest.

Barnum, Alex, "Forest Service Calls Logging-Road 'Timeout'; Conservation Groups Win Partial Victory," *San Francisco Chronicle*, Jan. 23, 1998, p. A9.

In a move to protect vast tracts of the nation's most pristine public lands, the Forest Service proposed yesterday an 18-month moratorium on building logging roads in the backcountry of national forests. The temporary ban, which could become final after a 30-day public-comment period, represents a partial victory for conservation groups. The groups have long battled the Forest Service's road-building program. Still, environmentalists criticized the proposal for exempting some of the most hotly contested forest land, including the Tongass National Forest in Alaska and parts of the Pacific Northwest and Northern California.

Bourne, Joel, "The End of the Roads?" *Audubon*, **July 1998, pp. 58-63.**

The United States is losing much of its pristine wilderness to pavement and gravel, and in the process wildlife habitat and watersheds are being lost as well. The author examines the effect of roads on wildlife.

Cushman, John H. Jr., "U.S. to Suspend Road Building In Many National Forest Areas," *The New York Times*, **Jan. 10, 1998, p. A1.**

The moratorium on building roads in national forests, designed by the Clinton administration, would be a partial victory for environmental advocates, who have long complained of the lasting damage done by bulldozers carving up old-growth forests.

Harmon, John, "'Roadless' Status Given to Forests Until Logging Policy Set," *Atlanta Journal-Constitution*, **Jan. 23, 1998, p. A7.**

From the sparkling cascades of Mountaintown Creek in North Georgia to the black bear haunts of Peters Mountain in southwestern Virginia, some of the most remote and endangered wild country remaining in the Southern Appalachians will get federal protection from logging and road building for the next 18 months. The U.S. Forest Service announced Thursday a proposal to protect 33 million acres of "roadless areas" in national forests, primarily in the West, while the agency revamps its controversial policy of building and maintaining timber roads.

Timber Industry

"Damaging Cuts for National Forests," *The Boston Globe*, **Aug. 17, 1998, p. A10.**

Congress runs the risk of shortchanging sensible national forest practices if it capitulates to logging interests in the budget for the Forest Service. Both House and Senate versions of the budget reduce the share of money going to a variety of environmentally important programs while raising the share that encourages commercial logging operations. When it returns from recess, Congress should restore the balance between these objectives.

"Senseless; Why are Taxpayers Subsidizing National Forest Logging?" *Houston Chronicle*, **July 9, 1998, p. A32.**

On one hand, national forests are viewed as an important source of lumber production and jobs. On the other, they are seen as lost-in-time remnants of America as the nation once was, untouched and unspoiled — a sanctuary for animals, birds, fish and plant life. While valid arguments can be made for limited, restricted and responsible logging in some areas of some national forests, no valid arguments can be made for taxpayers subsidizing such cuttings.

"Splintering the Forests," *The Washington Post*, **Nov. 28, 1997, p. A26.**

In recent years, the timber harvest from the national forests has dramatically declined. The decline may not yet be enough of a good thing. Congress should change the law to make it harder to cut on these public lands, particularly in areas never logged before. The problem is that the conservation of the forests is not the only consideration in deciding how much to cut. Nor is the timber industry, for all its power in the affected regions, the only source of pressure to cut more. Other groups also have their fortunes tied to an increase in the cut, and the proceeds from timber sales are shared in such a way that many people want to cut more.

"The Forests' Future," *The Christian Science Monitor*, **Feb. 23, 1998, p. 12.**

The Clinton administration recently announced an 18-month moratorium on road building on more than 30 million acres of national forest. This reverses decades of Forest Service efforts to make public land ever more accessible to the timber industry. The moratorium draws a line. It should herald an era in which the aesthetic and recreational value of unspoiled land eclipses its commercial value to industry.

Egan, Timothy, "Teddy Roosevelt is Rolling Over in His Grave," *Sports Afield*, **August 1998, pp. 84-88.**

With Western Republicans riding herd on key congressional committees, most legislation protecting wild lands has been corralled. These nature-hating members of Congress have been somewhat counteracted by more moderate members of the party, but they still hold considerable power.

Harmon, John, "National Forest Logging Under Fire; Treasury Losses Boost Case Against Cutting, Sierra Club Says," *Atlanta Journal-Constitution*, **Dec. 25, 1997, p. K14.**

The controversial logging of Georgia's two national forests took another hit with the release of a Sierra Club analysis that contends the U.S. Forest Service lost $4.5 million in 1996 on the Chattahoochee and Oconee national forests. The report joins a number of charges from other government agencies and numerous environmental groups that the selling of timber from America's 155 national forests costs the taxpayers.

Back Issues

Great Research on Current Issues Starts Right Here.
Recent topics covered by The CQ Researcher are listed below.
Now available on the Web
For information, call (800) 432-2250 ext. 279 or (202) 887-6279.

If you would like to have any of these CQ Researchers updated, or need more information about these topics, please call CQ Custom Research. Special rates for CQ subscribers. (202) 887-8600 or (800) 432-2250, ext. 600, or E-mail Custom.Research@cq.com

Back issues are available for $5.00 (subscribers) or $10.00 (non-subscribers). Quantity discounts apply to orders over 10. To order, call Congressional Quarterly Customer Service at (202) 887-8621.

Binders are available for $18.00. To order call 1-800-638-1710. Please refer to stock number 648.

Future Topics

▶ *Puerto Rico's Status*

▶ *Internet Privacy*

▶ *Human Rights*

THE CQ Researcher

PUBLISHED BY CONGRESSIONAL QUARTERLY INC.

Puerto Rico's Status

Statehood, commonwealth or independence?

P uerto Ricans go to the polls on Dec. 13 to vote on the island's political relationship with the United States. The plebiscite pits Puerto Rico's pro-statehood governor against groups that defend the island's current "commonwealth" status and groups that favor some form of sovereignty or independence. Statehooders say Puerto Ricans are entitled to the same political rights as other U.S. citizens, but advocates of commonwealth say the current arrangement gives Puerto Ricans economic benefits while protecting their cultural identity. Voters narrowly chose commonwealth over statehood in 1993; polls indicate a close contest again this year. Congress would have to approve any new status, but it has balked at making any changes since Puerto Rico became a commonwealth in 1952.

CQ   **October 23, 1998 • Volume 8, No. 40 • Pages 929-952**

Formerly Editorial Research Reports

COVER: SUPPORTERS FOR "STATEHOOD NOW" RALLY OUTSIDE THE SOUTHERN GOVERNORS ASSOCIATION MEETING IN DORADO, PUERTO RICO, ON AUG. 30, 1998. (AP/LYNNE SLADKY)

CQ Researcher

October 23, 1998
Volume 8, No. 40

EDITOR
Sandra Stencel

MANAGING EDITOR
Thomas J. Colin

STAFF WRITERS
Adriel Bettelheim
Mary H. Cooper
Kenneth Jost
Kathy Koch
David Masci

PRODUCTION EDITOR
Melissa Hall

EDITORIAL ASSISTANT
Laura S. Cavender

PUBLISHED BY
Congressional Quarterly Inc.

CHAIRMAN
Andrew Barnes

VICE CHAIRMAN
Andrew P. Corty

PRESIDENT AND PUBLISHER
Robert W. Merry

EXECUTIVE EDITOR
David Rapp

The CQ Researcher (ISSN 1056-2036). Formerly Editorial Research Reports. Published weekly, except Jan. 2, May 29, July 3, Oct. 30, by Congressional Quarterly Inc., 1414 22nd St., N.W., Washington, D.C. 20037. Annual subscription rate for libraries, businesses and government is $340. Additional rates furnished upon request. Periodicals postage paid at Washington, D.C., and additional mailing offices. POSTMASTER: Send address changes to The CQ Researcher, 1414 22nd St., N.W., Washington, D.C. 20037.

Puerto Rico's Status

BY KENNETH JOST

THE ISSUES

A string of fatal shootings topped the news in Puerto Rico early in September. Among the victims: two policemen and an 8-year-old boy.

The flurry of killings gave the leader of the opposition Popular Democratic Party (PDP) an opening to criticize the island's governor, Pedro J. Rosselló, for lax policies on crime. "The governor should recognize we are in a major crime wave," Anibal Acevedo Vilá, a member of the Puerto Rico House of Representatives and the PDP's president, told a news conference on Sept. 9. "Women and children are being shot down."

Rosselló was not in Puerto Rico to respond. Instead, he was finishing a three-day lobbying trip to the United States, working on the issue that he has made his highest priority: statehood for Puerto Rico. The two-term governor met with senators in Washington to urge passage of a bill authorizing a referendum for Puerto Ricans to choose between statehood, independence or the island's current commonwealth relationship with the United States.

But Rosselló came back empty-handed. Even before he returned to Puerto Rico, Senate Majority Leader Trent Lott, R-Miss., reiterated that the Senate would have no time to consider the issue in its final weeks before adjournment.

Rosselló tried to put a favorable spin on the trip. "I think it was a success," he told a Sept. 10 news conference just outside San Juan, Puerto Rico's capital city. "I didn't meet with anybody who was in disagreement with the proposition that Puerto Rico should be able to express itself" on its political status.

Despite the failure of the bill in Congress, Puerto Ricans will have a chance to vote on their political status later this year. Rosselló, whose pro-statehood New Progressive Party (NPP) controls both houses of Puerto Rico's legislature, signed a bill

in August to hold a local plebiscite on Dec. 13. Rosselló wanted federal legislation to give the vote greater weight, but he is confident that Puerto Ricans will opt for statehood in the balloting and that Congress will respond by setting in motion a process that could make Puerto Rico the 51st state within 10 years or less.

Opponents doubt both of Rosselló's predictions. Leaders of the PDP say they expect Puerto Ricans will again endorse commonwealth over statehood, just as they did by a substantial margin in 1967 and by a narrow margin in 1993. "We are the majority," Acevedo Vilá says.

Leaders of the Puerto Rican Independence Party and advocates of a fourth option — a semisovereign relationship with the United States called "free association" — are not predicting victory in the balloting. But, along with PDP leaders, they warn that even if Puerto Ricans vote for statehood, neither Congress nor the American people are ready to accept a Spanish-speaking state within the Union.

"The United States has more problems with Puerto Rico being a state than Puerto Rico has with being a state," says Eduardo Bhatia Gautier, a PDP senator from San Juan.

"What has been clear in the congressional process is that we're not

going to admit you as a state until you shed your Spanish skin and trade it for an Anglo-Saxon way of life and culture," says Luis Vega-Ramos, leader of the campaign organization called PROELA — after the Spanish initials for "free associated state," ELA.

The debate over the issue — already dominating Puerto Rico's talk radio stations during a week-long visit in early September — tracks arguments that have shaped Puerto Rico's politics since the United States acquired the island as part of the spoils for its victory in the Spanish-American War in 1898. *(See chart, p. 932.)* Many Puerto Ricans immediately advocated statehood, some called for independence and others worked to gain some degree of internal self-government within the colonial relationship with the U.S.

The establishment of the commonwealth arrangement in 1952 did not end the debate. Under commonwealth, Puerto Ricans have local self-government but are subject to federal laws even though they do not vote for members of Congress or president. They receive some federal benefits, but they do not pay federal taxes. *(See chart, p. 940.)*

In the years since commonwealth, support for independence has waned, while advocates of commonwealth and statehood have seemingly fought to a standstill. The two parties have "mutual vetoes" over any efforts by the other to change political status, one PDP veteran says. "We can stop statehooders from getting a majority that would impress Congress, while they have enough to stop our efforts to enhance commonwealth," says José Roberto Martínez, who headed Puerto Rico's Washington office from 1989-1992.

The status debate shapes Puerto Rico's politics, blurring ideological and political differences between the parties. "Within each of the three parties, you have people from far left to far right," Kenneth McClintock, an NPP senator, remarks over lunch in the Senate dining room. The

Major Political Parties in Puerto Rico

Puerto Rico's three major political parties are defined in terms of their positions on the island's governance status: statehood, commonwealth or independence.

New Progressive Party (NPP)
(Partido Nuevo Progresista, PNP)

CURRENT STATUS

• NPP members include Gov. Pedro J. Rosselló and Resident Commissioner Carlos A. Romero-Barceló

• NPP controls Puerto Rico's 54-member House (37 seats) and 28-member Senate (19 seats)

HISTORY

• The pro-statehood NPP was formed in 1968 out of Luis A. Ferré's United Statehooders organization, created for the 1967 plebiscite; NPP first brought to power in November 1968; has alternated power with PDP since then; traces history to pro-statehood Puerto Rican Republican Party founded by José Celso Barbosa in 1899; Republican Party shared power 1933-1941 as part of coalition with Socialists (Partido Socialista, now disbanded). NPP historically has been aligned with the U.S. Republican Party.

Popular Democratic Party (PDP)
(Partido Popular Democratico, PPD)

CURRENT STATUS

• Holds 16 House seats, 8 Senate seats

HISTORY

• The pro-commonwealth PDP was established by Luis Muñoz Marín in 1938 and won seven consecutive elections, 1940-1968; has alternated power with NPP since losing 1968 election after party split; traces history to pro-autonomy Unión de Puerto Rico, founded by Luis Muñoz Rivera in 1904; Unionists merged with some Republicans in 1924 to form the Alianza, which dissolved in 1929 and gave way in 1932 to the Liberal Party (Partido Liberal Puertorriqueño). The PDP historically has been aligned with the U.S. Democratic Party.

Puerto Rican Independence Party (PIP)
(Partido Independentista Puertorriqueño)

CURRENT STATUS

• Holds 1 House seat, 1 Senate seat

HISTORY

• The pro-independence PIP was founded in 1946 in split with PDP; reached maximum vote in 1952 (18.9 percent); party's forerunners date to 1912; has eschewed violence, unlike Puerto Rican nationalists (Partido Nacionalista, now all but defunct).

PDP's Bhatia agrees: "There ought to be a strong liberal party and a strong conservative party, but that just doesn't happen in Puerto Rico."

By contrast, Puerto Rico's status is a minor issue, at most, in Congress. Various proposals to strengthen the powers of

Puerto Rico's government within the commonwealth structure have gone unacted on since the 1950s. The legislation for a congressionally authorized referendum died this year despite the support of President Clinton and a majority of House Democrats and, among Republicans,

House Speaker Newt Gingrich of Georgia and the GOP chairmen of the House and Senate committees with jurisdiction over Puerto Rican affairs.

Even before the failure of the congressional legislation, Puerto Rico's major parties were trading accusations about

Puerto Rico: Isla del Encanto

Known as the Enchanting Island, Puerto Rico (Spanish for "rich harbor") lies about 1,000 miles southeast of Miami at the eastern end of the chain of islands known as the Greater Antilles, which also includes Cuba, Jamaica and Hispaniola (containing the Dominican Republic and Haiti).

At a Glance

- **Area**
  Puerto Rico — 3,508 sq mi.;
  U.S. — 3.7 million sq. mi.
  Puerto Rico is roughly the
  combined areas of
  Delaware, 2,396 sq. mi., and
  Connecticut, 1,231 sq. mi.

- **Population**
  Puerto Rico — 3.8 million;
  U.S. — 376 million
  Similar-size state: Arizona, 3.7 million

- **Birth rate**
  Puerto Rico — 17.4/1,000 inhabitants;
  U.S.: 15.2/1,000 inhabitants
  Three states have higher birth rates:
  Utah, Alaska, Texas

- **Life expectancy [at birth]**
  Puerto Rico: 73.5 years;
  U.S.: 75.7 years

- **Household income**
  Puerto Rico: $29,783;
  U.S., $36,656
  Lowest state: West Virginia, $26,657

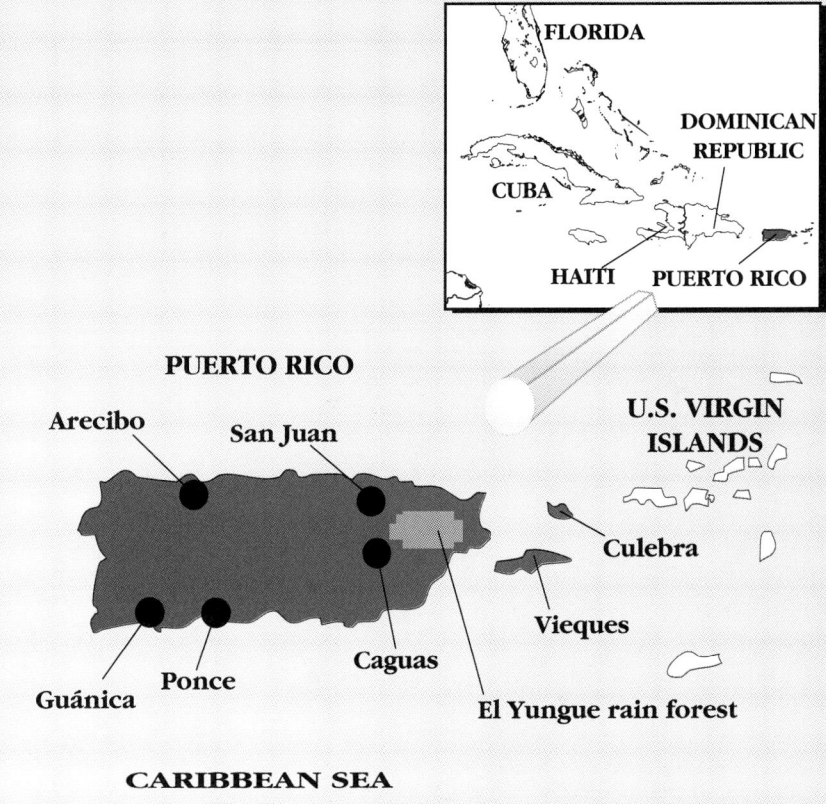

- **Gross state product**
  Puerto Rico: $38.6 billion
  U.S.: $6.8 trillion
  Next lowest state: New Mexico,
  $37.4 billion

- **Unemployment rate**
  Puerto Rico: 12.8%
  U.S.: 4.5%
  Highest state: West Virginia, 6.8%

- **Poverty rate**
  Puerto Rico: 55.3%
  U.S.: 13.5%
  Lowest state: New Mexico, 23.4%

- **Adults with high school degree or higher**
  Puerto Rico: 49.7%
  U.S.: 75.2%
  Lowest state: Mississippi, 64.3%;

Homicide rate
Puerto Rico:
15.4 per 100,000 population
U.S.: 7.4 per 100,000 population
Highest state: Louisiana,
17.5 per 100,000 population

Note: Data are from most current year available in each case.

Rosselló's decision to call a local plebiscite. PDP leaders say the definition of commonwealth to be listed on the ballot — written by the NPP-controlled legislature — is misleading.

"It's written in a way that people will have no other way but to vote for statehood," Acevedo Vilá says.

But Rosselló and other NPP leaders say the definition conforms to Supreme Court decisions that have upheld Congress' power to limit political rights for Puerto Rico under the Constitution's Territorial Clause. [1] "We used some Supreme Court decisions which intend to define what is statehood, and what is the present status, commonwealth," says Rep. Angel

Cintrón-García. "We take the main source as the Supreme Court. So you have a level playing field."[2]

The PDP is fighting the issue in court, claiming that the legislature's refusal to let the PDP write its own definition for the ballot violated the party's political and free-speech rights. But after suffering a setback in its lawsuit this month, the party decided on Oct. 15 to urge Puerto Ricans to vote for a fifth option on the ballot: "none of the above."

For Puerto Ricans, the choice between statehood, commonwealth, free association and independence poses issues both straightforward and complex. Statehooders emphasize issues of equal political rights, while supporters of the three other options all warn that Puerto Rico's separate identity would be submerged if it joined the union. Supporters of commonwealth say the current arrangement provides important economic benefits, but advocates of the other three options argue respectively that Puerto Rico would be better off economically if it were part of the United States or if it were free to be an independent player in the global economy.

As the campaigning gets under way, here are some of the questions that Puerto Ricans will be considering:

Should Puerto Rico's current commonwealth status be changed?

Puerto Ricans approved the creation of commonwealth in 1952 as a step forward in internal self-government, but the new status concealed divisions among Puerto Ricans and differing interpretations of commonwealth in Washington and San Juan.

Today, advocates of commonwealth argue that it gives Puerto Ricans an ideal political combination — autonomy plus ties to the United States — along with an exemption from federal taxes. But opponents from both sides, statehood and independence, attack commonwealth as a continuation of U.S. colonialism that denies Puerto Ricans full political rights and hinders the island's economic development.

PDP leaders say Puerto Rico's divisions underscore the advantages of the current status. "Commonwealth is hard to grasp,"

Gov. Pedro J. Rosselló, a statehood supporter, addresses a rally marking the centennial of U.S.-Puerto Rico relations.

Puerto Rico Federal Affairs Administration

says Bhatia, "but it is the best solution for a divided society." At the same time, they concede some of the critics' arguments that the current status needs to be changed in some respects: to use their terms, "perfected" or "developed."

"To perfect commonwealth, or to make commonwealth more perfect, is to make sure that Puerto Rico consents to federal laws that apply to Puerto Rico," Bhatia says. As one example, he suggests that the Puerto Rico legislature could vote at the end of each session of Congress on whether to accept application to Puerto Rico of newly enacted federal laws.

Advocates of statehood say that commonwealthers cannot have it both ways. "They want to be a sovereign country with U.S. citizenship," says the NPP's Cintron. "We are not a nation. We are a territory of the United States since 1898."

Leaders of the pro-independence party agree that trying to "perfect" commonwealth is futile. "You can always grant a larger degree of self-government," says Fernando Martin-García, the PIP's vice president and two-time candidate for governor. "But will the Congress reconsider its sovereignty over Puerto Rico, or will it merely delegate more powers? There is no middle way."

Advocates of the "free association" option on the Dec. 13 ballot say that status — called "ELA" for the Spanish words for "free associated state" — would both answer the arguments from commonwealth's critics and fulfill the intention of the creators of commonwealth. "We basically want to take it out of the power of Congress and place the relations on a basis of an international compact of free association," says Luis Vega. Vega's plan calls for the United States to continue to have responsibility for military affairs and to maintain a common currency with Puerto Rico, but for Puerto Rico to assume authority over other matters, including international commercial relations.

Leaders of the three established parties all dismiss the "free association" option. Leaders of the NPP and PDP both say the idea is unrealistic and, if adopted, would jeopardize U.S. citizenship for Puerto Ricans. Vega counters that provisions could be made to safeguard U.S. citizenship for Puerto Ricans and their heirs. He also says the proposal is comparable to the status that the United States granted to the Marshall Islands, Palau and the Micronesian States in the 1980s when it ended its control over the territories under a United Nations trusteeship.

For their part, *independentistas* say that "free association" would be an improvement over the current commonwealth status, but they dismiss it as a long-term goal. "I can't think of one governmental power that I think Puerto Rico should delegate to the United States," Martín says.

Whatever the arguments about commonwealth, PDP leaders face a difficult tactical decision unless the definition of commonwealth on the Dec. 13 ballot is changed. "If you put in the definition that we're a colony without dignity, that's not the commonwealth we believe in," says party President Acevedo.

But statehooders counter that the PDP is misleading Puerto Ricans about the limited powers granted Puerto Rico under commonwealth. "The commonwealth is asking for things that are just impossible," Cintrón says.

Would statehood be good for Puerto Rico? For the United States?

Statehood advocates emphasize the issue of political rights, but they also contend that both Puerto Rico and the United States would benefit from its joining the Union on an equal basis with the 50 states. Commonwealthers answer that statehood would hurt Puerto Rico economically and, along with advocates of independence, warn that it would risk a loss of Puerto Rico's cultural identity. In addition, opponents argue that statehood would exacerbate divisions within Puerto Rico and create lasting tensions with the rest of the United States.

NPP leaders begin and end their argument for statehood by stressing that Puerto Ricans are unrepresented in Washington even though they have been U.S. citizens — and subject to military service — since 1917. "I want the right to vote for the president who has sent me to war since

1917," Cintron says. "I want the right to vote for representatives in the Senate and the House. I want the right to be equal under the U.S. Constitution."

PDP leaders seek to counter the argument by suggesting some revisions in the commonwealth formula to correct what is sometimes called Puerto Rico's "democratic deficit." But they maintain that full statehood would be a disaster for the island's economy. "Statehood will destroy our economic sector by imposing [new] taxes on Puerto Rico," PDP President Acevedo Vilá says.

Statehood advocates insist that PDP officials have misled Puerto Ricans about the likely impact of federal taxes. "They say that everyone would pay federal taxes, but that's not so," Cintrón says. He notes that many Puerto Ricans have incomes so low that they would owe no federal income tax and, in fact, would be eligible for payments under the earned-income tax credit.

At the same time, NPP leaders say that statehood would represent a plus for the U.S. Treasury. In congressional testimony this summer, Cintrón cited an economic study that concluded statehood would result in a net benefit to the federal budget of more than $2 billion. "There's no worse scenario for the federal budget" than commonwealth, Cintrón says.

The tax issue emerges as a major concern about statehood in interviews with Puerto Ricans, but so, too, does the question of cultural identity. Opponents of statehood play to those fears by emphasizing the contrasts between the English-speaking mainland and the Spanish-speaking island. "You're either a *Yanqui* or a *Puertorriqueño*," says Manuel Rodríguez Orellana, the PIP's director of North American affairs. "There's nothing in-between."

NPP leaders discount the concern. "Statehood doesn't mean assimilation," Cintrón says. "Becoming or not becoming a state is not an issue with respect to changing the culture."

The language issue looms large in

debate in Washington about admitting Puerto Rico as a state. When the House in March approved the bill to authorize a status referendum, supporters had to counter an English-only amendment with a compromise that called for Puerto Rico to take steps to increase English proficiency if it became a state. [3]

Statehooders insist that representation in Congress would allow Puerto Rico to resist legislation to impose English as the island's only official language. "Laws can't change the way people feel," adds Leonides Diaz Urbina, who is directing the NPP's campaign for statehood in the Dec. 13 plebiscite.

Still, the debate underscores the continuing cultural differences between Puerto Rico and the United States. Opponents say those differences could produce a Quebec-type conflict in the United States. "Should Puerto Rico ever become a state, it would become a bleeding ulcer in the side of American federalism," PIP Vice President Martín says.

Cintron dismisses those fears, pointing to the United States' successful assimilation of such culturally diverse states as Texas, New Mexico and Hawaii. And he closes by returning to the question of political rights. "I want to be a first-class citizen," Cintron says, "the same as in the United States but living in Puerto Rico."

Could Puerto Rico succeed as an independent country?

Puerto Rico had no strong independence movement before the U.S. annexation, and the independence option attracted only 5 percent or so of the vote in the 1967 and 1993 plebiscites. But, as an often-quoted saying goes, "Scratch a Puerto Rican, and you find an *independentista* under the skin." [4]

Today, pro-independence advocates insist that Puerto Rico would be stronger economically and better off diplomatically and culturally if the island became an independent country. Supporters of the other three status options — statehood, commonwealth or free association —

Continued on p. 937

Se Habla Español — and Un Poco English

Spanish and English are interspersed in Puerto Rico — testimony to the island's four centuries as a Spanish colony and 100 years as an American territory. For example, the grocery store offers both "*leche fresca*" (fresh milk) and "light milk." The local beer lists ingredients in Spanish but displays the U.S. surgeon general's health warning in English. Local courts use Spanish, the federal court English.

The accelerating Americanization of the past few decades, however, has not changed Puerto Ricans' fundamental cultural identity: Puerto Rico remains today a predominantly Spanish-speaking territory with a predominantly Spanish- and Caribbean-influenced culture.

Language and cultural identity form an important issue in the debate over Puerto Rico's political status, both on the island and in the United States. Puerto Ricans opposed to statehood contend that becoming a state would force English on a society that has no desire to give up Spanish as its daily language. Supporters dismiss those fears as exaggerated.

In Washington, however, supporters of statehood seek to allay fears of a multilingual United States by saying that Puerto Ricans are already increasing their use and study of English. "People in the island, the majority, their first language is Spanish, but they are more than proficient in English," says Xavier Romeu, former executive director of the Puerto Rico Federal Affairs Administration in Washington.

For now, however, English is definitely a secondary language in Puerto Rico. About 25 percent of the population speak English easily, according to a 1990 Census Bureau survey. Another 24 percent speak English with difficulty, while a majority — 51 percent — speak no English. "From our perspective, 75 percent of the population speaks little or no English," says Eric Stone, a spokesman for the organization U.S. English, which advocates English as the official language of federal and state governments.

A week-long visit by a non-Spanish-speaking reporter confirms the statistics. Puerto Rico has more than 100 radio stations, but only one English-speaking outlet. Highway signs are mostly Spanish-only. (Stop signs, for example, say "*Pare*.") And, despite reassurances from Romeu, there were many times when no English-speakers could be found to provide information or assistance — including, on one occasion, a telephone call to the headquarters of the pro-statehood New Progressive Party.

"I speak English once every month," says Fernando Martín, vice president of the Puerto Rican Independence Party. "It is not part of anybody's daily life in any way.'

Language has been a sensitive issue between the United States and Puerto Rico since the establishment of colonial rule at the turn of the century. The U.S. made English an official language in 1902 along with Spanish. Public school classes were taught in English even though many — probably most — Puerto Rican students did not understand the language. Gov. Luis Muñoz Marín, the island's first elected governor, established Spanish as the language of instruction in public schools in 1949 — his first year in office.

Language was the pivotal issue when the U.S. House of Representatives considered a bill in March to hold a referendum in Puerto Rico on its political status. Rep. Gerald B.H. Solomon, a New York Republican and chairman of the powerful House Rules Committee, offered an amendment to require Puerto Rico to adopt English-only policies if it were admitted as a state. Lobbyists for U.S. English pointed out that Congress had imposed English-language requirements on other would-be states, including Arizona, Louisiana, New Mexico and Oklahoma.

Supporters of the referendum bill opposed Solomon's amendment. They countered with a compromise included in the bill as passed by the House that called on Puerto Rico to take steps to increase fluency in English if admitted as a state. The Senate did not take up the bill.

Public schools in Puerto Rico are also debating and struggling with the issue. Gov. Pedro J. Rosselló's administration is pushing a "Project for Developing a Bilingual Citizen" aimed at increasing the teaching of English in public schools. "We must equip each of our young people with the ability to communicate in both Spanish and English," Rosselló, a strong statehood supporter, said in a speech at Harvard University's John F. Kennedy School of Government in February.

Some teachers welcomed Rosselló's move, but others have resisted it. Teachers protesting the policy demonstrated in May 1997 in front of the Department of Education building in San Juan. "Math is difficult enough in Spanish, imagine in English," one of the protesters' signs read. [1]

The language issue has formed part of the debate in the campaigning for the Dec. 13 plebiscite that Rosselló decided to call after the legislation for a congressionally sanctioned referendum stalled. If statehood gains a majority or plurality of the votes, opponents are certain to revive the issue as Congress takes up any legislation aimed at admitting Puerto Rico as a state.

"Can a state in which over three-quarters of the population does not speak English integrate properly with a country in which 97 percent of the population speaks English?" asks Mauro Mujica, chairman of U.S. English.

But Luis Ferré, the 94-year-old former governor and patriarch of Puerto Rico's pro-statehood party, says language should not be an issue, either in Puerto Rico or in Washington.

"American democracy is supposed to be made up of equal rights," Ferré says. "There's no language in the Constitution. Americans are supposed to understand each other. That's all."

---

[1] See *The New York Times*, May 19, 1997, p. A12.

Continued from p. 935

generally avoid direct attacks on independence, but they all stress the value of continuing ties to the United States.

Supporters point out that Puerto Rico would be far from the smallest or least populated nation in the world if it became independent. "There are countries smaller than Puerto Rico, and more densely populated than Puerto Rico, that have developed more than Puerto Rico without food stamps, U.S. citizenship or federal funds," the PIP's Rodriguez says. "There is absolutely no reason that Puerto Rico cannot be a model of prosperity as well as democracy."

In fact, PIP leaders say, an independent Puerto Rico would be in a better position to promote the island's economic development by being able to negotiate commercial treaties on its own and give investment incentives to other countries besides the U.S. "At this point in our history," Martin says, "colonialism even from the economic point of view has become a straitjacket."

PROELA stresses a similar advantage in arguing for making Puerto Rico a free associated state. "The authority of Puerto Rico to be a player in the globalization of the 21st century would promote a transition from the dependency that we have today to a self-sustaining economy," Vega says.

Many economists, however, doubt that independence would prove beneficial for Puerto Rico. In testimony to the Senate Energy Committee in May, the General Accounting Office warned that independence would likely lower economic growth by reducing federal benefits and creating difficulty for government borrowing.

In addition, both PROELA and the PDP stress that full independence would jeopardize U.S. citizenship for Puerto Ricans and the island's ties to the states. "We appreciate our relationship with the United States," says PDP President Acevedo Vilá. "We are Puerto Ricans. We have our own language, our own identity. But we are U.S. citizens. We are proud

of that. The only way you can harmonize both things is by commonwealth."

For the United States, independence would represent a total break with the policies adopted since the Spanish-American War. The United States had renounced any intention of annexing Cuba before the outbreak of the war and committed itself to independence for the Philippines by 1916. But from the first of the military governors, the United States appeared determined to hold on to Puerto Rico.

Advocates of independence, however, say today that the United States may see less strategic value in holding on to Puerto Rico and some advantages in letting go. "Commonwealth is no longer useful to the U.S.," Martin says. "Puerto Rico costs too much money. Strategically, its value has been diminished. And the growth of nationalism has brought out the contradictions [of the current relationship]."

So far, however, independence supporters have not been able to show much strength at the polls. The PIP holds only one seat in each of the two chambers of the Puerto Rican legislature, and independence won only 4.4 percent of the vote in the 1993 plebiscite. [5]

PIP leaders say they hope to do better in this year's voting, but they vow to keep up their fight whatever the outcome. "We've been fighting for this for 100 years," Orellana says. "There is a nationality here that refuses to throw in the towel." ■

BACKGROUND

'The Oldest Colony'

Christopher Columbus' landing in 1493 on the island now called Puerto Rico opened the door to 400 years of largely neglectful Spanish colonial rule. [6] Ironically, Spain in 1897 granted Puerto

Ricans their largest measure of self-rule up to that time, just one year before the Spanish-American War. That "splendid little war" ended with Spain's cession of Puerto Rico to the United States. The United States ruled Puerto Rico as a colony for the next 54 years with a mixture of good intentions and oblivious paternalism until the creation of the current commonwealth status — which many Puerto Ricans continue to regard today as a form of colonialism.

Spanish colonizers led by Juan Ponce de Leon established a permanent foothold in what was then called San Juan Bautista in 1518. In short order, the combined effects of battles and disease essentially wiped out the native Taínos. The resulting colony served Spain well as a fortified garrison guarding access to Mexico and the rest of Spanish America. But Puerto Rico — the name originally was given just to the capital city in the 16th century — provided Spain little else of value and subsisted largely because of payments from Mexico.

Politically, Puerto Ricans were mostly quiescent: The only substantial pro-independence insurrection, in 1868, was easily quelled. Political battles in Spain between republicans and monarchists in the 19th century brought Puerto Rico alternating periods of liberalization and repression, but the changes mattered little to most Puerto Ricans. As José Trías Monge points out, Puerto Rico at the end of the 19th century was an extremely poor agricultural society, with a high illiteracy rate, few schools or other public services, and inadequate housing. [7] Even so, Spain in 1897 gave Puerto Ricans a measure of self-rule by providing in the Autonomic Charter for a bicameral parliament, with one chamber elected by universal suffrage, and a significant degree of autonomy over local affairs. [8]

The Spanish-American War of 1898 killed Puerto Rican autonomy at birth. Advocates of naval power in the United States saw Puerto Rico along with Cuba and Hawaii as valuable outposts for projecting U.S. power globally. Cuba and the

Philippines were the major theaters for the war that began in April 1898. The fighting in Puerto Rico lasted a mere 19 days: The U.S. troops that landed at Guanica, on the island's southwestern coast, were joyously received; resistance was minimal; and an armistice was proclaimed on Aug. 12. Spain had agreed five days earlier, after some hesitation, to cede Puerto Rico to the United States.

U.S. Rule

The United States ruled Puerto Rico for the next four decades through a succession of military and colonial governors who — with the notable exception of Theodore Roosevelt Jr. (1929-32) — ranged from insensitive to incompetent to venal. U.S. rule brought modest social and economic development, carefully limited doses of political reform and the mixed blessing of collectively imposed U.S. citizenship. Few Puerto Ricans were satisfied with their political status, but they were divided between favoring statehood, some form of autonomy or independence.

Congress narrowly approved the Treaty of Paris to end the Spanish-American War after debating the government's power under the Constitution to acquire territory as colonies. One year later, Congress passed the Foraker Act, the first organic act for Puerto Rico. The law gave Puerto Ricans the right to elect members of the lower chamber of a bicameral legislature, but no other say in their government. The president was to appoint the governor, six cabinet members who would also form a majority of the upper legislative chamber, and Supreme Court justices.

In 1917 Congress passed the second organic law for Puerto Rico: the Jones Act. The law provided for an elective Senate and gubernatorial appointment of most cabinet members subject to confir-

mation by the new upper chamber. Most important, it made all Puerto Ricans U.S. citizens. The Bureau of Insular Affairs, which oversaw U.S. relations with Puerto Rico, backed the move to discourage thoughts of independence.

From the start, the military and colonial governors appointed from Washington clamped down on any autonomist sentiment. Gen. Guy Henry, the second of three military governors, threatened the newspaper owned by Luis Muñoz Rivera, prime minister at the time of the invasion and later to be the leader of the pro-autonomy Union of Puerto Rico, because it called for the end of military government. The first of the civil governors, Charles Allen (1900-1902), began the practice of filling Cabinet posts with non-residents; he also removed all local judges who did not belong to the pro-statehood Republican Party.

Puerto Rican politics took shape around the status issue. The pro-statehood Republican Party, founded in 1899 by a black, U.S.-trained physician, José Barbosa, won the first three elections under U.S. rule by capitalizing on discontent with the old Spanish rule and prevalent pro-U.S. sentiment. The unpopularity of U.S. rule allowed Muñoz Rivera's Unionists to win the 1904 election and successive balloting until his death in 1916 and afterward.

The Republicans gained control of the legislature again only through an unlikely coalition with the Socialist Party in the 1930s. But the ups and downs of the Puerto Rican parties had limited impact. The Bureau of Insular Affairs, housed in the War Department until 1934 and thereafter in the Interior Department, exercised a dominant, consistently conservative influence on Puerto Rican affairs.

Creating Commonwealth

Puerto Rico remained poor and predominantly agricultural at the

end of the 1930s. [9] Two people played the major roles in the 1940s in laying the foundation for the island's economic development and transition to internal self-government: Rexford Tugwell, who served as governor from 1941 to 1946, and Luis Muñoz Marin, who put together a powerful political coalition within Puerto Rico and then conceived of commonwealth status and won approval for it from Congress and from Puerto Rican voters.

Tugwell was an economics professor and member of President Franklin D. Roosevelt's brain trust. [10] As governor, he instituted land reform, reduced the powers of the presidentially appointed auditor and attorney general, created a budget office and planning board and laid the basis for eventual creation of a civil service. In addition, he approved the 1942 law creating the Puerto Rico Development Company, the island legislature's first major initiative in the economic transformation from an agricultural to an industrialized economy.

Muñoz Marín, son of the Unionist leader Muñoz Rivera, began his rise to three decades of political dominance in Puerto Rico in 1931 after returning to the island from the United States, where he had spent most of his early life. [11] First elected as a senator from the short-lived Liberal Party, he formed a new, FDR-like party, the Popular Democratic Party, in 1938. The party adopted as its symbol the straw hat worn by the *jíbaros*, the agricultural laborers, and drew support as well from lower- and middle-class workers and upper-class intellectuals. Muñoz Marín's heart lay with independence, but he worked to give Puerto Rico more autonomy while also pushing a social justice agenda. The PDP gained a legislative majority in 1940 and won every election thereafter until 1968.

As president of the Puerto Rican Senate (1941-48), Munoz Marín sought to have Congress authorize a binding plebiscite on the island's status. Congress refused to pass a plebiscite bill, however,

Continued on p. 940

Chronology

Before 1900

Spain rules Puerto Rico as a colony for nearly 400 years before the United States' victory in the Spanish-American War.

1898
Spain cedes Puerto Rico to United States at end of Spanish-American War.

───── • ─────

1900-1949

United States rules Puerto Rico through military and colonial governors; Puerto Ricans are allowed to elect legislature and non-voting delegate to Congress, but appointed governor and U.S. president can veto local laws, and Congress retains right to legislate for island.

1900
Foraker Act establishes colonial government for Puerto Rico: president appoints governor, department heads and supreme court justices; Puerto Ricans elect only members of lower chamber of legislature.

1917
Jones Act makes Puerto Ricans U.S. citizens, provides for elected Senate.

1938
Luis Muñoz Marín founds Popular Democratic Party (PDP), which prevails in local elections from 1940-1968.

1947
Congress approves Elective Governor Act, giving Puerto Ricans right to elect their own governor; Muñoz Marín is chosen first governor in 1948.

───── • ─────

1950-1959

Puerto Ricans write internal constitution; with approval of charter by Congress, the Commonwealth of Puerto Rico — in Spanish, Estado Libre Asociado — is created.

1950
Congress passes Public Law 600, authorizing Puerto Rico to hold referendum on plan to draft internal constitution; plan wins approval in referendum on June 4, 1951, with 76.5 percent of vote.

1952
Congress gives final approval to Puerto Rico constitution; commonwealth is officially created on July 25, the 54th anniversary of the landing of U.S. troops on island in Spanish-American War.

1953
United Nations accepts Commonwealth of Puerto Rico as a self-governing territory.

───── • ─────

1960s-1989

Efforts to gain added power under commonwealth fail in Congress; new pro-statehood party organizes and ends PDP's control of Puerto Rico politics.

1967
Puerto Ricans, voting in congressionally authorized plebiscite on July 23, back enhanced commonwealth status over statehood.

1968
Luis Ferré organizes New Progressive Party (NPP) and wins election as first elected, pro-statehood governor; NPP and PDP alternate in power over next three decades.

───── • ─────

1990s

Pro-statehood NPP controls governorship and legislature, fails to win victory in local plebiscite in 1993, but schedules another vote in 1998; PDP complains definition of commonwealth on ballot is misleading.

1992
New Progressive Party candidate Pedro Rosselló, a U.S.-educated physician, wins governorship in three-way race with 49.9 percent of the vote; party captures control of both houses of Puerto Rican legislature. Rosselló is elected to a second term in 1996 with 51 percent of the vote — the first majority vote for a pro-statehood governor.

Nov. 14, 1993
Puerto Ricans, in local plebiscite, favor enhanced commonwealth status over statehood, 48.4 percent to 46.2 percent, with 4.4 percent voting for independence.

March 4, 1998
U.S. House passes bill authorizing referendum on status in Puerto Rico, 209-208; Senate Energy Committee holds hearings on similar legislation in May and July, but measure fails to reach Senate floor.

Aug. 17, 1998
Gov. Pedro Rosselló signs legislation authorizing local plebiscite on political status on Dec. 13, 1998.

Major Legislation Affecting Puerto Rico's Status

Congress established colonial rule over Puerto Rico in 1900 and approved creation of the commonwealth in 1952. Since then, Congress has taken no action on various proposals to change Puerto Rico's governance.

Legislation	Status	Provisions
Foraker Act	*Enacted in 1900*	*Provided for U.S. president to appoint governor and department heads; bicameral legislature, with one chamber elected under limited suffrage and second chamber of appointed members; supreme court appointed by president, lower court judges appointed by governor; federal court, Congress to have power to override local laws; Puerto Rico to have resident commissioner in Washington (given right to participate in congressional deliberations by House rules change in 1902). No provision in act on U.S. citizenship.*
Jones Act	*Enacted in 1917*	*Made Puerto Ricans U.S. citizens. Created elective Senate, with power to confirm governor's appointees for most departments; president retained power to name attorney general, minister of education, supreme court justices. Legislature given power to override gubernatorial veto, but president could still disapprove legislation, and Congress could annul any insular law at any time.*
Tydings bill	*Introduced in 1936; not acted on*	*Would have made Puerto Rico independent under unfavorable conditions: immediate termination of U.S. assistance; phase-in of U.S. tariffs; immigration restrictions; and mandatory selection of U.S. or Puerto Rican citizenship. A more favorable independence measure also was not acted on.*
Elective Governor Act	*Enacted in 1947*	*Provided for popular election of governor. President retained power to appoint auditor, supreme court justices; Congress retained power to legislate for Puerto Rico and review insular laws.*
Public Law 600	*Enacted in 1950*	*Provided, subject to approval in Puerto Rican referendum, for elected convention to draft constitution for Puerto Rico, subject to approval by Congress. Act described as "in the nature of a compact," but committee reports say U.S. "sovereignty" not affected. Approved in referendum June 4, 1951, with 76.5 percent of vote. The act renamed laws previously passed governing Puerto Rico as the Federal Relations Act.*

Continued from p. 938
and President Harry S. Truman — on Tugwell's recommendation — vetoed a bill passed by the Puerto Rican legislature in 1946 to call a local referendum. But Tugwell did recommend to Roosevelt that Puerto Ricans be allowed to elect their own governor. Roosevelt sent the recommendation to Congress in March 1943; the idea went through a presidential commission and became law four years later with Truman's signature on Aug. 5, 1947.

Easily elected governor in 1948, Muñoz Marín continued to work on the status issue. The PDP had backed legislation in May 1945 — the Tydings-Piñero bill — that called for Puerto Ricans to vote on three alternatives: statehood, independence, and what was called associated state. The associated state would have entailed a relinquishing of U.S. sovereignty along with provisions for U.S. military bases, a common market and reciprocal citizenship rights. The bill died, but

Muñoz Marín's support for the associated state led *independentistas* to quit the PDP in 1946 and form a new party, the Puerto Rican Independence Party.

Muñoz Marín's new proposal, which emerged in 1950 after several years of drafting, included two concepts: a constitution to be adopted by Puerto Rico and to be accepted by Congress as a binding compact. As finally enacted on July 3, 1950, Public Law 600 was described in its text as

Legislation	Status	Provisions
Public Law 447	*Enacted in 1952*	*Approved Puerto Rico Constitution, subject to deletion of Article 20 containing social and economic rights; provision added that no amendment could conflict with PL 600, the Federal Relations Act or U.S. Constitution. Puerto Rico's Constitution, as amended, approved by Puerto Rican voters, March 3, 1952.*
Fernós-Murray bill	*Introduced in 1959; not acted on*	*Would have provided for Puerto Rico to assume federal functions, set up new mechanism for determining applicability of federal laws, given Puerto Rico power over tariffs and redefined Puerto Rico-U.S. relationship into bilateral compact that could not be changed unilaterally by Congress.*
Status Commission Act	*Enacted in 1964*	*Created commission composed of equal U.S., Puerto Rican members to study relationship; original bill would have given commission power to draft new compact. Commission report, in 1966, recommends plebiscite on three status formulas. Plebiscite, on July 23, 1967, results in 60.5 percent vote for enhanced commonwealth status; no further action by Congress.*
Compact of Permanent Association	*Drafted in 1975; rejected by President Gerald R. Ford, 1976*	*Would have given the ``Free Associated State'' of Puerto Rico diplomatic rights in non-military areas, right to levy tariffs on non-U.S. products, power to control immigration. In rejecting proposal, Ford announces support for statehood.*
Johnston bill	*Introduced in Senate in 1989; died in 1990 along with related House bill*	*Backed by Puerto Rico's major parties, the measure would have provided for new referendum on status formulas as defined by each party, with winning formula to be implemented by Congress; similar House bill would not have been self-executing. House passes bill in October 1990, but proposals die in end-of-session impasse.*
Young, Craig bills	*Introduced in 1997; not enacted*	*Similar bills in House and Senate called for new plebiscite on status bill formulas, with definitions provided; House passes bill 209-208 on March 4, 1998, but efforts to get Senate to act fall short; Senate does pass non-binding resolution "supporting the right of United States citizens in Puerto Rico to express their desires regarding their political status."*

"in the nature of a compact." But it provided that, subject to approval by Puerto Rican voters, a convention would be called to draft an internal constitution that would be submitted to Congress and then to Puerto Ricans for adoption.

Opposition came from the Independence Party, some statehooders and the Nationalist Party. Some nationalists resorted to violence, initiating attacks that claimed 28 lives in Puerto Rico and that included an attempted assassination of Truman in Washington. But Puerto Ricans overwhelmingly approved the law on June 4, 1951, with 76.5 percent of the vote.

In elections for the convention in August, the PDP won 70 out of 92 seats; statehooders had 15, Socialists seven. The convention, which met from mid-September until Feb. 6, 1952, wrote a constitution for what was called in Spanish the "free associated state of Puerto Rico" and in English "commonwealth." Truman sent the charter to Congress with a recommendation of approval. Congress forced the deletion of one section dealing with social and economic rights, but amendments to limit Puerto Rican autonomy were either weakened or shelved. Three weeks after Truman's signature on the congressional resolution approving the constitution, the commonwealth was officially proclaimed on July 25, 1952 — the 54th

Many Options, Many Opinions

Lourdes Cruz teaches English as a second language in a Catholic school near San Juan. She thinks statehood would be a great boon for Puerto Rico, especially the island's less advantaged populations.

"Health care would be better," Cruz says. "Education would be better." Besides, she adds, "we're almost a state already."

But Linette Mondaldo, a fitness instructor in Ponce, Puerto Rico's second-largest city, strongly favors independence from the United States. "We are completely different," she says. "It's the right time to do it."

Between those two options, many Puerto Ricans say they are satisfied with the island's current political status. "We have all we need in commonwealth," says Carmen Flores, a retired secretary, as she shopped in the giant Plaza Las Américas mall, just outside San Juan. "We have American citizenship. We make laws in Puerto Rico. We have everything we want."

As campaigning gets under way for Puerto Rico's Dec. 13 plebiscite on political status, early polls show that residents are closely divided between statehood and commonwealth, with independence and the fourth option — free association — trailing. A poll in June showed statehood and commonwealth in a dead heat — with 40.9 percent and 40.2 percent of respondents, respectively — followed by 7.6 percent for independence.

Two months later, the same firm found statehood with a statistically insignificant lead over commonwealth — 38.8 percent to 35.5 percent — and independence with 7.6 percent. Significantly, the number of persons who answered undecided increased to 22 percent from 8.2 percent. [1]

An unscientific sampling of people questioned in the street in early September found parallel divisions, suggesting the likelihood of a muddled election in which neither statehood nor commonwealth receives a clear mandate from voters.

"It's probably going to be that nobody gets a majority," says Luis Vega-Ramos, leader of the organization PROELA, which wants the island to become a free associated state. That option was the last to be added to the ballot and could further confuse the final results.

The divisions on the issue defy easy categorization.

José Ramirez, a retired businessman who lived for many years in the United States, says he is "100 percent" for independence. "We don't want to disappear like the Hawaiians did," he says. A few steps away at Plaza Las Américas, Alberto Figueroa, a retired salesman and U.S. Army veteran, says he is "300 percent pro-statehood." Why? "Because I am pro-American," he says. More American than Puerto Rican? "Absolutely."

Commonwealthers give their opinions with less force, sometimes betraying a lingering sentiment for independence but doubts about its practicality. "I was born in the commonwealth," says Luis Zayas, a science teacher at a private school near Ponce. "And I don't know about independence."

Ramon Santiago, a retired businessman in Ponce, is similarly ambivalent. "I would like independence, of course, but I don't think it's viable at the moment," he says. He plans to vote for free association in the plebiscite.

As in the 1993 vote, commonwealth supporters are likely to find that "rice and beans" issues are most important for their voters. "We don't want to pay taxes," says Luis Maldonado, a security guard at a beachfront condominium near San Juan. Would he like to be able to vote for president and members of Congress? Yes, he says, but he is not particularly bothered about it.

But Puerto Rican nationalism is also an important factor in the support for commonwealth. "I like my own team in the Olympics, my flag, my customs," says Luis Padilla, a real estate agent in a San Juan suburb.

Statehood supporters minimize the fears of cultural assimilation. "All the states changed when they became states," says Augustín Colón, a resident of the small inland town of Aibonito. "I'm not afraid to become a state."

Instead, voters who favor becoming a state say they are eager to become full-fledged Americans. "I want to be a state," a San Juan cabdriver says. "I want to be American."

---

[1] The polls, conducted by Precision Research, Inc., surveyed 1,011 and 1,136 registered voters respectively. Results were published in *The San Juan Star*, June 8, 1998, and Aug. 22, 1998.

anniversary of the landing of U.S. troops in Puerto Rico.

Radical Changes

Puerto Rico's new commonwealth status accelerated a process of economic development that brought rapid economic growth through the 1960s. American investment in the island increased, as did American cultural influence. But Puerto Rico remained a jurisdiction and a society apart from the United States. And the status debate resumed within a few years, dominating Puerto Rican politics but resulting in no significant changes in the relationship from Congress.

Through the 1930s, Puerto Rico had essentially a monocultural economy consisting of sugar plantations owned by absentee corporations. [12] The transformation to an industrialized society began with a program by Muñoz Marín and Tugwell in the early 1940s to create state-owned industries. Within a few years, however, the government concluded the enterprises could not be made profitable and sold them to private concerns. Muñoz Marín, as PDP leader and president of the Senate, then made the critical decision to industrialize by seeking U.S. investment through tax incentives and other subsidies.

The Industrial Incentives Act of 1947 — the cornerstone of what Muñoz Marin dubbed "Operation Bootstrap" — provided an exemption from all insular income taxes until 1959 for any company manufacturing a good not produced in Puerto Rico as of Jan. 2, 1947. The tax-incentive strategy, extended and renewed periodically, remained a central feature of Puerto Rico's industrialization drive through the creation of commonwealth and to the present day.

The strategy succeeded in attracting outside capital to the island. Investment more than tripled in the 1950s from $111 million in 1950 to $354 million in 1960, then quadrupled over the next decade to reach $1.4 billion in 1970; imported capital amounted to more than half the amount in 1960 and the percentage continued to rise through the 1970s. Economic growth averaged 4.1 percent between 1955 and 1975. The benefits reached Puerto Rican workers: the average hourly wage rose from 42 cents in 1950 to 94 cents in 1960 and $1.78 in 1970. [13] But, as economic historian James Dietz points out, external capital, chiefly from the United States, played a disproportionate role in the growth. The result, many Puerto Ricans believed, was simply to change Puerto Rico from a political colony to an industrial colony of the U.S.

U.S. influence in Puerto Rico also increased because of the traffic of Puerto Ricans between the island and the states. As agriculture shrank, Puerto Ricans moved to the cities; but many could not find jobs there and instead emigrated to the United States. "We exported our surplus labor problem," says Martínez of the Muñoz Marín Foundation. From 1950 through 1970, the net emigration to the states amounted to 605,550 persons, about one-fourth of the island's 1950 population. The total migration flows were much larger: in 1970, for example, more than 2 million persons left Puerto

Rico for the U.S., and a nearly equal number returned to the island from the states. [14]

Politically, the status question remained the defining issue for Puerto Rican politics, but four major initiatives over the first four decades of commonwealth produced only stalemate in Washington. Muñoz Marín, now governor, pushed at the end of the 1950s for legislation to transfer federal functions to Puerto Rico and establish a mechanism for determining the applicability of U.S. laws to the island; Congress took no action. In the 1960s Muñoz Marín used his close ties to President John F. Kennedy's administration to try again along the same lines; but he had to settle for a status commission that recommended a new plebiscite. The 1967 voting produced a 60.5 percent majority for an enhanced commonwealth status, but Congress never acted on the changes envisioned. A new, U.S.-Puerto Rican commission in the 1970s recommended a "compact of permanent association." President Gerald R. Ford nixed the idea in 1976, however; instead, he unexpectedly declared his support for statehood.

President Ronald Reagan also professed support for Puerto Rican statehood, but his administration did nothing on the issue. The administration's only serious attention to Puerto Rico came in 1982 when United Nations Ambassador Jeanne J. Kirkpatrick succeeded in defeating an effort to put the question of the island's status before the U.N.'s "decolonization" committee.

By the end of the decade, the three major political parties on the island joined in asking for federal legislation to hold a new plebiscite on status, with the winning formula then to be adopted by Congress. A Senate committee endorsed the bill in 1990, while the House passed a weaker version calling for Congress to act on any plan approved by Puerto Rican voters. Both bills died at the end of the 1990 session.

Push for Statehood

The pro-statehood New Progressive Party regained the governorship in Puerto Rico's 1992 election after promising to hold a new local referendum on status within a year. Gov. Rosselló made good on his promise, but statehooders fell short of their anticipated victory in the 1993 balloting. Undeterred, Rosselló continued to push both in Washington and Puerto Rico for a new vote. He failed this year to get Congress this year to authorize a referendum, but he went ahead anyway with plans to hold a local advisory vote on the issue.

Turnout in the 1993 plebiscite was high: about 1.7 million votes, or 73.6 percent of those eligible. Statehooders gained 785,859 votes or 46.2 percent. Commonwealth fell below a majority for the first time, but edged out statehood with 823,258 votes or 48.4 percent. Independence garnered 75,253 votes or 4.4 percent.

Political analysts attributed the results to economic issues — chiefly, Puerto Ricans' concerns about paying taxes or losing jobs. "This was an issue of rice and beans," Luis Dávila Colón, a political commentator, said afterward. [15] But statehooders concluded that they lost because the PDP wrote its own definition of commonwealth. The ballot definition included four proposed enhancements in commonwealth status: full restoration of an important federal tax break for subsidiaries of mainland companies; extension of the federal Supplemental Security Income program to Puerto Rico; removal of caps on food stamp benefits; and special protection for the island's major agricultural product.

For that reason, Rosselló and other NPP leaders made the definition of commonwealth a major issue in pushing for a new referendum after the governor won re-election with 51 percent of the vote in 1996. Legislation in Congress — introduced by Republican lawmakers

At Issue:

What political status is best for Puerto Rico?

REP. LEONIDES DÍAZ URBINA
New Progressive Party

*O*n April 11, 1898, the United States ratified the Treaty of Paris, which put an end to the Spanish-American War. Through this treaty, Puerto Rico, along with other former Spanish possessions, was formally ceded to the United States. From thereon, Puerto Rico has been subject to the plenary powers of Congress, as provided in Article IV, Section 3, clause 2, of the Constitution, known as the Territorial Clause.

Throughout the years, Congress provided an ever larger degree of internal self-government, including the granting of U.S. citizenship by statute in 1917. Then in 1950, Congress, by means of Public Law 600, allowed the people of Puerto Rico the opportunity to draft a constitution of their own.

STATEHOOD

This year, Puerto Ricans will have an opportunity to vote in only the third plebiscite conducted in our island. We are confident that in this the 100th anniversary of our relationship with the United States, Puerto Ricans will express their intention of initiating the process that will allow us to become the 51st state of the Union.

Even though the United States has been very good to us, 100 years of political inequality is more than enough. It is inappropriate that the beacon of world democracy allows 4 million U.S. citizens to be politically disenfranchised. We want to share in the benefits and responsibilities of U.S. citizenship, just as we do when any of us decides to move to any state of the Union.

Statehood has been good for the 50 states that form our Union. There is no reason to believe that Puerto Rico would be any different from any of the other 50 states in experiencing a socioeconomic boom upon joining the Union. We want to stop being an endless drain of resources to our fellow taxpayers in the 50 states and instead become our nation's "Bridge to the Americas."

SEN. EDUARDO BHATIA GAUTIER
Popular Democratic Party

*t*he 100-year quest for the people of Puerto Rico has been how to craft a political and economic relationship with the United States that safeguards two fundamental aspirations. First, Puerto Ricans want to assert and strengthen their distinct and unique national identity. Second, a vast majority of Puerto Ricans want to continue the close political and economic association with the United States, including U.S. citizenship by birth.

Since 1952, the Caribbean island has been blessed with a carefully crafted and well-balanced political status called commonwealth. The commonwealth relationship — the Puerto Rican people's freely chosen form of government in all referenda held since 1952 — affords Puerto Ricans a greater degree of cultural and economic autonomy than states enjoy, but a lesser degree of participation in national affairs. The flexibility and dynamism of commonwealth has given

COMMONWEALTH

Puerto Rico the tools to achieve dramatic progress. The island's association with the United States has given it stability and access to the largest market in the world, and its fiscal autonomy has permitted Puerto Rico to attract industry to the island through low effective tax rates.

The productive economic vitality enjoyed by Puerto Rico under commonwealth is impossible under statehood. Statehood requires the imposition of federal income taxes, individual and corporate, which would destroy Puerto Rico's continued economic prosperity. Every single study conducted on this issue, including the Congressional Budget Office's, has established that the elimination of Puerto Rico's fiscal autonomy would entail massive capital flight and job loss.

Commonwealth is far from perfect. Today, it needs to be changed to deal with the broadening scope of congressional influence and to enhance Puerto Rico's ability to enter into commercial treaties with other countries. But, it still holds the promise to allow Puerto Rico to have a beneficial association with the United States without losing its own identity.

and supported by the NPP — included definitions of three options: commonwealth, statehood, or "separate sovereignty." The definition of commonwealth stated that U.S. citizenship for Puerto Ricans was "secured by statute" — raising what PDP leaders say is the unrealistic possibility that it might be

revoked by Congress. When that legislation stalled, Rosselló pushed a bill through the NPP-controlled Puerto Rican legislature for a local plebiscite with what PDP leaders said was a more slanted definition of commonwealth.

The House approved the bill for a congressionally authorized referendum

on March 4 by the narrowest of margins: a single vote. The measure called for a referendum on "self-determination" in Puerto Rico by the end of 1998. If statehood received a majority, President Clinton was to submit a transition plan to Congress within six months; Puerto Ricans would get another chance

LUIS VEGA-RAMOS
President, PROELA

*i*n September, Puerto Rico felt the force of Hurricane Georges. Sense and sensibility dictated that the status plebiscite of Dec. 13 be postponed. Gov. Rosselló thought differently, and Puerto Ricans are now in the dual process of rebuilding and self-determining. Tough choices are often made in the most adverse circumstances.

The main defect of the U.S.-Puerto Rico relationship is the applicability of the Territorial Clause of the Constitution.

FREE ASSOCIATION

Under Congress' plenary power, Puerto Rico is subject to legislation approved by a body in which it has no vote.

The best way to correct this democratic deficit is empowering the commonwealth through a compact of free association — ELA is the Spanish acronym — that recognizes Puerto Rico's sovereignty.

A compact is a contract between equals. Territories cannot make compacts with the federal government. Puerto Rico's aspirations for mutuality and prosperity, along with its strong desire to affirm its national identity, make this type of arrangement a perfect vehicle for its relations with the United States.

The United States has entered into compacts with the Marshall Islands, Palau and the Micronesian States. Contrary to the current commonwealth arrangement, these compacts are comprehensive documents that delegate specific powers to the United States, such as defense and security, instead of general ones. They are now in the process of being updated by Congress.

For Puerto Ricans, it should be noted that there is no legal impediment to including a provision in a compact that preserves the U.S. citizenship of those who have it, along with the right to transmit citizenship to future generations. Dual citizenship could also be agreed upon.

Through free association, dependence and uncertainty would give way to dignity, self-sufficiency and stability. Puerto Rico and the United States would reach the 21st century with a mutually beneficial relationship that sensibly averts the political threats of annexing a different nation into the federal Union.

FERNANDO MARTÍN-GARCÍA
Vice President, Puerto Rican Independence Party

*i*ndependence is not only the best political status for the people of Puerto Rico but also the only political status that can avoid what will otherwise be an inevitable crisis for American federalism.

Puerto Rico's fundamental problem is one of colonialism, not of individual civil rights. Full enfranchisement did not solve the Irish question, nor has it served even to blunt the struggle for Quebec's sovereignty. If the electoral franchise were the solution to Puerto Rico's colonial status, then becoming a prefecture of Japan or a department of France would also be a decolonizing alternative.

Obviously, the critical reality for any analysis of Puerto Rico is the recognition that we are a nation different and

INDEPENDENCE

distinct from the United States, as different as Jamaica or Costa Rica. The second step in this analysis must be the recognition of Puerto Rico's colonial status.

Once one comes to grips with these facts — a separate nationality subject to colonial rule — the inescapable conclusion is that only independence can provide a permanent solution both for the colony and for the colonial power.

Both the administration and Congress have gone a long way these past two years in recognizing the colonial nature of the relationship and making clear the undesirability of its continuation. This is an important first step.

Yet if the colonial problem is going to be solved once and for all, Congress must make clear that statehood for Puerto Rico is not a real option and at the same time express a policy that points to independence as the solution for the future.

As colonialism becomes fully discredited and as the insurmountable obstacles to statehood are made clear, the tremendous strength of Puerto Rican national identity will coalesce into an overwhelming sentiment for political independence.

After 100 years of nurturing dependence and subordination, the time for a new American policy toward Puerto Rico has arrived.

---

to vote on the final statehood plan approved by Congress.

The measure was sponsored by Rep. Don Young, Republican of Alaska and chairman of the House Resources Committee, and supported by the Speaker of the House Gingrich. But most Republicans opposed the bill, and most Demo-

crats supported it. And it was a Democratic representative — North Dakota's Earl Pomeroy — who switched his vote at the last minute to give the bill a 209-208 victory. News accounts said Pomeroy was persuaded by two staunch supporters: Puerto Rico's non-voting delegate to Congress, Carlos Romero Barceló, and Rhode

Island Democrat Patrick J. Kennedy. [16]

The Senate Energy Committee followed the House action with hearings in May and July on a comparable measure. But Senate Majority Leader Lott repeatedly said there would be no time for the Senate to act on the measure. Lott stuck to that position even after the committee's chairman, Sen. Frank Murkowski, Republican from Alaska, came out with a compromise version of the legislation at the end of July.

By that time, Rossello had turned his attention to the Puerto Rico legislature. The measure approved by the legislature on Aug. 13 and signed into law on Aug. 17 defines commonwealth in narrow and unfavorable terms. The 1950 law providing for commonwealth is said to delegate "limited self-government to the island in strictly local affairs." The definition emphasizes that Congress may treat Puerto Rico differently from other states, that U.S. citizenship for Puerto Ricans is "statutory," and that English is the "official language" of federal agencies and courts in Puerto Rico.

By contrast, the definition of statehood says that Puerto Rico would have "complete equality of rights, responsibilities, and benefits" with other states while Puerto Rico would "retain sovereignty" on "those affairs not delegated by the U.S. Constitution to the federal government." The law also sets out definitions of independence and a fourth option: "free association," which is described as a "non-colonial, non-territorial association" with the United States that would allow Puerto Rico to enter into international agreements on its own but would also end automatic U.S. citizenship for Puerto Ricans.

Once the legislation was signed, PDP leaders continued to attack the definition of commonwealth and vowed to challenge it in court. "By prohibiting the PDP from defining the commonwealth status, the NPP is violating the party's right to petition the government in whatever way we see fit on the island's status grievances," Sen. Bhatia said. But the NPP's campaign director insisted the commonwealth supporters were simply afraid of losing the plebiscite. "They are afraid that we will get the majority of votes," Díaz said. "They don't want to let it happen." [17] ■

CURRENT SITUATION

Contentious Issues

Both of Puerto Rico's major parties faced contentious issues this month about their strategies for the Dec. 13 political-status plebiscite:

• The governing New Progressive Party faced the simple question of whether to postpone the balloting because of the destruction caused by Hurricane Georges last month. The decision: Go forward with the vote as scheduled.

• The Popular Democratic Party had a more intricate problem: What stance to take toward a ballot that had what PDP leaders regarded as an unacceptable definition of commonwealth. It decided to urge voters to cast their ballots for a fifth option: "none of the above."

The calls to postpone the Dec. 13 plebiscite came not only from opposition parties but also from NPP leaders, including Senate President Charlie Rodríguez, a longtime rival of Rossello's, and Héctor O'Neill, mayor of Guaynabo and president of the party's association of mayors. But Rosselló — who apologized in his second inaugural speech last year to those who found him "stubborn" or "intransigent" — brooked no opposition to the schedule.

Rosselló firmly declared that the hurricane was no reason to postpone or cancel the vote on Puerto Rico's future. And when the NPP's governing board met on the issue on Oct. 6, it voted unanimously to proceed with the plebiscite as scheduled. Even so, O'Neill called the board's vote "a bad decision," and Rodríguez declined to attend the news conference announcing the move.

For its part, the PDP was beset with internal disagreements about the best strategy for the plebiscite in the days before a scheduled Oct. 15 party conference. Some PDP officials — including Rafael Cordero Santiago, mayor of Ponce, a traditional PDP stronghold — favored a boycott of the plebiscite. Some others said the party should get behind the "free association" option as the closest ballot option to the PDP's conception of commonwealth.

The party suffered a setback on the eve of the party's conference in its legal fight either to block the plebiscite or alter the definition of commonwealth. U.S. District Judge Juan Pérez-Giménez refused the PDP's effort to have the case tried in Puerto Rico's court system in a 25-page opinion that gave the party scant hope of succeeding with its claim in federal court.

"The issue raised . . . is inescapably and in reality one about the power of Congress to legislate for the island pursuant to the Territorial Clause," Pérez-Giménez wrote in the opinion filed Oct. 13. "This very issue . . . raises a fundamental, essential, decisive and outcome-determinative question of federal law that warrants the exercise of federal jurisdiction over the case."

Lawyers for the PDP said they would appeal the ruling to the 1st U.S. Circuit Court of Appeals in Boston, which has jurisdiction over Puerto Rico. But appellate courts have only limited authority to entertain appeals at intermediate stages of a lawsuit. At press time, no appeal had been filed.

With its legal strategy in doubt, the PDP's board of governors decided Oct. 15 that its best political tactic was to urge Puerto Ricans to vote for none of the four options — statehood, commonwealth, free association or independence — and instead mark the fifth column on the ballot: "none of the above."

PDP President Acevedo Vilá said the vote was the best way to "repudiate the plebiscite, Pedro Rosselló and statehood." A boycott, he said, would allow Rosselló to win "a 60, 70 or 80 percent favorable result in favor of statehood" and then "go to Washington and tell them that this is the will of the people."

The PDP's stance could cost the party the $500,000 in public funds it would have been entitled to receive if it campaigned for the commonwealth option and also might jeopardize its right to station party observers at polling places. More broadly, if party leaders fail to sell the tactic to rank-and-file members, the stance could further fracture the anti-statehood vote in the plebiscite.

For his part, Rosselló took a hands-off stance toward the PDP position when asked for reaction the next day. In a telephone interview from Boston, where he was campaigning for Democratic Party candidates, Rosselló told an Associated Press reporter that he did not want to get involved in the inner workings of another party. "Puerto Rico is a society based on law and order," Rosselló said. "We are forced to follow what the law stipulates." ■

OUTLOOK

Inertia and Impasse

When Hurricane Georges tore through the Caribbean last month, the havoc in Puerto Rico was front-page news in the mainland United States. But the debate about Puerto Rico's political status conducted over the past year both in Washington and on the island has barely registered as news for most Americans.

Puerto Rico has simply not been an important political issue within the United States since U.S. rule was established in the early part of the century. Historian Raymond Carr says U.S. governance of the island has been a monument to "the politics of selective inattention." [18] Gov. Rosselló

FOR MORE INFORMATION

If you would like to have this CQ Researcher updated, or need more information about this topic, please call CQ Custom Research. Special rates for CQ subscribers. (202) 887-8600 or (800) 432-2250, ext. 600, or E-mail Custom.Research@cq.com

New Progressive Party [statehood], P.O. Box 1992, Fernández Juncos Station, San Juan, P.R. 00910; (787) 721-1998.

Popular Democratic Party [commonwealth], P.O. Box 9065788, San Juan, P.R. 00906-5788; (787) 721-2000.

PROELA [free association], P.O. Box 194066, San Juan, P.R. 00919-4066; (787) 753-3748.

Puerto Rico Independence Party, 963 Roosevelt Ave., San Juan, P.R. 00920-2901; (787) 782-1455.

Puerto Rico Federal Affairs Administration, 1100 17th St., N.W., Suite 800, Washington, D.C. 20036; (202) 778-0710.

made a similar point when he told a Harvard University audience earlier this year that Puerto Rico has gone through "100 years of solitude" and that Puerto Ricans remain "disenfranchised stepchildren within the great American family." [19]

In the congressional debate over the status referendum bill this year, Republican and Democratic lawmakers alike stressed the importance of "self-determination" for Puerto Ricans. In introducing the measure during the House floor debate in March, Rep. Young described it as "a step for freedom."

Two of the three members of Congress of Puerto Rican extraction voted against the bill, however, arguing that the measure as written was tilted in favor of statehood. "Make no mistake," Rep. Nydia M. Velázquez, D-N.Y., said. "By voting on this legislation, we are again imposing statehood on the people of Puerto Rico."

The bill's failure can be attributed in part to the debate over the language issue and to the press of other legislative business. But partisan considerations were also a factor. Puerto Rico would seem most likely to send a predominantly Democratic congressional delegation to Washing-

ton — two senators and perhaps seven out of the expected eight House members it would be allotted — if it were admitted as a state.

Pro-statehood lobbyists tried to allay the fears of the Republican-controlled Congress by recalling that Alaska and Hawaii confounded partisan predictions after they attained statehood in the 1950s: Alaska has been predominantly Republican, and Hawaii predominantly Democratic, exactly the opposite of expectations at the time. In addition, advocates of Puerto Rican statehood presented the issue this year as an opportunity for the GOP to appeal to the growing Hispanic population within the U.S. Despite those arguments, most GOP members voted against the House bill, and the Senate's Republican leader decided not to take up the House-passed measure in the upper chamber.

In Puerto Rico, the status issue suffers not from inattention but from intractability. The two major parties are so closely balanced that each has a "mutual veto" over the other, according to PDP veteran Martínez. "We can stop statehooders from getting a majority that would impress the Congress, but they had enough [power] in 1989 and 1991 to stop our attempts to enhance commonwealth," Martínez says.

All three parties are predicting that the Dec. 13 plebiscite will resolve this impasse. Rosselló and other PNP leaders, professing confidence of victory, say the vote will impel Congress to start the process toward admitting Puerto Rico as a state. PDP leaders also predict victory in the balloting and tentatively suggest the result could clear the way for action on "perfecting" commonwealth. For their part, PIP leaders say the plebiscite simply underscores the irreconcilable conflict of U.S. rule. "This is part of the process that will force the United States to face the contradictions of the U.S. presence in Puerto Rico," Martín says.

More realistically, however, a close election may have little impact either in Puerto Rico or, more importantly, in Washington. "It's a futile exercise," says Trías, a former PDP-appointed chief justice of Puerto Rico's supreme court. "Puerto Rico cannot will itself into enhanced commonwealth or statehood."

A victory for the status quo — whether it results from the action of the Puerto Rican people or from the inaction of U.S. lawmakers — would come in the face of widespread dissatisfaction among Puerto Ricans with their relationship with the United States. But Trías says that neither statehood, enhanced commonwealth nor independence is likely any time soon. "We are debating between dreams and impossibilities," he says.

All three parties nonetheless vow to press harder for their respective status solutions whatever the results of the Dec. 13 balloting. Asked what the NPP will do if statehood loses, Cintrón responds, in imperfect English, "We still fight. We'll begin again and again and again. We are waiting for a century."

"We can be in that game forever," Martínez concludes. "I don't see any end to it." ■

Notes

[1] The Territorial Clause provides, "The Congress shall have Power to dispose of and make all needful Rules and Regulations respecting the Territory or other Property belonging to the United States; . . . " (Art. IV., Section 3, clause 2).

[2] For a critical account and analysis of Supreme Court decisions regarding Puerto Rico, see Juan R. Torruella, *The Supreme Court and Puerto Rico: The Doctrine of Separate and Unequal* (1985). Torruella, a Puerto Rican, is the chief judge of the 1st U.S. Circuit Court of Appeals, which has jurisdiction over Puerto Rico.

[3] See *The Washington Post*, March 5, 1998, p. A1.

[4] See Raymond Carr, *Puerto Rico: A Colonial Experiment* (1984), p. 13.

[5] For background, see Patrick G. Marshall, "Puerto Rico: The Struggle Over Status," *Editorial Research Reports*, Feb. 8, 1991, pp. 81-96.

[6] Background is drawn primarily from Carr, *op. cit.*, and José Trías Monge, *Puerto Rico: The World's Oldest Colony* (1997). See also

Arturo Morales Carrión, *Puerto Rico: A Political and Cultural History* (1983).

[7] Trias, *op. cit.*, pp. 15-20.

[8] See *ibid.*, pp. 12-15.

[9] See Trias, *ibid.*, p. 99.

[10] *Ibid.*, pp. 101-102. See Rexford G. Tugwell, *The Stricken Land: The Story of Puerto Rico* (1947).

[11] See Trías, *op. cit.*, pp. 92, 100-101. For English-language biographies, see ??? Aitken, *Poet in the Fortress: The Story of Luis Muñoz Marín* (1964), and Thomas G. Matthews, *Luis Muñoz Marín: A Concise Biography* (1967).

[12] Background drawn from James L. Dietz, *Economic History of Puerto Rico: Institutional Change and Capitalist Development* (1986), pp. 182-239 (1940s), 240-310 (1950s on). For a more favorable account of the industrialization process, see A. W. Maldonado, *Teodoro Moscoso and Puerto Rico's Operation Bootstrap* (1997).

[13] See *ibid.*, pp. 244, 260 (investment), p. 248 (wages). Growth rates are taken from testimony of J. Thomas Hexner before Senate Energy Committee, May 19, 1998. See J. Thomas Hexner and Glenn Jenkins, "Puerto Rico: The Economic and Fiscal Dimensions," report prepared for the Citizens Educational Foundation, 1998.

[14] Dietz, *op. cit.*, pp. 285-286.

[15] Quoted in *The New York Times*, Nov. 16, 1993, p. A24.

[16] *The New York Times*, March 5, 1998, A24. The final tally showed 43 Republicans, 165 Democrats, and one independent voting for the bill; 177 Republicans and 31 Democrats voting against it.

[17] Quoted in *The San Juan Star*, Aug. 20, 1998.

[18] Carr, *op. cit.*, pp. 12-13.

[19] Pedro Rosselló, "After '100 Años de Soledad,' a Date with Destiny," John F. Kennedy School of Government, Harvard University, Feb. 17, 1998.

Bibliography

Selected Sources Used

Books

Carr, Raymond, *Puerto Rico: A Colonial Experiment*, Vintage, 1984.

Carr, a historian and former professor at St. Antony's College, Oxford University, wrote this well-regarded political history under a commission from the Twentieth Century Fund. The book includes a two-page summary of Puerto Rico's political parties, detailed source notes and a six-page reading list.

Dietz, James L., *Economic History of Puerto Rico: Institutional Change and Capitalist Development*, Princeton University Press, 1986.

Dietz, a professor at California State University in Fullerton, surveys the economic history of Puerto Rico from the Spanish-colonial era into the 20th century, including the early period of U.S. control, the "transformation" of the 1930s, Operation Bootstrap and what he calls "growth and misdevelopment" since the 1950s. The book includes detailed source notes and a 16-page bibliography.

López, Adalberto, and James Petras (eds.), *Puerto Rico and Puerto Ricans: Studies in History and Society*, 1974.

The book includes 16 essays by various contributors examining, from a generally pro-independence perspective, Puerto Rico's colonial history, Puerto Rico in the 20th century and Puerto Ricans on the mainland. The book includes a detailed chronology and a six-page bibliography. Lopez, a historian, and Petras, a sociologist, are both professors at the State University of New York in Binghamton.

Maldonado, A. W., *Teodoro Moscoso and Puerto Rico's Operation Bootstrap*, University Press of Florida, 1997.

Journalist Maldonado traces the life of Teodoro Moscoso, his role in the creating and directing Operation Bootstrap from the late 1940s on and its impact on what he calls Puerto Rico's "economic miracle." The book — funded in large part by a grant from Chase Manhattan Bank — includes a seven-page bibliography.

Morales Carrión, Arturo, *Puerto Rico: A Political and Cultural History*, Norton, 1983.

Morales, a Puerto Rican historian, wrote the major parts of this history, commissioned by the American Association for State and Local History, with additional chapters covering the Spanish-colonial period by other scholars. Detailed source notes and a seven-page bibliography are included.

Trías Monge, José, *Puerto Rico: The World's Oldest Colony*, Yale University Press, 1997.

Trías, a distinguished Puerto Rican scholar and former supreme court justice, provocatively analyzes Puerto Rico's history as a Spanish and then U.S. colony. He ends with a strong call for immediate "decolonization" through a political status chosen respectively by Puerto Rico and the U.S. The book includes a chronology, source notes, a glossary and a six-page bibliography.

Tumin, Melvin M., with Arnold S. Feldman, *Social Class and Social Change in Puerto Rico* (2d ed.), Bobbs-Merrill, 1971.

This sociological examination of the effects of the industrialization of the 1950s on Puerto Rican society, originally published in 1961, found a more diverse class structure, increased educational and occupational mobility and tensions between Puerto Ricans' traditional cultural patterns and changed attitudes resulting from increased interactions with the United States.

Wagenheim, Kal, with Olga Jiménez de Wagenheim (eds.), *The Puerto Ricans: A Documentary History*, Praeger, 1973.

This collection of original sources covers political and social history from Columbus' landing and the Spanish-colonial period through the establishment of commonwealth status and the continuing strains created by the uncertain relationship with the United States in the 1970s. The book includes an eight-page bibliography.

The Next Step

Additional information from UMI's Newspaper & Periodical Abstracts™ database

Congressional Action

"A Matter of Self-Determination," *The Washington Post*, Sept. 12, 1998, p. A18.

Senate Majority Leader Trent Lott, R-Miss., is deciding whether to send to the floor a bill drafted by Sen. Frank Murkowski, R-Alaska, authorizing a self-determination process for Puerto Rico. Lott hasn't acted on the bill yet, possibly because the island is poor and its linguistic preference makes it a poor fit as a state. Also, it might send Democrats to Congress.

"Let Puerto Ricans Decide," *The Denver Post*, June 13, 1998, p. B9.

This editorial lauds Colorado Republican Sens. Wayne Allard and Ben Nighthorse Campbell for cosponsoring a measure that would let Puerto Ricans determine whether they want statehood, independence or to continue functioning as an unincorporated U.S. territory.

"The Puerto Rican Asterisk," *The Washington Post*, Aug. 4, 1998, p. A14.

The large and important burden of removing the asterisk from the American citizenship of residents of Puerto Rico now rests on the Senate. The House has done its bit by agreeing for the first time not simply to define the island's political options but also to commit Congress to honor Puerto Rico's choice among them. President Clinton is eager to proceed. But 100 years after the United States took the territory from Spain, the Senate still isn't sure. Republican Majority Leader Trent Lott, R-Miss., doubts there's time to legislate before Congress adjourns in October.

Alvarez, Lizette, "In Push for Puerto Rico Vote, Conservative Bent Is Stressed," *The New York Times*, July 24, 1998, p. A1.

Sen. Larry E. Craig, R-Idaho, never fails to point out that Puerto Rico passed the "Contract with America" in 1994. Craig is pushing legislation for a congressionally sanctioned referendum on Puerto Rico's status. It is an uphill battle to persuade his fellow Republican senators, especially the majority leader, Sen. Trent Lott of Mississippi, to take the chance that Puerto Rico will not, as a state, send two Democratic senators and six Democratic representatives to Washington. That fear, along with the fact that Puerto Rico is Spanish-speaking, has kept the Republican-controlled Congress from acting quickly in accordance with the party's 1996 pledge to support the right of Puerto Rico's citizens to be admitted to the Union as a fully sovereign state if they so determine.

Alvarez, Lizette, "Senator's Draft Bill Defines Options in Puerto Rico Plebiscite," *The New York Times*, Aug. 1, 1998, p. A14.

As Puerto Rico prepares for a plebiscite in December, a Senate committee chairman today released a scaled-back draft bill that defines the three options: commonwealth, statehood or independence. The bill was released by Sen. Frank H. Murkowski, the Alaska Republican who heads the Committee on Energy and Natural Resources. Murkowski said he had tried to use "accurate" and "neutral" definitions in the bill for the plebiscite, which is to be held on Dec. 13. But Puerto Rico's governor, Pedro J. Rossello, said he did not expect the plebiscite to be approved by Congress because the Senate would probably not pass a bill this year.

Colón, Rafael Hernandez, "Doing Right by Puerto Rico: Congress Must Act," *Foreign Affairs*, July 1998, pp. 112-114.

The question of self-determination for Puerto Rico remains unresolved. The author argues that Congress should offer the people of Puerto Rico the chance to vote on amending the commonwealth to enable their land to be governed in a fully democratic manner.

Dorning, Mike, "Puerto Rico Closer to Statehood; Vote Opposed by Reps. Gutierrez, Rush; Measure Narrowly Passed in House, Faces Senate Hurdle," *Chicago Tribune*, March 5, 1998, p. 3.

By a one-vote margin and a last-minute switch of sides by Democratic Illinois Rep. Bobby Rush, the House voted Wednesday night to begin the steps toward deciding if there will be statehood for Puerto Rico. One hundred years after the United States won the island in the war against Spain, the House voted to authorize a plebiscite on Puerto Rico's future status.

Gugliotta, Guy "Puerto Rico 'Fast Track' Plans Fade; Narrower Bill on Status Vote Possible," *The Washington Post*, July 17, 1998, p. A19.

Senators studying Puerto Rico's future have all but abandoned plans for elaborate legislation that could put the island on a "fast track" to statehood, but they held out hope that Congress this year could pass a stripped-down bill to establish how Puerto Ricans can vote on homeland status.

Hitt, Greg, "'English Only' Amendment to House Bill On Puerto Rico Exposes GOP Fissures," *The Wall Street Journal*, March 5, 1998, p. A24.

Conservative Republicans reopened the issue of whether English should be the United States' official language, embarrassing party leaders who have been trying to rebuild ties to Hispanics. Rep. Gerald B.H. Solomon, R-N.Y., sidetracked House debate yesterday on legislation intended to establish a statehood plebiscite in Puerto

Rico by offering the divisive "English only" amendment. The bill was approved 209-208 last night after Solomon's amendment failed in favor of a watered-down substitute, backed by most House Democrats and less than a third of House Republicans, that removed the teeth from the Solomon approach.

History

"For Every Puerto Rican, a Political Rally," _The New York Times_, July 26, 1998, p. 26.

Tens of thousands of Puerto Ricans celebrated and condemned the landing of American troops in Guanica 100 years ago, while thousands more traveled to a historic fortress in San Juan to pay homage to the political status that has defined Puerto Rico's relationship to the United States for nearly a half-century.

"Puerto Rico Deserves a Clean Choice," _Chicago Tribune_, Sept. 8, 1997, p. 10.

The prickly and awkward union between Puerto Rico and the United States began in 1898 much like a shotgun wedding — Spain simply handed the island over to the U.S. after the Spanish-American War — and the relationship hasn't changed much over the years. Congress next month will consider a proposal by Rep. Don Young, R-Alaska, that would let both partners re-examine and perhaps restructure their relationship. Young proposes to hold the first congressionally sanctioned plebiscite on the political status of Puerto Rico to offer voters in the island a choice of statehood, independence or the status quo, commonwealth.

Edgardo Rodriguez, Julia, "A Look At Puerto Rico: Escaping a Colonial State of Mind," _The Washington Post_, July 26, 1998, p. C3.

Only a year before U.S. troops came ashore, Puerto Rico had taken a tentative first step toward a degree of self-government, signing a carta autonomica (Charter of Autonomy) with Spain. That treaty promised what many in Puerto Rico saw, and still see, as a kind of truncated utopia — self-rule without full sovereignty, a "limited"colonialism. And it was against that achievement, gained entirely in the diplomatic arena, that the young American empire was to array its proud militarism, its political ignorance of the way imperial power is supposed to behave.

Navarro, Mireya, "A New Debate on the Fate (And State) of Puerto Rico," _The New York Times_, March 30, 1998, p. A1.

A century after Spain ceded Puerto Rico to United States rule after losing the Spanish-American War, Americans and Puerto Ricans are not so certain of their feelings for each other. Prodded by the centennial of the Spanish-American War this year, international disapproval of any vestiges of colonialism and the failings of the status quo, both the United States and Puerto Rico seem to want change.

Puerto Rican Culture

Gugliotta, Guy, "Phone Battle Mirrors Puerto Rico's Identity Crisis," _The Washington Post_, July 9, 1998, p. A1.

In the 100 years since the United States claimed Puerto Rico after the Spanish-American War, islanders have wrestled with the ambiguity of their political status — adrift between two cultures, not entirely comfortable with either. Nowhere has this identity crisis been more starkly drawn than in a recent general strike to protest the sale of the state-owned Puerto Rico Telephone Co. But it is far from clear whether the strike was just another skirmish in the century-old status war or the prologue to Armageddon. Puerto Ricans may begin to learn the answer next week when the Senate Energy and Natural Resources Committee takes up a bill, a version of which already has passed in the House, that could put Puerto Rico on the road to becoming the 51st state.

Lester, Joan Steinau, "Don't Force Puerto Rico Into Statehood," _San Francisco Chronicle_, March 29, 1998, p. E11.

I sat in the cool, breezy home of Margarita Ostolaza in Puerto Rico as I pondered, What is a nation? I met Ostolaza, a political science professor, 10 years ago. Now she's returned to San Juan from Washington, where she lobbied Congress to retain Puerto Rico's status as a U.S. "commonwealth," the form repeatedly favored in Puerto Rican referendums. The set of compromises allows Puerto Ricans to retain a national identity — and to value their unique status. A poll by _El Nueva Dia_, San Juan's major newspaper, found most people consider their nation to be Puerto Rico, not the United States; simultaneously, most regard their U.S. citizenship as very important.

MacDonald, Christine, "Statehood Issue Divides Area's Puerto Ricans," _The Boston Globe_, March 15, 1998, p. W1.

Puerto Ricans who live in the United States give their views on statehood vs. independence.

Spanish vs. English

Espenshade, Thomas J., and Haishan Fu, "An Analysis of English-Language Proficiency Among U.S. Immigrants," _American Sociological Review_, April 1997, pp. 288-305.

A study examines the factors that influence the process by which foreign-born persons whose mother tongue is not English acquire English-language proficiency. The results confirm that both pre- and post-immigration phases of the life cycle contain elements that are associated with how well immigrants to the United States speak English.

Navarro, Mireya, "Puerto Rico Teachers Resist Teaching in English," _The New York Times_, May 19, 1997, p. A12.

Teacher organizations say they oppose the Puerto Rico Department of Education's "Project for Developing a Bilingual Citizen," calling it a political rather than pedagogic move by a pro-statehood government that wants to make the island more palatable to Congress.

Back Issues

Great Research on Current Issues Starts Right Here.
Recent topics covered by The CQ Researcher are listed below.
Now available on the Web
For information, call (800) 432-2250 ext. 279 or (202) 887-6279.

If you would like to have any of these CQ Researchers updated, or need more information
about these topics, please call CQ Custom Research. Special rates for CQ subscribers.
(202) 887-8600 or (800) 432-2250, ext. 600, or E-mail Custom.Research@cq.com

JULY 1997
Transportation Policy
Executive Pay
School Choice Debate
Aggressive Driving

AUGUST 1997
Age Discrimination
Banning Land Mines
Children's Television
Evolution vs. Creationism

SEPTEMBER 1997
Caring for the Dying
Mental Health Policy
Mexico's Future
Youth Fitness

OCTOBER 1997
Urban Sprawl in the West
Diversity in the Workplace
Teacher Education
Contingent Work Force

NOVEMBER 1997
Renewable Energy
Artificial Intelligence
Religious Persecution
Roe v. Wade at 25

DECEMBER 1997
Whistleblowers
Castro's Next Move
Gun Control Standoff
Regulating Nonprofits

JANUARY 1998
Foster Care Reform
IRS Reform
The Black Middle Class
U.S.-British Relations

FEBRUARY 1998
Patients' Rights
Deflation Fears
Caring for the Elderly
The New Corporate Philanthropy

MARCH 1998
Israel at 50
The Federal Judiciary
Drinking on Campus
The Economics of Recycling

APRIL 1998
Biology and Behavior
Liberal Arts Education
Income Inequality
High-Tech Labor Shortage

MAY 1998
Census 2000
Child-Care Options
Alzheimer's Disease
U.S.-Russian Relations

JUNE 1998
Student Journalism
Antitrust Policy
Environmental Justice
Sleep Deprivation

JULY 1998
Encouraging Teen Abstinence
Population and the Environment
Democracy in Asia
Baby Boomers at Midlife

AUGUST 1998
Oil Production in the 21st Century
Flexible Work Arrangements
Coastal Development
Student Activism

SEPTEMBER 1998
Organic Farming
Cancer Treatments
Hispanic Americans' New Clout
The Future of Baseball

OCTOBER 1998
School Violence
Social Security
National Forests

Back issues are available for $5.00 (subscribers) or $10.00 (non-subscribers). Quantity discounts apply to orders over 10. To order, call Congressional Quarterly Customer Service at (202) 887-8621.

Binders are available for $18.00. To order call 1-800-638-1710. Please refer to stock number 648.

Future Topics

▶ *Internet Privacy*

▶ *Human Rights*

▶ *Drug Testing*

THE

CQ Researcher

PUBLISHED BY CONGRESSIONAL QUARTERLY INC.

Internet Privacy

Is more government regulation needed?

Privacy advocates warn that many Web sites try to collect personal information from on-line users, but few guarantee how that data will be used. They say the federal government should establish standards to protect privacy on-line. But Internet businesses and others contend that they can safeguard users' privacy without resorting to government interference. Law-enforcement agencies, meanwhile, favor government limitations on the use of sophisticated encryption technology, which makes on-line communications secure — even from the police. They fear that strong encryption software will aid criminals in hiding their activities. But privacy advocates argue that encryption technology assures companies and consumers that their on-line communications are not being tampered with.

November 6, 1998 • Volume 8, No. 41 • Pages 953-976

Formerly Editorial Research Reports

CQ Researcher

Nov. 6, 1998
Volume 8, No. 41

EDITOR
Sandra Stencel

MANAGING EDITOR
Thomas J. Colin

STAFF WRITERS
Adriel Bettelheim
Mary H. Cooper
Kenneth Jost
Kathy Koch
David Masci

PRODUCTION EDITOR
Melissa Hall

EDITORIAL ASSISTANT
Laura S. Cavender

PUBLISHED BY
Congressional Quarterly Inc.

CHAIRMAN
Andrew Barnes

VICE CHAIRMAN
Andrew P. Corty

PRESIDENT AND PUBLISHER
Robert W. Merry

EXECUTIVE EDITOR
David Rapp

The CQ Researcher (ISSN 1056-2036). Formerly Editorial Research Reports. Published weekly, except Jan. 2, May 29, July 3, Oct. 30, by Congressional Quarterly Inc., 1414 22nd St., N.W., Washington, D.C. 20037. Annual subscription rate for libraries, businesses and government is $340. Additional rates furnished upon request. Periodicals postage paid at Washington, D.C., and additional mailing offices. POSTMASTER: Send address changes to The CQ Researcher, 1414 22nd St., N.W., Washington, D.C. 20037.

COVER: NANCY EVERIST, ADVERTISING DIRECTOR OF THE NEW MEXICO TOURISM DEPARTMENT, PROMOTES LOCAL TOURISM VIA THE INTERNET. PRIVACY ADVOCATES WARN THAT ON-LINE BROWSERS CAN INADVERTENTLY DISCLOSE PERSONAL INFORMATION WHEN THEY VISIT WEB SITES. (AP PHOTO/MURRAE HAYNES)

Internet Privacy

THE ISSUES

Every day, millions of on-line consumers turn to the Internet to find everything from tips on travel to advice on healthy eating.

Many click on the popular GeoCities site. Not surprisingly, GeoCities wants something in return: marketable personal information. To encourage visitors to fill out questionnaires and reveal their names, incomes and other personal data, GeoCities offers them free E-mail accounts and their own Web home page.

In the past, GeoCities promised that the personal information being collected would not be shared "with anyone without your permission." But on Aug. 13, 1998, the Federal Trade Commission (FTC) accused GeoCities of breaking its promise.

"GeoCities has misled its customers, both children and adults, by not telling the truth about how it was using their personal information," said Jodie Bernstein, director of the FTC's Bureau of Consumer Protection, in a statement released that day.

According to the commission, GeoCities shared information about more than 2 million of its Web users with outside parties without receiving or even asking for permission. The data was used to create advertisements and solicitations personalized to appeal to the original GeoCities visitors.

"GeoCities was collecting all this sensitive information and the people [who had completed questionnaires] didn't realize what was going on," says Deirdre Mulligan, staff counsel at the Center for Democracy and Technology. "They didn't know what they were giving away."

Of course, much of the Internet, almost by definition, is not private. Indeed, the new medium connects

people around the world in a way that few could have dreamed about. Created by the Pentagon in the 1970s as an alternate means of communication during wartime, the net now offers tens of millions of ordinary people access to an amount of information that would dwarf what is stored in the Library of Congress.

The Internet has been hailed as the most important communications development since Guttenburg invented movable type more than 500 years ago. As with the advent of printing, the creation of the Internet has led to an information explosion that is rapidly transforming almost every sphere of life, from education to communications to retail commerce.

The number of people on-line is growing exponentially. Just four years ago, there were only about 3 million Internet users around the world, mostly in the United States. At the beginning of this year, the number had ballooned to nearly 60 million in the U.S. alone and more than 100 million worldwide. [1]

Along with an increase in the number of people on-line has come a corresponding growth in commercial use. Established retailers and a host of newcomers have created Web sites to hawk everything from rare books to sex toys. By the end of last year, 10 million people worldwide had purchased a product or service on-line. [2]

But the Internet, like most new technologies, presents challenges as well as

tremendous opportunities for society. Every day, millions of Americans disclose personal information about themselves when they buy goods or services from an on-line business or simply visit Web sites. In many cases, companies that operate these sites offer few or no assurances as to how this information will be used. Many, in fact, trade or sell consumers' names and addresses and other data to retailers and marketers. Other companies have sprung up solely for the purpose of collecting and selling personal information.

The growth of such on-line enterprises has prompted many policymakers and others to question whether they have the right to acquire and, more importantly, pass on personal data to third parties. And if so, should the Web sites be required to tell consumers what they intend to do with the birth dates, E-mail addresses and telephone numbers they are collecting?

According to an FTC study released on June 4, only 14 percent of commercial Web sites publicly disclosed their privacy policies. At the same time, 92 percent, collected personal information from users who visited them. [3] Another survey, conducted by *Business Week* in March, found that non-users of the Internet cite privacy concerns as their main reason for not going on-line. [4]

For its part, GeoCities acknowledged no wrongdoing and paid no fine. Yet, as part of a settlement with the FTC, it did agree to establish and enforce a new privacy policy. Now, when on-line consumers complete the GeoCities' questionnaire, they are told that the information will be released to outside parties.

Indeed, the FTC could not force GeoCities to stop passing on personal information. It is only empowered to act against what it sees as "deceptive practices," such as claiming you're not

CQ on the Web: www.cq.com

November 6, 1998   955

Most Web Sites Collect Personal Information

The vast majority of Web sites collect personal information from on-line consumers, and most collect several types of information, such as name, address, Social Security number and birth date.

Percent of Web Sites Collecting Personal Information

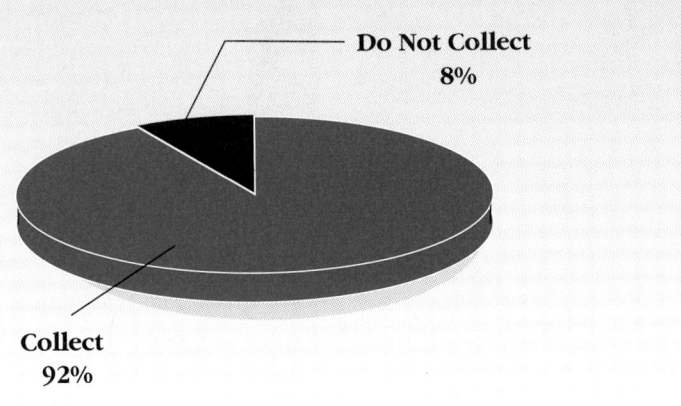

Do Not Collect
8%

Collect
92%

Source: "Privacy Online: A Report to Congress," Federal Trade Commission, June 1998.

on-line sites offer consumers little or no protection when it comes to maintaining the confidentiality of personal information.

The computer and retail industries argue, however, that government regulation is unnecessary and unrealistic. To begin with, they say, the Internet is still taking shape, making talk of rigid rules on privacy unrealistic. "At this stage, trying to nail down some policy with legislation might not work and could end up retarding the growth of on-line commerce," says Russ Bodoff, the general manager for the Better Business Bureau On-line, an industry group that aims to make self-regulation work.

Bodoff says that his organization and others like it have helped hundreds of Web sites create and enforce privacy standards. Already, supporters of self-regulation say, most of the biggest and most well-known sites have privacy policies. "With a little bit of guidance, self-regulation can be as effective as legislation," Bodoff claims.

Finally, self-regulation boosters argue, the on-line industry has an interest in guaranteeing privacy since consumers who feel abused by Web sites won't visit them again. Says Chet Dalzell, a spokesman for the Direct Marketing Association: "Marketers and retailers on-line know that they have to extend a certain amount of privacy and make sure transactions are secure in order to ensure that customers will visit or shop at their Web site."

As Dalzell suggests, privacy doesn't just entail creating a policy or rules to protect the confidentiality of information. Transactions and other communications must be secure from those who do not want to follow any rules that might be set.

Computers, as well as phones and other communications tools, secure the transfer of data by using encryption technology. Encryption software protects information by scrambling it into an unreadable code at its source and

passing on private information when you actually are. "We are not trying to tell them what their privacy policies ought to be," said Toby Levin, staff counsel at the FTC. [5]

That's part of the problem, say many privacy advocates. They point out that because there is no law protecting privacy on-line, Web sites are not obligated to do so. In fact, say some, the GeoCities case may end up doing more harm than good. "It has had a perversely undesirable effect in that it has convinced companies on-line not to post privacy policies so as to avoid any [FTC] scrutiny," says Jason Catlett, president of Junkbusters Corp., a New Jersey on-line-privacy protection firm. In other words, if there is no posted policy, there can be no deceptive practices.

Privacy advocates like Catlett say that the current system, where Web sites establish and enforce their own privacy policies if at all, is terribly flawed. They are urging the Clinton administration and Congress to step in with legislation aimed at protecting consumer privacy on-line. "We need to lay down some rules, simple do's and don'ts, for on-line privacy," says Jerry Berman, executive director at the Center for Democracy and Technology, a civil liberties group that focuses on technology issues. Among other things, such rules would give consumers the right to see the information collected about them and the ability to stop its dissemination to third parties.

In addition, Berman and others favor the creation of a privacy agency within the federal government to enforce the new rules and advise businesses on how to establish effective privacy policies. The FTC, they say, does not have the staff to police the Internet for evidence of deceptive practices (its current mandate), let alone enforce new privacy laws. [6]

Privacy advocates admit that there are Web sites, usually created by large businesses, that do have adequate privacy policies. But the majority of

unscrambling it when it is received.

Encryption is already widely used on-line in the United States to protect everything from sensitive E-mail to credit card numbers. But the intelligence and law-enforcement communities are wary of the potential for the misuse of this technology.

Currently, the United States bans the export of powerful encryption technology. The intelligence community argues that such controls are needed to keep powerful technology out of the hands of America's enemies, who would use it to thwart U.S. intelligence-gathering efforts.

"If this were easily obtainable, our ability to keep apprised of what terrorists and other enemies were doing would be severely hampered," says Dan Smith, chief of research for the Center for Defense Information, a pro-defense think tank. The ban should be kept in place even if it only delays states like Iraq and Libya from acquiring sophisticated encryption technology. "At least we have more time . . . to stay one step ahead of them," he says.

At the same time, the law-enforcement community is pressing Congress to require software makers to install a "key" or "back door" in their encryption programs, making it possible for state and federal officers to decode encrypted data. "When we obtain a court-ordered warrant, we should be able to access the encrypted information, just like we can wiretap phones and search homes today," says Charles Barry Smith, a special agent and encryption expert at the FBI. Most programs today contain no such key, often making data retrieval difficult if not impossible.

Smith and others say that criminals and terrorists are increasingly using computers to store information and to communicate with each other. And, they claim, strong encryption programs are already hampering law enforcement's efforts to conduct sur-

Few Sites Disclose Information Policy

Less than 15 percent of the Web sites that collect personal information tell consumers who is collecting the information and how it will be used.

Percent of Web Sites With an Information Disclosure

Disclosure
14%

No disclosure
86%

Source: "Privacy Online: A Report to Congress," Federal Trade Commission, June 1998

veillance and gather evidence in many cases.

But privacy advocates and the computer industry oppose both existing and proposed limits on encryption technology. To begin with, they argue, export controls are merely hurting American companies, which are losing this segment of the overseas software market to European and Asian corporations. "By hamstringing U.S. companies, we've simply created an opportunity for foreign firms to take over a market that should be ours," says Solveig Singleton, director of information studies at the CATO Institute. Some of this advanced, foreign encryption is available to America's enemies, defeating the purpose of the export limits in the first place.

In addition, privacy advocates argue, the proposed "key" to allow law enforcement to unlock encrypted information defeats the whole purpose of protecting your data. "It doesn't make any sense: Why would you want encryption that could be opened by a third party?" asks Marc Rottenberg, director of the Electronic

Privacy Information Center, which promotes on-line privacy and other civil liberties.

Questions concerning encryption or the regulation of Web sites will take on increasing importance as more and more people spend more and more time on-line. Other privacy concerns also have come to the fore. For instance, many experts, including some in the business community, supported the recent successful effort in Congress to enact legal protections for children's privacy on-line. Many of the same people also favor some sort of special protection for medical records and other very sensitive information.

As these and other issues are debated, here are some of the questions Internet experts are asking:

Should the federal government set privacy standards for the Internet?

On Friday, July 31, Vice President Al Gore delivered what was dubbed as a "major" speech on Internet privacy at the White House. Gore, who

Data-Collection Business Is Booming

In today's hyperconnected world, it's not difficult to find personal information about someone. Most search engines have "people finders" or "personal locators" that supply telephone numbers, street addresses, and even directions to people's houses. For a little money, say $25, one can obtain someone's Social Security number, previous addresses and possibly their driving record.

And that's just the tip of the iceberg. "Most people don't realize how much information about them is out there," says Deirdra Mulligan, staff counsel at the Center for Democracy and Technology.

"We should be worried about this," agrees Mary Griffin, counsel for the Consumers Union of the United States. "People just don't know how little privacy protection they have when it comes to this stuff."

Particularly worrisome, say privacy advocates like Griffin, are the hundreds of companies in the United States today that devote themselves to collecting an unfathomable amount of information about almost everyone in the country. Some can provide detailed financial histories, including information about bank accounts, credit card balances and loans. Others offer employment records or track buying habits.

"They have gone on an information-collecting binge," says Charles Morgan Jr., chief executive for Arkansas-based Acxiom Co., one of the largest information-collection firms in the country. "There's just this insatiable appetite for more information to make better decisions." [1]

The information these firms collect is used for a variety of purposes, from running credit checks to creating marketing campaigns. And the data comes from a huge number of sources. When someone fills out a credit-card application, registers with a club, completes a survey or enters a contest, there is a good chance that the information they have given will end up with one or more of these firms. Much of the information also comes from government agencies. "With so much public information on-line, it's easy to find out a lot about someone," says Pamela Rucker, a spokeswoman for the National Retail Federation.

There has long been a wealth of information available about Americans. After all, the United States has always been a consumer-driven and legalistic society. But until recently, there was no affordable way to collect, store and retrieve this data. Computers — and later the Internet — changed that. "The information was always there, but it took technology to enable them to use it properly," Rucker says.

And the opportunities offered by technology have led to an explosion of new data-collection firms. In the last five years alone — the period paralleling Internet growth — the number of firms has increased by a factor of 10. Today, there are more than 1,000 companies collecting and selling information. [2]

Many observers complain that the rush to collect personal information that has followed the computer and Internet revolutions has not been accompanied by proper efforts to protect privacy. "Technology is clearly ahead of policy here," Griffin says. Jason Catlett, president of Junkbusters Corp., a privacy-protection firm, agrees. "What we have is really a form of surveillance."

Griffin and others think that anyone who collects information from a consumer should be required to give the consumer the option of prohibiting disclosure to outside parties. For example, she says, "When you filled out a credit-card application, there would be a box you could check giving you the right to stop the transfer of that information to others."

But those who collect and use the information counter that the services they provide are integral to the flow of modern commerce in the Information Age. For example, they say, when people apply for credit cards or auto insurance, credit checks can be run almost instantaneously. Consumers may value their privacy, but they value convenience even more. "Consumers don't want it tomorrow, they want it now or yesterday," Rucker says.

---

[1] Quoted in Robert O'Harrow, "Data Firms Getting Too Personal?" *The Washington Post*, March 8, 1998.

[2] *Ibid.*

---

has long had an interest in the Net and is the administration's point man on technology issues, addressed computer industry executives, privacy advocates and others. "Privacy is a basic American value — in the Information Age and in every age," Gore said. "And it must be protected." [7]

The vice president went on to say that the nation needed a "Privacy Bill of Rights," so as to guarantee that Web sites do not acquire and use informa-

tion in ways that are unfair to consumers. "You should have the right to choose whether your personal information is disclosed," Gore said. "You should have the right to know how, when and how much of that information is being used; and you should have the right to see it yourself."

But while Gore called for new legislation to protect children's privacy on-line, he stopped short of asking Congress to codify his Bill of

Rights. Instead, he urged the on-line industry to step up its efforts at self-regulation, a policy long supported by the Clinton administration. [8]

For many privacy advocates in attendance that day, like the Electronic Privacy Information Center's Rottenberg, Gore's speech "came up short." According to Rottenberg and others, the vice president should have used the address to call for comprehensive privacy legislation. "The time has come to establish certain privacy protections in law, period," Rottenberg says.

Rottenberg and others argue that legal protections are needed because the on-line industry has shown — after being given years to establish and enforce effective privacy standards — that it is incapable of policing itself. "The industry is clearly not doing enough on its own," says Berman of the Center for Democracy and Technology.

While Berman admits that there are "some companies, usually big, established ones, that play by the rules, many don't recognize privacy concerns at all." A lot of these bad actors are "small start-ups that aren't aware that they have a responsibility to consumers." Like Rottenberg, Berman argues that "we will probably need some legislation to establish some minimum privacy benchmarks."

Those benchmarks, Berman says, include the protections mentioned by Gore: the right to choose whether your personal information can be disseminated and, if permission is given, to know how the data will be used. In addition, Berman says, "there has to be accountability, some sort of punishment for [the site] or remedy for the individuals" who have had their privacy violated.

Finally, opponents of self-regulation

say, there should be an agency or office to oversee and, if necessary, enforce privacy protections. "You need an office with some staff and resources and authority to make some decisions," Rottenberg says, adding that the president could appoint a "privacy czar" patterned after the drug czar, a position created in 1987 to coordinate the war against illegal narcotics.

Currently, the FTC has a role in overseeing privacy issues on-line. But

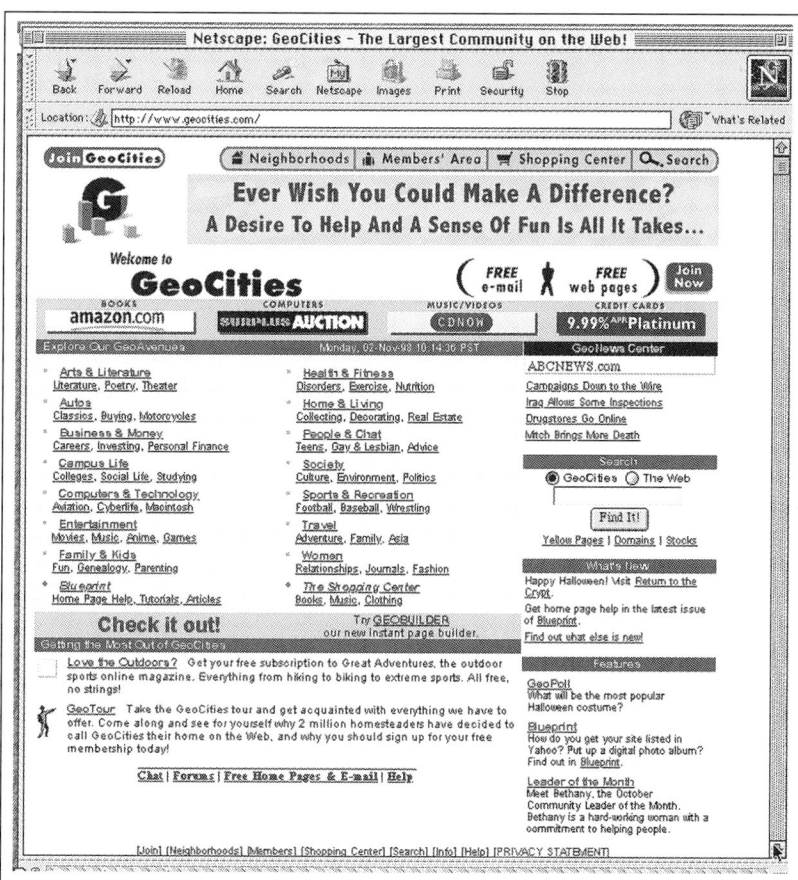

After the Federal Trade Commission accused the popular GeoCities Web site of misleading on-line visitors, it agreed to disclose that it releases personal information about visitors to outside parties.

while the agency has studied the issue and made recommendations, it has no authority to regulate the fair use of information on the Internet. Indeed, all it can do is prosecute deceptive or fraudulent practices. In the case of privacy, that means that if a Web

site posts a policy but does not follow its own rules, the agency can prosecute it for deceiving the site's users.

But, says Beth Givens, director of the Privacy Rights Clearinghouse, a privacy advocacy group in San Diego, even in the deceptive-practices arena, the agency does not have the resources to prosecute any but the most egregious cases. "If the FTC gets enough complaints about someone, they may eventually decide to do something," she says. "But if Jane or John Q. Grievance wants redress, the FTC is not strong enough to help."

The FTC's weakness points to the need for a new privacy agency, she and others say. It would not only enforce new privacy laws but also represent the United States in the international arena. "This is something that could actually be good for business," says Robert Gellman, a privacy consultant in Washington, D.C., who opposes comprehensive privacy legislation but favors a privacy agency. For instance, he says, such an office could negotiate with the European Union as it begins implementing the on-line privacy directive that it put into effect in October. (See story, p. 962.) "Right now, we really have no one to speak for us on this issue except the FTC, and they're only interested in privacy when they get a headline out of it," Gellman says, adding that most other developed countries already have a privacy agency or office.

But many supporters of self-regula-

Types of Personal Information Collected

More than half of the nation's Web sites collect four types of personal information from on-line customers.

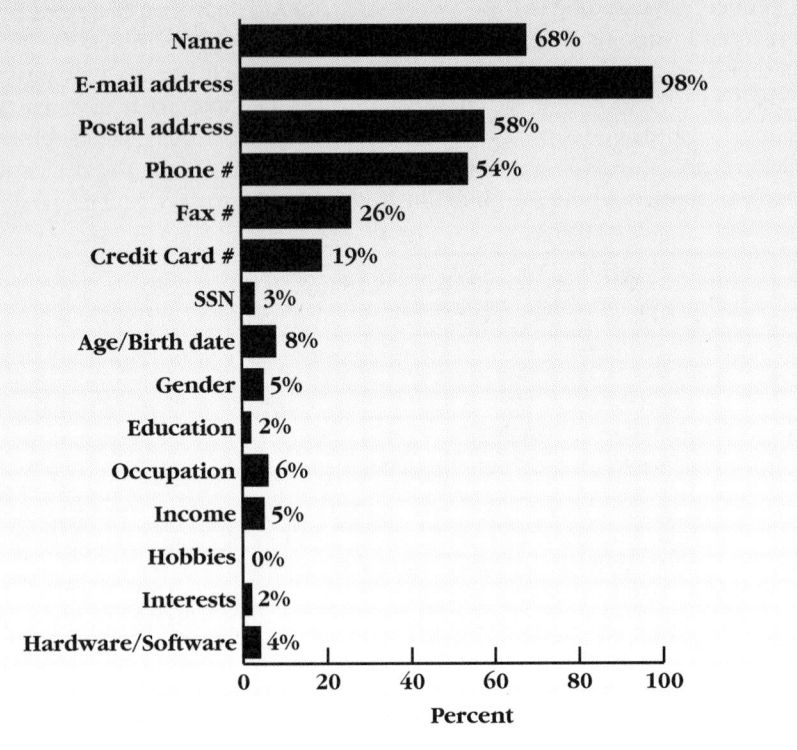

Name	68%
E-mail address	98%
Postal address	58%
Phone #	54%
Fax #	26%
Credit Card #	19%
SSN	3%
Age/Birth date	8%
Gender	5%
Education	2%
Occupation	6%
Income	5%
Hobbies	0%
Interests	2%
Hardware/Software	4%

Percent

Source: "Privacy Online: A Report to Congress," Federal Trade Commission, June 1998

tion claim that privacy agencies and laws would be nothing less than Orwellian. "The government shouldn't try to be big brother," said Ira Magaziner, one of President Clinton's leading advisers on the Internet. Regulations, Magaziner said recently, are "a knee-jerk reaction of the industrial age, when government was expected to protect you. In the digital age, there are new paradigms; one of them is to empower people by giving them the tools to protect themselves." [9]

Others who oppose government action point out that most Web sites are now trying to post and enforce privacy policies. "The majority of Web sites where there is shopping and things like that have privacy policies posted," says Dalzell of the Direct Marketing Association (DMA). Indeed, several organizations, including the DMA and the Better Business Bureau (BBB), have created privacy guidelines for members. Some groups, like the BBB, even have a "seal of approval" for sites that meet their standards.

Supporters of self-regulation also point out that Web sites will protect consumer privacy if for no other reason than it's good business. "Consumers will only go where they feel comfortable, and businesses on-line and elsewhere know that," says Mark Uncapher, vice president of the Information Technology Association of America, an industry group. "That fact, more than anything else, will drive self-regulation."

Other opponents of government action argue that privacy restrictions might put many sites out of business, since the personal information they receive is sometimes a substantial source of revenue, especially for less well-established businesses. According to CATO's Singleton, people who favor protecting privacy sometimes forget that it also "entails limiting the kind of information businesses can exchange with each other," she says. "Now that may not sink a big company, but many businesses on the Web are small and not profitable," she adds.

For example, Singleton says, many magazines are trying to stay afloat by selling targeted advertising, which appeals to the specific interests of each user. "Regular banner ads aren't lucrative," she says. But in order to sell targeted adds, the site must know something about the users, such as their interests, age and education.

Finally, and perhaps most important, self-regulation boosters argue, it is premature to talk about privacy regulation because the Internet is still in its infancy. "E-commerce was born just a few years ago, so this is a new area where marketers are still learning and struggling to determine the right formula," Dalzell says.

Gellman, while less optimistic about the promise of self-regulation, agrees that a comprehensive law on privacy would be hard, if not impossible, to write for the Internet at this or any time. "It's so hard to distinguish between industries, types of records and other things that writing rules would be very difficult," he says. "I mean, should the rules for access to medical records be the same as those for pizza delivery records?"

Uncapher agrees, adding that even if effective rules for today could be drafted, it would be counterproductive at this stage in the Internet's development to try to pin down a lasting policy. "The medium is growing so quickly," he says, "that it's impossible to come up with hard-and-fast rules on something like privacy."

But privacy advocates counter that the Internet is not beyond the grasp of effective regulation. "That argument is a cop-out because no change that would come, no growth in the Net, would obviate the need for basic protections, like requiring [Web sites] to disclose how they're using the information they gather," Givens says.

Rottenberg agrees that the argument against regulation is specious. "They don't think it's possible to enact legal safeguards for privacy because the technical changes are coming too fast," he says. "But they do believe in legal safeguards for copyrights and patents, which also concern fast-changing technology."

In addition, Givens, Rottenberg and others argue, consumers alone will not drive privacy policy. For one thing, they say, many people don't think or care about privacy issues. Others are simply not aware that their personal information is being taken and used by the Web sites they visit. "We could do all the best consumer education in the world," Givens says, "but there will always be people who will be vulnerable to abuse and deception."

Should encryption technology be free from export and other restrictions?

A recent television advertisement depicts a man working at a computer while his wife reads the newspaper. "Hon, do we have encryption software on our computer?" she asks. "Yeah," he says. "That makes it safe to do our bills on here. Encryption locks our private information." His wife then points out that "Washington" wants

to acquire the "key" to encryption programs, making everyone's sensitive information open to possible government scrutiny. "Should we trust Washington bureaucrats with the key to our private lives?" she asks. [10]

The commercial is reminiscent of the famous "Harry and Louise" spot, in which another anxious husband and wife worried about President Clinton's plans to overhaul the nation's health-care system. That advertisement is credited with helping kill the health-reform initiative.

The fact that "Harry and Louise"

Today, with millions of shoppers using credit cards on-line and millions more sending important information via E-mail, encryption has become a major tool of commerce.

---

are now talking about encryption at all is testament to how far the Information Age has penetrated daily life. Until the 1990s, encryption technology was largely the provenance of the national-security community, a technology used to protect sensitive data from the Soviet Union and other unfriendly powers. Today, with millions of shoppers using credit cards on-line and millions more sending important information via E-mail, encryption has become a major tool of commerce.

Encryption software protects data by scrambling it into an unreadable code. Only someone with companion software can decode the message and read the data. As the husband in the television commercial says, this allows consumers to send their credit card number or a sensitive document on the Internet, secure in the knowledge that it will be seen only by those authorized to see it.

And security is important. When someone sends an E-mail message or purchases something with a credit card on-line, the information is often routed through a number of computers — sometimes more than a dozen. At any one of these junctures, the data can be intercepted and downloaded by a third party without anyone else's knowledge.

Currently, there are no limits on the use of encryption technology in the United States. Any person or company can buy the most powerful program available. Indeed, many companies that have a presence on the Web are employing powerful encryption programs to ensure that transactions are secure.

But export controls limit the sale of much of the more powerful encryption programs overseas, even to America's closest allies in Europe and Asia. These controls, which have been in place for decades, are meant to keep the technology out of the hands of America's enemies by keeping it close to home. Less powerful encryption programs can be exported. Indeed, the Clinton administration recently eased up on some of these export restrictions. Still, the most powerful, and hence popular, U.S. encryption products are generally not available overseas.

In addition to export controls, the law-

Europe Protects On-line Privacy

While policy-makers in the United States debate the need for formal on-line privacy protection, their counterparts in the European Union (EU) have already embraced it.

The Directive on Personal Data Protection has been hailed as a model for the United States. It incorporates the basic principles espoused by American privacy advocates, giving individuals significant control over the use of sensitive personal information about them, such as health and financial records.

The directive gives EU citizens the right to see any information a Web site has collected about them. It also requires data collectors to inform citizens how the information will be used and empowers individuals to prohibit sites from passing on data to third parties.

But American businesses, and others, argue that the EU directive could severely hamper both traditional and Internet commerce in Europe and the United States. In particular, American companies complain about a provision in the law prohibiting the export of sensitive information to countries, like the U.S., that do not have similar privacy protections.

If that provision were enforced and the United States did not enact its own privacy-protection law, the flow of credit card numbers, addresses and similar information from Europe could grind to a halt, and with it much transatlantic commerce. "The potential for disruption here is enormous," says Chet Dalzell, a spokesman for the Direct Marketing Association.

Hoping to avoid a trade war, U.S. Commerce Department officials have proposed what is known as a "safe harbor" approach, allowing continued export of information to those U.S. companies with in-house privacy policies that meet EU standards. "We say, 'Let's create a situation where, if companies agree to follow certain data practices, they can be held harmless under the new directive,' " says David Aaron, under secretary of Commerce.

But, so far, U.S.-E.U. negotiations have produced no agreement. European officials call the safe harbor approach impractical. "The prevailing message from Brussels right now is that the EU is unwilling to do a deal with each American company," says Jason Catlett, president of Junkbusters, an on-line privacy-protection firm based in Green Brook, N.J. Catlett and others say that the Europeans hope that the United States will enact its own Internet privacy law.

Officials in both camps say that for the time being, no action is likely to be taken against American companies and others on-line. For one thing, the new directive, which went into effect on Oct. 25, still must be approved by the legislatures in each of the 15 member states of the European Union. So far, only two countries, Greece and Portugal, have formally ratified the directive, although, according to the European Union, 10 others are in the process of doing so presently.

Still, many predict, there could be trouble as early as next year if no agreement is reached. "I don't think the EU would cut off American Web sites, because we so dominate the Web right now," Catlett says. "But I do think they would pursue big, individual companies like Citibank or IBM and force them to shut down a large part of their Web traffic to and from Europe."

---

enforcement community, led by the FBI, has been pushing for new laws that would allow government officials to unscramble encrypted data, so long as they obtained a search warrant. Many existing programs allow only those who have purchased the encryption software to unscramble the data. Not even the manufacturer of the program has the means to decode what its customers have encrypted. The law-enforcement community wants encryption makers to be required to include a "key" or "back door" that would allow the company to unscramble data encrypted by its product in cases where the authorities obtained a valid search warrant.

Many high-technology companies and privacy advocates argue that restrictions on encryption of any kind — both existing and desired — are unnecessary and harmful. To begin with, they say, the current export restrictions are shortchanging consumers who buy encryption programs either alone or bundled into a software package. This is done to ensure that the software can be exported to other markets.

"If they installed stronger encryption features in the software, they would have to repackage these things for export," Rottenberg says. In other words, companies are intentionally "dumbing down" encryption protection to ensure that it is not affected by the export controls.

As a result, Rottenberg and others say, many on-line consumers and businesses are now much more vulnerable to an invasion of privacy, even though the technology to better protect them is readily available. Indeed, they point out that the Justice Department estimates that computer security breaches cost American companies and consumers $7 billion in 1997.

Intentionally putting weak encryption into larger software packages is also hurting the software makers, who are losing markets to companies in other technologically sophisticated countries in Europe and Asia. These foreign software makers are already filling the niche in the encryption market left open by the absence of competition from the United States. "Other countries are happy to use U.S. export controls as an excuse to outsell U.S. companies in this field," says CATO's Singleton.

In addition, opponents argue, export controls are not preventing the technology from falling into the wrong hands. "Today there are companies in other countries with strong encryption technology, much of it developed by software engineers who were educated in the United States," Singleton says. "So it's foolish to think that preventing strong encryption from leaving the United States is going to stop people from getting their hands on this technology."

But others disagree, arguing that America's strong encryption technology is still the world's best and thus should not be fully exportable. "It's clear that this technology could do great harm if it fell into the wrong hands, and so must be controlled," says Eugene "Red" McDaniel, president of the American Defense Institute.

McDaniel worries that the U.S. intelligence community would be unable to keep track of the nation's enemies if encryption technology were exported. "It could be devastating," he says.

The Center for Defense Information's Smith agrees. "This stuff could severely hamper our efforts to collect foreign intelligence by making it hard to nearly impossible to listen in on what our enemies are doing," he says.

Smith acknowledges that other companies in other nations undoubtedly are working on strong encryption and that American export controls may only delay the technology from falling into the wrong hands. Still, he argues, delay is reason enough to maintain the tight controls.

"We are clearly the most advanced in this area, and so even if we only delay the wrong people from getting hold of strong encryption," he says, "something good will have come from the [export] restrictions. If, say, Iraq doesn't get good encryption for a few more years because of these controls, at least the NSA [National Security Agency] has more time to come up with ways to crack these stronger [encryption] codes."

Others point out that American in-

dustries that need strong encryption, like banking, are able to buy the best in the world. And, says the FBI's Smith, echoing the industry argument, since most ordinary people don't buy software solely for encryption, export controls will be less likely to hurt software companies. "You buy Lotus Notes for what it does, not because it has strong encryption," he says, referring to a popular IBM software program. "The U.S. dominates about 70 percent of the world software market, not because it makes good encryption but because of the quality of the software and what it does."

And if some consumers get weaker encryption protection as a result of the export laws? "That's a small price to pay for our keeping this stuff away from potential enemies," says Smith of the Center for Defense Information.

Similarly, the FBI's Smith and others in the law-enforcement community argue that their proposal to require all encryption technology to have a "back door" is a small price for businesses and consumers to pay for protection against society's dangerous criminals. FBI Director Louis Freeh told the House Select Committee on Intelligence in September 1997 that without "a viable key management infrastructure that supports immediate decryption capabilities for lawful purposes, our ability to investigate and sometimes prevent the most serious crimes and terrorism will be severely impaired." [11]

Freeh and others point out that gaining access to computer records has helped solve or prevent countless crimes. For example, he says, World Trade Center bomber Ramsey Youseff used a computer to store his plans to destroy 11 U.S. airliners. If the information had been protected by a strong encryption program, it might not have been recoverable.

Now, they say, commercially available encryption technology is beginning to thwart investigations. "We're starting to see its use in the area of terrorism, where both domestic and

international terrorists are using commercially available encryption software to encrypt stored files and E-mails, and we're being frustrated at being able to gain plain-text access," Smith says. "In some of these cases, we don't know what they're talking about," he adds.

Law enforcement officials say that being prevented from accessing encrypted information upsets the balance between the need for privacy and the legitimate needs of the police. "We have the right to engage in a reasonable search after showing probable cause and pursuant to a warrant," Smith says. "This takes that away from us."

But privacy advocates argue that providing a "key" to encryption programs defeats the whole purpose of securing information in the first place. "The idea that you regulate encryption because it might cause the FBI problems is nonsense," Rottenberg says. "It's like saying that we should regulate typewriters because they may be used in a criminal act."

CATO's Singleton agrees, adding that requiring software makers to include a "key" to access encrypted messages in "real time," or as they're being sent, could be terribly burdensome for the software maker. "To allow the intercept of real-time communications is a technical feat that would require a lot of money and work," she says. ∎

BACKGROUND

Early Privacy Efforts

The value of privacy, or the right to be left alone, has long been recognized in the United States as a fundamental right. The U.S. Constitution's Bill of Rights recognizes privacy a number of times when it prohibits what it terms "unreasonable" search and seizure and allows defendants to refuse to incriminate themselves. Today, there is large body of statute and common law aimed at safeguarding individuals from unreasonable state interference.

But, according to privacy advocates, statute and common law have not kept apace with technological change. "There basically is no right to privacy on the Internet," Givens says. Still, there are principles that have come down during the last 25 years governing the fair use of a person's personal information or data.

The first glimmer of recognition that some sort of fair-use standards were needed came in 1973, when the Department of Health, Education and Welfare (HEW) created a task force to study the effect that computerization of medical records would have on privacy. The task force produced a "Code of Fair Information Practices," which set down several basic principles aimed at safeguarding personal privacy, including:

• Ensuring that the existence of personal databases is publicly known;

• Providing ways for people to learn what kind of information about them is in a database and how it is being used;

• Ensuring that individuals can check the accuracy of information about themselves and prevent the administrators of the database from using that information for purposes other than those for which it was collected;

• Providing guarantees that the information will not be misused. [12]

The HEW principles have formed the basis for later efforts to protect information privacy. For instance, Congress largely codified them when it passed the Privacy Act of 1974. Although the act's title implies broad, sweeping privacy coverage, it actually only applies to federal agencies when they collect data from individuals.

In 1980, the HEW principles were again largely incorporated in another set of privacy standards, this time drafted by the Organization of Economic Cooperation and Development (OECD). The Paris-based organization, which is a forum for some of the world's richest countries (including the United States), adopted "Guidelines on the Protection of Privacy and Transborder Flows of Personal Data." The guidelines did not have the force of law and instead were developed to aid nations in harmonizing their privacy policies. [13] They have been influential, most notably within the European Union, which issued its Directive on Protection of Personal Data in June 1995.

The 'Cookie' Monster

According to privacy advocates like Rottenberg, the phenomenal rise of Internet use has not been accompanied by a corresponding increase in the level of privacy awareness. "It hasn't kept pace with the technology," he says. Mulligan of the Center for Democracy and Technology agrees, adding: "A lot of people, when they're typing this stuff into their computers, think it's private, like they're using a typewriter or something."

But what exactly happens when someone logs on and begins "surfing the Net?" Just as there is a lack of consumer awareness of the extent to which personal data may be used by third parties, there is often a corresponding fear that by simply visiting a Web site one forfeits one's E-mail address and other confidential information.

In fact, when users visit a Web site, their browser usually releases very little detailed, personal information about them. From the visitors' Web browser, the site can determine

what kind of computer and Web browser is being used. The visitors' browser also reveals the last site they visited and, if they're at work, the name of their company. [14]

In addition, someone's browser releases its host E-mail address, such as aol.com or nyu.edu. With this information, the Web site could send an E-mail to everyone at the host address, a technique known as "spraying."

Not revealed is what would be considered more personal information: someone's name, phone number and home address. In almost all cases, E-mail addresses also remain confidential, unless the visitor is using a very old Web browser, some of which do reveal the user's E-mail in full.*

But Web sites do have ways of extracting a little more information about on-line users without asking anyone to disclose anything. For instance, the site can deposit a small amount of code in the user's hard drive, known as a "cookie." While a cookie cannot pry a person's name or E-mail address from them, it can track everything they do each time they're on the site.

The cookie allows the site to determine if the user is a return visitor and, if so, what they have done each time they have visited. So, for instance, Yahoo or another commonly used search engine might know that, say, user No. 8954 reads the Bible, has an interest in sailing and checks the stock price of IBM each day. This, in turn, allows the site to select specific advertisements to suit the particular user's interests. [15]

"People pick up all kinds of cookies all the time and immediately begin collecting all kinds of information about you," says Catlett, comparing them with parasites.

---

*There are a number of special programs capable of retrieving some E-mail addresses, but they are not commonly used.

Chronology

1960s-1980s

Early computer networks created by the military and universities eventually evolve into the Internet. The federal government and others begin considering privacy rights in the Information Age.

1969
Pentagon's Defense Advanced Research Projects Agency (DARPA) establishes ARPANET, a precursor to the Internet.

1973
A privacy task force created by the Department of Health, Education and Welfare (HEW) develops basic principles to safeguard personal health information stored on computers.

1974
Congress passes the Privacy Act, which applied the HEW task force's principles to government records.

1980
The Organization of Economic Cooperation and Development establishes privacy standards based largely on the HEW principles.

1984
Pentagon gives up control of the Internet.

1990-2000

The increased use of personal computers and modems leads to the dramatic growth of Internet use. Privacy advocates begin calling for legal protections for Internet users.

1991
The Center for Media Education is founded.

1992
The Privacy Rights Clearinghouse is founded.

1994
There are 3 million Internet users worldwide.

1995
The European Union (EU) adopts the Directive on Personal Data Protection.

1996
Congress passes the Health Insurance Portability Act, which requires new federal standards to protect health records to be in place by August 1999.

1997
According to the FTC, Internet businesses spent almost $1 billion for on-line advertising.

March 1997
FBI Director Louis J. Freeh urges a Senate committee to set limits on encryption software.

December 1997
An estimated 10 million people have purchased something over the Internet.

January 1998
The number of Internet users is estimated at 60 million in the United States alone.

June 1998
The FCC releases a report to Congress on Internet privacy.

August 1998
The FCC settles with the Web site GeoCities for alleged privacy violations.

Oct. 21, 1998
Congress passes legislation aimed at protecting children's privacy on-line.

Oct. 25, 1998
The EU's Directive on Personal Data Protection takes effect.

1999
Deadline for Congress to enact new standards to protect health records.

2000
FTC estimates that Internet advertising spending will total $4.35 billion.

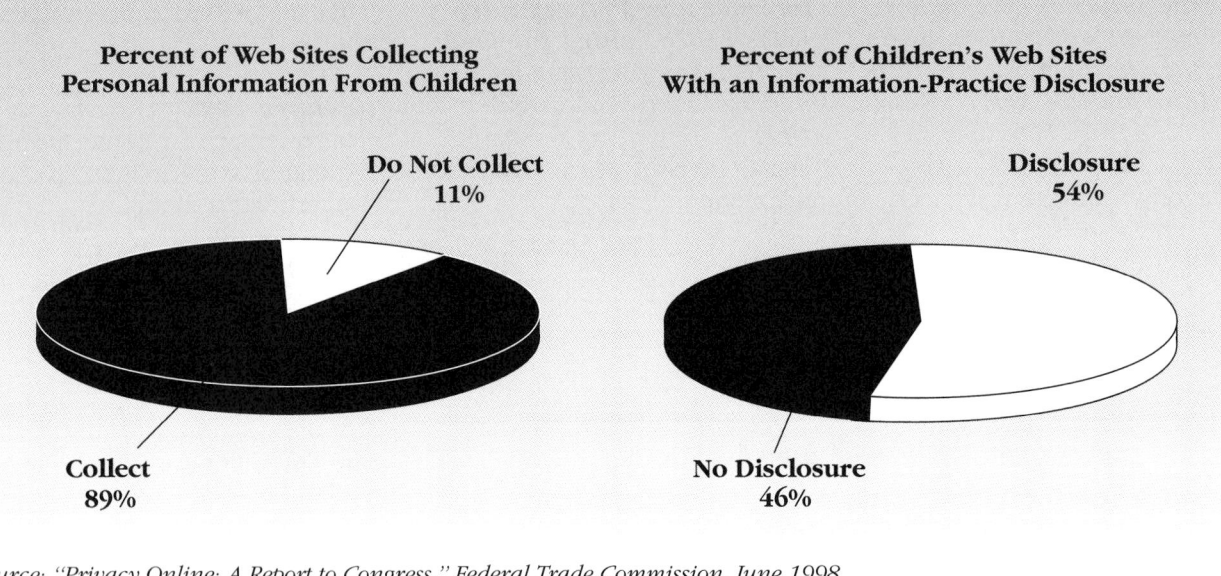

Many Children's Sites Don't Provide Disclosure

Nearly 90 percent of the Web sites targeted at children collect personal information from children, but nearly half don't provide information-disclosure statements.

Percent of Web Sites Collecting Personal Information From Children

Do Not Collect
11%

Collect
89%

Percent of Children's Web Sites With an Information-Practice Disclosure

Disclosure
54%

No Disclosure
46%

Source: "Privacy Online: A Report to Congress," Federal Trade Commission, June 1998

But there are ways to fight back. A program offered free by the Junkbusters Corp. prevents cookies, blocks out banner ads and protects attempts to pry an E-mail address from the user.

Some Internet experts say that the obsession with on-line confidentiality is misplaced. "What are we protecting consumers from, free coupons?" asks CATO's Singleton. "Targeted advertisements are actually an advantage to consumers because they speak to their interests."

But Catlett says the idea that consumers are being so closely tracked on-line is scary. "They're building these enormous profiles of where people are browsing and what they're looking at, that can be used to hurt them," he says. For example, Catlett predicts, on-line browsing records will be subpoenaed. "You know, it's like leaving behind radioactive material that can be traced," Catlett says. "The only reason it exists is because it's a windfall for the marketers." ■

CURRENT SITUATION

Medical Records

A family member is suddenly hospitalized while on vacation, thousands of miles from home. Instead of calling hometown doctors and hospitals in a search for relevant health records, the treating physician simply pulls up the patient's medical history on the Internet.

If the scenario sounds a little far-fetched, it shouldn't. Health-care providers, insurance companies and others are already putting personal medical information on-line. Indeed, there are companies that provide secure sites on the Web where individuals can store medical information for themselves and their families. "Because my kids have allergic reactions to medication, I have always been concerned over what would happen if they needed care when I wasn't available," says Leslie Lee, a housewife from Menlo Park, Calif., who recently put her family's health records on-line. [16]

For many consumers like Lee, on-line access to health records is a valuable and worthwhile service. But privacy advocates worry that using the Internet to store and access sensitive medical information could lead to profound breaches of privacy. "Many health-care providers and others already sell or give medical records away," Rottenberg says, pointing out, for example, that a lot of pharmacies sell prescription lists to pharmaceutical companies. "The Internet, of course, raises a host of new privacy concerns," he adds.

These concerns range far and wide. For instance, epidemiologists have recently expressed interest in tapping medical record databases for research purposes. Should they gain access and, if so, how would the information be controlled? And what rules would govern access for law-enforcement officials?

Computer-industry representatives say that while there are legitimate concerns, the situation should not turn into a privacy nightmare. "There is already a consensus today that parties that have no role in the person's health-care process — basically if they're not in the payment stream — shouldn't have access to the records." says Uncapher of the Information Technology Association.

Today, the presence of medical records on-line is still small, but growing fast. For instance, while only 16 percent of the nation's hospitals use the Internet to store and access patients' records, the number is almost double what it was two years ago. [17]

Currently, there are no nationwide laws to protect the confidentiality of medical records, although some states, like California, offer limited privacy protections. That is likely to change in the near future. In 1996, Congress passed the Health Insurance Portability Act, which among other things, mandated new federal standards to protect the confidentiality of medical records by August of 1999. If Congress doesn't act by that date (and so far it hasn't), the law authorizes the Department of Health and Human Services (HHS) to do the job for them via regulations.

In August, HHS announced standards that it would like to see either passed by Congress or promulgated as regulations. Among the proposals put forth by the agency were requirements that companies lock access to records, train employees in privacy standards and develop a security plan to ensure medical-record safety.

"Electronic medical records can give us greater efficiency and lower cost, but those benefits must not come at the cost of loss of privacy," said HHS Secretary Donna Shalala.

Protecting Children

Children who visit the Liberty Financial Company's Web site for

The Federal Trade Commission says 89 percent of all children's Internet sites collect personal information on children, but only 23 percent advise children to get a parent's permission before releasing information. Above, sixth-graders log-on in DeepHaven, Minn.

young people can learn a number of things about managing money, from how to open a savings account to the rudiments of investing. The site also offers kids a chance to win prizes, but only after they complete a survey that asks their E-mail address, age, sex and whether they own any stocks, bonds or other forms of wealth.

Peter P. Morgan, senior vice president for Liberty, says that the survey allows his company to better tailor the site to children's needs and that the information is not sold or even saved. "From our perspective, this site was meant to be an educational site for the benefit of kids and parents who want to teach [them] about economics,'" he says. [18]

But others see tremendous potential for sites like Liberty's to violate a child's privacy. "Children are so easily manipulated and their good will can be abused," says Katharina Kopp, a senior policy analyst at the Center for Media Education, a children's advocacy group. "When it comes to protecting their privacy, they cannot make rational decisions and are incapable of protecting their rights," she adds.

Kopp and other children's advocates say that there are a huge number of sites directed at kids. Some, like the Liberty site, are owned by companies that don't generally sell products or services to children. So why worry about them? According to Kopp, "marketers have long realized that kids can influence purchases, not only of children's items but adult purchases too." For instance she says, oil giant Chevron has created a Web site for children because the company knows that kids can convince their parents to buy their gasoline. In addition, she says, sites like Chevron's can acclimate children to a company brand so that when they become adults they will choose Chevron over other products."

Currently, about 10 million children under age 18 use the Internet regularly, more than five times more than in 1995. A recent survey by the Westin group found that 97 percent of parents oppose the selling or use

Protecting Yourself On-Line

Many Web sites post privacy policies aimed at allaying any concerns that on-line visitors might have. But others don't have such policies or, if they do, don't post them. Still, privacy advocates say, there are some things that Internet users can do to protect their privacy, such as:

• Check to see if the Web site you are visiting has a posted privacy policy. If it doesn't, there is no way of knowing how the information you give will be used. If a site does post a policy, check to see the limits it places on their ability to transfer your information to others.

• Download one of the many privacy-protection programs available on the Internet. They can block attempts to "steal" your E-mail address or shield your hard drive from "cookies," the code that many Web sites use to track someone's past and present activity on the site. Some, like the Junkbusters program cost nothing.

• Clean out your Web browser's memory cache after each session. The cache keeps a record of the Web sites you've visited, making it easy for others to trace your steps. Your browser's Preference folder should offer the option to empty the cache.

• Encrypt your on-line messages. Intercepting and reading E-mail is not that difficult. A good encryption program can make snooping much harder.

---

of information gathered from children. In the same survey, 80 percent of parents objected to Web sites requesting a child's name and address, even if that information is only going to be used internally. [19]

In a report released in June, the FTC determined that 89 percent of all children's sites it surveyed collected information on children. Of these, only 23 percent advised children to get their parents' permission and fewer than 10 percent attempted to require such permission. [20]

In the same report, FTC Chairman Robert Pitofsky called on Congress to act to protect children's privacy. "The Commission recommends legislation that would place parents in control of the on-line collection and use of personal identifying information from their children," he wrote. He went on to recommend that Web sites receive parental consent before getting information from children 12 and under. For older children, the commission recommended that the site notify parents before taking any information.

Pitofsky's call did not go unheeded on Capitol Hill. In October Congress added language that closely paralleled the FTC proposal to its fiscal 1999 omnibus spending bill. That measure was signed into law on Oct. 21. ■

OUTLOOK

Will Government Act?

Most privacy advocates predict that legal protection will eventually be extended to personal information on-line. "It is generally the case that when a new technology comes along, it takes time to sort the rules out," Rottenberg says. "But we usually end up with some sort of privacy protection, and I think that will be the case here."

Congress already has acted to protect children's privacy. Some action on medical record privacy is expected in the near future.

But Rottenberg and others also believe that more comprehensive privacy protections may be enacted soon. Their optimism stems in part from a belief that the Clinton administration is slowly shifting its position on Internet privacy from one of self-regulation to at least limited government oversight. "I think Gore may be in the process of changing his mind," Rottenberg says. "His hope is still that self-regulation will work, but that we should prepare for something else

if it doesn't."

Givens of the Privacy Rights Clearinghouse agrees that government is likely to soon lose patience with industry attempts at self-regulation. "The government is starting to say, 'We've given you a chance and it hasn't worked out all that well,'" she says. Indeed, in testimony in July, FTC Chairman Pitofsky told a House Commerce subcommittee that Congress should give the on-line industry until the end of 1998 to have an effective privacy policy in place. "If it does not work out, we believe Congress should seriously consider legislation," he said.

Others think that the European Union's new directive on on-line privacy may prod the business community into focusing more closely on privacy protection. "U.S. [on-line] firms may face some fines as the [EU] member states begin implementing the directive, and that might get them on board in favor of some sort of privacy regulation," Rottenberg says.

But others say that talk of imminent regulation is premature. "I think for now, legislative energy will be focused on protecting children and medical records," says Uncapher of the Information Technology Association. "I think the government is going to give self-regulation more of a

Continued on p. 970

At Issue:

Should the federal government set privacy standards for the Internet?

DEIRDRE MULLIGAN
Staff counsel, Center for Democracy and Technology

FROM TESTIMONY BEFORE THE SENATE COMMERCE, SCIENCE AND TRANSPORTATION SUBCOMMITTEE ON COMMUNICATIONS, SEPT. 23, 1998.

*t*he Center for Democracy and Technology (CDT) believes that it is time for Congress and relevant stakeholders to develop a bipartisan, national privacy policy for the Internet. While efforts at self-regulation continue, and are a necessary component of the electronic marketplace, legislation will speed the adoption of Fair Information Practices across the market, provide a level playing field, and ensure that bad actors are deterred.

Toward this end, CDT has called for legislation enabling the Federal Trade Commission to develop rules to protect the privacy of both adults and children. . . .

The Federal Trade Commission Report "Privacy Online: A Report to Congress" found that, despite increased pressure from the White House to develop meaningful self-regulation and growing public anxiety about privacy on the Internet, companies continue to collect personal information on the World Wide Web without providing even a minimum of consumer protection. . . .

While self-regulation is a necessary part of any effective privacy regime on the global Internet, structural flaws in a purely self-regulatory system and specific difficulties that arise from the nature of the Internet suggest that self-regulation alone will result in incomplete protection. The four primary shortcomings of industry self-regulation in the privacy area have been: 1)the failure to incorporate core elements of fair information practice into substantive guidelines; 2) the lack of oversight and enforcement; 3) the absence of legal redress to harmed individuals; and, 4) the inability to set enforceable limits on government access to personal information.

Self-regulatory efforts to provide privacy protections on the Internet, to date, continue to exhibit these structural flaws. . . .

If Congress acts soon, it can protect privacy, build upon and improve the ongoing activities in the private sector, establish a level playing field and create a structure for oversight and enforcement of privacy practices on the Internet. Failure to act will result in continuing consumer distrust of the Internet, inadequate attention to individual privacy in the marketplace, and a legal framework that in some instances actually punishes those moving in the right direction while creating no incentive for self-regulatory activities. . . . However, we must also recognize that legislation will not on its own provide complete privacy protection. Privacy protection must build upon the strengths of existing efforts — self-regulatory and technical — but fold them into a comprehensive system of enforceable privacy protections.

STEVEN J. COL
Senior vice president and general counsel, Council of Better Business Bureaus Inc. and BBBOnline Inc.

FROM TESTIMONY BEFORE THE HOUSE COMMERCE SUBCOMMITTEE ON TELECOMMUNICATIONS, TRADE AND CONSUMER PROTECTION, JUNE 21, 1998.

*t*he question posed so frequently in recent weeks by many in the executive and legislative branches, probably including some committee members, and by others closely following the on-line privacy-protection issue, is "has self-regulation of online privacy worked?" . . .

The better question for the subcommittee and the Congress as a whole to ask itself is not whether self-regulation of on-line privacy "has" worked, but rather whether self-regulation of on-line privacy "can" work, and is it "likely" to work sooner and better than other alternatives?

Let me explain. The Internet is moving at warp speed. What we know now about the technology, the type and number of content and marketing and advertising providers, the marketing techniques used, consumer access to and use of the medium and the extent to which privacy is jeopardized and is protected, is very, very different than the state of our knowledge just a year ago. . . .

Add to this equation the fact that the so-called Internet industry is many industries, and is not the cohesive force some would suggest. It is ISPs and browsers, and software companies, and on-line "cookie" companies and stockbrokers, and auto dealers, and computer sellers, and so on. Users are equally diverse, including sophisticated computer users, mainstream novices, business personnel, grandmothers and children.

Expectations that this environment would produce in this, the consumer Internet's infancy, a cohesive, organized, fully developed, comprehensive, ubiquitous and completely effective and funded program to protect and enforce on-line privacy may be naive. The point is, we are all learning, and we are developing techniques and responses to emerging issues as our learning progresses.

And, make no mistake about it, an exclusive legislative alternative to a self-regulatory approach is no better, and maybe is much worse. It won't be speedy and it won't have the nimbleness required to respond to the changing technology and cast of players. I dare say that had the Congress passed an omnibus privacy-protection law last year, covering all aspects of the Internet marketplace as it existed at that time, we would be testifying today before an oversight committee to discuss whether the government has adequately enforced the law, or whether the law required substantial change to accomplish its purposes.

Continued from p. 968

chance, give it more time."

CATO's Singleton agrees, adding that government attempts to enact comprehensive privacy regulation on the Internet would be fiercely resisted. "For years and years, businesses have enjoyed tremendous freedom in this area," she says, "and they're not going to let it go easily." ■

Notes

[1] Figures cited in Federal Trade Commission Associate Director David Medine's testimony before the House Judiciary Subcommittee on Courts and Intellectual Property, March 26, 1998.

[2] *Ibid.*

[3] Federal Trade Commission, "Privacy On-Line: A Report to Congress," June 1998, p. 23.

[4] Medine, *op. cit.*

[5] Quoted in Joel Brinkley, "Web Site Agrees to Safeguards in First On-Line Privacy Deal," *The New York Times,* Aug. 14, 1998.

[6] For background, see "Regulating the Internet," *The CQ Researcher,* June 30, 1995, pp. 561-584.

[7] Quoted in Ed Murrieta, "Gore: Protect Privacy," *Wired News,* July 31, 1998.

[8] Quoted in *Ibid.*

[9] Quoted in Deborah Scoblionkov and James Glave, "Magaziner: Back Off, Big Brother," *Wired News,* July 22, 1998.

[10] Quoted in Rajiv Chandrasekaran, "Harry

and Louise Have a New Worry: Encryption," *The Washington Post,* July 28, 1998.

[11] Testimony before the Senate Judiciary Subcommittee on Technology Terrorism, and Government Information, Sept. 3, 1997.

[12] Beth Givens, "A Review of the Fair Information Principles: The Foundation of Privacy Policy," Privacy Rights Clearinghouse, October 1997.

[13] *Ibid.*

[14] Elizabeth Weise, "Revealing Secrets About Privacy on the Web," *USA Today,* June 24, 1998.

[15] *Ibid.*

[16] Quoted in "Doctors and Patients Now Access Medical Records On-Line," *Business Wire,* Aug. 24, 1998.

[17] Milt Freudenheim, "Medicine at the Click of a Mouse; On-Line Health Files are Convenient. Are They Private?" *The New York Times,* Aug. 12, 1998.

[18] Quoted in Pamela Mendels, "Internet Sites for Children Raise Concerns on Privacy," *The New York Times,* July 4, 1998.

[19] Cited in testimony by David Medine, associate director, FTC, before the House Judiciary Subcommittee on Courts and Intellectual Property, March 26, 1998.

[20] FTC Report, *op. cit.*

FOR MORE INFORMATION

If you would like to have this CQ Researcher updated, or need more information about this topic, please call CQ Custom Research. Special rates for CQ subscribers. (202) 887-8600 or (800) 432-2250, ext. 600, or E-mail Custom.Research@cq.com

Business Software Alliance, 1150 18th St. N.W. Suite 700, Washington, D.C. 20036; (202) 872-5500; www.bsa.org. This organization of software companies promotes the growth of the software industry worldwide.

Center for Democracy and Technology, 1634 Eye St., N.W. Suite 1100, Washington, D.C. 20006; (202) 637-9800; www.cdt.org. The center lobbies for civil liberties, including the right of privacy, in the computer and communications media.

Center for Media Education, 1511 K St., N.W. Suite 518, Washington, D.C. 20005; (202) 628-2620; www.cme.org/cme. The center promotes the responsible use of new technologies for children.

Electronic Privacy Information Center, 666 Pennsylvania Ave. S.E. Suite 301, Washington, D.C. 20003; (202) 544-9240; www.epic.org. The center conducts research on the impact of the computer revolution on civil liberties, such as privacy.

Bibliography
Selected Sources Used

Books

Brin, David, "The Transparent Society: Will Technology Force Us to Choose Between Privacy and Freedom?" Addison Wesley (1998).

Brin, known more as a science fiction writer than a social commentator, argues that it is not possible to protect privacy in our technologically advanced society. But instead of limiting the ability of technology to guard privacy, the author proposes what he calls "reciprocal transparency," or complete openness. If companies or the government can collect information about citizens, Brin argues, they should fully know what that information is and where it's going.

Articles

Clark, Charles S., "Regulating the Internet," *The CQ Researcher*, June 30, 1995.

Clark's piece, while a bit dated, is an excellent introduction to the debate over Internet policy, including privacy protection.

Clausing, Jeri, "Critics Contend U.S. Policy on the Internet Has Two Big Flaws," *The New York Times*, June 15, 1998.

Clausing outlines the problems privacy advocates and others have with the Clinton administration's decision not to push for formal privacy protections on-line. This passivity, they say, will ultimately slow the commercial growth of on-line commerce.

Freudenheim, Milt, "Medicine at the Click of a Mouse; On-Line Health Files Are Convenient. Are They Private?" *The New York Times*, Aug. 12, 1998.

The article discusses the privacy implications of putting people's health records on-line.

Glover, K. Daniel, "Do You Have the Right to Be Left Alone?" IntellectualCapital.com, Aug. 27, 1998.

This on-line article gives a good overview of some parts of the basic debate over privacy protection in the Information Age.

Gruenwald, Juliana, "Who's Minding Whose Business on the Internet?" *CQ Weekly*, July 25, 1998.

Gruenwald chronicles recent efforts in Congress to regulate privacy on-line. She writes that lawmakers are facing increasing pressure to do something to guard consumer privacy, especially with regard to children.

Hansell, Saul, "Big Web Sites to Track Steps of Users," *The New York Times*, Aug. 16, 1998.

Hansell describes how big Web sites like Lycos-Tripod are collecting and storing information about Internet users' likes and dislikes in order to produce targeted advertisements.

O'Harrow Jr., Robert, "Data Firms Getting Too Personal?" *The Washington Post*, March 8, 1998.

O'Harrow gives a detailed and well-researched account of the data-warehousing industry. The article makes clear how easy it is for data-collection firms to collect even very personal information about almost anyone.

Mendels, Pamela, "Internet Sites for Children Raise Concerns on Privacy," *The New York Times*, July 4, 1998.

The article chronicles the growing concern over the potential for Web sites to violate the privacy of minors. Particularly worrisome for privacy advocates are those sites directed specifically at young people.

Quittner, Joshua, "No Privacy on the Web," *Time*, June 2, 1997.

Quittner gives a good summary of the debate over whether to regulate privacy on-line.

Wise, Elizabeth, "Revealing Secrets About Privacy on the Web," *USA Today*, June 24, 1998.

Wise provides an easy-to-read account of what can and cannot be learned about someone when they visit a Web site.

Reports and Studies

Federal Trade Commission, "Privacy On-Line: A Report to Congress," June 1998.

An exhaustive examination of on-line privacy issues by the closest thing the United States has to a privacy agency. In particular, the report details concerns regarding the privacy of children on the Internet.

Smith, Robert Ellis, "War Stories: Accounts of Persons Victimized by Invasions of Privacy," *Privacy Journal*, 1997.

Smith, publisher of the journal, has collected hundreds of tales of privacy invasions, both on- and off-line.

The Next Step

Additional information from UMI's Newspaper & Periodical Abstracts™ database

Computer and Retail Sales

"Internet Ad Growth," *USA Today*, **Sept. 23, 1998, p. B1.**

Among industries spending more than $5 million a year to advertise on the Internet, according to InterMedia Advertising Solutions, those with the greatest spending increase in 1997 over 1996 are: Business and technology, 401 percent increase; games, toys and hobbycraft, 342 percent increase; retail 290 percent increase; financial, 286 percent increase; and local amusements and services, 267 percent increase.

Barlow, Jim, "Retail's Next Wave Arriving by Wire," *Houston Chronicle*, **Sept. 13, 1998, p. D1.**

In past decades we've seen giant department stores in the cities replace the old general emporiums as the place where the middle class shops. In more rural areas, the discount Wal-Marts of the world have done a similar number on the small-town specialty store. Meanwhile, those who seek a middle way are having problems. Joining that mix is yet another distribution channel — the offering of goods over the Internet via your home or office computer. Right now, there's more promise than performance in wired shopping. Only about 5 percent of Americans have ever bought goods over the Internet.

Miller, Greg, "The Cutting Edge; More Retailers Testing Virtual Waters; Electronic Commerce: Toys R Us, Tower Records and Other Chains of the Physical World are Entering Cyberspace; But Smaller On-line Companies are Giving Them a Run for Their Money," *Los Angeles Times*, **Sept. 28, 1998, p. D1.**

Profits remain a pipe dream across much of on-line retailing, but the giant chains of the physical world are on a cyberspace building binge. Toys R Us, Borders Books, Tower Records and many others have either rolled out or revamped their virtual superstores in recent months.

Miller, Greg, "Firms to Set Standards for On-line Privacy; Internet: Proposal Will Ask Companies to Develop and Post Policies; Critics Worry About Lack of Enforcement Mechanism," *Los Angeles Times*, **June 20, 1998, p. D1.**

An unprecedented roster of on-line business giants, including America On-line, IBM and Microsoft is expected to unveil on Monday an extensive plan for protecting consumers' privacy on the Internet. The proposal, which comes on the heels of a Federal Trade Commission report finding widespread problems with on-line privacy protections, seeks to set guidelines for handling personal information increasingly culled from consumers over the Net. The plan calls for companies to post their privacy policies on their Web sites and estab-

lish a means of handling complaints about privacy issues. It also calls for setting up separate policies for collecting data from children, possibly requiring parental consent.

Data Collection

"Congress Passes Anti-Piracy Bill," *The New York Times*, **Oct. 13, 1998, p. C6.**

Legislation intended to protect books, music, computer software and other works from Internet pirates cleared its last congressional hurdle today, winning unanimous approval by the House of Representatives. The Senate approved the measure last week. It will now go to the White House, where President Clinton is expected to sign the bill into law.

Caruso, Denise, "An On-Line Tug-of-War Over Consumers' Personal Information," *The New York Times*, **April 13, 1998, p. D5.**

On March 30, in what both parties called "the most widespread initiative undertaken by members of the Internet industry," the Internet Content Coalition — a group of high-powered on-line and traditional media companies, including *The New York Times* — and Trust-E, an on-line privacy group, announced that they would jointly promote Trust-E's program as the industry standard for disclosing to consumers on the World Wide Web what information is being gathered about them and how it is being used.

Greene, Marvin V., "Who's Zoomin' Who on the Web," *Black Enterprise*, **October 1997, pp. 40-42.**

Privacy has become a major concern for avid Internet users because cookies, mechanisms that allow a Web site to deliver data to a client, often leave behind bits of information that other users could find. It has become easier to access this information because on-line databases do not need human input or clarification.

Hayes, Frank "Dangerous Web Data," *Computerworld*, **Oct. 12, 1998, p. 12.**

Companies need to make decisions on how data that is collected over the Web is going to be protected and used. Getting value from this data is discussed.

Miller, Leslie, "PC Users Want Net Laws for Privacy," *USA Today*, **June 12, 1997, p. D1.**

The majority of computer users are so worried about privacy on the Internet that 58 percent want the government to pass laws about how data can be collected and used, according to a survey. Half of computer users are not on-line and are more likely to favor laws than those now on-line (65 percent vs. 47 percent). But almost all (94 percent) think companies collecting data on kids should be held legally liable for violations of stated policies.

Electronic Commerce

Judice, Mary, "Internet Shopping Made Safer," *New Orleans Times-Picayune*, **Sept. 26, 1998, p. C1.**

If you are afraid to order from an Internet shopping site for fear your credit card number will end up in the wrong hands, you're not alone. A survey conducted by the American Institute of Certified Public Accountants found that 55 percent of those responding had shopped on-line but only 24 percent had actually made a purchase. The reason: 60 percent said they were concerned about the security of a financial transaction on-line.

Manes, Stephen, "How Much Privacy Do You Really Want," *PC World*, **September 1998, p. 316.**

Although Americans may think they cherish privacy, they are all-too-willing to swap it for bargains or convenience. The author comments on the erosion of privacy and the Internet's role in it.

McAndrews, James J., "Making Payments on the Internet," *Federal Reserve Bank of Philadelphia Business Review*, **January 1997, pp. 3-7.**

For the Internet to become an active market in goods and services, a way must be devised for buyers and sellers to securely and conveniently exchange payment. The author explores efforts to develop methods that will allow people to pay over the Internet .

Wang, Huaiqing; Matthew K.O. Lee and Chen Wang, "Consumer Privacy Concerns About Internet Marketing," *Communications of the ACM*, **March 1998, pp. 63-70.**

The authors provide a consumers' view of the worries of electronic commerce. Consumers are mostly concerned about their perceived loss of privacy because they do not trust the new mechanisms of electronic commerce.

Encryption

"To Be a Satisfied Customer, Be Cautious," *USA Today*, **Dec. 10, 1997, p. D4.**

The authors recommend using encryption in all transactions. Many sites offer various encoding systems that shield personal information as it traverses the Internet. The codes are not unbreakable, but they do help. Both Netscape's and Microsoft's new browsers include security icons (a solid key and a padlock, respectively) that tell you your transaction is protected. Don't send your naked credit card number onto the Internet.

Bly, Laura, "Sites Seek to Quell Unease About Credit-Card Transactions," *Denver Post*, **Aug. 16, 1998, p. T9.**

For every vacationer willing to plunk down a Visa card for a steeply discounted, last-minute weekend fare to Miami, thousands more are balking at the notion of buying on the Web. They're leery about sending credit information through cyberspace. They worry that Web sites and E-mail come-ons are proving to be fertile territories for scam artists. In an attempt to raise that comfort level, two of the Web's largest travel ticketing sites, Travelocity and Expedia, have launched insurance policies against unauthorized credit card use.

Clark, Don, "TriStrata Security to Launch Software for Protecting Computer Information," *The Wall Street Journal*, **Sept. 8, 1998, p. B6.**

Computer company TriStrata says its software, under development for five years, is hundreds of times as fast as conventional encryption techniques that banks and companies have used since the 1970s and that are the current favorites for protecting electronic commerce on the Internet . The company's claims have caused controversy in security circles. Bruce Schneider, an expert at security-consulting firm Counterpane Systems in Minneapolis, criticizes the company for being stingy with technical details and doubts it offers speed or security advantages. "These guys have no clue," he says.

Davidson, Paul, "House Passes Bill Protecting Net Copyrights," *USA Today*, **Oct. 13, 1998, p. B3.**

The House passed a bill this week that is expected to strengthen copyright protections on the Internet and make it easier to crack down on digital pirates. The bill makes it illegal to create or sell any technology used to break electronic copyright protection, such as encryption. The electronic locks make it impossible to copy software or games, movies, music or other content on the Internet .

Keyworth, G.A. II, "The Future of the Net: Computer Security Doesn't Hamper U.S. Security," *The Wall Street Journal*, **Aug. 5, 1998, p. A14.**

Today, the government invokes the alleged public-security hazard posed by encryption as a reason to impose controls, and in doing so it risks crippling the Internet. The central dilemma is a simple one: The encryption methods that make computer-to-computer communication over a public network valuable and secure also make eavesdropping difficult. This worries FBI Director Louis Freeh, who claims that "the increased use of encryption by terrorists, pedophiles, drug pushers and other criminals could jeopardize public safety."

Quick, Rebecca, "IBM Discovers Web-Hacking Preventative," *The Wall Street Journal*, **Aug. 24, 1998, p. B5.**

A new method promises to address a potential vulnerability in encryption systems used by many Web sites to protect credit-card numbers and other personal information while en route over the Internet. That flaw, discovered in June, sent Netscape Communications Corp. and Microsoft Corp. scrambling for a solution that would reassure consumers and businesses conducting electronic commerce. The software makers moved swiftly to address the problem in the encryption system known as the secure-sockets layer, or SSL. But while the fix apparently works, security experts noted its effectiveness can't be proved mathematically. IBM said its new system takes care of the problem in a way that is incontrovertibly effective.

Schwartz, John, "U.S. Wants Access to 'Keys' For Encrypted Messages," *The Washington Post*, March 27, 1997, p. A25.

Encryption, used to protect computerized information, has been one of the most contentious battles in the high-tech field for the Clinton administration. A new proposal regulating the computer software "keys" that unscramble encrypted data has drawn criticism from businesses and advocates of privacy. "To put a bill like this out indicates that our government is clueless on what to do about security on the Internet," said Jerry Berman, executive director of the Center for Democracy and Technology, a high-tech policy group. Advocates of strong encryption call it a necessity for privacy and security in the digital age. But law enforcement officials have warned that strong encryption will provide a haven for criminals and terrorists to work in secrecy.

Valigra, Lori, "Making the 'Net Safe for Business," *The Boston Globe*, Sept. 20, 1998, p. E4.

Massachusetts high-tech companies are sowing seeds in a growing hotbed of software technology: electronic commerce products that provide security for companies and consumers doing business over the Internet. As electronic commerce grows, so does the need for security to protect consumers' credit card and account information.

Federal Trade Commission

Bray, Hiawatha, "FTC Urges Step to Guard Privacy on the Internet," *The Boston Globe*, June 5, 1998, p. A1.

After visiting 1,400 of the most popular Web sites, the FTC found that the great majority requested personal information from visitors — names, addresses, phone numbers and sometimes even Social Security numbers and medical information. But there are no legal restrictions on how companies can use this data, and the FTC said most companies don't even bother to tell consumers how their personal information will be used. The study's results have led the FTC to abandon its previous policy that self-regulation by Internet-based businesses would be sufficient to protect the privacy rights of citizens. Instead, the agency is calling for a new federal law to strictly limit the ability of Internet businesses to collect personal information from children.

James, Frank "FTC Urges Internet Privacy Laws It Seeks to Limit Collection of Personal Data from Kids," *Chicago Tribune*, June 5, 1998, p. 14.

Concerned by the apparent failure of some commercial Web sites to observe voluntary privacy guidelines, the Federal Trade Commission asked Congress to require that companies put restrictions on collecting personal information from children. In a report to Congress, the commission concluded that the Internet is awash with commercial sites on the World Wide Web that ask users to provide personal information without explaining their plans for it.

Segal, David, "FTC Backs Industry's Internet Privacy Rules," *The Washington Post*, Dec. 18, 1997, p. E2.

The Federal Trade Commission yesterday released a report endorsing a wide-ranging set of principles on privacy-related issues drafted by the biggest players in the computerized database industry. The endorsement is a major victory for the industry, including the well-known Lexis-Nexis on-line search service, which recently devised its own rules in hopes of staving off legislative oversight by Congress. The companies have been criticized by the government and privacy rights groups for allowing access to personal information such as Social Security numbers, birth dates and driving records.

Privacy Laws and Standards

"Consumer Demand, Not New Laws, Will Protect Web Privacy," *USA Today*, July 7, 1998, p. A12.

On-line providers are starting to offer customers more options for security. Next week, America Online customers will get a new set of principles from the largest U.S. on-line service. Included will be promises that AOL won't read your E-mail, collect any information about your Web travels or give key data to others without personal authorization. The European Union threatens to block commercial Internet transactions with the United States by October if the administration fails to adopt privacy laws like its own. Among the requirements: Businesses must get permission to collect and share any information about consumers, no matter how trivial. Such measures would increase red tape and costs for both consumers and Web sites.

Anason, Dean "Legislators, Bankers Spar On Internet Privacy Law," *American Banker*, Sept. 19, 1997, p. 1.

Banking officials are clashing with government representatives over the need for financial privacy laws in cyberspace. Maintaining a united front at a House Banking subcommittee hearing, bank lobbyists set forth eight privacy principles adopted last week by four national, banking trade groups.

Gillin, Paul, "Private Thoughts," *Computerworld*, Oct. 19, 1998, p. 36.

Internet companies' stab at self-regulation in the touchy area of on-line privacy may only hasten the onset of dreaded government regulation.

Kutler, Jeffrey "Privacy Broker: Likely Internet Role for Banks," *American Banker*, Oct. 8, 1998, p. 1.

Experts inside and outside the banking industry agree that at the operational core of on-line trust are the techniques of digital certification. It is the closest thing to signature verification that virtual-world technologists have come up with. In theory, when fully developed and appropriately deployed, this derivative of data encryption technology, binding intricate mathematical codes to a consumer's or company's identity, could be even more reliable and secure than written signatures.

Lohr, Steve, "Study Sees Holes in Internet Security Plan," *The New York Times*, May 22, 1997, p. D9.

A panel of computer scientists said yesterday that the government's plans for unlocking data-scrambling software to pursue criminals and terrorists on the Internet could actually increase security risks and raise the costs of on-line commerce. The researchers, in a study coordinated by the Center for Democracy and Technology , a nonprofit policy group in Washington, examined the technical challenges of the government's Internet security proposal. The plan would permit American computer companies to export powerful data-scrambling software, but only if they established a system that would enable the keys to the code to be obtained by law-enforcement officials with a court warrant.

Lochhead, Carolyn, "Coalition Battles For Privacy; Boxer, Schlafly Unite to Guard Computer Data," *San Francisco Chronicle*, March 5, 1998, p. C1.

An unlikely coalition including Sen. Barbara Boxer, a liberal California Democrat, and anti-feminist Phyllis Schlafly formed yesterday to battle the Clinton administration over computer privacy. The coalition's aim is twofold: to defeat efforts by the FBI and other law enforcement agencies to gain access to private encryption codes, and to tear down U.S. restrictions on the export of encryption technology.

Miller, Leslie, "For Now, Privacy Protection is Up to You," *USA Today*, June 16, 1998, p. E11.

People who are not on-line often cite concerns about privacy as a reason for their hesitancy, not realizing that simply being careful can greatly reduce their risk. Children's advocate Kathryn Montgomery of the Center for Media Education and privacy experts David Sobel of the Electronic Privacy Information Center and Deirdre Mulligan of the Center for Democracy and Technology offer this suggestion: Read the fine print. Before registering your name, address or other personal information with a Web site, look for its privacy policy.

O' Harrow, Robert Jr., "Firms Prepare Plan for Protecting Privacy on Internet," *The Washington Post*, June 20, 1998, p. D3.

In a bid to head off federal privacy legislation, a group of companies that do business on the Internet are preparing a plan for self-regulation, even though orga-

nizers continue to squabble over how to enforce the voluntary rules. The new Online Privacy Alliance includes America Online Inc., Microsoft Corp., International Business Machines Corp. and almost 50 other companies and associations. The alliance started meeting in the spring after the White House and privacy advocates accused industry leaders of failing to develop consistent privacy protections on the sprawling computer network. Alliance members will announce guidelines urging companies to tell World Wide Web users how information is gathered and used and offer them a way to ensure that data are correct, according to several people involved. The group also would generally restrict members' collection of data about children younger than 13 without parental approval, these people said.

O' Harrow, Robert Jr., "White House Effort Addresses Privacy; Gore to Announce Initiative Today," *The Washington Post*, May 14, 1998, p. E1.

Administration officials said Vice President Al Gore will use a commencement speech at New York University to announce a White House directive requiring every federal agency to name a person to assess whether existing privacy laws are being followed. He also plans to unveil a consumer clearinghouse of privacy tools and information on the World Wide Web, including one to help people to remove private information from public lists of drivers' licenses. And he will call on consumer, government and information industry officials to gather at a privacy conference in Washington next month to begin developing an "electronic bill of rights," which would seek to ensure privacy for the millions of people using the Internet.

Quick, Rebecca, "Internet Giants Plan Campaign to Teach Consumers Their Online Privacy Rights," *The Wall Street Journal*, Oct. 7, 1998, p. B9.

Eight leading Internet companies plan to announce an online privacy awareness campaign, a move aimed at demonstrating to policy-makers that the industry can regulate itself. The companies, including America Online Inc., Microsoft Corp. and Netscape Communications Corp., each have agreed to donate space on their Web sites for banner ads promoting the campaign, which informs consumers about their privacy rights on-line. The campaign, called Privacy Partnership, is to be announced today at the Internet World trade show in New York.

Weintzen, Robert, and Lauren Weinstein, "Sound Off: Public Records — Public Lives," *Computerworld*, Sept. 8, 1997, pp. 88-90.

The authors discuss whether the United States should revisit federal regulations on accessing public records via the Internet.

Back Issues

Great Research on Current Issues Starts Right Here.
Recent topics covered by The CQ Researcher are listed below.
Now available on the Web
For information, call (800) 432-2250 ext. 279 or (202) 887-6279.

If you would like to have any of these CQ Researchers updated, or need more information about these topics, please call CQ Custom Research. Special rates for CQ subscribers. (202) 887-8600 or (800) 432-2250, ext. 600, or E-mail Custom.Research@cq.com

JULY 1997
Transportation Policy
Executive Pay
School Choice Debate
Aggressive Driving

AUGUST 1997
Age Discrimination
Banning Land Mines
Children's Television
Evolution vs. Creationism

SEPTEMBER 1997
Caring for the Dying
Mental Health Policy
Mexico's Future
Youth Fitness

OCTOBER 1997
Urban Sprawl in the West
Diversity in the Workplace
Teacher Education
Contingent Work Force

NOVEMBER 1997
Renewable Energy
Artificial Intelligence
Religious Persecution
Roe v. Wade at 25

DECEMBER 1997
Whistleblowers
Castro's Next Move
Gun Control Standoff
Regulating Nonprofits

JANUARY 1998
Foster Care Reform
IRS Reform
The Black Middle Class
U.S.-British Relations

FEBRUARY 1998
Patients' Rights
Deflation Fears
Caring for the Elderly
The New Corporate Philanthropy

MARCH 1998
Israel at 50
The Federal Judiciary
Drinking on Campus
The Economics of Recycling

APRIL 1998
Biology and Behavior
Liberal Arts Education
Income Inequality
High-Tech Labor Shortage

MAY 1998
Census 2000
Child-Care Options
Alzheimer's Disease
U.S.-Russian Relations

JUNE 1998
Student Journalism
Antitrust Policy
Environmental Justice
Sleep Deprivation

JULY 1998
Encouraging Teen Abstinence
Population and the Environment
Democracy in Asia
Baby Boomers at Midlife

AUGUST 1998
Oil Production in the 21st Century
Flexible Work Arrangements
Coastal Development
Student Activism

SEPTEMBER 1998
Organic Farming
Cancer Treatments
Hispanic Americans' New Clout
The Future of Baseball

OCTOBER 1998
School Violence
Social Security
National Forests
Puerto Rico's Status

Back issues are available for $5.00 (subscribers) or $10.00 (non-subscribers). Quantity discounts apply to orders over 10. To order, call Congressional Quarterly Customer Service at (202) 887-8621.

Binders are available for $18.00. To order call 1-800-638-1710. Please refer to stock number 648.

Future Topics

▶ *Human Rights*

▶ *Drug Testing*

▶ *European Monetary Union*

Human Rights

How much progress after 50 years?

uman rights advocates are preparing to mark the 50th anniversary of the United Nations' Universal Declaration of Human Rights, the first comprehensive charter of individual freedoms. Fifty years later, most of the world's countries have ratified a series of binding treaties committing them to respect key civil, political, social and economic rights. Human rights advocates say that conditions have improved since 1948 and that the U.N.'s human rights machinery has been strengthened. But they also say that flagrant abuses continue to occur in countries throughout the world. The United States itself has been criticized for failing to ratify many human rights treaties and for opposing a new proposal to create an International Criminal Court for serious human rights violations.

C_Q   **Nov. 13, 1998 • Volume 8, No. 42 • Pages 977-999**

Formerly Editorial Research Reports

CQ Researcher

Nov. 13, 1998
Volume 8, No.42

EDITOR
Sandra Stencel

MANAGING EDITOR
Thomas J. Colin

ASSOCIATE EDITOR
Sarah M. Magner

STAFF WRITERS
Adriel Bettelheim
Mary H. Cooper
Kenneth Jost
Kathy Koch
David Masci

PRODUCTION EDITOR
Melissa Hall

EDITORIAL ASSISTANT
Laura S. Cavender

PUBLISHED BY
Congressional Quarterly Inc.

CHAIRMAN
Andrew Barnes

VICE CHAIRMAN
Andrew P. Corty

PRESIDENT AND PUBLISHER
Robert W. Merry

EXECUTIVE EDITOR
David Rapp

Bibliographic records and abstracts included in The Next Step section of this publication are the copyrighted material of UMI, and are used with permission.

The CQ Researcher (ISSN 1056-2036). Formerly Editorial Research Reports. Published weekly, except Jan. 2, May 29, July 3, Oct. 30, by Congressional Quarterly Inc., 1414 22nd St., N.W., Washington, D.C. 20037. Annual subscription rate for libraries, businesses and government is $340. Additional rates furnished upon request. Periodicals postage paid at Washington, D.C., and additional mailing offices. POSTMASTER: Send address changes to The CQ Researcher, 1414 22nd St., N.W., Washington, D.C. 20037.

COVER: WIDESCALE HUMAN RIGHTS VIOLATIONS HAVE BEEN DOCUMENTED IN YUGOSLAVIA, WHERE MUSLIM REFUGEES WANT THE U.S. TO HELP THEM RETAKE THEIR HOMES FROM SERBIANS WHO FLED SARAJEVO. (REUTERS)

Human Rights

THE ISSUES

The jungle in eastern Congo was so thick, Roberto Garretón recalls today, that you could not thread a needle through the trees. But after making his way through the dense foliage, the Chilean human rights lawyer came upon a clearing that was "upholstered with stones."

Garretón, guided to the site by a refugee from neighboring Rwanda, recognized the site as a mass grave — evidence of massacres committed by the rebel forces that controlled much of what was then called Zaire. The rebel leader, Col. Laurent Kabila, had heatedly denied allegations of mass killings. Now Garretón, on a United Nations mission to investigate the accusations, had proof before his eyes.

"Here was the grave where they buried their dead," Garretón says. "You have people telling you that there had been massacres there, and you have a person telling you, 'I buried them here.' "

Garretón's 16-page report on his discoveries, submitted to the United Nations Human Rights Commission in April 1997, was the first independent confirmation of atrocities being committed by Kabila's rebels as they sought to topple the government of longtime strongman Mobutu Sese Seko. Less than six weeks later, the rebels took over the capital city of Kinshasa and installed Kabila as the head of a new government. In one of his first actions, Kabila declared Garretón persona non grata and ordered him out of the country.

In the 18 months since then, Garretón has continued in his role as the United Nations' so-called "special rapporteur" on the situation in Congo — supervising, in absentia, a team of U.N. investigators that has remained in the country but under significant limitations imposed by Kabila's government.

The U.N.'s critiques of human rights practices in Congo have not stopped the killings or had any noticeable effect on Kabila's policies. But the reports prepared by Garretón and a growing number of other U.N. special rapporteurs investigating human rights issues have helped document abuses around the world and may have helped improve human rights practices in some countries. (*See story, p. 988.*)

The mixed record helps explain why the international human rights community has mixed feelings as it prepares this year to mark an important milestone: the 50th anniversary of the Universal Declaration of Human Rights. The declaration, adopted by the United Nations General Assembly on Dec. 10, 1948, was the first comprehensive international charter of individual freedoms (*see p. 989*). It set the stage for dozens of major human rights treaties and the creation and later expansion of a United Nations apparatus that has sought to set human rights standards for individual countries to follow; assist governments in improving human rights conditions; and investigate, document and deter violations.

Human rights conditions have vastly improved in much of the world

since 1948, advocates and policy-makers agree. But with gross human rights abuses fresh in mind — as seen most recently, for example, in the wartime killings of civilians in Congo and Kosovo — human rights groups are tempering their celebrations with somber notes.

"We think that as we look back over 50 years, many of the promises have not been delivered," says Pierre Sané, secretary general of Amnesty International.

"Human rights groups are reluctant to talk about celebrating," says Kenneth Roth, executive director of Human Rights Watch. "There's so much left to be done."

On the positive side of the ledger, human rights advocates and experts list the development and broad acceptance of a growing body of international standards. "Fifty years ago, there were many, many governments that viewed human rights as interference in their internal affairs," says Roth. "That excuse is utterly discredited today."

A second major accomplishment is the growth of the human rights movement itself — not only international groups like Amnesty International and Human Rights Watch but also domestic organizations that operate in relatively free countries and in countries with more repressive regimes. "Today, you find human rights groups in almost every country in the world," says Roth. "Only the most repressive countries lack an indigenous human rights organization today."

Despite those accomplishments, human rights advocates acknowledge that the U.N. and advocacy groups have often been powerless to prevent the most blatant instances of human rights violations or to ensure compliance from governments that profess commitments to human rights.

"We see in the 1990s genocide in

Universal Declaration of Human Rights

The broadly phrased Universal Declaration of Human Rights covers civil and political rights (Articles 3-21) and social and economic rights (Articles 22-27). The United Nations General Assembly adopted the declaration 48-0, with eight abstentions, on Dec. 10, 1948.

Article 1 — All people 'born free and equal in dignity and rights.'

Article 2 — Everyone entitled to all freedoms set forth 'without distinction of any kind.'

Article 3 — Right to life, liberty, and security of person.

Article 4 — No slavery or servitude.

Article 5 — No torture or 'cruel, inhuman or degrading treatment or punishment.'

Article 6 — Right to recognition everywhere as a person before the law.

Article 7 — Equal protection of the law against 'any discrimination' and 'against any incitement to such discrimination.'

Article 8 — Right to effective remedy by competent national tribunals for violations of fundamental rights.

Article 9 — No arbitrary arrest, detention, or exile.

Article 10 — Right to a fair and public hearing by an independent and impartial tribunal in criminal cases.

Article 11 — Presumption of innocence until proved guilty in a public trial with 'all guarantees necessary for [a] defense.'

Article 12 — No 'arbitrary interference' with privacy, family, home or correspondence; no 'attacks' on 'honor or reputation.'

Article 13 — Freedom of movement and residence within national borders; right to leave and return to one's country.

Article 14 — Right to seek and enjoy in other countries asylum from prosecution, but not from non-political crimes.

Article 15 — Right to a nationality.

Article 16 — Men and women 'of full age' have a right to marry and found a family, without limitation due to race, nationality, or religion.

Bosnia and Rwanda right in front of our eyes," Sané says, "with total inaction by the international community."

'We are going through a very isolationist, complacent period in our history," Roth says, "where it's been all too difficult to mobilize attention to problems in Kosovo, Afghanistan, Congo or China.

"Human rights principles are broadly accepted, but human rights are nonetheless violated widely," Roth says.

The United Nations has been deeply involved in human rights since its founding in 1945. The Universal Declaration — 30 articles long — was one of the U.N.'s first major accomplishments. But the declaration was not binding, and it took another two decades to draft the two major human rights covenants: the International Covenant on Civil and Political Rights and the International Covenant on Social, Economic and Cultural Rights.

Most of the major U.N. treaties have been ratified by more than 100 countries each, but human rights groups note that the United States has failed to ratify many of them because of opposition within Congress and from conservative advocacy groups. "The United States has been one of the most reluctant countries to allow itself to be bound by international law," says Richard Reoch, who was an official with Amnesty International in London for 23 years before leaving in 1993 to head an environmental advocacy group.

Critics, however, say that the U.N. treaties are often vague or overly ambitious or

Article 17 — Right to own property 'alone or in association with others.'

Article 18 — Right to freedom of thought, conscience, and religion, including freedom to change one's religion or belief; right to manifest one's religion or belief in 'teaching, practice, worship and observance.'

Article 19 — Right to freedom of opinion and expression, including freedom 'to seek, receive and impart information and ideas through any media and regardless of frontiers.'

Article 20 — Right to freedom of peaceful assembly and association.

Article 21 — Right to take part in the government of one's country, 'directly or through freely chosen representatives'; equal access to public service; 'periodic and genuine elections' held by 'universal and equal suffrage' and secret vote.

Article 22 — Right to social security and to 'realization . . . of the economic, social and cultural rights indispensable for [one's] dignity' through national and international efforts and 'in accordance with the organization and resources of each State.'

Article 23 — Right to work, 'free choice of employment,' 'just and favorable conditions of work,' and 'protection against unemployment'; 'equal pay for equal work'; right to form and join trade unions.

Article 24 — Right to 'rest and leisure,' including 'reasonable limitation of working hours' and 'periodic holidays with pay.'

Article 25 — Right to a standard of living 'adequate for the health and well-being of [one's self] and [one's] family,' including food, clothing, housing and medical care; right to 'security' in event of unemployment, disability, sickness, or old age; all children entitled to protection whether born in or out of wedlock.

Article 26 — Right to education, including free education 'at least in elementary and fundamental stages'; compulsory elementary education; parents have 'a prior right to choose the kind of education' for their children.

Article 27 — Right to 'freely participate' in cultural life; right to protection of 'the moral and material interests' resulting from one's scientific, literary, or artistic works.

Article 28 — Everyone entitled to a social and international order in which rights set forth can be realized.

Article 29 — Everyone has duties to the community; rights and freedoms can be limited only to secure 'due recognition and respect' for rights of others and for 'the just requirements of morality, public order and the general welfare.'

Article 30 — Nothing in Declaration gives any state, group or person right to take action aimed at destruction of any of listed rights.

---

both and that the U.N. has proved to have little power — or political will — to enforce them anyway. "As a rule, the treaties are less important than either the willingness of private-sector groups to organize and fight and raise hell and of governments to be willing to make an issue about human rights even when that makes for diplomatic discomfort," says Joshua Muravchik, a self-described neoconservative human rights expert at the American Enterprise Institute.

The U.N. has moved to strengthen its human rights machinery in recent years, however. The most visible of the changes came in 1994 when then Secretary General Boutros Boutros-Ghali created the post of High Commissioner for Human Rights to direct the U.N.'s work in the area. The current commissioner, Mary Robinson, former president of Ireland, has been both visible and outspoken since assuming the post in September 1997.

As for the human rights groups, they are often criticized for taking an overly simplistic view of how to achieve their goals. "They tend to demand that these rights be respected instantly, without taking into account the longer processes of liberalization and democratization," says Catharin Dalpino, a visiting scholar at the Brookings Institution who served as deputy assistant U.S. secretary of State for human rights in President Clinton's first term. "Their lack of patience, or lack of realism, weakens their position."

U.S. Faulted on Executions, Police Practices

The murder case against Dwayne Allen Wright for a 1989 killing spree that left four people dead proceeded through Virginia courts much like other capital punishment cases. After his conviction and sentence to death, his final plea for executive clemency was rejected. On Oct. 14, 1998, he was executed in the electric chair.

For human rights groups, though, the Wright case put Virginia in the unsavory company of only five countries besides the United States — Iran, Nigeria, Pakistan, Saudi Arabia and Yemen — that defy international standards by executing people for offenses committed as juveniles.

The use of the death penalty against juvenile offenders is one of several issues that the human rights group Amnesty International is highlighting in a yearlong campaign against what it calls "a persistent and widespread pattern of human rights violations" in the United States.

"The United States prides itself as being a human rights leader," William Schulze, executive director of Amnesty International-USA, told a Washington, D.C., news conference to kick off the campaign on Oct. 7. "If our own house is not in order, that voice is diminished, less powerful."

But a prominent neoconservative human rights expert sharply attacked Amnesty for putting the United States in the same league as non-democratic countries with notorious records on human rights.

"In the interest of a false objectivity, they go about a distortion of reality," says Joshua Muravchik, a fellow at the American Enterprise Institute. "It's nonsense, and it does grave harm to the cause of human rights."

Amnesty launched the campaign by publishing a 150-page report that criticized the United States for "entrenched and nationwide police brutality," "physical and sexual abuse of prisoners" and the rising number of people executed and awaiting execution on death rows around the country. "It is time for the USA to deliver rights for all its people," the report concludes. [1]

On capital punishment, Amnesty noted that the International Covenant on Civil and Political Rights prohibits the death penalty for juvenile offenders. In ratifying the treaty, the United States added a number of so-called "reservations," including one to allow continued use of the death penalty for crimes committed by juveniles.

Wright, who was 17 years old at the time of the 1989 killings and had a history of mental illness, was the thirteenth person executed in the U.S. since 1990 for murders committed while they were juveniles. [2] In declining to commute the death sentence, Virginia Gov. James S. Gilmore III made no reference to the issue of executing juvenile offenders.

Amnesty's report said that police in the United States often use excessive force against suspects and that complaint procedures are "inadequate or wholly absent in some areas." Schultze and others at the news conference in particular criticized the growing use of electroshock devices — so-called "stun guns" — to control suspects, saying they inflict serious injury and their long-term effects are not known.

The National Association of Chiefs of Police dismissed the report as unfair. "Most U.S. law officers act in appropriate accordance with the intense level of danger their responsibilities present," the group's director, Gerald Arenberg, said in a statement. He also defended the use of stun guns. "It's actually one of the better devices, if used properly," Arenberg told The Associated Press.

The report also faulted prison conditions in the United States, saying that facilities are overcrowded, abuse of prisoners common and legal safeguards inadequate. It specifically criticized the housing of juveniles with adult offenders and the use of shackles for women prisoners in labor or while giving birth.

Muravchik said Amnesty's critique showed an anti-law enforcement bias. "Only in a lawful society are rights protected," he said after being given a summary of the issues raised. "A system of law entails restraints and punishments aimed at lawbreakers."

In releasing the report, however, Amnesty's international secretary-general, Pierre Sané, said the United States was lagging on human rights.

"Human rights practices in the United States have not kept pace with the evolving standards of decency," Sané said. "If the United States does not clean its own house," he added, "its credibility among the general population of the world will be tarnished."

---

[1] Amnesty International, *United States of America: Rights for All*, October 1998.

[2] *The New York Times*, Oct. 15, 1998, p. A19.

President Clinton himself was widely expected to put a strong emphasis on human rights in foreign policy, but advocacy groups are generally disappointed with his record in office. They complain, for example, of his decision midway in his first term to delink human rights and trade in dealing with China. More recently, they have sharply attacked the administration's refusal to approve a draft treaty completed this summer to establish an international criminal court. (*See "At Issue," p. 993.*)

Despite these controversies, the human rights community is likely to put aside some of those differences next month as they commemorate the Universal Declaration's 50th anniversary. Afterward, however, here are some of the issues that will continue to generate debate:

Is it realistic to expect all countries to comply with the Universal Declaration of Human Rights?

When the United States led the way in drafting and promulgating the Universal Declaration of Human Rights, racial segregation was still pervasive in America, women had few legal protections against discrimination, and the rights of criminal defendants were often ignored in police stations and in courtrooms. Today, countries with even graver human rights problems are among the nations that have endorsed the Universal Declaration and ratified many of the treaties written to implement its provisions.

The gap between rhetoric and reality gives critics and skeptics ample opportunity to question the value of the Universal Declaration. "Anyone who wants to damn it can do so by stressing the hypocrisy, the apathy, and the degree to which for the major powers human rights has been tucked into a larger framework of more material interests, like national security and economic matters," says Harvard Law School Professor Henry Steiner.

"It's worth celebrating, but with the understanding that the problems out there remain pretty much the same as they were 50 years ago," says Charles S. Lichenstein, a former deputy U.S. ambassador to the United Nations in the early 1980s and now a distinguished fellow at the conservative Heritage Foundation in Washington.

Human rights groups and advocates say that even though the declaration itself did not establish any binding obligations, it has helped reshape attitudes among governments and among the peoples of the world. "It established a common standard for all mankind," Steiner says.

"It was valuable to be able to say that this is something that is accepted everywhere, more or less," says Muravchik.

Some human rights experts, however, question the practical value of the declaration. "It's a fine goal, but the Universal Declaration is not in itself a roadmap," says Dalpino. "It does not begin to suggest how countries get to that level of recognition of human rights."

Dalpino sees greater value in the more specific provisions of the various U.N. treaties that have been negotiated since 1948, such as the two major covenants on civil and political rights and economic, social, and cultural rights. She says that even though many countries, including the United States, attach significant reservations to the treaties, ratification helps by giving domestic groups a standard to hold the government accountable to. In addition, some of the treaties, such as the covenant on civil and political rights, require countries to provide periodic reports on their compliance with the provisions. "That's very helpful internally too," Dalpino says.

Many conservatives, however, sharply attack the treaties, especially the covenant on economic rights and the more recent Covenant on the Rights of the Child. "The economic and social covenant seems to me to be very questionable," Muravchik says. "It boils down to saying that every country should be a relatively well-off country in which everyone shares the benefits. The problem is there's no way to decree that, there's no way to just make that happen."

Despite the limitations, liberal human rights experts maintain that the Universal Declaration remains valuable today in setting forth standards for all countries to be held to. "There are certain things that a government should refrain from doing, to refrain from transgressing moral values that are held around the world," says Roth of Human Rights Watch. "And if a government is determined to transgress them, the world has a duty to speak out against it."

These experts insist that the declaration's influence can be seen both in real events and in people's attitudes toward freedom around the world. "A discourse has been introduced that over 50 years has become so rooted that it cannot be uprooted," Steiner says.

"The fundamental themes show in the People's Republic of China. They showed in the breakup of the Soviet Union. They showed in the Velvet Revolution [in Czechoslovakia]. They show in the conflict in Nigeria. They showed in South Africa," Steiner continues. "It's in the air. More than in the air, it's in people's psyches."

Has the United Nations been effective in promoting international human rights?

The 50 years since the adoption of the Universal Declaration have witnessed the end of colonialism, the collapse of most of the world's communist regimes, and the gradual, if fitful, spread of democracy in the developing world. The United Nations' role in these developments is debatable: some advocates and experts credit it with helping to promote the spread of human rights, while others regard its impact as minimal or even counterproductive.

The U.N.'s principal human rights organ, the Human Rights Commission, was created in 1946 and now consists of 53 countries serving rotating three-year terms. The commission meets annually at its headquarters in Geneva, and the weeklong sessions serve as a forum for debating human rights issues, often focused on individual countries.

Some experts say those debates have been useful in promoting debate and encouraging progress on human rights in specific countries. "If you look at international relations in 1998, and if you compare it to 1948, there's much more attention to human rights," says David Forsythe, a law professor at the University of Nebraska. "Human rights violators are under much greater pressure. So, in the long run, the U.N. Human Rights Commission has been quite important in

Major U.N. Human Rights Treaties

The United Nations adopted two major human rights treaties in 1966 and five others since then along with an optional protocol to abolish the death penalty. The United States has ratified only three of the treaties.

Treaty	Date Adopted	Number of Countries to Ratify	U.S. Position
International Covenant on Economic, Social and Cultural Rights	1966	138	Signed; not ratified
International Covenant on Civil and Political Rights	1966	140	Ratified, 1992
CCPR: Optional Protocol #2 [Abolition of death penalty]	1989	92	No action
International Convention on the Elimination of All Forms of Racial Discrimination	1966	151	Ratified, 1994
Convention on the Elimination of All Forms of Discrimination Against Women	1979	162	Signed; not ratified
Convention against Torture and Other Cruel, Inhuman or Degrading Treatment or Punishment	1984	109	Ratified, 1994
Convention on the Rights of the Child	1989	191	Signed; not ratified
International Convention on the Protection of the Rights of All Migrant Workers and Their Families	1991	9	No action

Source: U.N. Commission on Human Rights

keeping this discourse on human rights fairly salient."

Other experts, however, say the Human Rights Commission's debates have been too political — slanted against Western countries and Israel, for example, while failing to confront human rights issues in communist countries or dictatorial regimes in the Third World.

"The U.N. has been a fudge factory," says Muravchik. "Every single one of the most vicious and most abusive governments in the world has served as a member of the Human Rights Commission: Cuba, Iraq, Syria, China, the Soviet Union, and on and on," he continues. "It's just

meant that the U.N. arena has not been a very fertile one for the advancement of human rights."

Dalpino says she sees no evidence that the Human Rights Commission's resolution process has been linked to any positive action in the countries being considered. "It tends to back abusive countries into a corner, and certainly doesn't do anything to make them want to liberalize," she says. "They're feel-good exercises and rather costly ones."

Most human rights groups, however, want the U.N. commission to be more willing to censure countries with poor records on human rights.

Roth complains, for example, of the commission's repeated refusal over the past several years to approve a resolution — supported by the United States up until this year — criticizing China for its human rights practices.

"Under any objective standard, China would have been repeatedly condemned," Roth says. "But China has been able to cajole or bribe several governments to oppose any condemnation effort, and this year even the U.S. government was willing to succumb to that bribery."

Reoch says the weaknesses are built into the U.N. system. "The United Na-

Probes Cover Torture, Children, Racism

United Nations human rights investigators — variously called special rapporteurs, special representatives or independent experts — are currently conducting inquiries in 12 individual countries and examining 19 broad "thematic" issues in countries throughout the world. The U.N. Human Rights Commission also provides advice, such as how to run a fair election, through technical-cooperation programs in four countries.

Country-specific investigations

Afghanistan • Burundi • Congo • Equitorial Guinea • Iran • Iraq • Myanmar • Nigeria Palestinian territories occupied since 1967 • Rwanda • Sudan • Territory of the former Yugoslavia

Technical-cooperation programs

- Cambodia
- Haiti
- Somalia
- Chad

Thematic investigations

Racism, racial discrimination and xenophobia • Extrajudicial, summary or arbitrary executions • Freedom of opinion and expression • Impact of armed conflict on children • Independence of judges and lawyers • Internally displaced persons • Mercenaries • Religious intolerance • Sale of children, child prostitution and child pornography • Torture and other cruel, inhuman or degrading treatment or punishment • Illicit movement and dumping of toxic waste • Violence against women • Effects of foreign debt • Restitution, compensation and rehabilitation for victims of grave violations of human rights • Extreme poverty • Education • Right to development • Working group on arbitrary detention • Working group on enforced or involuntary disappearances

Source: United Nations Commission on Human Rights

tions is nothing more than a club of governments," the former Amnesty official says. "It's often like asking the police to police themselves. In some ways, it's a miracle that it has produced the level of human rights commitment that it has produced."

Human rights groups are encouraged, however, by changes at the United Nations over the past few years — in particular, by the appointment of a high commissioner for human rights after more than a decade of lobbying for the post. The first high commissioner, Ecuadorean diplomat José Ayala Lasso, was criticized as weak and ineffectual in the position, but Robinson has drawn wide praise when she was appointed and since then. "It now has

better leadership," says Roth.

In addition, human rights groups and experts say that what Roth calls the U.N.'s "fact-finding capacity" has improved over the past few years. Currently, the Human Rights Commission has some 31 special rapporteurs at work: 12 on individual countries and another 19 on such broad themes as torture, judicial independence, and extrajudicial executions and disappearances.

Dalpino, the former Clinton administration official, says that in addition to providing factual documentation of human rights conditions, the special rapporteurs can often achieve positive results in the countries they are investigating. "They negotiate with the host government to a

certain extent," she says. "The report-writing is the end of a process. It tends to be less confrontational."

Human rights groups have also applauded the increased attention to human rights within the U.N.'s peacekeeping machinery, as in Bosnia and Rwanda. "The Security Council now deals with human rights on a regular basis as linked to peace and security issues," says Forsythe. Human rights groups want to see more money for the U.N.'s human rights machinery, and they complain about the limitations on the two U.N.-established war crimes tribunals for the former Yugoslavia and Rwanda.

Overall, however, human rights groups and experts say they are encouraged by the U.N.'s recent moves.

"International relations is fundamentally different in the 1990s on human rights, and the U.N. is frequently at the center of these activities," Forsythe concludes.

Has the Clinton administration done enough to support human rights around the world?

As the human rights community prepared last year to begin observing the Universal Declaration's 50th anniversary, President Clinton went before an audience of diplomats and activists to affirm the United States' commitment to the cause. "Advancing human rights must always be a central pillar of America's foreign policy," Clinton said at the Dec. 9 speech at the Museum of Jewish Heritage in New York City.

The Clinton administration's record on human rights, however, has been sharply criticized from all sides of the political spectrum. Conservatives and liberals alike say the administration has failed to back up its rhetorical commitment with concrete action to promote human rights from issues ranging from China and Bosnia to land mines and the proposed international criminal court for war crimes.

"Terrific rhetoric, no follow-through," says Lichenstein. "The Clinton administration never follows through. All it does it make threats, and now the threats are empty because the bad guys are pretty clear in their head that we don't mean it."

"Bill Clinton uses human rights like a bad cook uses spices," says Schultze of Amnesty International-USA. "He sprinkles a little bit of human rights on foreign policies when he wants to make them look good."

Conservatives and liberals have joined in sharply criticizing the administration's policies toward China. They fault Clinton for his decision midway in his first term to delink human rights and trade with China and for the decision this year to drop the effort at the U.N. Human Rights Commission to censure China. The administra-

tion has also been criticized for not doing enough to try to apprehend war crimes suspects in the former Yugoslavia, including Yugoslav President Slobodan Milosevic.

Liberal groups have also focused on the administration's stance on the land mine treaty and the international criminal court. In its annual report last December, Human Rights Watch charged that the administration had "actively obstructed" the effort to create the international tribunal and renewed the criticism this summer after a U.N. conference reached agreement on a draft treaty to be submitted to countries for ratification.

The administration has stoutly defended its record on the various issues. It has contended that its policy of "engagement" with China is more likely to produce human rights improvements than a more confrontational stance. It has also insisted that NATO peacekeeping troops should not have been given the additional responsibility of actively searching out war crimes suspects in the former Yugoslavia. And, when the Human Rights Watch report came out last year, State Department spokesman James Rubin said it was "obviously ridiculous" to accuse the U.S. of obstructing the international criminal court. [1]

Even so, the United States found itself in a small minority in July when the U.N. conference completed work on a treaty to create the new court. The conference, held in Rome, ended with a 120-7 vote in favor of the draft treaty.* The United States exerted strong pressure at the conference to modify the agreement, but the changes were rejected in a lopsided 113-17 vote.

Afterward, Rubin said the treaty was "deeply flawed and will produce a flawed court." He complained that the proposed court would subject U.S. service personnel to "politically motivated or ill-consid-

---

* The seven countries that voted against the treaty were China, Iraq, Israel, Libya, Qatar, the United States and Yemen.

ered or unjustified prosecutions." Among the changes the United States sought unsuccessfully was one that would have allowed countries ratifying the treaty to bar prosecutions of their nationals for war crimes or crimes against humanity for the first 10 years after creation of the court.

Human rights advocates have continued to sharply criticize the U.S. stance — contrasting it with the U.S. role in creating the two special U.N. war crimes tribunals for the former Yugoslavia and Rwanda. "It's OK for Yugoslavs, it's OK for Rwandans, but not for Americans," says Forsythe. "There's a real double standard there."

Despite those criticisms, administration officials insist that the United States has been — and remains today — at the forefront of the effort to promote human rights around the world. "I think that if you look around the world and you ask the people of the world which nation they look to as the beacon for human rights, democracy and freedom, there's no question the answer will be the United States," Rubin remarked last year. [2] ■

BACKGROUND

Universal Rights

The Universal Declaration of Human Rights represents the first comprehensive effort to establish global standards for individual freedoms, but the idea of "natural rights" began to emerge in the so-called Age of Enlightenment in the 17th and 18th centuries. The English philosopher John Locke and the French thinkers Montesquieu, Rousseau and Voltaire all articulated natural rights theories that influenced the writing of such national rights charters as the English

Continued on p. 988

Chronology

Before 1940
Political philosophers develop theories about universal human rights.

1919
League of Nations is founded after end of World War I, but proves unable to prevent a second world war.

— • —

1941-1965 *The United Nations adopts a non-binding "declaration" of human rights, then spends nearly two decades drafting two major treaties.*

1948
United Nations General Assembly adopts Universal Declaration of Human Rights, 48-0, with eight abstentions, on Dec. 10. Convention on the Prevention and Punishment of the Crime of Genocide is approved a day earlier.

1950
Council of Europe adopts U.N. adopts European Convention of Human Rights.

1952
General Assembly adopts Convention on Political Rights of Women.

1961
Amnesty International is founded.

— • —

1965-1980 *Two major international covenants are approved by General Assembly and take effect.*

Dec. 21, 1965
International Convention on the Elimination on All Forms of Racial Discrimination is adopted by U.N. General Assembly.

1966
U.N. General Assembly on Dec. 16 adopts the International Covenant on Economic, Social and Cultural Rights and the International Covenant on Civil and Political Rights; treaties come into force in 1976.

1975
Human rights provisions are included in Helsinki accord signed by 35 Western and Eastern European countries, as well as the Soviet Union, United States and Canada.

1978
U.N. Human Rights Commission appoints special rapporteur (investigator) on human rights conditions in Chile.

Dec. 18, 1979
Convention on the Elimination of All Forms of Discrimination against Women.

— • —

1980s *Use of special rapporteurs is expanded to more countries.*

1981
U.N. General Assembly adopts non-binding declaration against religious intolerance and discrimination.

1982
Special rapporteur on summary executions is appointed.

1984
International convention against torture is adopted by General Assembly on Dec. 10.

1989
General Assembly adopts Convention on the Rights of the Child; also adds optional protocol for abolition of death penalty to International Covenant on Civil and Political Rights.

— • —

1990s *Human rights components are added to U.N. peacekeeping operations.*

1993
Security Council creates war crimes tribunal for former Yugoslavia; World Conference on Human Rights held in Vienna; General Assembly approves post of high commissioner for human rights.

1994
José Ayala Lasso is appointed by Secretary General Boutros Boutros-Ghali as first high commissioner for human rights; Security Council creates war crimes tribunal for Rwanda.

1997
Lasso resigns amid criticism; Secretary General Kofi Annan names as his successor Mary Robinson, former president of Ireland; President Clinton calls human rights "central pillar" of U.S. foreign policy.

1998
U.N. conference completes draft of resolution to create International Criminal Court, with United States opposed; Universal Declaration celebrates its 50th anniversary on Dec. 10.

U.N. Investigators Uncover Harsh Conditions . . .

Nigel Rodley had been told that the use of leg irons, or "bar fetters," was common in Pakistani jails. So two days before he was to inspect the Lahore central jail in 1996, he urged the country's minister of justice to end the practice.

But Rodley, then an English lawyer serving as the United Nations' "special rapporteur," or investigator, on "torture and other cruel, inhuman or degrading treatment or punishment," didn't find a single inmate in irons on his visit. When he talked with the inmates in confidence, however, they told him that 300 sets of shackles had been removed the previous night.

Rodley asked officials to see the jail's registry. There, carefully recorded, was evidence that many of the inmates had been "awarded" bar fetters and that some had been shackled for months at a time. Jail officials admitted their ruse. Today, the Pakistani government says it is abolishing the practice.

The episode provides an unaccustomedly clear example of a positive result achieved by the U.N.'s human rights machinery. For the most part, though, Rodley, now a professor at the University of Essex, acknowledges that the work rests "pretty much on an act of faith that doing something is likely to be better than doing nothing."

"What effect one has on this or that particular case, one doesn't know," says Rodley, who worked for Amnesty International for 17 years and has served as the U.N.'s special rapporteur on torture since 1993. "One just intuits that the drip, drip, drip of pressure eventually erodes the resisting stone of the torturers."

Rodley is one of 31 people — mostly law professors or longtime human rights lawyers — currently directing U.N. human rights investigations either as special rapporteurs, special representatives or independent experts. Twelve are investigating individual countries; the other 19 are dealing with broad thematic issues. In addition, the U.N. Human Rights Commission has technical-cooperation programs with Cambodia, Chad, Haiti and Somalia.

The history of such U.N. human rights investigations dates to the 1960s, according to Rodley, when ad hoc groups of experts — as they were formally called — were created to examine human rights issues in southern Africa (1967) and the Israeli-occupied territories (1968). The U.N. created a special rapporteur on Chile in 1978 — the first formal use of that title — five years after Gen. Augusto Pinochet came to power in a bloody civil war.

Broader, thematic investigations were created in the 1980s: a working group on involuntary disappearances (1980), followed by a special rapporteur on summary executions (1982). The special rapporteur on torture was created in 1985, one year after the U.N. General Assembly adopted the international convention against torture.

Rodley's position is unusual in that it deals with individual allegations of torture as well as broader investigations. The special rapporteur is authorized to receive so-called urgent appeals in cases where an individual is being detained under circumstances that indicate a risk of torture; letters are then sent under Rodley's signature to the authorities asking for assurances that no ill treatment will occur. Specific allegations of

Continued from p. 986

Bill of Rights (1688) and the French Declaration of the Rights of Man and the Citizen (1789). Their writings also influenced such Americans as Thomas Jefferson and James Madison and through them the writing of the Declaration of Independence (1776) and the U.S. Bill of Rights (1791).

Before World War II, however, the few international treaties on human rights issues dealt only with specific issues, such as the 1817 treaty to ban the slave trade and the Geneva accords of the late 19th and early 20th centuries governing the conduct of war and the treatment of prisoners of war. The International Labor Organization, created along with the League of Nations after the end of World War

I, approved a treaty in 1930 restricting the use of forced labor. But the League of Nations itself did little work on human rights questions and proved unable as well to prevent a second world war.

The horrors of World War II convinced the international community of the need for concerted action to prevent aggressive war and violations of human rights by totalitarian governments. [3] The United Nations Charter, signed in San Francisco on June 26, 1945, established the U.N.'s major bodies for international consultation and peacekeeping but contained only a few, general references to human rights. The charter, however, included a provision that the Economic and Social Council create

a Commission on Human Rights with instructions to draft a comprehensive charter of individual freedoms for the General Assembly to consider and vote on.

Eleanor Roosevelt, widow of President Franklin D. Roosevelt, took the lead in the two-year effort to draft and adopt the declaration. The movement took inspiration in part from President Roosevelt's famous Four Freedoms speech in January 1941; it also built on the writings and advocacy of human rights activists in a number of other countries. Several of those served on the 18-member commission, including France's René Cassin, Lebanon's Charles Malik and Chile's Hernán San Cruz. Mrs. Roosevelt was elected chairman, a

... And Sometimes Bring About Change

torture can also be investigated in individual cases, but Rodley says the money and staff available for such investigations is "egregiously limited."

Finally, Rodley, accompanied by a small number of staff members, visits individual countries to examine conditions. Within the past year, for example, Rodley visited Russia, where he says he found "unbelievably barbaric conditions in places of pretrial detention." He has also visited Rwanda and several countries in Latin America, including Colombia and Mexico. One limitation: Rodley cannot visit an individual country without an invitation. Among the countries that have declined to issue invitations are the world's two most populous nations: China and India.

The reports by U.N. investigators often provoke negative reactions in the countries being examined. When a special rapporteur visited the United States to study the death penalty, some federal and state officials refused to see him; Senate Foreign Relations Committee Chairman Jesse Helms, R-N.C., called the mission "an absurd U.N. charade." The report, issued April 6, criticized the United States for the unfair, arbitrary and racist use of capital punishment.[1]

In another investigation, the United States refused, along with most other industrial countries, to provide information to the special rapporteur on the illicit movement and dumping of toxic wastes. African countries pushed for the creation of the post in 1995, saying that the export of toxic wastes to the continent threatened Africans' rights to life and health. But U.S. officials argued the investigation marginalized the significance of human rights. An initial report, nonetheless, identified the United States, along with Germany, Australia, Great Britain and the Netherlands, as the largest exporters of toxic wastes.[2]

The Human Rights Commission sometimes uses the reports in drafting and approving resolutions critical of individual countries or broad practices. The commission, for example, has passed several resolutions urging the new government in Congo to improve human rights conditions there. So far, the reports and resolutions appear to have had little effect on the government of President Laurent Kabila.

Even so, Roberto Garretón, the Chilean human rights lawyer serving as special rapporteur for Congo, says his experiences during the struggle against the Pinochet government demonstrate that the U.N.'s human rights work can have "enormous political and moral importance."

"I was a lawyer against the dictatorship for 16 years," Garretón says. "I never won a trial. I never liberated a prisoner. I was never able to convict a torturer. But we always won, twice a year" — referring to resolutions by the General Assembly in New York and the Human Rights Commission in Geneva.

"To the dictatorship and its ambassadors, this was what most annoyed them," Garretón continues. "We photocopied the reports and distributed them throughout the country, so that people could see that the truth was recognized somewhere."

---

[1] *The New York Times,* April 7, 1998, p. A17.

[2] *The New York Times,* April 5, 1998, p. A10.

---

post she held through 1952.

The final declaration emerged from two major drafting sessions by the commission and detailed debates and voting by the General Assembly in Paris in August 1948. The commission worked through a host of drafting questions and political mine fields: Anti-colonial countries, for example, forced the inclusion of a paragraph stating that "no distinction" was to be made between individual rights in independent countries and those recognized in "non-self-govering" territories. The commission intended to draft binding treaties at the same time, but that goal proved to be overly ambitious — and, in fact, was not completed until 1954. But the declaration went before the General Assembly on Dec. 10, 1948, and won approval on a 48-0 vote, with eight countries (Saudi Arabia, South Africa and Soviet-bloc countries) abstaining and two countries not present.

The drafters of the declaration cheered its adoption. Mrs. Roosevelt predicted it might become "the international Magna Carta of all mankind." Some other human rights advocates, however, professed sharp disappointment with its generality and its lack of binding provisions When the Economic and Social Council was discussing plans in 1949 to mark the first anniversary of its adoption, the observer from the International Law Association said the best way to celebrate the Universal Declaration of Human Rights was to forget it.[4]

Writing the Covenants

The United Nations approved the first of the more than 60 binding human rights treaties in force today on Dec. 9, 1948, the day before the adoption of the Universal Declaration. The Convention on Genocide — approved by the General Assembly without dissenting vote — sought to prevent a recurrence of anything like the Nazi Holocaust; it prohibited the killing, serious injury, or forced relocation of members of any national, ethnic, racial, or religious group "with intent to destroy" that group "in whole or in part" A second treaty followed just four years later: the Convention on the Political Rights of Women, a bare-bones document guaranteeing women the right to vote, hold public office, and exercise other public functions "on equal terms with men."

By contrast, the effort to put into effect the sweeping provisions of the Universal Declaration took more than a quarter-century. The Commission on Human Rights itself took six years to produce drafts of two covenants — not one, as originally contemplated. The General Assembly decided in 1951 to divide the two treaties because of the significant differences between the two types of rights: civil and political rights could be expressed in more nearly absolute terms and enforced by courts, while social and economic rights needed to be phrased in aspirational terms and their achievement depended mostly on legislative and executive branches than on the courts.

The two covenants follow the Universal Declaration's general structure, but both are significantly longer: 31 articles for the economic and social rights covenant, 53 for the one on civil and political rights. Some of the civil rights are prescribed as absolutes: the prohibition against slavery, the right "to have or to adopt" a religion, and the mandatory notice to a criminal defendant of the charges brought. Many others, however, contain significant qualifications. The right to counsel in criminal cases, for example, applies "in any case where the interests of justice so require" (Article 14). And the right to freedom of expression may be restricted "for respect of the rights and reputations of others" or "for the protection of national security or of public order, or of public health and morals" (Article 19).

The covenant on economic and social rights opens in explicitly aspirational terms: it calls on each signatory country to take steps "to the maximum of its available resources, with a view to achieving progressively the full realization of the rights" specified. Some provisions are nonetheless stated as absolutes — for example, the "right to social security, including social insurance." Working mothers are to be accorded "paid leave" or "leave with adequate social security

---

The Convention on Genocide — approved by the General Assembly without dissenting vote — sought to prevent a recurrence of anything like the Nazi Holocaust

---

benefits" during "a reasonable period before and after childbirth."

Most of the provisions, however, recognize inherent limits on a government's ability to put them into effect. The covenant, for example, requires universal free primary education but only the "progressive introduction" of free secondary education (Article 13). It calls on states to recognize "the right of everyone to the enjoyment of the highest attainable standard of physical and mental health" (Article 12). And it calls on signatory countries to use their own resources and "international cooperation" to provide "adequate food,

clothing, and housing" (Article 11).

Even after the drafting was completed in 1954, approval of the two covenants took another 12 years. The General Assembly adopted both treaties without dissenting vote on Dec. 16, 1966. It also approved an "optional protocol" to the civil and political covenant aimed at strengthening the enforcement powers of the Commission on Human Rights. In its earliest years, the commission had declined to consider individual complaints of human rights violations; by the mid-1950s, it agreed to consider specific incidents but kept any deliberations confidential.

The new protocol provided that countries could agree to permit citizens to file a so-called communication with the commission alleging a violation of any of the covenant's provisions; the commission was then empowered to "examine" the communication, in closed meetings, and "forward its views" to both the individual filing the complaint and the government concerned. There were again no dissenting votes on the protocol, but a substantial number of countries — 38 — abstained.

Stronger Machinery

Another decade passed before the two human rights treaties were ratified by the specified minimum number of countries — 35 — to come into force. [5] The United States did not ratify the covenant on civil and political rights until 1992 and so far has only signed but not ratified the covenant on economic and social rights. In the meantime, the General Assembly has gone on to approve several other major human rights covenants, including a treaty banning torture (1984), prohibiting "all forms" of discrimination against women (1988), and establishing rights for children (1989).

In addition to these international treaties, the U.N. had also used economic sanctions to deal with two specific human rights issues: the denial of political rights to black Africans by white minority governments in Rhodesia and South Africa. The U.N. Security Council voted to impose sanctions against Rhodesia on the same day that the General Assembly approved the two human rights covenants in 1966. The campaign against apartheid took form in an international convention approved by the General Assembly in 1973 that defined South Africa's system as a "crime against humanity." The Security Council followed in 1977 with an arms embargo against South Africa, though it stopped short of broader economic sanctions. The U.N.'s measures are credited, even by critics of economic sanctions, with playing some role in the eventual creation of representative democracies in Zimbabwe and South Africa.

The priority that the U.N. attached to the South Africa issue attested to the growing power of the African and Asian countries that gained independence in the decolonization period of the 1950s and '60s. The emergence of the so-called Third World ended the United States' dominance of the U.N. Critics of the U.N. contend that the shift resulted in an anti-Western bias reflected, for example, in opposition to Israel and a double standard toward human rights issues in many non-aligned nations and the communist bloc.

In an evaluation written at the end of the 1980s, Forsythe agreed that the Human Rights Commission devoted disproportionate attention to apartheid and to Israeli practices in the territories it occupied after the 1967 Arab-Israeli War. But he also said that the United States has been guilty of a double standard — for example, focusing far more attention on Cuba than on the death squads in El Salvador, a U.S. ally. [6]

More broadly, Forsythe contended, many Third World countries had come to show more genuine support for human rights issues despite a continuing concern about non-intervention in internal affairs. He noted that since 1978 the Human Rights Commission had been publishing a list of countries that had been the subject of human rights complaints. Despite a lack of specifics, the list has become more balanced over time, he wrote. He also found evidence of greater balance and greater resolve in the work of other U.N. human rights organs as well as in the General Assembly itself.

As one example, Forsythe noted a General Assembly debate in 1982 between competing resolutions sponsored by Cuba and Ireland on the relative importance of collective or individual rights. While the Cuban resolution passed with only one no vote — from the United States — many non-aligned countries then followed by joining the U.S. and other Western countries in adopting the second resolution as well — in effect, giving equal priority to individual rights.

The end of the Cold War eased the ideological divisions that had complicated the U.N.'s human rights work. By the end of the 1980s, the U.N.'s human rights machinery itself was also expanding. Besides receiving reports from individual countries, the Human Rights Commission had also begun to appoint independent experts — so-called special rapporteurs — to investigate claims of human rights violations both in specific countries, such as Chile and Iran, and on general subjects, such as religious persecution.

Human rights activists were disappointed by the General Assembly's continued refusal to create the post of High Commissioner for Human Rights. But as the 1990s began, the U.N.'s prospects for a stronger and more coherent approach to human rights appeared to be better than at any time in its history.

New Post Created

The United Nations continued to build its human rights machinery through the 1990s — in particular, with the creation of the high commissioner post in 1993. In addition, the U.N. broadened the human rights agenda by creating two special war crimes tribunals and by moving to incorporate human rights initiatives in peacekeeping operations. The two tribunals, however, have struggled against an array of difficulties, from limited funding to the difficulty of apprehending suspects in the former Yugoslavia. And human rights activists were generally disappointed with the low-key approach taken by the first high commissioner, José Ayala Lasso, who served for three years until resigning last year to become his country's foreign minister.

The General Assembly adopted the resolution establishing the high commissioner's post in December 1993 following a recommendation from a worldwide conference on human rights in Vienna in June. [7] The Clinton administration helped ensure passage by giving the proposal higher priority than the U.S. had done in the past. In an important concession to developing countries, the resolution included a clause reaffirming "the importance of promoting a balanced and sustainable development for all people." The resolution provided that the high commissioner would serve a four-year term, hold the rank of under-secretary general, and be responsible for improving the "coordination, effectiveness, and efficiency" of all U.N. human rights activities.

Upon his appointment, Lasso was viewed with suspicion by human rights groups because he had served in Ecuador's military government in the 1970s. When he resigned, he was given some credit for consolidating the office and for dispatching U.N.

monitors to Rwanda to try to stop the massacres there. But he was also criticized for having refused to speak out about human rights abuses, even in private. "He had no clout behind him except his moral voice, which he refused to use," says Roth. By contrast, Secretary General Kofi Annan was widely praised for picking Robinson for the post and for promising to integrate human rights issues into the range of the U.N.'s work.

The creation of the U.N. war crimes tribunals for the former Yugoslavia in 1993 and Rwanda in 1994 stemmed from the worldwide revulsion over the documented evidence of widespread killings of civilians and other human rights violations in those two conflicts. [8] The tribunals were the first courts ever created by the United Nations to try individuals for war crimes: the victorious Allies had conducted the trials of German and Japanese officials after World War II. Their work has been slow. So far, the tribunal for the former Yugoslavia — sitting in The Hague, Netherlands — has won only three convictions; the court for Rwanda — which sits in Ashura, Tanzania — has taken one guilty plea and not held any trials.

Meanwhile, an increasing number of U.N. special rapporteurs were working — and producing detailed reports — on a growing agenda of human rights issues. "Over the past five years [the Human Rights Commission] has developed an enhanced fact-finidng ability," Roth says. In addition, the commission was examining with greater care reports that individual countries were supposed to file on their compliance with human rights treaties. Forsythe said the accountability process sometimes paid off. "Human rights reports indicate that a number of states have changed their domestic legislation when questioned," he says.

Forsythe sees a more dramatic potential for change in what he calls the U.N.'s recent blending of human rights and security issues. In addition

to the two war crimes tribunals, Forsythe notes that the Security Council has authorized what he calls "complex peacekeeping" operations in Cambodia and El Salvador — deploying peacekeeping forces at the same time that human rights teams were dispatched to help supervise elections. "The new peacekeeping is designed to create a liberal democratic peace," he says. "In places like El Salvador and Cambodia, it's worked fairly well." ∎

CURRENT SITUATION

Enter Mary Robinson

The 40-year-old civil war in Colombia has claimed more than 120,000 lives and has been marked by pervasive human rights abuses by the government and paramilitary forces on one side and the leftist guerrillas on the other. So the international human rights community was cheered last year when the United Nations Commission on Human Rights opened an office in the capital city of Bogotá to help demonstrate the worldwide concern about conditions there.

But when the U.N.'s high commissioner for human rights, Mary Robinson, visited Colombia last month, she got dramatic reminders of the limits on the international body's ability to control events. In the days before her visit, some 56 people were killed by a rebel bombing of an oil pipeline, and the vice president of the country's largest trade union was assassinated outside his home. Robinson herself received a

telephone call warning that a bomb had been placed in the hotel where she was to attend a seminar on protecting human rights defenders.

Robinson issued statements condemning both of the incidents, and the seminar went ahead as scheduled. The 54-year-old former president of Ireland also went ahead with the rest of her schedule, which included meetings with Colombia's president, Andres Pastrana, and other ranking officials, including the country's human rights ombudsman. They assured Robinson that the government intended to implement a "national action plan" on human rights. Robinson was "happy to hear of that commitment," says spokesman José Diaz.

After one year in office, Robinson has collected a few other, similar assurances of cooperation on human rights issues, most notably in a 10-day visit to China in September. Chinese leaders used the visit to signal their intention to sign the International Covenant on Civil and Political Rights and to sign a letter of understanding with the U.N. Human Rights Commission requesting technical assistance on human rights matters. Robinson told an end-of-trip news conference that she was "interested in the awareness of and willingness to admit human rights problems among China's leaders." [9]

Robinson has traveled widely in the 14 months since assuming the U.N.'s top-ranking human rights post on Sept. 12, 1997. The other trouble spots she has visited include Cambodia, Iran, and Rwanda. She has also spoken out on a range of issues — for example, calling the civil war in Algeria an "intolerable" catastrophe and criticizing the pace of executions in the United States. [10]

In appointing Robinson, Secretary General Kofi Annan charged the one-time human rights lawyer not only with strengthening the U.N. Human Rights Commission itself but also with streamlining and coordinating human rights functions throughout the U.N. In a speech at Oxford University two months after

Continued on p. 994

At Issue:

Should the United States join the proposed International Criminal Court?

HELEN DUFFY

Counsel to the Campaign for an International Criminal Court at Human Rights Watch

*t*he International Criminal Court contributes to American foreign policy objectives in a number of ways. First, it's the most important development in human rights since the Universal Declaration of Human Rights 50 years ago. The new court will be able to hold perpetrators of genocide, crimes against humanity and serious war crimes personally to account. For the victims and survivors of future atrocities, the court will offer justice. And for those who commit heinous crimes, and hitherto have done so with impunity, the court will signal that they can no longer act without fear of prosecution. In and of itself, promoting human rights is obviously a central tenet of U.S. foreign policy.

At the same time, the court will have some good practical effects. It will encourage, even pressure, domestic courts to investigate and prosecute the worst human rights crimes themselves. Far from being a Hydra-headed harbinger of world government, the court should actually strengthen domestic court systems. This will fill an important practical gap in humanitarian law enforcement internationally.

Moreover, this kind of proactive judicial enforcement by national courts and the international court might forestall the next Rwanda or Yugoslavia.

So what's the problem? Clinton administration representatives have insisted on ironclad guarantees that no American would ever be prosecuted without U.S. government approval. That would gut the court's effectiveness. At the Rome conference finalizing the court's statute, other delegations conceded to U.S. demands for extremely strong guarantees against unwarranted prosecution and for multiple checks and balances on prosecutorial discretion and judicial decisions. All of these provisions were sufficient to satisfy France and the United Kingdom, among other close allies.

But not the United States. In Rome, the final vote was 120-7, with the U.S. delegation finding itself in the embarrassing company of Iraq, China, Libya and other frequent enemies of human rights.

If the United States wants to write the rules of international behavior, it also has to play by them. Washington seems to think that it can dictate the terms of institutions such as the International Criminal Court without actually participating in them. The next round of talks on the International Criminal Court will take up some critically important questions, such as the rules of evidence and procedure. The United States has key contributions to make to this debate. But those contributions will not count for much if Washington continues a policy of hostility to the court.

CHARLES M. LICHENSTEIN

Distinguished Fellow, The Heritage Foundation; deputy U.S. ambassador to the U.N., 1981-1984

*t*he short answer is, of course not. Not yet at any rate, and probably not at all. But I propose a fair and reasonable trade-off. If proponents of this triumph of good intentions can show me that an International Criminal Court (ICC) would likely bring Slobodan Milosevic to the bar of justice, and mete out some appropriate punishment, I vow to become its principal advocate — reserving the right to recommend major revisions in the court's processes.

The jurisdiction of the court embraces genocide, aggression, and an undifferentiated category of "crimes against humanity." With Hitler, Stalin, and Mao Tse-tung gone, who better than Milosevic to test the court's efficacy?

Obviously, though, it is not the absence of an ICC that leaves Milosevic free to commit genocide. It is the absence of political will on the part of some of the court's most ardent founding state parties: the United Kingdom, Canada and Germany, to name a few. In the language of the street, it is the absence of guts.

The United States, equally lacking in guts, at least has not yet compounded the hypocrisy by signing on to the Treaty of Rome. As soon as 60 countries do sign on, the ICC is in business.

It is scary to note, moreover, that the ICC as proposed would trash the constitutional protections of Americans who might get caught up in its limitless reach. The court itself will be the sole judge of whether it will defer to the prior jurisdiction of judicial systems party or non-party to the treaty. The court would be its own prosecutorial arm and its own appellate branch.

It is one thing to suggest that "there oughta be a law" or, in this case, a court. Maybe there ought to be a way of policing the boundaries of civilization against genocide and "crimes against humanity." But the terms would have to be defined with precision, legal procedures put in place, and institutions established — all within the context of a broad consensus about the purposes of the undertaking, the legitimacy, and the limits of the processes and institutions, and with protections against abuse.

In fact, there already is such a way, and it is called democracy or the democratic ethos. That is the necessary foundation. The institutional elaboration follows.

It may be that, if present trends toward democratization were to continue and strengthen, an International Criminal Court would be one of its byproducts. When the world is ready for an ICC, that is to say, it may not need one.

Mary Bourke Robinson: United Nations High Commissioner for Human Rights

Born: May 21, 1944.

Education: Bachelor's and law degrees, Trinity College, Dublin, 1967; master of law, Harvard University, 1968.

Career in Ireland: Member of Irish Senate (1969-89), Dublin City Council (1969-75); law professor, Trinity College (1969-75); twice defeated in elections for the Dail, major chamber in Irish Parliament; president of Ireland, 1990-1997 — first woman to hold position.

Human rights activities: Special rapporteur to European regional meeting on human rights, 1993; first head of state to visit Rwanda in aftermath of genocide there; appointed U.N. High Commissioner for Human Rights by Secretary-General Kofi Annan on June 12, 1997; took office, Sept. 12, 1997. As high commissioner, Robinson supervises the Geneva-based U.N. Center for Human Rights and 22 field offices, with about 300 employees and an annual budget of $21 million in regular U.N. funds and about $30 million in additional, voluntary payments by governments.

Source: U.N. Commission on Human Rights

Continued from p. 992

taking office, Robinson appeared to agree with criticisms of the U.N. bureaucracy as "being out of touch and, certainly, of being resistant to change." In the same speech, she had a downbeat assessment of the U.N.'s accomplishments on human rights.

"Count up the results of 50 years of human rights mechanisms, 30 years of multibillion-dollar development programs and endless high-level rhetoric," Robinson said, "and the global impact is quite underwhelming." [11]

Robinson has not been visibly daunted by the scope of her assignment or the number of obstacles. In a speech in Sweden last month, for example, she complained that human rights efforts were hampered by a "compartmentalized" international system and endorsed what is called "mainstreaming" human rights issues into other international organizations, including the two major lending institutions, the International Monetary Fund and the World Bank. In the same speech, Robinson made clear that her view of human rights extends beyond civil and political freedoms to include economic issues. "If we are serious about the right to life, we must equally be serious about the right to food, health care, education and shelter," Robinson said. [12]

Human rights groups generally cheered Robinson's appointment. Today, they are still positive, but cautious. "She is much more willing to be outspoken," says Human Rights Watch Executive Director Roth. But, he adds, "To some degree the jury is still out."

Concrete results, though, are still hard to find. Winifred Tate, a fellow with the Washington Office on Latin America, an advocacy group, says the establishment of the U.N. human rights office in Colombia "demonstrated concern" about the situation, but she notes that so far it has filled only six out of 12 budgeted staff positions.

"Unfortunately, the situation [in the country] has not improved," Tate adds. "That's not something you can expect."

Seeking Justice

Augusto Pinochet came to power in Chile in a bloody civil war in 1973 and ruled the South American country with an iron hand for the next 17 years before making way for a democratic government and retiring with what he thought was immunity from prosecution. But last month Pinochet was arrested in London under a warrant issued by a Spanish judge investigating the former leader's role in abduction, torture, and murder of political opponents.

Pinochet's arrest by British police on Oct. 16 touched off a vigorous debate not only in the countries directly involved — Chile, Britain, and Spain — but throughout the world. Supporters of the move hailed the effort to bring Pinochet to justice as vindication for the victims and a signal to other repressive leaders around the world. Critics said it risked reopening political tensions in Chile and deterring future dictators from leaving office peacefully for fear of criminal prosecutions years later. [13]

The debate is now on hold pending an appeal of a British court's Oct. 28 ruling that Pinochet has immunity from civil or criminal prosecution in England because he was a head of state during the events in question. Regardless of the outcome, though, Pinochet's case dramatizes the growing effort to bring human rights violators to justice either in national courts or through the use of international law and international tribunals.

So far, those efforts have produced relatively meager results, at least in terms of prosecuting high-ranking officials. National courts typically lack the resources or institutional strength to carry out legal proceedings. "There are always going to be all sorts of local and political pressures for courts within the country not to take the lead on these issues," says Michael Posner, executive director of the Lawyers Committee for Human Rights. Posner notes as one example that six one-time members of the ruling Argentine military junta were among those convicted for their parts in the so-called "dirty war" against suspected leftists in the late 1970s and early '80s, but they were given presidential pardons in late 1990. [14]

An alternative is represented by the South African Truth and Reconciliation Commission, which was established to investigate political crimes committed by the former apartheid government as well as by the African National Congress before the creation of a multiracial democracy in 1994. The commission had the power to issue an amnesty for crimes up to and including political assassinations, but only if an individual testified truthfully about his or her role in the offenses. The commission's final report, issued Oct. 29, strongly criticized both the government and the anti-apartheid movement for their actions during the liberation struggle. "Atrocious things were done on all sides," the report said.

Posner says the Spanish judge's actions represent a largely untested idea of prosecuting someone in a national court for offenses committed in another country. Over the past decade or so, however, U.S. courts have recognized civil claims in suits brought under a 1789 law, the Alien Tort Claims Act, against officials of foreign governments by victims of torture or other political offenses. A 1995 law also allows federal prosecutors to bring

criminal charges in U.S. courts against foreign torturers if they are found in the United States. So far, no prosecutions have been brought under the law, and the few judgments won in civil suits have proved difficult to collect.

Those difficulties have led human rights advocates to turn to the idea of international tribunals for prosecuting the most serious offenses: genocide, crimes against humanity, and war crimes. Even as the U.N. was creating the two special war crimes tribunals for the former Yugoslavia and Rwanda, human rights groups and experts were trying to hammer out an agreement on a permanent international court. The draft treaty approved in Rome on July 17 calls for a court of 18 judges, each from a different country and serving nine-year terms, and a full-time prosecutor with authority to initiate cases. The maximum punishment that could be imposed would be life imprisonment.

The Clinton administration initially supported creating the court, but came to oppose the proposal taking shape because of what the Defense Department saw as the risk that U.S. military personnel might be prosecuted for war crimes. To guard against that possibility, the U.S. wanted prosecutions to be initiated by the U.N. Security Council, where the U.S. has a veto. It also opposed a final provision that allows citizens of a country to be brought before the court even if it has not ratified the treaty.

Human rights advocates minimize the risk that Americans would ever be prosecuted before the new court. They note that the treaty calls for the tribunal to take a case only if the country's own courts cannot or will not prosecute. They also say that despite the U.S. position, the treaty is likely to be ratified in the relatively near future by the number of countries — 60 — needed to bring the court into existence. "We're now a couple of years away, probably three to four years at most, from 60 countries ratifying the treaty," Posner says. ■

Universal Rights?

China has gone to great lengths over the past month to try to improve its human rights image in international circles. It signed the International Covenant on Civil and Political Rights on Oct. 5, hosted an international human rights symposium the same week, and issued official communiqués afterward stressing its support for the Universal Declaration of Human Rights on the occasion of its 50th anniversary.

The declaration "plays an important role in promoting the development of the cause of human rights in the world," Chinese President Jiang Zemin said in a letter to U.N. Secretary General Annan publicized Oct. 22. But even as Jiang's letter was being released, the government was reported to be cracking down on political debate by closing a democracy-minded think tank and barring distribution of a book on political reform. The incidents showed that "sharp limits on what is permissible continue to exist," the U.S. State Department declared. [15]

China is far from the only country where human rights words are not matched by deeds. "Many governments subscribe to the [Universal Declaration] only nominally, but don't respect it at home," Roth says.

Robinson sounded a similar note in her annual report to the U.N. General Assembly. "The last 50 years has generated much hope," Robinson told the assembly's so-called Third Committee on Nov. 4. "Yet, I am afraid that in terms of practical reality of how human rights are lived, we must admit that the vision of the Universal Declaration is still far from reality."

Despite the unfulfilled promise on

such basic human rights issues as ensuring religious freedom or preventing torture, the United Nations is making its human rights agenda both broader and more ambitious. One recent initiative deals with the rights of indigenous people. In her report last week, Robinson stressed economic concerns. "The elimination of poverty and social exclusion may well be the most important human rights objective of the coming century," she said.

At the same time, Robinson told the General Assembly that the commission may not be able to carry out its responsibilities without "additional resources" for the coming year. The budget approved for the commission in 1997 allotted $42.2 million from regular U.N. funds for the two-year period 1998 and 1999. The commission also received voluntary contributions from member countries totaling about $31 million for 1998. "Further improvement would be at risk if resources remain inadequate," Robinson said.

Some critics see the emphasis on economic issues as a distraction from more genuine human rights concerns. "If you say every citizen should have a decent home to live in, I can't imagine that there's anyone who disagrees with that aspiration," Muravchik says. "But if you're saying this is a right, then what exactly do you mean by that?"

Liberal human rights experts sharply disagree, saying that the critique reflects a bias of the affluent West. "If you're talking to someone from the global South, they don't agree that economic rights are marginal," Forsythe says. "They don't agree that right to food, shelter, health care are in any way inferior to the civil and political rights that are well known in the West. If you're starving, don't have adequate nutrition or health care, then a lot of the civil and political rights become quite marginal."

Despite the differences and disagreements, human rights experts are generally optimistic about the future as they prepare to mark next month's historic milestone.

"There is an unstoppable momen-

FOR MORE INFORMATION

If you would like to have this CQ Researcher updated, or need more information about this topic, please call CQ Custom Research. Special rates for CQ subscribers. (202) 887-8600 or (800) 432-2250, ext. 600, or E-mail Custom.Research@cq.com

Amnesty International, USA, 322 Eighth Ave., New York, N.Y. 10001; (212) 807-8400; www.amnesty-usa.org.

Human Rights Watch, 350 Fifth Ave., 34th floor, New York, N.Y. 10018; (212) 290-4700; 1522 K St., N.W., Suite 910, Washington, D.C. 20005; (202) 371-6592; www.hrw.org.

Lawyers' Committee for Human Rights, 333 Seventh Ave., 13th floor, New York, N.Y. 10001; (212) 845-5200; www.lchr.org.

United Nations Commission on Human Rights, Palais Wilson, Room 2-016, 1211 Geneva, Switzerland; [011] 41-22-917-1239; www.unhchr.ch.

United Nations, Development and Human Rights Section, Department of Public Information, The United Nations, Room S-1040, New York, N.Y. 10017; (212) 963-1234; www.un.ch.

tum in this area," says Reoch, the former Amnesty International official. "There is a growing expertise in international human rights. The number of countries that are signing up for international treaties is increasing. The pressure on the U.N. to be effective in this area is increasing. And more and more and more governments are facing increasing pressure at home."

"I think we're seeing in the last 50 years only the start of a human rights revolution," he concludes. ∎

Notes

[1] See *The New York Times*, Dec. 5, 1997, p. A13.

[2] *Ibid.*

[3] Background on the drafting and adoption of the Universal Declaration, drawn from *The United Nations and Human Rights, 1945-1995* (1995), pp. 5-28; John P. Humphrey, *Human Rights and the United Nations: A Great Adventure* (1984), pp. 12-77. For background on the U.N., see Mary H. Cooper, "United Nations at 50," *The CQ Researcher*, Aug. 18, 1995, pp.729-752.

[4] Humphrey, *op. cit.*, p. 75.

[5] For evaluations of the U.N.'s work, see Patrick James Flood, *The Effectiveness of UN Human Rights Institutions* (1998), pp. 31-48, 116-132;

David P. Forsythe, *The Internationalization of Human Rights* (1991), pp. 55-86.

[6] Forsythe, *op. cit.*, pp. 65-69.

[7] See Flood, *op. cit.*, pp. 118-124, 156-159 (text of resolution). Flood, a retired career foreign service officer, served in the U.S. mission to the Human Rights Commission in Geneva during the 1980s.

[8] For background, see Keneth Jost, "War Crimes," *The CQ Researcher,* July 1995, pp. 585-608.

[9] See *The New York Times*, Sept. 16, 1998, p. A8.

[10] Some background drawn from a profile by Craig Turner, "At Swords' Point With Repression," *Los Angeles Times*, July 2, 1998, p. A1. For a biography, see John Horgan, *Mary Robinson: A Woman of Ireland and the World,* Roberts Rinehart, 1998.

[11] Mary Robinson, "Realizing Human Rights," Romanes Lecture, Oxford University, Nov. 11, 1997.

[12] Mary Robinson, "Human Rights: Challenges for the 21st Century," First Annual Dag Hammarskjold Lecture, Uppsala, Sweden, Oct. 1, 1998.

[13] For opposing points of view, see Diane F. Orenthicher, "Putting Limits on Lawlessness," *The Washington Post*, Oct. 25, 1998, p. C1; Adrian Karatnycky, "Pinochet's Rights and Ours," *The Wall Street Journal*, Oct. 26, 1998, p. A23. Orenthlicher is a professor of international law at American University's Washington College of Law; Karatnycky is president of Freedom House, a human rights organization.

[14] See *The New York Times*, Dec. 31, 1990, p. A4.

[15] See *The New York Times*, Oct. 28, 1998, p. A1.

Bibliography

Selected Sources Used

Books

Eide, Asbjorn, Gudmundur Alfredsson, Göran Melander, Lars Adam Rehof and Allan Rosas (eds.), *The Universal Declaration of Human Rights: A Commentary,* Scandinavian University Press, 1992.

The book proceeds from a brief history of the writing of the Universal Declaration of Human Rights to a chapter-by-chapter exposition of each of its 30 articles. Each chapter contains a list of references. Eide, the lead editor, is director of the Norwegian Institute of Human Rights; the other editors each represent other Scandinavian countries: Iceland, Sweden, Denmark, and Finland, respectively.

Flood, Patrick James, *The Effectiveness of UN Human Rights Institutions,* Praeger, 1998.

Flood, a retired U.S. foreign service officer, provides an overview and three case studies to examine the effect that United Nations' human rights bodies have had in improving human rights conditions. The book includes chapter notes, texts of some recent U.N. resolutions or instruments and a six-page bibliography.

Forsythe, David P., *The Internationalization of Human Rights,* Lexington Books, 1991.

Forsythe, a professor of political science at the University of Nebraska, gives an overview of the growing acceptance of human rights at the international level. Each chapter includes detailed source notes; there is also a six-page list of basic research and reference sources.

Hannum, Hurst, and Dana D. Fischer (eds.), *U.S. Ratification of the International Covenants on Human Rights,* Transnational Publishers, 1993.

The book provides legal and political perspectives on the issues created by the United States' consideration of the two major human rights treaties: the international covenants on civil and political rights and economic, social and cultural rights. Hannum is a professor at the Fletcher School of Law and Diplomacy, Tufts University; Fischer is a U.S. foreign service officer.

Humphrey, John P., *Human Rights and the United Nations: A Great Adventure,* Transnational Publishers, 1984.

Humphrey, a Canadian law professor who served as the first director of the United Nations' division on human rights, provides a personal memoir of the U.N.'s human rights work in its first two decades.

Steiner, Henry J., and Philip Alston, *International Human Rights in Context: Law, Politics, Morals,* Clarendon Press, 1996.

This comprehensive law school textbook covers the theoretical and historical background of international human rights law; human rights institutions and processes; the role of nation states in protecting and enforc-

ing human rights; and some current topics, including proposals for an international criminal court. Steiner is a professor at Harvard Law School and founder of the school's human rights program; Alston is professor of international law at the European University Institute in Florence and has served as chairman of the U.N.'s Committee on Economic, Social and Cultural Rights. The book includes a six-page bibliography.

***The United Nations and Human Rights:* 1945-1995, The United Nations: Department of Public Information, 1995.**

The book traces the history of the United Nations and human rights from the drafting of the U.N. Charter and the adoption of the Universal Declaration of Human Rights through the adoption of the various international human rights treaties and the integration of human rights components in current U.N. peacekeeping efforts. The book includes a six-page chronology and texts of nearly 100 U.N. resolutions, declarations or conventions on human rights from 1945 through 1994. Texts of major human rights treaties can also be found in Ian Brownlie (ed.), *Basic Documents on Human Rights*, Clarendon Press, 1992.

Reports and Studies

Jost, Kenneth, "Religious Persecution," *The CQ Researcher,* Nov. 21, 1997, pp. 1009-1032.

The report covers issues of religious persecution around the world, focusing in particular on the campaign against alleged mistreatment of Christians.

Jost, Kenneth, "War Crimes," *The CQ Researcher,* July 7, 1995, pp. 585-608.

The report, written as the United Nations' war crimes tribunal for the former Yugoslavia was about to begin its first trial, traces the development of international law regarding war crimes and the events leading to the establishment of the two U.N. tribunals — one dealing with Bosnia, the other with Rwanda.

Articles

Frum, David, "The International Criminal Court Must Die," *The Weekly Standard,* Aug. 17, 1998, p. 27.

Frum strongly argues against creation of the proposed International Criminal Court.

Stanley, Jonathan, "Focus: International Criminal Court — A Court That Knows No Boundaries?", *The Lawyer,* Aug. 11, 1998, p. 8.

This 1,200-word article in a British legal publication analyzes the proposed international criminal court from a supportive perspective. It also provides an address for the Web site maintained by the coalition campaigning for the new court: www.igc.apc.org/icc.

The Next Step

Additional information from UMI's Newspaper & Periodical Abstracts™ database

50th Anniversary of Universal Declaration

Robinson, Mary, "Shame of Failure on Human Rights," *World Today,* February 1998, pp. 45-48.

Robinson, the U.N.'s high commissioner for human rights, argues that the record on human rights hardly gives cause for celebrating the 50th anniversary of the Universal Declaration of Human Rights. Robinson also addresses the challenge of creating a culture throughout the U.N. where human rights drive decision-making.

"The Universal Declaration of Human Rights," *Social Education,* September 1998, p. 302.

The U.N. is celebrating the 50th anniversary of the Universal Declaration of Human Rights with Human Rights in Action, a project of the U.N. CyberSchoolBus [http://www.un.org/pubs/cyberschoolbus].

U.N. Commission on Human Rights

Dennis, Michael J., "The Fifty-Third Session of the U.N. Commission on Human Rights," *American Journal of International Law,* January 1998, pp. 112-124.

The article analyzes events at the 1997 session of the U.N. Commission on Human Rights. The commission adopted 78 resolutions and 26 decisions, most by consensus.

Lehrer, Jeremy, "Mary Robinson Brings a Determined Faith to the Role of United Nations Commissioner for Human Rights," *Human Rights,* summer 1998, pp. 8-11.

The article in this American Bar Association publication profiles Robinson and presents selected quotes on such issues as the Universal Declaration of Human Rights and the death penalty in the United States.

Olson, Elizabeth, "U.N. Panel Defeats U.S. Move to Censure Cuba on Human Rights," *The New York Times,* April 23, 1998, p. A5.

A U.S.-led effort to rebuke Cuba for its human rights practices was voted down by the U.N. Human Rights Commission, 19-16 with 18 abstentions. The commission did approve, 32-0, a resolution criticizing Iraq.

Shenon, Philip, "Annual U.N. Ritual Condemning China Loses U.S. Support," *The New York Times,* March 14, 1998, p. A1.

The Clinton administration gave China an important boost by dropping U.S. sponsorship of an annual United Nations resolution condemning China's record on human rights. The move effectively kills a resolution before the U.N. Human Rights Commission.

Turner, Craig, "At Swords' Points With Repression: New U.N. Human Rights Commissioner Mary Robinson Brings Tenacity and Toughness to the Post, Already Clashing With Several Governments," *Los Angeles Times,* July 2, 1998, p. A1.

The in-depth profile by the newspaper's U.N. bureau chief says that Mary Robinson demonstrated persistence in the face of opposition throughout her 25-year political career in Ireland and now will need all that tenacity as U.N. high commissioner for human rights in seeking to reverse the U.N.'s sorry record as an advocate for civil rights and rule of law around the world.

Children's Rights

Gill, Charles D., "So-called Leaders Shortchange Children of Rights," *Detroit News,* p. C6.

The author argues that America's children are worse off today than they were 20 years ago and complains that both the White House and the advocacy group Children's Defense Fund have failed to work for U.S. ratification of the U.N. Convention on the Rights of the Child.

International Criminal Court

Karatnycky, Adrian, "Don't Worry War Criminals — The New Court Won't Work," *The Wall Street Journal,* July 27, 1998, p. A15.

The author, president of the human rights group Freedom House, argues that the proposed International Criminal Court has no chance of doing the job it is setting out to accomplish but that it could deter the United States from intervening against tyrants, aggressors and perpetrators of ethnic cleansing and other serious crimes.

Neuffer, Elizabeth, "War Crimes Tribunal Adopted as U.S. Votes 'No'," *The Boston Globe,* July 18, 1998, p. A1.

Rebuffing U.S. objections, delegates from 120 countries resoundingly approved a treaty establishing a permanent International Criminal Court. The action was hailed as a historic step toward ending impunity for the world's most heinous crimes.

Orentlicher, Diane F., "The World: U.S. Cheats Justice in Opposing World Court," *Los Angeles Times,* Aug. 30, 1998, p. M2.

The law school professor and human rights activist argues that the lopsided vote in favor of the treaty for an International Criminal Court despite the United States' opposition marked a humiliating failure for the U.S. delegation and evoked a failure of U.S. leadership in support of efforts to combat impunity in crimes against conscience.

Pear, Robert, "Officials Accused of Atrocities Losing Places to Hide, Scholars Say," *The New York Times*, Oct. 19, 1998, p. A8.

The arrest of Gen. Augusto Pinochet shows the growing significance of international human rights law, suggesting that officials accused of atrocities have fewer places to hide these days.

Stanley, Alessandra, "U.S. Specifies Terms for War Crimes Court," *The New York Times*, July 10, 1998, p. A7.

The U.S. delegation to the international conference on creating an International Criminal Court for the first time specified its position on limiting the tribunal's jurisdiction. The U.S. said it could agree to the court only if its automatic jurisdiction were limited to genocide and applied only if the suspect's country had signed the treaty creating the tribunal.

U.S. Practices

Branigin, William, "Group Criticizes INS For Detaining Minors; Human Rights Watch Says Children Lack Access to Information, Counsel," *The Washington Post*, April 10, 1997, p. A23.

A human rights group charged the Immigration and Naturalization Service with violating the rights of hundreds of detained children each year and called for the shifting of its detention functions to "appropriate child-welfare authorities." The charges, contained in a 120-page report by the Human Rights Watch Children's Rights Project, were disputed by the INS.

Goshko, John M., "U.N. Panel Calls On U.S. To Halt Death Penalty," *The Washington Post*, p. A2.

The U.N. Human Rights Commission called on the United States to adopt a moratorium on executions after receiving a report that criticized its arbitrary and discriminatory use of the death penalty. The report was written by Bacre Waly Ndiaye of Senegal, an investigator for the Geneva-based rights commission, who carried out a fact-finding mission in the United States last October that triggered considerable criticism from congressional conservatives.

Henry, Charles P., and Tunua Thrash, "U.S. Human Rights Petitions Before the U.N.," *Black Scholar*, fall 1996, pp. 60-73.

The authors contend that the United States has demonstrated a callous indifference to its own human rights abuses and has weakened the U.N.'s ability to act upon reports concerning both foreign and domestic abuses.

Massimino, Elisa, "Perspective on Human Rights: Torture in the U.S. Is Still Torture," *Los Angeles Times*, Oct. 14, 1998, p. B7.

The author notes Amnesty International's launching of a yearlong campaign aimed at addressing human rights violations in the United States, including police brutality and brutality in prisons. But she says the report misses an important opportunity to call for these acts to be prosecuted as torture — as required by the United Nations Convention Against Torture, which the United States has ratified.

"Murder and the U.N.," *The Wall Street Journal*, April 21, 1998, p. A22.

The editorial criticizes the report by a United Nations investigator that called the United States' use of capital punishment unfair and arbitrary.

War crimes

"A Massacre Without Knives," *The Washington Post*, Sept. 16, 1998, p. A16.

The editorial says that when starvation and exposure begin to claim the lives of thousands of women and children in Kosovo, no one will be able to claim ignorance as an excuse for inaction. "Massive war crimes have been committed here," John Shattuck, U.S. assistant secretary of State for human rights, said during a recent visit to the Serbian province.

Women's Rights

Okin, Susan Moller, "Feminism, Women's Human Rights, and Cultural Differences," *Hypatia*, spring 1998, pp. 32-52.

The author argues that the recent global movement for women's human rights has achieved considerable re-thinking of human rights as previously understood. Since many women's rights violations occur in the private sphere of family life and are justified by appeals to cultural or religious norms, both families and cultures (including their religious aspects) have come under critical scrutiny.

Back Issues

Great Research on Current Issues Starts Right Here.
Recent topics covered by The CQ Researcher are listed below.
Now available on the Web
For information, call (800) 432-2250 ext. 279 or (202) 887-6279.

If you would like to have any of these CQ Researchers updated, or need more information about these topics, please call CQ Custom Research. Special rates for CQ subscribers. (202) 887-8600 or (800) 432-2250, ext. 600, or E-mail Custom.Research@cq.com

AUGUST 1997
Age Discrimination
Banning Land Mines
Children's Television
Evolution vs. Creationism

SEPTEMBER 1997
Caring for the Dying
Mental Health Policy
Mexico's Future
Youth Fitness

OCTOBER 1997
Urban Sprawl in the West
Diversity in the Workplace
Teacher Education
Contingent Work Force

NOVEMBER 1997
Renewable Energy
Artificial Intelligence
Religious Persecution
Roe v. Wade at 25

DECEMBER 1997
Whistleblowers
Castro's Next Move
Gun Control Standoff
Regulating Nonprofits

JANUARY 1998
Foster Care Reform
IRS Reform
The Black Middle Class
U.S.-British Relations

FEBRUARY 1998
Patients' Rights
Deflation Fears
Caring for the Elderly
The New Corporate Philanthropy

MARCH 1998
Israel at 50
The Federal Judiciary
Drinking on Campus
The Economics of Recycling

APRIL 1998
Biology and Behavior
Liberal Arts Education
Income Inequality
High-Tech Labor Shortage

MAY 1998
Census 2000
Child-Care Options
Alzheimer's Disease
U.S.-Russian Relations

JUNE 1998
Student Journalism
Antitrust Policy
Environmental Justice
Sleep Deprivation

JULY 1998
Encouraging Teen Abstinence
Population and the Environment
Democracy in Asia
Baby Boomers at Midlife

AUGUST 1998
Oil Production in the 21st Century
Flexible Work Arrangements
Coastal Development
Student Activism

SEPTEMBER 1998
Organic Farming
Cancer Treatments
Hispanic Americans' New Clout
The Future of Baseball

OCTOBER 1998
School Violence
Social Security
National Forests
Puerto Rico's Status

NOVEMBER 1998
Internet Privacy

Back issues are available for $5.00 (subscribers) or $10.00 (non-subscribers). Quantity discounts apply to orders over 10. To order, call Congressional Quarterly Customer Service at (202) 887-8621.

Binders are available for $18.00. To order call 1-800-638-1710. Please refer to stock number 648.

Future Topics

► *Drug Testing*

► *European Monetary Union*

► *AIDS Update*

THE
CQ Researcher

PUBLISHED BY CONGRESSIONAL QUARTERLY INC.

Drug Testing

Does it deter drug abuse?

D rug testing has become a major weapon in the war on drugs. Nearly three-quarters of America's biggest companies require job applicants to undergo urinalysis — up from only 21 percent a decade ago. Proponents say drug testing protects public safety and deters drug use, but opponents say neither can be proved. Until recently, most companies only tested job applicants and public-safety employees. But now employers randomly test all employees. Some state and local governments require random testing of public employees, high school students participating in after-school activities, prisoners and welfare and student-loan recipients. Many employee groups and civil libertarians see such expanded drug testing as a dangerous erosion of Americans' constitutional right to privacy.

CQ • Nov. 20, 1998 • Volume 8, No. 43 • Pages 1001-1024

Formerly Editorial Research Reports

DRUG TESTING

CQ Researcher

Nov. 20, 1998
Volume 8, No.43

EDITOR
Sandra Stencel

MANAGING EDITOR
Thomas J. Colin

ASSOCIATE EDITOR
Sarah M. Magner

STAFF WRITERS
Adriel Bettelheim
Mary H. Cooper
Kenneth Jost
Kathy Koch
David Masci

PRODUCTION EDITOR
Debra James

EDITORIAL ASSISTANT
Laura S. Cavender

PUBLISHED BY
Congressional Quarterly Inc.

CHAIRMAN
Andrew Barnes

VICE CHAIRMAN
Andrew P. Corty

PRESIDENT AND PUBLISHER
Robert W. Merry

EXECUTIVE EDITOR
David Rapp

The CQ Researcher (ISSN 1056-2036). Formerly Editorial Research Reports. Published weekly, except Jan. 2, May 29, July 3, Oct. 30, by Congressional Quarterly Inc., 1414 22nd St., N.W., Washington, D.C. 20037. Annual subscription rate for libraries, businesses and government is $340. Additional rates furnished upon request. Periodicals postage paid at Washington, D.C., and additional mailing offices. POSTMASTER: Send address changes to The CQ Researcher, 1414 22nd St., N.W., Washington, D.C. 20037.

COVER: OLYMPIC SNOWBOARDER ROSS REBAGLIATI LOST HIS GOLD MEDAL AFTER TESTING POSITIVE FOR MARIJUANA, BUT IT WAS REINSTATED AFTER HE CLAIMED SECONDHAND SMOKE CAUSED A FALSE-POSITIVE TEST READING. (AP PHOTO)

Drug Testing

BY KATHY KOCH

THE ISSUES

For Julie Izard, just married and looking for part-time work, organizing social activities at her apartment complex in Alexandria, Va., sounded perfect. Since the pay was minimal and the job only involved a few evenings a week, she viewed it almost as a volunteer position.

So she was surprised when she was sent to a nearby laboratory for a drug test. "I thought it was kind of funny," Izard says, since it wasn't a high-security job and she wouldn't be in charge of people's safety.

Drug testing has become a prime weapon in the nation's war on drugs, and more and more typical citizens like Izard — not just drivers, pilots, train operators and high-security government employees — are being asked to provide urine samples.

Nearly three-quarters of America's biggest companies hand job applicants a plastic cup as part of the recruiting process. A decade ago, only 21 percent of U.S. companies drug-tested recruits.

Most companies only test job applicants. Others screen both applicants and "safety-sensitive" employees — such as those who operate machinery. Still others test any employees who appear to be using drugs.

Increasingly, however, employers are requiring random testing of all employees — raising the hackles of some employees, unions and civil libertarians.

Momentum for the exponential growth in drug testing has come from several sources:

• The federal government — Transportation and Defense Department rules require drug testing for certain safety-sensitive jobs in both the public and private sectors; and the 1988 Drug-Free Workplace Act requires federal contractors or grant recipients to maintain drug-free workplaces.

• Courts — A series of decisions recognizes private employers' right

to test employees and applicants.

• Insurance companies — Insurers favor testing as a means of reducing accident liability and controlling health-care costs.

• Testing laboratories — Laboratories aggressively market their testing services to companies, schools and government agencies.

But clearly, much of the momentum for drug testing has come from Congress. "Over the past 15 years, Congress has passed laws requiring workplace drug testing of more than a tenth of the work force, or about 12 million individuals," says J. Michael Walsh, who designed the federal employee drug-testing regime.

Yet the same Congress has refused to undergo drug testing itself. Judges and political candidates are also exempt from mandatory drug testing, the courts have said (see p. 1016).

Meanwhile, federal, state and local governments are widening their drug-testing net to cover even more citizens. Besides government employees, drug tests are now given to welfare mothers, prisoners, college-loan recipients and, sometimes, students wanting to join school clubs. And at the urging of President Clinton, Congress and some states are considering requiring all teenagers applying for a driver's license to be tested.

Some experts predict that eventually anyone receiving public money of any sort will have to be tested. Louisiana already requires random drug testing of anyone who receives anything of economic value from the

state — and those who balk can lose their job, license, loan, scholarship, contract or public assistance.

Local school boards also are expanding drug testing. For years, middle- and high-school athletes have undergone testing. [1] Now some school districts are requiring anyone participating in extracurricular activities to be tested. A few districts test any student who parks a car on school property. A handful of private schools have tested their entire student bodies, something public schools so far have been prohibited by the Constitution from doing, although at least two Texas school districts are toying with the idea.

Perhaps nowhere are the "bladder cops" — as some critics call drug testers — more prevalent than in the scandal-plagued sports world. (*See story, p. 1012.*)

Civil libertarians and privacy advocates complain that the ever-widening drug-testing net dangerously erodes Americans' constitutional rights. While polls show most people agree that testing workers in safety-sensitive positions is appropriate, the trend toward testing new groups is "an evisceration of the Fourth Amendment in the name of the drug war," says Ethan Nadelmann, director of the Lindesmith Center, a drug-policy think tank.

Other critics call drug testing "chemical McCarthyism" because an improperly administered test could yield a false-positive result from the use of legitimate prescription drugs or even eating a poppy-seed bagel. Innocent job seekers or employees can lose their jobs. Sixty percent of companies fire an employee who tests positive for drugs; only 23 percent retain them, referring them for drug treatment.

If fired for a positive drug test, an employee usually cannot collect unemployment insurance. And employees who are injured on the job and test positive after the accident will probably be fired and become

Marijuana Was Most Frequently Detected

More than half of the employees who tested positive for drugs in 1997 had used marijuana.

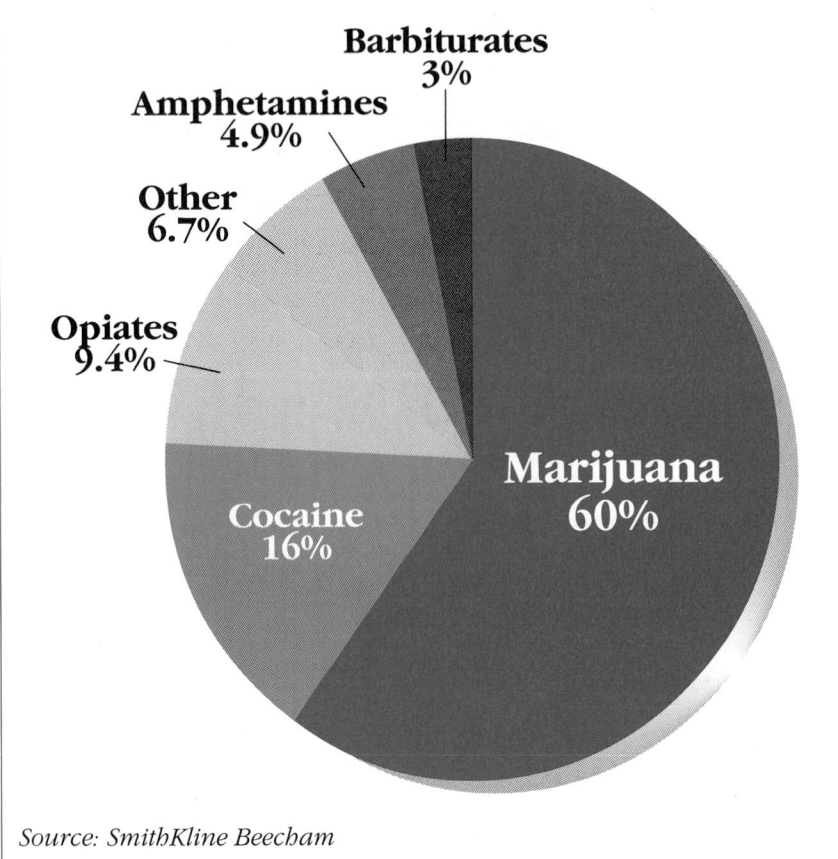

Barbiturates 3%

Amphetamines 4.9%

Other 6.7%

Opiates 9.4%

Cocaine 16%

Marijuana 60%

Source: SmithKline Beecham

ineligible for health benefits, workers' compensation or unemployment insurance.

Critics complain workplace drug testing gives employers unprecedented police power over what employees do during off-duty hours and unfairly targets those who use marijuana, which can remain in the system weeks longer than other "hard" drugs.

Proponents, however, say the magnitude of the nation's drug-abuse problem, and the cost of drug abuse to society — in lost productivity, workplace accidents, tardiness, absenteeism, workplace theft and in-

creased health-care costs — justifies testing, even if it infringes on individual privacy rights. [2]

"This problem is bleeding America," says Mark de Bernardo, executive director of the Institute for a Drug-Free Workplace, a coalition of businesses, business organizations and individuals. "The United States is the world's leader in substance abuse. We have 6 percent of the world's population, but we engage in 60 percent of the world's illicit drug use."

Last year, 13.9 million Americans — 6.4 percent of the population — used illicit drugs on a regular basis, a 10 percent increase from the 1992

record low of 5.8 percent. But the current rate is about half the 25 million who used illicit drugs in 1979, when drug use in America reached its peak and began declining, a decade before drug testing came into vogue.

Drug-testing advocates argue that because 74 percent of illicit drug users are employed, the workplace is an excellent place to catch them. "Employers have the most effective weapon in the war on drugs," de Bernardo says. "If your job is contingent on your being drug-free, it creates a powerful incentive for you to get off and stay off drugs.

Moreover, de Bernardo says, "Once an employer has a drug-testing policy, fewer drug abusers apply, and some [abusing] employees voluntarily leave."

Many abusers then seek work in small companies, he says, because only 3 percent of small firms — which employ half the nation's work force — have drug-testing programs. But twice as many employees in small firms use illegal drugs as in large firms.

To close the small-business "escape hatch," Congress last month appropriated $10 million for the Drug-Free Workplace Act of 1998 to encourage small companies to establish testing programs.

Polls show employees generally accept drug testing as a necessary evil, although there are still those who chafe at what they see as an unwarranted invasion of their privacy. Employees have filed dozens of court suits in the last 15 years, along with a handful of students, even though most students and parents favor drug testing because it gives students an excuse to resist peer pressure to use drugs. (*See story, p. 1006.*)

These are some of the questions being asked by those debating this issue:

Does drug testing deter drug use?

"There are lots of books and research to show that drug testing deters drug use," de Bernardo says. "Individual companies have seen dramatic decreases in positive drug-test rates."

He is quick to add that drug testing alone isn't a deterrent. It must be accompanied by a comprehensive substance-abuse prevention program that includes four other components: a written anti-drug policy, an anti-drug education program, rigorous enforcement and a treatment program for addicted employees.

Drug-testing proponents often cite a 1988 U.S. Navy study showing that drug use among enlisted men went down from 48 percent in 1980 to 5 percent in 1988 after a comprehensive substance-abuse prevention program with random drug testing was instituted. [3]

Indeed, a 1987 Navy personnel survey showed 83 percent considered random testing the Navy's strongest deterrent to drug abuse. "Significantly, 27 percent also said that they would resume their use of illicit drugs if the Navy discontinued its drug-testing program," according to the Institute for a Drug-Free Workplace. [4]

Another study showed a 50 percent drop in positive drug tests — from 22.9 percent to 11.6 percent — at the Southern Pacific Railroad after a year of "reasonable-suspicion" drug testing. [5]

Walsh says drug testing "keeps mainstream working folks from casual recreational use."

Workplace drug testing will deter drug use among those recreation users, most of whom are employed suburbanites, said Rep. Gerald B.H. Solomon, R-N.Y., as he argued for the bill to encourage small businesses to start drug testing. "If we were to solve that problem," he said, it would eliminate U.S. demand for drugs, "and in Colombia they would be making bathtubs instead of [exporting] drugs into this country."

Proponents also point to American Management Association (AMA) statistics showing the percentage of

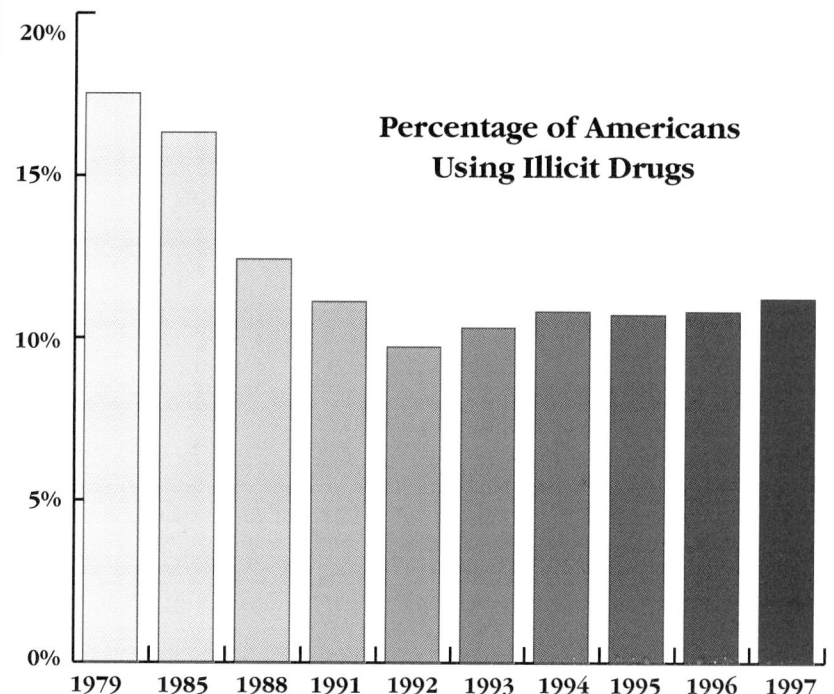

Americans' Drug Use Is Rising

Americans' drug use has been rising since 1992, but it was still 35 percent less in 1997 than it was in 1979, when U.S. drug use reached an all-time high.

Percentage of Americans Using Illicit Drugs

Source: Department of Health and Human Services, "National Household Survey on Drug Abuse," 1997

employees testing positive for drugs declined from 8.1 percent in 1989 to 1.9 percent in 1995. [6]

But Eric Greenberg, AMA's director of management studies, says the declining figures do not prove drug use is actually declining. That's because employers have been expanding the total pool of persons tested to include all employees, not just those suspected of drug use. If you test more employees who show no obvious signs of drug use, "Naturally, the test-positive ratios will go down," he says.

"When companies didn't expand the pool of employees covered, the percentages stayed the same," he says. "This is why I say those statis-

tics do not show that drug testing is a deterrent."

Lewis Maltby, director of the Office of Workplace Rights at the American Civil Liberties Union (ACLU), which opposes random drug testing, agrees. "When you go from suspicion-based testing to random testing, the number of hits are going to go down," he says.

Maltby argues that anti-drug education programs may be more of a deterrent. Companies that combine drug testing with education programs consistently have lower test-positive ratios than firms that rely solely on testing.

But some companies are cutting both their drug-education and supervisor-training programs, which teach

They Decided to Fight the System . . .

Hollister Gardner is hardly a rebellious teenager. He maintained an "A" average while serving as president of the National Honor Society, drum major in the band and treasurer of Future Farmers of America (FFA) at his West Texas high school.

But Gardner rebelled last year when he was told that he would have to pass a drug test to keep participating in such extracurricular activities.

Having never been involved in drugs, he chafed at the implication that he was guilty unless proven innocent. He believes the Fourth Amendment of the Bill of Rights protects U.S. citizens from such warrantless searches without "reasonable suspicion" that someone is guilty.

So he never signed the consent form. His 12-year-old sister, Sarah, and his 13-year-old cousin Molly also refused to sign theirs.

When the school notified Hollister that he could no longer attend after-school activities, he sued the Tulia Independent School District board, whose members include his father, Gary, the only board member who opposed drug testing when it was instituted. Representing himself in federal court, Hollister argued the board's drug-testing policy is unconstitutional.

"The school district can't test just because they feel like testing," he said. "People fought and died for these rights, and they are not to be given up to the Tulia School Board just because they think they can take them from you." [1]

The elder Gardner agreed with his son's decision. "To my eyes, it's almost a duty," he says. "It was something he just had to do." No trial date has been set in the case, which is pending in Amarillo's federal court.

The school district contends its policy is legal because in 1995 the U.S. Supreme Court upheld the Veronia, Ore., school district's policy of randomly testing all high school athletes. In that case, the court said random, suspicionless drug tests were justified because the drug crisis in the Veronia district had reached "epidemic proportions."

Gardner, now a sophomore at Angelo State University, says the drug problem in rural Tulia was not severe enough to justify warrantless searches. "I don't use drugs," he told

a newspaper reporter at the time, "and no one I know in my organizations uses them." [2]

Tulia School Superintendent Mike Vinyard says the school board instituted drug testing after a 1994 survey showed 27 percent of students in grades 7-12 had used drugs at least once, and 10 percent said they had used marijuana prior to the survey. Six percent of junior high kids said they had smoked marijuana before class.

Although the survey showed Tulia's drug use was below the state average, Vinyard says, "We think any drug use is serious." He said "about a dozen students" have tested positive since the program began in January 1997.

Most parents like the policy, he says, because fear of random testing gives students an excuse to resist peer pressure to use drugs. "The Gardner family is really the only critic of the program," Vinyard says. "Most parents would like to randomly test all students rather than only those in extracurricular activities."

Hollister Gardner

At least two other Texas school districts apparently feel the same way. The Texas Association of School Boards has reviewed at least two proposals from school districts wanting to require all students to be randomly drug tested. Shellie Hoffman, the association's director of legal services, would not reveal the names of the districts.

If adopted, they would become the first public school districts in the country to test all students. The policy would undoubtedly be challenged legally, says Jim Harrington, director of the nonprofit Texas Civil Rights Project. "The Supreme Court has made it very clear that drug testing can only be applied in certain cases, such as where there is a pervasive drug culture, violence or physical danger for athletes, or where students are considered role models," he says.

Hollister says that while parents may favor drug testing, many students supported him. "I had quite a few people come up to me and thank me for sticking up for their rights," he says.

But standing up for one's rights is costly, he says. Not unexpectedly, he and his family have paid emotionally,

managers to spot drug abuse — a policy that could prove "penny-wise but pound-foolish," Maltby says. Only 6 percent of surveyed companies rely only on drug testing, says

the AMA report.

Drug-testing opponents say there are no peer-reviewed, scientific studies to show that drug testing deters drug use. "The decline in drug use in

this country began in 1979," says Maltby. "Nobody was doing drug testing in 1979."

"The era of drug testing began in 1985-1986, yet since 1991, drug use

... When Ordered to Take Drug Tests

academically and financially for their stand. "I warned him if he refused to sign, he would get more flak than he ever thought about, and that they might not even let him graduate," remembers Hollister's father.

Hollister was not allowed to show his pig at the agricultural fair with other members of his FFA group, and his sister Sarah was told she could not play in the band. The school later allowed protesting students to stay in after-school activities until the case is settled.

The family also paid about $6,000 for transportation, court fees and administrative costs, says Gary Gardner, who calls himself "just a small dirt farmer." The costs were especially burdensome because of the huge losses Texas farmers suffered due to bad weather this year. "Any other year it wouldn't have been so bad," he says.

Hollister has even greater respect for the Constitution now. "Our family has always understood what the Constitution meant," he says. "Now I've really developed a love for it."

A lifelong love for the Constitution also led Georgia history teacher Sherry Hearn to stand up against drug testing. And she, too, has paid a high price.

Three years away from retirement, the award-winning Savannah, Ga., high school teacher lost her job — and nearly lost her pension — when she refused to take a drug test on demand.

For 27 years Hearn, who was her county's Teacher of the Year in 1994, had taught her American history students that the Fourth Amendment protects citizens against unreasonable searches and seizures by police. Not surprisingly, she had been an outspoken critic of her district's policy of allowing "lockdowns," or periodic, unannounced, schoolwide searches — using drug-sniffing dogs — to ferret out illegal guns or drugs. Many school districts, including 400 in Texas alone, use drug-sniffing dogs to search school grounds.

During the two-hour lockdowns in Savannah, students and teachers must stand in the hallways, while dogs search each room, bookbag and purse, and students are scanned with metal detectors.

Hearn maintains such searches without specific information that someone may possess drugs or weapons are an invasion of constitutional rights and a dreadful message to be sending students. She had opposed the tactics at faculty meetings, to her principal, the school board and to police officers who conducted the lockdowns.

Then during a lockdown on April 4, 1996, police say they found a partially smoked marijuana cigarette in Hearn's car. But police refused to show her the evidence, claiming it had been accidentally destroyed. Hearn refused to submit to a drug test without first seeing her lawyer, especially since the officers had searched her car without her permission, in clear violation of the school's written policy.

School board officials claim Hearn was fired for insubordination. She claims she was targeted by police because she had objected to the lockdowns.

No action was taken against the officers who searched her car without permission. And the school board never investigated a tip police received giving them the initials of a student who had bragged to classmates that he had "planted" the marijuana in Hearn's car.

"The board feels very strongly about its drug-free workplace policy, and we feel equally strongly that we can't pick and choose who gets to follow the rules," Chatham County School Board President Karen Matthews told The Associated Press. [3] Hearn's case is pending before the U.S. District Court in Atlanta.

Since she was fired, Hearn has been unable to find a full-time job at any Georgia public school. She believes she was blackballed for standing up for her rights. "How else would you explain someone with my qualifications not being able to find a job, when we have a teacher shortage in Georgia?" she asks.

She finally was hired at a juvenile detention center, and is enrolled again in the state's pension program.

Knowing how much standing up for her rights has cost her, if she had to do it over again would she take the test? She hopes not. "It would endanger my credibility with my students, which I spent 27 years building up."

More important, she says, "I would be voluntarily surrendering my rights. Anytime you accept any sort of violation — no matter how minor — of your basic liberties there are those who will take increasing liberties. Eventually, you won't have any left."

---

[1] Allan Turner, "Defending his rights; Student risking all to oppose drug testing," *The Houston Chronicle*, Feb. 2, 1997.

[2] *Ibid.*

[3] John Cheves, "Fired Chatham teacher sues," *Florida Times-Union*, April 17, 1997.

---

among teenagers has been going up," points out Allen St. Pierre, executive director of the NORML Foundation, which wants to legalize marijuana.

Critics like St. Pierre claim the statistics used to "prove" that testing deters drug abuse are "twisted and manipulated" by proponents, many of whom are connected to the testing industry.

"It's really hard to prove that drug testing is a deterrent in itself," says William Sonnenstuhl, professor of industrial labor relations at Cornell University. "If you look at the railroad industry, the first industry in which drug testing was implemented, they were not successful until the unions started educating their members to stop drinking and covering up for members who used alcohol or drugs on the job."

"I don't think drug testing deters anyone, except for the novices," Sonnenstuhl continues. "Skillful drug users know how to beat the tests. It just becomes a game they have to play."

In 1994, the National Academy of Sciences (NAS) reviewed all of the literature on drug testing and found "no conclusive scientific evidence from properly controlled studies that employment drug-testing programs widely discourage drug use or encourage rehabilitation." [7]

Drug-testing opponents say that rather than testing teenagers for drug abuse, it is cheaper to teach them how to say no to drugs.

"There are lots of peer-pressure resistance classes available to schools," says Jim Harrington, director of the Texas Civil Rights Project. "And they are much cheaper than drug testing."

Proponents say the "tough love" zero-tolerance approach encourages abusers to get treatment.

But skeptics point out that when an applicant fails a drug test, 98 percent of large employers reject his application, and 63 percent fire existing employees who test positive, rather than referring them to a company-supported drug rehab program. [8] Those fired workers are then usually ineligible for unemployment or health benefits, as well as workers' compensation if they were injured on the job before testing positive. Thus, say critics, most can't afford to join a drug-treatment program.

The "dumping" of drug abusers back into the community, unemployed and without benefits, "encourages their entry into illegal economies," says Paul M. Roman, research professor of sociology and director of the Center for Research on Deviance and Behavioral Health at the University of Georgia.

Workplace testing also misses those most seriously addicted to drugs who are usually unemployed, say critics. Other argue that some drug abusers merely substitute alcohol or harder drugs, such as heroin or cocaine, that are more difficult to detect through urinalysis because they only stay in the body for a few hours.

Nadelmann says, "If you want to get bombed on Saturday night now, and you need to be 'clean' on Monday morning, instead of smoking a joint, which will stay in your system longer, you'll switch to cocaine or heroin."

Does drug testing protect worker and public safety?

Proponents say companies with drug-testing policies have safer workplaces, better overall job performance, reduced liability for accidents and injuries and reduced medical and insurance costs.

"Without question, substance abusers account for higher rates of accidents in the workplace," says de Bernardo. "Lots and lots of studies link illicit drug use to impairment, and impairment to safety and health concerns."

"No one doubts that employers with effective substance-abuse policies have fewer workplace accidents," said Thomas J. Donohue, president of the U.S. Chamber of Commerce. As a result they have fewer workers'-compensation claims. Several states, he said, now offer employers who have such programs discounted rates on insurance premiums. [9]

In addition, "Employers consistently report reduced rates of employee violence and crime" after implementing a comprehensive substance-abuse policy, Donohue added.

Dan Wurzburg, corporate safety director for Sordoni Skanska construction-management firm in Parsippany,

N.J., said, "In the construction industry, having a drug-free workplace program means that the company can absolutely be assured that it will have a better safety record, and fewer accidents mean lower costs and lower insurance premiums."

According to data in the recent bill to encourage small businesses to set up workplace drug-testing programs, accidents involving drug users are 300-400 percent higher than among non-users.

In the Southern Pacific Railroad study, personal injuries and accidents dropped dramatically after drug testing was implemented. Personal injuries, for instance, dropped from 2,234 in 1983 to 322 in the first six months of 1988. Train accidents caused by human error decreased from 911 to 54 during the same period. [10]

But opponents question the statistics used by advocates to show that drug abusers cause more workplace accidents. For instance, the claim that 47 percent of workplace accidents are caused by drug abusers — used by Congress in October to justify spending $10 million to encourage workplace drug testing in small companies — "is absurd on the face of it," Sonnenstuhl says. "Such statistics are based on a series of assumptions "inferring causation where what has been shown is only correlation."

Workplace accident reports show that most accidents result from "a series of management or supervisory decisions that create or tolerate unsafe work environments, equipment and practices," Sonnenstuhl says.

"To blame drug users is to shift focus and remedial efforts from a strategy that has been proven successful [ie., reducing hazards and educating workers about workplace safety] to one of dubious assumptions, merits and promise," sociologist Staudenmeier says.

Sonnenstuhl says drug testing is being sold to employers and employees as a question of job safety. But

Experts Question Hair Testing

New drug-testing techniques being introduced are considered less invasive than urinalysis and almost impossible to "beat." Hair testing, for instance, can detect drug use as far back as three months. By comparison, urinalysis only detects heroin and cocaine within hours or days of use, and marijuana for up to 70 days.

Not surprisingly, some of the new techniques raise thorny questions about accuracy, privacy and the purpose of drug testing.

Ethan Nadelmann, director of the Lindesmith Center, a drug-policy think tank, argues that testing hair, sweat and saliva is more — not less — invasive because it delves more deeply into one's past history. And because hair and saliva contain DNA, they reveal information about medical conditions and genetic makeup that some employees may not want to reveal to their bosses.

"Hair testing opens the door to genetic testing by employers," says Lewis Maltby, director of the Office of Workplace Rights at the American Civil Liberties Union (ACLU), noting that companies could refuse to hire someone based on inherited medical conditions, which the applicant may not even know about. Although hair testers claim they wouldn't look at DNA, the procedure stirs controversy on several other fronts.

In hair testing, a snippet of hair from the back of the neck (or the armpit of a bald person) is tested for drug residues. The developer of the technique, Boston-based Psychemedics Corp., says it detects four times more drug users than urinalysis.

Florida entrepreneur H. Wayne Huizenga, founder of Blockbuster Entertainment and Waste Management Inc. and owner of the Miami Dolphins, is a major stockholder in Psychemedics and helped raise the company out of debt in 1989. With Blockbuster and Waste Management as major clients, the firm has grown to more than 1,400 clients today, including General Motors and The Sports Authority.

"Hair testing will continue to grow dramatically," says company General Counsel William Thistle. "It's inevitable once companies see the advantages."

Sales have more than doubled in the last five years, as more firms adopted the process. Several police departments have signed on as well, including New York City and Chicago. At least 40 private schools have begun testing students' hair, among them De la Salle High School in New Orleans, which randomly tests its entire 860-member student body.

(Public schools are generally thought to be prohibited by the Fourth Amendment from testing entire student bodies.)

Psychemedics has lobbied Congress to require the Health and Human Services Department (HHS) to adopt hair testing for all federal employees, but so far the agency has resisted.

"We in the federal government are not confident of it at this time," says Donna Bush, chief of drug testing for the Substance Abuse and Mental Health Services Administration (SAMHSA).

The National Institute on Drug Abuse, the Food and Drug Administration, the College of American Pathologists and the Society of Forensic Toxicologists are all concerned that hair testing may be unfairly biased against persons with coarse black hair, such as African-Americans, Asians or Hispanics. Some tests have shown that coarse hair shows much higher concentrations of drugs than lighter hair after ingestion of the same amount of drugs.

"There is no study, any time, any place, anywhere, that shows that Psychemedics' testing procedures have a racial bias," Thistle says. "I've been involved in hair testing since 1989, and at no time has there been a racial-discrimination lawsuit on the grounds that hair testing is racially biased."

Other scientists claim hair testing doesn't differentiate between drugs absorbed into the hair from environmental contamination, such as being at a concert where marijuana is smoked.

For these reasons, the ACLU strongly opposes hair testing. "Every reputable scientific organization in America rejects the use of hair testing for employment purposes," Maltby says.

Thistle says the ACLU should favor hair testing because it is not biased against marijuana users like urine testing. "With a urine test, the chances of finding a marijuana user are greater than finding a cocaine or heroin user," he says. "With hair testing, all drug users are uniformly caught."

Further, he says, the company's special decontamination procedure, which includes washing hair samples in various solutions for nearly two hours before conducting the tests, eliminates contamination due to passive absorption.

While Psychemedics' decontamination procedures may be carefully performed, critics say no one knows whether other hair testing labs are being as careful, because hair testing is unregulated. There are no national standards for hair analysis as there are for urinalysis.

John Baenziger, special commissioner of toxicology at the College of American Pathologists, says his group does not support hair testing yet because it is "not being done uniformly" and the procedures being used in labs "are not being looked at in a critical fashion."

more and more, all employees are being tested, including clerks and receptionists. As a result, "drug testing becomes just a moral cover for 'You shouldn't be using drugs.' "

Critics argue vociferously that drug testing does not test one's current fitness for duty, especially in the case of marijuana, which can show up in the urine for up to 70 days after consumption, long after the effects of the drug have worn off. Meanwhile, other drugs and alcohol are washed out of the system within a few hours, they point out. And cocaine doesn't show up immediately after being ingested.

Because of these discrepancies, "Most people who fail tests are totally sober, and most who are stoned pass," Maltby says.

"We've got reams and reams from the government itself that show urinalysis doesn't test impairment," St. Pierre says. "All the testimony before Congress has said that having marijuana metabolites in your urine does not prove impairment."

"So drug testing is not done to protect the public health, it is mainly done for the symbolism," he says. "Logic has totally been thrown out the door, as it has for most of this war on drugs."

If companies really wanted to protect workplace safety, they would go after alcohol use, say critics. "The biggest problem regarding workplace safety, bar none, is alcohol," St. Pierre says. Most urinalysis does not check for alcohol levels.

"Alcohol is an enormous problem," de Bernardo acknowledges. "Any employer who addresses drug abuse and not alcohol is foolish."

Critics of drug testing often favor impairment testing as the best way to protect public safety. "There are better ways to protect the public safety than to invade somebody's privacy," Maltby says. "It is absolutely clear that impairment testing protects the public safety better than urine testing."

Impairment testing, also called performance testing, involves using computerized video programs to test eye-hand coordination by requiring the employee to use a "joy stick" to keep a cursor in the middle of a screen. An employee takes several practice tests to establish his "baseline" capability, and then is tested randomly — or daily for those with safety-sensitive positions — to see whether he is impaired.

Yet, Donna Bush, chief of drug

testing for SAMHSA, says, "At this time we've not seen evidence in the peer-reviewed scientific literature that impairment testing works." "Performance testing is easily manipulated," says de Bernardo.

Walsh agrees. "There's not much data to show that it really works. And there's no data at all to show that it would detect drug use. If I'm an illicit drug user, I would have every incentive not to do well on the baseline."

Walsh and de Bernardo say such tests do not detect illegal drug use because they do not differentiate as to whether someone is impaired because he has been using drugs or he is merely fatigued because he was up all night with a sick child.

"Performance testing doesn't determine whether someone is engaged in illegal behavior," says de Bernardo. "It protects people's jobs who don't deserve that protection."

For that reason, urinalysis advocates also do not favor another method being used by police officers in some states to test driver impairment. They use new devices shaped like binoculars, which test the reactions of the pupils to flashes of light. "It shows if you are under the influence of something," says Maltby, but it doesn't determine whether it's alcohol or illegal drugs. ∎

BACKGROUND

War on Drugs

In 1971, President Richard M. Nixon declared the nation's first "war on drugs." But drug use continued, especially among youths, until it peaked in 1979.

By then, drugs like marijuana and cocaine had become socially acceptable in many quarters. For instance, in 1979, 19 percent of Americans 18-25 had used cocaine in the preceding 12 months, according to the National Institute on Drug Abuse. [11] As marijuana became regarded as a "soft drug" like alcohol and tobacco, 11 states decriminalized possession of small amounts, one legalized it and 29 others made possession of small amounts a misdemeanor, writes Beverly Potter, co-author of *Drug Testing at Work*. In 1977, President Jimmy Carter even called for decriminalization of marijuana possession.

In 1978-79, as drug use was reaching its peak in America, an anti-drug backlash developed, led by the "parents movement," which later became the Atlanta-based anti-drug group National Families in Action. In 1980-81, the military vowed to clean up its ranks and began random, suspicionless drug testing.

By 1982, President Ronald Reagan had declared a second "war on drugs," and drug testing outside the military came into vogue. In 1986, the president and his senior advisers submitted urine samples to be screened for the presence of illegal drugs. The symbolic gesture was designed to encourage private employers to test their workers, and to reduce employee opposition to testing.

Sociologist Staudenmeier calls Reagan's push for private employers to do drug testing "privatized social control." The Fourth Amendment prohibits the government from requiring the general population to provide urine samples, he points out. "We find the president of the United States appealing to employers to use their power to accomplish what the state cannot: widespread urine testing of American citizens," he wrote. [12]

But there was scant public outcry as companies increasingly began asking

Continued on p. 1013

Chronology

1960s *Marijuana, hallucinogens and other drugs become widespread among middle-class youth during the counterculture revolution. Drug use becomes rampant among Vietnam soldiers.*

1968
Mandatory drug testing in the military begins as addicted Vietnam vets begin returning home.

1970s *Marijuana and cocaine become socially acceptable in many quarters, even as the country launches its first "war on drugs."*

1971
President Richard M. Nixon declares the first "war on drugs."

Aug. 3, 1977
President Jimmy Carter calls for decriminalization of marijuana possession.

1979
Drug use peaks. Eleven states decriminalize possession of small amounts of "pot," one legalizes it and 29 others make possession a misdemeanor. Anti-drug backlash develops, led by the "parents movement."

1980s *Cocaine becomes the drug of choice among urban professionals. Crack cocaine, a highly addictive form of cocaine, causes skyrocketing crime rates. Only 5 percent of high-* school seniors smoke marijuana daily, compared with 10 percent in 1978.

1982
President Ronald Reagan declares a second "war on drugs."

July 1985
Arkansas court rules that "the excessive intrusive nature" of drug testing student athletes without reasonable suspicion is not justified by its need.

1986
In a symbolic gesture, Reagan and his senior advisers submit urine samples to be screened for the presence of illegal drugs. In September Reagan issues Executive Order 12564, calling for a "drug-free workplace" in all federal agencies.

November 1988
Congress passes Drug-Free Workplace Act, requiring federal contractors or grant recipients to maintain drug-free workplaces. Many employers set up voluntary testing programs. Employees begin suing, claiming drug testing is a violation of individual privacy rights. Courts allow suspicionless drug testing.

1989
President George Bush unveils his National Drug Control Strategy, encouraging comprehensive drug-free workplace policies in the private sector and in state and local government. In *National Treasury Employees Union v. Von Raab* decision, Supreme Court upholds random drug testing when a "special need" outweighs individual privacy rights.

1990s *President Bush expands the federal drug-testing program to include all White House personnel. Clinton expands the Reagan-Bush drug- testing policies. Drug use increases.*

1991
Congress passes the Omnibus Transportation and Employment Testing Act, extending drug and alcohol testing to 8 million private-sector pilots, drivers and equipment operators.

1992
Drug use begins increasing. Clinton is elected president.

1995
In *Veronia School District v. Acton*, the Supreme Court rules that random urinalysis of high school athletes is justified because the drug crisis in the school district has reached "epidemic proportions."

1996
Marijuana arrests are up 80 percent, mostly for possession. Teenage drug use becomes a hot campaign issue. Just before the election, Clinton proposes mandatory drug tests for all teens seeking driver's licenses.

1998
In June Congress rescinds federal student loans to any student convicted of a drug charge. In August Congress refuses to order tests for members of Congress and their staffs. In October the Supreme Court lets stand a rural Indiana high school's policy of testing all students in extracurricular activities and passes the Drug-Free Workplace Act of 1998.

Athletes vs. Drug Testers

Athletes have long been subjected to drug testing for performance-enhancing drugs, which are often dangerous to an athlete's long-term health and give users an unfair advantage over athletes that don't use them. [1]

But the use of banned performance-enhancing drugs appears to be on the rise, despite stepped-up testing. Athletic drug testing has become a constant cat-and-mouse game, as athletes continually try to outsmart the drug testers, and the laboratories keep improving their detection technology.

This year several drug-testing scandals have rocked the sports world, including:

• In July the top team in the prestigious Tour de France bicycle race was disqualified amid news that some cyclists were using the banned synthetic hormone EPO. The hormone, which increases the red blood cell count, gives athletes greater endurance by putting extra oxygen into the blood. But it is extremely dangerous and has been blamed for dozens of athletes' deaths.

• Irish swimmer Michelle de Bruin was banned for four years from swimming competitions after manipulating a test sample.

• Chinese swimmer Yuan Yuan was arrested at Sydney airport on her way to the World Swimming Championships in Perth. She was carrying 13 vials of human growth hormone, which her coach later said were his. He was suspended for 15 years.

• In February Canadian snowboarder Ross Rebagliati's Olympic gold medal was taken away after he tested positive for marijuana; it was returned after he appealed, claiming it was due to secondhand smoke.

Closer to home, controversy swirled around Mark McGwire, the record-breaking St. Louis Cardinals slugger who broke Roger Maris' single-season home-run record on Sept. 27. McGwire was using the controversial performance enhancer androstenedione, a testosterone-boosting precursor to anabolic steroids developed by East Germany's state-sponsored athletic drug program in the 1970s.

"Andro" rapidly elevates testosterone levels, producing a temporary energy surge described by East German swimmer Raik Hannemann as a "volcanic eruption." [2] It is sold in U.S. health food stores as a nutritional supplement.

Because andro is allowed in Major League Baseball (MLB), McGwire was cheered on to victory while taking the drug. But Olympic shotputter Randy Barnes was banned for life by the International Amateur Athletic Federation (IAAF) in July after he tested positive for the same substance, which some scientists say is extremely dangerous.

Because experts disagree over whether androstenedione should be considered an anabolic steroid and thus be banned because it is available only by prescription, sports organizations treat it differently. The IAAF, the International Olympic Committee (IOC), the National Football League and the National Collegiate Athletic Association have all banned it.

But MLB and the National Basketball Association have not, and the National Hockey League prohibits only illegal drugs. [3]

Such dramatic inconsistencies in athletic drug testing have led many to call for reform of international drug-testing laws so they are clear, consistent and enforceable.

Complicating the situation was the U.S. government's loosening of laws governing food supplements in 1994, which allowed products like androstenedione to be marketed in the U.S. as a food. Such products were not available over-the-counter under old Food and Drug Administration rules. Now, foreign athletes come to the United States shopping for banned performance-enhancers.

Other supplements, like the muscle-building amino acid creatine, are now widely used by high school and professional athletes alike. Creatine hit the headlines last summer, when both McGwire and his closest home run competitor, Sammy Sosa of the Chicago Cubs, admitted using it. Creatine is considered safe, but the long-term effects are unknown.

With new "natural" performance drugs and masking agents constantly being developed, drug testers have difficulty figuring out how to detect the new substances, and deciding whether they should be legal.

"In today's world, athletes who are determined to cheat know that natural substances are the way to go," said Don Catlin, a professor of medicine and pharmacology at the University of California at Los Angeles and a member of the IOC medical commission. The new substances, including androstenedione, are popular with athletes because they are currently undetectable through testing, and so new that many leagues have not formed policies about their use, he said. [4]

The IOC has called for establishment of an independent international agency to coordinate drug testing for Olympic athletes. The proposal will be discussed at a sports drug summit in February in Lausanne, Switzerland.

The Association of Professional Team Physicians recently called on MLB to ban androstenedione. Even if it does, there will probably be other questionable supplements on the market soon.

"There's a whole cornucopia of other things right behind it," said Catlin. "That's where things are going." [5]

---

[1] See Richard L. Worsnop, "Athletes and Drugs," *The CQ Researcher*, July 26, 1991, pp. 513-536.

[2] Quoted in Scott M. Reid, "Special Report: Slugger's drug widely banned," *The Denver Post*, Aug. 25, 1998

[3] Under federal law, anabolic steroids are a controlled substance, available only by prescription.

[4] Kirk Johnson, "Mac's use of drug raises issues beyond sports," *The* (Charleston, S.C.) *Post and Courier*, Sept. 1, 1998.

[5] *Ibid.*

Continued from p. 1010

employees for urine samples. Following a barrage of press articles in 1986 about crack cocaine and crack babies, public attitudes about drugs took a sharp right turn. A *Time*/CBS survey found that 72 percent of full-time workers said they would voluntarily submit to drug testing, and 25 percent of full-time factory workers said they had a colleague who used drugs. [13]

Several high-profile accidents in the 1980s involving drugged or drunken drivers and pilots added fuel to the national anti-drug sentiment. In 1981, a Navy pilot, apparently high on marijuana, crashed into the deck of the U.S.S. *Nimitz*, destroying several planes and causing more than $100 million in damages. Marijuana was also implicated in the 1987 Conrail-Amtrak train collision in Maryland, which killed 16 people. And alcohol was blamed for the 1989 *Exxon Valdez* accident in Alaska, which caused one of the worst oil spills in U.S. history. [14]

The public began to demand that those responsible for the safety of others — such as pilots, surgeons and police officers — be drug-free. In addition, the highly publicized deaths of University of Maryland basketball star Len Bias and Cleveland Browns' footfall player Don Rogers led to a public outcry about drug use among sports stars. Drug testing was touted as part of the solution to both problems.

Meanwhile, with increased availability bringing lower costs, cocaine had became the drug of choice among successful young urban professionals. Crack cocaine had also entered the picture, a highly addictive form of free-base cocaine, blamed for skyrocketing urban crime rates.

In the late 1980s, then-Attorney General Richard L. Thornburgh called drug testing by employers the moral thing to do. "That's really what started this whole process and has been driving it all along," Sonnenstuhl says. "The responsibility has to be put at the foot of the federal government for inciting all of this stuff."

Despite all the hysteria about skyrocketing drug use in the 1980s and Reagan's push for drug testing, total drug use nationwide had begun a steady decline in 1979 that continued until 1992. Cocaine and crack use continued to flourish in the 1980s among a small percentage of the population, but marijuana use, particularly among students, declined. By the late 1980s, for instance, only 5 percent of high-school seniors smoked marijuana every day, compared with 10 percent in 1978. [15]

Workplace Testing

Nonetheless, in September 1986 President Reagan issued Executive Order 12564, calling for a "drug-free workplace" in all federal agencies and ordering that employees in "sensitive positions" be tested for illegal drug use. The rule allowed anyone who tested positive to be fired after a single offense, but mandated that second offenders must be fired. President George Bush later expanded the program to include testing for all White House personnel. Today, 1.7 million employees in 111 federal agencies are tested, with those in safety-sensitive positions usually tested on a random basis.

Congress expanded the drug testing net with the Drug-Free Workplace Act of 1988, which required federal contractors or grant recipients to maintain drug-free workplaces. Although drug testing wasn't mandated, many employers set up testing programs.

In 1989, President Bush unveiled his National Drug Control Strategy. It said the federal government "has a responsibility to do all that it can to promote comprehensive drug-free workplace policies."

Two years later, Congress passed the Omnibus Transportation and Employment Testing Act of 1991, which extended mandatory drug and alcohol testing to 8 million private-sector pilots, drivers and equipment operators.

President Clinton has expanded the Reagan-Bush drug-testing policies to prisons, where those "who commit a lion's share of the crimes in this country are in a controlled environment," said White House senior adviser Rahm Emanuel. "We have to slam shut the revolving door between drugs and crime. Through mandatory testing, you will force a change in their behavior that will break the link." [16]

Arguing that most drug offenders get arrested sooner or later, the administration pushed through Congress a law requiring states to test and treat prisoners and parolees for drugs before they can receive federal prison-construction funds. It also increased the number of residential treatment centers in federal prisons and more than tripled the number of inmates being treated for substance abuse. [17]

Critics say the administration's anti-drug policies are nothing more than a war on casual marijuana users, because they are the ones most often "caught" with current drug-testing methods.

"Despite criticism that this administration is soft on drugs, FBI data clearly demonstrate that Clinton's war on marijuana smokers is the toughest ever waged in our nation's history," says St. Pierre of the NORML Foundation. Marijuana arrests have risen 80 percent since 1990, according to the FBI. Nearly 642,000 people were arrested for marijuana offenses in 1996, St. Pierre says, 85 percent for possession.

Legal Challenges

As soon as drug tests began appearing in schools and workplaces, individuals, unions and the American Civil Liberties Union (ACLU) began challenging the practice in court. Plaintiffs typically claimed drug testing violated individual privacy rights or Fourth Amendment protections against unreasonable search and seizure by government agents.

Until the mid-1980s, the lower courts had consistently ruled that — except in the military — it was unconstitutional to randomly drug test without "reasonable suspicion" that someone was using drugs.

But in the mid-1980s, as the "war on drugs" gained momentum and public attitudes toward drugs shifted, courts began allowing suspicionless drug testing when the state was seen to have an administrative interest that overrode an individual's right to privacy. This "administrative exception" was applied to jockeys, prison guards, nuclear plant employees, public school teachers and Customs Service employees.

In a precedent-setting 1989 case involving customs inspectors — *National Treasury Employees Union v. Von Raab* — the Supreme Court for the first time allowed random, suspicionless drug testing when there is a "special need" that outweighs the individual's privacy rights. The courts spent the next decade defining "special need."

Civil rights scholars viewed the *Von Raab* ruling as a major departure for the court because it was holding individual privacy rights as less important than the state's interest in winning the war on drugs. [18]

The decision is tantamount to jettisoning the need to establish probable cause before searching private homes because the state has a strong interest in eliminating crime, argued law scholar Jeannette C. James. [19]

But perhaps no case shocked civil libertarians more than *Veronia School District v. Acton*, in which the Supreme Court ruled in 1995 that suspicionless,

random urinalysis of high-school athletes was justified because the drug crisis in the school district had reached "epidemic proportions." Yet the Veronia district had found only 12 positive drug tests in four and a half years. Just 10 years earlier the court had struck down as unreasonable a New Jersey school's athlete drug-testing program in a school district where 28 students tested positive for drugs in a single year.

Justice Antonin Scalia — who had written a scathing dissent in *Von Raab* — wrote the majority opinion in the *Veronia* case.

Scalia argued that student athletes have even less privacy rights than the general student body because they are role models and because they dress and shower in close proximity to one another. He also said that school drug testing was a response to drug usage by athletes.

"Obviously his view of the evils of drugs had changed between 1989 and 1995," says Paul Armentano, publication director of NORML. ∎

CURRENT SITUTATION

Teen Drug Use Rises

After the *Veronia* ruling, more school districts instituted random drug testing of athletes, driven in part by new national surveys showing that declining teen drug use had suddenly reversed itself in 1992 and was rising steadily.

Indeed, drug use among teenagers became a hot campaign issue in 1996, after the annual "National Household Survey on Drug Abuse" showed that teen drug use had more than doubled

during Clinton's first term. [20] Republican presidential candidate Bob Dole blamed Clinton for the upswing, pointing out that he had slashed funding for the White House drug-policy office (which Clinton later restored) and had hired employees who had used drugs in the past.

Clinton pointed out that the increase in teen drug use was a multiyear trend that started before he was even sworn into office. Administration officials also noted that from 1992-1995 Congress consistently cut anti-drug education funds administered under the Safe and Drug-Free Schools program. Critics have called the program ineffective because there are few restrictions on how the money is spent, and it is allocated on a per-capita basis, rather than targeted at districts with severe drug problems.

Officials in the White House Office of National Drug Control Policy also pointed to opinion polls showing student attitudes about the dangers of marijuana had begun to change in 1990. Clinton's drug czar, Barry R. McCaffrey, said that from 1990-1993, the percentage of high-school seniors viewing marijuana use as risky fell. [21]

Joseph A. Califano, Jr., president of the National Center on Addiction and Substance Abuse at Columbia University, blamed the increased teen drug use on baby boomer parents' complacency about drugs. Califano released a survey showing that two-thirds of babyboomer parents who used drugs in their youth expected their children to do the same, and 40 percent felt they had little influence over their teenagers' decisions about drugs.

"What is infuriating about the attitudes revealed in this survey is the resignation of so many parents to the present mess," Califano said. [22]

Shortly before the election, Clinton proposed encouraging states to impose mandatory drug tests for all teens seeking driver's licenses. "Our message should be simple: no drugs, or no driver's license," Clinton said in his weekly radio address. Republicans called the proposal an election-year gimmick.

Since the 1996 election, teen drug use has continued rising, even as more schools have implemented or expanded testing programs. The percentage of youths ages 12-17 using illicit drugs increased from 9 percent to 11.4 percent from 1996-1997, still far below 1979's record high of 16.3 percent. Teen drug use had dropped to an all-time low of 5.3 percent in 1992.

Perhaps even more worrisome for parents and officials are the latest statistics showing that drug use among 12- and 13-year-olds increased from 2.2 percent to 3.8 percent from 1996-97. [23]

Some schools have responded to rising teen drug use by requiring testing not only for athletes but also for all students participating in extracurricular activities, such as band, drama and student council. Other schools test students who drive to school.

Privacy Issues Raised

Parents generally like testing programs, and some even want all students tested.

"The majority of kids support drug testing because it gives them an excuse to say 'no' to drugs," says Robert Weiner, spokesman for the White House Office of National Drug Control Policy. "The administration has been strongly supportive of giving schools that tool," he says.

But some parents and teenagers have sued their local school boards, claiming testing is an unconstitutional invasion of privacy.

However, on Oct. 5 the Supreme court let stand a rural Indiana high school's policy of requiring mandatory drug testing for all students in extracurricular activities. After a concerned parent sued the Rush County School Board, an Indiana appellate court had ruled that the policy does not violate students' privacy rights, even though the school district is not experiencing a serious drug problem. [24]

"We're getting closer to that line where you can expect to be tested just because you show up at school," said Kenneth J. Falk, an attorney for the Indiana Civil Liberties Union, which represented the plaintiffs. [25]

On the other hand, "Kids now can say, 'I can't experiment because my number may come up,' " said Rush County School Board lawyer Rodney V. Taylor. [26]

Although the court's inaction is not a precedent-setting decision, the ruling it left in place remains binding in Indiana, Illinois and Wisconsin. Critics say it opens the door for similar policies in other states. Several school districts had been waiting for the court to decide the case before they expanded their testing programs.

Civil libertarians and some editorial writers were stunned by the court's inaction.

"Drug abuse among teenagers is alarming, but so is the ease with which the Rehnquist court has disregarded fundamental constitutional protections guaranteed to citizens under the Fourth Amendment," said a *St. Petersburg Times* editorial. "Historically, suspicionless searches have been deemed to violate personal privacy and the protection against unreasonable searches and seizures. There may be compelling reasons to allow such searches, such as when public safety mandates it. But that's certainly not the case here." [27]

Critics point out that besides infringing on the Constitution, such programs target the wrong kids. High achievers who spend their free time playing in the band are not likely to be using drugs, they argue.

Politicians Not Tested

In other recent Supreme Court action on drug testing, the court last March 2 denied an appeal by two government economists who balked at taking random drug tests because they have access to the Old Executive Office Building next-door to the White House.

But the court has rejected drug testing for judges and politicians. The justices struck down a Georgia law requiring candidates for state office to take drug tests. Because urinalysis intrudes on a person's right to privacy, it should be used only when the risk to public safety "is substantial and real," the high court said. [28]

Meanwhile, lawmakers in the last two years introduced more than 60 bills requiring drug testing in one form or another; most were never acted upon.

The law providing $10 million to help small businesses establish drug-free workplaces was the only major drug-testing legislation approved. It also ordered the Small Business Administration to study the extent and costs of drug use in the workplace.

While Congress pushed for more small businesses to do drug testing, it refused to submit to drug testing for congressmen and their staffs, claiming it was too undignified and possibly unconstitutional.

"It's not fair to require more and more Americans to undergo drug testing, when the same Congress that passed the laws expanding the practice over the last 15 years won't submit to the same level of scrutiny themselves," St. Pierre says.

On the opening day of the 105th Congress, the House had passed a rules package requiring all representatives and their staffs to undergo random drug testing. But the rule was never implemented, due to opposition from both Republican and Democratic leaders, some of whom feared that the results of positive drug tests might be used against them by a political opponent.

"Of course, the information would be used against them," St. Pierre says. "That's exactly the way drug testing is being used across the country. We deny welfare mothers custody of their children, we deny students access to student loans, we deny employee access to workers' compensation or health benefits. Everybody is being punished for positive drug tests except the people who forced these laws on the country. It's rank hypocrisy."

"We have a few well-placed people who don't want this," said Rep. Joe L. Barton, R-Texas, who co-sponsored the bill with House Rules Committee Chairman Solomon.[29]

OUTLOOK

Questions of Fairness

Under the Drug-Free Workplace Act of 1998, more small companies are expected to begin asking their employees for urine samples. Some fear that cash-strapped firms may cut corners by only performing the one-step screening test, which is more likely to turn up false-positives. Congress recommended that the more comprehensive two-step testing be done, but many employers already reject job applicants based solely on the single-screening tests.

In large companies, drug testing is here to stay, predicts de Bernardo of the Institute for a Drug-Free Workplace. "There will be no retreat on drug testing," he says. "The numbers of companies testing increases every year." He predicts more large companies will expand their "for-cause"

testing programs to include universal random testing.

"It's by far the fairest type of testing you can do," he says. "It is inherently objective and has a greater deterrent impact." Testing only for "reasonable suspicion" is inherently subjective and open to abuse by an employer with a grudge, he adds.

But as employers expand their testing, they may run into a new obstacle: hemp seed oil. Sold in health food stores, hemp oil reportedly lowers cholesterol, fights viruses, increases calcium absorption and reduces inflammation. Because it comes from the same family as the marijuana plant, hemp oil can cause a user to test positive for marijuana.

Observers predict that marijuana smokers will start using the supplement to mask their marijuana use.

Others worry that as drug testing becomes more widespread, the confidentiality of the results may be compromised. "This information will become part of student records, insurance records and other databases, regardless of the reason that someone tested positive and how long ago it happened," says Alexander Robinson, public policy director of the Drug Policy Foundation.

Questions about fairness are already being raised about new tests using hair, sweat and saliva. The new techniques are considered less intrusive than urinalysis, and thus less subject to legal challenge. They are also expected to detect more drug users, because they are almost impossible to "beat."

Some say the expanding use of hair and urine testing is leading the country closer to a police state.

"You have a police-state mentality," Robinson says. "Incentives have been established in schools rewarding students who turn in other students. State and local ordinances reward kids who turn in their parents."

At the White House, Weiner ac-

knowledges that a "vocal few" see drug testing as moving toward a police state.

"People are making a huge deal out of this *horrendous* violation of individual rights," he says, "but it's also a violation of civil liberties to go through an X-ray machine at an airport, or to wear a seat belt. Their concerns about Americans' civil liberties are important, but the law has to support the general good. There's nothing wrong with drug testing when you have a national consensus."

Some opponents hope for a public backlash. "The hope is that proponents will go so far there will be some backlash," Nadelmann says. If not, drug testing could lead a desensitized public down "a slippery slope to greater and greater loss of freedom. Bit by bit, we are slowly getting used to greater and greater intrusion."

Some observers are concerned that so many students nationwide have acquiesced to drug testing without thinking much about its long-term impact on their privacy rights.

"As these students, now inoculated with an intolerant attitude, take power, invasions of privacy will become more widely implemented because they will be seen as prime American values," wrote Arnold Trebach and Scott Ehlers of the Drug Policy Foundation.[30]

Cornell's Sonnenstuhl argues that rather than curtailing constitutional rights, invading privacy and turning employers into policemen, "The best way to prevent alcohol and drug abuse in the workplace is for supervisors to do the job they were hired to do — monitor job performance and use discipline to encourage abusers to get treatment," he says. "Most large corporations are not training their supervisors to do their jobs."

But at a steel foundry in Portland, Ore., Pat Bishop has no doubts about testing.

Continued on p. 1020

At Issue:

Is workplace drug-testing effective?

Michael Walsh

President, the Walsh Group, P.A., a Bethesda, Md., research and consulting firm, and former executive director of the President's Drug Advisory Council.

FROM HR NEWS, APRIL 1996.

In 1994, the National Academy of Sciences (NAS) issued a report, "Under the Influence: Drugs and the American Workforce," in which the principal finding was that there is little or no data in the scientific literature to demonstrate the effectiveness of drug-free workplace programs in reducing substance abuse.

My colleagues at the American Civil Liberties Union have taken this to mean that these programs don't work. The fact is that the NAS found no evidence that the programs don't work either; there simply wasn't conclusive evidence one way or the other.

But from a national perspective, there are positive signs of success. Since the widespread implementation of drug-free workplace programs in the mid-1980's, we have seen a significant decline in the use of drugs by employed individuals. Data from the "National Household Survey on Drug Abuse" (conducted by the National Institute on Drug Abuse and, more recently, by the Substance Abuse and Mental Health Services Administration) indicate that the number of full-time workers that are current users of illegal drugs has dropped by more than 6 million over the last 10 years.

Over the last 15 years "employee drug testing" has become a standard business practice in the American workplace. A recent survey conducted by the American Management Association (AMA) indicates that nearly 80 percent of surveyed firms test employees for drugs.

Since 1987, company drug testing in the United States has increased by more than 300 percent. With the increased prevalence of illegal drug use, most executives believe that the absence of pre-employment testing would be an open invitation to drug users. The approximately 80 "Forensic Urine Drug Testing" laboratories certified by the U.S. Department of Health and Human Services are currently processing about 60,000 specimens a day, and many employers who conduct employee testing programs use labs certified by other organizations or use on-site test procedures.

This phenomenon of workplace drug testing evolved slowly over more than a decade. During that time policies, procedures, and technology have changed considerably. In general, most organizations don't have "drug-testing programs." Rather, "testing" has become the foundation for a comprehensive programmatic approach to substance abuse. Prevention and deterrence are the key concepts of most workplace programs, not detection, but when a worker develops a problem the standard practice is to get the substance-abusing employee into treatment, and back to work.

Lewis L. Maltby

Director, American Civil Liberties Union National Task Force on Civil Liberties in the Workplace.

FROM HR NEWS, APRIL 1996

Mounting evidence suggests that drug testing does not work, or at least that the claims of those who make their living selling testing are greatly exaggerated.

The most important evidence comes from the National Academy of Sciences. The academy's Institute of Medicine recently released a report which examines all the major studies regarding drugs and the workplace and summarizes the state of our knowledge. This report casts doubt on the effectiveness of drug testing. The critical assumption on which all drug-testing programs are based is that those who use illegal drugs are less productive than other employees.

The academy, after reviewing all the evidence, found no consistent relationship between drug use and the quality of an employee's work. No relationship was found between drug use and productivity, or between drug use and the rate of workplace accidents. In some areas, drug use did make a difference. Drug users had slightly higher rates of absenteeism.

The ultimate question for an employer is whether urine testing is cost-justified. Here, too, the academy found little support of the industry claims. Some studies found that drug testing was not cost-effective. Others reached the opposite conclusion, but were described by the academy as "deeply flawed." Overall, the academy concluded that, "decisions by organizations to adopt drug testing programs have often been made without a well-grounded consideration of the likely benefits."

One reason the benefits of drug testing are so hard to justify is that few drug users are ever identified. According to the National Institute on Drug Abuse, only 3 percent of all random drug tests are positive. When one considers the cost of programs required to identify these few people, serious questions emerge. The federal government recently found that the average cost of a confirmed positive test result is $77,000. Is it really worth this much money to learn that a file clerk is smoking marijuana on a Saturday night?

Non-testing employers do not ignore the problem of drug abuse. They simply choose to deal with it differently. Many companies rely on careful employee selection and thorough performance evaluation and quality-control systems to create a high-quality workforce, avoiding those with any performance-impairing problems, including drug abuse.

The truth is that there are many strategies for dealing with employee drug abuse. Urine testing is one strategy, but is not the only one. There are other approaches, and mounting evidence from impartial sources indicates that urine testing may not be the best way.

The Marijuana Debate Goes on

Discussions about drug testing invariably turn to marijuana and the age-old questions: Is it harmful? Addictive? Does it act as a "gateway" to harder drugs? Marijuana residues stay in the body longer than other drugs, thus causing more marijuana users to get "caught" by urinalysis than users of other drugs.

"Drug testing is all about marijuana," says John P. Morgan, professor of pharmacology at City University of New York Medical School, who supports legalization of marijuana. "It's a critical weapon in the government's war on recreational marijuana users," he adds, noting that more people have been arrested for possession of marijuana during the Clinton administration than any other.

Critics like Morgan say drug testing should focus on more dangerous and addictive drugs like cocaine and heroin, or alcohol and tobacco, rather than "pot."

But testing proponents contend that marijuana is dangerous, addictive and a gateway to harder drugs and that cracking down on marijuana will indirectly stem the demand for heroin and cocaine.

"It's easy for people to underestimate the impact that marijuana has,"says Mark de Bernardo, executive director of the Institute for a Drug-Free Workplace, which promotes workplace testing. "There are a lot more casual users of alcohol, who don't get addicted, than there are users of illicit drugs" who don't get addicted."

According to a recent report by the National Center on Addiction and Substance Abuse (CASA) at Columbia University, teens 12-17 who use marijuana are 85 times more likely to use cocaine than non-marijuana users. [1]

CASA President Joseph A. Califano contends that the gateway effect means that recent increases in marijuana use among teens will translate into 820,000 more children who will try cocaine in their lifetime, of whom 58,000 will become addicts. Califano wrote that the statistical link between smoking pot and using harder drugs presents "a convincing case for a billion-dollar-a-year investment to move biomedical research on substance abuse and addiction into the big leagues at the National Institutes of Health, along with heart disease, cancer and AIDS." [2]

But Morgan calls the addiction and gateway arguments the "Big Lie" being promulgated by "more and more people, including urine testers and prevention, treatment and education specialists, whose livelihoods depend on the war on marijuana."

"For the large majority of people," Morgan says, "marijuana is a terminus rather than a gateway drug. More than 72 million Americans have tried marijuana at some point in their lives," including the president, the Speaker of the House and the secretary of Health and Human Services, he points out. "Yet in the over-30 population, only 0.8 percent of the population is continuing to use marijuana on a daily or even near-daily basis." [3]

"The lies and exaggerations about marijuana's dangers do little to discourage young people from trying marijuana, and may even have the opposite effect," Morgan writes in his new book, *Marijuana Myths, Marijuana Facts, A Review of the Scientific Evidence.*

Co-authored with Lynn Zimmer, associate professor of sociology at Queens College, the book analyzes the data supporting each of 20 arguments against marijuana used by government agencies and drug testing proponents. "Over and over, we discovered that government officials, journalists and even many 'drug experts' had misinterpreted, misrepresented or distorted the scientific evidence," wrote the authors.

The gateway theory tries to establish a causal relationship when only a statistical association exists, Morgan says. "Most people who ride a motorcycle have ridden a bicycle," he writes. "However, bicycle riding does not cause motorcycle riding."

Regarding marijuana dependence, Morgan cites a study by two pharmacologists who independently ranked the dependence potential of caffeine, nicotine, alcohol, heroin, cocaine and marijuana. Both ranked marijuana and caffeine as the least addictive, and one said marijuana was less addicting than caffeine. [4]

However, treatment specialists report anecdotal evidence of psychological dependence on marijuana, especially by heavy marijuana users. [5] But drug-testing opponents contend that almost all heavy marijuana users are also heavy alcohol users, who probably self-medicate to deaden pre-existing emotional pain.

A study released last March by the National Institute on Drug Abuse (NIDA) apparently supports that finding. It found that teenagers with prior serious anti-social problems are at high risk for marijuana dependence. "This study provides additional important data to better illustrate that marijuana is a dangerous drug that can be addictive," said Alan I. Leshner, director of the institute. [6]

Yet in its "Facts Parents Need to Know" fact sheet on its Web site, NIDA concedes that "Most marijuana users do not go on to use other illegal drugs."

The government also says marijuana is "a hugely significant cause of car crashes," and that marijuana users are "jamming hospital emergency rooms and drug treatment centers," according to White House Office of National Drug Control Policy spokesman Robert Weiner.

"Those are all absolutely false statements," Morgan says. "There's no scientific basis for them." He cites a 1993 Department of Transportation study that said, "Of the many psychoactive drugs, licit and illicit, that are available and used by people who drive, marijuana may well be among the least harmful." [7]

In the largest such study ever undertaken, Australian

researchers at the University of Adelaide found that drivers using marijuana were no more likely to be involved in an accident than those who were drug-free. [8]

Morgan concedes that "inexperienced marijuana users and inexperienced drivers, in particular, may be unable to drive safely even after small doses of marijuana."

Weiner's claim that hospital emergency rooms are "jammed" with marijuana users is based on federal Drug Abuse Warning Network (DAWN) statistics showing recent increases in the number of patients mentioning marijuana in hospital emergency rooms.

Morgan points out that marijuana use is on the increase, and inexperienced users may suffer acute anxiety the first time they use it. But, he says, even though marijuana is the most widely used illicit drug in America, it is mentioned in emergency cases less often than most other illicit drugs, and less than over-the-counter drugs. For instance, in 1993, 47 percent of the drug "mentions" by adolescents were for over-the-counter pain medications, compared with about 8 percent for marijuana.

In addition, he points out, marijuana is rarely mentioned alone. About 80 percent of the marijuana "mentions" also involved alcohol use, he says. "When a patient mentions marijuana, it does not mean marijuana caused the hospital visit," Morgan writes.

Out of more than 500,000 drug-abuse episodes reported by emergency rooms in 1994, only 1.6 percent — or slightly more than 8,000 — involved only marijuana. "And none of the marijuana-only mentions were hospitalized," he says.

Further, he says, evidence of marijuana use was found in only 587 of the 8,426 drug-related deaths in 1993. "In all of those cases, other drugs were found as well," he says. "Marijuana did not cause a single overdose death."

But, argues de Bernardo, "Today's marijuana has 22 times the THC [9] that it had in the 1960s. It's much stronger, more addictive and more dangerous."

After examining statistics from the University of Mississippi's Potency Monitoring Project (PMP), Morgan concludes, "There is no reason to believe that today's marijuana is stronger or more dangerous than the marijuana smoked during the 1960s and '70s." [10]

Independent analyses of marijuana in the 1970s showed an average purity of 2-5 percent. Since 1980, average marijuana potency has fluctuated between 2-3.5 percent, he writes, with no consistent upward or downward trend. But comparing potency data across the 1970s and '80s is misleading, he says, because PMP samples in the '70s were typically from low-potency sources. Improved storage practices and measurement methods in the '80s may have increased the amount of THC detected.

Even if today's marijuana were more potent than in the 1960s, it would not necessarily be more dangerous or produce more intense effects on the body, Morgan says.

"There is no possibility of a fatal overdose from smoking marijuana, regardless of THC content," he writes. In fact,

he says, since the main danger from marijuana is damage to the lungs, higher-potency marijuana may be slightly less harmful than lower-potency marijuana, because users tend to smoke less of it to achieve the same "high."

The NIDA Web site points out that marijuana smoke contains the same cancer-causing ingredients as tobacco, sometimes in higher concentrations. "Studies show that someone who smokes five joints per week may be taking in as many cancer-causing chemicals as someone who smokes a full pack of cigarettes every day," it says.

Morgan concedes that marijuana smokers are at risk because they inhale more deeply and retain smoke in their lungs longer than tobacco smokers, and "joints" are not filtered. But he says there are no epidemiological studies showing higher rates of lung cancer in marijuana smokers than in tobacco smokers, probably because they inhale less smoke overall than cigarette smokers. But, he wrote, heavy smokers of both marijuana and tobacco possibly "have an increased risk of lung cancer." [11]

Drug-testing proponents also point out that about 100,000 people seek treatment for marijuana dependency each year. Morgan argues that many of those were referred to treatment centers by employers or courts, after they tested positive for marijuana. Most do not meet the official definition for "dependency," Morgan says, but either the court or the boss has given them the choice of seeking treatment, being fired or serving time, he says.

"Which would you choose?" he asks.

---

[1] "Cigarettes, Alcohol, Marijuana: Gateways to Illicit Drug Use," Center on Addiction and Substance Abuse, Columbia University, October 1994.

[2] From an editorial written by Califano in September 1997 and distributed to several newspapers.

[3] Morgan's statistics come from the "1994 National Household Survey on Drug Abuse, Population Estimates," Substance Abuse and Mental Health Services Administration, 1995.

[4] P.J. Hilts, "Is Nicotine Addictive? It Depends on Whose Criteria You Use," The New York Times, Aug. 2, 1994.

[5] For background, see Sarah Glazer, "Preventing Teen Drug Use," The CQ Researcher, July 28, 1995, pp. 666-689.

[6] Thomas Crowley, et. al, "Cannabis Dependence, Withdrawal and Reinforcing Effects Among Adolescents with Conduct Symptoms and Substance Use Disorders," Drug and Alcohol Dependence, spring 1998.

[7] H. Robbe and J. O'Hanlon, "Marijuana and Actual Driving Performance," Department of Transportation, 1993, p. 107.

[8] See C.E. Hunter et. al., "The Prevalence and Role of Alcohol, Cannabinoids, Benzodiazepines and Stimulants in Non-fatal Crashes," University of Adelaid, Department of Forensic Science, 1998; Robbe, op. cit. (Netherlands study).

[9] THC is the chief psychoactive ingredient in marijuana.

[10] The PMP has been monitoring the potency of marijuana samples submitted by law enforcement agencies since the early 1970s.

[11] Marijuana smokers are only 3 percent more likely than non-smokers to visit doctors for respiratory illnesses like bronchitis, according to researchers at the Kaiser Permanente Medical Care Program, he says.

Continued from p. 1016

"We've been randomly testing everyone in the company for the past five years, and during that time the percentage of employees testing positive has gone down from about 5 percent to 1," says Bishop, manager of health services for ESCO Corp.

"We work with molten metal, and our employees support drug testing overwhelmingly. No one wants to work with someone who is drug-impaired." ■

Notes

[1] For background, see Richard L. Worsnop, "High School Sports," *The CQ Researcher*, Sept. 22, 1995, pp. 825-858.

[2] For background, see Richard L Worsnop, "Privacy in the Workplace," *The CQ Researcher*, Nov. 19, 1993, pp. 1021-1044.

[3] "Winning the War on Drugs — Check the Military," *The Drug-Free Workplace Report*, fall 1990, p. 4.

[4] Marci M. DeLancey, "Does Drug Testing Work?" Institute for a Drug-Free Workplace, 1994.

[5] Robert W. Taggart, "Results of the Drug Testing Program at Southern Pacific Railroad," *Drugs in the Workplace: Research and Evaluation Data*, National Institute on Drug Abuse, 1989.

[6] "Workplace Drug Testing and Drug Abuse Policies: Summary of Key Findings," American Management Association, 1996.

[7] "Under the Influence? Drugs and the American Work Force," National Academy of Sciences, 1994.

[8] American Management Association, *op. cit.*

[9] Chamber of Commerce press release.

[10] Taggart, *op. cit.*

[11] Beverly A. Potter and Sebastian Orfali, *Drug Testing at Work: A Guide for Employers and Employees (1990).*

[12] William J. Staudenmeier Jr., "Urine Testing: The Battle for Privatized Social Control

During the 1986 War on Drugs," from *Images of Issues, Typifying Contemporary Social Problems,* Joel Best, ed. (1989).

[13] Potter, *op. cit.*

[14] *Under the Influence? Drugs and the American Work Force,* National Research Council, 1994.

[15] Potter, *op. cit.*

[16] Quoted in Christopher S. Wren, "Clinton to Require State Efforts to Cut Drug Use in Prisons," The *New York Times,* Jan. 12, 1998.

[17] *Ibid.*

[18] Paul Armentano, "A Look at the Historical Legal Basis for Urine Testing," *NORML Reports,* December 1995.

[19] Jeannette C. James, "The Constitutionality of Federal Employee Drug Testing," The *American University Law Review,* fall 1988.

[20] The survey is published each year by the Substance Abuse and Mental Health Services Administration.

[21] For background, see Sarah Glazer, "Preventing Teen Drug Use," *The CQ Researcher,* July 28, 1995, pp. 674-697.

[22] Quoted in Roberto Suro, "Boomers ex-

pect teen drug use, survey finds," *The Washington Post,* Sept. 19, 1996.

[23] Substance Abuse and Mental Health Services Administration.

[24] The case is *Todd v. Rush County Schools.*

[25] Quoted in Frank J. Murray, "High court declines to debate school drug testing," *The Washington Times,* Oct. 6, 1998.

[26] *Ibid.*

[27] "Opening the way to drug tests," *The St. Petersburg Times,* Oct. 13, 1998.

[28] Joan Biskupic, "Court allows drug tests for OEOB pass holders," *The Washington Post,* March 3, 1998.

[29] Quoted in "Different Sauces for Geese and Ganders?" The Associated Press, Aug. 7, 1998.

[30] Arnold Trebach and Scott Ehlers, "The war on our children: destroying the rights of America's youth to save them from drugs," "The Playboy Forum"; *Playboy,* February 1997. Trebach is a professor at American University and editor-in-chief of *The Drug Policy Letter,* published by the Drug Policy Foundation; Ehlers is associate editor.

Bibliography

Selected Sources Used

Books

Holtorf, Kent, *Ur-ine Trouble*, Vandalay Press, 1998.

Holtorf, a physician, has spent years reviewing the scientific data about drug testing. He describes how poorly trained personnel in uncertified laboratories can erroneously cause a job seeker to test positive for drugs and how common foods and medicines can cause false-positive test results.

Jacques Normand, et al., *Under the Influence? Drugs and the American Work Force*, National Academy of Sciences, 1994.

This National Academy of Sciences analysis of all the studies done before 1994 on the effectiveness of workplace drug testing found that "there is as yet no conclusive scientific evidence from properly controlled studies that employment drug-testing programs widely discourage drug use or encourage rehabilitation."

Potter, Beverly A., and Sebastian Orfali, *Drug Testing at Work, A Guide for Employers and Employees*, Ronin Publishing, 1990.

The authors describe how tests work, the civil rights issues involved, how to set up a program and how employees can protect themselves from false-positive results.

Zimmer, Lynn, and John P. Morgan, *Marijuana Myths, Marijuana Facts,* Lindesmith Center, 1997.

The 241-page book, published by billionaire George Sorros' drug-law reform think tank, includes more than 60 pages of bibliography and footnotes listing scores of studies on marijuana and its effects on the human body. Each chapter deals with one of the arguments against marijuana use.

Articles

Armentano, Paul, "A Look at the Historical Legal Basis for Urine Testing," *NORML Reports,* December 1995.

The publications director for the National Organization to Reform Marijuana Laws (NORML) writes about the legal history of drug testing, reviewing major court decisions and how the Supreme Court's position on privacy rights has shifted.

DeLancey, Marci M., "Does Drug Testing Work?" Institute for a Drug-Free Workplace, 1994.

This 116-page report by the institute — a coalition of businesses and individuals that promotes workplace drug testing — provides pages of statistics about the prevalence, cost and effectiveness of alcohol, drug and substance abuse. It also offers testimonials from companies that have established drug-testing programs.

James, Jeannette C., "The Constitutionality of Federal Employee Drug Testing," *The American University Law Review,* fall 1988.

James, a lawyer, focuses on the controversial Supreme Court decision in *National Treasury Employees Union v. Von Raab.* She contends the decision was tantamount to jettisoning the need to establish probable cause before searching private homes because the state has a strong interest in eliminating crime.

Murray, Frank J., "High court declines to debate school drug testing," *The Washington Times,* Oct. 6, 1998.

The author discusses the controversial Oct. 5 decision by the court to let stand a rural Indiana high school's policy of requiring mandatory drug-testing for all students in extracurricular activities, regardless of whether they are suspected of using drugs.

Staudenmeier, William J., Jr., "Urine Testing: The Battle for Privatized Social Control During the 1986 War on Drugs," from *Images of Issues, Typifying Contemporary Social Problems*, edited by Joel Best, 1989.

Sociologist Staudenmeier calls President Ronald Reagan's push for private employers to start drug testing "privatized social control." The Fourth Amendment prohibits the government from requiring the general population to be tested for drugs, he points out.

Trebach, Arnold, and Scott Ehlers, "The war on our children: destroying the rights of America's youth to save them from drugs," *Playboy*, February 1997.

Two Drug Policy Foundation editors argue that current U.S. drug-testing policy is indoctrinating several generations of children with the belief that venerable constitutional privacy guarantees are less important than the need for drug control.

Reports

***National Household Survey on Drug Abuse*, Substance Abuse and Mental Health Services Administration, 1997.**

The annual survey shows that teen drug use has been climbing since 1992.

Taggart, Robert W., *Results of the Drug Testing Program at Southern Pacific Railroad*, Drugs in the Workplace: Research and Evaluation Data, National Institute on Drug Abuse, 1989.

This study showed a 50 percent drop in positive drug tests after a year of "reasonable suspicion" drug testing.

The Next Step

Additional information from UMI's Newspaper & Periodical Abstracts™ database

Home Drug Tests

"FDA Approves Home Drug Testing System," *Healthcare Financing Review*, spring 1997, p. 296.

The first non-prescription drug test system has been approved by the FDA. Marketed as "Dr. Brown's Home Drug Testing System," it will detect marijuana, PCP, amphetamines, cocaine, heroin, codeine and morphine.

"FDA Removes Roadblock to Home Drug Testing," *Alcoholism & Drug Abuse Weekly*, Feb. 17, 1997, p. 1.

The U.S. Food and Drug Administration has decided that it will not subject home drug-testing kits to a rigorous approval process but instead will allow the marketing of drug-testing products without prior approval as long as they meet basic safety, accuracy and privacy standards.

Day, Kathleen, "Persistence Comes Up Positive; The Maker of a Drug-Testing Kit Finally Wins FDA Approval," *The Washington Post*, Feb. 10, 1997, p. W13.

The Food and Drug Administration gave Jacob Brown's company the first approval ever for the development and sale of a non-prescription drug test on Jan. 21. At $30 a kit, Brown is betting his product will appeal to parents and employers, not only because it is one-third the cost of other drug tests but because it is more convenient than having to go to a doctor for a test or to get a prescription for one.

Marijuana

Brook, Judith S., David W. Brook, Mario de la Rosa, Luis Fernando Duque, et al., "Pathways to Marijuana Use Among Adolescents: Cultural, Ecological, Family, Peer, and Personality Influences," *Journal of the American Academy of Child & Adolescent Psychiatry*, July 1998, pp. 759-766.

In this study, researchers found that family, personality and peer factors had a direct effect on adolescents' marijuana use. The article also addresses implications for prevention of marijuana use.

Chapman, Stephen, "What's So Bad About Marijuana? Not Much, Actually," *Chicago Tribune*, May 22, 1997, p. 31.

The author stipulates that if marijuana were killing substantial numbers of people, Americans would hear about it from the media and government officials. He says that the government's reaction to initiatives that would legalize medicinal marijuana — such as California's — is unfounded.

Langreth, Robert, "Studies Say Marijuana Affects Brain in Same Ways as Heroin and Cocaine," *The Wall Street Journal*, June 27, 1997, p. B6.

Marijuana use is on the rise, buoyed by its long-held reputation as a comparatively benign recreational drug, but new research shows it affects the brain in the same ways that highly addictive drugs like heroin and cocaine do.

Naylor, Janet, "In Macomb County: Students' Use of Marijuana Rising Again; Alarmed Officials Plan Billboard Drive to Educate Parents on Danger of Drug," *Detroit News*, Jan. 14, 1998, p. D5.

Alarmed that the use of marijuana among children is creeping up again, a coalition of drug-abuse prevention groups has started a campaign to educate parents about how to handle the issue. The campaign features 13 billboards across the county with the message: "Are you waiting for your kids to talk to YOU about pot?" The boards give parents a toll-free number to call for a booklet on how to start a dialogue with their children about drug abuse.

Wren, Christopher S., "Fewer Youths Report Smoking Marijuana," *The New York Times*, Aug. 7, 1997, p. A18.

Marijuana use by younger teenagers declined slightly last year for the first time in five years, but overall use of illegal drugs showed no change, according to an annual government survey released today. Drug use among young adults 18 to 25 years old continued to rise, the survey said, and increasing numbers of young people said they doubted that drug use was risky. Administration officials were heartened by the survey's report of an unexpected decline in overall drug use for youths between the ages of 12 to 17 but they did not claim that drug use, which has accelerated since 1992, had been reversed.

Wren, Christopher S., "Survey Finds More Children Being Offered Marijuana," *The New York Times*, March 5, 1997, p. A14.

The rising popularity of illegal drugs among teenagers is trickling down to their younger brothers and sisters, who are becoming more tolerant of drug use and are starting to try marijuana themselves, according to a survey released yesterday by the Partnership for a Drug-Free America. The annual Partnership Tracking Study for 1996, which focuses on children 9 through 12 years of age, found those children to be influenced by teenagers' use of drugs, primarily marijuana. Nearly one-fourth of the younger children interviewed said they were offered drugs last year, the survey said, an increase of five percentage points from the 19 percent who reported the experience in 1993. Only 7 percent of the parents thought their children were offered drugs.

Urinalysis in Schools

Issari, Philia, and Robert Holman Coombs, "Women, Drug Use, and Drug Testing," *Journal of Sport & Social Issues*, May 1998, pp. 153-169.

The drug-related attitudes and behaviors of female intercollegiate athletes and their views on drug testing were assessed and contrasted with those of male athletes.

Linshaw, Michael A., and Alan B. Gruskin, "The Routine Urinalysis: To Keep or Not to Keep, That is the Question," *Pediatrics*, December 1997.

The authors comment on the costs of routine urinalysis in children using the "dipstick" method.

Perry, Patrick, "Teen Drug Abuse: Bringing the Message Home," *Saturday Evening Post*, May 1998, p. 16.

Despite all the drug-abuse campaigns in recent years, drug use among American teenagers continues to rise. A school in Texas is having students take voluntary drug tests; there is talk of more widespread, random drug testing.

Taylor, Robert, "Compensating Behavior and the Drug Testing of High School Athletes," *Cato Journal*, winter 1997, p. 351-364.

The author explores the conditions under which the random drug testing of athletes will lead to the perverse outcome of increased student drug usage.

Turner, Allan, "Defending his Rights; Student Risking all to Oppose Drug Testing," *Houston Chronicle*, Feb. 2, 1997, p. D1.

A Texas honor student, Hollister Gardner, supported by his father, school board member Gary Gardner, filed suit in January 1997 against the Tulia school district in federal court, contending that the drug-testing policy it introduced in 1996 violates his Fourth Amendment protection against unreasonable search.

Urinalysis at Work

Biskupic, Joan, "Drug Testing of Candidates Struck Down by High Court; Georgia Law Held to Violate 4th Amendment," *The Washington Post*, April 16, 1997, p. A1.

Georgia's drug-testing policy was struck down by the Supreme Court because of its propensity to diminish personal privacy. Justice Ruth Bader Ginsburg wrote that although the practice may have been well-meant, it wasn't the answer to the country's illicit drug-use problem. The ruling was a triumph for opponents of broad-scale government drug testing, an increasingly common practice in an era of heightened concern for narcotics abuse. However, the court emphasized that the unique Georgia law, covering the governor, lieutenant governor, other top officials, judges and legislators, was not enacted in response to any reported illegal drug use among politicians. When the risk to public safety is real, the justices said, blanket searches would be allowed.

Brown, Nathan A., "Reining in the National Drug Testing Epidemic," *Harvard Civil Rights-Civil Liberties Law Review*, winter 1998, pp. 253-272.

In Chandler v. Miller, the Supreme Court held that a Georgia statute requiring candidates for statewide office to pass a drug test was unconstitutional under the Fourth Amendment.

Ellement, John, "Fired Employees Sue Company Over Drug Testing Bid," *The Boston Globe*, Oct. 25, 1996, p. D1.

Saying they lost their jobs because they wanted to protect their privacy, two former employees of Global Access Telecommunications Inc. in Boston, sued the company in 1996 for demanding they give hair samples the company wanted to test for illegal drug use and "medical research."

Forrest, Alexander R.W., "Ethical Aspects of Workplace Urine Screening for Drug Abuse," *Journal of Medical Ethics*, February 1997, pp. 12-17.

The author says that workplace screening for drug abuse raises many ethical issues. If the process is not part of medical practice, employees should have the same rights as they would have if required to provide intimate body samples in the course of a criminal investigation.

Gatland, Laura, "Controversial Drug Testing Riles Chicago Police Officers," *Christian Science Monitor*, July 1, 1998, p. 3.

Chicago's police department is considering random drug testing of the entire 13,000-member force using hair clippings. The department would join a handful of city and state police departments and hundreds of companies nationwide that are using hair analysis. Although urinalysis is still the most common drug test, employers are turning to hair analysis despite controversy surrounding the technology. The biggest advantage is that hair analysis can detect drug use as far back as three months. Urine testing has a window of just a few days.

Strosnider, Kim, "Federal Appeals Court Upholds Drug Testing for Medical Residents," *Chronicle of Higher Education*, Aug. 1, 1997, p. A33.

Texas Tech University Health Sciences Center did not violate the rights of a medical resident when requiring her to submit to a drug test, according to a federal appeals court. Information on the trial and the ruling is presented.

Back Issues

Great Research on Current Issues Starts Right Here.
Recent topics covered by The CQ Researcher are listed below.
Now available on the Web
For information, call (800) 432-2250 ext. 279 or (202) 887-6279.

If you would like to have any of these CQ Researchers updated, or need more information about these topics, please call CQ Custom Research. Special rates for CQ subscribers. (202) 887-8600 or (800) 432-2250, ext. 600, or E-mail Custom.Research@cq.com

AUGUST 1997
Age Discrimination
Banning Land Mines
Children's Television
Evolution vs. Creationism

SEPTEMBER 1997
Caring for the Dying
Mental Health Policy
Mexico's Future
Youth Fitness

OCTOBER 1997
Urban Sprawl in the West
Diversity in the Workplace
Teacher Education
Contingent Work Force

NOVEMBER 1997
Renewable Energy
Artificial Intelligence
Religious Persecution
Roe v. Wade at 25

DECEMBER 1997
Whistleblowers
Castro's Next Move
Gun Control Standoff
Regulating Nonprofits

JANUARY 1998
Foster Care Reform
IRS Reform
The Black Middle Class
U.S.-British Relations

FEBRUARY 1998
Patients' Rights
Deflation Fears
Caring for the Elderly
The New Corporate Philanthropy

MARCH 1998
Israel at 50
The Federal Judiciary
Drinking on Campus
The Economics of Recycling

APRIL 1998
Biology and Behavior
Liberal Arts Education
Income Inequality
High-Tech Labor Shortage

MAY 1998
Census 2000
Child-Care Options
Alzheimer's Disease
U.S.-Russian Relations

JUNE 1998
Student Journalism
Antitrust Policy
Environmental Justice
Sleep Deprivation

JULY 1998
Encouraging Teen Abstinence
Population and the Environment
Democracy in Asia
Baby Boomers at Midlife

AUGUST 1998
Oil Production in the 21st Century
Flexible Work Arrangements
Coastal Development
Student Activism

SEPTEMBER 1998
Organic Farming
Cancer Treatments
Hispanic Americans' New Clout
The Future of Baseball

OCTOBER 1998
School Violence
Social Security
National Forests
Puerto Rico's Status

NOVEMBER 1998
Internet Privacy
Human Rights

Future Topics

► *European Monetary Union*

► *AIDS Update*

► *Iran: 20 Years After The Revolution*

Back issues are available for $5.00 (subscribers) or $10.00 (non-subscribers). Quantity discounts apply to orders over 10. To order, call Congressional Quarterly Customer Service at (202) 887-8621.

Binders are available for $18.00. To order call 1-800-638-1710. Please refer to stock number 648.

European Monetary Union

Will it stabilize prices and boost global trade?

O
n Jan. 1, 1999, 11 of the 15 members of the European Union will take a giant stride toward economic integration by adopting a single currency, the euro. Initially, it will be used for non-cash transactions such as stock purchases, but in three years the nations in the new monetary union will begin using euros for all transactions. Supporters of European integration hope that the demise of the mark, the franc and other venerable European currencies will remove a major obstacle to economic unification. Achieving economic integration brings uncertainties and risks, however. The countries involved must cede sovereignty over monetary policy to the new European Central Bank, while the United States must confront a new competitor in the world-trade arena.

CQ Nov. 27, 1998 • Volume 8, No. 44 • Pages 1025-1048

Formerly Editorial Research Reports

Nov. 27, 1998
Volume 8, No.44

EDITOR
Sandra Stencel

MANAGING EDITOR
Thomas J. Colin

STAFF WRITERS
Adriel Bettelheim
Mary H. Cooper
Kenneth Jost
Kathy Koch
David Masci

PRODUCTION EDITOR
Debra James

EDITORIAL ASSISTANT
Laura S. Cavender

PUBLISHED BY
Congressional Quarterly Inc.

CHAIRMAN
Andrew Barnes

VICE CHAIRMAN
Andrew P. Corty

PRESIDENT AND PUBLISHER
Robert W. Merry

EXECUTIVE EDITOR
David Rapp

Cover: The European Union flag

Bibliographic records and abstracts included in The Next Step section of this publication are the copyrighted material of UMI, and are used with permission.

The CQ Researcher (ISSN 1056-2036). Formerly Editorial Research Reports. Published weekly, except Jan. 2, May 29, July 3, Oct. 30, by Congressional Quarterly Inc., 1414 22nd St., N.W., Washington, D.C. 20037. Annual subscription rate for libraries, businesses and government is $340. Additional rates furnished upon request. Periodicals postage paid at Washington, D.C., and additional mailing offices. POSTMASTER: Send address changes to The CQ Researcher, 1414 22nd St., N.W., Washington, D.C. 20037.

European Monetary Union

BY Mary H. Cooper

THE ISSUES

Around the world, the countdown to the new millennium has begun. But in Brussels, Belgium, the huge digital clock in front of European Union (EU) headquarters is ticking off the hours until another momentous event.

On Jan. 1, 1999, a new economic powerhouse will debut on the world stage. Eleven of the EU's 15 member states will start using a new common currency — the euro.

Moreover, Germany, France, Spain and the eight other charter members of the Economic and Monetary Union (EMU) — dubbed Euroland —will hand over considerable policy-making control to a new European Central Bank.* If all goes according to plan, the euro will foster a new era of prosperity in Europe and a formidable new challenge to U.S. dominance of global trade and finance.

"Eleven European states, joining 290 million inhabitants, will share the same currency for the first time since the fall of the Roman Empire," said Yves-Thibault de Silguy, a member of the European Commission, the EU's executive branch. "This is undeniably a historic event. It is also a sweeping economic and monetary event: The euro zone will be the world's leading trading power, and it will carry an economic weight comparable to that of the United States." [1]

All 15 members of the EU were invited to apply for membership in the EMU. But Greece failed to meet the criteria for membership, and the United Kingdom, Denmark and Sweden chose not to join, at least initially. (*See map, p. 1028.*)

Even without the other EU members, Euroland will be a major player in the

global economy. Its members account for 20 percent of global trade, even more than the United States (16 percent). Exports from the 11 members are 25 percent greater than those of the United States and twice those of Japan, the world's second-largest exporter. Euroland's combined gross domestic product (GDP) is 80 percent that of the United States but half again greater than Japan's. [2] (*See table, p. 1029.*)

At first, the new currency will be used only for non-cash transactions, such as purchases of stocks and bonds, government accounting and some business invoicing. But on Jan. 1, 2002, ordinary citizens will start using euro notes and coins for all exchanges. And six mounths later, in July 2002, national currencies such as the German mark, French franc and Italian lira will disappear altogether, marking the demise of powerful symbols of national identity.

Monetary union came to fruition so quickly that it caught many Europeans by surprise, but the idea is hardly new. Europeans had wrangled for decades as they tried to create what British Prime Minister Winston Churchill envisioned as a United States of Europe as early as 1946. Until recently, however, progress was blocked by bickering over agricultural subsidies, trade barriers and other issues, as well as the Continent's sluggish economy and high inflation and unemployment.

But the end of the Cold War and subsequent economic growth jumpstarted consolidation. In December 1991, even as former Soviet-bloc nations in Eastern Europe were clamoring to join the EU, its member nations were meeting in a small city in the Netherlands to create the common currency. The resulting Maastricht Treaty set strict economic standards that all participating countries would have to meet before joining the EMU and adopting the euro. Mainly, applicants had to reduce inflation and budget deficits and stabilize their exchange and interest rates (*see p. 1038*).

Efforts to meet Maastricht's strict criteria have paid off. "Europessimism" has given way to "Euro-optimism" as Italy, Spain and other nations with lackluster economies have made unprecedented strides toward reining in inflation and government spending.

In fact, the continent's overall economy has grown so strong in the past few years that Europe is being touted as the most economically stable region in the world, a safe haven for investors burned by the Asian financial crisis and the roller-coaster ride stock prices have taken in the United States.

Monetary union offers a number of potential benefits to member countries. Adoption of a single currency is designed to help stabilize prices, the main objective of EMU and the European Central Bank's foremost obligation under its charter. A single currency will eliminate trading against swings in currency values, reducing a major cost of trade both within Europe and with non-European importers and exporters. A single currency also will make it harder for companies to charge more for their products in one country than another, thus making it easier for consumers to pay fair prices.

Prices also should fall as inefficient European companies, long protected from outside competition, are forced either to become competitive

---

*The 11 nations are Austria, Belgium, Finland, France, Germany, Italy, Ireland, Luxembourg, the Netherlands, Spain and Portugal.

A New Alliance in Europe

The 11 charter members of the new Economic and Monetary Union (EMU) form a powerful trading alliance that will begin using the new euro currency in 1999; all are members of the European Union.* Four EU members are not in the monetary union: Greece sought membership but was rejected, and the United Kingdom, Denmark and Sweden chose not to join. Six other nations seek to join the EU and may then seek membership in the monetary union.**

**The 11 members are Austria, Belgium, Finland, France, Germany, Italy, Ireland, Luxembourg, the Netherlands, Spain and Portugal.*
** *The six are the Czech Republic, Estonia, Hungary, Poland, Slovenia and Cyprus (not shown).*

Source: European Union

in the larger European market or fail. Both consumers and businesses are expected to enjoy lower borrowing costs. And tourists traveling in Euroland will no longer have to trade currencies at every border crossing.

Many American analysts predict that the euro will also benefit the United States. U.S. exports to the European Union totaled more than $140 billion in 1997, accounting for a fifth of U.S. exports. Although European firms are rapidly becoming more efficient by entering into cross-border mergers and shedding government ownership through privatization, American companies retain a competitive edge in Europe.

"Most U.S. companies have already gone through the hard decisions on bringing costs under control," says Charles Ludolph, deputy assistant secretary for Europe at the Commerce Department's International Trade Administration. "In the aftermath of the 1980s, anybody still standing had brought costs under control, and this was reflected in the prices of their products. In Europe, they haven't gone through that at all."

If there is a downside to euro membership, it is the budget cuts and higher taxes that Italians, Spaniards and other Europeans endured to join Euroland and will have to endure in the future, lest inflation return and force governments to pay steep penalties.

The call for lower public spending also challenges a deep-rooted culture throughout most of Europe that looks to the government for generous unemployment compensation and pensions and other social-welfare programs. Unemployment, which remains a key concern for many Europeans and is thought to have helped unseat German Chancellor Helmut Kohl, may remain high for some time to come.

And there is another downside to monetary union. By adopting the single currency, Euroland governments will lose control over a vital instrument for managing a national economy — the power to mint money and influence its value by adjusting interest rates. If a euro nation's economy goes into recession, its government can no longer lower interest rates to spur borrowing and thus help boost production and employment. It will have to await action from the European Central

European Economies at a Glance

In meeting strict economic criteria for membership in the new Economic and Monetary Union (EMU), members instituted austerity measures that had the unwanted effect in many cases of increasing unemployment.

EU Countries	Population (in millions)	GDP (in $ billions)	Inflation Rate	Unemployment Rate	Deficit (% of GDP)	Debt (% of GDP)
Germany	82.1	1,452	0.6	9.5	-2.7	61.3
France	58.6	1,200	0.5	11.9	-3	58
*United Kingdom	57.6	1,190	1.5	6.5 (est.)	-1.9	53.4
Italy	56.8	1,080	2.1	12.0 (est.)	-2.7	121.6
Spain	39.1	593	1.6	18.5	-2.6	68.8
Netherlands	15.6	302	1.3	4.4 (est.)	-1.4	72.1
Belgium	10.2	197	0.8	8.8	-2.1	122.2
*Sweden	8.9	184	-0.1	7.7	-0.8	76.6
Austria	8.0	152	0.6	4.5	-2.5	66.1
Portugal	9.9	116	2.2	4.6	-2.5	62
*Denmark	5.3	113	1.1	4.3	0.7	65.1
*Greece	10.6	102	5.0	9.2 (est.)	-4	108.7
Finland	5.1	92	1.4	11.2	-0.9	55.8
Ireland	3.6	55	2.8	8.8	0.9	66.3
Luxembourg	0.4	10	0.7	2.2	1.7	6.7

Sources: *European Union, The New York Times 1998 Almanac*
*Not members of the Economic and Monetary Union
Note: Population and GDP figures are from 1997; all other data are from 1998.

Bank in Frankfurt, and there is no guarantee that the bank will lower rates if the recession is localized. Without the power to lower interest rates or devalue its currency, the country in recession would face rising unemployment. The loss of sovereignty is an especially sensitive issue in Britain, whose currency, the sterling, was the dominant currency in world trade before the dollar superseded it after World War I.

There are signs of discord in Euroland as well. While the political leaders of all 11 member countries express enthusiastic support of the new currency, not all citizens of Euroland are convinced. The euro enjoys wide support in Italy and in the smaller countries involved, such as Luxembourg, the Netherlands and Belgium. But ironically, support for the euro is weak in Germany and France, the two countries whose leaders have led the push toward European unification. Kohl, who was succeeded by Gerhard Schroeder in the Sept. 27 election, counted monetary union as one of the crowning achievements of his 16-year tenure. "The previous government and, to a somewhat lesser degree, the new government are formally very much for the euro," says Meinhard Miegel, director of the Bonn Institute for Economic and Social Research. "But this very optimistic approach to the new currency somehow has not convinced the majority of the population. Germans are still very hesitant when it comes to this change."

Signs of conflict are evident even at the official level. On May 2, when European heads of state announced the admission of the 11 members to the euro club, a crack in the veneer of official accord suddenly developed over the leadership of the European Central Bank. Although it was agreed that Wim Duisenberg, a former central banker from the Netherlands, would become the bank's first president, as expected, France suddenly blocked the appointment. A compromise was reached with an informal agreement that Duisenberg would

Expansion of the European Union . . .

As the European Union becomes stronger, many countries now outside the EU see membership as a ticket to security and prosperity. Eleven countries are seeking admission to the exclusive club of Europe's wealthiest countries. Admission to the EU would be a first step tward membership in the new Economic and Monetary Union (EMU).

Expansion has always been central to the EU's ultimate vision of creating a continental federation, a kind of United States of Europe. From its founding membership of six countries in 1958, the EU has expanded to 15 countries. Turkey has been trying to join since 1963, and the disintegration of the Soviet bloc after 1989 freed Central and Eastern European countries to apply for membership as the surest way to embrace the Western economic and political model, and Western military protection.

Not everyone covets EU membership. Switzerland has stayed away to preserve its traditional neutrality. And Norwegian voters chose not to join when the Scandinavian countries put EU membership to a referendum in 1997. Together with Iceland and Liechtenstein, they belong to a free-trade area of their own called the European Free Trade Association (EFTA). Talks now under way to include Canada in the EFTA may soon result in the first transatlantic trade agreement.

But most non-member countries are eager to join the EU. At a summit on enlargement held last December in Luxembourg, the EU invited six countries to become candidates for EU membership. Five others — Bulgaria, Latvia, Lithuania, Romania and Slovakia — were encouraged to improve conditions with an eye to gaining EU admission at a later date. On March 31, negotiations began with the six — the Czech Republic, Cyprus, Estonia, Hungary, Poland and Slovenia — which were picked for early admission on the basis of their economic, political and social conditions.

"These negotiations will take time," cautioned European Commission member Yves-Thibault de Silguy of France. "It's a matter of integrating more than 100 million people whose average income is far below the EU average."[1]

Even after they gain admission to the EU, unlikely to occur before 2003, the new members will have to meet a new set of criteria to join the EMU and adopt its new currency, the euro.

There are several obstacles to EU expansion, the most obvious concerning the euro itself. For monetary union to work, participating countries must have relatively sound economies. The criteria for adopting the euro include low interest rates, low inflation and little government red ink. Even among the relatively wealthy members of the EU, meeting the criteria has proved difficult. Greece failed to satisfy the criteria in time to join Jan. 1, and it will be even harder for less advanced economies, especially those that are still struggling to shift from Soviet-style state ownership to a system based on private enterprise.

The Czech Republic, one of the six candidates for early admission to the EU, has greatly reduced its budget deficit, but at the cost of worsening unemployment. And the Czechs have made little progress in privatizing companies

---

resign halfway through his eight-year term to make way for French central banker Jean-Claude Trichet.

Indeed, some economists say support for greater European union is eroding, even as the Jan. 1 start-up date approaches. "Increasing numbers of people in Europe are beginning to be Euroskeptics, not just on the currency itself, but on the entire European concept," says Bruce Alan Johnson, a senior fellow at the Hudson Institute, a public policy research organization in Indianapolis. "The currency is scaring them because it's so close to home. This is an issue that's beginning to feel like a barbed arrow piercing their hides."

But many other economists say the willingness of Italy, Spain and some other faltering European econo-mies to lower inflation and reduce government spending bodes well for the new arrangement. "I'm not a Eurofanatic in any sense," says Richard Portes, an economics professor at the London Business School, "but I've become increasingly convinced over time, as we've seen the adjustments that have been made, that this is going to work."

Another source of optimism for the euro has been Europe's ability thus far to weather the financial crises in Asia and Russia, though there are signs that the crises have begun to cut into European exports. "For now, at least, we have withstood a trial by fire over the past few months," says Angelo Cigona, financial attaché at the Italian Embassy in Washington. "The financial markets in Europe have shown no sign of con-cern about the prospects of monetary union. The fact that things have gone so well in such a difficult situation is very encouraging."

As the euro's introduction fast approaches, these are some of the issues that economists and policy-makers are considering:

Is Europe ready for monetary union?

The Maastricht Treaty, ratified in 1992, set five strict "convergence criteria" for EMU membership:

• Inflation within 1.5 percentage points of the three best-performing EU countries;

• annual budget deficits of no more than 3 percent of gross domestic product (GDP);

• exchange-rate stability for two

... Is Key to Federation

and financial markets and passing laws necessary to meet the EU's labor and environmental standards.

Another obstacle to expansion lies in the EU's institutions and programs. For example, EU decision-making relies on unanimous approval, and if membership expanded beyond the current 15 members, the EU's policy-making apparatus could become paralyzed.

In addition, expensive EU programs such as agricultural subsidies and development assistance to economically depressed countries could be swamped when poor, rural countries are admitted. Poland's overwhelmingly agricultural economy is based on roughly 2 million small, family-owned farms that are ill-equipped to compete with the EU's advanced agribusinesses. Absent a wrenching consolidation of the farming sector, Poland's admission would overwhelm the EU's agricultural program. [2] The EU already plans to spend $80 billion to help the new applicants make necessary reforms, and there are calls to greatly reduce the subsidy programs before they join.

There are also political complications involved in admitting new members. Opposition to expansion runs high in Germany, the main contributor to the EU's budget, where expansion is seen as a further drag on the economy. Germans are especially worried that the early admission of neighboring Poland, Hungary and the Czech Republic would encourage immigration from these countries, worsening unemployment.

Another divisive issue involves Turkey, whose application for EU membership dates back to 1963. Turkey was again rebuffed last year, ostensibly because of its poor record on human rights and its ongoing dispute with Greece over the status of Cyprus. Many Turks see their continued exclusion from the EU as nothing more than an act of European racism against a Muslim country. Indeed, opposition to Turkey's membership runs high in Germany, where the presence of millions of Turkish migrant workers is already a controversial political issue.

Many critics of the latest enlargement decision view Turkey's admission to the EU as a vital way to tie Turkey, a key NATO ally, more solidly to Europe. "Few things could be more important for our security than that Turkey should remain democratic and well-disposed toward the West," writes Michael Portillo, who served in former British Prime Minister John Major's Cabinet. "It is very difficult for the Turkish government to sell to its people the merits of being a good member of NATO, and it is difficult for us to persuade Turkey to be reasonable over the Cyprus problem, when it is offered so little and treated so brusquely by the EU." [3]

---

[1] Speaking at a Sept. 25 meeting of the European Commission in Vienna, Austria.

[2] See Peter Finn, "Poland's Family Farms Face Being Plowed Under," *The Washington Post*, Oct. 20, 1998.

[3] Michael Portillo, "Europe on the Brink," *The National Interest*, spring 1998, p. 36.

---

years;

• long-term interest rates within 2 percentage points of rates in countries with the lowest interest rates; and

• government debt of no more than 60 percent of GDP.

With less than seven years to meet the criteria, countries with large budget deficits and high inflation and interest rates adopted painful austerity measures. In Italy and Spain, for example, qualifying for the euro meant imposing tough budget cuts and tax increases, which have been especially painful at a time of persistently high unemployment.

By the May 1998 deadline, all but one of the 12 countries that had sought admission to the EMU had met the standards. Greece, whose budget deficit remained too high for admission in the first wave of applications, will try to qualify by 2001.

The quest to meet the Maastricht criteria has given Europe's financial health a big boost over the past few years. While the Asian financial crisis sent U.S. stocks into a nose dive last summer, and Russia defaulted on its loans, international investors poured money into European stocks and bonds. Though Europe's stock markets also took a hit in late summer, projected growth for the EU in 1999 stands at around 2 percent, down only slightly from last year's 2.5 percent growth rate.

The rosy economic picture, combined with the unprecedented convergence of economic and financial conditions in most of the EU, leads many economists to agree with Europe's political leaders that the time is ripe for monetary union. "There's very little doubt in my mind that they are ready," says Portes of the London Business School. "They have satisfied the formal criteria, which I always believed to be excessively precise and have relatively little economic justification."

But other experts are concerned that several countries are less prepared for monetary union than the statistics would suggest. They say that only a few countries actually met the criteria but that the numbers were fudged to enable Italy and some other countries into the union to bolster confidence in the euro.

"If they had been going by the letter of the Maastricht Treaty, they

AGENDA so nicht

German farmers at European Union headquarters in Brussels, Belgium, last March protest plans to expand the EU, known as Agenda 2000. To help pay for expansion, tariff protection and price supports for EU farmers would be eliminated or reduced. The placard reads "Agenda, not that way."

government debt below 60 percent of GDP. The rest — including such economic giants as Germany — slipped in through a loophole in the Maastricht Treaty that exempted countries where debt ratios are falling "at a satisfactory pace." [3]

"Clearly, not all the euro participants are ready," says Miegel of the Bonn Institute for Economic and Social Research. "The weak man in the whole thing is Italy. Everybody knew that, but when the final meeting came about, the heads of state and government decided to take Italy in."

A clear sign of Italy's inability to live by the Maastricht agreement, Miegel says, was the Oct. 9 collapse of Prime Minister Romano Prodi's government, which introduced the policies that enabled Italy to qualify for the EMU. "The communists were not willing to support his stringent budgetary policies, and that is why he had to leave," Miegel says. "The majority of the Italian parliament said they were not willing to fulfill the Maastricht agreement's requirements."

Prodi's successor, Massimo D'Alema, has promised to continue Prodi's program. However, D'Alema's role as leader of the Democratic Party of the Left, which succeeded the defunct Italian Communist Party, would suggest support for more government spending, not less.

Miegel questions D'Alema's ability to keep Italy on track with the EMU requirements. "If he wants to get a majority in parliament, he will have to be rather lenient in regard to his policies," Miegel says, "and that is not a good omen for the euro."

Italian officials reject these criticisms out of hand, citing a halving of inflation and a cut in the budget deficit from 7 percent of GDP to 3 percent over the past three years. "Italy's readiness on the economic-front is apparent from the statistics," says Cicogna at the Italian Embassy. "Italy fully satisfied all the economic convergence criteria for public fi-

would have gone for about six countries, not 11," says John Grahl, an economist at the University of North London Business School. "The others haven't met the required fiscal constraints, and their inclusion was a political override."

The European Commission itself acknowledged that only three of the applicant states managed to reduce

AP Photo/Yves Logghe

nance, inflation, interest rates and exchange rates.

"If it were true that the numbers were just an aberration, that would have become apparent later, but the economic trends continue to be strongly positive. Inflation remains very low and fell even lower recently, interest rates are completely in line with those of other European countries, and the exchange rate is very stable, as it was throughout this summer's turmoil."

While governments have been tightening their belts, European companies have also been gearing up for the increased competition that is expected to result from monetary union. Many of Europe's biggest companies are state-owned and have been sheltered from the competition that forced American companies to shed unprofitable divisions in the 1980s. But in preparation for the EMU, governments have been privatizing some of their biggest concerns, including telecommunications giants Deutsche Telekom AG and France Telecom and Italian oil and gas producer ENI SpA.

While the privatizations are still under way, other companies are seeking to capture market share by cutting costs and merging with partners in other Euroland countries. Some of the biggest are extending their reach beyond the region, notably Germany's Daimler-Benz, which bought Chrysler Corp. this year. Largely as a result of the merger activity, 38 of the world's largest 100 companies are European, up from 27 only a year ago. [4]

Can monetary union work without greater fiscal and political integration?

Viewed strictly from the American experience, the answer may well be no. After all, the Federal Reserve Board, the U.S. equivalent of the new European Central Bank, controls the money supply and interest rates in a single economic and political entity. Most of its citizens share a common language and a national culture of mobility — social, economic and physical. When regional economies fail, as did the manufacturing Midwest in the 1970s and the Texas oil patch in the 1980s, many workers move to areas where jobs are more plentiful. A common fiscal policy also means that a region in recession will pay less in federal taxes and receive more in federal welfare benefits, further easing the blow of economic hardship.

Euroland, by contrast, is a patchwork of sovereign nations with distinct languages, cultures and histories that have more often been at war with each other than in search of common ground. Today, just one European in three speaks English, the most commonly spoken foreign language on the Continent, and just 15 percent of non-French Europeans speak French. [5]

In fact, when Germany emerged as the strongest economy in the EC in the 1970s and '80s, language and cultural differences prevented many jobless workers from southern Italy, Greece and other poor regions from moving to Germany, even after new policies favoring labor mobility made it possible for EU citizens to work anywhere in the union. This labor immobility, together with the lack of a common fiscal policy, makes it all the more likely that regional recessions will escalate, creating what economists call asymmetric shocks that monetary union alone cannot prevent.

"Just to have monetary policy and nothing else won't work," says Grahl of the University of North London. "It will be hard to get an efficient system if you don't coordinate fiscal policy with monetary policy.* But all that exists at the moment is a constraint on deficits. There are no procedures

---

* Monetary policy involves setting interest rates; fiscal policy deals with spending and taxing.

for coordinating fiscal policies or for aligning fiscal policy with monetary policy. The danger is that the monetary policy will be announced, and then each country will have to adapt its own fiscal policy without asking, or even being able to ask, what the implications of everybody's fiscal policies are for the macroeconomy."

Grahl supports expansion of the European Union's budget, which is now used primarily to pay agricultural subsidies to member farmers. A small portion of the budget is used to help compensate for unemployment or low income in economically depressed regions and to help Spain, Greece, Portugal and Ireland — the "poor four" — reach EMU eligibility. The EC budget would have to be about five times its current size and used mostly to help regions cope with economic downturns, Grahl says, to have a macroeconomic impact.

But expansion of the EU budget would require agreement among all 15 members, a prospect that seems less likely than consensus on monetary union. "The feeling at the moment is that Germany, which is the biggest paymaster, would want reform of the way in which the budget is financed before it would consider an expansion of the budget," Grahl says. "And there are some countries, including Britain, which are just flatly opposed to [budgetary] expansion and want to continue to have a small budget."

Other experts say the risk of asymmetric shocks under EMU have been overblown. "It's very hard to think of shocks that would hit just one national economy and not the others in the system because European economies are not terribly specialized," says Portes of the London Business School. "There's a lot of differentiation among regions in individual countries, such as the Northeast and Southeast of England, not to mention Scotland, where conditions are very, very different. We have a one-size-fits-all monetary policy, and yet somehow we have survived."

Some economists emphasize that while the EMU is limited to monetary union, EC members are continuing to build closer links in other policy areas that will enable them to overcome regional downturns. "Economic policy consists of more than monetary policy," says Cicogna of the Italian Embassy. "Policies related to budgets, competition, strengthening the Common Market and other instruments can all be used to deal with this kind of problem, and these are areas in which member countries are now improving coordination. So I don't see any incompatibility between the creation of a single monetary and anti-inflationary policy on the one hand and problems that may affect the various countries in different ways."

Whether the EMU will lead to closer economic or even political union is a matter of even greater controversy. Churchill's vision of a United States of Europe is still acknowledged as the ultimate goal of the 40-year-old process of European integration. "The construction of economic and monetary union is a step in a much broader vision whose goal is to strengthen the political links among the nations of Europe," says Cicogna of the Italian Embassy, reflecting his country's strong support of the process. "Certainly the direction in which public opinion is headed in Italy points to stronger ties with the rest of Europe, though how this will or can happen on an institutional level is hard to say."

Euroskeptics counter that the economic and political basis for monetary union does not yet exist. "One of the bricks in the wall of Europe is the euro, but it won't stand because they are building on a foundation of sand," says Johnson of the Hudson Institute. A currency's success, he says, relies on confidence in

---

> "Euroland will have a huge economy, massive reserves and a huge trade surplus.
> If it's a success, it ought to be the second currency behind the dollar, without any shadow of a doubt."
>
> — *Caesar Bryan,*
> *senior vice president,*
> *Gabelli Asset*
> *Management Co.*

---

the issuer's political stability. "The Swiss franc is essentially the strongest currency in the world because people are confident about the stability of the Swiss government and the degree of gold backing. There's nothing backing the euro except the mixed basket of currencies, which includes not only the Deutschmark but the Spanish peseta, and that shakes people up."

Some critics predict that going ahead with EMU in the absence of closer fiscal and political union dooms the euro to failure from the outset. "Political union must precede monetary union — that is what historical experience keeps stressing," writes Josef Joffe, an editor of the Munich daily newspaper *Süddeutsche Zeitung*.

"Nor is monetary union a kind of furtive shortcut to political union, as Europe's federalists might presume," Joffe continues. "Money, in fact, does not bind what pulls apart. The first thing secessionist states do is to print their own tender — as the American Confederacy did in 1861, as Slovakia did in 1993. Money, as every unhappy family knows, is a prime cause of discord and divorce." [6]

Does European monetary union threaten the United States?

The U.S. dollar has reigned as the world's leading currency for more than a half-century. Most international trade, including non-U.S. trade, is conducted in dollars, and foreign governments hold more dollars in reserve than any other currency. But the new euro, by essentially incorporating the currencies of 11 European countries — including the mighty Deutschmark — may be poised to challenge the dollar's supremacy. At stake is not only the competitive edge held by U.S. banks and other financial institutions and lower transaction costs for American companies but also the political clout that comes with ownership of the world's pre-eminent currency.

"If the birth of the single currency lives up to its expectations," writes Italian financial columnist Isabella Bufacchi, "Euroland will not only develop to resemble the U.S. market,

Visitors to Europe won't see the new euro currency until Jan. 1, 2002. But beginning in 1999, the euro will be used for non-cash transactions, such as stock and bond purchases. Coins valued at one euro, above, will be worth slightly more than $1.

but it may even aspire to dethrone the dollar and its financial products from their dominion, thus far uncontested, on a global scale. How? The EMU meets all the requirements to become one of the biggest and most efficient markets in the world for stocks, bonds and derivatives denominated in what could well be a currency of refuge." [7]

Some American analysts agree that the euro has the makings to challenge, if not eclipse, the dollar. "Euroland will have a huge economy, massive reserves and a huge trade surplus," writes Caesar Bryan, senior vice president of Gabelli Asset Management Co. in Rye, N.Y. "Inflation is very low. If it's a success, it ought to be the second currency behind the dollar, without any shadow of a doubt." [8]

Other economists dismiss the euro as a threat to the greenback's dominance. "The dollar is still the major trading currency because commodities that are traded worldwide, from oil to pork bellies, are denominated in dollars at the end of the transaction," Johnson says. "Also, Europe is not a serious player in the Asian markets, and it's a non-player in South America," regions where dollar transactions dominate.

Not only the U.S. currency but also American companies may face stronger rivals as a result of the euro's arrival. Monetary union is forcing European companies to become more efficient, and thus potentially stronger competitors with U.S. companies for market share, both in the EU and abroad. Long before the euro's arrival, the pace of cross-border mergers between large European companies picked up in preparation to compete with U.S. giants in the global marketplace. Even longstanding rivals like the London and Frankfurt stock exchanges plan to start cooperating Jan. 4, the first day of trading in euros. [9]

But many American analysts say U.S. producers will flourish under the new currency regime, just as they have since the removal of internal trade barriers under the EU's single market. "U.S. manufacturers already benefit enormously from the economies of scale in Europe," says Marino Marcich, director of international investments and finance at the National Association of Manufacturers. By providing "one-stop shopping" for U.S. producers, he says, the single market means that "You can take a product, and if you have market access to a country like Ireland, you can market the exact same product across borders in 14 other countries."

In this view, large American companies, especially multinationals already present in Euroland, will actually gain a competitive edge over their European rivals under the euro. That's because the process of privatization is still very much under way in Europe, where many of the largest companies still retain the inefficiencies of partial or total state ownership and have yet to penetrate markets outside their borders.

"Unlike large European companies, which are mostly single-state companies, U.S. multinationals are all multi-European national companies," says Ludolph of the International Trade Administration. "Because the euro will be more stable [than national currencies], there will be less cost associated with changes among the various currencies that a U.S. multinational deals in. So they really are in a position to reap most of the benefits of the single currency."

U.S. multinationals may also be better placed than their European competitors to take advantage of the increase in price "transparency" the euro will bring. Up to now, companies selling goods on the European market have been able to charge different prices among countries and hide the differences behind the veil of frequently adjusted exchange rates.

"Starting Jan. 1, companies will no longer be able to mask their lack of competitiveness behind the differences between, say, lire and marks,"

Ludolph says. "They will have to be able to explain to Italian and German customers what exactly is in the price, and price competition will begin in a serious way. Companies caught at high price levels will have to come down to whatever the average price is in Europe. With the euro, we will see the beginning of the kind of cost sensitivity that you see in the United States, where price is the primary factor in competition."

American multinationals may be well-prepared for the euro's arrival. But the same cannot be said for the majority of American exporters, who shipped more than $140 billion in goods and services to EU countries last year, accounting for a fifth of total U.S. exports. Since June, the Commerce Department has held seminars-around the country and in September created a Web site to help exporters deal with the change, including the need to shift their contracts from marks and francs into euros.

But only weeks before the euro goes into effect on Jan. 1, Ludolph says, "U.S. exporters are, as a practical matter, totally uninformed and unprepared for the euro. Most exporters really don't read the newspapers, so they're unaware that the euro is going to change the currency that they're going to be dealing with. When they start getting orders in euro, there will be quite a bit of turmoil."

On balance, however, the Clinton administration has concluded that the euro's benefits for the U.S. economy far outweigh its potential threat to the dollar's supremacy. In the administration's view, the benefits are twofold. "The euro would force Europe to make macroeconomic decisions that are more market-oriented," Ludolph explains, "and this would make Europe a stronger economic partner for the United States."

"Also," Ludolph continues, "instead of 15 members of the EU making decisions on exchange rates, there would be a

single exchange-rate policy, one based on sound monetary and fiscal policy. We're really glad to see these governments adopting the same kind of structure that we have with the Federal Reserve Board." ∎

BACKGROUND

Early Union Efforts

The euro is the end result of repeated efforts to coordinate Europe's economic policies that predate the postwar push toward European Union. More than 130 years ago, France established a monetary system that linked the franc with the currencies of Belgium, Bulgaria, Greece, Italy and Switzerland. The Latin Monetary Union was intended to tame the volatility of members' exchange rates, which had disrupted trade.

The union did not last. But efforts to stabilize Europe's exchange rates did, initially by fixing currencies to the gold standard. After World War II, calls for greater economic and political collaboration among the countries of Western Europe mounted. France and West Germany took the lead, creating the European Coal and Steel Community in 1952 to coordinate coal and steel production under a supranational authority. Belgium, Italy, Luxembourg and the Netherlands also joined.

Under the 1958 Treaties of Rome, the same six countries established the European Economic Community with the goal of removing barriers to the free movement of capital, products and people. Together with a third entity, the European Atomic Energy Community, these institutions were known collectively as the European Community (EC), or the Com-

mon Market. Britain, Ireland and Denmark joined the EC in 1973, followed by Greece in 1981 and Portugal and Spain in 1986. In 1990, German unification added an additional 18 million people to the 12-nation community.

In addition to broadening the EC's reach with new members, the community gradually strengthened the bonds linking them. In 1968 a new agreement removed all customs duties on trade within the EC, setting a common external tariff on imports to the community. The EC also adopted a common agricultural policy. In 1979, EC citizens elected the first European Parliament.

Searching for Stability

In 1944, a new system of fixed exchange rates was set up, supported by a newly created multilateral institution, the International Monetary Fund (IMF). Using the dollar as the dominant currency, the Bretton Woods system reduced the volatility of exchange rates and enhanced the postwar economic boom and expansion in world trade for the next 27 years.

At the same time, efforts grew to more closely integrate monetary policy within the EC, and in 1962 the European Commission first proposed establishing a single currency. In 1971, EC heads of government endorsed a plan drawn up by a committee of experts headed by Luxembourg Prime Minister Pierre Werner that called for full economic and monetary union with a common currency by 1980.

The Werner Report's strategy was thwarted the same year when President Richard M. Nixon suspended convertibility of the dollar into gold, causing the Bretton Woods system of

Continued on p. 1038

Chronology

1950s-1960s
After World War II, Western European countries take steps to coordinate economic policy.

1952
The European Coal and Steel Community is set up to coordinate coal and steel production in France and Germany. Belgium, Italy, Luxembourg and the Netherlands also join.

1957
The same six countries sign the Treaties of Rome establishing the European Economic Community (EC), or Common Market, to remove trade barriers.

1968
A customs union goes into effect removing all duties on trade within the EC and setting a common external tariff on imports to the community. The EC also adopts a common agricultural policy.

1970s-1980s
Enlargement brings more Western European countries into the Common Market.

1971
President Richard M. Nixon abandons the Bretton Woods system of fixed exchange rates, resulting in chaos on European exchange markets and the creation of an exchange-rate system tying European curren-cies to the Deutschmark.

1973
The United Kingdom, Denmark and Ireland join the EC.

1979
A new European Monetary System is established to curb fluctuations in currency values. Community citizens elect the first European Parliament.

1981
Greece joins the EC, followed in 1986 by Portugal and Spain.

June 1988
EC members endorse a plan by Commission President Jacques Delors of France to achieve a single European market by 1992.

1990s-2000s
European integration proceeds with economic and monetary union.

1990
German unification adds 18 million people to the 12-member EC.

December 1991
Meeting in Maastricht, the Netherlands, EC members agree to establish a common currency and establish the economic criteria for countries wishing to join the monetary union.

January 1992
All internal border checks on the flow of people, goods, services and capital fall. The community renames itself the European Union (EU).

1995
Austria, Finland and Sweden join the EU, bringing the membership to 15 countries.

Dec. 12-13, 1997
Meeting in Luxembourg, the EU invites six countries — the Czech Republic, Cyprus, Estonia, Hungary, Poland and Slovenia — to become candidates for admission, but rebuffs Turkey, which first applied in 1963.

May 2, 1998
European heads of state meeting in Brussels agree that 11 EU member states will adopt the euro on Jan. 1, 1999. Greece fails to meet the criteria, and the United Kingdom, Denmark and Sweden choose not to join for the present. Wim Duisenberg, a former central banker from the Netherlands, is chosen to be the first president of a new European Central Bank.

Jan. 1, 1999
Eleven EU members will adopt a single currency, the euro, and hand over much of their power to make monetary and economic policy to the European Central Bank.

Jan. 1, 2002
Euro notes and coins are to be issued, replacing all national currencies in the 11 countries participating in monetary union within six months.

Wim Duisenberg of the Netherlands was chosen as the first president of the new European Central Bank.

Continued from p. 1036

fixed exchange rates to collapse. Left to the vagaries of the marketplace, European currencies gyrated in value until 1972, when EC governments devised an alternative mechanism to stabilize them.

The new system, known as the "snake," tied currencies loosely to the mark, which by then had replaced the pound sterling as Europe's strongest currency, thanks in large part to Germany's strong anti-inflationary policy. But domestic policy differences, which caused broad swings in currency values, weakened the system. Britain, France and Ireland joined and then dropped the snake.

In 1979, EC members replaced the snake with the European Monetary System and established a new exchange-rate mechanism (ERM) that strictly limited fluctuations in currency values. Member countries agreed to take the policy steps necessary to keep their currencies within a narrow range of a central rate denominated in a new European currency unit (ECU), whose value was based on the weighted average of all member countries' currencies.

But the new system was unable to prevent France and some other countries from repeatedly devaluing their currencies, and Britain and Italy eventually abandoned it. By 1993, EU members were forced to widen the allowable range of exchange-rate fluctuation.

Maastricht Treaty

By the early 1990s, the EC boasted 12 members and a complex of supranational institutions overseeing efforts to integrate Europe's diverse economies. But exchange-rate stability continued to elude the community. Dissatisfied with the ERM, EC members in June 1988 endorsed a plan by Commission President Jacques Delors of France to achieve a single European market by 1992. [10]

With the arrival of the "single market" in January 1992, EC members eliminated internal border checks on the flow of people, goods, services and capital. The community renamed itself the European Union and continued the process of enlargement by admitting Austria, Finland and Sweden in 1995, bringing the total membership to 15 countries. (Norwegians declined admission in a referendum.)

An integral part of Delors' plan was the creation of economic and monetary union as the first step toward political union. Included in the plan were common policies on foreign affairs, defense, justice and internal affairs. At the 1991 Maastricht conference, EC heads of government established five criteria for adoption of the single currency: a budget deficit of no more than 3 percent of GDP; a national debt of no more than 60 percent of GDP; stable currencies; and limits on inflation and interest rates.

As governments worked toward meeting these strict conditions, EU leaders in 1995 set the Jan. 1, 1999, deadline for monetary union and replacement of the ECU with the new currency, which they dubbed the euro.

Britain, long the most vocal skeptic of European integration, opted out of the treaty and was joined later by Denmark, whose citizens rejected the single currency in a referendum, and Sweden. ■

CURRENT SITUATION

Policy Differences

The ability of the 11 countries of Euroland to overcome deeply rooted economic problems has surprised the experts. Italy, for example, slashed its budget deficit from 11 percent in 1990 to less than 3 percent of GDP, as required by the Maastricht Treaty. They also have cut inflation and the ratio of government debt to GDP.

To achieve this performance, however, governments have had to make painful adjustments in public benefits and policies that have long been considered a right of citizenship. In addition, the same austerity measures that have enabled many countries to gain admission to the monetary union have blocked noticeable improvement in Europe's high unemployment rate. Unemployment averages 10.9 percent throughout the EU, ranging from a negligible 3.6 percent in Luxembourg to a severe 19.6 percent in Spain. Even as many Europeans welcome the euro's advent, the joblessness that has accompanied preparations for its arrival may undermine popular support for monetary union.

This is especially true in Germany, where government enthusiasm for the euro has never been matched by popular opinion. "Italy and the smaller states, such as Luxembourg, the Netherlands and Belgium, are very much in favor of the new currency," Miegel says. "But Germany, like France, is particularly hesitant. Germany has little history as a nation-state, so our economic situation, including our currency, means a lot to most Germans. For them, the mark is the symbol of Germany's resurrection after the Second World War as well as the symbol of identity when East and West Germany were united eight years ago. These are episodes in our history which are of great importance."

In exchange for giving up the mark, former Chancellor Kohl insisted that the European Central Bank adopt Germany's strict anti-inflationary monetary policy. But that may not satisfy popular opinion in Germany, Europe's economic powerhouse, where unemployment exceeds 11 percent of the work force.

Analysts attribute Kohl's defeat in September in part to concern about unemployment. His successor, Social Democrat Schroeder, promises to follow a political "Third Way" between traditional European socialism and American-style, free-market capitalism with a pledge to maintain Germany's generous welfare benefits while fostering industrial competitiveness.

But Schroeder's powerful finance minister, party leader Oskar Lafontaine, supports higher corporate taxes and berates the "casino quality" of free-market capitalism, alarming German businessmen over the new government's true agenda. Schroeder has further unnerved corporate leaders by calling for a cut in the retirement age from 65 to 60, with no loss of Germany's generous

---

> **"Italy and the smaller states, such as Luxembourg, the Netherlands and Belgium, are very much in favor of the new currency. But Germany, like France, is particularly hesitant."**
>
> — *Meinhard Miegel, Director, Bonn Institute for Economic and Social Research*

---

mandated benefits, as a way to generate new jobs.

Other governments, forced to adopt austerity measures to gain admission to the monetary union, face even more daunting problems. As unemployment topped 12 percent in the wake of efforts to reduce France's budget deficit, French voters last year replaced the ruling conservatives with a socialist government led by Prime Minister Lionel Jospin, who pledged to make job creation his main priority. In February, the National Assembly approved Jospin's initiative to shorten the workweek to 35 hours by 2000, in hope that more workers

will be required to produce the same amount of goods and services. Jospin's job-creation efforts have begun to pay off, as unemployment dropped to 11.7 percent in September.

Dissatisfaction with high unemployment also helped bring down the government of Italian Prime Minister Romano Prodi, whose policies had forced the Italian economy into compliance with the Maastricht criteria. Prodi's successor, the former communist D'Alema, pledged that his center-left government would maintain Prodi's budget and other policies governing Italy's adoption of the euro.

But the fall of Prodi's government showed how concern over the country's 12.5 percent unemployment rate runs high, even in a country where popular support for the euro has thus far been strong. D'Alema himself predicted that his government's survival will depend on its ability to create jobs, and he pledged to pursue Prodi's earlier goal of shortening the workweek.

"In the final analysis, the hope is to be able to restore sustainable growth in Italy," Cicogna says. "Now that we have achieved financial and monetary stability, we have to try to get some dividends here at home with job growth. Unemployment is undoubtedly the No. 1 problem in Italy right now."

Skeptics Opt Out

A sign of weakness in Europe's support for monetary union remains the decision by the United

Kingdom, Denmark and Sweden to opt out, at least for now. Disagreement over European integration has long dominated British politics, contributing to the 1990 resignation of Conservative Prime Minister Margaret Thatcher, who had reservations about the UK's place in the European Union, and the 1997 electoral victory of the Labor Party. Skepticism over monetary union continued to run so strong that even pro-Europe Conservative Prime Minister Tony Blair ruled out joining until after the next national election, expected to be held in 2001, and a referendum on monetary union shortly thereafter. Polls show a majority of Britons still opposed to adopting the euro.

The government cited Britain's high interest rates as the main reason for its decision to postpone immediately adopting the euro and the fear that taking the steps needed to meet the membership criteria would destabilize the economy. That fear has continued as economic growth has since stalled, putting Britain out of sync with much of the rest of Europe. [11]

Unlike Germany, where opposition to the euro is based on the mark's symbolic value, British Euroskepticism has arisen mainly from a reluctance to yield sovereignty over its monetary policy and cast its lot irrevocably with the rest of Europe, a move some see as jeopardizing Britain's longstanding partnership with the United States.

"The sterling is a very weak currency," Grahl says. "We're always going to have to relate our policy either to the United States or to Western Europe. We can cut adrift from one, but only by attaching ourselves more closely to the other."

In Grahl's view, Britain will even-tually adopt the euro, despite strong opposition among Conservatives and their supporters, including media magnate Rupert Murdoch and his vast news empire. "Probably it will be more advantageous to link up with

---

> "The devastating American Civil War shows that a formal political union is no guarantee against an intra-European war."
>
> — *Martin Feldstein*
> *Professor of economics,*
> *Harvard University*

Western Europe than to base our policy on dollar interest rates," Grahl says, "because we have a lot more trade with Western Europe and because, typically, interest rates would be rather lower."

OUTLOOK

Interest Rate Fight

On Jan. 1, 1999, the euro will be established as the official cur-rency of the European monetary union. The new currency will be denominated in 100 cents to the euro, and its conversion rate in national currencies will be permanently set. Over the next three years, national currencies will still circulate, but all capital, foreign exchange and interbank markets will convert their operations to euros. Retail businesses will accept national currencies, but prices will be quoted in both national currency and euro values.

The final phase will begin Jan. 1, 2002, when euro notes and coins will be issued throughout Euroland. Over the next six months, retailers will have to accept both currencies, as national currencies are gradually withdrawn from circulation. On July 1, 2002, they will cease to be legal tender altogether, and the euro will stand alone.

Just weeks before the euro's introduction, disagreement over optimal interest-rate levels is dividing Euroland. Europe has finally begun to feel the effects of the financial crises in Asia and Russia, mainly in terms of reduced exports. The forecast for the region's economic growth next year has been lowered by a half-point, to just over 2 percent. [12] To help restore economic growth, a number of Euroland's leaders have started calling for a reduction in interest rates.

Meeting in Austria in late October, several EU leaders called for lower interest rates together with government programs to stimulate the economy. Their request was dismissed by Duisenberg as well as his likely successor, Trichet of France, as nothing more than politically moti-

Continued on p. 1042

At Issue:

Will monetary union help solve Europe's economic problems?

KLAUS FRIEDRICH
Chief economist, Dresdner Bank Group

From testimony before the House Banking and Financial Services Subcommittee on Domestic and International Monetary Policy, April 28, 1998.

*W*ith the growing globalization of markets, Europe has to seize every opportunity if it wants to compete successfully in global markets. . . . Competition between the three economic powers — Europe, the United States and Japan — will become even fiercer: New competitors, for example from fast-growing Southeast Asia, are entering the market. A large Economic and Monetary Union will increase Europe's growth, market and job potential, thereby strengthening its global, competitive position.

Competition within Europe will also stiffen. Germany has to face up to that challenge, too, while at the same time taking advantage of the opportunities a bigger market provides. A single currency will not only spare tourists and business travelers the inconvenience and cost of having to exchange their national currencies. An important direct effect will also be that companies operating in the European market will no longer have to deal with exchange-rate risks and hedging costs. This will make the flow of goods, services and capital more efficient, thereby pushing down prices.

Monetary union will also facilitate long-term investment planning; capital will flow more readily into areas where it can be used efficiently. Above all, the elimination of exchange rates will increase market transparency, which will particularly benefit small- and medium-sized firms. Price lists will become more transparent, and internal cost accounting will become easier. Finally, monetary union should step up the pressure on economic policy-makers to abolish existing protectionist mechanisms and to break up monopolies and rigid market structures within the [European Union].

EMU is the monetary counterpart to the liberalization of trade within the framework of the European single market. The elimination of trade barriers and the mutual recognition of technical norms and standards in the European single market are widening our continent's product markets. Hence, it seems only logical after the removal of physical impediments to trade to also provide the necessary monetary "lubricant" in the form of a single currency. Europe still needs to improve further as a business location, and the euro could act as a catalyst in this respect.

German companies in particular will benefit from monetary union. They have time and again been profoundly affected by the real overvaluation of the D-mark. . . . A single European currency will significantly reduce such exchange-rate-related competitive distortions, thereby strengthening the international competitiveness of German exporters.

Robert Dujarric
Research fellow, Hudson Institute, Indianapolis, Ind.

From Robert Dujarric, "Europe's Continental Drift," American Outlook, *summer 1998, pp. 60-62.*

*t*he new currency will create additional problems for the EU. . . . Optimists about [European Monetary Union] hope that it will lead to political union because a monetary union creates requirements for greater economic union. This notion, however, underestimates the resiliency of the nation-state in Europe. There is still no such thing as a "European people" or European solidarity. Note that whereas western German taxpayers transfer $75 billion annually (net) to eastern Germany, Germany's contribution to the EU is only $12 billion, and increasing it has become politically unacceptable.

It is probably wishful thinking to believe that a European Union could order massive transfer payments across borders of the sort common within nation-states. European integration efforts in the past half-century show that economic integration does not automatically create momentum toward political union. Europe has made enormous progress in economic integration, but on the political front there has been almost none. . . .

[M]onetary union will do very little to solve Europe's economic and social problems. It will not foster political union and is unlikely to increase the pace of necessary economic deregulation and reform. Moreover, the risks associated with EMU are very high. A failure of monetary union would create the most acrimonious intra-Western European dispute since the 1950s and could paralyze Europe for years as states disagreed over financial and economic matters while lacking institutional mechanisms through which to resolve them effectively. . . .

Eventually, Europe's governments will be unable to finance the continental welfare state as its costs rise faster than their ability to tax. This may well destabilize political systems when governments no longer have generous benefits with which to pacify the electorate, which could induce a protectionist, inflationary and anti-deregulation backlash. . . .

Continental Europe is rich, democratic and bourgeois. Decay and instability will not overturn its liberal democratic order, nor is war between Western European states conceivable. . . . It is probable, however, that Europe's economic and social woes will increase during the next 10 years and that its ability to help stabilize the regions of the former communist world in the Balkans, Eastern Europe and the former Soviet Union will diminish. That will increase possibilities for conflict in those regions because the former communist states need a dynamic, prosperous and strong European Union to help them make the transition to freedom.

The new euro currency goes into general circulation in January 2002, and in July the German mark, Italian lira and other currencies will be withdrawn.

vated statements that Europe's central banks should ignore. More recently, German Chancellor Schroeder and his finance minister, Lafontaine, have joined the chorus, asking the Bundesbank, Germany's central bank, to lower its short-term rate of 3.3 percent. The same call has been heard in France, where the short-term rate also stands at 3.3 percent.

But not everyone endorses interest-rate drops. If Germany and France, whose interest rates serve as the standard for Euroland convergence, cut their rates, it will become that much harder for countries with higher rates, notably Ireland, Italy, Portugal and Spain, to stay in line. Italy cut its benchmark discount rate by a full percentage point in October, but that still left it at 4 percent, while Ireland's securities-repurchase rate stands considerably higher, at 4.9 percent.

Among Euroskeptics, Martin Feldstein, a Nobel Prize-winning economics professor at Harvard University, goes so far as to suggest that current differences over the relative importance of price stability and job creation and other issues may escalate under monetary union, in part because there is no acknowledged provision for countries to leave Euroland once they enter. "[C]ontrary to the hopes and assumptions of [French champion of European union Jean] Monnet and other advocates of European integration, the devastating American Civil War shows that a formal political union is no guarantee against an intra-European war," he writes. "Although it is impossible to know for certain whether these conflicts would lead to war, it is too real a possibility to ignore in weighing the potential effects of EMU and the European political integration that would follow." [13]

But supporters of the euro, including recent convert Portes of the London Business School, predict that the ongoing controversies over interest rates and job creation will soon be forgotten, as the euro's salutary effects on the European economy become apparent. Portes expects monetary union will provide a boost to capital markets in Europe, where companies have thus far relied mostly on bank loans to finance their business.

"You hear a lot of moaning about European labor markets," he says, "but there is increasing evidence that the major problem of the European economy is not over labor markets, but rather capital markets. We have lacked a single, broad, unified, liquid capital market in which firms can get away from the dead hand of bank financing and go into the markets."

Portes predicts the euro will permit the emergence of a thriving junk-bond market. "That kind of market doesn't exist here," he explains. "In Europe, it's only the big firms that can go into the capital markets, while the rest have to deal with the banks, and the banks are conservative."

As the capital market takes off, Portes predicts, big institutional investors will play the dominant role in financial markets, as in the United States.

"We will see the pension funds, insurance companies and asset managers take a pan-European view of their investment position and take on major roles in corporate governance and in exerting pressure on firms to improve their game," he says. "There will be integration of stocks markets, and this is really going to change the face of European business." ∎

Notes

[1] Speaking before a European Commission meeting held in Vienna, Austria, on Sept. 25, 1998.
[2] Eurostat, "New EUR 11: 'World's Greatest Trading Power,'" May 1, 1998; Eurostat is the EU's statistical branch.
[3] "European Commission Says 11 EU Member States Ready for Euro," *European Union News*, March 25, 1998.
[4] "The Global Giants," *The Wall Street Journal*, Sept. 28, 1998.
[5] See "Euro-Tongues Wag in English," *The Economist*, Oct. 25, 1997, p. 60.
[6] Josef Joffe, "The Euro: The Engine That Couldn't," *The New York Review of Books*, Dec. 4, 1997, p. 30.
[7] Isabella Bufacchi, "Le Borse degli Undici preparano l'attacco al trono di Wall Street," Il *Sole-24 Ore*, Sept. 28, 1998.
[8] Quoted by Christopher Gay and Sara Calian, "Ask the Pros," *The Wall Street Journal*, Sept. 28, 1998.
[9] See Dagmar Aalund, "What's the Euro?" *The Wall Street Journal*, Sept. 28, 1998.
[10] For background, see Mary H. Cooper, "Europe 1992," *The CQ Researcher*, June 28, 1991, pp. 417-440.
[11] See "Who Wants the Euro, and Why," *The Economist*, May 2, 1998, pp. 51-52.
[12] See Anne Swardson, "On the Verge of the Euro, a Continental Divide," *The Washington Post*, Nov. 7, 1998.
[13] Martin Feldstein, "EMU and International Conflict," *Foreign Affairs*, November/December 1997, p. 62.

Bibliography

Selected Sources Used

Books

Eichengreen, Barry, and Jeffry Frieden, eds., *Forging an Integrated Europe*, The University of Michigan Press, 1998.

In this collection of essays, economists and political scientists examine the potential for further European integration in the face of controversy over the degree of autonomy member states will retain.

Newhouse, John, *Europe Adrift*, Pantheon Books, 1997.

Newhouse, a consultant to the State Department, predicts that divisions within Europe over policy toward the Balkans, the decades-old feud between Greece and Turkey and other foreign policy issues will undermine the European Union's efforts to unify the continent.

Yergin, Daniel, and Joseph Stanislaw, *The Commanding Heights: The Battle Between Government and the Marketplace That is Remaking the Modern World*, Simon & Schuster, 1998.

Deregulation and privatization of industries worldwide are shifting power away from governments. In Europe, monetary union is accelerating the change as governments sell off unprofitable enterprises to help meet strict economic criteria for adopting the euro.

Articles

"An Awfully Big Adventure," *The Economist*, April 11, 1998, 22 pp.

This special survey of European monetary union examines the risks and potential benefits to Europe, the history leading up to the 1991 decision to adopt a single currency and the timetable for the euro's introduction.

Ash, Timothy Garten, "Goodbye to Bonn," *The New York Review of Books*, Nov. 5, 1998, pp. 41-43.

The September election of Social Democrat Gerhard Schroeder as Germany's new chancellor marks the beginning of a new era in Germany. The downfall of Helmut Kohl's 16-year Conservative government coincides closely with the replacement of the powerful Deutschmark by the euro and next year's move of the government from Bonn to Berlin.

Bergsten, C. Fred, "The Dollar and the Euro," *Foreign Affairs*, July/August 1997, pp. 83-95.

Unless the United States and the European Union cooperate to achieve a smooth transition from the dollar-denominated monetary regime, the new system created by the euro could create tensions between the two, sparking a round of trade protectionism that would disrupt world trade.

Feldstein, Martin, "EMU and International Conflict," *Foreign Affairs*, November/December 1997, pp. 60-73.

The Nobel Prize-winning economist warns that Europe is not ready for monetary union and that adoption of the euro will lead to disputes among European countries with different economic conditions that may spill over into neighboring countries outside the EU.

Fox, Justin, "Europe Is Heading for a Wild Ride," *Fortune*, Aug. 17, 1998, pp. 145-149.

Europe's businesses and citizens may be unprepared for the confusion and change that await them with the euro's introduction, beginning Jan. 1, 1999. Businesses will face unprecedented competition from rivals in other European countries, while unemployed workers may be unwilling to move abroad to find jobs.

Frieden, Jeffrey, "The Euro: Who Wins? Who Loses?" *Foreign Policy*, fall 1998, pp. 24-40.

The new European Central Bank may face conflicts in crafting monetary policy if some member countries slip into recession. Some groups, such as financial centers, stand to benefit from a strong euro, while workers and farmers would benefit from a weak euro, which would make European goods more competitive on world markets.

Joffe, Josef, "The Euro: The Engine That Couldn't," *The New York Review of Books*, Dec. 4, 1997, pp. 26-31.

A German journalist predicts that monetary union will not pave the way to political union in Europe: "Frenchmen and Germans don't want to be like the citizens of Michigan and New York; nor do Italians, Spaniards or Britons. They like Europe, but they like even better their national homelands, which have been around for one or two millennia. They don't speak each other's languages; they do not share each other's memories."

Malcolm, Noel, "The Case Against 'Europe,'" *Foreign Affairs*, March/April 1995, pp. 52-68.

A columnist for *The Daily Telegraph* of London opines that the costs of European integration outweigh any benefits. "'Europe,'" he writes, "will stumble under the weight of its costs like a woolly mammoth sinking into a melting tundra."

Portes, Richard, and Hélène Rey, "The Emergence of the Euro as an International Currency," *Economic Policy*, April 1998, pp. 307-343.

Two British economists predict that the euro will end the dollar's uncontested dominance in world trade and financial markets, bringing political and economic benefits to Europe.

The Next Step

Additional information from UMI's Newspaper & Periodical Abstracts™ database

The Euro

Aalund, Dagmar, "Investing in Euroland — What's the Euro? And Other Commonly Asked Questions About the Planned Single Currency," *The Wall Street Journal,* Sept. 28, 1998, p. R6.

For European big business, the euro is seen as a way to cut transaction costs and encourage cross-border mergers, enabling Europe to compete in the race for globalization. It is already encouraging once bitter rivals to come together: The London and Frankfurt stock exchanges, sensing that the euro will make regional exchanges irrelevant, plan to start cooperating on Jan. 4, 1999, the first day of trading in euros.

Collis, Roger, "Euro Translates Currency Babel," *The New York Times,* Sept. 13, 1998, p. 4.

From Jan. 1 — the start of a three-year transition period — double price lists will show French Coke costing, say, 98 euro-cents compared with 1.3 euros in Germany. During this transition, the rates of exchange between the euro and the particular currency of each nation that uses it will be irrevocably fixed, so there will not be a daily euro-franc exchange rate, for example, to worry about. Consumer organizations will publish price comparisons of popular items in the 11 countries of the euro zone. With euro notes and coins not due to enter circulation for another three years, transactions in euros may seem unreal: An invisible currency that everyone is talking about and more and more people are using — even the British, whose self-imposed exclusion from the euro means that they won't join the European monetary union (the agreement that created the euro) until at least 2002.

Gay, Christopher, and Sara Calian, "Investing in Euroland — Ask the Pros: How Some Top Money Managers are Changing Their European Strategies to Take Advantage of the Euro," *The Wall Street Journal,* Sept. 28, 1998, p. R14.

The introduction of a single currency will change the face of investing in Europe. It's forcing the pros to reassess stocks, bonds and currencies across the board. Currently, U.K. pension funds on average invest 55-60 percent of their assets in U.K. equities. But financial advisers see that trend possibly reversing, with funds investing as much as 70 percent in Europe in a few years.

McDowell, Edwin, "That Old American Express Standby, the Check, Will Soon be Out in That New Currency, the Euro," *The New York Times,* Sept. 9, 1998, p. C5.

American Express said yesterday that it would print euro-denominated traveler's checks in time for sales to start on Jan. 1, 1999, the beginning of the European monetary union. While the euro becomes the official currency of the 11-nation euro zone next Jan. 1, with national currency exchange rates fixed to the euro, the circulation of euro notes and coins will not begin until Jan. 1, 2002. During the three-year transition, consumers will be able to use the American Express euro traveler's checks — in denominations of 50, 100 and 200 euro — to pay for goods and services while merchants begin to convert to euro pricing.

Mundell, Robert, "Making the Euro Work," *The Wall Street Journal,* April 30, 1998, p. A18.

The European Council will meet tomorrow in London to announce its final decisions regarding which countries are eligible to proceed to European monetary union, and Saturday the selected countries will meet in Brussels to implement the decision. The designated countries will lock their exchange rates to each other on July 1, 1998; the European Currency Unit will become the euro on Jan. 1, 1999, when the process of replacing national currencies by euros within banks will begin. On Jan. 1, 2002, the circulation of euro banknotes and coins will begin, and six months later, the legal tender status of national banknotes and coins will end. By the middle of 2002, the technical transition will be complete.

Mundell, Robert, "The Case for the Euro — I," *The Wall Street Journal*, March 24, 1998, p. A22.

Tomorrow at a press conference in Frankfurt, the European Monetary Institute will list countries eligible for membership, pending a final decision by European Union heads of state at a summit in London on May 1. A single-currency European monetary union is set to go into effect next year.

Steinmetz, Greg, "Design: The Euro Designer's Art Is Sure to Have Wide Currency," *The Wall Street Journal,* July 7, 1998, p. B1.

As the winner of a competition to design the first series of euro bank notes, Robert Kalina has already begun to taste celebrity. A French magazine recently ranked the 43-year-old Austrian designer alongside singer Mick Jagger and German Chancellor Helmut Kohl as one of the "100 most important Europeans." Kalina's victory came with no prize money except for a small bonus from his employer, the Austrian National Bank. But his euro notes will be used by some 280 million Europeans in 11 countries.

European Central Bank

Aalund, Dagmar, and Brian Coleman, "Germany's Lafontaine Renews Call for Rate Cut — Shift Left May

Lead To Clash on Euro," *The Wall Street Journal*, Sept. 30, 1998, p. A13.

For years, German Chancellor Helmut Kohl's support of central bank independence served as a counterweight to the jobs-oriented policies championed by France and other socialist-led countries in the European Union. But that could change under the new government, suggesting the potential for clashes with the European Central Bank, which will guide monetary policy for the new euro currency.

Dahlburg, John-Thor, "European Union Leaders Approve Common Currency; Economy: 11 of 15 member Nations at Summit will Begin Phasing in the Euro in 1999; Accord Follows French-German Flap Over Who Should Head Central Bank," *Los Angeles Times*, May 3, 1998, p. A1.

On one of Europe's most momentous days since the Berlin Wall was sledgehammered into dust, leaders of the European Union agreed Saturday to launch a single and shared currency in 11 of their countries next Jan. 1, a giant stride toward greater economic and political integration. But they argued bitterly past midnight over who would head the bank that is to manage the new money.

Kamm, Thomas, Brian Coleman and Cacilie Rohwedder, "EMU Is Born Amid Battle Over Central Bank — Summit Picks Duisenberg In Compromise at ECB, Sets Course for the Euro," *The Wall Street Journal*, May 4, 1998, p. A17.

The European Central Bank, or ECB, will define and manage monetary policy in the euro zone. Dutchman Wim Duisenberg will be appointed to an eight-year-term as leader, but will step down "voluntarily" in 2002 to make way for France's Jean-Claude Trichet. Though the fight leads some to question the ECB's credibility and the ability of governments to define common economic policies, most analysts believe it will soon be forgotten as markets focus on the almost revolutionary step that is being taken.

European Monetary Union

Ascarelli, Silvia, "European Stock Markets Rush to Form Alliances — Euro May Spell An End for Some," *The Wall Street Journal*, May 6, 1998, p. A17.

In the headlong rush to a common European currency, the euro, stock exchanges are forming alliances that could be the precursor to giving up one of these potent symbols of national sovereignty possibly in just a few years. The Germans, French and Swiss are teaming up to create an electronic network called EURO Alliance and are in talks with the Italian and Spanish exchanges. The Netherlands, Belgium and Luxembourg are forming an alliance of their own. Denmark and Sweden — two countries that won't be part of the so-called euro zone next year — are creating a third block and are inviting other Scandinavian exchanges to join. London is stand-

ing aloof, but is ready to quote stock prices and keep separate order books — one in pounds, the other in euros — for the country's 100 biggest blue chips to avoid losing business to continental Europe.

Bray, Nicholas, "Chase Hopes to Profit From New European Currency — Big U.S. Bank Plans to Adopt the Euro on Jan. 1 for Internal Operations," *The Wall Street Journal*, Aug. 26, 1998, p. B4.

When economic and monetary union, or EMU, begins Jan. 1, Chase Manhattan Bank officials say, the New York-based bank will adopt the euro for all internal operations in Europe now conducted in the currencies of the 11 countries that will take part in EMU. "We won't be holding marks or francs any more," said Anthony Davies, Chase's London-based global project manager for EMU. "Our books and records will be in euros, our risks will be in euros and our payments will be in euros. Basically, we will be consolidating our accounts from day one in euros."

Impact on Europe

Atkinson, Mark, "Farewell to the Fast Buck New Currency for Top-Dollar Crime," *The Guardian*, April 20, 1998, p. 16.

A new study says that once euro banknotes begin circulating in 2002, they will quickly rival dollar bills as the underworld's currency of choice because they will be issued in higher denominations, allowing the same value of dirty money to be concealed in smaller places. The European Central Bank, which will manage the euro on behalf of the 11 countries expected to use the currency, is aiming to issue notes for 100, 200 and 500 euros — each worth much more than the highest-denomination U.S. bill, $100. Instead of lugging thick wads of $100 bills in suitcases, as they do now, they will be able to pack $1 million worth of 500 euro notes into a purse.

Elliott, Larry, "Tax 'Will Go Up' in Euro Nations," *The Guardian*, June 30, 1998, p. 23.

Consumers and businesses in some of the smaller member states of the new euro zone are likely to face higher tax bills as a result of joining a single currency dominated by Germany and France, the head of the European Central Bank, Wim Duisenberg, warned yesterday. Although he insisted that the deliberations of the central bank would remain secret, Duisenberg admitted that the needs of monetary union's two biggest economies would hold sway in euro-zone decisions on interest rates.

Impact on United States

"Dollar Surges Against Mark As a Weak Euro Is Foreseen," *The New York Times*, July 1, 1997, p. D17.

The dollar surged to its highest level against the German mark in more than three years yesterday, buoyed by concerns about the European monetary union.

"Worry About Trade and Euro Pushes Dollar Sharply Lower," *The New York Times,* June 10, 1997, p. D17.

The dollar fell sharply yesterday for a second session as concerns mounted over Japan's growing trade surplus and over Europe's plan for a single currency. Since reaching a three-and-a-half year high of 127.47 yen on May 1, the dollar has fallen about 11 percent against the Japanese currency.

Donnelly, Alan, "One Europe, One Currency, One Market: Implications for the U.S.," *Vital Speeches of the Day,* Dec. 15, 1997, pp. 130-133.

The author discusses the importance of Europe's single-currency plan to the United States. The economies of the United States and the EU are so intimately linked that there is not a choice between disengagement or further integration.

Elstein, Aaron, "Euro Seen Spelling Confusion for Bankers In the United States," *American Banker,* June 12, 1997, p. 26.

To drive home his point, lawyer Jeffrey B. Golden raised a toilet plunger as an illustration of how American bankers feel about Europe veering toward a common currency. "The concerns are primarily about the plumbing," said Golden. In other words, the European Union's plans for adopting a single currency called the euro by 1999 may look good, but beware of leaks.

Gilpin, Kenneth N., "Uncertainties For Dollar: Trade, Euro, U.S. Growth," *The New York Times*, June 28, 1997, p. A35.

The combined weight of a strong economy, low inflation and comparatively high interest rates in the United States buttressed the dollar for much of the first half of the year, helping it continue a rally in which it climbed back from historic lows. Although many of the positive fundamentals remain in place, three big uncertainties — the trade deficit with Japan, the outlook for European currency union and the U.S. economy — have weighed on the dollar after its rebound, and currency traders and analysts expect these factors to continue to play critical roles for the rest of the year.

Tavlas, George S., "The International Use of Currencies: The U.S. Dollar and the Euro," *Finance & Development*, June 1998, pp. 46-49.

The author discusses why the international monetary system needs only one or, at most, a few national currencies to carry out international transactions. The euro possesses the potential to challenge the hegemonic role now played by the dollar in international transactions.

Walker, Martin, "The Euro: Why It's Bad for the Dollar but Good for America," *World Policy Journal,* fall 1998, pp. 1-12.

The coming of the euro should put an end to the irrational currency fluctuations witnessed between the dollar/yen and dollar/D-mark rates, which will be good for the global economy, the United States and the Atlantic alliance.

Impact on World Trade

Andrews, Edmund L., "Currency Markets Largely Discount Maneuvers Over Euro," *The New York Times*, May 5, 1998, p. D6.

World currency traders today largely disregarded embarrassing political squabbles among European leaders this past weekend over plans to introduce a common European currency on Jan. 1. On the first business day after 11 European nations signed an agreement to adopt the euro, traders initially sold currencies such as the German mark but later bought them back at the expense of the dollar, leaving them little changed for the day. Many European stock markets posted big gains.

Bigelow, Michael, "Experts Worry Over Costs Of Using Euro; Restructuring Economies Could Prove Too Painful," *San Francisco Chronicle*, May 9, 1998, p. A1.

"Welcome to the land of euro skepticism," David Heathcoat-Amory, Britain's shadow secretary of the Treasury and Conservative member of Parliament, told a group of visiting American journalists recently in London. Chief among the questions is the issue of convergence, or getting individual economies to operate in sync. EMU designers set up entrance goals — acceptable interest rates, debt and deficit levels and low inflation rates — and made it clear that member states must adhere to these standards if they expect the union to succeed. Over time, the economies are supposed to become more integrated, a plus in the eyes of the new European Central Bank, whose primary mandate is currency stability.

Cooper, Helene, "Euro Whets Global Business Appetites; Producing, Explaining New Currency Lures Many Firms," *The Wall Street Journal,* Dec. 3, 1997, p. A19.

As Europe moves steadily toward a common currency, big bucks await the thousands who labor at Europe's various national coin-minting operations. France alone plans to mint 7.5 billion coins for the launch of the euro. The Hotel de la Monnaie, the state-owned mint in Pessac, just hired 25 extra people to help its 400 workers handle the load. There are promises of overtime and pay raises. "The euro will be a huge job," a spokeswoman says. "But we're not complaining." Neither are a host of lucky industries. In Paris, consultants are mass-producing board games on how companies can make money off Europe's new money. In London, lawyers are toting up billable hours giving advice on whether contracts need to be renegotiated. Farther away, in high-tech meccas in Israel, India, Ireland and America's Silicon Valley, computer gurus are salivating.

Back Issues

Great Research on Current Issues Starts Right Here.
Recent topics covered by The CQ Researcher are listed below.
Now available on the Web
For information, call (800) 432-2250 ext. 279 or (202) 887-6279.

If you would like to have any of these CQ Researchers updated, or need more information about these topics, please call CQ Custom Research. Special rates for CQ subscribers. (202) 887-8600 or (800) 432-2250, ext. 600, or E-mail Custom.Research@cq.com

Back issues are available for $5.00 (subscribers) or $10.00 (non-subscribers). Quantity discounts apply to orders over 10. To order, call Congressional Quarterly Customer Service at (202) 887-8621.

Binders are available for $18.00. To order call 1-800-638-1710. Please refer to stock number 648.

Future Topics

▶ *AIDS Update*

▶ *Searching for Jesus*

▶ *Iran: 20 Years After the Revolution*

PUBLISHED BY CONGRESSIONAL QUARTERLY INC.

AIDS Update

Are researchers closer to a cure?

Multiple-drug "cocktails" have transformed the once-deadly HIV infection into a manageable chronic condition for many people. Last year, AIDS fell out of the top 10 causes of death in the U.S. for the first time since 1990. But the news about AIDS isn't all positive. While the new treatments allow some infected people to live longer, they don't actually cure the disease, they have unpleasant side effects and can cost upward of $15,000 per year. Some activists and health officials worry that the heartening news is giving rise to complacency and a perception that the epidemic is over. And while science may be controlling the disease in the West, AIDS continues to ravage the developing world, where more than 11 million people have already died in the epidemic.

C_Q Dec. 4, 1998 • Volume 8, No. 45 • Pages 1049-1072

Formerly Editorial Research Reports

Cover: The "No Obits" headline in the Aug. 14, 1998, issue of the *Bay Area Reporter* refers to the lack of obituaries of AIDS victims. It was the first time in 17 years that no death notices were mailed to the weekly newspaper. (AP Photo/Ben Margot)

CQ Researcher

Dec. 4, 1998
Volume 8, No.45

EDITOR
Sandra Stencel

MANAGING EDITOR
Thomas J. Colin

ASSOCIATE EDITOR
Sarah M. Magner

STAFF WRITERS
Adriel Bettelheim
Mary H. Cooper
Kenneth Jost
Kathy Koch
David Masci

PRODUCTION EDITOR
Debra James

EDITORIAL ASSISTANT
Laura S. Cavender

PUBLISHED BY
Congressional Quarterly Inc.

CHAIRMAN
Andrew Barnes

VICE CHAIRMAN
Andrew P. Corty

PRESIDENT AND PUBLISHER
Robert W. Merry

EXECUTIVE EDITOR
David Rapp

The CQ Researcher (ISSN 1056-2036). Formerly Editorial Research Reports. Published weekly, except Jan. 2, May 29, July 3, Oct. 30, by Congressional Quarterly Inc., 1414 22nd St., N.W., Washington, D.C. 20037. Annual subscription rate for libraries, businesses and government is $340. Additional rates furnished upon request. Periodicals postage paid at Washington, D.C., and additional mailing offices. POSTMASTER: Send address changes to The CQ Researcher, 1414 22nd St., N.W., Washington, D.C. 20037.

AIDS Update

THE ISSUES

It's dawn, and Paul Wisotzky's daily battle with AIDS is about to begin. An hour before breakfast, the San Francisco business consultant swallows the first of 18 pills he'll take that day. The medications are part of a four-drug regimen designed to shut down the human immunodeficiency virus (HIV) that causes the disease.

Some of the drugs are taken twice a day, others three times. Certain ones need to be swallowed on an empty stomach, so Wisotzky carefully times his meals. The mix of medications leaves Wisotzky suffering from multiple side effects, including numbness in his hands and feet, nausea, headaches, diarrhea and a racing metabolism that prevents him from getting any rest unless he takes sleeping pills.

Wisotzky views it all as a small price to pay for staying alive. "I'm fairly convinced that if I wasn't on these drugs, I'd be dead," says Wisotzky, who was first diagnosed with HIV in 1985, at age 22, and developed AIDS three years later. "It's kind of bittersweet because I haven't experienced some kind of miraculous return to health, and I still have the virus. But I also never thought I'd live to see the year 2000, let alone 1995."

Wisotzky represents the positive side of the battle against AIDS. Since the mid-1990s, aggressive multiple-drug "cocktails" featuring a new class of drugs known as protease inhibitors have turned the once-lethal infection into a manageable chronic condition and dramatically reduced AIDS deaths in the United States and other developed countries. [1]

U.S. public health officials reported in October that the number of Americans who died from AIDS fell to 16,865 in 1997, a 45.8 percent decline from the 31,130 people who died from the illness in 1996 and significantly below the 43,000 deaths in the peak

year of 1995. AIDS also fell out of the top 10 causes of death in the United States for the first time since 1990. [2]

But the news about AIDS isn't all positive. While the new treatments can restore some health and make infected people live longer, they don't actually rid the body of the disease, they have unpleasant side effects and can cost upward of $15,000 per year. They aren't available in poor nations, particularly in Africa, where more than 80 percent of the world's AIDS deaths occur. Moreover, health officials say the drugs haven't yet slowed the rate of people becoming infected with HIV or made a dent in the global epidemic. Each day, about 16,000 more people are estimated to be infected, and more than 33 million adults and children are now believed to be living with the disease. (*See map, p. 1052.*)

"The bottom line is, although the results have been impressive, there's still a lot of work to be done," says Anthony Fauci, director of the National Institute of Allergy and Infectious Diseases (NIAID) in Bethesda, Md. "What I'm concerned about . . . is that the positive news reports can create the perception that HIV and AIDS are no longer a very ominous threat. That's a big mistake."

Officials say the only realistic long-term solution is development of an AIDS vaccine similar to the ones that contained or eradicated conditions like polio, measles and smallpox. But despite substantial federal spending on AIDS research, scien-

tists are still years away from producing usable results. Among other things, researchers are hampered by a lack of knowledge about precisely how HIV interacts with the body's immune system. The researchers acknowledge they will have to rely on a certain amount of trial and error until they hit on an approach that consistently works. [3]

In the meantime, the best hope of forestalling the disease is by encouraging prevention. Because sex and intravenous-drug use are the primary means of HIV transmission, public health officials rely on counseling and education programs for high-risk groups, as well as expanded HIV testing. They also are turning to politically controversial measures, such as condom distribution, clean-needle exchanges for drug addicts and comprehensive sex education in schools.

The focus on prevention dominated the 12th World AIDS Conference in Geneva, Switzerland, last July, where scientists repeatedly stressed that even the most aggressive new AIDS treatments don't work all of the time. Recent studies show that HIV can survive in the body in a latent state and be switched on when something causes the virus to be active again. Genes in the HIV virus also mutate after repeated exposure to the drugs, creating multiple strains of the disease and frustrating the pharmaceutical attack. Drug-resistant strains can also be spread from person to person. The scientists concluded that the only certain way of preventing new cases of the disease is to encourage people to behave more responsibly.

Finding a way to do that isn't simple. Some politicians question the need to spend heavily on prevention, reluctant to appear to be encouraging sexual promiscuity and drug habits. The dilemma divided the Clinton administration last spring,

CQ on the Web: www.cq.com   **Dec. 4, 1998   1051**

Worldwide AIDS Epidemic

AIDS has spread across the globe in the past 20 years, but sub-Saharan Africa has suffered by far the greatest toll. More than 11 million Africans have died from HIV/AIDS since the beginning of the epidemic in the late 1970s. About 2 million Africans will die this year alone from HIV/AIDS, and 22.5 million are infected. Worldwide, 33.4 million adults and children are living with HIV/AIDS.

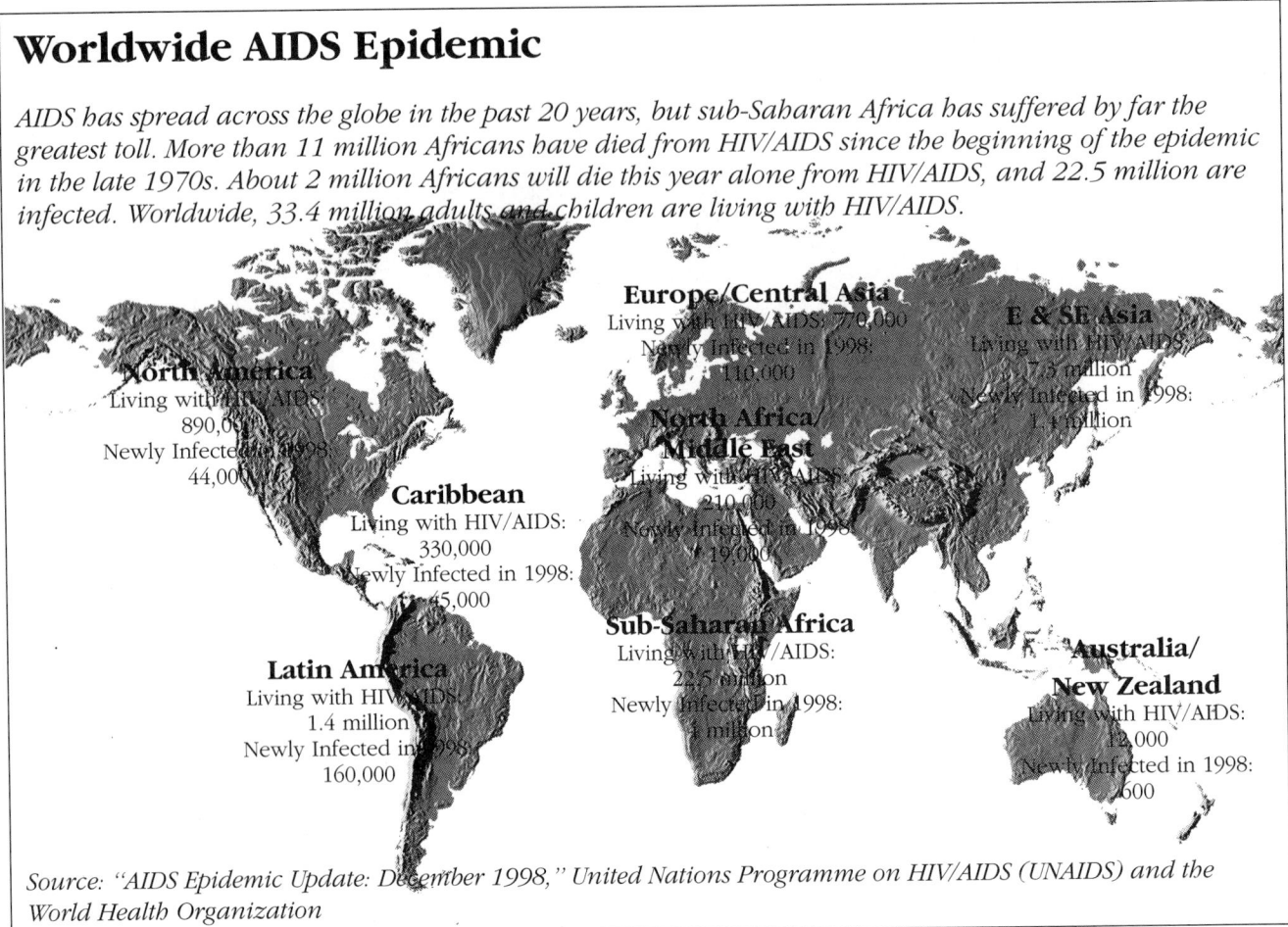

North America
Living with HIV/AIDS:
890,000
Newly Infected in 1998:
44,000

Caribbean
Living with HIV/AIDS:
330,000
Newly Infected in 1998:
45,000

Latin America
Living with HIV/AIDS:
1.4 million
Newly Infected in 1998:
160,000

Europe/Central Asia
Living with HIV/AIDS: 770,000
Newly Infected in 1998:
110,000

North Africa/Middle East
Living with HIV/AIDS:
210,000
Newly Infected in 1998:
19,000

Sub-Saharan Africa
Living with HIV/AIDS:
22.5 million
Newly Infected in 1998:
4 million

E & SE Asia
Living with HIV/AIDS:
7.5 million
Newly Infected in 1998:
1.4 million

Australia/New Zealand
Living with HIV/AIDS:
12,000
Newly Infected in 1998:
600

Source: "AIDS Epidemic Update: December 1998," United Nations Programme on HIV/AIDS (UNAIDS) and the World Health Organization

when officials certified the effectiveness of needle-exchange programs in reducing the spread of AIDS among drug addicts but balked at allowing federal funds to pay for them.

The budget for developing new AIDS treatments at the National Institutes of Health (NIH) has increased 30 percent since 1995 and will reach $1.79 billion next year. On the other hand, federal funding for AIDS prevention efforts has remained relatively flat for the past three years — at just over $600 million per year — leading local AIDS advocacy groups to complain that they are being stretched thin while dealing with an expanding roster of clients, many from low-income and minority neighborhoods.

AIDS activists say prevention needs to be placed on an even footing with drug development because the encour-

aging news about AIDS treatments appears to send the message that the epidemic is over and inadvertently encourages people to relax their safe-sex standards. Many of the new cases of the disease are found in minority women who contracted the disease through heterosexual contact. Activists say many of these women have less access to good health care, live in poverty and lack sufficient education and information about how the disease is spread. [4]

"Public health officials need to realize that [AIDS prevention] isn't as simple as providing pills to people," says Regina Aragon, public policy director of the San Francisco AIDS Foundation and a member of President Clinton's advisory council on HIV/AIDS. "When people hear AIDS deaths are down, they think we're

winning the battle. The flip side is the disease continues to be spread, and people need access to drugs, medical care and social services."

Congress is expected to address some of the concerns next year when it takes up legislation dealing with AIDS programs and HIV testing. One closely watched piece of legislation is the Ryan White CARE Act, named after an Indiana teenager who died of AIDS in 1990. Among other things, the act awards billions of dollars to local agencies that help AIDS patients with financial difficulties. The annual spending package is often a flashpoint for lawmakers to argue over controversial proposals, such as reporting the names of HIV-positive patients to public health officials.

State governments are grappling with the same issues. More states are mandat-

Search for AIDS Vaccine Accelerates

Over the past 15 years, scientists have come to know more about HIV than any other virus. But they haven't been able to break the chain of transmission with a vaccine — the only surefire way to stop the spread of the disease.

An effective AIDS vaccine would train the immune system to fight off the HIV infection by giving it a taste of the deadly invader. This would give the body a kind of immunological "head start" by priming it to attack the virus as soon as it appears instead of taking time to marshal a defense.

But vaccine development is a difficult, time-consuming task, mainly because scientists have a relatively poor understanding of just how HIV and the immune system interact. The scientists are still unsure exactly how to stimulate the body's disease-fighting cells and what cellular material to use to do the stimulating.

"We believe that, in the next nine years, we will have a vaccine that will have some impact," says Anthony Fauci, director of the National Institute of Allergy and Infectious Diseases (NIAID) in Bethesda, Md. "We may not hit a home run right away; it's an iterative process. But I think we'll see the first round of some measurable success."

Four years ago, Fauci's institute declined to fund trials on AIDS vaccines because administrators deemed none promising enough to justify the expense. But President Clinton's 1997 challenge to scientists to develop an AIDS vaccine by 2007 and new research developments have led to a change of heart. The NIAID is participating in upcoming trials of a vaccine it rejected four years ago called gp120, which consists of genetically engineered fragments of HIV's outer coat.

The trials will be the first large-scale test of an AIDS vaccine. The U.S. Food and Drug Administration in June approved a version of gp120 called Aidsvax, manufactured by VaxGen of South San Francisco, Calif., for testing on 5,000 volunteers in the United States and 2,500 more in Thailand. The trials will take at least three years. Earlier small-scale trials showed the vaccine built up some measurable viral resistance in more than 90 percent of patients who received the product.

The gp120 vaccine works by stimulating a so-called humoral response, in which the immune system smothers the invader with antibodies before it can infiltrate healthy cells. The advantages are that gp120 is safe and relatively simple to prepare. The problem is that antibodies produced in response to the vaccine's genetically engineered HIV fragments often fail to recognize active HIV when the "wild" virus turns up in patients.

Another approach is to use vaccines to prompt a second kind of reaction, known as a cellular response. This usually involves implanting HIV genes in non-HIV viruses, spurring disease-fighting cells to kill the HIV-infected cells. These vaccines are more complicated to prepare and, to date, have prompted only modest immune responses. Some researchers also worry that integrating HIV genes into human cells could harm patients.

Several combination vaccines are in early trials. One would use live canarypox virus loaded with HIV genes, followed by a booster shot of gp120. But the vaccines again are complicated to prepare, and the virus could potentially cause disease.

"It is unlikely that we will develop a vaccine suitable for wide-scale use in humans within the next five years," David Baltimore, president of the California Institute of Technology and chairman of NIH's Vaccine Research Committee, wrote recently in *Scientific American*. "But there is hope . . . even a partially effective vaccine could be valuable in limiting the amount of virus in patients, thus potentially reducing their infectiousness and the symptoms they suffer."[1]

---

[1] David Baltimore and Carole Heilman, "HIV Vaccines: Prospects and Challenges," *Scientific American*, July 1998, pp. 98-103.

---

ing HIV testing for segments of the population, especially pregnant women, newborns and prisoners. At least 29 states now also make it a crime to knowingly expose someone to HIV, with one-third of the states having enacted their laws within the last two years.

Legal experts say the trend represents a shift from earlier policies — which protected the rights of people with HIV and AIDS — to laws that attempt to identify those with HIV and, in some cases, punish those who place others at risk of contracting the virus.

"Mandatory screening [and other measures] may seem to be ways of 'getting tough' in the fight against the epidemic, but in reality they do not go to the heart of the problem," says Lawrence Gostin, director of the Georgetown University-Johns Hopkins University Program on Law and Public Health in Washington.[5]

As public health officials and policy-makers continue to examine the scope of the disease and its ramifications, here are some of the questions they are asking:

Has the effectiveness of new HIV/AIDS treatments been overstated?

Until recently, an HIV infection was one of medicine's most feared diagnoses — an almost-always-fatal condition that slowly destroyed the human immune system and made patients susceptible to tuberculosis, pneumonia and other "opportunistic diseases." The most doctors could do was treat the infections stemming from the immune failure or tinker with the chemical makeup of HIV

Federal Funding for AIDS Prevention and Care

Total federal spending on AIDS treatment and prevention will be $7.7 billion in fiscal 1999. Nearly $1.8 billion will fund research on treatments and vaccines at the National Institutes of Health. The Ryan White CARE Act, which provides federal support to communities and states with high incidences of AIDS, will receive more than $1.4 billion in fiscal '99.

Federal AIDS Programs: FY 1999 Funding
(numbers in millions)

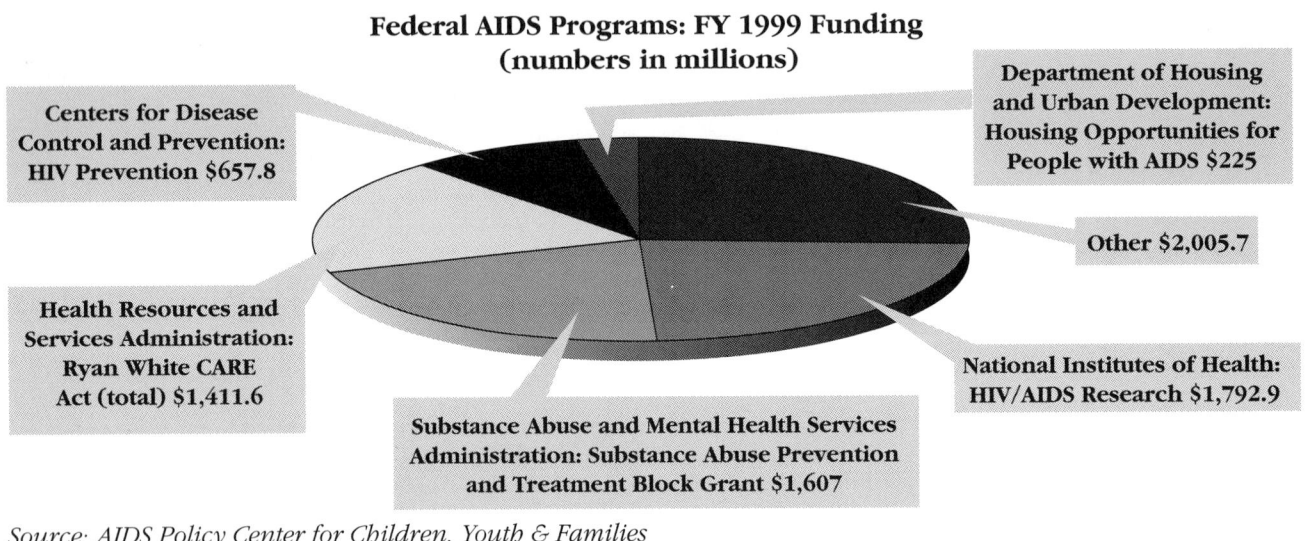

Centers for Disease Control and Prevention: HIV Prevention $657.8

Department of Housing and Urban Development: Housing Opportunities for People with AIDS $225

Other $2,005.7

Health Resources and Services Administration: Ryan White CARE Act (total) $1,411.6

National Institutes of Health: HIV/AIDS Research $1,792.9

Substance Abuse and Mental Health Services Administration: Substance Abuse Prevention and Treatment Block Grant $1,607

Source: AIDS Policy Center for Children, Youth & Families

through first-generation drugs, such as AZT, to try to delay death.

But over the past three years, aggressive multiple-drug therapies have been shown to suppress the virus more effectively and prevent it from infiltrating and killing the body's disease-fighting T-cells.* The key weapons are drugs called protease inhibitors, which interfere with an important enzyme in the HIV virus' molecular machinery.

HIV works by docking with T-cells and chemically invading their nuclear material. Slowly, the virus takes over the cells' genetic machinery and begins to churn out copies of itself, similar to the way a computer virus multiplies in a program. The duplicate HIV viruses are then gradually dispatched to other T-cells.

The protease inhibitors work by

---

*According to the U.S. Centers for Disease Control and Prevention's 1993 guidelines, an HIV-infected person is said to have AIDS when concentrations of T-cells fall below 200 cells per microliter of blood.

blocking an enzyme that splices a large protein inside HIV to form smaller pieces that the virus uses to make new copies of itself. This effectively destroys HIV's ability to replicate. But that in itself isn't enough to kill the virus. The protease inhibitors must be combined with two or more AZT-like drugs that jam another enzyme called reverse transcriptase, which helps HIV integrate itself into the healthy cell's nucleus.

Such combination therapies have dramatically improved the outlook for AIDS patients over the past three-and-a-half years, even those with advanced stages of infection. [6] The HIV clinics at San Francisco General Hospital and Johns Hopkins University Hospital in Baltimore have recorded a 50-80 percent decline in hospitalizations for HIV-related problems and a 50-70 percent drop in incidence of serious AIDS-related opportunistic infections.

But the treatments haven't worked

for everyone. Some patients haven't been able to adhere to rigorous schedules like the one Wisotzky maintains, or find they can't absorb all of the drugs because of AIDS-related intestinal disorders. Missing even a few doses can be fatal, because the interruption can cause drug-resistant strains of HIV to take over the body.

HIV first demonstrated its ability to thwart drugs by developing a resistance to AZT, which was introduced in 1987. The virus has an ability to signal its genetic material to chemically alter key enzymes, making it more difficult for drugs to bind and inactivate the enzymes. Because the HIV virus replicates quickly and relatively sloppily, the altered versions produce copies with even more chemical glitches that can proliferate unchecked at a rate of roughly 10 billion new viral particles each day. The result is myriad versions of the mutated virus, each capable of killing T-cells.

"Even if a patient has never been treated, any [drug] that is delivered will encounter some HIV variant that is already resistant or is on its way to accumulating the full set of mutations needed for resistance," says Douglas Richman, co-director of the AIDS Research Institute at the University of California at San Diego School of Medicine.

For this reason, doctors prescribe combinations of drugs that maximize potency and reduce the chance of resistance. The combinations simultaneously deliver multiple body blows to the HIV virus, enabling one drug to pick up the slack if another fails.

Still, HIV finds ways to evade even the most aggressive treatments. Researchers at last summer's World AIDS Conference presented evidence that HIV can retreat into crevices and reservoirs in inactive T-cells and lay dormant for years, undetected even by sensitive tests that screen for the virus in the blood. Scientists originally thought resting T-cells only had a short life span, reducing the danger of recurring HIV. New findings, however, suggest many of the virus-bearing cells live on and pose a threat for years. "We have overestimated the potency of our medical regimens," concluded David Ho, director of the Aaron Diamond AIDS Research Center in New York. [7]

Virtually everyone agrees that development of a vaccine is the only reliable way to permanently eliminate the threat of HIV. Vaccines work by stimulating the immune system to recognize an invading body. Because of the deadly nature of HIV, scientists can't use a weakened or killed version of the whole virus for immunizations as was done with the polio vaccine. That is because even if only one virus out of a million survived, it could kill the vaccinated person. Hence, AIDS vaccines use other viral substances to prime the immune system to produce protective antibodies, or directly expose T-cells to genetically engineered fragments of HIV to help them recognize the invader and mount a cellular defense. (*See story, p. 1053.*)

Vaccine development has been a slow and controversial process. Four years ago, NIH decided not to fund large-scale trials of AIDS vaccines then under development because government researchers concluded none was promising enough to justify the expense. The move generated intense criticism from AIDS activists, who said the government wasn't doing enough.

Facing lingering criticism, President Clinton last year challenged government scientists to develop an AIDS vaccine within 10 years and announced plans to establish a vaccine research center to bring researchers from different disciplines together on the NIH campus. NIH announced last summer it would also participate in trials on one of the vaccines it rejected four years ago, gp120, manufactured by VaxGen of South San Francisco, Calif. [8]

"What we know now is this is a much more complicated virus than we expected 10 years ago," says Margaret Johnston, an immunochemist who runs NIAID's AIDS vaccine program. "The worldwide urgency of HIV and AIDS is too great for us to make decisions [on which vaccines to test] based on guesswork. Some of the new approaches we've arrived at by understanding the biochemistry of HIV are now worth moving to larger-scale clinical trials."

Should condom-distribution and needle-exchange programs be part of federally funded AIDS-prevention efforts?

When AIDS first began ravaging Africa in the mid-1980s, officials in predominantly Islamic Senegal decided to mount a counterattack. The government immediately sought support from religious leaders for nationwide sex education in schools and programs to sell condoms at heavily discounted prices. The clergy gave its blessing, leading officials to launch a campaign particularly targeted at prostitutes, their clients and young men in the army.

Results suggest that the prevention strategy worked. Campaign director Ibrahim Ndoye told the World AIDS Conference that, while a recent survey showed nearly half the men from ages 15-24 and 15 percent of the women in that age group reported having casual sex, more than 60 percent of the women and 40 percent of the men claimed to have used condoms. Condom sales in the country have risen from 800,000 to 7 million per year over the past decade, and HIV infection in Senegal has fallen below 2 percent of the population, compared with more than 10 percent in neighboring Burkina Faso and Ivory Coast. [9]

Countries as disparate as Switzerland and Thailand have also developed prevention programs that appear to have limited the spread of sexually transmitted diseases without an observed decline in promiscuity. But developing a comprehensive prevention strategy remains difficult in the United States and some other countries because politicians are split on whether to spend public money on efforts that appear to encourage illicit or improper behavior.

"AIDS is a chronic disease of sexually promiscuous people," Sen. Jesse Helms, R-N.C., proclaimed during a 1995 U.S. Senate debate, in which he tried to cut funding for AIDS prevention. Helms blamed gay men for perpetuating the disease and said lawmakers who favored expanding the prevention programs were buckling to pressure from homosexual groups. [10]

AIDS activists dispute Helms' argument by pointing to statistics showing many of the new AIDS cases are caused by heterosexual contact. The activists add that spending more on AIDS prevention now will avoid having to spend larger sums later treating people who contract the disease. "AIDS drugs cost $40 a day. Condoms cost 40 cents, and are proven to prevent the spread of AIDS," says Daniel Zingale, executive director of Washington-based AIDS Action, which represents 2,400 local

Battle Over a T-Cell: New Drugs vs. the AIDS Virus

Researchers now think that drugs can suppress the AIDS virus as it attacks the body's disease-fighting T-cells in the bloodstream. The drugs attack the virus as it tries to enter the T-cell or during the virus' life cycle inside the T-cells. Viruses that successfully reproduce kill the host T-cells, lowering the body's resistance to disease and eventually bringing on full-blown AIDS.

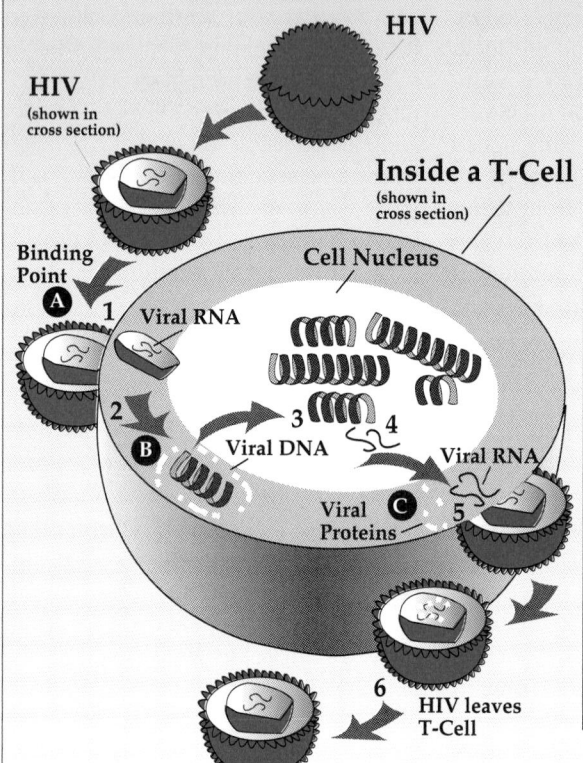

How the AIDS Virus Attacks a T-Cell

1. Virus enters cell, losing its protein coat
2. Viral RNA is converted to viral DNA
3. Viral DNA is replicated
4. DNA is converted back to RNA
5. Viral proteins are produced
6. New viruses, produced when proteins and RNA combine, leave demolished T-cell and enter bloodstream

New Drugs That Fight AIDS

A gp120 vaccine seeks to prevent binding of HIV to cell wall

B AZT and other drugs known as nucleoside analogs attack virus by blocking conversion of viral RNA into DNA

C Antiviral drugs called protease inhibitors block production of HIV enzyme essential to virus replication

Source: Roche Laboratories

AIDS groups nationwide.

The debate has intensified over the past six months with the release of two government studies that each conclude it's worthwhile to expand efforts to reach populations at greatest risk of contracting HIV. The U.S. Centers for Disease Control and Prevention (CDC) last summer released a cost-benefit analysis that concluded that only about 4,000 infections need to be averted in the United States to cover the CDC's annual AIDS-prevention budget of about $600 million. [11]

The National Institute of Mental Health in June released a study of 3,706 women and men in 37 inner-city clinics that found that, even among urban populations that typically are hardest to reach, targeted prevention messages in counseling sessions cut high-risk behavior in half and doubled regular condom use. [12]

Still, prevention remains a touchy issue — especially when dealing with proposals to distribute free sterile syringes to illegal-drug users. AIDS advocates say more than 60 percent of new AIDS cases in many urban areas come from drug users who share needles and transmit the disease through tainted blood. However, opponents fear handing out clean needles will increase and encourage illicit-drug use, pointing to

conclusions from Canadian studies in Montreal and Vancouver. [13]

Congress nine years ago passed a law barring federal funding of needle-exchange programs unless the secretary of Health and Human Services (HHS) presents scientific evidence that they cut the spread of AIDS and don't increase drug use. Local health organizations and private donors continue to sponsor needle exchanges, with the CDC estimating the programs distributed 17.5 million syringes last year.

The sensitivities over a federal role split health officials in the Clinton administration in April, when Gen. Barry McCaffrey, director of the White House Office on National Drug Control Policy, succeeded in killing a plan that would have used federal money for pilot needle-exchange programs in 10 cities. U.S. Surgeon General David Satcher and NIH Director Harold Varmus, among others, had spoken in favor of the programs, pointing to at least seven government studies concluding the exchanges reduced risky needle-sharing behavior with a resulting greater reduction in HIV transmission. HHS Secretary Donna E. Shalala certified that the programs were effective but, bending to political pressure, declined to lift the ban. Several Republicans in Congress had indicated that they would reintroduce the ban if the White House funded any programs. [14]

While political disagreements linger, some in the AIDS community are rethinking their prevention policies. Some AIDS groups are now openly promoting expanded HIV testing, a reversal from a decade ago when most groups urged HIV-positive people to avoid tests, fearing repercussions affecting health insurance coverage and the patients' job status.

"The fact that AIDS is hitting a broader cross-section of society, including a lot more women, means the face of the epidemic is changing," says Helene Gayle, director of the CDC's National Center for HIV Prevention. "A lot of people are rethinking how to deal with HIV and what's the most valid way of dealing with the health crisis."

Have the public and politicians grown less sympathetic to AIDS victims?

University of California-Davis psychologist Gregory Herek was taken aback when he recently decided to contrast public opinions and knowledge about AIDS with what people knew in 1991.

Using similar survey questions, Herek polled 1,712 adults and found 55 percent incorrectly believed AIDS can

The Changing Face of AIDS

The spread of the AIDS virus among intravenous-drug users in urban communities helps account for the disproportionate percentage of new AIDS cases found among African-Americans and Latinos.

U.S. AIDS Cases by Race/Ethnicity, 1981-1997

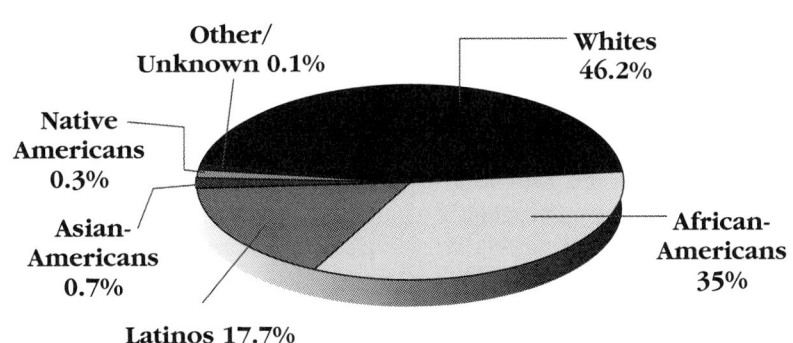

Other/Unknown 0.1%
Whites 46.2%
Native Americans 0.3%
Asian-Americans 0.7%
African-Americans 35%
Latinos 17.7%

Proportion of Newly Reported AIDS Cases 1985 & 1995

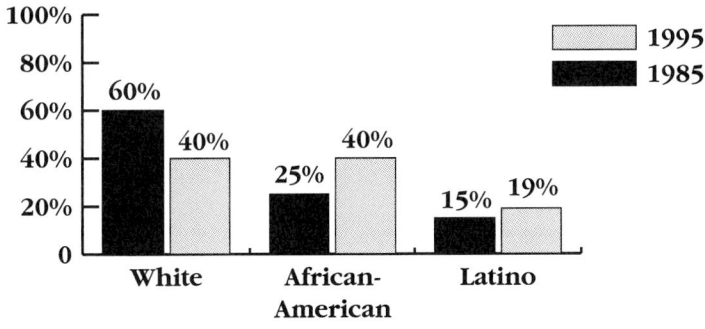

1995
1985

	White	African-American	Latino
1985	60%	25%	15%
1995	40%	40%	19%

Sources: San Francisco AIDS Foundation; Centers for Disease Control and Prevention

be spread by sharing a drinking glass, up from 48 percent in 1991. Twenty-seven percent said they would be less likely to put on a sweater that had been worn once by a person with AIDS, even if the clothing was first cleaned and repackaged. One-third said they would avoid shopping at a grocery store if it were owned by a person with AIDS.

When asked about the victims of AIDS, 29 percent of the survey respondents agreed that people who contracted AIDS through drug use or sex "got what they deserved," up from 20 percent in 1991. [15]

"I was very disturbed. I was appalled," Herek says. "I hear a lot of people saying that stigma is a thing of the past. People know how AIDS is transmitted. What they don't know is how you can't get AIDS."

Herek's poll was just one snapshot of public opinion. But activists say the numbers are evidence that, more than 15 years into the epidemic, HIV and AIDS remain misunderstood. Some of this is due to past contradictory statements about the ways HIV can be transmitted. More details about how the disease progresses also haven't reassured the general public. The activists worry that policy-makers and public health officials increasingly are translating their apprehension and frustration with the disease into laws that seek to identify people with the virus and punish those who put others at risk of contracting it.

More than two dozen state legislatures have passed laws making it a crime to transmit or knowingly expose others to HIV. More states are also mandating HIV testing for certain segments of the population, such as prisoners and newborns, and strengthening programs to identify HIV-positive people.

Sentiment for more stringent HIV laws has been fueled by several high-profile cases in which HIV-infected people knowingly exposed partners to the virus. One outbreak involving a New York teenager, Nushawn Williams — accused of knowingly infecting more than a dozen girls and young women — prompted New York's legislature in June to pass a tough, new law to notify partners of people known to have HIV.

In Arkansas, the state Supreme Court this summer upheld the conviction of a 24-year-old man, Pierre Weaver, who was sentenced to the maximum of 30 years in prison for knowingly transmitting the virus to a woman through unprotected sex. In Tennessee, an HIV-positive mother was jailed and charged with two counts of criminal exposure after telling police she slept with 50 men to get revenge for contracting the disease. [16]

The most intense debate currently surrounds state and federal efforts to implement so-called "names testing," in which names of HIV-positive people are reported to public health officials. (See "At Issue," p. 1065.) Epidemiologists say the most effective way to collect information needed to monitor and prevent the spread of AIDS is by logging the names of people carrying the virus — a method long used for other contagious diseases, such as syphilis and tuberculosis.

"Since the early 1980s, HIV has been treated like a civil-rights issue instead of a public-health crisis. As a result, thousands of people have tragically died of AIDS," says Rep. Tom Coburn, R-Okla., a physician who introduced a names-reporting measure in the 105th Congress.

Coburn's bill would have required doctors to report names of individuals testing positive for HIV to health officials, who could then notify partners that they also may have become infected. Supporters of the bill, including the American Academy of Family Physicians, say reporting names is preferable to using anonymous codes, which they say are unreliable.

However, AIDS activists and some state health officials strenuously oppose such measures, saying they will discourage people from getting tested and are tantamount to putting a "scarlet letter" on people with the virus. Former Surgeon General C. Everett Koop, the National Governors' Association and groups representing state health officials and AIDS program directors fought the recent Coburn effort, which failed to pass in the last session of Congress. The issue of names testing is likely to come up again in the 106th Congress.

"Names reporting is scary to me; we don't have the social infrastructure to handle it," says Dawn Averitt, a 29-year-old North Carolina woman who was diagnosed with HIV 10 years ago and didn't tell anyone for the first five years that she had the infection. "If you make names public, some people who test positive may be at risk of losing their job or their insurance or even their children, because some courts have ruled against custody for HIV-positive people," she says. "You can end up punishing people for coming forward."

Some 30 states require the reporting of HIV-positive patients' names. Another half-dozen have developed alternative systems that use anonymous codes instead of names. Advocates say the codes ensure privacy. But critics say codes lead to instances in which the same people are inaccurately reported multiple times. They also make it more difficult to track how often HIV/AIDS is responsible for a person contracting communicable diseases, such as tuberculosis or meningitis.

The CDC has implicitly endorsed names reporting and even lobbied some state health officials to adopt the system, though the Clinton administration has yet to put a policy in writing. "This is how surveillance is usually done; you use names as an entry point," epidemiologist Gayle says, adding that states should continue to have the option of offering anonymous tests.

Experts are only beginning to assess which of the systems works the best. Researchers at the University of California-San Francisco recently studied policies in six states and concluded that people who used anonymous code testing got tested earlier and obtained medical care sooner. However, they said it was unclear how many people who were tested anonymously would opt for names testing if it were the only option offered.

"Public health departments should maintain and in some instances en-

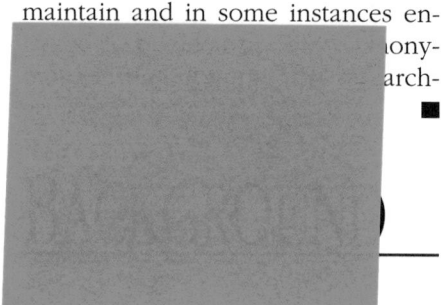

Epidemic's Origins

In July 1981, a small article in *The New York Times* reported the outbreak of a rare type of "cancer" among

Continued on p. 1060

Chronology

1980s *AIDS first appears and develops into an epidemic, spawning fears and a global health crisis.*

June 1981
U.S. Centers for Disease Control documents the first cases of a mysterious immune system disorder in five homosexual men in Los Angeles.

July 1982
After determining the disease is also expressed in heterosexual women and drug users, the CDC gives it the new name AIDS — acquired immune deficiency syndrome.

1984
Scientists at the Institute Pasteur in France and the National Cancer Institute in Bethesda, Md., announce that they have separately isolated the virus that causes AIDS, later named the human immunodeficiency virus (HIV). By year's end, 7,000 Americans have AIDS.

1985
The Food and Drug Administration (FDA) approves the first blood tests to detect the presence of antibodies to HIV. To reduce the risk of spreading the disease through transfusions of tainted blood, U.S. blood banks introduce blood-screening tests. Actor Rock Hudson, the first major public figure known to have AIDS, dies.

1987
The FDA approves the first anti-AIDS drug, AZT (zidovudine), marketed under the name Retrovir by Burroughs Wellcome. President Ronald Reagan gives his first speech on AIDS. By year's end, an estimated 36,000 Americans have been diagnosed with the disease and 20,000 have died.

1988
Surgeon General C. Everett Koop distributes 107 million copies of the pamphlet "Understanding AIDS," marking the launch of the first nationwide AIDS education campaign in the U.S.

———— • ————

1990s *AIDS research gradually yields information about the virus and ways to slow its progression, but a cure remains elusive.*

1990
Ryan White dies at age 19. The Indiana teenager, a hemophiliac infected with the AIDS virus through a tainted blood transfusion, gained national attention for his fight to attend public school despite concerns his condition might be contagious. Within months, Congress passes the Ryan White CARE Act, which offers better care for AIDS patients who don't have adequate health insurance or financial resources. By year's end, more than 307,000 AIDS cases worldwide have been reported to the World Health Organization; public health officials estimate 8-10 million people have the disease.

1991
Basketball star Earvin "Magic" Johnson announces he has tested positive for HIV. The FDA approves Videx, a drug marketed by Bristol-Myers Squibb that has similar disease-fighting abilities to AZT. In November, the number of AIDS cases in the U.S. reaches 200,000, having doubled in just over two years.

1994
AIDS becomes the leading cause of death in Americans ages 25 to 44. The number of AIDS cases in the U.S. doubles again, surpassing 400,000. A National Institutes of Health committee decides that a genetically engineered AIDS vaccine called gp120 is not promising enough to warrant large-scale testing.

1996
The FDA approves a series of drugs called protease inhibitors that, taken alone or in combination with others, prompt a new type of chemical attack on the HIV virus. The multiple-drug treatments make AIDS patients live longer, though they don't rid the body of the disease. The first AIDS hospice in San Francisco closes because fewer people are dying.

1997
The Joint United Nations Programme on HIV/AIDS reports that the disease is more widespread than previously thought, estimating 30 million people may be living with HIV/AIDS and that 16,000 new infections are spawned each day.

1998
The U.S. Supreme Court, in *Bragdon v. Abbott*, rules 5-4 that HIV-infected people are protected under the Americans with Disabilities Act. Researchers report drug-resistant strains of HIV can be transmitted from person to person. The CDC reports in October that the number of U.S. AIDS deaths fell 45.8 percent in 1997 and that the disease fell out of the top 10 causes of death for the first time since 1990.

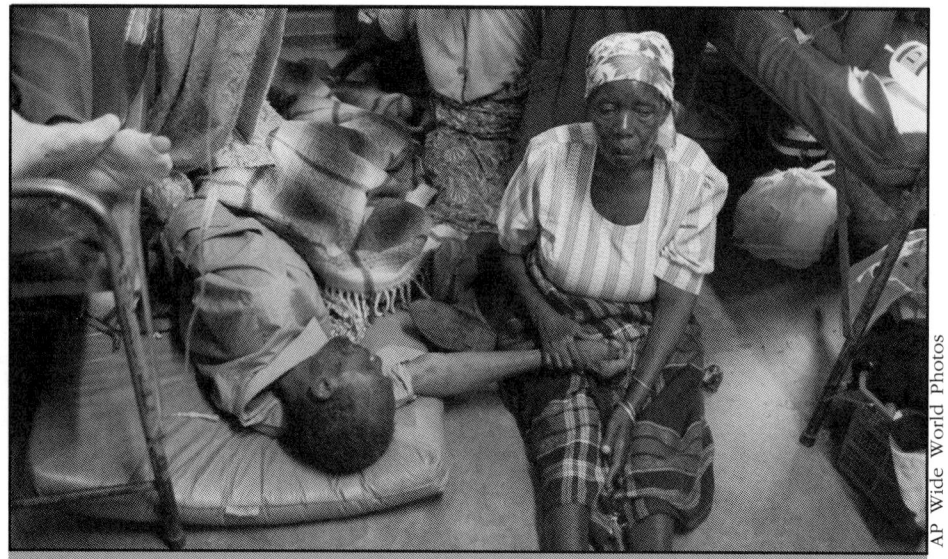

Snapshot of an Epidemic
Global estimates as of December 1998

People living with HIV/AIDS	33.4 million
New HIV infections in 1998	5.8 million
Deaths due to HIV/AIDS in 1998	2.5 million
Cumulative number of deaths *	13.9 million

* Total number of deaths since the beginning of the AIDS epidemic through 1998

Source: "AIDS Epidemic Update: December 1998," UNAIDS/World Health Organization

Continued from p. 1058
41 gay men in California and New York. Few at the time guessed it would be the beginning of a global epidemic.

CDC scientists in Atlanta first noticed the disease from the opportunistic infections it spawned, particularly a variety of pneumonia called *Pneumocystis carinii* and the lesion-forming Kaposi's sarcoma. Initially, the collection of ailments was thought to be confined to the gay community and came to be known as GRID, or gay-related immune deficiency. But by the following year — after similar cases were observed in heterosexual women, drug addicts and Haitian refugees in Miami — the CDC became convinced that the symptoms were evidence of a more widespread type of failure of the immune system and gave the disease a new name: AIDS, or acquired immune deficiency syndrome. [18]

Although the origins of AIDS are still not concrete and some theories are controversial, the disease is generally believed to have existed in sub-Saharan Africa since the 1950s and may have gradually spread through the use of unsterilized needles during vaccination campaigns. David Ho of the Aaron Diamond AIDS Research Center recently found fragments of the HIV genome in a 1959 blood sample of a man living in Leopoldville, Belgian Congo (now Kinshasa, Democratic Republic of the Congo) in what's believed to be the earliest confirmed case of HIV. The HIV virus that causes AIDS was formally identified by American and French researchers working separately in 1984 and designated the human immunodeficiency virus, or HIV, by an international committee of scientists in 1986.

The disease's emergence among homosexuals, intravenous-drug users and recipients of blood transfusions soon led scientists to understand how HIV is transmitted. Most now agree that the virus is transmitted through infected blood or semen that enters the body through mucosal tissues during sexual intercourse, or through the injection of contaminated blood or needles into blood vessels. Mothers also can transmit the virus to their babies, either before birth or through breast-feeding.

There are two major strains of HIV: HIV-1 and HIV-2. Both are spread the same way, but HIV-2 is less easily transmitted, and the period between the initial infection and illness is longer. HIV-1 is the predominant virus worldwide and has numerous subtypes, all distributed unevenly by geography. Routine antibody tests can detect the various subtypes.

In the laboratory, an HIV virus can be kept alive for two weeks or longer. However, such optimal conditions aren't found in the outside world, where the virus is easily killed by soap, hot water, bleach or alcohol. Because the virus can't live long outside the body, HIV is not spread through casual day-to-day contact, such as sharing a glass or sandwich, swimming in the same pool as an infected person or through inhalation of airborne viruses.

Combating AIDS

It is at the cellular level that HIV is a potent and insidious killer. Once introduced into the immune system, the virus attacks the very T-cells, or lymphocytes, that human bodies use to fight infections, instead of attacking the cells of the throat or lungs, like cold and flu viruses. By destroying T-cells over a decade or longer, HIV steadily reduces the body's ability to resist other diseases.

A diagnosis of full-blown AIDS is made when the body's T-cell count drops below 200 cells per cubic milliliter of blood, when the person contracts an opportunistic infection, such as pneumonia, meningitis or tuberculosis, or when the person gets a non-infectious condition, such as Kaposi's sarcoma. Death may result from any of these causes, as well as from dementia and wasting syndrome, which are believed to be caused by the virus itself.

Despite a good understanding of how the virus works, producing drugs to combat the disease has been a slow, frustrating process. The first antiviral AIDS drug, AZT, helped some patients suffering from *Pneumocystis carinii,* but it is toxic and only works for about two years, after which the virus usually becomes resistant. Other antiviral agents, such as dideoxyinosine and dideoxycytidine, help patients who cannot tolerate AZT or whose HIV becomes resistant to AZT. But these drugs only slow development of the disease by jamming the enzyme reverse transcriptase and don't provide a cure.

Beginning in 1995, a new class of drugs known as protease inhibitors gave researchers new hope that they could turn HIV into a treatable condition. These drugs interrupt another key enzyme, protease, and suppress replication of the virus. The drugs — indinavir, ritonavir, nelfinavir and saquinavir — have proven effective, even in AIDS patients who are very ill, and with less toxic side effects than AZT. However, large doses of protease inhibitors are required to shut down the viral infection, and the drugs often must be administered in tandem with AZT-like drugs to reduce the presence of HIV over extended periods.

The present strategy is to treat patients with regularly changing batteries of three- and four-drug AIDS "cocktails" to reduce the chance of viral mutations. This has cut the AIDS death rate without actually providing a cure. The heavy doses of multiple drugs often leave patients suffering from side effects ranging from kidney stones to hepatitis to high levels of cholesterol and triglycerides, increasing the risk of heart attack. Patients also suffer from a shift of body fat to the abdomen, or fat deposits on the back of the neck called "buffalo humps," which can be so disfiguring patients need surgery to have them removed. Recent attempts to reduce the amount and variety of medication and avoid some side effects failed, allowing the resurgence of the virus.

Many of the current AIDS treatments became available under a change in Food and Drug Administration (FDA) testing policies designed to give patients with life-threatening illnesses quicker access to experimental drugs. The FDA typically requires nine years of testing before approving drugs for specific conditions. An "accelerated approval" process instituted by then-FDA Administrator David Kessler in 1992 allows AIDS patients to get experimental drugs before the approval process is completed. Another policy change, called parallel track, allows HIV-positive individuals who can't participate directly in clinical trials to take the drug while the trial is under way.

President Clinton's 1997 challenge to scientists to develop an AIDS vaccine has accelerated interest in that branch of drug development. Researchers in recent years have identi-fied at least seven ways that an AIDS vaccine can be made, five of which have been tested in small-scale human trials. All seek to prime the human immune system by helping it recognize HIV and respond rapidly. The most popular approach is to try to spur the immune system's response with a vaccine made of the gp120 protein that coats the surface of HIV. Scientists believe attacking the protein should prevent HIV from entering T-cells in the first place. But thus far, disease-fighting antibodies generated from the vaccine in labs often fail to recognize HIV in patients.

A second popular vaccine approach uses genetic engineering to insert two actual HIV genes into a non-lethal virus, such as canarypox, a relative of smallpox. This host virus is then used to infect cells and prompt an immune response. To date, canarypox vaccines have proved safe in humans but only elicited a modest HIV-fighting response. [19]

Public's Response

While scientists labor over potential cures, society continues to grapple with how to respond to AIDS. Since the beginning of the epidemic, there has been little consensus about the extent of the danger, and a frequent tendency to label AIDS as a disease of certain groups. New York University sociologist Dorothy Nelkin, an authority on science and society, deems this an effort "to deny the vulnerability and responsibility of the wider population." [20]

Early perceptions that AIDS was primarily a "gay disease" led to public indifference or a lack of acknowledgment of the broader public health threat, some experts say. This led many organizations in the gay community, such as the Gay Men's Health Crisis in New York, to craft

The Scourge of Africa . . .

People in Zimbabwe call it *iyoyo*, or "that thing" — an appropriate, but chilling, way of referring to the HIV virus that causes AIDS. Public health officials estimate that the affliction may now infect as many as 25 percent of all adults in the impoverished African nation.

The situation is equally grim in neighboring countries such as Zambia and Botswana, where governments typically have less than $10 to spend on each person's health per year. Most residents have no idea whether they are infected with HIV, and no access to the tests and drugs that have become hallmarks of AIDS treatment and prevention in the developed world. [1]

Poverty, contaminated blood supplies, a lack of education and assorted cultural factors have combined to make AIDS the scourge of Africa. It's been nearly 20 years since the first reports of "slim disease," as AIDS was known then, starting making their way out of Uganda. Today, the continent is home to 83 percent of the world's AIDS deaths. By the end of 1998, 22.5 million of the 33.4 million adults and children living with HIV/AIDS worldwide will be Africans, according to new estimates from the Joint United Nations Programme on

Mourners wait outside a mortuary in Harare, Zimbabwe.

AP Photo/Denis Farrell

HIV/AIDS (UNAIDS) and the World Health Organization. [2]

"AIDS remains one of the most serious development problems to confront the world in decades, if not centuries," Peter Piot, executive director of UNAIDS, told the House International Relations Committee in September. "In Africa, comparisons with the medieval bubonic plague are not misplaced." [3]

The epidemic has already killed 11.5 million people in the countries of sub-Saharan Africa, and because there is little hope of access to the best drugs, doctors expect at least 20 million more will probably die. AIDS has also fueled a variety of preventable diseases that are beginning to overcome the region, including tuberculosis, hepatitis, malaria, measles, cholera and sexually transmitted diseases.

The situation is so severe that it's prompting demographers to scale back predictions for population growth over the next century. In October, the United Nations forecast a worldwide population of 8.9 billion by 2050 — a 50 percent increase from today's 5.9 billion people but significantly less than the 9.4 billion population that

their own prevention programs that preached personal responsibility.

Revelations that sports stars Earvin "Magic" Johnson and Arthur Ashe contracted the HIV virus in the early 1990s changed public opinion about the condition and made people aware that the disease can be spread to a wider population through unprotected heterosexual activities or transfusions of tainted blood. More recently the disease has become prominent among the urban poor and minorities, who typically have little political clout and elicit less public sympathy than other groups.

Public health officials also are concerned about AIDS victims in some rural areas, where various societal obstacles impede teaching prevention in schools or giving patients emotional support and information about complying with intricate drug regimens. Some believe the

prevalence of the disease in small towns is badly underreported because HIV-positive people are reluctant to admit that they have the virus. [21]

"The [disease's] impact in the urban areas is actually coming down a bit, whereas the impact in rural areas and small cities is actually going up," says Gary West, deputy director of the CDC's division of HIV/AIDS prevention.

Gostin of the Georgetown-Johns Hopkins program sees parallels between public reaction to the AIDS epidemic and the outbreak of venereal diseases between the 1930s and '50s. Then repulsion against infected people, particularly prostitutes, led people to view the situation as more of a problem of criminal law than health and medicine. Various laws were passed imposing criminal penalties for knowingly exposing people to venereal diseases.

The U.S. Supreme Court in June clarified the legal status of HIV-infected people, ruling 5-4 in *Bragdon v. Abbott* that Americans with the virus are protected from discrimination under the Americans with Disabilities Act, even if they do not have symptoms of AIDS. The landmark case was brought by an HIV-infected patient in Maine who was refused treatment by her dentist in his office.

Some analysts believe the ruling will extend beyond HIV/AIDS to affect patients with other conditions that some day may be disabling. Jennifer Middleton, staff attorney with the American Civil Liberties Union AIDS Project, says individuals with epilepsy, psychiatric illnesses and, possibly, terminal cancer may gain easier access to legal remedies as courts shift the burden of proof from whether a disability actually exists to whether discrimination

officials were predicting only two years ago.[4]

"Some developing countries with rapidly growing populations are now headed for population stability — not because of falling birth rates, but because of rapidly rising death rates," says Lester Brown, founder of the Washington-based Worldwatch Institute.

Crafting a strategy to keep more people healthy can be an exercise in frustration. U.N. officials in August moved to cut down on the number of infants infected with HIV through their mothers' milk by recommending that women infected with the virus consider feeding their babies formula instead. Last year alone there were more than 600,000 new cases among babies, most of whom received the virus from drinking infected breast milk. But funds for formula are scarce, and the water with which to prepare it often is unsafe.

Another option is administering AZT to women during the final stages of pregnancy, a treatment that has been shown to cut the risk of transmission to the child by half. The cost of such treatments is about $200 per person — a figure U.N. officials are trying to bring down by working with drug companies, local health officials and aid agencies.

Scenes of countries struggling to cope with an epidemic that threatens to destroy an entire generation are prompting some extraordinary efforts. In Uganda, where 20 percent of the population is HIV-infected, officials in October began an unprecedented AIDS vaccine trial in the hope of making the disease less deadly.

New vaccines with sometimes risky side effects are usually tested in developed nations with strong health-care programs. But citizens in the developing world actually make better subjects because scientists can gauge how well a vaccine reduces the amount of HIV that is already in an infected person. Such a test would be difficult in the West because most HIV-positive people are taking drugs that are unavailable in Africa.

Piot of the U.N. AIDS program acknowledges there are ethical dilemmas, such as using poor nations to test a vaccine that ultimately will benefit people in the developed world. But he says the situation is too dire to turn away. "In Africa they need a vaccine. Should we just tell them we have too many ethical problems to help them find one?" he asks.

---

[1] For background, see Michael Specter and Suzanne Daley, "Dead Zones," a series of articles on how AIDS ravages Africa and other continents, *The New York Times*, Aug. 6, 19, Sept. 18, 1998, p. A1.

[2] "AIDS Epidemic Update: December 1998," Joint United Nations Programme on HIV/AIDS and World Health Organization.

[3] Testimony before the House International Relations Committee, Sept. 16, 1998.

[4] See Joby Warrick, "AIDS' Long Shadow Cools Global Population Forecast," *The Washington Post*, Oct. 28, 1998, p. A2.

---

occurred.

The ruling "means that employers, businesses and health-care providers have to rely on objective, scientific facts about risk — not on their own individual judgment — before turning away someone with HIV," Middleton says. ∎

CURRENT SITUATION

Medicaid Eligibility

The Supreme Court decision in *Bragdon v. Abbott* made it clear that HIV-infected people can't be denied access to health-care services. But it's unclear whether the ruling will affect a simmering battle over expanding Medicaid coverage to currently ineligible people who have the virus.

AIDS activists and their allies in Congress complain that current Medicaid policies prevent many low-income, HIV-positive people from obtaining access to treatments that can prevent them from developing AIDS. Medicaid, the federal-state health insurance program for poor and disabled people, now covers people with HIV only if they have an AIDS-defining condition, are sick with the disease or are unable to be gainfully employed.

"It means you have to have full-blown AIDS before you can have access to AIDS-preventing drugs," complains AIDS Action's Zingale. "If you had rules like that for traffic safety, you'd put airbags in the car after it crashes."

Sixty-eight U.S. House members drafted a letter in August asking the Clinton administration to designate people with HIV as disabled so they can qualify for Medicaid and get multiple-drug AIDS cocktails. Sen. Robert G. Torricelli, D-N.J., is considering legislation requiring Medicaid to pay for drugs for HIV-infected people. Vice President Al Gore has also endorsed such a Medicaid expansion.

HHS Secretary Shalala has the authority to expand Medicaid if she can show such a step would not add costs to the program. Some Democratic lawmakers believe this criteria could be met because earlier drug treatment could avert having to pay treatment costs for late-term AIDS conditions. Others are skeptical, noting that the drug cocktails typically cost

$12,000 to $15,000, not including frequent blood tests and visits to the doctor that can drive the total annual cost of treatment to more than $35,000.

HHS spokesman Richard Sorian says Shalala's office is "examining all of the more recent data to see whether or not a change in policy is called for."

One way around the problem is for states to apply for waivers that would give expanded access to AIDS cocktails. Maine took such a step last year. The state requested nearly $18 million over five years in additional funding to expand Medicaid eligibility to cover protease inhibitors for HIV-positive people with incomes above the federal poverty level. Colorado, New Hampshire, Rhode Island, Texas, Vermont and Washington, D.C., are contemplating similar action, or have already applied for waivers. [22]

Clients are taught to cleanse hypodermic needles with water and bleach at the Lower East Side Harm Reduction Center — one of nine needle-exchange locations in New York. Several government studies have concluded that such programs can reduce HIV transmissions. But opponents fear handing out clean needles will encourage illicit-drug use.

Testing Controversy

Another controversial and evolving area of HIV/AIDS policy is HIV testing of pregnant women. This fall, the National Academy of Sciences' Institute of Medicine issued a landmark recommendation that HIV tests be a routine part of prenatal care for all women. The institute called on health-care providers to provide such tests and urged insurers to cover them. The tests would cost about $3 apiece if they were done in conjunction with other prenatal blood tests.

"If it is followed, women would not have to deal with the burden of disclosing personal risks or potential stereotyping; the test would simply be part of prenatal care that is the same for everyone," said the institute's panel of physicians, epidemiologists and ethicists. [23]

The move generated controversy because some experts believe testing should be concentrated on high-risk populations, not the general public. Others worry that general testing will somehow decrease counseling about HIV or compromise the privacy of prospective mothers. The policy recommendation was requested by Congress, but it is expected to primarily affect state legislators, who are responsible for most laws governing AIDS testing.

The Institute of Medicine's recommendation was only the latest effort by lawmakers and public health officials to reduce the number of pediatric AIDS cases. In 1994, researchers showed that administering AZT to pregnant women cut the risk of transmitting the virus to children by two-thirds or better. The following year, the U.S. Public Health Service recommended routine AIDS counseling for pregnant women, as well as voluntary testing. New York state passed a landmark law in 1997 requiring newborn testing for HIV, also mandating mothers be notified when their babies test positive.

U.S. health statistics show about 1,600 of the nearly 4 million babies born in the United States in 1996 — the last year for which complete figures were available — were infected with HIV. Full-blown AIDS is diagnosed in about 400 babies each year.

Minority Outreach

Another sign that the government is rethinking its response to the AIDS crisis comes via new federal outreach efforts to black and Latino communities, increasingly ravaged by the disease. President Clinton in October announced a $156-million initiative to create HIV-prevention campaigns in minority neighborhoods. It also would place more addicts in drug treatment and help local health workers assess the needs of people who are sick. [24]

NIH officials estimate blacks are six times as likely as whites and more than twice as likely as Hispanics to develop AIDS, largely due to injection-drug use. Reports that AIDS re-

Continued on p. 1066

At Issue:

Should the names of those who test positive for HIV/AIDS be given to public health officials?

REP. TOM COBURN, R-OKLA.

FROM TESTIMONY BEFORE THE HEALTH AND ENVIRONMENT SUBCOMMITTEE OF THE HOUSE COMMERCE COMMITTEE, FEB. 5, 1998.

yes

from the onset of this disease, proven medical and public health practices which have been successful . . . in curtailing other contagious diseases have been abandoned. It was decided that HIV, the deadliest disease of the 20th century, would be treated as a civil rights issue, instead of a public health issue. As a result, our response has been based almost exclusively on the rights of those infected to the detriment of those [who] are uninfected.

A test to detect HIV has been available for more than a decade, but the medical community has been forbidden to use it for routine screening. Therefore, in the course of a physical examination, a physician is prohibited from conducting a routine HIV test. No other disease is given such protection against diagnosis. . . .

The Centers for Disease Control and Prevention has relied on blind tests to determine the extent of the disease. . . . These tests, which do not identify the individual from whom the blood samples were taken, deny those who test positive the knowledge of their status, and thus prevent them from seeking medical care which can improve their lives. . . .

We should implement the public health practices which have been successful in helping curtail the spread of other infectious diseases to limit the spread of HIV. These include both disease reporting and partner notification. The latest therapies now available make reporting, notification and early diagnosis critical. . . . Many of the world's top scientists believe . . . that it's going to be possible to transform HIV into a chronic disease similar to that of diabetes. . . . However, the success of [new drug therapies] depends on starting treatment early. Sadly, most of those infected do not know they are infected until they become sick. By this point, they've been denied the medical care that could have prolonged their lives and [they] may have unknowingly infected others whom they love. . . .

As someone who has cared for AIDS patients, I want to do everything that I can do to prevent one more person from becoming infected with this horrible disease. The means to this end is available to us; throughout history epidemics have been stopped by identifying the infected, notifying the exposed, guaranteeing access to treatments and educating those who are infected about how to prevent transmission.

DANIEL ZINGALE
Executive director, AIDS Action

WRITTEN FOR THE CQ RESEARCHER, NOVEMBER 1998.

no

AIDS Action opposes proposals requiring states to establish new bureaucracies that collect and maintain the names of everyone with HIV as well as implement an oxymoronic mandatory partner-notification measure.

The names-reporting proposal is a bureaucratic scheme that could act as a disincentive to HIV testing at a time when as many as 300,000 HIV-positive Americans are unaware of their status. It's like a theater owner trying to attract crowds with tear gas.

AIDS Action supports reinvigorated voluntary HIV testing efforts, including better access to rapid testing. We don't need lists and an HIV police force. We need an effective law to encourage people at risk for HIV to get tested, get counseled and get the tools to protect their health and the health of others.

Not only do names-reporting and mandatory partner-notification plans act as a disincentive to testing, but they also fail to address deficiencies in access to health care as well as new life-prolonging AIDS drugs. Currently, Medicaid, the federal health program for the poor, is not eligible to low-income people with HIV until they develop AIDS.

Our voluntary testing and prevention structure would be decimated if people fear that getting a positive test could mean their name is reported to the government and they would be denied access to life-prolonging drugs and adequate care.

Instead of enacting a names-listing bureaucracy, AIDS Action is urging Congress to pass its Virtual Vaccine prevention plan, which is designed to ensure that HIV prevention and education efforts receive the same attention as the race to find a medical vaccine.

Mandatory partner notification is simply oxymoronic since effective partner notification requires the full cooperation and participation of people with HIV in consultation with health care professionals. To be effective, partner notification must be voluntary, consensual and run by experienced, trusted health care professionals, not a new government police force.

If passage of effective HIV prevention fails and names reporting prevails, people with HIV could once again be driven underground, people at-risk for infection might avoid testing and we could witness a tragic new crisis in the epidemic, just as we are beginning to make progress.

mains the No. 1 killer of African-American men and women ages 25 to 44 — despite the dramatic declines in overall AIDS deaths — led black members of Congress in May to ask President Clinton to declare that AIDS had created a "state of emergency" in African-American communities. Administration officials hesitated to go that far but pledged to find extra money for initiatives targeted at minorities.

"Like other epidemics before it, AIDS is now hitting hardest in areas where knowledge about the disease is scarce and poverty is high," Clinton said in announcing the program. "We must use all our power to end the growing disparities in HIV and AIDS."

The campaign is part of an $865 million increase in the government's fiscal 1999 investment in fighting AIDS, which will bring total federal spending on the disease to $7.7 billion. ∎

OUTLOOK

The Bottom Line

While thousands of researchers work on hopeful AIDS treatments, many big pharmaceutical companies sit on the sidelines, unconvinced that entering the AIDS market is a sound business decision. Many researchers and advocates believe their participation ultimately could lead to development of vaccines or other agents that would permanently halt the epidemic.

"Too many companies are reluctant to become involved in this work because they cannot envision making reasonable profits from products that would be primarily used in the developing world, where people can afford to buy very little," says Mark

Wainberg, a retrovirologist at McGill University in Montreal and president of the International AIDS Society.

So far, a handful of big companies have invested in developing AIDS vaccines, including Pasteur Merieux Connaught, a division of French drug giant Rhone-Poulenc; Merck & Co. of Whitehouse Station, N.J.; the Swiss pharmaceutical giant Novartis; and Philadelphia-based Wyeth-Ayerst Laboratories. A few firms are also considering development of easily administered topical microbicides that could be used in conjunction with existing drugs and help cut the rate of new infections.

But many companies see major disadvantages in developing new AIDS drugs. HIV vaccines would probably not have a big market in developed nations, where most people are deemed to be in low-risk groups. It would be difficult to charge enough in the developing world to recoup the companies' hefty research and development costs.

Because HIV doesn't infect non-humans (except chimpanzees), drug companies would encounter technical problems and, possibly, strong opposition testing promising drugs on animals. [25] Finding thousands of high-risk subjects for large-scale human trials could be even more daunting. And even if a drug showed promise, it would cost hundreds of millions of dollars to build a manufacturing plant that could produce enough of the product to meet demand.

Faced with these realities, some organizations are trying to make it more lucrative for companies to take on AIDS. The New York-based International AIDS Vaccine Initiative (IAVI) has held talks with the World Bank and other funding agencies about creating a $1 billion vaccine purchase fund to ensure that profit-driven drug companies have a guaranteed market.

In November, the IAVI also offered a novel twist on biotechnology

funding, providing about $4.5 million to underwrite vaccine research projects in North Carolina and Oxford, England. Instead of getting a cut of future profits, the organization won a commitment limiting the price the vaccine makers can charge in developing nations to no more than 10 percent above the cost of production. The vaccine makers can charge whatever they wish for their products in the industrialized world. [26]

Both vaccine makers — Alpha Vax Inc. of Durham, N.C., and the English team led by virologist Andrew McMichael — agreed to use African strains of HIV in their experimental treatments, presumably increasing the chances that any vaccines they develop will be useful in combating the disease in Africa.

In a separate development, NIH director Varmus has convened a working group of scientists to explore new ways of evaluating medical research to speed up the drug-approval process. This could include identifying early signs of a drug's eventual effect, such as reduced levels of HIV in the blood as a marker for AIDS.

The expedited approach is not in direct response to the AIDS crisis and would differ from the 1992 effort to accelerate approval of AIDS drugs. However, it would seek to establish more ironclad connections between a drug and its effects than the 1992 process, while conceivably helping drug companies avoid some of the lengthy and expensive clinical trials that are now required. [27]

"We can do the research and testing, but we need a collaboration with industry to make something in a bottle that people can use," says NIAID vaccine director Johnston. "We're very concerned about developing a healthy pipeline [of drugs]. We have to be willing to take risks. Even if some fail, I tell people, if I'm going to fail, I'd like to fail at something really big." ∎

Notes

[1] For background, see Mary H. Cooper, "Combating AIDS," *The CQ Researcher*, April 21, 1995, pp. 345-368.

[2] See U.S. Centers for Disease Control and Prevention, "Trends in the HIV & AIDS Epidemic, 1998," U.S. Department of Health and Human Services.

[3] For background, see David Baltimore and Carole Heilman, "HIV Vaccines: Prospects and Challenges," *Scientific American*, July 1998, pp. 98-103.

[4] For background, see Mary H. Cooper, "Women and AIDS," *The CQ Researcher*, Dec. 25, 1992, pp. 1121-1144.

[5] For background, see Lawrence Gostin and David Webber, "HIV Infection and AIDS in the Public Health and Health Care Systems: The Role of Law and Litigation," *Journal of the American Medical Association*, Vol. 279, April 8, 1998, pp. 1108-1113.

[6] For background, see Bernard Hirschel, "Progress and Problems in the Fight Against AIDS," *New England Journal of Medicine*, Vol. 338, No. 13, March 26, 1998, p. 906.

[7] Quoted in Mark Schoofs, "The Virus Fights Back," *The Village Voice*, July 14, 1998, p. 39.

[8] For background, see Jon Cohen, "NIH Concocts a Booster Shot for HIV Vaccines," *Science*, Vol. 281, No. 5381, Aug. 28, 1998.

[9] See "An Ounce of Prevention," *The Economist*, July 4, 1998, pp. 79-81.

[10] See Sue Kirchhoff, "Senate Votes Voluntary AIDS Testing for Pregnant Women," Reuters News Service, July 26, 1995.

[11] The study assumed the lifetime cost of treating HIV is $154,402. See "CDC Researchers Present Mounting Evidence that HIV Prevention Saves Lives and Dollars," U.S. Centers for Disease Control and Prevention press release and background materials, July 1, 1998.

[12] See "The NIMH Multisite HIV Prevention Trial: Reducing HIV Sexual Risk Behavior," *Science*, Vol. 280, June 19, 1998, pp. 1889-1894.

[13] See "HIV Epidemic in Vancouver Fuels Debate Over Needle Exchange," *Alcoholism and Drug Abuse Weekly*, Aug. 18, 1997.

[14] See Richard Knox, "Needle Exchanges Endorsed But Won't Get Federal Funds," *The Boston Globe*, April 21, 1998, p. A1.

[15] The poll was taken by the Survey Research Center for the University of California from September 1996 to March 1997. The findings are available on the Internet at http://psychology.ucdavis.edu/rainbow.html.

[16] See Lynda Richardson, "Wave of Laws Aimed at People With HIV," *The New York Times*, Sept. 25, 1998, p. A1.

[17] Quoted in Andrew Bindman, et al. "Anonymous HIV Testing is Important for Early Care," *Journal of the American Medical Association*, Vol. 280, Oct. 28, 1998, pp. 1416-1420.

[18] For background, see Karen Bellenir and Peter Dresser, eds., "AIDS Sourcebook: Health Reference Series No. 4," Omnigraphics Inc., 1995.

[19] Baltimore and Heilman, *op. cit.*, pp. 100-103.

[20] See Dorothy Nelkin, ed., *A Disease of Society: Cultural and Institutional Responses to AIDS* (1991), pp. 1-13.

[21] See Pam Belluck, "In Small Town, U.S.A., AIDS Presents New Set of Hardships," *The New York Times*, Oct. 12, 1998, p. A1.

[22] See "Maine to Expand Eligibility for AIDS Drugs with 1115 Waiver," *Managed Medicare & Medicaid*, No. 41, Vol. 3, Nov. 23, 1997.

[23] See "Reducing the Odds: Preventing Perinatal Transmission of HIV in the United States," Institute of Medicine, National Academy of Sciences, 1998.

[24] See Amy Goldstein, "U.S. to Begin Minority AIDS Initiative," *The Washington Post*, Oct. 29, 1998, p. A3.

[25] For background, see David Masci, "Fighting Over Animal Rights," *The CQ Researcher*, Aug. 2, 1996, pp. 673-696.

[26] See David Brown, "AIDS Research Grants Tied to Pledge in Vaccine Costs," *The Washington Post*, Nov. 20, 1998, p. A6.

[27] See Marlene Cimons, "Scientists Plan Faster Approval for New Drugs," *Los Angeles Times*, Oct. 12, 1998, p. A1.

FOR MORE INFORMATION

U.S. Centers for Disease Control and Prevention, 1600 Clifton Road, N.E., Atlanta, Ga. 30333; (404) 639-3534; www.cdc.gov. This branch of the U.S. Department of Health and Human Services surveys national and international HIV/AIDS trends, administers block grants to states for preventive health services and promotes AIDS education programs.

National Institute of Allergy and Infectious Diseases, 6003 Executive Blvd., Solar Building, #2A18, Rockville, Md. 20852; (301) 496-0545; www.niaid.nih.gov. This is the primary institute at the National Institutes of Health for AIDS research. It conducts a network of AIDS clinical trials and preclinical drug development research and supports epidemiological studies and research into AIDS vaccines.

Office of National AIDS Policy, 808 17th St., N.W., Suite 820, Washington, D.C. 20006; (202) 632-1090. This branch of the Executive Office of the President advises the president and formulates policy on matters related to AIDS and AIDS treatment.

Joint United Nations Programme on HIV/AIDS (UNAIDS), 20 Avenue Appia, CH-1211 Geneva 27, Switzerland; (41-22) 791 3666; www.unaids.org. This umbrella organization coordinates responses to the global AIDS epidemic, using United Nations organizations with complementary mandates and expertise.

AIDS Action, 1875 Connecticut Ave., N.W., Suite 700, Washington, D.C. 20009; (202) 986-1300; www.aidsaction.org. This nonprofit organization monitors and promotes legislation dealing with AIDS research, education and related public policy issues.

Bibliography

Selected Sources Used

Books

Bartlett, John and Ann Finkbeiner, *The Guide to Living With HIV Infection*, Developed at the Johns Hopkins AIDS Clinic, Johns Hopkins University Press, 1998.
A thorough and up-to-date guide to HIV and AIDS. Bartlett, director of the infectious disease program at the Johns Hopkins University Hospital in Baltimore, and science writer Finkbeiner cover breakthroughs in understanding how HIV reproduces and new strategies to track infections and suppress the virus.

Shilts, Randy, *And the Band Played On: Politics, People and the AIDS Epidemic*, Penguin, 1995 (Reissue edition).
The late San Francisco Chronicle reporter's critically acclaimed account of the early years of the AIDS epidemic examines the societal impact of the disease and assesses the responses of the Reagan administration, the U.S. medical establishment and the gay community.

Articles

"An Ounce of Prevention," *The Economist*, July 4, 1998, pp. 79-81.
Presentations from the 12th World AIDS Conference demonstrate there is a huge gap between the ways the disease is dealt with in rich and poor countries.

Brandt, Allan, "AIDS in Historical Perspective: Four Lessons from the History of Sexually Transmitted Diseases," *American Journal of Public Health*, Vol. 78, No. 4, 1988, pp. 367-371.
A Harvard University Medical School professor asserts the United States has had relatively little recent experience dealing with health crises, which contributed to the uncertain early responses to the AIDS epidemic.

Cohen, Oren and Anthony Fauci, "HIV/AIDS in 1998 — Gaining the Upper Hand?" *Journal of the American Medical Association*, Vol. 280, No. 1, July 1, 1998, pp. 87-88.
Researchers at the National Institute of Allergy and Infectious Diseases conclude that new advances in HIV therapies are helping AIDS patients live longer, though they can't rid patients' bodies of the disease. The authors conclude that developing a safe, effective vaccine is the "holy grail" of AIDS research.

"Defeating AIDS: What Will It Take?" *Scientific American*, July 1998, pp. 81-107.
A lengthy special report that includes articles by leading researchers on HIV therapy, drug resistance, HIV vaccines and the outlook for controlling the disease.

Flexner, Charles, "HIV-Protease Inhibitors," *New England Journal of Medicine*, Vol. 338, No. 18, April 30, 1998, pp. 1281-1291.
A not-too technical, very thorough description of how the new generation of AIDS drugs work, written by a Johns Hopkins University physician.

Schoofs, Mark, "HIV Down Among IV-Drug Users," *The Village Voice*, Aug. 4, 1998, p. 34.
Studies indicate that the rate of new HIV infections among injection-drug users in New York City is on the decline, but the good news is tenuous. The decline could be reversed by changes in AIDS prevention and drug treatment policies, such as the hotly contested issue of needle exchanges.

Schultz, Stacey and Ellen Licking, "AIDS: No More Silver Bullet," *U.S. News & World Report*, July 13, 1998, pp. 20-21.
The AIDS virus is fighting back against new treatments, and on many fronts it seems to be winning. This article explains how drug-resistant strains of HIV can be transmitted from one person to another.

Specter, Michael, "Urgency Tempers Ethics Concerns in Uganda Trial of AIDS Vaccine," *The New York Times*, Oct. 1, 1998, p. A1.
The frightening spread of AIDS in African nations is prompting public health officials to rethink ethical guidelines and conduct trials of promising drugs on some of the world's most at-risk populations.

Reports and Studies

Gostin, Lawrence, "Confidentiality, Privacy and the Right to Know," *Journal of the American Medical Association* HIV/AIDS Information Center, 1996.
A Georgetown University law school professor presents an overview of the conflicting legal and ethical obligations in testing HIV-positive patients.

National Academy of Sciences, "Preventing HIV Transmission: The Role of Sterile Needles and Bleach," National Academy Press, 1995.
One of the more comprehensive of at least a half-dozen government studies that conclude that needle-exchange programs reduce HIV infections and don't increase the amount of illicit-drug use.

"Reducing the Odds: Preventing Perinatal Transmission of HIV in the United States," Institute of Medicine, National Academy Press, 1998.
A panel of physicians, ethicists and epidemiologists urges HIV tests for all pregnant women.

The Next Step

Additional information from UMI's Newspaper & Periodical Abstracts™ database

AIDS in the Developing World

Annas, George J., and Michael A. Grodin, "Human Rights and Maternal-Fetal HIV Transmission Prevention Trials in Africa," *American Journal of Public Health*, **April 1998, pp. 560-563.**

The human rights issues raised by the conduct of maternal-fetal human immunodeficiency virus transmission trials in Africa are not unique to either acquired immunodeficiency syndrome or Africa, but public discussion of these trials presents an opportunity for the United States and other wealthy nations to take the rights and welfare of impoverished populations seriously.

Bessis, Sophie, "AIDS: Prevention or Care," *UNESCO Courier*, **July 1998, pp. 66-68.**

The ethical question of whether AIDS victims in poor African and Asian countries should be denied expensive treatment is discussed. Though treatment would not be cost-effective, a moral case is increasingly being made against such thinking.

Brown, David, "AIDS Study Emphasizes Prevention Worldwide; Researchers Estimate Effects of Past Programs, Benefits of Future Ones in Developing Nations," *The Washington Post*, **Nov. 4, 1997, p. A13.**

About 2.3 billion people, roughly half the population of the developing world, live in places where the AIDS epidemic has barely begun, and even mildly successful prevention programs could have enormous benefits, according to a new study. The 353-page World Bank study attempts to describe the effects AIDS already has had on the developing world and to predict what might happen under various future scenarios. It also evaluates numerous countries' responses to the epidemic and makes general policy recommendations.

Coggins, Christiana, "HIV Prevention and AIDS Care in Africa: A District Level Approach," *Population & Development Review*, **March 1998, pp. 178-179.**

The author reviews "HIV Prevention and AIDS Care in Africa: A District Level Approach," edited by Japheth Ng'weshemi, Ties Boerma, John Bennett and Dick Schapink.

Over, Mead, "Coping with the Impact of AIDS," *Finance & Development*, **March 1998, pp. 22-24.**

The AIDS epidemic is straining the limited resources available to many developing countries. The author suggests how governments can provide support to those affected by AIDS without neglecting others in need or abandoning important development goals.

AIDS and Minority Groups

Bockting, W.O.; B.E. Robinson; and B.R.S. Rosser, "Transgender HIV Prevention: A Qualitative Needs Assessment," *AIDS Care*, **August 1998, pp. 505-526.**

Although clinical experience and preliminary research suggest that some transgendered people are at significant risk for HIV, this stigmatized group has so far been largely ignored in HIV prevention.

Charles, Nick, "Brothers' Well-Being," *Essence*, **November 1998, pp. 58-60.**

Health information on four major disorders that black men face — HIV/AIDS, heart attacks, prostate cancer and impotence — is presented.

Takahashi, Lois M., and Gayla Smutny, "Health Journal: View from Vancouver: Cautiously Celebrating New AIDS Treatment; Community Planning for HIV/AIDS Prevention in Orange County, California," *Journal of the American Planning Association*, **Autumn 1998, pp. 441-456.**

HIV/AIDS remains a critical social concern in the United States. Although much progress has been made in terms of medical research, public awareness and prevention strategies, HIV/AIDS continues to affect more and differing groups of people.

Zimmerman, Marc A.; Jesus Ramirez-Valles; Enrique Suarez; Graciela de la Rosa; and Marco A. Castro, "An HIV/AIDS Prevention Project for Mexican Homosexual Men: An Empowerment Approach," *Health Education & Behavior*, **April 1997, pp. 177-190.**

In an intervention, participants design and implement an HIV/AIDS prevention project for Mexican homosexual men. The results suggest that the participants' HIV/AIDS knowledge and preventive behavior improved when compared with individuals who did not participate in the intervention.

Prevention and Education

Auslander, Wendy F.; Vered Slonim-Nevo; Diane Elze; and Michael Sherraden, "HIV Prevention for Youths in Independent Living Programs: Expanding Life Options," *Child Welfare*, **March 1998, pp. 208-221.**

The incidence of HIV among adolescents is increasing. Changing the behavior of these youngsters is necessary to avoid HIV, and this includes educational planning that will expand the future life options of these youths.

De Zoysa, Isabelle; Christopher J. Elias; and Margaret E. Bentley, "Ethical Challenges in Efficacy Trials of Vaginal Microbicides for HIV Prevention," *American Journal of Public Health*, April 1998, pp. 571-575.

The authors discuss some of the ethical challenges raised by advanced clinical trials designed to guess the safety and efficacy of vaginal microbicides in protecting women from HIV infection. The ethical principles that guide clinical research involving human subjects require that all participants in such trials be provided available measures known to reduce the risk of HIV infection.

Hobfoll, Stevan E., "Ecology, Community and AIDS Prevention," *American Journal of Community Psychology*, February 1998, pp. 143-144.

The author explores the role that may be played by an ecological view of AIDS prevention and AIDS-related social concerns. Sexual behavior and associated risks are not tied just to people's personal behavior.

Janz, Nancy K.; Marc A. Zimmerman; Patricia A. Wren; Barbara A. Israel; et al, "Evaluation of 37 AIDS Prevention Projects: Successful Approaches and Barriers to Program Effectiveness," *Health Education Quarterly*, February 1996, pp. 80-97.

The authors present results from a survey of 37 AIDS prevention and service projects. A variety of intervention activities were rated effective in AIDS education services by project staff.

Laidlaw, Kelly, "World AIDS Conference Stresses Prevention," *American Fitness*, September 1998, p. 23.

Prevention is the only realistic method to stop the spread of AIDS, according the 12th World AIDS Conference, held in Geneva, Switzerland. More than 30 million people worldwide are now infected, and doctors say a cure is a long way off.

Rosser, B.R. Simon, "New Directions in HIV Prevention," *SIECUS Report*, December 1997/January 1998, pp. 5-7.

The author reviews the four forces that appear to have influenced current change in HIV prevention: new treatment advances, a paradigm shift in theory and understanding, a scientific consensus on direction and the impact of the community-planning process on prevention.

Rowe, Paul M., "Case for Behavioural Studies for AIDS Prevention," *Lancet*, March 16, 1996, p. 750.

Thomas J. Coates, director of the Center for AIDS Prevention Studies at the University of California, San Francisco, indicated last month that halving the rates of risky sexual behavior could halt the AIDS epidemic. There are strong political barriers to the progress of research on sexual behavior.

Selwyn, Peter A., "Prospects for Improvement in Physicians' Communication Skills and in Prevention of

HIV Infection," *Lancet*, Aug. 15, 1998, p. 506.

An effective vaccine against HIV, improvements in the socioeconomic status of women in developing countries and prevention and treatment of drug addiction will contribute more to the retreat of the HIV epidemic than changes in physician consultations, but physicians should not avoid or overlook opportunities to help patients protect themselves against disease.

Sternberg, Steve, "Groups Seek More Funding for HIV Prevention Efforts," *USA Today*, July 21, 1998, p. A9.

Alarmed at the spread of AIDS nationwide, AIDS advocates have demanded millions for HIV prevention and decried the nation's "paralyzed" prevention efforts. Officials estimate that as many as 900,000 people in the United States now carry HIV, the virus that causes AIDS. Roughly 40,000 people get the lethal virus each year, half of them younger than 25. New cases add $6.2 billion in lifetime treatment costs to the nation's AIDS-care bill each year.

St. Louis, Michael E.; Judith N. Wasserheit; and Helene D. Gayle, "Janus Considers the HIV Pandemic; Harnessing Recent Advances to Enhance AIDS Prevention," *American Journal of Public Health*, January 1997, pp. 10-12.

An editorial discusses advances in HIV clinical care and prevention and the possibility that they may usher in an era in which the personal health concerns of people with HIV are aligned with the public health imperative to prevent the spread of the disease.

Walls, Carla T.; Jennifer Lauby; Karlene Lavelle; Tara Derby; and Lisa Bond, "Exposure to a Community-Level HIV Prevention Intervention: Who Gets the Message," *Journal of Community Health*, August 1998, pp. 281-299.

As part of the evaluation of a community-level HIV prevention program for women, this study examined predictors of exposure to print media and community outreach and assessed the relationship between exposure to the intervention and condom-use behavior.

Wilfert, Catherine; Donna T. Beck; Alan R. Fleischman; Lynne M. Mofenson; et al, "Human Immunodeficiency Virus/Acquired Immunodeficiency Syndrome Education in Schools," *Pediatrics*, May 1998, pp. 933-935.

The authors stipulate that education remains critical in the fight to prevent HIV infection and AIDS, particularly in schools. Accurate teaching of prevention needs to be included in K-12 health education curriculum.

Treating AIDS Patients

"Cost a Major Concern with Protease Inhibitors," *AIDS Alert*, April 1996, pp. 41-42.

The new protease inhibitors for AIDS treatment are very expensive. A call is ringing out for insurance companies to cover the new medications.

"FDA Research Unveils Clues on Serious Diseases," *FDA Consumer*, **March 1998, p. 4.**

FDA scientists have released the results of two studies that may change the way some life-threatening illnesses are treated. One study concerns the role of chemokines, and the other discusses factors that may make certain strains of HIV-1 more likely than others to be transmitted through sexual contact.

"Potential New AIDS Treatment Looks Very Promising," *Morning Edition*, **NPR, Nov. 4, 1994.**

A drug that has been in use for more than 30 years as a treatment for leukemia looks promising as a treatment for AIDS. Researchers have begun testing the drug on human subjects and hope to publish results in 1995.

Brink, Susan, "Closer, but Still no Cure," *U.S. News & World Report*, **Feb. 16, 1998, p. 73.**

For a while, AIDS activists wondered if an experimental HIV therapy might translate into a cure. While the therapy shows great promise as a treatment, it did not get rid of the virus.

Chase, Marilyn, "Health Journal: View from Vancouver: Cautiously Celebrating New AIDS Treatment," *The Wall Street Journal*, **July 15, 1996, p. B1.**

The author comments on the 11th International Conference on AIDS, and the promise shown by three new protease inhibitor drugs, which, when combined with older AIDS drugs like AZT, can almost purge the blood of circulating virus. However, the new therapy is very expensive.

Des Jarlais, Don C., "Stages in the Response of the Drug Abuse Treatment System to the AIDS Epidemic in New York City," *Journal of Drug Issues*, **spring 1990, pp. 335-347.**

In responding to the challenges of providing drug abuse treatment to people who are likely to die, drug-abuse treatment programs in New York City seem to have gone through four stages: denial, panic, coping and potential burnout.

Hutchcraft, Chuck, "Abbott AIDS Drug OK'd for Children; Norvir Can Be Used for 2-Year-Olds and Up," *The Chicago Tribune*, **March 15, 1997, p. 1.**

The U.S. Food and Drug Administration has given the green light to use HIV protease inhibitors, the powerful new class of AIDS drugs, in the treatment of children. The FDA approved the use of North Chicago-based Abbott Laboratories' Norvir to treat AIDS-infected children ages 2 to 13. At the same time, it approved the use of Viracept, made by La Jolla, Calif.-based Agouron Pharmaceutical Inc., in the treatment of adults and children. The action won the applause of the Pediatric AIDS Foundation.

Parini, Sue M., "Understanding Sexually Transmitted Diseases, Part II," *Nursing*, **April 1998, pp. 26-28.**

Information about sexually transmitted diseases is offered. The organisms that cause the infections, the infection's incubation period, symptoms, treatment and complications are described.

Perlman, David, "Quarter of AIDS Patients Not Getting Best Therapy," *San Francisco Chronicle*, **June 4, 1998, p. A9.**

Despite the availability of new AIDS drug combinations that are saving thousands of lives, at least one-quarter of HIV-infected patients are not being given the most effective therapy by their doctors, a national survey shows. Less than a year ago, the nation's leading AIDS physicians, working with the Department of Health and Human Services, published guidelines urgently recommending that all doctors prescribe a three-way combination of new and old drugs when they begin treating AIDS patients.

Richardson, Sarah, "Hope at a Price," *Discover*, **January 1998, pp. 90-91.**

After years of despair, hope is returning to HIV-infected patients. In a 1997 report, microbiologists showed that a combination of three drugs dramatically reduces virus levels.

Starr, Cynthia, "The Latest Recommendations for Antiretroviral Therapy," *Patient Care*, **Aug. 15, 1998, pp. 154-171.**

Patients with HIV infection are living longer, healthier lives, thanks largely to advances in antiretroviral therapy. Finding the right combination of drugs for each patient is essential.

Condom Distribution and Needle-Exchange Programs

Fuller, Jon, "AIDS Prevention: A Challenge to the Catholic Moral Tradition," *America*, **Dec. 28, 1996, pp. 13-20.**

The global AIDS epidemic is proving to be a challenge to the Catholic moral tradition. The use of condoms and needle-exchange programs runs contrary to many church beliefs.

Pinkerton, Steven D., and Paul R. Abramson, "Condoms and the Prevention of AIDS," *American Scientist*, **July 1997, pp. 364-373.**

The authors trace the history of the condom and sexually transmitted diseases, and explain why condoms are so important now.

Span, Paula, "Needle Exchanges Inject Controversy in AIDS Prevention," *The Washington Post*, **July 16, 1996, p. A1.**

The Lower East Side Needle Exchange Program in New York City, which operates three hours a day, six days a week, is dedicated to making sterile needles available to intravenous-drug users who are at risk of contracting the AIDS virus by using dirty or shared needles.

Back Issues

APRIL 1997
Declining Crime Rates
The FBI Under Fire
Gender Equity in Sports
Space Program's Future

MAY 1997
The Stock Market
The Cloning Controversy
Expanding NATO
The Future of Libraries

JUNE 1997
FDA Reform
China After Deng
Line-Item Veto
Breast Cancer

JULY 1997
Transportation Policy
Executive Pay
School Choice Debate
Aggressive Driving

AUGUST 1997
Age Discrimination
Banning Land Mines
Children's Television
Evolution vs. Creationism

SEPTEMBER 1997
Caring for the Dying
Mental Health Policy
Mexico's Future
Youth Fitness

OCTOBER 1997
Urban Sprawl in the West
Diversity in the Workplace
Teacher Education
Contingent Work Force

NOVEMBER 1997
Renewable Energy
Artificial Intelligence
Religious Persecution
Roe v. Wade at 25

DECEMBER 1997
Whistleblowers
Castro's Next Move
Gun Control Standoff
Regulating Nonprofits

JANUARY 1998
Foster Care Reform
IRS Reform
The Black Middle Class
U.S.-British Relations

FEBRUARY 1998
Patients' Rights
Deflation Fears
Caring for the Elderly
The New Corporate Philanthropy

MARCH 1998
Israel at 50
The Federal Judiciary
Drinking on Campus
The Economics of Recycling

APRIL 1998
Biology and Behavior
Liberal Arts Education
Income Inequality
High-Tech Labor Shortage

MAY 1998
Census 2000
Child-Care Options
Alzheimer's Disease
U.S.-Russian Relations

JUNE 1998
Student Journalism
Antitrust Policy
Environmental Justice
Sleep Deprivation

JULY 1998
Encouraging Teen Abstinence
Population and the Environment
Democracy in Asia
Baby Boomers at Midlife

AUGUST 1998
Oil Production in the 21st Century
Flexible Work Arrangements
Coastal Development
Student Activism

SEPTEMBER 1998
Organic Farming
Cancer Treatments
Hispanic Americans' New Clout
The Future of Baseball

OCTOBER 1998
School Violence
Social Security
National Forests
Puerto Rico's Status

NOVEMBER 1998
Internet Privacy
Human Rights
Drug Testing
European Monetary Union

Future Topics

▶ *Searching For Jesus*

▶ *Iran: 20 Years After the Revolution*

▶ *The Crisis in American Journalism*

Searching for Jesus

Are scholars undermining Christians' faith?

Most Christians literally believe the biblical accounts of the miraculous birth of Jesus told every Christmas in homes around the world: the story of Joseph and Mary, the appearance of the Star of Bethlehem, the adoration of the shepherds and the Wise Men. Many religious scholars, however, view the traditional nativity story as myth rather than history. Some of these scholars want to use historical techniques to reconstruct the actual events of Jesus' life, ministry and death. Some say the "quest for the historical Jesus" can lead to a better understanding of Jesus' spiritual message and its relevance for today. But others say it diverts Christians from the essential beliefs — and the central mystery — of their faith.

Dec. 11, 1998 • Volume 8, No. 46 • Pages 1073-1096

Formerly Editorial Research Reports

Searching for Jesus

Cover: A crèche from Guatemala is among the nativity scenes on display at the Washington National Cathedral. (Washington National Cathedral)

Dec. 11, 1998
Volume 8, No.46

EDITOR
Sandra Stencel

MANAGING EDITOR
Thomas J. Colin

STAFF WRITERS
Adriel Bettelheim
Mary H. Cooper
Kenneth Jost
Kathy Koch
David Masci

PRODUCTION EDITOR
Debra James

EDITORIAL ASSISTANT
Laura S. Cavender

PUBLISHED BY
Congressional Quarterly Inc.

CHAIRMAN
Andrew Barnes

VICE CHAIRMAN
Andrew P. Corty

PRESIDENT AND PUBLISHER
Robert W. Merry

EXECUTIVE EDITOR
David Rapp

Bibliographic records and abstracts included in The Next Step section of this publication are the copyrighted material of UMI, and are used with permission.

The CQ Researcher (ISSN 1056-2036). Formerly Editorial Research Reports. Published weekly, except Jan. 2, May 29, July 3, Oct. 30, by Congressional Quarterly Inc., 1414 22nd St., N.W., Washington, D.C. 20037. Annual subscription rate for libraries, businesses and government is $340. Additional rates furnished upon request. Periodicals postage paid at Washington, D.C., and additional mailing offices. POSTMASTER: Send address changes to The CQ Researcher, 1414 22nd St., N.W., Washington, D.C. 20037.

Searching for Jesus

BY KENNETH JOST

THE ISSUES

ary and Joseph stand beside the infant Jesus, lying in the familiar manger. There are camels and sheep, and the three Magi approach with their gifts. But the needlepoint nativity scene stitched for former President George Bush also contains a less familiar figure: a Texas longhorn steer.

The traditional nativity scenes from around the world on exhibit at Washington National Cathedral this Christmas are full of surprises. Jesus is depicted variously with Caucasian, Negroid or Oriental features. Kenyan woodcarvers added a rhinoceros and an elephant. Navajo craftsmen show the Magi with traditional Native American gifts, such as bread and cornmeal dough. The *nacimiento* from Costa Rica is fashioned from coffee root; the Holy Family from Appalachia is made out of corn husks.

"I am so moved by the way the story of the Incarnation touches people in so many cultures and so many places," says the Rev. Nathan Baxter, dean of the landmark Episcopal church .

For most Christians, the story of the Nativity is more than just a familiar and comforting holiday myth. According to a recent poll, a substantial majority of Americans strongly believe that Jesus was born in a stable to a virgin mother, that the star of Bethlehem announced his birth and that three Wise Men from the east brought him gifts.

But to many religious scholars, the accounts of the Nativity that Christians learn from childhood cannot be

taken as literally true.

"We all pretty much agree that there's no history in the birth and childhood stories," says Robert W. Funk, head of the Jesus Seminar. The controversial group of scholars sharply challenges the biblical accounts of Jesus' life and death.

Moreover, the seminar contends in two recent books that most of the words and deeds attributed to Jesus in the New Testament cannot be historically substantiated. Funk himself, a divinity-school graduate and former professor of religion, has stirred additional controversy by questioning Jesus' divinity and Christians' worship of him as the son of God. "Jesus is not the proper object of faith," Funk writes in *Honest to Jesus*, combining historical reconstruction of Jesus' life with a strongly written attack on institutionalized Christianity. [1]

The seminar is helping to lead a renewed effort by scholars to reconstruct the events of Jesus' life using history and reason rather than theology and faith. The so-called "quest for the historical Jesus" dates to the 1700s and has engaged the efforts of such diverse thinkers as Thomas Jefferson, philosopher Immanuel Kant and humanitarian Albert Schweitzer. The work has stirred controversy by questioning the literal accounts of Jesus' life in the four Gospels — Matthew, Mark, Luke and John — and assailing established church doctrine.

Today, the idea of using the few available historical sources to get at

an account of Jesus' life is more widely accepted than in the past. "There was considerable controversy at first over the notion of scholars discussing what ought to be considered authentic of Jesus' teaching and Jesus' deeds," says Bruce Chilton, a professor of religion at Bard College in Annandale, N.Y., and a member and sometime critic of the Jesus Seminar. "But over the course of time, this has come to be recognized as an appropriate question."

Still, some religious scholars continue to attack both the historical quest in general and the Jesus Seminar in particular. Luke Timothy Johnson, a professor of theology at Emory University in Atlanta, calls the historical quest "a paper chase" with no validity. "A lot of what passes for history in the New Testament guild is really a kind of literary manipulation," he says.

As for the Jesus Seminar itself, Johnson accuses the group — and Funk in particular — of shoddy scholarship and fraudulent promotion. "The vast majority of scholars do not basically buy what the Jesus Seminar is selling," he says.

Some members do criticize the seminar or seek to distance themselves from Funk's outspoken views. "Bob would like to use [the seminar's] findings to prod, provoke and reform the church," says Perry Kea, a professor of religion at the private, Methodist-affiliated University of Indianapolis. "I would make a distinction between the task and the use to which those results can be put."

Still, Kea and other seminar members who do not share all of Funk's views agree that the historical inquiry into Jesus' life is both legitimate and important. "It is the life of Jesus, and the death of Jesus, which is vindicated by the resurrection," says John Dominic Crossan, who co-founded the seminar with Funk and has written several books on Jesus' life.

The Life of Jesus According to All the Gospels

The word gospel, Greek for "good news," refers to the accounts of Jesus' life and teachings written in the early years of Christianity. The four Gospels of the New Testament are recognized in the official church canon and thus are called the "Canonical Gospels." Three of the Gospels — by the Evangelists Matthew, Mark and Luke — present similar accounts of Jesus' birth, ministry and death and are called "Synoptic Gospels." Some other gospels appear in complete manuscripts, but some are only fragmentary. Two "gospels" — the Sayings Gospel Q and the Signs Gospel — are hypothetical reconstructions based on literary examinations of other gospels that may have derived from the earlier, unconfirmed documents. Jewish-Christian gospels — circulated by early groups that considered themselves both Jewish and Christian — are known only through citation in later manuscripts; no known texts exist.

The Canonical Gospels

Matthew — Traditionally the most quoted and most influential of the three Synoptic Gospels; 28 chapters; account of nativity relates visitation by the Magi; includes the Sermon on the Mount and four other sermons, the Lord's Prayer, well-known parables and accounts of "miracles," and the passion, crucifixion and resurrection; believed to derive in part from Mark.

Mark — Thought to be the first of the Gospels written — perhaps 66-70 Common Era (C.E.) — and to have been a source for Matthew and Luke; 16 chapters; opens with baptism of Jesus by John the Baptist; includes scene of Jesus driving the money-changers from the temple; ends with the discovery of Jesus' empty tomb.

Luke — Longest of the Gospels and, along with Acts, part of a two-volume narrative; opens with the Annunciation; nativity account relates visitation by shepherds; includes stories of the Good Samaritan and the Prodigal Son; lengthy Travel Narrative relates Jesus' teachings as he travels to Jerusalem before his arrest and crucifixion; ends with Jesus appearing to followers and being carried to the sky.

Gospel of the Signs — A hypothetical gospel thought by some scholars to have been a source for John; reconstructed account of Jesus' deeds meant to be understood as 'signs' of Jesus' messianic status.

John — Consists mainly of discourses by Jesus, with less emphasis on narratives; most significant for "I am" statements ("I am the light of the world"), akin to divine statements of Hebrew scriptures; probably written in last 15 years of first century C.E.

Sayings Gospels

Sayings Gospel Q — A hypothetical collection of sayings of Jesus thought to be the source ("quelle" is German for source) of passages found in nearly identical form in Matthew and Luke but not in their major source, Mark.

Gospel of Thomas — Collection of sayings, totaling 114 verses, likely compiled in latter decades of first century C.E.; manuscript, in Coptic, discovered near Nag Hammadi, Egypt, in 1945; meaning of some passages obscured by paradox or metaphor; interpretation "still in its infancy."

Greek Fragments of Thomas — Several small fragments of Thomas, in Greek, were found in 1897, before the Nag Hammadi discovery; some differences with Coptic version, but not known whether there were two distinct gospels or simply different versions.

Secret Book of James — Consists of 11 short chapters introduced as "secret book" revealed by "the Savior"; one of the Nag Hammadi manuscripts; ends with Jesus' ascension and an attempt by James and Peter to follow, thwarted by inquisitiveness of other disciples.

Dialogue of the Savior — Dialogue between "the Lord" and several disciples, presented in 41 short chapters; another of the Nag Hammadi manuscripts.

Gospel of Mary — Presents story of Mary Magdalene recounting words of the Savior to non-comprehending male disciples, Peter and Andrew; three fragmentary manuscripts, perhaps half original text; written perhaps around 150 C.E.

Infancy Gospels

Infancy Gospel of Thomas — Consists of 19 short chapters said to describe "boyhood deeds" of Jesus; in circulation by second century C.E.; depicts Jesus as having supernatural powers in his youth; viewed as heretical by orthodox Christians of the era.

Infancy Gospel of James — Relates Mary's birth as answer to prayers by childless couple, her infancy and childhood and the announcement of Mary's pregnancy before recounting the nativity in passages parallel to but in some respects different from Matthew and Luke.

Fragmentary Gospels

Gospel of Peter — Papyrus manuscript found in Upper Egypt in 1886; includes portions of passion story, empty-tomb story and introduction to resurrection story; could date to second century C.E.

Secret Gospel of Mark — Two fragments are cited in letter by Clement of Alexandria (150-215 C.E.); includes reference to mysterious young man who appears to Jesus in Garden of Gethsemanae dressed only in linen cloth; account appears in canonical Mark, but not in Matthew or Luke.

Egerton Gospel — Fragment includes miracle stories, controversy dialogues and incidents of violence toward Jesus; copied in second half of second century C.E.

Oxyrhynchus 840 — Fragment of otherwise unknown narrative gospel found in Upper Egypt.

Gospel Oxyrhynchus 1224 — Fragments of Jesus' sayings discovered in 1903.

Jewish-Christian Gospels

Gospel of the Hebrews — Fragments are quoted by five authors and cited by three others; written perhaps in early second century C.E.

Gospel of the Ebionites — Seven fragments suggest narrative close to Matthew, also with connection to Mark and Luke.

Gospel of the Nazoreans — Fragments quoted or cited by three authors suggest narrative parallel to Matthew.

Source: Robert J. Miller (ed.), The Complete Gospels *(1994)*

"If Jesus was a human being, then history matters, and what the Jesus of history said and did matters to the church," Kea says. "It may not be the only thing that's part of the equation, but it's part of it"

For most Americans, these historical debates may seem remote. This Christmas — as in holiday seasons of the past — Christians will re-enact the nativity in countless church pageants according to the accounts in Matthew and Luke. They will thrill to the soaring crescendos of Handel's "Messiah" and sing familiar carols that incorporate the traditional images: manger, stable, star, angels, wise men. [2]

Still, Christian and general bookstores alike report robust sales of scholarly books on the life of Jesus. And a prominent English cleric who frequently visits the United States finds that interest in the issues is high among Christian laity in America.

"One of the things that impresses me is how many lay Christians read serious scholarship in this area," says N. T. Wright, dean of Litchfield Cathedral and a former New Testament professor at Oxford University. "I think quite a lot of ordinary church folk read these books and expect their clergy to know about them."

Here are some of the biblical-scholarship issues being debated:

Can a reliable, historical account of the life of Jesus be written?

The Jewish historian Josephus, writing in what is now known as the first century, devoted a single paragraph to Jesus in his work *Jewish Antiquities*. Josephus described Jesus as "a wise man" and "a doer of startling deeds" who "gained a following both among many Jews and among many of Greek origin." Along with this straightforward description, the paragraph also contains passages stating flatly that Jesus was "the Messiah" and that he "appeared" to

his followers three days after his death "just as the divine prophets had spoken of." [3]

Josephus' passage — written in about 70 Common Era (C.E.),* at the time of the Romans' destruction of the Second Temple — is significant as one of the few independent, nearly contemporaneous pieces of evidence of Jesus' ministry and its impact.

But the Josephus passage also illustrates the challenge for historians: Most biblical scholars today believe that the explicit affirmations of Jesus' messianic status and the resurrection were not written by Josephus but added later by early Christians — presumably to buttress their doctrinal views of Jesus' divinity.

History and evangelism are also combined in the early accounts of Jesus' life written by his followers, including the four so-called Canonical Gospels of the New Testament. None of them is a contemporary account. Mark, believed to be the earliest of the four, is thought to have been written around 70 C.E. — four decades after Jesus' death. Matthew and Luke followed later in the first century and may have used Mark as a source. Historical-quest scholars also believe that Matthew and Luke used an earlier gospel — known as "Q" after the German word for source, "quelle" — that either was oral or, if written, has not been found.

As history, the Gospels are lacking both because of omissions and discrepancies. None describes Jesus' physical appearance. Only one — Luke — includes any mention of Jesus' life between the nativity and the beginning of his ministry at age 30. And that mention, reporting on Jesus' visit to a temple at age 12, may have been included only to fulfill the scriptural prophecy of the messiah.

---

* "Common Era" is the preferred scholarly designation for the period after the birth of Christ that had been designated as "A.D." ("Anno Domini," Latin for "year of our Lord").

More troublingly to scholars, the Gospels differ in significant details. One telling discrepancy: Mark relates that Jesus hung on the cross for six hours before he died; Matthew and Luke say it was three hours. [4]

The analysis of the Gospels has been aided by recent archaeological finds, including the discoveries of the gospels of Peter and Thomas in the late 1800s and a trove of early manuscripts in a cave near Nag Hammadi in Upper Egypt in 1945. Even with these new manuscripts, however, some critics of the historical question insist that the sources for Jesus' life are simply inadequate ever to construct a reliable account.

"It can't be called history," Johnson says. "Any reconstruction of Jesus inevitably is an exercise in imagination."

Other critics, however, accept the idea of the quest, but question the approach. Gregory Boyd, a professor of theology at Baptist Bethel College and Seminary in St. Paul, Minn., says the research has too often been conducted with "a strong bias against the biblical portrayal. It's almost as though they're assuming that to get to the historical Jesus, you have to get behind the biblical documents."

Members of the Jesus Seminar counter that historical reconstructions are possible despite the limitations on the sources. "In some sense, one could view the seminar as the optimists in the group," Kea says. "We're clear that what we've got is a reconstruction," he continues. "But we do not despair of knowing, even with minimal certainty, what Jesus actually said or did."

Chilton agrees that despite the limitations the historical study is important. "Christian faith is grounded in a simple proposition: that in the form of Jesus, God became human," Chilton says. "Anything that one can understand about Jesus in historical terms must contribute to our assessment of Jesus in

Jesus as a Troubled, Gay Teenager

He is born to a virgin mother, rejects Satan in the wilderness, performs miracles, preaches love and selflessness and dies mocked on a wooden cross.

But playwright Terrence McNally's Son of God is different from the Jesus of the New Testament. His "Joshua" grew up as a troubled teenager in Corpus Christi, Texas, in the 1960s. He likes to party. He loves James Dean movies. And he's gay.

The Christ figure in McNally's controversial play "Corpus Christi" loves his disciples in body, not just in spirit. He blesses the marriage of two of them, Bartholomew and James, and condemns the "fag-haters in priests robes" who denounce him as a blasphemer. The plaque that hangs over his head on the cross proclaims him to be "King of the Queers."

Anson Mount as the Christ-figure Joshua with the rest of the ensemble cast of "Corpus Christi" during its 10-week run in New York City.

McNally's recreation of Jesus as a fun-loving homosexual and a martyr to homophobia played to sold-out audiences in New York City for 10 weeks from its opening on Oct. 13 until its final performance Nov. 29. But the play had scandalized many American Christians even before its opening.

The Catholic League for Decency denounced the play as blasphemous after word of the script leaked out in May. The Manhattan Theatre Club, which planned to mount the production at New York's City Center, initially backed out after receiving bomb threats, only to be embarrassed by a coalition of playwrights and free-speech advocates into going ahead with the production after all.

An estimated 2,000 religious protesters demonstrated outside the theater on opening night — countered by a much smaller group of several hundred people supporting the production. League President William Donohue called the play "a filthy attack on Christianity."

Many critics were harsher. "The terrible truth about 'Corpus Christi' is that it is simply not good enough to be blasphemous," wrote Fintan O'Toole of the *New York Daily News*. Ben Brantley of The *New York Times* called the play "about as threatening, and stimulating, as a glass of chocolate milk." Favorable reviews were scarce. *Time* magazine's Richard Zoglin called the production "a marvel of spare inventiveness" and the negative reviews "a sad injustice." [1]

Fictional retellings of the Jesus story have been a staple of American popular culture for more than a century. Some of the most famous — like Lew Wallace's 1880 novel *Ben-Hur* and Lloyd Douglas' 1940 novel *The Robe* — used Jesus' death to inspire self-sacrifice by Roman characters

who witnessed the crucifixion. Both were adapted into successful films. Other novelizations retold the story of Jesus' life in popular but reverential style. More recent works have tended to the unconventional. Two rock-inspired stage productions in the early 1970s — "Jesus Christ Superstar" and "Godspell" — depicted Jesus as a counter-culture flower child. Both went on to be popular films, but they also stirred controversy among some Christians as demeaning.

The controversy over McNally's play had quieted by the time of the play's next-to-last evening performance in November. Only a few demonstrators stand outside the theater.

Inside, the cast of 13 neatly scrubbed, handsome young men mill about the stage as the audience files in. The play begins as one of the actors steps forward and promises to tell "an old and familiar story" that "bears repeating." The play has campy touches: "Pontius Pilate High School"; a red-shirted James Dean as the devil. Joshua struggles with his heavenly father over his fate. "Why me?" he asks. "Why not?" God responds.

The play lasts under two hours, without intermission. The scenes track the Gospels: the Sermon on the Mount, the miracle of the loaves and fishes, the raising of Lazarus.

The production builds to Joshua's climactic entry into the unnamed city, his cacophonous trial and agonizing crucifixion. Joshua is mocked, stripped, flogged and nailed to the cross. He wears a crown of thorns, his palms painted red. The cast — now playing roles as Roman soldiers — raise Joshua to face the audience. With arms outstretched, Joshua slowly descends to a crouch. In Hebrew, he cries out, "My God, my God, why hast thou forsaken me?"

The applause at the end is polite but less than enthusiastic. Most of the audience files out in silence. "Interesting," one woman says noncommittally. "Good and bad," says another. "I thought it would never end," her companion says.

The playwright has anticipated a negative reception. "This is our story; perhaps other actors have told it better," one of the cast says in ending the performance. "If we have offended, so be it."

[1] See *The Washington Times*, Oct. 16, 1998, p. A2 (quoting *Daily News* and other reviews); *The New York Times*, Oct. 14, 1998, p. E1; *Time*, Nov. 2, 1998, p. 106. For an account of opposing demonstrations on opening night, see NPR's "Weekend Edition," Oct. 18, 1998.

religious terms."

Has the Jesus Seminar produced worthwhile studies of Jesus' life and teachings?

At the first meeting of the Jesus Seminar in 1985, Robert Funk set as the group's goal "a new narrative of Jesus, a new gospel, if you will." [5]

Thirteen years later, the seminar has produced three major works that purport to tell what Jesus actually said and did during his ministry and to compile all of the known "gospels" — the four Canonical Gospels as well as other early accounts of Jesus' life. Individual seminar members, including Funk and fellow co-founder Crossan, have written their own interpretations of Jesus, often setting out provocative views at some tension with established Christian denominations and traditionalist scholars and clergy.

Funk also vowed to "see to it that the public is informed of our judgments." On that score, at least, the seminar has succeeded. The books have been widely reviewed. And the seminar has been the subject of substantial news coverage over the years, including major articles in *Time* and *Macleans*, Canada's leading newsweekly. [6]

Predictably, the seminar has also drawn heavy criticism. Television evangelist Pat Robertson, host of the "700 Club," was quoted as calling the seminar "outrageous," while one Georgia minister called the seminar's work "totally un-Christian." Theology professor Johnson, who has become the most visible critic, not only has called the seminar "fraudulent" but also denounced the entire quest for the historical Jesus as "misguided." [7]

Today, Johnson continues to see no value in the seminar's work or in the quest for the historical Jesus. Asked if he has learned anything from the seminar, he says flatly, "No." The seminar, he continues, "represents a

---

Most Americans Believe in Christmas Miracles

More than three-quarters of the Americans surveyed believe "absolutely" or "mostly" in the miracles associated with the Christmas story of Jesus, including his birth to a virgin mother and the appearance of angels from heaven.

	Absolutely Believe	Mostly Believe	Do Not Believe
• Jesus was a real person who lived about 2,000 years ago.	73.6%	18.1%	4.7%
• Jesus was born in the small town of Bethlehem.	75.0%	20.4%	4.8%
• A star in the sky appeared over Bethlehem as a sign of the birth.	60.8%	21.2%	11.5%
• Jesus was born to a virgin mother.	61.0%	16.8%	15.4%
• Angels from heaven announced the birth to nearby shepherds.	60.8%	18.7%	13.9%
• Three Wise Men traveled from Eastern lands to bring gifts to the child.	62.3%	22.6%	8.6%

Note: Percentages do not add to 100 because those who did not answer are not included.

Source: Scripps Howard News Service and Ohio University; 1,033 people were contacted in the 1996 random-sample telephone poll.

---

reductio ad absurdum of tendencies in New Testament scholarship that have been there a long time. They haven't been improved by being reduced."

Johnson and other critics attack both the qualifications and the methods of the seminar as well as its conclusions. Johnson calls the seminar a "self-selected group" of academics who teach at relatively undistinguished universities. He accuses seminar members of being "media-savvy" promoters trying to use history as "a wedge against traditional belief."

As for the seminar's conclusions, Johnson says its two major works

pose a false question by asking whether the accounts of Jesus' life can be taken as literal. "I want to avoid the option of literal true, non-literal non-true," he says, "because that's a false option."

Funk gives well-rehearsed answers to the attacks. Self-selected group? "A stupid criticism," he says. "Any kind of group is better than single-voice judgments."

Lackluster credentials? "An *ad hominem* [attack] not worthy of scholars," he says. "I put my credentials up against any of them." (Funk has a doctorate from Vanderbilt University School of Divinity.)

The most common complaint centers on the seminar's use of color-coded voting by members in deciding which of Jesus' words and deeds were substantiated (*see p. 1086*). Funk insists the technique is in line with scholarly practice. "These guys [the critics] do it every time they go to a meeting," he says. "The only difference is I insisted we make some kind of report" after finishing. "Most scholars hate any kind of conclusions," he adds, "especially humanists."

Other seminar members voice similar defenses of the group's work. But they also stress that some of the criticisms stem from a misunderstanding of what the seminar claims to have accomplished. "What we can do is to measure the degree of consensus within this group of scholars," says Marcus Borg, a professor of religion at Oregon State University. "Once someone understands what the seminar has been doing, most of the criticisms vanish."

Does the search for "the historical Jesus" threaten Christians' faith?

Since their inception, the historical studies of Jesus have generally questioned many of the stories that traditional Christians accept as literal and view as central to their beliefs. Members of the Jesus Seminar voice the same kind of doubts today.

The nativity stories are "certainly not literally true," Chilton says. The accounts of miracles "are all black," says Funk, referring to the color code used to denote deeds believed to be "largely or entirely fictive." As for the story of the resurrection, Borg says it is "irrelevant what happened to the corpse of Jesus."

Members of the Jesus Seminar acknowledge that those views can be unsettling for many Christians. "Those churches that come out of a fundamentalist orientation are going to be threatened by this," Kea says. "There

are also going to be a number of Christians who are not quite fundamentalists but have a more conservative orientation and regard the Bible as divinely inspired, and therefore any critical analysis of the text would be challenging or intimidating."

Critics, however, say nothing in the historical research should be taken as undermining the central tenets of Christians' faith. "If it could prove that Jesus wasn't a miracle-working person who was divine, who rose again from the dead, then I think the Christian faith is in deep trouble," Boyd says. "As it stands, this scholarship doesn't pose a risk at all because they haven't shown anything of the sort."

Johnson calls the historical studies "a distraction" that is "irrelevant to Christians' faith."

"Even if we could determine exactly what Jesus did and what Jesus said, or even what Jesus thought, there would be absolutely no reason for me to take that as normative for my life," he says. "If he were not the Jesus of the Gospels, if he were not the risen Lord, Jesus would be just another dead guy from the past."

The Christian scholars who have devoted their academic lives to the search for Jesus sharply disagree. They say that the historical quest is supportive of and even essential to their faith. "If we don't make the distinction between the historical Jesus and the Jesus of religious faith, we risk losing both," Borg says.

In his biographies of Jesus, for example, Crossan, who previously taught at DePaul University, emphasizes the political context of the times. Palestine, homeland of the Jews, was ruled from Rome by an emperor who claimed to be the son of a Roman god. Crossan says that in that sense Jesus' use of the phrase "kingdom of God" is "an explicitly social-political-religious term."

"When Jesus talks about the kingdom of God, he is opposing a 100 per-

cent political term — kingdom — and a 100 percent theological term — God," Crossan says. "He is saying that what is going on here is not that. It is an ideological attack on the status quo."

For his part, Kea says that the historical studies of Jesus can help sustain faith for some Christians who have doubts about the literal accounts in the Gospels. "There are some Christians who say those conservative approaches don't work for them, who have difficulty with being told, 'You have to say the words and accept them,'" he says.

Borg himself says the historical approach helped him return to Christianity. Raised as a Lutheran, Borg says that in his 20s he found Christianity "harder and harder to believe." Examining the Gospels as history, he says, allowed him to go beyond a "literalistic approach."

"Jesus and the Gospels and the Bible as a whole point beyond themselves to God," says Borg, who is now Episcopalian. "The point is not to believe the Bible or the Gospels or Jesus, but to see them all together as a lens though which we see God."

Borg is confident, moreover, that the historical studies of Jesus have done nothing to diminish the number of Christian believers. "My strong impression is that very few people have lost their faith because of the Jesus Seminar and Jesus scholarship," Borg says. "And for every one who has lost their faith, maybe 100 have found their way back in." ■

BACKGROUND

Getting to Know Jesus

The undisputed historical facts about Jesus are relatively few, but sufficient to form the essential picture of his life, his ministry and his death. [8] He was born in the Roman-ruled Jewish homeland of Palestine during the reign of King Herod the Great. Scholars now say that the best guess for the year of his birth is 4 B.C.E. (before the Common Era), the year of Herod's death. He was publicly executed by crucifixion in Jerusalem on the orders of the Roman procurator Pontius Pilate when he was around age 30 — sometime between the years 27 C.E. and 33 C.E. — after a wandering ministry in and around his home region of Galilee that lasted two to three years.

The rest of Jesus' biography from the Gospels is either blank — what he did in childhood, how he earned his living — or problematic because of evident discrepancies. In Matthew, for example, the family flees Bethlehem with the infant Jesus to Egypt to escape Herod's wrath, while in Luke they simply return to their home in Nazareth. In addition, the Gospels — Greek for "good news" — are necessarily suspect because of their overt proselytizing purpose.

The limitations of the historical sources about Jesus combine with the inherent difficulties of studying ancient societies to force scholars into speculation about any number of intriguing questions. Some scholars believe Galilee was a relatively primitive, agrarian society — "a backwater," as Charlotte Allen writes in her recent book, *The Human Christ*. [9] Others believe Galilee was a more urbanized society, influenced by Hellenistic culture. Could Jesus read and write? Could he speak Greek in addition to the vernacular Aramaic? What about Hebrew? The only answers are speculative.

More significantly, the Gospels' presentatio°example, in their treatment of Jesus and Judaism. Jesus was a Jew throughout his life. Luke reports that he was circumcised after eight days, in accordance with Jewish custom; and at his crucifixion he was identified as "Jesus of Nazareth, King of the Jews" in a plaque affixed to the cross. Matthew recounts Jesus' life with features parallel to Judaism: the Sermon on the Mount hearkens to Moses receiving the Ten Commandments on Mount. Sinai. Luke, by contrast, explicitly uses the word "Christians" to describe Jesus' followers.

The Gospels differ, too, in their accounts of Jesus' passion, crucifixion and events afterward. Some of the discrepancies — as related by Allen — appear relatively minor. For example, the number of women who went to Jesus' tomb is variously said to be more than three (Luke), three (Mark), two (Matthew) or only Mary Magdalene (John). [10] More significantly, they differ in recounting Jesus' trial and execution: Matthew and Mark relate that he was convicted by Jewish authorities for blasphemy, while John says he was turned over to Roman authorities for trial. [11]

Early Christians

Jesus' followers did not separate from Judaism immediately, but there were scattered Christian communities — using that term — by the time of the Romans' suppression of the Jewish rebellion and the destruction of the Second Temple in 70. Scholars today emphasize the diversity of beliefs among early Christians. Some believed in the bodily resurrection; others did not. Some believed Jesus had preached a so-called eschatological message — a prediction that the world would end soon and the Kingdom of God would be established on Earth; others did not.

Disputes over Jesus' identity formed the basis for three dissident sects — Marcionites, Ebonites and Gnostics — that did not share the fundamental belief espoused by Paul and the other early apostles that Jesus was simultaneously both human and divine.

One early milestone in the development of an orthodox Christianity was a pronouncement in the year 180 by Irenaeus, bishop of Lyons, that of the various Christian texts in circulation four would be recognized as official gospels: Matthew, Mark, Luke and John.

Among the texts barred from the official canon as a result were the so-called gnostic gospels, including the gospels of Thomas and Mary Magdalene, which were unearthed in the cave near Nag Hammadi in Upper Egypt in 1945. In these gospels, Jesus' message centers on self-awareness — "gnosis" is Greek for knowledge — as a path toward knowledge of God. [12]

The critical events for the development of orthodox Christianity and its eventual growth into the world's dominant religion came in the fourth century. The Roman general Constantine launched a campaign in 311 to make himself emperor.

On the eve of a battle at Rome's Milvian Bridge in 312, Constantine had a vision of his soldiers' marching into battle carrying banners with the Christian cross and the words "by this, conquer." He credited his victory the next day to the dream. After becoming emperor, he moved to end the persecution of Christians and over time to make Christianity something of a state religion.

In 325, as emperor of both the eastern and western Roman empires, Constantine convened a council of bishops in Nicea in what is now Turkey. The council, in what became known as the Nicene Creed, proclaimed as Christian doctrine that Jesus was both human and divine: "one in essence with Father."

Continued on p. 1085

Chronology

Before 100
Jesus is born, conducts his ministry and dies on the cross; the first Gospels are written.

Approx. 30 C.E. (Common Era) Jesus is about 33 when he is crucified in Jerusalem by the Romans after a two- or three-year ministry in Galilee.

70-100
Four Gospels are written, with Mark followed by Matthew and Luke and then John. Scholars believe there may have been an earlier, possibly written, collection of sayings attributed to Jesus — called "Q" after the German word for source ("quelle").

101-325
Christianity separates from Judaism, grows despite persecution by Roman authorities, then becomes a state religion under Emperor Constantine.

180
Bishop Irenaeus of Lyons recognizes four Gospels — Matthew, Mark, Luke and John — as official church canon.

312
Constantine, a Roman general, uses a Christian symbol in his army's victory at the battle of Milvian Bridge; the next year, after becoming emperor, he adopts policy of toleration for Christians.

325
Council of Nicea adopts creed that declares Christ is "one in essence with Father."

1700-1930
The first "quest for the historical Jesus."

1774
Hermann Samuel Reimaris' posthumously published *Fragments of an Unknown* depicts Jesus as deceiving followers into believing that he worked miracles.

1819-1834
Friedrich Schleiermacher's lectures at the University of Berlin seek to counter skeptics while appealing to liberals by depicting Jesus as embodying the idea of human perfection but with no superhuman powers; first published in book form in 1864.

1835
David Friedrich Strauss' two-volume *Life of Jesus Critically Examined* discounts Gospels' accounts of Jesus' birth, speeches, miracles, death and resurrection.

1863
Ernest Renan's *La Vie de Jesus* romanticizes Jesus and becomes a best-seller in several languages.

1906
Albert Schweitzer's *The Quest of a Historical Jesus* traces the efforts to reconstruct Jesus' life; Schweitzer himself views Jesus as a mystic who expected the imminent end of the world.

1920s
German theologian Rudolf Bultmann argues that the historical Jesus is unknowable and irrelevant; his views help halt quests for three decades.

1950-present
The second and third historical quests are launched; the center of Jesus scholarship shifts from Europe to the United States.

1953
Ernest Kasemann, a former Bultmann student, argues in *The Problem of the Historical Jesus* that a historical portrait can be reconstructed from the Gospels' accounts of Jesus' life.

1970
The rock opera "Jesus Christ Superstar" appears; the play opens on Broadway in 1971, with a film adaptation in 1973.

1971
James Robinson sets forth his "trajectory theory" — examining the development of Christian thought by tracing the "trajectory" of any Christian text either backward or forward.

1985
The Jesus Seminar is founded.

1993
The Jesus Seminar's *The Five Gospels* concludes that fewer than one-fifth of the sayings attributed to Jesus in the Gospels can be authenticated.

1996
Prof. Luke Timothy Johnson's *The Real Jesus* strongly criticizes the methods and conclusions of the Jesus Seminar

1998
The Jesus Seminar's *The Acts of Jesus* questions most of the deeds attributed to Jesus in the Gospels; the play "Corpus Christi" depicts Jesus as a homosexual, drawing fire from religious groups.

A Jewish Scholar's Search for Jesus

Growing up in southeastern Massachusetts, Amy-Jill Levine was fascinated by Christianity. She was intrigued by Christmas trees and Easter bunnies. She liked Christmas music. She enjoyed the stories she heard when she accompanied Catholic friends to catechism.

But Levine also remembers the moment when one of her friends confronted her with the accusation: "You killed my Lord." Years later, the memory still hurts. "I couldn't fathom how this religion that I found so beautiful could have such hateful things in it," Levine says.

Today, Levine combines her interest in Christianity with her Jewish faith as one of the relatively small number of Jewish scholars who specialize in studying the life and teachings of Jesus.

"He makes perfectly good sense within the Jewish context," says Levine, a professor at Vanderbilt University's School of Divinity in Nashville. "If he did not make sense to Jews within a Jewish context, no one would have followed him."

Christianity's roots lie in Judaism, but Jesus criticized some of the views and practices of the Jewish priests of his time — for example, public fasting. In the past, Christian scholars emphasized the differences — often crudely depicting Christianity as an enlightened reform of an overly legalistic religion. Today, scholars are more likely to stress the commonalities: a belief in one god and a moral code stressing love of one's fellow man.

Christianity separated from Judaism within a few decades after the crucifixion. Jesus' followers came to believe that he was the Messiah prophesied by the Jewish scriptures. Jews came to view him as a false prophet. The differences were accentuated by Christian accounts that placed the major blame for Jesus' death on the Jewish priests and leaders rather than the Roman governor, Pontius Pilate.

The implication of Jewish blame for Jesus' death underlies the long history of Christian anti-semitism. "There's so much Jewish blood on Christians' hands," says Paula Fredriksen, a professor of religion at Boston University and a former Catholic who converted to Judaism at age 28.

"Historically, I think it likely there would have been some priestly involvement just as there would have been some Roman involvement," Levine says. "What is unhistorical is to say that 'the Jews' killed Jesus. Not all Jews were there; not all Jews who were there acquiesced — the women looking from afar, as Matthew tells us. I wasn't there."

As part of the Second Vatican Council in 1965, the Roman Catholic Church adopted a statement saying that Jesus' crucifixion "cannot be blamed on all the Jews living without distinction, nor upon the Jews of today."

Among Jewish audiences today, Levine says she finds "an enormous amount of curiosity" about Jesus and relatively limited knowledge. Fredriksen generally agrees.

"Orthodox Jews really don't know anything," she adds. "That's because there's a principled aversion to false prophecy and because of the costs that Christianity has imposed on Judaism."

A handful of so-called messianic Jewish groups today do combine beliefs in Judaism and in Jesus as the Messiah. The best known, Jews for Jesus, was founded in San Francisco in 1973 and has offices in six U.S. cities, branches in seven other countries and a reported 1996 annual budget of $16 million.[1]

Jews for Jesus proclaims on its Web site that its members are Jews who came to believe in Jesus but "refused to reject their Jewish heritage. Rather, in Christ they discovered the meaning of their own Jewishness." Established Jewish groups have criticized the messianic Jewish organizations — contending, for example, that their advertisements sometimes create the misleading impression that they are inviting Jews to traditional Jewish services.

"Most Jews I know don't stay up late at night worrying about Jews for Jesus," Fredriksen says. "It's a form of Christianity, not a form of Judaism."

Levine credits the Jesus Seminar with emphasizing the distinctions between Jesus' ethical teachings and his claims of messianic status. "Jesus' ethical pronouncements would be almost entirely congenial to Jewish communities," Levine says. "The messianic proclamations would not be."

Some recent "biographies" of Jesus by Christian scholars emphasize his Jewish identity: *A Marginal Jew* by John Meier, a professor at Notre Dame University; John Dominic Crossan's *The Historical Jesus: The Life of a Mediterranean Jewish Peasant*. In her survey of the quest for the historical Jesus, author Charlotte Allen concludes by seeing in the most recent, so-called third quest an emphasis on "the continuity" between Judaism and Christianity.

"Jews and Christians will probably never reach a religious consensus on who Jesus *was*," Allen writes, "but the importance placed by the third-questers on the ancient Jewish prophetic tradition offers a way in which Jews and Christians might reach a historical consensus on what Jesus *was like*."[2]

In similar vein, Levine sees increased dialogue today between Judaism and Christianity. "Today, thankfully, Jews and Christians are able to talk to each other and agree to disagree," she says. "We can talk across the table about what we have in common and what are our unique features."

---

[1] See Amanda Onion, "Goy Story," *The New Republic*, Jan. 8 & 15, 1996, pp. 31-33. The organization's Web site is www.jews-for-jesus.org.

[2] Charlotte Allen, *The Human Christ: The Search for the Historical Jesus* (1998), p. 328. For general background, see E.P. Sanders, *Jesus and Judaism* (1985).

The Historical Quest

The Jesus of the Nicene Creed endured with few significant doctrinal changes for more than 1,000 years, even as Christianity spread throughout the world. By the 1700s, however, two developments — the Protestant Reformation and the Age of Enlightenment — paved the way for a re-examination of Jesus' life. The result was the first "quest for the historical Jesus" — a flurry of books written over a 150-year period, primarily by German and French academics, that sought to reconstruct the historical person at the heart of Christianity.

In his history of the quest, written in 1906, the Alsatian-German medical missionary Albert Schweitzer divided the chroniclers of Jesus' life into "Jesus-haters" and "Jesus-lovers." The haters, Schweitzer wrote in *The Quest of a Historical Jesus*, disliked the "supernatural nimbus" surrounding Jesus, and their hate ironically "sharpened their historical insight." By contrast, Schweitzer said, the Jesus-lovers "found it a cruel task to be honest." [13]

The Jesus-haters included the author whose work is regarded as the beginning of the historical quest: Hermann Samuel Reimaris (1694-1768), a professor of Oriental languages at a secondary school in Hamburg, Germany. A collection of Reimaris' writings was published anonymously in 1774, six years after his death, under the title *Fragments of an Unknown*. In the seventh of the fragments, "Concerning the Intention of Jesus and His Teaching," Reimaris accused Jesus of deceiving his followers into believing he was a miracle worker and pointed out contradictions in the Gospel accounts of Jesus' resurrection. Charlotte Allen describes Reimaris as a churchgoing Lutheran "who secretly detested Christianity." Schweitzer called his work a "master-

piece" of anti-Christian polemic. [14]

The next of the major milestones in the quest is a monumental two-volume work, *Life of Jesus Christ Critically Examined*, by David Friedrich Strauss (1808-1874), a liberal theologian later turned democratic revolutionary and Prussian nationalist. Strauss developed a skepticism of traditional Christianity while a seminarian. In his 1,500-page work — completed in 1835, at age 27 — he discounted the Gospels' accounts of Jesus' birth, miracles, speeches, death and resurrection. Strauss, according to Allen's account, expected the book to be welcomed by other Christians discontented with old dogmas. Instead, the book "offended Christians of every stripe," Allen says, and Strauss was sacked from his university position even before the second volume appeared. [15]

Parallel to these dogma-debunking accounts came what Allen calls "a century-long spate" of biographies by German philosophers and theologians intended to "rescue" Jesus from "skeptics' ridicule." [16] All of them bowed to the scientism of the age by trying to find natural explanations for the supernatural events depicted in the Gospels. Karl Friedrich Bahrdt (1741-1792), for example, argued in his 11-volume work, *An Explanation of the Plans and Aims of Jesus*, that Jesus had actually not died on the cross, but had only fallen into unconsciousness and was then spirited away to a cave where, in hiding, he directed the course of the new Christian church.

Other authors of these so-called liberal biographies included Heinrich Gottlob Paulus (1761-1851), Karl August von Hase (1800-1890) and, the most celebrated of the group, Friedrich Ernst Daniel Schleiermacher (1768-1834), whose lectures on the historical Jesus were published in book form as *The Life of Jesus* in 1864. These are the "Jesus-lovers" so

derided by Schweitzer. "The sentimentality of their portraiture is boundless," Schweitzer wrote. "More objectionable," he said, was their modernist paraphrasings of Jesus' language. "None of the speeches are allowed to stand as spoken," he said. [17]

The two strands of sentimentality and skepticism combined in the next of the major 19th-century studies of Jesus: *The Life of Jesus* by Joseph Ernest Renan (1823-1892). [18] Renan was a graduate of a Catholic seminary in France, but by the time his book was published in 1863 he had lost his faith and had stopped going to Mass. In a first, Renan actually did research for his quest: During a monthlong trip to the Holy Land in 1861, he retraced what he was convinced were the actual steps of Jesus. Renan depicted Jesus as "a beautiful young man" who was attractive to women and who — in Allen's phrasing — "roamed the byways of Galilee on the back of a gentle donkey, attracting crowds of dreamy followers."

Renan's book became one of the best-selling books of the 19th century. His questioning of Jesus' divinity also got him fired from his position as professor of Hebrew at the College de France. Ironically, however, the anti-clerical government of France's Third Republic reinstated him as director of the college in 1873.

Time Out

By the end of the 19th century, the search for Jesus had lasted long enough to gain its own historian: Schweitzer. [19] Best-known today for his missionary work in Africa, Schweitzer (1875-1965) was a man of Renaissance versatility: a musician and theologian as well as a doctor. The son of a Lutheran pastor, he began his study of some 200 books about Jesus at the age of 26; the result, *The Quest of a Historical Jesus*, was published in 1906. The book, Allen says, suffers from a lack of structure, with "a tendency to read like a compilation of book reports." It also presents a vision of Jesus that differs both from traditional Christianity and from the "liberal lives" presented by German authors in the preceding century.

In Schweitzer's rendering, Jesus becomes a Jewish mystic fixated on the end of the world. Schweitzer, Allen says, accepts the accounts in the Synoptic Gospels as essentially historical, though he explains away the miraculous feeding of the 5,000 by suggesting that the crowd actually received only symbolic crumbs rather than a full meal. He views Jesus' teachings as an "interim ethic" to be followed until the coming of the Kingdom of Heaven. The crucifixion amounts to a failure of sorts, since the eschatological prediction does not come to pass. Still, Schweitzer depicts Jesus as "an immeasurably great Man" whose death on the cross "is His victory and His reign."

Schweitzer's book — like Renan's — became a best-seller and was followed by additional attacks by German theologians on the liberal Jesus-searchers of the previous century. But the whole enterprise — the quest and the critique — came to a halt in the 1920s with the work of another German scholar: Rudolf Bultmann (1884-1976). The son of a Lutheran pastor who studied for the ministry but was then persuaded to pursue an academic career, Bultmann came to believe — as Allen writes — that the New Testament was a collection of myths that told little about the historical Jesus. But he went on to conclude, in a 1929 essay, that the history is irrelevant to Christian faith. "It is not the historical Jesus, but Jesus Christ, the one who is preached,

who is Lord," Bultmann writes. [20]

Bultmann's views proved to be influential enough to effectively stop the historical quest for the next three decades. But the quest resumed after World War II, first in Germany among some of Bultmann's former students and, in the past few decades, most actively in the United States.

The New Quests

The so-called New Quest was pioneered by two of Bultmann's former students in Germany: Ernest Käsemann (1906-1998) and Günther Bornkamm (1905-1990). [21] Käsemann argued in a 1953 paper, "The Problem of the Historical Jesus," in contradiction to his former teacher, that a historical portrait could be reconstructed from the words attributed to Jesus in the Gospels. Bornkamm followed with a work in 1954, *Tradition and Interpretation in Matthew*, that used an analytic technique called "redaction criticism" to focus on the individual evangelist's role in arranging the stories in his gospel.

The New Quest theories were introduced in the United States by James Robinson, who heads the Institute for Antiquity and Christianity at Claremont College in California. Robinson's short 1959 book, *A New Quest for the Historical Jesus*, argued that historical methods provided an independent means for learning about Jesus. Twelve years later, Robinson set forth an influential new technique called trajectory theory. In a 1971 collection of essays co-authored with Harvard Divinity School Professor Helmut Koester, *Trajectories Through Early Christianity*, Robinson sought to demonstrate that any Christian text could be used — as Allen puts it — "to plot a trajectory, backward or forward, of

the thinking of early Christian groups."

In founding the Jesus Seminar in 1985, Funk took note of the new scholarship but complained that it had achieved little public visibility because of opposition from "the religious establishment." With about 30 members at its founding, the seminar grew over time to include some 200 scholars — although, as Funk acknowledges, some of the members "came and went." As its first project, Funk said the seminar should "determine what [Jesus] really said — not his literal words, perhaps, but the substance and style of his utterances." [22]

Culture Wars

Over the next seven years, the seminar met twice annually, reviewing papers and voting — aphorism by aphorism, parable by parable — on the probable authenticity of Jesus' sayings. The effort culminated in 1993 in the publication of *The Five Gospels: What Did Jesus Really Say?* The results, presented through the color-coding system used in voting, sharply challenged literalist readings of the Gospels. [23]

In fact, only 18 percent of Jesus' sayings were presented as red or pink — "undoubtedly" or "probably" uttered by Jesus. These included many familiar passages: the parables of the prodigal son, the good Samaritan, the mustard seed, the lamp and the bushel, God and the sparrows; and the admonitions to love your enemies, to turn the other cheek.

But only parts of the Sermon on the Mount were deemed probably reliable, and only a fragment of the Lord's Prayer. And the vast majority of Jesus' supposed words were either "gray" (Jesus did not say them, but the ideas are close to his own) or black (Jesus

Jesus: Star of Stage, Screen and Literature

Jesus has been an icon of American popular culture for more than a century, starring in countless novels, plays and movies. Below, some of the better-known works:

Ben-Hur: A Tale of the Christ (1880)

Jesus' crucifixion inspires the Roman soldier Ben-Hur to convert and dedicate his fortune to the Christian cause. Lewis Wallace's best-selling novel was adapted into an 1899 stage play and at least two film versions: Metro-Goldwyn-Mayer's 1926 version (bottom photo) and a 1959 remake, which won the Oscar for "Best Picture."

King of Kings (1927)

Jesus inspires the harlot Mary Magdalene to forsake her jewels, finery and sinful ways in the Cecil B. De Mille film.

The Nazarene (1939)

Jesus is a slightly built, poetically eloquent teacher in this best-selling novel by the Jewish writer Sholem Asch.

The Robe (1942)

The Roman soldier who wins Jesus' robe after the crucifixion converts and dies a happy martyr in Lloyd C. Douglas' best-seller, adapted for film in 1953.

The Greatest Story Ever Told (1949)

Jesus grows from a sensitive youth to a joyless evangelist in Fulton Oursler's novel, adapted for film in 1955.

The Last Temptation of Christ (1952)

Jesus is a tormented artist and the object of Mary Magdalene's unrequited desire in Nikos Kazantzakis' novel, adapted for film in 1988.

Jesus Christ Superstar (1970)

Jesus leads a singing band of followers into Jerusalem before his arrest and execution in the rock opera by Tim Rice and Andrew Lloyd Webber; produced in New York in 1971; film adaptation, 1973.

Godspell (1971)

Jesus and his followers dress and act as clowns in this musical adaptation of Matthew's gospel conceived and directed by John-Michael Tebelak.

The Gospel According to the Son (1997)

Jesus narrates his own story in this novelization by the Jewish author Norman Mailer

Corpus Christi (1998)

A troubled, gay, Texas teenager is a Christ-like figure in Terence McNally's controversial play, which closed in New York City on Nov. 29 after a 10-week run.

Sources: Allene Stuart Phy, "Retelling the Greatest Story Ever Told: Jesus in Popular Fiction," in The Bible in Popular Culture in America *(1985); Charlotte Allen,* The Human Christ: The Search for the Historical Jesus *(1998).*

did not say them, and the ideas represent a later or collective tradition). Included in those categories, for example, were Jesus' admonition in Matthew to go out and make disciples — the so-called Great Commission — and virtually all of Jesus' sayings in John, including all of the so-called "I am" statements — "I am the way, the truth and the life."

The book drew immediate criticism that continues to this day. "Very low-grade scholarship," says Wright, the author recently of a monumental, traditionalist biography of Jesus. [24] The color coding became a focal point of the criticism. Critics scorned the whole idea of trying to determine "the truth" by ballot and the specific tabulation methods — a weighted voting system that classified some statements as gray or black even though a plurality of the seminar had voted red or pink.

Funk and others contended that the use of color coding was akin to the "red letter" edition of the New Testament prepared by a 19th-century publisher that showed some but not all of Jesus' sayings in red. "There is nothing unusual about the conclusion that Jesus may not have actually said what's attributed to him," Crossan says.

The Jesus Seminar has published two other works. *The Complete Gospels*, which first appeared in 1992 and then in an annotated version in 1994, presents the texts of 21 gospels altogether — the Canonical Gospels, the Gnostic Gospel of Thomas and others, many of them known only through fragments of manuscripts unearthed in recent archaeological expeditions. ("An enormously useful volume," Wright says, despite his other criticisms.)

The seminar's other book, *The Acts of Jesus*, which appeared earlier this year, applied the same color-coding technique to the deeds attributed to Jesus in the four Gospels. The conclusion: Only 29 out of 176 reported events — 16 percent of the total — were deemed probably authentic.

Many members of the seminar have written their own individual accounts of Jesus' life or teachings, including Borg and Crossan. Other religion experts have also advanced some new interpretations. Among them are a number of feminist scholars, such as Elisabeth Schussler Fiorenza, a professor at the Harvard Divinity School, who criticize what they regard as the patriarchal nature of Christianity as it developed after Jesus' death. In her recent book, *Jesus: Miriam's Child, Sophia's Prophet*, Fiorenza emphasizes the role that women played in the Jesus story — the unwed mother Mary, the women at the tomb — and interprets Jesus' teaching as a message of liberation for all oppressed groups, including women in particular. [25]

In his book attacking the Jesus Seminar, Johnson accused Funk of maintaining a "pretense" of scientific discovery while actually conducting an inquiry "biased against the authenticity of the Gospel traditions." He also accused Funk of "hucksterism" and complained that news media had fallen prey to his manipulation. "The press helped stimulate precisely the sort of controversy that the Jesus Seminar sought," Johnson concluded, "and became the arena for a confused culture war between church and academy." [26] ∎

CURRENT SITUATION

Jesus on the Road

Robert Funk spends an hour telling his audience at the Unitarian Universalist church in Reston, Va., some of the things that the Jesus

Seminar believes Jesus said during his ministry. Now, to sharpen the point, Funk ends by listing 11 things that Jesus did not say.

Jesus did not think that a cosmic holocaust was about to occur, Funk tells the group of 80 people at the church, just outside Washington. He did not tell his followers to believe that he was the Messiah. In fact, he rarely referred to himself at all. Nor did he believe that he was born "without male sperm," the child of a virgin mother. Indeed, he was born in Nazareth, not Bethlehem — that was "a Christian fiction designed to fulfill the prophecy" of Hebrew scriptures.

The list goes on: Jesus did not suggest that his death would be a blood sacrifice to atone for humanity's sins. He did not predict his resurrection. He never organized a church or advocated celibacy. He never predicted his own second coming. And, Funk concludes, "Jesus was not the first Christian. He died a Jew."

The list contradicts many of the doctrines that traditional Christians regard as basic to the faith. But the audience at this Nov. 13 running of the Jesus Seminar road show is unfazed. No one gasps or rises to object. And no one seriously challenges Funk during the 45-minute question-and-answer period that follows.

Instead, the audience displays a sophisticated knowledge of biblical criticism. The first two questions, for example, ask Funk about "Q" — the hypothetical gospel that is the supposed source for the first known written gospels. "They clearly have done their homework," says Gretchen Woods, the church's minister. About one-fourth of the audience are congregation members, Woods estimates. Many of the others are students from the Methodist Wesley Seminar in Washington, she says.

The Jesus that emerges from Funk's talk differs from the one emphasized by televangelists and

Continued on p. 523

At Issue:

Is history essential for Christians to understand the "real" Jesus?

ROBERT W. FUNK
Director, Westar Institute, and founder of the Jesus Seminar

WRITTEN FOR THE CQ RESEARCHER, *DECEMBER 1998.*

j im Jones claimed that he knew the "real" Jesus and that Jonestown was the destiny to which that Jesus beckoned. David Koresh believed the Branch Davidians were the true followers of Jesus. In the first century, Matthew and Luke created new gospels by editing Mark and adding a collection of Jesus' aphorisms and parables. In the second century, Marcion reduced the story of Jesus to a truncated Gospel of Luke, while Tatian combined all four New Testament gospels into one harmonized construction called the Diatesseraron. In the fourth and fifth centuries, the councils of the emerging church, at the behest of a pagan emperor, adopted statements of faith about Jesus of Nazareth designed to identify heretics. In the wake of the Protestant Reformation, dozens of denominations advanced competing claims about Jesus as the Christ.

How are we to know which of these claims is congruent with the Jesus who lived in Galilee in the 30s of the Common Era? How are we to test whatever faith we have against the links posited between that faith and Jesus of Nazareth?

The study of history — the careful, critical evaluation of all the surviving ancient texts containing information about Jesus of Nazareth — is the only means we have. History, of course, is not enough. Historians can only assemble such facts as fall within the spectrum of probability in relation to the evidence and contemporary parallels. Historians cannot determine whether Jesus died for the sins of the world. But they can investigate how he died and under what circumstances.

It is important to know that when Pilate exonerates Jesus as innocent, while the Jewish authorities demand his death, we are dealing with Christian propaganda and not history. It is significant that the earliest texts do not support the view that the resurrection of Jesus involved the resuscitation of a corpse. It is worth knowing that Jesus may not have expected the world to end in his own time. It is equally important to understand that the council of Nicea in 325 formulated its propositions in relation to a symbolic universe no longer tenable.

History is the great disillusioner. Historians have a way of exposing illusions about the past. They do not determine ultimate truth, of course, but they can relativize excessive claims, such as those made by Nicea, Rome, Wittenberg, Nazi Germany, Waco and the Southern Baptist Convention.

Those who want certainty at the expense of knowledge can and will adopt some institution or person as the ultimate arbiter of truth. The rest of us will continue to quest for the historical Jesus and be satisfied with provisional results.

LUKE TIMOTHY JOHNSON
Professor, Candler School of Theology
Emory University

WRITTEN FOR THE CQ RESEARCHER, *DECEMBER 1998.*

t he answer to the question above depends on definition. Christians, for example, traditionally believed that Jesus of Nazareth died and then by resurrection entered fully into God's life and rule over creation. For them, Jesus is not simply a figure of the past but above all a powerful personal presence to be encountered and engaged in the present.

All the writings of the New Testament provide witness and interpretation of this human person Jesus from the perspective of the resurrection. The Gospels are truthful representations of Jesus precisely because of their interpretation of him as more than merely human.

From the perspective of faith, historical study of the New Testament world is important as enabling a richer and more responsible engagement with the ancient witnesses. Historical knowledge helps counter the natural tendency to reshape the Gospels — and Jesus — according to changing contemporary fashions. As historical awareness is tribute to incarnation, so is historical study of the New Testament appropriate and useful.

But it is not essential, for two reasons. First, our sources do not enable an adequate historical reconstruction of Jesus, as the multiple images constructed by contemporary questers — all using the same materials and same methods — attest. Jesus the mystic, the revolutionary, the sage, the gay magician, the eschatological prophet: The images are not only irreconcilable but each is as much a portrait of the particular historian as it is of Jesus. Historical reconstructions that are so fragmentary and various cannot provide the ground and therefore cannot be essential to Christian faith.

Second, any portrait of Jesus that stops short of his resurrection and continuing existence as life-giving Spirit misses the point about Christian faith, which bases itself explicitly on this living Lord who is worshipped by believers. Efforts to reform Christianity by reshaping the words and deeds of Jesus in patterns not provided by the Gospels not only fail historically but also miss the point theologically.

I started by saying the answer to the question posed above depended on definition. The present debate involves differences on several key terms in the question: What is the nature of history; what are the rules of historiography; and what are the limits of historical knowing? These come to sharp focus on the most fractious question of all: Can authentic Christianity be based on a historical reconstruction of Jesus that bypasses the resurrection and systematically deconstructs the New Testament witnesses?

Contemporary questers say yes; I say no. They invoke in support the Enlightenment. I call on the testimony of the saints.

conservative preachers. "He believed in a trust ethic, not a work ethic," Funk says. He quotes a saying the seminar does attribute to Jesus: "Ask — it'll be given to you; seek — you'll find; knock — it'll be opened for you" (Matthew 7:7).

Jesus believed that life should be celebrated, Funk says. He believed in a kingdom of God "without social compartments" — no divisions between rich and poor, free and slave, men and women, or heterosexual and homosexual. It is also a "brokerless kingdom." Believers can find God on their own, without a spiritual leader to mediate for them. And he frowned on public piety. "I sometimes wonder," Funk says, "if those who advocate public prayer have even read the Gospels."

Funk's Jesus is both a very human figure and a very shrewd teacher. "Very little of what Jesus says can be taken literally," Funk says. "The parable of the leaven is not about baking bread," he says. "The parable of the Good Samaritan is not about a robbery on the road to Jericho." Funk also likes Jesus' use of humor. "I sometimes refer to him as the first Jewish stand-up comic," Funk says.

As he turns to questions, Funk says with a smile that he expects a "brawl." Nothing of the sort occurs. The only confrontational questioner asks Funk to answer the charge that the members of the seminar were "self-selected." "We've never excluded anybody," Funk says. He shares the lectern with a colleague, Lane McGaughy. They offer different perspectives on some of the questions, but have only one disagreement — on the role of organized churches. Funk is disaffected from organized religion — "I quit," he says, matter-of-factly — while McGaughy still sees a role for churches as "a platform" for discussing social issues.

Afterward, Funk agrees that the reception was friendly. "We really

haven't had many hostile people in our audiences," he says. The Reston appearance was one of seven over a three-month period. Funk himself spoke in New York City and Charlotte, N.C. Others were held in Boulder, Colo.; Indianapolis; Madison, Wis.; Tulsa, Okla.; and Vancouver, British Columbia, in Canada. Turnout tonight is somewhat low: Funk says the audience in Charlotte one week earlier numbered about 200.

Some of the questions in Charlotte were more critical, Funk says. One person asked whether the seminar was trying to use historical study to settle theological issues. Funk said no. "What people do with the historical material as a theological matter is something else," he says.

A couple of people challenged him on the question of the bodily resurrection, Funk recalls. And one young man pressed the question of Jesus' divinity. McGaughy responded by asking the youth whether he believed in Jesus' commandment to sell all your property and give the proceeds to the poor. No, the questioner said. "If you don't honor that," McGaughy concluded, "what does it mean that you think Jesus is divine?"

Jesus in the Church

The Rev. Craig Barnes turned to the prologue of the Gospel of John — "In the beginning was the Word . . ." — for the theme of his Nov. 29 sermon on the first Sunday of Advent, the monthlong observance of the coming of Jesus' birth. John "identifies Jesus with the creativity of God," says Barnes, senior pastor of the 2,200-member National Presbyterian Church in Washington. "The purpose of that is to make a statement about the creativity of Jesus."

Barnes, a graduate of Princeton

Theological Seminary and the University of Chicago Divinity School, has read some of the recent literature in the historical quest for Jesus. In his view, the authors "start off on the wrong journey." The dissection of the Gospels, he says, risks "distracting people from that which nurtures faith."

"These documents are written as expressions of faith by people who experienced the living Jesus," Barnes says. "I buy that. My life has been changed dramatically by that, and so have [the lives] of my parishioners."

Other Washington ministers voiced similar feelings. "Getting hung up and debating the historicity [of the Gospels] in some narrow legalistic way is really diversionary," says the Rev. Lynn Bergfalk, pastor of Calvary Baptist Church in Washington's Chinatown. "I object to it because it detracts people from the fundamental nature of the message."

Bergfalk and Barnes are equally critical of liberal scholars like those in the Jesus Seminar and fundamentalists who insist on a literal reading of the Bible. Both groups "miss the spiritual dynamism" of the Gospels, Barnes says. "I wish both the fundamentalists and the liberals would quiet down and wrestle with the content of the message," Bergfalk says.

Among the small cross-section of local ministers interviewed, none defended the literal truth of the accounts of the Nativity presented in Matthew and Luke.

"The church has tended to accept a remarkably creative and interesting conflation of the two New Testament stories," says the Rev. William Lawrence, pastor of Metropolitan Memorial National Methodist Church in Washington. "The church is quite comfortable in seeing those two very different stories as part of one consistent narrative."

"The foundation of our belief is in the virgin birth and the resurrection," says the Rev. Norman Handy, pastor of

Ward Memorial A.M.E. (African Methodist Episcopal) Church in inner-city Washington. "If the Wise Men did not come, that does not negate our belief in the virgin birth and the resurrection."

Bergfalk says questions about other parts of the accounts of Jesus' life are also inconsequential. "If God really came in Christ, that alters reality so radically that all the other questions about the miracles, the details in the story are somewhat penultimate," Bergfalk adds.

Bergfalk, who trained at the Baptist-affiliated Bethel College, Yale Divinity School and the Methodist-affiliated Wesley Theological Seminary, says he has read some of the accounts of the Jesus Seminar's work.

"They seem to take a very liberal, radical position," he says. "I disagree with most of their conclusions," he says, but quickly adds: "To encourage people to struggle with their beliefs is essentially a positive, rather than a negative."

For his part, Handy confesses to little knowledge of the debate about the historical Jesus. But he says his church uses historical and sociological materials about Jesus' time to supplement their study of the Bible. "It strengthens what we believe in," he says.

The Rev. W. Ronald Jameson, monsignor at the 1,400-member St. Matthew's Cathedral in downtown Washington, similarly has little familiarity with the historical-quest literature. As to the Jesus Seminar, he read a magazine article about it over the summer, but recalled few details. "I thought that some of the questions raised were interesting," Jameson says. "I would have some problems with their conclusions."

For his first Advent sermon, Bergfalk chose the theme "Sleepwalking Through Life." The message: "Waking up to the radical call to follow Christ and live as a follower of Christ in our daily lives."

"The presupposition was that Jesus

FOR MORE INFORMATION

American Academy of Religion, 1703 Clifton Rd., NE, Suite G5, Atlanta, Ga. 30329-4019; (404) 727-7920; www.aar-site.org. The academy is the country's major professional society of religion scholars.

Society of Biblical Literature, 825 Houston Mills Road, Suite 825, Atlanta, Ga. 30329; (404) 727-3100; www.sbl-site.org. The society seeks to stimulate the critical investigation of biblical literature.

Westar Institute (the Jesus Seminar), P.O. Box 6144, Santa Rosa, Calif. 95406; (707) 523-1323; www.westarinstitute.org. The institute, home of the Jesus Seminar and the Polebridge Press, was founded in 1986 "as an advocate for religious literacy."

is the person who the church has confessed him to be for the last two millennia," Bergfalk says. "That's a living reality that calls for response in the contemporary world and in our practical living."

Jameson also emphasized the present-day meaning of Jesus' coming in his homily for the first week of Advent. "Jesus came upon this Earth in order to show us how to live, to give us the values that we need, and then he told us, 'Live them out,'" Jameson says.

OUTLOOK

Voices of Faith

King of Kings! The audience, following a centuries-old tradition, is on its feet as Handel's "Hallelujah Chorus" fills the vast sanctuary of Washington National Cathedral.

Lord of Lords! Bellowing organ, rolling timpani, fortissimo orchestra and chorus proclaim the Messiah's reign "for ever and ever."

Hallelujah! Hallelujah! George Frederick Handel's monumental oratorio "Messiah" takes Jesus' story from prophecy to nativity, from crucifixion to resurrection. Composed within the span of three weeks in 1741, the English-language work is a Christmas-time staple, performed countless times each season in formal concerts or informal sing-alongs. [27]

A stately overture opens the first of three parts in the two-and-a-half-hour work. Midway through, a brisk chorus proclaims the nativity: "For unto us a child is born." The second part darkens. The Messiah is "wounded for our transgressions," "cut off out of the land of the living." But the Messiah is raised to heaven, the word triumphs on Earth and God reigns omnipotent in the eagerly anticipated "Hallelujah Chorus." The third part opens with gentle reassurance — "I know that my Redeemer liveth" — and moves quickly to a majestic choral finale.

Handel's composition combines "grand exuberance" with "gentle and touching reflections on the mystery of faith," conductor Douglas Major says in the program notes for this year's cathedral performance. The historical Jesus, however, never appears: The oratorio is a masterwork of belief rather than presentation of fact.

The varied images of Jesus that emerge from the rest of the seasonal music are in the same vein: "holy infant so tender and mild, newborn king, dear savior, Christ the Lord." They are powerful images for Christians: durable despite the secularization and commercialization of the holiday, durable despite doubts of scholars and skeptics.

To Funk, the popular acceptance of unhistorical accounts of Jesus' life and death reflects badly on the church, on the academy and on the public itself. American Christianity is in "a defensive posture," he says. "Any time there is rapid social change, people become defensive."

Religious scholars have been reluctant to engage the public in debate on the issues, Funk continues. "The scholarship of the Bible has been kept a secret largely because of the controversy over Darwin," he explains. "What scholars learned about that was to stay out of public view when it came to talking about the Bible."[28]

As for the public, Funk says even self-professed Christians are ill informed about the Bible. Fewer than half could name all four Gospels in one recent poll, he says. In addition, "the general public always is more credulous than scientific elites," he says.

In his view, the quest for the historical Jesus can strengthen Christianity by displacing "the myth" of Jesus as a divine figure. "We need to transform it into the old story that can last into the third millennium," Funk concludes. "It's a myth of an external redeemer, where what we need is an internal redeemer."

Critics, however, say that Funk and other "questers" are misusing history to advance a cultural and theological agenda. "They seek to change Christianity as a cultural phenomenon by changing — or, to be more generous to them, finding — a Jesus more suited to that reformation," Johnson says. "The logic is that if the central symbol of Jesus is reduced to human dimensions, with appropriate social agendas, then Christianity ought to reform itself along those same lines."

"The agenda is not to get back to the past," he concludes. "It's to get to the present."

Despite their disagreements, schol-

ars on both sides say they find inspiration in the images of Jesus that the Christmas holiday conjures up.

Johnson starts with the Nativity itself: the infant Jesus, born of a single parent, in scandalous circumstances, refused a place of lodging, delivered in a place where the animals live. "God in Jesus has chosen to associate with the homeless and the outcast," he says.

"Images like the Prince of Peace are wonderful images," Funk says. "There are a lot of pictures of the Christmas scene that are valuable, that are worth emphasizing and renewing." ■

Notes

[1] Robert W. Funk, *Honest to Jesus: Jesus for a New Millennium* (1996).

[2] For background, see Charles S. Clark, "Religion in America," *The CQ Researcher*, Nov. 25, 1994, pp. 1033-1056.

[3] See John Meier, *A Marginal Jew: Rethinking the Historical Jesus (Vol. I): The Roots of the Problem and of the Person* (1991), pp. 56-69. The complete text of Josephus' passage about Jesus appears on p. 60.

4 See Charlotte Allen, *The Human Christ: The Search for the Historical Jesus* (1998), p. 86.

[5] Funk's remarks, delivered on March 21, 1985, in Berkeley, Calif., can be found in the seminar's newsletter, "The Issues of Jesus," *Forum*, Vol. 1, p. 1 (1985).

[6] See David Van Biema, "The Gospel Truth?" *Time*, April 8, 1996, pp. 52-60; Sharon Doyle Dreidger, "Is Jesus Really God?" *Macleans*, Dec. 15, 1997, pp. 40-47. For other representative coverage, see *U.S. News & World Report*, Aug. 4, 1997, pp. 35-36, and *The New York Times*, Nov. 25, 1996, p. A12.

[7] Luke Timothy Johnson, *The Real Jesus: The Misguided Quest for the Historical Jesus and the Truth of the Traditional Gospels* (1996). Critical quotations about the seminar are collected at p. 17, with citations. For a profile of Johnson, see *The New York Times*, April 29, 1996, p. A14.

[8] Background drawn in part from Allen, *op.*

cit., and "From Jesus to Christ: The Early Christians," an episode of "Frontline," Public Broadcasting System, April 6-7, 1998. A transcript and supplementary information about the PBS program can be found at www.pbs.org.

[9] Allen, *op. cit.*, p. 9.

[10] *Ibid.*, p. 80.

[11] For a detailed discussion, see E.P. Sanders, *Jesus and Judaism* (1985), pp. 294-318.

[12] See Elaine Pagels, *The Gnostic Gospels* (1979), pp. 119-141.

[13] See John Dominic Crossan, *The Birth of Christianity* (1998), p. 23.

[14] Allen, *op. cit.*, pp. 73, 113-116. Allen argues that the quest for a historical Jesus can be traced to English and French deists of the 1700s. She credits Thomas Chubb (1679-1747) — "a glovemaker from Salisbury who knew neither Latin nor Greek but who read voraciously in rationalist philosophy" — with originating the quest for the historical Jesus in a posthumously published essay, "Of the Personal Character of Jesus Christ" (see pp. 75-77).

[15] See *ibid.*, pp. 150-168.

[16] *Ibid.*, pp. 132-142.

[17] Albert Schweitzer, *The Quest for a Historical Jesus* (1910 translation), p. 29, cited in Allen, *op. cit.*, p. 132.

[18] *Ibid.*, pp. 183-195.

[19] *Ibid.*, pp. 73, 236-239.

[20] Rudolf Bultmann, "The Significance of the Historical Jesus," cited in Allen, *op. cit.*, pp. 244-245.

[21] For this section, see Allen, *op. cit.*, pp. 249-284.

[22] Funk, "The Issue of Jesus," *op. cit.*

[23] For a complete description of the methodology, see *The Five Gospels*, pp. 34-38.

[24] N. T. Wright, *Jesus and the Victory of God* (1993).

[25] See Elisabeth Schüssler Fiorenza, *Jesus: Miriam's Child, Sophia's Prophet: Critical Issues in Feminist Christology* (1995).

[26] Johnson, *op. cit.*, p. 20.

[27] King George II is said to have created the tradition of the audience rising for the "Hallelujah Chorus" by spontaneously standing when he first heard Handel's work. Some scholars, however, consider the story to be apocryphal. See *The Sunday Oklahoman*, Nov. 29, 1998, Entertainment/Travel section, p. 1 (citing David Burrows).

[28] For background, see David Masci, "Evolution vs. Creationism," *The CQ Researcher*, Aug. 22, 1997, pp. 745-768.

Bibliography

Selected Sources Used

Books

Allen, Charlotte, _The Human Christ: The Search for the Historical Jesus_, Free Press, 1998.

Allen, a Washington journalist, traces the written treatments of Jesus' life from the Gospels and the theological debates of the first centuries after his death through the various "historical" searches for Jesus beginning in Europe in the 18th and 19th centuries and continuing through the Jesus Seminar. The book includes detailed source notes and a 20-page bibliography.

Borg, Marcus J., and N.T. Wright, _The Meaning of Jesus: Two Visions_, Harper/San Francisco, 1998.

The book consists of eight pairs of opposing essays about Jesus on such topics as his birth, his teachings and his death. Borg is a professor of religion at Oregon State University and a member of the Jesus Seminar; Wright is dean of Lichfield Cathedral in England and a critic of the Jesus Seminar.

Crossan, John Dominic, _Jesus: A Revolutionary Biography_, Harper/San Francisco, 1994; _The Historical Jesus: The Life of a Mediterranean Jewish Peasant_, Harper/San Francisco, 1991.

Crossan, a retired professor at DePaul University in Chicago and founding co-chair of the Jesus Seminar, depicts Jesus as a social revolutionary who preached a message of radical egalitarianism and challenged existing social rules. The first book includes detailed scriptural citations and an 18-page bibliography; the second is a popularized distillation of the earlier work.

Funk, Robert W., _Honest to Jesus: Jesus for a New Millennium_, Polebridge Press/Harper/San Francisco, 1996.

Funk, a founder of the Jesus Seminar, argues that Jesus' views have been obscured by the Gospels and the growth of institutionalized Christianity; he ends with a list of 21 "theses" that sharply question many central views of traditional Christianity. The book includes source notes and a four-page list of suggested readings.

Funk, Robert W., Roy W. Hoover and the Jesus Seminar, _The Five Gospels: What Did Jesus Actually Say?_ Harper/San Francisco, 1993; Funk, Robert W., and the Jesus Seminar, _The Acts of Jesus: What Did Jesus Really Do?_ Polebridge Press/Harper/San Francisco, 1998.

These two volumes represent the major work products of the Jesus Seminar: their controversial attempts to recount, based on historical reconstruction, the "actual" teachings and acts of Jesus. Both volumes contain notes, suggestions for further reading and a roster of the seminar's members.

Johnson, Luke Timothy, _The Real Jesus: The Misguided Quest for the Historical Jesus and the Truth of the Traditional Gospels_, HarperCollins, 1996.

Johnson, a professor of New Testament at the Chandler School of Theology at Emory University in Atlanta, sharply attacks the Jesus Seminar on grounds of bias, methodology and fundamental approach. Citations to the writings and news coverage of the Jesus Seminar appear within the text.

McManners, John (ed.), _The Oxford Illustrated History of Christianity_, Oxford University Press, 1992.

This richly illustrated volume traces the history of Christianity through 1990. The book includes a 19-page list of readings and a 17-page chronology through 1990. McManners is a professor emeritus at Oxford University.

Meier, John, _A Marginal Jew: Rethinking the Historical Jesus: The Roots of the Problem and the Person (Vol I)_, Doubleday, 1991; _Mentor, Message and Miracle_ (Vol. II), Doubleday, 1994.

Meier, a professor at Notre Dame University, describes in the first volume the historical evidence available to construct an account of Jesus' life and, in the second volume, analyzes and interprets Jesus' teachings. Both volumes are carefully annotated; each one also contains maps of Palestine and of Galilee in Jesus' time.

Miller, Robert J. (ed.), _The Complete Gospels; Annotated Scholars Version_ [rev. edition], Polebridge Press, 1994.

The book — compiled and edited by members of the Jesus Seminar — provides new versions of the four Canonical Gospels (Matthew, Mark, Luke and John) along with 11 other "complete" gospels and five "fragmentary" gospels. The book includes a three-page glossary.

Pagels, Elaine, _The Gnostic Gospels_, Random House, 1979.

Pagels, a professor of religion at Princeton University, relates the discovery of the so-called Gnostic Gospels at Nag Hammadi in Egypt in 1945 and then examines what they revealed about the differences between gnostic and orthodox Christianity in the early centuries after Jesus' death. The book includes detailed source notes.

Sanders, E.P., _Jesus and Judaism_, Fortress Press, 1985.

A professor at Oxford University examines Jesus' intentions and his relationship to his contemporaries in Judaism. The book includes detailed source notes and scriptural citations and a 14-page bibliography.

The Next Step

Additional information from UMI's Newspaper & Periodical Abstracts™ database

Quest for the Historical Jesus

Dirda, Michael, "Man of Nazareth," *The Washington Post*, May 10, 1998, p. W1.

New Testament scholars, learned amateurs and diverse "crackpots" have attempted to paint a portrait of the historical Jesus. Each has found the Galilean he was looking for — whether a reform rabbi, Gnostic sage, political revolutionary, mythological being, gentle hippie, hysterical madman or gay magician. In her book The Human Christ, Charlotte Allen presents a skeptical popular history of the quest for "the historical Jesus."

"Easter," *The Detroit News*, April 12, 1998, p. B6.

This year's celebration of Easter is accompanied by renewed controversy. A recent Public Broadcasting Service documentary on efforts by historians and archaeologists to document the life of the historical Jesus and examine the early development of Christianity has been criticized by some for scanting the resurrection, thus missing the essential point of Christ's message.

Lattin, Don, "Looking for Jesus; Three Books Search from Different Angles — Historical, Skeptical and Mystical," *San Francisco Chronicle*, April 12, 1998, p. R1.

Christians' understanding of Jesus is inseparable from the preconceptions brought to the rich and varied portrayals of him in the Gospels of Matthew, Mark, Luke and John. Not surprisingly, readers of the Bible often find the Jesus they seek — Jesus as the teacher of wisdom, Jesus as apocalyptic messiah or Jesus as social revolutionary.

Martini, Carlo Maria, "A Christian Community: Toward the Third Millennium," *America*, May 2, 1998, pp. 8-12.

Even though millions throughout the world don't accept the central place of Christ, they recognize that a new time in history began with his birth. The author considers the third millennium's implications for Christianity.

Osiek, Carolyn, "The Birth of Christianity," *America*, Nov. 14, 1998, pp. 23-24.

The author reviews John Dominic Crossan's book, *The Birth of Christianity.*

Sheler, Jeffery L., "In Search of Jesus," *U.S. News & World Report*, April 8, 1996, pp. 46-53.

Some modern scholars claim that historical evidence reveals a much different portrait of Jesus than the one in Christian creeds. While the historical quest has been denounced by some as a frontal assault on the Christian faith and an attempt to undermine the Bible, its proponents find in it hope for a more rational basis for belief.

Steinke, Darcey, "Cross Currents," *The Village Voice*, Nov. 25, 1997, p. S16.

The author describes her first experience with the Christian faith and the development of her faith in Jesus Christ. She discusses various books that influenced her quest, including *Meeting Jesus Again for the First Time* by theologian Marcus Borg.

Willimon, William H., "Encountering Jesus: An Exchange," *The Christian Century*, Nov. 5, 1997, p. 1.

The author criticizes some of the theological conclusions about Jesus made by theologian Marcus Borg. He wishes Borg would ponder how to follow Christ, rather than reinterpreting Jesus to help modern man understand Him.

The Jesus Seminar

Budziszewski, J., "Divided Hearts," *National Review*, July 29, 1996, pp. 50-51.

The author reviews *The Real Jesus: The Misguided Quest for the Historical Jesus* and the *Truth of the Traditional Gospels* by Luke Timothy Johnson, a leading critic of the Jesus Seminar.

Galloway, Paul, "Listening for the Word of God; Religious Historians Take a Fine-Toothed Comb to Uncover What Jesus Really Said," *The Chicago Tribune*, May 1, 1997, p. 1.

Galloway interviews Robert W. Funk, founder of the controversial Jesus Seminar, a group of some 200 religious historians that has concluded that 82 percent of the declarations, aphorisms, parables and stories attributed to Jesus in the Gospels were actually composed by the authors of Matthew, Mark, Luke and John.

Hutchinson, Robert J., "The Jesus Seminar Unmasked," *Christianity Today*, April 29, 1996, pp. 28-30.

The author reviews *The Real Jesus* by Luke Timothy Johnson.

Johnson, Luke Timothy, "Who Is Jesus?" *Commonweal*, Dec. 15, 1995, pp.12-14.

The author examines the historical Jesus found in the New Testament. He also maintains that the "historical-critical method" of Jesus scholarship has tended to be overly critical of tradition and far less critical of itself.

Kay, James F., "Honest to Jesus: Jesus for a New Millennium," *Theology Today*, July 1997, pp. 262-266.

The author reviews *Honest to Jesus: Jesus for a New Millennium*, a book by Robert W. Funk, head of the Jesus Seminar.

Niebuhr, Gustav, "Iconoclastic Scholars of Jesus to Consider Doctrinal Revision," *The New York Times*, Nov. 25, 1996, p. A12.

For more than a decade, the biblical scholars who belong to the Jesus Seminar have provoked excitement, apprehension and outrage, among lay people and academics alike, in their attempt to sift the New Testament to discover what they say is a purely historical picture of Jesus. But now the seminar's founder, Robert W. Funk, says it will enter a new phase in which it will consider whether the New Testament should be revised to include other ancient Christian texts.

Celebrating Christmas

Bookbinder, Maxine Kopel, "Holidays: Strangers in Our Own Land," *USA Today*, Dec. 9, 1992, p. A14.

The author contends that the celebration of Christmas at some schools is unfair for children who are not Christian and feel left out. She argues that schools should either teach about the celebrations of many different cultures or not observe any holidays.

Lenhard, Elizabeth, "U.S. Christmas Traditions Amaze Immigrants," *The Atlanta Constitution*, Dec. 14, 1993, p. E1.

To some immigrants, Christmas in the United States is the ultimate manifestation of America as the Land of Plenty. These newcomers often adopt certain aspects of the holiday, putting up trees and giving gifts. Others are shocked by the commercialism and secularization of a holiday that continues to be a spiritual time in much of the Christian world.

Rogers, Kathryn, "'December Dilemma': It's Touchy," *The St. Louis Post-Dispatch*, Dec. 20, 1992, p. A1.

The article examines the dilemmas of Jewish-Christian families during the holiday season.

Christians and Jews

Kugel, James, "What the Dead Sea Scrolls Do Not Tell," *Commentary*, November 1998, pp. 49-53.

The author discusses the initial promise that the Dead Sea Scrolls held for providing insights on ancient Judaism and Christianity, and their later value when it was determined that the significant insights would not be forthcoming.

Novak, Michael, "Taste: New World, New Life _ The Meaning of Passover and Easter in America," *The Wall Street Journal*, April 10, 1998, p. W11.

Easter and Passover are in a sense one holiday, for the Christian Easter service is a new form of Passover, beginning with the re-enactment of the Last Supper of Jesus and his apostles (itself a Passover meal). Both celebrate the passage from captivity to liberation, from death to new life. Both holidays celebrate a new covenant of a people with their Creator. In this, they offer the original model for American compacts and constitutions.

Rice, Patricia, "Christians and Jews Will Celebrate with Seders as Part of the Holy Week," *St. Louis Post-Dispatch*, April 9, 1998, p. B1.

The word Seder appears on the calendars of both Christians and Jews this week. Christians celebrate their version of Jesus' Paschal Seder or Last Supper. Jews begin the celebration of the Festival of Pesah — the Hebrew word for passed over. It recalls the night that the plague that caused the death of each first-born male in Egypt "passed over" the Jews. Tens of thousands of area Christians will celebrate some form of a Jewish Seder — much the way Jesus celebrated it.

Jesus in Popular Culture

Soukup, Paul A., "Imaging the Divine: Jesus and Christ-Figures in Film," *Theological Studies*, June 1998, pp. 346-347.

The author reviews *Imaging the Divine: Jesus and Christ-Figures in Film* by Lloyd Baugh.

Eskridge, Larry, "'One Way:' Billy Graham, the Jesus Generation and the Idea of an Evangelical Youth Culture," *Church History*, March 1998, pp. 83-106.

The article examines the New Year's Day 1971 appearance of evangelist Billy Graham as grand marshal of the Tournament of Roses Parade. The episode is instructive for understanding Graham, the Jesus Movement's relationship to the times as a vast spiritual awakening among American youth and the evangelical subculture itself.

Lattin, Don, "Mailer Tackles the Greatest Story Ever Told; A Fictional Account of the New Testament — with Jesus as the Narrator," *San Francisco Chronicle*, April 27, 1997, p. R5.

In his new novel, *The Gospel According to the Son*, Norman Mailer not only retells the story of Jesus Christ — he writes it in the first person. Mailer, who is Jewish, read such Jesus scholars as Elaine Pagels and John Dominic Crossan, whose efforts to uncover "what Jesus really said" have produced a historical Jesus far too human for many Christians. But Mailer's Jesus is no mere teacher of wisdom, no social critic or Jewish revolutionary. Mailer's Jesus is born to a virgin, performs miracles and gradually comes to see himself as not just a carpenter from Nazareth but the Son of God, the Messiah for both Gentile and Jew.

Back Issues

Great Research on Current Issues Starts Right Here.
Recent topics covered by The CQ Researcher are listed below.
Now available on the Web
For information, call (800) 432-2250 ext. 279 or (202) 887-6279.

Back issues are available for $5.00 (subscribers) or $10.00 (non-subscribers). Quantity discounts apply to orders over 10. To order, call Congressional Quarterly Customer Service at (202) 887-8621.

Binders are available for $18.00. To order call 1-800-638-1710. Please refer to stock number 648.

Future Topics

▶ *Reform in Iran*

▶ *The Crisis in American Journalism*

▶ *Death Penalty Update*

PUBLISHED BY CONGRESSIONAL QUARTERLY INC.

Reform in Iran

Are moderates changing the Islamic Republic?

I n 1979, religious dissidents deposed the shah of Iran, casting aside his attempts to Westernize the oil-rich nation. Twenty years later, some scholars say that Iran is once again on the verge of profound change. They point to the election of moderate Mohammad Khatami to the presidency as proof that most Iranians reject the conservatism of the Islamic Republic. But other Iran-watchers say that Khatami has no desire to reverse the changes brought by the 1979 revolution, nor could he. Meanwhile, there is growing disagreement over whether U.S. economic sanctions against Iran bolster Iranian moderates and discourage Iran from supporting terrorism or encourage hard-liners within Iran.

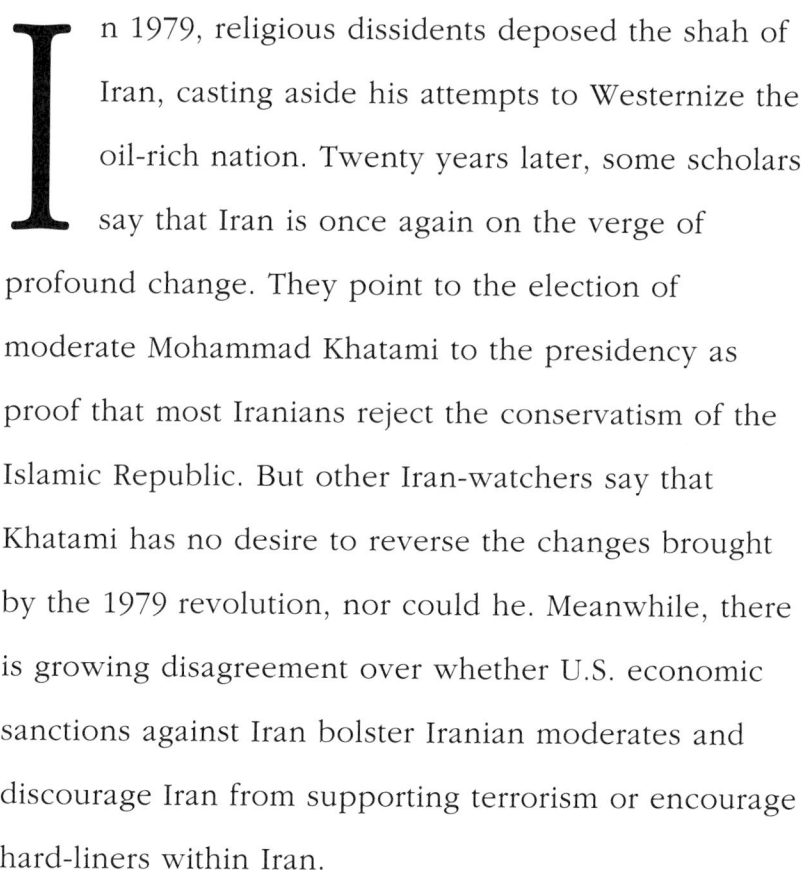

CQ | Dec. 18, 1998 • Volume 8, No. 47 • Pages 1097-1120

Formerly Editorial Research Reports

Dec. 18, 1998
Volume 8, No.47

EDITOR
Sandra Stencel

MANAGING EDITOR
Thomas J. Colin

STAFF WRITERS
Adriel Bettelheim
Mary H. Cooper
Kenneth Jost
Kathy Koch
David Masci

PRODUCTION EDITOR
Debra James

EDITORIAL ASSISTANT
Laura S. Cavender

PUBLISHED BY
Congressional Quarterly Inc.

CHAIRMAN
Andrew Barnes

VICE CHAIRMAN
Andrew P. Corty

PRESIDENT AND PUBLISHER
Robert W. Merry

EXECUTIVE EDITOR
David Rapp

Bibliographic records and abstracts included in The Next Step section of this publication are the copyrighted material of UMI, and are used with permission.

The CQ Researcher (ISSN 1056-2036). Formerly Editorial Research Reports. Published weekly, except Jan. 2, May 29, July 3, Oct. 30, by Congressional Quarterly Inc., 1414 22nd St., N.W., Washington, D.C. 20037. Annual subscription rate for libraries, businesses and government is $340. Additional rates furnished upon request. Periodicals postage paid at Washington, D.C., and additional mailing offices. POSTMASTER: Send address changes to The CQ Researcher, 1414 22nd St., N.W., Washington, D.C. 20037.

Cover: Outgoing Iranian President Hashemi Rafsanjani (right) meets with President-elect Mohammad Khatami in May 1997. (Reuters/Aladin Abdel)

Reform in Iran

By David Masci

THE ISSUES

The U.S. wrestlers did not know what to expect when they arrived in Tehran last February. Competing in a 17-nation tournament, they were the first Americans to formally represent the United States in Iran in almost 20 years. "We were all a little bit nervous," admitted team member Melvin Douglas. [1]

In the nation that popularized the phrase "Death to America," the athletes were especially wary about appearing overly patriotic. They were so concerned, in fact, that they brought two sets of uniforms — one with the American flag and one without it.

But the wrestlers' fears were unfounded. "Once we got there and went through opening ceremonies, and we held the [American] flag up . . . we received an unbelievable amount of applause and ovations," said wrestler Kevin Jackson. [2]

The emotional highlight of the trip was yet to come. On Feb. 23, Larry "Zeke" Jones delighted the crowd by picking up and waving an Iranian flag after accepting a silver medal. The arena shook as 12,000 Iranian fans responded with chants of "America! America!" [3]

Such a public display of affection for the United States in Iran was nothing short of amazing. Even more startling, the Americans had been invited to Iran by the new president of the Islamic Republic.

To many people in the United States, Iran is a land of terrorists and religious fanatics with a deep hatred for America. These impressions stem from the 1979 Islamic revolution and, in particular, the 444-day hostage crisis that followed. Many Americans have not forgotten the humiliation they felt while watching Iranian students, with their new government's blessing, publicly parading around

handcuffed and blindfolded personnel from the U.S. Embassy in Tehran.

Moreover, the mutual distrust and hostility has been reinforced by subsequent events, such as Iran's reported role in the 1983 bombing of the U.S. Marine barracks in Beirut, Lebanon, and America's downing of an Iranian airliner in 1990, just before the Persian Gulf War. Indeed, in the almost 20 years since the release of the American hostages, the United States has sparred repeatedly with the Islamic Republic over issues ranging from Iran's alleged support of terrorism to her quest for nuclear and other weapons of mass destruction. A U.S. economic embargo has added to the tension.

But in January, Iran's newly elected president, Mohammad Khatami, sought to defuse the historically tense U.S.-Iranian relations. In an interview with CNN reporter Christian Amanpour on Jan. 7, Khatami, a Shi'ite cleric, called for a new dialogue between the peoples, though not the governments, of Iran and the United States in order to "crack . . . the wall of mistrust." As part of the dialogue, Khatami proposed "exchanges" of artists, scholars and others in order to create a new understanding. [4] The wrestling tournament was the first of these exchanges.

Even more surprising, Khatami apologized for the hostage crisis, saying he understood that "the feelings of the great American people have been hurt" by the incident. "And,

of course, I regret it," he added. [5]

Khatami's conciliatory words have given rise to hope both inside Iran and beyond that the Islamic Republic is becoming more moderate. Khatami has spoken frequently of the need to protect human rights, respect the rule of law and improve Iran's relations with the West. Indeed, his surprising victory in the presidential election — he trounced the government's hand-picked, conservative candidate — was seen by many as another signal from the Iranian people that they wanted change.

Some Iran-watchers go so far as to predict the eventual downfall of the Islamic Republic. "I don't see this regime lasting much longer in its current form," says David Wurmser, a research fellow at the American Enterprise Institute (AEI).

To begin with, Wurmser argues, average Iranians no longer support the religious, ruling elite who came to power with the fall of Iran's autocratic shah, or king, in 1979. "As with any revolution, people rapidly lose faith with it, and that has already happened in Iran," he says. This natural process was accelerated in Iran, Wurmser and others say, by the government's profound mismanagement of the economy, which in turn has drastically lowered living standards.

On top of this, Wurmser and others point out, young Iranians (who make up the majority of the population) do not share their parents' revolutionary fervor. They were born after the shah's departure and know little of his rule or that of Ayatollah Ruhollah Khomeini, the founder of the Islamic Republic. "These kids don't care about that stuff," he says. "They're more interested in what's coming out of the U.S., like movies or music."

Those who predict the regime's downfall often point to Khatami as a possible catalyst for change. "Khatami represents the aspirations of the vast majority of Iranians, who want to move forward and create a more liberal and flexible society," says Sandra Mackey, an Iran scholar and author of *The Iranians: Persia, Islam and the Soul of a Nation.*

But other experts argue that such scenarios are overly optimistic, particularly in light of the recent killings of several prominent critics of clerical repression. They doubt that the revolution will be brought down any time soon because Khatami, for all his popularity, does not hold the reins of power in Iran. For instance, the military, police and judiciary are all controlled by the nation's spiritual leader, Ayatollah Ali Khamenei, who opposes radical change. "The system is structured in a way that makes it impossible for Khatami to really make big changes, no matter how popular he is," says Mohsen Milani, a professor of government and international affairs at the University of Florida at Tampa.

In addition, says Bahman Baktiari, a professor of political science at the University of Maine at Orono, Khatami is not some sort of Western liberal in a Shi'ite cleric's cloak. "Khatami is part of a system with many factions and constituencies," he says, "and he is working within that system, not trying to overturn it."

Some observers say it is the United States, and not Khatami and other moderates, that may ultimately provide the catalyst for change in Iran. But they disagree about how much pressure for change the United States should exert. Much of the disagreement focuses on the stringent economic sanctions the United States has imposed on Iran for what the American government alleges are a catalog of misdeeds from terrorism to human rights abuses. [6]

Many policy-makers argue that the restrictions have had a profoundly negative impact on Iran's economy

A Tough Neighborhood

Iran fought a war with Iraq from 1980-1988 that devastated Iran's oil industry and killed up to a half-million Iranian men. Recently Iran and Afghanistan exchanged threats after several Iranian diplomats were slain in Afghanistan.

Iran at a Glance

Population: 67.5 million (July 1997 est.)

Population growth rate: 2.1%

Area: 627,320 sq. mi.

Gross domestic product (GDP): $343.5 billion (1996 est.); per capita GDP, $5,200 (1996 est.)

Ethnic groups: Persian 51%, Azerbaijani 24%, Gilaki and Mazandarani 8%, Kurd 7%, Arab 3%, Lur 2%, Baluchi 2%,

Religions: Shi'a Muslim 89%, Sunni Muslim 10%, Zoroastrian, Jewish, Christian and Baha'i 1%

Languages: Persian and Persian dialects 58%, Turkic and Turkic dialects 26%, Kurdish 9%, Luri 2%, Baluchi 1%, Arabic 1%, other 2%,

Infant mortality rate: 50.8 deaths/1,000 live births (1997 est.)

Literacy: male, 78.4%; female, 65.8% (1994 est.)

and pride. They believe sanctions should be kept in place in order to leverage positive changes from Iran, both domestically and internationally. "Sanctions are the only real leverage we have, and we should use them to influence Iran on a host of issues," says Geoffrey Kemp, director of regional strategic programs at the Nixon Center a Washington-based foreign policy research organization.

Kemp and others say that sanctions ultimately aid moderates like Khatami because Iranians know that the embargo grew out of policies promulgated by hard-liners. In addition, they say, unilaterally lifting sanctions would boost conservatives like Khamenei, who likely would see the gesture as one of weakness on the part of the U.S. and hence an excuse to continue hard-line policies. "It's just like Germany before the war," Wurmser says. "Every time the Allies made a concession, Hitler took it as a green light to go further."

But others argue that sanctions strengthen hard-line factions in Iran at the expense of reformers like Khatami. According to Milani, sanctions reinforce the siege mentality prevalent among Iran's more conservative elements, so lifting them will give moderates the upper hand. "Goodwill begets goodwill," he says. "So when we make a positive gesture, they will be tempted to respond with a positive gesture too."

Moreover, Milani and others say, sanctions actually have little practical effect on Iran's economy because the United States is the only major country to impose restrictions on the Islamic Republic. Since Iran trades with everyone else, they say, U.S. restrictions only penalize American businesses, which can't tap into an oil-rich market with 67 million consumers.

As the Islamic Republic approaches its 20th anniversary, these are some of the questions being asked about the economic sanctions and Iran's political and social system:

Is Iran's Islamic revolution fading?

In May 1997, Iranians shocked the world and their own government by overwhelmingly electing Khatami to the presidency with a whopping 70 percent of the vote. Khatami's opponent, the government's hand-picked candidate, parliamentary Speaker Ali Akbar Nateq-Noori, had been heavily favored to win.

During pre-election campaigning, Khatami had called for more openness in society and a greater reliance on the rule of law. Khatami's victory, according to the authors of a recent article in *Foreign Policy*, "represented an unmistakable and overwhelming mandate for change, underlining the desire of Iranians from all classes for an easing of state restrictions on social and cultural life, for a greater say in political affairs and for a better economy." [7]

But it would be a mistake to view Khatami's election as the ascension of a hostile outsider. Iran's new president is no Jeffersonian democrat. He is a high-ranking Shi'ite cleric who has always supported the Islamic revolution. In fact Khatami was one of only four candidates (out of over 200) deemed "acceptable" by the regime to run for the presidency.

Moreover, in Iran, the presidency is not the highest office in the land, in theory or practice. That honor goes to Iran's spiritual leader, Khamenei. Khamenei is thought to be the most powerful man in the country, followed by former President Hashemi Rafsanjani, who holds a number of powerful appointed offices. Khatami, Milani says, "doesn't have many of the powers other presidents do, like control over the military or police."

And yet, while Khatami may not be a Western-style president, he does have power and has shown a willingness to use it in the service of reform. Much of Khatami's clout is derived from his tremendous popularity, which in turn has been nourished by the perception among the people that he is a moderate who favors change.

But when Iranian voters selected Khatami, did they see him as someone who would reform and save Iran's Islamic revolution? Or did they vote for an agent of radical change, someone who would begin overturning the existing order and create a new one?

Many observers see Khatami's election as a stunning rebuke to the regime. Some go so far as to say that it is the beginning of the end. "For all intents and purposes, this revolution is dead," says the Nixon Center's Kemp. "I mean, people don't believe in it anymore."

The American Enterprise Institute's Wurmser agrees. "Many of the mullahs are beginning to openly question the ideals of the revolution," he says. "When that happens, you know that the end is not far off."

Kemp, Wurmser and others say average Iranians have lost faith in part because they have gained little or nothing from the revolution. Sanctions, corruption, falling oil prices and general mismanagement have slowed the economy and hurt living standards, they say. In most cases, citizens are worse off now than they were under the shah (*see p. 1106*). "People have experienced the revolution for 20 years and have paid dearly for it," Wurmser says. "You can't maintain this level of sacrifice for a utopian ideal and expect people to deal with it indefinitely."

Moreover, many observers say most Iranians are sick of political, cultural and other restrictions established in the name of the revolution. "Iranians long for change, for a more open, freer society," Mackey says.

Indeed, as *Washington Post* correspondent John Lancaster recently observed, the same people who used to chant "Death to America" now have an insatiable appetite for U.S. cultural offerings: "Though officially banned, bootleg copies of the latest U.S. films are widely available in Iran, and it is rare to find a teenager who lacks at least a passing familiarity with the music of Michael Jackson or Madonna. Anti-American slogans share wall space with spray-painted odes to Metallica and Guns N'Roses. Bookstores are filled with Persian translations of novels by John Grisham, Sidney Sheldon and Danielle Steele." [8]

Finally, Wurmser and others argue, Khatami's election may prove to be a real catalyst for change in Iran. "I think the hard-liners let Khatami run [for president] to allow people to let off some steam," Wurmser says. "But once you let off some pent-up steam, you want to let off more." He predicts that the regime will "collapse sometime within the next five, or at most 10, years."

Similarly, Mackey predicts that moderates like Khatami, supported by the majority of the Iranian people, will begin pushing harder for wholesale changes that relegate religious hard-liners and their supporters into the background. "I think there will be a great upheaval, although not a revolution, against the powers that be," she says. There could be "a very different government in Iran in two or three years."

But other Iran-watchers read the tea leaves differently, arguing that Khatami's election should not be interpreted as the beginning of some great transformation in Iran. To begin with, they say, many Western analysts mistakenly interpret factional fighting within Iran as a sign that the Islamic Republic is crumbling. "People [outside the country] look at Khatami as some sort of glorious accident because they think of Iran as a totalitarian system," Milani says. In fact, he argues, "Iran has a lively parliamentary and political system

that accommodates factions with set ideas and agendas that compete with each other."

The University of Florida's Baktiari agrees. "Iran is not a straight democracy, but the system allows various factions to contend for power," he says. "It's like a continuous basketball game: The strategy is to score as many points as possible and win." But Baktiari contends that no one player, including Khatami, wants to end the game. "Everyone is on the same side in that they all want to preserve the system," he says.

The differences come over strategy. "One group, the moderates, thinks the masses need to participate more to help the system while the [conservatives] think that the leadership should make all the decisions," Baktiari says.

In this environment, Milani says, it is only natural that leaders with different ideas and methods are elected sooner or later. "It was inevitable that a reformer like Khatami would come to power — if not now, then in the future," he says.

Other Iran-watchers concur with Baktiari and Milani's contention that the Islamic Republic is not likely to collapse or change radically in the near future. But they are less sure that the country's political system is open to new ideas. Instead, they view Khatami and his supporters as a largely marginalized force. "Khatami and the moderates are not in control," says an official with a prominent Jewish organization in Washington. "All the power is in the hands of [the hard-liners], and they have the security apparatus in place to keep it for a long time."

Azar Nafisi, a professor of cultural studies at the Johns Hopkins University School for Advanced International Studies, agrees that Khatami has little room to maneuver. "They will only let him go so far, and he knows it," she says. Nafisi argues that Khatami's

election should not be viewed as a great new awakening in Iran, nor as a sign that the revolution is over. Instead, like Milani, she sees his election as part of a repeating cycle in the history of the revolution.

"When you look at the history of the Islamic Republic," Nafisi says, "you see that it's like the old Soviet Union in that there are periods of real repression, and then they loosen up before tightening everything again. Academics said the same things about Rafsanjani that they're saying about Khatami — 'he's a reformer, a moderate, etc.' "

Should the United States ease or eliminate the sanctions it has imposed on Iran?

The United States usually has viewed the Islamic Republic with a mixture of wariness and hostility. Relations got off to a bad start with the 1979 hostage crisis and have never recovered. From the American point of view, Iran under the mullahs has been responsible for misdeeds ranging from supporting international terrorism to trying to build nuclear bombs and other weapons of mass destruction.

For the last 20 years, American strategy has been to "contain" Iran. Toward that end, the United States has maintained almost airtight economic sanctions against the Islamic Republic, except for a brief period during the early 1980s.

Diplomatic relations were broken and sanctions first imposed in April 1980, during the hostage crisis. President Jimmy Carter had already frozen Iranian assets in the United States. These restrictions were partially eased after the hostages were released on the day Carter left office in January 1981. But sanctions were once again tightened by President Ronald Reagan in January 1984 after it was determined that Iran had assisted in the

Continued on p. 1104

Life Under the Chador for Iranian Women

Some strange things occurred in Tehran during the early morning hours of June 22. Iran's soccer team had just defeated the United States in the World Cup, generating spontaneous public celebrations. But as the crowds poured into the streets, some Iranian women defied Islamic law and removed their scarves and chadors, traditional, floor-length veils. Others danced with and even kissed men who were not their husbands. Still others pounded on cars, joyously urging drivers to honk their horns. [1]

Such behavior is forbidden in the strict Islamic Republic, but police and army units on patrol took no action. "Many women took off their chadors as a sign not only of celebration but also of disenchantment — with their lives and with this regime," says Azar Nafisi, a professor of cultural studies at Johns Hopkins University's School for Advanced International Studies in Washington, D.C.

Since the 1979 Islamic revolution overthrew the moderate shah of Iran, women have been subjected to a variety of rules, including a dress code, known as *hejab*. While men can essentially wear what they like, women must wrap their bodies in layers of dark clothing so as to not unnecessarily tempt the opposite sex by showing their feminine features. The code calls for all adult women to cover their heads and part of their faces with either a chador or scarf.

In addition, women are virtually segregated from men in public life, from schools and universities to buses and mosques. Recently, Iran's Majlis, or parliament, approved legislation segregating hospitals by sex.

Socializing is even more restricted. Men and women who are not married cannot hold hands or otherwise touch affectionately in public. Dating does not occur, at least in the open, and most women marry a husband of their parents' choosing.

Laws regarding marriage also leave women at a distinct disadvantage. For instance, men can take multiple wives, as is the custom in many Islamic countries. And they enjoy the right of automatic divorce as well as advantages in cases where both parents want custody of the children. Women, on the other hand, can only obtain a divorce for cause (such as adultery or the taking of a second wife) and must get the approval of the judge.

Under the last shah and his father, the situation was partly reversed. As part of their broader effort to secularize and Westernize Iran, women were encouraged to attend school, even university, and to work outside the home. The wearing of the chador in public was actually prohibited. Edicts were passed giving women more social and economic freedom, including the 1967 Family Protection Bill, which strengthened women's rights in divorce and custody battles.

Many of these changes, including the 1967 law, were reversed after the Islamic Republic was established. According to Johns Hopkins' Nafisi, many Iranian women fought the changes. "This was a modern society, and we did not approve of what they were doing," she says. "You know, it took four years to enforce the wearing of the chador because there was so much opposition to it among women."

Even today, says Nafisi, who fled Iran two years ago, many women bristle at the requirement. "When you see a wisp of hair in front," she says, "it is a form of protest."

Chador-wearing Iranian girls greet Iranian President Mohammad Khatami during his visit to Turkmenistan in December 1997.

But women have not been shut out of Iranian society completely. Suffrage is universal, women hold seats in parliament and there is a female Cabinet member, Environment Minister Massoumeh Ebtekar. There are even authorized women's groups and publications seeking to increase women's rights. In addition, most career paths are open to women. And at home, many women wear jeans, skirts and makeup and can be more relaxed with men.

"Women are clearly dissatisfied with the situation," says Patrick Clawson, director for research at the Washington Institute for Near East Policy. "That being said, I think they also realize that they live in a more open society than the Gulf states, like Saudi Arabia, where women aren't even allowed to drive."

---

[1] Elaine Sciolino, "Singing, Dancing and Cheering in the Streets of Teheran," *The New York Times,* June 22, 1998.

Anti-American Iranians demonstrate outside the U.S. Embassy in Tehran during the fourth week of the 1979 hostage crisis. Placards depict Uncle Sam as a warmonger, and Ayatollah Ruhollah Khomeini.

1983 bombing of the U.S. Marine Barracks in Beirut. [9]

During the Clinton administration, further limitations were imposed. In 1995, the president prohibited American companies from helping Iran develop its oil industry. The follow-ing year, Congress passed the so-called Iran-Libya Sanctions Act, re-quiring the president to punish for-eign companies that invest in Iran's energy industry.

Today, no U.S. goods may be exported to Iran, even through third countries. Americans may import Ira-nian goods worth less than $100. Investments in Iran and other finan-cial transactions are prohibited. [10]

But in the last year or so, U.S. policy-makers and others have be-gun to openly question the need for sanctions. "We need to encourage the moderates, and lifting the sanc-tions will do that," says the University of Florida's Milani.

Mackey agrees that removing sanc-tions could embolden reformers. "We could really send some effective sig-nals to Khatami and others in Iran that we understand and appreciate what they are trying to do," she says.

Mackey, Milani and others argue that by maintaining stiff sanctions, the United States is creating a situa-tion in Iran that plays to the strengths of more conservative elements in the government. "When the chief policy-makers in Iran see another country constantly trying to undermine them," Milani says, "the hard-liners gain the upper hand."

Those who favor lifting U.S. sanc-tions also argue that they have not yielded any concrete results. "For the past 20 years, people have been talking about using sanctions to modify Iran's behavior, and where have they gotten?" Milani asks. "The only thing these sanctions do is make us [Americans] feel better."

The biggest reason American sanc-tions have little or no bite, Milani and others point out, is due to the fact that the United States is the only major country that has significant restrictions on Iran. "The Iranians can get anything they want from other countries in Europe and Asia, and so the sanctions are not really having much effect," says the University of Maine's Baktiari.

In fact, opponents of sanctions say, they only penalize American corpora-tions. "All we're doing is giving an ad-vantage to our business competitors in Europe and Asia," says John Howard, director of international policy and programs for the U.S. Chamber of Commerce. Howard points out, for example, that U.S. companies have been unable to bid on lucrative contracts in Iran's energy industry.

But others argue that American businesses are not the only party penalized by the sanctions. "Of course the sanctions matter to Iran," says Patrick Clawson, research director at the Washington Institute for Near East Policy. "If they didn't affect the country, Iran wouldn't be trying to get them lifted." In particular, he argues, the ban on direct investment has slowed Iran's efforts to jump-start its stagnant economy by developing its oil and gas industry with foreign help (*see p. 1110*).

While Wurmser of the AEI agrees that sanctions hurt Iran's economy, he argues they also have tremendous symbolic weight. "The U.S. is the big player in the Middle East," he says, "and what it does matters to everyone in the region. The fact that the Americans have tagged Iran as an outlaw regime discredits them in the eyes of other countries, and that bothers them very much."

The sanctions also carry great symbolic weight within the country, Wurmser argues, because, contrary to popular impression, Iranians have great affection and admiration for America. "Iranians may buy things from Europe and other countries," he says, "but they love the United States, our people, our culture. The conflicts between the regime and the U.S. don't play well with the common people."

All of these pressures give the United States leverage that should not be wasted by empty, goodwill gestures, says the Nixon Center's Kemp. "They should never be lifted unilaterally," he says. "There needs to be some sort of quid pro quo every time."

Kemp and others also dispute the notion that sanctions bolster hard-liners at the expense of moderates. In fact, they argue, sanctions prop up moderate elements in Iranian society because everyone knows that deprivation caused by American sanctions are the result of Iran's hard-line policies.

"Sanctions tell conservatives: 'The more you pursue these [hard-line] policies, the more you will pay for it,' " Wurmser says. "The more we keep the pressure up, the more impetus there will be for change."

Lifting sanctions unilaterally, on the other hand, would actually help the conservatives in Iran. "If you make a gesture like that, it will be interpreted by hard-liners as a sign of weakness," Kemp says. "The hard-liners will say that the West is afraid and doesn't have the will to fight."

The Clinton administration has steered a middle course in the sanctions debate. While it has not called for their unilateral removal, it has indicated a willingness to consider easing them in conjunction with appropriate Iranian gestures. "The Islamic Republic should consider parallel steps," said Secretary of State Madeleine K. Albright in a now famous speech before the Asia Society in New York on June 17. "If such a process can be initiated and sustained in a way that addresses the concerns of both sides, then we in the United States can see a very different relationship. As the wall of mistrust comes down, we can develop with the Islamic Republic, when it is ready, a road map leading to normal relations." [11]

In addition, the White House of late has shown no interest in stiffening restrictions against Iran, especially when third countries are involved. For instance, earlier this year the administration decided not to exercise its authority under the Iran-Libya Sanctions Act to punish a foreign consortium — made up of companies from France, Russia and Malaysia — that was investing in the development of an Iranian natural-gas field. President Clinton also vetoed legisla-

tion that would have imposed sanctions against foreign firms that provided missile technology to Iran. ■

BACKGROUND

The Revolution

Today's Iran is built on a number of foundations. The first is ancient Persia, a civilization that arose more than 2,500 years ago to conquer much of Central Asia and the Middle East. At one point, under Kings Darius the Great and Xerxes, Persia stretched from India's western border to Greece. Although the empire was shattered in the 4th century B.C.E. (before Common Era) by Alexander the Great, it created a culture and sense of nationhood that survives to this day.

Iran's second foundation is Islam, which was brought by Arab invaders in the 7th century C.E. But unlike 90 percent of the world's Muslims, who belong to the Sunni sect, most Iranians follow Shi'ism. Shi'ites broke away from the main body of Islam following a leadership struggle after the Prophet Mohammad's death. Although Shi'ism is not uniquely Iranian, most Shi'ites are from Iran.

In the centuries leading up to the revolution, Iran was ruled by a series of kings, or shahs, from a number of familial dynasties. The last (Pahlavi) was founded in 1925 by Reza Khan, an Iranian military leader who had seized power. In an effort to modernize Iran, he set about improving the country's social services and infrastructure and trying to restrict the influence of Islam in everyday life. [12]

During World War II, Reza Shah's German sympathies got him into trouble with the British and the Soviets, who removed him from power and placed his son Mohammad Reza Shah Pahlavi on the throne. After the war, the new shah adopted pro-Western policies, allying Iran with Britain and the United States. A 1953 attempt to remove the shah from power was turned back with U.S. help. [13]

Although oil had been discovered in Iran in 1908, the country's petroleum industry didn't fully blossom until the postwar era. By the 1960s, the shah was using much of the nation's oil revenue to finance another modernization drive. Women were given new rights as part of a broader effort to secularize and Westernize Iranian society. Money was lavished on programs to promote education, health care and employment. Agricultural land was confiscated from richer farmers and redistributed.

Over time, the policies, known as the "White Revolution," angered many in Iran. Clergymen and other religious people bristled at efforts to secularize society, particularly in areas such as education and the rights of women. Landowners fought agricultural reform, and merchants were unhappy with the heavy-handed way in which the shah micromanaged the economy. [14]

By the late 1960s, the opposition began to coalesce around Ayatollah Ruhollah Khomeini, a religious leader who had been exiled in 1964 for his outspoken opposition to the shah. From abroad, Khomeini decried secularization, but he did not call for the establishment of a theocracy, which would have scared off non-religious opposition to the shah. Instead, Khomeini argued that the role of the clergy was to provide the Iranian people and government with moral guidance. [15]

As the 1970s wore on, opposition to the shah's rule seeped into almost every segment of society. The shah

Ayatollah Ruhollah Khomeini

Betmann-UPI

alienated many by brutally repressing dissent, regardless of its intent or intensity. In 1976, mass protests around the country were harshly put down by government forces.

Less than two years later, in January 1978, an article attacking Khomeini's character in a government newspaper sparked a new round of demonstrations. Security forces killed protesters by the hundreds, but this time the crackdown backfired. As the weeks and months dragged on, the size, frequency and intensity of the demonstrations increased. By November the country was engulfed in strikes, and chaos reigned.

Hoping to restore credibility to his regime, the shah stepped down as leader of the government (while remaining as shah) and on Dec. 29 appointed opposition politician Shahpur Bakhtiar, as prime minister. But the move did nothing to placate the people.

On Jan. 16, 1979, the shah announced that he was leaving for Egypt on vacation and went into exile. On Feb. 1, Khomeini arrived back in Iran to a hero's welcome. Less than two weeks later, Bakhtiar re-

signed as prime minister and fled the country. On April 1, the Islamic Republic of Iran was born, becoming one of the world's only theocracies. The shah died the following year in Cairo, having never returned to Iran. [16]

Chaos and Crisis

A common foe can bind together many different segments of a society. But when the enemy is vanquished, the victors often take up or renew disparate agendas, turning allies into bitter rivals.

Such a situation plagued Iran in the months following the shah's departure. The most powerful faction in the new republic was the mullahs, who under Khomeini's leadership set about building a new Islamic society. Backed by the army and their loyal, well-trained militia, the Revolutionary Guards, the mullahs proceeded — efficiently and at times brutally — to eliminate other elements of the revolutionary coalition.

Liberal and more secular intellectuals, who had been at the forefront of the opposition to the shah, held many important posts in the early years of the republic, including its first post-shah prime minister, Mehdi Bazargan, and first popularly elected president, Abolhassan Bani-Sadr. But by 1981, both Bazargan and Bani-Sadr had been forced from office and were in exile. During the next two years, Khomeini and the other clerics consolidated power by violently suppressing opposition. The Revolutionary Guards imprisoned and executed thousands, from Marxists to merchants. Many of the victims had helped to overthrow the shah just a few years before.

The political maneuvering during the

Continued on p. 1108

Chronology

1900-1960
Iran is an authoritarian state ruled by shahs, or kings.

1925
Reza Khan, a military officer, seizes power and proclaims himself as shah.

1936
In his drive to Westernize Iran, the shah prohibits women from wearing the chador in public.

1941
The shah is forced to abdicate by the British and Soviets over his pro-German sympathies. His son Mohammad Reza Pahlavi becomes shah.

1953
The United States helps thwart an attempt to depose the shah.

1960s-1970s
Opposition to the shah's rule grows, culminating in the Islamic Revolution.

1961
The shah announces a plan to modernize the economy, known as the "White Revolution."

1963
Islamic clerics, led by Ayatollah Ruhollah Khomeini and wealthy landowners, oppose the White Revolution's call for land reform and expanded women's rights.

1964
Khomeini is exiled by the shah.

1976
Protests against the shah's rule are violently put down.

January 1979
The shah goes into exile in Egypt.

February 1979
Khomeini returns from exile.

April 1979
The Islamic Republic of Iran is proclaimed.

November 1979
Militant students, with government backing, occupy the U.S. Embassy and hold 54 Americans hostage.

1980-Present
After a decade of revolutionary fervor and war, the Islamic Republic slowly begins to moderate its policies.

January 1980
Abolhassan Bani-Sadr, a nonclerical intellectual, is elected the first president of the new republic.

September 1980
Iraq invades Iran, setting off an eight-year war that will claim the lives of up to a half-million Iranians.

Jan. 21, 1981
Iran releases the American hostages after 444 days in captivity.

June 22, 1981
Conservative clerics force Bani-Sadr from office. Hojatolislam Ali Khamenei becomes president.

1982
The Iranian army drives Iraqi troops out of Iran. An attempted invasion of Iraq succeeds at first but soon stalls, resulting in years of trench warfare.

1985
Khamenei is re-elected to a second term as president.

1986-7
At great human cost, Iran besieges the southern Iraqi city of Basra but does not succeed in capturing it.

1988
New defeats at the hands of the Iraqis force Khomenei. to agree to a cease-fire, ending the war.

February 1989
Ayatollah Khomeini condemns Salmon Rushdie to death for his novel *The Satanic Verses*.

June 1989
Khomeini dies and is replaced as the nation's spiritual leader by President Khamenei. The Speaker of Iran's parliament, Ali Akbar Hashemi Rafsanjani, replaces Khamenei as president.

1990
Iraq invades Kuwait, sparking the Persian Gulf War.

1993
Rafsanjani is re-elected as president, promising to reform the country's moribund economy.

1997
Mohammad Khatami is overwhelmingly elected president, defeating a conservative, government-supported cleric. He promises greater freedom and respect for the rule of law.

January 1998
Khatami appears on CNN and calls on Iran and the U.S. to "crack . . . the wall of mistrust."

Continued from p. 1106

republic's early years was influenced by a number of other events. In November 1979, less than a year after the shah's departure, militant students occupied the U.S. Embassy compound in Tehran and imprisoned all but nine of the 61 diplomats and others who had been inside at the time. The students, with the tacit support of Khomeini, held the Americans for 444 days. President Carter tried unsuccessfully to free the captives with a variety of carrots and sticks, including a botched military raid. They finally were released on Jan. 20, 1981, the day that Ronald Reagan was sworn in as the new president.

Inside Iran, the hostage crisis strengthened hard-liners at the expense of more moderate elements in the government. Before the embassy takeover, some Iranian officials had been trying to repair relations with the United States, which had been severely strained during the fall of the shah, a key, longtime American ally in the region. Now, in the midst of intense anti-American feeling, these officials and their policies were discredited. Other moderates who refused to support the students also became suspect. Many lost political power or were purged from government. [17]

The new Islamic Republic faced an even graver threat than the United States: a September 1980 invasion by Iraq. Iraqi documents captured by Iran indicate that Iraqi leader Saddam Hussein believed that the ensuing chaos and political infighting would allow him to easily topple the Islamic Republic. At first, his tactic seemed to be working. The well-equipped Iraqi army pushed into Iran, making great territorial gains. But the Iranians cobbled together an effective fighting force, including remnants of the shah's old army and huge numbers of militant volunteers, and succeeded in pushing Saddam back. [18]

After losing most of the territory he had conquered, the Iraqi leader withdrew his troops from Iran and de-

Friendly crowds surround Iran's supreme leader, Ayatollah Ali Khamenei, during a funeral procession in September 1998 for Iranian diplomats killed in Afghanistan.

(AP Photo/Pedram Sayyad)

clared a cease-fire. But the Iranians, flush with victory and bent on revenge, refused to consider ending the conflict. In July 1982, Khomeini launched his own invasion, vowing that the war would not end until Saddam had been driven from power. But the offensive soon ground to a halt. Despite high morale, the Iranian troops were unable to dislodge Iraq's army, with its superior firepower and well-fortified positions.

For the next four years, the conflict settled into a stalemate, with both sides fighting a costly war of attrition along a static line inside Iraq. The situation closely resembled the First World War, complete with miles of trenches, human-wave assaults and nerve-gas attacks. Iranian attempts to regain the offensive in 1986 and '87 near the southern Iraqi town of Basra failed in spite of courageous efforts by Iranian troops.

By early 1988, the Islamic Republic's military was a spent and demoralized force. Saddam's soldiers,

after years on the defensive, began pushing the Iranians back. By July, the Iraqis had recaptured almost all of the territory that had been lost in 1982 and prepared to re-invade Iran. At this stage, Khomeini agreed to a U.N.-brokered cease-fire. The conflict was finally over.

For Iran, the war was a disaster. Up to a half-million young men had died for no appreciable gain. The entire economy, and the oil industry in particular, were decimated by the years of missile and air attacks on the nation's oil wells and refineries.

Presidential Moderation

For Iran, 1989 was a year of political turmoil and change. In March, Khomeini forced his designated successor, Ayatollah Hussein Ali Montazeri, to resign. Montazeri was thought to be a social and economic moderate, and his ouster was interpreted in the West as a triumph for hard-liners.

A few months later, the 89-year-old Khomeini died, throwing the country into a state of panic and grief. Like India's Ghandi or Egypt's Nasser, Khomeini defined an entire era in his country. Many predicted that his death would lead to political infighting and even civil war.

But the transition to a post-Khomeini era went surprisingly smoothly. The day after the Ayatollah's death, President Ali Khamenei was chosen to succeed Khomeini as the nation's spiritual leader, a post he still holds. The Speaker of the Majlis, or parliament, Ali Akbar Hashemi Rafsanjani, replaced Khamenei as president. Rafsanjani was elected to the job in his own right in August. [19]

Throughout the next two years, Khamenei and Rafsanjani worked to consolidate their political power while at the same time trying to lift Iran's standard of living. Both men were more pragmatic than Khomeini and worked, with some success, to purge the government of its most radical elements. Meanwhile, Rafsanjani tried to jump-start Iran's economy by implementing a five-year plan aimed at redirecting state resources away from the military and toward reconstructing the country's war-shattered industrial infrastructure.

While the leaders focused on domestic issues, new challenges were emerging internationally. Since the 1988 cease-fire, Iran and Iraq had been slowly negotiating a formal end to the war. The process received a boost on Aug. 2, 1990, when Iraq invaded and occupied Kuwait. Within a week of the invasion, Saddam found himself facing the threat of military action from the United States, Western Europe and even Arab countries such as Egypt and Syria. With such a powerful coalition arrayed against him, Hussein moved to ease tensions with Iran by offering favor-

able terms in exchange for a quick peace settlement. Iran accepted, and on Sept. 10, the two countries re-established diplomatic relations. [20] Throughout the ensuing Persian Gulf War, Iran maintained strict neutrality, condemning Iraq for invading Kuwait and the U.S.-led coalition for trying to liberate it.

In 1993, Iranians returned to the polls to elect a president. The incumbent was heavily favored in spite of the fact that his five-year economic plan had done little to improve the lives of average Iranians. But with weak opponents and the machinery of government (including most media) firmly behind him, Rafsanjani coasted to victory with 63.2 percent of the vote. [21]

During his second four-year term, Rafsanjani attempted to push Iran's largely state-run and inefficient economy toward a more market-oriented model. He cut subsidies on a variety of essentials, like gasoline and food. But the move inflicted tremendous hardship on ordinary people, generating popular resentment toward the government. By the summer of 1994, Iran was experiencing outbreaks of rioting.

Amid growing tension, Rafsanjani faced new political challenges. As the government grew less and less popular, emboldened conservatives in parliament worked to stop the economic-reform program. Even the president's one-time ally, Khamenei, began to attack Rafsanjani and other more pragmatic officials in his administration. Not surprisingly, new reform initiatives were either watered down or shelved. By 1997, when a new president was to be chosen, many Iranians were completely disenchanted with the government, angry over everything from the price of rice to the continuing enforcement of social restrictions.

The leading candidate to replace Rafsanjani (who was limited to two

terms under the Iranian Constitution) was Ali Akbar Nateq-Noori, a conservative cleric and Speaker of parliament. Nateq-Noori had the support of the government, including Khamenei.

Nateq-Noori's primary challenger was Khatami. As a descendent of the Prophet Mohammad and former Cabinet minister under Rafsanjani, Khatami was most certainly an insider in Islamic Iran. But he was also, in a way, an outsider as well, having been forced by conservatives from his post as minister of culture for being too pro-Western. For many Iranians, Khatami's dismissal by the establishment was reason enough to vote for him. But he had other appealing qualities: He was charismatic and friendly looking, and he campaigned as an agent of change. He also had the backing of the still powerful Rafsanjani and his allies.

During the campaign, Khatami attracted huge, enthusiastic crowds. And on election day in May, he crushed Nateq-Noori, winning 70 percent of the vote. Conservatives also lost ground in the Majlis, where they had previously had a comfortable majority. ■

CURRENT SITUATION

Changing Society

Iran's leadership is made up of veterans of the Islamic revolution. And yet, there are signs that the country is becoming a somewhat freer, more open society. Many of the strictures of the Islamic Republic are still in place, but they are enforced less rigorously or even, in a few cases, ignored.

"The regime is running behind the people, trying to catch up," says Nafisi of Johns Hopkins. "Iran is really a modern society controlled by a reactionary, fundamentalist government, and that's becoming increasingly more evident as time passes."

For instance, public religious fervor, once the hallmark of revolutionary Iran, has decreased dramatically in the last decade. "People now refrain from public displays of religion," Baktiari says. "Mosque attendance in Iran has really dropped off." Instead, Baktiari and others say, religion has become much more of a private activity.

Attitudes toward public morality also are slowly changing. It is still forbidden for unmarried couples to dance or hold hands in public. Women must cover their heads and legs, and in many public places, including schools and buses, they are segregated from men. And Iran's guardians of public morality, the Islamic Revolutionary Committees, still patrol the streets trying to prevent improper behavior. But young people are skirting or even flouting the rules with greater frequency. "There are parties where women dress like they do in the West, with makeup and skirts, and there is drinking and dancing," Nafisi says, adding that when representatives from the Revolutionary Committees show up, "you just bribe them to leave you alone."

Changes have come in the cultural realm as well. Iran now has a much livelier press than it once did, with newspapers and magazines representing different points of view. And television, once a drab collection of state-run channels, has begun adding soap operas and other Western-style shows to its usual lineup of religious programming. Some channels have even aired American films, such as "Dances with Wolves" and "Robocop." [22]

But Iranians don't need broadcast television to see American movies. Thanks to the Internet and video-cassette recorder (VCR), the country is awash in Western culture. Illegally imported videotapes as well as Western music, books and other cultural fare are readily available. A growing number of Iranians also have defied the ban on satellite dishes and are picking up an array of international television stations. "The Iranians love everything to do with the West, and America in particular," Wurmser says. "They think that anything that comes from the United States must be good, certainly better than what the regime offers."

The love of all things American may seem strange in a country where the United States is often derided as "the Great Satan." But, Iran-watchers explain, the urge to replace the mosque with MTV is largely due to the relative youth of Iranian society. "You have to understand that the majority of people are under 25 and don't remember the revolution or Khomeini or the shah," Nafisi says. "To them, everything good comes from abroad, especially the United States."

Economic Troubles

Like many countries in the Middle East, Iran is heavily dependent on oil. Petroleum generates some 80 percent of the nation's export earnings and accounts for about 17 percent of the GDP. [23]

When the price of oil was high, as it was in the 1970s, waste and corruption mitigated the positive impact of petroleum profits. Nonetheless, government-sponsored industrial development and infrastructure projects helped modernize the country and create jobs. [24] But the last few years

have not been kind to oil exporters. Energy prices are at their lowest level in years, and Iran is strapped for cash at a time when unemployment is rising and living standards, already low, are dropping. "They're in terrible shape because of the price drop," Baktiari says.

Unlike other countries, Iran is not able to make up the revenue shortfall by increasing oil output. Although Iran's proven petroleum reserves — estimated at 93 billion barrels — are on a par with big producers like the United Arab Emirates, its pumping capacity has been diminished. For instance, in 1997, Iran pumped 3.6 billion barrels of oil, much less than the 5.7 billion barrels produced in 1978, the last year of the shah's reign. [25]

Much of Iran's oil industry was destroyed during the 1980-88 Iran-Iraq War, when both countries targeted each other's wells, pipelines and refineries. After the war, Iran restored some of its oil-producing capacity, but the rebound has been hampered by a lack of funds and skilled labor. Moreover, outside oil companies have been reluctant to help the country rebuild its energy sector, given Iran's shaky relations with the United States and, at times, even Europe.

Similarly, Iran has had trouble capitalizing on its vast natural gas deposits. As with oil, shortages of money and technical expertise have stymied Iran's efforts to extract and export its gas — the second-largest proven reserves in the world after Russia. Currently, only a tiny amount of gas is exported; almost all is used for domestic consumption.

As the all-important energy sector sags, so does the rest of Iran's economy. Economic growth slowed from 3.2 percent last year to an estimated 2 percent in 1998. Such growth rates are normal, even healthy in the developed world. But in developing countries like Iran, a 2 percent

Soldiers guard the border between Iraq and Iran. In September, for the first time since the 1980-88 Iran-Iraq War, Iraqi President Saddam Hussein said Iranians could visit holy shrines in Iraq.

increase in GDP does not translate into a rise in the standard of living. For instance, economists estimate that to provide enough jobs to those entering the labor force and keep the unemployment rate from rising, Iran's economy must grow at 6 percent a year. [26]

Meanwhile, the jobless rate is already very high, estimated at 13 percent by the government and at up to 20 percent by outside economists. [27] And Iran's demographics are likely to make the situation even worse. Almost half the country's 67 million people were born after the 1979 revolution, meaning that an inordinately large number of young people will enter adulthood and the

labor market in the coming years. "Since Iran has 37 million young people under 25 years of age, the country is going to experience a 100 percent increase in unemployment," said Ali Reza Mahjub, secretary-general of the Union of Workers earlier this year. [28]

Economic problems have dramatically increased the demand for hard currency. As a result, Iran's currency, the *rial*, has fallen in value against the dollar, which in turn has led to a rise in consumer prices for many goods and services. According to Deputy Finance Minister Morteza Qarah-Baqian, average monthly family income has dropped to $70 dollars, while the cost of living is $160. [29]

But ordinary people are not the only ones feeling the pinch. Indeed, the government is said to be teetering on the edge of bankruptcy due to falling oil prices and general mismanagement. It has already borrowed heavily — including taking advances on future oil sales — and owes $6.3 billion, or about one-third of its annual budget. As a result, the government is having difficulty meeting its obligations. [30] "It is so bad that they did not even pay the government workers in October," Milani says.

In August, President Khatami announced plans to restructure Iran's economy with the aim of creating a more market-oriented system. A cornerstone of the plan is a proposal to privatize 6,000 state-owned com-

Iranian exiles who support the anti-government National Council for Resistance protest during President Mohammad Khatami's visit to the United Nations in September 1998.

(Reuters/John Levy)

by the government and making it easier for foreigners to repatriate profits.

Khatami's attempts at economic liberalization are expected to run into great opposition. For one thing, privatizing state industries would almost certainly lead to massive job cuts, which in turn would strengthen Khatami's conservative opponents and possibly provoke widespread social unrest.

Yet as the Nixon Center's Kemp recently wrote, "without economic reform, the economy is likely to deteriorate further which, in turn, will produce further domestic frustration, instability and political violence." [31]

Khatami's plan faces yet another problem, according to Baktiari. Even if reforms were embraced, he says, the Iranian government could very well botch the effort. "There is this huge, corrupt, inefficient bureaucracy that is really incapable of responding to a crisis with competence or vision," he says. ∎

OUTLOOK

'Everything Is Possible'

The old Persian saying, "Everything is difficult, but everything is possible," might well describe U.S.-Iranian relations today. Difficult hurdles must be overcome before normalizing relations can even be contemplated. But, for the first time in almost two decades, there is the possibility that progress can be made.

"I think there will be an end to hostilities and the beginnings of normal relations because I think Iran is ready for a real dialogue with the

panies by offering stock to workers. Since Iran's economy is largely government-owned — less than 20 percent of the GDP is generated by the private sector — a sell-off would

amount to a huge transfer of wealth. Khatami also wants to create a friendlier environment for foreign investment by lowering taxes, instituting protections against nationalizations

Continued on p. 1114

At Issue:

Should the United States consider easing or lifting the economic sanctions against Iran?

Rep. Lee H. Hamilton, D-Ind.

From a speech before the Council on Foreign Relations, April 15, 1998.

i believe we need to begin a policy of engagement with Iran. It will not be easy, and it will take time to produce results, but I am persuaded that such a policy serves the American national interest far better than our current posture of containment and isolation. The challenge is to find ways to begin talking with Iran, without preconditions, so that we can begin to address the many issues that divide us. . . .

Current U.S. policy is straightforward: to contain Iran because of its opposition to the Middle East peace process, its support for terrorism and its development of weapons of mass destruction. Supporters of that policy point to certain accomplishments: Iran's revolution has not spread; the Gulf is stable, and oil continues to flow out of it; Iran's economy is in trouble; foreign investment in Iran has slowed; and arms purchases and oil production by Iran are less than Iran intended.

But no one who looks at U.S. policy toward Iran since 1979 can be satisfied with this situation. Our central problems with Iran's foreign policy remain unaddressed. Our policy has been static. Our animosity toward Iran is as deeply ingrained as is Iran's animosity toward us. . . .

We want a government-to-government dialogue with Iran, but, over the years, we have been unwilling to take steps to help make that dialogue happen. We want Iran to change its policies, but we have been unwilling to pursue a strategy likely to promote changes in those Iranian policies that threaten our interests. . . .

[A] major step in U.S.-Iran relations must be to pursue an economic opening. The prime obstacle is the president's own Executive Order banning trade with Iran. The United States should signal to Iran that, once an authoritative dialogue begins and progress is made, the United States is prepared to ease that Executive Order, step-by-step.

A first step — a step we should take soon — is to license U.S. companies to resume discussions in Iran. Right now, U.S. firms — especially energy firms — are falling behind not only in the Iran market, but in efforts to develop Caspian energy resources. U.S. firms are penalized because they can't even hold talks with their Iranian counterparts. Third countries are sewing up contracts and markets from which we have excluded ourselves.

We should not treat U.S. firms worse than we treat foreign firms. We should allow U.S. firms to talk to Iran, so the can be ready to go — if and when U.S. sanctions against Iran are lifted.

Martin S. Indyk

Assistant Secretary of State for Near Eastern Affairs

From testimony before the Senate Foreign Relations Subcommittee on Near Eastern and South Asian Affairs, May 14, 1998.

u .S. concerns regarding some aspects of Iranian foreign policy practices remain intact, as does our determination to effectively address them. As the department's recently published annual report on terrorism made clear, Iran continues to be the most active state sponsor of terrorism. Throughout 1997, Iran continued to train and equip known terrorist groups . . . and to support their violent opposition to the Middle East peace process. . . .

The Iranian regime still seeks to project its regional influence through a conventional military buildup and through the development of weapons of mass destruction and advanced missile systems. Iran continues to pursue nuclear technologies, chemical and biological weapons components and production materials. Iran's acquisition of ever-more sophisticated missile technology presents an increasing threat to our friends and allies as well as our own military presence in the Gulf. In particular, Iran's pursuit of an indigenous capability to produce long-range ballistic missiles poses a threat to the stability of the Middle East, a region of vital interest to the United States.

The international community remains deeply concerned by Iran's human rights record. While the Special Representative has documented some progress, particularly in the area of freedom of speech, the U.N. High Commission on Human Rights once again this year adopted a resolution expressing concern regarding continuing human rights abuses such as severe restriction on freedom of religion and the use of brutal and inhuman punishments such as stoning, and the use of the death penalty for non-violent offenses. . . .

We continue to apply unilateral economic pressure on Iran to make the point that there is a price to be paid for pursuing policies which violate international norms: Unilateral sanctions have proven costly to U.S. business. However, we believe that Iran poses threats so significant that we have no choice but to accept these costs. Economic pressure has an important role in our efforts to convince Iran to cease its efforts to acquire weapons of mass destruction and missiles and to support terrorism. . . .

Our basic purpose is to persuade Iran that it cannot have it both ways: It cannot benefit from participation in the international community while at the same time going around threatening the interests of its member states. That it cannot improve its relations and standing in the West and in the Middle East while at the same time pursuing policies that threaten the peace and stability of a vital region.

Continued from p. 1112

United States," says the University of Florida's Milani.

But, Milani warns, the Americans must make the next move. "Khatami has already taken the first step by calling for a dialogue between peoples," Milani says, "and he has gotten nothing in return for it, just words." Milani argues that Khatami cannot move too far too fast because of hard-line opposition at home. "He needs something to show for his efforts," he says, like the lifting of some sanctions.

Others take a more guarded view. "I'm optimistic that the level of dialogue will improve — fewer harsh words, fewer burned flags," Baktiari says. "But as far as real policy is concerned, I don't think either president is in a position to take concrete steps forward because neither Clinton nor Khatami have anything to gain by making a serious move."

Baktiari argues that the woeful state of Iran's economy will force Khatami to expend his political capital on domestic reforms. As for Clinton, he says, gestures toward the Islamic Republic would "cost him support among [American] Jewish voters," an important constituency for the Democratic president.

Others are even more pessimistic, arguing that Khatami really isn't interested in making the kinds of changes that would be necessary to build a lasting relationship with the United States. "He's found a much better way to express traditional Iranian policy by repackaging the old message and presenting it as new thinking," says Clawson of the Washington Institute for Near East Policy.

In essence, Clawson argues, Khatami is taking advantage of what he senses is an American yearning to improve relations.

The official from the Washington Jewish organization agrees with Clawson that Iran and the United

FOR MORE INFORMATION

Middle East Institute, 1761 N St., N.W., Washington, D.C. 20036; (202) 785-1141; www.mideasti.org/mei. Conducts research and holds conferences on issues of import in the Middle East.

The Nixon Center, 1615 L St., N.W. Suite 1250, Washington, D.C. 20036; (202) 887-1000. The center conducts research on foreign policy issues through the prism of American national interest.

Washington Institute for Near East Policy, 1828 L St., N.W. Suite 1050, Washington, D.C. 20036; (202) 452-0650; www.washingtoninstitute.org. The institute conducts research and provides information on the Near East with the aim of improving American policy in the region.

States won't reach accommodation any time soon. "All of these academics listen to Khatami, and they're full of hope, thinking wonderful things are going to happen," the official says. "But words are not actions, and if you look at Iran's policy on issues like terrorism or weapons [development], there's no real change." ∎

Notes

[1] Quoted on "CNN Today," Feb. 25, 1998.

[2] Quoted in *Ibid*.

[3] Thomas Omestad, "Wrestling with Tehran," *U.S. News & World Report*, March 2, 1998.

[4] Quoted in Ibid.

[5] Quoted in Barbara Slavin, "Iranian Leader Extends a Hand," *USA Today*, Jan. 8, 1998.

[6] For background, see Mary H. Cooper, "Economic Sanctions," *The CQ Researcher*, Oct. 28, 1994, pp. 937-960.

[7] Robin Wright and Shaul Bakhash, "The U.S. and Iran: An Offer They Can't Refuse?" *Foreign Policy*, fall 1997.

[8] John Lancaster, "Barbie, 'Titanic' Show Good Side of 'Great Satan,'" *The Washington Post*, Oct. 27, 1998.

[9] Miles Pomper, "Warmer U.S.-Iranian Relations Get Cold Shoulder in Congress," *CQ Weekly*, May 16, 1998, pp. 1321-1323.

[10] *Ibid*.

[11] Quoted in Barbara Crossette, "Albright, in Overture to Iran, Seeks a 'Road Map' to Amity," *The New York Times*, June 18, 1998.

[12] Sandra Mackey, *The Iranians: Persia, Islam and the Soul of a Nation* (1998), p. 170.

[13] *Ibid*, pp. 202-207.

[14] *Ibid*. pp. 220-230.

[15] Daniel C. Diller (ed.), *The Middle East* (1994), p. 216.

[16] *Ibid*. p. 217.

[17] *Ibid*. p. 219.

[18] *Ibid*. p. 220. For background on Iraq, see Patrick G. Marshall, "Calculating the Costs of the Gulf War," *Editorial Research Reports*, March 15, 1991, pp. 145-168, and Mary H. Cooper, "Chemical and Biological Weapons," *The CQ Researcher*, Jan. 31, 1997, pp. 84-107.

[19] Mackey, *op. cit.*, pp. 356-359.

[20] Diller, *op. cit.*, p. 223.

[21] *Ibid*., p. 224.

[22] Lancaster, *op. cit.*

[23] Patrick Clawson, Michael Eisenstadt, Eliyahu Kanovsky and David Menashri, "Iran Under Khatami: A Political, Economic, and Military Assessment," Washington Institute for Near East Policy, 1998, p. 54.

[24] *Ibid*., p. 55.

[25] *Ibid*.

[26] Robin Wright, "Iran's Khatami Fosters Climate of Change," *Los Angeles Times*, May 27, 1998.

[27] *Ibid*.

[28] Quoted in *Ibid*.

[29] "Iran's Economic Crisis Deepens as Government Gropes for Stable Policy," Agence France Presse, Nov. 13, 1998.

[30] *Ibid*.

[31] Geoffrey Kemp, "America and Iran: Road Maps and Realism," The Nixon Center, 1998, p. 31.

Bibliography

Selected Sources Used

Books

Diller, Daniel (ed.), *The Middle East*, Congressional Quarterly Press (1994).

A slightly dated but still useful guide to the politics and culture of the Middle East. The chapter on Iran contains particularly useful information on the country in the 20th century.

Mackey, Sandra, *The Iranians: Persia, Islam and the Soul of a Nation*, Plume Press (1998).

Mackey, an Atlanta-based expert on the Middle East, provides an in-depth look at the Iran of yesterday and today, going back to ancient Persia in exploring the roots of Iranian culture. Her chapters on the Pahlavis are particularly clear and insightful. The 1998 edition (the book was originally published in 1996) contains an additional chapter on recent events in Iran, including the election of President Khatami.

Articles

Jehl, Douglas, "Iranians Still Warily Await Reforms They Voted For," *The New York Times*, Oct. 11, 1997.

Jehl examines the expectations of the Iranians who voted for and support President Khatami.

Lancaster, John, "Barbie, 'Titanic,' Show Good Side of 'Great Satan,'" *The Washington Post*, Oct. 27, 1998.

Lancaster details the impact of Western culture — but particularly the United States — on Iran. He observes that ordinary Iranians love all things American, from movies and music to computers and other high-tech gadgets.

Omestad, Thomas, "Wrestling with Tehran," *U.S. News & World Report*, March 2, 1998.

Omestad examines how sporting events and other opportunities for cultural contact are beginning to melt the usually icy relations between the United States and the Islamic Republic.

Perkovich, George, "In Iran, Whispers of Moderation," *The Washington Post*, Nov. 30, 1997.

Perkovich details a growing sense in Iran, especially among intellectuals, that the country is entering a period that will be characterized by moderation and a striving for normalcy.

Pomper, Miles, "Warmer U.S.-Iranian Relations Get Cold Shoulder in Congress," *CQ Weekly*, May 16, 1998.

Pomper examines the debate within the United States over its relations with Iran, focusing on the strong opposition from Capitol Hill to the Clinton administration's efforts to foster greater dialogue with the Iranians.

Sciolino, Elaine, "The Post-Khomeini Generation," *The New York Times*, Nov. 1, 1998.

Sciolino focuses on the hopes of young Iranians, who make up the majority of the nation's population. She concludes that "while not rebelling outright, [the young] reject the stern restrictions of the Islamic Republic and demand more freedom and prosperity."

Wright, Robin, "Iran Says U.S. is Imperiling Move Toward Rapprochement," *Los Angeles Times*, May 5, 1998.

Wright details the trip-wires and mines on the path toward better relations between the U.S. and Iran.

Wright, Robin, and Shaul Bakhash, "The U.S. and Iran: An Offer They Can't Refuse," *Foreign Policy, fall*, 1997.

Wright and Bakhash, a reporter for the *Los Angeles Times* and a professor of history at George Mason University, respectively, appraise the opportunities presented to Iran and the United States by the election of President Khatami. They argue that Khatami must make gestures on human rights and other issues and that Washington "must be alert to these shifts and help to accelerate them by responding appropriately."

Reports and Studies

Clawson, Patrick, Michael Eisenstadt, Eliyahu Kanovsky and David Menashri, "Iran and Khatami: A Political, Economic, and Military Assessment," The Washington Institute for Near East Policy, 1998.

This is a good geopolitical assessment of Iran today. In particular, Kanovsky, a professor of economics at Bar Ilan University in Israel, offers a lucid analysis of Iran's grave economic problems.

Kemp, Geoffrey, "America and Iran: Road Maps and Realism," The Nixon Center, 1998.

Kemp, director of regional strategic programs at the Nixon Center, takes a close look at U.S.-Iran relations. He is not very optimistic about the short-term prospects for better relations. "So long as there is domestic turmoil in Tehran and a pervasive anti-Iranian sentiment in the U.S. Congress, neither Khatami nor Clinton can go much further than they have today in improving relations," he writes.

The Next Step

Additional information from UMI's Newspaper & Periodical Abstracts™ database

Ayatollah Ali Khamenei

Hirst, David, "Khamenei Calls for Trial of Rival," *The Guardian*, Nov. 27, 1997, p. 16.

Iran's supreme leader, Ayatollah Ali Khamenei, yesterday urged that Grand Ayatollah Hussein Ali Montazeri, an influential opponent widely regarded as the "conscience" of the Islamic Revolution, stand trial for treason. It is a dangerous move in a power struggle between Khamenei, with his conservative clerical establishment, and the Islamic Republic's liberals, who look to the new president, Mohammad Khatami, as their champion. Khamenei said on state television he had "nothing personal" against Montazeri, a 75-year-old former pupil and companion of the late Ayatollah Khomeini. All he was doing was "defending the status of the Velayat e-Faqih," the guardianship of Islamic jurisprudence.

Lancaster, John, "Iranian Cleric Disputes Ayatollah's Right to Rule; Dissident's Challenge of Khamenei on Religious Grounds Stirs Violence, Demonstrations," *The Washington Post*, Dec. 23, 1997, p. A10.

Never far from the surface in Iran, the debate over the role of religion in politics erupted last month into public view, when a leading dissident cleric, Ayatollah Hossein Ali Montazeri, openly questioned the legitimacy of Iran's supreme leader, Ayatollah Ali Khamenei. In a speech to followers, which was reproduced on leaflets and widely distributed, Montazeri suggested that Khamenei is insufficiently qualified for his post. Even more audaciously, he seemed to question the basis of Iran's theocratic government, a system known as velayat-e faqih, a form of individual rule based on Islamic jurisprudence. Khamenei's hard-line backers reacted with fury, giving a green light to thugs who ransacked Montazeri's home and office and orchestrating a week-long series of pro-Khamenei demonstrations around the nation.

Wright, Robin, "Iran Leader Vows to Resist U.S. Reconciliation; Mideast: Ayatollah Ali Khamenei's Vehemence Alarms Washington," *Los Angeles Times*, Nov. 7, 1997, p. A12.

Iran's supreme leader, Ayatollah Ali Khamenei, has given his toughest anti-American speech in years, vehemently condemning rapprochement with the United States in an attempt to halt the growing policy debate on the issue within the new Iranian government. Khamenei, in a speech Wednesday to Iranian students, declared that the nation's "destiny" now depends on resisting recent suggestions that Iran change its long-standing policy toward the United States.

Economic Sanctions

Balz, Dan, "U.S. Eases Stand on Cuba, Iran Sanctions; Helms Condemns, Europe Hails Move," *The Washington Post*, May 19, 1998, p. A15.

The United States and European nations today settled festering trade disputes over U.S. sanctions against foreign companies doing business in Cuba, Iran and Libya. The accords, announced in London, affect the controversial Helms-Burton Act, which requires U.S. sanctions against foreign firms that make use of confiscated property in Cuba, and the Iran-Libya Sanctions Act, which is designed to punish Iran and Libya for sponsoring terrorism. As part of the accord on Iran-Libya sanctions, the Clinton administration agreed not to impose economic sanctions on three major foreign energy companies that have signed a contract to develop an offshore gas field in Iran.

Greenberger, Robert S., "U.S. Sees Limits to Economic Sanctions — Major Changes Are Expected, Though Probably Not This Year," *The Wall Street Journal*, Sept. 9, 1998, p. A2.

With President Clinton weakened by scandal and about a month left before Congress adjourns, prospects have dimmed for quick passage of legislation limiting the use of economic sanctions in foreign policy. But lawmakers from both parties, under pressure from U.S. business interests, believe that in the long run, major changes in U.S. sanctions policy are all but inevitable.

Griffin, Jennifer, and David Makovsky, "Tehran Takes Aim," *U.S. News & World Report*, May 6, 1996, pp. 49-50.

U.S. officials are blaming Iran for provoking the latest round of Middle East hostilities, but domestic problems are tempering Iran's ability to make trouble abroad. The country's social and economic problems are discussed.

Lippman, Thomas W., "U.S. Rethinking Economic Sanctions; State Department Team Weighs Costs, Impact of Trade Restrictions," *The Washington Post*, Jan. 26, 1998, p. A6.

Lucio A. Noto, the outspoken chairman of Mobil Corp., warned President Clinton a few months ago that the United

States "will lose strategically and economically" if the U.S. embargo on trade with Iran limits the ability of American firms to explore for oil in the Persian Gulf and Caspian Sea while foreign competitors have free rein. According to senior officials, the proliferating use of economic sanctions as a foreign policy tool is creating regulatory chaos, confusion about objectives, strains in relations with allies and sometimes counterproductive responses often without achieving the purpose for which the sanctions were designed.

"Road Map: Route to Better Relations with Iran Worth Studying," *Houston Chronicle*, July 15, 1998, p. A24.

In June, Secretary of State Madeleine K. Albright invited the government of Iran to join with the United States in drawing up a road map to a resumption of normal diplomatic relations. Iran's ruling mullahs quickly rejected the overture, but Rice University's Baker Institute has provided some useful directions for the route the United States might take.

In a report on Iran and its strategic role in the Persian Gulf, the James A. Baker III Institute for Public Policy recommends that the U.S. government take a more "nuanced and sophisticated" approach toward Iran.

Wright, Robin, "U.S. Expected to Waive Sanctions for Iran Trade," *Los Angeles Times*, May 15, 1998, p. A1.

To signal interest in rapprochement with Iran and to avert a trade war with Europe, President Clinton is likely to announce within days that the United States will waive economic sanctions against a Russian, French and Malaysian consortium for the biggest foreign investment in Iran since its 1979 revolution, according to U.S. and European officials. But the Clinton administration is now seeking a course that would coordinate Iran policy with Europe, prevent new friction with Russia and send a tangible message to the new, reformist government in Tehran that Washington genuinely seeks better relations, European officials say.

Iran-Iraq War

Daniel, Ben A., "New Iraq-Iran War May be Brewing," *Chicago Tribune*, Dec. 15, 1993, p. 22.

In a letter to the editor, Daniel, of the Assyrian Guardian, responds to an article published in the Tribune on Nov. 13, 1993. Daniel says that Iranian President Hashemi Rafsanjani's actions indicate that a new war with Iraq may be brewing.

Peterson, Scott, "Iran Hears Echoes of a 'Sacred' War; A Decade of Brutal Conflict with Iraq Shaped Iran's Relations with Other Islamic States, and West," *The Christian Science Monitor*, Oct. 2, 1998, p. 1.

Ali Zakani told of the spiritual and ideological import of the Iran-Iraq War of the 1980s — a conflict that for some Iranians sparked a revolutionary zeal and a commitment to Islam that has only increased over time.

"We didn't enter the battlefield to become martyrs, only to defend Islam and the revolution," says the bearded Zakani. "But we knew that if we died, we were going to be martyrs, and that was important to us," he says. "So we would have victory either way."

Peterson, Scott, "Iran, Iraq: Old Foes Warm Up; POW Exchange Began Over the Weekend," *The Christian Science Monitor*, April 6, 1998, p. 1.

Iraq and Iran are taking their first cautious steps toward rapprochement. Iraqis and diplomats say that there are mutual tactical reasons now for detente between the two giants of the Persian Gulf. At the moment, some 6,000 Iraqi prisoners of war are being released by Iran, most after more than a decade in captivity. But with more than 1 million from both sides killed in the war, the list of differences is long and likely to prevent any strategic alliance.

Struck, Doug, "POWs' Story a Reminder of the Brutal Iran-Iraq War," *The Washington Post*, April 12, 1998, p. A22.

The recent return of almost 6,000 Iraqi prisoners of the Iran-Iraq war evoked sharp memories here of the brutal war that saw an eight-year stream of taxis returning from the front with coffins tied to their roofs. Those casualties were a powerful anesthesia for mercy, a justification for keeping these prisoners for a decade after the war ended. The war was an inconclusive draw. Two years later, Iraqi President Saddam Hussein turned his guns toward Kuwait. In the international isolation that followed the Persian Gulf War, Iraq is seeking to improve relations with Iran.

Hashemi Rafsanjani

"An Interview with President Hashemi Rafsanjani of Iran," *CNN Specials*, July 2, 1995.

In a rare interview, Iranian President Hashemi Rafsanjani discusses his nation's military intentions.

"Rafsanjani's Complaint," *The Boston Globe*, June 9, 1994, p. 18.

Reflecting on Iranian President Hashemi Rafsanjani's accusation that the United States reneged on an agreement to release frozen Iranian assets for hostages, an editorial encourages the Clinton administration to avoid making any new deals with the "clerical despots in Tehran."

Hirst, David, "Rafsanjani Undermined in Defiance," ***The Guardian*, May 11, 1995, p. 13.**

The effects that the United States' trade and investment ban on Iran has had on the country's government are examined. Iranian President Ali Akbar Hashemi Rafsanjani has adopted an anti-American tone that is indistinguishable from his main political rivals.

Nader, George A., "From Tehran to Waco: Rafsanjani Talks Tough on Clinton, Rushdie and the Rights of Branch Davidians," ***The Washington Post*, July 9, 1995, p. C3.**

Excerpts from an interview with Iranian President Ali Akbar Hashemi Rafsanjani on a full range of issues at stake in the U.S.-Iran impasse. Rafsanjani stated that President Clinton's trade embargo would hurt only America and accused the United States of ignoring human rights violations in the Waco siege.

Oil and the Iranian Economy

Bahree, Bhushan, and Steve Liesman, "OPEC Appears Unable to Support Prices — On Eve of Crucial Meeting, Iran and Saudi Arabia Develop a Fresh Row," ***The Wall Street Journal*, Nov. 25, 1998, p. A2.**

On the eve of one of its most crucial meetings in recent memory, the Organization of Petroleum Exporting Countries (OPEC) appears unable to act to keep oil prices from a potential free fall. Ministers were meeting late into the night yesterday to find some way to prop up prices, which are hovering just above 12-year lows.

But further production cuts appear unlikely when ministers meet today, and it appears possible that the oil producers will leave Vienna without an agreement even to extend existing output cuts through the end of 1999.

Among OPEC's other considerable troubles, a fresh row erupted between Saudi Arabia and Iran, the group's two largest producers, which are now at odds over which of the two should cut output further to stop the oil-price slide.

Feld, Lowell, and Douglas MacIntyre, "OPEC Nations Grappling with Plunge in Oil Export Revenues," ***Oil & Gas Journal*, Sept. 21, 1998, pp. 29-35.**

Oil-export revenues for OPEC members are expected to drop in 1998 to $80.5 billion, the lowest level since 1972 and less than a fifth of the peak revenue year of 1980.

Ijaz, Mansoor, "Islamic Unity, Oil Clout: A One-Two Punch," ***The Christian Science Monitor*, Dec. 17, 1997, p. 19.**

The air of reconciliation at last week's world Islamic conference in Tehran should serve as a wake-up call for the West. The show of Islamic unity — led by Saudi Arabia, leader of the world's Sunni Muslims, and Iran, leader of the world's Shi'ite Muslims — may have direct implications for American economic and national security interests that are not being adequately considered. Until now, Persian Gulf states have shown little interest in any greater geo-strategic consideration than selfish maneuvering for market share.

Knott, David, "OPEC at the Crossroads with Non-OPEC Nations," ***Oil & Gas Journal*, June 15, 1998, pp. 19-25.**

The next OPEC meeting in Vienna on June 24 is a potential watershed; if OPEC's energy ministers come up with an agreement that pleases the markets, crude oil prices will likely be shored up after months of uncertainty. If the wrong call is made, however, prices could continue drifting down slowly or even plummet.

Persian Gulf War

Quinn, Mary Ellen, "Encyclopedia of the Persian Gulf War," ***Booklist*, Sept. 15, 1998, p. 262.**

The author reviews the *Encyclopedia of the Persian Gulf War* by Richard A. Schwartz.

Cushman, John H. Jr., "Pentagon Report on Persian Gulf War: A Few Surprises and Some Silences," ***The New York Times*, April 11, 1992, p. A4.**

The Pentagon issued a report to Congress on April 10, 1992, about the Persian Gulf War. It indicates that before the war began, the U.S. command anticipated that allied casualties may reach 10 percent of ground forces, or upwards of 10,000 soldiers. The report also credits the victory partly to high-technology weapons. Other details of the report are examined.

Jeffrey, Nancy Ann, "Persian Gulf War: One Year Later — Reserves Still Find Enough Recruits," ***Detroit News & Free Press*, Jan. 12, 1992, p. F5.**

Michigan recruiters say the Persian Gulf War didn't scare away potential recruits or veteran soldiers; the success of Operation Desert Storm and the poor economy and employment outlook have prompted many skilled people to join the reserves.

McAllister, Bill, "1991 Increase in Terrorism Reported: State Department Attributes 22 Percent Rise to the Persian Gulf War," ***The Washington Post*, May 1, 1992, p. A24.**

International terrorism incidents jumped 22 percent in

1991, largely because of ineffective acts linked to the Persian Gulf War.

President Muhammad Khatami

"Iran's President Khatami Calls for Investment by the United States," *The Wall Street Journal,* **Sept. 23, 1998, p. A19.**

Iranian President Mohammad Khatami called for U.S. investment in Iran but said his government remains cautious about improving ties with Washington. Khatami, who addressed the United Nations General Assembly on Monday, told reporters he sensed a more positive U.S. tone toward Iran but that it wasn't enough to improve formal ties.

Bloomfield, Lincoln P. Jr., "President Khatami's Discourse With the American People," *The Christian Science Monitor,* **Oct. 8, 1998, p. 11.**

The author comments on Iranian President Muhammad Khatami's overtures to the United States.

Darwish, Adel, "Iran at the Crossroads," Middle East, July 1998, pp. 4-6.

Hardliners in Iran, critical of what they interpret as a softening attitude by the Islamic Republic toward Western powers, have forced a showdown with President Khatami in the hope of sabotaging his rapprochement with the West.

Marcus, David L., "Iran's President Offers Americans Friendship," *The Boston Globe,* **Jan. 8, 1998, p. A1.**

President Mohammed Khatami of Iran publicly extended a hand of friendship to Americans yesterday, a move that could prompt Washington to reconsider its Persian Gulf policy. In a first for an Iranian official,

Khatami also issued a lukewarm apology for the 1979 hostage crisis that led the United States to break relations with Iran. The comments, the boldest move by an Iranian leader in two decades to bring a rapprochement with Washington, were made after Khatami had made several remarks in recent months to distance himself from hard-line clerics in Iran who call America the "great Satan."

Peterson, Scott, "Power Struggle in Iran Clouds View for U.S. Policymakers As President Khatami Tries to Leverage his Mandate for Reform, Hard-Line Clerics Offer Deep-Rooted Resistance," *The Christian Science Monitor,* **Oct. 16, 1998, p. 7.**

During these days of conflict between reform and hard-line clerics in the Islamic Republic — which is still singled out by the U.S. State Department as the "most active" state sponsor of terrorism — seeing through the "impenetrable shroud" is reminiscent of the Cold War days of Kremlinology. Iran is not a rival superpower sitting atop a nuclear arsenal. But as Iran asserts its strategic importance in a volatile region, and looms as a natural conduit for Caspian oil riches, understanding its mysterious ways of rule becomes crucial. No one can even say whether moderate President Mohammad Khatami is winning his drive to end Iran's isolation and restore what he calls a "civil society" to Iran, or whether conservatives are successfully thwarting him at every turn.

Seib, Gerald F., "Washington Insight: Iran Won't Be Sudden Pal of United States, Despite the End of Hostage Crisis," *The Wall Street Journal,* **Dec. 9, 1991, p. A11.**

The author explains why the release of U.S. hostages in the Middle East is not likely to be followed by improved relations between the United States and Iran. The country has embarked on an ambitious rearmament program and has done much to disrupt the peace talks between Israel and its neighbors.

Back Issues

Great Research on Current Issues Starts Right Here.
Recent topics covered by The CQ Researcher are listed below.
Now available on the Web
For information, call (800) 432-2250 ext. 279 or (202) 887-6279.

MAY 1997
The Stock Market
The Cloning Controversy
Expanding NATO
The Future of Libraries

JUNE 1997
FDA Reform
China After Deng
Line-Item Veto
Breast Cancer

JULY 1997
Transportation Policy
Executive Pay
School Choice Debate
Aggressive Driving

AUGUST 1997
Age Discrimination
Banning Land Mines
Children's Television
Evolution vs. Creationism

SEPTEMBER 1997
Caring for the Dying
Mental Health Policy
Mexico's Future
Youth Fitness

OCTOBER 1997
Urban Sprawl in the West
Diversity in the Workplace
Teacher Education
Contingent Work Force

Back issues are available for $5.00 (subscribers) or $10.00 (non-subscribers). Quantity discounts apply to orders over 10. To order, call Congressional Quarterly Customer Service at (202) 887-8621.

Binders are available for $18.00. To order call 1-800-638-1710. Please refer to stock number 648.

NOVEMBER 1997
Renewable Energy
Artificial Intelligence
Religious Persecution
Roe v. Wade at 25

DECEMBER 1997
Whistleblowers
Castro's Next Move
Gun Control Standoff
Regulating Nonprofits

JANUARY 1998
Foster Care Reform
IRS Reform
The Black Middle Class
U.S.-British Relations

FEBRUARY 1998
Patients' Rights
Deflation Fears
Caring for the Elderly
The New Corporate Philanthropy

MARCH 1998
Israel at 50
The Federal Judiciary
Drinking on Campus
The Economics of Recycling

APRIL 1998
Biology and Behavior
Liberal Arts Education
Income Inequality
High-Tech Labor Shortage

MAY 1998
Census 2000
Child-Care Options
Alzheimer's Disease
U.S.-Russian Relations

JUNE 1998
Student Journalism
Antitrust Policy
Environmental Justice
Sleep Deprivation

JULY 1998
Encouraging Teen Abstinence
Population and the Environment
Democracy in Asia
Baby Boomers at Midlife

AUGUST 1998
Oil Production in the 21st Century
Flexible Work Arrangements
Coastal Development
Student Activism

SEPTEMBER 1998
Organic Farming
Cancer Treatments
Hispanic Americans' New Clout
The Future of Baseball

OCTOBER 1998
School Violence
Social Security
National Forests
Puerto Rico's Status

NOVEMBER 1998
Internet Privacy
Human Rights
Drug Testing
European Monetary Union

DECEMBER 1998
AIDS Update
Searching for Jesus

Future Topics

▶ *Crisis in American Journalism*

▶ *Death Penalty Update*

▶ *Obesity and Health*

Journalism Under Fire

Can the media regain the public's trust?

A challenging, new era is dawning in American journalism. The Internet is forcing the news media to contend with revolutionary changes in technology as well as heightened competition from new sources of news. In addition, profound changes in media-ownership patterns have created pressure to maintain high profits, which has led to downsizing, increased coverage of "soft" and sensationalistic news and a de-emphasis on coverage of government and foreign news. Critics worry that the changes are seriously undercutting traditional journalistic values. Others say as journalism moves from newsprint to cyberspace, previously unheard voices will be able to participate in a public debate once dominated by media elites.

Dec. 25, 1998 • Volume 8, No. 48 • Pages 1121-1144

Formerly Editorial Research Reports

Cover: Surrounded by members of the press, Monica Lewinsky leaves the Federal Building in Los Angeles on May 28, 1998, during the investigation of her affair with President Clinton. (AP Photo/Chris Pizzello)

CQ Researcher

Dec. 25, 1998
Volume 8, No. 48

EDITOR
Sandra Stencel

MANAGING EDITOR
Thomas J. Colin

STAFF WRITERS
Adriel Bettelheim
Mary H. Cooper
Kenneth Jost
Kathy Koch
David Masci

PRODUCTION EDITOR
Debra James

EDITORIAL ASSISTANT
Laura S. Cavender

PUBLISHED BY
Congressional Quarterly Inc.

CHAIRMAN
Andrew Barnes

VICE CHAIRMAN
Andrew P. Corty

PRESIDENT AND PUBLISHER
Robert W. Merry

EXECUTIVE EDITOR
David Rapp

Bibliographic records and abstracts included in The Next Step section of this publication are the copyrighted material of UMI, and are used with permission.

The CQ Researcher (ISSN 1056-2036). Formerly Editorial Research Reports. Published weekly, except Jan. 2, May 29, July 3, Oct. 30, by Congressional Quarterly Inc., 1414 22nd St., N.W., Washington, D.C. 20037. Annual subscription rate for libraries, businesses and government is $340. Additional rates furnished upon request. Periodicals postage paid at Washington, D.C., and additional mailing offices. POSTMASTER: Send address changes to The CQ Researcher, 1414 22nd St., N.W., Washington, D.C. 20037.

Journalism Under Fire

BY KATHY KOCH

THE ISSUES

At the *Times-News* in Cumberland, Md., reporter Jeff Alderton doesn't check daily police reports in person anymore. He doesn't have time. His expanded beat includes courts and fire departments in a half-dozen counties.

Now Alderton checks the new fax machine in the newsroom for police department press releases.

"I guess they're telling us what they want us to know," acknowledges News Editor John Smith. "We make routine calls every night, and sometimes they tell us nothing is going on when we know that something is happening."

For former *New York Times* managing editor Gene Roberts, who heads the Project on the State of American Newspapers,* the *Times-News'* fax machine is just a symbol of the "sweeping changes taking place at America's newspapers" that he says threaten to undermine democracy in America.

Journalists at newspapers, news magazines, broadcast and cable networks and radio stations across the country say American journalism is having an identity crisis. "Go into any bookstore, and you will see book after book by prominent journalists bemoaning the death of journalism as we know it," says Robert McChesney, associate journalism professor at the University of Wisconsin.

Many ruefully agree with the British journalist Harold Evans, who said when he first arrived in the U.S., "The challenge of the American newspaper is not to stay in business, it is to stay in journalism." [1]

On the cusp of the next millennium, a new era has indeed dawned in American journalism. "Journalism

is changing to something new, but we don't know what the damn 'new' thing is," says James Carey, a professor at the Columbia University Graduate School of Journalism.

Many say the "new" journalism is clearly evident in the violence-saturated 11 o'clock news and the constant focus on sensationalistic stories, such as the O.J. Simpson murder trial, the death of Jon-Benet Ramsey, the young beauty pageant contestant, and the White House sex scandal involving Monica Lewinsky and President Clinton.

To optimists read younger and more cyber-savvy Americans — the new journalism means moving away from newsprint to cyberspace and the emergence of a vastly democratized journalistic free-for-all with previously unheard voices participating in a debate once dominated by media elites.

To pessimists — read old-line journalists — the future looks dark. The angst and hand-wringing are palpable at countless symposia, workshops, cyber-debates and media-watchdog discussions. They note that many newspapers, squeezed by the desire to keep profits constantly high in a notoriously cyclical industry, have slashed staff and the size of the "news hole," the space devoted to news coverage.

Indeed, Roberts says, they are taking shortcuts that could one day be "suicidal." "Newspapers are disconnecting from covering the things that make them essential to democracy," he says. "There are newspapers out there that no longer cover

government meetings of any kind on a regular basis."

Marvin Kalb, director of the Joan Shorenstein Center on Press, Politics and Public Policy at Harvard University, notes that the technological revolution of the last 20 years and a new business-oriented approach to newsgathering have "transformed the ethics, values and standards of journalism." In addition, he says, heightened anti-government cynicism and the end of the Cold War also helped popularize the tabloidized, poorly sourced stories in today's scandal-dominated "new" news. [2]

"There are serious questions today about what kind of information we are focusing on and whether we are losing sight of what our real purpose is," says Tom Kunkel, director of the Project on the State of American Newspapers. "There is astonishing pressure to maintain extraordinarily high profit margins, even as readership continues to decline."

The desire to maintain high profits has led the networks to cut staff, eliminate bureaus and require individual news programs to produce a profit. "Twenty-five years ago, a news program rarely made any money at all," Kalb says. "Today each program must make money."

Only about 60 percent of American households subscribe to a newspaper today. In an effort to hold on to readers, Kunkel says, editorial content has shifted from watching government to softer stories about lifestyle, sex, scandal and gossip. [3]

While a relative handful of prestige papers like *The Wall Street Journal*, *The New York Times* and *The Washington Post* still produce quality journalism, says McChesney, "those papers mostly serve the needs of the upper classes. For the great bulk of the population, we have schlock journalism."

Journalism's current ills are caused

* The results of the two-year study, funded by the Pew Charitable Trusts, are being featured in a series of in-depth articles in the *American Journalism Review.*

Daily Newspaper Circulation Dropped

Circulation of morning and evening U.S. daily papers fell from 62.8 million papers in 1987 to 56.7 million in 1997.* The 10 percent decline reflects the decreasing interest in evening papers as well as growing competition from other news sources.

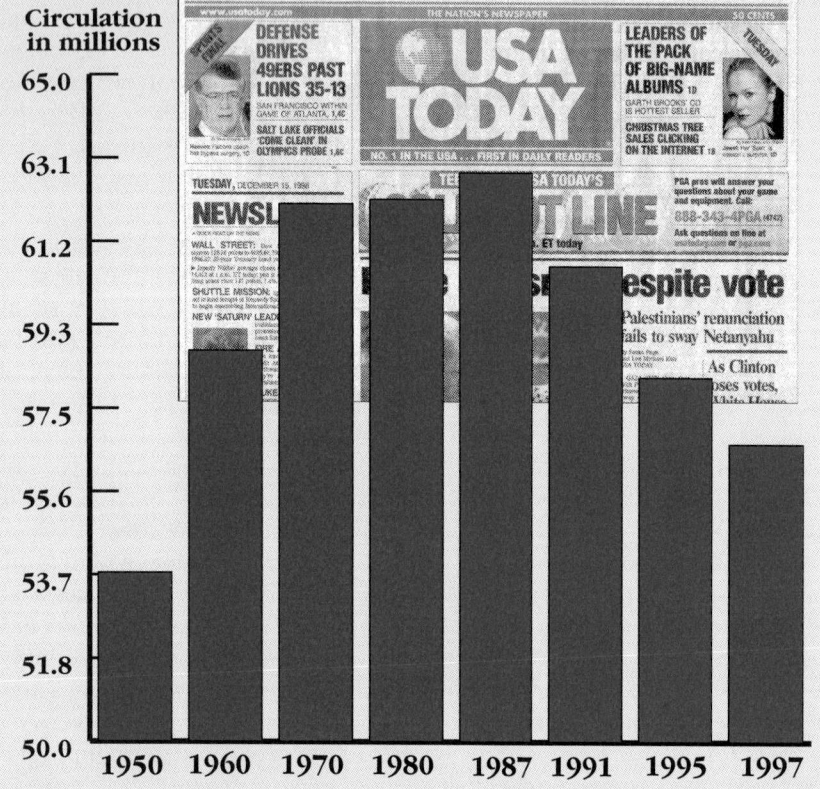

Circulation in millions

65.0
63.1
61.2
59.3
57.5
55.6
53.7
51.8
50.0

1950 1960 1970 1980 1987 1991 1995 1997

* Circulation is the actual number of papers sold, not the total number of readers (readership).

Source: Editor and Publisher

by numerous factors. But at the top of most critics' lists is the claim that journalistic values have been sacrificed on the alter of profits as traditional media outlets have increasingly been bought up by publicly owned corporations, answerable primarily to stockholders rather than to the public interest. In addition, many news organizations are now owned by global conglomerates and manufacturers with diverse holdings and interests,

like General Electric. News departments become tiny entities in such huge companies. In the past, media corporations—like Gannett or the Tribune Company—have primarily focused on news-gathering.

"The business side of the news is corrupting the body and soul of our profession—particularly as it's practiced on television," said Phil Balboni, president of the New England Cable News Network. Balboni spoke at a

May 1998 symposium at Harvard University sponsored by the Committee of Concerned Journalists.

In a scathing cover story in July titled "Money Lust," the *Columbia Journalism Review* said corporate pressure to produce unreasonable profits—two to three times higher than the national average for all industries—has diminished journalism to a point "that hasn't been seen in this country until now." The result could be "a fatal erosion of the ancient bond between journalists and the public," the article said. [4]

Many complain that these changes grew out of the crumbling of the invisible, sacrosanct wall that once separated the marketing and editorial departments of media outlets. Former General Mills President Mark Willes became the poster boy for those advocating destruction of the wall when he took over the Times Mirror Co. in 1995. Willes scandalized the journalism community when he declared he would use a "bazooka" to blow up the sacred wall at the company's flagship, the *Los Angeles Times*. [5]

Concern about high profits has led media executives to cut newsroom staffs and news holes while filling newspapers, magazines and airtime with more advertising and cheap-to-produce soft news, critics say. In addition, they say, companies have failed to reinvest profits in staff training, investigative reporting, salaries, plant and equipment. Such bottom-line journalism has dramatically reduced news quality, they argue.

But Dean Singleton, president of Denver-based Media News, a privately held chain of 151 papers, strongly disagrees. "Newspapers are probably better today than they've ever been editorially," he says.

Similarly, Stewart Garner, president of the Canadian-based Thomson newspaper chain, says, "Newspapers are a business, and no department can be immune from the fact. The only way to ensure their future is to make a healthy profit. For us that means an overall 20 percent profit margin. . . .To do anything else is to stick our heads in the sand." [6]

Besides profit pressures, America's traditional news outlets are competing with a plethora of new competitors, including three all-news cable networks, 10 weekly, prime-time TV news magazines, three cable business-news networks and two sports-news networks, not to mention thousands of newsletters, weeklies, alternative newspapers and hundreds of on-line news sources.

Under the onslaught of ferocious competition, newspapers and network news have watched readership and audience share melt away. In the late 1970s, more than 80 percent of Americans watched one of the three network newscasts; now fewer than 40 percent do.

Changing American lifestyles are another nail in traditional journalism's coffin, Columbia's Carey says. "Established patterns and routines of American life—including watching network news or reading the newspaper—have been destabilized," he says. We haven't settled into a new pattern."

America's media face other problems, as well, including:

• Declining public confidence in media organizations and journalists.

• Editors spending more time as marketers and promoters than as journalists.

• Editors increasingly being compensated with stock options, tying their financial well-being to the company's short-term performance on Wall Street.

• Journalists shrinking from covering corporate misdeeds because they are fearful of jeopardizing advertising income, or offending corporate parents.

• The "dumbing down," or softening, of the news, with dramatically

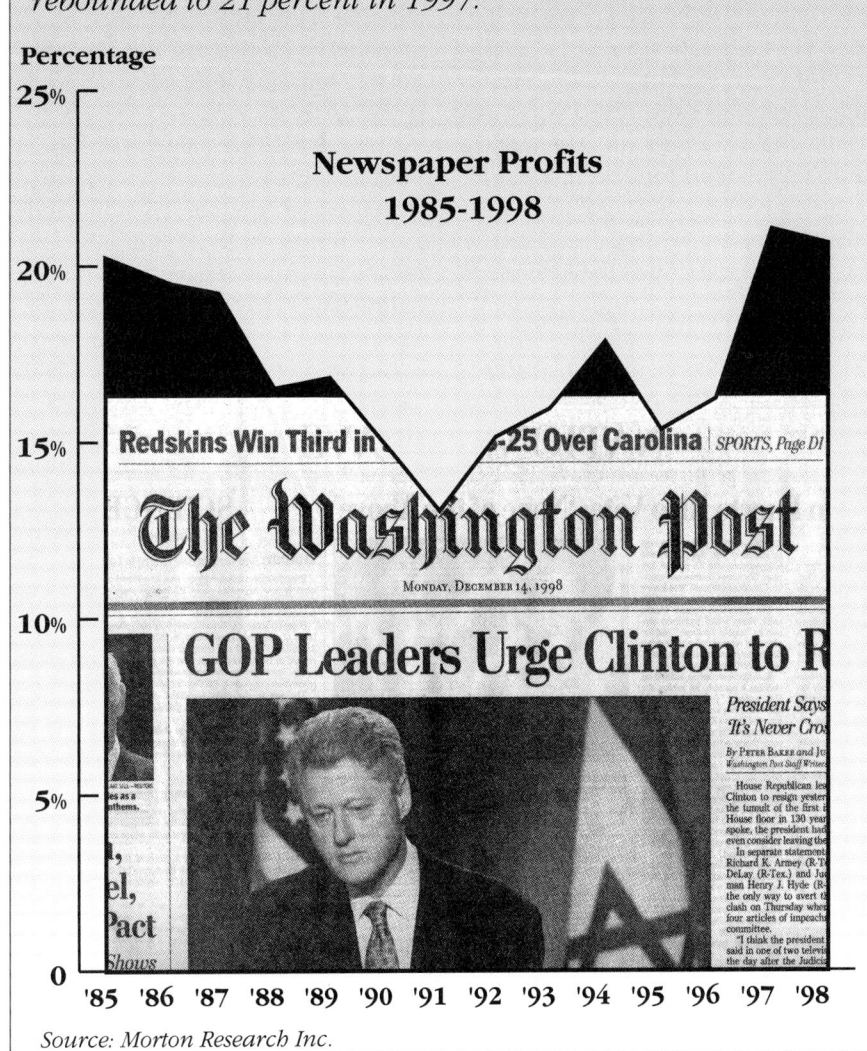

Newspaper Profits Rebound

An economic downturn in the 1980s pushed newspaper profits from 20.2 percent in 1985 to 13 percent in 1991. Profits rebounded to 21 percent in 1997.

Percentage

Newspaper Profits 1985-1998

Source: Morton Research Inc.

less coverage of government and foreign news. [7]

Recent media-ethics scandals have only reinforced the notion that something is rotten in the journalism world. And the perception that the media was in a feeding frenzy over the Lewinsky-Clinton sex scandal further turned off many readers and viewers.

"You could probably walk down the street and talk to nine or 10 people, and eight would tell you the

media are getting worse," says Steven Rendall, senior analyst for the media watchdog organization FAIR (For Accuracy in Media). "The scandal-mongering can be dated to the O.J. Simpson case," he says. "Since then, it has been just one scandal after another."

A recent poll backs up Rendall. According to *New York* magazine, 71 percent of respondents agreed that "legitimate news organizations and outlets are sinking to the level of tabloids in reporting gossip and unsubstantiated stories." [8]

The long-term impact of all these changes in the quality of the news, McChesney says, is an uninformed electorate. "Nowadays, when Jay Leno tells a political joke, he has to set it up and explain what he's talking about," he says. "He cannot assume there's even an elementary knowledge of current events. But he could have 50 years ago."

As journalism enters the 21st century, these are some of the key issues being debated:

Has the pressure to maximize profits hurt the quality of news coverage?

"There's no question that corporations with exaggerated conceptions of what a profit should be have put unhealthy pressure on news organizations," Kalb says. "News is no longer regarded as a public service. Instead, it's a profit center."

Local TV news stations in large markets today make 20-40 percent annual profit margins, he adds. "In the old days, 10 percent was regarded as first-rate. If you got up to 15 percent, you were doing magnificently." For American industry in general, profit margins average about 8 percent.

To Kalb and other observers, news is no longer defined by editorial judgment but by what will attract the most readers and viewers. "So content has changed to more fluff, sex and sensationalism," Kalb says.

Further, he says, the line between news and entertainment has been blurred as editors redefine news. From 1977-1997, the amount of "soft" news (celebrity, scandal, gossip and other human interest stories) in the American news media increased from 15 percent to 43 percent, according to a survey by the Project for Excellence in Journalism. [9]

Partly because of the scramble for

profits and the lack of sufficient staff in streamlined newsrooms, Kalb says, today's "new" news contains too many unnamed sources, too much editorializing or "attitude," too much scandal coverage, an immediate presumption of guilt and too much coverage of stories just because they are "out there," without first properly verifying them.

Editors today are uncertain about what to choose as news, how to present it and whether it is sufficiently entertaining to hold an audience, critics say. "Journalists have always been marketers," says James M. Naughton, president of the Poynter Institute for Media Studies in St. Petersburg, Fla. "Deciding what goes on Page One is a marketing judgment. But now more of those decisions are made with the lowest common denominator in mind, rather than giving the audience what it should read."

"For example, if editors at their daily news meetings are asked whether to run something going on in a distant part of the world, like Algeria, vs. the latest goings-on in the Lewinsky-Clinton scandal, the scandal will win out," he says. "More people will connect to it than to news about Algeria.

"But there are wonderful, important stories we need to be telling about Algeria and the Middle East that would enrich the understanding of people in an increasingly smaller world," he says. "Yet a news meeting is more apt to go for the safer, surer, sexier story that is closer to home."

Singleton argues that the switch to less hard news is a response to what the reader wants. "The definition of news is determined market by market," he says. "It's not a generic term. Most newspapers do a lot of research about what their readers want, and they want more and more sports, business and entertainment. They are not crying out for more local government news."

He bristles at the suggestion that editors know what's best for readers. "I have never subscribed to the theory that we should give the reader what they 'need.' I think editors that say that are arrogant. If you don't give the reader what he wants, you're not going to stay in business."

Thomson's Garner agrees. "Readers' definitions of news are broader than those of journalists," he wrote, citing recent research showing that grocery ads were more important to some readers than other parts of the newspaper. "Some journalists appear to have a bigger desire to save the world than report issues that really touch people. There is a traditional arrogance in some newsrooms that journalists always know best."

Naughton further argues that there are countless places where maximizing profits has reduced the quality of today's news. "When you reduce the number of people in the newsroom," he says, "they just run faster to keep doing all their jobs. Eventually you diminish what they're doing for their audience."

Short-changing the news is most apparent at local TV stations, where news shows draw 60 percent of the ad revenues for local stations, says James L. Baughman, journalism professor at the University of Wisconsin and author of *The Republic of Mass Culture*. "Most of us used to laugh at the local news and tell ourselves the networks will never sink to that level," he says. "Now the national news is more like the local news. Their audience share keeps plummeting, and they keep dumbing down their news, but the audience keeps shrinking."

Media executives say the networks have cut back on politics and foreign news not so much as a cost-cutting measure but as a response to what viewers want. William Wheatley, vice president of NBC News, said, "It's fair to say we're doing less politics than we once did. Part of it is a reaction to the fact that the viewers have turned thumbs down in a lot of ways on politics."

Norman Pearlstein, editor-in-chief of *Time* Inc., acknowledged that his magazine is publishing fewer hard-news cover stories but said it's less because of profit pressures and more because the economy is thriving, "so there's probably less concern with what has traditionally been the hard news story." [10]

Further, he said, since the collapse of communism and the end of the Cold War, "it's not surprising that the country has turned more inward. We're not getting a lot of demand for international coverage these days." [11]

Wheatley argued at a journalism forum last May that many of the cutbacks in TV network news were long overdue. "Journalism wasted a lot of money before," he said.

Besides cutting back on government and foreign news, critics say, television has dramatically reduced its coverage of political campaigns. The Rocky Mountain Media Watch (RMMW) organization monitored 128 evening broadcasts in 25 states and found that local broadcasts showed 5.5 political ads for each 1.3 news items on the election. RMMW said the lack of meaningful coverage is partly to blame for voter apathy and decreasing voter turnout. "In 1998, the country was bombarded by dubious political ads, and there were virtually no journalists critiquing these ads," McChesney says. "These [media] companies aren't going to bite the hand that feeds them."

"What serves advertisers and stockholders isn't necessarily what serves citizens best," he continues. "Journalism needs to go back to serving citizens."

The Times Mirror's Willes said journalism companies can both make money and produce quality news. "I don't think you have to make a tradeoff," he said. "It's not a choice of either high quality, independent journalism or a very successful business enterprise." [12]

Publicly held corporations have a fiduciary responsibility to their shareholders, he said. "Therefore, earning an adequate rate of return is not a 'nice to do,' it's a 'must do.'"

Rather than profit-making causing journalism quality to suffer, "I think just the opposite is true," he continued. "I think the more compelling the journalism, the more successful we'll be as a business enterprise."

That's a nice sentiment, Singleton says, but the hard reality is that "companies with the lowest profit margins have the best newspapers, and the ones with the highest margins have the lower-quality news."

Robert Kasabian, executive director of the International Newspaper Financial Executives Association, in Sterling, Va., says that cutting costs will only work for a while, before the product starts to suffer. "I don't think journalism is being sacrificed for the sake of impressing Wall Street. Chrysler isn't going to impress Wall Street if they turn out a cruddy product. Neither will newspapers. If you cut too much, the customer base will begin to erode."

Michael Schudson, a communications professor at the University of California at San Diego, says today's newspapers are better than they were 30 years ago. "In 1960, *The Washington Post* was not a great paper," he says. "Everybody assumes TV news is worse, but by editing more carefully, what gets left out is a lot of fluff." For instance, he says, in 1968, when convention coverage was gavel-to-gavel, the networks broadcast Sen. Hubert H. Humphrey's Democratic Convention speech in its entirety. "Looking at it by today's standards," he says, "you just want the poor man to shut up."

Bill O'Reilly, executive producer and anchorman for Fox News' "The O'Reilly Factor," argues that the public is better served now than it was 30 years ago. Back then, an "elite, power center of white guys in Manhattan" ran the three TV networks and three major news magazines and decided what news the American people received. They did not tell the public the truth about President John F. Kennedy's philandering and Mafia connections, the Bay of Pigs invasion or the Gulf of Tonkin, among other things, O'Reilly said. [13]

Has on-line journalism hurt the overall quality of journalism?

Traditional media face new, competitive pressure from cyber-journalists.

"Newspapers are now competing with other newspapers that are not even in their geographic distribution area," says Mark Stencel, politics editor of *The Washington Post's* Web site. For instance, even though *The New York Times* has a significantly larger circulation than *The Washington Post*, their on-line circulations are about the same.

On-line journalism has also sped up the news cycle, imposing deadlines 24 hours a day, seven days a week on news organizations that previously had daily or weekly deadlines. Thus newspapers with Web sites are competing with TV in breaking news, Stencel says.

But often those new, 24-hour deadlines have caused inaccuracies. "It has hurt journalism standards at places that weren't used to round-the-clock deadlines," says Adam C. Powell, vice president of technology and programs at the Freedom Forum, a journalism education and research organization. "It has turned daily reporters into wire editors. That's a different set of reflexes."

In two high-profile examples during coverage of the Lewinsky-Clinton scandal, the *Dallas Morning News* and *The Wall Street Journal* were forced to retract stories after rushing them to the Internet before verifying them.

Newspaper Readership Plummeted

Newspaper readership fell from more than three-quarters of Americans age 18 and over in 1970 to under 60 percent in 1997. Experts blame the decline on increasing competition from other news sources and declining leisure time.

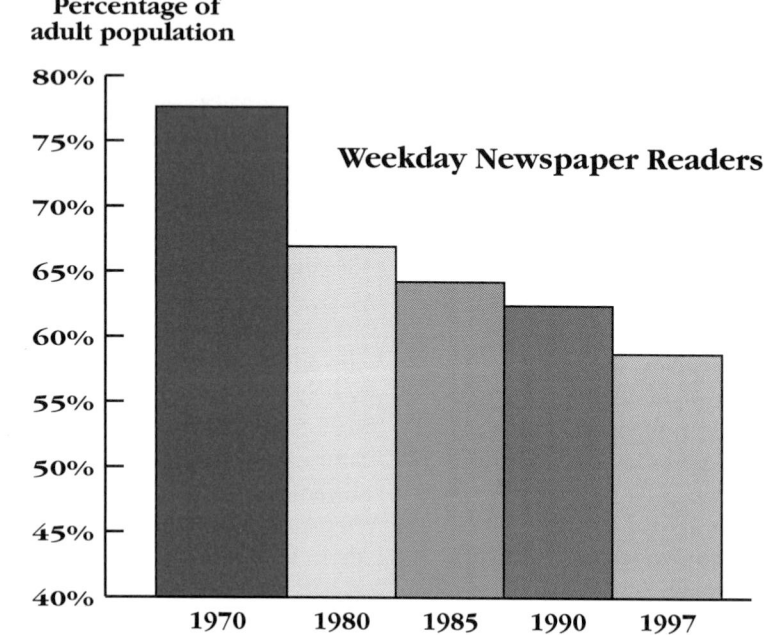

Percentage of adult population

Weekday Newspaper Readers

Sources: W.R. Simmons & Associates Research; Simmons Market Research Bureau; Scarborough Reports

"There is a lot of pressure on traditional media to be as current as the technology allows on-line publications to be," Naughton says. "There is a great temptation to substitute speed for care and meticulous gatekeeping and editing." Further, he warns, "When journalists have 24-hour deadlines, they may be inclined to incorporate other people's information into their own stories."

Traditional news organizations with high standards should refuse to let speed predominate, he says.

David Weir, managing editor of the on-line magazine *Salon*, insists that most on-line news sources are as committed to quality as traditional journalists are. "I don't know any major Internet sites that made serious errors" during the Lewinsky-Clinton scandal,

he says. "It was the traditional news organizations that had to retract stories they had rushed to the Web."

"All the digital news organizations that I've worked with act in a very restrained manner," he continues. "We get all kinds of rumors, but we check them out thoroughly first. We know we'll make our reputation by not making mistakes. So we are disinclined to go with things unless we have them sourced and documented."

The digital flubs got more attention because it's a new medium, Stencel says, pointing out that most major newspapers run corrections from time to time. "And sometimes they are pretty embarrassing," he says.

On-line proponents argue that it was not the Internet that caused most of the problems during the Lewinsky-Clinton

scandal but the abandonment of reporters' age-old practice of acquiring two reliable sources before printing something. Instead reporters "back-doored" stories—attributing information to other news sources without doing their own independent checking.

They also printed material that bordered on gossip, Weir says. Much of that was prompted by Internet reporter Matt Drudge, who was the first to publish the Lewinsky story. Although Drudge's stories eventually turned out to be true, the fact that he broke the story first prompted other media outlets to publish stories before they had independently verified them, simply because the story was already "out there."

Most say that it will take time before Internet news sources prove their credibility. "Some of the stuff on the Internet has no basis in fact whatsoever," says Richard Coles, dean of the journalism school at the University of North Carolina. "We teach our students to check anything they get off the Internet." [14]

"You have very reliable traditional news sources on-line, like *The New York Times*, CNN and *CQ*," Kalb says. "But then you have other news organizations for whom profit is terribly important and reliability is not. Eventually the standards drop."

"It's the credibility of the people who are posting the information that counts," Powell says. "And they range from *The New York Times* and *Congressional Quarterly* to those who are deliberately posting misinformation. It's all there. The good, the bad and the ugly. You just have to know where to look." But since it all looks more or less alike, he concedes, "It places more of a burden on the reader to develop a sense of skepticism about what to trust."

Kalb notes that most Web-page staffs are young, inexperienced reporters. "And they're not making much money, so when they cut back on salaries, that attracts even less experienced reporters."

Jon Katz, media columnist for the Freedom Forum, concedes that the Internet as a whole is not as accurate or reliable as the traditional media. "It's much too big and democratic," he says. "But it's not hard to find reliable information on the Internet."

He says the Lewinsky-Clinton mistakes were just "growing pains" while journalists adjust to the speed of the Internet. "You had one culture colliding with another and learning how to live with it. At first there was a tendency to just throw things onto the Internet. I think it's shocking that more mistakes weren't made," Katz says. "I think reporters learned their lesson quite well. Now they are scrupulous about what they do."

Katz argues that much of the concern about Internet reliability is coming from traditional journalists who see their power base eroding. "Traditional journalists are very unnerved by the Internet because they have been setting the agenda in politics for a long time," he says. "The Internet is free, open, inclusive. It's the antithesis of traditional journalism. So traditional journalists are not as powerful as they were. They are still much more powerful than a hacker with a Web site," he adds. "Yet they are running around screaming, 'The sky is falling! Who's going to be accurate anymore?'

"The question is whether journalists can share power with people on the Internet," he says. "Internet sources that are not accurate will not be powerful," Katz says. "That's what democracy is about."

Are journalism ethics eroding?

A series of ethical scandals gave journalism black eyes in 1998:

• In May, *The New Republic* fired 25-year-old writer Stephen Glass for including inaccurate or fabricated information in 27 of his 41 articles for the magazine.

• Two *Boston Globe* columnists, including popular Mike Barnicle, were dismissed for fabricating people and quotes, and plagiarism.

• CNN and *Time* magazine retracted a controversial story charging the U.S. military used nerve gas to kill American defectors in Laos during the Vietnam War, acknowledging "serious faults in the reporting."

• *The Cincinnati Enquirer* retracted an 18-page investigative exposé of the Chiquita Brands company, apologized and agreed to pay $10 million in damages after learning the reporter had stolen company voice-mail messages.

"In the midst of all the changes going on in American journalism, ethical norms we used to take for granted seem to be shaky," Carey says. He describes a recent "60 Minutes" episode showing Jack Kevorkian assisting in a suicide on the air as an example of the "slippery slope" on which journalism ethics are teetering.

"I think journalism ethics are in a great deal of difficulty," says Dan Hallin, a University of California at San Diego journalism professor. "It's clear we're in a period where the balance between the business side and the news side has shifted over to the business side—a period when ethics are eroding in significant ways."

Howard Kurtz, media critic for *The Washington Post*, blames the spate of ethical lapses on a combination of slipping media standards in some cases and greater scrutiny of the media in others. "Twenty or 30 years ago, there was plenty of plagiarism, embellishment and other ethical shortcuts," he says. "But they didn't always come to light, in part because journalists were reluctant to expose one another."

McChesney worries that today's corporatized media are much more hesitant to investigate corporate behavior because they are integrated into the society's power structure to an unprecedented extent. "Going

after powerful people has been elevated to a much higher state. The golfing buddy of the media owner isn't just the guy who owns the hardware store anymore. He's the guy who owns the $60 billion multinational corporation," he says.

McChesney cited numerous episodes of corporate media backing down from stories that upset the parent company. ABC News, for example, recently killed an investigative story alleging that Walt Disney Co., its parent, was not properly screening job applicants' to weed out pedophiles at its theme parks.

"When corporations are the stewards of journalism, they will put the bottom line first," McChesney says. "And if I were a shareholder in Disney, I'd want them to do the same thing. But it's not good for a democratic society."

Media defenders point to *Time's* two-part investigative series on corporate welfare in November to counter McChesney's point. But McChesney argues that, "What's striking about the *Time* piece is that it is so striking."

Kurtz says McChesney's concerns about intimidation by big business ring true in light of the behavior of *The Cincinnati Enquirer* in the Chiquita case.

"The amazing thing about this case is that *The Cincinnati Enquirer* has still not said what, if anything, it published about Chiquita was untrue," Kurtz says. "All the attention has focused on the reporter's controversial methods. The question of the accuracy of this extraordinarily long series of articles has sort of been taken off the table. Yet it's disturbing that a newspaper would pay $10 million and apologize before the company has even filed suit."

Former *New York Times* reporter Richard Reeves views journalists today as more ethical than they were in his younger years, when they were a "pretty roguish bunch." He remembers breaking into a school to get some documents he needed to expose a scandal. "A lot of people did that kind of thing in those days," he says. "Today, you'd end up in jail."

Many say it only appears that media ethics have eroded because it's being covered more. "For years, human-interest columnists were given latitude," Roberts says. "Now everyone is being watched. On the whole, if we really cover each other, I think the public will benefit. The problem is it's only the big papers that attract the scrutiny."

There are many more magazines now, and so much more competition for flashy, young writers, Kunkel says. "People who haven't really learned their trade, probably aren't up to it," he says. "And there are so many TV news magazines that they are rushing these things onto the air."

In some ways, journalism ethics have improved over the last half-century, Naughton says. "We've had scandals involving individuals in journalism throughout history. The latest scandals are just because there's more pressure for journalists to be stars, public figures and experts. That goes on in Washington more than anywhere else." ■

BACKGROUND

Journalism's Heyday

The concept that journalism's business side should be separate from its news side only developed about 100 years ago. Before 1800, the most common name for an American newspaper was *The Advertiser,* and its purpose was to publish commodity prices, quantities and availabilities.

"Every paper was, in a way, *The Wall Street Journal*," Carey says. "And the relationship between business and journalism was an intimate one." [15]

Throughout the 1800s, American journalism acted as the mouthpiece of political parties, so there was no conflict between the business office and the news operation, "because the source of one's subsidy was also the source of one's news," Carey says.

But at the end of the 19th century, the press declared its independence, and the problem of the separation of news and business erupted. "Once the press declared its independence from political parties, it also had to declare independence from its own business office," Carey says.

Since then, the tradition in American journalism "was that journalism companies were journalism companies, and they did not have a lot of business side involvements," he says. Unlike in other countries where manufacturers own the media, American journalism companies were not owned by corporations as a secondary business.

All of that began to change with the advent of broadcasting. Suddenly the church-state separation of the editorial and business offices became problematic, because broadcasting organizations were usually in the business of entertainment, not news-gathering, Carey says. Broadcasters' commitment to news was imposed on them by the Communications Act of 1934, which required them to provide news as a public service.

The tug-of-war between news and business seemed in balance in the 1960s and '70s, often viewed as the zenith of American journalism standards. CBS' William S. Paley, for instance, told a group of correspondents in 1962, "You guys cover the news; I've got Jack Benny to make money for me." [16]

Reeves says modern journalism distinguished itself during those years

by its coverage of the civil rights movement in the South, the Vietnam War and Watergate. But the media's performance brought about a pervasive change in public attitudes about government and, eventually, about the media itself.

"We as a people are more cynical about government since Vietnam and Watergate," Kunkel says. "And the mass media is much less respectful toward government and the system than it was 20 years ago."

Another impact of Watergate, writes former *Washington Post* Executive Editor Ben Bradlee, was that it "marked the final passage of journalists into the best seats of the establishment." [17]

Once in those seats, journalists were expected to deliver opinions, and their opinions carried weight in a universe dominated by televised celebrities, according to Kalb. The age of the journalist pundit had been born. "The upshot is that journalists have become too big for their britches," Kalb writes.

Rise of 'Soft' News

The 1980s brought revolutionary changes in both newspaper and broadcast journalism, led by the explosion of technology.

"When Ronald Reagan became president, the terms CNN, CD, PC and VCR didn't even exist," Reeves says.

The era of deregulation ushered in by Reagan led to the Telecommunications Act of 1996, which brought about "huge disruptive changes" in broadcasting, Hickey wrote. "Its deregulatory effects and the resultant seismic shift to corporate giantism have been at the public's expense, especially in the way the nation's information needs are met." [18]

Continued on p. 1134

Chronology

Late 1700s
American newspapers are mostly flyers listing prices, quantities and availabilities of commodities.

1800s
American newspapers serve as the mouthpieces of political parties until the end of the century, when the press declares its independence from political parties and its own business offices.

1900s
For most of the century, the news media are owned predominantly by journalism companies without secondary interests. An invisible wall separates the editorial and business offices of most media organizations. The wall weakens when radio begins broadcasting news, since broadcasting organizations are usually in the business of entertainment.

1934
The Communications Act of 1934 requires broadcasters to provide news as a public service.

1960s-1970s
The tug-of-war between news and business seems in balance during what many regard as the zenith of American journalism. Press credibility rises over coverage of the civil rights movement, the Vietnam War and Watergate. In the late '70s newspapers become increasingly interested in "soft" news, or lifestyle stories.

1980s
Cynicism about government and the media begins to increase, partly as fallout from the Vietnam and Watergate eras. The 1980s bring about revolutionary changes in both newspaper and broadcast journalism, primarily because of the explosion of technology. The Reagan administration launches a wave of deregulation efforts.

1982
Gannett Publisher Al Neuharth launches *USA Today*, with its combination of colorful graphics, short, punchy stories and less government reporting. As the paper gains nationwide readership, other editors copy its format.

1990s
Eighty percent of America's papers are owned by chains or groups, many of which are publicly traded. Newspaper readership declines to only 58.7 percent of adults.

1991
During the Persian Gulf War, millions of Americans turn to an upstart cable company, CNN, to watch the war occurring in real time. CNN is the only television news organization with correspondents and a direct satellite hookup in Baghdad. The three traditional networks, which had dramatically cut back their overseas news bureaus in the late 1980s, cover the beginning of the war by having their anchors interview military "experts" in New York studios. The pattern of turning to CNN for breaking international news is established.

1993
The end of the three-network monopoly is clearly signaled when Bill Clinton is inaugurated as president and begins to ignore the traditional news media and White House correspondents, cutting their access and hosting fewer news conferences in favor of direct access through alternative media like Larry King, MTV and televised town meetings.

1994
The trial of former football star O.J. Simpson for the murders of his ex-wife and her friend generates unprecedented press coverage, contributing to the impression that the mainstream media has been tabloidized. Meanwhile, foreign news on the evening newscasts decreases by 50 percent since 1984.

1996
The Telecommunications Act of 1996 brings about huge changes in broadcasting, including what some say is a seismic shift to ownership by giant corporations.

1998
Ethics scandals at *The Boston Globe*, *The New Republic* and other media outlets add to journalism's credibility woes.

With the Media in the Doghouse...

While the media are busy acting as society's watchdog, a burgeoning number of publications and groups are watching the watchdogs. In June a new magazine of press criticism, *Brill's Content*, hit newstands nationwide. PBS' "NewsHour With Jim Lehrer" recently hired CBS news reporter Terence Smith as its media observer. On cable, CNN has the new "Reliable Sources" show, and Fox has "News Watch."

Media critics today have a tougher job than they did a decade ago, given the proliferation of new sources of news, including three cable news networks, 10 weekly TV news magazines, plus thousands of newsletters, weeklies, alternative newspapers and on-line news sources.

Tom Goldstein, dean of the Columbia University Graduate School of Journalism, says there are so many new sources of news today that it's almost impossible to monitor them all. "Ten years ago, when I was writing about media, it was much easier," he recalls. "I'd look at the *Times*, the *Village Voice*, the *Journal* and other papers. The world was much more finite. I don't know how people who cover the media today can do their jobs with the confidence that they haven't missed something." [1]

David Shenk, author of *Data Smog: Surviving the Information Glut*, said covering the media is important in the digital age because "the proliferation of information has forced nearly everyone to become a very self-conscious media consumer." [2]

Others say the proliferation of media-monitoring groups is a sign that the industry is in trouble. "There hasn't been a time in modern American history when the media were as unpopular or controversial as they are right now," says *Washington Post* media critic Howard Kurtz. Given last summer's flurry of media scandals involving plagiarism and questionable reporting tactics, it would seem that there's no time like the present for monitoring the press' behavior, says on-line media critic Jon Katz of the Freedom Forum, a journalism education and research organization.

In addition to criticism and commentary in the daily press, the media in the United States are monitored in four basic ways:

Ombudsmen — About three dozen newspapers and a handful of television networks employ ombudsmen, or media critics, to write columns or commentary analyzing

Controversial Internet gossip reporter Matt Drudge.

AP Photo/Brian K. Diggs

the media's performance. Derisively called media navelgazers by some, Kurtz nonetheless would like to see more of them, especially at smaller and medium-sized newspapers. "The press is the most uncovered business in America," he says. "It stirs strong emotions and affects the lives of every American by shaping the national agenda. But the majority of newspapers don't have media critics."

Admittedly, he says, some of the new crop of media critics are "blatantly ideological," and some are "merely an effort to fill up some of those 24 hours on allnews cable stations. But whatever the shortcomings, it's about time people in my profession got a dose of the same scrutiny that we love to inflict on everyone else."

Watchdog Groups — Mediawatchdog groups represent all points on the political spectrum — from the conservative Accuracy in Media (AIM) to the liberal Fairness and Accuracy in Reporting (FAIR). FAIR senior analyst Steven Rendall says some groups that call themselves media watchdogs are merely "anti-journalist and antiinformation." Sometimes they bash journalists for simply printing something the group doesn't agree with, he says.

Launched in 1969, AIM is closely associated with its founder, conservative commentator Reed Irvine, who lately has alleged that the mainstream media is helping the Clinton administration and the Congress cover up charges that the TWA 800 flight was shot down by a missile. AIM board member James L. Tyson once proposed that government ombudsmen be stationed at each major network to ensure accuracy and fairness of newscasts.

Another conservative media-watchdog group, the Media Research Center, is headed by L. Brent Bozell III, former director of the National Conservative Political Action Committee and former finance chairman for Patrick Buchanan's primary challenge to President George Bush. The group monitors the daily TV news broadcasts for anti-conservative or pro-liberal bias.

FAIR, meanwhile, views the media through a different lens. The group recently surveyed the mainstream American media and says the popularly held view that most American media are liberal is a myth. Instead, says FAIR, it has a centrist, pro-business bias.

FAIR also conducts a yearly survey of how the media use quotes from think tanks and found that conservative

... Media-Monitoring Groups Are Keeping Busy

groups were quoted 53 percent of the time in 1997, compared with 16 percent for "progressive or left-leaning" think tanks.

The Denver-based Rocky Mountain Media Watch (RMMW) grades media coverage of violence, "fluff" and election news. For instance, it found that while the national crime rate has dropped in recent years, the amount of murder, assaults and robbery covered by the nightly news has not. In fact, the amount of news about violence has remained the same during the past four years, the group complained, giving the public a false sense of danger. [3]

The group also found that during the recent elections, political ads on local TV newscasts were five times more prevalent than news coverage about the elections. [4]

Press Reviews — The *Columbia Journalism Review*, published by the Columbia University Graduate School of *Journalism*, and the University of Maryland Journalism School's *American Journalism Review* have been around for years. The newest kid on the block is *Brill's Content*, first published last June. Vowing that "the media's free ride has come to a screeching halt," publisher Steven Brill ambitiously aims to monitor all media, including Web sites, mainstream newspapers and 24-hour cable. [5]

"I think this is a good thing," said Alan Murray, *The Wall Street Journal's* Washington bureau chief. "I think it's about time that somebody covered us as aggressively as we cover everybody else." [6]

"The rap always has been that only journalists are interested in the media," says Brill, who founded *American Lawyer* magazine and Court TV. "But in our subscription base, only about 5 percent are journalists. Non-fiction media is a huge, huge force in our society, affecting commerce, our family lives and our entertainment. We're operating on the premise that the key product in the next century will be information. So we are the business book about the most important business of the next century." [7]

Some cyber-journalists say media-monitoring groups may become unnecessary as the media shifts more and more to electronic distribution. Internet users are generally quick to express their displeasure with items they read on the Web and would not hesitate to flood a Web site that published erroneous or unfair reports with angry e-mail, they argue.

"As access to the Web grows, more people will be able to give us immediate feedback," wrote Tom Regan, associate editor of *The Christian Science Monitor's* electronic edition. "Which also means we've got to be on our toes. That will make us better journalists." [8]

Now the Internet has a watchdog of its own. Last March a group of journalists and graduate students at the Annenberg School of Communication at the University of Southern California in Los Angeles launched *OJR*, the *Online Journalism Review* (www.ojr.org).

"What the *Columbia Journalism Review* has done for

the [traditional] media world is what we hope the *Online Journalism Review* will do for the online world," says Geoffrey Cowan, Annenberg dean and *OJR's* publisher. [9]

Adam Clayton Powell III, director of technology and programs at The Freedom Forum, thinks the birth of *OJR* could open the door for other new media reviews. "This could be just the beginning," Powell says. "Every university across the country could begin to analyze Web sites in their communities." [10]

News Councils — Common in Europe and Canada, news councils allow the public to air complaints about alleged unfairness or inaccuracy in the media. Although overseas news councils often have some government connection, in the U.S. they are independent forums. They also conduct seminars and workshops on media-related issues to better explain the news business to the public.

"We are not a media 'watchdog' organization," says Gary Gilson, executive director of the Minnesota News Council, the granddaddy U.S. news councils. "That word has a punitive connotation, and that's not what we are about." Rather, he says, the group's role is to "get two sides that have a dispute to air them at a public hearing." Of the 120 or so public hearings the Minnesota council has held over the last 29 years, he says, about half have been decided in favor of the journalists.

There are only three other U.S. news councils: in Honolulu, Central Florida and Washington state.

"I think every state should have a news council," says John Hamer, executive director of the fledgling Washington council. "The media's reputation, credibility and trust level among the public are at their lowest point in years. A news council is one way to rebuild their credibility."

---

[1] Quoted in "Media on Media: Does the Public Really Care?" *Mediaweek*, Nov. 9, 1998.

[2] *Ibid.*

[3] Alexandra Marks, "Bit by bit, Americans feel safer," *The Christian Science Monitor*, Nov. 27, 1998.

[4] Dan Trigoboff, "Political ads outnumber election stories, study finds," *Broadcasting & Cable*, Nov. 2, 1998.

[5] Quoted in Lloyd Grove, "The Watchdogs' Watchdog; Steve Brill Grills Ken Starr About Other Reporters," *The Washington Post*, May 1, 1998.

[6] Quoted in *Ibid.*

[7] Quoted in *Mediaweek, op. cit.*

[8] Tom Regan, "How the Internet Is Turning the Public Into a Media Watchdog," *The Christian Science Monitor* July 16, 1998.

[9] Quoted in Dirk Smillie, "A Media Watchdog Let Loose on Cyberspace," *The Christian Science Monitor*, June 4, 1998.

[10] Quoted in *Ibid.*

Continued from p. 1130

Meanwhile, the roots of newspapers' obsession with soft news were being planted. In the late 1970s, to determine why newspapers were losing readership, the American Society of Newspaper Editors (ASNE) and the Newspaper Advertising Bureau (NAB) jointly commissioned two market research studies. A scientifically structured telephone survey of 3,000 newspaper readers, conducted by pollster Leo Bogart, found that people read newspapers primarily for hard news.

The other study, led by focus group researcher Ruth Clark, concluded that readers wanted "news you could use" — known in the industry as lifestyle stories.

But Clark's study contained a caveat. It did not say that readers wanted *only* softer news. All the focus groups "recognized that editors have a responsibility to inform and educate the public, and not merely to provide the public with what is popular or wanted," her report said. [19]

Predictably, perhaps, newspaper editors across the country embraced Clark's study — even though it contradicted Bogart's more scientific survey. But they ignored Clark's comments about the need for hard news. "Papers went soft," Roberts says, "and they're still going soft."

Bogart later wrote that by proclaiming that the public wanted "fun rather than facts," the Clark report "legitimized the movement to turn newspapers into daily magazines with the pelletized, palatable characteristics of TV news." [20]

'McPaper' Leads the Way

Newspapers began making substantial content changes, adding lifestyle sections and more features. Following the lead of the Gannett chain's highly successful *USA Today* — derisively dubbed "McPaper" when it was launched in 1982 — edi-

tors added colorful graphics, kept stories under 500 words and discouraged government reporting. One Gannett publisher in Montana would scribble a big "G" over every article that was "too governmental" and send the tearsheets back to the editor each day, Roberts recalls.

Even Clark was surprised by how many papers went overboard with her advice. In a subsequent telephone survey of 1,202 people in 1983, she found that consumers wanted "hard news, real news, whether it's national, state, regional or local." Lifestyle features, she said, "are perceived as add-on benefits." [21]

But the new report, and others like it, fell on deaf ears. Perhaps the editors were more convinced by the healthy operating profits they saw at Gannett. For most of this decade, Gannett has earned more than 20 percent; last year it made 25.3 percent.

By the late 1980s, hit by an economic downturn, the industry was downsizing along with the rest of corporate America. About 200 papers went out of business. Corporate groups and chains began gobbling up independent, family-owned papers. Today 80 percent of America's papers are owned by chains or vast corporate conglomerates.

Many of the new groups are publicly owned, which added a new dimension to editorial board discussions — the financial interests of shareholders. Publicly held companies now control 45 percent of the nation's daily newspaper circulation, says newspaper analyst John Morton.

As newspaper managers began worrying about stock market performance, they started looking at the bottom line. The traditional wall that had existed between the news and business departments began crumbling.

One of the first things to be examined was productivity. "The great journalism operations of the past had terrible productivity," Reeves says.

"Reporters would go out for three weeks to check out a story, and come back and say, 'There's no story there.' Those days are gone forever."

Many newspapers today have productivity meetings on Monday morning and review how many inches each reporter produced the previous week. Some papers, like the *Winston Salem Journal*, even established daily production quotas. A typical *Journal* reporter was expected to produce 40 stories a week, taking 0.9 hours each, using a press release and one or two "cooperative sources." The much-ridiculed system was later scrapped. [22]

Such assembly-line journalism enraged many reporters, among them Patti Epler of the *News Tribune* in Tacoma, Wash. She was once criticized in an annual review for producing too many in-depth pieces. "I kid you not," she told the *Columbia Journalism Review*. "They would count your bylines. . . . Not once did they talk about the quality of your stories." [23]

In their cost-cutting fervor, newspapers de-emphasized local government reporting. A recent study by the Project on the State of American Newspapers found that in 27 out of 50 states there are fewer statehouse reporters now than nine years ago.

Roberts worries that the decline in government reporting is happening in the midst of devolution—the Republican-inspired transfer of billions of federal dollars to state governments for distribution through block grants. "State government has never been more important," he says.

But while the vast sums being sent to the states have attracted 50,000 registered lobbyists to the nation's statehouses, Roberts says, there are only 513 full-time journalists covering them. In contrast, 3,000 reporters receive credentials every year to cover the Super Bowl, he points out.

Much the same is happening in Washington, Roberts says. "Some companies have cut way back on their Washington bureaus, and almost everybody has cut back on the 'beat' method of covering the news," he says. Now reporters cover broad subject areas. The result is that —as in the statehouses—agencies aren't being watched on a regular basis.

Climbing Profits

During the recession in the 1980s and early '90s, newspaper profits declined from a high of 20.2 percent in 1985 to 13 percent in 1991. Then, as depressed advertising revenues began rising again, profits began climbing, too, hitting 21 percent last year.

"Advertising rates are rising faster than GNP," Morton says, to a large extent because head-to-head competition between newspapers was virtually eliminated after the shakeout that occurred during downsizing. Mergers and buyouts further reduced the number of towns with two competing newspapers from 142 a decade ago to only eight today. "When you're the only game in town, ad rates tend to escalate," Morton says.

Two other trends—synergy and clustering—have contributed to the loss of competition and news quality in some local markets. Synergy occurs when a single corporation owns all the news media in town—the newspaper, radio and TV stations and even the on-line Web site. Typically, the editors of all the properties meet together each day to decide what the news is. "This is considered more efficient and better," Roberts says. "I don't doubt that it is more efficient, but what happens if the owners of all these appendages decide they're bored with government news. Then, suddenly, no one in town is printing government news."

The second trend is the clustering, or swapping, of newspapers by non-competing media companies to achieve regional dominance. "We're not sure yet exactly what the impact of clustering has been on the news," Roberts says.

Despite the changes, newspaper readership continues to decline. In 1970, nearly 78 percent of adult Americans read a daily paper, compared with only 58.7 percent today. "People read a daily newspaper to get information that they can't get anywhere else," Morton says. "It's local information, in detail, that bonds the reader to their newspapers. But some papers don't do a very good job of that anymore."

Some of that local bond has been broken by the transient nature of today's population, he concedes.

The decade-long stress on high profits has "undermined the industry," Morton says, particularly some "ill-advised" cost-cutting in 1991-92 and again in '94-'95. In 1994-95, when newsprint prices shot up 30-40 percent, many newspapers slashed newsroom budgets again, rather than see profits drop. "I think they overdid it, and did harm to the industry," he says.

Many publicly held companies acted out of "fear that their earnings would look bad, and their stock would suffer," Morton says. But he warns against generalizing.

"*The New York Times*, the *Boston Globe* and the *L.A. Times* are all public companies," Morton says, "and they're not known for stinting on quality. It's many of the smaller newspapers, rather than the famous ones," that are cutting corners.

Many family-owned companies are just as cost-conscious. "Most privately held companies have an awful lot of relatives that don't give a whit about the company except collecting their dividend checks," he says.

But today, critics complain, media companies expect excessive profits—

two to three times the rate of industry as a whole—and want them to increase every quarter, even though the newspaper business is cyclical.

"The media have never been charities," McChesney says. "But profit pressures have increased since the 1980s."

Media Consolidation

As newspapers were being bought up and streamlined by chains, the broadcast media were also being gobbled up by larger and larger media corporations. Since 1992, there has been an unprecedented wave of mergers and acquisitions among media giants, including Time Warner's purchase of Turner Broadcasting and Disney's acquisition of ABC.

The impact of the cuts and mergers on the content and quality of network news has been profound, McChesney says. In fact, the number of broadcast journalists was slashed 50 percent from the mid-1980s to the mid-'90s. As a result, he says, journalists became more reliant on the public relations industry, which exists to provide reporters with information favorable to their clients. There are now 20,000 more PR agents than there are editors or reporters, he says.

By the late 1990s, after another round of mergers and acquisitions, the media conglomerates had changed. They were no longer huge American companies but rather global media giants. The world's media are now dominated by nine giant transnational firms, including *Time Warner* (1997 sales: $24 billion) and Disney ($22 billion).

McChesney fears that journalists under corporate control will no longer take on powerful interests. "All journalists worth their salt antagonize the 'powers that be' at some point in their careers," McChesney says. "But that's seen by corporate media as bad for business."

FAIR's Rendall fears that conglomerate-owned media outlets will just become mouthpieces for capitalism. "A lot of these corporations decided years ago that they could get a two-for-one deal by buying up media outlets," Rendall says. "They got a very profitable business, and they got a propaganda organ through which they could shape policy and public discussion."

McChesney agrees, claiming today's media exhibit a new corporate bias, but that no one seems to care, least of all the business community.

Others are not so worried. Schudson at the University of California points out that quality media outlets like CNN and National Public Radio take up the slack. And, he adds, "We have nationwide home delivery of *The Wall Street Journal* and *The New York Times,* even on the West Coast. So on balance I'd say we're a little better off."

And even with corporate ownership, local papers retain a certain degree of autonomy, Morton says. Corporate owners can drive what happens through the budget process, Morton says, "But they won't tell you who to endorse for city council."

Baughman, too, is skeptical about the dangers of media consolidation. "We forget that in the 1950s and '60s the TV network oligarchy was very real," he says. "We didn't have much choice. You waited for the *Time* magazine to arrive because it was your window on the world."

Now, thanks to cable, he says, "We'll always have choices. If they put on very bad shows, we don't have to watch them. Look at ABC. Until recently it has performed quite badly—in ratings, profits, everything—since Disney bought it."

Carey agrees. "Just because powerful centralized interests take over those

organizations doesn't mean they will prevail. People can turn away, or companies can go broke." ■

CURRENT SITUATION

New News Sources

The result of all the corporate changes, critics say, is a confusing array of news from a variety of non-traditional sources, much of it poorer quality. But the "new news" is less diverse. Due to the "pack mentality" of today's highly competitive journalism, fewer stories get covered, and those being covered are invariably sensationalistic and often covered without restraint, such as the O.J. Simpson story, the Monica Lewinsky scandal and the death of Princess Diana.

Talk is cheap, so that's what passes for news these days, others complain. "Talk shows are cheaper to produce, so they pour money into those while they cut their news bureaus," Baughman says.

McChesney agrees, citing the proliferation of "pundit" panel discussions about the Lewinsky-Clinton scandal. "They can pontificate endlessly, but it is basically mindless, pointless commentary ad nauseum."

Besides punditry, the public is being inundated with TV news magazines and talk shows. There are so many information shows now besides those produced by the news divisions, Naughton says, "that people confuse them as news." For instance, Oprah Winfrey has a lot of authority, but she is not a journalist, he says.

He praises former Chicago anchor-

woman Carol Marin, who quit her job at the local NBC station in May 1997 when it hired controversial talk show host Jerry Springer as a news commentator. "God love her, that's the kind of spine journalists need," Naughton says. "They need to say 'No, I will not take part in confusing this drivel with legitimate news.'"

Weir of *Salon* magazine says the convergence of news and entertainment has "changed this whole game. You could argue that shows like 'Dateline' are more important than the NBC 'Nightly News' because they are attracting larger audiences."

Some observers envision the day when the networks replace the nightly news with news magazines. At the least, others see the network news shows becoming even more tabloidy.

" 'Hard Copy' — that's where the TV news business is going," Weir says.

The danger is that when politics and news are taken less seriously by the media, people withdraw from citizenship, Baughman says. "In 1956, citizenship was taken more seriously," he says. "Conventions were covered in full by the networks. You didn't have advertising agencies standing around with buckets of cash to give you, and there was still a lot of relatively unsold time. Now, conventions aren't covered, except in a sarcastic and mocking way."

But in 1996, the opportunity to maximize profits was even greater, he says. The networks actually turned down some political advertising because they had other more lucrative ads they could run.

The Shrinking Soundbite
Likewise, the average soundbite on TV news has dropped dramatically over the years, says the University of California's Hallin. In 1968, soundbites averaged 43 seconds, compared with about eight seconds today.

Continued on p. 1139

At Issue:

Are media mergers bad for consumers?

Todd Gitlin

Professor of culture, journalism and sociology, New York University

FROM "NOT SO FAST," MEDIA STUDIES JOURNAL, SUMMER 1996, PUBLISHED BY THE FREEDOM FORUM. REPRINTED WITH PERMISSION.

*t*he case against the ill effects of conglomeration is strongest and best-researched in the case of newspapers. The 12 largest chains control almost half of daily circulation. Chains, especially those that trade on the stock market, are more eager than single-paper proprietors to raise profit margins. They tend to cut costs by firing reporters and editors. As the number of newspapers in a chain goes up, the size of the newshole tends to shrink. Soft-news coverage goes up. Local coverage may increase or decrease as a percentage of the whole, but the articles tend to get shorter in either case. . . .

The point is not that the media were once fearless and are suddenly in danger of becoming fearful, or that entertainment was once stupendous and is suddenly in danger of dumbing down. . . .

The point is that the changes now in progress are largely irreversible, potentially consequential, and they are being left to marketeers whose commitment to the public is dubious. . . .

Now it is true that two phenomena have grown simultaneously in America's media. One is conglomeration. The other is segmentation. Demographic slices are the targets in cable TV, radio, magazines. If choice is the champion goal, then the more choice the better; and clearly Manhattan's Time Warner Cable, with 76 channels, cannot be worse for consumers than the pre-cable array of seven VHF channels. Can it?

Not in the obvious sense, although the proprietors of cable TV have a lock on access. These effective monopolies permit and deny access just as they choose. Accountability is not their game. Giving preferences to their corporate partners is. So is catering to high-spending demographics. But even beyond cable, the standard of comparison ought not to be the impoverished past. The relevant question is about democratic potential. No one who worries about media trusts proposes a return to the narrow pipeline of yesteryear. The question is, What variety of diversity will the titans indulge? Most likely, immense varieties of segmented entertainment.

The thoughtful discussion of ideas is at a premium. The spiral of triviality winds onward. When the possible harms are great and potentially irreversible, is this not a matter for public inquiry? Surely Congress and the press might spare 10 percent of the time, money and energy they have devoted to petty scandals involving the onetime governor of a small state for the rather more momentous question of the impact of centralized power on the nation's sluggish flow of ideas.

Steven Rattner

Managing director, Lazard Freres & Co. LLC.

FROM "A GOLDEN AGE OF COMPETITION," MEDIA STUDIES JOURNAL, SUMMER 1996, PUBLISHED BY THE FREEDOM FORUM. REPRINTED WITH PERMISSION.

*i*t is truly ironic to be assessing the impact of mergers on media competition just as we are entering what may well prove to be the golden age of competition in communications industries.

Look in almost any direction and you see developments that will benefit consumers. In Washington, Congress has just enacted long overdue legislation that will rationalize an outmoded regulatory apparatus and free giant telecommunications and cable companies to battle each other. In New York, an array of news and financial services is being launched by equally giant media companies. Around the country — particularly on the West Coast — smaller, fast-growing companies are fighting to dominate the Internet. . . .

Nor do I despair that many of our journalistic enterprises are owned by large corporations. If anything, companies like Cap Cities have demonstrated that the result of corporate ownership can be freer and better journalism than we had when a few press lords controlled many of our newspapers and television networks. And the basic difference between the press lords of yesterday and the media moguls of today is that the press lords often ran their papers as vehicles for their own ideology and personal ambition. Today's moguls, with a few exceptions, seem more interested in making money than in seeing the triumph of their own ideology or personal ambition. . . .

Beyond not diminishing competition or quality, many of the media mergers have brought benefits. In some cases, they have provided the capital needed to launch exciting but expensive new undertakings. For example, the sales of cable companies have in many instances provided the financial resources to upgrade the systems so that all of the aforementioned new services could be provided. . . .

I agree that the nature of the media industry suggests a special need for attentiveness on everyone's part. Maintaining a diversity and plentitude of views — as well as freedom of expression — is critical to our democratic process. There may be a few instances, like the Newspaper Preservation Act, where a special role on the part of government is appropriate in order to maintain the greatest possible diversity of views. But these situations should be few and far between because the more that government views itself as having a special role with regard to the media, the greater the risk of government interference with the free expression of views.

Are the Media Out of Touch?

Decades ago, when veteran reporter Richard Reeves was just starting out at *The New York Times*, medicine was covered by a police reporter who had never been to college. "Now the people who cover medicine at the *Times* are all MDs," says Reeves, who teaches journalism at the University of Southern California.

As the American press has become better-paid and better-educated than ever before, they are increasingly being criticized as being too elitist and disconnected to the common man.

"Journalists are out-of-touch, arrogant and judgmental," says Jon Katz, media critic for the Freedom Forum, a Gannett-funded education and research foundation. Nowhere was this more glaringly apparent than last spring, he says, in the midst of the Lewinsky-Clinton scandal, "when 181 papers were calling for the president's resignation, and the public was going completely in the opposite direction."

Journalists have always been criticized as aloof, although reporters argue that what some call "aloofness" is actually "objectivity." And ever since former Vice President Spiro T. Agnew called the press "nattering nabobs of negativism," complaints have persisted about the media's cynicism.

But the claim that journalists are out-of-touch is fairly new, and appears to stem partly from the extraordinary growth of the journalist-as-pundit phenomenon.

"Journalists have become too big for their britches," former CBS correspondent Marvin Kalb wrote recently. "For journalists who want to offer commentaries on television, deliver speeches for hefty fees, even appear in the movies in cameo roles, the once glorious if somewhat mundane pursuit of the truth now seems too humble a calling." [1]

"Journalists are being paid fabulous amounts of money to hear themselves talk," says James M. Naughton, president of the Poynter Institute for Media Studies in St. Petersburg, Fla. "It's epidemic in Washington."

Indeed, for the handful of journalists who've become paid political commentators, salaries are reaching unimaginable levels. In his new study "The Rise of the 'New News,'" Kalb found that TV network "beat" reporters in Washington make from $100,000 to $350,000 a year, which can be supplemented with lucrative television contracts and lecture fees if they break into the talk-show circuit. For instance, *Newsweek* senior political reporter Howard Fineman makes $160,000 a year at *Newsweek*, and will make an additional $65,000 a year as an MSNBC commentator, wrote Kalb.

"You see reporters on a TV talk show giving their opinion, and then you see them on a newscast supposedly giving the straight news — but you remember the opinion," says Richard Cole, dean of the University of North Carolina Journalism School. "Reporters should report the news and not become celebrities."

As pundits and journalists have become more affluent, said Ben Bradlee, former *Washington Post* executive editor, the American press has become more conservative on economic issues. "Reporters are more conservative than the previous generation. There is a good reason for that. They get paid a hell of a lot better. It's hard to be a conservative on $75 a week; but $75,000 a year and you begin to think of the kids and the bank account and the IRA." [2]

The liberal media-watchdog group Fairness and Accuracy in Reporting (FAIR) agrees. "While Americans as a whole have been opposed to GATT, NAFTA and fast track, every newspaper in the country was supporting it," says FAIR senior analyst Steven Rendall.

Many are quick to point out that reporters' and pundits' salaries in Washington and other large cities are much higher than the average American journalists' pay. For instance, reporters at small newspapers (with 30,000-70,000 circulation) earn about $23,000 a year, compared with a *New York Times* starting salary of $67,000. [3]

Others see a more disturbing trend causing the media's more conservative economic leanings and the perception that it is out of touch: the increasingly popular practice of compensating editors through bonuses and stock options based on the performance of the company's stock.

"Fueled in large measure by incentive bonuses, editors' compensation for decades has been rising much faster than wages in the overall economy, and much faster than the paychecks of their newsroom colleagues," wrote former *Des Moines Register* Editor Geneva Overholser, who conducted an extensive study on the role of American newspaper editors for the *American Journalism Review*. [4]

In the past decade, for instance, editors' total compensation has skyrocketed 50 percent, to an average of $106,124, according to a 1998 Inland Press Association survey. Compensation for editors at larger newspapers (250,000-500,000 circulation) reached $250,000 this year, according to the survey. Editors at the 100,000-250,000 circulation papers, who averaged $17,500 in 1968, today make $157,000.

John Carroll, editor of the *Baltimore Sun*, said when editors make so much money they don't have the same financial concerns as the average reader. "I never expected to make this kind of money when I came into the business as a reporter on $75 a week," he said. "I can't really say that my problems are the same problems as the people in this community." [5]

---

[1] Marvin Kalb, "The Rise of the 'New News,'" The Joan Shorenstein Center on Press, Politics and Public Policy, October 1998.

[2] Quoted in Alexander Cockburn, "We've met the establishment and it is us," *Los Angeles Times*, July 2, 1998.

[3] Kalb, *op. cit.*

[4] Geneva Overholser, "Editor Inc.," *American Journalism Review*, December 1998.

[5] Quoted in *Ibid.*

Continued from p. 1136

Especially in political news, Hallin says, "Journalists felt they should move to a more interpretive, active kind of journalism, and you couldn't do that without tighter soundbites."

The ratings chase also helped shrink the soundbite. Local stations first began using shorter soundbites to pick up the pace of TV news to garner higher ratings. "A two-minute clip of a politician is not the way to do that," Hallin says.

As a result, "Voters don't get to hear the candidates speak at length anymore," Hallin says. "It's harder to make up your mind about the logic of [the candidate's] ideas."

On the other hand, he says, broadcasts today deal more seriously with issues in some ways, such as background pieces, "reality checks" of candidates' statements, film clips of past statements that contradict current positions and interviewing experts about policy implications.

But many critics say election coverage is too focused on campaign strategy—"the horse race as opposed to the issues," says Kunkel. "So the politicians say less and less about what they're going to do."

"The 'new news' doesn't cost you much in the short-term, so you make a lot of money," McChesney says. "But the notion of journalism as a public service, providing crucial information that people need in a democracy, is lost." ∎

OUTLOOK

Saved by the Internet?

At the dawn of the new millennium, American journalism is at a crossroads. "It will take us a while to find our bearings in the current competitive, downscale, bottom-line marketplace," Naughton says. "I don't think it's going to be easy. It takes very strong leaders to pull this off. But we mustn't throw up our hands and say we are all doomed."

Grass-roots organizations like the Committee of Concerned Journalists have sprung up to speak out for professional values in American journalism, Naughton noted, and individual journalists can try to influence their bosses, owners and publishers. At the corporate levels, he says, corporations can try to persuade their institutional investors and Wall Street that short-term profit-taking in companies that need a long-term strategic view will hurt those companies eventually.

"We've got to come up with a better system than what we have now," McChesney says. "We need to get control of journalism back into the hands of journalists." Among the reforms he suggests are preventing broadcasters from accepting political advertising and divesting all TV news from corporate control.

In the absence of reform, some see America's information universe becoming a split system. "I think we'll move more and more to a two-tiered system here like they have in England, with a quality press and a mass press," Hallin says. "I don't think it's good for democracy. It makes society more unequal, because information is power."

Others say the Internet ultimately will save democracy. "I thank God every day for the Internet," says Katz of the Freedom Forum. "Increasingly, the media is run by mass marketers and greedy media moguls who don't care about the moral principles of journalism. But that [journalistic] spirit is present overwhelmingly on the Internet."

"Many people say the Internet will save democracy from the conglomerates because anyone can start a Web site," McChesney says. "There's some element of truth to that."

But Disney and other corporations will get on the Internet bandwagon, he predicts. "The Internet will be dominated by the largest media/telecommunications firms in the world," he says.

Katz thinks that will never happen. "Everyone with a computer is a publisher on the Internet. Sixty-five million Americans are used to speaking freely on the Internet. I don't think they want this scoffed up the way traditional media has been."

The Internet is changing the economics of the newspaper business so dramatically that to keep the presses rolling it's essential to be on-line.

"The Internet hasn't had significant impact on newspapers yet," Morton says. But clearly that will change. As computers become more ubiquitous, he sees the media's current high profit margins eroding somewhat. The Internet is much more competitive, he says, and "competition inevitably means lower profit margins."

Morton says no one knows what will happen when the Internet generation comes of age. "The elementary schools are basically teaching kids how to get information off the computer. It's really hard to predict what will happen to newspapers when these kids are all over 30," he says. "Newspapers need to be accessible with a keyboard and a screen."

Baughman says teachers starting in elementary school need to encourage students to be active consumers of news. "Many of my journalism students don't read newspapers," he says. "To many of them, if you're informed, you're a geek or a nerd."

Reeves fears that modern Internet technology opens the way for what he calls "ATM journalism." Under such a system, politicians, entertainers and corporations will simply put into cyberspace the information they want the public to have. "The next morning people who want information will punch in what they want," he says.

There will be no middlemen, no editors and no filters, he says. "Admittedly, the consumers will have a tough time figuring out where the information comes from or what the motivation is behind it," he says, "but we kid ourselves to think that others can't collect information and distribute it to society. They can, they are and they will."

Journalists are being backed into a corner and must adjust to survive, Reeves says. "We must make our corner one in which people will come to verify information in a society that is under data siege."

"If people lose confidence in the reliability of their mass media, there will be a price paid for that by our democracy," Naughton says, "which depends upon reliable information being presented to citizens.

Perhaps scariest of all, Naughton says, is the possibility that the special protections granted to the media by the First Amendment might someday be challenged if the media are perceived as "just another business."

The solution, Reeves says, is for "journalists to go back to the core of what we were hired to do—watch the parade go by, and every now and then yell out that the emperor has no clothes." ■

Notes

[1] Quoted in Geneva Overholser, "Editor Inc.," *American Journalism Review*, December 1998. For background, see Chris Conte, "Civic Journalism," *The CQ Researcher*, Sept. 20, 1996, pp. 817-840.

[2] Marvin Kalb, "The Rise of the 'New News,'" The Joan Shorenstein Center for Press, Politics and Public Policy, October 1998.

[3] For background, see Kenneth Jost, "Political Scandals," *The CQ Researcher*, May 27, 1994, pp. 457-480, and Kenneth Jost, "Talk

Show Democracy," *The CQ Researcher*, April 29, 1994, pp. 361-384.

[4] Neil Hickey, "Money Lust: How Pressure for Profit is Perverting Journalism," *Columbia Journalism Review*, July/August 1998.

[5] Quoted in Howard Kurtz, "Chex and Balance," *The Washington Post*, Dec. 2, 1997.

[6] Comments submitted to the Harvard symposium.

[7] See Peter Arnett, "Goodbye World," *American Journalism Review*, November 1998.

[8] "Off With Their Talking Heads," *New York*, Nov. 23, 1998.

[9] Quoted in Hickey, *op. cit.*

[10] Quoted in *Ibid.*

[11] Quoted in *Ibid.*

[12] Willes spoke at the Harvard forum.

[13] O'Reilley appeared on "The Diane Rehm Show," National Public Radio, Dec. 3, 1998.

[14] For background, see Susan Philips, "Student Journalism," *The CQ Researcher*, June 5, 1998, pp. 481-504.

[15] Remarks at the May 22 Harvard symposium.

[16] Quoted in Kalb, *op. cit.*

[17] Ben Bradlee, *A Good Life* (1996), p. 207.

[18] Hickey, *op cit.*

[19] Quoted in Charles Layton and Mary Walton, "Missing the Story at the Statehouse," *American Journalism Review*, July/August 1998.

[20] Quoted in *Ibid.*

[21] Quoted in *Ibid.*

[22] Richard Reeves, *What the People Know* (1998), p. 60.

[23] Doug Underwood, "Assembly-Line Journalism," *Columbia Journalism Review*, July/August 1998.

Bibliography

Selected Sources Used

Books

Barnouw, Erik, et al., ***Conglomerates and the Media,*** **The New Press, 1997.**

Essays by nine leading media critics discuss how increasing ownership of the U.S. media by conglomerates affects the creation and dissemination of the news. The authors discuss the decline of journalistic integrity and the effects of increasing profit expectations in the newsroom.

Baughman, James L., ***The Republic of Mass Culture: Journalism, Filmmaking, and Broadcasting in America Since 1941,*** **Johns Hopkins University Press, 1997.**

A University of Wisconsin journalism professor discusses how new, competitive realities of the 1990s have affected mass culture. Marketplace values have helped fragment the mass audience, encouraged record-breaking mergers between media companies and precipitated an alarming decline in the quality of journalism, he says.

Fuller, Jack, ***News Values: Ideas for an Information Age,*** **University of Chicago Press, 1996.**

Fuller, a Pulitzer Prize-winning journalist and *Chicago Tribune* publisher examines newsroom ethics, asking whether marketing decisions affect decisions about what constitutes "news" and what future newspapers have in a digital age.

Kurtz, Howard, ***Hot Air: All Talk, All the Time,*** **Times Books, 1996.**

The media critic for *The Washington Post* examines the world of talk, from journalism pundits to Howard Stern. He looks at how electronic democracy is changing the nature of political discourse in America.

McChesney, Robert W., ***Corporate Media and the Threat to Democracy,*** **Seven Stories Press, 1997.**

A journalism professor at the University of Wisconsin argues that the takeover of the American media by global conglomerates threatens political democracy. The profit-maximizing mentality of the global companies does not serve the public interest, he says.

Reeves, Richard, ***What the People Know: Freedom and the Press,*** **Harvard University Press, 1998.**

The veteran journalist reports on the state of the American media. Journalism "is in a crisis of change and redefinition," he writes, due to changes in technology and media ownership. The media have responded by dumbing down the news, reporting on what the public wants, he contends.

Underwood, Doug, ***When MBAs Rule the Newsroom,*** **Columbia University Press, 1993.**

This behind-the-scenes look at modern newspapers discusses the impact on news-gathering when corporations demand high profits, adopt "reader-friendly" journalism and follow a customer-driven approach to news.

Articles

Hickey, Neil, "Money Lust: How Pressure for Profit is Perverting Journalism," ***Columbia Journalism Review,*** **July/August 1998.**

In a scathing cover story, Hickey argues that cutbacks in staff and coverage of hard news in favor of softer features and celebrity news is eroding the press' credibility and the industry's performance of its role in a democracy.

Layton, Charles, and Mary Walton, "Missing the Story at the Statehouse," ***American Journalism Review,*** **July/Augst, 1998.**

This extensive study by the Project on the State of American Newspapers found that in 27 out of 50 states there are fewer statehouse reporters now than nine years ago, even though the Republican-dominated U.S. Congress since 1995 has transferred billions of federal dollars from Washington to state governments for distribution through block grants.

"Off With Their Talking Heads," ***New York,*** **Nov. 23, 1998.**

A *New York* magazine poll finds that 71 percent of respondents agreed that "legitimate news organizations and outlets are sinking to the level of tabloids in reporting gossip and unsubstantiated stories."

Overholser, Geneva, "Editor Inc.," ***American Journalism Review,*** **December 1998.**

Editors' compensation has been rising much faster than wages in the overall economy, and much faster than the paychecks of their newsroom colleagues, says the former *Des Moines Register* editor. This extensive study on the role of American newspaper editors was part of the two-year State of American Newspapers Project, funded by the Pew Charitable Trusts.

Reports and Studies

Kalb, Marvin, "The Rise of the 'New News,'" The Joan Shorenstein Center for Press, Politics and Public Policy, October 1998.

Kalb, director of the Harvard-based center, says the technological revolution of the last 20 years and a new business-oriented approach to news-gathering have transformed the standards of American journalism.

The Next Step

Additional information from UMI's Newspaper & Periodical Abstracts™ database

Ethics

Dashiell, Edith A., "Media Ethics: A Philosophical Approach," *Journalism & Mass Communication Quarterly*, **spring 1998, p. 216.**

The author reviews *Media Ethics: A Philosophical Approach* by Matthew Kieran.

Ferdinand, Pamela, "Tufts Forum Focuses on Jewell Case, Media Ethics," *The Boston Globe*, **Dec. 5, 1996, p. B10.**

A panel discussion at Tufts University examines the media coverage of former Olympic Park bombing suspect Richard Jewell.

Lieberman, Paul, "Death on the Small Screen Puts Spotlight on TV Ethics; Media: Debate over '60 Minutes' Kevorkian Episode is Likely to Affect how Television Addresses Right-to-Die Issue," *Los Angeles Times*, **Nov. 25, 1998, p. A1.**

Television journalist Mike Wallace of "60 Minutes," who had never met Jack Kevorkian, viewed the doctor as "kind of shopworn and a publicity seeker." And Don Hewitt, the show's executive producer, "had no interest, none whatsoever," recalled Wallace. The tape showed that Kevorkian had taken his right-to-death campaign to a new level — from assisted suicide to euthanasia, "death triggered directly by a doctor," as Wallace eventually described it on the air. Indeed, it showed Kevorkian personally injecting a lethal dose of drugs into the right hand of Thomas Youk, 52, a victim of paralyzing Lou Gehrig's disease.

Local TV News

Johnson, Steve, "How Low Can TV News Go?" *Columbia Journalism Review*, **July 1997, pp. 24-27.**

When daytime TV host Jerry Springer was hired to do nightly commentaries about local issues on WMAQ in Chicago, two news anchors quit in protest.

Nimmer, David, "News Fix," *Minneapolis St. Paul*, **October 1998, pp. 66-69.**

The author, a journalism professor and former reporter, discusses ways in which local TV news could be improved. Among other things, he suggests banning the use of superlatives, limiting weather hype and improving scripts.

Media Mergers

Conrad, Keith, "Media Mergers: First Step in a New Shift of Antitrust Analysis?" *Federal Communications Law Journal*, **April 1997, pp. 675-700.**

The alarming trend toward concentration of media ownership and the current state of antitrust laws are examined.

Jaquet, Janine, "Cornering Creativity," *The Nation*, **March 17, 1997, p. 10.**

The proliferation of synergy-inspired mergers among media conglomerates is discussed. Creative expression should not be controlled by a few corporations and showcased only when it is profitable.

Keating, Stephen, "Satellite-TV Deal Blocked; Justice Department Cites 'Cable Monopoly,' " *The Denver Post*, **May 13, 1998, p. C1.**

Taking its first major action against a media merger in recent memory, the Department of Justice filed an antitrust suit to block Primestar Inc. from acquiring $1.1 billion in satellite assets owned by News Corp. and MCI. Justice Department officials cited the "cable monopoly" and rising cable prices as the main reason to prevent Primestar, which is primarily owned by cable companies, from controlling satellite assets owned by American Sky Broadcasting, the News Corp./MCI venture. Primestar, based in the Denver area, claims its deal with American Sky Broadcasting would foster satellite-TV competition and says that it is prepared to "vigorously contest" the antitrust action in court.

Kerwin, Ann Marie, "Execs Predict '98 Mergers Aplenty for Magazines," *Advertising Age*, **June 15, 1998, p. S30.**

Those who keep an eye on the consumer, business-to-business and information industries are predicting that 1998 will be as strong as 1997 when it comes to media mergers and acquisitions. Results of a survey of 1,000 media and financial organization executives are discussed.

News Quality

Bash, Alan, "New Owners Turn CBS' Eye to News, Quality," *USA Today*, **Nov. 29, 1995, p. D1.**

The new owners of CBS are making preparations to change the TV lineup in an effort to revive the struggling network. The once top-rated company has languished in third place for the second season running.

Bodle, John V., "Assessing News Quality: A Comparison Between Community and Student Daily Newspapers," *Journalism & Mass Communication Quarterly*, **autumn 1996, pp. 672-686.**

Community daily newspapers were quantitatively compared with student dailies to determine the relative quality of the newswriting and news content.

Jurkowitz, Mark, "Lewinsky Saga Adds New Chapter to Media Ethics Book," *The Boston Globe*, Jan. 28, 1998, p. A17.

Every day, if not every hour, the Monica Lewinsky saga seems to rewrite the book on journalistic practice and standards. Yesterday, a story that did not even survive one day in *The Dallas Morning News* — or on the paper's Web site — became the newest fodder for the insatiable media appetite for the scandal. The story, reporting that independent counsel Kenneth W. Starr's staff had spoken with a Secret Service agent who would testify to seeing Lewinsky and President Clinton in a compromising situation, appeared on the Web site on Monday and made an early edition of yesterday's paper before being withdrawn. In a striking showcase of the immediacy of electronic journalism, the paper used the Web to quickly correct a story the site carried.

Montalbano, William D., "Diana's Death Gives Life to Ethics Debate; Media: British Press Wrestles with its Conscience, and Biographer Fends Off Blows from Royal Family, Charities," *Los Angeles Times*, Oct. 11, 1997, p. A21.

For the nation she held in thrall through public glamour and private misery, Princess Diana is proving as magnetic and vexatious in death as she did in life. In the predictable aftermath of CDs, T-shirts and Diana teacups, there is also the spectacle of British newspapers publicly wrestling with their consciences — and one another — about the hounding of public figures.

On-Line Journalism

Maddox, Kate, "Web Rivals' Plan to Merge Draws Cheers," *Advertising Age*, Oct. 19, 1998, pp. 48-50.

Media buyers and sellers are happy about the planned merger between Web rivals Media Metrix and Relevant Knowledge. Media Metrix is currently evaluating its marketing and advertising strategy for the combined company.

Pavlik, John V., "The Future of Online Journalism," *Columbia Journalism Review*, July 1997, pp. 30-31.

More than 1,600 daily newspapers are carried online every day, and the number of people getting their news on-line increases daily. Speculation on the future of on-line news and journalism is presented, and some Web sites to find up-to-the-minute news are discussed.

Profits

"Guardian Sees Record Profits," *The Guardian*, June 24, 1998, p. 23.

The Guardian Media Group, which publishes *The Guardian* and *The Observer*, yesterday reported profits before tax rising 76 percent in the year to end in March. The results were attributed to strong advertising growth, lower newsprint prices and tight cost control.

Alexander, Keith L., "Analysts Pan Media Companies' Prospects," USA Today, Sept. 30, 1998, p. B3.

Some top Wall Street analysts are getting nervous about prospects for media businesses. Several pessimistic reports, which hit the market Tuesday, rocked three of the nation's leading media companies: Viacom, Seagram and CBS.

Public Confidence

"Media Doing Their Job?" *USA Today*, April 28, 1998, p. A1.

According to the Marist Institute for Public Opinion, in February 1998, 41 percent of people felt the media were doing their jobs in covering the scandal involving President Clinton, while 59 percent felt the media were overstepping their role.

Greene, Bob, "Some Young Eyes Can Lower the Wall Between Media, Public," *Chicago Tribune*, July 8, 1998, p. 1.

The American public's disillusionment with newspapers and TV newscasts is growing.

Back Issues

Great Research on Current Issues Starts Right Here.
Recent topics covered by The CQ Researcher are listed below.
Now available on the Web
For information, call (800) 432-2250 ext. 279 or (202) 887-6279.

MAY 1997
The Stock Market
The Cloning Controversy
Expanding NATO
The Future of Libraries

JUNE 1997
FDA Reform
China After Deng
Line-Item Veto
Breast Cancer

JULY 1997
Transportation Policy
Executive Pay
School Choice Debate
Aggressive Driving

AUGUST 1997
Age Discrimination
Banning Land Mines
Children's Television
Evolution vs. Creationism

SEPTEMBER 1997
Caring for the Dying
Mental Health Policy
Mexico's Future
Youth Fitness

OCTOBER 1997
Urban Sprawl in the West
Diversity in the Workplace
Teacher Education
Contingent Work Force

Back issues are available for $5.00 (sub-scribers) or $10.00 (non-subscribers). Quantity discounts apply to orders over 10. To order, call Congressional Quarterly Customer Service at (202) 887-8621.

Binders are available for $18.00. To order call 1-800-638-1710. Please refer to stock number 648.

NOVEMBER 1997
Renewable Energy
Artificial Intelligence
Religious Persecution
Roe v. Wade at 25

DECEMBER 1997
Whistleblowers
Castro's Next Move
Gun Control Standoff
Regulating Nonprofits

JANUARY 1998
Foster Care Reform
IRS Reform
The Black Middle Class
U.S.-British Relations

FEBRUARY 1998
Patients' Rights
Deflation Fears
Caring for the Elderly
The New Corporate Philanthropy

MARCH 1998
Israel at 50
The Federal Judiciary
Drinking on Campus
The Economics of Recycling

APRIL 1998
Biology and Behavior
Liberal Arts Education
Income Inequality
High-Tech Labor Shortage

MAY 1998
Census 2000
Child-Care Options
Alzheimer's Disease
U.S.-Russian Relations

JUNE 1998
Student Journalism
Antitrust Policy
Environmental Justice
Sleep Deprivation

JULY 1998
Encouraging Teen Abstinence
Population and the Environment
Democracy in Asia
Baby Boomers at Midlife

AUGUST 1998
Oil Production in the 21st Century
Flexible Work Arrangements
Coastal Development
Student Activism

SEPTEMBER 1998
Organic Farming
Cancer Treatments
Hispanic Americans' New Clout
The Future of Baseball

OCTOBER 1998
School Violence
Social Security
National Forests
Puerto Rico's Status

NOVEMBER 1998
Internet Privacy
Human Rights
Drug Testing
European Monetary Union

DECEMBER 1998
AIDS Update
Searching for Jesus
Reform in Iran

Future Topics

▶ *Death Penalty Update*

▶ *Obesity and Health*

▶ *Foundations and Public Policy*

The CQ Researcher

Subject-Title Index

January 1991-December 1998

NOTE: Weekly *CQ Researcher* reports are indexed by title under boldface subject headings. Titles are followed by the date of the report and the number of the first page. Page numbers followed by asterisks refer to sidebars or the "At Issue" pro/con feature. Issues dated before May 10, 1991, were published under the name of *Editorial Research Reports*.

1